Stephen M. Stahl

CURRENT DIAGNOSIS & TREATMENT

Stephen M. Stahl

current
DIAGNOSIS
& TREATMENT

By

MARCUS A. KRUPP, MD

Clinical Professor of Medicine
Stanford University School of Medicine (Palo Alto)
Director of Research, Palo Alto Medical Research Foundation
Director of Laboratories, Palo Alto Medical Clinic

MILTON J. CHATTON, MD

Clinical Associate Professor of Medicine
Stanford University School of Medicine (Palo Alto)
Senior Attending Physician
Santa Clara Valley Medical Center (San Jose)
Research Associate, Palo Alto Medical
Research Foundation (Palo Alto)

And Associate Authors

Lange Medical Publications

LOS ALTOS, CALIFORNIA

1972

International Standard Book Number: *0–87041–122–5*
Library of Congress Catalogue Card Number: *62–10400*

A Concise Medical Library for Practitioner and Student

Current Diagnosis & Treatment 1972 $11.00

Current Pediatric Diagnosis & Treatment. Edited by C.H. Kempe, H.K. Silver, and D. O'Brien. 883 pp, *illus.*	1970
Review of Physiological Chemistry, 13th ed. H.A. Harper. 529 pp, *illus.*	1971
Review of Medical Physiology, 5th ed. W.F. Ganong. 573 pp, *illus.*	1971
Review of Medical Microbiology, 9th ed. E. Jawetz, J.L. Melnick, and E.A. Adelberg. 484 pp, *illus.*	1970
Review of Medical Pharmacology, 2nd ed. F.H. Meyers, E. Jawetz, and A. Goldfien. 663 pp, *illus.*	1970
General Urology, 6th ed. D.R. Smith. 416 pp, *illus.*	1969
General Ophthalmology, 6th ed. D. Vaughan, T. Asbury, and R. Cook. 316 pp, *illus.*	1971
Correlative Neuroanatomy & Functional Neurology, 14th ed. J.G. Chusid. 453 pp, *illus.*	1970
Principles of Clinical Electrocardiography, 7th ed. M.J. Goldman. 400 pp, *illus.*	1970
Handbook of Psychiatry, 2nd ed. Edited by P. Solomon and V.D. Patch. 648 pp.	1971
Handbook of Surgery, 4th ed. Edited by J.L. Wilson. 781 pp, *illus.*	1969
Handbook of Obstetrics & Gynecology, 4th ed. R.C. Benson. 774 pp, *illus.*	1971
Physician's Handbook, 16th ed. M.A. Krupp, N.J. Sweet, E. Jawetz, and E.G. Biglieri. 660 pp, *illus.*	1970
Handbook of Medical Treatment, 12th ed. Edited by M.J. Chatton, S. Margen, and H. Brainerd. 789 pp.	1970
Handbook of Pediatrics, 9th ed. H.K. Silver, C.H. Kempe, and H.B. Bruyn. 713 pp.	1971
Handbook of Poisoning: Diagnosis & Treatment, 7th ed. R.H. Dreisbach. 528 pp.	1971

Table of Contents

Preface

This book is intended to serve the practicing physician as a useful desk reference on the most widely accepted technics currently available for diagnosis and treatment. It is not intended to be used as a textbook of medicine. Specific current references to the clinical literature and general bibliographies are included as a guide to further study.

The wide acceptance of this book since its first appearance in 1962 has been most gratifying. Annual revisions will continue to be prepared for distribution in January of each year. A Spanish edition is available from El Manual Moderno in Mexico City, an Italian edition from Piccin Editore in Padua, a Romanian edition from Editura Medicala in Bucharest, and a Serbo-Croatian edition from Savremena Administracija in Belgrade. An English language edition for distribution in Asia is now printed in Tokyo by the Maruzen Company.

Although we have dealt primarily with internal medical disorders, discussions of other disorders commonly encountered in certain other specialties are included also.

The authors and editors have been careful to recommend those drug dosages that are in agreement with current official pharmacologic standards and responsible medical literature. Since there may be considerable variation in available preparations and dosages of particular drugs offered by individual manufacturers, all clinicians are advised to refer to the drug manufacturer's product information (eg, package inserts), especially in the case of new or infrequently prescribed medications.

The editors wish to express their sincere thanks to their associate authors for participating so effectively in this venture, and to the many students and physicians who have contributed suggestions and criticisms for this and previous editions.

Marcus A. Krupp
Milton J. Chatton

January, 1972

The Authors

J. Ralph Audy, MD, PhD
Director, G.W. Hooper Foundation; Chairman, Department of International Health, University of California School of Medicine (San Francisco).

Ralph C. Benson, MD
Professor of Obstetrics & Gynecology and Chairman, Department of Obstetrics & Gynecology, University of Oregon Medical School, Hospitals and Clinics (Portland).

Lloyd L. Brandborg, MD
Chief, Gastroenterology, Veterans Administration Hospital (San Francisco); Clinical Professor of Medicine, University of California School of Medicine (San Francisco).

Henry B. Bruyn, MD
Clinical Professor of Pediatrics & Medicine, University of California School of Medicine (San Francisco); Director of Student Health, University of California (Berkeley).

John V. Carbone, MD
Professor of Medicine, University of California School of Medicine (San Francisco).

Milton J. Chatton, MD
Clinical Associate Professor of Medicine, Stanford University School of Medicine (Palo Alto); Senior Attending Physician, Santa Clara Valley Medical Center (San Jose); Research Associate, Palo Alto Medical Research Foundation.

Joseph G. Chusid, MD
Associate Clinical Professor of Neurology, College of Physicians & Surgeons, Columbia University (New York City); Director of Department of Neurology, St. Vincent's Hospital and Medical Center (New York City); Associate Attending Neurologist, Columbia-Presbyterian Medical Center (New York City).

Wayne W. Deatsch, MD
Associate Clinical Professor of Otorhinolaryngology, University of California School of Medicine (San Francisco).

Robert H. Dreisbach, MD
Professor (Emeritus) of Pharmacology, Stanford University School of Medicine (Palo Alto).

Frederick L. Dunn, MD, DTM&H
Professor, Department of International Health & G.W. Hooper Foundation, University of California School of Medicine (San Francisco).

Harry K. Elkins, MD
Director, Santa Clara County Alcoholic Rehabilitation Clinic (San Jose).

Ephraim P. Engleman, MD
Clinical Professor of Medicine; Head, Rheumatic Disease Group, Department of Medicine, University of California School of Medicine (San Francisco).

John M. Erskine, MD
Assistant Clinical Professor of Surgery, University of California School of Medicine (San Francisco); Associate in Surgery, Stanford University School of Medicine (Palo Alto).

Joseph E. Giansiracusa, MD
Clinical Assistant Professor of Medicine, Stanford University School of Medicine (Palo Alto); Associate Clinical Professor of Medicine, University of California School of Medicine (San Francisco); Senior Attending Physician, Santa Clara Valley Medical Center (San Jose).

Robert S. Goldsmith, MD, DTM&H
Assistant Professor of Tropical Medicine & Epidemiology, University of California School of Medicine (San Francisco).

Carlyn Halde, PhD
Associate Professor, Department of Microbiology, University of California School of Medicine (San Francisco).

George B. Hamilton, MD
Chief, Gastroenterology, Letterman General Hospital (San Francisco); Assistant Clinical Professor of Medicine, University of California School of Medicine (San Francisco).

Gerald G. Hirschberg, MD
Associate Clinical Professor of Physical Medicine and Rehabilitation, University of California School of Medicine (San Francisco); Chief of the Physical Medicine & Rehabilitation Service, Contra Costa County Hospital (Martinez).

Ernest Jawetz, PhD, MD
Professor of Microbiology & Chairman, Department of Microbiology; Professor of Medicine, Lecturer in Pediatrics, University of California School of Medicine (San Francisco).

Floyd H. Jergesen, MD
Clinical Professor of Orthopedic Surgery, University of California School of Medicine (San Francisco).

Felix O. Kolb, MD
Clinical Professor of Medicine, Research Physician and Associate Director, Metabolic Research Unit, University of California School of Medicine (San Francisco); Chairman, Division of Endocrinology and Metabolism, Mount Zion Hospital (San Francisco).

Margaret S. Kosek, MD
Research Associate, Palo Alto Medical Research Foundation.

Marcus A. Krupp, MD
Clinical Professor of Medicine, Stanford University School of Medicine (Palo Alto); Director of Research Palo Alto Medical Research Foundation; Director of Laboratories, Palo Alto Medical Clinic.

Sidney Levin, MD
Associate Clinical Professor of Medicine, University of California School of Medicine (San Francisco); Chief of Medicine, Mount Zion Hospital and Medical Center (San Francisco).

R. Morton Manson, MD
Director, Clinical Services, Santa Clara Valley Medical Center (San Jose); Clinical Assistant Professor of Medicine, Stanford University School of Medicine (Palo Alto).

Frederick H. Meyers, MD
Professor of Pharmacology, University of California School of Medicine (San Francisco).

Perry A. Olsen, MD
Clinical Assistant Professor of Anesthesiology, Stanford University School of Medicine (Palo Alto); Director of Anesthesiology, Santa Clara Valley Medical Center (San Jose).

Rees B. Rees, Jr., MD
Clinical Professor of Dermatology & Radiology, University of California School of Medicine (San Francisco).

Sydney E. Salmon, MD
Assistant Professor of Medicine, Department of Medicine, and Research Associate, Cancer Research Institute, University of California School of Medicine (San Francisco).

Sol Silverman, Jr., DDS
Professor of Oral Biology (Chairman of the Division), University of California School of Dentistry (San Francisco).

Maurice Sokolow, MD
Professor of Medicine, University of California School of Medicine (San Francisco).

Phyllis Ullman, MA
Consultant Dietitian, Preventive Medicine Center (Palo Alto).

Daniel Vaughan, MD
Associate Clinical Professor of Ophthalmology, University of California School of Medicine (San Francisco).

Ralph O. Wallerstein, MD
Clinical Professor of Medicine, University of California School of Medicine (San Francisco).

John L. Wilson, MD
Professor of Surgery, Stanford University School of Medicine (Palo Alto).

John H. Windesheim, MD
Assistant Clinical Professor of Medicine, University of California School of Medicine (San Francisco).

1...

General Symptoms

Milton J. Chatton

FEVER

The body temperature is normally subject to individual variation as well as to fluctuation due to physiologic factors. Exercise, digestion, sudden increase in environmental temperature, and excitement (eg, medical examination) may cause a transient increase in temperature. There is a slight sustained temperature rise following ovulation during the menstrual cycle and in the first trimester of pregnancy. The normal diurnal variation may be as much as 2° F, being lowest in the early morning and highest in the late afternoon.

Careful readings with a reliable thermometer will prevent errors in clinical interpretation. Oral temperatures may be unreliable in "mouth-breathers" or in patients who are uncooperative, debilitated, or in shock. Rectal or vaginal temperatures are taken in these circumstances. Tympanic temperature determinations have recently been found to be even more reliable for measuring body temperature than rectal determinations, but tympanic thermometers are not presently applicable for general use.

The average normal oral body temperature is 98.6° F (range 96.7°–99° F), or 37° C (range 36°–37.4° C). The normal rectal or vaginal temperature is 1° F (0.5° C) higher than the oral temperature, and the normal axillary temperature is lower to a corresponding degree.

Prolonged elevation of rectal temperature over 106° F (41° C) may result in permanent brain damage; when the rectal temperature is over 109° F (43° C), heat stroke occurs and death is common.

The characteristics of the temperature pattern (graphic record), especially when viewed in light of other clinical findings, may be of prognostic value and a guide to the effectiveness of therapy.

Diagnostic Considerations

The outline below illustrates the wide variety of clinical disorders which may cause fever. Most febrile illnesses are short-lived or relatively easy to diagnose. In certain instances, however, the origin of the fever may remain obscure ("fever of undetermined origin," FUO). In the USA, prolonged fevers of undetermined origin are most frequently due to infectious diseases. About 20% are due to neoplastic disease; about 15% are due to connective tissue disease; and the remainder are due to miscellaneous causes. The 2 most commonly missed causes are pyelonephritis and thromboembolism. Extensive laboratory studies may be indicated: examination and culture of body fluids, exudates, and excretions; serologic tests, skin tests, tissue biopsy, and toxicologic studies. In addition to x-rays of the chest and conventional studies of the gastrointestinal and urinary tracts, useful information may be obtained from studies such as the liver scan, lymphangiography, angiocardiography, and celiac aortography. If clinical, laboratory, and radiologic studies suggest intra-abdominal disease, exploratory laparotomy may be required.

Use of the so-called therapeutic test for the diagnosis of a fever is justified only when a specific disease is suspected (eg, chloroquine for malaria). Hasty, empirical use of broad-spectrum antibiotics or of polypharmaceutical measures (eg, multiple antimicrobials, corticosteroids, antipyretics, analgesics) may seriously interfere with rational diagnosis and therapy and may actually be hazardous. Although mild fevers may be of psychogenic origin, this diagnosis should be made with extreme caution and should be based not only upon positive psychiatric criteria but after careful exclusion of the possibility of organic disease.

Clinical Classification of Causes of Fever (With Examples)

(1) Infections: Viral, rickettsial, bacterial, fungal, and parasitic infections are the commonest causes of fever. (a) Generalized infections without localizing signs (eg, septicemia). (b) Generalized infections with localizing signs (eg, pharyngitis, scarlet fever). (c) Localized infections (eg, pyelonephritis).

(2) Diseases of undetermined etiology: (a) Collagen diseases (eg, disseminated lupus erythematosus, polyarteritis nodosa, dermatomyositis, rheumatoid arthritis, rheumatic fever). (b) Other miscellaneous disease (eg, sarcoidosis, amyloidosis).

(3) Central nervous system disease: Cerebrovascular accidents, head injuries, brain and spinal cord tumors, degenerative CNS disease (eg, multiple sclerosis), spinal cord injuries.

(4) Malignant neoplastic disease: Primary neoplasms (eg, of thyroid, lung, liver, pancreas, and genitourinary tract). Secondary neoplasms, carcinoid.

(5) Hematologic disease: Lymphomas, leukemias, multiple myeloma, pernicious anemia, hemolytic anemias, hemorrhagic disease (eg, hemophilia).

(6) Cardiovascular disease: Myocardial infarction, thromboembolic diseases, bacterial endocarditis, congestive heart failure, paroxysmal tachycardias.

(7) Endocrine disease: Hyperthyroidism, pheochromocytoma.

(8) Diseases due to physical agents: Heat stroke, radiation sickness, trauma (eg, surgery), crushing injuries.

(9) Diseases due to chemical agents: Drug reactions, anesthesia, anaphylactic reactions, serum sickness, chemical poisoning, pyrogen reactions (following intravenous fluids).

(10) Disorders of fluid balance: Dehydration, acidosis.

(11) Psychogenic fever.

(12) Factitious or "false" fever.

Treatment

A. Removal of the Specific Cause of the Fever: The principal problem is to determine and eradicate the cause of the fever. Symptomatic measures directed toward depression of an elevated body temperature are usually not indicated except for high, prolonged fevers.

B. Reduction of the Fever by Nonspecific Means: When the body temperature is greater than 40° C (104° F), particularly if prolonged, the following measures may be utilized:

1. Increased fluid intake—By oral or parenteral routes.

2. Alcohol sponges—Cooling is due to evaporation.

3. Warm or tepid baths—These cause peripheral vasodilatation.

4. Cold sponges—Provide prompt cooling of skin and psychologic relief but interfere with heat loss.

5. Ice bags—Provide local comfort, eg, for headache.

6. Antipyretic drugs—These drugs are quite effective in reducing fever and have a simultaneous analgesic effect. They may, however, obscure the clinical picture, and may cause undesirable side-effects such as sweating, nausea and vomiting, and, rarely, skin eruptions and hematologic changes. Such drugs, therefore, are to be employed cautiously in fevers due to infectious diseases and are preferably not used in the enteric fevers (eg, typhoid fever). Aspirin, 0.3–0.6 gm every 4 hours as needed, is most commonly used. Other antipyretic analgesic drugs are listed below in the section on pain.

7. For reduction of very high fever (over 41.1° C [106° F]), see Heat Stroke.

Benzinger, M.: Tympanic thermometry in surgery and anesthesia. JAMA 209:1207–1211, 1969.

Molavi, A., & L. Weinstein: Persistent perplexing pyrexia: Some comments on etiology and diagnosis. M Clin North America 54:379–396, 1970.

Petersdorf, R.G.: Fever of unknown origin. Ann Int Med 70:64–66, 1969.

Roe, C.F.: Surgical aspects of fever. Curr Prob Surg 1–43, Nov 1968.

Tumulty, P.A.: Topics in clinical medicine: The patient with fever of undetermined origin. A diagnostic challenge. Bull Johns Hopkins Hosp 120:95–106, 1967.

SHOCK
(Circulatory Failure or Collapse)

"Shock" is a complex and incompletely understood syndrome which defies precise definition. It is practical, however, to consider shock as a disturbance of circulation resulting in ineffective perfusion or critical reduction of perfusion of vital tissues and a wide range of systemic effects. The term is descriptive of a pattern of signs and symptoms which usually includes systemic arterial hypotension, ashen pallor, cold and moist skin, collapse of superficial veins of the extremities, rapid and weak pulse, air hunger, thirst, oliguria, and a tendency to steadily progress toward a so-called "irreversible" phase.

Numerous pathophysiologic mechanisms are involved in the production of shock, such as lack of effective blood volume, reduction of cardiac output, altered peripheral vascular tone, increased capillary permeability, decreased urine output, acidosis, elevated blood lactate, and other alterations of the physicochemical characteristics of the blood. Little is known regarding the actual mechanisms leading to "irreversible" shock. Factors which unfavorably influence the prognosis in shock states include coma, acidosis (pH < 7.30), sepsis, anuria, heart disease, hepatic disease, and advanced age (> 70 years).

In so-called "warm shock" there is a normal blood volume, yet massive dilatation increases the capacity of the circulation. This may be caused by endotoxin from gram-negative bacterial infections, emotional stress, trauma, and certain drugs.

Shock is not a single clinical entity. Because widely different etiologic factors and multiple pathophysiologic mechanisms may result in systemic arterial hypotension, and because there is great confusion in defining the term "shock," there is serious question concerning the desirability of retaining a catch-all term which has such variable diagnostic and therapeutic meanings.

Classification

The shock syndromes may be arbitrarily classified clinically according to etiology and pathophysiology as follows:

A. Neurogenic Shock (Psychogenic Shock; Fainting, Syncope): This form of shock is usually vasovagal and caused by neurogenic or psychogenic factors, eg, spinal cord injury, pain, trauma, fright, unpleasant sights, sounds, or odors, or vasodilator drugs. Debility, asthenia, emotional instability, prolonged standing, excessive heat, alcohol, hypotensive drugs, and disorders of the autonomic nervous system predispose to neurogenic shock. The sudden autonomic overactivity results in vasodilatation or inhibition of constriction of the arterioles and rapid peripheral and splanchnic pooling of blood. Following a period of anxiety and signs of epinephrine release (tachycardia, tremors, and pallor), there is a sudden reflex vagal stimulation with decreased cardiac output, hypotension, and decreased cerebral blood flow. In the absence of spinal cord injury, the patient usually revives promptly in the recumbent position or following the administration of simple forms of treatment (eg, spirits of ammonia, physical stimuli), but observation is necessary to prevent recurrence and possible progression. Ephedrine sulfate, 15—30 mg subcut, may be required. If there is spinal cord injury, vasopressor drugs and other antishock measures are required. (See Chapter 16 for a discussion of the various types of syncope.) If the condition persists, consider other and more significant underlying causes of shock.

B. Hypovolemic Shock (Oligemic, Hemorrhagic, Traumatic, or Surgical Shock): In this form of shock there is a true diminution of blood volume due to loss of whole blood or plasma from the circulation. Compensatory vasoconstriction reduces the size of the vascular bed and may temporarily maintain the blood pressure, but if fluid is not replaced immediately hypotension occurs and the tissues become progressively more anoxic. Since the vascular space is the smallest of the body fluid compartments, even a moderate sudden loss of circulating fluids can result in severe and sometimes irreversible damage to vital centers. Rapid loss of 50% of blood volume is usually fatal.

Hypovolemic shock may result from (1) loss of whole blood by hemorrhage due to external or internal injuries, (2) loss of whole blood through nontraumatic internal hemorrhage (eg, bleeding peptic ulcer, ruptured varices), (3) loss of blood and plasma in extensive fractures and crushing injuries, (4) loss of plasma and hemolysis of red cells in extensive burns, (5) loss of plasma into serous body cavities (eg, peritonitis), (6) loss of plasma due to nephrotic syndrome, or (7) dehydration with electrolyte imbalance.

Debility, malnutrition, senility, hypotensive drugs (eg, coronary vasodilators), local anesthetics, general anesthetics, and adrenocortical insufficiency all predispose to hypovolemic shock.

The classical signs of pallor, coldness, cyanosis, sweating, tachycardia, and arterial hypotension may appear suddenly and often represent fully-developed shock. Since advanced shock is often refractory to even the most vigorous antishock therapy, early recognition or anticipation of shock is imperative.

C. Shock Due to Infection (Septic, Endotoxic, or Exotoxic Shock): The peripheral vascular collapse which follows the toxemia of overwhelming infection is characterized by an initial vasoconstriction followed by (or alternating with) vasodilatation, with venous pooling of blood. There is often a direct toxic action on the heart and adrenals. The mortality rate is high (40—80%). Septic shock is most commonly caused by infection due to gram-negative organisms (*Escherichia coli,* klebsiella, proteus, pseudomonas, meningococci) and less frequently by pneumococci, staphylococci, and clostridia. Septic shock occurs more often in the very young and the very old. Frequent predisposing factors include diabetes, hematologic malignancies, diseases of the genitourinary, hepatobiliary, and intestinal tracts, and corticosteroid, immunosuppressive, or radi-

ation therapy. Immediate precipitating factors may be urinary, biliary, or gynecologic manipulations. Septic shock may be obscured by ineffective antibiotic therapy.

Septic shock should always be suspected when a febrile patient has chills associated with hypotension. Early, the skin may be warm and the pulse full. Hyperventilation may occur and result in respiratory alkalosis. The sensorium and urinary output are often initially normal. The classic signs of shock are manifest later. The symptoms and signs of the inciting infection are not invariably present.

Early leukopenia followed by leukocytosis often occurs in gram-negative sepsis. The infecting organisms may often be isolated (eg, from blood, urine, genital tract).

D. Cardiogenic Shock: Shock due to ineffective circulation associated with inadequate cardiac output may occur in myocardial infarction, severe tachycardia, serious cardiac arrhythmias, pulmonary embolism, cardiac tamponade, terminal congestive failure, or as a complication of other forms of severe shock. Shock associated with myocardial infarction or other serious cardiac disease carries a very high mortality rate.

E. Metabolic Shock: Metabolic disorders which cause significant alteration in fluids and electrolytes (eg, diabetic acidosis, hypoadrenalcorticalism, uremia) may predispose to or result in shock.

F. Allergic Shock: See Anaphylactic Reactions, below.

Treatment

It is of vital importance to determine the specific cause or causes, contributing factors (eg, age, prior physical status, complications), severity, and duration of shock. Prompt, calculated, and decisive action is essential. Prevention or early recognition of shock is simpler and considerably more effective than the treatment of established shock.

A. General Measures:

1. Position—Place patient in the "shock position" (recumbent with head lower than the rest of the body) unless there is head injury. Some clinicians feel that simple elevation of the legs is more desirable since it is less apt to interfere with cerebral blood flow.

2. Airway—Maintain an adequate airway. Pull out the tongue; remove dental plates from the mouth, and blood, mucus, and foreign bodies from the nose and mouth. Ensure adequate ventilation by mouth-to-mouth breathing if necessary. If arterial P_{O_2} is below normal or if dyspnea or cyanosis is present, administer oxygen, 8—10 liters/minute, by nasal catheter or mask.

3. Temperature—Keep the patient comfortably warm. Avoid chilling (to prevent heat loss), and excessive externally applied heat, which will further dilate the peripheral vessels.

4. Analgesics—Control pain (particularly if severe) promptly by the use of appropriate first aid measures and analgesic drugs. Give morphine sulfate, 10—30 mg subcut for pain, but remember that subcutaneous absorption is poor in patients in shock. In case of severe pain, morphine sulfate, 10–15 mg IV, may be used to greatest advantage. ***Caution:*** Do not give morphine to unconscious patients, patients who have head injuries, those with respiratory depression, or those without pain.

Avoid overdosage with morphine; substitute barbiturates and salicylates for sedation and analgesia whenever possible.

5. Allay apprehension by reassuring word and action. Oral or parenteral sedatives may be necessary.

6. Laboratory studies—Determine blood hemoglobin, hematocrit, and red cell count immediately for base-line and follow-up values. Laboratory studies for rapid serial determination of serum electrolytes, pH, P_{O_2}, and P_{CO_2} may be invaluable. Blood lactate and pyruvate determinations may be indicated. Blood volume studies when performed by persons skilled in the technic are very useful.

7. Urine flow—Insert an indwelling catheter to monitor urine flow (which should be kept above 50 ml/hour). Urine flow less than 20 ml/hour indicates inadequate renal circulation which, if not corrected, can cause renal tubular necrosis.

8. Central venous pressure—Monitor central venous pressure continuously in all shock patients. Central venous pressure determination is a simple and relatively reliable measure of adequacy of vascular volume and of the pumping action of the heart. A catheter is inserted percutaneously (or by cutdown) through the antecubital or external jugular vein near or into the right atrium and is connected to a manometer. Normal values range from 5–8 cm of water. A low central venous pressure is suggestive of low blood volume and need for fluid replacement, whereas a high central venous pressure (above 15–17 cm) suggests either insufficient cardiac output or fluid overload. The central venous pressure may be normal in left ventricular failure due to myocardial infarction and neurogenic shock. Central venous pressure changes in response to appropriate, cautious administration of intravenous fluids may increase the value of central venous pressure as an indicator of blood volume and cardiac efficiency.

9. Parenteral fluid therapy—*Replace and maintain adequate blood volume.* Initial or emergency needs may be determined by the history, general appearance, vital signs and other physical findings, hemoglobin, and hematocrit, although these are not reliable guides for volume replacement. Under ordinary clinical conditions, determination of effective blood volume may be difficult and is subject to considerable variation. There is no simple technic or rule by which to accurately judge the fluid requirements. Continuous central venous pressure monitoring (normal: 5–8 cm of water) and blood volume determinations, when performed by persons skilled in the technics, may be useful for the evaluation of shock and as a guide to safe fluid replacement. Response to therapy is a valuable index. Selection of the replacement fluid which is most appropriate for the individual case is based upon consideration of what type of fluid has been lost (whole blood, plasma, water and electrolytes), the availability of the various solutions, laboratory facilities, and, to a lesser extent, expense. Whole blood is usually the most effective replacement fluid, especially if the hematocrit is < 35%, but other readily available parenteral fluids should be given immediately pending preliminary laboratory work and the procurement of whole blood. If the central venous pressure is low and the hematocrit is > 35%, replace blood volume with plasma or plasma expanders.

(1) Saline or dextrose solutions—Give immediately 500–2000 ml of sodium chloride injection (physiologic saline), lactated Ringer's injection, 5–10% dextrose injection, or 5% dextrose in saline rapidly intravenously while making preparations for plasma expanders, plasma, serum albumin, or whole blood. The latter exert a more sustained increase in blood volume through their colloidal osmotic pressure effects than do dextrose or electrolyte solutions. Saline should be used cautiously if the patient is known to have cardiac failure.

(2) Whole blood—Whole blood may sometimes be of value in the treatment of severe or refractory shock even in the face of an apparently good hematocrit figure; this is because of the misleading effect of hemoconcentration. (a) For **impending shock**, administer 250–500 ml of blood immediately and follow closely clinically and with hematocrit and blood volume studies to determine need for further plasma. (b) For **early or advanced shock**, administer 500 ml whole blood immediately and repeat with 500 ml every half hour up to a total of 2 liters or more, depending upon the presence of continued hemorrhage, clinical course, and hematocrit and blood volume findings. If overloading is feared, determine central venous pressure before and after the administration of each unit of blood. If shock persists, the prognosis is very poor.

(3) Plasma or serum albumin—Any of the various plasma preparations, such as lyophilized or reconstituted plasma, may be employed. Plasma is usually readily procurable, may be rapidly set up for administration, and does not require preliminary blood typing. The quantity of plasma to be given depends upon the stage of shock and the response to therapy, based upon both clinical and laboratory studies.

(4) Dextrans—Dextrans are fairly effective plasma "substitutes" for the emergency treatment of shock, but they cannot replace treatment with whole blood (or its derivatives) when the latter is necessary. These water-soluble biosynthetic polysaccharides have high molecular weights, high oncotic pressures, and the necessary viscosity, but they have not proved to be as useful as plasma and their use is not without hazard. They have the advantages of ready availability, of compatibility with other preparations used in intravenous solutions, and of not causing infectious hepatitis.

Dextran 40 (Rheomacrodex®), a low molecular weight dextran, is available as a 10% solution in either isotonic saline or 5% dextrose in water for intravenous use. It decreases blood viscosity and appears to improve the microcirculation. Rapid initial infusion of approximately 100–150 ml within the first hour is followed by slow maintenance for a total of 10–15 ml/kg/24 hours (preferably less than 1 liter/day).

Use dextrans cautiously in patients with cardiac disease, renal insufficiency, or marked dehydration to avoid pulmonary edema, congestive heart failure, or renal shutdown. Observe for possible anaphylactoid reactions. Prolongations of bleeding time have been reported. Use with caution in thrombocytopenic patients. Obtain blood for typing and cross-matching before dextran therapy since dextran may interfere with these tests.

10. Vasopressor drugs—Because of their remarkable ability to raise the blood pressure, several of the adrenergic drugs (sympathomimetic amines) have been used extensively, on a largely empiric basis, for the treatment of all types of shock. It is now known that in many instances it is doubtful whether the blood pressure elevation produced by the vasopressor drugs has a beneficial effect on the underlying disturbances, and there is good evidence to show that where these drugs are used unwisely the effect may be detrimental. Their routine use in all cases of shock is to be deplored.

So-called "pure" alpha-adrenergic receptor stimulating drugs (eg, phenylephrine, methoxamine) produce an increase in blood pressure due to marked vasoconstriction. However, they have little or no direct (inotropic) action on the heart; they decrease the cardiac output and visceral blood flow; and they increase the central venous pressure. On the other hand, the purely beta-adrenergic drugs (eg, isoproterenol) do not cause a marked increase in blood pressure but do increase myocardial contractility, cardiac output, and visceral blood flow and decrease central venous pressure. Most of the other sympathomimetic drugs have mixed alpha- and beta-mimetic effects which vary not only with the drugs but also with dosage, interaction with other drugs, and with the status of the patient. Although the alpha- and beta-mimetic effects of the various adrenergic drugs cannot always be sharply delineated, certain of the known pharmacologic effects of currently available agents can nevertheless be utilized for more selective therapy of shock.

Vasopressor drugs are most effective in hypotensive shock without associated decrease in blood volume (eg, spinal anesthesia or overwhelming systemic intoxication) although they may be of at least transient value in severe shock due to any cause. They may be utilized (with questionable value) for their cardiotonic effect in the shock associated with myocardial infarction or to increase the cardiac output which may occur in certain forms of shock. They should be considered as interval supportive therapy as a temporary expedient to protect vital areas of the body until fluid volume restoration and other antishock measures can be instituted and the patient is able to mobilize his own compensatory mechanisms.

Disadvantages of the vasopressor drugs include cardiac arrhythmias, peripheral vasoconstriction, increased tissue metabolism, and the uncertainty of perfusion of vital body tissues as well as other possible unknown deleterious effects. There is considerable experimental and clinical evidence that vasopressors have a deleterious effect in endotoxin shock. Careful monitoring of the patient including vital signs, mentation, skin color and temperature, central venous pressure, and urine flow are required. When vasopressors which have a cardiotonic action (beta-adrenergic effect) are employed, continuous cardiac monitoring is advisable.

Actually, there is experimental evidence that in advanced shock it is more physiologic to use vasodilator drugs such as adrenergic blocking agents (eg, phenoxybenzamine [Dibenzyline®], chlorpromazine [Thorazine®]) or hydrocortisone in order to provide maximum blood flow to vital tissues rather than simply maintain blood pressure. The beneficial effects of hydrocortisone are also related to improved cardiac efficiency and, in the case of septic shock, decreased sensitivity to endotoxin (see below). The use of adrenergic blocking vasodilators, however, is still undergoing evaluation, and they should be employed discreetly.

The principal vasopressor drugs used for shock are the following:

(1) Levarterenol bitartrate (norepinephrine, Levophed®), is a mixed alpha- and beta-mimetic agent, a powerful vasopressor, and a cardiotonic (inotropic) drug. Give 4–16 mg (4–16 ml of 0.2% solution) in 1 liter of dextrose in water IV. Avoid extravasation (may cause tissue necrosis and gangrene). Constant supervision with regular determination of blood pressure is essential. With concentrations greater than 4 mg/liter, an inlying polyethylene catheter is required.

(2) Mephentermine sulfate injection (Wyamine®) is primarily a cardiotonic drug, due to its predominantly beta-adrenergic effects. Give 5–20 mg at a rate of 1 mg/minute by continuous IV infusion of 0.1% solution in 5% dextrose in water; or 15–20 mg IM.

(3) Metaraminol bitartrate (Aramine®) is both an alpha- and a beta-mimetic agent with cardiotonic as well as vasopressor effects. Give 2–10 mg IM, or 0.5–5 mg cautiously IV, or 15–100 mg by slow infusion in 250–500 ml of 5% dextrose solution IV.

(4) Phenylephrine hydrochloride (Neo-Synephrine®), is an alpha-adrenergic stimulator which acts as a vasopressor without appreciable cardiotonic effect. Give 0.25–1 mg IV, or 5 mg IM, or by slow IV infusion of 100–150 mg/liter of 5% dextrose solution.

(5) Isoproterenol (Isuprel®), a beta-adrenergic stimulator, increases cardiac output by its action on the myocardial contraction mechanism and produces peripheral vasodilatation. Give 1–2 mg in 500 ml 5% dextrose in water IV. Because of its inotropic effect, an increased incidence of cardiac arrhythmias precludes its use if the cardiac rate is greater than 120/minute.

11. Diuretics—The cautious early administration of mannitol, an inert 6-carbon polyalcohol, as a 10–25% solution in 500–1000 ml of normal saline or Ringer's injection, has been recommended in selected patients after treatment with vasoactive compounds, in whom oliguria is present or anticipated. Furosemide (Lasix®), 200 mg IV, has also been recommended for this purpose. Urine flow and central venous pressure must be carefully monitored. The effectiveness of these agents in shock is still being studied, but it is felt that acute tubular necrosis may be prevented by preventing oliguria.

B. Specific Measures:

1. Hemorrhage and anemia—Although plasma is usually given as an emergency measure in shock complicating hemorrhage, acute anemia must be corrected by replacement with whole blood to prevent hypoxia. It is the hemorrhage, not the blood pressure, which requires treatment. The quantity of whole blood to be given will depend upon clinical response, hematocrit, and, when available, blood volume studies.

2. Anoxia (or hypoxia)—Oxygen may be indicated for hypoxia due to disorders such as cardiac failure and pneumonia. However, the patient in impending shock is apprehensive, and the mask or tent may increase his apprehension. The value of hyperbaric oxygen therapy is still under investigation.

3. Dehydration—Administer 500–2000 ml of sodium chloride injection or 5% dextrose injection IV as needed. As soon as the patient can swallow, give fluids by mouth.

4. Acid-base balance—Abnormalities of electrolyte and acid-base balance should be corrected. If acidosis is evidenced by an arterial blood pH of less than 7.35, give sodium bicarbonate, 40–100 mEq IV initially, and gauge further therapy by serial arterial pH determinations.

5. Adrenocortical failure—Adrenocortical steroid therapy has been found to be effective in shock-like states associated with serious medical emergencies. Although steroid treatment is most specifically applicable to shock of Addison's crisis, it may also be of spectacular value in certain acute allergic emergencies. Corticosteroids are usually less effective but may be employed in treating septic shock and overwhelming intoxications. Give hydrocortisone sodium succinate (Solu-Cortef®) (or equivalent), 100–300 mg as a 5% solution in sterile water or isotonic saline solution, rapidly IV. Subsequent doses of 50 mg may be given as required. Doses of 500–1000 mg daily for 3–5 days may be necessary.

6. Cardiac disorders—Digitalis is indicated only for those patients with pre-existing or presenting evidence of cardiac failure, increased central venous pressure, digitalis responsive arrhythmias, and, controversially, in myocardial infarction. Digitalis is of no value in shock due to other causes. Atropine may be of value in treating the bradycardias, predisposing to cardiogenic shock. Parenteral fluid for volume expansion may be necessary but should be used cautiously (especially sodium-containing solutions). Phlebotomy is sometimes useful in case of cardiac failure. The use of vasopressor drugs in myocardial infarction is controversial; if there is evidence of clinical shock (not merely mild hypotension), many physicians feel that mortality can be reduced by maintaining the blood pressure at levels of approximately 85 mm Hg (no more than 100 mm Hg). Continuous cardiac monitoring is highly desirable (especially when using beta-mimetic adrenergic drugs).

7. Infection—Immediate measures should be taken to combat infection, if present. Early recognition of incipient shock is critical. The mortality rate in gram-negative shock remains at about 50% despite advances in treatment. Initiate bacteriologic studies immediately and before therapy, if possible. If there are any indications of shock, institute preliminary broad-spectrum antibiotic therapy until bacteriologic studies reveal the identity of the organism. "Prophylactic" antibiotics, when there is no evidence of infection, are of doubtful value and may even be harmful, except when the hazard of infection is great (eg, extensive burns).

a. Antimicrobial therapy—Give any of the following: Kanamycin (Kantrex®), 0.5 gm every 6–12 hours IM (15 mg/kg/day); streptomycin, 0.5 gm every 6 hours IM; and chloramphenicol, 0.5 gm every 6 hours IM; or colistin, penicillin (up to 24–40 million units of penicillin IV have been used), ampicillin, gentamicin, or cephalothin in appropriate doses depending upon the nature of the infecting organism and antibiotic sensitivity tests.

b. Special supportive measures—In addition to general measures for the treatment of various forms of shock, certain measures may be of special value in septic shock: (1) If the initial central venous pressure is high or if shock persists after central venous pressure becomes normal, administer isoproterenol (Isuprel®), 2.5 mg in 5% dextrose in water, at a rate of 0.5–1 ml/minute. If shock persists after 15 minutes, urine output remains less than 30 ml/minute, or central venous pressure is elevated, double the infusion rate. Monitor cardiac rhythm and other vital signs. (2) In peripheral vascular failure (low central venous pressure and blood pressure after apparently adequate fluid replacement), give hydrocortisone, 0.5–1 gm every 4–6 hours IV for 24–48 hours. (3) Heparinization should be considered if intravascular clotting is present.

C. Evaluation of Therapy: Constant observation of the patient is imperative. The pulse, respiration, temperature (rectal), and blood pressure should be taken immediately and every 15–30 minutes or oftener thereafter until peripheral circulation has definitely improved.

1. Rapid recovery—If clinical appearance and vital signs return rapidly to normal, keep the patient under close observation but withhold further antishock therapy. Check vital signs every half hour. Determine hematocrit if there is any suspicion whatever that shock persists. Remember that hemoconcentration usually precedes blood pressure and pulse changes. After eliminating potential or existing shock-producing factors, the patient may be managed expectantly until it is reasonably certain that the danger has passed.

2. Delayed recovery—If the vital signs remain abnormal for even a brief period after initial measures have been taken, or if there is evidence of progression of peripheral circulatory failure, institute further vigorous antishock therapy as soon as possible. Blood hemoglobin, red blood count, hematocrit, central venous pressure, blood volume, and urine output should be determined as often as necessary to evaluate the results of therapy.

Cherry, J.W.: Endotoxin shock. S Clin North America 50:403–408, 1970.

Christy, J.H.: Treatment of gram-negative shock. Am J Med 50:77–88, 1971.

Hardaway, R.M., III: Clinical management of shock. Cincinnati J Med 52:45–53, 1971.

Hill, G.J., II: Central venous pressure technique. S Clin North America 49:1351–1359, 1969.

Jacobson, E.D., & G.F. Brobmann: The "adrenergic theory" of shock revisited. Med Counterpoint 2(15):23–26, 1970.

Lefer, A.M., & others: Mechanism of the lack of a beneficial response to inotropic drugs in hemorrhagic shock. Clin Pharmacol Therap 12:506–516, 1971.

Lefer, A.M., & R.L. Verrier: Role of corticosteroids in the treatment of circulatory collapse states. Clin Pharmacol Therap 11:630–655, 1970.

Mannitol: An osmotic diuretic. Med Lett Drugs Ther 10:5–6, 1968.

Mills, L.C., & J.H. Moyers (editors): *Hahnemann Symposium. Shock and Hypotension: Pathogenesis and Treatment.* Grune & Stratton, 1966.

Perloth, M.G., & D.C. Harrison: Cardiogenic shock: A review. Clin Pharmacol Therap 10:449–467, 1969.

Prout, W.G.: Relative value of central venous pressure monitoring and blood volume measurement in the management of shock. Lancet 1:1108–1112, 1968.

Thal, A.P., & others: *Shock: A Physiologic Basis for Treatment.* Year Book, 1971.

Weil, M.H., & H. Shubin: *The Diagnosis and Treatment of Shock.* Williams & Wilkins, 1967.

Wilson, R.F., & R. Krome: Factors affecting prognosis in clinical shock. Ann Surg 169:93–101, 1969.

PAIN

Pain is a very important symptom, not only because it is often the primary complaint for which the patient seeks relief but also because it provides the clinician with critical diagnostic information. In taking a history from the patient with pain, there should be a careful elicitation of characteristics such as chronology, nature, location, radiation, and aggravating and alleviating factors which influence the pain.

The reaction to pain, a function of the higher centers, is extremely variable and influenced by many factors depending upon the individual patient and the situation. It is important to determine, whenever possible, the primary etiology (eg, infection, toxins) and the pathogenesis (eg, inflammation, ulceration, distention, anoxia, spasm) of pain.

The relief of pain is achieved by removal of the primary cause (eg, cure of infection), neutralization of the effect of the stimulus (eg, antacids for hyperacidity of peptic ulcer), and, when these are not feasible, by dulling or obliteration of the sense of pain (eg, palliative narcotics for terminal cancer).

The hazards of administering analgesics without first attempting to establish a diagnosis cannot be over-emphasized (eg, acute abdominal pain). Analgesics, particularly narcotics, may mask the symptoms of serious acute or chronic illness.

Pain may be treated nonspecifically with drugs, physical measures (eg, heat, cold, immobilization), or surgery (eg, nerve resection, chordotomy). Since pain occurs in different intensities, drugs of corresponding potencies should be used. Narcotic analgesics should be avoided unless nonnarcotic drugs (in adequate dosage) would be ineffective. When narcotics are required, the relatively less addictive drugs (eg, codeine) should be employed first. One should prescribe the lowest effective dosage of narcotics and discontinue as soon as possible.

Because psychic or emotional factors may greatly influence the pain threshold, it is important to consider the "placebo" role of all therapeutic measures for the control of pain. Pharmacologically inactive drugs may be surprisingly effective in alleviating the pain of organic as well as functional disorders. Reassurance and explanation are, therefore, important factors in relieving pain, with or without analgesic drugs.

Nonnarcotic Analgesics

A. Salicylates: The salicylate drugs are analgesic, antirheumatic, uricosuric, and antipyretic. They are useful in relieving myalgias, neuralgias, arthralgias, headaches, and dysmenorrhea. Untoward reactions are usually mild, consisting of dizziness and dyspepsia, but large doses may cause tinnitus, deafness, blurring of vision, nausea and vomiting, diarrhea, diaphoresis, headache, and delirium. In sensitive patients, salicylates may cause urticarias and acute laryngeal edema.

1. Aspirin, plain, buffered, or enteric-coated, 0.3 gm tablets. Ordinary dosage is 0.3–0.6 gm every 4 hours as needed; 0.3 gm every 2–3 hours is said to be more effective and to cause fewer untoward reactions. Aspirin may cause gastrointestinal irritation and bleeding; this may be reduced by administration of the drug on a full stomach or with ½–1 tsp of baking soda or other antacid. Buffered aspirin usually available contains only small amounts of antacid, and the incidence of side-effects and the blood levels achieved are not appreciably different than with ordinary aspirin. The enteric-coated preparation is slower acting, but it prevents gastric irritation and is also useful for those patients who might be skeptical of the analgesic value of "ordinary aspirin."

Aspirin ingestion increases the bleeding tendency in patients with a wide variety of bleeding problems (eg, anticoagulant therapy, von Willebrand's disease).

2. Sodium salicylate, enteric-coated, 0.3–0.6 gm every 4 hours as needed.

3. Aspirin compound (APC) contains aspirin, phenacetin, and caffeine. No advantage of this combination over ordinary aspirin has been demonstrated. The large amounts of phenacetin ingested by habitual users of this combination may possibly cause serious renal damage.

B. Phenacetin, 0.3 gm every 3–4 hours, may be employed in case of salicylate intolerance; in general, however, this drug is more toxic. Prolonged or excessive use is not advised. (See above.)

C. Acetaminophen (Tylenol®, Tempra®), 325–650 mg orally 3–4 times daily, has analgesic potency comparable to aspirin for many painful conditions. It is the substance into which phenacetin is rapidly converted. It is less effective than aspirin in rheumatoid arthritis and other inflammatory disorders. Its antipyretic action is comparable to that of aspirin. Acetaminophen may be especially useful as a mild analgesic and antipyretic in aspirin allergy. It apparently does not produce coagulation defects, nor does it cause gastric irritation and mucosal bleeding.

D. Colchicine: The "analgesic" properties of colchicine are probably due to its anti-inflammatory effects. It is used clinically almost exclusively for gouty arthritis, but it has also been reported to be effective in sarcoid arthritis.

E. Phenylbutazone (Butazolidin®) and its metabolite or parahydroxy analogue, **oxyphenbutazone (Tandearil®),** exert a potent "analgesic" effect in painful disorders associated with inflammatory diseases. Although useful in a variety of acute rheumatic conditions, they are most effective in the treatment of acute gouty arthritis and active rheumatoid spondylitis. Because of their relatively high potential for toxicity, they should be reserved for patients who do not respond to salicylates and other simple therapeutic measures. They should be used cautiously within the recommended dosage range, usually 300–400 mg/day, or less, in divided doses. Follow the manufacturer's directions carefully. If, after a trial period of 1 week, the drugs fail to produce a favorable response, therapy should be discontinued. Toxic reactions include skin rash, hypersensitivity reaction of the serum sickness type, nausea, vomiting, stomatitis, peptic ulceration, sodium retention, blood dyscrasias, and prothrombin depression (when the drugs are used concurrently with anticoagulants of the coumarin type). As a precaution, blood counts are recommended twice weekly for the first month, weekly for the second month, and monthly thereafter. In general, the drugs should not be used in patients with gastrointestinal, renal, cardiac, or hematopoietic disease or in those receiving anticoagulant therapy. They should not be given for prolonged periods, and all patients should be observed frequently for evidence of toxicity.

F. Propoxyphene (Darvon®), 30–65 mg orally, and **ethoheptazine (Zactane®),** 65–150 mg: Although related chemically to the narcotics, these drugs are less potent in all respects. A few cases of propoxyphene abuse have been reported. Side-effects are uncommon (dizziness, epigastric pain, nausea). The problem of addiction is minimal, but the claim that their analgesic potency is equal to that of codeine is questionable. Their principal use is in patients who are allergic to or who cannot tolerate aspirin or codeine.

G. Indomethacin (Indocin®): This analgesic and anti-inflammatory agent is said to be useful in the rheumatic disorders, although its advantages over aspirin, if any, remain controversial. It appears to be most effective in ankylosing spondylitis and in osteoarthritis of the hip. The usual dose is 25 mg 2–4 times daily, increasing the dosage, if tolerated, up to no more than 200 mg daily. Untoward effects include headache, dizziness, lightheadedness, tinnitus, psychiatric disturbances (including depression and psychosis), drug rash, stomatitis, anorexia, dyspepsia, nausea, vomiting, peptic ulceration, gastrointestinal bleeding, and diarrhea. Hematologic or hepatotoxic effects are relatively uncommon. Because of the above side-effects and toxicity, patients under treatment should be observed carefully for any evidence of toxicity. Indomethacin should not be used as a "routine" mild analgesic (eg, instead of aspirin).

H. Pentazocine (Talwin®): Pentazocine is a weak narcotic antagonist of the benzomorphan series which has both morphine-like and nalorphine-like characteristics. A dose of 30 mg subcut approaches the analgesic effectiveness of 10 mg of morphine sulfate, and produces similar side-effects except for a slightly higher incidence and severity of drowsiness and respiratory depression. Pentazocine will not suppress abstinence symptoms in morphine-dependent subjects. Side-effects are similar to those of the narcotic group. A dose of 50 mg orally is approximately equivalent to 60 mg of codeine in analgesic effect, with a slightly more rapid onset and a slightly shorter duration of action. Adverse effects are somewhat comparable to those of codeine. Pentazocine has recently been found to cause addiction and is subject to drug abuse. Future legislative control may be required. Caution should be exercised in administration of this drug to pregnant women and to children under 12 years of age.

Narcotic Analgesics

The narcotic analgesics alter the perception of pain by their effects on the CNS. They are indicated for the relief of pain which is too intense to be controlled with nonnarcotic drugs or when pain is of a type not relieved by the salicylates (eg, visceral pain).

The narcotics are also mildly sedative in small doses; larger doses produce sleep, stupor, and respiratory depression. They are addictive and should be used cautiously and with careful attention to federal and state laws. Except for codeine, they should not be used for chronic illnesses except when necessary for the control of otherwise intractable pain in terminal illness.

Addiction and withdrawal are discussed in Chapter 17.

The specific treatment of intoxication with these drugs is discussed in Chapter 28.

Note: Always use the least potent narcotic drug which will control the pain, eg, codeine is preferable to meperidine, and meperidine to morphine.

A. Morphine: This drug is the most valuable of the potent narcotics for general clinical use. It causes CNS depression which results in powerful analgesia associated with sedation, euphoria, and hypnosis; selective respiratory center depression, and dulling or abolition of the cough reflex. It increases intracranial pressure. Morphine is useful for relief of acute severe pain. It is also valuable in the treatment of severe cardiac dyspnea (eg, pulmonary edema or cardiac asthma of "left ventricular failure"). It is a commonly used and valuable preoperative drug. Morphine is contraindicated in morphine sensitivity, bronchial asthma, undiagnosed surgical abdominal disease, hepatic insufficiency, hypothyroidism, morphinism, head injury, Addison's disease, and whenever vomiting may be dangerous. Untoward reactions include hypnosis (may be undesirable), respiratory depression, nausea and vomiting, severe constipation, urticaria, and pruritus. The addiction tendency is great.

1. **Morphine sulfate**, 8–15 mg orally or subcut. In cases of severe agonizing pain, especially pain associated with impending neurogenic shock (eg, acute pancreatitis), it may be given slowly in 5 ml physiologic saline intravenously. It is probable that only increased duration of effect is gained by increasing the dose above 10 mg.

2. **Morphine adjuncts**—Belladonna alkaloids, such as atropine and scopolamine, in dosages of 0.3–0.6 mg (1/200–1/100 gr) subcut administered simultaneously with morphine, may reduce some of the untoward effects of morphine. The phenothiazine tranquilizers may enhance the sedative effect of morphine.

B. **Morphine Congeners:** A number of drugs equivalent to morphine but offering no advantages are available. Claims of fewer side-effects should be regarded with skepticism.

The following subcutaneous doses are equivalent to 10 mg of morphine: hydromorphone (Dilaudid®), 2 mg; levorphanol (Levo-Dromoran®), 2 mg; oxymorphone (Numorphan®), 1 mg; phenazocine (Prinadol®), 1 mg; piminodine (Alvodine®), 7.5 mg.

C. **Methadone:** Methadone, 5–10 mg subcut, provides analgesia similar to that achieved with morphine. It is only ½ as effective when given orally. The onset is slower and the effect is more prolonged. It has powerful addictive properties. The only situation in which methadone is preferred is in the authorized treatment of addiction; withdrawal symptoms are ameliorated if methadone is first substituted for heroin or whatever opiate the addict has been taking (see Chapter 17).

D. **Meperidine (Demerol®):** 75–150 mg orally or IM (not subcut) every 3–4 hours provides analgesia and causes less intense side-effects than morphine. It is also less addictive than morphine, but addiction to meperidine is nevertheless very common.

E. **Meperidine Congeners:** Alphaprodine (Nisentil®), 60 mg subcut, and anileridine (Leritine®), 50 mg subcut, are equivalent to meperidine, 100 mg, except that their duration of action is shorter.

F. **Oxycodone (Dihydrohydroxycodeinone):** Usually given in dosages of 3–5 mg, this drug is available only in combinations with other ingredients in analgesic and cough mixtures (Percodan®, etc). It is frequently misused because the name suggests a similarity to codeine. It is more potent and more addictive than codeine.

G. **Codeine:** Codeine is pharmacologically similar to morphine but is less potent. Codeine diminishes the cough reflex and decreases bowel motility (constipating). It is preferred to morphine for relief of moderate degrees of pain because it is much less habit-forming and causes fewer untoward reactions (urticaria, nausea and vomiting, pruritus, dermatitis, anaphylactoid reactions).

1. Codeine phosphate, 8–65 mg orally or subcut every 3–4 hours as needed. If 65 mg is ineffective, use stronger narcotics, since larger doses of codeine are attended by increasing side reactions without increasing analgesia.

2. Codeine in dosages ranging from 8–65 mg is often used in combination with aspirin or ASA compound to produce an additive analgesic effect. The dosage is 1 tablet orally 3–4 times daily as necessary. In such mixtures codeine is the active ingredient; the aspirin is added for convenience in prescribing.

Eade, N.R., & L. Lasagna: Comparison of acetophenetidin and acetaminophen. II. Subjective effects in healthy volunteers. J Pharmacol Exper Therap 155:301–310, 1967.

Eckenhoff, J.E. (editor): Symposium on pain and its clinical management. M Clin North America 52:1–228, 1968.

Eddy, N.B.: Codeine and its alternates for pain and cough relief. Ann Int Med 71:1209–1212, 1969.

Finneson, B.E.: *Diagnosis and Management of Pain Syndromes,* 2nd ed. Saunders, 1969.

Jasinski, D.R., & others: Effects of short- and long-term administration of pentazocine in man. Clin Pharmacol Therap 11:385–403, 1970.

Melmon, K.L., Rowland, M., & H. Morelli: The clinical pharmacology of salicylates. California Med 110:410–422, 1969.

Miller, R.R., Feingold, A., & J. Paxinos: Propoxyphene hydrochloride: A critical review. JAMA 213:996–1006, 1970.

Shelley, J.H.: Phenacetin, through the looking glass. Clin Pharmacol Therap 8:427–471, 1967.

Wang, R.I.H. (editor): Symposium on treatment of pain. Mod Treat 5:1061–1208, 1968.

Wang, R.I.H.: Potent analgesics. Mod Treat 5:1136–1153, 1968.

ALLERGIC DISORDERS

Allergic disorders may be manifested by generalized systemic reactions or by localized reactions in any organ system of the body. The reactions may be acute, subacute, or chronic, and may be caused by an endless variety of offending agents (antigens). Many of the obscure or so-called idiopathic disorders are considered to have a possible allergic origin.

Allergic Reactions in Otherwise Nonallergic ("Normal") Individuals

Development of sensitization through contact with the antigen is more or less apparent. These reactions occur in a large percentage of "normal" individuals without evident hereditary predisposition. The diagnosis may be readily confirmed by appropriate skin testing or therapeutic trial *(caution)*. Examples are serum sickness, drug anaphylaxis, dermatitis venenata, and tuberculous sensitization.

Coombs, R.R.A., & P.G.H. Gell: The classification of allergic reactions underlying disease. In: *Clinical Aspects of Immunology*. Gell, P.G.H., & R.R.A. Coombs (editors). Davis, 1963.

Rhyne, M.B.: Skin testing: Concepts and realities. P Clin North America 16:227–241, 1969.

Sheldon, J.M., Lovell, R., & K.P. Matthews: *A Manual of Clinical Allergy*, 2nd ed. Saunders, 1967.

Atopic Disorders

These "natural or spontaneous" allergies occur in about 10% of the population, often with a family history of the same or a similar disorder; the incidence of atopy appears to be increasing. Antigenic etiology is much more obscure than in the case of the "normal" allergies. Determination of the allergens is much more difficult since complete reliance cannot be placed upon clinical history, skin tests, or elimination diets. Eosinophilia is characteristic but not pathognomonic of atopic disorders. The atopic disorders include hay fever (allergic rhinitis), eczema, urticaria, angioneurotic edema, allergic purpura, allergic migraine, allergic asthma, and anaphylactic reactions.

Anaphylactic Reactions (Anaphylactic Shock)

Anaphylactic reactions are the immediate shock-like and frequently fatal reactions which occur within minutes after administration of foreign sera or drugs. Although there is occasionally no history of previous exposure to the foreign substance, these acute reactions undoubtedly represent induced hypersensitivity. Anaphylactic reactions may occur following the injection of sera, penicillin and other antibiotics, and practically all repeatedly administered parenteral diagnostic and therapeutic agents. Anaphylaxis may rarely occur following ingestion of food and orally administered foods and drugs. *Note:* For this reason alone, sensitizing drugs should not be administered indiscriminately by oral, topical, or parenteral routes. Emergency drugs should be available whenever injections are given.

Three syndromes of anaphylaxis may be recognized, based upon the most conspicuous presenting clinical features: (1) laryngeal edema, (2) bronchospasm, and (3) vascular collapse.

Symptoms of anaphylaxis include apprehension, paresthesias, generalized urticaria or edema, choking sensation, cyanosis; wheezing, cough, incontinence, shock, fever, dilatation of pupils, loss of consciousness, and convulsions; death may occur within 5–10 minutes.

A. Emergency Treatment:

1. Epinephrine solution, 1 ml of 1:1000 solution (1 mg) IM, repeated in 5–10 minutes and later as needed. If the patient does not respond immediately, give 0.1–0.4 ml of 1:1000 solution diluted in 10 ml saline *slowly* IV.

2. Place in shock position. Keep warm.

3. Maintain adequate airway. Emergency tracheostomy may be necessary.

4. Diphenhydramine hydrochloride (Benadryl®), aqueous, 5–20 mg IV, after epinephrine if necessary.

5. Hydrocortisone sodium succinate (Solu-Cortef®), 100–250 mg, or prednisolone hemisuccinate (Metacortelone®), 50–100 mg in water or saline IV over a period of 30 seconds, after epinephrine or diphenhydramine for prolonged reactions.

6. Positive pressure oxygen therapy (see Chapter 6).

7. Aminophylline injection, 250–500 mg in 10–20 ml of saline *slowly* IV, may be of value.

8. Vasopressor agents—If arterial hypotension is severe, vasopressor agents (eg, levarterenol, 4 mg in 1 liter dextrose in water) by infusion may be required.

B. Prevention:

1. Precautions—Be aware of the danger. Do not use potentially dangerous drugs unless there is a definite need. Avoid giving drugs to patients with a history of hay fever, asthma, or other allergic disorders unless necessary. Whenever possible, determine by inquiry whether the patient previously has been given the drug he is about to receive. If there is a report of any allergic reaction on prior administration, the hazard of giving the drug, *either orally or by injection,* must be carefully considered. Scratch or conjunctival tests with dilute solutions of the test substance and intradermal tests are unreliable and not without hazard.

One of the commoner forms of drug anaphylaxis reported is that due to penicillin. Avoidance of use of penicillin is the only sure method of avoiding allergic reactions. Semisynthetic penicillins and related compounds are, in varying degree, cross-allergenic with natural penicillins. The indirect basophil degranulation test and the penicilloyl-polylysine conjugate intradermal skin test may not be as sensitive tests for penicillin allergy as the patient's history of previous reactions. A negative history or a negative skin test does not always imply safety. Conversely, a history of "allergy" or a positive skin test does not necessarily establish intolerance. If penicillin must be given as a lifesaving measure to a patient reasonably suspected of having penicillin allergy, (1) the patient must be under close observation, (2) a semisynthetic penicillin offers some slight advantage over natural penicillin, and (3) provision must be made for emergency treatment of anaphylaxis.

Patients who are known to be sensitive to insect bites should avoid areas where such insects are apt to be present. Protective garments (eg, gloves, netting, full-length clothing) may be necessary. Sensitized patients should always carry an insect-sting first aid kit containing a pre-loaded syringe of epinephrine, 1:1000, ephedrine sulfate tablet (25 mg), antihistamine tablet, and a tourniquet, and should be familiar with its use.

2. Prior administration of antihistaminic drugs (for selected patients)—Reduction of frequency and severity of anaphylactic reactions by means of the anti-

histaminic drugs has been reported. The antihistamines, however, do not provide safety against anaphylaxis in certain hypersensitive individuals.

3. Corticotropin and corticosteroids—Cautious administration of corticotropin and corticosteroids before administration of drugs to which the individual may be sensitive has been suggested. Clinical experience is limited, uncertain, and at best difficult to evaluate.

4. Desensitization—See p 906.

Marks, M.B.: Stinging insects: Allergy implications. P Clin North America 16:177–191, 1969.

Stewart, G.T.: Penicillin allergy. Clin Pharmacol Therap 11:307–311, 1970.

Valentine, M.D.: The anaphylactic syndromes. M Clin North America 53:249–257, 1969.

"Serum Sickness"

"Serum sickness" is a systemic allergic reaction which occurs within 1–3 weeks after injection of any foreign serum (eg, tetanus or diphtheria antitoxin), and even more frequently as a result of administration of many widely prescribed drugs. It is characterized by malaise, fever, urticaria, patchy or generalized rash, lymphadenopathy, musculoskeletal aches and pains, nausea and vomiting, and abdominal pain. It is usually mild and lasts about 2–3 days. Serious neurologic complications occur very rarely. In previously sensitized individuals the reaction may be severe or even fatal, and the onset may occur immediately after the injection or after a latent period of several hours to a few days (anaphylaxis).

A. Prevention:

1. Diagnosis—Recognition of individual hypersensitivity is based upon a history of allergic diathesis or previous drug or serum reactions and warrants special preliminary testing for sensitivity and careful precautions in administering immunizing sera.

2. Testing for serum sensitivity—See p 906.

3. Desensitization—If there is any evidence of sensitivity by either the conjunctival or intradermal sensitivity testing technics, it is imperative that the patient be desensitized with graded doses of the serum to be employed (see p 906).

B. Treatment:

1. Mild reactions—Antihistamines (eg, tripelennamine [Pyribenzamine®] or diphenhydramine [Benadryl®]), 25–50 mg every 4 hours as needed, or salicylates as needed.

2. Moderate or prolonged reactions—Antihistamines, epinephrine, ephedrine, or the corticosteroids may be required.

3. Severe reactions—See Anaphylactic Reactions, above.

Terr, A.I., & J.D. Bentz: Skin sensitizing antibodies in serum sickness. J Allergy 36:433–445, 1965.

Drugs Used in Allergic Disorders

Many manifestations of allergic reactions are due to the liberation of histamine from storage sites in the body. The treatment of allergies may thus consist of administering drugs which (1) prevent the effects of histamine (antihistaminic drugs); (2) reverse the effects of histamine (epinephrine, ephedrine, and related sympathomimetic drugs); or (3) suppress the allergic inflammatory reaction (corticosteroids).

A. The Antihistamines: The antihistaminic drugs do not prevent the release of histamine caused by the antigen-antibody reaction but they do, to a limited extent, prevent the histamine from acting on blood vessels, bronchioles, and other end organs.

The antihistamines are most effective in urticaria, angioneurotic edema, hay fever, and serum sickness. They are less predictably useful in vasomotor rhinitis and contact dermatitis, and are least apt to be effective in atopic dermatitis.

The most common side-effect is sedation of the type produced by the tranquilizers; this effect may be useful, but is often regarded as unpleasant by the patient. All patients receiving antihistaminic drugs should be cautioned against driving motor vehicles or airplanes. Other side-effects are feelings of weakness, dizziness, various gastrointestinal complaints, atropine-like effects such as dry mouth or blurred vision, and photodermatosis. Larger doses cause excitement, ie, insomnia and tremulousness progressing to confusion and convulsions.

The antihistamines should not be used topically since they are not locally effective and are common sensitizers.

In a given patient the choice of preparation depends upon trial and error and a decision about whether sedation is desired or not.

Some commonly used antihistaminic drugs and their usual dosages are as follows:

1. Sedation infrequent—
   *Chlorpheniramine (Chlor-Trimeton®, Teldrin®), 4 mg 4 times daily.
   *Brompheniramine, parabromdylamine (Dimetane®), 4 mg 4 times daily.

2. Sedation often prominent—
   *Diphenhydramine (Benadryl®), 25–50 mg 4 times daily.
   *Tripelennamine (Pyribenzamine®), 25 mg 4 times daily.
   Pyrilamine (Neo-Antergan®; contained in many combinations and brands), 50 mg 4 times daily.
   *Promethazine (Phenergan®), 12.5–25 mg twice daily. Give twice daily only. About twice as expensive as others.
   Methapyrilene (Semikon®, Histadyl®, Thenylene®), 25–50 mg 4 times daily. (Used in proprietary "sleeping tablets.")
   Thonzylamine (Anahist®, Neohetramine®), 50–100 mg 4 times daily.

3. Other antihistamines (long-acting)—
   Triprolidine (Actidil®), 2.5 mg twice daily.
   Pyrrobutamine (Pyronil®), 15 mg twice daily.

---

*Parenteral preparation available.

B. Sympathomimetic Drugs: The sympathomimetic drugs have actions opposite to those of histamine. The antihistamines may prevent further histamine effects; the sympathomimetics can counteract changes that have already occurred. Therefore, in emergency situations epinephrine is the drug of choice (see Anaphylactic Reactions, above). In chronic situations, ephedrine is useful either by itself or to supplement the effects of the antihistamines. (For dosages and other information about ephedrine and epinephrine, see Bronchial Asthma.)

C. Anti-inflammatory Steroids: In some acute allergic reactions (eg, contact dermatitis), drug and serum reactions, and in chronic allergies in which the severity justifies the use of an agent with diverse and profound effects, corticosteroids are very effective. (For dosages and other information about these drugs, see Bronchial Asthma and the discussions in Chapters 3 and 18.)

Special Elimination Diets for Allergic Patients

Patients with allergies may be given a normal diet containing no foods suspected of causing allergic reactions. Such reactions are produced most frequently by wheat, eggs, and milk; less frequently by citrus fruits, nuts, chocolate, and fish. Other foods may infrequently cause reactions.

More specialized diets have been prepared by allergists and are used both diagnostically and therapeutically. Consult books on allergy for these diets.

Grayson, L.D., & H.M. Shair: Atopic dermatitis. III. The correct choice of antihistaminic agents. Ann Allergy 21:168–170, 1963.

Rowe, A.H.: *Elimination Diets and the Patient's Allergies: A Handbook of Allergy.* Lea & Febiger, 1941.

Rowe, A.H., & A.H. Rowe, Jr.: *Bronchial Asthma: Its Diagnosis and Treatment.* Thomas, 1963.

Thompson, T.S.: Urticaria and angioedema. Ann Int Med 69:361–380, 1968.

•   •   •

2...
Fluid & Electrolyte Disorders

Marcus A. Krupp

Normally, the body fluids have a specific chemical composition and are distributed in discrete anatomic compartments of relatively fixed volumes. Disease produces associated or independent abnormalities in the amounts, distribution, and solute concentrations of the body fluids. Correct diagnosis and treatment of fluid and electrolyte disorders depends upon an understanding of the chemical laws and physiologic processes which control volume, distribution, and composition. In addition, the pharmacologic or physiologic action of some components of body fluids must be considered.

TABLE 2–1. TBW (as percentage of body weight) in relation to age and sex.*

Age	Male	Female
10–18	59%	57%
18–40	61%	51%
40–60	55%	47%
Over 60	52%	46%

*Modified and reproduced, with permission, from Edelman & Liebman: Anatomy of body water and electrolytes. Am J Med 27:256, 1959.

BASIC CONSIDERATIONS

VOLUME & DISTRIBUTION OF BODY WATER

The volume of body water in an individual is quite constant with intake (food, water consumed, and water produced by combustion) balanced by output (respiratory water vapor, perspiration, urine). Body water content among individuals differs inversely with obesity. Since fat cells contain very little water and lean tissue is rich in water, it follows that bodies heavy with fat will contain a smaller ratio of water/body weight than lean bodies. Sex differences also exist because, after childhood, females usually have a higher ratio of fat/lean tissue. As humans age, they tend to lay down more fat. In the average well nourished population of the United States, total body water varies as shown in Table 2–1.

The distribution of water among the body fluid compartments is dependent upon the distribution and content of solute. The ability of membranes and cells to restrict movement of solute into and from capillaries, interstitial fluid, and cells results in compartmentalization of solute with resultant distribution of water by osmosis to sustain (1) equal osmolal concentrations of solute in compartments and (2) equal concentrations of water in compartments. Differences in composition of solute in various compartments exist, but osmolality (concentration in compartment water) is

equal on both sides of the membrane separating 2 compartments.

Solute concentration is expressed in terms of osmols. The term osmol refers to the relationship between molar concentration and osmotic activity of a substance in solution. The osmolarity of a substance in solution is calculated by multiplying the molar concentration by the number of particles per mol provided by ionization. Glucose in solution provides 1 particle per molecule; NaCl in solution—for all practical purposes—totally dissociates into Na^+ and Cl^-, yielding 2 particles per molecule. One mol of glucose in solution thus yields 1 osmol; 1 mol of NaCl, 2 osmols. As with electrolyte concentrations, the milliunit is more convenient. Osmols-per-kilogram-of-water is termed osmolal; osmols-per-liter-of-solution is termed osmolar. The normal osmolarity of body fluids is 285–293 mOsm/liter.

In all problems of altered osmolality, the alteration exists in all body compartments, and the excess or deficit of solute or of water must be calculated on the basis of total body water (TBW).

ELECTROLYTES

In clinical medicine, the measurement of concentrations of electrolyte in body fluids is expressed in milliequivalents per liter of the fluid. Salts in solution dissociate into ions with positive charges (cations) and with negative charges (anions). The numbers of positive and negative charges are equal, ie, a divalent cation (++) will be balanced by 2 monovalent anions or 1 divalent anion (- -).

One mol (gram-molecule) of a substance is the molecular weight of the substance expressed in grams. One mol of a substance contains 6.023×10^{23} molecules of that substance. If the substance can exist in ionized form, its combining capacity with a substance of opposite charge will be determined by its valence, ie, the number of charges per atom or molecule. One mol of a monovalent ion is defined as an equivalent. Thus, 1 mol of a divalent ion will yield 2 equivalents, or, to put it otherwise, 1 equivalent of a divalent ion will be provided by ½ mol of the substance. The term equivalent, therefore, is an expression of concentration in terms of electrical charge. The concentrations of ions in body fluids are small and better expressed in terms of 0.001 equivalents or milliequivalents per liter. Dissociation of some complex ions such as phosphate and protein varies with pH, thus precluding the assignment of a specific valence. (At pH 7.4, the normal pH of plasma, phosphate exists as a buffer mixture of $H_2PO_4^-$ and $HPO_4^=$ to yield an effective valence of 1.8.)

TABLE 2–3. Body water distribution in an average normal young adult male.*

	ml/kg† Body Weight	% of Total Body Water
Total extracellular fluid	270	45
Plasma	45	7.5
Interstitial fluid	120	20
Connective tissue and bone	90	15
Transcellular fluid	15	2.5
Total intracellular fluid	330	55
Total body water	600	100

*Modified from Edelman & Liebman: Anatomy of water and electrolytes. J Med 27:256, 1959.

†$\dfrac{ml/kg}{10}$ = %, eg, 45 ml/kg = 4.5% body weight.

TABLE 2–2. Molar and milliequivalent weights.

	Valence	Molar Weights (gm)	Milliequivalent Weights (mg)
Cations			
Na^+	1	23	23
K^+	1	39	39
Ca^{++}	2	40	20
Mg^{++}	2	24	12
Anions			
Cl^-	1	35.5	35.5
HCO_3^-	1	61	61
$H_2PO_4^-$ $HPO_4^=$	$\{ \begin{matrix} 1 \\ 2 \end{matrix} \}$	31 (as P)	
$SO_4^=$	2	96	48

BODY FLUID COMPARTMENTS

The principal fluid compartments include plasma and interstitial fluid, which comprise the extracellular fluid, and intracellular fluid. Body fluids also are distributed to dense connective tissue, bone, and "transcellular" spaces (gut lumen, CSF, intraocular fluid), but these are relatively inaccessible and usually do not enter into clinical situations involving body fluid abnormalities.

The clinical simplification of considering body water or fluid as intracellular (ICW) or extracellular (ECW) is justified by the fact that sodium salts constitute the bulk of osmotically active solute in ECW whereas potassium salts constitute the bulk of osmotically active solute in ICW. Furthermore, almost all other solutes present in body water can be considered to be either freely diffusible between ICW and ECW (such as urea) or osmotically inactive (such as ICW magnesium, which is largely bound to protein) and consequently

are not osmotically active in either compartment, ie, they do not produce an osmotic gradient because their osmolar concentration is equal in both compartments.

The composition of the body fluids differs among the compartments. Characteristics of the electrolyte concentrations within the compartments are shown in Table 2–4.

Interstitial fluids are not readily available for assay. Clinically, one relies on determinations on plasma or serum which will provide adequate information to assess water and electrolyte derangements in the light of the clinical situation.

PHYSIOLOGY OF WATER & ELECTROLYTE & TREATMENT OF ABNORMAL STATES

In keeping with the basic considerations reviewed above, it is useful to describe the role of body fluids in support of homeostasis in terms of 3 closely related factors: volume, concentration, and pharmacologic activity. The ensuing discussion will consider the following:

Water Volume

(1) Extracellular fluid: Plasma, interstitial fluid, transcellular fluid (CSF, intraluminal intestinal fluid, ocular fluid).

(2) Intracellular fluid.

Concentration

(1) Osmolality: Total solute concentration.

(2) Concentration of individual electrolytes.

TABLE 2—4. Concentrations of cations and anions present in plasma, interstitial water (ISW), and intracellular water (ICW).

| | Plasma, mEq/liter | | ISW, mEq/liter* | ICW, mEq/liter |
	Average	Range	Average	Average
Na$^+$	140	138—145	144	10
K$^+$	4	3.5—4.5	4	150
Ca^{++}	5	4.8—5.65	5	
Mg^{++}	2	1.8—2.3	2	38
Total	151		*	198
Cl$^-$	103	97—105	117	3
HCO$_3^-$	27	26—30	30	10
Protein$^-$	16	14—18		65
HPO$_4^=$	2	1.2—2.3	2.3	100
SO$_4^=$	1		1.1	20
Undetermined anions	2		2.3	
Total	151		*	198

*Concentrations derived by converting plasma concentrations to mEq/liter of serum water and applying Donnan factors of 0.95 for cations and 1.05 for anions.

Pharmacologic Activity

(1) Concentration of hydrogen ion (pH).

(2) Concentration of electrolytes which exert pharmacologic actions.

WATER VOLUME

"Volume" and "water" are substantially interchangeable in the context of this discussion. Volume of body water is maintained by a balance between intake and excretion. Water as such, in foods and as a product of combustion, is excreted by the kidneys, skin, and lungs. Electrolytes important in maintaining volume and distribution include the cations sodium for extracellular fluid and potassium and magnesium for intracellular fluid, and the anions chloride and bicarbonate for extracellular fluid and phosphate and protein for intracellular fluid.

Loss of water or excess of water results in corresponding change in volume in both extra- and intracellular compartments. Loss of sodium (with accompanying anion) or excess of sodium results in decrease or increase, respectively, of the volume of extracellular fluid, with water moving out of the extracellular compartment with sodium loss and into the extracellular compartment with sodium retention.

In response to changes in volume, appropriate servo or feedback mechanisms come into play. The principal elements in regulation are antidiuretic hormone for water, aldosterone and other corticosteroids for sodium (and potassium), vascular responses affecting glomerular filtration rate for water and sodium, and, perhaps, a natriuretic hormone ("third factor") originating in the kidney.

The average adult requires at least 800—1300 ml of water per day to cover obligatory water needs. A normal adult on an ordinary diet requires 500 ml of water for renal excretion of solute in a maximally concentrated urine plus an additional amount of water to replace that lost via the skin and respiratory tract.

Fluid losses most often include electrolyte as well as water. Sweat, gastrointestinal fluids, urine, and fluid escaping from wounds contain significant quantities of electrolyte. In order to ascertain deficits of water and electrolytes, one must consider the history, change in body weight, clinical state, and appropriate determinations in plasma of concentration of each of the electrolytes, osmolality, protein, and pH. Assessment of renal function is required before repair and maintenance requirements can be determined and prescribed. Fig 2—1 indicates the variation in water required to excrete different loads of solute. The capacity of the kidney to excrete a concentrated or a dilute urine sets the limits of water requirement.

1. WATER DEFICIT

Water deficit results in a decrease in volume of both extracellular and intracellular fluids with a corresponding increase in concentration of both extracellular and intracellular solute in these fluids. In the blood, the loss of body water is reflected in an increased plasma osmolality as concentrations of plasma electrolyte and protein rise. With decreased blood volume, renal blood flow is reduced and excretion of urea falls, resulting in an elevation of urea in body fluids. Antidiuretic hormone secretion is stimulated, providing some protection from water loss by the kidney.

Water deficit results from reduced intake or unusual losses. Reduced intake is likely when the patient is unconscious, disabled, unable to ingest water because of esophageal or pyloric obstruction, or receives inadequate fluids to meet maintenance and replacement needs. Fever or a hot environment increases loss

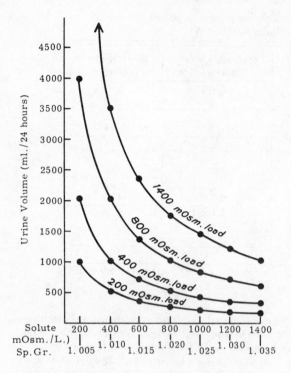

FIG 2–1. Total solute excretion and urine volume per given sp gr. (Redrawn and reproduced, with permission, from John H. Bland: *Clinical Recognition and Management of Disturbances of Body Fluids.* Saunders, 1956.)

from the lungs and skin. The kidney fails to conserve water when there is inadequate ADH (diabetes insipidus) or insensitivity to ADH (nephrogenic diabetes insipidus), osmotic diuresis in diabetes mellitus, inadequate tubule function due to renal disease, and impaired capacity to reabsorb water secondary to potassium depletion, hypercalcemia, correction of obstructive uropathy, or from intensive diuretic therapy.

Water deficit is characterized by thirst, flushed skin, acute weight loss, "dehydrated" appearance, dry mucous membranes, tachycardia, and oliguria. As dehydration increases, hallucinations and delirium, hyperpnea, and coma ensue.

Treatment

An essential guideline for treatment is acute change in weight, which is directly related to change in fluid volume.

Water may be provided with or without electrolyte. If water alone is needed, 2.5% dextrose solution may be given intravenously; the dextrose is oxidized to yield water.

In the presence of normal renal function, 2000–3000 ml of water per day (1500 ml/sq meter of body surface) will provide a liberal maintenance ration. If dehydration is present with increased serum sodium concentration and osmolality, extra water replacement can be estimated on the basis of restoring normal osmolality for the total body fluid volume. The need for intracellular water is reflected in the extracellular fluid

with which it is in osmotic equilibrium; therefore, any correction of deviation in osmolality must be considered on the basis of the total volume of body water.

The water requirement is increased in the presence of fever as a result of increased loss via the skin and lungs.

2. WATER EXCESS

Water excess (overhydration, dilution syndrome) results in expansion of the volume of body fluid and decreased concentration (dilution) of plasma electrolyte and protein, a reduced osmolality of plasma. Similar dilutions occur intracellularly. Normally, ADH secretion is inhibited, enabling the kidneys to excrete the excess water. Water excess results from intake in excess of capacity for excretion, usually from too large a water ration during parenteral administration; or from impaired excretory capacity resulting from acute or chronic renal insufficiency, renal functional changes (lowered glomerular filtration and increased water reabsorption) accompanying heart failure, liver disease with ascites, or administration of ADH or inappropriate secretion of "ADH-like" substance by neoplasms or in complex endocrine disturbances.

Water excess, particularly if severe or if it develops acutely, produces the syndrome of water intoxication, characterized by headache, nausea, vomiting, abdominal cramps, weakness, stupor, coma, and convulsions.

Treatment

The basic treatment consists of water restriction. If a real deficit of sodium exists as well, saline solutions should be employed. In the presence of severe water intoxication, administration of hypertonic saline solution may be useful to promote movement of excess intracellular water to the extracellular space, ie, to increase osmolarity and diminish intracellular water volume.

CONCENTRATION

The total concentration of solute (osmolarity) is apparently the same in intracellular and extracellular water. In the intracellular compartment, protein concentration plays a more important osmolar role than in the plasma. The protein content of interstitial fluid is small, and osmolar effects are therefore negligible. The most accessible and best index of osmolarity is the measurement of the solute concentration in the plasma by ascertaining the depression of the freezing point. An indirect and useful measurement is that of plasma sodium concentration, provided due attention is paid to hyperglycemia and high urea concentrations, which cause a significant increase in osmolality; and lipemia and hyperproteinemia, which provide a nonaqueous addition to plasma volume. In the latter situations, sodium concentration determinations yield low values which must be interpreted with consideration of the concentration of the other constituents, ie, in terms of plasma or serum water rather than of the plasma specimen per se.

1. HYPERNATREMIA

Increased concentration of sodium in extracellular fluid and hyperosmolality may result from water loss without equivalent sodium loss (pure water volume deficit) or from excessive sodium administration with inadequate water replacement. Hypernatremia may be due to inappropriate regulation of osmolality, occasionally present with intracranial tumors.

Hypernatremia is not an index of total body content of sodium. Increased total body sodium is usually due to retention of sodium with heart failure, cirrhosis of the liver, and nephrosis. In these states, sodium concentration in extracellular fluid is usually normal or low as a result of expansion of the total volume of body fluid.

Treatment

Treatment must be based on accurate appraisal of the significance of the alteration of the plasma sodium concentration. The clinical history and examination and corroborating laboratory data provide a guide for therapy. Hypernatremia due to water deficit is treated by replenishing water deficit (see above). If treatment with excessive quantities of sodium salts produces hypernatremia, withholding sodium may suffice. Natriuretic drugs (diuretics) may be employed to hasten excretion of the excess sodium; attention must be paid to replacement of water when diuretics are so employed.

2. HYPONATREMIA

A decreased concentration of sodium in extracellular fluid may result from loss of sodium or from dilution by retention of water. Sodium loss occurs with adrenocortical insufficiency, vigorous diuretic therapy, unusual losses of gastrointestinal secretions, renal insufficiency, and unusual sweating. When the deficit of water is replaced with inadequate sodium replacement, hyponatremia ensues. Retention of water

TABLE 2–5. Relationship of serum sodium to total body sodium in various clinical states.*

Serum Sodium	Total Body Sodium	Clinical States	Fluid and Electrolyte Therapy
Low (hyponatremia) < 130 mEq/liter	High	Edematous states (eg, nephrosis, cirrhosis, cardiac disease). May also occur after severe burns and in the immediate postoperative period.	Not indicated to raise serum sodium.
	Normal	Patients on low sodium intake retaining water as a metabolic response to trauma or surgery, particularly if given excess water (dilution syndrome; water intoxication). May also occur in cirrhotic patients after paracentesis.	**Mild:** Restrict fluids. **Severe:** Hypertonic (3–5%) sodium chloride solution may be needed.
	Low	Addison's disease; salt-wasting nephritis; gastrointestinal fluid and electrolyte losses; prolonged sweating with free access to water; perhaps in prolonged use of diuretic agents and on salt-free diets.	Isotonic sodium chloride solution.
Normal 135–145 mEq/liter	High	Renal, cardiac, or hepatic disease; also carcinoma involving pleural or peritoneal cavities. Caused by renal retention of water and salt in the same osmotic ratio.	
	Low	In the early stages of rapid salt depletion from gastrointestinal losses, renal excretion of a dilute urine preserves osmolarity of body fluids. A similar situation prevails in diabetic acidosis.	
High (hypernatremia) > 150 mEq/liter	High	Excess administration of sodium salts.	Water by mouth or dextrose and water intravenously. Withhold electrolytes.
	Normal	Simple dehydration due to deprivation of water; diabetes insipidus (congenital, or acquired, as in the diuretic phase of acute renal insufficiency or after cerebral trauma).	
	Low	Prolonged sweating without access to water.	Hypotonic sodium chloride solution.

*Reproduced, with permission, from Wilson & McDonald: *Handbook of Surgery,* 4th ed. Lange, 1969.

Chapter 2. Fluid & Electrolyte Disorders

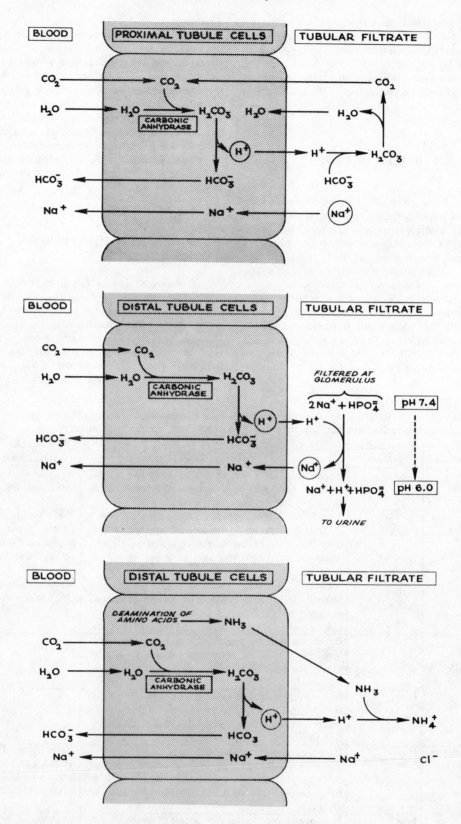

FIG 2–2. *Top:* Mobilization of hydrogen ions in proximal tubule. *Middle:* Secretion of hydrogen ions in distal tubule. *Bottom:* Production of ammonia in distal tubule.

occurs with the therapeutic use of ADH or with the secretion of excess antidiuretic substances by some types of carcinoma of the lung, with chronic severe heart failure, cirrhosis of the liver with ascites, and nephrotic syndrome. These states produce dilution syndromes characterized by hyponatremia (dilutional hyponatremia) and usually normal or high total body sodium.

Treatment

If there is a deficit of sodium, sodium chloride with or without sodium bicarbonate may be used for replacement. For replacement of moderate deficits, 0.9% sodium chloride (155 mEq of Na^+ and Cl^- per liter), or Ringer's solution with or without lactate, may be employed. For severe sodium deficit, 3% sodium chloride (513 mEq/liter) or 5% sodium chloride (855 mEq/liter) may be used with caution. More comprehensive texts on water and electrolyte metabolism must be consulted for specific information on treatment.

Hyponatremia due to dilution of electrolyte because of water retention should be treated by restriction of intake of water. In states associated with dilutional hyponatremia, total body sodium is elevated or normal and, therefore, sodium should not be administered.

The concentrations of other electrolytes in extracellular fluids have insignificant osmolar effects.

PHARMACOLOGIC ACTIVITY OF FLUIDS & ELECTROLYTES

HYDROGEN ION CONCENTRATION

The hydrogen ion concentration (H^+) of body fluids is closely regulated with intracellular concentrations of 10^{-7} molar (pH 7.0) and extracellular fluid concentrations of 4×10^{-8} molar (pH 7.4). In spite of accumulation or loss of H^+, these concentrations are maintained at nearly normal by buffer substances which remove or release H^+. The capacity of buffers is limited, however, and regulation is accomplished principally by the lungs and kidneys. The principal buffer substances include proteins, the oxyhemoglobin-reduced hemoglobin system, primary and secondary phosphate ions, some intracellular phosphate esters, and the carbonic acid-sodium bicarbonate system.

Most of the food used for energy is completely utilized, with production of water, CO_2, and urea. Sulfate and, to a limited extent, phosphate end-products are strong acid anions which must be "neutralized" by cation such as sodium. In the utilization of fat and carbohydrate, intermediate products include the strong acids acetoacetic acid and lactic acid. Buffers provide

cation and remove H^+, which is ultimately excreted by the kidneys as acid or as ammonium ion and by the lung as CO_2 and H_2O, equivalent to carbonic acid. The anions of strong acids with cation such as sodium and ammonium are eliminated by the kidney.

The role of the lung and kidney in removal of H^+ and in regulation of H^+ concentration can be viewed as,

$$\frac{[H^+] \quad [HCO_3^-] \rightleftharpoons P_{CO_2} \quad \text{lung}}{[HCO_3^-] \quad \quad \text{kidney}}$$

Respiratory control of the partial pressure of CO_2 (P_{CO_2}) in the pulmonary alveoli and therefore in the arterial plasma determines the H_2CO_3 concentration in body fluids:

$$CO_2 + H_2O \rightleftharpoons H_2CO_3$$

The elimination of CO_2 via the lung in effect removes carbonic acid. The kidney is responsible for $BHCO_3$ concentration in body fluids, which, with H_2CO_3, constitutes one of the buffer systems for regulation of pH.

The kidney tubule cells produce carbonic acid for metabolic CO_2 and water by the following reaction:

$$CO_2 + H_2O \underset{\boxed{\text{Carbonic anhydrase}}}{\rightleftharpoons} H_2CO_3$$

The carbonic acid serves as a source of H^+ which can be exchanged for Na^+ in the tubular urine so that H^+ is excreted and Na^+ reabsorbed. The exchange affects anions of weak acids: H^+ is excreted by the tubule cell into the tubular urine, and Na^+ is reabsorbed. The H^+ in the presence of HCO_3^- in the tubular urine forms H_2CO_3, which $\rightarrow H_2O$ and CO_2, which are reabsorbed. Similarly, H^+ is exchanged for 1 Na^+ of 2 $Na^+HPO_4^=$ to $\rightarrow Na^+H_2PO_4^=$. (See Fig 2-2.)

Although the pH of urine cannot be lowered below pH 4.5, additional H^+ ion can be excreted by combination with NH_3, generated principally from glutamine within the tubule cell. NH_3 diffuses from the tubule cell into the urine within the tubule where it combines with $H^+ \rightarrow NH_4^+$, providing cation for excretion with anions of strong acids with no increase in H^+ concentration (no lowering of pH). These exchanges in the renal tubule involve active transport systems capable of maintaining a gradient in concentration of extracellular fluid H^+ of 4×10^{-8} molar (pH 7.4) against a tubular urine H^+ of 32×10^{-6} molar (pH 4.5), an 800-fold increase in H^+ concentration. (See Fig 2-2.)

CLINICAL STATES OF ALTERED H⁺ CONCENTRATION

The clinical term acidosis signifies a decrease in pH (increase in H^+) of extracellular fluid; the term alkalosis signifies an increase in pH (decrease in H^+) of extracellular fluid. The change in H^+ concentration may be the result of metabolic or respiratory abnormalities.

1. RESPIRATORY ACIDOSIS

Respiratory acidosis follows ventilatory abnormalities resulting in CO_2 retention and elevation of P_{CO_2} in alveoli and arterial blood (hypercapnia). Inadequate ventilation during anesthesia, following suppression of the respiratory center by CNS disease or drugs or resulting from respiratory muscle weakness or paralysis, produces CO_2 retention. Anatomic changes in structure of the lung (emphysema) or pulmonary circulation and abnormal thoracic structure (kyphoscoliosis) may alter alveolar-capillary blood exchange or diminish effective ventilation to prevent CO_2 excretion. In association with impaired CO_2 excretion there may be impaired O_2 exchange with low alveolar and arterial P_{O_2} (hypoxia). In the presence of CO_2 retention and the resultant increase in H_2CO_3 concentration, compensatory reabsorption of HCO_3^- by the kidney provides buffer to reduce H^+ concentration, but this protection cannot be accomplished rapidly and is effectively available only in chronic situations that develop slowly.

The hazard of acute hypercapnia cannot be overemphasized. Buffer protection is severely limited, and renal response is very slow. Thus, an increase in P_{CO_2} can quickly produce sharp increases in H^+ concentration (decrease in pH) to levels incompatible with life. Respiratory inadequacy resulting in sudden increase in P_{CO_2} will usually result in a severe decrease in P_{O_2}, compounding the threat to life. It is apparent that periods of hypoventilation constitute a serious and often lethal complication in the immediate postoperative state, in thoracic surgery, in severe illness or shock accompanied by obtunded consciousness, in trauma to the CNS, and in the presence of heart failure, cardiac arrhythmias, and myocardial infarction.

Treatment
Treatment is directed toward improving ventilation with mechanical aids, bronchodilators, correction of heart failure, and antidotes for anesthetics or drugs suppressing the respiratory center. Tracheostomy or tracheal intubation is often required. Close monitoring of P_{CO_2}, P_{O_2}, and pH of arterial blood is essential. The respiratory center is readily rendered unresponsive by high P_{CO_2} (hypercapnia), and recovery may be very slow. In the presence of hypercapnia, relief of hypoxia

with oxygen therapy may deprive the patient of the only remaining stimulus to the respiratory center and produce more severe hypoventilation with resultant CO_2 narcosis and death. Assistance with respiration is required until the respiratory center becomes normally responsive to normal CO_2 concentrations.

2. RESPIRATORY ALKALOSIS

Respiratory alkalosis is a result of hyperventilation which produces lowered P_{CO_2} and elevated pH of extracellular fluid. Anxiety is the usual cause. Hyperventilation during anesthesia or from incorrectly used mechanical respiratory aids occurs more commonly than is generally appreciated. Renal compensation by excretion of HCO_3^- (with Na^+ predominantly) is too slow a response to be effective, and elevation of pH may reach a point at which asterixis, tetany, and increased neuromuscular irritability appear.

Treatment
Treatment of spontaneous hyperventilation consists of reducing anxiety by drugs or psychotherapy. Tetany may be alleviated by rebreathing exhaled air, which will increase P_{CO_2} and lower blood pH. Regulation of devices used in assisting with respiration should be determined by measurement of the P_{CO_2} and pH of arterial blood.

3. METABOLIC ACIDOSIS

Metabolic acidosis occurs with starvation, uncontrolled diabetes mellitus with ketosis, electrolyte (including bicarbonate) and water loss with diarrhea or enteric fistulas, and renal insufficiency or tubular defect producing inadequate H^+ excretion. Cation loss (Na^+, K^+, Ca^{++}) and organic acid anion retention occur with starvation and uncontrolled diabetes mellitus. In the presence of renal insufficiency, phosphate and sulfate are retained and cation (especially Na^+) is lost because of limited H^+ secretion for exchange with cation in the renal tubule. A rare cause of metabolic acidosis is the ingestion of acid salts such as NH_4Cl or mandelic acid or acid precursors such as methyl alcohol; these are particularly likely to produce acidosis in the presence of renal insufficiency. Respiratory compensation for metabolic acidosis by hyperventilation provides reduction of P_{CO_2} and thereby reduction of H_2CO_3 in extracellular fluid.

Treatment
Treatment is directed toward correcting the metabolic defect (eg, insulin for control of diabetes) and replenishment of water and of deficits of Na^+, K^+,

HCO_3^-, and other electrolytes. Anion replacement should include bicarbonate or lactate (bicarbonate equivalent), but large quantities of bicarbonate are needed only in unusual and threatening states. The "maintenance" solution described above is adequate for most needs; lactated Ringer's solution may be preferred if larger quantities of Na^+ are required. A mixture of half 0.9% saline and half 1/6 molar sodium lactate (or bicarbonate) provides an even greater fraction of HCO_3^-. Renal insufficiency requires careful replacement of water and electrolyte deficit and closely controlled rations of water, sodium, potassium, calcium, chloride, and bicarbonate to maintain normal extracellular fluid concentrations; the elevated serum phosphate may be lowered by interfering with phosphate absorption from the gut by oral administration of aluminum hydroxide preparations. In the presence of renal insufficiency, elevated extracellular K^+ concentrations may be reduced by either oral administration of ion exchange resins which bind K^+, either ingested or secreted, and prevent absorption in the intestine (see Hyperkalemia, below), or by hemodialysis or peritoneal dialysis.

Lactic Acidosis

A rare and serious form of acidosis is that due to large quantities of lactic acid. It is presumed that severe tissue anoxia (eg, in shock) leads to anaerobic glucose metabolism with production of lactic acid. Acidosis develops abruptly and is usually severe and highly resistant to therapy with HCO_3^-. Plasma lactate concentration may rise to 8 mM/liter.

Lactic acidosis must be considered in anoxic states, hypovolemic or endotoxin shock, severe pulmonary insufficiency or pulmonary edema, heart failure, severe hepatic failure, nonketotic diabetic acidosis, following phenformin therapy, and following poisoning with paraldehyde or salicylates. Diagnosis is confirmed in states of overt acidosis by actual lactate levels or by demonstrating that a large amount of unidentified anion is present in the serum (ie, not Cl^-, HCO_3^-, $HPO_4^=$, or ketone bodies).

Treatment is often ineffectual. The primary and contributing causes must be treated vigorously and sodium bicarbonate administered in large quantities despite the dangers of sodium overload.

4. METABOLIC ALKALOSIS

Metabolic alkalosis results from loss of gastric juice rich in HCl and occurs also in association with K^+ deficit (diuretics, adrenocortical excess, abrupt correction of hypercapnia) which is characteristically accompanied by increased urinary excretion of H^+. All of these result in renal retention of HCO_3^-, producing elevated extracellular fluid bicarbonate. Respiratory compensation by hypoventilation produces an elevation in P_{CO_2}, increasing the H_2CO_3 fraction of the bicarbonate buffer system.

Treatment

Alkalosis of metabolic origin requires adequate water, K^+, and Na^+. The anion should be exclusively Cl^- to replace the HCO_3^- excess and Cl^- deficit; no lactate or bicarbonate should be employed until normal blood pH and bicarbonate levels are obtained.

POTASSIUM

Potassium is one of the major intracellular cations, occupying a role that is parallel to that of sodium in extracellular fluid. Physiologic actions of potassium are related primarily to concentration of the cation in extracellular fluid, although the intracellular concentration may have some influence. Potassium plays an important part in muscular contraction, conduction of nerve impulses, enzyme action, and cell membrane function.

Cardiac muscle excitability, conduction, and rhythm are markedly affected by changes in concentration of K^+ in extracellular fluid. Both an increase and a decrease of extracellular K^+ concentration diminish excitability and conduction rate. Higher than normal concentrations produce a marked depression of conductivity with cardiac arrest in diastole; in the presence of very low concentrations, cardiac arrest occurs in systole. The effects of abnormal K^+ concentrations in extracellular fluid upon cell membrane potential of cardiac muscle and upon depolarization and repolarization are manifested in the ECG.

Membrane potential and excitability of skeletal and smooth muscle are profoundly affected by the concentrations of K^+, Ca^{++}, and Mg^{++}, with H^+ and Na^+ also involved. Conduction across the myoneural junction is under the influence of these cations as well. At both extremes of abnormal concentration of K^+ in extracellular fluid, muscle contractility is impaired and flaccid paralysis ensues.

Potassium concentration of extracellular fluid is closely regulated between 3.5–5 mEq/liter. Excretion of the 35–100 mEq of potassium contained in the daily diet of the average adult is predominantly via the kidney. There is good evidence that the potassium in glomerular filtrate is reabsorbed in the proximal tubule and that active secretion of potassium into the tubular fluid occurs in the distal portion of the tubule.

1. HYPERKALEMIA

Causes of increased extracellular K^+ concentration include failure of the kidney to excrete ingested potassium (acute and chronic renal failure, severe oliguria due to severe dehydration or trauma); unusual release of intracellular potassium in burns, crushing injuries, or severe infections; and overtreatment with potassium

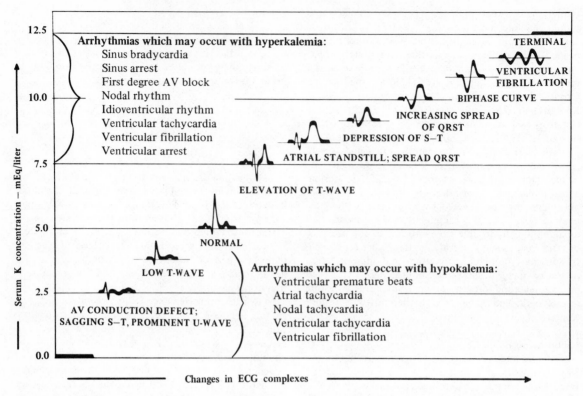

FIG 2–3. Correlation of serum potassium concentration and ECG. (Provided there is no parallel change in sodium and calcium.)

salts. In metabolic acidosis, extracellular K^+ concentration is increased as K^+ shifts from cells.

The elevated K^+ concentration interferes with normal neuromuscular function to produce weakness and paralysis; abdominal distention and diarrhea may occur. As extracellular concentration of K^+ increases, the ECG reflects impaired conduction by peaked T waves of increased amplitude, atrial arrest, spread in the QRS, biphasic QRS–T complexes, and finally ventricular fibrillation and cardiac arrest.

Treatment

Treatment consists of withholding potassium and employing cation exchange resins by mouth or enema. Kayexalate®, a sodium cycle sulfonic polystyrene exchange resin, 40–80 gm/day in divided doses, is usually effective. In an emergency, insulin may be employed to deposit K^+ with glycogen in the liver, and Ca^{++} may be given intravenously as an antagonist ion. Sodium bicarbonate can be given intravenously as an emergency measure in severe hyperkalemia; the increase in pH so induced results in a shift of K^+ into cells. Hemodialysis or peritoneal dialysis may be required to remove K^+ in the presence of protracted renal insufficiency.

2. HYPOKALEMIA

Potassium deficit may or may not be accompanied by lowered extracellular fluid K^+ concentration; however, when hypokalemia is present, total potassium deficit is usually profound. Exceptions to this common circumstance include the hypokalemia of alkalosis and that following administration of insulin. Causes of potassium deficit include reduced intake due to starvation or upper gastrointestinal obstruction; poor absorption in steatorrhea, short bowel syndrome, and regional enteritis; loss via the gastrointestinal tract due to emesis, diarrhea, and suction; loss via the kidney due to congenital tubule malfunction, diuresis resulting from diabetes or diuretics, accompanying metabolic alkalosis, and following excessive treatment with saline solutions containing little or no potassium; loss of interstitial fluid with burns or freezing; loss of K^+ due to adrenocortical hormone (cortisol or aldosterone) excess; and intracellular shifts in bouts of familial periodic paralysis. A low concentration of K^+ in extracellular fluid results in impaired neuromuscular function with profound weakness of skeletal muscle, leading to impaired ventilation, and of smooth muscle, producing ileus. The ECG shows decreased amplitude and broadening of T waves, prominent U waves, sagging S–T segments, atrioventricular block, and, finally, cardiac arrest. Metabolic alkalosis with elevated plasma pH and bicarbonate concentration develops as a result of potassium deficit which is accompanied by renal excretion of H^+ and reabsorption of bicarbonate and by movement of Na^+ and H^+ from extracellular fluid into cells as K^+ is lost. A defect of water reabsorption by the renal tubule also occurs, producing polyuria and hyposthenuria; this is only slowly ameliorated following treatment.

Treatment

Treatment requires replacement of potassium orally or parenterally. Because of the toxicity of potassium, it must be administered cautiously to prevent hyperkalemia. Furthermore, confirmation of adequate renal function is important when potassium is administered since the principal route of excretion is via the kidney. KCl in a total dose of 1–3 mEq/kg/24 hours may be given parenterally in glucose or saline solutions (or both) at a rate that will not produce hyperkalemia. Except in an emergency in which serum K^+ is extremely low and cardiac muscle and respiratory muscle activity seriously impaired, the administration of K^+ should be at a rate of 10–20 mEq per hour or less. Cl^- is always needed to relieve the hypochloremia that is associated with the accompanying metabolic alkalosis.

CALCIUM

Calcium constitutes about 2% of body weight, but only about 1% of the total body calcium is in solution in body fluid. In the plasma, calcium is present as a nondiffusible complex with protein (33%); as a diffusible but undissociated complex with anions such as citrate, bicarbonate, and phosphate (12%); and as Ca^{++} (55%). The normal total plasma (or serum) calcium concentration is 4.5–5.5 mEq/liter (9–11 mg/100 ml). The serum calcium level is responsive to 2 hormones: parathyroid hormone elevates and calcitonin lowers the concentration. Bone serves as a reservoir of calcium available to body fluids. Excretion of Ca^{++} is via the kidney.

Calcium functions as an essential ion for many enzymes. It is an important constituent of mucoproteins and mucopolysaccharides, and is essential in blood coagulation.

Along with other cations, calcium exerts an important effect on cell membrane potential and permeability manifested prominently in neuromuscular function. It plays a central role in muscle contraction as it is released from the sarcolemma to enter into the ATP-ADP reaction. During muscle relaxation, the calcium is actively transferred back to the sarcolemma and sarcoplasmic reticulum.

Neural function is sensitive to Ca^{++} concentration of interstitial fluid. Excitability is diminished by high Ca^{++} concentration and increased by low concentration. Signs of elevated Ca^{++} concentration include dulling of consciousness and stupor and muscular flaccidity and weakness. Low Ca^{++} concentration increases excita-

bility to produce hyperirritability of muscle, tetany, and convulsions.

Cardiac muscle responds to elevated Ca^{++} concentration with increased contractility, ventricular extrasystoles, and idioventricular rhythm. These responses are accentuated in the presence of digitalis. With severe calcium toxicity, cardiac arrest in systole may occur. Low concentration of Ca^{++} produces diminished contractility of the heart and a lengthening of the Q–T interval of the ECG by prolonging the S–T segment.

1. HYPERCALCEMIA

Hypercalcemia results from hyperparathyroidism, invasion of bone by neoplasm (lung, breast, kidney, thyroid), production of a parathyroid-like hormone by isolated neoplasms (ovary, kidney, lung), sarcoidosis, multiple myeloma, and vitamin D intoxication.

Hypercalcemia affects neuromuscular function to produce weakness, and causes polyuria, dehydration, thirst, anorexia, vomiting, and constipation. Stupor, coma, and azotemia ensue.

Treatment

Treatment consists of control of the primary disease. Symptomatic hypercalcemia is associated with a high mortality rate; treatment must be promptly instituted. Until the primary disease can be brought under control, renal excretion of calcium with resultant decrease in serum Ca^{++} concentration can be promoted with a variety of agents. Excretion of Na^+ is accompanied by excretion of Ca^{++}; therefore, inducing natriuresis by giving Na^+ salts intravenously and by adjunctive use of diuretics is the emergency treatment of choice. Sodium chloride or sodium sulfate in large quantities (70–80 mEq/hour) with or without diuretics (furosemide) for 12–48 hours may be required. Replacement of water and of K^+ and Mg^{++} is usually necessary. The use of phosphate is hazardous and should be reserved for unusual cases refractory to saline therapy. When elevated Ca^{++} concentrations result from sarcoidosis or neoplasm, corticosteroids such as prednisone may be effective. Mithramycin is useful if elevated Ca^{++} is the result of neoplasm metastatic to bone.

2. HYPOCALCEMIA

Hypocalcemia results from hypoparathyroidism (idiopathic or postoperative), chronic renal insufficiency, rickets and osteomalacia, and malabsorption syndromes. Serum Ca^{++} concentration is reduced in association with decreased serum albumin concentrations (a physiologic relationship).

Hypocalcemia affects neuromuscular function to produce muscle cramps and tetany, convulsions, stridor and dyspnea, diplopia, abdominal cramps, and urinary frequency. Personality changes may occur. In chronic hypoparathyroidism and pseudohypoparathyroidism, cataracts may appear and calcification of basal ganglia of the brain may occur. Mental retardation and stunted growth are common in childhood.

Treatment

Treatment depends on the primary disease. Treatment of hypoparathyroidism with vitamin D and calcium is discussed in Chapter 18. For tetany due to hypocalcemia, calcium gluconate, 1–2 gm, may be given IV. A continuous infusion to sustain plasma calcium concentration may be required. Oral medication with the chloride, gluconate, levulinate, lactate, or carbonate salts of calcium will usually control milder symptoms or latent tetany. The low serum Ca^{++} associated with low serum albumin concentration does not require replacement therapy.

MAGNESIUM

About 50% of total body magnesium exists in the insoluble state in bone. Only 5% is present as extracellular cation; the remaining 45% is contained in cells as intracellular cation. The normal plasma concentration is 1.5–2.5 mEq/liter, with about 1/3 bound to protein and 2/3 as free cation. Excretion of magnesium ion is via the kidney, with no evidence of active tubule secretion.

Magnesium is an important prosthetic or activator ion, participating in the function of many enzymes involved in phosphate transfer reactions, including those requiring ATP or other nucleotide triphosphate as coenzymes.

Magnesium exerts physiologic effects on the nervous system resembling those of calcium. Elevated Mg^{++} concentration of interstitial fluid produces sedation and central and peripheral nervous system depression. Low concentrations produce increased irritability, disorientation, and convulsions.

Magnesium acts directly upon the myoneural junction. Elevated levels produce blockage by decreasing acetylcholine release, reducing the effect of acetylcholine on depolarization, and diminishing excitability of the muscle cell. Calcium ion exerts an antagonistic action. Low levels of magnesium increase neuromuscular irritability and contractility, partly by increasing acetylcholine release. Tetany and convulsions may occur.

Cardiac muscle is affected by large increases in magnesium concentration in the range of 10–15 mEq/liter. Conduction time is increased, with lengthened duration of P–R and QRS components of the ECG. As the concentration of Mg^{++} increases further, cardiac arrest in diastole occurs.

Elevated magnesium concentrations produce vasodilatation and a drop in blood pressure by blockade of sympathetic ganglia as well as a direct effect on smooth muscle.

1. HYPERMAGNESEMIA

Magnesium excess is almost always the result of renal insufficiency and inability to excrete what has been absorbed from food or infused. Occasionally, with the use of magnesium sulfate as a cathartic, enough magnesium is absorbed to produce toxicity, particularly in the presence of impaired renal function. Manifestations of hypermagnesemia include muscle weakness, fall in blood pressure, and sedation and confusion. The ECG shows increased P–R interval, broadened QRS complexes, and elevated T waves. Death usually results from respiratory muscle paralysis.

Treatment

Treatment is directed toward alleviating renal insufficiency. Calcium acts as an antagonist to Mg^{++} and may be employed parenterally for temporary benefit. Extracorporeal or peritoneal dialysis may be indicated.

2. HYPOMAGNESEMIA

Magnesium deficit may be encountered in chronic alcoholism in association with delirium tremens, starvation, diarrhea, malabsorption, prolonged gastrointestinal suction, vigorous diuresis, primary hyperaldosteronism, and hypoparathyroidism, particularly after parathyroidectomy for hyperparathyroidism and when large doses of vitamin D and calcium are consumed.

Magnesium deficit is characterized by neuromuscular and CNS hyperirritability with athetoid movements; jerking, coarse, and flapping tremors; positive Babinski response, nystagmus, tachycardia, hypertension, and vasomotor changes.

Treatment

Treatment consists of the use of parenteral fluids containing magnesium as chloride or sulfate, 10–40 mEq/day during the period of severe deficit followed by 10 mEq/day for maintenance. Magnesium sulfate may also be given IM, 4–8 gm (66–133 mEq) daily in 4 divided doses.

THE APPROACH TO DIAGNOSIS & TREATMENT OF WATER, ELECTROLYTE, & ACID-BASE DISTURBANCES

In the diagnosis and treatment of water and electrolyte derangements, one must rely upon clinical appraisal of the patient, including details of the history, the presenting disease and its complications, recent and abrupt change in weight, the physical examination, and the laboratory data bearing upon altered volume, osmolarity, distribution, and physiologic manifestations. Although a thorough knowledge of the physiologic principles of water and electrolyte metabolism and of renal function is essential to sound management and direction of therapy, the science of therapy is far from exact, and the physician must always consider and be grateful for the homeostatic resources of the patient. If renal function is reasonably good, the range between acceptable lower and upper limits of amounts of water and electrolytes is broad and the achievement of "balance" not difficult. In the presence of renal insufficiency, some endocrinopathies influencing water and electrolyte metabolism, shock, heart failure, hepatic insufficiency, severe gastrointestinal fluid loss, pulmonary insufficiency, and some rarer diseases, the patient is deprived of his homeostatic resources and the physician is called upon to substitute as best he can with close observation and meticulous quantitative therapy.

Some general principles will be included here. For difficult and complicated problems, more specialized and more complete texts must be consulted.

MAINTENANCE

Most of those who require water and electrolyte are relatively normal people who cannot take orally what they require for maintenance.

It is apparent from Table 2–6 that the range of tolerance for water and electrolytes (homeostatic limits) permits reasonable latitude in therapy provided normal renal function exists to accomplish the final regulation of volume and concentration.

An average adult whose entire intake is parenteral would receive his maintenance ration in 2500–3000 ml of 5% or 10% dextrose in 0.2% saline solution (34 mEq Na^+ + Cl^-/liter). To each liter, 30 mEq KCl could be added. In 3 liters, the total chloride intake would be 192 mEq, which could be tolerated. An alternative would be to eliminate the KCl if parenteral fluids would be required for only 2–3 days. After 3 days of potassium-free parenteral fluids, total potassium loss may become significant and replacement is desirable. Other solutions available for maintenance therapy contain electrolyte mixtures designed to meet average adult requirements: in one example, each liter contains dextrose, 50 gm; Na^+, 40 mEq; K^+, 35 mEq; Cl^-, 40 mEq; HCO_3^- equivalent, 20 mEq; and $PO_4^{\equiv}$, 15 mEq. The daily administration of 2500–3000 ml satisfies the needs listed in Table 2–6.

In situations requiring maintenance or maintenance plus replacement of fluid and electrolyte by parenteral infusion, the total daily ration should be administered continuously over the 24-hour period in

TABLE 2–6. Daily maintenance rations for patients requiring parenteral fluids.

	Per sq M Body Surface	Average Adult (60–100 kg)
Glucose	60–75 gm	100–200 gm
Na^+	50–70 mEq	80–120 mEq
K^+	50–70 mEq	80–120 mEq
Water	1500 ml	2500 ml

order to ensure the best utilization by the patient. Periodic large infusions result in responsive excretion by the kidney, reducing the opportunity for precise regulation by the kidney. Continuous infusion is desirable, particularly when losses are large and the total volume of the daily infusion is correspondingly large. With modern technics for continuous infusions, around-the-clock administration imposes little discomfort or hardship on the patient.

DEFICITS

To the maintenance ration one must add water and appropriate electrolyte for replacement of losses previously incurred and water and electrolytes to, replace current losses. The amounts of water and electrolytes are dictated by clinical evaluation of deficits of each, and a further choice of anion would be dictated by the presence of metabolic acidosis or alkalosis and in some instances of respiratory acidosis.

The severity of dehydration (volume depletion) is assessed by means of the history, the magnitude of acute weight loss, and, on physical examination, the loss of elasticity of the skin and subcutaneous tissues, dry mucous membranes, tachycardia and hypotension, lethargy, and weakness. As dehydration becomes more severe, the decrease in plasma volume results in progression of hypotension and shock. Hemoconcentration progresses with loss of plasma water; electrolyte concentrations differ according to the losses incident to the primary disease; the increase in BUN reflects the decrease in glomerular filtration rate incident to circulatory changes associated with low blood volume.

Effective extracellular fluid volume and circulating blood volume accompany acutely occurring redistribution of fluid following burns, bowel obstruction, peritonitis, venous obstruction, and, rarely, lymphatic obstruction.

Treatment consists of replacement of water deficit with appropriate electrolyte replacement according to serum osmolarity (Na^+ concentration), blood pH, and serum K^+ concentration. In the presence of hyperosmolarity (hypernatremia), electrolyte-free or hypotonic solutions should be employed; if serum Na^+ concentration is normal, repletion can be accomplished with isotonic solutions. If hypo-osmolarity (hyponatremia) exists due to sodium loss, hypertonic (3–5%)

TABLE 2–7. Volume and electrolyte content of gastrointestinal fluid losses.*

	Na⁺ (mEq/liter)	K⁺ (mEq/liter)	Cl⁻ (mEq/liter)	HCO₃⁻ (mEq/liter)	Volume (ml)
Gastric juice, high in acid	20 (10–30)	10 (5–40)	120 (80–150)	0	1000–9000
Gastric juice, low in acid	80 (70–140)	15 (5–40)	90 (40–120)	5–25	1000–2500
Pancreatic juice	140 (115–180)	5 (3–8)	75 (55–95)	80 (60–110)	500–1000
Bile	148 (130–160)	5 (3–12)	100 (90–120)	35 (30–40)	300–1000
Small bowel drainage	110 (80–150)	5 (2–8)	105 (60–125)	30 (20–40)	1000–3000
Distal ileum and cecum drainage	80 (40–135)	8 (5–30)	45 (20–90)	30 (20–40)	1000–3000
Diarrheal stools	120 (20–160)	25 (10–40)	90 (30–120)	45 (30–50)	500–17,000

*Average values/24 hours with range in parentheses.

TABLE 2–8. Examples of solutions for parenteral infusion.

	Electrolyte Content in mEq/liter								Glucose (gm/liter)
	Na⁺	K⁺	Ca⁺⁺	Mg⁺⁺	NH₄⁺	Cl⁻	HCO₃⁻ Equiv*	PO₄⁼	
5% glucose in water									50
10% glucose in water									100
Isotonic saline (0.9%)	155					155			
Sodium chloride (5%)	855					855			
Ringer's solution	147	4	4			155			
Ringer's lactate (Hartmann's)	130	4	3			109	28		
Darrow's solution (KNL)	121	35				103	53		
Potassium chloride									
0.2% in dextrose 5%		27				27			50
0.3% in dextrose 5%		40				40			50
"Modified duodenal solution" with dextrose, 10%	80	36	5	3		64	60		100
"Gastric solution" with dextrose, 10%	63	17			70	150			100
Ammonium chloride, 0.9%					170	170			
Sodium lactate, 1/6 molar	167						167		
Sodium bicarbonate, 1/6 molar	167						167		
Examples of "maintenance solutions":									
Pediatric electrolyte "No. 48" with dextrose 5%	25	20		3		22	23	3	50
Maintenance electrolyte "No. 75" with dextrose 5%	40	35				40	20	15	50
Levulose and dextrose with electrolyte (Butler's II)	58	25		6		51	25	13	100
5% dextrose in 0.2% saline	34					34			50
10% dextrose in 0.45% saline	77					77			100

HCO₃⁻ equivalent may be lactate, acetate, gluconate, or citrate, or combinations of these.
A variety of modifications of multiple electrolyte solutions are commercially available.

TABLE 2–9. Examples of electrolyte concentrates.

	Ampule Volume	Electrolyte Content in mEq per Ampule								
		Na^+	K^+	Ca^{++}	Mg^{++}	NH_4^+	Cl^-	HCO_3^-	Lactate	$PO_4^{\equiv}$
Potassium chloride*	10 ml		20				20			
KMC*	10 ml		25	10	10		45			
Potassium phosphate*	20 ml		40							40
Calcium gluconate, 10%	10 ml			4.5					4.5 (gluconate)	
Sodium bicarbonate, 7.5%†	50 ml	45						45		
Sodium lactate, molar†	40 ml	40							40	
Ammonium chloride*	30 ml					120	120			
Magnesium sulfate, 50%	—				8‡					

Note: The physician should always check the contents of the ampule as listed by the manufacturer.
*Dilute to 1 liter or more.
†Dilute as indicated by the manufacturer.
‡8 mEq/ml.

$NaCl$ solutions or hypertonic $NaHCO_3$ solutions may be required. In addition to replacement needs, maintenance requirements must be met, requiring correlation of volume, electrolyte concentration, and rate of administration to effect a normal state.

One should aim for total replacement in 48–72 hours. Time is required for circulation, diffusion, equilibration, renal response, and restoration of normal homeostatic mechanisms; a general rule is to provide daily maintenance needs plus half the deficit in the first 24 hours and a quarter of the deficit daily for 2 days thereafter to complete restitution in 72 hours. To this must be added the equivalent of continuing losses.

Common situations in which deficits may be large are discussed below. Other less common derangements are beyond the scope of this chapter. For therapeutic guidance, consult more detailed texts and specific treatises.

1. DIABETIC KETOSIS

Characterized by significant losses of water, sodium, and potassium in addition to retention of ketone body acids and a decrease in bicarbonate and pH in the extracellular fluid. Therapy is outlined in Chapter 18.

2. GASTROINTESTINAL DISEASE

Often accompanied by large losses of water, sodium, and potassium. Loss of chloride or bicarbonate is related to site of the disease or obstruction, eg, in pyloric obstruction with loss of HCl; small bowel fluid losses with loss of bicarbonate. (See Table 2–7.) Fol-

TABLE 2–10. Examples of oral electrolyte preparations.

Preparation	Supplied As	Electrolyte Content*					
		Na^+	K^+	NH_4^+	Ca^{++}	Cl^-	HCO_3^-
NaCl	Salt	17				17	
NaHCO₃	Salt	12					12
KCl	Salt		14			14	
K-triplex®	Elixir		15 mEq/ 5 ml				
K gluconate (Kaon®)	Elixir		7 mEq/ 5 ml				
Ca gluconate	Salt				4.5		
Ca lactate	Salt				10		
NH₄Cl (acidifying salt)	Salt			19†		19	
Kayexalate® (ion-exchange resins)	Salt	1‡	‡				

*mEq/gm unless otherwise specified.
†NH_4^+ is converted to H^+ in the body, mEq for mEq.
‡1 gm resin removes 1 mEq K^+ and contributes 3 mEq Na^+ to patient.

TABLE 2–11. Equivalent values of salts used for therapy.*

Salt	gm	mEq of Cation per Amount Stated
IV or oral		
NaCl	9	155
NaCl	5.8	100
NaCl	1	17
NaHCO$_3$	8.4	100
Na lactate	11.2	100
KCl	1.8	25
K acetate	2.5	25
{ K$_2$HPO$_4$	1.84	25
{ KH$_2$PO$_4$	0.4	
CaCl$_2$	0.5	10
Ca gluconate	2	10
MgCl$_2$	0.5	10
Oral		
K citrate	3	25
K tartrate	5	27

*Reproduced, with permission, from Krupp, Sweet, Jawetz, & Biglieri: *Physician's Handbook,* 16th ed. Lange, 1970.

lowing intubation, the collected secretions should be assayed to determine the volume and losses of electrolyte that must be replaced.

3. BURNS

Edema accompanying the trauma to tissue results in sequestration of fluids in tissues beneath the burns with consequent decrease in circulating plasma volume and circulatory collapse. Therapy is described in Chapter 27.

4. PERITONITIS

Inflammation may produce a large collection of fluid in the peritoneal cavity. Prompt restoration of plasma volume and extracellular fluid is essential.

5. ASCITES

The association of liver disease with ascites and the consequences of therapy with diuretics may produce complex alterations of fluid distribution and electrolyte concentrations. (See Chapter 10.)

• • •

SUMMARY OF CLINICAL APPROACH

The following outline summarizes an approach to therapy with water and electrolytes. Listed are factors essential to an assessment of the state of the patient, of the urgency for treatment, and of the choice of the therapeutic agents and the quantities to be administered. This outline has been useful in planning the therapeutic attack and averting the omission of essential elements of treatment.

Problems
    1. Simple maintenance.
    2. Repair of deficit plus maintenance.
    3. Repair plus replacement of continuing losses plus maintenance.
    4. Replacement of continuing losses plus maintenance.

Situations: Acute or Chronic
    A. Acute:
    1. Respiratory—P$_{CO_2}$ and pH. Often overlooked. H$^+$ concentration can change rapidly to life-threatening levels. **Therapy must be immediate and adequate.**
    2. Organic ion acidosis (lactate, ketones), "anion gap." Normally, Cl$^-$ + CO$_2$ + 12 = Na$^+$ in mEq/liter, or Cl$^-$ + ½ CO$_2$ + 25 = Na$^+$ in mEq/liter.
    3. Plasma K$^+$ concentration deficit or excess.
    4. Hyper- or hypo-osmolality, often iatrogenic.
    5. Explosive gastrointestinal loss, Addison's disease in crisis.
    6. Acute renal shutdown.
    B. Chronic:
    1. Renal insufficiency.
    2. Pulmonary insufficiency.
    3. Chronic gastrointestinal disease (gut, liver).
    4. Endocrine abnormality, especially myxedema.

Determinants in Establishing Therapy
    Sex: Females are usually fatter and, therefore, have lower total body water ratios (per kg) than males.
    Size: Fat or lean; more fat means lower ratios of total body water/kg.
    Renal and pulmonary function.
    Cause of abnormal state, ie, shock, gastrointestinal obstruction, third space sequestration, diabetes or other endocrine abnormality, malnutrition, induced by drug effect or therapeutic error.

Observations
    Weight.
    Intake, output, and loss record.
    Serum electrolytes, osmolality, urea or creatinine, protein, glucose.
    Arterial blood P$_{CO_2}$, pH, P$_{O_2}$ as indicated.
    Urine specific gravity, osmolality, volume.

• • •

Tables 2–8, 2–9, 2–10, and 2–11 indicate the wide choices open to the physician in planning the restoration of water and electrolyte in the variety of clinical problems that may occur. A sound understanding of the physiologic mechanisms discussed above enables the physician to direct therapy rationally and with considerable skill. If renal and pulmonary function are compromised, the task becomes difficult and hazardous for even the best informed clinicians.

• • •

Bibliography

General

Black, D.A.K.: Symptoms and signs in disorders of body fluid. J Chronic Dis 11:340–347, 1960.

Bland, J.H.: *Clinical Metabolism of Body Water and Electrolytes.* Saunders, 1963.

Pitts, R.F.: *Physiology of the Kidney and Body Fluids,* 2nd ed. Year Book, 1968.

Robinson, J.R.: Metabolism of intracellular water. Physiol Rev 40:112–149, 1960.

Sunderman, F.W., & F.W. Sunderman, Jr.: *Clinical Pathology of the Serum Electrolytes.* Thomas, 1966.

Windhazer, E.E.: Kidney, water, and electrolytes. Ann Rev Physiol 31:117–172, 1969.

Fluid Volume

Bricker, N.S., & S. Klahr: The physiologic basis of sodium excretion and diuresis. Advances Int Med 16:17–41, 1970.

Clift, G.V., & others: Syndrome of inappropriate vasopressin secretion. Arch Int Med 118:453–460, 1966.

Earley, L.E., & T.M. Daugharty: Sodium metabolism. New England J Med 281:72–86, 1969.

Githers, J.H.: Hypernatremic dehydration. Clin Pediat 2:453–462, 1963.

Kleeman, C.R., & M.P. Fichman: The clinical physiology of water metabolism. New England J Med 277:1300–1307, 1967.

Kleeman, C.R., : Hypo-osmolar syndromes secondary to impaired water excretion. Ann Rev Med 21:259–268, 1970.

Leaf, A.: The clinical and physiologic significance of the serum sodium concentration. New England J Med 267:24–30, 77–83, 1962.

Maffly, R.H., & I.S. Edelman: The role of sodium potassium and water in the hypo-osmotic states of heart failure. Progr Cardiovas Dis 4:88–104, 1961.

Warhol, R.M., Eichenholz, A., & R.O. Mulhausen: Osmolality. Arch Int Med 116:743–749, 1965.

Welt, L.G.: Hypo- and hypernatremia. Ann Int Med 56:161–164, 1962.

Hydrogen Ion

Albert, M.S., Dell, R.B., & R.B. Winters: Quantitative displacement of acid-base equilibrium in metabolic acidosis. Ann Int Med 66:312–322, 1967.

Blumentals, A.S. (editor): Symposium on acid-base balance. Arch Int Med 116:647–742, 1965.

Diarrhea and acid-base disturbances. Leading article. Lancet 1:1305–1306, 1966.

Elkinton, J.R.: Hydrogen ion turnover in health and disease. Ann Int Med 57:660–684, 1962.

Kassirer, J.P., & W.B. Schwartz: The response of normal man to selective depletion of hydrochloric acid. Correction of metabolic alkalosis in man without repair of potassium deficiency. Am. J Med 40:10–26, 1966.

Manfredi, F.: Effects of hypocapnia and hypercapnia on intracellular acid-base equilibrium in man. J Lab Clin Med 69:304–312, 1967.

Schwartz, W.B., & W.C. Waters: Lactate versus bicarbonate. Editorial. Am J Med 32:831–834, 1962.

Statement of acid-base terminology. Ann Int Med 63:885–890, 1965; Anesthesiology 27:7–12, 1966; Ann New York Acad Sc 133:251–258, 1966.

Steinmetz, P.R.: Excretion of acid by the kidney-functional organization and cellular aspects of acidification. New England J Med 278:1102–1109, 1968.

Tranquada, R.E., Grant, W.J., & C.R. Peterson: Lactic acidosis. Arch Int Med 117:192–202, 1966.

Van Ypersele de Strihou, C., Brasseur, L., & J. McConinck: The "carbon-dioxide response curve" for chronic hypercapnia in man. New England J Med 275:117–122, 1966.

Potassium

Bellet, S.: The cardiotoxic effects of hyperpotassemia and its treatment. Postgrad Med 25:602–609, 1959.

Kassirer, J.P., & others: The critical role of chloride in the correction of hypokalemic alkalosis in man. Am J Med 38:172–189, 1965.

Leaf, A., & R.F. Santos: Physiologic mechanisms in potassium deficiency. New England J Med 264:335–341, 1961.

Papper, S., & R. Whang: *Hyperkalemia and Hypokalemia.* Disease-A-Month. Year Book, June 1964.

Surawicz, B.: Electrolytes and the electrocardiogram. Am J Cardiol 12:656–662, 1963.

Weatherall, M.: Ions and the actions of digitalis. Brit Heart J 28:497–504, 1966.

Calcium

Breuer, R.I., & L. Bauer: Caution in the use of phosphates in the treatment of severe hypercalcemia. J. Clin Endocrinol 27:695–698, 1967.

Chakmakjian, Z.H., & E. Bethune: Sodium sulfate treatment of hypercalcemia. New England J Med 275:862–869, 1966.

Foster, G.V.: Calcitonin (thyrocalcitonin). New England J Med 279:349–360, 1968.

Goldsmith, R.S., & S.H. Ingbar: Inorganic phosphate treatment of hypercalcemia of diverse etiologies. New England J Med 274:1–7, 284, 1966.

Howard, J.E., & W.C. Thomas: Clinical disorders of calcium homeostasis. Medicine 42:25–45, 1963.

Perlia, C.P., & others: Mithramycin treatment of hypercalcemia. Cancer 25:389–394, 1970.

Singer, F.R., & others: Mithramycin treatment of intractable hypercalcemia due to parathyroid carcinoma.
New England J Med 283:634–636, 1970.

Suki, W.N., & others: Acute treatment of hypercalcemia
with furosemide. New England J Med
283:836–840, 1970.

Magnesium

Gitelman, H.J., & L.G. Welt: Magnesium deficiency. Ann
Rev Med 20:233–242, 1969.

MacIntyre, I.: Magnesium metabolism. Advances Int Med
13:143–154, 1967.

Wacker, W.E.C., & A.F. Parisi: Magnesium metabolism.
New England J Med 278:772–776, 1968.

3...

Skin & Appendages

Rees B. Rees, Jr.

Diagnosis of Skin Disorders

Take a thorough case history from every patient with a skin disease. Do not neglect the role of constitutional factors in production or aggravation of skin diseases (eg, internal disease, emotional factors, dietary aberrations). Inquire about systemic and topical medications. Examine the entire body surface in good (preferably natural) light.

Planning the Treatment

Many topical agents are available for the treatment of dermatologic disorders. In general, it is better to be thoroughly familiar with a few drugs and treatment methods than to attempt to use a great many.

In planning the treatment it is necessary to consider the individual character of the patient's skin. Dry skins usually require lubricating or softening agents; moist or oily skins usually require greaseless drying agents.

Begin treatment with mild, simple remedies. In general, acute, inflamed lesions are best treated with soothing, nonirritating agents; chronic, thickened lesions with stimulating or keratolytic agents. Apply a small amount of medicament to a small area and observe for several hours for skin sensitivity.

Do not change remedies before the agent has had time to demonstrate its effectiveness. However, discontinue the drug immediately if an untoward local reaction develops.

Instruct the patient carefully on how to apply medicaments.

When in doubt about the proper method of treatment, **undertreat** rather than overtreat.

Note: Prescription numbers in the text refer to Tables 3–1 to 3–6 at the end of the chapter.

General Rules Governing Choice of Topical Treatment of Various Stages of Dermatoses

Note: The choice of treatment will vary with the individual case depending upon the characteristics of the dermatosis, the extent of the lesions, the general character of the patient's skin, previous medication and drug allergies, and other factors.

A. Acute Lesions: (Recent onset, red, burning, swollen, itching, blistering, or oozing.) Use wet preparations (Table 3–1), such as soaks, for lesions localized to extremities; cool wet dressings for localized lesions of the head, neck, trunk, or extremities; or baths for generalized lesions (see below under Pruritus).

B. Subacute Lesions: (Intermediate duration, subsiding lesions, and lesions which are less angry in appearance.) Use wet preparations as outlined above, shake lotions (Table 3–3), or both.

C. Chronic Lesions: (Longer duration, quiescent, thickened, encrusted, fissured, scaly.) Use wet preparations or shake lotions (or both) as outlined above, or any of the following: emulsions (Table 3–3); hydrophilic ointments (Table 3–4); pastes (high powder content) (Table 3–4); creams such as cold cream and vanishing creams (Table 3–4); or greasy ointments (Table 3–5).

Prevention of Complications

The most common complications of skin diseases are pyoderma, local or systemic spread of infection, overtreatment dermatitis, drug sensitivity reactions, and cosmetic disfiguration.

A. Pyoderma: Infected, inflamed, or denuded areas of skin are receptive environments for pyogenic organisms introduced by scratching, rubbing, or squeezing of skin lesions. Patients should be instructed to wash their hands frequently and to avoid manipulation of infected areas. Medications should be kept in closed containers and applied with sterile applicators, which should be discarded after use. Crusts and scabs should not be removed except by the physician. If an infection occurs in a hairy portion of the body, special care should be taken in cleansing and shaving the area.

B. Local or Systemic Spread of Infection: Almost any skin infection may spread by extension or through blood vascular or lymphatic channels. In most cases this complication is a much greater threat to the patient's health and life than the primary skin infection. A most striking and serious example is the extension of staphylococcal infections of the face to the cavernous sinuses. Lymphangitis, lymphadenitis, septicemia, renal carbuncle, bladder infections, and glomerulonephritis may occur as sequelae to primary skin infection. For these reasons it is important to institute vigorous local and systemic measures for the control of skin infections. Systemic antibiotics are ordinarily reserved for serious skin infections or infections associated with systemic reactions, and should be selected on the basis of bacteriologic studies.

C. Overtreatment Dermatitis: This may be avoided if the physician and the patient are aware that undertreatment is preferable to overtreatment and if the patient is warned to avoid overenthusiastic application of topical remedies (either too much or too long).

D. Exfoliative Dermatitis: This complication cannot always be anticipated or avoided but it may be minimized if a careful history of drug sensitivity is obtained before institution of drug therapy. In allergic individuals it is imperative to apply a small amount of topical medication in order to determine hypersensitivity. Drugs which may be required for systemic use (eg, sulfonamides, antibiotics, or antihistamines) should preferably not be used in topical preparations. Sodium sulfacetamide and the tetracyclines appear to be safe for topical use.

E. Cosmetic Disfiguration: Disfiguration due to skin disorders may be avoided by early, careful treatment of skin lesions and by appropriate dermatologic operative technics. Self-manipulation of skin lesions, especially on the face and exposed skin areas, should be avoided.

Rees, R.B.: Topical dermatologic medication. Cutis 5:431–437, 1969.

Rook, A., Wilkinson, D.S., & F.J. Ebling: *Textbook of Dermatology.* Davis, 1968.

Shuster, S.: Systemic effects of skin disease. Lancet 1:907–912, 1967.

PRURITUS
(Itching)

"Pruritus is that disagreeable sensation that excites the desire to scratch." (Haffenreffer.) It is the commonest presenting symptom in dermatology, and includes localized or generalized itching, stinging, crawling, and burning sensations. Pruritus is far less well tolerated than pain.

Itching is a modified form of pain, carried on slow afferent fibers.

Transient, mild pruritus may be physiologic. Pruritus may be a symptom of specific dermatologic disorders; may be idiopathic; or may foreshadow or accompany serious disease of internal origin (lymphomas and other neoplasms, hepatic or biliary disease, diabetes mellitus [generalized itching in an undiagnosed case is rare], nephritis, or drug intoxication or habituation). Perhaps the most common cause of generalized pruritus is excessive dryness of the skin, as in borderline forms of ichthyosis, senile degeneration complicated by irritation with soaps, and low humidity due to artificial heating and cold weather. Other causes are pressure and chafing; chemical irritants (including drugs); food and other allergies; and emotional factors.

Treatment

A. General Measures: Foods should be simple; avoid rich and spicy foods. Test diets or elimination diets are indicated for suspected food allergies. If pruritus is believed to be primarily a manifestation of an emotional disorder, direct therapy accordingly.

External irritants (eg, rough clothing, occupational contactants) should be avoided. Soaps and detergents should not be used by persons with dry or irritated skin. Starch baths may be used. Nails should be kept trimmed and clean. Avoid scratching, if possible. Unnecessary medications should be discontinued since medication itself often produces pruritus.

B. Specific Measures: Remove or treat specific causes whenever possible.

C. Local Measures:

1. Shake lotions, emulsions, and ointments, incorporating the volatile analgesics and antipruritics listed in Table 3–1, may be of value in relieving itching.

2. If the skin is too dry, softening agents may afford relief, eg, rose water ointment (R 30). An excellent principle for dry skin is to wet it, as in a bath (to hydrate the keratin), and then apply petrolatum to the wet skin to trap the moisture.

3. If the skin is too moist, drying agents may afford relief, eg, wet dressings, soaks (R 1–5, R 7); shake lotions (R 13–15); and powders (R 8–11) (especially if the process is acute). Remember that silver nitrate and potassium permanganate may stain the skin.

4. Tub baths–Generalized pruritus may often be effectively controlled by lukewarm baths, 15 minutes 2–3 times daily. After bathing, the skin should be blotted (not rubbed) dry. (*Caution:* Avoid excessive drying of skin by overbathing, prolonged bathing periods, and exposure to drafts after bathing.) Useful bath formulations are as follows: (1) Starch and soda bath: 1–3 cups of starch and 1 cup of sodium bicarbonate dissolved thoroughly in 1 tubful (50 gallons) of lukewarm water. (Soda may be omitted.) (2) Tar bath: Dissolve 50–100 ml coal tar solution USP in 1 tubful (50 gallons) of warm water. (Watch for sensitivity.) (3) Bath oils: 5–25 ml in 1 tubful (50 gallons) of warm water (Alpha-Keri®, Nivea® skin oil, Lubath®, Domol®, or Mellobath®).

D. Potentiation of Topical Corticosteroid Creams or Ointments: By covering selected lesions of psoriasis, lichen planus, and localized eczemas each night, first with the corticosteroid, then with a thin plastic pliable film (eg, Saran Wrap®), between 1–2% of the medicament may be absorbed. Complications include miliaria, pyoderma, heat stroke, adrenal cortical suppression, local skin atrophy, malodor, fungal infection, and urticarial erythema.

E. Systemic Antipruritic Drugs:

1. Antihistaminic and "antiserotonin" drugs may be tried in certain cases of pruritus of allergic or undetermined etiology.

2. Epinephrine injection, 0.25–1 ml of 1:1000 solution every 4 hours, may be of value in certain severe acute cases which may be due to allergy (eg, urticaria).

3. Phenobarbital, 15–30 mg 2–4 times daily, may provide useful sedation in agitated or distracted patients. Barbiturates themselves rarely produce dermatitis.

4. Corticotropin or the corticosteroids (see Chapter 18).

Prognosis

Elimination of external factors and irritating agents is often successful in giving complete relief of pruritus. Pruritus accompanying specific skin disease will subside when the disease is brought under control. Idiopathic pruritus and that accompanying serious internal disease may not respond to any type of therapy.

Editorial: Scratching the surface of the itch. New England J Med 279:715–716, 1968.

Holti, G.: Management of pruritus and urticaria. Brit MJ 1:155–157, 1967.

Kenshalo, D.R. (editor): *The Skin Senses.* Thomas, 1968.

Witten, V.H.: Present status of topical corticosteroid therapy. Pages 25–35 *in:* Waisman, M.: *Pharmaceutical Therapeutics in Dermatology.* Thomas, 1968.

COMMON DERMATOSES

CONTACT DERMATITIS
(Dermatitis Venenata)

Essentials of Diagnosis

- Erythema and edema, often followed by vesicles and bullae in area of contact with suspected agent.
- Later weeping, crusting, and secondary infection.
- Often a history of previous reaction to suspected contactant.
- Patch test with agent usually positive in the allergic form.

General Considerations

Contact dermatitis is an acute or chronic dermatitis which results from direct skin contact with chemicals or other irritants (eg, poison ivy). Lesions are most often on exposed parts. Four-fifths of such disturbances are due to excessive exposure to or additive effects of primary or universal irritants (eg, soaps, detergents, organic solvents). Others are due to actual contact allergy or idiosyncrasy. The most common allergies to dermatologic agents include antimicrobials, antihistamines, and anesthetics.

Clinical Findings

A. Symptoms and Signs: Itching, burning, and stinging are often extremely severe, distributed on exposed parts or in bizarre asymmetric patterns. The lesions consist of erythematous macules, papules, and vesicles. The affected area is often hot and swollen, with exudation, crusting, and secondary infection. The pattern of the eruption may be diagnostic (eg, typical linear streaked vesicles on the extremities and erythema and swelling of the genitals in poison oak dermatitis). The location will often suggest the cause: scalp involvement suggests hair tints, lacquer, shampoos, or tonics; face involvement, creams, soaps, shaving materials; neck involvement, jewelry, fingernail polish; etc.

B. Laboratory Findings: The patch test may be useful but has serious limitations. In the event of a positive reaction, a control test must be done on another individual to rule out primary irritation. Photopatch tests may be necessary in the case of suspected photosensitivity contact dermatitis. These are done by exposing the traditional patch test site to sunlight after 48 hours.

Differential Diagnosis

Asymmetric distribution and a history of contact help distinguish contact dermatitis from other skin lesions. Eruptions may be due to primary irritation from chemicals or allergic sensitization to contactants. The commonest sensitizers are poison oak and ivy, rubber antioxidants and accelerators, nickel and chromium salts, formalin, and halogenated salicylanilide antiseptics. Differentiation may be difficult if the area of involvement is consistent with that seen in other types of skin disorders such as scabies, dermatophytid, atopic dermatitis, and eczema on the body.

Prevention

Prevent reexposure to irritants. Avoid soaps and detergents. Use so-called "hypoallergenic cosmetics" or eliminate cosmetics entirely. Protective rubber gloves may be used. In such cases an inner cotton glove must be used. Protective (barrier) creams are almost useless. It may be necessary to change occupation or duties if occupational exposure is otherwise unavoidable.

Plant irritants (especially Rhus species, eg, poison ivy) should be destroyed by manual removal or by chemical means (2,4-D or dichlorophenoxyacetic acid) near dwellings and in frequented areas.

Prompt and thorough removal of irritants by prolonged washing or by removal with solvents or other chemical agents may be effective if done very shortly after exposure. In the case of Rhus toxin, thorough washing with soap and water must be done within a few minutes if it is to be of any value.

Most well-controlled studies indicate that injection or ingestion of Rhus antigen is of no practical clinical value.

Treatment

A. General Measures: For acute severe cases, one may give prednisone, 35 mg immediately, then 30, 25, 20, 15, 10, and 5 mg on successive days. Triamcinolone (Kenalog®) IM, 40 mg once intragluteally, may be used instead. (See Chapter 18.)

B. Local Measures: Treat the stage and type of dermatitis (see p 37).

1. Acute weeping dermatitis—Do not scrub lesions with soap and water. Apply soothing solutions (Table 3–1). If eruption becomes generalized, use the soothing starch and soda antipruritic bath described on p 32. Shake lotions (℞ 13–15) may be indicated instead of wet dressings or in intervals between wet dressings, especially for involvement of intertriginous areas or when oozing is not marked. Lesions on the extremities may be bandaged with wet dressings. Hydrocortisone and related preparations in lotion, cream, or ointment applied sparingly 2–4 times daily may be very helpful. Corticosteroid sprays may be best (avoid the eyes).

2. Subacute dermatitis (subsiding)–Use shake lotions.

3. Chronic dermatitis (dry and lichenified)–Treat with hydrophilic, greasy ointments or creams. Tars are perhaps most useful in this stage of the dermatitis.

Prognosis

Contact dermatitis is self-limited if reexposure is prevented. Spontaneous desensitization may occur. Increasing sensitivity to industrial irritants may necessitate a change of occupation.

Agrup, G., & others: Value of history and testing in suspected contact dermatitis. Arch Dermat 101:212–215, 1970.

Fisher, A.A.: *Contact Dermatitis.* Lea & Febiger, 1967.

Hjorth, N., & others: Time-saving patch test antigen dispenser. Arch Dermat 102:300–303, 1970.

ERYTHEMA NODOSUM

Essentials of Diagnosis

- Painful red nodules on anterior aspects of legs.
- No ulceration seen.
- Slow regression over several weeks to resemble contusions.
- Some cases associated with infection or drug sensitivity (eg, iodides, bromides, sulfonamides).

General Considerations

Erythema nodosum is a symptom complex characterized by tender, erythematous nodules which appear most commonly on the extensor surfaces of the legs. It usually lasts about 6 weeks, and may be recurrent. It may be associated with various infections (primary coccidioidomycosis, primary tuberculosis, streptococcosis, rheumatic fever, or syphilis) or may be due to drug sensitivity (notably sulfathiazole). It may accompany leukemia, sarcoidosis, and ulcerative colitis.

Clinical Findings

A. Symptoms and Signs: The swellings are exquisitely tender, and are usually preceded by fever, malaise, and arthralgia. The nodules are most often located on the anterior surfaces of the legs below the knees but may occur (rarely) on the arms, trunk, and face. The lesions, 1–10 cm in diameter, are at first pink to red; with regression, all the various hues seen in a contusion can be observed. The nodules occasionally become fluctuant, but they do not suppurate.

B. Laboratory Findings: The histologic finding of fat replacement atrophy in the corium or dermis is strongly suggestive of erythema nodosum. Hilar adenopathy is often seen on chest x-ray.

Differential Diagnosis

Syphilitic gummas and sporotrichosis are usually unilateral. Erythema induratum is seen on posterior legs and shows ulceration. Nodular vasculitis is usually on calves and is associated with phlebitis. Erythema multiforme occurs in generalized distribution. In the late stages, erythema nodosum must be distinguished from simple bruises and contusions.

Treatment

A. General Measures: Eliminate or treat the "specific" cause, eg, systemic infection and exogenous toxins. Rest in the hospital may be advisable. Focal infections should be treated, although this does not appear to influence the course of the disease. Systemic therapy directed against the lesions themselves may include tetracycline drugs, 250 mg 4 times daily for several days; or corticosteroid therapy (see Chapter 18) unless it is contraindicated (tuberculosis must be ruled out).

B. Local Treatment: This is usually not necessary. If the lesions are troublesome, treat according to stage and type of dermatitis (see p 31).

Prognosis

The lesions usually disappear after about 6 weeks, but they may recur. The prognosis depends in part on that of the primary disease.

Fine, R.M., & H.D. Meltzer: Chronic erythema nodosum. Arch Dermat 100:33–38, 1969.

Naish, P.F.: Erythema nodosum. Practitioner 202:637–642, 1969.

ERYTHEMA MULTIFORME

Essentials of Diagnosis

- Sudden onset of symmetric erythematous skin lesions with history of recurrence.
- May be macular, papular, urticarial, bullous, or purpuric.
- "Target" lesions with clear centers and concentric erythematous rings may be noted.
- Mostly on extensor surfaces; may be on palms, soles, or mucous membranes.
- History of herpes simplex, systemic infection or disease, and drug reactions may be associated.

General Considerations

Erythema multiforme is an acute inflammatory, polymorphic skin disease of multiple or undetermined origin. It may occur as a primary skin disorder or as a skin manifestation of systemic infection, malignant or chronic disease of the internal organs (including chronic ulcerative colitis, rheumatoid state, lupus erythematosus, and dermatomyositis), or as a reaction to an ingested drug or injected serum. Long-acting sulfonamides are particularly likely to cause erythema multiforme. Herpes simplex virus and infestations such as ascariasis have also been implicated. The lesions occur predominantly in the spring and fall, and are most common in young people. Unfortunately, very little is known about the pathogenesis.

Clinical Findings

A. Symptoms and Signs: The onset is sudden, often accompanied by burning sensations. There may be soreness of the oral, ocular, and genital mucous membranes. Several lesions may be present with relatively little discomfort. Slight to severe headache, backache, and malaise may occur, and slight to moderate fever.

The principal sign is the symmetric distribution of grouped or isolated crops of violaceous, edematous papules, macules, or nodules, 0.5–1 cm in diameter, with dome-shaped surfaces. The lesions enlarge and become purplish. The term "multiforme" signifies that the lesions may have many varieties. In addition to those just listed, there may be vesicles, bullae, pustules, urticarial lesions, and hemorrhagic alterations. The bullae may resemble those of pemphigus, but usually are surrounded by an erythematous halo. A rather characteristic lesion is the erythema iris (herpes iris), the "bull's eye" pattern formed by an erythematous papule with central clearing. Lesions are usually on the extensor surfaces but may appear anywhere, such as the palms and soles. Mucous membrane ulcerations (aphthae) are frequent. The tracheobronchial mucosa may be involved in severe cases (Stevens-Johnson variant), causing bronchitis and atelectasis. A rare type, erythema perstans, may be present for months or years.

B. Laboratory Findings: There are no characteristic laboratory findings. Histologic changes may be suggestive but are not pathognomonic.

Differential Diagnosis

Secondary syphilis, urticaria, drug eruptions, and toxic epidermal necrolysis must be ruled out. The bullous variety of erythema multiforme is more severe and should be differentiated from dermatitis herpetiformis, pemphigus, and pemphigoid. In erythema multiforme there is usually some constitutional reaction, including fever.

Complications

Erythema multiforme may be complicated by visceral lesions (eg, pneumonitis, myocarditis, nephritis).

Prevention

Avoid all unnecessary medications in patients with a history of erythema multiforme.

Treatment

A. General Measures: Bed rest and good nursing care when fever is present.

B. Specific Measures: Eliminate causative factors such as chronic systemic infections (eg, tuberculosis), focal infections, and sensitizing drugs. Tetracycline, 250 mg 4 times daily for several days, may be useful. Corticosteroids may be tried, as for erythema nodosum. Sulfapyridine, 0.5 gm 4 times daily, may succeed where other measures fail.

C. Local Measures: Treat the stage and type of dermatitis (see p 31). For acute lesions, employ simple wet dressings and soaks or soothing lotions. (For treatment of buccal lesions, see Aphthous Ulcer in Chapter 10.) Subacute lesions require soothing lotions.

Prognosis

The illness usually lasts 2–6 weeks and may recur. The Stevens-Johnson syndrome, a variant of this process (with associated visceral involvement), may be serious or even fatal. The prognosis depends in part on that of the primary disease.

Konzelman, J.L., & others: Oral ulcerations–their differential diagnosis. Cutis 7:27–31, 1971.

Löffler, A.: Erythema multiforme. Dermatologica, Suppl 138, 1969.

PEMPHIGUS

Essentials of Diagnosis

- Relapsing crops of bullae appearing on normal skin.
- Often preceded by mucous membrane bullae, erosions, and ulcerations.
- Nikolsky's sign (superficial detachment of skin after pressure or trauma) variably present.
- Acantholysis (Tzanck's test) presumably is diagnostic.

General Considerations

Pemphigus is an uncommon skin disease of unknown etiology which is always fatal within 2 months to 5 years if untreated. The bullae appear spontaneously and are relatively asymptomatic, but the complications of the disease lead to great toxicity and debility. There is a surprising lack of pathologic internal medical or laboratory findings; no primary lesions are found in internal organs at biopsy. The disease occurs almost exclusively in adults, and is more common among Jews. Recent studies have demonstrated the presence of autoantibodies.

Clinical Findings

A. Symptoms and Signs: Pemphigus is characterized by an insidious onset of bullae in crops or waves. The lesions may appear first on the mucous membranes, and these rapidly become erosive. Toxemia and a "mousy" odor may occur soon. Rubbing the thumb on the surface of uninvolved skin may cause easy separation of the epidermis (Nikolsky's sign).

B. Laboratory Findings: On a smear taken from the base of a bulla and stained with Giemsa's stain (Tzanck's test) one may see a unique histologic picture of disruption of the epidermal intercellular connections, called acantholysis. There may be leukocytosis and eosinophilia. As the disease progresses, low serum protein levels may be found as well as serum electrolyte changes. The sedimentation rate may be elevated, and anemia may be present.

Differential Diagnosis

Acantholysis is not seen in other bullous eruptions such as erythema multiforme, drug eruptions, contact dermatitis, or bullous impetigo, or in the less common dermatitis herpetiformis and pemphigoid. All of these diseases have gross clinical characteristics which distinguish them from pemphigus.

Complications

Secondary infection commonly occurs, often causing extreme debility. Terminally there may be shock, septicemia, disturbances of electrolyte balance, cachexia, toxemia, and pneumonia.

Treatment

A. General Measures: Hospitalize the patient at bed rest and provide antibiotics, blood transfusions, and intravenous feedings as indicated. Anesthetic troches may be used before eating to ease painful oral lesions.

B. Specific Measures: Begin therapy with large initial doses of corticosteroids, eg, 120–150 mg or more of prednisone (or equivalent) to suppress blistering within 3 or 4 days. Maintain with corticosteroids by mouth, and reduce dosage as rapidly as possible to a daily minimum maintenance level sufficient to control local or systemic manifestations. Methotrexate, azathioprine (Imuran®), and cyclophosphamide (Cytoxan®) are being used investigationally with some success.

C. Local Measures: Skin and mucous membrane lesions should be treated as for vesicular, bullous, and ulcerative lesions due to any cause (see p 31). Complicating infection requires appropriate local antibiotic therapy.

Prognosis

Pemphigus was at one time invariably fatal, but the disease can now be controlled indefinitely in many cases. Steroid therapy may induce a complete and permanent remission, in which case maintenance therapy can be discontinued. One-half of all deaths are now related to the complications of steroid therapy.

Beutner, E.H., & others: *Autosensitization in Pemphigus and Bullous Pemphigoid.* Thomas, 1970.

Lever, W.F.: Diagnosis and treatment of pemphigus. California Med 114:37–38, Feb 1971.

ATOPIC DERMATITIS
(Eczema)

Essentials of Diagnosis

- Pruritic vesicular, papular, exudative, or lichenified eruption on face, neck, upper trunk, wrists, and hands and in the folds of knees and elbows.
- Personal or family history of allergic manifestations (eg, asthma, allergic rhinitis, eczema).
- Tendency to recur, with remission from age 2 to early youth and beyond.

General Considerations

Atopic dermatitis is a chronic superficial inflammation of the skin due to a genetic predisposition. These individuals often react to allergens (notably wool and animal epidermals). It is part of the triad of hay fever-asthma-eczema. The disease usually appears in infancy, disappears at the age of 2 or 3 years, recurs in early youth, and thereafter tends to come and go. Personal or family histories of allergic disease are usually obtained. Recent evidence shows a high level of norepinephrine bound in the skin.

Clinical Findings

A. Symptoms and Signs: Itching may be extremely severe and prolonged, leading often to emotional disturbances which have been erroneously interpreted by some as being causative. The distribution of the lesions is characteristic, with involvement of the face, neck, and upper trunk ("monk's cowl"). The bends of the elbows and knees are involved. An abortive form may involve the hands alone (in which case the history of atopy is all-important). In infants the eruption usually begins on the cheeks and is often vesicular and exudative. In children (and later) it is dry, leathery, and lichenified, although intraepidermal vesicles are occasionally present histologically. Adults generally have dry, leathery, hyperpigmented or hypopigmented lesions in typical distribution.

B. Laboratory Findings: Scratch and intradermal tests are disappointing. Eosinophilia may be present. The delayed-blanch reaction to methacholine may help in diagnosing atypical atopic dermatitis.

Differential Diagnosis

Distinguish from seborrheic dermatitis (frequent scalp and face involvement, greasy and scaly lesions, and quick response to therapy), contact dermatitis (especially that due to weeds), and lichen simplex chronicus (flat, more circumscribed, less extensive lesions).

Complications

Kaposi's varicelliform eruption, which includes superimposed skin infection with herpes simplex virus (eczema herpeticum) or the vaccine virus (eczema vaccinatum) may be serious. The patient should be protected from these viruses if possible.

Treatment

A. General Measures: Corticotropin or the corticosteroids may provide spectacular improvement in severe or fulminant eczema (see Chapter 18). Triamcinolone acetonide suspension, 20–40 mg IM every 3 weeks (or less often), may exert control (*caution*). The Scholtz regimen includes cleansing with Cetaphil® lotion (no soap), avoidance of wool and other irritants, 0.01% fluocinolone acetonide solution topically, water-soluble vitamin A, 100,000 units daily by mouth (*caution*), oral antihistamines, and small doses of thyroid.

B. Specific Measures: Avoidance of temperature stress may help to minimize abnormal cutaneous vascular and sweat responses.

The diet should be adequate and well balanced. There is no evidence that standardized or routine dietary restrictions are of value, especially in adults.

Attempts at desensitization to various allergens by graded injections are disappointing, and may cause severe flares.

An attempt should be made to identify and treat emotional disturbances, but this is of little practical value in the management of the dermatitis.

C. Local Treatment: Avoid all unnecessary local irritations to the skin, such as may occur from excessive bathing or as a result of exposure to irritating drugs, chemicals, greases, and soaps. Soapless detergents are not advisable. Clear up skin infections promptly (particularly those with exudates) by appropriate measures (see Chapter 18). Corticosteroids in lotion, cream, or ointment form applied sparingly twice daily may be very helpful. X-ray or grenz ray therapy (by a specialist) may be used effectively, if only temporarily, in many stages.

Treat the clinical type and stage of the dermatitis:

1. For acute weeping lesions use the solutions listed in Table 3–1 as soothing or astringent soaks, baths, or wet dressings for 30 minutes 3 or 4 times daily. Shake lotions (R 13, 14) may be employed at night or when wet dressings are not desirable. Lesions on extremities, particularly, may be bandaged for protection at night.

2. Subacute or subsiding lesions may be treated with shake lotions, which may incorporate mild antipruritic or mild stimulating agents. Shake lotions are usually preferred for widespread lesions. Ointments (Table 3–5) containing mild tar may be used.

3. Chronic, dry, lichenified lesions are best treated with ointments, creams, and pastes (Table 3–4) containing lubricating, keratolytic, antipruritic, and mild keratoplastic agents as indicated. Topical corticosteroids and tars are the most popular agents in chronic eczema. Useful corticosteroids are fluocinolone acetonide (Synalar®) and triamcinolone acetonide (Aristocort®, Kenalog®) in creams, ointments, lotions, solutions, and sprays. Coal tar is available as 2–5% ointments, creams, and pastes. Iodochlorhydroxyquin (Vioform®), 3%, or chlorquinaldol (Sterosan®) ointment or cream may be used in hairy areas or if there is an idiosyncrasy to tar.

Prognosis

The disease runs a chronic course, often with a tendency to disappear and recur.

Ayres, S., Jr., & R. Mihan: Atopic dermatitis–success or failure with the Scholtz regimen. Australian J Dermat 9:16–22, 1968.

Fishman, H.: Atopic eczema–practical aspects of therapy. Cutis 5:438–451, 1969.

Rostenberg, A., Jr., & L.M. Solomon: Infantile eczema and systemic disease. Arch Dermat 98:41–46, 1968.

CIRCULATORY OR STASIS DERMATITIS

Essentials of Diagnosis

- Pruritic red, weeping, swollen areas of eczema and ulceration on the lower legs.
- Older persons with history or evidence of varicose veins, arterial insufficiency, trauma, or episodes of thrombophlebitis.
- Atrophic pigmented skin with scars of old ulcerations.

General Considerations

Eczema of the legs, also called gravitational or hemostatic eczema, is common in older persons, especially men. Most cases are due to impaired circulation, as in varicose veins and arterial disorders, but the disease may be initiated or made worse by the slightest injury, excessive exposure to soap, medication, cold, low humidity, and even malnutrition. After an injury or reaction to medication in a patch of stasis dermatitis, a generalized pruritic vesicular eruption may occur (autosensitization, "toxic absorption phenomenon"). Autoimmune diseases may cause leg ulcers. The reaction may occur spontaneously also. It is considered to be due to reaction with a heat-labile, complement-dependent, 7S γ-globulin specific for epidermal cells.

Post-phlebitic syndrome may cause stasis dermatitis and ulcers at any age.

Clinical Findings

Severe itching is the only symptom. Red, oozing, swollen patches of eczema are present on the backs or outer surfaces of one or both legs (often over the malleoli). Ulcers in the centers of the patches of eczema are rounded and sharply circumscribed, with dirty gray bases and thickened borders. There may be considerable edema. A variant is the hypertensive ischemic ulcer, which may be surprisingly painful.

Differential Diagnosis

Differentiate from other causes of leg ulcers such as sickle cell anemia, hypertension, erythema induratum, and the syphilitic ulcers of late syphilis. The eczema itself must be distinguished from that due to contact dermatitis (eg, overtreatment and stocking dyes).

Treatment

A. General Measures and Prevention: Maintain general health (by proper diet, rest, and sleep) and good skin hygiene. Avoid prolonged sitting, standing, or walking, and constricting garters. Wear properly fitted shoes and stockings. Protect from trauma.

B. Specific Measures: Treat the underlying specific disease, eg, varicose veins, obstructive arterial disease amenable to surgery, thrombophlebitis, and congestive heart failure and hypertension. Autosensitization reaction may be treated with internal and topical corticosteroids.

C. Local Measures: For acute weeping dermatitis use continuous cool wet dressings (Table 3–1). Avoid sensitizing or irritating topical medicaments. For infected eczema or ulcers use topical antibiotic powders (Achromycin® surgical powder, Terramycin® topical powder). Combinations of topical corticosteroids with antibiotics in the form of creams, lotions, and ointments may be useful for more chronic processes.

Painting indolent ulcers with Castellani's solution, 1% aqueous gentian violet, or 10% silver nitrate solution may hasten healing.

Pressure dressings with foam rubber pads and the use of pressure gradient support (Jobst® stockings) may be vital in the healing of indolent stasis ulcers and stubborn stasis dermatitis.

Prognosis

The prognosis depends in great part upon the improvement of the circulation to the limb (eg, repair of varicose veins) and adequacy of treatment. There is a great tendency toward chronicity and recurrence.

Pascher, F.: Symposium on chronic ulcers of the leg. Arch Dermat 98:670–676, 1968.
Perera, P.: An investigation of varicose ulcers. Tr St John Hosp Dermat Soc 56:174–176, 1970.

LICHEN SIMPLEX CHRONICUS
(Localized Neurodermatitis)

Essentials of Diagnosis

- Chronic itching associated with pigmented lichenified skin lesions.
- Exaggerated skin lines overlying a thickened, well circumscribed scaly plaque.
- Predilection for nape of neck, wrists, external surfaces of forearms, inner thighs, genitalia, post-popliteal and antecubital areas.

General Considerations

Lichen simplex chronicus is a persistent, usually well localized plaque several cm in diameter, commonly located on the side of the neck, the flexor aspect of the wrist, or the ankle. A "scratch-itch" cycle is a prominent feature. The lesions may arise out of normal skin, or the disease may occur as a complication of contact dermatitis or any irritative dermatitis. It is par-

ticularly common in persons of Oriental extraction living in the USA, but is said to be rare in their countries of origin. It is more common in women over 40 years of age. Only one person in 5 is born with skin which has the ability to lichenify following chronic manipulation or scratching.

Clinical Findings

Intermittent itching incites the patient to manipulate the lesions. Dry, leathery, hypertrophic, lichenified plaques appear on the neck, wrist, perineum, thigh, or almost anywhere. The patches are well localized and rectangular, with sharp borders, and are thickened and pigmented. The lines of the skin are exaggerated and divide the lesion into rectangular plaques.

Differential Diagnosis

Differentiate from other plaque-like lesions such as psoriasis, lichen planus, seborrheic dermatitis, and nummular dermatitis.

Treatment

The area should be protected and the patient encouraged to avoid stressful and emotionally charged situations if possible. Topical corticosteroids give relief. The injection of triamcinolone acetonide suspension into the lesion may occasionally be curative. Application of triamcinolone acetonide, 0.1%, or fluocinolone, 0.025%, cream nightly with Saran Wrap® covering may be helpful. Roentgen or grenz radiation may be used conservatively by an expert in the technic.

Prognosis

The disease tends to be chronic, and will disappear in one area only to appear in another. Itching may be so intense as to interfere with sleep.

DERMATITIS MEDICAMENTOSA
(Drug Eruption)

Essentials of Diagnosis

- Usually abrupt onset of widespread, symmetric erythematous eruption.
- May mimic any inflammatory skin condition.
- Constitutional symptoms (malaise, arthralgia, headache, and fever) may be present.

General Considerations

Dermatitis medicamentosa is an acute or chronic inflammatory skin reaction to a drug. Almost any drug, whether ingested, injected, inhaled, or absorbed, may cause a skin reaction. This entity does not include dermatitis caused by a drug acting locally (contact dermatitis). The eruption usually recurs upon reexposure to the same or a related drug, although identical reactions may be produced by unrelated drugs and the same drug may produce different types of reactions in different individuals. Reexposure to a suspected drug may be hazardous.

Clinical Findings

A. Symptoms and Signs: The onset is usually abrupt, with bright erythema and often severe itching, but may be delayed (penicillin, serum). Fever and other constitutional symptoms may be present. The skin reaction usually occurs in symmetric distribution. In a given situation the physician may suspect one specific drug (or one of several) and must therefore inquire specifically whether it has been used or not.

Drug eruptions may be briefly classified, with examples, as follows: (1) erythematous (bismuth, arsenicals, barbiturates, sulfonamides, antihistamines, atropine), (2) eczematoid or lichenoid (gold, quinacrine), (3) acneiform or pyodermic (corticotropin, iodides, corticosteroids, bromides), (4) urticarial (penicillin, antibiotics, sera), (5) bullous (iodides), (6) fixed (phenolphthalein, barbiturates), (7) exfoliative (arsenicals, gold), (8) nodose (sulfathiazole, salicylates). (9) Exanthematous eruptions may be caused by many drugs. Ampicillin for infectious mononucleosis causes a morbilliform eruption. (10) Photosensitization may also occur (phenothiazines, chlorothiazides, demethylchlortetracycline, griseofulvin).

B. Laboratory Findings: The complete blood count may show leukopenia, agranulocytosis, or evidence of aplastic anemia.

Differential Diagnosis

Distinguish from other eruptions usually by history and subsidence after drug withdrawal, although fading may be slow.

Complications

Blood dyscrasias may occur.

Prevention

People who have had dermatitis medicamentosa should avoid analogues of known chemical "allergens" as well as known offenders.

Treatment

A. General Measures: Treat systemic manifestations as they arise (eg, anemia, icterus, purpura). Antihistamines may be of value in urticarial and angioneurotic reactions (see p 44), but use epinephrine, 1:1000, 0.5–1 ml IV or IM, as an emergency measure. Corticosteroids (see Chapter 18), may be used as for acute contact dermatitis in severe cases.

B. Specific Measures: Stop all drugs, if possible, and hasten elimination from the body by increasing fluid intake. Dimercaprol (BAL) may be tried in cases due to heavy metals (eg, arsenic, mercury, gold) (see Chapter 28). Sodium chloride, 5–10 gm daily orally, may hasten elimination of bromides and iodides in cases due to those drugs (see Chapter 28).

C. Local Measures: Treat the varieties and stages of dermatitis according to the major dermatitis which is simulated. Watch for sensitivity.

Prognosis

Drug rash usually disappears upon withdrawal of the drug and proper treatment. If systemic involvement is severe (notably with arsenicals), the outcome may be fatal.

Fellner, M.J., & others: The usefulness of immediate skin tests to haptenes derived from penicillin. Arch Dermat 103:371–374, 1971.

Jelinek, J.E.: Cutaneous side effects of oral contraceptives. Arch Dermat 101:181–186, 1970.

Kligman, A.M., & R. Breit: The identification of phototoxic drugs by human assay. J Invest Dermat 51:90–99, 1968.

Rees, R.B.: Cutaneous drug reactions. Texas Med 66:92–93, 1970.

Savin, J.A.: Current causes of fixed drug eruptions. Brit J Dermat 83:546–549, 1970.

Weary, P.E., & others: Eruptions from ampicillin in patients with infectious mononucleosis. Arch Dermat 101:86–91, 1970.

EXFOLIATIVE DERMATITIS

Essentials of Diagnosis

- Scaling and erythema over large area of body.
- Itching, malaise, fever, weight loss.
- Primary disease or exposure to toxic agent (contact, oral, parenteral) may be evident.

General Considerations

Exfoliative dermatitis, a disorder in which a considerable portion of the skin is reddened and covered with lamellated scales which exfoliate freely, may be due to leukemia, lymphoma, or other internal malignancy; may occur as a sequel to dermatitis medicamentosa or contact dermatitis; or may be idiopathic (most cases).

Variants of ichthyosis may resemble exfoliative dermatitis.

Clinical Findings

A. Symptoms and Signs: Symptoms include itching, weakness, malaise, fever, and weight loss. Exfoliation may be generalized or universal, and sometimes includes loss of hair and nails. Generalized lymphadenopathy may be due to lymphoma or leukemia or may be part of the clinical picture of the skin disease (dermatopathic lymphadenitis). There may be mucosal sloughs.

B. Laboratory Findings: Blood and bone marrow studies and lymph node biopsy may show evidence of leukemia or lymphoma. Skin biopsy may show evidence of mycosis fungoides or a specific dermatosis (ie, psoriasis or lichen planus). Hypoproteinemia (a grave sign) and anemia may be present.

Differential Diagnosis

Differentiate from other scaling eruptions such as psoriasis, lichen planus, severe seborrheic dermatitis, and dermatitis medicamentosa, which may themselves develop into exfoliative dermatitis.

Complications

Septicemia, debility (protein loss), pneumonia, high output cardiac failure, masking of fever, hypermetabolism, and thermoregulatory disorders.

Prevention

Patients receiving sensitizing drugs should be watched carefully for the development of skin reactions of all types. The drug should be withheld until the nature of the skin reaction is determined. Proved sensitization should be considered an absolute contraindication to further administration of the drug. Dermatitis or dermatoses should not be overtreated.

Treatment

A. General Measures: Hospitalize the patient at bed rest with talc on bed sheets. Keep room at warm, constant temperature, and avoid drafts. Transfusions of whole blood or plasma may be required. Avoid all unnecessary medication.

Systemic corticosteroids may provide spectacular improvement in severe or fulminant exfoliative dermatitis, but long-term therapy should be avoided if possible (see Chapter 18). Suitable antibiotic drugs should be given when there is evidence of bacterial infection; pyoderma is a common complication of exfoliative dermatitis.

B. Specific Measures: Stop all drugs, if possible, and hasten elimination of offending drug by all means, eg, by increasing fluid intake. Dimercaprol (BAL) may lessen the severity or duration of reactions due to arsenic or gold (see Chapter 28).

C. Local Measures: Observe careful skin hygiene and avoid irritating local applications. Treat skin as for acute extensive dermatitis first with wet dressings, soothing baths (see p 32), powders (Table 3–2), and shake lotions (Table 3–3); and later with soothing oily lotions (Table 3–3) and ointments (Table 3–4).

Topical anti-infective drugs (eg, oxytetracycline, chlortetracycline, erythromycin, or polymyxin B ointment) should be used when necessary.

Prognosis

The prognosis is variable, depending often upon the prognosis of the primary disease (eg, lymphoma). Idiopathic exfoliative dermatitis is unpredictable in its duration and recurrence.

Abrahams, I.: Dermatitis, exfoliative, and erythroderma. Pages 82–83 in: *Current Dermatologic Management.* S. Madden (editor). Mosby, 1970.
Shuster, S., & J. Marks: *Systemic Effects of Skin Disease.* Heinemann, 1970.

PHOTODERMATITIS
(Dermatitis Actinica, Erythema Solare or Sunburn, Polymorphous Light Sensitivity, Contact Photodermatitis)

Essentials of Diagnosis

- Painful erythema, edema, and vesiculation on sun-exposed surfaces.
- Fever, gastrointestinal symptoms, malaise, or prostration may occur.
- Proteinuria, casts, and hematuria may occur.

General Considerations

Photodermatitis is an acute or chronic inflammatory skin reaction due to overexposure or hypersensitivity to sunlight or other sources of actinic rays (cold or hot quartz), photosensitization of the skin by certain drugs, or idiosyncrasy to actinic light as seen in some constitutional disorders including the porphyrias and many hereditary disorders (phenylketonuria, xeroderma pigmentosum, and others). Contact photosensitivity may occur with perfumes, antiseptics, and other chemicals.

Clinical Findings

A. Symptoms and Signs: The acute inflammatory skin reaction is accompanied by pain, fever, gastrointestinal symptoms, malaise, and even prostration. Signs include erythema, edema, and possibly vesiculation and oozing on exposed surfaces. Exfoliation and pigmentary changes often result.

B. Laboratory Findings: Proteinuria, casts, hematuria, and hemoconcentration may be present. Look for porphyrins in urine and stool, protoporphyrins in blood, and findings in other inborn errors of metabolism.

Differential Diagnosis

Differentiate from contact dermatitis which may develop from one of the many substances in suntan lotions and oils. Sensitivity to actinic rays may also be part of a more serious condition such as porphyria, erythropoietic protoporphyria, lupus erythematosus, or pellagra. Phenothiazines, sulfones, chlorothiazides, griseofulvin, and antibiotics may photosensitize the skin. Polymorphous light sensitivity eruptions include several distinct clinical syndromes of unknown etiology. Contact photodermatitis may be caused by bithionol and chlorosalicylanilides (weak antiseptics in soaps, creams, etc).

Complications

Delayed cumulative effects in fair-skinned people include keratoses and epitheliomas. Some individuals become chronic light-reactors even when they apparently are no longer exposed to photosensitizing or phototoxic drugs.

Prevention

Persons with very fair, sensitive skins should avoid prolonged exposure to strong sun or ultraviolet radiation. Preliminary conditioning by graded exposure is advisable.

Protective agents should be applied before exposure, the best of which is 5% para-aminobenzoic acid in 50% ethyl alcohol (℞ 50).

The use of psoralens orally is controversial.

Treatment

A. General Measures: Treat constitutional symptoms by appropriate supportive measures. Control pain, fever, and gastrointestinal and other symptoms as they arise. Aspirin may have some specific value.

B. Local Measures: Treat as for any acute dermatitis (see p 31). First use cooling and soothing wet dressings (Table 3–1), and follow with lotions (Table 3–3). Greases must be avoided because of their occlusive effect.

Prognosis

Dermatitis actinica is usually benign and self-limiting unless the burn is severe or when it occurs as an associated finding in a more serious disorder.

Fisher, D.A., & others: Polymorphous light eruption and lupus erythematosus. Arch Dermat 101:458–461, 1970.

Goldstein, N.: PABA in Hawaii–clinical experience with an alcoholic para-aminobenzoic acid sunscreen. Cutis 7:537–546, 1971.

Kalivas, J.: A guide to the problem of photosensitivity. JAMA 209:1706–1709, 1969.

Reed, W.B.: The genetics of the photodermatoses. Cutis 7:645–653, 1971.

LICHEN PLANUS

Essentials of Diagnosis

- Pruritic, violaceous, flat-topped papules with fine white streaks and symmetric distribution.
- Commonly seen along linear scratch mark (Koebner phenomenon).
- Anterior wrists, sacral region, penis, legs, mucous membranes.
- Usually occurs in an otherwise healthy but emotionally tense person.
- Histopathology is diagnostic.

General Considerations

Lichen planus is a chronic inflammatory disease associated with emotional tension or stress. It is more common after the second decade of life and is rare in children.

Clinical Findings

Itching is mild to severe. The lesions are violaceous, flat-topped, angulated papules, discrete or in clusters, on the flexor surfaces of the wrists and on the penis, lips, tongue, and buccal and vaginal mucous membranes. The papules may become bullous or ulcerated. The disease may be generalized. Mucous membrane lesions have a lacy white network overlying them which is often confused with leukoplakia. Papules are 1–4 mm in diameter, with white streaks on the surface (Wickham's striae).

Differential Diagnosis

Distinguish from similar lesions produced by quinacrine or bismuth sensitivity and other papular lesions such as psoriasis, papular eczema, and syphiloderm. Lichen planus on the mucous membranes must be differentiated from leukoplakia. Certain photo-developing or duplicating solutions may produce contact eruptions which mimic lichen planus.

Treatment

A. General Measures: Patients are often "high-strung" or tense and nervous, and episodes of dermatitis may follow emotional crises. Measures should be directed at relieving anxiety, eg, with phenobarbital, 15–30 mg 2–4 times daily orally for 1 month. Corticosteroids (see Chapter 18) may be required in severe cases.

B. Local Measures: Use shake lotions containing tar (℞ 16). X-ray or grenz ray therapy (by a specialist) may be used in severe cases. Intralesional injection of triamcinolone acetonide is useful for localized forms. Corticosteroid cream or ointment may be used nightly under thin pliable plastic film.

Prognosis

Lichen planus is a benign disease, but it may persist for months or years and may be recurrent. Oral lesions tend to be especially persistent.

Irgang, S.: Lichen planus. Cutis 6:887–897, 1970.

Samman, P.D.: Lichen planus: A dermatological centenary. Brit J Dermat 81:306–307, 1969.

Zaias, N.: The nail in lichen planus. Arch Dermat 101:264–271, 1970.

PSORIASIS

Essentials of Diagnosis

- Silvery scales on bright red plaques, usually on the knees, elbows, and scalp.
- Stippled nails.
- Itching uncommon unless psoriasis is eruptive or occurs in body folds.
- Psoriatic arthritis may be present.
- Histopathology is specific.

General Considerations

Psoriasis is a common benign, acute or chronic, inflammatory skin disease which apparently is based upon genetic predisposition. A genetic error in the mitotic control system has been postulated. Injury or irritation of a psoriatic skin tends to provoke lesions of psoriasis in the site. Psoriasis occasionally is eruptive, particularly in periods of stress.

Clinical Findings

There are usually no symptoms. Eruptive psoriasis may itch, and psoriasis in body folds itches severely (inverse psoriasis). The lesions are bright red, sharply outlined plaques covered with silvery scales. The elbows, knees, and scalp are the most common sites. Nail involvement may resemble onychomycosis. Fine stippling in the nails is pathognomonic. There may be associated arthritis which resembles the rheumatoid variety.

Differential Diagnosis

Differentiate in the scalp from seborrheic dermatitis; in body folds from intertrigo and candidiasis; and on the nails from onychomycosis.

Treatment

A. General Measures: Warm climates seem to exert a favorable effect. Nonspecific internal medication is of little value with the exception of arsenic, which is hazardous in view of the recurrent nature of the lesions and the delayed effect of excessive use of arsenic (keratoses, epitheliomas). Severe psoriasis calls for hospitalization and treatment with topical corticosteroids under a plastic suit or by means of the Goeckerman or Ingram routine.

Corticotropin or corticosteroids may be necessary to give relief in fulminating cases.

Reassurance is important since these patients are apt to be discouraged by the difficulties of treatment. An attempt should be made to relieve anxieties.

B. Local Measures:

1. Acute psoriasis—Avoid irritating or stimulating drugs. Begin with a shake lotion (℞ 13, 14) or bland ointment (Table 3–4) containing 5% detergent solution of coal tar. As the lesions become less acute, gradually incorporate mild keratoplastic agents into lotions (Table 3–3) and hydrophilic ointments (Table 3–4).

2. Subacute psoriasis—Give warm baths daily, scrubbing the lesions thoroughly with a brush, soap, and water. Apply increasing concentrations of keratoplastic or stimulating agents incorporated in lotions (Table 3–3) and hydrophilic ointments (Table 3–4). Solar or ultraviolet irradiations may be applied in gradually increasing doses.

3. Chronic psoriasis—Administer the following ultraviolet irradiation and tar regimen daily as needed (modified from Goeckerman): Smear 2–5% coal tar ointment thickly on the skin and leave for 12–24 hours. Wipe off ointment with mineral oil, leaving a light stain. Follow with gradually increasing suberythema doses of ultraviolet light as tolerated.

Apply ammoniated mercury ointment, 5%, locally twice daily (watch for mercurialism), or anthralin ointment, 0.5%, locally once a day (avoid the eyes). Mercury is unpopular now because of consumer attitudes, but it may be effective topically when other measures fail.

For localized lesions, triamcinolone acetonide suspension, 2.5 mg/ml, may be injected intralesionally. Apply triamcinolone acetonide, 0.1%, or fluocinolone, 0.025%, cream nightly and cover with Saran Wrap®. Betamethasone valerate, 0.1% ointment, may be superior.

Prognosis

Individual manifestations can often be cleared, although the tendency to regression and recurrence persists. Psoriasis is a prolonged and recalcitrant disease.

Farber, E.M., & D.R. Harris: Hospital treatment of psoriasis. Arch Dermat 101:381–389, 1970. [Ingram routine.]

Mandy, S., & others: Topically applied mechlorethamine in the treatment of psoriasis. Arch Dermat 103:272–276, 1971.

Rees, R.B., & J.D. Jacobitz: Methotrexate for psoriasis. Dermat Digest 10:40–48, 1971.

See also Witten reference under Pruritus, p 33.

PITYRIASIS ROSEA

Essentials of Diagnosis

- Oval, fawn-colored, scaly eruption following cleavage lines of trunk.
- Herald patch commonly precedes eruption by 1–2 weeks.
- Occasional pruritus.

General Considerations

Pityriasis rosea is a common mild, noncontagious, acute inflammatory skin disease of unknown etiology. It behaves like an infectious exanthem in that it runs a definite course (usually 6 weeks) and confers a solid "immunity" (second attacks are rare). It occurs usually during the spring or fall. A chronic form of the disease occurs rarely. A good tan suppresses the eruption (in the tanned areas only).

Clinical Findings

Occasionally there is severe itching. The lesions consist of oval, fawn-colored macules 4–5 mm in diameter following cleavage lines on the trunk. Exfoliation of the lesions causes a crinkly scale which begins in the center. The proximal portions of the extremities are involved. A "herald patch" is usually evident. This is the initial lesion, which usually precedes the later efflorescence by 1–2 weeks.

Differential Diagnosis

Differentiate from secondary syphilis, especially when lesions are numerous or smaller than usual. Tinea corporis, seborrheic dermatitis, tinea versicolor, and drug eruptions may simulate pityriasis rosea.

Treatment

Acute irritated lesions (uncommon) should be treated as for acute dermatitis with wet dressings (Table 3–1) or shake lotions (R 13–16). Apply coal tar solution, 5% in starch lotion, twice daily. Ultraviolet light is helpful.

Prognosis

Pityriasis rosea is usually an acute self-limiting illness which disappears in about 6 weeks.

Cohen, E.L.: Pityriasis rosea. Brit J Dermat 79:533–537, 1967.

SEBORRHEIC DERMATITIS

Essentials of Diagnosis

- Dry scales or dry yellowish dandruff with or without underlying erythema.
- Scalp, central face, presternal, interscapular areas, umbilicus, and body folds.

General Considerations

Seborrheic dermatitis is an acute or chronic papulosquamous dermatitis. It is based upon a genetic predisposition mediated by an interplay of such factors as hormones, nutrition, infection, and emotional stress. The role of pityrosporon organisms is unclear.

Clinical Findings

Pruritus may be present but is an inconstant finding. The scalp, face, chest, back, umbilicus, and body folds may be oily or dry, with dry scales or oily yellowish scurf. Erythema, fissuring, and secondary infection may be present.

Differential Diagnosis

Distinguish from other skin diseases of the same areas such as intertrigo and fungal infections; and from psoriasis (location).

Treatment

A. General Measures: Prescribe a well-balanced, adequate diet and restrict excess sweets, spices, hot drinks, and alcoholic beverages. Regular working hours, recreation, sleep, and simple cleanliness are recommended. Treat aggravating systemic factors such as infections, overwork, emotional stress, constipation, and dietary abnormalities.

B. Local Measures:

1. Acute, subacute, or chronic eczematous lesions—Treat as for dermatitis or eczema (see p 37). An emulsion base containing 0.5% hydrocortisone and 10% sodium sulfacetamide is useful for all forms and stages. Corticosteroid creams, lotions, or solution may be used in all stages (R 20, 39, 40).

2. Seborrhea of the scalp—Use one of the following: (1) Selsun® (selenium sulfide) suspension or Capsebon® once a week after shampoo. Fostex® cream (containing soapless cleansers, wetting agents, hexachlorophene, sulfur, and salicylic acid) may be used as a weekly shampoo for oily seborrhea. (2) Sebulex® is similar to Fostex® and is also effective. Sebizon® lotion (sodium sulfacetamide) may be applied once daily. (3) Sebical® shampoo, containing tar and allantoin, may succeed where other fail.

3. Seborrhea of nonhairy areas—Mild stimulating lotion (R 16), ointment (R 35), or 3–5% sulfur in hydrophilic ointment (Table 3–5) may be used. (The addition of 1% salicylic acid aids in removing scales.)

4. Seborrhea of intertriginous areas—Avoid greasy ointments. Apply astringent wet dressings (R 1–5, 7) followed by 5% ammoniated mercury in hydrophilic ointment (Table 3–5).

Prognosis

The tendency is to life-long recurrences. Individual outbreaks may last weeks, months, or years.

Brotherton, J.: Relative effectiveness of different classes of fungicides against *Pityrosporum ovale*. Brit J Dermat 80:749–757, 1968.

Derbes, V.J.: Seborrheic dermatitis. Cutis 4:553–558, 1968.

ACNE VULGARIS

Essentials of Diagnosis

- Pimples (papules or pustules) over the face, back, and shoulders occurring at puberty.
- Cyst formation, slow resolution, scarring.
- The most common of all skin conditions.

General Considerations

Acne vulgaris is a common inflammatory skin disease of unknown etiology apparently caused by a genetic predisposition and activated by androgens. It may occur at any time from puberty through the period of sex hormone activity. Eunuchs are spared, and the disease may be provoked by giving androgens to a predisposed individual. Identical involvement may occur in identical twins.

The disease is more common in males. Contrary to popular belief, it does not always clear spontaneously when maturity is reached. If untreated, it may persist into the 4th and even 6th decade of life. The skin lesions are the result of sebaceous overactivity, retention of sebum, overgrowth of the acne bacillus (*Corynebacterium acnes*) in incarcerated sebum, irritancy of fatty acids, and foreign body reaction to extrafollicular sebum. The role of antibiotics in controlling acne is not clearly understood, although they reduce lipases which produce irritating free fatty acids.

Clinical Findings

There may be mild soreness, pain, or itching; inflammatory papules, pustules, ectatic pores, acne cysts, and scarring. The lesions occur mainly over the face, neck, upper chest, back, and shoulders. Comedones are common.

Self-consciousness, embarrassment, and shame may be the most disturbing symptoms.

Differential Diagnosis

Distinguish from acneiform lesions caused by bromides, iodides, and contact with chlorinated naphthalenes and diphenyls.

Complications

Cyst formation, severe scarring, and psychic trauma.

Treatment

A. General Measures:

1. Education of the patient—The patient should be carefully instructed about the nature of his skin disorder, the objectives of treatment, and the necessity for faithful adherence to the treatment program. It should be explained that treatment is essential not only to produce an acceptable cosmetic result while the condition is active but also to prevent permanent scarring.

2. Diet—The diet should be adequate and well-balanced. Forbid chocolate, nuts (including peanut butter), fatty or fried foods, seafoods, alcoholic beverages, spicy foods, and excess carbohydrates. Foods are less important than formerly thought.

3. Eliminate all possible medication, especially bromides or iodides.

4. Avoid exposure to oils and greases.

5. Treat anemia, malnutrition, infection, gastrointestinal disorders, or other factors which may aggravate acne.

6. Aggravating or complicating emotional disturbances must be taken into consideration and treated appropriately.

7. Antibiotics—Tetracycline, 250 mg orally every day, may exert better long-term control than any other treatment in some cases. Tetracycline may permanently discolor growing teeth.

Clindamycin (Cleocin®), 150 mg daily by mouth, may work when tetracycline fails. Chloramphenicol (Chloromycetin®) should not be used internally for acne.

B. Local Measures: Ordinary soap is adequate for cleansing, but pHisoHex® may be used. Avoid greasy cleansing creams and other cosmetics. Shampoo the scalp 1—2 times a week (℞ 48). Extract blackheads with a comedo extractor. Incise and drain fluctuant cystic lesions with a small sharp scalpel.

1. Keratoplastic and keratolytic agents—Acne lotion (sulfur-zinc lotion, ℞ 18) may be applied locally to the skin at bedtime and washed off in the morning.

2. Keratolytic ointments and pastes—Begin with weak preparations and increase strength as tolerated. Apply one of the following at bedtime and remove in the morning: (1) Sulfur, 2—10% in hydrophilic ointment. (2) Quinolor® compound ointment.

3. Commercial preparations for acne include Fostex® cream and cake, Fostril Hc® cream, Cort Acne® lotion, Rezamid® lotion. Acne-Dome® cleanser, cream, and lotion, Resulin® lotion, Sulforcin® cream and lotion, and Clantis® lotion.

4. Dermabrasion—Cosmetic improvement may be achieved by abrasion of inactive acne lesions, particularly flat, superficial scars. The skin is first frozen and anesthetized with ethyl chloride or Freon® and then carefully abraded with fine sandpaper or special motor-driven abrasive brushes. The technic is not without untoward effects, since hyperpigmentation, grooving, and scarring have been known to occur.

Gentle daily abrasion may be accomplished with abrasive particles incorporated in a suitable vehicle (Pernox®, Brasivol®).

5. Superficial chemosurgery—Liquid phenol or 25—50% trichloroacetic acid applied carefully to acne scars with an applicator and removed immediately with 70% alcohol may produce favorable cosmetic results.

6. Irradiation—Simple exposure to sunlight in graded doses is often beneficial. Ultraviolet irradiation may be used as an adjunct to other treatment measures. Use suberythema doses in graded intervals up to the point of mild erythema and scaling. X-ray radiation (by a specialist) should be reserved for the most severe cases after other measures have been tried without success.

7. Oral contraceptives are said to help some young women with acne. Apparently it is the mestranol contained in them which is beneficial. Hyperpigmentation (melasma) is an occasional complication. (Topical occlusive corticosteroids may produce acne.)

Prognosis

Untreated acne vulgaris may persist throughout adulthood and may lead to severe scarring. The disease is chronic and tends to recur in spite of treatment.

Ashton, H., & others: Lincomycin and clindamycin. Brit J Dermat 83:604—606, 1970.

Freinkel, R.K.: Acne vulgaris: Follicles, fats and flora. Cutis 7:409—412, 1971.

Fulton, J.E., Jr., & others: Effect of chocolate on acne vulgaris. JAMA 210:2071—2074, 1969.

Pedace, F.J., & R. Stoughton: Topical retinoic acid in acne vulgaris. Brit J Dermat 84:465—469, 1971.

Reisner, R.: Rational therapy of acne vulgaris. Cutis 7:175—184, 1971.

URTICARIA (HIVES) & ANGIONEUROTIC EDEMA (GIANT HIVES)

Essentials of Diagnosis

- Wheals with marked itching.
- Fever, malaise, and nausea may occur.

General Considerations

Hives is an acute or chronic inflammatory skin reaction of allergic origin. Most acute forms are caused by ingestion of foods to which the patient is sensitive.

Chronic urticaria requires the same sort of exhaustive investigation indicated for a long-continued unexplained fever. Common causes are foods (shellfish, pork, strawberries, wheat, eggs, milk, tomatoes, chocolate), drugs (antibiotics, especially penicillin, salicylates, belladonna, iodides, bromides, serum, vaccines, phenolphthalein, opium derivatives), insect bites, parasitic infestation, and emotional disturbances. In chronic urticaria, the cause will rarely be found.

Clinical Findings

A. Symptoms and Signs: In addition to intolerable itching, there may also be malaise and slight fever. Nausea may result from involvement of the gastrointestinal mucosa. The wheals vary greatly in size, shape, and amount of swelling.

B. Laboratory Findings: There may be transient eosinophilia. In chronic urticaria, extensive laboratory investigations may be required in the search for occult foci of infection, food and drug sensitivity, and other possible causes. ECG abnormalities have been reported in a few cases.

Differential Diagnosis

Distinguish from contact dermatitis, poison oak, and dermographia.

Complications

Laryngeal obstruction is the most important complication, especially in the angioedema variant of urticaria. Hereditary angioneurotic edema due to lack of $C'1^a$ esterase inhibitor is frequently fatal.

Prevention

Avoid reexposure to sensitizing drugs or foods and aggravating physical, systemic, or emotional factors. In the penicillin-sensitive patient exposure to occult sources of penicillin may occur, eg, in milk and other foods.

Treatment

A. General Measures: Initial castor oil purgation to remove possible antigenic substances has been recommended in acute cases. Stools may be examined for parasites. During the acute phase the diet should be simple and free of such common offenders as yeast, wheat, milk, eggs, pork, fish, shellfish, tomatoes, strawberries, and chocolate. The past history, food diaries, trial diets, and elimination diets may be helpful in determining offending foods. The patient should not remain on a restricted diet unless food sensitivity can be demonstrated. Avoid unnecessary medication. (Suspect **all** drugs.)

1. Antihistaminic drugs often give prompt and sustained symptomatic relief. Hydroxyzine (Atarax®, Vistaril®) may have special value.

2. Epinephrine injection, 0.3−1 ml of 1:1000 solution, subcut, for acute lesions when laryngeal edema is suspected or present, when urticaria is intense, or when antihistaminic drugs have failed to give relief.

3. Ephedrine sulfate, 25 mg orally 4 times daily, or ephedrine-sedative mixtures.

4. Systemic corticosteroids (see Chapter 18) may provide spectacular improvement in severe or fulminant angioneurotic edema. These drugs should be used only if it is apparent that the patient will not respond to more conservative measures.

5. Fresh plasma may be life-saving during an acute attack of hereditary angioneurotic edema.

B. Local Measures: Topical antipruritic preparations are frequently of benefit (see p 32 and Table 3−2).

Prognosis

The disease is usually self-limited and lasts only a few days. The chronic form may persist for years.

Africk, J., & K.M. Halprin: Infectious mononucleosis presenting as urticaria. JAMA 209:1524−1525, 1969.

Champion, R.H., & others: Urticaria and angioedema: Review of 554 patients. Brit J Dermat 81:588−597, 1969.

Urticaria. Lancet 2:1344−1345, 1969.

INTERTRIGO

Intertrigo is caused by the macerating effect of heat, moisture, and friction. It is especially likely to occur in obese persons and in humid climates. Poor hygiene is an important etiologic factor. There is often a history of seborrheic dermatitis. The symptoms are itching, stinging, and burning. The body folds develop fissures, erythema, and sodden epidermis, with superficial denudation. Urine and blood examination may reveal diabetes mellitus, and the skin examination may reveal candidiasis. A direct smear may show abundant cocci. Intertrigo is the commonest cause of disability in American troops in tropical areas.

Treatment is as for tinea cruris (see p 55), but fungicidal agents should not be used. Recurrences are common.

MILIARIA
(Heat Rash)

Essentials of Diagnosis

- Burning, itching, superficial aggregated small vesicles or papules on covered areas of the skin.
- Hot moist climate.
- May have fever and even heat prostration.

General Considerations

Miliaria is an acute dermatitis which occurs most commonly on the upper extremities, trunk, and intertriginous areas. A hot, moist environment is the most frequent cause, but individual susceptibility is important and obese persons are most often affected. Plugging of the ostia of sweat ducts occurs, with consequent ballooning and ultimate rupture of the sweat duct, producing an irritating, stinging reaction.

Clinical Findings

The usual symptoms are burning and itching. Fever, heat prostration, and even death may result in severe forms. The lesions consist of small superficial, reddened, thin-walled, discrete but closely aggregated vesicles, papules, or vesicopapules. The reaction occurs most commonly on covered areas of the skin.

Differential Diagnosis

Distinguish from similar skin manifestations occurring in drug rash.

Prevention

Provide optimal working conditions when possible, ie, controlled temperature, ventilation, and humidity. Avoid overbathing and the use of strong, irritating soaps. Graded exposure to sunlight or ultraviolet light may benefit persons who will later be subjected to a hot, moist atmosphere. Susceptible persons should avoid exposure to adverse atmospheric conditions.

Treatment

An antipruritic cooling lotion such as the following should be applied 2–4 times daily:

R	Menthol	1.0
	Phenol	2.0
	Glycerin	15.0
	Alcohol, q s ad	240.0

Alternative measures which have been employed with varying success are drying shake lotions (R 13 with 1% phenol, or R 14) and antipruritic powders or other dusting powders. Treat secondary infections (superficial pyoderma) with potassium permanganate soaks, compresses, or baths (Table 3–1). Ammoniated mercury, 2–5% in hydrophilic ointment (Table 3–4), may be employed advantageously. Tannic acid, 10% in 70% alcohol, applied locally twice daily, serves to toughen the skin. Anticholinergic drugs given by mouth may be very helpful in severe cases.

Prognosis

Miliaria is usually a mild disorder, but death may result in the severe forms (tropical anhidrosis and asthenia) as a result of interference with the heat-regulating mechanism. The process may also be irreversible to some extent, requiring permanent removal of the individual from the humid or hot climate.

Champion, R.H.: Disorders of the sweat glands. Practitioner 200:625–631, 1968.

Sulzberger, M.B., & T.B. Griffin: Induced miliaria, postmiliarial hypohidrosis, and some potential sequelae. Arch Dermat 99:145–151, 1969.

PRURITUS ANI & VULVAE

Essentials of Diagnosis

- Itching, chiefly nocturnal, of the anogenital area.
- There may be no skin reactions; or inflammation of any degree may occur up to lichenification.

General Considerations

Most cases have no obvious cause, but multiple specific causes have been identified. Anogenital pruritus may be due to the same causes as intertrigo, lichen simplex chronicus, seborrheic dermatitis, contact dermatitis (from soap, colognes, douches, contraceptives), or may be due to irritating secretions, as in diarrhea, leukorrhea, trichomoniasis, or local disease (candidiasis, dermatophytosis). Diabetes mellitus must be ruled out. Psoriasis or seborrheic dermatitis may be present. Uncleanliness may be at fault.

Clinical Findings

A. Symptoms and Signs: The only symptom is itching, which is chiefly nocturnal. Physical findings are usually not present, but there may be erythema, fissuring, maceration, lichenification, excoriations, or changes suggestive of candidiasis or tinea.

B. Laboratory Findings: Urinalysis and blood sugar determination may reveal diabetes mellitus. Direct microscopic examination or culture of tissue scrapings may reveal yeasts, fungi, or parasites. Stool examination may show intestinal parasites.

Differential Diagnosis

Distinguish among the various causes of this condition, such as Candida organisms, parasites, local irritation from contact with drugs and irritants, and other primary skin disorders of the genital area such as psoriasis, seborrhea, or intertrigo.

Prevention

Treat all possible systemic or local causes. Instruct the patient in proper anogenital hygiene.

Treatment (See also Pruritus, p 32.)

A. General Measures: Avoid "hot," spicy foods, and drugs which can irritate the anal mucosa. Treat constipation if present (see p 301). Instruct the patient to use very soft or moistened tissue or cotton after a bowel movement and to clean thoroughly. Women should apply the same precautions after urinating. Instruct the patient regarding the harmful and pruritus-inducing effects of scratching.

B. Local Measures: Corticosteroid creams (see R 40) or Vioform® hydrocortisone cream are quite useful. Sitz baths twice daily are of value if the area is acutely inflamed and oozing, using silver nitrate, 1:10,000–1:200; potassium permanganate, 1:10,000; or aluminum subacetate solution, 1:20. Underclothing should be changed daily. Paint fissured or ulcerated areas with Castellani's carbolfuchsin solution.

X-ray or grenz ray therapy (by a specialist) may be used if other measures fail.

Prognosis

Although usually benign, anogenital pruritus may be persistent and recurrent.

Verbov, J.L.: Pruritus ani. Practitioner 205:67—69, 1970.

CALLOSITIES & CORNS
(OF FEET OR TOES)

Callosities and corns are caused by pressure and friction due to faulty weight-bearing, orthopedic deformities, or improperly fitting shoes. Some persons are hereditarily predisposed to excessive and abnormal callus formation.

Tenderness on pressure and "after-pain" are the only symptoms. The hyperkeratotic well-localized overgrowths always occur at pressure points. On paring, a glassy core is found (which differentiates these disorders from plantar warts, with multiple bleeding points upon cutting across capillaries). A soft corn often occurs laterally on the proximal portion of the fourth toe as a result of pressure against the bony structure of the interphalangeal joint of the fifth toe.

Treatment consists of correcting mechanical abnormalities which cause friction and pressure. Shoes must be properly fitted, and orthopedic deformities corrected. Callosities may be removed by careful paring of the callus after a warm water soak, or with keratolytic agents, eg,

℞	Salicylic acid	4.0
	Acetone	4.0
	Collodion, qs ad	· 15.0

Sig: Apply locally to callus every night and cover with a strip of adhesive. Remove adhesive in the morning. Repeat until corn or callus is removed.

A metatarsal leather bar, ½ inch wide and ¼ inch high, may be placed on the outside of the shoe just behind the weight-bearing surface of the sole. "Ripplesole" shoes may be effective.

Women who tend to form calluses and corns should not wear confining footgear.

Murray Space-Shoes® (expensive) may be specially fitted. For those who cannot afford them, shoes with sponge rubber soles may be used, with the shoemaker cutting cavities on the insides of the soles to correspond with the calluses.

Carney, R.: Confusing keratotic lesions of the sole. Cutis 7:32—34, 1971.
Montgomery, R.: Dermatoses of the hands and feet. Cutis 5:452—456, 1969.

CHRONIC DISCOID
LUPUS ERYTHEMATOSUS

Essentials of Diagnosis
- Red, asymptomatic, localized plaques, usually on the face, often in butterfly distribution.
- Scaling, follicular plugging, atrophy, and telangiectasia of involved areas.
- Histology distinctive.

General Considerations

Lupus erythematosus is a superficial, localized discoid inflammation of the skin occurring most frequently in areas exposed to solar or ultraviolet irradiation. The etiology is not known. The disseminated type is discussed in Chapter 13.

Clinical Findings

A. Symptoms and Signs: There are usually no symptoms. The lesions consist of dusky red, well localized, single or multiple plaques, 5—20 mm in diameter, usually on the face and often in a "butterfly pattern" over the nose and cheeks. There is atrophy, telangiectasia, and follicular plugging. The lesion is usually covered by dry, horny, adherent scales.

Where indicated, a complete medical study should be made to rule out systemic lupus erythematosus.

B. Laboratory Findings: There are usually no significant laboratory findings in the chronic discoid type. If there is leukopenia or proteinuria, with or without casts, one must suspect the disseminated or systemic form of the disease. Histologic changes are distinctive. The antinuclear antibody test is perhaps best for ruling out systemic lupus erythematosus.

Differential Diagnosis

The scales are dry and "tack-like," and can thus be distinguished from those of seborrheic dermatitis. Differentiate also from the morphea type of basal cell epithelioma and, by absence of nodules and ulceration, from lupus vulgaris.

Complications

Dissemination may occur. There may be scarring.

Treatment

A. General Measures: Treat chronic infections. Provide protection from sunlight and all other powerful radiation. *Caution:* Do not use any form of radiation therapy.

Maintain optimal general health by well-balanced diet with supplementary vitamins and iron as indicated. Ensure adequate rest, and prescribe bed rest when the patient is febrile.

B. Medical Treatment: (For discoid type only.) *Caution:* Any of the following drugs may cause serious eye changes. If the medication is continued, ophthalmologic examination should be done every 3 months. Wherever possible, chronic discoid lupus erythematosus should be considered a cosmetic defect only and should be treated topically or with camouflaging agents.

1. Chloroquine phosphate, 0.25 gm daily for 1 week, then 0.25 gm twice weekly. Watch for signs of toxicity.

2. Hydroxychloroquine sulfate (Plaquenil®), 0.2 gm orally daily, then twice weekly, may occasionally be effective when quinacrine and chloroquine are not tolerated.

3. A triple synthetic antimalarial (Triquin®), 1 tablet daily, then twice weekly, may be more effective and better tolerated than the above.

4. Quinacrine hydrochloride (Atabrine®), 0.1 gm orally daily for 2 weeks, then 0.1 gm twice weekly for 3 months or more. Watch for signs of toxicity.

C. Local Infiltration: Triamcinolone acetonide suspension, 10 mg/ml, may be injected into the lesions once a week or once a month. This should be tried before internal treatment (see above).

D. Corticosteroids: Corticosteroid creams applied each night and covered with airtight, thin, pliable plastic film may be useful.

Prognosis

The disease is persistent but not life-endangering unless it turns into the disseminated variety.

Kay, D.M., & D.L. Tuffanelli: Lupus erythematosus: Newer aids in diagnosis. Dermat Digest 7:69–75, 1968.

Tuffanelli, D.L., & others: Dermal-epidermal junction in lupus erythematosus. Arch Dermat 99:652–662, 1969.

VIRAL INFECTIONS OF THE SKIN

HERPES SIMPLEX
(Cold or Fever Sore)

Essentials of Diagnosis

- Recurrent small grouped vesicles on an erythematous base, especially around oral and genital areas.
- May follow minor infections, trauma, stress, or sun exposure.
- Regional lymph nodes may be swollen and tender.

General Considerations

Herpes simplex is an acute viral infection. Clinical outbreaks, which may be recurrent in the same location for years, are provoked by fever, sunburn, indigestion, fatigue, windburn, menstruation, or nervous tension.

Chronic virus multiplication, rather than latency, may account for recurrent herpes simplex.

Clinical Findings

The principal symptoms are burning and stinging. Neuralgia may precede and accompany attacks. The lesions consist of small, grouped vesicles which can occur anywhere but which most often occur on the lips, mouth, and genitals. Regional lymph nodes may be swollen and tender.

Differential Diagnosis

Distinguish from other vesicular lesions, especially herpes zoster and impetigo. In the genital area, differentiate from syphilis, lymphogranuloma venereum, and chancroid.

Complications

Pyoderma, Kaposi's varicelliform eruption (eczema herpeticum or disseminated herpes simplex), encephalitis, keratitis.

Treatment

For persistent or severe, recurrent herpes:

A. General Measures: Eliminate precipitating agents when possible.

B. Local Measures: Apply a moistened styptic pencil several times daily to abort lesions. Dust vesicles twice daily with bismuth formic iodide (BFI) powder or use shake lotions (R 13, 14); camphor spirit locally twice daily; or epinephrine, 1:100 locally twice daily. Topical corticosteroids are contraindicated. Treatment of dendritic keratitis is discussed on p 75.

If there is associated cellulitis and lymphadenitis, apply cool compresses. Treat stomatitis with mild (saline) mouth washes. X-ray or grenz ray therapy (by a specialist) may be indicated in selected cases.

Application of neutral red or proflavine to the lesion, followed by a 15-minute exposure to a cool white 15-watt fluorescent desk lamp, is said to be effective treatment.

Prognosis

Individual attacks last 1–2 weeks. Recurrences are common.

Catalano, P.M.: Broadening spectrum of herpesvirus hominis (herpes simplex). Arch Dermat 101:364–366, 1970.

Felber, T., & others: Photodynamic inactivation of herpes simplex. Presented at AMA Section on Dermatology, June 1971.

HERPES ZOSTER
(Shingles)

Essentials of Diagnosis

- Pain along course of nerve followed by painful grouped vesicular lesions.
- Involvement is unilateral. Lesions are usually on face and trunk.
- Swelling of regional lymph nodes (inconstant).

General Considerations

Herpes zoster is an acute vesicular dermatitis of viral origin. There is considerable evidence that this virus and the virus of varicella are identical. The 2 diseases may be concurrent.

Clinical Findings

Pain usually precedes the eruption by 48 hours or more and may persist and actually increase in intensity after the lesions have disappeared. The lesions consist of grouped, tense, deep-seated vesicles distributed unilaterally along the neural pathways of the trunk. The commonest distributions are on the trunk or face. Regional lymph glands may be tender and swollen.

Differential Diagnosis

Since poison oak and poison ivy dermatitis may be produced unilaterally and in a streak by a single brush with the plant, it must be differentiated at times from herpes zoster. Differentiate also from similar lesions of herpes simplex, which is usually less painful.

Complications

Persistent neuralgia, anesthesia of the affected area following healing, facial or other nerve paralysis, and encephalitis may occur.

Treatment

A. General Measures: Barbiturates may help control tension and nervousness associated with neuralgia. Aspirin or APC compound with or without codeine phosphate, 30 mg, usually controls pain. A single intragluteal injection of triamcinolone acetonide suspension, 40–60 mg, may give prompt relief. Ophthalmologic consultation should be considered for supraorbital involvement to avoid serious ocular complications.

B. Local Measures: Wet dressings may be necessary for acute and extensive inflammatory lesions (see p 68). Calamine lotion or other shake lotions (see p 69) are often of value. Apply the lotion liberally and cover with a protective layer of cotton. Do not use greases.

X-ray therapy (by an expert) may be helpful.

C. Post-zoster Neuralgia: Infiltration of involved skin with triamcinolone acetonide suspension and lidocaine (Xylocaine®) may be worth trying.

Prognosis

The eruption persists 2–3 weeks and does not recur. Motor involvement may lead to temporary palsy. Post-zoster neuralgia, which usually occurs in elderly individuals in supraorbital distribution, is extraordinarily persistent and devastating and does not respond to treatment. Ocular involvement may lead to blindness.

Campbell, E.W., Jr., & others: Therapy of disseminated herpes zoster. Cutis 7:581–583, 1971.
Eaglstein, W.H., & others: The effects of early corticosteroid therapy on the skin eruption and pain of herpes zoster. JAMA 211:1681–1683, 1970.

Juel-Jensen, B.E., & others: Treatment of zoster with idoxuridine in dimethyl sulfoxide: Results of two double-blind controlled trials. Brit MJ 4:776–780, 1970.

WARTS

Essentials of Diagnosis

- Warty elevation anywhere on skin or mucous membranes, usually no larger than 0.5 cm in diameter.
- Prolonged incubation period (average 2–18 months).
- Spontaneous "cures" are frequent (50%), but warts are often unresponsive to any treatment.
- "Recurrences" (new lesions) are frequent.

General Considerations

Warts are usually seen as solitary or clustered lesions, all presumably due to the same virus, most often on the exposed parts such as the fingers or hands. The incubation period is 2–18 months. No age group is exempt, but warts are perhaps more commonly seen in children and young adults. The virus is intranuclear, arranged in icosahedron symmetry, and 40–55 nm in diameter. It has not yet been grown in the laboratory.

Clinical Findings

There are usually no symptoms. Tenderness on pressure occurs with plantar warts; itching with anogenital warts. Occasionally a wart will produce mechanical obstruction (eg, nostril, ear canal).

Warts vary widely in shape, size, and appearance. Flat warts are most evident under oblique illumination. Subungual warts may be dry, fissured, and hyperkeratotic, and may resemble hangnails or other nonspecific changes. Plantar warts resemble plantar corns or calluses.

Prevention

Avoid contact with warts. A person with flat warts should be admonished not to scratch the areas. Occasionally an electric shaver will prevent the spread of warts in razor scratches.

Treatment

A. Removal: Remove the warts whenever possible by one of the following means:

1. Surgical excision—Inject a small amount of local anesthetic into the base and then remove the wart with a dermal curet or scissors or by shaving off at the base of the wart with a scalpel. Trichloroacetic acid or Monsel's solution on a tightly wound cotton-tipped applicator may be painted on the wound, or electrocautery may be applied.

2. Liquid nitrogen applied with a cotton-tipped applicator until the wart is thoroughly blanched causes after-pain, but large numbers of warts may be so treated bloodlessly.

3. Keratolytic agents—Either of the following may be used:

℞ Salicylic acid   4.0
   Ethyl aminobenzoate (Benzocaine®)   0.15
   Acetone
   Flexible collodion, a̅a̅   15.0

Sig: Paint on warts each night.

℞ Salicylic acid   3.6
   Alcohol, 40%, qs ad   120.0

Sig: Paint on flat warts with cotton swab daily.

4. Anogenital warts are best treated by painting them weekly with 25% podophyllin in compound tincture of benzoin *(caution).*

B. Internal Medical Treatment: There is no specific internal remedy.

Prognosis

There is a striking tendency to the development of new lesions. Warts may disappear spontaneously or may be unresponsive to treatment.

Almeida, J.D., & J.D. Oriel: Wart viruses. Brit J Dermat 83:698–699, 1970.
Hurstone, M.: Treatment of warts with 5-fluorouracil. Brit J Dermat 83:218, 1970.

BACTERIAL INFECTIONS OF THE SKIN

IMPETIGO

Impetigo is a contagious and auto-inoculable infection of the skin caused by staphylococci or, less commonly, streptococci. The infected material may be transmitted to the skin by dirty fingernails. In children, the source of infection is often a pyogenic nasal infection or another infected child.

Itching is the only symptom. The lesions consist of macules, vesicles, pustules, and honey-colored gummy crusts which when removed leave denuded red areas. The face and other exposed parts are most often involved.

Impetigo must be distinguished from other vesicular and pustular lesions such as herpes simplex, varicella, and contact dermatitis (dermatitis venenata).

Treatment is as for folliculitis. Response to local treatment for infection and to systemic antibiotics is usually good. Systemic treatment should be given if there is fever or unresponsiveness. The nephritis which occasionally develops may be fatal (particularly in infants). Erythromycin may be preferable to the penicillins for impetigo.

Parker, M.T.: Streptococcal skin infection and acute glomerulonephritis. Brit J Dermat 81 (Suppl 1):37–46, 1969.
Rees, R.B.: Bacterial infections of the skin. Pages 583–585 in: *Current Therapy 1971.* H.F. Conn (editor). Saunders, 1971.

ECTHYMA

Ecthyma is a deeper form of impetigo, with ulceration. It occurs frequently on the legs and other covered areas, often as a complication of debility and infestations.

Kelly, C., & others: Streptococcal ecthyma: Treatment with benzathine penicillin G. Arch Dermat 103:306–310, 1971.

BOCKHART'S IMPETIGO

Bockhart's impetigo is a staphylococcal infection which produces tense, globular painful pustules at the follicular orifices. It is a form of folliculitis (see below).

IMPETIGO NEONATORUM

Impetigo neonatorum is a highly contagious, potentially serious form of impetigo occurring in infants. It requires prompt systemic treatment and protection of other infants (isolation, exclusion from the nursery of personnel with pyoderma, etc). The lesions are bullous and massive, and accompanied by systemic toxicity. Death may occur.

FOLLICULITIS
(Including Sycosis Vulgaris or Barber's Itch)

Essentials of Diagnosis
- Itching and burning in hairy areas.
- Pustules in the hair follicles.
- In sycosis, inflammation of surrounding skin area.

General Considerations

Folliculitis is caused by staphylococcal infection of a hair follicle. When the lesion is deep-seated, chronic, and recalcitrant, it is called sycosis. Sycosis is usually propagated by the auto-inoculation and trauma of shaving. The upper lip is particularly susceptible to involvement in men who suffer with chronic nasal discharge from sinusitis or hay fever.

Clinical Findings

The symptoms are slight burning and itching, and pain on manipulation of the hair. The lesions consist of pustules of the hair follicles. In sycosis the surrounding skin becomes involved also and so resembles eczema, with redness and crusting.

Differential Diagnosis

Differentiate from acne vulgaris and infections of the skin, such as impetigo.

Complications

Abscess formation.

Prevention

Correct precipitating or aggravating factors: systemic (eg, diabetes mellitus) or local causes (eg, mechanical or chemical skin irritations, discharges).

Treatment

A. Specific Measures: Systemic anti-infectives may be tried if the skin infection is resistant to local treatment; if it is extensive or severe and accompanied by a febrile reaction; if it is complicated; or if it involves the so-called "danger areas" (upper lip, nose, and eyes).

Local anti-infective agents are of proved value and should be tried in sequence until a favorable response is obtained (allowing 3–4 days for evaluation). They should be applied initially at night and protected by dressings; soaks should be applied during the day. After the area has cleared, any of the following preparations may be applied 2–4 times daily: (1) Neomycin sulfate, 1% cream or ointment, locally 4 times daily. (2) Iodochlorhydroxyquin (Vioform®), 3% in cream or ointment form, locally twice daily. (3) Other antibiotics, alone or in combination, as ointments locally 2–4 times daily. These include polymyxin B in combination with bacitracin or oxytetracycline, neomycin, chloramphenicol, and erythromycin.

Penicillin and sulfonamides should not be used topically, with the exception of sodium sulfacetamide.

B. Local Measures: Cleanse the area gently with a weak soap solution and apply soaks or compresses to the involved area for 15 minutes twice daily (Table 3–1). When skin is softened, gently open the larger pustules and trim away necrotic tissue.

Prognosis

Folliculitis is often stubborn and persistent, lasting for months and even years.

Leading Article: Bacteria and the skin. Lancet 2:860–869, 1968.

FURUNCULOSIS (BOILS) & CARBUNCLES

Essentials of Diagnosis

- Extremely painful inflammatory swelling of a hair follicle which forms an abscess.
- Primary predisposing debilitating disease sometimes present.
- Antibiotic-resistant strains of "hospital staph" are responsible for an increasing percentage of cases.

General Considerations

A furuncle (boil) is a deep-seated infection (abscess) involving the entire hair follicle and adjacent subcutaneous tissue. The most common sites of occurrence are the hair parts exposed to irritation and friction, pressure, or moisture, or to the plugging action of petroleum products. Because the lesions are auto-inoculable, they are often multiple. Thorough investigation usually fails to uncover a predisposing cause, although an occasional patient may have uncontrolled diabetes mellitus, nephritis, or other debilitating disease.

A carbuncle is several furuncles developing in adjoining hair follicles and coalescing to form a conglomerate, deeply situated mass with multiple drainage points.

Clinical Findings

A. Symptoms and Signs: The extreme tenderness and pain are due to pressure on nerve endings, particularly in areas where there is little room for swelling of underlying structures. The pain, fever, and malaise are more severe in carbuncles than with furuncles. The follicular abscess is either rounded or conical. It gradually enlarges, becomes fluctuant, and then softens and opens spontaneously after a few days to 1–2 weeks to discharge a core of necrotic tissue and pus. The inflammation occasionally subsides before necrosis occurs.

A carbuncle is much larger than a boil. Instead of having only one core it has 2 or more.

B. Laboratory Findings: There may be slight leukocytosis.

Differential Diagnosis

Differentiate from deep mycotic infections such as sporotrichosis and blastomycosis; from other bacterial infections such as anthrax and tularemia; and from acne cysts.

Complications

Fatal cavernous sinus thrombosis may occur as a complication of a manipulated furuncle on the central portion of the upper lip or near the nasolabial folds. Perinephric abscess, osteomyelitis, and other hematogenous staphylococcal infections may also occur.

Treatment

A. Specific Measures:

1. Systemic anti-infective agents are indicated (chosen on the basis of cultures and sensitivity tests if possible).

2. Bacterial recolonization with a harmless staphylococcus may be tried for recurrent furunculosis.

B. Local Measures: Immobilize the part and avoid overmanipulation of inflamed areas. Use moist heat to help larger lesions "localize." Use proper surgical incision, epilation, or debridement **after** the lesions are "mature." Do not incise deeply. Apply anti-infective ointment and bandage the area loosely during drainage.

Prognosis

Recurrent crops may harass the patient for months or years. Carbunculosis is more severe and more hazardous than furunculosis.

Fritsch, W.C.: Therapy of impetigo and furunculosis. JAMA 214:1862–1866, 1970.

Shinefield, H.R., & others: Bacterial interference between strains of *Staphylococcus aureus,* 1960 to 1970. Am J Dis Child 121:148–152, 1971.

ERYSIPELAS

Essentials of Diagnosis

- Edematous, spreading, circumscribed, hot, erythematous area, with or without vesicle or bulla formation.
- Pain, malaise, chills and fever.
- Leukocytosis, increased sedimentation rate.

General Considerations

Erysipelas is an acute inflammation of the skin and subcutaneous tissue caused by infection with beta-hemolytic streptococci. It occurs classically on the cheek.

Clinical Findings

A. Symptoms and Signs: The symptoms are pain, malaise, chills, and moderate fever. A bright red spot appears first, very often near a fissure at the angle of the nose. This spreads to form a tense, sharply demarcated, glistening, smooth, hot area. The margin characteristically makes noticeable advances from day to day. The patch is somewhat edematous and can be pitted slightly with the finger. Vesicles or bullae occasionally develop on the surface. The patch does not usually become pustular or gangrenous, and heals without scar formation. The disease may complicate any break in the skin which provides a portal of entry for the organism.

B. Laboratory Findings: Leukocytosis and increased sedimentation rate almost invariably occur.

Differential Diagnosis

Distinguish from cellulitis, with its less definite margin and involvement of deeper tissues, and from erysipeloid, a benign bacillary infection producing redness of the skin of the fingers or the backs of the hands in fishermen and meat handlers.

Complications

Unless erysipelas is promptly treated, death may result from extension of the process and systemic toxicity, particularly in the very young and in the aged.

Treatment

Place the patient at bed rest with the head of his bed elevated, apply hot packs, and give aspirin for pain and fever. Penicillin is specific for beta-hemolytic streptococcus infections.

Prognosis

Erysipelas formerly was very dangerous to life, particularly in the very young and in the aged. With antibiotic therapy the disease can now usually be quickly controlled. Prompt and adequate treatment usually will limit it to one attack.

Robinson, R.C.V.: Antibiotics and other anti-infectious drugs. Pages 49–64 *in:* Waisman, M. (editor): *Pharmaceutical Therapeutics in Dermatology.* Thomas, 1968.

CELLULITIS

Cellulitis, a diffuse spreading infection of the skin, must be differentiated from erysipelas (a superficial form of cellulitis) because the 2 conditions are quite similar. Cellulitis involves deeper tissues and may be due to one of several organisms, usually cocci. The lesion is hot and red but has a more diffuse border than does erysipelas. Cellulitis usually occurs after a break in the skin. Recurrent attacks may sometimes affect lymphatic vessels, producing a permanent swelling called "solid edema."

The response to systemic, anti-infective measures (penicillin, broad-spectrum antibiotics, or sulfonamides) is usually prompt and satisfactory.

ERYSIPELOID

Erysipelothrix rhusiopathiae infection must be differentiated from erysipelas and cellulitis. It is usually a benign infection commonly seen in fishermen and meat handlers, which is characterized by redness of the skin, most often of a finger or the back of the hand, and which gradually extends over a period of several days. Systemic involvement which occurs rarely, is manifested by reversal of the albumin-globulin ratio and other serious changes. Endocarditis may occur.

Penicillin is usually promptly curative. Broad-spectrum antibiotics may be used instead.

DECUBITUS ULCERS
(Bedsores)

Bedsores (pressure sores) are a special type of ulcer caused by impaired blood supply and tissue nutrition due to prolonged pressure over bony prominences. The skin overlying the sacrum and hips is most commonly involved, but bedsores may also be seen over the occiput, ears, elbows, heels, and ankles. They occur most readily in aged, paralyzed, and debilitated patients in whom an adequate underlying fat pad is lacking. Low-grade infection may occur.

Good nursing care and nutrition and maintenance of skin hygiene are important preventive measures. The skin and the bed linens should be kept clean and dry. Bedfast, paralyzed, moribund, or listless patients who are candidates for the development of decubiti must be turned **frequently** (at least every hour) and must be examined at pressure points for the appearance of small areas of redness and tenderness. Inflated rubber rings, rubber pillows, and an alternating pressure mattress, all of which are essential in the treatment of early lesions, are of value also in prevention.

Early lesions should also be treated with topical antibiotic powders and adhesive absorbent bandage (Gelfoam®). Established lesions require surgical consultation and care. A spongy pad called "Feathersoft" may be placed under the patient and may work best in some cases. It may be laundered often.

Adams, L.A., & S.M. Bluefarb: How we treat decubitus ulcers. Postgrad Med 44:269–271, 1968.
Walden, R.H., & others: Inoperable pressure sores. Prevention and management. New York J Med 71:657–662, 1971.

FUNGAL INFECTIONS
OF THE SKIN

Mycotic infections are traditionally divided into 2 principal groups: superficial and deep. In this chapter we will discuss only the superficial infections: tinea capitis, tinea corporis, and tinea cruris; dermatophytosis of the feet and dermatophytid of the hands; tinea unguium (onychomycosis, or fungal infection of the nails); and tinea versicolor. Candidiasis belongs in an intermediate group but will be considered here as well as with the deep mycoses.

The diagnosis of fungal infections of the skin is usually based on the location and characteristics of the lesions and on the following laboratory examinations:

(1) Direct demonstration of fungi in 10% potassium hydroxide preparations of scrapings from suspected lesions. (2) Cultures of organisms. Dermatophytes responsive to griseofulvin are easily detectable, with color change from yellow to red on dermatophyte test medium (DTM) medium. (3) Skin tests, eg, trichophytin (not reliable) for superficial mycoses. (This test has exclusion value in suspected dermatophytid.) (4) Examination with Wood's light (an ultraviolet light with a special filter), which causes hairs to fluoresce a brilliant green when they are infected by microsporum organisms (cause about 90% of cases of tinea capitis in some areas of the USA). The lamp is also invaluable in following the progress of treatment. Ringworm of the scalp may be totally unsuspected yet discovered easily with Wood's light in mass surveys of school children. Trichophyton-infected hairs do not fluoresce. (5) Histologic sections stained with periodic acid-Schiff (Hotchkiss-McManus) technic. Fungal elements stain red and are easily found.

Serologic tests are of no value in the diagnosis of superficial fungal infections.

Principles of Local Treatment

Treat acute active fungal infections initially as for any acute dermatitis (see p 31). *Note:* It may be necessary to treat the dermatitis before applying topical fungicidal medication.

Most topical fungicidal agents are strong skin irritants. **It is easy to overtreat.**

General Measures & Prevention

Keep the skin dry, since moist skin favors the growth of fungi. A cool climate is preferred. Reduce exercise and activities to prevent excessive perspiration. Dry the skin carefully after bathing or after perspiring heavily. Socks and other clothing should be changed often. Sandals or open-toed shoes should be worn. Skin secretions should be controlled with talc or other drying powders or with drying soaks (Table 3–1). Sedatives (eg, phenobarbital) may be effective in reducing skin secretions in tense, nervous people. Toughen the skin with graded daily sunbaths or with a quartz lamp.

Wilson, J.W., & others: Superficial fungous infections of the skin. Hosp Med 7:98–114, 1971.

Griseofulvin

Griseofulvin is an antibiotic obtained by fermentation of several species of penicillia. It is water-soluble and thermostable, and is not related chemically to any other antibiotic in current use. Cross-sensitization with other antibiotics has not been a problem. The drug is deposited in keratinous structures and apparently acts by interfering with reproduction of the fungal elements.

Griseofulvin is employed in oral dosage against dermatophyte or "ringworm" fungal infections. It is most effective for ringworm infections of the scalp and quite effective for involvement of the face, neck, and trunk; reasonably effective against ringworm of the groin; and less effective for involvement of hands and feet. Nail infections are least responsive to griseofulvin therapy.

The drug is supplied in tablets of 250 and 500 mg. Microcrystalline forms are now available in 250 mg capsules and 500 mg tablets, and are apparently better absorbed. The average daily dose is 1 gm orally for adults and comparably less for children. Absorption is allegedly better after a fatty meal. Prolonged treatment may be required for onychomycosis.

Toxic reactions include headache, urticaria, dizziness, drowsiness, morbilliform and hemorrhagic eruptions, gastrointestinal distress, and loose stools, as well as photosensitivity and interference with the action of bishydroxycoumarin (Dicumarol®). Although severe reactions are occasionally reported, hematologic studies and assays of kidney and liver function have shown the drug to be essentially free of severe side reactions.

Taplin, D., & others: Isolation and recognition of dermatophytes on a new medium (DTM). Arch Dermat 99:203–209, 1969.

TINEA CAPITIS
(Ringworm of Scalp)

Essentials of Diagnosis

- Round, gray, scaly "bald" patches on the scalp.
- Usually in prepuberal children.
- Often fluorescent under Wood's lamp.
- Microscopic examination or culture identifies the fungus.

General Considerations

This persistent, contagious, and sometimes epidemic infection occurs almost exclusively in children and disappears spontaneously at puberty. Two genera (Microsporum and Trichophyton) cause ringworm infections of the scalp. Microsporum accounts for many of the infections, and hairs infected with this genus fluoresce brilliantly under Wood's light. Trichophyton species account for some of the very resistant infections, which may persist into adulthood.

Clinical Findings

A. Symptoms and Signs: There are usually no symptoms, although there may be slight itching. The lesions are round, gray, scaly, apparently bald patches on the scalp. (The hairs are broken off and the patches are not actually bald.) Scalp ringworm may be undetectable with the naked eye, becoming visible only under the Wood's light, in which case the hairs exhibit a brilliant green fluorescence extending down into the hair follicle.

B. Laboratory Findings: Microscopic or culture demonstration of the organisms in the hairs may be necessary.

Differential Diagnosis

Differentiate from other diseases of scalp hair such as pediculosis capitis, pyoderma, alopecia areata, and trichotillomania (voluntary pulling out of one's own hair).

Prevention

Exchange of headgear must be avoided, and infected individuals or household pets must be vigorously treated and reexamined for determination of cure. The scalp should be washed after haircuts.

Complications

Kerion (a nodular, exudative pustule), possibly followed by scarring, is the only complication.

Treatment

Griseofulvin, preferably microcrystalline, 0.25–0.5 gm by mouth daily or twice daily for 2 weeks, will cure most cases.

Prognosis

Tinea capitis may be very persistent, but usually clears spontaneously at puberty. Most ringworm infections of the scalp will clear spontaneously in 1–2 years even if not treated.

Harrell, E.R.: Fungus diseases. Pages 111–118 *in:* Yaffee, H.S. (editor): *Newer Views of Skin Diseases.* Little, Brown, 1966.

TINEA CORPORIS OR TINEA CIRCINATA
(Body Ringworm)

Essentials of Diagnosis

- Pruritic, ringed, scaling, centrally clearing lesions; small vesicles in a peripherally advancing border.
- On exposed skin surfaces.
- History of exposure to infected domestic animal.
- Laboratory examination by microscope or culture confirms diagnosis.

General Considerations

The lesions are often on exposed areas of the body such as the face and arms. A history of exposure to an infected cat may be obtained. All species of dermatophytes may cause this disease, but some are more common than others.

Clinical Findings

A. Symptoms and Signs: Itching is usually intense, which serves to distinguish the disease from other ringed lesions. The lesions consist of rings of vesicles with central clearing, grouped in clusters and distributed asymmetrically, usually on an exposed surface.

B. Laboratory Findings: Hyphae can be demonstrated readily by removing the cap of a vesicle and examining it microscopically in a drop of 10% potassium hydroxide. The diagnosis may be confirmed by culture.

Differential Diagnosis

Itching distinguishes tinea corporis from other skin lesions with annular configuration, such as the annular lesions of psoriasis, erythema multiforme, and pityriasis rosea.

Complications

Complications include extension of the disease to the scalp hair or nails (in which case it becomes much more difficult to cure), overtreatment dermatitis, pyoderma, and dermatophytid.

Prevention (See also p 54.)

Avoid contact with infected household pets and avoid exchange of clothing without adequate laundering.

Treatment

A. Specific Measures: Griseofulvin (microcrystalline), 0.5 gm orally daily for children and 1 gm orally daily for adults.

B. Local Measures: *Caution:* Do not overtreat.

R	Salicylic acid	0.3
	Sulfur, ppt	0.9
	Hydrophilic ointment, q s ad	30.0

Sig: Apply locally twice daily.

Compound undecylenic acid ointment may be used in the less chronic and nonthickened lesions.

Tolnaftate (Tinactin®) solution (R 21) applied topically is effective against dermatophyte infections other than of the nails.

Prognosis

Body ringworm usually responds promptly to griseofulvin by mouth or to conservative topical therapy.

Blank, H., & others: Cutaneous *Trichophyton mentagrophytes* infections in Vietnam. Arch Dermat 99:135–144, 1969.
Gilgor, R.S., & others: Lupus erythematosus-like tinea of the face (tinea faciale). JAMA 215:2091–2094, 1971.

TINEA CRURIS
(Jock Itch)

Essentials of Diagnosis

- Marked itching in intertriginous areas.
- Peripherally spreading, sharply demarcated, centrally clearing erythematous macular lesions, with or without vesicle formation.
- May have associated tinea infection of feet.
- Laboratory examination with microscope or culture confirms diagnosis.

General Considerations

Tinea cruris lesions are confined to the groin and gluteal cleft and are as a rule more indolent that those of tinea corporis and tinea circinata. The disease often occurs in athletes as well as in persons who are obese or who perspire a great deal. Any of the dermatophytes may cause tinea cruris, and it may be transmitted to the groin from active dermatophytosis of the foot. Intractable pruritus ani may occasionally be caused by tineal infection.

Clinical Findings

A. Symptoms and Signs: Itching is usually more severe than that which occurs in seborrheic dermatitis or intertrigo. Inverse psoriasis, however, may itch even more than tinea cruris. The lesions consist of erythematous macules with sharp margins, cleared centers, and active, spreading peripheries in intertriginous areas. There may be vesicle formation at the borders, and satellite vesicular lesions are sometimes present.

B. Laboratory Findings: Hyphae can be demonstrated microscopically in 10% potassium hydroxide preparations. The organism may be cultured readily.

Differential Diagnosis

Differentiate from other lesions involving the intertriginous areas, such as candidiasis, seborrheic dermatitis, intertrigo, and psoriasis of body folds ("inverse psoriasis").

Treatment

A. General Measures: (See also p 31.) Drying powder (Table 3–2) should be dusted into the involved area 2–3 times a day, especially when perspiration is excessive. Keep the area clean and dry but avoid overbathing. Prevent intertrigo or chafing by avoiding overtreatment, which predisposes to further infection and complications. Rough-textured clothing should be avoided.

B. Specific Measures: Griseofulvin (see p 53) is indicated for severe cases. Give 1 gm orally daily for 1–2 weeks.

C. Local Measures: Treat the stage of dermatosis (see p 31). Secondarily infected or inflamed lesions are best treated with soothing and drying solutions, with the patient at bed rest. Use wet compresses of potassium permanganate, 1:10,000 (or 1:20 aluminum acetate solution), or, in case of anogenital infection, sitz baths.

Fungicidal preparations: Any of the following may be used: (1) Weak solutions of iodine (not more than 1% tincture) twice daily. (2) Carbolfuchsin solution (Castellani's paint), 1/3 strength, once a day. (3) Compound undecylenic acid ointment twice daily. (4) Sulfur-salicylic acid ointment (R 35). (5) Tolnaftate (Tinactin®) solution (R 21).

Prognosis

Tinea cruris usually responds promptly to topical or systemic treatment.

Kuflik, E.G., & others: An evaluation of topical antifungal therapy in servicemen. Cutis 7:287–290, 1971.

TINEA MANUUM & TINEA PEDUM
(Dermatophytosis,
Tinea of Palms & Soles, "Athlete's Foot")

Essentials of Diagnosis

- Itching, burning, and stinging of interdigital webs, palms, and soles.
- Deep vesicles in acute stage.
- Exfoliation, fissuring, and maceration in subacute or chronic stages.
- Skin scrapings examined microscopically or by culture may reveal fungus.

General Considerations

Tinea of the feet is an extremely common acute or chronic dermatosis. It is possible that the causative organisms are present on the feet of most adults at all times. Certain individuals appear to be more susceptible than others. Most infections are caused by Trichophyton and Epidermophyton species.

Clinical Findings

A. Symptoms and Signs: The presenting symptom is usually itching. However, there may be burning, stinging, and other sensations, or frank pain from secondary infection with complicating cellulitis, lymphangitis, and lymphadenitis. Tinea pedum often appears as a fissuring of the toe webs, perhaps with denudation and sodden maceration. However, there may also be grouped vesicles distributed anywhere on the soles or the palms, a generalized exfoliation of the skin of the soles, or destructive nail involvement in the form of discoloration and hypertrophy of the nail substance with pithy changes. Acute reddened, weeping vesicular lesions are seen on the skin in the acute stages.

B. Laboratory Findings: Hyphae can often be demonstrated microscopically in skin scales treated with 10% potassium hydroxide. Culture with Sabouraud's medium is simple and often informative, but does not always demonstrate pathogenic fungi.

Differential Diagnosis

Differentiate from other skin conditions involving the same areas such as interdigital intertrigo, candidiasis, psoriasis, contact dermatitis (from shoes, powders, nail polish), atopic eczema, and scabies.

Prevention

The essential factor in prevention is personal hygiene. Rubber or wooden sandals should be used in community showers and bathing places. Open-toed shoes and sandals are best for general wear. Careful drying between the toes after showering is recommended. Socks should be changed frequently. Apply dusting and drying powders as necessary (Table 3–2), and place small wads of cotton between the toes at night.

Treatment

A. Specific Measures: Griseofulvin (see p 53) has been disappointing in the treatment of dermatophytosis of the feet and should be used only for severe cases or those which are recalcitrant to topical therapy.

B. Local Measures: *Caution:* Do not overtreat.

1. Acute stage (lasts 1–10 days)—Give aluminum subacetate solution soaks (℞ 4) for 20 minutes 2–3 times daily. If secondary infection is present, use soaks of 1:10,000 potassium permanganate. If secondary infection is severe or complicated, treat as described on p 31.

2. Subacute stage—Any of the following may be used: (1) Zincundecate ointment twice daily. (2) Whitfield's ointment, ¼–½ strength (℞ 33). (3) Solution of coal tar, 5% in starch lotion, or ℞ 16. (4) Coal tar, 1–2% in Lassar's paste.

3. Chronic stage—Use any of the following: (1) Sulfur-salicylic acid ointment or cream (℞ 35). (2) Whitfield's ointment, ¼–½ strength (℞ 33). (3) Compound undecylenic acid ointment twice daily. (4) Alcoholic Whitfield's solution (℞ 46). (5) Carbolfuchsin solution (Castellani's paint). (6) Tolnaftate (Tinactin®) solution (℞ 21).

C. Mechanical Measures: Carefully remove or debride dead or thickened tissues after soaks or baths.

D. X-Ray or Grenz Ray: Radiation therapy (by a specialist) may be of value when other measures fail.

Prognosis

Tinea of the hands and feet usually responds well to treatment, but recurrences are common in strongly predisposed persons.

Kuflik, E.G., & others: An evaluation of topical antifungal therapy in servicemen. Cutis 7:287–290, 1971.

DERMATOPHYTID
(Allergy or Sensitivity to Fungi)

Essentials of Diagnosis

- Pruritic, grouped vesicular lesions involving the sides and flexor aspects of the fingers and the palms.
- Fungal infection elsewhere on body, usually the feet.
- Trichophytin skin test positive. No fungus demonstrable in lesions.

General Considerations

Dermatophytid is a sensitivity reaction to an active focus of dermatophytosis elsewhere on the body, usually the feet. Fungi are present in the primary lesion but are not present in the lesions of dermatophytid. The hands are most often affected, but dermatophytid may occur on other areas of the body also.

Clinical Findings

A. Symptoms and Signs: Itching is the only symptom. The lesions consist of grouped vesicles, often involving the thenar and hypothenar eminences. Lesions are round, up to 15 mm in diameter, and may be present on the side and flexor aspects of the fingers. Lesions occasionally involve the backs of the hands or may even be generalized.

B. Laboratory Findings: The trichophytin skin test is positive, but it may also be positive with other disorders. A negative trichophytin test rules out dermatophytid. Repeated negative microscopic examinations of material taken from the lesions is necessary before the diagnosis of dermatophytid can be established.

Differential Diagnosis

Differentiate from all diseases causing vesicular eruptions of the hands, especially contact dermatitis, dyshidrosis, and localized forms of atopic dermatitis.

Prevention

Treat fungal infections early and adequately, and prevent recurrences (see p 53).

Treatment

General measures are as outlined on p 31. The lesions should be treated according to type of dermatitis. The primary focus should be treated with griseofulvin (see p 53) or by local measures as described for dermatophytosis (see above). A single injection of triamcinolone acetonide suspension, 40 mg intragluteally, may suppress the eruption until the causative focus is controlled.

Prognosis

Dermatophytid may occur in an explosive series of episodes, and recurrences are not uncommon; however, it clears with adequate treatment of the primary infection elsewhere on the body.

TINEA UNGUIUM & CANDIDAL ONYCHOMYCOSIS

Essentials of Diagnosis

- Lusterless, brittle, hypertrophic, friable nails.
- Fungus demonstrated in nail section by microscope or culture.

General Considerations

Tinea unguium is a destructive trichophyton or epidermophyton infection of one or more (but rarely all) fingernails or toenails. The species most commonly found are *Trichophyton mentagrophytes, T rubrum,* and *Epidermophyton floccosum. Candida albicans* causes candidal onychomycosis.

Clinical Findings

A. Symptoms and Signs: There are usually no symptoms. The nails are lusterless, brittle, and hypertrophic, and the substance of the nail is friable and even pithy. Irregular segments of the diseased nail may be broken.

B. Laboratory Findings: Laboratory diagnosis is mandatory. Portions of the nail should be cleared with 10% potassium hydroxide and examined under the microscope for branching hyphae or collections of spores. Fungi may also be cultured, using Sabouraud's medium. Periodic acid-Schiff stain of a histologic section will also demonstrate the fungus readily.

Differential Diagnosis

Distinguish from nail changes caused by contact with strong alkalies and certain other chemicals and from those due to psoriasis, lichen planus, and candidiasis.

Treatment

A. General Measures: See p 31.

B. Specific Measures: Griseofulvin (see p 53) in full dosages daily for 3–8 months may be necessary for tinea unguium, and even this may not result in cure. Candida infection may be treated specifically with nystatin (Mycostatin®), cream or powder, amphotericin B (Fungizone®) lotion, or Onycho-Phytex® solution (a borotannic complex in alcoholic ethyl acetate). Thymol, 4% in chloroform, may be applied morning and night.

C. Local Measures: Sandpaper or file the nails daily (down to nail bed if necessary). Surgical avulsion of the nail may be required.

Fungicidal agents: Apply one of the following twice daily on affected nails: (1) 1% tannic acid and 2% salicylic acid in 40% isopropanol or (2) 10% aqueous solution of glutaraldehyde, freshly prepared.

Prognosis

Cure is difficult, even with microcrystalline griseofulvin by mouth in a dose of 1–2 gm daily for months.

Ashton, H., & others: Topical antifungal agents. Brit J Dermat 82:539–541, 1970.

Editorial: Problems of chronic paronychia. Brit MJ 4:257–258, 1970.

Suringa, D.W.R.: Treatment of superficial onychomycosis with topically applied glutaraldehyde. Arch Dermat 102:163–167, 1970.

TINEA VERSICOLOR

Essentials of Diagnosis
- Pale macules which will not tan.
- Velvety, chamois-colored macules which scale with scraping.
- Trunk distribution the most frequent site.
- Fungus on microscopic examination of scales.

General Considerations
Tinea versicolor is a mild, superficial *Malassezia furfur* infection of the skin (usually of the trunk). The eruption is called to the patient's attention by the fact that the involved areas will not tan, and the resulting pseudoachromia may be mistaken for vitiligo. The disease is not particularly contagious and is apt to occur more frequently in those who wear heavy clothing and who perspire a great deal.

Clinical Findings
A. Symptoms and Signs: There may be mild itching. The lesions are velvety, chamois-colored macules which vary from 4–5 mm in diameter to large confluent areas. Scales may be readily obtained by scraping the area with the fingernail. Lesions may appear on the trunk, upper arms, neck, and face.

B. Laboratory Findings: Large, blunt hyphae and thick-walled budding spores may be seen under the low power objective when skin scales have been cleared in 10% potassium hydroxide. *M furfur* is difficult to culture.

Differential Diagnosis
Distinguish from vitiligo on basis of appearance. Differentiate also from seborrheic dermatitis of the same areas.

Treatment & Prognosis
Encourage good skin hygiene. Tinea versicolor responds readily to selenium sulfide suspension (Selsun®), lathered on daily. Relapses are frequent. Newer topical treatments include tolnaftate (Tinactin®; O-2-naphthyl-m,N-dimethylthiocarbanilate) solution, and acrisorcin (Akrinol®) cream.

Sulfur-salicylic acid soap used on a continuing basis may be the best treatment.

McCabe, R.J.: Variations of tinea versicolor. Cutis 6:1343–1345, 1970.

McGinley, K.J., & others: Microbiology of tinea versicolor. Arch Dermat 102:168–171, 1970.

CUTANEOUS CANDIDIASIS
(Moniliasis)

Essentials of Diagnosis
- Severe pruritus of vulva, anus, or body folds.
- Superficial, denuded, beefy red areas with or without satellite vesicopustules.
- Whitish curd-like concretions on the surface.
- Fungus on microscopic examination of scales or curd.

General Considerations
Cutaneous candidiasis is a superficial fungal infection which may involve almost any cutaneous or mucous surface of the body. It is particularly likely to occur in diabetics, during pregnancy, and in obese persons who perspire freely. Antibiotics may be contributory. Hypoparathyroidism may be complicated by candidiasis.

Clinical Findings
A. Symptoms and Signs: Itching may be intense. Burning sensations are sometimes reported, particularly around the vulva and anus. The lesions consist of superficially denuded, beefy red areas in the depths of the body folds such as in the groin and the intergluteal cleft, beneath the breasts, at the angles of the mouth, and in the umbilicus. The peripheries of these denuded lesions are superficially undermined, and there may be satellite vesicopustules. Whitish, curd-like concretions may be present on the surface of the lesions (particularly in the oral and vaginal mucous membranes). Paronychia and interdigital erosions may occur.

B. Laboratory Findings: Clusters of budding cells and short hyphae can be seen under the high power lens when skin scales or curd-like lesions have been cleared in 10% potassium hydroxide. The organism may be isolated on Sabouraud's medium.

Differential Diagnosis
Differentiate from intertrigo, seborrheic dermatitis, and tinea cruris involving the same areas.

Complications
Candidiasis may spread from the skin or mucous membranes to the bladder, lungs, and other internal organs. Fungemia may cause shock and coma without mucocutaneous lesions.

Treatment
A. General Measures: Treat associated diabetes, obesity, or hyperhidrosis. Keep the parts dry and exposed to air as much as possible. If possible, discontinue systemic antibiotics; if not, give nystatin (Mycostatin®) by mouth concomitantly in a dose of 1.5 million units 3 times daily.

B. Local Measures:

1. Nails and skin—Apply nystatin (Mycostatin®) cream, 100,000 units/gm, or amphotericin B (Fungizone®) lotion, 3–4 times daily. Gentian violet, 1%, or carbolfuchsin paint (Castellani's paint) may be applied 1–2 times weekly as an alternative. Onycho-Phytex® solution (a borotannin complex in alcoholic ethyl acetate), may be applied to candidal paronychia twice daily. Thymol, 4% in chloroform, may be applied to paronychia twice daily.

2. Vulva, anal mucous membranes—Insert 1 nystatin (Mycostatin®) vaginal tablet (100,000 units) nightly for 2 weeks, or apply nystatin dusting powder (100,000 units/gm) once or twice daily onto moist mucous membrane areas. Amphotericin B, gentian violet, or carbolfuchsin (see above) can also be used.

Prognosis

Cutaneous candidiasis may be intractable and prolonged, particularly in children, in whom the disturbance may take the form of a granuloma which resists all attempts at treatment.

Barlow, A.J.E., & others: Chronic paronychia. Brit J Dermat 82:448–453, 1970.

Calnan, C.D.: Chronic mucocutaneous candidiasis. Brit J Dermat 83:423–424, 1970.

Editorial: Candidiasis: Colonization versus infection. JAMA 215:285–286, 1971.

Maibach, H.I., & R.B. Rees: Candidiasis. Pages 208–209 in: *Current Dermatologic Management.* S. Madden (editor). Mosby, 1970.

Montes, L.F., & others: Generalized cutaneous candidiasis. JAMA 204:351–354, 1968.

Valdimarsson, H.: Lymphocyte abnormality in chronic mucocutaneous candidiasis. Lancet 1:1259–1262, 1970.

PARASITIC INFESTATIONS OF THE SKIN

SCABIES

Essentials of Diagnosis

- Nocturnal itching.
- Pruritic vesicles and pustules in "runs" or "galleries," especially on the sides of the fingers and the heels of the palms.
- Mites, ova, and black clots of feces visible microscopically.

General Considerations

Scabies is a common dermatitis caused by infestation with *Sarcoptes scabiei.* An entire family may be affected. The infestation is generalized but usually spares the head and neck (although even these areas may be involved in infants). The mite is barely visible with the naked eye as a white dot. Scabies is usually acquired by sleeping or other close contact with an infested individual. This infestation is less common in the United States now than formerly.

Clinical Findings

A. Symptoms and Signs: Itching occurs almost exclusively at night. The lesions consist of more or less generalized excoriations with small pruritic vesicles, pustules, and "runs" or "galleries" on the sides of the fingers and the heels of the palms. The run or gallery appears as a short irregular mark (perhaps 2–3 mm long), as if made by a sharp pencil. Characteristic lesions may occur on the nipples in females and as pruritic papules on the scrotum in males. Pruritic papules may be seen over the buttocks. Pyoderma is often the presenting sign.

B. Laboratory Findings: The adult female mite may be demonstrated by probing the fresh end of a run or gallery with a pointed scalpel. The mite tends to cling to the tip of the blade. One may shave off the entire run or gallery (or, in the scrotum, a papule) and demonstrate the female mite, her ova, and small black dots of feces. The diagnosis should be confirmed by microscopic demonstration of the organism, ova, or feces.

Differential Diagnosis

Distinguish from the various forms of pediculosis and from other causes of pruritus.

Treatment & Prognosis

Unless the lesions are complicated by severe secondary pyoderma (see p 31), treatment consists primarily of disinfestation. If secondary pyoderma is present, potassium permanganate soaks (1:10,000), one-half hour 2–3 times daily, may be indicated before definitive treatment is given.

Disinfestation with gamma benzene hexachloride (lindane, Gexane®, Kwell®), 0.5% in cream base, applied each night for 3 nights, is the treatment of choice. This preparation can be used before secondary infection is controlled. Some recent evidence indicates that strains of *Sarcoptes scabiei* resistant to this drug may be developing. Alternative very effective drugs are Topocide® (benzyl benzoate) lotion or crotamiton (Eurax®) cream or lotion, either of which may be applied in the same way as gamma benzene hexachloride.

Unless treatment is aimed at all infected persons in a family group, reinfestations will probably occur.

Haydon, J.R., Jr., & R.M. Caplan: Epidemic scabies. Arch Dermat 103:168–173, 1971.

Lyell, A.: Diagnosis and treatment of scabies. Brit MJ 3:223–224, 1967.

PEDICULOSIS

Essentials of Diagnosis

- Pruritus with excoriation.
- Nits on hair shafts; lice on skin or clothes.
- Occasionally sky-blue macules (maculae caeruleae) on the inner thighs or lower abdomen in pubic louse infestation.

General Considerations

Pediculosis is a parasitic infestation of the skin of the scalp, trunk, or pubic areas. It usually occurs among people who live in overcrowded dwellings with inadequate hygiene facilities, although pubic lice may be acquired by anyone who sits on an infested toilet seat. There are 3 different varieties: (1) Pediculosis pubis caused by *Phthirus pubis* (pubic louse, "crabs"); (2) pediculosis corporis, by *Pediculus humanus* var *corporis* (body louse); (3) pediculosis capitis, by *P humanus* var *capitis* (head louse).

Head and body lice are similar in appearance, 3–4 mm long. Head louse infestations may be transmitted by shared use of hats or combs. The body louse can seldom be found on the body, as the insect comes on the skin only to feed, and must be looked for in the seams of the underclothing.

Trench fever, relapsing fever, and typhus may be transmitted by the body louse.

Clinical Findings

Itching may be very intense in body louse infestations, and scratching may result in deep excoriations over the affected area. The clinical appearance is of gross excoriation. Pyoderma may be present and may be the presenting sign in any of these infestations. Head lice can be found on the scalp or may be manifested as small nits resembling pussy-willow buds on the scalp hairs close to the skin. They are easiest to see above the ears and at the nape of the neck. Body lice may deposit visible nits on the lanugo hair of the body. Pubic louse infestations are occasionally generalized, particularly in a hairy individual; the lice may even be found on the eyelashes and in the scalp.

Differential Diagnosis

Distinguish head louse infestation from seborrheic dermatitis, body louse infestation from scabies, and pubic louse infestation from anogenital pruritus and eczema.

Treatment

One may use the same remedies described for scabies (see above).

Prognosis

Pediculosis responds promptly to topical treatment.

Ackerman, A.B.: Current concepts: Crabs–the resurgence of *Phthirus pubis.* New England J Med 278:950–951, 1968.
Duffy, D.M.: Ectoparasitic infections. Cutis 7:161–168, 1971.

SKIN LESIONS
DUE TO OTHER ARTHROPODS

Essentials of Diagnosis

- Localized rash with pruritus.
- Furuncle-like lesions containing live arthropods.
- Tender erythematous patches which migrate ("larva migrans").
- Generalized urticaria or erythema multiforme.

General Considerations

Some arthropods (eg, most pest mosquitos and biting flies) are readily detected as they bite. Many others are not, eg, because they are too small, there is no immediate reaction, or they bite during sleep. Reactions may be delayed for many hours; many severe reactions are allergic. Patients are most apt to consult a physician when the lesions are multiple and pruritus is intense. Severe attacks may be accompanied by insomnia, restlessness, fever, and faintness or even collapse. Rashes may sometimes cover the body.

Many persons will react severely only to their earliest contacts with an arthropod, thus presenting pruritic lesions when traveling, moving into new quarters, etc. Body lice, fleas, bedbugs, and local mosquitos should be borne in mind. Spiders are often incorrectly believed to be the source of bites; they rarely attack man, although the brown spider (Loxosceles) may cause severe necrotic reactions and death due to intravascular hemolysis, and the black widow spider (*Latrodectus mactans*) may cause severe systemic symptoms and death.

In addition to arthropod bites, the most common lesions are venomous stings (wasps, hornets, bees, ants, scorpions) or bites (centipedes), dermatitis due to urticating hairs of caterpillars, dermatitis due to vesicating agents, furuncle-like lesions due to fly maggots or sandfleas in the skin, and a linear creeping eruption due to a migrating larva.

Clinical Findings

The diagnosis may be difficult when the patient has not noticed the initial attack but suffers a delayed reaction. Individual bites are frequently in clusters and tend to occur either on exposed parts (eg, midges and gnats) or under clothing, especially around the waist or at flexures (eg, small mites or insects in bedding or clothing). The reaction is often delayed for 1–24 hours or more. Pruritus is almost always present, and may be all but intolerable once the patient starts to scratch. Secondary infection, sometimes with serious consequences, may follow scratching. Allergic manifestations, including urticarial wheals, are common. Papules may become vesicular. The diagnosis is greatly aided by searching for possible exposure to arthropods and by considering the occupation and recent activities of the patient. The principal arthropods are as follows:

(1) Bedbugs: In crevices of beds or furniture; bites tend to occur in lines or clusters. The closely related kissing bug has been reported with increasing frequency as attacking man.

(2) Fleas: In beds and floors. Rat fleas may attack the legs. Stick-tight fleas from poultry in the southern United States may be found actually attached to the skin. Tunga or chigoe fleas in South America and Africa burrow into the skin and swell, and secondary infection occurs readily following maltreatment.

(3) Ticks: Usually picked up by brushing against low vegetation. Larval ticks may attack in large numbers and cause much distress; in Africa and India they have been confused with chiggers. Ascending paralysis may occasionally be traced to a tick bite, and removal of the embedded tick is essential.

(4) Chiggers or red-bugs are larvas of trombiculid mites. A few species confined to particular countries and usually to restricted and locally recognized habitats (eg, berry patches, woodland edge, lawns, brush turkey mounds in Australia, poultry farms) attack man, often around the waist, on the ankles, or in flexures, raising intensely itching erythematous papules after a delay of many hours. The red chiggers may sometimes be seen in the center of papules which have not yet been scratched. Chiggers are the commonest cause of distressing multiple lesions (trombidiasis) due to arthropods.

(5) Bird mites: Larger than chiggers, infesting chicken houses, pigeon lofts, or nests of birds in eaves. Bites are multiple anywhere on the body, although poultry handlers are most often attacked on the hands and forearms. Room air conditioning units may suck in bird mites and infest the inhabitants of the room.

Rodent mites from mice or rats may cause similar effects. In the case of bird mites and rodent mites the diagnosis may readily be overlooked and the patient treated for other dermatoses or for psychogenic dermatosis. Intractable "acarophobia" may result from early neglect or misdiagnosis.

(6) Mites in stored products: These are white and almost invisible, and infest products such as copra ("copra itch"), vanilla pods ("vanillism"), sugar, straw, cotton seeds, and cereals. Persons who handle these products may be attacked, especially on the hands and forearms and sometimes on the feet. Infested bedding may occasionally lead to generalized dermatitis.

(7) Caterpillars of moths with urticating hairs: The hairs are blown from cocoons or carried by emergent moths, causing severe and often seasonally recurrent outbreaks after mass emergence, eg, in some southern states of the USA.

(8) Tungiasis is due to the burrowing flea known as *Tunga penetrans* (also known as chigoe, jigger; not the same as chigger) found in Africa, the West Indies, and South America. The female burrows under the skin, sucks blood, swells to the size of 0.5 cm, and then ejects her eggs onto the ground. Ulceration, lymphangitis, gangrene, and septicemia may result, possibly with fatality. Chloroform or ether on a cotton pledget will kill the insect when applied to the lesion, and disinfestation may be accomplished with insecticide applied to the terrain.

Differential Diagnosis

Arthropods should be considered in the differential diagnosis of skin lesions showing any of the above symptoms.

Prevention

Arthropod infestations are best prevented by avoidance of contaminated areas, personal cleanliness, and disinfection of clothing, bed clothes, and furniture as indicated. Lice, chiggers, red-bugs, and mites can be killed by DDT applied to the head and clothing. (It is not necessary to remove clothing.) Benzyl benzoate and dimethylphthalate are excellent acaricides; clothing should be impregnated by spray or by dipping in a soapy emulsion.

Treatment

Caution: Avoid local overtreatment.

Living arthropods should be removed carefully with tweezers after application of alcohol. Heat (lighted cigarette held near the skin) may make ticks and leeches detach themselves. Preserve in alcohol for identification. (*Caution:* In endemic Rocky Mountain spotted fever areas, do not remove ticks with the bare fingers for fear of becoming infected.) Children in particular should be prevented from scratching.

Apply corticosteroid lotions or creams. If they are not available, crotamiton (Eurax®) cream or lotion may be used; it is a miticide as well as an antipruritic. Calamine lotion or a cool wet dressing is always appropriate. Antibiotic creams, lotions, or powders may be applied if secondary infection is suspected.

Localized persistent lesions may be treated with intralesional corticosteroids.

Avoid exercise and excessive warmth.

Codeine may be given for pain. Creams containing local anesthetics are not very effective and may be sensitizing. If an anesthetic cream is desired, lidocaine should be used since it is the least sensitizing.

See also Myiasis in Chapter 24.

Marshall, J.: Ticks and the human skin. Dermatologica 135:60–65, 1967.

Perlman, F.: Arthropod sensitivity. Pages 222–244 in: *Dermatologic Allergy*. L.H. Criep. Saunders, 1967.

Schreiber, M.M., & S.I. Shapiro: Necrotic arachnidism in the southwestern United States. Cutis 7:674–680, 1971.

Smith, J.D., & E.B. Smith: Multiple fire ant stings. Arch Dermat 103:438–441, 1971.

TUMORS OF THE SKIN

General Considerations

Areas exposed to chronic irritation (sun, chemicals, friction) are especially susceptible to neoplastic disease. The blue-eyed, sandy-complexioned person living under conditions of excessive sun exposure is a most likely candidate for skin cancer, especially of the squamous cell or basal cell variety. In the southwestern United States skin cancer is the commonest skin problem, being even more common than acne vulgaris.

Classification

The following classification is admittedly oversimplified; almost any tumor arising from embryonal cells in the various stages of their development can be found in the skin.

A. Malignant:

1. Squamous cell carcinoma and senile keratoses usually occur on exposed parts in blue-eyed, sandy-complexioned persons. Squamous cell carcinoma may develop very rapidly, attaining a diameter of 1 cm within 2 weeks. It appears as a small red, conical, hard nodule which quickly ulcerates. Metastasis may occur early. Keratoacanthomas are benign growths which resemble squamous cell carcinoma.

2. Basal cell carcinomas also occur mostly on exposed parts. They grow slowly, attaining a size of 1–2 cm in diameter only after a year's growth. They present a waxy appearance, with telangiectatic vessels easily visible. Metastases either almost never occur or are caused by a squamous cell component of the tumor.

3. Paget's disease, considered by some to be a manifestation of apocrine sweat gland carcinoma, may occur around the nipple, resembling chronic eczema, or may involve apocrine areas such as the genitalia.

B. Premalignant: Keratoses and leukoplakia have a marked tendency to be malignant. Actinic keratoses occur on exposed parts of the body in persons of fair complexion, and nonactinic keratoses may be provoked by exposure to arsenic systemically or occupational irritants such as tars. In keratoses the cells are atypical and similar to those seen in squamous cell epitheliomas, but these changes are well contained by an intact epidermal-dermal junction. Leukoplakia is the counterpart of keratoses occurring on mucous membranes. One sees similar changes microscopically, plus the development of granular and horny layers which are not seen normally in mucous membranes or transitional epithelium. Leukoplakia may occur on the basis of individual predisposition or may be provoked by exposure to irritants such as excessive sunlight (lower lip), associated disease (eg, syphilitic glossitis), excessive pipe smoking, and chewing tobacco.

C. Benign:

1. Seborrheic warts, considered by some to be nevoid, consist of benign overgrowths of epithelium which have a pigmented velvety or warty surface. They are extremely common, both on exposed and covered parts, and are commonly mistaken for melanomas or other types of cutaneous neoplasms.

2. Bowen's disease (intraepidermal squamous cell epithelioma) is relatively uncommon and resembles a plaque of psoriasis. The course is relatively benign, but malignant progression may occur.

D. Nevi:

1. Cellular nevi are almost always benign, and almost everyone has at least a few of these lesions. They usually appear in childhood, and tend to spontaneous fibrosis during the declining years.

2. Junctional nevi, which consist of clear nevus cells and usually some melanin, have nevus cells on both sides of the epidermal junction. They are possible forerunners of malignant melanoma. If a nevus is on the palm, sole, or genitalia, or is subjected to continuous irritation, the possibility of melanomatous degeneration should be considered.

3. Compound nevi, composed of junctional elements as well as clear nevus cells in the dermis, may also tend to develop into malignant melanoma. Dermal cellular nevi are quite benign.

4. Blue nevi are benign, although they have been said to give rise occasionally to malignant melanoma. They are small, slightly elevated, and blue-black.

5. Epithelial nevi include several types of verrucous epithelial overgrowths, usually in linear distribution. Microscopically, cells found normally in the epidermis are present. Such lesions rarely degenerate into squamous or basal cell carcinomas.

6. Freckles consist of excess amounts of melanin in the melanocytes in the basal layer of the epidermis. Ephelides, or juvenile freckles, may be evanescent; lentigines, or senile freckles, are usually larger and more persistent.

Clinical Findings

A. Symptoms and Signs: The very absence of symptoms such as itching should lead one to suspect skin neoplasm when a growth is present. Soreness or pain (from ulceration or rapid growth) is occasionally reported.

Tumors of the skin consist of small nodules of varying rates of growth. The more rapid the growth, the more urgent the diagnosis. Any change in the texture or appearance of the skin should at least make the physician think of premalignant or malignant change. Whitish patches on mucous membranes, especially if their surfaces are rough, may suggest leukoplakia. Ulceration, crusting, or bleeding of any swollen area may point to cutaneous malignancy.

B. Laboratory Findings: Microscopic examination of biopsied or excised tissue usually is diagnostic for any of the lesions listed above. When malignant melanoma is suspected, the biopsy incision should include the entire lesion and a wide margin of normal skin.

Complications

Squamous cell carcinoma is particularly likely to metastasize to regional lymph glands and then to distant sites. Basal cell carcinomas, if neglected, may cause extensive local destruction; or occult spread may occur. Death may eventually take place with these "locally malignant" tumors as a result of invasion of vital structures. Melanomas spread similarly to the way in which squamous cell carcinomas do, and frequently spread hematogenously also.

Treatment

A. Surgical Measures: Both benign and malignant tumors of the skin may be removed surgically by any of the following technics:

1. Electrosurgery—Curettage with a dermal curet followed by electrodesiccation; removal with a cutting current; or electrocoagulation.

2. Scalpel surgery.

3. Chemosurgery (Mohs technic)—In this microscopically controlled technic the tissues are fixed with zinc chloride, dissected bloodlessly, and then examined histologically. Tissue sites in which malignant cells persist are re-treated until tumor-free. This method should be considered only when other methods of treatment have failed.

B. Radiation: (By a specialist.)

1. X-ray therapy is successful for squamous cell and basal cell carcinomas. In general, malignant melanomas are unresponsive.

2. Radium and its products used interstitially or in contact may give excellent results.

C. Topical Chemotherapy: Application of 5-fluorouracil, 1% in propylene glycol, to keratoses nightly for one month, is effective. Protect the eyes. Treat complicating dermatitis with topical corticosteroids.

Prognosis

Cancer of the skin accounts for about 2% of all cancer fatalities in the United States. With the exception of melanomas, in which the outlook is grave, all cases are potentially curable if treated early. However, even with the best care a 100% cure rate has never been attained.

Premalignant lesions such as senile, arsenical, and occupational keratoses and leukoplakia have a favorable prognosis if treated early. Arsenical keratoses and leukoplakia sometimes progress to squamous cell carcinoma and death despite the best of care.

Only one in 0.1–1 million cellular nevi develops into a malignant melanoma.

Eaglstein, W.H., & others: Fluorouracil: Mechanism of action in human skin and actinic keratoses. Arch Dermat 101:132–139, 1970.

Freeman, R.G., & J.M. Knox: Recent experience with skin cancer. Arch Dermat 101:403–408, 1970.

Helm, F.: The treatment of skin cancer: Indications for selection among the various therapeutic methods. Dermat Digest 7:70–75, 1968.

Tromovitch, T.A., & others: Mohs' technique (cancer chemotherapy): Treatment of recurrent cutaneous carcinomas. Cancer 19:867–868, 1966.

Zacarian, S.A.: *Cryosurgery of Skin Cancer.* Thomas, 1969.

MISCELLANEOUS SKIN, HAIR, & NAIL DISORDERS

PIGMENTARY DISORDERS

Melanin is formed in the melanocytes in the basal layer of the epidermis. Its precursor, the amino acid tyrosine, is slowly converted to dihydroxyphenylalanine (DOPA) by tyrosinase, and there are many further chemical steps to the ultimate formation of melanin. This system may be affected by external influences such as exposure to sun, heat, trauma, ionizing radiation, heavy metals, and changes in oxygen potential. These influences may result in hyperpigmentation, hypopigmentation, or both. Local trauma may destroy melanocytes temporarily or permanently, causing hypopigmentation, sometimes with surrounding hyperpigmentation as in eczema and dermatitis. Internal influences include melanocyte-stimulating hormone (MSH) from the pituitary gland, which is increased in pregnancy and in states in which there is an inadequate normal output of hydrocortisone by the adrenal cortex. Melatonin, a pineal hormone, regulates pigment dispersion and aggregation.

Other pigmentary disorders include those resulting from exposure to exogenous pigments such as carotenemia, argyria, deposition of other metals, and tattooing. Other endogenous pigmentary disorders are attributable to metabolic substances, including hemosiderin (iron), in purpuric processes; mercaptans, homogentisic acid (ochronosis), bile pigments, and carotenes.

Classification

Pigmentary disorders may be classified as primary or secondary and as hyperpigmentary or hypopigmentary.

A. Primary Pigmentary Disorders: These are nevoid or congenital, and include pigmented nevi, Mongolian spots, and incontinentia pigmenti, vitiligo, albinism, and piebaldism. Vitiligo is a genetically determined lack of pigmentation in which inhibited melanocytes are present in involved areas. Vitiligo, found in approximately 1% of the population, may be associated with hyperthyroidism and hypothyroidism, pernicious anemia, diabetes mellitus, addisonism, and carcinoma of the stomach. Albinism, partial or total, occurs as a genetically determined recessive trait. Piebaldism, a localized hypomelanosis, is an autosomal dominant trait.

B. Secondary Pigmentary Disorders: Hyper- or hypopigmentation may occur following overexposure to sunlight or heat or as a result of excoriation or direct physical injury. Hyperpigmentation occurs in arsenical melanosis or in association with Addison's disease (due to lack of the inhibitory influence of hydrocortisone on the production of MSH by the pituitary gland). Several disorders of clinical importance are as follows:

1. Chloasma (melasma)—This is essentially a nevoid disorder occurring as patterned hyperpigmentation of the face. It is often associated with exaggeration of normal pigmentation elsewhere, such as in the axillas, the linea alba, the groins, and around the nipples. It is common during pregnancy as a result of the stimulus of MSH and tends to fade following each pregnancy. Oral progestins (contraceptive) may cause chloasma.

2. Berlock hyperpigmentation can be provoked by hypersensitivity to essential oils in perfumes, and these should be excluded wherever possible.

3. Leukoderma or secondary depigmentation may complicate atopic dermatitis, lichen planus, psoriasis, alopecia areata, lichen simplex chronicus, and such systemic conditions as myxedema, thyrotoxicosis, syphilis, and toxemias. It may follow local skin trauma of various sorts, or may complicate dermatitis due to exposure to gold or arsenic. Antioxidants in rubber goods, such as monobenzyl ether of hydroquinone, can cause leukoderma from the wearing of gauntlet gloves, rubber pads in brassieres, etc. This is most likely to occur in Negroes.

4. Ephelides (juvenile freckles) and **lentigines** (senile freckles).

5. Drugs—Pigmentation may be produced by chloroquine and chlorpromazine.

Differential Diagnosis

One must distinguish true lack of pigment from pseudoachromia such as occurs in tinea versicolor, pityriasis simplex, and seborrheic dermatitis. It may be difficult to differentiate true vitiligo from leukoderma and even from partial albinism.

Complications

The development of solar keratoses and epitheliomas is more likely to occur in persons with vitiligo and albinism. Vitiligo tends to create pruritus in anogenital folds. There may be severe emotional trauma in extensive vitiligo and other types of hypo- and hyperpigmentations, particularly in naturally dark-skinned persons.

Treatment & Prognosis

There is no return of pigment in partial or total albinism; return of pigment is rare in vitiligo; in leukoderma repigmentation may occur spontaneously. The only effective treatment for vitiligo (with some response in 10–15% of patients only) is topical therapy with methoxsalen (Oxsoralen®) and systemic therapy with trioxsalen (Trisoralen®). The topical preparation should be used in no greater than 1:10,000 concentration, as it may cause severe phototoxic effects and blisters. Trioxsalen is given in a dosage of 10 mg orally each morning (2–4 hours before exposure to sunlight) for weeks or months, and in combination with judicious exposure to sunlight may bring about repigmentation in vitiligo. Liver function tests are not necessary.

Localized ephelides and lentigines may be destroyed by careful application of a saturated solution of liquid phenol on a tightly wound cotton applicator. Chloasma and other forms of hyperpigmentation may be treated by protecting the skin from the sun and with cosmetics such as Covermark® (Lydia O'Leary Company) or A-Fil® (Texas Pharmacal Company). Cosmetics containing perfumes should not be used.

Bleaching preparations are of 2 principal types: 5% ammoniated mercury in a cream base, and hydroquinone in liquid or cream form. This is not without hazard, and it is best to start with the weakest preparation offered by the manufacturer. The use of any bleach may result in unexpected hypo- or hyperpigmentation, particularly with prolonged use.

Treatment of other pigmentary disorders should be directed toward avoidance of the causative agent if possible (as in carotenemia) or treatment of the underlying disorder.

Africk, J., & J. Fulton: Treatment of vitiligo with topical trimethylpsoralen and sunlight. Brit J Dermat 84:151–156, 1971.

Dawber, R.P.R.: Clinical associations of vitiligo. Postgrad MJ 46:276–277, 1970.

Fitzpatrick, T.B., & others: The evolution of concepts of melanin biology. Arch Dermat 96:305–323, 1967.

Kenney, J.A., Jr.: Vitiligo treated by psoralens. Arch Dermat 103:475–480, 1971.

BALDNESS
(Alopecia)

Baldness Due to Scarring

Cicatricial baldness may occur following chemical or physical trauma, lichen planopilaris, severe bacterial or fungal infections, severe herpes zoster, chronic discoid lupus erythematosus, scleroderma, and excessive ionizing radiation. The specific cause is often suggested by the history, the distribution of hair loss, and the appearance of the skin, as in lupus erythematosus and other infections. Biopsy may be necessary to differentiate lupus from the others.

Scarring alopecias are irreversible and permanent. There is no treatment.

Baldness Not Due to Scarring

Noncicatricial baldness may be classified according to distribution as alopecia universalis (generalized but not total hair loss), alopecia totalis (complete hair loss), and alopecia areata (patchy baldness).

Nonscarring alopecia may occur in association with various **systemic diseases** such as disseminated lupus erythematosus, cachexia, lymphomas, uncontrolled diabetes, severe thyroid or pituitary hypofunction, and dermatomyositis. The only treatment necessary is prompt and adequate control of the underlying disorder, in which case hair loss may be reversible.

Male pattern baldness, the most common form of alopecia, is of genetic predetermination. The earliest changes occur at the anterior portions of the calvarium on either side of the "widow's peak." Associated seborrhea is common, and is evident as excessive oiliness and erythema of the scalp, with scaling. Premature loss of hair in a young adult male may give rise to a severe neurotic reaction. The extent of hair loss is variable and unpredictable. There is no treatment, and the patient should be cautioned not to spend money on advertised lotions or massage devices. Seborrhea may be treated as described on p 43.

Diffuse idiopathic alopecia of women seems to be increasing in incidence. The cause is not known. The disease may not be apparent until about 80% of the hair is lost, and is then manifest as a diffuse thinning of the hair over the entire scalp (especially over the calvarium). Testosterone excretion has been shown to be elevated. These women may develop a neurotic reaction comparable in severity to cancerophobia. Associated seborrhea should be controlled. Estrogens internally and topically may be tried, as may low-dose interrupted courses of corticosteroids. Deficiency of iron storage may play a role.

Alopecia areata is of unknown cause and no pathologic scalp changes have been identified. The bare patches may be perfectly smooth, or a few hairs may remain. Severe forms may be treated by injection of triamcinolone acetonide suspension into the patches or by judicious use of systemic corticosteroid therapy, although systemic therapy is rarely justified unless the disease is of serious emotional or economic significance.

Systemic corticosteroids have also been used in the treatment of generalized and total alopecia. Alopecia areata is usually self-limiting, with complete regrowth of hair, but some mild cases are permanent and the extensive forms are usually permanent, as are the totalis and universalis types also.

Cataracts may complicate extensive alopecia areata.

In **trichotillomania** (the pulling out of one's own hair) the patches of hair loss are irregular and growing hairs are always present since they cannot be pulled out until they are long enough.

Triparanol (no longer available) and excessive prolonged intake of vitamin A may cause hair loss and dry skin.

Comaish, S.: Metabolic disorders and hair growth. Brit J Dermat 84:83–85, 1971.

Mehregan, A.H.: Trichotillomania. Arch Dermat 102:129–133, 1970.

Wechsler, H.L.: Diseases of the scalp and hair. Cutis 5:415–422, 1969.

HIRSUTISM

Hirsutism may be diffuse or localized, acquired or congenital. Essential hirsutism of women is most clearly manifested in the bearded area and on the upper lip, but it may be present on the chest and around the nipples as well. Endocrinologic studies may be necessary to rule out excessive androgen secretion. Suppression of androgenic adrenocortical output by the inhibitory pituitary action of small doses of oral corticosteroids may be indicated in some cases. If hirsutism is due to excessive androgen excretion, extirpation of the offending gland may be followed by disappearance of excessive hair. Wax depilation of unwanted hair may be satisfactory for some women. Papillary damage thereby may discourage hair growth.

Dalla Pria, S., & others: Antiandrogen in acne and idiopathic hirsutism. J Invest Dermat 52:348–352, 1969.

Ridley, C.M.: A critical evaluation of the procedures available for the treatment of hirsutism. Brit J Dermat 81:146–153, 1969.

KELOIDS & HYPERTROPHIC SCARS

Keloids are tumors consisting of actively growing fibrous tissue which occur as a result of trauma or irritation in predisposed persons, especially those of Negro ancestry. The trauma may be relatively trivial, such as an acne lesion. Keloids behave as neoplasms, although they are not malignant. Spontaneous digitations may project from the central growth, and the tumors may become large and disfiguring. There may be itching and burning sensations with both types of tumor.

Hypertrophic scars, usually seen following surgery or accidental trauma, tend to be raised, red, and indurated. After a few months or longer they lose their redness and become soft and flat. Removal should not be attempted until all induration has subsided.

Intralesional injection of a corticosteroid suspension is effective against hypertrophic scars. The treatment of keloids is less satisfactory; surgical excision, x-ray therapy, and freezing with solid CO_2 or liquid nitrogen are used, as well as injection of corticosteroid suspensions into the lesions.

Rees, R.B.: Keloids. Pages 566–567 in: *Current Therapy, 1970.* H.F. Conn (editor). Saunders, 1970.

NAIL DISORDERS

Nail changes are never pathognomonic of a specific systemic or cutaneous disease. All of the nail manifestations of systemic disorders may be seen also in the absence of any systemic illness.

Nail dystrophies cannot usually be related to changes in thyroid function, hypovitaminosis, nutritional disturbances, or generalized allergic reactions.

Classification

Nail disorders may be classified as (1) local, (2) congenital or genetic, and (3) those associated with systemic or generalized skin diseases.

A. Local Nail Disorders:

1. Onycholysis (distal separation of the nails, usually of the fingers) is caused by excess exposure to water, soaps, detergents, alkalies, and industrial keratolytic agents. Nail hardeners and demethylchlortetracycline may cause onycholysis. Hypothyroidism is said to play a part.

2. Distortion of the nail occurs as a result of chronic inflammation of the nail matrix underlying the eponychial fold.

3. Discoloration and pithy changes, accompanied by a musty odor, are seen in ringworm infection.

4. Grooving and other changes may be caused by warts, nevi, and other growths impinging on the nail matrix.

5. Allergic reactions (to formaldehyde and resins in undercoats and polishes) involving the nail bed or matrix formerly caused hemorrhagic streaking of the nails, accumulation of keratin under the free margins of the nails, and great tenderness of the nail beds.

6. Beau's lines (transverse furrows) may be due to faulty manicuring.

B. Congenital and Genetic Nail Disorders:

1. A longitudinal single nail groove may occur as a result of a genetic or traumatic defect in the nail matrix underlying the eponychial fold.

2. Nail atrophy may be congenital.

3. Hippocratic nails (club fingers) may be congenital.

C. Nail Changes Associated With Systemic or Generalized Skin Diseases:

1. Beau's lines (transverse furrows) may follow any serious systemic illness.

2. Atrophy of the nails may be related to trauma or vascular or neurologic disease.

3. Hippocratic nails (club fingers) are occasionally related to prolonged anoxemia brought about by cardiopulmonary disorders.

4. Spoon nails are often seen in patients with anemia.

5. Stippling of the nails is seen in psoriasis.

6. Nail changes may be seen also with alopecia areata, lichen planus, and keratosis follicularis.

Differential Diagnosis

It is important to distinguish congenital and genetic disorders from those caused by trauma and environmental disorders. Nail changes due to ringworm or dermatophyte fungi may be difficult to differentiate from onychia due to candida infections. Direct microscopic examination of a specimen cleared with 10% potassium hydroxide, or culture on Sabouraud's medium, may be diagnostic. Ringworm of the nails may be closely similar to the changes seen in psoriasis and lichen planus, in which case careful observation of more characteristic lesions elsewhere on the body is essential to the diagnosis of the nail disorders.

Complications

Secondary bacterial infection occasionally occurs in onychodystrophies, and leads to considerable pain and disability and possibly more serious consequences if circulation or innervation is impaired. Toenail changes may lead to ingrown nail, in turn often complicated by bacterial infection and occasionally by exuberant granulation tissue. Poor manicuring and poorly fitting shoes may contribute to this complication. Cellulitis may result.

Treatment & Prognosis

Treatment consists usually of careful debridement and manicuring and, above all, reduction of exposure to irritants (soaps, detergents, alkali, bleaches, solvents, etc). Antifungal measures may be used in the case of onychomycosis and candidal onychia, antibacterial measures may be used for bacterial complications. When nail changes are associated with specific diseases, such as psoriasis and lichen planus, one may use appropriate measures, but the nail changes are usually very slow to reverse themselves. Congenital or genetic nail disorders are usually uncorrectable. Longitudinal grooving due to temporary lesions of the matrix, such as warts, synovial cysts, and other impingements, may be cured by removal of the offending lesion.

Bean, W.B.: Nail growth. Arch Int Med 122:359–361, 1968.

Fox, E.C.: Onycholysis: Association with hypothyroidism. Cutis 2:767–776, 1966.

Marks, R., & J.P. Ellis: Yellow nails. Arch Dermat 102:619–623, 1970.

MANIFESTATIONS INVOLVING THE SKIN DUE TO PARASITIC DISEASES

Pruritus, perianal: Enterobiasis, hymenolepiasis, *Taenia saginata* infection.

Pruritus, with or without rash (often transient): Cercarial dermatitis (schistosomal), strongyloidiasis, hookworm disease, early onchocerciasis, trichinosis, loiasis, flea bites, pediculosis, tungiasis.

Rash, nonirritating: Macular, maculopapular, or annular-serpiginous in early (rarely late) African trypanosomiasis, trichinosis, toxoplasmosis.

Urticaria: Helminthiases, especially strongyloidiasis, early schistosomiasis, echinococcosis, ascariasis, loiasis.

Edema of eyelids, face: Early trypanosomiasis (unilateral in Chagas' disease—Romaña's sign; transient in African, with Winterbottom's sign), trichinosis, loiasis, fasciolopsiasis, ocular sparganosis.

Ulcers (exposed areas): Cutaneous and mucocutaneous leishmaniasis, trypanosomal chancre, emergence site of Dracunculus, myiasis, amebiasis.

Splinter hemorrhages: Trichinosis.

Purpura: Flea bites.

Chronic papular, vesicular, weeping dermatitis: Pediculosis.

Nodules and local swellings: Onchocerciasis, early leishmaniasis, loiasis (Calabar "nodules," transient edema), American trypanosomiasis (chagoma, painful), *Dermatobia hominis*, spargana, cysticercosis.

Creeping eruption: Cutaneous larva migrans, gnathostomiasis, strongyloidiasis (usually buttocks or trunk), Gastrophilus myiasis (mimicking).

Pigmentation: Visceral leishmaniasis, onchocerciasis, chronic pediculosis.

Skin thickening: Filariasis (elephantiasis), post-kala-azar leishmaniasis.

Ears and nose, swelling: Leishmaniasis (Chiclero's ear; tapir nose with leishmanial granuloma; ulcerations of cutaneous and mucocutaneous leishmaniasis).

• • •

General Bibliography

Arnold, H.L., Jr., & R.B. Rees: American Academy of Dermatology—Chicago, Illinois, Dec 5—10, 1970. (Meeting review.) Cutis 7:327—343, 1971.

Braverman, I.M.: *Skin Signs of Systemic Disease.* Saunders, 1970.

Cipollaro, A.C., & P. Crossland: *X-Ray and Radium in the Treatment of the Skin,* 5th ed. Lea & Febiger, 1967.

Criep, L.H.: *Dermatologic Allergy: Immunology, Diagnosis, Management.* Saunders, 1967.

Fisher, A.A.: *Contact Dermatitis.* Lea & Febiger, 1967.

Kay, D.M., & D.L. Tuffanelli: Immunofluorescent techniques in clinical diagnosis of cutaneous disease. Ann Int Med 71:753—762, 1969.

Kopf, A.W., & R. Andrade: *Year Book of Dermatology.* Year Book, 1970.

Lever, W.F.: *Histopathology of the Skin,* 4th ed. Lippincott, 1967.

Lewis, G.M., & C.E. Wheeler: *Practical Dermatology.* Saunders, 1967.

Madden, S.: *Current Dermatologic Management.* Mosby, 1970.

Newbold, P.C.H.: Skin markers of malignancy. Arch Dermat 102:680—692, 1970.

Pillsbury, D.M.: *A Manual of Dermatology.* Saunders, 1971.

Rees, R.B.: Dermatologic advances: 1968—1969. Arch Dermat 101:12—20, 1970.

Rees, R.B.: Management of common skin diseases. Texas Med 66:94—99, 1970.

Rook, A., Wilkinson, D.S., & F.J. Ebling: *Textbook of Dermatology.* Davis, 1968.

Shuster, S., & J. Marks: *Systemic Effects of Skin Disease.* Heinemann, 1970.

Stewart, W.D., Danto, J.L., & S. Madden: *Synopsis of Dermatology.* Mosby, 1970.

Waisman, M. (editor): *Pharmaceutical Therapeutics in Dermatology.* Thomas, 1968.

Zubrod, C.G.: The skin and antitumor drugs. Arch Dermat 96:560—564, 1967.

TABLE 3–1. Simple solutions: For soaks and wet dressings.

Indications: For acute, red, swollen, itching, infected, weeping, or vesicular lesions.
Technic: Solutions must be applied cool (hot for infections).

    (1) Basin soaks (2–5 quarts of solution) for hands and feet, ¼ hour twice daily.
    (2) Wet dressings (for localized lesions). Use Turkish towel; keep saturated with solution.
        (a) Open dressings for very acute lesions and when marked cleansing and soothing action is desired. Frequent applications are necessary (eg, ½ hour 2–3 times daily).
        (b) Covered dressings should not be used.

Agent	Action*	Range of Concentrations Used	Most Common Strength Used	Preparation of Solution of Most Commonly Employed Strength
Plain tap water	*	—	—	—
R 1 Sodium chloride	*	6:1000–15:1000 (0.6–1.5%)	0.9%	2 tsp to 1 liter of water.
R 2 Sodium bicarbonate	Antipruritic	1:50–1:20 (2–5%)	3%	8 tsp to 1 liter of water.
R 3 Magnesium sulfate	Antipruritic	1:50–1:25 (2–4%)	3%	8 tsp to 1 liter of water.
R 4 Aluminum subacetate solution	Astringent	1:200–1:10 (0.5–10%)	5%	Domeboro® powder, 2¼ dr (2 tsp), or 50 ml (1 2/3 oz) Burow's solution to 1 liter of water.
R 5 Silver nitrate	Astringent, antiseptic, stains the skin	1:10,000–1:200 (0.01–0.5%)	1:400 0.25%	10 ml of 25% Ag-NO₃ solution or 2.5 gm (38 gr) Ag-NO₃ to 1 liter of water.
R 6 Neomycin, 0.1% solution	Antibacterial		0.1%	0.1%. As wet dressings for exudative pyodermas.
R 7 Potassium permanganate	Antipruritic, oxidizing, antiseptic, astringent, stains the skin	1:10,000–1:400 (0.01–0.25%)	1:10,000 0.01%	One 0.3 gm (5 gr) tablet to 3 liter of water or 0.1 gm (1½ gr) tablet to 1 liter of water.

*All of the solutions listed have a drying, soothing, and cleansing action also.

TABLE 3–2. Powders.

Name	Prescription	Instructions and Remarks
R 8 Absorbable gelatin sponge (nonsterile)	Gelfoam® powder, 10 gm	For leg ulcers and other indolent ulcers. It is absorbable hemostatic gelatin. Apply twice daily. Use antibiotic topical powder also.
R 9 Talc		Simple dusting powder.
R 10 Antibiotic powder, topical	Oxytetracycline (Terramycin®), neomycin-polymyxin-bacitracin (Neosporin®), or tetracycline (Achromycin®) topical powder.	For pyodermas. Dust on lesions twice daily.
R 11 Nystatin (Mycostatin®)	R Nystatin, 100,000 U/gm dusting powder, 15 gm	Dusting powder twice daily for candidiasis.

TABLE 3−3. Lotions and emulsions.

Liquid mixtures containing medicaments in solution or suspension are useful in a wide variety of localized and generalized skin lesions because they are easy to apply and remove. They often have a marked drying effect and must not be used if this effect is undesirable. The following are some useful, well-known lotions:

Lotion and Action	Prescription		Instructions and Remarks
R 12 Topocide® lotion	Benzyl benzoate lotion		For generalized application. Scabicide and lousicide.
R 13 Calamine lotion (soothing, drying)	R Prepared calamine Zinc oxide Glycerin Magma of bentonite Lime water, q s ad	8.0 8.0 2.0 25.0 100.0	Apply locally 3−4 times daily or as needed. Use for acute dermatitis. Avoid excessive drying by prolonged use of this lotion (as with other nonoily lotions). Add 1% phenol for antipruritic effect.
R 14 Starch lotion (antipruritic, soothing, drying)	R Starch, corn Zinc oxide Glycerin Lime water, q s ad	24.0 24.0 12.0 120.0	Apply locally twice daily and as needed. Use for acute dermatitis. Useful basic lotion to which other agents may be added.
R 15 Oily lotion (soothing, drying, lubricating)	R Zinc oxide Olive oil Lime water, $\overline{aa}$ q s ad	10.0 120.0	Apply locally 3−4 times daily or as needed. Use for acute dermatitis. Less drying than R 13 and 14.
R 16 Coal tar lotion (soothing, drying, keratoplastic)	R Solution of coal tar Zinc oxide Starch Glycerin Water, q s ad	12.0 24.0 24.0 36.0 120.0	Apply locally at night. Scrub in a.m. Use for subacute dermatitis. Useful mild stimulating lotion. Do not use on hairy or infected areas.
R 17 Sun screen emulsion (protective)	R Para-aminobenzoic acid Emulsion base, q s ad	3.0 30.0	Apply locally to skin before each exposure to the sun.
R 18 Acne lotion	R Sulfur, ppt Zinc sulfate $\overline{aa}$ Sodium borate Zinc oxide $\overline{aa}$ Acetone Camphor water Rose water, $\overline{aa}$ q s ad	 3.6 6.0 30.0 120.0	Apply locally at night for acne.
R 19 Amphotericin B (Fungizone®)	R Fungizone® lotion	30.0	Apply twice daily and as needed for muco-cutaneous candidiasis.
R 20 Fluocinolone acetonide, 0.01% solution	Synalar® solution	20.0	Apply twice daily for scalp dermatitis and atopic dermatitis. Avoid eyes and genitalia.
R 21 Tolnaftate solution	Tinactin® solution	10.0	Apply twice daily for dermatophyte (tinea) fungal infections. Ineffective for onycho-mycosis.
R 22 Underarm lotion (antiperspirant)	R Aluminum chloride Glycerin Distilled water, q s ad	60.0 30.0 240.0	Apply small quantity to underarms each morning. Useful antiperspirant.

TABLE 3–4. Ointment bases.

Indications:
1. To trap moisture in a dry skin.
2. To provide mechanical protection to the underlying lesions.
3. To help absorb or imbibe transudates from underlying lesions. (This holds true only for the hydrophilic preparations.)
4. To apply active medicinal agents to the skin.

Contraindications:
1. Acute, inflamed, oozing lesions.
2. Hairy areas (except the hydrophilic preparations).

Preparation	Prescription		Properties
	Ointments		
R 23 Petrolatum, white			Chemically inert. Retards penetration of incorporated medicaments in some cases.
R 24 Petrolatum, hydrophilic	3% cholesterol in petrolatum, white wax, and stearyl alcohol.		Favors penetration of incorporated medicaments. Imbibes water (hydrophilic).
R 25 Wool fat, hydrous (lanolin)			Adheres well to skin; stable; favors penetration. Watch for sensitization.
R 26 Wool fat (anhydrous lanolin)			Imbibes water. Favors penetration. Watch for sensitization.
R 27 Zinc oxide ointment	20% zinc oxide in liquid petrolatum, wool fat, wax, and white petrolatum.		Mechanical protection; imbibes water; stiffens ointment (gives "body" to ointment) and makes it adhere to skin.
R 28 Theobroma oil (cocoa butter)			Melts at body temperature.
	Creams		
	(Contain water; more softening and soothing than ointments.)		
R 29 Hydrophilic ointment	R Methylparaben	0.025	Favors penetration; imbibes water; good vehicle for water-soluble medicaments. Parabens may sensitize the skin (rarely).
	Propylparaben	0.015	
	Stearyl alcohol	25.0	
	White petrolatum	25.0	
	Propylene glycol	12.0	
	Polyoxyl 40 stearate	5.0	
	Purified water, q s ad	100.0	
R 30 Rose-water ointment	R Spermaceti	12.5	"Cold cream" (water in oil); cooling and soothing effect.
	White wax	12.0	
	Expressed almond oil	56.0	
	Sodium borate	0.5	
	Rose water	5.0	
	Distilled water	14.0	
	Rose oil	0.02	
R 31 Emulsion base	R Duponal® C	1.6	Nonheating and nonirritating. Less messy than other creams and ointments.
	Cetyl alcohol	7.0	
	Stearyl alcohol	7.0	
	White petrolatum	20.0	
	Heavy liquid petrolatum	2.0	
	Butoben®	0.05	
	Distilled water, q s ad	100.0	
	Pastes		
	(High powder content. Promote evaporation and cooling; decrease vesiculation.)		
R 32 Zinc oxide paste (Lassar's paste)	R Zinc oxide	25.0	Mechanical protective. Increases adhesion but decreases penetration of medicaments.*
	Starch	25.0	
	Petrolatum, white, q s ad	100.0	

*Add 2% cholesterol on 5% acetyl alcohol to increase water-imbibing power.

TABLE 3—5. Ointments: Miscellaneous standard prescriptions.

Common Name	Prescriptions		Instructions and Remarks
℞ 33 Ointment of benzoic and salicylic acid (Whitfield's)	℞ Benzoic acid Salicylic acid Polyethylene glycol ointment, q s ad	6.0 3.0 100.0	Apply locally at bedtime. Fungicide. Often prescribed in ½–¼ strength. Not for acute or subacute lesions.
℞ 34 Aluminum acetate ointment ("1-2-3")	℞ Aluminum acetate solution Wool fat Zinc oxide paste	10.0 20.0 30.0	Apply locally to skin as needed. Valuable on receding inflammatory processes.
℞ 35 Sulfur-salicylic acid ointment	℞ Sulfur Salicylic acid Petrolatum, q s ad	1.0–3.0 1.0–3.0 100.0	Apply locally as needed. Potent fungicide. *Note:* Not for acute or subacute lesions.
℞ 36 Acrisorcin cream	Akrinol® cream	50.0	Apply twice daily for tinea versicolor. Avoid eyes and genitalia.
℞ 37 Ammoniated mercury ointment	℞ Ammoniated mercury Liquid petrolatum Petrolatum, q s ad	5.0 3.0 100.0	Apply locally to skin as needed. For seborrheic dermatitis and psoriasis. Watch for mercurialism or pigmentary changes.
℞ 38 Gamma benzene hexachloride	℞ Kwell® ointment	60.0	Apply as directed. Useful scabicide.
℞ 39 Hydrocortisone ointment or cream	Available as 0.25, 1.5, 1, and 2.5% ointment in 5 gm to 120 gm quantities.		Apply a thin film twice daily. Combined with tar, antibiotics, or iodochlorhydroxyquin. Do not use in dendritic keratitis.
℞ 40 Triamcinolone (0.025 or 0.1%) or fluocinolone (0.01 or 0.25%) or	℞ Ointment or cream	15.0	Apply each night and cover with thin plastic film (Saran Wrap®) for localized eczema or psoriasis. May be used overnight under a plastic suit for generalized psoriasis. *(Caution.)*
Betamethasone valerate (0.1%)	℞ Ointment	45.0	Has special value for psoriasis.

TABLE 3—6. Solutions, tinctures, and paints.

℞ 41 Gentian violet	1% aqueous solution.		Antiseptic (gram-positive organisms) and fungicide (candida).
℞ 42 Sodium thiosulfate	10% aqueous solution.		Fungicide (especially for tinea versicolor).
℞ 43 Silver nitrate	1–10% aqueous solution.		Cauterizing and astringent for fissures and ulcers.
℞ 44 Chrysarobin	4% in chloroform.		For candidal paronychia.
℞ 45 Nitromersol	0.5% (1:200 tincture) (Metaphen®)		Bacteriostatic and germicidal.
℞ 46 Alcoholic "Whitfield's" solution	℞ Salicylic acid Benzoic acid Alcohol 40% q s ad	2.0 4.0 120.0	Apply locally. Effective fungicidal combination. May substitute bay rum for alcohol.
℞ 47 Benzoin, compound tincture	Full strength.		Useful for abraded, fissured, or ulcerated areas.
℞ 48 Soft soap liniment	65% soap.		Useful detergent.
℞ 49 Antiseborrheic shampoo	Selsun®, Fostex®, Sebulex®, Capsebon®, Alvinine®, Sebical®.		Contain detergents, salicylic acid, sulfur compounds, tar and allantoin, or quinolone. Some may cause excess oiliness.
℞ 50 Sun-blocking tincture	℞ 5% para-aminobenzoic acid in 50% ethanol.		More effective than most sunscreens.

4...

Eye

Daniel Vaughan

NONSPECIFIC MANIFESTATIONS OF EYE DISEASES

Pain

The 2 most serious eye disorders which cause pain are iritis and acute glaucoma. If neither is present, look for a corneal abrasion or foreign body, or a foreign body concealed beneath the upper eyelid.

Blurred Vision

The most important causes of blurred vision are refractive error, corneal opacities, cataract, vitreous clouding, retinal detachment, macular degeneration, central retinal vein thrombosis, central retinal artery occlusion, optic neuritis, and optic atrophy.

Conjunctival Discharge

Discharge is usually caused by bacterial or viral conjunctivitis.

"Eyestrain"

This is a common ocular complaint which usually means eye discomfort associated with prolonged reading or close work. Significant refractive error, early presbyopia, inadequate illumination, or phoria (usually exophoria with poor convergence) should be ruled out.

Photophobia

Photophobia suggests iritis, keratitis, corneal ulcer, or ocular albinism.

"Spots"

"Spots before the eyes" are vitreous opacities which usually have no clinical significance; in unusual instances they signify impending retinal detachment or posterior uveitis.

Headache

Headache is only occasionally due to ocular disorders. The causes of ocular headache are in general the same as for "eyestrain" (above).

TABLE 4–1. Differential diagnosis of common causes of inflamed eye.

	Acute Conjunctivitis	Acute Iritis*	Acute Glaucoma†	Corneal Trauma or Infection
Incidence	Extremely common	Common	Uncommon	Common
Discharge	Moderate to copious	None	None	Watery or purulent
Vision	No effect on vision	Slightly blurred	Markedly blurred	Usually blurred
Pain	None	Moderate	Severe	Moderate to severe
Conjunctival injection	Diffuse; more toward fornices	Mainly circumcorneal	Diffuse	Diffuse
Cornea	Clear	Usually clear	Steamy	Clarity change related to cause
Pupil size	Normal	Small	Moderately dilated and fixed	Normal
Pupillary light response	Normal	Poor	None	Normal
Intraocular pressure	Normal	Normal	Elevated	Normal
Smear	Causative organisms	No organisms	No organisms	Organisms found only in corneal ulcers due to infection

*Acute anterior uveitis.
†Angle closure glaucoma.

Diplopia

Double vision is due to muscle imbalance or to paralysis of an extraocular muscle as a result of inflammation, hemorrhage, tumefaction, or infection of the 3rd, 4th, or 6th nerves. The 6th nerve is most commonly affected.

Levene, R.: Glaucoma: Annual review. Arch Ophth 85:227–251, 1971.

Williams, D.J., Gills, J.P., Jr., & G.A. Hall: Results of 233 peripheral iridectomies for narrow-angle glaucoma. Am J Ophth 65:548–552, 1968.

OCULAR EMERGENCIES

ACUTE (ANGLE-CLOSURE) GLAUCOMA

Acute glaucoma can occur only with the closure of a preexisting narrow anterior chamber angle. If the pupil dilates spontaneously or is dilated with a mydriatic or cycloplegic, the angle will close and an attack of acute glaucoma is precipitated; for this reason it is a wise precaution to examine the anterior chamber angle before instilling these drugs. About 1% of people over age 35 have narrow anterior chamber angles, but many of these never develop acute glaucoma.

A quiet eye with a narrow anterior chamber angle usually converts spontaneously to angle-closure glaucoma. The process can be precipitated by anything that will dilate the pupil, eg, indiscriminate use of mydriatics or cycloplegics by the patient or the physician. The cycloplegic can be administered in the form of eyedrops or systemically, eg, by the anesthetist ordering scopolamine or atropine prior to a cholecystectomy. Increased circulating epinephrine in times of stress can also dilate the pupil and cause acute glaucoma. Sitting in a darkened movie theater can have the same effect.

Patients with acute glaucoma seek treatment immediately because of extreme pain and blurring of vision. The eye is red, the cornea is steamy, and the pupil is moderately dilated and does not react to light. Intraocular pressure is elevated (tonometry).

Acute glaucoma must be differentiated from conjunctivitis and acute iritis.

Peripheral iridectomy within 12–48 hours after onset of symptoms will usually result in a permanent cure. Untreated acute glaucoma results in complete and permanent blindness within 2–5 days after onset of symptoms. Before surgery, the intraocular pressure must be lowered by means of miotics instilled locally and osmotic agents and carbonic anhydrase inhibitors administered systemically.

Three different osmotic agents (urea, mannitol, and glycerol) are available for lowering intraocular pressure preoperatively in angle-closure glaucoma. Urea and mannitol are administered intravenously. Glycerol is gaining popularity because it is given orally. The dosage of all 3 of these osmotic drugs is about 1.5 gm/kg.

FOREIGN BODIES

If a patient complains of "something in my eye" and gives a consistent history, he usually has a foreign body even though it may not be readily visible. Almost all foreign bodies, however, can be seen under oblique illumination with the aid of a hand flashlight and loupe.

Note the time, place, and other circumstances of the accident. Test visual acuity before treatment is instituted as a basis for comparison in the event of complications.

Conjunctival Foreign Body

Foreign body of the upper tarsal conjunctiva is suggested by pain and blepharospasm of sudden onset in the presence of a clear cornea. After instilling a local anesthetic, evert the lid by grasping the lashes gently and exerting pressure on the midportion of the outer surface of the upper lid with an applicator. If a foreign body is present it can be easily removed by passing a sterile wet cotton applicator across the conjunctival surface.

Corneal Foreign Body

When a corneal foreign body is suspected but is not apparent on simple inspection, instill fluorescein into the conjunctival sac and examine the cornea with the aid of a magnifying device and strong illumination. The foreign body may then be removed with a sterile wet cotton applicator. An antibiotic should be instilled, eg, polymyxin-bacitracin (Polysporin®) ointment. It is not necessary to patch the eye, but the patient must be examined in 24 hours for secondary infection of the crater. If it is not possible to remove the corneal foreign body in this manner, it should be removed by an ophthalmologist. If there is no infection, a layer of corneal epithelial cells will line the crater within 24 hours. It should be emphasized that the intact corneal epithelium forms an effective barrier to infection. Once the corneal epithelium is disturbed, the cornea becomes extremely susceptible to infection.

Early infection is manifested by a white necrotic area around the crater and a small amount of gray exudate. These patients should be referred immediately to an ophthalmologist.

Untreated corneal infection may lead to severe corneal ulceration, panophthalmitis, and loss of the eye.

Intraocular Foreign Body

A patient with an intraocular foreign body should be referred immediately to an ophthalmologist. With delay the ocular media become progressively more cloudy, and a foreign body visible shortly after the injury may not be visible several hours later. The foreign body can often be removed through the point of entry with a magnet if this is attempted soon enough.

The visual prognosis is generally poor.

Bronson, N.R., II: Management of intraocular foreign bodies. Am J Ophth 66:279–283, 1968.

may cause intractable glaucoma with permanent visual loss. Any patient with traumatic hyphema should be put at bed rest for 6–7 days with both eyes bandaged. Secondary hemorrhage rarely occurs after this time.

Coles, W.H.: Traumatic hyphema: An analysis of 235 cases. South MJ 61:813–816, 1968.

Hoefle, F.B.: Initial treatment of eye injuries. Arch Ophth 79:33–36, 1968.

Lerman, S.: Blowout fracture of the orbit. Brit J Ophth 54:90–98, 1970.

Paton, D., & M.F. Goldberg: *Injuries of the Eye, the Lids, and the Orbit: Diagnosis and Management.* Saunders, 1970.

CORNEAL ABRASIONS

A patient with a corneal abrasion complains of severe pain, especially with movement of the lid over the cornea.

Record the history and visual acuity. Examine the cornea and conjunctiva with a light and loupe to rule out a foreign body. If an abrasion is suspected but cannot be seen, instill sterile fluorescein into the conjunctival sac; the area of corneal abrasion will stain a deeper green than the surrounding cornea.

Instill polymyxin-bacitracin (Polysporin®) ophthalmic ointment and apply a bandage with firm pressure to prevent movement of the lid. The patient should rest at home, keeping the fellow eye closed, and should be observed on the following day to be certain that the cornea has healed. Recurrent corneal erosion is frequently a result of improper treatment of corneal abrasions.

Laibson, P.R.: Cornea and sclera: Annual review. Arch Ophth 85:738–761, 1971.

CONTUSIONS

Contusion injuries of the eye and surrounding structures may cause ecchymosis ("black eye"), subconjunctival hemorrhage, edema or rupture of the cornea, hemorrhage into the anterior chamber (hyphema), rupture of the root of the iris (iridodialysis), paralysis of the pupillary sphincter, paralysis of the muscles of accommodation, cataract, subluxation or luxation of the lens, vitreous hemorrhage, retinal hemorrhage and retinal edema (most common in the macular area), detachment of the retina, rupture of the choroid, fracture of the orbital floor ("blowout fracture"), and optic nerve injury. Many of these injuries are immediately apparent; others may not become apparent for days or weeks. Patients with moderate to severe contusions should be seen by an ophthalmologist.

Any injury severe enough to cause hyphema involves the danger of secondary hemorrhage which

ULTRAVIOLET KERATITIS
(Actinic Keratitis)

Ultraviolet burns of the cornea are usually caused by exposure to a welding arc or to the sun when skiing ("snow blindness"). There are no immediate symptoms, but about 12 hours later the patient complains of agonizing pain and severe photophobia. Slit lamp examination after instillation of sterile fluorescein shows diffuse punctate staining of both corneas.

Treatment consists of local steroid therapy, systemic analgesics, and sedatives as indicated. All patients recover within 24–48 hours without complications.

See reference under Corneal Abrasions, above.

CORNEAL ULCER

Corneal ulcers constitute a medical emergency. The typical gray, necrotic corneal ulcer is preceded by trauma, usually a corneal foreign body. The eye is red with lacrimation and conjunctival discharge, and the patient complains of blurred vision, pain, and photophobia.

Prompt treatment is essential to prevent complications. Otherwise, visual impairment may occur due to corneal scarring or infection.

Corneal ulcers have many causes including bacterial, viral, fungal, and allergic. Only the most serious types will be discussed here.

Pneumococcal ("Acute Serpiginous") Ulcer

Diplococcus pneumoniae is a common bacterial cause of corneal ulcer. The early ulcer is gray and fairly well circumscribed.

Since the pneumococcus is sensitive to both sulfonamides and antibiotics, local therapy is usually effective. If untreated, the cornea may perforate. Concurrent dacryocystitis, if present, should also be treated.

Pseudomonas Ulcer

A less common but much more virulent cause of corneal ulcer is *Pseudomonas aeruginosa.* The ulceration characteristically starts in a traumatized area and spreads rapidly, frequently causing perforation of the cornea and loss of the eye within 48 hours. *Pseudomonas aeruginosa* usually produces a pathognomonic bluish-green pigment.

Early diagnosis and vigorous treatment with gentamicin locally is essential if the eye is to be saved.

Herpes Simplex (Dendritic) Keratitis

Corneal ulceration caused by herpes simplex virus is more common than any bacterial ulcer. It is almost always unilateral, and may affect any age group of either sex. It is often preceded by upper respiratory tract infection with fever and facial "cold sores."

The commonest finding is of one or more dendritic ulcers (superficial branching gray areas) on the corneal surface. These are composed of clear vesicles in the corneal epithelium; when the vesicles rupture, the area stains green with fluorescein. Although the dendritic figure is its most characteristic manifestation, herpes simplex keratitis may appear in a number of other configurations.

Treatment consists of removing the virus-containing corneal epithelium without disturbing Bowman's membrane or the corneal stroma. This is best done by an ophthalmologist. *Caution:* Do not give local corticosteroids, as they enhance the activity of the virus by impairing the natural inflammatory response. This may lead to perforation of the cornea and loss of the eye.

IUDR (5-iodo-2-deoxyuridine; idoxuridine; Herplex®, Stoxil®, Dendrid®) is quite effective against herpes simplex keratitis. It is instilled locally as 0.1% solution, 2 drops in the affected eye every hour day and night for about 3 days; if improvement is noted after that time, give the drug approximately every 2 hours for 2 days and then gradually withdraw over a period of 3 more days.

Many ophthalmologists still prefer to remove the affected corneal epithelium mechanically and apply a pressure bandage for a few days until the epithelium regenerates.

Burns, R.P.: *Pseudomonas aeruginosa* keratitis: Mixed infections of the eye. Am J Ophth 67:257–262, 1969.

Laibson, P.R.: Cornea and sclera: Annual review. Arch Ophth 85:738–761, 1971.

Smolin, G., & M. Okumoto: Herpes simplex keratitis. Arch Ophth 83:746–751, 1970.

CHEMICAL CONJUNCTIVITIS & KERATITIS

Chemical burns are treated by irrigation of the eyes with saline solution or plain water as soon as possible after exposure. Do **not** neutralize an acid with an alkali or vice versa, as the heat generated by the reaction may cause further damage. Alkali injuries require prolonged irrigation since alkalies are not precipitated by the proteins of the eye as are acids. The pupil should be dilated with 0.2% scopolamine or 2% atropine. A combination corticosteroid and antibiotic solution or ointment is instilled frequently. Complications include symblepharon, corneal scarring, tear duct obstruction, and secondary infection.

Girard, L.J., & others: Severe alkali burns. Tr Am Acad Ophth 74:787–803, 1970.

Levine, R.A., & C.J. Stahl: Eye injury caused by tear-gas weapons. Am J Ophth 65:497–508, 1968.

Schultz, G., Henkind, P., & E.M. Gross: Acid burns of the eye. Am J Ophth 66:654–657, 1968.

GONOCOCCAL CONJUNCTIVITIS

Gonococcal conjunctivitis, which may cause corneal ulceration, is manifested by a copious purulent discharge. The diagnosis may be confirmed by a stained smear and culture of the discharge. Prompt treatment with local and systemic penicillin is required.

SYMPATHETIC OPHTHALMIA
(Sympathetic Uveitis)

Sympathetic ophthalmia is a rare, severe bilateral granulomatous uveitis. The cause is not known, but the disease may occur at any time from 1 week to many years after a penetrating injury through the ciliary body. The injured (exciting) eye becomes inflamed first and the fellow (sympathizing) eye second. Symptoms and signs include blurred vision with light sensitivity and redness.

The best treatment of sympathetic ophthalmia is prevention by removing the damaged eye. Any severely injured eye (eg, one with perforation of the sclera and ciliary body, with loss of vitreous and retinal damage) should be enucleated within 1 week after the injury. Every effort should be made to secure the patient's reasoned consent to the operation. In established cases of sympathetic ophthalmia, systemic corticosteroid therapy may be helpful. Without treatment, the disease progresses gradually to bilateral blindness.

Morse, P.H., & J.R. Duke: Sympathetic ophthalmitis. Am J Ophth 68:508–512, 1969.

LACERATIONS

Lids

If the lid margin is lacerated the patient should be referred for specialized care since permanent notching may result. Lid lacerations not involving the margin may be sutured just as any other skin laceration.

Conjunctiva

In superficial lacerations of the conjunctiva, sutures are not necessary. In order to prevent infection, instill a broad-spectrum antibiotic ointment into the eye 2–3 times a day until the laceration is healed.

Cornea or Sclera

Keep examination and manipulation at an absolute minimum, since pressure may result in extrusion of the intraocular contents. Bandage the eye lightly and cover with a metal shield which rests on the orbital bones above and below. Instruct the patient not to squeeze his eyes shut and to remain as quiet as possible. Transfer him to an ophthalmologist for further care.

Tredici, T.J.: Management of ophthalmic casualties in Southeast Asia. Mil Med 133:355–362, 1968.

ORBITAL CELLULITIS

Orbital cellulitis is manifested by an abrupt onset of fever, proptosis, and swelling and redness of the lids. It is usually caused by a pyogenic organism. Immediate treatment with systemic antibiotics is indicated to prevent brain abscess. The response to antibiotics is usually excellent.

Howard, G.M.: The orbit: Annual review. Arch Ophth 84:839–854, 1970.

VITREOUS HEMORRHAGE

Hemorrhage into the vitreous body may obscure a retinal detachment. Treatment by an ophthalmologist is indicated.

Freeman, H.M.: The lens and vitreous: Annual review. Arch Ophth 82:551–566, 1969.

COMMON OCULAR DISORDERS

CONJUNCTIVITIS

Conjunctivitis is the most common eye disease in the Western Hemisphere. It may be acute or chronic. Most cases are exogenous and due to bacterial or viral infection, though endogenous inflammation may occur (eg, phlyctenular conjunctivitis, a sensitive response to circulating tuberculoprotein). Other causes are allergy, chemical irritations, and fungal or parasitic infection. The mode of transmission of infectious conjunctivitis is usually direct contact, ie, via fingers, towels, or handkerchiefs, to the opposite eye or to other persons.

Conjunctivitis must be differentiated from iritis, glaucoma, corneal trauma, and keratitis.

Bacterial Conjunctivitis

The organisms found most commonly in bacterial conjunctivitis are *Diplococcus pneumoniae* and *Staphylococcus aureus.* Both produce a copious, purulent discharge. There is no pain or blurring of vision. The disease is usually self-limited, lasting about 10–14 days if untreated. A sulfonamide or antibiotic ointment instilled locally 3 times daily will usually clear the infection in 2–3 days. Do not use antibiotic-corticosteroid combinations.

Viral Conjunctivitis

One of the commonest causes of viral conjunctivitis is adenovirus type 3, which is usually associated with pharyngitis, fever, malaise, and preauricular adenopathy. Locally, the palpebral conjunctivas are red and there is a copious watery discharge and scanty exudate. Children are more often affected than adults, and contaminated swimming pools are frequently the source of the virus. There is no specific treatment, although local sulfonamide therapy may prevent secondary bacterial infection. The disease usually lasts about 10 days.

Trachoma & Inclusion Conjunctivitis

Trachoma, although rare in the USA except among American Indians, is the most common disease known to man with the exception of the common cold. It is a type of bilateral keratoconjunctivitis caused by an organism *(Chlamydia trachomatis)* similar to that which causes psittacosis and lymphogranuloma venereum, and only occurs under conditions of poor hygiene and overcrowding. Trachoma is manifested by chronic bilateral conjunctival redness and mild itching, a watery discharge, and scanty (except during exacerbations) exudate. Epidemiologic considerations are important in the diagnosis.

Trisulfapyrimidines are the drugs of choice; the adult dosage is 4 gm daily for 3 weeks. Treatment with one of the tetracyclines, 1 gm stat and then 250 mg 4 times daily for 3 weeks, is also effective. Topical therapy is much less satisfactory than oral sulfonamides or tetracyclines. When used, it consists of instilling erythromycin or tetracycline ointment 4 times daily. Without treatment, trachoma progresses to cause corneal scarring with moderate to severe visual loss.

Inclusion blennorrhea is manifested by bilateral conjunctival redness and a copious exudate. It is becoming an increasingly more frequent cause of ophthalmia neonatorum but occurs rarely in adults. On a stained smear the organism *(Chlamydia oculogeni-talis)* is indistinguishable from that which causes trachoma. Clinically, inclusion blennorrhea is easily differentiated from trachoma by its profuse discharge and the near absence of corneal involvement. It responds well to local sulfonamide ointment therapy 4 times daily; local tetracycline therapy is equally effective. With treatment, the disease can be cleared in 1 week; otherwise it may persist for 3 months to 1 year.

Allergic Conjunctivitis

Allergic conjunctivitis is common, and is most often associated with hay fever. It causes bilateral tearing, itching, and redness, and a minimal stringy discharge. It is usually chronic and recurrent. Local corticosteroid therapy is often effective.

Fungal & Parasitic Conjunctivitis

Fungal and parasitic conjunctivitides are rare in most parts of the world, and are usually unilateral. They often present with a localized inflammatory granuloma. A more common example is leptothrix conjunctivitis, which occurs in persons in close contact with cats.

Ophthalmia Neonatorum

Ophthalmia neonatorum is any infection of the conjunctiva in the newborn. Common types are chemical (silver nitrate), bacterial (staphylococcal, pneumococcal, gonococcal), and chlamydial (inclusion blennorrhea).

The diagnosis can often be made by knowing the date of onset of symptoms. Silver nitrate conjunctivitis occurs within 24 hours after birth, bacterial conjunctivitis within 2–5 days, and inclusion blennorrhea within 5–10 days. The diagnosis is confirmed by cultures and by microscopic examination of a smear of the conjunctival scrapings.

Silver nitrate conjunctivitis will clear in a few days without treatment, or corticosteroid ointment may be applied to hasten healing. Bacterial conjunctivitis and inclusion blennorrhea respond well to specific antibiotic or sulfonamide therapy.

Bacterial conjunctivitis in newborn infants may be prevented by instilling silver nitrate solution, 1%, or penicillin ointment, 100,000 units/gm, into the conjunctival sac of each eye immediately after birth. More concentrated silver nitrate solutions will cause permanent corneal scarring, and even 1% solution frequently causes chemical conjunctivitis; many ophthalmologists therefore recommend that penicillin be substituted. The disadvantage of penicillin prophylaxis is that it may favor the emergence of penicillin-resistant strains of staphylococci in the nursery. In most states of the USA some form of prophylaxis is required, usually either silver nitrate or penicillin.

Conference on trachoma and allied diseases. Am J Ophth 63:1027–1657, 1967.

Giffin, R.B., Jr.: Eye damage in newborns from use of strong silver nitrate solutions. California Med 107:178–180, 1967.

Kazdan, J.J., Schachter, J., & M. Okumoto: Inclusion conjunctivitis. Am J Ophth 64:116–124, 1967.

Sexton, R.R.: Eyelids, lacrimal apparatus, and conjunctiva: Annual review. Arch Ophth 85:379–396, 1971.

Thygeson, P., & C.R. Dawson: Trachoma and follicular conjunctivitis in children. Arch Ophth 75:3–13, 1968.

PINGUECULA

Pinguecula is a yellow nodule of hyaline and elastic tissue on either side of the cornea (more commonly on the nasal side) in the area of the lid fissure. The nodules rarely grow, but inflammation is common. No treatment is indicated. Pinguecula is common in persons over 35 years of age.

PTERYGIUM

Pterygium is a fleshy, bilateral, triangular encroachment of a pinguecula onto the nasal side of the cornea and is usually associated with constant exposure to wind and dust. Excision is indicated if the growth threatens vision by approaching the pupillary area.

UVEITIS

Uveitis is any inflammation of the uveal tract (iris, ciliary body, and choroid). Inflammation of the iris primarily is called anterior uveitis, iridocyclitis, or iritis; inflammation of the choroid (and usually the retina as well) is called posterior uveitis or chorioretinitis.

Uveitis may be either granulomatous (exogenous) or nongranulomatous (endogenous); the latter is more common. The disease is usually unilateral, and signs and symptoms are similar in both types, varying only in intensity. Early diagnosis and treatment are important to prevent the formation of posterior synechias.

Uveitis must be differentiated from conjunctivitis, acute glaucoma, and corneal ulcer.

Nongranulomatous Uveitis (Endogenous)

Most cases of nongranulomatous uveitis are of apparently spontaneous onset, but there is a fairly close correlation with rheumatoid arthritis. Nongranulomatous uveitis occurs in about 10% of all patients with rheumatoid arthritis. The iris and ciliary body are primarily affected, but occasional foci are found in the choroid. Exacerbations parallel the rheumatic process.

The onset is acute, with marked pain, redness, photophobia, and blurred vision. A circumcorneal flush, caused by dilated limbal blood vessels, is present. Fine white keratic precipitates (KP) on the posterior surface of the cornea can be seen with the slit lamp or with a loupe. The pupil is small, and there may be a collection of fibrin with cells in the anterior chamber. If posterior synechias are present, the pupil will be irregular and the light reflex will be absent.

Local and systemic corticosteroid therapy tends to shorten the course. Warm compresses will decrease pain. Atropine, 2%, 2 drops into the affected eye twice daily, will prevent posterior synechia formation and alleviate photophobia. Recurrences are common, but the prognosis is good.

Granulomatous Uveitis (Exogenous)

Granulomatous uveitis usually follows invasion by the causative organism, eg, *Mycobacterium tuberculosis* or *Toxoplasma gondii*, although these pathogens are rarely recovered. Any or all parts of the uveal tract may be affected, but there is a predilection for the choroid.

Granulomatous uveitis is more subtle than nongranulomatous uveitis in that there is usually less pain and redness, but the permanent eye damage is relatively devastating. The onset is usually slow, and the affected eye may be only slightly and diffusely red. Because of vitreous haze and retinal involvement, vision may be more blurred than would be expected in view of the apparent mildness of the process. Pain is minimal or absent and photophobia is slight. The pupil may be normal or, if posterior synechias are present, slightly smaller than normal and irregular. Large gray "mutton fat" keratic precipitates on the posterior surface of the cornea may be seen with the slit lamp or loupe. The anterior chamber may be cloudy. Iris nodules are commonly present, and there may be vitreous haze. Fresh lesions of the choroid appear yellow when viewed with the ophthalmoscope.

Treatment is usually unsatisfactory since the causative agent is rarely identified. The pupil should be kept dilated with atropine and associated systemic disease treated as indicated. The visual prognosis is fair.

Anderson, B., Sr.: Rheumatoid syndromes. Am J Ophth 64:35–50, 1967.

Brockhurst, R.J., & C.L. Schepens: Uveitis. 4. Peripheral uveitis: The complication of retinal detachment. Arch Ophth 80:747–753, 1968.

Killen, B.U.: Gout and uveitis. Brit J Ophth 710–712, 1968.

Maumenee, A.E.: Clinical entities in "uveitis": An approach to the study of intraocular inflammation. Am J Ophth 69:1–27, 1970.

Schlaegel, T.F., Jr.: The uvea: Annual review. Arch Ophth 85:524–535, 1971.

HORDEOLUM

Hordeolum is a common staphylococcal abscess which is characterized by a localized red, swollen, acutely tender area on the upper or lower lid. Internal hordeolum is a meibomian gland abscess which points to the skin or to the conjunctival side of the lid; external hordeolum or sty (infection of the glands of Moll or Zeis) is smaller and on the margin.

The primary symptom is pain, the intensity of which is directly related to the amount of swelling.

Warm compresses are helpful. Incision is indicated if resolution does not begin within 48 hours. An antibiotic or sulfonamide instilled into the conjunctival sac every 3 hours is beneficial during the acute stage. Without treatment, internal hordeolum may lead to generalized cellulitis of the lid.

CHALAZION

Chalazion is a common granulomatous inflammation of a meibomian gland, characterized by a hard, nontender swelling on the upper or lower lid. It may be preceded by a sty. The majority point toward the conjunctival side.

If the chalazion is large enough to impress the cornea, vision will be distorted. The conjunctiva in the region of the chalazion is red and elevated.

Treatment consists of excision by an ophthalmologist.

Sexton, R.R.: Eyelids, lacrimal apparatus, and conjunctiva: Annual review. Arch Ophth 85:379–396, 1971.

TUMORS

Verrucae and papillomas of the skin of the lids can usually be excised by the general physician. Malignancy should be ruled out by microscopic examination of the excised material.

BLEPHARITIS
(Granulated Eyelids)

Blepharitis is a common chronic, bilateral inflammation of the lid margins. It may be ulcerative *(Staphylococcus aureus)* or nonulcerative (seborrheic). The latter type may be caused by *Pityrosporum ovale,* although the relationship is not definite. Both types are usually present. Seborrhea of the scalp, brows, and frequently of the ears is almost always associated with seborrheic blepharitis.

Symptoms are irritation, burning, and itching. The eyes are "red-rimmed," and scales or "granulations" can be seen clinging to the lashes. In the staphylococcal type, the scales are dry, the lid margins are red and ulcerated, and the lashes tend to fall out; in the seborrheic type the scales are greasy, ulceration is absent, and the lid margins are less red. In the more common mixed type, both dry and greasy scales are present, and the lid margins are red and may be ulcerated.

Cleanliness of the scalp, eyebrows, and lid margins is essential to effective local therapy. Scales must be removed from the lids daily with a damp cotton applicator.

An antistaphylococcal antibiotic or sulfonamide eye ointment is applied with a cotton applicator once daily to the lid margins. The treatment of both types is similar except that in severe staphylococcal blepharitis antibiotic sensitivity studies may be required.

Thygeson, P.: Complications of staphylococcic blepharitis. Am J Ophth 68:446–449, 1969.

ENTROPION & ECTROPION

Entropion (inward turning of the lid, usually the lower) occurs occasionally in older people as a result of degeneration of the lid fascia. Surgery is indicated if the lashes rub on the cornea.

Ectropion (outward turning of the lower lid) is fairly common in elderly people. Surgery is indicated if ectropion causes excessive tearing, exposure keratitis, or a cosmetic problem.

DACRYOCYSTITIS

Dacryocystitis is a common infection of the lacrimal sac. It may be acute or chronic and occurs most often in infants and in persons over 40. It is usually unilateral, and is always secondary to obstruction of the nasolacrimal duct.

Adult Dacryocystitis

The cause of obstruction is usually unknown, but a history of trauma to the nose may be obtained. In acute dacryocystitis the usual infectious agent is *Staphylococcus aureus* or *Streptococcus pyogenes;* in the chronic form, *Diplococcus pneumoniae* or, occasionally, *Hemophilus influenzae* is found. Mixed infections do not occur.

Acute dacryocystitis is characterized by pain, swelling, tenderness, and redness in the tear sac area; purulent material may be expressed. In chronic dacryocystitis tearing and discharge are the principal signs. Mucus or pus may be expressed from the tear sac.

Acute dacryocystitis responds well to systemic antibiotic therapy, but recurrences are common if the obstruction is not surgically removed. The chronic form may be kept latent by using antibiotic eye drops, but relief of the obstruction is the only cure.

Infantile Dacryocystitis

Normally the nasolacrimal ducts open spontaneously during the first month of life. Occasionally one of the ducts fails to canalize and a secondary pneumococcal dacryocystitis develops. When this happens, forceful massage of the tear sac is indicated, and antibiotic or sulfonamide drops should be instilled in the conjunctival sac 4–5 times daily. If this is not successful after a few weeks, probing of the nasolacrimal duct is indicated regardless of the infant's age. To minimize spread of the infection, penicillin is sometimes given intramuscularly 2 days before probing; the tear sac is irrigated freely just before probing. One probing is effective in about 75% of cases; in the remainder cure can almost always be achieved by repeated probings.

Sexton, R.R.: Eyelids, lacrimal apparatus, and conjunctiva: Annual review. Arch Ophth 85:379–396, 1971.

CHRONIC (OPEN-ANGLE) GLAUCOMA

Essentials of Diagnosis
- Insidious onset in older age groups.
- No symptoms in early stages.
- Gradual loss of peripheral vision over a period of years.
- Persistent elevation of intraocular pressure associated with pathologic cupping of the optic disks.
- *Note:* "Halos around lights" are not present unless the intraocular tension is markedly elevated.

General Considerations

In chronic glaucoma the intraocular pressure is consistently elevated. Over a period of months or years this results in optic atrophy with loss of vision varying from a slight constriction of the peripheral visual fields to complete blindness.

The cause of the decreased rate of aqueous outflow in chronic glaucoma has not been clearly demonstrated. The disease is bilateral and is genetically determined, most likely as an autosomal recessive trait which is so common that it is easily confused with dominant inheritance (pseudo-dominant). Infantile glaucoma usually has an autosomal recessive mode of inheritance.

In the USA it is estimated that there are 2 million people with glaucoma; about half of these cases are undetected. About 90% of all cases of glaucoma are of the chronic open-angle type.

Clinical Findings

Patients with chronic glaucoma have no symptoms initially. There may be slight cupping of the optic disk. The visual fields gradually constrict, but central vision remains good until late in the disease.

Tonometry, ophthalmoscopic visualization of the optic nerve, and central visual field testing are the 3 prime tests for the diagnosis and continued clinical evaluation of glaucoma. The normal intraocular pressure is about 10–25 mm Hg. Except in acute glaucoma, however, the diagnosis is never made on the basis of one tonometric measurement, since various factors can influence the pressure (eg, diurnal variation). Transient elevations of intraocular pressure do not constitute glaucoma (for the same reason that periodic elevations of blood pressure do not constitute hypertensive disease).

Prevention

All persons over age 20 should have tonometric and ophthalmoscopic examinations every 3–5 years. They may be done by the general physician, internist, or ophthalmologist. If there is a family history of glaucoma, annual examination is indicated. Mydriatic and cycloplegic drugs should not be used until the anterior chamber angle has been evaluated by gonioscopy.

Treatment

Most patients can be controlled with miotics, eg, pilocarpine, 1–2%, 3–4 times daily. Pilocarpine increases the rate of outflow of aqueous. Carbonic anhydrase inhibitors—eg, acetazolamide (Diamox®), ethoxzolamide (Cardrase®)—decrease the rate of aqueous production. Epinephrine eyedrops, 0.5–2%, decrease aqueous production and increase outflow. (*Caution:* Epinephrine is contraindicated if the anterior chamber angle is narrow.) Treatment must be continued through life.

Prognosis

Untreated chronic glaucoma which begins at age 40–45 will probably cause complete blindness by age 60–65. Early diagnosis and treatment will preserve useful vision throughout life in most cases.

Drance, S.M.: The early field defects in glaucoma. Invest Ophth 8:84–91, 1969.

Fisher, R.F., Carpenter, R.G., & C. Wheeler: Assessment of established cases of chronic simple glaucoma. Brit J Ophth 54:217–228, 1970.

Kronfeld, P.C.: Functional characteristics of surgically produced outflow channels. Am J Ophth 67:451–463, 1969.

Lazenby, G.W., Reed, J.W., & W.M. Grant: Short-term tests of anticholinergic medication in open-angle glaucoma. Arch Ophth 80–443–448, 1968.

Levene, R.Z.: Glaucoma: Annual review. Arch Ophth 85:227–251, 1971.

Norskow, K.: Primary glaucoma as a cause of blindness. Acta ophth 46:853–859, 1968.

Peczon, J.D., & W.M. Grant: Diuretic drugs in glaucoma. Am J Ophth 66:680–683, 1968.

RETINAL DETACHMENT

Essentials of Diagnosis

- Blurred vision in one eye becoming progressively worse. ("A curtain came down over one of my eyes.")
- No pain or redness.
- Visible detachment ophthalmoscopically.

General Considerations

Detachment of the retina is usually spontaneous but may be secondary to trauma. Spontaneous detachment occurs most frequently in persons over 50 years old. Predisposing causes such as aphakia and myopia are common.

Clinical Findings

As soon as the retina is torn, a transudate from the choroidal vessels, mixed with vitreous, combines with abnormal vitreous traction on the retina and the force of gravity to strip the retina from the choroid. The superior temporal area is the most common site of detachment. The area of detachment rapidly increases, causing corresponding progressive visual loss. Central vision remains intact until the macula becomes detached.

On ophthalmoscopic examination the retina is seen hanging in the vitreous like a gray cloud. One or more retinal tears, usually crescent-shaped and red or orange, are always present, and can be seen by an experienced examiner.

Differential Diagnosis

Sudden partial loss of vision in one eye may also be due to vitreous hemorrhage or thrombosis of the central retinal vein or one of its branches.

Treatment

All cases of retinal detachment should be referred immediately to an ophthalmologist. If the patient must be transported a long distance, his head should be positioned so that the detached portion of the retina will recede with the aid of gravity. For example, a patient with a superior temporal retinal detachment in the right eye should lie on his back with his head turned to the right. Position is less important for a short trip.

Treatment consists of drainage of the subretinal fluid and closure of the retinal tears by diathermy or scleral buckling (or both). This produces an inflammatory reaction which causes the retina to adhere to the choroid. Photocoagulation is of value in a limited number of cases of minimal detachment. It consists of focusing a strong light ("burning glass") through the pupil to create an artificial inflammation between the choroid and the retina.

The **laser** (light amplification by stimulated emission of radiation) is occasionally used in the same manner as the photocoagulator.

The main use of the photocoagulator and laser is in the prevention of detachment by sealing small retinal tears before detachment occurs.

Cryosurgery is also being used effectively in the treatment of retinal detachment. A supercooled probe is applied to the sclera to cause a chorioretinal scar with minimal scleral damage. This decreased scleral damage (as compared with diathermy) makes the operation less hazardous and, because scar formation is minimal, greatly facilitates reoperation. Cryosurgery may eventually replace diathermy completely.

Prognosis

About 80% of uncomplicated cases can be cured with one operation; an additional 10% will need repeated operations; the remainder never reattach. The prognosis is worse if the macula is detached, if there are many vitreous strands, or if the detachment is of long duration. Without treatment, retinal detachment almost always becomes total in 1–6 months. Spontaneous detachments are ultimately bilateral in 20–25% of cases.

Brockhurst, R.J., & Criswick, V.G.: Retinal detachment. Arch Ophth 82:641–651, 1969.

Kaufmann, T.: Myopia and ablation of the retina: Statistical analysis of 800 cases. Ophthalmologica 157:249–262, 1969.

L'Esperance, F.A., Jr.: The retina and optic nerve: Annual review. Arch Ophth 83:771–794, 1970.

CATARACT

Essentials of Diagnosis

- Blurred vision, progressive over months or years.
- No pain or redness.
- Lens opacities, which may be grossly visible.

General Considerations

A cataract is a lens opacity. Cataracts are usually bilateral. They may be congenital or may occur as a result of trauma or, less commonly, systemic disease. Senile cataract is by far the most common type; most persons over 60 have some degree of lens opacity.

Clinical Findings

Even in its early stages a cataract can be seen through a dilated pupil with an ophthalmoscope, a slit lamp, or an ordinary hand illuminator. As the cataract matures the retina will become increasingly difficult to visualize, until finally the fundus reflection is absent. At this point the pupil is white and the cataract is mature.

The degree of visual loss corresponds to the density of the cataract.

Treatment

Only a small percentage of senile cataracts require surgical removal. Degree of visual impairment is the prime surgical criterion; other factors include age, general health, and occupation. Treatment of senile cataract consists of removal of the entire lens followed by refractive correction with a spectacle cataract lens. Contact lenses are replacing the heavy cataract lenses mainly in younger patients and patients of any age requiring surgery in one eye only.

Cryoextraction, using a supercooled metal probe, is probably the commonest method now being employed for surgical removal of cataracts. Originally the prime indications for cryoextraction were dislocated cataractous lenses and any cataract which was difficult to grasp with the lens capsule forceps.

Prognosis

If surgery is indicated, lens extraction improves visual acuity in 95% of cases. The remainder either have preexisting retinal damage or develop postoperative complications such as glaucoma, hemorrhage, retinal detachment, or infection.

Chandler, P.A.: Surgery of congenital cataract. Am J Ophth 65:663–674, 1968.

Freeman, H.M.: The lens and vitreous: Annual review. Arch Ophth 82:551–566, 1969.

Swan, K.C., & J.T. Flaxel: Limbal wound healing after cataract extraction. Arch Ophth 81:653–660, 1969.

Worthen, D.M., & R.E. Brubaker: An evaluation of cataract cryoextraction. Arch Ophth 79:8–9, 1968.

STRABISMUS

Essentials of Diagnosis

- History of eyes deviating.
- Demonstration of deviation by corneal reflection and cover tests.
- Reduced visual acuity in the deviating eye.

General Considerations

About 5% of children are born with or develop a malfunction of binocular coordination known as strabismus. In descending order of frequency, the eyes may deviate inward (esotropia), outward (exotropia), upward (hypertropia), or downward (hypotropia). The cause is not known, but fusion is lacking in almost all cases. If a child is born with straight eyes but has inherited "weak fusion," he may develop strabismus.

Clinical Findings

Children with frank strabismus first develop diplopia. They soon learn to suppress the image from the deviating eye and the vision in that eye therefore fails to develop. This is the first stage of amblyopia ex anopsia.

Most cases of strabismus are obvious, but if the angle of deviation is small or if the strabismus is intermittent, the diagnosis may be obscure. The best method for detecting strabismus is to direct a light toward each pupil from a distance of 1—2 feet. If the corneal reflection is seen in the center of each pupil, the eyes can be presumed to be straight at that moment.

As a further diagnostic test ("cover test"), cover the right eye with an opaque object ("cover") and instruct the patient to fix his gaze on the examining light with the left eye. If fusion is weak, covering the right eye will disturb the fusion process sufficiently to allow the right eye to deviate, and this can be observed behind the cover. The right eye may swing back into alignment when the cover is removed (phoria). In obvious strabismus, the covered eye will maintain the deviated position after the cover is removed (tropia). Ask the patient to follow the examining light with both eyes to the right, left, up, and down to rule out extraocular muscle paralysis. If there is a history of deviation but it cannot be demonstrated, the patient should be reexamined in 6 months.

Prevention

Amblyopia due to strabismus can be detected by routine visual acuity examination of all **preschool** children. Visual acuity testing is best done with an illiterate E card close to the 4th birthday by the child's mother, but is often performed in the physician's office as a routine procedure. Treatment by occlusion of the good eye is simple and effective.

The prevention of blindness by these simple diagnostic and treatment procedures is one of the most rewarding experiences in medical practice.

Treatment

The objectives in the treatment of strabismus are (1) good visual acuity in each eye; (2) straight eyes, for cosmetic purposes; and (3) coordinate function of both eyes.

The best time to initiate treatment is around the age of 6 months. If treatment is delayed beyond this time the child will favor the straight eye and suppress the image in the other eye; this results in failure of visual development (amblyopia ex anopsia) in the deviating eye.

If the child is under 7 years of age and has an amblyopic eye, the amblyopia can be cured by occluding the good eye. At 1 year of age, patching may be successful within 1 week; at 6 years it may take a year to achieve the same result, ie, to equalize the visual acuity in both eyes. Prolonged patching does not impair vision in the good eye.

Surgery is usually performed after the visual acuity has been equalized. If the visual acuity is the same in both eyes and the eyes can be made reasonably straight through surgery (or with glasses, as in the case of accommodative esotropia), eye exercises (orthoptics) may assist the patient in learning to use his eyes together (fusion).

Prognosis

The prognosis is more favorable for strabismus which has its onset at age 1—4 than for strabismus which is present at birth; better for divergent (outward

deviation) than for convergent strabismus; and better for intermittent than for constant strabismus.

Burian, H.M.: Pathophysiological basis of amblyopia and its treatment. Am J Ophth 67:1—12, 1969.

Von Noorden, G.K.: Strabismus: Annual review. Arch Ophth 84:103—122, 1970.

Von Noorden, G.K., & A.E. Maumenee: *Atlas of Strabismus.* Mosby, 1967.

•   •   •

PRINCIPLES OF TREATMENT
OF OCULAR INFECTIONS

Identification of Pathogen

Before one can determine the drug of choice, the causative organism must be identified. For example, a pneumococcal corneal ulcer will respond to treatment with a sulfonamide, penicillin, or any broad-spectrum antibiotic, but this is not true in the case of corneal ulcer due to *Pseudomonas aeruginosa,* which requires vigorous treatment with polymyxin or gentamicin. Another example is staphylococcal dacryocystitis, which, if it does not respond to penicillin, is most likely to respond to erythromycin.

Choice of Alternative Drugs

In the treatment of infectious eye disease, eg, conjunctivitis, one should always use the drug which is the most effective, the least likely to cause complications, and the least expensive. It is also preferable to use a drug which is not usually given systemically, eg, sulfacetamide or bacitracin. Of the available antibacterial agents, the sulfonamides come closest to meeting these specifications. Two reliable sulfonamides for ophthalmic use are sulfisoxazole (Gantrisin®) and sodium sulfacetamide (Sulamyd®). The sulfonamides have the added advantages of low allergenicity and effectiveness against the chlamydial group of organisms. They are available in ointment or solution form.

Two of the most effective broad-spectrum antibiotics for ophthalmic use are gentamicin (Garamycin®) and neomycin. Both of these drugs have some effect against gram-negative as well as gram-positive organisms; allergic reactions to neomycin are common. Other antibiotics frequently used are erythromycin (Ilotycin®, Erythrocin®), the tetracyclines, bacitracin, and polymyxin (Aerosporin®). Combined bacitracin-polymyxin (Polysporin®) ointment is often used prophylactically after corneal foreign body removal for the protection it affords against both gram-positive and gram-negative organisms.

Method of Administration

Most ocular anti-infective drugs are administered locally. Systemic administration as well is required for all intraocular infections, corneal ulcer, orbital cellulitis, dacryocystitis, and any severe external infection which does not respond to local treatment.

Ointment vs Liquid Medications

Ointments have greater therapeutic effectiveness than solutions since contact can be maintained longer. However, they do cause blurring of vision; if this must be avoided, solutions should be used.

Havener, W.H.: Ophthalmic antibiotic therapy. Tr Penn Acad Ophthal 21:69–73, 1968.

Havener, W.H.: *Ocular Pharmacology,* 2nd ed. Mosby, 1970.

Leopold, I.H.: Ocular complications of drugs. JAMA 205:631–633, 1968.

Macri, F.J.: Pharmacology and toxicology of ophthalmic drugs: Annual review. Arch Ophth 82:707–719, 1969.

TECHNICS USED IN THE TREATMENT OF OCULAR DISORDERS

Instilling Medications

Place the patient in a chair with his head tilted back, both eyes open, and looking up. Retract the lower lid slightly and instill 2 drops of liquid into the lower cul-de-sac. Have the patient look down while finger contact on the lower lid is maintained. Do not let him squeeze his eye shut.

Ointments are instilled in the same general manner.

Self-Medication

The same technics are used as described above, except that drops are usually better instilled with the patient lying down.

Eye Bandage

Most eye bandages should be applied firmly enough to hold the lid securely against the cornea. An ordinary patch consisting of gauze-covered cotton is usually sufficient. Tape is applied from the cheek to the forehead. If more pressure is desired, use 2 or 3 bandages. The black eye patch is difficult to sterilize and therefore is seldom used in modern medical practice.

Warm Compresses

A clean towel or washcloth soaked in warm tap water is applied to the affected eye 2–4 times a day for 10–15 minutes.

Removal of a Superficial Corneal Foreign Body

Record the patient's visual acuity, if possible, and instill sterile local anesthetic drops. With the patient sitting or lying down, an assistant should direct a strong light into the eye so that the rays strike the cornea obliquely. Using either a loupe or a slit lamp the physician locates the foreign body on the corneal surface. He may remove it with a sterile wet cotton applicator or, if this fails, with a spud, holding the lids

apart with the other hand to prevent blinking. An antibacterial ointment (eg, Polysporin®) is instilled after the foreign body has been removed. It is preferable not to patch the eye, but the patient must be seen on the following day to make certain healing is under way.

PRECAUTIONS IN THE MANAGEMENT OF OCULAR DISORDERS

Use of Local Anesthetics

Unsupervised self-administration of local anesthetics is dangerous because the patient may further injure an anesthetized eye without knowing it.

Pupillary Dilation

Cycloplegics and mydriatics should be used with caution. Dilating the pupil can precipitate an attack of acute glaucoma if the patient has a narrow anterior chamber angle.

Local Corticosteroid Therapy

Repeated use of local corticosteroids presents 4 serious hazards: herpes simplex (dendritic) keratitis, fungal overgrowth, open-angle glaucoma, and cataract formation. Furthermore, perforation of the cornea may occur when the corticosteroids are used for herpes simplex keratitis.

Contaminated Eye Medications

Ophthalmic solutions must be prepared with the same degree of care as fluids intended for intravenous administration.

Tetracaine (Pontocaine®), proparacaine (Ophthaine®, Ophthetic®), physostigmine, and fluorescein are most likely to become contaminated. The most dangerous is fluorescein, as this solution is frequently contaminated with *Pseudomonas aeruginosa,* an organism which can rapidly destroy the eye. Sterile fluorescein filter paper strips are now available and are recommended in place of fluorescein solutions.

The following rules should be observed in handling eye medications for use in the diagnostic examination of uninjured eyes: (1) Obtain solutions in small amounts from the pharmacy. (2) Be certain that the solution is sterile as prepared and that it contains an effective antibacterial agent. (3) Date the bottle at the time it is procured.

Plastic dropper bottles are becoming more popular each year. Solutions from these bottles are safe to use in uninjured eyes. Whether in plastic or glass containers, eye solutions should not be used for long periods of time after the bottle is first opened. Two weeks is a reasonable time to use a solution before discarding.

If the eye has been injured accidentally or by surgical trauma, it is of the greatest importance to use sterile medications supplied in sterile, disposable, single use eye-dropper units.

Fungal Overgrowth

Since antibiotics, like corticosteroids, when used over a prolonged period of time in bacterial corneal ulcers, favor the development of secondary fungal corneal infection, the sulfonamides should be used whenever they are adequate for the purpose.

Sensitization

A significant portion of a soluble substance instilled in the eye may pass into the blood stream. This suggests that an antibiotic instilled into the eye can sensitize the patient to that drug and cause a hypersensitivity reaction upon subsequent systemic administration.

Macri, F.J.: Pharmacology and toxicology of ophthalmic drugs: Annual review. Arch Ophth 82:707–719, 1969.

•   •   •

MANIFESTATIONS INVOLVING THE EYES DUE TO PARASITIC DISEASES

Chorioretinitis: Congenital toxoplasmosis, amebiasis.

Ophthalmitis: Onchocerciasis, gnathostomiasis, toxocariasis, cysticercosis.

Iritis, iridocyclitis: Onchocerciasis, acquired toxoplasmosis.

Conjunctivitis, photophobia, etc: Loiasis, onchocerciasis, cysticercosis, sparganosis.

Punctate keratitis: Onchocerciasis.

Palpebral edema: American trypanosomiasis, trichinosis, cysticercosis, sparganosis.

•   •   •

General Bibliography

Adler, F.H.: *Physiology of the Eye*, 5th ed. Mosby, 1970.

Allen, J.H.: *May's Manual of Diseases of the Eye*, 24th ed. Williams & Wilkins, 1968.

Aronson, S.B., & others (editors): *Clinical Methods in Uveitis. The Fourth Sloan Symposium on Uveitis.* Mosby, 1968.

Beard, C.: *Ptosis.* Mosby, 1969.

Becker, B., & R. Burde: *Current Concepts in Ophthalmology,* Vol 2. Mosby, 1969.

Chandler, P., & W.M. Grant: *Lectures on Glaucoma.* Lea & Febiger, 1965.

Donaldson, D.D.: *Stereo-Atlas of External Diseases of the Eye.* Vol 1. *Congenital Anomalies of Systemic Diseases.* Mosby, 1966.

Duke-Elder, S.: *Parson's Diseases of the Eye,* 14th ed. Little, Brown, 1964.

Ellis, P.P., & D.L. Smith: *Handbook of Ocular Therapeutics and Pharmacology,* 3rd ed. Mosby, 1969.

Havener, W.H.: *Ocular Pharmacology,* 2nd ed. Mosby, 1970.

Hughes, W.F. (editor): *Year Book of Ophthalmology.* Year Book, 1971.

Keeney, A.H.: *Ocular Examination: Basis and Technique.* Mosby, 1970.

Kolker, A.E., & T. Hetherington: *Becker-Schaefer's Diagnosis & Therapy of the Glaucomas,* 3rd ed. Mosby, 1970.

Lyle, T.K., Cross, A.G., & C.A.G. Cook: *May and Worth's Diseases of the Eye,* 13th ed. Davis, 1968.

Martin-Doyle, J.L.C.: *Synopsis of Ophthalmology,* 3rd ed. Williams & Wilkins, 1967.

Newell, F.W.: *Ophthalmology: Principles and Concepts,* 2nd ed. Mosby, 1969.

Scheie, H.G., & D.M. Albert: *Adler's Textbook of Ophthalmology,* 8th ed. Saunders, 1969.

Trevor-Roper, P.D.: *Lecture Notes on Ophthalmology,* 3rd ed. Blackwell, 1968.

Vaughan, D., Asbury, T., & R. Cook: *General Ophthalmology,* 6th ed. Lange, 1971.

Von Noorden, G.K., & A.E. Maumenee: *Atlas of Strabismus.* Mosby, 1967.

Walsh, F.B., & W.F. Hoyt: *Clinical Neuro-ophthalmology,* 3rd ed. 3 vols. Williams & Wilkins, 1969.

5...

Ear, Nose, & Throat

Wayne W. Deatsch

DISEASES OF THE EAR

HEARING LOSS

Classification

A. Sensorineural Deafness (Perceptive, Nerve): Disturbance in the inner ear neural structures or nerve pathways leading to the brain stem.

B. Conductive Deafness: Disturbance of the sound transmission mechanism of the external or middle ears prevents sound waves from reaching the inner ear.

C. Mixed Type: Disturbance in both the conductive and nerve mechanisms.

D. Functional Deafness: Hearing loss for which no organic lesion can be detected.

General Considerations

Five to 10% of people have a hearing defect, temporarily or permanently, which is severe enough to impair their normal function. Hearing loss may occur at any age and produces disability depending upon the degree of loss, the age at which it occurs (interference with language and speech development), and whether one or both ears are affected.

Nerve type (sensorineural) hearing loss may be congenital, due to birth trauma, maternal rubella, erythroblastosis fetalis, or malformations of the inner ear; or it may be due to traumatic injury to the inner ear or 8th nerve, vascular disorders with hemorrhage or thrombosis in the inner ear, toxic agents (streptomycin, neomycin, polymyxin, kanamycin, quinine, aspirin, chloroquine), bacterial and viral infections (mumps, etc), severe febrile illnesses, Ménière's disease, posterior fossa tumors, multiple sclerosis, presbycusis, and exposure to loud sound.

Conductive hearing loss may also be congenital, due to malformations of the external or middle ear. Trauma may produce perforation of the eardrum or disruption of the ossicular chain. Inflammatory middle ear disease may produce serous otitis media, acute or chronic purulent otitis media, or adhesive otitis media. Otosclerosis, a common familial conductive hearing loss with onset in middle life, produces ankylosis of the stapes by overgrowth of new spongy bone; the etiology is not known.

Clinical Findings

The older patient will usually be aware of hearing loss of significant degree, and an accurate history is of importance to determine etiology. All the causes of hearing loss listed above must be investigated. In particular, the age at onset, degree of loss, progression, associated tinnitus or vertigo, exposure to head trauma, sound trauma, ototoxic drugs, previous infection, and severe febrile illnesses must be checked.

In infants and young children the diagnosis is often suggested by failure of speech development, lack of cooperation, inability to concentrate, and slow progress in learning.

A complete ear, nose, and throat examination is essential in all patients with hearing loss. Most important is examination of the ear canal, eardrum, and middle ear with the magnifying otoscope to detect even slight abnormalities. Attention must be given to obstructing or infected adenoid and tonsils, nasal and sinus infection, and evidences of other cranial nerve disturbance.

Special tests of value are as follows:

(1) Spoken voice test.

(2) Watch tick test.

(3) Tuning fork tests: The 500 and 1000 cps forks are the most important. These tests detect lateralization of the sounds of the fork and demonstrate comparative disturbances of air conduction and bone conduction (to distinguish conductive loss and nerve type loss).

(4) Audiometric tests (pure tone, speech tests, and other highly specialized audiometric tests) give accurate quantitative estimates of the degree of hearing loss.

(5) Labyrinthine tests give valuable objective evidence of inner ear function. An absent or altered labyrinthine response is quite significant. The test is done by irrigating the ear canals with hot or cold water to produce nystagmus and vertigo. The response in each ear should be equal.

Treatment

A. Hearing Loss in Children:

1. **Nerve deafness**—There is no medical or surgical treatment for most types of nerve deafness. Prompt treatment of bacterial infections of the CNS (meningitis, etc) and the prompt treatment of severe febrile illnesses may prevent some development of nerve deafness. During treatment with known ototoxic drugs,

hearing should be checked regularly and the drug discontinued if hearing begins to be impaired. If other equally effective drugs are available, ototoxic drugs should not be used. Management consists of rehabilitation and education. A hearing aid is valuable if there is residual hearing. Speech reading and speech training must be incorporated into the educational program.

2. Conductive deafness—Acute suppurative otitis media should be treated with early myringotomy in addition to medical management. Acute catarrhal otitis media may be treated medically, but the patient must be carefully followed to ensure that the infection completely resolves. Otherwise, residual fluid in the middle ear may produce a conductive hearing loss due to persistent serous otitis media, glue ear, or adhesive otitis media. Antibiotics in adequate doses and nasal decongestants should be administered for at least 7 days and often longer. This is necessary to prevent smoldering, partially eradicated infections that may recur in a few days with antibiotic-resistant organisms. Paracentesis and aspiration may be necessary.

Serous otitis media is common in children as well as in adults. Vigorous early treatment will usually reverse the hearing loss. Investigation and treatment of contributing nasal allergy or infection combined with aspiration of fluid from the middle ear is effective. Removal of obstructing or infected tonsils and adenoidal tissue is often necessary. In protracted and recurrent cases, repeat adenoidectomy or myringotomy and insertion of indwelling ventilating tubes may be necessary. Follow-up eustachian tube inflations are often required. The progress of each case must be carefully followed by audiometric testing.

Chronic otitis media in childhood should be treated vigorously to attempt to cure the disease and preserve or restore hearing. Many cases respond to cleansing followed by instillation of powders (eg, chloramphenicol and boric acid) or antibiotic solutions. Attention must again be directed to underlying nasal or sinus disease and infected or obstructing tonsils and adenoid. Other cases require surgery of the middle ear or mastoid (or both). Bilateral congenital anomalies of the external ear canal and middle ear can sometimes be corrected surgically. This should be done before plastic repair of the external ear is made. Small central perforations of the eardrum can be closed by patching with a paper or other membrane as an office procedure. Larger central perforations may be closed with a vein graft or skin graft. Marginal perforations usually require skin grafting and mastoid exploration.

B. Hearing Loss in Adults:

1. Nerve deafness—Nerve loss due to acoustic trauma will sometimes improve over a period of 6 months if the patient can avoid exposure to loud noise. The best treatment is prevention of exposure to loud noise either by avoiding the sources of noise (industry, recreation, military) or by wearing suitable protective ear plugs or other noise attenuators. Recent observations of hearing loss after exposure to highly amplified "rock" music should be noted. The nerve loss of Ménière's disease often improves with treatment and

between attacks. There is no medical or surgical treatment for other forms of nerve deafness except as mentioned above, prompt treatment of bacterial CNS infections and severe febrile illnesses, and the avoidance (if possible) or discontinuance of ototoxic drug administration if hearing loss begins to develop. A hearing aid should not be recommended for a patient with nerve deafness unless audiometric testing (pure tone and speech) indicates that the patient will probably learn to use the instrument satisfactorily. The learning of speech reading (lip reading) as well as auditory training by a hard-of-hearing patient is of definite value in his rehabilitation.

2. Conductive deafness—Important advances have been made recently in the surgical treatment of middle ear deafness. Otosclerosis may be treated successfully by the fenestration operation or by a direct operation on the fixed stapes through the ear canal and middle ear. The most recent technics involve removal of the stapes and replacement of the foot plate with a graft (vein, fat, or gelfoam) and replacement of the stapes crura with a prosthesis (wire or plastic strut).

Perforations of the eardrum can be repaired by vein, fascia, or skin grafting (myringoplasty).

Mastoid and middle ear operations have been designed for the treatment of suppuration and the removal of cholesteatoma and to preserve or improve hearing by skin grafting and by replacing or realigning the ossicular chain (tympanoplasty).

Serous otitis media in adults is treated in the same manner as in children.

Nerve deafness due to Ménière's disease will sometimes respond to early, adequate, and prolonged treatment. A fluctuating loss has a more favorable prognosis than a sudden severe loss. The basis of medical management is sodium restriction (1 gm sodium diet), antihistamines (eg, diphenhydramine or dimenhydrinate 4 times daily for 1–2 months), potassium substitution for sodium (KCl, 1 gm 3 times daily for 1–2 weeks), vasodilators (nicotinic acid in flushing doses 4 times daily), and reassurance.

Hilger, J.: The aging ear. Postgrad Med 44:219–228, 1968.

House, H.P., Linthicum, F.H., Jr., & E.W. Johnson: Current management of hearing loss in children. Am J Dis Child 108:677–696, 1964.

Jerger, J.: Review of diagnostic audiometry. Ann Otol Rhin Laryng 77:1042–1053, 1968.

Juers, A.L.: Non-organic hearing problems. Laryngoscope 76:1714–1723, 1966.

Landau, G.D.: Diagnosis and treatment of hearing loss. GP 34:128–172, Dec 1966.

Lebo, C.P., & K.P. Oliphant: Music as a source of acoustic trauma. Laryngoscope 78:1211–1218, 1968.

Lindsay, J.R., & G.H. Conner: Microsurgery of the ear. S Clin North America 46:111–130, 1966.

Sheehy, J.L., Gardner, G., Jr., & W.M. Hambley: Tuning fork tests in modern otology. Arch Otol 94:132–138, 1971.

DISEASES OF THE EXTERNAL EAR

1. IMPACTED CERUMEN

Cerumen is the normal secretion of the cartilaginous part of the ear canal which serves a protective function. Normally it dries and falls out of the ear canal, but it may accumulate within the canal because of dryness or scaling of the skin, narrowing or tortuosity of the ear canal, or excess hair in the ear canal. It may be packed in deeper by repeated unskilled attempts to remove it. There are usually no symptoms until the canal becomes completely occluded, when a feeling of fullness, deafness or tinnitus, or a cough due to reflex stimulation of the vagus nerve may occur. Otoscopy reveals the mass of yellow, brown, or black wax which may be sticky and soft or waxy, or stony hard.

If the mass is firm and movable, it may be removed through the speculum with a dull ring curette or a cotton applicator. If this is painful, the impaction may be removed by irrigation with water at body temperature, directing the stream of water from a large syringe at the wall of the ear canal and catching the solution in a basin held beneath the ear. If the impaction is very hard and adherent and cannot be readily removed by irrigation, it must be softened by repeated instillations of oily ear drops, glycerin, or peroxide, and irrigated again in 2–3 days.

2. EXTERNAL OTITIS

Differential Diagnosis

Diffuse eczematoid dermatitis of the ear canal, diffuse infected dermatitis, and furuncle of the ear canal must be distinguished from dermatitis due to contact with foreign objects (hearing aids, earphones) or infected material draining from the middle ear through a perforated eardrum.

External otitis may vary in severity from a diffuse mild eczematoid dermatitis to cellulitis or even furunculosis of the ear canal. It is frequently referred to as a fungal infection of the ear, although in many cases there is no infection and the reaction is a contact dermatitis (earphones, earrings) or a variant of seborrheic dermatitis. Infections of the ear canal are usually bacterial (staphylococcal and gram-negative rods), although a few are caused by fungi (aspergillus, mucor, penicillium). Predisposing factors are moisture in the ear canal in a warm, moist climate or due to swimming or bathing, trauma due to attempts to clean or scratch the itching ear, and seborrheic and allergic dermatitis.

Clinical Findings

A. Symptoms and Signs: Itching and pain in the dry, scaling ear canal are the chief symptoms. There may be a watery or purulent discharge and intermittent deafness. Pain may become extreme when the ear canal becomes completely occluded with edematous skin and debris. Preauricular, postauricular, or cervical adenopathy or fever indicate increasing severity of infection.

Examination shows crusting, scaling, erythema, edema, and pustule formation. Cerumen is absent. There may be evidence of seborrheic dermatitis elsewhere.

B. Laboratory Findings: The white count may be normal or elevated.

C. Special Examinations: After the canal is cleansed so that the eardrum is visible, otitis media can often be excluded if tuning fork tests indicate normal or nearly normal hearing.

Treatment

A. Systemic Treatment: If there is evidence of extension of infection beyond the skin of the ear canal (lymphadenopathy or fever), systemic antibiotics may be necessary. Systemic analgesics are required for pain.

B. Local Treatment: The objectives of local treatment are to keep the ear canal clean and dry and to protect it from trauma. Debris may be removed from the canal by gently wiping it with a cotton applicator or with suction or, occasionally, irrigation. The use of glycerite of peroxide with urea ear drops 3 times daily often helps to remove debris.

Topical antibiotic ointments and ear drops (eg, neomycin polymyxin, bacitracin) applied to the ear canal with a cotton wick for 24 hours followed by the use of ear drops twice daily help to control infection. Topical corticosteroids aid in decreasing inflammatory edema and controlling the often underlying dermatitis. Many antifungal and antimicrobial agents may be used topically, but some must be used with caution because of the possibility of local sensitivity reactions. Compresses of Burow's solution or 0.5% acetic acid are sometimes effective against acute weeping infected eczema when other measures fail. Seventy percent alcohol frequently controls itching in the dry, scaling ear canal.

Prognosis

External otitis is often refractory to treatment, and recurrences are frequent.

Jenkins, B.H.: Otitis externa: Prophylaxis and treatment. Eye Ear Nose Throat Monthly 43:47–50, 1964.

DISEASES OF THE MIDDLE EAR

1. ACUTE OTITIS MEDIA

Essentials of Diagnosis

- Ear pain, a sensation of fullness in the ear, and hearing loss; aural discharge.

- Onset following an upper respiratory infection.
- Fever and chills.

General Considerations

Acute otitis media most commonly occurs in infants and children, but it may occur at any age. Suppuration of the middle ear usually occurs following or accompanying disease of the upper respiratory tract. Beta-hemolytic streptococci, staphylococci, pneumococci, and *Hemophilus influenzae* are the usual infecting organisms. The acute inflammation of the middle ear mucosa is followed by acute suppuration and then a more severe suppuration with perforation of the tympanic membrane and occasionally with necrosis of the middle ear mucosa and eardrum.

Clinical Findings

A. Symptoms and Signs: The principal symptoms are ear pain, deafness, fever, chills, and a feeling of fullness and pressure in the ear. The eardrum at first shows dilatation of the blood vessels on the malleus and at the annulus; this is followed by diffuse dullness and hyperemia of the eardrum and loss of normal landmarks (short process of malleus) and bulging of the drum as the pressure of retained secretions increases in the middle ear. If the eardrum ruptures, discharge is found in the ear canal; the discharge may be pulsating. Fever is usually present.

B. Laboratory Findings: The white count is usually increased. Culture of the drainage will reveal the infecting organism.

C. Special Examinations: Hearing tests will show a conductive hearing loss.

Differential Diagnosis

Acute otitis media with bulging of the eardrum must be distinguished from myringitis bullosa, usually by the presence of more than one bleb in the ear canal and the absence of marked hearing loss. Acute otitis media with drainage must be distinguished from acute external otitis. The history of a preceding upper respiratory tract infection and hearing loss confirm the diagnosis of otitis media. Acute exacerbation of chronic otitis media is diagnosed by a history of otorrhea and hearing loss and by finding scar tissue on the eardrum. Reflex otalgia (pharyngitis, laryngitis, dental disease, temporomandibular joint disease) is present if there are no acute inflammatory changes in the ear canal or eardrum and no fever.

Complications

Acute mastoiditis, labyrinthitis, or meningitis may occur as complications.

Treatment

A. Systemic Treatment: Bed rest, analgesics, and systemic antibiotics are usually required. Penicillin or a broad-spectrum antibiotic is usually the drug of choice, and should be continued for at least 6 days to minimize the likelihood of recurrence of an incompletely resolved infection after a latent period. Nasal decongestants, topical and systemic, help restore eustachian tube function.

B. Local Treatment: Ear drops are of limited value except in the mildest cases. Local heat may hasten resolution. Local cold applications relieve pain occasionally. The most important aspect of treatment is myringotomy when the infection does not resolve promptly or when bulging of the eardrum indicates that a discharge is present and is under pressure. Myringotomy should also be promptly performed if there is continued pain or fever, increasing hearing loss, or vertigo.

Prognosis

Acute otitis media adequately treated with antibiotics and myringotomy if indicated resolves with rare exceptions. Complicating mastoiditis occurs most commonly following inadequate or no treatment. Persistent conductive hearing loss with or without middle ear fluid may occur following incomplete resolution of the infection. It is imperative to examine the ears and to test the hearing after otitis media to prevent persistent conductive hearing loss with serous otitis media or "glue ear."

Beales, P.H.: Acute otitis media. Practitioner 199:752–760, 1967.

Dysart, B.R.: Progress report: Otitis media and complications. Arch Otolaryng 84:468–472, 1966.

Feingold, M., & others: Acute otitis media in children. Am J Dis Child 111:361–365, 1966.

Hambley, W.M.: External otitis versus otitis media. GP 34:136–138, Oct 1966.

Palmer, B.W.: Hemorrhagic bullous myringitis: Recent concepts of etiology and complications. Eye Ear Nose Throat Monthly 47:562–565, 1968.

2. CHRONIC OTITIS MEDIA

Chronic inflammation of the middle ear is nearly always associated with perforation of the eardrum. It is important to distinguish the relatively benign chronic otitis associated with eustachian tube disease—characterized by central perforation of the eardrum and often mucoid otorrhea occurring with an upper respiratory tract infection—from the chronic otitis associated with mastoid disease that is potentially much more dangerous; the latter is characterized by perforation of Shrapnell's membrane or posterior marginal perforation of the eardrum, often with foul-smelling drainage and cholesteatoma formation. Drainage from the ear and impaired hearing are frequent symptoms.

Treatment of the chronic "tubal ear" should be directed at improving eustachian tube function by correcting nasal or sinus infection, infected or hypertrophied tonsils or adenoid, or nasal polyps or deviated nasal septum and nasal allergy. Ear drops (alcohol and boric acid, or antibiotic solutions) or dusting powders (iodine, boric acid, or antibiotics) and frequent cleansing of the ear are of value. Systemic antibiotics have limited value. If there is evidence of continued suppuration or if mastoiditis or other complications occur, radical or modified radical mastoidectomy should be done. In some cases of chronic otitis media where hearing loss has occurred—and if the middle ear infection is quiescent and eustachian tube function is adequate—reconstructive middle ear operations (tympanoplasty) can be attempted to improve the hearing.

Diamant, M.: Chronic middle ear discharge. Eye Ear Nose Throat Month 44:77–83, 1965.

Goodwin, M.R.: Acute mastoiditis and acute labyrinthitis without mastoidectomy. Laryngoscope 78:227–235, 1968.

Hill, F.T.: Comprehensive care in the treatment of chronic suppurative otitis media. Laryngoscope 71:587–595, 1961.

Juers, A.L., Patterson, C.N., & J.B. Farrior: Symposium on tympanoplasty. I. Office closure of tympanic perforations—passé. II. Silastic sponge implants in tympanoplasty. III. Tympanoplasty: The anterior atticotympanotomy. Surgery of the posterior tympanic recesses. Laryngoscope 78:756–779, 1968.

Macbeth, R.: Chronically discharging ear. Practitioner 199:735–743, 1967.

Ruggles, R.L., & C.A. Koconis: Tympanic perforations: Safe or not? Laryngoscope 77:337–340, 1967.

Thomas, G.L.: Cholesteatoma of the ear. California Med 108:205–208, 1968.

3. SEROUS OTITIS MEDIA

Serous otitis media may occur at any age. It is characterized by the accumulation of sterile fluid (serous or mucoid) in the middle ear, producing symptoms of hearing loss, a full, plugged feeling in the ear, and an unnatural reverberation of the patient's voice. It may be caused by (1) an obstruction of the eustachian tube which prevents normal ventilation of the middle ear and subsequent transudation of serous fluid; (2) an incompletely resolved exudate of purulent otitis media; or (3) an allergic exudate of serous fluid into the middle ear.

Examination shows a conductive hearing loss and a retracted eardrum, often with a characteristic "ground glass" amber discoloration and impaired mobility of the eardrum with the pneumatic otoscope. Air-fluid bubbles or a fluid level can sometimes be seen through the eardrum.

The absence of fever, pain, and toxic symptoms distinguish serous otitis media from acute otitis media. Cancer of the nasopharynx must be ruled out in persistent unilateral serous otitis media in an adult.

Local treatment consists of eustachian tube inflations, paracentesis of the eardrum with aspiration of the middle ear contents, and nasal decongestants (0.25% phenylephrine nasal spray or phenylpropanola-

mine, 25–50 mg orally 3 times daily). Antihistamines should be given if there is any suggestion of contributing nasal allergy. Underlying factors must be corrected by tonsillectomy, adenoidectomy, control of nasal allergy, and treatment of nasal or sinus infection. Indwelling plastic ventilating tubes after myringotomy and local or systemic use of corticosteroids may help in persistent cases.

Amiri, C.S.: Fluid in the middle ear: Classification of cases. Eye Ear Nose Throat Month 47:319–320, 1968.

Chan, J.C.M., Logan, G.B., & J.B. McBean: Serous otitis media and allergy. Am J Dis Child 114:684–692, 1967.

Draper, W.L.: Secretory otitis media in children: A study of 540 children. Laryngoscope 77:636–653, 1967.

Feuerstein, S.S.: Surgery of serous otitis media. Laryngoscope 76:686–708, 1966.

Oppenheimer, R.P., & J.R. Siegel: Treatment of serous otitis in children. GP 35:105–107, March 1967.

4. MASTOIDITIS

Acute mastoiditis is a complication of acute suppurative otitis media. Bony necrosis of the mastoid process and breakdown of the bony intercellular structures occur in the second to third week. When this occurs there is evidence of continued drainage from the middle ear, mastoid tenderness, systemic manifestations of sepsis (fever, headache), and x-ray evidence of bone destruction.

If suppurative mastoiditis develops in spite of antibiotic therapy, mastoidectomy must be done. Acute mastoiditis is rarely seen since chemotherapeutic and antibiotic therapy has become available for the treatment of acute suppurative otitis media.

Chronic mastoiditis is a complication of chronic otitis media. If the disease occurs in infancy the mastoid bone does not develop cellular structure but becomes dense and sclerotic. Infection is usually limited to the antral area. However, x-ray findings of a sclerotic mastoid does not necessarily mean that a chronic infection is present, only that an infection was present in infancy and that as a result the mastoid air cells are not well developed. The presence of infection must be determined by clinical findings. In some cases of marginal perforation or Shrapnell's membrane perforation (attic perforation) of the eardrum, cholesteatomas develop. Cholesteatoma is produced by the ingrowth of squamous epithelium from the skin of the external ear canal into the middle ear or mastoid, forming an epithelial cyst. Desquamation and laminated growth of the cyst may produce erosion of adjacent bone or soft tissue.

Antibiotic drugs are usually of limited usefulness in clearing the infection in chronic mastoiditis, but they may be effective in the treatment of complications. Many cases of chronic otitis media and mastoiditis can be managed by local cleansing of the ear and instillation of antibiotic powders or solutions. Other cases may require radical or modified radical mastoidectomy or tympanoplasty.

Ronis, B.J., Ronis, M.L., & E.P. Liebman: Acute mastoiditis as seen today. Eye Ear Nose Throat Monthly 47:502–507, 1968.

COMPLICATIONS OF MIDDLE EAR INFECTIONS

Following Acute Suppurative Otitis Media & Mastoiditis

A. Subperiosteal abscess following acute otitis media and mastoiditis is infrequent. Simple mastoidectomy is required.

B. Facial nerve paralysis developing in the first few hours or days after the onset of acute otitis media is due to edema of the nerve in the bony facial canal. Conservative treatment is usually indicated (antibiotics, myringotomy, supportive measures).

C. Meningitis, epidural, subdural, and brain abscess, and sigmoid sinus thrombosis are serious complications of suppurative otitis media and mastoiditis which may be masked by antibiotic drugs. Surgical treatment of the mastoid disease and its complications is required.

Following Chronic Otitis Media

A. Acute exacerbations of chronic otitis media and mastoiditis may lead to meningitis, epidural, subdural, and brain abscess, and sigmoid sinus thrombosis, requiring antibiotic therapy and surgery.

B. Facial nerve paralysis is usually the result of direct pressure on the nerve by cholesteatoma or granulation tissue. Mastoidectomy and decompression of the facial nerve are necessary.

Dysart, B.R.: Progress report: otitis media and complications. Arch Otolaryng 84:468–472, 1966.

Myers, E.N., & H.T. Ballantine, Jr.: The management of otogenic brain abscess. Laryngoscope 75:273–288, 1965.

Proctor, C.A.: Intracranial complications of otitic origin. Laryngoscope 76:288–308, 1966.

DISEASES OF THE INNER EAR

1. MÉNIÈRE'S SYNDROME
(Paroxysmal Labyrinthine Vertigo)

Essentials of Diagnosis

- Intermittent attacks of vertigo, nausea, vomiting, profuse sweating.
- Progressive, often unilateral nerve type hearing loss and continuous tinnitus.

General Considerations

Ménière's syndrome is characterized by recurrent episodes of severe vertigo associated with deafness and tinnitus. It is encountered most often in men in the age group from 40–60. The cause is not known, but "endolymphatic hydrops" with marked dilatation of the cochlear duct is the pathologic finding. Ménière's syndrome may follow head trauma or middle ear infection, but many cases develop without apparent damage to the nervous system or ear.

Clinical Findings

Intermittent severe vertigo, which may appear to throw the subject to the ground, is the principal symptom. Brief loss of consciousness occasionally occurs in an attack. "Spinning" of surrounding objects is often noted. Nausea, vomiting, and profuse perspiration are often associated. The attacks may last from a few minutes to several hours. The frequency of attacks varies considerably even in the same patient. Headache, nerve type hearing loss, and tinnitus occur during and persist between attacks. Hearing loss is apt to be progressive, and is unilateral in 90% of cases. Nystagmus may occur during attacks of vertigo. An altered labyrinthine response is often demonstrated by means of the caloric or Bárány test. There is increased sensitivity to loud sounds. Audiometric tests show recruitment, decreased speech discrimination, and a nerve type hearing loss.

Differential Diagnosis

Distinguish the vertigo from that produced by posterior fossa tumors (other findings such as papilledema, increased CSF pressure and protein, and brain stem signs). Differentiate dizziness and lightheadedness from those seen in some systemic diseases, brain stem vascular disease, and psychiatric disorders.

Treatment

Reassurance is important, since many of these patients have a marked psychic overlay. A salt-free diet and ammonium chloride, 1–2 gm 4 times daily, may be helpful. Diuretics such as acetazolamide (Diamox®) and chlorothiazide (Diuril®) may also be used. Nicotinic acid, 50–100 mg IV 2–3 times daily, or 100 mg orally 5–6 times daily, has been found useful. The antihistamines, especially diphenhydramine hydrochloride (Benadryl®) and dimenhydrinate (Dramamine®), in doses of 50–100 mg 3–4 times daily, appear to be of benefit to some patients. Parenteral diphenhydramine or dimenhydrinate—or atropine sulfate, 0.6 mg—may stop the acute attack.

Destructive surgery on the labyrinth or vestibular nerve may be necessary in a few severe cases which do not respond to medical measures.

Prognosis

Ménière's syndrome is a chronic recurrent disease which persists for several years. Remission or improvement of vertigo after treatment is often noted; however, tinnitus and deafness usually are unaffected and permanent. Progression is slow and sometimes stops before complete deafness occurs.

Cessation of attacks of vertigo may follow complete loss of hearing.

Procedures which destroy or interrupt an affected vestibular portion of acoustic nerve (such as destruction of the labyrinth or section of the acoustic nerve) may prevent further attacks of vertigo.

Leivers, E.: Vertigo. Arch Otolaryng 88:373–376, 1968.
Lindsay, J.R., Kohut, R.I., & P.A. Sciarra: Ménière's disease: Pathology and manifestations. Ann Otol Rhin Laryng 76:5–22, 1967.
McCabe, B.F.: Clinical aspects of the differential diagnosis of end-organ vertigo. Ann Otol Rhin Laryng 77:193–198, 1968.
Proud, G.O.: Practical testing methods for vestibular disorders: Office tests. Ann Otol Rhin Laryng 77:199–202, 1968.
Simonton, K.M.: Ménière's disease and medical treatment of vertigo. Mayo Clin Proc 44:81–84, 1969.
Symposium on vertigo. Arch Otolaryng 85:497–560, 1967.

2. TINNITUS

Tinnitus is a sensation of noise in the ears or head that may be objective (heard by the examiner) or subjective. Objective tinnitus is uncommon, and is usually caused by transmitted vascular vibrations in the blood vessels of the head and neck or by rhythmic rapid contractions of the muscles of the soft palate or middle ear. The examiner can often hear the sound through a stethoscope placed over the ear or can see movements of the eardrum or palate.

Subjective tinnitus usually accompanies hearing loss or other disorders of the external, middle, or inner ear. Although the etiology is unknown, it is presumed to be due to irritation of nerve endings in the cochlea by degenerative vascular or vasomotor disease. Most patients state that the noise is bearable during the day but is much louder and more disturbing at night when the masking effect of environmental sounds is not present.

If possible, treatment is directed at the underlying cause. If the etiology cannot be determined, reassurance may be all that is necessary. An air conduction hearing aid during the day and a pillow speaker for music or other masking sound during the night may be necessary in severe cases. Sedation may be used sparingly. Difficult cases may require the close cooperation of an otolaryngologist, internist, neurologist, and psychiatrist.

Fowler, E.P.: Subjective head noises. (Tinnitus aurium.) Genesis and differential diagnostic significance. A few facts and several speculations. Laryngoscope 75:1610–1618, 1965.
Harpman, J.A.: Vascular tinnitus. Arch Otolaryng 86:53–54, 1967.

3. ACUTE NONSUPPURATIVE LABYRINTHITIS

Acute inflammation of the inner ear characteristically follows respiratory tract infections and is manifested by intense vertigo, usually with marked tinnitus, a staggering gait, and nystagmus. Hearing loss is often not present.

Bed rest, preferably in a darkened room, is indicated until severe symptoms subside. Antibiotics are of little value unless there is associated infection of the middle ear or mastoid bone. Antihistamine drugs (as for motion sickness) may be of value. Sedation is generally helpful. Give phenobarbital, 15–60 mg 3–4 times daily. Chlorpromazine hydrochloride (Thorazine®), 50 mg IM (or other phenothiazine derivative), is useful in the acute early phase.

Attacks of labyrinthitis may last for several days. Recovery is usually complete.

Sheehy, J.L.: The dizzy patient. Arch Otolaryng 86:18–19, 1967.
Smith, J.L.: Evaluation of the dizzy patient. Eye Ear Nose Throat Monthly 45:58–59, 1966.
Symposium on vertigo. Arch Otolaryng 85:497–560, 1967.

4. ACUTE SUPPURATIVE LABYRINTHITIS

Acute suppurative labyrinthitis is an infection of the intralabyrinthine structures. It may occur following acute otitis media and mastoiditis, acute exacerbations of chronic otitis media and mastoiditis, or meningitis unrelated to ear diseases. There is usually total destruction of labyrinthine function in the affected area and complete unilateral deafness.

Antibiotics and surgical drainage are indicated.

5. CHRONIC LABYRINTHITIS

Chronic labyrinthitis is secondary to erosion of the bony labyrinthine capsule (usually the lateral semicircular canal) by cholesteatoma. The patient has chronic episodes of vertigo, and attacks of vertigo can be reproduced by increasing the air pressure in the ear canal with a pneumatic otoscope (positive fistula test).

Mastoidectomy and removal of the cholesteatoma are required.

DISEASES OF THE NOSE

VESTIBULITIS

Inflammation of the nasal vestibule may occur as a dermatitis of the skin of the nose, often as a result of irritation from a nasal discharge; as a fissure resulting from chronic dermatitis or the trauma of picking or wiping the nose; or as a furuncle, usually after pulling hairs from the nose. Symptoms vary from scaling and weeping to edema, hyperemia, intense pain, and abscess formation. Fissures usually occur at the junction of the columella with the ala or with the floor of the nose. Careful cleansing of nasal discharge, avoidance of pulling nasal hairs, and protection with petrolatum or boric acid ointment may prevent these problems.

The application of soothing, protective, and antimicrobial ointments (eg, 5% ammoniated mercury, 3% iodochlorhydroxyquin cream, neomycin, polymyxin, or bacitracin ointments) several times daily for several days after symptoms disappear is usually adequate treatment. For more severe infections, systemic antibiotics, local heat, and general supportive measures may be necessary.

NASAL SEPTAL HEMATOMA & ABSCESS

Septal hematoma occurs following trauma to the nose. The swollen septum produces nasal obstruction and frontal headache. Septal abscess usually is the result of an infected septal hematoma. It may occur following a furuncle in the vestibule, and produces nasal obstruction, headache, fever, malaise, pain in the nose, and tenderness over the nasal dorsum.

Septal hematoma may be treated conservatively by observation for possible infection; it should resolve in 4–6 weeks. It may also be relieved by aspiration with a large-bore needle or by incision and drainage, in both cases taking extreme precautions to prevent infection.

Septal abscess must be drained by wide incision of one side of the septum and suction. Necrotic pieces of cartilage may be cautiously removed. The incision must be wide enough to prevent early closure or must be spread open daily. Nasal packing may be necessary to control bleeding. Systemic antibiotics are required. Destruction of cartilage causes saddle deformity.

Fearon, B., McKendry, J.B., & J. Parker: Abscess of the nasal septum in children. Arch Otolaryng 74:408–412, 1961.

"COMMON RESPIRATORY DISEASE"
(Common Cold, Grippe, Acute Bronchitis, Tracheobronchitis)

This group of diseases includes the numerous self-limited, usually viral infections of the upper respiratory tract. Children 1–5 years old are most susceptible, and adults from 25–35 next most susceptible. The incidence is lowest during the summer months. Exposure to cold, chilling, and dampness are probably of little etiologic significance.

Known agents which may cause this syndrome include the rhinoviruses (30 different serologic types), adenovirus, ECHO virus, coxsackievirus, influenza viruses, parainfluenza viruses, and mycoplasmal organisms. This great diversity probably explains the frequent recurrence of "colds" in many individuals.

Clinical Findings

A. Symptoms and Signs: The patient complains of malaise, "feverishness" with usually little or no fever, and headache. Nasal discomfort (burning, fullness, itching) is a prominent feature, with watery discharge and sneezing followed shortly by mucoid to purulent discharge and nasal obstruction. Throat symptoms include "dryness," mild to moderate "soreness" rather than actual pain, hoarseness, and "tickling." Cough with scanty sputum and substernal aching may occur. Serious obstruction may occur in infants and young children or in adults with underlying bronchopulmonary disease (eg, emphysema).

The nasal mucosa is reddened and edematous. The external nares are red. The pharynx and tonsils usually show mild to moderate injection without edema or exudate. Cases of pharyngitis with considerable injection and exudate which fail to yield beta-hemolytic streptococci on repeated culture should probably be included in this group.

Cervical lymph nodes may be enlarged and slightly tender. Herpes labialis is common.

B. Laboratory Findings: The white count may be slightly elevated, but in most cases this is due to secondary bacterial infection.

Differential Diagnosis

Many specific infectious diseases present initial manifestations indistinguishable from those of common respiratory disease. Vigilance is required to avoid diagnostic errors of omission (eg, meningococcal infection, diphtheria).

Influenza is recognized by its epidemic occurrence and by serologic confirmation.

Exanthematous diseases (especially measles and chickenpox) may simulate common respiratory disease in their preeruptive phase.

In the initial phase, beta-hemolytic streptococcal pharyngitis may be clinically indistinguishable from acute nonstreptococcal exudative pharyngitis. Cultures make the diagnosis.

Complications

Complications result from secondary bacterial infections, often aided by the obstruction of respiration passages (eg, sinus ostia, bronchioles). They include purulent sinusitis, otitis media, bacterial pneumonia, and tonsillitis.

Treatment

No specific treatment is available. Antibiotics are used only to prevent secondary infection in patients with low pulmonary and cardiac reserves and to treat complicating secondary infections.

General measures consist of rest, sufficient fluids to prevent dehydration, and a light, palatable, well balanced diet. Aspirin may be given for headache, sore throat, muscle soreness, and fever. Vasoconstrictors give temporary relief of nasal obstruction and rhinorrhea. Phenylephrine hydrochloride (Neo-Synephrine®), 0.25%, several drops in each nostril every 2–3 hours; or phenylpropanolamine hydrochloride (Propadrine®), 25–50 mg every 4–6 hours, is satisfactory for this purpose. Antihistamines may relieve the early symptoms of mucous membrane inflammation. Cough may be reduced by inhaling steam or with codeine phosphate, 8–15 mg orally every 2–4 hours. Heat to the area of the sinuses may relieve nasal obstruction.

Johnson, H.E., & others: Viral infections and the common cold (panel discussion). Dis Chest 45:46–53, 1964.

Kneeland, Y., Jr.: Common upper respiratory infection including the common cold. M Clin North America 43:1327–1334, 1959.

ALLERGIC RHINITIS
(Hay Fever)

Essentials of Diagnosis

- Watery nasal discharge, sneezing, itching eyes and nose.
- Pale, boggy mucous membranes.
- Eosinophilia of nasal secretions and blood.

General Considerations

See discussion under Bronchial Asthma.

Clinical Findings

A. Symptoms and Signs: The principal symptoms are nasal congestion, a profuse, watery nasal discharge, itching of the nasal mucosa leading to paroxysms of violent sneezing, conjunctival itching and burning, and lacrimation. The nasal mucosa are pale blue and boggy. Polyps may be present. The conjunctivas are often reddened and swollen.

B. Laboratory Findings: A smear of the nasal secretions reveals increased numbers of eosinophils. (In infections, neutrophils predominate.) The peripheral blood may reveal mild (5–10%) or occasionally marked (30–40%) eosinophilia, even between clinical episodes.

Skin tests may be of aid in the detection of the allergens but must be correlated with the clinical picture to determine their significance.

Differential Diagnosis

A history of an allergy aids in distinguishing allergic rhinitis from the common upper respiratory infections; hay fever should be suspected in young children as the real cause of repeated "colds."

Treatment

A. Specific Measures: There is no true specific treatment. Hyposensitization or desensitization is sometimes beneficial and consists of administering the allergen (usually pollen) in gradually increasing doses to induce an "immunity." For best results, therapy should be started 3–6 months before the beginning of the hay fever season.

B. General Measures:

1. Antihistamines give relief in 60–80% of patients, but their effectiveness often wanes as the season continues.

2. Sympathomimetic drugs such as ephedrine and phenylpropanolamine are effective by themselves or in combination with the antihistamines.

3. Sedation may be of value for tense or nervous patients.

4. The corticosteroids are useful in severe hay fever which cannot be controlled by the agents mentioned above. Prednisone, 20–40 mg by mouth daily in divided doses, may be used for several days until symptoms are controlled. Dosage should then be reduced gradually (over a period of 7–10 days) to the smallest daily dose that will suppress symptoms. Discontinue steroid therapy as soon as possible.

5. Maintenance of an allergen-free atmosphere and the use of dust-proof respirator masks and room air filters are often of value during the pollen season if the patient must remain in the area. When dust is the offending agent, prepare a dust-free bedroom as follows: Cover the mattress and pillow with an air-tight nonantigenic material (plastic or sheet rubber). Remove all carpets, drapes, bedspreads, and other lint-producing materials, and all ornate furniture or other objects which are not easily dusted. Blankets should be of synthetic material if possible.

Household pets must be considered possible sources of allergens.

Prognosis

Allergic rhinitis is a self-limited though recurrent disorder with mild morbidity and no mortality.

Criep, L.H.: Nasal allergy–an interdisciplinary problem. Eye Ear Nose Throat Monthly 44:70–76, 1965.

Taylor, L.: Perennial nasal allergy. Practitioner 197:775–779, 1966.

Williams, R.I.: Modern concepts in clinical management of allergy in otolaryngology. Laryngoscope 76:1389–1415, 1966.

SINUS INFECTION

Essentials of Diagnosis: Acute

- History of acute upper respiratory infection, dental infection, or nasal allergy.
- Pain, tenderness, redness, swelling over the involved sinus.

- Nasal congestion and purulent nasal discharge.
- Clouding of sinuses on x-ray or transillumination.
- Fever, chills, malaise, headache.
- Teeth hurt or feel "long" (maxillary sinusitis), or swelling occurs near the nasal canthus of eye (ethmoid sinusitis).

Essentials of Diagnosis: Chronic
- Nasal obstruction.
- Postnasal discharge.
- Clouding of sinus on x-ray or transillumination.
- Pain is not a common finding.

General Considerations

Acute sinus infection usually follows an acute upper respiratory infection, swimming or diving, dental abscess or extractions, or nasal allergies, or occurs as an exacerbation of a chronic sinus infection. Isolated acute frontal sinus infection is rare. Acute ethmoiditis is most common in infants and children. Chronic pyogenic infections of single sinuses do occur, but this is less common than pansinusitis.

Clinical Findings

A. Symptoms and Signs:

1. Acute sinusitis–The symptoms resemble those of acute rhinitis but are more severe. There is headache and facial pain, tenderness and swelling with nasal obstruction, and a purulent nasal and postnasal discharge, sometimes causing sore throat and cough. The headache typically is worse during the day and subsides in the evening. Acute maxillary sinusitis may cause pain in the teeth and a feeling of "long teeth." Acute ethmoiditis causes headache between and behind the eyes, and eye motion increases the pain. Tenderness medially in the roof of the orbit occurs with frontal sinusitis. Fever and systemic symptoms vary with the severity of the infection.

2. Chronic sinusitis–Chronic sinus infection may produce no symptoms. A mild postnasal discharge and a musty odor or nonproductive cough may be the only symptoms. Nasal obstruction and sometimes profuse purulent nasal and postnasal discharge may also occur.

B. Laboratory Findings: In acute sinusitis the white count may be elevated, and culture of nasal discharge usually shows the pyogenic organisms.

C. Other Examinations: X-ray and transillumination show clouding of the involved sinuses.

Differential Diagnosis

Acute dental infection usually produces greater facial swelling lower in the face with more marked tenderness of the involved tooth than does maxillary sinusitis. The more localized swelling and tenderness and greater involvement of the eyelids with absence of nasal discharge distinguishes an infected tear sac from ethmoiditis. X-ray examination gives more definite evidence of sinus involvement.

An isolated chronic maxillary sinusitis without obvious underlying cause suggests dental disease or neoplasm.

Complications

Chronic sinusitis is the commonest complication of acute sinusitis. Orbital cellulitis and abscess may follow ethmoiditis or frontal sinusitis. Frontal sinusitis may be complicated by meningitis or extradural, subdural, or brain abscess. Osteomyelitis of the facial or frontal bones may occur.

Treatment

A. Acute Sinusitis: Place the patient at bed rest and give sedatives, analgesics, a light diet, and fluids. Oral nasal decongestants (eg, phenylpropanolamine, 25–50 mg 3 times daily) and systemic antibiotics frequently produce prompt resolution of the infection. Broad-spectrum antibiotics appear to be most beneficial, but nearly all antibiotics have been effective.

Local heat, topical nasal decongestants (eg, 0.25% phenylephrine), and gentle spot suctioning of the nasal discharge are helpful.

The sinuses must not be manipulated during the acute infection. Antrum irrigation is of value after the acute inflammation has subsided. Acute frontal sinusitis is treated medically and conservatively; cannulation is rarely warranted. Trephining of the sinus floor may occasionally be indicated in acute fulminating infections. Acute ethmoid infections respond to medical management; if external fluctuation develops incision and drainage is indicated.

B. Chronic Sinusitis: When the infecting organism has been identified the suitable antibiotic is given systemically. Irrigation of the antra or Proetz displacement may help drainage. Conservative surgery to promote drainage is of value (removal of polyps, submucous resection of an obstructing septum, intranasal antrotomy). If conservative treatment is not effective, more radical sinus surgery by the external approach may be considered.

C. Treatment of Complications:

1. Osteomyelitis, meningitis, abscess–Give supportive measures and antibiotics. Remove necrotic bone and drain abscesses as required.

2. Orbital fistulas–Treat the underlying sinus disease and close the tract surgically.

3. Oroantral fistula–Remove underlying sinus infection by the Caldwell-Luc operation and close the tract.

4. Mucoceles (mucopyoceles)–Surgical excision.

Prognosis

Acute infections usually respond to medical management and irrigation.

Chronic infections often require surgical correction. Chronic frontal sinusitis is especially likely to persist or recur.

Bryant, F.L.: Conservative surgery for chronic maxillary sinusitis. Laryngoscope 77:575–583, 1967.

Davison, F.W.: Chronic sinus disease: Differential diagnosis. Laryngoscope 78:1738–1745, 1968.

Haynes, R.E., & H.G. Cramblett: Acute ethmoiditis. Am J Dis Child 114:261–267, 1967.

Macbeth, R.: Chronic sinusitis. Practitioner 197:765–774, 1966.

McCabe, B.F.: "I've got sinus." GP 32:135–139, Sept 1965.

Mills, C.P.: Acute sinusitis. Practitioner 197:757–764, 1966.

Wassermann, D.: Acute paranasal sinusitis and cavernous sinus thrombosis. Arch Otolaryng 86:205–209, 1967.

NASAL TUMORS

Benign Tumors

Angioma, fibroma, papilloma, chondroma, and osteoma are the most common types of benign neoplasms of the nose and sinuses. Nasal tumors produce obstruction and nasal discharge when they become large enough. Severe epistaxis occurs with angioma. Secondary infection may occur. Pressure atrophy of surrounding structures, widening of the nasal bridge, and displacement of the eye may occur. X-rays and biopsy usually establish the diagnosis.

Treatment consists of complete removal with permanent intranasal drainage of involved sinuses.

Malignant Tumors

Many nasal malignancies originate in the sinuses and extend into the nose. Sarcoma and carcinoma occur. Symptoms and signs may not occur until late; the most common are obstruction, discharge, epistaxis, pain, swelling of the face, and diplopia. X-ray shows clouding of the sinuses that may suggest infection; secondary infection is frequently present. Bony destruction may show on x-rays. Cytologic smears of antrum irrigation fluid and "cell buttons" may show malignant cells. Biopsy is diagnostic.

Surgical excision is usually the treatment of choice. Some cases may be treated by biopsy followed by x-ray therapy or, occasionally, surgery plus irradiation or cautery.

Choa, G.: Nasopharyngeal carcinoma. Some observations on the clinical features and techniques of examinations. Pacific Med Surg 75:172–174, 1967.

Holsti, L.R., & R. Rinne: Treatment of malignant tumors of paranasal sinuses. Acta radiol 6:337–350, 1967.

Oliver, P.: Cancer of the nose and paranasal sinuses. S Clin North America 47:595–600, 1967.

Sisson, G.A., Johnson, N.E., & C.S. Amiri: Cancer of the maxillary sinus. Clinical classification and management. Ann Otol Rhin Laryng 72:1050–1090, 1963.

EPISTAXIS
(Nosebleed)

The most common sites of nasal bleeding are the mucosal vessels over the cartilaginous nasal septum (Kiesselbach's area or Little's area) and the anterior tip of the inferior turbinate. Bleeding is usually due to external trauma to the nose, nasal infection (especially with vigorous nose-blowing), or drying of the nasal mucosa when humidity is low. Minor trauma such as nose-picking may lead to ulcerations of the nasal septum and subsequent hemorrhage. Up to 5% of nosebleeds originate posteriorly in the nose where the bleeding site cannot be seen; these can cause great problems in management.

Nosebleed may escape diagnosis if the blood drains into the pharynx and is swallowed. In these cases bloody or "coffee-ground" vomitus may be the first clue.

Underlying causes of nosebleed such as blood dyscrasias, hypertension, hemorrhagic disease, nasal tumors, and certain infectious diseases (measles or rheumatic fever) must be considered in any case of recurrent or profuse nosebleed without obvious cause.

Treatment

A. Specific Measures: Treatment of the underlying disease depends upon an adequate examination to detect cardiovascular, renal, or liver disease, blood dyscrasias, coagulation defects, or other systemic disorders contributing to the nosebleed. Give transfusions as necessary if blood loss is excessive.

B. Local Measures: Have the patient sit up and forward with his head tipped downward to prevent swallowing and aspiration of blood. Good illumination (with a head mirror or headlight) is essential to proper examination and treatment.

1. **Anterior epistaxis**—Pressure over the area (pinching the nose) for 5 minutes is often sufficient to stop bleeding. This may be combined with packing the bleeding nostril with a pledget of cotton moistened with hydrogen peroxide, 0.25% phenylephrine, or 1:1000 epinephrine solution.

After active bleeding has stopped (or if pressure fails to stop bleeding), a cotton pledget moistened with a topical anesthetic (1% tetracaine or 5% cocaine) applied to the bleeding area will provide anesthesia for cauterization with a chromic acid bead, trichloroacetic acid, or an electrocautery. After cauterization, lubrication with petrolatum helps prevent crusting. A second cauterization is infrequently necessary.

If the source of bleeding is not accessible to cauterization (beneath the inferior turbinate, behind septal spurs, or high in the vault) or is not controlled by cauterization, the nasal cavity must be packed. After maximum shrinkage of the mucosa has been achieved with a suitable decongestant (0.25% phenylephrine or 2% ephedrine) and topical anesthesia, the nasal cavity can be tightly packed with half-inch gauze lubricated with petrolatum or cod liver oil. Pack the gauze into the nose in layers, starting either in the vault or on the floor of the nasal cavity. The packing may be left in place as long as 5–6 days if the patient is given adequate analgesics for pain and antibiotic medication to help prevent suppurative otitis media and sinusitis.

2. Posterior epistaxis—Posterior bleeding can sometimes be controlled only by means of a posterior nasal pack. This accomplishes 2 things: it compresses and controls bleeding sites in the nasopharynx or posterior choana, and it provides a "backstop" for very firm anterior packing that might otherwise be dislodged into the pharynx.

The postnasal pack is prepared as follows: (1) Sew 3 strings (No. 1 braided silk) through and through the center of a rolled 4 × 4 gauze sponge. (2) Pass a soft rubber catheter through the bleeding nostril into the pharynx and out through the mouth. (3) Attach 2 of the strings to the catheter tip and draw them through the mouth and out through the bleeding nostril. (4) Guide the gauze pack with a finger into the nasopharynx and posterior choana, taking care not to roll the uvula upward beneath the pack. (5) Anchor the 2 strings over a gauze bolster at the anterior nares. (6) Allow the third string to remain in the mouth and tape it to the face, or cut it about 4 inches long and allow it to dangle in the pharynx; it is used later to remove the pack.

The pack should not be left in place more than 4 days. The patient's ears should be examined daily for evidence of acute otitis media. Bleeding may recur when the pack is removed, or may even continue with the packing in place. If this occurs, the pack must usually be changed or reinserted under general anesthesia.

If the bleeding persists beneath or behind an inaccessible nasal septal spur, submucous resection of the septum may be necessary to relieve traction on the mucosal vessels and to permit more effective packing.

If bleeding persists from a site low in the nasal cavity, external carotid artery ligation in the neck must be considered. Uncontrolled bleeding from high in the vault of the nose may necessitate ligation of the anterior or posterior ethmoidal artery (or both) as it passes from the orbit into the ethmoidal labyrinth.

Prognosis

Most anterior nosebleeds are easily treated as an office procedure; complicated nosebleed or posterior nosebleed may require hospitalization for 2–3 weeks.

Severe nosebleed in cirrhotics or patients with borderline coronary arterial insufficiency may produce severe complications.

Fenn, A.C.: Radiopaque filled Foley balloon in posterior epistaxis. Arch Otolaryng 87:171–173, 1968.

McDevitt, T.J., Goh,A.S., & M.J. Acquarelli: Epistaxis: Management and prevention. Laryngoscope 77:1109–1115, 1967.

Middleton, P.: Surgery for epistaxis. Laryngoscope 77:1011–1015, 1967.

Reading, P.: Epistaxis. Practitioner 197:785–792, 1966.

DISEASES OF THE PHARYNX

SIMPLE PHARYNGITIS

Acute simple (catarrhal) pharyngitis is an acute inflammation of the mucosa of the pharynx which to some extent involves the lymphatic structures also. It usually occurs as part of an upper respiratory tract disorder which may also affect the nose, sinuses, larynx, and trachea. The most common causes are bacterial or viral infection; rarely, it is due to inhalation of irritant gases or ingestion of irritant liquids. Pharyngitis may occur as part of the syndrome of an acute specific infection (eg, measles, scarlet fever, whooping cough).

The inflammation may be diffuse or localized (lateral pharyngitis). Drying of the mucosa occurs in pharyngitis sicca.

In acute pharyngitis the throat is dry and sore. Systemic symptoms are fever and malaise. The pharyngeal mucosa is red and slightly swollen, with thick, sticky mucus. The disease lasts only a few days.

Chronic pharyngitis may produce few symptoms, eg, throat dryness with thick mucus and cough; or recurrent acute episodes of more severe throat pain, dull hyperemia and mild swelling of the mucosa (especially the tonsil pillars), and thick tenacious mucus often in the hypopharynx.

The treatment of acute pharyngitis is symptomatic: rest, light diet, analgesics, and warm, nonirritating gargles or throat irrigations. Antibiotics may be used for initial or complicating bacterial infection.

Chronic pharyngitis is treated by removing underlying causes such as infections of the nose, sinuses, or tonsils and by restricting irritants such as alcohol, spicy foods, and tobacco. Local removal of the tenacious secretion with suction or saline irrigation and application of 2% silver nitrate are helpful.

ACUTE TONSILLITIS

Acute tonsillitis is nearly always a bacterial infection, often due to streptococci. It is a contagious airborne or food-borne infection which can occur in any age group but is more common in children. Associated adenoidal infection in children is usual.

The onset is sudden, with sore throat, fever, chills, headache, anorexia, and malaise. The tonsils are swollen and red; the tonsillar pillars and pharynx are red, and pus or exudate is present on the tonsils or in the crypts. The cervical lymph nodes frequently are tender and enlarged. The white count may be elevated, and throat cultures will show the infecting organism.

Other causes of sore throat and fever which must be distinguished from acute tonsillitis include simple pharyngitis, infectious mononucleosis, Vincent's angina, diphtheria, agranulocytosis, and mycotic infections. Smear and culture from the throat identify the bacterial and mycotic infections. The white count helps distinguish viral infections and blood dyscrasias. The white count and heterophil antibody titer will make the diagnosis of infectious mononucleosis.

The complications of local extension are chronic tonsillitis, acute otitis media, acute rhinitis and sinusitis, peritonsillar abscess or other deep neck abscess, and cervical lymph node abscess. Nephritis, osteomyelitis, rheumatic fever, or pneumonia may follow streptococcal tonsillitis.

Treatment consists of bed rest, fluids, a light diet, analgesics, and antibiotics as required. Local relief of pain may be obtained with frequent gargles or throat irrigations using hot, nonirritating solutions (eg, saline, 30% glucose, aspirin).

Spontaneous resolution usually occurs after 5—7 days. Vigorous treatment may shorten the course, prevents many complications, and makes the patient more comfortable.

Elmendorf, D.M.F., & J.V. Skiff: Antimicrobials: role in treatment of ear, nose, and throat infections, group A streptococcal disease. New York J Med 67:252—254, 1967.

Malcomson, K.G.: Tonsillitis: Acute and chronic. Practitioner 199:777—784, 1967.

CHRONIC TONSILLITIS

Chronic tonsillitis usually results from repeated or unresolved acute infection. It is manifested by persistent dull hyperemia. Mild edema and scarring of the tonsils and tonsillar pillars may occur, and the crypts may contain abnormal secretions. Other symptoms and signs may range from a mild scratching sensation in the throat to cough, fetid breath, and a pharyngeal exudate. An enlarged cervical lymph node is common. The size of the tonsils is of little significance in determining the presence of chronic infection. Chronic infection may predispose to recurrent acute infections.

The treatment of significant chronic tonsillar infection is surgical excision (see below). Intercurrent acute infections and chronic infections in people who are poor operative risks (because of advanced age or severe systemic or hemorrhagic diseases) are treated medically as outlined above for acute infections. Chronic infection can rarely be eradicated by conservative treatment.

Adenotonsillectomy (T & A)

The value of adenotonsillectomy, the indications for and the contraindications to the operation, and the optimal time for the operation when it is indicated have been the subject of much controversy. Most surgeons agree that there are occasions when the operation is of definite benefit to the patient and that there are circumstances in which it is definitely contraindicated. Even when a strong indication for surgery is present, however, the decision to operate must not be made until all pertinent restraining factors (eg, medical, psychologic, social) have been evaluated.

Surgery is contraindicated during episodes of acute tonsillar infection. Many surgeons prefer to withhold the operation during the peak months of the poliomyelitis "season."

A. Strong Indications: Whenever the infected or hypertrophied tonsils and adenoid are almost certainly the underlying or only cause of the disease:

1. Recurrent acute infection or chronic infection of tonsils and adenoid.
2. Recurrent acute ear infections.
3. Persistent or recurrent serous otitis media.
4. Peritonsillar abscess.

B. Equivocal Indications: When the infected or hypertrophied tonsils are likely to be the cause of the disease or are contributing to or aggravating the disease: (Other possible contributing factors must first be investigated and ruled out or treated.)

1. Snoring and mouth breathing.
2. Large tonsils.
3. Poor eating habits in a frail, often anemic child.
4. Allergic rhinitis and asthma.
5. Systemic disease, eg, nephritis, rheumatic or congenital heart disease, rheumatic fever (considered a strong indication by some, even in the absence of local disease).
6. Frequent upper respiratory tract infections.

C. Relative Contraindications: When the operation may do more harm than good unless special precautions are taken:

1. Cleft palate—Further speech impairment can occur following adenotonsillectomy. The lateral adenoidal masses only should be removed.
2. The mere presence of tonsils and adenoid.
3. Systemic disease, eg, uncontrolled diabetes, tuberculosis, heart disease.
4. Intercurrent infection.

D. Absolute Contraindications: When the operation will certainly do more harm than good:

1. Hemorrhagic disease, eg, hemophilia.
2. Far-advanced, severe systemic disease.

Boyle, W.F.: Adenotonsillectomy in children: Modern indications and preparation. Postgrad Med 40:489—491, 1966.

Poydhouse, N.: A controlled study of adenotonsillectomy. Arch Otol 92:611—616, 1971.

Ritter, F.N.: Tonsillectomy and adenoidectomy: Indications and complications. Postgrad Med 41:342—347, 1967.

Roy, A., & others: Tonsillectomy. Arch Otolaryng 87:167—170, 1968.

PERITONSILLAR ABSCESS
(Quinsy)

Peritonsillar abscess is a complication of acute tonsillitis which occurs when the infection spreads to the potential peritonsillar space deep to the tonsil between the tonsillar capsule and the constrictor pharyngis muscle. Mixed pyogenic organisms (streptococci, staphylococci, pneumococci) are usually obtained upon culture. The sore throat of tonsillitis suddenly becomes more severe on one side when the infection breaks through the tonsillar capsule; dysphagia increases, trismus may be present, and one-sided swelling pushes the tonsil and tonsillar pillar toward or across the midline. The swelling extends to the soft palate, and the uvula is displaced. Fluctuation develops between the 3rd and 5th days.

Symptomatic care and antibiotic therapy are indicated. After the abscess becomes fluctuant, it must be incised and drained. The walls of the abscess should be spread daily to prevent re-formation of the abscess. After the infection subsides, tonsillectomy should be done to prevent recurrences.

Hora, J.F.: Deep-neck infections. Arch Otolaryng 77:129–136, 1963.

LUDWIG'S ANGINA
(Cellulitis of the Floor of the Mouth)

Ludwig's angina is a severe pyogenic infection of the sublingual and submaxillary spaces of the floor of the mouth and the anterior neck. A rapidly spreading diffuse cellulitis or abscess formation pushes the tongue upward against the roof of the mouth, limiting its motion and causing pain. The airway may become obstructed, or the infection may spread downward in the neck.

Supportive treatment and large doses of antibiotics are necessary. If abscess occurs, external incision and drainage should be performed. Local anesthesia avoids the danger of immediate obstruction of the airway, which may occur if general anesthesia is used. Because of the diffuse nature of the infection, large quantities of free pus are seldom obtained. Incision must be adequate and the fascial spaces above and below the hyoglossus muscle must be opened by blunt dissection. A tracheostomy may be necessary.

RETROPHARYNGEAL ABSCESS

Retropharyngeal abscess is a pyogenic infection which occurs most often in infants and children. Suppuration occurs in the fascial space between the posterior pharyngeal wall and the prevertebral fascia as a result of suppurative lymph node infection, usually following tonsillar, nasal, or sinus infection. The symptoms are difficulty in swallowing and breathing, and fever. The posterior pharyngeal wall is tender and swollen.

Early treatment (antibiotics, hydration) may produce resolution. If fluctuation occurs incision and drainage are required, with the patient in full Trendelenburg position, adequate lighting, and suction equipment at hand. General anesthesia is avoided because of the danger of laryngeal obstruction and aspiration. Tracheostomy may be necessary.

Hora, J.F.: Deep-neck infections. Arch Otolaryng 77:129–136, 1963.

PARAPHARYNGEAL ABSCESS

Parapharyngeal abscess is a pyogenic infection which occurs as a complication of acute tonsillitis, peritonsillar abscess, dental infection, or acute pharyngitis. It is localized in the fascial space outside the constrictor pharyngis muscle and deep to the investing cervical fascia, in close relationship to the carotid sheath and the stylopharyngeus and stylohyoid muscles. Infection can spread along the carotid sheath into the mediastinum. There are signs and symptoms of sepsis, bulging of the lateral pharyngeal wall, and trismus. The veins of the neck and scalp may be distended as a consequence of pressure upon the jugular vein. Brawny swelling and redness may develop later in the neck below the angle of the mandible.

Early treatment consists of hydration and antibiotics in large doses. Intraoral incision and drainage should be done only by a surgeon familiar with this area because of the danger of hemorrhage from large blood vessels. External incision and drainage at the angle of the jaw and upper neck can be done if pus is sought deep in the neck by blunt dissection.

Caution is required in giving general anesthesia because of the hazard of airway obstruction. Local anesthesia or a tracheostomy for general anesthesia should be considered.

Alexander, D.W., Leonard, J.R., & M.L. Trail: Vascular complications of deep neck abscesses. A report of four cases. Otolaryngology 78:361–370, 1968.

DISEASES OF THE LARYNX

ACUTE LARYNGITIS

Acute inflammation of the laryngeal mucosa due to bacterial or viral infection may occur singly or in association with acute rhinitis, pharyngitis, or tracheitis. It may also occur with influenza, measles, or diphtheria, or as a result of inhalation of irritants. Hoarseness is the chief symptom. Pain and cough are often present. Stridor and dyspnea may occur if edema is marked. Examination of the larynx shows redness of the mucosa and edema with or without exudate. The acute inflammation may extend into the bronchi and lungs, and slight hemoptysis may occur if coughing ruptures small blood vessels.

Treatment consists of voice rest, decreased smoking, control of underlying nasal, sinus, or throat infections, and control of cough. Steam inhalations and local cold or heat to the neck may provide relief. Systemic antibiotics are helpful in bacterial infections. If marked edema produces dyspnea and stridor, parenteral steroids may decrease the edema sufficiently so that tracheostomy can be withheld.

Andrew, J.D., Tandon, O.P., & D.C. Turk: Acute epiglottitis: Challenge of a rarely recognized emergency. Brit MJ 3:524–526, 1968.
Skowron, P.N., Turner, J.A.P., & G.A. McNaughton: The use of corticosteroid (dexamethasone) in the treatment of acute laryngotracheitis. Canad MAJ 94:528–531, 1966.

CHRONIC LARYNGITIS

Chronic inflammation of the laryngeal mucosa may be due to many causes, including repeated acute laryngitis, chronic vocal abuse, chronic inhalation of irritants (including smoking), chronic sinus and throat infection, syphilis and tuberculosis (rare today), allergy, and hypometabolic states. Chronic hoarseness is the chief symptom. Cough, expectoration of tenacious secretions, and a feeling of dryness in the throat are often present. Examination shows signs of chronic inflammation; a thickened, dull, edematous mucosa of the vocal cords; and polypoid changes, whitish plaques, and thickened secretions. Ulceration is occasionally seen.

Chest x-ray and other tests for signs of tuberculosis, serologic tests for syphilis, and biopsy to rule out carcinoma may be required.

Treatment consists of correcting the underlying cause, if any; antibiotics for sinus and throat infections; antiallergenic measures when indicated; decreased smoking, and voice rest.

Gabriel, C.E., & D.G. Jones: The importance of chronic laryngitis. J Laryng Otol 74:349–357, 1960.

TUMORS OF THE LARYNX

Essentials of Diagnosis
- Hoarseness is the principal symptom.
- Respiratory obstruction.
- Sore throat, "sticking" sensation in throat, pain referred to the ear.
- Cough or hemoptysis.
- Dysphagia.

General Considerations
Tumors of the larynx may be benign or malignant. Both produce similar symptoms and may be considered together. The symptoms depend upon the size and location of the tumor.

Benign laryngeal tumors may be neoplastic (eg, papilloma, fibroma), may be due to allergy or metabolic disturbance (polyps), or may be due to extrinsic or intrinsic trauma (singer's nodules, intubation granuloma). Ninety-five percent of malignant laryngeal tumors are squamous cell carcinomas, but sarcoma, adenocarcinoma, and others occur.

Clinical Findings
Hoarseness is the earliest and principal manifestation of vocal cord tumor. As the tumor enlarges, stridor and dyspnea may occur, usually late. With tumors elsewhere in the larynx (false cord, epiglottis, arytenoepiglottic fold, pyriform sinus), voice change may be a late symptom and minor throat discomfort (sometimes referred to the ear), dysphagia, or mild cough may be the only early symptoms. Laryngeal examination usually shows a mass or ulceration at the tumor site. Submucosal tumors may be manifested only as a fullness or swelling of the affected area. Biopsy examination establishes the diagnosis.

Differential Diagnosis
Tumors of the larynx must be distinguished from chronic laryngitis, tuberculosis, syphilis, contact ulcer, granulomas, and laryngeal paralysis. Laryngeal symptoms lasting longer than 2–3 weeks must be investigated. Direct or indirect laryngoscopy is often diagnostic. Chest x-ray and other tests for tuberculosis, serologic tests for syphilis, laryngeal biopsy, and bacteriologic cultures usually establish a firm diagnosis.

Treatment & Prognosis
Almost all of the technics involved in intralaryngeal manipulation and surgery require the skills of an otolaryngologist.

Small, asymptomatic benign tumors may require no treatment other than diagnosis to rule out malignancy. Vocal cord polyps or ulcers due to metabolic disturbances (allergy or hypothyroidism) or to vocal misuse or other trauma may improve when the underlying problem is treated. Small benign tumors of the vocal cord producing hoarseness may be locally excised under direct or indirect laryngoscopy. Larger benign tumors—especially papillomas, which have a great tendency to recur—may require laryngotomy for adequate excision.

Malignant tumors are treated by external irradiation or surgical excision. Irradiation is suitable for superficial malignancies confined to the vocal cord which show no evidence of invasion of muscle or cartilage. More extensive tumors require surgical excision and often en bloc neck node dissection.

McCoy, G.: Cancer of the larynx. California Med 100:192–195, 1964.
Peres, C.A., & others: Irradiation of early carcinoma of the larynx. Arch Otol 93:465–472, 1971.

Shaw, H.J.: Cancer of the larynx. Practitioner 199:785–796, 1967.

Work, W.P., & W.F. Boyle: Cancer of the larynx. Laryngoscope 71:830–846, 1961.

TRACHEOSTOMY

There are 4 indications for tracheostomy: (1) respiratory obstruction at the level of the larynx or above; (2) inability to clear tracheobronchial secretions; (3) for administration of anesthesia; and (4) to place the larynx at rest.

The causes of airway obstruction at or above the larynx include infections (laryngotracheobronchitis, epiglottitis, and diphtheria), tumors, edema (allergic, infectious, post-irradiation), trauma, and foreign bodies. Upper airway obstruction produces suprasternal, intercostal, and epigastric retraction and signs of hypoxia, including restlessness, increasing pulse, and, as a late finding, cyanosis. Disorders which interfere with normal sphincter action of the larynx, permit aspiration of pharyngeal secretions, and prevent effective cough include loss of consciousness and organic muscular paresis due to poisoning, cerebrovascular accidents, postoperative state, poliomyelitis, and organic CNS disease. There are some surgical situations, especially in surgery of the head or neck, where an endotracheal tube cannot be introduced through the nose or mouth but can be introduced through a tracheostomy. Intralaryngeal disease rarely may require tracheostomy to place the larynx at rest.

Two kinds of tracheostomies are performed: emergency and elective. **Emergency tracheostomy** must be done immediately even if proper equipment and assistance is not available. In these circumstances, **cricothyrotomy** is a safe procedure which can be performed rapidly as follows: With a scissors or knife the skin is cut vertically over the cricothyroid membrane (the part of the airway nearest the skin), a transverse incision is made in this membrane, and the wound is spread with the knife handle or other dilator. It is essential to stay in the midline and to promptly replace this emergency airway with a proper tracheostomy. If a laryngoscope and endotracheal tube or a bronchoscope are available, the airway may be established with one of these devices and a deliberate tracheostomy then performed.

Elective tracheostomy is done under general or local anesthesia while the patient's airway is still adequate or has been reestablished with an endotracheal tube or bronchoscope. The precise surgical technic may vary, eg, with midline or horizontal incision, blunt or sharp dissection, retraction or division of the thyroid isthmus; but the principles are the same in all: (1) avoid trauma to the cricoid cartilage, (2) stay in the midline to avoid trauma to lateral neck structures, and (3) do not close the incision tightly, thus minimizing subcutaneous emphysema.

Post-tracheostomy care must include humidifying the inspired air to keep secretions loose and prevent the formation of mucus plugs and crusts, frequent cleaning (every 2–4 hours) of the inner tube, avoidance of heavy sedation, and constant attention during the first 24–48 hours. Uninterrupted observation may not be necessary with some adults, but with small children it is absolutely necessary that a nurse, hospital attendant, or member of the family be in constant attendance as long as the tracheostomy is maintained.

The use of cuffed tracheostomy tubes facilitates positive pressure assisted or controlled respiration. Prolonged inflation of the cuff may result in tracheal mucosal ulceration and subsequent granuloma formation or tracheal stenosis. The cuff must be deflated intermittently.

Beatrous, W.P.: Tracheostomy (tracheotomy). Its expanded indications and its present status. Based on an analysis of 1,000 consecutive operations and a review of the recent literature. Laryngoscope 78:3–55, 1968.

Bryant, L.R., Trinkle, J.K., & L. Dubilien: Reappraisal of tracheal injury from cuffed tracheostomy tubes. JAMA 215:625–631, 1971.

Pratt, L.W.: Complications of tracheotomy. Eye Ear Nose Throat Monthly 48:119–127, 1969.

Taillens, J-P.: Modern indications for tracheotomy in cases of acute and chronic asphyxia. Advances Oto-Rhino-Laryng 15:1–31, 1968.

FOREIGN BODIES IN THE AIR & FOOD PASSAGES

Foreign bodies may lodge in the larynx, bronchi, or esophagus, usually while eating, following sudden inspiration caused by surprise, as a result of simple carelessness while holding something in the mouth, or while unconscious. Eighty percent of cases of inhaled or swallowed foreign bodies occur in children under 15 years of age. In adults most foreign bodies are large boluses of food or bones lodged in the esophagus as a result of hasty eating or full dentures which impair normal sensation in the mouth.

Esophageal foreign bodies are usually found at the thoracic inlet, less commonly at the cardia or midesophagus. If laryngeal foreign bodies completely block the airway, asphyxia is imminent. A foreign body small enough to pass the glottis will seldom lodge in the trachea but will be found in the bronchi. The relatively sharp angle of the left bronchus and the straight right bronchus cause most bronchial foreign bodies to be found in the right side. Nearly all foreign bodies that enter food or air passages through the mouth and do not enter the stomach can be removed by the same route.

Laryngeal Foreign Bodies

Laryngeal foreign bodies may produce hoarseness, stridor, cough, and gagging; may obstruct the airway partially or completely and cause dyspnea, stridor, or asphyxia; and may produce inflammatory symptoms of fever, pain, tenderness, and swelling. They can be removed with a grasping forceps through a direct laryngoscope under topical or general anesthesia. The patient should be in the Trendelenburg position to prevent the foreign body from entering the trachea or esophagus, and a bronchoscope and esophagoscope of proper size should be available in case this happens.

A small laryngeal foreign body may become lodged in the bronchi (see below).

Bronchial Foreign Bodies

Bronchial foreign bodies usually produce an initial episode of coughing followed by an asymptomatic ("silent") period varying from a few hours (some vegetable foreign bodies) to months or years (less irritating nonvegetable foreign bodies) before obstructive and inflammatory symptoms occur (cough, wheezing, atelectasis, and pulmonary infection). If the foreign body lodges in such a way as to create a valve effect, obstructive emphysema of a pulmonary segment or lobe may be present. Recurrent episodes of cough and pulmonary infection, especially if unilateral, are suggestive of foreign body. X-rays will show a foreign body if it is radiopaque. Nonradiopaque foreign bodies will be revealed on x-ray only by the signs of bronchial obstruction and infection. Vegetable foreign bodies produce earlier and more severe inflammatory symptoms than nonvegetable objects.

In the differential diagnosis it is necessary to consider pneumonia, bronchiectasis, lung abscess, and tuberculosis.

Bronchial foreign bodies are removed through a bronchoscope with suitable forceps by a skilled endoscopist. General anesthesia is usually employed. In the case of very small radiopaque foreign bodies (eg, straight pins) in the periphery of the lung which cannot be located with the bronchoscope alone, a biplane fluoroscope can sometimes be used. Thoracotomy is occasionally necessary to remove foreign bodies in the periphery of the lung.

Unrecognized bronchial foreign bodies may produce severe and progressive pulmonary infection, with pneumonia, abscess, and empyema. In children, bronchoscopic manipulation may produce laryngeal edema severe enough to require tracheostomy.

Esophageal Foreign Bodies

Esophageal foreign bodies usually produce immediate symptoms of coughing and gagging; pain in the neck at the level of the thyroid cartilage, with a sensation of something "stuck in the throat"; and difficulty in swallowing or inability to swallow food or saliva. Occasionally, however, especially in children, weeks or months may pass before symptoms of infection or obstruction occur. Pooling of saliva in the pyriform sinuses is suggestive of esophageal obstruction. X-rays will show opaque objects, but often will not show a bolus of meat or a bone. Fluoroscopic observation as the patient swallows a capsule filled with barium sulfate or a wisp of cotton impregnated with barium sulfate is a useful means of locating suspected foreign bodies, since the radiopaque test object will be delayed by the foreign body in its transit through the esophagus.

Esophageal foreign bodies near the cardia may produce pain in the interscapular area.

Esophageal foreign bodies should be removed through the esophagoscope by a skilled endoscopist. Only rarely does an esophageal foreign body constitute an emergency, and so the delay involved in referral is not usually hazardous. Blind probing in an effort to dislodge a foreign body is extremely hazardous.

Perforation of the esophagus by an esophageal foreign body or during endoscopic removal may lead to mediastinal infection (fatal in 50% of cases) or, rarely, severe hemorrhage.

Goff, W.F.: What to do when foreign bodies are inhaled or ingested. Postgrad Med 44:135—142, 1968.

Kallay, F., Hirschberg, J., & G. Csermely: Treatment of airways with foreign bodies in infants. Arch Otolaryng 88:303—306, 1968.

●   ●   ●

General References

Coates, G.M., Schenck, H.P., & M. Miller: *Otolaryngology.* 5 vols. Prior, 1960.

De Weese, D.D., & W.H. Saunders: *Textbook of Otolaryngology,* 2nd ed. Mosby, 1964.

Reading, P.: *Common Diseases of the Ear, Nose and Throat.* Little, Brown, 1966.

6...

Respiratory Tract & Mediastinum

R. Morton Manson, Sidney Levin, Ernest Jawetz, & Perry A. Olsen

NONSPECIFIC MANIFESTATIONS

Cough

Cough is probably the most common symptom of respiratory disease. It may be produced by disturbances anywhere from the oropharynx to the terminal bronchioles. Cough may also occur in diseases not primarily respiratory in nature, eg, congestive heart failure, mitral valve disease, otitis media, or subdiaphragmatic irritation. Patients often overlook or minimize a chronic cough, and detailed interrogation is sometimes necessary.

Paroxysmal cough suggests bronchial obstruction.

The best treatment for cough is to treat the underlying disease. The patient should avoid irritations such as smoking, allergens, dusts, fumes, and air pollutants. Bronchial spasm may be relieved with bronchodilating drugs given orally or by nebulization (or both). Antihistamines and, in severe cases, corticosteroids may be used to reduce inflammation of mucous membranes. To liquefy tenacious sputum, give potassium iodide, saturated solution, 10–15 drops in water 4 times daily. Antitussive drugs, eg, codeine phosphate, 15–30 mg every 3–4 hours, may be given as needed.

Dyspnea

Exertional dyspnea may appear with impaired ventilation (eg, restrictive or obstructive defects), inefficient mechanics of breathing (eg, high oxygen cost of breathing), or with diffusion defects. Early pulmonary disease seldom produces dyspnea.

Dyspnea at rest is more characteristic of congestive heart failure than of chronic pulmonary disease, but it does appear in diffuse pulmonary diseases causing alveolar-capillary block and when secondary factors are superimposed on a low pulmonary reserve (eg, bronchitis in an emphysematous patient). Acute illnesses (pneumonia, spontaneous pneumothorax, bronchial asthma, massive atelectasis) can produce marked dyspnea at rest.

Orthopnea is usually considered to be presumptive evidence of congestive heart failure, but some pulmonary patients breathe easier in a sitting position (bronchial asthma).

Expectoration

The characteristics of the sputum must not be neglected. Mucoid sputum is seen in tracheobronchitis and asthma. A yellow or greenish sputum suggests bacterial infection. Foul-smelling sputum suggests anaerobic infection (eg, putrid lung abscess). Pink, frothy sputum is seen in pulmonary edema. "Rusty" sputum is typical of pneumococcal pneumonia. Copious sputum separating into layers is characteristic of bronchiectasis.

The production of large amounts of sputum with a change of posture (eg, upon arising in the morning) occurs when dependent cavities or bronchiectatic spaces suddenly empty into the bronchial tree.

Wheezing

Wheezing is the characteristic sign of bronchial narrowing. In bronchial asthma, it is paroxysmal and diffuse. Acute left ventricular failure may produce diffuse wheezing which is differentiated from asthma and bronchitis by associated signs of congestive failure and prolonged arm-to-tongue circulation time. A persistent localized wheeze is evidence of local bronchial obstruction (eg, carcinoma, inflammatory stenosis, foreign body).

Chest Pain

Pain due to lung disease occurs with involvement of the parietal pleura (the visceral pleura is insensitive to pain) or the chest wall, including its bony and cartilaginous structures. Pleural pain is usually unilateral and aggravated by changes in intrathoracic pressure (cough, sneeze, deep breathing). Diaphragmatic irritation may cause pain referred to anterior shoulder (central irritation) or to the upper abdomen (peripheral irritation). Involvement of the chest wall structures is usually accompanied by tenderness, and pain from this location is more constant and less affected by breathing and coughing.

Localized swelling, pain, and tenderness of one or more costosternal cartilages, caused by a nonspecific inflammation, occurs occasionally (Tietze's syndrome) and may be mistaken for cardiac or pulmonary disease.

Cardiac pain is usually substernal and frequently radiates to the neck, jaw, left shoulder, or arm. Such pain produced by exercise and relieved by rest is almost always due to myocardial ischemia. Pericardial inflammation produces substernal or precordial pain that is aggravated by deep breathing. Pain from esophageal irritation or spasm is deep and central and is altered by swallowing. Deep, persistent, aching chest pain may be caused by localized neoplasms.

A careful history is essential to the identification of chest pain.

Hemoptysis

Bleeding may occur in many bronchopulmonary diseases. Tuberculosis, carcinoma, bronchiectasis, and bronchitis are the commonest causes. Fatal hemorrhage is rare. Bleeding from the nose or pharynx may lead to a history of blood-spitting. Collateral circulation between the bronchial and pulmonary veins may cause hemoptysis in mitral stenosis. When associated with chest pain and shock, hemoptysis suggests pulmonary infarction.

Cyanosis

Cyanosis represents increased concentration of reduced hemoglobin in the blood, which can result from a number of defects of function in pulmonary disease: (1) Impaired diffusion from alveoli to capillaries; (2) inadequate gross ventilation of alveoli; and (3) disturbed perfusion-ventilation relationships (increased intrapulmonary "shunts").

Reduced hemoglobin in the blood may not be manifested as frank cyanosis even when present to a significant degree.

Polycythemia

Increase in the total erythrocyte mass may be very striking as a compensatory response to the chronic anoxemia of pulmonary insufficiency. Primary polycythemia (erythremia) is usually associated with a normal arterial oxygen saturation, but differentiation from the symptomatic variety is not always easy on this or any other basis.

Polycythemia is discussed in Chapter 9.

Pulmonary Osteoarthropathy

Pulmonary osteoarthropathy refers to those changes in the bones and soft tissues of the extremities seen in some patients with chronic pulmonary disease. These include clubbing of the fingers and toes, subperiosteal proliferation in the long bones, arthralgia, and nonpitting edema of the skin. Such manifestations have been known to disappear with correction of the pulmonary pathology (eg, resection of a localized bronchial carcinoma). The pathogenesis of pulmonary osteoarthropathy is not understood.

Clubbing is frequently seen in bronchiectasis, bronchial carcinoma, and lung abscess; it is unusual in tuberculosis. It may also be caused by such diverse nonpulmonary disorders as congenital heart disease and hepatic cirrhosis; and it may occur as a congenital trait.

DISORDERS OF THE BRONCHI

BRONCHITIS

Bronchial infection or inflammation may occur as a primary disorder or may be a prominent finding in many pulmonary diseases (eg, tuberculosis, bronchiectasis, emphysema), but its clinical importance in certain situations is often underemphasized.

Acute bronchitis is characterized by productive (mucopurulent to purulent) cough and absence of x-ray densities. On examination, musical rhonchi are commonly heard, and wheezing is occasionally present. Acute bronchitis is common in viral infections and in the healthy adult is rarely serious, but in infants and small children respiratory obstruction may be severe and life-threatening. In the adult with chronic pulmonary insufficiency (especially emphysema), superimposed acute bronchitis may lead to critical impairment of ventilation and death. Sputum cultures usually yield the common mouth organisms. Occasionally, specific pathogens such as pneumococci or beta-hemolytic streptococci are found. *Hemophilus influenzae* may cause bronchitis in children.

Chronic bronchitis is characterized by similar features of long duration without a clear prodrome of acute upper respiratory infection. Very commonly, in older patients there is coexisting emphysema; and the terms emphysema and bronchitis have been used to designate the same clinical entity. For this reason, some physicians prefer the term chronic obstructive bronchopulmonary disease in these patients.

Sputum cultures are usually not helpful and contain only a mixture of mouth organisms.

Infections involving the small bronchial structures (ie, bronchiolitis) can produce a very severe and occasionally a fatal disease in adults as well as in children (the latter having been recognized for many years). On occasion, acute bronchitis appears to produce the clinical and electrocardiographic manifestations of cor pulmonale, which may be reversed with improvement of the bronchitis.

Treatment

A. Acute Bronchitis: Bed rest is advisable, and smoking should be prohibited. Sufficient fluids should be provided to prevent dehydration. Steam inhalation is usually helpful. An antihistamine may help relieve bronchial inflammation. Severe cough should be controlled with an antitussive agent such as codeine phosphate, 15–30 mg every 3–4 hours. Ephedrine, 25 mg orally, or a similar bronchodilator, is helpful if bronchospasm is present. Aspirin will help reduce fever and make the patient more comfortable. Antibiotics should be used in an attempt to prevent secondary infection in patients with impaired respiratory or cardiac function or debility from other illness, and in infants and children with severe symptoms. Sputum cultures are

TABLE 6–1. Pulmonary function tests most useful to the clinician.

Test	Clinical Significance	Normal Values
Vital capacity (VC) Maximum volume that can be expelled after a maximum inspiration. No time limit.	Repeated abnormal values (more or less than 20% of predicted) may be significant. Main value is in following course of cardiopulmonary or respiratory disease with serial tests.	Male: VC = (27.63–[0.112 × age in years]) × height in cm. Female: VC = (21.78–[0.101 × age in years]) × height in cm. (Baldwin, E. de F., & others: Medicine 27:243, 1948.)
Forced expiratory volume (FEV) "Timed vital capacity." Maximum volume expelled in a timed interval, usually 1 or 3 seconds.	A reduced time volume usually indicates obstructive bronchopulmonary disease. Improvement after a bronchodilator indicates some degree of reversibility.	FEV_1 sec = 83% of actual VC. FEV_3 sec = 97% of actual VC.
Maximal expiratory flow rate (MEFR) Measurement of maximal flow rate of a single expelled breath, expressed in liters/minute.	A reduced flow rate has the same significance as a reduced FEV. The test requires little effort, and several types of small, portable instruments are available. Suitable for screening tests.	Adult male = > 400 liters/minute. Adult female = > 300 liters/minute.
Maximal voluntary ventilation (MVV) "Maximal breathing capacity." Maximal volume expelled in 12–15 seconds of forced breathing, expressed in liters/minute.	Measures essentially the same function as FEV and MEFR. An additional confirmation test of FEV and MEFR. Requires sustained effort and cooperation of patient to a greater degree.	There is a wide variation of normal values depending upon age, size, and sex. The following formulas can be used as a guide for predicted values. Male (86.5–[0.522 × age in years]) × sq M body surface. Female (71.3–[0.474 × age in years]) × sq M body surface.
	When low values are obtained, the above tests should be repeated after administration of a bronchodilator.	
O_2 tension (arterial) (PO_2)	Hypoxemia which is not apparent clinically can be detected and its cause can often be determined by serial measurements after certain maneuvers such as exercise and O_2 breathing. In effect, we now measure the arterial O_2 tension in assessing pulmonary function; because of the shape of the dissociation curve, hypoxemia is more accurately reflected.	Arterial O_2 tension (PO_2) = 90–100 mm Hg
CO_2 tension (PCO_2) **Plasma bicarbonate (HCO_3^-)** **pH of arterial blood**	Important values in the diagnosis and management of respiratory acidosis due to CO_2 retention. (Now readily measured in arterial blood by the method of Astrup: Clin Chem 7:1–15, 1969.)	PCO_2 40 mm Hg Plasma HCO_3^- 24 mEq/liter pH 7.40

not usually helpful. When an antibiotic is indicated, use penicillin procaine G, 600,000 units IM twice daily; penicillin G tablets, 400,000 units or 250 mg, 4 times daily; one of the tetracycline drugs, 250–500 mg 4 times daily; or ampicillin, 250–500 mg 4 times daily.

B. Chronic Bronchitis: The possibility that the "bronchitis" is secondary to some serious underlying disease must always be kept in mind. Sources of possible chronic irritation should be avoided (eg, smoking, allergenic agents, fumes or other irritants). A change of climate may sometimes be warranted. Nonproductive cough should be suppressed with codeine phosphate, 15–30 mg every 3–4 hours, or a comparable antitussive agent. Thick sputum should be liquefied by adequate fluid intake and saturated solution of potassium iodide, 10–15 drops orally 4 times daily. Bronchial spasm (frequently present with paroxysmal coughing) should be relieved with ephedrine sulfate, 8–25 mg, or related drugs, orally every 4 hours, or isoproterenol hydrochloride (Isuprel®, Aludrine®), 1:200 solution by nebulization every 2–4 hours. Ephedrine and isoproterenol may be used together. Bronchial inflammation may be reduced by the use of antihistamine drugs; in severe, intractable cases, the use of corticosteroid drugs such as prednisone is justified. Prednisone is given orally in an initial dosage of 5–10 mg 4 times daily for 3–4 days, and then gradually reduced to a small maintenance dose or, preferably, eliminated over the next 7 days.

Antibiotics are indicated if the sputum is purulent. Penicillin, one of the tetracyclines, or ampicillin given orally are the drugs of choice. (See treatment of acute bronchitis for dosage.) If improvement does not occur in several days; sputum culture to determine the predominating organisms and antibiotic sensitivities may be helpful. After initial control is achieved, prolonged maintenance treatment with ½ the usual dosage may be necessary to prevent relapse. The use of maintenance antibiotic therapy may decrease the severity and duration, but not the frequency, of intercurrent acute respiratory infections. This is especially so where pneumococci are repeatedly recovered during acute episodes.

Bates, D.V.: Chronic bronchitis and emphysema. New England J Med 278:546–561, 600–604, 1968.

Brinkman, G.L., & D.L. Block: The prognosis in chronic bronchitis. JAMA 197:1–7, 1966.

Eadie, M.D., Stott, E.J., & N.R. Grist: Virological studies in chronic bronchitis. Brit MJ 2:671–673, 1966.

Filley, G.F.: Emphysema and chronic bronchitis: Clinical manifestations and their physiologic significance. M Clin North America 51:283–292, 1967.

Fletcher, C.M.: Recent clinical and epidemiological studies of chronic bronchitis. Scandinav J Resp Dis 48:285–293, 1967.

Holdaway, D., Romer, A.C., & P.S. Gardner: The diagnosis and management of bronchiolitis. Pediatrics 39:924–928, 1967.

Malone, D.N., Gould, J.C., & I.W.B. Grant: A comparative study of ampicillin, tetracycline hydrochloride, and methacycline hydrochloride in acute exacerbations of chronic bronchitis. Lancet 2:594–595, 1968.

Stuart-Harris, C.H.: Pulmonary hypertension and chronic obstructive bronchitis. Ann Rev Resp Dis 97:9–17, 1968.

ASTHMA

Essentials of Diagnosis

- Recurrent acute attacks of wheezing, dyspnea, cough, and mucoid sputum.
- Prolonged expiration with generalized wheezing and musical rales.
- Eosinophilia of sputum and blood.

General Considerations

Familial susceptibility, environmental exposure, and such modifying factors as psychogenic stimuli must all be considered in the etiologic evaluation of an allergic patient. Half of these patients give a definite history of family allergy (rhinitis, asthma, eczema, urticaria). Seventy-five percent of children with 2 allergic parents will be allergic. A familial history gives no information, however, about the specific clinical expression of the allergy.

Most allergic disorders of the respiratory tract are caused by inhalant allergens, principally pollens (especially the ragweed family), animal danders, and house-dusts.

Modifying factors (psychic stress, infections, endocrine disturbances) may precipitate symptoms by upsetting the "balance" between the patient and his allergenic environment. The antigen-antibody reaction then results, and leads to the rapid appearance of reversible tissue changes: increased capillary permeability, increased secretion of mucus, spasm of smooth muscle, and increased numbers of eosinophils in the tissues, secretions, and peripheral blood.

The onset of allergic asthma is usually before 20 years of age.

The asthma syndrome also occurs in the absence of clear-cut allergy. Hypersensitivity to bacteria ("intrinsic" asthma) has been proposed, but the evidence is not convincing. The onset is often later in life. Asthma may also occur as a feature of systemic diseases such as polyarteritis nodosa and eosinophilic infiltrations of the lungs (Loeffler's syndrome).

Clinical Findings

A. Symptoms and Signs: Bronchial asthma is characterized by recurrent acute attacks of wheezing, dyspnea, cough, and expectoration of mucoid sputum (especially at the end of an attack). Coughing at night, coughing and wheezing on exertion, and a history of frequent "colds" may be more prominent in children than clear-cut paroxysms of wheezing. Nasal symptoms (itching, congestion, and watery discharge) may precede attacks of wheezing.

The acute attack presents a characteristic picture. The patient sits up, "fighting for air," with his chest fixed in the inspiratory position and using his accessory muscles of respiration. Great difficulty is evident with expiration. Wheezing may be audible across the room and usually overshadows other pulmonary signs. In the young asthmatic wheezing characteristically disappears or diminishes markedly soon after the injection of epinephrine.

When bronchial asthma becomes prolonged, with acute, severe, intractable symptoms, it is known as **status asthmaticus.**

B. Laboratory Findings: The sputum is characteristically tenacious and mucoid, containing "plugs" and "spirals." Eosinophils are seen microscopically. The differential blood count may show eosinophilia. (Skin testing is discussed in Chapter 21.) In severe, acute bronchospasm, arterial hypoxemia may be present due to disturbed perfusion/ventilation relationships, alveolar hypoventilation, or functional right-to-left shunts.

C. X-Ray Findings: Chest films usually show no abnormalities. Emphysema may be acute (reversible) in severe paroxysms or chronic (irreversible) in longstanding cases. Transient, migratory pulmonary infiltrations have been reported. Pneumothorax may complicate severe attacks.

Differential Diagnosis

Distinguish wheezing from that due to bronchitis, obstructive emphysema, and congestive heart failure.

Complications

Chronic bronchial asthma may lead to such complications as chronic pulmonary emphysema and chronic cor pulmonale. Other complications are atelectasis, pulmonary infection, and pneumothorax.

Treatment

The treatment may be divided into 2 phases: (1) Treatment of the acute attack, and (2) interim therapy, which is aimed at preventing further attacks. Epinephrine and intravenous aminophylline are the drugs of choice for the emergency management of acute bronchial asthma. However, for status asthmaticus or for acute attacks in epinephrine-resistant patients, the adrenal corticosteroids and corticotropin are usually necessary. Intravenous hydrocortisone (Solu-Cortef®) and methylprednisolone (Solu-Medrol®) are the preparations of choice. Corticotropin is equally effective, but the response is slower. *Note:* Epinephrine must be used cautiously in patients with "cardiac asthma," hypertension, or angina.

A. Treatment of the Acute Attack: Eliminate known allergens from the patient's environment. Maintain adequate rest and relieve apprehension by reassurance and sedatives. Treat respiratory infections vigorously with antibiotics. Give fluids orally or parenterally as necessary to prevent dehydration.

Of the expectorants available, only the iodides have demonstrated capacity to liquefy or increase the secretions of the lower respiratory tract. For this purpose potassium iodide, saturated solution, 10–15 drops in water 4 times daily, is often added to the treatment program.

1. Mild or moderate attacks—Epinephrine is the drug of choice.

a. Epinephrine injection (1:1000), 0.2–0.5 ml subcut. For moderate attacks, repeat every 1–2 hours.

b. Epinephrine inhalation (1:100) or isoproterenol (Isuprel®, Aludrine®) inhalation (1:200 in aqueous solution) by nebulizer, 1 or 2 inhalations every 30–60 minutes as necessary. Isoproterenol is also available in tablets of 10 and 15 mg for sublingual administration, but most patients find inhalation therapy preferable because it is associated with fewer cardiovascular side-effects. Isoproterenol microcrystals for inhalation are useful but are more expensive.

c. Sterile epinephrine suspension (1:500 in oil), 0.2–1 ml IM, may also be given at onset (and repeated in 10–14 hours as necessary) if a prolonged effect is desired.

d. If the attack is not controlled with epinephrine or isoproterenol, give aminophylline, 0.25–0.5 gm in 10–20 ml saline **slowly IV;** or 0.5 gm added to 500–1000 ml of saline and given by IV drip. Aminophylline may also be given in solution rectally or as rectal suppositories.

e. Ephedrine sulfate or hydrochloride, 25–50 mg orally, with or without a barbiturate, may relieve mild attacks.

f. Sedation—Phenobarbital, 0.1 gm; may repeat 0.03 gm 4 times daily.

2. Severe attack in epinephrine-responsive patients—(May also treat as for Status Asthmaticus, below.) Use epinephrine, aminophylline, and sedation as for a mild or moderate attack. Inhalations of 100% oxygen by mask at a rate of 6–12 liters/minute may give great relief from dyspnea. When available, oxygen by intermitent positive pressure breathing (eg, Bennett apparatus) and bronchodilating aerosols administered simultaneously through the same apparatus often afford relief. As a bronchodilator, isoproterenol, 1:400, is preferred because it produces fewer systemic reactions than epinephrine. IPPB may be used 15–20 minutes of every hour.

If the response to the above measure is not satisfactory, use intravenous hydrocortisone or corticotropin as described below.

Adequate hydration with intravenous fluids is very important in the treatment of severe asthma.

3. Status asthmaticus—Hospitalization is mandatory, but treatment should not be delayed while awaiting transportation. Give aminophylline, 0.25–0.5 gm in 10–20 ml of diluent **slowly IV.** Also give hydrocortisone sodium succinate (Solu-Cortef®), 100 mg IV, or methylprednisolone (Solu-Medrol®), 80 mg IV. Give oxygen by mask or nasal cannula as soon as it is available.

Treatment should be continued with intravenous fluids, using 2–3 liters of 5% dextrose in water in the first 24 hours, with each bottle containing aminophylline, 0.5 gm. Also give another 100 mg of hydrocortisone sodium succinate (Solu-Cortef®). (In desperate situations, as much as 1000 mg of hydrocortisone can be used in the first 8–12 hours. Infusions of hydrocortisone should be separated from other fluids.) The next most effective drug is corticotropin injection, 20–40 mg by IV infusion over a 6–8 hour period. Simultaneously with the intravenous drugs, give prednisone, 10–15 mg, every 6 hours. Improvement should be noted in 4–6 hours; the attack will usually subside in 24–48 hours.

Sedation should be used to allay apprehension. Pentobarbital sodium, 0.1–0.2 gm orally, or paraldehyde, 8–15 ml in 30 ml of oil by rectum, should be used.

Adequate hydration should be continued with intravenous fluids until sufficient oral intake is possible. Serum electrolytes must be monitored and adjusted during prolonged administration of intravenous fluids.

If hydrocortisone or corticotropin is not available, administer epinephrine cautiously, 1 ml of 1:1000 solution in 1 liter of 5% dextrose by IV drip, 60–80 drops/minute. If improvement does not occur, a general anesthetic may be lifesaving. If an anesthesiologist is not available, give ether, 30–90 ml in equal quantities of olive oil rectally, and repeat in 12–24 hours if necessary.

Bronchoscopy and tracheostomy to remove tenacious secretions and maintain a clear airway are sometimes necessary, but these can usually be avoided by the proper use of corticosteroid drugs.

B. Interim Therapy: Attempt to identify the offending allergens and treat accordingly. Emotional disturbances should be eliminated if possible. Good living hygiene should be promoted. Patients with "intrinsic" asthma (usually associated with bronchitis) may be helped by antibiotic therapy.

Ephedrine hydrochloride or sulfate, 25–50 mg, with or without phenobarbital, 15–30 mg every 3–6 hours, may prevent or reduce recurrences. The following is a useful prescription incorporating aminophylline.

Aminophylline-ephedrine-phenobarbital capsules:

℞ Aminophylline	0.2
Ephedrine hydrochloride or sulfate	0.025
Phenobarbital	0.015

Sig: One capsule every 4 hours.

Nebulized isoproterenol (Isuprel®, Aludrine®), 1:200, from a pocket nebulizer, is useful in controlling mild symptoms and preventing more severe episodes.

Antihistamines may give relief in some patients, but their use in bronchial asthma has generally been disappointing.

Patients who are not helped by other measures may be treated on a long-term basis with prednisone or a similar corticosteroid. The dosage employed should be just sufficient to keep the patient comfortable and relatively free of symptoms. Begin with 5 mg 3–4 times daily.

A new agent, cromolyn sodium (Intal®), has shown some promise in experimental trials in cortico-steroid-resistant asthma. This drug is not available for general use in the USA but has been used for several years in Great Britain and elsewhere. It acts to specifically inhibit the liberation of mediators of anaphylaxis initiated by the antigen-antibody reaction. It is administered as a micronized powder by inhalation. Occasional pharyngeal and tracheal irritation has been noted, but no systemic side-effects have been reported.

The beneficial effects attributed by some investigators to removal of the glomus (carotid body) have not been confirmed, and this procedure cannot be recommended.

Prognosis

Most patients with bronchial asthma adjust well to the necessity for continued medical treatment throughout life. Inadequate control or persistent aggravation by unmodifiable environmental conditions favors the development of incapacitating or even life-threatening complications.

Curran, W.S., & others: Glomectomy for severe bronchial asthma: A double-blind study. Am Rev Resp Dis 93:84–89, 1966.

Dulfarro, M.J.: Bronchodilators, pulmonary function, and asthma. Ann Int Med 68:955–956, 1968.

Freedman, B.J., Meisner, P., & G.B. Hill: A comparison of different bronchodilators in asthma. Thorax 23:590–597, 1968.

Johnstone, D.E.: A study of the natural history of bronchial asthma in children. Am J Dis Child 115:213–216, 1968.

Mannsell, K., Pearson, R.S.B., & J.L. Livingstone: Long-term corticosteroid treatment of asthma. Brit MJ 1:661–664, 1968.

Mathison, D.A., & others: Cromolyn treatment of asthma. JAMA 216:1454–1458, 1971.

Segal, M.S., & E.B. Weiss: Current concepts in the management of the patient with status asthmaticus. M Clin North America 51:373–390, 1967.

Siegal, S.: Current trends in bronchial asthma. New York J Med 67:621–629, 1057–1062, 1967.

BRONCHIECTASIS

Essentials of Diagnosis

- Chronic cough with expectoration of large amounts of purulent sputum, hemoptysis.
- Rales and rhonchi over lower lobes.
- X-ray of chest reveals little; bronchograms show characteristic dilatations.

General Considerations

Bronchiectasis is a dilatation of the medium-size bronchi with destruction of bronchial elastic and muscular elements. It may be caused by pulmonary infections (eg, pneumonia, pertussis, or tuberculosis), or by bronchial obstruction (eg, due to foreign bodies or extrinsic pressure). Atelectasis and congenital defects in children (eg, situs inversus, pulmonary cysts, absent frontal sinuses) are commonly associated with bronchiectasis. The incidence of the disease has been greatly reduced by the improved treatment of pulmonary infections with antibiotics.

Since infection and bronchial obstruction do not regularly produce significant bronchiectasis, unknown intrinsic factors are presumed to play a role. In many patients, a history of onset following a single pulmonary disease (usually in childhood) is obtained. Sinusitis is present in most patients, but its relation to the bronchial disease is not well understood.

Clinical Findings

A. Symptoms and Signs: Symptoms arise as a result of impaired bronchial function (ie, loss of expansile and ciliary function) and stasis, which permits secretions to accumulate in the dilated segments. The patient gives a history of a chronic productive cough and "bronchitis-like" symptoms associated with repeated bouts of pneumonia. The usual etiologic agents of pneumonia are found. (Delayed resolution of a pneumonia should always suggest underlying bronchial disease.) Chronic cough and expectoration are characteristic. Large amounts of purulent sputum, which often separates into 3 layers (sediment, fluid, foam) on standing, are produced. Expectoration is greatest with changes of posture (allowing sudden drainage of bronchiectatic segments), such as arising from bed.

Hemoptysis occurs in about 50% of cases; it is occasionally severe but rarely fatal. Even in tuberculosis, secondary bronchiectasis may be the main source of bleeding. This may be the only symptom.

Weight loss, asthenia, night sweats, and fever are the result of chronic and acutely exacerbating pulmonary infection.

Pulmonary insufficiency may result from recurrent destruction of pulmonary tissue with resulting fibrosis and emphysema.

Rales and rhonchi over the lower lobes are the most prominent physical findings, and the diagnosis of bronchiectasis is uncertain if they are persistently absent. They are more frequently elicited if the examination is carried out before and after postural drainage with coughing (head-down position). Retraction of the chest wall, diminished thoracic excursion, and mediastinal shift toward the side of major involvement will be noted in long-standing disease with loss of lung tissue. Varying signs of pneumonia are present during acute infection.

Emaciation, cyanosis, and clubbing of the fingers are seen in advanced cases, as with other chronic suppurative pulmonary diseases.

B. Laboratory Findings: Not characteristic. Polycythemia, secondary to pulmonary insufficiency, may be present in advanced disease. Sputum smears and cultures help to rule out active tuberculosis (especially important in bronchiectasis of the upper lobe). Pneumococci are found in some cases. Pseudomonas and aerobacter strains may become established after repeated use of antibiotics.

C. X-Ray Findings: Plain chest films are at times helpful. Increased pulmonary markings at the lung bases together with multiple radiolucencies strongly suggest the diagnosis. Patches of chronic inflammation may be present.

Selective instillation of iodized contrast media into the bronchial tree (bronchograms) reveals sacculated, cylindric, or fusiform dilatations with loss of the normal "tree-in-full-bloom" pattern of the terminal bronchi.

Caution: Bronchographic examination is contraindicated during acute infections and in patients who are sensitive to iodine.

D. Instrumental Examination: Although bronchoscopy does not allow visualization of the bronchiectatic areas, it may reveal bronchial obstruction as the underlying pathology, may identify pulmonary segments giving rise to sputum, and can be utilized for bronchography.

Differential Diagnosis

Differentiate from chronic bronchitis, tuberculosis (which also may cause bronchiectasis), and lung abscess; other causes of hemoptysis such as carcinoma and adenoma.

Complications

Recurrent infection in poorly drained pulmonary segments leads to chronic suppuration and pulmonary insufficiency. Complications include severe or fatal hemoptysis, progressive pulmonary insufficiency, chronic cor pulmonale, and amyloidosis.

Treatment

A. General Measures: Postural drainage is the most effective measure for the relief of symptoms due to bronchiectasis. The patient should assume the position that gives maximum drainage (usually lying on the bed in the prone, supine, or either lateral position with the hips elevated by 3–5 pillows and no pillow under the head), maintaining this position for 10–15 minutes 2–4 times a day. The first drainage is upon awakening and the last at bedtime.

Thick sputum should be liquefied with saturated solution of potassium iodide, 10–15 drops in water 4 times daily. Mucolytic agents such as acetylcysteine (Mucomyst®) given by aerosol may also be effective.

Bronchoscopic drainage is of value initially to eliminate bronchial stenosis or obstruction. It may be necessary to dilate the stenosed bronchus, but repeated bronchoscopy is not advised.

Prompt attention to upper respiratory infections is very important in preventing bronchial infection. Many patients with bronchiectasis suffer from chronic upper respiratory tract infections with postnasal drip. This must be corrected whenever possible.

Although climate does not cure, a warm, dry climate often is of benefit, especially since it tends to reduce the incidence of upper respiratory infections. Avoid a dusty, smoke-filled atmosphere.

Patients with severe disease should have adequate rest in bed. Elevating the foot of the bed 4–6 inches is sometimes helpful in promoting drainage. Good nutrition and health are very important. Smoking must be prohibited.

When resectional surgery is not feasible and a large sputum volume is present, a permanent tracheostomy or tracheal fistula may permit better drainage by allowing frequent catheter aspiration.

B. Specific Measures: Antibiotic therapy reduces cough, sputum, and other symptoms, especially during acute exacerbations, but these benefits may be transient and the antibiotics are best used intermittently as exacerbations occur. Prolonged use of antibiotics in maintenance dosage (usually ½ the regular dose) is sometimes indicated.

1. Penicillin may be used parenterally (best for attacks of acute pneumonia; see below) or orally. Give 250 mg (400,000 units) penicillin G 4 times daily.

2. Tetracycline drugs, 250 mg 4 times daily.

3. The use of other antibiotics should be guided by sensitivity studies.

4. Aerosol antibiotics (penicillin, streptomycin) are of no value.

5. Mucolytic agents—See above.

C. Surgical Treatment: Pulmonary resection is indicated (1) for younger patients in otherwise good health with recurring symptoms, and (2) for patients up to 60 years of age with severe symptoms (especially recurrent hemorrhage) due to localized unilateral disease who are otherwise good surgical risks. The results following incomplete removal of bronchiectasis are poor.

Prognosis

The judicious use of antibiotics and surgery has greatly improved the prognosis in bronchiectasis.

Borrie, J., & I. Lichter: Surgical treatment of bronchiectasis: A ten-year survey. Brit MJ 2:908–912, 1965.
Bradford, J.K., & P.T. DeCamp: Bronchiectasis. S Clin North America 46:1485–1492, 1966.
Crofton, J.: Prognosis and treatment of bronchiectasis. Brit MJ 1:721–723, 783–784, 1966.
Ferguson, T.B., & T.H. Burford: The changing pattern of pulmonary suppuration: Surgical implications. Dis Chest 53:396–406, 1968.
Sealey, W.C., Bradham, R.R., & W.C. Young, Jr.: The surgical treatment of multisegmental and localized bronchiectasis. Surg Gynec Obst 123:80–90, 1966.

DISEASES OF THE LUNGS

PNEUMOCOCCAL PNEUMONIA

Essentials of Diagnosis

- Sudden onset of shaking chills, fever, chest pain, and cough with rust-colored sputum.
- X-rays show infiltration, often lobar in distribution.
- Pneumococci are present in the sputum and often in blood.
- Leukocytosis.

General Considerations

Pneumonia is an inflammatory process in lung parenchyma most commonly caused by infection. The consolidation of pneumonia must be differentiated from pulmonary infarction, atelectasis with bronchial obstruction, and congestive heart failure, but it may coexist with any of these conditions. The pneumococcus accounts for 80% or more of primary bacterial pneumonias; types I–VIII are most commonly found in adults, whereas type XIV is common in children. These pathogenic organisms are frequently present among the normal flora of the respiratory tract. The development of pneumonia must therefore usually be attributed to an impairment of natural resistance. Conditions leading to aspiration of secretions include obliteration of the cough or epiglottal reflex, impairment of upward migration of mucus sheets (propelled by cilia), and impairment of alveolar phagocyte function. Among conditions which predispose to pneumonia are viral respiratory diseases, malnutrition, exposure to cold, noxious gases, alcohol intoxication, depression of cerebral functions by drugs, and cardiac failure. Pneumonic consolidation may be in one or more lobes, or patchy in distribution.

Clinical Findings

A. Symptoms and Signs: The onset is usually sudden, with shaking chills, "stabbing" chest pain (exaggerated by respiration but sometimes referred to the shoulder, abdomen, or flank), high fever, cough and "rusty" sputum, and occasionally vomiting. A history of recent respiratory illness can often be elicited.

The patient appears severely ill, with marked tachypnea (30–40/minute) but no orthopnea. Respirations are grunting, nares flaring, and the patient often lies on the affected side in an attempt to splint the chest. Herpes simplex lesions are often present.

Initially, chest excursion is diminished on the involved side, breath sounds are suppressed, and fine inspiratory rales are heard. Later, the classical signs of consolidation appear. A pleural friction rub or abdominal distention may be present. During resolution of the pneumonia, the signs of consolidation are replaced by rales. Physical findings are often inconclusive, and repeated x-ray examination is helpful.

B. Laboratory Findings: Blood cultures are positive for pneumococci in about 25% of cases. In peripheral blood, leukocytosis (20–35 thousand/cu mm) is the rule, and a low white count carries a poorer prognosis.

Expectorated sputum must be examined by Gram's stain and by culture. In the smears, the presence of many squamous epithelial cells suggests heavy contamination with saliva and nasopharyngeal secretions, and such specimens are of doubtful value. Typical sputum from pneumococcal pneumonia contains many red and white cells and many pneumococci. If good sputum specimens are not obtainable, a transtracheal aspirate may reveal the etiologic agent.

C. X-Ray Findings: Initially, there may be no findings or a vague haziness across the involved part of the lung field. Later, typical consolidation is well defined either in lobar or in patchy distribution. Fluid shadows in the costophrenic angles may appear before pleural exudate can be detected by physical examination. During resolution of the consolidation, areas of radiolucency may appear, suggesting "pseudocavitation."

Treatment

A blood culture and a good sputum specimen for smear and culture should always be obtained before treatment is started. The dosage and route of administration of antimicrobial drugs are influenced to some extent by the clinical severity of the disease, the presence of unfavorable prognostic signs (see below), and the presence of complications.

A. Antibacterial Therapy: Penicillin G is the drug of choice. It is given parenterally at first in dosages ranging from procaine penicillin, 600,000 units every 12 hours IM for moderate illness, to aqueous penicillin G, 10 million units per 24 hours by IV infusion in the most severe cases. Only after there has been a definite response to treatment should oral penicillin G or V (400,000 units every 4–6 hours) be considered. All pneumococci are susceptible to penicillin at present. Some strains resistant to tetracyclines, erythromycin, or lincomycin have been encountered. Therefore, these alternatives to penicillin (eg, in patients with documented hypersensitivity) may fail, but they (or cephalexin, 0.5 gm every 4–6 hours) can be tried orally in mildly ill patients (for dosages, see Chapter 25). In more severely ill persons, cephalothin (Keflin®), 8–12 gm IV, or cephaloridine (Keflordin®, Loridine®), 4 gm IV or IM, would be reasonable alternatives.

Sulfonamides have not been in favor recently because the therapeutic response is slower than with penicillin. However, sulfisoxazole diolamine or sodium sulfadiazine, 4–6 gm IV, followed by maintenance doses IV or orally, is adequate (if not optimal) treatment for many cases of pneumococcal pneumonia. The usual sulfonamide precautions (see Chapter 26) should be observed.

B. General Supportive Treatment:

1. Ventilation and oxygenation—An adequate airway must be maintained—if necessary, by tracheal suction, endotracheal tube, or tracheostomy. Oxygen must be supplied to any patient with severe pneumonia, cyanosis, or marked dyspnea; this will also help to prevent pulmonary edema. Oxygen may be supplied by nasal catheter, soft rubber mask, or oxygen tent. With masks, a 95% oxygen concentration can be maintained, whereas with nasal tubes or tents the concentration will reach only 40–50%. However, masks are difficult to tolerate because of cough and expectoration. Oxygen must be humidified to prevent drying of secretions.

2. Shock and pulmonary edema—These are the most frequent causes of death in pneumonia. Oxygen administration tends to prevent pulmonary edema; impending right heart failure must be managed, and digitalization is urgent. Treat shock as outlined in Chapter 1.

3. Toxic delirium—This occurs in any severe pneumonia and may be particularly difficult to manage in alcoholics. It must be controlled to prevent exhaustion and circulatory failure. This is best done by means of a phenothiazine (eg, promazine [Sparine®], 50–100 mg IM) or paraldehyde (8–12 ml orally, repeated as necessary every 4 hours; or 5 ml IM, repeated in 30 minutes if necessary). Anxiety and restlessness during waking hours may also be treated with phenobarbital, 15–30 mg every 4 hours. Pentobarbital, 0.1 gm at bedtime, helps to ensure adequate rest. While administering sedatives or tranquilizers, it is helpful to check the patient's sensorium frequently for any change suggestive of pneumococcal meningitis, which would make a diagnostic lumbar puncture mandatory.

4. Fluids—Patients with pneumococcal pneumonia may perspire profusely and lose much fluid and salt. Sufficient fluid must be given to maintain a daily urinary output of at least 1500 ml. Electrolytes must be kept in balance.

5. Diet—Initially, the dyspneic patient will be anorexic, and a liquid diet will be preferred. With improvement, a normal diet will be tolerated. If complications suggest a long illness, a high-protein, high-caloric diet with vitamin supplementation is indicated.

6. Cough—If cough interferes with sleep and rest, it may be suppressed with codeine phosphate, 15–30 mg every 3–4 hours subcut or orally; or by elixir of terpin hydrate with codeine, 1 tsp every 3–4 hours as necessary.

7. Pleuritic pain—For mild pain, spray ethyl chloride over the area of greatest pain for about 1 minute, and then along the long axis of the body through the entire area of pain, so that a line of frost about 1 inch wide is formed. This gives relief for 1–10 hours in the great majority of patients. Codeine phosphate, 15–30 mg, may be given as necessary for pain. For severe pain, give procaine hydrochloride solution, 0.5–1%, subcut, in a series of injections passing through the area of greatest pain and 5 cm higher and lower. For very severe pain, use meperidine (Demerol®), 50–100 mg, or morphine sulfate, 10–15 mg.

8. Abdominal distention—Abdominal distention is usually due to air swallowing in severe dyspnea, and is a frequent problem in patients with pneumonia. Breathing oxygen in high concentrations (90–100%) is useful because oxygen is rapidly absorbed from the intestines. Neostigmine methylsulfate, 1:2000, 1 ml subcut, and insertion of a rectal tube will usually produce rapid initial decompression. Gastric dilatation can be relieved by suction through a nasal tube passed into the stomach.

9. Congestive failure—(Distinguish from shock and pulmonary edema.) In elderly patients or patients with preexisting heart disease, congestive failure may be precipitated by pneumonia. Rapid digitalization is indicated.

10. Cardiac arrhythmias—Extrasystoles usually require no treatment. If atrial fibrillation or flutter develops, rapid failure may be precipitated. Rapid digitalization is usually indicated in these cases.

C. Evaluation of Treatment: With proper selection of antimicrobial drugs, there should be marked improvement and defervescence in 72 hours or less. If this fails to occur, one must consider 3 main possibilities: (1) the presence of a serious complication such as empyema, pulmonary suppuration associated with bronchial obstruction, endocarditis, or meningitis; (2) that the infection may be caused by an organism other than the pneumococcus and resistant to the drug used; and (3) possible drug fever or other associated disease. If there is evidence of pleural fluid, it must be aspirated promptly, smeared, and cultured to detect infection or empyema which requires drainage. If an organism other than the pneumococcus is shown by laboratory examination to be the probable etiologic agent, treatment must be directed against it.

Complications

Complications of pneumococcal pneumonia occur with the following approximate frequencies: sterile pleural effusion (4–8%), empyema (0.5–2%), endocarditis and meningitis (0.1–0.3%), and pericarditis (0.1%). Other complications, eg, pneumococcal arthritis, are even more rare. Fibrous organization of the pneumonia (in place of resolution) occurs sometimes but rarely causes disability. All pleural fluid collections must be aspirated and examined by smear and culture to permit early treatment of empyema.

Prognosis

Untreated pneumococcal pneumonia has a mortality rate of 20–40% depending upon the presence or absence of the following unfavorable prognostic signs: age over 45 years, presence of other disease (eg, heart failure, cirrhosis), pregnancy, absence of leukocytosis, bacteremia, marked proteinuria, pulmonary edema, and shock.

With early and adequate penicillin treatment, the fatality is about 5%. Virtually all fatalities occur in the age groups under 2 years and over 45–50 years. In untreated, uncomplicated cases, resolution by crisis (or more gradually) occurs 7–10 days after onset.

Anderson, R., & others: Lincomycin and penicillin G in the treatment of mild and moderately severe pneumococcal pneumonia. Am Rev Resp Dis 97:914–918, 1968.

Percival, A., & others: Increased incidence of tetracycline-resistant pneumococci in Liverpool in 1968. Lancet 1:998–1000, 1969.

Turck, M.: Current therapy of bacterial pneumonias. M Clin North America 51:541–548, 1967.

OTHER BACTERIAL PNEUMONIAS

Primary bacterial pneumonias caused by single bacterial species other than the pneumococcus may ac-count for up to 15% of all bacterial pneumonias at present. All of these pneumonias may have somewhat similar physical findings and x-ray evidence of pulmonary infiltration or consolidation. For proper treatment it is crucial to identify the etiologic agent by blood culture and by sputum examination with stained smear and culture. Transtracheal aspiration or even lung puncture may be needed for specific diagnosis and treatment.

Klebsiella Pneumonia

Klebsiella pneumoniae (Friedländer's bacillus) occurs as a member of the normal bacterial flora in the respiratory tract or gut of 5–20% of the population. Primary pneumonia due to this organism occurs mainly in persons between 40–60 years of age with a history of alcoholism, malnutrition, or debilitating diseases. Klebsiella pneumonia is also a frequent type of superinfection in persons hospitalized for serious disease, including other types of pneumonia treated with antimicrobial drugs.

The onset is usually sudden, with chills, fever, dyspnea, cyanosis, and profound toxicity. The sputum is often red ("currant jelly"), mucoid, sticky, and difficult to expectorate. Physical findings and white counts are variable. The disease may be fulminating and progress rapidly to a fatal outcome. In subacute forms, there is a tendency to necrosis of lung tissue and abscess formation.

The diagnosis is based on finding short, encapsulated gram-negative bacteria in sputum smears as the predominant organism (in poorly stained smears they may be mistaken for pneumococci) and klebsiellae in blood and sputum cultures. Immediate intensive antimicrobial treatment is essential. Kanamycin (Kantrex®), 0.5 gm, is injected IM every 6–8 hours (15 mg/kg/day); and cephalothin (Keflin®), 6–10 gm IV, is sometimes given in addition. When drug-resistant klebsiella infections occur in a hospital environment, gentamicin, 3–5 mg/kg/day, may be injected IM in 3 equal doses. Antimicrobial treatment may have to be continued for more than 2 weeks to avoid relapses. General supportive treatment is the same as for pneumococcal pneumonia.

The fatality rate in untreated klebsiella pneumonia is near 80%. Even with apparently adequate treatment, the fatality rate may be near 40%.

Manfredi, F., Daly, W.J., & R.H. Behnke: Clinical observations of acute Friedländer pneumonia. Ann Int Med 58:642–653, 1963.

Hemophilus Influenzae Pneumonia

This is a rare form of primary bacterial pneumonia in adults. It has occurred in the presence of cardiac disease, hypogammaglobulinemia, and chronic lung disease. Symptoms and signs do not distinguish this from other bacterial pneumonias. The sputum may be bloody, but gram-stained smears may be misinterpreted. The diagnosis ultimately rests on the results of cultures of blood and sputum.

Treatment with ampicillin, 1–1.5 gm orally every 6 hours or 150 mg/kg/day IV, may be expected to cure the infection. An alternative method of treatment is with chloramphenicol, 0.5 gm orally every 6 hours. General measures are the same as for pneumococcal pneumonia.

Johnson, W.D., & others: *Hemophilus influenzae* pneumonia in adults. Report of five cases and review of the literature. Am Rev Resp Dis 97:1112–1117, 1968.

Pseudomonas Pneumonia & Proteus Pneumonia

Pneumonias caused by *Pseudomonas aeruginosa* and by various species of proteus occur with increasing frequency in debilitated persons with chronic lung or heart disease and alcoholism, or as superinfections in patients who have required inhalation therapy or tracheal suction and have received antimicrobial drugs. Contaminated equipment may be an important etiologic factor.

These pneumonias are associated with early delirium, massive consolidation often proceeding to necrosis and multiple abscess formation, and a high fatality rate. Gentamicin, 3–5 mg/kg/day IM in 3 divided doses, plus carbenicillin, 18–30 gm/day by IV infusion, appears to be a possible method of treatment. With renal failure, the dosage must be adjusted downward to prevent nephrotoxicity.

Fetzer, A.E., & others: Pathologic features of pseudomonas pneumonia. Am Rev Resp Dis 96:1121–1130, 1967.

Tillotson, J.R., & A.M. Lerner: Characteristics of pneumonias caused by *B proteus*. Ann Int Med 68:287–294, 1968.

Tillotson, J.R., & A.M. Lerner: Characteristics of nonbacteremic pseudomonas pneumonia. Ann Int Med 68:295–307, 1968.

Streptococcal Pneumonia

Pneumonia due to hemolytic streptococci occurs usually as a sequel to viral infection of the respiratory tract, especially influenza or measles, or in persons with underlying pulmonary disease. The patients are usually severely toxic and cyanotic. Pleural effusion develops frequently and early and progresses to empyema in 1/3 of untreated patients. The diagnosis rests on finding large numbers of streptococci in smears of sputum and culturing hemolytic streptococci from blood and sputum.

The treatment of choice is with penicillin G in a dosage similar to that for pneumococcal pneumonia (see above). If treatment is started early, the prognosis is good.

Staphylococcal Pneumonia

Pneumonia caused by *Staphylococcus aureus* occurs as a sequel to viral infections of the respiratory tract (eg, influenza) and in debilitated (eg, postsurgical) patients or hospitalized infants, especially after antimicrobial drug administration. There is often a history of a mild illness with headache, cough, and generalized aches which abruptly changes to a very severe illness with high fever, chills, and exaggerated cough with purulent or blood-streaked sputum and deep cyanosis. There may be early signs of pleural effusion, empyema, or tension pneumothorax. X-ray examination reveals lung consolidation, pneumatoceles, abscesses, empyema, and pneumothorax. The demonstration of pyopneumothorax and of cavities with air-fluid levels by x-ray is highly suggestive of staphylococcal pneumonia. The diagnosis must be made by examination of sputum by smear (masses of white cells and gram-positive cocci, many intracellular), culture (predominantly *S aureus*), pleural fluid culture, and blood culture. The white count is elevated, usually to more than 20,000/cu mm.

Initial therapy (based on sputum smear) consists of full systemic doses of a cephalosporin, a penicillinase-resistant penicillin, or vancomycin. The dosages are as follows: cephalothin (Keflin®), 8–14 gm/day IV; methicillin, 8–16 gm/day IV; vancomycin (Vancocin®), 2 gm/day IV; nafcillin, 6–12 gm/day IV. If the staphylococcus proves to be penicillin-sensitive by laboratory test, penicillin G, 20–60 million units/day IV, is the antibiotic of choice. If empyema develops, drainage must be established. If pneumothorax develops, it is treated as described on pp 139–140.

The prognosis varies with the underlying condition of the patient and the drug susceptibility of the organism.

Bacteroides Pneumonia

Pneumonias caused by anaerobic Bacteroides species occur as complications of abdominal or pelvic bacteroides infections and in patients with chronic lung disease. Pleural effusions and empyema develop early and are a main feature of the disease, which is often subacute or chronic. The diagnosis is based on the foul odor of the empyema and the demonstration of pleomorphic gram-negative anaerobes. Drainage of empyema must be combined with intensive penicillin or tetracycline treatment.

Tillotson, J.R., & A.M. Lerner: Bacteroides pneumonias: Character of cases with empyema. Ann Int Med 68:308–317, 1968.

Winterbauer, R.H., & others: Recurrent pneumonia. Predisposing illness and clinical patterns in 158 patients. Ann Int Med 70:689–699, 1969.

Pneumocystis Carinii Pneumonia

This is a rare disorder which occurs in debilitated children or in patients who are immunosuppressed or suffer from leukemia. The diagnosis can be made by lung biopsy and the demonstration of typical cysts of the parasite *P carinii* in Giemsa-stained impression smears from lung tissue. Pentamidine isethionate (Lomidine®), 4 mg/kg/day IM, may be curative.

Lillehei, J.P., & others: *Pneumocystis carinii* pneumonia. JAMA 206:596–600, 1968.

"MIXED" BACTERIAL PNEUMONIAS
(Hypostatic Pneumonia, "Terminal" Pneumonia, Bronchopneumonia)

Essentials of Diagnosis
- Variable onset of fever, cough, dyspnea, expectoration.
- Symptoms and signs often masked by primary (debilitating) disease.
- Greenish-yellow sputum (purulent) with mixed flora.
- Leukocytosis (often absent in aged and debilitated).
- Patchy infiltration on chest x-ray.

General Considerations
Mixed bacterial pneumonias include those in which culture and smear reveal several organisms, not one of which can clearly be identified as the etiologic agent. They usually appear as complications of surgery or other trauma, various chronic illnesses (cardiac failure, advanced carcinoma, uremia), and certain acute illnesses (eg, measles, influenza). They are common complications of chronic pulmonary diseases such as bronchiectasis and emphysema. Old people are most commonly affected ("terminal" pneumonia). Patients treated with intermittent positive pressure breathing apparatus or immunosuppressive drugs may develop pneumonia due to gram-negative rods.

The following findings in a debilitated, chronically ill, or aged person suggest a complicating pneumonia: (1) worsening of cough, dyspnea, cyanosis; (2) low-grade, irregular fever; (3) purulent sputum; and (4) patchy basal densities on a chest film (in addition to previously noted densities caused by a primary underlying disease, if any).

Clinical Findings
A. Symptoms and Signs: The onset is usually insidious, with low-grade fever, cough, expectoration, and dyspnea which may become marked and lead to cyanosis. The physical findings are extremely variable and may not be impressive against a background of chronic cardiac or pulmonary disease. Those signs listed under other bacterial pneumonias may also be present with this type.

B. Laboratory Findings: The appearance of a greenish or yellowish (purulent) sputum should suggest a complicating pneumonia. Smears and cultures reveal a mixed flora. Predominant types should be noted as a guide to therapy. Leukocytosis is often absent in the aged and debilitated patient.

C. X-Ray Findings: X-ray shows patchy, irregular infiltrations, most commonly posterior and basal (in bedridden patients). Abscess formation may be observed. Careful interpretation is necessary in order to avoid confusion with shadows due to preexisting heart or lung disease.

Differential Diagnosis
Mixed bacterial pneumonias must be differentiated from tuberculosis, carcinoma, and other specific mycotic, bacterial, and viral pulmonary infections (to any of which they may also be secondary).

Treatment
Where no specific etiologic microorganisms are present in the sputum, broad-spectrum antibiotics can be used. Give ampicillin, 1–1.5 gm, or tetracycline, 0.5 gm, every 6 hours orally. If staphylococci are present in the sputum in large numbers, treat as for staphylococcal pneumonia. If gram-negative rods are prevalent, their identification and drug sensitivity guide treatment.

Prognosis
The prognosis depends upon the nature and severity of the underlying pulmonary disease and varies with the predominating organism.

Hahn, H.H., & H.N. Beaty: Transtracheal aspiration in the evaluation of patients with pneumonia. Ann Int Med 72:183–187, 1970.
Klein, J.O.: Diagnostic lung puncture in the pneumonias of children. Pediatrics 44:486–492, 1969.

ASPIRATION PNEUMONIA

Aspiration pneumonia is an especially severe type of pneumonia with a high mortality rate. It results from the aspiration of gastric contents. Important predisposing factors include impairment of the swallowing mechanism (eg, esophageal disease), inadequate cough reflex (eg, anesthesia, postoperative state, CNS disease, drug abuse), and impaired gastric emptying (eg, pyloric obstruction). Pulmonary injury is due in large part to the low pH (< 2.5) of gastric secretions.

Scattered areas of pulmonary edema and bronchospasm occur, and the x-ray appearance may be confused with that of pulmonary emboli, atelectasis, bronchopneumonia, and congestive heart failure.

Treatment is as for "mixed" bacterial pneumonias. The use of corticosteroids in full doses seems to be of value in reducing the severity of the inflammatory reaction (eg, hydrocortisone, 200 mg IM initially and 50 mg IM every 6 hours for 2 days; then 25 mg IM every 6 hours for the next 2 days).

Bronchoscopic aspiration may be attempted, but it may be possible to remove only a small amount of the aspirated fluids.

Harris, M.S.: Aspiration disease in the elderly. Dis Chest 47:487–491, 1965.
Ribando, C.A., & W.J. Grace: Pulmonary aspiration. Am J Med 50:510–519, 1971.
Vandam, L.D.: Current concepts: Aspiration of gastric contents in the operative period. New England J Med 273:1206–1207, 1965.

PRIMARY ATYPICAL PNEUMONIA

Essentials of Diagnosis

- Gradually increasing cough with scanty sputum and fever.
- Minimal physical signs on chest examination.
- X-ray evidence of infiltration.
- White blood count in normal range or low.

General Considerations

The PAP syndrome may be caused by a variety of viral, rickettsial, chlamydial, and mycoplasmal agents. It must be differentiated from specific bacterial, mycobacterial, and fungal pneumonias and from neoplastic diseases. An attempt should be made to diagnose the specific agent causing the infection (virus, rickettsia, chlamydia, mycoplasma) by means of appropriate laboratory tests and epidemiologic investigations. Prominent causative agents include adenoviruses (especially types 4, 7, and 14 in military personnel), influenza viruses; the rickettsia of Q fever, *Coxiella burnetii*; the chlamydiae of the psittacosis group; the fungi coccidioides, histoplasma, and cryptococcus; and *Mycoplasma pneumoniae* ("Eaton agent"). Transmission of Q fever requires contact with cattle, goats, or sheep; transmission of psittacosis requires contact with birds. The mycotic infections are acquired from contaminated soil or dust, whereas viral and mycoplasmal pneumonias are transmitted by droplets from person to person. Only 10–20% of *M pneumoniae* infections produce pneumonia; the others are asymptomatic or present as upper respiratory disease. However, mycoplasmal pneumonia is probably the commonest type of pneumonia encountered in otherwise healthy young adults (eg, university students).

Clinical Findings

A. Symptoms and Signs: The clinical picture varies widely, both in the spontaneous and experimentally induced forms. Symptoms may be mild, as in the "common cold" or "flu"; hence the likelihood that many diseases previously diagnosed as "upper respiratory infection" were in fact pneumonias. Occasional severe cases occur which may be fatal.

The disease often begins as a mild upper respiratory tract infection proceeding to a dry cough which grows worse, increasing fever, hoarseness, headache, and generalized aching. Extreme fatigue is common. Pleuritic pain and effusion are uncommon.

Physical findings are frequently sparse and sometimes completely absent in the face of a surprising degree of infiltration as seen on x-ray. Rales are usually heard. Diminished breath sounds over the involved areas may be noted in early cases.

B. Laboratory Findings: The sputum is scanty, rarely blood-tinged. The smear shows a striking lack of bacteria and yields only the usual flora of the mouth on culture. The white count may be normal or may show mild to severe leukopenia. Mild leukocytosis may appear later in the course of the disease.

Autohemagglutinins for human type O erythrocytes (cold agglutinins) appear in the convalescent phase of mycoplasmal pneumonia (seldom before the second week) in about 50% of cases. To be significant, a rise in titer must be > 1:10 during the second week.

Specific antibodies to mycoplasma may be demonstrated. *M pneumoniae* can be grown from respiratory secretions on special media.

C. X-Ray Findings: Linear infiltrates tend to appear first at hilar areas, extending later into the middle and basal portions of both lungs. The initial appearance of these changes may be delayed, and clearing on x-ray usually occurs within 3 weeks. There is considerable variation in the x-ray pattern, and no configuration is diagnostic.

Complications

Pleural effusions occur in 5–20% of cases. Atelectasis, pneumothorax, pericarditis, myocarditis, secondary bacterial pneumonia, and acute hemolytic anemia may occur. Bronchiectasis also has been seen as a late complication.

Treatment

General measures are as for pneumococcal pneumonia.

In mild cases of mycoplasmal pneumonia antimicrobial drugs are not indicated. Severe cases may be treated with erythromycin (0.5 gm orally every 6 hours) or tetracycline (0.5 gm orally every 6–8 hours). Rarely is it necessary to administer these drugs intravenously.

Prognosis

Mortality in untreated cases is low. Fever usually disappears by the 10th day, although x-ray abnormalities persist for longer periods.

Alexander, E.R., & others: Pneumonia due to *Mycoplasma pneumoniae.* New England J Med 275:131–136, 1966.
See also references under Pneumococcal Pneumonia.

LIPOID PNEUMONIA

This disease is an aspiration pneumonia associated with the use of oily medications. Fibrosis and the presence of macrophages containing oil droplets are the histologic features.

Symptoms and signs vary widely, at times resembling those of acute pneumonia (fever, productive cough) or chronic lung disease (weight loss, night sweats). There may be no symptoms but striking x-ray densities. Patients must be carefully questioned about the use of mineral oil, oily nose drops, or ointments used in the nose. Physical signs vary accordingly and are not diagnostic. Peribronchial infiltrations, diffuse lobar densities, scattered discrete densities, and even central cavitation have all been described on x-ray.

Leukocytosis may occur with acute symptoms. Proper examination of the sputum for oil droplet-laden macrophages will often establish the diagnosis.

Treatment is nonspecific and symptomatic. Use of the oil-containing preparation should be discontinued. When this is done, further progression of the disease usually does not occur and the prognosis is good. Large solitary masses may require resection.

Hinshaw, H.C., & L.H. Garland: *Diseases of the Chest,* 3rd ed. Saunders, 1969.

Schwindt, W.D., Barbee, R.A., & R.J. Jones: Lipoid pneumonia. Arch Surg 95:652–657, 1967.

PNEUMONIAS DUE TO SPECIFIC VIRUSES, RICKETTSIAE, & CHLAMYDIAE

The important specific viral, rickettsial, and chlamydial (bedsonial) infections which may produce pneumonia include influenza, Q fever, Rocky Mountain spotted fever, typhus, and psittacosis (ornithosis). The exanthematous viral diseases (rubeola, varicella, variola, and vaccinia) all give rise occasionally to specific pneumonias.

These pneumonias are indistinguishable from primary atypical pneumonia on the basis of pulmonary physical and x-ray findings. Diagnosis depends upon recognition of the specific systemic disease by extrapulmonary features (eg, rash), a history of exposure to vectors (eg, parrots, ticks), epidemiologic information, and demonstration of a significant rise in specific antibody titers.

The treatment of viral pneumonia is symptomatic. Anti-infective chemotherapy for chlamydial diseases is discussed in Chapter 21. Treat rickettsial pneumonias as outlined in the discussion of rickettsioses.

See references under Pneumococcal Pneumonia.

PULMONARY INFILTRATION WITH EOSINOPHILIA (PIE Syndrome)

This relatively uncommon syndrome is characterized by migratory multiple pulmonary infiltrates, eosinophilia (up to 80%) in the peripheral blood, and variable symptomatology. It is believed to represent an allergic response to a number of diseases, including parasitic infections (*Entamoeba histolytica,* Trichuris, *Fasciola hepatica*), bacterial and mycotic infections (tuberculosis, brucellosis, coccidioidomycosis), and certain of the "collagen" diseases. It often occurs without an apparent cause.

Treatment and prognosis depend upon the underlying disease. When specific infections have been excluded, corticosteroid treatment may cause dramatic resolution.

Carrington, C.B., & others: Chronic eosinophilia pneumonia. New England J Med 280:787–798, 1969.

Ford, R.M.: Transient pulmonary eosinophilia and asthma. A review of 20 cases occurring in 5,702 asthma sufferers. Am Rev Resp Dis 93:797–803, 1966.

PULMONARY TUBERCULOSIS

Essentials of Diagnosis

- Presenting signs and symptoms are usually minimal: malaise, lassitude, easy fatigability, anorexia, mild weight loss, afternoon fever, cough, apical rales, hemoptysis.
- Symptoms and signs may be entirely absent.
- Positive tuberculin skin test; especially a recent change from negative to positive.
- Apical or subapical infiltrates, often with cavities.
- *Mycobacterium tuberculosis* in sputum or in gastric or tracheal washings.

General Considerations

Pulmonary tuberculosis is a specific pulmonary infection caused by the acid-fast organism, *Mycobacterium tuberculosis,* and characterized by the formation of tubercles in the lung. The first or primary infection is usually a self-limited disease in children which escapes detection. A few develop progressive primary tuberculosis. Another small percentage of patients, after a latency period of months to years, develop progressive pulmonary disease of the adult type. Primary infection occurring in adults may evolve into adult type disease without developing the characteristic changes of primary disease seen in children. While most people who are infected at any age never develop the disease, it is not always possible to predict which ones are at risk. Malnutrition, diabetes, measles, chronic corticosteroid administration, silicosis, and general debility may predispose to the progression of infection to disease. Once primary infection has occurred, the person's future risk is from those same tubercle bacilli. Superinfection ("exogenous reinfection") occurs rarely if at all.

Clinical Findings

A. Symptoms and Signs: Symptoms may be absent—or mild and nonspecific—in the presence of active disease. When present, the most frequent symptoms are cough, malaise, easy fatigability, weight loss, low-grade afternoon fever, night sweats, and pleuritic pain. Cough, when present, has no specific characteristics. Blood in the sputum is strongly suggestive of tuberculosis. Patients with pulmonary tuberculosis occasionally present with symptoms due to extrapulmonary complications such as laryngeal, intestinal, renal, or CNS involvement.

Pulmonary signs may be difficult to elicit even in the presence of active disease. Fine persistent rales over the upper lobes may be found. These are best heard during inspiration after a slight cough. Advanced disease may lead to retraction of the chest wall, deviation of the trachea, wheezes, rales, and signs of pneumonic consolidation. Signs of cavitation are unreliable.

Pulmonary tuberculosis cannot be ruled out by physical examination alone. A chest x-ray is the minimum requirement.

B. Laboratory Findings:

1. Tuberculin skin test—This test is based on skin hypersensitivity to a specific bacterial protein obtained from culture media. Tuberculin may be administered intracutaneously (Mantoux) and by multiple puncture methods (eg, tine test, Heaf test). The intracutaneous method employing purified protein derivative (PPD) in the intermediate strength (5 tuberculin units) is the most reliable. The patch test (Vollmer) should not be used.

a. Positive reaction—A positive reaction (induration 10 mm or more in diameter) indicates past or present infection. The skin test becomes positive 2–8 weeks after infection with the tubercle bacillus. The incidence of positive reactions varies with population groups and is higher among disadvantaged segments in all countries. False-positive reactions may occur as a result of cross-sensitivity to atypical mycobacteria (see below).

b. Negative reaction—A negative reaction, for all practical purposes, rules out tuberculous etiology of pulmonary disease. Anergy (disappearance or marked decrease in the tuberculin reaction) is a rare phenomenon which occurs with overwhelming tuberculosis, exanthematous diseases, corticosteroid treatment, and sarcoidosis. The possibility of defective testing material must also be considered.

c. Conversion reaction—A conversion reaction is a negative reaction which becomes positive during observation. It implies recent infection and is an important finding because the risk of developing disease is greatest during the first 1–2 years after infection.

2. Bacteriologic studies—Recovery of the tubercle bacillus from sputum or gastric or tracheal washings is the only incontrovertible diagnostic finding. Tracheal wash with saline or sputum induction by inhalation of a heated aerosol (5% saline) produces a more reliable specimen for bacteriologic examination if there is no spontaneous sputum production.

a. Sputum—Direct smears are positive when the bacterial count is high. Positive smears should always be confirmed by culture, although treatment is usually started before culture results are completed. Sensitivities to the major antituberculosis drugs should be determined for organisms obtained by culture.

Whenever possible, fresh sputum should be obtained for culture although tubercle bacilli will usually survive several days in specimens transmitted by mail.

Culture is more sensitive than smear examination, but the time required for growth of organisms (4–6 weeks) is a disadvantage. Certain atypical acid-fast organisms may cause confusion. Newer bacteriologic

methods usually permit the differentiation of *Myco tuberculosis* from atypical mycobacteria as well as differentiation of the several groups of the latter (see below).

b. Gastric washings—Stained smears of gastric washings are of no value because of the occurrence of nontuberculous acid-fast organisms. Culture of gastric contents is especially useful for patients who cannot cooperate (eg, children, senile patients).

3. Biopsies—Enlarged lymph nodes in supraclavicular or cervical areas should be searched for carefully, since they may reveal an extension of the underlying pulmonary disease easily accessible by biopsy. In addition to histologic examination, excised nodes should always be cultured for tubercle bacilli and fungi. Pleural and pulmonary biopsy may also give valuable diagnostic information.

C. X-Ray Findings: Chest films disclose disease in almost all cases. Failures occur where lesions are hidden behind ribs, cardiovascular structures, and the diaphragm. A single film is usually insufficient for diagnosis. Although many features suggest the likelihood of tuberculosis, there is no pathognomonic x-ray pattern.

Hilar lymph node enlargement associated with a small parenchymal lesion which heals with calcification is the usual picture of primary infection. Many "primaries" (proved by change of tuberculin skin test from negative to positive) do not present x-ray abnormalities. Very large nodes are unusual in adults, in whom "primary" infection cannot be distinguished from postprimary progression by x-ray findings.

Apical and subapical infiltrations are the usual presenting x-ray features of "adult" (postprimary progression) tuberculosis. Lordotic views may be required to reveal such lesions where uncertainty exists in the posteroanterior projection.

Cavitation is presumptive evidence of tuberculous activity. Tomograms are occasionally necessary for the demonstration of cavities.

Fibrotic disease, with dense, well delineated strands, may dominate the picture. The physician should not be deluded into considering such lesions inactive ("scars").

Solitary nodules, miliary lesions, and lobar consolidation (acute caseous pneumonia) present difficult problems in differential diagnosis.

Tuberculous pleural effusion has no characteristic x-ray appearance that differentiates it from other effusions.

Lower lung field tuberculosis in the absence of upper lobe lesions is uncommon (about 3% of all cases).

Bronchial tuberculosis may lead to obstruction and bronchiectasis, with corresponding x-ray findings.

Serial films are often crucial in the establishment of activity and are indispensable in the selection and evaluation of therapy.

Differential Diagnosis

Tuberculosis can mimic nearly any pulmonary disease. Important diseases to be considered are bacterial and viral pneumonias, lung abscess, pulmonary mycoses, bronchogenic carcinoma, sarcoidosis, pneumoconioses, and "atypical" (nontuberculous) mycobacterial infections.

Recovery of tubercle bacilli by culture establishes the diagnosis of tuberculosis. If carcinoma is suspected and cannot be promptly excluded, early tissue diagnosis by thoracotomy may be indicated without waiting for culture results.

A negative tuberculin skin test makes the diagnosis of tuberculosis very unlikely.

Prevention

A. Isolation Precautions: Persons in contact with patients with active tuberculosis should protect themselves by wearing a mask. Patients who are cooperative and who have no cough (or cover their mouths when coughing) and who have been on antituberculosis drug treatment for at least 2 weeks are not hazardous to be around even without special precautions. Hospital personnel with negative tuberculin skin tests who are in contact with tuberculosis patients should have repeat skin tests twice a year.

B. Examination of Contacts: Close contacts must be examined by skin test when an active case is discovered. Those with positive tests should have a chest x-ray. Those who have negative skin tests should be retested 2 months after contact with the active case has been broken. Those with positive skin tests and negative x-rays should receive preventive treatment with isoniazid (see ¶ D, below). Some recommend giving all close contacts (with negative x-rays) isoniazid for 1 year whether the skin test is positive or netgative.

C. BCG vaccination: Although it is generally agreed that BCG vaccination offers some protection to tuberculin-negative persons, several factors limit its usefulness. In most parts of the world, the risk of developing tuberculosis is slight among tuberculin-negative persons. Converting tuberculin-negative people to positive reactors by vaccination deprives the clinician of an important tuberculosis control measure, ie, the discovery of early infection by skin testing and treatment of converters with isoniazid. For these reasons, BCG vaccination is recommended only where exposure to tuberculosis is great and the usual tuberculosis control measures are not operative.

D. Treatment of Tuberculin Reactors (Without Other Evidence of Disease): Certain tuberculin reactors, especially the newly infected, should be given preventive treatment with isoniazid. Most authorities now recommend the preventive treatment of anyone known to have been infected with tuberculosis within the preceding year as well as those reactors who are at increased risk of developing tuberculosis (ie, those with diabetes, silicosis [life-time treatment], and those receiving prolonged corticosteroid treatment). This "preventive" treatment consists of isoniazid, 5 mg/kg/day orally in a single daily dose for 1 year. Activities need not be restricted. Pretreatment x-rays must show no evidence of tuberculosis. X-rays should be repeated in 6 months and annually thereafter.

Treatment

A. Drug Therapy: (See Table 6–2.) Drug treatment is the most important single measure in the management of tuberculosis and is indicated in all cases of active disease.

Bed rest is advisable if there are symptoms such as fever, hemoptysis, or severe cough, and usually is needed only for a few weeks. In general, return to normal physical activity is permitted following a brief period of observation after an effective drug regimen has been established.

Patients with positive sputum must be isolated until sputum cultures are negative for tubercle bacilli.

The present recommendation is for prolonged administration of combinations of the major drugs listed below. Many patients seem to benefit from prolonged treatment even after moderate resistance of the organisms to the drugs has been shown by sensitivity tests. Most authorities advise a minimum of 12 months of drug treatment after the "inactive" status has been attained (x-ray lesions stable, no cavitation, and cultures negative—all for at least 6 months).

The principal drugs currently used in the treatment of pulmonary tuberculosis are isoniazid (INH), rifampin, streptomycin, ethambutol, and aminosalicylic acid (PAS). The simultaneous use of isoniazid and 2 of the other drugs is recommended in the initial treatment of advanced disease or whenever the sputum contains tubercle bacilli. When tubercle bacilli are no longer present in the sputum, treatment should be continued with isoniazid plus one of the other oral agents.

Sensitivity tests on tubercle bacilli recovered by culture should be started, using the major drugs, before treatment is initiated. When the results of these studies are obtained (4–6 weeks later), it may be necessary to modify the drug regimen.

1. Isoniazid (INH)—This is the most effective drug currently available. However, when used alone its effectiveness is decreased by the early emergence of bacterial resistance.

Isoniazid is indicated for any active tuberculosis lesion, including primary tuberculosis in children. It is of particular value in miliary tuberculosis, tuberculous meningitis, and other forms of extrapulmonary tuberculosis. Adverse reactions to the drug are infrequent with the usual dose of 5/mg/kg/day. Hypersensitivity reactions may occur. With large doses, peripheral neuropathy and, rarely, CNS irritability may occur. There is evidence that the latter are related to pyridoxine depletion. Supplementary doses of pyridoxine (25–50 mg/day orally) should be given.

2. Rifampin (Rifampicin®, Rifadin®)—Rifampin is the newest antituberculosis agent available, and early reports seem to indicate that it will be another major drug. It is a semisynthetic derivative of the antibiotic rifamycin. It is given orally and is said to be well tolerated except for occasional gastrointestinal irritation and rare hypersensitivity reactions. Its teratogenic potential when used in pregnant women is not yet known. Its place in the spectrum of antituberculosis drugs is not yet established, but at present its use with one or more of the major drugs, preferably including isoniazid, can be recommended for the initial treatment or the retreatment of tuberculosis.

The adult dose is 600 mg daily orally in one dose; for children, give 10–20 mg/kg/day orally, not to exceed 600 mg/day.

3. Streptomycin sulfate—The indications for this drug are the same as for isoniazid except that it is less effective than isoniazid in advanced tuberculosis. Like isoniazid, it is less effective when used alone, and whenever possible should be given in combination with other drugs.

Streptomycin may cause 8th nerve damage (vertigo and, rarely, deafness), especially with prolonged daily use. This may become irreversible if the drug is continued.

Toxic reactions to streptomycin are few when the drug is given twice weekly. This regimen produces a therapeutic effect comparable to that of other streptomycin schedules (except in the more serious forms of the disease, where daily dosage may be necessary). Generalized dermatitis occasionally occurs, in which case the drug must be discontinued. Perioral numbness often appears shortly after injection and may last for several hours. By itself it can be ignored.

4. Ethambutol (Myambutol®)—Ethambutol is a new antituberculosis drug which appears to be a valuable addition to the major drugs listed above. It is relatively free of side-effects. Retrobulbar neuritis has been noted, but when the drug is used in the recommended dosage this has been a minor and reversible complication. Visual acuity should be determined before and monthly during treatment; the drug should be stopped if a decrease in visual acuity occurs. Its use should be avoided in infants and young children in whom visual acuity cannot be monitored. At present, the principal indication for use of ethambutol is as a substitute for aminosalicylic acid. Ethambutol is given orally, 15 mg/kg/day. The daily amount should be rounded off to the nearest 100 mg and given as a single dose.

5. Aminosalicylic acid (PAS) or its calcium or sodium salt—This drug has a low level of antituberculosis activity, but when used with the other drugs it delays the emergence of resistant organisms. Toxic reactions include nausea, vomiting, and diarrhea; a febrile reaction; and, occasionally, generalized dermatitis and hepatitis. The gastrointestinal symptoms may sometimes be overcome by using a different preparation or by stopping the drug for several days and then resuming it in small doses, gradually increasing to the regular dose in 2–3 weeks. When fever, dermatitis, or hepatitis due to PAS toxicity occurs, the drug must be stopped.

6. Other antituberculosis drugs—These are more toxic and less effective than those described above. They are used in various combinations in the treatment of disease resistant to the primary drugs. Retreatment in the presence of resistant organisms should be guided by drug sensitivity tests. The addition of a single effective drug to a failing regimen is usually fruitless. A planned program using at least 3 carefully selected drugs simultaneously is recommended. The reader should consult the references cited below for further information.

The other drugs include the following:

a. Ethionamide (Trecator®) is the most useful and least toxic of the second-line drugs. Early reports were encouraging, but it now appears that the status of ethionamide will be limited to that of a drug of occasional value.

b. Cycloserine (Seromycin®) has limited antituberculosis activity but is useful when bacterial resistance to the major drugs is present, especially in connection with resectional surgery. The usual adult dose is 250 mg twice daily orally. It may cause CNS irritability. When larger doses are used, pyridoxine hydrochloride, 50 mg/day, and diphenylhydantoin (Dilantin®), 100 mg/day, should be given.

c. Pyrazinamide (Aldinamide®, PZA) is a drug which occasionally produces severe toxic hepatitis. Observe carefully for symptoms and laboratory evidence of liver dysfunction, and stop the drug promptly if any abnormality appears. The usual adult dose is 0.75 gm orally twice daily.

d. Viomycin sulfate (Vinactane®, Viocin®), a less effective and more toxic drug than the foregoing, has limited usefulness where chemotherapy is needed and the above-mentioned drugs cannot be used (hypersensitivity, resistant organisms). The usual dose is 2 gm IM daily or twice weekly for up to 6 weeks.

7. Corticosteroids—The corticosteroids are used effectively in conjunction with antituberculosis drug treatment in certain extrapulmonary forms of tuberculosis. Their use in pulmonary tuberculosis is beneficial only in certain cases of very extensive disease with severe toxic symptoms.

B. Collapse Therapy (Pneumothorax, Pneumoperitoneum): This type of treatment is no longer used in the treatment of tuberculosis.

C. Surgery:

1. Pulmonary resection—Resection is an important mode of treatment in selected cases, although very few patients now require surgery for pulmonary tuberculosis. Pulmonary resection is indicated in any of the following circumstances: (1) When there is a localized pulmonary nodule and the possibility of cancer cannot be excluded. (2) For bronchial stenosis. (3) For old thoracoplasty failures. (Some of these can be successfully treated by resection.) (4) For any localized chronic focus which has not improved substantially after 3–6 months of adequate drug therapy, especially if tubercle bacilli persist in the sputum.

2. Thoracoplasty—This operation is no longer used as a primary treatment measure. It is occasionally used (1) to reduce the pleural "dead space" after a large pulmonary resection and thus minimize distention of the remaining lung, or (2) to close a chronic empyema space.

D. Diet: The diet should be adequate in calories and high in proteins and vitamins. No special diets have been shown to be of benefit. Normal weight should be maintained.

TABLE 6—2. Primary antituberculosis drugs.

Drug	Adult dose	Remarks
Isoniazid (INH)	5—10 mg/kg/day orally*	The only indication for using these drugs singly
Rifampin	600 mg/day orally†	is hypersensitivity of the patient to the other
Streptomycin	1 gm IM daily or twice weekly	drugs or for the treatment of tuberculin reac-
Ethambutol (Myambutol®)‡	15 mg/kg/day orally in a single dose	tors (see text).
Aminosalicylic acid (PAS)	4—5 gm orally 3 times daily after meals	
Combined therapy		Use 3 drugs (including INH) initially until spu-
Isoniazid	As above	tum cultures are negative, and then continue
and		with 2 drugs. In severe disease, use strepto-
Rifampin	As above	mycin daily until improvement is established
and		(and then twice weekly), and use INH in the 10
Streptomycin	As above	mg/kg/day dose.
or		
Ethambutol	As above	
or		
Aminosalicylic acid	As above	

*In divided doses. When 10 mg/kg/day are used, give also pyridoxine, 25—50 mg/day orally.
†In children, 15—20 mg/kg daily, 600 mg maximum.
‡Monitor visual acuity (see text).

E. Climate: There is little evidence that climate is of any significance in the management of tuberculosis. The availability of good medical care is far more important.

F. Symptomatic Treatment: The patient should be reassured that his symptoms will disappear as the illness is brought under control.

1. Cough—In general, cough in tuberculosis should not be abolished with drugs. Productive cough should be encouraged, and the patient should be taught to cover his mouth and cough with minimal effort. If it becomes necessary to suppress exhausting cough, codeine phosphate, 8—15 mg orally, or other antitussive agents every 4—6 hours as necessary may be helpful. Patients with large cavities who produce copious sputum may be helped by postural drainage. When secondary infection is present, penicillin or broad-spectrum antibiotics may be indicated.

2. Night sweats—Avoid excessive bed clothing.

3. Hemorrhage—The chief danger of hemorrhage in tuberculosis is not sudden death but aspiration of the infected blood and spread of the disease to other parts of the lungs. Antishock therapy should be instituted if bleeding is severe and shock is imminent. Reassurance is most important in allaying apprehension. Phenobarbital sodium, 60—120 mg subcut, may be of value in quieting the apprehensive patient. Use cough inhibitors carefully in the treatment of hemorrhage. Codeine phosphate, 8—15 mg every 4—6 hours, should be given to suppress (but not to abolish) cough. *Caution:* Do not give morphine.

Continued severe bleeding can sometimes be controlled with posterior pituitary injection, 1 ml (10 IU) **slowly** IV in 10 ml of normal saline.

Absolute bed rest is essential during periods of hemorrhage, but complete immobilization is unwise.

Moving from time to time helps bring up secretions. Instruct the patient in the proper method of coughing (see above).

G. Response to Treatment: A favorable symptomatic response to treatment is usually reported within 2—3 weeks; improvement can usually be observed on x-rays within 4 weeks; and positive sputum usually becomes negative within 2 months. Repeat x-ray examination and sputum tests, preferably cultures, should be done at monthly intervals during the first few months of treatment. When improvement is established, the interval between x-ray can be lengthened. When sputum has been negative on 3 consecutive cultures, and surgery is not indicated, a rapid return to normal activities can be permitted. If there is no x-ray improvement or sputum conversion within 3 months, the treatment program should be reevaluated. Tuberculosis is considered "inactive" when the following criteria (National Tuberculosis Association Diagnostic Standards) have been satisfied for at least 6 months: (1) No symptoms; (2) x-ray appearance stable, without evidence of cavitation; and (3) sputum (or gastric or bronchial washings) negative for tubercle bacilli by culture. It should be emphasized that patients who are on a good chemotherapy regimen and are asymptomatic may resume their normal physical activities before the criteria for "inactive" disease have been met.

Prognosis

Very few people die of pulmonary tuberculosis when modern treatment methods are used before the disease reaches a very advanced stage. Most patients, including those with advanced disease, can be restored to a normal state of health within 12 months.

A good treatment program should result in a 95% cure rate in all cases of initially treated disease. Of those who remain inactive 2 years after cessation of proper treatment, less than 1% can be expected to relapse. Lifelong surveillance is advisable for all patients who have had more than minimal disease.

Bobrowitz, I.D., & D.E. Robins: Ethambutol-isoniazid vs PAS-isoniazid in original treatment of pulmonary tuberculosis. Am Rev Resp Dis 96:428–438, 1967.

Cohen, A.G.: *The Drug Treatment of Tuberculosis*. Thomas, 1966.

Committee on Revision of Diagnostic Standards, American Thoracic Society: *Diagnostic Standards and Classification of Tuberculosis*. National Tuberculosis and Respiratory Diseases Association, 1969.

Committee on Therapy, American Thoracic Society: Adrenal corticosteroids and tuberculosis. Am Rev Resp Dis 97:484–485, 1968.

Committee on Therapy, American Thoracic Society: Ethambutol in the treatment of tuberculosis. Am Rev Resp Dis 98:320–321, 1968.

Committee on Therapy, American Thoracic Society: Treatment of drug resistant tuberculosis. Am Rev Resp Dis 94:125–127, 1966.

Crofton, J.: The chemotherapy of bacterial respiratory infections. Am Rev Resp Dis 101:841–859, 1970.

Fox, W.: Changing concepts of the chemotherapy of pulmonary tuberculosis. Am Rev Resp Dis 97:767–790, 1968.

Hinshaw, H.C., & L.H. Garland: *Diseases of the Chest*, 3rd ed. Chap 26–29. Saunders, 1969.

Johnson, R.F., & P.C. Hopewell: Chemotherapy of tuberculosis. Ann Int Med 70:359–367, 1969.

Lester, W.: Tuberculosis: An urban problem. Ann Int Med 68:947–948, 1968.

Mitchell, R.S.: Control of tuberculosis. New England J Med 276:905–910, 1967.

Myers, J.A., Bearman, J.E., & A.C. Botkins: The natural history of tuberculosis in the human body. Dis Chest 53:687–698, 1968.

Newman, R., & others: Rifampin in initial treatment of pulmonary tuberculosis. A USPHS tuberculosis therapy trial. Am Rev Resp Dis 103:461–476, 1971.

Pfuetze, K.H., & D.B. Radner (editors): *Clinical Essentials of Diagnosis and Treatment*. Thomas, 1966.

Public Health Service recommendations on the use of BCG vaccination in the United States. Morbidity Mortality 15:350–351, 1966.

Pyle, M.M., & others: A four-year clinical investigation of ethambutol in initial and retreatment cases of tuberculosis: Efficacy, toxicity, and bacterial resistance. Am Rev Resp Dis 93:428–441, 1966.

Riska, N.: Scandinavian symposium concerning BCG vaccination. Scandinav J Resp Dis 49 (Suppl 65):11–62, 1968.

Stead, W.W.: The clinical spectrum of primary tuberculosis in adults: Confusion with reinfection in the pathogenesis of chronic tuberculosis. Ann Int Med 68:731–745, 1968.

Steele, J.D.: The surgical treatment of pulmonary tuberculosis. Ann Thoracic Surg 6:484–502, 1968.

Strieder, J.W., Laforet, E.G., & J.P. Lynch: Surgery of pulmonary tuberculosis. New England J Med 276:960–965, 1967.

PULMONARY DISEASE DUE TO UNCLASSIFIED ("ATYPICAL") MYCOBACTERIA

It is now recognized that certain mycobacteria other than the tubercle bacillus, which are ordinarily saprophytic, under certain circumstances produce chronic progressive pulmonary disease that is clinically similar to pulmonary tuberculosis. Cervical lymphadenitis is now more commonly due to these organisms (in the USA) than to tuberculosis, and is very similar clinically.

These organisms are identical with tubercle bacilli microscopically and are differentiated by certain cultural characteristics. The atypical mycobacteria are divided into 4 groups, designated groups I, II, III, and IV. Group I mycobacteria are photochromogens, ie, when cultured in vitro they develop a yellow color on exposure to light. The best known group I mycobacteria are *Myco kansasii* and *Myco marinum*. Group II mycobacteria are scotochromogens, characterized by the appearance of yellow-orange coloration in in vitro culture even if grown in the dark. One of the species of this group is *Myco scrofulaceum,* known to cause cervical adenitis. Group III mycobacteria are nonphotochromogens. Like *Myco tuberculosis,* they generally remain a buff color when cultured in vitro. The best known member of this group is *Myco intracellulare* (the Battey organism). Group IV mycobacteria are distinguished by a relatively rapid rate of growth (days instead of weeks) and hence are designated "rapid growers." This group is seldom pathogenic and often appears as a contaminant. *Myco fortuitum,* however, can cause disease in humans.

Groups I and III and, more rarely, group II organisms may produce pulmonary disease which is clinically similar to "typical" tuberculosis but can be distinguished from it by bacterial culture technics. Because atypical acid-fast bacilli may exist as nonpathogenic saprophytes in man, care must be taken to identify them as the cause of disease.

Drug resistance of mycobacteria organisms from a patient who has never been treated suggests that they are atypical mycobacteria. In spite of the in vitro drug resistance, patients with atypical mycobacteriosis may show marked response to these drugs. This is especially true of *Myco kansasii*; more than 80% of patients with this infection may expect cure on the triple drug regimen of isoniazid, aminosalicylic acid, and streptomycin. Group III disease responds less favorably, but with the use of additional drugs a high rate of success may be achieved.

Infection with atypical mycobacteria and subsequent delayed hypersensitivity to them may result in cross-sensitivity to the tuberculin skin test (PPD-tuberculin). The size of these reactions to PPD-T is considerably less than those caused by typical tuberculosis. Further clarification may be obtained by dual testing with PPD-T and PPD-B (antigen derived from the Battey bacillus, or type III atypical mycobacteria).

Skin test antigens from atypical mycobacteria are available. However, their use to precisely identify the specific atypical organism causing infection is very limited, and reliance on bacteriologic results is preferred.

Transmission of atypical disease from man to man has not been reported, so that spread of infection among humans need not be feared. Atypical mycobacteriosis is more frequently seen in people with chronic pulmonary and systemic diseases. As greater numbers of these people survive longer, and with the successful treatment of "typical" tuberculosis, atypical mycobacteriosis may become a more frequent clinical problem.

Treatment with the chemotherapeutic agents which are effective in tuberculosis has been generally less predictable, and surgery may be required.

Fischer, S.A., & others: Retreatment of patients with isoniazid-resistant tuberculosis. Am Rev Resp Dis 97:392–398, 1968.

Goldman, K.P.: Treatment of mycobacterial infection of the lungs. Thorax 23:94–99, 1968.

Johanson, W.G., Jr., & D.P. Nicholson: Pulmonary disease due to *Mycobacterium kansasii.* An analysis of some factors affecting prognosis. Am Rev Resp Dis 99:73–85, 1969.

Palmer, C.E., & L.B. Edwards: Identifying the tuberculous infected. The dual-test technique. JAMA 205:167–169, 1968.

LUNG ABSCESS

Essentials of Diagnosis

- Development of pulmonary symptoms about 2 weeks after possible aspiration, bronchial obstruction, or previous pneumonia.
- Septic fever and sweats, periodic sudden expectoration of large amounts of purulent, foul-smelling or "musty" sputum. Hemoptysis may occur.
- X-ray density with central radiolucency and fluid level.

General Considerations

Lung abscess is an inflammatory lesion which has caused necrosis of lung tissue. It is characterized by the onset of pulmonary symptoms 10–14 days after certain disruptions of bronchopulmonary function or alteration of bronchopulmonary structure by any of the following means: (1) Aspiration of infected material (eg, during oral surgery). (2) Suppression of cough reflex (eg, in coma or with drugs). (3) Bronchial obstruction (eg, postoperative atelectasis, foreign bodies, neoplasms). (4) Pneumonias, especially certain bacterial types. (5) Ischemia (eg, following pulmonary infarction). (6) Septicemia (especially staphylococcal). Infection with pyogenic or anaerobic bacteria in any of these situations causes lung abscess. The usual location is the superior segment of the lower lobe or the lower

portion of the upper lobe of the right lung. Pleuritis and at times rupture into the pleural space, with bronchopleural fistula (empyema, pyopneumothorax), may occur.

If inadequately treated, lung abscess usually becomes chronic.

Clinical Findings

A. Symptoms and Signs: Onset may be abrupt or gradual. Symptoms include fever (septic type), sweats, cough, and chest pain. Cough is often nonproductive at onset. Periodic sudden expectoration of large amounts of purulent, foul-smelling sputum followed by a remission of systemic symptoms is characteristic of lung abscess. Hemoptysis is common.

Pleural pain, especially with coughing, is common because the abscess is often subpleural.

Weight loss, anemia, and pulmonary osteoarthropathy may appear when the abscess becomes chronic (8–12 weeks after onset).

Physical findings may be minimal. Consolidation due to pneumonitis surrounding the abscess is the most frequent finding. Rupture into the pleural space produces signs of fluid or pneumothorax.

B. Laboratory Findings: Sputum is foul-smelling and dirty gray or brown in anaerobic ("putrid") infections; greenish or yellowish with a "musty" but not offensive odor in pyogenic ("nonputrid") infections. Smear and cultures for tubercle bacilli are required, especially in lesions of the upper lobe and in chronic abscess.

Routine and anaerobic sputum cultures are of aid in selection of appropriate antibiotic therapy. Blood cultures may reveal septic embolization as a source of lung abscess.

C. X-Ray Findings: A dense shadow is the initial finding. A central radiolucency, often with a visible fluid level, appears as surrounding densities subside. Tomograms (section films) may be necessary to demonstrate cavitation.

Chest films may also reveal associated primary lesions (eg, bronchogenic carcinoma); allow accurate assessment of response to therapy; provide anatomic localization where surgery is contemplated; and give information on pleural complications. Pleural effusions should be aspirated promptly to detect the presence of empyema.

D. Instrumental Examination: Bronchoscopy should be performed routinely, since up to 10% of lung abscesses are secondary to bronchogenic carcinoma.

Differential Diagnosis

Differentiate from other causes of pulmonary cavitation: tuberculosis, bronchogenic carcinoma, mycotic infections, and staphylococcal pneumonia.

Treatment

Postural drainage and bronchoscopy are important to promote drainage of secretions.

A. Acute Abscess: Intensive antibacterial therapy is necessary to prevent destruction of lung tissue. If the patient improves, long-term treatment (1–2 months) is necessary to assure a cure. If the patient fails to respond, surgery is indicated without delay. Failure of fever to subside after 2 weeks of therapy, abscess diameter of more than 6 cm, and very thick cavity walls are all factors which lessen the likelihood of success with nonsurgical treatment alone.

B. Chronic Abscess: Although some patients with chronic lung abscess can be cured with antibacterial agents, antibiotic therapy is most often employed as a means of reducing infection in preparation for surgery.

Complications

Rupture of pus into the pleural space (empyema) causes severe symptoms: increase in fever, marked pleural pain, and sweating; the patient becomes "toxic" in appearance. In chronic abscess, severe and even fatal hemorrhage may occur. Metastatic brain abscess is a well-recognized complication. Bronchiectasis may occur as a sequel to lung abscess even when the abscess itself is cured. Amyloidosis may occur if suppuration has continued for a long time.

Prognosis

The prognosis is excellent in acute abscess with prompt and intensive antibiotic therapy. The incidence of chronic abscess is consequently low. In chronic cases, surgery is curative.

Ferguson, T.B., & T.H. Burford: The changing pattern of pulmonary suppuration: Surgical implications. Dis Chest 53:396–406, 1968.

Flavell, G.: Respiratory tract disease: Lung abscess. Brit MJ 1:1032–1036, 1966.

Perlman, L.V., Lerner, E., & N. D'Esopo: Clinical classification and analysis of 97 cases of lung abscess. Am Rev Resp Dis 99:390–398, 1969.

Weiss, W., & H.F. Flippin: Treatment of nonspecific primary lung abscess. Arch Int Med 120:8–11, 1968.

BRONCHOGENIC CARCINOMA

Essentials of Diagnosis

- Insidious onset with cough, localized wheeze, or hemoptysis; often asymptomatic.
- May present as an unresolved pneumonia, atelectasis, or pleurisy with bloody effusion, or as a pulmonary nodule seen on x-ray.
- Metastases to other organs may produce initial symptoms.
- Endocrine, biochemical, and neuromuscular disorders (see below) may be the presenting features of bronchogenic carcinoma.

General Considerations

Cancer arising in the mucous membranes of the bronchial tree is the most common intrathoracic malignancy. It occurs predominantly in men (8:1), and may

appear at any age; but most cases occur in the cancer age group (over 40).

The importance of genetic and environmental factors in the etiology of bronchogenic carcinoma is not known. However, the disease is rare in nonsmokers. Local invasion of ribs, mediastinal structures, and nerve plexuses, and distant metastases to the liver, adrenals, kidneys, and brain are common.

Clinical Findings

A. Symptoms and Signs: Persistent, nonproductive cough, hemoptysis, and localized persistent wheeze are the major symptoms produced by bronchial irritation, erosion, and partial obstruction (although there may be no symptoms). These are often attributed to "cigarette cough" or "chronic bronchitis."

Pulmonary infections (pneumonitis, lung abscess) occurring distal to a bronchial obstruction frequently dominate the clinical picture and mask an underlying neoplasm. Any atypical pulmonary infection (persisting, recurring, or responding incompletely to therapy) should suggest carcinoma.

Metastases frequently give rise to the first symptoms, eg, bone or chest pain in osseous or pleural involvement; neurologic symptoms due to brain involvement. ("No craniotomy without a chest film.")

In general, pulmonary signs result from the sequelae of bronchial obstruction, pleural involvement, and mediastinal invasion. When a solitary small lesion does not produce significant bronchial obstruction or pleural involvement, there are no findings. If the lesion is large enough there may be physical (and x-ray) signs of partial or complete bronchial obstruction with associated atelectasis and infection.

Clubbing of the fingers, nonpitting edema of the extremities, and periosteal overgrowth (seen on x-ray) may appear rapidly (and have even been known to precede x-ray signs) with a localized carcinoma and may regress spectacularly following surgical removal.

Local spread is characterized by pleural fluid (bloody effusion is commonly present), signs of mediastinal invasion (pericardial effusion, hoarseness and brassy cough, stridor, dysphagia), and signs of extension to neck structures. Bronchogenic carcinoma in the upper part of the lung may produce Pancoast's syndrome (ipsilateral Horner's syndrome and shoulder-arm pain).

Particular attention must be paid to involvement of scalene nodes and the development of liver nodules, both common sites of metastases. Careful neurologic examination must be performed for evidence of brain metastases.

Certain uncommon metabolic manifestations of bronchogenic carcinoma have been recognized: myasthenic symptoms resembling myasthenia gravis; peripheral neuritis involving both sensory and motor components; clubbing of the digits; a renal sodium-losing picture; Cushing's syndrome; carcinoid syndrome (hyperserotoninemia), even when the tissue is not carcinoid; hypercalcemia not due to osseous metastases; and hyponatremia due to inappropriate excessive secretion of antidiuretic hormone (ADH). The mechanisms of these manifestations are poorly understood. They may disappear when the tumor is removed and do not necessarily signify a grave prognosis.

B. Laboratory Findings: (The definitive stage of diagnosis.)

1. Sputum cytology—In the hands of an expert cytologist, a positive diagnosis of bronchogenic carcinoma can be made in 60—70% of cases on the basis of sputum cytology. Several fresh specimens should be studied.

2. Bronchoscopy—Visualization and biopsy of the tumor is possible in 75% of cases; diagnosis is extended to over 80% with cytologic studies of bronchial washings.

3. Biopsy of the scalene fat pad may reveal lymph nodes containing metastatic carcinoma. This procedure is indicated in the presence of possible hilar or mediastinal node involvement.

4. Mediastinoscopy is an extension of the scalene node biopsy concept by which tissue from deeper nodes (and therefore of greater diagnostic value) is obtained. In experienced hands, it is a valuable procedure.

5. Needle aspiration biopsy of localized lesions under careful fluoroscopic control with an image amplifier appears to be a useful and safe procedure.

6. Exploratory thoracotomy may be the only way to establish the nature of a mass when other studies are negative. The risk is small in the hands of an experienced thoracic surgeon.

C. X-Ray Findings: The chest film offers the greatest possibility of early diagnosis and cure. Solitary nodules which do not cause symptoms or signs can be detected only by this method. Thirty to 60% of these "coin" lesions have proved to be carcinomas at thoracotomy.

The varied x-ray patterns with which bronchogenic carcinoma may present include: perihilar mass (34—36%), atelectasis (segmental or lobar) (21—23%), pleural effusion (5—15%), and mediastinal lymph node enlargement (5—15%).

The follow-up investigation of a pulmonary infection should include search for evidence of delayed or incomplete resolution, associated masses, and hilar or mediastinal lymph node enlargement. The latter can best be demonstrated with barium in the esophagus. Chest films at weekly intervals are mandatory for pneumonias not responding satisfactorily to therapy.

Treatment

Early detection and surgical removal offer the only hope of cure. For this reason, a routine chest x-ray once a year for all men over 40 who are smokers is strongly recommended. Symptoms due to inoperable lesions may be temporarily controlled by nonoperative means. Currently, there is interest in preoperative treatment with supervoltage radiation, with the hope that this will increase operability. The studies to date are inconclusive.

Prognosis

Early diagnosis is important if the lesion is to be found in an operable stage. At present only about 8% of all patients are alive 5 years after diagnosis. Undifferentiated tumors have the worst prognosis. Squamous cell and adenocarcinomas have the same (somewhat better) prognosis.

Adams, W.E.: Current concepts of surgical management of carcinoma of the lung. Dis Chest 51:233—240, 1967.

Caldwell, W.L., & M.A. Bagshaw: Indications for and results of irradiation of carcinoma of the lung. Cancer 22:999—1004, 1968.

Flynn, J.R., Rossi, N.P., & R.L. Lawton: Mediastinoscopy in carcinoma of the lung. Arch Surg 94:243—246, 1967.

Gobbel, W.G., Sawyers, J.L., & W.G. Rhea: Experience with palliative resection and irradiation therapy for carcinoma of the lung. J Thoracic Cardiovas Surg 53:183—191, 1967.

LeRoux, B.T.: Bronchial carcinoma. Thorax 23:136—143, 1968.

Morton, O.L., Itabashi, H.H., & O.F. Grimes: Nonmetastatic neurological complications of bronchogenic carcinoma: The carcinomatous neuromyopathies. J Thoracic Cardiovas Surg 51:14—29, 1966.

Paulson, D.L.: *Carcinoma of the Lung.* Curr Prob Surg, Nov 1967.

Pearson, F.G.: An evaluation of mediastinoscopy in the management of presumably operable bronchogenic carcinoma. J Thoracic Cardiovas Surg 55:617—625, 1968.

Remington, J.: Smoking, sputum and lung cancer. Brit MJ 1:732—734, 1968.

Stenseth, J.H., Clagett, O.T., & L.B. Woolner: Hypertrophic pneumonary osteoarthropathy. Dis Chest 52:62—68, 1967.

Stevens, G.M., & others: Needle aspiration biopsy of localized pulmonary lesions. California Med 106:92—97, 1966.

Valaitis, J., & others: Bronchogenic carcinoma in situ in asymptomatic high-risk population of smokers. J Thoracic Cardiovas Surg 57:325—332, 1969.

Watson, W.L.: *Lung Cancer. A Study of 5000 Memorial Hospital Cases.* Mosby, 1968.

Weiss, W., Boucot, K., & D.A. Cooper: The Philadelphia Pulmonary Neoplasm Research Project. JAMA 216:2119—2123, 1971.

BRONCHIAL ADENOMA

Bronchial adenoma (neoplasm arising in the glandular structures of the bronchial mucous membranes) is the most common (80%) "benign" bronchopulmonary neoplasm. Sex distribution is equal; age incidence is somewhat lower than that of bronchogenic carcinoma. It is locally invasive.

The great majority of bronchial adenomas arise in the proximal bronchi. The onset is insidious. Cough and localized wheeze are similar to those of bronchogenic carcinoma. These tumors are quite vascular; hemoptysis is common, occurring in 25—30% of cases.

Since bronchial adenoma does not tend to exfoliate, sputum examination is not helpful. Differentiation from bronchogenic carcinoma thus depends upon bronchoscopic biopsy or exploratory thoracotomy.

In many cases bronchial adenoma can be distinguished from bronchogenic carcinoma only by histologic and cytologic study. Distinguish also from other benign obstructions, eg, foreign body, tuberculous bronchial stenosis.

Treatment

Pedunculated and locally noninvasive adenomas may sometimes be removed by bronchoscopy, but serious bleeding can occur (even with biopsy alone). It is usually necessary to perform an exploratory thoracotomy and remove the neoplasm surgically.

The prognosis is good. The tumor tends to be locally invasive, but 5–10% metastasize slowly. Fatalities are not usually due to metastases but are associated with bronchiectasis, pneumonitis, hemorrhages, the complications of surgery, or asphyxiation secondary to obstruction by the tumor.

Baldwin, J.N., & O.F. Grimes: Bronchial adenomas. Surg Gynec Obst 124:813–818, 1967.

Batson, J.F., Gale, J.W., & R.C. Hickey: Bronchial adenomata. Arch Surg 92:623–630, 1966.

Donahue, J.K., Weichert, R.F., & J.L. Ochsner: Bronchial adenoma. Ann Surg 167:873–885, 1968.

BRONCHIOLAR CARCINOMA
(Alveolar Cell Carcinoma, Pulmonary Adenomatosis)

Bronchiolar carcinoma is a relatively uncommon pulmonary malignancy (1–5% of lung cancers) which grows slowly and metastasizes late. In contrast to bronchogenic carcinoma, it is often bilateral. Pulmonary architecture is not altered. The neoplastic cells line the alveoli and bronchioles. Sex distribution is equal. Most cases occur in the age group from 50–60.

Since this neoplasm originates in the bronchiolar or alveolar lining, the major bronchi are not involved and symptoms develop late. Copious watery or mucoid sputum is the major sign. With widespread lung involvement, dyspnea, cyanosis, dullness to percussion, clubbing, and cor pulmonale develop.

Cytologic examination of sputum is valuable since this tumor commonly exfoliates.

The usual x-ray picture is of bilateral multiple lung nodules or areas of consolidation (or both), but solitary nodules may be present and calcification may occur.

The bilateral occurrence, long survival, and relative absence of symptoms help distinguish bronchiolar carcinoma from bronchogenic carcinoma and bronchial adenoma; however, bronchiolar carcinoma may present as a single nodule and with calcification, thus requiring differentiation also from tuberculomas, metastatic lesions, and mycotic infections (granulomas).

Treatment

If involvement is unilateral and there is no evidence of extrapulmonary extension, surgical excision may be warranted.

Prognosis

With treatment, survival may be up to 6 or 7 years. Widespread pulmonary involvement is the usual cause of death. Metastases occur in 50% of cases.

Hewlett, T.H., & others: Bronchiolar carcinoma of the lung: Review of 39 patients. J Thoracic Cardiovas Surg 48:614–624, 1964.

Knudson, R.J., & others: Unusual cancer of the lung. II. Bronchiolar carcinoma of the lung. Dis Chest 48:628–633, 1965.

Kress, M.B., & W.B. Allan: Bronchiolo-alveolar tumors of the lung. Bull Johns Hopkins Hosp 112:115–133, 1963.

ALVEOLAR PROTEINOSIS

Alveolar proteinosis is a chronic, progressive, often fatal disease of unknown etiology (and unrecognized before 1958) characterized by progressive dyspnea, cough, intermittent fever, pulmonary infiltrations on x-ray, and pulmonary insufficiency of the alveolar-capillary block syndrome type. The diagnosis is based on the histologic findings (at biopsy or autopsy) of striking replacement of the alveolar air spaces with a granular, amorphous material which stains characteristically with periodic acid-Schiff stain. The chemical similarity between this material, which appears to be a phospholipid (palmitoyl lecithin), and the surface-active agent normally secreted by the alveolar epithelium suggests the possibility of an abnormal hypersecretion of this substance. These patients seem to be prone to the development of nocardiosis and other fungus infections.

Ramirez has described a method of irrigating the involved lung with heparin solution via an endobronchial catheter. Large quantities of the proteinaceous material can thus be removed, and this results in clearing by x-ray and improvement in pulmonary function.

Gerard has recently reported a case treated successfully with intensive IPPB and nebulized proteolytic enzyme.

Gerard, F.P., Sabety, A.M., & W. Lurie: Pulmonary alveolar proteinosis: Practical management. J Thoracic Cardiovas Surg 57:273–275, 1969.

Ramirez-R, J.: Pulmonary alveolar proteinosis. Arch Int Med 119:147–156, 1967.

Ramirez-R, J., & W.R. Harlan, Jr.: Pulmonary alveolar proteinosis. Nature and origin of alveolar lipid. Am J Med 45:502–512, 1969.

Ramirez-R, J.: Alveolar proteinosis: Importance of pulmonary lavage. Am Rev Resp Dis 103:666–678, 1971.

DESQUAMATIVE INTERSTITIAL PNEUMONIA

This is apparently a distinct type of interstitial pneumonia of unknown etiology. It occurs predominantly in adults, with an equal sex distribution. Gradually increasing exertional dyspnea and chronic cough with little or no sputum production are the principal symptoms, and the characteristic x-ray changes are diffuse "ground glass" densities in the periphery of the lower lobes. Pulmonary function measurements show "alveolo-capillary block" to be the principal physiologic disturbance. Histologically, masses of large desquamated alveolar cells fill the alveoli without disturbing the basic architecture and without necrosis. The natural course of the disease has not been determined. A favorable response to corticosteroids has been noted in most cases.

Klocke, R.A., & others: Desquamative interstitial pneumonia. Ann Int Med 66:498–506, 1967.
Liebow, A.A., Steer, A., & J.G. Billingsley: Desquamative interstitial pneumonia. Am J Med 39:369–404, 1965.

SILICOSIS

Essentials of Diagnosis

- History of exposure to dust containing silicon dioxide (eg, hard-rock mining, sandblasting).
- Characteristic x-ray changes: Bilateral nodules, fibrosis, hilar lymphadenopathy.
- Recurrent respiratory infections.
- **Note:** Tuberculosis is a common complication.

General Considerations

The pneumoconioses are chronic fibrotic pulmonary diseases caused by inhalation of inorganic occupational dusts. Free silica (silicon dioxide) is by far the most common offender. Prolonged exposure is usually required.

Clinical Findings

A. Symptoms and Signs: Symptoms may be absent or may consist only of unusual susceptibility to upper respiratory tract infections, "bronchitis," and pneumonia. Dyspnea on exertion is the commonest presenting complaint. It may progress slowly for years. Cough usually develops and is dry initially but later becomes productive, frequently with blood-streaked sputum. Severe and, occasionally, fatal hemoptysis may occur.

Physical findings may be absent in patients with advanced silicosis.

B. Laboratory Findings: Sputum studies for acid-fast bacilli are indicated to rule out silicotuberculosis.

Lung biopsy is occasionally indicated to establish the diagnosis for compensation purposes.

C. X-Ray Findings: Chest x-rays are not diagnostic but often strongly suggest the diagnosis. Abnormalities are usually bilateral, symmetric, and predominant in the inner midlung fields. Small nodules tend to be of uniform size and density. Enlargement of hilar nodes is a relatively early finding. Peripheral calcification of the nodes, giving an "eggshell" appearance, may occur later. Fibrosis is manifested by fine linear markings and reticulation. Coalescence of nodules produces larger densities. Associated emphysema gives an x-ray picture of increased radiolucency, often quite striking at the lung bases.

Treatment

No specific treatment is available. Symptomatic treatment is indicated for chronic cough and wheezing. When tuberculosis occurs, antituberculous drugs must be continued for life. In the presence of a positive tuberculin skin test and no other evidence of active tuberculosis, isoniazid, 300 mg daily, should be given indefinitely.

Prognosis

Gradually progressive dyspnea may be present for years. The development of complications, especially tuberculosis, markedly worsens the prognosis.

Gaensler, E.A., & W.W. Addington: Current concepts: Asbestos or ferruginous bodies. New England J Med 280:488–491, 1969.
Gaensler, E.A., & others: Graphite pneumoconiosis of electrotypers. Am J Med 41:864–882, 1966.
Schepers, G.W.H.: Lung disease caused by inorganic and organic dust. Dis Chest 44:133–140, 1963.
Therdos, P.A.: Lung biopsy in the diagnosis of the pneumonoconioses. Dis Chest 53:271–281, 1968.
Whipple, H.E. (editor): Biological effects of asbestosis. Ann New York Acad Sc 132:1–766, 1965.

OTHER PNEUMOCONIOSES

The following substances, when inhaled, cause varying degrees of pulmonary inflammation, fibrosis, emphysema, and disability, usually to a lesser degree than silicon dioxide: coal dust, bauxite (aluminum and silicon), asbestos (dehydrated calcium-magnesium silicate), mica dust (aluminum silicates), talc (hydrous magnesium silicate), graphite (crystallized carbon plus silicon dioxide), beryllium, and diatomaceous earth. The latter is almost pure silicon dioxide but produces effects essentially like those of silicosis only when heated (flux calcined) in the manufacture of abrasives.

Identification of these pulmonary dust diseases depends upon a careful inquiry into possible occupational or casual exposure.

Treatment is symptomatic.

See references under Silicosis, above.

TABLE 6–3. Pneumoconioses.*

Disease and Occupation	Causative Particle and Pathology	Clinical Features	X-Ray Findings
Silicosis (mining, drilling, blasting, grinding, abrasive manufacture; various other processes exposing silica to high temperatures, such as iron moulding or ceramic manufacture)	Free silica (SiO_2, particle size about 3 μ), crystobalite, and tridymite (toxic isomers produced by exposure of silica to high temperatures) cause tissue reactions producing nodules, fibrosis, lymphatic blockage emphysema, and hilar adenopathy.	Required exposure is 2–20 years. Dyspnea on exertion, dry cough. Frequent infections, especially tuberculosis. Pulmonary insufficiency, chronic cor pulmonale.	Hilar adenopathy; peripheral ("eggshell") calcification of hilar nodes; nodules (inner, midlung fields), overall increased radiolucency, fibrosis. Signs of associated tuberculosis.
Asbestosis (asbestos mining and processing)	Magnesium silicate (particle size 20–200 μ), rod-shaped bodies visible in tissue sections and sputum, causing obstruction of bronchioles, distal atelectasis, fibrosis (little nodulation).	Required exposure 2–8 years. Dyspnea early. Productive cough. Pulmonary insufficiency. "Corns" on skin of extremities (imbedded particles). Possible increased incidence of bronchogenic carcinoma and malignant mesothelioma.	Fine reticular markings in lower lung fields. Thickening of pleura ("ground glass" appearance), obliteration of costophrenic angles. Bilateral pleural calcifications.
Berylliosis (beryllium production, manufacture of fluorescent powders)	Beryllium particles. **Acute:** Patchy infiltrations, resembling bronchial pneumonia. **Chronic:** Alveolar septal granuloma causing fine nodules. Fibrosis not prominent. Elastic tissue damaged, causing emphysema. No hilar adenopathy.	**Acute:** After a few weeks of exposure, upper respiratory symptoms; "bronchitis," "pneumonia" later. **Chronic:** Required exposure 6–18 months. Dyspnea, cough, weight loss, cyanosis, skin lesions, pulmonary insufficiency, cor pulmonale.	**Acute:** Clear at first, then patchy infiltrations. **Chronic:** Scattered minute ("sandpaper") nodules. Later, larger nodules, diffuse reticular markings. No hilar adenopathy.
Bauxite pneumoconiosis (Shaver's disease; aluminosis)	May be due to other toxic contaminants (eg, crystobalite, tridymite) rather than aluminum dust per se, causing fibrosis, hilar adenopathy, atelectasis.	Required exposure is several months to 2 years. Dyspnea (marked pulmonary insufficiency). Attacks of spontaneous pneumothorax.	Hilar and mediastinal adenopathy, irregularity of diaphragms, fibrosis, emphysema.
Anthracosis (rarely dissociated from silicosis) (mining, city dwellers)	Coal dust, causing black discoloration of lungs, nodes, distant organs (nodules rare).	Progressive disease (fibrosis, emphysema) reported in Welsh soft-coal workers. Silica may be an important factor.	"Reticulation," fine nodules. Coal dust may produce large densities by deposition without fibrosis.
Siderosis (iron ore processing, metal drilling, electric arc welding)	Iron oxides, metallic iron, causing "red" (oxides) and "black" (metallic) discoloration of lung. "Red" type leads to fibrosis. "Black" type associated with silicosis.	Symptoms are those of associated silicosis.	Dependent mainly on associated silicosis.

*Actual exposure is rarely to one dust alone.

PULMONARY GRANULOMATOSIS DUE TO INHALED ORGANIC ANTIGENS
("Farmer's Lung")

Inhalation of various organic dusts can produce an acute granulomatous interstitial pneumonitis, usually in agricultural workers. Causative agents include moldy hay, mushroom compost, bagasse (moldy sugar cane residue), avian excreta and feathers, redwood sawdust ("sequoiosis"), and maple bark.

The onset is acute, 6–8 hours after inhalation, with fever, chills, cough, dyspnea, and rales and rhonchi. The disease is usually reversible on removal from the irritating agent, but repeated exposure may lead to progressive emphysema and pulmonary fibrosis.

Extremely rapid onset, immunologic studies, and dramatic response to adrenocortical steroids suggest that this is a hypersensitivity phenomenon, possibly to fungi associated with the dust.

Hapke, E.J., & others: Farmer's lung. A clinical, radiographic, functional, and serologic correlation of acute and chronic stages. Thorax 23:451–468, 1968.

Nicholson, D.P.: Bagasse worker's lung. Am Rev Resp Dis 97:546–560, 1968.

Rankin, J., & others: Pulmonary granulomatoses due to inhaled organic antigens. M Clin North America 51:459–482, 1967.

SILO-FILLER'S DISEASE

Silo-filler's disease is a recently recognized agricultural industrial pulmonary disease caused by inhalation of nitrogen dioxide fumes emanating from silos which have been freshly filled (eg, with corn or alfalfa).

The initial phase, appearing promptly after exposure, consists of cough, dyspnea, and weakness. This is followed by a quiescent phase, with some persistence of dyspnea and weakness, followed by a second acute phase with fever, chills, malaise, increasing cough and dyspnea, tachypnea and tachycardia, and diffuse rales and rhonchi. Extensive miliary infiltrates are present on x-ray. Death may occur within 2–3 weeks after onset, or there may be gradual recovery over a period of 1–2 months.

Oxygen (including intermittent positive pressure breathing), antibiotics, and corticosteroids have been used in treatment.

Preventive measures include avoiding entry into silos if fumes are present and assuring good ventilation of silos by means of open doors and mechanical blowers.

Donoghue, F.E., & H.W. Schmidt: Farmer's lung and silo-filler's disease. M Clin North America 48:903–910, 1964.

IDIOPATHIC PULMONARY HEMOSIDEROSIS

Idiopathic pulmonary hemosiderosis is a chronic, relapsing, often fatal disease of unknown cause characterized by recurrent hemoptysis, cough, frequently dyspnea, and marked hypochromic anemia with the usual hematologic features of iron deficiency anemia. In some instances it has been associated with fatal glomerulonephritis (Goodpasture's syndrome). Typical nephrotic syndrome has also been reported. Nodular or reticular infiltrates are characteristically present on chest x-rays during exacerbations and usually clear during remissions. The chest findings in association with severe hypochromic anemia should suggest the diagnosis. The characteristic hematologic feature is the presence of hemosiderin-laden macrophages in the lungs.

There is no treatment.

Ognibene, A.J., & D.E. Johnson: Idiopathic pulmonary hemosiderosis in adults. Arch Int Med 111:503–509, 1963.

PULMONARY ATELECTASIS

Essentials of Diagnosis

- Acute: sudden marked symptoms of dyspnea, cyanosis, fever, even if area is small.
- Chronic: almost no symptoms even if area is large.
- Homogeneous density on x-ray.
- Mediastinal shift toward involved side, diaphragm up, narrowing of intercostal spaces.

General Considerations

Pulmonary atelectasis is a collapse and nonaeration of lung segments distal to a complete bronchial obstruction produced by a wide variety of diseases. A clinical history consistent with retention of secretions, aspiration of a foreign body, or bronchial infection can usually be obtained.

Postoperative atelectasis is the most common variety (occurs in 2–5% of patients after major surgery). The onset is usually 24–72 hours after operation.

Bronchial obstruction prevents entry of air into the distal segment lobe or even the entire lung.

Compensatory changes occur to "fill in the space" previously occupied by the collapsed lung: (1) shift of the mediastinum toward the side of collapse, (2) upward displacement of the diaphragm on the involved side, and (3) overexpansion of remaining lung tissue on both sides ("compensatory emphysema").

Compression of the lung from without (eg, pleural effusion) is of far less physiologic significance than atelectasis due to obstruction.

Clinical Findings

A. Symptoms and Signs: The severity of symptoms depends upon the site of obstruction and the rate at which it develops, and the presence or absence of infection in the atelectatic area. The more acute the onset (eg, postoperative atelectasis), the more marked the symptoms. Massive collapse in acute atelectasis causes marked dyspnea, cyanosis, tachycardia, chest pain, and fever. Lesser degrees of collapse produce variable symptoms, but even a small acute atelectasis may produce symptoms.

Symptoms, eg, wheezing and cough, are often due to the obstruction itself or to infection distal to the block.

The physical findings in acute atelectasis include tachycardia (often out of proportion to the amount of fever), decrease of chest motion on the affected side, with narrowing of intercostal spaces; displacement of the mediastinum to the involved side, as shown by the shift of the trachea, cardiac apex, and dullness; percussion dullness; and decreased to absent vocal fremitus, breath sounds, and voice sounds. Bronchial breath sounds are occasionally present over the atelectatic area and may alternate with diminished breath sounds.

In chronic atelectasis, displacement of the mediastinum is modified by the slowness of compensatory changes, rigidity of the mediastinum due to the underlying disease, and changes of the elasticity of the surrounding diseased lung.

B. X-Ray Findings: The collapsed segment is visible as a homogeneous "ground glass" density. The atelectatic portion of lung is denser than a comparable area of consolidation because no air is present with the fluid. The volume of the collapsed lobe diminishes markedly. The diaphragm is displaced upward on the side of the collapse. Mediastinal shift to the involved side is a major diagnostic feature. Pleural fluid is not infrequently noted on the affected side, but it fails to displace the mediastinum back to the midline and the fluid line is seen to run downward and laterally from the midline instead of upward and laterally (as in fluid without atelectasis).

C. Instrumental Examination: Bronchoscopy is very helpful in diagnosis and treatment.

Differential Diagnosis

Pulmonary atelectasis must be distinguished from lobar pneumonia, other pulmonary infections, pulmonary infarction, and pleural effusion.

Complications

The sequelae of unrelieved obstruction with atelectasis are infection, destruction of lung tissue with fibrosis, and bronchiectasis.

Treatment

A. Postoperative Atelectasis: Force the patient to cough and to hyperventilate. Bronchodilatation by aerosol with an intermittent positive pressure apparatus (eg, Bennett, Bird, or other machines) has been demonstrated to resolve many cases of postoperative atelectasis. The addition of a mucolytic agent such as acetylcysteine (Mucomyst®) may help dissolve plugs of mucus. The apparatus should be used for 30 minutes every 2–3 hours for 24 hours before deciding that other measures are necessary. The use of IPPB postoperatively in patients with chronic pulmonary disease is also effective in preventing atelectasis.

Aspiration of the tracheobronchial tree with a soft rubber catheter passed blindly through the nasopharynx or with the aid of a laryngoscope is often effective.

If the above fail or atelectasis is massive, aspiration of mucus by bronchoscopy is indicated.

Give procaine penicillin G, 600,000 units IM, twice daily, or tetracycline, 250 mg orally 4 times daily.

B. Spontaneous Atelectasis: Bronchoscopy is indicated to determine the nature of the obstruction and to institute appropriate treatment.

Prognosis

Although the outlook is usually good, unrelieved collapse may result in death (when massive) or in prolonged morbidity (when lobar or segmental).

Thomas, P.A., Lynch, R.E., & E.H. Merrigan: Incidence of contralateral pulmonary atelectasis after thoracotomy: An evaluation of preventive after care. Dis Chest 51:288–292, 1967.

ADULT RESPIRATORY DISTRESS SYNDROME
("Shock" Lung, "Pump" Lung)

This condition is being more frequently recognized, and its pathogenesis and causes are becoming clearer. It occurs after massive injury with shock, heart-lung perfusion procedures, fat embolism, aspiration pneumonia, and certain viral pneumonias. The pathogenesis appears to involve a leak in the pulmonary capillary endothelium with interstitial edema and alveolar hemorrhage and loss of surfactant, resulting in atelectasis, the formation of a hyaline membrane, and plugging of small arteries. This results in a severe diffusion defect and disturbance of the perfusion-ventilation ratio (physiologic shunting). Loss of pulmonary compliance (stiff lungs) and a decrease in functional residual capacity occur.

A common aggravating factor is overloading of the circulation with blood and fluids in the treatment of traumatic shock. Dependence on central venous pressure measurements as a guide to fluid replacement will cause this error in this situation. Urine output, state of consciousness, stable vital signs, and warm extremities are safer guides.

Clinical Findings

A. Symptoms and Signs: The principal symptoms are progressive dyspnea and cyanosis following one of the predisposing conditions listed above. Physical examination usually shows dyspnea, cyanosis, grunting respiration, intercostal retraction, and signs of progressive pulmonary consolidation. When assisted ventilation is instituted, progressively higher pressures are needed to maintain the tidal volume.

B. Laboratory Findings: Laboratory studies typically show a reduced PaO_2, a normal or decreased $PaCO_2$ (elevated $PaCO_2$ is an ominous sign), and a normal or elevated arterial blood pH.

C. X-Ray Findings: Chest x-rays show patches of pneumonia initially which coalesce to form larger areas of consolidation. There is usually a 12–24 hour delay between the injury and the appearance of infection.

Treatment

A. Oxygen: Maintain oxygenation with assisted respirations. A volume controlled machine is often necessary because of the increased airway resistance. In this condition the use of continuous positive pressure throughout the breathing cycle has been shown to be helpful. In addition to providing adequate tidal volume (15–20 mg/kg is desirable), the aim is to maintain a pressure of about 5 cm water at the end of expiration. The newer positive pressure machine such as the Bennett MA-1 and the Ohio-560 have this ability. (Other machines can provide a variable resistance to expiration but without a sustained pressure between the end of expiration and the next breath. A simple system can be improvised, using a large flex tube attached to the exhalation port of a pressure-controlled ventilator and placing the other end 5 cm under water.)

Oxygen is given in a high enough concentration to maintain the PaO_2 between 60–80 mm Hg. The concentration of oxygen in the inspired air should be reduced as soon as feasible.

B. Fluid Therapy: Blood and sodium-containing intravenous infusions should be kept to the minimum needed to sustain circulation. If pulmonary edema develops, salt-poor albumin and intravenous furosemide (Lasix®) may be used.

C. Antibiotic Therapy: Antibiotics should be used specifically–if possible, according to sensitivity results. The danger of superinfection following the use of broad-spectrum antibiotics is great in these patients.

D. Corticosteroids: Corticosteroids in large doses intravenously are helpful when pneumonia, fat embolism, or aspiration is the underlying cause. They have not been effective in "shock" lung secondary to trauma.

Course & Prognosis

These patients may require many days of this type of support before the process is reversed. Serial x-rays and blood gas studies are the best guides to treatment. The mortality rate remains high.

Ashbaugh, D.G., & others: Acute respiratory distress in adults. Lancet 2:319–323, 1967.

Ashbaugh, D.G., & others: Continuous positive pressure breathing (CPPB) in adult respiratory distress syndrome. J Thoracic Cardiovas Surg 57:31–41, 1969.

Bredenberg, C.E., & others: Respiratory failure in shock. Ann Surg 169:392, 1969.

Murray, J.F.: Shock lung. California Med 112:43–50, Feb, 1970.

CHRONIC PULMONARY EMPHYSEMA

Essentials of Diagnosis

- Insidious onset of exertional dyspnea; dyspnea at rest only in late stages; no orthopnea.
- Prolonged expiratory phase and wheezing are common.
- Productive cough, often ineffective in clearing the bronchi.
- Barrel chest; use of accessory muscles of respiration.
- Over-aerated lung fields and flattened diaphragm on chest x-ray are frequently seen.

General Considerations

Emphysema is characterized by diffuse distention and over-aeration of the alveoli, disruption of intra-alveolar septa, loss of pulmonary elasticity, increased lung volume, and associated impairment of pulmonary function due to disturbed ventilation and altered gas and blood flow. Partial obstruction of smaller bronchi is frequently present.

Emphysema may occur (1) in the absence of a history of preceding chronic lung disease (etiology is unknown, although an inherent defect in pulmonary elastic tissue has been suggested); (2) secondary to chronic diffuse bronchial obstruction (eg, bronchitis, asthma); or (3) in association with fibrotic pulmonary disease (eg, silicosis, fibrosis). There is no justification for the view that glass-blowing, wind-instrument playing, and similar occupations cause emphysema. Many investigators feel that cigarette smoking is a major cause.

A predilection for chronic obstructive pulmonary disease has been noted in certain families. In 1964, the association between a deficiency of the glycoprotein, alpha$_1$ antitrypsin, and obstructive pulmonary disease was reported, suggesting a genetic factor. More recently, a hereditary association has been described which was independent of alpha$_1$ antitrypsin deficiency. Both hereditary factors and smoking appear to be important in the causation of emphysema.

Emphysema is the most common cause of chronic pulmonary insufficiency and chronic cor pulmonale. It is predominantly a disease of men over the age of 45.

Localized areas of emphysema occur in many pulmonary diseases and are usually of no importance. Giant bullae sometimes occur and may cause spontaneous pneumothorax. When these are localized and not associated with generalized emphysematous changes, surgical excision may be indicated.

The term bronchitis has often been used to designate this clinical entity (especially in Britain), and some authors prefer the term chronic obstructive bronchopulmonary disease.

Clinical Findings

A. Symptoms and Signs: The diagnosis of physiologically significant emphysema depends upon a history of exertional dyspnea and chronic productive cough (the most frequent presenting symptoms). Onset is usually insidious. Dyspnea at rest and orthopnea are unusual even with advanced emphysema (except with superimposed acute bronchial disease). Productive cough is common. Cough is frequently aggravated by intercurrent respiratory infections. Bouts of wheezing are not unusual. Minor respiratory infections which would be of no consequence to patients with normal lungs can produce fatal or near-fatal disturbances of respiratory function in the patient with emphysema.

Weakness, lethargy, anorexia, and weight loss are due to hypoxia, the increased muscular activity required for breathing, and respiratory acidosis. When ventilatory insufficiency is severe, headache, impaired sensorium, asterixis (flapping tremor), papilledema, and miosis may be encountered.

In the typical patient with advanced emphysema the chest is maintained in a fixed inspiratory position ("barrel-shaped") with increased anteroposterior diameter. The neck appears shortened. Accessory muscles of respiration (sternomastoids, pectorals, scaleni) are employed along with overuse of abdominal and upper intercostal muscles. Palpation confirms decreased costal motion, with a tendency of the entire thorax to move vertically as a unit. Diffuse hyperresonance, especially at the bases, masks the normal cardiac and hepatic dullness. Descent of diaphragms is decreased to absent. Breath sounds are diminished, with a prolonged and high-pitched expiratory phase. Scattered musical wheezes and rhonchi are frequently present.

In the absence of measuring equipment, several simple procedures can be used during the physical examination to confirm the presence of significant ventilatory obstruction. The total vital capacity should normally be exhaled in 3 seconds with maximum effort. This can easily be timed with a stopwatch or second hand. If emptying time is 5–6 seconds, moderate obstructive disease is present; if greater than 7 seconds, severe obstruction is present.

The match test is also helpful. If the patient is unable to blow out a match held 6 inches from the open mouth, severe ventilatory obstruction is usually present.

The liver is depressed by the flattened diaphragm and may be palpable 2–3 cm below the costal margin. The lips and nail beds are frequently cyanotic. The face is frequently ruddy to ruddy-cyanotic, reflecting anoxia and compensatory polycythemia. Clubbing of the fingers and toes is occasionally encountered, along with other manifestations of pulmonary osteoarthropathy.

Peripheral edema and venous distention occur if right heart failure (cor pulmonale) is present.

B. X-Ray Findings: Hyper-illumination of lung fields is most marked at the bases and behind the sternum. The anteroposterior chest diameter is increased. Low, flat diaphragms move poorly on fluoroscopy. Bullae may appear as annular translucencies, occasionally of immense size. Scintillation scanning and pulmonary angiography are helpful in evaluating the non-affected lung when excision of large bullae is being considered.

C. Laboratory Findings: Vital capacity may be normal in emphysema even though extensive disease is present. Increased residual air volume is the most characteristic abnormality, but its determination is not a clinical procedure. A reduction in the timed vital capacity is a simple and direct measure of obstruction and air-trapping.

Ventilatory insufficiency causes alveolar hypoxia and decreased Pa_{O_2} in the blood. If this condition persists, the Pa_{CO_2} increases as a result of the inability of the lungs to blow off CO_2. Initially, this developing acidosis is compensated for by retention of bicarbonate by the kidneys. When this mechanism fails, the pH of the blood falls and there is progressive respiratory acidosis. Measurement of these blood gases and the blood pH is now readily available in most hospitals. The determinations should be done on arterial blood. Pa_{O_2} less than 50 mm Hg or a Pa_{CO_2} greater than 50 mm Hg signifies respiratory failure. The pH may remain normal in the presence of respiratory acidosis (elevated Pa_{CO_2}) until the compensatory mechanisms are overcome.

The red blood count and packed cell volume may be increased (secondary polycythemia), but marked polycythemia is not a frequent finding in emphysema. Absence of the usual $alpha_1$ globulin peak in the serum protein electrophoretic pattern may be a clue to the hereditary origin of the emphysema ($alpha_1$ antitrypsin deficiency).

Differential Diagnosis

The dyspnea of chronic pulmonary emphysema must be distinguished from that due to congestive heart failure, chronic bronchitis, and asthma.

Complications

Recurrent acute, suppurative infections of the bronchioles are manifested by increase in dyspnea, cyanosis, fever, and the production of purulent sputum. Such infections are a grave matter in patients with poor pulmonary function.

Indiscriminate prolonged administration of oxygen at ambient pressure to patients in respiratory acidosis may remove the last remaining stimulus to respiration, ie, hypoxia, resulting in hypoventilation, increasing acidosis, and coma. Sedatives must be avoided.

Spontaneous pneumothorax may result from rupture of an emphysematous bleb into the pleural space.

Congestive right heart failure (cor pulmonale) may result from chronic emphysema, worsening the prognosis.

Treatment

Since many patients have an associated chronic bronchitis with some elements of spasm, therapy is generally similar to that outlined for chronic bronchitis or chronic asthma. Give bronchodilators to relieve spasm and sputum liquefiers (saturated solution of potassium iodide, oral fluids, aerosols) to thin tenacious secretions. Control infection with specific antibiotics (or tetracycline if bacterial sensitivity cannot be determined). Prolonged antimicrobial therapy may be necessary.

If the above methods fail to relieve bronchial obstruction, corticosteroids may give dramatic relief. For long-term use they should be used in minimum dosage with careful attention to the dangers and precautions outlined in Chapter 18.

Oxygen therapy is usually necessary but must be used cautiously and the patient observed frequently to prevent hypoventilation or coma due to CO_2 retention. Low-flow nasal O_2 (2–3 liters/minute) can be used if the patient is closely observed for hypoventilation. Monitoring of the PaO_2, $PaCO_2$, and arterial blood pH should be done initially and repeated in 2–3 hours if possible. Early acidosis can sometimes be corrected by the use of low-flow oxygen alone. In the absence of monitoring, intermittent positive pressure ventilatory assistance should also be used (15–30 minutes every 1–4 hours) until clinical improvement occurs.

Maintain optimal mechanical efficiency of the diaphragm. Exercises to strengthen the abdominal muscles and permit more complete exhalation should be encouraged. There is renewed interest in the use of long-term oxygen therapy during exercise since improved portable, light-weight containers for liquid oxygen have been developed. Improvement in exercise tolerance and decreased morbidity have been reported in selected patients with chronic lung disease. Long-term results from the commoner methods of treatment mentioned above have not been impressive.

For the treatment of chronic pulmonary heart disease, see discussion in Chapter 7.

Respiratory failure: When alveolar hypoventilation occurs as a result of chronic pulmonary disease or a number of other causes and the compensatory mechanisms are overcome, severe respiratory acidosis occurs. *This is a medical emergency.* The general principles of treatment are as follows: (1) Improve ventilation and provide sufficient oxygen to sustain tissue needs. (2) Correct electrolyte and fluid imbalance. (3) Treat infection, bronchospasm, heart failure, and other contributory factors. These are discussed in the following paragraphs.

(1) Ventilation and oxygen therapy: Ventilation must be improved immediately. A clear airway is essential. If this cannot be assured—especially if the patient cannot cooperate—an oral or nasal endotracheal tube or a tracheostomy tube should be inserted immediately. Emergency ventilation can be provided by a self-inflating bag or even mouth-to-mouth resuscitation until proper equipment can be obtained.

The commonest devices for prolonged assisted ventilation are the pressure cycled IPPB machines (eg, Bennett, Bird). These will assist spontaneous respiration or can be set to cycle automatically in the presence of apnea or feeble respiratory efforts. When using pressure-sensitive machines, the total volume being produced should be measured by a Wright respirometer. When airway resistance is too great (> 30 cm H_2O), machines that deliver a predetermined volume (Air Shields, Bennett MA-1, Emerson, Engstrom, Ohio-560) are necessary.

Arterial blood should be drawn for blood gas and pH determinations as soon as possible and should be repeated at least hourly until the patient's condition has been stabilized.

Oxygen is given either via an oxygen-driven IPPB device (use the air dilution setting) or by adding supplemental oxygen to an IPPB system driven by compressed air. Some believe that the latter method gives more precise control of the oxygen administered. An attempt should be made to maintain the arterial PaO_2 at 60–80 mm Hg during treatment.

If the patient can cooperate, assisted ventilation should be given initially by face mask. If there is clinical improvement or improvement in blood gas measurements after 1 hour, intubation may be avoided.

When intubation is necessary, an oral or nasal cuffed endotracheal tube can be tolerated for several days and a tracheostomy can be done electively later if necessary. A cuffed tracheostomy tube should be used. Cuffed tubes should be deflated every 20–30 minutes to prevent damage to the mucosa. A new type of endotracheal tube with a soft, low pressure cuff is now available to further minimize the problems. If sudden respiratory distress occurs in any patient with a cuffed tube in the trachea, the cuff should be deflated immediately until the problem is located. Endotracheal and tracheostomy tubes must be suctioned at least hourly, using gentle, aseptic technic.

Proper attention must be given to humidification whenever assisted respiration devices are used. Nebulized water is the most effective agent for thinning secretions. A main-stream system should be used.

(2) Electrolytes and fluids: Severe acidosis (pH < 7.15) is life-threatening, and sodium bicarbonate, 88–132 mEq, should be given IV immediately. The pH should be rechecked in 15 minutes and further treatment adjusted accordingly.

Many patients with chronic respiratory failure have potassium depletion which is greatly aggravated by acute respiratory failure, and potassium must be replaced in the form of potassium chloride. Dehydration must be corrected by cautious fluid replacement to help mobilize secretions. Beware of overadministration of parenteral fluids.

(3) Complicating factors: Infection is frequently the precipitating cause of respiratory failure in chronic lung disease. In critical situations, penicillin (or cephalothin) and kanamycin can be started pending the culture and sensitivity reports. In less urgent cases, tetracyclines or ampicillin can be used.

Bronchospasm which is identified by diffuse pulmonary wheezing heard during the expiratory phase of respiration should be eliminated if possible. The most effective agents are aminophylline, 500 mg in 500 ml dextrose and water IV every 4–6 hours, and isoproterenol (Isuprel®), 1:200, diluted with 3 parts of water and given by IPPB nebulization for 15 minutes every 2 hours.

If these measures are insufficient, prednisone, 40 mg orally daily (or equivalent), can be used for a few days. Prolonged use should be avoided.

The most effective treatment for the right heart failure of chronic pulmonary disease is improved ventilation and correction of hypoxemia. The patient should also be digitalized after hypoxemia has been corrected, and diuretics may be used in severe failure.

Prognosis

The prognosis for morbidity and mortality depends upon the extent of pulmonary insufficiency, which is best judged by the patient's tolerance for exercise and by pulmonary function studies.

Bates, D.V.: Chronic bronchitis and emphysema. New England J Med 278:546–551, 600–604, 1968.

Bigelow, D.B., & others: Acute respiratory failure. M Clin North America 51:323–340, 1967.

Burrows, B., & R.H. Earle: Course and prognosis in chronic obstructive lung disease. New England J Med 280:397–404, 1969.

Committee on Therapy, American Thoracic Society: Current status of surgical treatment of pulmonary emphysema and asthma. Am Rev Resp Dis 97:486, 1968.

Ebert, R.V., & J.A. Pierce: Pathogenesis of pulmonary emphysema. Arch Int Med 111:34–43, 1966.

Emirgil, C., & others: A study of the long-term effect of therapy in chronic obstructive pulmonary disease. Am J Med 47:367–377, 1969.

Falk, G.A., & W.A. Briscoe: Alpha$_1$-antitrypsin deficiency in chronic obstructive pulmonary disease. Ann Int Med 72:427–429, 1970.

Filley, G.F.: Emphysema and chronic bronchitis: Clinical manifestations and their physiologic significance. M Clin North America 51:283–292, 1967.

Larson, R.K., & others: Genetic and environmental determinants of chronic obstructive pulmonary disease. Ann Int Med 72:627–632, 1970.

Levine, B.E., & others: The role of long-term continuous oxygen administration in patients with chronic airway obstruction with hypoxemia. Ann Int Med 66:639–650, 1967.

Lopez-Majano, V., & others: Pulmonary resection in bullous disease. Am Rev Resp Dis 99:554–564, 1969.

Petty, T.L., Bigelow, D.B., & B.E. Levine: The simplicity and safety of arterial puncture. JAMA 195:693–695, 1966.

Reid, L.: *The Pathology of Emphysema.* Year Book, 1967.

Rodman, T., & F.H. Sterling: *Pulmonary Emphysema and Related Lung Diseases.* Mosby, 1969.

Schloerb, P.R., & others: Potassium depletion in patients with chronic respiratory failure. Am Rev Resp Dis 102:53–59, 1970.

Stevens, P.M., & others: Pathophysiology of hereditary emphysema. Ann Int Med 74:672–680, 1971.

Tomashefski, J.F., & P.C. Pratt: Pulmonary emphysema: Pathology and pathogenesis. M Clin North America 51:269–282, 1967.

OBESITY & HYPOVENTILATION

This syndrome has been described in extremely obese individuals who show no evidence of primary disease of the lungs or heart. It is characterized by somnolence, cyanosis, periodic respirations, hypoxia, hypercapnia, secondary polycythemia, right ventricular hypertrophy, and heart failure. It has been called the "Pickwickian syndrome" because of its similarity to Dickens' description of the fat boy in *The Pickwick Papers*.

Weight reduction appears to reverse the abnormalities.

Grant, J.L., & W. Arnold, Jr.: Idiopathic hypoventilation. JAMA 194:119–122, 1965.

Lyons, H.A., & C.T. Huang: Therapeutic use of progesterone in alveolar hypoventilation associated with obesity. Am J Med 44:881–888, 1968.

THE ALVEOLAR-CAPILLARY BLOCK SYNDROME

This clinical syndrome, due to impaired oxygen-diffusing capacity of the lungs, occurs in a variety of diseases which involve the alveolar-capillary interface. Prominent among these are sarcoidosis, berylliosis, scleroderma, bronchiolar carcinoma, miliary tuberculosis, idiopathic fibrosis and granulomatosis, mitral stenosis, and asbestosis. Recent studies suggest that decrease in the total pulmonary capillary bed, decrease in the total pulmonary diffusing surface, and disturbance in the ventilation/blood flow relationship may be more important in pathogenesis than thickening of the alveolar walls.

The principal clinical features are hyperventilation, tachypnea, dyspnea, cyanosis, and basal rales. Signs of bronchial obstruction (eg, wheezing) are usually absent. Chest films almost always reveal striking and diffuse infiltration.

Precise definition is made by pulmonary function tests, which reveal the following: (1) uniform reduction in lung volume with normal residual volume/total lung capacity ratio, (2) well-preserved maximal breathing capacity, (3) decreased diffusing capacity, (4) anoxemia, and (5) normal or decreased arterial CO_2 tension.

Treatment is directed at the underlying cause of the impaired oxygen diffusion. If this is reversible, improvement can be anticipated. Miliary tuberculosis and some forms of pulmonary edema are reversible with appropriate treatment. Diffuse pulmonary sarcoidosis in its acute form and some types of nonspecific granuloma respond dramatically to corticosteroid drugs. When fibrosis is well established, improvement usually does not occur.

Burrows, B.: Pulmonary diffusion and alveolar-capillary block. M Clin North America 51:427–438, 1967.

ACUTE PULMONARY EDEMA OF EXTRINSIC ORIGIN

Typical acute pulmonary edema in the absence of the usual underlying cardiac disease and arising *de novo* in previously healthy lungs has been described after the use of certain drugs (nitrofurantoin, hydrochlorothiazide, heroin), and after rapid ascent to altitudes exceeding 8000 feet ("altitude pulmonary edema").

In view of the rarity of symptoms in relation to the frequency of these situations, there appears to be an individual idiosyncrasy which is as yet poorly understood.

Nicklaus, J.M., & A.B. Snyder: Nitrofurantoin pulmonary reaction. Arch Int Med 121:151–155, 1968.

IDIOPATHIC INTERSTITIAL FIBROSIS

This entity was first described by Hamman and Rich in 1933. Since then, many cases with similar pathology but varying clinical manifestations have been described. The characteristic clinical findings are chronic cough, progressive dyspnea, and diffuse pulmonary infiltrations by x-ray. Recently, several proved cases of interstitial fibrosis have been found by lung biopsy in dyspneic patients before x-ray changes have occurred.

All of the known causes of this picture—eg, infection, inhalation or systemic use of toxic substances, and various systemic diseases—must be excluded. The pathology is confirmed by lung biopsy.

The prognosis is generally poor. The course is relentlessly progressive over a period of months to years.

Corticosteroids appear to be of benefit in some cases, especially for the early stages. Use prednisone, 60 mg daily orally with a gradual reduction to a main-. tenance dose of 5–10 mg over a 3-month period. If improvement has not occurred within 30 days, the drug should be discontinued.

Ford, W.B., & others: Interstitial pulmonary fibrosis. J Thoracic Cardiovas Surg 47:799–808, 1964.

Williams, M.H., Jr., Adler, J.J., & C. Colp: Pulmonary function studies as an aid in the differential diagnosis of pulmonary hypertension. Am J Med 47:378–383, 1969.

SARCOIDOSIS
(Boeck's Sarcoid)

Essentials of Diagnosis

- Hilar adenopathy and nodular or fibrous infiltration of both lungs on the chest x-ray.
- Tuberculin reaction usually negative; no bacteriologic evidence of tuberculosis.
- Biopsy (most commonly the lymph nodes and skin) reveals noncaseating granuloma.
- Hyperglobulinemia and hypercalcemia may occur.
- Occasionally, the skin, bones, joints, salivary glands, and uvea (uveoparotid fever) are also involved.

General Considerations

Boeck's sarcoid is a chronic noncaseating granuloma which may involve any tissue of the body. The tissue changes seen in this condition are nonspecific and can apparently be caused by exposure to any of a variety of infectious and noninfectious agents. When no specific cause can be determined, the clinical entity is called Boeck's sarcoid or sarcoidosis. There is growing evidence than an unidentified viral agent may be involved in this "idiopathic" form. Distribution is worldwide, but the incidence is highest in the temperate zones, especially in southeastern USA. The incidence in the black population is 17 times that in whites. The usual age range is 20–40.

Since the lungs are most commonly involved, sarcoidosis is an important entity in the differential diagnosis of chest diseases. Extrapulmonary lesions are uncommon and diverse, but skin lesions causing atrophic scars, "punched out" lesions of the small bones of the hands and feet, uveitis, and swelling of the salivary glands are suggestive of sarcoidosis.

Clinical Findings

A. Symptoms and Signs: Pulmonary symptoms and signs are commonly absent in spite of marked x-ray abnormalities. Constitutional symptoms, such as night sweats, fever, and loss of weight, are often minimal or absent. Cough and dyspnea occur late in patients with progressive pulmonary lesions, although they may occasionally occur early in the presence of an acute onset.

Skin lesions consist of nodules and diffuse infiltrations, especially of the face, ears, nose, and extensor surfaces. Atrophic scars may follow healing. Erythema nodosum may occur.

Other clinical manifestations are very uncommon. Enlargement of the tracheal bronchial nodes may produce cough and dyspnea due to compression. Uveo-parotid fever is characterized by fever and malaise as well as firm, painless, persistent involvement of the parotid and other salivary glands. There is also lacrimal gland involvement; variable involvement of the eyes with conjunctivitis, iritis, and corneal and vitreous opacities; and involvement of the retina.

Polyarthritis may occur.

Myocardial lesions may result in arrhythmias, conduction defects, and even cardiac failure.

Paralysis of the facial muscles, soft palate, and vocal cords and peripheral neuritis may be encountered.

B. Laboratory Findings: There are no diagnostic hematologic findings. Serum globulin is often increased (absolute). Serum calcium and alkaline phosphatase may be elevated.

Pulmonary function tests usually show a restriction of the vital capacity without significant evidence of obstruction. The carbon monoxide diffusion capacity is usually decreased in the presence of parenchymal pulmonary lesions.

Tuberculin and various fungus antigen skin tests are usually negative.

Antigen prepared from sarcoid nodes and injected intracutaneously reproduces the sarcoid tubercle locally, usually after weeks or months, in most patients with sarcoidosis (Kveim reaction). The value of this test is questionable because positive reactions may occur in the presence of lymphadenopathy due to diverse causes.

Biopsy is the definitive diagnostic procedure. Skin and lymph nodes are the most accessible sites. Even small, inconspicuous nodes may reveal typical lesions. Lymph nodes anterior to the scalenus anticus muscle are "connected" to the mediastinal nodes, and biopsy of these nodes reveals the highest incidence of positive results (70%). Conjunctival biopsy has been recommended as a routine examination for tissue confirmation of sarcoidosis. When more superficial sites fail to produce the lesion, needle biopsy of the liver (which is frequently involved) may be of value.

C. X-Ray Findings: The principal finding is hilar adenopathy, which is bilateral and striking ("potato nodes"). Paratracheal nodes also are frequently enlarged. Accentuation of perihilar markings may be noted in association with adenopathy. Pulmonary nodules are diffuse and may be small, resembling those of miliary tuberculosis. Hilar nodes usually regress or disappear as parenchymatous lesions appear. Progressive, advanced disease results in numerous linear and reticular densities (fibrosis). Characteristic "punched out" areas in the small bones of the hands and feet may be seen but are uncommon.

Differential Diagnosis

The most important diseases to be differentiated are tuberculosis, the collagen diseases, mycotic infections, the malignant lymphomas (especially Hodgkin's disease), and other diseases producing x-ray patterns of hilar lymphadenopathy or miliary pulmonary nodules.

The relative clinical "silence" of sarcoidosis is an important differential feature.

Treatment

There is no specific treatment. Corticosteroid therapy may produce a prompt regression of symptoms and signs, although relapses may occur and prolonged treatment may be necessary. Symptomatic treatment is used as necessary.

Prognosis

Sarcoidosis is a relatively benign disease. The overall mortality is about 5%. Pulmonary lesions usually stabilize or regress without treatment. Complications may include pulmonary tuberculosis, cardiac failure (due to actual myocardial involvement or cor pulmonale), and pulmonary insufficiency when pulmonary lesions are progressive. The altered diffusion capacity tends to persist even after other signs and symptoms have cleared.

Buckley, C.E. III, & F.C. Dorsey: A comparison of serum immunoglobulin concentrations in sarcoidosis and tuberculosis. Ann Int Med 72:37–42, 1970.

Deenstra, H., & M.J. Van Ditmars: Sarcoidosis. Dis Chest 53:57–61, 1968.

Hoyle, C., Smyllie, H., & D. Leak: Prolonged treatment of pulmonary sarcoidosis with corticosteroids. Thorax 22:519–524, 1967.

Israel, H.L., & A. Ostrow: Sarcoidosis and aspergilloma. Am J Med 47:243–250, 1969.

Israel, H.L., & others: Kveim reaction and lymphadenopathy in sarcoidosis and other diseases. New England J Med 284:345–349, 1971.

Norberg, R.: Studies in sarcoidosis. Acta med scandinav 181:497–504, 1967.

GOODPASTURE'S SYNDROME
(Hemorrhagic Pulmonary-Renal Syndrome)

The combination of pulmonary hemorrhage and glomerulonephritis is now recognized as a distinct clinical and pathologic syndrome. This disorder principally affects young men and pursues a rapidly progressive and, in most cases reported to date, fatal course, with death occurring as a result of respiratory or renal failure. The cause is not known, and the relationship between this disorder and those associated with diffuse vasculitis is uncertain. Goodpasture's syndrome may be a variant of glomerulonephritis, of greater severity or with a greater extension of the streptococcal hypersensitivity to the pulmonary alveoli.

Pathologic findings consist of diffuse pulmonary intra-alveolar hemorrhage and severe proliferative glomerulonephritis. Clinical manifestations include hemoptysis, pulmonary infiltrates, anemia, arterial hypertension, hematuria, and proteinuria.

A similar clinical and pathologic picture is seen in older patients of both sexes who have diffuse vasculitis due to polyarteritis nodosa or Wegener's granulomatosis, but the arterial lesions in Goodpasture's syndrome are sufficiently at variance to warrant its identification as a separate clinical entity.

Treatment is as for glomerulonephritis and pneumonia, but is only palliative. Azathioprine (Imuran®) is reported to have induced a very favorable partial remission in one patient.

Bloom, V.R.: Lung purpura and nephritis (Goodpasture's syndrome) complicated by the nephrotic syndrome. Ann Int Med 63:752–759, 1965.

Proskey, A.J., & others: Goodpasture's syndrome: A report of five cases and review of the literature. Am J Med 48:162–173, 1970.

WEGENER'S GRANULOMATOSIS

This is a necrotizing granuloma of unknown etiology which involves the upper respiratory tract and the lungs and is associated with a diffuse vasculitis involving both arteries and veins. Renal failure due to glomerulitis and pulmonary failure are the usual causes of death. Recently, a clinical form characterized by pulmonary lesions with little or no systemic involvement has been described. The sex distribution is equal, and the disease usually appears in the 4th and 5th decade in previously healthy people. The condition may be a variant of disseminated polyarteritis.

Clinical manifestations include epistaxis, severe sinusitis, hemoptysis, pulmonary consolidation, blood eosinophilia, hemorrhagic skin lesions, and progressive renal failure.

Treatment with corticosteroids has been unsuccessful, but recent reports suggest that treatment with cytotoxic agents (eg, cyclophosphamide, chlorambucil, azathioprine) may be effective.

Israel, H.L., & A.S. Patchefsky: Wegener's granulomatosis of lung: Diagnosis and treatment. Ann Int Med 74:881–891, 1971.

Novack, S.N., & C.M. Pearson: Cyclophosphamide therapy in Wegener's granulomatosis. New England J Med 284:938–942, 1971.

Raitt, J.W.: Wegener's granulomatosis: Treatment with cytotoxic agents and adrenocorticoids. Ann Int Med 74:344–356, 1971.

PULMONARY EMBOLISM

Essentials of Diagnosis

- Sudden onset of dyspnea and anxiety, with or without substernal pain, is characteristic of a large pulmonary embolus. Signs of acute right heart failure and circulatory collapse may follow shortly.

- Less severe dyspnea, pleuritic pain, cough, hemoptysis, and an x-ray density in the lung are characteristic of pulmonary infarction.

- Gradually developing unexplained dyspnea with or without pulmonary x-ray densities may indicate repeated minor embolization to the lungs.

- A history or clinical findings of thrombophlebitis is common in patients with pulmonary embolism.

General Considerations

Most emboli arise from thromboses in the deep veins of the lower extremities. (Emboli of air, fat, and tumor cells are not discussed here.) This event is so common in the older, bedridden, or postoperative patient (especially after extensive abdominal or pelvic surgery) that any sudden appearance of pulmonary or cardiac symptoms and signs in such patients should at once suggest this diagnosis. Such symptoms in the early postpartum period also strongly suggest pulmonary embolism.

Clinical Findings

The clinical and laboratory manifestations of pulmonary embolism depend largely on the level at which the obstruction occurs, hence on the size of the embolus. In a terminal artery the findings may be minimal or absent until repeated embolization has occurred; in a medium-sized artery, predominantly pulmonary symptoms and signs and x-ray densities; in a large artery, predominantly cardiac signs of acute right heart failure with distention of neck veins and liver, and ECG changes, progressing to shock, syncope, cyanosis, and sudden death. The latter symptoms and signs are those of the embolism per se; hemoptysis, pleuritic pain, and infiltrates on x-ray result from lung infarction, and appear 12–36 hours after embolism.

The source of a pulmonary embolus is frequently clinically "silent."

A. Symptoms and Signs: These are characteristically sudden and episodic, interspersed with "silent" intervals. Chest pain (present in 75% of cases) may be pleuritic or anginal (not dependent upon pre-existing coronary disease). Dyspnea (50% of cases) varies from mild wheezing to frank pulmonary edema. Sudden dyspnea in the absence of obvious evidence of cardiac or pulmonary disease is a characteristic of pulmonary embolism. Cough occurs in about 30% of cases, hemoptysis in about 25%. Syncope is a much more frequent symptom in pulmonary embolism than in acute myocardial infarction.

Temperature commonly rises sharply at the onset of symptoms; this may be the sole manifestation of pulmonary embolism. Shaking chills are rare.

Cardiac signs include tachycardia, prominent pulsations in the second and third left intercostal spaces (rare), accentuation of the second pulmonic sound, loud systolic murmur, protodiastolic gallop, vascular collapse ("shock"), and cyanosis.

Pulmonary signs, which may be transient, include rales, signs of consolidation, pleural friction rub, and (occasionally) signs of pleural fluid.

B. Laboratory Findings: Moderate leukocytosis occurs in 70% of cases, hyperbilirubinemia in 50%. The sedimentation rate is elevated. Serum LDH is usually elevated, and SGOT may or may not be elevated.

The arterial PaO_2 (breathing room air) is usually less than 80 mm Hg.

C. X-Ray Findings: Abnormalities usually result from pulmonary infarction. Enlargement of main pulmonary artery, elevated diaphragm, small pleural effusion, and a density in the lung, which may be delayed several days, are frequent findings. There is no characteristic shape of the pulmonary density.

The technic of scanning for radioactivity from ^{131}I-labeled macroaggregated albumin injected intravenously characteristically reveals negative defects in the lung areas distal to pulmonary artery obstruction, and has been especially useful as a screening technic where ordinary x-rays reveal no lesions. (Negative defects may appear in many lung diseases, but usually there are obvious associated x-ray densities. Also, crescent-shaped defects applied to the lateral lung border are quite characteristic of pulmonary infarctions.) Pulmonary angiography is a more definitive procedure for confirming the diagnosis and estimating the extent of involvement of the pulmonary vasculature.

D. ECG Findings: These are often transient, evolve rapidly in at least 10–20% of cases, and would probably be encountered oftener if more frequent tracings were obtained. Standard leads show a deep S in lead I; prominent Q with inverted T in lead III; tall P in lead II (occasionally); and right axis deviation. Precordial leads show inverted T waves in V_{1-4}; transient, incomplete right bundle branch block; prominent R waves over the right precordium; and displacement of the transitional zone to the left ("clockwise rotation").

Differential Diagnosis

Differentiate from myocardial infarction, acute pneumonias, atelectasis, pneumothorax, and obscure cardiac and pulmonary causes of dyspnea and chest pain.

Treatment

A. Emergency Measures:

1. Give oxygen in high concentration (preferably 100%) by mask to overcome anoxia. This also helps prevent cardiorespiratory failure.

2. Heparin, 10,000 units IV every 6 hours for 6 doses, has been shown to be helpful, apparently through vasodilatation. (Do not use if contraindication to anticoagulant exists.) Anticoagulation should be continued with one of the coumarin derivatives.

3. For severe pain, give meperidine hydrochloride (Demerol®), 50–100 mg subcut or IV; or morphine sulfate, 8–15 mg subcut or IV. These agents should be avoided in the presence of shock. (Intramuscular medications should not be used in heparinized patients.)

4. Treat shock, if present, with vasopressor drugs such as levarterenol bitartrate (Levophed®), 4 mg/liter;

or metaraminol bitartrate (Aramine®), 15–100 mg in 500 ml 5% dextrose solution IV. Adjust the rate of infusion to maintain the systolic pressure at about 90 mm Hg.

5. Pulmonary embolectomy is feasible with modern cardiopulmonary bypass technics, and a number of successful cases have been reported. This procedure must be considered when embolization is massive and life-threatening if facilities are available. The ultimate role of surgery and precise means of selecting candidates for this approach are now being explored.

B. Follow-Up Treatment: Observe carefully for secondary infection, and institute antibiotic treatment promptly if signs occur. If pleural effusion occurs and embarrasses respiration, remove fluid by paracentesis. Recurrence of emboli in spite of adequate anticoagulation may require vena caval interruption.

Prognosis

Pulmonary embolism is a common cause of sudden death. The prognosis is grave when acute cor pulmonale or vascular collapse (shock) occurs. Recovery from small emboli is frequent. The mortality rate rises with each episode of embolism.

Amador, E., & E. Potchen: Serum lactic dehydrogenase activity and radioactive lung scanning in the diagnosis of pulmonary embolism. Ann Int Med 65:1247–1255, 1966.

Berger, R.L., & others: Diagnosis and management of massive pulmonary embolism. S Clin North America 48:311–326, 1968.

Crane, C., & others: The management of major pulmonary embolism. Surg Gynec Obst 128:27–36, 1969.

Dalen, J.E., & L. Dexter: Pulmonary embolism. JAMA 207:1505–1507, 1969.

Davis, W.C., & A.A. Sasahara: Management of pulmonary embolism in the postoperative patient. S Clin North America 48:869–876, 1968.

Fleming, H.A., & S.M. Bailey: Massive pulmonary embolism in healthy people. Brit MJ 1:1322–1326, 1966.

Gray, F.D.: *Pulmonary Embolism: Natural History and Treatment.* Lea & Febiger, 1966.

Kafer, E.R.: Respiratory function in pulmonary thromboembolic disease. Am J Med 47:904–915, 1969.

Sabiston, D.C., Jr., & W.G. Wolfe: Experimental and clinical observations on the natural history of pulmonary embolism. Ann Surg 168:1–15, 1968.

Secker-Walker, R.H.: Scintillation scanning in diagnosis of pulmonary embolism. Brit MJ 1:206–208, 1968.

Szucs, M.M., Jr., & others: Diagnostic sensitivity of laboratory findings in acute pulmonary embolism. Ann Int Med 74:161–166, 1971.

DISEASES OF THE PLEURA

FIBRINOUS PLEURISY

Deposition of a fibrinous exudate on the pleural surface is the cardinal pathologic feature of fibrinous pleurisy. This is usually secondary to a pulmonary disease; pneumonia, pulmonary infarction, and neoplasm are the most frequent causes. Fibrinous pleurisy may precede the development of pleural effusion.

Chest pain is typically "pleuritic," ie, it is greatest during inspiration. Pain is minimal or absent when the breath is held or when the ribs are splinted. Referred pain may occur from the diaphragmatic pleura to the shoulder and neck (central diaphragm) or upper abdomen (peripheral diaphragm).

Pleural friction rub ("to-and-fro," "squeaky-leather" or "grating" sounds) with respirations is pathognomonic. It may occur without pleuritic pain and vice versa. Splinting of the involved chest is characteristic, with decreased motion and shallow, "grunting" respirations. The patient lies on the painful side. Other findings reflect the underlying pulmonary disease.

Treatment is aimed at the underlying disease. The treatment of the pleurisy consists only of relieving pain. Analgesics may be used as necessary. Strapping the chest with adhesive tape may give relief by restricting movement. Procaine intercostal block may be used in more severe cases.

Fibrinous pleurisy clears promptly with the resolution of the primary process. Pleural scars may remain and create minor diagnostic difficulties on future chest x-rays.

PLEURAL EFFUSION

Essentials of Diagnosis

- Dyspnea if effusion is large; may be asymptomatic.
- Pain of pleurisy often precedes the pleural effusion.
- Decreased breath sounds, flatness to percussion, egophony.
- The underlying cardiac or pulmonary disease may be the major source of symptoms and signs.
- X-ray evidence of pleural fluid.

General Considerations

Any fluid collection (transudate or exudate) in the pleural space constitutes a pleural effusion. Because there is considerable variation in the type of effusion produced by a given disease, diagnostic rules—such as "tuberculous effusions are never bloody"—are of statistical significance but are not binding upon the diagnostic evaluation of individual cases.

Numerous disease processes of inflammatory, circulatory, and neoplastic origin can cause pleural effusion. Every effort should be directed toward the diagnosis of the primary disease. "Idiopathic" pleural effusion often proves to be of tuberculous origin.

Clinical Findings

A. Symptoms and Signs: There may be no symptoms. Chest or shoulder pain may be present at onset, especially when fibrinous pleurisy precedes the effusion. Dyspnea may be mild or, with large or rapidly forming effusions, prominent. Cardiac failure may be associated with effusion. Fever, sweats, cough, and expectoration may occur, depending upon the underlying cause.

Physical findings include decreased motion of the chest and decreased to absent vocal fremitus on the side of the fluid, flat percussion note and decreased to absent breath sounds over the fluid, and egophony (*e-to-a* sound) at the upper level of the fluid. With large effusions the mediastinum shifts away from the fluid (as shown by displacement of the trachea and the cardiac apex), although underlying atelectasis may result in a shift toward the fluid. Signs resembling those of consolidation (dullness, bronchial breath sounds, bronchophony) are occasionally elicited over the fluid, presumably as a result of compression of the underlying lung by large, rapidly forming effusions.

B. X-Ray Findings: Three hundred ml or more must be present before fluid can be demonstrated by x-ray. Obliteration of the costophrenic angle is the earliest sign. Later, a homogeneous triangular density with a concave medial border extends upward to the axilla; other borders are formed by the lateral chest wall and the diaphragm. The mediastinum shifts away from the fluid (displaced heart and tracheal air shadow). The mobility of the fluid shadow, which "pours" into dependent areas of pleural space when the patient is placed on the involved side, may aid in the demonstration of small effusions. An atypical distribution of fluid along the interlobar fissures or in loculated areas may be noted.

C. Thoracentesis: This is the definitive diagnostic procedure. It demonstrates conclusively the presence of fluid, and provides samples for study of physical characteristics, protein content, cells, and infectious agents. Thoracentesis should be performed carefully to avoid introducing infection and puncturing the visceral pleura.

1. Removal of fluid for examination—Remove 50–1000 ml. Use a 2-way stopcock to avoid introduction of air. Care must be exercised to avoid contaminating the pleural space.

2. Pleural fluid examination—(Specimen must be fresh.) Measurement of specific gravity or determination of protein content should be done to distinguish a transudate from an exudate (specific gravity of 1.015 and protein of 3 gm/100 ml are the approximate division points.) Smear and stain for the detection of organisms and nature of the cellular content. Collect a specimen in an anticoagulant tube for cell count. Cultures on appropriate media are indicated for all fluids from unexplained pleural effusions to demonstrate the presence of tubercle bacilli, other bacteria, or fungi. Perform pathologic examination of a centrifuged "button" in suspected cases of malignancy.

LDH levels have frequently been found to be increased in effusions due to malignancy.

D. Pleural Biopsy: This procedure has become very simple and valuable as a result of the development of better biopsy needles (eg, Abrams' needle) which permit thoracentesis and removal of one or more tissue specimens with the same needle. Pleural biopsy is indicated whenever the diagnosis is in doubt. If the tissue is not diagnostic, several more specimens should be taken.

Prevention of Postpneumonic & Other Sterile Effusions

Preventive measures are directed at the primary disease. Begin or continue antibiotics as for treatment of pneumonia until the patient has been afebrile for 10–14 days or fluid is almost entirely resorbed.

Treatment

A. Postpneumonic and Other Sterile Effusions: Remove readily obtainable fluid by multiple thoracentesis, at daily intervals if necessary. Removal of more than 1000 ml at a time is not advisable. Reexamine pleural fluid to rule out empyema if the pleurisy does not respond to treatment. Bed rest is essential until the patient is afebrile.

B. Tuberculous Effusion: Uncomplicated pleural effusion due to tuberculosis is treated essentially as minimal pulmonary tuberculosis. A course of isoniazid (INH) plus one of the other major antituberculosis drugs (see Table 6–2) is recommended. Many patients with untreated tuberculous effusions develop pulmonary tuberculosis later, usually within 5 years.

Removal of all readily available fluid by thoracentesis is advisable to minimize later pleural fibrosis. When high fever persists for longer than 2 weeks, hematogenous dissemination should be suspected.

Prognosis

The prognosis is that of the underlying disease.

Arrington, C.W., & others: Management of undiagnosed pleural effusions in positive tuberculin reactors. Am Rev Resp Dis 93:587–593, 1966.

Committee on Therapy, American Thoracic Society: Therapy of pleural effusion. Am Rev Resp Dis 97:479–483, 1968.

Gaensler, E.A.: "Idiopathic" pleural effusion. New England J Med 283:816–817, 1970.

Poppins, H., & K. Kokkola: Diagnosis and differential diagnosis in tuberculous pleurisy. Scandinav J Resp Dis 49 (Suppl 63):105–110, 1968.

PLEURAL EMPYEMA
(Nontuberculous)

Acute infection of the pleural space may result from (1) direct spread from adjacent bacterial pneumonia (especially pneumococcal, streptococcal, and staphylococcal, (2) rupture of lung abscess into the pleural space, (3) invasion from subphrenic infection, or (4) traumatic penetration. The availability of early and specific therapy for these conditions has made empyema an uncommon disease.

The clinical findings are often obscured by the primary underlying disease. Pleural pain, fever, and "toxicity" after clinical improvement of the primary disease, in association with physical and x-ray signs of pleural fluid, are characteristic. Thoracentesis reveals a frankly purulent exudate from which the etiologic organism may be cultured. Empyema, like lung abscess, may become chronic, with a prolonged course and little tendency to spontaneous resorption (especially in bronchiectasis and tuberculosis).

The key to successful nonsurgical treatment of an acute empyema is early diagnosis. Any collection of fluid appearing in the course of a pulmonary inflammatory disease should be aspirated at once. If pus is present, a specimen should be obtained for culture. The fluid is then aspirated as completely as possible and the pleural space irrigated with sterile physiologic saline solution until the irrigating solution returns clear. Aqueous penicillin, 1 million units, and streptomycin, 0.5 gm, in 10 ml of saline, are left in the pleural space following the irrigation. Aspiration, irrigation, and instillation of antibiotics are repeated daily until no further fluid can be obtained. When cultures of the pleural fluid are reported, the antibiotics may be adjusted accordingly. The same antibiotic is given parenterally or orally (or both), and should be continued for 10–14 days after the patient has become afebrile. (*Caution:* Prolonged use of streptomycin should be avoided because of the danger of 8th nerve damage.)

If the pus is initially too thick to be aspirated through a needle, or if the patient's condition is worsening despite treatment, surgical drainage is indicated. Chronic empyema usually results from inadequately treated acute empyema or from a bronchopleural fistula. When the latter complication is present, surgical intervention may be required.

Snider, G.L., & S.S. Soleh: Empyema of the thorax in adults: Review of 105 cases. Dis Chest 54:410–415, 1968.

Thomas, D.F., & others: Management of streptococcal empyema. Ann Thoracic Surg 2:658–664, 1966.

HYDROTHORAX

The term hydrothorax generally denotes the presence of a collection of serous fluid having a specific gravity of less than 1.015 or a protein content of less than 3 gm/100 ml (transudate). The most common cause is congestive heart failure, but lymphatic obstruction and obstruction of the superior vena cava or vena azygos may also cause hydrothorax. The not unusual finding of hydrothorax in hepatic cirrhosis with ascites (6%) is explained by recent observations of ready transfer of radioiodine-labeled albumin from the peritoneal to the pleural spaces. The initial examination of the pleural fluid should be as described above.

The fluid should be removed by thoracentesis when it causes dyspnea.

The prognosis is that of the underlying disease.

HEMOTHORAX

Hemothorax (pooling of blood in a pleural space) is most commonly due to trauma. The findings are as for pleural effusion. World War II experience has shown that aspiration and irrigation of the blood from the pleural cavity is the treatment of choice. Repeated aspirations are performed as necessary. If bleeding continues, thoracotomy is indicated. Great care must be taken during aspiration to avoid bacterial contamination of the pleural cavity. Surgical removal of residual blood clots may be necessary.

SPONTANEOUS PNEUMOTHORAX

Essentials of Diagnosis

- Sudden onset of chest pain referred to the shoulder or arm on the involved side; associated dyspnea.
- Hyperresonance, decreased chest motion, decreased breath and voice sounds on involved side; mediastinal shift away from involved side.
- Chest x-ray revealing retraction of the lung from the parietal pleura is diagnostic.

General Considerations

The cause of spontaneous pneumothorax is unknown in 90% of cases, but it may be secondary to pulmonary disease. The idiopathic form typically occurs in healthy young males with no demonstrable pulmonary disease other than the subpleural blebs usually found on thoracotomy or (rarely) autopsy.

Entry of air into the pleural space from a rent in the visceral pleura causes partial to complete collapse of the underlying lung. Collapse usually is self-limited by rapid sealing of the tear. Occasionally a "valve effect" occurs, with progressive entry of air on inspiration and failure of exit on expiration, and with increasing intrapleural pressure (tension pneumothorax). This has a profound effect on cardiorespiratory dynamics and may be fatal if not treated promptly.

Clinical Findings

A. Symptoms and Signs: Symptoms are occasionally minimal (vague chest discomfort, dry cough) or may even be overlooked. Characteristically, however, the onset is sudden, with chest pain referred to the shoulder and arm on the affected side. Pain is aggravated by physical activity and by breathing, producing dyspnea. Fever is usually not present. Shock and cyanosis occur in tension pneumothorax, where high intrapleural pressure interferes with venous return to the heart.

Physical findings consist of decreased chest motion and decreased to absent vocal fremitus and breath sounds on the affected side. (Breath sounds may be abnormally loud and harsh on the normal side.) The percussion note is hyperresonant over the involved side. With large pneumothorax, the mediastinum shifts away from the affected side and a metallic "close to" sound can be heard with the stethoscope when one coin is tapped against another held to the chest ("coin sign"). A "tapping sound" roughly synchronous with the heart beat is occasionally heard in left-sided pneumothorax.

B. X-Ray Findings: Air in the pleural space with a visible border of retracted lung (difficult to see if the collapse is small) is best seen over the apex and in films taken in expiration. Retraction may be confined to one area of the lung (pleural adhesions in other areas). Contralateral shift of the mediastinum is demonstrated by displacement of the tracheal air shadow and cardiac apex. (Great amounts of air are present with tension pneumothorax.) Pleural fluid (bleeding from a ruptured area or torn adhesion) is occasionally visible, but is seldom present in large quantity.

Differential Diagnosis

Spontaneous pneumothorax may be secondary to a diseased pleura (eg, tuberculosis, neoplasm) or pulmonary disease (eg, tuberculosis, abscess, bullous emphysema); but it is most commonly due to unexplained rupture of small blebs on the visceral lung surface. The cause of bleb formation and the exact mechanism of rupture in idiopathic cases are not known. Fifty percent of cases occur in the age group from 20–24; 85% in men. Onset may occur during exercise or at complete rest. Chest pain must be differentiated from that of myocardial infarction (especially when there is shoulder-arm radiation), pulmonary embolism, and acute fibrinous pleurisy.

Treatment

A. Emergency Measures for Tension Pneumothorax: *Note:* This is a medical emergency. Insert a trocar or large bore, short-beveled needle into the anterior part of the affected chest (just into the pleural space to avoid trauma to the expanding lung). After tension has been relieved, a simple one-way valve made from a rubber glove finger, slit at the end, can be tied to the hub of the trocar or needle. As soon as possible, a catheter should be introduced into the pleural space via a trocar and attached to a water trap with the end of the tubing under 1–2 cm of water. (A plastic catheter mounted on a disposable aluminum stylet and packaged ready to use is now available. It obviates the need for a trocar and is suitable for both emergency and definitive treatment.) A suction pump (with a maximum vacuum of −30 cm of water) may be attached to the water trap.

If pain is severe, give morphine sulfate, 8–15 mg subcut or IV. Treat shock if present.

Follow-up treatment is as for spontaneous pneumothorax.

B. Spontaneous Pneumothorax Without Increased Intrathoracic Pressure: Bed rest is essential until air has been largely resorbed. If tuberculosis is present, treat accordingly. Pleural pain should be treated with analgesics or strapping. If cough is annoying, codeine sulfate, 15–60 mg every 3–4 hours, should be used. Aspirate air if dyspnea is present or if the pneumothorax space is large enough to aspirate safely. If air leakage continues, an intercostal catheter (see above) or an inlying needle (eg, Clagett S needle) attached to a water trap and suction pump (see above) may be necessary. Continue suction until the lung has been reexpanded for 24 hours. Administer oxygen if dyspnea is present. In some cases of spontaneous pneumothorax where the lung does not expand or if there are repeated episodes of collapse, exploratory thoracotomy may be necessary.

Prognosis

The outlook is very good in "idiopathic" cases but is more serious in secondary cases because of the danger of infection of the pleural space. Recurrence occurs in 15–20%, usually on the same side. After 2 episodes, surgical correction should be considered. Patients with a history of spontaneous pneumothorax should be advised to avoid flying in unpressurized aircraft and high altitudes. Hemothorax occurs in about 10% of cases. Empyema may occur where underlying disease, especially tuberculosis, is present. Failure of lung to reexpand, with fibrothorax, is rare in the idiopathic type.

Tension pneumothorax is a true emergency.

Fuchs, H.S.: Idiopathic spontaneous pneumothorax and flying. Aerospace Med 38:1283–1285, 1967.

Inouye, W.Y., Berggren, R.B., & J. Johnson: Spontaneous pneumothorax: Treatment and mortality. Dis Chest 51:67–73, 1967.

Killen, D.A., & W.G. Gobbel, Jr.: *Spontaneous Pneumothorax.* Little, Brown, 1968.

Spontaneous pneumothorax. Editorial. Brit MJ 1:720–721, 1968.

Vogt-Moykopf, I., & O. Haiderer: Current views on the management of spontaneous pneumothorax. Surg Gynec Obst 123:313–316, 1966.

TRAUMATIC PNEUMOTHORAX

Note: This is an emergency. Open chest wounds (sucking wounds) must be made airtight by any available means (eg, bandage, handkerchief, shirt, or other material) and closed surgically as soon as possible.

Traumatic pneumothorax due to lung puncture or laceration (fractured rib, bullet, etc) is managed like spontaneous pneumothorax (above). Surgery is frequently required.

DISEASES OF THE MEDIASTINUM

MEDIASTINAL MASS

Mediastinal masses are often clinically "silent" until they become large. They are frequently discovered on routine chest x-rays and fluoroscopy, where their position, density, and mobility are of aid in differential diagnosis. Biopsy is often the only way to make a differential diagnosis.

Because of their proximity to the heart, great vessels, esophagus, air passages, and surrounding nerves, even benign lesions are potentially serious.

The symptoms and signs are usually due to compression and distortion of surrounding structures. Pain is usually substernal. It originates in the afferent lower cervical and upper thoracic segments (may mimic "cardiac" pain), and occasionally radiates to the shoulder, neck, arms, or back. Cough suggests tracheal and bronchial involvement. Dyspnea is due to airway obstruction (which may lead to pulmonary infections). Respirations may be stertorous, with suprasternal retraction on inspiration. Hoarseness is associated with compression paralysis of the thoracic portion of the left recurrent laryngeal nerve. Dysphagia is due to extrinsic compression of the esophagus with obstruction; it varies from mild to severe.

Compression of the heart or great vessels is an unusual cause of symptoms.

Tracheal shift is due to displacement by mass. Tracheal tug is associated with adjacent aortic aneurysms with transmitted pulsations.

The superior vena cava syndrome consists of dilated neck veins, fullness of the neck and face (collar of Stokes), and collateral veins on the thoracic wall. It is caused by compression of the superior vena cava.

Horner's syndrome (ipsilateral miosis, ptosis, and enophthalmos) is due to compression of sympathetic outflow pathways.

Chest x-rays after a swallow of barium are essential. Fluoroscopy should be done to detect pulsations. Angiography may be helpful to identify vascular stricture. Lymph node biopsy of palpable (eg, cervical, supraclavicular) or nonpalpable (anterior scalene, paratracheal) nodes may be definitive. Mediastinoscopy is being used with increasing frequency. Exploratory thoracotomy is often necessary.

Treatment will depend upon the primary disease. The prognosis is variable, depending upon the cause and the histologic characteristics of the mass.

Boyd, D.P., & A.I. Midell: Mediastinal cysts and tumors: An analysis of 96 cases. S Clin North America 48:493–506, 1968.

Burke, W.A., Burford, T.H., & R.F. Dorfman: Hodgkin's disease of the mediastinum. Ann Thoracic Surg 3:287–295, 1967.

Holmes-Sellors, T., Thackery, A.C., & A.D. Thomson: Tumours of the thymus: A review of 88 operational cases. Thorax 22:193–220, 1967.

TABLE 6–4. Differential diagnosis of mediastinal masses.

Metastases may occur in any portion of the mediastinum. Among infrequent mediastinal masses are thymus enlargement (superior), lipoma, pericardial cyst (anterior), meningocele, and aneurysm of the descending aorta (posterior). Thymus enlargement is in the anterior superior mediastinum. It is physiologic in infants, usually malignant in adults. Benign enlargement is present in up to 15% of cases with myasthenia gravis.

Lesion	Density	Mobility (Fluoroscopy)	Clinical Features
Anterior			
Aneurysm, ascending aorta	May show calcification.	Vigorous expansile pulsation. Often difficult to demonstrate.	Pulsating mass may be palpable on the anterior chest wall. Erosion of vertebrae may produce back pain. Associated evidence of late syphilis is present.
Dermoid	Translucent upper area merging with denser underlying shadow. Presence of teeth or bone is pathognomonic. Tend to calcify.	May change in shape with respirations (fluid contents compressible).	Often clinically silent. Occasional rupture into bronchus with coughing up of hair and sebaceous material. May be associated with other congenital anomalies.
Substernal thyroid	Merges with soft tissues of neck. May have hazy calcification.	Moves with swallowing. Usually displaces trachea.	Upper portion is often palpable in the neck. Signs of thyrotoxicosis may be present.
Superior			
Bronchogenic cyst	May contain air over fluid (communication with bronchus).	May be seen to rise with swallowing.	May become infected, simulating ordinary lung abscess.
Middle			
Lymphoma (Hodgkin's disease, lymphosarcoma)	Dense, rounded masses. Usually bilateral.	May show transmitted pulsations when close to vessels. Relatively fixed.	Prominent systemic symptoms (eg, Pel-Ebstein fever, cachexia, anemia, pruritus). Lymphadenopathy in palpable areas.
Posterior			
Neurofibroma	Close relationship to thoracic spine.	Fixed.	Often "silent" when discovered. Radicular pain may be prominent. Usually not associated with generalized neurofibromatosis (Von Recklinghausen). May produce compression of spinal cord.

Joseph, W.L., Murray, J.F., & D.G. Mulder: Mediastinal tumors: Problems in diagnosis and treatment. Dis Chest 50:150–160, 1966.

PNEUMOMEDIASTINUM

Essentials of Diagnosis

- Sudden onset of severe retrosternal pain.
- Crepitus on palpation of neck and chest.
- Crunching sound simultaneous with heart beat.
- X-ray is diagnostic.

General Considerations

Free air in the mediastinum may be secondary to perforation of the intrathoracic esophagus or respiratory tract or may be caused by spontaneous rupture of an alveolus into the perivascular interstitial tissues of the lung. Air may also be sucked into the mediastinum through an open neck wound or from an area of emphysema in the neck resulting from a chest wound. Spontaneous pneumomediastinum is often associated with spontaneous pneumothorax, most often of the tension type.

Clinical Findings

A. Symptoms and Signs: Symptoms are usually minimal. Typically, the air escapes into the subcutaneous tissues of the neck and then over the rest of the body and retroperitoneally. If pneumothorax (especially tension pneumothorax) is present also, there is usually a sudden onset of severe retrosternal pain radiating to the neck, shoulders, and anus (retroperitoneal dissection).

Dyspnea is not usually severe. Uncommonly, high intramediastinal pressure results in compression of the heart and blood vessels with marked dyspnea, shock, and even death ("air block"); hemodynamics are similar to those of pericardial tamponade.

Subcutaneous emphysema with crepitus on palpation of the skin of the neck or upper chest is common. Air may cause grotesque puffing of the neck and face.

"Crackling" or "crunching" sounds (Hamman's sign) in the substernal and precordial areas synchronous with the heart beat are characteristic, but are occasionally due to left-sided pneumothorax.

B. X-Ray Findings: These are definitive, showing radiolucency surrounding the heart border and streaking of the upper mediastinum; and radiolucency of the retrosternal area on a lateral film taken at full expiration and in the subcutaneous tissues of the neck and shoulder areas.

Differential Diagnosis

The pain of pneumomediastinum may simulate that of myocardial infarction.

Treatment

No treatment is usually required, but a prompt search should be made for the underlying cause (eg, pneumothorax, ruptured bronchus, perforated esophagus).

Prognosis

Spontaneous recovery is the rule. Unrelieved intramediastinal tension occasionally causes death.

Gray, J.M., & G.C. Hanson: Mediastinal emphysema: Aetiology, diagnosis, and treatment. Thorax 21:325–332, 1966.

ACUTE MEDIASTINITIS

Acute inflammation of the mediastinal space may be due to traumatic perforation of the esophagus or trachea (eg, during instrumentation or by lodged foreign bodies); spontaneous perforation of the esophagus (as in carcinoma); or lymphatic and direct spread from an infection of the neck or head, eg, retropharyngeal and cervical abscess.

Onset is usually within 24 hours after perforation. Findings include substernal and neck pain; progressive dysphagia, dyspnea, fever, chills, prostration, and "toxicity"; and signs of pneumomediastinum.

There may be no radiographic findings. Mediastinal widening is visible as a diffuse soft tissue density. Mediastinal mass (abscess), with or without a fluid level, may be visible.

Treatment

Treatment consists of large doses of penicillin plus kanamycin until organism sensitivities are determined. Surgical drainage in the cervical region is indicated when a collection of pus bulges in that area.

Prognosis

Without treatment, the mortality rate is high; with treatment, the prognosis is markedly improved.

CHRONIC MEDIASTINITIS

Granulomatous and fibrous mediastinitis accounts for about 10% of the lesions presenting a mediastinal mass by x-ray. The most common causes are histoplasmosis, tuberculosis, and sarcoidosis (in that order).

The clinical manifestations include widening of the mediastinum by x-ray, superior vena caval obstruction, and, occasionally, partial esophageal or tracheobronchial obstruction.

Scalene or mediastinal node biopsy may establish the cause, or mediastinal exploration may be necessary.

Granulomatous disease may respond to specific treatment and corticosteroids. Obstruction due to fibrosis may be amenable to surgical decompression.

Schowengerdt, C.G., & others: Granulomatous and fibrous mediastinitis. A review and analysis of 180 cases. J Thoracic Cardiovas Surg 57:365–379, 1969.

OXYGEN THERAPY & VENTILATORY ASSISTANCE

Oxygen therapy is the administration of oxygen in concentrations greater than found in the ambient atmosphere. The percentage of oxygen administered is not critical if the respiratory system is intact but is of great importance in respiratory failure.

Respiratory failure can be said to exist when the arterial oxygen tension (Pa_{O_2}) is less than 50 mm Hg. Ventilatory failure is present when the arterial CO_2 tension (Pa_{CO_2}) is greater than 50 mm Hg. These conditions usually coexist, but hypoxemia may occur in the absence of CO_2 retention.

The normal ranges of the partial pressures of the gases in the arterial blood is as follows: Pa_{O_2} = 80–100 mg Hg; Pa_{CO_2} = 35–45 mm Hg.

The clinical manifestations of respiratory failure include restlessness, headache, confusion, tachycardia, diaphoresis, impaired motor function, asterixis, central cyanosis, hypotension or hypertension, miosis, and coma. Unfortunately, these symptoms may be absent or difficult to detect in significant respiratory failure and are often missed if blood gases are not measured.

Facilities for the rapid measurement of the Pa_{O_2}, Pa_{CO_2}, and arterial blood pH are available in most general hospitals. Arterial blood can be easily and safely obtained from a radial, brachial, or femoral artery. (See Petty reference, below).

Patients who are anemic should have transfusions of packed red cells to increase the oxygen carrying capacity of the blood.

USE OF OXYGEN IN RESPIRATORY FAILURE

The commonest methods of administering oxygen are listed in Tables 6–5 and 6–6. The percentages of oxygen delivered are only approximate; when the concentration must be carefully controlled, the gas delivered to the patient should be monitored with an oxygen meter. (Some of the newer, more sophisticated positive pressure respirators provide oxygen in accurately measured amounts.) The Venturi mask (Venti-Mask®) is a simple disposable mask that dilutes 100% oxygen to various selected concentrations with reasonable accuracy. Maintenance of the Pa_{O_2} between 60–80 mm Hg is usually sufficient to correct hypoxia.

Mechanical ventilators are used when it is necessary to assist or control breathing. In the former case, the patient's inspiratory effort triggers the flow of positive pressure; in the latter, automatic cycling is provided by the machine. (See section below on Ventilatory Assistance.)

Oxygen therapy must include humidification of the gas delivered. This is especially important when tracheal airways are used. Heated aerosol delivered with a mainstream nebulizer is preferred. Plain sterile water is as effective as the various mucolytic and surface tension lowering agents and is less irritating.

Complications of Oxygen Therapy

A. Aggravation of Respiratory Acidosis: In patients with chronic respiratory insufficiency and CO_2 retention, the use of oxygen at ambient pressures may inhibit the respiratory drive and further depress breathing, thus increasing CO_2 retention and acidosis. However, these patients are hypoxic and require oxy-

gen. The safest method of administration is with a positive pressure machine which also provides increased ventilation and removal of CO_2.

Many such patients who are awake and able to cooperate may be treated with low-flow oxygen (2–3 liters/minute) given at ambient pressures via nasal prongs or catheter, but they must be observed closely for signs of respiratory depression (decreasing rate or depth of breathing and decreasing level of consciousness). If possible, arterial blood gases should be monitored before and during such treatment. If deterioration occurs, increased ventilation (see below) is essential.

B. Oxygen Toxicity: Oxygen given at high concentrations for more than 24 hours can apparently cause alveolar damage as well as cerebral symptoms. Patients being maintained on respirators are most often exposed to this hazard. (The danger of producing retrolental fibroplasia in newborns, especially the premature, by administering oxygen in concentrations greater than 40% is well known.)

Oxygen should be used only in concentrations sufficient to maintain the Pa_{O_2} between 60–80 mm Hg.

C. Infection: Oxygen equipment, especially equipment of the positive pressure type, is subject to contamination with pseudomonas and other organisms. Aerosol generators, tubing, manifolds, masks, and mouth pieces should be replaced with sterilized equipment before they are used on a different patient and should be changed daily when in continuous use.

Ventilatory Assistance

When adequate oxygenation cannot be achieved with supplemental oxygen at ambient pressure or when the Pa_{CO_2} level remains elevated (above 60 mm Hg), ventilatory assistance with intermittent positive pressure (IPPB) breathing is required.

Mechanical ventilators providing IPBB are of 2 general types: pressure controlled or volume controlled. With the pressure controlled devices (Bennett,

TABLE 6–5. Oxygen therapy equipment at ambient pressure.*

Equipment	Flow (liters/min)	Approximate O_2 Concentration Delivered (%)	Remarks
Nasal cannula (prongs)	4–6	30–40	Nasal obstruction interferes.
Nasal catheter	4–6	30–40	Misplaced catheter may cause gastric dilatation.
Mask (with exhalation valve)	6–8 8–12	35–45 45–65	May be difficult to fit and uncomfortable for prolonged use.
Mask (with bag)	6–8 8–12	40–60 60–90	
Venturi mask (Venti-Mask®)	4–8	24, 28, 35†	Accurate concentrations delivered over wide range by Venturi principle. Light plastic mask.

*See also Table 6–6. Both types may be used for assisted ventilation (patient cycled) and controlled ventilation (machine cycled).

†Disposable mask for each concentration.

TABLE 6–6. Oxygen therapy with positive pressure units.*

Equipment	Approximate O_2 Concentration Delivered (%)	Remarks
Pressure controlled (Bennett, Bird, and others)	40–100 (when driven by oxygen).	"Air dilution" setting usually delivers more than 40% O_2 specified. Most commonly used. Not effective when airway resistance (mask pressure) exceeds 30 cm H_2O.
Volume controlled (Air Shields, Bennett MA-1, Emerson, Engstrom, Ohio-560)	21–100. (Newer models have more accurate O_2 concentration controls.)	Most effective for controlled ventilation. Can overcome high airway resistance.

*See also Table 6–5. Both types may be used for assisted ventilation (patient cycled) and controlled ventilation (machine cycled).

Bird, etc), the flow of positive pressure stops when a preset pressure is reached in the airway (10–30 cm water). The volume controlled devices (Air Shields, Bennett MA-1, Emerson, Engstrom, Ohio-560) deliver a predetermined tidal volume regardless of the pressure in the airway (within physiologic limits). Most of these devices can provide either assisted or controlled ventilation.

Assisted ventilation is triggered by the patient's own inspiratory effort. If the patient is conscious and able to cooperate, this can be applied with a pressure controlled IPPB device using a simple mouth piece or tight-fitting mask. Depending on the urgency, the assisted ventilation can be used without interruption or periodically (eg, 20–30 minutes per hour), alternating with ambient pressure oxygen sufficient to correct hypoxia. If the patient's inspiratory effort is too weak to cycle the machine regularly, the automatic cycling control must be set to ensure an adequate rate. When the patient is unconscious, paralyzed, or unable to cooperate, ventilation must be controlled and a tracheal airway is essential. A nasal or oral endotracheal tube may be used for several days. For longer periods, a tracheostomy is usually substituted. Both endotracheal and tracheostomy tubes should be cuffed. Damage to the trachea from prolonged cuff pressure is avoided by deflating the cuff for 1 minute every 20–30 minutes. New soft low-pressure cuffs are now available to further minimize this problem.

Patients who are intubated and fight the machine should be sedated sufficiently with parenteral morphine, meperidine (Demerol®), or diazepam (Valium®) to permit unhindered controlled ventilation.

The administration of bronchodilator drugs to control bronchospasm is frequently indicated during assisted ventilation. Nebulized isoproterenol (Isuprel®), 0.5 ml of 1:200 solution in 2–3 ml water every 4–6 hours, may be used. Aminophylline may also be added to the intravenous infusion bottles (500 mg/liter).

When airway resistance is too great (usually above 30 cm water mask pressure) to provide an adequate tidal volume (500–800 ml), a volume controlled ventilator is required. The reader should consult the manufacturers' literature for a more detailed description and instructions in the operation of the various machines.

When tracheal airways are used, particular attention must be paid to humidification. A warmed supersaturated water vapor delivered in the mainstream is preferred. The airway must also be suctioned at regular intervals, using aseptic technic, to ensure patency.

Prolonged positive pressure ventilation may be harmful to patients with impaired cardiac function because of the decrease in venous return that may occur. Therefore, further administration requires additional caution.

Discontinuing prolonged assisted ventilation can be accomplished by giving the treatment intermittently and then gradually extending the time the patient is off the machine.

Bendixin, H.H., Hedley-Whyte, J., & M.B. Laver: Impaired oxygenation in surgical patients during general anesthesia with controlled ventilation: A concept of atelectasis. New England J Med 269:991–996, 1963.

Brummer, D.L.: Oxygen therapy in cardiopulmonary disease. (Committee on Therapy, American Thoracic Society.) Am Rev Resp Dis 101:811–814, 1970.

Fletcher, G., & J.P. Bunker: Physiologic basis of prolonged artificial ventilation. Ann Rev Med 17:473–482, 1966.

Hedley-Whyte, J., & P.M. Winter: Oxygen therapy. Clin Pharmacol Therap 8:696–737, 1967.

Hirschberg, G.G., Lewis, L., & D. Thomas: *Rehabilitation Manual for the Care of the Disabled and Elderly.* Lippincott, 1964.

Mushin, W.W., & others: *Automatic Ventilation of the Lungs,* 2nd ed. Davis, 1969.

Nunn, J.F., & J. Freeman: Problems of oxygenation and oxygen transport during hemorrhage. Anaesthesia 19:206–216, 1964.

Petty, T.L., Bigelow, D.B., & B.E. Levine: The simplicity and safety of arterial puncture. JAMA 195:693–695, 1966.

Rosen, M., & E.K. Hilliard: The use of suction in clinical medicine. Brit J Anesth 32:486–504, 1960.

•   •   •

MANIFESTATIONS INVOLVING THE RESPIRATORY SYSTEM DUE TO PARASITIC DISEASE

Cough (usually dry, perhaps with some degree of asthma: Early schistosomiasis japonicum (Katayama's syndrome), ascariasis (Löffler's syndrome), paragonimiasis, amebic abscess, filariasis, including animal filariids (tropical eosinophila, Löffler's syndrome). (See also Pneumonitis and Eosinophilic lung, below).

Eosinophilic lung, PIE, or Löffler's syndrome: Ascariasis (transient) or filariid infections, trichuriasis, fascioliasis, amebiasis (rarely), toxocariasis.

Asthma: Ascariasis, visceral larva migrans.

Pneumonitis (at times with hemoptysis): Larval migrations in ascariasis, hookworm, strongyloidiasis, paragonimiasis, schistosomiasis, secondary to amebic abscess liver, pulmonary amebiasis.

Hemoptysis: Paragonimiasis, amebic abscess.

Dyspnea: Advanced schistosomiasis (especially japonicum), visceral leishmaniasis, paragonimiasis, hookworm disease.

Abscess: Amebiasis, paragonimiasis.

Tumor: Echinococcosis (hydatid cyst).

• • •

General Bibliography

Cheney, F.W., Jr., & J. Butler: The affects of ultrasonically-produced aerosols on airway resistance in man. Anesthesiology 29:1099–1106, 1968.

Comroe, J.H., Jr.: *Physiology of Respiration.* Year Book, 1965.

Kirby, W.M.M. (editor): Modern management of respiratory diseases. M Clin North America 51:267–572, 1967.

Levine, E.R.: Inhalation therapy: Aerosols and intermittent positive pressure breathing. M Clin North America 51:307–322, 1967.

Morton, J.W., & K.W. Turnbull: Reversibility of chronic bronchitis, asthma, and emphysema: Response to bronchodilators quantitated and compared. Dis Chest 53:126–132, 1968.

Public Health Service, US Department of Health, Education, & Welfare: Management of chronic obstructive lung disease. Public Health Service Publication No. 1457, May 1966.

7...

Heart & Great Vessels

Maurice Sokolow & Ernest Jawetz

The diagnosis of any cardiovascular disease consists of (1) determining the etiology, (2) identifying the structural changes, (3) defining the physiologic abnormalities, and (4) assessing the remaining functional capacity of the heart. Treatment and the estimation of prognosis are both based upon a clear understanding of these 4 factors.

Etiology is established by considering the patient's age, the history, the specific abnormalities present, and appropriate laboratory studies, such as antistreptolysin O titer, serologic test for syphilis, protein-bound iodine, or level of serum enzymes. Abnormalities of cardiac structure and function are identified by careful physical examination combined with radiologic and ECG studies. Cardiac catheterization is needed to determine the extent of shunts and to measure the pressures in the heart chambers, aorta, or pulmonary artery. Dye-dilution tests are useful in some otherwise undetectable right-to-left or left-to-right shunts. Biplane angiography and cineangiography are of great value in outlining the anatomy of congenital and acquired abnormalities, the degree of valvular insufficiencies, and cardiac tumors as well as assessing left ventricular function by calculation of left ventricular volumes, left ventricular ejection fraction, and similar data.

Radioisotope scanning of the heart with pertechnetate ^{99m}Tc may be of value in demonstrating intracardiac shunts. Ultrasound (echoencephalography) may be of value in diagnosing pericardial effusion and valvular disease (particularly mitral) and for determining the relative thickness of left and right ventricular muscle. Radarkymography—a new, noninvasive technic for recording horizontal movements of the cardiac silhouette—has been recently described as a method of detecting regional ventricular dysfunction.

NONSPECIFIC MANIFESTATIONS

The most common symptoms resulting from heart disease are dyspnea, fatigue, chest pain, and palpitation. However, because any of these symptoms may be due to noncardiac disorders (even in patients with known heart disease), the proper interpretation of their significance depends upon systematic inquiry and diagnostic studies.

Dyspnea

Dyspnea due to heart disease is almost always associated with cardiac enlargement and other structural or physiologic changes.

The most common type of dyspnea due to heart disease is **exertional dyspnea**—distinct shortness of breath upon moderate exertion which is relieved by rest.

Orthopnea is dyspnea in recumbency which is promptly relieved by sitting up.

Paroxysmal nocturnal dyspnea suddenly awakens the patient and forces him to sit on the side of the bed or stand up for relief. It may be the first symptom of left ventricular failure or tight mitral stenosis.

Noncardiac causes of exertional dyspnea include poor physical condition, obesity, debility, advanced age, chronic lung disease, anemia, and obstruction of the nasal passages. Orthopnea occurs in extreme obesity, tense ascites due to any cause, abdominal distention due to gastrointestinal disease, and in the third trimester of pregnancy. Paroxysmal nocturnal dyspnea can be simulated by bronchial asthma appearing in adult life for the first time and by airway obstruction due to paratracheal tumors.

Anxiety states and cardiac neuroses can produce any form of dyspnea, but such patients often describe sighing respirations and complain of inability to take in a satisfying breath. Psychogenic dyspnea is also associated with acute respiratory alkalosis, which causes lightheadedness or mental clouding, paresthesias of the limbs or around the mouth, and at times frank tetany, tremulousness, and apprehension.

Fatigue

Easy fatigability which is relieved by rest is common in low-output states and heart failure. It may be the chief complaint (rather than dyspnea) in congenital heart disease, cor pulmonale, or mitral stenosis complicated by pulmonary hypertension. Asthenia—chronic exhaustion and lethargy which are not improved by rest—is due to such psychologic disorders as depression, cardiac neuroses, and chronic anxiety; or may be a component of effort syndrome ("neurocirculatory asthenia"). Noncardiac organic causes of fatigue include chronic infections, anemia, endocrine and metabolic disorders, chronic poisoning, habitual use of depressant or sedative drugs, malignancy, collagen diseases, and any debilitating illness.

Chest Pain

Chest pain occurs in the following cardiovascular disorders: angina pectoris (in which the pain is due to intermittent ischemia of the myocardium); myocardial infarction; myopericarditis, pericardial effusion or tamponade; aortic dissection or aneurysm; and pulmonary embolism or infarction.

Chest pain is one of the most common presenting complaints in medicine. Careful evaluation includes inquiry concerning its quality, location, radiation, duration, and the factors which precipitate, aggravate, or relieve it. Serial examinations are often required, as well as laboratory tests. Exercise tests, therapeutic tests, and selective coronary cineangiography are sometimes required.

The following noncardiac disorders are often associated with chest pain which resembles or is indistinguishable from that of heart disease: (1) Arthritis or disk disease of the lower cervical and upper thoracic spine (dorsal or ventral nerve root pain). (2) Cardiac neurosis. (3) Neurocirculatory asthenia and other emotional disorders. (4) Sliding hiatus hernia, acute or chronic cholecystitis, acute pancreatitis, cardiospasm, peptic ulcer, esophageal pain. (5) Disorders causing local chest wall pain, eg, costochondritis, strain or inflammation of the pectoral and intercostal muscles and ligaments, postmyocardial infarction syndrome, "shoulder-hand" syndrome. (6) Periarthritis of the left shoulder. (7) Spontaneous pneumothorax. (8) Pleurisy, spinal cord disease, mediastinal tumor, neoplastic invasion of ribs or vertebrae. (9) Mediastinal emphysema.

Palpitation

Consciousness of rapid, forceful, or irregular beating is the most common complaint referable to the heart. In the vast majority of instances palpitation is due to increased awareness of normal heart action, either because of anxiety about the presence of heart disease or secondary to long-standing emotional disorders such as neurocirculatory asthenia. Organic causes are anemia, thyrotoxicosis, debility, and paroxysmal arrhythmias.

Two types of palpitation are most often described: **Sinus tachycardia**, a rapid, forceful pounding which may begin gradually or suddenly but invariably slows gradually, occurs normally on exertion or during excitement. **Premature ventricular systoles** cause a sensation of the heart "skipping a beat" or "stopping and turning over."

Patients with true paroxysmal tachycardia describe a rapid, regular palpitation or "fluttering" sensation which begins suddenly, lasts minutes or hours, and then ceases abruptly. In younger patients there are no other symptoms unless the attacks are prolonged. In older patients paroxysmal arrhythmias may produce angina pectoris, congestive heart failure, dizziness, or syncope. Paroxysmal atrial fibrillation is felt as a rapid irregular pounding which begins and ends suddenly.

Chronic atrial fibrillation and flutter are in themselves usually not perceived by the patient except after exercise or excitement when the ventricular rate increases.

An ECG taken during an episode of palpitation establishes the diagnosis. However, clinical observation of the heart rate and rhythm and the effect of exercise and carotid sinus pressure, together with an assessment of the overall clinical picture (age of patient, associated heart and other diseases), permits diagnosis in the great majority of cases without electrocardiograms.

SIGNS OF HEART DISEASE

Valuable information pertaining to the etiology, nature, and extent of heart disease is often found on general physical examination, eg, Argyll Robertson pupils, splinter hemorrhages, splenomegaly, diffuse goiter, large kidneys, congenital anomalies, or epigastric bruit. Abnormal pulsations of the neck veins or precordium, cyanosis, clubbing, and edema should be carefully noted. Careful palpation may disclose right or left ventricular hypertrophy, thrills, and diastolic movements.

Edema

Edema caused by heart failure appears first in the ankles and lower legs of ambulatory patients and over the sacrum, flanks, buttocks, and posterior thighs of bedridden patients.

The mere presence of edema does not establish a diagnosis of heart failure in a patient who also complains of dyspnea. Significant edema occurs often in obese patients and those with incompetent leg veins and healed thrombophlebitis. Garters, rolled or elastic-top stockings, tight girdles, prolonged sitting or standing, premenstrual fluid retention, and "idiopathic edema of women" are other common noncardiac causes. Nephrosis or terminal nephritis, cirrhosis with tense ascites, congenital or acquired lymphedema, hypoproteinemia, severe malnutrition or anemia, and obstruction of the inferior vena cava can produce dependent edema.

Cyanosis

Cyanosis is classified as central or peripheral. Central cyanosis results from low arterial oxygen saturation caused by intracardiac right-to-left shunts, pulmonary arteriovenous fistula, certain chronic lung diseases, or pneumonia. It is differentiated from peripheral cyanosis by being present also on warm mucous membranes such as the insides of the lips and cheeks and on the tongue and conjunctivas, and is established by determining the arterial oxygen tension (P_{O_2}) and saturation. Polycythemia vera may produce central cyanosis despite normal oxygen saturation since the larger numbers of red cells produce a proportionately greater increase in the amount of reduced hemoglobin. A useful means of differentiating cyanosis caused by a shunt in the heart or lung from that caused by primary lung disease is to administer 100% oxygen: Cyanosis caused by shunt will be unaffected, whereas that due to parenchymal lung disease will disappear or decrease.

Peripheral cyanosis occurs in the presence of normal arterial oxygen saturation. It only occurs on cool portions of the body, such as the fingertips, nose, ears, and cheeks. It is caused by slowed circulation through peripheral vascular beds, which allow the capillary blood to give up more than normal amounts of oxygen. Reduced cardiac output due to mitral stenosis, pulmonary stenosis, or heart failure causes peripheral cyanosis. The most common causes, however, are nervous tension with cold, clammy hands, and exposure to cold.

Murmurs, Sounds, & Clicks

Auscultation permits the examiner to determine the presence of structural or functional abnormalities by noting changes in the first or second heart sounds, the presence of additional heart sounds, extracardiac sounds, systolic pulmonary or aortic ejection clicks, mid and late systolic clicks associated with mitral disease, and by analysis of murmurs. The examiner must also recognize the sounds which have no known pathologic significance: normally split first sound, normal third sound, cardiorespiratory murmurs, and the innocent heart murmurs. Accurate interpretation of murmurs is difficult in the presence of gross heart failure with very low cardiac output or rapid ventricular rates. In these situations restoration of compensation or slowing of the ventricular rate may cause prominent murmurs to decrease in intensity; previously faint or inaudible murmurs may in turn become loud. Murmurs are graded on the basis of intensity into grades I (least intense) to VI (most intense). With experience, most examiners rarely differ by more than one grade in evaluating a murmur.

A. Systolic Murmurs: A soft short systolic murmur at any valve area may be innocent if there are no other abnormalities and if it changes markedly with respiration and position. Exercise and tachycardia increase the intensity of any murmur. This so-called innocent or functional systolic murmur, usually present at the mitral or pulmonary area, is "ejection" in type (crescendo-decrescendo, ending before systole is complete, and related to the ejection of blood from the right or left ventricle into the pulmonary artery or aorta, respectively). It is most easily heard in recumbent, thin-chested individuals; full inspiration causes it to disappear or diminish markedly, whereas full expiration may accentuate it considerably. The louder a systolic murmur, the more likely it is to be organic in origin. Any systolic murmur associated with a thrill at that valve area is due to valvular or outflow tract disease unless there is gross anemia. An apical pansystolic murmur (a "regurgitant" murmur) which merges with and replaces the first sound and which is well transmitted into the left axilla or left infrascapular area is organic, ie, is due to deformity of the mitral valve or dilatation of the mitral valve ring with regurgi-

tation. An aortic systolic murmur is "ejection" in type and midsystolic. It is transmitted into the carotids or upper interscapular area when due to organic disease of the aortic valve or to dilatation of the base of the aorta. This murmur is often heard well at the apex of the heart.

B. Diastolic Murmurs: Diastolic murmurs may result from dilatation of the heart (acute myocarditis, severe anemia), dilatation of the aortic ring (marked hypertension), deformity of a valve, or intracardiac shunts. When listening for diastolic murmurs, attention should be focused only on diastole, excluding from awareness as far as possible (once one has determined the timing) the first heart sound and any systolic murmurs.

C. Systolic Time Intervals: It has been demonstrated that left ventricular function can be assessed indirectly by quantitating the ratio (PEP/LVET; pre-ejection period/left ventricular ejection time) by simultaneous phonocardiography, indirect carotid pulse tracing, and ECG. The LVET is prolonged by impaired left ventricular function (as in patients with angina pectoris after exercise), and the ratio makes correction for heart rate unnecessary.

Braunwald, E., & H.J.C. Swan (editors): Cooperative study on cardiac catheterization. Circulation 37 (Suppl 3), 1968.

Carlsson, E.: *Measurement of Cardiac Chamber Volumes and Dimensions by Radiographic Methods: A Methodological Study With Some Physiological Applications.* Univ of Calif Press, 1970.

Cohn, J.N.: Diagnostic and therapeutic value of bedside monitoring of left ventricular pressure. Am J Cardiol 23:107–108, 1969.

Fredrickson, D.S.: On cultivating prognosis on cardiovascular research. Am J Cardiol 21:853–858, 1968.

Friedberg, C.K.: *Diseases of the Heart,* 3rd ed. Saunders, 1966.

Gorlin, R., & E.H. Sonnenblick: Regulation of the performance of the heart. Am J Cardiol 22:16–23, 1968.

Gould, L., & A.F. Lyon: Pulsus alternans, an early manifestation of left ventricular dysfunction. Angiology 19:103–109, 1968.

Guyton, A.C.: Regulation of cardiac output. Anesthesiology 29:314–326, 1968.

Haber, E., & A. Leatham: Splitting of heart sounds from ventricular asynchrony in bundle-branch block, ventricular ectopic beats, and artificial pacing. Brit Heart J 27:691–696, 1965.

Harrison, T.R., & T.J. Reeves: *Principles and Problems of Ischemic Heart Disease.* Year Book, 1968.

Hurst, J.W., & R.B. Logue: *The Heart, Arteries and Veins,* 2nd ed. McGraw-Hill, 1970.

Kahler, R.L., & E. Braunwald: The contribution of modern hemodynamic techniques to the diagnosis of acquired heart disease. M Clin North America 46:1519–1554, 1962.

Kazamias, T.M., & others: Detection of left-ventricular-wall motion disorders in coronary-artery disease by radarkymography. New England J Med 285:63–71, 1971.

Leatham, A.G.: Auscultation of the heart. Lancet 2:703–707, 1958.

Leatham, A.G.: *Auscultation of the Heart and Phonocardiography.* Churchill, 1970.

Marshall, R.J., & J.T. Shepherd: *Cardiac Function in Health and Disease.* Saunders, 1968.

Mason, D.T.: The autonomic nervous system and regulation of cardiovascular performance. Anesthesiology 29:670–680, 1968.

Mason, D.T., & B. Segal (editors): Symposium on ventricular function: Clinical applications based on new understanding of pathophysiology. Am J Cardiol 23:485–584, 1969.

Mendel, D.: *A Practice of Cardiac Catheterization.* Blackwell, 1968.

Mounsey, P.: Praecordial pulsations in health and disease. Postgrad MJ 44:134–139, 1968.

Scheinman, M., Abbott, J., & E. Rapaport: Clinical uses of a flow-directed right heart catheter. Arch Int Med 124:19–24, 1969.

Scheinman, M., & E. Rapaport: Critical assessment of the use of central venous O_2 saturation as a mirror of mixed venous oxygen in severely ill cardiac patients. Circulation 40:165, 1969.

Silverman, M.E., & J.W. Hurst: The hand and the heart. Am J Cardiol 22:718, 1968.

Starmer, C.F., McIntosh, H.D., & R.E. Whalen: Electrical hazards and cardiovascular function. New England J Med 284:181–186, 1971.

Sutton, G.H.A., & A. Lesson: Second heart sound and pulmonary hypertension. Brit Heart J 30:743–756, 1968.

Swan, H.J., & others: Catheterization of the heart in man with use of a flow-directed balloon-tipped catheter. New England J Med 283:447–451, 1970.

Tavel, M.E.: *Clinical Phonocardiography and External Pulse Recording.* Year Book, 1967.

Watson, H.: *Pediatric Cardiology.* Lloyd-Luke Ltd, 1968.

Weissler, A.M., Harris, W.S., & C.D. Schoenfeld: Systolic time intervals in heart failure in man. Circulation 37:149–159, 1968.

Weissler, A.M., & C.L. Garrard, Jr.: Systolic time intervals in cardiac disease. Mod Concepts Cardiovas Dis 40:1–8, 1971.

Werko, L.: Can we prevent heart disease? Ann Int Med 74:278–288, 1971.

.   .   .

FUNCTIONAL & THERAPEUTIC CLASSIFICATION OF HEART DISEASE*

Functional Capacity (Four classes.)

Class I: No limitation of physical activity. Ordinary physical activity does not cause undue fatigue, palpitation, dyspnea, or anginal pain.

Class II: Slight limitation of physical activity. Comfortable at rest, but ordinary physical activity results in fatigue, palpitation, dyspnea, or anginal pain.

Class III: Marked limitation of physical activity. Comfortable at rest, but less than ordinary activity causes fatigue, palpitation, dyspnea, or anginal pain.

Class IV: Unable to carry on any physical activity without discomfort. Symptoms of cardiac insufficiency, or of the anginal syndrome, may be pres-

*Criteria Committee, New York Heart Association.

ent even at rest. If any physical activity is undertaken, discomfort is increased.

Therapeutic Classification (Five classes.)

Class A: Physical activity need not be restricted.

Class B: Ordinary physical activity need not be restricted, but unusually severe or competitive efforts should be avoided.

Class C: Ordinary physical activity should be moderately restricted, and more strenuous efforts should be discontinued.

Class D: Ordinary physical activity should be markedly restricted.

Class E: Patient should be at complete rest, confined to bed or chair.

CONGENITAL HEART DISEASES

Congenital lesions account for about 2% of all heart disease in adults.

The following classification and relative frequency of defects is based on a study by Paul Wood (Wood, P.: *Diseases of the Heart and Circulation,* 3rd ed. Lippincott, 1968).

Classification

A. Without Shunt:
  1. **Right-sided**—Pulmonary stenosis (12%).
  2. **Left-sided**—Coarctation of aorta (9%); aortic stenosis (3%).

B. With Shunt:
  1. **Acyanotic**—
    Atrial septal defect (20%).
    Patent ductus arteriosus (13%).
    Ventricular septal defect (9%).
  2. **Cyanotic**—
    Tetralogy of Fallot (11%).
    Pulmonary stenosis with reversed interatrial shunt (3%).
    Eisenmenger's syndrome (3%).
    Tricuspid atresia (1.5%).

Other congenital anomalies are present in an estimated 20% of cases. Particularly common are mongolism, Marfan's syndrome, and chromosomal abnormalities such as Turner's syndrome.

Pathogenesis of Clinical Manifestations

Congenital heart disease produces symptoms and signs by one or more of the following mechanisms:

A. **Stenosis of a Valve or Vessel (A, above):** Hypertrophy of the proximal ventricle occurs and there is eventual heart failure with the usual manifestations.

B. **Left-to-Right Shunt (B 1, above):** Shunting of blood from the left atrium or ventricle to the right atrium or ventricle increases the work of the right ventricle and the amount of pulmonary blood flow at the expense of systemic flow. In large shunts, and in smaller ones during exercise, this discrepancy is exaggerated, and dyspnea and fatigue occur. For unknown reasons, some of these shunts cause pulmonary hypertension; reversal of shunt then occurs, converting the original left-to-right shunt into a right-to-left shunt (Eisenmenger's syndrome). Hemoptysis may occur.

C. Right-to-Left Shunt (B 2, above): Shunting of "venous" blood from the right atrium or ventricle into the aorta, left atrium, or left ventricle, bypassing the pulmonary circulation, causes arterial unsaturation which beyond a certain point is recognizable clinically as cyanosis. Squatting may bring relief of exertional dyspnea and fatigue. Syncope occurs when pulmonary blood flow is very low. Compensatory polycythemia results from the persistent unsaturation, and this in turn may be responsible for cerebral thrombosis in severe cases. Clubbing usually accompanies gross cyanosis.

In addition to the specific hemodynamic effects of the lesions themselves, metastatic brain abscess is a hazard in right-to-left shunts and bacterial endocarditis may develop, especially in ventricular septal defect, patent ductus arteriosus, and bicuspid aortic valve.

In addition to x-ray and ECG study, cardiac catheterization, biplane or cineangiocardiography, or dye-dilution curves are often necessary to delineate the exact nature and magnitude of existing defects.

Differential Diagnosis

A. Auscultatory Signs: A history of a murmur present in infancy, congenital anomalies elsewhere in the body, and the finding of murmurs and thrills in areas separate from those of valve lesions found in rheumatic heart disease are helpful. A thrill and murmur along the left sternal border are most often due to congenital heart disease, although acquired aortic stenosis may confuse the diagnosis. Soft to prominent apical mid-diastolic murmurs are present in septal defect and patent ductus arteriosus but none of the other characteristics of mitral stenosis are present. Venous hum over the upper parasternal area may be confused with the continuous murmur of patent ductus arteriosus or aortic-pulmonary communication, but the former is markedly diminished by recumbency.

B. Cyanosis With Clubbing: Cyanosis, clubbing, and polycythemia may also occur in chronic cor pulmonale secondary to lung disease, and in congenital pulmonary arteriovenous fistula. When there is serious question regarding the origin of cyanosis and clubbing, measurement of response of arterial oxygen to inhalation of 100% oxygen is helpful, because the arterial oxygen saturation cannot rise to normal if a shunt is present.

C. Cyanosis Without Clubbing: Cyanosis without clubbing and polycythemia is usually "peripheral," secondary to reduced cardiac output, or slowed peripheral circulation. Arterial oxygen saturation is normal.

If after careful study potentially remediable congenital heart disease remains a diagnostic possibility, the patient should be referred for cardiac catheterization, angiocardiography, and dye dilution studies.

Keith, J.D., Rowe, R.D., & P. Vlad: *Heart Disease in Infancy and Childhood,* 2nd ed. Macmillan, 1967.

Perloff, J.K.: *Clinical Recognition of Congenital Heart Disease.* Saunders, 1970.

Rudolph, A.M.: The changes in the circulation after birth: Their importance in congenital heart disease. Circulation 41:343–361, 1970.

PURE PULMONARY STENOSIS

Stenosis of the pulmonary valve or infundibulum increases the resistance to outflow, raises the right ventricular pressure, and limits the amount of pulmonary blood flow. Since there is no shunt, arterial saturation is normal, but severe stenosis causes peripheral cyanosis by reducing cardiac output. Clubbing or polycythemia does not develop unless a patent foramen ovale or atrial septal defect is present, permitting shunting of blood from the right to the left atrium.

Clinical Findings

A. Symptoms and Signs: Mild cases (right ventricular-pulmonary artery gradient < 50 mm Hg) are asymptomatic. Moderate to severe stenosis (gradients exceeding 80 mm Hg) causes dyspnea on exertion (in the absence of heart failure), fainting, and chest pain. Right ventricular failure develops eventually in severe cases, producing edema, increased dyspnea, and fatigue.

There is a palpable right ventricular heave. A loud, harsh systolic murmur and a prominent thrill is present in the left second and third interspaces parasternally; the murmur is in the third and fourth interspaces in infundibular stenosis. The second sound is obscured by the murmur in severe cases; the pulmonic component is diminished, delayed, or absent. Both components are audible in mild cases. A presystolic gallop and a prominent "a" wave in the venous pulse are present in severe cases.

B. X-Ray Findings and Fluoroscopy: The heart size may be normal, or there may be a prominent right ventricle and atrium or gross cardiac enlargement, depending upon the severity. The pulmonary artery is dilated with weak or absent pulsations in valvular stenosis, normal in infundibular stenosis. Pulmonary vascularity is normal or (in severe cases) diminished.

C. ECG Findings: Right axis or right ventricular hypertrophy; peaked P waves.

D. Special Studies: Cardiac catheterization permits estimation of the gradient across the pulmonic valve, determines whether the stenosis is valvular or infundibular, and, together with dye studies, demonstrates the presence or absence of associated shunts. Angiography delineates the anatomy of the defect, including the infundibulum of the right ventricle.

Treatment

Pure pulmonic stenosis with evidence of progressive hypertrophy and resting gradients over 75–80 mm Hg is treated surgically with low operative mortality and excellent results in most cases. All lesions are corrected under direct vision; those with associated outflow tract hypertrophy are often approached through a ventriculotomy.

Prognosis

Patients with mild stenosis may have a normal life expectancy unless bacterial endocarditis occurs. Severe stenosis causes refractory heart failure in the twenties and thirties. Moderate stenosis may be asymptomatic in childhood and adolescence, but cardiac symptoms and cardiac failure occur with increasing frequency as the patient becomes older. Only 12% of patients survive past age 50. In patients with pure pulmonic stenosis, the incidence of bacterial endocarditis is about 1% per year.

Campbell, M.: Natural history of congenital pulmonary stenosis. Brit Heart J 31:394, 1969.

Hoffman, J.: Natural history of congenital outflow obstructions. Ann Rev Med 22:15, 1968.

Moller, J.H., & P. Adams, Jr.: The natural history of pulmonary valvular stenosis. Serial cardiac catheterizations in 21 children. Am J Cardiol 16:654–664, 1965. Snellen, H.A., & others: Pulmonic stenosis. Circulation 38 (Suppl 5):93–101, 1968.

Shem-Tov, A., & others: Corrected transposition of the great arteries: A modified approach to the clinical diagnosis in 30 cases. Am J Cardiol 27:99, 1971.

Tandon, R., Nadas, A.S., & R.E. Gross: Results of open-heart surgery in patients with pulmonic stenosis and intact ventricular septum: A report of 108 cases. Circulation 31:190–201, 1965.

PULMONARY STENOSIS WITH REVERSED INTERATRIAL SHUNT

The elevated pressure in the right ventricle causes right ventricular hypertrophy and decreased distensibility. Venous blood therefore passes more readily from the right atrium through the atrial defect into the left atrium. Arterial unsaturation results, and may be sufficient to produce all the consequences of "cyanotic congenital heart disease."

Clinical Findings

A. Symptoms and Signs: Exertional dyspnea and fatigue; cyanosis, clubbing, and polycythemia; a long, harsh pulmonic systolic murmur and thrill; and slight to prominent right pulmonary artery pulsation and right ventricular heave.

B. X-Ray Findings: Slight to moderate cardiac enlargement, decreased pulmonary vascularity, and a dilated pulmonary artery (in valvular stenosis).

C. ECG Findings: Right ventricular hypertrophy and prominent P waves.

D. Special Studies: Cardiac catheterization and angiocardiography are helpful in distinguishing this lesion from tetralogy.

Treatment

Correction of pulmonic stenosis decreases right ventricular pressure and permits the atrial shunt to again become left to right if it is not closed. The shunt is usually corrected at the same operation.

Prognosis

Without surgical treatment, survival beyond early adult life is rare.

COARCTATION OF THE AORTA

The adult type of coarctation of the aorta consists of localized narrowing of the aortic arch just distal to the origin of the left subclavian artery in the region of the ligamentum arteriosum. A bicuspid aortic valve is present in 25% of cases. Blood pressure is elevated in the aorta and its branches proximal to the coarctation and decreased distally. Collateral circulation between the high and low pressure aortic segments develops through the intercostal arteries and branches of the subclavian arteries.

Clinical Findings

A. Symptoms and Signs: There are no symptoms until the hypertension produces left ventricular failure or cerebral hemorrhage. Strong arterial pulsations are seen in the neck and suprasternal notch. Hypertension is present in the arms but the pressure is normal or low in the legs. This difference is exaggerated by exercise, which is helpful in the diagnosis of doubtful cases. Femoral pulsations are absent or weak and delayed in comparison with the brachial pulse. Visible or palpable collateral arteries are present in the intercostal spaces and along the borders of the scapulas. Late systolic ejection murmurs at the base are often heard better posteriorly, especially over the spinous processes.

B. X-Ray Findings: X-ray shows scalloping of the ribs due to enlarged collateral intercostal arteries; dilatation of the left subclavian artery and poststenotic aortic dilatation ("3" sign); and left ventricular enlargement.

C. ECG Findings: The ECG shows left ventricular hypertrophy; it may be normal in mild cases.

Treatment

Resection of the coarcted site is a more difficult operative procedure than ligation of a patent ductus arteriosus, and the surgical mortality is in the neighborhood of 1–3%. The risks of the disease are such, however, that if a skilled heart surgeon is available all coarctations in patients up to the age of 20 years should be resected. In patients between the ages of 20 and 35, surgery is advisable if the patient is showing evidence of left ventricular strain. The mortality rises considerably in patients over 50 years of age, and surgery in this age group is of doubtful value.

Prognosis

Most patients with the adult form of coarctation die before the age of 40 from the complications of hypertension, rupture of the aorta, bacterial endocarditis, or cerebral hemorrhage (congenital aneurysms). However, 25% of patients have a normal cardiovascular prognosis and die of causes unrelated to the coarctation.

Campbell, M.: Natural history of coarctation of the aorta. Brit Heart J 32:633–641, 1970.

Karnell, J.: Coarctation of the aorta. Circulation 38 (Suppl 5):35–44, 1968.

Sellors, T.H., & M. Hobsley: Coarctation of the aorta. Lancet 1:1387–1392, 1963.

ATRIAL SEPTAL DEFECT

The most common form of atrial septal defect is persistence of the ostium secundum in the mid-septum; less commonly, the ostium primum (which is low in the septum, involving the endocardial cushion) persists, in which case mitral or tricuspid abnormalities may also be present. In both instances, normally oxygenated blood from the left atrium passes into the right atrium, increasing the right ventricular output and the pulmonary blood flow. In the primum defect, mitral valve insufficiency produces, additionally, strain on the left ventricle.

Clinical Findings

A. Symptoms and Signs: Most patients with moderate secundum defects are asymptomatic. With large shunts, exertional dyspnea or cardiac failure may develop. Prominent right ventricular pulsations are readily visible and palpable. A moderately loud systolic ejection murmur can be heard in the second and third interspaces parasternally due to increased flow across the pulmonic valve, as well as an apical or xiphoid mid-diastolic soft murmur due to increased flow across the tricuspid valve, especially on inspiration. Thrills are uncommon. The second sound is widely split, and does not vary with respiration.

B. X-Ray Findings: Large pulmonary arteries with vigorous pulsations, increased pulmonary vascularity, an enlarged right atrium and ventricle, and a small aortic knob.

C. ECG Findings: Right axis or right ventricular hypertrophy may be present in ostium secundum defects. Incomplete or complete right bundle branch block is present in most cases, and left superior axis deviation with counterclockwise rotation in the frontal plane in ostium primum defect.

D. Special Studies: Cardiac catheterization permits calculation of the amount of blood shunted, the intracardiac and pulmonary pressures, and the pulmonary vascular resistance. The catheter may pass through the defect into the left atrium. Angiocardiography may reveal primum defects or mitral insufficiency.

Treatment

Small atrial septal defects do not require surgery. Lesions with a large left to right shunt (more than 2 or 3 times systemic flow) with slight or no increased pulmonary arterial resistance should be operated upon. The surgical risks now are sufficiently low so that patients with a pulmonary to systemic flow rate of 1.5:1 should probably be operated on.

Surgery should be withheld from patients with pulmonary hypertension with reversed shunt because of the risk of acute right heart failure.

Prognosis

Patients with small shunts may live a normal life span; with larger shunts, they survive to middle or late life before pulmonary hypertension or heart failure appear. The latter is precipitated most often by atrial fibrillation, or raised pulmonary vascular resistance. Large shunts cause disability by age 40. Raised pulmonary vascular resistance secondary to pulmonary hypertension rarely occurs in childhood or young adult life in secundum defects but is common in primum defects; after age 40, pulmonary hypertension may occur in secundum defects.

The surgical mortality with cardiac bypass is small (< 1%) in patients under 45 years of age who are not in cardiac failure and have pulmonary artery pressures < 60 mm Hg. It increases to 6–10% in patients over age 40 with cardiac failure or pulmonary artery pressures > 60 mm Hg. Most of the survivors show considerable improvement.

Campbell, M.: Natural history of atrial septal defect. Brit Heart J 32:820–827, 1970.

Cohn, L.H., Morrow, A.G., & E. Braunwald: Operative treatment of atrial septal defect: Clinical and haemodynamic assessments in 175 patients. Brit Heart J 29:725–734, 1967.

Dalen, J.E., Haynes, F.W., & L. Dexter: Life expectancy with atrial septal defect. Influence of complicating pulmonary vascular disease. JAMA 200:112, 1967.

Flamm, M.D., Cohn, K.E., & E.W. Hancock: Ventricular function in atrial septal defect. Am J Med 48:286, 1970.

Gault, J.H., & others: Atrial septal defect in patients over the age of 40 years: Clinical and hemodynamic studies and the effects of operation. Circulation 37:261–272, 1968.

Kimball, K.G., & M.B. McIlroy: Pulmonary hypertension in patients with congenital heart disease. Am J Med 41:883–897, 1966.

Kulbertus, H.E., Coyne, J.J., & K.A. Hallidie-Smith: Electrocardiographic correlation of anatomical and haemodynamic data in ostium primum atrial septal defects. Brit Heart J 30:464–469, 1968.

Rahimtoola, S.H., Kirklin, J.W., & H.B. Burchell: Atrial septal defect. Circulation 38(Suppl 5):2–12, 1968.

Saksena, F.B., & H.E. Aldridge: Atrial septal defect in the older patient: A clinical and hemodynamic study in patients operated on after age 35. Circulation 42(Suppl 6):1009, 1970.

Tikoff, G., & others: Clinical and hemodynamic observations after surgical closure of large atrial septal defect complicated by heart failure. Am J Cardiol 23:810–817, 1969.

PATENT DUCTUS ARTERIOSUS

The embryonic ductus arteriosus fails to close normally and persists as a shunt connecting the left pulmonary artery and aorta, usually near the origin of the left subclavian artery. Blood flows from the aorta through the ductus into the pulmonary artery continuously in systole and diastole; it is a form of arteriovenous fistula, increasing the work of the left ventricle. In some patients, obliterative changes in the pulmonary vessels cause pulmonary hypertension. Then the shunt is bidirectional or right-to-left.

Clinical Findings

A. Symptoms and Signs: There are no symptoms until or unless left ventricular failure develops. The heart is of normal size or slightly enlarged with a forceful apex beat. Pulse pressure is wide and diastolic pressure is low. A continuous, rough "machinery" murmur, accentuated in late systole, is heard best in the left first and second interspaces at the sternal border. Thrills are common. Paradoxic splitting of the second sound may be present if there is considerable left ventricular hypertrophy.

B. X-Ray Findings: The heart is normal in size and contour, or there may be left ventricular and left atrial enlargement. The pulmonary artery, aorta, and left atrium are prominent.

C. ECG Findings: Normal pattern or left ventricular hypertrophy, depending upon the width of the ductus.

D. Special Studies: Cardiac catheterization establishes the presence of a left-to-right shunt. The catheter may be passed through the ductus into the aorta from the pulmonary artery, and, when combined with angiography, excludes other lesions (such as ruptured sinus of Valsalva into the right heart), which may cause a similar murmur.

Treatment

Because of the low operative mortality rate (< 1%) in skilled hands, division and closure is recommended in both children and adults. The mortality rate becomes higher as the patient becomes older. This necessitates caution in recommending surgery in older adults who are asymptomatic and have no left ventricular hypertrophy. Subacute bacterial endocarditis is the major hazard in this group.

The indications for ligation or division of a patent ductus arteriosus in the presence of pulmonary hypertension are controversial, but current opinion favors ligation whenever the flow through the ductus is permanently or intermittently from left to right, ie, when pulmonary blood flow is increased, and the pulmonary artery pressure is < 100 mm Hg.

Prognosis

Large shunts cause a high mortality from cardiac failure early in life. Smaller shunts are compatible with long survival, congestive heart failure being the most common complication. Bacterial endocarditis may also occur. A small percentage of patients develops pulmonary hypertension and reversal of shunt, such that the lower legs, especially the toes, appear cyanotic in contrast to normally pink fingers. At this stage, the patient is inoperable.

Campbell, M.: Natural history of persistent ductus arteriosus. Brit Heart J 30:4–14, 1968.

Espino-Vela, J., Cardenas, N., & R. Cruz: Patent ductus arteriosus: With special reference to patients with pulmonary hypertension. Circulation 38 (Suppl 5):45–60, 1968.

Rudolph, A.M., & others: Hemodynamic basis for clinical manifestations of patent ductus arteriosus. Am Heart J 68:447–458, 1964.

VENTRICULAR SEPTAL DEFECT

In this lesion a persistent opening in the upper interventricular septum due to failure of fusion with the aortic septum permits blood to pass from the high-pressure left ventricle into the low-pressure right ventricle. In 1/4–1/3 of cases the shunt is not large enough to strain the heart. With large shunts, both left and right ventricular strain may develop.

Clinical Findings

A. Symptoms and Signs: The clinical features are dependent upon the size of the defect and the presence or absence of a raised pulmonary vascular resistance. If the latter is normal and the defect is small, the left-to-right shunt is small; if the defect is large, the resistance to flow between the ventricles is small and the left-to-right shunt is large; a rise in pulmonary vascular resistance decreases the left-to-right shunt and converts the pansystolic murmur into a "lopsided" diamond ejection murmur. A long, loud, harsh systolic murmur and thrill are found in the left 3rd and 4th interspaces along the sternum, and may be the only finding in small defects. In large shunts a right ventricular heave is palpable and a mid-diastolic "flow murmur" and a third heart sound may be heard at the apex.

B. X-Ray Findings: With large shunts the right or left ventricle (or both), the left atrium, and the pulmonary arteries are enlarged, and pulmonary vascularity is increased.

C. ECG Findings: May be normal or may show right, left, or biventricular hypertrophy.

D. Special Studies: Cardiac catheterization permits a definitive diagnosis in all but the most trivial defects. Infants with cardiac failure should be studied to establish the diagnosis and determine the appropriate treatment.

Treatment

Ventricular septal defects vary in severity from trivial asymptomatic lesions with normal cardiac hemodynamics to extensive lesions causing death from cardiac failure in infancy. The former do not require surgery. The ideal case for curative repair with cardiac bypass technics is one with a large left-to-right shunt, left ventricular hypertrophy, and only moderate pulmonary hypertension. When severe pulmonary hypertension is present (pulmonary arterial pressures > 85 mm Hg) and the left-to-right shunt is small, the surgical mortality risk is at least 50%. If the shunt is reversed, surgery is contraindicated. If surgery is required because of unrelenting cardiac failure in infancy due to a large left-to-right shunt, pulmonary artery banding may decrease the shunt and tide the patient over until age 5 or 6, when definitive repair can be done. It has become increasingly evident that some defects (perhaps as many as 30–50%) close spontaneously. Therefore, surgery should be deferred until late childhood unless the disability is severe or unless pulmonary hypertension is observed to progress or to develop.

Prognosis

Patients with the typical murmur as the only abnormality have a normal life expectancy except for the threat of bacterial endocarditis. With large shunts, congestive heart failure may develop early in life and survival beyond age 40 is unusual. Shunt reversal occurs in an estimated 25%, producing Eisenmenger's syndrome.

Clarkson, P.M., & others: Prognosis for patients with ventricular septal defect and severe pulmonary vascular obstructive disease. Circulation 38:129–135, 1968.

Gotsman, M.S., & others: Haemodynamic studies after repair of ventricular septal defect. Brit Heart J 31:63–71, 1969.

Hallidie-Smith, K.A., & others: Effects of surgical closure of ventricular septal defects upon pulmonary vascular disease. Brit Heart J 31:246–260, 1969.

Hoffman, J.I.E.: Medical history of congenital heart disease: Problems in its assessment with special reference to ventricular septal defect. Circulation 37:97–125, 1968.

Lillehei, C.W., Anderson, R.C., & Y. Wang: Clinical and hemodynamic changes after closure of ventricular septal defects. JAMA 205:114–118, 1968.

TETRALOGY OF FALLOT

Pulmonary stenosis together with a high interventricular septal defect, which allow the right ventricle to empty into the aorta, prevent venous blood from passing normally into the pulmonary artery. Instead, blood passes from the right ventricle into the aorta and into the left ventricle. Aortic blood is therefore markedly unsaturated, and cyanosis, polycythemia, and clubbing appear early. Exercise causes cyanosis to deepen.

Clinical Findings

A. Symptoms and Signs: Physical development is retarded in severe cases. Dyspnea is common; squatting relieves fatigue and dyspnea; and syncope occasionally occurs. Prominent signs are cyanosis and clubbing, a slight right ventricular heave and absent apical impulse, and a short, harsh systolic murmur and thrill along the left sternal border. The heart is not enlarged. A single loud second sound is heard unless the lesion is mild, when the second sound is split with the pulmonary component decreased in amplitude.

B. X-Ray Findings: The lung fields are abnormally clear. The apex of the heart is blunted, with a concavity in the pulmonary artery segment (boot-shaped heart). A right aortic arch is present in 25% of cases.

C. ECG Findings: Moderate right ventricular hypertrophy is almost always present. Prominent P waves are occasionally present.

D. Special Studies: Cardiac catheterization and right ventricular angiocardiography together establish the diagnosis and define the anatomy. Aortography has been recommended as a routine procedure in patients considered for radical corrective surgery to show the aortic branches and unexpected associated defects.

Treatment

Tetralogy of Fallot is treated surgically using extracorporeal circulation, and the operative mortality rate is reasonably low. Patients with underdeveloped pulmonary arteries and those weighing less than 15 kg should be given a preliminary Blalock type shunt if severe oxygen deprivation (as indicated by cyanosis) threatens survival. Propranolol (Inderal®) has been used with benefit for episodes of syncope due to infundibular contraction.

Prognosis

Tetralogy is the commonest cause of cyanotic congenital heart disease in adults, and survival to adult life is not common. Severe hypoxemia is the commonest cause of death. Vascular thromboses secondary to polycythemia are also common. The severity of the syndrome is dominated by the magnitude of the pulmonic stenosis; the greater the stenosis, the greater the right-to-left shunt and the smaller the pulmonary blood flow.

Cole, R.B., & others: Long-term results of aortopulmonary anastomosis for tetralogy of Fallot: Morbidity and mortality, 1946–69. Circulation 43(Suppl 2):263, 1971.

Crawford, D.W., Simpson, E., & M.B. McIlroy: Cardiopulmonary function in Fallot's tetralogy after palliative shunting operations. Am Heart J 74:463–472, 1967.

Eriksson, B.O., Thoren, C., & P. Zitterquist: Long term treatment with propranolol in selected cases of Fallot's tetralogy. Brit Heart J 31:37–44, 1969.

Goldman, B.S., Mustard, W.T., & G.S. Trusler: Total correction of tetralogy of Fallot: Review of ten years' experience. Brit Heart J 30:563–568, 1968.

Gotsman, M.S., & others: Results of repair of tetralogy of Fallot. Circulation 40:803–823, 1969.

Kirklin, J.W.: The tetralogy of Fallot. Am J Roentgenol 102:253–266, 1968.

Rees, S., & J. Somerville: Aortography in Fallot's tetralogy and variants. Brit Heart J 31:146–153, 1969.

EISENMENGER'S SYNDROME
(Pulmonary Hypertension in Congenital Heart Disease)

This lesion was originally defined as ventricular septal defect, right ventricular hypertrophy, and over-riding of the aorta, producing cyanosis, but it is now thought of as pulmonary hypertension causing reversal of any originally left-to-right shunt. In order of frequency the defects most commonly resulting in this mechanism of shunt reversal are ventricular septal defect, patent ductus arteriosus, and atrial septal defect (rare under age 21 or in secundum defects). The cause of the pulmonary hypertension is not known; in many cases it may have been present from birth. The increased pulmonary vascular resistance causes right ventricular hypertrophy, and variable shunt reversal occurs. Blood still passes from left to right as well as from right to left.

Clinical Findings
A. Symptoms and Signs: Moderate to severe exertional dyspnea is common. Ventricular septal defect and atrial septal defect cause cyanosis with clubbing and polycythemia. Reversed ductus causes cyanosis of the lower legs and toes. Right ventricular and pulmonary artery pulsations are palpable; a systolic murmur can be heard along the left sternal border; and there may be an early pulmonic systolic ejection click.

B. X-Ray Findings: Large, actively pulsating central pulmonary arteries with reduced peripheral pulmonary vascularity are noted on fluoroscopy.

C. ECG Findings: Right ventricular hypertrophy with peaked P waves is the usual finding.

D. Special Studies: Cardiac catheterization, angiocardiography, and dye dilution studies may be necessary to establish the site of the shunt.

Treatment
No surgical treatment is effective in Eisenmenger's syndrome.

Prognosis
Most patients die of heart failure, vascular thrombosis, or endocarditis before 30 years of age.

Wood, P.: The Eisenmenger syndrome. Brit MJ 2:701–709, 755–762, 1958.

TRICUSPID ATRESIA

Atresia of the tricuspid valve may occur (1) as an isolated lesion; (2) with stenosis of the pulmonary arteries together with atrial septal defect; or (3) in association with ventricular septal defect or patent ductus arteriosus. Blood from the right atrium passes into the left atrium and reaches the lungs by passing through a ventricular septal defect into the right ventricle or, when the right ventricle and the pulmonary artery are rudimentary, by shunting from the aorta into the pulmonary circulation through a patent ductus.

Examination reveals a strong apical impulse, a systolic murmur and thrill along the left sternal border, cyanosis, clubbing, and polycythemia. The ECG reveals left axis deviation or left ventricular hypertrophy. Angiocardiography and cardiac catheterization are necessary for definitive diagnosis. Anastomosis of the subclavian artery to the pulmonary artery (Blalock) is probably the procedure of choice if the pulmonary blood flow is low. The benefits of anastomosis of the right atrium to the pulmonary artery have not yet been established.

The prognosis for life is poor. Only an occasional patient survives to adulthood.

Campbell, M.: Tricuspid atresia and its prognosis with and without surgical treatment. Brit Heart J 23:699–710, 1961.

ACQUIRED HEART DISEASES

RHEUMATIC FEVER

Criteria for Diagnosis (Modified After Jones)
A. Major Criteria:
1. Carditis.
2. Sydenham's chorea.
3. Subcutaneous (fascial) nodules.
4. Erythema marginatum.
5. Polyarthritis.

B. Minor Criteria:
1. Fever.
2. Polyarthralgia.
3. Prolongation of P–R interval.
4. Increased sedimentation rate or C-reactive protein.
5. Evidence of antecedent beta-hemolytic streptococcus infection.
6. Verified history of previous rheumatic fever or presence of rheumatic valvular disease.

The diagnosis of rheumatic fever is almost certain when 2 or more major criteria are present. Nevertheless, rheumatoid arthritis, neurocirculatory asthenia, bacterial endocarditis, collagen diseases, serum sickness, penicillin reaction, and chronic infectious disease can reproduce the early manifestations of rheumatic fever.

General Considerations

Rheumatic fever is a subacute or chronic systemic disease which for unknown reasons may either be self-limiting or lead to slowly progressive valvular deformity. Rarely, it is acute and fulminant.

Rheumatic fever is the commonest cause of heart disease in people under 50 years of age. In overall incidence, it ranks third behind hypertension and atherosclerotic coronary disease. It is somewhat more common in males than in females, but chorea is seen more frequently in females. The peak incidence occurs between the ages of 5 and 15; rheumatic fever is rare before the age of 4 and after 50.

Rheumatic fever is initiated by an infection with group A hemolytic streptococci, appearing usually 1–4 weeks after tonsillitis, nasopharyngitis, or otitis.

The acute phase of rheumatic fever may involve the endocardium, myocardium, pericardium, synovial joint linings, lungs, or pleura. The characteristic lesion is a perivascular granulomatous reaction and vasculitis. The mitral valve is attacked in 75–80% of cases, the aortic valve in 30%, the tricuspid and pulmonary valve in less than 5%. Small pink granules appear on the surface of the edematous valve. Healing may be complete, or a progressive scarring due to subacute or chronic inflammation may develop over months and years.

Clinical Findings

A. Major Criteria:

1. Carditis—The presence of carditis establishes the diagnosis of rheumatic fever whenever there is (1) a definite history of rheumatic fever, or (2) valvular disease clearly of rheumatic origin, or (3) whenever a streptococcal infection of the upper respiratory tract is known to have occurred within the preceding 4 weeks. Carditis is most apt to be evident in children and adolescents; in adults, it is often best detected by serial ECG study. Any of the following establishes the presence of carditis:

a. Pericarditis—Either fibrinous (with a pleuritic type of precordial, epigastric, or left shoulder pain; friction rub; characteristic ST–T changes on the ECG) or with effusion of any degree. It is uncommon in adults and is at times diagnosed by the progressive increase in "heart shadow" on serial chest x-rays.

b. Cardiac enlargement, detected by physical signs or x-ray, indicating dilatation of a weakened, inflamed myocardium. Serial x-rays are often needed to detect the change in size.

c. Frank congestive failure, right- and left-sided—Right heart failure is more prominent in children, and painful engorgement of the liver is a valuable sign.

d. Mitral or aortic diastolic murmurs, indicative of dilatation of a valve ring or the myocardium with or without associated valvulitis.

In the absence of any of the above definite signs the diagnosis of carditis depends upon the following less specific abnormalities considered in relation to the total clinical picture.

(1) ECG changes: P–R prolongation greater than 0.04 second above the patient's normal is the most significant abnormality; changing contour of P waves or inversion of T waves is less specific.

(2) Changing quality of heart sounds.

(3) Pansystolic apical murmur which persists or becomes louder during the course of the disease and is transmitted into the axilla. The Carey Coombs short mid-diastolic murmur should be carefully sought.

(4) Gallop rhythm: Difficult to differentiate from the physiologic third sound in children and adolescents.

(5) Sinus tachycardia out of proportion to the degree of fever, persisting during sleep and markedly increased by slight activity.

(6) Arrhythmias, shifting pacemaker, ectopic beats.

2. The 2 following signs occur most often in association with severe carditis and so are of little value in initial diagnosis; occasionally, however, they appear before carditis is evident and constitute strong presumptive evidence of rheumatic fever.

a. Erythema marginatum (annulare)—Frequently associated with skin nodules. The lesions begin as rapidly enlarging macules which assume the shape of rings or crescents with clear centers. They may be slightly raised and confluent. The rash may be transient or may persist for long periods.

b. Subcutaneous nodules—These are uncommon except in children. The nodules may be few or many, are usually small (2 cm or less in diameter), firm, nontender, and are attached to fascia or tendon sheaths over bony prominences such as the elbows, the dorsal surfaces of the hands, the malleoli, the vertebral spines, and the occiput. They persist for days or weeks, are usually recurrent, and are clinically indistinguishable from the nodules of rheumatoid arthritis.

3. Sydenham's chorea may appear suddenly as an isolated entity with no "minor criteria" or may develop in the course of overt rheumatic fever. Eventually 50% of cases have other signs of rheumatic fever. Girls are more frequently affected, and occurrence in adults is rare. Chorea consists of continual, nonrepetitive, purposeless jerky movements of the limbs, trunk, and facial muscles. Milder forms masquerade as undue restlessness as the patient attempts to convert uncontrolled movements into seemingly purposeful movements. Facial grimaces of infinite variety are common. These movements are made worse by emotional tension and disappear entirely during sleep. The episode lasts several weeks, occasionally months.

4. Arthritis—The arthritis of rheumatic fever is characteristically a migratory polyarthritis of gradual or sudden onset which involves the large joints sequentially, one becoming hot, red, swollen, and tender as the inflammation in the previously involved joint subsides. The body temperature rises progressively as each successive joint becomes inflamed. In adults only a single or a small joint may be affected. The acute arthritis lasts 1–5 weeks and subsides without residual deformity. *Note:* Joint involvement is considered a major criterion only when definite effusion and signs of inflammation are present. This is in contrast to arthralgia, in which pain or stiffness is present without these objective signs. Prompt response of arthritis to therapeutic doses of salicylates is characteristic (but not diagnostic) of rheumatic fever.

With respect to arthritis, the dictum, "one major and 2 minor criteria," is a source of diagnostic confusion. Arthritis and arthralgia are common in children and young adults, often accompanied by fever and an increased sedimentation rate. Streptococcal infection or "sore throat" is also common. Coincidental association of these factors thus often leads to an unwarranted diagnosis of rheumatic fever. A definite diagnosis requires bona fide evidence of carditis or the appearance of additional rheumatic manifestations such as erythema marginatum or chorea.

B. Minor Criteria: The following common nonspecific manifestations are of diagnostic help only when associated with other more specific features:

1. Fever is always present with arthritis and carditis. In subacute or chronic phases it is low-grade and may be continuous or intermittent. Fever is important only as evidence of an inflammatory process. Certain children and even adults may have normal peak temperatures of 37.5–37.8° C (99.5–100° F), and this should not be construed erroneously as "fever."

2. Malaise, asthenia, weight loss, and anorexia may be the only overt effects of a smoldering rheumatic state, but are also characteristic of any chronic active disease.

3. Abdominal pain is common. It is variable in site and severity and occasionally leads to an unnecessary laparotomy. It may result from liver engorgement, sterile rheumatic peritonitis, or rheumatic arteritis, or may be referred from the pleura or pericardium.

4. Recurrent epistaxis is believed by some clinicians to be a sign of "subclinical" rheumatic fever.

5. "Growing pains" in joints, periarticular tissues, or muscle insertions may be a symptom of rheumatic fever ("arthralgia").

C. Laboratory Findings: These are helpful in 3 ways:

1. As nonspecific evidence of inflammatory disease—Sedimentation rate and C-reactive protein are almost always increased during active rheumatic fever except when chorea is the only clinical sign. Variable leukocytosis and normochromic anemia may appear. Slight proteinuria and microhematuria are occasionally seen and may not indicate concomitant glomerulonephritis.

2. As evidence of antecedent beta-hemolytic streptococcal infection—A high titer or increasing antistreptolysin O titer indicates recent infection but does not mean that rheumatic fever is present. Throat culture is positive for beta-hemolytic streptococci in 50% of cases of active rheumatic fever.

3. As strong evidence against the diagnosis—A low antistreptolysin O titer (50 Todd units) which does not rise on repeated tests tends to rule out rheumatic fever. A normal sedimentation rate is rare in the presence of active rheumatic fever.

Differential Diagnosis

Rheumatic fever may be confused with the following: rheumatoid arthritis, osteomyelitis, traumatic joint disease, neurocirculatory asthenia or cardiac neurosis, bacterial endocarditis, pulmonary tuberculosis, chronic meningococcemia, acute poliomyelitis, disseminated lupus erythematosus, serum sickness, drug sensitivity, leukemia, sickle cell anemia, inactive rheumatic heart disease, congenital heart disease, and "surgical abdomen."

Complications

Congestive heart failure occurs in severe cases. Other complications include cardiac arrhythmias, pericarditis with large effusion, rheumatic pneumonitis, pulmonary embolism and infarction, cardiac invalidism, and early or late development of permanent heart valve deformity.

Prevention of Recurrent Rheumatic Fever

The principles of prevention are to avoid beta-hemolytic streptococcal infections if possible and to treat streptococcal infections promptly and intensively with appropriate antibiotics.

A. General Measures: Avoid contact with persons who have "colds" or other upper respiratory infections. Patients with rheumatic fever do better in an equable climate, where streptococcal infections are less common.

B. Prevention of Infection: Two methods of prevention are now advocated:

1. Penicillin, 200–250 thousand units orally every day before breakfast, or benzathine penicillin G (Bicillin®), 1 million units IM once a month. This is advocated especially for children who have had one or more acute attacks and should be given throughout the school year. Adults should receive preventive therapy for about 5 years after an attack. It is most important to give preventive penicillin between September and June.

2. Sulfonamides—If the patient is sensitive to penicillin, give sulfadiazine, 0.5–1 gm daily throughout the year. *Caution:* Patients receiving sulfonamides should have periodic blood counts and urinalyses. If there is any tendency toward leukopenia, the drug should be stopped immediately.

C. Treatment of Streptococcal Sore Throat: It has been shown that prompt therapy (within 24 hours) of streptococcal infections will prevent most attacks of acute rheumatic fever. (See Chapter 21.)

Treatment

A. Medical Treatment:

1. Salicylates—The salicylates markedly reduce fever and relieve joint pain, and may reduce joint swelling. There is no evidence that they have any effect on the natural course of the disease. *Note:* The salicylates should be continued as long as necessary to relieve pain, swelling, or fever. If withdrawal results in a recurrence of symptoms, treatment should immediately be reinstituted.

a. Sodium salicylate is the most widely used of this group of drugs. Maximum dose is 1–2 gm every 2–4 hours orally to allay symptoms and fever; 4–6 gm/day suffices in most adults. In an occasional patient maximum doses may not be completely effective. There is no evidence that intravenous administration has any advantage over the oral route. Early toxic reactions to the salicylates include tinnitus, nausea, and vomiting. Antacids are usually given with salicylates to reduce gastric irritation. *Caution:* Never use sodium salicylate or sodium bicarbonate in patients with acute rheumatic fever who have associated cardiac failure.

b. Aspirin may be substituted for sodium salicylate, with the same dosages and precautions.

2. Penicillin should be employed in the treatment as well as the prevention of rheumatic fever to reduce the incidence of long-term sequelae. See Chapter 21 for intensive penicillin therapy schedules.

3. Corticosteroids—Careful studies have shown no clear or consistent proof that cardiac damage is prevented or minimized by corticosteroids even when they are given early in large doses. Corticosteroids are effective anti-inflammatory agents for reversing the acute exudative phase of rheumatic fever and are probably more potent for this purpose than salicylates. A short course of corticosteroids usually causes rapid improvement in the acute manifestations of rheumatic fever and is indicated in severe cases. There may be prompt disappearance of fever, malaise, tachycardia, and polyarthritis. Abnormal ECG changes (prolonged P–R interval) and sedimentation rates may return to normal limits within a week.

A suggested schedule, to be started as soon as severe rheumatic fever is diagnosed, is as follows: Give prednisone, 5–10 mg orally every 6 hours for 3 weeks, and then gradually withdraw over a period of 3 weeks by reducing and then discontinuing first the nighttime, then the evening, and finally the daytime doses. In severe cases the dosage should be increased, if necessary, to levels adequate to control symptoms (see the discussion of the methods, dangers, and precautions in the use of corticosteroids in Chapter 18).

B. General Measures: Bed rest should be enforced until all signs of active rheumatic fever have disappeared. The criteria for this are as follows: Return of the temperature to normal with the patient at bed rest and without medications; normal sedimentation rate; normal resting pulse rate (under 100 in adults); return of ECG to normal or fixation of abnormalities. The patient may then be allowed up slowly, but several months should elapse before return to full activity unless the rheumatic fever was exceedingly mild. Maintain good nutrition.

C. Treatment of Complications:

1. Congestive failure—Treat as for congestive failure, with the following variations:

a. A low-sodium diet and diuretics are of particular value in promoting diuresis and treating failure in acute rheumatic fever.

b. Digitalis is usually not as effective in acute rheumatic fever as in most cases of congestive failure and may accentuate the myocardial irritability, producing arrhythmias which further embarrass the heart. Digitalis should be given, but with extreme care.

c. Many cases of congestive failure are due to acute myocarditis. These often respond dramatically to corticotropin (ACTH) or the corticosteroids. When sodium-retaining hormonal agents are employed, rigorous sodium restriction (< 200 mg daily) or thiazide drugs are imperative.

2. Pericarditis—Treat as any acute nonpurulent pericarditis. The rheumatic effusion is sterile, and antibiotics are of no value. The general principles include relief of pain, by opiates if necessary, and removal of fluid by cardiac paracentesis if tamponade develops. This, however, is rarely necessary. If paracentesis is performed it should be preceded and followed by a short course of penicillin therapy to prevent infection of the pericardium. Corticotropin (ACTH) and the corticosteroids as well as salicylates should be continued or started, as they seem to have a specific favorable effect in aiding resorption of the fluid.

Prognosis

Initial episodes of rheumatic fever last months in children and weeks in adults. Twenty percent of children have recurrences within 5 years. Recurrences are uncommon after 5 years of well-being, and rare after the age of 21. The immediate mortality is 1–2%. Persistent rheumatic activity with a greatly enlarged heart, heart failure, and pericarditis indicate a poor prognosis; 30% of children thus affected die within 10 years of the initial attack. Otherwise the prognosis for life is good. Eighty percent of all patients attain adult life, and half of these have little if any limitation of activity. Approximately 1/3 of young patients have detectable valvular damage after the initial episode, most commonly a combination of mitral stenosis and insufficiency. After 10 years, 2/3 of surviving patients will have detectable valvular disease. In adults, residual heart damage occurs in less than 20% and is generally less severe. Mitral insufficiency is the commonest residual, and aortic insufficiency is much more common than in children. The influence of steroids on prognosis is as yet not known. Twenty percent of patients who have chorea develop valvular deformity even after a long latent period of apparent well-being.

Combined Rheumatic Fever Study Group: A comparison of short-term, intensive prednisone and acetylsalicylic acid therapy in the treatment of acute rheumatic fever. New England J Med 272:63–69, 1965.

Feinstein, A.R., & M. Spagnuolo: The clinical patterns of acute rheumatic fever: A reappraisal. Medicine 41:279–305, 1962.

Markowitz, M., & A.G. Kuttner: *Rheumatic Fever: Diagnosis, Management and Prevention.* Saunders, 1965.

Sokolow, M., & A. Snell: Atypical features of rheumatic fever in young adults. JAMA 133:981, 1947.

RHEUMATIC HEART DISEASE
(Rheumatic Valvulitis, Inactive)

Chronic rheumatic heart disease results from single or repeated attacks of rheumatic fever which produce rigidity and deformity of the cusps, fusion of the commissures, or shortening and fusion of the chordae tendineae. Stenosis or insufficiency results and both often coexist, although one or the other predominates. The mitral valve alone is affected in 50–60% of cases; combined lesions of the aortic and mitral valves occur in 20%; pure aortic lesions in 10%. Tricuspid involvement occurs only in association with mitral or aortic disease in about 10% of cases. The pulmonary valve is rarely affected.

Clinical Findings

A history of rheumatic fever is obtainable in only 60% of patients with rheumatic heart disease.

The earliest evidence of organic valvular disease is a significant murmur. The earliest evidence of hemodynamically significant valvular lesions is found on x-ray, fluoroscopy, and ECG study, since these will reveal the earliest stages of specific chamber enlargement. Careful physical examination also permits accurate diagnosis of advanced valve lesions.

The important findings in each of the major valve lesions are summarized in Table 7–1. Hemodynamic changes, symptoms, associated findings, and course are discussed below.

Management of Asymptomatic Valvular Heart Disease
A. Prevention:
1. Recurrences of acute rheumatic fever can be prevented by (1) avoiding exposure to streptococcal infections; (2) continuous antibiotic prophylaxis in selected patients under 35 and those who have been exposed to known hemolytic streptococcal infections; and (3) prompt and adequate treatment of infections due to hemolytic streptococci.

2. The patient should be given advice regarding dental extraction, urologic procedures, surgical procedures, etc to prevent bacteremia and possible subacute bacterial endocarditis.

B. General Measures: Vocational guidance is necessary to anticipate possible reduced exercise tolerance in later life. Follow-up observations should emphasize early recognition of disturbances of thyroid function, anemia, and arrhythmias; maintenance of general health, and avoidance of obesity and excessive physical exertion.

1. MITRAL STENOSIS

Over 75% of patients with mitral stenosis are women below the age of 45. Relatively slight degrees of narrowing are sufficient to produce the auscultatory

signs. When the valve has narrowed to less than 1.5 cm, patients experience dyspnea and fatigue whenever their heart rate increases. The short diastolic interval during tachycardia results in inadequate ventricular filling. Consequently, the cardiac output falls and blood accumulates in the atrium and the pulmonary veins and capillaries. Eventually, pulmonary congestion is present continually, and symptoms increase in severity. Recumbency at night further increases the pulmonary blood volume, causing orthopnea, paroxysmal nocturnal dyspnea, or actual transudation of fluid into the alveoli, leading to acute pulmonary edema. Severe pulmonary congestion may also be initiated by acute bronchitis or any acute respiratory infection, by development of subacute bacterial endocarditis, or recurrence of acute rheumatic carditis. As a result of long-standing pulmonary venous hypertension, anastomoses develop between the pulmonary and bronchial veins in the form of bronchial submucosal varices. These often rupture, producing mild or severe hemoptysis.

Fifty to 80% of patients develop paroxysmal or chronic atrial fibrillation which, until controlled, may precipitate dyspnea or pulmonary edema. Twenty to 30% of these patients in turn will later have major emboli in the cerebral, visceral, or peripheral arteries as a consequence of thrombus formation in the left atrium.

Right ventricular hypertrophy, dilatation, and failure appear eventually in 40–50% of patients, producing the typical signs of "right heart failure."

In a few patients, for unknown reasons, the pulmonary arterioles become narrowed or constricted; this greatly increases the pulmonary artery pressure and accelerates the development of right ventricular failure. These patients have relatively little dyspnea but experience great fatigue and weakness on exertion because of the markedly reduced cardiac output.

Treatment

Closed mitral valvulotomy is advisable only if symptoms are due to a mechanical obstruction of the mitral valve and not due to mitral insufficiency. Some surgeons prefer to perform all mitral valvulotomies under "open bypass," believing that a better repair is possible under direct vision. Replacement of the valve is indicated when combined stenosis and insufficiency are present, or if anatomically the mitral valve is so distorted and calcified that a satisfactory fracture, even if the operation is performed "open" under cardiopulmonary bypass, is not possible (see Mitral Insufficiency). Systemic embolism probably is an indication for open operation. If the signs of mitral stenosis are present but there is no systolic murmur, mitral regurgitation is exceedingly unlikely. If there is a loud pansystolic murmur at the apex in association with an accentuated, often early third heart sound, a soft first sound, and no opening snap, the diagnosis of predominant mitral regurgitation is likely even if a short mid-diastolic murmur can be heard at the apex. Unless hypertension or an aortic valvular lesion is present, left ventricular hypertrophy shown on ECG should make

TABLE 7–1. Differential diagnosis of rheumatic heart disease.

	Mitral Stenosis	Mitral Insufficiency	Aortic Stenosis	Aortic Insufficiency	Tricuspid Stenosis	Tricuspid Insufficiency
Inspection	Malar flush. Precordial bulge and diffuse pulsation in young patients.	Usually forceful apical impulse to left of MCL.	Localized heaving PMI. Carotid pulsations weak, exhibiting slow rise.	Generalized pallor. Strong, abrupt carotid pulsations. Forceful PMI to left of MCL and down. Capillary pulsations.	Giant "a" wave in jugular pulse with sinus rhythm. Often olive-colored skin (mixed jaundice and local cyanosis).	Large "v" wave in jugular pulse.
Palpation	"Tapping" sensation over area of expected PMI. Mid-diastolic and/or presystolic thrill at apex. Small pulse. Right ventricular pulsation left 3rd–5th ICS parasternally when pulmonary hypertension is present.	Forceful, brisk PMI; systolic thrill over apex. Pulse normal, small, or slightly collapsing.	Powerful, heaving localized PMI to left of MCL and slightly down. Systolic thrill over aortic area (best felt with patient leaning forward, breath held in maximum expiration). Plateau pulse; small and slowly rising.	Apical impulse forceful and displaced significantly to left and down. Water-hammer pulses.	Mid-diastolic thrill between lower left sternal border and PMI. Presystolic pulsation of liver (sinus rhythm only).	Right ventricular pulsation. Occasionally systolic thrill at lower left sternal edge. Systolic pulsation of liver.
Percussion	Dullness in left 3rd ICS parasternally. ACD normal or slightly enlarged to left only.	ACD increased to left of MCL and slightly down.	ACD slightly enlarged to left and down.	Definite cardiac enlargement to left and down.		Usually cardiac enlargement to left and right.
Heart sounds, rhythm, and BP	Loud snapping M$_1$. Opening snap along left sternal border or at apex. Atrial fibrillation common. BP normal.	M$_1$ normal or buried in murmur. 3rd heart sound. Delayed opening snap occasionally present. Atrial fibrillation common. BP normal.	A$_2$ normal, or delayed and weak; may be absent. BP normal or systolic pressure normal with high diastolic level. Ejection click occasionally present just preceding murmur.	Sounds normal or A$_2$ loud. Wide pulse pressure with diastolic pressure < 60 mm Hg.	M$_1$ often loud.	Atrial fibrillation usually present.

MCL = Midclavicular line
PMI = Point of maximal impulse
ICS = Intercostal space
ACD = Area of cardiac disease

P$_2$ = Pulmonary second sound
M$_1$ = Mitral first sound
A$_2$ = Aortic second sound
BP = Blood pressure

Murmurs: Location and transmission	Sharply localized at or near apex. Graham-Steell murmur along lower left sternal border in severe pulmonary hypertension.	Loudest over PMI; transmitted to left axilla, left infrascapular area.	Right 2nd ICS parasternally and/or at apex; heard in carotids and occasionally in upper interscapular area.	Loudest along left sternal border in 3rd–4th interspace. Also heard over aortic area and apex.	3rd–5th ICS along left sternal border out to apex.	As for tricuspid stenosis.
Timing	Onset at opening snap ("mid-diastolic") with presystolic accentuation if in sinus rhythm. Graham-Steell begins with P_2 (immediate diastolic).	Pansystolic: begins with M_1 and ends at or after A_2.	Midsystolic: begins after M_1, ends before A_2, reaches maximum intensity in midsystole.	Begins immediately after aortic 2nd sound and ends before 1st sound.	As for mitral stenosis.	As for mitral insufficiency.
Character	Low-pitched, rumbling; presystolic murmur merges with loud M1 in a "crescendo." Graham-Steell high-pitched, blowing.	Blowing, high-pitched; occasionally harsh or musical.	Harsh, rough.	Blowing, high-pitched.	Blowing, often faint.	Blowing, coarse, or musical.
Optimum auscultatory conditions	After exercise, left lateral recumbency. Bell chest piece lightly applied.	After exercise, left lateral recumbency. Bell chest piece lightly applied.	Patient resting, leaning forward, breath held in full expiration. Bell chest piece, lightly applied.	Slow heart rate; patient leaning forward, breath held in full expiration. Diaphragm chest piece.	Murmur usually louder during and at peak of inspiration. Patient recumbent. Bell chest piece.	Murmur usually becomes louder during inspiration.
X-ray and fluoroscopy*	Straight left heart border. Large left atrium sharply indenting esophagus. Large right ventricle and pulmonary artery if pulmonary hypertension present.	Enlarged left ventricle and left atrium; systolic expansion of left atrium if enlargement not extreme.	Concentric left ventricular hypertrophy. Prominent ascending aorta, small knob. Calcified valve common.	Moderate to great left ventricular hypertrophy. Prominent aortic knob. Strong aortic pulsation on fluoroscopy.	Enlarged right atrium only.	Enlarged right atrium and ventricle.
ECG	Left axis deviation or frank left ventricular hypertrophy. P waves broad, tall, or notched in standard leads; broad negative phase of diphasic P in V_1.	Broad P waves in standard leads; broad negative phase of diphasic P in V_1. Normal axis. If pulmonary hypertension is present, tall peaked P waves, right axis deviation or right ventricular hypertrophy appear.	Left ventricular hypertrophy.	Left ventricular hypertrophy.	Wide tall peaked P waves. Normal axis.	Right axis usual.

*Pertechnetate radioisotope scans and ultrasound are being increasingly used to augment x-ray studies.

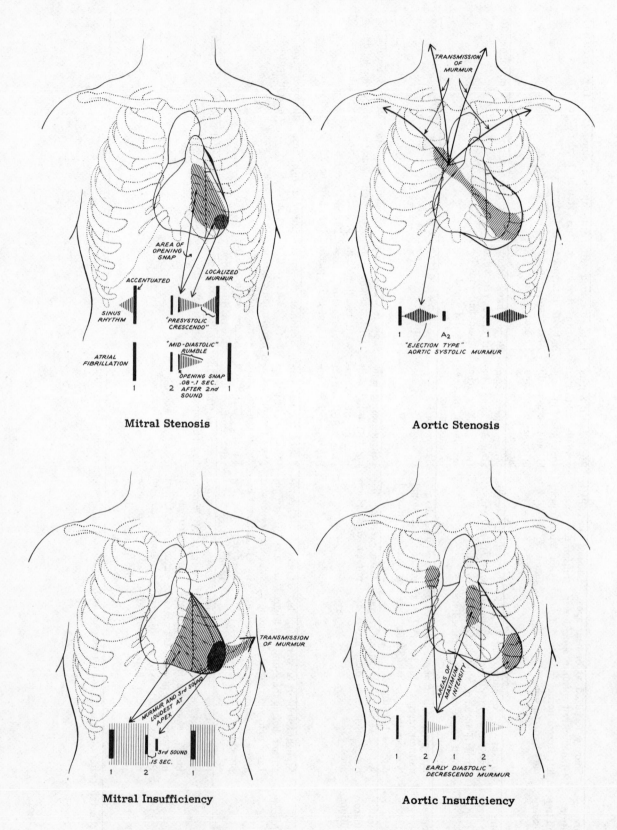

FIG 7–1. Murmurs and cardiac enlargement in common valve lesions.

one very cautious in recommending closed operation for mitral stenosis because in this circumstance the mitral valve is probably regurgitant. If there is a moderate systolic murmur at the apex, the diagnosis depends upon a consideration of the total findings.

Special diagnostic studies such as angiocardiography, dye dilution, and pressure curves from the left ventricle and left atrium during left heart catheterization or left ventricular puncture may prove helpful in difficult cases.

Because the course of mitral stenosis is highly variable and because of the significant mortality (3–5%) as well as morbidity of mitral valvulotomy and the frequency of restenosis, surgery is not advised in mild cases with slight exertional dyspnea and fatigue only. Indications for surgery include the following: (1) Signs of mitral stenosis with a pliable valve (opening snap, snapping first sound). (2) Uncontrollable pulmonary edema. (3) Disabling dyspnea and occasionally pulmonary edema. (4) Evidence of pulmonary hypertension with right ventricular hypertrophy and early congestive failure. (5) Increased pulmonary arteriolar resistance, with marked dyspnea and increased P_2. These patients are apt to develop right heart failure and emboli. (6) Right heart failure or tricuspid incompetence (or both) when secondary to marked mitral valve disease.

Continuous anticoagulant therapy is required for patients treated by valve replacement.

Fishman, N.H., & others: Follow-up evaluation of 100 consecutive mitral prosthesis implants. Arch Surg 97:691–695, 1968.

Granath, A.: Mitral valvulotomy. A clinical and hemodynamic pre- and postoperative study. Acta med scandinav 178 (Suppl 433):1–133, 1965.

Kittle, C.F., & others (editors): Symposium on cardiovascular surgery, 1968. Circulation 39 (Suppl 1), 1969.

McGoon, D.C.: Surgery of the heart and great vessels. New England J Med 278:143–148, 194–198, 1968.

Reppert, E.H.: Surgical treatment of valvular heart disease. Part I. Criteria for operability in rheumatic heart disease. Am Heart J 75:838–842, 1968.

Starr, A., Herr, R.H., & J.A. Wood: Mitral replacement: Review of six years' experience. J Thoracic Cardiovas Surg 54:333–358, 1967.

2. MITRAL INSUFFICIENCY

During ventricular systole, the mitral leaflets do not close normally and blood is forced back onto the atrium as well as through the aortic valve. The net effect is an increased work load in the left ventricle. The left atrium enlarges progressively, but the pressure in pulmonary veins and capillaries rises only transiently during exertion. Patients have exertional dyspnea and fatigue which usually progress slowly over many years. Left ventricular failure eventually develops, and orthopnea and paroxysmal dyspnea may appear, followed rapidly by the symptoms of right heart failure.

When heart failure is fully developed, the response to therapy is incomplete and the patient remains incapacitated. Mitral insufficiency, like stenosis, predisposes to atrial fibrillation; but this arrhythmia does not provoke acute pulmonary congestion, and fewer than 5% of patients have peripheral arterial emboli. Mitral insufficiency especially predisposes to subacute bacterial endocarditis.

Clinically, mitral insufficiency is characterized by a pansystolic murmur maximal at the apex, radiating to the axilla and occasionally to the base; a hyperdynamic left ventricular impulse and a brisk carotid upstroke; and a prominent third heart sound. When there is slight associated mitral stenosis, a short middiastolic murmur and a late opening snap may be present. The magnitude of the left ventricular hypertrophy is usually moderate, both clinically and electrocardiographically, and most of the enlargement of the cardiac shadow seen on x-ray is due to considerable diffuse enlargement of the left atrium. Calcification of the mitral valve is common, though less common than in pure mitral stenosis. The same is true of enlargement of the main pulmonary artery on x-ray.

Hemodynamically, the most striking feature of severe rheumatic mitral insufficiency is an elevated left atrial pressure with a large v wave and a rapid y descent due to rapid filling of the left ventricle. Overwork of the left ventricle ultimately leads to left ventricular failure and reduced cardiac output.

Patients with rheumatic mitral insufficiency have systemic emboli and pulmonary hypertension less often—and atrial fibrillation more often—than do patients with mitral stenosis. Because of the frequency of combined mitral stenosis and insufficiency, and because of the difficulty in some patients with fixed valves to specify which is dominant, dogmatic differentiation is unwise.

When mitral insufficiency is combined with aortic stenosis or aortic insufficiency, patients may become symptomatic with lesser hemodynamic abnormalities of both valves than if the valves were diseased separately.

Nonrheumatic mitral insufficiency. Mitral insufficiency may be due to causes other than rheumatic fever and have different clinical findings and a different clinical course, perhaps the most common being secondary to papillary muscle dysfunction or necrosis following acute myocardial infarction. When the mitral insufficiency is due to papillary dysfunction, it may subside as the infarction heals. Other causes include rupture of the chordae tendineae, usually secondary to bacterial endocarditis but occasionally occurring spontaneously or after trauma; the so called "floppy valve syndrome" or "click" syndrome (a connective tissue disorder related to Marfan's syndrome in which a peculiar late systolic "whoop" is heard); mitral insufficiency secondary to bacterial endocarditis with perforation of a cusp; cardiac tumors, especially left atrial myxoma; or surgically acquired mitral insufficiency. In contrast to rheumatic mitral insufficiency, the other varieties usually develop cardiac failure more rapidly, are in sinus rhythm rather than atrial fibrillation, occur in males more often than females, have little or no enlargement of the left atrium, have no calcification of the mitral valve, have no associated mitral stenosis, and often present an angiographic appearance which may be helpful. Part of the distinction in the clinical picture may be due to the fact that the nonrheumatic causes of mitral insufficiency are more acute and patients get into trouble within months or 1–2 years, whereas in rheumatic mitral insufficiency the course develops over a period of many years. Because the course of non-rheumatic mitral insufficiency may be more fulminant, surgical treatment with replacement of the valves is often more urgent.

Treatment

Reconstructive operations on the mitral valve are infrequent today and usually performed for a perforated leaflet in bacterial endocarditis or, rarely, because of ruptured chordae. When the disability is great enough to warrant the surgical risk, open heart surgery using cardiopulmonary bypass is almost always required, with replacement of the diseased valve with a prosthetic device. Various types of prosthetic devices have been employed, the most common being the Starr-Edwards ball valve. Late complications have occurred, however, including degenerative changes in the silastic ball, so that many of the ball valves are now completely covered by cloth. Alternatively, low profile disk type valves, homografts, and heterografts are being used by some surgeons. It is still too soon to determine which is the best design and type of valve replacement, and the decision in any particular case should be left to the experienced surgeon. In addition to changes in the valve itself, late complications include systemic embolization, leaks of the valve, hemolytic anemia, and, occasionally, sudden death, particularly in aortic valve replacements.

Prognosis

The early and late embolic complications must be recognized, but the surgical mortality has declined with greater experience. The fate of the prosthesis over the long term is uncertain. Follow-up studies have shown considerable clinical and hemodynamic improvement in surviving patients, including reversal of pulmonary and left atrial hypertension. Usually, however, some hemodynamic abnormality persists.

Barlow, J.B., & others: Late systolic murmurs and nonejection ("mid-late") systolic clicks. Brit Heart J 30:203, 1968.

Brigden, W.W., & A. Leatham: Mitral incompetence. Brit Heart J 15:55, 1963.

Brittar, N., & J.A. Sosa: The billowing mitral valve leaflet. Circulation 38:763–770, 1968.

Cline, M.J., & H.E. Williams: University of California School of Medicine Medical Staff Conference: Atrial myxoma. California Med 3:200–207, 1969.

Ellis, L.B., & A. Ramirez: The clinical course of patients with severe "rheumatic" mitral insufficiency. Am Heart J 78:406–419, 1969.

Gerbode, F., Kerth, W.J., & G.H. Puryear: The surgery of non-rheumatic acquired insufficiency of the mitral valve. Progr Cardiovas Dis 11:173–197, 1968.

Goodwin, J.F. (editor): Symposium on cardiac tumors. Am J Cardiol 11:34, 1968.

Harvey, W.P.: Clinical aspects of cardiac tumors. Am J Cardiol 21:328–343, 1968.

Hodam, R., & others: Totally cloth covered prosthesis: A review of two years of clinical experience. Circulation 41 (Suppl 2):33–39, 1970.

Morrow, A.G., & others: Prosthetic replacement of the mitral valve: Preoperative and postoperative clinical and hemodynamic assessments in 100 patients. Circulation 35:962, 1967.

Perloff, J.K., & W.P. Harvey: Auscultatory and phonocardiographic manifestations of pure mitral regurgitation. Progr Cardiovas Dis 5:172–194, 1962.

Raphael, M.J., Steiner, R.E., & E.B. Raferty: Acute mitral incompetence. Radiology 18:126–136, 1967.

Roberts, W.C., & A.G. Morrow: Causes of early postoperative death following cardiac valve replacement: Clinicopathologic correlations in 64 patients studied at necropsy. J Thoracic Cardiovas Surg 54:422–437, 1967.

Ross, J., Jr., Braunwald, E., & A.G. Morrow: Clinical and hemodynamic observations in pure mitral insufficiency. Am J Cardiol 2:11, 1958.

Sanders, C.A., & others: Diagnosis and surgical treatment of mitral regurgitation secondary to ruptured chordae tendineae. New England J Med 276:943, 1967.

Spencer, F.C.: Surgical treatment of valvular heart disease. 7. Prosthetic cardiac valves. Am Heart J 76:839–845, 1968.

Steiner, R.E.: Radiological aspects of cardiac tumors. Am J Cardiol 21:344–357, 1968.

Wigle, E.D., & P. Auger: Sudden, severe mitral insufficiency. Canad MAJ 96:1493–1503, 1967.

Williams, J.F., Jr., Morrow, A.G., & E. Braunwald: The incidence and management of "medical" complications following cardiac operations. Circulation 32:608–619, 1965.

Yao, S.T., & others: Penetrating wounds of the heart: A review of 80 cases. Ann Surg 168:67–78, 1968.

3. AORTIC STENOSIS

Over 80% of patients with aortic stenosis are men. Slight narrowing, roughened valves, or aortic dilatation may produce the typical murmur and thrill without causing significant hemodynamic effects. In mild to moderate cases, the characteristic signs are an ejection systolic murmur at the aortic area transmitted to the neck and apex and an ejection systolic click at the aortic area; in severe cases, a palpable left ventricular heave, often reversed splitting of the second sound, and a weak aortic second sound. The chest film reveals dilatation of the ascending aorta in valvular stenosis. When the valve area is less than 1/5 of normal, ventricular systole becomes prolonged and the typical plateau pulse develops. At this stage exertional dyspnea, fatigue, and pounding of the heart are noted. Cardiac output is ultimately markedly reduced so that patients have angina pectoris, great weakness or giddiness on exertion, or syncope. Survival beyond 3 years is uncommon if any of these appear. Many patients develop myocardial infarction, and 30% or more die suddenly. The stenosis may be valvular, subvalvular, or supravalvular, requiring identification and differential surgical procedures.

Most patients require complete preoperative study, including right and left heart catheterization and aortic, coronary, and left ventricular angiograms to evaluate the presence and degree of associated valve regurgitation and coronary stenoses.

Aortic valvular stenosis must be distinguished from supravalvular and from outflow obstruction of the left ventricular infundibulum (muscular subaortic obstruction; idiopathic hypertrophic subaortic stenosis). The former is congenital and uncommon; surgical experience is limited, and results depend on the findings in the ascending aorta. In the latter variety, the obstruction may be intermittent, aggravated by digitalis or inotropic influences, and relieved by propranolol (Inderal®) or sedation. If the patients are symptomatic, have severe obstruction to left ventricular flow, and achieve no benefit from propranolol, surgery is advised. Myotomy and limited resection of the hypertrophied muscle have produced gratifying results.

Treatment

The indications for surgical correction of aortic stenosis are progressive left ventricular failure, attacks of syncope due to cerebral ischemia, angina pectoris when it is thought to be due to the decreased cardiac output of aortic stenosis and not to associated coronary artery disease, or hemodynamic and clinical evidence of severe aortic stenosis even in patients with few symptoms. In the presence of both mitral and aortic stenosis, surgical correction or replacement of both valves can be performed at the same procedure.

The lesion must be severe before surgery can be recommended. Aortic valve replacement with a prosthetic or homograft valve is now the procedure of choice. Reconstructive procedures have proved unsatisfactory but may be necessary in severe congenital aortic stenosis when small enough prostheses are not available.

Follow-up of patients who have had valve replacement reveals an early surgical mortality of 4–20% and a late mortality of 16–30%, with an average 23% over a 5-year period. Good results occurred in 85% of the surviving patients. Striking hemodynamic improvement has been documented in those judged clinically to have a good result.

Barratt-Boyes, B.G., & others: Aortic homograft valve replacement: A long-term follow-up of an initial series of 101 patients. Circulation 40:753–777, 1969.

Campbell, M.: The natural history of congenital aortic stenosis. Brit Heart J 30:514–526, 1968.

Dexter, L., & L. Werko (editors): Evaluation of results of cardiac surgery. Circulation 38 (Suppl 5), 1968.

Friedman, W.F., Modlinger, J., & J.R. Morgan: Serial hemodynamic observations in asymptomatic children with valvar aortic stenosis. Circulation 43(Suppl 1):91, 1971.

Herr, R.H., & others: Aortic valve replacement: A review of six years' experience with the ball-valve prosthesis. Ann Thoracic Surg 6:199, 1968.

Hultgren, H.N., Hubis, H., & N. Shumway: Cardiac function following prosthetic aortic valve replacement. Am Heart J 77:585–598, 1969.

Kerzacky, A.K., & others: Combined mitral and aortic valve disease. Am J Cardiol 25:588–602, 1970.

Lee, S.J.K., & others: Hemodynamic changes following correction of severe aortic stenosis using the Cutter-Smeloff prosthesis. Circulation 42:719, 1970.

Morrow, A.F., & others: Obstruction to left ventricular outflow: Current concepts of management and operative treatment. Ann Int Med 69:1255–1285, 1968.

Mundth, E.D., & W.G. Austen: Postoperative intensive care in the cardiac surgical patient. Progr Cardiovas Dis 2:229–261, 1968.

Oakley, C.M., & K.A. Hallidie-Smith: Assessment of site and severity in congenital aortic stenosis. Brit Heart J 29:367–380, 1967.

Perloff, J.K.: Clinical recognition of aortic stenosis: The physical signs and differential diagnosis of the various forms of obstruction to left ventricular outflow. Progr Cardiovas Dis 10:323–352, 1968.

Ross, J., Jr., & E. Braunwald: Aortic stenosis. Circulation 38 (Suppl 5):61–67, 1968.

Salzman, S.H., & others: Epinephrine infusion in man: Standardization, normal response and abnormal response in idiopathic hypertrophic subaortic stenosis. Circulation 43(Suppl 1):137, 1971.

Wood, P.: Aortic stenosis. Am J Cardiol 1:553–571, 1958.

4. AORTIC INSUFFICIENCY

For many years the only sign may be a soft aortic diastolic murmur, ie, "auscultatory" aortic insufficiency, indicating regurgitation of a very small amount of blood through the incompetent leaflets during diastole. As the valve deformity increases, larger and larger amounts regurgitate, diastolic blood pressure falls, the pulse wave assumes its characteristic contour, and the left ventricle progressively enlarges. This is the stage of "dynamic" aortic insufficiency. Many patients remain asymptomatic even at this point, or experience exertional dyspnea. Left ventricular failure often begins abruptly with acute pulmonary edema or recurrent paroxysmal nocturnal dyspnea and orthopnea; fatigue, weakness, and exertional dyspnea are then incapacitating. Angina pectoris, or protracted chest pain simulating angina, appears in many. The heart failure is refractory to treatment and is the chief cause of death. Ten to 15% of these patients die suddenly.

Although rheumatic aortic insufficiency is the most common variety, other causes must be considered such as dissecting aneurysm of the aorta, bacterial endocarditis, rheumatoid arthritis, and ruptured aneurysm of the sinus of Valsalva. When aortic insufficiency develops acutely (as in dissecting aneurysm or perforated cusp during bacterial endocarditis), left ventricular failure may develop rapidly and surgery may be urgently required.

Treatment

Aortic insufficiency usually requires prosthetic replacement of the entire valve. The substantial surgical risk and the uncertain prognosis limit the indications to patients with class III or class IV lesions. The ideal time for replacement is uncertain because many patients survive for 5–10 years on medical treatment despite substantial insufficiency and left ventricular hypertrophy. The long-term "survival" of the prosthetic or homograft valve is not known. Emboli are less frequent than with mitral valve replacement, but require continuous anticoagulants unless a homograft has been used. The surgical risk is less with aortic insufficiency than with aortic stenosis.

Aortic insufficiency which appears or worsens after subacute bacterial endocarditis may lead to severe cardiac failure in weeks or months even though the infection is controlled. Surgical removal of the valve is indicated even during the infection if cardiac failure worsens despite medical treatment. Patients should be observed closely for many months after endocarditis.

Replacement of the valve may become a surgical emergency if perforation of a cusp or rupture of the sinus of Valsalva or of the subaortic valvular structure occurs, causing acute severe left ventricular failure. Great judgment is required to determine the timing of and need for physiologic studies.

Baronders, J.A., & M. Sarde: Some changing aspects of aortic regurgitation. Arch Int Med 124:600, 1969.

Bigelow, J.C., & others: Multiple valve replacement: Review of five years' experience. Circulation 38:656–664, 1968.

Duvoisin, G.E., & D.C. McGoon: The advantages and disadvantages of prosthetic valves for aortic valve replacement. Progr Cardiovas Dis 11:294–303, 1969.

Gault, J.H., & others: Left ventricular performance following correction of free aortic regurgitation. Circulation 42:773, 1970.

Hamby, R.I., Gulotta, S.J., & A.Z. Hassen: Immediate hemodynamic effects of aortic regurgitation in man. Am J Cardiol 21:478, 1968.

Reppert, E.H.: Surgical treatment of valvular heart disease. Part II. Criteria for operability in rheumatic heart disease aortic valve lesions. Am Heart J 76:136, 1968.

Scheu, H., Rothlin, M., & R. Hegglin: Aortic insufficiency. Circulation 38 (Suppl 5):77–92, 1968.

Shein, K.I., & others: Combined aortic and mitral incompetence: Clinical features and surgical management. Am Heart J 76:728–736, 1968.

Wigle, E.D., & C.J. Labrosse: Sudden, severe aortic insufficiency. Circulation 32:708–720, 1965.

5. TRICUSPID STENOSIS

Most patients with tricuspid stenosis are women, and mitral valve disease is usually present also. Tricuspid stenosis acts as a mechanical block to the return of blood to the heart, and the systemic venous engorgement is analogous to the pulmonary venous engorgement caused by mitral stenosis. Tricuspid stenosis should be suspected when "right heart failure" appears early in the course of mitral disease, marked by hepatomegaly, ascites, and dependent edema. These are more prominent when atrial fibrillation is present. Severe fatigue is usual. Cardiac cirrhosis develops early, and patients acquire a characteristic complexion which is a blend of peripheral cyanosis and slight jaundice. Careful examination is needed to differentiate the typical diastolic rumble along the lower left sternal border from the murmur of mitral stenosis. In the presence of sinus rhythm, a presystolic liver pulsation can be found in half of the patients. In atrial fibrillation only the slow emptying of the jugular vein during diastole is noted. A giant right atrium on a chest film or angiogram confirms the diagnosis of tricuspid valve disease.

Treatment

Congenital tricuspid stenosis is associated with an underdeveloped right ventricle and does not lend itself to valvotomy. Diversion of the superior vena caval flow into the right lung is a relatively safe closed procedure which confers a significant degree of palliation.

Acquired tricuspid stenosis is rare and may be amenable to valvotomy under direct vision, but it usually requires a prosthetic valve replacement.

Lillehei, C.W., & others: Valve replacement for tricuspid stenosis or insufficiency associated with mitral valvular disease. Circulation 33:34, 1966.

Sanders, C.A., & others: Tricuspid stenosis: A difficult diagnosis in the presence of atrial fibrillation. Circulation 33:26, 1966.

6. TRICUSPID INSUFFICIENCY

Tricuspid insufficiency affects the right ventricle just as mitral insufficiency affects the left ventricle. The symptoms and signs of organic tricuspid valve disease due to rheumatic heart disease are identical with those resulting from right ventricular failure due to any cause. The valvular lesion can be suspected in the presence of mitral disease by noting a relatively early onset of right heart failure and a harsh systolic murmur along the lower left sternal border which is separate from the mitral murmur and which often increases in intensity during and just after inspiration.

Treatment

Replacement of the tricuspid valve is being performed with increasing frequency with fair results. Tricuspid insufficiency secondary to severe mitral valve disease may regress when only the mitral valve is replaced.

•   •   •

Prognosis of Rheumatic Heart Disease

Recurrent rheumatic fever may produce fatal heart failure at any time, and bacterial endocarditis is a constant threat.

A. Mitral Stenosis: In general, patients with severe mitral stenosis die of intractable congestive failure in the 30's or 40's after a prolonged period of disability.

B. Mitral Insufficiency and Aortic Valve Lesions: These patients become symptomatic later in life, but death occurs within a few years after the onset of symptoms of congestive heart failure.

C. Aortic Stenosis: When angina, left ventricular failure, or syncope is present, death usually occurs within 3 years.

D. Tricuspid Lesions: These are usually associated with mitral valve disease. The prognosis is surprisingly good, with survival for up to 10 years after the onset of edema, but patients are incapacitated by fatigue.

BACTERIAL ENDOCARDITIS

Essentials of Diagnosis

Subacute:

- Patient with rheumatic, congenital, or atherosclerotic heart disease.
- Continuous fever, weight loss, joint and muscle pains, fatigue, anemia.
- Heart murmur, splenomegaly, petechiae, embolic phenomena.
- Blood culture positive.

Acute:

- Patient with acute infection or recent history of surgery or instrumentation, or narcotic addict.
- High fever, sudden change or appearance of new murmurs, embolic phenomena, petechiae, splenomegaly, and toxic appearance.

General Considerations

Subacute bacterial endocarditis (SBE) is a smoldering bacterial infection of the endocardium usually superimposed on preexisting rheumatic or calcific valvular or congenital heart disease. Bacteremia following a respiratory infection, dental work, or cystoscopy is often the initiating event, but in many instances the source of infection is not known. Nonhemolytic streptococci, especially *Streptococcus viridans* and *S faecalis,* are the usual etiologic agents; staphylococci are occasionally responsible, but virtually any microorganism, including fungi, can be encountered.

Bacteria lodge on the endocardium of valves (usually aortic and mitral) and multiply. Fibrin and platelet thrombi are deposited, forming irregular friable vegetations which break off to give emboli to the brain, peripheral arteries, or viscera. Embolic nephritis or true glomerulonephritis sometimes produces renal failure. Shedding of bacteria into the blood stream from the involved valves may produce mycotic aneurysms which, however, rarely rupture. Active rheumatic carditis may be present. SBE produces mild to moderate systemic symptoms; cerebral, renal, splenic, or mesenteric emboli; heart failure; or any combination of these. The onset usually follows bacteremia from one of the sources cited above within days or weeks.

Acute bacterial endocarditis (ABE) is a rapidly progressive infection of normal or abnormal valves, usually developing in the course of heavy bacteremia from acute infections such as pneumococcal pneumonia, postabortal pelvic infection, abscesses, or intravenous injection of narcotics. It may also occur as a complication of cardiac surgery, transurethral prostatectomy, or surgery on infected tissue. Pneumococci, hemolytic staphylococci, beta-hemolytic streptococci, and gram-negative coliform organisms are the most common pathogens.

Acute endocarditis produces large, friable vegetations, severe embolic episodes with metastatic abscess formation, and rapid perforation, tearing, or destruction of the affected valves or rupture of chordae tendineae.

Clinical Findings

A. Symptoms and Signs: Fever is present in most cases, although afebrile periods may occur, especially in the aged. Any or all of the following may occur also: night sweats, chills, malaise, fatigue, anorexia, weight loss; vague muscle aching, arthralgia, or redness and swelling of the joints; sudden visual disturbances, aphasia, or hemiplegia due to cerebral emboli; pain in the abdomen, chest, or flanks due to mesenteric, splenic, pulmonary, or renal emboli; nosebleeds, easy bruisability, and symptoms of heart failure. In ABE, the course is more fulminating and the patient is very toxic.

In SBE, evidence of rheumatic, congenital, or calcific heart disease is usually present. Findings include tachycardia, splenomegaly; petechiae of the skin, mucous membranes, and ocular fundi, or beneath the nails as "splinter hemorrhages"; clubbing of the fingers and toes; pallor or a yellowish-brown tint of the skin; neurologic residuals of cerebral emboli; and tender red nodules of the finger or toe pads. Heart murmurs may be considered "insignificant" in infection of the tricuspid and pulmonary valve, where recurrent pulmonary infarction suggesting pneumonia may be a prominent feature. The clinical picture is often atypical in older persons, since fever, chills, and leukocytosis may be absent.

ABE presents as a severe infection associated with chills, high fever, prostration, and multiple, serious embolic phenomena. These may be superimposed on the antecedent causative infection (eg, pneumonia, furunculosis, pelvic infection) or may appear abruptly following instrumentation or surgery. Heart murmurs may change rapidly, and heart failure occurs early.

ABE or SBE may develop during "prophylactic" or inadequate therapeutic antibiotic administration. In these circumstances the onset is "masked" and a sudden embolic episode, the appearance of petechiae, unexplained heart failure, changing murmurs, or a rising temperature may be the first clue.

B. Laboratory Findings: In suspected SBE, take 2 blood cultures daily for 3–5 days. Within 2–7 days of incubation, 85–95% of these cultures will grow organisms and permit specific drug selection. In ABE, take 2 or 3 cultures during the emergency work-up; then begin antibiotic treatment. In the presence of repeated negative blood cultures (eg, in uremic patients), bone marrow should be cultured.

The administration of an antimicrobial drug may interfere with positive blood cultures for 7–10 days.

Normochromic anemia, a markedly elevated sedimentation rate, variable leukocytosis, microscopic hematuria, proteinuria, and casts are commonly present in SBE and ABE. Nitrogen retention may be the first clue, especially in older patients. Rheumatoid factor is demonstrable in 50–60% of cases of SBE of more than 6 weeks' standing.

Complications

The complications of ABE or SBE include peripheral arterial emboli (producing hemiplegias or aphasia; infarction of the bowel, kidney, or spleen; or acute arterial insufficiency of an arm or leg); congestive heart failure, renal failure, hemorrhagic tendency, anemia, and metastatic abscess formation (especially ABE). Splenic abscess may cause lack of response to therapy, or relapse.

Differential Diagnosis

SBE must be differentiated from various seemingly primary disease states. Hemiplegia, intractable heart failure, anemia, a bleeding tendency, or uremia may be caused by SBE. If a patient presenting with any of these illnesses has fever and a heart murmur, blood cultures should be taken.

Specific diseases that require differentiation are the lymphomas, thrombocytopenic purpura, leukemia, acute rheumatic fever, disseminated lupus erythematosus, polyarteritis nodosa, chronic meningococcemia, brucellosis, disseminated or miliary tuberculosis, and nonbacterial thrombotic endocarditis or chronic wasting disease.

ABE masquerades as a severe systemic response to an obvious preexisting infection. It can be recognized only by noting rapid clinical deterioration, bacteremia, the appearance or sudden change of heart murmurs, heart failure, and major embolic accidents, especially to the CNS, simulating meningitis.

Prevention

A. Medical Measures: Some cases of endocarditis arise after dental procedures or surgery of the oropharynx and genitourinary tract. Patients with known cardiac anomalies who are to have any of these procedures should be prepared in one of the following ways, although it should be noted that failures sometimes occur:

(1) 600,000 units procaine penicillin with 600,000 units crystalline penicillin, IM, 1 hour before

surgery, and then 600,000 units procaine penicillin IM daily for 2 days.

(2) 500,000 units penicillin G or V orally 4 or 5 times daily on the day of surgery and for 2 days after surgery.

(3) In case of penicillin sensitivity, or in persons receiving penicillin prophylaxis for rheumatic fever, give erythromycin, 250 mg orally 4 times daily on the day of surgery and for 2 days afterward.

(4) For genitourinary or gastrointestinal surgery, give streptomycin or kanamycin, 1–2 gm daily in addition to (1).

B. Surgical Measures: Surgery may be warranted for the prevention of bacterial endocarditis in selected patients with surgically correctable congenital lesions (eg, patent ductus arteriosus) or acquired lesions (eg, symptomatic aortic and mitral valvular disease). Preoperative antibiotic therapy should be instituted as above.

Treatment

A. Specific Measures: The most important consideration in the treatment of bacterial endocarditis is a bactericidal concentration of antibiotics in contact with the infecting organism, which is often localized in avascular tissues or in vegetations. Penicillin, because of its high degree of bactericidal activity against the great majority of bacteria which produce bacterial endocarditis, and because of its low incidence of side reactions, is by far the most useful drug. Synergistic combinations of antibiotics have proved valuable at times. Few cases have been cured by bacteriostatic drugs used alone.

Positive blood cultures are invaluable to confirm the diagnosis and to guide treatment with tests of susceptibility of the infecting organism to various antibiotics or combinations of antibiotics. Two blood cultures should be obtained daily for 3–5 days before instituting treatment, except in desperately ill patients in whom antibiotic therapy is started after emergency work-up including 2–3 blood cultures.

Note: **Control of antimicrobial treatment.** Negative blood cultures are a minimal initial requirement of effective therapy. An assay of serum bactericidal activity is the best guide to support the selection of drugs and the daily dose, after treatment has been started. During therapy, the patient's serum diluted 1:5 or 1:10 should be rapidly bactericidal in vitro

TABLE 7–2. Approximate dosage schedules.

Penicillin Inhibition (Bactericidal at 72 Hours) (units/ml)	Total Daily Penicillin Dosage (Parenteral) (millions of units)	
< 0.1	1–3	(penicillin procaine)
0.1–0.5	3–5	(aqueous)
0.5–0.9	5–10	(aqueous)
1–5	10–20	(aqueous)
> 5	20–500	(aqueous)

under standardized laboratory conditions for the organisms initially grown from the patient's blood stream.

1. Penicillin is the drug of choice in a large majority of cases of bacterial endocarditis. It should be administered parenterally at first to all patients until adequate serum bactericidal activity has been established. A shift to oral administration can be considered only in patients with exquisitely susceptible infecting organisms where control over oral drug intake (about 5 times the parenteral dose) and adequacy of serum levels can be maintained.

The dosage of penicillin is a function of the susceptibility of the organism. Viridans streptococci susceptible to 0.1 unit penicillin/ml (more than 80%) can be eradicated from bacterial endocarditis by administering penicillin G, 3—5 million units daily for 3—4 weeks. This is given conveniently by IM injection of 1.2 million units procaine penicillin 3 times daily. Streptococci killed by 1.0 but not by 0.1 unit/ml require penicillin G (aqueous), 5—10 million units daily for 3—4 weeks. This can be given IM or IV. Streptococci and other organisms killed by penicillin in concentrations greater than 1.0 unit/ml require more than 10 million units penicillin G, usually administered by continuous intravenous drip in part of the daily fluid requirement of 5% glucose in water or saline. The following complications must be considered: (a) Each million units of potassium penicillin contains about 1.7 milliequivalents of potassium, which arouses concern about potassium toxicity. (b) At very high concentrations of penicillin, there is enough diffusion into the CNS to cause neurotoxicity. (c) With intravenous antibiotic therapy of long duration, there is a significant risk of superinfection; to minimize this possibility, injection sites must be changed each 48 hours and must be kept scrupulously aseptic.

If bacteremia and signs of bacterial endocarditis activity persist, the dosage can be increased (500 million units penicillin G have been given daily) until serum assay and clinical response are satisfactory. If blood cultures are negative and serum assay suggests adequate drug effect, continuing symptoms or signs may have to be attributed to causes other than active infection.

2. Combined penicillin and aminoglycoside—The addition of streptomycin, kanamycin, or gentamicin enhances the bactericidal activity of penicillins for many streptococci, particularly enterococci *(S faecalis)*. In bacterial endocarditis due to viridans streptococci, streptomycin sulfate, 0.5 gm, can be injected IM 2 or 3 times daily for 10 days (in addition to penicillin given as above). The total time of treatment can then be reduced to 18—22 days (instead of 3—4 weeks). In bacterial endocarditis due to enterococci, streptomycin, 0.5 gm, or kanamycin, 0.5 gm, is injected every 8—12 hours while penicillin G (10—60 million units daily) or ampicillin (8—20 gm daily) is injected IV for 4—5 weeks. This combined treatment has a better record of eradicating enterococci from bacterial endocarditis than penicillin alone, and represents one of the best accepted examples of antibiotic

synergism. Other drug combinations can occasionally be discovered by laboratory test to treat occasional cases of bacterial endocarditis caused by particularly resistant microorganisms, but this must be done under strict laboratory control.

3. Cephalothin, 6—12 gm daily IV, has been used for streptococcal and staphylococcal bacterial endocarditis as a substitute for penicillin in allergic individuals. Hypersensitivity to cephalothin and a variety of other untoward reactions may occur. Enterococci are often resistant.

4. Methicillin, 6—24 gm daily IV for 4—6 weeks, has been used in bacterial endocarditis caused by penicillinase-producing staphylococci. Alternate drugs are nafcillin, 8—16 gm IV, and oxacillin, 8—16 gm IV daily, given for the same period. Vancomycin, 2—4 gm IV daily, has been given for 2—4 weeks in staphylococcal bacterial endocarditis.

5. Tetracyclines, erythromycin, and similar drugs which are mainly bacteriostatic are not drugs of choice in bacterial endocarditis. If administered to patients with fever of unknown origin, these drugs suppress bacteremia temporarily and produce symptomatic improvement. However, they generally fail to eradicate the infection, permit progression of the lesion, and interfere with specific diagnosis. In bacterial endocarditis caused by Bacteroides species, other anaerobes, or rickettsiae, tetracyclines may be the drugs of choice. Dosage must be judged by serum assay and patient tolerance.

6. In bacterial endocarditis caused by gram-negative bacteria of the enteric flora, **kanamycin,** 0.5 gm IM every 6—12 hours, or **gentamicin,** 3—4 mg/kg/day IM in 3 divided doses, may be the principal drug, sometimes combined with cephalothin, 6—12 gm IV, or carbenicillin, 12—30 gm IV, to give bactericidal combinations by laboratory test. Polymyxin B and colistin have not proved to be clinically useful in bacterial endocarditis caused by Pseudomonas species in spite of marked susceptibility of the organisms in vitro. Only surgical removal of the infected site (eg, patch over septal defect, prosthesis) in the cardiovascular system has led to cure of pseudomonas bacterial endocarditis. With all these drugs, constant vigilance regarding nephro-, neuro- and ototoxicity is essential, and dosages may have to be adjusted if renal function is impaired.

7. In patients with a clinical picture typical of bacterial endocarditis but persistently negative blood cultures, empirical treatment with **penicillin G,** 20—50 million units/day IV, plus **streptomycin,** 1 gm/day IM, can be given for 4 weeks. Several of the manifestations of the disease should show marked improvement with such treatment. If there is no clinical improvement in 3—5 days, a therapeutic trial of other drugs (see above) is warranted.

8. Follow-up and recurrences—At the end of the established treatment period of 3—6 weeks, all antimicrobial therapy should be stopped. After 3 days, blood cultures are taken daily for 4 days and then once weekly for 4 weeks while the patient is observed carefully. Most bacteriologic relapses occur during this time, but some recurrences are delayed for several months. Embolic phenomena and fever may occur both during and after successful treatment and—by themselves—are not adequate grounds for retreatment. An initial adequate course of therapy in bacteriologically proved bacterial endocarditis can result in up to 90% bacteriologic cure. If bacteriologic relapse occurs, the organism must be isolated and tested again, and a second—often longer—course of treatment administered with properly selected drugs.

In spite of bacteriologic cure, a majority of patients treated for bacterial endocarditis progress to cardiac failure in 5—10 years. This mechanical failure can be attributed in part to valvular deformities (eg, perforation of cusp, tearing of chordae) caused by the bacterial infection and in part to the healing and scarring process. Therefore, surgical correction of abnormalities in cardiovascular dynamics must be considered as part of the follow-up.

B. General Measures: Supportive treatment, as for any severe infection, must be given. Anemia, if severe, may require transfusion of blood or red cell mass. Anticoagulants (eg, heparin, bishydroxycoumarin) are not indicated in uncomplicated bacterial endocarditis and may contribute to hemorrhagic complications.

C. Treatment of Complications:

1. Infarctions of organs in the systemic circulation usually result from emboli originating in vegetations in the left heart. Emboli derived from right heart lesions may produce pulmonary infarction. Treatment is symptomatic and anticoagulants are sometimes helpful. Embolectomy can be attempted if an accessible site can be located.

2. Cardiac failure—Myocarditis, which frequently accompanies bacterial endocarditis of long duration, and increasing deformity of heart valves may precipitate cardiac failure and require digitalization and sodium restriction. In such patients, the sodium salts of penicillins are undesirable, and potassium or calcium salts are preferred. Early valve replacement may have to be considered even during antimicrobial therapy if there is evidence of progressive severe heart failure. Because of the bad prognosis of progressive aortic insufficiency developing with bacterial endocarditis, insertion of an aortic valve prosthesis may be essential after only 2—3 weeks or less of satisfactory antimicrobial drug therapy.

3. Many patients with bacterial endocarditis develop **nitrogen retention** due to focal embolic nephritis or glomerulonephritis. This requires adjustment of drug dosage and—rarely—temporary treatment of uremia until renal function improves during antimicrobial therapy.

Prognosis

Bacterial endocarditis is uniformly fatal unless the bacterial infection can be eradicated, but in a few cases surgical removal of an infected A-V fistula or patent ductus arteriosus has been curative. The poorest prognosis for bacteriologic cure exists in patients with con-

sistently negative blood cultures and long delay in therapy; in those with very highly resistant organisms; and in those with an infected prosthesis. If bacteriologic cure is accomplished, the prognosis depends on the adequacy of cardiovascular function as mechanical distortions and impairment of dynamics develop during infection and healing. Only about 50% of patients with bacteriologically cured bacterial endocarditis are well 5 years after treatment. Among valve lesions, aortic insufficiency carries the worst outlook and merits the most prompt surgical consideration. Among embolic events, those to the brain have the poorest prognosis. Cerebral emboli and rupture of mycotic aneurysms may occur even after bacteriologic cure. Renal functional impairment is generally reversible by early adequate antimicrobial therapy.

Bennett, W.M., Singer, I., & C.H. Coggins: A practical guide to drug usage in adult patients with impaired renal function. JAMA 214:1468—1475, 1970.

Cliff, M.M., Soulen, R.L., & A.J. Finestone: Mycotic aneurysms: A challenge and a clue. Arch Int Med 126:977—982, 1970.

Green, G.R., Peters, G.A., & J.E. Geraci: Treatment of bacterial endocarditis in patients with penicillin hypersensitivity. Ann Int Med 67:235—249, 1967.

Jawetz, E., & M. Sonne: Penicillin-streptomycin treatment of enterococcal endocarditis. New England J Med 274:710—715, 1966.

Lerner, P.L., & L. Weinstein: Infective endocarditis in the antibiotic era. New England J Med 274:199—206, 259—265, 323—331, 388—393, 1966.

Ramsey, R.G., Gunnar, R.M., & J.R. Tobin, Jr.: Endocarditis in the drug addict. Am J Cardiol 25:608—619, 1970.

Shaffer, R.B., & W.H. Hall: Bacterial endocarditis following open-heart surgery. Am J Cardiol 25:602—608, 1970.

Stason, W.B., & others: Cardiac surgery in bacterial endocarditis. Circulation 38:514—524, 1968.

Tumulty, P.A.: Management of bacterial endocarditis. Geriatrics 22:122—139, 1967.

Werner, A.S., & others: The bacteremia of bacterial endocarditis. JAMA 202:199—203, 1967.

HYPERTENSIVE CARDIOVASCULAR DISEASE

The criteria for the diagnosis of hypertension are arbitrary, because the arterial pressure rises with age and varies from one occasion of measurement to another. Most authorities consider hypertension to be present when the diastolic pressure consistently exceeds 100 mm Hg in a person more than 60 years of age, or 90 mm Hg in a person less than 50 years of age. The vascular complications of hypertension are thought to be the consequence of the raised arterial pressure.

Hypertension which has not demonstrably affected the heart is called "hypertensive vascular disease." When left ventricular hypertrophy, heart failure, or coronary artery disease is present, "hypertensive cardiovascular disease" is the appropriate term.

Hypertension in any form is uncommon before age 20. In young people it is commonly caused by chronic glomerulonephritis, renal artery stenosis, pyelonephritis, or coarctation of the aorta.

Transient elevation of blood pressure caused by excitement, apprehension, or exertion and the purely systolic elevation of blood pressure in elderly people caused by loss of elasticity in their major arteries do not constitute hypertensive disease.

Etiology & Classification

A. Primary Hypertension: In about 85% of cases of hypertensive vascular or cardiovascular disease, no cause can be established. The onset of essential hypertension is usually between ages 25 and 55. The family history is usually suggestive of hypertension (stroke, "sudden death," heart failure). Women are affected more often than men. Elevations in pressure are transient early in the course of the disease but eventually become permanent. Even in established cases the blood pressure fluctuates widely in response to emotional stress, especially anger, resentment, and frustration. The resting blood pressure is lower than single casual office readings, and can be determined after several hours' rest in bed. Blood pressures taken by the patient at home or during daily activities using a portable apparatus are lower than those recorded in the office, clinic, or hospital. It is not established which readings are most reliable in estimating prognosis.

Note: All of the foregoing may be true in other forms of hypertension also. A diagnosis of essential hypertension is warranted only after repeated and thorough search for specific causes has been unsuccessful.

B. Secondary Hypertension:

1. Renal hypertension—

a. Vascular—Narrowing of one or both renal arteries due to atherosclerosis, fibromuscular hyperplasia, or other causes has come to be recognized as perhaps the most common cause of curable hypertension. It may present in the same manner as essential hypertension but may be suspected in the following circumstances: (1) if the onset is after age 50; (2) if there are epigastric or renal artery bruits; (3) if there is atherosclerosis elsewhere; (4) if there are variations in the size and appearance, time of appearance of contrast media, or delayed hyperconcentration of contrast material in the involved kidney on the intravenous urogram; (5) if there are increased amounts (relative to the other kidney) of renin activity in renal vein blood; (6) if there is abnormal excretion of radioactive materials by renal scan; or (7) if atherosclerosis or fibromuscular hyperplasia can be demonstrated by renal artery angiogram.

The functional significance of an established lesion is determined (1) by means of the Howard-Stamey test with decreased sodium concentration and increased osmolality in the urine on the involved side, and (2) by demonstrating increased renal vein renin on the involved side as compared to the opposite side. When both tests are positive in the presence of a severely stenosed proximal renal artery lesion, reconstructive surgery offers a very good prognosis.

b. Parenchymal—Chronic glomerulonephritis and pyelonephritis have in the past accounted for the largest group of known causes of hypertension. Unilateral pyelonephritis is rare but can often be cured by surgery. Polycystic kidney disease and congenital or acquired obstructive hydronephrosis are rare causes. Acute glomerulonephritis is often associated with hypertension.

2. Endocrine—Pheochromocytoma, a tumor of the adrenal medulla or (rarely) of chromaffin tissue along a sympathetic chain, causes sustained or intermittent hypertension by releasing norepinephrine and epinephrine into the blood stream. Cushing's syndrome, primary aldosteronism, 17-hydroxylase deficiency, congenital adrenal hyperplasia with virilism, and deoxycorticosterone overtreatment of patients with adrenal insufficiency regularly cause hypertension. An eosinophilic tumor of the pituitary, producing acromegaly, may also cause hypertension.

3. Coarctation of the aorta—Congenital constriction of the arch of the aorta produces hypertension in the upper extremities and carotid arteries. Blood pressure in the legs is normal or low.

4. Miscellaneous—Hypertension of varying severity is present in toxemias of pregnancy, increased intracranial pressure due to tumor or hematoma, overdistention of a neurogenic bladder, and in the late stages of polyarteritis nodosa, disseminated lupus erythematosus, and scleroderma.

C. Malignant Hypertension: Any form of sustained hypertension may abruptly become more severe. The diastolic pressure rises above 130 mm Hg, causing widespread arteriolar necrosis, rapidly progressive renal failure, and papilledema. Papilledema may precede renal impairment and is the best definitive clinical sign; the height of the blood pressure alone may be misleading. The term "malignant" is used because mortality approaches 100% in 2 years if the disease is not treated.

Pathogenesis

Essential and renal hypertension are due to increased peripheral arteriolar resistance of unknown mechanism. Unless heart failure or edema is present, cardiac output and blood volume are not affected in well-established cases. Renal pressor substances may play a role in essential and renal hypertension, but this has not been demonstrated in humans.

In pheochromocytoma hypertension is due to varying combinations of increased cardiac output and peripheral resistance caused by epinephrine and norepinephrine, respectively.

The mechanism of production of hypertension by adrenal glucocorticoids, aldosterone, and deoxycorticosterone is not known.

The hypertension of coarctation of the aorta is thought to result directly from the constriction, which causes the left ventricle to eject blood into a "short chamber," although the renal mechanism may be involved.

Pathology

Sustained hypertension causes the initially reversible arteriolar narrowing to become permanent as a result of intimal thickening, hypertrophy of the muscular coats, and hyaline degeneration. In malignant hypertension, arteriolar necrosis (especially in the renal vessels) develops rapidly and is responsible for the acute onset of renal failure. The dominant manifestations of hypertension are secondary to left ventricular hypertrophy and failure and to the widespread arteriolar lesions. Hypertension accelerates the development of coronary and cerebral artery atherosclerosis; myocardial infarction and cerebral hemorrhage or thrombosis are common sequelae.

Clinical Findings

The clinical and laboratory findings are mainly referable to the degree of vascular deterioration and involvement of the "target organs": heart, brain, kidneys, eyes, and peripheral arteries.

A. Symptoms: Mild to moderate essential hypertension is compatible with normal health and well being for many years. Vague symptoms usually appear after the patient learns he has "high blood pressure." Suboccipital headaches, characteristically occurring early in the morning and subsiding during the day, are common, but any type of headache may occur (even simulating migraine). Other common complaints are lightheadedness, tinnitus, "fullness in the head," easy fatigability, loss of energy, and palpitations. These symptoms are caused by anxiety about hypertension or by associated psychologic disturbances.

Patients with pheochromocytoma which secretes predominantly norepinephrine usually have sustained hypertension. Intermittent release of catechol causes attacks (lasting minutes to hours) of acute anxiety, palpitation, profuse perspiration, pallor, trembling, and nausea and vomiting; blood pressure is markedly elevated during the attack, and angina or acute pulmonary edema may occur. In primary aldosteronism, patients may have recurrent episodes of generalized muscular weakness or paralysis, paresthesias, polyuria, and nocturia due to associated hypokalemia.

Cardiac involvement often leads to paroxysmal nocturnal dyspnea or cardiac asthma with or without symptoms of chronic left ventricular failure. Angina pectoris or myocardial infarction may develop.

Progressive renal involvement may not produce striking symptoms, but nocturia or intermittent hematuria may ultimately occur.

Peripheral arterial disease most commonly causes intermittent claudication. When the terminal aorta is narrowed or occluded, pain in the buttocks and low back pain appear on walking and men become impotent.

Cerebral involvement causes (1) hemiplegia or aphasia due to thrombosis or (2) sudden hemorrhage leading to death in hours or days. In malignant hypertension (and occasionally in its absence), severe headache, confusion, coma, convulsions, blurred vision, transient neurologic signs, and nausea and vomiting may occur ("hypertensive encephalopathy"). The mechanism of their production is not known. Cerebral edema may play a role, and the findings are usually reversible with treatment.

B. Signs: Physical findings depend upon the cause of hypertension, its duration and severity, and the degree of effect on target organs.

1. Blood pressure—The diagnosis of hypertension is not warranted in patients under the age of 50 unless the blood pressure exceeds 140/90 mm Hg on at least 3 separate occasions after the patient has rested 20 or more minutes in familiar, quiet surroundings. Casual readings (ie, those taken in the usual fashion) may be much higher than this in the absence of hypertensive disease, since with rest the pressures return to normal; this is vascular hyperreactivity, not hypertension.

2. Retinas—The Keith-Wagener (KW) classification of retinal changes in hypertension has prognostic significance and correlates well with the clinical course.

KW1 = Minimal arteriolar narrowing.

KW2 = More marked narrowing and arteriovenous nicking.

KW3 = Flame-shaped or circular hemorrhages and fluffy "cotton wool" exudates.

KW4 = Any of the above plus papilledema, ie, elevation of the optic disk, obliteration of the physiologic cup, or blurring of the disk margins. By definition, malignant hypertension is always associated with papilledema.

3. Heart and arteries—A loud aortic second sound and an early systolic ejection click may occur. Evidence of left ventricular enlargement with a left ventricular heave indicates well established disease. With onset of left ventricular failure, pulmonary basal rales, gallop rhythm, and pulsus alternans may be noted; a presystolic gallop alone does not necessarily imply failure.

4. Pulses—Direct comparison should be made of both carotid, radial, femoral, popliteal, and pedal pulses, and the presence or absence of bruits over major vessels, including the abdominal aorta and iliacs, should be determined. Blood pressure should be taken in both arms and legs.

5. Cerebrum—Neurologic residuals of cerebral thrombosis or hemorrhage may be present, ranging from only a positive Babinski or Hoffman reflex to frank hemiplegia or hemianopsia.

6. Endocrine status—The signs of Cushing's disease should be noted if present: trunk obesity, hirsutism, acne, purple striae, and finely-grained skin. One kidney may be displaced by an adrenal tumor. In primary aldosteronism, flaccid paralysis or muscular weakness and hypoactive or absent tendon reflexes may be noted as well as diminished or absent vasomotor circulatory reflexes.

7. Coarctation of aorta—Weak or delayed femoral pulses (in comparison with radial pulses) in younger people justify a diagnosis of coarctation of the aorta. Confirmatory signs are a basal systolic murmur transmitted to the interscapular area and palpable collateral arteries along the inferior rib margins and especially around the scapular borders.

8. Renal artery stenosis—A characteristic arterial bruit may be heard with a diaphragm stethoscope in the left or right epigastrium, transmitted from the affected renal artery. The bruit can often be traced into the flank and to the costovertebral angle.

9. Renal parenchymal disease—The patient may have a "uremic" appearance and odor. Polycystic kidneys are large and readily palpable.

C. Laboratory Findings: Routine urinalysis may disclose a low fixed specific gravity compatible with advanced renal parenchymal disease or hypokalemic nephropathy of primary aldosteronism. In both, NPN is elevated and anemia due to advanced azotemia may be present. In aldosteronism, however, the serum potassium is low and the serum sodium and CO_2 elevated; the reverse is true in uremia associated with primary renal disease.

Proteinuria, granular casts, and occasionally microhematuria occur in nephrosclerosis; differentiation from chronic nephritis on this basis alone is impossible.

Demonstrable bacilluria in a fresh clean specimen suggests chronic pyelonephritis; white cell casts are rarely found. Pyuria is frequently absent. Quantitative culture of a clean specimen must be performed on all patients and repeated at intervals, since bacilluria in chronic pyelonephritis may be intermittent.

Quantitative determination of urinary excretion of 17-hydroxycorticosteroids or catecholamines and vanillylmandelic acid is indicated if the clinical picture suggests Cushing's disease or pheochromocytoma, respectively. Urinary aldosterone need not be determined routinely; except in very early or borderline instances, the diagnosis usually can be strongly suspected by blood chemistry.

Tests for pheochromocytoma:

(1) Determine 24-hour urinary catecholamines (see Appendix) or vanillylmandelic acid (normal: 0.7–6.8 mg/24 hours). In most centers, catechol excretion has replaced the provocation tests (histamine and phentolamine [Regitine®]) as a screening method.

(2) Test in presence of sustained hypertension due to pheochromocytoma: The baseline blood pressure should be determined while the patient rests for 20 minutes. It should exceed 170/110 mm Hg. Phentolamine (Regitine®), 2.5–5 mg rapidly IV, best given into the tubing of an infusion during which the levels of the blood pressure have been stabilized, should produce a sustained fall of at least 35/25 mm Hg within 2–5 minutes in patients with pheochromocytoma. *Note:* Sedatives, antihypertensive drugs, and uremia may cause a false-positive test.

(3) Provocative test for a patient with normal blood pressure: Give 0.01–0.025 mg of histamine base in 0.5 ml of normal saline in a tuberculin syringe rapidly IV, leaving the needle in the vein (so that phentolamine can be given to lower excessive blood pressure rise in response to histamine). A blood pressure rise of 60/30 mm Hg or a rise greater than that following a cold pressor test occurs within 2 minutes when pheochromocytoma is present.

D. X-Ray Findings: Chest x-ray may disclose rib notching and the small aortic knob of coarctation and indicate the degree of cardiac enlargement caused by hypertension. Intravenous urograms yield valuable information on relative renal size, relative rate of appearance and disappearance of the contrast material, renal displacement, the presence of obstruction, and pyelonephritis, and are diagnostic of polycystic disease.

E. ECG Findings: ECG can estimate the degree of left ventricular hypertrophy and will show signs of coronary artery disease with conduction disturbances and significant Q waves. In aldosteronism the Q–T interval is prolonged.

F. Special Studies: Presacral oxygen studies may be useful in visualizing adrenal tumors. If renal artery stenosis is suspected, intravenous urograms are indicated. It may also be necessary to perform transfemoral aortography with the contrast medium introduced at a level at or just below the orifices of the renal arteries; differential radioisotope excretion studies on the 2 kidneys; or differential urinary function studies on each kidney (differential water, electrolyte, inulin, PAH, and dye excretion measurements).

G. Follow-up Studies: If specific causes have been excluded, periodic ophthalmoscopic study and evaluation of cardiac and renal status by ECG, chest x-ray, PSP excretion, creatinine clearance, BUN, urinary specific gravity, and urine protein determinations are advised to observe the progression of the disease.

Treatment With Hypotensive Drugs

Many patients with hypertension, especially middle-aged women, live years in comfort without treatment. Great care should therefore be exercised before subjecting these patients to the disagreeable side-effects and potential dangers of a continuous program of drug therapy.

Hypertension varies strikingly in severity in different patients; treatment at present should be varied depending upon the severity of the hypertension and the presence of complications.

Factors which unfavorably influence the prognosis in chronic arterial hypertension and which accordingly determine the nature of drug therapy include the following: (1) high diastolic and systolic blood pressure levels; (2) male sex (worse in men than women); (3) early age at onset; (4) Negro race; (5) retinal abnormalities (see p 172); (6) cardiac abnormalities (eg, ECG changes, cardiomegaly, angina); (7) cerebrovascular accidents; and (8) renal abnormalities.

Recent large-scale studies demonstrate rather convincingly that appropriate drug treatment of asymptomatic mild to moderate degrees of chronic hypertension results in significantly lower morbidity and mortality rates than are reported in untreated control patients. Current insurance data have shown that even slight increases in blood pressure decrease survival, especially by causing premature atherosclerosis.

There is considerable variation of opinion among clinicians about the preference for and the proper sequence of administration of the several drugs that are available. A certain amount of trial and error is involved in selection of the proper agents for each patient, depending upon response to treatment, tolerance of the medication, and the ability of the patient to cooperate. None of the drugs are devoid of undesirable side reactions. The least toxic drugs should be used for mild hypertension. Combinations of drugs working by different mechanisms are frequently necessary to sustain reduced blood pressure and minimize toxicity, but this may make it difficult to evaluate treatment. Fixed-dose combinations should be avoided, especially early in the course of treatment.

In mild to moderate hypertension, therapy is usually initiated with thiazides or (less frequently) other classes of diuretics. If blood pressure is not controlled by diuretics alone after a period of 1–3 weeks, the second drug may be either reserpine, hydralazine, or methyldopa. In moderate arterial hypertension (diastolic pressure of 110–130 mm Hg), it may be advisable to initiate treatment with a combination of thiazides and reserpine plus, if indicated, hydralazine. In severe cases or when patients fail to respond to other agents, the combination of a thiazide and guanethidine should be used. In general, guanethidine should replace rather than be added to reserpine or methyldopa when the latter have proved to be ineffective. If hypertension is complicated by renal failure, methyldopa and perhaps hydralazine are usually the most effective agents. In the treatment of malignant hypertension, it may be necessary to combine a rapidly acting ganglioplegic drug such as trimethaphan with the potent but slower acting sympatholytic drug guanethidine.

The monoamine oxidase inhibitors should not be used in combination with any of the antihypertensive drugs because of the possibility of provoking hypertensive crises. Amphetamines and tricyclic antidepressants (eg, amitriptyline [Elavil®]) block the effectiveness of guanethidine and may occasionally aggravate hypertension.

A. Indications for Hypotensive Drugs:

1. Definite indications—Hypotensive drug therapy is definitely indicated in malignant hypertension; in hypertensive cardiac failure (pulmonary edema) when "fresh" acute myocardial infarction has been excluded; for rapidly increasing diastolic blood pressure with left ventricular hypertrophy and dilatation; hypertensive encephalopathy; when there is evidence of deterioration in the heart and fundi (exudates and hemorrhages), especially in young (particularly male and Negro) patients; in dissecting aneurysm in hypertensives; or when there are persistent diastolic pressures exceeding 105 mm Hg.

2. Probable indications—Hypotensive drugs are indicated in recurrent mild cerebral thrombosis with neurologic sequelae and high diastolic pressure; in intractable coronary insufficiency with high diastolic pressure; when the diastolic blood pressure varies between 100–110 mm Hg without evidence of the complications of hypertension, especially in patients under age 50; or for severe intractable hypertensive headaches (in the absence of obvious emotional stress).

3. Doubtful indications—Hypotensive drug therapy is probably not indicated for mild benign essential hypertension in elderly women or for early transient hypertension in young people in whom there is no objective evidence of vascular deterioration or complications.

B. Drugs Available:

Antihypertensive agents, once begun for significant hypertension, should be continued indefinitely, especially in those with severe hypertension before treatment.

1. Oral diuretic agents—Thiazides such as chlorothiazide reduce the dose required of blocking agents to about half, and synergize with other agents such as rauwolfia. Give chlorothiazide (Diuril®), 0.5–1 gm/day in divided doses, with due caution for electrolyte depletion, especially in patients receiving digitalis; or hydrochlorothiazide (Hydro-Diuril®, Esidrix®), 50 mg 1–2 times daily. Other oral diuretic agents are probably as effective, but the more potent ones (ethacrynic acid [Edecrin®] or furosemide [Lasix®]) may lead to electrolyte depletion more readily than the thiazides. To avoid hypokalemia, some authorities advise adding potassium-retaining drugs such as spironolactone (Aldactone®), 25 mg 3 times daily, or triamterene (Dyrenium®) when oral diuretics are used. If this is done, serum potassium must be checked frequently to avoid hyperkalemia. It is best to avoid adding these potassium-retaining drugs, giving instead a high-potassium diet (fruits and vegetables). Hyperuricemia and hyperglycemia may occur with the use of thiazides, and probenecid (Benemid®), allopurinol (Zyloprim®), or oral hypoglycemic agents may be necessary.

2. Rauwolfia drugs—Rauwolfia has a relatively slight hypotensive action but may be useful because of its mild sedative effect and its value as an adjunct when combined with ganglionic or postganglionic blocking compounds, veratrum, hydralazine (Apresoline®), or chlorothiazide. Nasal stuffiness, gastric hyperacidity, sodium retention, and severe depression may occur, in which case the drug should be withdrawn. Give either of the following: (1) Reserpine, 0.1–0.25 mg 3 times daily orally at onset and maintain on 0.25 mg/day. *Caution:* Do not use if there is a history of previous mental depression. Reserpine may also be given IM, 1–2.5 mg every 8–12 hours, for a short time in hypertensive emergencies. (2) Rauwolfia (Raudixin®), 100–200 mg daily.

3. Hydralazine hydrochloride (Apresoline®)—The initial dosage of this drug is 10–25 mg orally twice daily, progressively increasing to a total dosage of 200 mg/day. The results of the oral use of this drug as a sole method of therapy are often not impressive, but some patients obtain a hypotensive effect. Because hydralazine does not decrease the renal blood flow, it is useful as an adjunct to oral postganglionic or ganglionic blocking agents as well as to the oral diuretics, especially if there is impaired renal function.

Toxic side-effects are common when large doses of hydralazine are used alone but uncommon when the drug is used in combination with chlorothiazide in doses not exceeding 200 mg/day or with rauwolfia. The most important are headache and palpitations with tachycardia. A syndrome resembling systemic lupus erythematosus has occurred, usually after large doses have been given for many months.

4. Methyldopa (Aldomet®)—An initial dose of 250 mg 2 or 3 times daily orally is gradually increased at intervals of 2–3 days to a total daily dose (divided into 2–4 doses) of 0.75–2.5 gm. Both supine and standing pressures are reduced in about 2/3 of cases of moderate hypertension; the postural effect may predominate, especially in patients receiving reserpine. Concomitant thiazide therapy is desirable both to potentiate the hypotensive effects of the drug and to counteract the fluid retention which (with drowsiness) is its main side-effect. As with other hypotensive agents, methyldopa should be given under close supervision by the physician until a stable dose schedule is established. A positive Coombs test and uncommon hemolytic anemia may occur. Fever is a rare toxic reaction.

5. Postganglionic and ganglionic blocking agents—

a. Postganglionic blocking agents—Guanethidine (Ismelin®) acts by blocking the postganglionic adrenergic neurons; tolerance rarely occurs. The drug can be given in a single daily dose; it is effective and well tolerated; and it does not produce parasympathetic blockage. The initial dose is 10 mg orally, increasing gradually to tolerance at weekly intervals. Postural hypotension (especially in the morning on awakening and after exercise), diarrhea, muscle aching, and lack of ejaculation in men are the major symptoms of toxicity.

b. Ganglionic blocking agents—These agents are used very infrequently today because they block parasympathetics and have been superseded by guanethidine in most clinics. Pentolinium tartrate (Ansolysen®), chlorisondamine chloride (Ecolid®), and mecamylamine hydrochloride (Inversine®) can be used orally or subcutaneously. The initial doses of the oral ganglionic blocking compounds are as follows: Hexamethonium (Methium®), 125 mg; pentolinium tartrate (Ansolysen®), 10–20 mg; chlorisondamine chloride (Ecolid®), 10–20 mg. Mecamylamine (Inversine®) is given in doses beginning with 1–2.5 mg once or twice daily and increased by increments of 2.5 mg per dose until a satisfactory standing pressure is achieved. The effects of these types of drugs are enhanced by concurrent thiazide administration. With the exception of mecamylamine, absorption following oral administration is small and irregular, with resultant unpredictable falls in blood pressure.

c. Basic principles in the use of the ganglionic and postganglionic drugs—(1) Hospitalize the patient under close supervision except when using guanethidine (Ismelin®), in which case treatment can be started on an outpatient basis. (2) Start with a small initial dose and increase gradually, depending upon the tolerance and response of the patient. (3) The degree of reduction of blood pressure should be only moderate in the first week or so, and no attempt should be made to reduce the pressure to normal until it has been demonstrated that the patient can tolerate systolic pressures of about 160 mm Hg without hypotensive symptoms. (4) Postural hypotension, which is greatest at the height of the effect of the drug, should be considered not only as a potential danger to the patient but also as a therapeutic weapon to prolong the hypotensive action of the drug after the peak effect has worn off. (5) Minimize the dose of ganglionic blocking agent required (and thereby minimize side-effects) by prior administration of reserpine, 0.25 mg/day, or thiazide drugs (see above), or both. (6) Minimize constipation by use of laxatives or, if necessary, neostigmine by mouth. (7) Minimize diarrhea (from guanethidine) by the use of small doses of codeine. (8) Warn the patient of the effects of additional vasodilatation due to heat, including hot baths, alcohol, and immobility following exercise. The effect of these drugs should be evaluated in an ambulatory patient in the erect position. Otherwise, excessive doses will be given.

d. Determination of adequate dosage—A trial of 1–2 weeks is usually required to determine the dose necessary to lower the blood pressure to about 160/100 mm Hg. The patient may then be seen on an outpatient basis and the dose gradually increased to that level which produces the desired fall of blood pressure. Opinion is divided about whether the desired pressure at the time of peak action of the drug is 150–160 mm Hg systolic or whether it is that which results in mild hypotensive symptoms on standing. Constipation is to be avoided in patients receiving oral methonium compounds because it increases the absorption of the drug; laxatives should be given to ensure a daily bowel movement.

Although the determination of the proper drug dosage is difficult, it is usually considered satisfactory if standing diastolic pressures of 90–100 mm Hg or less are achieved. Since the effectiveness of the drug cannot be determined by casual blood pressure readings in the physician's office, the following methods have been used to determine effective dosage: (1) Home blood pressure readings are recorded and shown to the physician at his regular visits. The physician may increase or decrease the dose, and the patient is instructed to decrease the dose whenever the blood pressure falls below 150/90, and not to take a dose if the blood pressure is below 130/80 in the recumbent position. (2) Motionless standing for 1 minute before taking the drug is advocated to prevent excessive hypotension. Blood pressure will then be sufficiently high so that an additional quantity can be taken without harm. This only guards against excessive dosage; it does not indicate when the dose has been inadequate. (3) Periodic hospitalization is advisable for 1–2 days to determine basal blood pressure readings. These readings are often 25–50 mm Hg less than readings obtained in the doctor's office and can be used for more accurate control of the blocking compounds. (4) Blood pressure recordings throughout the day, using portable equipment, give a more representative record of the patient's usual pressures, but the apparatus is not generally available.

e. Side-effects and hazards of ganglionic and post-ganglionic blocking agents—

(1) Acute hypotensive reactions are manifested by faintness, weakness, and nausea and vomiting. The patient should be instructed to lie down immediately and place his feet higher than his head. Unless the hypotensive effect is too severe, the symptoms pass rapidly with this postural assistance. If the symptoms persist, give a vasopressor drug such as phenylephrine hydrochloride (Neo-Synephrine®) or methoxamine (Vasoxyl®) subcutaneously, or a slow, continuous intravenous infusion of levarterenol bitartrate (Levophed®), 4 mg/liter, titrated carefully, because occasional patients are unusually sensitive to some vasopressors.

(2) Acute or progressive renal failure due to decreased renal blood flow or filtration pressure may necessitate discontinuing the drug.

(3) Vascular thromboses and renal failure are hazards in older patients who suffer severe and abrupt falls of blood pressure.

(4) A low-sodium diet potentiates the action of blocking compounds. If an individual receiving fixed doses of the drug is given a low-sodium diet, hypotensive symptoms may occur. It is usually desirable to place the patient on a 2 gm sodium diet at the onset of therapy.

(5) Alcohol, hot climate, vasodilator drugs, vigorous exercise, and salt depletion potentiate the action of ganglionic and postganglionic compounds.

(6) Parasympatholytic effects due to parasympathetic blocking by the ganglionic blocking agents (but not guanethidine) will cause blurring of vision, constipation, and dryness of the mouth; these can be corrected in part by the use of neostigmine orally in doses of 7.5–15 mg. Simple laxatives should be tried initially for constipation.

6. Veratrum compounds—These drugs have not received wide acceptance because of the narrow margin between their therapeutic and toxic effects—nausea, vomiting, and weakness—and are rarely used today.

7. Propranolol (Inderal®)—Decrease in the cardiac output after propranolol by decreasing the heart rate without changing the stroke volume has led to its use in hypertension. A modest fall in pressure may occur, but diuretics are more effective and probably safer.

C. Acute Hypertensive Crises: Patients with acute severe hypertension (diastolic blood pressure > 150 mm Hg) must be hospitalized and treated on an emergency basis with parenteral hypotensive drugs. The most important of the hypertensive "crises" are those of acute hypertensive encephalopathy, acute pulmonary edema associated with a marked rise in blood pressure in hypertensive patients with left ventricular failure, malignant hypertension, acute dissecting aneurysm of the aorta with a high arterial pressure, and hemorrhagic stroke with marked elevation of blood pressure.

Constant monitoring of the blood pressure, preferably in an intensive care unit, is required. The patient should be sitting up or the head of the bed should be elevated to 30°. BUN and serum creatinine should be determined daily if BUN is > 50 mg/100 ml. Advance preparation should be made to treat excessive pressure drop (see Chapter 1).

Several parenteral antihypertensive drugs are available, but no single agent can be classified as the drug of choice.

1. Rapidly acting agents—

a. The ganglionic blocking agent trimethaphan (Arfonad®), 1 ampule of 500 mg in 1 liter 5% dextrose in water, is given IV at a rate of 1–4 ml/min. It takes effect within a few minutes and lasts for the duration of the infusion. The objective should be to reduce the diastolic blood pressure to about 110 mm Hg over a period of about 1 hour.

b. An alternative rapidly acting ganglioplegic drug, pentolinium tartrate (Ansolysen®), 1–2 mg subcut or IM, may be given every 1–2 hours, depending upon response.

2. Delayed acting agents—

a. Reserpine, 1–2.5 mg IM every 8 hours.

b. Hydralazine (Apresoline®), 5–20 mg IM every 2–4 hours.

c. Methyldopa (Aldomet®), 500 mg IV every 2–4 hours, takes effect more slowly than the ganglioplegics, and its effect lasts for 8–12 hours.

d. Diazoxide (Hyperstat®), 300 mg IV in a single dose, acts promptly as a vasodilator without decreasing cardiac output or renal blood flow. It has been used especially in toxemia of pregnancy.

D. Subsequent Therapy: When the blood pressure has been brought under control, guanethidine (Ismelin®) is given orally combined with thiazides or other oral antihypertensive agents and parenteral drugs are tapered off over a period of 2–3 days.

E. Other Methods of Treatment: A rigid low-sodium diet (containing 350 mg of sodium or less per day) has been made unnecessary by the introduction of chlorothiazide (Diuril®); 2 gm of sodium are usually allowed.

Attempts to treat hypertensive patients with psychoanalytic methods have not been successful, although attention to the emotional needs of such patients is an important adjunct to treatment.

For nervousness, give phenobarbital, 15–30 mg 3–4 times daily, or similar mild sedatives. Tricyclic depressants should be avoided if guanethidine is used because they compete with guanethidine uptake and the antihypertensive effect of the latter is diminished.

Treatment of Complications

The cardiac, cerebral, and renal complications of hypertension are discussed under congestive failure, angina pectoris, myocardial infarction, cerebral hemorrhage, cerebral thrombosis, and renal failure.

The headache of hypertension is of unknown cause but is often of emotional origin except in the presence of accelerated or malignant hypertension.

Suggestion and explanation are often helpful. Hypotensive drugs are most effective in relieving severe headache associated with the malignant or premalignant phase of hypertension.

Prognosis

Although many patients with slight elevation of blood pressure live a normal span, most patients with untreated hypertensive cardiovascular disease die of complications within 20 years of onset. Before the effective antihypertensive drugs were available, 70% of patients died of heart failure or coronary artery disease, 15% of cerebral hemorrhage, and 10% of uremia. Heart failure is now an uncommon cause of death; cerebrovascular, coronary artery, and renal artery complications of the basic atherosclerotic process account for the majority of deaths.

The survival of patients with malignant hypertension has been markedly improved by modern drug therapy; 50–60% are now alive 5 years after diagnosis, whereas at most about 10% were alive after 2 years before the newer drugs became available.

The underlying cause of hypertension may be responsible for death, as in Cushing's disease, polyarteritis, and terminal nephritis.

Amsterdam, E.A., & others: Renal vein renin activity in the prognosis of surgery for renovascular hypertension. Am J Med 47:860–869, 1969.

Aokie, B.S., & W.R. Wilson: Hydralazine and methyldopa in thiazide treated hypertensive patients. Am Heart J 79:798–805, 1970.

Barham-Carter, J.: Hypotensive therapy in stroke survivors. Lancet 1:486–489, 1970.

Bengtsson, U., Hogdahl, A.M., & B. Hood: Chronic non-obstructive pyelonephritis and hypertension: A long-term study. Quart J Med 37:361, 1968.

Bourgoignie, J., & others: Renal venous renin in hypertension. Am J Med 48:332–342, 1970.

Breckenridge, A., Dollery, C.T., & E.H.O. Parry: Prognosis of treated hypertension: Changes in life expectancy and causes of death between 1952 and 1967. Quart J Med 39:411–429, 1970.

Breckenridge, A., & others: Hypertension in the young. Quart J Med 36:549–563, 1967.

Channick, B.J., Adlin, E.V., & A.D. Marks: Suppressed plasma renin activity in hypertension. Arch Int Med 123:131–140, 1969.

Cole, F.M., & P.O. Yates: Comparative incidence of cerebrovascular lesions in normotensive and hypertensive patients. Neurology 18:255–259, 1968.

DeBakey, M.E., & others: Abnormalities of the sinuses of Valsalva: Experience with 35 patients. J Thoracic Cardiovas Surg 54:312–332, 1967.

Deming, Q.B.: Blood pressure: Its relation to atherosclerotic disease of the coronaries. Bull New York Acad Med 44:968–984, 1968.

Dollery, C.T.: Drugs and the regulation of the blood pressure. Chap 12, pages 301–327, in: *Modern Trends in Pharmacology and Therapeutics.* W.F.M. Fulton (editor). Appleton-Century-Crofts, 1967.

Dollery, C.T.: Treatment of malignant hypertension. Mod Treat 3:39–49, 1966.

Dustan, H.P., & others: Arterial pressure responses to discontinuing antihypertensive drugs. Circulation 37:370–379, 1968.

Fishman, L.M., & others: Incidence of primary aldosteronism in "essential" hypertension. JAMA 205:497–502, 1969.

Foster, J.H., & others: Renovascular hypertension secondary to atherosclerosis. Am J Med 46:741–750, 1969.

Freis, E.D.: Hypertensive crisis. JAMA 208:338–342, 1969.

George, J.M., & others: The syndrome of primary aldosteronism. Am J Med 48:343, 1970.

Gifford, R.W., Jr.: Hypertensive cardiovascular disease: Effect of antipressor therapy on the course and prognosis. Am J Cardiol 17:656–662, 1966.

Gilmore, H.R.: The treatment of chronic hypertension. M Clin North America 55:317–324, 1971.

Goldfien, A.: Treatment of pheochromocytoma. Mod Treat 3:1360–1376, 1966.

Gross, F. (editor): *Antihypertensive Therapy: Principles and Practice.* Springer, 1966.

Gunnells, J., Jr., & others: Peripheral and renal venous plasma renin activity in hypertension. Ann Int Med 71:555–575, 1969.

Haber, E.: Pathophysiologic studies of the renin-angiotensin system. New England J Med 280:148–155, 1969.

Haber, E.: The renin-angiotensin system in curable hypertension. Mod Concepts Cardiovas Dis 38:17–22, 1969.

Hamby, W.M., & others: Intravenous use of diazoxide in the treatment of severe hypertension. Circulation 37:169–174, 1969.

Hunt, J.C., & others: Diagnosis and management of renovascular hypertension. Am. J. Cardiol 23:434–445, 1969.

Julius, S., & others: Relationship between cardiac output and peripheral resistance in borderline hypertension. Circulation 43(Suppl 3):382, 1971.

Kannel, W.B., & others: Epidemiologic assessment of the role of blood pressure in stroke. The Framingham Study. JAMA 214:301–310, 1970.

Khatri, I.M., & E.D. Freis: Hemodynamic changes during sleep in hypertensive patients. Circulation 39:785–790, 1969.

Laragh, J.H.: Recent advances in hypertension. Am J Med 39:616–645, 1965.

Leishman, A.W.D., & G. Sandler: Guanethidine and hypertension after five years. Angiology 18:705, 1967.

Liddle, G.W., & A.M. Shute: The evolution of Cushing's syndrome. Advances Int Med 15:41, 1969.

Lindsay, J., & J.W. Hurst: Drug therapy of dissecting aortic aneurysms. Circulation 37:216–219, 1968.

Locksley, H.B.: Hemorrhagic strokes: Principal causes, natural history, and treatment. M Clin North America 52:1193–1212, 1968.

McQueen, E.G.: Management of hypertension in pregnancy. Med Today 4:102, 1970.

Mohamed, S., & others: The effects of alpha-methyldopa on renal function in hypertensive patients. Am Heart J 76:21–28, 1968.

Mroczek, W.J., & others: The value of aggressive therapy in the hypertensive patient with azotemia. Circulation 40:893–905, 1969.

Nicotero, J.A., & others: Prevention of hyperuricemia by allopurinol in hypertensive patients treated with chlorothiazide. New England J Med 282:133–135, 1970.

Perloff, D., & others: Renal vascular hypertension: Further experiences. Am Heart J 74:614–631, 1967.

Pickering, G.: Hyperpiesis: High blood pressure without evident cause: Essential hypertension. Brit MJ 2:959–968, 1965.

Sannerstedt, R., Bjure, J., & E. Varnauskas: Correlation between electrocardiographic changes and systemic hemodynamics in human arterial hypertension. Am J Cardiol 26:117–123, 1970.

Shapiro, A.P.: Hypertension in renal parenchymal disease. Disease-A-Month, Sept 1969.

Smith, W.M., & others: Co-operative clinical trial of alpha-methyldopa. III. Double-blind control comparison of alpha-methyldopa and chlorothiazide, and chlorothiazide and rauwolfia. Ann Int Med 65:657–671, 1966.

Sokolow, M., & D. Perloff: The prognosis of essential hypertension treated conservatively. Circulation 23:697–713, 1961.

Sokolow, M., & D. Perloff: The choice of drugs and the management of essential hypertension. Progr Cardiovas Dis 8:253–277, 1965.

Sokolow, M., & others: Relationship between level of blood pressure measured casually and by portable recorders and severity of complications in essential hypertension. Circulation 34:279–298, 1966.

Temple, T., Jr., & others: Treatment of Cushing's disease: Correction of hypercortisonism by o,p'DDD without induction of aldosterone deficiency. New England J Med 281:801–848, 1969.

Vaamonde, C.A., David, N.J., & R.F. Palmer: Hypertensive emergencies. M Clin North America 55:325–334, 1971.

Veterans Administration Cooperative Study Group on Antihypertensive Agents: I. Effects of treatment on morbidity in hypertension. II. Results in patients with diastolic pressure averaging 90 through 114 mm Hg. JAMA 202:1028–1034, 1967; 213:1143–1152, 1970.

Weir, R.J., & others: Blood-pressure in women after one year of oral contraception. Lancet 1:467, 1971.

Wheat, M.W., Jr., & others: Acute dissecting aneurysms of the aorta: Treatment and results in 64 patients. J Thoracic Cardiovas Surg 58:344, 1969.

ARTERIOSCLEROTIC HEART DISEASE
(Arteriosclerotic Coronary Artery Disease; Ischemic Heart Disease)

Arteriosclerotic heart disease, or obliterative atherosclerosis of the coronary arteries, is the commonest underlying cause of cardiovascular disability and death. A disorder of lipid metabolism is thought to be responsible for the localized subintimal accumulations of fatty and fibrous tissue which progressively obstruct the epicardial portions of the coronary arteries and their main branches.

Risk factors (established by prospective studies) which predispose to the development of ischemic heart disease include genetic predispositions, arterial hypertension, diabetes mellitus, hypercholesterolemia and hypertriglyceridemia, and cigarette smoking (> 1 pack/ day). Other factors of less importance include obesity and possibly physical fitness.

Men are more often affected than women by an overall ratio of 4:1; before the age of 40 the ratio is 8:1, and beyond age 70 it is 1:1. In men the peak incidence of clinical manifestations is age 50–60; in women, age 60–70. Advanced stages of atherosclerotic coronary artery disease, even complete occlusion, may remain clinically silent, being discovered incidentally after death due to other causes. At present, the only means of determining the location and extent of narrowing is coronary angiography. There is no correlation between the clinical symptoms and signs and the extent of disease.

The pathophysiology underlying the clinical manifestations of arteriosclerotic heart disease may be listed as follows:

Clinical Expression	Mechanism
1. Angina pectoris	1. Transient, localized myocardial ischemia.
2. Acute myocardial infarction.	2. Arterial occlusion.
3. Pre-infarction angina.	3. Prolonged myocardial ischemia, with or without myocardial necrosis.
4. Heart failure, acute and chronic arrhythmias, conduction disturbances, abnormal ECG.	4. Gradual fibrosis of myocardium or conduction system. May result from (2) or (3) also.
5. Sudden death.	5. Any of the above.

1. ANGINA PECTORIS

Essentials of Diagnosis

- Squeezing or pressure-like pain, retrosternal or slightly to the left, which appears quickly during exertion, may radiate in a set pattern, and subsides with rest.
- Seventy percent have diagnostic ECG abnormalities after mild exercise; the remaining 30% have normal tracings or nondiagnostic abnormalities.

General Considerations

Angina pectoris is usually due to arteriosclerotic heart disease, but in rare instances it may occur in the absence of significant disease of the coronary arteries as a result of severe aortic stenosis or insufficiency, syphilitic aortitis, increased metabolic demands as in hyperthyroidism or after thyroid therapy, marked anemia, or paroxysmal tachycardias with very rapid ventricular rates. The underlying mechanism is a discrepancy between the myocardial demands for oxygen and the amount delivered through the coronary arteries. The 3 groups of variables which determine the production of relative or absolute myocardial ischemia are as follows:

(1) Limitation of oxygen delivered by the coronary arteries: (a) Vessel factors include atherosclerotic narrowing, lack of collateral circulation, and reflex narrowing in response to emotion, cold, upper gastrointestinal disease, or smoking. (b) Blood factors consist of anemia, hypoxemia, and polycythemia (increased viscosity). (c) Circulatory factors are fall in blood pressure due to arrhythmias, orthostatic hypotension, bleeding, and Valsalva's maneuver; and decreased filling pressure of or flow to the coronary arteries due to aortic stenosis or insufficiency.

(2) Increased cardiac output: Physiologic factors are exertion, excitement, digestion and metabolism following a heavy meal. Pathologic factors (high-output states) include anemia, thyrotoxicosis, arteriovenous fistula, and pheochromocytoma.

(3) Increased myocardial demands for oxygen: May be due to increased work of the heart, as in aortic stenosis, aortic insufficiency, and diastolic hypertension; or increased oxygen consumption due to thyrotoxicosis or in any state characterized by increased catecholamine excretion (pheochromocytoma, strong emotion, and hypoglycemia).

Physiologic changes in patients developing exercise-induced angina during cardiac catheterization have shown a considerable rise in left ventricular end-diastolic pressure just before the angina and the ischemic changes in the ECG appeared. Myocardial oxygen consumption increased similarly. The changes indicate that left ventricular failure or decreased compliance coincides with the appearance of angina.

Clinical Findings

A. History: The diagnosis of angina pectoris depends almost entirely upon the history, and it is of the utmost importance that the patient be allowed to describe the symptoms in his own way, using his hands to demonstrate the location and quality of the symptom. The history should specifically include the following categories:

1. Circumstances that precipitate and relieve angina—Angina most commonly occurs during walking, especially up an incline or a flight of stairs. Exertion which involves straining, closing the glottis, and immobilizing the thorax precipitates an attack most rapidly. Regardless of the type of activity, angina occurs *during* exertion and subsides promptly if the patient stands or sits quietly. Patients prefer to remain upright rather than lie down. Some patients obtain relief by belching, and for this reason may attribute their distress to "stomach trouble." The amount of activity required to produce angina varies with each patient, but it is always less after meals, during excitement, or on exposure to a cold wind. Heavy meals and strong emotion can provoke an attack in the absence of exertion.

2. Characteristics of the discomfort—Patients often do not refer to angina as a "pain" but as a sensation of squeezing, burning, pressing, choking, aching, bursting, "gas," or tightness. It is commonly attributed to "indigestion." The distress of angina is never a sharply localized or darting pain which can be pointed to with a finger. It appears quickly during exertion, and increases rapidly in intensity until the patient is compelled to stop and rest even though the initial discomfort may not be severe.

3. Location and radiation—The distribution of the distress may vary widely in different patients but is always the same for each individual patient. In 80–90% of cases the discomfort is felt behind or slightly to the left of the sternum. When it begins farther to the left or, uncommonly, on the right, it characteristically moves centrally and is felt deep in the chest. Although angina may radiate to any segment from C2 to T10, it radiates most often to the left shoulder and upper arm, frequently moving down the inner volar aspect of the arm to the elbow, forearm, wrist, or 4th and 5th fingers. Radiation to the right shoulder and distally is less common, but the characteristics are the same. Occasionally angina may be referred to, or felt initially in, the lower jaw, the base or back of the neck, the interscapular area, or high in the left back.

Angina may almost certainly be excluded when the patient designates the only site of pain by pointing to the area of the apical impulse with one finger.

4. Duration of attacks—Angina is of clearly defined short duration, and subsides completely without residual discomfort. If the attack is precipitated by exertion and the patient promptly stops to rest, the distress of angina usually lasts less than 3 minutes (although most patients think it is longer). Attacks following a heavy meal or which are brought on by anger often last 15–20 minutes.

5. Effect of glyceryl trinitrate—The diagnosis of angina pectoris is strongly supported (1) if 0.4 mg of glyceryl trinitrate (nitroglycerin) invariably shortens an attack and (2) if that amount taken immediately beforehand invariably permits greater exertion before the onset of angina or prevents angina entirely. However, this source of diagnostic information is less reliable than the characteristic history.

6. Unrelated disorders that intensify angina should be considered. Cholecystitis, sliding hiatus hernia, thyrotoxicosis, paroxysmal arrhythmias, orthostatic hypotension, or left ventricular failure may account for unusual variants of angina pectoris.

B. Signs: Examination during a spontaneous or induced attack frequently reveals a significant elevation in systolic and diastolic blood pressure; occasionally gallop rhythm is present during pain only. Carotid sinus massage often causes the pain to subside more quickly than usual if it slows the cardiac rate, and is a helpful maneuver in instances of "atypical angina."

It is important to detect signs of diseases that may contribute to arteriosclerotic heart disease, eg, diabetes mellitus (retinopathy or neuropathy), xanthomatosis (tuberosa, plana, or tendinosa); or disorders that intensify the angina, such as hypertension, thyrotoxicosis, orthostatic hypotension, and aortic stenosis or mitral stenosis.

The cardiovascular examination is normal in 25–40% of patients with angina. In the remainder, evidence of occlusive disease of the peripheral arteries,

TABLE 7–3. The five major categories of primary hyperlipidemia.*

Appearance of Plasma	Cholesterol Elevation	Triglyceride Elevation	Origin, Possible Mechanism	Clinical Presentation	Usual Age at Detection	Rule Out
I. Rarest. Exogenous hyperlipidemia, or hyperchylomicronemia.						
Creamy layer over clear infranate on standing	↑	Often 1000 mg/100 ml or above. ↑↑↑	Genetic. Defective lipoprotein lipase activity.	"Cream of tomato soup" blood. White retinal vessels. Hepatosplenomegaly. Xanthomas. Abdominal pain on normal diet.	Early childhood.	Pancreatitis, diabetes.
II. Relatively common.						
Clear or only slightly opalescent	Usually 300–500 mg/100 ml in genetic; usually <400 in sporadic.	↑ or normal	Genetic (dominant gene); sporadic.	Tendon and tuberous xanthomas. Corneal arcus. Accelerated atherosclerosis.	Early childhood (in severe cases).	Hypothyroidism, obstructive liver disease, nephrotic syndrome.
III. Relatively uncommon.						
Turbid, moderately lactescent	↑↑ Highly variable (from nearly normal to over 1000 mg/100 ml and weight-sensitive).	↑ Highly variable (175–1500 mg/100 ml in same patient) and weight-sensitive.	Genetic (recessive gene?); sporadic.	Xanthomas (especially yellow streaks on palms). Abnormal glucose tolerance. Hyperuricemia.	Adulthood (over age 20).	Hepatic disease, dysglobulinemia, uncontrolled diabetes.
IV. Most common. Endogenous hyperlipidemia.						
Turbid, lactescent	↑	↑↑ 200–5000 mg/100 ml	Genetic; sporadic. Excessive endogenous glyceride synthesis. Deficient glyceride removal.	Accelerated vascular disease (especially coronary in young adults). Abnormal glucose tolerance ("mild" diabetes in most).	Adulthood.	Hyperthyroidism, diabetes, pancreatitis, glycogen storage disease, nephrotic syndrome, pregnancy, multiple myeloma.
V. Uncommon. Mixed exogenous and endogenous hyperlipidemia.						
Creamy layer over milky infranate on standing	↑	↑↑	Probably genetic.	Abdominal pain (sometimes leading to surgery, at which the only finding is milky peritoneal fluid).	Early adulthood.	Insulin-dependent diabetes, pancreatitis, alcoholism.

*Reproduced, with permission, from: Fredrickson, D.S.: New drugs in the treatment of hyperlipidemia. Hospital Practice 3:54–57, June 1968.

hypertensive retinopathy and cardiomegaly, significant murmurs, or signs of cardiac failure may be noted.

C. Laboratory Findings: Anemia, hypercholesterolemia, diabetes mellitus, hypoglycemia, hyperthyroidism, and upper gastrointestinal diseases should be investigated as possible contributory factors. STS should be done routinely. A chest film should be taken to exclude pulmonary, cardiac, and skeletal abnormalities.

D. ECG Findings: The resting ECG is normal in 25% of patients with angina. In the remainder, abnormalities include atrioventricular or intraventricular conduction defects, patterns of left ventricular hypertrophy, old myocardial infarction, or nonspecific ST–T changes.

An exercise test may be warranted if the diagnosis is seriously in doubt. Do not do an exercise test unless the resting ECG is normal, the patient has had no digitalis for 3 weeks, and the onset of the pain is not of recent origin. These precautions are necessary to prevent exercising a patient with acute or subacute myocardial ischemia. A positive ECG exercise test consists of at least a 1 mm horizontal depression or definite sag of the entire ST segment in one or more leads. Depression of the ST junction alone ("J"), flattening of T waves, or minor ST segment depression is not diagnostic. In the standardized test significant changes occur in only 50–60% of patients with angina. The percentage is much higher when tracings are taken during a spontaneous attack or if a more extensive exercise test is used.

E. Selective Coronary Cineangiography: (See also discussion of surgery for coronary heart disease, p 185.) Increasing experience has shown that angiography is relatively safe and defines the localization and magnitude of the anatomic disease in the coronary arteries. However, patients with definite angina pectoris rarely have normal coronary angiograms, so a normal study does not necessarily exclude coronary disease. The indications are not established, but the procedure is being performed with increasing frequency, especially since newer bypass surgical procedures (see below) are so promising. Coronary angiography should not be used solely for diagnosis, because a carefully taken history plus an electrocardiogram usually suffice.

Differential Diagnosis

Psychophysiologic cardiovascular reactions are a loosely defined group of disorders having in common dull aching chest pains often described as "heart pain," lasting hours or days, often aggravated by exertion but not promptly relieved by rest. Darting, knifelike pains of momentary duration at the apex or over the precordium are often present also. Emotional tension and fatigue make the pain worse. Dyspnea of the hyperventilation variety, palpitation, fatigue, and headache are also usually present. Continual exhaustion is a frequent complaint.

The "anterior chest wall syndrome" is characterized by sharply localized tenderness of intercostal muscles, pressure on which reproduces the chest pain. Sprain or inflammation of the chondrocostal junctions, which may be warm, swollen, and red (so-called Tietze's syndrome), may result in diffuse chest pain which is also reproduced by local pressure. Intercostal neuritis (herpes zoster, diabetes mellitus, etc) may confuse the diagnosis.

Xiphoid tenderness and lower sternal pain may arise from and be reproduced by pressure on the xiphoid process.

Any of the above may occur in a patient with angina.

Cervical or thoracic spine disease (degenerative disk disease, postural strain, "arthritis") involving the dorsal roots produces sudden sharp, severe chest pain similar to angina in location and "radiation" but related to specific movements of the neck or spine, recumbency, and straining or lifting. Pain due to cervical thoracic disk disease involves the outer or dorsal aspect of the arm and the thumb and index fingers rather than the ring and little fingers.

Peptic ulcer, chronic cholecystitis, cardiospasm, and functional gastrointestinal disease are often suspected because some patients indisputably obtain relief from angina by belching. In these disorders symptoms are related to food intake rather than exertion. X-ray and fluoroscopic study are helpful in diagnosis. The pain is relieved by appropriate diet and drug therapy.

Hiatus hernia is characterized by lower chest and upper abdominal pain after heavy meals occurring in recumbency or upon bending over. The pain is relieved by bland diet, antacids, semi-Fowler position, and walking.

Degenerative and inflammatory lesions of the left shoulder, cervical rib, and the scalenus anticus syndrome are differentiated from angina by the fact that the pain is precipitated by movement of the arm and shoulder, paresthesias are present in the left arm, and postural exercises and pillow support to the shoulders in bed give relief.

"Tight" mitral stenosis or pulmonary hypertension resulting from chronic pulmonary disease can on occasion produce chest pain which is indistinguishable from angina pectoris, including ST segment sagging or depression. The clinical findings of mitral stenosis or of the lung disease are evident, and the ECG invariably discloses right axis deviation or frank right ventricular hypertrophy.

Prevention of Ischemic Heart Disease: Management of the Patient With High Risk Factors

Although it has been shown that individuals who have the risk factors listed in the introductory paragraph to this section—especially if they are present in combination and if the patient is under age 50—have a high risk of developing clinical disease, there is little evidence that correcting them will prevent further progression of the disease once it has occurred. Emphasis should therefore be given to prevention. Hypertension and diabetes should be adequately treated; cigarette smoking should be discouraged; and optimal weight

TABLE 7–4. Dietary management of familial hyperlipoproteinemias.*

Disorder	Type	Dietary Therapy
Exogenous lipemia (fat-induced lipemia, hyperchylomicronemia)	I	(1) Fat restriction to less than 30 gm daily. Medium-chain triglycerides (eg, Portagen®) added for calories. (2) No restriction of protein, cholesterol, or carbohydrate. Alcohol contraindicated.
Familial hypercholesterolemia (hyperbetalipoproteinemia)	II	(1) Low cholesterol (not more than 300 mg daily). Increased polyunsaturated to saturated fatty acid ratio (2:1). For diet, see Table 7–5.) Only one portion (3 oz) cooked red meat daily; more fish and chicken. Restricted egg yolks, shellfish, organ meats, and animal fats. (2) Use of safflower, soybean, corn, cottonseed, sunflower, sesame oils, 1–2 oz daily (increase by 1 oz when red meat taken). Special (soft) margarines allowed to replace oils–those whose primary ingredient is listed as liquid oil.
Broad beta disease (dysbetalipoproteinemia)	III	(1) Weight reduction and maintenance of "ideal" weight. Low cholesterol: 20% calories from protein, 40% from carbohydrate, 40% from fat. (For diet, see Table 7–5.) (2) Dietary cholesterol limited to less than 300 mg/day–only source to be from one portion (3 oz) lean meat. Restricted egg yolks, shellfish, organ meats, and animal fats. Increased polyunsaturated to saturated fatty acid ratio (2:1). Use of oils and soft margarines. (3) Elimination of concentrated sweets, sugars.
Endogenous lipemia (carbohydrate-induced lipemia, hyperprebetalipoproteinemia)	IV	(1) Weight reduction and maintenance of "ideal" weight. Controlled carbohydrate. (For diet, see Table 7–6.) (2) Carbohydrate (40%) calories limited to fruits, vegetables, breads, cereals, starches, elimination of concentrated sweets (sugars). (3) Animal fats or foods containing cholesterol limited to less than 500 mg daily. Eggs, shellfish, organ meats allowed in limited amounts. Special oils and margarines recommended.
Mixed lipemia	V	(1) Weight reduction and maintenance of "ideal" weight. Restricted fat and controlled carbohydrate. (For diet, see Table 7–6.) (2) Fat limited to 30% calories; preference given to polyunsaturated fats. Cholesterol limited to 300–500 mg daily. (3) Carbohydrate (50%) limited to fruits, vegetables, breads, cereals, starches, with elimination of concentrated sweets (sugars). (4) Alcohol contraindicated.

*Adapted from Bagdade, J.D., & E.L. Bierman: Diagnosis and dietary treatment of blood lipid disorders. M Clin North America 54:1393–1398, 1970; and from Levy, R.I., & others: Dietary management of hyperlipoproteinemia. J Am Dietet A 58:406–416, 1971.

and physical fitness should be encouraged. Management of the hyperlipidemias requires a knowledge of the different types of abnormalities. Table 7–3 summarizes our most authoritative classification (Fredrickson, D.S.: New drugs in the treatment of hyperlipidemia. Hospital Practice 3:54–57, June 1968). Treatment, according to Fredrickson, is as follows:

Type I: Reduce fat intake to 35 gm/day.

Type II: Reduce saturated fats and cholesterol in the diet (Table 7–5) and try one of the following drugs: Cholestyramine (Cuemid®), 16–32 gm daily in divided doses with meals; beta-sitosterol (Cytellin®), 12–18 gm/day in divided doses before meals; clofibrate (Atromid-S®), 500 mg 4 times daily. Cholestyramine binds bile acids, increasing their excretion; beta-sitosterol interferes with the absorption of cholesterol; and clofibrate interferes with the synthesis of cholesterol. Side-effects include gastrointestinal upsets. Careful follow-up by the physician for unexpected side-effects is essential.

Type III: Reduce body weight to ideal weight and prescribe a low-fat, low-cholesterol diet as for type II (Table 7–5). Clofibrate (Atromid-S®), 2 gm daily, may reduce cholesterol levels 25–50% and triglyceride levels 40–80%.

Type IV: Reduce body weight with a high-protein, low-fat, low-carbohydrate diet (Table 7–6) to ideal weight and substitute polyunsaturated fats for saturated fats. Clofibrate may be of value, but dietary treatment is more effective.

Type V: Same as for type IV (Table 7–6).

TABLE 7—5. Dietary plan for low-cholesterol, modified fat diet: For types II and III.*

Foods to Use	Foods to Avoid	1200 Calories (40% Cal From Unsaturated Fat) Polyunsaturated:Saturated Fat Ratio 2:1	1800 Calories (40% Cal From Unsaturated Fat) Polyunsaturated:Saturated Fat Ratio 2:1
Milk, nonfat	Whole and low-fat milk	2 cups (16 oz) daily	2 cups (16 oz) daily
Fruits (without sugar), fresh, canned, or juices—at least one to be citrus or tomato	Avocado, olives	3 servings daily	3—5 servings daily
Vegetables—at least one to be leafy green or yellow		3 or more servings daily	3 or more servings daily
Breads, cereals, starches, enriched white or whole grain		2—4 servings daily	7 servings daily
Eggs (with yolks)		Limited to 2 per week (in any form)	Limited to 2 per week (in any form)
Egg whites		As desired	As desired
Poultry, fish, veal (3 oz cooked per serving)†	Skin and fat on poultry, duck, and goose; shellfish, spare ribs, corned brisket, frankfurters, pan-fried or deep fat-fried meats, sausage, luncheon meats, organ meats	9—11 of the main meals per week	9—11 of the main meals per week
Lean beef, lamb, pork, ham, or Canadian bacon (3 oz cooked per serving)	Fat meats, prime cuts, meat drippings and gravies	3—5 servings per week	3—5 servings per week
Fats and oils: Soft margarines (those listing primary ingredient as "liquid oil"), oils such as safflower, soybean, corn, cottonseed, sesame, or sunflower	Butter, cream, hydrogenated shortenings or margarines or cream substitutes	2 tbsp daily	4 tbsp daily
Sugars and sweets: Gelatin dessert, sherbet, fruit ices, angelfood cake, fruit pies made with allowed shortenings	Desserts made with cream, butter, sweet rolls	1 serving per day if substituted for 1 serving bread or cereal	2 servings daily if substituted for 1 serving bread or cereal
Coffee, tea, coffee substitutes, artificial sweeteners, "diet drinks," usweetened gelatin, lemon juice, vinegar, herbs, spices, condiments, fat-free broths or bouillon, sour pickles and relishes		As desired	As desired

*Tables 7—5 and 7—6 adapted from: *Planning Fat-Controlled Meals for 1200 and 1800 Calories*. American Heart Association, 1969; and from Levy, R., & others: Dietary management of hyperlipoproteinemia. J Am Dietet A 58:406—416, 1971.

†Poultry, fish, or veal substututes: ½ cup cottage cheese (low-fat), 1 cup cooked dried peas or beans, 4 tbsp peanut butter, 1/3 cup nuts (especially walnuts). *Avoid* cheddar type cheeses, hydrogenated nut butters.

Treatment

A. Treatment of the Acute Attack:

1. Glyceryl trinitrate (nitroglycerin) is the drug of choice; it acts in about 1—2 minutes. As soon as the attack begins, place one 0.3 mg tablet under the tongue and allow it to dissolve. The dose may be increased to 0.4—0.6 mg if no relief is obtained from a smaller dose. Glyceryl trinitrate may be used freely whenever an attack occurs or may be used in order to prevent an attack (see below). It may cause headache and hypotension.

2. Amyl nitrite, 1 pearl crushed and inhaled, acts in about 10 seconds. This drug usually causes flushing of the face, pounding of the pulse, and sometimes dizziness and headache. These reactions may be minimized by inhaling the drug from a distance or by rapid-

TABLE 7–6. Dietary plan for modified fat, controlled carbohydrate, low-cholesterol diet: For types IV and V.

Foods to Use	Foods to Avoid	1200 Calories (40–50% CHO) Polyunsaturated:Saturated Fat Ratio 1:1	1800 Calories (40–50% CHO) Polyunsaturated:Saturated Fat Ratio 1:1
Milk, nonfat		2 cups (16 oz) daily	3 cups (24 oz) daily
Fruits (without sugar), fresh, canned, or juices—at least one to be citrus or tomato	Avocado, olives	3 servings daily	4 servings daily
Vegetables—at least one to be leafy green or yellow		3 or more servings daily	3 or more servings daily
Breads, cereals, starches, enriched white or whole grain*		3 servings daily	7 servings daily
Eggs (with yolks)†		3 per week	3 per week
Egg whites		As desired	As desired
Cooked lean meats, fish, poultry: Beef, lamb, pork, veal, ham, Canadian bacon‡	Skin and fat on poultry, duck, and goose; shellfish,† fish roe (caviar), pan-fried or deep fat-fried meats, marbled or fatty meats, cold cuts or luncheon meats, sausage, frankfurters, corned brisket, spare ribs, organ meats,† gravies	5 oz daily	6 oz daily
Fats and oils: Soft margarines (those listing primary ingredient as "liquid oil"); oils such as safflower, soybean, corn, cottonseed, sesame, or sunflower	Butter, cream, hydrogenated shortenings or margarines, cream substitutes	2 tbsp daily	4 tbsp daily
Sugars and sweets	All desserts, confections, candies made with sugar (white or brown), syrups, honey, jellies, preserves (except as substitutes for bread*)		
Coffee, tea, coffee substitutes, artificial sweeteners, "diet drinks," unsweetened gelatin, lemon juice, vinegar, sour pickles and relishes, herbs, spices, condiments, fat-free broth or bouillon		As desired	As desired

*Substitutes for 1 serving of bread (not to be used more than 3 times a week): 1/3 cup gelatin dessert, 1 tsp honey, jelly, or preserve, ¼ cup sherbet, ½ cup skimmed milk pudding, 1½ inch cube angelfood cake, 1 oz hard sugar candy, 1 oz rum, vodka, whiskey, 1½ oz sweet wine, 2½ oz dry wine, 5 oz beer.
†Substitute for 1 egg yolk: 2 oz shellfish, liver or other organ meat.
‡Substitutes for 1 oz meat: 1½ tbsp peanut butter, ¼ cup low-fat cottage cheese, 1 oz low-fat cheese (less than 2% fat).

ly passing the crushed pearl before the nose. The patient soon learns how to vary the amount of drug he wishes to inhale.

3. Longer-acting nitrates and other drugs have no place in the therapy of the acute attack.

4. Alcohol—One or 2 oz of whisky or brandy may be a helpful home remedy.

5. General measures—The patient should stand still or sit or lie down as soon as the pain begins and remain quiet until the attack is over. This is the natural reaction of most patients, but some try to "work the attack off" and patients should be warned against this.

B. Prevention of Further Attacks:

1. Angina may coexist with or be aggravated by left ventricular failure, obvious or incipient. Treatment

of the cardiac failure with diuretics or digitalis or both, as well as by other methods such as prolonged rest, etc, may be extremely helpful in the treatment of angina pectoris.

2. Glyceryl trinitrate (nitroglycerin), 0.3–0.6 mg under the tongue just before activity.

3. Long-acting nitrates—Pentaerythritol tetranitrate (Peritrate®), 10 mg orally 3 times daily before meals; erithrityl tetranitrate (Cardilate®), 10–15 mg sublingually 3 times daily; and isosorbide dinitrate (Isordil®), 10 mg 4 times daily. There is no convincing evidence that these agents prolong life in patients with coronary heart disease or are better than placebos.

4. Propranolol (Inderal®), 10–30 mg 3 times daily, has been given with benefit to patients with angina provided left ventricular failure, past or present, is absent. Care must be exercised during its use, and the precautions noted on p 194 should be observed. Combinations with long-acting nitrates such as isosorbide dinitrate have been shown to be significantly better than either drug used alone.

5. Xanthines may be of some benefit, given preferably by rectal suppository (250–500 mg).

6. The objective of production of myxedema by means of thiouracil compounds or radioactive iodine (see Chapter 18) is to reduce the work of the heart. Good results have been reported in about ½ of cases of intractable angina, but this method should not be used until prolonged rest and attention to the emotional needs of the patient have ruled out a transient reversible coronary insufficiency.

7. General measures—The patient must avoid all habits and activities that he knows will bring on an attack. Coexisting disorders (especially anemia) which may lead to increased cardiac ischemia must be treated. Most patients with angina do not require prolonged bed rest, but rest and relaxation are beneficial. Adequate mental rest is also important. Obese patients should be placed on a reducing diet low in animal fats and their weight brought to normal or slightly subnormal levels. Tobacco is best avoided or used in moderation because it produces tachycardia and elevation in blood pressure, and because cigarette smoking has been shown to be a risk factor in coronary heart disease. Physical fitness resulting from a regular exercise program has been thought to be helpful, but the benefits may be mainly psychologic. There is little conclusive evidence supporting such a program.

8. Sedatives or tranquilizers may reduce the frequency of attacks.

9. Control hyperlipidemia—See above.

SURGERY FOR CORONARY HEART DISEASE

In the past 2 years considerable progress has been made in the indications and modifications of bypass procedures for coronary artery stenosis. The procedure most commonly used is anastomosis of a graft of the saphenous vein from the aorta to the distal portion of the obstructed coronary artery, beyond the stenosis. Single, double, or even triple bypass grafts have been made in the same patient, and the initial results are most promising. The data show improvement of left ventricular function, increased cardiac output, improved cardiac contraction, and relief of angina pectoris. The grafts have remained patent in about 70% of the patients, but the period of observation has been short and it remains to be seen how long the grafts will remain patent.

The indications for bypass surgery include major stenosis (at least 50–70%) of the proximal segment of a coronary artery, combined with a distal segment without significant disease and with a circumference of more than 4 mm that permits a satisfactory anastomosis. The preoperative determination of whether the distal portion of an artery is suitable for bypass requires coronary angiograms of high quality.

The availability of this new surgical procedure, which shows considerable promise in the treatment of coronary heart disease, has sharpened and broadened the indications for coronary angiography. The most common indication is severe angina pectoris, unimproved by restricted activity and nitroglycerin. Most recently, the indications for coronary angiograms and possible bypass surgery have been extended to include preinfarction angina and possibly angina which follows a myocardial infarction. Because of the frequent coexistence of dyskinesia or aneurysm of the left ventricle, dysfunction of the papillary muscle, or ventricular septal defect, patients studied by coronary angiography should have concurrent left ventricular cineangiography to determine localized areas of dyskinesia or mitral insufficiency. Some surgeons have done infarctectomies if the patient following an acute myocardial infarction has shock or pump failure, but the mortality rate is very high and these operations must be considered experimental. The same can be said of doing bypass surgery in the presence of apparent extension of an acute myocardial infarction.

Ventricular aneurysms and areas of dyskinesia and akinesia have been found to occur more frequently than previously thought, primarily because they may not be obvious on a plain film of the chest but can be seen in a left ventricular cineangiogram. At present it is not considered wise to resect the aneurysm unless the patient is in cardiac failure. Patients with left ventricular failure of undetermined cause should have a coronary angiogram and a left ventricular cineangiogram to exclude left ventricular aneurysm or localized areas of impaired contraction secondary to coronary heart disease.

Implantation of the internal mammary arteries into the myocardium, the so-called Vineberg procedure, is being performed less and less often as the results have been shown to be inadequate; in many institutions, the procedure has been abandoned in favor of bypass surgery.

Prognosis

The course is prolonged, with variable frequency and severity of attacks punctuated by periods of complete remission and episodes of myocardial infarction, or terminated by sudden death. The average survival after onset of angina is 8–10 years, and the annual mortality attributable to angina is 5–8% above that expected on the basis of age and sex. Diabetes mellitus, hypertension, cardiomegaly, congestive failure, myocardial infarction, arrhythmias, and conduction defects (as shown on ECG) shorten the life expectancy. Onset prior to age 40 or a family history of early cardiac death is prognostically unfavorable.

Half of all patients die suddenly, and an additional 1/3 after myocardial infarction. Heart failure accounts for a portion of the remainder of deaths.

Fallon, H.J., & J.W. Woods: Response of hyperlipoproteinemia to cholestyramine resin. JAMA 204:1161–1164, 1968.

Favaloro, R.G., & others: Severe segmental obstruction of the left main coronary artery and its divisions. J Thoracic Cardiovas Surg 60:469–482, 1970.

Havel, R.J.: Pathogenesis, differentiation and management of hypertriglyceridemia. Advances Int Med 15:117, 1969.

Havel, R.J.: Typing of hyperlipoproteinemias. Atherosclerosis 11:3–6, 1970.

Hunninghake, D.B., Tucker, D.R., & D.L. Azarnoff: Long-term effects of clofibrate (Atromid-S®) on serum lipids in man. Circulation 39:675–684, 1969.

Judkins, M.P.: Percutaneous transfemoral selective coronary arteriography. Radiol Clin North America 6:467, 1968.

Lees, R.S., & D.E. Wilson: Treatment of hyperlipidemia. New England J Med 284:186–195, 1971.

Morgan-Jones, A.: The nature of the coronary problem. Brit Heart J 32:583–592, 1970.

Parker, J.O., & others: Reversible cardiac failure during angina pectoris. Circulation 39:745–757, 1969.

Pouget, J.M., & others: Abnormal responses of the systolic time intervals to exercise in patients with angina pectoris. Circulation 43:289–299, 1971.

Riseman, J.E.F.: The clinical course of angina pectoris. Am J M Sc 252:146–158, 1966.

Robinson, B.F.: Mode of action of nitroglycerine in angina pectoris: Correlation between hemodynamic effects during exercise and prevention of pain. Brit Heart J 30:295–303, 1968.

Saltups, A., & others: Left ventricular hemodynamics in patients with coronary artery disease and in normal subjects. Am J Med 50:8–19, 1971.

Silverman, M.E., & J.W. Hurst: Abnormal physical findings associated with myocardial infarction. Mod Concepts Cardiovas Dis 38:69–72, 1969.

Slack, J.: Risks of ischaemic heart disease in familial hyperlipoproteinaemic states. Lancet 2:1380–1382, 1969.

Varnauskas, E., & others: Hemodynamic effects of physical training in coronary patients. Lancet 2:8, 1966.

Welch, C.C., & others: Cinecoronary arteriography in young men. Circulation 42:647–652, 1970.

Wiener, L., Dwyer, E.M., Jr., & J.W. Cox: Hemodynamic effects of nitroglycerin, propranolol and their combination in coronary heart disease. Circulation 39:623–632, 1969.

2. VARIANTS OF ANGINA PECTORIS

Angina Decubitus

Patients with otherwise typical angina may on occasion have an attack shortly after going to bed or may be awakened by an attack. Sitting or standing up brings relief slowly, and glyceryl trinitrate is not as effective as usual. Such episodes are usually brief and infrequent. If this variant appears suddenly, occurs nightly, and especially if pain recurs during the night, conditions that intensify angina must be sought. If none are found, this type of angina decubitus is indicative of impending myocardial infarction, and the death rate is high if patients are not treated as for pre-infarction angina (see below).

Intractable Angina (Status Anginosus, Coronary Failure, Coronary Insufficiency)

Aggravating factors such as thyrotoxicosis and undue emotional tension must be diligently sought, for they account for 5–10% of cases. A high percentage of patients with prolonged anginal-type pain develop frank myocardial infarction or die suddenly. Some patients suddenly revert to their usual pattern of angina or become asymptomatic. Only rarely does a patient continue to have prolonged chest pain, presumably from myocardial ischemia, without evidence of myocardial necrosis.

If adequate doses of glyceryl trinitrate are not effective, treat as for myocardial infarction. If pain persists after myocardial infarction has been ruled out, therapeutic myxedema with thiouracil compounds or radioactive iodine should be considered.

Anginal Pain as a Precursor to Myocardial Infarction (Pre-infarction Angina)

Patients should be treated as for myocardial infarction in the following situations: (1) Sudden onset of angina pectoris. (2) Rapid crescendo in frequency, severity, and duration. (3) Abrupt change in location or radiation. (4) Association of nausea or vomiting with pain. (5) Persistent or repetitive angina decubitus. (6) Complete refractoriness to glyceryl trinitrate.

Reappearance of angina after a long asymptomatic interval may or may not require treatment as for myocardial infarction.

Blankenhorn, D.H., Chin, H.F., & F.Y.K. Lou: Ischemic heart disease in young adults. Ann Int Med 69:21, 1968.

Bruce, R.A., & T.R. Hornsten: Exercise stress testing in evaluation of patients with ischemic heart disease. Progr Cardiovas Dis 11:371–390, 1969.

Dawber, T.R., & H.E. Thomas, Jr.: Prophylaxis of coronary heart disease, stroke, and peripheral atherosclerosis. Ann New York Acad Sc 149:1038–1057, 1968.

Doan, A.E., & others: Myocardial ischemia after maximal exercise in healthy men. One year follow-up of physically active and inactive men. Am J Cardiol 17:9–19, 1966.

Frick, M.H., & others: Hemodynamic effects of nitroglycerin in patients with angina pectoris. Studies by an atrial pacing method. Circulation 37:160–169, 1968.

Gordon, T., & W.B. Kannel: Premature mortality from coronary heart disease. JAMA 215:1617–1625, 1971.

Kannel, W.B., & others: Serum cholesterol, lipoproteins, and the risk of coronary heart disease. Ann Int Med 74:12, 1971.

Kasser, I.S., & R.A. Bruce: Comparative effects of aging and coronary heart disease on submaximal and maximal exercise. Circulation 39:759, 1969.

Kattus, A.A., Jr., & others: Diagnosis, medical and surgical management of coronary insufficiency. Ann Int Med 69:115–136, 1968.

Katz, L.N.: Physical fitness and coronary heart disease: Some basic views. Circulation 35:405–415, 1967.

Lee, G.B., & others: Correlation of vectorcardiogram and electrocardiogram with coronary arteriogram. Circulation 38:189–200, 1968.

Lees, R.S., & D.E. Wilson: The treatment of hyperlipidemia. New England J Med 284:186–195, 1971.

Levy, R.I., & D.S. Fredrickson: Diagnosis and management of hyperlipoproteinemia. Am J Cardiol 22:576–583, 1968.

Morris, J.N., & M.J. Gardner: Epidemiology of ischemic heart disease. Am J Med 46:683, 1969.

Seltzer, C.C.: Smoking and coronary heart disease. JAMA 203:193–200, 1968.

Weinblatt, E., & others: Prognostic factors in angina pectoris: A prospective study. J Chronic Dis 21:231–246, 1968.

Weiner, L., Dwyer, E.M., Jr., & J.W. Cox: Left ventricular hemodynamics in exercise-induced angina pectoris. Circulation 38:240–249, 1968.

ACUTE MYOCARDIAL INFARCTION

Essentials of Diagnosis

- Sudden but not instantaneous development of crushing anterior chest pain producing hypotension or shock.
- Rarely painless, masquerading as acute congestive heart failure, syncope, cerebral thrombosis, or "unexplained" shock.
- Fever, leukocytosis, rising sedimentation rate, elevated SGOT and LDH within 24–48 hours.
- ECG: Abnormal Q waves, elevated ST; later, symmetric inversion of T waves.

General Considerations

Myocardial infarction is ischemic necrosis of a localized area of the myocardium due to occlusion of a coronary artery by thrombus formation or subintimal hemorrhage at the site of atheromatous narrowing. Less often, complete occlusion by proliferation of the intimal plaques or by hemorrhage into a plaque is responsible. Infarction may occur in the absence of complete occlusion if coronary blood flow is temporarily reduced, as in postoperative or traumatic shock, gastrointestinal bleeding or hypotension due to any cause, or dehydration. Rarely, embolic occlusion, syphilitic aortitis, or acute vasculitis cause infarction.

The location and extent of infarction depend upon the anatomic distribution of the vessel, the site of current and previous occlusions, and the adequacy of collateral circulation. Thrombosis occurs most commonly in the anterior descending branch of the left coronary artery, resulting in infarction of the anterior left ventricle. Occlusion of the left circumflex artery produces anterolateral infarction. Right coronary thrombosis leads to infarction of the posteroinferior portion of the left ventricle.

Clinical Findings

A. Symptoms:

1. Premonitory pain—In over 1/3 of patients, alteration in the pattern of angina, sudden onset of atypical angina, or unusual "indigestion" felt in the chest precedes myocardial infarction by hours, days, or several weeks.

2. Pain of infarction—This may begin during rest (even in sleep) or activity. It is similar to angina in location and radiation but is more severe, does not subside with rest, and builds up rapidly or in waves to maximum intensity in the space of a few minutes or longer. Glyceryl trinitrate has no effect. The pain may last for hours if unrelieved by narcotics, and is often unbearable. The patient breaks out in a cold sweat, feels weak and apprehensive, and moves about, seeking a position of comfort. He prefers not to lie quietly. Lightheadedness, syncope, dyspnea, orthopnea, cough, wheezing, nausea and vomiting, or abdominal bloating may also be present, singly or in any combination.

3. Painless infarction—In 5–15% of cases, pain is absent or minor and is overshadowed by the immediate complications, notably acute pulmonary edema or rapidly developing heart failure, profound weakness, shock, syncope, or cerebral thrombosis.

B. Signs: Physical findings are highly variable, and the apparent clinical severity of the episode does not necessarily correlate well with the extent or location of the infarction.

1. Shock—Shock may be described as a systolic blood pressure below 80 mm Hg (or slightly higher with prior hypertension) along with gray facial color, mental dullness, cold clammy skin, peripheral cyanosis, tachycardia or bradycardia, and weak pulse. Shock is present only in severe attacks (incidence about 8–14%). Shock may be caused primarily by the pain rather than the hemodynamic effects of the infarction; if so, distinct improvement occurs within 30–60 minutes after relief of pain and administration of oxygen.

2. Cardiac effects—In the severe attack, the first and second heart sounds are faint, often indistinguishable on auscultation, and assume the so-called "tic-tac" quality. Gallop rhythm, distended neck veins, and basal rales are often present. Acute pulmonary edema or rapidly progressive congestive failure may dominate the picture. In less severe attacks, examination is normal or there may be diminished intensity of the first sound or low systolic blood pressure. Pericardial friction rub appears in 20–30% of cases between the second and fifth days; it is often transient or intermittent.

3. Fever—Fever is absent at the onset (in contrast to acute pericarditis) and during prolonged shock. It usually rises to 37.8–39.4° C (100–103° F)—rarely to 40.6° C (105° F)—within 24 hours and persists for 3–7 days (rarely longer).

C. **Laboratory Findings:** Leukocytosis of 10–20 thousand cells/cu mm usually develops on the second day and disappears in 1 week. The sedimentation rate is normal at onset, rises on the second or third day, and remains elevated for 1–3 weeks. SGOT activity increases in 6–12 hours, reaches a peak in 24–48 hours, and returns to normal in 3–5 days. Serum lactic acid dehydrogenase may remain elevated for 5–7 days. Serial determinations are helpful in equivocal instances. Creatine phosphokinase (CPK) activity may increase earliest but is volatile and less reliable.

D. **ECG Findings:** ECG changes do not correlate well with the clinical severity of the infarction. The characteristic pattern consists of specific changes which undergo a stereotyped "evolution" over a matter of weeks in the average case. At the onset there is elevation of ST segment and T wave and abnormal Q waves; the ST segment progressively returns to the baselines as T waves become symmetrically inverted. An unequivocal ECG diagnosis of infarction can only be made in the presence of all 3 abnormalities. Serial ST–T changes alone are compatible with but not diagnostic of infarction. The characteristic changes are not seen in the presence of left bundle branch block or when a previous infarct has permanently altered the ECG. Even in these instances an ECG taken early in an attack often shows ST segment displacement.

Differential Diagnosis

In acute pericarditis, fever often precedes the onset of pain, which is predominantly pleuritic and is significantly relieved by breath-holding and specific body positions. The friction rub appears early, is louder, is heard over a greater area, and is more persistent than in infarction, and a pleuropericardial rub is often also present. There are no QRS changes, and T wave inversion is more widespread without reciprocal changes (except in aVR). SGOT and LDH are rarely elevated.

Dissecting aneurysm causes violent chest pain which is often of maximum severity at onset. It typically spreads up or down the chest and back over a period of hours. Changes in pulses, changing aortic murmurs, and left pleural effusion or cardiac tamponade are distinctive features. Blood pressure does not fall early. Syncope or neurologic abnormalities are common. ECG changes are not diagnostic of infarction unless the coronary ostia are involved in the proximal dissection.

Acute pulmonary embolism may cause chest pain indistinguishable from myocardial infarction as well as hypotension, dyspnea, and distended neck veins, but the ECG, regardless of coronary-like changes, will usually show right axis deviation or right ventricular conduction defect early in the course of the acute process. SGOT, CPK, and LDH are often elevated, as in myocardial infarction. If the attack is not fatal, pulmonary infarction follows, frequently causing pleuritic pain, hemoptysis, and localized lung findings. Thrombophlebitis is often found on careful examination of the legs, groins, and lower abdomen.

Cervical or thoracic spine disease produces sudden, severe chest pain similar to myocardial infarction; but orthopedic measures give relief and the ECG is normal.

Hiatus hernia may simulate the pain of infarction, and the T waves may be flat or even inverted during the attack, but there is no hypotension or subsequent fever, leukocytosis, or increase in sedimentation rate, SGOT, or LDH.

Acute pancreatitis and acute cholecystitis may superficially mimic infarction. A past history of gastrointestinal symptoms, present findings in the abdomen, jaundice, elevated serum amylase, and x-ray findings differentiate these. Most helpful is the absence of diagnostic serial ECG changes.

Spontaneous pneumothorax, mediastinal emphysema, pre-eruptive herpes zoster, and severe psychophysiologic cardiovascular reactions may also have to be differentiated from myocardial infarction.

Complications

Congestive heart failure and shock may be present at onset of infarction or may develop insidiously or abruptly following an arrhythmia or pulmonary embolization. Sedation and weakness may mask the presence of dyspnea and orthopnea. Distention of neck veins, persistent basal rales, gallop rhythm, the appearance of the murmur of mitral insufficiency, abnormal cardiac pulsations, an enlarging tender liver, and sacral edema should be sought daily. Portable chest films to recognize pulmonary venous congestion are desirable.

If anticoagulants are not given, pulmonary embolism secondary to phlebitis of the leg or pelvic veins occurs in 10–20% of patients during the acute and convalescent stage.

Arrhythmias occur commonly after myocardial infarction and are thought to be the cause of death in about 40% of patients. The mechanism is either cardiac arrest or ventricular fibrillation; the former occurs following shock or heart failure, and the latter is more apt to be a primary event (although it can be secondary). Continuous monitoring has revealed a higher incidence of ventricular tachycardia, complete AV block, and other less serious arrhythmias than was formerly suspected. Ventricular premature beats often precede more serious arrhythmias in late or secondary but not in early or primary ventricular fibrillation. Atrial arrhythmias are less common and often transient, as is the case with atrial fibrillation. The prompt recognition of arrhythmias is essential in order to initiate treatment.

Cerebrovascular accident may result from a fall in blood pressure associated with myocardial infarction or from embolism secondary to a mural thrombus. It is advisable to take an ECG in all patients with "cerebrovascular accident."

Recurrent myocardial infarction or extension of the infarction occurs in about 5% of patients during recovery from the initial attack.

Rupture of the heart is uncommon. When it occurs it is usually in the first week.

Perforation of the interventricular septum is very rare, characterized by the sudden appearance of a loud, harsh systolic murmur and thrill over the lower left parasternal area or apex and acute heart failure. This must be distinguished from mitral insufficiency caused by papillary muscle infarction or dysfunction. Both may precipitate cardiac failure and require cardiac surgery when the patient's condition has stabilized in weeks or months and right and left heart catheterization reveals a significant hemodynamic lesion. Emergency cardiac surgery is sometimes required.

Ventricular aneurysm and peripheral arterial embolism may occur early or not for months after recovery. The spectrum of ventricular aneurysm is now recognized to extend from frank outpocketing of an area of myocardium to localized noncontraction or paradoxical pulsation seen on cineangiography. Approximately 20% of patients develop some form of aneurysm or left ventricular akinesis, recognized clinically by abnormal paradoxical precordial pulsations and proved by cinefluoroscopy or left ventricular cineangiography. Some of these patients develop refractory cardiac failure and benefit from surgical excision.

The shoulder-hand syndrome is a rare preventable disorder caused by prolonged immobilization of the arms and shoulders, possibly due to "reflex sympathetic dystrophy." Early pain and tenderness over the affected shoulder is followed by pain and swelling and weakness of the hand, with excessive or deficient sweating.

Oliguria, anuria, or, rarely, tubular necrosis may result if shock persists.

Treatment

A. Immediate Treatment: There is convincing evidence that patients are treated best in a special coronary care unit equipped with continuous monitoring, alarm, recording, pacemaker, and resuscitation equipment, and with specially trained nurses and physicians. It is now clear that the risk of ventricular fibrillation and sudden death is much greater in the first few hours after the onset of the myocardial infarction. Every effort should be made to admit these patients to the coronary care unit as soon as possible to decrease the incidence of death outside the hospital. Some cities (notably Belfast, Ireland) are using specially equipped coronary ambulances to minimize the fatalities. Prophylactic anti-arrhythmia programs are also undergoing research study and trial.

1. Rest—Attempt to allay apprehension and anxiety. Physical and mental rest in the most comfortable position is essential during the first 2–3 weeks, when rupture of the heart is most apt to occur. The patient should not be allowed to feed or care for himself during the first few days unless the attack is mild, without shock or other complications. Special nursing care is highly desirable. A bedside toilet probably requires less effort than the use of a bedpan.

Adequate sleep is as vital in patients with myocardial infarction as it is with those suffering from cardiac failure. Sedatives should be used as necessary to provide sufficient sleep, and morphine derivatives should not be withheld in the first few days if they are indicated.

2. Analgesia—When pain is severe, give morphine sulfate, 5–10 mg slowly IV. If the pain is not relieved in 15 minutes, repeat this dosage. Further injections can be given subcut, 5–10 mg as necessary for continued relief. The subcutaneous route is used unless the attack is severe or the patient is in shock. If the patient is in shock with severe pain, slow intravenous administration may be necessary. *Caution:* Do not give a second dose of morphine if respirations are below 12/minute. Morphine may cause venous pooling and decreased cardiac output with fainting if the patient is allowed to sit or stand.

Meperidine and dihydromorphinone are preferred by some because they are said to produce less nausea and vomiting. The dosage of dihydromorphinone (Dilaudid®) is 4 mg IM or IV. The dosage of meperidine (Demerol®) is 50–100 mg IV or IM as needed.

Aminophylline, 0.5 gm IV very slowly (1–2 ml per minute), may be helpful if the pain is not relieved by opiates or oxygen (see below).

3. Oxygen is often useful and sometimes necessary for the relief of dyspnea, cyanosis, pulmonary edema, shock, and chest pain.

4. Shock (see p 190) is a frequent and serious complication, with an estimated mortality of 80%, particularly when it is delayed until after the pain has subsided. Treatment of shock is unsatisfactory, and the best results are achieved when shock is treated early. A hypotonic myocardium often accompanies acute myocardial infarction, and shock may be associated with an increased venous pressure. Some clinicians therefore favor digitalization as for congestive failure in the shock of acute myocardial infarction. The increased cardiac output increases coronary flow, and the pressure may rise. Similarly, an inotropic drug such as isoproterenol (Isuprel®) has proved effective. Monitoring of pulmonary artery or "wedge" pressure and arterial pressure permits better control of the use of inotropic agents as well as of the use of fluids such as plasma and dextran if these are given. Vasopressor drugs such as levarterenol (Levophed®) are thought by some to be helpful.

Shock may be the result of undetected ventricular tachycardia or other arrhythmias, and prompt treatment of this complication (see below) may be lifesaving. Venous and arterial transfusions have not been very effective but should be kept in mind as adjuncts if diminished blood volume is a factor.

4. Anticoagulant therapy is a controversial matter in the milder cases (rapid relief of pain, minimal signs of myocardial necrosis, absence of shock or cardiac failure). In severe cases of myocardial infarction, anticoagulants are generally recommended.

B. Follow-Up: Alert clinical observation for evidence of extension of the infarction, new infarction, the appearance of complications, or symptoms requiring treatment is essential. Recurrent pain days or weeks after the initial pain has subsided suggests extension of the myocardial necrosis; confirmation should be sought in the ECG and in other clinical features. The same methods of treatment are used as for the first infarction, but a further period of rest is required. Preventive methods to decrease the risk of progressive coronary disease (unproved) are discussed on p 184.

C. Treatment of Complications:

1. Cardiac failure—If cardiac failure develops, treat as for failure due to any cause. Oxygen, low-sodium intake, diuretics, inotropic agents such as isoproterenol (Isuprel®), and cautious digitalization are the essential features of treatment. Potassium salts should be employed (potassium chloride, 1 gm 3 times daily) if diuretics are given to a patient receiving digitalis and a low-sodium diet. *Caution:* Avoid enteric-coated potassium tablets because of the risk of small bowel ulceration. The patient should be digitalized in such a manner as to avoid toxic reactions if possible. Rapid digitalization is best avoided unless the need is urgent. If the cardiac failure is mild and manifested solely by pulmonary rales and increased dyspnea, restriction of sodium and the administration of diuretics may be sufficient. Digitalis is avoided by some authorities because of the hazard of ventricular arrhythmias, but its well-controlled administration should not be deferred if cardiac failure demands it.

2. Shock is a frequent and serious complication, with an estimated mortality of 80%, particularly when it is delayed until after the pain has subsided. Treatment of shock is unsatisfactory, and the best results are achieved when shock is treated early. A hypotonic myocardium often accompanies acute myocardial infarction, and shock may be associated with an increased venous pressure. Some clinicians therefore favor digitalization as for congestive failure in the shock of acute myocardial infarction. The increased cardiac output increases coronary flow, and the pressure may rise. Similarly, an inotropic drug such as isoproterenol (Isuprel®) has proved effective. Monitoring of direct arterial pressures and pulmonary artery diastolic pressures (by flow-directed catheters) as a means of estimating left ventricular end-diastolic pressures, and blood gas measurement permit better hemodynamic analysis of the clinical situation and better control of the use of inotropic agents as well as of the use of fluids such as plasma and dextran if these are given. Clinical appraisal of adequate perfusion of the vital organs (sensorium, urine output, appearance of the skin, and arterial pressure) must not be neglected. Vasopressor drugs such as levarterenol (Levophed®) are thought by some to be helpful, but inotropic drugs are usually more effective.

Shock may be the result of undetected ventricular tachycardia or other arrhythmias, and prompt treatment of this complication (see below) may be life-saving. Venous and arterial transfusions have not been very effective but should be kept in mind as adjuncts if diminished blood volume is a factor.

3. Arrhythmias—Ventricular premature beats are common. They indicate increased irritability of the damaged myocardium and may presage ventricular tachycardia or fibrillation. Lidocaine (Xylocaine®), 50–100 mg IV, followed by an intravenous infusion at a rate of 1–2 mg/minute, is the drug of choice. Alternatives are procainamide, quinidine sulfate, or, if digitalis is thought to be responsible for the arrhythmia, potassium salts. Aggressive treatment of ventricular arrhythmias may prevent ventricular fibrillation and cardiac arrest.

Ventricular tachycardia is an emergency (see p 197). Ventricular fibrillation should be instantly recognized on the alarm system at the nursing station, and defibrillation should be accomplished within 30 seconds. In most coronary care units, defibrillation is performed by specially trained nurses if a skilled physician is not immediately available. Lidocaine (Xylocaine®) should be given by intravenous infusion (1–2 mg/minute) to prevent recurrence.

Atrial fibrillation is usually transient. If this persists, if the patient tolerates it poorly, or if congestive heart failure occurs, digitalize with care or treat by cardioversion.

4. Stokes–Adams attack with heart block—(See p 200.) *This is an emergency.* Complete heart block complicates acute myocardial infarction in 6–10% of cases. It has a high mortality, usually lasts less than a week, and often can be treated by artificial pacing through a transvenous catheter placed in the right ventricle. Pacing at a rate of 70–80 may greatly improve the cardiac output and tissue perfusion and prevent Stokes-Adams attacks. Asystole may occur unpredictably, so electrode catheters should be placed prophylactically in patients with complete AV block with anterior infarctions, type II Mobitz AV block, or in inferior infarctions with complete AV block. Some question arises in type I Mobitz block in inferior infarctions. Infusions of lidocaine should be given to prevent ventricular fibrillation if AV block subsides and competition occurs with the patient's own pacemaker.

Ventricular fibrillation is the major hazard associated with pacing in acute myocardial infarction; for this reason, patients with first degree AV block or with type I second degree AV block with Wenckebach pauses and narrow QRS complexes in inferior infarction are not routinely paced. Demand pacemaker, activated by a delay in the appearance of the QRS complex, may be preferred, so that, when AV conduction is unstable and intermittent, competition between the normal and artificial pacemaker will not occur.

Sinus bradycardia, especially in inferior infarcts, may presage AV block and should be treated with passage of a transvenous pacemaker electrode (prophylactically) and atropine, 0.5–1 mg IV. The externally generated pacemaker can be attached if complete block occurs.

5. Thromboembolic phenomena are common during the course of myocardial infarction. Anticoagulants should be administered promptly. For treatment of pulmonary embolism, see discussion in Chapter 6.

6. Oliguria, anuria, acute tubular necrosis—See Chapter 15.

7. Rupture, perforation of the interventricular septum, mitral insufficiency from papillary muscle dysfunction or rupture, and aneurysm—Surgical repair of perforated ventricular septum or mitral insufficiency after the lesion has stabilized, if cardiac failure has persisted. Resection of aneurysm is recommended in the presence of major ventricular aneurysm with persistent cardiac failure but not for minor asymptomatic aneurysm. No treatment is available for cardiac rupture.

8. Shoulder-hand syndrome—Best treated by preventive physical therapy instituted early.

9. Activity status in convalescence—The minimum period of rest should be at least 3 weeks; if the infarction has been very severe, this should be increased to about 6 weeks. The programs for most patients is 1 month of complete rest, 1 month of slowly increasing activity, and 1 month of restricted activity before returning to work. The amount of rest should be individualized according to the severity of the myocardial infarction and the response of the patient.

The patient should not be permitted to walk freely about the room for about 7–10 days after he is first allowed out of bed. Gradual resumption of activity is most important. He should remain on the same floor, with gradually increasing periods of walking, slowly and without producing chest pain, dyspnea, undue tachycardia, or fatigue. When first allowed out of doors, usually not until 2 months after the infarction, he should avoid hills and stairs for another month.

Prognosis

The overall mortality during the first month after the infarction averages 30%. Most of the deaths occur in the first 12 hours. In the mild attack clinical manifestations subside promptly and the initial mortality is less than 5%. Clinically severe myocardial infarction may require 6–12 weeks for full recovery. The mortality rises to 60–90% with prolonged shock, severe early heart failure, leukocytosis over 25,000 with eosinophilia, fever above 40° C (104° F), uncontrolled diabetes mellitus, old age, and previous definite infarction, especially if these occur in combination. Pulmonary embolism which is not treated with anticoagulants, persistent arrhythmias, and extension of the infarct superimpose a mortality of 15–20% during early convalescence.

Long-term survival is related to the availability of medical care and the presence of other chronic diseases in addition to the residuals of infarction. Complete clinical and ECG recovery is compatible with survival of 10–15 years. Patients with residual heart failure, arrhythmia, or angina die within 3–6 years.

Aspenstrom, G., & others: Collaborative analysis of long-term anticoagulant administration after acute myocardial infarction. Lancet 1:203–209, 1970.

Assessment of short-term anticoagulant administration after cardiac infarction. Brit MJ 1:335–341, 1969.

Baxley, W.A., & T.J. Reeves: Abnormal regional myocardial performance in coronary artery disease. Progr Cardiovas Dis 13:405, 1971.

Beregovich, J., & others: Management of acute myocardial infarction complicated by advanced atrioventricular block. Am J Cardiol 23:54, 1969.

Chamberlain, D.A., & others: Sequential atrioventricular pacing in heart block complicating acute myocardial infarction. New England J Med 282:578–582, 624–625, 1970.

Cheng, T.O.: Incidence of ventricular aneurysm in coronary artery disease: An angiographic appraisal. Am J Med 50:340, 1971.

Cooley, D.A., & G.L. Hallman: Surgical treatment of left ventricular aneurysm: Experience with excision of post-infarction lesions in 80 patients. Progr Cardiovas Dis 2:222–228, 1968.

DeBusk, R.F., & D.C. Harrison: The clinical spectrum of papillary muscle disease. New England J Med 281:1458–1467, 1969.

Dewar, H.A., & M. Floyd: Deaths from ischaemic heart disease outside hospital and experience with a mobile resuscitation unit. Brit Heart J 31:389, 1969.

Favaloro, R.G., & others: Direct myocardial revascularization by saphenous vein graft Ann Thoracic Surg 10:97–111, 1970.

Friedberg, C.K., Cohen, H., & E. Donoso: Advanced heart block as a complication of acute myocardial infarction: Role of pacemaker therapy. Progr Cardiovas Dis 10:466–481, 1968.

Gareth, R., & others: Influence of aorto-coronary bypass surgery on left ventricular performance. New England J Med 284:1116–1120, 1971.

Gianelly, R., & others: Effect of lidocaine on ventricular arrhythmias in coronary heart disease. New England J Med 277:1215–1218, 1967.

Grace, W.J., & P.M. Yarvote: Acute myocardial infarction: The course of the illness following discharge from the coronary care unit. Chest 59:15–17, 1971.

Gregory, J.J., & W.J. Grace: The management of sinus bradycardia: Nodal rhythm and heart block for the prevention of cardiac arrest and acute myocardial infarction. Progr Cardiovas Dis 10:505–518, 1968.

Haddy, F.J.: Pathophysiology and therapy of the shock of myocardial infarction. Ann Int Med 73:809–827, 1970.

Han, J.: Mechanisms of ventricular arrhythmias associated with myocardial infarction. Am J Cardiol 24:800–814, 1969.

Heikkila, J.: Mitral incompetence as a complication of acute myocardial infarction. Acta med scandinav 182(Suppl 475):1–139, 1967.

James, T.N.: Pathogenesis of arrhythmias and acute myocardial infarction. Am J Cardiol 24:791–800, 1969.

Judkins, M.P.: Percutaneous transfemoral selective coronary arteriography. Radiol Clin North America 6:467, 1968.

Johnson, W.D., Flemms, R.J., & D. Upley, Jr.: Direct coronary surgery utilizing multiple vein bypass grafts. Ann Thoracic Surg 9:436, 1970.

Killip, T.: Management of the patient with acute myocardial infarction. M Clin North America 52:1061–1075, 1968.

Kimball, J.T., & T. Killip: Aggressive treatment of arrhythmias in acute myocardial infarction: Procedures and results. Progr Cardiovas Dis 10:483–505, 1968.

Lassers, B.W., & others: Left ventricular failure and acute myocardial infarction. Am J Cardiol 25:511–523, 1970.

Leren, P.: The effect of plasma cholesterol lowering diet in male survivors of myocardial infarction. Acta med scandinav 100(Suppl 446), 1966.

Ljungström, B., Johansson, B.W., & J. Sievers: Arterial P_{O_2}, P_{CO_2}, pH and standard bicarbonate in patients with an acute myocardial infarction. Cardiologia 51:138–147, 1967.

Lown, B., Klein, M.D., & P.I. Hershberg: Coronary and precoronary care. Am J Med 46:705–724, 1969.

McGinn, F.S., Gould, L., & A.F. Lyon: The phonocardiogram and apexcardiogram in patients with ventricular aneurysm. Am J Cardiol 21:467–478, 1968.

Moran, N.C.: Evaluation of the pharmacologic basis for the therapy of circulatory shock. Am J Cardiol 26:570, 1970.

Morris, G.C., & others: The distal coronary bypass. Ann Surg 172:652, 1970.

Mourdjinis, A., & others: Clinical diagnosis and prognosis of ventricular aneurysm. Brit Heart J 30:497–513, 1968.

Mundth, E.D., & others: Circulatory assistance and emergency direct coronary artery surgery for shock complicating acute myocardial infarction. New England J Med 283:1382–1384, 1970.

Perloff, J.K., Talano, J.V., & J.A. Ronan, Jr.: Noninvasive techniques in acute myocardial infarction. Progr Cardiovas Dis 13:437, 1971.

Perry, L.W., & L.P. Scott: Anomalous left coronary artery from pulmonary artery: Report of 11 cases; review of indications for and results of surgery. Circulation 41:1043–1053, 1970.

Porter, C.McG.: Pulmonary artery pressure monitoring in cardiogenic shock. Arch Int Med 127:304–306, 1971.

Ramo, B.W., & others: Hemodynamic findings in 123 patients with acute myocardial infarction on admission. Circulation 42(Suppl 4):567, 1970.

Rosen, H.S.L., & others: Site of heart block in acute myocardial infarction. Circulation 42(Suppl 5):925, 1970.

Sampson, J.J., & J.C. Hutchinson: Heart failure in myocardial infarction. Progr Cardiovas Dis 10:1–29, 1967.

Scheidt, S., Ascheim, R., & T. Killip III: Shock after acute myocardial infarction: A clinical and hemodynamic profile. Am J Cardiol 26:556, 1970.

Scheinman, M.M.: Heart block complicating acute myocardial infarction. Nebraska State Med J 54:694, 1969.

Schimert, G., & others: Excision of a kinetic left ventricular wall for intractable heart failure. Ann Int Med 70:437–446, 1969.

Schluger, J., & others: Cardiac pacing in acute myocardial infarction complicated by complete heart block. Am Heart J 80:116, 1970.

Selzer, A., Gerbode, F., & W.J. Kerth: Clinical, hemodynamic and surgical considerations of rupture of the ventricular septum after myocardial infarction. Am Heart J 78:598, 1969.

Solomon, H.A., Edwards, A.L., & T. Killip: Prodromata in acute myocardial infarction. Circulation 40:463–473, 1969.

Spencer, F.C.: Venous bypass grafts for occlusive disease of the coronary arteries. Am Heart J 79:568–572, 1970.

Whalen, R.E., & C.F. Stamer: Electric shock hazards in clinical cardiology. Mod Concepts Cardiovas Dis 36:7–12, 1967.

Whalen, R.E., Ramo, B.W., & A.G. Wallace: The value and limitations of coronary care monitoring. Progr Cardiovas Dis 13:422, 1971.

Young, E., & C. Williams: The frontal plane vectorcardiogram in old inferior myocardial infarction: Criteria for diagnosis and ECG correlation. Circulation 37:604–624, 1968.

Young, W.G., Jr., & D.C. Sabiston, Jr.: Preoperative assessment of left ventricular function in patients selected for direct myocardial revascularization. Ann Thoracic Surg 11:395–402, 1971.

Zipes, D.P.: The clinical significance of bradycardic rhythms with acute myocardial infarction. Am J Cardiol 24:814–826, 1969.

DISTURBANCES OF RATE & RHYTHM

The presence of a significant arrhythmia should be suspected in any of the following circumstances: (1) when there is a history of sudden onset and sudden termination of palpitation or rapid heart action; (2) when the heart rhythm is grossly irregular; (3) when the heart rate is below 40 or above 140/minute; (4) when the heart rate does not change with breath-holding or exercise; (5) when a rapid heart rate suddenly slows during carotid sinus massage; (6) when the first heart sound varies in intensity; or (7) when a patient develops sudden anginal pain, shock, congestive heart failure, or syncope.

The complete diagnosis of an arrhythmia consists of accurate identification of the site of origin of the abnormality and proper assessment of its significance. The most common arrhythmias are sinus arrhythmia, sinus tachycardia, sinus bradycardia, atrial and ventricular premature beats, and paroxysmal atrial tachycardia. These occur in normal and diseased hearts alike and have no significance except insofar as they alter circulatory dynamics. Atrial fibrillation and flutter occur most commonly in patients with arteriosclerotic or rheumatic heart disease, but thyrotoxicosis, acute infections, or trauma may precipitate them in the absence of heart disease. Ventricular tachycardia is a serious disorder of rhythm and appears most often in the presence of advanced coronary artery disease. Partial or complete heart block also results from coronary heart disease but is most commonly due to fibrosis of the conduction system. Digitalis toxicity is a frequent cause of many types of arrhythmia.

From the physiologic standpoint, arrhythmias are harmful to the extent that they reduce cardiac output, lower blood pressure, and interfere with perfusion of the vital territories of the brain, heart, and kidney. Rapid heart rates may cause any or all of these changes and, in the presence of heart disease, may precipitate acute heart failure or pulmonary edema, angina pectoris or myocardial infarction, syncope, poor cerebration with confusion, or cerebral thrombosis. Patients with otherwise normal hearts may tolerate rapid rates with no symptoms other than palpitation or fluttering, but prolonged attacks usually cause weakness, exertional dyspnea, and precordial aching. The rate at which slow heart rates produce symptoms at rest or on exertion depends upon the underlying state of the cardiac muscle and its ability to increase its stroke output. If the heart rate abruptly slows, as with the onset of complete heart block or transient standstill, syncope or convulsions may result.

If possible, elicit a history of previous attacks and precipitating factors, symptoms of heart failure, and anginal pain. Examine for cardiac enlargement, significant murmurs, signs of heart failure, and hypotension. Count the heart rate for 1 minute. If the rate is seemingly regular, repeat the count twice to determine if the rate is absolutely regular; if irregular, determine whether pulse deficit is present. If there is no severe failure, angina, or recent infarction, determine the effects of breath-holding, exercise, and change of position on the heart rate and rhythm. Massage the right and left carotid sinus successively for 30 seconds while listening to the heart; cease massage as soon as a change in rate occurs. Note whether the first heart sound varies in intensity. Examine the neck veins for abnormal pulsations or cannon waves.

The final diagnosis of arrhythmias depends upon the ECG. However, consideration of the patient's age, the type of associated heart disease, and the results of the examination permit a diagnosis in most cases before the ECG is taken.

His bundle recordings are a new method of analyzing arrhythmias and AV block (see p 196).

Anderson, R., & others: Relation between metabolic acidosis and cardiac dysrhythmias in acute myocardial infarction. Brit Heart J 30:493–496, 1968.

Ayres, S.N., & W.J. Grace: Inappropriate ventilation in hypoxemia as causes of cardiac arrhythmias: The control of arrhythmias without antiarrhythmic drugs. Am J Med 46:495–506, 1969.

Bigger, J.T., Jr., Bassett, A.L., & B.F. Hoffman: Electrophysiological effects of diphenylhydantoin on canine Purkinje fibers. Circulation Res 22:221–236, 1968.

Bigger, J.T., Jr., & C.C. Jaffe: The effect of bretylium tosylate on the electrophysiologic properties of ventricular muscle and Purkinje fibers. Am J Cardiol 27:82, 1971.

Bigger, J.T., Jr., & W.J. Mandel: Effect of lidocaine on the electrophysiological properties of ventricular muscle and Purkinje fibers. J Clin Invest 49:63, 1970.

David, L.D., & J.V. Temte: Effects of propranolol on the transmembrane potentials of ventricular muscle and Purkinje fibers of the dog. Circulation Res 2:661, 1968.

Durrer, D., Schuilenburg, R.M., & H.J.J. Wellens: Pre-excitation revisited. Am J Cardiol 25:690–698, 1970.

Epstein, S.E., & E. Braunwald: Beta-adrenergic receptor blocking drugs: Mechanisms of action and clinical applications. New England J Med 275:1106–1112, 1966.

Escher, D.J.W., & S. Furman: Emergency treatment of cardiac arrhythmias. JAMA 214:2028–2034, 1970.

Frieden, J., & others: Propranolol treatment of chronic intractable supraventricular arrhythmias. Am J Cardiol 22:711–718, 1968.

Massumi, R.A., & N. Ali: Accelerated isorhythmic ventricular rhythms. Am J Cardiol 26:170–186, 1970.

McIntosh, H.D., & J.J. Morris, Jr.: The management of supraventricular arrhythmias. Med Ann District of Columbia 35:525, 1966.

Pamintuan, J.C., Dreyfus, L.S., & Y. Watanabe: Comparative mechanisms of antiarrhythmic agents. Am J Cardiol 26:512–520, 1970.

Pick, A., & R. Langendorf: Recent advances in the differential diagnosis of AV junctional arrhythmia. Am Heart J 76:553–576, 1968.

Singer, D.H., Lazzara, R., & B.S. Hoffman: Interrelationships between automaticity and conduction in Purkinje fibers. Circulation Res 21:537, 1967.

Sokolow, M., & D. Perloff: The clinical pharmacology and use of quinidine in heart disease. Progr Cardiovas Dis 3:316–331, 1961.

Watanabe, Y., & L.S. Dreyfuss: Newer concepts in the genesis of cardiac arrhythmias. Am Heart J 76:114–136, 1968.

SINUS ARRHYTHMIA

Sinus arrhythmia is a cyclical increase in normal heart rate with inspiration and decrease with expiration. It results from reflex changes in vagal influence on the normal pacemaker and disappears with breath-holding or increase of heart rate due to any cause. It has no significance except in older persons, when it may be associated with coronary artery disease.

SINUS TACHYCARDIA

Sinus tachycardia is a heart rate faster than 100 beats/minute due to rapid impulse formation by the normal pacemaker secondary to fever, exercise, emotion, anemia, shock, thyrotoxicosis, or drug effect. The rate may reach 180 in young persons but rarely exceeds 160. The rhythm is basically regular, but serial 1-minute counts of the heart rate indicate that it varies 5 or more beats/minute with changes in position, breath-holding, sedation, or correction of the underlying disorder. The rate slows gradually, but tachycardia may begin abruptly in response to sudden emotional stimuli.

SINUS BRADYCARDIA

Sinus bradycardia is a heart rate slower than 60 beats/minute due to increased vagal influence on the normal pacemaker. The rate increases after exercise or administration of atropine. Slight degrees have no significance unless there is underlying heart disease, especially coronary heart disease or acute myocardial infarction. Elderly patients may develop weakness, confusion, or even syncope with slow heart rates. Atrial and ventricular ectopic rhythms are more apt to occur with slow ventricular rates. It may be desirable to use atropine in some patients to speed the heart rate. Rarely, artificial pacemakers are necessary.

Goel, B.G., & J. Han: Atrial ectopic activity associated with sinus bradycardia. Circulation 42(Suppl 5):853, 1970.

Easley, R.M., Jr., & S. Goldstein: Sino-atrial syncope. Am J Med 50:166, 1971.

ATRIAL PREMATURE BEATS

Atrial premature beats occur when an ectopic focus in the atria fires off before the next expected impulse from the sinus node. Ventricular systole occurs prematurely, and the compensatory pause following this is only slightly longer than the normal interval between beats. Such premature beats occur with equal frequency in normal or diseased hearts and are never sufficient basis for a diagnosis of heart disease. Speeding of the heart rate by any means usually abolishes premature beats.

PAROXYSMAL ATRIAL TACHYCARDIA

This is the commonest paroxysmal tachycardia. It occurs more often in young patients with normal hearts. Attacks begin and end abruptly, and usually last several hours. The heart rate may be 140–240/minute (usually 170–220/minute) and is perfectly regular, ie, the rate will not vary more than 1–2 beats/minute. Exercise, change of position, and breath-holding have no effect. Carotid sinus massage or induced gagging or vomiting either have no effect or promptly abolish the attack. Patients are asymptomatic except for awareness of rapid heart action unless there is underlying heart disease, especially mitral stenosis and coronary heart disease. In prolonged attacks with rapid rates, dyspnea or tightness in the chest may be felt. Paroxysmal atrial tachycardia may result from digitalis toxicity, and then is associated with AV block so that only every second or, rarely, every third atrial impulse reaches the ventricles (so-called PAT with block).

Prevention of Attacks

A. **Specific Measures:** Attempt to find and remove the cause, especially emotional stress, fatigue, or excessive use of alcohol or tobacco.

B. **Drugs:**

1. Quinidine sulfate, 0.2–0.6 gm 3–4 times daily, may be used to prevent frequent and troublesome attacks. Begin with small doses and increase if the attacks are not prevented and toxic effects do not occur.

2. If quinidine is not effective or not tolerated, full digitalization and maintenance may prevent or decrease the frequency of attacks.

3. Procainamide hydrochloride (Pronestyl®) in a maintenance dosage of 250–500 mg 3 times daily may be tried if quinidine and digitalis are not successful.

4. Propranolol (Inderal®), 10–40 mg 3–4 times daily, has been shown to prevent recurrent atrial arrhythmias even in patients refractory to quinidine and procainamide. Use *cautiously* (if at all) in patients with early heart failure, heart block, or bronchospasm.

Treatment of the Acute Attack

In the absence of heart disease, serious effects are rare. Most attacks subside spontaneously, and the physician should not use remedies that are more dangerous than the disease. Particular effort should be made to terminate the attack quickly if it persists for several days; if cardiac failure, syncope, or anginal pain develops; or if there is underlying cardiac disease.

A. **Mechanical Measures:** A variety of methods have been used to interrupt attacks, and the patient may learn to do these himself. These include Valsalva's maneuver (holding the breath and contracting the chest and abdominal muscles), stretching the arms and body, lowering the head between the knees, and breath-holding.

B. **Vagal Stimulation:**

1. **Carotid sinus pressure**—With the patient relaxed in the semi-recumbent position, firm but gentle pressure and massage are applied first over one carotid sinus for 10–20 seconds and then over the other. Pressure should not be exerted on both carotid sinuses at the same time. Continuous auscultation of the heart is required so that carotid sinus pressure can be withdrawn as soon as the attack ceases. Carotid sinus pressure will interrupt about half of the attacks, especially if the patient has been digitalized or sedated.

2. **Bilateral eyeball pressure** has been recommended, but it is rarely as effective as carotid sinus pressure and involves the risk of detaching the retina.

3. **Induced vomiting** (except in cases of syncope, anginal pain, or severe cardiac disease).

C. **Drug Therapy:** If mechanical measures fail and the attack continues (particularly if the above symptoms are present), drugs should be employed. There is no unanimity of opinion about the most effective drugs, but the following are satisfactory: (1) Digitalis orally or, if no digitalis has been given in the preceding 2 weeks, intravenously. (2) Pressor agents. (3) Procainamide hydrochloride (Pronestyl®). Continuous ECG's or continuous monitoring of the heart rate and blood pressure is essential. (4) Propranolol (Inderal®), 10–30 mg 3 times daily before meals and at bedtime, or 1 mg IV slowly, and with clinical and ECG monitoring until therapeutic effects begin. The drug should then be stopped. A second dose of 1 mg may be given in 2–5 minutes if no untoward effects have occurred. Atropine, 0.5–1 mg, should be given IV if excessive bradycardia occurs. *Caution:* Propranolol should be given intravenously only if other measures fail and the clinical situation is serious and warrants the risk. (5) Neostigmine (Prostigmin®), 1 mg subcut. (6) Quinidine sulfate. (7) Syrup of ipecac, 4–8 ml, may be used to induce vomiting. It may be repeated if unsuccessful. (8) Methacholine chloride (Mecholyl®), 10 mg subcut, is often effective but produces unpleasant side-effects and should rarely be used.

D. **Cessation of Drug Therapy:** Paroxysmal atrial tachycardia, usually with 2:1 block, may be due to digitalis toxicity (increased dosage or excessive potassium diuresis). Treatment consists of stopping digitalis and diuretics and treating the patient for digitalis toxicity with potassium.

E. Cardioversion (see below) may be used if the clinical situation is severe enough to warrant anesthesia and electric precordial shock. Because of the possibility of digitalis intoxication as the cause of atrial or nodal tachycardia (especially if there is associated AV block), electric shock should be used in progressively increasing amounts beginning with 25 watt-seconds. If ventricular premature beats develop, use lidocaine (Xylocaine®), 50–100 mg IV and, if the premature beats disappear, one can repeat the shock. Cardioversion should be abandoned for the time being if the premature beats recur.

ATRIAL FIBRILLATION

Atrial fibrillation is the commonest chronic arrhythmia. It occurs most frequently in rheumatic heart disease, especially mitral stenosis, and arteriosclerotic heart disease. It may appear paroxysmally before becoming the established rhythm in thyrotoxicosis. Infection, trauma, surgery, poisoning, or excessive alcohol intake may cause attacks of atrial fibrillation in patients with normal hearts. It is the only common arrhythmia in which the ventricular rate is rapid and the rhythm irregular. An ectopic atrial pacemaker fires 400–600 times/minute. The impulses pass through the atria at varying speeds and are mostly blocked at the AV node. The ventricular response is completely irregular, ranging from 80–160 beats/minute in the untreated state. Because of the varying stroke volumes induced by the varying periods of diastolic filling, not all ventricular beats result in a palpable peripheral pulse. The difference between the apical rate and pulse rate is the "pulse deficit"; this deficit is greater when the ventricular rate is high. Exercise intensifies the irregularity when the heart rate is slow. Carotid sinus massage has no effect or causes only slight slowing.

Prevention
See Paroxysmal Atrial Tachycardia, above.

Treatment
A. Paroxysmal Atrial Fibrillation:

1. Digitalis—Digitalis is the drug of choice, especially when the arrhythmia occurs in persons with organic heart disease (particularly mitral stenosis) or with rapid ventricular rates, or when the symptoms or signs of cardiac failure have appeared. In case of doubt about whether to use quinidine or digitalis first, digitalis should be given because it controls the ventricular rate by producing an AV block, which is the immediate objective of treatment. The objective of treatment with quinidine or DC cardioversion is to abolish the atrial ectopic rhythm, and it is quite safe to wait until the ventricular rate is brought under control with digitalis. Give full digitalizing doses, with the objective of slowing the ventricular rate to 70–80/minute and avoiding toxic manifestations. In paroxysmal fibrillation there is no clear evidence that the use of digitalis will result in established fibrillation.

2. Cardioversion—In cases where an attack of atrial fibrillation persists in an otherwise normal heart with a ventricular rate under 140 and with no other symptoms or signs of cardiac failure, cardioversion may be used at once to convert the rhythm to sinus rhythm. Quinidine is used rarely today to effect conversion to sinus rhythm.

B. Chronic Atrial Fibrillation: Opinion varies, but the following indications for conversion of atrial fibrillation serve as a general guide. Each case must be individualized. In general, conversion is attempted whenever it is thought that the patient will be better off with sinus rhythm than with atrial fibrillation: (1) Atrial fibrillation persisting after thyrotoxicosis has been treated surgically or by other means. (2) Atrial fibrillation of a few weeks' duration in an individual with no or only slight cardiac disease. (3) Atrial fibrillation associated with frequent embolic phenomena. (4) Refractory cardiac failure induced by the atrial fibrillation. (5) Severe palpitations due to inability to decrease the ventricular rate with digitalis; this may be obvious only on exertion. (6) Atrial fibrillation appearing for the first time postoperatively in patients with a technically successful mitral valvulotomy.

1. Digitalis—Thorough digitalization is the first step. The patient is then usually placed on maintenance digitalis indefinitely. The object of digitalization is to slow the ventricular rate and to improve myocardial efficiency, but digitalis toxicity is to be avoided and digitalis is stopped for 2 days before cardioversion.

2. Countershock—Synchronized DC countershock, 2.5 msec, 50–400 watt-seconds, under general anesthesia, has converted many patients to sinus rhythm even when quinidine has failed or was not tolerated in adequate dosage. It is now the procedure of choice in converting chronic atrial fibrillation (or flutter). DC shock should be avoided in the presence of digitalis toxicity. Relapses have been a problem, and further work is required to determine the long-term benefits.

3. Quinidine is used to abolish the ectopic rhythm once the ventricular rate is controlled with digitalis if the countershock is not available. It is potentially hazardous and should be used only in carefully selected cases by a physician thoroughly familiar with the drug and by a method which ensures close medical supervision (preferably in the hospital), while conversion to sinus rhythm is being attempted. Maintenance doses are used following conversion with countershock to maintain sinus rhythm. *Caution:* See p 221 for dangers of quinidine therapy.

4. Propranolol (Inderal®), 10–40 mg 3–4 times daily, may be used to slow the ventricular rate when this fails to occur satisfactorily with digitalis. Use *cautiously* (if at all) in the presence of cardiac failure, heart block, or bronchospasm.

Cramer, G.: Early and late results of conversion of atrial fibrillation with quinidine. A clinical and hemodynamic study. Acta med scandinav, Suppl 490, 1968.

Hornsten, T.R., & R.A. Bruce: Effects of atrial fibrillation on exercise performance in patients with cardiac disease. Circulation 37:543–549, 1968.

Hurst, J.W., & others: Management of patients with atrial fibrillation. Am J Med 37:728–741, 1964.

Irons, G.V., Jr., Ginn, W.N., & E.S. Orgain: Use of a beta adrenergic receptor blocking agent (Propranolol) in the treatment of cardiac arrhythmias. Am J Med 43:161–170, 1967.

Kleiger, R., & B. Lown: Cardioversion and digitalis. II. Clinical studies. Circulation 33:878–887, 1966.

Lown, B.: Electrical reversion of cardiac arrhythmias. Brit Heart J 29:469–489, 1967.

Scott, M.E., & G.C. Patterson: Cardiac output after direct current conversion of atrial fibrillation. Brit Heart J 31:87–90, 1969.

Sokolow, M., & R.E. Ball: Factors influencing conversion of chronic atrial fibrillation with special reference to serum quinidine concentration. Circulation 14:568, 1956.

Vassaux, C., & B. Lown: Cardioversion of supraventricular tachycardias. Circulation 39:791–802, 1969.

ATRIAL FLUTTER

Atrial flutter is uncommon and usually occurs in patients with rheumatic or coronary heart disease, cor pulmonale, atrial septal defect, or as a result of quinidine effect on atrial fibrillation. Ectopic impulse formation occurs at rates of 250–350, with transmission of every 2nd, 3rd, or 4th impulse through the AV node to the ventricles. The ventricular rate is usually ½ the atrial rate (2:1 block), or 150/minute. Carotid sinus massage causes sudden slowing or standstill, with rapid return of the rate to the original level on release of pressure. When the ventricular rate is 75 (4:1 block), exercise may cause sudden doubling of the rate to 150 (2:1 block). The first heart sound varies slightly in intensity from beat to beat.

Prevention

Similar to prevention of atrial tachycardia.

Treatment

A. **Paroxysmal Atrial Flutter:** Treatment is similar to that of paroxysmal atrial tachycardia except that digitalis is the drug of choice. The arrhythmia tends to become established more often than does atrial or nodal tachycardia.

B. **Chronic Atrial Flutter:**

1. **Digitalis** is the drug of choice. It increases the AV block and prevents a 2:1 or 1:1 conduction. In about ½ of cases atrial fibrillation or sinus rhythm results from full digitalization. Digitalis may be given by any of the usual methods. Oral medication is usually sufficient, although the intravenous route may be used if the situation is critical and DC cardioversion is not available. Digitalis must often be given in larger doses than are usually required for cardiac failure. When a fixed 4:1 conduction is produced by digitalis, a slightly increased dose may convert the flutter to atrial fibrillation or sinus rhythm; or DC countershock may be used.

2. **Propranolol (Inderal®)** may be used as in atrial fibrillation to slow the ventricular rate if this is difficult with digitalis. (See Atrial Fibrillation, above.)

3. **DC countershock** as in atrial fibrillation (see above). This is rapidly becoming the treatment of choice because of the ease and effectiveness of the procedure in restoring sinus rhythm and because the toxic effects of large doses of digitalis and quinidine can be avoided.

4. **Quinidine** should not as a rule be used to treat atrial flutter unless the patient is fully digitalized with a slow ventricular rate, because of the danger of producing a 1:1 conduction. If digitalis results in only a 4:1 conduction or produces atrial fibrillation which does not spontaneously convert to sinus rhythm, quinidine may be given if DC cardioversion is not available.

AV NODAL (JUNCTIONAL) RHYTHM

The AV node or the atrial-nodal junction or the nodal-His bundle junction may assume pacemaker activity for the heart, usually at a rate of 40–60 beats/minute. This may occur in normal hearts, myocarditis, coronary artery disease, or as a result of digitalis therapy. The rate responds normally to exercise, and the diagnosis is often a surprise finding on ECG. Careful examination of the jugular pulse may reveal the presence of cannon waves. Patients are often asymptomatic. Digitalis toxicity must be considered in each case.

AV NODAL (JUNCTIONAL) TACHYCARDIA

This arrhythmia is due to rapid, perfectly regular impulse formation in the AV node or bundle of His with regular transmission to the ventricles. The usual rates are 140–240/minute. Nodal or junctional tachycardia may be a benign condition or may reflect serious myocardial disease; it is more common than other arrhythmias in cor pulmonale and may often be the result of digitalis toxicity, which increases the rate of impulse formation in subsidiary pacemaker cells. Aberrant conduction often makes the distinction from ventricular tachycardia difficult, especially if there is retrograde conduction for the atria.

In the diagnosis of supraventricular arrhythmias with aberrant conduction and their differentiation from ventricular arrhythmias, His bundle electrograms may be very helpful. A bipolar or tripolar catheter can be inserted percutaneously via the femoral vein and positioned in the right ventricle in the region of the tricuspid valve. It is then possible to record impulses from the atria, bundle of His and His-Purkinje-ventricular impulses. In any given arrhythmia, one can see whether the His bundle spikes precede each QRS complex, in which case the rhythm originates above the ventricles in the region of the bundle of His. If the ventricular complex is not preceded by a His spike or atrial activity, the ectopic focus arises distal to the bundle of His. One can determine the interval between the atrial spike and the His spike and between the His spike and the beginning of the QRS to determine where AV conduction delays occur. His bundle recordings are also valuable in atrial fibrillation to distinguish between aberrant conduction from a rapid ventricular rate and ventricular premature beats, or ventricular tachycardia. If the His spike precedes each ventricular ECG, ventricular tachycardia is excluded.

If the diagnosis can be made by clinical and routine electrocardiography, the cost and hazards of cardiac catheterization should be avoided.

Treatment is along the same lines as for atrial tachycardia.

Easley, R.M., Jr., & S. Goldstein: Differentiation of ventricular tachycardia from junctional tachycardia with aberrant conduction: The use of competitive atrial pacing. Circulation 37:1015, 1968.

Marriott, H.J.L.: Differential diagnosis of supraventricular and ventricular tachycardia. Geriatrics 25:91, 1970.

VENTRICULAR PREMATURE BEATS

Ventricular premature beats are similar to atrial premature beats in mechanism and manifestations but are much more common. Together, they are the commonest causes of a grossly irregular rhythm with a normal heart rate. Ectopic impulse formation causes ventricular contraction to occur sooner than the next expected beat. The sound of this contraction is audible and is followed by a longer than normal pause since the next expected beat does not occur (compensatory pause). The interval between the preceding normal beat and the beat following the compensatory pause is exactly twice the normal interval between beats in the case of ventricular premature beats, and slightly less than this with atrial premature beats. Single premature beats which occur after every normal beat produce bigeminy. Exercise generally abolishes premature beats, and the rhythm becomes regular.

Premature beats have no definite significance unless they arise from multiple foci, occur with rapid ventricular rates or in runs, or appear when digitalis is given. Severe myocardial disease or digitalis toxicity may then be responsible, but in the vast majority of instances no organic heart disease can be found.

Treatment

If no associated cardiac disease is present and if the ectopic beats are infrequent and produce no palpitations, no specific therapy is indicated.

If ventricular premature beats are due to digitalis toxicity, withdraw digitalis and diuretics for 3—5 days or until the arrhythmia disappears and then resume medication in smaller dosage. Diphenylhydantoin (Dilantin®) may be of value (see below). At times, however, patients with cardiac failure who are receiving digitalis may develop ventricular premature beats which are due not to digitalis toxicity but to inadequate digitalization and cardiac failure. If in doubt as to the cause, withdraw digitalis for several days and treat the cardiac failure with other available methods (see p 203). In these circumstances, the ventricular premature beats often disappear as the cardiac failure improves.

Potassium chloride, 1—3 gm 4 times daily, is often helpful in ventricular premature beats of digitalis origin.

Quinidine or procainamide should be used orally to abolish ventricular premature beats when they occur in runs or from several foci in patients with heart disease. For premature beats in myocardial infarction, see p 190.

Watanabe, Y.: Reassessment of parasystole. Am Heart J 81:451, 1971.

PAROXYSMAL VENTRICULAR TACHYCARDIA

This is an uncommon serious arrhythmia due to rapid ectopic impulse formation in the ventricles. The rate may be 160—240. It usually lasts hours but may persist for days if untreated. The rhythm is almost completely regular, but less so than in atrial tachycardia, and the first sound may vary slightly in intensity from beat to beat. Carotid sinus massage has no effect.

Paroxysmal ventricular tachycardia usually occurs after myocardial infarction or as a result of digitalis toxicity. Pain due to myocardial ischemia, fall in blood pressure, and shock are common.

Prevention

The drugs of choice are quinidine and procainamide or, if ventricular premature beats occur during acute myocardial infarction, a constant infusion of lidocaine (Xylocaine®) at a rate of 1—2 mg/minute.

Treatment

　　A. Average Case:

　　1. DC countershock has replaced pharmacologic methods of treatment of ventricular tachycardia in all but the mildest cases.

　　2. Lidocaine (Xylocaine®), 50—100 mg IV followed by 1—4 mg/minute IV, has largely replaced quinidine and procainamide because of its short duration of action and infrequent hypotensive effect (see below).

　　3. Quinidine, 0.4 gm orally every 2 hours for 3 doses, if the attack is well tolerated and the patient is not in shock and if DC cardioversion is not available. If the attack continues and there is no toxicity from the quinidine, increase the dose to 0.6 gm orally every 2 hours for 3 doses or use DC countershock. If countershock is not available and the larger oral dosage of quinidine is not successful, change to procainamide.

4. Procainamide hydrochloride (Pronestyl®), 0.5–1.5 gm orally every 4–6 hours, may be substituted for quinidine if quinidine is ineffective or produces toxic symptoms.

5. Diphenylhydantoin (Dilantin®), 5 mg/kg IV or 100–250 mg IV very slowly, has been used with success in ventricular arrhythmias, especially when they are due to digitalis. Sinus rhythm may be induced, and digitalis-induced ventricular arrhythmias may be prevented when DC shock is given. Slow administration and careful ECG and blood pressure monitoring are necessary.

B. More Severe Case: (Or when other medication has failed.)

1. DC countershock (see above).

2. Lidocaine (Xylocaine®), 50–100 mg IV, repeated if necessary.

3. Procainamide hydrochloride (Pronestyl®), 0.5–1 gm, may be given IM and repeated in 4 hours; or IV, 100 mg every 5 minutes.

4. Quinidine gluconate, 0.8 gm or 0.5 gm of quinidine base, may be given IM and repeated every 2 hours for 2–3 doses.

5. Propranolol (Inderal®) may be given slowly IV in 1 mg doses under constant clinical ECG monitoring. The precautions noted under the atrial arrhythmias should be observed. Propranolol is rarely used in ventricular tachycardia unless cardioversion is not available.

C. Urgent Case:

1. DC countershock, depolarizing the entire heart, has proved of great value in patients not responding to lidocaine or procainamide, even in acute myocardial infarction. Under general anesthesia, a DC shock, synchronized to the downstroke of the R wave of the ECG, 2.5 msec in duration, and 50–400 watt-seconds, can be given.

2. Lidocaine (Xylocaine®), 1 mg/kg in 1 or 2% solution (50–100 mg for an adult), given IV has proved effective. If the arrhythmia recurs, one may give an IV infusion of 50 mg/hour (1 gm diluted to 1 liter of 5% glucose) (about 1–2 mg/minute) or repeat the intravenous injection twice at 20-minute intervals.

3. Procainamide hydrochloride (Pronestyl®), 1 gm *slowly* IV (at a rate not to exceed 100 mg/minute). During the infusion, continuous ECG or, at least, repeated blood pressure determinations are essential. Severe hypotension may result from the medication.

4. Quinidine may be given IV as quinidine gluconate, 0.8 gm diluted with 50 ml of 5% glucose *slowly* (1 ml/minute), with continuous ECG and determination of blood pressure. When giving intravenous quinidine in severe cases (particularly when the previous rhythm was complete AV block), the physician should be alert to the possibility of precipitating ventricular fibrillation or asystole. (See Heart-Lung Resuscitation.)

5. Propranolol (Inderal®) may be given as for more severe cases (above).

6. Vasopressor drugs for shock—If shock is present as a result of ventricular tachycardia or results from the drugs given intravenously, it can be treated with vasopressor drugs as described under the treatment of shock (see Chapter 1).

7. Other drugs—(1) Magnesium sulfate, 10 ml of a 20% solution, may be given *slowly* IV. Calcium salts should be readily available to counteract magnesium toxicity. (2) Intravenous morphine or meperidine (Demerol®) is sometimes successful.

8. Digitalis is usually contraindicated in ventricular tachycardia; however, in some patients with cardiac failure in whom the above-mentioned drugs have failed to restore sinus rhythm, full digitalization, given carefully, has been successful.

9. Temporary transvenous cardiac pacing may capture the rhythm from the ectopic ventricular tachycardia and has been used when anti-arrhythmia drugs have failed.

Bigger, J.T., Jr., & R.H. Heissenbuttel: Clinical use of antiarrhythmic drugs. Postgrad Med 47:119, 1970.

Fowler, N.: Symposium on the treatment of cardiac arrhythmias. Mod Treat 7:1, 1970.

Helfant, R.H., & others: The clinical use of DPH (Dilantin) in the treatment and prevention of cardiac arrhythmias. Am Heart J 77:315, 1969.

Hornbaker, J.H., Jr., Humphries, J.O., & R.S. Ross: Permanent pacing in the absence of heart block: An approach to the management of intractable arrhythmias. Circulation 39:189–196, 1969.

Kiss, Z.S., Smith, D., & G. Sloman: Electrical cardiac pacing in patients without heart block. Australian Ann Med 19:220–225, 1970.

Massumi, R.A., Tawakkol, A.A., & A.D. Kistin: Reevaluation of electrocardiographic and bedside criteria for diagnosis of ventricular tachycardia. Circulation 36:628–636, 1967.

Norris, R.M., Mercer, C.J., & S.E. Yeates: Idioventricular rhythm complicating acute myocardial infarction. Brit Heart J 32:617–622, 1970.

Raftery, E.B., & others: Incidence and management of ventricular arrhythmias after acute myocardial infarction. Brit Heart J 31:273–280, 1969.

Zypes, D.P., & others: Artificial atrial and ventricular pacing in the treatment of arrhythmias. Ann Int Med 70:885, 1969.

VENTRICULAR FLUTTER & FIBRILLATION

These arrhythmias represent more advanced stages of ventricular tachycardia in which the rate of impulse formation is more rapid and transmission becomes irregular, resulting in ineffective ventricular contractions. Diagnosis can be established only by ECG. Ventricular flutter-fibrillation is rapidly fatal unless terminated by defibrillation. It is usually associated with severe myocardial damage, but may be precipitated by epinephrine, quinidine, or digitalis.

Treatment

A. Surgical and Mechanical Measures: External cardiac massage, prompt ventilation, and electric defibrillation is the treatment of choice (see Appendix). Continuous monitoring of patients with acute myocardial infarction has shown at least half of sudden expected deaths to be due to ventricular fibrillation. Prompt treatment may be lifesaving. Surgical exposure of the heart with direct cardiac massage is infrequently performed today except during cardiac operations.

B. Medical Treatment: Usually ineffective. In paroxysmal episodes, try to prevent (as in ventricular tachycardia).

DISTURBANCES OF CONDUCTION

SINO-ATRIAL (S-A) BLOCK

In S-A block the normal pacemaker fails to initiate the depolarizing impulse at irregular or regular intervals or, rarely, in a fixed 2:1 ratio. This failure is apparently due to heightened vagal tone and is not related to the presence of heart disease. Exercise and atropine therefore abolish S-A block. This arrhythmia can be recognized by the fact that no sound is audible during the prolonged interval between beats (in contrast to ventricular premature beats). There are no symptoms unless the period of standstill extends over the span of several beats, in which case momentary faintness or even syncope may occur. In susceptible individuals, carotid sinus massage induces S-A block.

Treatment

In most cases no treatment is required. The causative factors, especially digitalis, should be eliminated if possible. The following drugs may be tried: (1) Atropine sulfate, 0.6 mg 4 times daily orally. (2) Ephedrine sulfate, 25 mg orally 4 times daily. In more prolonged cases, give atropine, 0.5–1 mg IV. Transvenous pacing rarely is required.

ATRIOVENTRICULAR (AV) BLOCK
(See also p 192.)

AV block consists of prolongation of the conduction time of the normal impulse from the atria to the ventricles. It is classified, according to the degree of block, as (1) prolonged conduction (latent heart block), (2) incomplete or partial heart block, and (3) complete heart block.

Prolonged conduction (latent heart block): The P–R interval is prolonged to 0.22 seconds or more, but every atrial impulse reaches the ventricles. Its presence can be suspected clinically when the first heart sound is faint in the presence of a vigorous apical impulse. There may be a presystolic gallop rhythm due to audible atrial contraction. AV block is most commonly seen in acute rheumatic fever and coronary artery disease, and as a result of treatment with digitalis or quinidine.

Incomplete or partial heart block: In incomplete heart block the delay in conduction increases to the point where an impulse does not reach the ventricles, resulting in failure of a ventricular contraction, ie, every so often a beat is dropped. When a beat is skipped, the bundle recovers for a while; the cycle may therefore be repeated regularly or irregularly, in the former producing a 2:1 or 3:1, etc, rhythm. The diagnosis is made by noting that the intervals between heart beats in which no sound is audible is twice as long as normal (see Ventricular Premature Beats). Incomplete heart block occurs most often in arteriosclerotic heart disease. Diphtheria is a rare cause.

Some authorities divide partial (second degree) AV block into Mobitz type I, with partial progressive AV block and Wenckebach pauses; and type II, with intermittent dropped beats. It is thought that, following myocardial infarction, type I requires no specific treatment, whereas type II often leads to complete AV block and Stokes-Adams attack and therefore requires pacing. His bundle recordings (see p 196) have demonstrated that in partial AV block it is possible to determine if the block is above or below the bundle of His. If above, the course is usually benign; if below, pacing should be considered more definitely.

Complete heart block: This usually occurs only in older patients with fibrosis of the cardiac skeleton involving the conduction system. Less frequently, it is due to coronary heart disease. Occasionally it is congenital. Transmission of atrial impulses through the AV node is completely blocked, and a ventricular pacemaker maintains a slow, regular ventricular rate, usually less than 45 beats/minute. Exercise does not increase the rate. The first heart sound varies greatly in loudness; wide pulse pressure, changing systolic blood pressure level, and cannon venous pulsations in the neck are also present. Patients may be asymptomatic or complain of weakness or dyspnea if the rate is less than 40/minute—at times at even higher rates if the left ventricle cannot increase its stroke output. During periods of transition from partial to complete heart block, certain patients have ventricular asystole which lasts several seconds to minutes. Syncope occurs abruptly, and if the asystole is prolonged beyond a few seconds convulsive movements appear (Stokes-Adams syndrome). Asystole of 2–3 minutes is usually fatal.

Treatment

A. Prolonged Conduction and Incomplete Heart Block: In the absence of Stokes-Adams syndrome (see below), treatment of AV conduction defects is rarely successful except by elimination of drugs, if they are causative, or by the subsidence of acute myocarditis.

Prolongation of the AV conduction itself usually needs no treatment (except careful observation) unless there is complete heart block (see below). Cardiac failure or weakness may occur with slow ventricular rates. Ephedrine or isoproterenol (Aludrine®, Isuprel®) should be given to increase the rate of the ventricular pacemaker (see below).

See p 201 for a discussion of the danger of complete AV block in patients with partial AV block and bundle branch block.

B. Complete Heart Block and Stokes-Adams Syndrome: Try to eliminate or treat the cause. The objective of treatment is to obtain an idioventricular pacemaker discharging at a rate of at least 40/minute or more, but recent data with artificial pacing indicate that a ventricular rate of 70 is far superior.

1. Artificial transvenous or transventricular pacemaker—Implantation of myocardial electrodes with platinum wires tunneled to a zinc-cadmium battery placed subcutaneously in the abdomen has been largely replaced by transvenous introduction of the electrode catheter into the right ventricle. Dramatic improvement in cardiac failure, cerebral symptoms, and syncopal attacks has resulted in earlier use of artificial pacing in many patients. Cardiac stimulation via an electrode left in the right ventricle via a cardiac catheter introduced from the superior vena cava is a useful temporary recourse, and may be lifesaving, especially when syncopal attacks have occurred.

Pacemakers are now introduced following a single proved Stokes-Adams attack, and are used with increasing frequency when slow ventricular rates induce cerebral or cardiac insufficiency. Follow-up of patients with pacemakers is essential to establish early the presence of faulty functioning.

When AV block is intermittent but causing syncope, a demand pacemaker is preferable because it is activated only during bradycardia, thus decreasing the likelihood of ventricular fibrillation caused by stimulation of the heart during the vulnerable period resulting from competition between the natural and artificial pacemakers.

2. Isoproterenol hydrochloride (Aludrine®, Isuprel®), 5–15 mg, may be given sublingually 3 or 4 times daily or oftener, or by IV infusion, 2–15 mg/500 ml.

3. Ephedrine sulfate, 25–60 mg orally 4 times daily, is often effective. The dose must be sufficient to prevent the attacks. If necessary, secobarbital sodium (Seconal®), 30 mg, may be given with each dose of ephedrine.

4. Epinephrine—If attacks are frequent and are not controlled with ephedrine or isoproterenol, epinephrine, 0.5 ml of 1:1000 solution, may be given every 8 hours as needed, or 0.2 ml of a 1:1000 solution may be given subcutaneously every 2 hours. Epinephrine is used less often than (1) and (2) above, but is valuable if procedures (1) and (2) are not available.

5. Intracardiac epinephrine injection, 0.5 ml of a 1:1000 solution, may be given if cardiac standstill persists.

6. Corticosteroids occasionally reverse complete AV block if it is of recent onset.

Beregovich, J., & others: Management of acute myocardial infarction complicated by advanced atrioventricular block: Role of artificial pacing. Am J Cardiol 23:54–65, 1969.

Berkowitz, W.D., & others: The use of His bundle recordings in the analysis of unilateral and bilateral bundle branch block. Am Heart J 81:340, 1971.

Bernstein, V., Rotem, E., & D.I. Peretz: Permanent pacemakers: Eight-year follow-up study. Ann Int Med 74:361–369, 1971.

Chamberlain, D.A., & others: Sequential atrioventricular pacing in heart block. New England J Med 282:577–582, 1970.

Criscitiello, M.G.: Current concepts: Therapy of atrioventricular block. New England J Med 279:808, 1968.

Friedberg, C.K., Cohen, H., & E. Donoso: Advanced heart block as a complication of acute myocardial infarction: Role of pacemaker therapy. Progr Cardiovas Dis 10:466–481, 1968.

Gadboys, H.L., Lukban, S., & R.S. Litwak: Long term follow-up of patients with cardiac pacemakers. Am J Cardiol 21:55–60, 1968.

Gilcrest, A.R.: Clinical aspects of high grade heart block. Scottish MJ 3:53, 1958.

Harris, A., & others: Aetiology of chronic heart block: A clinico-pathological correlation of 65 cases. Brit Heart J 31:206–218, 1969.

Harris, A., & others: Causes of death in patients with complete heart block and artificial pacemakers. Brit Heart J 30:14–20, 1968.

Hudson, R.E.B.: Surgical pathology of the conducting system of the heart. Brit Heart J 29:646–670, 1967.

Kistuk, W.J., & D.S. Beanlands: Complete heart block associated with acute myocardial infarction. Am J Cardiol 26:380, 1970.

Langendorf, R., & A. Pick: Atrioventricular block, type II: Mobitz—Its nature and clinical significance. Circulation 38:819–822, 1968.

Lassers, B.W., & others: Hemodynamic effects of artificial pacing in complete heart block complicating acute myocardial infarction. Circulation 38:308–323, 1968.

Narula, O.S., & others: Atrioventricular block: Localization and classification by His bundle recordings. Am J Med 50:146, 1971.

Norris, R.M.: Heart block in posterior and anterior myocardial infarction. Brit Heart J 31:352–369, 1969.

Pomerantz, B., & R.A. O'Rourke: The Stokes-Adams syndrome. Am J Med 46:941–961, 1969.

Rosen, K.M., Rahimtoola, S.H., & R.M. Gunnar: Pseudo A-V block secondary to premature nonpropagated His bundle depolarizations: Documentation by His bundle electrocardiography. Circulation 42(Suppl 3):367, 1970.

Siddons, H., & E. Sowton: *Cardiac Pacemakers.* Thomas, 1967.

Sowton, E.: Implantable cardiac pacemakers. Brit Heart J 30:587–591, 1968.

Spritzer, R.C., & others: Arrhythmias induced by pacemaking on demand. Am Heart J 77:619–628, 1969.

See also references for Paroxysmal Ventricular Tachycardia.

BUNDLE-BRANCH BLOCK (BBB)

BBB is purely an ECG diagnosis based on widening of the QRS interval to 0.12 second or more. It is caused by delayed conduction through the right or left branch of the bundle of His or the myocardium. Heart rate and rhythm are not affected. Coronary heart disease is a frequent cause, but fibrosis of the conduction system and congenital lesions may be responsible. BBB (especially RBBB) may be benign and not influence life expectancy. Left BBB, reflecting left ventricular disease, is thought to have a worse prognosis than RBBB. The blocks may be due to local fibrosis and may precede AV block.

Recent clinical and pathologic data indicate that the combination of right bundle-branch block and left anterior hemiblock (left axis deviation exceeding −30°) represents bilateral bundle-branch (bivascular) block, and, especially when combined with AV block, involves a substantial likelihood of complete AV block and possible sudden death. Studies are in progress to determine whether to use a transvenous pacemaker prophylactically to prevent Stokes-Adams attacks. A more conservative approach is to follow the patients closely and use a pacemaker only when complete AV block develops.

There is no specific treatment. Treat the underlying disease, if possible.

Baragan, J., & others: Chronic left complete bundle-branch block: Phonocardiographic and mechanocardiographic study of 30 cases. Brit Heart J 30:196, 1968.

Rosenbaum, M.B.: The hemiblocks: Diagnostic criteria and clinical significance. Mod Concepts Cardiovas Dis 39:141−146, 1970.

ACCELERATED CONDUCTION SYNDROME
(Wolff-Parkinson-White)

The Wolff-Parkinson-White syndrome is a rare condition in which there is a rapid atrial to ventricular conduction producing a characteristic ECG with a P−R interval of less than 0.1 second and slurring of the upstroke of the QRS, resulting in an apparently abnormally prolonged QRS interval. Patients are subject to attacks of paroxysmal supraventricular tachycardia but generally do not have underlying heart disease.

CONGESTIVE HEART FAILURE

Essentials of Diagnosis
Left ventricular failure:
- Exertional dyspnea and fatigue, orthopnea, paroxysmal nocturnal dyspnea.

Right ventricular failure:
- Elevated venous pressure, hepatomegaly, dependent edema.

Both:
- Cardiomegaly, gallop rhythm, prolonged arm-to-tongue circulation time.

General Considerations

Congestive heart failure is a clinical syndrome which develops eventually in 50−60% of all patients with organic cardiovascular disease. It is defined as the clinical state resulting from inability of the heart to expel sufficient blood for the metabolic demands of the body. Heart failure may therefore be present when cardiac output is high, normal, or low; regardless of the absolute level, the cardiac output is reduced relative to metabolic demands.

The left or right ventricle alone may fail initially, but combined failure is the rule in most cases. Failure of the right ventricle secondary to pulmonary parenchymal or vascular disease is termed "cor pulmonale" or "pulmonary heart disease" and is discussed on p 212.

The most common underlying causes of cardiac insufficiency are hypertension, coronary atherosclerosis, and rheumatic heart disease. Less common causes are chronic pulmonary disease, congenital heart disease, syphilitic aortic insufficiency, calcific aortic stenosis, cardiomyopathies, and bacterial endocarditis. Numerous rare causes of heart failure include collagen diseases, arteriovenous fistula, myocarditis, beriberi, and myocardial involvement by tumors or granulomas.

In 50% of cases there are demonstrable precipitating diseases or factors. The commonest of these are arrhythmias, respiratory infection, myocardial infarction, pulmonary embolism, rheumatic carditis, excessive or rapid administration of parenteral fluids, pregnancy, thyrotoxicosis, anemia, and excessive salt intake.

Etiology

The basic causes of ventricular failure are as follows:

A. Myocardial Weakness or Inflammation: Coronary artery disease, myocarditis.

B. Excess Work Load:

1. Increased resistance to ejection−Hypertension, stenosis of aortic or pulmonary valves.

2. Increased stroke volume−Mitral insufficiency, tricuspid insufficiency, aortic insufficiency, congenital left-to-right shunts.

3. Increased body demands−Thyrotoxicosis, anemia, pregnancy, arteriovenous fistula.

Pathogenesis

The ventricle responds to each of the mechanisms listed above initially by dilatation followed by hypertrophy. When increased strength of contraction is no longer sufficient, the diastolic filling pressure and volume increase, maintaining normal cardiac output for a time. Eventually, however, the cardiac output is insufficient to meet the metabolic demands of the body tissues. At this point cardiac insufficiency exists.

Clinical Findings

A. Symptoms and Signs:

1. Left ventricular failure—Left ventricular failure is characterized predominantly by symptoms: dyspnea, exertional fatigue and weakness, and nocturia. **Exertional dyspnea,** which is caused by pulmonary vascular engorgement, resembles the normal ventilatory response to exercise but is associated with increased awareness of breathlessness and difficulty in breathing. In heart failure, the patient regularly becomes short of breath during an amount of exertion which previously caused no difficulty. As the pulmonary engorgement progresses, less and less activity brings on dyspnea until it is present even when the patient is at rest (rest dyspnea). **Orthopnea,** or shortness of breath occurring in recumbency which is promptly relieved by propping up the head or trunk, is precipitated by the further increase in pulmonary engorgement on recumbency. **Paroxysmal nocturnal dyspnea** may appear at any time and is often the first indication of left ventricular failure caused by severe hypertension, aortic stenosis or insufficiency, or myocardial infarction. It also occurs in patients with tight mitral stenosis in advanced stages. It is an exaggerated form of orthopnea, the patient awakening from sleep gasping for breath, and compelled to sit or stand up for relief. Cough is frequently present. For unknown reasons, patients may have inspiratory and expiratory wheezing (so-called cardiac asthma). The paroxysmal cough and dyspnea may pass in a few minutes to several hours, or may progress to acute pulmonary edema. Patients become pale or frankly cyanotic, sweat profusely, and complain of great air hunger. Cough productive of frothy white or pink sputum is characteristic. The attack may subside in 1 to several hours, or the left ventricle may progressively weaken, leading to shock and death.

These forms of dyspnea must be distinguished from those occurring commonly in many other conditions. Advanced age, debility, poor physical conditioning, obesity, chronic pulmonary disease, or severe anemia commonly produce exertional dyspnea. Extreme obesity (Pickwickian syndrome), ascites from any cause, abdominal distention from gastrointestinal disease, or advanced stages of pregnancy may produce orthopnea in the absence of preexisting heart disease. Bronchial asthma appearing in middle life may be symptomatically indistinguishable from the paroxysmal nocturnal dyspnea of left ventricular failure. Patients with neurocirculatory asthenia or anxiety states with psychophysiologic cardiovascular reactions may suffer from many kinds of dyspnea.

Accurate determination of the arm-to-tongue circulation times and systemic venous pressure is sometimes helpful in differential diagnosis of dyspnea if its cardiac origin is in question.

Exertional fatigue and weakness due to reduced cardiac output are early symptoms and disappear promptly on resting. Severe fatigue, rather than dyspnea, is the chief complaint of patients with mitral stenosis who have developed pulmonary hypertension and low cardiac output.

Nocturia occurs as a result of the excretion of edema fluid accumulated during the day and the increased renal perfusion in the recumbent position; it reflects the decreased work of the heart at rest and often the effects of diuretics administered during the day.

In the absence of overt right ventricular failure, examination should disclose the following: (1) the basic cause of the left ventricular failure (hypertension, aortic or mitral valve disease, myocardial infarction); (2) left ventricular hypertrophy, in which the apical impulse is forceful or heaving, displaced to the left and downward, confirmed by ECG and chest x-ray; and (3) a prolonged arm-to-tongue circulation time. The following may or may not be present, and are not necessary for diagnosis: basilar parenchymal rales which do not clear on coughing, gallop rhythm, pulsus alternans, and an accentuated pulmonary component of the second sound ("P2"). The chest x-ray may reveal left atrial enlargement in the case of mitral stenosis, and pulmonary vascular congestion; and shows unquestioned left ventricular enlargement in the usual case.

2. Right ventricular failure—Right ventricular failure is characterized predominantly by signs. It develops after left ventricular failure of even short duration. Mitral stenosis, pulmonary valve stenosis, cor pulmonale, and tricuspid insufficiency, and such complications of congenital disease as Eisenmenger's syndrome resulting from interventricular or interatrial septal defect may produce relatively pure right ventricular failure. Tricuspid stenosis produces the same effects as right ventricular failure. **Anorexia, bloating,** or **exertional right upper abdominal pains** are common, reflecting hepatic and visceral engorgement secondary to elevated venous pressure. **Oliguria** is present in the daytime, polyuria at night. Headache, weakness, and mental aberration are present in severe cases.

The venous pressure can be estimated by noting the extent of jugular filling (during normal expiration) above the level of the clavicles when the patient is propped up so that his trunk makes a 30° angle with the bed. A simple water manometer allows serial determinations of the venous pressure at the bedside (zero level junction of lower and middle thirds of the AP diameter of the chest is a commonly used reference point). Normal pressure is 6–10 cm H_2O. Right ventricular hypertrophy in pure right failure is easily demonstrated by lower sternal or left parasternal systolic lift or forceful pulsations independent of the apical impulse. The liver is enlarged. Ascites is rarely prominent; when it appears early and in massive amounts, cardiac tamponade, constrictive pericarditis, or tricuspid stenosis should be considered. Dependent edema caused by heart failure usually is first noted in (or is more prominent in) the left leg. The edema subsides overnight initially, but eventually persists and increases in extent. Pleural effusion is more common on the right side. Coolness of the extremities and cyanosis of the nail beds are due to reduced peripheral blood flow. Sinus tachycardia is present.

The ECG findings indicate pure right ventricular hypertrophy in pure right-sided failure, mixed hypertrophy in Eisenmenger's syndrome, and, usually, evidence of left ventricular hypertrophy or coronary artery disease when left-sided failure is predominant.

Right atrial and ventricular enlargement are readily seen in pure right heart failure, but specific chamber enlargement is difficult to define when right failure is secondary to left heart failure.

Determination of systolic time intervals (see p 148) may provide an indirect means of assessing impaired left ventricular function prior to the development of cardiac failure. Left ventricular cineangiograms (see p 146) provide a direct visual picture of left ventricular contraction and ejection.

B. Laboratory Findings: Red and white cell counts, hemoglobin, packed cell volume, and sedimentation rate are normal in uncomplicated left heart failure. Polycythemia may occur in chronic cor pulmonale. Urinalysis often discloses significant proteinuria and granular casts. The BUN may be elevated because of reduced renal blood flow, but the urine specific gravity is high in the absence of primary renal disease. The serum sodium, potassium, CO_2, and chloride are within normal limits in ordinary congestive heart failure before diuretics are used. Specific tests should be made for any suspected unusual etiologies or complications contributing to heart failure, eg, thyrotoxicosis, bacterial endocarditis, syphilis, collagen disease, pheochromocytoma.

Differential Diagnosis

Congestive heart failure must be differentiated from neurocirculatory asthenia, acute and chronic pulmonary disease, bronchial asthma, cirrhosis, carcinoma of the lung, nephrosis or nephritis, mediastinal tumor, repeated pulmonary emboli, obstruction of the vena cava, and anemia.

Consideration of the history together with physical findings of organic cardiovascular disease, enlarged heart, gallop rhythm, pulsus alternans, elevated venous pressure in the absence of collateral venous circulation, and prolonged circulation time differentiate congestive heart failure from these conditions.

Potentially curable causes of congestive heart failure must be specifically considered: constrictive pericarditis, mitral stenosis, pulmonary stenosis, tricuspid stenosis, subacute bacterial endocarditis, thyrotoxicosis, peripheral arteriovenous fistula, beriberi, and recurrent arrhythmias.

Treatment

The objectives of treatment are to increase the force and efficiency of myocardial contraction and to reduce the abnormal retention of sodium and water. The patient shares a significant responsibility in the management of his disease, because treatment is long-term and involves restrictions in diet and activity.

Specific search should be made for reversible noncardiac causes of failure, eg, thyrotoxicosis, anemia, myxedema, nutritional disturbances (especially vitamin B deficiency), arteriovenous fistulas, polycythemia vera, and Paget's disease.

Determine and eliminate, if possible, the factor precipitating the cardiac failure, eg, infection (especially respiratory), pulmonary infarction, overexertion, increased sodium intake, discontinuation of medication (especially digitalis); the onset of arrhythmia, particularly with rapid ventricular rates (eg, atrial fibrillation); myocardial infarction, and anemia.

A. Rest: Rest in bed or sitting in a chair decreases the work of the heart and promotes sodium diuresis. Morphine- or barbiturate-induced sleep comes as a welcome relief to a patient who has spent many sleepless, dyspneic nights with his disease. Adequate rest should be maintained until compensation has occurred and then should be replaced by progressive ambulation. Most patients can use a bedside toilet with no more effort than is required for a bedpan.

Rest should be continued as long as necessary to permit the heart to regain reserve strength, but should not be so prolonged as to cause generalized debility of the patient.

Patients are usually more comfortable in a cool room.

Cardiac patients at bed rest are prone to develop phlebitis. They should be given passive or active leg exercises and an elastic stocking to prevent phlebothrombosis.

B. Diet: (See Table 7–7.) At the onset of therapy, give frequent (4–6) small, bland, low-caloric, low-residue meals with vitamin supplements. The degree of sodium restriction depends upon the severity of the failure and the ease with which it can be controlled by other means. Even with the use of diuretics, unlimited sodium intake is considered unwise. Evaluation of the previous intake of sodium will provide a baseline upon which to gauge the degree of restriction required. Before drastic sodium restriction is instituted, the renal function should be evaluated to determine if the kidneys can conserve sodium. In an occasional case, 350 mg or less of sodium may be the maximum tolerated without development of edema, although such extreme restriction is usually necessary only when failure is first treated. Vitamin supplements may be indicated. Restricted diets and anorexia may lead to malnutrition and avitaminosis, with a superimposed beriberi type of failure.

If sodium restriction is observed faithfully, there is no indication or need for strict fluid restriction.

C. Digitalis: (See p 217.) Digitalis increases the speed and force of cardiac contraction. Increased cardiac output, decreased cardiac size and ventricular diastolic pressure, and a fall in right atrial and peripheral venous pressure follow digitalization in patients with cardiac failure. The glycosides available are qualitatively similar. They differ in speed of action, dosage, and rate of excretion. It is advisable to become familiar with a rapid intravenous and a rapid oral method.

TABLE 7–7. Dietary plan for low-sodium diet: 1800 calories.
(Adapted from: *Sodium Restricted Diets.* American Heart Association, 1969.)

Food	Average Sodium per Serving	Sodium Levels/Day 500 mg	1000 mg	1500–3000 mg*
Milk: whole, low-fat, nonfat	120 mg/8 oz	1 glass (8 oz) daily†	2 glasses (16 oz) daily†	2 glasses or more daily
Egg, prepared in any way without salt	57 mg/egg	1	1	1
Meat, poultry, fish, fresh or frozen; beef, lamb, veal, pork, fish, chicken, turkey‡	25 mg/oz	6 oz cooked or substitute	6 oz cooked or substitute	6 or more oz cooked (small amounts regular cheese)
Fruits, all kinds: fresh, frozen, canned, dried, or juices	2 mg/half-cup	4 or more servings daily	4 or more servings daily	4 or more servings daily
Vegetables: fresh, frozen, or dietetic canned, green or yellow	9 mg/half-cup	3 or more servings daily §	3 or more servings daily	3 or more servings daily**
Breads, enriched white or whole grain	120 mg/slice	None	None	3 or more servings daily
Breads, low-sodium	5 mg/slice	4 or more slices daily	4 or more slices daily	As desired
Cereals, regular cooked (without salt, nonenriched)	1 mg/cup	As desired	As desired	As desired
Cereals, dry, prepared (cornflakes, etc)	165–300 mg/cup	None	None	1 serving daily
Cereals: shredded wheat, puffed wheat, puffed rice	1 mg/cup	As desired	As desired	As desired
Starches: potatoes (white or sweet), corn, lima beans, peas, mixed vegetables††	5–10 mg/half-cup	1 or more servings daily	1 or more servings daily	As desired
Starches: rice, macaroni, spaghetti, noodles	1 mg/half-cup	As desired	As desired	As desired
Butter, margarine	40 mg/tsp	None	None	4 or more servings daily
Unsalted butter, margarine	0.04 mg/tsp	4 or more tsp daily	4 or more tsp daily	As desired
Oils	None	As desired	As desired	As desired
Salad dressings	80–200 mg/tsp	None	None	In moderation
Unsalted salad dressings	Up to 0.4 mg/tsp	As desired	As desired	As desired
Homemade soups, with allowed milk, meats, vegetables	Varies with the sodium content of ingredients	As desired	As desired	As desired
Sugars, syrups, jellies, honey, candies (hard sugar)	None	As desired	As desired	As desired
Desserts: homemade (salt-free) gelatin, ice cream, sherbet, meringues, puddings, pound cakes	10–50 mg/serving	As desired	As desired	As desired

TABLE 7–7 (cont'd). Dietary plan for low-sodium diet: 1800 calories.

Food	Average Sodium per Serving	500 mg	Sodium Levels/Day 1000 mg	1500–3000 mg*
Salt	2300 mg/tsp	None	None	½ tsp daily*
Monosodium glutamate (Accent®, Ajino-moto®)	750 mg/tsp	None	None	In place of salt
Baking soda (sodium bicarbonate)	1000 mg/tsp	None	None	Moderate use in cooking
Baking powder	370 mg/tsp	None	None	Moderate use in cooking

Avoid: Canned vegetables or vegetable juices unless low-sodium dietetic canned; canned soups, soda crackers, potato chips, pretzels, "snack foods," quick or hot breads, waffles, pancakes, olives, pickles, relishes, condiments such as ketchup, mustard, chili sauce, salted nuts, sauerkraut.

*Small amounts of salt (up to ½ tsp/day) may be used in cooking or at the table.

†Buttermilk should not be used.

‡*Avoid* salted or cured or smoked meats, fish, or chicken; ham, bacon, sausage, luncheon meats, frankfurters, sardines, canned tuna or salmon (unless without salt), shellfish, regular cottage cheese and cheddar type cheeses. **Substitutes:** Low-sodium cheese or dietetic peanut butter.

§On 500 mg sodium diet, avoid the following vegetables: Artichokes, beet greens, beets, carrots, celery, chard, dandelion greens, hominy, kale, mustard greens, spinach, sauerkraut, white turnips.

**May use any fresh, frozen, or drained regular canned vegetables except sauerkraut. ††Only fresh or dietetic canned lima beans and peas. The frozen are packed with salt.

Rapid digitalization is indicated in atrial flutter and fibrillation with fast ventricular rates and in acute pulmonary edema; otherwise, slow digitalization is preferred.

D. Removal of Sodium and Water:

1. Thiazide diuretics—Sodium diuresis is most conveniently accomplished by the use of an orally active agent such as chlorothiazide (Diuril®) or any of its analogues (see p 222). The diuretics can be given daily or intermittently depending on the need. Dietary or supplementary potassium must be adequate to prevent potassium depletion and digitalis toxicity.

2. Mercurial diuretics—The mercurial diuretics (see p 223) are slightly more potent than the thiazide diuretics. In general, they are reserved for use only when the oral preparations have been tried without success. They act by decreasing the sodium and chloride reabsorption in the renal tubules. Clinical effect is noted in about 2 hours following intramuscular or subcutaneous injection and is essentially complete in 10–12 hours. Small quantities of mercurials (0.5–1 ml) may result in adequate diuresis and should be used initially. They should be given in the morning so that their effect will have largely subsided by nightfall. Large doses may initiate massive diuresis with extensive fluid and electrolyte losses. This can be very distressing and can produce untoward symptoms, particularly in older people. The action of the mercurial diuretics can be potentiated by giving chlorides, eg, ammonium chloride, 2 gm 4 times daily on the day before mercurial administration, or lysine monohydrochloride, 5 gm 4 times daily, if there is associated severe liver disease. The use of ammonium chloride for periods longer than 48 hours has no advantage and increases the danger of acidosis. Acetazolamide

(Diamox®), 0.25 gm once or twice daily for 2–3 days before the mercurial is given, also potentiates its action.

3. Aldosterone antagonists—Spironolactone (Aldactone®) causes sodium diuresis without potassium loss and can be combined with a thiazide to neutralize the potassium-wasting effect of thiazides. The onset of effect may be delayed for 1 week. Response is variable but may be striking. The initial dosage is 25 mg 4 times daily. Drowsiness, hyperkalemia, hypovolemia, hypotension, and breast tenderness may occur. Similar potassium sparing may occur with triamterine (Dyrenium®; see p 223), which may be used in combination with thiazides, ethacrynic acid, or furosemide (see below). *Caution:* Check serum potassium.

4. Ethacrynic acid (Edecrin®), 25–100 mg orally, and **furosemide (Lasix®)**, 40–80 mg orally (see p 223), are potent diuretics of short duration. They cause nausea and diarrhea more often than the thiazides, especially with regular dosage. The considerable diuresis may cause a significant fall in glomerular filtration rate and hypokalemia, and these drugs must therefore be used with considerable caution. The rapid onset of action (within 30 minutes) makes them valuable on occasion for treatment of acute pulmonary edema, but their potency increases the hazards and the thiazides are probably preferable for the average patient with congestive failure unless there is associated renal failure.

E. Oxygen Therapy: Useful when respiratory distress is present.

F. Sympathetic and Other Inotropic Agents: Isoproterenol (Isuprel®) and glucagon may have a place in therapy if digitalis is contraindicated, especially in the postoperative period after open heart surgery or following acute myocardial infarction.

G. Mechanical Measures: Paracentesis of fluid in the chest and abdomen should be undertaken if respiration is embarrassed. Since sodium retention may occur as a result of fluid collection in the chest, abdomen, and legs, diuresis may occur following the procedure. Venesection (in low-output failure in the absence of anemia), rotating tourniquets, Southey tubes, and acupuncture may be beneficial if the more conventional forms of treatment fail. Southey tubes and acupuncture are especially valuable in severe right heart failure with obstinate dependent edema. Care must be taken to avoid a severe low-sodium syndrome with hyperkalemia.

H. Peritoneal Dialysis: Hypertonic peritoneal dialysis is an effective method, reserved for patients with severe heart failure, dilutional hyponatremia, and renal failure. Some remissions have been dramatic; and the method should be given a greater trial.

I. Observation During Treatment of Cardiac Failure: Record the following observations on every visit:

1. Status of original symptoms.
2. New symptoms.
3. Morning weight or weight with same clothes.
4. Presence of the signs of congestive failure (venous engorgement and pulsations, pulmonary rales, pleural fluid, engorgement of the liver, presence of edema).
5. Examination of the heart and blood vessels (cardiac sounds, gallop rhythm, friction rub, cardiac rhythm and apical rate, cardiac size, peripheral arterial pulsations, and status of the veins).
6. Blood pressure and presence of pulsus alternans.

Prognosis

Heart failure is most often complicated by pulmonary embolization secondary to venous thrombosis occurring in the leg veins. Pulmonary infections, cardiac cirrhosis, and peripheral arterial embolization may occur. In general, the speed and adequacy of response to therapy is the most reliable guide to prognosis. Detection and removal of a precipitating condition prolongs survival. The age of the patient, the degree of cardiac enlargement, the extent of myocardial damage, and the severity of underlying cardiac and associated diseases must all be considered. Survival for 5–8 years is common. Survival is longer in failure due to mitral insufficiency or that precipitated by atrial fibrillation. Survival is shorter when failure is due to mitral stenosis, syphilitic aortic insufficiency, calcific aortic stenosis, myocardial infarction, chronic pulmonary disease, and severe hypertension.

See also section on digitalis and diuretics (pp 216–220; 222).

Avery, W.G., Samet, P., & M.A. Sackner: The acidosis of pulmonary edema. Am J Med 48:320, 1970.

Bank, N.: Physiological basis of diuretic action. Ann Rev Med 19:103–118, 1968.

Brest, A.N., & others: Symposium on congestive heart failure. II. Clinical selection of diuretic drugs in the management of cardiac edema. Am J Cardiol 22:168–176, 1968.

Cairns, K.B., & others: Clinical and hemodynamic results of peritoneal dialysis for severe cardiac failure. Am Heart J 76:227–234, 1968.

Dodge, H.T., & W.A. Baxley: Hemodynamic aspects of heart failure. Am J Cardiol 22:24–34, 1968.

Early, L.E.: Current concepts: Diuretics. New England J Med 276:966–968, 1023–1025, 1967.

Eichna, L.W.: Circulatory congestion and heart failure. In: *American Heart Association Symposium on Congestive Heart Failure,* 2nd ed. American Heart Association, 1966.

Krasnow, N.: Biochemical and physiological response to isoproterenol in patients with left ventricular failure. Am J Cardiol 27:73–82, 1971.

Laragh, J.H.: Ethacrynic acid and furosemide. Am Heart J 75:564–566, 1968.

Laragh, J.H.: The proper use of newer diuretics. Ann Int Med 67:606, 1967.

Mahabir, R., & S.T. Laufer: Clinical evaluation of diuretics in congestive heart failure. Arch Int Med 124:1–7, 1969.

Mason, D.T., & E. Braunwald: Symposium on congestive heart failure. II. Digitalis: New facts about an old drug. Am J Cardiol 22:151–161, 1968.

Mitchell, J.H., Wallace, A.G., & N.S. Skinner, Jr.: Intrinsic effects of heart rate on left ventricular performance. Am J Physiol 205:41–48, 1963.

Pool, P.E., & G. Braunwald: Fundamental mechanisms in congestive heart failure. Am J Cardiol 22:7–15, 1968.

Porter, G.A., Bennett, W.H., & H.E. Griswold: Mode of action of ethacrynic acid in congestive heart failure. Arch Int Med 121:235–242, 1968.

Salmon, S.E., & R.W. Schrier: Edema formation and the use of diuretics. California Med 114:56–63, March 1971.

Sarnoff, S.J., & E. Berglund: Ventricular function. I. Starling's law of the heart studied by means of simultaneous right and left ventricular function curves in the dog. Circulation 9:706, 1954.

Spann, J.F., Jr., Mason, D.T., & R.F. Zelis: Recent advances in the understanding of congestive heart failure. Mod Concepts Cardiovas Dis 39:73–78, 79–84, 1970.

Stampfer, M., & others: Hemodynamic effects of diuresis at rest and during intense upright exercise in patients with impaired cardiac function. Circulation 37:900–912, 1968.

Walker, W.G.: Indications and contraindications for diuretic therapy. Ann New York Acad Sc 139:481–496, 1966.

SPECIAL PROBLEMS IN THE MANAGEMENT OF CONGESTIVE HEART FAILURE

Acute Pulmonary Edema

Acute pulmonary edema is a grave emergency. Treatment may vary depending upon the cause and severity. For example, in a mild attack, morphine and rest in bed alone may suffice; in an attack due to atrial fibrillation with rapid ventricular rate, lanatoside C or digoxin given intravenously may be required.

The patient should be elevated to the semi-Fowler position or placed in a chair; this decreases the venous return to the heart. Morphine sulfate, 5–10 mg IV or IM, relieves anxiety, depresses pulmonary reflexes, and induces sleep. Relief from forceful respiration decreases the negative intrathoracic pressure and the venous return to the heart.

Oxygen should be administered in high concentrations by mask or (for children) by hood or tent. Moderate concentrations (40–60%) can be achieved with an oxygen tent or nasal catheter. Oxygen relieves hypoxia and dyspnea and decreases pulmonary capillary permeability.

Positive-pressure breathing for short periods may be of great value in improving ventilation. Antifoaming agents to lower the surface tension of the bronchial secretions may be helpful.

Soft rubber tourniquets or blood pressure cuffs, applied with sufficient pressure to obstruct venous but not arterial flow and rotated every 15 minutes, will effectively reduce the venous return to the heart. The tourniquets should be removed gradually as the attack subsides. About 700 ml of blood may be trapped in the extremities by this method. Venesection (300–700 ml) is the most direct way of reducing the venous return to the heart and may strikingly increase cardiac output and decrease right atrial and peripheral venous pressure in low-output cardiac failure. It is contraindicated if anemia is present.

Ethacrynic acid (Edecrin®), 25–100 mg orally or 25–50 mg IV, or furosemide (Lasix®; see above), may be useful because of its potent and prompt diuretic action.

Rapid digitalization is of great value. Extreme care should be taken in giving digitalis intravenously to a previously digitalized patient.

Aminophylline, 0.25–0.5 gm slowly IV, is often helpful. It increases cardiac output, renal blood flow, glomerular filtration rate, and urine output of water and sodium. Rectal aminophylline suppositories, 0.25–0.5 gm, are often helpful and are more convenient for the patient.

In the acute recurrent pulmonary edema of hypertensive heart disease and in the presence of severe hypertension, reserpine, 1–2.5 mg IM every 8–12 hours (in addition to other measures outlined for acute hypertensive emergencies on p 176), may be helpful. Care must be taken not to produce hypotension.

Refractory Cardiac Failure

When the treatment measures outlined above do not result in clinical improvement, re-evaluate the total situation with particular attention to the following questions:

(1) Has bed rest been adequate? Is the patient receiving more sodium than ordered? Have treatment measures been carefully and properly administered? A review of the patient's activities, diet, and medications is essential.

(2) Are unrecognized recurrent pulmonary infarction, anemia, masked hyperthyroidism, vitamin deficiency, bacterial endocarditis, abrupt worsening or production of valvular insufficiencies, silent myocardial infarction, or arrhythmias present?

(3) Have complications such as acute rheumatic myocarditis or subacute bacterial endocarditis been superimposed upon a rheumatic heart?

(4) Are there electrolyte abnormalities which may have resulted from diet or diuretics? Electrolyte disturbances may lead to mercurial resistance, produce a low-sodium syndrome, or, in the case of a low potassium, enhance digitalis intoxication.

Management of Convalescence

Provide adequate rest and exercise within tolerance. Careful attention should be paid to the treatment of noncardiac causes of cardiac failure and to the avoidance of precipitating factors.

A. Digitalization: Once digitalis is started it is usually necessary to continue it for life.

B. Low-Sodium Diet: Allow 1.5 gm sodium chloride (600 mg of sodium) per day. It is advisable to check the patient's serum sodium or urinary sodium frequently to be certain that sodium deficiency is not occurring. An inadequate sodium intake in the presence of severe renal impairment can precipitate fatal renal failure. If thiazide compounds are used it is wise to allow the ambulatory patient at least 2 gm of sodium a day in his diet.

A high-sodium diet is particularly apt to maintain cardiac failure if the patient concurrently is up and about, stimulating aldosterone secretion. Dietary review often reveals that the patient is not restricting his sodium adequately.

C. Diuretics: The adequately digitalized patient on a sodium-restricted diet may still accumulate edema fluid. Diuretic drugs should be added to his regimen in the amounts necessary to prevent this accumulation.

The thiazide diuretics, because of the greater convenience of oral administration, are most widely used. Any one of the agents listed in Table 7–10 can be given several times each week or even daily. Because potassium depletion is a hazard in the use of the thiazide diuretics, potassium must be added, either as potassium chloride, 1 gm 3 times daily, or by the use of fruit juices, fruits (bananas), and vegetables.

Electrolyte Disturbances in Cardiac Failure

During treatment of cardiac failure, 3 types of electrolyte disturbance may be seen.

A. Hypochloremic Alkalosis: This is due to chloride excretion out of proportion to sodium loss following diuresis, producing a low serum chloride and a high serum bicarbonate. Serum sodium and potassium levels may be normal or low. Symptoms of dehydration may be present: dry mucous membranes and loss of tissue turgor and a latent or manifest tetany.

Treatment is with ammonium chloride, 4–6 gm/day for 3–4 days, repeated after an interval of 3–4 days. This must be done with *caution* if there is associated severe liver disease. Potassium salts may be given if a potassium deficit exists (see below). If tetany is present, calcium salts must be given concurrently.

Low serum sodium may be dilutional and may occur in association with hypokalemic alkalosis; restriction of fluids and administration of potassium salts such as potassium chloride may be helpful. Hypokalemic and hypochloremic alkalosis may coexist.

B. Low-Sodium Syndrome: In the absence of edema, the onset of weakness, oliguria, sweating, and azotemia heralds the "low-salt syndrome." Hot weather, fever, and vomiting are additional predisposing factors. Low serum sodium may be present without alkalosis or acidosis, or it may be complicated by dehydration and acidosis. It may follow severe sodium restriction accompanied by diuresis.

In mild cases treatment consists merely of increasing the sodium intake. For severe cases, treat with intravenous hypertonic saline.

The total body sodium is usually increased when edema is present in spite of hyponatremia. In such cases sodium should not be administered, but water should be restricted to counteract the dilutional hyponatremia.

C. Hypokalemia: This may result from excessive potassium excretion due to the administration of mercurial, thiazide, or the newer potent diuretics, or acetazolamide (Diamox®), or following the administration of acid or ammonia resins to patients receiving a low-sodium diet. Hypokalemia may induce digitalis intoxication.

Treatment consists of giving potassium chloride, 3–6 gm daily orally, provided renal function is adequate. *Caution:* Parenteral potassium salts should not be given in the presence of acidosis or renal failure.

High-Output Failure

The term "high-output failure" means that, in the presence of fully developed congestive heart failure, the cardiac output is greater than normal but still insufficient for the needs of the body. It occurs characteristically when pre-existing heart disease is complicated by thyrotoxicosis, severe anemia (hemoglobin < 8 gm/100 ml), pregnancy, arteriovenous fistula, beriberi, and occasionally by Paget's disease of bone, or chronic pulmonary disease or liver disease with arterial oxygen unsaturation.

The clinical picture of congestive heart failure is present except for more marked tachycardia, overactive heart, bounding pulses, and warm hands and skin generally. The circulation time may be short or normal in the face of greatly elevated venous pressure. This combination is never found in uncomplicated heart failure except when fever or one of the disorders listed above is present.

Treatment is directed at the failure as well as at the associated illness, eg, anemia, thyrotoxicosis.

Friedberg, C.K.: Prevention of heart failure. Am J Cardiol 22:190–194, 1968.

Goldberg, L.I.: Use of sympathomimetic amines in heart failure. Am J Cardiol 22:177–182, 1968.

Haber, E.: Current techniques for serum or plasma digitalis assay, and their potential clinical application. Am J Med Sc 259:301, 1970.

Hultgren, H.N., & M.D. Flamm: Pulmonary edema. Mod Concepts Cardiovas Dis 38:1–6, 1969.

Leonard, J.J., & W.J. deGroot: The thyroid state and the cardiovascular system. Mod Concepts Cardiovas Dis 38:23–28, 1969.

Salmon, S.E., & R.W. Schrier: Congestive heart failure after acute myocardial infarction. California Med 114:23–28, Feb 1971.

Scheinman, M., Brown, M., & E. Rapaport: Hemodynamic effects of ethacrynic acid in patients with refractory acute left ventricular failure. Am J Med 50:291, 1971.

Smith, T.W.: Measurement of serum digitalis glucosides, clinical applications. Circulation 43:179–181, 1971.

See also references for Congestive Heart Failure.

DISEASES OF THE PERICARDIUM

ACUTE PERICARDITIS

Essentials of Diagnosis

- Pleuritic or persisting substernal or precordial pain referred to the left neck, shoulder, or back.
- Pericardial friction rub.
- ECG: Early, concordant ST elevation; late, general symmetric T inversion without Q waves or reciprocal changes except in aVR.

General Considerations

In approximate order of frequency, **infectious pericarditis** is caused by viruses, *Mycobacterium tuberculosis,* pyogenic bacteria associated with bacteremia or septicemia (pneumococcus, hemolytic streptococcus, *Staphylococcus aureus,* meningococcus, gonococcus), and brucella. **Inflammatory pericarditis** includes all diseases associated with acute vasculitis, most commonly disseminated lupus erythematosus, acute rheumatic fever, and serum sickness. A miscellaneous group includes pericarditis which occurs after pericardiectomy, myocardial infarction, or trauma; pericarditis associated with uremia, metastatic tumors, and the lymphomas; and hemorrhagic pericarditis due to dissecting aneurysm.

Acute pericarditis is traditionally classified as fibrinous pericarditis with effusion, in which the pericardial cavity contains significant amounts of transudate, blood, exudate, or pus. Varying degrees of myocarditis accompany pericarditis and are responsible for the ECG changes in ST–T contours.

Clinical Findings

A. Symptoms and Signs: Acute viral pericarditis is more common in men 20–50 years of age and frequently follows a "viral" respiratory infection. The onset of pain is usually rapid or sudden; pain is precordial or substernal, pleuritic or steady (or both), and radiates to the left neck, shoulder, back, or epigastrium. It is worse in the supine position and may be accentuated by swallowing. Tachycardia and a pericardial (often pleuropericardial) friction rub are present.

Fever is 37.8–39.4° C (100–103° F) or higher in infectious pericarditis, and is determined by the febrile pattern of the underlying disease in the other varieties.

B. Laboratory Findings: Leukocytosis of 10–20 thousand is always present in acute viral pericarditis; leukopenia may be noted in pericarditis associated with disseminated lupus erythematosus. LE cells should be sought in isolated acute pericarditis.

C. X-Ray Findings: Chest x-rays may show cardiac dilatation, associated pneumonitis, and pleural effusion.

D. ECG Findings: Initially, ECG changes consist only of ST–T segment elevation in all leads, with preservation of normal upward concavity. Return to the baseline in a few days is followed by T wave inversion. Reciprocal changes are absent except in aVR, and Q waves do not appear.

Differential Diagnosis

A. Acute Myocardial Infarction: Acute viral pericarditis usually follows a respiratory infection, occurs in the age group from 20–50 years, and characteristically presents with pleuritic pain. Fever, friction rub, leukocytosis, and an elevated sedimentation rate are found at the onset rather than 24–72 hours later. ECG changes are usually distinctive. SGOT or LDH are only rarely elevated even in severe pericarditis.

B. Acute Pleurisy: Pericardial friction rub is differentiated from pleural friction rub by its persistence when the breath is held, although there may also be a pleuro-pericardial friction sound which is related to respiration. ECG changes are diagnostic of pericarditis in the absence of a rub.

C. Confusion of Rub With Murmurs: Pericardial friction rubs are differentiated by their changing character, lack of association with the usual areas of murmurs, high-pitched or "scratchy" quality, and asynchrony with the heart sounds.

Complications

Pericardial effusion is the only noteworthy complication. Cardiac dilatation accompanying acute viral pericarditis rarely produces heart failure but may cause arrhythmias.

Treatment

Treat the underlying condition and give analgesics as necessary for relief of pain. Salicylates and corticotropin (ACTH) or the corticosteroids are useful in rheumatic pericarditis.

Prognosis

The prognosis of viral pericarditis is usually excellent; recovery occurs in 2 weeks to 3 months; recurrences are uncommon; and residual pericardial thickening or persistent ECG abnormalities are rare. The promptness and adequacy of antibiotic and surgical treatment determine the outcome in tuberculous and purulent pericarditis. Other manifestations of disseminated lupus erythematosus may become apparent after an attack of presumed "viral" pericarditis. In the miscellaneous group, the basic disorder determines the prognosis.

Baily, G.L., & others: Uremic pericarditis: Clinical features and management. Circulation 38:582–592, 1968.
Schrire, V.: Pericarditis (with particular reference to tuberculous pericarditis). Australasian Ann Med 16:41–51, 1967.

PERICARDITIS WITH EFFUSION

Essentials of Diagnosis

- Aspiration of fluid from the pericardial sac is the only infallible diagnostic procedure in pericarditis with effusion.
- Chest pain, dyspnea, weakness, distended neck veins, a large, quiet heart, and paradoxic pulse.

General Considerations

The most common causes of pericardial effusion are uremia, tuberculosis, malignancy, purulent pericarditis, and inflammatory diseases. Rare types include chylous and "chronic idiopathic" pericarditis. Myxedema may produce significant effusion.

The speed of accumulation determines the physiologic importance of the effusion. Massive pericardial effusions, if they accumulate slowly, may produce no symptoms. However, sudden hemorrhage into the pericardium or sudden accumulation of relatively small effusions may raise the intrapericardial pressure to the point of cardiac tamponade, in which the fluid limits venous inflow and diastolic filling of the heart. In tamponade the cardiac output falls, and tachycardia and elevation of venous pressure appear as compensatory mechanisms. Shock and death may result if tamponade is not relieved.

Clinical Findings

A. Symptoms and Signs: Pain is often absent but may be present as in acute pericarditis and as a dull, diffuse, oppressive precordial or substernal distress. Dyspnea and cough cause the patient to sit up and lean forward for relief. Dysphagia is prominent. Fever and other symptoms depend upon the primary disease (eg, septicemia, empyema, malignancy).

The area of "cardiac" dullness is enlarged and the apex beat is not palpable or is well within the lateral border of dullness. Friction rub may persist despite a large effusion. In tamponade, distended neck veins, paradoxic pulse, and narrow pulse pressure are present. Liver enlargement, ascites, and leg edema depend upon the degree and duration of tamponade. Acute tamponade produces the clinical picture of shock.

B. Laboratory Findings: The etiology of acute effusion is determined by bacteriologic and cytologic study of aspirated fluid; of chronic effusion, by pericardial biopsy. Leukocytosis and a rapid sedimentation rate are present when the effusion is infectious or inflammatory. The arm-to-tongue circulation time is normal in the presence of large effusion without tamponade; this is often a clue to the correct interpretation of a "large heart shadow" on chest x-ray. In myxedema, pericardial effusion and prolongation of the circulation time are present without tamponade.

C. X-Ray Findings: A rapidly enlarging "cardiac" silhouette with sharply defined margins, an acute right cardiophrenic angle, clear lung fields, and pleural effusion are common. Cardiac pulsations are feeble or absent. Intravenous CO_2 administration allows estimation of the distance between the atrial cavity and the pericardial sac by x-ray, as does also the position of a catheter in the right atrium. Angiocardiography is usually helpful in establishing the diagnosis of pericardial effusion.

D. ECG Findings: T waves are low, flat, diphasic, or inverted in all leads; QRS voltage is uniformly low.

Differential Diagnosis

Cardiac dilatation with congestive heart failure may be impossible to differentiate from pericarditis with effusion if pleural effusion is also present. However, rapid changes in heart size as seen by x-ray, clear lung fields with normal hilar vessels, definite paradoxic pulse, and absent cardiac pulsations on fluoroscopy are rare in congestive failure. In a patient with "heart failure," the absence of significant murmurs, arrhythmia, and hypertension should suggest pericarditis with effusion.

Complications

Cardiac tamponade is a serious complication. Rapidly developing pericardial effusions or hemorrhage into the pericardial sac may so impede venous return and cardiac filling that cardiac output falls and irreversible shock occurs. Anticoagulant therapy creates a serious hazard of hemorrhage.

Purulent pericarditis is usually secondary to other infection elsewhere but is at times caused by contamination of a previous pericardial tap.

Treatment

A. Emergency Treatment (Paracentesis): The indications for pericardial paracentesis are the symptoms and signs of cardiac tamponade. As the pericardial fluid increases in amount, and particularly when it increases rapidly, the venous pressure may rise toward its limit of 22–24 cm water and the cardiac output may progressively fall. When this occurs, the patient becomes weak, pale, and dyspneic, and the pulse pressure becomes very narrow and the pulse rapid and thready, ie, the patient goes into shock. Under these circumstances removal of the pericardial fluid may be lifesaving; the fluid should be removed slowly to avoid cardiac dilatation or sudden reflex changes in rate and rhythm.

1. Sites of puncture–(*Caution:* Avoid puncture of the ventricular muscle.) Puncture may be made at the left 5th or 6th interspace about 1 cm within the area of cardiac dullness or 1–2 cm inside the left heart border as localized by x-ray (roughly 7–8 cm) outside the left sternal line. The needle is pushed slowly inward and slightly upward. If effusion is present, one should find fluid within 3–5 cm–at times 7–8 cm. Puncture may also be made in the epigastric area between the xiphoid process and the left sternal margin. Insert the needle upward at an angle of about 30°, pointed toward the midline. The pericardium is reached at about 3–4 cm.

2. Equipment–No. 16 or 18 needle with short bevel and fitting stylet; No. 26 or 27 needle to infiltrate the skin with procaine; and a 20–30 ml syringe to remove fluid. The syringe should be connected to the needle with a 4-inch piece of rubber tubing to prevent excessive movement of the needle. A sterile ground wire is connected between the needle and the V lead of a well grounded ECG machine in order to indicate when the myocardium is entered. Proper grounding of the patient and the ECG is essential to prevent accidental induction of ventricular fibrillation.

3. Technic–Clean and sterilize skin over the area to be punctured. Drape the surrounding area with sterile towels. Infiltrate the skin with 1–2% procaine solution. Insert the needle (detached from the syringe and without a stylet) slowly into the skin, following the directions according to the site selected. When the fluid is encountered it must be withdrawn slowly. When the needle encounters the epicardium, the monitoring ECG will show a sudden upward shift of the ST segment, indicating the limit to which the needle may be advanced. This technic greatly decreases the likelihood of cardiac puncture. A small polyethylene catheter can be introduced through the needle for removal of large amounts of fluid.

After the needle is removed, a simple dressing over the needle puncture is adequate.

B. Specific Measures:

1. Tuberculous pericarditis–The current treatment is to treat the systemic infection with bed rest, attention to nutrition and other general factors, and intensive antituberculosis chemotherapy. If fever and signs of pericardial effusion do not rapidly subside and are still obvious in 1 month, surgical decortication of the pericardium should be considered in order to prevent chronic constrictive pericarditis. Good judgment is required to determine when the disease is progressing despite medical treatment and when signs of constriction are appearing.

2. Rheumatic pericarditis with effusion–Treat as for rheumatic fever. The salicylates may help in causing fluid resorption. Paracentesis is usually unnecessary but should be performed if tamponade occurs.

3. Hydropericardium due to heart failure–Treatment of the congestive failure is usually sufficient.

4. Hemopericardium due to rupture of adjacent structure (usually post-traumatic)–If fluid accumulation is excessive, remove fluid **at once.**

5. Infection–Treat infection with appropriate chemotherapeutic agents and perform paracentesis as needed to relieve pressure. When fluid is being removed instill 50,000–150,000 units of penicillin or the equivalent topical amount of streptomycin or other indicated antibiotic into the pericardial sac, and repeat whenever a tap is performed. Chemotherapeutic agents should be continued as long as purulent effusion is present. If fluid is encapsulated or the patient is not responding to therapy, surgical drainage via pericardiotomy may be necessary.

6. Uremic pericarditis often clears clinically after beginning therapy with chronic dialysis. Severe tamponade may require pericardiectomy.

Prognosis

Tuberculous pericarditis causes death in the majority of untreated cases and results in chronic constrictive pericarditis in many that survive. The mortality rate is very low with early and adequate treatment; the long-term effect on the incidence of constrictive pericarditis is not known.

Acute benign pericarditis is rarely fatal.

Rheumatic pericarditis, if severe and protracted, is associated with myocarditis, and this determines the immediate prognosis. Residual pericardial disease of clinical significance does not occur.

Purulent pericarditis, since it is usually associated with a blood stream infection or infection elsewhere, is usually fatal if not treated; however, it responds satisfactorily to antibiotics.

Gotsman, M.S., & V. Schrire: A pericardiocentesis electrode needle. Brit Heart J 28:566–569, 1966.

Hollenberg, M., & J. Daugherty: Lymph flow and ^{131}I albumin reabsorption from pericardial effusion in man. Am J Cardiol 24:514–522, 1969.

Shabetai, R., & others: Hemodynamics, cardiac tamponade and constrictive pericarditis: Symposium on pericardial disease. Am J Cardiol 26:445–488, 1970.

CHRONIC CONSTRICTIVE PERICARDITIS

Essentials of Diagnosis

- Markedly elevated venous pressure.
- Slight to moderate cardiac enlargement and quiet heart action.
- Paradoxic pulse.
- Ascites out of proportion to ankle edema.

General Considerations

Encasement of the myocardium by an adherent, dense fibrous pericardium may be asymptomatic or may prevent ventricular expansion during diastole. If this happens the stroke volume is low and fixed and cardiac output can be increased only by tachycardia. Venous pressure rises as in congestive heart failure, and this, together with renal retention of sodium and water, produces the peripheral signs of right heart failure.

Clinical Findings

A. Symptoms and Signs: The principal symptoms are slowly progressive dyspnea, fatigue, and weakness on exertion, abdominal distention, and leg edema. Examination shows markedly distended neck veins with weak or absent systolic pulsations but prominent diastolic retraction, a moderately enlarged heart with a quiet precordium in the presence of tachycardia, faint heart sounds, a palpable and audible pericardial knock in early diastole, a low pulse pressure with a high diastolic level, paradoxic pulse, enlarged liver, ascites, and edema of both legs and the scrotum. Atrial fibrillation is frequently present.

B. Laboratory Findings: The arm-to-tongue circulation time is prolonged. Rarely, tuberculous infection of the lungs or other organ is noted.

C. X-Ray and Fluoroscopic Findings: The "heart" is usually moderately enlarged. Its shape is not consistent with valvular or hypertensive heart disease. Pulsations are weak or absent. Lung fields are clear. Pericardial calcification is very common but is not diagnostic of constrictive pericarditis. Diagnostic ultrasound may be of assistance.

D. ECG Findings: T waves are flat or inverted; low voltage of QRS complexes is variable. Atrial fibrillation is common.

Differential Diagnosis

Marked venous engorgement in the neck without systolic pulsation, slight to moderate cardiac enlargement, absence of significant murmurs or hypertension, paradoxic pulse, and ECG changes distinguish chronic constrictive pericarditis from tricuspid stenosis, congestive heart failure from any cause, especially cardiomyopathy, cirrhosis of the liver, mediastinal tumor, nephrosis, and obstruction of the vena cava.

Complications

In cases of tuberculous origin, a miliary spread or acute flare-up of the intrapericardial infection may occur.

Thrombophlebitis of the leg veins may occur secondary to elevated venous pressure, venous stasis, and inactivity.

Treatment

Give a low-sodium diet and diuretics as in cardiac failure to combat ascites and congestive failure. Digitalis is usually of little value unless the patient has atrial fibrillation.

Surgical removal of the constricting pericardium can frequently restore a patient to normal health. If congestive phenomena are chronic or the pericarditis is progressive, surgical intervention is the only method offering possible cure. In a large London hospital, the recent surgical mortality was 4%, and 85% of patients were greatly benefited by the procedure.

Prognosis

Constrictive pericarditis known to be due to tuberculosis is usually fatal without antituberculosis drugs and surgery. Most patients with constrictive pericarditis due to any cause have increasing disability because of ascites and edema and die of mechanical "heart failure." A few patients show no progression of symptoms or signs for years. Spontaneous regression is rare.

Conti, C.R., & G.C. Friesinger: Chronic constrictive pericarditis: Clinical and laboratory findings in 11 cases. Johns Hopkins Med J 120:262–273, 1967.

Dayem, M.K.A., & others: Investigation and treatment of constrictive pericarditis. Thorax 22:242–252, 1967.

Fitzpatrick, D.P., & others: Restoration of normal intracardiac pressures after extensive pericardiectomy for constrictive pericarditis. Circulation 25:484–492, 1962.

Golinko, R.J., & others: The mechanism of pulsus paradoxicus during acute pericardial tamponade. J Clin Invest 42:249, 1963.

Kloster, F.E., & others: Hemodynamic studies following pericardiectomy for constrictive pericarditis. Circulation 32:415, 1965.

Lindell, S.E., & others: Haemodynamic changes in chronic constrictive pericarditis during exercise and histamine infusion. Brit Heart J 25:35, 1963.

Somerville, W.: Constrictive pericarditis, with special reference to the change in natural history brought about by surgical intervention. Circulation 38 (Suppl 5):102–111, 1968.

DISEASES OF THE MYOCARDIUM

CHRONIC OR SUBACUTE PULMONARY HEART DISEASE
(Chronic or Subacute Cor Pulmonale)

Essentials of Diagnosis

- Symptoms and signs of chronic bronchitis and pulmonary emphysema.
- No significant murmurs or hypertension.
- ECG: tall peaked P waves and right axis deviation.
- Chest x-ray: enlarged right ventricle, pulmonary conus and artery.

General Considerations

Cor pulmonale refers to the right ventricular hypertrophy and eventual failure resulting from pulmonary parenchymal or vascular disease. It may be acute, subacute, or, most commonly, chronic, and its clinical features depend both upon the primary disease and its effects on the heart.

Chronic cor pulmonale is most commonly caused by chronic obstructive pulmonary emphysema, often referred to as "chronic asthmatic bronchitis." Less common or rare causes include pneumoconiosis, pulmonary fibrosis, kyphoscoliosis, primary pulmonary hypertension, repeated episodes of subclinical pulmonary embolization, and obliterative pulmonary capillary infiltration from metastatic carcinoma. Emphysema and associated fibrosis result in obliteration of capillaries and disturbance of pulmonary function with resultant hypoxia. Compensatory polycythemia and increased cardiac output also appear. The combined effect of these changes is increased pulmonary artery pressure, which in turn leads to right ventricular hypertrophy and eventual failure of the "high-output" variety.

Clinical Findings

A. Symptoms and Signs: The dominant symptoms of compensated cor pulmonale are respiratory in origin: chronic productive cough, exertional dyspnea, wheezing respirations, undue fatigability, and weakness. When the pulmonary disease has advanced sufficiently to cause right ventricular failure, these symptoms are intensified. In addition, dependent edema, right upper quadrant pain, and digestive disturbances may appear. Signs include cyanosis, clubbing, distended neck veins, pulmonary emphysema, prominent lower sternal or epigastric pulsations, an enlarged tender liver, and dependent edema. The heart size cannot be determined because of emphysema, but there is no evidence of valvular disease. Pulses are full and the extremities warm unless the patient is terminal or in shock.

B. Laboratory Findings: Polycythemia is usually present in cor pulmonale secondary to emphysema. The arterial oxygen saturation is below 85%; P_{CO_2} is often elevated. Venous pressure is significantly elevated in right ventricular failure, but the circulation time may be normal or only slightly prolonged.

C. ECG Findings: The ECG shows right axis deviation, peaked P waves. Deep S waves are present in lead V_6. Left axis deviation may occur in patients with pulmonary emphysema. Frank right ventricular hypertrophy is uncommon except in "primary pulmonary hypertension," in which this is the rule.

D. X-Ray Findings: Chest x-ray discloses the presence or absence of parenchymal disease and a prominent or enlarged right ventricle, pulmonary conus, and artery.

Differential Diagnosis

In its early stages cor pulmonale can be diagnosed only on x-ray or ECG evidence. When frank congestive signs appear, differentiation from primary left ventricular failure is possible by considering the predominant history of respiratory complaints, the absence of orthopnea, the degree of cyanosis, bounding pulses, and warm extremities in the presence of edema. ECG demonstration of right axis deviation, normal or only moderately prolonged circulation time, and absence of demonstrable factors pointing to left failure are helpful.

Complications

Intercurrent respiratory infections increase dyspnea, cough, and cyanosis and may precipitate a dangerous degree of respiratory acidosis in advanced emphysema. Neurologic manifestations of CO_2 narcosis may appear: disorientation, somnolence, coma, and occasionally convulsions.

Treatment

A. Specific Measures: Give appropriate antibiotic therapy for the respiratory infection that so commonly precedes failure in this type of case. The patient may be afebrile.

B. General Measures:

1. Intermittent positive-pressure mask breathing, eg, with the Bennett, Emerson, Bird, or similar respirator, at pressure settings of +10 to +15 (inspiration) may be helpful. Patients who do not breathe spontaneously may be treated advantageously with the automatic Bird respirator; the other nonautomatic apparatuses may be operated manually. These devices provide a convenient, effective method of administering bronchial dilators, antifoaming agents, and aerosols (see chapter 7). None of the intermittent devices controlled by the patient lower the cardiac output.

2. In cor pulmonale, intermittent positive-pressure breathing, especially when combined with effective bronchial dilators, is probably the most effective therapeutic measure. The use of mechanical devices in acute respiratory distress may not be helpful and should perhaps be postponed until other measures have improved the situation.

3. CNS depressants, especially narcotics, barbiturates, and hypnotics, are strongly **contraindicated** in the treatment of cardiac failure secondary to primary pulmonary disease (cor pulmonale) due to their marked depressant action on the respiratory centers.

4. Treat heart failure in the usual way with bed rest, restriction of sodium, diuretics, and digitalis. Digitalis may not be effective if cardiac output is high.

5. Give acetazolamide (Diamox®), 250 mg daily, after adequate ventilation has been restored, ie, when CO_2 elimination is effective.

Prognosis

Compensated cor pulmonale has the same outlook as the underlying pulmonary disease. Once congestive signs appear, the average life expectancy is 2–5 years, but survival is significantly longer when uncomplicated emphysema is the cause. Left ventricular failure secondary to coronary artery disease, hypertension, or aortic valve lesions may develop and shorten expectancy accordingly.

Comroe, J.H., Jr., & others: *The Lung: Clinical Physiology and Pulmonary Function Tests,* 2nd ed. Year Book, 1962.

Dexter, L.: Thromboemboli as a cause of cor pulmonale. Bull New York Acad Med 41:981–993, 1965.

Emirgil, C., & others: Routine pulmonary function studies as a key to the status of the lesser circulation in chronic obstructive pulmonary disease. Am J Med 50:191, 1971.

Gilbert, R., Keighley, J., & J.H. Auchincloss: Mechanisms of chronic carbon dioxide retention in patients with obstructive pulmonary disease. Am J Med 38:217, 1965.

Harvey, R.M., Enson, Y., & M.I. Ferrer: A reconsideration of the origins of pulmonary hypertension. Chest 59:82–94, 1971.

Lyons, H.A., Becker, W.H., & G.E. Torres: The management of severe pulmonary emphysema. Am J Med 36:62, 1964.

Oakley, C.M., & J.F. Goodwin: Current clinical aspects of cor pulmonale. Am J Cardiol 20:842–852, 1967.

Sleeper, J.C., Orgain, E.S., & H.D. McIntosh: Primary pulmonary hypertension. Review of clinical features and pathologic physiology with a report of pulmonary hemodynamics derived from repeated catheterization. Circulation 26:1358–1369, 1962.

SYPHILITIC CARDIOVASCULAR DISEASE

Essentials of Diagnosis

- Linear calcification or localized dilatation of the ascending aorta on x-ray.
- Aortic valvular insufficiency without stenosis or mitral valve disease.
- Evidence of syphilitic etiology: history of infection, positive STS, or presence of other forms of late syphilis.

General Considerations

Syphilitic "heart disease" may consist of aortic valvular insufficiency (most common), aortic dilatation or aneurysm, or narrowing of the coronary ostia. It comprises less than 5% of all heart disease in population groups which have ready access to effective treatment of syphilis. It is more common in men (3:1) and is usually diagnosed between the ages of 35 and 55 (10–20 years after the primary infection). STS are positive in about 85% of untreated cases. The ascending aorta, arch, and descending aorta are most commonly affected; the abdominal aorta is rarely involved. Aortic valve insufficiency occurs in about 10% of cases of untreated syphilitic aortitis. One or both of the coronary ostia may be partially occluded.

Clinical Findings

A. Aortitis: There are no symptoms, and physical signs are absent unless dilatation has occurred. In a man under the age of 40 without hypertension or demonstrable arteriosclerosis, a ringing or accentuated second aortic sound with or without a soft aortic systolic murmur is "suggestive" of syphilitic aortitis. Fluoroscopic evidence of increased width and pulsation of the ascending aorta, best seen in the left anterior oblique view, in the absence of elongation, is also suggestive. Heavy linear calcification limited to the root of the aorta and arch is almost diagnostic.

B. Aortic Insufficiency: Clinical, x-ray, and ECG manifestations are as for rheumatic aortic insufficiency. Ten percent of cases are associated with saccular aneurysm. Aortic insufficiency may produce no symptoms for surprisingly long periods; once heart failure develops, however, it soon becomes refractory to treatment and death usually occurs within 2–5 years.

C. Aortic Aneurysm: Symptoms and signs are dependent upon the site and size of the aneurysm. Aneurysm of the ascending aorta is characterized by visible pulsation or dullness of the manubrium and in the first to third interspaces parasternally; lowered blood pressure in the right arm; and an aortic systolic murmur and thrill without peripheral signs of aortic stenosis. Aneurysm of the aortic arch is characterized by cough, dyspnea, and recurrent pulmonary infections (compression of trachea or right main stem bronchus); hoarseness (compression of recurrent laryngeal nerve); edema of the face and neck, distended neck veins, and prominent veins over upper chest (compression of superior vena cava); and dysphagia (compression of the esophagus). Aneurysm of the descending aorta is usually asymptomatic; when it is large it may erode the ribs or spine, producing pain which is worse in recumbency and visible or palpable pulsations medial to the left scapula.

X-ray findings consist of saccular or sharply defined fusiform bulging of the thoracic aorta with increased pulsation. Clot formation or periaortic fibrosis may dampen the pulsations and simulate a solid tumor. Transaxillary or retrograde femoral artery injections of radiopaque contrast media differentiate the 2 by demonstrating continuity of the aorta with the lumen of the aneurysm.

D. Narrowing of the Coronary Artery Ostia: Angina pectoris is identical to that seen in coronary heart disease. Its syphilitic origin can only be inferred in the presence of one of the other manifestations of syphilitic aortitis.

Differential Diagnosis

The clinical picture can mimic rheumatic and arteriosclerotic heart disease and rheumatoid arthritis. Syphilitic aneurysms are indistinguishable clinically from those caused by arteriosclerosis.

Treatment

A. Specific Measures: Treat syphilis as outlined in Chapter 22. Several subsequent courses of penicillin are advised by some authorities at intervals of 6 months or 1 year, especially if the STS remains positive.

B. General Measures: Bed rest may be desirable during treatment with penicillin to prevent Herxheimer's reaction.

C. Surgical Measures: Surgical repair of the aneurysm has been attempted but is hazardous. Successful surgical endarterectomy for coronary ostia stenosis has been accomplished. Surgical correction of aortic insufficiency may be necessary.

Complications

A. Aortic Insufficiency: Left ventricular hypertrophy, which may progress to failure.

B. Aortic Aneurysm: Recurrent pulmonary infection, bronchiectasis, atelectasis, bronchial hemorrhage, and rupture or dissection of the aneurysm.

Prognosis

A. Aortitis: Ten to 20% of patients develop aortic insufficiency and other manifestations of syphilitic cardiovascular disease; in the remainder, life expectancy is not affected.

B. Aortic Insufficiency: If penicillin is given when the signs of aortic insufficiency are purely ausculta-

tory, the progress of the lesion may be slowed or even arrested; this significantly improves the prognosis for survival.

C. Aortic Aneurysm: Once aneurysms have reached sufficient size to produce symptoms by compression of adjacent structures, life expectancy is measured in months. Longer survival is possible when the aneurysm is small and effective therapy for syphilis has been given. Death is usually due to rupture of the aneurysm.

D. Narrowing of the Coronary Artery Ostia: This condition tends to aggravate the heart failure due to syphilitic aortic insufficiency and predisposes to sudden death. Surgical correction has been successfully accomplished.

Beck, W.: Syphilitic obstruction of coronary ostia successfully treated by endarterectomy. Brit Heart J 27:911, 1965.

ACUTE & CHRONIC MYOCARDITIS & ENDOMYOCARDIAL DISEASES (Cardiomyopathies)

Essentials of Diagnosis

- Persistent tachycardia, low systolic blood pressure, diminished first heart sound, changing systolic murmurs, gallop rhythm, pulsus alternans, prominent "right heart" failure.
- Absence of recognizable common etiology of heart failure.
- ECG: atrioventricular or intraventricular conduction defect, abnormal T waves, low voltage QRS; no characteristic pattern.

General Considerations

Acute myocarditis is a focal or diffuse inflammation of the myocardium occurring during or after many viral, bacterial, rickettsial, spirochetal, fungal, and parasitic diseases. Mild forms are very common and are recognizable only by serial ECG changes. Severe myocarditis producing signs and symptoms occurs most commonly in acute rheumatic fever, diphtheria, scrub typhus, and Chagas' disease (*Trypanosoma cruzi* infection). Bacteremia, viral pneumonia and encephalitis, and trichinosis may be associated with myocarditis of varying severity.

Endomyocardial disease includes a wide variety of noninfectious myocardial diseases whose clinical manifestations are similar to those of myocarditis except that peripheral embolization and refractory heart failure are more common and the process is more chronic. A partial list of these includes alcoholic cardiomyopathy, Fiedler's isolated myocarditis, isolated hypertrophy of the septum, subaortic muscular stenosis of the left ventricle, subendocardial fibroelastosis, idiopathic cardiac hypertrophy (congenital and adult), familial cardiomegaly, idiopathic myocardial failure in pregnancy, collagen diseases (scleroderma, disseminated lupus erythematosus, polyarteritis nodosa), serum sickness, and amyloidosis.

Clinical Findings

A. Symptoms and Signs: Mild forms of myocarditis are asymptomatic and are overshadowed by the underlying disease. Severe myocarditis may result in weakness, syncope, dizziness, dyspnea, nausea, vomiting, chest pain, and shock or sudden death. In endomyocardial diseases the course may be acute, subacute, or chronic, but the symptoms are similar. Fiedler's myocarditis, idiopathic cardiac hypertrophy, idiopathic heart failure of pregnancy, and other primary myocardial diseases are characterized by peripheral emboli and heart failure. Noncardiac manifestations of the basic disease may be noted, as in carcinoid syndrome, Friedreich's ataxia, and the collagen diseases.

In addition to those of the underlying disease (eg, hemochromatosis, scleroderma), signs include fever, tachycardia, cardiac enlargement, faint heart sounds, changing systolic murmurs, arrhythmias, variable congestive heart failure (predominantly right-sided), with hepatomegaly, gallop rhythm, pulsus alternans, and distended neck veins; and signs of cerebral or peripheral embolization. The obstructive cardiomyopathies may present as idiopathic left ventricular failure and may simulate aortic stenosis, chronic constrictive pericarditis, beriberi heart disease, etc.

B. ECG Findings: Partial to complete atrioventricular block and intraventricular conduction defects; diffusely flat to inverted T waves; and low voltage QRS. In mild myocarditis, only transient flattening or inversion of T waves may be noted.

Differential Diagnosis

Myocarditis and endomyocardial disorders vary so much in clinical signs that they are confused with thyrotoxicosis, bacterial endocarditis, "painless" coronary artery disease, rheumatic heart disease with faint or atypical murmurs, pericardial tamponade, and neoplastic disease of the heart. Sinus tachycardia and minor ECG changes are an insufficient basis for diagnosis.

Treatment

No specific therapy is available except in the obstructive cardiomyopathies of the left ventricle. Surgical excision of the subaortic stenosis or ventricular septectomy is now feasible under cardiopulmonary bypass. Corticosteroids are occasionally helpful in the collagen group of diseases. Anticoagulant therapy may be indicated for patients with embolization. The general principles of treatment of cardiac failure and anemia are to be followed as they apply in specific cases.

In the presence of cardiac failure, left ventricular cineangiography and coronary angiography are frequently necessary to exclude coronary heart disease with dyskinesia or aneurysm which are amenable to surgical excision.

Prognosis

A. Acute Myocarditis: The common forms rarely produce disability or death. The overall mortality rate in diphtheritic myocarditis is 25%; the death rate approaches 100% if shock or congestive heart failure occurs and is 50–75% with complete heart block. Mortality is similarly high in Chagas' disease. Myocarditis is the chief cause of death in scrub typhus. With the exception of rheumatic fever, there are no late sequelae after recovery.

B. Primary Myocardial Disease or Cardiomyopathy: This group of diseases, often of unknown cause, usually develops insidiously, although it may occasionally follow acute myocarditis. Various names have been given to the entity, eg, primary myocardial disease, primary cardiomyopathy, idiopathic cardiac hypertrophy. The left ventricle is usually dominantly involved, although in some cases the right ventricle as well as the septum may be involved. There is usually no obstructive disease, but in some varieties there may be obstruction of the left or right ventricular outflow tracts. The dividing line between primary cardiomyopathy and so-called obstructive idiopathic hypertrophic subaortic stenosis is not clear.

Patients with primary cardiomyopathy usually present with unexplained left ventricular hypertrophy or left ventricular failure which usually progresses over a period of months or a few years. Associated symptoms include embolic phenomena, cardiac arrhythmias, and clinical and hemodynamic evidence of either obstructive or restrictive left ventricular disease.

Among known causes of cardiomyopathy, alcoholic cardiomyopathy is perhaps the most common, although opinion differs about whether alcohol directly affects the myocardial cells (producing cardiomyopathy) or whether it operates via the mechanism of thiamine deficiency (beriberi heart). The former opinion is most widespread and is perhaps supported by the best evidence. Other generalized diseases often associated with cardiomyopathy are primary amyloidosis, scleroderma, sarcoidosis, and endocardial fibrosis in Africa. Postpartum myocarditis and heart failure are thought to be a variant of the cardiomyopathies, but the evidence is not clear. Glycogen storage disease and various neurologic disorders also may be associated with primary myocardial disease.

Primary cardiomyopathy is often diagnosed by eliminating all known causes and will probably continue to be so until its cause becomes known.

Abelmann, W.H.: Myocarditis. New England J Med 275:832–834, 1966.

Adelman, A.G., & others: Long-term propranolol therapy in muscular subaortic stenosis. Brit Heart J 32:804–812, 1970.

Goodwin, J.F.: Disorders of the outflow tract of the left ventricle. Brit MJ 2:461–467, 1967.

Gould, L., & others: Nonobstructive primary myocardial disease: Hemodynamic studies in fourteen cases. Am J Cardiol 22:523–531, 1968.

Hamm, B.R.I., & others: Primary myocardial disease: Clinical, hemodynamic, and angiographic correlates in 50 patients. Am J Cardiol 25:625–635, 1970.

Harvey, W.P., Segal, J.P., & T. Gurel: The clinical spectrum of primary myocardial disease. Progr Cardiovas Dis 7:17, 1964.

Morrow, A.G., & others: Operative treatment in idiopathic hypertrophic subaortic stenosis: Techniques, and the results of preoperative and postoperative clinical and hemodynamic assessments. Circulation 37:589–596, 1968.

Nellen, M.: Effects of prompt squatting on the systolic murmur in idiopathic hypertrophic obstructive cardiomyopathy. Brit MJ 3:140–143, 1967.

Sommers, K., & others: Hemodynamic features of severe endomyocardial fibrosis of the right ventricle, including comparison with constrictive pericarditis. Brit Heart J 30:322–333, 1968.

Steiner, R.E.: Radiology of hypertrophic obstructive cardiomyopathy. Proc Roy Soc Med 57:444, 1964.

THE CARDIAC PATIENT & SURGERY

Major surgery in the cardiac patient is inevitably more hazardous than in patients with normal hearts. When shock, hemorrhage, hypoxia, struggling during induction, thromboembolism, and hypoventilation occur in a patient with heart disease the danger of coronary occlusion, myocardial infarction, cardiac failure, and arrhythmias is increased.

The major cardiac lesions which increase the risks of surgery are rheumatic heart disease (especially aortic stenosis); coronary heart disease (about 5% additional hazard); and syphilitic cardiovascular disease, especially if there is involvement of the coronary ostia (as suggested by associated angina). Hypertension without cardiac or renal involvement does not usually add to the surgical risk.

If possible, surgery of important magnitude and duration in patients with recent congestive failure should be delayed 3 weeks after recovery; in patients with recent myocardial infarction a delay of 3–6 months is advisable. The patient should be brought into the best cardiac state possible before surgery with medications, diet, and vitamin supplements. Anemia should be corrected. Presurgical electrolyte management is also very important in the cardiac patient.

In inducing and maintaining anesthesia in a cardiac patient, adequate ventilation, oxygenation, and smooth induction without struggling are important.

During surgery hypotension should be treated promptly if it occurs; anemia should be avoided; and fluid therapy should be given to maintain optimal cardiac reserve.

Improvements in anesthesia and surgical skill have reduced the risk of major surgery in recent years. The presence of cardiac disease increases the risk but should not per se deny patients the benefits of elective but necessary surgery.

THE CARDIAC PATIENT & PREGNANCY

The following information will assist in estimating the likelihood of cardiac failure in a pregnant woman: (1) functional class before pregnancy; (2) the age of the patient; (3) the size of the heart; (4) the structural lesion of the heart; (5) the presence of arrhythmias; (6) the patient's socioeconomic status (eg, if children are at home or if the patient must work); (7) the intelligence and cooperation of the patient; and (8) the presence of associated disease.

Assessment of Risk of Heart Disease in Pregnancy

A. Little or No Functional Incapacity: Almost all patients who are asymptomatic or who have only mild symptoms with ordinary activities can continue to term under close medical supervision. If the patient develops more severe symptoms with activity she should be hospitalized, treated for failure, and kept in bed until term.

B. Moderate or Marked Functional Incapacity: If the patient has pure mitral stenosis and develops acute pulmonary edema or has moderate to marked symptoms with activity, mitral valvulotomy should be considered. This has been successfully accomplished up to the 8th month. If the patient does not have an operable lesion, she should be hospitalized, treated for cardiac failure, and kept in bed until term.

C. Severe Functional Incapacity: All patients seen during the first trimester who have symptoms on little or no activity and who do not have an operable cardiac lesion should be aborted, because of the high incidence of recurrent failure and death in this group of patients. Tubal ligation should be considered.

Physiologic Load Which Pregnancy Imposes on the Heart

The work of the heart increases by about 50% at the beginning of about the third month, when the blood volume and cardiac output increase. The placenta acts as an arteriovenous fistula. Cardiac failure may occur at any time from the end of the first trimester up to 2–3 weeks before term, at which time the load for some unaccountable reason decreases.

Sodium should be restricted after the second month.

Management of Labor

Current opinion holds that vaginal delivery is to be preferred except when there is an obstetric indication for cesarean section. Coarctation of the aorta may be the only cardiac disease which contraindicates vaginal delivery, because of the danger of rupture of the aorta.

The second stage should be made as short as possible, using forceps when possible. Ergonovine maleate (Ergotrate®) should probably not be used because of the increased work of the heart which it causes.

Burwell, C.S., & J. Metcalfe: *Heart Disease and Pregnancy. Physiology and Management.* Little, Brown, 1958.

Gilchrist, A.R.: Cardiological problems in younger women including those of pregnancy and the puerperium. Brit MJ 1:209, 1963.

Kincaid-Smith, P., Bullen, M., & J. Mills: Prolonged use of methyldopa in severe hypertension in pregnancy. Brit MJ 1:274–276, 1966.

CARDIOVASCULAR DRUGS

DIGITALIS & DIGITALIS-LIKE PREPARATIONS*

Action of Digitalis & Digitalis-Like Preparations

The fundamental action of digitalis glycosides is to increase the force and velocity of cardiac contraction, whether or not the heart is failing. When the heart is not failing, augmentation of the contractile state of the heart can be demonstrated by the increased peak rate of change of the ventricular pressure curve even if there is no increase of cardiac output. It is not established how, at the cellular level, digitalis increases contractility, but one theory (Braunwald) proposes that it does so by potentiating excitation-contraction coupling by increasing the intracytoplasmic calcium ion concentration during activation as the sarcoplasmic reticulum releases calcium ions. Electrophysiologically, digitalis increases the automaticity of secondary pacemakers in the atrial-AV nodal junction and in the AV node-His bundle junctions, as well as in secondary pacemakers throughout the entire Purkinje system. Digitalis also decreases impulse conduction of the heart, which may lead to reentry phenomena and ventricular irritability. Digitalis blocks conduction through the AV node, and this action is most helpful in slowing the ventricular rate in atrial fibrillation, but it also may produce partial or complete AV block. The drug may induce junctional tachycardia or AV dissociation by enhancing the automaticity of the junctional pacemakers or may cause ventricular premature beats, ventricular tachycardia, or ventricular fibrillation.

In congestive heart failure, digitalis, by enhancing the force of contraction of the ventricle, significantly increases cardiac output, decreases right atrial pressure, decreases the venous pressure, and increases the excretion of sodium and water and so corrects some of the hemodynamic and metabolic alterations in cardiac failure. The inotropic effect of digitalis fortunately occurs before the toxic manifestations, although the therapeutic-toxic ratio often is quite narrow. All of the digitalis preparations seem to be similar with respect to the relative inotropic action as compared to the effect on impulse formation and impulse conduction.

*See also Congestive Heart Failure, p 201.

Principles of Administration

A. Digitalis Saturation (Digitalization): Traditionally, it is thought that digitalis must be administered initially in large doses to achieve tissue saturation and produce a therapeutic effect. Smaller doses (representing the amount metabolized and excreted) are administered daily thereafter as long as the indications for digitalis persist (usually for life).

B. Criteria of Adequate Digitalization: Digitalis is administered until a therapeutic effect has been obtained (eg, relief of congestive failure or slowing of the ventricular rate in atrial fibrillation), or until the earliest toxic effect (anorexia or arrhythmia) appears.

1. In congestive failure with normal rhythm—Digitalization is adequate if: (1) diuretic action is adequate, and edema fluid is lost; (2) cardiac size is decreased as dilatation becomes less; (3) venous pressure and circulation time return to normal; (4) the heart rate decreases (if increase was due to failure); (5) an engorged tender liver becomes smaller and nontender.

2. In atrial fibrillation—When the rate is below 80 after exercise, one can usually consider the patient adequately digitalized. Exercise consists of requiring bed patients to sit up 5 times and ambulatory patients to hop up and down on 1 foot 5 times.

C. ECG Effects: The most characteristic change which digitalis produces in the ECG is sagging of the ST segment and displacement of the T waves in a direction opposite to that of the main deflection. Later the P–R interval may be prolonged. The ST–T changes cannot be used as criteria of digitalis toxicity, for the effects appear before saturation is present and persist for 2–3 weeks after digitalis has been discontinued. However, the ECG is often of value in determining whether digitalis has been administered in the past 2–3 weeks and may give an idea of the amount.

D. Toxic Effects of Digitalis: There are no non-toxic digitalis preparations, and the difference between the therapeutic and toxic level is very small.

1. Slight toxicity—Anorexia, ventricular ectopic beats, bradycardia.

2. Moderate toxicity—Nausea and vomiting, headache, malaise, ventricular premature beats.

3. Severe toxicity—Diarrhea, blurring of vision, confusion, disorientation, junctional (nodal) tachycardia, AV dissociation, paroxysmal atrial tachycardia with block, atrial fibrillation, ventricular tachycardia, S-A or AV block.

4. Extreme toxicity—High-degree conduction blocks and ventricular fibrillation.

Because many arrhythmias occur in the absence as well as in the presence of digitalis toxicity, it is often difficult for the physician to know whether the drug has caused the arrhythmia. A high degree of probability exists with respect to multifocal ventricular beats, junctional AV nodal tachycardia, AV dissociation not associated with AV block, and paroxysmal atrial tachycardia with block. Ventricular tachycardia is common in acute myocardial infarction but may be due to digitalis toxicity. When digitalis is con-

TABLE 7–8. Digitalis and digitalis-like preparations.*

Glycoside and Preparations Available	Dose		Method of Administration	Speed Maximum Action and Duration
	Digitalizing	**Maintenance**		
Parenteral preparations Ouabain, 1 and 2 ml ampules, 0.25 mg (1/240 gr)	0.25–0.5 mg (1/240–1/120 gr)	Not used for mainte-nance	0.25–0.5 mg (1–2 ml) diluted in 10 ml saline slowly IV; follow with another drug (see below).	½–1½ hours; dura-tion, 2–4 days.
Deslanoside (Cedi-lanid-D®), 2 and 4 ml ampules, 0.4 and 0.8 mg	8 ml (1.6 mg)	0.2–0.4 mg (1–2 ml)	1.2 mg (6 ml) IV or IM and follow with 0.2–0.4 mg (1–2 ml) IV or IM every 3–4 hours until effect is obtained.	1–2 hours; duration, 3–6 days.
Digitoxin (dilute before use), 1 and 2 ml ampules, 0.2 and 0.4 mg	1.2 mg (6 ml)	0.05–0.2 mg	0.6 mg (3 ml) IV or IM fol-lowed by 0.2–0.4 mg every 4–6 hours until 1.2 mg has been given.	3–8 hours; duration, 14–21 days.
Digoxin (Lanoxin®), 2 ml ampules, 0.25 mg/ml	1.5 mg (6 ml)	0.25–0.75 mg (1–3 ml)	0.5–1 mg (2–4 ml) IV and 0.25–0.5 mg (1–2 ml) in 3–4 hours; then 0.25 mg (1 ml) every 3–4 hours until effect is obtained.	1–2 hours; duration, 3–6 days.
Oral preparations Digitalis, 0.03, 0.06, and 0.1 gm tablets (½, 1, and 1½ gr)	1–1.5 gm (15–22½ gr)	0.05–0.2 gm (¾–3 gr)	0.6 gm (10 gr) at once; 0.4 gm (6 gr) in 6–8 hours; 0.2 gm (3 gr) every 6 hours for 2–3 doses; then 0.1 gm (1½ gr) twice daily until effect is achieved.	6–8 hours; duration, 18–21 days.
Digitoxin, 0.1, 0.15, and 0.2 mg tab-lets	1.2 mg	0.05–0.2 mg	0.6 mg at once and repeat in 12 hours and then 0.2 mg twice daily until effect is obtained.	6–8 hours; duration, 14–21 days.
Digoxin, 0.25 and 0.5 mg tablets	1.5–3 mg	0.15–0.5 mg	1 mg at once, and then 0.25–0.5 mg every 6 hours. Total, 3 mg.	4–6 hours; duration, 2–6 days.
Lanatoside C (Cedi-lanid®), 0.5 mg tablets	7.5 mg	0.5–1.5 mg	2.0 mg at once, and then 0.5–0.75 mg every 6 hours until effect is obtained.	
Acetyldigitoxin (Acylanid®), 0.1 and 0.2 mg tablets	1.6–2.4 mg	0.1–0.2 mg	1.6 mg in 24 hours or 0.6–1 mg daily until effect is ob-tained.	4–6 hours; duration, 14–21 days.
Gitalin (Gitaligin®), 0.5 mg tablets	4–6 mg	0.5 mg	1 mg 3 times first day fol-lowed by 0.5 mg every 6 hours until effect is obtained.	4–6 hours; duration, 8–14 days.

*Check manufacturers' descriptive literature. Dosage sizes of tablets and ampules change from time to time.

tinued despite the presence of the above arrhythmias (thought likely as an index of digitalis toxicity), the mortality is very high.

In the past several years, quantitative methods for determining digitalis in the serum or plasma have been perfected. The most promising technic seems to be radioimmunoassay. Although there is an overlap in the serum concentrations of digoxin as determined by radioimmunoassay, Smith found that the serum levels in patients considered to be digitalis toxic averaged 2 (± 1.5) ng/ml, as compared to 1 (± 0.7) in patients judged to be nontoxic. Serum levels may prove helpful in the case of doubtful digitalis toxicity, especially since results can be available in about 1 hour.

E. Relationship of Digitalis to Potassium Ion: There is an antagonism between potassium and digi-talis, and digitalis toxicity is more likely to occur in any clinical situation in which potassium is decreased in the cells or serum, eg, as a result of potassium diure-sis due to mercurial or thiazide diuretics, or following corticosteroid therapy. In these circumstances, potassium ion should be given.

F. Treatment of Severe Digitalis Toxicity: Withhold digitalis and diuretics until the manifestations of toxicity have subsided, and treat the cardiac failure, if present, with other means. Give potassium salts, 4–8 gm orally per day in divided doses, or, depending upon the clinical urgency, well-diluted intravenous potassium salts slowly (not more than 20–30 mEq/hour). In emergency circumstances, potassium may be given more rapidly under ECG control. Do not give potassium salts intravenously in the presence of high-grade AV block or renal failure. One can treat premonitory ventricular arrhythmias with lidocaine (Xylocaine®), diphenylhydantoin (Dilantin®), propranolol (Inderal®), or procainamide (Pronestyl®). *Caution:* Cardioversion should be used with great caution if digitalis toxicity is suspected. It may precipitate digitalis-induced arrhythmias or be followed by more serious arrhythmias such as ventricular tachycardia. If essential, administer electrical cardioversion in small graded increments.

The differentiation of digitalis toxicity and inadequate digitalization is sometimes quite difficult. The only safe procedure, if uncertain, is to withhold digitalis and diuretics and treat the cardiac failure with restriction of sodium and other means to improve cardiac function. Nausea, vomiting, and arrhythmias which are in fact due to digitalis toxicity will subside in 2–3 days. *Caution:* Do not give rapid-acting intravenous digitalis preparations to a patient taking digitalis who is apparently in failure unless it is certain that the manifestations observed are not due to digitalis toxicity.

G. Choice of Digitalis Preparation: (See Table 7–8.) All of the cardiac glycosides have similar pharmacologic properties, differing only in dose, absorption, speed of onset of action, and duration of action. With digitalis leaf and digitoxin there is a long latent period before maximal effect is achieved, and the duration of effect is long. Digoxin (Lanoxin®), lanatoside C (Cedilanid®), and deslanoside (Cedilanid-D®) have a much more rapid onset of action and briefer duration of effect. Acetyldigitoxin (Acylanid®) is recommended only for oral administration and is equivalent to digoxin. Gitalin (Gitaligin®) has properties intermediate between those of digitoxin and digoxin. Ouabain exerts its effect within a few minutes, but it is rarely used in the USA because other parenteral glycosides are available.

Indications for Administration of Digitalis

(1) Cardiac failure (left, right, or combined), with sinus rhythm or atrial fibrillation.

(2) Atrial fibrillation or flutter with a rapid ventricular rate.

(3) Supraventricular paroxysmal tachycardia.

(4) Before cardiac surgery, especially mitral valvulotomy, in patients with sinus rhythm, so that if paroxysmal atrial fibrillation occurs during or following surgery the ventricular rate will not be too rapid.

TABLE 7–9. Oral administration of the digitalis drugs.

Urgency	Drug	Dosage
Moderate	Digitalis	0.4 gm (6 gr) every 8 hours for 3 doses.
	Digitoxin	0.4 mg every 8 hours for 3 doses.
	Digoxin	0.5 mg every 8 hours for 3 doses.
Intermediate	Digitalis	0.2 gm (3 gr) 3 times daily for 2 days, or 0.1 gm (1½ gr) 4 times daily for 3 days.
	Digitoxin	0.2 mg 3 times daily for 2 days.
	Digoxin	0.5 mg twice daily for 2 days, or 0.25 mg 3 times daily for 3 days.
Least	Digitalis	0.1 gm (1½ gr) 3 times daily for 4–5 days.
	Digitoxin	0.1 mg 3 times daily for 4–6 days.
	Digoxin	0.25–0.5 mg twice daily for 4–6 days.

(5) Prevention of paroxysmal atrial arrhythmias in patients in whom quinidine has failed or cannot be tolerated.

Routes of Administration of Digitalis

A. Parenteral Administration:

1. Emergency digitalization–(1) Acute pulmonary edema or other severe failure. Caution should be used in giving the full digitalizing dose in a single injection intravenously under these circumstances. The drug should be given slowly, in divided doses. (2) Treatment of atrial arrhythmias when the need for control of the ventricular rate is urgent.

2. Inability to take digitalis orally, eg, in nausea and vomiting due to any cause, in coma, and postoperatively.

B. Oral Administration: Oral administration is used unless parenteral administration is indicated.

Methods of Digitalization

A. Untreated Cases: (When the patient has received no digitalis in the preceding 2 weeks.)

1. **Parenteral digitalization—***Caution:* Never administer a full digitalizing dose intravenously unless it is certain that no digitalis has been given in the preceding 2 weeks. Always give intravenous preparations slowly.

Select the drug on the basis of the rapidity of effect needed. Except in extreme emergencies do not give the entire average digitalizing dose in a single dose. A good general rule is to give 1/2 to 2/3 of the average digitalizing dose immediately and then give the remainder in 2–4 hours. Observe carefully for digitalis toxicity. When the initial dose is given parenterally, it is advisable to give also an average maintenance dose of a digitalis preparation if the patient is able to swallow. Optimal digitalization can thus be achieved and maintained from the start. It is not necessary to give the same glycoside orally that was used for the initial medication (eg, may digitalize with intravenous lanatoside C and give digitalis leaf for maintenance).

A history of digitalis therapy is often difficult to obtain, and digitalis toxicity has occurred in patients who have denied or were unaware of having received the drug. This is another reason for not giving a full digitalizing dose in a single injection.

Individualize the dosage schedule for each patient.

2. Rapid oral digitalization (within 24 hours)—It is usually unwise to attempt to digitalize with a single oral dose, since nausea and vomiting are common and make it very difficult to estimate the degree of digitalization. Multiple oral doses are usually adequate for initial digitalization. Close medical observation is required before each dose is given, and further doses should be withdrawn at the first sign or symptom of toxicity.

3. Slow digitalization—At times it is desirable to digitalize slowly over the course of a week, especially if the patient cannot be closely observed during this period. Any of the digitalis preparations can be given in daily doses 2 or 3 times the average maintenance dose for 5–7 days. The total digitalizing dose may be somewhat greater than when digitalization is rapid. As soon as toxic symptoms appear the drug should be stopped for 1 day and the patient given the average maintenance dose.

B. Partially Treated Cases: If a digitalis preparation has been taken within 2 weeks, give ¼ of the estimated digitalizing dose and then give additional digitalis cautiously, observing the response.

Maintenance Doses & Methods

The oral route is preferred in maintaining digitalization. The exact maintenance dose must be determined clinically for each patient.

Bennett, W.M., Singer, I., & C.H. Coggins: A practical guide to drug usage in adult patients with impaired renal function. JAMA 214:1468–1476, 1970.

Bigger, J.T., & others: Relationship between plasma level of diphenylhydantoin sodium and its cardiac antiarrhythmic effects. Circulation 38:363, 1970.

Fisch, C.: Treatment of arrhythmias due to digitalis. J Indiana MA 60:146–152, 1967.

Hoffman, B.F., & D.H. Singer: Effects of digitalis on electrical activity in cardiac fibers. Progr Cardiovas Dis 7:226–261, 1964.

Jacobs, D., Donosco, E., & C. Friedberg: A-V dissociation. A relatively frequent arrhythmia. Medicine 40:101, 1961.

Selzer, A.: The use of digitalis in acute myocardial infarction. Progr Cardiovas Dis 10:518–529, 1968.

Smith, T.W., Butler, V.P., Jr., & E. Haber: Determination of therapeutic and toxic serum digoxin concentrations by radioimmunoassay. New England J Med 281:1212–1244, 1969.

QUINIDINE*

Quinidine is a valuable drug in the management of most cardiac arrhythmias. It increases the effective refractory period of cardiac muscle; slows the rate of atrial and ventricular conduction; decreases the excitability of the myocardium; reduces vagal tone; and has a general depressant action on smooth muscle, causing vasodilatation. As far as conversion of atrial fibrillation is concerned, several of these pharmacologic actions oppose each other; the clinical effect depends upon which action predominates.

Quinidine can be given orally, intramuscularly, or intravenously, as occasion demands. The intravenous route should be used only in urgent situations by physicians experienced in the use of the drug. Quinidine is rapidly absorbed following oral administration, reaches a peak level of effectiveness in about 2 hours, and is excreted slowly; about 30% of the peak level remains after 12 hours. Only 10–20% of orally administered quinidine is excreted in the urine; the remainder is metabolized in the body.

After 5 or 6 doses have been given at 2-hour intervals, no significant rise in blood level occurs with further doses at the same interval. When a fixed dose of quinidine is given 4 times a day, as in a maintenance schedule, the blood level rises progressively but more slowly, reaching a maximum in about 48–72 hours. The midday blood levels then remain more or less the same as long as this same schedule is maintained. If higher blood levels are desired, the individual dose must be increased or the interval between doses shortened. Because 30–40% of the peak blood level of quinidine is still present in the serum 12 hours after the last of a series of repeated doses of quinidine, a fixed dosage schedule such as 0.4 gm every 2 hours for 5 doses can be repeated for several days to produce increasing concentrations of quinidine in the blood.

Long-acting quinidine preparations are available and permit 2 or 3 rather than 4 daily doses of quinidine sulfate to obtain the desired effect. They should be used only to prevent recurrence and not for conversion of chronic arrhythmias.

Indications & Contraindications

Conflicting opinions have been expressed by cardiologists on the indications, dosages, and dangers in the use of quinidine. It must be remembered that patients taking quinidine have organic cardiac disease; unpredictable accidents occur even when quinidine is not given.

A. Indications: The use of quinidine as the primary agent to convert established atrial and ventricular arrhythmias has been superseded by the use of DC cardioversion because of its greater effectiveness and safety. If DC conversion is not available or is contraindicated for any reason, one should recall that quini-

---

*Quinine may be used, but it is only about 30% as effective as quinidine. Only quinidine will be discussed here.

dine can be used for the conversion of established atrial fibrillation, atrial flutter, and ventricular and nodal tachycardia. Quinidine is valuable in the prevention of recurrent paroxysmal arrhythmias and the suppression of frequent premature beats, especially following myocardial infarction, after surgery, and in similar clinical situations.

B. Contraindications: Quinidine idiosyncrasy and complete heart block are absolute contraindications to the use of quinidine. Relative contraindications are bundle branch block, thyrotoxicosis, acute rheumatic fever, and subacute bacterial endocarditis.

Preparations & Routes of Administration

(1) Quinidine sulfate should be given orally except when parenteral quinidine is specifically indicated.

(2) The intramuscular preparation can be used if the patient is unable to take the medication orally and the situation is not critical. Quinidine gluconate, 0.8 gm in 10 ml ampules, is available.

(3) An intravenous preparation should be used only when great urgency requires it and only by a physician familiar with the use of the drug. Quinidine gluconate, 0.8 gm in 10 ml ampules, can be diluted with 50–100 ml of 5% glucose and given slowly IV at a rate of 1 ml/minute.

Toxicity

A. Myocardial Toxicity: The myocardial toxicity is the most important and should be specifically looked for when quinidine is used. The earliest effects are seen on ECG: prolongation of the Q–T interval and QRS interval, and ventricular premature beats or ventricular tachycardia.

B. Nausea, vomiting, and diarrhea may be sufficiently severe to require cessation of the drug.

C. Cinchonism: Tinnitus, vertigo, and headache may be severe enough to necessitate withdrawal of the drug. *Caution:* When the QRS interval becomes more than half again as wide as before treatment, or when runs of ventricular premature beats or ventricular tachycardia occur, quinidine should be stopped immediately. In rare instances ventricular tachycardia may progress to ventricular fibrillation and sudden death.

In patients with atrial fibrillation who are converted with quinidine, transient sino-atrial block may occur at the time of conversion and nodal rhythm may be temporarily noted. This has no clinical significance. Transient prolongation of the P–R interval occasionally occurs when sinus rhythm follows quinidine conversion of atrial fibrillation; this usually subsides spontaneously with smaller maintenance doses.

D. Other Cardiovascular Effects:

1. Hypotension may occur when large doses of quinidine are used or if the drug is given parenterally. It rarely is significant with ordinary oral doses.

2. Emboli occur in about 1% of patients with chronic atrial fibrillation converted with quinidine. The incidence is higher in untreated atrial fibrillation; in fact, atrial fibrillation with frequent emboli is an important reason for attempting to convert to sinus rhythm. Anticoagulants are advised for 1–2 weeks before conversion to prevent the development of new thrombi in the atria in patients with a history of recent emboli.

E. Idiosyncrasy: Fever, purpura, rash, or severe hypotension following a test dose of 0.1 gm.

Conversion to Sinus Rhythm

Cardioversion is preferable to quinidine for this purpose (see above). If cardioversion is not available or is contraindicated, quinidine may be used.

The patient should be under constant observation, preferably in a hospital. Give a test dose of 0.1 gm and wait 2 hours to exclude the possibility of idiosyncrasy.

If the patient has atrial fibrillation or atrial flutter, complete digitalization is advised to slow the ventricular rate and to improve cardiac function. If digitalis is not used, the altered atrioventricular conduction resulting from quinidine may cause a rise in ventricular rate of 30–50 beats per minute and may force cessation of quinidine therapy.

For a patient with chronic arrhythmia in cardiac failure in whom immediate conversion is not essential, additional measures (eg, sodium restriction, diuretics) are indicated before quinidine is given. The patient should be ambulatory for 2 weeks to decrease the likelihood of venous thrombosis. One week of anticoagulant therapy may be desirable, but the data are incomplete regarding its value.

In elective cases, 0.2–0.4 gm every 6 hours can be given for 2–3 days, increasing the dose if no toxic effects have occurred and the arrhythmia persists. If reversion to sinus rhythm is required more quickly, give 0.4 gm every 2 hours for 5–6 doses on the first day; this produces an average blood level of 6–7 mg/liter. Each succeeding dose produces a smaller increment in the blood level, and if conversion does not occur after 5–6 doses larger amounts must be given. In urgent circumstances, begin immediately after the 5th dose; otherwise it is best to wait until the next morning and begin again with 0.6 gm every 2 hours. Giving the drug more frequently than every 2 hours is not warranted since it takes that long for the peak effect of the preceding dose to be reached. In most cases 0.6 gm every 2 hours for 5 doses will convert the arrhythmia to sinus rhythm. If it does not, higher doses can be used if no toxicity has been encountered and it is urgent to convert the arrhythmia. Eighty percent of the successful conversions occur with daily doses of 3 gm or less.

Increasing quinidine effect can be roughly estimated by serial determinations of blood quinidine levels; by determining the atrial rate of fibrillation; and by measurement of the Q–T and QRS intervals. Rate of fibrillation is best determined on V_1, the right precordial lead in the ECG. The atrial rate is slowed markedly in atrial fibrillation; as the rate approaches 200–250/minute, conversion is near. As Q–T and

QRS widen up to 25—30% above the initial values, significant quinidine effects can be predicted.

Braunwald, E., & P.E. Pool: Mechanism of action of digitalis glycosides. Mod Concepts Cardiovas Dis 38:129—132, 1968.

Goldstein, A., Aronow, L., & S.M. Kalman: *Principles of Drug Action: The Basis of Pharmacology.* Harper, 1968.

Lown, B., & S. Wittenberg: Cardioversion and digitalis. III. Effect of change in serum potassium concentration. Am J Cardiol 21:513—517, 1968.

Mason, D.T., Spann, J.F., Jr., & R. Zelis: New developments in the understanding of the actions of the digitalis glycosides. Progr Cardiovas Dis 11:443, 1969.

Sokolow, M., & D.B. Perloff: The clinical pharmacology and use of quinidine in heart disease. Progr Cardiovas Dis 3:316—330, 1961.

Wallace, A.G., & others: Electrophysiologic effects of quinidine. Circulation Res 19:960, 1966.

NITRITES & NITRATES

The nitrites are smooth muscle relaxants. Whether diseased coronary arteries are able to dilate in response to nitrite administration has recently been questioned. The relief of angina is probably due to a decrease in cardiac work resulting from a decrease in venous return and subsequent cardiac output secondary to venous pooling due to relaxation of the capacitance vessels.

Rapid-Acting

The rapid-acting preparations (glyceryl trinitrate and amyl nitrite) are useful in terminating an episode of angina or in preventing it if given just before exercise.

A. Glyceryl Trinitrate Tablets (Nitroglycerin): Place 1 tablet (0.3—0.6 mg) under the tongue as necessary. Effective in 1—2 minutes; effect lasts 15—40 minutes.

B. Amyl Nitrite "Pearl": Break pearl (contains 0.2 ml) in cloth and inhale as necessary. Effective in 10 seconds; effect lasts 5—10 minutes.

Long-Acting Nitrates

The usefulness of these preparations has not been clearly established. The onset of their effect after single doses is delayed for 15—60 minutes but persists for 4—6 hours. Repeated doses may lead to tolerance, and the results of clinical trials are, at best, conflicting.

The following organic nitrates are administered orally or sublingually 4 times a day. (1) Pentaerythritol tetranitrate (Peritrate®), 10—20 mg. (2) Erythrol tetranitrate (Cardilate®), 15 mg (sublingually). (3) Mannitol hexanitrate (Nitranitol®), 15—60 mg. (4) Trolnitrate phosphate (Metamine®, Nitretamin®), 2—4 mg. (5) Isosorbide dinitrate (Isordil®), 10 mg.

The effect of concurrently administered propranolol is enhanced by the nitrates.

XANTHINES

Cardiac catheterization and metabolic balance studies have demonstrated that intravenous xanthines increase the cardiac output, increase renal blood flow and glomerular filtration rate, and enhance the excretion of sodium and water; they therefore may be valuable in the treatment of cardiac failure. They have also been shown to increase the coronary blood flow when used in large doses, and may on occasion be helpful in angina pectoris.

Preparations

Oral preparations are not useful.

A. Parenteral: Aminophylline injection, 0.25—0.5 gm IV slowly over a 5-minute period, or IM; may repeat in 2—4 hours.

B. Rectal: Rectal suppositories containing aminophylline, 0.3—0.5 gm, may be valuable in an impending attack of cardiac asthma or in nocturnal angina pectoris.

DIURETICS

Diuretics are drugs which suppress renal tubular reabsorption of sodium. They are used in the treatment of diseases associated with excess sodium retention and consequent fluid accumulation (edema), eg, congestive heart failure. The orally active diuretics have also been used in the treatment of hypertension, since sodium depletion (as well as other mechanisms) potentiates the effects of hypotensive drugs.

Thiazide (Thiodiazine, Disulfonamide) Diuretics

Drugs of this class have the great advantage of being effective in oral form. The marked sodium loss which they cause is accompanied by potassium diuresis of a potentially toxic degree, especially if digitalis is being given concurrently. These sulfonamide derivatives have only a slight carbonic anhydrase inhibiting effect.

The thiazide diuretics are useful in potentiating the effect of hypotensive drugs and in the treatment of edema due to congestive heart failure, renal disease, cirrhosis, and other sodium retention states. They also may be used in the treatment of diabetes insipidus.

The thiazides are contraindicated in acute renal failure and must be used in smaller doses and with careful observation in cirrhotic patients and in patients receiving digitalis.

Potassium depletion is the principal toxic effect, and is most likely to occur early in the use of these drugs when diuresis is most marked. If the diet is deficient in fresh fruits and vegetables, potassium chloride, 1 gm 3—4 times daily, should be given. Intermittent diuretic therapy or the concomitant use of potassium-sparing diuretics may prevent hypokalemia. The possi-

TABLE 7−10. Useful oral diuretics.

	Daily Dose
Benzthiazide (Exna®)	25−100 mg
Benzydroflumethiazide (Naturetin®)	5−10 mg
Chlorothiazide (Diuril®)	250−1000 mg
Chlorthalidone (Hygroton®)	50−200 mg
Cyclothiazide (Anhydron®)	1−2 mg
Ethacrynic acid (Edecrin®)	100−200 mg
Flumethiazide (Ademol®)	250−1000 mg
Furosemide (Lasix®)	40−80 mg
Hydrochlorothiazide (Esidrix®, Hydro-Diuril®, Oretic®)	25−100 mg
Hydroflumethiazide (Saluron®)	25−100 mg
Methyclothiazide (Enduron®)	2.5−10 mg
Polythiazide (Renese®)	1−4 mg
Quinethazone (Hydromox®)	50−100 mg
Spironolactone (Aldactone®)	50−100 mg
Triamterene (Dyrenium®)	100−200 mg
Trichloromethiazide (Naqua®, Metahydrin®)	2−8 mg

bility of precipitating digitalis toxicity by potassium diuresis must be considered in patients receiving digitalis.

Other toxic effects are allergic reactions such as skin rashes, pruritus, and, rarely, bone marrow depression; gastrointestinal disturbances; photosensitization; elevated serum uric acid, with the precipitation of gout; and impaired glucose tolerance.

It is agreed that the amount of sodium in the diet should be kept reasonably constant. One can restrict sodium in order to reduce the dose of the diuretic.

The available thiazides are listed below. Outside of the laboratory there is no basis for preferring one to another. Chlorthalidone (Hygroton®) is not a thiodiazine but a sulfonamide which is otherwise similar to the other drugs listed. In treating edema a large dose may be used initially if necessary, but the dose should be decreased rapidly and doses given at longer than daily intervals if "dry" weight is maintained.

If potassium supplements are used because of K^+ loss, use liquid or nonenteric coated potassium salts.

Ethacrynic Acid (Edecrin®) & Furosemide (Lasix®)

Ethacrynic acid is a new potent diuretic, a derivative of aryloxyacetic acid, which can be used for the same indications as the thiazides (see p 222). It is more potent, more rapid in action (30−60 minutes), and causes a greater depletion of sodium and potassium and hence a danger of hyponatremia and hypokalemic alkalosis. Intermittent therapy is advised, beginning with small doses (25−50 mg) with caution in patients with impaired renal function and those receiving digitalis.

Similar effects can be obtained with furosemide, a new nonthiazide, nonmercurial diuretic which can be given orally or intravenously. It has the advantage, apart from its rapid action, of not affecting carbohydrate metabolism. The initial daily dosage is 20−40

mg. *Caution:* Observe patient for hearing impairment and discontinue ethacrynic acid if there is any evidence of hearing loss.

Mercurial Diuretics

Intramuscularly or subcutaneously administered mercurial diuretics, which were standard drugs for many years, are slightly more potent than the thiazide diuretics. They cause less potassium diuresis, but are more often responsible for sodium depletion. No satisfactory oral preparations are available. The mercurial diuretics are now used only for an occasional difficult patient with congestive heart failure and usually only after a trial with an oral diuretic.

The dose of each of the following mercurial diuretics is 0.5−2 ml of the prepared solution given no oftener than once daily: chlormerodrin (Neohydrin®), meralluride (Mercuhydrin®), mercaptomerin (Thiomerin®), mercurophylline (Mercuzanthin®), mercumatilin (Cumertilin®), merethoxylline procaine (Dicurin Procaine®), and mersalyl (Salyrgan®).

Carbonic Anhydrase Inhibitors

These drugs, exemplified by acetazolamide (Diamox®), are sulfonamide derivatives which depress the renal tubular reabsorption of bicarbonate. This action leads to only a transient and minor sodium diuresis but a persistent decrease of plasma bicarbonate concentrations and increase of plasma chloride concentration. Administered once or twice a week, these drugs are sometimes useful in the treatment of congestive failure associated with cor pulmonale or to potentiate the action of mercurial diuretics.

Carbonic anhydrase inhibitors may cause drowsiness, paresthesias, and minor allergic reactions.

For diuresis, acetazolamide (Diamox®) is given in doses of 250−500 mg 2−3 times per week. Ethoxzolamide (Cardrase®) is used in 62.5−125 mg doses. Experience with dichlorphenamide (Daranide®) and methazolamide (Neptazane®) is limited to their use in glaucoma.

Aldosterone Antagonist

Spironolactone (Aldactone®) is an antagonist to aldosterone, the adrenal steroid which controls renal tubular reabsorption of sodium. It therefore causes sodium diuresis without potassium loss. It can be combined with a thiazide to neutralize the potassium-wasting effect of the latter drug. The onset of effect may be delayed for as long as a week. The response of patients with congestive failure and primary aldosteronism has been variable. The drug should be regarded as a promising supplementary diuretic in the resistant edema of cirrhosis and nephrosis, but it is expensive and may cause hyperkalemia. Serial serum potassium determinations and ECG observation is advised. Initial dosage is 25 mg 4 times daily. Drowsiness, breast tenderness, hyponatremia, hyperkalemia, and hypotension may occur.

Triamterene (Dyrenium®)

Like spironolactone, triamterene may be valuable when combined with the thiazides to prevent hypokalemia as well as to provide a slightly additive diuretic effect. It may be added to the mercurial diuretics in the same way. The BUN as well as the serum potassium may rise following triamterene administration, and these components should be monitored during treatment. Mild gastrointestinal side-effects may occur. The usual dose is 100 mg twice daily after meals initially, followed by 50–100 mg daily as a maintenance dose depending upon response.

PROCAINAMIDE HYDROCHLORIDE

Procainamide (Pronestyl®) depresses ectopic pacemakers, prevents arrhythmias under cyclopropane anesthesia following epinephrine, and is useful in the treatment of nodal and ventricular arrhythmias. To a lesser degree, it can be used to prevent these arrhythmias. It has a much less potent effect on the atrial than on the ventricular arrhythmias. Whether procainamide or quinidine is the drug of choice in the ventricular arrhythmias has not been settled.

Dosage & Administration
A. Oral Preparations: Supplied as 250 mg capsules. 0.25–1 gm orally every 4–6 hours is the recommended dose.

B. Intramuscular Preparations: Supplied as 1 gm ampules in 10 ml diluent. The peak effect occurs within 15–60 minutes, and a significant blood level is still present after 6 hours. The blood level is higher and the decrease is slower in patients with congestive failure and renal insufficiency. Hypotension is infrequent with intramuscular use of the drug in the above dosage.

C. Intravenous Preparations: Supplied as 1 gm ampules in 10 ml diluent. Can be used for ventricular tachycardia of a severe or urgent nature. The drug should be given very slowly, 50–100 mg/minute up to a dose of 1 gm with continuous blood pressure and, if possible, ECG control.

Toxicity
The toxicity of procainamide is the same as that of quinidine (with the exception of cinchonism).

(1) Severe hypotension is noted, particularly with the parenteral use of procainamide, and may be severe enough to require withdrawal of the drug or the use of concurrent pressor therapy. This is why frequent blood pressure determinations are necessary.

(2) Prolongation of the QRS interval may occur, as with quinidine.

(3) Ventricular arrhythmias may occur, as with quinidine.

(4) Systemic lupus erythematosus may be initiated or aggravated by procainamide.

Koch-Weser, J., & S.W. Klein: Procainamide dosage schedules, plasma concentrations, and clinical effects. JAMA 215:1454–1460, 1971.

ADRENERGIC BETA RECEPTOR BLOCKADE

Norepinephrine, the specific neurotransmitter liberated at the sympathetic nerve terminals, as well as other drugs and hormones, exert their effects via effector sites known as receptors. The concept of alpha and beta receptor sites was conceived by Ahlquist to explain differing effector responses to different chemical agents, although no anatomic or chemical structure has been identified which is a receptor. Adrenergic receptors are those parts of effector cells which allow them to detect and respond to epinephrine and related compounds. They can be described only in terms of the effector response to drug application. Ahlquist showed that beta receptors are associated with cardiac stimulation, vasodilatation, and relaxation of smooth muscle in the bronchi, myometrium, and intestine. Alpha receptors are associated with vasoconstriction, relaxation of the intestinal muscle, and contraction of the dilator muscles of the pupil. The specific agonist for alpha receptors is phenylephrine; adrenergic alpha receptor blocking agents are substances that specifically block responses to phenylephrine. The specific agonist for beta receptors is isoproterenol; beta-adrenergic blockers are substances which block the responses to isoproterenol but have no effect on the response to phenylephrine. There may be a third or other receptors to explain some of the responses observed in man.

Chemical agents that interfere with the action of sympathetic amines at the receptor site have been found to have therapeutic use in conditions in which adrenergic beta receptor activity is excessive or undesirable. The adrenergic beta receptor blocking agent utilized most frequently today is propranolol (Inderal®), which competitively and specifically blocks the responses of the beta receptor to isoproterenol and other sympathomimetic amines.

Administration
Propranolol (Inderal®) can be used orally, 10 mg 4 times daily, increasing to 180–200 mg/day with close follow-up; or intravenously, 1–5 mg, 1 mg/minute, with careful ECG monitoring. *Caution:* Because sympathetic activity is important for left ventricular function, particularly in the failing heart, beta blockers may be hazardous in the presence of cardiac failure and should be used with great caution or not at all if incipient or actual failure is present. Beta blockers prolong AV conduction and may aggravate high-grade AV block; the presence of AV block should be considered a contraindication. Beta blockers may produce bronchospasm by blocking the bronchial relaxation of the catecholamines and should be used with great caution in patients who have a tendency to bronchial asthma. Do not use if patients are receiving MAO inhibitors.

Clinical Use of Propranolol
A. Anti-Arrhythmic Activity: There is good evidence that propranolol converts some atrial and ven-

tricular arrhythmias to normal and may prevent the recurrence of paroxysmal atrial and ventricular arrhythmias, especially when they are caused by digitalis. Because of its negative chronotropic action, propranolol may slow the ventricular rate in patients with atrial fibrillation and flutter whose ventricular rate cannot be slowed with digitalis. The negative inotropic action of propranolol should be appreciated even when the heart rate is controlled. The drug supplements and does not replace other established anti-arrhythmic agents.

B. Angina Pectoris: Propranolol may increase exercise tolerance, reduce the frequency of attacks, and prevent the ischemic ECG changes with exercise because it reduces cardiac work and myocardial oxygen consumption as well as preventing ventricular premature beats and slowing the heart after exercise. Some authors believe that the beneficial effect is enhanced when propranolol is combined with long-acting nitrates. Treatment of angina pectoris is a controversial subject because of the subjective nature of the symptom and the frequent improvement resulting from the use of placebos.

C. Idiopathic Hypertrophic Subaortic Stenosis: Propranolol reduces the obstructive gradient caused by endogenous and exogenous catecholamines, producing clinical improvement in many patients and thus avoiding the necessity of surgical treatment; surgical treatment should be delayed until the response to propranolol is determined.

D. Hypertension: Propranolol has a slight antihypertensive action, usually less than that obtained from diuretics; patients may require large doses of the drug.

E. Pheochromocytoma: Although alpha adrenergic blocking drugs—phentolamine (Regitine®) or phenoxybenzamine (Dibenzyline®)—restore the blood volume and diminish the risk of abrupt rises in pressure before and during surgical treatment, they do not prevent the tachycardia produced by the release of catecholamines. Therefore, propranolol is a useful adjunct in the preparation of patients with pheochromocytoma for surgery.

F. Tetralogy of Fallot: Spells of increased cyanosis and of syncope may be due to increased contraction of the infundibulum of the right ventricle, presumably from sympathetic impulses. Propranolol has been helpful in relaxing the infundibulum, decreasing the frequency of these serious episodes.

Abboud, F.M.: Concepts of adrenergic receptors. M Clin North America 52:1009–1016, 1968.

Ahlquist, R.P.: Agents which block adrenergic B-receptors. Ann Rev Pharmacol 8:259–272, 1968.

Aronow, W.S., & M.A. Kaplan: Propranolol combined with isosorbide dinitrate versus placebo in angina pectoris. New England J Med 280:847–850, 1969.

Battock, D.J., Alvarez, H., & C.A. Chidsey: Effects of propranolol and isosorbide dinitrate on exercise performance and adrenergic activity in patients with angina pectoris. Circulation 39:157–171, 1969.

Bjorntorp, P.: Treatment of angina pectoris with beta-receptor blockage, mode of action. Acta med scandinav 184:259–262, 1968.

Cohen, L.S., & E. Braunwald: Amelioration of angina pectoris in idiopathic hypertrophic subaortic stenosis with beta-adrenergic blockade. Circulation 35:847, 1967.

Cohen, L.S., & E. Braunwald: Chronic beta adrenergic receptor blockade in the treatment of idiopathic hypertrophic subaortic stenosis. Progr Cardiovas Dis 11:211–221, 1968.

Cullhed, I., & A. Parrow: Acute hemodynamic changes following beta-adrenergic blockade in hyperthyroidism. Acta med scandinav 184:235–239, 1968.

Dwyer, E.M., Jr., Wiener, L., & J.W. Cox: Effects of beta-adrenergic blockade (propranolol) on left ventricular hemodynamics and the electrocardiogram during exercise-induced angina pectoris. Circulation 38:250–260, 1868.

Epstein, S.E., & E. Braunwald: Inhibition of the adrenergic nervous system in the treatment of angina pectoris. M Clin North America 52:1031–1039, 1968.

Epstein, S.E., & E. Braunwald: Beta-adrenergic receptor blockade. Propranolol and related drugs. Ann Int Med 67:1333, 1967.

Furgerg, C.: Adrenergic beta-blockade and physical working capacity. Acta med scandinav 182:119–127, 1967.

Gibson, D., & E. Sowton: The use of beta-adrenergic receptor blocking drugs in dysrhythmias. Progr Cardiovas Dis 12:16–39, 1969.

Lewis, C.M., & A.J. Brink: Beta-adrenergic blockade. Hemodynamics and myocardial energy metabolism in patients with ischemic heart disease. Am J Cardiol 21:846–859, 1968.

Lucchesi, B.R., & L.S. Whitsitt: The pharmacology of beta-adrenergic blocking agents. Progr Cardiovas Dis 11:410–430, 1969.

Mason, D.T.: Autonomic nervous system and regulation of cardiovascular performance. Anesthesiology 29:724, 1968.

Nicotero, J.A., & others: Effects of propranolol on the pressor response to noxious stimuli in hypertensive patients. Am J Cardiol 22:657–666, 1968.

Parker, J.O., West, R.O., & S. DiGiorgi: Hemodynamic effects of propranolol in coronary heart disease. Am J Cardiol 21:11–20, 1968.

Pitt, B., & R.S. Ross: Beta adrenergic blockade in cardiovascular therapy. Mod Concepts Cardiovas Dis 38:47–54, 1969.

Richardson, D.W., & others: Effect of propranolol on elevated arterial blood pressure. Circulation 37:534–542, 1968.

Russek, H.I.: Propranolol and isosorbide dinitrate synergism in angina pectoris. Am J M Sc 254:406–415, 1967.

Somany, P.: Anti-arrhythmic activity of the beta-adrenergic blocking agent, ICI 45763. Am Heart J 77:63–72, 1969.

Symposium on catecholamines in cardiovascular physiology and disease. Circulation Res 21, Suppl 3, 1967.

Theilen, E.O., & W.R. Wilson: Beta adrenergic receptor blocking drugs in the treatment of cardiac arrhythmias. M Clin North America 52:1017–1029, 1968.

Whalen, R.E., Morris, J.J., Jr., & H.B. MacIntosh: Hemodynamic effects of beta-adrenergic blockade at controlled ventricular rates. Am Heart J 76:775–784, 1968.

ACIDIFYING SALTS
(Chlorides)

Chlorides alone are rarely effective diuretics, but they enhance the action of mercurial diuretics, especially when the patient becomes refractory to repeated injections of mercurials. It is thought that chlorides act by producing acidosis and by serving as anions to enhance the excretion of sodium ions. Ammonium chloride, 2 gm 3 times daily, may be given 2—4 days before a mercurial injection and then omitted for 3—4 days before repeating the drug in cyclic fashion. Other chlorides are equally effective, and if the patient has hepatic disease—in which case ammonium ions are potentially toxic—one can give lysine monohydrochloride (Darvyl®, Lyamine®) in similar cyclic fashion. It is given in powder form, 5 gm 3—4 times daily, dissolved in any palatable fluid. Each gram of lysine monohydrochloride provides about 5 mEq of chloride.

The chlorides in large doses and if continued may produce hyperchloremic acidosis with severe dyspnea and gastrointestinal symptoms. Because of the hazard of acidosis, chlorides should not be used in the presence of impaired renal function and the ammonium ion should not be used in hepatic disease.

•   •   •

CARDIAC MANIFESTATIONS OF PARASITIC DISEASES

Shock: Malaria (falciparum).

Myocarditis with cardiac arrhythmias; enlargement, insufficiency: American trypanosomiasis, toxoplasmosis.

Cor pulmonale: Schistosomiasis haematobium.

•   •   •

General Bibliography

See list of texts on p 148.

8 . . .

Blood Vessels & Lymphatics

John M. Erskine & John H. Windesheim

DEGENERATIVE & INFLAMMATORY ARTERIAL DISEASES

Arteriosclerosis accounts for most of the forms of degenerative arterial disease. Its incidence increases with age; although manifestations of the disease may appear in the 4th decade, people over 40 (particularly men) are most commonly affected. Diseases which predispose to arteriosclerosis include the hyperlipidemic states, diabetes mellitus, and hypertension. Arteriosclerosis tends to be a generalized disease with some degree of involvement of all major arteries, but it produces its major clinical manifestations by critical involvement of one essential artery at a time. Gradual narrowing and ultimate occlusion of the artery is the most common course of the disease, but weakening of the arterial wall, aneurysmal dilatation of the arterial segment, and, ultimately, rupture of that segment of artery also occurs.

Less common forms of degenerative and inflammatory arterial disease which must be considered are cystic medial necrosis of the aorta, syphilitic aortitis and arteritis, arteritis of both large and small arteries of undetermined etiology, thromboangiitis obliterans (Buerger's disease), and fibromuscular hyperplasia of visceral arteries.

DISEASES OF THE AORTA

ANEURYSMS OF THE THORACIC AORTA

Progress in antibiotic therapy has reduced the incidence of syphilitic aneurysms; most thoracic aneurysms are now due to arteriosclerosis. Very rapid deceleration, as in an automobile or airplane accident, can result in a tear of the thoracic aorta just beyond the origin of the left subclavian artery with the formation of an aneurysm in those that survive the initial injury. Cystic medial necrosis, a poorly understood and rela-

tively rare degenerative condition, may lead to a thoracic aneurysm in relatively young people.

Clinical Findings

Manifestations depend largely on the position of the aneurysm and its rate of growth.

A. Symptoms and Signs: There may be no symptoms. Substernal, back, or neck pain may occur, as well as symptoms and signs due to pressure on (1) the trachea (dyspnea, stridor, a brassy cough), (2) the esophagus (dysphagia), (3) the left recurrent laryngeal nerve (hoarseness), or (4) the superior vena cava (edema in the neck and arms; distended neck veins). The findings of regurgitation at the aortic valve may be present.

B. Laboratory Findings: The serology may be positive if the aneurysm is syphilitic.

C. X-Ray Findings: X-ray examination (several views) and perhaps fluoroscopy, tomography, esophagography, and angiocardiography are the chief means of arriving at a diagnosis.

Differential Diagnosis

The differential diagnosis between an aneurysm and a mediastinal tumor can sometimes be made only at thoracotomy, and even then the diagnosis may be difficult since some aneurysms are so filled with thrombus that pulsations may not be a prominent feature.

Treatment

Aneurysms of the thoracic aorta often progress with increasing symptoms and finally rupture. Resection of aneurysms is now considered the treatment of choice if technically feasible and if the patient's general condition is such that the major surgical procedure usually required can be done with an acceptable risk. This is especially true if an aneurysm is large, associated with symptoms and signs, and limited to the ascending or descending aorta. Small, asymptomatic aneurysms, especially in poor risk patients, are perhaps better followed and treated only if progressive enlargement occurs.

Saccular aneurysms with narrow necks can often be excised without occluding the aorta. Fusiform aortic aneurysms require resection and grafting of the aortic defect, usually with the patient on partial or complete cardiac bypass.

Prognosis

Small aneurysms and those discovered months or years following an episode of rapid deceleration may change very little over a period of years, and death may result from causes other than rupture in many cases. If the aneurysm is large—and (especially) if it is symptomatic and associated with hypertension or arteriosclerotic cardiovascular disease—the prognosis is poor. In general, 1/3 will be dead in 3 years, ½ in 5 years, and 2/3 in 10 years, but only about 1/3 of all deaths will result from rupture. Saccular aneurysms, those distal to the left subclavian artery, and even those limited to the ascending aorta can now be removed with an acceptable mortality rate. Resection of aneurysms of the arch carries a very high mortality.

Bennett, D.E., & J.K. Cherry: The natural history of traumatic aneurysms of the aorta. Surgery 61:516–523, 1967.

Björk, V.O., & L. Björk: Surgical treatment of aneurysms of the descending thoracic aorta. J Cardiovas Surg 7:50, 1966.

Garrett, H.E., & others: Surgical treatment of aneurysm of the thoraco-abdominal aorta. S Clin North America 46:913–918, 1966.

Joyce, J.W., & others: Aneurysms of the thoracic aorta. A clinical study with special reference to prognosis. Circulation 29:176–181, 1964.

Kahn, A.M., Joseph, W.K., & R.K. Hughes: Traumatic aneurysms of the thoracic aorta. Ann Thoracic Surg 4:175, 1967.

DISSECTING ANEURYSMS OF THE AORTA

Essentials of Diagnosis

- Sudden severe chest pain with radiation to the back, abdomen, and extremities.
- Shock may be present, though often not until the later stages.
- CNS changes may occur.
- A history of hypertension is usually present.
- Dissection occurs most frequently in males.

General Considerations

Dissection may begin as a primary tear of the intima of an atherosclerotic ascending aorta or, less commonly, of the aorta distal to the arch. Hypertension is present in the majority of patients and may thus be an etiologic factor. Dissection may arise as a result of degenerative changes in the media of the aorta (cystic medial necrosis) with intramural hemorrhage, followed later by a tear of the intima; the blood is thus allowed to flow out of the lumen into the wall of the aorta. (The disorder is therefore common in patients with Marfan's syndrome.) In either case, the blood dissects in the media of the artery, both proximal and distal to the original tear, and may involve some of the branches. External rupture followed by death usually occurs in hours, days, or weeks. Intraluminal rupture

may occur with the establishment of a reentry opening, and the patient may survive with blood flowing through both the lumen of the aorta and the new channel in the aortic wall.

Clinical Findings

A. Symptoms and Signs: Severe, persistent pain of sudden onset is usually present, most often in the chest and occasionally radiating to the back, abdomen, and hips, often in an orderly, progressive fashion. Shock may be present though often there is only a relative decrease in the prerupture hypertensive levels. Partial or complete occlusion of the arteries to the brain or spinal cord may lead to such CNS findings as convulsions, hemiplegia, or paralysis of the lower extremities. Peripheral pulse and blood pressure may be diminished and unequal. Murmurs may appear over the arteries, and signs of acute arterial occlusion may be present. An aortic diastolic murmur due to functional insufficiency caused by dissection into the region of the aortic valve may be noted. Fever is frequently present.

B. Laboratory Findings: Leukocytosis is usually present. ECG changes may not be present unless dissection involves a coronary ostium or unless cardiac failure results from insufficiency of the aortic valve or from cardiac tamponade as a result of leakage into the pericardial sac.

C. X-Ray Findings: X-ray may show widening of the thoracic aorta with progressive changes. Angiocardiography may demonstrate the double lumen. There may be findings of pericardial or pleural effusion.

Differential Diagnosis

A dissecting aneurysm is most commonly confused with acute myocardial infarction. Patients with dissecting aneurysm may also have heart disease with recent or old ECG changes, however.

Treatment

A. Medical: Controlled hypotension through the use of drugs is now an established approach, particularly if the individual, as is so often the case, is hypertensive. Lowering the blood pressure and diminishing the pulsatile flow from the heart is successful in a high percentage of the cases that reach the hospital and may convert an acute, progressive dissection into a relatively stable condition which may be studied, followed, and dealt with, if necessary, by means of elective surgery. Medical therapy is also indicated in patients with stable subacute or chronic dissection.

One recommended approach is to start with trimethaphan (Arfonad®) intravenously to reduce the systolic blood pressure to about 100 mm Hg. This infusion is maintained for approximately 48 hours, by which time reserpine, 1 or 2 mg IM or orally twice daily, and guanethidine (Ismelin®), 25–50 mg orally twice daily (also started with trimethaphan), will have taken effect to maintain a relative hypotension. Occasionally, propranolol (Inderal®) and hydrochlorothiazide (Hydro-Diuril®) may also be employed. Subsequently, an effort is made to maintain the blood pressure as near normal as possible, usually with reserpine and guanethidine, and the patient is followed carefully.

Chest x-rays, peripheral pulses and murmurs, heart sounds, and the CNS must be checked frequently; if the condition fails to stabilize—especially if the blood pressure will not respond to medication promptly, if progression of the dissection is not controlled, or if uncontrolled aortic valve insufficiency develops—surgery may still be employed.

B. Surgical: Operative intervention may sometimes interrupt a progressive dissection, particularly if the dissection is limited to the ascending aorta or starts distal to the left subclavian artery and involves only the descending aorta, in which case resecting and grafting of the involved aortic segment may be possible. Sometimes the establishment of a reentry opening from the false to the true aortic lumen may arrest the dissection and prevent aortic rupture. If equipment for partial or complete cardiac bypass is not available or if the patient is a very poor operative risk, surgery should not be attempted.

Prognosis

Without treatment the mortality rate is very high. Death occurs suddenly in approximately 1/3 of patients; in another 50–60%, death usually occurs in days or weeks unless treatment is prompt and adequate. Some patients can be saved by surgical means or by hypotensive therapy. The occasional untreated patient may survive for months or years.

Austen, W.G., & others: Therapy of dissecting aneurysms. Arch Surg 95:835–842, 1967.
Kuipers, F.M., & I.J. Schatz: Prognosis in dissecting aneurysm of the aorta. Circulation 27:658–661, 1963.
Lindsay, J., Jr., & J.W. Hurst: Clinical features and prognosis in dissecting aneurysm of the aorta: A reappraisal. Circulation 35:880–888, 1967.
Neptune, W.B.: Dissecting aneurysms of the thoracic aorta. Dis Chest 52:233–239, 1967.
Shuford, W.H., & others: Problems in the aortographic diagnosis of dissecting aneurysms of the aorta. New England J Med 280:225–231. 1969.
Wheat, M.W., Jr., & R.F. Palmer: Drug therapy for dissecting aneurysms. Dis Chest 54:372–377, 1968.

ANEURYSMS OF THE ABDOMINAL AORTA

The vast majority of aneurysms of the abdominal aorta are below the origin of the renal arteries and generally involve the bifurcation of the aorta and thus the proximal end of the common iliac arteries. Aneurysms of the upper abdominal aorta are rare. Most aneurysms of the distal aorta are arteriosclerotic in origin and fusiform in shape.

Clinical Findings

A. Symptoms and Signs: Three phases can be recognized:

1. Asymptomatic—A pulsating mid and upper abdominal mass may be discovered on a routine physical examination, most frequently in men over 50. The calcification which frequently exists in the wall of the aneurysm may be discovered at the time of an abdominal x-ray examination. As a general rule, surgical resection should be advised even for an asymptomatic aneurysm, particularly if it is large. Although small aneurysms (< 7 cm) also rupture, surgery may occasionally be withheld if the patient is a poor operative risk and especially if he has a significant cardiac, renal, or distal peripheral obliterative vascular disease. If the aneurysm later increases in size or becomes symptomatic, operative intervention should be seriously considered.

2. Symptomatic—Pain varies from mild midabdominal or lumbar discomfort to severe constant or intermittent abdominal and back pain requiring narcotics for relief. Intermittent pain may be associated with a phase of enlargement or intramural dissection. Pain is an unfavorable prognostic sign which usually justifies early surgery. Peripheral emboli and thrombosis, which commonly complicate the more distal aneurysms, are infrequent in abdominal lesions.

3. Rupture—Rupture of an aneurysm almost always causes death in a few hours or days and is therefore an indication for immediate surgical intervention. Pain is usually severe. Because the dissection is most often into the retroperitoneal tissues, which offer some resistance, shock and other manifestations of blood loss may at first be mild or absent; but free uncontrolled bleeding inevitably follows, resulting in death. There is an expanding, pulsating abdominal and flank mass, and subcutaneous ecchymosis is occasionally present in the flank or groin. About half of such patients can be saved by immediate surgery.

B. Laboratory Findings: Cardiac and renal function should be evaluated by means of ECG, urinalysis, and BUN determination.

C. X-Ray Findings: Calcification in the wall of the aneurysm usually outlines the lesion on anteroposterior and lateral plain films of the abdomen. In some cases the position of the aneurysm in relation to the renal arteries can be identified by intravenous urograms, but more often the examination is inconclusive. Bony erosion of the vertebrae does not usually occur in abdominal aneurysms. Translumbar aortograms are seldom employed; the aneurysm may be ruptured by the procedure, and the information gained regarding the upper limits of the lesion may be inaccurate since a solid thrombus often occupies most of the aneurysm, except for a central channel through which the blood flows. If distal occlusive disease or renovascular hypertension is suspected, an aortogram may be indicated to obtain more accurate knowledge of the extent of the distal disease or the condition of the renal arteries.

Treatment

Surgical excision and grafting of the defect is indicated on all aneurysms of the distal aorta except when the lesion is very small and asymptomatic or when the general condition of the patient is so poor that the surgical risk is greater than the risk of rupture.

Prognosis

The mortality following elective surgical resection is around 10%; of those that survive surgery, approximately 60% are alive 5 years later and 30% 10 years later. Among unoperated patients, approximately 9% survive 5 years and all are dead in 10 years, although rupture of aneurysm does not account for all deaths.

Blum, L.: Ruptured aneurysm of abdominal aorta. New York State J Med 68:2061–2066, 1968.

Campbell, G.S.: Physiological and technical factors in the surgical treatment of abdominal aortic aneurysms. Surgery 62:789, 1967.

Crawford, E.S., & others: Aneurysm of the abdominal aorta. S Clin North America 46:963–978, 1966.

Haimovici, H.: Abdominal aortic aneurysm: A critical clinical reappraisal. J Cardiovas Surg 8:181–194, 1967.

Schatz, I.J.:, Fairbairn, J.F., & J.L. Juergens: Abdominal aortic aneurysms: Reappraisal. Circulation 26:200–205, 1962.

Szligyi, D.E., & others: Contribution of abdominal aortic aneurysmectomy to prolongation of life: 12-year review of 480 cases. Ann Surg 164:678–699, 1966.

·   ·   ·

FEMORAL & POPLITEAL ANEURYSMS

Aneurysms of the femoral or popliteal arteries are not uncommon. They are usually arteriosclerotic in origin, in which case they may be multiple and are often bilateral. They may also be due to trauma. Syphilitic or mycotic aneurysms occur occasionally, the latter after an episode of bacteremia or, more often, from a septic embolus.

The diagnosis is usually not difficult, although a lesion in the popliteal area may go unnoticed until attention is focused on the area by a complication of the aneurysm. The cardinal finding is a firm, pulsating mass in the femoral or popliteal area, often associated with a bruit. Pulsation may not be present if thrombosis has already taken place. The distal circulation may be impaired, especially if the gelatinous thrombus which so frequently fills most of the aneurysm has partially or completely occluded the central lumen or if emboli from this thrombus have blocked one or more of the distal vessels. Arteriography may be helpful in outlining the extent of the aneurysm and the status of the peripheral vessels.

Rupture can occur, and it may result in death or loss of the limb. Complete thrombosis causes distal gangrene in about 1/3 of popliteal aneurysms. Emboli to the distal vessels from the thrombus lining the wall of the aneurysm often cause ischemic changes or gangrene. Thrombophlebitis can occur as a result of pressure obstruction of a neighboring vein. Pressure on the tibial or peroneal nerves may produce pain in the lower leg.

Surgical excision of the aneurysm with grafting of the defect is the treatment of choice in all except very small femoral or popliteal aneurysms or in patients who are poor surgical risks. Bypassing a popliteal aneurysm by means of a vein graft with proximal and distal ligation of the aneurysm is perhaps a more satisfactory approach. The incidence of loss of limb following resection and grafting is low. Thrombophlebitis may occur postoperatively from manipulation or damage of the neighboring veins.

Baird, R.J., & others: Popliteal aneurysms: A review and analysis of 61 cases. Surgery 59:911–917, 1966.

Howell, J.F., & others: Surgical treatment of peripheral arteriosclerotic aneurysm. S Clin North America 46:979–990, 1966.

ARTERIOSCLEROTIC OCCLUSIVE DISEASE

OCCLUSIVE DISEASE OF THE AORTA & ILIAC ARTERIES

Occlusive disease of the aorta and the iliac arteries begins most frequently just proximal to the bifurcation of the common iliac arteries and at or just distal to the bifurcation of the aorta. Atherosclerotic changes occur in the intima and media, often with associated perivascular inflammation and calcified plaques in the media. Progression is usually in a proximal direction, involving first the complete occlusion of one or both common iliac arteries, then the aortic bifurcation, and finally the abdominal aorta up to the segment just below the renal vessels. Although atherosclerosis is a generalized disease, occlusion tends to be segmental in distribution, and when the involvement is in the aorto-iliac vessels there may be minimal atherosclerosis in the more distal external iliac and femoral arteries. The best candidates for direct arterial surgery are those with localized occlusions with relatively normal vessels above and below.

Men between the ages of 30 and 60 are most commonly affected. Cardiac and renal diseases and hypertension are often associated with this defect.

Clinical Findings

Intermittent claudication is almost always present in the calf muscles and is usually present in the thighs and buttocks also. It is most often bilateral and progressive, so that by the time the patient seeks help the pain may be produced by walking a block or less. Difficulty in having or sustaining an erection is a common complaint in men. Coldness of the feet may be present; rest pain is infrequent.

Femoral pulses are absent or very weak. Pulses distal to the femoral area are usually absent. Pulsation of the abdominal aorta may be palpable. A bruit may be heard over the aorta or one or both of the iliac or femoral arteries. Atrophic changes of the skin, subcutaneous tissues, and muscles of the distal leg are usually minimal or absent. Dependent rubor and coolness of the skin of the foot are minimal unless distal arterial disease is also present.

A translumbar aortogram gives much valuable information regarding the level and extent of the occlusion and the condition of the vessels distal to the block. In general, the amount of occlusive arterial disease found at surgery is more marked that what is demonstrated by arteriography. An arteriogram which reveals only minimal occlusive iliac disease does not rule out significant narrowing since the major plaques often involve only the posterior wall of the artery, in which case significant narrowing may not be noted on anteroposterior arteriograms. The possibility of a complication from this procedure must be weighed against the importance of the information to be gained, but it is usually indicated. Anteroposterior and lateral films of the abdomen and sometimes of the thighs will give some information regarding the degree of calcification in the vessels.

Treatment

Surgical treatment is indicated if claudication interferes appreciably with the patient's essential activities or work. The objective of treatment is reestablishment of blood flow through the narrowed or occluded aorto-iliac segment. This can be achieved by arterial prosthesis or thrombo-endarterectomy.

A. Arterial Graft (Prosthesis): An arterial prosthesis, bypassing the occluded segment, is the treatment of choice in the more extensive aorto-iliac occlusions, and in general the bifurcation graft extends from the abdominal aorta to the distal common femoral arteries.

B. Thrombo-endarterectomy: This is perhaps of most value when the occlusion is limited to the common iliac arteries and the external iliac and common femoral arteries are free of occlusive disease.

C. Sympathectomy: A bilateral lumbar sympathectomy should be added to the direct arterial procedure in most cases.

Prognosis

Operative mortality is relatively low and the immediate and long-term benefits are often impressive. Improvement is both subjective and objective, with relief of all or most of the claudication and in many cases return of all of the pulses in the legs.

Garrett, H.E., & others: Surgical considerations in the treatment of aorto-iliac occlusive disease. S Clin North America 46:949–962, 1966.

Humphries, A.W., & others: Experiences with aortoiliac and femoropopliteal endarterectomy. Surgery 63:48–58, 1969.

Kouchoukos, N.T., & others: Operative therapy for aortoiliac arterial occlusive disease. Arch Surg 96:628–635, 1968.

OCCLUSIVE DISEASE OF THE FEMORAL & POPLITEAL ARTERIES

In the region of the thigh and knee the vessels most frequently blocked by occlusive disease are the superficial femoral artery and the popliteal artery. Atherosclerotic changes usually appear first at the most distal point of the superficial femoral artery where it passes through the adductor magnus tendon into the popliteal space. In time the whole superficial femoral artery and the proximal popliteal artery may become occluded. In general, the common femoral and deep femoral arteries are patent and relatively free of disease; the distal popliteal and its 3 terminal branches may also be relatively free of occlusive disease.

Clinical Findings

As a rule, the changes are initially more advanced in one leg than the other, although similar changes often appear later in the other extremity.

A. Symptoms and Signs: Intermittent claudication, which often appears upon as little exertion as walking ½–1 block, is confined to the calf and foot. If rest pain is also present, arterial disease is extensive and the prognosis is poor. Atrophic changes in the lower leg and foot may be quite definite, with loss of hair, thinning of the skin and subcutaneous tissues, and diminution in the size of the muscles. Dependent rubor and blanching on elevation of the foot are usually present. When the leg is lowered after elevation, venous filling on the dorsal aspect of the foot may be slowed to 15–20 seconds or more. The foot is usually cool or cold. If these findings are marked, significant occlusive disease in the aorto-iliac or lower leg vessels also should be suspected. The common femoral pulsations are usually of fair or good quality, but no popliteal or pedal pulses can be felt.

B. X-Ray Findings: X-rays of the thigh and leg may show calcification of superficial femoral and popliteal vessels. A femoral arteriogram will show the location and extent of the block as well as the status of the distal vessels, but often it is important to know the condition of the aorto-iliac vessels also since a relatively normal inflow as well as an adequate distal "run off" is important in determining the success of an arterial procedure; if there is any question, a translumbar aortogram will often give information on the condition of the iliac, femoral, and popliteal vessels (see above).

Treatment

Surgery is indicated (1) if intermittent claudication interferes significantly with the patient's essential physical activities or (2) if pregangrenous or gangrenous lesions appear on the foot and it is hoped that a major amputation can be avoided.

A. Arterial Graft: An autogenous vein graft using a reversed segment of the great saphenous vein can be placed, bypassing the occluded segment. Synthetic arterial prostheses have not proved to be very satisfactory in this area because of the relatively high incidence of early or late thrombosis.

B. Thrombo-endarterectomy: Thrombo-endarterectomy with removal of the central occluding core may be successful, particularly if the occluded segment is short.

When iliac or common femoral occlusive disease exists as well as distal femoral and popliteal occlusions, it is better to relieve the obstructions in the larger, proximal arteries and thus to deliver more blood to the profunda femoris than to operate on the smaller distal vessels where the chances of success are less favorable. This is especially true if the inflow of blood is significantly diminished by the more proximal occlusive disease.

C. Sympathectomy: Lumbar sympathectomy may be used as an adjunct to grafting or endarterectomy or as the sole measure if a direct operation is thought inadvisable. It can be done a few days before or at the same time as a direct procedure; the vasodilator effect of sympathectomy may improve the circulation to the foot and lower leg, especially if there is considerable arterial disease in the vessels of the lower leg or foot.

Prognosis

Thrombosis of the "bypass" graft or of the endarterectomized vessel either in the immediate postoperative period or months or years later is relatively frequent in the superficial femoral-popliteal area. This is particularly true if one or more of the 3 terminal branches of the distal popliteal artery are occluded or badly diseased or if endarterectomy or a synthetic prosthesis is used. For this reason, operation is usually not recommended for mild or moderate claudication, and many of these patients will go for years without much progression of their symptoms or the development of ischemia or gangrene. Some may improve as collateral circulation develops. The chances of success are even less in patients with ischemia or early gangrene, but the procedure is often justified because some limbs can be saved from amputation. Failure of the graft or the endarterectomy does not usually make the condition of the limb worse than it was before the procedure.

Darling, R.C., & others: Saphenous vein bypass grafts for femoropopliteal occlusive disease. Surgery 61:31–40, 1967.

Vollmar, J., & others: Principles of reconstructive procedures for chronic femoro-popliteal occlusions. Ann Surg 168:215–223, 1968.

OCCLUSIVE DISEASE OF THE ARTERIES IN THE LOWER LEG & FOOT

Occlusive processes in the lower leg and foot may involve, in order of incidence, the tibial and common peroneal arteries and their branches to the muscles, the pedal vessels, and occasionally the small digital vessels. Symptoms depend upon the vessels that are narrowed or thrombosed, the suddenness and extent of the occlusion, and the status of the proximal and collateral vessels. The clinical picture may thus vary from slowly developing vascular insufficiency coming on over months or years and sometimes resulting ultimately in atrophy, ischemic pain, and finally gangrene, to a rapidly progressive and extensive thrombosis resulting in acute ischemia and often gangrene.

Clinical Findings

Although all of the possible manifestations of vascular disease in the lower leg and foot cannot be described here, there are certain significant clinical aspects which enter into the evaluation of these patients.

A. Symptoms:

1. Claudication—Intermittent claudication is the commonest presenting symptom. Aching fatigue during exertion usually appears first in the calf muscles; in more severe cases a constant or cramping pain may be brought on by walking only a short distance. Less commonly, the feet are the site of most of the pain. Pain that lasts longer than 10 minutes after rest suggests some other disease, such as arthritis. The distance that the patient can walk before pain becomes severe enough to necessitate a few minutes' rest gives a rough estimate of circulatory inadequacy: 2 blocks (400–500 yards) or more is mild, 1 block is moderate, and ½ block or less is severe.

2. Rest pain—Rest pain may be due to sepsis or ischemia. The former is usually throbbing, whereas ischemia usually produces a persistent, gnawing ache with occasional spasms of sharp pain. Rest pain often comes on in bed at night when the cardiac output is less. The foot is warm and some relief may be obtained by uncovering the foot and placing it in a dependent position. In more advanced stages the pain may be constant and so severe that even narcotics may not relieve it. Ischemic neuropathy is an important factor in this condition. The patient may request amputation.

3. Muscle cramps—Sudden painful contractions that last only a few minutes but leave a soreness for minutes or days in a pulseless leg are usually related to the arterial disease.

B. Signs:

1. Absence of pulsations—Careful palpation over the femoral, popliteal, dorsalis pedis, and posterior tibial arteries should be done to determine which pulsations are present. Although the popliteal pulse may be present, both pedal pulses are usually absent. The dorsalis pedis pulse is congenitally absent in 8% of people, but the posterior tibial pulse is always present unless the artery is diseased even though obesity or edema may make it difficult to feel. The examiner may have trouble telling which pulsations are his own and which are the patient's. Exercise or nitroglycerin may speed the patient's pulse and make the difference more apparent. Exercise in certain patients with arterial disease may make pedal pulses disappear. If a popliteal pulse is present, a direct surgical approach on the vessels of the leg is not likely to be of any value.

2. Color changes in the feet—Normally the skin of the feet is warm and pale as a result of the rapid flow of blood through the arterioles, and few of the capillaries are filled. Skin irritation leads to capillary filling and the skin becomes red. Defective blood supply causes anoxic paralysis of the capillaries and a bluish-red skin (rubor).

The rate of return of color following blanching induced by local pressure is an inaccurate index to circulatory adequacy because the blood which returns on release of the pressure does not necessarily represent true circulation.

a. Pallor upon elevation—If pallor appears rapidly upon elevation of the foot from the horizontal—or if it appears when the leg is only slightly raised—the circulatory status is poor.

b. Flushing time—Color normally returns in a few seconds to a foot placed in a dependent position after 1–2 minutes of elevation with the patient lying on his back. The poorer the collateral circulation, the longer the interval before flushing begins to appear in the toes. In general, if dependent flushing (or reactive hyperemia) begins in the toes within 20 seconds, the arterial disease is mild and the collateral circulation probably adequate, and the extremity may be salvaged by lumbar sympathectomy. If flushing time is over 20 seconds—and especially if it appears only after 45–60 seconds—the arterial disease is extensive and sympathectomy will be of little or no value.

c. Dependent rubor—Beefy redness of the toes or foot on dependency is frequently present in occlusive disease of this area, but it may not reach its full extent until a minute or more after the leg has been placed in the dependent position. Dependent rubor implies moderate or severe arterial occlusive disease.

d. Rubor of stasis—When almost complete stasis in the distal vessels occurs, with venous as well as arterial thrombosis and extravasation of red blood cells, redness of the toes and forefoot may develop which may not completely disappear on elevation of the leg. Usually, however, there is pallor of the skin surrounding the red area in the elevated leg. This disorder is often associated with severe pain and is more commonly noted in thromboangiitis obliterans than in atherosclerosis.

e. Patchy cyanosis and pallor indicates a severe degree of ischemia; it is seen frequently following acute thrombosis or recent embolus.

3. Venous filling time—If the valves in the saphenous system are competent, venous filling is a valuable gauge of collateral circulation of the foot. If the veins on the dorsum of the foot begin to fill in 30 seconds or less after the leg is placed in a dependent position after having been elevated for about 1 minute, the borderline pregangrenous extremity can probably be saved by sympathectomy. After complete obstruction of a major artery, the venous filling time may be as long as 90 seconds.

4. Local tissue changes—Diminished arterial flow causes wasting of the subcutaneous tissues of the digits, foot, and lower leg. Hair is lost over these areas, the skin becomes smooth and shiny, and the nails become thickened and deformed. Infections are common following minor injuries or even without injury at the edge of a nail or under a thick callus. Once established,

infection may become indolent and chronic with the formation of an ischemic ulcer which is often located over a pressure point of the foot; or the infection may lead to localized or progressive gangrene. Local heat should not be used in the treatment of such an infection.

5. Skin temperature studies—Skin temperature and plethysmographic studies may be of value in calibrating the degree of vasoconstrictor activity, and in certain borderline cases may help determine whether lumbar sympathectomy will be of value. A rough clinical test may be carried out by exposing the leg to room temperature for a few minutes. If arterial circulation is inadequate the leg will feel quite cool, especially if there is considerable vasoconstrictor activity or if the leg is quite ischemic.

6. Sweating—Sweating is under the control of the sympathetic nervous system and is therefore an index of the degree of autonomic activity in the extremity. If a patient with occlusive disease still notes sweating of his feet, some degree of sympathetic activity is present and lumbar sympathectomy is more likely to be of benefit.

C. X-Ray Findings: Films of the lower leg and foot may show calcification of the vessels and thinning of the bones. If there is a draining sinus or an ulcer close to a bone or joint, osteomyelitis may be apparent on the film. If fairly strong popliteal pulses can be felt, arteriography is not likely to be of much value as a guide to surgical treatment; sometimes, however, the status of the femoral or popliteal arteries must be evaluated in this way.

D. Arterial Disease in Diabetic Patients: Atherosclerosis develops oftener and earlier in patients with diabetes mellitus, especially if the disease has been poorly controlled over a period of years. Either the large or small vessels may be involved, but occlusion of the smaller vessels is relatively more frequent than in the nondiabetic forms. These are the vessels that do not qualify for direct arterial surgery. The care of the diabetic patient who develops occlusive arterial disease of the foot and lower leg is more difficult. The resistance to infection seems to be less, and the control of diabetes may be more difficult in the presence of infection. Anesthesia of the toes and distal foot (due to diabetic neuropathy) predisposes to injury; in those patients with neurogenic ulcers, pain may be minimal and the peripheral circulation may be perfectly adequate so that local healing may take place at a relatively normal rate. Recurrent trouble is frequent, however, and, because of the sensory deficit, injury and secondary infection may be advanced before medical attention is sought. Visual defects due to diabetic retinopathy make care of the feet more difficult and injuries more likely.

Ulcers and gangrene, when present, are more likely to be moist and infected and progress more rapidly, often with a more generalized inflammatory response.

Treatment

A. Intermittent Claudication: The patient should be instructed to walk slowly, take short steps, avoid stairs and hills, and to stop for brief rests to avoid pain. Walking, however, is the most effective way to develop collateral circulation, and walking up to the point of claudication followed by a 3-minute rest should be done at least 8 times a day.

Lumbar sympathectomy is the surgical treatment of choice. It is most likely to be of benefit if the popliteal pulse is palpable, but it may still be of value when only the femoral pulse can be felt in the leg. A flushing time or venous filling time of 20 seconds or less when the leg, blanched by a period of elevation, is placed in the dependent position is a favorable sign; if flushing or venous filling is delayed more than 30 seconds, there is much less chance that sympathectomy will be of any benefit. If sweating of the feet occurs, the operative result is likely to be favorable. More refined objective evidence for or against the operation may be obtained in constant temperature rooms and by means of the plethysmograph. Walking capacity following sympathectomy may never improve or may not improve for weeks or months since the increased collateral flow to the muscles develops gradually. The improvement in skin circulation, with a dry, warm foot, is often apparent within a few hours.

A frequent and annoying sequel to sympathectomy is an unexplained neuralgia down the lateral aspect of the thigh and leg which develops usually by about the 10th postoperative day. The pain may be mild or severe, and may last for days or weeks. The treatment is symptomatic, and the neuralgia always ultimately disappears.

B. Circulatory Insufficiency in the Foot and Toes: Sympathectomy may be indicated even when the femoral pulse is absent or when pregangrenous changes are present in the toes. Moderate or marked rest pain usually implies such advanced changes that the procedure will often be of little or no benefit. The operation usually results in a dry, warmer foot, and is of value for patients whose marginally adequate circulation becomes dangerously reduced by normal vasoconstrictive reflexes. The additional collateral flow serves to protect the leg should further vascular occlusions occur. Vasodilator drugs are usually of little or no value and, unless there is abnormal vasoconstriction, may actually be harmful. Blood flow studies show a decrease in the blood supply to the ischemic limb of the elderly arteriosclerotic at the height of systemic vasodilatation due to drugs. Other measures as outlined under Instructions in the Care of the Feet should also be employed (see Chapter 18).

C. Infections, Ulcers, and Gangrene of the Toes or Foot:

1. Early treatment of acute infections–Place the patient at complete bed rest with the leg in a horizontal or slightly depressed position. An open or discharging lesion should be covered with a light gauze dressing, but tape should not be used on the skin. Culture and sensitivity studies should be obtained if there is any purulent discharge, but if advancing infection is present an appropriate antibiotic should be started immediately. Purulent pockets should be drained.

Ulcerations covered with necrotic tissue can often be prepared for spontaneous healing or grafting with wet dressings of sterile saline changed 3–4 times a day. Petrolatum or Xeroform® gauze and a bacitracin-neomycin ointment may also help soften crusted infected areas and aid drainage.

Treat diabetes and anemia, if present.

2. Early management of established gangrene–In most instances an area of gangrene will progress to a point where the circulation provided by the inflammatory reaction is sufficient to prevent progressive tissue death. The process will at least temporarily demarcate at that level. This can be encouraged by measures similar to those outlined in the preceding section on the treatment of acute infection. If the skin is intact and the gangrene is dry and due only to arterial occlusion, antibiotics should be withheld. If infection is present or if the gangrene is moist, antibiotics should be used in an effort to limit the process and prevent septicemia.

If the gangrene involves only a segment of skin and the underlying superficial tissue, sympathectomy and, if possible, an artery graft may reverse the process. The necrotic tissue can be removed and the ulcer grafted or allowed to heal as outlined above in the section on ulcers. If the hoped for healing does not occur and amputation is required, it can sometimes be carried out at a more distal level because of those procedures.

3. Amputations for gangrene–

(1) A toe which is gangrenous to its base can sometimes be amputated through the necrotic tissue and left open; this procedure may be employed to establish adequate drainage when there is active infection with undrained pus in addition to the gangrene.

(2) When the distal part of the toe is gangrenous and there is sufficient circulation in the proximal toe, a closed amputation can be carried out after the area has become well demarcated and inflammation has subsided.

(3) Transmetatarsal amputation can be considered if the gangrene involves one or more toes down to but not into the foot and if the circulation in the distal foot seems adequate to support healing.

(4) Amputation below the knee may be employed in patients with a palpable popliteal pulse or even without one if there is good collateral circulation around the knee (as indicated by a warm and well-nourished lower leg) when gangrene or ischemia in the foot is so severe or so distributed that local amputation (as outlined above) is not feasible. The preservation of the knee and proximal part of the lower leg is most important in that a more useful prosthesis can then be applied and the patient can turn in bed with greater ease, and amputation at that level should be attempted provided there is a reasonable chance of success.

(5) Amputation above the knee (through the distal thigh in the supracondylar area) is indicated in patients with very advanced peripheral vascular disease requiring amputation because of gangrene or severe ischemic pain. It is also employed if an attempted below-knee amputation has failed to heal. Even if the

femoral artery is obliterated, there will be sufficient collateral circulation to allow healing provided gentle technic with good hemostasis is used.

(6) Guillotine amputation–Infection with bacteremia or septicemia occasionally develops secondary to gangrene of the lower extremity. This usually requires emergency amputation above or below the knee. In such a situation, it is often wise to leave the stump open so that it can heal by secondary intention or be revised or reamputated when the infection has been controlled.

Crawford, E.S., & others: Occlusive disease of the femoral artery and its branches. S Clin North America 46:991–1000, 1966.

Gomes, M.R., Berratz, P.E., & J.C. Juergens: Aortoiliac surgery. Arch Surg 95:387–394, 1967.

Moore, W.S., & others: Below knee amputation for vascular insufficiency. Arch Surg 97:886–893, 1968.

Shaw, R.S., Austen, W.G., & S. Stipa: A ten year study of lumbar sympathectomy on the peripheral circulation of patients with arteriosclerotic occlusive disease. Surg Gynec Obst 119:486–494, 1964.

Szilagyi, D.E., & others: Lumbar sympathectomy: Current role in treatment of arteriosclerotic occlusive disease. Arch Surg 95:753–761, 1967.

OCCLUSIVE DISEASE OF THE EXTRACRANIAL ARTERIES

The symptoms of cerebrovascular insufficiency may vary from gradual mental deterioration to sudden complete hemiplegia and death. In the majority of patients the stenosis or occlusion is in the intracranial arteries and thus is not amenable to surgical correction, but in approximately 1/3 of cases disease of one or more of the extracranial vessels is responsible for either the major stroke or, more frequently, the recurrent "little strokes" or ischemic episodes.

Arteriosclerosis is the usual cause of extracranial arterial occlusive disease and the process is frequently segmental in nature, involving typically the common carotid bifurcation and the proximal portions of the internal carotid and vertebral arteries; less commonly, the intrathoracic segments of the major aortic branches may be involved. The significant occlusive process may be limited to a short segment of one vessel, or 4 vessels may be involved. Consequently, the integrity of all the vessels supplying the brain should be assessed in evaluating symptoms thought to be due to cerebral or brain stem ischemia on the basis of a reduction below a critical point of the total blood flow to the brain.

Occlusions of the great vessels at the aortic arch can also occur as a result of syphilitic aortitis or of a nonspecific arteritis which may occur in young women.

Clinical Findings

A. Symptoms and Signs: There is no completely consistent correlation between the clinical findings and the degree and location of the occlusive arterial processes. Therefore, arteriography is of major importance.

1. Carotid vessels–In insufficiency related primarily to the carotid vessels, the symptoms are usually those of supratentorial involvement: weakness of the extremities or face, anesthesia, aphasia, mental confusion, memory deterioration, personality changes, hemiplegia, and coma. Pulsation in the internal carotid artery cannot be accurately palpated clinically, but a bruit over the carotid bifurcation is an indication of stenosis of the internal carotid in that area. Occlusive disease may exist in the absence of a bruit, and a bruit may be present in the absence of significant obstruction.

2. Vertebral and basilar vessels–Insufficiency related primarily to the vertebral and basilar vessels results in subtentorial symptoms such as vertigo (especially on standing up) and unsteady gait.

3. Eye manifestations–Transient episodes of altered vision or blindness (especially when walking) may occur, and there may be decreased intraoptic arterial pressure on the side of the major carotid occlusive disease as measured by ophthalmodynamometry. (Use of a tilt table, with measurements made in both supine and upright positions, increases the value of this eye examination.) Microemboli of fibrin, platelet thrombi, or fragments of arteriosclerotic material which may arise from arteriosclerotic ulcers in the carotid artery may be noted in the retinal arteries in association with a transient episode of altered vision.

4. Great vessels–Occlusive lesions of the great vessels arising from the aortic arch may produce intermittent claudication in the arm, diminished or absent pulsations in the common carotid or axillary vessels, blood pressure differences in the 2 arms, or a bruit over the supraclavicular areas.

5. Subclavian steal syndrome–When the proximal left subclavian or the innominate artery is completely occluded, some of the collateral blood flow to the arm may come through the vertebral artery on the involved side as a retrograde flow, resulting in reduction of the total blood supply to the brain. Exercise of the arm may thus be associated not only with claudication but also with dizzy spells or other CNS symptoms.

B. X-Ray Findings: Arteriography is the most accurate diagnostic procedure and usually consists of a series of studies which include all 4 arteries to the brain. An aortic arch study may be done first, usually by means of a catheter inserted into the arch through the right axillary or brachial artery or through one of the femoral arteries. The percutaneous method of catheterization (Seldingen technic) is customarily used. Direct injection through a needle inserted into the carotid artery may be necessary for more detailed views of the carotid bifurcation. The inclusion of the intracranial arteries in the study may help to rule out a neoplasm or occlusive disease in the cerebral arteries.

Treatment

A. Indications: Surgery may restore a more normal blood flow to the brain, and improvement may result if the collateral flow has not been adequate. Surgery may provide some future protection to the brain from damage due to a progression of the arterial disease with further reduction of total blood flow, or from emboli to the brain originating in the areas of stenosis. Stenoses that narrow the lumen less than 50% are not significant and should be left alone. "Prophylactic" surgery on stenotic vessels in patients with no CNS symptoms is seldom indicated.

1. Emergency surgery–Emergency surgery for acute stroke has been disappointing, and fatal postoperative bleeding into an area of infarcted brain is not infrequent. In general, arterial studies and surgery should be deferred for at least several weeks until the condition has stabilized and collateral circulation has become better established.

2. Elective surgery–Patients with suspected extracranial arterial stenosis with intermittent symptoms or constant mild neurologic defects should be evaluated for surgery.

3. Withhold surgery–Patients with hemiplegia who show no signs of recovery will not be benefited by an operation to improve the blood supply to the damaged brain.

B. Surgical Treatment: Thrombo-endarterectomy is generally employed to relieve a stenosis of the bifurcation of the common carotid artery which is considered to be clinically significant (over 60% occlusion). Carotid occlusions at the level of the aorta are generally treated by means of a bypass graft; a procedure limited to the neck is usually sufficient.

The period of complete occlusion of the carotid while the arterial procedure is in progress may occasionally (5–10%) result in temporary or permanent brain damage and sometimes in death.

There is evidence that general anesthesia provides some protection to the brain provided the preoperative blood pressure is maintained throughout the surgical procedure. Some advocate an internal shunt to maintain internal carotid flow during the endarterectomy procedure, especially in patients with bilateral carotid stenoses. Reliable criteria are still being sought to determine which patients require an internal shunt during endarterectomy.

Prognosis

Although the surgical procedure can be done in carefully selected patients with an acceptable mortality and complication rate, it has not been proved conclusively that surgery results in prolongation of life. Transient ischemic attacks can usually be eliminated, even though the individual may not be permanently protected from a major stroke in the future.

Egan, R.W., & J.F. Upson: Carotid artery surgery for cerebral vascular insufficiency. Angiology 16:698, 1965.
Hohf, R.P.: The clinical evaluation and surgery of internal carotid insufficiency. S Clin North America 47:71–89, 1967.
Santschi, D.R., & others: The subclavian steal syndrome: Clinical and angiographic considerations in 74 cases in adults. J Thoracic Cardiovas Surg 51:103, 1966.

Schwartz, W.S., Ramseyer, J.C., & R.N. Baker: Management of transient cerebral ischemic attacks. California Med 107:471–480, 1967.
Yashon, D., & others: Long term results of carotid bifurcation endarterectomy. Surg Gynec Obst 122:517–523, 1966.

RENAL ARTERY STENOSIS

Stenosis of a renal artery can cause progressive hypertension, which may be relieved by restoring a more normal blood flow to the kidney. The renal pressor mechanism functions whenever all or a portion of the kidney is inadequately perfused. Atherosclerosis is the most common cause, but congenital stenosis of the renal artery does occur and may account for hypertension in children and young adults. Stenosis of one or both renal arteries can result from thickening of the media of the artery (fibromuscular hyperplasia), and this condition can account for hypertension in the young or the middle-aged (especially women).

Clinical Findings

A. Symptoms and Signs: Renal artery stenosis should be considered in any patient with rapidly developing, severe hypertension, especially if the diastolic pressure is high or if a bruit can be heard in the upper abdomen over the area of a renal artery, and in the following types of cases: hypertension which has its onset either in old people or in those under 30; hypertension which develops or progresses after an episode of flank or abdominal pain; and hypertension in patients in whom intravenous urograms reveal a definite difference in the size of the kidneys (more than 1 cm) or a difference in the time taken for the nephrogram to appear or for the first sign of the contrast media to appear in each renal pelvis. (Frequent films for the first 10 minutes are necessary to determine the degree of difference.)

B. Laboratory Findings: Isotope renography, using one, 2, or 3 different isotopes to define separate aspects of renal blood flow and function by means of the scintillation camera, is a relatively simple screening procedure. Differential renal excretion studies are now generally considered too difficult to perform with sufficient accuracy to yield reliable results. Measurement of circulating renin or angiotensin may become of value as a screening test.

C. X-Ray Findings: Although a difference between the 2 kidneys may be seen on intravenous urogram, as noted above (and, if present, may be a significant finding), a normal study does not rule out renal artery disease, particularly if bilateral renal artery stenosis exists. Renal arteriography, preferably by the retrograde femoral approach, is the definitive method for demonstrating the presence, nature, location, and extent of an obstructing renal artery lesion. If the simpler screening studies such as the rapid sequence intravenous urogram and the isotope renogram are suggestive of renal artery stenosis in a young or middle-aged individual, the study is probably indicated.

Treatment

The treatment of choice in the carefully selected patient is to remove or bypass the stenosis; if this cannot be done, nephrectomy should be performed provided the other kidney is free from disease.

If the diagnosis is accurate and surgical correction of the defect is successful, a normotensive state is achieved in many cases. In the very arteriosclerotic patient over 50 or 60, the surgical mortality is such that medical management or nephrectomy rather than direct arterial surgery should be seriously considered.

Foster, J.H., & others: Hypertension and fibromuscular dysplasia of the renal arteries. Surgery 65:157–181, 1969.

Hunter, J.A., & others: Problems in management of renovascular hypertension. S Clin North America 47:91–107, 1967.

Morris, G.C., & others: Late results of surgical treatment for renovascular hypertension. Surg Gynec Obst 122:1–7, 1966.

Perloff, D., & others: Renal vascular hypertension: Further experiences. Am Heart J 74:614–631, 1967.

Winter, C.C.: *Correctable Renal Hypertension.* Lea & Febiger, 1964.

CELIAC & SUPERIOR MESENTERIC ARTERY DISEASE

Aneurysms or occlusive disease occasionally occur in the visceral branches of the abdominal aorta. Arterial insufficiency to the intestine is generally manifested by postprandial pain and malabsorption leading to weight loss. A bruit is generally audible. Catheter angiography may define the extent of the occlusive disease and show whether arterial surgery—such as endarterectomy or bypass graft—is indicated. Thrombosis of the superior mesenteric artery generally results in infarction of the bowel. (See Acute Mesenteric Vascular Occlusion in Chapter 10.)

Rob, C.: Surgical diseases of the celiac and mesenteric arteries. Arch Surg 93:21–32, 1966.

Stoney, R.J., & E.J. Wylie: Recognition and surgical management of visceral ischemic syndromes. Ann Surg 164:714–722, 1966.

ACUTE ARTERIAL OCCLUSION

Essentials of Diagnosis

- Symptoms and signs depend on the artery occluded, the organ or region supplied by the artery, and the adequacy of the collateral circulation to the area primarily involved.
- Occlusion in an extremity usually results in pain, numbness, tingling, weakness, and coldness. There is pallor or mottling; motor, reflex, and sensory alterations or loss; and collapsed superficial veins. Pulsations in arteries distal to the occlusion are absent.
- Occlusions in other areas result in such conditions as cerebral vascular accidents, intestinal ischemia and gangrene, and renal or splenic infarcts.

Differential Diagnosis

The primary diagnosis is between arterial embolism and thrombosis. In an older individual with both arteriosclerotic vascular disease and cardiac disease, the differentiation may be very difficult. Acute thrombophlebitis with arterial spasm can be distinguished on the basis of a normal or elevated skin temperature, distended veins, and edema.

1. ARTERIAL EMBOLISM

Arterial embolism usually occurs as a complication of rheumatic heart disease, myocardial infarction, bacterial endocarditis, or congestive heart failure; about 2/3 of cases are associated with atrial fibrillation. In about 10% of patients no source of the embolus is clinically evident, and in this group the differential diagnosis between embolism and thrombosis may be difficult.

Occasionally an arterial thrombus may dislodge, resulting in an embolus to a distal arterial segment; aneurysms, arteriosclerotic plaques or ulcers, or inflammatory conditions such as thromboangiitis obliterans may be the source of such emboli; if the emboli are small, the symptoms may be localized and transient.

Emboli tend to lodge at the bifurcation of an artery and usually occur in the arteries of the lower extremities, although the arteries of the upper extremities, brain, or viscera are occasionally involved.

Clinical Findings

In an extremity, the initial symptoms are usually pain (sudden or gradual in onset), numbness, coldness, and tingling. Symptoms may have a sudden onset, though they may develop gradually over a period of several hours. Signs include absence of pulsations in the arteries distal to the block; coldness, pallor or mottling; hypesthesia or anesthesia; and weakness or paresis of the limb. The superficial veins are collapsed. Later, blebs and skin necrosis may appear, and gangrene may occur.

Treatment

Immediate embolectomy is the treatment of choice in almost all early cases. It should be done within 12 hours of the embolic episode if possible. If a longer delay has occurred or if there is clinical evidence of tissue necrosis, embolectomy may be associated with too high a mortality; in such circumstances, nonoperative measures (as outlined below) should be depended upon, accepting amputation at a later date in some of these cases.

A. Emergency Preoperative Care:

1. Heparin—Heparin sodium, 5000 units IV, should be given as soon as the diagnosis is made or suspected in an effort to prevent distal thrombosis. The effect of this dose will usually be dissipated by the time the patient has been moved to surgery. If a 4–5 hour delay is anticipated, 3000–4000 units should also be given IM.

2. Sympathetic block—A sympathetic block should not be attempted once heparin has been given, and it is better to emphasize heparin treatment and surgery at the earliest moment rather than to risk the delay involved in a blocking procedure. If surgery must be delayed or if the patient is considered inoperable, a sympathetic block may be tried before heparin is given.

3. Protect the part—Keep the extremity at or below the horizontal plane. Do not apply heat or cold to the involved extremity (but heat to an uninvolved extremity may help produce reflex vasodilatation). Protect from hard surfaces and overlying bedclothes.

4. Vasodilators—Papaverine, 60 mg IV every 2–3 hours, or 30 mg intra-arterially proximal to the site of occlusion, may be given. Whisky, 1½ oz 4 times daily, nicotinic acid, 50 mg 4 times daily, or tolazoline (Priscoline®), 12.5–25 mg 3–4 times daily, may also be tried if surgery is not considered possible.

5. Analgesics—Pain should be relieved with an analgesic.

6. Arteriography—Arteriography may be of value either before or during surgery. There may be more than one embolus in an extremity; x-ray studies may help locate a distal embolus or determine the extent of the thrombosis.

B. Surgical Treatment: Local anesthesia is generally used if the occlusion is in an artery to an extremity. After removing the embolus through the arteriotomy, the proximal and distal artery should be explored for additional emboli or secondary thrombi by means of a specially designed catheter with a small inflatable balloon at the tip (Fogarty catheter). An embolus at the aortic bifurcation or in the iliac artery can often be removed under local anesthesia through common femoral arteriotomies with the use of these same catheters.

Prognosis

Arterial embolism is a threat not only to the limb but also to the life of the patient. Emergency surgery is poorly tolerated by patients with major cardiac disease and the hospital mortality is high.

Mortality increases with the size and location of the embolus; aortic and iliac emboli are the most dangerous. Concomitant cerebral or mesenteric embolism may occur, as well as progressive cardiac failure. Emboli associated with hypertensive or arteriosclerotic heart disease have a poorer prognosis than those arising from rheumatic valvular disease in younger patients. Emboli recur in almost half of the entire group of patients, and in over half of those with atrial fibrillation.

In patients with atrial fibrillation an attempt should be made to restore normal rhythm with quinidine or cardioversion, although restoration of normal rhythm tends to be permanent only in patients with recent or transitory fibrillation. Long-term anticoagulant therapy may diminish the danger of further emboli. Correction of mitral stenosis with the patient on cardiopulmonary bypass is indicated in selected individuals. Heart surgery done in the earlier stages of mitral stenosis diminishes the chance of later embolic complications.

2. ACUTE ARTERIAL THROMBOSIS

Acute arterial thrombosis generally occurs in an artery in which the lumen has become almost obliterated by the gradual deposition of atherosclerotic material in the wall of the artery, often resulting in a channel which is 90% or more obliterated. Blood flowing through such a narrow, irregular, or ulcerated lumen may clot, leading to a sudden, complete occlusion of the narrow segment. The thrombosis may then propagate either up or down the artery to a point where the blood is flowing rapidly through a somewhat less diseased artery, usually into a significant arterial branch. Occasionally the thrombosis is precipitated when the blood stream displaces an arteriosclerotic plaque, blocking the lumen. Inflammatory involvement of the arterial wall, with narrowing of the channel as in thromboangiitis obliterans, will also lead to acute thrombosis. Chronic mechanical irritation of the subclavian artery compressed by a cervical rib may also lead to a complete occlusion. Thrombosis in a diseased artery may be secondary to an episode of hypotension, trauma to the area of the artery, or cardiac failure. Polycythemia also increases the chance of thrombosis.

Chronic, incomplete arterial obstruction usually results in the establishment of some collateral flow, and further flow will develop relatively rapidly through the collaterals once complete occlusion has developed. The extremity may go through an extremely critical period of hours or days, however, while the additional collateral circulation develops around the block. The survival of the tissue distal to the block depends on the development of adequate collateral circulation, which in turn depends on the location and length of the arterial thrombosis and whether undesirable conditions such as shock, heart failure, anemia, or hemoconcentration can be corrected promptly.

Clinical Findings

The local findings in the extremity are usually very similar to those described in the section on arterial embolus. The following differential points should be checked: (1) Are there manifestations of advanced occlusive arterial disease in other areas, especially the opposite extremity (bruit, absent pulses, secondary changes as described on p 232)? Is there a history of intermittent claudication? These clinical manifestations are suggestive but not diagnostic of thrombosis. (2) Is there a history or are there findings of a recent episode of atrial fibrillation or myocardial infarction? If so, an embolus is more likely than a thrombosis. (3) ECG and serum enzyme studies may give added information regarding the cardiac state and its likelihood as a source of an embolus. (4) An emergency arteriogram may be of value in making a more accurate differential diagnosis and in planning the therapy.

Treatment

Whereas emergency embolectomy is the usual approach in the case of an early occlusion from an embolus, a nonoperative approach is frequently used in the case of thrombosis for 2 reasons: (1) The segment of thrombosed artery may be quite long, requiring rather extensive and difficult surgery (thromboendarterectomy or artery graft). The removal of a single embolus in a normal or nearly normal artery is, by comparison, relatively quick and definitive. (2) The extremity is more likely to survive without development of gangrene because some collateral circulation has usually formed during the stenotic phase before acute thrombosis. With an embolus, this is not usually the case; the block is most often at a major arterial bifurcation, occluding both branches, and the associated arterial spasm is usually more acute.

Treatment is therefore as outlined under emergency preoperative care for the arterial embolus (see above), with observation for hours or days. Gradual improvement in the circulation of the distal areas of the extremity is usually noted. If this does not occur and if tissue necrosis seems likely, emergency surgery may be considered, particularly if x-ray studies reveal that there is a reasonable chance of success. Sympathectomy may occasionally tip the balance in a borderline situation and save the extremity.

Prognosis

Limb survival usually occurs with acute thrombosis of the iliac or superficial femoral arteries; gangrene is more likely if the popliteal is suddenly occluded, especially if the period between occlusion and treatment is long or if there is considerable arterial spasm or proximal arterial occlusive disease. If the limb does survive the acute occlusion, a period of observation and evaluation will usually be possible and the late treatment and prognosis is outlined above in the section on occlusive disease of the femoral and popliteal arteries.

Darling, R.C., & others: Arterial embolism. Surg Gynec Obst 124:106–114, 1967.

Deterling, R.A., Jr.: Acute arterial occlusion. S Clin North America 46:587–604, 1966.

Fogarty, T.J.: Catheter technic for arterial embolectomy. J Cardiovas Surg 8:22–28, 1967.

Hallman, G.L., & others: Surgical considerations in arterial embolism. S Clin North America 46:1013–1020, 1966.

Wessler, S., & others: Studies in peripheral arterial occlusive disease. III. Acute arterial occlusion. Circulation 17:512–525, 1958.

• • •

THROMBOANGIITIS OBLITERANS (TAO)
(Buerger's Disease)

Essentials of Diagnosis

- Almost always in young men who smoke.
- Extremities involved with inflammatory occlusions of the more distal arteries, with circulatory insufficiency of the toes or fingers.
- Thromboses of superficial veins may also occur.
- Course is intermittent and amputation may be necessary, especially if smoking is not stopped.

General Considerations

Buerger's disease is an episodic and segmental inflammatory and thrombotic process of the arteries and veins, principally in the limbs. It is seen most commonly in men between the ages of 25 and 35. The effects of the disease are almost solely due to occlusion of the arteries. The symptoms are primarily due to ischemia, complicated in the later stages by infection and tissue necrosis. The inflammatory process is intermittent, with quiescent periods lasting weeks, months, or years.

The clinical differential diagnosis between Buerger's disease and atherosclerotic peripheral vascular disease may be difficult or impossible.

The arteries of the legs are most commonly affected. The plantar and digital vessels and those in the lower leg (especially the posterior tibial artery) are most frequently involved. Occlusion of the femoral-popliteal arteries does not often occur. In the upper extremity, the distal arteries are most commonly affected. Different arterial segments may become occluded in successive episodes; a certain amount of recanalization occurs during quiescent periods.

Superficial migratory thrombophlebitis is a common early indication of the disease.

The cause is not known, but alteration in the collagen in the vessels suggests that it may be a collagen disorder. A history of smoking is almost always obtained and little or no progress can be made in treatment if the patient continues to smoke.

Clinical Findings

The signs and symptoms are primarily those of arterial insufficiency, and the differentiation from arteriosclerotic peripheral vascular disease may thus be difficult. Although the 2 diseases are similar in many ways, the following findings suggest Buerger's disease:

(1) The patient is a man between the ages of 20 and 40 who smokes.

(2) There is a history or finding of small, red, tender cords resulting from migratory superficial segmental thrombophlebitis, usually in the saphenous tributaries rather than the main vessel. A biopsy of such a vein often gives microscopic proof of Buerger's disease.

(3) Intermittent claudication is common and is frequently noted in the palm of the hand or arch of the foot. Rest pain is common and, when present, is persistent. It takes the form of gnawing or aching, often interferes with sleeping and eating, and tends to be more pronounced than in the patient with atherosclerosis. Numbness, diminished sensation, and pricking and burning pains may be present as a result of ischemic neuropathy.

(4) The digit or the entire distal portion of the foot may be pale and cold or there may be rubor which may remain relatively unchanged by posture; the skin may not blanch on elevation, and on dependency the intensity of the rubor is often more pronounced than that seen in the atherosclerotic group. The distal vascular changes are often asymmetric, so that not all of the toes are affected to the same degree. Absence or impairment of pulsations in the dorsalis pedis, posterior tibial, ulnar, or radial artery is frequent.

(5) Trophic changes may be present, often with painful indolent ulcerations along the nail margins.

(6) There is usually evidence of disease in both legs and possibly also in the hands and lower arms. There may be a history or findings of Raynaud's phenomenon in the finger or distal foot.

(7) The course is usually intermittent, with acute and often dramatic episodes followed by rather definite remissions. When the collateral vessels as well as the main channels have become occluded, an exacerbation is more likely to lead to gangrene and amputation. The course in the patient with atherosclerosis tends to be less dramatic and more persistent.

Differential Diagnosis

Arteriosclerosis obliterans occurs in an older age group, sometimes with associated hyperlipidemia and vessel calcification and without associated phlebitis.

Scleroderma causes characteristic skin changes prior to definite vascular findings.

Raynaud's disease causes symmetric bilateral color changes, primarily in young women. There is no impairment of arterial pulsations.

Livedo reticularis and acrocyanosis are vasospastic diseases which do not affect peripheral pulsations.

Frostbite may produce superficial gangrene. Pulsations proximal to the region of gangrene are not impaired, and there is a history of exposure to cold. Nonvascular trophic ulcers may occur in tabes dorsalis, syringomyelia, and other diseases associated with sensory loss. In these disorders pulsations are present and there are no postural color changes.

Among the neuromuscular conditions, the lesions most commonly confused with Buerger's disease are protruded intervertebral disks, metatarsalgia, and other mechanical foot derangements. None of these cause typical claudication or changes in peripheral pulsations.

Treatment

The principles of therapy are the same as those outlined for atherosclerotic peripheral vascular disease, but the long-range outlook is better in patients with Buerger's disease, so that when possible the approach should be more conservative and tissue loss kept to a minimum.

A. General Measures: Smoking must be given up; the physician should be emphatic and insistent on this point. The disease is almost sure to progress if this advice is not heeded.

See Instructions in the Care of the Feet in Chapter 18.

B. Surgical Treatment:

1. Sympathectomy—Sympathectomy is useful in eliminating the vasospastic manifestations of the disease and aiding in the establishment of collateral circulation during the acute phase. It is also helpful in relieving the milder or moderate forms of intermittent claudication and rest pain; if amputation of a digit is necessary, it may aid in the healing of the surgical wound.

2. Arterial grafts—If the femoral pulse is present and the popliteal pulse is absent, a femoral arteriogram should be taken to assess the feasibility of using a graft. However, arterial grafting procedures are not often indicated in patients with Buerger's disease because they do not usually have a complete block in the ileofemoral region.

3. Amputation—The indications for amputation are similar in many respects to those outlined for the atherosclerotic group (see above), although the approach should be somewhat more conservative from the point of view of the preservation of tissue. Most patients with Buerger's disease who are managed carefully do not require amputation. The results of amputation of the middle 3 toes are better than the results which can be achieved by amputation of the great and little toes. It is almost never necessary to amputate the entire hand, although fingers must occasionally be removed.

If there is evidence of both large and small vessel disease, the results of conservative management are poor and amputation is frequently necessary. Pain may become so severe that the conservative approach must be discarded.

Prognosis

Except in the case of the rapidly progressive form of the disease—and provided the patient stops smoking and takes good care of his feet—the prognosis for survival of the extremities is good. Buerger's disease rarely results in death.

Abramson, D.I., & others: Thromboangiitis obliterans: A true clinical entity. Am J Cardiol 12:107–118, 1963.

Eadie, D.G.A., & others: Buerger's disease. Brit J Surg 55:452–456, 1968.

Goodman, R.M., & others: Buerger's disease in Israel. Am J Med 39:601–615, 1965.

Schatz, I.J., Fine, G., & W.R. Eyler: Thromboangiitis obliterans. Brit Heart J 28:84–91, 1966.

IDIOPATHIC ARTERITIS OF TAKAYASU
("Pulseless Disease")

Pulseless disease, most frequent in young women, is a polyarteritis of unknown etiology, with particular predilection for the aortic arch and its branches. It occurs particularly in the Orient. Manifestations, depending upon the vessel or vessels involved, may include evidence of cerebrovascular insufficiency, syncope or dizziness, marked collateral circulation in the neck, chest, and shoulders, absence of pulsations in the upper extremities, visual disturbances, and ophthalmologic changes compatible with chronic hypoxia of the ocular structures. Systemic symptoms, such as are encountered in systemic lupus erythematosus, do not occur.

Pulseless disease must be differentiated from vascular lesions of the aortic arch due to syphilis and atherosclerosis.

The arteritis leads to progressive occlusion of the proximal carotid, innominate, or subclavian arteries and, unless treated by bypass grafts of the involved vessels, can lead to blindness and hemiplegia.

Austen, W.G., & R.S. Shaw: Surgical treatment of pulseless (Takayasu's) disease. New England J Med 270:1228–1231, 1964.

Johnson, C.D., Ziakle,T.J., & L.L. Smith: Occlusive disease of the vessels of the aortic arch: Diagnosis and management. California Med 108:20–24, 1968.

TEMPORAL ARTERITIS
(Giant Cell Arteritis)

Temporal arteritis is a disease of unknown cause that occurs in the elderly. Because the characteristic giant cells are frequently present not only in the temporal arteries but in the aorta and its branches as well, the condition is frequently called giant cell arteritis. The arterial manifestations may be preceded by musculoskeletal symptomatology identical to that of polymyalgia rheumatica and presumably represent different clinical manifestations of the same disease.

Clinical Findings
A. Symptoms and Signs: Prodromal symptoms consisting of aches and pains of joints or muscles and malaise may exist for several years. A low-grade fever, anorexia, fatigue, and weight loss may also precede the development of localizing symptoms by weeks or months. Severe throbbing frontal or occipital headaches may then appear and persist for some time. Ocular complications consisting of sudden or gradual loss of vision in one or both eyes (50% bilateral) may then appear as a result of involvement of the central retinal artery. Systemic complications from arterial lesions in the cerebral or coronary vessels or the aorta may lead to a cerebral or myocardial infarction or aortic dissection.

The involved temporal or occipital arteries are firm, tender cords which may be nodular and are usually pulseless. Erythema in the same region is usually present. Vascular abnormalities may be present in the retinas.

B. Laboratory Findings: Mild anemia, leukocytosis, and a markedly elevated sedimentation rate are usually present. Biopsy of the involved temporal artery will yield a microscopic diagnosis (though occasionally the temporal artery is not involved even in advanced cases).

C. X-Ray Findings: Temporal arteriography may be useful as a screening procedure and may also help to determine the proper biopsy site.

Treatment
Smoking should be discontinued.

A. Analgesia: Relief of pain with analgesics is indicated, but the stronger narcotics should not be used because of the danger of addiction in chronic cases. Local infiltration with lidocaine (Xylocaine®) may be of value.

B. Corticosteroid Therapy: Corticosteroid therapy should be begun as soon as the diagnosis is made. The prodromal symptoms and headaches respond promptly to this therapy, and the ocular complications can be prevented. Large doses should be used initially (300 mg of cortisone daily or comparable amounts of the newer analogues). Maintain on 200 mg of cortisone (or equivalent) until symptoms are controlled (usually 2–5 weeks) and then reduce the dosage gradually but maintain on 25–75 mg of cortisone (or equivalent) until the disease has run its course. Symptoms can reappear after therapy has been diminished or discontinued, so continued observation is necessary.

Prognosis
Temporal arteritis is often a self-limited disease which may persist for 2 months to 2 years. If diagnosed and treated early, the ocular and grave systemic complications can be prevented. Blindness and death may result if the disease is not diagnosed and treated.

Andrews, J.M.: Giant-cell ("temporal") arteritis: A disease with variable clinical manifestations. Neurology 16:963–971, 1966.

Bevan, A.T., Dunnill, M.S., & M.J.G. Harrison: Clinical and biopsy findings in temporal arteritis. Ann Rheumat Dis 27:271–277, 1968.

Birkhead, N.C., Wagener, H.P., & R.M. Shick: Treatment of temporal arteritis with adrenal corticosteroids: Results in fifty-five cases in which lesion was proved at biopsy. JAMA 163:821–827, 1967.

Goodman, J.A.: Polymyalgia rheumatica. California Med 111:484–485, 1969.

Harrison, M.J.G., & A.T. Bevan: Early symptoms of temporal arteritis. Lancet 2:638–640, 1967.

VASOSPASTIC DISORDERS

RAYNAUD'S DISEASE & RAYNAUD'S PHENOMENON

Essentials of Diagnosis

- Paroxysmal bilateral symmetrical pallor and cyanosis followed by rubor of skin of the digits.
- Precipitated by cold or emotional upset; relieved by warmth.
- Absence of or only minimal gangrene.
- Primarily a disorder of young women.

General Considerations

Raynaud's disease is the primary or idiopathic form of paroxysmal digital cyanosis. Raynaud's phenomenon is the secondary form.

In Raynaud's disease the digital arteries respond excessively to vasospastic stimuli. The cause is not known, but some abnormality of the sympathetic nervous system seems to be active in this entity. The disease occurs primarily in females between puberty and age 40, and a family history of a vasospastic phenomenon can often be obtained.

Clinical Findings

Raynaud's disease and Raynaud's phenomenon are characterized by intermittent attacks of pallor or cyanosis—or pallor followed by cyanosis—in the fingers (and rarely the toes), precipitated by cold or occasionally by emotional upsets. Early in the course of the disease, only 1–2 fingertips may be affected; as the disease progresses, all the fingers down to the distal palm may be involved. The thumbs are rarely affected. General as well as local body cooling is usually necessary. Recovery usually begins near the base of the fingers as a bright red return of color to the cyanotic or pale digit. During recovery there may be intense rubor, throbbing, paresthesia, and slight swelling. Attacks usually terminate spontaneously or upon returning to a warm room or putting the extremity in warm water. Between attacks there may be no abnormal findings. For diagnosis, an attack should be induced by exposure of the hand or the whole body to cold. Sensory changes which often accompany vasomotor manifesta-

tions include numbness, stiffness, diminished sensation, and aching pain. The condition may progress to atrophy of the terminal fat pads and the digital skin, and gangrenous ulcers may appear near the fingertips and then heal during warm weather.

Raynaud's disease is much rarer than Raynaud's phenomenon and appears first between the ages of 25 and 45, almost always in women. It tends to be progressive, and, unlike Raynaud's phenomenon (which may be unilateral and may involve only 1–2 fingers), symmetric involvement of the fingers of both hands is ultimately the rule. Spasm gradually becomes more frequent and prolonged. Gangrene of the whole finger is rare, and the peripheral pulses are normal.

Differential Diagnosis

Differentiation must be made between Raynaud's disease and the numerous disorders which may be associated with Raynaud's phenomenon. These include thromboangiitis obliterans, arteriosclerosis obliterans, cervical rib (scalenus anticus) syndrome, collagen diseases, and disorders characterized by cold agglutinins and cryoglobulinemia.

The differentiation from thromboangiitis obliterans is usually not difficult, since thromboangiitis obliterans is a disease of men, and when Raynaud's phenomenon occurs in thromboangiitis obliterans it is usually in only 1–2 digits. The absence of weakness of peripheral pulses rules out the possibility of Raynaud's disease and is essential also in differentiating Raynaud's disease from arteriosclerosis obliterans. Arteriosclerosis obliterans occurs generally in an older age group, and Raynaud's phenomenon in this condition is rarely bilateral or symmetric.

Raynaud's phenomenon may occur in patients with cervical ribs (scalenus anticus syndrome). The symptoms in these disorders are generally unilateral, and brachial plexus compression symptoms tend to dominate the clinical picture. The various maneuvers and tests helpful in diagnosing these conditions should be performed on any patient with unilateral Raynaud's phenomenon.

It may be difficult to differentiate the skin thickening in Raynaud's disease from the early stages of scleroderma with Raynaud's phenomenon. If Raynaud's phenomenon has been present for some years but sclerodermatous changes are minimal, the diagnosis of Raynaud's disease is more likely. The skin of the face, neck, and chest is involved in the later stages of scleroderma, and esophageal involvement is manifested by dysphagia.

Raynaud's phenomenon is occasionally the presenting complaint in systemic lupus erythematosus.

Cryoglobulins (abnormal proteins which are precipitated on exposure to cold) cause a disorder simulating Raynaud's disease. They are usually found in serious systemic diseases, and the diagnosis is not difficult. Testing for cryoglobulins may be worthwhile in atypical cases of Raynaud's phenomenon.

In acrocyanosis, cyanosis of the hands is permanent and diffuse.

Frostbite may lead to chronic changes with Raynaud's phenomenon. Ergot poisoning, particularly the prolonged or excessive use of ergotamine (Gynergen®), must also be considered.

Treatment

A. General Measures: The body should be kept warm, and the hands especially should be protected from exposure to cold; gloves should be worn when out in the cold and when reaching into the refrigerator. The hands should be protected from injury at all times; wounds heal slowly, and infections are hard to control. Softening and lubricating lotion to control the fissured dry skin (Polysorb Hydrate® lotion) should be applied to the hands frequently. Smoking should be stopped.

B. Vasodilators: Vasodilator drugs such as papaverine (Povabid Plateau® capsules), 150 mg every 12 hours, nicotinyl alcohol tartrate (Roniacol®), 1 or 2 tablets every 12 hours, tolazoline (Priscoline®), 25–50 mg 3–4 times daily, or nylidrin (Arlidin®), 6 mg 3–4 times daily after meals, may be tried, although generally they have been disappointing and the latter 2 are contraindicated in the presence of peptic ulcer or coronary artery disease. Nitroglycerin, 0.3 mg (1/200 gr) sublingually 4 times daily and 10 minutes before exposure to cold, is helpful.

C. Methyldopa (Aldomet®): Since methyldopa depletes sympathetic nerve storage of norepinephrine, it may inhibit reflex arteriolar and venous constriction in response to cold. Clinically, it has been found helpful in doses of 1–2 gm daily orally.

D. Surgical Treatment: Although the duration of benefit of dorsal sympathectomy to dilate the cutaneous vessels of the fingers may be limited, this is still the most effective method of treatment for Raynaud's disease or phenomenon. Symptoms tend to recur in 2–5 years with the gradual return of sympathetic activity, and, for that reason, surgery should not be resorted to in the early, mild stages. Sympathectomy is of no value in advanced, severe cases.

Prognosis

Raynaud's disease is usually benign, causing mild discomfort on exposure to cold and progressing very slightly over the years. In a few cases rapid progression does occur, so that the slightest change in temperature may precipitate color changes. It is in this situation that sclerodactylia and small areas of gangrene may be noted, and such patients may become quite disabled by severe pain, limitation of motion, and secondary fixation of distal joints.

Gifford, R.W., Jr.: The clinical significance of Raynaud's phenomenon and Raynaud's disease. M Clin North America 42:963–970, 1958.

Kirtley, J.A., & others: Cervicothoracic sympathectomy in neurovascular abnormalities of the upper extremities. Ann Surg 165:869–879, 1967.

Varad, D.P., & A.M. Lawrence: Suppression of Raynaud's phenomenon by methyldopa. Arch Int Med 124:13–18, 1969.

See also reference under Acrocyanosis, below.

LIVEDO RETICULARIS

Livedo reticularis is a vasospastic disorder of unknown etiology which causes constant mottled discoloration on large areas of the extremities. It occurs primarily in young women. It may be associated with occult malignancy.

Patients with this disorder complain of persistent bluish mottling of the lower extremities, at times involving only the lower portions but occasionally involving the thighs and the hands and arms (usually to a lesser degree). The color may change to a reddish hue in warm weather but never entirely disappears spontaneously. A few patients complain of paresthesias, coldness, or numbness in the involved areas. Rarely, a history of recurrent ulcerations in the lower extremities can be obtained.

Bluish mottling of the extremities is diagnostic. The peripheral pulses are normal. The extremity may be cold, with increased perspiration.

Livedo reticularis must be differentiated from acrocyanosis, Raynaud's disease, and organic occlusive diseases.

Treatment consists of protection from exposure to cold, and use of vasodilators (see above) in more severe cases. If ulceration or gangrene is present, bed rest, compresses, vasodilators, and occasionally sympathectomy may be indicated.

In most instances livedo reticularis is entirely benign. In a few patients recurrent ulceration and even gangrene may require periodic hospitalization.

Barker, N.W., Hines, E.A., & W. McK. Craig: Livedo reticularis: A peripheral arterial disease. Am Heart J 21:592–604, 1941.

See also reference under Acrocyanosis, below.

ACROCYANOSIS

Acrocyanosis is an uncommon vasospastic disturbance which is possibly related to defects in the reflexes in the venules, leading to secondary arteriolar constriction. It may occur at any age, and is most common in women. It is characterized by coldness, clamminess, and marked cyanotic discoloration of the skin. There may be some swelling, but no pain. The symptoms are usually worse during cold months, are not paroxysmal, and are usually persistent. There are no helpful laboratory findings.

Treatment consists of reassuring the patient that acrocyanosis is an entirely benign condition and of protecting him from cold. Rarely, in severe cases, sympathectomy is warranted.

The color changes may persist for life.

Gifford, R.W., Jr.: Arteriospastic disorders of extremities. Circulation 27:970–975, 1963.

• • •

ERYTHROMELALGIA
(Erythermalgia)

Erythromelalgia is a paroxysmal bilateral vasodilative disorder of unknown etiology. Idiopathic (primary) erythromelalgia occurs in otherwise healthy persons, rarely in children, and affects men and women equally. A secondary type is occasionally seen in patients with polycythemia vera, hypertension, gout, and organic neurologic diseases.

The chief symptom is bilateral burning distress which lasts minutes to hours, first involving circumscribed areas on the soles or palms (or both) and, as the disease progresses, the entire extremity. The attack occurs in response to stimuli producing vasodilatation (eg, exercise, warm environment), especially at night when the extremities are warmed under bedclothes. Reddening or cyanosis as well as heat may be noted. Relief may be obtained by cooling the affected part and by elevation.

No findings are generally present between attacks. On induction of the syndrome, heat and redness are noted in association with the typical pain. Skin temperature and arterial pulsations are increased, and the involved areas may sweat profusely.

Erythromelalgia must be differentiated from peripheral neuritis and organic occlusive diseases as well as from acrocyanosis.

In primary erythromelalgia, aspirin may give excellent relief. The patient should avoid warm environments. In severe cases, if medical measures fail, section or crushing of peripheral nerves may be necessary to relieve pain.

Primary idiopathic erythromelalgia is uniformly benign. The prognosis in secondary erythromelalgia depends upon the underlying disease.

Babb, R.R., & others: Erythermalgia. Review of 51 cases. Circulation 29:136–141, 1964.

Pepper, H.: Primary erythermalgia. Report of a patient treated with methysergide maleate. JAMA 203:1066–1067, 1968.

VASOMOTOR DISORDERS ASSOCIATED WITH TRAUMA

REFLEX SYMPATHETIC DYSTROPHY
(Causalgia)

Essentials of Diagnosis

- Burning pain and hyperesthesia in an extremity, associated with red and cool extremity.
- Atrophy of skin and muscle may be present.
- History of trauma to a peripheral nerve of the extremity.

General Considerations

Causalgia, which is characterized by intense burning pain and vasodilatation in an extremity, is a rare disorder caused by partial division or bruising of a peripheral nerve (usually the median nerve) or involvement of the nerve in scar tissue. The injury may be trivial. An operation on the extremity may precede the development of the condition.

Clinical Findings

A. Symptoms and Signs: The pain is distal to the point of injury but not confined to the course of the nerve, and it may not appear for a few days or weeks. Pain is initiated by light touch, temperature changes, movement of the limb, or dependency. The skin becomes red, smooth, devoid of wrinkles and hair, scaly, cold, and moist. Limitation of joint movements and deformity may develop later. The patient's life may be dominated by the effort to avoid the slightest trauma to the extremity and especially to various trigger points that may develop.

B. X-Ray Findings: Osteoporosis of bone is commonly seen on x-ray.

Prevention

All unnecessary trauma to peripheral nerves should be carefully avoided during surgical procedures on the extremities. Splinting an injured extremity for an adequate length of time during the acutely painful phase may help prevent development in some cases.

Treatment and Prognosis

A. Conservative Treatment: Since the disorder usually subsides after a year or so, the treatment of choice involves keeping the affected area cool and protected from stimuli, even though the patient often demands more aggressive therapy. Analgesics may be given, but narcotics should be avoided if possible.

B. Surgical Treatment: Sympathectomy may be of value if a sympathetic block gives relief, and this is usually the treatment of choice if operative measures are required. Division of the nerve proximal to the site of irritation gives relief but denervates the area supplied by the nerve. Reamputation of a painful stump is often followed by recurrence of symptoms in the new stump. Spinothalamic tractotomy is a desperate measure that is not always successful. If severe nervous and mental manifestations are prominent, local or operative procedures will probably be of no value. The prognosis for a useful life in the more advanced forms is poor.

Owens, J.C.: Causalgia. Am Surgeon 23:634–643, 1957.

SUDECK'S ATROPHY

Sudeck's atrophy is an acute atrophy of the bones of an extremity which usually develops after minor injury, especially to the ankle or wrist. Symptoms and signs of vasomotor hyperactivity include pain of a burning type made worse by movement, edema, local heat, and swelling. The limb may ultimately become cold, cyanotic, and wasted, with stiffness of the joints. Secondary fractures occasionally occur in the atrophic bones.

Prophylaxis consists of adequate early treatment of sprains. The early manifestations are usually treated by physical therapy: mild heat, light massage, and gentle movement of the joints. A walking type of plaster cast for the foot and ankle region may be of value.

In severe and chronic forms, sympathectomy may give relief.

DEGENERATIVE & INFLAMMATORY VENOUS DISEASE

VARICOSE VEINS

Essentials of Diagnosis

- Dilated, tortuous superficial veins in the lower extremities.
- Varicose veins may be asymptomatic or they may be associated with fatigue, aching discomfort, or pain.
- Secondary changes in the skin and subcutaneous tissue may develop.

General Considerations

Varicose veins develop predominantly in the lower extremities. They consist of abnormally dilated, elongated, and tortuous alterations in the saphenous veins and their tributaries. These vessels lie immediately beneath the skin and superficial to the deep fascia; they therefore do not have as adequate support as the veins deep in the leg, which are surrounded by muscles. In many cases there is an inherited abnormality of the vein wall allowing increased distensibility, incompetence of the valves, and formation of varicosities. Other contributory factors are prolonged standing over a number of years, pregnancy, obesity, and, perhaps, aging.

Secondary varicosities can develop as a result of obstructive changes and valve damage in the deep venous system following thrombophlebitis, or occasionally as a result of proximal venous occlusion due to neoplasm. Congenital or acquired arteriovenous fistulas are also associated with varicosities.

The long saphenous vein and its tributaries are most commonly involved, but the short saphenous vein is occasionally affected. There may be one or many incompetent perforating veins in the thigh and lower leg, so that blood can reflux into the varicosities not only from above, by way of the saphenofemoral junction, but also from the deep system of veins through the incompetent perforators. Largely because of these valvular defects, venous pressure in the superficial veins does not fall appreciably on walking; over the years the veins progressively enlarge and the surrounding tissue and skin develop secondary changes such as fibrosis, chronic edema, and pigmentation. Atrophic changes take place in the skin.

Clinical Findings

A. Symptoms: Extensive varicose veins may produce no subjective symptoms, whereas minimal varicosities may produce many symptoms. Aching or burning discomfort, fatigue, or pain in the lower leg brought on by periods of standing are the most common complaints. Cramps may occur, but intermittent claudication and coldness of the feet are not associated with varicose veins. One must be careful to distinguish between the symptoms of arteriosclerotic peripheral vascular disease and those of venous disease, since occlusive arterial disease usually contraindicates the operative treatment of varicosities. Itching from an associated eczematoid dermatitis may occur in the region of the veins.

B. Signs: Dilated, tortuous, elongated veins beneath the skin in the thigh and lower leg are generally readily visible in the standing individual, although in very obese patients palpation and percussion may be necessary to detect their presence. Secondary tissue changes may be absent even in extensive varicosities; but if the varicosities are of long duration, brownish pigmentation and thinning of the skin above the ankle are often present. Swelling may occur, but extensive swelling and fibrosis in the subcutaneous tissue of the lower leg usually denote the postphlebitic state.

C. Trendelenburg's Test: Of use in determining the competence of the valves at the proximal end of the long saphenous vein close to the saphenofemoral junction and in the communicating veins between the superficial and deep vessels.

1. With the patient supine, elevate the leg. If there is no organic venous obstruction, varicosities will empty immediately.

2. Place a rubber tourniquet around the upper thigh and ask the patient to stand.

a. If the long saphenous vein remains empty for 30 seconds or more and then fills very slowly from below over a period of 1–2 minutes, the valves close to the saphenofemoral junction are incompetent, the valves in the communicating veins are competent, and the blood is flowing through them in the right direction (superficial to deep). On release of the tourniquet, if the veins fill rapidly from above, the incompetence of the proximal valves is confirmed.

b. If the varicosities fill rapidly, the communicating veins between the deep and the superficial vessels are incompetent and blood is refluxing into the varicosed vessels. If, on release of the tourniquet, no additional filling of the varicosities occurs, the valves in the saphenous vein close to the saphenofemoral junction are competent; if, on the other hand, further distention of the varicosities occurs when the tourniquet is released, the valves at the upper end of the long saphenous vein are also incompetent. The precise site of these defective perforating veins can often be determined by repetition of this maneuver while placing the tourniquet at successively lower levels or using 2 or 3 tourniquets at different levels.

Differential Diagnosis

Primary varicose veins should be differentiated from those secondary to (1) chronic venous insufficiency of the deep system of veins, (2) extrinsic or occlusive retroperitoneal vein obstruction, (3) arteriovenous fistula (congenital or acquired), and (4) congenital venous malformation. Venography may be of value in the investigation of some of these problems. If significant occlusion of the deep venous system is suspected and extensive vein surgery is being considered, phlebography of the deep system should be performed to be certain that the deep veins are patent before the superficial veins are removed.

Complications

Ulceration often results from a blow to the thin, atrophic, pigmented skin of the lower leg or ankle region, and such a lesion frequently becomes chronic, scarred, and painful. Occasionally, an ulcer will penetrate into a varix, and profuse hemorrhage from the fistula will occur.

Treatment of the ulcer consists of rest and elevation of the leg and application of saline compresses. A skin graft may be necessary. If the patient must remain ambulatory, firm compression of the lower leg and foot as afforded by Unna's boot or some other form of a compression boot dressing (see p 252) may be used. Recurrent ulcerations are common.

Thrombophlebitis, starting in the varicosities and occasionally extending into the deep system by way of the perforating veins or the saphenofemoral junction, is not uncommon, particularly in pregnant women or in those receiving contraceptive medication (see below).

Stasis dermatitis may also be a problem (see p 252).

Treatment

Varicosities tend to progress, and when the disease is relatively advanced some form of therapy should be considered if progressive changes and complications are to be avoided.

A. Conservative Treatment:

1. Elastic stockings and intermittent elevation of the legs constitute the best therapeutic approach in very old or poor risk patients, in patients who refuse surgery or have to put it off, and sometimes in women with mild or moderate varicosities who are going to have more children (since better long-term results can be obtained in women who are not going to become pregnant again). Elastic stockings may also be of value in those patients who show early a tendency toward varicosities or whose families have a high incidence of varicosities, especially if they must spend many hours standing.

2. Injection treatment of varicosities with sclerosing solutions to produce thrombosis of the segment of vein should generally be reserved for treatment of short segments which remain after adequate surgery. The recurrence rate after injection therapy is high, and complications can occur (eg, local or systemic reactions and infections around the vein, or deep thrombophlebitis).

B. Surgical Treatment: High ligation at the saphenofemoral junction, often with stripping of the saphenous vein, is the treatment of choice for moderate or extensive varicosities. This should be combined with ligations of the secondary veins which are varicosed and interruption of all incompetent perforating veins. The short saphenous vein may also require ligation at its junction with the popliteal vein. In older individuals or those with mild involvement, stripping may be avoided and local anesthesia may be used throughout the procedure. Ambulation with elastic bandages is encouraged as soon as recovery from the anesthesia permits. Standing and sitting are contraindicated for 1−2 weeks postoperatively; in bed, the legs should be elevated.

Prognosis

Patients should be informed that even extensive and carefully performed surgery may not prevent the development of additional varicosities and that further (though usually more limited) surgery may be necessary later. If extensive varicosities reappear after previous surgery, the completeness of the high ligation should be questioned and reexploration of the saphenofemoral area may be necessary. Even after adequate treatment of varicose veins, the secondary tissue changes may not regress.

Burges, C.M.: A practical approach to the treatment of varicose veins. S Clin North America 43:1385−1392, 1963.

Gerson, L.: The treatment of varicose veins: A critical study of choice of method. Angiology 13:260−264, 1962.

Lev, H.D.: The modern conception of therapy of varicose veins. Angiology 15:371−378, 1964.

Lofgren, K.A.: Vein surgery. JAMA 188:17−21, 1964.

Sherman, R.S.: Varicose veins. S Clin North America 44:1369−1381, 1964.

THROMBOPHLEBITIS
OF SUPERFICIAL VEINS

Essentials of Diagnosis

- Red, painful, tender, raised areas involving the skin and subcutaneous tissue, usually in linear distribution along the course of visible veins.
- No constitutional reaction.

General Considerations

Superficial thrombophlebitis may occur spontaneously, as in pregnant or postpartum women or in individuals with varicose veins or thromboangiitis obliterans; or it may be associated with trauma, as in the case of a blow to the leg or following intravenous therapy with irritating solutions. In the migratory or recurrent form, thromboangiitis should be suspected. It may also be a manifestation of abdominal malignancy such as carcinoma of the pancreas and may be the earliest sign. The long saphenous vein is most often involved. Superficial thrombophlebitis is usually not associated with thrombosis in the deep leg veins. Pulmonary emboli are infrequent but do occur.

Short-term venous catheterization is extremely common now. Small peripheral arm veins are most commonly used. The catheter should be observed daily for signs of local inflammation. It should be removed if a local reaction develops in the vein, and in any case it should be removed within 48—72 hours. Serious septic complications can occur if these rules are not followed.

Clinical Findings

The patient usually experiences a dull pain in the region of the involved vein. Local findings consist of induration, redness, and tenderness along the course of a vein. The process may be localized, or it may involve most of the long saphenous vein and its tributaries. The inflammatory reaction generally subsides in 1—2 weeks; a firm cord may remain for a much longer period. Edema of the extremity is absent.

Differential Diagnosis

The linear rather than circular nature of the lesion, and the distribution along the course of a superficial vein, serve to differentiate superficial phlebitis from erythema nodosum, erythema induratum, panniculitis, and fibromyositis.

Treatment

If the process is well localized and not near the saphenofemoral junction, local heat and bed rest with the leg elevated are usually satisfactory. Phenylbutazone (Butazolidin®), 100 mg 3 times daily for 5 days, may aid in the resolution of the inflammatory process but is contraindicated in individuals with peptic ulcer.

If the process is very extensive or shows a tendency to proceed upward toward the saphenofemoral junction, or if it is in the proximity of the saphenofemoral junction initially, ligation and division of the saphenous vein at the saphenofemoral junction is indicated. The inflammatory process usually regresses following this procedure, though removal of the involved segment of vein (stripping) may result in a more rapid recovery.

Anticoagulation therapy is seldom indicated unless there seems to be a rapid progression of the disease. It is indicated. if there seems to be extension into the deep system.

Prognosis

The course is generally benign and brief, and the prognosis depends on the underlying pathology. Phlebitis of a saphenous vein occasionally extends to the deep veins, in which case pulmonary embolism may occur.

Bentley, D.W., & M.H. Lepper: Septicemia related to indwelling venous catheter. JAMA 206:1749—1752, 1968.

Wilmore, D.W., & S.J. Dudrick: Safe long-term venous catheterization. Arch Surg 98:256—258, 1969.

THROMBOPHLEBITIS
OF DEEP VEINS

Essentials of Diagnosis

- Pain and swelling in the involved extremity.
- Calf tenderness and positive Homans' sign.
- Deep venous thrombosis may exist without any clinical manifestations.

General Considerations

Thrombophlebitis is partial or complete occlusion of a vein by a thrombus with a secondary inflammatory reaction in the wall of the vein. It is encountered most frequently in the deep veins of the legs and pelvis in postoperative or postpartum patients during the 4th—14th days, and in patients with fractures or other trauma, cardiac disease, or a stroke, especially if prolonged bed rest is involved. In the postoperative patient, the initial thrombosis generally occurs during the major surgical procedure or in the first 24 hours following operation (or injury).

The deep veins of the calf are most frequently involved, but the thrombotic process may start in or progress to the femoral and iliac veins. The site of origin is at times in the pelvic veins or in the long saphenous vein.

Predisposing factors are aging, malignancy, shock, dehydration, anemia, obesity, and chronic infection. Perhaps the most prominent etiologic factors in thrombophlebitis are venous stasis and the pressure changes produced in the endothelium of the vein wall as the legs lie for hours supported by the mattress of the bed or operating table. Exposed subendothelial tissue or a variety of intravascular stimuli affecting the blood result in the release of platelet constituents; platelet aggregates form, followed by the deposition of fibrin, leukocytes, and, finally, red cells, and a thrombus is formed which can then propagate in the vein.

Pregnancy and the oral contraceptive drugs are associated with thrombophlebitis in some women; the medication should be permanently discontinued in those who develop phlebitis and should not be prescribed for those with a history of venous thrombosis.

Clinical Findings

There may be no symptoms or signs in the extremity in the early stages. The patient not infrequently suffers a pulmonary embolus, presumably from the leg veins, without symptoms or demonstrable abnormalities in the extremities.

A. Symptoms: The patient may complain of a dull ache, a tight feeling, or frank pain in the calf or, in more extensive cases, the whole leg, especially when walking. A feeling of anxiety is not uncommon.

B. Signs: Typical findings, though variable, are as follows: tenderness and induration or spasm in the calf muscles; slight swelling in the involved calf, as noted by careful measurements; pain in the calf produced by dorsiflexion of the foot (Homans' sign); and slight fever and tachycardia. When the femoral and iliac veins are also involved, the swelling in the leg may be marked (phlegmasia alba dolens). The skin may be cyanotic if venous obstruction is severe (phlegmasia cerulea dolens), or pale and cool if a reflex arterial spasm is superimposed.

Symmetrical pitting edema of the lower legs and ankles, particularly if there is no associated tenderness, is generally secondary to heart, kidney, or liver disease. Thrombophlebitis may be present in both legs, but the involvement may not produce symmetrical changes. Contusions, with or without hematoma, and muscle strain may be hard to differentiate from deep thrombophlebitis, and thrombophlebitis may develop in a contused leg. Phlebography is of value in confirming the diagnosis of thrombophlebitis.

Complications

The major complication of deep thrombophlebitis is pulmonary embolism.

A small or moderately large pulmonary embolism may be present without any associated pulmonary symptoms, signs, or x-ray findings. Clinical manifestations, when present, take the form of pleuritic pain (often with a transient friction rub), a dry cough (sometimes associated with hemoptysis), local rales in the area of involvement, a small amount of pleural fluid, and often x-ray evidence of pulmonary consolidation or diminished vascular markings. Fever and increased pulse and respiration rates are frequently present. The serum LDH and bilirubin may be elevated, and the isotope lung scan may reveal perfusion defects consistent with emboli.

Massive pulmonary embolism is associated with shock, dyspnea, and cyanosis, and often with transient ECG changes characteristic of cor pulmonale. Death may occur in minutes or hours. The pulmonary artery pressure is elevated, and pulmonary angiography will demonstrate the embolus in the pulmonary vascular tree.

Chronic venous insufficiency and varicose veins ultimately occur in some cases. (See Chronic Venous Insufficiency, below.)

Prevention

Great attention must be devoted to the effective prevention of this complication.

(1) The legs, well padded, should be elevated 10–20° during a long operation.

(2) Patients with a history of phlebitis or with varicose veins should have elastic supports on the legs during and after operation or delivery or when an illness demands many days in bed.

(3) Preoperative correction of anemia, dehydration, congestive failure, or metabolic disturbances diminishes the incidence of thrombophlebitis.

(4) Postoperative exercises of the legs should be started at the close of the operative procedure while the patient is still on the operating table or in the delivery room and continued for several days. Early ambulation (but not standing or sitting) is likewise of value and should be started as soon as possible after operation or acute illness. If bed rest is necessary, passive or active bed exercises should be instituted and continued as long as the patient must remain in bed (eg, active or passive flexion of the toes, ankles, knees, and hips repeated frequently while the patient is awake). The bedclothes should be kept loose so that the legs can be moved freely and turning in bed can be done with ease. Deep breathing should be encouraged.

(5) Elevation of the foot of the bed to 15–20° may be of value in patients predisposed to thrombophlebitis. Venous stasis may be diminished by keeping the head of the bed near the horizontal and avoiding bed adjustments or pillows which result in prolonged flexion of the knees.

(6) Prophylactic use of anticoagulants may occasionally be indicated, particularly in patients with a fracture of the femur or tibia. If anticoagulants are to be used they should be started within 1–2 days after the injury and should be continued for several weeks. (See below.)

(7) Brief but regular periods of walking during long airplane and automobile trips should be encouraged since venous thromboses do occur during such times even in active, healthy adults.

Treatment of Acute Thrombophlebitis

A. Local Measures: The legs should be elevated 15–20°; the trunk should be kept horizontal; and the head and shoulders may be supported with pillows. After 5–10 days, when the inflammatory aspects have had time to produce a more adherent thrombus (and provided the swelling and local symptoms have largely subsided), walking but not standing or sitting is permitted. The time out of bed and walking is increased each day.

Elastic bandages or stockings are applied from the toes to just below the knees as soon as the diagnosis is made and continued until the swelling tendency has disappeared, often for months. Bandages and anticoagulants initially, and intermittent elevation of the legs subsequently, help prevent postphlebitic changes. These measures are perhaps even more important if surgical ligation of the femoral vein or the vena cava has been necessary.

B. Medical Treatment (Anticoagulants): Anticoagulant therapy is considered to be definitive in most cases of deep thrombophlebitis with or without pulmonary embolism. There is evidence that the relatively high incidence of fatal pulmonary embolism secondary to venous thrombosis is significantly reduced by adequate anticoagulant therapy. Progressive thrombosis with its associated morbidity is also reduced considerably, and the chronic secondary changes in the involved leg are probably also less severe. Heparin acts rapidly and seems to be the most effective drug, and it should be used at least during the initial phase of treatment. Later, especially if a prolonged period on anticoagulants is thought advisable, one of the longer acting drugs such as warfarin (Coumadin®) or bishydroxycoumarin (Dicumarol®) can be used.

The rate of subsidence of symptoms is variable, and occasional cases are quite refractory to therapy. Therapy should probably be continued for at least 12–14 days for venous thrombosis and 21–28 days for pulmonary embolism. It may have to be continued for a longer period if signs and symptoms of active or unresolved thrombosis persist or if the patient has a marked thrombotic tendency with a history of recurrent acute episodes. In the patients who were active at the time the thrombophlebitis developed (ie, those with a significant thrombotic tendency), long-term anticoagulant therapy over a period of 6 or more months is probably advisable. This is particularly true if there has been an associated pulmonary embolus.

1. Heparin–The Lee-White clotting time or the new and more precise whole blood partial thromboplastin time (WBPTT) and the prothrombin time should be determined before initiating therapy.

The dose required may vary considerably with individuals or even with a single patient at different stages of therapy (smaller doses are often required as time goes on). Therapy must be followed closely by means of clotting time or WBPTT determinations. A clotting time of 20–30 minutes immediately before the next dose of heparin is a satisfactory level; if it is more than 35 minutes, the next injection should probably be delayed and the dose lowered somewhat; if it is less than 18, a somewhat larger dose may be indicated. After the dose for an individual patient has been established, a clotting time once every 24 hours taken just before the next scheduled dose is probably sufficient in most cases, and the results should determine the next heparin dose. Several methods of administration are available.

a. Deep subcutaneous–Intermittent administration of sodium heparin every 6 hours, with a clotting time at least once every 24 hours done ½ hour before the next scheduled dose. For the adult of average size, 6000–8000 units every 6 hours is a convenient starting dose; after 1 or 2 days of therapy, the required dose usually drops to a range of 4000–6000 units. Some prefer an 8-hour schedule with somewhat larger doses (10,000–12,000 units) and some use still larger doses on a 12-hour schedule. Hematomas at the injection site can be expected.

b. Intravenous–Intermittent intravenous injections of heparin sodium on a 4-hour basis may be used. The usual initial dose is 5000 units followed by an individualized dose of 5000–10,000 units every 4 hours depending on the laboratory studies. Occasionally, a continuous intravenous infusion may be used, beginning with 10,000 units in 1 liter of 5% glucose at 15–25 drops/minute and alternating the rate of flow depending on the laboratory studies done approximately every 3–4 hours. Control is more difficult by this route, but its use is sometimes worthwhile in a patient manifesting extreme thrombotic tendencies and in those that must be anticoagulated very rapidly with a large dose, eg, the patient who has just had a massive pulmonary embolus. (The postembolic reflex bronchial constriction appears to be blocked by large doses of heparin in the range of 15,000 units initially and 80–100 thousand units in the first 24 hours.)

At present the most general use of heparin is during the first phase of anticoagulant therapy. Many physicians shift to the prothrombin depressant drugs for the final phase. They consider heparin a more adequate and reliable anticoagulant and defer shifting until the symptoms and signs of thrombosis have largely or completely subsided. Heparin may thus be used for the first 7–14 days (sometimes even longer), and it is only withdrawn when the prothrombin time has been depressed to the therapeutic range. Some prefer to use only heparin.

2. Prothrombin depressants–Prothrombin depressants (Table 8–1) differ in rapidity of onset and duration of effect.

A good therapeutic effect has been achieved when prothrombin activity has fallen to at least 25%, preferably between 20% and 10%, or when the prothrombin time is 2–2½ times the control. At the beginning of treatment, daily prothrombin activities should be determined and the subsequent dose withheld until the report is received. In well-stabilized patients, weekly or even monthly determination may be adequate.

The usual starting doses and maintenance doses of 2 antiprothrombin drugs are shown in Table 8–1. Patients with initial activities below 80–100% should receive smaller doses. Interaction of these drugs with other drugs does occur; those reducing the anticoagulant effect include barbiturates, glutethimide (Doriden®), meprobamate, and griseofulvin. Potentiation may occur with phenylbutazone (Butazolidin®), diphenylhydantoin (Dilantin®), salicylates, sulfisoxazole, tetracyclines, chloramphenicol, neomycin, quinidine, chloral hydrate, and certain other drugs. Careful attention to the dose is required both

TABLE 8–1. Prothrombin depressants.

	Dosage (Oral)*			Approximate Time to Peak Effect (Days)	Approximate Duration of Effect (Days)
	1st Day	2nd Day	Usual Daily Maintenance and Range		
Bishydroxycoumarin (Dicumarol®)	200–400 mg	100–200 mg	100 mg (25–150)	2–3	4
Warfarin (Coumadin®, Panwarfin®, Athrombin®)	30–50 mg	10–15 mg	7 mg (5–15)	1–2	2–3

*Only warfarin may be given intravenously. The oral route is almost always used. Dosages given are single daily doses unless otherwise specified.

during administration and following withdrawal of drugs which potentiate or inhibit anticoagulant effects, and interacting drugs should be avoided if possible.

3. Treatment of bleeding and overdosage—The principal danger from anticoagulant therapy is abnormal bleeding. In bleeding due to heparin excess the coagulation time can be rapidly returned to normal by administering 1% protamine sulfate in physiologic saline IV to neutralize the heparin. Give a dose in mg equal to 1/100 of the number of units of heparin administered.

Bleeding due to an excess of the prothrombin depressant drug is more difficult to control since the prothrombin activity rises slowly after therapy is discontinued. Phytonadione (Konakion®, Mephyton®, AquaMephyton®) is indicated in patients receiving the prothrombin depressant drugs who must have the prothrombin activity returned to normal—either because they are bleeding or because emergency surgery is necessary. Phytonadione, 5–10 mg orally, may be used to correct excessive hypoprothrombinemia with or without minor hemorrhage when continued anticoagulant therapy is anticipated. AquaMephyton®, 10–40 mg, may be given slowly IV in cases of serious hemorrhage and an excessively low prothrombin time, and its effectiveness can be evaluated by serial prothrombin time determinations. If the liver is normal, a safe range may be achieved in 4–24 hours, but repeated injections over 2–3 days may be required. Transfusions of fresh citrated blood may also be necessary to restore blood volume if active hemorrhage is present and to replace clotting factors during the latent period of phytonadione's action.

C. Surgical Measures:

1. Vein ligation—Vein ligation is recommended for any instance in which anticoagulant therapy is contraindicated. Examples are patients with active peptic ulcer or ulcerative colitis, certain blood dyscrasias, significant liver disease, and patients in the first 2–3 postoperative days, especially if the operation has involved extensive dissections. Vein ligation is also indicated if there are signs of propagation of the thrombus or if emboli continue to occur during adequate anticoagulant therapy; or if septic phlebitis is present.

The chance of a second, possibly fatal pulmonary embolism is appreciably reduced after ligation or plication of the inferior vena cava.

Although some degree of chronic edema of the legs may develop as a result of ligation, it can usually be minimized if anticoagulant therapy is resumed 1–2 days following surgery and if follow-up care, consisting of elastic supports to the lower legs and elevation of the legs at intervals, is continued for at least 1 year (see next section).

2. Femoral vein thrombectomy—In certain cases of massive venous occlusion (phlegmasia cerulea dolens) which have not responded to a trial of sympathetic block, elevation of the leg, heparin, and fluid and electrolyte replacement, a femoral vein thrombectomy to remove the iliofemoral thrombosis may be indicated. This has also been advocated for cases of massive edema without vasospasm (phlegmasia alba dolens). If the thrombus has not become adherent (less than 48 hours from the time of onset), function of the venous system may be restored and maintained by postoperative heparin. Massive edema (and the danger of secondary gangrene, requiring later amputation) has been reduced by this procedure; rethrombosis or pulmonary embolus can occur postoperatively, and this approach may not stand the test of time.

Prognosis

With adequate treatment the patient usually returns to normal health and activity within 3–6 weeks. The prognosis in most cases is good once the period of danger of pulmonary embolism has passed, but for the first 2–3 weeks it is guarded. Occasionally, recurrent episodes of phlebitis occur in spite of good local and anticoagulant management. Such cases may even have recurrent pulmonary emboli. Chronic venous insufficiency may result, with its associated complications.

Estes, J.E.: Thrombophlebitis. Thomas, 1964.

Freeark, R.J., & others: Posttraumatic venous thrombosis. Arch Surg 95:567–575, 1967.

Gray, F.D., Jr.: Pulmonary Embolism. Lea & Febiger, 1966.

Haller, J.A., Jr.: Deep Thrombophlebitis: Pathophysiology & Treatment. Saunders, 1967.

Hershey, F.B., & others: Phlebography in diagnosis and management of venous diseases of the legs. M Clin North America 51:161–174, 1967.

Little, J.M., & others: Venous thromboembolic disease. Brit J Surg 53:657–667, 1966.

Mozes, M., & others: Inferior vena cava ligation for pulmonary embolism: Review of 118 cases. Surgery 60:790–794, 1966.

Mustard, J.F., & others: Thromboembolism: A manifestation of the response of blood to injury. Circulation 42:1–21, 1970.

Negus, D., & others: ^{125}I-Labelled fibrinogen in the diagnosis of deep vein thrombosis and its correlation with phlebography. Brit J Surg 55:835–839, 1968.

Nusbaum, M., & W.S. Blakemore: Treatment of acute phlebitis. Surg Gynec Obst 119:1107–1118, 1964.

Pierucci, L., Jr., & G.S. Nicoll: Thromboembolism. S Clin North America 47:1173–1186, 1967.

Sevitt, S.: The acutely swollen leg and deep vein thrombosis. Brit J Surg 54:886–889, 1967.

Sevitt, S., & N. Gallagher: Venous thrombosis and pulmonary embolism. Brit J Surg 48:475–489, 1961.

Skinner, D.B., & others: Anticoagulant prophylaxis in surgical patients. Surg Gynec Obst 125:741–746, 1967.

Spittell, J.A., Jr.: Thrombophlebitis and pulmonary embolism. Circulation 27:976–980, 1963.

CHRONIC VENOUS INSUFFICIENCY

Essentials of Diagnosis

- A history is often obtained of phlebitis or leg injury.
- Ankle edema is the earliest sign.
- Stasis pigmentation, dermatitis, subcutaneous induration, and often varicosities occur later.
- Ulceration at or above the ankle is common (stasis ulcer).

General Considerations

Chronic venous insufficiency generally results from changes secondary to deep thrombophlebitis although a definite history of phlebitis can often not be obtained. It can also occur as a result of neoplastic obstruction of the pelvic veins or congenital or acquired arteriovenous fistula.

When insufficiency is secondary to deep thrombophlebitis (the postphlebitic syndrome), the valves in the deep venous channels (and sometimes in the perforating veins) have been damaged or destroyed by the thrombotic process. The recanalized, valveless, irregular deep veins are functionally inadequate, and the pumping action of the contracting calf muscles does not lower the venous pressure during walking. Thus, the venous pressure remains high at all times and secondary changes eventually take place in the venules, capillaries, subcutaneous tissues, skin, and superficial veins. Primary varicose veins with no abnormalities of the deep venous system may also result in the changes of chronic venous stasis.

Clinical Findings

Chronic venous insufficiency is characterized by progressive edema of the leg (particularly the lower leg) and secondary changes in the skin and subcutaneous tissues. The usual symptoms are itching, a dull discomfort made worse by periods of standing, and pain if an ulceration is present. The skin is usually thin, shiny, atrophic, and cyanotic, and a brownish pigmentation often develops. Eczema is often present, and there may be large areas of superficial weeping dermatitis. The subcutaneous tissues are thick and fibrous. Recurrent ulcerations are common, usually just above the ankle, on the medial or anterior aspect of the leg; healing results in a thin scar on a fibrotic base which breaks down with minor trauma. Varicosities often appear and are usually associated with incompetent perforating veins in the mid and upper part of the leg.

Differential Diagnosis

The edema of congestive failure is usually bilateral and symmetrical and may involve the sacral region; other signs of congestive failure should make the differentiation from venous insufficiency rather simple.

Renal diseases may cause widespread edema. Urinary and blood studies aid the diagnosis.

Lymphedema causes a brawny edema which does not subside easily with elevation. The other signs of venous insufficiency (eg, varicosities, pigmentation, ulceration) are absent in lymphedema, and a history of episodes of acute cellulitis may be obtained.

Ulcers of chronic arterial insufficiency are much more painful than those of venous insufficiency. They generally occur on the toes or the foot, and pedal pulsations are absent.

Erythema induratum begins as a painful nodule followed by ulceration. This is usually bilateral and symmetric, and the ulcers occur primarily on the posterior surface of the lower part of the leg.

Numerous other leg ulcers (eg, those of trauma, sickle cell anemia, and fungal infections) can usually be differentiated from venous insufficiency by absence of varicose veins, congestion of the skin, and chronic swelling.

Prevention

Irreversible tissue changes and associated complications in the lower legs can be minimized through adequate treatment of acute thrombophlebitis with anticoagulants and energetic measures to avoid chronic edema in subsequent years. The latter can be done by elastic supports to the lower legs during the day and evening, intermittent periods of elevation of the legs, and elevation of the legs throughout the night.

Treatment

A. General Measures: Bed rest, with the legs elevated to diminish chronic edema, is fundamental in the treatment of the acute complications of chronic venous insufficiency. Measures to control the tendency toward edema include (1) intermittent elevation of the legs during the day and elevation of the legs at night,

(2) avoidance of long periods of sitting or standing, and (3) the use of well-fitting elastic supports worn from the mid foot to just below the knee during the day and evening if there is any tendency for swelling to develop.

B. Stasis Dermatitis: Eczematous eruption may be acute or chronic, and the treatment varies accordingly.

1. Acute weeping dermatitis—

a. Wet compresses for 1 hour 4 times daily of either boric acid solution (1 tbsp/liter of water), potassium permanganate solution (100 mg/liter of water), or aluminum acetate buffered solution (Burow's solution) (2 tablets/liter of water).

b. Compresses are followed with 0.5% hydrocortisone cream in a water-soluble base. (Neomycin may be incorporated into this cream.)

c. Systemic antibiotics may be indicated if active infection is present.

2. Subsiding or chronic dermatitis—

a. Continue the hydrocortisone cream for 1–2 weeks or until no further improvement is noted. Cordran® tape, a plastic, corticosteroid impregnated tape, is a convenient way to apply both medication and dressing.

b. Zinc oxide ointment with ichthammol (Ichthyol®), 3%, 1–2 times a day, cleaned off as desired with mineral oil.

c. Carbolfuchsin (Castellani's) paint to the toes and nails 1–2 times a week may help control dermatophytosis and onychomycosis. Desenex® powder, ointment, or aerosol may also be used.

3. Energetic treatment of chronic edema, as outlined in sections A and C, with almost complete bed rest during the acute phase.

C. Ulceration: Ulcerations are preferably treated with compresses of isotonic saline solution, which aid the healing of the ulcer or may help prepare the base for a skin graft. A lesion can sometimes be treated on an ambulatory basis by means of a semirigid boot applied to the leg after much of the swelling has been reduced by a period of elevation. Such a boot must be changed every 1–2 weeks, depending to some extent on the amount of drainage from the ulcer. The ulcer, tendons, and bony prominences must be adequately padded. Special ointments on the ulcer are not necessary. The semirigid boot may be made with Unna's paste or with Viscopaste® (a bandage impregnated with gelatin and zinc oxide) or Gauztex® bandage (impregnated with a nonallergenic self-adhering compound).

D. Secondary Varicosities: Varicosities secondary to damage to the deep system of veins may in turn contribute to undesirable changes in the tissues of the lower leg. Varicosities should occasionally be removed and the incompetent perforators ligated, but the tendency toward edema will persist and the measures outlined above (¶ A) will be required for life. Varicosities can often be treated along with edema by elastic stockings and other nonoperative measures. If the obstructive element in the deep system is severe, it may be most undesirable to remove superficial chan-

nels which may be carrying most of the blood out of the leg. In the more complicated forms of postphlebitic conditions (and even, in certain instances, in acute phlebitis), phlebography may be of value in mapping out by means of x-rays the areas of obstruction or incompetence of the deep veins of the leg. The selection of the correct treatment may depend on such a study.

Prognosis

Individuals with chronic venous insufficiency often have recurrent problems, particularly if measures to counteract persistent venous hypertension, edema, and secondary tissue changes are not conscientiously adhered to throughout life. Additional episodes of acute thrombophlebitis can occur.

Cranley, J.J., & others: Chronic venous insufficiency of the lower extremity. Surgery 49:48, 1961.

De Takats, G.: Postphlebitic syndrome. JAMA 164:1861–1867, 1957.

Haeger, K.: The treatment of the severe post-thrombotic state. A comparison of some surgical and conservative methods. Angiology 19:439–449, 1968.

Lofgren, K.A., & others: Extensive ulcerations in the postphlebitic leg. S Clin North America 44:1383–1402, 1964.

SUPERIOR VENA CAVA OBSTRUCTION

Obstruction of the superior vena cava is a relatively rare condition which is usually secondary to the neoplastic or inflammatory process in the superior mediastinum. The most frequent causes are (1) neoplasms, such as lymphomas, primary malignant mediastinal tumors, or carcinoma of the lung with direct extension; (2) chronic fibrotic mediastinitis, either of unknown origin or secondary to tuberculosis or pyogenic infection; (3) thrombophlebitis, often by extension of the process from the axillary or subclavian vein into the innominate and vena cava; (4) aneurysm of the aortic arch; and (5) constrictive pericarditis.

Clinical Findings

A. Symptoms and Signs: Initially, the cutaneous veins may be dilated and the eyelids may be edematous. Later, there may be rather general swelling of the head and arms. If the venous congestion is marked, there may be a degree of cyanosis of that area with engorged veins and even some CNS symptoms. All signs and symptoms may be exaggerated by bending over or lying down so that the patients spend their time sitting up and avoiding physical exertion.

B. Laboratory Findings: The venous pressure in the arm is elevated (often over 20 cm water) and is normal in the leg. A supraclavicular lymph node biopsy may supply a tissue diagnosis.

C. X-Ray Findings: Chest x-rays and venograms may be quite helpful in defining the nature of the primary problem.

Treatment

If the primary problem is due to a malignant neoplasm, radiation therapy or chemotherapy may relieve the pressure on the superior vena cava. Surgery is usually not indicated, though it may be necessary in order to arrive at a diagnosis. If the process results from tuberculosis, antituberculosis chemotherapy is indicated. In cases secondary to mediastinal fibrosis, excision of the fibrous tissue around the great vessels may reestablish flow; if complete thrombosis has occurred, a graft may be tried, though such grafts generally thrombose.

Prognosis

The prognosis depends upon the nature of the obstructive lesion; it is especially bad when malignancy or aortic aneurysm is the cause. Even with mediastinitis and primary thrombophlebitis, the mortality is high.

Failor, H.J., Edwards, J.E., & C.H. Hodgson: Etiologic factors in obstruction of the superior vena cava: A pathologic study. Proc Staff Meet Mayo Clin 33:671–678, 1958.
Lowenberg, E.L., & others: The superior vena cava syndrome. Dis Chest 47:323–333, 1965.

DISEASES OF THE LYMPHATIC CHANNELS

LYMPHANGITIS & LYMPHADENITIS

Essentials of Diagnosis

- Red streak from wound or area of cellulitis toward regional lymph nodes, which are usually enlarged and tender.
- Chills and fever often present.

General Considerations

Lymphangitis and lymphadenitis are common manifestations of a bacterial infection which is usually caused by the hemolytic streptococcus and usually arises from an area of cellulitis, generally at the site of an infected wound. The wound may be very small or superficial or an established abscess may be present, feeding bacteria into the lymphatics. The involvement of the lymphatics is often manifested by a red streak in the skin extending in the direction of the regional lymph nodes which are, in turn, generally tender and enlarged. Systemic manifestations include fever, chills, and malaise. The infection may progress rapidly, often in a matter of hours, and may lead to bacteremia or septicemia and even death.

Clinical Findings

A. Symptoms and Signs: Throbbing pain is usually present in the area of cellulitis at the site of bacterial invasion. Malaise, anorexia, sweating, chills, and fever (37.8–40° C [100–104° F]) develop rapidly. Pain or discomfort is noted in the regional nodes. The red streak, when present, may be definite but it may be very faint and easily missed. It is not usually tender or indurated, as is the area of cellulitis. The involved regional lymph nodes may be enlarged 2–3 times and are often acutely tender. The pulse is often rapid.

B. Laboratory Findings: Leukocytosis with an increase in immature cells is usually present. Later, a blood culture may be positive. Culture and sensitivity studies on the wound exudate or pus may be helpful in treatment of the more severe or refractory infections.

Differential Diagnosis

Lymphangitis may be confused with superficial thrombophlebitis, but the erythematous reaction associated with thrombosis overlies the induration of the venous thrombus and the inflammatory reaction in and around the vein. Venous thrombosis does not result in lymphadenitis, and a wound of entrance with the associated cellulitis is generally not present. Superficial thrombophlebitis frequently arises as a result of intravenous therapy, particularly when catheters are left in place for more than 2 days.

Cat scratch fever should be considered when multiple, superficial cat scratches are noted on the extremity and the lymphadenitis, though often very large, is relatively nontender.

Neither of these conditions is accompanied by the systemic manifestations that often occur with acute lymphadenitis and lymphangitis.

Treatment

A. General Measures: Rest and perhaps splinting and elevation of the area, as well as heat and symptomatic treatment of local pain and systemic reaction, are useful.

B. Specific Measures: Antibiotic therapy should always be instituted when local infection becomes invasive, as manifested by cellulitis and lymphangitis. A culture of any purulent discharge available should be obtained (often there is nothing to culture), and antibiotic therapy should be started in full doses at once. Because the causative organism is so frequently the streptococcus, penicillin is usually the drug of choice. If the patient is allergic to penicillin, erythromycin or one of the other drugs that are effective against grampositive bacteria may be used. (See Chapter 26.)

C. Wound Care: Drainage of pus from an infected wound should be carried out, generally after the above measures have been instituted, and only when it is clear that there is an abscess associated with the site of initial infection; an area of cellulitis should not be incised.

Prognosis

With proper therapy and particularly with the use of an antibiotic effective against the invading bacteria, control of the infection can usually be achieved in a few days and septicemia prevented. Delayed or inadequate therapy can still lead to overwhelming infection and death.

Shick, R.M.: Recurrent lymphangitis and cellulitis of the extremities. M Clin North America 49:1089–1098, 1949.

LYMPHEDEMA

Essentials of Diagnosis

- Painless edema of one or both lower extremities, primarily in young females.
- Initially, pitting edema, which becomes brawny and often nonpitting with time.
- Ulceration, varicosities, and stasis pigmentation do not occur.
- There may be episodes of lymphangitis and cellulitis.

General Considerations

The underlying mechanism in lymphedema is impairment of the flow of lymph from an extremity. When due to congenital developmental abnormalities of the lymphatics, it is referred to as the primary form. The secondary form results when an inflammatory or mechanical obstruction of the lymphatics occurs such as from trauma, regional lymph node resection or irradiation, or extensive involvement of regional nodes by malignant disease or filariasis. Secondary dilatation of the lymphatics that occurs in both forms leads to incompetence of the valve system, disrupting the orderly flow along the lymph vessels, and results in progressive stasis of a protein-rich fluid with secondary fibrosis. Episodes of acute and chronic inflammation may be superimposed, with further stasis and fibrosis. Hypertrophy of the limb results, with markedly thickened and fibrotic skin and subcutaneous tissue and diminution in the fatty tissue.

Lymphangiography and radioactive isotope studies are sometimes useful in defining the specific lymphatic defect.

Treatment

There is no very satisfactory treatment for lymphedema, but the following measures can be instituted: (1) The flow of lymph out of the extremity, with a consequent decrease in the degree of stasis, can be aided through intermittent elevation of the extremity, especially during the sleeping hours (foot of bed elevated 15–20°, achieved by placing pillows beneath the mattress); the constant use of elastic bandages or carefully fitted heavy duty elastic stockings; and massage toward the trunk—either by hand or by means of pneumatic pressure devices designed to milk edema out of an extremity. (2) Secondary cellulitis in the extremity should be avoided by means of good hygiene and treatment of any trichophytosis of the toes. Once an infection starts, it should be treated by very adequate periods of rest, elevation, and antibiotics. Infection can be a serious and recurring problem and often difficult to control. Intermittent prophylactic antibiotics may occasionally be necessary. (3) Intermittent courses of diuretic therapy, especially in those with premenstrual or seasonal exacerbations. (4) Surgery is indicated in severe cases when conservative management fails to control the size of the limb or when recurrent attacks of infection cannot be prevented by other means. It is not indicated for cosmetic reasons since the cosmetic results are poor. There is no truly satisfactory operation.

Battezzati, M., Donini, I., & E. Marsili: The morphologic and physiologic basis for a new classification of lymphoedema. J Cardiovas Surg 8:52–61, 1967.

DeRoo, T.: The value of lymphography in lymphedema. Surg Gynec Obst 124:755–765, 1967.

Gough, M.H.: Primary lymphoedema: Clinical and lymphangiographic studies. Brit J Surg 53:917–925, 1966.

Kinmonth, J.B., & others: Primary lymphoedema: Clinical and lymphangiographic studies of a series of 107 patients in which the lower limbs were affected. Brit J Surg 45:1–10, 1957.

Love, L., & S.E. Kim: Clinical aspects of lymphangiography. M Clin North America 51:227–248, 1967.

Smith, R.D., Spittell, J.A., Jr., & A. Schirger: Secondary lymphedema of the leg: Its characteristics and diagnostic implications. JAMA 185:80–82, 1963.

Thompson, N.: The surgical treatment of chronic lymphoedema of the extremity. S Clin North America 47:445–503, 1967.

•   •   •

MANIFESTATIONS INVOLVING THE BLOOD VESSELS DUE TO PARASITIC DISEASES

Regional perivasculitis and fibrosis: Schistosomiasis.

Varicocele: Filariasis bancrofti.

•   •   •

General Bibliography

Abramson, D.I.: Drugs used in peripheral vascular disease. Am J Cardiol 12:203–215, 1963.

Allen, E.V., Barker, N.W., & E.A. Hines, Jr.: *Peripheral Vascular Diseases,* 3rd ed. Saunders, 1962.

Barker, W.F.: *Surgical Treatment of Peripheral Vascular Disease.* McGraw-Hill, 1962.

Barker, W.F.: *Peripheral Arterial Disease.* Saunders, 1966.

Darling, R.C.: Peripheral arterial surgery. New England J Med 280:27–30, 84–90, 141–145, 1969.

DeBakey, M.E.: Symposium on vascular surgery. S Clin North America 46:823–1071, 1966.

Haller, J.A., Jr.: *Deep Thrombophlebitis.* Saunders, 1967.

Julian, O.C. (editor): Symposium on peripheral vascular diseases. S Clin North America 40:1–240, 1960.

Winsor, T.: *Peripheral Vascular Diseases: An Objective Approach.* Thomas, 1959.

Winsor, T., & C. Hyman: *A Primer of Peripheral Vascular Disease.* Lea & Febiger, 1965.

9 ...

Blood

Ralph O. Wallerstein

ANEMIAS
(See Table 9–1.)

Diagnosis of Anemia

Anemia is a common clinical finding which must be explained. Extensive investigations are sometimes required to determine the cause. The answers to the following 4 fundamental questions are always relevant to a complete evaluation of the anemia patient: (1) Is there evidence of iron deficiency? (2) Is the anemia megaloblastic? (3) Is there evidence of hemolysis? (4) Is the bone marrow hypoactive?

Iron deficiency must be considered in all anemias of obscure origin—regardless of red cell morphology. Staining for marrow hemosiderin is the most reliable technic; marrow hemosiderin is always absent in iron deficiency anemia and is normal or increased in all other forms. Determination of serum iron and total iron-binding capacity is almost as useful. The combination of low serum iron and elevated total iron-binding capacity is seen only in iron deficiency anemia. If these tools are not available, recourse must be had to obtaining a history of blood loss or evidence of it by stool guaiac determination.

The diagnosis of moderately severe megaloblastic anemia (fewer than 3 million red cells/cu mm) can always be made by examination of the blood and bone marrow. The blood shows oval macrocytes and hyper-segmented granulocytes; the bone marrow contains megaloblasts.

The major hemolytic disorders, regardless of type, have in common reticulocytosis, slightly increased serum bilirubin (indirect), and an increased number of nucleated red cells in the marrow.

In hypoplastic anemia the bone marrow is fatty and contains relatively few nucleated red cells.

In any case of undiagnosed normocytic normochromic anemia which does not fall into the above 4 groups, the following causes must be considered: infection, azotemia, malignancy, myxedema, and liver disease.

IRON DEFICIENCY ANEMIA

Essentials of Diagnosis
- Pallor, lassitude.
- Hypochromia, microcytosis; red blood count less reduced than hemoglobin.
- Serum iron low; total iron-binding capacity increased.
- Bone marrow hemosiderin absent.
- Blood loss usually occult.

General Considerations

Iron deficiency anemia in the adult is almost always due to blood loss. Excessive menstrual flow and gastrointestinal bleeding (due to hiatus hernia, gastritis, peptic ulcer, previous gastrectomy, polyps, malignancy, hemorrhoids, or excessive salicylate intake) are the principal causes. Gastrointestinal bleeding is usually chronic and occult. Rare causes include hemosiderinuria, pulmonary hemosiderosis, excessive blood donation, faulty diet, and habitual starch eating.

A normal daily diet contains 12–15 mg of iron, or approximately 6 mg of iron per 1000 calories, of which 5–10% (0.6–1.5 mg) is absorbed. (More iron is absorbed in iron deficiency anemia.) Because less than 1 mg of iron is excreted normally per day, normal persons are in positive iron balance. Chronic bleeding of as little as 2–4 ml of blood per day may lead to a negative iron balance and iron deficiency anemia.

TABLE 9–1. The anemias.

Type	Characteristic Findings
Iron deficiency	Low serum iron, high TIBC, absent marrow hemosiderin.
Megaloblastic	Characteristic red cell, white cell, and marrow morphology.
Hemolytic	High reticulocyte count, low or absent haptoglobin, high indirect bilirubin.
Marrow failure Absolute (eg, aplastic anemia)	Pancytopenia; normal marrow tissue replaced by fat.
Relative (eg, infection, azotemia, cancer, liver disease, myxedema)	Red cell, white cell, and serum factors often have no distinguishing characteristics. The marrow picture is not striking.

Clinical Findings

A. Symptoms and Signs: In addition to symptoms of the primary disease (if any), symptoms due to anemia may be present: easy fatigability, dyspnea, palpitation, angina, and tachycardia. Waxy pallor, brittle hair and nails, smooth tongue, cheilosis, and dysphagia are late findings.

B. Laboratory Findings: The hemoglobin may fall to as low as 3 gm/100 ml, but the red cell count is rarely below 2.5 million/cu mm and the red cells are usually microcytic and hypochromic (although in approximately 20% of adults the red cells are normocytic and nearly normochromic). Reticulocytes and platelets are normal or increased. The white count is normal. Serum iron is usually below 30 μg/100 ml (normal is 90–150 μg/100 ml); total iron-binding capacity is elevated to 350–500 μg/100 ml (normal is 250–350 μg/100 ml). Percent saturation is 10% or less.

The most critical test is the bone marrow stain for hemosiderin; stainable iron is always absent in iron deficiency anemia. The bone marrow aspirate contains increased numbers of nucleated red cells; the normoblasts have only scanty cytoplasm.

Differential Diagnosis

Iron deficiency anemia is the only anemia in which hemosiderin is absent in bone marrow; in all other types of anemia iron is present in bone marrow in normal or increased amounts. In thalassemia minor (which is also manifested by a hypochromic, microcytic anemia) the red cells are smaller and have a more abnormal appearance (for a given degree of anemia); the red count may be above normal and the hemoglobin is rarely below 9 gm/100 ml, and the bone marrow hemosiderin, serum iron, and total iron-binding capacity are normal.

Iron deficiency anemia must be differentiated from other hypochromic anemias.

A. Anemia of Infection: (See p 275.) Red cells are normocytic and mildly hypochromic. Serum iron is low, but total iron-binding capacity is also decreased. Bone marrow hemosiderin is present.

B. Sideroachrestic Anemias: See p 268.

C. Some Hemoglobinopathies: All hemoglobin abnormalities involving the thalassemia gene are microcytic and hypochromic, eg, S-thalassemia, hemoglobin C-thalassemia, and hemoglobin H disease (see p 274); the red cells in hemoglobin E disease may be quite small. The diagnosis is made by hemoglobin electrophoresis.

Complications

Severe dysphagia (Plummer-Vinson syndrome) develops in some patients. Iron deficiency anemia may be the presenting finding in gastrointestinal cancer. In patients with heart disease, severe anemia may precipitate angina pectoris or congestive heart failure.

Treatment

Iron is specific for this type of anemia. It should be started as soon as an etiologic diagnosis has been made. Transfusions are rarely needed.

A. Oral Preparations and Dosages: The maximum absorption is considered to be about 25 mg/day. Give one of the following: (1) ferrous sulfate, 0.2 gm 3 times daily after meals; or (2) ferrous gluconate, 0.3 gm 3 times daily after meals. Oral iron should be continued for 3 months after hemoglobin values return to normal in order to replenish iron stores.

Many other iron salts and chelates, often mixed with other metals or vitamins, are promoted, but none are more useful in iron deficiency anemia than ferrous sulfate. The degree of gastrointestinal irritation and the amount absorbed are functions of the iron content of the salt or complex.

B. Parenteral Iron: The indications are intolerance to oral iron, refractoriness to oral iron (poor absorption), gastrointestinal disease precluding the use of oral iron, continued blood loss, and replacement of depleted iron stores when oral iron fails. Parenteral iron should be given only in the amounts necessary to correct the deficiency. Calculate the total dosage as follows: 250 mg for each gm of hemoglobin below normal. (Normal: men, 14–16 gm; women, 12–16 gm.)

Iron-dextran injection (Imferon®) for intramuscular use contains 5% metallic iron (50 mg/ml). Give 50 mg (1 ml) immediately and then 100–250 mg IM daily or every other day until the total dose has been given. Inject deeply with a 2-inch needle into the upper outer quadrant of the buttock, using the "Z" technic (pulling the skin to one side before inserting the needle) to prevent leakage of the solution and discoloration of the skin. Imferon® may also be given intravenously. It is best administered in doses of 250–500 mg; a test dose of 0.5 ml should be given first; if the patient experiences no unusual reaction, the entire amount may be given over 3–5 minutes.

Prognosis

Following iron therapy all the signs and symptoms of iron deficiency anemia are reversible unless blood loss continues. Bleeding in excess of 500 ml/week over a period of weeks or months probably cannot be treated successfully by iron medication alone.

Committee on Iron Deficiency: Iron deficiency in the United States. JAMA 203:407–412, 1968.

Crosby, W.H.: Iron and anemia. Disease-A-Month, Jan 1966.

Kasper, C.K., Whissell, D.Y.E., & R.O. Wallerstein: Clinical aspects of iron deficiency. JAMA 191:359–363, 1965.

PERNICIOUS ANEMIA
(Addisonian Anemia)

Essentials of Diagnosis

- Anorexia, dyspepsia; smooth, sore tongue.
- Constant, symmetric numbness and tingling of the feet.
- Pallor and a trace of jaundice.
- Oval macrocytes, pancytopenia, hypersegmented neutrophils.
- Megaloblastic bone marrow.

General Considerations

Pernicious anemia is a conditioned vitamin B_{12} deficiency due to an absorption defect, not dietary lack. Intrinsic factor is absent. The defect is rare before age 35; it is more common in persons of Scandinavian, English, and Irish extraction, and is very rare in Orientals. Predisposition to pernicious anemia is probably inherited as a single, dominant, autosomal factor. About 40% of patients have a 7S gamma "autoantibody" with activity against intrinsic factor in their serum; approximately twice that many have antibody against parietal cells. A precipitable antibody to intrinsic factor may also be present in their gastric juice.

Intrinsic factor is secreted by the gastric mucosa; it makes possible absorption of vitamin B_{12}, mostly at the distal ileum, in the presence of calcium and at a pH of 5–7. It is probably a mucopolypeptide or mucopolysaccharide with a molecular weight of 50,000.

Total body vitamin B_{12} content is estimated to be 5 mg; daily loss is approximately 2.5 μg. Clinical and hematologic evidence of pernicious anemia appears when the body vitamin B_{12} pool has been reduced to 10% of normal.

Clinical vitamin B_{12} deficiency may also be caused by gastrectomy, regional ileitis, certain intestinal malformations involving the ileum, resection of the ileum, and fish tapeworm disease.

Clinical Findings

A. Symptoms and Signs: Patients with pernicious anemia may tolerate their disease well and have few symptoms. Anemia may cause easy fatigability, dyspnea, palpitation, angina, and tachycardia. Vitamin B_{12} deficiency may lead to glossitis, gastrointestinal symptoms such as belching, indigestion, anorexia, and diarrhea; CNS symptoms occur in approximately 10% of patients and include constant symmetric numbness and tingling of the lower extremities, ataxia, mental disturbances, and loss of vibration sense and deep reflexes; sensory symptoms usually appear before the motor symptoms and signs.

B. Laboratory Findings:

1. Blood—In addition to the characteristic large oval red cells there are a few small misshapen red cells. The white blood count is usually under 5000/cu mm. The granulocytes, which constitute less than 50% of white cells, tend to be hypersegmented. Platelets usually are reduced (40–100 thousand/cu mm). Reticulocytes range from less than 1% to 3%. The icterus index is increased, but is rarely higher than 15 units.

2. Bone marrow—The bone marrow is hyperactive and is easily entered with the aspiration needle. The characteristic megaloblastic abnormalities are particularly evident in the more mature forms. Giant metamyelocytes are prominent. Megakaryocytes are hypersegmented and reduced in number. Hemosiderin is increased and in the form of fine granules.

3. Other laboratory tests—Patients secrete no free gastric acid and very little gastric juice, even after injection of histamine or betazole hydrochloride (Histalog®), 50 mg (1 ml). Serum LDH (lactate dehy-

drogenase) activity is excessively elevated. Haptoglobin is usually absent. Serum vitamin B_{12} concentration (normally 300–400 $\mu\mu$g/ml) is less than 100 $\mu\mu$g/ml. Absorption of ^{57}Co-labeled vitamin B_{12} is greatly impaired. This is demonstrated by the Schilling test, which involves the oral administration of a small (0.5 μg) dose of radiocobalt-labeled vitamin B_{12} followed 2 hours later by the parenteral administration of 1000 μg of unlabeled vitamin B_{12}. Less than 5% of the radioactive vitamin B_{12} is excreted in the urine in 24 hours (normal: 15–40%), but simultaneous administration of intrinsic factor increases the excretion of vitamin B_{12} 5-fold or more. Vitamin B_{12} absorption may also be measured by externally monitoring hepatic uptake after oral administration of ^{57}Co-labeled vitamin B_{12}. The Schilling test is useful only in (1) differentiating addisonian pernicious anemia from megaloblastic anemias due to folic acid deficiency; (2) diagnosing addisonian pernicious anemia in remission; and (3) diagnosing defective vitamin B_{12} absorption in patients with combined system disease before the onset of anemia. The Schilling test may give a false low value (decreased urinary radioactivity) in the following situations: inadequate urine collection, impaired kidney function, diarrhea, and occasionally in hypothyroidism. Low values which are not improved by simultaneous administration of intrinsic factor are characteristically seen with malabsorption involving disease of the ileum and with fish tapeworm disease (even in asymptomatic carriers).

Some patients with pernicious anemia in relapse may have intestinal malabsorption as well; their Schilling test is not improved by intrinsic factor until after several months of vitamin B_{12} therapy.

Differential Diagnosis

Pernicious anemia must be differentiated from folic acid deficiency (see below) by means of vitamin B_{12} absorption tests.

Large red cells are not seen exclusively in the megaloblastic anemias, but their oval appearance is characteristic, as are the hypersegmented white cells and the megaloblasts of the marrow.

In the various hemolytic anemias some young nucleated red cells in the marrow may resemble megaloblasts; however, there are no oval macrocytes and no hypersegmented PMN's, and the reticulocytes are above 3%.

Treatment

Pernicious anemia in relapse is treated with vitamin B_{12} (cyanocobalamin), 100 μg IM 1–3 times per week until blood values return to normal. Thereafter, 100 μg IM monthly are given. The patient must be impressed that the need for vitamin B_{12} injections will continue for the rest of his life.

Patients who have undergone total gastrectomy should receive maintenance doses of vitamin B_{12} (100 μg IM monthly).

Prognosis

Untreated pernicious anemia is fatal. With parenteral vitamin B_{12} therapy the reticulocytes begin to increase on the 4th day and reach a peak between the 6th and 10th days. The magnitude of the reticulocyte peak correlates well with the degree of anemia; with an initial red count of 1 million/cu mm, a maximum reticulocyte count of 40% may be anticipated. Normal hemoglobin values are obtained in about 6 weeks. CNS symptoms are reversible if they are of relatively short duration (less than 6 months), but may be permanent if they have existed longer. Histamine-fast achlorhydria persists; the Schilling test remains abnormal.

Castle, W.B.: Current concepts of pernicious anemia. Am J Med 48:541–548, 1970.

Chanarin, I.: *The Megaloblastic Anemias.* Blackwell, 1969.

Herbert, V.: Megaloblastic anemia. New England J Med 268:201–203, 368–371, 1963.

Heinrich, H.C.: Metabolic basis of the diagnosis and therapy in vitamin B_{12} deficiency. Pages 199–249 in: *Seminars in Hematology*, vol 1. Grune & Stratton, 1964.

FOLIC ACID DEFICIENCY

Folic acid deficiency produces the same hematologic findings as pernicious anemia, but blood changes occur sooner because folate storage lasts for only 1–2 months. The most common cause is malnutrition, especially in association with alcoholism ("nutritional megaloblastic anemia"). Folic acid deficiency may develop in sprue and may complicate certain chronic hemolytic anemias (eg, sickle cell anemia). It is occasionally seen in epileptics receiving primidone (Mysoline®), diphenylhydantoin (Dilantin®), or phenobarbital; in patients following treatment with methotrexate (amethopterin) or pyrimethamine (Daraprim®); and in pregnancy (especially when associated with vomiting and inadequate diet, toxemia, and twins). In megaloblastic anemias due to folic acid deficiency, CNS symptoms are lacking, free gastric acid may be present, and the vitamin B_{12} absorption test (Schilling) is normal. In sprue, vitamin B_{12} absorption may be impaired even after administration of intrinsic factor. Serum folate activity is less than 3 μg/ml (normal is 7 μg/ml or more), and urine formiminoglutamic acid after histidine loading is increased.

"Pernicious" or megaloblastic anemia of pregnancy is caused by folic acid, not vitamin B_{12} deficiency. Poor nutrition is the major factor in its development. The requirement for folic acid increases markedly during pregnancy. Low serum folate levels are found in approximately 20% of pregnancies; the incidence of deficiency is much higher with twins, toxemia, or abruptio placentae. Only a small percentage of women with low levels of folic acid have megaloblastic anemia.

The diagnosis is made by finding hypersegmented polymorphonuclear leukocytes in the blood and megaloblastic maturation in the marrow. Oval macrocytes are found less consistently than in other megaloblastic anemias; the red cell MCV is usually normal and may even be low.

For therapy, give folic acid, 5 mg daily orally, until hematologic remission occurs.

In megaloblastic anemia of infancy and in megaloblastic anemia due to malnutrition or antiepileptic therapy, folic acid is given only until a hematologic remission is obtained. No maintenance therapy is necessary.

A patient with sprue or malabsorption syndrome may require initial therapy with parenteral folic acid and maintenance with oral folic acid. Some of these patients have an associated vitamin B_{12} or iron deficiency and have to be treated accordingly. Others require the addition of corticosteroids for relief of symptoms.

Folic acid is given orally or IM, 5 mg daily. The intramuscular preparation contains 15 mg/ml.

Herbert, V.: Diagnosis and treatment of folic acid deficiency. M Clin North America 46:1365–1379, 1962.

Herbert V.: *The Megaloblastic Anemias.* Grune & Stratton, 1959.

APLASTIC ANEMIA

Essentials of Diagnosis

- Lassitude, pallor, purpura, bleeding.
- Pancytopenia, fatty bone marrow.
- History of exposure to an offending drug or x-ray radiation.

General Considerations

Aplastic anemia may occur at any age. Its incidence is approximately 4 per million population. It is characterized by pancytopenia or a selective depression of red cells, white cells, or platelets. In over ½ of cases the etiology is not known. It may occur as a toxic reaction to many chemicals and drugs, eg, chloramphenicol (Chloromycetin®), benzene, phenylbutazone (Butazolidin®), and mephenytoin (Mesantoin®). Hair dyes, plant sprays, insecticides, volatile solvents, large doses of antileukemic drugs, and excessive x-ray or ionizing radiation may also cause this disease. Rarely, an associated thymoma is found.

Clinical Findings

A. Symptoms and Signs: Anemia may cause lassitude, pallor, fatigue, tachycardia, thrombocytopenia, purpura, bleeding, neutropenia, and infections with high fever.

B. Laboratory Findings: The red cell count may be below 1 million/cu mm. The cells are usually slightly macrocytic. The reticulocyte count is often low, but may be normal or even slightly elevated. The white count may be less than 2000/cu mm and the platelet count less than 30,000/cu mm. The icterus index is usually below normal. The bone marrow is fatty, with very few red cells, white cells, and megakaryocytes. Hemosiderin is present.

Fixed tissue section made from the marrow aspirate and stained with hematoxylin and eosin are best for demonstrating the characteristic architecture of an aplastic bone marrow; smears of the aspirate stained with Wright's stain are not adequate for diagnosis.

Differential Diagnosis

In hypersplenism, the marrow is hyperactive and the spleen is large.

In myelofibrosis the spleen and liver are enlarged; red cells vary in size and shape; bizarre and tear-shaped cells may be seen; leukocytosis is common; the platelet count may be low, normal, or even elevated, and giant platelets are common; the marrow is fibrotic rather than fatty and is difficult to aspirate; and evidence of extramedullary hematopoiesis may be seen in the liver and spleen.

Aleukemic leukemia and, on occasion, lymphosarcoma may be indistinguishable clinically from aplastic anemia, especially when the smear of the marrow aspiration does not show many cells. Paraffin sections of the aspirate or biopsy are needed for diagnosis.

Complications

Long-term transfusion therapy may lead to development of leuko-agglutinins and hemosiderosis. Overwhelming infection secondary to the leukopenia and hemorrhage secondary to thrombocytopenia are frequently terminal events.

Some patients make a partial recovery and develop a syndrome resembling paroxysmal nocturnal hemoglobinuria.

Treatment

A. General Measures: Eliminate exposure to suspected toxins and discontinue all unnecessary medication. No agents are known that will predictably stimulate marrow function, but the following may be tried:

1. Androgens—Give one of the following: (1) Fluoxymesterone (Halotestin®), 40–100 mg daily orally. (2) Oxymetholone (Adroyd®, Anadrol®), 2.5 mg/kg/day orally. (3) Testosterone enanthate (Delatestryl®), 200–400 mg/kg/day given twice weekly IM. (4) Methandrostenolone (Dianabol®), 40–100 mg/day orally.

2. Cobaltous chloride, 100–150 mg orally daily for at least 3 weeks.

3. If a thymoma is present, its removal may be considered.

B. Transfusions: Give preferably as packed red cells only, less than 1 week old. Five ml of packed red cells/kg will raise the red cell count by 10%. (For example, 500 ml of red cells will raise the hemoglobin of a 50 kg patient by 20%, or 3 gm/100 ml.) The average requirement for adults is 5 units (2500 ml whole blood or 1250 ml red cells) every 2 months. Post-transfusion hemoglobin levels of 11–12 gm/100 ml are satisfactory. Many patients do not have to be transfused until the hemoglobin level falls to less than 7 gm/100 ml. If a febrile transfusion reaction develops, serum should be checked for leuko-agglutinins; if these white cell antibodies have developed, the buffy coats should be removed from all subsequent transfusions.

C. Treatment of Complications:

1. Infections—Antibiotics should not be given prophylactically, even when leukopenia is severe. When infections occur, specific antibiotics are used if possible. If the bacterial agent cannot be identified, a broad-spectrum antibacterial agent (eg, kanamycin, 0.5 gm twice daily) and a penicillinase resistant bactericidal agent (eg, cloxacillin, 4 gm daily orally) are used. Patients must pay meticulous attention to personal hygiene and avoid exposure to infections.

2. Bleeding—When bleeding occurs in association with severe thrombocytopenia, prednisolone (or equivalent), 10–20 mg orally every 8 hours, may be tried. Hemorrhagic manifestations may be relieved even without a rise in the platelet count. Acute bleeding episodes are sometimes successfully controlled by platelet-rich transfusions. This is best accomplished by giving fresh (less than 4 hours old) whole blood, carefully collected in siliconized bottles or plastic equipment.

3. Hemolytic anemia—If an associated hemolytic anemia with splenic sequestration of red cells develops, splenectomy may have to be considered.

Prognosis

The mortality with severe bone marrow depression is over 50%; hemorrhage and overwhelming infection are the main causes of death. The course—from onset of anemia to death—is usually only a few months. Some patients can be maintained on transfusions for years. Partial or complete spontaneous remission may occur.

Lewis, S.M.: Course and prognosis in aplastic anaemia. Brit MJ 1:1027–1030, 1965.

Scott, J.L., Cartwright, G.E., & M.M. Wintrobe: Acquired aplastic anemia: An analysis of thirty-nine cases and review of the pertinent literature. Medicine 38:119–172, 1959.

ANEMIA OF LEAD POISONING

Lead poisoning in the adult may produce a mild anemia, and pallor but no jaundice; the spleen is not enlarged. The red cells are normocytic, slightly hypochromic, and may show coarse or fine basophilic stippling. Reticulocytes are slightly elevated. The white cells and platelets are normal. The bone marrow shows normal activity. Red cell ^{51}Cr survival shows moderately diminished red cell life spans (half-life, 18–26 days). The osmotic fragility is decreased. Urine coproporphyrin is greatly increased. After treatment with a chelating agent, there is a 5- to 10-fold increase of coproporphyrin and lead in the urine.

Lead interferes with hemoglobin synthesis at several levels. It inhibits heme synthesis and prevents the proper utilization and incorporation of iron into protoporphyrin. It also inhibits globin synthesis. As a result, the following substances accumulate in the urine of patients with lead poisoning: delta-aminolevulinic acid, coproporphyrin, and lead. Protoporphyrin accumulates in the red cells.

Byers, R.K.: Lead poisoning. Review of the literature and report on 45 cases. Pediatrics 23:585–603, 1959.
Chisolm, J.J.: Disturbances in the biosynthesis of heme in lead intoxication. J Pediat 64:174–187, 1964.

ANEMIA OF MYXEDEMA

Some patients with very low thyroid function have a moderately severe anemia. A similar blood picture may be seen in hypopituitary disease. The red blood cell count is rarely below 3 million/cu mm and the hemoglobin is rarely less than 9 gm/100 ml. The anemia tends to be macrocytic and normochromic. However, iron deficiency, a frequent complication, especially in women with menorrhagia, will produce hypochromic microcytic anemia. Bone marrow cellularity is decreased with increase in fat spaces. Nucleated red cells are normoblastic. White cells and platelets are normal.

Thyroid medication induces a gradual return to normal hemoglobin levels and red blood count in 3–4 months.

Tudhope, J.R.: Anemia in hypothyroidism. Quart J Med 29:513, 1960.

PURE RED CELL APLASIA

This is a relatively rare condition (less common than aplastic anemia) characterized by moderate to severe anemia, very low reticulocyte counts, aplasia of red cell precursors, and normal white blood cells and platelets. It may occur as a congenital disorder, presenting as profound anemia in the first 3 months of life (Blackfan-Diamond syndrome).

The adult form may be secondary to several causes. Preleukemic leukemia must always be considered and the granulocytic series carefully scrutinized for abnormalities. Selective red cell hypoplasia develops in most patients with renal failure. Some cases are associated with thymoma. Some degree of red cell aplasia occasionally accompanies infections. Acute red cell aplasia may develop during the course of hemolytic anemia, eg, in hereditary spherocytosis or sickle cell anemia ("aplastic crisis"). Rarely, autoimmune hemolytic anemia may have an aplastic phase. A form of this disorder occurs in severe protein malnutrition (kwashiorkor). Under experimental conditions, riboflavin (vitamin B_2) deficiency has led to selective red cell aplasia. These disorders do not usually show the degree of red cell aplasia seen in the idiopathic cases and those that result from the toxic effects of drugs. Drugs that have been implicated on occasion as the causative agent in this anemia are chloramphenicol (Chloromycetin®), diphenylhydantoin (Dilantin®), quinacrine (Atabrine®), sulfathiazole, benzol, and antituberculosis agents. These drugs usually produce pancytopenia and total marrow aplasia but occasionally cause only selective red cell aplasia.

The only signs and symptoms are those of anemia. The red count may be as low as 1 million/cu mm, but the red cells look normal under the microscope and have no unusual shape or inclusions. Reticulocytes are reduced to 0.1% or even less. White cells and platelets are normal in number and appearance. Serum iron may be elevated.

The marrow is aspirated easily. It has a normal architecture and normal or increased iron stores confined to histiocytes. Nucleated red cells usually total less than 100 per 1000 white cells. They are normoblastic. White cells, megakaryocytes, and stromal cells are unremarkable.

Serum creatinine and chest x-ray should be obtained. A leukocyte alkaline phosphatase and bone marrow chromosome cultured for Philadelphia chromosome may be worthwhile. Erythropoietin is usually greatly increased.

Underlying conditions must be corrected. Corticosteroids are very effective in children but are less consistently beneficial in adults. Prednisone, 10–20 mg 3–4 times daily, may be tried. Testosterone is helpful in some patients. Benefits from cobalt or vitamin B_2 have been reported on occasion.

If a thymoma is found, its removal does not necessarily produce a hematologic remission.

Finkel, H.E., Kimber, R.J., & W. Dameshek: Corticosteroid-responsive acquired pure red cell aplasia in adults. Am J Med 43:771–776, 1967.
Tsai, S.Y., & W.C. Levin: Chronic erythrocytic hypoplasia in adults. Review of the literature and report of a case. Am J Med 22:322–330, 1957.

HEMOLYTIC ANEMIAS

1. ACQUIRED HEMOLYTIC ANEMIA

Essentials of Diagnosis
- Fatigue, malaise, pallor, jaundice.
- Splenomegaly.
- Persistent anemia and reticulocytosis.
- Coombs test usually positive.

General Considerations
A positive direct Coombs test (Table 9–2) means that a plasma protein, usually either IgG or comple-

TABLE 9–2. Positive Coombs test.
(Most common examples of specific causes.)

Neoplastic	
Chronic lymphatic leukemia	G
Lymphosarcoma	G
Reticulum cell sarcoma	G and C
Hodgkin's disease	G
Collagen diseases	
Lupus erythematosus	G and C
Rheumatoid arthritis	G and C
Infectious diseases	
Cytomegalic virus disease	G
Viral pneumonia	C
Infectious mononucleosis	C
Drugs	
Penicillin	G
Methyldopa (Aldomet®)	G

Legend: G = anti-IgG
       C = anticomplement

ment, has become fixed abnormally and relatively irreversibly to the red cell surface. The protein is detected by the Coombs serum, which is prepared by immunizing certain laboratory animals against human immunoglobulins or complement.

When done with the usual "broad-spectrum" antiglobulin serum, a positive Coombs test indicates attachment to the red cell membrane of gamma globulin, compounds of complement, transferrin, a complex of certain drugs, and gamma globulin, or possibly other globulins. A "nonspecific" positive direct Coombs test without hemolysis may be found occasionally in a variety of unrelated clinical conditions, eg, rheumatoid arthritis, ulcerative colitis, and leukemia. Appropriate clinical information and a few serologic tests usually lead to the correct diagnosis.

Two major types of red cell coating with protein exist—the IgG type ("gamma Coombs") and the anticomplement type ("nongamma Coombs"), often associated with a cold antibody. The former is found in lymphoma, systemic lupus erythematosus, and certain drug reactions, but in 2/3 of cases no specific cause is found. In the nongamma type, a component of complement rather than of gamma globulin is fixed to the red cell surface; the concentration of complement in the patient's serum is correspondingly low. These antibodies may develop after viral pneumonia, with reticulum cell sarcoma, and with certain drugs; in ½ of cases, no cause is found.

Occasionally, auto-antibodies have Rh specificity, eg, some patients with autoimmune hemolytic anemia or a positive direct Coombs test have antibodies against a specific antigen present on their own red cells; this occurs in approximately 1/3 of cases and usually involves anti-E, anti-c, or anti-e antibodies.

Red cell coating in vivo as described above is always referred to as the "direct" Coombs test. In approximately ½ of these, the indirect Coombs test is also positive. This test measures circulating antibody in patients' serum. In the autoimmune hemolytic anemias, the indirect Coombs test is, of course, only positive when the direct Coombs test is positive, the positive indirect test merely indicating an excess of antibody.

Autoimmune hemolytic anemia may occur following exposure to certain agents. Three different mechanisms are recognized:

(1) Penicillin in large doses can produce this type of hemolytic anemia; it becomes firmly fixed to the red cell membrane and acts as a hapten to stimulate antibody formation. The antibody "coats" red cells, and a positive direct Coombs test with hemolytic anemia may develop.

(2) Several drugs can bring some immune injury to red cells, platelets, and white cells without first attaching to the cell surface. These agents stimulate antibody formation; the drug and its appropriate antibody then combine, attach to red cells, and damage them. The role of the red cells has been referred to as that of an "innocent bystander." The antibody is usually of the anticomplement or IgM type. Stibophen (Fuadin®), quinidine, and quinine are among the drugs implicated in this type of reaction.

(3) A third mechanism for the development of a positive Coombs test has been observed with the use of the antihypertensive agent methyldopa (Aldomet®). Approximately 20% of patients who take this drug develop a positive Coombs test, but only 1–2% of these develop hemolytic anemia. The drug, while of prime etiologic importance, does not itself participate in the ultimate reaction. It perhaps produces some subtle changes on the red cell surface, possibly by interfering with normal biosynthesis of membrane components, causing alterations which result in "new" antigens.

A positive Coombs test in a patient who has been transfused recently (within a few weeks) must be interpreted with great caution. The "coated" cells may be incompatible donor cells in a patient who has antibodies from a prior transfusion. The incompatibility occasionally leads to delayed (by 4–14 days) transfusion reactions that may simulate "autoimmune" hemolytic anemia.

Hemolysis without antibody (negative Coombs test) may develop in uremia, cirrhosis, diffuse vasculitis, cancer, and in some bacterial infections.

Clinical Findings

A. Symptoms and Signs: Manifestations of anemia (weakness, pallor, dyspnea, palpitation, dizziness) or hemolysis (fever, jaundice, splenomegaly, hepatomegaly) may be present.

B. Laboratory Findings: Acquired hemolytic anemia is usually normocytic and normochromic. Spherocytes and nucleated red cells may be seen. White cell and platelet counts are frequently elevated, but leukopenia and thrombocytopenia may occur. The reticulocyte count is usually over 10%, often very high (50% or even more), but occasionally low. The bone marrow shows marked erythroid hyperplasia and ample hemosiderin. Indirect bilirubin may be elevated to 2 mg/100 ml. There is no bile in the urine. Stool urobilinogen may be greatly increased. Haptoglobin may be low or absent. Normal donor blood has short survival.

Differential Diagnosis

The hemoglobinopathies are differentiated by electrophoresis. In hemolytic anemia associated with cirrhosis the primary disease is usually evident. In hereditary spherocytosis and in congenital nonspherocytic hemolytic anemia the Coombs test is negative. In refractory normoblastic anemia with intramedullary hemolysis, the reticulocyte count is not elevated, bone marrow shows many sideroblasts, and donor blood survives normally.

Complications

The hemolytic anemia may become acute, with shock, upper abdominal pain, and prostration. Thrombocytopenic purpura may develop.

Treatment

Treatment must often be directed against the underlying disease. Transfusions are only palliative, and their effects are dissipated rapidly since donor cells are also destroyed at an accelerated rate.

A. Medical Treatment: Prednisolone (or equivalent), 10–20 mg 4 times daily, is given orally until normal hemoglobin values are reached or undesirable side-effects develop. The dose may be reduced rapidly to 20 mg/day and then decreased by 5 mg each week until the smallest dose needed to maintain normal hemoglobin levels is being given. Occasionally, medication can then be discontinued. Patients must be reexamined every 4 weeks even when in remission because there is always a danger of sudden relapse.

B. Surgical Treatment: When corticosteroids fail or when large doses are required for maintenance, splenectomy must be considered. Preliminary ^{51}Cr red cell life span determinations and body surface counting over the spleen to determine splenic radioactivity should be done before the decision to operate is made. When splenic radioactivity is more than twice normal, as compared to the liver, splenectomy is likely to be of value.

Prognosis

In idiopathic acquired hemolytic anemia, prolonged remissions may occur spontaneously or following splenectomy or corticosteroid therapy; some cases are fatal. Often the prognosis depends upon that of the underlying disorder.

Allgood, J.W., & H. Chaplin: Idiopathic acquired autoimmune hemolytic anemia. Am J Med 43:254–273, 1967.

Dacie, J.V.: Autoimmune hemolytic anemia. Brit J Med 2:381–386, 1970.

Drugs and the Coombs antiglobulin test. Editorial. New England J Med 277:157–158, 1967.

2. HEREDITARY SPHEROCYTOSIS
(Congenital Hemolytic Anemia;
Congenital Hemolytic Jaundice)

Essentials of Diagnosis

- Malaise, abdominal discomfort.
- Jaundice, anemia, splenomegaly.
- Spherocytosis, increased osmotic fragility of red cells, negative Coombs test.

General Considerations

In hereditary spherocytosis, the red cells have a defective membrane which is abnormally permeable to sodium. To prevent excessive intracellular sodium accumulation, which in turn would lead to influx of water and cell rupture, increased metabolic work must be done by the cells. The necessary energy is derived from increased glycolysis. Glucose deprivation, as it occurs in the spleen—and in vitro during the performance of the autohemolysis or incubated osmotic fragility tests—leads to red cell destruction. When red cells from a patient with hereditary spherocytosis are transfused to a normal recipient, they are destroyed in the (normal) spleen. On the other hand, normal donor blood survives almost normally in a patient with hereditary spherocytosis. The disease is chronic, hereditary, and transmitted by a dominant autosomal gene; and is seen in all races. In 25% of cases no family involvement can be demonstrated. It may be first manifested in the newborn period, and may resemble hemolytic disease due to ABO incompatibility; but in some patients the disease is not discovered until after the age of 80.

Clinical Findings

A. Symptoms and Signs: There may be easy fatigability and moderate and constant jaundice; the spleen is almost always enlarged and may cause left upper quadrant fullness and discomfort. Splenic infarction may cause acute pain. The anemia may be intensified during infections, following trauma, and during pregnancy.

On rare occasions an acute "aplastic" anemia develops with profound anemia and, in some cases, fever, headache, abdominal pain, and pancytopenia with hypoactive marrow. In occasional instances there may be no clinical findings; the diagnosis is made only because the discovery of the disease in a more severely afflicted relative has led to an intensive search and laboratory testing of the blood.

B. Laboratory Findings: The red blood count is moderately decreased (3–4 million/cu mm). The red cells are small (MCV = 70–80 cu μ) and hyperchromic (MCHC = 36–40%). Spherocytes in varying numbers are seen on the smear. The reticulocyte count is usually increased; the white cell and platelet counts may be only moderately increased.

In the bone marrow there is marked erythroid hyperplasia; hemosiderin is present in only moderate amounts since the spleen is the main reservoir of iron in this disorder.

Indirect serum bilirubin and stool urobilinogen are usually elevated; haptoglobins often decreased or even absent. The Coombs test is negative.

Osmotic fragility is characteristically increased; hemolysis of 5–10% of cells may be observed at saline concentrations of 0.6% or even higher. The response may be normal in some patients, but a sample of defibrinated blood incubated at 37° C for 24 hours ("incubated fragility test") will show increased hemolysis when compared to normal blood similarly treated.

Autohemolysis of defibrinated blood incubated under sterile conditions for 48 hours is usually greatly increased (10–20% compared to a normal value of less than 5%).

The addition of 10% glucose prior to incubation will decrease the amount of autohemolysis.

Red cell survival studies, using the patient's own blood labeled with ^{51}Cr, will show a greatly shortened red cell life span and sequestration in the spleen.

Differential Diagnosis

Spherocytes in large numbers occur in many patients with autoimmune hemolytic anemia. Osmotic fragility and autohemolysis are similarly increased, but are less consistently improved by glucose. The positive Coombs test, negative family history, and sharply reduced survival of normal donor blood in these patients establish the diagnosis.

Spherocytes are also seen in hemoglobin C disease, in some drug-induced hemolytic anemias, in some alcoholics, and with burns.

Complications

Gallstones composed principally of bile pigments (reflecting increased metabolism of hemoglobin) occur in up to 85% of adults and may develop even in children. Leg ulcers are occasionally seen. During febrile illnesses, aplastic crises may occur with profound anemia and decreased white cell and platelet counts, but little jaundice.

Treatment

There is no specific medical treatment for this disorder.

A. Surgical Treatment: Splenectomy is indicated in all cases once the diagnosis is definitely established, even if the anemia is minimal and there is no jaundice. Preoperative transfusion is rarely necessary. When there is associated cholelithiasis, splenectomy should precede cholecystectomy unless both procedures are done at the same time. Splenectomy is usually deferred until after the first few years of life.

B. Treatment of Aplastic Crisis: Prompt and adequate transfusion therapy is necessary to prevent cardiovascular collapse. Antibiotics may be necessary to treat precipitating infections.

Prognosis

Splenectomy eliminates anemia and jaundice, but abnormal red cell morphology and abnormal osmotic fragility persist. Red cell life span is almost normal after splenectomy.

Jacob, H.S.: Abnormality in the physiology of the erythrocyte membrane in hereditary spherocytosis. Am J Med 41:734–743, 1966.

3. OVALOCYTOSIS
(Hereditary Elliptocytosis)

Ovalocytosis is inherited as a dominant trait with variable clinical expressions. It is equally common in males and females, and occurs in all ethnic groups. The determining gene is on the same chromosome that carries the Rh blood group gene. Twenty-five to 90% of the red cells may be oval. It is thought to occur in 4 out of 10,000 individuals in the USA. About 12% of subjects have moderate anemia, a palpable spleen, and slight jaundice. Reticulocyte counts are elevated. Patients may have marked poikilocytosis and some spherocytes. Incubated osmotic fragility and autohemolysis may be increased but are restored to normal by glucose. Splenectomy is usually beneficial in patients with overt hemolysis.

The disorder is usually asymptomatic, without anemia and with normal red cell indices, but red cell survival is often shortened. In some patients the red cells are more oval than elliptical; a few spherocytes may be seen.

Cutting, H.O., & others: Autosomal dominant hemolytic anemia characterized by ovalocytosis. Am J Med 39:21–34, 1965.

Greenberg, L.H., & R.K. Tanaka: Hereditary elliptocytosis with hemolytic anemia: A family study of five affected members. California Med 110:389–393, 1969.

Geerdink, R.A., & others: Hereditary spherocytosis and hyperhemolysis. Acta med scandinav 179:715–728, 1966.

4. ACUTE HEMOLYTIC ANEMIA

Essentials of Diagnosis

- Sudden onset with chills, fever, nausea, vomiting, or pain in abdomen or back.
- Pallor, slight jaundice, splenomegaly.
- Red or black urine.

General Considerations

Acute hemolytic anemia may be drug-induced, especially in sensitive individuals (see Primaquine-Sensitive Hemolytic Anemia); it may be due to certain infections, eg, *Escherichia coli* infections, hemolytic streptococcal septicemia, *Clostridium welchii* infections, and malaria; it may be seen in some forms of cancer and malignant lymphomas, and in some diseases of uncertain origin, eg, lupus erythematosus and infectious mononucleosis. It is usually seen during the course of paroxysmal nocturnal hemoglobinuria, thrombotic thrombocytopenic purpura, paroxysmal cold hemoglobinuria, and when high titered cold agglutinins develop during convalescence from viral pneumonia. Sometimes the cause is not known.

Clinical Findings

A. Symptoms and Signs: The onset is fulminating, with chills, fever, abdominal pain, pallor, jaundice, weakness, and tachycardia.

B. Laboratory Findings: The anemia is usually normocytic and normochromic, but spherocytes, burr cells, microspherocytes, and nucleated red cells may be seen. The red cell count and hemoglobin are lowest several days after the onset of symptoms. The white count may reach 50,000/cu mm and the platelet count 1 million/cu mm, but occasionally both are decreased. A blood smear stained with methyl violet may show small granules (Heinz bodies), which are not visible with Wright's stain. Reticulocytes may be greatly increased. The Coombs test is usually negative.

The bone marrow is hyperplastic, with a predominance of nucleated red cells. There may be hemoglobinemia lasting a few hours, followed by methemalbuminemia (manifested by a brown discoloration of the serum) for a few days and usually a moderately elevated indirect bilirubin value. Haptoglobin, a glycoprotein migrating electrophoretically with alpha$_2$ globulin, which can normally bind 50−150 mg/100 ml of free hemoglobin, disappears from the serum.

The urine may contain hemoglobin and hemosiderin; urobilinogen may be elevated, but not bile. Stool urobilinogen is increased. Red cell enzyme studies may show a deficiency of glucose-6-phosphate dehydrogenase; cold agglutinins may be found in atypical pneumonia; slightly acid serum may hemolyze the cells in paroxysmal nocturnal hemoglobinuria (Ham's test); and a circulating hemolysin may be found in paroxysmal cold hemoglobinuria (Donath-Landsteiner test).

Differential Diagnosis

The fulminating onset of acute hemolytic anemia, with chills and fever, may simulate an infection. The abdominal pain may suggest surgical illness; the profound anemia suggests blood loss. In acute hemolytic anemia, however, the serum is invariably pigmented as a result of the products of hemolysis. A pink serum indicates free hemoglobin; a brown serum, methemalbumin; and a yellow serum, bilirubin.

Complications

Shock may occur if the development of anemia is sufficiently abrupt or severe. Acute tubular necrosis secondary to profound ischemia may lead to acute renal failure.

Treatment

Acute hemolytic anemia may be a medical emergency. The patient should be hospitalized, all medications discontinued, and possible causes investigated.

Spontaneous remission frequently occurs. Even patients who are not critically ill are observed for a few days for a gradual decline of reticulocytosis, followed by a hemoglobin rise of 1−2 gm/100 ml/week. Under these circumstances only supportive therapy need be given.

A. General Measures: Since acute renal failure is a potential hazard, serum electrolytes and BUN are determined and strict attention is paid to fluid intake and output and electrolyte administration.

B. Transfusions: Transfusions are used only to combat shock or anoxia; packed red cells are preferable to whole blood. Rarely is it necessary or desirable to raise the hemoglobin level above 8 gm/100 ml with transfusions.

C. Corticosteroids: If reticulocytosis persists and hemoglobin levels do not rise, if there is a continuous drop in hemoglobin, or if the patient is severely ill, give prednisolone (or equivalent), 10−20 mg 4 times daily. Corticosteroids are continued until serum and urine are clear of hemolytic products and the hemoglobin level is normal. The dose may be reduced rapidly at first to 20 mg/day and then decreased by 5 mg each week. Splenectomy is rarely if ever indicated in acute hemolytic anemia.

Prognosis

Acute hemolytic anemia usually remits spontaneously, either because the offending agent is removed or because only a portion of the patient's red cells, usually the older ones, are sensitive to the toxin. Hemolytic anemias secondary to serious underlying disorders such as metastatic cancer, thrombotic thrombocytopenic purpura, or *Clostridium welchii* infection (as seen with induced abortion) are often rapidly fatal.

Wallerstein, R.O., & P.M. Aggeler: Acute hemolytic anemia. Am J Med 37:92−104, 1964.

5. PAROXYSMAL NOCTURNAL HEMOGLOBINURIA

Paroxysmal nocturnal hemoglobinuria is a chronic hemolytic anemia of variable severity, characterized by rather constant hemoglobinemia and hemosiderinuria and recurrent episodes of acute hemolysis with chills, fever, pain, and hemoglobinuria.

The basic disorder is an unknown intracellular defect; hemolysis is produced by interaction between the abnormal cells and several factors present in normal serum: magnesium, properdin, and complement-like components.

The onset is usually in adult life, and the disease is not familial. Spleen and liver may be slightly enlarged. White cell and platelet counts are often decreased; the reticulocyte count is increased. The bone marrow is usually hyperactive but may be hypoplastic; aplastic anemia occasionally precedes the clinical development of this disorder.

The indirect serum bilirubin is elevated. Hemoglobinemia and methemalbuminemia are often present.

TABLE 9–3. Differential diagnosis of paroxysmal hemoglobinuria.

	Attacks Precipitated By	Site of Pain	Plasma Discoloration	Anemia	Urinary Pigment	Specific Tests
Paroxysmal nocturnal hemoglobinuria	Sleep	Lumbar, abdominal, legs, shoulder girdle.	Prominent	Chronic	Hemoglobin	Ham's test; sugar water test.
Cold hemoglobinuria	Cold	Abdominal cramps, backache.	Prominent	During attacks only.	Hemoglobin	Serologic test for syphilis. Donath-Landsteiner.
March hemoglobinuria	Exercise	Lumbar	Prominent	None	Hemoglobin	Provocative exercise test.
Idiopathic myoglobinuria	Usually exercise	Muscles	None	None	Myoglobin	Spectroscopic examination of myoglobin.

Haptoglobins are absent, LDH markedly elevated, the red cell acetylcholinesterase level is low. The intrinsic red cell defect is demonstrated by finding hemolysis on incubation of the patient's red cells in normal acidified serum (Ham's test). The "sugar water test" is an excellent screening method. Hemoglobin electrophoresis, osmotic fragility, and the Coombs test are normal.

Complications consist of overwhelming infection, aplastic crises, and thromboses. After years of hemosiderinuria, iron deficiency may develop.

Transfusion reactions occur where the donor blood (plasma) hemolyzes the patient's red cells.

Transfusions are given for severe anemia or complications such as trauma, infections, thromboses, or leg ulcers. The administration of 1 liter of 6% dextran solution, preferably of relatively high molecular weight (150,000), before transfusion may prevent hemolysis of the patient's own cells by donor serum.

Crosby, W.H.: Paroxysmal nocturnal hemoglobinuria. Relation of the clinical manifestations to underlying pathogenic mechanisms. Blood 8:769–812, 1953.

Hartman, R.C., & D.E. Jenkins: The sugar-water test for paroxysmal nocturnal hemoglobinuria. New England J Med 275:155–157, 1966.

6. HEREDITARY NONSPHEROCYTIC HEMOLYTIC ANEMIA

Essentials of Diagnosis

- Moderate anemia.
- Familial and congenital.
- Spleen slightly enlarged.
- No spherocytes; osmotic fragility normal.
- High reticulocyte count.

General Considerations

This is a heterogeneous group of hemolytic anemias caused by intrinsic red cell defects. The onset is in childhood; many of these disorders are inherited as a mendelian dominant trait. In some patients the underlying abnormality is unknown; others have severe deficiency of glucose-6-phosphate dehydrogenase activity, indicating a defect in the pentose phosphate pathway. The severity varies considerably in different ethnic groups. Qualitative as well as quantitative differences in the enzyme may exist. Caucasians of Mediterranean origin are principally affected, but Sephardic Jews and Iranians, among others, are also commonly affected.

Anemia and jaundice are often discovered early in life; patients may even be jaundiced at birth, suggesting hemolytic anemia of the newborn; other family members may have a similar defect. A hemolytic crisis may be precipitated by certain drugs such as phenacetin, some sulfonamides, antimalarials, nitrofurantoin, and naphthalene (mothballs).

Clinical Findings

A. Symptoms and Signs: Severe anemia may be fatal in infancy. The disorder is usually recognized in childhood. There may be symptoms of anemia, slight jaundice, and a palpable spleen.

B. Laboratory Findings: The red cells may be normal or slightly enlarged. Howell-Jolly bodies and Pappenheimer bodies (iron particle inclusions visible with Wright's stain) and stippling may be prominent, especially after splenectomy. The reticulocyte count is greatly elevated even if the anemia is only mild. White cell and platelet counts are normal. The marrow shows tremendous erythroid hyperplasia and normal hemosiderin. Osmotic fragility and hemoglobin electrophoresis are normal.

A useful maneuver, especially during an acute hemolytic phase, is a test for Heinz bodies. A positive result implies drug-induced hemolytic anemia. Heinz bodies are not visible on Wright's stain. In some patients, autohemolysis may be greatly increased and is not repaired by glucose.

A hereditary enzyme defect can sometimes be demonstrated and a specific diagnosis made on that basis. Glucose-6-phosphate dehydrogenase deficiency has been studied most extensively.

Other forms of congenital enzyme defects resulting in nonspherocytic hemolytic anemia include deficiencies of pyruvate kinase, glutathione, glutathione reductase, diphosphoglyceromutase, ATPase, and triosephosphate isomerase. These abnormalities can be discovered only by relatively sophisticated biochemical technics.

Differential Diagnosis

In hereditary spherocytosis the red cells are small and round, osmotic fragility is increased, and jaundice is often prominent.

In acquired hemolytic anemia the Coombs test is positive. In refractory normoblastic anemia the reticulocyte count is low and the spleen is not palpable. In the hemoglobinopathies the diagnosis is made by hemoglobin electrophoresis.

In the newborn this condition may be very difficult to differentiate from hemolytic anemia due to ABO incompatibility.

Complications

There may be associated cholelithiasis and cholecystitis.

Treatment

Transfusions may be necessary. Splenectomy is of no benefit.

Valentine, W.N.: Hereditary hemolysis anemias associated with specific erythrocyte enzymopathies. California Med 108:280–294, 1968.

7. PRIMAQUINE-SENSITIVE HEMOLYTIC ANEMIA (And Anemias Due to Other Drug Sensitivities)

This is a drug-induced acute hemolytic anemia which occurs in persons of particular racial groups who have genetically transmitted errors of metabolism. The most important defect is thought to be a deficiency of glucose-6-phosphate dehydrogenase in the erythrocytes and, to a variable degree, in other tissues. There is also a deficiency of catalase and, in the reduced form, glutathione. The trait is sex-linked and of intermediate dominance; it finds its full expression in males and homozygous females and intermediate expression in heterozygous females. Ten to 15% of American Negro males and 1–2% of American Negro females have this disorder.

When not challenged by a drug, the red blood count, red cell indices, and red cell morphology are entirely normal although the red cell survival time is slightly shortened. More than 40 drugs and other substances are capable of inducing hemolysis, including antimalarials, sulfonamides, eg, salicylazosulfapyridine (Azulfidine®), sulfamethoxypyridazine (Kynex®), sul-

fisoxazole (Gantrisin®); nitrofurans, antipyretics, analgesics, sulfones, water-soluble vitamin K, and uncooked fava beans. Favism occurs principally in the Mediterranean area and is most common in Sardinia. Hemolytic episodes in the absence of drug administration may be produced by hepatitis, other viral or bacterial infections, and diabetic acidosis. These drugs accelerate the oxygen consumption of red cells, thereby activating the pentose phosphate pathway. An enzyme defect in this pathway leads to oxidation of TPNH (reduced triphosphopyridine nucleotide; now called dihydronicotinamide adenine dinucleotide phosphate [NADPH]), an important source of cellular energy; permits oxidation of protein sulfhydryl groups in the cell membrane; and eventually causes oxidation of hemoglobin with irreversible changes and Heinz body formation.

Several laboratory methods have been devised for identifying susceptible individuals. There is a glutathione stability test, a dye reduction test using cresyl blue, a methemoglobin reduction test, and a commercially available dye reduction spot test.

Management consists of withdrawal of the drug or toxic substance. Recovery is the rule.

Burka, E.R., Weaver, Z., & P.A. Marks: Clinical spectrum of hemolytic anemia associated with glucose-6-phosphate dehydrogenase deficiency. Ann Int Med 6:817–825, 1966.

Carson, P.E., & H. Fisher: G6PD deficiency and related disorders of the pentose phosphate pathway. Am J Med 41:744–761, 1966.

Grimes, A.J.: Laboratory diagnosis of enzyme defects in the red cell. Brit J Haemat 17:129–137, 1969.

Tarlov, A.R., & others: Primaquine sensitivity. Arch Int Med 109:209–234, 1962.

8. MICROANGIOPATHIC HEMOLYTIC ANEMIA

This term describes a group of acquired hemolytic anemias due to various causes that are characterized by fragmented or helmet-shaped red cells, burr cells, or microspherocytes. Associated thrombocytopenia is common; normal donor cells are destroyed rapidly. This form of red cell distortion may be seen in association with the following conditions: thrombotic thrombocytopenic purpura, metastatic cancer, post-cardiotomy, drug toxicity (perhaps in association with glucose-6-phosphate dehydrogenase deficiency), the hemolytic-uremic syndrome of infancy and pregnancy, in postpartum malignant nephrosclerosis, malignant hypertension (rare), acute nephritis (rare), and uremia.

In some of these, small thrombi in arterioles and capillaries, especially in the kidney, may be found. Some degree of intravascular coagulation may be present.

Except for those that are drug-induced, these anemias carry a very poor prognosis.

Brain, M.C., & others: Microangiopathic hemolytic anaemia. New England J Med 281:833—835, 1969.

Hammond, D., & others: Hemolytic-uremic syndrome. Am J Dis Child 114:440—449, 1967.

ANEMIAS WITH INTRAMEDULLARY HEMOLYSIS*
(Ineffective Erythropoiesis)

An important pathologic process in several anemias is the destruction of immature, nucleated red cells while still in the marrow. The erythroblasts apparently are defective in some way and are sequestered by reticuloendothelial cells. Some of these disorders (eg, pernicious anemia) may be associated with frank megaloblastosis; others (eg, refractory normoblastic anemias) show erythroblasts that resemble megaloblasts.

These disorders are characterized by marked erythroid hyperplasia in the marrow without elevation of reticulocyte counts. Radio-iron studies show greatly increased iron turnover and uptake by the marrow; delayed release from the marrow; and poor incorporation into circulating red cells with secondary accumulation in the liver. Red cell survival as measured with ^{51}Cr is usually only moderately shortened; the peripheral erythrocytes apparently represent the best cells made by the disordered marrow.

Examples of anemia with intramedullary hemolysis are the following:

Refractory Normoblastic Anemia

This is a heterogeneous group of chronic, moderate to severe anemias. Patients may have symptoms of anemia and perhaps slight splenic enlargement, but no other abnormal physical findings are present. Red cells are mostly normocytic and normochromic, but a few hypochromic microcytic cells may be seen. White cells and platelets may be slightly decreased. The bone marrow shows considerable erythroid hyperplasia and some erythrophagocytosis. Marrow hemosiderin is greatly increased and tends to aggregate in granules in normoblasts and histiocytes. Some of these patients respond to pyridoxine (see below).

Sideroachrestic Anemias

In this often familial group, most of the red cells are hypochromic and microcytic, serum iron is high, and iron deposits in the marrow, liver, and spleen are excessive. Many erythrocytes and erythroblasts contain nonhemoglobin iron ("ringed sideroblasts") in their mitochondria. The spleen is usually enlarged. Some of these patients respond to pyridoxine (see below).

Pyridoxine Responsive Anemias

In some of the above groups of anemias, hemoglobin may be restored to normal by large doses (50—200

*Pernicious anemia, folic acid deficiency, and thalassemia are discussed elsewhere in this chapter.

mg IM daily) of pyridoxine; the microcytosis and hypochromia may persist. The patients have no other signs of pyridoxine deficiency such as CNS and skin involvement. A few patients have macrocytic anemia and megaloblastic bone marrow that do not respond to vitamin B_{12} or folic acid.

Dacie, J.V., & others: Refractory normoblastic anemia. Brit J Haemat 5:56—82, 1959.

Horrigan, D.L., & J.W. Harris: Pyridoxine responsive anemia. An analysis of 61 cases. Advances in Internal Medicine XII, 1964.

Kushner, J.P., & others: Idiopathic refractory sideroblastic anemia. Medicine 50:139—159, 1971.

Symposium on sideroblastic anemia. Brit J Haemat 11:41—113, 1965. [See especially D.L. Mollin: Introduction, Sideroblasts, and Sideroblastic Anemia, pp 41—48.]

ABNORMAL HEMOGLOBINS

The human red cell contains 200—300 million molecules of hemoglobin. Each molecule contains 4 heme groups and one globin molecule. The globin molecule is composed of 2 pairs of polypeptide chains. One pair has been designated arbitrarily as alpha chain and the other beta chain on the basis of many differences involving long amino acid sequences. The members of each pair are identical. Each chain is made up of 28 peptides. The production of alpha and beta chains is under the control of 2 different genetic loci, which are independent (that is, not closely linked).

Three different types of hemoglobin are normally present; 97% is hemoglobin A. The other 2 normal hemoglobins are present in trace amounts of 1—3%. Hemoglobin A_2 possesses an alpha chain but, in place of the beta chain, a pair of delta polypeptides which differ from the beta chain probably in less than 10 amino acids. Fetal hemoglobin (hemoglobin F) contains a gamma chain instead of a beta chain and differs from the latter in numerous amino acid substitutions. Beta, delta, and gamma chains seem to be the result of closely linked alleles.

Hemoglobinopathies involve abnormalities in the hemoglobin chains. These are due to changes in the DNA template (a different order of bases in the one locus resulting in the production of different amino acids—and therefore faulty protein). Differences between normal and abnormal hemoglobins are relatively minute. For instance, sickle (S) hemoglobin differs from normal hemoglobin in the single amino acid of peptide No. 4 of the beta chain, ie, one out of 300 amino acids. Yet this small difference has far-reaching clinical effects which produce sickle cell disease. Most of the well-known hemoglobinopathies involve abnormalities of the beta chains. A few alpha chain abnormalities are known.

In thalassemia erythroid cells have decreased ability to synthesize normal adult hemoglobin (A). The defect apparently results from an intrinsic abnormality of the gene controlling the rate of hemoglobin synthesis ("regulatory" gene). The hemoglobin structure, ie, the amino acid sequence of the globin moiety (under control of a "structural" gene), is not abnormal.

The thalassemia gene may affect the synthesis of either the α-chain or the β-chain of the hemoglobin molecule. In α-chain thalassemia there will be a surplus of chains potentially combining with the α-chain, and this could be the basis for pure β-chain hemoglobin—Hb H(β^4)—or pure γ-chain hemoglobin—Hb Bart's (γ^4). In the presence of a gene affecting the β-chain, there will be an excess of α-chains available for combination with delta chains, resulting in an increase of A_2 hemoglobin; or, with gamma chains, with an increase in F hemoglobin.

Beta thalassemia is allelic with hemoglobins S and C, and interacts with them (hemoglobin S or C constitutes 60–80% of the total hemoglobin). Alpha thalassemia is not allelic with hemoglobins S and C and does not interact (hemoglobin S or C constitutes 50% of the total hemoglobin).

Combined Staff Clinic from Department of Medicine, Columbia University: The thalassemia syndrome. Am J Med 36:919–935, 1964.

Jensen, W.N.: The hemoglobinopathies. Disease-A-Month. Year Book, 1961.

Ranney, H.: Clinically important variants of human hemoglobin. New England J Med 282:144–152, 1970.

1. HEREDITARY HEMOGLOBINOPATHIES

Certain hereditary hemolytic anemias seen almost exclusively in Negroes are characterized by the genetically determined presence of an abnormal type of hemoglobin in the red cells.

The heterozygous hemoglobin trait syndromes usually represent asymptomatic carriers, eg, in sickle cell trait, which occurs in about 9% of American Negroes, there is no anemia. With hemoglobin C trait, which occurs in about 3% of American Negroes, there is no anemia but target cells are common. The relative frequency of some hemoglobinopathies (per 1000 Negroes) is as follows: A/S, 90; S/S, 2; A/F, ·10; S/C, 0.66; A/C, 30; C/C, 0.166.

The homozygous hemoglobin disorders usually cause some anemia. The most common and the most serious is sickle cell anemia, which occurs in 1 in 500 American Negroes. Homozygous hemoglobin C disease occurs only in 1 in 6000, and is a relatively mild disease. Double heterozygous diseases, eg, combinations of hemoglobins S and C, occur with an incidence of 1 in 1500. In addition, S-thalassemia or C-thalassemia may occur, but they are much less severe than sickle cell anemia. Target cells are prominent in all, especially when the C trait is present.

In general, all of the homozygous disorders with the exception of sickle cell anemia and all of the double heterozygous disorders are characterized by splenomegaly.

Fetal hemoglobin is increased in double heterozygous disorders when one of the genes is a thalassemia gene. Some fetal hemoglobin is also present in sickle cell anemia.

Table 9–4 lists some of the more common hemoglobinopathies.

2. SICKLE CELL ANEMIA

Essentials of Diagnosis

- Recurrent attacks of fever, and pain in the arms, legs, or abdomen since early childhood in a Negro patient.
- Anemia, jaundice, reticulocytosis, positive sickle cell test, and demonstration of abnormal (S) hemoglobin.

General Considerations

Sickling of the chemically abnormal hemoglobin occurs at low oxygen tension, especially at a low pH. The S (sickle) hemoglobin is less soluble in deoxygenated (reduced) form, the viscosity of the whole blood consequently increases, and the result is stasis and obstruction of blood flow in the capillaries, terminal arterioles, and veins. Localized sickling, vascular occlusion, and perivascular edema cause pain and swelling in the involved organs.

Sickle cell anemia is a hereditary disorder, essentially confined to Negroes; the abnormal hemoglobin is transmitted as a single dominant gene. Heterozygous carriers have mixtures of normal and sickle hemoglobin in all of their red blood cells.

Clinical Findings

A. Symptoms and Signs: The diagnosis is usually made in childhood, but occasionally a patient will reach adult life before a well documented crisis develops. Patients with sickle cell anemia tend to be of asthenic build with long spindly legs. Constant scleral icterus of moderate degree is common. The crisis consists of attacks of bone and joint pain or abdominal pain, sometimes with fever, lasting hours or days. The tender, rigid abdomen may resemble surgical illness and may last for hours or days. Cerebral thrombosis may occur, producing headaches, paralysis, and convulsions.

B. Laboratory Findings: Anemia is moderately severe (red blood count is usually 1.5–2.5 million/ cu mm), normocytic, and normochromic. Some sickle cells are usually present on the blood smear. Reticulocytes may be 15–20%. When a drop of fresh 2% solution of sodium metabisulfite is mixed on a slide with a drop of blood, sickling of most of the red cells occurs in a few minutes. A white count of 20–30 thousand is not unusual during painful crisis, and there may be as many as 100 nucleated red cells per 100 white cells. The hemoglobin values may remain constant even during a clinical crisis. The bone marrow shows marked

TABLE 9–4. Hematologic findings in the hemoglobinopathies.*

Hemoglobin Disorder	Erythrocytes (mill/ cu mm)	Hemoglobin (gm/ 100 ml)	RBC Size	RBC Hgb Content	Reticulocytes (%)	Target Cells (%)	Hemoglobins (%)		Fetal Hemoglobins (%)
Normal (adult men and women A/A)	4.2–6.2	12–18	82–92 cu μ	32–36 %	0.5–1.5	0	A A_2	97 2–3	0–2
A/S	N	N	N	N	N	0	A_2 S	2–3 22–48	0–2
S/S	1.5–4.0	2–11	N	N	5–30	Some	A_2 S	2–3 80–100	0–20
S/Thalassemia	2.0–5.0	6–14	Small	Decr	4–20	Many	A_2 S A	2–6 50–90 2–3	1–26
S/C	2.5–5.5	8.1–15.1	N	N	0.2–10	5–85	C S	37–67 30–60	0–8
S/D	2.5–4.0	7–12	N	N	7–13	2– Some	D S	23–75 25–77	Trace
S/Persistent F	3.5–5.0	11–15	N	N	N	0	S A_2	75 0–1	25
A/C	N	N	N	N	N	0–40	A C	50–70 30–50	0–2
C/C	3.1–5.0	7–14.5	N	Incr	1–12	20–100	C	97–100	0–3
A/D	N	N	N	N	N	0	D	< 50	0–2
D/D	5.5–7.1	12–13	Small	N	1–1.5	50–80	D	100	0–2
H/Thalassemia	1.6–6.4	8–11	Small	Decr	2–22	1–30	A H A_2	60–85 15–40 0–1	Trace–4
Thalassemia minor	4.0–7.5	8.3–13.2	Small	Decr	0.5–9.0	0–10	A A_2	90+ 2–9	0–10
Thalassemia major	1.0–4.0	2–8	Small	Decr	1.5–38	0–50	A A_2	10–30 2–3	70–90
Hereditary persistence of fetal hemoglobin (A/F)	N	N	N	N	N	0	A A_2	70–90 0–1	10–30

*Modified from Dacie: *The Hemolytic Anemias, Congenital and Acquired,* 2nd ed. Part I. Grune & Stratton, 1960.

erythroid hyperplasia, with more nucleated red cells than white cells. Hemosiderin is present. The indirect bilirubin may be elevated to 2 mg/100 ml, and there may be a slight elevation of the plasma hemoglobin. Haptoglobin is usually absent. The specific gravity of the urine is relatively fixed at 1.010, and there may be hemosiderinuria. X-rays of the bones may show varying degrees of cortical thinning, diffuse osteoporosis, and thickening of the trabecular markings.

Differential Diagnosis

Sickle cell anemia is differentiated from other hemoglobinopathies by hemoglobin electrophoresis, the sickle cell test, and fetal hemoglobin determination. Hematuria may simulate genitourinary tumor, tuberculosis, or vascular disease. Bone and joint pain may resemble rheumatic fever. The abdominal pain may simulate surgical abdominal conditions; persistence of normal bowel sounds in sickle cell crisis may be a helpful differential diagnostic finding.

The spleen is not enlarged in adult sickle cell anemia. An anemic Negro patient with an enlarged spleen and a positive sickle cell preparation probably has a double heterozygous disorder instead (eg, "sickle thalassemia" rather than sickle cell anemia). The sickle cell test does not reliably differentiate between sickle cell anemia (the homozygous disorder) and sickle cell trait (the heterozygous carrier state). In sickle cell anemia the red count is always low; the finding of a low hemoglobin with a normal red count in a Negro patient with a positive sickle cell preparation is not compatible with sickle cell anemia but suggests iron deficiency anemia plus sickle cell trait.

An electrophoretic pattern indistinguishable from that of sickle cell anemia may be found in the following: (1) Sickle cell-hemoglobin D disease: Hemoglobin D has the same electrophoretic mobility as hemoglobin S, but electrophoresis on agar gel at pH 6.0 differentiates these 2 hemoglobins. Hemoglobins A and D migrate together and ahead of hemoglobin S. (2) Some instances of sickle thalassemia: Hemoglobin A is sometimes absent in sickle thalassemia because its formation is suppressed by the thalassemia gene. Family studies may distinguish sickle thalassemia from sickle cell anemia. Hemoglobin A_2 is usually elevated in S-thalassemia but normal in S-S. (3) Sickle cell-persistent fetal hemoglobin syndrome.

Complications

Complications include leg ulcers, bone infarction, aseptic necrosis of the femoral head, osteomyelitis (especially due to salmonella), cardiac enlargement with auscultatory findings similar to those of mitral stenosis, recurrent gross hematuria, and cholelithiasis. Following infection there may be an aplastic crisis.

Treatment

Treatment is symptomatic. There is considerable variation in the frequency and severity of clinical manifestations.

A. Treatment of Clinical Crisis: Place the patient at bed rest and give analgesics. Local measures, cobalt, nasal oxygen, carbonic anhydrase inhibitors, and vasodilators have been employed with little success. Sodium bicarbonate, 3.5 mEq/kg/hour IV, or plasma expanders (eg, dextran), plasma, and glucose solution with 0.45% sodium chloride solution have been said to be occasionally successful in relieving pain.

B. Treatment of Hemolytic and Aplastic Crisis: Transfusions are mandatory. The hemoglobin level should be raised to 12–14 gm/100 ml. Adequate hydration is necessary. A careful search for infections should be made and appropriate antibiotic therapy instituted.

C. Treatment of Complications:

1. Leg ulcers—The legs are immobilized and elevated under a heat cradle. The ulcer area is cleansed and debrided. The patient is given sufficient blood to raise the hemoglobin level to 12–14 gm/100 ml.

2. Cholelithiasis or orthopedic disorders requiring surgery—Give sufficient preoperative blood to raise the hemoglobin level to 12–14 gm/100 ml.

3. Sickle cell anemia appearing during pregnancy—Transfuse to 10–12 gm/100 ml in the third trimester.

4. Pulmonary thrombosis and osteomyelitis—Treat by standard methods.

Prognosis

Many patients die in childhood of cerebral hemorrhage or shock. Others live beyond the age of 50 years. There is a tendency to progressive renal damage, and death from uremia may occur.

Diggs, L.W.: Sickle cell crisis. Am J Clin Path 44:1–19, 1965.

3. SICKLE CELL TRAIT

Sickle cell trait rarely causes symptoms or signs. Blood counts, red cell morphology, and red cell life span are normal. Gross hematuria occurs in 3–4% of cases; renal concentrating capacity is usually impaired; and pregnant women with the trait have an increased susceptibility to pyelonephritis. Splenic infarcts on high altitude flying as well as pulmonary infarcts develop occasionally. Under the stress of anoxia, as in congestive heart failure, acute alcoholism, or shock due to any cause, massive, fatal infarct may occur.

McCormick, W.F.: The pathology of sickle cell trait. Am J Med Sc 241:329–335, 1961.

4. S-C HEMOGLOBIN DISEASE

Essentials of Diagnosis

- Recurrent attacks of abdominal, joint, or bone pain.
- Enlarged spleen.
- Minimal anemia.
- Positive sickle cell test; many target cells.

General Considerations

The racial incidence and mode of inheritance of hemoglobin S-C disease are similar to those of sickle cell anemia. It represents a double heterozygous state, ie, the patient must receive the gene for S from one parent and the gene for C from the other. The incidence is 1 in 1500 in the American Negro population.

Clinical Findings

A. Symptoms and Signs: The average age at time of diagnosis is 11 years. In addition to abdominal, bone, joint, or chest pain, there may be painless hematuria, vitreous hemorrhages, and pulmonary thromboses. Jaundice is minimal. The liver is slightly enlarged and the spleen is large in 2/3 of patients. Heart murmurs are uncommon.

B. Laboratory Findings: Red blood count and hemoglobin values are nearly normal unless a complication is present. Target cells are very prominent, but red cell indices are normal; a few sickled cells may be seen. The sickle cell test is positive. Red cell survival is slightly shortened. White cell and platelet counts are normal. The marrow shows increased erythropoiesis. On electrophoresis the percentages of hemoglobin S and hemoglobin C are nearly equal. Hemoglobin F is normal.

Differential Diagnosis

S-C hemoglobin disease is differentiated from sickle cell anemia by its more benign clinical picture and splenic enlargement and by its characteristic migration on hemoglobin electrophoresis. Sickle thalassemia is also more severe than S-C hemoglobin disease, and is identified by hemoglobin electrophoresis. Other conditions with target cell formation include hemoglobin C disease and C trait, thalassemia minor, and jaundice, especially when due to cirrhosis and in patients who have undergone splenectomy.

Complications

Eye manifestations (eg, vitreous hemorrhages, retinal detachment), splenic infarcts, gross hematuria, or pulmonary thromboses may occur.

Treatment

Management is similar to that given for sickle cell anemia. Most patients require no therapy.

Prognosis

The outlook for these patients is considerably better than in sickle cell anemia. Some patients live into their 70's.

River, G.L., Robbins, A.B., & S.O. Schwartz: S-C hemoglobin: A clinical study. Blood 18:385–416, 1961.

5. S-THALASSEMIA

Some patients with this disease may have frequent episodes of jaundice, enlargement of the liver and spleen, recurrent bouts of fever, joint pain, and occasional abdominal pain. Others may have no symptoms and no splenic enlargement. The blood shows hypochromic, microcytic red cells varying in size and shape, with target and sickle forms. Different electrophoretic patterns are recognized. Patients may have relatively large amounts of hemoglobin S and increased amounts of hemoglobin A_2 (up to 6%) and F (up to 15%), and hemoglobin A varies from none to 40%; these probably represent hemoglobin S-beta thalassemia disease. Others have more hemoglobin A than S, and normal or low fractions of A_2 and F; they are classified as hemoglobin S-alpha thalassemia, and are clinically much milder. The severity of anemia varies from patient to patient and even may fluctuate in a given patient; normal hemoglobin values may be found.

Aksoy, M.: Alpha S-thalassemia. Blood 22:757–769, 1963.
Monti, A., & others: The S-thalassemia syndrome. *In:* Problems of Cooley's anemia. Ann New York Acad Med 119:474–484, 1964.

6. HEREDITARY PERSISTENCE OF FETAL HEMOGLOBIN

Individuals with this condition have no clinical abnormalities and are not anemic. They are characterized by the presence, throughout life, of large amounts of fetal hemoglobin in the erythrocytes. The trait is transmitted as a single factor allelic with the gene for hemoglobins S and C. The heterozygous (hemoglobin A-F) form occurs in 1 in 1000 American Negroes.

The red cells appear normal, and the reticulocytes and icterus index are not elevated. Fetal hemoglobin varies between 20–40% (average, 26%) and is uniformly distributed among the erythrocytes. Hemoglobin A_2 is decreased.

Patients with hereditary persistence of fetal hemoglobin must be distinguished from hemoglobin S-F and C-F heterozygotes, who are also clinically well and not anemic; and from thalassemia-F heterozygotes, who resemble individuals with thalassemia minor. In these 3 conditions fetal hemoglobin values are appreciably higher than in the hemoglobin A-F group.

Conditions with lesser elevation of hemoglobin F include occasional cases of thalassemia minor and rare cases of aplastic anemia. Fetal hemoglobin values in this group may reach 20%.

Conley, C.L., & others: Hereditary persistence of fetal hemoglobin. Blood 21:261–281, 1963.

7. THALASSEMIA MINOR

Essentials of Diagnosis
- Mild but persistent anemia.
- Red blood count normal or elevated.
- Similar blood findings in one of the parents.
- Patient usually has a Mediterranean or southern Chinese racial background.

General Considerations

Thalassemia major (Cooley's anemia) represents the homozygous state of the thalassemia genes, whereas thalassemia minor represents the heterozygous form. It is probable that more than a single set of alleles is involved in thalassemia. This may account for the various clinical gradations between the major and minor forms of the disease. Thalassemia is both congenital and familial.

Clinical Findings

A. Symptoms and Signs: There are usually no symptoms. The spleen may be slightly enlarged. Patients occasionally complain of upper left quadrant pain.

B. Laboratory Findings: The red count may exceed 6 million/cu mm. The hemoglobin does not fall below 9 gm/100 ml in uncomplicated cases. The red cells are very small (MCV = 50–70 cu μ), and hemoglobin concentration often is only moderately reduced (MCHC = 29–31%). Target cells and stippled cells are common. Red cells vary considerably in size and shape—more than in iron deficiency anemia of a comparable hemoglobin level. Some hypochromic macrocytes may be seen. Red cell patterns vary from one family to another. One group may have many target cells; another group may have stippled cells. Reticulocytes vary from 1–9%; platelets and white cells are not remarkable.

The bone marrow shows increased numbers of nucleated red cells. White cells and megakaryocytes are normal. Hemosiderin is present. In patients of Mediterranean ancestry, hemoglobin A_2 (a slow-moving normal hemoglobin component demonstrated on starch or agar gel electrophoresis) is usually increased 2- or 3-fold. It is allelic to hemoglobin S, and represents a beta hemoglobin chain abnormality. Fetal hemoglobin may be increased up to 6% in about ½ of patients; it is unevenly distributed among the red blood cells. In a much less common form of beta thalassemia, hemoglobin F levels are increased to 10–20%, but A_2 levels are normal. Clinically these patients are similar to those with A_2 variant. Rarely, thalassemia minor is associated with normal A_2 and F components, is nonallelic to hemoglobin S (both traits may appear in the same child), and probably represents an alpha chain abnormality.

Differential Diagnosis

Thalassemia minor must be differentiated principally from iron deficiency anemia. It is not a severe anemia; the hemoglobin level is almost always above 9 gm/100 ml, and serum iron, total iron-binding capacity, and marrow hemosiderin are normal.

Other hypochromic, microcytic anemias with normal or even increased serum iron and marrow hemosiderin are as follows:

A. Certain hemoglobinopathies, especially hemoglobin H and hemoglobin E disease and the so-called Lepore trait, are diagnosed by hemoglobin electrophoresis.

B. Sideroachrestic anemia, characterized by increased iron values, many sideroblasts, and biochemical evidence of disordered heme synthesis. Hemoglobin electrophoresis is normal.

Complications

Thalassemia does not respond to iron therapy, and unnecessary and prolonged treatment with parenteral iron could lead to excess iron storage.

Treatment & Prognosis

No treatment is required, and unnecessary iron therapy must be avoided. During pregnancy, transfusions may be necessary to maintain hemoglobin above 9 gm/100 ml. Patients with thalassemia minor have normal life spans.

Fink, H. (editor): Second conference on the problems of Cooley's anemia. Ann New York Acad Sc 165:1–508, 1969.

Marks, P.A.: Thalassemia syndromes. New England J Med 275:1363–1369, 1966.

Nathan, D.G., & R.B. Gunn: Thalassemia. Am J Med 41:815, 1966.

Stamatoyannopoulos, G., & others: F-Thalassemia. Am J Med 47:194–208, 1969.

8. THALASSEMIA MAJOR
(Cooley's Anemia; Mediterranean Anemia)

Essentials of Diagnosis

- Severe anemia starting in early infancy.
- Very large liver and spleen.
- Hypochromic, microcytic red cells with many erythroblasts.
- Greatly elevated fetal hemoglobin.

General Considerations

This is a hereditary disorder characterized by increased hemolysis due to an intracorpuscular defect involving abnormal hemoglobin synthesis and ineffective erythropoiesis. Two incomplete dominant abnormal alleles are present in this homozygous form of thalassemia; in thalassemia minor (the heterozygous form), only one such abnormal allele is present. The disease is found in patients of Mediterranean ancestry and from an area forming a wide band extending over northern Africa and southern Europe to Thailand and including Iran, Iraq, Indonesia, and southern China. Among the various peoples involved the incidence of thalassemia trait is up to 50% (usually about 5%).

Clinical Findings

A. **Symptoms and Signs:** Severe anemia and a huge liver and spleen are usually recognized in early childhood. Jaundice is usually present.

B. **Laboratory Findings:** Severe microcytic, hypochromic anemia is present. Target cells and bizarre-shaped red cells are seen. Nucleated red cells are numerous. The reticulocyte count is moderately elevated. The platelet count and white count are normal or increased. Serum bilirubin is elevated. Haptoglobins are absent. Paper hemoglobin electrophoresis is normal. A_2 is not elevated, but fetal hemoglobin may be increased to 90%. The bone marrow shows tremendous erythroid hyperplasia and ample stainable iron.

C. **X-Ray Findings:** Skeletal lesions (evident on x-ray) are most prominent in the skull and long bones and consist of increase of the medullary portion and thinning of the cortex, the so-called hair on end appearance.

Differential Diagnosis

Other hemoglobinopathies involving varying mixtures of hemoglobin S, hemoglobin C, and others with thalassemia may give similar but less severe clinical pictures. Congenital nonspherocytic hemolytic anemia may resemble this disorder. Hemoglobin electrophoresis, determination of fetal hemoglobin, and family studies make the correct diagnosis.

Treatment

Regularly spaced transfusions are often necessary to maintain life. Rarely, folic acid may be helpful for associated folic acid deficiency. When secondary hemolytic anemia develops with evidence of accelerated splenic sequestration of transfused red cells, splenectomy may be helpful.

Complications

There may be cardiorespiratory symptoms due to the chronic anemia. Leg ulcers and cholelithiasis may develop. Transfusion induced iron overload, with myocardial hemosiderosis, may lead to cardiac arrhythmia; intractable heart failure is a fairly common cause of death. Few patients survive into adult life.

Weatherall, D.J.: *The Thalassemia Syndromes.* Blackwell, 1965.

9. HEMOGLOBIN H DISEASE

Hemoglobin H disease is a microcytic hypochromic anemia that resembles thalassemia minor morphologically. It is a congenital, familial hemoglobin disorder. One parent usually has thalassemia minor with a normal level of A_2 hemoglobin; the other parent appears normal but is a silent carrier of an alpha chain defect. Hemoglobin H disease is seen most often in Filipinos and Chinese, and sometimes in Greeks. Hemoglobin H combines more rapidly with oxygen than normal hemoglobin, but does not yield it readily; it is more readily oxidized than normal hemoglobin.

The spleen is enlarged; a moderate degree of anemia is present, and the reticulocyte count is elevated. The patient may have periods of acute exacerbation of anemia during infection. Hemoglobin H differs from normal hemoglobin by its more rapid electrophoretic mobility and by its instability. When blood from a patient with hemoglobin H disease is incubated for 30 minutes at room temperature with 2% sodium metabisulfite, precipitates form in the red cells which are demonstrable by reticulocyte stain. Hemoglobin H, unlike hemoglobin I, the other "faster than normal" hemoglobin, migrates to the anode even at pH 6.5. Its iso-electric point is pH 5.6. Osmotic fragility is decreased; red cell life span is shortened to a half-life of 12–24 days; marrow erythropoiesis is effective; and glycolytic enzyme levels are normal. Hemoglobin H varies from a few percent up to 40% of the patient's hemoglobin. (It is composed of 4 beta chains.) A_2 hemoglobin is decreased.

Splenectomy may be helpful if anemia is severe.

Rigas, D.A., & others: Hemoglobin H. J Lab Clin Med 47:51–64, 1956.
Wai Kan, Y., & others: Globin chain synthesis in the alpha thalassemia syndromes. J Clin Invest 47:2515–2522, 1968.

HYPERSPLENISM

Essentials of Diagnosis

- Large spleen.
- Pancytopenia.
- Active marrow.

General Considerations

The most common form of hypersplenism is congestive splenomegaly, often due to portal hypertension secondary to cirrhosis. Other causes are thrombosis, stenosis, atresia, or angiomatous deformity of the portal or splenic vein, external pressure due to cysts, and aneurysm of the splenic artery.

The spleen may be enlarged because of a specific infiltrate, as in Gaucher's disease, Niemann-Pick disease, Letterer-Siwe disease, tuberculosis, or Boeck's sarcoid. Nonspecific enlargement may occur, as in rheumatoid arthritis (Felty's syndrome).

In hypersplenism the platelet count, white count, and to some extent the red count are reduced because of pooling in or sequestration by the enlarged spleen.

Clinical Findings

A. Symptoms and Signs: Patients affected with hypersplenism due to congestive splenomegaly are usually under 35 years of age. Some have little difficulty; others may have sudden hematemesis due to esophageal varices. Gastrointestinal bleeding occurs in about half.

The large spleen may cause abdominal fullness. Sometimes the spleen is found accidentally during a routine examination. Some patients have purpura. In primary splenic neutropenia, fever and pain over the splenic region occur.

B. Laboratory Findings: The anemia is often mild, normocytic and normochromic; the reticulocyte count may be elevated. The ^{51}Cr red cell life span is decreased, with evidence of increased splenic sequestration. Platelets and white cells, particularly the granulocytes, are greatly decreased, with a shift to the left.

The bone marrow shows varying degrees of generalized hyperactivity.

Differential Diagnosis

Hypersplenism is characterized by "empty blood," "full marrow," and a large spleen.

Leukemia and lymphoma are diagnosed by marrow aspiration or lymph node biopsy and examination of the peripheral blood (white count and differential). In hereditary spherocytosis there are spherocytes, osmotic fragility is increased, and platelets and white cells are normal. The hemoglobinopathies with splenomegaly are differentiated on the basis of hemoglobin electrophoresis. Thalassemia major becomes apparent in early childhood, and the blood smear morphology is characteristic. In myelofibrosis marrow biopsy shows proliferation of fibroblasts and replacement of normal elements. In idiopathic thrombocytopenic purpura the spleen is not enlarged. In aplastic anemia, the spleen is not enlarged and the marrow is fatty.

Complications

Gastrointestinal hemorrhage due to bleeding from esophageal varices may be fatal. Granulocytopenia may cause persistent leg ulcers or overwhelming infection.

Treatment

Therapy is usually that of the underlying condition. When the hematologic abnormalities are not severe, no treatment is required.

Splenectomy may be advisable for congestive splenomegaly due to a splenic vein abnormality alone and when leukopenia with recurrent infections or thrombocytopenic purpura are associated with the splenomegaly of tuberculosis, Gaucher's disease, Felty's syndrome, or sarcoidosis.

If congestive splenomegaly is due to liver or portal vein disease, splenectomy should be done only in conjunction with a splenorenal, splenocaval, or portacaval shunt.

Prognosis

The prognosis is that of the underlying disorder. The course in congestive splenomegaly due to portal hypertension depends upon the degree of venous obstruction and liver damage. Without hematemesis, the course may be relatively benign and splenectomy may not be necessary.

Jandl, J.H., & R.H. Aster: Increased splenic pooling and the pathogenesis of hypersplenism. Am J M Sc 253:383–397, 1967.

SECONDARY ANEMIAS

Under this heading are listed several diseases frequently accompanied by moderate to severe anemia. The anemia is usually caused by a combination of shortened red cell life span and inadequate bone marrow compensation, so-called relative bone marrow failure or sick cell syndrome. The red cells may be normal in appearance. The reticulocyte count may be slightly elevated. White cells are normal. Platelet counts may be elevated. No abnormal serum factors are demonstrable. The bone marrow is active and erythropoiesis may be increased. Some of these disorders have their own characteristics which are described below. It is important to recognize complicating iron deficiency or folic acid deficiency, which can be treated specifically.

1. ANEMIA OF CIRRHOSIS

Some degree of anemia is almost invariably seen in the patient with cirrhosis.

(1) Iron deficiency due to blood loss may occur with gastritis, esophageal varices, hemorrhoids, or associated peptic ulcer.

(2) Folic acid deficiency and the characteristic megaloblastic picture is seen in only 5% of cirrhotic patients with anemia, but some degree of folic acid deficiency can be demonstrated in most patients by sensitive methods, eg, serum folate levels or FIGLU (see p 259) excretion.

(3) A moderately severe hemolytic anemia is seen most frequently. The red cells are thin, flat, macrocytic, and slightly hypochromic, and vary greatly in size but not in shape. Target cells are common, and the reticulocyte count is moderately elevated. The white count is normal or elevated, and the platelet count is usually increased. In some patients, particularly when the spleen is enlarged, white cell and platelet counts are decreased. ^{51}Cr red cell survival studies show a half-life of 15–25 days. The Coombs test is negative. The bone marrow is hyperplastic and contains many erythroblasts, frequent plasma cells, and increased numbers of megakaryocytes. With acute exacerbation of chronic hepatitis, histiocytes filled with fat may be seen.

The hemolytic anemia of cirrhosis does not respond to any specific measures nor to corticosteroid therapy. The treatment is that of the underlying disorder.

(4) Acute hemolytic anemia develops occasionally after excessive alcohol intake. Jaundice, hyperlipemia, hypercholesterolemia, and spherocytosis are associated findings. Liver biopsy shows fatty infiltration and only minimal fibrosis. The syndrome improves rapidly with abstinence from alcohol.

Eichner, E.R., & R.S. Hillman: The evolution of anemia in alcoholic patients. Am J Med 50:218–232, 1971.

Jandl, J.H.: The anemia of liver disease: Observations on its mechanism. J Clin Invest 34:390–404, 1955.

Zieve, L.: Jaundice, hyperlipemia and hemolytic anemia. Ann Int Med 48:471, 1958.

2. ANEMIA OF CANCER

Anemia of cancer may be due to any of the following:

(1) Chronic blood loss with subsequent development of iron deficiency anemia.

(2) Hemolysis, usually moderate and demonstrable only by ^{51}Cr red cell survival studies. Occasionally, hemolysis is severe and acute (see Acute Hemolytic Anemia).

(3) Replacement of functional marrow by the malignant tissue ("myelophthisic anemia").

Hyman, G.A., & J.L. Harvey: The pathogenesis of anemia in patients with carcinoma. Am J Med 19:350–356, 1955.

3. ANEMIA OF INFECTION

Anemia usually develops only in chronic infections which are clinically obvious, eg, in patients with lung abscess, empyema, pelvic inflammatory disease, tuberculosis, or rheumatoid arthritis. The anemia in these cases is only moderately severe, and the hemoglobin rarely falls below 9 gm/100 ml. The cells are normocytic and may be slightly hypochromic. The reticulocyte count is normal, low, or slightly elevated. Platelets and white cells are not remarkable, although there may be toxic granulation of polymorphonuclear cells. The serum iron is low, but (in contrast to iron deficiency anemia) the total iron-binding capacity is also low. The red cell life span is moderately shortened and there is an insufficient increase in erythropoiesis. The bone marrow contains decreased, normal, or increased numbers of cells. Hemosiderin appears fuzzy and diffuse. Severe anemia with a marked degree of hemolysis may develop during the course of subacute bacterial endocarditis, *Escherichia coli* infection, hemolytic streptococcus infection, or *Clostridium welchii* infection.

Cartwright, G.E., & M.M. Wintrobe: The anemia of infection. XVII. A review. Advances Int Med 5:165–226, 1952.

4. ANEMIA OF AZOTEMIA

Anemia commonly develops during the course of renal insufficiency due to any cause. The red cells are normocytic and normochromic, and there is little variation from normal in size and shape. "Acanthocytes" (cells with thorny outpocketings) are occasionally seen. The reticulocyte count is normal, low, or slightly elevated. The bone marrow is normal or hypoplastic. Ferrokinetic measurements show decreased red cell life span and an inadequate increase in bone marrow erythropoiesis. Hemolysis is occasionally severe, with greatly shortened red cell survival time. Renal failure may be considered responsible for anemia if the NPN is above 75 mg/100 ml, the BUN above 50 mg/100 ml, or the serum creatinine above 2 mg/100 ml.

Adamson, J.W., Eschbach, J., & C.A. Finch: The kidney and erythropoiesis. Am J Med 44:725–734, 1967.
DesForges, J.F.: Anemia in uremia. Arch Int Med 126:808–811, 1970.
Eisler, A.: Anemia of chronic renal disease. Arch Int Med 126:774–807, 1970.

·   ·   ·

ACUTE LEUKEMIA

Essentials of Diagnosis
- Weakness, malaise, anorexia, bone and joint pain.
- Pallor, fever, petechiae, lymph node swelling, splenomegaly.
- Leukocytosis; immature, abnormal white cells in peripheral blood and bone marrow.
- Anemia, thrombocytopenia.

General Considerations
Acute leukemia is a disorder of the blood-forming tissue characterized by proliferation of abnormal white cells. It is generally considered to be neoplastic, occurs in all races, and may develop at any age. Peak incidence is in the first 5 years of life.

Clinical Findings
A. Symptoms and Signs: Presenting complaints are often general, consisting of weakness, malaise, anorexia, fever, and purpura. Pain in the joints, lymph node swelling, or excessive bleeding after dental extraction may also be initial complaints. Petechiae are frequently seen early in the course of the disease. Spleen, liver, and lymph nodes are usually enlarged in acute lymphatic leukemia but in less than ½ of patients with acute myeloblastic leukemia. Sternal tenderness is common. Any organ may be involved.

B. Laboratory Findings: Normochromic, normocytic anemia occurs early. The platelet count is usually below 100,000/cu mm, while the white count varies from less than 10,000 to over 100,000/cu mm. One-third are leukopenic. On the blood smear immature and abnormal cells may be seen; on a thick or overstained smear they may be mistaken for lymphocytes.

Auer bodies, red-staining rods in the cytoplasm of myeloblasts or monoblasts, occur in 10–20% and are pathognomonic of acute leukemia. Acute myelocytic leukemia may be differentiated from acute lymphocytic leukemia by the presence of peroxidase-staining cytoplasmic granules in the former.

There is massive proliferation of primitive malignant cells in the bone marrow even when leukopenia exists.

Radiologic involvement can be seen in almost all of the children and in ½ of the adults. Diffuse osteoporosis, periosteal elevation, osteolytic lesions, and radiolucent metaphyseal bands are the most common lesions.

Complications
Fatal gastrointestinal tract hemorrhage, pressure symptoms on the brain stem, brain hemorrhage, and overwhelming infection are the chief causes of death. Intracerebral hemorrhage occurs more frequently in patients with very high white cell counts (over 300,000/cu mm). Bacterial (pseudomonas) infections, fungal (candida and aspergillus) infections, and virus diseases such as disseminated cytomegalic inclusion disease have become the major causes of death.

Differential Diagnosis
The combination of anemia, thrombocytopenia, and bone marrow proliferation of primitive white cells is found only in leukemia. Leukocytosis may or may not be present. Among the other features, petechiae may be seen in idiopathic thrombocytopenic purpura

or in aplastic anemia, but there is no enlargement of lymph nodes, liver, or spleen. Enlarged lymph nodes and splenomegaly may be found in infectious mononucleosis, Hodgkin's disease, or in lymphosarcoma, but the bone marrow and peripheral red cells and platelets are usually normal. Marked lymphocytosis is often seen in whooping cough and infectious lymphocytosis, but the white cells are mature and red cell and platelet counts are normal. Malignant tumors, eg, neuroblastoma, osteosarcoma, and metastatic cancer, may cause bone pain, anemia, and leukocytosis; if there is marrow invasion, these conditions may resemble leukemia.

Treatment

Treatment is aimed at symptomatic relief and remission of the disease process.

A. General Measures: Once the diagnosis has been established, a conference is held with the patient or his family and the nature of the disease, its treatment and cost, the prognosis, and the need for follow-up care are discussed in detail. It is important that the patient lead as normal a life as possible, with maintenance of work or school activities. Hospitalization is essential only for transfusions, severe complications, or terminal involvement.

In young patients antileukemic therapy is begun as soon as the diagnosis is established. In some elderly patients with only moderate anemia and leukopenia, specific antileukemic therapy may not be indicated. The antimetabolites are not well tolerated by this group and are not very effective. These patients can usually be supported with occasional transfusions for anemia and antibiotics for infection. Oral fluid intake must be increased for patients receiving antileukemic agents to prevent precipitation of uric acid crystals in the kidneys.

At first patients are followed with weekly blood counts, including platelet counts; during remissions they are seen every 2–3 weeks.

B. Transfusions: Hemoglobin should be maintained at 8–10 gm/100 ml. Whole blood or packed red cells less than a week old are satisfactory.

C. Chemotherapy: (L = effective in acute lymphatic leukemia; M = effective in acute myeloblastic leukemia.) Toxic effects are common with most of these agents. All may produce serious marrow depression. Vincristine fairly regularly causes constipation and peripheral neuritis; Cytoxan®, hemorrhagic cystitis; daunorubicin, cardiotoxicity; methotrexate, ulcerations of the oral mucous membranes and hepatitis; mercaptopurine, hepatitis. All may cause some alopecia.

1. **For rapid control of overt disease—**

a. Vincristine (Oncovin®), 0.05 mg/kg IV once a week (L and M).

b. Cyclophosphamide (Cytoxan®), 3 mg/kg orally daily (L).

c. Cytosine arabinoside (Cytosar®), 100 mg IV daily for 4 days. (L and M).

d. Daunorubicin, 1 mg/kg IV daily for 4 days (L and M).

Prednisone, 1–3 mg/kg (children) or 60–100 mg orally daily (adults), may be used with any of the above (L).

2. **For maintenance—**

a. Mercaptopurine, 2.5 mg/kg orally daily (L and M). This is also a good inducing agent in patients who are not too severely ill. (*Caution:* When used in conjunction with allopurinol [Zyloprim®], reduce to 1/3 the calculated dose.)

b. Methotrexate, 1.25–5 mg orally daily (L).

c. Thioguanine, 2 mg/kg orally daily (L and M).

D. Treatment of Complications:

1. **Local manifestations—**Severe bone pain, massive lymph node enlargement interfering with respirations and swallowing, and CNS involvement with signs of increased intracranial pressure may be treated successfully with local irradiation. Intrathecal methotrexate, 5 mg dissolved in 10 ml of spinal fluid administered every 3 days until the spinal fluid is clear, may be a valuable adjunct to oral or intramuscular methotrexate.

2. **Fever—**Careful search is made for a bacterial agent, and specific antibiotics are instituted. Prophylactic antibiotics are not used.

3. **Hemorrhage—**Corticosteroids in the above doses and transfusions of fresh whole blood (platelet-rich) may be necessary.

4. **Hyperuricemia—**Allopurinol, which inhibits the formation of uric acid, should be administered to patients with high uric acid or high white count along with chemotherapy. A high fluid intake is also important. The usual dose of allopurinol (Zyloprim®) is 100 mg 3–4 times daily. The dose of mercaptopurine must be reduced to 25–35% of the usual dose when allopurinol is being given.

Prognosis

Average survival for untreated acute leukemia is about 2–6 months; for treated acute leukemia, about 6–12 months. Patients with acute lymphoblastic leukemia, regardless of age, and with a white count of less than 10,000/cu mm have a better prognosis than patients with myeloblastic leukemia. In adults remissions often last only a few months; in children remissions occasionally last from one to several years.

Boggs, D.R., Wintrobe, M.M., & G. Cartwright: The acute leukemias. Medicine 41:163–225, 1962.

Clarkson, B., & others: Changing concepts of treatment in acute leukemia. M Clin North America 55:561–600, 1971.

Henderson, E.S.: Treatment of acute leukemia. Seminars Hemat 6:271–319, 1969.

Zuelzer, W.W.: Acute stem cell leukemia. Blood 24:477–494, 1964.

CHRONIC MYELOCYTIC LEUKEMIA

Essentials of Diagnosis

- Weakness, lassitude, fever, abdominal discomfort.
- Painless enlargement of spleen.
- Unexplained leukocytosis, immature white cells in peripheral blood and bone marrow.
- Anemia.

General Considerations

Chronic leukemia is characterized by proliferation of abnormal white cells, which invade the blood stream and may infiltrate any part of the body to cause local symptoms. It is inevitably fatal.

In addition to their immaturity, leukemic cells have certain distinguishing biochemical characteristics. Leukemic neutrophilic cells have less glycogen and alkaline phosphatase than normal or polycythemia white cells, whereas their histamine content is higher. Many of the immature myeloid cells in blood and marrow characteristically show the so-called Philadelphia chromosome, an abnormally small autosome.

Chronic myelocytic leukemia is primarily a disease of young adults, but it may be found at any age.

Clinical Findings

A. Symptoms and Signs: Pallor, weakness, sternal tenderness, fever, purpura, skin nodules, and retinal hemorrhages or exudate may be seen. There may be abdominal discomfort secondary to splenomegaly. Gum bleeding after dental extraction, or large ecchymoses or muscle bleeding after trauma—presumably manifestations of thrombasthenia—may be the presenting sign.

Some patients are diagnosed accidentally before the onset of symptoms when a high white count is found during a routine examination.

B. Laboratory Findings: The white count may exceed 500,000/cu mm, but fewer than 5% of the cells are "blasts." Nonfilamented neutrophils, metamyelocytes, and myelocytes predominate; the neutrophils are alkaline phosphatase negative; basophils, eosinophils, and platelets are increased; and a few normoblasts may be seen. Some degree of anemia is common. The marrow shows complete replacement of fat by cellular elements, mostly granulocytes, but few blasts.

Differential Diagnosis

In leukemoid reactions due to infection or metastatic cancer, eosinophils and basophils are decreased rather than increased, the leukocyte alkaline phosphatase is strongly positive, and the marrow is only moderately hyperplastic. In myelofibrosis, the spleen may be quite large but leukocytosis only moderate; the marrow is fibrotic, the granulocytes are usually alkaline phosphatase positive; and the Philadelphia chromosome is not seen.

Complications

Probably no part of the body is exempt from leukemic infiltration. Complications will depend upon the area infiltrated, eg, pressure symptoms or hemorrhage if the CNS is infiltrated. The spleen may become very large and painful. Half of the patients die in a "blastic" crisis.

Treatment

A. General Measures: The aim of therapy is palliation of symptoms and correction of anemia. Initial manifestations and each exacerbation should be treated promptly. Specific treatment of the anemia is unnecessary, as it is usually corrected by treatment directed at the leukemic process. Blood counts are checked weekly at first and then once or twice a month until a satisfactory remission is obtained. During remission patients are encouraged to resume normal activity, but follow-up visits are necessary every 1–3 months. The nature of the disease should be explained to the patient and the necessity for periodic observation and lifelong treatment should be impressed upon him.

B. Irradiation: X-ray therapy consists of total body irradiation or local therapy to the spleen, liver, or local infiltrates. (X-ray therapy localized to the spleen has a beneficial general effect on the hematopoietic system by mechanisms which are still unknown. Localized high-voltage x-ray over the spleen in doses of 50–100 r daily until a total of 600 r has been given is usually sufficient for clinical hematologic remission.) X-ray therapy (by a radiologist) is given over a period of a few weeks. X-ray is most effective in the treatment of local manifestations.

The results of treatment with radiophosphorus (^{32}P) are comparable to those of total body irradiation; it is less effective in the treatment of local manifestations. There is no radiation sickness. The dosage of ^{32}P depends upon the degree of leukocytosis. One mc (millicurie) is equivalent to 15 r. If the white count is above 50,000/ cu mm, the initial dosage of ^{32}P is 1–2.5 mc IV; 2 weeks later, 1–1.5 mc are given. Similar doses are given every 2 weeks until the white count is less than 20,000/cu mm. During remission patients are seen every 1–3 months. When the white count rises above 25,000, an additional 1–1.5 mc are given.

C. Chemotherapy: Busulfan (Myleran®), an alkylating agent, is the drug of choice. Initial dosage is 2 mg 2–4 times daily, continued until the white count is less than 10,000/cu mm. As a rule the white count begins to drop within a week and normal values are reached in 4–6 weeks. When the white count reaches about 10,000/cu mm the drug may be discontinued, or administered intermittently. Remissions may last for several months to more than a year. When relapse occurs, a course of busulfan may be repeated. Overtreatment results in general depression of myelopoiesis; irreversible thrombocytopenia may develop. Since thrombocytopenia may occur before any significant drop in hemoglobin, platelet counts should always be done as part of the routine count. The drug should be withheld if platelet values are below normal.

Melphalan (Alkeran®) is also quite effective. Mercaptopurine (Purinethol®) is used for blastic crises.

Prognosis

The average life expectancy in chronic myelocytic leukemia is about 3–4 years. With appropriate therapy the course is frequently remittent, with periods of months during which the patient is free of symptoms.

Haut, A., & others: Busulfan in the treatment of chronic myelocytic leukemia. The effect of long term intermittent therapy. Blood 17:1–19, 1961.
Haut, A., Wintrobe, M.M., & G.E. Cartwright: The clinical management of leukemia. Am J Med 28:777–793, 1960.

CHRONIC LYMPHATIC LEUKEMIA

Essentials of Diagnosis

- Pallor.
- Superficial lymph node enlargement.
- Absolute lymphocytosis in adults.

General Considerations

This disorder involves progressive accumulation of aged, small lymphocytes which have lost the capacity to divide. The life span of these metabolically abnormal cells may be considerably lengthened to several years; the total body lymphocyte mass expands considerably, and may reach enormous proportions. The cells, which originate in lymph nodes, aggregate chiefly in the lymph nodes, spleen, blood, and marrow. The decline in levels of immunoglobulins commonly observed during the course of the disease may represent the replacement of normal, immunologic competent cells by cells that are functionally inert and have lost the ability to react to antigenic stimuli. These lymphocytes have a strikingly low mitotic rate.

The disorder may remain relatively quiescent for several years, free of symptoms and signs and with relatively stable lymphocyte counts; or it may become progressive, with various clinical manifestations and a rising blood count.

Chronic lymphatic leukemia is rare under the age of 30 and extremely rare in Orientals.

Clinical Findings

A. Symptoms and Signs: The onset is insidious, and the diagnosis is usually made accidentally during routine examination. Weakness and symptoms of hypermetabolism may be present. Enlarged lymph nodes may cause pressure symptoms (eg, tracheal compression with respiratory difficulty). The spleen, liver, and lymph nodes are not tender.

B. Laboratory Findings: At the time of diagnosis, the hemoglobin may be normal. Anemia develops as the disease progresses. Lymphocytosis usually precedes the rise in total white count. Eventually, the white count rises and may reach 100–500 thousand/cu mm.

Over 90% of the cells are mature lymphocytes; "smudge" cells are common. The platelet count tends to be below normal. Early in the disease, the marrow architecture may be normal; lymphocytes make up more than 30% of cells.

Differential Diagnosis

Similar lymph node enlargement may be seen in lymphosarcoma and infectious mononucleosis. Differentiation is usually readily made on the basis of the blood smear.

Lymphocyte counts of 50–100 thousand/cu mm may be seen in children with whooping cough or infectious lymphocytosis. Lymphatic leukemoid reactions of moderate degree (with white counts of 20–30 thousand/cu mm) are occasionally seen with tuberculosis. Diffuse lymph gland enlargement may be found in lymphosarcoma and infectious mononucleosis, and rarely in tuberculosis, syphilis, carcinomatosis, hyperthyroidism, brucellosis, lupus erythematosus, and toxoplasmosis. In Hodgkin's disease, lymph node enlargement is usually asymmetric or only in a single site.

Complications

Severe hemolytic anemia, frequently with a positive Coombs test, develops in 1/3 of the patients. Thirty percent of patients have hypogammaglobulinemia and may be susceptible to infection.

Treatment

A. General Measures: It may be desirable to withhold therapy until clinical manifestations appear or until hematologic complications develop. Many older patients with this disorder remain relatively asymptomatic despite high leukocyte levels. All symptomatic patients and all patients with anemia or thrombocytopenia must be treated.

B. Irradiation: As for chronic myelocytic leukemia, but systemic control with splenic radiation is less frequent.

C. Chemotherapy:

1. Chlorambucil (Leukeran®) is widely used. The dosage is 0.1–0.2 mg/kg daily in divided doses after meals. Clinical and hematologic improvement may not be evident for 3–4 weeks and maximum improvement may not be achieved for 2–4 months. When the white count falls below 25,000/cu mm, the dose should be reduced, usually to a maintenance level of 2–4 mg daily. The drug should be discontinued when the white count falls to 5000–10,000/cu mm. Side-effects are relatively uncommon, although gastrointestinal irritation occurs. Pancytopenia may develop, but recovery usually occurs when the drug is discontinued.

2. Triethylenemelamine (TEM), 2.5–5 mg in a single dose on an empty stomach with 1–2 gm of sodium bicarbonate, is a useful alkylating agent. It has the advantage of simplicity of administration, but the effects are less predictable than with other agents.

3. Cyclophosphamide (Cytoxan®), 50–100 mg orally 1–3 times daily, causes less platelet depression than other agents and may be used when other agents have produced thrombocytopenia.

D. Corticosteroids: Some patients respond well to relatively small doses of corticosteroids. Initially one may give prednisone (or equivalent), 40 mg daily until a response occurs; maintenance may be as little as 10–20 mg every 48 hours.

E. Treatment of Complications:

1. Anemia—Anemia is caused by a combination of 2 factors: increased rate of red cell destruction and inadequate bone marrow compensation. It often fails to respond to antileukemic therapy and transfusions have to be given. Prednisolone (or equivalent), 10–20 mg 4 times daily, is usually required. With remission of the anemia, corticosteroids may be gradually withdrawn. With severe hemolytic anemia and splenic sequestration of the red cells, splenectomy may have to be considered. Intercurrent anemia due to blood loss and iron deficiency is treated with iron.

2. Hemorrhage—Abnormal bleeding in leukemia is usually due to thrombocytopenia, which may be secondary to either the leukemic process or to therapy. If due to the leukemia, it may be improved by appropriate chemotherapy; if due to chemotherapy, the marrow-depressing drugs must be discontinued and corticosteroid therapy instituted until the marrow has had a chance to recover.

3. Infections—Infections are treated with specific antibiotics. Prophylactic use of antibiotics is not recommended. Some patients develop low levels of gamma globulin. With gamma globulin levels of 0.7 gm/100 ml or less, prophylactic gamma globulin is needed. Initially, 0.3 ml/lb is given in divided doses of 5 ml each; a maintenance dose of ½ this amount is administered once or twice a month.

Prognosis

The average life expectancy in chronic lymphatic leukemia is about 3–4 years. Most patients respond well to chemotherapy or x-ray therapy, and long periods of remission are the rule. There is a group of patients with this disorder, usually the more elderly ones, in whom the disease remains relatively inactive without treatment, sometimes for many years.

Boggs, D.R., & others: Factors influencing the duration of survival of patients with chronic lymphocytic leukemia. Am J Med 40:243–254, 1966.

Galton, D.A.G.: The pathogenesis of chronic lymphocytic leukemia. Canad MAJ 94:1005–1010, 1966.

Zacharski, L.R., & J.W. Linman: Chronic lymphocytic leukemia versus chronic lymphosarcoma cell leukemia. Am J Med 47:75–81, 1969.

MULTIPLE MYELOMA

Essentials of Diagnosis

- Weakness, weight loss, recurrent pneumonia.
- Constant, severe bone pain aggravated by motion.
- Anemia, rapid sedimentation rate, and elevated serum globulin.
- Immature, atypical plasma cells in bone marrow.

General Considerations

Multiple myeloma is a malignant disease characterized by neoplastic proliferation of cells normally responsible for synthesis of gamma globulins or immunoglobulins. The group of immunoglobulins include gamma G (formerly called 7S gamma, gamma 2, or gamma ss) and gamma A (formerly gamma 1A or B_2A). The gamma G globulin molecule is known to consist of 2 pairs of polypeptide chains. One pair, the "L" (light) chain, has an approximate molecular weight of 20,000 and determines the globulin's antigenic behavior; it is probably identical with Bence Jones protein. Normally, 2 antigenically distinct types are recognized by immunoelectrophoresis; type I is approximately twice as common as type II. In multiple myeloma all the abnormal globulin belongs to either type I or type II, but not to both.

Amyloidosis, whether primary or secondary, is probably always associated with plasma cell neoplasia; abnormal gamma globulin products, particularly those of the Bence Jones (L-polypeptide) type, are directly involved in these tissue ("amyloid") infiltrates.

The "H" (heavy) chain has a molecular weight of approximately 55,000; its specific subunits determine whether the globulin belongs to the gamma G, gamma A, or macroglobulin class.

Abnormal protein is found in the blood and often in the urine. The type of abnormal protein produced varies with each myeloma patient. In any one patient it will remain the same, however, varying only in quantity.

The disease appears in later life and is twice as common in males as in females. It is seen in all races.

Clinical Findings

A. Symptoms and Signs: Symptoms of anemia may be the only complaint, or there may be constant bone pain, especially on motion, and tenderness (especially of the back) and spontaneous fractures. Spleen and liver are usually not enlarged. Extramedullary plasma cell tumors are occasionally found in the oropharynx, on the skin, or near the spinal cord. Marked weight loss is common.

B. Laboratory Findings: Anemia is moderate and of the normocytic, normochromic type. Rouleau formation is marked and interferes with the technic of the red count, blood smear, typing, and cross-matching. The sedimentation rate is greatly elevated; white count, platelet count, and morphology are usually normal. The bone marrow may show sheets of plasma cells with large nuclei and nucleoli.

Serum globulin may exceed 10 gm/100 ml. The electrophoretic pattern is characterized by a tall, sharp peak in contrast to the broad gamma peaks seen in other illnesses with hyperglobulinemia. The abnormal globulin peak may be in the $alpha_2$, beta, or gamma range for immunoglobulin gamma G, and in the gamma to beta range for gamma A. Cryoglobulin, a serum protein which precipitates in the cold, may be found.

Serum calcium levels are often elevated, but phosphorus and alkaline phosphatase values remain normal. Nitrogen retention, proteinuria, and renal casts also occur. Bence Jones proteinuria is found in about 40% of myeloma patients.

The bony lesions appear on x-rays as rounded, punched-out, or mottled areas. New bone formation is lacking. Sometimes there is merely diffuse osteoporosis. In about 10% of cases x-rays are normal early in the disease.

Differential Diagnosis

Pathologic fractures and osteolytic lesions are also found in reticulum cell sarcoma, lymphosarcoma, and in metastatic cancer, particularly if the origin is the breast, kidney, prostate, or thyroid. These lesions are usually single, however, and some attempt at new bone formation is evident. Lymphosarcoma is particularly difficult to differentiate from multiple myeloma when there are bony tumors, oral cavity tumors, cord compression with paraplegia, or invasion of the bone marrow by atypical cells. Electrophoresis usually provides the answer.

Hyperparathyroidism is differentiated by low serum phosphorus and high alkaline phosphatase values. In primary macroglobulinemia (Waldenström), the electrophoretic pattern is similar to that of multiple myeloma, but hemorrhagic phenomena are prominent, bone lesions are, rare, and the pathologic cells resemble lymphocytes rather than plasma cells. The diagnosis is made by demonstration of "specific" macroglobulin paraprotein by serum ultracentrifugation.

In cirrhosis of the liver, cancer, infections, and hypersensitivity reactions, up to 25% of plasma cells may be seen in the bone marrow, but they tend to aggregate near histiocytes and blood vessels and do not form sheets of cells. Hyperglobulinemia may be seen in sarcoidosis, lupus erythematosus, cirrhosis, lymphogranuloma venereum, and kala-azar infections. In most of these disorders, however, the basic disorder is obvious, the plasma cells are adult, and the electrophoretic pattern shows a broad gamma elevation rather than a sharp peak.

A monoclonal "spike" on serum electrophoresis may be observed occasionally in patients who have no other clinical or laboratory stigmas of myeloma or macroglobulinemia. Lymphoma, leukemia, and cancer may be associated disorders; in some cases, no disease is found.

Complications

Complications include paraplegia due to cord tumor, hemorrhage due to thrombocytopenia or interference with the normal coagulation mechanism, recurrent infections due to disturbance of antibody formation, and renal failure without hypertension or hematuria due to renal tubule casts.

Treatment

A. General Measures: Treatment is supportive only, with the principal aims being control of pain and reduction of tumor masses. Antimetabolites are ineffective. Good urine output must be maintained to prevent protein precipitation. Ambulation is encouraged to combat negative calcium balance, but patients must avoid exposure to trauma because of their susceptibility to fractures. Frequent blood transfusions may be necessary to combat the anemia. Analgesics may be necessary for control of pain.

B. Irradiation: X-ray therapy is valuable in controlling pain and decreasing tumor mass.

C. Alkylating Agents: Melphalan (Alkeran®) is probably the most effective agent available now. It is structurally similar to nitrogen mustard but is administered orally. The usual dose is 6 mg daily for 2–3 weeks; the maintenance dose is 1–4 mg daily.

D. Cyclophosphamide (Cytoxan®): This is another alkylating agent effective at times in the therapy of multiple myeloma. Give 50–100 mg orally 1–3 times daily for maintenance. Side-effects are nausea, alopecia (20%), and leukopenia.

E. Treatment of Complications: Hypercalcemia with nausea and vomiting may be combated with corticosteroids. Vertebral fracture and cord compression may require laminectomy for decompression. For recurrent infection it may be necessary to give gamma globulin, 10 ml IM every 2 weeks, in spite of high "gamma globulin" values. Antibiotic therapy is indicated for specific infections.

Prognosis

The average survival time after diagnosis is 1½–2 years. Occasionally a patient may live for many years in apparent remission.

Combined Staff Clinics: Plasma cell dyscrasias. Am J Med 44:256–269, 1968.

Kunkel, H.G.: Myeloma proteins and antibodies. Am J Med 39:1–3, 1965.

McArthur, J.R., & others: Melphalan and myeloma. Ann Int Med 72:665–670, 1970.

Osserman, E.F., & K. Takatsuki: Plasma cell myeloma: Gamma globulin synthesis and structure. Medicine 42:357–384, 1963.

MACROGLOBULINEMIA

Macroglobulinemia is a chronic neoplastic disease of the bone marrow which bears some clinical resemblance to both multiple myeloma and chronic lymphocytic leukemia. It is characterized by excessive production of gamma M (IgM) globulin. The disorder usually develops after the age of 50. Symptoms of anemia (weakness, easy fatigability), hemorrhagic phenomena (petechiae and ecchymoses), or signs of hypermetabolism (fever and weight loss) may be the presenting findings. Some patients have a moderately enlarged spleen or diffuse lymphadenopathy. The blood may show some degree of pancytopenia; rarely, abnormal white cells, and often some rouleau formation. The marrow may be difficult to aspirate, and biopsy may be neces-

TABLE 9–5. Nomenclature for the human immunoglobulins.

Present Terms	New Terms
$7S\gamma$, γ_2, γ_{SS}	γG or IgG
$\gamma_{1\,A}$, $B_2 A$	γA or IgA
$19S\gamma$, $\gamma_{1\,M}$, $B_2 M$	γM or IgM
Type I or B proteins	K
Type II or A proteins	L
Type I or B L chains	κ (kappa)
Type II or A L chains	λ (lambda)
Heavy chains $7S\gamma$	γ (gamma)
Heavy chains $\gamma_{1\,A}$	α (alpha)
Heavy chains $\gamma_{1\,M}$	μ (mu)
Fragment A, C, S, I, II	Fab-fragment
Fragment B, F, III	Fc-fragment
A piece	Fd-fragment

sary to demonstrate a diffuse infiltrate with lymphoid elements and some plasma cells. Precipitated protein may be seen on the marrow smear. Total serum globulin may exceed 7 gm/100 ml. Most sera with a concentration of macroglobulins greater than 2 gm/100 ml and with an electrophoretic mobility in the gamma region will give a positive Sia water (euglobulin) test. Paper electrophoresis shows a sharp peak and is indistinguishable from multiple myeloma. Differentiation from multiple myeloma is made by (1) ultracentrifugation, which shows the globulin to be of the S (Svedberg) 19 type or greater, implying a molecular weight in excess of 1 million; (2) immunoelectrophoresis; (3) finding an altered electrophoretic pattern by splitting the macromolecule with penicillamine; or (4) selectively precipitating the macroglobulin with rivanol (6,9-diamino-2-ethoxyacridine lactate). About 10% of patients have Bence Jones protein in their urine, but renal involvement is rare. Osteolytic lesions are not seen. Many patients have greatly increased blood volumes. Smaller amounts of macroglobulin, usually less than 15% of the total globulin, may be seen in malignant lymphomas, collagen diseases, sarcoidosis, cirrhosis, and nephrosis.

In some patients the course is benign over a period of several years. The average survival is about 4 years.

Treatment is with chlorambucil (Leukeran®), 0.1–0.2 mg/kg daily, as described on p 312; or melphalan (Alkeran®), as described on p 314.

Cohen, R., Bohannon, R.A., & R.O. Wallerstein: Waldenström's macroglobulinemia. Am J Med 41:278–284, 1966.
McCallister, B.D., & others: Primary macroglobulinemia. Review with a report on thirty-one cases and notes on the value of continuous chlorambucil therapy. Am J Med 43:394–434, 1967.

CRYOGLOBULINEMIA

Serum globulins that precipitate on cooling and redissolve on warming may occur in a variety of disorders (eg, myeloma, macroglobulinemia, malignant lymphoma, collagen diseases, glomerulonephritis, infectious mononucleosis, syphilis, and cytomegalovirus disease). They may represent homogeneous proteins that have become physically altered (myeloma), mixtures of immunoglobulins, or immune complexes (eg, IgG and IgM)—ie, antigen and antibody, possibly with complement (eg, lupus erythematosus). The finding of cryoglobulinemia is often without any apparent significance. It is assumed that when symptoms do occur as a result of cryoglobulinemia, the abnormal protein, on cooling, precipitates in smaller vessels and causes increased viscosity, stasis, thrombosis, or hemorrhage.

Clinical manifestations may include a Raynaud-like phenomenon on exposure to cold, oronasal bleeding, purpura, petechiae, retinal vascular constriction and hemorrhage, urticaria, and mottling, ulcerations, necrosis, and gangrene, especially in dependent areas. Cryoglobulins in significant concentrations (30 mg/100 ml) may be demonstrated in the blood.

Treatment consists of preventing exposure to cold and, when possible, treatment of the underlying disease. Penicillamine and immunosuppressive agents have been tried. In general, treatment is unsatisfactory.

Barnett, E.V., & others: Cryoglobulinemia and disease. Ann Int Med 73:95–107, 1970.
Spalluto, L.O., & others: Cryoglobulinemia based upon interaction between a gamma macroglobulin and 7S gamma globulin. Am J Med 32:142–147, 1962.

MYELOFIBROSIS
(Myelosclerosis, Agnogenic Myeloid Metaplasia)

Essentials of Diagnosis
- Weakness and fatigue.
- Large spleen.
- Anisocytosis and poikilocytosis of red cells.
- Leukocytosis.
- "Dry tap" on bone marrow aspiration.

General Considerations

Myelofibrosis is a proliferative neoplastic disorder of the mesenchymal tissue and is probably related to other myeloproliferative disorders such as chronic myelocytic leukemia and polycythemia vera. There is progressive fibrosis of the marrow and myeloid metaplasia in the liver and spleen. The disease is usually seen in adults beyond middle age. In about 10% of cases it is preceded by polycythemia vera. Occasionally it is associated with tuberculosis or metastatic cancer.

Clinical Findings

A. Symptoms and Signs: Patients may complain of fatigue, weakness, weight loss, occasionally bone pain, abdominal discomfort, and symptoms of anemia. The spleen is almost always enlarged, usually markedly so. The liver may be enlarged. The lymph nodes are not affected.

B. Laboratory Findings: Anemia may be severe. The red cells vary greatly in size and shape; teardrop-shaped, distorted red cells, nucleated and stippled cells may be seen. The reticulocyte count is often slightly elevated. The white count may be high (20–50 thousand/cu mm), with a marked shift to the left and many basophils. The white cell alkaline phosphatase reaction is usually strongly positive, but may be negative in 10% of patients. The platelet count may be greatly increased initially, and giant platelets and megakaryocyte fragments may be seen. Bone marrow aspiration is usually unsuccessful, yielding only sheets of platelet and megakaryocyte fragments and a few erythroblasts and granulocytes. Bone marrow biopsy shows fibrous tissue replacing normal marrow spaces. Splenic puncture may show erythroblasts, megakaryocytes, and young granulocytes.

Complications

Rapid splenic enlargement may be painful. The patient may develop symptoms of hypermetabolism with fever, sweating, and weight loss.

Secondary hypersplenism may lead to thrombocytopenia and bleeding and to hemolytic anemia with splenic sequestration of red cells. Some patients die in an acute "blastic" crisis.

Differential Diagnosis

In chronic myelocytic leukemia the white cell alkaline phosphatase reaction is negative. Hemolytic anemias are readily differentiated by the great number of reticulocytes, hypercellularity, and red cell hyperplasia of the bone marrow. Lymphosarcoma and metastatic cancer with "dry tap" are differentiated by marrow biopsy.

Treatment

If the spleen is not painful and the anemia only moderate, no treatment may be required. For severe anemia, one of the following may be tried: (1) testosterone enanthate (Delatestryl®), 1–2 mg/kg twice weekly IM; (2) fluoxymesterone (Halotestin®), 40–100 mg daily orally; or (3) methandrostenolone (Dianabol®), 40–100 mg daily orally. Many patients have to be maintained on multiple transfusions. For painful enlargement of the spleen give busulfan (Myleran®), 2 mg 1–3 times daily, or local x-ray radiation. For hemolytic anemia with splenic sequestration give prednisolone (or equivalent), 10–20 mg 4 times daily orally, or even consider splenectomy. For "blastic crisis" mercaptopurine (Purinethol®), 2.5 mg/kg/day, may be tried.

Prognosis

The average survival from the time of diagnosis is 2–3 years. In some patients the disease remains quiescent for several years even without transfusions. Death is due to hemorrhage, secondary infection, or acute blastic crisis.

Bouroncle, B.A., & C.A. Doan: Myelofibrosis. Clinical, hematologic, and pathologic study of 110 patients. Am J M Sc 243:697–715, 1962.

Nakai, G.S., & others: Agnogenic myeloid metaplasia. Ann Int Med 57:419–440, 1962.

HODGKIN'S DISEASE

Essentials of Diagnosis

- Regional lymph nodes enlarged, firm, non-tender, painless.
- Fever, weight loss, excessive sweating, pruritus, fatigue.
- Exacerbations and remissions.

General Considerations

Hodgkin's disease is seen in all races and occurs most commonly in young adults. It is characterized by abnormal proliferation, in one or several lymph nodes, of lymphocytes, histiocytes, eosinophils, and Reed-Sternberg giant cells. It starts most likely as a regionally localized process which tends to spread to contiguous lymphatic structures. Accurate measurement of the extent, or "staging," of the disease when first diagnosed is essential for proper management and prognosis. The "stage" of the disease is more important than its microscopic lymph node pattern in determining its course.

Clinical Findings

A. Symptoms and Signs: Regional unilateral lymphadenopathy (especially swelling of cervical nodes) is usually the presenting sign. The nodes are firm, nontender, and of various sizes. They may adhere to the deeper tissues, but the skin remains freely movable. If the mediastinum is involved early, respiratory difficulty may be the initial complaint. Hepatosplenomegaly and constitutional complaints usually appear late, and there may be fever, excessive sweating, fatigue, and pruritus.

B. Laboratory Findings: Specific diagnosis is made by lymph node biopsy. The blood count usually shows an absolute lymphopenia and, occasionally, some eosinophilia. Anemia is a late finding (stage IV). Patients with Hodgkin's disease often lose the ability to show delayed hypersensitivity; eg, they cannot react to the tuberculin skin test.

C. X-Ray Findings: Osteolytic lesions may be seen.

Differential Diagnosis

Hodgkin's disease must be distinguished from other diseases which involve lymph tissue, eg, tuberculosis, syphilis, brucellosis, infectious mononucleosis, metastatic cancer, leukemia, sarcoidosis, lupus erythematosus, and serum sickness. Anticonvulsive agents may produce lymph node changes similar to those seen in Hodgkin's disease. Differential diagnosis is made by biopsy, blood smear, or serologic tests.

Complications

Hemolytic anemia, intractable itching, superior vena cava obstruction, and pleural effusion occur. Painful and tender Hodgkin's sarcoma may develop. Paraplegia from extradural cord compression may occur.

Treatment

Radiation is used for stages I, II, and III in an effort to eradicate the disease. Chemotherapy is palliative for patients with advanced disease, especially if they have constitutional symptoms. Occasionally, the 2 methods are combined.

A. Irradiation: The treatment of choice for regionally localized disease is wide-field megavoltage radiotherapy to 3500–4000 r in 4 weeks. Some radiotherapists give similar doses to the involved areas in stage III disease. For proper staging of the disease a chest x-ray is a minimum requirement. Inferior vena cavagraphy and lymphangiography are indicated to determine possible retroperitoneal involvement. Almost half of patients with apparent stage I or II disease are shown to be stage III by proper diagnostic x-ray studies. Involvement of the bone marrow or liver is rare in early Hodgkin's disease.

B. Antitumor Chemotherapy (for Stage III or IV):

1. Mechlorethamine (nitrogen mustard)–0.4 mg/kg of the powder is dissolved in sterile water and given within 5 minutes into an infusion of physiologic saline. Patients are best treated in the evening after a light lunch and no supper. The unpleasant immediate side-effects of nausea and vomiting should be controlled by premedication with sedatives and antiemetic agents. Improvement of symptoms and reduction in size of lymph node masses may begin in 1–3 days. Medication may be repeated every 2 months as long as there is no marrow depression.

2. Chlorambucil (Leukeran®)–Used for maintenance for 3–6 weeks after mechlorethamine therapy in severe cases or instead of mechlorethamine in less severe cases. Give 0.2 mg/kg orally in divided doses after meals. Improvement may not begin for 3–4 weeks, and maximum improvement may not be achieved for 2–4 months. Side-effects are rare, but medication must be discontinued if bone marrow depression occurs. Patients should be followed with weekly blood counts at first and less frequently thereafter (but at least once a month).

3. Cyclophosphamide (Cytoxan®), 2–3 mg/kg IV daily for 6 days followed by 50–100 mg orally 1–3 times daily for maintenance. The principal disadvantage of this drug is the high incidence (20%) of alopecia it causes.

4. Vinblastine sulfate (Velban®) may be tried in resistant cases. The dosage is 0.1–0.15 mg/kg IV once a week, depending upon the white count. Untoward reactions include nausea, peripheral neuropathy, and alopecia.

5. Procarbazine (Matulane®), 50–200 mg daily orally.

6. Combination chemotherapy–To obtain maximal antitumor effect with minimal damage to healthy tissue, combinations of drugs with different mechanisms of action and various dose-limiting toxicities have been employed in preference to a large dose of a single drug. The following scheme ("MOPP") has been used: mechlorethamine, 6 mg/sq m IV on days 1 and 8; vincristine (Oncovin®), 1.4 mg/sq m IV on days 1 and 8; procarbazine (Matulane®), 100 mg/sq m orally daily for 14 days in each cycle; and prednisone, 40 mg/sq m orally daily during cycles 1 and 4. This dosage schedule is given in 6 two-week cycles over 6 months. A complete cycle consists of these 2 weeks of intensive therapy followed by a rest period of 2 weeks without any treatment. Cyclophosphamide (Cytoxan®), 650 mg/sq m IV, may be substituted for mechlorethamine.

C. Treatment of Complications:

1. Autoimmune hemolytic anemia–See p 261.

2. Intractable pruritus and fever–If alkylating agents fail, colchicine may be used. Dilute 3 mg in 20 ml of sterile normal saline solution and give very slowly IV at intervals of 3 days for 3 doses.

3. Pleural effusion–Triethylenemelamine (TEM), 5 mg dissolved in 5 ml of sterile physiologic saline solution, may be injected into the pleural cavity. After administration the patient's position is changed every 5 minutes for 30 minutes to allow maximum contact of the drug with the pleura.

4. Mediastinal or spinal cord compression is treated with mechlorethamine, 0.4 mg/kg IV, followed 24 hours later by x-ray therapy.

TABLE 9–6. Staging of Hodgkin's disease.

Stage*	Definition
0	No detectable disease due to prior excisional biopsy
I	Single abnormal lymph node
II	Two or more discrete abnormal nodes, limited to one side of diaphragm
III	Disease on both sides of diaphragm but limited to the lymph nodes, spleen, or Waldeyer's ring
IV	Involvement of bone, bone marrow, lung parenchyma, pleura, liver, skin, gastrointestinal tract, CNS, renal or sites other than lymph nodes, spleen, or Waldeyer's ring

*All stages are subclassified as A or B to describe the absence or presence of systemic symptoms, respectively.

Prognosis

Patients with true stage I or II disease who receive intensive radiotherapy and who have no new manifestations for 5 years (about 50% of patients so treated) have at least a 95% chance of being cured. New manifestations, usually by extension of disease from the original site, occur in the other 50%, but usually within 2 years after initial therapy. In some centers attempts are now being made to reduce the incidence of extension by prophylactically radiating apparently uninvolved contiguous areas. The overall 5-year survival in Hodgkin's disease appears to be approximately 30% at the present time.

Aisenberg, A.C.: Primary management of Hodgkin's disease. New England J Med 278:93–95, 1968.

Devita, V.T., & others: Combination chemotherapy in the treatment of advanced Hodgkin's disease. Ann Int Med 73:881–895, 1970.

Kaplan, H.S.: Role of intensive radiotherapy in the management of Hodgkin's disease. Cancer 19:356–367, 1966.

Perry, S., & others: Hodgkin's disease. Ann Int Med 67:424–442, 1967.

LYMPHOSARCOMA

Lymphosarcoma is a malignant disease of lymphatic tissue. It may arise in any lymphoid aggregate. Lymphadenopathy, usually painless, is the initial abnormality in most patients, occurring most frequently in the neck and usually unilaterally at first. Initial nasopharyngeal, mediastinal, or intra-abdominal involvement is not infrequent. The skin, gastrointestinal tract, nervous system, and bones are involved occasionally. Malaise, fever, weight loss, and sweating are the presenting findings. The liver or spleen is enlarged during the course of the illness in about 1/3 of patients. The diagnosis is made by lymph node biopsy, which shows destruction of node architecture and replacement with tightly packed lymphocytes or lymphoblasts.

This is a disease of middle age, but it may also occur in children. The median survival is 2 years in adults, but less than a year in patients under 16 years of age.

Unlike Hodgkin's disease, which is often unifocal initially and may be cured by intensive local or "mantle" irradiation, lymphosarcoma is usually multifocal from the beginning, and therapy is merely palliative; local irradiation should rarely exceed 2500 r (in air). However, if careful staging indicates localized disease, intensive radiotherapy, as described in the section on Hodgkin's disease, is worthwhile to attempt a cure. Corticosteroids are often helpful in generalized disease. Chemotherapy is used as in Hodgkin's disease. Combination chemotherapy ("COP") may be more effective than single agents: Cyclophosphamide (Cytoxan®), 15

mg/kg IV once a week; vincristine (Oncovin®), 0.025 mg/kg IV once a week; and prednisone, 0.6 mg/kg orally daily. This is given as a 6-week course.

Kaplan, H.S.: Clinical evaluation and radiotherapeutic management of Hodgkin's disease and the malignant lymphomas. New England J Med 278:892–899, 1968.

Rosenberg, S.A., Diamond, H.D., & L.F. Craver: Lymphosarcoma: The effects of therapy and survival in 1,269 patients in a review of 30 years' experience. Medicine 40:31–84, 1961.

Ultman, J.E., & others: The therapy of lymphoma. Seminars Hemat 6:376–403, 1969.

GIANT FOLLICULAR LYMPHOMA

In giant follicular lymphoma there is painless enlargement of groups of superficial lymph nodes; they are discrete, rubbery, and not fixed. Involvement of the inguinal areas is relatively common. Systemic symptoms are less prominent than in other malignant lymphomas, and the spleen and liver are less often enlarged. Some degree of anemia is seen in 25% of cases. The disease is seen primarily in middle age. Spontaneous remissions may occur. Approximately 50% of patients live more than 5 years. Chlorambucil or local x-ray irradiation is the treatment of choice.

Blumenberg, R.M., & others: Giant follicular lymphoma—a review of 46 cases. Am J Med 35:832–841, 1963.

Rappaport, H., Winter, W.J., & E.B. Hicks: Follicular lymphoma. Cancer 9:792–821, 1956.

MYCOSIS FUNGOIDES

Mycosis fungoides is a chronic, fatal disease of the reticuloendothelial cells of the skin which may progress to secondary involvement of lymph nodes and internal organs. The initial lesions resemble chronic, benign, nonspecific dermatitis or psoriasis. At this stage histologic changes do not indicate a malignant process. Later findings include infiltration, lichenification and plaque formation, and tumors.

The characteristic pathologic findings at these later stages of the disease are pleomorphic cellular infiltrates in the skin, with focal collections in the epidermis of mononuclear cells with large amounts of clear cytoplasm and small, dense nuclei. When the cellular aggregates form tumors, they may break through the epidermis and ulcerate. At this stage, histologic distinction from reticulum cell sarcoma and Hodgkin's disease may be impossible.

Generalized itching and lymph node involvement are frequent systemic manifestations. Some patients show large mononuclear cells, resembling histiocytes or reticulum cells in the blood (Sézary cells).

The interval between the first appearance of a seemingly benign chronic skin eruption and the diagnosis of mycosis fungoides may be several years. Most patients die within 3 years after the tissue diagnosis is made.

Treatment is palliative, but very good results may be obtained with radiation applied by electron beam, to give very little skin penetration and permit total body irradiation without visceral damage. Chemotherapy with nitrogen mustard or its analogues is the alternative. Dosage considerations are similar to those for Hodgkin's disease.

Block, J.B., & others: Mycosis fungoides. Am J Med 34:228–235, 1963.

• • •

POLYCYTHEMIA VERA

Essentials of Diagnosis
- Malaise, fatigue, weakness.
- Florid facies, dusky redness of mucosa.
- Greatly increased red cell values and increase in total red cell mass.

General Considerations
Polycythemia vera is a myeloproliferative disorder which often involves one or several formed elements, such as red cells, white cells, or platelets in varying degrees. Symptoms are probably due to increased blood viscosity and hypermetabolism. Although the disease may occur at any age, it is usually a disorder of middle age. It is more common in men than in women. Erythropoietin production is greatly depressed.

Clinical Findings
A. Symptoms and Signs: Patients may complain of headache, inability to concentrate, some hearing loss, itching (especially after bathing), pain in the fingers and toes, and redness of the conjunctivas. They may have a decreased feeling of well-being and a loss of efficiency and energy. A dusky redness is particularly noticeable on the lips, fingernails, and mucous membranes. The retinal veins are frequently tortuous and black. There is no clubbing of the fingers. The spleen is palpable in about half of cases at initial examination.

B. Laboratory Findings: The red cell count is 6–10 million/cu mm; the hemoglobin is above 18 gm/100 ml in men and above 16 gm/100 ml in women; and the hematocrit is over 55%. The white count is normal to 20,000/cu mm, and there may be an increase in basophils. The leukocyte alkaline phosphatase content is increased; platelets often are elevated and may be above 1 million/cu mm, but may be normal. Some patients with greatly elevated platelet counts

(over 1 million/cu mm) but hemoglobin concentrations in the normal range may have masked polycythemia vera. In these cases the increased red cell volume may be obscured by a simultaneous rise in plasma volume. In others, chronic gastrointestinal bleeding may keep the red cell volume within the normal range.

The bone marrow shows hyperactivity of all elements; the increase in megakaryocytes may be striking.

The arterial oxygen saturation is normal or slightly low, but always above 91%. The uric acid is frequently elevated to 5–10 mg/100 ml. The red cell volume is increased above the upper normal of 33 ml/kg.

Differential Diagnosis
Polycythemia vera must be differentiated especially from high normal values (see below), which remain relatively stable and do not increase; and from stress erythrocytosis, a state of decreased plasma volume, normal red cell volume, and rapid fluctuations in blood values seen occasionally in tense individuals.

The upper limits of normal for males are as follows: Hemoglobin, 18 gm/100 ml; red blood cell count, 6.2 million; hematocrit, 54%. For women: Hemoglobin, 16 gm/100 ml; red blood cell count, 5.4 million; hematocrit, 47%.

In secondary polycythemia the basic pulmonary or cardiac disorder is usually obvious, as in cyanotic heart disease and pulmonary fibrosis. In marked obesity (Pickwickian syndrome), which may also result in hypoventilation, the arterial oxygen saturation is distinctly decreased, leukocytosis and thrombocytosis are absent, and bone marrow hyperplasia is limited to the erythroid series. (Emphysema rarely raises the hemoglobin more than 1–2 gm/100 ml above normal.)

Occasionally a structural hemoglobin abnormality is responsible for tight oxygen binding; only partial pressure of blood oxygen is decreased, and dissociation at the tissue level is below normal.

Polycythemia may occur in association with renal tumors or cysts, pyelonephritis, renal obstructive disease, cerebellar hemangioblastoma, uterine fibroids, and hepatoma. Some of these disorders may be responsible for excessive erythropoietin production. The spleen usually is not enlarged, and the white cells and platelets are not affected.

Complications
Hemorrhage (particularly gastrointestinal bleeding) and thrombosis (cerebral, pulmonary, or deep vein) may occur in uncontrolled polycythemia vera. Excessive bleeding at surgery is common. Secondary gout occurs in about 10% of patients.

Treatment
A. Radiophosphorus (^{32}P): The initial dosage varies from 3–5 mc IV. If ^{32}P is given orally, the dose is increased by 25%.

After therapy the patient should be seen at intervals of 3–4 weeks until a remission has occurred. Platelets begin to fall at 2 weeks and reach a low point in 3–5 weeks. Red cells begin to decrease at 1 month and reach a low point at 3–4 months. At 2 months, if there has been no effect on platelets or red cells, patients are re-treated with an additional 2–3 mc or with ^{32}P. If necessary, another 2–3 mc dose is given at 6 months. When blood counts have returned to normal, patients are re-examined every 3 months.

Remissions may last 6 months to 2 years, and occasionally much longer. Relapse is treated by the total initial effective dose but should not exceed 5 mc.

B. Venesection (Phlebotomy): Remove 500–2000 ml of blood per week until the hematocrit reaches 45%, and repeat phlebotomy whenever the hematocrit rises 4–5%. The average maintenance is 500 ml every 2–3 months. When phlebotomy is the only therapy, medicinal iron must not be given. A low-iron diet is not practical, but certain foods of very high iron content should be avoided (clams, oysters, liver, legumes).

C. Chemotherapy: As an alternative to radiation, myelosuppressive agents may be used. Dosages for initial therapy, until response occurs (which may require 3–5 months) are about twice as large as maintenance dosages. Some patients stay in remission without maintenance therapy.

1. Chlorambucil, 10–12 mg/day initially and then 3–4 mg/day.

2. Cyclophosphamide (Cytoxan®), 100–150 mg/day initially and then 50–75 mg/day.

3. Melphalan (Alkeran®), 4–6 mg/day initially and then 2 mg/day or less for maintenance.

D. Treatment of Complications: Surgery in patients with polycythemia vera is frequently complicated by hemorrhage. Patients should be in hematologic remission before operation. Blood loss at surgery is replaced by whole blood transfusions. Fibrinogen (human), 4–6 gm, is given if the bleeding is due to fibrinogen deficiency. Gout is treated the same as primary gout.

Prognosis

In properly treated patients, survival averages approximately 13 years. Three stages of the disease can be recognized: (1) the "florid" stage, with a high red count and hemoglobin, may last many years; (2) compensated myelofibrosis, not requiring treatment, may continue for several more years; (3) the anemic phase, with severe myelofibrosis, megakaryocytic hyperplasia, and a very large spleen lasts for a few months up to 2 years. About 5% of patients die of acute leukemia.

Gardner, F. (editor): Polycythemia. Seminars in Hematology 3:175–234, 1966.

Pollycove, M., & others: Classification and evaluation of patterns of erythropoiesis in polycythemia vera studied by iron kinetics. Blood 28:807–829, 1966.

Treatment of polycythemia: A panel discussion. Blood 32:483–500, 1968.

Wasserman, L.R., & H.S. Gilbert: The treatment of polycythemia vera. M Clin North America 50:1501–1518, 1966.

AGRANULOCYTOSIS

Essentials of Diagnosis

- Chills, fever, sore throat, prostration.
- Ulceration of oral mucosa and throat.
- Granulocytopenia with relative lymphocytosis.
- Increased sedimentation rate.

General Considerations

Agranulocytosis may be secondary to the use of certain drugs and chemicals, eg, antithyroid drugs, sulfonamides, phenothiazines, phenylbutazone (Butazolidin®), and aminopyrine. Some of these agents lead to the production of circulating agglutinins against granulocytes; in other cases the cause of agranulocytosis is not known. Some drugs, eg, aminopyrine, cause an explosive onset of symptoms and leukopenia; others, eg, the antithyroid drugs and the phenothiazines, produce leukopenia only gradually after several days or weeks, even on readministration.

Clinical Findings

A. Symptoms and Signs: Onset is often sudden, with chills, fever, and extreme weakness. There may be a brownish-gray exudate of the throat and greenish-black membranous ulcers of the oral mucosa, respiratory tract, vagina, and rectum. Regional adenopathy is common. Macules and papules developing into bullae may develop on the skin. The spleen and liver are not enlarged, and there is no bone tenderness.

B. Laboratory Findings: Granulocytes disappear from the blood, and monocytes and lymphocytes may also be reduced in absolute numbers. Red cells and platelets are not affected. The bone marrow appears hypoplastic; only a few early myeloid cells are seen, but red cell series and megakaryocytes are normal. After the offending drug is removed, recovery takes place in 8–10 days; lymphocytes and monocytes reappear before the granulocytes. During recovery, a transient excess of lymphocytes followed by a phase of primitive granulocyte proliferation may be observed in the marrow.

Differential Diagnosis

Differentiate from aplastic anemia (thrombocytopenia and anemia) and from acute aleukemic leukemia (hyperplastic marrow, predominance of malignant cells).

Complications

Complications include sepsis, bronchial pneumonia, hemorrhagic necrosis of mucous membrane lesions, and parenchymal liver damage with jaundice.

Treatment

A. General Measures: Discontinue suspected chemical agents or drugs. Obtain a blood sample for bacterial culture and antibiotic sensitivity testing. Supportive measures include good oral hygiene, adequate fluid intake, and reduction of fever. Patients should be isolated if possible to reduce exposure to infection.

B. Antibiotics: Penicillin is the most effective agent against the common invaders, the gram-positive cocci. If there is evidence of bacterial infection, give 0.6–1.2 million units daily while the white count is low. Penicillin or other antibiotics should not be used "prophylactically." Broad-spectrum antibiotics are used only when specifically indicated on the basis of culture and sensitivity tests.

C. Corticosteroids: If the patient appears toxic, corticosteroids may have to be considered.

Prognosis

The mortality rate may approach 80% in untreated cases. With antibiotic therapy mortality is much lower and when recovery occurs it is complete. Patients must be cautioned against re-exposure to offending agents.

Pisciotta, A.V.: Studies in agranulocytosis: Patterns of recovery. J Lab Clin Med 63:445, 1964.

Pisciotta, A.V., & others: Agranulocytosis following administration of phenothiazine derivatives. Am J Med 25:210–223, 1958.

Pretty, H.M., & others: Agranulocytosis: A report of 30 cases. Canad MAJ 93:1058–1064, 1965.

HEMORRHAGIC DISORDERS

Diagnosis of Coagulation Problems

In the study of a coagulation problem the history is of utmost importance. The following questions must be answered:

(1) How long is the history of bleeding? Has bleeding been noted since early childhood, or is onset relatively recent? How many previous episodes have there been?

(2) What are the circumstances of the bleeding? Has it occurred after minor surgery, such as tonsillectomy or tooth extraction? Has it occurred after falls or participation in contact sports?

(3) What is the duration of the bleeding episode? (Prolonged oozing is more significant than massive hemorrhage.)

(4) Is there a family history of bleeding?

(5) What is the type or character of the bleeding? Purpuric spots suggest a capillary or platelet defect; they are not characteristic of hemophilia. Hematomas, hemarthroses, or large ecchymoses at the site of trauma suggest hemophilia. Sudden, severe bleeding from multiple sites after prolonged surgery or during obstetric procedures suggests acquired fibrinogen deficiency. Massive bleeding from a single site without a history of purpura or previous bleeding suggests a surgical or anatomic defect rather than a coagulation defect.

Gaston, L.W.: The blood clotting factors. New England J Med 270:236–242, 290–298, 1964.

Ratnoff, O.D.: The therapy of the hereditary disorders of blood coagulation. Arch Int Med 112:92–111, 1963.

Ratnoff, O.D.: The blood clotting mechanism and its disorders. Disease-A-Month, Nov 1965.

HEMOPHILIA

Essentials of Diagnosis

- Lifelong history of bleeding in a male; usually congenital and familial.
- Slow, prolonged bleeding after minor injury.
- Recurrent hemarthroses and hematomas.
- Prolonged coagulation time; bleeding time normal.

General Considerations

Classical hemophilia is due to a deficiency of antihemophilic factor (AHF), a constituent of normal plasma which is essential for thromboplastin formation. The disorder is transmitted as a sex-linked recessive gene by clinically unaffected female carriers to male offspring. AHF levels are decreased in 1/3 to 1/2 of female carriers. About 85% of congenital bleeders have classical hemophilia. One-third of these cases are sporadic, ie, a family history of bleeding is not obtained.

Clinical Findings

A. Symptoms and Signs: Patients with hemophilia rarely have massive hemorrhages. Bleeding is charac-

Coagulation Factor Synonyms	
Factor V:	Proaccelerin, labile factor, AC globulin.
Factor VII:	Proconvertin, stable factor, serum prothrombin conversion accelerator (SPCA).
Factor VIII:	Antihemophilic factor (AHF), antihemophilic globulin (AHG), antihemophilic factor A (AHF-A).
Factor IX:	Plasma thromboplastin component (PTC), antihemophilic factor B (AHF-B), Christmas factor
Factor X:	Stuart factor, Stuart-Power factor.
Factor XI:	Plasma thromboplastic antecedent (PTA).
Factor XII:	Hageman factor.
Factor XIII:	Fibrin stabilizing factor.

TABLE 9–7. Differential diagnosis of some bleeding disorders.

	Hemophilia (AHF, PTC)*		Idiopathic Thrombocytopenic Purpura	Vascular Hemophilia	Thrombasthenia (Glanzmann's)	Prothrombin Complex Deficiency	Defibrination Syndrome
	Severe	Mild					
Clinical Features:†							
Petechiae	–	–	++++	+	++	Ecchymoses	Ecchymoses
Hematoma, large	++++	++	–	–	–	–	–
Hemarthrosis	++++	±	–	±	–	–	–
Postsurgical bleeding	++++	++++	+	+++	+	++	++++
Onset in childhood	+	±	–	+	+	±	–
Hereditary	+	+	–	+	+	–	–
Laboratory:							
Bleeding time	N	N	Incr	Incr	N or incr	N	N
Clotting time	Incr	N	N	N	N	N or incr	No clot
Clot retraction time	N	N	Incr	N	Incr	N	No clot
Prothrombin time	N	N	N	N	N	Incr	Incr
Partial thromboplastin time (PTT)	Decr	Decr	Only platelets abnormal	Abnormal	Incr. Only platelets abnormal	N	Incr
Platelet count	N	N	Decr	N	Platelets look abnormal	N	Decr

*AHF = Antihemophilic factor. PTC = Plasma thromboplastin component.
†Frequency expressed on a scale of – to ++++.

teristically a delayed and prolonged oozing or trickling, occurring after minor trauma or surgery, eg, tonsillectomy or tooth extraction. With extravasation of blood, painful hematomas form in the deep subcutaneous or intramuscular tissue. Joint deformity results from repeated hemorrhage into joint spaces. Gastrointestinal bleeding and hematuria are also prominent findings.

The frequency of bleeding episodes is variable. There may be periods of spontaneous bleeding from multiple sites followed by a phase during which there is neither spontaneous bleeding nor bleeding following minor trauma.

In mild cases a bleeding history may be lacking; the disease is suspected only after dental or surgical procedures.

B. Laboratory Findings: In patients with severe hemophilia, the coagulation time may range from 30 minutes to several hours. Partial thromboplastin time (PTT) is greatly prolonged. Antihemophilic factor (AHF) is virtually absent from the plasma. During clinically silent periods these laboratory tests remain abnormal. Capillary fragility, bleeding time (except after ingestion of aspirin), prothrombin time, fibrinogen content, and platelet values are normal.

In mild cases the coagulation time is normal, but the PTT is prolonged. The plasma contains only 5–40% of antihemophilic factor (normal = 50–150%).

Differential Diagnosis

Plasma thromboplastin component deficiency (Christmas disease), which accounts for about 2–3% of congenital bleeders (15% of hemophiliacs), has the same clinical manifestations and hereditary transmission as classical hemophilia. Differentiation is by special coagulation studies and is essential if appropriate therapy is to specifically correct each of these deficiencies.

Plasma thromboplastin antecedent (PTA) deficiency accounts for 1% of hemophiliacs. It is an autosomal recessive trait, therefore affecting both males and females. It occurs almost exclusively in Jews. Patients have only mild bleeding tendencies. Spontaneous bleeding is unusual, though some patients bruise easily. Bleeding usually only occurs after injury and some surgical procedures; hemarthroses do not occur. The differentiation from factor VIII and IX deficiency is made by special coagulation studies. Treatment consists only of administering fresh frozen plasma; no therapeutic concentrate exists as yet.

Prothrombin complex disorders are characterized by a prolonged prothrombin time and a normal coagulation time.

In fibrinogen deficiency, the blood does not clot at all in the test tube, or a clot may form at a normal rate and then contract to a tiny residue.

Complications

Repeated hemarthroses may lead to ankylosis. Hematoma formation around the peripheral nerves may cause permanent damage with pain, anesthesia, or muscle atrophy. Retroperitoneal bleeding may be fatal. Autoimmune anticoagulants (anti-AHF) following repeated transfusions develop in approximately 5% of patients.

Treatment

A. General Measures: Treatment is based on raising the level of AHF in the patient's blood and maintaining it at this level until hemostasis is obtained. AHF is very labile in blood collected in the usual manner. Blood should be used within 6 hours after taking it from the donor, or the plasma should be separated and frozen or lyophilized. The half-disappearance time of AHF in vivo is about 12 hours.

Treatment is evaluated by the clinical response. Coagulation time and prothrombin consumption values cannot be used as guides during treatment. Correction of abnormal PTT is a useful indicator.

The management of factor IX deficiency is similar; however, since factor IX is stable at blood bank conditions for long periods, plasma need not be fresh.

B. AHF Concentrates: See Table 9–8.

C. Plasma: (Fresh frozen plasma, 140 units/200 ml.) Just prior to infusion the plasma is thawed at 37° C (98.6° F) until all solid material is liquefied. For maximum response it is administered as an initial dose of 15–20 ml/kg over a period of 1–2 hours, then ½ the dose every 12 hours for the next 3 days. Smaller amounts may be satisfactory in some cases.

D. Factor IX Complex: Konyne® (Cutter) contains factors II, VII, IX, and X, 500 in vitro units/20 ml bottle. Give 10–20 units/kg. Repeat every 24 hours.

E. Special Problems:

1. Bleeding—For the simpler bleeding episodes (eg, hemarthroses or dental extraction), give enough AHF concentrate to raise the plasma level to 50% (eg, cryoprecipitate, 1 bag/6 kg).

No further therapy is usually needed. In more severe cases (eg, abdominal or retroperitoneal bleeding), one must raise the AHG level to 75% (1 bag/4 kg); this dose may have to be repeated in 24 and 48 hours.

2. Surgical procedures—Patients are prepared by infusion of AHF concentrates to reach a 50% AHF level.

Aminocaproic acid (Amicar®, EACA) may be a valuable adjunct to therapy. Give 6 gm IV 2 hours before surgery and then 6 gm 4 times daily IV for 1 week.

3. Hemarthroses—During the bleeding phase the joint must be put at rest, in position of comfort, and possibly packed with ice or put into a protective cast. If pain is severe, aspiration may be necessary.

As soon as pain and bleeding have been controlled, usually within 3–5 days, muscle-setting exercises are begun. When swelling subsides, active motion of the joint is encouraged. Weight bearing is not permitted until the periarticular soft tissues have returned to nearly normal and motion and muscle power of the joint are normal.

Prognosis

Spontaneous hemorrhages into joints and bleeding from minor injuries or surgery are rarely dangerous. Major trauma and bleeding into loose tissues, eg, the retroperitoneal space, may be fatal despite therapy with plasma. Fatal, uncontrollable hemorrhage may also occur if inhibitors (anti-AHF factor) develop following multiple transfusions.

Aggeler, P.M., & others: The mild hemophilias. Occult deficiencies of AHF, PTC and PTA frequently responsible for unexpected surgical bleeding. Am J Med 30:89–94, 1961.

Biggs, R., & R.G. MacFarlane: Haemophilia and related conditions. A survey of 148 cases. Brit J Haemat 4:1–27, 1958.

Dallman, P.R., & J.G. Pool: Treatment of hemophilia with factor VIII concentrates. New England J Med 278:199–202, 1968.

Ratnoff, O.D.: The biology and pathology of the initial stages of blood coagulation (factors XII and XI deficiencies). Pages 220–245 in: *Progress in Hematology.* Vol 5. Grune & Stratton, 1966.

Strauss, H.S.: *Diagnosis and Treatment of Hemophilia.* Children's Hospital & Medical Center, Boston, 1967.

Walsh, P.N., & others: Epsilon-aminocaproic acid therapy for dental extractions in hemophilia. Brit Haemat 20:463–475, 1971.

IDIOPATHIC (PRIMARY) THROMBOCYTOPENIC PURPURA

Essentials of Diagnosis

- Petechiae, ecchymoses, epistaxis, easy bruising.
- No splenomegaly.
- Decreased platelet count, prolonged bleeding time, poor clot retraction, normal coagulation time.

General Considerations

The thrombocytopenia is the result of increased platelet destruction; the platelet count is closely related to the rate of destruction. Normal platelet survival is 8–10 days. Survival is usually only 1–3 days in chronic idiopathic thrombocytopenic purpura, and even less in the acute form. An antiplatelet factor with

TABLE 9–8. AHF concentrates.

	AHF Units		Usual Dose to Reach 50% AHF	Storage Requirement
	Per Package	Per ml		
Cryoprecipitate	100–150	4–6	1 bag/6 kg	Freeze
Hemofil® (Hyland)	230 725	33 28	1 pkg/10 kg 1 pkg/36 kg	Refrigerate
AHF (Courtland)	200	8	1 vial/10 kg	Room temperature
Fibro-AHG® (Merck)	75	0.75	1 vial/3–4 kg	Refrigerate

the characteristics of antibody may be present in the plasma. Despite an apparent increase in the number of megakaryocytes in the marrow, platelet production is usually not increased; antibodies may disturb mega-karyocytic development and lead to ineffective pro-duction. The disorder may be secondary to viral infec-tion, drug hypersensitivity, platelet isoimmunity, dis-seminated lupus erythematosus, lymphoproliferative disorders, infectious mononucleosis, or other condi-tions. The spleen is thought to act in 2 ways: It seques-ters damaged platelets and contributes to antibody for-mation.

Acute thrombocytopenic purpura is more com-mon in children. Eighty-five percent of patients are less than 8 years old; it usually remits spontaneously in 2 weeks to a few months. Chronic thrombocytopenic purpura may start at any age and is more common in females. At onset it cannot be distinguished from the acute form by any known laboratory test; there may be clinical remissions and exacerbations, but the plate-let count is always low.

Drug hypersensitivity may occur following the use of quinidine, quinine, chlorothiazide derivatives, sulfonamides, phenylbutazone (Butazolidin®), and sev-eral other agents. When the offending drug is with-drawn, the platelet counts begin to rise within a few days and return to normal within a few weeks.

Clinical Findings

A. Symptoms and Signs: The onset may be sud-den, with petechiae, epistaxis, bleeding gums, vaginal bleeding, gastrointestinal bleeding, or hematuria. In the chronic form there may be a history of easy bruising and recurrent showers of petechiae, particularly in pressure areas. The spleen is not palpable.

B. Laboratory Findings: The platelet count is al-ways below 100,000/cu mm and may be below 10,000/cu mm. The absence of platelets on the periph-eral blood smear is striking. White cells are not af-fected; and anemia, if present, is secondary to blood loss.

The bone marrow megakaryocytes are increased in number but not surrounded by platelets; they are abnormal, with single nuclei, scant cytoplasm, and often vacuoles. The chief value of the marrow exami-nation is to rule out leukemia and aplastic anemia.

The bleeding time is prolonged, but coagulation time is normal. Clot retraction is poor. Prothrombin consumption is decreased in severe cases. Capillary fragility (Rumpel-Leede test) is greatly increased. An LE test and a prothrombin time should be done to look for lupus, which may present as purpura or with bleeding due to an anticoagulant.

Differential Diagnosis

Purpura may be the first sign of acute leukemia or macroglobulinemia. The diagnosis is made by finding the characteristic malignant cells in the blood or bone marrow. In thrombocytopenia accompanying aplastic anemia, the marrow fat is increased and megakaryo-cytes are decreased or absent. Thrombotic thrombo-cytopenic purpura is associated with hemolytic ane-mia, jaundice, and CNS symptoms.

Thrombocytopenic purpura may also be seen in association with a variety of disorders causing spleno-megaly and hypersplenism: congestive splenomegaly, Felty's syndrome, Gaucher's disease, tuberculosis, sar-coidosis, and myelofibrosis. Lupus erythematosus may be associated with thrombocytopenic purpura with or without splenomegaly. Other conditions that may have to be ruled out before making the diagnosis of idio-pathic thrombocytopenic purpura include septicemia (especially with gram-negative organisms) and intravas-cular coagulation (sometimes associated with micro-angiopathic disorders).

In the newborn, thrombocytopenic purpura may also be caused by septicemia, congenital syphilis, cyto-megalic inclusion disease, hemolytic disease of the newborn, a congenital lack of megakaryocytes, or a congenital giant hemangioma. In the Aldrich syn-drome, thrombocytopenic purpura is associated with eczema, increased susceptibility to infection, and defi-ciency of isoagglutinins, immunoglobulins, and lymphocytes; it is a sex-linked recessive disorder.

Scurvy may cause purpura and massive skin and muscle hemorrhage, especially into hair follicles of the legs and extensor surfaces of the arms. Coagulation tests are normal.

The Henoch-Schönlein syndrome (anaphylactoid purpura) is associated with widespread inflammatory reactions of the capillaries and small arterioles. It may be associated with abdominal pain and gastrointestinal bleeding, hematuria, proteinuria, and polyarthritis.

Vascular hemophilia (von Willebrand's disease) is characterized by prolonged bleeding time and capillary fragility with normal platelet count and clot retraction.

In thrombasthenia (Glanzmann's syndrome), the platelet count is normal but the platelet morphology is abnormal and clot retraction is poor.

In autoerythrocyte sensitization patients develop painful, raised purplish spots which tend to enlarge and can be reproduced by injecting a few of the patient's red cells under the skin.

Complications

Fatal cerebral hemorrhage occurs in 1–5% of cases; hemorrhage from the nose and gastrointestinal and urinary tracts may be dangerously severe. Pressure of a hematoma on nerve tissue may cause pain, anes-thesia, or paralysis. Children born to mothers with idi-opathic thrombocytopenic purpura may have transient neonatal purpura.

Treatment

A. General Measures: Patients should avoid trau-ma, contact sports, elective surgery, and tooth extrac-tion. All unnecessary medications and exposure to po-tential toxins must be discontinued.

Children with mild purpura following viral infec-tions do not require any therapy. They should be ob-served until petechiae disappear and the platelet count returns to normal.

B. Corticosteroids: Corticosteroids are warranted in patients with moderately severe purpura of short duration, especially when there is bleeding from the gastrointestinal or genitourinary tract. Corticosteroids are also given to patients with purpura who have complications contraindicating surgery. Prednisolone (or equivalent), 10–20 mg 4 times daily, is usually required to control bleeding. The dosage is continued until the platelet count returns to normal, and then is gradually decreased.

C. Splenectomy: Splenectomy is indicated for all patients with well-documented thrombocytopenic purpura of more than 1 year's duration; for all patients with moderately severe purpura who have relapsed 2–3 times after corticosteroid therapy; and for all patients with severe idiopathic thrombocytopenic purpura who do not respond to corticosteroids.

Corticosteroids should not be used immediately before surgery unless bleeding is severe. If splenectomy must be performed on a patient who has been on corticosteroids, full doses of corticosteroids should be maintained for 3 days after surgery and then decreased gradually.

The platelet count rises promptly following splenectomy, and often doubles within the first 24 hours. Maximum values are reached 1–2 weeks postoperatively. Sometimes the platelet count will exceed 1 million/cu mm before leveling off. Anticoagulant therapy is not necessary with even higher platelet counts. Splenectomy may be considered successful only when counts stay normal for at least 2 months.

Prognosis

Spontaneous and permanent recovery occurs in 75% of all childhood idiopathic thrombocytopenic purpura and in 25% of all adult cases. Splenectomy is curative in 70–90% of all patients.

Baldini, M.: Idiopathic thrombocytopenic purpura. New England J Med 274:1245–1251, 1301–1306, 1360–1367, 1966.

Cream, J.J., & others: Henoch-Schönlein purpura in the adult. Quart J Med 39:461–484, 1970.

Doan, C.A., Bouroncle, B.A., & B.K. Wiseman: Idiopathic and secondary thrombocytopenic purpura: Clinical study and evaluation of 381 cases over a period of 28 years. Ann Int Med 53:861–876, 1960.

HEREDITARY HEMORRHAGIC TELANGIECTASIA
(Rendu-Osler-Weber Disease)

Essentials of Diagnosis

- Telangiectatic lesions on face, mouth, nose, hands.
- Epistaxis or gastrointestinal bleeding.
- Familial involvement.

General Considerations

This is a vascular abnormality involving primarily the veins; vessels are dilated and their walls are thin. Lesions may be visible in childhood but usually do not bleed severely until adulthood. The disorder is inherited as a dominant trait. Males and females are involved equally. A positive family history can be obtained in 80% of cases.

Skin and mucous membrane lesions may be asymptomatic for many years; the diagnosis is established by inference when telangiectases and angiomas are noted in patients with otherwise inexplicable attacks of epistaxis or gastrointestinal bleeding.

Clinical Findings

A. Symptoms and Signs: Multiple bright red lesions 1–4 mm in diameter that blanch on pressure are seen on the face, oral or nasopharyngeal membranes, and upper extremities in over 90% of patients. The lesions are often first noticed in childhood, but severe bleeding is unusual before the age of 30; the peak incidence of severity is in the 6th decade. Approximately 5% of patients have pulmonary arteriovenous fistulas.

Epistaxis is the most common form of bleeding; gastrointestinal bleeding occurs in about 15% of cases; it may be severe enough to require surgery, but the actual gastrointestinal lesions may be difficult to demonstrate at operation.

B. Laboratory Findings: The usual laboratory tests are helpful only in ruling out other causes of bleeding; bleeding and clotting times, prothrombin time, platelet count, clot retraction, and tourniquet tests are normal. Secondary iron deficiency anemia may be present.

Differential Diagnosis

Petechiae do not blanch on pressure, are more purple, and are not particularly common on the lips and tongue. Spider angiomas are arteriolar, can be shown to pulsate on pressure, and have several fine channels extending from their centers.

Complications

Severe bleeding may cause chronic iron deficiency anemia. Bleeding may exceed 1000 ml per week from the gastrointestinal tract.

Treatment

There is no cure.

Asymptomatic lesions require no therapy. Local pressure and topical hemostatic agents may be tried in accessible bleeding areas. Cauterization of the nasal mucous membranes may be necessary.

For uncontrollable gastrointestinal bleeding, unsuitable for surgery, iron therapy is indicated. If bleeding is severe (50–100 ml/day), give iron dextran injection (Imferon®), 5–10 ml IV once weekly. For more severe bleeding, transfusions are necessary.

Halpern, M., & others: Hereditary hemorrhagic telangiectasia. Radiology 90:1143–1149, 1968.

Smith, C.R., & others: Hereditary hemorrhagic telangiectasia and gastrointestinal hemorrhage. Gastroenterology 44:1–6, 1963.

THROMBOTIC THROMBOCYTOPENIC PURPURA

This is a severe, acute illness with a poor prognosis. The major clinical manifestations are fever, jaundice, purpura, drowsiness with fluctuating neurologic signs, thrombocytopenia, hemolytic anemia with characteristically fragmented red blood cells, and renal abnormalities. Any one of these features may be absent, especially initially. Coombs' test is negative, red cell enzymes are not decreased, and Heinz bodies are absent.

The pathologic diagnosis depends upon vascular lesions located at arteriolocapillary junctions, with widespread distribution in many organs. The lesions consist of subintimal deposition of PAS positive material, hyaline thrombi, and vessel wall weakening, leading to aneurysmal dilatations. The thrombotic phenomena are thought to be secondary reactions to the damaged vascular walls.

Treatment is usually of no avail. Occasional successes have been reported with large doses of corticosteroids, 6% clinical dextran, and heparin. Splenectomy does not help.

Amorosi, E.L., & J.E. Ultmann: Thrombotic thrombocytopenic purpura: Report of 16 cases and review of the literature. Medicine 45:139–159, 1966.
Lerner, R.C., Rapaport, S.I., & J. Melitzer: Thrombotic thrombocytopenic purpura. Serial clotting studies, relation to the generalized Schwartzman reaction, and remission after adrenal steroid and dextran therapy. Ann Int Med 66:1180–1190, 1967.

VASCULAR HEMOPHILIA
(Pseudohemophilia, Von Willebrand's Disease)

Essentials of Diagnosis

- History of excessive bruising and frequent nosebleeds since childhood.
- Prolonged bleeding time, normal platelet count.

General Considerations

This relatively common disorder resembles hemophilia in that it causes prolonged bleeding, particularly after oropharyngeal surgery or trauma; however, it occurs in both sexes, the bleeding time is prolonged, and the coagulation time is usually normal.

The hemostatic defect results from lack of a plasma factor necessary for platelets to adhere to each other and to cut vessel walls, and from an associated decrease in factor VIII production. The disorder is transmitted as an autosomal dominant to both sexes. The incidence of familial involvement approaches 80%. Factor VIII levels are usually decreased.

Clinical Findings

A. Symptoms and Signs: There is a history of frequent nosebleeds in childhood, prolonged bleeding from small cuts (eg, kitchen knife, razor cuts while shaving), excessive menstrual flow, prolonged oozing following oropharyngeal or minor gynecologic surgery, and easy bruisability. Other family members are usually affected also. Childbirth is usually uncomplicated by bleeding, and these patients can often undergo major abdominal surgery without hemorrhagic complications. Skin bleeding is ecchymotic rather than petechial.

B. Laboratory Findings: A prolonged bleeding time (Ivy) is essential for diagnosis; it is greatly prolonged following the ingestion of as little as 0.6 gm of aspirin. PTT is usually prolonged, reflecting low factor VIII. If factor VIII levels are very low (less than 5%), even the coagulation time may be prolonged. Platelet adhesiveness, as measured by the Salzman test, in which blood is passed through a tube with fine glass beads, is characteristically decreased (ie, more platelets than normal pass through the tube without adhering). Platelet count, platelet aggregation, prothrombin time, and clot retraction are all normal.

Differential Diagnosis

Vascular hemophilia must be differentiated from conditions with qualitative platelet defects. Glanzmann's syndrome is also characterized by a prolonged bleeding time and a normal platelet count; platelet morphology is abnormal; bleeding is often severe and may even be fatal. In macroglobulinemic purpura, ecchymoses and prolonged bleeding time may occur. In the recently described platelet-collagen interaction defect, platelet aggregation is faulty. In all of these conditions, factor VIII levels are normal.

Treatment

For serious bleeding episodes, give fresh frozen plasma, 15 ml/kg. If the bleeding site is accessible, bleeding is controlled by local pressure with thrombin-soaked gelfoam. Whole blood replacement may be necessary.

Prognosis

Bleeding is usually self-limited, although it may be prolonged. Fatal bleeding may occur, especially after minor surgical procedures. Childbirth and major abdominal procedures are less likely to be complicated by excessive bleeding. Bleeding tends to become less severe with increasing age.

Barrow, E.M., & J.B. Graham: Von Willebrand's disease. Progr Hemat 4:203–221, 1964.
Caen, J.P.: Congenital bleeding disorders with long bleeding time and normal platelet count. I. Glanzmann's thrombasthenia. Am J Med 41:4–26, 1966.
Larrieu, M.J., & others: Congenital bleeding disorders with long bleeding time and normal platelet count. II. Von Willebrand's disease. Am J Med 45:354–372, 1968.

Sahud, M.: Differential diagnosis of platelet dysfunction. California Med 112:66–76, March 1970.

INTRAVASCULAR COAGULATION
(Defibrination Syndrome, Consumption Coagulopathy)

Essentials of Diagnosis

- Diffuse bleeding from the skin and mucous membranes.
- Poor, small clot.
- Reduced platelets or on smear.
- Prolonged prothrombin time.

General Considerations

This is a pathologic form of coagulation which differs from normal clotting in 3 principal ways: (1) it is diffuse rather than localized; (2) it damages the site of clotting instead of protecting it; and (3) it consumes several clotting factors to such a degree that their concentration in the plasma becomes so low that diffuse bleeding may occur. It is seen in certain obstetric catastrophes and following some types of surgery, particularly involving the lung, brain, or prostate. In some of these conditions and in malignancies (especially of the prostate), septicemia, hemolytic transfusion reaction, and hemolytic uremic syndrome in infancy, deposition of fibrin in small blood vessels may lead to serious and even fatal tissue necrosis. Examples are (1) glomerular capillary thrombosis leading to cortical necrosis or a pattern similar to that of acute tubular necrosis, (2) adrenal sinusoidal thrombosis with resultant hemorrhagic necrosis of the adrenals (Waterhouse-Friderichsen syndrome); and (3) hemorrhagic skin necrosis in purpura fulminans. These conditions are caused in part by a failure to clear fibrin. Some relationship may exist between irreversible endotoxin shock and disseminated intravascular clotting.

Unexpected, profuse, or uncontrollable bleeding in certain surgical or obstetric situations suggests acute defibrination. Multiple coagulation factors are involved. The syndrome is acquired and results from intravascular coagulation.

Clinical Findings

A. Symptoms and Signs: The most common manifestations are diffuse bleeding from many sites at surgery and from needle puncture. Minimal trauma may cause severe bleeding, or there may be spontaneous ecchymoses, epistaxis, or gastrointestinal hemorrhage. Uncontrollable postpartum hemorrhage may be a manifestation of intravascular coagulation.

B. Laboratory Findings: The combination of a poor, small clot, reduced platelets on the blood smear, and a prolonged prothrombin time is very suggestive of this disorder. Clotting time is usually normal. With a marked fibrinogen depletion (fibrinogen < 75 mg/ml), the clot that forms in a test tube may be quite flimsy and friable. It may be so small and retracted that it

may not even be visible, thus simulating fibrinolysis. The contents of the test tube should be poured into a Petri dish or onto a piece of filter paper for closer examination. If a clot can be demonstrated, it suggests that fibrinogen depletion, and not fibrinolysis, is the primary process.

A form of hemolytic anemia associated with fragmentation of the red blood cells (microangiopathic hemolytic anemia) may accompany some of these conditions.

Platelet counts usually vary from 30–120 thousand/cu mm. Prothrombin time is usually less than 40% and may be less than 10%. Screening tests for fibrinogen (Hyland Laboratories Fi test) usually indicate values of less than 100 mg/100 ml. The activated PTT (normal: < 47 seconds) is prolonged to as much as 100 seconds. The thrombin time is prolonged. The bleeding time is usually prolonged when platelet levels are below 70,000.

It is usually quite helpful to obtain laboratory evidence of fibrinolysis when investigating a case of suspected intravascular coagulation. Acute fibrinolysis, while occasionally a primary process, is most commonly seen in association with intravascular coagulation. The 2 most commonly used tests are demonstration of fibrin degradation products in plasma or serum and the determination of euglobulin clot lysis.

Fibrin degradation products result from the digestion of fibrinogen or fibrin by plasmin or other enzymes. These products cannot be coagulated by thrombin; they actually inhibit the thrombin-fibrinogen reaction and cause a prolonged thrombin time, and also inhibit platelet aggregation, thromboplastin formation, and fibrin polymerization. They make the Fi test for fibrinogen difficult to interpret. Fibrin degradation products are usually demonstrated by immunologic methods and can be quantitated by a tanned red cell hemagglutination inhibition test.

The time necessary for a euglobulin clot to lyse is a measure of fibrinolytic activity. In normal individuals more than 2 hours is required for the clot to lyse. Significant fibrinolysis is evident when a euglobulin clot liquefies in less than 60 minutes.

Plasminogen levels are low; plasminogen is the inactive precursor of fibrinolysin (plasmin). Since it is activated to plasmin in acute fibrinolysis, its activity is characteristically low in this disorder.

Demonstration of the characteristic clotting factor pattern by individual factor assay is of great help in differential diagnosis. In primary fibrinolysis, in fibrinogen deficiency from underproduction rather than excessive utilization, in hepatic necrosis, and following heparin administration (eg, excessive dose by error), clot formation or retraction may be grossly abnormal, but factor VII levels are not decreased.

Differential Diagnosis

Disseminated intravascular coagulation—which, like all clotting, is associated with secondary fibrinolysis—must be distinguished from primary fibrinolysis, a much rarer clinical phenomenon requiring very different management. This latter syndrome may occur with disseminated carcinoma (especially of the prostate), with septicemia, and with very severe liver disease. Diffuse bleeding similar to that encountered in intravascular coagulation does not occur, and platelets, factor V, and factor VIII are less strikingly decreased; a clot may form initially but dissolves completely in less than 2 hours. As in secondary fibrinolysis, fibrinogen is low or absent; consequently, prothrombin and thrombin times are prolonged, plasminogen is low, and plasmin levels are increased.

Other conditions where clots fail to form in vitro are circulating anticoagulant and heparin administration. In vitro clotting may be greatly prolonged to 1 hour or more in the hemophilias and in factor XII deficiency.

Treatment

If possible, treat the underlying disorder, eg, shock or sepsis. Heparin may be effective to stop pathologic clotting, and it may also control bleeding. In adults, the usual dose of heparin is 100 USP units/ kg every 4–6 hours IV; in children, 50 units/kg every 4 hours after an initial dose of 100 units. If the diagnosis of intravascular coagulation was correct and therapy is effective, fibrinogen levels, PTT, and PT should rise within 24 hours and platelet count within a few days. Whole blood may be necessary to combat shock. With severe fibrinogen deficiency, human fibrinogen in doses of 4–6 gm may be given IV, but the risk of hepatitis is considerable. Platelet concentrates may be used in severe platelet deficiency.

Prognosis

In fibrinogen deficiency due to liver disease or cancer, the prognosis is usually that of the underlying disorder. Excessive bleeding during brain or lung surgery or at delivery may be completely and permanently corrected by intravenous administration of fibrinogen if fibrinolysins have not been activated.

Abildgaard, C.F.: Recognition and treatment of intravascular coagulation. J Pediat 74:163–176, 1969.
Deykin, D.: The clinical challenge of disseminated intravascular coagulation. New England J Med 283:636–644, 1970.
Verstraete, M., & others: Excessive consumption of blood coagulation components as cause of hemorrhagic diathesis. Am J Med 38:899, 1965.

ACQUIRED PROTHROMBIN COMPLEX DISORDERS
(Factors V, VII, X, & Prothrombin)

Essentials of Diagnosis

- Ecchymoses and epistaxis, spontaneously or after minimal trauma.
- Postoperative wound hemorrhage.
- Bleeding from venepuncture.

General Considerations

In all of these disorders an underlying process is usually evident, eg, liver disease or anticoagulant therapy. Regardless of which member of the prothrombin complex is deficient (prothrombin, factors V, VII, or X), the Quick prothrombin time is prolonged.

There are 3 forms of prothrombin complex deficiency.

A. Vitamin K Deficiency: This may be seen in obstructive jaundice, in the malabsorption syndrome, after prolonged antibiotic therapy, in hemorrhagic diseases of the newborn, and following continued ingestion, therapeutic or surreptitious, of coumadin anticoagulants. The pattern of vitamin K deficiency is characterized by reduction of factors II, VII, and X but not of factor V.

B. Severe Liver Disease: There is primarily a deficiency of factor V, but factors II, VII, IX, and X may also be low.

C. Excessive Utilization: See Intravascular Coagulation.

Clinical Findings

A. Symptoms and Signs: There is no previous history of hemorrhagic manifestations. Ecchymoses and epistaxis may occur spontaneously or after minimal trauma. Gastrointestinal bleeding and postoperative wound hemorrhage are common. Bleeding into joints does not occur.

B. Laboratory Findings: The Quick prothrombin time measures deficiencies in any member of the prothrombin complex, ie, if there is a deficiency in prothrombin, factor V, factor VII, or factor X, or if the fibrinogen levels are less than 125 mg/100 ml, the prothrombin time will be prolonged. Conversely, if the prothrombin time is normal one can assume that all prothrombin complex components are adequate. Specific tests for these factors are of value when a congenital defect is suspected or when the underlying cause of the prolonged prothrombin time is not evident.

In these acquired prothrombin complex disorders the prothrombin time is usually below 40–50%; surgical bleeding may occur below 50%; spontaneous bleeding at 10–15%. Prothrombin consumption, coagulation time, bleeding time, capillary fragility, and clot retraction are normal unless there is associated thromboplastin deficiency.

Treatment

A. General Measures: Deficiency due to vitamin K lack or coumarin compound excess is successfully treated by cessation of coumarin therapy and administration of appropriate medication. The deficiency of liver disease, however, does not respond to vitamin K. Replacement therapy with whole blood or plasma is generally unsatisfactory because of the lability of factor V in vitro and the very rapid disappearance rate of factor VII in vivo.

B. Vitamin K:

1. Phytonadione (fat-soluble vitamin K_1; Mephyton®) for the treatment of coumadin excess—To re-

store prolonged prothrombin time to normal, give 5 mg orally. For major bleeding, 10—15 mg of Aqua-Mephyton® given slowly IV at a rate not exceeding 10 mg/minute will shorten the prothrombin time in 2 hours and produce safe therapeutic levels in 4—6 hours.

2. Synthetic, water-soluble vitamin K (menadione sodium bisulfite [Hykinone®], menadiol [Synkayvite®]) is used for the treatment of vitamin K deficiency due to malabsorption. The dosage is 5 mg daily.

Prognosis

Vitamin K deficiency and the effect of coumarin excess can be corrected by parenteral or oral administration of vitamin K. The prognosis in other conditions depends upon the underlying disorder.

Deykin, D.: Heparin therapy. New England J Med 283:691—694, 801—803, 1970.

O'Reilly, R.A., & P.M. Aggeler: Surreptitious ingestion of coumarin anticoagulant drugs. Ann Int Med 64:1034—1041, 1966.

CIRCULATING ANTICOAGULANTS

Essentials of Diagnosis

- Ecchymoses.
- Gastrointestinal bleeding.
- Hemarthroses.
- Prolonged coagulation time.

General Considerations

A circulating anticoagulant is an abnormal blood component which inhibits the coagulation of normal blood. Most circulatory anticoagulants interfere with thromboplastin formation, probably by immune antibody production; the majority are directed against AHF and occur either in patients with hemophilia after many transfusions or spontaneously and transiently 8—10 weeks after obstetric delivery. Other circulatory anticoagulants interfere with the action of thromboplastin and may be associated with lupus erythematosus and similar disorders. Circulating anticoagulants may appear at any age and in either sex.

Clinical Findings

A. Symptoms and Signs: Patients develop sudden spontaneous hemorrhages characterized by ecchymoses, subcutaneous and intramuscular hematomas, hematuria, hemarthroses, gastrointestinal bleeding, and bleeding into the tongue and pharynx. Abnormal uterine bleeding may occur in women.

B. Laboratory Findings: In all patients the coagulation time is prolonged (30 minutes to several hours), but once a clot forms it is of good quality and contracts normally. Prothrombin consumption is decreased. Prothrombin time is normal in the hemophilia-like group but may be prolonged in the type of circu-

lating anticoagulants seen in lupus erythematosus. Bleeding time and platelet counts are normal. The thromboplastin generation test shows abnormal plasma phase but normal serum phase. The existence of circulatory anticoagulants can only be proved if relatively small amounts (20—40%) of patient's blood or plasma inhibit coagulation of normal blood or plasma. If circulating anticoagulants are present only in small amounts, more refined methods of demonstrating the inhibitor effect are necessary.

Differential Diagnosis

Coagulation time is prolonged also in hemophilia, fibrinogen deficiency, and in the presence of fibrinolysins. However, in fibrinogen deficiency or in the presence of fibrinolysins, either no clot forms at all or it forms at a normal rate and then lyses or contracts to a small nubbin. Another group of inhibitors of coagulation causing hemorrhagic phenomena (chiefly petechiae, epistaxis, and abnormal uterine bleeding) are the abnormal proteins, macroglobulins, myelomas, and cryoglobulins.

Treatment

The therapy of a bleeding hemophiliac with a circulating anticoagulant to AHF may require massive doses of AHF concentrate (Hyland Antihemophilic Factor-Method Four) to overload the inhibitor.

Prednisolone orally in relatively large doses (15—20 mg 4 times daily) may be tried, especially in cases associated with autoimmune phenomena, eg, lupus erythematosus.

Prognosis

The presence of circulating anticoagulants in the blood is a severe and dangerous disorder. If anticoagulants develop in the course of hemophilia, the outcome is often fatal. Circulating anticoagulants which develop after pregnancy disappear spontaneously after several months.

Margolius, A., & others: Circulating anticoagulants. Medicine 40:145—202, 1961.

BLOOD TRANSFUSIONS

Blood transfusions are used to restore blood volume after hemorrhage; to improve the oxygen carrying capacity of the blood in severe chronic anemia; and to combat shock in acute hemolytic anemia. Blood volume or red cell mass should be restored to approximately 70% of normal after hemorrhage. Adequate oxygen-carrying capacity can usually be maintained in chronic anemia by raising the hemoglobin value to 50—70% of normal. Shock in acute hemolytic or acute aplastic anemia can be prevented by maintaining hemoglobin values at 50—70% of normal.

Amount of Blood for Transfusion

A. Adults: Two units of whole blood or red cell mass will raise the hemoglobin by 2—3 gm in the average adult (70 kg) (red blood count 0.8—1 million/cu mm, hematocrit 8—9%). (Ten ml/kg of whole blood or 5 ml/kg of cells will produce a 10% hemoglobin rise.)

B. Children:

1. Over 25 kg—Give 500 ml of whole blood or 400 ml of red cells.

2. Under 25 kg—Give 20 ml/kg of whole blood or 15 ml/kg of red cells.

3. Premature infants—Give 10 ml/kg of whole blood or red cells.

Rate of Transfusion

Except in the case of emergencies, blood should be given at a rate of 80—100 drops/minute, or 500 ml in 1½—2 hours. For rapid transfusions, it is best to use a 15 gauge needle and allow the blood to run freely. The use of pressure is dangerous unless it can be applied by gentle compression of collapsible plastic blood containers.

Serologic Considerations

The antigens for which routine testing should always be performed in donors and recipients are A, B, and D (Rh_o). Pretransfusion compatibility tests use the serum of the recipient and the cells of the donor (major cross-match). To ensure a maximal margin of safety, each transfusion should be preceded by a 3-part compatibility procedure: (1) at room temperature in saline; (2) at 37° C fortified by the addition of albumin; and (3) at 37° C followed by an antiglobulin test.

Miscellaneous Considerations

The age of the blood (within the expiration period) is relatively unimportant in restoring volume deficits or repairing oxygen-carrying capacity defects. Fresh blood is required only if functioning platelets are needed; relatively fresh blood (less than 4 days old) is used in exchange transfusions. Red cell mass (hematocrit about 70%), infused through 17—18 gauge needles, is the treatment of choice in chronic anemias. Precipitates of platelets, leukocytes, and fibrinogen or fibrin in some bank bloods may clog the filters in administration sets and cause the infusion rate to slow down; when this happens, the filters should be replaced.

General principles of blood transfusion. Transfusion 3:301—346, 1963.

TRANSFUSIONS IN BLEEDING DISORDERS

Blood plasma is not adequate for the treatment of coagulation disorders. Even though the various clotting factors, except platelets and factors V and VIII, are stable in bank blood, they are not present in sufficient concentration to repair a deficiency. The various con-

centrates described above (Table 9—8) may have to be used. No concentrates exist for factors V and XI.

When over 10 units of bank blood have to be given in a few hours, the levels of factors V and VIII may decrease sufficiently to cause prolongation of the PTT, but they usually do not fall below hemostatically adequate levels. Thrombocytopenic bleeding may become a problem and may have to be treated. Platelet concentrates are available in 30 ml volumes and contain 3/4 of the platelets formed in a unit of fresh blood. Two units of platelet concentrate will raise the platelet count by approximately 15,000/cu mm 1 hour after infusion in an average sized adult; 8 units are the minimum effective dose. Compatibility tests are not necessary for platelet concentrates; either type-specific or type O blood should be given.

Aggeler, P.M.: Physiologic basis for transfusion therapy in hemorrhagic disorders. Transfusion 1:71—86, 1961.

HEMOLYTIC TRANSFUSION REACTIONS

Essentials of Diagnosis

- Chills and fever during blood transfusion.
- Pain in the back, chest, or abdomen.
- Hemoglobinemia and hemoglobinuria.

General Considerations

In all significant hemolytic transfusion reactions there is immediate, grossly visible hemoglobinemia. A normal serum color during or immediately after a transfusion rules out hemolysis as the cause of even severe symptoms.

In transfusion reaction due to ABO incompatibility the donor cells are hemolyzed instantaneously in the general circulation. In reactions due to incompatibility in some of the other blood groups (such as Rh), hemolysis is more gradual and may last hours, most of the destruction occurring in the reticuloendothelial tissues.

Serious transfusion reactions are often caused by clerical errors such as improper labeling of specimens or improper identification of patients.

Incompatibility due to the less common blood group antibodies may be detected only by a Coombs test.

Clinical Findings

A. Symptoms and Signs: There may be chills and fever, and pain in the vein at the local injection site or in the back, chest, or abdomen. Anxiety, apprehension, and headache are common. In the anesthetized patient, spontaneous bleeding from different areas may be the only sign of a transfusion reaction.

B. Laboratory Findings: Post-transfusion blood counts fail to show the anticipated rise in hemoglobin; spherocytes may be present on the blood smear; and initial leukopenia at 1—2 hours is followed by a slight leukocytosis. Free hemoglobin can be detected within a few minutes. Methemalbumin, an acid hematin-albumin complex giving a brown color to the serum, may appear after a few hours and persist for several days. Elevated bilirubin levels, when present, are usually greatest 3—6 hours after the transfusion. Haptoglobin disappears from the serum. Hemoglobinuria and oliguria may occur.

After the reaction occurs it is essential to draw a fresh specimen from the patient, perform a direct Coombs test, and check it against the blood in the transfusion bottle (not the pilot tube) by the indirect Coombs test. If the indirect Coombs test is positive, exact identification of the offending antibody may be made by matching the patient's serum against a panel of known test cells. Unusual antibodies found in transfusion reactions are anti-c, anti-K (Kell), anti-E, anti-Fy^a (Duffy), anti-Le^a (Lewis), anti-Jk^a (Kidd), anti-C, and anti-P.

Differential Diagnosis

Transfusion in the presence of leukoagglutinins, which usually develop after 5 or more transfusions or after previous pregnancy, may cause severe chills and high fever. There is no fall in hematocrit, a cross-match is compatible, there are no pigmentary changes in the serum, and leuko-agglutinins can be demonstrated in vitro when the patient's serum is matched against several white cell donors. In allergic transfusion reactions, the above tests also are negative and no leuko-agglutinins are present.

Complications

Acute tubular necrosis and azotemia may follow a severe transfusion reaction.

Treatment

Hives, chills, and fever following the transfusion of blood are not necessarily due to hemolysis; if the patient's serum remains clear, the transfusion may be continued. However, once the diagnosis of hemolysis is well established by appropriate tests the main problems are to combat shock and treat possible renal damage.

A. Treatment of Shock: After antibody screening of the patient's serum, transfusions with properly matched blood may be advisable. If no satisfactory answer can be found to the reason for the transfusion reaction, plasma expanders, such as dextran, and plasma may have to be used instead of whole blood. Pressor agents may be necessary.

B. Treatment of Renal Failure: Some studies suggest that osmotic diuretics such as mannitol can prevent renal failure following a hemolytic transfusion re-action. After an apparent reaction and in oliguric patients, a test dose of 12.5 gm of mannitol (supplied as 25% solution in 50 ml ampules) is administered IV over a period of 3—5 minutes; this dose may be repeated if no signs of circulatory overload develop. A satisfactory urinary output following the use of mannitol is 60 ml/hour or more. Mannitol can be safely administered as a continuous intravenous infusion; each liter of 5—10% mannitol should be alternated with 1 liter of normal saline to which 40 mEq of KCl have been added to prevent serious salt depletion. If oliguria develops despite these efforts, treat as for acute renal failure.

Prognosis

The hemolysis is self-limited. Renal involvement is comparatively infrequent. The death rate from hemolytic transfusion reactions is about 10%.

Davidsohn, I., & K. Stern: Blood transfusion reactions: Their causes and identification. M Clin North America 44:281—292, 1960.

•   •   •

MANIFESTATIONS INVOLVING THE BLOOD & LYMPHATIC SYSTEM DUE TO PARASITIC DISEASES

Severe anemias: Malaria, trypanosomiasis, visceral leishmaniasis, schistosomiasis, hookworm disease, fish tapeworm (Diphyllobothrium), trichinosis.

Leukopenia: Visceral leishmaniasis, malaria.

Eosinophilia: Helminthiases, especially clonorchiasis, strongyloidiasis, trichinosis, echinococcosis, ascariasis, schistosomiasis, fasciolopsiasis, onchocerciasis, filariasis, larva migrans, and gnathostomiasis.

Generalized lymph node enlargement: African trypanosomiasis, acquired toxoplasmosis, filariasis.

Regional lymph node enlargement: African (posterior cervical, Winterbottom's sign) and American (chancral) trypanosomiasis; filariasis.

Lymphadenitis: American trypanosomiasis, filariasis (recurrent).

Lymphangitis: Filariasis (recurrent).

Lymphatic obstruction and elephantiasis: Filariasis.

Splenomegaly: Malaria (especially chronic), visceral leishmaniasis, schistosomiasis japonicum, trypanosomiasis, toxoplasmosis, ascariasis (with Löffler's syndrome), filariasis.

Conrad, M.E.: Hematologic manifestations of parasitic diseases. Seminars Hematol 8:267—303, 1971.

• • •

General Bibliography

Biggs, R., & R.G. MacFarlane: *Treatment of Haemophilia and Other Coagulation Disorders.* Davis, 1966.

Cartwright, G.E.: *Diagnostic Laboratory Hematology,* 4th ed. Grune & Stratton, 1967.

Dacie, J.V.: *The Hemolytic Anemias. I. Congenital Hemolytic Anemias. II. The Auto-immune Hemolytic Anemias. III. Secondary and Symptomatic. IV. Drug-induced, PNH, Hemolytic Disease of the Newborn.* Churchill, 1960, 1962, 1967.

DeGruchy, G.C.: *Clinical Haematology in Medical Practice,* 3rd ed. Blackwell, 1970.

Harris, J.W., & R.W. Kellermeyer: *The Red Cell: Production, Metabolism, Destruction, Normal and Abnormal,* rev ed. Harvard, 1970.

Karnowsky, D.C., & R.W. Rawson: Symposium on medical advances in cancer. M Clin North America 50:611–912, 1966.

Mollison, P.L.: *Blood Transfusion in Clinical Medicine,* 4th ed. Davis, 1967.

Rapaport, H.: *Tumors of the Hematopoietic System.* Armed Forces Institute of Pathology, 1966.

Wintrobe, M.M.: *Clinical Hematology,* 6th ed. Lea & Febiger, 1967.

10 . . .

Gastrointestinal Tract & Liver

John V. Carbone, Lloyd L. Brandborg, George B. Hamilton,
Sol Silverman, Jr., Milton J. Chatton, & John L. Wilson

NONSPECIFIC MANIFESTATIONS

HALITOSIS
("Bad Breath")

Halitosis can result from many causes, including improper oral hygiene; chronic nasal and sinus disease; dental caries, gum infections, tonsillar infections; systemic diseases, fevers, and toxemias; chronic pulmonary disease (eg, lung abscess); gastrointestinal disease at almost any level of the gastrointestinal tract; and neuropsychiatric disorders where only the subjective complaint of "bad breath" is present.

Treatment is directed at the underlying cause. Thorough brushing of the teeth after each meal and the use of mouth washes may provide transient benefit.

PYROSIS
("Heartburn")

Pyrosis, a disagreeable substernal burning pain, may result from any irritating stimulus of the distal esophagus. Its most important association is with reflux of acid-peptic gastric contents, ie, peptic esophagitis. The incidence of heartburn in pregnancy is very high (42–48%). Heartburn tends to improve in the final weeks of pregnancy and to disappear shortly after delivery.

Antacids are often effective in relieving symptoms, although it is not clear that they act by neutralizing gastric hydrochloric acid. The treatment is usually small dry meals, elevation of the head of the bed, maintaining an erect position after eating, weight reduction, and avoidance of tight clothing (eg, girdles and belts).

Briggs, D.W.: Heartburn of pregnancy. Practitioner 200:824–857, 1968.

NAUSEA & VOMITING

These symptoms may occur singly or concurrently, and may be due to a wide variety of causes. Reflex causes excite the vomiting center by disturbing gastrointestinal structures and other viscera. Correction is therefore dependent upon treatment of the underlying cause: irritation, inflammation, or mechanical disturbance at any level of the gastrointestinal tract (from pharynx to rectum); irritating impulses arising in any diseased viscera, eg, cholecystitis; disturbances of semicircular canals, eg, seasickness; and toxic action of cardiac drugs, eg, digitalis. Central (vomiting center) causes include central emetics (emetine, apomorphine, morphine); exogenous and endogenous toxins, increased intracranial pressure, and cerebral hypoxia due to cerebral anemia or hemorrhage. Psychic causes may have either a superficial or deep-seated basis.

Treatment

A. Acute: Simple acute vomiting such as occurs following dietary indiscretion or in the morning sickness of early pregnancy may require little or no treatment. When necessary, treatment consists of prescribing simple tolerated foods and, occasionally, mild sedative and antispasmodic drugs.

B. Prolonged: Severe or prolonged nausea and vomiting requires careful medical management. Specific causes must be corrected. The following general measures may be utilized as adjuncts to specific medical or surgical measures:

1. Fluids and nutrition—Maintain adequate hydration and nutrition. Withhold foods temporarily and give 5–10% glucose in saline solution or water intravenously. When oral feedings are resumed, begin with dry foods in small quantities, eg, salted crackers, graham crackers. With "morning sickness" these foods may best be taken before arising. Later, change to frequent small feedings of simple, palatable foods. Hot beverages (tea and clear broths) and cold beverages (iced tea and carbonated liquids, especially ginger ale) are tolerated quite early. Avoid lukewarm beverages. Always consider the patient's food preferences.

2. Medical measures—*Note:* All unnecessary medication should be withheld from pregnant women during the critical early phase of fetal development. Unless the nausea and vomiting of pregnancy is severe or progressive, caution should be observed in using medication for this purpose. The possible teratogenic effects of many classes of drugs are now being investigated.

(1) Sedative-antispasmodic drugs may be of value.

(2) Chlorpromazine hydrochloride (Thorazine®) and promazine hydrochloride (Sparine®) may be administered deeply IM in doses of 25–50 mg every 4–6 hours as necessary, or orally in doses of 10–50 mg every 4–6 hours as necessary.

(3) Prochlorperazine (Compazine®), 5 mg 3–4 times daily orally when feasible; 25 mg by rectal suppository twice daily; or 5–10 mg deeply into buttocks every 3–4 hours (not exceeding 40 mg/24 hours), has been reported to be valuable.

(4) Triflupromazine (Vesprin®), 5–10 mg IM; 10 mg every 6–8 hours orally.

(5) Fluphenazine (Permitil®, Prolixin®), 1–3 mg IM; 1–3 mg orally.

(6) Perphenazine (Trilafon®), 2–4 mg 4 times daily.

(7) Trifluoperazine (Stelazine®), 1–2 mg daily.

3. Psychotherapy may be of value if emesis appears to have a psychic basis. Isolation of the patient is recommended if symptoms become chronic. Hospitalization may be necessary. Visiting should be restricted. Avoid unpleasant psychic stimuli such as strange odors, foul-smelling or foul-tasting medication, emesis basins or other unattractive objects, and foods which are improperly prepared or served. Place the patient on a definite treatment program and let it be known that something is being done. "Hard-boiled" or brutal technics are to be avoided. Attempt to determine the psychic basis of the nausea and vomiting, but avoid aggressive psychotherapy during the acute phase of the illness.

Lumsden, K., & W.S. Holden: The act of vomiting in man. Gut 10:173–179, 1969.

HICCUP
(Singultus)

Hiccup, usually a benign, transient phenomenon, may occur as a manifestation of many diseases. It is important to rule out specific causes such as neuroses, CNS disorders, cardiorespiratory disorders, gastrointestinal disorders, renal failure, infectious diseases, and other diseases. It may be the only symptom of peptic esophagitis.

Treatment

Countless measures have been suggested for interrupting the rhythmic reflex that produces hiccup. None of these may be successful, however, and the symptom may be so prolonged and severe as to jeopardize the patient's life.

A. Simple Home Remedies: These measures probably act by diverting the patient's attention; they consist of distracting conversation, fright, painful or

unpleasant stimuli, or of having the patient perform such apparently purposeless procedures as holding his breath, sipping ice water, or inhaling strong fumes.

B. Medical Measures:

1. Sedation–Any of the common sedative drugs may be effective, eg, pentobarbital sodium, 0.1 gm orally or 0.13 gm by rectal suppository.

2. Local anesthetics (viscous lidocaine [Xylocaine®]) may be of some use. General anesthesia may be tried in intractable cases.

3. Antispasmodics–Atropine sulfate, 0.3–0.6 mg, may be given subcut.

4. Amyl nitrite inhalations may be effective.

5. CO_2 inhalations–Have the patient rebreathe into a paper bag for 3–5 minutes, or give 10–15% CO_2 mixture by face mask for 3–5 minutes.

6. Tranquilizers–Chlorpromazine hydrochloride (Thorazine®) and promazine hydrochloride (Sparine®) have been used successfully for prolonged or intractable hiccup.

7. Antacids.

C. Surgical Measures: Various phrenic nerve operations, including bilateral phrenicotomy, may be indicated in extreme cases which fail to respond to all other measures and which are considered to be a threat to life.

Souadjian, J.V., & J.C. Cain: Intractable hiccup: Etiologic factors in 220 cases. Postgrad MJ 43:72–80, 1968.

CONSTIPATION

Specific causes of constipation include colonic or rectal lesions, hypometabolism, and neuroses. Be especially suspicious of organic causes when there are sudden unexplained changes in bowel habits. Inadequate fluids and low-residue diets may have a constipating effect. Constipation is a frequent complication of physical inactivity or prolonged bed rest. The following commonly used drugs may cause constipation: belladonna and derivatives, narcotics, diuretics, salts of bismuth, calcium, and iron, and aluminum hydroxide or aluminum phosphate gels.

Treatment

The patient should be told that a daily bowel movement is not essential to health or well-being. So-called "auto-intoxication" theories are unfounded, and many symptoms (eg, lack of "pep") attributed to constipation have no such relationship.

A. Reestablishment of Regular Evacuation: Set aside a regular period after a meal (preferably breakfast) for a bowel movement, even when the urge to defecate is not present. Cathartics and enemas should not be used for simple constipation since they interfere with the normal bowel reflexes. If it seems inadvisable to withdraw such measures suddenly from a patient who has employed them for a long time, bland laxatives and mild enemas (see below) can be used temporarily. Cathartic and enema "addicts" often defy all medical measures, and treatment is especially difficult when there is a serious underlying psychiatric disturbance.

B. Diet: The diet may be modified to satisfy the following requirements:

1. Adequate volume—Often "constipation" is merely due to inadequate food intake.

2. Adequate bulk or residue—This does not necessarily imply "roughage" such as bran. Smooth or bland foods may be preferred in "spastic" constipation.

3. Vegetable irritants—Unless there is a specific contraindication (eg, intolerance), stewed or raw fruits or vegetables may be of value, especially in the "atonic" type of constipation.

4. Adequate fluids—The patient should be encouraged to drink adequate quantities of fluids so that sufficient water will be available in the intestinal tract for passage of intestinal contents. Six to 8 glasses of fluid per day, in addition to the fluid content of foods, are ordinarily sufficient. A glass of hot water taken ½ hour before breakfast seems to exert a mild laxative effect.

C. Exercise: Moderate physical exercise is essential. Bed patients may require active and passive exercises. Good tone of the external abdominal muscles is important. Corrective physical therapy may be employed in patients with protuberant abdomens.

D. Medications: Bland laxatives may be employed temporarily. They should be withdrawn as soon as the constipation improves. The bulk-producing laxatives must be administered with an adequate or high fluid intake.

1. Liquid petrolatum (mineral oil), 15—30 ml 1—2 times daily as needed. Do not use mineral oil over prolonged periods, since it may interfere with intestinal absorption, particularly fat-soluble vitamins. There is also a slight risk of lipoid pneumonia, even from its oral use.

2. Agar with mineral oil, 15—30 ml 1—2 times daily as needed.

3. Olive oil, 15—30 ml 1—2 times daily as needed.

4. Vegetable mucilages, eg, psyllium hydrophilic mucilloid (Metamucil®), 4—12 ml 2—3 times daily after meals in a full glass of water.

5. Cascara sagrada aromatic fluid extract, 4—8 ml at bedtime.

6. Magnesia magma (milk of magnesia), 15—30 ml at bedtime.

7. Sodium phosphate, 4—8 gm in hot water before breakfast.

8. Dioctyl sodium sulfosuccinate (Colace®, Doxinate®), a surface wetting agent, in recommended doses varying from 50—480 mg/day.

9. Bisacodyl (Dulcolax®), a colonic contact laxative, 10—15 mg at bedtime.

E. Enemas: Because they interfere with restoration of a normal bowel reflex, enemas should ordinarily be used only as a temporary expedient in chronic constipation or fecal impaction. In some instances it may be necessary to administer enemas, as required, for a prolonged period.

1. Saline enema (nonirritating)—Warm physiologic saline solution, 500—2000 ml as necessary.

2. Warm tap water (irritating)—500—1000 ml as necessary.

3. Soapsuds (SS) enema (irritating)—75 ml of soap solution per liter of water.

4. Oil retention enema—180 ml of mineral oil or vegetable oil instilled in the rectum in the evening and retained overnight. The oil is evacuated the following morning. This is continued until a "bowel rhythm" is reestablished.

Hinton, J.M., & J.E. Lennard-Jones: Constipation: Definition and classification. Postgrad MJ 44:720—723, 1968.

FECAL IMPACTION

Hardened or putty-like stools in the rectum or colon may interfere with the normal passage of feces; if the impaction is not removed manually, by enemas, or by surgery, it can constitute partial or complete intestinal obstruction. The impaction may be due to organic causes (painful anorectal disease, tumor, or neurogenic disease of the colon) or to functional causes (bulk laxatives, antacids, residual barium from x-ray study, low-residue diet, starvation, drug-induced colonic stasis, or prolonged bed rest and debility). The patient may give a history of obstipation, but more frequently there is a history of watery diarrhea. There may be blood or mucus in the stool. Physical examination may reveal a distended abdomen, palpable "tumors" in the abdomen, and a firm stool in the rectum. The impaction may be broken up digitally or dislodged with a sigmoidoscope. Cleansing enemas (preferably in the knee-chest position) or, in the case of impaction higher in the colon, colonic irrigations may be of value. Daily oil retention enemas followed by digital fragmentation of the impaction and saline enemas may be necessary.

FLATULENCE
(Tympanites)

Eliminate specific causes of flatulence. Gastrointestinal gas is in large part due to swallowed air (aerophagia). However, flatulence may be due to dietary causes and functional and organic disease of the digestive system.

Treatment

A. Correction of Aerophagia: Anxiety states are often associated with deep breathing and sighing and the consequent swallowing of considerable quantities of air. When possible, treat underlying anxiety features.

B. Correction of Physical Defects: These sometimes interfere with normal swallowing or breathing. (1) Structural deformities of the nose and nasopharynx, eg, nasal obstruction and adenoids. (2) Spatial defects of the teeth or ill-fitting dentures.

C. Good Hygiene and Eating Habits: Instruct the patient to avoid dietary indiscretions, eating too rapidly and too much, eating while under emotional strain, drinking large quantities of liquids with meals, taking laxatives, and chewing gum.

D. Diet: The diet should be nutritious as tolerated and enjoyed by the patient. Milk and milk products such as milk shakes may lead to excessive flatulence.

E. Medications: Drugs are, in general, unsatisfactory, and at times are only of placebo value.

1. Anticholinergic-sedative drugs—These agents serve to diminish the flow of saliva (which is often excessive in these patients), thereby reducing the aerophagia which accompanies swallowing.

2. Spirit of peppermint, 0.5 ml 3 times daily in a small glass of water after meals.

3. Sedatives.

Berk, J.E. (editor): Gastrointestinal gas. Ann New York Acad Sc 150:1–190, 1968.

Weinstein, L., & others: Diet as related to gastrointestinal function. JAMA 176:935–941, 1961.

DIARRHEA

Etiology

The causes of diarrhea may be classified as follows:

(1) Psychogenic disorders: "Nervous" diarrhea.

(2) Intestinal: Viral enteritis, amebiasis, heavy metal poisoning, catharsis habituation, gastrocolic fistula, fecal impaction, carcinoma, chronic ulcerative colitis; salmonellosis, shigellosis, giardiasis, coccidiosis, and other parasitic diseases.

(3) Malabsorption: Celiac sprue, vagotomy, small bowel syndrome.

(4) Pancreatic disease: Pancreatic insufficiency.

(5) Biliary tract disorders: Choledochoduodenostomy.

(6) Reflex from other viscera: Pelvic pathology (extrinsic to gastrointestinal tract).

(7) Neurologic disease: Tabes dorsalis, diabetic neuropathy.

(8) Metabolic disease: Hyperthyroidism.

(9) Globulin deficiencies.

(10) Unknown cause: Diarrhea of travelers.

Treatment

Eliminate the specific cause whenever possible.

A. Correct Physiologic Changes Induced by Diarrhea: In addition to the necessity for control of hyperperistalsis, it is essential that the following secondary or complicating features be treated.

1. Fluid imbalance (dehydration).

2. Mineral imbalance (eg, hypocalcemia, hypokalemia, hyponatremia).

3. Nutritional disturbances (eg, hypoproteinemia and other deficiencies).

4. Psychogenic disturbances (eg, fixation on gastrointestinal tract or anxiety regarding sphincter mishaps in cases of long-standing diarrhea).

B. Diet:

1. Acute—Most clinicians feel that food should be withheld for the first 24 hours or restricted to clear liquids. Frequent small soft feedings are added as tolerated.

2. Convalescent—Food should be incorporated into the diets of patients convalescing from acute diarrhea as tolerated. Nutritious food, preferably all cooked, in small frequent meals, is usually well tolerated. *Avoid* raw vegetables and fruits, fried foods, bran, whole grain cereals, preserves, syrups, candies, pickles, relishes, spices, coffee, and alcoholic beverages.

A diet free of milk and milk products and all foods cooked is a restricted diet. These patients may require vitamin supplements if this diet is prolonged.

C. Antidiarrheal Agents:

1. Bismuth preparations—Any of the following may be used for acute or chronic diarrheas:

a. Bismuth subcarbonate, 1–2 gm, after liquid bowel movements or 4 times daily.

b. Bismuth magma (bismuth hydroxide and subcarbonate), 4 ml after liquid bowel movements or 4 times daily.

c.

℞ Bismuth subcarbonate	15–30.0
Paregoric, q s ad	120.0

Sig: Shake well. One tsp after liquid bowel movements or 4 times daily.

d. Milk of bismuth and paregoric (equal amounts of each) may be substituted for the above mixture, using the same dose.

e. (Modified after Bockus)

℞ Belladonna extract	0.5
Bismuth subcarbonate	
Calcium lactate	
Kaolin, $\overline{aa}$	30.0
Peppermint oil	2 drops

Sig: One tsp 3 times daily, before meals and at bedtime, or after liquid bowel movements as needed.

2. Pectin-kaolin compounds—Useful proprietary mixtures are available (eg, Kaopectate®). Give 15–30 ml 3 times daily, before meals and at bedtime, or after liquid bowel movements as needed.

3. Diphenoxylate with atropine (Lomotil®), 2.5 mg 3–4 times daily as needed, is an effective antidiarrheal agent, but it must be used cautiously in patients with advanced liver disease and in those taking barbiturates and other addicting drugs.

4. Opiates must be avoided in chronic diarrheas and are preferably avoided in acute diarrheas unless there is intractable diarrhea, vomiting, and colic. Always exclude the possibility of acute surgical abdominal disease before administering opiates. Give either of the following:

a. Paregoric, 4–8 ml after liquid movements as needed or with bismuth (see above).

b. Codeine phosphate, 15–65 mg subcut after liquid bowel movements as needed.

5. Strong opiates—Morphine and dihydromorphinone should be reserved for selected patients with severe acute diarrhea who fail to respond to more conservative measures.

a. Morphine sulfate, 8–15 mg subcut after liquid bowel movements as needed. This drug may produce nausea and vomiting.

b. Dihydromorphinone hydrochloride (Dilaudid®) may be substituted for morphine. Give 2–3 mg IM after liquid bowel movements as needed.

6. Antispasmodic-sedative drugs are frequently useful. The antispasmodic drugs, particularly when used in combination with the barbiturates, exert a mild antiperistaltic action in acute and chronic diarrheas associated with anxiety tension states. It may be necessary to administer the various belladonna or belladonna-like alkaloids to a point near toxicity in order to achieve the desired effect.

D. Psychotherapy: Many cases of chronic diarrhea are of psychogenic origin. A survey of anxiety-producing mechanisms should be made in all patients with this complaint.

Conn, H.O., & R. Quintiliani: Severe diarrhea controlled by gamma globulin in a patient with agammaglobulinemia, amyloidosis and thymoma. Ann Int Med 65:528–541, 1966.

Eichenwald, H.F., & G.H. McCracken, Jr.: Acute diarrheal disease. M Clin North America 54:443–453, 1970.

Fordtran, J.S.: Speculations on the pathogenesis of diarrhea. Fed Proc 26:1405–1414, 1967.

Turner, A.C.: Traveller's diarrhoea: A survey of symptoms, occurrence, and possible prophylaxis. Brit MJ 2:653–654, 1967.

PSYCHOLOGIC GASTROINTESTINAL DISORDERS

This common group of disorders has many names, eg, nervous indigestion, functional dyspepsia, pylorospasm, colonic irritability, spastic colitis, functional colitis, mucous colitis, intestinal neurosis, and laxative or cathartic colitis. All or a portion of the gastrointestinal tract may be involved. These disorders are characterized by hyperirritability and altered motility and secretion of the gastrointestinal tract, and they have a common origin in psychic factors or abnormal living habits (or both).

It is essential to eliminate the possibility of organic gastrointestinal disease. A history of "nervousness," neuropathic traits, and emotional disturbances can usually be obtained. The patient's living habits are irregular and unhygienic, eg, improper diet and irregular meals. Bowel consciousness and cathartic and enema habits are a prominent feature. There is a highly variable complex of gastrointestinal symptoms: nausea and vomiting, anorexia, foul breath, sour stomach, flatulence, cramps, and constipation or diarrhea, and a definite relationship can usually be established between symptoms and emotional stress or strain.

Nocturnal diarrhea, awakening the patient from a sound sleep, almost invariably is due to organic disease of the bowel.

Examination discloses generalized abdominal tenderness (variable), particularly along the course of the colon. X-ray shows sphincter spasm and altered gastrointestinal motility without other evidence of abnormalities.

Treatment

A. Diet: No single diet is applicable to all of these patients. Exclusion of milk and milk products may prove helpful. All foods should be cooked.

B. Personal Habits and Hygiene: Regular hours and meals and adequate sleep, exercise, and recreation are important. Restriction of alcohol and tobacco may be indicated.

C. Symptomatic Treatment: Sedative-antispasmodic medication is of particular value in these disorders.

(1)

R Tincture of belladonna   10–30.0
Elixir of phenobarbital, q s ad   120.0

Sig: One tsp in ½ glass of water 3 times daily 20–30 minutes before meals and at bedtime as needed.

(2)

R Belladonna extract   0.008
Phenobarbital   0.015

Sig: One tablet 3 times daily 20–30 minutes before meals and at bedtime as needed.

D. Psychotherapy: This may consist of simple reassurance or more intensive technics. Reassurance as to the absence of organic disease, after careful examination, is most important.

Advances in methods and concepts of gastrointestinal motility. Gastroenterology 54:768–780, 1968.

Connell, A.M.: The irritable colon syndrome. Postgrad MJ 44:668–673, 1968.

De Lor, C.J.: The irritable bowel syndrome. Am J Gastroenterol 47:427–434, 1967.

Hill, O.W.: Psychogenic vomiting. Gut 9:348–352, 1968.
Schuster, M.M.: Functional gastrointestinal disorders. GP 35:131–139, March 1967.

MASSIVE UPPER GASTROINTESTINAL HEMORRHAGE

Massive gastrointestinal hemorrhage is a common emergency. It may be defined as rapid loss of sufficient blood to cause hypovolemic shock. The actual volume of blood loss required to produce shock varies with the size, age, and general condition of the patient and with the rapidity of bleeding. Sudden loss of 20% or more of blood volume (blood volume is approximately 75 ml/kg of body weight) produces hypotension, tachycardia, and other signs of shock. For example, a previously well 70 kg man who develops shock as a result of gastrointestinal hemorrhage will have lost at least 1000–1500 ml of blood. The immediate objectives of management are (1) to restore an effective blood volume and (2) to establish a diagnosis on which definitive treatment can be based.

The major causes of gastrointestinal bleeding are peptic ulceration of the duodenum or stomach, esophageal varices, and gastritis. In addition, hemorrhagic gastritis due to an ulcerogenic drug such as aspirin is an extremely important cause of gastrointestinal bleeding.

Clinical Findings

A. Symptoms and Signs: There is usually a history of sudden weakness or fainting associated with or followed by tarry stools or vomiting of blood. Melena occurs in all patients, and hematemesis in over 50%. Hematemesis is especially common in esophageal varices (90%), gastritis, and gastric ulcer. The patient may or may not be in shock when first seen, but he will at least be pale and weak if major blood loss has occurred.

There is usually no pain, and the pain of peptic ulcer disease often stops with the onset of bleeding. Abdominal findings are not remarkable except when hepatomegaly, splenomegaly, or a mass (neoplasm) is present. There may be a history of peptic ulcer, cirrhosis, or other predisposing disease, but the history often gives no clue to the source of bleeding.

The etiology of bleeding should be established promptly, if possible, since the decision whether to operate or to continue with medical measures will often depend upon the diagnosis. The most critical differentiation is between peptic ulcer and esophageal varices, since emergency surgery may be indicated and successful in peptic ulcer but less often indicated or successful in varices. Specific diagnosis is of value also because of the difficulties of entering the abdomen in search of the unknown bleeding point.

A history of peptic ulcer or ingestion of antacids favors a diagnosis of peptic ulcer. A history of alcoholism or jaundice favors liver disease. Jaundice, hepatosplenomegaly, spider angiomas, liver palms, fetor hepaticus, ascites, and hepatic encephalopathy are suggestive of liver disease.

The principal diagnostic procedures in the investigation of upper gastrointestinal bleeding, to be carried out after instituting necessary emergency treatment, are outlined below.

B. Laboratory Findings: When the cause of the massive gastrointestinal hemorrhage cannot be established, certain laboratory studies should be conducted:

1. Liver function studies–Bilirubin, transaminases, serum protein electrophoresis, alkaline phosphatase, prothrombin time, and BSP retention determinations on the blood are useful in diagnosis of liver disease (portal hypertension and varices) as a possible cause of bleeding. Normal BSP retention practically excludes liver disease severe enough to produce varices.

2. Blood studies–Studies of the clotting mechanism, bleeding time, prothrombin concentration, and platelet count may prove useful in the obscure case of massive gastrointestinal bleeding.

C. Endoscopy: When varices are suspected, esophagoscopy may be useful. The procedure can be done on the operating table just before laparotomy if necessary. When both varices and peptic ulcer are seen on x-ray, esophagoscopy may help to decide the source of bleeding. Gastroscopy may also prove useful in certain instances where esophagoscopy and x-ray examination of the upper gastrointestinal tract have not established the source or location of the bleeding.

D. X-Ray Findings: The cause of upper gastrointestinal bleeding can be demonstrated on x-ray in about 75% of cases. All patients with upper gastrointestinal bleeding should have an upper gastrointestinal barium study at the earliest possible time. The examination is postponed only if there is active bleeding or shock. Selective angiography may be of value in localization of gastrointestinal hemorrhage.

Treatment

A. General Measures: The patient should be under the observation of both an internist and a surgeon from the outset. Blood is obtained immediately for complete blood count and hematocrit, as well as grouping and cross-matching of at least 3 or 4 units of blood. In interpreting the red blood count and hematocrit it should be kept in mind that, after acute blood loss, a period of 24–36 hours may be required for reequilibration of body fluids. Meanwhile, the hematocrit poorly reflects extent of blood loss. Blood volume determination may occasionally be helpful in estimating acute blood loss. Replacement therapy through a large intravenous needle (18 gauge minimum) or catheter is started immediately with lactated Ringer's solution or 5% dextrose in normal saline. If shock is severe, dextran or plasma is given while blood transfusion is being prepared. Blood pressure, pulse, and respiration are recorded every 15–60 minutes. Bed rest and charting of fluid intake, urine output, and temperature are ordered. Mild barbiturate sedation is provided if necessary, and vitamin K (menadiol sodium diphosphate [Synkayvite®], 5 mg orally daily) is given empirically if liver disease is suspected. Restlessness may be symptomatic of continued hemorrhage, shock, or hypoxia.

B. Blood Replacement: Treatment of shock by blood transfusion is begun without delay. Hematocrit or hemoglobin determinations are done every few hours until stabilized. The objective of blood replacement is to relieve shock and restore effective blood volume. The volume of blood required to accomplish this must be estimated empirically. Assume that blood volume is 75 ml/kg of body weight and calculate the patient's normal blood volume. If moderate shock is present (eg, blood pressure is 70–90, pulse rate 110–130, and there are clinical signs of hypovolemia such as faintness, pallor, cold and moist skin), transfusion equivalent to 25% of the normal blood volume will probably be required for resuscitation. If shock is severe, with blood pressure below 70, the initial volume of blood transfusion required may be 40–50% of normal blood volume. Shock should be controlled promptly and completely by rapid administration of blood. When blood pressure and pulse have been restored to relatively normal levels and clinical signs of hypovolemia have been relieved, blood transfusion may be slowed and the total volume of blood to be given is then determined by the course of the disease. A poor response usually means continued bleeding (see below) or inadequate replacement. A central venous pressure catheter is useful in gauging blood replacement and detection of over-transfusions and congestive heart failure.

C. Medical Measures: Acid peptic digestion is a causative or aggravating factor in many cases of massive upper gastrointestinal hemorrhage, including varices. Feedings and oral medications for ulcer are begun as soon as shock and nausea have subsided. Continued slight bleeding is no contraindication to the following regimen:

1. Diet–Liquid diet for the first 24 hours, followed by mechanically soft diet.

2. Antacids–Aluminum hydroxide-magnesium hydroxide mixture, 30 ml every hour. The clinician must be aware of the possibility of severe constipation and fecal impaction.

3. Other medications indicated include mild barbiturate sedation or chlordiazepoxide (Librium®).

4. Nasogastric tube insertion may be useful to permit evacuation of blood by lavage with ice water or an ice water-antacid mixture until returns are clear. Antacids may then be administered hourly through the tube, which is aspirated periodically to determine the presence of fresh blood.

D. Management of Bleeding Esophageal Varices: When varices are the cause of bleeding, special measures are indicated (see discussion of cirrhosis, p 350).

E. Indications for Emergency Operation: Except when esophageal varices are the cause of bleeding, emergency surgery to stop active bleeding should be considered under any of the following circumstances: (1) When the patient has received 2 liters or more of blood but shock is not controlled or recurs promptly. (2) When acceptable blood pressure and hematocrit cannot be maintained with a maximum of 500 ml of blood every 8 hours. (3) When bleeding is slow but persists more than 2–3 days. (4) When bleeding stops initially but recurs massively while the patient is receiving adequate medical treatment. (5) When the patient is over 50. It has been shown that the death rate from exsanguination in spite of conservative measures is greater in the older age group and rare in patients under 40. Massive bleeding is less well tolerated and is less likely to stop in older patients or small children, who will therefore require operative intervention more frequently.

Prognosis

The overall mortality of about 14% indicates the seriousness of massive upper gastrointestinal hemorrhage. Fatality rates vary greatly, depending upon the etiology of the bleeding and the presence of other serious systemic disease. Overall operative mortality for emergency surgery to stop bleeding is high, and best results are obtained when bleeding can be controlled medically and surgery deferred until the patient has recovered from the effects of the bleeding. Hemorrhage from duodenal ulcer causes death in about 3% of treated cases, whereas in bleeding varices the mortality rate may be as high as 50%.

Conn, H.O., & W.W. Lindenmuth: Prophylactic portacaval anastomosis in patients with esophageal varices. New England J Med 279:725–731, 1968.

Freeark, R.J., Norcross, W.J., & R.J. Baker: Exploratory gastrotomy in management of massive upper gastrointestinal hemorrhage. Arch Surg 94:684–695, 1967.

Frey, C.F., Reuter, S.R., & J.J. Bookstein: Localization of gastrointestinal hemorrhage by selective angiography. Surgery 67:548–555, 1970.

Goodman, A.A., & C.F. Frey: Massive upper gastrointestinal hemorrhage following surgical operations. Ann Surg 167:180–184, 1968.

Halmagyi, A.F.: A critical review of 425 patients with upper gastrointestinal hemorrhage. Surg Gynec Obst 130:419–430, 1970.

Mark, J.B., & others: Further experience with general body hypothermia in the treatment of massive gastrointestinal hemorrhage. Am J Surg 116:286–292, 1968.

Orloff, M.J.: Emergency portacaval shunt, varix ligation and nonsurgical treatment of bleeding esophageal varices in unselected patients with cirrhosis. Ann Surg 166:456–478, 1967.

Palmer, E.D.: The vigorous diagnostic approach to upper gastrointestinal tract hemorrhage. JAMA 207:1477–1480, 1969.

Sedgewick, C.E., & J.K. Vernon: Gastrointestinal bleeding: Diagnosis and management. S Clin North America 48:523–541, 1968.

Udall J.A.: Don't use the wrong vitamin K. California Med 112:65–67, April 1970.

Zollinger, R.M., & W.V. Nick: Upper gastrointestinal tract hemorrhage. JAMA 212:2251–2254, 1970.

DISEASES OF THE MOUTH

CARIES
(Dental Decay)

It is well established that 3 essentials are required to produce the carious lesion: bacteria, a substrate, and a susceptible tooth. Although animal studies indicate a relationship between caries and certain metabolic disorders, this association has not been confirmed in humans. Conditions that predispose to xerostomia (eg, tranquilizers and belladonna type drugs, Sjögren's syndrome, head and neck irradiation) may promote caries.

The diagnosis is based on x-ray examination (radiolucencies of the enamel and dentin) and clinical observation of an area of tooth structure that is soft, necrotic, discolored, and often sensitive. Both types of examination are necessary to a complete evaluation of the presence and extent of dental caries. There is no absolute correlation between extent of caries and symptoms. Absence of dental pain does not imply absence of caries.

Prevention & Treatment*

The following empiric approach is suggested:

(1) Restorative dentistry to remove decay is the single most important measure. Do not neglect caries in deciduous teeth, since bone infection or premature loss of these teeth affects the health and eventual positions of the permanent dentition.

(2) Proper mouth hygiene will reduce bacterial flora and substrate. Frequent brushing with dentifrices and the use of mouth rinses are both helpful. Electric toothbrushes increase efficiency in cleansing tooth surfaces, but a relationship to reduced caries incidence has not been proved. Therapeutic ingredients other than fluoride added to dentifrices have no recognized beneficial effects.

(3) Reduction of carbohydrate (mainly sucrose) and sticky foods (eg, jams, cookies, foods that tend to adhere to tooth surfaces for prolonged periods) will reduce available substrate and acid production and decalcification.

(4) Topical applications (by a dentist) of fluoride will form a more acid-resistant tooth structure (fluoroapatite instead of hydroxyapatite). This procedure should be considered if a clinical problem of caries control exists even if the patient has been exposed to a fluoridated water supply during dental development. If water supplies are not fluoridated, daily oral fluoride supplements are recommended for the child up to age 12 (during tooth development). (The amount of supplementation depends upon the concentration of fluoride occurring naturally in the water supply and should not exceed a total daily intake of 1 mg.)

The evidence available does not give clear support to the use of fluoride as a prenatal supplement for caries prevention in children.

Horowitz, H.S., & S.B. Heifetz: The current status of topical fluorides in preventive dentistry. J Am Dent A 81:166–177, 1970.
Keyes, P.H.: Present and future measures for dental caries control. J Am Dent A 79:1395–1404, 1969.

DISCOLORED TEETH

The most common causes of discolored teeth are food stains, bacteria, habits (such as tobacco use), and drugs. These can be managed by altering habits and by dental prophylaxis. There may be pulpal hemorrhage induced by trauma, resulting in a deposition of hemosiderin on the internal crown surface. This causes a darkening of the tooth which usually remains sterile and asymptomatic but nonvital. These teeth can be effectively bleached for esthetic reasons. Occasionally, however, discoloration is due to changes in tooth structure due to tetracyclines, erythroblastosis fetalis, congenital defects of enamel or dentin, and fluorosis.

Tetracyclines

Tetracycline discoloration occurs in some patients when these antibiotics (tetracycline, oxytetracycline, chlortetracycline, and demethylchlortetracycline) are given by mouth during the period of tooth development (infancy and childhood). Since an entire layer of dentin may be calcified in a few days, a small dosage over a short period may be incorporated into and appear to involve an entire tooth. The discoloration is gray-brown or yellow-brown. A typical yellow fluorescence is seen under ultraviolet light in undecalcified sections. A history of tetracycline ingestion can almost always be obtained.

The teeth are not harmed. Treatment (by a crown) is indicated only for esthetic reasons. Preliminary reports indicate that bleaching technics may be effective.

Because of the risk of discoloration, the use of tetracyclines during the period of tooth development should be avoided if possible.

Witkop, C.J., Jr., & R.P. Wolf: Hypoplasia and intrinsic staining of enamel following tetracycline therapy. JAMA 185:100–111, 1963.

*The ADA Council on Dental Therapeutics has classified Crest® toothpaste (stannous fluoride) and Colgate Dental Cream® (monofluorophosphate) under Group A, which consists of accepted products which will be listed in Accepted Dental Remedies. The ADA Council on Dental Materials and Devices has classified the Water Pik Oral Irrigating Device® (Aqua Tec Corp) and Aqua Pulse® (General Electric) as acceptable for use as effective aids to the toothbrush in a program of good oral hygiene.

Erythroblastosis Fetalis

Tooth discoloration due to erythroblastosis fetalis may be indistinguishable from that due to tetracyclines. The diagnosis is made on the basis of the history. Treatment (by means of a crown) is required only for esthetic reasons.

Congenital Defects

Dentinogenesis imperfecta is a hereditary condition involving both primary and secondary teeth, which appear grayish-brown. Very rarely, osteogenesis imperfecta is present also. The diagnosis can be made on the basis of a typical x-ray picture of peg-shaped dental roots without pulp chambers or canals. The teeth are usually soft and wear down rapidly; therefore, protection of the teeth with crowns is ultimately required.

Amelogenesis imperfecta is a hereditary condition which causes defects in the tooth enamel and a yellow-brown discoloration. The diagnosis is made by the history and the presence of enamel defects. Treatment is primarily for esthetic reasons.

Fluorosis

Dental fluorosis occurs most frequently when the fluoride in the water supply exceeds 2 ppm (1 ppm is the recommended concentration). The frequency and intensity of the discoloration is proportionate to the concentration in the water and the amount consumed during tooth development. The discoloration can vary from chalky-white to yellow-brown stains, often irregular in appearance. Deciduous teeth are not affected, possibly because the amount of fluorine available in utero is very low. These teeth can be effectively bleached as required with 30% hydrogen peroxide (Superoxol®).

PREMATURE LOSS OF TEETH

Deciduous teeth are usually shed between the ages of 6 and 12. When teeth become loose or are lost prior to age 5 (and trauma is not a factor), histiocytosis X, childhood hypophosphatasia, and precocious periodontal disease must be considered.

Histiocytosis X

In histiocytosis X, only the posterior deciduous teeth are involved. Occasionally this is the first sign of the disease, and the diagnosis is suggested by gingival erosion and a roentgenolucency involving one or more teeth. Confirmation is by examination of a biopsy specimen taken from the jaw lesion.

Curettage of the involved jawbone is often adequate treatment. Irradiation may be necessary; but also it may interfere with the development of the permanent teeth.

Hypophosphatasia

Childhood hypophosphatasia is an inborn error of metabolism in which the anterior deciduous teeth are selectively lost, usually before age 3. The roots show only minimal resorption. There is usually no other involvement, although bony demineralization may occur. The diagnosis is made by finding a low serum alkaline phosphatase and the presence of phospho-ethanolamine in the urine. The condition is self-limited, and no treatment is required. The permanent teeth are not affected.

Pimstone, B., Eisenberg, E., & S. Silverman: Hypophosphatasia: Genetic and dental studies. Ann Int Med 65:722–729, 1966.

Precocious Periodontal Disease

Precocious periodontal disease is manifested by loose teeth as well as inflamed and edematous gingivas. The etiology is not known. All the deciduous and permanent teeth are usually involved. Supportive treatment should be given until extractions are required.

ABSCESSES OF THE TEETH
(Periapical Abscess)

Dental decay is not self-limiting; unless it is removed it will lead to infection of the pulp and subsequent periapical abscess. Death of the pulp and periapical infection may also result from physical and chemical trauma. The only treatment is root canal therapy (cleansing and filling of the entire canal) or extraction.

In the early stage of pulp infection the symptoms may not be localized to the infected tooth. Intermittent throbbing pain is usually present, and is intensified by local temperature change. In the later putrescent stage the pain is extreme and continuous, and may be accentuated by heat but is often relieved by cold. After the infection reaches the bone, the typical syndrome is localization, pain upon pressure, and looseness of the tooth. Symptoms may then disappear completely, and, if drainage occurs, a parulis (gum boil) may be the only finding. When drainage is inadequate, swelling, pain, lymphadenopathy, and fever are often present. At this stage antibiotics are advisable before local therapy is undertaken. Diagnosis depends upon symptoms, pulp testing (hot, cold, electricity), percussion, x-rays (may not show the diagnostic periapical radiolucency), looseness, deep decay or fillings, parulis, and swelling. Care should be taken to rule out sinusitis, neuralgia, and diseases affecting the cervical lymph nodes.

Incision and drainage are indicated whenever possible. Antibiotics and analgesics may be given as necessary. Unless contraindicated from a history of hypersensitivity, penicillin is the antibiotic of choice. Do not use antibiotic troches.

If not eventually treated by root canal therapy or extraction, the abscess may develop into a more extensive osteomyelitis or cellulitis (or both), or may eventually become cystic, expand, and slowly destroy bone without causing pain.

Johnson, R.H., Dachi, S.F., & J.V. Haley: Pulpal hyperemia: A correlation of clinical and histologic data from 706 teeth. J Am Dent A 81:108–117, 1970.

VINCENT'S INFECTION
(Necrotizing Ulcerating Gingivitis, Trench Mouth)

Vincent's infection is an acute inflammatory disease of the gums which may be accompanied by pain, bleeding, fever, and lymphadenopathy. The etiology is not known, and it is doubtful if the disease is communicable. It may occur as a response to many factors, such as poor mouth hygiene, inadequate diet and sleep, alcoholism, and various other diseases such as infectious mononucleosis, nonspecific viral infections, bacterial infections, thrush of mouth, blood dyscrasias, and diabetes mellitus. The presence of fusiform and spiral organisms is of no importance since they occur in about 1/3 of clinically normal mouths and are absent in some cases of Vincent's infection.

Management depends upon ruling out underlying systemic factors and treating the signs and symptoms as indicated with systemic antibiotics, oxygenating mouth rinses (3% hydrogen peroxide in an equal volume of warm water), analgesics, rest, and appropriate dietary measures. Refer the patient to a dentist for further treatment (eg, curettage).

PERIODONTAL DISEASE

Food, bacteria, and calculi which are present between the gums and teeth in areas called "dental pockets" may cause an inflammatory process and the formation of pus (pyorrhea) with or without discomfort or other symptoms. If this continues unchecked, the involved teeth will become loose and eventually will be lost as a result of resorption of supporting alveolar bone. If there is no drainage, accumulation of pus will lead to acute swelling and pain (lateral abscess).

The diagnosis depends upon a combination of findings, including localized pain, loose teeth, demonstration of dental pockets, erythema, and swelling or suppuration. X-ray may reveal destruction of alveolar bone.

As in periapical abscess, the severity of signs and symptoms will determine the advisability of antibiotics. Local drainage and oxygenating mouth rinses (3% hydrogen peroxide in an equal volume of warm water) will usually reverse the acute symptoms and allow for routine follow-up procedures. Curettage or gingivectomy (or both) to reduce excess gum tissue help prevent formation of the "dental pockets" which predispose to acute periodontal infections. In some cases, because of the advanced nature of the lesion (bone loss) or the position of the tooth (third molars in particular), extraction is indicated.

In some cases, periodontal disease occurs even in the presence of good hygiene and without obvious cause. In these instances, even intensive care only slows the process of alveolar bone destruction.

Glickman, I.: Periodontal disease. New England J Med 284:1071–1077, 1971.

ULCERATIVE STOMATITIS

Ulcerative stomatitis is a general term for multiple ulcerations on an inflamed oral mucosa. It may be secondary to blood dyscrasias, erythema multiforme, inflammatory bowel disease, bullous lichen planus, acute herpes simplex infection, pemphigoid lesions, drug reactions, and allergies. Frequently no contributory factor can be identified. A general physical examination and history are required to establish a diagnosis if possible. Until this is done, treatment should be strictly palliative.

When a causative factor cannot be determined, or if the lesions are not self-limiting, prolonged treatment on an empiric basis may be necessary. The diet should consist of soft bland foods as tolerated, with vitamin supplementation. The use of alcohol and tobacco must be strictly forbidden. Mild mouth washes, preferably salt solution (4 times a day and after meals), promote optimal hygiene and relieve discomfort. Give analgesics as necessary for pain.

Adour, K.K.: Oral manifestations of systemic disease. M Clin North America 50:361–369, 1966.

APHTHOUS ULCER
(Canker Sore, Ulcerative Stomatitis)

An aphthous ulcer is a shallow mucosal ulcer with flat, fairly even borders surrounded by erythema. The ulcer may or may not be covered with a pseudomembrane. It has never been adequately demonstrated that this lesion is due to a virus or any other specific chemical, physical, or microbial agent. One or more ulcers may be present, and they tend to be recurrent. They are often painful. Nuts, chocolates, and irritants such as citrus fruits often cause flare-ups of aphthous ulceration, but abstinence will not prevent recurrence.

Stresses of various types have also been shown to be contributory. The diagnosis depends mainly upon ruling out similar but more readily identifiable disease; a history of recurrence; and inspection of the ulcer.

Bland mouth rinses and hydrocortisone-antibiotic ointments reduce pain and encourage healing. Hydrocortisone in an adhesive base (Orabase®) has been particularly useful. Sedatives, analgesics, and vitamins may help indirectly. Vaccines and gamma globulins have not proved significantly beneficial. Although caustics relieve pain by cauterizing the fine nerve endings, they also cause necrosis and scar tissue, which prolong healing and often prepare the site for chronic recurrences. Systemic antibiotics are contraindicated. Systemic corticosteroids in high doses for a short period of time may be very helpful for severe debilitating recurrent attacks.

Healing, which usually occurs in 1–3 weeks, may be only slightly accelerated with treatment. Occasionally, aphthous ulcers take the form of periadenitis, in which they are larger, persist sometimes for months, and may leave a residual scar. This form can be confused with carcinoma.

Brody, H.A., & S. Silverman, Jr.: Studies on recurrent aphthae. I. Clinical and laboratory comparisons. Oral Surg 27:27–34, 1969.
Francis, T.C.: Recurrent aphthous stomatitis and Behçet's disease. Oral Surg 30:476–487, 1970.

CANDIDIASIS
(Moniliasis, Thrush)

Thrush of the mouth is due to overgrowth of *Candida albicans.* It is characterized by creamy-white, curd-like patches anywhere in the mouth. The adjacent mucosa is usually erythematous, and scraping the lesions usually uncovers a raw bleeding surface. Pain is commonly present, and fever and lymphadenopathy are sometimes present also. Although this fungus occurs in about 1/3 of normal appearing mouths, overgrowth does not occur unless the "balance" of the oral flora is disturbed, eg, by debilitating or acute illnesses or as a result of anti-infective therapy. Concomitant candidiasis of the gastrointestinal tract may occur.

The diagnosis is based upon the rather typical clinical picture, and may be confirmed by cultures.

Treatment is not uniformly successful; the infection usually persists in spite of treatment as long as the causative factors are present. The patient should have a nutritious diet with vitamin supplementation, and should receive sufficient rest. Saline solution mouth rinses every 2 hours give local relief and promote healing. Specific antifungal therapy consists of nystatin (Mycostatin®) mouth rinses, 500,000 units 3 times daily (100,000 units/ml in a flavored vehicle), held in the mouth and then swallowed; vaginal troches (100,000 units) to be dissolved orally 4 times daily;

and 1% aqueous gentian violet solution painted on affected areas 3 times daily.

In some instances, primarily under dentures, a candidal lesion may appear as a slightly granular or irregularly eroded erythematous patch. In these cases, a diagnosis can be established by a heavy overgrowth of *Candida albicans* in culture or a biopsy revealing hyphae of candida invading epithelium (PAS stain). Nystatin (Mycostatin®) powder, 100,000 units/gm, applied 4 times daily for several weeks, is frequently effective in reversing signs and symptoms.

Chronic angular cheilitis is often a manifestation of candidiasis. It is best treated with nystatin (Mycostatin®) powder.

Silverman, S., Jr.: Diagnosis and treatment of commonly occurring oral mucosal lesions. D Clin North America, pp 111–123, March 1968.

LEUKOPLAKIA

Leukoplakia (a white patch) of the oral mucous membranes is occasionally a sign of carcinoma; it is important to rule out malignancy.

The most common cause of leukoplakia is epithelial hyperplasia and hyperkeratosis, usually in response to an irritant. Such conditions as white spongy nevi and lichen planus can be confused with leukoplakia, but they have no malignant tendencies. Keratosis of the tongue is often a finding in tertiary syphilis, and there is a significant statistical correlation between cancer of the tongue and a history of syphilis. In many cases the cause cannot be determined.

Leukoplakia is usually asymptomatic. It is often discovered upon routine examination or by patients feeling roughness in their mouths. Because there is no reliable correlation between clinical features and microscopic findings, a definitive diagnosis may be established only by histopathology. However, because of the extensiveness of some intraoral leukoplakias, cytologic smears from the surface are helpful in supplementing both clinical and biopsy information.

Treatment consists of removing all irritants (eg, tobacco, ill-fitting dentures). If the leukoplakia is not reversible, excision should be performed when feasible. However, since some leukoplakias occur so diffusely that complete excision is often impractical, careful clinical examination and follow-up are essential. It must be remembered that the diagnosis must be reaffirmed periodically, since a leukoplakia may unpredictably transform into a malignancy. Electrodesiccation, vitamin A, and proteolytic enzymes have not given predictably favorable results. Preliminary studies utilizing cryosurgery appear promising.

Silverman, S., Jr., & R.D. Rozen: Observations on the clinical characteristics and natural history of oral leukoplakia. J Am Dent A 76:772–777, 1968.

SIALADENITIS

Acute inflammation of a parotid or submandibular salivary gland is usually due to viral or bacterial infection or, less commonly, blockage of the duct. The gland is swollen and tender. Observation of Wharton's and Stenson's ducts may show absent or scanty secretion with fluctuation of swelling, especially during meals, which indicates blockage; or a turbid secretion, which suggests infection. Clinical examination and x-ray may disclose ductal or glandular calcific deposits. Sialograms are of help in differentiating normal and diseased glands. Probing the ducts may reveal an inorganic plug or organic stenosis.

Inflammation of the salivary glands due to bacterial, chemical, or other unidentified factors may also cause xerostomia. When the dryness is not responsive to therapy and acute signs are not apparent, systemic sialagogues or local troches may stimulate salivation.

Tumors may be confused with nonneoplastic inflammation. In these situations biopsy (usually excisional) should be performed, but only after other diagnostic and therapeutic procedures have failed to yield a diagnosis. Neoplasms are usually not associated with an acute onset and, at least in the early phases, are not painful. The lymph nodes are intimately associated with the salivary glands, and consideration must be given to diseases in which lymphadenopathy is a prominent finding, eg, lymphomas and metastatic malignancy. Such lesions as glandular hyperplasia and Mikulicz's disease may be confused with salivary or parotid gland disorders. The cause is not known, and no treatment is required.

In the acute stage, antibiotics, heat, and analgesics are indicated. Ductal stones which are too large for removal by massage and manipulation must be removed surgically (when the acute phase has subsided). If calcification or infection of the gland recurs often, extirpation of the gland must be considered. Radiation therapy may be effective in curing acute or recurrent sialadenitis which does not respond to other types of therapy.

GLOSSITIS

Inflammation of the tongue (usually associated with partial or complete loss of the filiform papillae, which creates a red, smooth appearance) may be secondary to a variety of diseases such as anemia, nutritional deficiency, drug reactions, systemic infection, and physical or chemical irritations. Treatment is based on identifying and correcting the primary cause if possible and palliating the tongue symptoms as required. Many obscure cases are due to such conditions as geographic tongue and median rhomboid glossitis.

The diagnosis is usually based on the history and laboratory studies, including cultures as indicated. Empiric therapy may be of diagnostic value in obscure cases.

When the cause cannot be determined and there are no symptoms, therapy is not indicated.

Dreizen, S.: Oral indications of the deficiency states. Postgrad Med 49:97–102, 1971.

GLOSSODYNIA, GLOSSOPYROSIS
(Chronic Lingual Papillitis)

Burning and pain, which may involve the entire tongue or isolated areas and may occur with or without glossitis, may be associated findings in hypochromic or pernicious anemia, nutritional disturbances, diabetes mellitus, or other disorders, and may be the presenting symptoms. In those cases due to diabetes the 2-hour glucose tolerance test is often positive when the screening urinalysis is negative. Allergens (eg, in dentifrices) are rare causes of tongue pain. Certain foods may cause flare-ups, but are not the primary causes. Dentures, poor oral hygiene, and dental infections are usually of no etiologic significance.

Although most cases occur in postmenopausal women, these disorders are not restricted to this group.

In most cases a primary cause cannot be identified. Cultures are of no value since the offending organisms are usually present also in normal mouths. Many clinicians believe that these symptoms occur on a primarily functional basis.

Treatment is mainly empiric. Antihistamines, sedatives and tranquilizers, and vitamins are occasionally of value. The injection of hydrocortisone in an oil base directly into the tongue has been of some help in puzzling cases. Local anesthetic injections and placebo injections are of value in differentiating functional and organic disease. Ointments and mouth rinses are of no value.

Partial xerostomia occasionally contributes to the symptoms. This may be remedied by sucking on nonmedicated troches or the administration of pilocarpine, 10–20 mg daily in divided doses. Estrogen supplementation in the postmenopausal patient is sometimes helpful.

Brody, H.A., Prendergast, J.J., & S. Silverman, Jr.: The relationship between oral symptoms, insulin release, and glucose intolerance. Oral Surg 31:777–782, 1971.
Silverman, S., Jr.: Oral changes in metabolic diseases. Postgrad Med 49:106–110, 1971.

PIGMENTATION OF GINGIVAS

Abnormal pigmentation of the gingiva is most commonly a racially controlled melanin deposition in the epithelial cytoplasm. It is most prevalent in non-Caucasian peoples. The color varies from brown to black, and the involvement may be in isolated patches or a diffuse speckling. Nongenetic causes include epithelial or dermal nevi (rare), drugs (eg, bismuth, arsenic, mercury, or lead), and amalgam fragments which become embedded in the gums during dental work. Similar lesions may also appear during the menopause or in Addison's disease, intestinal polyposis, neurofibromatosis, and several other disorders associated with generalized pigmentations.

The most important consideration is to rule out malignant melanoma (extremely rare in the mouth), which is suggested by rapid growth and slight elevation.

Hansen, L.S., Silverman, S., Jr., & J. Beumer: Primary malignant melanoma of the oral cavity. Oral Surg 26:352—359, 1968.

GINGIVAL HYPERTROPHY

Gingival hypertrophy or enlargement is usually due to epithelial and fibroblastic hyperplasia. Erythema, hemorrhage, and pain are not usually present. (This is in contrast to acute or subacute gingivitis, an inflammatory process usually caused by bacterial infection and poor oral hygiene; see Vincent's Infection.) It may be congenital (gingival fibromatosis), or it may be due to a drug reaction (commonly to diphenylhydantoin or one of the other anticonvulsants). In many instances the cause cannot be determined.

If the hyperplasia cannot be reversed by correcting a causative factor and if a problem of hygiene or tooth movement is present, gingivectomy is indicated. Recurrence is common.

ORAL CANCER

Cancers of the lips, tongue, floor of the mouth, buccal mucosa, palate, gingivas, and oropharynx account for about 5% of all malignancies. Estimates from various surveys indicate that the average 5-year survival rate for all patients with oral cancer is less than 30%. However, with early detection, the 5-year survival rates are almost doubled. (By definition, detection is "early" when lesions are less than 2 cm in diameter without evidence of metastases.) Therefore, early diagnosis followed by adequate treatment appears to be the most effective means of controlling oral cancer.

The lips and tongue are the most frequent sites of involvement. Squamous cell carcinoma is the most common type, accounting for over 90% of all oral cancers. Oral cancer is a disease of older people; over 90% occur in persons over 45, and the average age is about 60. The male-female ratio is about 2:1.

The etiology of oral cancer is not known. A genetic factor is not apparent. There is a definite increased risk with the use of tobacco and alcohol. Oral leukoplakia is an important precancerous lesion. A history of syphilis seems to increase the risk of cancer of the tongue.

There are no reliable signs or symptoms in early oral carcinoma, although pain is the most frequent first complaint. An early cancer may appear as a small white patch (leukoplakia), an aphthous-like or traumatic ulcer, an erythematous plaque, or a small swelling. Because of the variability of signs and symptoms, even clinical judgment and experience will not preclude diagnostic errors. Biopsy is the only method of definitely diagnosing a carcinoma. However, immediate biopsy of every ill-defined or innocuous appearing lesion is impractical and not indicated. Exfoliative cytology is a simple, reliable, and acceptable means of differentiating benign and early malignant neoplasms. In the case of small lesions whose gross appearance would be altered by a biopsy, the clinician who will give the treatment should see the lesion before the biopsy is taken so he can judge the extent of resection or radiation required. Lymph nodes should not be incised for biopsy for fear of causing dissemination of tumor cells.

Curative treatment consists of surgery and radiation, alone or in combination. Teeth within the primary beam of radiation and any other teeth with advanced caries or periodontal disease should be removed in order to minimize subsequent osteomyelitis, but these generalizations may be modified in individual cases depending upon the prognosis and the patient's age and preferences. The risk of osteoradionecrosis is much greater in the mandible than in the maxilla. After tooth removal, the alveolar bone must be trimmed evenly so that a primary closure is permitted. One week is arbitrarily allowed for initial healing before radiation treatment is started. Since the dosages are fractionated, more time is still available for healing before damaging levels of radiation are delivered to a surgical area.

Antibiotics and adequate pretreatment dentistry will minimize postoperative infection. An attempt should be made to save the teeth necessary to support prostheses. Many teeth exposed to irradiation remain relatively free of disease and functional for long periods. The periodontium is maintained in optimal condition by periodic routine dental procedures. When areas that have been directly in the beam of irradiation are treated, extreme care is exercised and antibiotics may be selectively administered. Frequent fluoride applications appear to aid in minimizing tooth decalcification and caries. Alterations of taste and saliva are usually reversible; if not, there is no effective remedy.

If metastasis to the cervical lymph nodes occurs, surgical dissection (usually radical) of these nodes may be indicated.

Shedd, D.P., & others: Ten year survey of oral cancer in a general hospital. Am J Surg 114:844—852, 1967.
Silverman, S., Jr.: Oral cancer. Hosp Med 7:36—51, 1971.

DISEASES OF THE ESOPHAGUS*

ACHALASIA OF THE ESOPHAGUS

Achalasia is an idiopathic neural disturbance resulting in dilatation of the esophagus without organic stenosis. It causes severe but often intermittent swallowing difficulties. Although the peak onset is in men between the ages of 20 and 40, achalasia may occur in both sexes at any age.

There seem to be 2 types of achalasia of the esophagus. They can be recognized by characteristic differences in symptomatology, x-ray findings, and pathologic findings at surgery. The more common type exhibits a narrowing within the distal 5 cm (2 inches) of the esophagus. The esophagus above is widely dilated, and its muscle layer greatly thickened. The esophagus may assume a sigmoid configuration. This type of achalasia is usually painless, and the esophagus appears atonic after a barium swallow. These patients are prone to pulmonary complications (atelectasis, pneumonitis, and fibrosis) as a result of repeated aspiration of stagnant esophageal contents.

The second variety of achalasia is characterized by hypertrophy of the circular muscle layer in the lower esophageal segment. The esophagus is only moderately dilated. These patients experience retrosternal pain as an early or persistent symptom. On fluoroscopic examination the esophagus appears hypertonic, ie, peristaltic activity is increased and disordered.

Obstruction to the passage of both liquids and solids results in difficulty with swallowing and regurgitation of food (food seems to stick at the level of the xiphoid), aggravated by extremely cold or hot liquids, carbonated beverages, or emotional upset.

Pain is generally located at the xiphoid, but may radiate to the back substernally and to the neck, and may occur with or without swallowing.

X-ray of the esophagus reveals a smooth obstruction at the cardia with dilatation of the esophagus above the area of stenosis. Peristaltic waves are small and irregular.

If the patient with achalasia is given 1–5 mg of methacholine (Mecholyl®), IM, the esophagus will undergo violent tonic contractions. This response is not seen in normal individuals or patients with other esophageal lesions. Atropine should be available to modify this response.

*Kramer, P.: Esophagus. Gastroenterology 54:1171–1192, 1968.

Wilkins, E.W., Jr., & D.B. Skinner: Surgery of the esophagus. New England J Med 278:887–891, 1968.

Zboralske, F.F., & G.W. Friedland: Diseases of the esophagus: Present concepts. California Med 112:33–51, Jan. 1970.

Aspiration of regurgitated material may cause pulmonary infections or even strangulation. Because of difficult alimentation, malnutrition may result.

Treatment consists of administration of soft or liquid foods until definitive treatment is possible. Brusque dilatation of the cardia with a pneumatic dilator or a myotomy may be indicated.

Ellis, F.H., Jr., & others: Esophagomyotomy for esophageal achalasia: Experimental, clinical and manometric aspects. Ann Surg 166:640–656, 1967.

Gillies, M., Nicks, R., & A. Skyring: Clinical, manometric, and pathological studies in diffuse esophageal spasm. Brit MJ 1:527–530, 1967.

Just-Viera, J.O., & C. Haight: Achalasia and carcinoma of the esophagus. Surg Gynec Obst 128:1081–1095, 1969.

Misiewicz, J.J., & others: Achalasia of the cardia: Pharmacology and histopathology of isolated cardia sphincteric muscle from patients with or without achalasia. Quart J Med 38:17–30, 1969.

ESOPHAGEAL WEBS

Congenital webs may occur at various levels of the esophagus, causing narrowing and the symptoms and signs of obstruction. The webs are demonstrable by esophagoscopy or x-ray, or may be seen at surgery. Upper esophageal webs may be associated with anemia (Plummer-Vinson syndrome), which is manifested by dysphagia, glossitis, spooning of nails, splenomegaly, and hypochromic anemia. Treatment consists of divulsion of the webs by bougienage, esophagoscopy, or, occasionally, surgery. Iron deficiency anemia, when present, is treated with iron salts.

Postlethwait, R.W., & W.C. Sealy: Experiences with the treatment of 59 patients with lower esophageal web. Ann Surg 165:786–796, 1967.

Seaman: W.B.: The significance of webs in the hypopharynx and upper esophagus. Radiology 89:32–38, 1967.

LOWER ESOPHAGEAL RING

An anatomic ring in the lower esophagus causes intermittent dysphagia of solid food when the lumen of the esophagus is decreased to 14 mm (¾ inch) or less in diameter. X-ray shows a clearly defined diaphragm-like narrowing of the distal esophageal lumen. Anatomic studies reveal this diaphragm to be located at the esophagogastric junction.

If symptoms are present, rupture or surgical divulsion of the ring is indicated.

Goyal, R.K., Glancy, J.J., & H.M. Spiro: Lower esophageal ring. New England J Med 282:1298–1305, 1355–1362, 1970.

ESOPHAGEAL CYSTS

Esophageal cysts probably result from buds of the primitive foregut or tracheobronchial branches. They may be asymptomatic but can cause dysphagia, dyspnea, cough, cyanosis, or chest pain, either because of their location or because they tend to contain acid-secreting epithelium which may produce peptic ulceration. The cysts are in the lower half of the esophagus between the muscle layers of the esophageal wall. Diagnosis is made by demonstration of a mediastinal mass on x-ray or at surgery. Surgical excision may be necessary.

Desforges, G., & J.W. Strieder: Esophageal cysts. New England J Med 262:60–64, 1960.

DIVERTICULUM OF THE ESOPHAGUS
(Zenker's Diverticulum)

Essentials of Diagnosis
- Dysphagia progressing as more is eaten; bad breath, foul taste in mouth.
- Regurgitation of undigested or partially digested food representing first portion of a meal.
- Irritating cough.
- Swelling in neck with eating.
- Increased salivation.
- Gurgling.
- X-ray (barium) confirms diagnosis.

General Considerations
Diverticula are classified as true or pulsion diverticula, which occur at either end of the esophagus (most commonly at the hypopharynx); or false or traction diverticula, located in the middle 1/3 of the esophagus (at the level of the left main bronchus) adjacent to hilar lymph nodes. Pulsion diverticulum is a herniation of the mucosa, due to internal pressure, through a weakness in the muscle wall of the esophagus, either at the pharyngoesophageal junction (inferior pharyngeal constrictors) or the epiphrenic region. Traction diverticulum is usually due to external traction on a normal esophageal structure by inflammatory adhesions. It does not cause symptoms and is an incidental x-ray finding. Pulsion diverticulum usually causes symptoms. Pulsion diverticulum may also occur as a result of a local esophageal injury, eg, a lye burn.

Clinical Findings
A. Symptoms and Signs: Symptoms and signs are related to the size of the diverticulum, the amount of food stasis that occurs, and the compression of nearby structures. Small diverticula are usually asymptomatic. The principal symptom is dysphagia due to increased mucus in the throat. The initial portion of a meal is generally swallowed well, but filling of the diverticulum causes pressure distress. Undigested food is then regurgitated. In small diverticula this may occur only on lying down. Swelling of the neck after eating and gurglings in the neck may occur. Halitosis and a foul taste in the mouth may be present. In the late stages, weight loss may occur.

B. X-Ray Findings: X-ray demonstration of the posterior diverticulum at the junction of the hypopharynx and esophagus is diagnostic of a pulsion diverticulum. Other diverticula are also readily demonstrated on x-ray examination.

Differential Diagnosis
The dysphagia and regurgitation associated with a diverticulum must be distinguished from that caused by neoplasm, strictures, or spasms of the esophagus, usually on the basis of the x-ray examination or the presence of a mass in the neck after eating.

Treatment & Prognosis
Surgical removal of the offending pouch is usually curative. If untreated, dysphagia progresses and pulmonary complications (due to aspiration of regurgitated material) and mediastinitis may occur.

Cross, F.S.: Esophageal diverticula and related neuromuscular problems. Ann Otol Rhin Laryng 77:914–926, 1968.

PEPTIC ESOPHAGITIS

Peptic esophagitis is related to reflux of gastric juices into the esophagus. Gastric reflux is counteracted by saliva and the alkaline secretion of the esophageal glands. Peptic esophagitis is believed to be due to the fact that the acid-pepsin activity of gastric juice destroys the effectiveness of the protective mechanisms of the esophagus. Contributing factors may include (1) unusual anatomic location of the cardia (short esophagus); (2) obstruction to outflow of the stomach with regurgitation proximally; (3) hiatus hernia; and (4) excessive vomiting. The essential pathophysiology is a malfunctioning distal esophageal sphincter with or without hiatus hernia.

Manifestations include dysphagia, substernal pain, and hypochromic anemia. Stricture and hemorrhage are late complications.

When the peptic disease is the important factor, dietary and medical treatment should be similar to that for peptic ulcer. The patient should be instructed to sleep with the head of his bed elevated 8–10 inches on blocks to promote gravity drainage of his esophagus. Esophagitis associated with a small hiatus hernia should be similarly treated; esophagitis associated with a large hiatus hernia, however, may require surgical repair. Peptic esophagitis associated with short esophagus, stricture, or traction type hiatus hernia often requires dilatation in addition to the ulcer regimen. In intractable cases, attempts to decrease gastric acidity by x-ray to the stomach, vagotomy, partial gastrectomy, esophagojejunostomy, and actual resection of the strictures may give relief.

Bombeck, C.T., Aoki, T., & L.M. Nyhus: Anatomic etiology and operative treatment of peptic esophagitis: An experimental study. Ann Surg 165:752–764, 1967.

Cocco, A.E., & O.C. Brantigan: Esophagitis: Diagnosis and surgical treatment. Ann Surg 169:857–866, 1969.

Hill, L.D., & others: New concepts of the pathophysiology of hiatal hernia and esophagitis. Am J Surg 111:70–78, 1966.

BENIGN STRICTURE OF THE ESOPHAGUS

Healing of any inflammatory lesion of the esophagus may result in a cicatricial stricture. Common causes are ingestion of corrosive substances, acute infectious diseases, foreign body or instrumentation injuries, and peptic esophagitis.

The characteristic symptom is slowly progressive dysphagia. In corrosive burns, the acute phase may be followed by a few weeks of improvement before the stricture becomes severe. Ability to swallow liquids is maintained longest.

Pain may occur and the sensation of food sticking in the chest is common. Localization of these sensations at the level of the lesion is often surprisingly accurate. X-ray demonstration of smooth narrowing with little or no dilatation above is characteristic. Esophagoscopy, biopsy, or cytologic examination may be required for confirmation in doubtful cases to rule out malignancy.

Careful dilatation with a string-guided bougie or a dilator (Mahoney or Hurst) is usually successful. However, dilatation requires skill and experience; if symptoms cannot be relieved by this means, resection of the stricture and esophagogastrostomy are indicated.

Benedict, E.B.: Peptic stenosis of the esophagus: A study of 233 patients treated with bougienage, surgery or both. Am J Digest Dis 11:761–770, 1966.

Holinger, P.H.: Management of esophageal lesions caused by chemical burns. Ann Otol Rhin Laryng 77:819–829, 1968.

Johnson, E.E.: A study of corrosive esophagitis. Laryngoscope 73:1651–1696, 1968.

MacDonald, W.C., & others: Esophageal exfoliative cytology. A neglected procedure. Ann Int Med 59:332–337, 1963.

HIATUS HERNIA
(Diaphragmatic Hernia)

Essentials of Diagnosis

- Pressure sensation, severe pain, burning behind lower sternum (any or all 3).
- Pain aggravated by recumbency or increase of abdominal pressure, relieved by upright position.
- Cough, dyspnea, palpitation, and tachycardia may be present.
- X-ray and esophagoscopy demonstrate the herniation.

General Considerations

Herniation of a portion of the stomach through the diaphragm can be divided into 2 types: paraesophageal and short esophageal. In paraesophageal hernia the esophagus is of normal length and herniation occurs through a large esophageal hiatus. In the short esophageal type (due to congenital or acquired esophageal shortening) a portion of the gastric cardia is pulled through the diaphragm. The large majority of patients with hiatus hernia are asymptomatic.

Clinical Findings

A. Symptoms and Signs: Distention of the pouch with air or food may cause a pressure sensation or severe pain behind the lower sternum which may radiate to the jaw and arms. The pain is precipitated by increase in abdominal pressure due to coughing, lifting, bending, or eating. Pulmonary or cardiac symptoms such as tachycardia, palpitation, cough, and dyspnea may occur. Incompetence of the cardio-esophageal sphincter mechanism leads to reflux of gastric contents into the esophagus. This may lead to substernal distress, cough, and aspiration when the patient reclines. Peptic esophagitis with ulceration, bleeding, or stricture may ensue.

B. X-Ray Findings: X-ray or cineradiographic demonstration of the hernia and reflux (with the patient in the Trendelenburg position or with abdominal compression) is usually possible.

C. Special Examinations: Esophagoscopy is of aid in diagnosis and better demonstrates associated esophagitis. Esophageal motility studies demonstrate location and adequacy of esophageal sphincters.

Differential Diagnosis

The retrosternal pain of hiatus hernia may radiate into the neck and arms and require differentiation from the pain of ischemic heart disease. Hiatus hernia may be an asymptomatic incidental finding.

Complications

Hemorrhage may occur from erosions or ulceration in the thoracic pouch.

Treatment

Give small, dry meals with liquids between meals. Antacids every hour usually provide relief from heartburn. The patient should be instructed to avoid lying down immediately after eating and to avoid exercising vigorously after eating. If reflux occurs, the patient should be instructed to elevate the head of his bed 8–10 inches.

Surgical correction of the hiatal defect should be considered if the symptoms are severe or if the hernia is associated with reflux or esophagitis. Surgical treatment frequently fails to relieve all of the symptoms.

Prognosis

Dietary management and weight reduction often relieve the symptoms. Surgical repair may be required for hernias which do not respond to conservative management.

Earlam, R.J., & F.H. Ellis, Jr.: The surgical repair of hiatal hernia: Current controversies. S Clin North America 47:813–826, 1967.

Menguy, R.: Esophageal hiatal hernia: Panel discussion. Am J Surg 113:91–101, 1967.

Palmer, E.D.: The hiatus hernia-esophagitis-esophageal stricture complex: Twenty-year prospective study. Am J Med 44:566–579, 1968.

Shatz, B., & A.E. Baue: Medical and surgical aspects of hiatus hernia. JAMA 214:125–129, 1970.

Wilkins, E.W., Jr., & D.B. Skinner: Surgery of the esophagus. New England J Med 278:824–828, 1968.

Wilkins, E.W., Jr., & D.B. Skinner: Recent progress in surgery of the esophagus. Part I. Pathophysiology and gastroesophageal reflux. J Surg Res 8:41, 1968.

BENIGN NEOPLASMS OF
THE ESOPHAGUS

Benign neoplasms of the esophagus occur infrequently. Long-standing nonprogressive dysphagia is the only symptom, and must be differentiated from other causes of dysphagia such as stricture, diverticulum, cardiospasm, and hysteria. They are accidentally found and are often asymptomatic. Esophagoscopic and x-ray findings are often diagnostic. The lesion itself must be differentiated from malignant neoplasm by biopsy.

Surgical resection of the tumor is curative.

Schmidt, A., & K. Lockwood: Benign neoplasms of the esophagus. Acta chir scandinav 133:640–644, 1967.

CARCINOMA OF THE ESOPHAGUS

Squamous cell carcinoma or adenocarcinoma of the esophagus is common in old men. The lower and middle portions of the esophagus are most often involved.

Clinical Findings

A. Symptoms and Signs: Vague discomfort and strange sensations in swallowing may precede more definite symptoms by months. In the classic syndrome, progressive dysphagia begins with sticking of large food particles, particularly with rapid eating, and progresses to inability to swallow even liquids. Pain and sensation of a lump may occur and at times are at the same level as the lesion. Regurgitation, belching, hoarseness, and cough occur late, when obstruction is nearly complete. Weight loss which may progress to extreme emaciation is usual.

B. X-Ray Findings: X-ray shows an irregular or annular obstruction.

C. Special Examinations: Esophagoscopic study and biopsy or lavage and cytologic study are necessary to prove the diagnosis.

Differential Diagnosis

Carcinoma of the esophagus must be differentiated from cardiospasm, diffuse esophageal spasm, and strictures. The x-ray picture may be similar to that found with spasm and stricture, and final differentiation often depends on biopsy.

Treatment & Prognosis

There is no satisfactory treatment for esophageal carcinoma. Soft or liquid food should be given as tolerated; gastrostomy feedings may be given in selected cases.

Surgical removal is reserved for the few patients who have no demonstrable metastases and are good surgical risks. Deep radiation therapy may be employed in selected cases.

In advanced cases dilatation may be palliative for short periods.

MacDonald, W.C., & others: Esophageal exfoliative cytology. A neglected procedure. Ann Int Med 59:332–337, 1963.

Nakayama, K., & others: Surgical treatment combined with preoperative concentrated irradiation for esophageal cancer. Cancer 20:778–788, 1967.

Nardi, G.L., & G.D. Zuidema: Surgical treatment of advanced esophageal carcinoma. Am J Surg 109:583–586, 1965.

Pearson, J.G.: The value of radiotherapy in the management of esophageal cancer. Am J Roentgenol 105:500–513, 1969.

Raphael, H.A., Ellis, F.H., Jr., & M.B. Dockery: Primary adenocarcinoma of the esophagus: 18 year review and review of the literature. Ann Surg 164:785–796, 1966.

Turnbull, A.D., & J.T. Goodner: Primary adenocarcinoma of the esophagus. Cancer 22:915–918, 1968.

DISEASES OF THE STOMACH

ACUTE SIMPLE GASTRITIS

Acute gastritis, probably the most common disturbance of the stomach, is frequently accompanied by generalized enteritis. It occurs in all age groups. The causes are as follows: (1) chemical irritants, eg, alcohol; (2) bacterial infections or toxins, eg, staphylococcal food poisoning, scarlet fever, pneumonia; (3) viral infections, eg, "viral gastroenteritis," measles, hepatitis, influenza; and (4) allergy, eg, to shellfish.

Clinical Findings

A. Symptoms and Signs: Anorexia is always present and may be the only symptom. More commonly there is epigastric fullness and pressure, nausea, and vomiting. Hematemesis occurs occasionally. Diarrhea and cramping pain (enteritis), malaise, chills, headache, and muscle cramps may be present. The patient may be prostrated and dehydrated. Examination shows mild epigastric tenderness.

B. Laboratory Findings: Mild leukocytosis may be present.

C. Special Examinations: Gastroscopy is rarely performed but shows diffuse erythema, occasional petechiae, and copious adherent mucus.

Treatment & Prognosis

Give nothing by mouth until acute symptoms of pain and nausea have subsided. Then give clear liquid and progress to a soft diet as tolerated. Sedatives, phenothiazine tranquilizers, or opiates may be used as indicated. Symptoms last 1–7 days.

ACUTE CORROSIVE GASTRITIS

Ingestion of corrosive substance is most common in children but may occur in attempted suicide. The substances most commonly swallowed are strong acids (sulfuric, nitric), alkalies (lye, potash), oxalic acid, iodine, bichloride of mercury, arsenic, silver nitrate, and carbolic acid. Gastric changes vary from superficial edema and hyperemia, deep necrosis and sloughing, to perforation.

Corrosion of the lips, tongue, mouth, and pharynx, and pain and dysphagia due to esophageal lesions are usually present. Nitric acid causes brown discoloration; oxalic acid causes white discoloration of mucous membranes. There is severe epigastric burning and cramping pain, nausea and vomiting, and diarrhea. The vomitus is often blood-tinged. Severe prostration with a shock-like picture and thirst may occur. Palpation of the abdomen may show epigastric tenderness or extreme rigidity.

Leukocytosis and proteinuria are present. X-ray and endoscopy are contraindicated during the acute phase because of the increased risk of perforation.

Immediate treatment consists of prompt administration of the appropriate antidote. Avoid emetics and lavage if corrosion is severe because of the danger of perforation. Treat gastritis as for acute simple gastritis.

After the acute phase has passed, place the patient on a peptic ulcer regimen. If perforation has not occurred, recovery is the rule. However, pyloric stenosis may occur early or late, requiring gastric aspiration, parenteral fluid therapy, and surgical repair.

The amount of the corrosive substance, its local and general effects, and the speed with which it is removed or neutralized determine the outcome. If the patient survives the acute phase, gastric effects are usually overshadowed by esophageal strictures, although chronic gastritis or stricture formation at the pylorus may follow.

Thompson, C.E., Ashurst, P.M., & T.J. Butler: Survey of haemorrhagic erosive gastritis. Brit MJ 3:283–284, 1968.

CHRONIC GASTRITIS

Essentials of Diagnosis

- Long-standing upper abdominal dyspeptic symptoms.
- Mild epigastric tenderness or no physical findings whatever.
- Gastric biopsy is the definitive diagnostic technic.

General Considerations

Chronic gastritis may be classified (on the basis of gastroscopic observation) as (1) chronic superficial gastritis, with hyperemia, edema, hemorrhages, and superficial erosions; (2) atrophic gastritis, with thin, pale mucosa, narrow gastric folds, and prominent submucosal vessels; and (3) chronic hypertrophic gastritis, with thick, dull, velvety mucosa and cobblestone nodularity of the mucosa. The cause is not known. Even in those types which are secondary to tumors, ulcers, or obstruction or which occur after surgery, the degree and extent of the process may not correlate well with the severity of the inciting factors.

Chronic gastritis is a waste-basket diagnosis which should never be made without the exclusion of all other causes of epigastric discomfort and positive demonstration by histologic means.

Clinical Findings

A. Symptoms and Signs: Gastrointestinal symptoms, if they occur, may include anorexia, epigastric pressure and fullness, heartburn, nausea, vomiting, specific food intolerance, peptic ulcer-like syndrome, and anemia or gross hemorrhage. The vast majority of persons with chronic gastritis do not have symptoms from this lesion.

Physical findings are often absent or consist only of mild epigastric tenderness.

B. Laboratory Findings: The laboratory findings may be entirely normal. The gastric analysis, although not diagnostic, frequently shows achlorhydria.

C. X-Ray Findings: Although the x-ray in chronic hypertrophic gastritis may show heavy folds, these findings are not diagnostic and not specific to the lesion.

Differential Diagnosis

Since clinical and pathologic findings correlate so poorly, the diagnosis of chronic gastritis should be made only on the basis of anatomic findings obtained via gastric biopsy, surgery, or autopsy.

Treatment & Prognosis

The treatment of chronic gastritis, except in those cases associated with pernicious anemia or iron deficiency anemia, is not very successful. However, the use of a peptic ulcer regimen, combined with the elimination of aggravating factors such as alcohol, salicylates, and caffeine, may reduce the severity of the symptoms.

Fisher, J.M., & others: An immunological study of categories of gastritis. Lancet 1:176–179, 1967.
Siurala, M., & others: Prevalence of gastritis in a rural population. Bioptic study of subjects selected at random. Scandinav J Gastroent 3:211–223, 1968.

PEPTIC ULCER

A peptic ulcer is an acute or chronic benign ulceration occurring in a portion of the digestive tract which is accessible to gastric secretions. Since an active peptic ulcer does not occur in the absence of acid-peptic gastric secretions, peptic ulcers are not found in conditions where acid is absent.

Other factors in peptic ulceration (besides the presence of gastric acidity) include hypersecretion and decreased tissue resistance.

Peptic ulcer may occur during the course of drug therapy (adrenocortical hormones, phenylbutazone, salicylates, reserpine, and indomethacin). It may occur as a result of severe tissue injury such as extensive burns or intracranial surgery, and may be associated with endocrine tumors producing gastrin, which stimulates hypersecretion of hydrochloric acid and a very refractory peptic ulcer diathesis (Zollinger-Ellison syndrome).

Kirsner, J.B.: Peptic ulcer: A review of the recent literature on various clinical aspects. Gastroenterology 54:611–641, 945–975, 1968.

1. DUODENAL ULCER

Essentials of Diagnosis

- Epigastric distress 45–60 minutes after meals, or noctural pain, both relieved by food, antacids, or vomiting.
- Epigastric tenderness and guarding.
- Chronic and periodic symptoms.
- Gastric analysis shows acid in all cases and hypersecretion in some.
- Ulcer crater or deformity of duodenal bulb on x-ray.

General Considerations

Duodenal ulcer occurs in about 10% of people at some time. Although the average age at onset is 33 years, duodenal ulcer may occur at any time from infancy to the later years. It is 4 times as common in males as in females. Occurrence during pregnancy is unusual.

Duodenal ulcer is 4 or 5 times as common as benign gastric ulcer. Morbidity due to peptic ulcer is a major public health problem.

About 95% of duodenal ulcers occur in the duodenal bulb or cap, ie, the first 5 cm (2 inches) of the duodenum. The remainder are between this area and the ampulla. Ulcers below the ampulla are rare. The majority are near the lesser curvature. The ulceration varies from a few mm to 1–2 cm in diameter and extends at least through the muscularis mucosa, often through to the serosa and into the pancreas. The margins are sharp, but the surrounding mucosa is often inflamed and edematous. The base consists of granulation tissue and fibrous tissue, representing healing and fibrinoid necrosis.

Clinical Findings

A. Symptoms and Signs: Symptoms may be absent or vague and atypical. In the typical case pain is described as gnawing, burning, cramp-like, or aching, or as "heartburn"; it is usually mild to moderate, located over a small area near the midline in the epigastrium near the xiphoid. The pain may radiate below the costal margins, into the back, or, rarely, to the right shoulder. Nausea may be present, and vomiting of small quantities of highly acid gastric juice with little or no retained food may occur. The distress usually occurs 45–60 minutes after a meal; is usually absent before breakfast; worsens as the day progresses; and may be most severe between 12 midnight and 2:00 a.m. It is relieved by food, milk, alkalies, and vomiting generally within 5–30 minutes.

Remissions often occur, followed by exacerbations precipitated by stress, infection, or emotional strain.

Signs are usually limited to tenderness in the epigastrium, superficial as well as deep (75% of cases), and voluntary epigastric muscle guarding.

B. Laboratory Findings: Bleeding, hypochromic anemia, and occult blood in the stools occur in chronic ulcers. Gastric analysis shows acid in all cases and hypersecretion in some.

C. X-Ray Findings: An ulcer crater is demonstrable by x-ray in 50–70% of cases but may be obscured by cicatricial distortion of the duodenal cap. When no ulcer is demonstrated, the following are suggestive of ulceration: (1) Irritability of the bulb with difficulty in retaining barium there; (2) point tenderness over the bulb; (3) pylorospasm; (4) gastric hyperperistalsis; and (5) hypersecretion or retained secretions.

Differential Diagnosis

When symptoms are typical the diagnosis of peptic ulceration can be made with assurance; when symptoms are atypical, duodenal ulcer may be confused clinically with functional gastrointestinal disease, gastritis, gastric carcinoma, and irritable colon syndrome. Final diagnosis often depends upon x-ray.

Complications

A. Intractability to Treatment: Most cases of apparently intractable ulcer are probably due to an inadequate medical regimen or failure of cooperation on the part of the patient. The designation "intractable" should be reserved only for those patients who have received an adequate supervised trial of therapy. The possibility of occult etiologic and aggravating factors as well as complications of the ulcer must always be considered.

B. Hemorrhage Due to Peptic Ulcer: Hemorrhage is caused either by erosion of an ulcer into an artery or vein or, more commonly, by bleeding from granulation tissue. The majority of bleeding ulcers are on the posterior wall. The sudden onset of weakness, faintness, dizziness, chilliness, thirst, cold moist skin, desire to defecate, and the passage of loose tarry or even red stools with or without coffee-ground vomitus is characteristic of acute gastrointestinal hemorrhage.

The blood findings (hemoglobin, red cell count, and hematocrit) lag behind the blood loss by several hours and may give a false impression of the quantity of blood lost.

C. Perforation: It occurs almost exclusively in males between the ages of 25 and 40. The symptoms and signs are those of peritoneal irritation and peritonitis; ulcers which perforate into the lesser peritoneal cavity cause less dramatic symptoms and signs. A typical description of perforated peptic ulcer is an acute onset of epigastric pain, often radiating to the shoulder or right lower quadrant and sometimes associated with nausea and vomiting, followed by a lessening of pain for a few hours, and then by board-like rigidity of the abdomen, fever, rebound tenderness, absent bowel sounds, leukocytosis, tachycardia, and even signs of marked prostration. X-ray demonstration of free air in the peritoneal cavity confirms the diagnosis.

D. Penetration: Extension of the crater beyond the duodenal wall into contiguous structures without extension into the free peritoneal space occurs fairly frequently with duodenal ulcer and is one of the important causes of failure of medical treatment. Penetration generally occurs in ulcers on the posterior wall, and extension is usually into the pancreas; but the liver, biliary tract, or gastrohepatic omentum may be involved.

Radiation of pain into the back, night distress, inadequate or no relief from eating food or taking alkalies, and, in occasional cases, relief upon spinal flexion and aggravation upon hyperextension—any or all of these findings in a patient with a long history of duodenal ulcer usually signify penetration.

E. Obstruction: Minor degrees of pyloric obstruction are present in about 20–25% of patients with duodenal ulcer, but clinically significant obstruction is much less common. The obstruction is generally caused by edema and spasm associated with an active ulcer, but it may occur as a result of scar tissue contraction even in the presence of a healed ulcer.

The occurrence of epigastric fullness or heaviness and, finally, copious vomiting after meals—with the vomitus containing undigested food from a previous meal—suggest obstruction. The diagnosis is confirmed by the presence of an overnight gastric residual of greater than 50 ml containing undigested food, and x-ray evidence of obstruction, gastric dilatation, and hyperperistalsis. A succussion splash on pressure in the left upper quadrant may be present, and gastric peristalsis may be visible.

Treatment

The rationale and efficacy of the various dietary and pharmacologic measures for the treatment of peptic ulcer have been seriously challenged. Despite the difficulty of documenting the influence of the different traditional treatment measures in inducing remissions or preventing recurrences of peptic ulcer, the clinician usually finds it necessary to provide symptomatic treatment by such measures. The limiting factor in therapy, in the light of present knowledge, is the fact that although ulcers may heal, the ulcer diathesis remains.

A. Acute Phase:

1. General measures—The patient should have 2 or 3 weeks' rest from work if possible. If the home situation is unsatisfactory or if the patient is unable to cooperate, hospitalization is recommended. If the patient must continue to work, he should be given careful instructions about the medical program. Arrangements should be made for rest periods and sufficient sleep. Anxiety should be relieved whenever possible, but active psychotherapy during the acute phase is usually not indicated.

Alcohol should be strictly forbidden. If the patient can quit smoking without too much distress, he should do so.

The following drugs may aggravate peptic ulcer or may even cause perforation and hemorrhage: corticotropin, the adrenal corticosteroids, rauwolfia, phenylbutazone, and large doses of salicylates. They should be discontinued.

2. Diet—Numerous dietary regimens have been designed for the treatment of peptic ulcer. There is considerable controversy regarding the value or advisability of the strict smooth, bland diets so widely used in the past. It is difficult, however, to disregard the beneficial effects of properly selected restricted diets. For the time being it would appear prudent to avoid the extremes of either overly restrictive or overly permissive diets.

The important principles of dietary management of peptic ulcer are as follows: (1) nutritious diet; (2) frequent small feedings; (3) regularity of meals; (4) restriction of substances which stimulate gastric secretion, especially coffee, tea, cola beverages, and alcohol; and

(5) avoidance of foods known to produce symptoms in a given individual.

In the acute phase of ulcer symptomatology, it is often useful to begin with hourly feedings of full liquids together with hourly antacids for a period of up to 24 hours. The quantity of liquids may then be increased and foods added as desired for satisfaction. After about a week of this preliminary routine, the diet should be liberalized. Many patients require and expect a modified bland diet until they are free of symptoms.

It is doubtful that dietary measures, other than for the elimination of known aggravating factors, play a significant role in preventing ulcer recurrence.

3. Antacids—Although antacids usually relieve ulcer pain promptly and are therefore of value in treatment, there is little evidence that they influence either the rate of ulcer healing or relapse. Many antacids are available, and in certain circumstances each of the agents listed below has special advantages and disadvantages. *Caution:* All patients on antacid therapy should be watched for diarrhea, constipation, fecal impaction, or "milk-alkali syndrome."

In order to be effective, antacids must be taken frequently. During the acute phase they must be taken every hour or ½ hour during the day and night if necessary. As improvement progresses the patient may increase the interval between doses to 2 hours. The drugs should be taken on a regular program; irregular and "as needed" antacid therapy is not effective.

a. Aluminum hydroxide gel—These agents have enjoyed popular use because they are convenient to administer, have less tendency to cause alkalosis, and have local adsorbent and demulcent actions. However, they are constipating, interfere with phosphate and vitamin absorption, may have to be given in large doses, and may fail to give relief. Give aluminum hydroxide gel (Amphojel®) (liquid), 1–2 tsp in ½ glass of water every 1–2 hours; or aluminum hydroxide gel-magnesium trisilicate mixtures (liquid), 1–2 tsp in ½ glass of water every 1–2 hours (less constipating). Aluminum hydroxide and magnesium hydroxide colloidal suspension (Aludrox®, Maalox®, Mylanta®) and monalium hydrate (Riopan®) are useful nonconstipating antacid mixtures which are given in doses comparable to those of other aluminum hydroxide preparations. Aluminum hydroxide tablets are not recommended since most are essentially inert in their properties.

b. Magnesium oxide-calcium carbonate mixtures—

R Magnesium oxide   15.0–60.0
    Calcium carbonate, q s ad   120.0

Sig: Take ½–1 tsp in ½ glass of water as directed.

Magnesium oxide is a laxative drug and calcium carbonate tends to produce constipation. By varying the amount of magnesium oxide in this prescription, the laxative or constipating effects of the 2 ingredients

may be effectively balanced. The powder may be given in alternating doses with aluminum hydroxide gels.

Calcium carbonate has an excellent neutralizing action, but renal stones and systemic disturbances of calcium metabolism may complicate calcium carbonate therapy.

4. Sedatives—Tense and apprehensive patients will usually profit greatly from sedation. The barbiturates are preferred, alone or in combination with antispasmodic drugs. Hypnotic doses of the barbiturates may be necessary to ensure sleep.

5. Belladonna preparations—The use of these agents should be restricted. The dosage necessary to produce an antisecretory effect may cause blurring of vision, constipation, urinary retention, and tachycardia. They may be used for refractory pain. Combining these agents with sedatives enhances their clinical effects. Belladonna preparations, when employed in proper dosage, are probably as effective as any of the anticholinergic preparations listed below and have the added advantage of being inexpensive.

a. Belladonna tincture, 0.3–0.6 ml (5–10 drops) in ½ glass of water 3 times daily, 20–30 minutes before meals, and at bedtime as necessary (0.6 ml of the tincture equals about 0.2 mg of atropine). This preparation permits rather delicate "titration" of desired antispasmodic effect by simply regulating the number of drops, but is a nuisance to the patient to measure each time.

b. Belladonna extract, 8–15 mg 20–30 minutes before meals and at bedtime (15 mg equals about 0.2 mg atropine alkaloid).

c. Belladonna with phenobarbital—See prescriptions on p 304.

6. Synthetic anticholinergic-antispasmodic drugs—These drugs should generally be given 3–4 times daily in dosages large enough to produce oral dryness. They also produce blurred vision, tachycardia, urinary retention, and other atropine-like side-effects due to blockage of parasympathetic activity. These atropine substitutes are, however, quaternary amines and do not cause CNS side-affects. They should not be used for patients with glaucoma, bladder neck obstruction, pyloric obstruction, marked gastric retention, and intestinal stasis. Examples of these drugs (together with an initial dose which can be given 4 times daily and increased until side-effects appear) are as follows: Diphemanil methylsulfate (Prantal®), 100 mg; glycopyrrolate (Robinul®), 1 mg (prolonged action); hexocyclium methylsulfate (Tral®), 25 mg; homatropine methylbromide, 5 mg; isopropamide iodide (Darbid®), 5 mg (twice daily only); mepenzolate bromide (Cantil®), 25 mg; methantheline bromide (Banthine®), 50 mg; methscopolamine bromide (Pamine®), 2.5 mg; oxyphencyclimine (Daricon®), 10 mg (prolonged action); oxyphenonium bromide (Antrenyl®), 5 mg; penthienate bromide (Monodral®), 5 mg; pipenzolate methylbromide (Piptal®), 5 mg; propantheline bromide (Pro-Banthine®), 15 mg; tridihexethyl chloride (Pathilon®), 25 mg.

B. Convalescent Phase:

1. Reexamination—When clinical quiescence of the lesion is evident (based on freedom from symptoms), a repeat gastrointestinal x-ray series is advisable to determine whether or not there is x-ray evidence of healing. Anticholinergic therapy, if used, should be discontinued 72 hours prior to x-ray examination for duodenal ulcer.

2. Education of patient regarding recurrences—The chronic and recurrent nature of the illness should be explained to the patient, and he should be warned about the complications of careless or improper treatment. It should be emphasized that the following factors are most frequently responsible for recurrence of ulcer: improper diet and irregular eating habits, irregular living habits (long or irregular hours), use of alcohol or tobacco, emotional stress, and infections, particularly of the upper respiratory tract. The patient should be instructed to return to the ulcer regimen or a modification of it if symptoms recur or if he recognizes that he is exposing himself to conditions known to aggravate the ulcer. Antacid and other medications should be readily available.

3. Rest and recreation—Provisions should be made for rest and recreation to promote physical and mental relaxation.

C. Treatment of Complications:

1. Hemorrhage—

a. Institute immediate emergency measures for treatment of hemorrhage and shock (see Chapter 1). Hospitalize the patient at absolute bed rest and keep him comfortably warm. If sedation is necessary, give one of the following: codeine phosphate, 30–65 mg subcut or orally; dihydromorphinone (Dilaudid®), 4 mg subcut every 4–6 hours as necessary; or sodium phenobarbital, 30–100 mg subcut or orally as necessary during the first 24–48 hours. Phenobarbital may be continued for several days if necessary. Avoid morphine, if possible, since it may cause nausea and predispose to shock.

Blood should be given to restore effective blood volume and maintain blood pressure and pulse. In severe hemorrhage the time, rate, and volume of blood administration should suit the physiologic needs, and large amounts of blood may be given when indicated. Transfusions must be given if hemorrhage is severe (hemoglobin < 8 gm/100 ml or red blood count < 2.5 million), if immediate surgery is contemplated, or if symptoms of anoxia or shock are not rapidly controlled.

Observe pulse, respirations, and blood pressure every 30–60 minutes since these data may give information regarding shock status in advance of blood changes. Observe all vomitus and stools for gross or occult blood. Type and cross-match the patient's blood carefully as soon as possible. Have whole blood or plasma available without delay. If blood or plasma is not available, saline or plasma expander may temporarily maintain intravascular volume until blood can be obtained. Take a complete blood count and determine hematocrit initially and serially as indicated. Determine blood NPN or urea nitrogen for comparison with later studies as an indication of blood in the gastrointestinal tract.

b. General measures—Correct dehydration and salt depletion with physiologic saline solution, 1–1.5 liters daily IV, and oral liquid feedings as soon as tolerated (see below). Sodium chloride, 3–6 gm/liter, may be added to the liquid food mixture to prevent salt depletion.

The policy of initial starvation is a matter of considerable controversy. Since the patient is often nauseated and anorexic, or even in shock on the first day, food may be safely withheld. If the patient is nauseated or vomiting, thirst may be controlled by fluids given parenterally. The patient may be permitted to dissolve ice chips or hard fruit-flavored candy under the tongue to relieve thirst. If the patient is hungry and is not vomiting, begin immediate administration of food. It is best to begin with a full liquid diet alternating with hourly antacids. Solid foods may be added when the patient has shown apparent clinical improvement.

c. Convalescent care—After the acute episode, the conservative medical regimen outlined for uncomplicated peptic ulcer should be instituted.

d. Surgery should be performed if hemorrhage persists and the patient's condition does not stabilize with 2–4 liters of blood in a 24-hour period. As soon as the patient's condition permits, endoscopy or a gastrointestinal x-ray (or both) should be performed to help localize the site of bleeding or identify the character of the bleeding lesion. Manipulation during such examinations should be as gentle as possible.

2. Perforation—Acute perforation constitutes a medical emergency. Immediate surgical repair, preferably by simple surgical closure, is indicated. More extensive operations are usually unwise at the time of the acute episode because of the increased operative hazard due to the patient's poor physical condition. If the patient has had no previous therapy or if previous therapy has been inadequate, he should be treated by means of a conservative medical regimen.

The morbidity and mortality depend upon the amount of spillage and especially the time lapse between perforation and surgery. Surgical closure of the perforation is indicated within 24 hours. After this time has elapsed, antibiotics and supportive measures are usually indicated rather than operative intervention.

3. Obstruction—Obstruction due to spasm and edema can usually be treated adequately by gastric decompression and ulcer therapy; obstruction due to scar formation requires surgery. It must be remembered that the obstruction may not represent a complication of an ulcer but may be due to a primary neoplastic disease, especially in those patients with no history or only a short history of peptic ulcer.

a. Medical measures (for obstruction due to spasm or edema) consist of bed rest, preferably in a hospital, continuous gastric suction for 48 hours, and parenteral administration of electrolytes and fluids. After 48 hours, begin hourly feedings. Aspirate gastric juice every 12 hours to measure gastric residual. Do not use anticholinergic drugs since they delay gastric emptying. Give sedative or sedative-tranquilizer drugs, and a progressive diet as tolerated. Hourly antacids should be employed as for treatment of uncomplicated ulcer.

b. Surgical measures (for obstruction due to scarring) are indicated only after a thorough trial of conservative measures. Various procedures have been recommended. It is currently the practice to perform gastric resection in most cases, or antrectomy and vagotomy.

Prognosis

Duodenal ulcer tends to have a chronic course with remissions and exacerbations. Many patients can be adequately controlled by medical management. About 25% develop complications, and 5–10% ultimately require surgery.

Babb, R.R.: Diagnosis of Zollinger-Ellison syndrome: Ulcerogenic tumor of the pancreas. California Med 113:1–3, July 1970.

Barreras, R.F.: Acid secretion after calcium carbonate in patients with duodenal ulcer. New England J Med 282:1402–1405, 1970.

Buchman, E., & others: Unrestricted diet in the treatment of duodenal ulcer. Gastroenterology 56:1016–1020, 1969.

Burdette, W.J., & B. Rasmussen: Perforated peptic ulcer. Surgery 63:576–585, 1968.

Conn, J.H., & others: Massive hemorrhage from peptic ulcer: Evaluation of methods of surgical control. Ann Surg 169:784–789, 1969.

Dragstedt, L.R.: Peptic ulcer: An abnormality in gastric secretion. Am J Surg 117:143–156, 1969.

Eiseman, B., & R.L. Heyman: Stress ulcers: A continuing challenge. New England J Med 282:372–374, 1970.

Fisher, R.D., Ebert, P.A., & G.D. Zuidema: Obstructing peptic ulcer: Results of treatment. Arch Surg 94:724–727, 1967.

Flick, A.L.: Acid content of common beverages. Digestive Dis 15:317–320, 1970.

Hinshaw, D.B., & others: Vagotomy and pyloroplasty for perforated duodenal ulcer: Observations in 180 cases. Am J Surg 115:173–176, 1968.

Medical treatment of peptic ulcer. Med Lett Drugs Therap 11:105–107, 1969.

Piper, D.W.: Antacid and anticholinergic drug therapy of peptic ulcer. Gastroenterology 52:1009–1018, 1967.

Pops, M.A.: Duodenal ulcer today. Ann Int Med 67:164–182, 1967.

Ruffin, J.N., & others: A co-operative double-blind evaluation of gastric "freezing" in the treatment of duodenal ulcer. New England J Med 281:16–19, 1969.

2. GASTRIC ULCER

Essentials of Diagnosis

- Epigastric distress on an empty stomach, relieved by food, alkalies, or vomiting.
- Epigastric tenderness and voluntary muscle guarding.
- Anemia, occult blood in stool, gastric acid.
- Ulcer demonstrated by x-ray or gastroscope.

General Considerations

Benign gastric ulcer is in many respects similar to duodenal ulcer. Acid gastric juice is necessary for its production, but decreased tissue resistance appears to play a more important role than hypersecretion.

About 60% of benign gastric ulcers are found within 6 cm of the pylorus. The ulcers are generally located at or near the lesser curvature and most frequently on the posterior wall. Another 25% of the ulcers are located higher on the lesser curvature.

Gastric ulcers are 2 or 3 times more common in males, usually over 40 years of age.

Clinical Findings

A. Symptoms and Signs: There may be no symptoms or only vague and atypical symptoms. Typically the epigastric distress is described as gnawing, burning, aching, or "hunger pangs," referred at times to the left subcostal area. Episodes occur usually 45–60 minutes after a meal and are relieved by food, alkalies, or vomiting. Nausea and vomiting are frequent complaints. There may be a history of remissions, with exacerbations occurring in the winter months. Weight loss, constipation, and fatigue are common.

Epigastric tenderness or voluntary muscle guarding is usually the only finding.

B. Laboratory Findings: If bleeding has occurred, there may be hypochromic anemia or occult blood in the stool. The gastric analysis always shows an acid pH after betazole (Histalog®) and the presence of low normal to normal secretion.

C. Other Examinations: X-rays or gastroscopic examination usually confirm the presence of an ulcer.

Differential Diagnosis

The symptoms of gastric ulcer, especially if atypical, need differentiation from those of irritable colon, gastritis, and functional gastrointestinal distress.

Most important is the differentiation of benign gastric ulcer from malignant gastric ulcer. A favorable response to hospital management is presumptive evidence that the lesion is benign and not malignant. Malignant ulcers may respond initially, but residual changes at the site usually demonstrate the true nature of the process.

Complications

Hemorrhage, perforation, and obstruction may occur (see Complications of Duodenal Ulcer, above).

Treatment

Since about 10% of gastric ulcers prove to be due to carcinoma, ulcer treatment (as for duodenal ulcer) should be intensive, and failure to respond in 3–4 weeks with complete healing should be regarded as an indication for surgical exploration and resection. However, even a carcinoma may show improvement on an ulcer regimen, and clinical relief does not necessarily mean that the ulcer is benign. Repeated follow-up at 6 weeks, 3 months, and 6 months after apparently complete healing is therefore indicated. In the event of recurrence under intensive medical management, perforation, obstruction, or massive uncontrollable hemorrhage, surgery is mandatory.

Prognosis

Gastric ulcers have a lesser tendency to recur than duodenal ulcers. There is no significant evidence that malignant degeneration of gastric peptic ulceration ever occurs.

Brandborg, L.L., & J. Wenger: Cytological examination in gastrointestinal tract disease. M Clin North America 52:1315–1328, 1968.

Doll, R., Langman, M.J., & H.H. Shawdon: Treatment of gastric ulcer with estrogens. Gut 9:46–47, 1968.

Kukral, J.C.: Gastric ulcer: An appraisal. Surgery 63:1024–1036, 1968.

Nelson, S.W.: The discovery of gastric ulcers and the differential diagnosis between benignancy and malignancy. Radiol Clin North America 7:5–25, 1969.

3. STOMAL (MARGINAL) ULCER
(Jejunal Ulcer)

Marginal ulcer should be suspected when there is a history of operation for an ulcer followed by recurrence of abdominal symptoms after a symptom-free interval of months to years. The marginal ulcer incidence after simple gastroenterostomy is 35–75%; after subtotal gastrectomy or vagotomy, about 5%. Approximately ½ of the ulcers are jejunal, and the others are located on the gastric side of the anastomosis. The abdominal pain is burning or gnawing, often more severe than the preoperative ulcer pain, and is located lower in the epigastrium, even below the umbilicus and often to the left. The pain often covers a wider area and may radiate to the back.

The "food-pain rhythm" of peptic ulcer distress frequently occurs earlier (within an hour) in marginal ulcer as a result of more rapid emptying time; and relief with antacids, food, and milk may be incomplete and of short duration. Nausea, vomiting, and weight loss are common. Hematemesis occurs frequently. Low epigastric tenderness with voluntary muscle guarding is usually present. An inflammatory mass may be palpated. Anemia and occult blood in the stool are common. On gastric analysis free hydrochloric acid can be demonstrated, although rapid emptying makes the procedure difficult. On x-ray the ulcer niche at the stoma is often difficult to demonstrate, although compression films are helpful and narrowing of the stoma is suggested. On gastroscopy the marginal ulcer may be visualized; jejunal craters can also be seen occasionally.

Stomal ulcer must be differentiated from functional gastrointestinal distress, especially in a patient concerned about the possibility of recurrence of an ulcer after surgery. Atypical symptoms must be differentiated from gastritis and pancreatic disease.

Complications include gross hemorrhage, perforation, stenosis of the stoma, and gastrojejunocolic fistula.

A course of ulcer therapy should be given as outlined for duodenal ulcer. Stomal ulcers are often resistant to medical therapy, however, and vagotomy or a more extensive gastrectomy is usually necessary to decrease the acid secretion of the stomach.

X-ray therapy to the stomach (1800–2000 r) will substantially reduce the gastric secretion of hydrochloric acid and in some instances may induce achlorhydria for varying periods of time. The use of x-ray therapy to the stomach should be restricted to those instances of complicating disease leading to increased surgical risk and to the elderly patients in whom temporary benefit may be optimal.

Andros, G., & others: Anastomotic ulcers. Ann Surg 165:955–966, 1967.

POSTGASTRECTOMY (DUMPING) SYNDROME

The postgastrectomy (dumping) syndrome probably occurs in about 10% of patients after partial gastrectomy. Its cause is not completely understood, but most evidence points to the following sequence of events: The ingestion and rapid hydrolysis of food, especially carbohydrates, results in hypertonicity in the jejunal contents; this causes a rapid inflow of fluid into the jejunum from the surrounding plasma and extracellular tissues, creating a drop in the circulating blood volume. This change in blood volume produces a sympathetic vasomotor response, ie, the symptoms the patient complains of. This sympathetic response, although possibly due in part to a distended jejunum, is mainly secondary to the diminished blood volume.

One or more of the following symptoms occurs within 20 minutes after meals: sweating, tachycardia, pallor, epigastric fullness and grumbling, warmth, nausea, abdominal cramps, weakness, and, in severe cases, syncope, vomiting, or diarrhea. Nonspecific ECG changes may be noted. Blood sugar is not low during an attack.

It is important to distinguish this syndrome from spontaneous hypoglycemia which occurs in some postgastrectomy patients and is associated with a low blood sugar. This latter syndrome occurs much later after the meal (1–3 hours) and is relieved by the ingestion of food.

Changing the diet to frequent, small, equal feedings high in protein, moderately high in fat, and low in carbohydrate usually reduces the severity of symptoms. Sedative and anticholinergic drugs may be of value. Serotonin antagonists (eg, phenothiazines) have been reported to relieve symptoms, but this has not been thoroughly evaluated.

Buchwald, H.: The dumping syndrome and its treatment. A review and presentation of cases. Am J Surg 116:81–88, 1968.

Silver, D., & others: The pathogenesis and management of the dumping syndrome. Monogr Surg Sc 3:365–406, 1966.

CARCINOMA OF THE STOMACH

Essentials of Diagnosis

- Upper gastrointestinal symptoms with weight loss in patients over age 40.
- Palpable abdominal mass.
- Anemia, occult blood in stools, positive cytology.
- Gastroscopic and x-ray abnormality.

General Considerations

Carcinoma of the stomach is a common cancer of the digestive tract. It occurs predominantly in males over 40 years of age. Delay of diagnosis is caused by absence of definite early symptoms and by the fact that patients treat themselves instead of seeking early medical advice. Further delays are due to the equivocal nature of early findings and to temporary improvement with symptomatic therapy.

A history of the following precancerous or possibly precancerous conditions should alert the physician to the danger of stomach cancer:

(1) **Atrophic gastritis of pernicious anemia:** The incidence of adenomas and carcinomas is significantly increased.

(2) **Chronic gastritis, particularly atrophic gastritis:** There is a wide variation in the reported incidence of gastritis with cancer, and a definite relationship has not been proved.

(3) **Gastric ulcer:** The major problem is in the differentiation between benign and malignant ulcer.

(4) **Achlorhydria:** The incidence of lowered secretory potential in early life is higher in those patients who later develop carcinoma.

Carcinoma may originate anywhere in the stomach. Grossly, lesions tend to be of 4 types (Boremann):

Type I: Polypoid, intraluminal mass.
Type II: Noninfiltrating ulcer.
Type III: Infiltrating ulcer.
Type IV: Diffuse infiltrating process (to linitis plastica).

Gross typing generally correlates better with prognosis than the histologic grading of malignancy, ie, type I has a better prognosis than type II, etc.

Clinical Findings

A. Symptoms and Signs: There is no characteristic symptom or symptom complex in early gastric carcinoma. The patient may complain of vague fullness, nausea, sensations of pressure, belching, and heartburn after meals, with or without anorexia, especially for meat. These symptoms in association with weight loss and decline in general health and strength in a man over 40 years of age should suggest the possibility of stomach cancer. Diarrhea, hematemesis, and melena may be present.

Specific symptom complexes may be determined in part by the location of the tumor. A peptic ulcer-like syndrome generally occurs with ulcerated lesions (types II and III) and in the presence of acid secretion, but may occur with complete achlorhydria. Unfortunately, symptomatic relief with antacids (even healing of the ulcer) tends to delay diagnosis. Symptoms of pyloric obstruction are progressive postprandial fullness to retention type vomiting of almost all foods. Lower esophageal obstruction causes progressive dysphagia and regurgitation.

Physical findings are usually limited to weight loss and, if anemia is present, pallor. In about 20% of cases a palpable abdominal mass is present; this does not necessarily mean that the lesion is inoperable. Liver or peripheral metastases may also be present.

B. Laboratory Findings: Achlorhydria after stimulation with betazole (Histalog®), 1.5 mg/kg subcut, in the presence of a gastric ulcer is pathognomonic of malignancy. The presence of acid does not exclude malignancy. If bleeding occurs, there will be occult blood in the stool and mild to severe anemia. With bone marrow invasion, the anemia may be normoblastic.

C. Other Examinations: X-ray or gastroscopic visualization of the lesion is important diagnostically. However, biopsy and positive pathologic examination of exfoliated cells is diagnostic.

Differential Diagnosis

The symptoms of carcinoma of the stomach are often mistaken for those of benign gastric ulcer, chronic gastritis, irritable colon syndrome, or functional gastrointestinal disturbance; x-ray and gastroscopic findings must be differentiated from those of benign gastric ulcer or tumor. In case of doubt, an exploratory operation is in order.

Stomach sarcoma is often clinically indistinguishable from gastric carcinoma until biopsy examination. Primary sarcoma of the stomach is rare, but it accounts for 10% of malignant gastric tumors in persons under 30 years of age. A palpable mass is more frequent in sarcomatous lesions than in gastric carcinoma, and the x-ray picture is characteristically that of a well-circumscribed intramural mass with, frequently, a central crater.

It is important to differentiate localized sarcomatous lesions from gastric lymphomas, which are best treated by resection followed by irradiation. The prognosis varies widely with the histologic type, but in general is better than that of gastric carcinoma.

Treatment

Surgical resection is the only curative treatment. Signs of metastatic disease include a hard, nodular liver, enlarged left supraclavicular (Virchow's) nodes, skin nodules, ascites, rectal shelf, and x-ray evidence of osseous or pulmonary metastasis. If none of these are present and there is no other contraindication to operation, exploration is indicated. The presence of an abdominal mass is not a contraindication to laparotomy, since bulky lesions can often be totally excised. Palliative resection or gastroenterostomy is occasionally helpful. High-voltage x-ray therapy may be of some value.

Prognosis

There is wide variation in the biologic malignancy of gastric carcinomas. In many the disease is widespread before symptoms are apparent; in a fortunate few a slow growth may progress over years and be resectable even at a late date.

Brandborg, L.L., Tankersley, C.B., & F. Vyeda: "Low" vs "high" concentration chymotrypsin in gastric exfoliative cytology. Gastroenterology 57:500–505, 1969.

Gilbertsen, V.A.: Results of treatment of stomach cancer. Cancer 23:1305–1308, 1969.

Kelsey, J.R.: *Cancer of the Stomach*. Thomas, 1967.

McNeer, G., & G.T. Pack: *Neoplasms of the Stomach*. Lippincott, 1967.

Prolla, J.C., Kobayashi, S., & J.B. Kirsner: Gastric cancer. Arch Int Med 124:238–246, 1969.

Ringerta, N.: The pathology of gastric carcinoma. Nat Cancer Inst Monogr 25:275–285, 1967.

BENIGN TUMORS OF THE STOMACH

Most benign tumors do not cause symptoms, and often are so small that they are overlooked on x-ray examination. Their importance lies in the problem of differentiation from malignant lesions, their precancerous possibilities, and the fact that they occasionally cause symptoms.

These tumors may be of epithelial origin (eg, adenomas, papillomas) or mesenchymal origin (eg, leiomyomas, fibromas, hemofibromas, lipomas, hemangiomas). The mesenchymal tumors, which are intramural, rarely undergo malignant change.

Clinical Findings

A. Symptoms and Signs: Large tumors may cause a vague feeling of epigastric fullness or heaviness; tumors located near the cardia or pylorus may produce symptoms of obstruction. If bleeding occurs it will cause symptoms and signs of acute gastrointestinal hemorrhage (eg, tarry stools, syncope, sweating, vomiting of blood). Chronic blood loss will cause symptoms of anemia (fatigue, dyspnea, syncope). If the tumor is large, a movable epigastric mass may be palpable.

B. Laboratory Findings: The usual laboratory findings may be present.

C. X-Ray Findings: The x-ray is characterized by a smooth filling defect, clearly circumscribed, which does not interfere with normal pliability or peristalsis. Larger tumors may have a small central crater visible on x-ray.

Treatment & Prognosis

If symptoms occur (particularly hemorrhage), surgical resection is necessary. Although adenomas have a very low malignant potential, many workers favor their removal even though they have been observed over a period of many years in certain patients without malignant change.

Beard, E.J., & others: Non-carcinomatous tumours of the stomach. Brit J Surg 55:535–538, 1968.

Trumbull, W.E., Uriu, M., & R.A. Weber: Surgical management of benign intramural gastric tumors. Pacific Med Surg 75:156–160, 1967.

DISEASES OF THE INTESTINES

BACILLARY DYSENTERY
(Shigellosis)

Essentials of Diagnosis

- Cramps and diarrhea, often with blood and mucus in the stools.
- Fever, malaise, myalgia, prostration.
- Pus in stools; organism isolated on stool culture.
- Characteristic sigmoidoscopic findings.

General Considerations

Shigella dysentery is a common disease, but it often occurs in mild or atypical forms and is unrecognized. Carriers often contribute to water- or milk-borne epidemics. Fly spread is important in areas of poor sanitation.

The infection may become localized and cause changes in the colon and the terminal ileum. Mucosal lymphoid hyperplasia, edema, and congestion progress to tiny follicular ulcers which enlarge and often become confluent. Mesenteric lymphadenitis is often present.

Clinical Findings

A. Symptoms and Signs: The onset is often abrupt, with diarrhea, lower abdominal cramps and tenesmus, anorexia, nausea, chills, malaise, myalgia, headache, and drowsiness. The disease may vary from almost asymptomatic, with a few soft stools daily, to quite severe, with frequent watery stools containing blood and mucus, severe general toxicity, and even convulsions. Prostration and dehydration are progressive. The abdomen is moderately tender but not rigid. Fever may be high, but is usually 38.9° C (102° F) or less.

B. Laboratory Findings: Polymorphonuclear leukocytosis; hemoconcentration; blood, mucus, and pus in the stools. Stool culture is positive for shigella strains (often difficult or impossible to isolate), and there is a transitory rise of agglutination titers, often with bizarre cross-reactions.

C. Special Examinations: On sigmoidoscopic examination there is early punctate follicular hyperplasia on an engorged mucosa progressing to punctate follicular bleeding ulcers and then large discrete or confluent ulcers.

Differential Diagnosis

Bacillary dysentery must be distinguished from functional diarrhea, parasitic and viral infections, and diarrhea associated with chronic ulcerative colitis; and from salmonella or staphylococcal food poisoning.

Complications

Complications include perforation and peritonitis (rare), anal excoriations and abscesses, and acute arthritis, manifested by painful effusion in a large joint.

Treatment*

A. Emergency Measures (for Severe Cases): Isolate the patient and use all contagious disease precautions. Combat dehydration and electrolyte imbalance by the liberal use of saline and dextrose solutions intravenously and, when necessary, potassium solutions. Urinary output should be kept at 1000–1500 ml/day. In the absence of specific severe intestinal infections which predispose to perforation, the cautious use of narcotics may be considered to reduce fluid loss and relieve pain. Watch for circulatory collapse and shock. Obtain a stool specimen for microscopic examination and culture.

B. Specific Measures: The broad-spectrum antibiotics are now considered the drugs of choice, since many strains are now resistant to the sulfonamides. There is a significant variation in response of specific organisms in different individuals. Give one of the tetracyclines or, if essential, chloramphenicol (Chloromycetin®), 0.25–1 gm every 6 hours. Ampicillin (Penbritin®, Polycillin®), 20–40 mg/kg body weight every 6 hours for 6–16 days, is reported to be effective. Sulfadiazine is the sulfonamide of choice if antibiotics are not available. Give 2–4 gm immediately with equal or double quantities of sodium bicarbonate, and follow with 1–2 gm every 4 hours. If diarrhea is severe, larger doses by mouth or parenteral sodium sulfadiazine may be necessary.

For very severe bacillary dysentery, serum treatment (in addition to antibiotics or sulfonamides) may be helpful: (1) Bacillary dysentery polyvalent antitoxin serum. Test for sensitivity and administer

*Chronic bacillary dysentery: Treat as for chronic nonspecific ulcerative colitis.

30–100 ml diluted 10-fold in physiologic saline solution IV 3 times daily until the toxemia is overcome. (2) Shiga antitoxin serum. Administer as above in doses of 40–80 ml in 500 ml saline solution IV twice daily.

C. General Measures: The patient should be isolated at bed rest and all body discharges, dirty bed linens, and bed clothing carefully disinfected. Rectal hygiene is important. When diarrhea is severe and the patient is weak, it may be advisable to have him defecate on disposable absorbent pads or sheets to avoid exertion. Initial purgation therapy is probably not advisable. Local heat may be applied to the abdomen for pain. Phenobarbital, 15–30 mg orally 3 or 4 times daily, or pentobarbital sodium, 0.1–0.13 gm orally as needed, may be used if sedation is required. For severe pain give codeine phosphate, 15–65 mg orally or subcut as needed. Give camphorated tincture of opium (paregoric), 4–8 ml as necessary for pain and frequent loose bowel movement. Atropine sulfate, 0.3–0.6 mg orally or subcut, is effective for relief of cramps.

Adequate fluid intake by oral and parenteral routes should be forced to the limit of tolerance. Total oral fluid intake should be about 3 liters/day during the acute phase. One liter or more of parenteral saline solution daily may be necessary to replace fluid and salt losses in profuse diarrhea.

Although starvation diets are undesirable, patients with severe bacillary dysentery should not be allowed to eat a "normal" diet for 6–8 weeks after the acute phase has subsided. Give parenteral feedings, if necessary, and evaluate bowel symptoms before adding the various dietary constituents. In the early acute stage, give clear broths, rice water, albumin water, tea with lactose, barley water, or apple juice (not cider) at frequent intervals. In the late acute stage, gradually add (as tolerated) boiled milk, cereals and strained fruit juices, toasted soda crackers or bread, and gelatin desserts. In the subacute stage, gradually add (as tolerated) mashed potatoes, boiled rice, boiled chicken, soft-cooked eggs, lean fish, scraped beef, and custards and puddings.

Prognosis

The uncomplicated disease lasts about 1 week. Antibiotics and general measures speed recovery and lower the mortality rate, which may be significant, particularly in infants and old people.

Barrett-Connor, E.: Shigellosis in the adult. JAMA 198:717–720, 1966.

FOOD POISONING

The term food poisoning here refers to the acute intoxication which results from the noxious agents or enterotoxins produced by bacteria. This is in contrast to gastrointestinal disturbances which are actually the result of infection of the gastrointestinal tract with microbial organisms or which are due to vegetable, animal, or chemical poisons. Food poisoning is a result of poor hygiene in preparation, processing, storage, distribution, or handling of food. Food poisoning should be suspected in febrile gastrointestinal disturbances of acute onset, especially when more than one person in a family, group, or community is involved. Diagnosis is aided by a careful history and collection of specimens of suspected food, vomitus, and stools for laboratory study. Reporting to local health authorities is essential.

Treatment is symptomatic and supportive except in botulism, for which specific antitoxin is indicated. Perform gastric lavage and withhold food and sedation. Correct disturbances of fluid and electrolyte balance. Liquid and soft diets are indicated in convalescence.

Patterson, M. (editor): Symposium on treatment of gastrointestinal infections. Mod Treat 3:965–1087, 1966.

Taylor, J.: Salmonella food poisoning. Practitioner 195:12–17, 1965.

TABLE 10–1. Differential diagnosis of bacterial food poisoning.

Organism	Onset After Ingestion	Severity
Clostridium botulinum	12–24 hours	Very severe; often fatal.
Staphylococcus aureus	1–6 hours	May be severe; usually recover in 1–4 days.
Salmonella enteritidis	8–24 hours	May be severe; usually recover in 1–2 days.
Streptococcus faecalis	5–20 hours	

REGIONAL ENTERITIS
(Regional Ileitis, Regional Enterocolitis, Granulomatous Ileocolitis, Crohn's Disease)

Essentials of Diagnosis

- Insidious onset.
- Intermittent bouts of diarrhea, low-grade fever, and right lower quadrant pain in a young adult.
- Fistula formation or right lower quadrant mass and tenderness.
- X-ray evidence of abnormality of the terminal ileum.

General Considerations

Regional enteritis is a chronic inflammatory disease of the small intestine causing fever, weight loss, and disturbed bowel function. It generally occurs in young adults and runs an intermittent clinical course with mild to severe disability and frequent complications.

The etiology is not known. The terminal ileum is the typical primary site, but involvement may extend up to the duodenum and into the colon, at times as "skip lesions" with normal intestine intervening. There is marked thickening of the submucosa with lymphedema, lymphoid hyperplasia, and nonspecific granulomas, and often ulceration of the overlying mucosa. A marked lymphadenitis occurs in the mesenteric nodes.

Clinical Findings

A. Symptoms and Signs: The disease is characterized by exacerbations and remissions. Abdominal pain, colicky or steady, in the right lower quadrant or periumbilical area, is present at some time during the course of the disease and varies from mild to severe. Diarrhea may occur, usually with intervening periods of normal bowel function or constipation. Fever may be low-grade or, rarely, spiking with chills. Anorexia, flatulence, malaise, and weight loss are present. Milk products and chemically or mechanically irritating foods may aggravate symptoms.

Abdominal tenderness, especially in the right lower quadrant, with signs of peritoneal irritation and an abdominal or pelvic mass in the same area, is usually present. The mass is tender and varies from a sausage-like thickened intestine to matted loops of intestine. The patient usually appears chronically ill.

B. Laboratory Findings: There is usually a hypochromic (occasionally macrocytic) anemia and occult blood in the stool. The x-ray shows mucosal irregularity, ulceration, stiffening of the bowel wall, and luminal narrowing in the terminal ileum. Sigmoidoscopic examination may show an edematous hyperemic mucosa or a discrete ulcer when the colon is involved.

Differential Diagnosis

Acute regional enteritis may simulate acute appendicitis. Location in the terminal ileum requires differentiation from intestinal tuberculosis and lymphomas. Regional enteritis involving the colon must be distinguished from idiopathic ulcerative colitis, amebic colitis, and infectious disease of the colon. The sigmoidoscopic and x-ray criteria distinguishing these various entities may not be absolute, and definitive diagnosis may require cultures, examinations of the stool for parasites, and biopsy in selected instances.

Complications

Ischiorectal and perianal fistulas occur frequently. Fistulas may occur to the bladder or vagina and even to the skin in the area of a previous scar. Mechanical intestinal obstruction may occur. Nutritional deficiency due to malabsorption may produce a sprue-like syndrome. Generalized peritonitis is rare because perforation occurs slowly.

Treatment & Prognosis

A. General Measures: The diet should be generous, high-calorie, high-vitamin, and adequate in proteins, excluding raw fruits and vegetables. Treat anemia, dehydration, diarrhea, and avitaminosis as indicated. The sulfonamides may exert a favorable effect. Give sulfisoxazole (Gantrisin®), phthalylsulfathiazole (Sulfathalidine®), or salicylazosulfapyridine (Azulfidine®) in an initial dosage of 1–1.5 gm 4–8 times daily in equal doses, preferably with meals or taken with food. With improvement, the dosage may be reduced to 0.5 gm 3 times daily. Penicillin and the tetracyclines are best avoided because of their tendency to produce candidal or enterococcal diarrhea. Corticotropin and the corticosteroids may be beneficial in some patients with diffuse regional enteritis; some clinicians use the corticosteroids in ileitis when suppurative complications are not present. Experience indicates that long-term use of these agents may not be without hazard.

B. Surgical Measures: Surgery may be necessary for the treatment of specific complications (eg, abscesses, fistulas, intestinal obstruction, or hemorrhage). Short-circuiting operations may be necessary when involvement is extensive and complications are present.

Crohn, B.B.: Granulomatous diseases of the small and large bowel: A historical survey. Gastroenterology 52:767–772, 1967.

Goldstein, M.J., & others: Ulcerative and "granulomatous" colitis: Validity of differential diagnostic criteria. Ann Int Med 72:841–851, 1970.

Law, D.H.: Regional enteritis. Gastroenterology 56:1086–1110, 1969.

Slaney, G.: Crohn's disease. Brit MJ 3:294–298, 1969.

Zetzel, L.: Granulomatous (ileo) colitis. New England J Med 282:600–605, 1970.

TUMORS OF THE SMALL INTESTINE

Benign and malignant tumors of the small intestine are rare. There may be no symptoms or signs, but bleeding or obstruction (or both) may occur. The obstruction consists either of an intussusception with the tumor in the lead or a partial or complete occlusion in the lumen by growth of the tumor. Bleeding may cause weakness, fatigability, lightheadedness, syncope, pallor, sweating, tachycardia, and tarry stools. Obstruction causes nausea, vomiting, and abdominal pains. The abdomen is tender and distended, and bowel sounds are diminished or absent. Malignant lesions produce weight loss and extra-intestinal manifestations (eg, pain due to stretching of the liver capsule, flushing due to carcinoid). In the case of a duodenal carcinoma, a peptic ulcer syndrome may be present. A palpable mass is rarely found.

If there is bleeding, melena and hypochromic anemia occur. X-ray may show the tumor mass or abnormality in the small bowel if obstruction is present; in the absence of obstruction, it is extremely difficult to demonstrate the mass.

Benign Tumors

Benign tumors may be symptomatic or may be incidental findings at operation or autopsy. Treatment consists of surgical removal.

Benign *adenomas* constitute 25% of all benign bowel tumors. *Lipomas* occur most frequently in the ileum; the presenting symptom is usually obstruction due to intussusception. *Leiomyomas* are usually associated with bleeding and may also cause intussusception. *Angiomas* behave like other small bowel tumors but have a greater tendency to bleed.

Malignant Tumors

The treatment of malignant tumors and their complications is usually surgical.

Adenocarcinoma is the most common malignancy of the small bowel, occurring most frequently in the duodenum and jejunum. Symptoms are due to obstructions or hemorrhage. The prognosis is very poor. *Lymphomas* are also first manifested by obstruction or bleeding. Perforation or sprue may also occur. Postoperative radiation therapy may occasionally be of value. *Sarcomas* occur most commonly in the mid small bowel, and may first be manifested by mass, obstruction, or bleeding. The prognosis is guarded.

Carcinoid tumors arise from the argentaffin cells of the gastrointestinal tract. Ninety percent of these tumors occur in the appendix and 75% of the remainder occur in the small intestine (usually the distal ileum). Carcinoids may arise in other sites, including the stomach, colon, bronchus, pancreas, and ovary. The tumor may secrete serotonin, and the systemic manifestations may consist of (1) paroxysmal flushing and other vasomotor symptoms, (2) dyspnea and wheezing, (3) recurrent episodes of abdominal pain and diarrhea, and (4) symptoms and signs of right-sided valvular disease of the heart. The diagnosis is confirmed by finding elevated levels of 5-hydroxyindoleacetic acid in the urine. The primary tumor is usually small, and obstruction is unusual. The metastases are usually voluminous and surprisingly benign. Treatment is symptomatic and supportive; surgical excision may be indicated if the condition is recognized before widespread metastases have occurred. Response to treatment with serotonin antagonists has been irregular. Repeated administration of corticotropin or the corticosteroids may occasionally be of value. The prognosis for cure is poor, but long-term survival is not unusual.

Marshak, R.H., & others: Metastatic carcinoma of the small bowel. Am J Roentgenol 94:385–394, 1965.

McPeak, C.J.: Malignant tumors of the small intestine. Am J Surg 114:402–411, 1967.

Ostermiller, W., Joergenson, E.J., & L. Weibel: A clinical review of tumors of the small bowel. Am J Surg 111:403–409, 1966.

MECKEL'S DIVERTICULITIS

Meckel's diverticulum, a remnant of the omphalo-mesenteric duct, is found in about 2% of persons, more frequently in males. It arises from the ileum 2 or 3 feet from the ileocecal valve and may or may not have an umbilical attachment. Most are silent, but various abdominal symptoms may occur. The blind pouch may be involved by an inflammatory process similar to appendicitis; its congenital bands or inflammatory adhesions may cause acute intestinal obstruction; it may induce intussusception; or, in the 16% which contain heterotopic islands of gastric mucosa, it may form a peptic ulcer.

The symptoms and signs of the acute appendicitis-like disease and the acute intestinal obstruction caused by Meckel's diverticulitis cannot be differentiated from other primary processes except by exploration. Ulcer-type distress, if present, is localized near the umbilicus or lower and, more important, is not relieved by alkalies or food. If ulceration has occurred blood will be present in the stool. Other laboratory findings often cannot be differentiated from those of appendicitis or other causes of obstruction. Massive gastrointestinal bleeding and perforation may occur.

Meckel's diverticulitis should be resected, either for relief or for differentiation from acute appendicitis. Surgery is curative.

Passaro, E., Jr., Richmond, D., & H.E. Gordon: Surgery for Meckel's diverticulum in the adult. Arch Surg 93:315–318, 1966.
Rutherford, R.B., & D.R. Ahers: Meckel's diverticulum: A review of 148 pediatric patients. Surgery 59:618–626, 1966.

MESENTERIC VASCULAR INSUFFICIENCY

1. MESENTERIC VASCULAR ISCHEMIA
(Abdominal Angina)

The syndrome of intestinal angina has received increasing attention of late. Progress in angiographic technics and vascular surgery has led to effective diagnostic and therapeutic approaches. The entity may be secondary to atherosclerosis and may precede vascular occlusion (see below). In some instances it is secondary to compression of the vessels either by the crura of the diaphragm or by anomalous bands.

Localized or generalized postprandial pain is the classical picture. The intensity of pain may be related to the size of the meal; the relationship to eating leads to a diminution in food intake and eventually weight loss. An epigastric bruit may be heard. Laboratory evidence of malabsorption may be present. The small bowel series may reveal a motility disorder. Visceral angiograms are necessary to confirm the narrowing of the celiac or mesenteric arteries.

Surgical revascularization of the bowel is the treatment of choice. In certain instances, small, frequent feedings prove helpful.

Corday, E., Gold, H., & J.K. Vyden: Gastrointestinal vascular syndromes. Hosp Practice 5:57–65, 1970.
Dick, A.P., & others: An arteriographic study of mesenteric arterial disease. Gut 8:206–220, 1967.
Dunbar, J.D., & S.W. Nelson: Nonangiographic manifestations of intestinal vascular disease. Am J Roentgenol 99:127–135, 1967.
Marston, A.: Mesenteric arterial disease: The present position. Gut 8:203–205, 1967.

2. MESENTERIC VASCULAR OCCLUSION

Essentials of Diagnosis
- Severe abdominal pain with nausea, fecal vomiting, and bloody diarrhea.
- Severe prostration and shock.
- Abdominal distention, tenderness, rigidity.
- Leukocytosis, hemoconcentration.

General Considerations
Mesenteric arterial or venous occlusion is a catastrophic abdominal disorder. Arterial occlusion is occasionally embolic but is more frequently thrombotic. Both occur more frequently in men and in the older age groups.

The superior mesenteric artery or its branches are often involved. The affected bowel becomes congested, hemorrhagic, and edematous, and may cease to function, producing intestinal obstruction. True ischemic necrosis then develops.

Clinical Findings
A. Symptoms and Signs: Generalized abdominal pain often comes on abruptly, and is usually steady and severe, but it may begin gradually and may be intermittent with colicky exacerbations. Nausea and vomiting occur; the vomitus is rarely bloody but frequently contains feces. Bloody diarrhea and marked prostration, sweating, and anxiety may occur. A history of abdominal surgery or inflammation or of an embolic source or arteriosclerosis may be elicited.

Shock may be evident. Abdominal distention occurs early, and audible peristalsis (evident early) may later disappear. Peritoneal irritation is demonstrated by diffuse tenderness, rigidity, and rebound tenderness.

B. Laboratory Findings: Hemoconcentration, leukocytosis (over 15,000 with a shift to the left), and often blood in the stool.

C. X-Ray Findings: A plain film of the abdomen shows moderate gaseous distention of the small and large intestines and evidence of peritoneal fluid.

Differential Diagnosis

Differentiate from acute pancreatitis, anoxic organic obstruction, and a perforated viscus. The elevated amylase in pancreatitis, the characteristic x-ray picture of obstruction, and free peritoneal air in perforation may differentiate these conditions.

Treatment & Prognosis

Treat shock. Surgical exploration is indicated with minimal delay. Gangrenous bowel should be resected and an end-to-end anastomosis performed if feasible. When the infarction is due to embolization or isolated thrombus of the superior mesenteric artery, embolectomy or thrombectomy may be possible and should be attempted. Anticoagulants are not indicated.

The mortality rate is extremely high in the acute disease.

Bergan, J.J., & others: Intestinal ischemic syndromes. Ann Surg 169:120–126, 1969.

Kittredge, R.D.: Ischemia of the bowel. Am J Roentgenol 103:400–404, 1968.

Ottinger, L.W., & W.G. Austen: A study of 136 patients with mesenteric infarction. Surg Gynec Obst 124:251–261, 1967.

Stoney, R.J., & E.S. Wylie: Recognition and surgical management of visceral ischemic syndrome. Ann Surg 164:714–722, 1966.

INTUSSUSCEPTION

Intussusception is the prolapse of intestine into the lumen of the adjoining portion, causing intestinal obstruction. It is primarily a disease of infants and young children, predominantly males, but it can occur at any age. The most frequent site of intussusception is around the ileocecal valve, with ileum prolapsing into the cecum or colon. There is a marked tendency for the invaginated portion to progress with peristalsis of the investing bowel, and this may compromise the circulation of the invaginated portion and cause congestion, edema, and gangrene. Any lesion of the intestine—Meckel's diverticulum, polyps, submucous tumors, ulcers—can provoke an intussusception, but in most cases in infants and children no such lesions are demonstrable.

Clinical Findings

A. Symptoms and Signs: The onset is with paroxysms of severe colicky abdominal pain and short periods of remission. Later the pain may be more steady. Vomiting often occurs early and may persist or may disappear. Diarrhea is usually present at the onset; blood and mucus are generally present in later stools. An abdominal mass is found in most cases when the examination is satisfactory (as under anesthesia) and varies from a small nodule to a sausage-shaped tumor, usually in the right abdomen and often more distinct

during periods of pain. The mass may move during the progress of the intussusception. On rectal examination one may be able to palpate the mass or the head of the intussusception or, rarely, see its actual prolapse. There may be blood and mucus in the rectum. Dehydration and fever are late signs.

B. Laboratory Findings: Blood and mucus in the stool may be present. With gangrene the white blood count is elevated.

C. X-Ray Findings: Barium contrast x-rays may show the obstruction in the colon or cecum (rarely in the terminal ileum), and the head of the prolapsed portion may be outlined. Higher enteric intussusceptions show only the intestinal obstruction pattern on a plain film of the abdomen.

Complications

Strangulation with gangrene, perforation, and peritonitis may occur in untreated intussusception.

Treatment

Decompression of the bowel by intubation or enterostomy may be sufficient to relieve the intussusception and should not be delayed for more than 24–36 hours. However, conservative decompression is usually not indicated in adults. Barium enema reduction may be attempted in the early stages and is successful in a limited number of cases. (See Acute Organic Intestinal Obstruction, below.) If there is no response to decompression or if signs of gangrene become apparent, surgical exploration and removal of the causative factor (eg, polyp, Meckel's diverticulum, foreign bodies, carcinoma) is mandatory.

Prognosis

Barium enema reduction in the early stage or operative reduction and resection, if necessary, give excellent results, and recurrence is rare in the absence of a precipitating lesion. Spontaneous reduction of an intussusception can occur with repeated attacks.

Dick, A., & G.S. Green: Large bowel intussusception in adults. Brit J Radiol 34:769–777, 1961.

ACUTE ORGANIC INTESTINAL OBSTRUCTION

Essentials of Diagnosis

- Colicky abdominal pain, fecal vomiting, constipation, borborygmus.
- Progressive shock, tender distended abdomen without peritoneal irritation.
- Audible high-pitched tinkling peristalsis or peristaltic rushes.
- X-ray evidence of gas or gas and fluid levels without movement of gas.
- Little or no leukocytosis.

General Considerations

Acute organic intestinal obstruction usually involves the small intestine, particularly the ileum. Major inciting causes are external hernia and band adhesions. Less common causes are gallstones, neoplasms, granulomatous processes, intussusception, volvulus, and internal hernia.

Clinical Findings

A. Symptoms and Signs: Colicky abdominal pain in the periumbilical area becomes more constant and diffuse as distention develops. Vomiting, at first of a reflex nature associated with the waves of pain, later becomes fecal. Borborygmus and consciousness of intestinal movement, obstipation, weakness, perspiration, and anxiety are often present. The patient is restless, changing position frequently with pain, and is often in a shock-like state with sweating, tachycardia, and dehydration. Abdominal distention may be localized, with an isolated loop, but usually is generalized. The higher the obstruction, the less the distention; the longer the time of obstruction, the greater the distention. Audible peristalsis, peristaltic rushes with pain paroxysms, high-pitched tinkles, and visible peristalsis may be present. Abdominal tenderness is absent to moderate, and generalized, and there are no signs of peritoneal irritation. Fever is absent or low-grade. A tender hernia may be present.

B. Laboratory Findings: With dehydration hemoconcentration may occur. Leukocytosis is absent or mild. Vomiting may cause electrolyte disturbances.

C. X-Ray Findings: Abdominal x-ray reveals gas-filled loops of bowel, and the gas does not progress downward on serial x-rays. Fluid levels may be visible.

Differential Diagnosis

Differentiate from other acute abdominal conditions such as inflammation and perforation of a viscus or renal or gallbladder colic. The absence of both rigidity and leukocytosis helps distinguish the obstruction from inflammation and perforation; the location, radiation, and the absence of distention or fecal vomiting distinguish the colic. Differentiate also from mesenteric vascular disease and torsion of an organ (eg, ovarian cyst). In the late stages of obstruction it may be impossible to distinguish acute organic intestinal obstruction from the late stage of peritonitis.

Complications

Anoxic changes may occur initially due to volvulus, external or internal hernia, band obstruction of the closed loop type, and intussusception.

Treatment

A. Conservative Measures: Fluid balance must be restored and maintained. The abdomen should be decompressed with a Levin tube or long intestinal tube and suction. If strangulation has not occurred, conservative treatment (decompression alone) may be tried for 24–36 hours and is frequently successful in partial obstruction caused by adhesions. The patient must be constantly observed and surgical correction undertaken at the first indication of strangulation or if there is no improvement after 24–36 hours. In general, however, definitive treatment by intubation should not be attempted in complete large or small bowel obstruction.

With signs of improvement (cessation of pain, decreased distention, decrease in the volume of suction drainage, passage of gas and feces per rectum), constant suction can be replaced by intermittent suction (2 hours on, 2 off) and, after 24 hours, by gravity drainage while oral fluids are permitted by mouth. If oral fluid therapy is well tolerated and bowel function is maintained, the tube may be removed.

The failure to tolerate oral fluids is an indication to resume suction or surgical correction.

B. Surgical Measures: Failure to respond to conservative therapy, the occurrence of strangulation, or the presence of a lesion frequently associated with strangulation (volvulus, hernia, obturation, intussusception in adults, or complete obstruction by adhesions) is usually an indication for immediate surgical correction after fluid and electrolyte balance has been restored. Surgery consists of relieving the obstruction and removing the cause, and resecting any gangrenous bowel with end-to-end anastomosis.

Prognosis

Prognosis varies with the causative factor and is definitely improved by early relief of obstruction. This may be possible by intestinal intubation with decompression, but surgery is usually required.

Greene, W.W.: Bowel obstruction in the aged: A review of 300 cases. Am J Surg 118:541–545, 1969.
Remenchik, A.P., & P.J. Talso: Medical management of intestinal obstruction. M Clin North America 48:67–74, 1964.

FUNCTIONAL OBSTRUCTION
(Adynamic Ileus, Paralytic Ileus)

Essentials of Diagnosis

- Continuous abdominal pain, distention, vomiting, and obstipation.
- History of a precipitating factor (surgery, peritonitis, pain).
- Minimal abdominal tenderness; decreased to absent bowel sounds.
- X-ray evidence of gas and fluid in bowel.

General Considerations

Adynamic ileus is a neurogenic impairment of peristalsis which may lead to intestinal obstruction. It is a common disorder due to a variety of intra-abdominal causes, eg, direct gastrointestinal tract irritation (surgery), peritoneal irritation (hemorrhage, ruptured viscus, pancreatitis, peritonitis), and anoxic organic obstruction. Renal colic, vertebral fractures, spinal cord injuries, pneumonia and other severe infections, uremia, and diabetic coma also may cause adynamic ileus.

Clinical Findings

A. Symptoms and Signs: There is mild to moderate abdominal pain, continuous rather than colicky, associated with vomiting (which may later become fecal) and obstipation. Borborygmus is absent. The symptoms of the initiating condition may also be present, eg, fever and prostration due to a ruptured viscus.

Abdominal distention is generalized and may be massive, with nonlocalized minimal abdominal tenderness and no signs of peritoneal irritation unless due to the primary disease. Bowel sounds are decreased to absent. Dehydration may occur after prolonged vomiting. Other signs of the initiating disorder may be present.

B. Laboratory Findings: With prolonged vomiting hemoconcentration and electrolyte imbalance may occur. Leukocytosis, anemia, and elevated serum amylase may be present depending upon the initiating condition.

C. X-Ray Findings: X-ray of the abdomen shows distended gas-filled loops of bowel in the small and large intestines and even in the rectum. There may be evidence of air-fluid levels in the distended bowel.

Differential Diagnosis

The symptoms and signs of obstruction with absent bowel sounds and a history of a precipitating condition leave little doubt as to the diagnosis. It is important to make certain that the adynamic ileus is not secondary to an organic obstruction, especially anoxic, where conservative management is harmful and immediate surgery may be lifesaving.

Treatment

Most cases of adynamic ileus are postoperative and respond to restriction of oral intake with gradual liberalization of the diet as the bowel function returns. Severe and prolonged ileus may require gastrointestinal suction and complete restriction of oral intake. Parenteral restoration of fluids and electrolytes is essential in such instances. When conservative therapy fails it may be necessary to operate for the purpose of decompressing the bowel by enterostomy or cecostomy and to rule out mechanical obstruction.

Those cases of adynamic ileus secondary to other diseases (eg, electrolyte imbalance, severe infection, intra-abdominal or back injury, pneumonitis) are managed as above plus treatment of the primary disease.

Prognosis

The prognosis varies with that of the initiating disorder. Adynamic ileus may resolve without specific therapy when the cause is removed. Intubation with decompression is usually successful in causing return of function.

Catchpole, B.N.: Ileus: Use of sympathetic blocking agents in its treatment. Surgery 66:811–820, 1969.

SPRUE SYNDROME
(Malabsorption Syndrome, Tropical Sprue, Nontropical Sprue, Idiopathic Steatorrhea)

Essentials of Diagnosis

- Bulky, pale, frothy, foul-smelling, greasy stools with increased fecal fat on chemical analysis of the stool.
- Weight loss and signs of multiple vitamin deficiencies.
- Impaired intestinal absorption of glucose, vitamins, fat; large amounts of free fatty acids and soaps in the stool.
- Hypochromic or megaloblastic anemia; "deficiency" pattern on small bowel x-ray.

General Considerations

Sprue syndromes are diseases of disturbed small intestine function characterized by impaired absorption, particularly of fats, and motor abnormalities. Celiac disease and nontropical sprue respond to gluten-free diets. The polypeptide gliadin is the offending substance in gluten. Tropical sprue does not respond to gluten-free diet. It is apparently a deficiency state which responds to folic acid and tetracyclines.

Pathologic changes are minimal other than the marked wasting and the signs of multiple vitamin deficiencies. A flat intestinal mucosa without villi in the small intestine is noted, and some observers have described degenerative changes in the myenteric nerve plexuses.

Rare secondary varieties of sprue syndrome in which the cause of the small intestine dysfunction is known include gastrocolic fistulas, obstruction of intestinal lacteals by lymphoma, Whipple's disease, extensive regional enteritis, and parasitic infections such as giardiasis, strongyloidiasis, and coccidiosis.

Clinical Findings

A. Tropical Sprue: The main symptom is diarrhea; at first it is explosive and watery; later, stools are fewer and more solid and characteristically pale, frothy, foul-smelling, and greasy, with exacerbations on high-fat diet or under stress. Indigestion, flatulence, abdominal cramps, weight loss (often marked), pallor, asthenia, irritability, paresthesias, and muscle cramps may occur. Quiescent periods with or without mild symptoms often occur, especially on leaving the tropics.

Vitamin deficiencies cause glossitis, cheilosis, angular stomatitis, cutaneous hyperpigmentation, and dry rough skin. Abdominal distention and mild tenderness are present. Edema occurs late.

Hypochromic microcytic anemia or macrocytic anemia with a megaloblastic marrow may be present. The fecal fat is increased, mainly as free saturated fatty acids and soaps. Absorption of other substances is decreased, giving flat oral vitamin A tolerance and glucose tolerance curves. The intravenous glucose tolerance, however, is normal. Plasma carotene and proteins and serum calcium, phosphorus, cholesterol, and prothrombin are low. Gastric hypochlorhydria is present. The pancreatic enzymes are normal.

If x-rays are taken with barium which flocculates, a deficiency pattern is noted—ie, dilatations, segmentation and irregular flocculation of barium, loss of the normal feathery mucosal pattern, and often excess gas in the dilated loops. If nonflocculating barium is used, dilatation of the gut is the main abnormality.

B. Celiac Sprue: This disorder is characterized by defective absorption of fat, protein, vitamin B_{12}, carbohydrate, and water. Absorption of fat-soluble vitamins A, D, and K is impaired. Osteomalacia may ensue. Protein loss from the intestine may occur. Elimination of gluten from the diet causes dramatic improvement.

In 1/3 of patients with celiac sprue, the onset is in early childhood, but symptoms may persist into adult life. The anemia is usually hypochromic and microcytic. The complications of impaired absorption are more severe: infantilism, dwarfism, tetany, vitamin deficiency signs, and even rickets may be seen. Low plasma carotene is often used as a diagnostic criterion.

Differential Diagnosis

It is necessary to distinguish primary sprue syndromes from those that are secondary to other gastrointestinal diseases, such as gastrocolic fistula, Whipple's disease, intestinal lymphoma, and extensive regional enteritis. These are usually easily differentiated by the characteristic x-ray patterns. Neutral stool fats, decreased pancreatic enzymes, and a normal to diabetic glucose tolerance curve differentiate the steatorrhea of pancreatic disease. Intestinal and mesenteric tuberculosis, although rare, may also mimic primary sprue. Small intestine suction biopsy is the most definitive way of establishing the diagnosis of celiac sprue.

Treatment

The anemia of sprue is treated by means of oral iron administration when the anemia is hypochromic. The macrocytic anemia of nontropical sprue usually responds to cyanocobalamin (vitamin B_{12}), $15-30~\mu g$ IM, $1-2$ times per week, and then $10-15~\mu g$ IM every $1-2$ weeks after remission is obtained; or folic acid, $10-15$ mg daily orally or IM.

The diet should be high-caloric, high-protein, low-fat, and gluten-free. If strict exclusion of gluten from the diet does not lead to improvement, the diagnosis is incorrect and another cause must be sought for the malabsorption syndrome. Prothrombin deficiency is treated by means of water-soluble vitamin K preparations orally or, if urgent, intravenously or intramuscularly. For hypocalcemia or tetany give calcium chloride, phosphate, or gluconate, 2 gm orally 3 times daily; and vitamin D, $5000-20,000$ units. Vitamin supplements by mouth are also advisable in sprue.

The corticosteroids may be advantageous in certain sprue patients since they increase the absorption of nitrogen, fats, and other nutrients from the gastrointestinal tract.

Prognosis

With proper treatment the clinical and hematologic response is good.

Brandborg, L.L.: Structure and function of the small intestine in some parasite diseases. Am J Clin Nutr 24:124–132, 1971.

Finkelstein, J.D.: Malabsorption. M Clin North America 52:1339–1354, 1968.

Greenberger, N.J., & T.G. Skillman: Medium-chain triglycerides: Physiologic considerations and clinical implications. New England J Med 280:1045–1058, 1969.

Isselbacher, K.J.: Biochemical aspects of fat absorption. Gastroenterology 50:78–82, 1966.

Jeffries, G.H., Weser, E., & M.H. Sleisinger: Malabsorption. Gastroenterology 56:777–797, 1969.

Klipstein, F.A.: Tropical sprue. Gastroenterology 54:275–293, 1968.

Kowlessar, O.D., & L.D. Phillips: Celiac disease. M Clin North America 54:647–656, 1970.

Krone, C.L., & others: Studies on the pathogenesis of malabsorption. Medicine 47:89–108, 1968.

Mann, J.G., Brown, W.R., & F. Kern, Jr.: The subtle and variable clinical expression of gluten-induced enteropathy (adult celiac disease, non-tropical sprue). Am J Med 48:357–366, 1970.

Roggin, G.M.: Malabsorption in the chronic alcoholic. Johns Hopkins Med J 125:321–330, 1969.

Rubin, C.E., & W.O. Dobbins, III: Peroral biopsy of the small intestine. A review of its diagnostic usefulness. Gastroenterology 49:676–697, 1965.

Rubin, C.E., Eidelman, S., & W.M. Weinstein: Sprue by any other name. Gastroenterology 58:409–413, 1970.

DISACCHARIDASE DEFICIENCY

The specific disaccharidase deficiencies in the intestinal mucosa have become increasingly important in our understanding of malabsorption. The congenital absence of these enzymes leads to an acidic diarrhea (fecal pH 4.5–6.0). There are large amounts of lactic acid in the stool. The infant fails to thrive. The onset of the clinical picture in the adult may follow intestinal surgery, regional enteritis, ulcerative colitis, or the sprue syndromes. The diagnosis is confirmed by a flat oral tolerance to the specific disaccharide and the onset of an acidic diarrhea with ingestion of the offending sugar.

Thus far lactose, sucrose-isomaltose, and glucose-galactose intolerances have been described as congenital defects. Secondary disaccharidase deficiencies have been described in both children and adults with giardiasis, celiac disease, ulcerative colitis, short bowel syndrome, cystic fibrosis, and after gastrectomy.

McCracken, R.D.: Adult lactose tolerance. JAMA
    213:2257–2260, 1970.

Peternel, W.W.: Disaccharidase deficiency. M Clin North Amer-
    ica 52:1355–1366, 1968.

Welsh, T.D., & others: Human intestinal disaccharidase activity.
    Arch Int Med 117:488–503, 1966.

INTESTINAL LIPODYSTROPHY
(Whipple's Disease)

Whipple's disease is an uncommon malabsorption
disorder of unknown etiology with widespread systemic manifestations. Histologic examination of the
small bowel mucosa and mesenteric and peripheral
lymph nodes reveals characteristic large, foamy mononuclear cells filled with cytoplasmic material which
gives a positive periodic acid-Schiff (PAS) staining reaction. Electron microscopic studies reveal bacterial
bodies in the macrophages. The disease occurs primarily in middle-aged men and is of insidious onset;
the course, without treatment, is usually downhill. The
clinical manifestations include abdominal pain, diarrhea, steatorrhea, gastrointestinal bleeding, fever,
lymphadenopathy, polyarthritis, edema, and gray to
brown skin pigmentation. Anemia and hypoproteinemia are common.

The response to treatment with broad-spectrum
antibiotics is often dramatic. The prognosis with antibiotics is markedly improved.

Clemett, A.R., & R.H. Marshak: Whipple's disease: Roentgen
    features and differential diagnosis. Radiol Clin North
    America 7:105–111, 1969.

Fearrington, E.L., & E.W. Monroe: Whipple's disease. Postgrad
    Med 44:103–109, 1968.

PSEUDOMEMBRANOUS ENTEROCOLITIS

Pseudomembranous enterocolitis is a necrotizing
lesion of the gut which may extend from the stomach
to the rectum. Grossly it is characterized by a friable,
grayish-yellow membrane loosely adherent to the
underlying mucosa or submucosa. Microscopically,
mucosal necrosis, leukocytes, and necrotic debris are
enmeshed in the fibrin membrane. Gram-positive cocci
and other bacteria may be present in the membrane.
The etiology is not completely understood, but the
evidence points to the enterotoxin of the hemolytic
Staphylococcus aureus as the precipitating factor. Suppression of other intestinal bacteria by antibiotics leads
to the overgrowth of staphylococci.

The disease usually becomes manifest from the
2nd–12th day after surgery or after antibiotic therapy.
The patient usually has had or is taking antibiotics.
The initial symptoms are usually diarrhea and fever.

Diarrhea is profuse and watery and the stools may
resemble serum and have a peculiar necrotic odor.
Some patients may show abdominal distention or
vomiting. The patient's condition rapidly deteriorates,
with tachycardia, hypotension, shock, dehydration,
oliguria, and electrolyte and protein loss. Liquid stools
may exceed 10 liters/day. Leukocyte counts are normal or elevated. Hemoconcentration frequently occurs.
Stools may contain membrane, leukocytes, and gram-
positive cocci.

Pseudomembranous enterocolitis must be distinguished from other postoperative complications such
as peritonitis, mesenteric thrombosis, and hypovolemia
due to blood loss. The history of antibiotic therapy
and major surgery (especially gastrointestinal) are
important in the differential diagnosis.

All antibiotics the patient is receiving at the outset of the disease must be discontinued. Combat the
marked dehydration and electrolyte depletion which
occurs with electrolyte solutions containing sodium
and potassium according to the patient's needs.
Administer plasma, whole blood, and corticosteroids
to combat shock. Vancomycin (Vancocin®), 250–500
mg IV, is the treatment of choice if the patient is not
vomiting and does not have profound illness; otherwise, give cephalothin (Keflin®), 1 gm IV, every 6
hours until toxicity subsides and staphylococci disappear from the stools. In noninfective pseudomembranous colitis failing to respond to treatment, colectomy has been suggested when the disease process is
confined to the colon.

Pseudomembranous enterocolitis is an extremely
grave condition. Mortality statistics vary from
30–90%.

Gelfand, M.D., & D.L. Krone: Nonstaphylococcal pseudomem-
    branous colitis. Am J Digest Dis 14:278–281, 1969.

Groll, A., & others: Fulminating noninfective pseudomembran-
    ous colitis. Gastroenterology 58:88–95, 1970.

Moore, H.D.: Diagnosis and natural history of gas cysts of the
    colon. Brit MJ 2:536–537, 1968.

APPENDICITIS

Essentials of Diagnosis

- Right lower quadrant abdominal pain and
  tenderness with signs of peritoneal irritation.
- Anorexia, nausea, vomiting, constipation.
- Low-grade fever and mild polymorphonuclear leukocytosis.

General Considerations

Appendicitis is initiated by obstruction of the
appendiceal lumen by a fecalith, inflammation, foreign
body, or neoplasm. Obstruction is followed by infection, edema, and frequently infarction of the appendiceal wall. Intraluminal tension develops rapidly and
tends to cause early mural necrosis and perforation. All

ages and both sexes are affected, but appendicitis is more common in males between 10 and 30 years of age.

Appendicitis is one of the most frequent causes of acute surgical abdomen. The symptoms and signs usually follow a fairly stereotyped pattern, but appendicitis is capable of such protean manifestations that it should be considered in the differential diagnosis of every obscure case of intra-abdominal sepsis and pain.

Clinical Findings

A. Symptoms and Signs: An attack of appendicitis usually begins with epigastric or periumbilical pain associated with 1–2 episodes of vomiting. Within 2–12 hours the pain shifts to the right lower quadrant, where it persists as a steady soreness which is aggravated by walking or coughing. There is anorexia, moderate malaise, and slight fever. Constipation is usual, but diarrhea occurs occasionally.

At onset there are no localized abdominal findings. Within a few hours, however, progressive right lower quadrant tenderness can be demonstrated; careful examination will usually identify a single point of maximal tenderness. The patient can often place his finger precisely on this area, especially if asked to accentuate the soreness by coughing. Light percussion over the right lower quadrant is helpful in localizing tenderness. Rebound tenderness and spasm of the overlying abdominal muscles are usually present. Psoas and obturator signs, when positive, are strongly suggestive of appendicitis. Rectal tenderness is common and, in pelvic appendicitis, may be more definite than abdominal tenderness. Peristalsis is diminished or absent. Slight to moderate fever is present.

B. Laboratory Findings: Moderate leukocytosis (10,000–20,000/cu mm) with an increase in neutrophils is usually present. It is not uncommon to find a few red cells on microscopic examination of the urine, but otherwise the urinalysis is not remarkable.

C. X-Ray Findings: There are no characteristic changes on plain films of the abdomen. However, visualization in the right lower quadrant of a radiopaque shadow consistent with fecalith in the appendix may heighten suspicion of appendicitis.

Factors Which Cause Variations From the "Classical" Clinical Picture

A. Anatomic Location of Appendix: Abdominal findings are most definite when the appendix is in the iliac fossa or superficially located. When the appendix extends over the pelvic brim, the abdominal signs may be minimal, greatest tenderness being elicited on rectal examination. Right lower quadrant tenderness may be poorly localized and slow to develop in retrocecal or retroileal appendicitis. Inflammation of a high-lying lateral appendix may produce maximal tenderness in the flank. Bizarre locations of the appendix may rarely occur in association with a mobile or undescended cecum; in such cases symptoms and signs may be localized in the right upper or the left lower quadrant.

B. Age:

1. Infancy and childhood—In infancy appendicitis is relatively rare, but when it occurs the diagnosis is difficult because of the problem of interpretation of history and physical findings. The disease tends to progress rapidly and, when rupture occurs, to result in generalized peritonitis because of poor localizing mechanisms.

2. Old age—Elderly patients frequently have few or no prodromal symptoms. Abdominal findings may be unimpressive, with slight tenderness and neglible muscle guarding until perforation occurs. Fever and leukocytosis may also be minimal or absent. When the white count is not elevated, a shift to the left is significant evidence of inflammation.

3. Obesity—Obesity frequently increases the difficulty of evaluation by delaying the appearance of abdominal signs and by preventing their sharp localization.

4. Pregnancy—See discussion in Chapter 12.

Differential Diagnosis

Acute gastroenteritis is the disorder most commonly confused with appendicitis. In rare cases it either precedes or is coincident with appendicitis. Vomiting and diarrhea are more common. Fever and white blood count may rise sharply and may be out of proportion to abdominal findings. Localization of pain and tenderness is usually indefinite and shifting. Hyperactive peristalsis is characteristic. Gastroenteritis frequently runs an acute course. A period of observation usually serves to clarify the diagnosis.

Mesenteric adenitis may cause signs and symptoms identical with appendicitis. Usually, however, there are some clues to the true diagnosis. Mesenteric adenitis is more likely to occur in children or adolescents; respiratory infection is a common antecedent; localization of right lower quadrant tenderness is less precise and constant; and true muscle guarding is infrequent. In spite of a strong suspicion of mesenteric adenitis, it is often safer to advise appendectomy than to risk a complication of appendicitis by procrastination.

Meckel's diverticulitis may mimic appendicitis. The localization of tenderness may be more medial, but this is not a reliable diagnostic criterion. Because operation is required in both diseases, the differentiation is not critical. When a preoperative diagnosis of appendicitis proves on exploration to be erroneous, it is essential to examine the terminal 5 feet of the ileum for Meckel's diverticulitis and mesenteric adenitis.

Regional enteritis, perforated duodenal ulcer, ureteral colic, acute salpingitis, mittelschmerz, ruptured ectopic pregnancy, and twisted ovarian cyst may at times also be confused with appendicitis.

Complications

A. Perforation: Appendicitis may subside spontaneously, but it is an unpredictable disease with a marked tendency to progression and perforation. Because perforation rarely occurs within the first 8 hours, diagnostic observation during this period is relatively safe. Signs of perforation include increasing severity of pain, tenderness, and spasm in the right lower quadrant followed by evidence of generalized peritonitis or of a localized abscess. Ileus, fever, malaise, and leukocytosis become more marked. If perforation with abscess formation or generalized peritonitis has already occurred when the patient is first seen, the diagnosis may be quite obscure.

Treatment of perforated appendicitis is appendectomy unless a well-localized right lower quadrant or pelvic abscess has already walled off the appendix. Supportive measures are as for acute peritonitis.

B. Generalized Peritonitis: This is a common sequel to perforation. Clinical findings and treatment are discussed elsewhere in this chapter.

C. Appendiceal Abscess: This is one of the possible complications of untreated appendicitis. Malaise, toxicity, fever, and leukocytosis vary from minimal to marked. Examination discloses a tender mass in the right lower quadrant or pelvis. Pelvic abscesses tend to bulge into the rectum or vagina.

Abscesses usually become noticeable 2–6 days after onset, but antibiotic therapy may delay their appearance. Appendiceal abscess is occasionally the first and only sign of appendicitis and may be confused with neoplasm of the cecum, particularly in the older age group in whom systemic reaction to the infection may be minimal or absent.

Treatment of early abscess is by intensive combined antibiotic therapy (eg, penicillin and streptomycin or tetracycline, or both). On this regimen, the abscess will frequently resolve. Appendectomy should be performed 6–12 weeks later. A well-established, progressive abscess in the right lower quadrant should be drained without delay. Pelvic abscess requires drainage when it bulges into the rectum or vagina and has become fluctuant.

D. Pylephlebitis: Suppurative thrombophlebitis of the portal system with liver abscesses is a rare but highly lethal complication. It should be suspected when septic fever, chills, hepatomegaly, and jaundice develop after appendiceal perforation. Intensive combined antibiotic therapy is indicated.

E. Other complications include subphrenic abscess and other foci of intra-abdominal sepsis. Mechanical intestinal obstruction may be caused by adhesions.

Treatment

A. Preoperative Care:

1. Observation for diagnosis–Within the first 8–12 hours after onset the symptoms and signs of appendicitis are frequently indefinite. Under these circumstances a period of close observation is essential. The patient is placed at bed rest and given nothing by mouth. *Note:* Laxatives should not be prescribed when appendicitis or any form of peritonitis is suspected. Parenteral fluid therapy is begun as indicated. Narcotic medications are avoided if possible, but sedation with barbiturates or tranquilizing agents is not contraindi-

cated. Abdominal and rectal examinations, white blood count, and differential count are repeated periodically. Abdominal films and an upright chest film are obtained on all difficult diagnostic problems. In most cases of appendicitis, the diagnosis is clarified by localization of signs to the right lower quadrant within 24 hours after onset of symptoms.

2. Intubation–Preoperatively, a nasogastric tube is inserted if there is sufficient peritonitis or toxicity to indicate that postoperative ileus may be troublesome. In such patients the stomach is aspirated and lavaged if necessary, and the patient is sent to the operating room with the tube in place.

3. Antibiotics–In the presence of marked systemic reaction with severe toxicity and high fever, preoperative administration of antibiotics (eg, penicillin and streptomycin) is advisable.

B. Surgical Treatment: In uncomplicated appendicitis, appendectomy is performed as soon as fluid imbalance and other significant systemic disturbances are controlled. Little preparation is usually required. Early, properly conducted surgery has a mortality of a fraction of 1%. Morbidity and mortality in this disease stem primarily from the complications of gangrene and perforation which occur when operation is delayed.

C. Postoperative Care: In uncomplicated appendicitis, postoperative gastric suction is usually not necessary. Ambulation is begun on the first postoperative day. The diet is advanced from clear liquids to soft solids during the 2nd–5th postoperative days, depending upon the rapidity with which peristalsis and gastrointestinal function return. Parenteral fluid supplements are administered as required. Enemas, except of the small oil retention type, are contraindicated. Mineral oil, milk of magnesia, or a similar milk laxative may be given orally at bedtime daily from about the third day onward if necessary. Antibiotic therapy (eg, penicillin with streptomycin or tetracycline, or both) is advisable for 5–7 days or longer if abdominal fluid at operation was purulent or malodorous, if culture was positive, or if the appendix was gangrenous. Primary wound healing is the rule, and the period of hospitalization is usually 1 week or less. Normal activity can be resumed in 2–3 weeks after surgery in uncomplicated cases, especially if a McBurney type incision was used.

D. Emergency Nonsurgical Treatment: When surgical facilities are not available, treat as for acute peritonitis. On such a regimen acute appendicitis will frequently subside and complications will be minimized.

Prognosis

With accurate diagnosis and early surgical removal of the appendix mortality and morbidity are minimal. Delay of diagnosis still produces significant mortality and morbidity if complications occur.

Recurrent acute attacks may occur if the appendix is not removed. "Chronic appendicitis" does not exist.

Brickman, I.D., & W. Leon: Acute appendicitis in childhood. Surgery 60:1083–1089, 1966.

Burgos, W.F., & D.G. Johnson: Appendicitis: A computer study. Postgrad Med 44:110–117, 1968.

Howie, J.G.R.: Death from appendicitis and appendectomy. Lancet 2:1334–1336, 1966.

Kazarian, K., Roeder, W.J., & W.L. Mersheimer: Decreasing mortality and increasing morbidity from acute appendicitis. Am J Surg 119:681–685, 1970.

Leffall, L.D., Jr., Cooperman, A., & B. Syphax: Appendicitis: A continuing surgical challenge. Am J Surg 113:654–659, 1967.

ACUTE MESENTERIC LYMPHADENITIS

Essentials of Diagnosis

- Constant right lower quadrant or periumbilical pain in a child.
- Anorexia, nausea, vomiting, fever up to 39.4° C (103° F).
- Right lower quadrant tenderness with minimal or no peritoneal irritation.
- Leukocytosis generally over 15,000/cu mm.
- History of recent or current upper respiratory infection.

General Considerations

Mesenteric lymphadenitis is an acute benign inflammation of the mesenteric lymph nodes causing fever and abdominal pain. It is usually a disease of children, may be recurrent, and presents a major problem in differentiation from acute appendicitis, Meckel's diverticulitis, renal infection or colic, and right lower lobe pulmonary infections in children with pain referred to the right lower quadrant. Episodes are frequently preceded by or accompanied by upper respiratory infections, and bacterial or viral etiology has been suggested. True suppuration is rare.

Clinical Findings

A. Symptoms and Signs: There is an acute onset of abdominal pain in the right lower quadrant of periumbilical area, generally steady from the onset rather than colicky, and associated with nausea, vomiting, and anorexia. Diarrhea often occurs. Abdominal tenderness is mild to severe and usually greatest in the right lower quadrant; point localization of pain is unusual. Peritoneal irritation and right vault rectal tenderness are mild or absent. Fever to 37.8–39.4° C (100–103° F) is usually present.

B. Laboratory Findings: There is a polymorphonuclear leukocytosis with a shift to the left, generally over 15,000/cu mm and higher than would be expected from the findings.

Treatment & Prognosis

Exploration may be warranted to be certain that the patient does not have appendicitis. Complete resolution is the rule.

Donhauser, J.L.: Primary acute mesenteric lymphadenitis. Arch Surg 74:528–535, 1957.

INTESTINAL TUBERCULOSIS
(Tuberculous Enterocolitis)

In the USA tuberculosis of the intestinal tract is almost always secondary to pulmonary tuberculosis. The incidence rises sharply in far-advanced lung disease.

The mode of infection is by ingestion of tubercle bacilli with the formation of ulcerating lesions in the intestine, particularly the ileocecal region, and involvement of the mesenteric lymph nodes.

Symptoms may be absent or minimal even with extensive disease. When present they usually consist of fever, anorexia, nausea, flatulence, distention after eating, and food intolerance. There may be abdominal pain and mild to severe cramps, usually in the right lower quadrant and often after meals. Constipation may be present, but mild to severe diarrhea is more characteristic.

Abdominal examination is not characteristic, although there may be mild right lower quadrant tenderness. Fistula-in-ano may be evident. Weight loss occurs.

There are no characteristic laboratory findings. The presence of tubercle bacilli in the feces does not correlate with intestinal involvement.

X-ray examination reveals irritability and spasm, particularly in the cecal region, irregular hypermotility of the intestinal tract; ulcerated lesions and irregular filling defects, particularly in the right colon and ileocecal region; and pulmonary tuberculosis.

The prognosis varies with that of the pulmonary disease. The intestinal lesions usually respond to chemotherapy and rest when reexposure to infecting material is prevented.

Abrams, J.S., & W.D. Holden: Tuberculosis of the gastrointestinal tract. Arch Surg 89:282–293, 1964.

DISEASES OF THE COLON & RECTUM

CHRONIC NONSPECIFIC ULCERATIVE COLITIS

Essentials of Diagnosis

- Bloody diarrhea with lower abdominal cramps.
- Mild abdominal tenderness, weight loss, fever.
- Anemia; no stool pathogens.
- Specific x-ray and sigmoidoscopic abnormalities.

General Considerations

Chronic ulcerative colitis is an inflammatory disease of the colon of unknown etiology characterized by bloody diarrhea, a tendency to remissions and exacerbations, and involvement mainly of the left colon. It is primarily a disease of adolescents and young adults but may have its onset in any age group.

The pathologic process is that of acute nonspecific inflammation in the colon, particularly the rectosigmoid area, with multiple, irregular superficial ulcerations. Repeated episodes lead to thickening of the wall with scar tissue and the proliferative changes in the epithelium may lead to polypoid structures. The etiology is not known, and may be multiple.

Clinical Findings

A. Symptoms and Signs: This disease may vary from mild cases with relatively minimal symptoms to acute and fulminating, with severe diarrhea and prostration. Diarrhea is characteristic; there may be up to 30 or 40 discharges daily, with blood and mucus in the stools, or blood and mucus may occur without feces. Blood in the stool is the cardinal manifestation of ulcerative colitis. Constipation may occur instead of diarrhea.

Nocturnal diarrhea is usually present when daytime diarrhea is severe. Rectal tenesmus may be severe, and anal incontinence may be present. Cramping lower abdominal pain often occurs but is generally mild. Anorexia, dyspeptic symptoms, malaise, weakness, and fatigability may also be present. A history of intolerance to dairy products can often be obtained, and there is a tendency toward remissions and exacerbations.

Fever, weight loss, and evidence of toxemia vary with the severity of the disease. Abdominal tenderness is generally mild and occurs without signs of peritoneal irritation. Abdominal distention may be present in the fulminating form and is a poor prognostic sign. Rectal examination may show perianal irritation, fissures, hemorrhoids, fistulas, and abscesses.

B. Laboratory Findings: Hypochromic microcytic anemia due to blood loss is usually present. In acute disease a polymorphonuclear leukocytosis may also be present. The sedimentation rate is elevated. Stools contain blood, pus, and mucus but no pathogenic organisms. Hypoproteinemia may occur. In the fulminating disease electrolyte disturbances may be evident.

C. X-Ray Findings: On x-ray the involvement may be regional to generalized and may vary from irritability and fuzzy margins to pseudopolyps, decreased size of colon, shortening and narrowing of the lumen, and loss of haustral markings. When the disease is limited to the rectosigmoid area, the barium enema may even be normal.

D. Special Examinations: Sigmoidoscopic changes are present in over 90% of cases and vary from mucosal hyperemia, petechiae, and minimal granularity in mild cases to ulceration and polypoid changes in severe cases. The mucosa, even when it appears grossly normal, is almost invariably friable when wiped with a cotton sponge.

Differential Diagnosis

Differentiate from bacillary dysentery and amebic dysentery on the basis of specific stool pathogens. When rectal strictures have developed, differentiate from lymphogranuloma venereum by history and Frei test. Other points in the differential are functional diarrhea, regional enteritis, intestinal neoplasm, and diverticulitis. It is imperative that cultures and parasitology specimens be taken prior to barium examinations or initiation of therapy.

Complications

Pericolitis may develop with fever, increased pain and tenderness, and, at times, even a palpable mass and x-ray evidence of narrowing. Frank perforation may occur.

Perianal disorders such as hemorrhoids, fissures, abscesses, strictures, prolapse, and rectovaginal or rectovesical fistulas can occur.

Malignant degeneration can take place, and the incidence of carcinoma is higher in people with chronic ulcerative colitis.

Ulcerative esophagitis may also occur.

Deficiency disease can occur, presenting as retarded physical and sexual maturity (in disease starting in childhood), vitamin deficiency, fatty metamorphosis and cirrhosis of the liver, and osteoporosis.

Erythema nodosum, pyoderma gangrenosum, and acute arthritis may develop.

Treatment

Ulcerative colitis is a chronic disease. Symptomatic remission is not the only index of response. Treatment should be prolonged until the sigmoidoscopic and x-ray appearance of the colon have returned to normal.

A. General Measures: Bed rest is necessary during the acute phase of the disease, and may substantially reduce intestinal cramping and diarrhea. The diet should be bland. Ask the patient whether he has any food idiosyncrasies. During the acute phase, elimination of milk, milk products, and wheat may reduce the diarrhea; these foods may be added to the diet when the disease process has improved.

These patients need understanding and reassurance. Mild sedation is often necessary for nervousness.

Care should be used in the administration of antiperistaltic agents so that excessive amounts are not used; dilation of the colon may occur. Narcotics should be avoided except for severe diarrhea.

B. Medical Measures: The pathogenesis of ulcerative colitis is unknown. The role of autoimmunity or bacteria and the nature of precipitating events have not yet been discerned. Whatever the pathogenesis, corticotropin, adrenocorticosteroids, and the sulfonamides have provided the best means of control.

1. Adrenocorticosteroid hormones—Corticotropin and hydrocortisone are the most effective drugs for inducing remissions, and are definitely indicated in the severe toxic form of the disease. The hospitalized patient may be given corticotropin as IV drip (20—40 units over a period of 8 hours), or 80—100 units of gel subcut. If corticotropin is unavailable or contraindicated, give hydrocortisone (100—300 mg/day), prednisone or prednisolone (20—80 mg/day), or equivalent, depending upon individual preference. These drugs may be given parenterally if oral therapy seems ineffective. If the response to corticotropin is satisfactory, the dosage may be reduced or oral therapy with prednisone (20—40 mg/day) may be substituted and gradually reduced at weekly intervals over a period of 1—3 months. General measures include diet, rest, and sulfonamide drugs. These are essential during this phase of the illness.

Long-term suppression of ulcerative colitis with these agents leads to hyperadrenocorticism, osteoporosis, toxic psychosis, peptic ulcer, hypokalemia, and hyperglycemia. Local therapy of the colon by enema makes possible the long-term treatment with steroids with a negligible risk of hyperadrenocorticism and other complications. Give hydrocortisone hemisuccinate (100 mg) or prednisolone-21-phosphate (20 mg) in 100 ml of saline once or twice daily by slow rectal drip or retention enema; or hydrocortisone in oil (100 mg/2 oz) every night as a retention enema. The patient should preferably lie on his left side with the buttocks elevated. Hydrocortisone is the least expensive and can be prepared for home use by mixing 1.6 gm of hydrocortisone powder in 1 quart of vegetable oil.

2. Anti-infective agents—Sulfonamides are not curative but may be useful in management. In one carefully controlled study, sulfonamide therapy reduced the incidence of recurrence and severity of individual attacks. Although the poorly absorbable sulfonamides are preferred by many clinicians, there are no critical data confirming the superiority of the nonabsorbable over the absorbable drugs or of one drug over another. Give any of the following: (1) succinylsulfathiazole (Sulfasuxidine®), 3 gm every 4 hours; (2) phthalylsulfathiazole (Sulfathalidine®), 1—5 gm every 4 hours; (3) sulfisoxazole (Gantrisin®), 2 gm/day; or (4) salicylazosulfapyridine (Azulfidine®), 2—8 gm/day.

Penicillin, streptomycin, chloramphenicol, or other selected antibiotics may be indicated in certain instances (eg, localized perforation or systemic infection).

C. Surgical Measures: Surgery may be required if medical therapy is not successful after an adequate trial. Subtotal or total colectomy is the procedure of choice. Colectomy may prevent or correct some of the extracolonic manifestations of ulcerative colitis such as arthritis, iritis, and pyoderma.

Prognosis

The disease may have many remissions and exacerbations over many years. At times the course is fulminant. Permanent and complete cure on medical therapy is unusual, and life expectancy is shortened. Medical measures control the majority of cases, but colectomy is necessary for severe disease and for complications.

Christopher, N.L., Watson, D.W., & E.R. Farber: Relationship of chronic ulcerative esophagitis to ulcerative colitis. Ann Int Med 70:971—976, 1969.

DeDombal, F.T.: Ulcerative colitis: Definition, historical background, aetiology, diagnosis, natural history and local complications. Postgrad MJ 44:684—692, 1968.

Eade, M.N.: Liver disease in ulcerative colitis. I. Analysis of operative liver biopsy in 138 consecutive patients having colectomy. Ann Int Med 72:475—487, 1970.

Edwards, F.C., & S.C. Truelove: The course and prognosis of ulcerative colitis. I. Short-term prognosis. II. Long-term prognosis. III. Complications. IV. Carcinoma of the colon. GUT 4:299—315, 1963; 5:1—22, 1964.

Fink, S.J., & R.F. Mais: Cell-mediated immune reaction to colon altered by bacteria. GUT 9:629—632, 1968.

Folley, J.H.: Ulcerative proctitis. New England J Med 282:1362—1364, 1970.

Glotzer, D.J., & others: Comparative features and course of ulcerative and granulomatous colitis. New England J Med 282:582—587, 1970.

Goligher, J.C.: Surgical treatment of ulcerative colitis. Brit MJ 2:671—673, 1968.

Jalan, K.N., & others: Influence of corticosteroid on the results of surgical treatment for ulcerative colitis. New England J Med 282:588—592, 1970.

Matts, S.G.F.: Local treatment of ulcerative colitis with prednisolone-21-phosphate enemata. Lancet 1:517—519, 1960.

Mendeloff, A.I., & others: Illness experience and life stresses in patients with irritable colon and with ulcerative colitis. New England J Med 282:14—17, 1970.

Misiewicz, J.J., & others: Controlled trial of sulphasalazine [salicylazosulfapyridine; Azulfidine®] in maintenance therapy for ulcerative colitis. Lancet 1:185—188, 1965.

Truelove, S.C.: Medical management of ulcerative colitis. Brit MJ 2:539—541, 605—606, 1968.

Watkinson, G.: The medical treatment of ulcerative colitis. Postgrad MJ 44:696—707, 1968.

Watkinson, G., Thompson, H., & J.C. Goligher: Right-sided or segmental ulcerative colitis. Brit J Surg 47:337—351, 1960.

CONGENITAL MEGACOLON
(Hirschsprung's Disease)

Hirschsprung's disease is a congenital disorder characterized by massive dilatation of the proximal colon due to loss of propulsive function in the distal sigmoid and rectum. The basic pathophysiologic abnormality is absent or reduced ganglion cells in the rectum and lower sigmoid with loss of propulsive activity in this segment. Dilatation and muscular hypertrophy above this level are compensatory.

Symptoms include recurrent fecal impactions that are relatively refractory to cathartics and more responsive to enemas, infrequent bowel movements, and an enlarging abdomen. The periods between defecations may be 3—4 weeks or longer. Stools are large and have an offensive odor. Secondary symptoms include displacement of the thoracic contents, causing dyspnea, edema of the extremities, and audible borborygmus.

Abdominal distention is often massive and associated with costal flaring. Fecal masses and gas-filled loops of bowel are palpable in the abdomen, and sluggish visible peristalsis may be evident. Signs of poor nutrition may be present, such as multiple vitamin deficiencies, emaciation, and retarded growth. Secondary signs such as abdominal hernia, thinning of the abdominal wall, and diastasis recti abdominis are frequently present.

X-ray shows a normal or narrowed segment in the lower sigmoid or rectum and a dilated proximal colon.

In mild forms treatment may consist only of dietary supervision (avoiding high-residue foods) and giving stool softeners and lubricating agents. Frequent enemas are necessary. Parasympathomimetic drugs are useful on occasion.

If surgery is necessary the colon must be completely emptied and the gastrointestinal tract sterilized preoperatively. Cecostomy or colostomy is not definitive, but is a useful preliminary step until definitive surgery is feasible or as a life-saving procedure in a critically ill child.

The surgical procedure of choice is abdominoperineal removal of the rectosigmoid, the so-called "pull-through" operation (Swenson).

Abdominoperineal resection and anastomosis will yield excellent results in 80% of cases.

Soper, R.T., & F.E. Miller: Congenital aganglionic megacolon (Hirschsprung's disease). Arch Surg 96:554–562, 1968.

Tobon, F., & others: Nonsurgical test for diagnosis of Hirschsprung's disease. New England J Med 278:188–193, 1968.

DIVERTICULOSIS & DIVERTICULITIS

Essentials of Diagnosis

- Older person with left lower quadrant pain, constipation, and fever.
- Left lower quadrant tenderness with or without a palpable tender mass.
- Leukocytosis; blood may be present in the stool.
- X-ray evidence of diverticula and area of narrowing.

General Considerations

Diverticula in the colon become frequent with advancing age and in themselves cause no symptoms. The inflammatory complication, diverticulitis, probably affects 20–25% of diverticula at some time.

Colonic diverticula occur primarily in the high pressure areas of the colon. They tend to dissect along the course of the nutrient vessels and consist of a mucosal coat and a serosa. Although diverticula may occur throughout the gut, they are most common in the sigmoid colon and occur with increasing frequency after age 40.

Inflammatory changes in diverticulitis vary from mild infiltration in the wall of the sac to extensive inflammatory changes in the surrounding area (peridiverticulitis) with perforation or abscess formation. The changes are comparable to those seen in appendicitis.

Clinical Findings

Diverticulosis without diverticulitis is asymptomatic.

A. Symptoms and Signs: There are commonly intermittent episodes of left lower quadrant cramping to steady and severe abdominal pain which may last for days. Relief is often obtained by passing flatus or a bowel movement. Constipation is usual but diarrhea may occur. Blood in the stool is found in about 20% of cases. Massive hemorrhage may occur and is more common in diverticulosis. Dysuria and frequency may occur.

Left lower quadrant and left rectal vault tenderness may be mild or severe and signs of peritoneal irritation may be present. In about ½ of cases there is a left lower quadrant mass. Low-grade fever is present with attacks.

B. Laboratory Findings: Polymorphonuclear leukocytosis occurs with acute attacks.

C. X-Ray Findings: Barium enema may show the diverticula, spasm, and hypermotility of the involved segment, or irregular narrowing of a long segment of the lumen with fusiform ends and gradual transition to normal bowel.

D. Special Examination: Sigmoidoscopic examination rarely demonstrates the diverticula and reveals fixation and narrowing at the rectosigmoid junction.

Differential Diagnosis

The constrictive lesion of the bowel shown on x-ray or sigmoidoscopic examination must often be differentiated from carcinoma of the colon. The x-ray appearance of a short lesion and abrupt transition to normal bowel, and the frequent occurrence of blood in the stool, usually point to a carcinoma, but final differentiation can sometimes be made only by biopsy or at surgery.

Complications

Perforation, peritonitis, and complete intestinal obstruction may occur but are rare. Abscess and fistula formation also occur. The fistula is usually vesicosigmoid, but may go to the skin, the small intestine, or the perianal area.

Treatment

The treatment of uncomplicated diverticular disease consists of (1) a diet high in residue; (2) bulk additives, eg, psyllium hydrophilic mucilloid (Metamucil®); (3) a stool softener such as dioctyl sodium sulfosuccinate (Colace®, etc), 240 mg/day; and (4) anticholinergic drugs such as Donnatal®, Librax®, and propantheline (Pro-Banthine®). Vegetable oils (olive oil), mineral oil, and vegetable gum laxatives may be used.

The treatment of acute diverticulitis requires antibiotic therapy. The antibiotic of choice is ampicillin. Other useful antibiotic drugs include cephalothin (Keflin®) and combined treatment with penicillin and streptomycin.

Recurrent attacks of diverticulitis or the presence of perforation, fistulization, or abscess formation require surgical resection of the involved portion of the colon.

Prognosis

The usual case is mild and responds well to dietary measures and antibiotics.

Botsford, T.W., & R.M. Zollinger, Jr.: Diverticulitis of the colon. Surg Gynec Obst 128:1209–1214, 1969.
Colcock, B.P.: Management of complicated diverticulitis. S Clin North America 48:543–551, 1968.
Judd, E.S.: Massive bleeding of colonic origin. S Clin North America 49:977–989, 1969.
Tagart, R.E.: Diverticular disease of the colon: Clinical aspects. Brit J Surg 56:417–423, 1969.
Williams, I.: Diverticular disease of the colon: A 1968 review. GUT 9:498–501, 1968.

POLYPS OF THE COLON & RECTUM
(Intestinal Polyps)

Adenomatous polyps of the colon and rectum are common benign neoplasms which are usually asymptomatic but may cause painless rectal bleeding. They may be single or multiple, occur most frequently in the sigmoid and rectum, and are found incidentally in about 9% of autopsies. The incidence of polyps increases with age. The diagnosis is established by sigmoidoscopy and double contrast barium enema. When a polyp is found in the rectum, the colon should be studied by x-ray.

Whether polyps are precancerous is an important question. Pedunculated, adenomatous polyps probably have negligible malignant potential and may usually be treated by simple polypectomy through the sigmoidoscope. In most patients, surgery is not indicated unless the polyp grows on repeated observation or causes symptoms such as bleeding. Papillary (villous) adenomas are sessile lesions which are known to become metastasizing carcinoma and should be removed. The overwhelming majority of cancers of the colon and rectum arise as cancer de novo.

Familial intestinal polyposis is a rare hereditary disease characterized by innumerable adenomatous polyps of the colon and rectum. Cancer frequently develops in the large bowel, sometimes at a very early age. Colectomy with ileoproctostomy is the treatment of choice and may be followed by spontaneous regression of the rectal polyps. The rectum should be examined regularly and residual polyps removed

through the sigmoidoscope. If this is not possible, the rectum should also be excised.

Culp, C.E.: New studies of the colonic polyp and cancer. S Clin North America 47:955–960, 1967.
Drexler, J.: Asymptomatic polyps of the rectum and colon. Arch Int Med 121:62–66, 1968.
Thomas, K.E., & others: Natural history of Gardner's syndrome. Am J Surg 115:218–226, 1968.

CANCER OF THE COLON & RECTUM

Essentials of Diagnosis

- Altered bowel function (constipation or diarrhea).
- Blood in the feces, unexplained anemia, weight loss.
- Palpable mass involving colon or rectum.
- Sigmoidoscopic or x-ray evidence of neoplasm.

General Considerations

Carcinoma is the only common malignancy of the colon and rectum. Lymphoma, carcinoid, melanoma, fibrosarcoma, and other types of sarcoma do occur but are very rare. The treatment of all is essentially the same.

Carcinoma of the colon and rectum causes more deaths than any other form of cancer. The only known predisposing causes are familial multiple polyposis, chronic ulcerative colitis, chronic lymphogranuloma venereum, chronic granuloma inguinale, and perhaps adenoma. Males are affected more commonly than females in a ratio of 3:2. The highest incidence is in patients about 50 years of age, but occasional cases have been reported in younger persons and even in children. The anatomic distribution of cancer of the large bowel (based on a study of about 5000 cases) is approximately 16% in the cecum and ascending colon, 5% in the transverse colon, 9% in the descending colon, 20% in the sigmoid, and 50% in the rectum.

Of all lesions of the colon and rectum, 1/2–2/3 lie within reach of the examining finger or sigmoidoscope and therefore can be biopsied on the first visit.

Clinical Findings

Symptoms vary depending upon whether the lesion is in the right or the left side of the colon. In either case, a persistent change in the customary bowel habits almost always occurs and should invariably alert the physician to investigate the colon. An acute abdominal emergency may be precipitated by perforation or intussusception. The definitive diagnostic procedures in all cases are sigmoidoscopy and barium enema.

A. Carcinoma of the Right Colon: Because the fecal stream is fluid and the bowel lumen large in the right half of the colon, symptoms of obstruction occur less frequently than in left-sided tumors. Vague abdominal discomfort is often the only initial complaint. This may progress to cramp-like pain, occasionally simulating cholecystitis or appendicitis. Secondary anemia with associated weakness and weight loss is found in ½ of patients with right colon lesions. The stools are usually positive for occult blood but rarely show gross blood. The patient is likely to have diarrhea. The first indication of cancer may be the discovery of a palpable mass in the right lower quadrant.

B. Carcinoma of the Left Colon: Obstructive symptoms predominate, particularly increasing constipation. There may be short bouts of diarrhea. Occasionally the first sign is acute colonic obstruction. A small amount of bright red blood with bowel movements is common, and anemia is found in about 20% of cases. At times a mass is palpable. About ½ of patients give a history of weight loss.

Differential Diagnosis

Cancer of the colon may need to be differentiated from diverticulitis, which is usually associated with fever and has a different x-ray appearance. Functional bowel distress may also simulate cancer of the colon.

Treatment

The only curative treatment in cancer of the large bowel is wide surgical resection of the lesion and its regional lymphatics after adequate bowel preparation and appropriate supportive measures. When a significant degree of mechanical obstruction is present, a preliminary transverse colostomy or cecostomy is necessary. Even in the presence of metastatic disease, palliative resection may be of value to relieve obstruction, bleeding, or the symptoms of local invasion.

Care of the Colostomy

The commonest permanent colostomy is the sigmoid colostomy made at the time of combined abdominoperineal resection.

Colostomy irrigation is begun about 1 week after operation. Each day, a well-lubricated catheter or rectal tube is gently inserted about 15 cm into the colostomy and 500–1000 ml of water are instilled from an enema can or bag held 30–60 cm above the colostomy. After the bowel has become accustomed to regular enemas, evacuation will occur within about ½ hour after the irrigation. Some individuals have regular movements without irrigation. A small gauze or disposable tissue pad worn over the colostomy, held in place by a wide elastic belt or ordinary girdle, is usually all the protection required during the day. If the stoma is tight, it is advisable for the patient to dilate it daily for several months by insertion of the index finger. Commercial colostomy kits make care simple and convenient.

Three important principles of colostomy management are routine time for bowel evacuation; complete emptying after irrigation; and regulation of diet to avoid diarrhea. The patient with a colostomy can live a normal life.

Stricture, prolapse, and wound hernia are late colostomy complications requiring surgical correction. Skin irritation is less likely to occur than with ileostomy.

Prognosis

Over 90% of patients with carcinoma of the colon and rectum are suitable for either curative or palliative resection, with an operative mortality of 3–6%. The overall 5-year survival rate after resection is about 50%. If the lesion is confined to the bowel and there is no evidence of lymphatic or blood vessel invasion, the 5-year survival rate is 60–70%. Local recurrence of carcinoma in the anastomotic suture line or wound area occurs in 10–15% of cases. The incidence of local recurrence can be decreased if special precautions are taken at operation to avoid implantation of malignant cells. About 5% of patients develop multiple primary colon cancers. Early identification of resectable local recurrence or a new neoplasm depends upon careful follow-up with sigmoidoscopy and barium enema every 6 months for 2 years and yearly thereafter.

Dwight, R.W., Higgins, G.A., & R.J. Keehn: Factors influencing survival after resection in cancer of the colon and rectum. Am J Surg 117:512–522, 1969.

Galante, M., Dunphy, J.E., & W.S. Fletcher: Cancer of the colon. Ann Surg 165:732–744, 1967.

Scudamore, H.H.: Cancer of the colon and rectum: General aspects, diagnosis, treatment and prognosis. A review. Dis Colon Rectum 12:105–114, 1969.

DISEASES OF THE ANUS

HEMORRHOIDS

Internal hemorrhoids are varices of that portion of the venous hemorrhoidal plexus which lies submucosally just proximal to the dentate margin. External hemorrhoids arise from the same plexus but are located subcutaneously immediately distal to the dentate margin. There are 3 primary internal hemorrhoidal masses: right anterior, right posterior, and left lateral. Three to 5 secondary hemorrhoids may be present between the 3 primaries. Straining at stool, constipation, prolonged sitting, and anal infection are contributing factors and may precipitate complications such as thrombosis. Diagnosis is suspected on the history of protrusion, anal pain, or bleeding, and confirmed by proctologic examination.

Carcinoma of the colon or rectum not infrequently aggravates hemorrhoids or produces similar complaints. Polyps may be present as a cause of bleeding which is wrongly attributed to hemorrhoids. For these reasons, the treatment of hemorrhoids is always preceded by sigmoidoscopy and barium enema. When portal hypertension is suspected as an etiologic factor, investigations for liver disease should be carried out. Hemorrhoids which develop during pregnancy or parturition tend to subside thereafter and should be treated conservatively unless persistent after delivery.

The symptoms of hemorrhoids are usually mild and remittent, but a number of disturbing complications may develop and call for active medical or surgical treatment. These complications include pruritus, incontinence, recurrent protrusion requiring manual replacement by the patient, fissure, infection, or ulceration, prolapse and strangulation, and secondary anemia due to chronic blood loss. Carcinoma has been reported to develop very rarely in hemorrhoids.

Conservative treatment suffices in most instances of mild hemorrhoids, which may improve spontaneously or in response to low-roughage diet and regulation of the bowel habits with mineral oil or other nonirritating laxatives to produce soft stools. Local pain and infection are managed with warm sitz baths and insertion of a soothing anal suppository such as Anusol® 2 or 3 times daily. Ethylaminobenzoate (benzocaine) and similar types of anal ointments should be avoided so as not to sensitize the patient to these agents. Prolapsed or strangulated hemorrhoids should be gently reduced with the lubricated gloved fingers, the buttocks strapped, and the prone position maintained for a few days; surgery is recommended when the local reaction has subsided.

For severe symptoms or complications, complete internal and external hemorrhoidectomy is advisable and is a highly satisfactory procedure when properly done. Excision of a single external hemorrhoid, evacuation of a thrombosed pile, and the injection treatment of internal hemorrhoids fall within the scope of office practice.

Evacuation of Thrombosed External Hemorrhoid

This condition is caused by the rupture of a vein at the anal margin, forming a clot in the subcutaneous tissue. The patient complains of a painful lump, and examination shows a tense, tender, bluish mass covered with skin. If seen after 24–48 hours when the pain is subsiding—or if symptoms are minimal—hot sitz baths are prescribed. If discomfort is marked, removal of the clot is indicated. With the patient in the lateral position, the area is prepared with antiseptic and 1% procaine or lidocaine (Xylocaine®) is injected intracutaneously around and over the lump. A radial ellipse of skin is then excised and the clot evacuated. A dry gauze dressing is held in place for 12–24 hours by taping the buttocks together, and daily sitz baths are then begun.

Rowe, R.J.: Symposium: Management of hemorrhoidal disease. Dis Colon Rectum 11:127–136, 1968.

CRYPTITIS & PAPILLITIS

Anal pain and burning of brief duration with defecation is suggestive of cryptitis and papillitis. Digital and anoscopic examination reveals hypertrophied papillae and indurated or inflamed crypts. Treatment consists of mineral oil by mouth, sitz baths, anal suppository (Anusol®) after each bowel movement, and local application of 5% phenol in oil or carbolfuchsin compound to the crypts. If these measures fail, surgical excision of involved crypts and papillae should be considered.

Hirschman, L.J., Nigro, N.D., & R.M. Burke: The scope of office proctology: Cryptitis and papillitis. S Clin North America 35:1506–1507, 1955.

FISSURE-IN-ANO
(Anal Fissure)

Acute fissures represent linear disruption of the anal epithelium due to various causes. They usually clear if bowel movements are kept regular and soft (eg, with mineral oil). The local application of a mild styptic such as 1–2% silver nitrate or 1% gentian violet solution may be of value.

Chronic fissure is characterized by (1) acute pain during and after defecation; (2) spotting of bright red blood at stool with occasional more abundant bleeding; (3) tendency to constipation through fear of pain; and (4) the late occurrence of a sentinel pile, a hypertrophied papilla, and spasm of the anal canal (usually very painful on digital examination). Regulation of bowel habits with mineral oil or other stool softeners, sitz baths, and anal suppositories (eg, Anusol®), twice daily, should be tried. If these measures fail, the fissure, sentinel pile, or papilla and the adjacent crypt must be excised surgically. Postoperative care is along the lines of the preoperative treatment.

Alexander, R.M., & S.D. Manheim: Anal fissures in infants and children. J Dis Child 96:29–31, 1958.
Hayden, E.P.: Proctology. New England J Med 260:420–429, 1959.

ANAL ABSCESS

Perianal abscess should be considered the acute stage of an anal fistula until proved otherwise. The abscess should be adequately drained as soon as localized. Hot sitz baths may hasten the process of localization. The patient should be warned that after drainage of the abscess he may have a persistent fistula. It is painful and fruitless to search for the internal opening of a fistula in the presence of acute infection. The presence of an anal abscess should alert the clinician to the possibility of inflammatory bowel disease.

FISTULA-IN-ANO

About 95% of all anal fistulas arise in an anal crypt, and they are often preceded by an anal abscess. If an anal fistula enters the rectum above the pectinate line and there is no associated disease in the crypts, ulcerative colitis, rectal tuberculosis, lymphogranuloma venereum, cancer, or foreign body should be considered in the differential diagnosis.

Acute fistula is associated with a purulent discharge from the fistulous opening. There is usually local itching, tenderness, or pain aggravated by bowel movements. Recurrent anal abscess may develop. The involved crypt can occasionally be located anoscopically with a crypt hook. Probing the fistula should be gentle because false passages can be made with ease, and in any case demonstration of the internal opening by probing is not essential to the diagnosis.

Treatment is by surgical incision or excision of the fistula under general anesthesia. If a fistula passes deep to the entire anorectal ring so that all the muscles must be divided in order to extirpate the tract, a 2-stage operation must be done to prevent incontinence.

Jackman, R.J.: Anorectal fistulas: Current concepts. Dis Colon Rectum 11:247–255, 1968.

ANAL CONDYLOMAS

These wart-like papillomas of the perianal skin and anal canal flourish on moist, macerated surfaces, particularly in the presence of purulent discharge. They are not true tumors but are infectious and auto-inoculable, probably due to a virus. They must be distinguished from condyloma lata caused by syphilis. The diagnosis of the latter rests on the positive serologic test for syphilis or the discovery of *Treponema pallidum* on dark-field examination.

Treatment consists of accurate application of 25% podophyllin in tincture of benzoin to the lesion (with bare wooden or cotton-tipped applicator sticks to avoid contact with uninvolved skin). Condylomas in the anal canal are treated through the anoscope and the painted site dusted with powder to localize the application and minimize discomfort. Electrofulguration under local anesthesia is useful if there are numerous lesions. Local cleanliness and the frequent use of a talc dusting powder are essential.

Condylomas tend to recur. The patient should be observed for several months and advised to report promptly if new lesions appear.

BENIGN ANORECTAL STRICTURES

Congenital

Anal contracture or stenosis in infancy may result from failure of disintegration of the anal plate in fetal life. The narrowing is treated by careful repeated dilatation, inserting progressively larger Hegar dilators until the anus admits first the little and then the index finger.

Traumatic

Acquired stenosis is usually the result of surgery or trauma which denudes the epithelium of the anal canal. Hemorrhoid operations in which too much skin is removed or which are followed by infection are the commonest cause. Constipation, ribbon stools, and pain on defecation are the most frequent complaints. Stenosis predisposes to fissure, low-grade infection, and occasionally fistula.

Prevention of stenosis after radical anal surgery is best accomplished by local cleanliness, hot sitz baths, and gentle insertion of the well-lubricated finger twice weekly for 2–3 weeks beginning 2 weeks after surgery. When stenosis is chronic but mild, graduated anal dilators of increasing size may be inserted daily by the patient. For marked stenosis a plastic operation on the anal canal is advisable.

Inflammatory

A. Lymphogranuloma Venereum: This infectious disease is the commonest cause of inflammatory stricture of the anorectal region. Acute proctitis due to lymphatic spread of the organism occurs early, and may be followed by perirectal infections, sinuses, and formation of scar tissue (resulting in stricture). Frei and complement fixation tests are positive.

The tetracycline drugs are curative in the initial phase of the disease. When extensive chronic secondary infection is present or when a stricture has formed, repeated biopsies are essential because epidermoid carcinoma develops in about 4% of strictures. Local operation on a stricture may be feasible, but a colostomy or an abdominoperineal resection is often required.

B. Granuloma Inguinale: This disease may cause anorectal fistulas, infections, and strictures. The Donovan body is best identified in tissue biopsy when there is rectal involvement. Epidermoid carcinoma develops in about 4% of cases with chronic anorectal granuloma.

The early lesions respond to tetracyclines. Destructive or constricting processes may require colostomy or resection.

Banov, L.: Rectal strictures of lymphogranuloma venereum. Am J Surg 88:761–767, 1954.

Santulli, T.V., Schulinger, L.N., & R.A. Amoury: Malformations of the anus and rectum. S Clin North America 45:1253–1271, 1965.

ANAL INCONTINENCE

Obstetric tears, anorectal operations (particularly fistulotomy), and neurologic disturbances are the most frequent causes of anal incontinence. When incontinence is due to surgery or trauma, surgical repair of the divided or torn sphincter is indicated. Repair of anterior laceration due to childbirth should be delayed for 6 months or more after parturition.

SQUAMOUS CELL CARCINOMA OF THE ANUS

These tumors are relatively rare, comprising only 1–2% of all malignancies of the anus and large intestine. Bleeding, pain, and local tumor are the commonest symptoms. Because the lesion is often confused with hemorrhoids or other common anal disorders, immediate biopsy of any suspicious lesion or mass in the anal area is essential. These tumors tend to become annular, invade the sphincter, and spread upward into the rectum.

Except for very small lesions (which can be adequately excised locally), treatment is by combined abdominoperineal resection. Radiation therapy is reserved for palliation and for patients who refuse or cannot withstand operation. Metastases to the inguinal nodes are treated by radical groin dissection when clinically evident. The 5-year survival rate after resection is about 50%.

Kuehn, P.G., Eisenberg, H., & J.F. Reed: Epidermoid carcinoma of the perianal skin and anal canal. Cancer 22:932–938, 1968.

Rosato, F.E., Buck, W., & E.F. Rosato: Squamous-cell carcinoma of the anal canal: A review of 21 cases. Dis Colon Rectum 11:209–212, 1968.

Wolfe, H.R., & H.J. Bussey: Squamous cell carcinoma of the anus. Brit J Surg 55:295–301, 1968.

DISEASES OF THE LIVER & BILIARY TRACT

JAUNDICE

Classification of Jaundice
A. **Prehepatic (Hemolytic):**
  1. **Intramedullary**–"Shunt" hyperbilirubinemia.

TABLE 10–2. Laboratory examination in hepatocellular and obstructive jaundice.

Tests	Normal Values	Hepatocellular Jaundice	Uncomplicated Obstructive Jaundice
Bilirubin Direct	0.1–0.4 mg/100 ml	Increased	Increased
Indirect	0.2–0.7 mg/100 ml	Increased	Increased
Urine bilirubin	None	Increased	Increased
Urine urobilinogen	0–4 mg/24 hours	Increased	Markedly decreased in complete obstruction
Stool urobilinogen	40–280 mg/24 hours	Unchanged or lowered	Decreased
Bromsulphalein® retention (5 mg/kg)	5% or less in 45 minutes	Increased	Increased
Protein electrophoresis (gm/100 ml)	Albumin, 3.3–6.5 Alpha$_1$ globulin, 0.04–0.41 Alpha$_2$ globulin, 0.3–0.9 Beta globulin, 0.7–1.5 Gamma globulin, 0.3–1.4 Total protein, 6.5–8.4	Albumin decreased	Unchanged
Alkaline phosphatase	2–4.5 Bodansky units	Increased (++)	Increased (++++)
Cholesterol Total	100–250 mg/100 ml	Decreased if damage severe	Increased
Esters	60–70% of total	Decreased if damage severe	Normal
Prothrombin time	40–100% after vitamin K, 15% increase in 24 hours.	Prolonged if damage severe	Prolonged if obstruction marked
SGPT, SGOT	SGPT, 5–35 units SGOT, 5–40 units	Increased in hepatocellular damage, viral hepatitis	Usually unchanged, may be increased

2. **Extramedullary**—Hemolysis due to drugs, infections, etc.

B. **Hepatic**:
   1. **Congenital**—
      a. **Indirect hyperbilirubinemia**—Constitutional hepatic dysfunction, glucuronyl transferase deficiency.
      b. **Direct hyperbilirubinemia**—Rotor's syndrome, Dubin-Johnson-Sprinz syndrome, benign intermittent cholestasis, intermittent jaundice of pregnancy.
   2. **Acquired**—
      a. **Cholestatic**—
         (1) Due to drugs, eg, chlorpromazine, methyltestosterone.
         (2) Due to infection—Viral hepatitis.
      b. **Noncholestatic**—
         (1) Due to drugs—Fluothane, iproniazid.
         (2) Due to infection—Viral, spirochetal.

C. **Posthepatic**: Extrahepatic obstruction.
   1. **Intermittent**, eg, stone.
   2. **Complete**, eg, carcinoma of pancreas.

Manifestations of Diseases Associated With Jaundice

A. **Prehepatic**: Hemolysis, weakness. Abdominal or back pain may occur with acute hemolytic crisis. Normal stool and urine color. Jaundice. Splenomegaly is usually prominent except in sickle cell disease. Hepatomegaly variable.

B. **Hepatic**:
1. **Acquired**—Malaise, anorexia, low-grade fever, right upper quadrant discomfort. Dark urine, jaundice, amenorrhea. Enlarged, tender liver, vascular spiders, palmar erythema, ascites, gynecomastia, sparse body hair, fetor hepaticus.
2. **Congenital**—May be asymptomatic; the intermittent cholestasis is often accompanied by pruritus and light-colored stools and occasional malaise.

C. **Posthepatic**: Colicky right upper quadrant pain, weight loss (carcinoma), jaundice, dark urine, light stool. Fluctuating jaundice and intermittently colored stools indicate intermittent obstruction due to stone or due to carcinoma of the ampulla or the junction of the common hepatic ducts. Blood in stools suggests malignancy. Hepatomegaly, visible and palpable gallbladder (Courvoisier's gallbladder). Ascites, rectal shelf, and weight loss indicate malignancy. Chills and fever suggest stone with cholangitis.

The serum glutamic-oxaloacetic transaminase (SGOT) test has proved to be of value in the diagnosis of liver disease. It will probably replace such tests as the cephalin flocculation test in following the progress of acute liver disease.

Liver biopsy is a safe and relatively accurate method for diagnosing a wide range of hepatic disorders. It is of limited value in differentiating intrahepatic from extrahepatic cholestasis.

Clermont, R.J., & T.C. Chalmers: The transaminase tests in liver disease. Medicine 46:197–208, 1967.
Lester, R., & R.F. Troxler: Recent advances in bile pigment metabolism. Gastroenterology 56:143–169, 1969.
Popper, H.: Cholestasis. Ann Rev Med 19:39–56, 1968.
Schimmel, E.M.: Diagnostic procedures in liver disease. M Clin North America 52:1407–1416, 1968.
Symposium on liver disease. Medicine 46, 1967.
Wise, R.E.: Radiology of the liver and biliary tract. Gastroenterology 53:312–325, 1967.
Zimmerman, H.J.: The differential diagnosis of jaundice. M Clin North America 52:1417–1444, 1968,

VIRAL HEPATITIS
("Infectious" [Short Incubation Period] Hepatitis; "Serum" [Long Incubation Period] Hepatitis)

Essentials of Diagnosis
- Anorexia, nausea, vomiting, malaise, symptoms of upper respiratory infection, aversion to smoking.
- Fever; enlarged, tender liver; jaundice.
- Normal to low white cell count, abnormal hepatocellular liver function tests.
- Liver biopsy shows characteristic hepatocellular necrosis and mononuclear infiltrate.

General Considerations

A. **Short Incubation Hepatitis**: Infectious hepatitis is a viral infection of the liver which may occur sporadically or in epidemics. The liver involvement is a part of a generalized infection but dominates the clinical picture. This disease is the most common infection of the liver, and often becomes a major health problem in crowded establishments, eg, military bases, mental hospitals, camps. Transmission of the virus is usually by the intestinal-oral route. The virus can also be transmitted by blood donors in the anicteric or preicteric phase of the disease. The virus is present in the feces and blood during the prodromal and acute phases of the icteric disease, and in the feces and blood in the anicteric form of the disease; occasionally it is present in an asymptomatic carrier state. The incubation period is 2–6 weeks.

B. **Long Incubation Hepatitis**: "Serum" hepatitis is a viral infection of the liver usually transmitted by the inoculation of infected blood or blood products, although recent studies have shown that serum hepatitis virus may be infective by the fecal-oral route. The virus is similar to that which causes infectious hepatitis but is immunologically distinct, and little or no cross-immunity exists between the 2 diseases. The virus is found only in the blood and tissues of an infected person and is not usually excreted via the intestinal tract. The incubation period is 6 weeks to 6 months. The pathologic findings are identical with those of infectious hepatitis. Clinical features are also similar, but there is usually a history of injection, the disease is more common in the older age groups, and the onset is more often insidious than abrupt. These facts, with the longer incubation period, often allow clinical differentiation, but in many cases the exact type cannot be determined. (See Table 10–3.)

TABLE 10–3. Differentiating features of infectious hepatitis and serum hepatitis.*

	Infectious Hepatitis (IH)	Serum Hepatitis (SH)
Incubation period	Relatively short (30–38 days)	Relatively long (41–108 days)
Onset	Acute	Insidious
Urticarial rash	Usually absent	Often present
Arthralgia	Usually absent	Often present
Abnormal transaminase activity	Brief (< 21 days)	Prolonged (35–200 days)
Thymol turbidity and IgM levels	Constantly elevated	Normal (75% of cases)
Hepatitis associated antigen (HAA or Australia antigen)	Not present	Present

*Prepared from data of Krugman, S.: Viral hepatitis: New clinical, epidemiological and immunological concepts. California Med 113:57–59, July 1970.

Pathologic findings in both diseases show varying degrees of necrosis of the parenchymal cells and variable numbers of lymphocytes and plasma cells in the portal cells and in the areas of necrosis. The reticulum framework is generally preserved, although it may become condensed. Healing is by regeneration from surviving cells, usually without distortion of the normal architecture.

Clinical Findings

The clinical picture is extremely variable, ranging from asymptomatic infection without jaundice to a fulminating disease and death in a few days.

A. Symptoms:

1. Prodromal phase—The speed of onset varies from abrupt to insidious with general malaise, myalgia, fatigability, upper respiratory symptoms (coryza, scratchy throat), and severe anorexia out of proportion to the degree of illness. Nausea and vomiting are frequent, and diarrhea or constipation may occur. Fever is generally present but is rarely over 103° F (39.4° C). Defervescence often coincides with the onset of jaundice. Chills or chilliness may mark an acute onset.

Abdominal pain is generally mild and constant in the upper right quadrant or right epigastrium, and is often aggravated by jarring or exertion. A distaste for smoking may occur early in the illness.

2. Icteric phase—Clinical jaundice occurs after 5–10 days but may be present at the onset, although many patients never develop clinical jaundice. With the onset of jaundice there is often an intensification of the prodromal symptoms followed by progressive clinical improvement.

3. Convalescent phase—There is an increasing sense of well being, return of appetite, and disappearance of jaundice, abdominal pain, and fatigability.

B. Signs: Hepatomegaly, rarely excessive and often variable from day to day, is present in over ½ of cases. Liver tenderness is often present. Splenomegaly is present in 15% of cases, and soft lymphadenopathy, especially cervical, may occur. Signs of general toxemia vary from minimal to severe.

C. Laboratory Findings: The white cell count is normal to low, and abnormal lymphocytes (virus lymphocytes) may be present. Mild proteinuria is common, and bilirubinuria often precedes the appearance of jaundice. Acholic stools are often present during the initial icteric phase. Liver function tests tend to reflect hepatocellular damage, with abnormal BSP, SGOT, and SGPT values, increased gamma globulin, and urobilinogenuria. In the cholangiolitic variety the liver function tests may indicate obstruction as well. The Australia antigen may be present in serum hepatitis.

Liver biopsy generally shows the characteristic pathology.

Differential Diagnosis

Differentiate viral hepatitis from other diseases that cause hepatitis or involve the liver such as Weil's disease, amebiasis, cirrhosis, infectious mononucleosis, and toxic hepatitis. The prodromal phase or the nonicteric form of the disease must be distinguished from other infectious diseases such as influenza, upper respiratory infection, and the prodromal stages of the exanthematous diseases. In the obstructive phase of viral hepatitis it is necessary to rule out other obstructive lesions such as choledocholithiasis, chlorpromazine toxicity, and carcinoma of the head of the pancreas. Homologous serum hepatitis is clinically indistinguishable from infectious hepatitis. The HAA (Australia antigen) may help in differentiating the two types.

Prevention

Isolation of infected individuals is recommended. Human immune globulin, 0.02–0.06 ml/lb, may attenuate the disease if given to exposed persons during the incubation period. The higher doses are usually justified only in special circumstances (eg, pregnancy, debility, previous liver disease, or complicating illness).

Avoid unnecessary transfusions, especially of possibly infected blood, serum, or plasma. In the USA, blood transfusions are responsible for an estimated 30,000 cases of hepatitis each year. Tests for the hepatitis-associated antigen to detect viral hepatitis carriers among blood donors are of value and may enable detection of about 1/3 of infected donors.

Treatment

A. General Measures: Bed rest should be at the patient's option during the acute initial phase of the disease. Bed rest beyond the most acute phase is not warranted. The return to activity during the convalescent period should be gradual. It is essential to keep a close check on the patient's actual intake and output during the acute phase. If (and only if) the patient is unable to take or retain food or fluids by mouth, give 10% glucose solution intravenously. If the patient shows signs of impending hepatic coma, protein should be restricted to 40 gm/day and increased as improvement progresses. In general, dietary management consists of giving a palatable diet as tolerated. Patients with infectious hepatitis should avoid vigorous physical exertion, alcohol, and all potentially hepatotoxic medication. Barbiturates and morphine may precipitate hepatocerebral intoxication.

B. Corticotropin and Corticosteroids: These agents are recommended only if the patient's condition is deteriorating. They should not be given routinely in viral hepatitis.

Prognosis

In the great majority of cases of infectious hepatitis clinical recovery is complete in 3–16 weeks. Laboratory evidences of disturbed liver function may persist longer. Overall mortality is less than 1%, but is higher in older people (particularly in postmenopausal women). In a few cases the course is prolonged or symptoms are recurrent, with eventual full recovery. Cirrhosis of the portal or postnecrotic types or chronic progressive hepatitis develops infrequently.

Hepatitis has a poor prognosis in severely ill and elderly patients. Post-transfusion hepatitis occurs as a complication in 0.25–3% of blood transfusions and up to 12% of pooled plasma transfusions. The asymptomatic carrier state and persistent viremia after acute disease make control of contamination in donor blood extremely difficult.

Grady, G.F., & others: Risk of posttransfusion viral hepatitis. New England J Med 271:337–341, 1964.

Havens, W.P., Jr.: Viral hepatitis. M Clin North America 54:455–466, 1970.

Koff, R.S., & K.J. Isselbacher: Changing concepts in the epidemiology of viral hepatitis. New England J Med 278:1371–1380, 1968.

Krugman, S., & J.P. Giles: Viral hepatitis: New light on an old disease. JAMA 212:1019–1029, 1970.

McCollum, R.W.: The natural history of hepatitis. Bull New York Acad Med 45:127–137, 1969.

Prince, A.M., & others: Immunologic distinction between infectious and serum hepatitis. New England J Med 282:987–991, 1970.

Repsher, L.H., & R.K. Freebern: Effects of early and vigorous exercise on recovery from infectious hepatitis. New England J Med 281:1393–1396, 1969.

Sherlock, S.: The treatment of hepatitis. Bull New York Acad Med 45:189–200, 1969.

Shulman, N.R., Hirschman, R.J., & L.F. Barker: Viral hepatitis. Ann Int Med 72:257–269, 1970.

Sutnick, A.I., & others: Viral hepatitis: Revised concepts as a result of the study of Australia antigen. M Clin North America 54:805–817, 1970.

VARIANTS OF INFECTIOUS HEPATITIS

Cholangiolitic Hepatitis

There is usually a cholestatic phase in the initial icteric phase of infectious hepatitis, but in occasional cases this is the dominant manifestation of the disease. The course tends to be more prolonged than that of ordinary hepatitis. The symptoms are often extremely mild, but jaundice is deeper and pruritus is often present. Laboratory tests of liver function indicate cholestasis with bilirubinuria and elevated alkaline phosphatase and cholesterol.

Differentiation from extrahepatic obstruction may be difficult even with liver biopsy. Liver biopsy should be undertaken with considerable caution in the presence of extrahepatic biliary obstruction.

Gall, E.A., & H. Braunstein: Hepatitis with manifestations simulating bile duct obstruction. (So-called "cholangiolitic hepatitis.") Am J Clin Path 25:1113–1127, 1955.

Fulminant Hepatitis

Hepatitis may take a rapidly progressive course terminating in less than 10 days. Extensive necrosis of large areas of the liver gives the typical pathologic picture of acute liver atrophy. Toxemia and gastrointestinal symptoms are more severe, and hemorrhagic phenomena are common. Neurologic symptoms of hepatic coma develop (see Cirrhosis). Jaundice may be absent or minimal, but laboratory tests show extreme hepatocellular damage.

Exchange transfusions have been advocated in fulminant hepatitis. Although hepatic coma may be transiently improved, the prognosis in this form of the disease is apparently unaffected. Since patients die in and not from hepatic coma, the procedure is not recommended.

Prolonged Hepatitis

The persistence of symptoms 6 months or more after an acute episode of hepatitis presents a problem of differentiation of psychoneurosis, persistent hepatitis, and chronic active hepatitis.

The pathologic findings in persistent hepatitis are identical to those of the acute disease irrespective of the duration of the illness. The prognosis is good, and complete recovery the rule. Liver function studies are similar to if not identical with the acute phase of the disease. In chronic active hepatitis, pathologic examination, in addition to hepatocellular necrosis, shows progressive fibrosis, and cirrhosis is almost invariably present.

The treatment of persistent hepatitis is symptomatic. A good nutritious diet, adequate rest, vitamin supplementation, and avoidance of potentially hepatotoxic substances such as alcohol and certain drugs are indicated. The treatment of chronic active hepatitis consists of general measures plus the use of corticosteroids or immunosuppressive drugs such as mercaptopurine (Purinethol®). The immunosuppressive drugs are at present experimental and should only be used under an approved protocol; their ultimate role in the long-term prognosis of this form of liver disease remains to be determined.

The natural history of chronic active hepatitis is ultimately cirrhosis or hepatic failure.

Mackay, I.R.: Chronic hepatitis: Effect of prolonged suppressive treatment and comparison of azathioprine and prednisolone. Quart J Med 37:379–392, 1968.

Mistilis, S.P., Skyring, A.P., & C.R. Blackburn: Natural history of active chronic hepatitis. I. Clinical features, course, diagnostic criteria, morbidity, mortality and survival. Australasian Ann Med 17:214–223, 1968.

Schaffner, F., & F.M. Klion: Chronic hepatitis. Ann Rev Med 19:25–38, 1968.

DRUG- & TOXIN-INDUCED LIVER DISEASE

The introduction of new drugs into medicine has resulted in an increase in toxic reactions of many types. Not infrequently, the site of the toxic reaction is the liver.

The diagnosis of drug-induced liver disease is not always easy, and in many instances the diagnosis is not made until long-term observation or repeated administration of an agent makes the relationship clear. Drug-induced liver disease can mimic infectious hepatitis or obstructive jaundice. The clinician must be aware of these reactions and carefully question the patient with respect to the use of various drugs before he can dismiss drug-induced liver disease as a possibility.

Although fatalities have occurred as a result of drug-induced liver disease, most patients recover without serious complications if the drug is discontinued promptly and, in most instances, permanently withheld thereafter. Deaths have occurred when hepatotoxic drugs have been reinstituted in susceptible patients.

Hepatotoxic Group

A. Substances Which May Act Like Poisons: Substances that lead to fatty metamorphosis and centrolobular necrosis are listed below. This list, although extensive, remains incomplete.

Alcohol	Poisonous mushrooms
Carbon tetrachloride	Tetracyclines
Chloroform	Stilbamidine and related
Heavy metals	stilbenes
Phosphorus	

B. Drugs Producing a Picture Similar to That of Viral Hepatitis:

Cinchophen (Atophan®)	Phenylacetylurea
Chloramphenicol	(Phenurone®)
(Chloromycetin®)	Phenylbutazone
Chlortetracycline	(Butazolidin®)
(Aureomycin®)	Pyrazinamide (PZA)
Halothane	Streptomycin
Iproniazid (Marsilid®)	Sulfamethoxypyridazine
Novobiocin	(Kynex®)
Penicillin	Zoxazolamine (Flexin®)

Cholestatic-Cholangiolitic Groups

The substances in this group, although unrelated structurally, cause a reaction resembling extrahepatic obstruction clinically, functionally, and occasionally histologically:

Arsenicals (organic)	Methyltestosterone
Aminosalicyclic acid (PAS)	Norethandrolone (Nilevar®)
Chlorpromazine (Thorazine®)	Para-aminobenzyl caffeine
Chlorpropamide (Diabinese®)	Phenindione (Hedulin®)
Chlorothiazide (Diuril®)	Prochlorperazine
Ectylurea (Nostyn®)	(Compazine®)
Erythromycin estolate (Ilosone®)	Promazine (Sparine®)
Mepazine (Pacatal®)	Sulfadiazine
Methimazole (Tapazole®)	Thiouracil
	Toluenediamine

Liver Dysfunction Due to Oral Contraceptives (Cholestatic)

Abnormalities of liver function, including elevated transaminases, serum bilirubin, and BSP retention, have been reported with the use of oral contraceptive agents. Histologic changes have been demonstrated. Serum transaminase abnormalities may revert to normal with continuing therapy. Studies suggest that the hepatotoxic effect of oral contraceptives is due primarily to their progesterone content.

Conney, A.H.: Drug metabolism and therapeutics. New England J Med 280:653–660, 1969.

Lewis, M., Schenker, S., & B. Combes: Studies on the pathogenesis of tetracycline-induced fatty liver. Am J Digest Dis 12:429–438, 1967.

Ockner, R.K., & C.S. Davidson: Hepatic effects of oral contraceptives. New England J Med 276:331–334, 1967.

Peters, R.L., & others: Hepatic necrosis associated with halothane anesthesia. Am J Med 47:748–764, 1969.

Read, A.E., Laidlaw, J., & C.F. McCarthy: Effects of chlorpromazine in patients with hepatic disease. Brit MJ 3:497–499, 1969.

Recknagel, R.O.: Carbon tetrachloride hepatotoxicity. Pharmacol Rev 145:145–208, 1967.

Roman, W., & R. Hecker: The liver toxicity of oral contraceptives: A critical review of the literature. MJ Australia 2:682–688, 1968.

Zimmerman, H.J.: The spectrum of hepatotoxicity. Perspect Biol Med 12:135–161, 1968.

FATTY LIVER

Fatty liver is due to chronic malnutrition. It is primarily the result of excessive alcohol ingestion (especially with poor dietary intake), but it is also seen in diabetes mellitus, obesity, kwashiorkor, and galactosemia. The diagnosis depends upon the observation of hepatomegaly with relatively normal liver function and the characteristic fatty liver changes on biopsy.

Berg, G.: Fatty liver: Pathogenesis and clinical significance. Digestion 1:61, 1968.

Lieber, C.S., & E. Rubin: Alcoholic fatty liver. New England J Med 280:705–708, 1969.

CIRRHOSIS

Essentials of Diagnosis

- Weakness, anorexia, gastrointestinal complaints, occasional right upper quadrant pain, hematemesis.
- Hepatosplenomegaly, spider angiomas, ascites, dependent edema, jaundice, weight loss.
- History of alcoholism.
- Hepatocellular dysfunction shown by liver function tests; esophageal varices.
- Liver biopsy.

General Considerations

Cirrhosis is the most common form of chronic liver disease. It is due to many causes, but in a significant number of cases no cause can be determined. The following may play a role in etiology: malnutrition (especially vitamin B complex deficiency), alcoholism, hepatitis (rarely), and chronic and repeated exposure to hepatotoxins.

The essential pathologic features are degeneration and necrosis of hepatic cells, often with fatty metamorphosis; nodular regeneration with loss of the normal lobular pattern and relationships to blood vessels and bile ducts; increased fibrous tissue, usually in thin strands; bile duct proliferation; and inflammatory cell infiltration during phases of active parenchymal degeneration. The major distinguishing characteristic (from other types of cirrhosis) is the uniformity of the process; the nodules are less than 0.5 mm in diameter. Alteration of portal blood flow leads to congestive splenomegaly and other evidences of portal hypertension such as esophageal varices.

The incidence is higher in males, and the age at onset is from 40–60 years.

Clinical Findings

A. Symptoms and Signs: Portal cirrhosis may cause no symptoms for long periods, both at the onset and later in the course (compensated phase). The onset of symptoms may be insidious or, less often, abrupt. Weakness, fatigability, and weight loss are common. Anorexia is always present and may be extreme, with nausea, flatulence, and often vomiting. Abdominal pain is due to gaseous or ascitic distention or, more characteristically, consists of aching in the right upper quadrant or right epigastrium as a result of hepatic enlargement. Diarrhea is frequently present, but some patients become constipated. Menstrual alteration (usually amenorrhea), impotence, loss of libido, sterility, and painful enlarged breasts in men (rare) may occur. Hematemesis is the presenting symptom in 15–25%.

In 70% of cases the liver is palpable, firm, and has a blunt edge. Skin manifestations consist of spider angiomas (generally only on the upper half of the body), palmar erythema (mottled redness of the thenar and hypothenar eminences), telangiectasis of exposed areas, and evidence of vitamin deficiency. Weight loss and the appearance of chronic illness are present. Jaundice, usually not a presenting sign, is generally mild except in the terminal phase. Ascites, hydrothorax, dependent edema, and purpuric lesions are late findings; the precoma state (tremor, dysarthrias, rigidity, sluggish pupils, delirium, drowsiness) and coma are very late findings. Gynecomastia, pectoral and axillary alopecia, and testicular atrophy may be present. Fever is present in 35% of cases and is a manifestation of alcoholic hepatitis; splenomegaly is present in 35–50% of cases. The superficial veins of the abdomen and thorax are dilated (collateral circulation).

B. Laboratory Findings: In latent disease, laboratory abnormalities may be absent or minimal. Anemia is a frequent finding. It is usually normocytic, rarely macrocytic. The white cell count may be low, elevated, or normal and may reflect hypersplenism. The sedimentation rate is increased. Coagulation abnormalities may be present as a result of failure of synthesis of clotting constituents in the liver. Proteinuria may be present, and oliguria is frequent in active disease with ascites formation.

Liver function tests show primarily hepatocellular dysfunction.

Needle or surgical biopsy of the liver shows cirrhosis. Serial biopsies may sometimes be required to follow the progress of the disease.

C. X-Ray Findings: X-ray may reveal splenomegaly and esophageal or gastric varices.

D. Special Examinations: Esophagoscopy and gastroscopy also demonstrate the varices when present.

Differential Diagnosis

Differentiation of portal cirrhosis from other types of cirrhosis may be difficult. Hemochromatosis occurs almost exclusively in males and is associated with pigmented skin. Postnecrotic cirrhosis occurs more often in women and in younger individuals, often with a history of infectious hepatitis. Biliary cirrhosis is marked by jaundice, hyperlipemia, and skin pigmentation.

Complications

Upper gastrointestinal tract bleeding may occur as a result of varices, hemorrhagic gastritis, or the not infrequently associated gastric and duodenal ulcers. Hemorrhage may be massive and fatal or may precipitate liver failure. Liver failure may also be precipitated by alcoholism, surgery, and infection. Primary carcinoma of the liver and portal vein thrombosis occur more frequently in patients with cirrhosis. Lower resistance often leads to serious infections, especially pulmonary.

Treatment

A. General Measures: The principles of treatment are abstinence from alcohol, rest during the acute phase, and adequate diet. The diet should be palatable, with adequate calories and protein (75—100 gm/day) and, in the acute phase, sodium restriction. In the presence of hepatic precoma or coma, protein intake should be restricted. Vitamin supplementation is indicated if deficiencies are present.

B. Special Problems:

1. Ascites and edema due to sodium retention, hypoproteinemia, and portal hypertension—Treatment of ascites, other than to relieve distressing symptoms, is usually not indicated. Even the mildest therapeutic measures carry the potential of significant discomfort or harm to the patient.

a. Reduce sodium intake to 0.5—2 gm NaCl daily, or even less if necessary.

b. Restoration of plasma proteins—This is most difficult and depends primarily upon adequate liver function. High-protein feedings may induce precoma or coma. Salt-poor albumin is expensive and transient in effect. Restriction of fluid intake and diuresis may be of some help.

c. Thiazide diuretics—If diuretics are necessary, it is generally preferred to initiate diuretic therapy with one of the thiazide drugs. Chlorothiazide (Diuril®), 250—500 mg orally 2—4 times daily—or any of the other thiazide diuretics (in equivalent doses)—produces a marked increase in the excretion of sodium, potassium, and chloride. Observe carefully for hypokalemia and possible precoma or coma. Potassium supplements should be administered daily.

d. Spironolactone (Aldactone®), an aldosterone antagonist, 25 mg orally 4 times daily, or **triamterine (Dyrenium®),** 100—200 mg orally daily, promotes sodium excretion with conservation of potassium. These agents are more effective when used in combination with other diuretics such as the thiazides, since potassium loss is reduced.

e. Ethacrynic acid (Edecrin®), 50 mg orally every 2—3 days, building up to a maximum daily dose of 150—200 mg if necessary, and **furosemide (Lasix®),** 40—80 mg orally daily, are both powerful diuretic agents. Their use should virtually be restricted to hospitalized patients. They should be used only if the milder agents are not effective since their toxicity, especially with chronic use, is greater because of their potency.

f. Abdominal paracentesis should be performed only for relief of pain, marked discomfort, respiratory embarrassment, or anorexia due to abdominal distention and not simply for cosmetic reasons.

2. Hepatic encephalopathy—Ammonia produced in bacterial decomposition of protein in the large bowel is either ineffectively removed by damaged liver cells or, because of portal obstruction, bypassed directly into the systemic circulation. The amount of ammonia produced is dependent upon the protein content, the bacterial flora, and the motility of the colon; and hepatic encephalopathy may be further aggravated by the invasion of colonic organisms through the blood stream. Bleeding into the bowel from varices or ulcerations—or as a result of bleeding tendencies—may significantly increase the amount of protein in the bowel and may precipitate rapid development of encephalopathy and coma. Other factors which may precipitate hepatic coma include potassium deficiency, thiazide diuretics, narcotics, hypnotics and sedatives, drugs containing ammonium or amino compounds, paracentesis, and hepatic or systemic infection.

a. Dietary protein may be drastically curtailed or completely withheld for short periods if necessary, especially in acute episodes. Parenteral nutrition is usually indicated.

b. Gastrointestinal bleeding should be treated by all necessary medical and surgical measures to remove blood and prevent further bleeding. Give milk of magnesia, 30 ml 4 times daily, or magnesium sulfate, 10—15 gm by indwelling nasogastric tube.

c. Control the intestinal flora with neomycin sulfate, 0.5—1 gm every 6 hours for 5—7 days.

d. Treat shock as outlined in Chapter 1.

e. Treat infection with antibiotics chosen on the basis of culture and sensitivity studies. In some instances broad-spectrum antibiotics are indicated if the patient's condition is deteriorating.

f. If agitation is marked, give sodium phenobarbital, 15—30 mg IM, or chloral hydrate, 0.25—0.5 gm by rectum *cautiously* as indicated. Avoid narcotics and CNS depressants.

3. Anemia—For hypochromic anemia, give ferrous sulfate, 0.2—0.3 gm enteric-coated tablets, 3 times daily after meals.

4. Hemorrhagic tendency due to hypoprothrombinemia may be treated with vitamin K preparations, although this treatment is ineffective when intrahepatic damage is severe. Blood transfusions may be necessary to control the bleeding tendency. Give menadione, 1—3 mg orally 3 times daily after meals; or menadione sodium bisulfite, 2 mg IV or IM every other day. If obstructive jaundice is present, give supplementary bile salts.

5. Hemorrhage from esophageal varices—Posterior pituitary injection for surgical use (Pituitrin S®), 10 units in 200 ml 5% dextrose and water by IV infusion over a period of 30—45 minutes, should be tried and repeated in an attempt to control hemorrhage due to esophageal varices. If this is not successful, bleeding can at times be controlled by the use of the triple-lumen (Sengstaken) tube. Surgical measures are usually hazardous and unsatisfactory, but surgery to relieve portal hypertension may be considered in selected patients. In patients in otherwise good condition in whom hepatocellular dysfunction is relatively slight, portacaval anastomosis may be of benefit.

6. Pruritus—Cholestyramine (Cuemid®, Questran®), a basic anionic exchange resin, binds bile salts in the intestine and may relieve itching in patients with cholestasis. The dosage is 4 gm in water or fruit juice, with meals, 3 times daily.

7. Hemochromatosis—Intermittent bleeding over a period of many years (phlebotomy) of patients with "primary" hemochromatosis may have a very beneficial effect.

Prognosis

The prognosis in portal cirrhosis has shown little change over the years. The major factor determining the prognosis is the patient's ability to discontinue the excessive use of alcohol. In advanced cases, only 50% survive 2 years and only about 35% survive 5 years. Hematemesis, jaundice, and ascites are unfavorable prognostic signs. Many latent cases, however, do not appear to shorten life, and often are diagnosed only at autopsy.

Anderson, R.P., & E.F. Wolfman, Jr.: Portal hypertension: Current status. California Med 111:25—37, 1969.

Chalmers, T.C.: The management of hepatic coma: A continuing problem. M Clin North America 52:1475—1482, 1968.

Epstein, F.H.: Ascites and its delivery. New England J Med 282:713—717, 1970.

Epstein, M., & others: Renal failure in patients with cirrhosis: The role of active vasoconstriction. Am J Med 49:175—185, 1970.

Joseph, R.R.: A rational approach to the treatment of ascites in Laennec's cirrhosis. M Clin North America 53:1359—1365, 1969.

Leevy, C.M., & H. Baker: Nutritional deficiencies in liver disease. M Clin North America 54:467—477, 1970.

Liebowitz, H.R.: Pathogenesis of ascites in cirrhosis of the liver. New York J Med 69:1895—2024, 1969.

Schaffner, F. (editor): Symposium on the treatment of liver disease. Mod Treat 6:121—214, 1969.

Steigmann, F., & R. Mejicano: The impact of diuretics on chronic liver disease. Am J Gastroenterol 52:37—44, 1969.

Stone, W.D., Islam, N.R., & A. Paton: The natural history of cirrhosis. Quart J Med 37:119—132, 1968.

POSTNECROTIC CIRRHOSIS

The clinical and laboratory findings in postnecrotic cirrhosis are indistinguishable from those of portal cirrhosis, but the following are valuable clues to the diagnosis: Postnecrotic cirrhosis is usually not related to alcoholism; its incidence is higher in women, and the age at onset is often below 40 in both sexes; the onset is frequently similar to that of acute viral hepatitis; jaundice is usually more intense and is present early in the course; ascites and peripheral edema are present early; and hyperglobulinemia (predominantly gamma globulin) is consistently present and may reach extreme values (10 gm/100 ml).

Treatment consists primarily of rest, a palatable diet with adequate caloric content, and restriction of sodium in the presence of fluid retention. Adrenal corticosteroids may make the patient feel better and decrease the severity of jaundice, but they are of doubtful value in the long-term management of this disease.

The present impression is that postnecrotic cirrhosis is more rapidly progressive and less responsive to treatment than portal cirrhosis. The complications, however, are the same. Latent cases do occur and may not progress, but after the onset of symptoms only 20% of patients survive 5 years.

HEMOCHROMATOSIS

Idiopathic hemochromatosis is characterized by excessive iron absorption, with deposition of hemosiderin in the liver, pancreas, heart, adrenals, testes, and kidneys. Eventually the patient may develop hepatic, pancreatic, and cardiac insufficiency. The disease usually occurs in males and is rarely recognized before the second or third decade. Clinical manifestations include hepatomegaly and hepatic insufficiency, skin pigmentation (slate gray due to iron and brown due to melanin), cardiac enlargement and insufficiency, and diabetes mellitus with its complications. Bleeding from esophageal varices and hepatic carcinoma may occur.

Laboratory findings include elevated plasma iron, saturated iron-binding protein in plasma, and the characteristic liver biopsy stain for iron.

Treatment consists of weekly phlebotomy of 500 ml of blood for many months (sometimes up to 2—3 years) until plasma iron and hematocrit determinations indicate depletion of iron stores. Symptomatic and supportive treatment of diabetic, hepatic, and cardiac complications may be necessary.

Although the long-term benefits of iron depletion therapy have not been completely established, available data indicate that the course of the disease may be favorably altered.

Heilmeyer, L.: Pathogenesis of hemochromatosis. Medicine 46:209—216, 1967.

MacDonald, R.A.: *Hemochromatosis and Hemosiderosis.* Thomas, 1964.

HYPERBILIRUBINEMIC STATES

Constitutional Hepatic Dysfunction (Gilbert's Disease)

This is a benign form of jaundice which must be distinguished from hemolytic disease and chronic hepatitis. The plasma bilirubin is primarily in the unconjugated form. The remainder of the laboratory examination is normal. Physical examination and liver biopsy are also normal. The symptoms are usually iatrogenic or psychoneurotic in origin. The prognosis is excellent.

Powell, L.W., & others: Idiopathic unconjugated hyperbilirubinemia (Gilbert's syndrome). New England J Med 277:1108—1112, 1967.

Familial Chronic Idiopathic Jaundice (Dubin-Sprinz-Johnson Syndrome)

This form of jaundice is believed to be due to a faulty excretory function of liver cells and is characterized by elevated serum bilirubin (conjugated form), elevated plasma BSP (conjugated form), and normal alkaline phosphatase. The gallbladder does not visualize on x-ray, and the liver biopsy shows a heavy pigmentation. Grossly, the liver appears deep brown to black; microscopically, it is heavily pigmented with a golden brown pigment.

The prognosis is good.

Mandemo, E., & others: Familial chronic idiopathic jaundice (Dubin-Sprinz disease) with a note on Bromosulphalein metabolism in this disease. Am J Med 28:42–50, 1960.

Rotor's Syndrome

This is similar to Dubin-Sprinz-Johnson syndrome and, in fact, may be a variant of it. Pigmentation of the liver, however, does not occur in Rotor's syndrome, and the gallbladder is readily visualized in cholecystography.

Dubin, I.N.: Rotor's syndrome and chronic idiopathic jaundice. Arch Int Med 100:823–824, 1962.

Crigler-Najjar Syndrome

This is a rare form of severe hereditary nonhemolytic jaundice, appearing shortly after birth, which is due to an absence of glucuronyl transferase. The baby accumulates unconjugated bilirubin and develops CNS disease resembling kernicterus.

There is no known treatment, and death usually occurs in infancy.

Crigler, J.F., Jr., & V.A. Najjar: Congenital familial nonhemolytic jaundice with kernicterus. Pediatrics 10:169–180, 1952.

Recurrent Jaundice of Pregnancy

This form of cholestatic liver dysfunction is manifested by the onset of pruritus and jaundice in the third trimester of pregnancy. In the milder forms the patients may experience only the pruritus. The hepatic dysfunction clears rapidly after delivery, and the jaundice and pruritus usually clear within 2 weeks after delivery. The condition is benign, but characteristically recurs with subsequent pregnancies. The liver shows cholestasis. These women may have an increased tendency to cholestasis with the use of agents employed to regulate ovulation.

Svanborg, A., & S. Ohlsson: Recurrent jaundice of pregnancy: A clinical study of 22 cases. Am J Med 27:40, 1959.

Benign Intermittent Cholestasis

The patient with intermittent cholestasis characteristically has prolonged periods of pruritus, jaundice, and malaise. Typically, the serum bilirubin, alkaline phosphatase, and BSP retention are increased. The onset occurs early in life and may persist throughout the patient's lifetime. The liver shows cholestasis; during remissions the liver is entirely normal.

Summerskill, W.H.J., & J.M. Walshe: Benign recurrent intrahepatic "obstructive" jaundice. Lancet 2:686, 1959.
Tygstrup, N.: Intermittent possibly familial intrahepatic cholestatic jaundice. Lancet 1:1171, 1960.

BILIARY CIRRHOSIS
(Primary & Secondary)

Essentials of Diagnosis

- Jaundice, pruritus, right upper quadrant aching.
- Hepatomegaly, xanthomas.
- Abnormal liver function tests indicative of obstruction.
- Good nutritional status with long-standing disease; history of extrahepatic obstructive lesion.
- Liver biopsy often diagnostic.

General Considerations

Biliary cirrhosis is a chronic disease of the liver clinically manifested by cholestasis. The bile flow is most commonly obstructed in an extrahepatic site by calculus, neoplasm, scarring, or congenital atresia. Stasis alone may produce cirrhosis, but the frequently superimposed infection hastens the process. The less common intrahepatic obstructions may have no identifiable cause but have been noted to follow viral hepatitis, particularly the cholangiolitic type, and intrahepatic cholangitis. Some cases may be due to toxins. The disease is far more common in women (particularly the intrahepatic type).

The pathologic findings vary with the cause and the stage of the process, but the following are characteristic: bile stasis with bile thrombi, pigmentation, extensive multiplication of bile ducts, nodular loss of normal architecture, marked cellular infiltration in the fibrous septa, little evidence of hepatic necrosis or regeneration, and absence of fatty metamorphosis. Bile lakes and bile infarcts are characteristic of extrahepatic obstruction.

Clinical Findings

A. Symptoms and Signs: In extrahepatic obstruction, symptoms of the primary lesion may predominate (eg, carcinoma of the pancreas, choledocholithiasis). Jaundice and pruritus are initial symptoms. Jaundice is often marked and of varying intensity. Cholangitis may cause chills and fever. Mild right upper quadrant aching may be present. Anorexia, weight loss, and weakness may occur late in the illness.

The liver is enlarged and firm but usually not tender. Splenomegaly is a late finding when it occurs. The general signs of cirrhosis—ascites, peripheral edema, hematemesis, hemorrhagic manifestations in the skin and mucous membranes, bleeding gums, and epistaxis—are usually late manifestations. Spider angiomas and palmar erythema are not usually present. Xanthomatous lesions may occur in the skin of the eyelids, around the joints, and within tendons. Nutrition may remain good until the terminal phase.

B. Laboratory Findings: The blood findings are normal except insofar as they reflect the inciting lesion. The stools are light-colored, frequent, and fatty, and stool urobilinogen is reduced. The urine is dark and contains bile. Liver function tests initially show a pattern of obstruction (elevated alkaline phosphatase and serum cholesterol, especially the free cholesterol fraction; decreased prothrombin, elevated bilirubin); but as obstruction persists—often complicated by infection—evidence of hepatocellular dysfunction appears. Hyperlipemia, with a predominant increase in cholesterol and phospholipids, may reach extreme levels of over 3 gm/100 ml. The serum, however, remains clear.

Liver biopsy, surgical or needle, usually demonstrates the typical pathologic findings, although in late stages differentiation from other types of cirrhosis may be difficult. Antimitochondrial antibodies may be helpful in establishing the diagnosis of biliary cirrhosis.

C. X-Ray Findings: X-ray may show the inciting lesion or esophageal varices or, not infrequently, osteoporosis.

Treatment

Exploration is indicated to establish the diagnosis of primary or secondary biliary cirrhosis. If no obstruction can be found with operative cholangiography, the only treatment is supportive: adequate nutrition, relief of itching, and, in some instances, adrenal corticosteroids. Extrahepatic obstruction should be relieved if found. Treat any infection that is present with appropriate antibiotic drugs.

Prognosis

The intrahepatic form is generally progressive in spite of therapy, though spontaneous improvement may occur. Death due to liver failure, infections, or hemorrhage generally occurs in 5–10 years.

The course and prognosis of biliary cirrhosis secondary to extrahepatic obstruction depends upon the course of the inciting lesion. If the obstruction can be relieved and any associated infection controlled, the cirrhosis in early stages will remain stationary.

Ahrens, E.H., Jr., & others: Primary biliary cirrhosis. Medicine 29:299–364; 1950.
Popper, H., Rubin, E., & F. Schaffner: The problem of primary biliary cirrhosis. Am J Med 33:807–810, 1962.

ACUTE CHOLECYSTITIS

Essentials of Diagnosis

- Nausea, vomiting.
- Severe right upper quadrant pain and tenderness.
- Fever and leukocytosis.

General Considerations

Cholecystitis is associated with gallstones in over 90% of cases. Acute cholecystitis is usually superimposed on a chronic process and is precipitated by obstruction of the cystic duct by a stone (or, rarely, by edema in the absence of calculi). There is rapid development of a tense, edematous, inflamed gallbladder. Infection often follows as a result of invasion by resident organisms.

Clinical Findings

A. Symptoms and Signs: A past history suggestive of gallbladder disease can often be obtained. The acute attack is frequently precipitated by a heavy meal and begins with right upper quadrant pain which usually radiates to the right infrascapular region. Pain is agonizingly severe and prostrating, and is associated with vomiting. Right upper quadrant tenderness is invariably present, and in most cases is associated with local muscle spasm and rebound tenderness. The tensely distended gallbladder may be palpable. Minimal jaundice is occasionally present in the absence of common duct obstruction. Marked jaundice indicates choledocholithiasis or liver damage. Low-grade or moderate fever is present.

B. Laboratory Findings: Moderate leukocytosis is typical. Serum bilirubin levels of 1–4 mg/100 ml may be seen in the absence of common duct obstruction; clinical jaundice appears when the bilirubin exceeds 2.5 mg/100 ml. Slight elevation of the serum amylase may rarely be noted.

C. X-Ray Findings: Gallstones are found on plain abdominal x-rays in about 25% of cases of acute cholecystitis. Intravenous cholecystography may be a useful emergency diagnostic procedure. If the gallbladder fills, acute cholecystitis is ruled out.

Differential Diagnosis

The disorders most likely to be confused with acute cholecystitis are perforated peptic ulcer, acute pancreatitis, appendicitis in a high-lying appendix, perforated carcinoma or diverticulum of the hepatic flexure, liver abscess, liver congestion, acute viral hepatitis, and pneumonia with pleurisy on the right side. The diagnosis of uncomplicated acute cholecystitis is usually not difficult because of the definite localization of pain and tenderness in the right upper quadrant and the characteristic right infrascapular radiation.

Complications

A. Gangrene of the Gallbladder: Continued marked or progressive right upper quadrant pain, tenderness, muscle spasm, fever, and leukocytosis after 24—48 hours are suggestive of severe inflammation and possibly gangrene of the gallbladder. Necrosis may occasionally develop without definite signs, especially in the obese abdomen.

B. Cholangitis: Intermittent high fever and chills are the major signs. Common duct stone may be a contributing cause.

Treatment

Acute cholecystitis will subside on a conservative regimen in the majority of cases. Cholecystectomy can then be scheduled 6 weeks to 3 months later when the patient's general condition is optimal and the technical difficulties of operation minimized. If, as occasionally happens, recurrent acute symptoms develop during this waiting period, cholecystectomy is indicated without further delay. When a program of conservative therapy is elected for acute cholecystitis, all patients (particularly the diabetic, the obese, and the elderly) must be watched carefully for signs of gangrene of the gallbladder.

Operation for acute cholecystitis is mandatory when there is evidence of gangrene or perforation. Operation during the acute stage is also justified as a means of reducing overall morbidity in good risk patients in whom the diagnosis is unequivocal. It is best to defer operation, if possible, in the presence of acute pancreatitis or common duct stone.

A. Conservative Treatment: During the acute period while the patient is being evaluated, the abdominal examination and white blood count should be repeated several times daily. The principles of treatment are the same as in acute peritonitis, with the addition of an anticholinergic drug such as parenteral atropine or oral belladonna. Meperidine (Demerol®) is the analgesic of choice, since morphine produces spasm of the sphincter of Oddi. Antibiotics (eg, penicillin and streptomycin; or tetracycline alone; or the 3 drugs together in severe cases) are administered in all except mild, rapidly subsiding cases.

B. Surgical Treatment: When surgery is elected for acute cholecystitis, cholecystectomy is the operation of choice. The common duct should also be explored if indicated. In the poor risk patient or when technical difficulties with cholecystectomy arise, cholecystostomy is the safest procedure.

Prognosis

Mild acute cholecystitis frequently subsides. However, the possibility of recurrence cannot be disregarded. Moderate or severe acute cholecystitis is an indication for surgery. Particularly in old people, it may result in serious complications which may be a threat to health and life. Surgery is most often curative.

Cafferata, H.I., Stallone, R.J., & C.W. Mathewson: Acute cholecystitis in a municipal hospital. Arch Surg 98:435—441, 1969.

Klingen Smith, W., & others: Cholecystectomy in acute cholecystitis. Arch Surg 92:689—694, 1966.

Meyer, K.A., Capos, N.J., & A.I. Mittelpunkt: Personal experiences with 1261 cases of acute and chronic cholecystitis and cholelithiasis. Surgery 61:661—668, 1967.

CHRONIC CHOLECYSTITIS

Essentials of Diagnosis

- Recurrent colicky right upper quadrant pain.
- Epigastric distress, nausea.

Clinical Findings

A. Symptoms and Signs: When significant complaints occur they fall into 2 general categories: (1) chronic epigastric distress, often postprandial; and (2) recurrent "biliary colic" characterized by attacks of right upper quadrant pain radiating to the right infrascapular region, lasting a few minutes or hours, occasionally accompanied by vomiting, and often precipitated by dietary indiscretion.

There are no specific physical findings except for transient, mild right upper quadrant tenderness during attacks of biliary colic. If hydrops of the gallbladder is present (rare), the tense, nontender organ can usually be palpated with ease.

B. Laboratory Findings: None are diagnostic. Serum bilirubin and liver function tests should be done, especially if common duct stone or liver disease is suspected.

C. X-Ray Findings: Oral cholecystography is the most important diagnostic procedure. The presence of gallstones on plain films or cholecystography is presumptive evidence of cholecystitis. When there is simply nonfilling of the gallbladder, cholecystography is repeated with a double dose of the test medium. Alternatively, an intravenous cholecystogram can be ordered, particularly if common duct stone is suspected. If the gallbladder fails to visualize on the second examination, it is probably diseased. Cholecystography is unreliable when there is significant liver dysfunction (BSP retention greater than 20%), common duct obstruction (serum bilirubin above 5 mg/100 ml), malabsorption of the test material, or in the presence of an acute abdomen due to any cause.

The noncalculous gallbladder which fills poorly and empties sluggishly is not a surgical problem, but because small stones may be easily overlooked in such cases cholecystography should be repeated if symptoms are especially suggestive of gallbladder disease. Sensitivity to iodine is the only contraindication to cholecystography.

Differential Diagnosis

If there are attacks of typical biliary colic and x-ray evidence of cholelithiasis or a nonfunctioning gallbladder, the diagnosis is not difficult. When nonspecific symptoms are the chief complaint, it is necessary to consider other gastrointestinal conditions. Among these are peptic ulcer, chronic pancreatitis, irritable colon, and carcinoma of the stomach, pancreas, hepatic flexure, liver, or gallbladder. It is often advisable to obtain an upper gastrointestinal barium study on patients with suspected gallbladder disease because of the frequent coexistence of other disorders (especially peptic ulcer).

Complications

The complications of chronic cholecystitis with cholelithiasis include acute cholecystitis, common duct stone, cholecystenteric fistula, pancreatitis, and carcinoma of the gallbladder.

Treatment

A. Medical Treatment: Conservative management is indicated for patients without clinical or x-ray evidence of stones; for patients who refuse surgery; for poor risk patients; and for patients with a short life expectancy.

1. Diet—Diets should be palatable and tolerable to the patient. Weight reduction programs are indicated if the patient is obese.

2. Antispasmodic medication—Any of the following can be given: tincture of belladonna, 10 drops 3 times daily before meals; belladonna extract, 15 mg 3 times daily before meals; phenobarbital-antispasmodic mixtures (see Treatment of Duodenal Ulcer); or atropine sulfate, 0.4–0.6 mg orally, sublingually, or subcut.

3. Sedative-antispasmodic mixtures—Give as necessary for symptomatic relief.

4. Dehydrocholic acid (Decholin®), 0.25–0.5 gm 3 times daily after meals, may be used as a hydrocholeretic. Do not use this drug if biliary stasis is due to complete mechanical obstruction.

B. Surgical Treatment: Surgery is indicated in the following circumstances if the patient is a good surgical risk: (1) For patients with biliary stones, with or without jaundice, who have recurrent attacks of right upper abdominal quadrant pain. (2) For patients with suspicion of gallbladder malignancy. In general, cholecystectomy is preferred to palliative procedures except for poor risk or seriously ill patients or when there are technical contraindications. Choledochostomy may also be indicated.

Prognosis

The overall mortality following cholecystectomy is less than 1%. However, biliary tract surgery is more complicated and hazardous in elderly patients; in patients over 70, cholecystectomy probably has a mortality of 5–10%.

After a properly performed operation, the patient usually is asymptomatic and requires no special diet or regimen.

Munster, A.M., & J.R. Brown: Acalculous cholecystitis. Am J Surg 113:730–734, 1967.

CHOLELITHIASIS

The high incidence of gallstones in the general population accounts for the clinical frequency of cholecystitis. Autopsy studies show that 32% of women and 16% of men past the age of 40 have gallstones. The incidence of calculi rises sharply at around 40 years of age. Pregnancy is an important predisposing cause of gallstones, and obesity may also be a contributing factor; hence the description of the typical gallbladder patient as "female, fat, and 40."

Gallstones usually consist of cholesterol, calcium bilirubinate, calcium carbonate, or a mixture of these. About 90% of the stones associated with chronic cholecystitis are of the mixed variety, whereas the preceding 3 types of "pure" calculi may be seen in a relatively normal gallbladder. Calcium bilirubinate stones tend to occur, sometimes at an early age, in such diseases as congenital hemolytic anemia and sickle cell anemia as a result of increased bilirubin in the bile.

Infection plays an important role in both cholelithiasis and cholecystitis. Chronic, low-grade bacterial involvement of the gallbladder produces cellular debris on which the various salts precipitate in the early stages of mixed stone formation. When mechanical obstruction of the cystic duct occurs, invasive infection of the distended gallbladder is common. Bacteria of intestinal origin (streptococci, coliform bacteria, and staphylococci) can be cultured from about half of calculous gallbladders removed at operation.

Cholelithiasis is asymptomatic in most patients, being discovered incidentally at operation or autopsy or on x-ray films. The management of asymptomatic gallstones is controversial, but most surgeons advise prophylactic removal of the gallbladder if the patient is a reasonably good surgical risk. This view is not shared by most gastroenterologists since the likelihood of developing malignancy of the gallbladder in the presence of cholelithiasis is probably negligible. Symptomatic cholelithiasis requires surgery.

DeMarco, A., Nance, F.C., & I. Cohn, Jr.: Chronic cholecystitis: Experience in a large charity institution. Surgery 63:750–756, 1968.

PRIMARY SCLEROSING CHOLANGITIS

Primary sclerosing cholangitis is a disease of unknown etiology. It may be associated with ulcerative colitis or regional enteritis. Slow-growing bowel duct carcinomas may mimic sclerosing cholangitis. The disorder is characterized by a diffuse inflammatory process leading to fibrosis and stenosis of the biliary tract. Clinically the disease presents as progressive obstructive jaundice. It may occur early in life. Treatment consists of surgical bypass of the stricture area when possible. Corticosteroids and broad-spectrum antibiotics may be useful.

Grua, O.E., & J.A. McMurrin: Sclerosing cholangitis: Review and presentation of an unusual pathologic variant. Am J Surg 116:659–663, 1968.

Manesis, J.G., & J.F. Sullivan: Primary sclerosing cholangitis. Arch Int Med 115:137–139, 1965.

Warren, K.W., Athanassiades, S., & J.I. Monge: Primary sclerosing cholangitis. A study of forty-two cases. Am J Surg 111:23, 1966.

CHOLEDOCHOLITHIASIS
(Biliary Colic)

Essentials of Diagnosis

- Often a history of colic or jaundice.
- Sudden onset of severe right upper quadrant or epigastric pain which may radiate to right scapula or shoulder.
- Nausea and vomiting.
- Fever, often followed by hypothermia or shock.
- Jaundice, sometimes delayed.
- Leukocytosis.
- Plain films of abdomen may reveal gallstones.

General Considerations

About 10% of patients with gallstones have choledocholithiasis. The percentage rises with age, and the incidence in elderly people may be as high as 50%. Common duct stones usually originate in the gallbladder but may also form in the common duct. The stones are frequently "silent," as no symptoms result unless there is some obstruction.

Clinical Findings

A. Symptoms and Signs: A history suggestive of chronic cholecystitis can usually be obtained. The additional features which suggest the presence of a common duct stone are (1) frequently recurring attacks of biliary colic, (2) chills and fever associated with the attacks of colic, and (3) a history of jaundice. Jaundice, which may be transient, is usually first noted within 1–2 days after an attack of colic. Occasionally there is no pain associated with the jaundice.

The presence of jaundice is strong evidence for common duct stone in a patient with a history of chronic gallbladder disease. Epigastric tenderness may occur during attacks of colic. Otherwise there are no specific abdominal signs.

B. Laboratory Findings: Liver function tests should be performed on all cases. Bilirubinuria and elevation of serum bilirubin are present if the common duct is obstructed. Elevation of the serum alkaline phosphatase is especially suggestive of obstructive jaundice. Because BSP retention is increased by duct obstruction, this test does not evaluate hepatocellular function under these circumstances. Prolongation of the prothrombin time begins to occur when bile is excluded for more than a few days from the gastrointestinal tract. When marked obstructive jaundice persists for several weeks, liver damage occurs and differentiation of obstructive from hepatocellular jaundice becomes progressively more difficult.

C. X-Ray Findings: If the serum bilirubin level is below 5 mg/100 ml and liver function is satisfactory, intravenous cholangiography may visualize the common duct. When jaundice is marked, plain abdominal x-rays are studied for biliary calculi.

Differential Diagnosis

The commonest cause of obstructive jaundice is common duct stone. Next in frequency is carcinoma of the pancreas, ampulla of Vater, or common duct. Metastatic carcinoma (usually from the gastrointestinal tract) and direct extension of gallbladder cancer are other important causes of obstructive jaundice. Hepatocellular jaundice can usually be differentiated on the basis of the history, clinical findings, and liver function tests.

Complications

A. Biliary Cirrhosis: Prolonged common duct obstruction causes severe liver damage; hepatic failure or portal hypertension may be the ultimate result in untreated cases.

B. Cholangitis: The incidence of bacteria in common duct bile is 75% when calculi are present; the organisms most frequently cultured are *Escherichia coli, Aerobacter aerogenes, Streptococcus faecalis,* and *Proteus vulgaris.* Ascending infection is frequent in common duct stone, adds to liver damage, and may rarely lead to multiple liver abscesses.

C. Hypoprothrombinemia: Patients with obstructive jaundice or liver disease may bleed excessively at operation as a result of hypoprothrombinemia. If the prothrombin deficiency is due to faulty vitamin K absorption, the following preparations are of value: (Parenteral administration is preferred to ensure complete absorption.)

1. Intravenously or subcutaneously–Give one of the following:

a. Phytonadione (AquaMephyton®, Konakion®) is the preparation of choice. The recommended dosage is 10 mg daily.

b. Menadione sodium bisulfite (Hykinone®) may be used if phytonadione is not available. The dosage is 10 mg daily.

2. Orally–Give one of the following:

a. Menadiol sodium diphosphate (Synkayvite®), 5 mg twice daily, is the preferred oral agent. It is water-soluble and is absorbed from the intestinal tract in the absence of bile.

b. Menadione, 5 mg twice daily, after meals.

Treatment

Common duct stone is treated by cholecystectomy and choledochostomy.

A. Preoperative Care: Emergency operation is rarely necessary; a few days devoted to careful evaluation are well spent.

1. Liver function should be evaluated thoroughly.

2. Prothrombin time should be restored to normal by parenteral administration of vitamin K preparations (see above).

3. Nutrition should be restored by a high-carbohydrate, high-protein diet.

4. Vitamin supplements should be given.

5. Cholangitis, if present, should be controlled with antibiotics (eg, tetracycline, ampicillin, or penicillin and streptomycin).

B. Indications for Common Duct Exploration: At every operation for cholelithiasis the advisability of exploring the common duct must be considered. Operative cholangiography via the cystic duct is a very useful procedure for demonstrating common duct stone. Any of the following evidences of common duct stone may be an indication for choledochostomy:

1. Preoperative findings suggestive of choledocholithiasis include a history (or the presence) of obstructive jaundice; frequent attacks of biliary colic; cholangitis; history of pancreatitis; and an intravenous cholangiogram showing stone, obstruction, or dilatation of the duct.

2. Operative findings of choledocholithiasis are palpable stones in the common duct; dilated or thick-walled common duct; gallbladder stones small enough to pass through the cystic duct; and pancreatitis.

C. Postoperative Care:

1. **Antibiotics**—Postoperative antibiotics are not administered routinely after biliary tract surgery. Cultures of the bile are always taken at operation. If biliary tract infection was present preoperatively or is apparent at operation, penicillin and streptomycin or a tetracycline is administered postoperatively until sensitivity tests on culture specimens are available.

2. **Management of the T-tube**—Following choledochostomy a simple catheter or T-tube is placed in the common duct for decompression. It must be attached securely to the skin or dressing because inadvertent removal of the tube may be disastrous. A properly placed tube should drain bile at the operating table and continuously thereafter; otherwise it is blocked or dislocated. The volume of bile drainage varies from 100–1000 ml daily (average, 200–400 ml). Above-average drainage may be due to obstruction at the ampulla (usually edema), increased bile output, low resistance or siphonage effect in the drainage system, or a combination of these.

3. **Cholangiography**—A cholangiogram through the T-tube should be done on about the 7th or 8th postoperative day. Under fluoroscopic control, a radiopaque medium (eg, 50% Hypaque®) is aseptically and gently injected until the duct system is outlined and the medium begins to enter the duodenum. The injection of air bubbles must be avoided since on x-ray they resemble stones in the duct system. Spot films are taken. If the cholangiogram shows no stones in the common duct and the opaque medium flows freely

into the duodenum, clamp the tube overnight and remove it by simple traction on the following day. A small amount of bile frequently leaks from the tube site for a few days. A rubber tissue drain is usually placed alongside the T-tube at operation. This drain is partially withdrawn on the 5th day and shortened daily until it is removed completely on about the 7th day.

CARCINOMA OF THE BILIARY TRACT

Carcinoma of the gallbladder occurs in approximately 2% of all people operated on for biliary tract disease. It is a notoriously insidious disease, and the diagnosis is usually made at surgery. Metastases—by direct extension into the liver or to the peritoneal surface—may be the initial manifestation.

Carcinoma of the bile duct is less common. It usually presents as acute obstructive jaundice. It may be associated with symptoms of ascending cholangitis.

Recurrent to continuous right upper quadrant pain, jaundice, and a right upper quadrant mass either due to a distended gallbladder, hepatomegaly, or tumor may be the presenting clinical picture. Ascites may occur with peritoneal implants. Pruritus is a prominent complaint.

Laboratory findings consist of abnormal liver function tests indicative of obstruction to bile flow.

The tumor is rarely resectable, and the prognosis is poor. Diversion of the bile stream is a palliative procedure.

Buckwalter, J.A., Lawton, R.L., & R.T. Tidrick: Bypass operations for neoplastic biliary tract obstruction. Am J Surg 109:100–106, 1964.

DenBesten, L., & R.D. Liechty: Cancer of the biliary tree. Am J Surg 109:587–589, 1965.

ElDomeiri, A.A., Brasfield, R.D., & J.L. O'Quinn: Carcinoma of the extrahepatic bile ducts. Ann Surg 169:525–532, 1969.

Litwin, M.S.: Primary carcinoma of the gallbladder. Arch Surg 95:236–240, 1967.

DISEASES OF THE PANCREAS

ACUTE PANCREATITIS
(Acute Hemorrhagic Pancreatitis, Acute Interstitial Pancreatitis)

Essentials of Diagnosis

- Abrupt onset acute epigastric pain, often with back radiation.

- Nausea, vomiting, prostration, sweating.
- Abdominal tenderness and distention, fever.
- Leukocytosis, elevated serum and urinary amylase and lipase.
- History of previous episodes or alcoholic or dietary excess.

General Considerations

Acute pancreatitis is a severe abdominal disease produced by acute inflammation in the pancreas and associated escape of pancreatic enzymes from the acinar cells into the surrounding tissue. The basic cause is not known, and multiple factors may be responsible. Acute pancreatitis is most commonly associated in the USA with alcoholism and biliary tract disease. The fact that acute pancreatitis can be precipitated by alcoholism or dietary excess suggests that a secretory stimulus factor (perhaps with associated intraductal obstruction) is at work. Vascular and allergic causes have also been postulated. Surgical manipulation in the upper abdomen may also be followed by acute pancreatitis.

Pathologic changes vary from acute edema and cellular infiltration to necrosis of the acinar cells, hemorrhage from necrotic blood vessels, and intra- and extrapancreatic fat necrosis. A portion of the gland or the entire pancreas may be involved.

Clinical Findings

A. Symptoms and Signs: Epigastric abdominal pain, generally abrupt in onset, is steady and severe, and is often made worse by lying supine and better by sitting and leaning forward. The pain usually radiates into the back but may radiate to the right or left. Nausea, vomiting, and constipation are present; and severe prostration, sweating, and anxiety are often present. There may be a history of alcoholic intake or a heavy meal immediately preceding the attack, or a history of similar, milder episodes in the past.

The abdomen is tender mainly in the upper abdomen, often with guarding or rigidity. The abdomen may be distended, and bowel sounds may be absent in associated paralytic ileus. Fever of $101-102°$ F ($38.3-38.9°$ C), tachycardia, hypotension (even true shock), pallor, and a cool clammy skin are often present. Mild jaundice is common in acute pancreatitis. An upper abdominal mass may be present but is not characteristic.

B. Laboratory Findings: Leukocytosis (10,000–30,000), proteinuria, casts (25% of cases), glycosuria (10–20% of cases), hyperglycemia and abnormal glucose tolerance curves (50% of cases), and elevated serum bilirubin may be present. NPN and serum alkaline phosphatase may be elevated, flocculation tests may be positive, and coagulation tests abnormal. A decrease in serum calcium correlates well with the severity of process; depression is greatest on about the 6th day; levels below 7 mg/100 ml are associated with tetany and are an unfavorable sign.

The serum enzymes are elevated. Serum amylase is elevated early (in 90% of cases) and returns to normal by the third day; serum lipase rises more slowly and persists a few days longer. Urine amylase and amylase activity in the peritoneal fluid (may be very high) remain elevated longer than serum amylase.

Peritoneal fluid is yellow to reddish brown, with microscopic fat globules, and its pancreatic enzyme content is very high.

C. X-Ray Findings: X-rays may show gallstones, a "sentinel loop" of gas-distended small intestine in the left upper quadrant, or linear focal atelectasis or pleural fluid in the left pleural cavity. All of these findings are suggestive of acute pancreatitis but are not diagnostic.

D. ECG Findings: ST–T wave changes may occur, but they usually differ from those of myocardial infarction.

Differential Diagnosis

Acute pancreatitis may be almost impossible to differentiate from common duct stone or perforated peptic ulcer with elevated serum amylase. It must be differentiated also from acute mesenteric thrombosis, renal colic, dissecting aortic aneurysm, acute cholecystitis, and acute intestinal obstruction. The serum amylase may also be elevated in high intestinal obstruction, mumps, and after abdominal surgery or administration of narcotics.

Complications

Pancreatic abscess is a suppurative process in necrotic tissue with rising fever, leukocytosis, and localized tenderness and epigastric mass.

Pseudocyst (a cystic structure formed from necrotic areas) develops outside the pancreas and may become very large.

Chronic pancreatitis develops in 10% of cases.

Permanent diabetes mellitus and exocrine pancreatic insufficiency occur uncommonly.

Prevention

All associated etiologic factors should be corrected, eg, biliary tract disease, duodenal ulcers. The patient should be warned not to eat large meals or foods which are high in fat content and not to drink alcohol. The most common precipitating factor in acute pancreatitis is alcoholic indulgence.

Treatment

A. Emergency Measures for Impending Shock: Place the patient at bed rest in the shock position and give morphine sulfate, 15–20 mg subcut or IV, or meperidine (Demerol®), 100–150 mg, as necessary for pain. Atropine sulfate, 0.4–0.6 mg subcut, should be given as an antispasmodic.

Give 250–500 ml of plasma IV immediately and follow with subsequent infusions as necessary to correct disturbed fluid balance and maintain normal hematocrit. Five percent glucose or normal saline (or both) may be used initially if plasma is not available or to correct fluid and mineral imbalance.

Withhold food and fluids by mouth and initiate continuous gastric suction.

The patient should be constantly attended, and vital signs should be checked every 15—30 minutes, as indicated, during the acute phase. Blood count, hematocrit, serum amylase, and serum lipase should be observed closely.

B. Follow-Up Care: After the patient has recovered from shock (or if shock does not develop) it is necessary to choose between conservative or expectant medical management and exploratory surgery. Conservative therapy is preferred. Observe the patient closely for evidence of continued inflammation of the pancreas or related structures. A surgeon should be consulted in all cases of suspected acute pancreatitis. If the diagnosis is in doubt and there is a possibility of a serious and surgically correctable lesion (eg, perforated peptic ulcer), exploration is indicated.

In general, conservative measures are indicated when the diagnosis of pancreatitis has been established. However, in patients with severe hemorrhagic pancreatitis not responding to conservative treatment, it may be advisable to perform a laparotomy in order to remove the fluid collection or drain an abscess from the abdominal cavity.

When acute pancreatitis is unexpectedly found on exploratory laparotomy, it is usually wise to close without intervention of any kind. If the pancreatitis appears mild and cholelithiasis is present, cholecystostomy or cholecystectomy may be justified. Patients with unsuspected pancreatitis who receive the least intra-abdominal manipulation have the least morbidity and mortality after laparotomy except that sump suction drainage as noted above may be indicated in severe hemorrhagic pancreatitis.

The development of a pancreatic abscess is an indication for prompt drainage, usually through the flank. If a pseudocyst develops and persists, surgical treatment may be required.

The patient should be examined frequently. Periodic blood counts, blood glucose determinations, and serum and urine enzyme determinations should be carried out as indicated. Antibiotic therapy should be reserved for patients with suppurative complications.

No fluid or foods should be given by mouth for at least 48 hours, and continuous nasogastric suction should be maintained for that period. After 48—72 hours, small quantities of liquid foods may be introduced gradually by mouth as tolerated. Gastric suction may be temporarily discontinued several times during the day for small oral feedings and then gradually discontinued, depending upon clinical progress. Give parenteral fluids as necessary to replace lost fluid, electrolytes, albumin, and whole blood.

Atropine sulfate, 0.4—0.6 mg subcut, may be administered 3 times daily.

C. Convalescent Care: When clinical evidence of pancreatic inflammation has cleared, place the patient on a low-fat diet and give belladonna extract, 15 mg 3 times daily, or atropine sulfate, 0.4—0.6 mg 3 times daily. Antacids should be given at hourly intervals until the acute attack subsides.

Prognosis

Recurrences are common. The mortality rate is over 10% with medical supportive therapy. Surgery is indicated only when the diagnosis is in doubt or in the presence of an associated disorder such as stones in the biliary tract.

Frey, C.F.: The operative treatment of pancreatitis. Arch Surg 98:406—417, 1969.

Louw, J.H., Marks, I.N., & S. Bank: The management of severe acute pancreatitis. Postgrad MJ 43:31—44, 1967.

Nugent, F.W., & S. Zuberi: Treatment of acute pancreatitis. S Clin North America 48:595—600, 1968.

Waterman, N.G., & others: The treatment of acute hemorrhagic pancreatitis by sump drainage. Surg Gynec Obst 126:963—971, 1968.

White, T.T.: *Pancreatitis.* Williams & Wilkins, 1966.

Zieve, L.: Relationship between acute pancreatitis and hyperlipemia. M Clin North America 52:1493—1501, 1968.

CHRONIC RELAPSING PANCREATITIS

Some individuals, about 1/3 of whom are alcoholics, have repeated attacks of pancreatitis. Once an attack of pancreatitis has occurred, the chance of recurrence is about 50%. Progressive fibrosis and varying degrees of destruction of functioning glandular tissue occur as a result. Pancreaticolithiasis and obstruction of the duodenal end of the pancreatic duct are often present. Cholecystitis is present in about 50% of patients with chronic pancreatitis. Hyperparathyroidism and familial hyperlipidemia should be ruled out. Males are affected 6 times as often as females.

Clinical Findings

A. Symptoms and Signs: Recurrent attacks of epigastric and left upper quadrant pain with referral to the upper left lumbar region are typical. Anorexia, nausea, vomiting, constipation, and flatulence are common. Abdominal signs during attacks consist chiefly of tenderness over the pancreas, mild muscle guarding, and paralytic ileus. Attacks may last only a few hours or as long as 2 weeks; pain may eventually be almost continuous. Steatorrhea (as indicated by bulky, foul, fatty stools) and other types of intestinal malabsorption may occur in chronic pancreatitis.

B. Laboratory Findings: Serum amylase and bilirubin may be elevated during acute attacks. Glycosuria may be present. Excess fecal fat may be demonstrated on chemical analysis of the stool.

C. X-Ray Findings: Plain films often show pancreaticolithiasis and mild ileus. A cholecystogram may reveal biliary tract disease, and upper gastrointestinal series may demonstrate a widened duodenal loop.

Complications

Narcotic addiction is common. Other frequent complications include diabetes mellitus, pancreatic pseudocyst or abscess, cholestatic liver disease with or without jaundice, steatorrhea, malnutrition, and peptic ulcer.

Treatment

Correctable coexistent biliary tract disease should be treated surgically.

A. Medical Measures: A low-fat diet and anticholinergic drugs should be prescribed. Alcohol is forbidden because it frequently precipitates attacks. Mild sedatives may be helpful. Narcotics are avoided. Malabsorption is treated with pancreatin (eg, Viokase®), 3–4 gm orally 3 times daily after meals. Every effort is made to manage the disease medically.

B. Surgical Treatment: When conservative measures fail, surgical intervention must be considered. There is no agreement as to the procedure of choice, and operations must be strictly individualized. The objectives of surgical intervention are to eradicate biliary tract disease, ensure a free flow of bile into the duodenum, and eliminate obstruction of the pancreatic duct. Sphincterotomy of the sphincter of Oddi has been favored by some. When obstruction of the duodenal end of the duct can be demonstrated by operative pancreatography, dilatation of the duct or resection of the tail of the pancreas with implantation of the distal end of the duct by pancreaticojejunostomy may be successful. Anastomosis between the longitudinally split duct and a defunctionalized limb of jejunum without pancreatectomy may be in order. In advanced cases it may be necessary, as a last resort, to do subtotal or total pancreatectomy.

Prognosis

This is a serious disease and often leads to chronic invalidism. The prognosis is best when patients with acute pancreatitis are carefully investigated with their first attack and are found to have some remediable condition such as chronic cholecystitis and cholelithiasis, choledocholithiasis, stenosis of the sphincter of Oddi, or hyperparathyroidism. Surgical relief of these aggravating conditions may prevent recurrent pancreatic disease.

Berk, J.E., & P.H. Guth: Chronic pancreatitis. M Clin North America 54:479–92, 1970.

Warren, K.W.: Surgical management of chronic relapsing pancreatitis. Am J Surg 117:24–32, 1969.

CARCINOMA OF THE HEAD OF THE PANCREAS & THE PERIAMPULLARY AREA

Essentials of Diagnosis

- Obstructive jaundice, which may be painless.
- Enlarged gallbladder may be painful.
- Upper abdominal pain with radiation to back, weight loss, and thrombophlebitis are usually late manifestations.

General Considerations

Carcinoma is the commonest neoplasm of the pancreas. About 75% are in the head and 25% in the body and tail of the organ. Carcinomas involving the head of the pancreas, the ampulla of Vater, the common bile duct, and the duodenum are considered together because they are usually indistinguishable clinically.

Clinical Findings

A. Symptoms and Signs: Abdominal pain, jaundice, weight loss, and a palpable gallbladder are the most frequent findings in these tumors. Pain, which is present in over 70%, is often vague and diffuse in the epigastrium and is rarely comparable to biliary colic. Later, more persistent, severe pain develops and often radiates to the back. This usually indicates that the lesion has spread beyond the pancreas and is inoperable. The jaundice is obstructive and must be differentiated from the hepatocellular type. Unfortunately, it is rarely possible to make the diagnosis before jaundice occurs. Diarrhea is seen occasionally, and thrombophlebitis in the legs is a rare sign. It is a useful clinical rule (Courvoisier's law) that jaundice associated with palpable gallbladder is indicative of obstruction by neoplasm. On rare occasions the gallbladder may not be palpable because of cystic duct obstruction or contraction of the gallbladder secondary to chronic infection.

B. Laboratory Findings: There may be mild anemia. Glycosuria, hyperglycemia, and impaired glucose ·tolerance or true diabetes mellitus are found in 10–20% of cases. The serum amylase or lipase is occasionally elevated. Liver function responses are those of obstructive jaundice. Steatorrhea is rare. The secretin test of exocrine secretion is usually abnormal in volume, bicarbonate, or amylase response. In a few cases, duodenal cytology has shown malignant cells. Occult blood in the stool is suggestive of carcinoma of the ampulla of Vater.

C. X-Ray Findings: Hypotonic duodenography and selective celiac and superior mesenteric arteriography may be most helpful by demonstrating either the encroachment of the duodenum or abnormal vessels in the region of the pancreas. X-ray examination is usually noncontributory in involvement of the body and tail. With carcinoma of the head of the pancreas, the gastrointestinal series may show a widening of the duodenal loop, mucosal abnormalities in the duodenum ranging from edema to invasion or ulceration, or spasm or compression of the second portion of the duodenum.

Treatment

Abdominal exploration is usually necessary to confirm the diagnosis and determine resectability, which is about 30%. Radical pancreaticoduodenal resection is indicated for lesions which are strictly limited to the head of the pancreas, periampullary zone, and duodenum. When radical resection is not feasible, cholecystojejunostomy is performed to relieve the jaundice. A gastrojejunostomy is also done if duodenal obstruction is expected to develop later.

Prognosis

Carcinoma of the head of the pancreas has a very poor prognosis; fewer than 10% of resected cases survive 5 years. Lesions of the ampulla, common duct, and duodenum are more favorable, with a 5-year survival rate of 20–40% after resection. The operative mortality of radical pancreaticoduodenectomy is 10–15%.

Ansari, A., & G.E. Burch: A correlative study of proven carcinoma of the pancreas in 83 patients. Am J Gastroenterol 50:456–475, 1968.

Smith, P.E., & others: An analysis of 600 patients with carcinoma of the pancreas. Surg Gynec Obst 124:1288–1290, 1967.

Warren, K.W., Braasch, J.W., & C.W. Thum: Carcinoma of the pancreas. S Clin North America 48:601–618, 1968.

CARCINOMA OF THE BODY & TAIL OF THE PANCREAS

About 25% of pancreatic cancers arise in the body or tail. There are no characteristic findings in the early stages. The initial symptoms are vague epigastric or left upper quadrant distress. Anorexia and weight loss usually occur. Later, pain becomes more severe and frequently radiates through to the left lumbar region. A mass in the mid or left epigastrium may be palpable. The spontaneous development of thrombophlebitis in the legs is suggestive. The diagnosis is usually made only by abdominal exploration. Resection is rarely feasible, and cure is rarer still.

Arlen, M., & A. Brockunier, Jr.: Clinical manifestations of carcinoma of the tail of the pancreas. Cancer 20:1920–1923, 1967.

Mani, J.R., Zboralske, F.F., & A.R. Margulis: Carcinoma of the body and tail of the pancreas. Am J Roentgenol 96:429–446, 1966.

ACUTE PERITONITIS

Essentials of Diagnosis

- History of abdominal illness.
- Abdominal pain, vomiting, fever, and prostration.
- Abdominal rigidity and diffuse or local tenderness (often rebound).
- Later, abdominal distention and paralytic ileus.
- Leukocytosis.

General Considerations

Localized or generalized peritonitis is the most important complication of a wide variety of acute abdominal disorders. Peritonitis may be caused by infection or chemical irritation. Perforation or necrosis of the gastrointestinal tract is the usual source of infection. Chemical peritonitis occurs in acute pancreatitis and in the early stages of gastroduodenal perforation. Regardless of the etiology, certain typical features are usually present.

Clinical Findings

A. Systemic Reaction: Malaise, prostration, nausea, vomiting, septic fever, leukocytosis, and electrolyte imbalance are usually seen in proportion to the severity of the process. If infection is not controlled, toxemia is progressive and toxic shock may develop terminally.

B. Abdominal signs:

1. Pain and tenderness—Depending upon the extent of involvement, pain and tenderness may be localized or generalized. Abdominal pain on coughing, rebound tenderness referred to the area of peritonitis, and tenderness to light percussion over the inflamed peritoneum are characteristic. Pelvic peritonitis is associated with rectal and vaginal tenderness.

2. Muscle rigidity—The muscles overlying the area of inflammation usually become spastic. When peritonitis is generalized (eg, after perforation of a peptic ulcer), marked rigidity of the entire abdominal wall may develop immediately. Rigidity is frequently diminished or absent in the late stages of peritonitis, in severe toxemia, and when the abdominal wall is weak, flabby, or obese.

3. Paralytic ileus—Intestinal motility is markedly inhibited by peritoneal inflammation. Diminished to absent peristalsis and progressive abdominal distention are the cardinal signs. Vomiting occurs as a result of pooling of gastrointestinal secretions and gas, 70% of which is swallowed air.

C. X-Ray Findings: Abdominal films show gas and fluid collections in both large and small bowel, usually with generalized rather than localized dilatation. The bowel walls, when thrown into relief by the gas patterns, may appear to be thickened, indicating the presence of edema or peritoneal fluid.

D. Diagnostic Abdominal Tap: Occasionally useful.

Differential Diagnosis

Peritonitis, which may present a highly variable clinical picture, must be differentiated from acute intestinal obstruction, acute cholecystitis with or without choledocholithiasis, renal colic, gastrointestinal hemorrhage, lower lobe pneumonias, porphyria, periodic fever, hysteria, and CNS disorders (eg, tabes).

Treatment

The measures employed in peritonitis as outlined below are generally applicable as supportive therapy in most acute abdominal disorders. The objectives are

(1) to control infection, (2) to minimize the effects of paralytic ileus, and (3) to correct fluid, electrolyte, and nutritional disorders.

A. Specific Measures: Operative procedures to close perforations, to remove sources of infection such as gangrenous bowel or an inflamed appendix, or to drain abscesses are frequently required. The cause of the peritonitis should always be identified and treated promptly.

B. General Measures: No matter what specific operative procedures are employed, their ultimate success will often depend upon the care with which the following general measures are performed:

1. Bed rest in the medium Fowler (semi-sitting) position is preferred.

2. Nasogastric suction is started as soon as peritonitis is suspected. It is important to prevent gastrointestinal distention by the prompt institution of suction, which is continued until peristaltic activity returns and deflation by rectum seems imminent or has begun. The gastric (eg, Levin) tube is usually adequate. In persistent paralytic ileus, the intestinal tract may be more adequately decompressed by means of a long intestinal tube (eg, Miller-Abbott), although passage of such a tube into the small bowel is frequently difficult because of poor intestinal motility. In rare cases combined gastric and long intestinal tube suction may be necessary to relieve or prevent distention.

3. Give nothing by mouth. Oral intake can be resumed slowly after nasogastric suction is discontinued.

4. Fluid and electrolyte therapy and parenteral feeding are required.

5. Narcotics and sedatives should be used liberally to ensure comfort and rest.

6. Antibiotic therapy—If infection with mixed intestinal flora is probably present, combined therapy with penicillin and streptomycin is begun empirically. When cultures are available, antibiotics are chosen according to sensitivity studies.

7. Blood transfusions are used as needed to control anemia.

8. Toxic shock, if it develops, requires intensive treatment.

Complications & Prognosis

The most frequent sequel of peritonitis is abscess formation in the pelvis, in the subphrenic space, between the leaves of the mesentery, or elsewhere in the abdomen. Antibiotic therapy may mask or delay the appearance of localizing signs of abscess. When fever, leukocytosis, toxemia, or ileus fails to respond to the general measures for peritonitis, a collection of pus should be suspected. This will usually require surgical drainage. Liver abscess and pylephlebitis are rare complications. Adhesions may cause early or, more frequently, late intestinal obstruction.

If the cause of peritonitis can be corrected, the infection, accompanying ileus, and metabolic derangement can usually be managed successfully.

Friedland, J.A., & M.N. Harris: Primary pneumococcal peritonitis in a young adult. Am J Surg 119:737–739, 1970.

. . .

PERIODIC DISEASE
(Benign Paroxysmal Peritonitis, Familial Mediterranean Fever, (Periodic Fever, Recurrent Polyserositis)

Periodic disease is a heredofamilial disorder of unknown pathogenesis, probably metabolic, characterized by recurrent episodes of abdominal or chest pain, fever, and leukocytosis. It is usually restricted to people of Mediterranean ancestry, primarily Armenians, Sephardic Jews, Turks, Arabs, Greeks, and Italians. The disease suggests surgical peritonitis, but the acute attacks are recurrent, self-limited, and not fatal. Amyloidosis of the primary type occurs in some cases, and death may result from renal or cardiac failure. Acute episodes may be precipitated by emotional upsets, alcohol, or dietary indiscretion. Treatment is symptomatic and supportive.

Sohar, E., & others: Familial Mediterranean fever: A survey and review of the literature. Am J Med 43:227–253, 1967.

. . .

GASTROINTESTINAL MANIFESTATIONS DUE TO PARASITIC DISEASES

Abdominal pain: Giardiasis, trichinosis, strongyloidiasis.

Diarrhea or dysentery: Amebiasis, malaria, giardiasis, balantidiasis, fasciolopsiasis, schistosomiasis mansoni and japonicum, trichinosis, strongyloidiasis, paragonimiasis, teniasis and hymenolepiasis, hookworm disease, *Dientamoeba fragilis* infection, kala-azar.

Diarrhea and constipation, alternating: Amebiasis, giardiasis, balantidiasis, strongyloidiasis.

Nausea and vomiting: Malaria, giardiasis, trichinosis, fasciolopsiasis.

Peptic ulcer (simulated): Giardiasis, fasciolopsiasis.

Peritonitis: Ascariasis, amebic dysentery.

Appendicitis: Amebiasis, ascariasis, trichinosis.

Intestinal obstruction: Ascariasis.

Megacolon, mega-esophagus: American trypanosomiasis.

Tumors: Ameboma.

Hepatitis: Amebiasis, schistosomiasis, clonorchiasis, fascioliasis, fasciolopsiasis.

Hepatomegaly (tender): Malaria, amebiasis (hepatitis or abscess), larval transit in schistosomiasis japonicum, ascariasis (ascaris and toxocara), filariasis.

Hepatomegaly (nontender): Hydatidosis, schistosomiasis, clonorchiasis, fascioliasis, visceral leishmaniasis, typanosomiasis, toxoplasmosis.

Hepatic abscess: Amebiasis, fasciolopsiasis, clonorchiasis, opisthorchiasis.

Cirrhosis: Schistosomiasis mansoni and japonicum, clonorchiasis.

Hepatic tumor: Carcinoma in clonorchiasis, schistosomiasis, cyst (hydatid) in echinococcosis.

Ascites: Schistosomiasis japonicum, bancroftian filariasis, fasciolopsiasis.

Jaundice: Falciparum malaria; carcinoma in clonorchiasis, schistosomiasis; fascioliasis. (*Note:* Yellowing of skin may occur with treatment by quinacrine, lucanthone, santonin).

Cholecystitis: Giardiasis, fascioliasis, fasciolopsiasis.

Cholelithiasis: Clonorchiasis.

• • •

General Bibliography

Badenoch, J., & B.N. Brooke (editors): *Recent Advances in Gastroenterology.* Little, Brown, 1965.

Banks, P.A., & H.D. Janowitz: Some metabolic aspects of exocrine pancreatic disease. Gastroenterology 56:601–617, 1969.

Bockus, H.L.: *Gastroenterology*, 2nd ed. Vol 1: *Examination of the Patient, The Esophagus and the Stomach.* Vol 2: *Small Intestine, Absorption and Nutrition, Colon, Peritoneum, Mesentery, Omentum.* Vol 3: *Liver, Biliary Tract, Pancreas, Parasites, Secondary Gastrointestinal Disorders.* Saunders, 1963–1965.

Burge, H.: *Vagotomy.* Williams & Wilkins, 1964.

Colby, R.A., Kerr, D.A., & H.B.G. Robinson: *Color Atlas on Oral Pathology*, 2nd ed. Lippincott, 1961.

Cope, Z.: *Early Diagnosis of the Acute Abdomen,* 13th ed. Oxford, 1968.

Cope, Z.: *A History of the Acute Abdomen.* Oxford, 1965.

Glas, W.W., & S.E. Gould: *The Acute Abdomen.* Williams & Wilkins, 1966.

Halsted, J.A., & H. Zimmerman (editors): Symposium on gastrointestinal and liver disease. M Clin North America 52:1265–1501, 1968.

Lumsden, K., & S.C. Truelove: *Radiology of the Digestive System.* Davis, 1965.

Margulis, A.R., & H.J. Burhenne: *Alimentary Tract Roentgenology.* 2 vols. Mosby, 1967.

Mellinkoff, S.M. (editor): *The Differential Diagnosis of Diarrhea.* Blakiston, 1964.

Naish, J.M., & A.E.A. Read: *Basic Gastro-enterology.* Williams & Wilkins, 1965.

Pack, G.T., & I.M. Ariel: *Treatment of Cancer and Allied Diseases: Tumors of the Gastrointestinal Tract, Pancreas, Biliary System, and Liver.* Hoeber, 1962.

Patterson, M. (editor): Symposium on the treatment of gastrointestinal infections. Mod Treat 3:965–1087, 1966.

Paulson, M. (editor): *Gastroenterologic Medicine.* Saunders, 1969.

Read, A.E.: Advances in liver disease. Abstr World Med 43:801–820, 1969.

ReMine, W.H., Priestley, J.T., & J. Berkson: *Cancer of the Stomach.* Saunders, 1964.

Schiff, L.: *Diseases of the Liver,* 3rd ed. Lippincott, 1969.

Schindler, R.: *Gastroscopy: The Endoscopic Study of Gastric Pathology*, 2nd ed. Hafner, 1966.

Sherlock, S.: *Diseases of the Liver and Biliary System,* 4th ed. Thomas, 1968.

Silverberg, M., & M. Davidson: Pediatric gastroenterology: A review. Gastroenterology 58:229–252, 1970.

Spiro, H.M.: *Clinical Gastroenterology.* MacMillan, 1970.

Thompson, C.M., & others: *The Stomach.* Grune & Stratton, 1967.

Truelove, S.C., & P.C. Reynell: *Diseases of the Digestive System,* 2nd ed. Davis, 1970.

11...

Diseases of the Breast

John L. Wilson

CARCINOMA OF THE FEMALE BREAST

Essentials of Diagnosis

- Early findings: Single, nontender, firm to hard breast mass with ill-defined margins.
- Later findings: Skin or nipple retraction, axillary lymphadenopathy, breast enlargement, hardness, redness, pain, fixation of mass to skin or chest wall.
- Late finding: Bone, lung, visceral, or brain metastasis.
- Nipple erosion may be the only indication of early Paget's carcinoma.

General Considerations

Carcinoma of the breast is among the most common malignant tumors and is a major cause of death in women. The peak incidence is between the ages of 40 and 50, but breast cancer occurs frequently at all ages past 30. The annual incidence of breast carcinoma is about 70 per 100,000, and the mortality rate is about 26 per 100,000. It is estimated that 5% of women develop the disease during their lifetime, and about 20% of deaths from cancer among women are attributable to breast cancer.

A predisposition to breast cancer is inherited; women with a family history of mammary carcinoma, particularly in mothers, sisters, and daughters, are more likely to develop the disease and to be affected at an earlier age. Because mammary dysplasia may possibly be associated with an increased incidence of malignancy, continuous follow-up of patients with mammary dysplasia is indicated. Women who have never been pregnant are more likely to develop breast cancer than multiparous females. Lactation probably does not protect from breast cancer, as formerly thought. Breast cancer patients do not differ from unaffected women with respect to lactation history if account is taken of the fact that breast cancer patients tend to be of low parity. There is a greater danger of developing a second primary lesion in the opposite breast, as 5–8% of all breast cancers occur consecutively and 1% concurrently. Robbins & Berg (Cancer 17:501, 1964), in a 20-year retrospective study, found that the risk increased about 10 times for the second breast; that bilaterality occurred more often in women under 50 years of age; and that it was more frequent when the tumor in the primary breast was multicentric or of comedo or lobular type. Inflammation, trauma, and benign neoplasms are not precancerous.

Although the mean duration of life in untreated carcinoma of the breast is about 3 years, the biologic behavior of the disease is highly variable; some untreated patients succumb in 3 months, whereas others survive for 5–30 years. In general, the course of mammary cancer is related to histologic type and grade: well-differentiated tumors tend to progress more slowly. However, the choice of treatment is based primarily upon the extent of the disease and not upon the microscopic pattern of the lesion.

It would appear that a significant percentage of women with breast cancer may have an abnormal hormonal environment as determined by deviations from normal in excretion of estrogens, androgens, and hydrocorticosteroids. However, evidence based on hormonal assays is still conflicting, and it is not possible to rely with confidence on such studies to identify individuals with a high risk of developing the disease or likely to respond to hormonal therapy when metastases have occurred.

The relative frequency of carcinoma in various anatomic sites in the breast is as follows: upper outer quadrant, 45%; lower outer quadrant, 10%; upper inner quadrant, 15%; lower inner quadrant, 5%; central (subareolar or diffuse), 25%. Metastasis to regional lymph nodes is the principal mode of spread. Axillary metastases are found on microscopic study in 50–60% of patients undergoing radical mastectomy. The internal mammary nodes are invaded in about 1/3 of patients who have clinically advanced disease of borderline operability. When the tumor is in the central or inner half of the breast and when the axillary nodes have already been invaded, the internal mammary chain is particularly likely to be involved.

Hematogenous spread of breast cancer is common; the bones (especially the pelvis, spine, femur, ribs, skull, and humerus), lungs, and liver are most frequently affected.

The high mortality rate of breast cancer can be most effectively reduced by early detection and adequate surgical treatment. The patient herself is best able to discover the early lesions. Regular monthly self-examination of the breasts after each menstrual period should be practiced by all women over 30. Periodic screening examination, including mammography, is proving effective in detecting early breast cancer. The general availability of such service should significantly reduce the mortality rate from carcinoma of the breast.

Clinical Findings

A. Symptoms and Signs: The primary complaint in about 80% of patients with breast cancer is a lump (usually painless) in the breast. Less frequent symptoms are breast pain; erosion, retraction, enlargement, discharge, or itching of the nipple; and redness, generalized hardness, enlargement, or shrinkage of the breast. Rarely, an axillary mass, swelling of the arm, or back pain (from metastases) may be the first symptom.

Examination of the breast should be meticulous, methodical, and gentle. Careful inspection and palpation—with the patient supine, arms at her sides and overhead; and sitting, arms at her sides and overhead—are essential; unless this procedure is followed at all physical examinations, early lesions will be missed. In some series, 5–10% of cases of breast carcinoma have been discovered during physical examinations performed for other purposes.

A lesion smaller than 1 cm in diameter may be difficult or impossible for the examiner to feel and yet may be discovered by the patient. She should always be asked to demonstrate the location of the mass; if the physician fails to confirm her suspicions, he should repeat the examination in 1 month. During the premenstrual phase of the cycle increased innocuous nodularity may suggest neoplasm or may obscure an underlying lesion. If there is any question regarding the nature of an abnormality under these circumstances, the patient should be asked to return after her period.

The axillary and cervical regions must be examined carefully for lymphadenopathy. The location, size, consistency, and other physical features of all lesions should be recorded on a drawing of the breast for future reference.

Breast cancer usually consists of a nontender firm or hard lump with poorly delimited margins (caused by local infiltration). Slight skin or nipple retraction is an important early sign. Minimal asymmetry of the breast may be noted. Very small (1–2 mm) erosions of the nipple epithelium may be the only manifestation of carcinoma of the Paget type. Watery, serous, or bloody discharge is an infrequent early sign. The following are characteristic of advanced carcinoma: edema, redness, nodularity, or ulceration of the skin; the presence of a large primary tumor; fixation to the chest wall; enlargement, shrinkage, or retraction of the breast; marked axillary lymphadenopathy; ipsilateral supraclavicular lymphadenopathy; and distant metastases.

B. Special Clinical Forms of Breast Carcinoma:

1. Paget's carcinoma—The basic lesion is intraductal carcinoma, usually well differentiated and multicentric in the nipple and breast ducts. The nipple epithelium is infiltrated, but gross nipple changes are often minimal and a tumor mass may not be palpable. The first symptom is often itching or burning of the nipple accompanied by a superficial erosion or ulceration. The diagnosis is readily established by biopsy of the erosion.

Paget's carcinoma is not common (about 3% of all breast cancers), but it is important because it appears innocuous. It is frequently diagnosed and treated as dermatitis or bacterial infection. This is disastrous, for the lesion metastasizes to regional nodes in up to 60% of cases and should be treated in the same manner as other forms of breast cancer.

2. Inflammatory carcinoma—This is the most malignant form of breast cancer and comprises about 3% of all cases. The clinical findings consist of a rapidly growing, sometimes painful mass which enlarges the breast. The overlying skin becomes erythematous, edematous, and warm. The diagnosis should be made only when the redness involves more than 1/3 of the skin over the breast. The inflammatory changes, often mistaken for an infectious process, are caused by carcinomatous invasion of the subdermal lymphatics with resulting edema and hyperemia. These tumors may be caused by a variety of histologic types. Metastases occur early and widely in all cases, and for this reason inflammatory carcinoma is virtually incurable. Radical mastectomy is rarely indicated. Radiation and hormone therapy are usually of little value, but may be tried.

C. Laboratory Findings: Carcinoma localized to the breast and axillary nodes causes no abnormalities detectable by clinical laboratory examinations. Certain tests may be useful as clues to the presence of more widespread disease. A consistently elevated sedimentation rate may be the result of disseminated cancer. Liver metastases may be associated with elevation of alkaline phosphatase. Hypercalcemia is an occasional important finding in advanced malignancy of the breast. Radionuclide scanning of liver, bone, or brain may be of assistance in the search for metastatic foci.

D. X-Ray Findings: Because of the frequency of metastases to the bones and lungs, preparation for a radical mastectomy should include posteroanterior and lateral chest films. Anteroposterior and lateral views of the lumbar spine and pelvis and lateral skull x-ray should also be taken preoperatively in all except very early lesions. Mammography of the unaffected breast, either preoperatively or after the diagnosis has been established in a potentially curable lesion of the opposite breast, is advisable as an aid in identifying occult carcinoma. A baseline mammogram of the unaffected breast may also be of value for comparison with future examinations.

E. Mammography: A mammogram is a soft tissue x-ray which requires special training and experience in taking and interpreting the films. Mammography is the only reliable means of detecting breast cancer prior to the appearance of signs and symptoms. Many breast cancers can be diagnosed by mammography as long as 2 years prior to their clinical recognition, and recent reports indicate that certain premalignant conditions of the breast may be identifiable in the future. These developments have led to increased interest in various experimental methods of earlier detection such as xeroradiography, thermography, ultrasonography, isotope scanning, and angiography. Wide practical application of certain of these new methods such as xeroradiography and thermography is imminent.

1. Indications—Indications for mammography include the following:

a. To survey the opposite breast at the time a diagnosis of breast cancer is made and annually thereafter.

b. To complement the annual physical examination of women, particularly those with a family history of breast cancer.

c. As an aid in evaluating breasts with ill-defined or questionable masses; multiple masses; nipple discharge, erosion, or retraction; skin changes; or pain.

d. As an aid in the search for occult primary cancer in the presence of metastatic disease from an unknown primary.

Both false-positive and false-negative results are obtained with mammography, but if mammography is employed proficiently and extensively the percentage of malignant lesions reported on biopsy remains around 35%—and this in spite of the fact that more biopsies are done. The safest course is to biopsy all suspicious masses found on physical examination and, in the absence of a mass, all suspicious lesions demonstrated by mammography.

2. Usefulness and limitations—The advantages of mammography are as follows: (1) It may demonstrate early and operable breast neoplasms when clinical findings are minimal or absent; (2) a negative result helps to confirm the surgeon's impression of the benign nature of a lesion; and (3) in proved carcinoma of the breast, mammography can at times demonstrate unsuspected carcinoma in the opposite breast.

Although false-negative and false-positive readings occur, the experienced radiologist can interpret mammograms correctly in about 90% of cases.

Differential Diagnosis

Differential diagnosis depends upon biopsy. The following lesions are most likely to be confused with carcinoma: mammary dysplasia (cystic disease of the breast), fibroadenoma, intraductal papilloma, and fat necrosis.

With rare exceptions, all breast lumps should be removed without delay for frozen section, to be followed immediately by modified or standard radical mastectomy if operable cancer is present. Needle biopsy may be substituted for open biopsy where facilities are adequate to process needle specimens.

Treatment of breast cancer should never be undertaken without an unequivocal histologic diagnosis. Fortunately, frozen section in this disease is highly reliable. On the rare occasion when diagnosis on frozen section or other type of histologic preparation is questionable, treatment should be deferred pending further tissue examination.

Indications for biopsy of the breast include the following: (1) persistent mass, (2) bloody nipple discharge, (3) eczematoid nipple, and (4) positive mammography. Thermography is an experimental procedure which is less reliable than mammography but potentially useful as a screening procedure. In the

absence of physical or mammographic findings, positive thermography is a relative indication for biopsy of the suspicious area. Unexplained axillary adenopathy calls for biopsy of the enlarged node. Random or mirror image biopsy of the contralateral breast is practiced in some centers when the diagnosis of operable breast cancer is established. In patients at high risk of developing breast cancer, biopsy of the breast for minimal or equivocal change is justified.

In experienced hands, needle aspiration of discrete, spherical lesions of the breast is a useful means of distinguishing the benign cysts of fibrocystic disease from a solid tumor which may be cancer. Turbid greenish or amber fluid is characteristic of a benign cyst which should disappear completely without residual mass when aspirated. Blood-tinged fluid or a persistent mass after aspiration is an indication for biopsy. In any case, patients who develop cysts have an increased risk of breast cancer and should be followed regularly. A baseline mammogram should be obtained. When in doubt regarding the diagnosis, biopsy should be performed.

Cytologic examination of nipple discharge is rarely helpful, and breast biopsy is preferred for bloody or questionable secretions.

Clinical Staging

Patients with breast cancer can be grouped into stages according to the characteristics of the primary tumor (T), regional lymph nodes (N), and distant metastases (M). Physical, radiologic, and other clinical examinations, usually including biopsy of the primary lesion, are used in determining the stage, which is based on all information available before therapy. Staging is useful in estimating the prognosis and deciding on the type of treatment to be advised. The International Union Against Cancer and the American Joint Committee on Cancer Staging and End Results Reporting have each formulated a standard TNM system to be used by physicians in breast cancer staging.

From the practical point of view, it is useful to remember that the International and American systems of staging differ only in detail from the following brief definition of stages:

Stage I: The tumor is confined to the breast. There may be early signs of skin involvement such as dimpling or nipple retraction, but there are no signs of axillary or distant metastases.

Stage II: The primary tumor is as in stage I, but there are movable, suspicious nodes in the ipsilateral axilla.

Stage III: The primary tumor is infiltrating the skin or chest wall, or the axillary nodes are matted or fixed.

Stage IV: Distant metastases are present.

The clinician must decide treatment and prognosis in breast cancer patients whose extent of disease ranges from minimal to advanced. Judgment on management and outlook is improved if patients are systematically classified or "staged" in a manner which

TABLE 11-1. Five-year survival after radical mastectomy according to stage of breast cancer.

Stage	International System	American System
I	80%	75%
II	70%	65%
III	50%	45%
IV	0	0

allows comparison with similar cases treated by others. Both the International and the American staging systems provide sound criteria for the clinical classification of patients with breast cancer (Table 11-1).

Curative Treatment

Treatment may be curative or palliative. Curative treatment is advised for clinical stage I and stage II disease and for selected patients in stage III. Palliative treatment by radiation, hormones, endocrine ablation, or chemotherapy is recommended for patients in stage IV (distant metastases), for stage III patients unsuitable for curative efforts, and for previously treated patients who develop distant metastases or ineradicable local recurrence.

A. Types of Curative Treatment:

1. Radical mastectomy—This operation involves *en bloc* removal of breast, pectoral muscles, and axillary nodes and has been the standard curative procedure for breast cancer since the turn of the century, when W.S. Halstead and Willy Meyer independently described their versions of the technic. Experience with radical mastectomy is extensive, and no other form of therapy has produced better results in properly selected patients. Radical mastectomy removes the local lesion and the axillary nodes with a wide safety margin of surrounding tissue. If the disease has already spread to the internal mammary or supraclavicular nodes or to more distant sites, radical mastectomy alone will not cure the patient.

2. Extended radical mastectomy—This procedure involves, in addition to standard radical mastectomy, the removal of the internal mammary nodes. The extended operation has been recommended by a few surgeons for medially or centrally placed breast lesions and for tumors associated with positive axillary nodes because of the known frequency of internal mammary node metastases under these circumstances. It does not appear that extended radical mastectomy is significantly more effective than irradiation in preventing recurrence from internal mammary metastases. For that reason, extended radical mastectomy has few advocates at this time.

3. Modified radical mastectomy—This procedure involves complete removal of all breast and subcutaneous tissue (as in standard radical mastectomy) and dissection in continuity of the axillary lymphatic bed up to the level of the coracoid process. The difference between the modified and the standard radical mastec-

tomy is that the standard operation also removes the pectoralis major and minor muscles and the highest group of axillary nodes just inferior to the clavicle. There is now considerable evidence that morbidity, mortality, survival, and local recurrence rates for standard and modified radical mastectomy are essentially the same for stage I and stage II breast cancer. Prospective controlled clinical studies will be needed to settle the issue in a definitive manner, but there is already a notable shift in major centers to the use of modified radical mastectomy in patients who, a few years ago, would have been treated by standard radical mastectomy.

4. Simple mastectomy—If the malignancy is confined to the breast without spread to the adjacent muscles or to the regional nodes or beyond (true clinical stage I disease), simple mastectomy (or even wide local excision) should be effective in eradicating the cancer. Clinical experience bears this out in certain cases. The problem is the inability to determine with certainty, prior to their resection and pathologic examination, that the axillary nodes are not involved. Physical examination is highly unreliable in detecting axillary metastases. Simple mastectomy must, therefore, be considered an inadequate operation for breast cancer until more is known about the risk associated with leaving axillary metastases until they become clinically evident.

5. Supervoltage irradiation—In recent years, the proved efficacy of supervoltage irradiation in sterilizing the primary lesion and the axillary and internal mammary nodes has made radiation therapy with or without simple mastectomy (or wedge resection) an important option for primary treatment of certain breast cancers, particularly those that are locally advanced or when the patient refuses mastectomy.

B. Choice of Primary Treatment for Breast Cancer: There is evidence that control of mammary cancer confined to the breast and axillary nodes can be achieved by a number of different approaches as outlined above. Variability in tumor-host relationships from patient to patient and the unpredictability of occult metastases make it difficult to determine with precision the relative merits of current competing forms of treatment without controlled prospective clinical trials. Relying on the evidence now at hand, modified radical mastectomy is recommended as the primary treatment of choice in stage I and stage II lesions.

Stage III lesions are a borderline group and may or may not be suitable for surgical treatment by standard or modified radical mastectomy. Radical surgical treatment is usually contraindicated in stage III lesions with the following characteristics: (1) Extensive edema involving more than 1/3 of the skin of the breast. (2) Satellite nodules on the skin. (3) Carcinoma of the inflammatory type. (4) Parasternal tumor nodules. (5) Edema of the ipsilateral arm. (6) Palpable ipsilateral infraclavicular lymph nodes (metastases suspected or proved by biopsy). (7) Two or more of the following grave signs of locally advanced carcinoma: (a) ulceration of the skin; (b) limited edema involving less than 1/3 of the skin of the breast; (c) fixation of axillary lymph nodes to the skin of the deep structures of the axilla; (d) axillary lymph nodes measuring 2.5 cm or more in transverse diameter; (e) pectoral muscle or chest wall attachment.

The features listed above are signs of advanced disease and are almost invariably associated with spread to the internal mammary or supraclavicular nodes or other distant sites outside the scope of either standard or modified radical mastectomy. Under these circumstances, operation is not curative and may actually encourage dissemination of the disease locally or systemically. Radiotherapy with or without simple mastectomy (or wedge resection) is a more effective approach in these advanced stage III cases.

There remain those stage III lesions which do not exhibit the advanced signs listed above. A modified radical mastectomy may be performed if the primary tumor and the enlarged axillary nodes can clearly be excised with an adequate margin by this procedure. Attachment to the pectoral muscles, high axillary nodes, large primary tumor or nodes, or other technically unfavorable conditions would make standard radical mastectomy the preferred operation.

C. **Radiotherapy as Adjunct to Radical Mastectomy:** The purposes of preoperative or postoperative radiotherapy in association with modified or standard radical mastectomy are (1) to reduce the incidence of local recurrence from residual cancer in the operative field and (2) to sterilize metastatic cancer in the internal mammary and supraclavicular lymph nodes. Patients are, therefore, selected for radiotherapy on the basis of the likelihood of local recurrence or of the existence of disease in unresected regional nodes. According to these criteria, completely resectable lesions confined to the breast (stage I) do not call for radiotherapy. On the other hand, stage II and stage III patients may be considered for radiotherapy before or after modified or standard radical mastectomy. Only supervoltage irradiation should be advised as adjunctive therapy. Orthovoltage irradiation for this purpose is outmoded.

1. **Postoperative radiotherapy**—The efficacy of postoperative irradiation in improving survival or recurrence rates has not been decisively demonstrated. However, in view of the proved ability of supervoltage radiotherapy to destroy cancer cells in the breast and regional nodes, postoperative radiotherapy is commonly recommended under the following conditions: (1) The tumor is cut through or there is a high likelihood that residual tumor has been left in the operative field. (2) The tumor is larger than 5 cm or is located in the central or medial portion of the breast. (3) There are metastases to the axillary nodes. Radiotherapy is begun as soon after operation as the patient's general condition and state of the wound permit. A tumor dose in the range of 4000–6000 rads is delivered in 4–5 weeks, primarily to the internal mammary and supra- and infraclavicular nodal areas. The chest wall may also be irradiated.

When irradiation is properly managed, delayed wound healing, pulmonary damage, and lymphedema of the arm are infrequent problems.

2. **Preoperative radiotherapy**—The beneficial results of preoperative radiotherapy are more definite than those of postoperative radiotherapy. Preoperative irradiation reduces the incidence of local recurrence. One investigator demonstrated a 5% local recurrence rate after preoperative radiotherapy—compared to a 16% local recurrence rate following postoperative radiotherapy. Preoperative radiotherapy is possibly also of value in making inoperable patients curable by radical mastectomy, although in such patients the results may not be superior to those obtainable by radiotherapy alone.

Indications for preoperative irradiation include the following: (1) Primary tumor larger than 5 cm. (2) Limited skin edema or direct skin involvement over tumor. (3) Multiple low or mid axillary nodes. (4) A prior surgical intervention which may have disseminated the tumor locally. A 4000–6000 rad tumor dose is delivered to the axillary, supraclavicular, and internal mammary nodes, and the chest wall and breast are treated tangentially. Radical mastectomy is performed 5–6 weeks after completion of radiotherapy.

Palliative Treatment

A. **Radiotherapy:** Palliative radiotherapy may be advised for locally advanced cancers with distant metastases in order to control ulceration, pain, and other manifestations in the breast and regional nodes. Radical irradiation of the breast and chest wall and the axillary, internal mammary, and supraclavicular nodes should be undertaken in an attempt to cure locally advanced and inoperable lesions when there is no evidence of distant metastases. A certain number of patients in this group are cured in spite of extensive breast and regional node involvement.

Palliative irradiation is also of value in the treatment of certain bone or soft tissue metastases to control pain or avoid fracture, particularly when hormonal, endocrine ablation, and chemical therapy are either inappropriate or ineffective.

B. **Hormone Therapy:** When distant metastases have occurred in breast cancer, the patient is incurable, but disseminated disease may be kept under control or made to regress for sustained periods by various forms of endocrine therapy including administration of hormones or ablation of ovaries, adrenals, or hypophysis. About 1/3 of breast cancer patients will respond to one or more of these endocrine measures. The incidence of hormonal responsiveness is approximately the same in premenopausal women as in older postmenopausal women, although the methods of treatment used may be quite different.

Ablation of ovarian secretion by oophorectomy or irradiation of the ovaries is, in the premenopausal patient, the simplest and most reliable method of obtaining tumor regression in advanced breast cancer. Administration of estrogen to premenopausal patients—or to patients whose tumor has responded favorably to castration—may stimulate tumor growth. These observations have led to the hypothesis of estrogen dependence to explain the tumor regression seen in some breast cancers after castration, bilateral adrenalectomy, or hypophysectomy. According to this hypothesis, reactivation of tumor growth after control by castration is due to increasing estrogen secretion from the adrenal cortex. Bilateral adrenalectomy at this stage is known to cause further tumor regression in some cases. Subsequently, when the tumor reactivates after control by adrenalectomy, hypophyseal ablation may have an effect by eliminating secretion of both FSH and ACTH, which are capable of activating ectopic adrenal sources of estrogen. The assumption of estrogen dependence thus appears to explain the clinical remission of tumor growth seen after endocrine ablation therapy in some patients with late breast cancer. However, biochemical methods of estrogen determination have failed to show a correlation between clinical response and quantitative change in estrogen secretion. Furthermore, the estrogen dependence hypothesis cannot explain regression of some tumors after estrogen, androgen, or progestin therapy. Therefore, a combination of direct effect by metabolic products of the steroid on the tumor and of indirect effect via the pituitary (eg, alteration in prolactin or other pituitary secretion) is a postulated cause of tumor regression in steroid therapy of breast cancer. Since different tumors probably vary in their response to hormonal therapy (depending on the hormonal environment in which they have developed), the choice of a suitable steroid for therapy in each patient may be difficult. Nevertheless, certain general principles can be followed as guides to endocrine therapy.

Endocrine therapy is employed when surgery and irradiation have failed or when widespread metastases have rendered them useless. Many patients are candidates for a trial of hormone treatment because about ½ of all patients with breast cancer and 60% of those having positive axillary nodes at the time of mastectomy will develop metastatic lesions. The major forms of hormone treatment are (1) estrogen, (2) androgen, and (3) corticosteroid therapy.

1. Estrogen therapy—Estrogens should be reserved for postmenopausal women. The best results of estrogen administration are obtained in women more than 5 years past the menopause. Estrogen is capable of causing exacerbation of tumor growth in 50% of premenopausal women and should not be given to them or to recently postmenopausal women until the vaginal smear ceases to show evidence of estrogenic activity. Tumor remission rates from estrogen (and androgen as well) tend to increase with increasing number of years past the menopause.

Estrogen administered as primary therapy will induce tumor regression in over 30% of postmenopausal patients with advanced breast cancer. Objective evidence of tumor regression is seen most commonly in soft tissue metastases in older patients, and over 40% of this group show remission of tumor growth. Both local soft tissue and visceral lesions show a higher remission rate from estrogen than from androgen therapy. The reverse is true for bone metastases.

Treatment usually consists of giving diethylstilbestrol, 5 mg 3 times daily orally (or equivalent) and should be continued as long as it is beneficial.

Initial evidence of regression of metastatic cancer is usually not seen until about 4 weeks after beginning estrogen therapy, but the trial of estrogen should not be abandoned in less than 2 months except in case of obvious exacerbation or serious side-effects. The average duration of remission is about 16 months, but remissions of soft tissue lesions of over 5 years are occasionally seen. The survival time of those who respond to estrogen therapy is about twice that of nonresponders.

The commonest side-effects are anorexia, nausea, and vomiting. These usually disappear within a few weeks, but when symptoms of toxicity are severe the dosage should be reduced temporarily until tolerance is acquired. Pigmentation of nipples, areolas, and axillary skin; enlargement of the breasts; and sodium and water retention are other side-effects of estrogen therapy. Uterine bleeding occurs in the majority of postmenopausal patients when estrogen therapy is stopped, and patients should be told of this possibility to avoid anxiety. Severe bleeding can usually be controlled by administration of testosterone proprionate, 100 mg IM daily for 3 or 4 doses.

2. Androgen therapy—Androgen administration causes temporary amenorrhea in premenopausal women. Tumor regression is noted in 10–20% of such patients with advanced breast cancer. However, because of the more frequent and prolonged remission from castration, this procedure is preferred as initial treatment in the premenopausal group. Androgen therapy may be usefully added to castration in patients under 35 years of age, or in the presence of bone metastases, because of the poor results from castration alone in such patients. Failure of response to castration may be considered an indication for a trial of androgen therapy because of the low likelihood of a favorable response by these patients to adrenalectomy or hypophysectomy.

Estrogen therapy is not advisable in recently postmenopausal women until the vaginal smear ceases to show evidence of estrogenic activity because of the danger of exacerbating the disease. A trial of androgen therapy is warranted in this group, but the expectation of favorable response is only about 15% of patients.

Since bone metastases are commonly more responsive to androgen than to estrogen therapy, a trial of androgen may be advantageous when osseous lesions are present, particularly before adrenalectomy or hypophysectomy is undertaken. About 25% of patients more than 5 years past the menopause with bone metastases will respond to androgen therapy. Patients failing to respond can still be subjected to operation if indicated, and surgery will usually have been delayed only about 6 weeks.

Postmenopausal patients who have shown a favorable response to castration or estrogen therapy and have then relapsed may be given a trial of androgen therapy with a 20–30% chance of favorable response. In patients more than 5 years past the menopause, bony metastases which have failed to respond to estrogens are more likely to regress on secondary androgen therapy than are soft tissue metastases. Occasionally, androgen administration will cause tumor regression in the completely hypophysectomized patient.

Androgen may be given continuously as long as tumor regression persists. It is probably preferable, however, to administer androgen until the tumor has regressed maximally and then discontinue administration until reactivation occurs, at which time resumption of androgen therapy will often lead to another regression. Intermittent therapy of this kind has the advantage of reducing the tendency to virilization while varying the hormonal environment of the tumor, thereby possibly postponing the development of autonomy in the tumor.

The androgen preparation frequently employed is testosterone proprionate, 100 mg IM 3 times a week. However, it is simpler and equally effective to give fluoxymesterone (Halotestin®), 20–40 mg daily orally. An orally administered nonvirilizing androgen, testolactone (Teslac®), is reported to be as effective as testosterone propionate is causing tumor regression. The major interest in this compound is that, since it appears to be relatively inert hormonally, it may have a direct effect on the breast cancer.

About 3 months of androgen therapy are usually required for maximal response. Pain relief may be achieved in up to 80% of patients with osseous metastases. In addition, androgen therapy usually results in a sense of well-being and an increase in energy and weight, particularly in postmenopausal patients. The principal adverse side-reactions are increased libido and masculinizing effects, eg, hirsutism, hoarseness, loss of scalp hair, acne, and ruddy complexion. Virilization occurs in practically all women taking testosterone proprionate for longer than 6 months but in only about 1/3 of patients on fluoxymesterone. Fluid retention, anorexia, vomiting, and hepatotoxicity are among the rarer side-effects of androgen therapy.

3. Corticosteroids–Corticosteroids are especially valuable in the management of the serious acute symptoms which may result from such conditions as hypercalcemia, brain and lung metastases, and hepatic metastases with jaundice. Corticosteroid therapy is also indicated for patients who are too ill for major endocrine ablation therapy and for those whose tumors do not respond to other endocrine therapy. The combination of systemic corticosteroid and the intracavitary injection of an alkylating agent (see Chapter 30) may be very effective in controlling pleural effusion due to metastatic breast cancer.

The patient's age and previous response to sex hormone therapy are not correlated with response to corticosteroid therapy, which probably acts through a local effect upon the tumor or the tumor bed. Previous response to corticosteroids does not predict a similar response to adrenalectomy. Objective evidence of tumor regression following corticosteroid administration is less than that following adrenalectomy. Remission on corticosteroid therapy averages about 6 months, whereas that following adrenalectomy is over 12 months.

The subjective response of the seriously ill patient to corticosteroid administration is often striking. Appetite, sense of well-being, and pain from bone or visceral metastases may be markedly improved. However, objective regression of soft tissue lesions occurs in only about 15% of patients. The relief of coma from brain metastases and dyspnea from lung metastases is often encouraging but transient. Hypercalcemia is probably improved by specific action on calcium metabolism.

Cortisone, 150 mg, or prednisone or prednisolone, 30 mg, is an average daily oral dose. Twice or 3 times this dosage may be required temporarily for control of severe, acute symptoms. A variety of other corticosteroids have been employed in equivalent dosage with similar results. The dosage of corticosteroids must be reduced slowly if they have been used for prolonged periods because of the adrenocortical atrophy induced.

Adrenocortical hormones may cause numerous undesirable systemic effects and serious complications such as uncontrollable infection, bleeding peptic ulcer, muscle weakness, hypertension, diabetes, edema, and features of Cushing's syndrome.

The best overall tumor remission rate from hormonal therapy in postmenopausal patients can probably be obtained when treatment is individualized. In general, those patients with soft tissue and intrathoracic metastases will respond best to estrogen therapy. Androgen therapy is usually more effective in patients with bone metastases. Corticosteroid therapy should be particularly considered for those with brain and liver metastases.

C. Therapeutic Endocrine Ablation:

1. Castration–Oophorectomy in premenopausal women with advanced, metastatic, or recurrent breast cancer results in temporary regression in about 35% of cases, with objective improvement lasting an average of about 10 months. Life is definitely prolonged in those who respond favorably. Patients not responding to castration usually fail to respond favorably to adrenalectomy, hypophysectomy, or specific hormones. Authorities differ on whether castration should be given a trial in all premenopausal women before advising bilateral adrenalectomy or hypophysectomy. Of those patients responding favorably to castration, 40–50% will respond to bilateral adrenalectomy or hypophysectomy. Of those not responding to oophorectomy, only 10–15% show tumor regression after one of the major procedures. According to some authorities, simultaneous oophorectomy and adrenalectomy is the palliative treatment of choice in premenopausal women with disseminated breast cancer. Prophylactic castration of all premenopausal women with breast cancer is not of proved value and is not recommended.

Castration can be performed by bilateral oophorectomy or irradiation. Surgical removal of the ovaries is preferable because it rules out the possibility of residual ovarian function. Therapeutic castration is essentially confined to premenopausal women and is of no value in truly postmenopausal women. Ovarian function may persist for a few years after cessation of menses, and this can be determined by means of the vaginal smear; if evidence of persistent estrogenic activity is found, castration may be beneficial.

2. **Adrenalectomy or hypophysectomy** – Regression of advanced breast cancer occurs in about 30% of patients after either of these procedures. Patients who respond to castration or to hormone administration are most likely to benefit from removal of the adrenals or pituitary. This information is helpful in the selection of patients for one of these major ablation procedures.

Adrenalectomy is preferred over hypophysectomy because of its wider availability and greater ease of postoperative endocrine management. The mortality rate of both procedures is in the range of 5%. Transsphenoidal implantation (under local anesthesia) of beta ray-emitting yttrium can now be performed with low morbidity and mortality in a few centers, and destruction of the pituitary with great precision by a proton beam is a possible future mode of therapy. Currently, however, adrenalectomy is the procedure of choice in most institutions.

Corticosteroid replacement therapy is required after bilateral adrenalectomy. The following regimen is suggested:

Day before operation, 6 pm: Hydrocortisone sodium succinate (Solu-Cortef®), 100 mg IM
Day of operation:
   Preoperatively: Solu-Cortef®, 100 mg IM
   During operation: Solu-Cortef®, 100 mg IM
   Postoperatively: Solu-Cortef®, 50 mg IM every 4 hours
Postoperative day:
   First day: Solu-Cortef®, 100 mg every 8 hours
   Second day: Solu-Cortef®, 50 mg IM every 6 hours
   Third day: Solu-Cortef®, 50 mg IM every 12 hours
   Fourth day: Solu-Cortef®, 25 mg IM every 8 hours, or cortisone acetate, 25 mg orally every 8 hours
   Fifth day and thereafter as maintenance dose: Cortisone acetate, 25 mg orally twice daily

Maintenance dose of cortisone must be supplemented in some patients by fludrocortisone, 0.1–0.25 mg orally daily or every other day for its sodium-retaining effect. Diet following adrenalectomy should include at least 3 gm of salt daily, which may be achieved by liberal salting of food. Adrenal insufficiency will occur if the cortisone maintenance regimen is inadequate or is neglected. Resulting symptoms may include extreme weakness, nausea and vomiting, rapid weight loss, or hypotension. Increased stress calls for increased cortisone dosage. Acute crises of adrenal insufficiency require immediate hospitalization and intensive treatment.

In premenopausal women, when oophorectomy alone is followed by a remission and adrenalectomy is withheld until progression of the tumor resumes, the overall palliation and length of survival are better than when adrenals and ovaries are removed at the same operation. Postmenopausal women should be treated by simultaneous oophorectomy and adrenalectomy.

The response of metastatic breast carcinoma to administration of hormones or to ablation of endocrine glands is most likely to be favorable under the following circumstances: (1) slowly growing tumor (eg, free interval between diagnosis and development of metastases exceeds 24 months); (2) hormone therapy is begun promptly when metastases appear; (3) metastases localized to soft tissues, bones, and pleuropulmonary region (as opposed to visceral areas such as liver and brain); (4) advanced age; and (5) previous response to hormone therapy or castration. However, favorable responses may occur occasionally when none of these conditions exist.

D. Chemotherapy:* Anticancer chemotherapy should be considered for palliation of advanced breast cancer when hormone treatment is not successful or when the patient becomes unresponsive to it. Chemotherapy is most likely to be effective in patients who previously responded to hormonal therapy. The most useful chemotherapeutic agent to date is fluorouracil (5-FU), but alkylating agents, particularly triethylenethiophosphoramide (Thio-TEPA®) and mechlorethamine (nitrogen mustard, HN_2) are also of value. These drugs are administered intravenously. Their side-effects include bone marrow depression and nausea and vomiting, which may be so severe as to limit or prevent their application.

Intrapleural injection of methotrexate will frequently control pleural effusion due to metastases. Control of pleural effusion due to metastatic breast cancer is best achieved by trocar thoracotomy to establish closed tube drainage. When the fluid has been practically completely removed, 20 mg of methotrexate, freshly dissolved in 50–100 ml of diluent, is injected through the tube and the tube is then clamped for 2 hours and then reopened to water-seal drainage. The tube is removed in a day or two when all the fluid has been evacuated and the lung fully expanded.

E. Hypercalcemia in Advanced Breast Cancer:* Hypercalcemia occurs transiently or terminally in about 10% of women with advanced breast cancer. The serum calcium level should be determined periodically in such patients or when suggestive symptoms occur. The cause of the elevated serum calcium is unknown, but there is a possible relation to (1) immobilization of the patient by progressive invalidism, (2) radiotherapy for osseous metastases, or (3) hormonal therapy. However, hypercalcemia develops in many women without these presumed causes and in the absence of bony

---

*A more detailed discussion is presented in Chapter 30.

metastases or changes in the parathyroid glands. This supports the theory that certain disseminated breast cancers elaborate on osteolytic substance. Some breast tumors have been found to produce parathormone; others elaborate a sterol with vitamin D-like activity.

The symptoms of hypercalcemia are protean, and its course is treacherous. Initial symptoms usually include diffuse CNS changes, alterations of renal function, vomiting, and dehydration. Rapid deterioration, anuria, coma, and death may occur.

Prevention is important and consists of (1) adequate hydration (at least 2 liters of fluid per day), (2) maintenance of as much physical activity as possible, and (3) a low-calcium diet (avoidance of milk, cheese, ice cream, and vitamin D).

Treatment of hypercalcemia is based on (1) immediate cessation of any hormone therapy, (2) increasing the rate of calcium excretion in the urine by maintaining a fluid intake of 5–6 liters per day, and (3) decreasing the mobilization of calcium from the bone by administration of corticosteroids in the form of 20–100 mg of prednisone (or equivalent) orally daily. Disodium edetate may be given intravenously. For acute, severe, potentially fatal elevations of serum calcium, the intravenous injection of isotonic sodium sulfate may be lifesaving. Major endocrine ablation may be required after the hypercalcemia is controlled or may (rarely) be necessary as a control measure.

After subsidence of an episode of hypercalcemia, many patients survive for months or years with essentially the same relationship to their disease.

Complications of Radical Mastectomy

Except for local recurrence, usually due to implantation of tumor cells in the wound at operation, the only important late complication of radical mastectomy is edema of the arm. Significant edema occurs in 10–30% of cases. When it appears in the early postoperative period it is usually caused by lymphatic obstruction due to infection in the axilla. Late or secondary edema of the arm may develop years after radical mastectomy as a result of infection in the hand or arm with obliteration of lymphatic channels. After radical mastectomy the lymphatic drainage of the arm is always compromised and the extremity is more susceptible to infection from minor injuries than formerly. The patient should be warned of this and treatment instituted promptly if infection occurs. Specific instruction should be given to the patient who has had radical mastectomy to avoid breaks in the skin of the hand and arm on the operated side and to refrain from tasks likely to cause superficial wounds and infections. Well-established chronic edema is treated by elevation and the wearing of an elastic sleeve tailored to fit the arm snugly. Periodic use of an intermittent positive pressure sleeve may be helpful in severe cases. These measures will not cure the condition but will reduce the edema and minimize its reaccumulation.

Prognosis

In the USA, the annual mortality rate for breast cancer is about 26 per 100,000 females. Death rates are slightly higher among the nonwhite population (92% black) than among whites through ages 45–49, but lower thereafter. Age-adjusted death rates for female breast cancer differ throughout the world. In general, reported rates are higher in developed countries (with the notable exception of Japan) and are low in underdeveloped countries. Reported differences may be due in part to underdiagnosis, underreporting, and variable certification practices.

When cancer is confined to the breast, the 5-year clinical cure rate by radical mastectomy is 75–90%. When axillary nodes are involved, the rate drops to 40–60%. Operative mortality is about 1%. The most unfavorable anatomic site for breast carcinoma is the medial portion of the inner lower quadrant. Breast cancer is probably more malignant in young than in old women, but the difference is not great. The prognosis of carcinoma of the breast occurring during lactation or pregnancy is generally poor, since over ¼ are inoperable; but when radical mastectomy is feasible and the axillary nodes are not involved, the overall 5-year clinical cure rate in this group of patients is 60–70%. The presence of axillary metastases in patients who are pregnant or lactating is an extremely poor prognostic sign and the 5-year clinical cure rate after radical mastectomy under these conditions is only 5–10%.

Most of the local and distant metastases occur during the first 3 years after radical mastectomy. During this period the patient should be examined every 3–4 months. Thereafter, a follow-up examination is done every 6 months for the life of the patient with special attention to the opposite breast because of the increased risk in such patients of developing a second primary lesion.

Barker, W.F., & others: Management of nonpalpable breast carcinoma discovered by mammography. Ann Surg 170:385–395, 1969.

Crowley, L.G.: Current status of the management of patients with endocrine-sensitive tumors. Part I. Introduction and carcinoma of the breast. California Med 110:43–60, 1969.

Egan, R.L.: Roles of mammography in the early detection of breast cancer. Cancer 24:1197–1200, 1969.

Farrow, J.H.: Current concepts in the detection and treatment of the earliest of the early breast cancers. Cancer 25:468–477, 1970.

Fisher, B.: Prospects for the control of metastases. Cancer 24:1263–1269, 1969.

Gershon-Cohen, J., & M.B. Hermel: Modalities in breast cancer detection: Xeroradiography, mammography, thermography, and mammometry. Cancer 24:1226–1230, 1969.

Greisbach, W.A.: Mammography as a possible screening examination using conventional techniques. Cancer 23:874, 1969.

Guttman, R.: Role of supervoltage irradiation of regional lymph node bearing areas in breast cancer. Am J Roentgenol 95:560–564, 1966.

Haagensen, C.D., & others: Treatment of early mammary carcinoma: A cooperative international study. Ann Surg 170:875–899, 1969.

Kennedy, B.J.: Hormone therapy in inoperable breast cancer. Cancer 24:1345–1349, 1969.

Moore, F.D., & others: Carcinoma of the breast: A decade of new results with old concepts. New England J Med 277:293–296, 343–350, 411–416, 460–468, 1967.

Seideman, H.: Cancer of the breast: Statistical and epidemiological data. Cancer 24:1355–1378, 1969.

Strax, P., Venet, L., & S. Shapiro: Mass screening in mammary cancer. Cancer 23:875–878, 1969.

Watson, T.A.: Cancer of the breast. The Janeway Lecture—1965. Am J Roentgenol 96:547–559, 1966.

CARCINOMA OF THE MALE BREAST

Male breast cancer, since it is rare and usually asymptomatic, is often ignored by the patient and overlooked by the physician. It may occur at any time after age 20, but the peak incidence is in the 50s. The chief local finding is a painless mass not infrequently associated with nipple retraction, encrustation, or discharge.

Treatment consists of radical mastectomy in operable patients, who should be chosen by the same criteria as for female breast carcinoma. Radiation therapy is also advised according to similar indications as in female patients. Irradiation is the first step in the treatment of localized metastases in the skin, lymph nodes, or skeleton which are causing symptoms. Since male breast cancer is so frequently a disseminated disease, endocrine therapy is of considerable importance in its management. Castration in advanced breast cancer is the most successful palliative measure and is more beneficial than the same procedure in the female. Objective evidence of regression may be seen in 60–70% of male patients who are castrated—approximately twice the proportion seen in the female. Bilateral adrenalectomy (or hypophysectomy) has been proposed as the procedure of choice when a tumor has reactivated after castration. Corticosteroid therapy is considered by some to be more efficacious than major endocrine ablation. Male breast cancer is too rare to enable this issue to be decided in a definitive manner at this time. Either approach may be temporarily beneficial. Estrogen therapy (5 mg of diethylstilbestrol 3 times daily orally) may rarely be effective, and androgen therapy may exacerbate bone pain. Castration, bilateral adrenalectomy, and corticosteroids are the main lines of therapy for advanced male breast cancer.

The absolute 5-year survival of men with breast cancer is about 30%. Following radical mastectomy, the 5-year survival is about 40%. Huggins & Taylor reported a 5-year survival in only 35% of 14 stage I cases of male breast cancer. Palliative therapy is frequently required in this disease due to the frequency of occult metastases and of the tendency to present in an advanced stage.

MAMMARY DYSPLASIA

Essentials of Diagnosis

- Painful, often multiple, frequently bilateral masses in the breast.
- Rapid fluctuation in size of mass is common.
- Frequently pain occurs or increases and size increases during premenstrual phase of cycle.
- Most common age is 30–50. Rare in postmenopausal women.

General Considerations

This disorder, also known as chronic cystic disease of the breast, is the most frequent lesion of the breast. It is common in women 30–50 years of age but rare in postmenopausal women, which suggests that it is related to ovarian activity. Estrogen hormone is considered an etiologic factor. The typical pathologic change in the breast is the formation of gross and microscopic cysts from the terminal ducts and acini. Large cysts are clinically palpable and may be several cm or more in diameter.

Clinical Findings

Mammary dysplasia may produce an asymptomatic lump in the breast which is discovered by accident, but pain or tenderness often calls attention to the mass. There may be discharge from the nipple. In many cases discomfort occurs or is increased during the premenstrual phase of the cycle, at which time the cysts tend to enlarge rapidly. Fluctuation in size and rapid appearance or disappearance of a breast tumor are common in cystic disease. Multiple or bilateral masses are not unusual, and many patients will give a past history of transient lump in the breast or cyclic breast pain. Pain, fluctuation in size, and multiplicity of lesions are the features most helpful in differentiation from carcinoma. However, if skin retraction is present, the diagnosis of cancer should be assumed until disproved by biopsy.

Differential Diagnosis

Pain, fluctuation in size, and multiplicity of lesions help to differentiate these lesions from carcinoma and adenofibroma. Final diagnosis often depends on biopsy. Mammography may be helpful.

Treatment

Mammary dysplasia can rarely be distinguished with certainty from carcinoma on the basis of the clinical findings. Therefore, it is usually necessary to prepare the patient for standard or modified radical mastectomy and to explore the lesion in the operating room under general anesthesia with provisions for immediate diagnosis by frozen section. Discrete cysts or small localized areas of cystic disease should be excised when cancer has been ruled out by microscopic examination. Surgery in mammary dysplasia should be conservative, since the primary objective of surgery is to exclude malignancy. Simple mastectomy or extensive removal of breast tissue is rarely, if ever, indicated.

When the diagnosis of mammary dysplasia has been established by biopsy or is practically certain because the history is classical, aspiration of a discrete mass is justifiable. The skin and overlying tissues are anesthetized by infiltration with 1% procaine and a No. 19 or 20 gauge needle is introduced. If a cyst is present, typical watery fluid (straw-colored, gray, greenish, brown, or black) is easily evacuated and the mass disappears. The patient is reexamined at intervals of 2—4 weeks for 3 months and every 6—12 months thereafter throughout life. If no fluid is obtained, if a mass persists after aspiration, or if at any time during follow-up an atypical persistent lump is noted, biopsy should be performed without delay.

Breast pain associated with generalized mammary dysplasia is best treated by avoidance of trauma and by wearing (night and day) a brassiere which gives good support and protection. Hormone therapy is not advisable because it does not cure the condition and has undesirable side-effects.

Prognosis

Exacerbations of pain, tenderness, and cyst formation may occur at any time until the menopause, when the symptoms of mammary dysplasia subside. The patient should be taught to examine her own breasts each month just after menstruation and to inform her physician if a mass appears.

Davis, H.H., Simons, M., & J.B. Davis: Cystic disease of the breast: Relationship to carcinoma. Cancer 17:957–978, 1964.

Fechner, R.E.: Fibrocystic disease in women receiving oral contraceptive hormones. Cancer 25:1332–1339, 1970.

Steinhoff, N.G., & W.C. Black: Florid cystic disease preceding mammary cancer. Ann Surg 171:501–508, 1970.

FIBROADENOMA OF THE BREAST

This common benign neoplasm occurs most frequently in young women, usually within 20 years after puberty. It is somewhat more frequent and tends to occur at an earlier age in black than in white women. Multiple tumors in one or both breasts are found in 10—15% of patients.

The typical fibroadenoma is a round, firm, discrete, relatively movable, nontender mass 1—5 cm in diameter. The tumor is usually discovered accidentally. Clinical diagnosis in young patients is generally not difficult. In women over 30, cystic disease of the breast and carcinoma of the breast must be considered. Fibroadenoma does not normally occur after the menopause, but postmenopausal women may occasionally develop fibroadenoma after administration of estrogenic hormone.

Treatment in all cases is excision and frozen section to determine if the lesion is cancerous.

Cystosarcoma phylloides is a type of fibroadenoma with cellular stroma which tends to grow rapidly. This tumor may reach a large size, and if inadequately excised will recur locally. The lesion is rarely malignant. Treatment is usually by local excision of the mass with a margin of surrounding breast tissue.

DIFFERENTIAL DIAGNOSIS OF NIPPLE DISCHARGE

In order of frequency, the following lesions cause nipple discharge: intraductal papilloma, carcinoma, mammary dysplasia, and ectasia of the ducts. The discharge is usually serous or bloody. It should be checked for occult blood with the benzidine or guaiac test. When papilloma or cancer is the cause, a tumor can frequently (but not always) be palpated beneath or close to the areola.

The site of the duct orifice from which the fluid exudes is a guide to the location of the involved duct. Gentle pressure on the breast is made with the fingertip at successive points around the circumference of the areola. A point will often be found at which pressure produces discharge. The dilated duct or a small tumor may be palpable here. The involved area should be excised by a meticulous technic which ensures removal of the affected duct and breast tissues immediately adjacent to it. If a tumor is present it should be biopsied and a frozen section done to determine whether cancer is present.

When localization is not possible and no mass is palpable, the patient should be reexamined every week for one month. When unilateral discharge persists, even without definite localization or tumor, exploration must be considered. The alternative is careful follow-up at intervals of 1—3 months. Mammography should be done. Cytologic examination of nipple discharge for exfoliated cancer cells occasionally may be helpful in differential diagnosis.

Although none of the benign lesions causing nipple discharge are precancerous, they may coexist with cancer and it is not possible to distinguish them definitely from malignancy on clinical grounds. Patients with carcinoma almost always have a palpable mass, but in rare instances a nipple discharge may be the only sign. For these reasons chronic nipple discharge, especially if bloody, is usually an indication for resection of the ducts.

Atkins, H., & B. Wolff: Discharges from the nipple. Brit J Surg 51:602–606, 1964.

Funderburk, W.W., & B. Syphax: Evaluation of nipple discharge in benign and malignant breast diseases. Cancer 24:1290–1296, 1969.

FAT NECROSIS

Fat necrosis is a rare lesion of the breast but is of clinical importance because it produces a mass, often accompanied by skin or nipple retraction, which is indistinguishable from carcinoma. Trauma is presumed to be the cause, although only about ½ of patients give a history of injury to the breast. Ecchymosis is occasionally seen near the tumor. Tenderness may or may not be present. If untreated, the mass associated with fat necrosis gradually disappears. As a rule the safest course is to obtain a biopsy. When carcinoma has been ruled out, the area of involvement should be excised.

BREAST ABSCESS

During nursing an area of redness, tenderness, and induration not infrequently develops in the breast. In the early stages the infection can often by reversed by discontinuing nursing with that breast and administering a broad-spectrum antibiotic. If the lesion progresses to form a localized mass with increasing local and systemic signs of infection, an abscess is present and should be drained.

A subareolar abscess may develop in young or middle-aged women who are not lactating. These infections tend to recur after incision and drainage unless the area is explored in a quiescent interval with excision of the involved collecting ducts at the base of the nipple.

Except for the subareolar type of abscess, infection in the breast is very rare unless the patient is lactating. Therefore, findings suggestive of abscess in the nonlactating breast require incision and biopsy of any indurated tissue.

Benson, E.A., & M.A. Goodman: An evaluation of the use of stilbesterol and antibiotics in the early management of acute puerperal breast abscess. Brit J Surg 57:255–258, 1970.

Benson, E.A., & M.A. Goodman: Incision with primary suture in the treatment of acute puerperal breast abscess. Brit J Surg 57:55–58, 1970.

Habif, D.V., & others: Subareolar abscess associated with squamous metaplasia of lactiferous ducts. Am J Surg 119:523–526, 1970.

●   ●   ●

General References

Ackerman, L.V., & J.A. del Regato: *Cancer–Diagnosis, Treatment, and Prognosis,* 3rd ed. Mosby, 1963.

Haagensen, C.D.: *Diseases of the Breast.* Saunders, 1956.

Spratt, J.S., Jr., & W.L. Donegan: *Cancer of the Breast.* Saunders, 1967.

Stoll, B.A.: *Hormonal Management in Breast Cancer.* Lippincott, 1969.

12 . . .

Gynecology & Obstetrics

Ralph C. Benson

GYNECOLOGY

NORMAL UTERINE BLEEDING

Menstruation is uterine bleeding which occurs at intervals of 24–32 days in the normal woman during the reproductive years. The pituitary gonadotropins and estrogen are responsible, although progesterone, thyroid hormones, and the adrenocorticosteroids also influence menstruation.

Ovulation and the resulting production of estrogen and progesterone result in bleeding (**ovulatory menstruation**) from a secretory endometrium when pregnancy does not occur. In the absence of ovulation, bleeding (**anovulatory menstruation**) is from a nonsecretory endometrium.

Menarche, which generally occurs between ages 11–14, marks the onset of menstrual periods. Menstruation ceases with the **menopause** at 45–55 years of age.

The average duration of menstrual bleeding is 3–7 days, and a blood loss of 50–100 ml is usual. Characteristically, menstrual blood will not clot because it has already clotted within the uterine cavity and has reliquefied. Uterine cramping often occurs with ovulatory cycles, but anovulatory bleeding is usually painless.

Menstrual aberrations are often early indications of disease or deficiency states, emotional tension, and pregnancy.

Chiazze, L., Jr., & others: The length and variability of the human menstrual cycle. JAMA 203:377–380, 1968.

Frisancho, A.R., & others: Age at menarche: A new method of prediction and retrospective assessment based on hand x-rays. Hum Biol 41:42–50, 1969.

Leary, P.M., & D. Obst: Nutrition and the menarche. South African MJ 43:324–325, 1969.

Moos, R.H., & others: Fluctuations in symptoms and moods during the menstrual cycle. J Psychosom Res 13:37–44, 1969.

Pasnan, R.O.: Psychosomatic aspects of menstrual disorders. Clin Obst Gynec 12:724–740, 1969.

Wallace, M.J.: Fluorescence microscopy of the vaginal smear during the menstrual cycle. Fertil Steril 20:299–311, 1969.

ABNORMAL PREMENOPAUSAL UTERINE BLEEDING

Abnormal uterine bleeding means either (1) excessive or prolonged bleeding during the normal time of flow (hypermenorrhea, menorrhagia) or (2) any bleeding during the intermenstrual interval (metrorrhagia). Abnormal uterine bleeding is a matter of concern to almost every woman at some time between the menarche and the menopause. The bleeding is always disturbing, often debilitating, and occasionally critical.

The causes of abnormal bleeding may be classified according to whether bleeding occurs during or between periods. Common causes of **hypermenorrhea** (menorrhagia) are myoma, endometrial polyposis, irregular shedding of the endometrium, functional hypertrophy of the uterus, blood dyscrasias, and psychologic syndromes. **Polymenorrhea** (uterine bleeding which occurs more often than once every 24 days) may be due to a short cycle (proliferative phase less than 10 days, or secretory phase less than 14 days), or to premature interruption of the cycle due to physical or emotional stress. **Metrorrhagia** (irregular flow at times other than the normal menstrual period) may be due to hormonal imbalance or miscellaneous pelvic abnormalities. Hormonal causes include endometrial cystic glandular hyperplasia, ovulation bleeding (mittelschmerz), administration of estrogens, anovulatory bleeding, and hypothyroidism. Pelvic abnormalities which cause metrorrhagia include cervical or endometrial polyposis, submucous myoma; carcinoma or sarcoma of the cervix, corpus uteri, or fallopian tubes; and endometritis (postabortion, or due to tuberculosis or cervical stenosis).

Clinical Findings

A. Symptoms and Signs: The diagnosis of the disorders underlying the bleeding usually depends upon a careful description of the extent and amount of flow, related pain, if any, relationship to LMP and PMP, and a past history or family history of pertinent illnesses. All medications the patient has taken during the previous month must be accounted for to rule out estrogenic stimulation or androgenic inhibition of flow. The following signs are significant: fullness of the abdomen, cutaneous lesions, edema, exaggerated vascular patterns, abdominal or pelvic floor herniation, tenderness or guarding of the abdomen, adenopathy, dullness or shifting dullness, and swelling, tenderness, or discharge in the vicinity of Skene's or Bartholin's glands. The rectovaginal examination may reveal tenderness, induration, nodulation, mass formation, and the presence of intraperitoneal fluid.

B. Laboratory Findings: Vaginal smears should be obtained (before digital examination) for cytologic and bacteriologic study. Vaginal smears taken during active bleeding and fixed in alcohol-ether can be laked of red cells (after fixation) with 1% HCl; the epithelial detritus which remains may reveal tumor or trophoblastic cells from a uterine abortion. In addition to urinalysis and routine hematocrit, STS, white and differential count, and sedimentation rate, blood studies (when necessary) should include bleeding time, clotting time, clot retraction time, platelet count, and a tourniquet test for capillary fragility. PBI or BEI tests are indicated to rule out abnormal thyroid function.

C. X-Ray Findings: X-rays should be ordered only if tumors, fluid collections, or anatomic deformities are suspected, in which case a plain film of the abdomen, hysterosalpingography, cystography, and barium enema studies are indicated.

D. Special Examination: Cervical biopsy and curettage are usually necessary to establish a definitive diagnosis of the cause of bleeding. Polyps, tumors, and submucous fibroids are commonly identified in this way. Cancer of the cervix or endometrium may require cone or multiple-quadrant biopsy of the cervix and differential curettage of the cervix and uterine cavity.

Complications

Continued or excessive blood loss leads to anemia, which favors local or systemic infection. Tumors may cause infertility. Cervical, uterine, or tubal neoplasm must be found and removed before metastasis occurs.

Treatment

A. Emergency Measures: If bleeding has been massive, place the patient in the Trendelenburg position and give sedation, intravenous fluids, and blood transfusions as required. Hemostasis is best achieved with surgical dilatation and curettage because this procedure has both therapeutic and diagnostic advantages. Temporary hemostasis (for 1–2 days) with diethylstilbestrol, 25 mg orally every 15 minutes for 8 doses or 100 mg twice daily for 2 days, is often effective.

B. Curettage: Surgical curettage is the treatment of choice. After biopsy and curettage hormonal therapy may be used for several months for the further control of bleeding.

C. Corrective Hormone Therapy After Proper Diagnosis:

1. Estrogens and progestogens–

a. To control **hypermenorrhea** (not metrorrhagia)–Progesterone aqueous suspension, 35 mg IM on the 24th day after the onset of LMP; hydroxyprogesterone caproate (Delalutin®), 125 mg IM on the 21st day; norethindrone (Norlutin®), 10 mg orally daily for 7 days beginning on the 21st day; norethynodrel with mestranol (Enovid®), 10 mg orally daily for 7 days beginning on the 21st day; medroxyprogesterone acetate (Provera®), 5 mg orally daily for 4 days beginning on the 21st day.

b. In **metrorrhagia** the following may be used–Estradiol valerate (Delestrogen®), 5 mg IM on the 14th day and hydroxyprogesterone caproate (Delalutin®), 250 mg IM on the 21st day; norethynodrel with mestranol (Enovid®), 10 mg orally daily from the 5th through the 20th days.

2. **Androgens**–Androgens should be administered cautiously to adolescent girls or young adult women because even minimal doses may cause permanent voice change and irreversible hirsutism. The following regimen should be used only in patients over 45 years of age: Testosterone enanthate (Delatestryl®), 200 mg IM on the 5th day of the cycle; after 7 days, methyltestosterone, 10 mg sublingually daily for 2 weeks; after 7 days, methyltestosterone, 10 mg sublingually every other day for 3 weeks of each month for 2 months.

3. **Thyroid hormone** is indicated if it is certain that hypothyroidism is present and is the only cause of abnormal bleeding.

4. **Chorionic gonadotropin,** 1000–2000 units IM daily for 12 days following ovulation, will extend the postovulatory (luteal) phase and may thus enhance fertility.

5. **Clomiphene citrate (Clomid®)** 50 mg orally daily for 5 days is of value in proved anovulatory bleeding states and in the Stein-Leventhal syndrome but is not effective for hypermenorrhea or metrorrhagia due to other causes.

D. Irradiation Therapy: X-ray or radium therapy to terminate menses is indicated only for poor-risk or menopausal patients. In women under 35 years of age, about 1250 r will be required; in older women, 800 r will usually suffice.

E. Surgical Therapy: Intractable bleeding, particularly in women over age 40, may require hysterectomy. Prior to the menopause, the ovaries should be preserved if they appear to be normal.

Prognosis

In the absence of cancer, large tumors, and salpingitis, about 50% of patients with hypermenorrhea and almost 60% of patients with metrorrhagia will resume normal menstrual periods after curettage alone. Giving thyroid hormone or progesterone when indicated will increase the recoveries by another 10–15%.

Arronet, G.H., & W.S.M. Arrata: Dysfunctional uterine bleeding: A classification. Obst Gynec 29:97–107, 1967.

Elwood, P.C., & others: Community study of menstrual iron loss and its association with deficiency anemia. Brit J Prev Soc Med 22:127–131, 1968.

Ghosh, B.K., & others: Histology of the ovary in functional uterine bleeding. J Obst Gynec India 19:18–26, 1969.

POSTMENOPAUSAL VAGINAL BLEEDING

Vaginal bleeding which occurs 6 months or more following cessation of menstrual function may be due to local or systemic causes. Carcinoma of the cervix or endometrium accounts for 35–50% of cases. Administration of estrogens in excessive amounts or in noncyclic manner is the second most important cause. Other causes include atrophic vaginitis, trauma, polyps, hypertensive cardiovascular disease, submucous myomas, trophic ulcers of the cervix associated with prolapse of the uterus, blood dyscrasias, and endogenous estrogen production by a feminizing ovarian tumor. Uterine bleeding is usually painless but pain will be present if the cervix is stenotic, if bleeding is severe and rapid, or in the presence of infection or torsion or extrusion of a tumor.

Bleeding varies from a bright ooze or brown discharge to frank hemorrhage. The patient may report a single episode of spotting or profuse bleeding for days or months. Laboratory examination of vaginal fluid may disclose exfoliated neoplastic cells, infection, or free basal epithelial cells and white cells (but no cornified epithelial cells in the absence of exogenous or endogenous estrogen). Passage of a sound into the uterus will demonstrate cervical stenosis and hematocolpos; will cause an intracervical or endometrial neoplasm to bleed (Clark test); or may outline a cervical or uterine tumor. Aspiration biopsy or suction curettage often provides sufficient endometrial tissue for the purpose of examining for cancer, endometrial hyperplasia, endometritis, and other local disorders.

Treatment

The patient should be hospitalized for thorough evaluation and definitive care. Dilatation and curettage (with polypectomy if indicated) will cure about ½ of all patients with postmenopausal bleeding. Withdraw all sex steroid drugs and do not reinstitute therapy until the cause of bleeding has been identified and bleeding has been controlled for at least 3 months. If bleeding recurs after a second curettage in a patient who is not taking estrogens, total hysterectomy and bilateral salpingo-oophorectomy may be indicated.

Prognosis

Curettage will cure many cases. The prognosis for women whose bleeding is due to neoplastic disease depends upon the extent of invasion and the success of antitumor therapy.

Copenhaver, E.W.: Postmenopausal bleeding related to estrogen therapy. Geriatrics 23:128–130, 1968.

Daly, J.J., & K. Balagh, Jr.: Hemorrhagic necrosis of the senile endometrium ("apoplexia uteri"). New England J Med 278:709–711, 1968.

McElin, T.W., & others: Diagnostic dilatation and curettage: A 20-year survey. Obst Gynec 33:807–812, 1969.

Paloucek, F.P., Graham, J.B., & C.L. Randall: Benign postmenopausal vaginal bleeding. JAMA 199:701–703, 1967.

PREMENSTRUAL TENSION SYNDROME

Essentials of Diagnosis

- Recurrent, marked, periodic weight gain, agitation, or depression prior to menstruation of ovulatory cycles.
- Emotional, unmarried, or nulliparous women between 30–40 years of age are most commonly affected.

General Considerations

The premenstrual tension syndrome is a recurrent (monthly) disorder characterized by obvious fluid retention, autonomic over-response, and hyper- or hypoactivity. It involves about 50% of women to some degree, especially during the 3rd and 4th decades of life. The disorder appears to be an exaggerated physiologic and psychologic reaction to the onset of menstruation, and is often accompanied by antisocial behavior (even crimes of violence).

Although slight hypoglycemia has been reported on occasion, no gross endocrine or other physical dysfunction distinguishes the patient with premenstrual tension syndrome. This disorder aggravates mental illness, hypermetabolism, chronic cystic mastitis, and obesity.

Dread of an impending period and concern regarding pregnancy, elimination, and femininity are basic problems. The woman experiences ego depreciation and often blames her mother for her menstrual difficulties. Atypical pelvic pain and primary dysmenorrhea may be associated problems.

Clinical Findings

A. Symptoms and Signs: Anxiety, agitation, insomnia, inability to concentrate, and a feeling of inadequacy are reported. Patients complain of mastalgia, nausea and vomiting, and diarrhea or constipation. Depression and self-pity may color the woman's affect, or she may be contentious and aggressive. Peculiar drives or unusual appetites are commonplace.

The emotional build-up parallels weight gain (edema) of up to 6–8 lb. The general and pelvic examinations are not otherwise specific. A prompt weight loss by diuresis follows the onset of the period.

B. Laboratory Findings: Blood counts and urinalysis are not diagnostic. Slight functional hypoglycemia may occasionally be noted during the period of tension. Estrogen and progestogen production and excretion studies generally relate to an ovulatory cycle.

C. Special Examinations: A high anxiety quotient (by Clyde Mood Scale, Taylor Anxiety Score, etc) by a labile, poorly oriented, or emotionally immature woman may be recorded.

Differential Diagnosis

Rule out hyperthyroidism, hyperaldosteronism, hyperinsulinism, extreme psychoneurosis, and psychosis.

Treatment

Prescribe diuretics together with tranquilizers for agitated patients, or diuretics and stimulant drugs for depressed patients. Reassurance, positive suggestion, and specific psychotherapy are most helpful. A medium caloric, low-sodium, high-protein diet with frequent small feedings is helpful. Encourage an active life and discourage invalidism. An attempt should be made to redirect the patient's attitudes, with emphasis on pride in her feminine role. Suppress ovulation by small doses of a progestin-dominant, combination type oral contraceptive when acceptable.

Prognosis

Considerable symptomatic relief and improvement in behavior can be achieved in responsive, cooperative patients.

Hain, J.D., & others: Menstrual irregularity: Symptoms and personality. J Psychosom Res 14:81–87, 1970.
Kane, F.J., Jr., & others: Amelioration of premenstrual mood disturbance with a progestational agent (Enovid®). Dis Nerv System 27:339–342, 1968.
Tonks, C.M.: Premenstrual tension. Brit J Hosp Med 1:383–387, 1968.

PRIMARY DYSMENORRHEA
(Essential or Functional Dysmenorrhea)

Essentials of Diagnosis

- Prodromal signs of breast engorgement, agitation, abdominal bloating, pelvic heaviness.
- Intermittent aching or cramping in lower midline of abdomen at onset of bleeding.
- Tenderness upon pelvic and abdominal examination.

General Considerations

Pain with menstrual periods for which no organic cause can be found (primary or essential dysmenorrhea) accounts for about 80% of cases of painful menses. The pain is always secondary to an emotional problem. Although primary dysmenorrhea is particularly common during adolescence, it may occur at any time from the menarche to the menopause. Dysmenorrhea and general menstrual discomfort are often described together as "menorrhalgia."

Clinical Findings

Agitation, abdominal bloating, breast engorgement, and pelvic heaviness often precede the flow. Intermittent aching to cramp-like discomfort in the lower midline usually accompanies the onset of bleeding. Circulatory engorgement of the vagina and cervix, slight patulousness of the os, and bogginess of the uterus (all evidence of the pelvic congestion syndrome) are frequently recorded before and during bleeding. Uterine, parametrial, and adnexal tenderness are often described as well.

Dysmenorrhea equivalents—periodic headache, nausea, diarrhea, urinary frequency and urgency—indicate monthly dysfunction of other organ systems.

Differential Diagnosis

Menstrual cramps which develop more than 5 years after the menarche are usually due to organic causes. Generalized abdominal pain or particularly well localized right- or left-sided pelvic pain are indicative of organic disease. Typical patterns of referred pain also suggest secondary dysmenorrhea.

Treatment

A. Specific Measures: The definitive management of primary dysmenorrhea must be directed at the underlying psychodynamics. The gynecologist who is interested in these problems must be prepared to spend considerable time with the patient at each visit and to pursue a cure over a long period of time. Patients with severe emotional disorders should be treated by a psychiatrist.

B. General Measures: Analgesics may be warranted until the diagnosis is established. The use of narcotics is contraindicated for fear of addiction. Warm douches may afford temporary relief. Ovulation can be suppressed and dysmenorrhea usually prevented by any of the oral contraceptives. Minimal dosage is recommended to reduce side-effects. Diethylstilbestrol, 0.5 mg orally daily for 14 days beginning with the first day of the period; or methyltestosterone, 5 mg orally 3 times daily from the 5th through the 10th days after the onset of menstruation (for 2 or 3 months), is a valuable temporary expedient. Methyltestosterone does not interfere with ovulation in this dosage.

C. Surgical Measures: Primary presacral neurectomy is rarely justified, and hysterectomy is never indicated.

Prognosis

In women with insight who are cooperative and want to be cured, the prognosis is good. Very little can be done for the patient who prefers to use menstrual symptoms as a monthly refuge from responsibility and participation.

Golub, L.J., & others: Exercise and dysmenorrhoea in young teenagers: A three-year study. Obst Gynec 32:508–511, 1968.
Matthews, A.E.B., & others: Double-blind trial of sequential oral contraceptive (C-Quens) in the treatment of dysmenorrhoea. J Obstet Gynaec Brit Common 75:1117–1122, 1968.
Muller, F.G., Jr.: The treatment of dysmenorrhoea by behavior therapy techniques. J Nerv Ment Dis 147:371–376, 1968.
Santamarina, B.A.G.: Dysmenorrhoea. Clin Obst Gynec 12:708–723, 1969.

LEUKORRHEA
("White Vaginal Discharge")

Leukorrhea may occur at any age and affects almost all women at some time. It is not a disease but the manifestation of ovulation or of a local or systemic disorder. The most common cause is infection of the lower reproductive tract; other causes are inflammation, estrogenic or psychic stimulation, tumors, and estrogen depletion.

Leukorrheic discharge is usually white because of the presence of exfoliated or inflammatory cells. The persistence of some vaginal mucus is normal. Nevertheless, when soiling of the clothing or distressing local symptoms occur, the discharge must be considered abnormal.

Any moisture may add to normal body odor and may be a source of self-consciousness. Frequent bathing and drying of the parts will suffice. In contrast, a seriously objectionable odor may be an indication of vaginal (or vulvar) infection.

Clinical Findings

A. Symptoms and Signs: Vaginal discharge, with or without discomfort, may be associated with itching when urine contaminates the inflamed introitus. The patient may complain of pudendal irritation, proctitis, vaginismus, and dyspareunia. There may be no symptoms in other cases.

Inflammation or ulceration of the vulvovaginal surfaces or cervix and a copious, white or colored, usually odorous discharge are usually present.

B. Laboratory Findings: Blood findings may suggest low-grade infection. Cytologic study of a smear of vaginal secretion is indicated for all parous patients and others over 25 years of age or whenever malignancy is suspected. The same preparation can be stained to show trichomonads, candida, or other organisms. Trichomonads are often seen in freshly voided urine contaminated with leukorrheic discharge. If these organisms are noted in a catheterized specimen, urethral and bladder involvement by the flagellate is likely. Culture of the trichomonad is difficult but may be successful when Trichosel® medium is used.

Leukorrhea associated with a positive serology may be due to syphilis; a positive Frei test suggests lymphogranuloma venereum; the dmelcos skin test is positive in chancroid.

Inspect a fresh wet preparation of the vaginal fluid first for motile *Trichomonas vaginalis*. Look for heavy clouding of the spread and especially the covering of epithelial cells ("clue cells") by myriads of small, darker bacteria; these will probably be *Hemophilus vaginalis*. Then add 10% potassium hydroxide to lake blood cells as an aid in visualization of candida hyphae and spores. Examination of a gram-stained smear will identify intracellular gram-negative diplococci (*Neisseria gonorrhoeae*), other predominant bacteria, and helminths. If possible, culture the vaginal fluid anaerobically and aerobically to identify bacterial pathogens. Thioglycollate bacterial medium is most useful in the culture of hemophilus microorganisms.

Inoculate Nickerson's, Sabouraud's, Pagano-Levin, or a similar medium to demonstrate candida.

Secure a vaginal smear for acid-fast staining and an inoculum for culture (or guinea pig inoculation) for *Mycobacterium tuberculosis* when tuberculosis is suspected.

Prevention

The husband should use a condom if infection or reinfection is likely. Sexual promiscuity and borrowing of douche tips, underclothing, or other possibly contaminated articles should be avoided.

Tetracycline therapy over long periods of time may cause candida vaginitis due to the overgrowth of these yeasts.

TABLE 12-1. Differential diagnosis of the causes of leukorrhea.

Color	Consistency	Amount	Odor	Probable Causes
Clear	Mucoid	+ to ++	None	Ovulation, excessive estrogen stimulation, emotional tension.
Milky	Viscid	+ to +++	None to acrid	Cervicitis, *Hemophilus vaginalis* vaginitis.
White	Thin with curd-like flecks	+ to ++	Fusty	Vaginal mycosis.
Pink	Serous	+ to ++	None	Hypoestrinism, nonspecific infection.
Yellow-green	Frothy	+ to +++	Fetid	*Trichomonas vaginalis* vaginitis.
Brown	Watery	+ to ++	Musty	Vaginitis, cervicitis. Cervical stenosis, endometritis; neoplasm of the cervix, endometrium, or tube. Post-irradiational.
Gray, blood-streaked	Thin	+ to ++++	Foul	Vaginal ulcer. Pyogenic vaginitis-cervicitis (trauma, long-retained pessary, forgotten tampon). Vaginal, cervical, endometrial, tubal neoplasm.

Treatment

A. Specific Measures: Treat infection with the specific drugs listed below. If sensitivity develops, discontinue medication and substitute another drug as soon as practicable. Continue treating the patient during menstrual flow. Choose a mode of therapy (eg, suppositories, oral therapy) which need not be discontinued because of bleeding.

1. *Trichomonas vaginalis* vaginitis—It may be necessary to treat the patient for several months; change the medication after 2–3 months in resistant cases: (1) Metronidazole (Flagyl®), 250 mg orally 3 times daily for 10 days. The physician should treat the husband similarly during the same interval. Insist upon condom protection against reinfection during coitus until both partners are free of *Trichomonas vaginalis* organisms. (*Caution:* This drug may encourage the growth of candida organisms. Rapid disappearance of leukorrhea due in part to trichomoniasis may mask gonorrhea.) (2) Diiodohydroxyquinoline (Diodoquin®), dextrose, lactose, and boric acid (Floraquin®), carbarsone, or Devegan® suppositories, 1 vaginally twice daily for 8 weeks. Additional vaginal insufflation with the same preparation in powder form twice weekly for the first month is also helpful. (3) Furazolidonenifuroxime (Tricofuron®) vaginal suppositories, 1 twice daily for 8 weeks.

2. *Candida albicans*—Discontinue oral contraception; substitute condom protection temporarily. (1) Nystatin (Mycostatin®) vaginal suppositories, each containing 100,000 units, 1 daily for 2 weeks, are most effective. (2) Propionic acid gel (Propion Gel®), 1 application vaginally daily for 3 weeks. (3) Gentian violet, 2% aqueous solution applied topically to the vulva, vagina, and cervical area twice weekly for 3 weeks. (4) Gentian violet, lactic acid, and acetic acid (Gentia Jel®), 1 application vaginally daily for 3 weeks.

3. *Hemophilus vaginalis* vaginitis—(1) Sulfathiazole, sulfacetamide, and benzylsulfanilamide in cream form (Sultrin®), 1 application daily for 2 weeks. (2) Acidified 0.1% hexetidine gel (Sterisil®), 1 application daily for 2 weeks.

4. Atrophic (senile) vaginitis—(1) Diethylstilbestrol, 0.5 mg vaginal suppository, 1 every third day for 3 weeks. Omit medication for 1 week (to avoid uterine bleeding); then resume cyclic therapy indefinitely unless contraindicated. (2) Dienestrol or Premarin® vaginal cream, 1/3 of an applicator every third day for 3 weeks. Omit medication for 1 week, then resume cyclic therapy. (3) Diethylstilbestrol, 0.2–0.5 mg (or equivalent), orally daily for 3 weeks each month.

5. Gonorrheal vaginitis—Treat as directed in Chapter 21. *Caution:* Treatment will be inadequate unless 3 sets of slides or, preferably, cultures of discharge from Skene's ducts and the cervical canal reveal no gonococci. Perform a serologic test for syphilis prior to treatment and repeat 2 months later.

B. General Measures: Utilize internal menstrual tampons to reduce vulvar soiling, pruritus, and odor. Coitus should be avoided until a cure has been achieved. Trichomonal and candidal infections require treatment of the husband also. Relapses are often reinfections. Re-treat both parties.

Antipruritic medications are disappointing unless an allergy is present. Specific and local therapy will usually control itching promptly.

C. Local Measures: Occasional acetic acid douches (2 tbsp of distilled [white] vinegar per liter of water) may be beneficial in the treatment of leukorrhea. *Caution:* Never prescribe alkaline (soda) douches. They are unphysiologic and often harmful because they discourage the normal vaginal flora by raising vaginal pH.

Douches are not essential to cleanliness or marital hygiene. Too frequent douches of any kind tend to increase mucus secretion. Irritating medications cause further mucus production.

In severe, resistant, or recurrent trichomonal or candidal vaginitis, treat the cervix (even when it is apparently normal) by chemical or light thermal cauterization. Investigate the urinary tract and Skene's and Bartholin's ducts and treat these areas if they appear to be reservoirs of reinfection.

D. Surgical Measures: Hospital cauterization, conization of the cervix, incision of Skene's glands, or bartholinectomy may be required. Cervical, uterine, or tubal disease (tumors, infection) may necessitate laparotomy, irradiation, or other appropriate measures.

Prognosis

Leukorrhea in pregnant, debilitated, or diabetic women is difficult to cure especially when due to *Trichomonas vaginalis, Candida albicans,* or *Hemophilus vaginalis.* Repeated or even continuous treatment over 3–4 months may be required until the patient is delivered or the diabetes is controlled.

The prognosis is good if the exact diagnosis is made promptly and intensive therapy instituted. Treatment of only one of several causes may be the reason for failure of therapy.

Catterall, R.D.: Diagnosis of vaginal discharge. Brit J Ven Dis 46:122–124, 1970.

Cohen, L.: Influence of the pH on vaginal discharges. Brit J Ven Dis 45:241–246, 1969.

Diddle, A.E., & others: Oral contraceptive medications and vulvovaginal candidiasis. Obst Gynec 34:373–377, 1969.

Driscoll, A.M., & others: Sexually transmitted disease in gynecological outpatients with vaginal discharge. Brit J Ven Dis 46:125, 1970.

Grewal, M.S., & others: Comparative therapeutic evaluation of mycostatin and lincomycin against vaginal candidiasis. Indian Pract 22:67–73, 1969.

Heller, R.H., & others: Vulvovaginitis in the premenarcheal child. J Pediat 74:370–377, 1969.

Mendel, E.B., & others: Mycoplasma species in the vagina and their relation to vaginitis. Obst Gynec 35:104–108, 1970.

CERVICITIS

Cervicitis is the most common of all gynecologic disorders. Over 60% of parous women have cervicitis, usually as a result of pre- or postpartum infections.

Gonorrhea and mixed infections frequently cause acute and chronic cervicitis in nonpregnant women. Chronic cervical infection is the most common cause of leukorrhea and a major etiologic factor in infertility, dyspareunia, abortion, and intrapartum infection. Chronic cervicitis may even predispose to cervical cancer. At least ¾ of all women have cervicitis at some time during their adult lives.

Vaginitis or cervical instrumentation and lacerations may initiate cervicitis.

Cervicitis is characterized by erosion (a transient ulceration of the endo- and ectocervix) and eversion (ectropion), which is due to outward growth of endocervical cells.

The characteristics of cervical mucus vary with the menstrual cycle. In the absence of infection, the cervical mucus is thin, clear, and acellular at the time of ovulation or after moderate estrogen stimulation. In cervicitis the mucus is mucopurulent, even blood-streaked, and may be tenacious and viscid at midcycle. Microscopic examination of a smear of cervical mucus from a patient with clinical cervicitis or bleeding never shows the normal "fern" formation. The acidity of the mucus and the presence of bacteria are noxious to sperm.

The symptoms include leukorrhea, low back pain, hypogastric pain, dyspareunia, dysmenorrhea, dysuria, urinary frequency and urgency, metrorrhagia, and cervical dystocia.

Cervical cancer, venereal infections, and cervical tuberculosis must be ruled out.

Treatment

A. Acute Cervicitis: Treat acute infections with appropriate antibiotics. Avoid instrumentation and vigorous topical therapy during the acute phase and before the menses, when an upward spread of the infection may occur.

B. Chronic Cervicitis: Replace and retain a free retroverted uterus (which both aggravates and predisposes to cervicitis) with a vaginal pessary to reduce chronic passive congestion of the cervix and corpus. Prescribe warm acetic acid douches or water-soluble acid vaginal creams (eg, Aci-Jel®).

1. For mild cervicitis, cauterize the ecto- and endocervix during the midcycle with 5% silver nitrate solution or 2% sodium hydroxide solution.

2. In more severe or resistant cases, give diethylstilbestrol, 0.1 mg orally, and sulfisoxazole (Gantrisin®), 0.5 gm orally twice daily for 15 days, beginning with the first day of menstruation.

3. In deep hypertrophic chronic cervicitis, cauterize the cervix with the galvanocautery ("hot" or nasal tip cautery) or by means of diathermy (high frequency or "cold" cautery), coagulating lightly with radial strokes of the instrument. Treat only portions of the canal and portio at any one visit, preferably during the first half of the cycle. Treatment may be repeated monthly if necessary. Immediately after cauterization, prescribe daily acetic acid douches or furazolidonenifuroxime (Tricofuron®) or sulfonamide cream or suppositories locally for 3–4 days to suppress infection. Sound and dilate the cervical canal periodically to prevent stenosis.

4. Trachelorrhaphy (cervical repair), conization, and hysterectomy are justified only occasionally for intractable cervicitis.

Prognosis

Mild chronic cervicitis usually responds to local therapy in 4–8 weeks; more severe chronic cervicitis may require 2–3 months of treatment. The prognosis for acute cervicitis is excellent if an accurate diagnosis by means of smears and cultures is made and appropriate antibiotic treatment given.

Elstein, M., & others: The relation of cervical mucous proteins to sperm penetrability. J Obstet Gynaec Brit Common 77:1123–1126, 1970.

Goldman, R.L., & others: Cytomegalovirus infection in the cervix: An incidental finding of possible clinical significance. Obst Gynec 34:326–329, 1969.

CYST & ABSCESS OF BARTHOLIN'S DUCT & GLAND

Gonorrhea and other infections often involve Bartholin's duct and, to a lesser degree, the gland itself. Obstruction prevents drainage of secretions and exudations, which leads to pain and swelling. The infection resolves and pain disappears, but stenosis of the distal portion of the duct and distention of the proximal duct persist. Reinfection causes recurrent tenderness and further enlargement of the duct.

The principal symptoms are periodic painful swelling on either side of the introitus and dyspareunia. Fullness in one or both of the labia and soft distortion of the introitus are apparent. A fluctuant swelling 1–4 cm in diameter in the inferior portion of either labium minus is a sign of occlusion of Bartholin's duct. Tenderness is evidence of active infection.

Differentiate from inclusion cysts (after laceration or episiotomy), large sebaceous cysts, hydradenoma, congenital anomalies, and cancer of Bartholin's gland or duct (rare).

Treat infection with broad-spectrum antibiotics and local heat. If an abscess develops, incise and drain. After the acute process has subsided, marsupialize the affected duct or excise the duct and gland.

The prognosis is excellent.

Goldberg, J.E.: Simplified treatment for disease of Bartholin's gland. Obst Gynec 35:109–110, 1970.

Kelly, J.: Bartholin's abscess. Brit J Hosp Med 2:1696–1698, 1969.

Pearson, A.E., & others: Genital bacteroidal abscesses in women. Am J Obst Gynec 107:1264–1265, 1970.

Word, B.: Office treatment of cysts and abscess of Bartholin's gland, duct. South MJ 61:514–518, 1968.

URETHRAL CARUNCLE

Urethral caruncles may occur at any age, but postmenopausal women are most commonly affected. Caruncle may be due to infection, ectropion, papilloma, angioma, or benign or malignant neoplasms. Most caruncles represent eversions of the urethral mucosa or bacterial infections at the meatus (or both). Consider cancer when the lesion is ulcerative or progressive.

Dysuria, frequency, tenderness, vaginal bleeding, leukorrhea, and dyspareunia are the usual complaints, but a few caruncles are asymptomatic. A small, bright red tumor or sessile mass protruding from the urethral meatus may bleed, exude, or cause pain depending upon its etiology and size.

Complications include local ulceration, urethritis, and vaginitis. Bleeding is rarely excessive. An occasional caruncle may represent malignant change in a granuloma or may be a primary urethral or vulvar cancer.

Treatment

Obtain tissue for biopsy and exudate for smear and culture. If the growth is benign and infection is minimal, fulgurate lightly under topical anesthesia and apply nitrofurazone (Furacin®) cream or other chemotherapeutic agent. Repeated light fulguration is preferred to extensive coagulation initially. A bladder sedative compound (see p 412) will usually relieve urinary distress. Excision may also be a valuable procedure, but care must be taken to avoid causing stenosis of the urethra. Local or systemic cyclic estrogen therapy is helpful before and after treatment in the postmenopausal patient. Prognosis in benign cases is excellent.

If the growth is malignant, the patient should receive radical surgery or irradiation therapy.

Gillenwater, J.Y., & H.M. Burros: Unusual tumors of the female urethra. Obst Gynec 31:617–619, 1968.

Nasah, B.T.: Urethral caruncle. J Obstet Gynaec Brit Common 75:781–783, 1968.

Zeigerman, J.G., & others: Cancer of the female urethra: A curable disease. Obst Gynec 36:785–789, 1970.

URETHRAL DIVERTICULUM

Essentials of Diagnosis

- Dysuria, frequency, urgency, chills and fever in middle-aged women.
- Urethral tenderness, dyspareunia.
- Doughy or cystic anterior vaginal mass.
- Dribbling of discharge after voiding or urethral stripping.

General Considerations

One or more diverticula occasionally develop in the urethra, generally in the mid or distal portion, as the result of inflammation, trauma, or a wolffian duct cyst. Most patients with a diverticulum are parous females 40–50 years of age. Urethritis, venereal disease, or trauma due to obstetric, surgical, or urologic procedures or the passage of a stone may be the immediate cause of the diverticulum.

Infection and abscess formation with drainage from the sacculation into the urethra may result in a single or multiloculated outpouching which may be 3–4 cm in diameter. Inflammation, closure of the ostium, or calcareous concretions within the diverticulum cause urinary symptoms, dyspareunia, and sub- or para-urethral fullness; spontaneous drainage is marked by leakage of pus, blood, or urine and relief of symptoms. Recurrent disability is the rule.

Clinical Findings

A. Symptoms and Signs: Exacerbations of urinary distress, postvoiding dribbling, painful coitus, and fullness in the anterior or mid urethra, perhaps dating from urethritis or trauma, are described. Parous women near the menopause are most commonly afflicted. Stones are found in 10% of diverticula, and carcinoma may develop in the sacculations also.

B. Laboratory Findings: Expression and examination of the purulent, sanguineous, or uriniferous discharge from the urethra will reveal local inflammation. Urinalysis is not diagnostic, and blood studies do not indicate the site of infection. Panendoscopy with catheterization of the diverticula generally will identify the problem.

C. X-Ray Findings: Fill the bladder with 60 ml of radiopaque material and 100 ml of sterile water. Require the patient to void but suddenly stop the stream by occluding the urethral meatus with the finger. Lateral and anteroposterior x-ray films generally will reveal the contrast medium in diverticula.

Differential Diagnosis

The symptomatology of urethral diverticulum is commonly overlooked or misdiagnosed, and is usually ascribed to chronic, resistant cystitis. Urethrocele—not a herniation but a sagging urethra—usually is associated with cystocele and is not a separate or discrete fullness. Gartner's duct and inclusion cysts are always lateral to and never communicate with the urethra. Firm, nontender masses may be urethral or para-urethral stones or benign or malignant tumors.

Treatment

A. Emergency Measures: Prescribe broad-spectrum antibiotic therapy, warm vinegar douches, and analgesics. Aspiration of the fluid from an occluded, acutely inflamed diverticulum may give marked relief.

B. Surgical Measures: Transvaginal diverticulectomy generally is required. Drain the bladder by means of an inlying catheter for 7–10 days postoperatively.

Prognosis

Excision of a diverticulum generally is successful, but fistula or stricture formation may occur and the diverticulum may recur.

Gruber, F.H.: Cinecystourethrography in the diagnosis of urethral diverticula of woman. Am J Obst Gynec 104:606–607, 1969.

Pathak, U.N., & others: Diverticulum of the female urethra. Obst Gynec 36:789–794, 1970.

CARCINOMA OF THE UTERINE CERVIX

Essentials of Diagnosis

- Abnormal uterine bleeding and vaginal discharge.
- Cervical lesion may be visible on inspection as a tumor or ulceration.
- Vaginal cytology usually positive; must be confirmed by biopsy.

General Considerations

Cancer of the cervix is the second most common malignancy in women (exceeded only by breast cancer). Squamous cell cancer accounts for about 95% of cases; adenocarcinoma is responsible for almost 5%.

Cancer appears first in the intra-epithelial layers (the preinvasive stage, or carcinoma in situ). Preinvasive cancer is a common diagnosis in women 30–40 years of age, but most patients with invasive carcinoma are 40–50 years old. Five to 10 years probably are required for carcinoma to penetrate the basement membrane and invade the tissues in most instances. After invasion, death usually occurs in 3–5 years in the untreated or unresponsive patient.

Invasion is associated with ulceration and spotting. Sanguineous vaginal discharge or abnormal bleeding does not occur until the cancer has penetrated into the substance of the cervix.

Clinical Findings

A. Symptoms and Signs: The most common findings are metrorrhagia and cervical ulceration. Hypermenorrhea occurs later. Leukorrhea (sanguineous or purulent, odorous, and nonpruritic) appears after the invasion. Vesical and rectal dysfunction or fistulas and pain are late symptoms. Anemia, anorexia, and weight loss are signs of advanced disease.

Cervical carcinoma in situ is not visible unless one employs the colposcope. Occasionally a small patch of leukoplakia may represent preinvasive carcinoma, or a thickened area in an everted cervix may show malignant changes. Punch biopsy or cold conization of the cervix is required for diagnosis.

Schiller test: Aqueous solutions of iodine stain the surface of the normal cervix mahogany-brown because normal cervical epithelial cells contain glycogen. Zones of cancer within the epithelium over the cervix do not contain glycogen and so fail to stain with Lugol's or Schiller's iodine reagent. Scars, areas of erosion or eversion, cystic mucus glands, and zones of nonmalignant leukoplakia also fail to take the stain, however, and so this test is useful only in identifying abnormal areas.

B. "Staging" or Estimate of Gross Spread of Cancer of the Cervix: The depth of penetration of the malignant cells beyond the basement membrane is a reliable clinical guide to the extent of primary cancer within the cervix and the likelihood of secondary or metastatic cancer. It is customary to stage cancers of the cervix as shown in Table 12–2. (Percentages given are approximations.)

C. Cytologic Examination (Papanicolaou): Vaginal cytology is usually suggestive or positive. If the smear is negative but cancer is still suspected, biopsy is required. Biopsy confirmation of a positive cytologic examination is always required before definitive treatment is given. Vaginal smears for cytologic examination should be prepared as requested by the pathologist who will examine the slides. A frequently used technic is as follows:

Material from the vagina can be obtained by aspiration or with a spatula or cut tongue depressor. After vaginal fluid is obtained, a vaginal speculum

TABLE 12–2. Clinical staging and lymph node metastases of cancer of the cervix.*

Stage	Direct Extension	Lymph Node Metastases
0	Preinvasive carcinoma (carcinoma in situ).	None
I	Carcinoma strictly confined to the cervix (extension to the corpus disregarded).	About 10%
Ia	Minimal stromal invasion (preclinical invasive carcinoma, ie, cases which cannot be diagnosed by routine clinical examination).	
Ib	All other cases of stage I.	
II	Carcinoma extends beyond the cervix but has not extended to pelvic wall; vagina (but not the lower third) is involved.	Slightly over 20%
IIa	Carcinoma has not infiltrated parametrium.	
III	Carcinoma has extended to pelvic wall. Rectal examination shows no cancer-free space between tumor and pelvic wall. Lower third of vagina is involved.	30–35%
IV	Carcinoma has extended beyond true pelvis or has involved the mucosa of the bladder or rectum. However, the presence of bullous edema is not sufficient evidence to classify a case as stage IV.	At least 75%

*Approved by the International Federation of Obstetricians and Gynecologists.

(moistened in warm water) is inserted and the cervix is visualized. No lubricant should be used. The second specimen is taken from the region of the squamo-columnar junction by scraping with a cut tongue depressor or plastic spatula. Because this is the focus from which most cancers of the cervix develop, these scrapings provide the most reliable specimen for finding carcinoma in situ. Specimens should always be taken from any area of the cervix which is clinically abnormal.

While the scrapings taken directly from the cervix provide material for highly accurate interpretation, the vaginal smear gives reliable results as well, ranging from 80–95%. The advantage of the vaginal smear is that it may reveal malignant cells not only from the cervix but also from the endometrium, the ovaries, and even other abdominal viscera.

Smears to be mailed to a laboratory for staining and interpretation should remain in the alcohol fixative for at least 1 hour. After fixation fit the slides into the mailing container. Wrap the history form around the container and secure with a rubber band for further protection of the slides against breakage in mailing.

If a serial study is desired, most patients can learn to aspirate, smear, and fix their own slides.

The cytologic report from the pathology laboratory (Table 12–3) usually describes the cell specimens as (1) "normal," repeat in 1 year; (2) "suspicious," repeat stage II smears in 6 months and stage III smears immediately; or (3) "positive," take biopsy. Any additional information of value is added—eg, degree of inflammation, the presence of pathogens, and hormonal evaluation.

Perhaps the most important caution relates to the "suspicious" smear. Repeat smears should be done to pinpoint the source of danger since trichomonas infection, atrophic changes, or other clinical conditions unreleated to cancer may be the reason for the abnormal or atypical cells.

Note: In no case, including that of the positive smear, is treatment justified until definitive diagnosis has been established through biopsy studies.

TABLE 12–3. American Cancer Society terminology of Papanicolaou smears.

American Cancer Society	Papanic-olaou Stage	Characteristics
Normal	I	Negative for malignant cells.
Suspi-cious	II	Negative for malignant cells but containing atypical benign elements (including evidences of infection or radiation changes).
	III	Markedly atypical cells suspicious of malignancy.
Positive	IV	Probably malignant cells.
	V	Cells cytologically conclusive of malignancy.

An excess of exudate can be dropped into Bouin's or Zenker's fixative (10% formalin causes too much shrinkage) and subsequently treated as a "button" for sectioning. The following information should be included with the request for cytologic examination: Patient's name, date, record of previous vaginal smear (Yes or No; Positive or Negative), age, marital status, gynecologic complaints, menstrual history, LMP, surgical procedures, endocrine administration, x-ray or radium irradiation, provisional diagnosis, and the purpose of the study.

D. Cold Conization and Differential Curettage: These procedures may be necessary to determine invasion and extent of the cancer.

E. X-Ray Findings: Chest and skeletal x-rays may reveal metastases in advanced disease.

Differential Diagnosis

Abnormal bleeding and vaginal discharge are also found in cervicitis, venereal cervical lesions, and cervical polyps. A visible suspicious cervical lesion may be found in benign cervical polyps, cervical ulceration, nabothian cyst, cervical endometriosis, and cervical pregnancy or tuberculosis.

Complications

Metastases to regional lymph nodes occur with increasing frequency from stage I to stage IV. Paracervical extension occurs in all directions from the cervix. The ureters are often obstructed lateral to the cervix, causing hydroureter and hydronephrosis and consequently impaired kidney function. Almost 2/3 of patients with carcinoma of the cervix die of uremia when ureteral obstruction is bilateral. Pain in the back and in the distribution of the lumbosacral plexus is often indicative of neurologic involvement. Gross edema of the legs may be indicative of vascular and lymphatic stasis due to tumor.

Pelvic infections which complicate cervical carcinoma are most often due to streptococci and staphylococci.

Vaginal fistulas to the gastrointestinal and urinary tracts are severe late complications. Incontinence of urine and feces are major complications, particularly in debilitated individuals.

Hemorrhage is the cause of death in 10–20% of patients with extensive invasive carcinoma of the cervix.

Prevention

The causes of cervical cancer are still unknown. Nevertheless, complete chastity is associated with almost total freedom from this malignancy. Theoretically, carcinoma of the cervix (and penis) before middle age may be considered to be a carcinogen-induced neoplasm. The incidence of cervical cancer should therefore be reduced by the following health measures: (1) Improved personal hygiene. Prevention and prompt treatment of vaginitis and cervicitis, male circumcision in infancy, and precoital washing of the penis or habitual use of condoms. (2) Avoidance of intercourse at an early age; limitation of the number of consorts. (3) Frequent cancer cytoscreening of all women, especially parous individuals in lower socio-economic groups and those who are sexually promiscuous. (4) Prompt removal of suspicious cervical lesions such as epithelial anaplasia, dysplasia, and atypical or equivocal foci.

Treatment

A. Emergency Measures: Vaginal hemorrhage originates from gross ulceration and cavitation in stage II–IV cervical carcinoma. Ligation and suturing are usually not feasible, but ligation of the uterine or hypogastric arteries may be lifesaving when other measures fail. Styptics such as Negatan®, 10% silver nitrate solution, and acetone are effective, although delayed sloughing may result in further bleeding. Vaginal packing is helpful. Irradiation therapy usually controls bleeding.

B. Specific Measures:

1. Noninvasive carcinoma (stage 0)—In a woman over 40 with in situ carcinoma of the cervix, total hysterectomy with removal of a wide vaginal cuff is the surgical treatment of choice; irradiation therapy may be used alternatively in women who are poor operative risks. In a younger woman who wishes to have another baby, deep conization of the cervix may be acceptable. This is a calculated risk and imposes the absolute necessity of vaginal smears every 6 months for an indefinite time.

2. Invasive carcinoma—Irradiation (by a specialist) is generally the best treatment for invasive carcinoma of the cervix. The objectives of irradiation treatment are (1) the destruction of primary and secondary carcinoma within the pelvis and (2) the preservation of tissues not invaded. Gamma emissions derived from x-rays, ^{60}Co, radium, the cyclotron, the linear accelerator, and comparable sources are employed. All stages of cancer may be treated by this method, and there are fewer medical contraindications to irradiation than to radical surgery. Optimal results have been achieved with externally applied roentgen therapy combined with intracavitary and paracervical vaginal radium therapy.

Prognosis

The overall 5-year arrest rate for squamous cell carcinoma or adenocarcinoma originating in the cervix is about 45% in the major clinics. Percentage arrest rates are inversely proportionate to the stage of the cancer: stage 0, 99%; stage I, 77%; stage II, 65%; stage III, 25%; stage IV, about 5%.

Ayer, J.E.: Proper taking and interpretation of Papanicolaou smear. Cancer Cytol 8:37–45, 1968.

Bond, M.R., & I.B. Pearson: Psychological aspects of pain in women with advanced cancer of the cervix. J Psychosom Res 13:13–19, 1969.

Boyes, D.A., & others: The results of treatment of 4389 cases of preclinical cervical squamous carcinoma. J Obstet Gynaec Brit Common 77:769–780, 1970.

Collins, J.A., & others: Surgical management of carcinoma of the cervix. Am J Obst Gynec 108:441–444, 1970.

Lewis, B.W., & others: Primary adenocarcinoma of the cervix. J Obstet Gynaec Brit Common 77:277–279, 1970.

Mikuta, J.J., & others: Carcinoma of the cervix and pregnancy. JAMA 204:763–766, 1968.

Muirhead, W., & L.S. Green: Carcinoma of the cervix: Five-year results and sequelae of treatment. Am Obst Gynec 101:744–749, 1968.

Ragon, T.W.: Microinvasive carcinoma of the uterine cervix. J Arkansas Med Soc 65:139–144, 1968.

Wells, A.H., & others: Smears from the cervix: Cancer cell detection. Minnesota Med 51:25–29, 1968.

CARCINOMA OF THE ENDOMETRIUM
(Corpus or Fundal Cancer)

Adenocarcinoma of the endometrium is the second most common malignancy of the female genital tract. It occurs with greatest frequency in women 60–70 years of age. Abnormal uterine bleeding is the presenting sign in 80% of cases. A watery, serous or sanguineous, malodorous vaginal discharge is occasionally present. Pyometra or hematometra may be due to carcinoma of the endometrium. Pain occurs late in the disease, with stasis, or when the uterus becomes infected.

Surgical dilatation and differential curettage and pathologic examination of curretings are the most reliable means of diagnosis. Cytologic examination of aspirated material from the upper endocervical canal is diagnostic in only 80–85% of cases. Uterine lavage of the endometrial cavity with 3–5 ml of normal saline (eg, using the Gravlee Jet Washer®) may yield cells identifiable as malignant elements in suspected endometrial cancer. However, curettage is essential for confirmation before definitive therapy is initiated.

The Clark test is performed by gently passing a blunt curved uterine sound through the endocervical os and into the uterine cavity, and then removing it without further manipulation. Bleeding constitutes a positive test, and is presumptive evidence of fundal cancer. However, benign polyps, submucous myomas, and even an early pregnancy may also cause bleeding. Tissue is therefore required to make the diagnosis of cancer. Hysterography shows hypertrophic folds of endometrium, an irregular bulky tumor tending to fill the cavity, or gross papillary growths within the cavity.

Prevention

Routine screening of all women by periodic vaginal smears and prompt dilatation and curettage of patients who report abnormal menstrual bleeding or postmenopausal uterine bleeding will uncover many incipient as well as clinical cases of endometrial cancer.

Treatment

A. General Measures: Patients with carcinoma of the uterus are often weak, anemic, obese, diabetic, or hypertensive; they should be restored to maximum health before surgery.

B. Specific Measures: Treatment usually consists of total hysterectomy and bilateral salpingo-oophorectomy. Preliminary external irradiation or intracavitary radium therapy is probably indicated if the cancer is poorly differentiated or if the uterus is definitely enlarged in the absence of myomas.

Prognosis

With early diagnosis and treatment, the 5-year cure rate is 80–85%.

Austin, J.H., & B. MacMahon: Indicators of prognosis in carcinoma of the corpus uteri. Surg Gynec Obst 128:1247–1252, 1969.
Barbaro, C.: The place of aspiration lavage in the early diagnosis of uterine malignancy. Australian New Zealand J Obstet Gynaec 10:49–50, 1970.
Delclos, L., & others: Adenocarcinoma of the uterus. Am J Roentgenol 105:603–608, 1969.
Geisler, H.E., & others: Carcinoma of the endometrium in premenopausal women. Am J Obst Gynec 104:657–663, 1969.
Hong, K.C.: Prognosis of endometrial carcinoma. Obst Gynec 34:680–684, 1969.
Kneale, B., & others: Progestogen therapy for advanced carcinoma of the endometrium. MJ Australia 2:1101–1104, 1969.
Lees, D.H.: An evaluation of treatment in carcinoma of the body of the uterus. Obst Gynec Surv 25:258–261, 1970.
Liu, W.: Cytologic and clinical observations in cancer of the corpus. Am J Obst Gynec 106:624–625, 1970.
Palmer, A.L., & others: Gross examination of curettings in endometrial carcinoma. Ohio Med J 66:44–45, 1970.
Schulz, A.E., & others: Isolated vaginal cuff recurrence following therapy of endometrial adenocarcinoma. Am J Obst Gynec 104:679–686, 1969.
Vougtama, V., & others: Second primary cancers of endometrial carcinoma. Cancer 26:842–846, 1970.

CERVICAL POLYPS

Cervical polyposis is a common disorder which may occur at any time after the menarche but which is only occasionally noted in postmenopausal women. The cause is not known, but inflammation may play a role in etiology. The principal symptoms are leukorrhea and abnormal vaginal bleeding. A cervical polyp is visible on pelvic examination unless it is high in the canal, in which case hysterosalpingography or sounding of the cervix may be required. Vaginal cytologic examination demonstrates infection and metaplasia.

Cervical polyp must be differentiated from neoplastic disease of the endometrium, small submucous pedunculated myoma, endometrial polyp, and the products of an aborted conception.

Treatment

A. Medical Measures: Cervical discharge should be submitted for culture and sensitivity tests and antibiotic therapy instituted as indicated.

B. Surgical Measures: All cervical polyps should be removed surgically. They can often be removed in the office by avulsion, scalpel excision, or high-frequency electrosurgery. All tissue recovered should be examined by a pathologist to rule out malignant change. If the cervix is soft, patulous, or definitely dilated and the polyp is large, surgical dilatation and curettage in a hospital is required (especially if the pedicle is not readily visible). Exploration of the cervical and uterine cavities with the polyp forceps and curet may reveal multiple polyps or other important lesions. Warm vinegar douches are indicated for 3–7 days after removal to reduce the inflammatory reaction.

Prognosis

Simple removal is almost always curative.

Aaro, L.A., Jacobson, L.J., & E.H. Steele: Endocervical polyps. Obst Gynec 21:659–665, 1963.
Newman, H.F., & J.S. Northrup: Mucosal cervical polyps. Am J Obst Gynec 84:1816–1819, 1962.
Overstreet, E.W.: Clinical aspects of endometrial polyps. S Clin North America 42:1013, 1962.

MYOMA OF THE UTERUS
(Fibroid Tumor, Fibromyoma)

Essentials of Diagnosis

- Irregular enlargement of the uterus (may be asymptomatic).
- Hypermenorrhea, metrorrhagia, dysmenorrhea, and leukorrhea (variable).
- Acute and recurrent pelvic pain if the tumor becomes twisted on its pedicle.
- Symptoms due to pressure on neighboring organs (large tumors).
- X-ray evidence of calcification of some degenerative myomas.

General Considerations

Myoma is the most common neoplasm of the female genital tract. It is a discrete, round, firm, benign uterine tumor composed of smooth muscle and connective tissue. At least 10% of all gynecologic disorders of women are related to myoma. Only 2% are solitary, and several hundred have been found in one uterus. Some myomas become quite large; the largest on record weighed over 45.5 kg (100 lb). The most convenient classification is by anatomic location: (1) intramural, (2) submucous, (3) subserous, (4) intraligamentous, (5) parasitic, ie, deriving its blood supply from an organ to which it becomes attached, and (6) cervical.

Clinical Findings

A. Symptoms and Signs: Intramural, subserous, and intraligamentary tumors may distort or obstruct neighboring viscera, causing pain and bleeding. Submucous myomas which become large enough to displace adjacent organs cause dysmenorrhea, leukorrhea, hypermenorrhea, and metrorrhagia. Cervical myomas cause vaginal discharge, bleeding, dyspareunia, and infertility. Parasitic myomas cause intestinal obstruction if they are large enough to involve the omentum or bowel.

In nonpregnant women the manifestations of myoma are often minimal, eg, pelvic pressure or distention, urinary frequency, menometrorrhagia, constipation, dysmenorrhea. Infertility may be due to a myoma which obstructs or distorts the genital tract.

In pregnant women myomas cause additional hazards: abortion, malpresentation, failure of engagement, premature labor, pain, dystocia, ineffectual labor, and postpartum hemorrhage.

B. Laboratory Findings: The red blood cell count may reveal polycythemia due (curiously) to the tumor or anemia as a result of blood loss.

C. X-Ray Findings: A flat film of the pelvis may demonstrate opacities if calcific degeneration has occurred. Hysterography (contraindicated during pregnancy) may reveal a cervical or submucous tumor.

D. Special Examination: In the nonpregnant woman, vaginal examination under general anesthesia and surgical dilatation and curettage can be used in doubtful cases to establish the diagnosis.

Differential Diagnosis

The irregular enlargement of the uterus observed with myomas must be differentiated from the similar but regular enlargement that may occur with uterine pregnancy, adenomyosis, benign uterine hypertrophy, sarcoma, and adherent adnexa or viscera. Uterine bleeding, dysmenorrhea, and leukorrhea may also occur with other types of neoplastic disease, cervicitis, cervical stenosis, and other gynecologic disorders. These possibilities must be considered even when the diagnosis of myoma has been established.

Treatment

A. Emergency Measures: Give blood transfusions if necessary. Emergency surgery is required for acute torsion of a pedunculated myoma or intestinal obstruction. The only emergency indication for myomectomy during pregnancy is torsion. Abortion is not inevitable.

B. Specific Measures:

1. Nonpregnant women—In nonpregnant women, small asymptomatic myomas should be left undisturbed and observed at intervals of 6 months. Intramural and subserous myomas do not require surgery unless they are larger than a 14 week pregnancy, multiple, or distorting. Cervical myomas should be removed when they become larger than 3–4 cm in diameter.

2. Pregnant patients—If the uterus is no larger than a 6 month pregnancy by the 4th month of gestation, an uncomplicated course can be anticipated. If the mass (especially a cervical tumor) is the size of a 5 or 6 month pregnancy by the second month of gesta-

tion, abortion will probably occur. Wherever possible, defer surgery until 6 months after delivery, at which time involution of the uterus and regression of the tumor will be complete.

C. Surgical Measures: Surgery is indicated for the removal of large, rapidly growing or seriously symptomatic myomas in the nonpregnant patient. The measures available for the treatment of myoma are myomectomy, total or subtotal abdominal or vaginal hysterectomy, and, if surgery is contraindicated, irradiation. Myomectomy is the treatment of choice during the childbearing years. The ovaries should be preserved if possible in women under age 45. Subtotal hysterectomy has been virtually abandoned because it is a difficult procedure and there is no advantage to leaving the cervix. Radium should not be used for submucous tumors.

Prognosis

Surgical therapy is curative. Future pregnancies are not endangered by myomectomy, although cesarean delivery may be necessary after wide dissection. Careful hysterectomy with retention of normal ovaries does not hasten menopause.

Fechner, R.E.: Atypical leiomyomas and synthetic progestin therapy. Am J Clin Path 49:697–703, 1968.

Gudgeon, D.H.: Leiomyosarcoma of the uterus. Obst Gynec 32:101–106, 1968.

Lock, F.R.: Multiple myomectomy. Am J Obst Gynec 104:642–650, 1969.

Loeffler, F.E., & others: Myomectomy at the Chelsea Hospital for Women. J Obstet Gynaec Brit Common 77:167–170, 1970.

Pietila, K.: Hysterography in the diagnosis of uterine myoma: Roentgen findings in 829 cases compared with the operative findings. Acta obst gynec scandinav 48 (Suppl 5):1–67, 1969.

ENDOMETRIOSIS & ADENOMYOSIS

Aberrant growth of endometrium outside the uterine cavity (endometriosis) and benign invasion of endometrium into the uterine musculature (adenomyosis) are common causes of abnormal uterine bleeding and dysmenorrhea. Endometriosis frequently causes dyspareunia, painful defecation, or rectal bleeding. The pain tends to be constant, beginning 2–7 days before the onset of menses and becoming increasingly severe until flow slackens. Pelvic examination may disclose tender indurated nodules in the cul-de-sac, especially if the examination is done at the onset of menstruation.

Endometriosis and adenomyosis must be distinguished from pelvic inflammatory disease (differentiated by the presence of fever and leukocytosis), from tuberculosis, and from myomas and other neoplasia of the reproductive organs. Only in pelvic inflammatory disease and endometriosis are the symptoms usually aggravated by menstruation. Dilatation and curettage will generally distinguish adenomyosis from submucous myoma and cancer of the endometrium. Bowel invasion by endometrial tissue may produce clinical findings which may be almost indistinguishable from bowel neoplasm; differentiation in these rare instances depends upon biopsy.

Laboratory findings are of no value in the diagnosis of these disorders. X-ray contrast studies are helpful in the delineation of colonic involvement in endometriosis; and contrast hysterography is diagnostic in adenomyosis if the medium penetrates the glands.

Endometriosis is a significant cause of infertility.

Treatment

A. Endometriosis:

1. Medical treatment—Young married women with mild but advancing endometriosis should be advised to become pregnant without delay to secure a family and retard the progress of the disease. If the patient does not want a child or cannot become pregnant, exogenous hormone therapy is indicated with one of the following regimens:

(1) Progestins, eg, norethynodrel and ethinyl estradiol 3-methyl ether (Enovid®), 10 mg orally daily for 2 weeks beginning on the 5th day of the menstrual period and increasing by 10 mg increments every 2 weeks until 40 mg daily are being taken. Continue for 6–9 months for optimal effect. This drug induces pseudopregnancy. Restrict sodium during administration of Enovid® to prevent fluid retention. If fluid does accumulate, give hydrochlorothiazide (Hydro-Diuril®), 50 mg orally every other day. Repeat courses may be given after an observation interval of 2–3 months.

(2) Diethylstilbestrol, 1 mg orally on the first day of the menstrual period and increasing by 1 mg increments every 3 days until 5 mg have been given. Then give 25 mg daily, increasing by 25 mg increments every week until 100 mg are being taken daily. Continue 100 mg daily for 4 months, decrease by 25 mg weekly to a daily dose of 5 mg over the next 2 months, and then give 1 mg daily for 1 month, and stop. This regimen (and ¶ 1, above) usually relieves symptoms completely, but about 30% of patients have recurrences when medication is withdrawn.

(3) Methyltestosterone, 5–10 mg sublingually daily, usually relieves pain and retards the growth of endometrial tissue. Ovulation is usually not impaired by the smaller dose, and many patients on androgen therapy become pregnant. Medication must be discontinued at the first signs of virilization, since voice changes induced by androgen therapy are not reversible.

Analgesics with codeine may be given as necessary for pain.

2. Surgical measures—The surgical treatment of moderately extensive endometriosis depends upon the patient's age and her desire to preserve reproductive function. If the patient is under 35, resect the lesions, free adhesions, and suspend the uterus. At least 20% of patients so treated will become pregnant, although half

must undergo surgery again when the disease progresses. If the patient is over 35 years old and both ovaries are involved, both ovaries, the tubes, and the uterus must be excised. If one ovary is normal, it need not be removed.

Extensive endometriosis almost invariably necessitates ablation of both ovaries and tubes and the uterus regardless of the patient's age, unless it is possible to improve the patient's condition by inducing pseudopregnancy with progestins (see above) so that a less radical procedure will suffice.

3. X-ray therapy—If surgery is contraindicated or refused, castration doses of x-ray will relieve the symptoms and cause almost complete regression of the lesions. X-ray therapy cannot be condoned unless the diagnosis of advanced endometriosis is unequivocal.

B. Adenomyosis: The only treatment is surgical. A distinct zone of involvement is rarely found at operation. Hysterectomy is the treatment of choice because adenomyosis is such a widespread process. Prior to the menopause, normal ovaries should be retained. X-ray or radium irradiation is therapeutically effective but should be avoided in young women because it induces menopause.

Prognosis

The prognosis for reproductive function in early or moderately advanced endometriosis is good with conservative therapy. Castration is curative in severe and extensive endometriosis; if it is refused, hormone therapy may be beneficial.

Complete relief of symptoms is the rule following corrective surgery for adenomyosis.

Chalmers, J.A.: Conservative management of endometriosis. Proc Roy Soc Med 61:360–361, 1968.

Porges, R.F.: Acute retrograde menstruation. Report of a case. Obst Gynec 35:524–526, 1970.

Pratt, J.H., & others: Spontaneous rupture of endometrial cysts of the ovary presenting as an acute abdominal emergency. Am J Obst Gynec 108:56–62, 1970.

Ranney, B.: Endometriosis. II. Emergency operations due to hemoperitoneum. Obst Gynec 36:437–442, 1970.

Rogers, S.F., & W.M. Jacobs: Infertility and endometriosis: Conservative surgical approach. Fertil Steril 9:529–536, 1968.

Simmons, C.A.: Some peculiarities of endometriosis. Proc Roy Soc Med 61:357–358, 1968.

Snaith, L.: The treatment of endometriosis by oral progestogens. Proc Roy Soc Med 61:358–360, 1968.

Sutton, E.C.: Etiological factors in endometriosis with report of a case with reflux menstruation. Univ Carolina MJ 31:45–47, 1970.

CYSTOCELE

Essentials of Diagnosis

- Feeling of vaginal fullness and looseness, and incomplete emptying of the bladder.

- Soft, reducible mass, bulging into the anterior vagina, increased by straining.
- Residual urine collection.
- Urinary frequency, dysuria, stress or urgency incontinence (frequently).

General Considerations

Herniation of the posterior bladder wall and trigone into the vagina almost always is the result of laceration, during parturition, of the subvesical fibroareolar pseudofascia. Birth of a large baby and multiple or operative delivery increase the likelihood and degree of cystocele. Cystocele may be accompanied by urethrocele, a sagging of the urethra stripped from its attachments beneath the symphysis during childbirth. Prolapse of the uterus and rectocele and enterocele may be associated with cystocele. Concomitant with involution, which is marked after the menopause, the pelvic floor supports become attenuated, so that cystocele often becomes symptomatic after middle life.

Residual urine (60 ml or more) commonly complicates cystocele. Chronic, recurrent cystitis may follow, and problems of voiding usually result. When the normal posterior urethrovesical angle becomes considerably reduced with enlarging cystocele, stress incontinence develops.

Clinical Findings

A. Symptoms and Signs: Patients with cystocele describe vaginal looseness and a sense of the presence of urine even after voiding. A thin, reducible, nontender bulge into the vagina is noted forward of the cervix when cystocele is present. The woman may learn to manually reduce the sagging bladder to void completely. Residual urine usually is contaminated by bacteria. Hence, urgency, frequency, and dysuria, symptomatic of chronic urinary infection, may persist or recur. Stress incontinence is likely when the bladder herniation is extensive.

B. Laboratory Findings: Catheter drainage of the bladder after voiding will reveal more than 60 ml of residual urine in moderate or marked cystocele. Urinalysis of a catheterized or "clean-catch" specimen may reveal evidence of urinary tract infection.

C. X-Ray Findings: Anteroposterior and, especially, lateral films following introduction of x-ray contrast medium or a metal bead chain into the bladder will demonstrate bladder herniation.

Differential Diagnosis

Large bladder stones and tumors are firm and easily outlined. The bulge of a prolapsed cervix is readily seen with a speculum. An anterior cul-de-sac hernia is rare, but the small bowel within the sac may be felt to crepitate. This intestinal hernia may be visualized during gastrointestinal x-ray studies.

Treatment

A. Emergency Measures: Acute urinary retention secondary to overfilling of the bladder or marked uterine prolapse requires bladder catheterization.

B. Surgical Measures: Anterior vaginal colporrhaphy is most effective for cystocele repair. Transabdominal cystocele correction or obliterative vaginal operations (Le Fort's operation or colpectomy) may be chosen for correction of cystocele in special instances.

C. Supportive Measures: Pessaries (Menge, Gellhorn, Gehrung, ball) may reduce and support cystocele in patients who refuse or cannot withstand surgery. In postmenopausal women, estrogen therapy, eg, conjugated estrogenic substances (Premarin®), 1.25 mg every other day (or equivalent) for an indefinite period, and the Kegel isometric exercises may improve urinary control.

D. Medical Measures: Treat urinary infections vigorously and adequately with antibiotics selected by culture and sensitivity tests.

Prognosis

The prognosis following surgery is excellent in the absence of pregnancy or stress due to increased intraabdominal pressure (chronic ascites, bronchitis, asthma, bronchiectasis) or degenerative neurologic disorders affecting the pelvic floor structures.

Pratt, J.H.: Surgical repair of pelvic relaxation. Chicago Med 69:1057–1062, 1966.

RECTOCELE

Essentials of Diagnosis

- Chronic constipation or painful evacuation of feces.
- Soft posterior vaginal fullness.

General Considerations

Rectocele is a rectovaginal hernia caused by rupture, during childbirth, of the fibrous connective tissue layer separating these 2 structures. It may be due to the trauma of rapid delivery or forceps or breech extraction, particularly of a large fetus. Multiparous women are commonly affected. The quality of the tissues, the degree of damage, and the elimination habits of the patient are important factors in the development of rectocele and in its symptomatology. Constipation is aggravated by feces collection in the rectocele pouch. Straining at stool increases the defect, and hemorrhoids, anal fissures, uterine prolapse, enterocele, and cystocele may develop also. Although rectocele occasionally is diagnosed soon after a particularly difficult delivery, the abnormality usually becomes apparent after age 35–40 years. Digital rectocele compression, enemas, or frequent laxatives may be required to facilitate regular, easy bowel movements.

Clinical Findings

A. Symptoms and Signs: A sense of vaginal and rectal fullness and the constant urge for a bowel movement are typical complaints. A soft, thin-walled, reducible, nontender fullness involving the lower 2/3 of the posterior vagina may be seen (even without a speculum) and felt, often while the patient is straining, by depression of the perineum. A rectal examination easily confirms sacculation of the rectum into the vagina.

B. X-Ray Findings: Lateral films during a barium enema will delineate the rectocele.

Differential Diagnosis

Enterocele may develop above a rectocele. The apex of the rectocele should be identified by digital examination. Rectovaginal examination with the patient standing is helpful for confirmation of the diagnosis of enterocele because this hernia may protrude only when the patient is erect. A vaginal speculum will usually expose a prolapsed cervix or soft cervical or pedunculated uterine tumor, which are rarely confused with rectocele.

Treatment

A. Surgical Measures: Posterior colpoperineorrhaphy (often with correction of a true or potential enterocele) usually is curative of rectocele.

B. Supportive Measures: Avoidance of straining, coughing, and heavy lifting, improved diet and bowel habits, laxatives, and rectal suppositories are helpful. Good muscular relaxation during the second stage of labor, episiotomy, and prophylactic forceps delivery will often avoid or limit rectocele occurrence.

Prognosis

The prospects for cure after surgery are good provided subsequent vaginal delivery and straining at stool are avoided.

Marek, C.B.: Transverse repair for rectocele. South MJ 62:749–752, 1969.

Nichols, D.H., & others: Surgical significance of the rectovaginal septum. Am J Obst Gynec 108:215–220, 1970.

ENTEROCELE

Essentials of Diagnosis

- Uncomfortable heaviness in the vagina.
- Abdominal cramping several hours after eating (occasionally); constipation.
- Fullness or bulge in the vaginal vault, usually in menopausal or older parous women.

General Considerations

Cul-de-sac hernias may involve the pouch of Douglas (common) or may be anterior to the uterus (rare). Either type may be congenital or, by far most commonly, acquired. The congenital form may be noted in nulliparous patients. Enterocele frequently appears after severe coughing or straining. Birth trauma (usually forceps or breech extraction) develops or extends a sacculation between the uterosacral ligaments involving especially the posterior wall of the cul-de-sac. The thin enterocele sac, lined by peritoneum, generally contains small bowel which rarely is adherent. Uterine prolapse often is associated with enterocele, and, if procidentia is progressive, the hernial pouch also becomes larger. A sense of weight in the pelvis and fullness in the vagina may be associated with gastrointestinal discomfort several hours after meals, or constipation may be troublesome. Spontaneous obstruction almost never occurs in an enterocele. The differential diagnosis involves rectocele (posterior hernia) or cystocele (anterior hernia) and uterine descensus.

Clinical Findings

A. Symptoms and Signs: The pelvic and abdominal symptoms are vague and nonspecific. A sense of weight and distention of the upper vagina rarely is severe. Vaginal palpation will reveal a fullness in the upper vagina with enterocele. To distinguish a posterior cul-de-sac hernia, the examiner should place one finger in the rectum and one in the vagina; when the patient strains, the enterocele may be felt between the fingers in the rectovaginal septum. The hernia ia always more marked when the patient is standing or is in the high Fowler position.

B. X-Ray Findings: Lateral (erect) pelvic x-rays taken during small bowel study may reveal an enterocele.

Differential Diagnosis

Distinguish enterocele from cystocele when an anterior enterocele is suspected, or from rectocele when a posterior cul-de-sac hernia is possible. Prolapse of the vaginal vault (colpocele) following hysterectomy is almost always an enterocele. Uterine descensus may be confusing until the cervix is visualized, palpated, and identified.

Treatment

A. Emergency Measures: If bowel obstruction occurs, immediate laparotomy and release will be required.

B. Surgical Measures: Enterocele excision may be done transvaginally or transabdominally after dissection of the sac, high ligation, and fixation of the point of closure and reinforcement of the zone of weakness. Rectocele and cystocele repair and correction of uterine prolapse (or hysterectomy) should be done concomitantly.

C. Supportive Measures: Treat cough and constipation and limit straining and heavy lifting. Help the obese patient reduce.

Prognosis

The prognosis following proper (complete) surgery is good. Hysterectomy without closure of a true or potential pelvic hernia will be followed by enterocele.

Uefelder, H.: Enterocele. Progr Gynec 5:447–454, 1970.

MALPOSITION OF THE UTERUS
("Tipped Uterus")

Various types of uterine malposition have been said to cause pelvic pain, backache, abnormal uterine bleeding, and infertility. However, current opinion holds that a relationship between malposition of the uterus and definite symptomatology can be established only after specific, careful evaluation. Back pain, for example, is usually due to an orthopedic disorder. Anteflexion of the uterus almost never causes symptoms and requires no treatment. Lateral displacements of the uterus are frequently due to far more serious pelvic disease (usually neoplasms). Retrodisplacements may cause symptoms and require treatment.

The diagnosis of any type of uterine malposition depends upon abdominal and rectovaginal examination, and can be confirmed and documented by hysterography. If a woman complaining of pain, bleeding, or infertility is found to have a retroverted or retroflexed uterus, and if other more common causes of these complaints have been ruled out, a trial of pessary support is warranted. If the vaginal pessary consistently relieves symptoms and the symptoms return when the pessary is removed, it may be advisable to suspend the uterus surgically. If surgery is contraindicated or refused, the pessary may be worn intermittently until the menopause, at which time regression of uterine tissue will probably relieve symptoms altogether.

Knee-chest exercises are of doubtful value.

Mahran, M.: Effect of bilateral excision of the round ligaments on the position of the uterus after labor. Am J Obst Gynec 105:495–497, 1969.

UTERINE PROLAPSE

Essentials of Diagnosis
- Firm mass in the lower vagina or protrusion of the cervix beyond the introitus.
- Sense of heaviness in the pelvis.
- Low backache or dragging sensation in the groins.

General Considerations
Uterine prolapse most commonly occurs as a delayed result of childbirth injury to the pelvic floor (particularly the transverse cervical and uterosacral ligaments). Unrepaired lacerations of the levator musculature and perineal body aggravate the weakness. Attenuation of the pelvic structures with aging, congenital weakness, neurologic injury to the sacral nerves, ascites, and internal genital tumors accelerate the development of prolapse.

Retroposition of the uterus usually develops with prolapse, whereupon the corpus, now in the axis of the vagina, exerts a piston-like action with each episode of increased intra-abdominal pressure. The cervix often becomes elongated for unknown reasons.

In slight prolapse the uterus descends only part way down the vagina. In moderate prolapse the corpus descends to the introitus and the cervix protrudes slightly beyond. In marked prolapse (procidentia) the entire cervix and uterus protrude beyond the introitus and the vagina is inverted.

Clinical Findings
A firm mass is palpable in the lower vagina. In moderate prolapse the cervix protrudes just beyond the introitus. The patient complains of a sense of heaviness in the pelvis, low backache, and a "dragging" sensation in the inguinal regions.

Pelvic examination with the patient bearing down or straining in the supine or standing position will demonstrate downward displacement of a prolapsing cervix and uterus. Herniation of the bladder, rectum, or cul-de-sac is diagnosed in a similar way. Consider uterine or adnexal neoplasms and ascites as possible causes of prolapse.

Rectovaginal examination may reveal rectal fullness (rectocele) or hernia of the pouch of Douglas behind and below the cervix. A metal sound or firm catheter within the bladder may be used to determine the extent of cystocele.

Differential Diagnosis
Uterine prolapse, a reducible sacropubic hernia, is the descensus of the cervix and uterus down the vagina to or beyond the introitus. If the uterus protrudes outside the introitus, the condition is known as uterine procidentia. Prolapse is generally associated with a compressible vaginal herniation of the bladder (cystocele), rectum (rectocele), and of the small bowel (enterocele). These defects may occur singly or in combination. Tumors of the cervix or uterus and fecal impaction in a rectocele must be differentiated from a sagging cervix and uterus.

Complications
Abnormal uterine bleeding and abortion may result from disordered uterine circulation. Ulceration in procidentia predisposes to cancer.

Prevention
Avoidance of obstetric trauma, and postpartum exercises to strengthen the levator musculature (Kegel), will prevent or minimize subsequent prolapse. Prolonged cyclic estrogen therapy for the postmenopausal woman will often conserve the strength and tone of the pelvic floor.

Treatment
Selection of the surgical approach depends upon the patient's age, the extent of prolapse, and her desire for menstruation, pregnancy, and coitus. Uterine suspension or ventrofixation is not effective in the treatment of prolapse.

Palliative therapy with a well-fitted vaginal pessary (eg, inflatable doughnut type, Gellhorn pessary) may give relief if surgery is refused or contraindicated.

Estrogen supplementation will improve the tissue tone and correct atrophic vaginitis in postmenopausal patients.

Prognosis

Prolapse may remain constant for months or years, but it never regresses and will ultimately become more extreme unless corrected surgically.

Diddle, A.W., & others: Partial colpocleisis for complete vaginal prolapse: Demonstration of a technique. J Reprod Med 4:94–96, 1970.

Fliegner, J.R.H.: Utero-vaginal prolapse during pregnancy. Australian New Zealand J Obstet Gynec 9:240–248, 1969.

Mueller, H.E.: Prolapsus uteri causing hydronephrosis. J Am Geriatrics Soc 17:1055–1063, 1969.

Piver, M.S., & J. Spezia: Uterine prolapse during pregnancy. Obst Gynec 32:765–769, 1968.

SALPINGITIS

Essentials of Diagnosis

- Severe cramp-like, nonradiating, lower abdominal pain; adnexal tenderness.
- Chills, moderately high intermittent fever.
- Venereal contact, leukorrhea.
- Abnormal menstruation or abortion.
- White count 20,000/cu mm with marked leukocytic preponderance; rapid sedimentation rate.
- Intracellular gram-negative diplococci in cervical, urethral, or Bartholin duct discharge with initial *Neisseria gonorrhoeae* infection.

General Considerations

Salpingitis, or inflammation of the fallopian tubes (also called pelvic inflammatory disease, PID), is directly or indirectly involved in almost 1/5 of all gynecologic problems. It may be acute or chronic and unilateral or bilateral. It is almost always due to bacterial infections, usually with gonococci, streptococci, tubercle bacilli, or a mixed bacterial flora. Tuberculous salpingitis usually occurs in prepuberal girls or in infertile or postmenopausal women. Women in the childbearing years are most susceptible to pyogenic infections. Predisposing factors include venereal contact, hysterosalpingography with excess of oily contrast media, degenerative cervical or uterine neoplasms, operative delivery, and peritonitis of bowel origin.

Clinical Findings

A. Symptoms and Signs: The manifestations of acute salpingitis include severe, cramp-like lower abdominal (usually bilateral) nonradiating pain, chills and fever, menstrual disturbances, leukorrhea, and adnexal tenderness. In the chronic stage, dysmenorrhea, dys-

pareunia, infertility, recurrent low-grade fever, and tender pelvic masses are described.

B. Laboratory Findings: The white count is elevated and the sedimentation rate is increased. The causative organisms may be demonstrated by appropriate smears and cultures of the vaginal discharge.

Differential Diagnosis

Acute appendicitis is typified by generalized lower abdominal pain, nausea, vomiting, and altered bowel function, with localization of pain in the right lower quadrant. Ectopic pregnancy is the preferred diagnosis when persistent lower quadrant pain of sudden onset is associated with a tender, soft adnexal mass, uterine bleeding, and a history of recent menstrual irregularity. In infected intrauterine abortion with adnexitis, the cervix is patulous, the lochia bloody and foul-smelling, and one or both ovaries are enlarged and tender.

Treatment

A. Specific Measures: For nontuberculous salpingitis give ampicillin, 500 mg orally 4 times daily for 5–7 days, or the equivalent in other antibacterial drugs. Tuberculous salpingitis is treated with streptomycin, 1 gm IM twice weekly; isoniazid, 150–300 mg orally daily; and aminosalicylic acid, 12–20 gm orally daily for at least 6 months.

B. General Measures: Control pain with hypnotics and analgesics. Delay or prevent menstruation for 1–2 months by oral sequential contraceptive hormone therapy such as Enovid®, 10–15 mg/day.

C. Surgical Measures: Defer surgery during the acute phase. Consider surgery for pelvic abscess, large pelvic inflammatory masses, demonstrable pelvic disease causing persistent pain which cannot be controlled by medication, repeated episodes of abnormal uterine bleeding unresponsive to therapy, and whenever tuberculous masses do not resolve or fistulas develop in spite of massive prolonged antibiotic therapy. Adnexectomy and perhaps hysterectomy may be required in extensive chronic incapacitating bilateral salpingitis.

Prognosis

Inflammation confined to one or both fallopian tubes, treated early and adequately, usually resolves rapidly, although obstruction occurs in many instances. If an abscess develops within or near the tube, recurrent salpingitis is the rule and infertility is almost a certainty.

McLone, D.G., & others: Gonorrhoea in females treated with one oral dose of tetracycline. Brit J Ven Dis 44:218–219, 1968.

Mickal, A.: Surgery for ruptured tubo-ovarian abscess. Am J Obst Gynec 100:432–436, 1968.

Rees, E., & others: Gonococcal salpingitis. Brit J Ven Dis 45:205–215, 1969.

Trussell, R.R.: Pelvic inflammatory disease. Proc Roy Soc Med 61:365–367, 1968.

Wright, N.H.: Acute pelvic inflammatory disease in an indigent population. Am J Obst Gynec 101:979–990, 1968.

OVARIAN TUMORS

Follicle (Retention) Cysts

Follicle cysts are common, frequently bilateral and multiple cysts which appear on the surface of the ovaries as pale blebs filled with a clear fluid. They vary in size from microscopic to 4 cm in diameter (rarely larger). These cysts represent the failure of an incompletely developed follicle to reabsorb. They are commonly found in prolapsed adherent ovaries or when a thickened previously inflamed ovarian capsule prevents extrusion of the ovum. Symptoms are usually not present unless torsion or rupture with hemorrhage occurs, in which case the symptoms and signs of an abdominal emergency are often present. Large or numerous cysts may cause aching pelvic pain, dyspareunia, and occasionally abnormal uterine bleeding. The ovary may be slightly enlarged and tender to palpation, and the vaginal smear will often show a high estrogen level and a lack of progesterone stimulation.

Pelvic inflammatory disease and endometriosis must be considered in the differential diagnosis.

Most follicle cysts disappear spontaneously within 60 days without any treatment; when symptoms are disturbing, warm douches, pelvic diathermy, and attempt at reestablishment of ovulation with progesterone medication may be helpful. Malignant change does not occur.

Any cyst which becomes larger than 5 cm in diameter or which persists longer than 60 days probably is not a follicle cyst.

Corpus Luteum Cysts

Corpus luteum cysts are functional, nonneoplastic enlargements of the ovary caused by the unexplained increase in secretion of fluid by the corpus luteum which occurs after ovulation or during early pregnancy. They are 4–6 cm in diameter, raised, and brown; and are filled with tawny serous fluid. An organizing blood clot is often found within the cavity.

Corpus luteum cysts may cause local pain and tenderness, and either amenorrhea or delayed menstruation followed by brisk bleeding after resolution of the cyst. They are usually readily palpable. Corpus luteum cyst may encourage torsion of the ovary, causing severe pain, or it may rupture and bleed, in which case laparotomy is usually required to control hemorrhage into the peritoneum. Unless these acute complications develop, symptomatic therapy is all that is required. The cyst will disappear within 2 months in nonpregnant women, and will gradually become smaller during the last trimester in pregnant women.

Theca Lutein Cysts

Theca lutein cysts range in size from minute to 4 cm in diameter. They are usually bilateral, are filled with clear straw-colored and occasionally bloody serous fluid, and are found only in association with hydatidiform mole and chorio-epithelioma or after excessive chorionic gonadotropin therapy. The cysts may rupture and bleed. The primary disease is suggested when an extremely high titer of chorionic gonadotropin is found in association with ovarian cysts. The remote possibility of bilateral papillary cystadenoma should be considered in the differential diagnosis.

These cysts disappear spontaneously following elimination of the molar pregnancy or destruction of the chorio-epithelioma.

Endometrial Ovarian Cysts

Ectopic endometrium which develops on the ovary causes periodic (nonhormonally induced) bleeding. Attempts at "healing" follow each period, but invasion of the endometrial tissue eventually results in cyst formation. These cysts vary from microscopic in size up to 10–12 cm in diameter. They are filled with thick, chocolate-colored (old) blood; and are often adherent to neighboring viscera. The symptoms are infertility, hypermenorrhea, dyspareunia, and secondary or acquired dysmenorrhea. Not all "chocolate cysts" are of endometrial origin, since bleeding into any cystic cavity will result in the accumulation of decomposed blood.

The treatment of large endometrial ovarian cysts is surgical removal, leaving as much functioning ovarian tissue as possible. Small cysts may be destroyed by electrocautery.

Czanobilsky, B., & others: Endometrioid carcinoma of the ovary: A clinicopathologic study of 75 cases. Obst Gynec 26:1141–1152, 1970.

Fibromas of the Ovary

About 5% of ovarian tumors are fibromas. They are unilateral, firm, nonfunctional (no hormone production), and benign, being composed principally of fibrous connective tissue. Fibromas are smooth, round, lobulated, nonadherent, and generally small, although a few have been reported which weighed as much as 2.25 kg (5 lb). Fibromatous tumors are the principal cause of **Demons-Meigs syndrome**. The ascitic fluid is thought to be ovarian tumor transudate which is transferred in an uncertain manner to the thoracic cavity. The abdomen enlarges and the patient complains of orthopnea, tachycardia, and chest oppression. Torsion often occurs, causing agonizing pain in the affected lower quadrant and nausea and vomiting. Larger tumors cause a sense of pelvic heaviness. The tumor is usually palpable on pelvic examination.

Demons-Meigs syndrome must be distinguished from primary pulmonary and abdominal disease causing hydrothorax and ascites.

Treatment consists of surgical removal. Hydrothorax and ascites disappear promptly after removal of the tumor. Unless sarcoma is found on pathologic examination, the prognosis is excellent.

Compton, H.L., & F.M. Finck: Serous adenofibroma and cystadenofibroma of the ovary. Obst Gynec 36:636–645, 1970.

Brenner Tumor

A Brenner tumor is a unilateral, firm, non-encapsulated, nonfunctioning neoplasm which consists of nests of epithelioid cells surrounded by whorls of dense connective tissue. It is often mistaken for fibroma. These tumors comprise 1% of all ovarian neoplasms. They are believed to arise from Walthard cell rests, but are occasionally found in the wall of a pseudomucinous cystadenoma. Brenner tumors may grow to 30 cm in diameter, although most are less than 2–3 cm. They are most common in women over 40 years of age, and are occasionally associated with Demons-Meigs syndrome. They are almost never malignant.

Brenner tumors produce symptoms only by virtue of their size and situation, ie, unilateral pelvic discomfort and a sense of fullness and heaviness in the lower abdomen. If torsion occurs it causes acute abdominal pain with nausea and vomiting.

Treatment consists of ovariectomy.

Teratoid Tumors

Teratoid tumors are of unknown origin. They are composed of 1, 2, or 3 germinal layers which may grow into any possible combination of imperfectly formed structures. If one type of tissue predominates, the appearance will be that of a single-tissue tumor; such is the case in struma ovarii, the thyroid (iodine-containing) tumor of the ovary. Dermoid cysts, the most common type of teratoid tumor, contain ectodermal (and often mesodermal) tissue in the form of macerated skin, hair, bone and teeth; the cyst is filled with a heavy, greasy sebaceous material and integumental structures. Teratoid tumors occur primarily in women 18–40 years of age. Orientals are prone to develop dermoids. Dermoids account for 10% and solid teratomas 0.1% of all ovarian tumors. About 15% are bilateral.

The clinical manifestations of teratoid tumor are produced when the freely shifting mass distorts and displaces neighboring viscera. A teratoid is relatively light and rarely adherent. It tends to "float" upward in the abdomen, which encourages the development of a long pedicle; when torsion occurs, sudden, excruciating, persistent pain results. Rupture of a dermoid due to trauma or during pregnancy results in chemical peritonitis. If the neoplasm is large, the patient may complain of constipation and urinary frequency. Calcification may be observed on x-ray in the form of teeth or bone.

Teratoid tumor must be differentiated from pedunculated uterine myomas.

The treatment of teratoma is surgical removal and examination and aspiration of the other ovary to make certain that another dermoid is not present. Care should be taken not to spill the contents into the pelvic cavity, and teratomas should never be needled through the cul-de-sac for therapeutic or diagnostic reasons since leakage into the abdomen causes irritation and peritonitis.

The prognosis is usually excellent. Malignant change, though uncommon, implies a guarded prognosis.

Bennington, J.L., & others: Incidence and relative frequency of benign and malignant ovarian neoplasms. Obst Gynec 32:627–632, 1968.

Moore, J.G., & others: Ovarian tumors in infancy, childhood and adolescence. Am J Obst Gynec 99:913–922, 1967.

Woodruff, J.D., & others: Ovarian teratomas: Relationship of the histologic and ontogenic factors to prognosis. Am J Obst Gynec 102:702–715, 1968.

Cystadenomas (Pseudomucinous & Serous Cystadenomas)

Cystadenomas are the most common of ovarian neoplasms, representing 70% of all ovarian tumors. These tumors produce no hormone and are most common in women between the ages of 45 and 65. Serous and pseudomucinous cystadenoma occur with about equal frequency.

Pseudomucinous cystadenoma grows more sluggishly and becomes larger than the serous type; some have been reported to weigh over 45.5 kg (100 lb). These tumors are in a sense teratomas composed entirely of entoderm. They are usually multilocular; contain a thick, viscid, brownish liquid; are lined by tall columnar epithelial and goblet cells; and are contained in a tough membranous capsule. About 5% are found to be malignant at surgery.

Serous cystadenomas do not become as large as pseudomucinous cystadenomas; most weigh 4.5–9 kg (10–20 lb). They are multilocular, filled with a thin yellowish fluid, are lined by cuboidal or short columnar cells, and tend to develop papillary excrescences on both their inner and outer surfaces. Serous cystadenoma's, like the pseudomucinous type, are also contained in a parchment-like capsule. Small sand-like, sharp, calcareous concretions (psammoma bodies) are often present within the tumor. Serous cystadenomas are believed to arise from invagination of the germinal epithelium of the surface of the ovary.

Cystadenomas are silent tumors because they do not produce hormones, pedicles form rarely, and the capsule does not rupture easily. Symptoms are produced only when the tumor becomes large enough to cause increased abdominal girth and weight gain, pelvic heaviness, constipation, and urinary frequency. The tumor is easily palpable on abdominal examination, and x-rays may show psammoma bodies. About 50% eventually become malignant.

Treatment consists of surgical removal of benign tumors by oophorocystectomy and, if malignant change has occurred, panhysterectomy and bilateral salpingo-oophorectomy. Radiation or systemic chlorambucil or another cancer chemotherapeutic drug is indicated if peritoneal or visceral metastases are found.

All ovarian cysts over 7 cm in diameter and those which persist for over 90 days should be removed.

Decker, D.G., & others: Cyclophosphamide in the treatment of ovarian cancer. Clin Obst Gynec 11:382–400, 1968.

Kottmeier, H.L.: Treatment of ovarian cancer with Thio-TEPA. Clin Obst Gynec 11:428–438, 1968.

Rutledge, F.: Chemotherapy of ovarian cancer with melphalan. Clin Obst Gynec 11:354–366, 1968.

Mesonephroma

Mesonephroma is an uncommon nonfunctioning ovarian tumor which clinically and grossly resembles papillary serous cystadenoma. Most cases occur in patients over 35 and are probably of teratogenous origin. The tumor is often 10–20 cm in diameter when first discovered. Thirty percent are malignant. Salpingo-oophorectomy is necessary for cure. If it is likely that malignant change has occurred, panhysterectomy is required. Radiation therapy should be considered also.

Anderson, M.C., & F.A. Langley: Mesonephroid tumours of the ovary. J Clin Path 23:210–218, 1970.

Tarride, J., & W.B. Kingsley: Mesonephroma of the ovary. Cancer 22:1208–1214, 1968.

Arrhenoblastoma

Arrhenoblastoma is a rare ovarian tumor (fewer than 175 cases have been reported). It occurs most frequently during the reproductive years, and is assumed either to arise from sexually ambivalent cells noted in the ovary of the 6–7 week embryo or to be of teratoid origin. The tumor is unilateral (slightly more often on the right side), and may be minute or may fill the entire pelvis. Twenty-five percent become malignant, but metastases are usually late.

Arrhenoblastomas are often hormonally active, producing androgenic substances which cause both defeminization and virilization, manifested by varying degrees of amenorrhea, acne, hirsutism, recession of the hairline at the forehead, slight alopecia, loss of feminine contour, breast and genital atrophy, clitoral hypertrophy, and deepening of the voice. The urinary excretion of 17-ketosteroids is slightly to moderately increased; urinary dehydroepiandrosterone levels are strikingly high. The urinary hydroxysteroids are not elevated. The FSH titer is normal or minimally reduced.

Arrhenoblastoma must be distinguished from the adrenocortical disorders, a much more frequent cause of virilization, which usually cause less virilization and a much more pronounced elevation of the urinary 17-ketosteroids.

Arrhenoblastoma should be removed surgically together with other pelvic reproductive organs unless the patient desires children and the tumor is clinically and histologically benign, in which case unilateral oophorectomy and salpingectomy are sufficient. Hormonal evaluation should be repeated after several months to determine recurrence.

Koss, L.G., & others: Masculinizing tumor of the ovary, apparently with adrenocortical activity: A histologic, ultrastructural, and biochemical study. Cancer 23:1245–1258, 1969.

Radman, H.M., & others: Arrhenoblastoma of the ovary: Presentation of a case report and discussion of the differential diagnosis. Am J Obst Gynec 106:1187–1190, 1970.

Virilizing Lipoid Cell Tumors

Virilizing lipoid cell tumors of the ovary are a group of rare small neoplasms occurring in women over 50 years of age and causing symptoms and signs of virilization, such as hirsutism, masculine hair distribution, odorous perspiration, acne, and clitoral hypertrophy. Obesity is common. Hypertension, polycythemia, and diabetes mellitus are sometimes associated. The tumor may be too small to be palpated. The excretion of 17-oxysteroids and 17-ketosteroids is elevated, and the urinary pregnanetriol level may be high.

These tumors must be differentiated from arrhenoblastoma and primary adrenal abnormalities. About 20% are malignant.

Treatment consists of surgical removal.

Lopez, J.M., Migeon, C.J., & G.E.S. Jones: Hirsutism and evaluation of the dexamethasone suppression and chorionic gonadotropin stimulation test. Am J Obst Gynec 98:749–758, 1967.

Stein-Leventhal Syndrome

Bilateral polycystic ovaries, secondary amenorrhea or oligomenorrhea, and infertility in females 15–30 years of age typify the classical Stein-Leventhal or polycystic ovarian syndrome. Hirsutism and obesity often are associated problems. Defective intermediate metabolism of sex steroids, perhaps familial, is postulated as the cause, and a deficiency of the enzymes 3β-ol-dehydrogenase and 10-hydroxylase in the ovary probably are responsible. Anovulation accounts for the menstrual aberration and infertility. Hirsutism probably is due to overstimulation by intrinsic androgen. The slightly enlarged gonads, often described as "oyster ovaries," are pearly-white, smooth, and firm. A condensation of tissue in the peripheral cortex forming a pseudocapsule with many small, persistent follicle cysts beneath luteinization of the theca interna (but rarely of the ovarian stroma) may be noted.

The history and palpably enlarged ovaries (in about ½ of cases) permit a presumptive diagnosis. Pelvic pneumography, culdoscopy, peritoneoscopy, or culdotomy add confirmatory evidence. Laboratory studies reveal slight elevation of the urinary 17-ketosteroids and plasma testosterone. The urinary estrogen, FSH, and adrenocorticosterone excretion remain normal. An increased output of Δ4-androstenedione, 17-a-hydroxyprogesterone, or dehydroepiandrosterone has been described.

Adrenocortical hyperplasia or tumor is ruled out by the normal hydroxycorticosteroid excretion. A masculinizing neoplasm is unlikely because of bilateral ovarian enlargement.

Initial treatment (still empiric) should be medical. Courses of clomiphene citrate (Clomid®), 50 mg orally daily for 5 days each month, or 50 mg daily for 3–4 months, may induce ovulation and correct the menstrual problem. Larger doses should not be given to avoid macrocystic ovaries, rupture, and hematoperitoneum. If the patient is unresponsive to clomiphene, wedge resection of 1/3–1/2 of each ovary may be beneficial. Unfortunately, the hirsutism and obesity do not respond to the above therapy but can be overcome by epilation and diet.

Allen, W.M., & others: Ovarian resection in the Stein-Leventhal syndrome. Obst Gynec 33:569–573, 1969.

Bamford, S.B., & others: Size variation of the late replicating X chromosome in polycystic ovarian disease. Acta cytol 12:283–289, 1968.

Gyves, M.T.: The significance of peripheral sclerosis in the Stein-Leventhal syndrome. Fertil Steril 21:502–507, 1970.

Lawrence, D.M.: Steroid excretion in the Stein-Leventhal syndrome. J Obstet Gynaec Brit Common 75:922–928, 1968.

Rhodes, P.: The effects of wedge resection of the ovaries in 63 cases of Stein-Leventhal syndrome. J Obstet Gynaec Brit Common 75:1108–1112, 1968.

Shuster, S., & others: Skin collagen and thickness in women with hirsuties. Brit MJ 4:772, 1970.

Tacchi, D., & T. Lind: In defense of the Stein-Leventhal syndrome. J Obstet Gynaec Brit Common 75:322–326, 1968.

Theca Cell Tumors*

Theca cell tumors are rare functional, feminizing ovarian neoplasms derived from ovarian stromal anlagen. They occur most frequently in young girls and postmenopausal women, and vary in size from minute nodules to masses 30 cm in diameter. The ratio of theca cell tumors to granulosa cell tumors is 1:8, and pure theca cell tumors are rare. About 1% become malignant. The tumor is almost invariably unilateral.

Clinical and laboratory findings are identical with those of granulosa cell tumors. As is true of granulosa cell tumors also, theca cell tumors may rarely virilize rather than feminize for obscure reasons.

As the cause of abnormal uterine bleeding, theca cell tumors must be differentiated from idiopathic precocious puberty, granulosa cell tumors, and uterine neoplasms.

Treatment for benign theca cell tumors is unilateral ovariectomy. Malignant tumors require total hysterectomy and bilateral salpingo-oophorectomy.

Granulosa Cell Tumor*

Granulosa cell tumors, the most common ovarian neoplasms of sex gland derivation, represent 3–4% of all ovarian tumors. They are solid tumors which vary in size from microscopic to 9 kg (20 lb), and often produce estrogens. A rare tumor may be virilizing, however. Granulosa cell tumors are most often seen in women 50–70 years of age. Ten percent are bilateral. Both granulosa and theca cells are always found together. About 15–20% are malignant, but metastasis is almost always confined to neighboring genital organs.

*Pure granulosa cell tumors of the ovary are rare; theca cells are almost always present also. It would be more appropriate to speak of granulosa-theca cell tumors or theca-granulosa cell tumors, depending upon which type of cell predominates. The 2 types are dealt with separately here in order to simplify discussion.

The clinical manifestations of granulosa cell tumors are secondary to the production of large amounts of estrogen. In children, this causes early development of pubic hair, hypertrophy of the breasts, and enlargement of the labia, cervix, and uterus (pseudoprecocious puberty). Advanced bone age and early epiphyseal closure (dwarfism) will occur if hormonal stimulation is continued for a long period. In the functional years menometrorrhagia is usually the only symptom. In postmenopausal women refeminization and reinstitution of uterine bleeding occur. Very large tumors may cause symptoms secondary to abdominal distention, displacement of the pelvic structures, or torsion of the pedicle. Ascites often occurs when the neoplasm is malignant. On pelvic examination a mobile, often soft and cystic mass is palpable in the adnexa. Laboratory findings consist of elevated urinary estrogens and a high degree of cornification as demonstrated in the vaginal smear.

Granulosa cell tumors must be differentiated from other causes of postmenopausal bleeding or abnormal menstruation, and other functional tumors (eg, lipoid cell tumors and theca cell tumors of the ovary).

Treatment consists of surgical removal. In patients in the functional or prepuberal years, benign tumors are removed by ovariectomy; in postmenopausal women, total hysterectomy and bilateral salpingo-oophorectomy is indicated.

Dinnerstein, A., & J.A. O'Leary: Granulosa-theca cell tumors. A clinical review of 102 patients. Obst Gynec 31:654–658, 1968.

Simmons, R.L., & J.J. Sciarra: Treatment of late recurrent granulosa cell tumors of the ovary. Surg Gynec Obst 124:65–70, 1967.

Dysgerminoma

Dysgerminoma is a nonfunctioning, potentially malignant ovarian tumor. About 4% of all primary malignant ovarian tumors are dysgerminomas and about 1/3 of dysgerminomas are cancerous. Dysgerminoma is bilateral in 1/3 of cases, and is most common in females 10–30 years of age. It is thought to be of teratoid origin. Although usually small when found (4–7 cm in diameter), dysgerminomas may grow rapidly to fill the entire pelvis. The tumor is often discovered in patients with underdeveloped secondary sex characteristics such as occur in female pseudohermaphrodites. The same tumor found in a male is called a seminoma.

Symptoms are usually due to abdominal enlargement caused by rapid tumor growth and ascites. Severe abdominal distress and acute pain may result if the thin capsule ruptures. Weakly false-positive pregnancy tests have been reported in some cases.

Other nonfunctioning ovarian tumors (eg, teratoma, cystadenoma) must be considered in the differential diagnosis.

Treatment usually consists of surgical removal of the tumor and all pelvic reproductive organs, but if the tumor is small, unilateral, and histologically benign, and if the patient desires to maintain reproductive function, partial oophorectomy may be feasible.

Underdeveloped secondary sex characteristics do not improve after removal of the tumor.

Dehner, L.P., & others: Comparative pathology of ovarian neoplasms. III. Germ cell tumors. J Comp Path 80:299–306, 1970.

Dozois, R.R., & others: Ovarian tumors associated with the Peutz-Jeghers syndrome. Ann Surg 72:233–238, 1970.

Jackson, S.M.: Ovarian dysgerminoma. Brit J Radiol 40:459–462, 1967.

Seligman, S.A.: Dysgerminoma. Postgrad MJ 43:400–405, 1967.

Serment, H., & others: Ovarian hormone tumors of female children. Internat J Gynec Obst 8:409–456, 1970.

Wider, J.A., & others: Dysgerminoma: A clinical review. Obst Gynec 31:560–565, 1968. s,

Secondary Ovarian Cancer

In 10% of cases of fatal malignant disease in women, the ovary is found to be secondarily involved by metastasis or extension of malignancy, usually from the uterus or the ovary. One-third represent metastasis from stomach cancer. The intestine, breast, thyroid, kidney, and adrenals may also be primary foci. One of the most important carcinomas which metastasizes to the ovaries is the Krukenberg tumor, which usually originates in the stomach, involves both ovaries, and presents as a large mucin-producing, buff-colored, solid, lobulated, often kidney-shaped, nonadherent tumor with a heavy capsule. At laparotomy it is important to distinguish these secondary ovarian cancers from primary ovarian tumors clinically and by frozen section.

Frick, H.C., II, & others: Disseminated carcinoma of the ovary treated by L-phenylalanine mustard. Cancer 21:508–513, 1968.

Heald, F.P., Craig, J.M., & P.M.L. Ming: Ovarian tumors in adolescence: Types and presenting features. Clin Pediat 6:401–404, 1967.

Long, R.T.L., & others: Variations in survival among patients with carcinoma of the ovary. Analysis of 253 cases according to histologic type, anatomical stage and method of treatment. Cancer 20:1195–1202, 1967.

URINARY STRESS INCONTINENCE

Involuntary leakage of urine during moments of increased intra-abdominal pressure is one of the most common gynecologic complaints. It may occur as a result of congenital or acquired disorders of the urinary tract, pelvic musculature, or nervous system. Compression of the bladder by the pregnant uterus, pelvic tumors, or ascites may also reduce the ability to retain urine. Leakage usually occurs upon coughing, sneezing, laughing, or sudden lifting of objects. Most women with urinary stress incontinence have suffered childbirth injuries or have developed weakness of the pelvic floor structures following menopause. Relaxation of the supports to the bladder and urethra is noted, often with cystocele, rectocele, and uterine prolapse. Lateral cystourethrograms generally reveal loss of the normal posterior urethrovesical angle.

Urinary stress incontinence must be differentiated from neurogenic bladder and bladder irritability. Paradoxic incontinence or overflow voiding may be due to neurologic disorders or to partial urethrovesical obstruction.

Treatment

A trial of medical treatment is always indicated before surgery is considered. Medical disorders such as myasthenia gravis, diabetes mellitus, extreme obesity, and asthma, which aggravates stress incontinence, should be controlled if possible. Postmenopausal women should receive cyclic estrogen therapy, eg, with diethylstilbestrol, 0.25 mg orally daily for 3 weeks each month. Patients who do not have serious neurologic disorders and have not sustained severe physical injury can be taught to contract the pubococcygeus and sphincter ani muscles repeatedly to reestablish urinary control (Kegel exercises).

Patients who fail to respond to exercises may be candidates for surgery, particularly when cystocele or prolapse of the bladder and uterus is present. A useful surgical prognostic test is to fill the bladder and elevate the anterior vaginal wall lateral to the urethra at the urethrovesical junction with the fingers or an instrument. If loss of urine does not occur with stress, the prognosis is good.

Medical therapy alone is curative in about half of cases. The overall surgical cure rate in patients who require operation is about 85%.

Benson, R.C.: Retropubic vesicourethropexy. Obst Gynec 35:665–669, 1970.

Burch, J.C.: Cooper's ligament urethrovesical suspension for stress incontinence. Am J Obst Gynec 100:764–774, 1968.

Frewen, W.K.: Urge and stress incontinence: Fact and fiction. J Obstet Gynaec Brit Common 77:932–934, 1970.

Habib, H.N.: Non-operative treatment of recurrent stress incontinence in female subjects: Preliminary report of a new device. J Urol 101:854–856, 1969.

Inglesi, J.J., & others: Surgical treatment for urinary stress incontinence in women: Experience in 300 cases with 10-year follow-up. Am J Obst Gynec 108:1072–1076, 1970.

Kohler, F.P., Uhle, C.A.W., & C.C. MacKinney: Long-term evaluation of retropubic urethropexy for stress incontinence in female patients. J Urol 99:50–52, 1968.

Marshall, F.J., & R.M. Segaul: Experience with suprapubic vesicourethral suspension after previous failures to correct stress incontinence in women. J Urol 100:647–648, 1968.

Skjaeraasen, J.S.: Stress incontinence: A follow-up study of operative treatment. Acta obst gynec scandinav 48:575–588, 1969.

Uhle, C.A.W., & others: Urinary stress incontinence in the female patient. J Urol 99:613–616, 1968.

FRIGIDITY

Failure on the woman's part to achieve normal emotional release or orgasm during coitus may be due to temporary situational problems; when the failure is chronic or recurrent, the problem is often evidence of deep-seated, unresolved psychosexual conflicts. Various degrees of relative frigidity occur commonly, but absolute frigidity is rare. In so-called facultative frigidity the patient is responsive to one partner but not to another.

Fear of pregnancy is an important factor in the reduction of sexual responsiveness. Marital disharmony due to ineptitude in sex technics, impotence of the husband (including premature ejaculation), or dyspareunia may be important factors. Vaginismus and, in extreme cases, vaginal hypesthesia may occur.

Frigidity may develop as a result of environmental difficulties such as living in a crowded household or with in-laws. Overwork, discouragement, or unhappiness may provoke or aggravate the problem.

Frigidity may be the result of arrested or distorted emotional development. Some patients exhibit homosexual tendencies, infantile fixations, asceticism, or hostility toward men. Social or religious taboos or prejudices may underlie the problem. Critical situations involving rape, perversion, venereal infection, or incest are occasionally described. Nymphomania is a type of frigidity characterized by a constant quest for sexual gratification, always without success.

Out of reluctance to admit that the problem exists, few women consult even the gynecologist with a complaint of frigidity. Most frigid women seeking medical advice describe other symptoms (often dyspareunia) as a subterfuge.

In most instances, frigidity is a far more intricate problem than the rather superficial causes often recorded would indicate. The background of the patient's sexual difficulty must be explored cautiously but carefully. Simple discussion may often be useful in correcting misconceptions and allaying fears, and the physician can sometimes give advice about sex practices that will be of value to both partners. Environmental factors should be manipulated favorably whenever possible. Contraceptive advice should be given if fear of pregnancy is a problem. If prompt improvement does not occur, however, an attempt should be made to refer the patient for psychiatric care.

Androgens and aphrodisiac drugs are absolutely worthless in the treatment of frigidity and may be harmful.

The prognosis in long-standing, marked frigidity is extremely poor.

Huffer, V., & others: Oral contraceptives: Depression and frigidity. J Nerv Ment Dis 15:35–41, 1970.

Kant, F.: *Frigidity*. Thomas, 1969.

Martin, M.J.: Frigidity, impotence and the family. Psychosom Med 9:225–228, 1968.

DYSPAREUNIA

Dyspareunia (painful coitus) may be functional or organic, or may be due to a combination of both causes. Either type may occur early (primary) or late (secondary) in marriage. The location of discomfort may be external (at the introitus) or internal (deep within the genital canal or beyond), and some women describe both types of pain.

External dyspareunia may be due to occlusive or rigid hymen, vaginal contracture due to any cause, or traumatic or inflammatory disorders of the vulva, vagina, urethra, or anus.

Organic causes of internal dyspareunia include hourglass contracture of the vagina, septate vagina, severe cervicitis or retroposition of the uterus, prolapse or neoplastic disease of the uterus, tubo-ovarian disease, and pelvic endometriosis.

Pelvic examination often reveals marked contraction of the perineal and levator musculature, with adduction of the thighs. Genital hypoplasia and other congenital disorders, urethral caruncle, scarring or contracture of the vagina, vulvovaginitis, kraurosis vulvae, and rectal or bladder abnormalities may be present.

Treatment

A. Specific Measures: Functional dyspareunia can only be treated by counseling and psychotherapy. Both partners should be interviewed. The treatment of organic dyspareunia depends upon the underlying cause.

B. General Measures: Mild sedation, eg, phenobarbital, 15 mg orally 3 times daily, or prochlorperazine (Compazine®), 15 mg orally daily, is of value for the relief of extreme emotional tension.

C. Local Measures: For functional dyspareunia, hymeneal-vaginal dilatations with a conical (Kelly) dilator or test tubes of graduated sizes may give relief. Anesthetic ointment applied to the introitus gives some relief but is of no permanent value. Organic dyspareunia due to vaginal dryness may be treated with a water-soluble lubricant. Estrogen therapy is indicated for senile vulvovaginitis.

D. Surgical Measures: Hymenectomy, perineotomy, and similar plastic procedures should be performed only on clear indications. Significant vaginal obstructive lesions should be corrected. Treat chronic symptomatic cervicitis by cauterization or shallow conization.

Prognosis

Few patients with functional dyspareunia are quickly and easily cured. Organic dyspareunia subsides promptly after elimination of the underlying cause of pain.

Ellison, C.: Psychosomatic factors in the unconsummated marriage. J Psychosom Res 12:61–65, 1968.

Graber, E.A.: Newlywed apareunia. Obst Gynec 33:418–421, 1969.

Kinch, R.A.H.: Painful coitus. Med Aspects Human Sexuality 1:6–12, Oct. 1967.

PSYCHOGENIC PELVIC PAIN

Functional pelvic pain is variously reported to occur in 5–25% of gynecologic patients. The diagnosis is established by ruling out organic causes and, wherever possible, by eliciting a consonant history. A fairly characteristic "profile" of the typical woman with psychogenic pain is as follows: she is egotistical and vain, demanding and self-indulgent, shallow, dramatic, emotionally labile and inconsistent, and coquettish but relatively frigid.

Treatment

Any woman who complains of pelvic pain must have a thorough diagnostic evaluation, in a hospital if necessary. Reassurance and symptomatic therapy are always indicated, and may be all that the physician can provide. Since the basic disorder is a psychic one, the physician must be prepared to spend a great deal of time with these women. Do not give narcotics and do not operate except upon definite surgical indications. Be wary of prescribing sedatives as these patients may commit suicide when depressed.

Prognosis

Since these women often refuse therapy, withdraw from a treatment program soon after it is well under way, and change physicians frequently, their medical future is bleak. In general, they are unwilling to abandon invalidism as a way of life.

TABLE 12–4. Differential diagnosis of organic and psychogenic pain.

	Organic Pain	Psychogenic Pain
Type	Sharp, cramping, intermittent.	Dull, continuous.
Time of onset	Any time. May awaken patient.	Usually begins well after waking, when social obligations are pressing.
Radiation	Follows definite neural pathways.	Bizarre pattern or does not radiate.
Localization	Localizes with typical point tenderness.	Variable, shifting, generalized.
Progress	Soon becomes either better or worse.	Remains the same for weeks, months, years.
Provocation	Often reproduced or augmented by manipulation, not by mood.	Not triggered or accentuated by examination but by interpersonal relationships.

Of those patients who can be persuaded to submit to psychiatric care, over ½ will show marked improvement and many will be cured. Reassurance and symptomatic therapy give temporary improvement in about ¾ of cases.

Osofsky, H.J., & S. Fisher: Pelvic congestion. Some further considerations. Obst Gynec 31:406–410, 1968.

GYNECOLOGIC BACKACHE

Gynecologic backache is usually due to a well-defined pelvic disorder. It is most often seen during the childbearing years, and is more common among women who have had several children. Multiple causes are the rule (gynecologic combined with orthopedic, urologic, or neurologic disease). Gynecologic causes include the following: (1) Traction or pulsion on the peritoneum, the supportive structures of the generative organs, or the pelvic floor (tumors, ascites, uterine prolapse). (2) Inflammation of the pelvic contents: bacterial infection (peritonitis, salpingitis) or chemical irritation (due to iodides used in salpingography, fluid from a ruptured dermoid cyst). (3) Invasion of pelvic tissues or bone by tumor or endometriosis. (4) Obstruction of the genital tract (cervical stenosis). (5) Torsion or constriction of pelvic viscera (ovary enmeshed in adhesions, twisted ovarian cyst). (6) Congestion of internal genitalia (turgescence of the retroposed uterus, backache during menstruation). (7) Psychologic tension (anxiety, apprehension). (8) Masters-Allen syndrome (avulsion of uterus from parauterine supports), also called the "universal joint syndrome."

Clinical Findings

A. Symptoms and Signs: Constant lumbosacral or sacral backache is often due to salpingitis, pelvic abscess, or a twisted ovarian cyst. Back pain due to endometriosis of the cul-de-sac is referred to the coccygeal region or rectum. Ovarian, renal, and ureteral backache commonly radiates down the back into the buttocks or along the distribution of the sciatic nerves.

The major symptoms and signs of the underlying pelvic disease are almost always present.

B. Laboratory Findings: Infection will be reflected in the routine blood studies. Cytologic study of vaginal exudate may reveal neoplastic cells or bacteria.

C. X-Ray Findings: Anteroposterior and lateral films of the spine often disclose a postural, degenerative, neoplastic, or other orthopedic cause of backache. Myelograms may be required to demonstrate a herniated intervertebral disk.

Treatment

Successful treatment of the underlying disease is the only curative procedure. Supportive measures include the following: (1) Bed rest on a firm mattress, permitting the patient to seek the most comfortable position. (2) Local heat as necessary. (3) Warm water douches twice daily. (4) Aspirin or aspirin with codeine as needed. (5) Sedatives, eg, phenobarbital, 15 mg 3 times daily to reduce emotional tension.

Prognosis

Gynecologic backache almost always subsides with treatment of the underlying pelvic disorder.

INFERTILITY

A couple is said to be infertile (1) if pregnancy does not result after 1 year of normal marital relations without contraceptives; (2) if the woman conceives but aborts repeatedly; or (3) if the woman bears one child but aborts repeatedly or fails to conceive thereafter. About 10% of marriages are infertile. Female infertility may be due to nutritional deficiencies, hormonal imbalance, developmental anomalies of the reproductive organs, infections, or tumors. Male infertility is usually due to sperm deficiencies (low sperm count, morphologic abnormalities, or impaired motility). The male partner is accountable for about 40% of cases of infertility.

Diagnostic Survey

Successful treatment of infertility is possible only if an early and accurate diagnosis can be established. Over a period of at least 3 months, with 4 office visits for the wife and 2–3 for the husband, both partners usually can be evaluated and the cause of infertility determined.

A. First Visit: (Wife and husband.) In a joint interview, the physician explains the problem of infertility and its causes to the husband and wife. Separate private consultations are then conducted, allowing appraisal of marital adjustments without embarrassment or criticism. Pertinent details (eg, venereal disease or prior illegitimate pregnancies) must be obtained concerning marital, premarital, and extramarital sexual activities. A complete medical, surgical, and obstetrical history must be taken. The gynecologic history should include queries regarding the menstrual pattern (eg, pain, metrorrhagia, and leukorrhea) and the type of menstrual protection worn, either internal or external. The present history includes marital adjustment, difficulties, use of contraceptives and types, douches, libido, sex technics, orgasm, frequency and success of coitus, and correlation of intercourse with ovulation. Family history includes familial traits, liabilities, illnesses, repeated abortions, and abnormal children.

The husband is instructed to bring a complete ejaculate for spermatozoal analysis at the next visit. Sexual abstinence for at least 4 days before the semen is obtained is emphasized. Semen may be collected either by coitus or masturbation. A clean, dry, wide-mouthed bottle for collection is preferred, but a vaginal (Doyle) spoon can be used. Condoms should not be employed. The stoppered bottle should be transported to the laboratory in a paper bag held away from the body. Chilling of the bottle should also be avoided.

Semen should be examined (by the physician himself) within 1–2 hours after collection.

B. Second Visit: (Wife and husband; 2–4 weeks after first visit.) The woman receives a complete physical and pelvic examination. Do not overlook irritations, discharges, tenderness, maldevelopments, and masses. The husband's general physical examination, with emphasis on the genital and rectal examination, is done next. Penile, urethral, testicular, epididymal, and prostatic abnormalities are sought. The results of the spermatozoal analysis are explained to the couple without undue optimism or pessimism. Laboratory studies for both husband and wife include urinalysis, complete blood count (including hematocrit determination), and STS. Thyroid function should be determined.

C. Third Visit: (Wife; 1 month after second visit. The husband is not required to return for a third visit if his physical examination and initial semen analysis are normal. Spermatozoal analysis is repeated on the third visit if the previous study was abnormal.)

1. Tubal insufflation (Rubin test)—Uterotubal insufflation in infertile patients has both diagnostic and therapeutic value. It is best done during the early preovulatory period. The test is a safe office procedure in properly selected patients if CO_2 is employed and if the pressure is kept below 200 mm Hg. Tubal insufflation at or about the time of ovulation is most likely to be revealing and successful. Pneumoperitoneum (and shoulder pain) is proof of tubal patency. Auscultation over the lower abdomen during insufflation may disclose the whistle of gas passing through one tubal ostium or the other. It is most helpful to secure a kymographic record of insufflation; tubal peristalsis, patency, leakage in the system, tubal spasm, partial obstruction, or release of tubal obstruction may be revealed in this way.

2. Hysterosalpingography is preferred by many but may not be required if gas insufflation is unimpeded.

D. Fourth Visit: (Wife; 1 month following the third visit.) The patient returns just prior to ovulation within 6 hours after coitus. The cervical mucus should be thin, clear, and alkaline. Spinnbarkeit or elasticity is an expression of the viscosity of mucus. When a drop of cervical fluid is placed between 2 fingers, for example, the mucus will stretch into a thin strand when the fingers are separated slowly. The mucus is more viscid before and after ovulation. At the time of ovulation, the mucus can often be stretched 10 cm or more. Infection and bleeding also reduce spinnbarkeit. A good spinnbarkeit (stretching to a fine thread 4 cm or more in length) is desirable. A small drop of cervical mucus should be obtained for the fern test and the Sims-Huhner test. The presence or absence of active sperms is noted. The presence in the cervical mucus of 10–15 active sperms per high power field constitutes a satisfactory Sims-Huhner test. The fern test should show clear arborizations: frond-like crystal patterns in the dried mucus. If no motile spermatozoa are found, the Sims-Huhner test should be repeated (assuming that active spermatozoa were present in the semen analysis).

E. Later Tests: (As indicated.) Testicular biopsy is indicated if azoospermia or oligospermia is present. A vaginal smear and an endometrial biopsy may be required to determine if ovulation is occurring. This is best taken from the side wall in the fundus to avoid a pregnancy which usually implants high in the uterus anteriorly or posteriorly. If tests of tubal patency were unsatisfactory, hysterosalpingography is done. Peritoneoscopy or culdoscopy may be required if tubal adhesions or endometriosis are suspected. Laparotomy will be necessary for salpingostomy, lysis of adhesions, and removal of ovarian abnormalities. Sterility on the basis of disorders of the sex chromosomes should be ruled out by examination for Barr bodies and sex chromatin analysis of desquamated buccal or vaginal cells.

Cystoscopy and catheterization of ejaculatory duct orifices, using a fluid x-ray contrast medium, may be required to demonstrate duct stenosis. Vasography by direct injection of the vas near its origin may demonstrate an occlusion. Needle aspiration of the upper pole of the epididymis (globus major) suggests inflammatory closure of the tract if no spermatozoa are recovered.

Treatment

Treatment in all cases depends upon correction of the underlying disorder or disorders suspected of causing infertility.

A. Infertility in the Female:

1. Medical measures—Fertility may be restored by proper treatment in many patients with endocrine imbalance, particularly those with hypo- or hyperthyroidism. The alleviation of cervicitis is of value in the return of fertility.

2. Surgical measures—Surgical correction of congenital or acquired abnormalities (including tumors) of the lower genital tract or uterus may frequently renew fertility. Surgical excision of ovarian tumors or ovarian foci of endometriosis frequently restores fertility. Surgical relief of tubal obstruction due to salpingitis will reestablish fertility in fewer than 20% of cases. In special instances of cornual or fimbrial block, the prognosis after surgery is much better.

3. Induction of ovulation—An attempt should be made to induce ovulation in cases of infertility due to anovulation which has persisted longer than 6 months (includes brief secondary amenorrhea, oligomenorrhea), galactorrhea, recurrent dysfunctional uterine bleeding, and polycystic ovarian disease (Stein-Leventhal syndrome).

a. Clomiphene citrate (Clomid®)—The mechanism of action of this drug is not clearly understood.

Give 50 mg orally daily for 5 days. If ovulation does not occur, increase the dosage to 100 mg orally daily for 5 days. If ovulation still does not occur, repeat the course of 100 mg daily for 5 days and add chorionic gonadotropin, 2000 units IM daily.

Ovulation is likely to occur in women with polycystic ovarian disease and those who are amenorrheic after having used oral contraceptive agents. In other types of patients, the results are unpredictable. Multiple pregnancies occur with a frequency of 1:16; abortion occurs in 20—25% of pregnancies. The long-range effectiveness of this treatment is poor.

b. Corticosteroids (glucocorticoids)—In patients with hyperadrenocorticism (hyperplasia) and polycystic ovarian disease, give prednisone (minimal sodium retention), 7.5—15 mg orally in 3—4 divided doses daily (or equivalent). Treatment must be continued indefinitely for women with adrenal hyperplasia; for others, a therapeutic trial of 6—8 months is indicated.

About 30% of patients with polycystic ovarian disease will ovulate as a result of corticosteroid therapy. Discontinue treatment if ovulation does not occur after 6—8 months. Polycystic ovarian disease patients are generally improved for months after cessation of therapy.

c. Ovarian wedge resection—Wedge resection is indicated when medical measures are not effective.

d. Human menopausal gonadotropins (HMG) (Pergonal®)—HMG is indicated in cases of hypogonadotropism and most other types of anovulation (exclusive of ovarian failure) after previous treatment failure. Begin with 75 IU of FSH plus 75 IU of LH (1 ampule) IM daily for 9—12 days. Determine 24-hour urinary estrogen. If < 100 μg, give 10,000 IU chorionic gonadotropin (HCG) IM when a good estrogen effect (clear, thin cervical mucus) indicates advanced follicle development. Arrange daily coitus following the last injection of HMG for 3 days. If pregnancy does not occur, repeat the cycle of treatment twice more. If pregnancy still does not result, increase the dosage to 2 ampules of HMG daily for 9—12 days plus HCG (if not contraindicated by elevated estrogen). The cost is considerable.

Ovulation is likely to occur, and multiple pregnancies (mostly twins) occur in 20% of pregnancies.

B. Infertility in the Male: Surgical correction of congenital or acquired abnormalities of the penis and urethra may permit successful vaginal penetration and normal insemination. Testicular hypofunction secondary to hypothyroidism or diabetes mellitus is often corrected by appropriate treatment. Surgical correction of varicocele and hydrocele may restore fertility.

Mumps orchitis requires prompt testicular decompression by surgical excision of the tunica albuginea to preserve fertility.

Artificial insemination using the husband's specimen (AIH), as in oligospermia, has been most disappointing. Artificial insemination with a donor's specimen (AID) is very successful—assuming normal female function and acceptability of AID by the couple.

Prognosis

The prognosis for conception and normal pregnancy is good if minor (even multiple) disorders can be identified and treated early; poor if the causes of infertility are severe, untreatable, or of prolonged duration.

No treatment is effective for infertility due to marked uterine hypoplasia. Congenital deficiency or absence of the ovaries is a hopeless sterility problem. Perioophoritis defies medical and surgical treatment. Agenesis or dysgenesis of the testes resists all treatment. Infertility due to prostatitis, seminal vesiculitis, and obstruction in the sperm conduit system rarely responds to treatment.

If treatment is not successful within 1 year, the physician must consider whether he should recommend adoption.

Davidson, H.A.: The post-coital test. Practitioner 201:467–473, 1968.

Donovan, J.C., & C.D. McGee: The Rubin test: Therapeutic aspects. Rocky Mountain MJ 65:65–71, 1968.

Hill, A.M.: Experiences with artificial insemination. Australian New Zealand J Obstet Gynaec 10:112–114, 1970.

Isojima, S., & others: Immunologic analysis of sperm-immobilizing factor found in sera of women with unexplained sterility. Am J Obst Gynec 101:677–683, 1968.

Jones, G.S.: Induction of ovulation. Ann Rev Med 19:351–372, 1968.

Marshall, J.R.: Ovulation induction. Obst Gynec 35:963–970, 1970.

Moore-White, M.: Pituitary irradiation therapy in infertility. Internat J Fertil 14:309–312, 1969.

Peterson, E.P., & S.J. Behrman: Laparoscopy of the infertile patient. Obst Gynec 36:363–367, 1970.

Shettles, L.B.: Cervix factor. J Reprod Med 3:147–150, 1969.

Whitelaw, J.M., & others: Hysterosalpingography and insufflation: A 35-year clinical study. J Reprod Med 4:56–65, 1970.

CONTRACEPTION

Contraception is the voluntary prevention of pregnancy either for medical or personal reasons. In the USA, the prescription, demonstration, and sale of contraceptives is legal in all states of the USA. All faiths accept the principle of family planning; the Roman Catholic Church alone requires that this be accomplished by total or periodic abstinence.

The "perfect" contraceptive should be simple, acceptable, effective, safe, economical, and reversible. No contraceptive method yet devised satisfies all of these criteria. The following is a selection based upon efficacy and general patient acceptance:

"Rhythm" Method

The "rhythm" method, using the basal body temperature to identify the period of ovulation ("unsafe period"), requires the cooperation of both parties and is moderately or highly effective depending upon the care with which it is used and the regularity of the woman's menstrual cycle. It is useless postpartum.

A. Method of Ogino: After the length of the menstrual cycle has been observed for at least 8 months (preferably for 1 year), the following calculations are made: (1) The first fertile day is determined by subtracting 18 days from the shortest cycle. (2) The last fertile day is determined by subtracting 11 days from the longest cycle. For example, if the observed cycles run from 24 to 28 days, the fertile period would extend from the 6th day of the cycle (24 minus 18) through the 17th day (28 minus 11). It is essential to base the calculations upon a written record of the woman's menstrual periods—not on her memory or testimony alone. Other variations of this method are also used.

B. Basal Body Temperature Method: A great deal of effort and interest are required on the part of the patient to make sure that a truly basal temperature chart is being recorded. (The temperature must be taken immediately upon awakening, before any activity whatever.) A drop in temperature usually occurs 1–1½ days before ovulation, and a rise of about 0.7° F occurs 1–2 days after ovulation. The high temperature continues throughout the remainder of the cycle. The third day after the rise marks the end of the fertile period.

1. HORMONAL SUPPRESSION OF OVULATION
(See Table 18–23.)

Inhibition of ovulation by means of estrogens or progestogens, alone or in combination, has been possible for many years, but only recently has the availability of potent synthetic progestational agents (mainly 19-nortestosterone and 17-hydroxyprogesterone compounds, now called "gestagens") made effective oral contraception generally practical and widely acceptable.

Methods of Suppression

A. Single Hormone Therapy: Moderate to large daily doses of estrogen for 3 weeks per month will prevent ovulation because the estrogen suppresses LTH, LH, and FSH. However, unpleasant side-effects, particularly nausea and menometrorrhagia, invariably develop. For this reason, this hormone alone is impractical for long-term use.

Combined daily small dosage gestagens are now under clinical investigation. Although ovulation usually continues with this "minipill" therapy, pregnancy does not occur mainly because the cervical mucus becomes hostile to sperm penetration. This promising new approach may soon be available to more patients.

B. Combined Hormone Therapy:

1. **The "classic pill"** is a synthetic progestin or gestagen plus Enovid®, Ortho-Novum®, etc. One tablet per day is prescribed, beginning on the 5th day from the start of the period and continuing for 20 days. Bleeding usually begins 1–4 days after cessation of the medication. The patient then resumes the same dosage on the 5th day of the cycle.

This type of hormonal contraception is effective because it (1) interferes with pituitary function by blocking LH release, (2) alters tubal motility to discourage fertilization, (3) modifies endometrial maturation, and (4) renders cervical mucus impervious to sperm migration.

2. The "sequential pill" (Oracon®) contains a higher daily dosage of estrogen than the "classic pill" alone. The estrogen is given alone for 15 days, and estrogen and gestagen are given each day for the last 5 days. The dosage program is similar to that outlined for (1) above. Estrogen inhibits ovulation, and progestogen is added at the end of the cycle to produce a more physiologic endometrium, normalize menstruation, and thicken the cervical mucus, adding to the contraceptive effect of the medication.

The sequential pill inhibits ovulation by suppressing release of FSH. It probably also affects the physiology of the tubes, endometrium, and cervix.

Caution: Maximal protection against pregnancy with combined therapy may not be assured until the second cycle because ovulation occasionally occurs early during the first month of medication.

In general, a dose of ≤ 50 µg of estrogen per pill is preferred as a means of avoiding serious side-effects.

Effects of Oral Contraceptives (Table 12–5.)

In general, most patients "feel better" on this medication, although libido remains about the same. Most women with dysmenorrhea and many with premenstrual tension are relieved by oral contraception. A few patients with premenstrual tension become worse when they are given this drug.

Some undesirable side-effects relating to dosage and tolerance develop in at least 25% of patients on oral contraceptives. Approximately 20% of women placed on this routine discontinue it, largely because of one or more of the following problems: Nausea (rarely emesis) affects 10–15% of all patients, but is most marked during the first few cycles and usually subsides thereafter. Headache and mastalgia occur initially in 3–5% of patients, but are less troublesome after 2–3 months of therapy. Initial weight gain (edema) of 2–5 lb or more is reported by about 50% of women. This weight is lost during menstruation but recurs each month despite fair control by diet and diuretics. Breakthrough bleeding develops in 5–8% of patients. This complication usually is controlled by the administration of an extra ½ or 1 tablet daily for the remainder of that cycle only. The next month, the patient may resume a 1 tablet per day regimen.

Some patients describe depression, abdominal cramps, lethargy, chloasma, or acne.

A. Effect on Menstrual Cycle: Oral contraceptive therapy helps to regulate and maintain normal menstrual bleeding. Many patients develop scanty periods, and a few cease to menstruate. However, an occasional patient will experience breakthrough bleeding. *Caution:* Cancer may cause abnormal uterine bleeding also, and vaginal cytology alone may not detect cancer. Women over 35 years of age who experience repeated breakthrough bleeding should cease taking oral contra-

---

TABLE 12–5. Hormone-related side-effects of oral contraceptives.*

Common side-effects	
Estrogen excess	**Estrogen deficiency**
Gastric disturbances	Nervousness, irritability
Fluid retention	Early and midcycle bleeding
Mucorrhea	Decreased menstrual flow
Premenstrual tension	
Increased size of fibroids	
Progestogen excess	**Progestogen deficiency**
Depression, lassitude, reduced libido	Delayed onset of menses
Decreased menstrual flow	Late breakthrough spotting and bleeding
Acne, hirsutism	Irregular cycles
Increased appetite; anabolic weight gain	Hypermenorrhea
Candidal vaginitis	
Melasma	
Mastodynia; leg cramps	
Uncommon side-effects	
Alopecia	Galactorrhea
Gingivitis (epulis)	Coronary or hypertensive disease
Visual disturbances	Jaundice (hypercholestasis)
Cerebral arterial insufficiency (stroke, severe headache)	Ureteral dilatation
	Venous thromboembolism
Cystic mastitis; fibroadenoma	Rheumatic symptomatology

*After R.M. Nelson.

ceptive therapy and submit to multiple cervical biopsy or conization and dilatation and curettage to rule out malignancy.

B. Thromboembolic Disorders: There may be a slight increase in the incidence of thromboembolic disorders in women over 35 who are on oral contraceptives. The mechanism of this process is uncertain, but prethrombotic plasma changes, including an increase in prothrombin, proconvertin, fibrinogen, and Stuart factor levels, have been blamed. The incidence of lipid anomalies of genotypic origin (ie, familial hyperlipidemia) is about 3% of the general population. It is possible that in such women anovulatory steroids may facilitate the occurrence of intravascular coagulation due to interference by anomalous lipids. Women with a history of varices or thrombophlebitis—especially those over 35 years of age—should use another contraceptive method.

C. Liver Dysfunction: Increase in serum transaminase levels and interference with bile secretion by hepatic cells—even cholestatic jaundice—are reported occasionally. Oral contraception should not be used by women with liver disorders or cholelithiasis.

D. Carbohydrate Intolerance: Reduced glucose tolerance may develop after several months of medication. Women with diabetes mellitus on oral contraceptives require especially close supervision of their metabolism.

E. Lactation: The amount of milk produced is decreased in about 1/3 of patients who are given oral contraceptives in the late puerperium. A rare nonpregnant woman may develop slight lactation when on oral contraceptives for unexplained reasons.

F. Effect on Endocrine System: (See also Table 12–5.) Even with long-term therapy, humans have not been found to be adversely affected by oral contraceptive drugs. Nevertheless, it is best to discontinue oral contraceptive therapy every year for approximately 2 months and to check pituitary, thyroid, and adrenal performance if normal function does not resume.

High-dosage or continuous administration of progestin-estrogen combinations finally results in gonadotropin repression to undetectable levels. Low-dosage combined oral contraceptives prevent the LH and FSH midcycle peaks. Sequential anovulants depress FSH.

G. Subsequent Fertility: Approximately ¾ of women desirous of pregnancy will conceive within 2 months following discontinuation of oral contraceptive therapy. This indicates prompt resumption of endocrine function, even after prolonged use of the pill. Unfortunately, a few develop amenorrhea for unexplained reasons.

H. Miscellaneous Effects: Oral contraceptives may cause plasma triglyceride levels to rise almost as high as those of men of comparable age. This has suggested that anovulatory drugs may have an atherosclerosis potential.

Increased plasma triglyceride levels in normal young women taking oral contraceptives may result from a decrease in postheparin lipolytic activity and impaired triglyceride removal. Concomitant elevation of serum insulin suggests the stimulation of endogenous hepatic triglyceride synthesis and its secretion into the plasma.

Oncology and "The Pill"

There is no convincing evidence that oral contraceptives are cancerogenic. Patients who have had an estrogen-dependent breast tumor or endometrial cancer should not be given an oral estrogen-containing contraceptive. On the other hand, progestogens encourage endometrial slough at the time of the period and may actually have an anti-cancer effect. Patients with uterine myomas should not receive continued gestagen-estrogen medications because these tumors often enlarge considerably after 2–3 months.

Contraceptive Effectiveness

Oral contraceptives are by far the most effective method of prevention of pregnancy now in use. (An occasional woman will forget to take one or more tablets.) The effectiveness of the various types of oral contraception has been reported to be 0.2–1.5 pregnancies per 100 woman years.

Selection of the Proper Oral Contraceptive

The initial choice of oral contraceptives should be based on (1) a thorough knowledge of the differences in composition of the various pills, (2) an estimate of the woman's natural hormone status and requirements, and (3) a consideration of her age and desire for future pregnancies.

For younger patients (16–20 years of age), endocrine maturity may lag behind social sophistication. These girls often have anovulatory, irregular menses. In young women and in older women (over 40 years of age) who do not have estrogen sensitivity, sequential regimens with an estrogen dominance are best. The patient should be asked about nausea and vomiting in previous pregnancies, fluid retention, weight gain, acne, etc. Keep the dosage low in both patient groups to avoid oversuppression of the pituitary in the young and thromboembolism in older women. Sequentials can be prescribed for most patients because intermenstrual spotting is not often associated with their use. Moreover, the duration of flow can be reduced by sequentials with 6 rather than 5 days of progestogen. Nevertheless, if oligomenorrhea occurs in the young patient, oral contraception is contraindicated.

If the patient has estrogen sensitivity, give a combination pill; the length of the cycle will determine the potency of the progestogen. A good index of the woman's progestogen requirement is the amount and duration of the menstrual flow. When bleeding is heavy and long, potent progestins are needed and a larger dose combination pill (eg, Norlestrin®, 2.5 mg; Norinyl®, 2 mg) is useful. This avoids breakthrough bleeding. Patients with a short flow do best with a weaker progestogen, estrogen dominant product. Intermediate progestogen products are Norlestrin®, 1 mg; Ovulen®; Ortho-Novum®, 1 mg; and Enovid®.

Side-effects are not inevitable but are due to too much or not enough estrogen or progestogen. Selection of the proper oral contraceptive is possible in most cases without impractical biochemical or cytologic studies. If the first choice is poor and the patient has unpleasant side-effects, select a better pill in an attempt to avoid the problems described.

If the patient has progestogen sensitivity, give a sequential with low progestogen content (eg, Oracon®).

The "minipill" (norethindrone acetate, 0.2 mg daily) can be given to most women with reasonably regular, average periods because side-effects, save for intermenstrual spotting, are virtually absent.

Contraindications to Oral Contraceptives
(After Stephens)

Oral contraceptives are contraindicated in the presence of (or if the patient has a past history of) any of the following:

(1) Strong family history of stroke
(2) Severe migraine
(3) Cerebral arterial insufficiency
(4) Cardiovascular disease
(5) Liver disease
(6) Severe diabetes mellitus
(7) Nephritis
(8) Genital or breast cancer
(9) Thrombophlebitis or thromboembolism
(10) Large uterine myomas

Arronet, G.H., & others: A study on ovulation inhibition by quinestrol. One dose a month. Internat J Fertil 14:295–299, 1969.

Connell, E.B.: A comparative study of oral contraceptives. J Reprod Med 5:38–41, 1970.

Depression as a side effect of oral contraceptives. Editorial. MJ Australia 56:884, 1969.

Dickey, R.P., & C.H. Dorr, II: Oral contraceptives: Selection of the proper pill. Obst Gynec 33:273–287, 1969.

Gambrell, R.D., Jr.: Immediate postpartum oral contraception. Obst Gynec 36:101–106, 1970.

Goldzieher, J.W.: An assessment of the hazards and metabolic alterations attributed to oral contraceptives. Contraception 1:409–445, 1970.

Haller, J.: A review of the long-term effects of hormonal contraceptives. Contraception 1:233–251, 1970.

Schoenberg, B.S., & others: Strokes in women of childbearing age: A population study. Neurology 20:181–189, 1970.

Scutchfield, F.D., & W.N. Long: Parenteral medroxyprogesterone as a contraceptive agent. Pub Health Rep 84:1059–1062, 1969.

Spellacy, W.N., & S.A. Birk: The development of elevated blood pressure while using oral contraceptives: A preliminary report of a prospective study. Fertil Steril 21:301–306, 1970.

Taber, B.L.: Oral contraceptives and future fertility. Internat J Fertil 13:427–430, 1968.

2. CERVICAL CAP

The cervical cap used alone is a simple, easy, and effective method, though fitting is required. The cap may not be satisfactory with a large cystocele, rectocele, or descensus uteri. The initial cost is moderate.

3. DIAPHRAGM & JELLY

The cervical diaphragm used in combination with spermatocidal vaginal jelly or cream is generally acceptable and quite effective. The cost of the fitting and materials is not insignificant to some couples.

4. FOAM

Spermatocidal foam (Delfen®, Emko®) transferred from an aerosol container to the vagina by an applicator is a good, esthetic contraceptive of moderate cost.

5. CONDOM

The male sheath of rubber or animal membrane affords good protection against pregnancy—equivalent to that of a diaphragm and spermatocidal jelly; it is also a venereal disease prophylactic. The disadvantages are expense, dulling of sensation, and sperm loss due to tearing, slipping, or leakage with detumescence of the penis.

INTRAUTERINE CONTRACEPTIVE DEVICE (IUCD)

Plastic or metal coils, spirals, or rings, when retained in the uterus for the prevention of pregnancy, are as effective as other methods excepting hormone suppression of ovulation. Fertilization may occur, but nidation is prevented because tubal mobility is so increased by IUCD that the endometrium is unprepared for implantation. The IUCD is particularly useful and popular among couples in the lower socioeconomic classes because it offers semipermanent, reversible protection at minimal cost and no personal effort or reference to the calendar. The most successful IUCD's are the Lippes loop and the double coil (Saf-T-Coil®). Insertion 6 weeks postpartum or immediately after a menstrual period is recommended; removal can be accomplished at any time. Difficulty in insertion and removal of the IUCD (especially in nulliparas), initial cramping, and extrusion of the IUCD (particularly within the first 2–3 months) are disadvantages.

Burnhill, M.S., & C.H. Birnberg: Improving the results obtained with current intrauterine contraceptive devices. Fertil Steril 20:232–240, 1969.

Davis, H.J., & J. Lesinski: Mechanism of action of intrauterine contraceptives in women. Obst Gynec 36:350–358, 1970.

Hingorani, V., & others: Lochia and menstrual patterns in women with postpartum IUCD insertions. Am J Obst Gynec 108:989–991, 1970.

Jennings, P.X.: Contraception using the Lippes loop. New Zealand MJ 69:27–31, 1969.

Kaufman, S.A., & others: Evaluation of the Lippes loop in planned parenthood. New York J Med 70:2103–2107, 1970.

Lehfeld, H., & others: Ovarian pregnancy and the intrauterine device. Am J Obst Gynec 108:1005–1009, 1970.

Lewit, S.: Outcome of pregnancy with intrauterine devices. Contraception 2:47–57, 1970.

Mukherjee, K., & S. Banerjee: Bleeding as a complication of the intrauterine contraceptive device and its management. J Indian MA 52:423–426, 1969.

COMMON SURGICAL PROCEDURES IN OBSTETRICS & GYNECOLOGY

SURGICAL DILATATION & CURETTAGE (D & C)

Curettage is the instrumental exploration of the cervical canal and endometrial cavity and the removal of tissue for diagnostic and therapeutic purposes. Curettage requires the use of dilators for the introduction of instruments beyond the internal os.

Surgical curettage is the most frequently performed of all gynecologic operations. In contrast to aspiration curettage, surgical curettage requires general anesthesia. The relaxation that occurs with anesthesia provides an excellent opportunity for examination and yields far more information and tissue than suction collection or biopsy of the endometrial cavity.

Curettage should not be done if there is any reason to suspect that an intrauterine pregnancy is present nor in the absence of definite indications. Hysterosalpingography can sometimes give the desired information. In septic shock due to late abortion, control of shock and hysterectomy without D & C may be lifesaving.

Indications for Surgical Dilatation & Curettage
  A. Childhood:
    1. Diagnostic indications—Suspected genital tract anomalies (hypoplastic uterus, bicornuate uterus); uterine bleeding (eg, due to endometrial tuberculosis, cancer).
    2. Therapeutic indications—Control of bleeding.
  B. Adolescence and Adulthood:

  1. Diagnostic indications—Suspected neoplasms of the cervix and uterus; abnormal uterine bleeding; investigation of possible malformations, including position of fundus; endometritis; confirmation of ovulation and determination of consistency of endometrial maturation relative to time in cycle (in study of infertility).
  2. Therapeutic indications—Removal of polyps and excessive tissue overgrowth (endometrial hyperplasia) in the management of abnormal uterine bleeding. Early therapeutic abortion.
  C. Postmenopausal Age Group:
    1. Diagnostic indications—Bleeding or discharge due to possible cancer, polyps, or infection.
    2. Therapeutic indications—Drainage of hematometra or pyometra. (Drain first and perform curettage when infection subsides and the uterus is reduced in size.)

Holt, E.M.: Outpatient diagnostic curettage. J Obstet Gynaec Brit Common 77:1043–1046, 1970.

Kahler, V.L., & others: Value of the endometrial biopsy. Obst Gynec 34:91–95, 1969.

McElin, T.W., & others: Study of uterine perforations occurring during 2991 instances of diagnostic curettage. Internat J Gynaec Obstet 7:243–251, 1969.

McLennan, C.E.: Endometrial regeneration after curettage. Am J Obst Gynec 104:185–194, 1969.

OVARIECTOMY

The ovary performs numerous functions. It is a repository for primordial sex cells, the woman's chromosomal endowment for procreation. During the functional years, it is the organ for the production, "ripening," and monthly release of mature ova. The ovary produces steroid sex hormones. Estrogens are produced from childhood until about age 65; after puberty until the menopause, ovulation is associated with the production of progestogens; and from maturity and into the climacteric, small amounts of androgens are produced. Estrogens, most of all, have specific effects on virtually every gland and tissue in the body.

In benign ovarian disease before the menopause, inspection, bisection, and, perhaps, frozen section of the other ovary at laparotomy are necessary in order not to miss serious abnormalities. If an ovary appears normal, it should not be removed until after the menopause. Ovarian hormones "cushion" the patient into the climacteric and help to prevent atherosclerosis, osteoporosis, and vaginitis.

Unless the ovaries are seriously diseased or obviously inactive, they should be protected and retained. Even though synthetic ovarian hormones can be given exogenously, they are expensive and troublesome and less satisfactory than natural estrogens.

Ovariectomy is not warranted in the case of small, unilateral, nontender ovarian enlargements in premenopausal women, nor for the management of asymptomatic postinflammatory tubo-ovarian cysts. There is no justification for ovariectomy for cancer prevention during the functional years. Unilateral ovariectomy for benign cystoma is followed by reoperation involving the other ovary in 5–10% of cases; nevertheless, the chance of the remaining ovary developing cancer is only about 6%. After age 50, the occurrence of ovarian cancer falls to about 1%.

Indications for Ovariectomy

(1) A persistent or enlarging ovarian tumor > 6–7 cm diameter in premenopausal women or > 4 cm in postmenopausal patients. The enlargement should be substantiated by 2 or more examinations over a 3-month period.

(2) Sudden acute and then persistent adnexal pain and tenderness associated with ovarian enlargement— all indicative of an ovarian tumor on a twisted pedicle.

(3) Unresectable ovarian dermoid, endometriosis, or obviously benign tumor.

(4) Ovarian inflammatory destruction or abscess.

(5) Serous cystadenoma containing numerous solid areas or exteriorization of papillary projections. Remove the other ovary and uterus if malignancy seems likely.

(6) Both ovaries should be removed when carcinoma of the ovary, fallopian tube, or endometrium is being treated by hysterectomy.

(7) An ovary that contains a functional ovarian tumor larger than 3–4 cm should be removed.

(8) Remove both ovaries for cancer prevention in women who undergo hysterectomy after the menopause or those over age 65 who are subjected to laparotomy for other reasons.

(9) Bilateral ovariectomy is justified premenopausally for palliation of estrogen-dependent mammary cancer.

Barlow, J.J., & others: Estradiol production after ovariectomy for carcinoma of the breast: Relevance to the treatment of menopausal women. New England J Med 280:633–637, 1969.

Randall, C.L., & others: The frequency of oophorectomy at the time of hysterectomy: Trends in surgical practice, 1928–1953. Am J Obst Gynec 100:716–726, 1968.

Wilson, R., & M.N. Kroch: The menopause: Symptomatology and replacement therapy. Ann Roy Coll Physic Surg Canada 3:47, 1970.

HYSTERECTOMY

The menstrual and procreative functions of the uterus have great psychologic significance for women, and the physician should attempt to preserve the uterus in premenopausal women if at all possible. There are absolute indications for hysterectomy such as uterine sarcoma and uncontrollable hemorrhage, but most hysterectomies are performed for less compelling reasons. The patient's age, marital status, and parity

must be considered in the decision whether or not to remove the uterus.

Hysterectomy is not warranted for control of pain or bleeding or for contraception or sterilization when other less extreme measures will suffice. It should be avoided if possible in those women who have a psychologic need for menstruation; in those who are inordinately apprehensive of major surgery; and in any case where the uterus is needed as a repository for radium in the management of residual pelvic cancer.

Indications for Hysterectomy

(1) **Gynecologic indications:** Chronic, disabling pelvic inflammatory disease or rupture of pelvic abscess; extensive endometriosis not amenable to hormone therapy or conservative surgery; generative tract anomalies of uncorrectable dysfunctional type causing habitual abortion (eg, hypoplastic uterus); uterine perforation at curettage, causing intraperitoneal or retroperitoneal hemorrhage, hematoperitoneum, pelvic floor lacerations, uterine prolapse, abnormal uterine bleeding that cannot be controlled by curettage or hormonal therapy, menometrorrhagia complicating sex steroid therapy for osteoporosis.

Bilateral adnexectomy for tubo-ovarian disease should include hysterectomy unless the uterus is required as a receptacle for radium therapy of pelvic malignancy.

(2) **Neoplastic diseases:** Symptomatic myoma or adenomyosis of the uterus; bilateral serous adnexal cystadenoma; sarcoma or carcinoma of the uterus; hemorrhagic chorio-epithelioma of the uterus unresponsive to chemotherapy; stage I epidermoid carcinoma of the cervix; in conjunction with bilateral oophorectomy for control of residual estrogen-dependent mammary carcinoma; as part of exenteration for pelvic recurrence of rectal carcinoma.

(3) **Obstetric indications:** Ruptured interstitial pregnancy, placenta accreta, advanced hydatidiform mole, sterilization, septic shock due to clostridia (correct shock first).

(4) **Medical indications:** Hypertensive cardiovascular disease causing abnormal bleeding due to "uterine apoplexy"; hypermenorrhea due to pseudohemophilia.

Types of Hysterectomy

A. Subtotal Hysterectomy: Subtotal (incomplete) hysterectomy is rarely justified because the cervix, a potentially serious focus of disease, is left behind.

B. Total Hysterectomy:

1. Abdominal hysterectomy is advisable for the treatment of inflammatory problems; large, multiple uterine tumors; adnexal neoplasms; obstetric complications; for wide exploration or dissection; or whenever previous surgery or scarring has restricted the uterus.

2. Vaginal hysterectomy usually is preferred for removal of a prolapsed uterus, especially when pelvic floor weakness and associated vaginal hernias require correction.

C. Extended hysterectomy (Wertheim, Schauta, Okabiachi) is warranted only for the elimination of invasive cancer by one fully qualified in this highly specialized area of surgery.

After hysterectomy. Editorial. Brit MJ 2:252, 1970.

Beavis, E.L.GG., & others: Ovarian function after hysterectomy with conservation of the ovaries in premenopausal women. J Obstet Gynaec Brit Common 76:969–978, 1969.

Johnson, C.G.: Vaginal hysterectomy and vaginectomy in personal retrospect. Am J Obst Gynec 105:14–19, 1969.

Neely, M.R.: Reducing the morbidity of vaginal hysterectomy. J Obstet Gynaec Brit Common 76:176–177, 1969.

Wright, R.C.: Hysterectomy: Past, present, and future. Obst Gynec 33:560–563, 1969.

OBSTETRICS

DIAGNOSIS & DIFFERENTIAL DIAGNOSIS OF PREGNANCY

In about 1/3 of cases it is difficult to make a definitive diagnosis of pregnancy before the second missed period because of the variability of the physical changes induced by pregnancy, the possibility of tumors, and because obesity and poor patient relaxation often interfere with the examination. Even experienced physicians sometimes make "false-positive" and "false-negative" diagnoses of pregnancy. The potentially grave emotional and legal consequences of an incorrect diagnosis of pregnancy should make the physician cautious; if he is in any doubt, he should schedule a reexamination in 3–4 weeks. If the patient demands earlier confirmation, a pregnancy test can be ordered (Tables 12–6 and 12–7).

Manifestations of Pregnancy

A. Presumptive Manifestations: The following symptoms and signs are usually due to pregnancy, but even 2 or more are not diagnostic. A record or history of time and frequency of coitus may be of considerable value.

1. Symptoms—Amenorrhea, nausea and vomiting (first trimester), breast tenderness and tingling (after 1–2 weeks), urinary frequency and urgency (first trimester), "quickening" (may appear at about the 16th week), weight gain.

2. Signs—Skin pigmentation (after 16th week), epulis (after first trimester), breast changes (enlargement, vascular engorgement, colostrum), abdominal enlargement, cyanosis of vagina and cervical portio (about the 6th week), softening of the cervix (4th or 5th week), softening of the cervicouterine junction (5th or 6th week), irregular softening and slight enlargement of the fundus (about the 5th week), generalized enlargement and diffuse softening of the corpus (after 8th week).

B. Probable Manifestations (After 28th Week): Uterine enlargement, uterine souffle (bruit), uterine contractions.

C. Positive Manifestations: Any of the following, none of which is usually present until the 4th month, is undeniable medical and legal proof of pregnancy: auscultation of the fetal heart, palpation of the fetal outline, recognition of fetal movements by the physician, demonstration of fetal skeleton by x-ray.

Differential Diagnosis of Pregnancy

All of the presumptive and probable symptoms and signs of pregnancy can be caused by other conditions, and all the clinical and laboratory tests indicative of pregnancy may be positive in the absence of conception. Clinical experience and often the passage of time with reexamination are required to establish the correct diagnosis. The most common disorders which may be confused with pregnancy are uterine and adnexal tumors.

TABLE 12–6. Immunodiagnostic tests for pregnancy.*

Name	Procedure	Interpretation and Remarks
Hemagglutination inhibition test (Pregnosticon®)	Red cells sensitized to human chorionic gonadotropin (HCG) + urine (?HCG) + anti-HCG serum.	Immunodiagnostic test depends upon: (1) HCG injected into a rabbit which develops anti-HCG serum. (2) Sheep red cells are tanned, formalinized, and sensitized to HCG. (3) When antibodies are bound or "coated" to red cells, hemagglutination results; but addition of urine from a pregnant woman blocks the reaction between antibody and red cells. Therefore, clumping (ring formation in bottom of test tube) indicates that the patient is not pregnant; no clumping, patient is pregnant.
Agglutination inhibition test (Gravindex®)	Anti-HCG serum + urine + HCG antigen (latex particles). Interpret in 3 minutes.	Similar to above but latex particles with adsorbed HCG used instead of red cells.

*Accuracy is satisfactory, with increasing reliability from the 40th day after the 1st day of LMP.

TABLE 12–7. Clinical pregnancy tests.*

Name	Procedure	Interpretation and Remarks
Estrogen-progesterone	Progesterone, 20 mg, and estradiol benzoate, 2 mg IM	If bleeding does not occur within 10 days after administration of estrogen-progesterone or 7 days after administration of progesterone, norethindrone, or norethynodrel, and if other causes of amenorrhea have been ruled out, pregnancy is probable. *Note:* If bleeding occurs, the test is negative for pregnancy.
Progesterone	Delalutin®, 250 mg (2 ml) IM	
Norethindrone	Norethindrone (Norlutin®), 20 mg orally	
Norethynodrel	Norethynodrel (Enovid®), 20 mg orally	

*Accuracy is high.

Bell, J.L.: Comparative study of immunological tests for pregnancy diagnosis. J Clin Path 22:79–83, 1969.

Cabrera, H.S.: A comprehensive evaluation of pregnancy tests. Am J Obst Gynec 103:32–38, 1969.

Graber, E.A., & others: A clinical test for pregnancy. Am J Obst Gynec 108:991–992, 1970.

Hobson, B.M.: Pregnancy diagnosis using the Pregnosticon haemagglutination inhibitor test. J Obstet Gynaec Brit Common 75:718–743, 1968.

Pyle, L.A., Jr.: The use of a pregnancy test in replacement of medical evaluation. J Occup Med 12:26–27, 1970.

Ravel, R., & others: Effects of certain psychotropic drugs on immunologic pregnancy tests. Am J Obst Gynec 105:1222–1225, 1969.

MINOR DISCOMFORTS OF NORMAL PREGNANCY*

Backache

Virtually all pregnant women suffer from at least minor degrees of lumbar backache during gestation. Postural and other back strain, especially during the last trimester, and relaxation of the pelvic joints due to the steroid sex hormones and perhaps relaxin are also responsible for backache.

The following measures are valuable both as prevention and treatment.

(1) Stress correct ("tall") posture, with abdomen flattened as much as possible, the pelvis tilted forward, and the buttocks "tucked under" to straighten the back.

(2) Daily body exercises to maintain normal muscle strength and tone.

(3) Heels for general wear should be of medium height to further strengthen the back, particularly when flat footwear has been worn extensively.

(4) A firm mattress. Avoid sag which may cause painful, prolonged flexion of the back (after exaggerated extension while erect). Bedboards between the springs and mattress often provide welcome support.

(5) Local heat and light massage to relax tense, taut back muscles.

(6) A maternity girdle may be indicated for patients with backache due to extreme lordosis or kyphoscoliosis or associated with obesity or multiple pregnancy.

(7) Analgesics will be adequate for mild distress. Carisoprodol (Rela®, Soma®), 350 mg orally 4 times daily (or a comparable sedative or muscle relaxant drug) gives temporary relief.

(8) Orthopedic evaluation is necessary when disability results from backache. Note neurologic signs and symptoms indicative of intervertebral disk syndrome or other nerve compression problems, radiculitis, and similar disorders.

Syncope & Faintness

Syncope and faintness are most common in early pregnancy. Vasomotor instability, often associated with postural hypotension, results in transient cerebral hypoxia and pooling of blood in the legs and in the splanchnic and pelvic areas, especially after prolonged sitting or standing in a warm room. Hypoglycemia before or between meals, more common during pregnancy, may result in "lightheadedness" or even fainting.

These attacks can be prevented by avoiding inactivity and utilizing deep breathing, vigorous leg motions, and slow change of position. Encourage the patient to take 6 small meals a day rather than 3 large ones. Stimulants (spirits of ammonia, coffee, tea, or amphetamines) are indicated for attacks due to hypotension; food for hypoglycemia.

Urinary Symptoms

Urinary frequency, urgency, and stress incontinence are quite common, especially in advanced pregnancy. They are due to reduced bladder capacity and the pressure of the presenting part upon the bladder.

Suspect urinary tract disease, especially infection, if dysuria or hematuria is reported.

When urgency is particularly troublesome, the patient should avoid tea, coffee, spices, and alcoholic beverages. Bladder sedatives are available in various forms. Levamine (Repetabs®), one orally twice daily, may be beneficial. The following mixture is often useful:

*Morning sickness is discussed with Vomiting of Pregnancy.

TABLE 12–8. Teratogenic and fetotoxic drugs.

Maternal Medication	Fetal or Neonatal Effect
Established teratogenic agents	
Antineoplastic agents	Multiple anomalies, abortion.
Antimetabolites (amethopterin, fluoro-uracil, DON, 6-azauridine, etc)	
Alkylating agents (cyclophosphamide, etc)	
Antibiotics (amphotericin B, mitomycin, etc)	
Sex hormones (androgens, progestogens, estrogens)	Masculinization, advanced bone age.
Thalidomide	Fetal death or phocomelia; deafness; cardiovascular, gastrointestinal, or genitourinary anomalies.
Possible teratogens	
Antihistamines	Anomalies
Antithyroid drugs (thioureas, potassium iodide)	Goiter, mental retardation
Corticosteroids	Cleft palate, harelip
Insulin (shock or hypoglycemia)	Anomalies
LSD	"Fractured chromosomes," anomalies
Sulfonylurea derivatives	Anomalies
Vitamin D	Cardiopathies
Fetotoxic drugs	
Analgesics, narcotics	
Heroin, morphine	Neonatal death or convulsions, tremors
Salicylates (excessive)	Neonatal bleeding
Cardiovascular drugs	
Ammonium chloride	Acidosis
Hexamethonium	Neonatal ileus
Reserpine	Nasal congestion, drowsiness
Coumarin anticoagulants	Fetal death or hemorrhage
Poliomyelitis immunization (Sabin)	Death or neurologic damage
Sedatives, hypnotics, tranquilizers	
Meprobamate	Retarded development
Phenobarbital (excessive)	Neonatal bleeding
Phenothiazines	Hyperbilirubinemia
Smallpox vaccination	Death or fetal vaccinia
Thiazides	Thrombocytopenia
Tobacco smoking	Undersized babies
Vitamin K (excessive)	Hyperbilirubinemia

> ℞ Tincture hyoscyamus   30.0
> Potassium citrate   50.0
> Water, q s ad   120.0
>
> **Sig:** One tsp in water orally
>   every 4 hours as necessary.

Heartburn

Heartburn (pyrosis or "acid indigestion") results from gastroesophageal regurgitation. In late pregnancy, this may be aggravated by displacement of the stomach and duodenum by the uterine fundus.

About 15% of all pregnant patients experience severe pyrosis (as well as nausea and vomiting) during the latter portion of pregnancy because of diaphragmatic hiatus hernia. This develops with "tenting" of the diaphragm and flaring of the lower ribs after the 7th or 8th month of pregnancy. The hernia is reduced spontaneously by parturition. Symptomatic relief, not surgery, is recommended.

A. Neostigmine Bromide (Prostigmin®): Give 15 mg orally 3 times daily as necessary to stimulate gastrointestinal secretion and motility.

B. Acidifying Agents: Glutamic acid hydrochloride, 0.3 gm 3 times daily before meals. (Hydrochloric acid solutions damage the teeth.) Avoid antacids during early pregnancy because gastric acidity is already low at this time.

C. Other Measures: Hard candy, hot tea, and change of posture are helpful. In late pregnancy, antacids containing aluminum hydroxide gel to reduce gastric irritation are beneficial.

Briggs, D.W.: Heartburn of pregnancy: Incidence and preliminary trial of "Alcin." Practitioner 200:824–827, 1968.

De Paula, C.L.: Reflux esophagitis as the cause of heartburn in pregnancy. Am J Obst Gynec 98:1–10, 1967.

Lind, J.F., & others: Heartburn in pregnancy: A manometric study. Canad MAJ 98:571–574, 1968.

Constipation

Bowel sluggishness is common in pregnancy. It is due to suppression of smooth muscle motility by increased steroid sex hormones, and pressure upon and displacement of the intestines by the enlarging uterus. Constipation frequently causes hemorrhoids and aggravates diverticulosis and diverticulitis.

A. General Measures: Stress good bowel habits. The patient should attempt to have an evacuation at the same time every day. The diet should consist of bulk foods, including roughage (unless contraindicated by gastrointestinal intolerance), laxative foods (citrus fruits, apples, prunes, dates, and figs), and a liberal fluid intake. Encourage exercise (walking, swimming, calisthenics).

B. Medical Treatment:

1. To soften the stool, give bulk laxatives and "smoothage" agents which are neither absorbed by nor irritating to the bowel. By accumulating fluid volume, they increase peristalsis. Dioctyl sodium sulfosuccinate (Colace®, Doxinate®) is detergent. Psyllium hydrophilic mucilloid (Metamucil®) is hydrophilic.

2. Prescribe mild laxatives in more severe cases. These include cascara and phenolphthalein. Milk of magnesia and Epsom salts are also useful in small doses.

3. Avoid purges for fear of inducing labor. Do not prescribe mineral oil since it prevents absorption of fat-soluble vitamins when administered in large amounts.

Hemorrhoids

Straining at stool and bearing down at delivery often cause hemorrhoids, especially in women prone to varicosities. For these reasons it is best to prevent or treat constipation early and to spare the patient's having to strain during the second stage of labor by elective low forceps delivery with episiotomy when feasible.

A. Medical Measures: Gently replace the hemorrhoid, if this can be done easily. Warm (or cool) sitz baths or compresses are helpful. Anesthetic ointments such as dibucaine (Nupercaine®) and cyclomethycaine (Surfacaine®) can be used for relief of pain. If used sparingly, the following ointment is safe and most effective in relieving rectal pain. (Avoid long-term use.)

R		
Cocaine hydrochloride	0.3	
Phenol	0.6	
Petrolatum		
Lanolin aa	15.0	

Sig: Apply a small amount to the anus 1–4 times daily as necessary.

Anusol® or other astringent, anesthetic emollient cones may be used rectally twice daily or at bedtime for symptomatic relief.

B. Surgical Treatment: Incise recently thrombosed, painful hemorrhoids under local anesthesia and evacuate the clot. Do not suture. Order sitz baths, rectal ointments, suppositories, and mild laxatives postoperatively.

Injection treatments to obliterate hemorrhoids during pregnancy are contraindicated. They may cause infection and extensive thrombosis of the pelvic veins, and are rarely successful because of the great dilatation of many vessels.

Breast Soreness

Physiologic breast engorgement may cause discomfort, especially during early and late pregnancy. A well-fitting brassiere worn 24 hours a day affords relief. Ice caps are temporarily effective. Hormone therapy is of no value.

Headache

Headache is most disturbing during the first and third trimesters. Emotional tension is the most common cause; consider anxiety, uncertainty, and similar psychic causes when headache is migrainous, band-type, occipital, or more or less constant. Refractive errors and ocular imbalance are not caused by normal pregnancy, but the pregnant woman tends to be sedentary and may read or sew more despite "eyestrain." Hormonal stimulation causes vascular engorgement of the nasal turbinates, and the resultant congestion and epistaxis contribute to sinusitis and headache.

Severe, persistent headache in the last trimester must be regarded first as symptomatic of toxemia of pregnancy.

The belief that pituitary swelling during normal pregnancy causes headache is without foundation.

Discuss the patient's difficulties in an attempt to relieve her fears and resolve psychologic conflicts.

Obtain ophthalmologic studies, which may reveal the need for corrective lenses or eye exercises. Insist on adequate illumination for reading and close work.

Nasopharyngeal examination may disclose abnormalities. Give phenylephrine (Neo-Synephrine®) nose drops, 0.25%, for catarrh and epistaxis. Oily solutions may soften crusts and prevent mucosal drying which predisposes to nosebleed.

Analgesics may be given as necessary for temporary relief. Sedative or tranquilizers may be required for very anxious or disturbed patients, but their use should be avoided if possible.

Callaghan, N.: The migraine syndrome in pregnancy. Neurology 18:197–199, 1968.

Ankle Swelling

Edema of the lower extremities not associated with toxemia develops in 2/3 of women in late pregnancy. Edema is due to sodium and water retention as a result of ovarian, placental, and adrenal steroid hormones and the normally increased venous pressure in the legs. Varicose veins develop from venous congestion, prolonged sitting or standing, and elastic garters and panty girdles.

Treatment is largely preventive and symptomatic, since nothing can be done about the level of the pregnancy hormones. The patient should elevate her legs frequently and sleep in a slight Trendelenburg position. Circular garters and clothing which interfere with venous return should not be worn.

Restrict salt intake and provide elastic support for varicose veins (see below).

Lees, M.M., & others: The circulatory effects of recumbent postural change in late pregnancy. Clin Sc 32:453–466, 1967.

Robertson, E.G.: Oedema in pregnancy. Med Today 2:12–18, 1968.

Thompson, A.M., Hytten, F.E., & W.Z. Billewicz: Epidemiology of edema during pregnancy. J Obstet Gynec Brit Common 74:1–10, 1967.

Varicose Veins

Varicosities are usually a problem of the multipara, and may cause severe complications. They are due to weakness of the vascular walls; increased venous stasis in the legs due to the hemodynamics of pregnancy; inactivity and poor muscle tone; and obesity, since the excessive tissue mass requires increased circulation and fatty infiltration of connective tissue impairs vascular support.

Serious phlebothrombosis and thrombophlebitis often complicate the puerperium, but they are uncommon during pregnancy. Pulmonary emboli are infrequent.

The vulvar, vaginal, and even the inguinal veins may be markedly enlarged during pregnancy. Damaged vulvovaginal vessels give rise to hemorrhage at delivery.

Large vulvar varices cause pudendal discomfort. A vulvar pad wrapped in plastic film, snugly held by a menstrual pad belt or T-binder and elastic leotards gives relief.

Anticoagulants may be required in acute thrombophlebitis. Heparin is preferred to bishydroxycoumarin since it does not cause fetal damage, is more easily controlled, and is not excreted in the milk. Fortunately, neither drug, whether administered before or during labor, causes increased bleeding from the uterus as efficient mechanical compression of the myometrial vessels prevents excessive blood loss despite increased blood coagulation time. Cervical, vaginal, and perineal lacerations may bleed more briskly if the patient has received heparin or bishydroxycoumarin.

Injection treatment of varicose veins during pregnancy is futile and hazardous.

Vascular surgery can be performed during the first 2 trimesters, but vein stripping is best delayed until after the puerperium. In all other respects management is the same as in nonpregnant women (see Chapter 8).

Fanfera, F.J., & L.H. Palmer: Pregnancy and varicose veins. Arch Surg 96:33–35, 1968.

Mabatoff, R.A., & J.A. Pincus: Management of varicose veins during pregnancy. Obst Gynec 36:928–934, 1970.

Leg Cramps

Cramping or "knotting" of the muscles of the calves, thighs, or buttocks may occur suddenly after sleep or recumbency after the first trimester of pregnancy. For unknown reasons it is less common during the month prior to term. Sudden shortening of the leg muscles by "stretching" with the toes pointed precipitate the cramp. It is believed that cramps are due to reduction in the level of diffusible serum calcium or increase in the serum phosphorus level (or both). This follows excessive dietary intake of phosphorus in milk, cheese, meat, or dicalcium phosphate, diminished calcium intake, or impaired calcium absorption. Fatigue and sluggish circulation in the extremities are contributory factors.

A. Immediate Treatment: Require the patient to stand barefooted on a cold surface (eg, a tiled bathroom floor). Rub and "knead" the contracted, painful muscle. Passively flex the foot to lengthen the calf muscles. Apply local heat.

B. Preventive and Definitive Treatment:

1. Reduce dietary phosphorus intake temporarily by limiting meat to one serving daily and milk to 1 pint daily. Discontinue dicalcium phosphate and other medications containing large amounts of phosphorus.

2. Eliminate excess phosphorus by absorption with aluminum hydroxide gel, 0.5–1 gm orally in liquid or tablet form with each meal.

3. Increase the calcium intake by giving calcium lactate, 0.6 gm (or equivalent) orally 3 times daily before meals. Even larger doses may be required if the absorption of calcium from the intestinal tract is impaired.

4. Walk with the toes pointed forward, but lead with the heel.

Abdominal Pain

Intra-abdominal alterations causing pain during pregnancy include the following:

A. Pressure: Pelvic heaviness, a sense of "sagging" or "dragging," relate to the weight of the uterus on the pelvic supports and the abdominal wall. Frequent rest periods in the supine or lateral recumbent position and a maternity girdle are recommended.

B. Round Ligament Tension: Tenderness along the course of the round ligament (usually the left) during late pregnancy is due to traction on this structure by the uterus with rotation of the uterus and change of the patient's position. Local heat and treatment as for pressure pain are effective.

C. Flatulence, Distention, and Bowel Cramping: Large meals, fats, gas-forming foods, and chilled beverages are poorly tolerated by pregnant women. Mechanical displacement and compression of the bowel by the enlarged uterus, hypotonia of the intestines, and constipation predispose to gastrointestinal distress. Correct and simplify the diet, and reduce food intake at any one meal. Maintain regular bowel functions and prescribe mild laxatives when indicated.

Recommend regular exercise and frequent change of body position.

D. Uterine Contractions: Braxton-Hicks contractions of the uterus are a normal phenomenon which may be startling to hyperreactive women. The onset of premature labor must always be considered when forceful contractions develop, but if contractions remain infrequent and brief the danger of early delivery is not significant. Analgesics and sedatives (including alcohol) may be of value. Codeine is rarely required.

E. Intra-abdominal Disorders: Pain due to obstruction or inflammation involving the gastrointestinal, urinary, nervous, or vascular system must be diagnosed and treated specifically.

F. Uterine or Adnexal Disease: Consider and treat pathologic pregnancy and tubal or ovarian disease appropriately.

VOMITING OF PREGNANCY
(Morning Sickness) &
HYPEREMESIS GRAVIDARUM
(Pernicious Vomiting of Pregnancy)

Essentials of Diagnosis

- Morning or evening nausea and vomiting usually begins soon after the first missed period and ceases after the 4th–5th month of gestation.
- Dehydration, acidosis, and nutritional deficiencies develop.

General Considerations

About ¾ of women, most of them primiparas, complain of nausea and vomiting during pregnancy ("morning sickness"). Persistent vomiting during pregnancy is called hyperemesis gravidarum when extreme. About one woman in 500 develops hyperemesis gravidarum and requires hospitalization. Hyperemesis gravidarum can be fatal if it is not controlled.

The etiology of vomiting during pregnancy is not known, although various physiologic mechanisms have been postulated to account for it. Psychogenic factors are prominent in most cases.

Clinical Findings

A. Symptoms and Signs: The onset is most commonly during the 5th or 6th week of pregnancy, and the disorder usually persists only until the 14th to 16th week. Symptoms are most severe in the morning upon arising. Nutritional deficiencies are almost never noted. Hyperemesis gravidarum which continues unchecked is characterized clinically by dehydration, weight loss, avitaminosis, and jaundice.

B. Laboratory Findings: Severe vomiting causes hemoconcentration, decreased serum proteins and alkali reserves, and elevation of BUN, serum sodium chloride, and serum potassium. Ketone bodies are pres-

ent in the concentrated urine specimen. Slight proteinuria is a common findings.

C. Ophthalmoscopic Examination: Retinal hemorrhages and retinal detachment are unfavorable prognostic signs.

Differential Diagnosis

Vomiting during pregnancy may be due to any of the diseases with which vomiting is usually associated, eg, infections, poisoning, neoplastic diseases, hyperthyroidism, gastric disorders, gallbladder disease, intestinal obstruction, hiatus hernia, diabetic acidosis, uremia due to any cause, and hydatidiform mole.

Complications

The most serious complication of hyperemesis gravidarum is jaundice due to so-called "toxic hepatitis." Intraocular hemorrhage and retinal detachment may cause permanent blindness.

Treatment

A. Mild Nausea and Vomiting of Pregnancy: Reassurance and dietary restrictions are all that is required in many instances. In general, dry foods at frequent intervals are indicated. Restrict fats, odorous foods, spiced dishes, and items which do not appeal to the patient.

Sedatives and antiemetics may be required. Vitamins are of no value unless deficiencies have developed. Antihistamines are useful for their sedative effect. Amphetamines may be given for their mood-elevating effect. Narcotics have no place in the treatment of digestive disorders of pregnancy.

Note: The possibility of teratogenicity of many drugs, including some antiemetics, cannot be overlooked in selecting patients for medical treatment of nausea of pregnancy and in deciding which drugs to use and in what dosages (Table 12–8). In general, it is probably best to give medical treatment only when urgently required; to avoid new and experimental drugs and all drugs which have been suggested as potential teratogens; and to give the lowest dosage which is consistent with clinical efficacy. Sedative-antispasmodic medication may be useful.

B. Hyperemesis Gravidarum: Hospitalize the patient in a private room at complete bed rest without bathroom privileges. Allow no visitors (not even the husband) until vomiting ceases and the patient is eating. Give nothing by mouth for 48 hours. and order appropriate parenteral fluids with vitamin and protein supplements as indicated. If there is no response after 48 hours, institute nasogastric tube feeding of a well-balanced liquid baby formula by slow drip. As soon as possible, place the patient on a dry diet consisting of 6 small feedings daily with clear liquids 1 hour after eating.

If the clinical situation continues to deteriorate in spite of therapy, therapeutic abortion may be required. The urgent indications are delirium, blindness, tachycardia at rest, jaundice, anuria, and hemorrhage.

Prognosis

Vomiting of pregnancy is self-limited, and the prognosis is good. Intractable hyperemesis gravidarum is a real threat to the life of the mother and the fetus.

Adams, R.H., & others: Hyperemesis gravidarum. I. Evidence of hepatic dysfunction. Obst Gynec 31:659–664, 1968.
Hazards of drug prescribing in pregnancy. Editorial. Brit MJ 3:220–223, 1967.
Tylden, E.: Hyperemesis and physiological vomiting. J Psychosom Res 12:85–93, 1968.

ECTOPIC PREGNANCY

Essentials of Diagnosis

- Abnormal menstrual bleeding with symptoms suggestive of pregnancy.
- Cramping pains in the lower abdomen.
- Vaginal bleeding, frequently with passage of decidual tissue.
- A tender mass palpable outside the uterus.

General Considerations

Any pregnancy arising from implantation of the ovum outside the cavity of the uterus is ectopic. Ectopic implantation occurs in about one out of 200 pregnancies. About 98% are tubal. Other sites of ectopic implantation are the abdomen, the ovary, and the cervix. Peritonitis, salpingitis, abdominal surgery, and pelvic tumors may predispose to abnormally situated pregnancy. Combined extrauterine and intrauterine pregnancy may occur. Only tubal ectopic pregnancy will be discussed in the following paragraphs.

Clinical Findings

A. Symptoms and Signs: The cardinal symptoms and signs of tubal pregnancy are (1) amenorrhea or a disordered menstrual pattern, followed by (2) uterine bleeding, (3) pelvic pain, and (4) pelvic (adnexal) mass formation. It may be acute or chronic.

1. Acute (about 40% of tubal ectopic pregnancies)—Severe lower quadrant pain occurs in almost every case. It is sudden in onset, lancinating, intermittent, and does not radiate. Backache is present during attacks. Abnormal uterine bleeding is present in 80% and a pelvic mass is palpable in 70%. Collapse and shock occur in about 10%, often after pelvic examination. Two-thirds of patients give a history of abnormal menstruation; most have been infertile.

2. Chronic (about 60% of tubal ectopic pregnancies)—Blood leaks from the tube over a period of days, and considerable blood may accumulate in the peritoneum. Slight but persistent vaginal spotting is reported, and a pelvic mass can be palpated. Discoloration of the umbilicus by blood pigment (Cullen-Hofstätter sign), although it is not commonly seen, is diagnostic of hematoperitoneum.

B. Laboratory Findings: Blood studies show anemia, increased icteric index, slight leukocytosis, elevated serum amylase (variable), and reticulocytosis. Urine urobilinogen is elevated in ectopic pregnancy with internal hemorrhage. Pregnancy tests are of little value in diagnosis.

C. X-Ray Findings: A plain posteroanterior film of the abdomen may reveal a pelvic mass or other evidence of ectopic pregnancy. Percutaneous retrograde femoral arteriography and hysterosalpingography are believed by most American physicians to be dangerous procedures which are unnecessary for diagnosis.

D. Special Examinations: Culdocentesis and similar procedures are of value principally for demonstrating hematoperitoneum.

Differential Diagnosis

The presence of clinical and laboratory findings suggestive or diagnostic of pregnancy will distinguish ectopic pregnancy· from many acute abdominal illnesses, such as acute appendicitis, a ruptured corpus luteum cyst or ovarian follicle, a twisted ovarian cyst, and urinary calculi. Uterine enlargement with clinical findings similar to those found in ectopic pregnancy is also characteristic of an aborting uterine pregnancy or hydatidiform mole.

Complications

The principal complications are hemorrhage and shock from acute ectopic tubal pregnancy. The most serious sequelae are chronic pelvic inflammatory disease, infertility, and urinary tract infection.

Treatment

Surgical treatment is imperative, since the patient may bleed to death if internal hemorrhage is not promptly brought under control. Devitalized tissue and blood must be removed to prevent complications.

An ectopic pregnancy is "neglected" if surgery is delayed more than a few hours after the first physician has examined the patient. Transfusion should be started before surgery is begun.

A. Emergency Treatment: Hospitalize the patient at once if there is a reasonable likelihood of ectopic pregnancy. Ideally, 6 pints of blood for transfusion should be available if the patient is in shock or if internal bleeding is suspected. Give blood under pressure into 2 large veins or intra-arterially. External heat, morphine, oxygen, slight Trendelenburg position, and moderately snug tourniquets around the upper legs may be lifesaving while preparations for surgery are being made.

B. Surgical Treatment: *Stop the bleeding!* The products of conception must be removed. Gross blood in the abdomen should be evacuated. If it is fresh and unclotted, autotransfusion is feasible, especially if adequate bank blood is not available. Blood for autotransfusion must be filtered through several layers of gauze into a flask containing a solution of 3.8% sodium citrate (1 part citrate solution to 5 parts blood).

Utilize an anesthetic agent which will stimulate respiration and ensure adequate oxygen, eg, ether or cyclopropane. Thiopental (Pentothal®) may cause depression of vital centers, and spinal or caudal anesthesia is often accompanied by severe, uncontrollable hypotension in patients verging upon shock. Most women with a ruptured ectopic pregnancy require only a light anesthetic for the brief procedure necessary to control hemorrhage.

1. Salpingectomy (not excision of a portion of the tube) is indicated if gross tubal damage has occurred. Cornual excision must be done to prevent subsequent tubal or cornual pregnancy and endosalpingosis in the tubal stump.

2. Salpingostomy—Enucleation of the products of conception, with ligation of bleeding points (but without closure of the tube), has many advocates. The tube heals readily without stenosis. This procedure is especially appropriate when the other tube is absent or diseased. Although pregnancy may occasionally recur in such a tube, the majority of these patients become normally pregnant.

Salpingostomy for the purpose of eliminating the pregnancy is not condoned by the Catholic Church.

C. Postoperative Care: Transfusions and iron therapy are indicated postoperatively, together with a high-vitamin, high-protein diet.

Prognosis

Maternal mortality in the USA from ectopic pregnancy is 1–2%. The mortality is lowest where adequate surgical facilities are available for immediate intervention.

Repeat tubal gestation occurs in about 10% of cases, but this should not be regarded as a contraindication to future pregnancy.

Campbell, J.S., & others: Chronic pelvic inflammation as a precursor to ectopic pregnancy: Fact or fancy? Ann Roy Coll Physic Surg Canada 3:47, 1970.

Douglas, E.S., Jr., & others: Surgical management of tubal pregnancy: Effect on subsequent fertility. Obst Gynec Surv 25:231–233, 1970.

Halpin, T.F.: Ectopic pregnancy: The problem of diagnosis. Am J Obst Gynec 106:227–236, 1970.

Lucas, C., & A.M. Hassin: Place of culdocentesis in the diagnosis of ectopic pregnancy. Brit MJ 1:200–202, 1970.

Miles, V.H.: Pathogenesis of tubal pregnancy. Am J Obst Gynec 105:1230–1234, 1969.

Morchandani, J., & P. Madan: Extra-uterine pregnancy: A 10-year survey. J Obst Gynec India 19:601–605, 1969.

Pathak, W.N., & D.B. Stewart: Autotransfusion in ruptured ectopic pregnancy. Lancet 1:961–964, 1970.

Wei, P.Y.: Occurrence of ectopic pregnancy in women with intrauterine devices. Am J Obst Gynec 101:776–778, 1968.

TOXEMIA OF PREGNANCY

Essentials of Diagnosis

- Headache, vertigo, irritability, convulsions, coma.
- Scintillating scotomas, partial or complete blindness, retinal hemorrhages.
- Nausea, vomiting, epigastric pain, hepatic enlargement and tenderness.
- Elevated blood pressure, edema, proteinuria, oliguria, anuria.

General Considerations

Toxemia of pregnancy usually occurs in the last trimester of pregnancy or early in the puerperium. The term **preeclampsia** denotes the nonconvulsive form; with the development of convulsions and coma, the disorder is termed **eclampsia**. Ten to 20% of pregnant women in the USA develop toxemia. Primigravidas are most commonly affected. Uncontrolled toxemia causes permanent disability and may be fatal. Five percent of cases of toxemia of pregnancy progress to eclampsia; 10–15% of women with eclampsia die.

The etiology is not known. Malnutrition—especially reduced protein ingestion—may play a role. Predisposing factors include vascular and renal disease and sodium retention, which seems to "sensitize" an otherwise healthy pregnant woman.

Clinical Findings

A. Preeclampsia: Headache, vertigo, malaise, and nervous irritability are due in part to cerebral edema; scintillating scotomas and visual impairment are due to edema of the retina, retinal hemorrhage, and retinal detachment; epigastric pain, nausea, and liver tenderness are due to congestion, thrombosis of the periportal system, and subcapsular hepatic hemorrhages.

Eclamptogenic toxemia is diagnosed by observing both of the following: (1) persistent hypertension or a sudden rise of blood pressure and (2) generalized edema and proteinuria during the last 4 months of pregnancy. Urine protein determinations are the only laboratory tests of positive value in the diagnosis. Ophthalmoscopic examination in severe preeclampsia and eclampsia reveals variable arteriolar spasm, edema of the optic disks, and, with increasing severity, cotton-wool exudates and even retinal detachment.

B. Eclampsia: The symptoms of eclampsia are those of severe preeclampsia. The signs are as follows: (1) generalized tonic-clonic convulsions; (2) coma followed by amnesia and confusion; (3) 3–4+ proteinuria; (4) marked hypertension preceding a convulsion, and hypotension thereafter (during coma or vascular collapse); (5) stertorous breathing, rhonchi, frothing at the mouth; (6) twitching of muscle groups (eg, face, arms); (7) nystagmus; and (8) oliguria or anuria.

Laboratory findings in eclampsia are hemoconcentration, greatly reduced blood CO_2 combining power and content, and increased serum uric acid, nonprotein nitrogen, and urea nitrogen.

Ophthalmoscopic examination generally reveals one or more of the following: papilledema, retinal edema, retinal detachment, vascular spasm, arteriovenous "nicking," and hemorrhages. Repeated ophthalmoscopic examination is helpful in judging the success of treatment.

Differential Diagnosis

The combination of renal, neurologic, and hypertensive findings in a previously normal pregnant woman distinguishes toxemia of pregnancy from primary hypertensive, renal, or neurologic disease.

Treatment

Treatment must be prompt and vigorous. The best form of treatment is termination of pregnancy by the most expeditious means available which is least harmful to the patient and her baby. Cesarean section after the 36th week of pregnancy may be indicated for patients who are not good candidates for induction of labor. Avoid delaying more than 3 weeks in severe preeclampsia because fetal death in utero and permanent maternal vascular damage may result.

A. Preeclampsia: The objectives of treatment are (1) to prevent eclampsia, permanent cardiovascular and renal damage, and vascular accidents; and (2) to deliver a normal baby that will survive. Place the patient at bed rest and give sedatives. Excess extracellular fluid should be mobilized with diuretics. Give antihypertensive drugs as indicated. Delivery should be delayed, if possible, until the disease is under control or until improvement is marked.

1. Home management—Most patients can be managed at home under alert supervision, including frequent blood pressure readings, daily urine protein determinations, and careful recording of fluid intake and output. Sodium retraction (less than 3 gm of salt per day) must be rigidly enforced. If improvement does not occur in 48 hours, transfer the patient to a hospital.

2. Hospital care—Any patient who does not respond to home management (as above) after 48 hours must be hospitalized at absolute bed rest in a single room with no visitors (not even the husband). Determine blood pressure and urine protein at frequent intervals. Examine the ocular fundi every day, noting particularly arteriolar spasm, edema, hemorrhages, and exudates. The diet should be salt-poor (less than 1 gm salt per day), low-fat, high-carbohydrate, and with a moderate protein content. If the urine output exceeds 500 ml/day a zero water balance is essential; limit fluid intake to 500 ml/day from all sources, plus salt-free fluids to compensate visible losses. Sedatives, diuretics, and antihypertensive drugs should be given as indicated.

B. Eclampsia:

1. Emergency care—If the patient is convulsing, turn her on her side to prevent aspiration of vomitus and mucus and to prevent the caval syndrome. Insert a padded tongue blade or plastic airway between the teeth to prevent biting the tongue and to maintain respiratory exchange. Aspirate fluid and food from the glottis or trachea. Give oxygen by face cone or tent. (Masks and nasal catheters produce excessive stimulation.) Give magnesium sulfate, 10 ml of 25% aqueous solution IV or IM; repeat half of this dose 4 times daily to prevent or control convulsions, lower blood pressure, and encourage diuresis. (Do not repeat magnesium sulfate if the urinary output is less than 100 ml/hour, the respirations are less than 16/minute, or the knee jerk reflex is absent.) In cases of overdosage, give calcium gluconate (or equivalent), 20 ml of a 10% aqueous solution IV slowly, and repeat every hour until urinary, respiratory, and neurologic depression have cleared. (Do not give more than 8 injections of a calcium salt within 24 hours.)

2. General care—Hospitalize the patient in a single, darkened, quiet room at absolute bed rest, with side rails for protection during convulsions. Allow no visitors. Do not disturb the patient for unnecessary procedures (eg, baths, enemas, douches), and leave the blood pressure cuff on her arm. Typed and crossmatched whole blood must be available for immediate use because patients in eclampsia often develop premature separation of the placenta with hemorrhage and are susceptible to shock.

3. Laboratory evaluation—Insert a retention catheter for accurate measurement of the quantity of urine passed. Determine the protein content of each 24-hour specimen until the 4th or 5th postpartum day. NPN, CO_2 combining power and content, and serum protein should be determined as often as the severity and progression of the disease indicate. If serum protein is below 5 gm/100 ml, give 250–500 ml of serum albumin. If salt-poor serum albumin is not available, give plasma or serum.

4. Physical examination—Check blood pressure frequently during the acute phase and every 2–4 hours thereafter. Observe fetal heart tones every time the blood pressure is obtained. Perform ophthalmoscopic examination once a day. Examine the face, extremities, and especially the sacrum (which becomes dependent when the patient is in bed) for signs of edema.

5. Diet and fluids—If the patient is convulsing, give nothing by mouth. Record fluid intake and output for each 24-hour period. If she can eat and drink, give a salt-poor (less than 1 gm salt per day), high-carbohydrate, moderate protein, low-fat diet. Provide potassium chloride as a salt substitute. If the urine output exceeds 700 ml/day, replace the output plus visible fluid loss with salt-free fluid (including parenteral fluid) each day. If the output is less than 700 ml/day, allow no more than 2000 ml of fluid per day (including parenteral fluid). Give 200–300 ml of a 20% solution of dextrose in water 2–3 times a day during the acute phase to protect the liver, to replace fluids, and to aid nutrition. (Do not give 50% glucose; it will sclerose the veins.) Use no sodium-containing fluids (eg, Ringer's injection). Give 25–50 ml salt-poor albumin or 250–500 ml of plasma or serum if the patient is oliguric or if the serum protein is low.

6. Diuretics—Hydrochlorothiazide (Hydro-Diuril®), 25–50 mg orally or IV, may be given to promote diuresis in patients who are not anuric or severely oliguric.

7. Sedatives—Give a sedative upon admission to the hospital and maintain mild sedation until improvement is established.

8. Delivery—Because severe hypertensive disease, renal disease, and toxemia of pregnancy are usually aggravated by continuing pregnancy, the most direct method of treatment of any of these disorders is termination of pregnancy. Control eclampsia before attempting induction of labor or delivery. Induce labor, preferably by amniotomy alone, when the patient's condition permits. Use oxytocin (Pitocin®) to stimulate labor if necessary. Regional anesthesia (preferably pudendal block) is the technic of choice. Nitrous oxide (70%) and oxygen (30%) may be given with contractions, but 100% oxygen should be administered between contractions.

Vaginal delivery is preferred. If the patient is not at term, if labor is not inducible, if she is bleeding, or if there is a question of disproportion, cesarean section may be necessary. If so, use procaine (or equivalent) for local infiltration of the abdominal wall. After the baby is delivered, give thiopental (Pentothal®) anesthesia for abdominal closure.

Prognosis

The maternal mortality rate in eclampsia is 10–15%. Most patients improve strikingly in 24–48 hours with appropriate therapy, but early termination of pregnancy is usually required.

Although babies of mothers with toxemia of pregnancy are small for their gestational age (probably because of placental malfunction), they fare better than premature babies of the same weight born of nontoxemic mothers.

Chandhuri, S.K.: Relationship of protein caloric malnutrition with toxemia of pregnancy. Am J Obst Gynec 107:33–37, 1970.

Chesley, L.C., & others: Long-term follow-up study of eclamptic women: Fifth periodic report. Am J Obst Gynec 101:886–898, 1968.

Elliott, P.M.: The management of eclampsia with intravenous diazepam and protoveratrine. Australian New Zealand J Obstet Gynaec 10:99–100, 1970.

Foster, H.W.: Toxemia of pregnancy: A continuing challenge. J Nat Med Ass 61:222–226, 1969.

Gray, M.J.: Use and abuse of thiazides in pregnancy. Clin Obst Gynec 11:568–578, 1968.

Mengert, W.F.: Lifetime observations on the etiology of eclampsia. South MJ 61:459–465, 1969.

Rogers, S.F., & others: Aggressive toxemia management (preeclampsia and eclampsia). Obst Gynec 33:724–728, 1969.

Zuspan, F.P.: Toxemia of pregnancy. J Reprod Med 2:116–139, 1969.

Zuspan, F.P., & E. Talledo: Factors affecting delivery in eclampsia: The condition of the cervix and uterine activity. Am J Obst Gynec 100:672–685, 1968.

ABORTION

Essentials of Diagnosis

- Vaginal bleeding in a pregnant woman.
- Uterine cramping.
- Disappearance of symptoms and signs of pregnancy.
- Negative or equivocal pregnancy tests.
- The products of conception may or may not be expelled.

General Considerations

Abortion is defined as termination of gestation before the fetus becomes viable. Viability is usually reached at 28 weeks, when the infant weighs slightly more than 1 kg (2.2 lb). About ¾ of abortions occur before the 16th week of gestation; of these, ¾ occur before the 8th week. At least 12% of all pregnancies terminate in spontaneous abortion; at least 15% of abortions are criminally induced.

About 50–60% of spontaneous abortions result from ovular defects; 15% are caused by maternal factors (trauma, infections, dietary deficiencies, diabetes mellitus, hypothyroidism, poisoning, anatomic malformations). There is no good evidence that abortion may be induced by psychic stimuli such as severe fright, grief, anger, or anxiety. In about ¼ of cases the cause of abortion cannot be determined.

Clinical Findings

A. Symptoms and Signs: Abortion is classified clinically as (1) inevitable, (2) complete, (3) incomplete, and (4) missed. In threatened abortion the previable gestation is in jeopardy but the pregnancy often continues.

1. Inevitable abortion—In inevitable abortion the passage of some or all of the products of conception is momentarily impending. Bleeding and cramps do not subside.

2. Complete abortion—In complete abortion all of the conceptus is expelled. When complete abortion is impending the symptoms of pregnancy often disappear; sudden bleeding then begins, followed by cramping. The fetus and the rest of the conceptus may be expelled separately. When the entire conceptus has been expelled, pain ceases but slight spotting persists.

3. Incomplete abortion—In incomplete abortion a significant portion of the pregnancy (usually a placental fragment) remains in the uterus. Only mild cramps are reported, but bleeding is persistent and often excessive.

4. Missed abortion—In missed abortion the pregnancy has been terminated for at least 1 month but the conceptus has not been expelled. Symptoms of pregnancy disappear and the BBT is not elevated. There is a brownish vaginal discharge but no free bleeding. Pain is not present. The cervix is semi-firm and slightly patulous; the uterus becomes smaller and irregularly softened; the adnexa are normal.

B. Laboratory Findings: Pregnancy tests are negative or equivocally positive. Blood and urine findings are those usually observed in infection and anemia if these complications have occurred.

C. X-Ray Findings: In late abortion a plain film of the abdomen may demonstrate a distorted angulated fetal skeleton and often intrauterine gas.

Differential Diagnosis

The bleeding which occurs in abortion of a uterine pregnancy must be differentiated from the abnormal bleeding of an aborting ectopic pregnancy, hyperestrinism in a nonpregnant woman, and membranous dysmenorrhea. The passage of hydropic villi in the bloody discharge is diagnostic of the abortion of a hydatidiform mole.

Complications

Hemorrhage in abortion is a major cause of maternal death. Infection is most common after criminally induced abortion; death results from salpingitis, peritonitis, septicemia, and septic emboli. Less common complications are perforation of the uterus, chorioepithelioma, and infertility.

Treatment

A. Emergency Measures: If abortion has occurred after the first trimester, the patient should be hospitalized. In all cases induce uterine contraction with oxytocics, eg, oxytocin (Pitocin®), IM or IV (not ergot preparations), to limit blood loss and aid in the expulsion of clots and tissues. Ergonovine maleate (Ergotrate®) should be given only if the diagnosis of complete abortion is certain. Give antishock therapy, including blood replacement, to prevent collapse after hemorrhage.

B. General Measures: Place the patient at bed rest and give sedatives to allay uterine irritability and limit bleeding. Coitus and douches are contraindicated. Antibiotics are indicated if criminal abortion is likely or if signs of infection are present.

C. Surgical Measures:

1. Cerclage (Shirodkar) during the second trimester for closure of an incompetent internal cervical os.

2. Dilatation and curettage for possible retained tissue. Start an IV drip of oxytocin (Pitocin®) before surgery to avoid uterine penetration.

3. Uterine packing to control bleeding and promote separation and evacuation of fragments. Remove the packing in 6–8 hours to allow drainage.

Prognosis

The prognosis is good if severe infection is avoided. If the maternal factors which caused an abortion can be corrected, future pregnancies often go to term without incident.

Brown, J.B., & others: Hormone levels in threatened abortion. J Obstet Gynaec Brit Common 77:690–700, 1970.

Carr, D.H.: Genetic factors in pregnancy wastage. Obst Gynec Surv 25:218–221, 1970.

Larson, S.L.: Chromosome studies in spontaneous abortions. Internat Surg 51:124–131, 1969.

Rashid, S., & P. Smith: Suction evacuation of the uterus for incomplete abortion. J Obstet Gynaec Brit Common 77:1047–1048, 1970.

Thiede, H.A.: Cytogenetics of abortion. M Clin North America 53:773–794, 1969.

HABITUAL ABORTION

Habitual abortion implies loss of 3 or more previable (< 1000 gm) pregnancies in succession. Emotionally immature women are prone to habitual abortion.

Habitual abortion is a clinical, not a pathologic diagnosis. Hormonal aberrations often seem to be responsible for habitual abortion. Habitual abortion occurs in about 0.4% of all pregnancies or 4% of all spontaneous abortions, and is usually the result of recurrent (persistent) rather than random (accidental) factors. Many habitual abortions result from abnormal genetic disorders. About 15% are due to maternal organic disease.

The clinical findings are similar to those observed in other types of abortion (see above).

Treatment

The entire program of therapy rather than any single aspect of it will be responsible for success or failure. Most regimens of therapy include psychotherapy. A special clinic or individualized therapy, preferably by one therapist who has established good rapport with the patient, is most desirable.

A. General Measures:

1. Preconception therapy is aimed at detection of maternal or paternal defects which may contribute to abortion. A thorough general and gynecologic examination is essential. Psychic factors, including emotional conflicts in marriage and during previous pregnancies, must be evaluated. The competence of the cervical os must be determined. Hysterography (for tumor or congenital anomalies), PBI, vaginal smears, and other tests should be performed as indicated. Endometrial tissue should be examined in the postovulation stage of the cycle to determine the adequacy of the response of the endometrium to hormones. Every attempt should be made to restore good physical and emotional health.

2. Postconception therapy—Provide early prenatal care and schedule frequent office visits. Repeated gentle abdominopelvic examinations are indicated so that abnormal uterine development can be noted early. Permit unrestricted telephone calls. Give adequate sedatives. Insert a vaginal pessary if retroposition of the uterus is a possible cause of symptoms. Be prepared to hospitalize the patient promptly at the first sign of impending abortion.

Prescribe an adequate diet high in vitamins (especially vitamins C and K). The patient should strive to achieve and maintain an appropriate pregnancy weight for her height and build. Give thyroid hormone only as indicated. Vitamin E is of no value.

Insist that the patient avoid intercourse during the entire pregnancy. Hot baths and douches are likewise contraindicated. Complete bed rest is justified, however, only for bleeding or pain. Empiric steroid sex hormone therapy is not warranted. Excessive smoking should be curbed.

If arborization of the cervical mucus occurs, with or without therapy, the pregnancy is lost.

B. Surgical Measures: Incompetency of the cervical os should be corrected by means of the Lash or Shirodkar type of operation. Trachelorrhaphy may be required for severe cervical lacerations. Uterine suspension, myomectomy, and a unification operation (for double uterus) may be justified for treatment of habitual abortion.

Prognosis

The prognosis is good if the cause of abortion can be corrected. If a woman has lost 3 previous pregnancies, she has a 70—80% chance of carrying a fetus to viability. If she has aborted 4 or 5 times, her likelihood of a successful pregnancy is 65—70%.

Contifaris, B.: Habitual abortion and premature labor due to incompetence of the internal os of the cervix: Cause, diagnosis, treatment. Internat Surg 51:156—162, 1969.

Kaskarelis, D., & others: Surgical treatment of cervical incompetence during pregnancy. Internat Surg 53:296—299, 1970.

Pergament, E., Kadotani, T.. & H. Sato: Chromosome studies in repeated spontaneous abortions and stillbirths. Am J Obst Gynec 100:912—917, 1968.

THERAPEUTIC ABORTION

The indications for and legal restraints on therapeutic abortion have been greatly liberalized in recent years, and all physicians should become familiar with the professional practices and standards in their communities. This discussion will be limited to a description of the methods employed and the complications that may arise.

Methods

A. Dilatation and Curettage: Almost 2/3 of therapeutic abortions are performed transvaginally by dilatation of the cervix and evacuation of the uterus. Before the 12th week of pregnancy, the vaginal route is usually chosen for therapeutic abortions unless sterilization is to be performed also, in which case laparotomy and abdominal hysterotomy are required. After the 12th week, abdominal hysterotomy is safer than dilatation of the cervix and evacuation of the uterus from below.

The preoperative preparation is similar to that employed for dilatation and curettage or cesarean section if hysterotomy is chosen. Postoperative management is comparable to postpartal care, although the patient can usually resume full activity in 2—3 weeks.

B. Suction Therapeutic Abortion: Suction curettage has supplanted mechanical curettage in many hospitals for the interruption of early pregnancy. The following advantages and disadvantages are recognized.

1. Advantages—Suction evacuation of the products of early conception has the following advantages:

a. Less dilatation of the cervix is necessary than for surgical dilatation and curettage (lessens likelihood of cervical tears and incompetent cervix).

b. The negative pressure is powerful enough so that the tip of the instrument need not come into contact with the entire uterine cavity surface (even the uterine "dead space" is denuded).

c. Separation of the placenta occurs at its surface contact, thus protecting the basalis and muscularis. Therefore, traumatic amenorrhea and intrauterine adhesion (Asherman's syndrome) is less likely.

d. Suction aspiration is much more rapid and expeditious than surgical dilatation and curettage (3 minutes average).

e. Less anesthesia and analgesia are required (basal analgesia and paracervical block may suffice).

f. When the uterine cavity is quickly evacuated, rapid contraction of the uterus occurs, minimizing blood loss. Measurement of blood lost is possible.

g. The short operating time and the minimal use and exchange of instruments reduce the danger of infection.

h. Blunt suction tubes are less traumatic than curets.

2. Disadvantages—

a. The suction tube is not delicate enough to distinguish minor changes in architecture of the uterus (small polyps, partial septa).

b. In pregnancy of more than 10 weeks' duration, the instrument can be blocked by fetal-placental fragments.

c. The negative pressure is produced by an electric motor, and mechanical or current failure may occur.

d. More distortion and fragmentation of the tissues occurs with suction.

e. If there is a tight fit at the cervix and prolonged suction is applied, excessive blood loss may occur.

C. Intra-amniotic Injection of Hypertonic Solutions: Therapeutic abortion after the 14th week and evacuation of the uterus following fetal death can be accomplished medically within 12—14 hours, almost without exception, by aseptic transabdominal aspiration of amniotic fluid and immediate very slow replacement by a similar amount of sterile aqueous 20% sodium chloride or 50% glucose solution. Saline should not be used for patients with eclamptogenic toxemia or other disorders in which sodium restriction is desirable. Labor generally requires only 2—3 hours; its cause is uncertain. Whether labor is the result of progestogen block or reduced progestogen production by the placenta is debated.

After voiding (to prevent injury to the bowel or bladder), the patient is placed in the slight Trendelenburg position. A site half-way between the symphysis and umbilicus and slightly lateral to the midline is chosen for amniocentesis. After preparation with antiseptic, the skin is anesthetized with procaine or comparable solution. A No. 14 or 16, 4–6 inch needle with obturator is inserted slowly into the uterine cavity. Ideally, 100–200 ml of fluid are withdrawn. In second trimester pregnancy and missed abortion, only small amounts of amniotic fluid may be available. In such instances, at least 60–90 ml of solution should be injected if possible.

The recovered placenta reveals extensive edema and submembranous degeneration. Signs of hypoxia are noted when fetal death follows injection of hypertonic solutions.

Complications

Therapeutic abortion is a potentially dangerous operation even in healthy women. Perforation of the uterus, pelvic infection, hemorrhage, and embolism are the most common complications. The primary mortality in elective first trimester abortion is 0.05–0.1% (Scandinavia). A 5% morbidity (fever, pelvic infection) is recorded in the first trimester and over 15–20% in such second-trimester, state-authorized interruptions of pregnancy.

The mortality is 1–2% in the seriously ill pregnant patient whose physical or emotional disease may justify abortion. The postoperative morbidity is proportionate.

Protracted feelings of guilt and remorse commonly result from interruption of pregnancy, particularly when religious and social conflicts complicate the decision to abort and the patient feels responsible for the loss of the baby.

Clinical indications for terminating pregnancy. Editorial. Brit MJ 1:133–134, 1968.

Genser, G., & others: Studies of therapeutic abortions induced by injection of hypertonic saline. J Obstet Gynaec Brit Common 75:1058–1062, 1968.

Kushner, D.H., & J Marlow: Therapeutic abortion by aspiration curettage. J Reprod Med 2:291–294, 1969.

Lederer, H.D.: Psychiatric issues in therapeutic abortion. Med Coll Virginia Quart 5:126–129, 1969.

Manabe, Y.: Artificial abortion at midpregnancy by mechanical stimulation of the uterus. Am J Obst Gynec 105:132–146, 1969.

McCoy, D.R.: The emotional reaction of women to therapeutic abortion and sterilization. J Obstet Gynaec Brit Common 75:1054–1057, 1968.

Schulman, H.: Induced abortion in a municipal hospital. Obst Gynec 36:616–620, 1970.

Sprague, C.: The role of RhoGAM in therapeutic and spontaneous abortion. Hawaii Med J 29:450–451, 1970.

STERILIZATION

Sterilization is any procedure which renders the individual, man or woman, incapable of reproduction. Sterilization may be done electively in all states but Utah (where a medical indication is required), to limit the number of children; or may be compulsory, if the individual or couple are considered unfit to bear children because of hereditary diseases or mental incapacity.

The indications for sterilization are usually grouped as neuropsychiatric, medical, surgical, obstetric, and socioeconomic. In general, when irremediable conditions constitute a bona fide indication for therapeutic abortion, prevention of subsequent pregnancy by sterilization is warranted. The Roman Catholic Church forbids sterilization without exception.

Surgical sterilization of women may be accomplished by the abdominal, vaginal, transuterine, or inguinal approach. The most commonly used technic is to occlude the tubes by ligation. However, part or all of the tubes may be excised or closed by coagulation. Hysterectomy may be the best means of sterilization if tumors, bleeding problems, or relaxation of the pelvic floor justifies the major procedure required.

The safety of tubal ligation, the sterilization operation most commonly employed, varies with the procedure, whether the woman has just been delivered, and by what route. If done at cesarean section, a 1–2% failure rate must be expected with the Pomeroy method. In the nonpregnant patient (or 24 hours following vaginal delivery), failures (Pomeroy) are about 1:300.

Sterilization by irradiation requires approximately 2000 r to the ovaries by external x-ray or intrauterine radium administration.

The effectiveness of sterilization depends upon the method employed. The only certain methods are irradiation in adequate dosage, bilateral oophorectomy, and hysterectomy.

Brenner, P., & others: Evaluation of cesarean section hysterectomy as a sterilization procedure. Am J Obst Gynec 108:335–339, 1970.

Haynes, D.M.: Tubal sterilization in an indigent population. Am J Obst Gynec 106:1044–1053, 1970.

Hayt, E.: Legal responsibility for unsuccessful sterilization. Hosp Manage 109:50–55, 1970.

Kroener, W.F., Jr.: Surgical sterilization by fimbriectomy. Am J Obst Gynec 104:247–254, 1969.

Svennerud, S., & B. Astedt: Sterilization during laparoscopy. Acta obst gynec scandinav 48 (Suppl 3):64–65, 1969.

Wheeless, C.R.: Outpatient tubal sterilization. Obst Gynec 36:208–211, 1970.

HYDATIDIFORM MOLE & CHORIO-EPITHELIOMA

Essentials of Diagnosis

- Uterine bleeding at 6–8 weeks.
- Excessive nausea and vomiting.
- Uterus larger than expected for duration of pregnancy.
- Presence of vesicles passed from vagina.
- Urinary chorionic gonadotropins high.

General Considerations

Hydatidiform mole is a degenerative disorder of the chorion which occurs as a complication of about one in 1500 pregnancies in the USA, usually during the first 18 weeks. It is characterized by prominent, pale yellow, grape-like vesicular enlargements of the villi and vascular incompetence of the villous tree. Although it is assumed to be of placental (fetal) origin, the precise cause is not known. Hydatidiform mole is more common among women over 40, and is over 5 times more prevalent in the Orient than in the Occident. Malignant change (chorio-epithelioma) occurs in about 4% of cases in the USA, and is often fatal when it does occur.

Clinical Findings

A. Symptoms and Signs: Excessive nausea and vomiting occur in over 1/3 of patients with hydatidiform mole. Uterine bleeding, beginning at 6—8 weeks, is observed in virtually all instances and is indicative of threatened or incomplete abortion. In about 1/5 of cases the uterus is larger than would be expected in a normal pregnancy of the same duration. Intact or collapsed vesicles may be passed through the vagina.

Eclamptogenic toxemia, frequently of the fulminating type, may develop during the second trimester.

Chorio-epithelioma may be manifested by continued or recurrent uterine bleeding after evacuation of a mole; or by the presence of an ulcerative vaginal tumor, pelvic mass, or evidence of distant metastatic tumor. The diagnosis is established by pathologic examination of curettings or by biopsy.

B. Laboratory Findings: Hydatidiform mole or chorio-epithelioma is probably present when the FSH exceeds 0.5 million rat units/liter of urine and the LH titer is above 0.2 million rat units/liter. The urinary 17-ketosteroid level is often twice the normal pregnancy level (10—15 μg/100 ml). The vaginal smear reveals distinct, heavy cell groupings, a predominance of superficial cells, acidophilia, and pyknosis in about half of the exfoliate cells.

C. X-Ray Findings: Hysterography after the third month, either by the transcervical or transcutaneous route, utilizing intravenous urographic media, may demonstrate a honeycomb appearance of the uterine contents.

D. Special Examinations: Preserve any tissue passed spontaneously. Identification of placental hydatids will establish the diagnosis.

Differential Diagnosis

The excessive nausea and vomiting which occurs in hydatidiform mole must be distinguished from hyperemesis gravidarum; the excessively large uterus from multiple pregnancy, hydramnios, and uterine tumors; and the vaginal bleeding from threatening or complete abortion. The presence of a large uterus and laboratory findings of pregnancy with the absence of a fetal skeleton by x-ray makes the diagnosis of a mole very probable.

Treatment

A. Emergency Measures: Hemorrhage indicative of abortion requires immediate hospitalization. Type and cross-match the patient's blood, and have at least 2 units of blood available for transfusion. Free bleeding will cease as soon as the uterine contents are evacuated and firm uterine contraction with oxytocin is established. Curettage will probably be required for removal of adherent tissue.

B. Specific (Surgical) Measures:

1. Empty the uterus as soon as possible after the diagnosis of hydatidiform mole is established. Suction evacuation followed by careful dilatation and curettage is the preferred method of treatment. If the uterus is larger than a 3-month pregnancy, pack the cavity for 6—12 hours after curettage to reduce bleeding and aid in the removal of tissue missed by the curet. Give ergonovine maleate (Ergotrate®), 0.2 mg orally every 4 hours after curettage for 4 doses. A second D & C in 3—4 weeks may be required if bleeding persists or fever develops.

2. Hysterotomy—If the uterus is larger than a 5-month pregnancy and the cervix is resistant to wide dilatation, hysterotomy may be indicated (vaginal if infection is clinically evident; otherwise, anterior abdominal). Do not resect ovarian cysts or remove the ovaries; spontaneous regression will occur with elimination of the mole.

3. Hysterectomy rarely is curative. If malignant tissue is found at surgery or follow-up, chemotherapy is indicated. Methotrexate is the most promising chemotherapeutic agent.

C. Antitumor Chemotherapy: Methotrexate (amethopterin), 3 mg/kg IM in divided doses over a 5-day period, is recommended. The side-effects—anorexia, nausea and vomiting, stomatitis, rash, diarrhea, and bone marrow depression—usually are reversible in about 3 weeks. They can be ameliorated by the administration of folic acid or folinic acid. Death occurs occasionally from agranulocytosis or toxic hepatitis. Repeated courses of methotrexate 1 month apart generally are required to destroy the trophoblast and maintain a zero chorionic gonadotropin titer. If liver disease complicates the problem or if the tumor is resistant, give dactinomycin (actinomycin D, Cosmegen®), 10 μg/kg IV (well-diluted) over a period of 5 days in monthly courses.

D. Supportive Measures: Replace blood and give iron and vitamins. If infection is suspected, give broad-spectrum antibiotics for 24 hours before and 3—4 days after surgery.

Prognosis

The risk of chronic abortion is not great in women who have had hydatidiform mole. A 5-year arrest after courses of chemotherapy, even when metastases have been demonstrated, can be expected in about 75% of cases of choriocarcinoma.

Aguero, O., & J. Zighelboim: Fetography and molegraphy. Surg Gynec Obst 130:649–654, 1970.

Beischer, W.A., & others: Hydatidiform mole and its complications in the state of Victoria. J Obstet Gynaec Brit Common 77:263–276, 1970.

Cline, M.J.: Choriocarcinoma. California Med 110:244–249, 1969.

Morrison, J., & others: Ultrasonic scanning in obstetrics. III. The Diagnosis of hydatidiform mole. Australian New Zealand J Obstet Gynaec 10:1–3, 1970.

Prophylaxis of choriocarcinoma. Editorial. Brit MJ 3:514, 1968.

Robinson, D.E., & others: The diagnosis of hydatidiform mole by ultrasound. Australian New Zealand J Obstet Gynaec 8:74–78, 1968.

Van Thiel, D., & others: Pregnancies after chemotherapy of trophoblastic neoplasms. Science 169:1326–1327, 1970.

THIRD TRIMESTER BLEEDING

Five to 10% of women have vaginal bleeding in late pregnancy. Multiparas are more commonly affected. Obstetric bleeding is the major cause of maternal mortality and morbidity. The physician must distinguish between placental causes of obstetric bleeding (placenta previa, premature separation of the placenta) and nonplacental causes (systemic disease or disorders of the lower genital tract).

In general, the approach to the problem of bleeding in late pregnancy should be conservative and expectant.

The patient should be hospitalized at once, preferably by ambulance, at complete bed rest. Perform a complete, gentle abdominal examination but no rectal or vaginal examination. Over 90% of patients with third trimester bleeding will cease to bleed in 24 hours on bed rest alone. If bleeding is profuse and persistent, however, vaginal examination is indicated after preparation and blood replacement. The operating room should be ready for cesarean section before this examination is done.

If the patient is less than 36 weeks pregnant and the fetus is too small for survival, it may be necessary to keep her in the hospital or at home at bed rest until the chances of delivering a viable infant are more favorable. If bleeding stops, it is likely that it will start again.

Casselden, P.A.: Soft tissue placentography and the uterine compressor. Radiography 36:125–131, 1970.

Goeditch, J.M., & N.E. Boyce, Jr.: Management of abruptio placentae. JAMA 212:288–293, 1970.

Hibbard, B.M.: Simplified placental localization (with technetium). Brit MJ 3:85–88, 1969.

Hibbard, L.T.: Placenta previa. Am J Obst Gynec 104:172–184, 1969.

McCullough, J.A., & others: Antepartum hemorrhage: Analysis of 304 patients in a private institution. Obst Gynec 31:836–839, 1968.

Pritchard, J.A.: Genesis of severe placental abruption. Am J Obst Gynec 108:22–27, 1970.

Pystynew, P., & others: Placental localization by different methods. Acta obst gynec scandinav 48 (Suppl 3):158–160, 1969.

Semmens, J.P.: Placenta previa and placental localization. GP (new series) 2:72–79, Sept 1970.

Sharma, S.D., & G. Jones: Amniography. East African MJ 47:1–13, 1970.

POSTPARTUM HEMORRHAGE

Postpartum hemorrhage has been defined arbitrarily as the loss of at least 500 ml of blood following delivery. However, since a small woman can lose blood less safely than a large one, it is felt that the loss of 1% or more of body weight (expressed in terms of ml of blood) would be a more proper definition. Postpartum hemorrhage is the major cause of maternal mortality in the USA.

The most common causes are uterine atony, lacerations during delivery, and blood dyscrasias or coagulation defects.

Prevention

The following types of patients are especially prone to develop postpartum bleeding: Women with multiple pregnancies, polyhydramnios, a history of postpartum hemorrhage, primary or secondary uterine inertia, desultory or prolonged labor, uterine infections, placenta previa, abruptio placentae, after heavy analgesia or anesthesia, and those who are delivered by cesarean section. Measures to prevent postpartum bleeding in these patients are as follows:

(1) Start 500 ml of 5% glucose in water slowly IV through a No. 18 needle near the end of the first stage of labor.

(2) Immediately after delivery, add 0.5 ml oxytocin (Pitocin®) to the infusion (not into the tubing).

(3) On completion of the third stage of labor, give ergonovine maleate (Ergotrate®), 0.2 mg IM. Avoid giving excessive amounts of analgesics and anesthesia.

(4) Maneuver the uterus up and out of the pelvis and, by raising it with a large sponge on a forceps in the vagina, massage it gently until it becomes firm and remains so.

(5) Keep the patient in the delivery room or recovery room for 1 hour after delivery.

Treatment

A. Emergency Measures: Control bleeding promptly by suture, manual recovery or expression of the placenta, or intravenous oxytocin (Pitocin®) as indicated. Packing of the uterus (and vagina) controls bleeding by the pressure applied to bleeding points and because packing stimulates uterine contractions. However, packing must be used with discretion for the following reasons: (1) The uterus relaxes slowly and bleeding often recurs, even when packing is very tight. (2) Tight packing may actually prevent uterine contractions. (3) If packing fails to check bleeding, further blood loss may make a necessary hysterectomy even more hazardous. (4) The risk of infection is greater with packing than when other methods of hemostasis are used.

B. General Measures: Reinspect the placenta for missing fragments. Examine for lacerations of the birth canal. Note the quality of contractions of the elevated uterus, determine bleeding and clotting time, and obtain typed and cross-matched blood for transfusion.

Prognosis

The mortality rate in postpartum hemorrhage depends upon the amount and rapidity of blood loss, the patient's general health, and the speed and adequacy of treatment.

Duckman, S., & others: Delayed postpartum uterine hemorrhage. Obst Gynec 36:568–573, 1970.

Fort, A.T.: Hemorrhagic complications of labor and delivery. Obst Gynec 34:717–720, 1969.

Greiss, F.C., Jr., & others: Maternal deaths from hemorrhage in North Carolina. North Carolina MJ 30:1–5, 1969.

Purcell, G., Jr., & H.L. Nossel: Factor XI (PTA) deficiency: Surgical and obstetric aspects. Obst Gynec 35:69–74, 1970.

Schneider, C.L.: Obstetric shock and shock in obstetrics. Postgrad Med 45:185–191, 1969.

Yussman, M.A., & D.M. Haynes: Rupture of the gravid uterus: A 12-year study. Obst Gynec 36:115–120, 1970.

INVERSION OF THE UTERUS

Inversion of the uterus at or following delivery (puerperal inversion) is an extreme medical and surgical emergency. It may occur as a result of straining; pulling by the infant on the cord and placenta; traction on the cord by the physician before placental separation; severe "kneading" of the fundus (overzealous Credé maneuver); or separation and extraction of an adherent placenta, especially during deep inhalation anesthesia, which causes extreme relaxation. The incidence is about one in 15,000 deliveries. The diagnosis is obvious if inversion is complete.

Nonpuerperal inversion is a less serious disorder which is due to extrusion or associated with extraction of a large uterine tumor (myoma). Treatment consists of hysterectomy if replacement is unsuccessful.

Prevention

Most cases of puerperal uterine inversion can be prevented by good obstetric care. Do not pull on the cord unless the placenta has separated. Do not push on the fundus or use the Credé maneuver. Use regional anesthesia whenever possible. Do not leave the patient until the uterus is contracted and rounded. Do not place a pad or roll beneath the abdominal binder after delivery.

Treatment

Note: Consultation and assistance are mandatory, since maternal mortality is about 30% unless treatment is prompt and appropriate.

A. Emergency Measures: Shock (out of proportion to blood loss) must be controlled with intravenous fluids, plasma, whole blood, and oxytocin (Pitocin®). Do not use ergot preparations during this stage of management, since they cause tetanic contractures of the cervix and uterus and interfere with manipulation.

B. Specific Measures: Replace the uterus by abdominovaginal manipulation, applying countertraction on the cervix while reinserting the inverted portion. Deep general (ether) anesthesia is required. Leave the placenta attached, compress the fundus in the anteroposterior diameter, and apply ring forceps to the cervix. Combat cervical constriction with amyl nitrite by inhalation or epinephrine, 5–10 minims of 1:1000 solution, IM. Leave the fist in the uterus and administer ergonovine maleate (Ergotrate®) or ergotamine tartrate (Gynergen®), which at this point have the advantage of causing cervical constriction and thus preventing recurrence after manual support is withdrawn. Packs are contraindicated since they tend to maintain uterine distention.

C. Surgical Measures: If manipulative treatment is not immediately successful, proceed at once to surgical correction to avoid infection.

1. Transabdominal replacement (Houltain)—Incise the posterior wall of the inverted uterus, replace the fundus with towel clamps applied hand-over-hand, and suture.

2. Transvaginal replacement—Two methods are available: (1) Transect the cervix anteriorly to replace the fundus from below, and suture (Spinelli). (2) Incise through the cervix posteriorly, replace the fundus, and suture (Küstner).

D. Postoperative Measures: Give broad-spectrum antibiotics; replace blood, fluids, and electrolytes; and decompress the stomach with a nasogastric tube.

Prognosis

Manual replacement, properly performed, is successful in about 75% of patients with inversion. Maternal mortality with inadequate management is about 30%.

Inversion of the uterus may recur after a subsequent delivery.

Balakreshna, H., & G.F. Marx: Inversion of the uterus during methoxyflurane anesthesia. Canad Anaesth Soc J 15:34–36, 1968.

Lascarides, E., & M. Cohen: Surgical management of nonpuerperal inversion of the uterus. Obst Gynec 32:376–381, 1968.

Moldofsky, L.F.: Management of inversion of the uterus: Report of 4 cases. Obst Gynec 29:488–494, 1967.

Pyko, B.E., & R.L. Chomov: Puerperal inversion of the uterus. J Am Osteopath Ass 68:604–609, 1969.

PUERPERAL SEPSIS

Essentials of Diagnosis
- Fever over 100.4° F for 2 days beginning 24 or more hours after delivery during the 4-week puerperium.
- Foul lochia (occasionally profuse).
- Pain and tenderness in pelvis or adnexa.

General Considerations
Puerperal sepsis is a general term for any infection in the genital tract resulting from abortion, labor, and delivery. Most cases are due to streptococci (principally the anaerobic group). The anaerobic streptococci are common inhabitants of the genital and intestinal tracts. The beta-hemolytic streptococci, not normally found in the genital and intestinal tracts, cause a particularly severe type of infection. Puerperal infection with staphylococci, gonococci, pneumococci, or clostridia is less common but very serious.

Hemorrhage and eclamptogenic toxemia have now surpassed puerperal sepsis as a cause of maternal death in regions where good medical care is available; in primitive areas, puerperal sepsis is still the major life-threatening obstetric disease.

Exogenous infection occurs via the oronasal droplet route or by means of direct contact. Inflammation and trauma commonly initiate endogenous sepsis. Medical complications such as diabetes mellitus or anemia, poor hygiene, premature rupture of membranes, prolonged labor, and operative intervention encourage puerperal sepsis.

Vaginitis, cervicitis, and intrapartum contamination of the genital canal lead to endometritis; lacerations of the cervix and vagina frequently lead to parametritis. Endometritis or parametritis may be followed by adnexitis and peritonitis. Pelvic or femoral thrombophlebitis, serious in itself, is often complicated by septic embolism.

Even while puerperal infection is developing in the genital tract, the infection may spread to the intestines or urinary tract. Adynamic ileus, for example, may occur in association with peritonitis.

Complications
The patient may die soon after delivery as a consequence of overwhelming infection within the pelvis or of septicemia. More often, the infection resolves to a pelvic abscess. Femoral thrombophlebitis ("milk leg") may lead to a postphlebitic syndrome characterized by protracted pain and swelling of the extremity. Chronic salpingitis and infertility are common late sequelae.

Clinical Findings
A. Symptoms and Signs: Fever ("childbed fever") of the intermittent type occurs but is not always a prominent sign. Other signs of infection are foul or profuse lochia, excessive bleeding, pelvic or abdominal pain, and general collapse. Genital tract ulceration, lacerations, and hematoma formation may be found on pelvic examination. The uterus is often sensitive and subinvoluted. Adnexal tenderness, induration, restriction, and mass formation may be present. Unilateral pelvic distress or pain and swelling of the leg usually indicate phlebitis. Sudden chest pain, cough, and shock may signify pulmonary embolism.

B. Laboratory Findings: The white count and sedimentation rate are usually elevated; PMNs are predominant. The red cell count, hemoglobin, and hematocrit will often reveal anemia. Aerobic and anaerobic cultures of material taken from the uterine cavity or endocervix together with antibiotic sensitivity tests are essential to determine definitive therapy. X-ray films of the chest may disclose pulmonary infarction due to embolism.

Differential Diagnosis
Differentiate from urinary tract infection, upper respiratory infection, mastitis, and enteritis.

Prevention
Preventive measures include good general hygiene, protection from contact with infection, and aseptic and antiseptic precautions in labor. Avoid prolonged labor and unnecessary surgical risks, and minimize trauma and blood loss. Deep, prolonged analgesia and anesthesia must be avoided if possible. The fetus and other products of conception should be delivered in the easiest manner possible.

Treatment
A. Emergency Measures and Antibiotics: Treat shock by all available means, including adrenocortical steroid therapy and transfusions as required (see Chapter 1), and give very large doses of appropriate antibiotics. Give tetanus toxoid and antitoxin if *Clostridium tetani* infection is likely. While awaiting the results of cultures and antibiotic sensitivity studies in serious, perhaps overwhelming infection, including septic shock, methicillin, 8 gm, and penicillin G, 12 million units IM per day in divided doses, should be administered. When a clostridial infection is suspected, 20 million units of penicillin G should be given during the first 24 hours. If pseudomonas infection is definite or likely, the above plus gentamicin, 3 mg/kg/day IM, is a most effective addition. When the circulatory perfusion is poor, gentamicin should be given intravenously. This program of therapy usually controls infection with streptococci, pneumococci, gonococci, or clostridia, at least until more specific therapy can be instituted.

Restore fluid and electrolyte balance, replace blood, and administer oxytocics.

B. General Measures: Restrict the patient to bed, force fluids, and encourage food intake. Give enemas as required for marked flatulence or constipation.

C. Surgical Measures: Hysterectomy is indicated for the treatment of a ruptured uterus with infection, neglected placenta accreta, and the rare case of uterine abscess following septic abortion, infected hydatidiform mole, or large myoma. Consider ligation of the vena cava and ovarian veins for repeated pulmonary emboli.

Prognosis

The prognosis depends upon the type of infection and the degree of exposure, the patient's resistance, and the promptness and adequacy of therapy. About a century ago, the maternal mortality in the USA was more than 50 per 10,000 live births. The majority of these deaths were due to puerperal sepsis. In 1962, with vastly better obstetrical care, the overall maternal mortality was 3.8 per 10,000.

Freel, J.H.: Intensive treatment of obstetric sepsis. Am J Obst Gynec 104:651–656, 1969.

Friend, J.R., & V.V. Kakkar: The diagnosis of deep vein thrombosis in the puerperium. J Obst Gynaec Brit Common 77:820–823, 1970.

Mead, P.B., & others: Group A streptococcal puerperal infection: Report of an epidemic. Obst Gynec 32:460–464, 1968.

O'Sullivan, J.F.: Puerperal venous thrombosis treated with phenylbutazone. Brit J Clin Pract 22:427–429, 1968.

MEDICAL COMPLICATIONS DURING PREGNANCY

Diabetes Mellitus

Changes in carbohydrate and fat metabolism and increased clearance of glucose complicate the management of diabetes in the pregnant woman. The prevention of common hazards of diabetes, such as hypoglycemia, ketosis, and diabetic coma, requires greater effort and attention to detail on the part of both the physician and the patient. Although pregnancy does not appear to alter the ultimate severity of diabetes, retinopathy and nephropathy may appear or become worse during pregnancy.

Even in carefully managed diabetics, the incidence of obstetric complications such as hydramnios, toxemia, infections, and prematurity are increased. The infants are larger than those of nondiabetic women. There is a marked increase in unexplained fetal mortality in the last few weeks of pregnancy as well as a high rate of neonatal deaths.

Optimal care requires cooperative management of the patient and offspring (by internist, obstetrician, and pediatrician) and delivery 2–4 weeks before term. Under these circumstances, maternal mortality is not significantly higher than in the nondiabetic. However, the fetal and neonatal mortality remains about 10–20%.

Caputo, N.T., & A.N. Pineda: Diabetes and pregnancy: Preliminary report. Michigan Med 68:221–222, 1969.

Corson, S.L., & R.J. Bolognese: Urinary estriol in the management of obstetric problems (including diabetes mellitus). Am J Obst Gynec 101:633–637, 1968.

High-Risk Obstetric Categories (Modified after Wigglesworth, 1968)

History of Any of the Following:

Hereditary abnormality (osteogenesis imperfecta, Down's syndrome, etc).

Premature or small-for-date neonate (most recent delivery).

Congenital anomaly, anemia, blood dyscrasia, toxemia, etc.

Severe social problem (teen-age pregnancy, drug addiction, etc).

Long-delayed or absent prenatal care.

Age < 18 or > 35 years.

Teratogenic viral illness or dangerous drug administration in the first trimester.

A 5th or subsequent pregnancy, especially when the gravida is > 35 years of age.

Prolonged infertility or essential drug or hormone treatment.

Significant stressful or dangerous events in the present pregnancy (critical accident, excessive exposure to irradiation, etc).

Heavy cigarette smoking.

Pregnancy within 2 months of a previous delivery.

Diagnosis of Any of the Following:

Height under 60 inches or a prepregnant weight of 20% less than or over the standard for height and age.

Minimal or no weight gain.

Obstetric complications (toxemia, multiple pregnancy, hydramnios, etc).

Abnormal presentation (breech, presenting part unengaged at term, etc).

A fetus that fails to grow normally or is disparate in size from that expected.

A fetus > 42 weeks gestation.

Kahn, C.B., & others: Clinical and chemical diabetes in offspring of diabetic couples. Obst Gynec Surv 25:234–237, 1970.

Notelovitz, M.: The obstetrician and the fetus of the diabetic mother. South African MJ 43:143–146, 1969.

Schwartz, R.H., & others: Timing of delivery in the pregnant diabetic patient. Obst Gynec 34:787–791, 1969.

Glomerulonephritis Complicating Pregnancy

The initial attack of acute glomerulonephritis rarely occurs during pregnancy; most obstetric problems relating to glomerulonephritis involve transitional chronic forms of the disease.

Pregnancy does not aggravate glomerulonephritis although infertility, abortion, premature delivery, fetal death in utero, premature separation of the normally implanted placenta, and placental dysmaturity occur with greater frequency in women with glomerulonephritis than in normal women. Nephritis causes hypertension, predisposes to eclamptogenic toxemia, and is associated with a high incidence of perinatal mortality and morbidity.

The medical treatment of glomerulonephritis is discussed in Chapter 15. Adrenocortical steroids may be harmful, and antibiotics are ineffectual. Therapeutic abortion may be justified for acute, severe exacerbation of glomerulonephritis with renal insufficiency. Glomerulonephritis may be an indication for cesarean section when placental dysmaturity or eclamptogenic toxemia occurs.

Felding, C.F.: Obstetric aspects in women with histories of renal disease. Acta obst gynec scandinav 48 (Suppl 2):1–42, 1969.

Gill, G.N., & J.P. Hayslett: Hereditary nephritis and pregnancy. Am J Obst Gynec 104:19–23, 1969.

Nadler, N., & others: Acute glomerular nephritis during late pregnancy: Report of a case. Obst Gynec 34:277–283, 1969.

Studd, J.W.W., & J.D. Blainey: Pregnancy and the nephrotic syndrome. Brit MJ 1:276–280, 1969.

Tuberculosis

Tuberculosis of the bronchi, lungs, and pleura is not directly affected by pregnancy but urologic tuberculosis may be. A pregnant patient with tuberculosis is slightly more prone to spontaneous abortion and premature delivery than other women. Tuberculous endometritis and placentitis occur in advanced cases, but congenital tuberculosis is rare. Interruption of pregnancy because of pulmonary tuberculosis is almost never justified on medical grounds since the advent of antituberculosis drugs. Babies born of tuberculous mothers are no more likely to develop the disease than others provided they are separated from the infected mother and unfavorable environment at birth.

Rasmussen, F.: The ototoxic effect of streptomycin and dihydrostreptomycin on the fetus. Scandinav J Resp Dis 50:61–67, 1969.

Rosemann, G.W.E.: Kidney tuberculosis in pregnancy. South African J Obst Gynaec 1:33–35, 1969.

Varpela, E., & others: Streptomycin and dihydrostreptomycin medication during pregnancy and their effect on the child's inner ear. Scandinav J Resp Dis 50:101–109, 1969.

Heart Disease Complicating Pregnancy

About 5% of maternal deaths are due to heart disease. Pregnancy causes a significant increase in pulse rate, an increase of cardiac output of more than 30%, a rise in plasma and blood volume, and expansion of the red cell mass. Both vital capacity and oxygen consumption rise only slightly during pregnancy.

Over 90% of cases of heart disease complicating pregnancy in the USA are of rheumatic origin, and ¾ of these have mitral stenosis. Congenital heart disease constitutes an obstetric problem in less than 5% of cardiac patients.

The physical stress of labor, delivery, and the puerperium imposes moderate to extreme burdens on the maternal heart. These increase to a peak at about 28–32 weeks, when maximal cardiac strain must be anticipated.

In general, patients with class I or class II functional disability (80% of pregnant women with heart disease) do well obstetrically. Over 80% of maternal deaths due to heart disease occur in women with class III or IV cardiac disability. Congestive failure is the usual cause of death. Three-fourths of these deaths occur in the early puerperium. The perinatal fetal death rate is greatly increased when the mother is a class III–IV cardiac.

Therapeutic abortion may be justified in certain cases of pregnancy associated with class III–IV cardiac disease. Cesarean section should be performed only upon obstetric indications. The indications for sterilization should be liberalized for women with class III–IV heart disease not amenable to surgery.

Chesley, L.C.: The remote prognosis for pregnant women with rheumatic cardiac disease. Am J Obst Gynec 100:732–743, 1968.

Collins, H.A., & others: Cardiac surgery during pregnancy. Ann Thoracic Surg 5:300–310, 1968.

D'Cruz, I.A.: Cardiac emergencies in pregnant and puerperal women. Indian Pract 21:31–34, 1968.

Handjani, A.M., & others: Grand multiparity and rheumatic heart disease. Obst Gynec 32:212–213, 1968.

MacDonald, H.N.: Pregnancy following insertion of cardiac valve prosthesis: A review and further case report. J Obstet Gynaec Brit Common 77:603–609, 1970.

Neill, C.A.: Pregnancy and congenital heart disease. Postgrad Med 44:118–122, 1968.

Richardson, P.M., & others: Pericardiectomy in pregnancy. Thorax 25:627–630, 1970.

Urinary Tract Infection During Pregnancy

The urinary tract is especially vulnerable to infections during pregnancy because the altered secretions of steroid sex hormones and the pressure exerted by the gravid uterus upon the ureters and bladder cause hypotonia and congestion and predispose to urinary stasis. Cervicitis and vaginitis also predispose to urinary infection. The trauma of labor and delivery and urinary retention postpartum may initiate or aggravate infection in the urinary system. *Escherichia coli* is an offending organism in over 2/3 of cases.

Almost 10% of pregnant women suffer from urinary tract infection. Chronic pyelonephritis, a major cause of death in older women, often follows recurrent acute urinary tract infections during successive pregnancies. Urinary tract infection increases the likelihood of premature delivery and the incidence of perinatal mortality.

The diagnosis should be based on stained smear and culture of a catheterized or clean-catch specimen of urine. Bacillary infection should be treated initially with sulfisoxazole (Gantrisin®), 2 gm orally and then 1 gm 4 times daily, or nitrofurantoin (Furadantin®), 75 mg orally 4 times daily. If cocci are present, give penicillin G, 1 million units IM and then 600,000 units IM twice daily. Mixed infections should be treated with streptomycin, 1 gm IM, and penicillin G, 600,000 units IM, and then 0.5 gm of streptomycin and 600,000 units of penicillin twice daily. Change to other drugs as dictated by the results of laboratory studies.

Force fluids and alkalinize the urine. Give analgesics, laxatives, and antipyretic drugs as indicated.

Felding, C.F.: Pregnancy following renal disease. Clin Obst Gynec 11:579–593. 1968.

House, T.E., & others: Pregnancy complicated by urinary tract infections. Obst Gynec 34:670–674, 1969.

Kincaid-Smith, P.: Bacteriuria and urinary infections in pregnancy. Clin Obst Gynec 11:533–549, 1968.

Paterson, L., & others: Suprapubic aspiration of urine in diagnosis of urinary tract infections during pregnancy. Lancet 1:1195–1196, 1970.

Anemia

Iron deficiency anemia occurs in about 20% of pregnancies in the USA. About 95% of pregnant women with anemia have the iron deficiency type. Pregnancy increases the body's iron requirement. Many nonpregnant women are iron deficient because of inadequate iron intake (diet), faulty iron absorption, or loss of iron in menstruation, dysfunctional uterine bleeding, or postpartum hemorrhage, or as a result of iron deprivation by the fetus during a previous pregnancy. Many women, anemic before pregnancy, never "catch up" during or after pregnancy. Iron deficiency anemia often develops or increases as pregnancy progresses.

Fetal and maternal morbidity are increased in proportion to the severity of the anemia. Most obstetric problems involving anemia relate to premature delivery and infection. Oral iron supplements are desirable during pregnancy; if iron deficiency anemia is marked, intravenous or intramuscular iron therapy may be required late in pregnancy.

Other types of anemia such as sickle cell anemia, megaloblastic anemia, and hemolytic anemia may complicate pregnancy more rarely.

Coopland, A.T., & others: Acute leukemia in pregnancy. Am J Obst Gynec 105:1288–1289, 1969.

Harrison, K.A.: Changes in blood volume produced by treatment of severe anemia of pregnancy. Clin Sc 36:197–207, 1969.

Hibbard, E.D., & W.J. Spencer: Low serum B_{12} levels and latent Addisonian anaemia in pregnancy. J Obstet Gynaec Brit Common 77:52–57, 1970.

Levin, N., & D. Tabanao-Mahusay: Sickle cell disease in pregnancy: A report on exchange transfusion. Maryland MJ 18:75–77, 1969.

Pakes, J.B., & others: Studies in beta thalassemia trait in pregnancy. Am J Obst Gynec 108:1217–1223, 1970.

Verley, K.W., & E.W. Lowe: The problem of anemia in obstetrical patients. J Nat Med Ass 60:217–220, 1968.

Vyas, R.B., & others: Correlation of various physiological factors with blood volume in severely anemic pregnant women. J Obst Gynec India 19:174–180, 1969.

Syphilis & Gonorrhea

Untreated syphilis acquired shortly before conception usually causes midtrimester abortion or fetal death in utero, and the fetus almost invariably bears the stigmas of syphilis. Syphilis contracted at conception often results in the premature delivery of an infant with congenital syphilis. If syphilis is acquired late in pregnancy, the infant may or may not have the disease at birth. Syphilis contracted in early pregnancy responds in a manner similar to syphilis contracted in late pregnancy but untreated; premature delivery of an infant with congenital syphilis is to be expected. Syphilis contracted during mid pregnancy often results in congenital syphilis in the infant. (See Chapter 22.)

Gonorrhea now is one of the most common infectious diseases in the USA. It must be diagnosed and treated successfully before delivery because gonococcal ophthalmia in neonates may occur even in babies who supposedly received silver nitrate drops in the conjunctival sacs immediately after birth (see p 759).

False-positive (and false-negative) serologic tests for syphilis are not uncommon. Isolation and intensive treatment with penicillin or, in the case of penicillin sensitivity, other antisyphilitic drugs are indicated whenever syphilis is proved or presumed to be present. The possibility that other venereal diseases may be present also must always be considered in any patient with syphilis.

Russell, E.H., & others: The FTA–ABS test in late syphilis. JAMA 203:545–548, 1968.

Thin, R.N.T., & A.M. Michael: Sexually transmitted disease in antenatal patients. Brit J Ven Dis 46:126–128, 1970.

Thyrotoxicosis

Toxic goiter is not common during pregnancy, but it often develops soon after delivery and may have serious consequences. Thyrotoxicosis during pregnancy may result in fetal maldevelopment and goiter.

Radioactive isotope therapy may cause athyreosis in the fetus and therefore must never be given during pregnancy. Antithyroid drugs may be given cautiously, but hypothyroidism must be avoided at all costs to ensure normal fetal development. Elective thyroidectomy following preparation with iodine is recommended by some clinicians in preference to medical management during and after pregnancy.

Hennen, G., & others: Human chorionic thyrotropin: Further characterization and study of its secretion during pregnancy. Clin Endocrinol 29:581–594, 1969.

Hung, W.: Effect of maternal thyrotoxicosis on the fetus and newborn. J Nat Med Ass 61:70–73, 1969.

Kaori, M., & I. Itelson: Management of thyrotoxicosis in pregnancy: Value of serial protein bound iodine and Homolski tests. Israel J Med Sc 5:43–48, 1969.

Parathyroid Dysfunction & Tetany

Pregnancy normally causes a slight (secondary) hyperparathyroidism. Severe, chronic hyperparathyroidism causing osteitis fibrosa cystica is rare during pregnancy except in patients with long-standing renal disease. The most serious problems relating to parathyroid dysfunction during pregnancy are hypoparathyroid tetany and muscle cramps. Tetany is usually associated with a deficiency of calcium or excess of phosphate (eg, due to intake of calcium phosphate prenatal capsules), or lack of vitamin D and parathormone. It may follow infection or the hypocalcemia which sometimes occurs during lactation, or may be seen during the latter months of pregnancy if calcium supplements are inadequate. Hyperventilation during labor may precipitate tetany. Tetany of the newborn is unusual in breast-fed infants, but it may occur transiently if phosphate intake is excessive (eg, if too much cow's milk is given or as a result of relative hypoparathyroidism in the neonatal period).

Osler, M.: Pregnancy and endocrine disorders: Incidence and obstetrical considerations. Acta obst gynec scandinav 46 (Suppl):49–57, 1967.

Rubin, A., & others: Maternal hyperparathyroidism and pregnancy. JAMA 206:128–130, 1968.

The Exanthematous Diseases

Maternal mortality is increased in smallpox and severe epidemic chickenpox. The effects of these viral diseases on the pregnant woman and on the fetus depend upon the virulence of the strain and the degree of the mother's immunity to the disease. High fever, toxicosis, and fetal viremia may result in death of the fetus.

Infants born of women with smallpox, measles, or chickenpox may have the disease at birth, but congenital malformations are rarely present. Congenital anomalies occur in up to 50% of infants born to women who contract sporadic rubella during the first trimester. Gamma globulin will not prevent deformity even if it is given to exposed women before the rash appears. Congenital disorders may result, however, even if the disease never becomes clinically apparent and gamma globulin is given.

Therapeutic abortion on a fetal indication is not permitted in the USA.

Dudgeon, J.A.: Immunization against rubella. Nature 223:674–676, 1969.

Hardy, J.B.: Adverse fetal outcome following maternal rubella after the first trimester. JAMA 207:2414–2420, 1969.

Heggie, A.D., & F.C. Robbins: Natural rubella acquired after birth: Clinical features and complications. Am J Dis Child 118:12–17, 1969.

McNeil, D.D.: Rubella: Its diagnosis, its role in teratogenesis and its prevention. Virginia M Month 95:488–491, 1968.

Plotkim, S.A., & W.J. Mellman: Rubella in the distant past as a possible cause of congenital malformations. Am J Obst Gynec 108:487–489, 1970.

Myopia

It is generally held that pregnant women with myopia have a definite increase in myopia during pregnancy. No large surveys have been done, but it is possible that the increase in refractive error has no relationship to the pregnancy but is merely a normal progression of the disorder occurring in a young woman and that it would have occurred with or without pregnancy.

SURGICAL COMPLICATIONS DURING PREGNANCY

Elective major surgery should be avoided during pregnancy. However, normal, uncomplicated pregnancy has no debilitating effect and does not alter operative risk except as it may interfere with the diagnosis of abdominal disorders and increase the technical problems of intra-abdominal surgery. Abortion is not a serious hazard after operation unless peritoneal sepsis or other significant complication occurs.

During the first trimester, congenital anomalies may be induced in the developing fetus by hypoxia. It is preferable to avoid surgical intervention during this period; if surgery does become necessary, the greatest precautions must be taken to prevent hypoxia and hypotension.

The second trimester is usually the optimum time for operative procedures.

Akasheh, F.: Rupture of the uterus: Analysis of 104 cases of rupture. Am J Obst Gynec 101:406–408, 1968.

D'Cruz, I.A., & others: Maternal deaths due to non-obstetric acute abdominal conditions. J Obst Gynec India 18:524–530, 1968.

Ledger, W.J., & others: Postoperative adnexal infections. Obst Gynec 31:83–89, 1968.

Ramoso-Jalbuena, J., & others: Complications and management of ovarian tumors during pregnancy. J Philippines MA 44:140–148, 1968.

Scott, J.S.: Coagulation failure in obstetrics. Brit M Bull 24:32–38, 1968.

Zilberman, A., & others: Evaluation of cesarian section scar by hysterography. Obst Gynec 32:153–157, 1968.

Ovarian Tumors in Pregnancy

Ovarian tumors in pregnancy are important because of (1) delay in diagnosis and palliation of possible malignant neoplasm; (2) obstruction of the birth canal by the tumor; and (3) the possibility of rupture and chemical peritonitis or intraperitoneal spread of tumor. Tumors with a high malignancy potential include the serous and pseudomucinous cystadenomas, which often are bilateral and large. Teratoid tumors may involve both ovaries, and when they rupture they may cause serious irritation and obstruction. Pelvic examination done early and repeated later in pregnancy may reveal discrete adnexal masses. If these are persistent, greater than 6 cm in diameter, and especially if they are increasing in size or bilateral, laparotomy is indicated despite an advancing pregnancy.

Achari, K., & V. Prasad: Ovarian tumors in pregnancy. J Obst Gynec India 18:444–449, 1968.

Chowdbury, R.: Ovarian tumors complicating pregnancy (a critical analysis of 30 cases). J Obst Gynec India 18:439–443, 1968.

Coates, A.: Cyclophosphamide in pregnancy. Australian New Zealand J Obstet Gynaec 10:33–34, 1970.

Colon & Rectal Carcinoma

Pregnancy increases the likelihood of spread of carcinoma of the colon or rectum. Malignant tumors of the lower bowel are often neglected or palliated during pregnancy with tragic results. The prognosis is extremely poor for the pregnant carcinoma patient unless prompt radical surgery is possible.

The symptoms of rectal and colon carcinoma include constipation of increasing severity, often alternating with transient diarrhea, and rectal bleeding or blood-streaked stools. Anemia and weight loss are late signs.

In almost 2/3 of cases of carcinoma of the colon and rectum, the lesion can be reached by the examining finger and biopsied through the sigmoidoscope even during pregnancy. Barium x-ray studies may reveal the site and extent of the lesion.

The treatment of apparently curable carcinoma of the rectum and colon during pregnancy depends upon the duration of the pregnancy at the time of the diagnosis as well as the extent of the malignancy.

(1) Four to 20 weeks: Radical resection and colostomy via the abdominoperineal approach is indicated, avoiding the pregnant uterus. In the absence of obstetric contraindications, vaginal delivery at term should be permitted.

(2) Twenty-one to 28 weeks: Sacrifice the pregnancy by hysterectomy and then do an abdominoperineal resection and colostomy.

(3) After the 28th week: Cesarean section should be done as soon as fetal viability seems likely. Resect the cancerous bowel and construct a colostomy 3–4 weeks after delivery.

For the incurable patient, cesarean section is indicated as soon as the fetus is viable. Palliative resection should be done at delivery or afterward to prevent intestinal obstruction.

Carcinoma of the Breast

Cancer of the breast is diagnosed approximately once in 3500 pregnancies and accounts for about 2.5% of breast cancers in women. Pregnancy accelerates the growth of cancer of the breast. Inflammatory carcinoma is an extremely serious type of breast cancer which occurs most commonly during lactation in young, obese women with pendulous breasts.

If breast biopsy confirms the diagnosis of cancer, radical mastectomy should be done regardless of the stage of the pregnancy. (An exception is inflammatory carcinoma, which invariably is far-advanced when correctly diagnosed. Surgery or irradiation will not benefit such a patient, for whom the prospect is hopeless.) If spread to the regional glands has occurred, x-ray therapy should be given also. Therapeutic abortion or interruption of pregnancy is usually of no value. Cesarean section should be performed only upon obstetric indications. After delivery, oophorectomy, adrenalectomy, and hypophysectomy may be considered for palliation of advanced breast cancer.

The 5-year survival rate in patients with stage I cancer of the breast diagnosed during pregnancy and treated by radical surgery is 60–70%; with stage II breast cancer, the survival rate drops to less than 10% even with radical surgery and x-ray therapy.

Lynch, G.A.: Breast cancer associated with pregnancy. Ulster MJ 38:34–46, 1969.
Zeigerman, J.H., & others: Inflammatory mammary cancer during pregnancy and lactation. Obst Gynec 32:373–375, 1968.

Choledocholithiasis & Cholecystitis

Severe choledocholithiasis and cholecystitis are not common during pregnancy despite the fact that women tend to form gallstones (1/3 of all women over 40 have gallstones). When they do occur, it is usually in late pregnancy or in the puerperium. About 90% of patients with cholecystitis have gallstones.

Symptomatic relief may be all that is required. Meperidine (Demerol®) and atropine are effective in alleviating pain and ductal spasm. Morphine is contraindicated in cholelithiasis or cholecystitis because it may induce spasm of the sphincter of Oddi.

Gallbladder surgery in pregnant women should be attempted only in extreme cases (eg, obstruction) because it greatly increases the fetal mortality rate (up to about 15%). Cholecystostomy and lithotomy may be all that is feasible during advanced pregnancy, deferring cholecystectomy until after delivery. On the other hand, withholding surgery when it is definitely needed may result in necrosis and perforation of the gallbladder and peritonitis. Intermittent high fever, jaundice, and right upper quadrant pain may indicate cholangitis due to impacted common duct stone. Surgical removal of gallstones and establishment of biliary drainage are essential in such cases.

Therapeutic abortion or early delivery (by induction or cesarean section) is not warranted.

O'Neill, J.P.: Surgical conditions complicating pregnancy. II. Diseases of the gallbladder and pancreas. Australian New Zealand J Obstet Gynaec 9:249–252, 1969.
Roszkowski, I., & S. Pisarek-Miedzinska: Jaundice in pregnancy. II. Clinical course of pregnancy and delivery and condition of the neonate. Am J Obst Gynec 101:500–503, 1968.

Ileus

Adynamic (paralytic) ileus is the result of diminished or absent contractility of the bowel and causes intestinal obstruction. Ileus is rare before delivery, but moderate ileus is common in the postpartum period, especially after cesarean section. Obstetric complications such as peritonitis, renal or ureteral stone, or torsion of the adnexa and bladder atony may be associated with adynamic ileus.

A "silent" bowel is indicative of reduced or absent peristalsis. Abdominal tenderness and pain are present. A "laddering" effect of gas in the bowel segments in the small and large intestine on x-ray films supports the diagnosis of adynamic ileus.

It is essential to differentiate paralytic ileus from ileus due to mechanical obstruction. In the latter form, the bowel is hyperactive and x-rays reveal distention of the intestine proximal to the obstruction.

The treatment of paralytic ileus is discussed in Chapter 10. Ileus due to mechanical obstruction usually requires surgery.

O'Neill, J.P.: Surgical complications of pregnancy. III. Intestinal obstruction and miscellaneous conditions. Australian New Zealand J Obstet Gynaec 10:10–17, 1970.
See reference under Hernia, below.

Hernia

Pregnancy gives temporary protection from umbilical, incisional, and often inguinal hernias even though it widens the hernial rings. The enlarging uterus displaces the intestines, so that the bowel will usually not enter a defect in the body wall. Many abdominal hernias are reduced spontaneously during pregnancy; a few irreducible ones may result in obstruction of the involved intestine. After delivery, hernia again becomes a hazard, but the chance of incarceration is not increased.

Incarcerated hernias must be reduced surgically during pregnancy if severe pain or obstruction develops. Elective herniorrhaphy should be deferred until after delivery. The necessity for repair of hernias is not an indication for cesarean section. Women with abdominal hernias should be delivered by the low forceps technic to prevent straining before and during labor.

Craddock, D.R., & J.I. Hall: Strangulated diaphragmatic hernia complicating pregnancy. Brit J Surg 55:559–560, 1968.
Utian, W.H.: Umbilical hernia containing a pregnant uterus at term. South Africa J Obst Gynec 6:18–20, 1968.

Ureteral Stone

Ureteral stone is more common during pregnancy than otherwise because of the dilatation of the renal pelvis and ureter which occurs in response to high titers of steroid sex hormones and the minor (physiologic) obstructive uropathy characteristic of pregnancy. Small stones, previously retained, are thus permitted to enter the proximal ureter. Most ureteral stones are passed in the urine, albeit painfully; others become impacted. Sudden, agonizing pain in the costovertebral angle and flank with radiation to the lower quadrant and vulva, urinary urgency, and hematuria without—initially—pyuria or fever are characteristic of ureteral stone. X-ray films rarely reveal a stone, but intravenous urography may demonstrate partial obstruction.

Symptomatic therapy with hypnotics and antispasmodics is always indicated. Paravertebral or caudal block may sometimes be used for relief of pain and to relax the spastic ureter. Retrograde catheter manipulation may dislodge the stone and permit it to pass, or the stone may be extracted transureterally. If such efforts are unsuccessful and if severe pain persists and progressive hydronephrosis develops, remove the stone by extraperitoneal ureterolithotomy irrespective of the patient's obstetric status. In the absence of dystocia, normal delivery at term is the rule.

Harris, R.E., & D.R. Dunnihoo: Incidence and significance of urinary calculi in pregnancy. Am J Obst Gynec 99:237–241, 1967.

Appendicitis During Pregnancy

Appendicitis occurs in about one of 1200 pregnancies. Management is more difficult than when the disease occurs in nonpregnant persons since the appendix is carried high and to the right, away from McBurney's point, and localization of infection does not usually occur. The distended uterus displaces the colon and small bowel; uterine contractions prevent abscess formation and walling-off; and the intestinal relationships are disturbed. In at least 20% of obstetric patients, the correct diagnosis is not made until the appendix has ruptured and peritonitis has become established. Delay may lead to premature labor or abortion.

Early appendectomy is indicated. If the diagnosis is made during labor at or near term, do an extraperitoneal cesarean section and appendectomy to minimize peritonitis. Therapeutic abortion is never indicated with appendicitis. If drains are necessary, they should be transabdominal, not transvaginal.

With early diagnosis and appendectomy, the prognosis is good for the mother and her baby.

Heera, P.: Acute appendicitis during pregnancy, labor and puerperium. J Obst Gynec India 18:496–499, 1968.
O'Neill, J.P.: Surgical conditions complicating pregnancy. I. Acute appendicitis real and simulated. Australian New Zealand J Obstet Gynaec 9:94–99, 1969.
Todd, D.W., & others: Chronic appendicitis: Report of a case coexistent with pregnancy. Am J Obst Gynec 107:650–651, 1970.

PREVENTION OF HEMOLYTIC DISEASE OF THE NEWBORN
(Erythroblastosis Fetalis)

The antibody anti-Rh_o(D) is responsible for most severe instances of hemolytic disease of the newborn (erythroblastosis fetalis). The Rh_o(D) antigen, also called the Rh factor, is inherited by approximately 85% of Caucasians. The remaining 15% are Rh-negative or, more properly, Rh_o(D)-negative. An Rh_o(D)-negative woman who carried an Rh_o(D)-positive fetus often develops the antibody anti-Rh_o(D). This antibody, once produced, remains in the woman's circulation during subsequent pregnancies. It poses a serious threat of hemolytic disease for subsequent fetuses whose red cells carry the antigen.

Immunization against hemolytic disease of the newborn now is possible with human Rh_o(D) immune globulin (RhoGAM®). This purified concentrate of antibodies against $Rh_0(D)$ antigen is obtained from Rh-negative women immune to the D-antigen. A passive immunity is conferred when such a preparation is injected into another individual. Unfortunately, passive immunity is brief. Nevertheless, passive antibodies can prevent active immunity from occurring, as in a mother who is producing anti-$Rh_0(D)$.

When fetal Rh-positive red cells enter the mother's blood stream, she does not begin to produce anti-$Rh_0(D)$ immediately. If passive anti-$Rh_0(D)$ is injected soon after delivery ($<$ 72 hours), therapeutically administered anti-$Rh_0(D)$ will attack and destroy fetal Rh-positive cells so that $Rh_0(D)$ antigen is removed from her circulation. Once the antigen is eliminated, the mother will not produce anti-$Rh_0(D)$ and she does not become actively immune to $Rh_0(D)$. Hence, during her next Rh-positive gestation, there will be no anti-$Rh_0(D)$ antibodies in her blood stream to react to fetal red cells, and erythroblastosis will be prevented during that pregnancy.

The immunizing dose of human $Rh_0(D)$ immune globulin is 2 ml IM.

Alvey, J., & others: Prevention of rhesus iso-immunization. J Irish Med Ass 61:311–314, 1968.

Diamond, L.K.: Protection against Rh sensitization and prevention of erythroblastosis fetalis. Pediatrics 41:1–4, 1968.

Horger, E.O., III: Prevention of Rh sensitization: A report on the effectiveness of Rh immunoglobulins in preventing Rh sensitization. Pennsylvania Med 71:75–78, 1968.

Prevention of Rh haemolytic disease, 1969. MJ Australia 1:1035–1036, 1969.

QUELLING LABOR

The successful prevention of premature labor and delivery would reduce perinatal mortality and morbidity enormously. Ethyl alcohol administered intravenously to the point of inebriation will inhibit pituitary release of oxytocin, the impetus for labor. Give as 0.5% solution in 500 ml of 5% dextrose in water. The first 100–200 ml must be run in rapidly and the drip then slowed to 10–20 ml/hour for maintained sedation. This dosage is safe for both the mother and the fetus.

Isoxsuprine (Vasodilan®) is a uterine relaxant and may also inhibit otherwise uncomplicated premature labor. Give 10 mg IV in 500 ml of 5% dextrose in water over a 1–2 hour period. This can be repeated over a 24-hour period, after which 10 mg orally every 3 hours may be substituted. Isoxsuprine may cause maternal hypotension or syncope or fetal bradycardia. Hence, this medication requires careful control.

Alcohol or isoxsuprine will not prevent or stop contractions when the membranes are ruptured or when the cervix is widely dilated. Other drugs such as the opiates and anesthetics, possibly harmful to the fetus, may slow uterine contractions, but they will not stop established labor.

Krapohl, A.J., Anderson, J.M., & T.N. Evans: Isoxsuprine suppression of uterine activity. Obst Gynec 32:178–187, 1968.

SUPPRESSION OF LACTATION

If the patient does not wish to suckle her infant and wishes to "dry up" her breasts, this can be done by estrogen or androgen administration or by mechanical inhibition of lactation. Hormones presumably suppress lactation by inhibiting the secretion of pituitary hormone. Hormonal suppression is effective only if started immediately after delivery. Postpartum bleeding may be increased.

Suppression With Estrogens

A. Oral Estrogens: Eg, ethinyl estradiol, 1.3 mg (26 tablets containing 0.05 mg each), administered as follows: (Diethylstilbestrol may be used in comparable doses.)

1. Four tablets (0.2 mg) twice daily on the first postpartum day.

2. Three tablets (0.15 mg) twice daily on the second day.

3. Two tablets (0.1 mg) twice daily on the third day.

4. One tablet (0.05 mg) twice daily on the 4th through the 7th days.

B. Depot Estrogens: Estradiol valerate (Delestrogen®), 3 ml of a solution containing 10 mg/ml immediately after delivery.

Suppression With Estrogen & Progestin

High-dosage estrogen-progestogen combinations with estrogen dominance (eg, Enovid®, 5 mg) are moderately effective in suppressing lactation. Inhibition is principally due to the suppressive effect of estrogen on hypothalamic-pituitary function.

Suppression With Androgens

Methyltestosterone, 10 mg buccal tablets dissolved in the cheek pouch 5 times daily on the second and third postpartum days.

Suppression With Estrogens & Androgens

Testosterone enanthate, 90 mg/ml, and estradiol valerate, 4 mg/ml, 3 ml injected IM immediately after delivery.

Mechanical Suppression of Lactation

If the patient begins to nurse and then for any reason wishes to transfer her baby to formula feedings and dry up her breasts (eg, if mastitis develops or the baby is to be weaned), hormones will not be effective and mechanical suppression is indicated. The patient should cease attempting to nurse and should not express milk or pump her breasts. Apply a tight compression "uplift" binder for 72 hours and a snug brassiere thereafter. Ice packs and analgesics, eg, aspirin and codeine, can be used as necessary. Fluid restriction and laxatives are of no value.

The breasts will become distended, firm, and tender. After 48–72 hours, lactation will cease and pain will subside. Involution will be complete in about 1 month.

The uncommon but impressive occurrence of thromboembolic phenomena in parturients on high-dosage estrogen or estrogen-progestogen medication is reminiscent of similar problems ascribed to the oral contraceptives. When the likelihood of vascular occlusion is increased, as in postcesarean section patients, those who have had a difficult vaginal delivery, a febrile course, etc, mechanical suppression of lactation is the logical choice when nursing is not elected.

Barbour, E.M., & N.K. Barnah: Inhibition of lactation with quinestrol. Scottish MJ 13:277–279, 1968.

Jeffcoate, T.N.A., & others: Puerperal thromboembolism in relation to the inhibition of lactation by estrogen therapy. Brit MJ 4:19–25, 1968.

Slotnick, E.A.: The use of a progestational agent in the immediate postpartum period for the suppression of lactation. J Am Osteopath Ass 68:705–708, 1969.

Sterrat, G.M., & others: The effectiveness of stilbestrol in the suppression of postpartum lactation. J Obstet Gynaec Brit Common 75:313–315, 1968.

Turnbull, A.C.: Puerperal thromboembolism and suppression of lactation. J Obstet Gynaec Brit Common 75:1321–1323, 1968.

PUERPERAL MASTITIS

Postpartum inflammation of the breast occurs most often in clinic patients after several weeks or more of nursing. Infection is via the ducts following contamination of the nipple, and is often related to fissures in the nipple or obstructed milk flow. The hemolytic *Staphylococcus aureus* is the causative agent in most cases. Inflammation is unilateral in 3/4 of patients; primiparas are most often affected.

The onset is with chills, fever, malaise, and regional pain, tenderness, and induration. Localization, mass formation, fluctuation, and axillary adenopathy occur later. In most cases, once infection is well established, abscess formation is unavoidable.

Treatment consists of suppression of lactation, constant support of the breasts, antipyretics and analgesics, and intensive broad-spectrum antibiotic therapy. Incision and drainage are required if abscess formation occurs.

Prevention consists of proper initial nursing procedure and breast hygiene.

Devereux, W.P.: Acute puerperal mastitis: Evaluation of its management. Am J Obst Gynec 108:78–81, 1970.

Richardsom, W.W.: Breast abscess. Brit J Hosp Med 2:1137, 1969.

• • •

General Bibliography

Baird, D.: *Combined Textbook of Obstetrics and Gynecology.* Livingstone, 1969.

Behrman, S.J., & J.R.G. Gosling: *Fundamentals of Gynecology,* 2nd ed. Oxford, 1966.

Benson, R.C.: *Handbook of Obstetrics & Gynecology,* 4th ed. Lange, 1971.

British Medical Journal: *Obstetrics in General Practice II.* Grune & Stratton, 1966.

Clayton, S.G., & others: *Obstetrics by Ten Teachers,* 11th ed. Williams & Wilkins, 1966.

Clinical Obstetricss and Gynecology. A Quarterly Book Series. Hoeber. [By subscription only, published 4 times a year.]

Danforth, D.N.: *Textbook of Obstetrics and Gynecology,* 2nd ed. Harper, 1971.

Dewhurst, C.: *Student's Guide to Obstetrics and Gynecology,* 2nd ed. Williams & Wilkins, 1966.

Eastman, N.J., & L.M. Hellman: *Williams' Obstetrics,* 14th ed. Appleton-Century-Crofts, 1971.

Garrey, M.M., & others: *Obstetrics Illustrated.* Livingstone, 1969.

Green, T.H., Jr.: *Gynecology,* 2nd ed. Little, Brown, 1971.

Greenhill, J.P.: *Obstetrics,* 13th ed. Saunders, 1965.

Jeffcoate, T.N.A.: *Principles of Gynecology,* 4th ed. Appleton-Century-Crofts, 1971.

Jones, H.W., Jr., & R.H. Heller: *Pediatric and Adolescent Gynecology.* Williams & Wilkins, 1966.

Kistner, R.W.: *Gynecology Principles and Practice,* 2nd ed. Year Book, 1971.

McLennan, C.E.: *Synopsis of Obstetrics,* 8th ed. Mosby, 1970.

Novak, E.R., Jones, G.S., & H.W. Jones: *Novak's Textbook of Gynecology,* 8th ed. Williams & Wilkins, 1970.

Novak, R.E., & J.D. Woodruff: *Novak's Gynecologic and Obstetric Pathology,* 7th ed. Saunders, 1970.

Pinker, G.D., & D.W.T. Roberts: *Short Textbook of Gynecology and Obstetrics.* Lippincott, 1967.

Reid, D.E.: *Textbook of Obstetrics.* Saunders, 1962.

Taylor, E.S.: *Essentials of Gynecology,* 4th ed. Lea & Febiger, 1969.

Taylor, E.S.: *Beck's Obstetric Practice,* 8th ed. William & Wilkins, 1966.

Willson, J.R., & others: *Obstetrics and Gynecology,* 4th ed. Mosby, 1970,

13 . . .

Arthritis & Allied Rheumatic Disorders

Ephraim P. Engleman, Joseph E. Giansiracusa, & Milton J. Chatton

Examination of the Patient

The specific diagnosis of a rheumatic disease can usually be made at the bedside or in the office.

The examination depends upon a careful history and physical examination, with special attention to articular signs of inflammation (eg, heat, soft tissue swelling, effusion) and the functional status of the joints (eg, range of motion, ankylosis, deformity, atrophy). Certain laboratory procedures, depending upon the suspected diagnosis, complete the study. These most commonly include a complete blood count, urinalysis, ESR, tests for rheumatoid factor and antinuclear antibodies, serum uric acid determination, and x-rays of key joints. These studies are important not only for diagnosis but also serve as a base-line for judging the results of therapy.

Examination of Joint Fluid

Synovial fluid examination may provide valuable diagnostic and prognostic information in the management of joint disease. It also demonstrates the severity of synovial tissue inflammation. The skin overlying the joint to be aspirated is cleansed with soap and water and then prepared with an antiseptic solution. With sterile technic the puncture site is infiltrated with a local anesthetic. The knee, by far the easiest joint to tap, is entered with an 18 gauge needle slightly superior and 2 cm (¾ inch) lateral (or medial) to the patella with the joint fully extended. From this position the suprapatellar space is entered. After removal of as much fluid as possible, the needle is withdrawn and the puncture site covered with a sterile bandage or adhesive dressing.

The following studies should then be performed:

(1) Gross examination: Carefully note consistency and appearance. If fluid is green or purulent, examination with Gram's stain may be indicated. If grossly bloody, consider a bleeding disorder, trauma, or "traumatic tap." Note if fluid is xanthochromic.

(2) Microscopic examination:

(a) Cytology: Collect 2–5 ml in a heparinized bottle (to prevent clotting). The red and white cells are counted, using the same equipment and technic as for a standard white count. The diluent, however, should be normal saline since the usual acidified diluent causes the fluid to clot in the pipet (see below). One drop of methylene blue added to the saline makes the cells distinguishable. Differential counts are performed on thin smears with Wright's stain.

(b) Crystals: Compensated polarized light microscopy identifies the existence and type of crystals.

(c) Examine for RA inclusion cells and LE cells.

(3) Mucin clot tests for hyaluronate: A small amount of fluid is placed in a test tube and enough acetic acid is added to make a final concentration of about 1% or more. The clot is graded from good to very poor according to its integrity. (See Table 13–1.)

(4) Culture: Collect 1 ml of fluid in a sterile culture tube and perform routine cultures as well as special studies for gonococci, tubercle bacilli, or fungi as indicated.

(5) Sugar: Collect 2–3 ml of fluid in a fluoride tube. The patient must be fasting, and the blood sugar must be determined at the time of joint aspiration.

(6) Examine synovial fluid for rheumatoid factor.

Interpretation: Synovial fluid studies are not diagnostic unless a specific organism is identified in the culture or unless the urate crystals of gouty synovitis or the calcium pyrophosphate crystals of pseudogout are demonstrated. Most of the latter patients have articular chondrocalcinosis and often evidence of arthritis. As shown in Table 13–1, there is considerable overlap in the cytologic and biochemical values obtained in different diseases. These studies do, however, make possible a differentiation according to the severity of inflammation. Thus joint fluids in inflammatory diseases such as infections and rheumatoid arthritis are often turbid with an elevated white count (usually well above 3000 cells/cu mm, with over 50% polynucleated forms), a poor mucin clot, and a synovial fluid sugar content which is considerably lower than the blood sugar. Diseases in which articular inflammation is relatively mild, such as osteoarthritis and traumatic arthritis, usually produce a clear fluid with a low white count (usually below 3000/cu mm) and a good mucin clot; and the synovial fluid and blood sugar levels are within 10 mg/100 ml of each other.

RHEUMATOID ARTHRITIS

Essentials of Diagnosis

- A systemic disease.
- Prodromal symptoms common: malaise, fever, weight loss, sweating or paresthesias (or both) of hands and feet, Raynaud's phenomenon, morning stiffness.

TABLE 13–1. Significant synovial fluid findings in common joint diseases.*

	Appearance	Clot	Range†	Leukocytes (/cu mm)	PMN's (%)	Type of Mucin‡ Ppt	Sugar Differences§ (mg/100 ml)	Crystals
Normal	Clear	0	Min / Avg / Max	13 / 63 / 180	0 / 7 / 25	G / G / G	<10	0
Traumatic arthritis	Clear	0 to +	Min / Avg / Max	50 / 1,250 / 10,400	0 / 5 / 36	F / G / G	−4 / 5 / 24	0
Osteoarthritis (degenerative joint disease)	Clear to slightly turbid	0 to ++	Min / Avg / Max	70 / 720 / 8,600	0 / 7 / 58	F / G / G	−6 / 0 / 17	Possible (calcium phosphate)
Rheumatic fever	Slightly turbid	0 to +++	Min / Avg / Max	300 / 17,820 / 98,200	2 / 50 / 98	F / G / G	−5 / 4 / 9	0
Gouty arthritis	Turbid	± to ++++	Min / Avg / Max	1000 / 13,317 / 70,600	0 / 71 / 99	VP / P / G	−12 / 12 / 74	Present (urate)
Rheumatoid arthritis	Clear to turbid	0 to ++++	Min / Avg / Max	450 / 14,000 / 66,000	0 / 65 / 96	VP / P / G	−14 / 26 / 87	Occasional (cholesterol)
Tuberculous arthritis	Turbid	0 to +++	Min / Avg / Max	2500 / 19,470 / 105,000	18 / 60 / 96	VP / P / G	−3 / 60 / 108	0
Specific infectious arthritis	Very turbid	0 to ++++	Min / Avg / Max	7800 / 73,370 / 266,000	46 / 90 / 100	VP / VP / F	−40 / 71 / 122	0

*Modified from M.W. Ropes: Bull Rheum Dis 7(Suppl):22, 1957.

†The values to the right of this column indicate the ranges found: min = minimum; avg = average; max = maximum.

‡VP = few flecks in cloudy solution; P = small friable mass in cloudy solution; F = soft mass in clear or slightly cloudy solution; G = tight, ropy clump in clear solution.

§The difference between serum and fluid concentration.

- Onset usually insidious and in small joints of hands and feet; progression is centripetal and symmetric; deformities common.
- Other extra-articular signs: atrophy of skin and muscle, lymphadenopathy, subcutaneous nodules, splenomegaly, iritis.
- Serologic tests for rheumatoid factor (RF) often positive.

General Considerations (See Table 13–2.)

Rheumatoid arthritis is a chronic, systemic inflammatory disease of unknown etiology. Its prevalence rate in the general population is 1–3%; female patients outnumber males almost 3:1. The usual age at onset is 20–40 years; the disease is relatively uncommon in children. Psoriasis is seen in about 5% of cases.

The pathologic findings in the joint include chronic synovitis with pannus formation. Cartilage erosion occurs early. In the acute phase, effusion and other manifestations of inflammation are common. In the late stage organization may result in fibrous ankylosis; true bony ankylosis is occasionally seen. In both acute and chronic phases, inflammation of soft tissues around the joints may be prominent. Granulomatous invasion of adjacent bone with resulting bony destruction may occur.

The most characteristic histologic lesion of rheumatoid arthritis is the subcutaneous nodule. This is a granuloma with a central zone of necrosis, a surrounding palisade of radially arranged elongated connective tissue cells, and a periphery of chronic granulation tissue. Pathologic alterations indistinguishable from those of the subcutaneous nodule are occasionally seen in the myocardium, pericardium, endocardium, heart valves, visceral pleura, lungs, sclera, dura mater, spleen, and larynx, as well as in the synovia, periarticular tissues, and tendons. Nonspecific pericarditis and pleuritis are found in 25–40% of autopsied patients. Additional nonspecific lesions include inflammation of small arteries, pulmonary fibrosis, round cell infiltration of skeletal muscle and perineurium, and hyperplasia of lymph nodes. Secondary amyloidosis is found in 20% or more of autopsied patients.

Clinical Findings

A. Symptoms and Signs: The onset of articular signs of inflammation is usually insidious, with prodromal symptoms of malaise, weight loss, vasomotor disturbances (eg, paresthesias, Raynaud's phenomenon),

TABLE 13–2. Diagnostic characteristics of the major features of arthritis.

	Rheumatoid Arthritis	Arthritis Due to Specific Infection	Osteoarthritis	Arthritis Due to Gout
Family history of similar illness	Often	No	Often	Yes
Sex prevalence	Most common in women.	Either sex.	Either sex.	Usually men (90–95%).
Age at onset	Any age, but usually 20–40.	Any age.	Usually over 40.	Usually over 35.
Type of onset	Insidious (subacute), usual. Acute, atypical.	Acute infection: sudden. Chronic infection: slow.	Insidious (slow).	Sudden (cessation of symptoms also sudden).
Fever	Yes	Yes (especially acute).	No.	Yes (during acute episodes).
Chills	Only in children.	Yes	No	No
Joints involved	Any; often symmetric; tendency to spread centripetally. Especially proximal finger joints.	Any; usually monarticular.	Usually the large and weight-bearing joints; also distal joints of fingers.	Any; mon- or polyarticular. Especially metatarsophalangeal joint of great toe.
Joint effusion	Yes	Yes	Slight if any.	Yes
Ankylosis	Yes	Yes	No	No
Muscle atrophy	Yes	Yes (local).	Yes (local).	Yes (late).
Deformities	Yes	Yes (late).	Yes (late).	Yes (late).
Skin changes	Atrophic, glossy over joints.	Similar to rheumatoid arthritis.	Senile changes.	Local desquamation and pruritus with recovery from acute attack.
Subcutaneous nodules	Yes	No	No	Yes (tophi with urate crystals).
Anemia	Yes	No (early), yes (chronic).	No	No
Leukocytosis	May be present.	May be present.	No	May be present during acute episode.
Sedimentation rate or C-reactive protein	Elevated	Elevated	Normal	Elevated
X-ray appearance of joints	Early: juxta-articular osteoporosis; joint effusion. Late: narrowing of joint spaces, bone destruction, ankylosis.	Similar to rheumatoid arthritis, but changes appear much faster and osteoporosis is more prominent near involved joints.	No changes until late; lipping, osteophytes, and narrowing of joint spaces.	Early: normal. Late: punched-out radiolucent areas of epiphyseal bone, not necessarily diagnostic.
Other diagnostic features	Positive "rheumatoid factor" agglutination tests (latex, bentonite, etc).	Bacteriologic evidence of specific infection.	Absence of related systemic manifestations	Serum uric acid > 7.5 mg/100 ml. Prompt relief of acute episode by colchicine.

and vague periarticular pain or stiffness. Less often, the onset is acute, apparently triggered by a stressful situation such as infection, trauma, or emotional strain. In any case there is characteristically symmetric joint swelling with associated stiffness, redness, warmth, tenderness, and pain. Pain and stiffness are prominent in the morning and subside during the day with moderate use. Stiffness may recur after daytime inactivity and may be much more severe after strenuous activity. Although any joint may be affected, the proximal interphalangeal and metacarpophalangeal joints of the fingers, wrists, knees, ankles, and toes are most often involved. Monarticular disease is occasionally seen early, especially in children. Palmar erythema is seen occasionally, as are tiny hemorrhagic infarcts in the nail folds or finger pulps and other signs of vasculitis. An evanescent morbilliform rash is commonly observed in children. Twenty percent of patients have subcutaneous nodules. These are most commonly situated over bony prominences, but are also observed in the bursas and tendon sheaths. Five to 10% of patients have an enlarged spleen, and about 30% have lymph node enlargement. Low-grade fever, anorexia, weight loss, fatigue, and weakness are often present; chills do not occur except in children with severe disease. After months or years, thickening of the periarticular tissue, flexion deformities, subluxation, and ankylosis may occur. Atrophy of skin or muscle is common. Dryness of the eyes, with corneal and conjunctival staining characteristic of keratoconjunctivitis sicca, is found especially in advanced disease (see Sjögren's syndrome). Other ocular manifestations include episcleritis and nongranulomatous iritis. Pericarditis and pleuropulmonary disease, when present, are frequently unsuspected clinically and found only at autopsy.

B. Laboratory Findings: Serum protein abnormalities are often present. Various serologic technics are used to detect certain macroglobulins which constitute the so-called rheumatoid factor. One of these, the F2 latex fixation test, is positive in 60–75% of cases. More sensitive tests will yield even higher percentages of positivity. False-positive reactions are not unusual, especially with old age, liver disease, and syphilis, and in symptom-free relatives of patients with rheumatoid arthritis. Antinuclear antibodies are often demonstrable, although their titers are usually lower in rheumatoid arthritis than in systemic lupus erythematosus.

During both the acute and chronic phases the C-reactive protein and the ESR are elevated. A moderate hypochromic normocytic anemia is common. The white count is normal or slightly elevated, but leukopenia may occur especially in the presence of splenomegaly. Joint fluid examination is valuable, reflecting abnormalities which are associated with varying degrees of inflammation.

C. X-Ray Findings: Early signs are osteoporosis around the involved joint and erosion of the cartilage at the periphery of the joint surface. Later, extensive erosion of cartilage produces joint space narrowing. Bony cysts result from invasion by granulation tissue. After some years the degenerative changes of secondary osteoarthritis may be superimposed.

Differential Diagnosis

The differentiation of rheumatoid arthritis from other diseases of connective tissue can be exceedingly difficult, even impossible. However, certain clinical features are often helpful. Rheumatic fever is characterized by the migratory nature of the arthritis, the dramatic and objective response to salicylates in adequate dosage, the more common occurrence of carditis, skin rashes, and chorea, and the elevated antistreptolysin titer. Butterfly rash, positive LE preparations, and renal disease point to the diagnosis of systemic lupus erythematosus. Osteoarthritis is not associated with constitutional manifestations and the joint pain of the latter is characteristically relieved by rest, frequently in contrast to the morning stiffness of rheumatoid arthritis. Signs of articular inflammation, prominent in rheumatoid arthritis, are usually minimal in osteoarthritis. Gouty arthritis may be confused with rheumatoid arthritis, but acute onset in one joint, hyperuricemia, the identification of urate crystals in the joint fluid, the presence of tophi, and the dramatic response to colchicine are helpful in diagnosis. Pyogenic arthritis can be distinguished by chills as well as fever, the demonstration of the causative organism in the joint fluid, and the frequent presence of a primary focus elsewhere, eg, gonococcal urethritis.

Treatment

A. Basic Program (Conservative Management): All evidence indicates that conservative management offers a long-term prognosis often as good as or better than that of more spectacular methods. Since none of these latter measures are curative, and because their administration is often accompanied by undesirable side effects, a conservative approach is usually the method of choice.

The primary objectives of treatment of rheumatoid arthritis are the reduction of inflammation and pain, preservation of function, and prevention of deformity. A simple regimen consisting of rest, physical therapy, and salicylates is the best means of rehabilitating the patient without trading existing problems for others which may be even more devastating. In any event, these measures are so basically necessary as to warrant their continuation even when more heroic steps must be taken. In other words, these measures constitute the basic program of treatment to which other treatment may be added if necessary.

1. Systemic rest–There is a great deal of empirical evidence for the benefits of systemic rest. That rheumatoid arthritis is a systemic disease and not a disease limited to the joints has been shown above. Rest may be considered a common therapeutic denominator, treating as it does the person as a whole. Although a recent clinical study has questioned the beneficial effects of prolonged bed rest, the preponderance of evidence supports the view that intermittent rest has definite value. Rest, in some measure, should be prescribed when the diagnosis of active disease is made. This assumes that bed rest is supervised and that other aspects of care are not neglected.

The amount of rest required depends upon the severity of the disease. Complete bed rest may be desirable and even imperative, particularly in patients with profound systemic and articular involvement. In mild disease 2–4 hours of rest each day may suffice, allowing the patient to continue his work by restricting only his avocational activities. The duration of the rest program depends upon the course. In general, rest should be continued until significant improvement is sustained for at least 2 weeks, at which time the program may be liberalized. However, the increase of physical activity must proceed gradually and with appropriate support for any involved weight-bearing joints. Recrudescence of the disease is an indication for retarding the rate of physical restoration.

2. Emotional rest–The importance of emotional factors in rheumatoid arthritis and the need for psychologic support cannot be overemphasized. This support depends upon rapport between the patient and his doctor. An understanding of the patient's personality and his emotional reactions to his illness (and to all the exigencies of his life) allows the doctor to guide him in his present problems and to anticipate many others.

3. Articular rest–Decrease of articular inflammation may be expedited by articular rest. Articular rest is accompanied by bed rest in the case of weight-bearing joints but is further enhanced by appropriate adjustable orthopedic supports or splints. These are of particular value in the presence of deformity, whether due to muscle spasm or soft tissue contracture. Splints not only provide rest for inflamed joints but also relieve spasm and thus pain, and also prevent deformities or reduce deformities already present. They must be removable to permit daily motion and exercise of the affected extremities (see below). When ambulation is started, care must be taken to avoid weight-bearing which will aggravate flexion deformities. This is accomplished with the aid of supports such as crutches and braces until the tendency to contracture has subsided.

4. Exercise—This is the most important modality in the physical therapy of rheumatoid arthritis. The management of rheumatoid arthritis is based on the concomitant administration of rest and therapeutic exercise, always in proper balance. Therapeutic exercises are designed to preserve joint motion and muscular strength and endurance. Most effective are exercises of the active-assistive type. These should be performed, within the limits of pain tolerance, from the outset of management. As tolerance for exercise increases and the activity of the disease subsides, progressive resistance exercises may be introduced. (Specific instructions for exercises are contained in *Home Care in Rheumatoid Arthritis,* a booklet published by the Arthritis Foundation, 1212 Avenue of the Americas, New York City.)

5. Heat—This is used primarily for its muscle relaxing and analgesic effect. Radiant or moist heat is generally most satisfactory. The ambulatory patient will find warm tub baths most convenient. Exercise may be better performed after exposure to heat.

6. Salicylates—Aspirin and sodium salicylate are the analgesic drugs of choice. There is evidence that salicylates also exert an anti-inflammatory effect. The proper dosage is that amount that provides optimal relief of symptoms without causing toxic reactions. Most adults can tolerate daily doses of 4–6 gm. Tinnitus and gastric irritation are early manifestations of toxicity. If tinnitus occurs, the daily dose should be decreased by decrements of 0.6 or 0.9 gm until this symptom disappears. The addition of antacids, especially at bedtime, may lessen symptoms of gastric irritation. This may also be accomplished by the ingestion of salicylates with meals and at bedtime with antacid. The use of enteric-coated tablets may also reduce gastric irritation, but enteric coating may interfere with the absorption of salicylates.

7. Other analgesic drugs—Anti-inflammatory analgesic drugs (see below) may be required for pain relief in progressive and severe disease. Codeine, in a bedtime dose of 30 mg, should be reserved for patients with severe nocturnal pain. Other narcotics should not be used. (See Chapter 1.)

8. Diet—The diet should be well balanced and adjusted to each individual's requirements. There is no specific food contraindication. If dietary intake is normal, there is usually no need to use supplemental vitamins.

9. Hematinic agents—These are not beneficial in the treatment of the anemia of rheumatoid arthritis. In the presence of coexisting iron deficiency, however, iron salts, eg, ferrous sulfate, 0.2 gm orally 3 times daily, are useful. Significant iron deficiency is not unusual following long-term loss of microscopic amounts of blood per rectum associated with the prolonged use of salicylates.

B. Anti-inflammatory Drugs: One or another of the drugs discussed below may be considered for use in patients with progressive disease following a reasonable trial (3–6 months) of conservative management. However, their use must be regarded as a supplement to and not a substitute for the comprehensive approach outlined above.

1. Gold salts (chrysotherapy)—Although the value of gold salts in the treatment of rheumatoid arthritis remains highly controversial, this form of therapy has regained some of its former popularity in recent years. The exact mode of action is not known, but these agents are known to be lysosomal stabilizers.

a. Indications—Active disease responding unfavorably to conservative management; patients who should not receive corticosteroids.

b. Contraindications—Previous gold toxicity; other drug allergy; systemic lupus erythematosus (misdiagnosed as rheumatoid arthritis); significant renal, hepatic, or hematopoietic dysfunction; general debility.

c. Preparations of choice—Gold thiomalate or gold thioglucose.

d. Weekly intramuscular dose—10 mg the first week; 25 mg the second week; and 50 mg weekly thereafter until toxic reactions appear, response is adequate, or a total dose of 1 gm has been given without improvement. If response is good, continue to give 50 mg every 2 weeks and, as improvement continues, every 3 and then every 4 weeks for an indefinite period.

e. Toxic reactions—About 37% of all patients (range in various series: 8–61%) experience toxic reactions to gold therapy; the mortality is about 0.4%. The manifestations of toxicity are similar to those due to poisoning with other heavy metals (notably arsenic), and include dermatitis (mild to exfoliative), stomatitis, agranulocytosis, purpura, hepatitis, nitritoid reactions, bronchitis, aplastic anemia, peripheral neuritis, nephritis, and photosensitization. In order to prevent or reduce the severity of toxic reactions, do not give gold salts to patients with any of the contraindicating disorders listed above and observe all patients carefully during the course of gold therapy. Before each injection, ask the patient how he has felt since the previous injection; examine the skin and mucous membranes for dermatitis or purpura; examine the urine for protein and microscopic hematuria; determine the hemoglobin and white count; and inspect a blood smear for differential white count values and for platelets. Platelet counts or liver function tests should be performed periodically. Warn the patient against exposure to strong light.

If signs of toxicity appear, withdraw the drug immediately. Corticosteroids or corticotropin control most toxic reactions. Chelating agents for gold such as penicillamine or dimercaprol (BAL) may be helpful.

2. Corticosteroids (cortisone, hydrocortisone, prednisone, prednisolone, triamcinolone, methylprednisolone, dexamethasone, betamethasone)—These agents represent an important advance in the management of rheumatoid arthritis. However, they must be considered as a supplement to and not a substitute for the comprehensive approach outlined above. Some clinicians feel that the corticosteroids should not be employed unless the patient is also receiving maximal doses of salicylates. Perhaps the greatest disadvantage which might stem from their use, aside from the serious problem of untoward reactions, lies in the tendency of patient and physician to neglect the less spectacular but proved benefits which may be derived from general supportive treatment, physical therapy, and orthopedic measures. These agents do not represent the long-awaited "specific" antirheumatic factor and do not cure the disease. While corticosteroids usually produce immediate and dramatic symptomatic relief, they do not alter the natural progression of the disease; furthermore, clinical manifestations of active disease commonly reappear when the drug is discontinued.

a. Indications—Active and progressive disease which does not respond favorably to conservative management; patients who should not receive gold salts.

b. Contraindications and precautions—See p 681.

c. Daily oral dose—Give the least amount which will permit functional improvement but not more than 10–15 mg of prednisone or equivalent. Many patients do reasonably well on 5–7.5 mg daily. (The use of 1 mg or 2.5 mg tablets is to be encouraged.) Efforts should be made every 3 or 4 weeks to lower the daily dose by decrements of 0.5–1 mg.

d. Intra-articular corticosteroids (hydrocortisone acetate or other) may be helpful if one or 2 joints are the chief source of difficulty. Intra-articular hydrocortisone in a dose of 25–50 mg may be repeated as required for symptomatic relief.

3. Chloroquines (antimalarials)—It appears probable that chloroquine phosphate and hydroxychloroquine sulfate have mild antirheumatic properties in selected patients with mild rheumatoid arthritis. However, toxic reactions occur in as many as 30–40% of patients: nausea, vomiting, leukopenia, rash, blanching of hair, ocular disturbances, and toxic psychosis. The disadvantages of these drugs seriously impair their clinical use in rheumatoid arthritis. Periodic ophthalmologic examination is required if they are employed.

4. Phenylbutazone (Butazolidin®)—This analgesic drug is of limited usefulness in peripheral rheumatoid arthritis (see Ankylosing Spondylitis, below).

5. Indomethacin (Indocin®)—This recently introduced drug is probably no more effective in rheumatoid arthritis than the salicylates, but its untoward effects are far greater (see p 441).

C. Cytotoxic Drugs: Cyclophosphamide (Cytoxan®), azathioprine (Imuran®), and chlorambucil (Leukeran®) have been used in a limited number of patients with severe rheumatoid arthritis. Response to treatment is not necessarily correlated with laboratory parameters of rheumatoid activity. These drugs are toxic and should not be used until further experimental studies have been carried out.

D. Orthopedic Measures: See p 455.

Prognosis

The course of rheumatoid arthritis is totally unpredictable, although spontaneous remissions and relapses are common early in the disease. Occasionally, in well-established cases, permanent spontaneous remission occurs with either return to normal function of the involved joints (if involvement is early and minimal) or some decrease in the amount of disability (if of a longer duration). In most cases, however, the disease is ultimately progressive; some degree of deformity is the usual end result of the disease. In 10 years, 15% are likely to be bedridden, 50% capable of self care and employable, and 35% ambulatory but unable to earn a living.

Bland, J.H. (editor): Symposium on rheumatoid arthritis. M Clin North America 52:477–769, 1968.

Cohen, B.S., & others: Home care program in the management of rheumatoid arthritis. J Chronic Dis 19:631, 1966.

Cooperating Clinics Committee of the American Rheumatism Association: A controlled trial of cyclophosphamide in rheumatoid arthritis. New England J Med 283:883–889, 1970.

Duthie, J.J.R., & others: Course and prognosis in rheumatoid arthritis: A further report. Ann Rheumat Dis 23:193–204, 1964.

Engleman, E.P.: Conservative management of rheumatoid arthritis. M Clin North America 52:699–702, 1968.

Fremont-Smith, K., & T.B. Bayles: Salicylate therapy in rheumatoid arthritis. JAMA 192:1133, 1965.

Goldman, J.A., & E.V. Hess: Treatment of rheumatoid arthritis—1970. Bull Rheum Dis 21:609–612, 1970.

Hamerman, D.: Views on the pathogenesis of rheumatoid arthritis. M Clin North America 52:593–605, 1968.

Hollander, J.L., & A.J. Rawson: Gamma globulin, rheumatoid factors and rheumatoid arthritis. Bull Rheum Dis 18:502–505, 1968.

Hollingsworth, J.W.: *Local and Systemic Complications of Rheumatoid Arthritis.* Saunders, 1968.

Katz, S., & others: Outpatient care in rheumatoid arthritis. JAMA 206:1249–1254, 1968.

Marmor, L.: Surgery for rheumatoid arthritis. Am J Surg 115:630–636, 1968.

Mills, J.A., & others: Value of bed rest in patients with rheumatoid arthritis. New England J Med 284:453–458, 1971.

Sharp, J.T., & others: Observations on the clinical, chemical and serological manifestations of rheumatoid arthritis, based on the course of 154 cases. Medicine 43:41–58, 1964.

Zuaifter, N.J.: Antimalarial treatment of rheumatoid arthritis. M Clin North America 52:759–764, 1968.

ANKYLOSING SPONDYLITIS
(Rheumatoid Spondylitis, Marie-Strümpell Disease, Rheumatoid Arthritis of Spine)

Essentials of Diagnosis

- Chronic backache in a young man.
- Progressive limitation of back motion and chest expansion.

- Transient (50%) or permanent (25%) peripheral joint involvement indistinguishable from peripheral rheumatoid arthritis.
- Diagnostic x-ray changes in sacroiliac joints.
- Uveitis in 5–10%.
- Accelerated sedimentation rate and negative serologic tests for rheumatoid factor.

General Considerations

Ankylosing spondylitis, frequently familial, is a chronic inflammatory disease of the joints of the axial skeleton, manifested clinically by pain and progressive stiffening of the spine. While the synovitis of ankylosing spondylitis is histologically identical with the synovitis of peripheral rheumatoid arthritis, certain features tend to distinguish this disease from rheumatoid arthritis: its preponderance among males (approximately 10:1); age at onset (usually in late teens or early 20's); the relatively high incidence of uveitis; a pathologically distinctive lesion of the aorta; and the absence of the "rheumatoid factor." In addition to the synovitis, a second pathologic feature of ankylosing spondylitis involves the intervertebral fibrocartilages; the annulus fibrosis may gradually ossify with resulting fusion of the vertebral bodies.

Clinical Findings

A. Symptoms and Signs: The onset is usually gradual, with intermittent bouts of back pain which may radiate down the thighs. As the disease advances, symptoms progress in a cephalad direction and back motion becomes limited, with the normal lumbar curve flattened and the thoracic curvature exaggerated. Atrophy of the trunk muscles is common. Chest expansion is often limited as a consequence of costovertebral joint involvement. Radicular symptoms may occur. In advanced cases the entire spine becomes fused, allowing no motion in any direction. Transient, acute arthritis of the peripheral joints occurs in about 50% of cases, and permanent changes in the peripheral joints—most commonly the hips, shoulders, and knees—are seen in about 25%. There is increasing awareness of cardiac involvement; aortic insufficiency is reported in about 4%. Nongranulomatous uveitis is seen in 5–10% of cases and may be a presenting feature. Constitutional symptoms similar to those of rheumatoid arthritis may occasionally be present.

B. Laboratory Findings: The sedimentation rate is accelerated in 85% of cases, but serologic tests for the rheumatoid factor are usually negative. There may be leukocytosis and anemia.

C. X-Ray Findings: The x-ray shows early erosion and sclerosis of the sacroiliac joints with later involvement of the apophysial joints of the spine, calcification of the anterior and lateral spinal ligaments, squaring and generalized demineralization of the vertebral bodies. The term "bamboo spine" has been used to describe the late radiographic changes.

Additional x-ray findings include periosteal new bone formation on the iliac crest, ischial tuberosities, and calcanei, and alterations of the symphysis pubis and sternomanubrial joint similar to those of the sacroiliacs. Radiologic changes in peripheral joints, when present, resemble those of rheumatoid arthritis.

Differential Diagnosis

Although peripheral rheumatoid arthritis may ultimately involve the spine, it is characteristically in the cervical region while the sacroiliac joints are usually spared. Other features which differentiate ankylosing spondylitis from peripheral rheumatoid arthritis are the absence of subcutaneous nodules and the negative serologic tests for the rheumatoid factor. The history and physical findings of ankylosing spondylitis serve to distinguish this disorder from other causes of low back pain such as degenerative disk disease, osteoarthritis, osteoporosis, soft tissue trauma, and tumors. The single most valuable distinguishing sign of ankylosing spondylitis is the x-ray appearance of the sacroiliac joints, although a similar x-ray picture may be seen in juvenile rheumatoid arthritis, in arthritis associated with psoriasis, with ulcerative colitis, regional enteritis, and Whipple's disease, and as a sequel to Reiter's syndrome, especially after frequent recurrences. The x-ray appearance of the sacroiliac joints in spondylitis should be distinguished from that in osteitis condensans ilii. In some areas and occupations, brucellosis and fluoride poisoning may be important in the differential diagnosis.

Treatment

A. Basic Program: As for rheumatoid arthritis. The importance of postural and breathing exercises should be stressed. When spondylitis is associated with chronic ulcerative colitis, regional enteritis, or psoriasis, appropriate treatment of these disorders may improve the spondylitis.

B. Drug Therapy: Phenylbutazone (Butazolidin®) and oxyphenbutazone (Tandearil®) are potent analgesic and anti-inflammatory agents which are often remarkably effective against ankylosing spondylitis in small doses and may be used cautiously if response to salicylates is inadequate. They are contraindicated in peptic ulcer, cardiac decompensation, and significant renal, hepatic, or hematopoietic dysfunction. Give the least amount which will provide symptomatic improvement. Start with 100 mg daily and increase if necessary to 100 mg every 12 hours or every 8 hours, but do not give more than 300 mg daily. The drug may be continued cautiously as long as required for symptomatic relief unless toxic reactions occur. Special precautions include blood counts twice weekly for 4 weeks, once weekly for the next 4 weeks, and once every 2 or 3 weeks thereafter.

Toxic reactions include salt and water retention, rash, agranulocytosis and other hematologic abnormalities, peptic ulcer, and hepatitis. If toxicity occurs, withdraw the drug immediately. Corticosteroids or corticotropin may be helpful in the treatment of agranulocytosis.

Indomethacin (Indocin®), another anti-inflammatory analgesic agent, 50–75 mg/day in divided doses, is often effective, and at this time appears to be less toxic than the butazones. However, this agent may produce a variety of untoward reactions including headache, giddiness, nausea, vomiting, peptic ulcer, depression, and psychosis. (See Chapter 1.)

C. X-ray radiation to painful areas of the spine often provides symptomatic relief, but has lost favor because of the high incidence of leukemia in patients so treated.

D. Corticosteroids may be given as for rheumatoid arthritis.

E. Physical Therapy and Orthopedic Measures: See p 455.

Prognosis

Spontaneous remissions and relapses are common and may occur at any stage. Occasionally the disease progresses to ankylosis of the entire spine. In general, the functional prognosis is good except in those instances where the hips are seriously and permanently involved.

Blumberg, B., & C. Ragan: The natural history of rheumatoid spondylitis. Medicine 35:1–31, 1956.

Calabro, J.J.: An appraisal of the medical and surgical management of ankylosing spondylitis. Clin Orthop 125:48, 1968.

Calabro, J.J., & B.A. Maltz: Ankylosing spondylitis. New England J Med 282:606–610, 1970.

Ogryzlo, M.A., & P.S. Rosen: Ankylosing (Marie-Strümpell) spondylitis. Postgrad Med 45:182–191, 1969.

OSTEOARTHRITIS
(Degenerative Joint Disease)

Essentials of Diagnosis

- A degenerative disorder without systemic manifestations.
- Pain relieved by rest.
- Articular inflammation minimal.
- X-ray findings: Narrowed joint space, osteophytes, increased density of subchondral bone, bony cysts.
- Commonly secondary to other articular disease.

General Considerations

Osteoarthritis is a chronic, progressive arthropathy which is characterized by degeneration of cartilage and by hypertrophy of bone at the articular margins. Hereditary and mechanical factors may be variably involved in the pathogenesis. Osteoarthritis is traditionally differentiated into 2 types: (1) primary osteoarthritis, which most commonly affects the terminal interphalangeal joints (Heberden's nodes), the metacarpophalangeal and carpometacarpal joints of the thumb, hip (malum coxae senilis), knee, the metatarsophalangeal joint of the big toe, and the cervical and lumbar spine; and (2) secondary osteoarthritis (clinically similar, but often more severe), which may occur in any joint as a sequel to articular injury resulting from either intra-articular (including rheumatoid arthritis) or extra-articular causes. The injury may be acute, as in a fracture; or chronic, as that due to overweight, bad posture, and occupational overuse of a joint. Pathologically, the articular cartilage is first roughened and finally worn away, and spur formation and lipping occur at the edge of the joint surface. The synovial membrane becomes thickened, with hypertrophy of the villous processes; the joint cavity, however, never becomes totally obliterated, and the synovial membrane does not form adhesions. Inflammation is characteristically minimal except for the occasional acute Heberden's node.

Clinical Findings

A. Symptoms and Signs: The onset is insidious. Initially there is articular stiffness which develops later into pain on motion of the affected joint and is made worse by prolonged activity and relieved by rest. Deformity may be absent or minimal; however, bony enlargement is occasionally prominent, and flexion contracture or valgus deformity of the knee is not unusual. There is no ankylosis, but limitation of motion of the affected joint or joints is common. Coarse crepitus may often be felt in the joint. Joint effusion and other articular signs of inflammation are mild. There are no systemic manifestations.

B. Laboratory Findings: Elevated sedimentation rate and other laboratory signs of inflammation or dysproteinemia are not present.

C. X-Ray Findings: X-rays may reveal narrowing of the joint space, sharpened articular margins, osteophyte formation and lipping of marginal bone, and damaged and thickened, dense subchondral bone. Bone cysts may also be present.

Differential Diagnosis

Because articular inflammation is minimal and systemic manifestations are absent, osteoarthritis should seldom be confused with other arthritides. The neurogenic arthropathy of Charcot is easily distinguished by x-ray and neurologic examination. Osteoarthritis may coexist with any other type of joint disease. Furthermore, one must be cautious in attributing all skeletal symptoms to degenerative changes in joints, especially in the spine, where metastatic malignancy, osteoporosis, multiple myeloma, or other bone disease may coexist.

Treatment

A. General Measures:

1. Rest—Physical activity which induces physiologic or traumatic strain should be avoided. Occupational or recreational overuse of an affected joint must be prevented. If weight-bearing joints are involved, such weight-bearing activities as climbing stairs, walking, or prolonged standing should be minimized. Postural strain should be corrected. Supports which relieve strain due to pendulous abdomen or breasts should be supplied.

2. Diet should be adjusted to meet the patient's needs. Weight reduction for obese patients helps to diminish stress on the joints.

3. Local heat in any form and other forms of physical therapy are often of symptomatic value.

B. Analgesic Drugs: Salicylates (as for rheumatoid arthritis) are indicated for the relief of pain. Indomethacin (Indocin®), 50–75 mg/day in divided doses, may be effective temporarily, especially in osteoarthritis of the hip joint (see p 441).

C. Intra-articular corticosteroids (as for rheumatoid arthritis) may give transient relief.

D. Orthopedic Measures: Orthopedic measures to correct developmental anomalies, deformities, disparity in leg length, and severely damaged joint surfaces may be required.

Prognosis

Although marked disability is less common than in rheumatoid arthritis, symptoms may be quite severe and limit activity markedly. This is especially true with involvement of the hips, knees, and cervical spine. Although there is no cure, proper treatment may greatly relieve symptoms and thereby improve function.

Bollet, A.J.: An essay on the biology of osteoarthritis. Arthritis Rheum 12:152–163, 1969.

Howell, D.S., & others: A comprehensive regimen for osteoarthritis. M Clin North America 55:457–469, 1971.

Moskowitz, R.W., Klein, L., & W.A. Mast: Current concepts of degenerative joint disease (osteoarthritis). Bull Rheum Dis 17:459–464, 1967.

Sokoloff, L.: The pathology and pathogenesis of osteoarthritis. Pages 849–870 *in:* Hollander, J.L.: *Arthritis and Allied Conditions.* Lea & Febiger, 1966.

GOUTY ARTHRITIS

Essentials of Diagnosis

- Acute onset, usually monarticular, involving the metatarsophalangeal joint of the big toe in about 50% of cases.
- Dramatic therapeutic response to colchicine.
- Postinflammatory desquamation and pruritus are almost pathognomonic.
- Hyperuricemia.
- Identification of urate crystals in joint fluid or tophi.
- Asymptomatic periods between acute attacks.
- Urate deposits in subcutaneous tissue, bone, cartilage, joints,·and other tissues.
- Familial disease; 95% males.

General Considerations

Gout is a metabolic disease of a heterogeneous nature, often familial, associated with abnormal amounts of urates in the body and characterized by an early, recurring acute arthritis, usually monarticular, and a late chronic deforming arthritis.

About 95% of patients with gout are men, usually over 30 years of age. In women the onset is usually postmenopausal. The characteristic histologic lesion is the tophus, a nodular deposit of sodium acid urate crystals and an associated foreign body reaction. This may be found in cartilage, subcutaneous and periarticular tissues, tendon, bone, the kidneys, and elsewhere. Urates have been demonstrated in the synovial tissues (and fluid) during acute arthritis; indeed, the acute inflammation of gout is believed to be activated by the phagocytosis by polymorphonuclear cells of urate crystals with the ensuing release from the PMN's of chemotactic and other substances capable of mediating inflammation. The precise relationship of hyperuricemia to acute gouty arthritis is still obscure, since hyperuricemia may occur in patients who never have gouty arthritis. Recent studies suggest that rapid fluctuations in serum urate levels, either increasing or decreasing, are important factors in precipitating acute gout. The mechanism of the late, chronic stages of arthritis is better understood. This is characterized pathologically by tophaceous invasion of the articular and periarticular tissues, with structural derangement and secondary degeneration (osteoarthritis).

Uric acid kidney stones are present in 10–20% of patients with gouty arthritis. Nephrosclerosis with renal dysfunction is common; so-called "renal gout" or "gouty nephritis," much less common, refers to kidney disease due to tophaceous deposition in the renal parenchyma, chiefly the pyramids and the renal vasculature.

Typical acute gouty arthritis may accompany other diseases, notably those of the hematopoietic system, eg, leukemia or polycythemia, where there is excessive breakdown of nucleic acids, and certain rare enzyme deficiency diseases. Although referred to as "secondary gout," these attacks are clinically indistinguishable from "primary gout." However, a family history of gout is usually not obtained, and women are affected more commonly than is the case with primary disease.

Hyperuricemia often occurs in patients without arthritis or urinary stones. Determination of the cause of the hyperuricemia in such cases (eg, thiazide drugs, psoriasis, lead intoxication, blood dyscrasias, "idiopathies") is of primary concern, and treatment, other than ensuring adequate fluid intake and urinary output, is usually not necessary unless uric acid levels are very high and there is danger of nephropathy. Allopurinol (see below) may be used in these circumstances.

Clinical Findings

A. Symptoms and Signs: The acute arthritis is characterized by its sudden onset, frequently nocturnal, either without apparent precipitating cause or following an infection, surgical procedure, or minimal trauma such as caused by ill-fitting shoes. The metatarsophalangeal joint of the great toe is the most susceptible joint, although other joints, especially those of the feet, ankles, and knees, are commonly affected. More than one joint may occasionally be affected during the same attack; in such cases the distribution of the arthritis is usually asymmetric. As the attack progresses the pain becomes intense. The involved joints are swollen and exquisitely tender, and the overlying skin tense, warm, and dusky red. Fever, headache, malaise, anorexia, and tachycardia are common. Local desquamation and pruritus during recovery from the acute arthritis are almost pathognomonic of gout but are not always present. Tophi may be found in the external ears, hands, feet, olecranon, and prepatellar bursas. They are usually seen only after several attacks of acute arthritis.

Asymptomatic periods of months or years commonly follow the initial acute attack. Later, gouty arthritis may become chronic, with symptoms of progressive functional loss and disability. Gross deformities, due usually to tophaceous invasion, are seen. Signs of inflammation may be absent or superimposed.

Hypertension, renal stones, and renal failure may be associated with gouty arthritis.

B. Laboratory Findings: The blood uric acid is practically always elevated (> 7.5 mg/100 ml) unless uricopenic drugs are being given (see p 916). During an acute attack the sedimentation rate and white count are usually elevated. Examination of the material aspirated from a tophus shows the typical crystals of sodium urate and confirms the diagnosis. Further confirmation is obtained by identification of urate crystals by compensated polariscopic examination of wet smears prepared from joint fluid aspirates. Such crystals are negatively birefringent and needle-like, and may be found free or in cells.

C. X-Ray Findings: Early in the disease x-rays show no changes; later, punched-out areas in the bone (radiolucent urate tophi) are seen.

Differential Diagnosis

Once the diagnosis of acute gouty arthritis is suspected it is easily confirmed by the presence of hyperuricemia, dramatic response to full doses of colchicine, local desquamation and pruritus as the edema subsides, positive identification of tophi, a positive family history, and polariscopic examination of joint fluid. Acute gout is often confused with cellulitis. Appropriate bacteriologic studies should exclude acute pyogenic arthritis. Acute chondrocalcinosis (pseudogout) may be distinguished by the identification of calcium pyrophosphate crystals in the joint fluid, usually normal serum uric acid, the x-ray appearance of chondrocalcinosis, and the relative therapeutic ineffectiveness of colchicine.

Chronic tophaceous arthritis may rarely mimic chronic rheumatoid arthritis. In such cases the diagnosis of gout is established conclusively by the demonstration of urate crystals in the contents of a suspected tophus. Biopsy may be necessary to distinguish tophi from rheumatoid nodules. An x-ray appearance similar to that of gout may be found in rheumatoid arthritis, sarcoid, multiple myeloma, hyperparathyroidism, and Hand-Schüller-Christian disease.

Treatment

A. Acute Attack:

1. Colchicine, which may inhibit the chemotactic property of leukocytosis and thus interfere with the inflammatory response to urate crystals, is the drug of choice, especially when used diagnostically as well as therapeutically. It should be given as early as possible in the acute attack or during the prodrome to obtain maximum benefit. Give 0.5 or 0.6 mg every hour or 1 mg every 2 hours until pain is relieved or until nausea or diarrhea appears; and then stop the drug. The usual total dose required is 4–8 mg, and the pain and swelling will subside in 24–72 hours. Once the patient knows how much will produce toxic symptoms, the drug should be given in a dose of about 1 mg less than the toxic dose. Colchicine-induced diarrhea is controlled with paregoric, 4 ml after each bowel movement. The gastrointestinal side-effects of colchicine can be avoided by intravenous administration in an initial dose of 1–3 mg in 10–20 ml of saline solution. This may be repeated in a few hours, but no more than 4–6 mg should be given IV within a period of 24 hours for a single attack. Colchicine causes local pain and tissue damage from occasional extravasation during injection. Furthermore, the toxicity of colchicine given intravenously may be substantial in patients with renal dysfunction. This route of administration of colchicine is rarely necessary and is inadvisable if the oral route can be used.

2. Phenylbutazone (Butazolidin®) is a remarkably effective anti-inflammatory agent in acute gout and is the drug of choice when the diagnosis is well established. The initial dose is 400 mg, followed by 200 mg every 6 hours until the attack subsides; do not continue for more than 3 days. Toxicity is rarely a problem in such short-term use of phenylbutazone.

3. Indomethacin (Indocin®) is said to be as effective as phenylbutazone in acute gout. A daily dose of 75–200 mg for 2–3 days is suggested.

4. Corticotropin (ACTH) and the corticosteroids often give dramatic symptomatic relief in acute episodes of gout, and if given for a sufficient length of time will control most acute attacks. However, when corticotropin and corticosteroids are discontinued shortly after termination of attacks, many patients promptly relapse unless colchicine is given. Since colchicine and phenylbutazone are equally or more effective and provide a more lasting effect, they are preferred.

5. Analgesics—At times the pain of an acute attack may be so severe that analgesia is necessary before a more specific drug becomes effective. In these cases codeine or meperidine (Demerol®) may be given. Cinchophen and neocinchophen should not be used because they cause severe liver damage.

6. Bed rest is very important in the management of the acute attack, and should be continued for about 24 hours after the acute attack has subsided. Early ambulation may precipitate a recurrence.

7. Physical therapy is often of little value during the acute attack, although hot or cold compresses to or elevation of the affected joints may make some patients more comfortable.

B. Management Between Attacks: Treatment during symptom-free periods is intended to minimize urate deposition in tissues, which causes chronic tophaceous arthritis, and to reduce the frequency and severity of recurrences. There is evidence that these objectives are in fact attainable.

1. Diet—From a dietary standpoint it would appear that it is most important simply to avoid obesity, fasting, dehydration, and acidosis. Rigid diets are nutritionally inadequate and often fail to influence the hyperuricemia or the course of gouty arthritis. Since dietary sources of purines contribute very little to the causation of the disease, restriction of foods high in purine (eg, kidney, liver, sweetbreads, sardines, anchovies, meat extracts) cannot be expected to contribute significantly to the management of the disease. Specific foods or alcoholic beverages which precipitate attacks should be avoided. However, there is little evidence that alcohol in moderation will precipitate attacks or is otherwise harmful in patients with gout. A high liquid intake and, more important, a daily urinary output of 2 liters or more will aid urate excretion and minimize urate precipitation in the urinary tract.

2. Colchicine—The daily administration of colchicine in a dose of 0.5 mg 3 times daily should be started simultaneously with uricosuric drugs or allopurinol in order to suppress the acute attack which may be precipitated by these drugs. After several weeks of such treatment it is usually possible to lower the daily dose of colchicine to 0.5 mg. There is some suggestion that colchicine, even in this small dosage, has preventive value and should be continued indefinitely.

3. Uricosuric drugs—These drugs, by blocking tubular reabsorption of filtered urate and reducing the metabolic pool of urates, prevent the formation of new tophi and reduce the size of those already present. Furthermore, when administered concomitantly with colchicine, they may lessen the frequency of recurrences of acute gout. The indications for uricosuric treatment are either the appearance of tophi on physical or x-ray examination, or increasing frequency or severity of the acute attacks.

Any one of several uricosuric drugs may be employed:

(1) Probenecid (Benemid®), starting with 0.5 gm daily and gradually increasing to 1–2 gm daily.

(2) Salicylates, 5–6 gm daily.

(3) Sulfinpyrazone (Anturane®), starting with 100 mg daily and gradually increasing to 200–400 mg daily. In any case, the maintenance dose is determined by observation of the serum uric acid response and the urinary uric acid response. Ideally, one attempts to maintain a normal serum urate level.

Precautions with uricosuric drugs: It is important to maintain a daily urinary output of 2000 ml or more in order to minimize the precipitation of uric acid in the urinary tract. This can be further prevented by giving alkalinizing agents to maintain a urine pH of above 6.0. If a significant uricosuric effect is not ob-

tained in the presence of overt renal dysfunction, do not increase the dose of the drug beyond the limits stated above. Avoid using salicylates with any other uricosuric drug, since they antagonize the action of other uricosuric agents.

4. Allopurinol—The xanthine oxidase inhibitor, allopurinol (Zyloprim®), is an important addition to the therapy of gouty arthritis. It promptly lowers plasma urate and urinary uric acid concentrations and facilitates tophus mobilization. The drug is of special value in uric acid overproducers; in patients unresponsive to the uricosuric regimen; and in gouty patients with renal insufficiency or uric acid renal stones. It should be used cautiously in patients with renal insufficiency. The major adverse effect is the precipitation of an acute gouty attack.

The daily dose is determined by the serum uric acid response. A normal serum uric acid level is often obtained with a daily dose of 200–400 mg. Occasionally (and in selected cases) it may be helpful to continue the use of allopurinol with a uricosuric drug. Neither of these drugs is of help in acute gout.

Severe and potentially fatal hypersensitivity reactions associated with allopurinol have been reported.

C. Chronic Tophaceous Arthritis: There is good evidence that in the presence of good renal function tophaceous deposits can be made to shrink in size and occasionally to disappear altogether. The treatment is essentially the same as that outlined for the intervals between acute attacks. Surgical excision of large tophi offers immediate mechanical improvement in selected deformities and may lessen the load on renal function.

Prognosis

Without treatment, the acute attack may last from a few days to several weeks, but proper treatment quickly terminates the attack. The intervals between acute attacks vary up to years, but the asymptomatic periods often become shorter if the disease progresses. Chronic tophaceous arthritis occurs after repeated attacks of acute gout and only after inadequate treatment. Although the deformities may be marked, only a small percentage of patients become bedridden. The younger the patient at the onset of disease, the greater the tendency to a progressive course. Destructive arthropathy is rarely seen in patients whose first attack is after age 50.

Allopurinol: A Symposium. Ann Rheumat Dis 25:No. 6 Suppl, 1966.

Grahame, R., & J.T. Scott: Clinical survey of 354 patients with gout. Ann Rheumat Dis 29:461–468, 1970.

Gutman, A.B. (editor): Proceedings of conference on gout and purine metabolism, 1964. Arthritis Rheum 8:599, 1965.

McCarty, D.J., Jr.: The pendulum of progress in gout: From crystals to hyperuricemia and back. Arthritis Rheum 7:534, 1964.

Mills, R.M., Jr.: Severe hypersensitivity reactions associated with allopurinol. JAMA 216:799–802, 1971.

Seegmiller, J.H.: The acute attack of gouty arthritis. Arthritis Rheum 8:714, 1965.

Talbot, J.H.: Gout. M Clin North America 54:431–441, 1970.

Wallace, S.L., Omokoku, B., & N.H. Ertel: Colchicine plasma levels: Implications as to pharmacology and mechanism of action. Am J Med 48:443–448, 1970.

Yü, T.-F., & A.B. Gutman: Principles of current management of primary gout. Am J M Sc 254:893, 1967.

ACUTE INFECTIOUS (PYOGENIC) ARTHRITIS

Essentials of Diagnosis

- Sudden onset of acute arthritis, usually mon-articular, most often in large weight-bearing joints and wrists, frequently preceded by migratory arthralgia.
- Frank chills and fever.
- Joint fluid findings often diagnostic.
- Dramatic therapeutic response to appropriate antibiotic.
- Similar infection commonly found elsewhere in body.

General Considerations

The pyogenic cocci (gonococcus, meningococcus, staphylococcus, pneumococcus, and streptococcus) are the usual causes of this form of arthritis. The organisms may enter the joints directly, as in local trauma or needling or by extension from adjacent bone; or indirectly, by hematogenous spread. In recent years this type of disease has been seen more commonly as a result of the development of resistant strains of organisms, the increasing therapeutic use of intra-articular injections, and the decreasing mortality of premature infants, in whom the incidence of septic arthritis is relatively high. The worldwide increase of gonococcal infections, particularly antibiotic-resistant, has posed a special problem. Pathologic changes include varying degrees of acute inflammation with synovitis, effusion, abscess formation in synovial or subchondral tissues, and, if treatment is not adequate, articular destruction.

Clinical Findings

A. Symptoms and Signs: The onset is usually sudden; the joint becomes acutely painful, hot, and swollen, and chills and fever are often present. The large weight-bearing joints and the wrists are most frequently affected. Although only one or 2 joints are affected, there may be a prodromal period of migratory arthralgia which may last for several days; this is especially true during the period of bacteremia.

B. Laboratory Findings: Leukocytosis of the synovial fluid may be as high as 100,000/cu mm, with 90% or more polymorphonuclear cells. Synovial fluid sugar is often low. The organisms can usually be demonstrated by smear or culture. (A notable exception is gonococcal arthritis, which can be identified bacteriologically in only ½ of cases.) Other laboratory findings of the infectious disease are present also.

C. X-Ray Findings: Radiologic evidence of demineralization may be present within days of onset; bony erosions and narrowing of the joint space followed by osteomyelitis and periostitis may be seen within 2 weeks.

Differential Diagnosis

The septic course with chills and fever, the acute systemic reaction, the joint fluid findings, evidence of similar infection elsewhere in the body, and the dramatic response to appropriate antibiotics are diagnostic of pyogenic arthritis. Gout is excluded by the absence of hyperuricemia and other signs of gout. Acute rheumatic fever and rheumatoid arthritis commonly involve many joints and are not associated with chills. Pyogenic arthritis may be superimposed on other types of joint disease, notably rheumatoid arthritis, and must be excluded (by joint fluid examination) in any apparent acute relapse of the primary disease.

Treatment

Prompt systemic treatment with penicillin or one of the broad-spectrum antibiotics (chosen on the basis of sensitivity studies) is usually effective. Local aspiration, irrigation with saline, intra-articular administration of antibiotics, and incision and drainage are sometimes indicated. Relieve pain with local hot compresses and by immobilization of the joint with a splint or traction (or both). Rest, immobilization, and elevation are used at the onset of treatment. Early active motion exercises within the limits of tolerance will hasten functional recovery.

Prognosis

With prompt antibiotic therapy (within 7–10 days of onset), functional recovery is usually complete. Bony ankylosis and articular destruction commonly occur if treatment is inadequate.

Keiser, H., & others: Clinical forms of gonococcal arthritis. New England J Med 279:234–240, 1968.

Medical Staff Conference, University of California, San Francisco: Gonococcal sepsis and arthritis. Calif Med 114:18–25, Jan 1971.

Nelson, J.D.: Antibiotic concentrations in septic joint effusions. New England J Med 284:349–353, 1971.

Partain, J.O., Cathcart, E.S., & A.S. Cohen: Arthritis associated with gonorrhoea. Ann Rheumat Dis 27:156–162, 1968.

Schmid, F.R., & R.H. Parker: Ongoing assessment of therapy in septic arthritis. Arthritis Rheum 12:529–534, 1969.

Willerson, J.T., Barth, W.F., & J.L. Decker: Septic arthritis, the unexpected complication. Postgrad Med 45:127–135, 1969.

CHRONIC PYOGENIC ARTHRITIS

Chronic pyogenic arthritis follows untreated or unsuccessfully treated acute primary or secondary pyogenic arthritis. Inadequacy of treatment can be manifest by persistence of infection, but its course is either intermittent or continuous at a slow rate. One or more pathogens may produce a purulent inflammatory response within a joint; pyogenic cocci and enteric gram-negative rods are more common. Although a previously identified pathogen is likely to persist, superinfection can occur, especially with open surgical treatment and antibiotics. The original bacterial strain may be eliminated by treatment only to be supplanted by another, or it may persist with the new invader to cause a mixed infection.

Chronic pyogenic arthritis is likely to produce variable but characteristic clinical pictures. An overt or manifest infection can be continuously or recurrently active. Uninterrupted progress from the acute stage is characterized by continued local pain and swelling, restriction of joint motion, sinus formation, and increasing deformity. X-rays show progressive destruction of cartilage manifest by narrowing of the joint cleft, erosion of bone, and even infraction or cavitation. Even though the course is indolent, it is that of continued deterioration. Apparent abatement may follow intermittent treatment, notably with antibiotics, in the recurrent type; but these episodes of comparative clinical quiescence only reflect temporary dormancy. Occult or covert infections are characterized by insidiousness and indolency. They may be unrecognized for long periods since they do not produce striking clinical findings. They may occur concomitantly with other joint lesions or complicate surgical operations on joints, especially after the use of surgical implants or antibiotic prophylaxis of postoperative infection.

Chronic pyogenic arthritis must be differentiated from all chronic nonpyogenic microbial infections of joints, gout, rheumatoid arthritis, and symptomatic degenerative arthritis.

The goal of treatment is eradication of infection and restoration of maximum joint function. Bacterial sensitivity tests provide a basis for selection of antimicrobial drugs to be used as an adjunct to surgical operations. Operative destruction of the joint by arthrodesis, debridement, saucerization of bone, or resection is often necessary to eliminate chronic infection.

Jergesen, F., & E. Jawetz: Pyogenic infections in orthopaedic surgery: Combined antibiotic and closed wound treatment. Am J Surg 106:152—163, 1963.

Warren, C.P.W.: Arthritis associated with salmonella infection. Ann Rheumat Dis 29:483—487, 1970.

ARTHRITIS & PSORIASIS

In many (possibly most) patients with coexisting joint disease and psoriasis, the arthritis component is indistinguishable from rheumatoid arthritis. There is, however, a group of individuals with psoriasis whose articular findings are sufficiently distinct to warrant classification as a separate category: psoriatic arthritis. In these persons, the psoriasis tends to precede the onset of arthritis and the articular and cutaneous lesions tend to recur together and to relapse simultaneously. The joint manifestations occur more frequently with generalized than with local psoriatic involvement. The articular disorder tends to involve the distal interphalangeal joints, which are occasionally the site of osteolysis with gross destruction, producing so-called "sausage digits." Additional x-ray signs may include widening of the interphalangeal joint spaces, resorption of the distal phalangeal tufts, and ankylosis of affected finger joints. Radiologic evidence of sacroiliac involvement may also be present. Subcutaneous nodules are absent, and tests for rheumatoid factor are negative. The blood uric acid may be elevated, especially if the psoriatic lesions are extensive.

The treatment of arthritis with psoriasis is similar to that of rheumatoid arthritis, although drugs causing skin reactions should be avoided when possible. Serious adverse effects (eg, cirrhosis) have tempered the early enthusiasm for treatment by cytotoxic agents such as methotrexate.

Jajic, I.: Radiological changes in the sacro-iliac joints and spine of patients with psoriatic arthritis and psoriasis. Ann Rheum Dis 27:1—6, 1968.

Muller, S.A., Farrow, G.M., & D.L. Martalock: Cirrhosis caused by methotrexate in the treatment of psoriasis. Arch Dermat 100:523—530, 1969.

Wright, V., & J. Moll: Psoriatic arthritis. Bull Rheum Dis 21:627—631, 1971.

ARTHRITIS & INFLAMMATORY INTESTINAL DISEASES

Arthritis is a common complication of ulcerative colitis, regional enteritis, and Whipple's disease. Occasionally the arthritis is indistinguishable from rheumatoid arthritis. More commonly, however, the arthritis is asymmetric, affects large joints, parallels the course of the bowel disease, and rarely leaves residual deformity. Tests for rheumatoid factor are negative. Ankylosing spondylitis is not infrequently seen.

The synovitis is pathologically nonspecific. Rheumatoid factor is usually absent from the serum. Treatment of the arthritis is supportive and symptomatic.

McEwen, C.: Arthritis accompanying ulcerative colitis. Clin Orthop 57:9—17, 1968.

Soren, A.: Joint affections in regional ileitis. Arch Int Med 117:78, 1966.

REITER'S SYNDROME

Reiter's syndrome is a clinical triad of unknown etiology, consisting of nonspecific urethritis, conjunctivitis, and arthritis, which occurs most commonly in young male adults. It may follow (within a few days to 4 weeks) sexual exposure or diarrhea, and is usually accompanied by a systemic reaction, including fever (without chills). The arthritis is most commonly symmetric and frequently involves the large weight-bearing joints (chiefly the knees and ankles); ankylosing spondylitis may occur. Additional clinical manifestations may include balanitis, ulcerations in the mouth, keratosis blennorrhagica, and carditis. While most signs of the disease disappear within days or weeks, the arthritis is apt to persist for several months or longer. Characteristically, the initial attack is self-limited and terminates spontaneously.

Recurrences involving any combination of the clinical manifestations are common and are sometimes followed by permanent sequelae, especially in the joints. X-ray signs of permanent or progressive joint disease may be seen in the sacroiliac as well as the peripheral joints.

Reiter's syndrome must be distinguished from gonococcal arthritis, postgonococcal rheumatoid arthritis, rheumatoid arthritis or ankylosing spondylitis which incidentally follow nonspecific urethritis, and psoriatic arthritis. The skin lesions of keratosis blennorrhagica may be undistinguishable from those of pustular psoriasis.

Treatment is symptomatic.

Engleman, E.P., & H.M. Weber: Reiter's syndrome: Rheumatic manifestations of systemic disease. Clin Orthop 57:19–30, 1968.

Weinberger, H.J., & others: Reiter's syndrome: Clinical and pathologic observations. A long-term study of 16 cases. Medicine 41:35–91, 1962.

CHONDROCALCINOSIS
(Pseudogout)

Chondrocalcinosis or "pseudogout" is characterized by acute recurrent arthritis, usually in large joints, principally the knees, and is often associated with systemic symptoms. The condition may be familial, and is usually seen in persons age 60 or older; but it may occur as a complication of a wide variety of metabolic disorders (eg, hyperparathyroidism, diabetes). Joint aspirates reveal calcium pyrophosphate crystals which, in the polarizing microscope, exhibit a weakly positive birefringence and, like gouty crystals, may be intracellular or extracellular. X-ray examination shows calcification, usually symmetric, of cartilaginous structures, and signs of degenerative joint disease (osteoarthritis). Unlike gout, chondrocalcinosis is usually associated with normal serum urate levels, and is not ordinarily benefited by the administration of colchicine.

Treatment is directed at the primary disease, if present. Some of the anti-inflammatory agents (eg, corticosteroids, salicylates, phenylbutazone, indomethacin) may be of benefit.

Moskowitz, R.W., & D. Katz: Chondrocalcinosis and chondrocalsynovitis (pseudogout syndrome). Analysis of twenty-four cases. Am J Med 43:322–334, 1967.

PALINDROMIC RHEUMATISM

Palindromic rheumatism is a disease of unknown etiology characterized by frequent recurring attacks (at irregular intervals) of acute arthritis. The attacks rapidly disappear in several hours to several days. The small joints of the fingers are most commonly affected, but any peripheral joint may be involved. Although hundreds of attacks may occur over a period of years, there is no permanent articular damage. Palindromic rheumatism must be distinguished from acute gouty arthritis and an atypical, acute onset of rheumatoid arthritis.

Symptomatic treatment is usually all that is required during the attacks. Chrysotherapy may be of value in preventing recurrences.

Hench, P.S., & E.F. Rosenberg: Palindromic rheumatism. Arch Int Med 73:293–321, 1944.

POLYMYALGIA RHEUMATICA

This disorder, seen most often in elderly women, often begins abruptly with severe pain and stiffness in the shoulders, hips, pectoral and pelvic girdles, and proximal limb muscles. It may be associated with fever, malaise, weight loss, elevated sedimentation rate, and some degree of anemia. Giant cell arteritis can sometimes be demonstrated by biopsy of the temporal artery. There appears to be a relationship between polymyalgia rheumatica and temporal or cranial arteritis. Blindness is a serious threat in the coexisting presence of arteritis.

Many patients respond well to high doses of salicylates or to small doses of corticosteroids. Large doses of corticosteroids are required in the presence of giant cell arteritis.

Fernandez-Herlihy, L.: Polymyalgia rheumatica. Intern Med Dig 5:42–50, 1970.

Fessel, W.J., & C.M. Pearson: Polymyalgia rheumatica and blindness. New England J Med 276:1403–1405, 1967.

Goodman, M.A., & C.M. Pearson: Polymyalgia rheumatica and associated arteritis: A review. California Med 111:453–460, 1969.

Healy, L., & others: Polymyalgia rheumatica and giant cell arteritis. Arthritis Rheum 14:138–141, 1971.

ARTHRITIS IN SARCOIDOSIS

The frequency of arthritis among patients with sarcoidosis is variously reported between 10% and 37%. Most commonly acute in onset and following the appearance of extra-articular signs of sarcoidosis, articular symptoms may appear insidiously and may antedate other manifestations of the disease. Knees and ankles are most commonly involved, but any joint may be affected. Distribution of joint involvement is usually, but not always, polyarticular and symmetric. The arthritis is commonly self-limiting after several weeks or months; infrequently, the arthritis is recurrent or chronic. Despite its occasional chronicity, the arthritis is rarely associated with joint destruction or significant deformity. Although sarcoid arthritis is commonly associated with erythema nodosum, the diagnosis is contingent upon the demonstration of other extra-articular manifestations of sarcoid and, notably, biopsy evidence of epithelioid tubercles or a positive Kveim test. In chronic arthritis, x-ray shows rather typical changes in the bones of the extremities with intact cortex and cystic changes. Typical sarcoid granulomas may be demonstrated by a biopsy of a chronically involved synovial membrane. Rheumatoid factor is sometimes present in low titers in the serum of patients with sarcoidosis, but this is a nonspecific finding and is unrelated to the joint disease.

Treatment of arthritis in sarcoidosis is usually symptomatic and supportive. A short course of corticosteroids may be effective in patients with severe and progressive joint disease.

The occurrence of joint disease is usually a favorable prognostic sign with respect to the course of sarcoidosis.

Siltzbach, L.E., & J. Duberstein: Arthritis in sarcoidosis. Clin Orthop 57:31–51, 1968.

INTERMITTENT HYDRARTHROSIS

Intermittent hydrarthrosis is a rare clinical entity of unknown etiology which is characterized by recurring, often painless joint effusions, particularly in the knee, usually occurring at regular intervals and lasting several hours to several days. The existence of this entity has been questioned, and other causes of joint effusion must be carefully excluded before the diagnosis is considered. A significant percentage later develop chronic rheumatoid arthritis.

Treatment is symptomatic, and may include removal of joint fluid.

NEUROGENIC ARTHROPATHY
(Charcot Joint)

Neurogenic arthropathy is joint destruction resulting from loss or diminution of proprioception, pain, and temperature perception. Although usually associated with tabes dorsalis, it is also seen in diabetic neuropathy, syringomyelia, spinal cord injuries, subacute combined degeneration of pernicious anemia, and peripheral nerve injuries. Prolonged administration of hydrocortisone by the intra-articular route may also cause Charcot joint. With loss of the normal muscle tone and loss of protective reflexes, a marked traumatic osteoarthritis ensues; this results in an enlarged, painless joint with extensive erosion of cartilage and osteophyte formation. X-ray changes, although sometimes "classical," may be degenerative or hypertrophic in the same patient.

Treatment is directed against the primary disease; mechanical devices are used to assist in weight-bearing and prevention of further trauma. In some instances, amputation becomes unavoidable.

Chandler, G.N., & others: Charcot's arthropathy following intra-articular hydrocortisone. Brit MJ 1:952–953, 1959.
Storey, G.: Charcot joints. Brit J Ven Dis 40:109, 1964.

"CONNECTIVE TISSUE" DISEASES

A variety of names (eg, collagen diseases, collagenoses, diffuse vascular diseases, visceral angiitides, diffuse connective tissue diseases, and diseases of immunologically embarrassed individuals) have been given to the group of diseases—protean in nature—which appear to have in common widespread fibrinoid alterations in connective tissues with varying degrees of vascular inflammation and necrosis and associated disturbances of immunologic mechanisms. Rheumatoid arthritis (discussed earlier in this chapter), rheumatic fever, disseminated lupus erythematosus, polyarteritis nodosa, scleroderma, dermatomyositis, Hashimoto's thyroiditis, nonthrombocytopenic purpuras, and perhaps glomerulonephritis are the chief members of this group of probably interrelated diseases of unknown etiology.

The differentiation of the collagen diseases into definite clinical categories is sometimes difficult, and in many instances the diagnosis can be established only after prolonged and painstaking observation. Anatomic, histologic, and immunologic findings often overlap in these disorders. Serologic tests for abnormal globulins (eg, rheumatoid factor), LE cell preparations, and fluorescent antinuclear staining reactions may assist in the differential diagnosis of the various collagen diseases, but they are not specific. Since these diseases, however, usually differ sufficiently in clinical pattern, response to treatment, and prognosis, the generally accepted specific terminology perhaps serves a useful purpose. There is some evidence that the various collagen syndromes not only overlap but may actually coexist (eg, systemic lupus erythematosus and rheumatoid arthritis).

There is clinical and immunologic evidence that a variety of triggering mechanisms (eg, infectious, traumatic, chemical, or metabolic alterations) in the genetically predisposed individual may be associated with the onset or exacerbations of these diseases, thereby suggesting a common relationship of etiology and pathogenesis. The relative roles of genetic and environmental factors remain uncertain. A number of connective tissue diseases of unknown etiology are accompanied by evidence of an autoimmune (the term "autosensitivity" is preferred by many clinicians) type of reaction (ie, when the immune mechanism of a given individual would appear to paradoxically injure, or even . destroy, specific tissues in his own body). In many instances (eg, lupoid hepatitis), there is evidence that progressive cellular injury and inflammation may result from such autoimmune disturbance. Hypergammaglobulinemia, low complement levels, multiple "auto-antibodies," accumulation of lymphocytes and plasma cells in damaged tissues, effectiveness of corticosteroid treatment, and coexistence of autoimmune disorders are considered to be reasonable indices of autoimmunity and further justification for the "natural" grouping of these diseases. However, there is evidence that the measurable antinuclear and anticytoplasmic reactions are not responsible for the lesions. It is of interest also that evidence of immunologic alterations (eg, rheumatoid factor, false-positive STS, positive Coombs test, and antinuclear antibodies) may be demonstrated in certain asymptomatic relatives of patients with connective tissue diseases. A positive STS should suggest the possibility of the presence of or future development of one of the connective tissue diseases.

SYSTEMIC (DISSEMINATED) LUPUS ERYTHEMATOSUS

Essentials of Diagnosis

- Occurs predominantly in young women.
- Symptoms and signs referable to multiple organ systems.
- Weakness, malaise, fever, joint pains, and weight loss.
- Erythematous rash on face or other areas exposed to sunlight.
- Anemia, leukopenia, thrombocytopenia, hyperglobulinemia, and increased ESR.
- LE cells may be demonstrated in blood and other tissues.
- Antinuclear antibodies often found.

General Considerations

Systemic lupus erythematosus is a noninfectious inflammatory syndrome which primarily involves the vascular and connective tissues of many organs with a resultant multiplicity of local and systemic manifestations. Although the etiology is not known, the disease may be initiated or aggravated by the use of drugs (eg, hydralazine, sulfonamides, procainamide, degraded tetracycline) or foreign proteins or exposure to solar or ultraviolet radiation, and possibly by psychic trauma. A viral cause has been suggested. An autoimmune mechanism is suggested by the finding of several abnormal serum protein fractions and antinuclear antibodies in patients with systemic lupus erythematosus. Antibody to DNA may be the cause of the acute manifestations. The type, severity, time of onset, and duration of the pathologic involvement may result in a highly variable clinical pattern and prognosis. Pathologic changes are nonspecific, but include widespread vascular and perivascular fibrinoid changes, disseminated arteritis, verrucous endocarditis, and focal or diffuse glomerulonephritis. Polyserositis and generalized lymphadenitis are found in over 50% of cases. A characteristic histologic finding is the so-called lupus erythematosus (LE) cell and the apparently related extracellular masses of homogeneous purple nuclear breakdown materials (hematoxylin bodies). Antinuclear antibodies have been found in families of patients with systemic lupus erythematosus.

Clinical Findings

A. Symptoms and Signs:

1. **Acute**—The onset is rapid and the course is fulminant. Prostration, fever, symmetric malar erythema ("butterfly rash"), generalized lymphadenopathy, basilar pneumonia, pleural effusion, tachycardia, gallop rhythm, pericarditis, hepatosplenomegaly, nephritis, musculoskeletal aches and pains, delirium, psychosis, convulsions, coma, and finally death may occur within a few weeks.

2. **Chronic**—In occasional instances the onset is rapid and the disease later becomes chronic, but most frequently the onset is insidious and the disease is subject to remissions and exacerbations over a period of many years.

a. Systemic reaction—Weakness, malaise, fever, and weight loss may occur.

b. Skin—Discoid lupus erythematosus may occasionally precede the systemic focus of the disease. Conversely, discoid lesions may develop during the course of the systemic disease. Erythema of exposed surfaces, especially symmetric malar erythema, is the most common manifestation of systemic lupus erythematosus, but purpura, subcutaneous nodules ("rheumatoid nodules"), angioneurotic edema, alopecia, vitiligo, or hyperpigmentation may occur.

c. Lymph nodes—Half of patients have generalized lymphadenopathy.

d. Eyes—Corneal involvement and severe retinopathy, including cotton wool retinal exudates, have been reported.

e. Hematopoietic system—Hematologic involvement occurs in all patients. There may be severe hemolytic anemia or thrombocytopenic purpura. Hypersplenism has been described. Splenomegaly occurs in about 20–25% of cases.

f. Lungs—Pulmonary dysfunction with basilar atelectatic pneumonitis, and pleurisy with or without effusion, are common.

g. Cardiovascular system—Pericarditis, with or without effusion, may occur. Myocarditis with tachycardia, gallop rhythm, and disturbances of rhythm may result in heart failure. Raynaud's phenomenon is common, and other peripheral vascular syndromes, including gangrene, may occur.

h. Gastrointestinal system—Ulcerative lesions of the mucous membranes, especially the mouth, are very common. There may be anorexia, nausea and vomiting, diarrhea, abdominal pains, and bloody stools. The intestinal involvement may be the result of extensive vasculitis, ulceration or perforation, or the result of coexisting ulcerative colitis or ileocolitis.

i. Liver—Hepatomegaly, often accompanied by evidence of hepatic dysfunction, occurs in a significant number of cases. A form of chronic, progressive liver disease, with continuing cellular injury and inflammation which may result from autoimmune disturbances, characterized by coarsely nodular cirrhosis, marked hypergammaglobulinemia, and unusual elevation of the serum transaminase, has been termed "lupoid hepatitis" because many of the extrahepatic manifestations mimic disseminated lupus.

j. Kidneys—Three different types of lupus nephritis have been described. Focal proliferative lupus nephritis is characterized by proteinuria and microscopic hematuria, but nephrotic syndrome and renal failure are rare. Response to corticosteroids is favorable. Diffuse proliferative lupus nephritis and membranous lupus nephritis are usually characterized by the nephrotic syndrome and renal insufficiency. Although remissions can be induced in some of these patients with corticosteroids, the prognosis is generally unfavorable, and most patients die of the complications of renal failure within 3 years.

k. Musculoskeletal system—Myalgia and arthralgia occur in almost all patients. About 1/3 of patients will develop a polyarthritis which is indistinguishable from rheumatoid arthritis. However, spinal involvement and advanced destruction of articular cartilage are uncommon.

l. CNS—Involvement of the CNS is common and may vary from mild neurotic traits to psychosis, convulsions, neuritis, hemiplegia, and coma.

B. Laboratory Findings: A mild to moderate normochromic normocytic anemia is found in the majority of patients. Hemolytic anemia occurs infrequently, but may be severe. Mild leukopenia with "shift to the left" is common. The sedimentation rate is high in almost all cases, often even during periods of remission. Serum globulin is increased in about 50% of cases, usually in the alpha$_2$ and gamma fractions. Many other serum protein abnormalities of unknown significance have been described. Antinuclear antibodies are often present. Liver function tests are frequently abnormal. Biologic false-positive STS (including FTA and TPI) are found in 20% of cases. Protein, white cells, red cells, and casts in the urine reflect the type and degree of renal involvement.

Finding the characteristic LE cell in venous blood or in other tissues may be of value in diagnosis, although the LE cell is not pathognomonic. An absence of LE cells does not rule out the diagnosis of systemic lupus erythematosus. The LE cell, which is apparently due to a specific antinuclear antibody, is typically a polymorphonuclear leukocyte containing a large globular mass of homogeneous reddish purple material (when stained with Wright's stain) which fills a large portion of the cell. This material may also occur extracellularly. The LE cell may be found in many other disease states. Skin biopsy and staining with fluorescein conjugated antihuman complement serum may show characteristic fluorescence.

Differential Diagnosis

Since systemic lupus erythematosus involves many organ systems it may be confused with a wide variety of diseases, especially musculoskeletal, dermatologic, and hematologic disorders. It must also be differentiated from many acute and chronic infectious diseases. The latter is particularly true of syphilis because of the positive STS.

Treatment

A. Corticosteroids and Corticotropin: These drugs may exert a very favorable and often remarkable effect, but the results are variable. Treatment is usually more effective in the early phases of the illness. Many patients obtain marked temporary benefits during acute episodes or when there is involvement of vital organs. Large doses may be necessary, and may be life-saving. Opinion still differs about whether these drugs should be withdrawn after acute attacks subside or continued indefinitely on a maintenance basis. Renal lesions, previously considered to be irreversible, may respond favorably to high doses of corticosteroids over a prolonged period. Alternate-day corticosteroid therapy has been reported to be useful in the treatment of lupus nephritis.

B. Other General Measures: A high-caloric, high-vitamin diet is advised. Iron salts or blood transfusions may be necessary to correct anemia. Patients should be advised against undue exposure to sunlight or to other ultraviolet radiation. If Raynaud's phenomenon exists, protect against exposure to cold. All drugs previously mentioned as causative should be avoided. Appropriate anti-infective treatment should be instituted for pneumonia or other infections. Salicylates and other analgesics and physical therapy may be indicated in the management of musculoskeletal aches and pains. Renal disease is treated according to the type and severity of the involvement.

In patients who fail to respond to adequate corticosteroid therapy, a trial of immunosuppressive agents such as the purine antagonists (eg, mercaptopurine or azathioprine) or alkylating agents (eg, nitrogen mustards, cyclophosphamide) is indicated. A guarded favorable response has been reported with these agents, but their value has not been proved. Severe gastrointestinal or bone marrow side reactions may occur.

Many clinicians feel that the antirheumatic effect of chloroquine and other antimalarials does not justify the risk of toxic retinopathy associated with their use; others maintain that the drugs are useful in selected patients who can be kept under frequent supervision by an ophthalmologist.

Course & Prognosis

The disease may be fulminant, with a rapid progression of severe symptoms leading to death in a few weeks even with treatment. More frequently, the disease follows an episodic pattern with recurrent involvement of one or more organ systems over a period of many years. After the 4th year there is a decreased mortality rate. Longevity of patients with the chronic illness may perhaps be increased by proper corticosteroid therapy.

Ackerman, G.L.: Alternate-day steroid therapy in lupus nephritis. Ann Int Med 72:511–519, 1970.

Baldwin, D.S.: The clinical course of the proliferative and membranous forms of lupus nephritis. Ann Int Med 73:929–942, 1970.

Blomgren, S.E., & others: Antinuclear antibody induced by procainamide: A prospective study. New England J Med 281:64–66, 1969.

Dubois, E.L.: *Lupus Erythematosus.* Blakiston, 1966.

Evans, A.S., Rothfield, N.F., & J.C. Niederman: Raised antibody titers to E-B virus in systemic lupus erythematosus. Lancet 1:167–168, 1971.

Hahn, B.H., Yardley, J.H., & M.B. Stevens: "Rheumatoid" nodules in systemic lupus erythematosus. Ann Int Med 72:49–58, 1970.

Interdepartmental Conference, University of California, Los Angeles: Systemic lupus erythematosus. California Med 111:467–481, 1969.

Kraus, S.J., Haserick, J.R., & M.A. Lantz: Fluorescent treponemal antibody-absorption test reactions in lupus erythematosus: Atypical beading pattern and probable false-positive reactions. New England J Med 282:1287–1290, 1970.

Mackay, J.R.: Lupoid hepatitis and primary biliary cirrhosis: Auto-immune disease of the liver? Bull Rheum Dis 18:487–494, 1968.

Smith, C.K., Cassidy, J.T., & G.G. Bole: Type I dysgammaglobulinemia, systemic lupus erythematosus and lymphoma. Am J Med 48:113–119, 1970.

Statsny, P., & M. Ziff: Cold insoluble complexes and complement levels in systemic lupus erythematosus. New England J Med 280:1376–1381, 1969.

POLYARTERITIS (PERIARTERITIS) NODOSA

Essentials of Diagnosis

- Symptoms and signs referable to multiple organ systems.
- Weakness, malaise, fever, weight loss.
- Renal involvement, hypertension, asthma, heart failure, cutaneous eruptions, abdominal pain, musculoskeletal aches and pains, peripheral neuritis.
- Proteinuria and hematuria, leukocytosis, eosinophilia, elevated sedimentation rate, hyperglobulinemia.
- Biopsy of painful areas may show necrotizing arteritis.

General Considerations

Polyarteritis nodosa is a noninfectious inflammatory syndrome of unknown etiology with varying manifestations of multiple organ systems characterized by widespread segmental inflammation and necrosis of small and medium-sized arteries with resultant granulomas. In a few cases there is a history of drug sensitization. A cytotoxic serum factor has been described. The arterial lesions occur most frequently in the kidneys, muscles, peripheral nerves, heart, gastrointestinal tract, and liver, although any organ may be involved. Microscopically, there is necrosis, fibrous changes, and leukocytic infiltration, with or without eosinophils.

Clinical Findings

A. Symptoms and Signs: The mode of onset, clinical findings, and the course of the disease may be highly variable. The most common findings are hypertension, renal disease, musculoskeletal aches and pains, and peripheral neuritis. Acute oliguric renal failure may develop early in the course of the disease, without significant evidence of other organ involvement. Other manifestations include fever, malaise, weakness, weight loss, bronchial asthma, bronchial pneumonia, angina, congestive failure, nausea, abdominal pain, hematemesis, and melena. Skin lesions may include papular eruptions, purpura, vesicles, bullae, or subcutaneous periarterial nodules.

B. Laboratory Findings; Leukocytosis and mild normocytic anemia are common. Eosinophilia may occur. The sedimentation rate and the serum globulin level are frequently elevated. Proteinuria, hematuria, pyuria, and casts are common urinary findings.

Biopsy of multiple sections of muscle from painful areas may establish the diagnosis, although negative pathologic findings do not necessarily rule out the possiblity of the disease. Vasculitis, as seen in a muscle biopsy, may occur in the other connective tissue diseases.

Differential Diagnosis

The diagnosis of polyarteritis is suggested by the very multiplicity of clinical involvement and the rapid progression of the illness. Polyarteritis must be differentiated from the other angiitides such as systemic lupus erythematosus, scleroderma, and Wegener's granulomatosis, and from rheumatic fever, rheumatoid arthritis, glomerulonephritis, and pyelonephritis. It may at times be confused with acute and chronic infections, the lymphomas, and other granulomatous diseases.

Treatment

Treatment is symptomatic and supportive. Corticosteroids may occasionally be beneficial, especially in cases of involvement of vital organs. The healing of arteritis may be accompanied by thrombosis. In socalled paradoxic adverse reactions, the corticosteroid dosage should be reduced. Intercurrent infections may be treated with antibiotics.

Prognosis

The disease usually runs a fulminating course, with death often occurring within a few months after diagnosis. In occasional instances the patient may live comfortably for several years, especially with corticosteroid therapy. Recovery is unpredictable.

Fronhert, P.P., & S.G. Sheps: Long-term follow-up study of periarteritis nodosa. Am J Med 43:8–14, 1967.
Ladefoged, J., & others: Acute anuria due to polyarteritis nodosa. Am J Med 46:827–831, 1969.
Yust, I., Schwartz, J., & F. Dreyfuss: A cytotoxic serum factor in polyarteritis nodosa and related conditions. Am J Med 48:472–476, 1970.

DIFFUSE SCLERODERMA
(Systemic Sclerosis)

Scleroderma is a chronic mesenchymal disease of undetermined origin characterized by connective tissue proliferation in the dermis and in multiple internal organs. The onset is insidious: Stiffness of the hands, sweating of the hands and feet, and Raynaud's phenomenon may at times be present for years before the condition becomes recognized. The skin eventually becomes hard, thick, parchment-like, and glossy without evidence of pitting edema, and the fingers and toes become fixed in position. Gradually the entire integument becomes involved, and ulceration, pigmentation and depigmentation, widespread or local calcification of the skin (especially around the joints), and paronychia and ulceration of the fingers and toes may occur. Esophageal involvement with dysphagia may occur early. Disturbance of gastrointestinal motility may occur. Respiratory movement may be impaired as a result of sclerodermatous constriction of the thorax, and pulmonary fibrosis and recurrent bronchial pneumonia may occur. Pulmonary function studies often show decreased vital capacity, decreased compliance, and low diffusing capacity, even in patients without

dysphagia or with normal chest films. The pericardium is frequently involved. Myocardial disease may result in arrhythmias or congestive heart failure. The sedimentation rate and serum globulin are elevated. The LE phenomenon or a rise in antinuclear antibodies may occur. Renal involvement is common and may lead to terminal uremia. Proteinuria, hematuria, and casts are found frequently in later stages of the disease. X-rays show subcutaneous calcification, osteoporosis of bone, and destruction of the distal phalanges. Gastrointestinal x-rays may show a loss of normal peristalsis.

Treatment is symptomatic and supportive. Corticosteroids are usually ineffective. Low molecular weight dextran (dextran 40) has proved to be of symptomatic value, but experience with this agent is limited.

The condition is usually slowly progressive for many years. Death is usually due to renal or cardiac failure or to sepsis.

D'Angelo, W.A., & others: Pathologic observations in systemic sclerosis (scleroderma): A study of 58 autopsy cases and 58 matched controls. Am J Med 46:428–440, 1969.
Norton, W.L., & J.M. Nardo: Vascular disease in progressive systemic sclerosis (scleroderma). Ann Int Med 73:317–324, 1970.

DERMATOMYOSITIS
(Polymyositis)

Dermatomyositis is a chronic, nonsuppurative inflammatory disease of undetermined origin which involves primarily the skin and striated muscles. The inflammatory process may be limited largely to the muscles—hence the term polymyositis. There is an unexplained high incidence of associated neoplastic disease (10–20%) in patients with dermatomyositis. Some workers have speculated that the dermatomyositis is a metabolic or immunologic manifestation of the primary neoplastic disease.

The onset, although usually insidious, may at times be acute. Weakness, fatigue, mild fever, weight loss, and muscular aching are early symptoms. Diffuse erythema of the face and neck may occur, and a purplish periorbital edema is often noted. Erythema, with or without edema, may occur in other skin areas, especially the extensor surfaces of the arms and legs. Desquamation, pigmentary changes, and subcutaneous induration and calcification may occur. Aching, tenderness, and weakness of muscles is characteristic. Muscular involvement may be generalized, but is most marked in the flexor muscles of the upper and lower extremities. Involvement of special muscle groups may result in ocular palsies, dysphagia, or respiratory embarrassment. Multiple gastrointestinal ulcers may occur. There may be a mild normocytic anemia, increased sedimentation rate, and increased serum globulin. Serum enzyme (eg, SGOT) levels are elevated and are useful not only in diagnosis but in following the effectiveness of therapy. Creatinuria parallels muscle destruction. Biopsies show variable dermatitis and non-suppurative inflammatory, degenerative changes in muscles. The electromyogram is useful for the early detection and differentiation of dermatomyositis from the neuromuscular disorders.

Treatment is symptomatic and supportive. High dosages of salicylates may be of value. Corticosteroids occasionally provide marked improvement. Emergency measures to provide an adequate airway may be necessary. Removal of associated malignancy may result in a regression of the disease.

The disease is usually moderately progressive, undulating in severity, and crippling over a period of years, but it may at times be fulminating in nature.

Appropriate investigations to rule out malignant neoplastic disease are indicated for all patients who develop dermatomyositis in adult life.

Medsger, T.A., Jr., Dawson, W.N., Jr., & A.T. Masi: The epidemiology of polymyositis. Am J Med 48:715–723, 1970.

Rose, A.L., & J.N. Watson: Polymyositis: A survey of 89 cases with particular reference to treatment and prognosis. Brain 89:747–768, 1966.

SICCA SYNDROME
(Sjögren's Syndrome)

Sjögren's syndrome is a generalized connective tissue disorder of undetermined etiology, with multiple systemic involvement. Dryness of the eyes, mouth, and nose, due to hypofunction of the lacrimal and parotid glands, is characteristic. Unilateral or bilateral parotid swelling may occur. Weakness, fatigue, and musculoskeletal aches and pains are common. Chronic polyarthritis, often of a rheumatoid type, may be present. Neuritis may occur. The syndrome has been described in association with such a wide variety of other diseases that manifestations may be quite variable. Increased sedimentation rate, hyperglobulinemia (usually gamma globulin), cryoglobulinemia, rheumatoid factor, thyroglobulin antibodies, antinuclear antibodies, and persistent hyposthenuria are frequently observed. Pathologic findings in the lacrimal, salivary, and submucous glands consist principally of lymphocytic and plasma cell infiltration with atrophy of the glandular tissue and diminution of secretions. Arteritis and periarteritis may occur in the viscera and lymph nodes.

Many treatment methods have been proposed, but results have not been uniformly good. Local treatment of eye dryness with irrigating solution or artificial tears (methylcellulose, 0.12% in saline) instilled into the eyes every 3 hours is simple and effective in minimizing keratoconjunctivitis and corneal ulceration. Treatment with corticotropin or the corticosteroids is warranted, especially in the systemic disease, but should be used with caution if corneal infection or ulceration is present. There is no known treatment for the mouth dryness.

The disease is subject to remissions and exacerbations, but is usually not progressive. The overall prognosis depends upon the associated systemic involvement or connective tissue disease.

Beck, T.S., & others: Antinuclear and precipitating auto-antibodies in Sjögren's syndrome. Ann Rheum Dis 24:16–22, 1965.

Hood, J., Burns, C.A., & R.E. Hodges: Sjögren's syndrome in scurvy. New England J Med 282:1120–1124, 1970.

Shioji, R., & others: Sjögren's syndrome and renal tubular acidosis. Am J Med 48:456–463, 1970.

WEGENER'S SYNDROME
(Wegener's Granulomatosis)

Wegener's syndrome is a rare generalized progressive granulomatous disorder of undetermined etiology characterized by severe sinusitis, pulmonary inflammation, multiplicity of symptoms due to generalized arteritis, and terminal renal insufficiency. The disease begins with nasal, paranasal sinus, or pulmonary symptoms, with chronic productive cough or hemoptysis. Fever, malaise, weakness, or weight loss may be severe. Progressive destruction of the cartilage of the nose and the bony structures around the paranasal sinuses occurs later. Chemosis, papillitis, and exophthalmos may occur. There may be parotitis, carditis, musculoskeletal aches and pains, prostatitis, and polyneuritis. Proteinuria, hematuria, and white cells and casts in the urine are evidence of marked renal involvement.

Immunosuppressive treatment with methotrexate has recently been reported to induce remissions lasting over 2 years. Combined treatment with corticosteroids and cytotoxic agents has resulted in remission of this disease for as long as 8 years. Corticosteroids alone may give temporary relief or induce temporary remissions early in the course of the disease.

Capizzi, R.L., & J.R. Bertino: Methotrexate therapy of Wegener's granulomatosis. Ann Int Med 74:74–79, 1971.

Raitt, J.W.: Wegener's granulomatosis: Treatment with cytotoxic agents and adrenocorticoids. Ann Int Med 74:344–356, 1971.

• • •

GENERAL PRINCIPLES IN THE PHYSICAL MANAGEMENT OF ARTHRITIC JOINTS

The following general principles apply to the treatment of any disease of the joints:

(1) Arrange or support the affected joints in comfortable positions which will permit optimal physical use if joint motion is subsequently lost.

(2) In the deforming types of arthritis, after the acute process has subsided, employ active exercises or passive mobilization early and regularly, as tolerated, in order to prevent deformity and to preserve joint motion.

(3) Avoid measures which cause persistent increase in symptoms. So-called "routine measures," eg, heat and massage, are not uniformly tolerated and there is no evidence that they improve function.

(4) Patients with joint disease (particularly rheumatoid or suppurative arthritis) are constantly threatened by deformity. Guard particularly against flexion deformities.

(5) The services of a specialist in physical therapy should be utilized whenever necessary.

(6) If the arthritis is severe, if the course of the disease seems unfavorable, or if deformity appears inevitable, early consultation with an orthopedist is imperative. Special orthopedic measures such as traction, casts, braces and corsets, and surgical measures including arthroplasty, capsulotomy, tenotomy, arthrodesis, and synovectomy may be required. There has been a trend in some centers toward earlier surgery in patients with progressive and deforming arthritis.

(7) Emphasize to the patient the importance of complete cooperation and his responsibility with the physical therapy program at home as well as in the office or hospital. Stress the importance of year-round continuance of treatment if necessary. Instruct the patient (or, if necessary, his family and friends) in the proper use of heat, immobilization, and passive mobilization under home conditions.

Licht, S. (editor): *Therapeutic Heat and Cold,* 2nd ed. E. Licht, 1965.

Lowman, E.W. (editor): Rehabilitation. M Clin North America 53:485–738, 1969.

Potter, T.A., & E.A. Nalebuff (editors): Surgical management of rheumatoid arthritis. S Clin North America 49:731–950, 1969.

·   ·   ·

MANIFESTATIONS OF THE MUSCULOSKELETAL SYSTEM DUE TO PARASITIC DISEASES

Elephantiasis: Filariasis.

Muscular pain, tenderness: Trichinosis.

Calcification: Cysticercosis, filariasis, loiasis, dracunculosis.

●   ●   ●

General Bibliography

American Rheumatism Association: Primer on the rheumatic diseases. JAMA 190:127–140, 425–444, 509–530, 741–751, 1964.

Anderson, J.R., Buchanan, W.R., & R.B. Goudie: *Autoimmunity: Clinical and Experimental.* American Lecture Series No. 673. Thomas, 1967.

Banks, H.H. (editor): Symposium on musculoskeletal disorders, II. P Clin North America 14:533–704, 1967.

Beetham, W.P., Jr., & others: *Physical Examination of the Joints.* Saunders, 1965.

Blumberg, B.S., & others: ARA nomenclature and classification of arthritis and rheumatism. (Tentative.) Arthritis Rheum 7:93–98, 1964.

Christian, C.L.: Seventeenth rheumatism review: Rheumatism and arthritis. Review of American and English literature for the years 1963 and 1964. Arthritis Rheum 9:93–266, 1966.

Corley, C.C., Jr., Lessner, H.E., & W.E. Larsen: Azathioprine therapy of "autoimmune" diseases. Am J Med 41:404–412, 1966.

Engleman, E.P., & M.A. Shearn: Recent advances in rheumatic diseases. Ann Int Med 66:199–220, 1967.

Ferguson, R.H., & J.W. Worthington: Recent advances in rheumatic diseases: 1967 through 1969. Ann Int Med 73:109–125, 1970.

Gardner, D.L.: *Pathology of the Connective Tissue Diseases.* Williams & Wilkins, 1965.

Garewal, G.S., & S.D. Deodhar: Antinuclear factor test: Diagnostic value. Cleveland Clin Quart 36:53–58, 1969.

Hill, A.G.S. (editor): *Modern Trends in Rheumatology.* Appleton-Century-Crofts, 1966.

Hollander, J.L. (editor): *Arthritis and Allied Conditions,* 7th ed. Lea & Febiger, 1966.

Prockop, D.J., & K.I. Kivirikko: Relationship of hydroxyproline excretion in urine to collagen metabolism. Ann Int Med 66:1243–1266, 1967.

Rosenberg, E.F. (editor): Symposium on muscle, bone and joint disorders. M Clin North America 49:1–300, 1965.

Rothermich, N.O.: An updated look at antirheumatic drugs. M Clin North America 51:1213–1222, 1967.

Rupe, E. (editor): Treatment of collagen diseases. Mod Treat 3:1243–1324, 1966.

Samter, M. (editor): *Immunological Disease,* 2nd ed. Little, Brown, 1971.

Swannell, A.J., & E.N. Coomes: Preliminary results of azathioprine treatment in severe rheumatic disease. Ann Phys Med 10:112–120, 1969.

Vaughn, J.H., Barnett, E.V., & J.P. Leddy: Autosensitivity diseases. New England J Med 275:1426–1432, 1486–1494, 1966.

Watson, D.W., & A.G. Johnson: The clinical use of immunosuppression. M Clin North America 53:1225–1241, 1969.

Windhorst, D.B., & others: New findings regarding auto-immune factors in skin disease. M Clin North America 54:95–105, 1970.

14...
Bone & Joint Diseases

Floyd H. Jergesen

INFECTIONS
OF BONES & JOINTS

OSTEOMYELITIS

Osteomyelitis is acute or chronic inflammation of bone due to infection. It may be classified according to the mechanism of introduction of the causative agent (ie, as primary or secondary) or on the basis of microbial etiology.

Primary osteomyelitis is caused by direct implantation of microorganisms into bone and is likely to be localized to the site of inoculation. Open (compound) fractures, penetrating wounds (especially those due to firearms), and surgical operations on bone commonly provide access for microbial contamination. Intramedullary aspiration or injection accounts for an occasional infection. Operative treatment is usually necessary; the principal adjunctive treatment is with antimicrobial drugs. The treatment of primary osteomyelitis is usually discussed in conjunction with open fractures or postoperative wound complications.

The route of infection of **secondary osteomyelitis** is usually through the arteries. Exceptions are spread through veins to the bones of the pelvis or spine and direct extension from neighboring articular or soft tissue infections.

1. ACUTE PYOGENIC OSTEOMYELITIS

Essentials of Diagnosis
- Fever, chills, malaise, sweating.
- Pain, tenderness, swelling, limitation of joint motion.
- Culture of the blood or lesion is essential for precise etiologic diagnosis.

General Considerations

About 95% of cases of acute secondary osteomyelitis are caused by pyogenic organisms, usually a single strain. Further contamination during open surgical treatment or "superinfection" during antibiotic treatment with a different organism may produce a mixed infection.

Acute hematogenous osteomyelitis occurs predominantly during the period of skeletal growth. Staphylococci account for about 75% of infections, and group A beta-hemolytic streptococci are the next most common pathogens. The remainder of cases are caused by a wide variety of organisms. Preexisting infection of other organ systems—most commonly the skin, respiratory tract, and genitourinary tract—can be identified in about ½ of cases. A history of trauma is frequently present.

Clinical Findings

A. Symptoms and Signs: In infants the onset is often precipitate, with alarming systemic symptoms of toxicity; an insidious onset may be characterized by subtle generalized symptoms. Voluntary movement of the extremity is likely to be inhibited. Tenderness in the region of the involved bone usually occurs before swelling or redness, which are later manifestations frequently associated with extra-osseous abscess formation.

In children, the onset may be accompanied by high fever, chills, and prostration; it may be less dramatic, especially when drug therapy for a predisposing infection has been given. Local pain may indicate an area of tenderness and even soft tissue swelling. Passive joint motion of the extremity may be inhibited because of muscle guarding.

The onset in adults is likely to be less striking than in infants and children. Generalized toxic symptoms of bacteremia may be absent, and vague, shifting, or evanescent local pain may be the earliest manifestation. Depending upon the duration and extent of bone involvement, tenderness may be present or absent. Limitation of joint motion may be marked, especially in patients with spine involvement or when lesions are near joints.

B. Laboratory Findings: The precise diagnosis at any age depends upon the recovery and identification of the causative organism. Early in the course—especially during the stage of invasion—blood cultures are likely to be positive; repeated cultures may be necessary. Acceleration of the ESR and leukocytosis occur commonly, but their absence does not rule out osteomyelitis.

When the infection is severe, secondary anemia is likely to occur early.

C. X-Ray Findings: Significant changes in bone cannot be identified by x-ray examination until 7–10 days after the onset in infants and 2–4 weeks after onset in adults. Extra-osseous soft tissue swelling (caused by exudates) adjacent to the osseous focus may be the earliest significant finding, appearing within 3–5 days after the onset of symptoms. Later, architectural alteration of cancellous bone and destruction of compact bone are indicative of processes that have been active for days or weeks. Subperiosteal new bone formation is a late manifestation of a healing reaction.

D. Special Examinations: Early diagnosis is facilitated by recovery of material from the local lesion for culture studies. Exudates may be recovered by aspiration of extra-osseous tissues in areas of tenderness. Otherwise, when localizing symptoms are clearly manifest—especially in the region of a metaphysis, where the cortex is comparatively thin—the medulla can be aspirated with a small bone trocar to obtain material for culture. If symptoms are severe and the process has been active for more than 48 hours, specimens for culture may be obtained during open surgical treatment.

Differential Diagnosis

Acute hematogenous osteomyelitis must be differentiated from suppurative arthritis, rheumatic fever, and cellulitis. The pseudoparalysis associated with acute osteomyelitis of infancy may simulate poliomyelitis at the onset. With mild symptoms, it may initially mimic transient synovitis of the hip joint or Legg-Perthes disease. Acute forms with mixed symptoms and subacute forms must be differentiated from tuberculosis and mycotic infections of bone and Ewing's sarcoma.

Complications

The most common complication of acute secondary osteomyelitis is chronic osteomyelitis, which can be due to delayed diagnosis or inadequate early treatment. Waiting for manifest x-ray evidence, treatment by nonspecific measures, or ineffective antimicrobial drug therapy may abet progressive destruction of bone and soft tissues.

Other complications include soft tissue abscess formation, septic arthritis from extension into joints, and metastatic infections from the initial osteomyelitic focus.

Pathologic fracture may occur at the site of extensive bone destruction.

Treatment

A. General Measures: The severity of systemic symptoms partly determines the general management. Attention must be given to fluid balance of the acutely toxic patient. Immobilization of the affected extremity by splinting, plaster encasement, or suspension in an orthopedic apparatus is advisable for relief of pain and protection against pathologic fracture. During the acute stage, secondary anemia is best corrected by whole blood replacement. Pain should not be completely abolished by uninterrupted use of drugs since its intensity can be an important clue to the effectiveness of treatment.

B. Specific Measures: Although the antibiotics have provided new concepts of treatment, rational therapy continues to rest upon surgical principles and drug therapy is mainly adjunctive. The selection of specific measures depends in part upon the type of infecting organism, the stage of progress of the lesion, and the general response of the patient. Treatment must be individualized, and only broad guides will be outlined here.

1. Operative treatment—During the first 2–3 days after the onset of acute infection, open surgical treatment can be avoided in many cases, especially in infants and children. If vigorous general care and appropriate antibiotic therapy are instituted promptly, the progress of the local lesion may be controlled and spread of the infection halted before suppuration and significant tissue destruction have occurred.

If an abscess has formed beneath the periosteum or has extended into soft tissues of infants and children, it should be drained at least once daily by aspiration. Pain and fever that persist longer than 2–3 days after initiating aspiration and antimicrobial therapy suggest spread of the infection. Surgical decompression of the medullary cavity by drilling or fenestration should be done promptly with the hope of minimizing progression of bone necrosis. Subsequent treatment of the local lesion may be by open or closed technics.

2. Antibiotics—Rational antibiotic treatment is based upon an understanding of the disease and laboratory isolation of the pathogen followed by antibiotic sensitivity studies. In the seriously ill patient, antibiotic therapy should be instituted as soon as culture material has been collected; treatment should not be withheld until laboratory studies have been completed. If the initial clinical findings are compatible with the understanding that the most common causes of acute osteomyelitis in infants and children are staphylococci or group A beta-hemolytic streptococci, drug treatment can be started promptly. If no contraindication (such as a history of drug sensitivity) exists, begin treatment immediately intravenously with a β-lactamase-resistant semisynthetic penicillin such as methicillin, oxacilllin, or nafcillin in dosages sufficient to produce a bactericidal serum level. The dosage of the appropriate antibiotic may be guided in part by the serum assay, which determines in vitro the comparative efficacy of the drug against the etiologic microbial strain. Broad-spectrum antibiotics alone, with the exception of semisynthetic penicillins or cephalosporins, should be avoided because prolonged treatment is required and resistant strains are likely to emerge rapidly.

In the seriously ill adult patient, it is often necessary to begin treatment before the causative organism has been isolated. The initial selection of drugs requires a critical clinical appraisal. The most common microbial causes of acute hematogenous osteomyelitis are gram-positive cocci and gram-negative enteric bacilli. A likely primary focus such as a skin, respiratory tract, or genitourinary tract infection may offer a clue. If a gram-positive coccal infection is suspected, a semisynthetic penicillin resistant to penicillinase (β-lactamase) is the drug of first choice. Cephalosporin (Cephalothin®) and vancomycin (Vancocin®) are alternatives. Gram-negative bacilli have widely different drug sensitivities, and combinations of drugs must be given until the causative microorganism has been isolated and its precise drug sensitivities determined. Various combinations have been advocated, eg, kanamycin (Kantrex®) plus polymyxin B given intravenously. Recent studies have indicated that gentamicin (Garamycin®), with or without cephaloridine (Keflordin®, Loridine®), may be effective for acute severe infections presumably caused by gram-negative bacteria. When endotoxic shock is present, specific measures for its treatment must be used in addition to chemotherapy.

Chemotherapy should be continued for about 2–3 weeks after the patient is afebrile or repeated wound cultures fail to show growth.

Rational drug therapy is based upon drug sensitivity tests. Properly executed disk sensitivity studies will give early guidance concerning the probable efficacy of drugs that might be selected for the treatment of infections due to staphylococci or group A streptococci. However, the disk sensitivity technic does not indicate the likely effective dosage, which should be in the bactericidal range. A more reliable laboratory guide is assay of the drug concentration in the patient's serum against the isolated strain. To provide an adequate opportunity for tissue saturation by the drug, the serum sample should not be taken until 24–48 hours after starting treatment. Adjustment of dosage or selection of alternate drugs may then be indicated. Although disk sensitivity studies may provide reliable guidance for treatment of infections caused by the microorganisms mentioned above (and others), this test cannot be relied upon for optimal help when enteric bacilli or enteric cocci are involved. Tube dilution sensitivity studies are more reliable under these circumstances. Other advantages of the tube dilution methods include a more realistic indication of drug dosage, determination of drug combinations that may have additive or synergistic effects, and indications of effective drug selections when the flora are mixed.

C. Treatment of Complications: Treatment of the common complications of acute hematogenous osteomyelitis is essentially as for acute suppurative arthritis and chronic osteomyelitis, which are discussed elsewhere. "Superinfection" in the form of bacteremia due to a different microbial strain requires, in addition, the same treatment as primary infection.

Course and Prognosis

The mortality rate in acute osteomyelitis is probably no more than 1%. Morbidity, however, continues to be high. If effective treatment can be instituted within 48 hours after onset, prompt recovery can be expected in about 2/3 of cases. Chronicity and recurrence of infection are likely when treatment is delayed.

Capitanio, M.A., & J.A. Kirkpatrick: Early roentgen observations in acute osteomyelitis. Am J Roentgenol 108:488–496, 1970.

Hall, J.E., & E.A. Silverstein: Acute hematogenous osteomyelitis. Pediatrics 31:1033–1038, 1963.
Jergesen, F., & E. Jawetz: Pyogenic infections in orthopaedic surgery. Am J Surg 106:152–163, 1963.
Martin, C.M., & others: Initial, presumptive therapy for serious acute gram-negative rod infections: Preliminary report of a controlled clinical trial. Trans New York Acad Sc (Series II) 29:589–605, 1967.

2. SALMONELLA OSTEOMYELITIS

Although the incidence of infection with *Salmonella typhi* has decreased in the USA during the past 25 years, the incidence of infection with other species of salmonella has increased. Infection of the bones or joints occurs as a complication in less than 1% of cases of typhoid fever. Skeletal infection due to salmonella may be associated with sickle cell disease. The common lesion is periostitis of the shafts of long bones without extensive destruction or abscess formation. Intervertebral disk space infection is the usual manifestation in the spine. A complication is bone abscess formation.

The onset of bone and joint infection may occur during the acute stage of the primary disease or during convalescence. Recurrence of fever, with pain and local tenderness, may suggest the late occurrence of bone infection. Extensive abscess formation does not tend to occur even without specific treatment. Previous antibiotic therapy may make recovery of the organism difficult to the point that a presumptive diagnosis must be based upon serologic agglutination titers (Widal).

Acute symptoms respond to chloramphenicol (Chloromycetin®) or ampicillin (Penbritin®, Polycillin®). The chronic lesion may require operative evacuation of the abscess in addition to antibiotics.

De Torregrosa, M. Vda., & others: Association of salmonella-caused osteomyelitis and sickle cell disease. JAMA 174:354–356, 1960.
Schulte, W.J., & K.R. Tucker: Surgical implications in salmonellosis. Arch Surg 96:593–598, 1968.
Simon, S.D., & C.M. Silver: Salmonella osteomyelitis: Report of 3 cases, 1 with fatal outcome and autopsy. J Int Coll Surg 28:197–205, 1957.

3. BRUCELLA OSTEOMYELITIS

Brucella infection of the skeletal system is not common, but it may occur as a complication or sequel of brucellosis. Infections both by *Brucella melitensis* and *Br abortus* have been reported. Skeletal lesions are likely to be found in the lumbar spine or sacroiliac joints. The lesion is usually granulomatous, although abscess formation may occur. Osteophytes may form early in the course of the disease and subsequently, by coalescence, cause spontaneous fusion of the spine.

It may not be possible to recover organisms from the blood or from specimens taken from the local lesion. Presumptive diagnosis of active infections will depend upon a rising titer of serologic agglutination tests during the acute stage or brucellergen skin tests which, when positive, do not indicate relative activity of the disease.

Bradstreet, C.M.P., & others: Intradermal tests and serological tests in suspected brucella infection in man. Lancet 2:653–656, 1970.

Ganado, W., & A.J. Craig: Brucellosis myelopathy. J Bone Joint Surg 40A:1380–1388, 1958.

Kelly, P.J., & others: Brucellosis of the bones and joints. JAMA 174:347–353, 1960.

Serre, H., & others: Sacro-illiitis due to brucellosis. Sem Hôp Paris 46:3311–3317, 1970.

4. CHRONIC PYOGENIC OSTEOMYELITIS

Essentials of Diagnosis

- Pain, tenderness, swelling, edema, and redness of overlying skin.
- Sinus tract formation.

General Considerations

Chronic pyogenic osteomyelitis may occur as a consequence of missed diagnosis or ineffective treatment of acute infection, or it may appear without preceding acute infection as an indolent, slowly progressive process with no striking symptoms. Recurrent infection is manifested by exacerbation of symptoms with or without drainage after a quiescent period of days, weeks, or years. Chronic osteomyelitis at the site of an unhealed fracture is generally discussed under the treatment of fractures.

Clinical Findings

A. Symptoms and Signs: Symptoms may be so mild and the onset so insidious that there is little or no disability. There may be a history of injury. Local manifestations are variable, ranging from no symptoms at all to unremitting pain and persistent discharge. A nidus of infection of bone or soft tissue may communicate through a sinus to the skin surface. Periodic or constant discharge of pus in small quantities may cause no great disability, and the patient may care for it himself by frequent dressing changes. Other manifestations of chronicity are recurrent fever, swelling, pain, and increased drainage.

B. Laboratory Findings: Leukocytosis, anemia, and acceleration of the ESR are inconstant and cannot be relied upon as diagnostic criteria.

C. X-Ray Findings: Architectural alterations of bone depend upon the stage, extent, and rate of progress of the disease. Destruction of bone may be diffuse or focal and may appear as areas of radiolucency. Bone necrosis, apparent as areas of increased density, is due to differentially increased absorption of calcium

from surrounding vascularized bone. Involucrum and new bone formation are healing responses which may be identified beneath the periosteum or within bone. Subperiosteal new bone may be seen as a lamellar pattern. Resorption of sclerotic bone and reformation of the normal trabecular pattern also suggest healing in cancellous bone.

Tomography may be helpful in identifying deep areas of bone destruction. Sinograms made with aqueous radiographic media (Hypaque®, 25%; Renografin®, 30%) frequently aid in localization of sequestra and points of persistent infection. They also demonstrate the anatomic course and configuration of sinus tracts. Occasionally, bone scanning with radioisotopes may aid in the localization of occult infection when x-ray examination by usual technics is inconclusive.

D. Special Examinations: The causative organisms should be determined by culture, and drug sensitivity studies performed. Culture of exudates from sinus orifices may be misleading because skin contaminants are likely to be present. More reliable specimens for culture can be recovered by taking multiple samples of suspected tissue at operation or by deep aspiration at a distance from points of external drainage.

Differential Diagnosis

Chronic pyogenic osteomyelitis should be differentiated from benign and malignant tumors; from certain forms of osseous dysplasia; from fatigue fracture; and from specific infections discussed later in this section.

Complications

The most common complication is persistence of infection and acute recurrences. Chronic infection may cause deterioration of health evidenced by anemia, weight loss, weakness, and amyloidosis. Chronic osteomyelitis may act as a focus of infection for seeding other areas.

Acute exacerbations can be complicated by sympathetic effusions into adjacent joints or frank purulent arthritis.

Constant erosion and progressive destruction of bone occasionally lead to pathologic fracture.

Prior to epiphyseal closure, overgrowth of a long bone may occur as a result of chronic hyperemia.

Rarely, and only after many years of drainage, squamous cell carcinoma or a fibrosarcoma arises in persistently and actively infected tissues.

Treatment

A. General Measures: Rigid rules of treatment cannot be laid down because of the varied clinical and pathologic manifestations of this disease. During the quiescent phase, no treatment is necessary and the patient lives an essentially normal life. Minor exacerbations accompanied by drainage may be managed adequately with changes of dressings. More acute episodes may require immobilization of the part, bed rest, local heat, and mild analgesics. Anemia and malnutrition should be treated as indicated.

B. Specific Measures: Occasionally, when the drug sensitivities of the causative organism are known, systemic antibiotic therapy is advantageous in conjunction with general measures. This is especially true during the early phase of a recurrence without external drainage or abscess formation.

Evidence is lacking at this time of the efficacy of hyperbaric oxygen therapy in the treatment of chronic osteomyelitis caused by aerobic microorganisms.

Copious drainage and clinical and x-ray evidence of progressive bone destruction and sequestration require more aggressive treatment.

1. Operative treatment—Soft tissue abscesses occasionally form with associated sequestration; they can be treated adequately by operative exploration and open or closed drainage. Such treatment may also suffice for **Brodie's abscess**, a unique and rare localized infection of bone.

More extensive and long-standing infections require more extensive surgery to remove sinus tracts, abscess walls, thick soft tissue scars, and infected bone which is either sequestered or attached. In very serious cases, destructive operations such as diaphysectomy or amputation are required.

Before antibiotic drugs became available, primary wound closure was generally followed by persistent drainage, and most surgeons preferred open wound treatment. With local and systemic antibiotic therapy, it is now possible to close the wound and drain it intermittently by tube suction. Obliteration of cavities is essential for successful early wound closure. Some deep cavities can be obliterated by transferring an adjacent muscle into the cavity. Defects in superficial bones can be closed by the early application of a temporary split skin graft when there is insufficient overlying skin and subcutaneous tissue for adequate coverage. The transfer of pedicle flaps of skin and subcutaneous fat from distant sites should be deferred until there is reasonable assurance that the infection has been suppressed. In occasional cases, it may be months or years before minor but frequent recurrences of infection can be eliminated.

2. Antibiotics—Rational antibiotic therapy is based upon careful sensitivity studies of material cultured from the wound. Antimicrobial drugs in high concentrations can be introduced intermittently into the wound for topical therapy. Although the systemic use of a single antibiotic is often successful for the treatment of staphylococcal and beta-hemolytic streptococcal infections, optimal treatment of gram-negative infections often necessitates combinations of drugs. The principle of combined antibiotic action can also be applied by using poorly absorbed, more toxic agents such as neomycin, vancomycin, or polymyxin B locally and well absorbed, less toxic drugs systemically. Periodic cultures of wound secretions are necessary to determine the effectiveness of treatment. Serum concentrations of systemically administered drugs should be determined periodically as a guide for drug selection and dosage.

Course & Prognosis

Even after vigorous treatment, recurrence of infection is likely. The most frequent technical cause of recurrence is failure to remove all areas of infected soft tissue scar or necrotic and unseparated bone no matter how small. It is assumed that these abnormal tissues harbor bacterial "persisters." The altered metabolic activity or (perhaps) the altered morphology of "persisters" probably permits them to remain in relatively unaggressive states in the tissues for prolonged periods. The mechanisms of survival of microorganisms are not well understood, but their causative roles in recurrence of infection are well recognized.

Compere, E.L.: Treatment of osteomyelitis and infected wounds by closed irrigation and a detergent-antibiotic solution. Acta orthop scandinav 32:324–333, 1962.

Dymling, J.-F., & B. Wendeberg: External counting of [85]Sr and [47]Ca in localized bone infections. Acta orthop scandinav 36:8–20, 1965.

Jergesen, F., & E. Jawetz: Pyogenic infections in orthopaedic surgery. Am J Surg 106:152–163, 1963.

Johnson, L.L., R.L. Kempson: Epidermoid carcinoma in osteomyelitis. J Bone Joint Surg 47A:133–145, 1965.

West, W.F., & others: Chronic osteomyelitis. I. Factors affecting the results of treatment in 186 patients. JAMA 213:1837–1842, 1970.

SPECIFIC INFECTIONS OF BONES & JOINTS*

MYCOTIC INFECTIONS

Fungus infections of the skeletal system are usually secondary to a primary infection, frequently of the lower pulmonary tract. Although skeletal lesions have a predilection for the cancellous extremities of long bones and the bodies of vertebrae, the predominant lesion—a granuloma with varying degrees of necrosis and abscess formation—does not produce a characteristic clinical picture.

Differentiation from other chronic focal infections depends upon culture studies of synovial fluid or tissue obtained from the local lesion. Serologic and skin tests and histologic studies provide presumptive support of the diagnosis.

Schwarz, J., & K. Salfelder: Diagnosis of surgical deep mycoses. Surg Gynec Obst 128:252–274, 1969.

1. COCCIDIOIDOMYCOSIS

Coccidioidomycosis of bones and joints is usually secondary to primary pulmonary infection. The focus

*Acute and chronic pyogenic arthritis is discussed in Chapter 13.

in the lungs may not be visible by x-ray examination when the skeletal lesion appears. During the initial phase of pulmonary infection, arthralgia with periarticular swelling, especially in the regions of the knees and ankles, should be differentiated from organic bone and joint involvement. Osseous lesions commonly occur in cancellous bone of the vertebrae or near the ends of long bones. Because of a predilection for the latter sites, redness and swelling of the skin over bony prominences may be the first to call attention to the local process; abscess and sinus formation follow. Joint infection may be due to direct spread via the blood stream, or it may be caused by extension from a nearby osseous focus. The granulomatous lesions of bone or the villonodular synovitis of the joints cannot be differentiated microscopically from other mycotic infections. Histologic demonstration of spherules containing endospores supports the diagnosis but is not pathognomonic. Changes in bone seen in x-rays simulate those of tuberculosis. Local atrophy of bone progresses to focal destruction, which may appear cystic, indicating coalescence of granulomas or abscess formation. Subperiosteal new bone formation and sclerosis characterize the healing response. Sequestration is uncommon.

Diagnosis depends upon the recovery of *Coccidioides immitis* from the lesion by mycotic culture. The organism may not be recovered from synovial fluid, especially after systemic treatment with amphotericin B.

Systemic treatment with amphotericin B (Fungizone®) should be tried for bone and joint infections. It may also be of value for instillation into joints during the early stages of infection or after synovectomy. Immobilization of joints by plaster casts and avoidance of weight bearing provide beneficial rest. Chronic infection of bone may respond to operative treatment by curettage or saucerization. Amputation may be the only solution for stubbornly progressive infections which do not respond to less drastic measures. Synovectomy and joint debridement are reserved for more advanced joint infections. Contaminated dressings and plaster casts should·be carefully handled to prevent spread of infection to others.

Eckmann, B.H., Schaefer, G.L., & M. Huppert: Bedside interhuman transmission of coccidioidomycosis via growth on fomites. Am Rev Resp Dis 89:175–185, 1964.

Mazet, R., Jr.: Skeletal lesions in coccidioidomycosis. Arch Surg 70:297–507, 1955.

Pollock, S.F., Morris, J.M., & W.R. Murray: Coccidioidal synovitis of the knee. J Bone Joint Surg 49A:1397–1407, 1967.

2. HISTOPLASMOSIS

Focal skeletal or joint involvement in histoplasmosis is rare and generally represents dissemination from a primary focus in the lungs. The granulomatous lesions are not characteristic, and the diagnosis depends upon culture studies of biopsy material recovered from skeletal foci. Complement fixation tests may provide presumptive support of a diagnosis. Skeletal lesions may be single or multiple.

Surgical debridement of the focal lesion has been recommended. Amphotericin B (Fungizone®) has been useful for treatment of some patients.

Omer, G.E., Lockwood, R.S., & L.O. Travis: Histoplasmosis involving the carpal joint. J Bone Joint Surg 45A:1699–1703, 1963.

3. CRYPTOCOCCOSIS
(Torulosis)

Cryptococcosis (torulosis or European blastomycosis) is an uncommon but worldwide chronic granulomatous pulmonary disease which may be disseminated to the nervous system and rarely to the skeletal system. The granulomatous lesions of bone are not characteristic. Diagnosis depends upon culture of the yeast-like fungus, *Cryptococcus neoformans*, from the osseous focus; agglutination tests for the specific antigen and antibody, when positive, give presumptive support to the diagnosis. Surgical removal of diseased bone is believed to enhance healing and minimize further dissemination.

Systemic treatment with amphotericin B (Fungizone®) is recommended.

Gosling, H.R., & W.S. Gilmer, Jr.: Skeletal cryptococcosis (torulosis). Report of cases and review of the literature. J Bone Joint Surg 38A:660–668, 1956.

Gordon, M.A., & D.K. Vedder: Serologic tests in diagnosis and prognosis of cryptococcosis. JAMA 197:961–967, 1966.

4. NORTH AMERICAN BLASTOMYCOSIS
(Gilchrist's Disease)

North American blastomycosis (Gilchrist's disease) of the skeletal system presumably represents dissemination from a primary pulmonary focus. The granulomatous and suppurative lesions may occur in any part of the skeleton, but appear most frequently in the cancellous extremities of long bones and the bodies of vertebrae. The clinical picture is essentially that of chronic osteomyelitis with a predominantly osteolytic character. Diagnosis depends upon identification by culture of *Blastomyces dermatitidis* from the osseous lesion. The budding spherules may be demonstrated in histologic preparations.

Conservative surgical treatment of the local lesion is advocated. Amphotericin B (Fungizone®) may be effective when given systemically.

Casad, D.E., & others: North American blastomycosis in California. California Med 106:20–27, 1967.

Furcolow, M.L., & others: Blastomycosis. An important medical problem in the Central United States. JAMA 198:529–532, 1966.

Cushard, W.G., & others: Blastomycosis of bone. Treatment with intramedullary amphotericin-B. J Bone Joint Surg 51A:704–712, 1969.

SYPHILIS OF BONES & JOINTS

Syphilitic arthritis or osteitis may occur during any stage of the congenital or acquired systemic disease. Although the incidence continually decreases in the USA, syphilis and its skeletal manifestations continue to be significant problems in some parts of Africa and southeast Asia.

In **infancy**, a typical manifestation of congenital syphilis is epiphysitis and metaphysitis. Radiologically, a zone of sclerosis appears adjacent to the growth plate but is separated from another similar zone by one of rarefaction. Partial replacement of the rarefied bone by inflammatory tissue precedes suppuration and abscess formation, which may in turn cause epiphyseal displacement because of structural weakening. Focal periosteal thickening about the anterior fontanel causes Parrot's nodes.

Periostitis and osteoperiostitis are manifestations of congenital syphilis in **childhood** and **adolescence**. Bone involvement is frequently symmetric, and periosteal proliferation along the tibial crest causes the classical "saber shin." A painless bilateral effusion of the knees (Clutton's joints) is a rare manifestation of the congenital disease.

In **adulthood**, a tertiary manifestation of either congenital or acquired syphilis is gumma formation. This granulomatous process is characterized by localized destruction of bone accompanied by surrounding areas of sclerosis of varying extent. Extensive destruction with accompanying rarefaction may cause pathologic fracture because of structural weakening. Periostitis in the adult is likely to occur in the bones of the thorax and in the shafts of long bones. The x-ray picture of syphilitic osteitis in the adult is not diagnostic, but bone production is generally more pronounced than bone destruction.

Clinical suspicion is diagnostically useful because syphilis can mimic so many diseases. When localized clinical symptoms with compatible x-ray studies are supported by a history of congenital or acquired infection, thorough serologic studies will probably provide confirmatory evidence. Biopsy is not necessary to establish a direct diagnosis, but it may differentiate a gumma from other lesions. A favorable response of the lesion to specific drug treatment supports the diagnosis and can be a useful method of differentiation from other lesions which would be refractory to the specific agent.

The only local treatment that is necessary for the skeletal lesion is immobilization to provide comfort or protection from fracture if extensive weakening of bone is judged to be present. Lesions of bones and joints respond favorably and promptly to adequate chemotherapy of the systemic disease.

McGladdery, H.: Osteolytic bone syphilis. J Bone Joint Surg 32B:226–229, 1950.

Slapinker, S., & deV. Minnaar: Syphilitic disease of the long bones in the Bantu. J Bone Joint Surg 33B:578–583, 1951.

TUBERCULOSIS OF BONES & JOINTS

Essentials of Diagnosis

- Pain, tenderness, swelling, limitation of joint motion.
- Known primary infection in another organ system.

General Considerations

Practically all tuberculous infections in the USA are caused by the human strain of *Mycobacterium tuberculosis*. Infection of the musculoskeletal system is commonly caused by hematogenous spread from a primary lesion of the respiratory or gastrointestinal tract. Tuberculosis of the thoracic or lumbar spine may be associated with an active lesion of the genitourinary tract. It is a disease of childhood, occurring most commonly before puberty. Adult infection is uncommon except in the debilitated geriatric patient.

Clinical Findings

A. Symptoms and Signs: The onset of symptoms is generally insidious and not accompanied by alarming general manifestations of fever, sweating, toxicity, or prostration. Pain in the region of an involved joint may be mild at onset and accompanied by a sensation of stiffness. It is commonly accentuated at night. Limping is a mechanism to protect a weight-bearing joint. Restriction of joint motion due to muscle guarding during the early phase of the infection is another protective mechanism. As the disease process progresses, limitation of joint motion becomes fixed because of muscle contractures, organic destruction of the joint, and the progressive healing response in soft tissue and bone.

Local findings during the early stages may be limited to tenderness, soft tissue swelling, joint effusion, and increase in skin temperature about the involved area. As the disease progresses without treatment, muscle atrophy and deformity become apparent. Abscess formation with spontaneous drainage externally leads to sinus formation. Progressive destruction of bone in the spine may cause a gibbus, especially in the thoracolumbar region.

B. Laboratory Findings: The precise diagnosis rests upon the recovery of the causative acid-fast pathogen from joint fluid, tissue exudates, or tissue specimens by artificial culture methods or animal inoculation. Biopsy of the lesion or of a regional lymph node may demonstrate the characteristic histologic picture of acid-fast bacillary infection but does not differentiate tuberculosis from other nontuberculous mycobacterial lesions.

C. X-Ray Findings: X-ray manifestations are not characteristic. There is a latent period between the onset of symptoms and the initial positive x-ray finding. The earliest changes of tuberculous arthritis are those of soft tissue swelling and distention of the capsule of effusion. Subsequently, bone atrophy causes thinning of the trabecular pattern, narrowing of the cortex, and enlargement of the medullary canal. As joint disease progresses, destruction of cartilage is manifested by narrowing of the joint cleft and focal erosion of the articular surface, especially at the margins. Extensive destruction of joint surfaces causes deformity. As healing takes place, osteosclerosis becomes apparent around areas of necrosis and sequestration. Where the lesion is limited to bone, especially in the cancellous portion of the metaphysis, the x-ray picture may be that of single or multilocular cysts surrounded by sclerotic bone. As intra-osseous foci expand toward the limiting cortex and erode it, subperiosteal new bone formation takes place.

D. Special Examinations: An important step toward establishment of a precise diagnosis is to obtain material from the focal lesion for animal inoculation or microbial culture studies. Exudates may be collected by aspiration or representative tissues removed by either percutaneous or open biopsy. Cutaneous reaction to protein derivatives of various mycobacteria are of presumptive diagnostic value insofar as the local lesion is concerned.

Differential Diagnosis

Tuberculosis of the musculoskeletal system must be differentiated from all subacute and chronic infections, rheumatoid arthritis, gout, and occasionally from osseous dysplasia. Infections caused by nontuberculous mycobacteria can be differentiated only by laboratory procedures which require expert knowledge.

Complications

Clinical infection probably occurs only in persons with inadequate immunologic defense following massive exposure to this ubiquitous pathogen. In people with inadequate defense mechanisms, children, and elderly people with other systemic disease, tuberculosis is likely to have an accelerated rate of progress. Destruction of bones or joints may occur in a few weeks or months if adequate treatment is not provided. Deformity due to joint destruction, abscess formation with spread into adjacent soft tissues, and sinus formation are common. Paraplegia is the most serious complication of spinal tuberculosis. As healing of severe joint lesions takes place, spontaneous fibrous or bony ankylosis follows.

Treatment

The modern treatment of tuberculosis of the skeletal system consists of 3 phases: general care, surgery, and chemotherapy.

A. General Measures: This is especially important when prolonged recumbency is necessary and includes skillful nursing care, adequate diet, and appropriate treatment of associated lesions (pulmonary, genitourinary, etc).

B. Surgical Treatment: No rigid recommendations can be made for the operative treatment of tuberculosis because the stage of the infection and the character of the lesion are the determinants. In acute infections where synovitis is the predominant feature, treatment can be conservative, at least initially: Immobilization by splint or plaster, aspiration, and chemotherapy may suffice to control the infection. This treatment is desirable for the management of infections of large joints of the lower extremities in children during the early stage of the infection. It may also be used in adults either as definitive treatment of early and mild infections or preliminary to operative management. Synovectomy may be valuable for less acute hypertrophic lesions which involve tendon sheaths, bursas, or joints.

Various types of operative treatment are necessary for chronic or advanced tuberculosis of bones and joints depending upon the location of the lesion and the age and general condition of the patient. The availability of effective drugs for systemic use has broadened the indications for synovectomy and debridement. Conversely, the need for more radical surgical procedures such as arthrodesis and amputation has diminished. Even though the infection is active and all involved tissue cannot be removed, supplementary chemotherapy permits healing to proceed. In general, arthrodesis of weight-bearing joints is preferred when useful function cannot be salvaged.

C. Chemotherapy: Modern chemotherapy of tuberculosis is based essentially on the systemic administration of drugs to which the strain of pathogen is susceptible. Isoniazid (INH) and aminosalicylic acid (PAS) have been the most reliable. Resistant strains are likely to emerge during administration of streptomycin. Other useful but more toxic drugs include viomycin, capreomycin, pyrazinamide, cycloserine, ethionamide, and ethambutol.

Allen, A.R., & A.W. Stevenson: A ten-year follow-up of combined drug therapy and early fusion in bone tuberculosis. J Bone Joint Surg 49A:1001–1003, 1967.

Falk, A.: A follow-up study of the initial group of cases of skeletal tuberculosis treated with streptomycin, 1946–1948. J Bone Joint Surg 40A:1161–1168, 1958.

Friedman, B.: Chemotherapy of tuberculosis of the spine. J Bone Joint Surg 48A:451–474, 1966.

Kelly, P.J., & others: Infection of synovial tissues by mycobacteria other than *Mycobacterium tuberculosis*. J Bone Joint Surg 49A:1521–1530, 1967.

Palmer, C.E., & L.B. Edwards: Identifying the tuberculous infected. JAMA 205:167–169, 1968.

Runyon, E.: Anonymous mycobacteria in pulmonary disease. M Clin North America 43:273–290, 1959.

GONORRHEAL ARTHRITIS

Gonorrheal arthritis (gonococcal arthritis, gonorrheal rheumatism) is an acute inflammatory disease caused by *Neisseria gonorrhoeae* which is almost always secondary to infection of the genitourinary tract. At one time, joint involvement occurred in 2–5% of all gonococcal infections. Currently, gonorrheal arthritis is encountered more frequently in women who have occult genitourinary infections and occasionally in children. Symptoms related to the musculoskeletal system are likely to appear during the third week of inadequately treated infection.

Joint infection is via the blood stream. Clinical evidence of involvement of multiple joints is often present at onset, but symptoms are likely to be transient in all joints except one. Large weight-bearing joints are affected most frequently. Systemic symptoms may accompany the essential clinical features of the local lesion, which are those of acute arthritis. Initially, the process may only consist of synovitis with effusion, but as it progresses the exudate becomes purulent and destruction of cartilage follows which may lead to fibrous or bony ankylosis.

The precise diagnosis is established by recovery of the causative microorganism from the involved joint by culture. A positive complement fixation test of joint exudate is said to be more significant than a positive reaction in the blood. Identification of gonococcal antibody in serum by the fluorescent technic is more reliable than the complement fixation test. Other presumptive evidence is obtained from positive cultures from the lower genitourinary tract.

Gonorrheal arthritis must be differentiated from rheumatoid arthritis, although there may be a concomitant gonococcal infection of the genitourinary system; from pyogenic arthritis caused by other organisms; from acute synovitis; from Reiter's disease; and from gout.

Nonspecific treatment includes immobilization of the joint, bed rest, and analgesics as necessary for pain. Systemic treatment of gonorrhea by antimicrobial drugs is discussed in Chapter 21. If the joint fluid is purulent, contains organisms, and recurs rapidly in large quantities, systemic treatment can be supplemented by instillation into large joints of 25–50 thousand units of penicillin G in 5 ml of saline, and repeated once or twice at daily intervals.

The prognosis for preservation of joint function is good if the diagnosis is established promptly and treatment is vigorous.

Cooke, C.L., & others: Gonococcal arthritis. JAMA 217:204–205, 1971.

Fink, C.W.: Gonococcal arthritis in children. JAMA 194:123–124, 1965.

Hess, E.V., Hunter, D.K., & M. Ziff: Gonococcal antibodies in acute arthritis. JAMA 191:531–534, 1965.

CERVICOBRACHIAL PAIN SYNDROMES

A large group of articular and extra-articular disorders is characterized by pain that may involve simultaneously the neck, shoulder girdle, and upper extremity. Diagnostic differentiation is often difficult. Some of these entities and clinical syndromes represent primary disorders of the cervicobrachial region; others are local manifestations of systemic diseases. The clinical picture is further complicated when 2 or more of these conditions occur coincidentally.

Some of the more common disorders in this category are discussed below.

OSTEOARTHRITIS OF THE CERVICAL SPINE
(Cervical Spondylosis, Degenerative Arthritis, Hypertrophic Arthritis)

This entity consists of degenerative disease of the apophyseal joints and intervertebral disk joints with or without neurologic manifestations. Osteoarthritis of the articular facets is characterized by progressive thinning of articular cartilage, subchondral osteosclerosis, and osteophytic proliferation around the joint margins.

Although degeneration of cervical disks does occur in adolescence, it increases in frequency after age 40 and is marked by gradual narrowing as demonstrated by x-ray examination. The nucleus pulposus may extrude through a tear in the annulus fibrosus, or a portion of the annulus may protrude; either can cause nerve root or spinal cord compression. Osteocartilaginous proliferation occurs around the margins of the vertebral body and gives rise to osteophytic ridges which may encroach upon the intervertebral foramens and the spinal canal, causing compression of the neurovascular contents. Pain may be limited to the posterior neck region or, depending upon the level of the symptomatic joint, may radiate to the occiput, shoulder girdle region, arm, forearm, and hand. It may be intensified by active or passive neck motions. The general distribution of pain and paresthesias, when they are a feature, correspond roughly to the involved dermatome in the upper extremity. Radiating pain in the upper extremity is often intensified by hyperextension of the neck and deviation of the head to the involved side. Limitation of cervical movements is the most common objective finding. Neurologic signs depend upon the extent of compression of nerve roots or the spinal cord. Severe compression of the spinal cord may cause long tract involvement resulting in paraparesis or paraplegia.

An early x-ray finding is loss of the normal anterior convexity of the cervical curve. Comparative reduction in height of the involved disk space is a frequent finding in adults, and characteristic changes around the apophyseal joint clefts are late changes observed predominantly in the lower cervical spine. The most common late x-ray finding is osteophyte formation anteriorly adjacent to the disk. Myelography is the single most valuable x-ray means of demonstrating nerve root or spinal cord compression.

This entity should be differentiated from other cervicobrachial pain syndromes, rheumatoid arthritis, ankylosing spondylitis, chronic cervical sprains ("whiplash" injuries), primary and metastatic tumors of bone, and other causes of cervical myelopathy intrinsic to the cord.

Acute symptoms usually respond to rest of the cervical spine, which may be provided by external cervical support with a felt collar or a neck brace. Cervical traction, either continuously in recumbency or periodic, may be necessary for severe pain. Analgesics may be given for temporary relief, but prolonged use of narcotics may only obscure and delay the recognition of a more serious associated disorder. Chronic pain, especially when it radiates into the upper extremity, usually requires more positive methods of providing cervical rest such as bracing.

Surgical fusion of the cervical spine alone is rarely necessary for control of pain. When compression of nerve roots or the spinal cord causes significant neurologic deficit, laminectomy or anterior disk removal (with or without spine fusion) is necessary to prevent further damage.

Osteoarthritis is progressive, and symptoms are likely to recur. The cervical segment that first caused symptoms may become asymptomatic, but symptoms may arise from a previously uninvolved segment.

Lang, E.F.: Management of cervical spondylosis. Postgrad Med 33:58–64, 1963.

THORACIC OUTLET SYNDROME

The thoracic outlet syndrome includes certain disorders with varied manifestations which are caused by compression of the neurovascular structures supplying the upper extremity: cervical rib syndrome, costoclavicular syndrome, scalenus anticus and scalenus medius syndromes, pectoralis minor syndrome, Wright's syndrome, and "effort thrombosis" of the axillary and subclavian veins. (Cervical rib syndrome is discussed in Chapter 16.)

Symptoms and signs may arise from intermittent or continuous pressure on elements of the brachial plexus and the subclavian or axillary vessels by a variety of anatomic structures of the shoulder girdle region. The neurovascular bundle can be compressed between the anterior or middle scalene muscles and a normal first thoracic rib or a cervical rib. Descent of the shoulder girdle may continue in adulthood and cause compression. Faulty posture, chronic illness, occupation, and advancing age are other predisposing factors. The components of the median nerve that encircle the axillary artery may cause compression and vascular symptoms. Sudden or repetitive strenuous physical activity may initiate "effort thrombosis" of the axillary or subclavian vein.

Pain may radiate from the point of compression to the base of the neck, the axilla, the shoulder girdle region, arm, forearm, and hand. Paresthesias are frequently present and are commonly distributed to the volar aspect of the 4th and 5th digits. Sensory symptoms may be aggravated at night or by prolonged use of the extremities for daily tasks. Weakness and muscle atrophy are the principal motor symptoms. Vascular symptoms consist of arterial ischemia characterized by pallor of the fingers on elevation of the extremity, sensitivity to cold, and, rarely, gangrene of the digits or venous obstruction marked by edema, cyanosis, and engorgement.

Deep reflexes are usually not altered. When the site of compression is between the upper rib and clavicle, partial obliteration of subclavian artery pulsation may be demonstrated by abduction of the arm to a right angle with the elbow simultaneously flexed and rotated externally at the shoulder so that the entire extremity lies in the coronal plane.

X-ray examination is most helpful in differential diagnosis. The value of clinical plethysmography as an objective method of recording brachial arterial pulsations has been emphasized by Winsor and Brow. When venous or arterial obstruction is thought to be intravascular, venography or arteriography is likely to demonstrate the location of the occlusion.

Thoracic outlet syndrome must be differentiated from symptomatic osteoarthritis of the cervical spine, tumors of the cervical spinal cord or nerve roots, periarthritis of the shoulder, and other cervicobrachial pain syndromes.

Conservative treatment is directed toward relief of compression of the neurovascular bundle. The patient is instructed to avoid any physical activity that is likely to precipitate or aggravate symptoms. Overhead pulley exercises are useful to improve posture. Shoulder bracing, although uncomfortable to many patients, provides a constant stimulus to improve posture. When lying down, the shoulder girdle should be bolstered by arranging pillows in an inverted "V" position.

Operative treatment may be necessary when conservative measures are not successful.

Symptoms may disappear spontaneously or may be relieved by carefully directed conservative treatment. Operative treatment is more likely to relieve the neurologic rather than the vascular component that causes symptoms.

Winsor, T., & R. Brow: Costoclavicular syndrome. Its diagnosis and treatment. JAMA 196:697–699, 1966.

SCAPULOHUMERAL PERIARTHRITIS
(Adhesive Capsulitis, Frozen Shoulder)

Periarthritis of the shoulder joint is an inflammatory disorder of multiple etiology involving primarily the soft tissues. It is most common in the minor shoulder among women after the 4th decade. It may be manifest as inflammation of the articular synovia, the tendons around the joint, the intrinsic ligamentous capsular bands, the paratendinous bursas (especially the subacromial), and the bicipital tendon sheath. Calcareous tendinitis and attritional disease of the rotator cuff, with or without tears, are common incidental lesions.

The onset of pain, which is aggravated by extremes of shoulder joint motion, may be acute or insidious. Pain may be most annoying at night and may be intensified by pressure on the involved extremity when sleeping in the lateral decubitus position. Tenderness upon palpation is often noted near the tendinous insertions into the greater tuberosity or over the bicipital groove. Although a sensation of stiffness may be noted only at onset, restriction of shoulder joint motion soon becomes apparent and is likely to progress unless effective treatment is instituted.

Opinion differs on how best to treat this disorder. Pain can usually be controlled with mild analgesics. Passive exercise of the shoulder by an overhead pulley mechanism should be repeated slowly for about 2 minutes 4 times daily. Forceful manipulation of the shoulder joint during this exercise should be avoided. Injection of tender areas with local anesthetics or corticosteroids gives at best only transitory relief. Some surgeons prefer closed manipulation of the shoulder under anesthesia, but this is likely to aggravate rather than relieve pain and restriction of motion. Operative treatment has been advocated by some but should be reserved for the occasional refractory case.

Neviaser, J.S.: Musculoskeletal disorders of the shoulder region causing cervicobrachial pain. Differential diagnosis and treatment. S Clin North America 43:1703–1714, 1963.

SCAPULOHUMERAL CALCAREOUS TENDINITIS

Calcareous tendinitis of the shoulder joint is an acute or chronic inflammatory disorder of the capsulotendinous cuff (especially the supraspinatous portion) characterized by deposits of calcium salts among tendon fibers. It is the most common cause of acute pain near the lateral aspect of the shoulder joint in men over age 30. The calcium deposit may be restricted to the tendon substance or may rupture into the overlying subacromial bursa.

Symptoms consist of pain (at times quite severe), tenderness to pressure over the deposit, and restriction of shoulder joint motion. Chronic symptoms may be intermittent and similar to those of scapulohumeral periarthritis.

X-ray examination confirms the diagnosis and demonstrates the site of the lesion.

Calcareous tendinitis must be differentiated from other cervicobrachial pain syndromes, pyogenic arthritis, osteoarthritis, gout, and tears of the rotator cuff.

The aim of treatment is to relieve pain and restore shoulder joint function. Pain is best treated by multiple needling of the lesion under local anesthesia or by operative evacuation of the calcium deposit. After either type of treatment, early recovery of shoulder joint function should be fostered by judiciously supervised exercises. Acute symptoms occasionally subside after spontaneous rupture of the calcium deposit into the subacromial bursa. Chronic symptoms may be treated by analgesics, exercises, injections of local anesthetics or corticosteroids with or without needling of the deposit, and x-ray therapy. Large deposits that appear dense on x-ray may require surgical evacuation.

When x-ray examination shows that a deposit has disappeared, recurrence of that deposit is rare. Symptoms of periarthritis may persist if shoulder joint motion is not completely regained.

Quigley, T.B.: Injection therapy of calcium deposits. S Clin North America 43:1495–1499, 1963.

SCAPULOCOSTAL SYNDROME

The scapulocostal syndrome has been attributed to fatigue associated with habitually faulty posture which exerts tension on the deep cervical fascia and adjacent muscles, causing dull, aching pain in the posterior cervical region. Pain may radiate to the occiput, the medial angle of the scapula, and down the arm and forearm to the ulnar side of the hand, or along the vertebral border of the scapula to the region of the 4th and 5th ribs posteriorly. Tenderness is commonly present near the insertion of the levator muscle into the vertebral border of the scapula. A sensation of stiffness around the shoulder girdle and diffuse tenderness in the region of the trapezius muscle may also be present.

This disorder must be differentiated from other cervicobrachial pain syndromes and from generalized disorders such as polymyositis and fibrositis.

Treatment consists of correction of faulty posture by exercise, periodic rest to relieve fatigue, local applications of heat or cold (whichever provides greater comfort) to the posterior cervical region, and infiltration with local anesthetics or spraying the skin overlying "trigger points" with ethyl chloride. If symptoms do not subside in response to these measures, the diagnosis should be reconsidered.

Michele, A.A., & J. Eisenberg: Scapulocostal syndrome. Arch Phys Med Rehab 49:383–387, 1968.

CAUSALGIA
(Reflex Sympathetic Dystrophy)

The term causalgia will be restricted here to denote an uncommon pain syndrome that affects either the lower or upper extremity. (A more complete discussion is offered in Chapter 8.) The precise cause is unknown, but upper extremity causalgia is most often due to complete or incomplete laceration of the median nerve or the brachial plexus. The cardinal symptom, which appears immediately or within a few weeks after injury, is severe, burning pain, often paroxysmally precipitated by friction or even drafts of air and commonly restricted to the area of sensory supply of the affected nerve. Intolerance to dryness and relief by cold, wet applications are characteristic. Vasomotor or trophic changes of skin appear and are evidenced by coolness, color changes (redness or cyanosis), glossiness, edema, and dryness. The small joints of the hand become stiff, and bone atrophy is demonstrable by x-ray. Relief of pain by stellate ganglion block is a useful confirmatory test.

In its major form, causalgia must be differentiated from pseudocausalgia (minor causalgia), Sudeck's atrophy (see Chapter 8), and other reflex dystrophies of the upper extremity.

Symptomatic treatment by protection of the part from irritation, wet dressings, analgesics, and repeated sympathetic blocks are temporizing measures. Operative sympathetic denervation gives permanent relief of intractable pain of true causalgia in the majority of critically selected patients (see reference).

Baker, A.G., & F.G. Winegarner: Causalgia. A review of twenty-eight cases. Am J Surg 117:690–694, 1969.

EPICONDYLITIS
(Tennis Elbow, Epicondylalgia)

Epicondylitis is a pain syndrome affecting the midportion of the upper extremity; no single causative lesion has been identified. It has been postulated that chronic strain of the forearm muscles due to repetitive grasping or rotatory motions of the forearm causes microscopic tears and subsequent chronic inflammation of the common extensor or common flexor tendon at or near their respective osseous origins from the epicondyles. Inflamed and redundant, synovium-covered fibrofatty projections in the posterior radio-humeral joint may also play an etiologic role.

Epicondylitis occurs most frequently during middle life in the major extremity. Pain is predominantly on the medial or lateral aspect of the elbow region; may be aggravated by grasping; and may radiate proximally into the arm or distally into the forearm. The point of maximal tenderness to pressure is 1–2 cm distal to the epicondyle. Resisted dorsiflexion or volar flexion of the wrist may accentuate the pain. X-ray examination generally reveals no significant change, but occasionally a discrete, amorphous deposit of calcium salts adjacent to the epicondyle in the tendinous fibers is demonstrated.

Epicondylitis must be differentiated from other cervicobrachial pain syndromes as well as from gout and rheumatoid arthritis.

Treatment is directed toward relief of pain and tenderness. Most acute or subacute symptoms can be relieved by avoidance of repetitive grasping. Chronic symptoms may require restrictive immobilization such as that provided by an Ilfeld elbow brace or a volar plaster splint. Physical therapy is ineffective except for relief of mild symptoms. Infiltration of "trigger points" by local anesthetic solutions with or without corticosteroids is advocated by some. Operative treatment is reserved for chronic, refractory cases.

Symptoms usually respond to rest and conservative measures.

Bosworth, D.M.: Surgical treatment of tennis elbow. A follow-up study. J Bone Joint Surg 47A:1533–1536, 1965.

CARPAL TUNNEL SYNDROME

Carpal tunnel syndrome is a painful disorder caused by compression of the median nerve between the volar carpal ligament and adjacent structures. Even though no anatomic lesion is apparent, flattening or even circumferential constriction of the median nerve may be observed during operative section of the ligament.

Pain in the distribution of the median nerve, which may be burning and tingling (acroparesthesia), is the initial symptom. Aching pain may radiate proximally into the forearm and even to the shoulder joint. Pain may be episodic or constant, and is exacerbated by manual activity. Impairment of sensation in the median nerve distribution may not be apparent when symptoms are recent, and subtle disparity between the affected and opposite sides can be demonstrated by requiring the patient to identify different textures of cloth by rubbing them between the tips of the thumb and the index finger. Muscle weakness or atrophy, especially of the abductor pollicis brevis, appears later than sensory disturbances. The most indicative special examination is determination of motor conduction delay, which is prolonged before muscle weakness or atrophy becomes obvious.

This syndrome should be differentiated from other cervicobrachial pain syndromes and from compression syndromes of the median nerve in the forearm or arm.

Treatment is directed toward relief of pressure on the median nerve. Conservative treatment usually relieves mild symptoms of recent onset. When a primary lesion is discovered, specific treatment should be given. When soft tissue swelling is a cause, elevation of the extremity may relieve symptoms. Splinting of the hand and forearm at night may be beneficial. When nonspecific inflammation of the ulnar bursa is thought to be a cause, some authors recommend injection of corticosteroids.

Operative division of the volar carpal ligament gives lasting relief when conservative treatment fails. Pain usually subsides within a few days. Muscle strength returns gradually but complete recovery cannot be expected when atrophy is pronounced.

Nicolle, F.V., & F.M. Woolhouse: Nerve compression syndromes of the upper limb. J Trauma 5:313–318, 1965.

SHOULDER-HAND SYNDROME

Shoulder-hand syndrome (accepted by some as a clinical entity) is a variable complex of symptoms and signs arising from various painful disorders of the shoulder joint and hand of the same extremity. According to the current view, it is a manifestation of reflex neurovascular dystrophy. The syndrome is essentially a combination of scapulohumeral periarthritis and Sudeck's atrophy of the hand and wrist.

Shoulder-hand syndrome occurs with increasing frequency during the middle years of life. Shoulder symptoms may precede or follow hand involvement, or both may begin at the same time. The elbow joint is usually spared; when the elbow is involved, painful restriction of motion is the principal manifestation.

This syndrome should be differentiated from other cervicobrachial pain syndromes and from rheumatoid arthritis, polymyositis, scleroderma, and gout.

In addition to specific treatment of the underlying disorder, treatment is directed toward restoration of function. Therapy described for scapulohumeral periarthritis (see above) and Sudeck's atrophy (see Chapter 8) is given simultaneously. The prognosis depends in part upon the stage in which the lesions of the shoulder joint and hand are encountered and the extent and severity of associated organic disease. Early treatment offers the best prognosis for maximal recovery.

Steinbrocker, O.: The shoulder-hand syndrome: Present perspective. Arch Phys Med Rehab 49:388–395, 1968.

CERVICOBRACHIAL PAIN OF INTRATHORACIC ORIGIN

Pain in the shoulder girdle region and upper extremity due to myocardial ischemia of arteriosclerotic heart disease is discussed in chapter 8. This is a frequent cause of shoulder-hand syndrome.

Bronchogenic carcinoma (see Chapter 6) in the region of the pulmonary apex is an uncommon cause of cervicobrachial pain. Because of the frequency of bronchogenic carcinoma among older people, it is likely to coexist with other organic lesions which cause pain in the anatomic regions under discussion here. X-ray examination of the upper thorax by lordotic projections or tomography may reveal lesions that are not demonstrated by routine x-ray technics employed for the diagnosis of lung, shoulder girdle, and cervical spine disorders.

TUMORS & TUMOR-LIKE LESIONS OF BONE

Tumors of bone have been categorized classically as primary and secondary, but there is some disagreement about which tumors are primary to the skeleton. Tumors of mesenchymal origin that reflect skeletal tissues (eg, bone, cartilage, and connective tissue) and tumors developing in bones that are of hematopoietic, nerve, vascular, fat cell, and notochordal origin should be differentiated from secondary malignant tumors that involve bone by direct extension or hematogenous spread.

Malignancy may be exhibited by local aggressiveness, manifested either by progressive growth in situ with infiltration and destruction of adjacent tissues, or by metastasis to distant sites via blood or lymph channels.

Lichtenstein has offered a practical classification of bone tumors that serves admirably as a framework of reference (see reference below).

The direct diagnosis of the tumors of bone discussed below can usually be established with greatest precision when it becomes a joint endeavor of clinician, radiologist, and pathologist.

Jaffe, H.L.: *Tumors and Tumorous Conditions of the Bones and Joints.* Lea & Febiger, 1958.
Lichtenstein, L.: *Bone Tumors.* Mosby, 1970.

OSTEOMA

The term osteoma is restricted to an uncommon benign tumor that arises from membranous bone, usually about the accessory nasal sinuses, in the mandible, or in the skull. Aegerter & Kirkpatrick consider the lesion to be nonneoplastic, a hamartoma. Histologically, the tumor is composed of varying quantities of compact bone which may contain osteoid, cancellous bone, and vascular connective tissue. The fibrous tissue capsule blends with adjacent normal periosteum. Symptoms tend to occur during adulthood and are likely to be caused by protrusion of the tumor mass superficially, where it becomes visible, or deeply, where it interferes with the function of adjacent structures. Osteoma must be differentiated from osteochondroma, osteophytes occurring in tendons and ligaments, and reactive hyperostosis of the skull. This benign tumor should not be confused with "parosteal osteoma," which may manifest aggressive tendencies. Surgical removal is curative.

OSTEOCHONDROMA
(Osteocartilaginous Exostosis, Osteochondromatosis, Hereditary Multiple Exostosis)

Osteochondroma can occur as a single lesion, but, because of the familial tendency, multifocal lesions are commonly referred to as hereditary multiple exostosis. Aegerter & Kirkpatrick have emphasized the hamartomatous nature of the lesions, but Lichtenstein prefers to classify it as a benign neoplasm.

This common benign bone tumor characteristically arises from the surface of bone of enchondral origin near an epiphyseal plate but does occur in flat bones. It may have a sessile or pedunculated configuration and arises from cortical deficient cancellous bone. The body or stalk of the tumor mass has a periphery of compact bone covered by periosteum; the interior is composed of spongy bone. The summit is covered by hyaline cartilage which may show active proliferation if enchondral ossification of the skeleton is not completed.

Symptoms are likely to be caused by protrusion of the tumor, especially when a thick layer of soft tissue does not cover it. Initial subjective symptoms may be tenderness caused by irritation or pain due to pressure on adjacent structures such as a neurovascular bundle or another bone. Occasionally, limitation of joint motion draws attention to the tumor mass. Chronic irritation may cause formation of an adventitious bursa that contains riziform bodies.

The x-ray picture is characteristic. A sessile lesion superimposed upon the underlying bone of origin may simulate nonosteogenic fibroma or chondromyxoid fibroma. The discovery of a solitary tumor invites an x-ray survey to determine the presence or absence of others.

Complications may arise from pressure on adjacent vital structures such as a major vessel or nerve trunk. Malignant transformation to chondrosarcoma is rare and likely to be slow in its manifestation.

Thorough surgical removal with the enveloping periosteum is curative.

OSTEOID OSTEOMA

Osteoid osteoma, a lesion lacking certain characteristics of neoplasia, has been defined as a tumor-like nidus composed of osteoid and trabeculas of newly formed bone deposited in a substratum of highly vascularized osteogenic connective tissue. It can occur in cancellous or campact bone. About ½ of reported cases have involved bones of the lower extremity. Although the diagnosis is established most frequently during adolescence or early adulthood, the lesion has been observed from childhood to senescence.

Pain varies in severity and is frequently intensified at night. Aspirin or other mild analgesics afford transitory relief. Where the lesion is superficial, localized tenderness may be a feature, and swelling may occur as a result of reactive osteosclerosis. Reactive sclerosis tends to be less intense about a lesion in spongy bone. When the comparatively radiolucent nidus occurs in compact bone, it may be obscured by surrounding reactive sclerotic bone and not be apparent on routine x-ray examination. Overexposed films or tomography may make the nidus visible under such circumstances.

Osteoid osteoma must be differentiated from other tumor-like lesions and benign tumors of bone (eg, benign osteoblastoma) and localized infections such as Brodie's abscess and chronic osteomyelitis.

Although spontaneous healing has been observed, pain is likely to persist during the prolonged phase of recovery. Surgical removal of the nidus, which is rarely more than 1 cm in its greatest dimension, gives prompt relief to pain and is curative.

Phelan, J.T.: Osteoid osteoma. Surg Gynec Obst 121:112–116, 1965.

NONOSTEOGENIC FIBROMA
(Nonossifying Fibroma, Fibrous Cortical Defect, Metaphyseal Fibrous Defect)

This common lesion of bone (or possibly related group of lesions with varying characteristics) is now considered to be nonneoplastic. Certain easily recognized examples—especially those encountered about the posteromedial aspect of the lower femoral metaphysis during infancy and childhood—which do not produce symptoms and tend to undergo spontaneous regression to the point of disappearance have been accorded a separate category (subperiosteal cortical defect) by Aegerter & Kirkpatrick. Grossly, the tissue is firm and may have a grayish-white, yellowish, or brownish color. Histologically, it is composed predominantly of compacted spindle cells, commonly arranged in a whorled pattern. The extent of vascularity of the stroma varies even within the same focus. Other stromal elements include giant cells and macrophages engorged with lipid. Although osteoid formation is not a feature, Morton has observed metaplastic bone formation and has raised the question of the relationship of this lesion to fibrous dysplasia.

This lesion occurs most frequently in the metaphyses of major long bones—especially those of the lower extremity—during childhood and adolescence, but it may be encountered from infancy through early adulthood. It may be discovered fortuitously by x-ray examination because of injury or on some other unrelated basis. In the metaphysis, it is likely to be located eccentrically, near the periosteum. An area of radiolucency involving compact bone of the cortex and adjacent spongiosa is oriented so that its greatest dimension parallels the long axis of the involved bone. In more slender bones (fibula and those of the forearm), larger lesions occupy a more central position and may cause fusiform expansion. Superficially, a thin wall of compact bone may be preserved although elevated beyond the level of the surrounding normal cortex. Deeply, it is demarcated by a layer of sclerotic bone which separates the tumor mass from spongy bone. Pain calls attention to the condition, and local tenderness or swelling may be noted. Occasionally pathologic fracture is the first sign. Biopsy of lesions that simulate other conditions, eg, fibrous dysplasia, solitary cysts, histocytosis X, bone infarct, chondromyxoid fibroma, and chronic osteomyelitis may be necessary to establish a precise differentiation.

Once the diagnosis is established, active treatment can be deferred because of the propensity of this lesion to heal spontaneously. Pain and signs of aggressiveness are indications for surgical treatment, which consists of removal of the focus either by curettement or excision.

Morton, K.S.: Bone production in non-osteogenic fibroma. J Bone Joint Surg 46B:233—243, 1964.

BENIGN OSTEOBLASTOMA
(Osteogenic Fibroma, Ossifying Fibroma, Osteofibroma, Fibrous Osteoma)

Benign osteoblastoma includes a group of incompletely understood benign, osteoblastic neoplasms with varied histologic and clinical features which may simulate giant cell tumor or osteogenic sarcoma. It is encountered most frequently during childhood and adolescence but may become manifest during adulthood. Although it is found in the skull and the vertebras, the long bones of the lower extremities are more common sites. The histologic picture is that of osteoid formation with varying degrees of calcification but without cellular atypism in a richly vascularized stroma containing a varying population of giant cells. Local pain, an important clinical feature, calls attention to the lesion. The x-ray picture is not distinctive but does demonstrate evidence of rarefying destruction of normal bone, cortical expansion, and focal osteosclerosis which gives an overall impression of mottling. Routine laboratory tests do not aid in the differential diagnosis. Because of inconstant clinical and histologic manifestations, microscopic differentiation from "giant osteoid osteoma," giant cell tumor, osteogenic sarcoma, and fibrous dysplasia may be difficult and may require expert opinion.

Surgical removal of the tumor by local resection followed by bone grafting, if necessary, is applicable to accessible lesions of the flat bones and those of the extremities. In the vertebras, complete removal by curettage or resection may not be feasible. In this circumstance, x-ray therapy has been recommended in addition to surgery.

Lichtenstein, L., & W.B. Sawyer: Benign osteoblastoma. J Bone Joint Surg 46A:755—765, 1964.

CHONDROMYXOID FIBROMA

Chondromyxoid fibroma of bone is a rare tumor of varying degrees of aggressiveness that contains both chondroid and myxoid elements. Local invasion and malignant transformation have been reported. The tumor may be encountered at any age but has been observed most frequently during adolescence and early childhood. It involves the metaphyses of major long bones, bones of the hand and foot, and flat bones. Grossly, the tumor is firm and may contain grit-like foci of calcified cartilage. Microscopically, the cartilage components show various states of differentiation, cellular pleomorphism, and cytologic activity. In the center of the mass, chondroblasts may predominate; elsewhere, greater maturation is characterized by sparseness of cartilage elements accompanied by chondroid production. The myxoid matrix contains spindle and stellate cells, and the fibrous stroma may exhibit varying degrees of collagenization. Giant cells are common. Lichtenstein & Bernstein have described the subtleties and deviations of the microscopic appearance of this tumor in the reference cited below.

Pain calls attention to the lesion, and swelling and tenderness may be apparent where its position is superficial. The x-ray appearance is not characteristic and may simulate that of nonosteogenic fibroma or malignant but indolent primary tumors of bone. Chondromyxoid fibroma may appear as an ovoid or elongated focus of rarefaction and cortical expansion with erosion. It may be demarcated from cancellous bone by a thin zone of osteosclerosis. In some instances, the appearance may be that of multiple foci of osteolysis incompletely and indistinctly separated from each other by ridges of sclerotic bone. The precise diagnosis must be established by biopsy.

Treatment is by surgical excision. Curettement has been observed to be followed by recurrence.

Feldman, F., & others: Chondromyxoid fibroma of bone. Radiology 94:249—260, 1970.
Lichtenstein, L., & D. Bernstein: Unusual benign and malignant chondroid tumors of bone. Cancer 12:1142—1157, 1959.

ENCHONDROMA

A solitary enchondroma is composed of a mass of cartilage cells that lack the characteristics of neoplastic cells. The multifocal manifestation is now referred to as enchondromatosis and includes dyschondroplasia, the term formerly used to designate the multiple variety (Ollier's disease), where skeletal involvement is predominantly unilateral; and Maffucci's syndrome, the simultaneous occurrence of enchondromatosis and multiple cavernous hemangiomas.

Solitary enchondroma involves predominantly phalanges, metacarpals, and metatarsals but may be encountered in the metaphyses of major long bones and in flat bones. Although the lesion probably begins to form before skeletal maturation is complete, it may not be discovered until adulthood. Grossly, the lesion is a globoid mass of pale, firm tissue that may appear lobulated when examined in its entirety. Microscopically, the cartilage cells of representative areas have single small, uniform nuclei and pale-staining cytoplasm. They tend to occupy lacunas within a hyaline matrix. Fibrous tissue and blood vessels separate the lobules. Foci of calcification or ossification may be interpreted as evidence of maturation.

Minor trauma may cause pathologic fracture, or indolent progression may cause mild pain, tenderness, or swelling. The characteristic x-ray picture of lesions of the hand or foot is that of a discrete focus of radiolucency with mottling or compartmentalization caused by incomplete ridges of sclerotic bone. Cortical expansion occurs without extensive erosion.

Microscopically, individual lesions of skeletal enchondromatosis cannot be differentiated from the solitary type, but Lichtenstein has noted the tendency to greater cellularity among the former. Multiple lesions are likely to cause bizarre deformity because of their size and to disturb longitudinal growth of the involved skeletal segments. Malignant transformation of solitary lesions of the hand or foot is unlikely, but in other locations—or in the multifocal variety—persons who are afflicted should be periodically examined for evidence of aggressiveness.

Treatment of a symptomatic solitary lesion of the hand or foot is by thorough curettement and supplemental bone grafting if significant loss of bone structure occurs.

CHONDROBLASTOMA
(Epiphyseal Chondromatous Giant Cell Tumor, Codman's Tumor)

Chondroblastoma is an uncommon benign tumor that is encountered predominantly in the epiphyseal regions of adolescents, usually in the major tubular bones but also in flat bones. Although the tumor involves the epiphysis primarily, it may involve the metaphysis adjacent to the epiphyseal plate and may erode articular cartilage. The chondroblast is a representative cell and it tends to occur closely packed without accompanying stroma. Lichtenstein has emphasized that focal areas of calcification with degenerative changes characterized by swelling and necrosis of cartilage cells are the hallmarks of this tumor. Multinucleated giant cells are likely to be found in areas of hemorrhage. Connective tissue that replaces necrotic cartilage may produce collagen, and areas of myxomatous appearance may also be identified. Pain in the region of a major joint is likely to be the subjective complaint that calls attention to the presence of the tumor. An ovoid focus of radiolucency in the epiphysis or adjacent metaphysis with a demarcating wall of sclerotic bone and punctate areas of mottling caused by calcification within the tumor are significant x-ray findings.

Although this tumor is considered to be benign, instances of aggressiveness have been reported (see reference, below).

Surgical treatment by thorough curettement is usually adequate.

Kahn, L.B., Wood, F.M., & L.V. Ackerman: Malignant chondroblastoma. Arch Path 88:371–376, 1969.

CHORDOMA

Chordoma, a rare skeletal tumor that apparently arises from notochordal elements, occurs predominantly at the base of the skull or in the sacrococcygeal region but occasionally involves other vertebral segments as well. The cytology is varied but reflects the supposed ectodermal or mesodermal origins of this tumor. Microscopically, some tumors contain cavities lined by cuboidal epithelium and others have vacuolated tumor cells that are distributed in a mucinous matrix. Subjective symptoms are related to the specific structures encroached upon since the tumor grows slowly, metastasizes late, and manifests local aggressiveness by destruction of adjacent bone and spread into contiguous soft tissues. Local pain and tenderness or peripheral neurologic deficit, depending upon the location, are the usual clinical features. X-ray findings are not characteristic but do demonstrate an osteolytic lesion with varying degrees of calcification. Biopsy establishes the diagnosis.

Surgical resection may be feasible for limited lesions in the coccyx or distal sacrum. Most lesions are surgically inaccessible but incomplete excision is palliative. The tumor is relatively radioresistant; for significant palliation, less than 4000 rads is likely to be ineffective (see reference below).

Pearlman, A.W., & M. Friedman: Radical radiation therapy of chordoma. Am J Roentgenol 108:333–341, 1970.

GIANT CELL TUMOR
(Osteoclastoma)

Giant cell tumor of bone apparently arises from connective tissue of the marrow. The characteristic microscopic picture is of stromal cells resembling fibroblasts with multinucleated giant cells distributed among them. Many authors consider the stromal cell to be primary and the giant cell to represent an agglomeration of the basic tumor cell. Osteoid and new bone may be encountered in areas of repair. Giant cell tumor is observed most commonly from late adolescence to middle adulthood. The majority occur in the ends of major long bones, especially about the knee or in the lower radius, but they have also been observed in other bones of the extremities and in the spine. Progressive intensification of localized pain and insiduous swelling call attention to the presence of the tumor. The x-ray finding of an osteolytic focus with a foam-like appearance in the cancellous ends of the femur or tibia about the knee or in the distal radial metaphysis, eccentrically located with expansion and erosion of the overlying cortex, may raise suspicion. Elsewhere, the x-ray picture is less indicative. Biopsy is necessary to differentiate this tumor from other lesions that may simulate it, especially unicameral bone cyst, aneurysmal cyst, chondromyxoid fibroma, osteoblastoma, and chondroblastoma. In addition, it must be differentiated from "brown tumor" of hyperparathyroidism.

The treatment of accessible tumors is by surgical operation. Whenever possible, excision is preferred to curettement. When the lesion is extensive and ominous, segmental resection is preferred and may require supplemental bone grafting. In surgically inaccessible areas, partial removal of the tumor supplemented by x-ray therapy is justified. This tumor tends to be locally aggressive and it does metastasize.

Dahlin, D.C., & others: Giant-cell tumor: A study of 195 cases. Cancer 25:1061–1070, 1970.
Goldenberg, R.R., & others: Giant-cell tumor of bone: An analysis of 218 cases. J Bone Joint Surg 52A:619–664, 1970.

EWING'S SARCOMA

Ewing's sarcoma is a fairly common primary malignant neoplasm of bone that apparently arises from the marrow, but the nature of the parent cell remains in dispute. The propensity for this tumor to metastasize to the viscera and the common finding of multiple skeletal lesions has raised the question whether it is multicentric or merely tends to metastasize to other bones. Grossly, the tumor tissue is soft, frequently becomes necrotic to the point of liquidity, and destroys surrounding bone. Microscopically, the tumor cells tend to be compacted and their morphology varies. The nuclei are small, round or oval, with varying amounts of cytoplasm, and the cell boundaries are frequently not discernible. Foci of degeneration are present, and necrosis of tumor cells occurs followed by hemorrhage and repair by fibrous tissue.

This tumor is encountered most frequently during adolescence and early adulthood, but it occurs in childhood as well. Initially, it is likely to be discovered in the shaft of a major tubular bone, a vertebra, or a flat bone of the trunk. Local pain is the outstanding symptom, and it is likely to increase with time. Tenderness and increase in skin temperature are localizing signs that accompany swelling and induration. Mild anemia and leukocytosis are frequently observed.

In the long bones, the tumor is located in the diaphysis. Diffuse osteosclerosis of the cortex with a fusiform configuration, subperiosteal lamination ("onion peel"), and, occasionally, periosteal reaction resembling the "sunburst" pattern are x-ray manifestations. Growth of the tumor causes medullary destruction which may be identified as diffuse rarefaction or nondescript mottling.

Although the course may be slow and marked by episodes of comparative quiescence, the general trend is toward progression with metastasis. The differential diagnosis includes osteomyelitis, osteogenic sarcoma, adrenal neuroblastoma, Hodgkin's disease, and lymphosarcoma. The precise diagnosis cannot be established by clinical and x-ray findings; biopsy with histologic study is necessary. Metastases are frequently present when the symptomatic lesion is discovered.

Supervoltage radiation and chemotherapy provide the most effective palliation. Radical surgery, resection, or amputation has little to offer because, in spite of prompt diagnosis and vigorous treatment, the mortality rate is estimated to be about 95%.

Boyer, C.E., Jr., & others: Ewing's sarcoma. Cancer 20:1602–1606. 1967.
Johnson, R., & S.R. Humphreys: Past failures and future possibilities in Ewing's sarcoma: Experimental and preliminary clinical results. Cancer 23:161–166, 1969.

PLASMA CELL MYELOMA

Plasma cell myeloma is a primary malignant tumor of bone that arises from the hematopoietic reticulum of marrow. It may be primary in the viscera or soft tissues. Although it may present as a solitary lesion, it usually demonstrates multifocal skeletal involvement. The tumor cell resembles a plasma cell, but its precise nature has not been certainly established. Grossly, the tumor tissue is soft, dark red or grayish in color, and richly vascularized. The characteristic compacted tumor cells resemble plasma cells, but the morphology varies to the point that some cellular elements resemble the myelocytic series. Stroma is sparse, and thin-walled blood vessels are numerous. This tumor is encountered predominantly after the age of 40 and is roughly twice as frequent in men as women. Pain is the most common symptom which draws attention to the lesion. Swelling and induration with tumor formation are local signs. Diffuse involvement of the spine is characterized by kyphosis and flattening of the lumbar curve with loss of body height. Pathologic fracture is common and may be the initial manifestation that draws attention to the underlying disease. When this condition is discovered early in its course, laboratory tests may not give positive help. As the disease progresses, organ systems other than the bone marrow become involved, and this is reflected by abnormal laboratory tests. Anemia, hypercalciuria, hypercalcemia, hyperglobulinemia, Bence Jones proteinuria, and hyperuricemia may be found. X-ray findings are variable, and, because of widespread involvement, diffuse osteoporosis may be the only significant manifestation. Focal lesions of bones appear essentially as diffuse or circumscribed areas of rarefaction without surrounding sclerosis, and in some cases with cortical expansion. Collapse of vertebral bodies caused by infraction secondary to extensive marrow replacement by tumor may be apparent at one or more levels. Although myeloma presents a fairly characteristic clinical picture in its florid state, marrow aspiration or biopsy of questionable lesions with microscopic study may be necessary to establish a precise diagnosis.

Complications arise from encroachment of the tumor on vital structures such as the spinal cord or cauda equina.

The rate of progress is variable, and periods of abatement with apparent remission are frequently observed. Palliative x-ray therapy is useful for the relief of intractable pain. Chemotherapy may ameliorate symptoms and prolong life in selected patients (see reference below).

Surgical removal of a solitary focus may cure that lesion, but the disease is fatal.

Alexanian, R., & others: Treatment for multiple myeloma. JAMA 208:1680–1685, 1969.

OSTEOGENIC SARCOMA

With the exception of myeloma, osteogenic sarcoma is the most common primary malignant tumor of bone. It is encountered most commonly in the age group from preadolescence through early adulthood but may occur also in later life. It is about twice as common in males as females. The site of primary appearance is almost always solitary, though multicentric foci are seen rarely. The metaphyses of major long bones are common locations, and about 50% involve the knee region. Less frequent sites include the pelvis, the more slender long bones, and the flat bones.

Clinical Findings

A. Symptoms and Signs: Constitutional symptoms of weight loss and anemia may be apparent by the time the diagnosis is made. Pain is of gradual onset but becomes progressively more severe. In occasional cases swelling, which may be a combination of tumor mass and edema, is the initial complaint. Increase in local heat, venous engorgement, and tenderness are variable local manifestations.

B. Laboratory Findings: Histologic examination of representative biopsy material is the most useful laboratory procedure. The histologic features vary among tumors, but unifying characteristics are anaplastic connective tissue stroma and the formation of tumor osteoid and bone directly from it. Elevation of the serum alkaline phosphatase level is significant, and the degree of elevation may be indicative of relative osteoblastic activity.

C. X-Ray Findings: The x-ray findings vary depending upon the osteolytic or sclerosing nature of the tumor. Diffuse rarefaction may reflect the comparative vascularity. Foci of osteolysis of spongy bone are caused by tumor destruction and incomplete replacement with less dense osteoid. Almost without exception, the cortex exhibits alteration of normal contour by erosion or replacement by disorderly new bone formation. Neoplastic and reactive bone spicules that are oriented perpendicularly to the normal cortical surface—the classical "sunburst" effect—are likely to appear in sclerosing lesions. X-ray examination of the chest should accompany local examination of bone when the presence of this tumor is suspected.

Radioactive isotopes—especially (because of their affinity for bone) isotopes of strontium, gallium, and fluorine—have been used to demonstrate occult lesions and metastases.

Differential Diagnosis

The differential diagnosis includes other primary malignant tumors of bone (chondrosarcoma, fibrosarcoma, and giant cell tumor), myositis ossificans, eosinophilic granuloma, and fibrous dysplasia.

Treatment

Specific treatment depends upon the primary location of the tumor and the presence of metastasis. Radiation therapy alone may relieve pain by decreasing the rate of growth of the tumor, but its curative value is doubtful; however, it is justifiable when a tumor is not amenable to operative treatment. The value of preoperative irradiation as an adjunct to ablative surgery has not been established.

Amputation offers the best possibility of control when the lesion is accessible and metastasis has not occurred. Five-year survival rates in large series have varied from zero to about 20%. When a solitary pulmonary metastasis is present, its removal is justifiable because of sporadic reports of 5-year survival afterward.

Prognosis

The more distant the lesion is from the trunk, the more favorable the outlook. In general, the prognosis is less favorable for large tumors. A greatly elevated preoperative serum alkaline phosphatase is a poor prognostic sign. The outlook for prolonged survival for tumors involving the trunk which cannot be radically excised is extremely poor. When osteogenic sarcoma complicates Paget's disease, the outlook is hopeless.

Nonsanchuk, J.S., & others: Osteogenic sarcoma: Prognosis related to epiphyseal closure. JAMA 208:2439–2441, 1969.

Marcove, R.C., & others: Osteogenic sarcoma under the age of 21. A review of 145 operative cases. J Bone Joint Surg 52A:411–423, 1970.

O'Hara, J.M., & others:. An analysis of 30 patients surviving longer than 10 years after treatment for osteogenic sarcoma. J Bone Joint Surg 50A:335–354, 1968.

PAROSTEAL SARCOMA
(Parosteal Osteoma, Parosteal Osteogenic Sarcoma, Juxtacortical Sarcoma, Desmoid of Bone)

Parosteal sarcoma is a primary tumor of extracortical origin which is seen most commonly in adolescents and young adults. The distal metaphysis of the femur, especially the popliteal aspect, is a common site; the tibia and humerus are other locations. The histologic picture is variable and somewhat dependent upon the area sampled.

Because of the indolent nature of this tumor, a mass is commonly the initial feature. Routine laboratory tests are not helpful in the diagnosis. X-ray demonstrates a mass–predominantly extracortical–and some lesions may demonstrate foci of nebulous calcification but with unmistakable distortion of adjacent soft tissue markings. Others may be so extensively ossified as to be radiopaque near the cortex while the more superficial zone demonstrates mottling. The diagnosis is dependent upon critical correlation of clinical and x-ray findings and microscopic study of carefully selected biopsy tissues.

This tumor must be differentiated from the osteoblastic variety of osteogenic sarcoma, myositis ossificans, calcified hematoma, and osteochondroma.

Once the diagnosis has been established, segmental resection with reconstruction of the resulting defect by bone grafting or prosthetic replacement has been found to be more reliable than local excision, which has been shown to be associated with recurrence. Extensive involvement of soft tissues and especially a neurovascular bundle may make amputation the treatment of choice.

This tumor is slowly aggressive, and pulmonary metastases have been reported even after a prolonged interval following apparent eradication of the local lesion. The 5-year survival rate has been estimated to be as high as 70% following ablative surgery.

Van der Heul, R.O., & J.R. von Ronnen: Juxtacortical osteosarcoma: Diagnosis, differential diagnosis, treatment, and an analysis of 80 cases. J Bone Joint Surg 49A:415–439, 1967.

FIBROSARCOMA

Fibrosarcoma of bone, a primary malignant tumor of fibroblastic origin, does not produce tumor osteoid or new bone. It is encountered predominantly during adult life in major long bones, especially those of the lower extremity. This tumor of intraosseous origin tends to destroy compact bone of the cortex and to invade adjacent soft tissues. Therefore, it must be differentiated from fibroblastic tumors (eg, periosteal fibrosarcoma and parosteal sarcoma) that arise extracortically and invade bone. Multicentric lesions have been reported.

The nonspecific presenting complaints of pain and swelling offer no help in differentiation from other tumors or tumor-like lesions. Likewise, x-ray findings of nonuniform osteolysis with cortical expansion and destruction and varying amounts of reactive new bone production suggest aggressiveness. Precise diagnosis depends upon microscopic study of representative tumor tissue.

Fibrosarcoma may complicate Paget's disease or fibrous dysplasia, or may occur in bone exposed to irradiation many years previously.

Depending upon its manifest aggressiveness, well differentiated tumors may be treated occasionally by local resection. In most cases, however, amputation with or without preliminary irradiation is indicated if metastasis cannot be demonstrated. Radiation therapy alone holds little promise of cure.

The prognosis of this formidable tumor is discouraging although some authors report slightly better long-term results than can be achieved in the case of osteogenic sarcoma.

Eyre-Brook, A.L., & C.H.G. Price: Fibrosarcoma of bone: Review of 50 consecutive cases from the Bristol Bone Tumour Registry. J Bone Joint Surg 51B:20–37, 1969.

CHONDROSARCOMA

Chondrosarcoma of bone is a primary malignant tumor that arises from cartilage cells and tends to exhibit its cartilaginous origin throughout its process of differentiation. Chondrosarcomas comprise about 5–10% of all malignant primary bone tumors.

This neoplasm is one of an extensive group of histologically related benign and malignant tumors that display characteristics of hyaline cartilage or chondroid elements and originate either from osseous or extraskeletal mesenchymal tissues.

Difficulty arises in proper interpretation of the histopathologic features and requires experience and judgment on the part of the pathologist, especially when radical surgery is the treatment of choice.

Clinical Findings

The initial symptom that calls attention to the presence of the tumor may be either pain or swelling, or a combination of both; neither is diagnostic. When pain occurs in the region of a previously known lesion that is of probable cartilaginous origin, prompt investigation is warranted. Progressive enlargement or interference with joint motion of a peripheral type of tumor also is ominous. The essential x-ray findings of central chondrosarcoma are those of destruction of bone, both the spongiosa and the cortex. Areas of mottled calcification in the osteolytic zone are common. Where the lesion involves the shaft of a tubular bone, the cortex may be thickened and expanded, giving a fusiform configuration. Peripheral chondrosarcoma is identified as a tumor that presents as a mass. Calcification in the tumor mass may have a nebulous, mottled, or occasionally a streak-like appearance. The site of origin of the tumor from the cortex may show evidence of erosion.

The most helpful special examination is microscopic study, especially those areas that are not extensively calcified or ossified or show degenerative changes. This examination should be completed before any radical surgical treatment is carried out.

Angiography may disclose the comparative vascularity of the tumor and may demonstrate criteria of malignancy. Because of its selective concentration in cartilage, radioactive sulfur has been used for scintigraphy and may be useful to detect occult metastatic deposits. Complications include pathologic fracture, recurrence after incomplete surgical removal, and dissemination of variable tumor cells in the wound during biopsy. For that reason, when amputation is probable, the surgical approach for biopsy should be planned so that it does not encroach upon the site of definitive surgery.

Treatment

Irradiation probably has no role in the curative treatment of this malignant tumor. Radical removal of the lesion by local excision, segmental resection, or amputation is the treatment of choice. Since no 2 lesions have the same anatomic peculiarities, the specific surgical technic must vary accordingly. In general, lesions farthest from the trunk offer the greatest possibility for initial surgical treatment by technics other than amputation. In lesions near the trunk, radical removal at the time of the initial attack is preferred because recurrence is practically incurable. Curettage is only palliative but has been used and repeated to control some indolent lesions that are not amenable to complete removal.

Prognosis

The slow growth of chondrosarcoma, the long intervals between recurrences, and the tendency toward late metastasis make evaluation of the success of surgical treatment unreliable unless the follow-up period is prolonged. It is generally agreed that an interval of 10 years between treatment and final evaluation is necessary. Metastasis may occur through lymph channels but is usually through the venous system. Death may also occur as a complication of encroachment on vital structures by local enlargement of the tumor.

In general, the prognosis of properly treated chondrosarcoma is much more favorable than for osteogenic sarcoma.

Henderson, E.D., & D.C. Dahlin: Chondrosarcoma of bone: A study of 288 cases. J Bone Joint Surg 45A:1450–1458, 1963.

METASTATIC TUMORS TO BONE

Most malignant tumors of bone represent metastases from a primary extraskeletal focus, and most are of epithelial origin. Occasionally, a primary malignant tumor of bone will metastasize to another osseous locus (eg, Ewing's sarcoma). With the exception of malignant tumors of the CNS, almost any tumor may metastasize to bone. The avenue is by the blood vessels or lymphatics.

Pain is usually the initial subjective complaint, but swelling occasionally occurs first. Although pathologic fracture without antecedent pain may be the first sign of a skeletal metastasis, mild or remittent pain usually occurs first. Occasionally, especially in the spine and proximal femur, fracture with gradual displacement of fragments can occur without dramatic increase of pain. Deformity as the result of angulation or collapse of the involved segment of bone then becomes an indicative objective finding. Other findings such as tenderness or discomfort from percussion may aid in the diagnosis. Although an accelerated sedimentation rate may accompany extensive bone metastasis, it is not of value in the direct diagnosis. Elevation of the serum alkaline phosphatase may be associated with widespread metastatic lesions of bone, especially those that are osteoblastic. With the exception of biopsy, the single most valuable diagnostic aid is x-ray examination. The x-ray negative during a routine bone survey study should be of the highest technical quality to demonstrate subtle changes of bone and soft tissue architecture which might otherwise not be apparent. Supplementary x-ray technics such as laminography, arteriography, and intra-osseous phlebography (osteography) may demonstrate lesions that are not ordinarily detectable. Radioisotope scanning may reveal the location of metastatic foci in the skeleton before they can be demonstrated by the usual x-ray technics. Biopsy is necessary for exact diagnosis. Representative and adequate samples of tissue must be obtained for proper histologic study, especially when the location of the primary lesion is unknown.

The chief x-ray finding of bone metastasis is that of destruction and replacement of bone by the invading tumor. Foci of involvement may be osteolytic, osteoblastic, or a combination of both. Fracture is especially likely to occur through osteolytic zones.

Treatment

The treatment of skeletal metastases depends upon the nature of the primary tumor and the extent of involvement. If the osseous focus is amenable to irradiation, chemotherapy, or hormonal therapy, such treatment is indicated, especially when progressive enlargement of the lesion causes pain or jeopardizes the integrity of the bone to the point of impending fracture. The management of fractures that complicate bone metastasis is perplexing. Since the primary tumor is likely to be extraskeletal, total care of the patient requires cooperation with other specialists. In general, if evaluation of the patient suggests that life expectancy is longer than a few weeks, definitive treatment of the fracture should be started promptly. The technic of treatment is directed toward relief of pain, restoration to maximal functional activity at the earliest time, return of the patient to an independent existence, and creation of conditions favorable to fracture healing. If life expectancy is limited to a few weeks, the most important goals are to provide comfort by the relief of pain and the simplification of nursing care by various orthopedic means.

Legge, D.A., & others: Radioisotope scanning of metastatic lesions of bone. Mayo Clin Proc 45:755–761, 1970.

Parrish, F.F., & J.A. Murray: Surgical treatment for secondary neoplastic fractures. J Bone Joint Surg 52A:665–686, 1970.

• • •

General Bibliography

Aegerter, E., & J.A. Kirkpatrick, Jr.: *Orthopedic Diseases,* 3rd ed. Saunders, 1968.

Baker, A.B.: *Clinical Neurology,* 2nd ed. Vol 3. Hoeber, 1962.

Dahlin, D.C.: *Bone Tumors,* 2nd ed. Thomas, 1967.

Ferguson, A.B., Jr.: *Orthopaedic Surgery in Infancy and Childhood,* 3rd ed. Williams & Wilkins, 1968.

Geschickter, C.F., & M.M. Copeland: *Tumors of Bone,* 3rd ed. Lippincott, 1949.

Hollander, J.L.: *Arthritis and Allied Conditions,* 7th ed. Lea & Febiger, 1966.

Jaffe, H.L.: *Tumors and Tumorous Conditions of the Bones and Joints.* Lea & Febiger, 1958.

Lichtenstein, L.: *Bone Tumors,* 3rd ed. Mosby, 1965.

Lichtenstein, L.: *Diseases of Bones and Joints.* Mosby, 1970.

Paul, L.W., & J.H. Juhl: *Essentials of Roentgen Diagnosis of the Skeleton.* Hoeber, 1967.

Shands, A.R., Jr., & R.B. Raney: *Handbook of Orthopaedic Surgery,* 7th ed. Mosby, 1967.

Turek, S.L.: *Orthopaedics,* 2nd ed. Lippincott, 1967.

15...

Genitourinary Tract

Marcus A. Krupp

NONSPECIFIC MANIFESTATIONS

Pain

The localization, pattern of referral, and type of pain are important clues to the diagnosis of genitourinary tract disease.

(1) Pain caused by **renal disease** is usually felt as a dull ache in the "flanks" or costovertebral angle, often extending along the rib margin toward the umbilicus. Because many renal diseases do not produce sudden distention of the capsules of the kidney, absence of pain is common.

(2) **Ureteral pain** is related to obstruction and is usually acute in onset, severe, and colicky, and radiates from the costovertebral angle down the course of the ureter into the scrotum or vulva and the inner thigh. The site of the obstruction may be determined by the location of the radiation of the pain: high ureteral pain is usually referred to the testicle or vulva; mid-ureteral pain to the right lower quadrant of the abdomen; and low ureteral pain to the bladder.

(3) **Bladder pain** accompanies overdistention of the bladder in acute urinary retention and distention of a bladder wall altered by tuberculosis or interstitial cystitis. Relief comes with emptying the bladder. Pain due to bladder infection is usually referred to the distal urethra and accompanies micturition.

(4) Pain caused by **chronic prostatic disease** is uncommon.

(5) Pain caused by **testicular inflammation or trauma** is acute and severe and is occasionally referred to the costovertebral angle. Pain associated with infection of the epididymis is similar to that associated with testicular inflammation.

Urinary Symptoms

Infection, inflammation, and obstruction produce symptoms associated with urination.

(1) **Frequency, urgency, and nocturia** are commonly experienced when inflammation of the urinary tract is present. Severe infection produces a constant desire to urinate even though the bladder contains only a few ml of urine. Frequency and nocturia occur when bladder capacity is diminished by disease or when the bladder cannot be emptied completely, leaving a large volume of residual urine. Nocturia associated with a large urine volume may occur with heart failure, renal insufficiency, mobilization of edema due to any cause,

diabetes insipidus, hyperaldosteronism, and ingestion of large amounts of fluid late in the evening.

(2) **Dysuria and burning pain in the urethra on urination** are associated with infection of the bladder and prostate.

(3) **Enuresis** may be due to urinary tract disease but is most often caused by neural or psychogenic disorders.

(4) **Urinary incontinence** may be due to anatomic abnormality, physical stress, the urgency associated with infection or nervous system disease, and the dribbling associated with an overdistended flaccid bladder.

Characteristics of Urine

(1) **Cloudy urine** is most frequently the result of the urates or phosphates which precipitate out as urine collects in the bladder, and is usually of no significance.

(2) **Hematuria** is always of grave significance. It may be due to neoplasms, vascular accidents, infections, anomalies, stones, or trauma to the urinary tract. When blood appears only during the initial period of voiding, the likely source is the anterior urethra or prostate. When blood appears during the terminal period of voiding, the likely source is the posterior urethra, vesical neck, or trigone. Blood mixed in with the total urine volume is from the kidney, ureters, or bladder.

Renal Function Tests

Recognition of renal diseases and evaluation of renal function are dependent on laboratory determinations. As renal function becomes impaired, laboratory observations provide reliable indices of the capacity of the kidney to meet the demands of excretion, reabsorption, and secretion and to fulfill its role in maintaining homeostasis.

Useful tests may be categorized according to the physiologic function measured, as follows:

A. Glomerular Filtration Rate (GFR): Inulin clearance is the most reliable measurement, but for clinical use the endogenous creatinine clearance is suitable. Urea clearance is less reliable. The plasma creatinine or urea levels reflect the GFR, rising as the filtration rate diminishes. Newer radioiodine compounds are suitable for clearance studies.

B. Renal Plasma Flow (RPF): A properly performed phenolsulphonphthalein (PSP) clearance test serves as a clinical measurement of renal blood (plasma) flow.

C. Tubular Transport: Proximal tubular transport is measured by the "15 minute" determination in the PSP excretion test. Distal tubular transport can be ascertained by concentration and dilution tests.

Renal Biopsy

Renal biopsy is a valuable diagnostic procedure which also serves as a guide to rational treatment. The technic has become well established, frequently providing sufficient tissue for light and electron microscopy and for immunofluorescent examination. Absolute contraindications include anatomic presence of only one kidney, severe malfunction of one kidney even though function is adequate in the other, bleeding diathesis, the presence of hemangioma, tumor, or large cysts, abscess or infection, hydronephrosis, and an uncooperative patient. Relative contraindications are the presence of serious hypertension, uremia, severe arteriosclerosis, and unusual difficulty in doing a biopsy due to obesity, anasarca, or inability of the patient to lie flat.

Clinical indications for renal biopsy, in addition to the necessity for establishing a diagnosis, include the need to determine prognosis, to follow progression of a lesion and response to treatment, to confirm the presence of a generalized disease (collagen disorder, amyloidosis, sarcoidosis), and to follow rejection response in a transplanted kidney.

DISORDERS OF THE KIDNEYS

ACUTE GLOMERULONEPHRITIS

Essentials of Diagnosis

- History of preceding streptococcal infection.
- Malaise, headache, anorexia, low-grade fever.
- Mild generalized edema, mild hypertension, retinal hemorrhages.
- Gross hematuria; protein, red cell casts, granular and hyaline casts, white cells, and renal epithelial cells in urine.
- Elevated antistreptolysin O titer, variable nitrogen retention.

General Considerations

Glomerulonephritis is a disease affecting both kidneys. In most cases recovery from the acute stage is complete, but progressive involvement may destroy renal tissue and renal insufficiency results. Acute glomerulonephritis is most common in children 3–10 years of age, although 5% or more of initial attacks occur in adults over the age of 50. By far the most common cause is an antecedent infection of the pharynx and tonsils or of the skin with group A β-hemolytic streptococci, certain strains of which are nephritogenic. Nephritis occurs in 10–15% of children and young adults who have clinically evident infection with a nephritogenic strain. In children under age 6, pyoderma (impetigo) is the most common antecedent; in older children and young adults, pharyngitis is a common and skin infection a rare antecedent. Nephritogenic strains commonly encountered include, for the skin, M types 49 (Red Lake), 2, and provisional 55; for pharyngitis, types 12, 1, and 4. Rarely, nephritis may follow infections due to pneumococci, staphylococci, some bacilli, and viruses. Rhus dermatitis and reactions to venom or chemical agents may be associated with renal disease clinically indistinguishable from glomerulonephritis.

The pathogenesis of the glomerular lesion has been further elucidated by the use of new immunologic technics (immunofluorescence) and electron microscopy. A likely sequel to infection by nephritogenic strains of β-hemolytic streptococci is injury to the mesangial cells in the intercapillary space. The glomerulus may then become more easily damaged by antigen-antibody complexes developing from the immune response to the streptococcal infection. Beta-1-C globulin of complement is deposited either alone or in association with IgG on the epithelial side of the basement membrane, and occasionally in subendothelial sites as well.

A clinical variant similar to poststreptococcal nephritis is Goodpasture's syndrome in which a severe acute glomerulonephritis is characteristically accompanied by diffuse hemorrhagic inflammation of the lungs. The cause is unknown, but antibody to glomerular basement membrane (GBM), which acts as an autologous antigen, has been demonstrated. The antibody (anti-GBM) also reacts with lung basement membrane. IgG and β-1-C complement have been demonstrated on the glomerular and lung basement membranes by immunofluorscent and electron microscopy.

Gross examination of the involved kidney shows only punctate hemorrhages throughout the cortex. Microscopically, the primary alteration is in the glomeruli, which show proliferation and swelling of the mesangial endothelial cells of the capillary tuft. The proliferation of capsular epithelium produces a thickened crescent about the tuft, and in the space between the capsule and the tuft there are collections of leukocytes, red cells, and exudate. Edema of the interstitial tissue and cloudy swelling of the tubule epithelium are common. As the disease progresses, the kidneys may enlarge. The typical histologic findings in glomerulitis are enlarging crescents which become hyalinized and converted into scar tissue and obstruct the circulation through the glomerulus. Degenerative changes occur in the tubules, with fatty degeneration and necrosis and ultimate scarring of the nephron. Arteriolar thickening and obliteration become prominent.

Clinical Findings

A. Symptoms and Signs: Often the disease is very mild, and there may be no reason to suspect renal involvement unless the urine is examined. In severe cases, about 2 weeks following the acute streptococcal infection, the patient develops headache, malaise, mild fever, puffiness around the eyes and face, flank pain, and oliguria. Hematuria is usually noted as "bloody" or, if the urine is acid, as "brown" or "coffee-colored." Respiratory difficulty with shortness of breath may occur as a result of salt and water retention and circulatory congestion. There may be moderate tachycardia and moderate to marked elevation of blood pressure. Tenderness in the costovertebral angle is common.

B. Laboratory Findings: The diagnosis is confirmed by examination of the urine, which may be grossly bloody or coffee-colored (acid hematin) or may show only microscopic hematuria. In addition, the urine contains protein (1–3+) and casts. Hyaline and granular casts are commonly found in large numbers, but the classical sign of glomerulitis, the erythrocyte cast (blood cast), may be found only occasionally in the urinary sediment. The erythrocyte cast resembles a blood clot formed in the lumen of a renal tubule; it is usually of small caliber, intensely orange or red, and under high power with proper lighting may show the mosaic pattern of the packed red cells held together by the clot of fibrin and plasma protein.

With the impairment of renal function (decrease in GFR and blood flow) and with oliguria, plasma or serum urea nitrogen and creatinine become elevated, the levels varying with the severity of the renal lesion. The sedimentation rate is rapid. A mild normochromic anemia may result from fluid retention and dilution. Infection of the throat with nephritogenic streptococci is frequently followed by increasing antistreptolysin O (ASO) titers in the serum, whereas high titers are usually not demonstrable following skin infections. Production of antibody against streptococcal deoxyribonuclease B (anti-DNase B) is more regularly observed following both throat and skin infections.

Confirmation of diagnosis is made by examination of the urine, although the history and clinical findings in typical cases leave little doubt. The finding of erythrocytes in a cast is proof that erythrocytes were present in the renal tubules and did not arise from elsewhere in the genitourinary tract.

Differential Diagnosis

Although considered to be the hallmark of glomerulonephritis, erythrocyte casts also occur along with other abnormal elements in any disease in which glomerular inflammation and tubule damage are present, ie, polyarteritis nodosa, disseminated lupus erythematosus, dermatomyositis, sarcoidosis, subacute bacterial endocarditis, "focal" nephritis, Goodpasture's syndrome, Henoch's purpura, or poisoning with chemicals toxic to the kidney.

Complications

In severe cases, signs compatible with cardiac failure appear as a result of salt and water retention rather than of myocardial failure per se: cardiac enlargement, tachycardia, gallop rhythm, pulmonary passive congestion, pleural fluid, and peripheral edema.

With severe hypertension, signs of left ventricular failure often develop and the symptoms and signs of hypertensive encephalopathy may predominate: severe headache, drowsiness, muscle twitchings and convulsions, vomiting, and at times papilledema and retinal hemorrhage.

Any infection occurring in a patient with glomerulonephritis must be regarded as a serious complication.

Treatment

A. Specific Measures: There is no specific treatment. Adrenocorticosteroids and corticotropin are of no value and may be contraindicated because they increase protein catabolism, sodium retention, and hypertension. Eradication of beta-hemolytic streptococci with penicillin or other antibiotic is desirable.

B. General Measures: In uncomplicated cases, treatment is symptomatic and designed to prevent overhydration and hypertension. Hospitalization is indicated if oliguria, nitrogen retention, and hypertension are present. Bed rest is of great importance and should be continued until clinical signs abate. Blood pressure and BUN should be normal for more than 1–2 weeks before activity is resumed. A guide to duration of bed rest is the urine: When protein excretion has diminished to near normal and when white and epithelial cell excretion has decreased and stabilized, activity may be resumed on a graded basis. Excretion of protein and formed elements in the urine will increase with resumption of activity, but such increases should not be great. Erythrocytes may be excreted in large numbers for months, and the rate of excretion is not a good criterion for evaluating convalescence. If the sedimentation rate increases or if urinary findings become more pronounced with activity, return to bed rest and restricted activity are indicated for 10 days to 2 weeks before trial of activity is repeated.

In the presence of elevated BUN and oliguria, severe dietary protein restriction is indicated. If severe oliguria is present, no protein should be given. If no nitrogen retention is apparent, the diet may contain 0.5 gm of protein/kg ideal weight. Carbohydrates should be given liberally to provide calories and to reduce the catabolism of protein and prevent starvation ketosis. With severe oliguria, potassium intoxication may occur.

Sodium restriction varies with the degree of oliguria; in severe cases no sodium should be allowed. As recovery progresses, sodium intake can be increased.

Fluids should be restricted in keeping with the ability of the kidney to excrete urine. If restriction is not indicated, fluids can be consumed as desired. Occasionally, when nausea and vomiting preclude oral consumption, fluids must be given intravenously in amounts depending upon the severity of the oliguria. Glucose must be given in sufficient quantities to spare protein and prevent ketosis.

If edema becomes severe, a trial of an oral diuretic such as furosemide is in order. Treatment of extreme fluid overload and oliguria may require dialysis.

If anemia becomes severe (hematocrit less than 30%), blood transfusions in the form of packed red cells may be given.

C. Treatment of Complications:

1. Hypertensive encephalopathy should be treated vigorously. Sedation with barbiturates or paraldehyde may suffice in mild cases. Magnesium sulfate (with its attendant hazardous side-effects) is no longer required because more effective agents are available. Reserpine, in doses of 0.05–0.1 mg/kg IM for children and a total dose of 2.5–5 mg IM for adults, may be repeated every 6–12 hours to reduce blood pressure. The common side-effects of reserpine therapy are not often a problem because treatment is usually not prolonged. Short-term therapy with hydralazine (Apresoline®), 20–40 mg IM for adults followed by oral or intramuscular doses as required, may be employed. Reserpine plus hydralazine, in smaller doses of each, may reduce the side-effects of each. If rapid reduction in blood pressure is mandatory, hydralazine may be given IV in a dose of 0.25–0.5 mg/kg. Other agents may be employed: The ganglionic blocking agents trimethaphan (Arfonad®) and pentolinium (Ansolysen®) and the postganglionic blocker guanethidine (Ismelin®). The use of these drugs must be closely supervised by physicians conversant with their pharmacologic characteristics and by experienced attendants.

Diphenylhydantoin (Dilantin®) may be of use in controlling seizures.

2. Heart failure should be treated as any case of left ventricular failure, ie, with severe restriction of fluid and sodium intake and the use of digitalis and oxygen. To reduce fluid overload, an oral diuretic such as furosemide may be helpful.

3. Infection should be promptly eradicated with appropriate antibiotics. Prophylactic penicillin for several months after the acute phase has been advocated, but its value is not proved.

Prognosis

The progression of glomerulonephritis to healing or advancing disease is depicted in Fig 15–1. Most patients with the acute disease recover completely within 1–2 years; 5–20% show progressive renal damage. If oliguria, heart failure, or hypertensive encephalopathy is severe, death may occur during the acute attack. Even with severe acute disease, however, recov-

ery is the rule, particularly in children. In Goodpasture's syndrome, recovery is rare.

See references under Latent Glomerulonephritis, below.

CHRONIC GLOMERULONEPHRITIS

Progressive destruction of the kidney may continue for many years in a clinically latent or subacute form. The subacute form is similar to the latent form (see below) except that symptoms occur, ie, malaise, mild fever, and sometimes flank pain and oliguria. Treatment is as for the acute attack. Exacerbations may appear from time to time, reflecting the stage of evolution of the disease.

LATENT GLOMERULONEPHRITIS

If acute glomerulonephritis does not heal within 1–2 years, the vascular and glomerular lesions continue to progress and tubular changes occur. In the presence of smoldering, active nephritis, the patient is usually asymptomatic and the evidence of disease consists only of the excretion of abnormal urinary elements.

The urinary excretion of protein, red cells, white cells, epithelial cells, and casts (including erythrocyte casts, granular casts, and hyaline and waxy casts) continues at levels above normal. As renal impairment progresses, signs of renal insufficiency appear (see below).

The differential diagnosis is the same as that given for acute glomerulonephritis.

Prevention

Treat intercurrent infections promptly and vigorously as indicated. Avoid unnecessary vaccinations.

Treatment

Treat exacerbations as for the acute attack, nephrotic state, or incipient renal insufficiency as indicated. A normal diet, adequate for growth in childhood and adolescence, is desirable. A protein intake of 0.5–1 gm/kg is permissible as long as renal function is adequate to maintain a normal BUN. A liberal fluid intake is desirable.

Strenuous exercise may be harmful; otherwise, normal activity is permitted.

Prognosis

Worsening of the urinary findings may occur with infection, trauma, or fatigue. Exacerbations may resemble the acute attack, and may be associated with intercurrent infection or trauma. Other exacerbations may be typical of the nephrotic syndrome (see below).

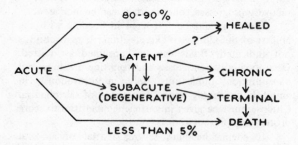

FIG 15–1. Prognosis in glomerulonephritis.

Death in uremia is the usual outcome, but the course is variable and the patient may live a reasonably normal life for 20–30 years.

Bricker, N.S.: Renal function in chronic renal disease. Medicine 44:263–288, 1965.

Carpenter, C.B.: Immunologic aspects of renal disease. Ann Rev Med 21:1–16, 1970.

Dixon, F.J.: The pathogenesis of glomerulonephritis. Am J Med 44:493–498, 1968.

Fish, A.J., & others: Epidemic acute glomerulonephritis associated with Type 49 streptococcal pyoderma. II. Correlative study of light, immunofluorescent and electron microscopic findings. Am J Med 48:28–39, 1970.

Kaplan, E.L., & others: Epidemic acute glomerulonephritis associated with type 49 streptococcal pyoderma. I. Clinical and laboratory findings. Am J Med 48:9–27, 1970.

Kark, R.M.: Renal biopsy and prognosis. Ann Rev Med 18:269–298, 1967.

Kushner, D.C., & others: Acute glomerulonephritis in the adult. Medicine 40:203–240, 1961.

Wannamaker, L.W.: Streptococcal infections of the throat and skin. New England J Med 282:78–85, 1970.

CHRONIC RENAL INSUFFICIENCY

Essentials of Diagnosis

- Weakness and easy fatigability, headaches, anorexia, nausea and vomiting, pruritus, polyuria, nocturia.
- Hypertension with secondary encephalopathy, retinal damage, heart failure.
- Anemia, azotemia, and acidosis, with elevated serum potassium, phosphate, and sulfate; and decreased serum calcium and protein.
- Urine specific gravity low and fixed; mild to moderate proteinuria; few red cells, white cells, and broad renal failure casts.

General Considerations

The pathologic picture varies with the cause of the damage to the kidney. Extensive scarring with decrease in kidney size, hyalinization of glomeruli, and obliteration of some tubules and hypertrophy and dilatation of others produce great distortion of renal architecture. The vascular changes are due to the effects of scar formation and of prolonged hypertension, with thickening of the media, fragmentation of elastic fibers, intimal thickening, and obliteration of the lumens in some areas. In diabetic nephropathy the typical glomerular lesions of intercapillary sclerosis are often distinct. The vascular lesions of periarteritis or of systemic lupus erythematosus often serve to establish these diagnoses. Obstructive uropathy presents the classical picture of hydronephrosis with compression and destruction of the renal parenchyma. Polycystic disease, multiple myeloma, amyloid disease, and other rarer causes of renal failure usually can be identified by characteristic pathologic lesions.

Clinical Findings

The clinical symptoms and signs of metabolic and hypertensive components of renal failure appear insidiously and may not be noted until the effects are severe.

A. Symptoms and Signs: Metabolic and vascular abnormalities incident to renal insufficiency produce typical symptoms and signs. The metabolic defect is due to failure of the kidney to excrete the daily load of nitrogenous waste and to excrete or conserve water and electrolytes as required to maintain balance. The result is the clinical picture of uremia with its 3 cardinal signs: anemia, azotemia, and acidosis. The uremic patient often is weak and tired, complains of anorexia and nausea and vomiting, and may have diarrhea. He is often short of breath. Pruritus is common and the excoriations may be purpuric. Pallor and a waxy appearance of the skin are often observed. Polyuria reflects the inability of the kidney tubules to absorb water; as glomerular filtration becomes greatly reduced, oliguria appears. Terminal manifestations are severe nausea, diarrhea, muscle twitching, hyperpnea, pruritus, bleeding from mucous membranes, and somnolence. Urea frost on the skin and fibrinous pericarditis and pleurisy are associated with marked elevations of BUN.

Hypertension may become severe and may produce headache, convulsions, and left heart failure. Retinopathy with papilledema, hemorrhages, exudates, and severe changes of the arterioles often produce impairment of vision. Encephalopathy produces convulsions. Left heart failure is often accompanied by overt pulmonary edema.

B. Laboratory Findings: Laboratory studies reveal the functional and chemical defects. The urine usually is dilute, contains small amounts of protein, few red cells, white cells, and epithelial cells, and a few granular and waxy casts some of which are broad in caliber (broad renal failure casts). The anemia is usually normochromic, and the hemoglobin often in the range of 6–9 gm/100 ml. BUN and creatinine are greatly elevated. Serum sodium concentration may be slightly lower than normal, serum potassium slightly to markedly elevated, and serum calcium concentration decreased. With retention of phosphate, sulfate, and (frequently) chloride, plasma bicarbonate concentration is decreased. Retention of organic acids and loss of sodium and of bicarbonate buffer is accompanied by a decrease of plasma pH. Deficient hydrogen ion secretion by damaged tubules contributes to acidosis.

Differential Diagnosis

Chronic renal insufficiency presents symptoms and signs related to the functional disability resulting from a reduction in the number of functioning nephrons rather than to the cause of the renal damage. It is often impossible to distinguish between renal insufficiency due to chronic glomerulonephritis, pyelonephritis, malignant hypertension, diabetic nephropathy, obstructive nephropathy, and collagen disease. The presence of large kidneys characteristic of polycystic disease should serve to identify this cause of renal failure.

Treatment

Hypertension or heart failure should be treated as indicated.

A. Diet and Fluids: Limitation of protein to 0.5 gm/kg/day helps to reduce azotemia, acidosis, and hyperkalemia.

The diet should include adequate calories. Sodium should not be restricted. Fluid intake should be sufficient to maintain an adequate urine volume, but no attempt should be made to force diuresis. Obligatory water loss may be quite high because of the large solute load (eg, sodium and urea) which must be excreted by a reduced number of nephrons; intake must be sufficient to maintain renal function without causing excessive diuresis or edema. *Caution:* Water restriction for laboratory examination or tests of renal function is hazardous.

B. Electrolyte Replacement:

1. Sodium supplements may be required to restore sodium losses resulting from failure of the kidney to provide NH_4^+ and H^+ for sodium conservation. A mixture of NaCl and $NaHCO_3$ in equal parts, 1–2 gm 2–3 times daily with meals, may be required in addition to dietary sources.

2. Potassium intake may have to be restricted or supplemented. In severe hyperkalemia, active measures to remove potassium may be required (see discussion in Chapter 2). Measurement of the serum potassium concentration will provide indications.

3. Calcium lactate, 4 gm 2–3 times daily, may be given to relieve hypocalcemic tetany. Intravenous administration of calcium gluconate may be required at times.

4. Serum phosphate levels may be lowered by reducing absorption of phosphate in the gastrointestinal tract with administration of aluminum hydroxide gel, 30 ml 3–4 times daily.

C. Transfusions: Transfusions of whole blood or packed red cells may be required for treatment of anemia. Iron is usually ineffective, and there is no indication that cobalt is of any use.

D. General Measures: Nausea and vomiting may be alleviated with chlorpromazine, 15–25 mg orally or 10–20 mg IM (or equivalent amounts of related compounds). The barbiturate drugs may be used for sedation as required. Hypertension may prove difficult to combat because of the hazards of sodium restriction and the use of drugs requiring renal excretion. Reserpine, 0.25 mg orally 2–4 times daily, is relatively safe. For convulsions it may be necessary to give barbiturates such as pentobarbital sodium, 0.25–0.5 gm IV or IM, or amobarbital sodium, 0.5 gm IV or IM. Paraldehyde is often well tolerated orally or rectally in doses of 4–15 ml.

E. Extracorporeal Dialysis and Kidney Transplants: These approaches to the treatment of renal insufficiency due to any cause have been under investigation for many years, and encouraging experience has prompted expansion of facilities for scheduled repeated extracorporeal dialysis. The growing success with renal transplantation holds promise for extending the life of the patient with chronic renal disease.

1. Simplified mechanisms for dialysis with the artificial kidney and ingenious cannulas permit periodic dialysis with a minimum of professional supervision in hospital centers and in the patient's home. Patients with creatinine clearances of 0–2 ml/minute have been kept alive for 3–4 years in reasonable health and activity by dialysis once or twice a week. The criteria for selection of patients are now clear. Centers are being established for the treatment of chronic renal insufficiency and home units are generally available, although considerable skill is demanded of those who operate the devices. A recent survey indicates a 1-year survival on dialysis of 87% and a 2-year survival of 73%. Peritoneal dialysis has been less useful than hemodialysis for long-term therapy.

2. Transplantation of kidneys from one human to another has been technically feasible for many years. Survival of such grafts has been limited by the rejection of the foreign organ by the recipient except when donor and recipient were identical twins. Blood typing and leukocyte typing for multiple antigens have improved the matching of donor and recipient, with an encouraging decrease in the rejection rate. Further experience with immunosuppressive drugs and adrenal corticosteroids has improved protection of the homologous transplant from rejection for extended periods. The use of antilymphocytic globulin (ALG) to suppress immunity has been impressively effective, but evaluation requires more experience. Survival data since January 1967 are much improved over prior experience. When transplantation is between siblings, the 1-year kidney survival is greater than 90% and the 2-year survival slightly over 80%. The survival of kidneys from unrelated donors is only 45% at 1 year and about 40% at 2 years, but with improved tissue typing and with new methods of preserving a donor kidney this experience should improve markedly.

Prognosis

The prognosis depends upon the degree of renal failure. Intercurrent infections will hasten the downhill course.

Bennett, W.M., & others: A practical guide to drug usage in adult patients with impaired renal function. JAMA 214:1468–1475, 1970.

Berlyne, G. M.: *Nutrition in Renal Disease.* Livingstone, 1968.

Curtis, J.R., & others: Maintenance hemodialysis. Quart J Med 38:49–89, 1969.

Donadio, J.V., Jr., & W.J. Johnson: Conservative management of chronic renal failure. M Clin North America 50:1175–1186, 1966.

Franklin, S.S.: Uremia: Newer concepts in pathogenesis and treatment. M Clin North America 54:411–430, 1970.

Hume, D.M.: Renal homotransplantation in man. Ann Rev Med 18:229–268, 1967.

Lange, K.: Nutritional management of kidney disorders. M Clin North America 55:513–520, 1971.

Merrill, J.P., & C.L. Hampers: Uremia. New England J Med 282:953–961, 1014–1021, 1970.

Merrill, J.P. (editor): Symposium on the treatment of acute renal failure. Mod Treat 6:923–1063, 1969. [Includes therapy of chronic renal failure.]

Milne, M.D. (editor): Management of renal failure. Brit M Bull 27:95–185, 1971.

Palmer, R.A., & others: Treatment of chronic renal failure by prolonged peritoneal dialysis. New England J Med 274:248–253, 1966.

Pendras, J.P., & R.V. Erickson: Hemodialysis: A successful therapy for chronic uremia. Ann Int Med 64:293–311, 1966.

Rapaport, F.T., & J. Dausset: *Human Transplantation.* Grune & Stratton, 1968.

Russell, P.S., & H.J. Winn: Transplantation. New England J Med 282:786–793, 848–854, 896–906, 1970.

Seventh International Transplantation Conference. F.T. Rapaport (editor). Proc New York Acad Sc 129:585–672, 1966.

Starzl, T.E., & others: The problems and prognosis of the chronically surviving patient after renal homotransplantation. Ann New York Acad Sc 129:598–614, 1966.

Stewart, J.H., & others: Peritoneal and haemo-dialysis: A comparison of their morbidity, and of the mortality suffered by dialysed patients. Quart J Med 35:407–420, 1966.

Welt, L.G. (editor): Symposium on uremia. Am J Med 44:653–802, 1968.

NEPHROTIC SYNDROME

Essentials of Diagnosis

- Massive edema.
- Proteinuria > 3.5 gm/day.
- Hypoalbuminemia < 3 gm/100 ml.
- Hyperlipidemia: Cholesterol > 300 mg/100 ml.
- Lipiduria: Free fat, oval fat bodies, fatty casts.

General Considerations

Tissue obtained by biopsy or at necropsy will show changes characteristic of the underlying disease, eg, disseminated lupus erythematosus, amyloidosis, diabetic nephropathy. Most of the cases of nephrotic syndrome, however, cannot be attributed to such diseases and are classified according to the nature of the lesion in the glomerulus:

(1) **Minimal glomerular lesion:** (About 20% of cases of idiopathic nephrosis.) No abnormality is visible by examination with the light microscope. With the electron microscope, alterations of the glomerular basement membrane can be seen. They are characterized by swelling and vacuolization and loss of organization of food processes of the epithelial cells. (So-called lipoid or pure nephrosis; Earle's epithelial cell disease; foot process disease.)

(2) **Membranous disease:** (About 70% of cases of idiopathic nephrosis.) By light microscopy there is thickening of the basement membrane. With the electron microscope, distortion, blunting, and fusion of epithelial cell foot processes can be distinguished in addition to the thickened basement membrane.

(3) **Proliferative lesions:** (About 5% of cases of idiopathic nephrosis.) Increase in numbers of epithelial cells and formation of crescents in Bowman's capsule with variable scarring of the glomerular tuft are readily identified with the light microscope.

(4) **Mixed membranous and proliferative lesions:** (About 5% of cases of idiopathic nephrosis.)

Clinical Findings

A. **Symptoms and Signs:** Edema may appear insidiously and increase slowly; often it appears suddenly and accumulates rapidly. As fluid collects in the serous cavities, the abdomen becomes protuberant and the patient may complain of anorexia and become short of breath. Symptoms other than those related to the mechanical effects of edema and serous sac fluid accumulation are not remarkable.

On physical examination massive edema is apparent. Signs of hydrothorax and ascites are common. Pallor is often accentuated by the edema, and striae commonly appear in the stretched skin of the extremities. Hypertension, changes in the retina and retinal vessels, and cardiac and cerebral manifestations of hypertension may be demonstrated more often when collagen disease, diabetes mellitus, or renal insufficiency is present.

B. **Laboratory Findings:** The urine contains large amounts of protein, 4–10 gm/24 hours or more. The sediment contains casts, including the characteristic fatty and waxy varieties; renal tubule cells, some of which contain fatty droplets (oval fat bodies); and variable numbers of erythrocytes. A mild normochromic anemia is common, but anemia may be more severe if renal damage is great. Nitrogen retention varies with the severity of impairment of renal function. The plasma is often lipemic, and the blood cholesterol is usually greatly elevated. Plasma protein is greatly reduced. The albumin fraction may fall to less than 2 gm or even below 1 gm/100 ml. Some reduction of gamma globulin occurs in pure nephrosis, whereas in systemic lupus erythematosus the protein of the gamma fraction may be greatly elevated. The serum electrolyte concentrations are often normal, although the serum sodium may be slightly low; total serum calcium may be low, in keeping with the degree of hypoalbuminemia and decrease in the protein-bound calcium moiety. During edema forming periods, urinary sodium excretion is very low and urinary aldosterone excretion elevated. If renal insufficiency (see above) is present, the blood and urine findings are usually altered accordingly.

Renal biopsy is essential to confirm the diagnosis and to indicate prognosis.

Differential Diagnosis

The nephrotic syndrome (nephrosis) may be associated with a variety of renal diseases, including glomerulonephritis (membranous and proliferative), collagen disease (disseminated lupus erythematosus, polyarteritis, etc), amyloid disease, thrombosis of the renal vein, diabetic nephropathy, syphilis, and reaction to toxins such as bee venom. Rhus antigen, drugs such as trimethadione (Tridione®), and heavy metals. In small children, nephrosis may occur without clear evidence of any cause.

Treatment

There is no specific treatment except for syphilis or for heavy metal poisoning. Bed rest is indicated for patients with severe edema or those who have infections. Infections should be treated vigorously and promptly with appropriate antibiotics. Hospitalization is desirable if corticosteroid therapy is given. The diet should provide a normal protein ration (0.75–1 gm/kg/day), with adequate calories. Sodium intake should be restricted to 0.5–1 gm/day. Potassium need not be restricted.

Experience over the last decade has proved the value of adrenocorticosteroids in treating the nephrotic syndrome in children and in adults when the underlying disease is the minimal glomerular lesion (lipoid nephrosis), systemic lupus erythematosus, glomerulonephritis, or idiosyncrasy to toxin or venom. Corticosteroid therapy is less often efficacious in the presence of membranous disease, proliferative lesions, or mixed lesions of the glomerulus. It is of little or no value in amyloidosis or renal vein thrombosis, and is contraindicated in diabetic nephropathy.

The goals of therapy are (1) to induce diuresis, (2) to produce a protein-free urine, (3) to elevate the serum albumin to normal levels, and (4) to reduce lipidemia toward normal. With increasing experience, the trend has been toward longer courses of therapy extending well into periods of clinical remission.

Although prednisone is widely used, other corticosteroids may be employed in equivalent doses. Give prednisone (1–2 mg/kg/day for children or 80–120 mg daily for adults) in divided doses orally for 10 days to 3 or 4 weeks. If diuresis begins early in the course of treatment, the dosage of corticosteroid may be reduced slowly over a period of 3–4 weeks, seeking the smallest dose that will fulfill the goals of therapy and maintain the remission. When there is no response to corticosteroid therapy, rapid reduction of intake of corticosteroid may be followed by diuresis and improvement. If there is no response upon withdrawal of the corticosteroid, additional courses using high doses daily should be tried before concluding that the patient's disease is refractory to corticosteroids.

When diuresis is well established and proteinuria and edema are diminishing, therapy can be altered from daily to intermittent administration of corticosteroid. Alternate day therapy appears to maintain remission satisfactorily. The total dose administered for 48 hours on the daily schedule is administered orally as one dose at breakfast every other day. On this regimen there is usually no evidence of adrenal suppression; normal growth may be expected in children; and cushingoid changes and hypertension are very rare. In some instances, initiation of therapy on the 48-hour schedule has been successful.

Another form of intermittent therapy consisting of prednisone, 60 mg orally daily in divided doses on 3 consecutive days of the week, with no corticosteroid on the succeeding 4 days, has been employed extensively. Disadvantages include the high incidence of the customary side-effects of high doses of corticosteroid with signs of adrenal suppression manifest during the 4 days of rest.

At present it is considered justifiable to continue intermittent therapy for a year if the patient remains edema-free and if proteinuria is reduced to negligible amounts. If exacerbations occur, therapy can be intensified. Potassium supplements may be desirable during corticosteroid therapy, although none may be required on the alternate day schedule.

Diuretics are often ineffective. The most useful are the chlorothiazide derivatives, eg, hydrochlorothiazide, 50–100 mg every 12 hours; other chlorothiazide derivatives, chlorthalidone, or other diuretics, may be employed in comparable effective dose levels. Aldosterone antagonists may be helpful when employed concurrently with thiazides. Salt-free albumin, dextran, and other oncotic agents are of little help and their effects are transient.

Caution: Elevation of serum potassium, development of hypertension, and sudden severe increase in edema contraindicate continuation of corticosteroid therapy. Such complications usually arise during the first 2 weeks of continuous therapy.

Immunosuppressive drugs, including alkylating agents, cyclophosphamide, mercaptopurine, azathioprine (Imuran®), and others, are under trial in the treatment of the nephrotic syndrome. The use of corticosteroids plus immunosuppressive agents is similar to that employed in reversing rejection of homotransplants in man. Experience is still meager, but increasingly encouraging results have been reported in children and adults with proliferative, membranous, and mixed lesions and with systemic lupus erythematosus. Those with minimal lesions refractory to corticosteroid therapy did no better when immunosuppressive agents were added. Improvement was shown in the glomerular changes and renal function in many responding well to treatment. The incidence of improvement has not been established.

Serious side-effects related both to corticosteroids and to the cytotoxic agents were common. At present this form of therapy should be employed only by those experienced in treating the nephrotic syndrome in patients who have proved refractory to well established treatment regimens.

For renal vein thrombosis, the treatment is directed against progress of thrombus formation with heparin and long-term use of coumarin drugs.

Prognosis

The course and prognosis depend upon the basic disease responsible for the nephrotic syndrome. In about 50% of cases of childhood nephrosis, the disease appears to run a rather benign course when properly treated, and to leave insignificant sequelae. Of the others, most go inexorably into the terminal state with renal insufficiency. Adults with nephrosis fare less well, particularly when the fundamental disease is glomerulonephritis, systemic lupus erythematosus, amyloidosis, renal vein thrombosis, or diabetic nephropathy. In those with minimal lesions, remissions, either spontaneous or following corticosteroid therapy, are common. Treatment is more often unsuccessful or only ameliorative when the other glomerular lesions are present. Hypertension and nitrogen retention are serious signs.

Bhorade, M.S., & others: Nephropathy of secondary syphilis: A clinical and pathological spectrum. JAMA 216:1159—1166, 1971.

Etteldorf, J.N., & others: Cyclophosphamide in the treatment of idiopathic lipoid nephrosis. J Pediat 70:758—766, 1967.

Gresham & others: Pathology of lupus nephritis. J Mt Sinai Hosp 30:117—126, 1963.

Grupe, W.E., & W. Heymann: Cytotoxic drugs in steroid-resistant renal disease. Am J Dis Child 112:448—458, 1966.

Hamilton, C.R., Jr., & others: Renal vein thrombosis and pulmonary embolism. Johns Hopkins Med J 124:331—338, 1969.

Kark, R.M., & others: The nephrotic syndrome in adults: A common disorder with many causes. Ann Int Med 49:751—774, 1958.

McCarthy, L.J., Titus, J.L., & G.W. Daugherty: Bilateral renal-vein thrombosis and the nephrotic syndrome in adults. Ann Int Med 58:837—857, 1963.

Medical Research Council Working Party: Controlled trial of azathioprine and prednisone in chronic renal disease. Brit MJ 2:239—241, 1971.

Michael, A.F., & others: Immunosuppressive therapy of chronic renal disease. New England J Med 276:817—828, 1967.

Moncrieff, M.W., & others: Cyclophosphamide therapy in the nephrotic syndrome in childhood. Brit MJ 1:666—671, 1969.

Muehrcke, R.C., & others: Lupus nephritis: A clinical and pathological study based on renal biopsies. Medicine 36:1—145, 1957.

Pollack, V.E., Rosen, C., & C.L. Pirani: Natural history of lipoid nephrosis and of membranous glomerulonephritis. Ann Int Med 69:1171—1196, 1968.

Rosenmann, E., Pollak, V.E., & C.L. Pirani: Renal vein thrombosis in the adult: A clinical and pathological study based on renal biopsies. Medicine 42:269—335, 1968.

Soyka, L. F.: Nephrotic syndrome: Current concepts in diagnosis and therapy. Clin Pediat 6:77, 1967.

White, R.H.R., Cameron, J.S., & J.R. Trounce: Immunosuppressive therapy in steroid-resistant proliferative glomerulonephritis accompanied by the nephrotic syndrome. Brit MJ 2:853—859, 1966.

ARTERIOLAR NEPHROSCLEROSIS

Intimal thickening of the afferent arteriole of the glomerulus is the characteristic finding. Obliteration of the arteriole or severe narrowing of the lumen deprives the nephron of its blood supply and produces areas of infarction and scar formation. Obliteration of glomeruli is common. If the disease is "malignant" and rapidly progressive, points of hemorrhage are found and vascular changes, resembling an endarteritis with severe intimal thickening associated with malignant hypertension, become marked. Renal insufficiency occurs when the kidney is scarred and contracted.

The symptoms and signs are those of hypertension and renal insufficiency and, occasionally, heart failure and hypertensive encephalopathy.

Treatment is directed against hypertension and chronic renal insufficiency.

The course is progressively downhill. The patient usually succumbs to renal failure, and death is sometimes hastened by intercurrent infection.

ACUTE RENAL FAILURE

Essentials of Diagnosis

- Sudden onset of oliguria; urine volume 20—200 ml/day.
- Proteinuria and hematuria; isosthenuria with a specific gravity of 1.010—1.016.
- Anorexia, nausea and vomiting, lethargy, elevation of blood pressure. Signs of uremia.
- Progressive increase in serum BUN, creatinine, potassium, phosphate, sulfate; decrease in sodium, calcium, CO_2.
- Spontaneous recovery in a few days to 6 weeks.

General Considerations

Acute renal failure is a term applied to a state of sudden cessation of renal function following a variety of insults to normal kidneys. Among the causes of acute renal failure are the following: (1) Toxic agents, eg, carbon tetrachloride, mercury bichloride, arsenic, diethylene glycol, sulfonamides, and mushroom poisoning. (2) Traumatic shock due to severe injury, surgical shock, or myocardial infarction, and ischemia associated with surgery on the abdominal aorta. (3) Tissue destruction due to crushing injury, burns, intravascular hemolysis (transurethral resection of the prostate, incompatible blood transfusion). (4) Infectious diseases, eg, leptospirosis, hemorrhagic fever, septicemia due to gram-negative bacteria with shock. (5) Severe water and electrolyte depletion. (6) Complications of pregnancy, eg, bilateral cortical necrosis.

Return of renal function can be expected, but even with the best treatment the mortality rate is high.

Renal tubular necrosis is the characteristic finding. In some instances, after exposure to a specific toxin, the proximal tubule may be primarily damaged; and renal tubule cell disintegration and desquamation with collection of debris in the lumens of the tubules are found uniformly throughout both kidneys. In other cases, tubule cell destruction and basement membrane disruption are scattered throughout both kidneys. In cases due to hemolysis or crushing injury, heme or myoglobin casts may be present, but it is unlikely that such casts produce tubule cell destruction. The spotty distribution of the damage is consonant with alterations in blood flow which produce ischemic necrosis. In bilateral cortical necrosis, ischemic infarcts are distributed throughout both kidneys.

Clinical Findings

The cardinal sign of acute renal failure is acute reduction of urine output following injury, surgery, a transfusion reaction, or other causes listed above. The daily volume of urine may be reduced to 20–30 ml/day or may be as high as 400–500 ml/day. After a few days to 6 weeks the daily urine volume slowly increases. Anorexia, nausea, and lethargy are common symptoms. Other symptoms and signs are related to the causative agent or event.

The course of the disease may be divided into the oliguric and diuretic phases.

A. Oliguric Phase: During the oliguric phase, the urine excretion is greatly reduced. The urine contains protein, red cells, and granular casts, and the specific gravity of the urine is usually 1.010–1.016. The rate of catabolism of protein determines the rate of increase of metabolic end products in body fluids. In the presence of injury or fever, the serum BUN, creatinine, potassium, phosphate, sulfate, and organic acids increase rapidly. Typically, because of dilution and intracellular shifts, the serum sodium concentration drops to 120–130 mEq/liter with a corresponding fall in serum chloride. As organic acids and phosphate accumulate, serum bicarbonate concentration decreases. Normochromic anemia is common. With prolonged oliguria, signs of uremia appear with nausea, vomiting, diarrhea, neuromuscular irritability, convulsions, somnolence, and coma. Hypertension frequently develops and may be associated with retinopathy, left heart failure, and encephalopathy. During this phase of the disease, therapy modifies the clinical picture significantly. Overhydration produces signs of water intoxication with convulsions, edema, and the serious complication of pulmonary edema. Excess saline administration may produce edema and congestive failure. Failure to restrict potassium intake or to employ agents to remove potassium at the proper time may result in potassium intoxication. High extracellular potassium levels produce neuromuscular depression which progresses to paralysis and interference with the cardiac conduction system, resulting in arrhythmias; death may follow respiratory muscle paralysis or cardiac arrest. The ECG changes as the potassium level rises, first showing peaked T waves, then broadening of the QRS complex and lack of P waves; later, a biphasic ventricular complex; and, finally, cardiac arrest or ventricular fibrillation. With proper treatment, potassium intoxication is almost always reversible, and death should seldom occur because of it.

B. Diuretic Phase: After a few days to 6 weeks of oliguria, the diuretic phase begins, signifying that the nephrons have recovered to the point that urine excretion is possible. The urine volume usually increases in increments of a few ml to 100 ml/day until 300–500 ml/day are excreted, after which the rate of increase in flow is usually more rapid. Rarely, the urine volume increases rapidly during the first day or so of diuresis. Diuresis may be the result of impaired nephron function, with loss of water and electrolytes; but this is uncommon and true deficits of water, sodium, and potassium seldom occur. More often, diuresis represents an unloading of excess extracellular fluid which has accumulated during the oliguric phase, either as a result of overhydration during therapy or unusual metabolic production of water. Diuresis usually occurs when the total nephron function is still insufficient to excrete nitrogenous metabolic products, potassium, and phosphate, and the concentration of these constituents in the serum may continue to rise for several days after urine volumes exceed 1 liter/day. Renal function returns slowly to normal, and blood chemical findings become normal.

Differential Diagnosis

Because acute glomerulonephritis, ureteral obstruction due to edema at the ureterovesical junction following ureteral catheterization, ureteral obstruction by neoplasm, bilateral renal artery occlusion due to embolism or dissecting aneurysm, and, rarely, a ruptured bladder may present with symptoms and signs indistinguishable from those of tubular necrosis, appropriate diagnostic procedures should be employed as suggested by the history and by physical examination. Occasionally a profound state of dehydration may produce severe oliguria; rapid infusion of 500–1000 ml of 0.45% saline will restore blood volume temporarily to the point that glomerular filtration will increase and urine will be excreted.

Treatment

A. Specific Treatment: Immediate treatment of the cause of oliguria is essential.

1. Shock—Vigorous measures to restore normal blood pressure levels are mandatory in order to overcome renal ischemia. *Caution:* When it becomes apparent that tubular necrosis has occurred, the volume of fluids administered must be sharply curtailed; if vasopressor drugs are required, they must be given in the limited amount of fluid permitted.

2. Transfusion reaction—See discussion in Chapter 9.

3. Obstruction of ureters—Cystoscopy and catheterization of ureters may be necessary.

4. Heavy metal poisoning—Dimercaprol (BAL) may be of use in mercury or arsenic poisoning, although by the time the renal lesion is apparent it may be too late.

B. General Measures: The following discussion of conservative medical management often serves adequately for the uncomplicated case. If oliguria persists beyond a week or if the patient has sustained severe trauma or is in a severe "catabolic state," from infection or toxic materials, dialysis is indicated. Hemodialysis is more effective, but peritoneal dialysis may be adequate. Indications for dialysis include threatening hyperkalemia, serious electrolyte or water excess, or inability to maintain a relatively stable state with continuing oliguria.

1. Oliguric phase—The objectives of therapy are to maintain normal body fluid volume and electrolyte concentration, reduce tissue catabolism to a minimum, and prevent infection until healing occurs.

a. Bed rest—"Reverse isolation" to protect the patient from exposure to hospital infections.

b. Fluids—Restrict fluids to a basic ration of 400 ml/day for the average adult. Additional fluid may be given to replace unusual losses due to vomiting, diarrhea, sweating, etc. The metabolism of fat, carbohydrate, and protein provides water of combustion; and catabolism of tissues provides intracellular water. These sources must be included in calculations of water balance, thus leaving only a small ration to be provided as "intake" (see ¶ e, below).

c. Diet—In order to limit sources of nitrogen, potassium, phosphate, and sulfate, no protein should be given. Glucose, 100–200 gm/day, should be given to prevent ketosis and to reduce protein catabolism. Although fat may be given as butter or as an emulsion for oral or intravenous use, it is usually better to permit the patient to fulfill caloric needs from his own fat deposits.

The fluid and glucose may be given orally or intravenously. When administered intravenously as a 20–50% glucose solution, the 400 ml of fluid should be given continuously through the 24-hour period through an intravenous catheter threaded into a large vein to reduce the likelihood of thrombosis. Vitamin B complex and vitamin C should be provided.

d. Electrolyte replacement—Replace preexisting deficits. Otherwise, electrolyte therapy is not necessary unless clear-cut losses are demonstrable, as in vomiting, diarrhea, etc. *Note:* Potassium must not be administered unless proved deficits exist, and then only with caution.

e. Observations—Daily records of fluid intake and output are essential; an indwelling catheter is usually required to permit accurate measurement of urine output. Weight should be recorded daily whenever possible. Because the patient is consuming his own tissues, he should lose about 0.5 kg/day. If he fails to lose weight, he is receiving too much fluid. Frequent (often daily) measurements of serum electrolytes (especially potassium) and creatinine are essential. The ECG may be helpful in evaluating potassium levels.

f. Infection—Treat vigorously with appropriate antibiotics, bearing in mind that the drug may not be excreted. "Reverse isolation" is a useful protective measure.

g. Congestive heart failure—See discussion in Chapter 7.

h. Anemia—A hematocrit of less than 30% is an indication for cautious transfusion with a small volume of packed fresh red blood cells.

i. Potassium intoxication—See discussion in Chapter 2.

j. Uremia—The artificial kidney and peritoneal dialysis are effective, but require expert management in a well-equipped hospital. With appropriate facilities, dialysis has proved to be of great value if employed "prophylactically" when it is evident that conservative therapy is inadequate to prevent acidosis, advance of azotemia, and clinical deterioration.

k. Convulsions and encephalopathy—Give paraldehyde rectally. Barbiturates should be restricted to pentobarbital sodium or amobarbital sodium, which are metabolized by the liver. Chlorpromazine and promazine are also useful.

2. Diuretic phase—Unless water and electrolyte deficits clearly exist, no attempt should be made to "keep up" with the diuresis; collections of excess water and electrolyte are usually being excreted. Fluid and diet intake can be liberalized as diuresis progresses until a normal daily intake is reached. Protein restriction should be continued until serum BUN and creatinine levels are declining. Infection is still a hazard. Occasionally diuresis will be accompanied by sodium retention, hypernatremia, and hyperchloremia associated with confusion, neuromuscular irritability, and coma. When this happens, water and glucose must be given in sufficient quantities to correct hypernatremia. Serum electrolytes and BUN or creatinine should be measured frequently.

Prognosis

If severe complications of trauma and infection are not present, skillful treatment often will tide the patient over the period of oliguria until spontaneous healing occurs. Death may occur as a result of water intoxication, congestive heart failure, acute pulmonary edema, potassium intoxication, and encephalopathy. With recovery there is little residual impairment of renal function.

Burns, R.O., & others: Peritoneal dialysis: Clinical experience. New England J Med 267:1060–1066, 1962.

Franklin, S.S., & J.P. Merrill: Acute renal failure. New England J Med 262:711–718, 761–767, 1960.

Handa, S.P., & P.A.F. Morrin: Diagnostic indices in acute renal failure. Canad MAJ 96:78–82, 1967.

Kiley, J.E., Powers, S.R., Jr., & R.T. Beebe: Acute renal failure: Eighty cases of renal tubular necrosis. New England J Med 262:481–486, 1960.

Lewers, D.T., & others: Long-term follow-up of renal function and histology after acute tubular necrosis. Ann Int Med 73:515–521, 1970.

Maher, J.F., & G.E. Schreiner: Cause of death in acute renal failure. Arch Int Med 110:493–504, 1962.

Merrill, J.P.: Kidney disease: Acute renal failure. Advances Int Med 10:127–150, 1960.

Muehrcke, R.C.: *Acute Renal Failure: Diagnosis and Management.* Mosby, 1969.

Nienhuis, L.I.: Clinical peritoneal dialysis. Arch Surg 93:643–653, 1966.

Papper, S.: Renal failure. M Clin North America 55:335–357, 1971.

Teschan, P.E., & others: Prophylactic hemodialysis in the treatment of acute renal failure. Ann Int Med 53:992–1016, 1960.

HEREDITARY RENAL DISEASES

The importance of inheritance and the familial incidence of disease warrants inclusion of the classification of hereditary renal diseases suggested by Perkoff (see reference below). Although relatively uncommon in the population at large, hereditary disease must be recognized to permit early diagnosis and treatment in other family members and to prepare the way for genetic counseling.

Many of the renal diseases that can occur as heritable abnormalities are listed in Chapter 29 (Some Diseases With Known Modes of Inheritance). Selected diseases are discussed briefly below.

1. HEREDITARY CHRONIC NEPHRITIS

Evidence of the disease usually appears in childhood, with episodes of hematuria often following an upper respiratory infection. Renal insufficiency commonly develops in males but only rarely in females. Survival beyond the age of 40 is rare.

In many families, deafness and abnormalities of the eyes accompany the renal disease. Another form of the disease is accompanied by polyneuropathy. Infection of the urinary tract is a common complication.

The anatomic features resemble glomerulonephritis. There are often fat-filled cells (foam cells) which are either macrophages or of tubule cell origin. These occur characteristically at the corticomedullary junction.

Laboratory findings are commensurate with existing renal function.

Treatment is symptomatic.

2. CYSTIC DISEASES OF THE KIDNEY

Congenital structural anomalies of the kidney must always be considered in any patient with hypertension, pyelonephritis, or renal insufficiency. The manifestations of structural renal abnormalities are related to the superimposed disease, but management and prognosis are modified by the structural anomaly.

Polycystic Kidneys

Polycystic kidney disease is familial and often involves not only the kidney but the liver and pancreas as well.

The formation of cysts in the cortex of the kidney is thought to result from failure of union of the collecting tubules and convoluted tubules of some nephrons. New cysts do not form, but those present enlarge and, by pressure, cause destruction of adjacent tissue. Cysts may be found in the liver and pancreas.

The incidence of cerebral vessel aneurysms is higher than normal.

Cases of polycystic disease are discovered during the investigation of hypertension, by diagnostic study in patients presenting with pyelonephritis or hematuria, or by investigating the families of patients with polycystic disease. At times, flank pain due to hemorrhage into a cyst will call attention to a kidney disorder. Otherwise the symptoms and signs are those commonly seen in hypertension or renal insufficiency. On physical examination the enlarged, irregular kidneys are easily palpable.

The urine may contain leukocytes and red cells. With bleeding into the cysts there may also be bleeding into the urinary tract. The blood chemical findings reflect the degree of renal insufficiency. X-ray examination shows the enlarged kidneys, and urography demonstrates the classical elongated calyces and renal pelves stretched over the surface of the cysts.

No specific therapy is available, and surgical interference is contraindicated unless ureteral obstruction is produced by an adjacent cyst. Hypertension, infection, and uremia are treated in the conventional manner.

Although the disease may become symptomatic in childhood or early in early adult life, it usually is discovered in the 4th or 5th decades. Unless fatal complications of hypertension or urinary tract infection are present, uremia develops very slowly and patients live longer than with other causes of renal insufficiency.

Cystic Disease of the Renal Medulla

Two syndromes have been recognized with increasing frequency as their diagnostic features have become better known.

Medullary cystic disease is a familial disease which may become symptomatic during adolescence. Anemia is usually the initial manifestation, but azotemia, acidosis, and hyperphosphatemia soon become evident. Hypertension may develop. The urine is not remarkable, although there is often an inability to produce a concentrated urine. Many small cysts are scattered through the renal medulla.

Sponge kidney is asymptomatic and is discovered by the characteristic appearance of the urogram. Enlargement of the papillae and calyces and small cavities within the pyramids are demonstrated by the contrast media in the excretory urogram. Many small calculi often occupy the cysts, and infection may be troublesome. Life expectancy is not affected.

Dalgaard, O.Z.: Bilateral polycystic disease of the kidneys: A follow-up of 284 patients and their families. Acta med scandinav 158(Suppl 328), 1957.

Goldman, S.H., & others: Hereditary occurrence of cystic disease of the renal medulla. New England J Med 274:984–992, 1966.

MacDougall, J.A., & W.G. Prout: Medullary sponge kidney: Clinical appraisal and report of 12 cases. Brit J Surg 55:130–133, 1968.

Osathanondh, V., & E.L. Potter: Pathogenesis of polycystic kidneys. Arch Path 77:459–512, 1964.

Perkoff, G.T.: Hereditary renal diseases. New England J Med 277:79–85, 1967.

Strauss, M.B.: Clinical and pathological aspects of cystic disease of the renal medulla. Ann Int Med 57:373–381, 1962.

Wahlqvist, L.: Cystic disorders of kidney: Review of pathogenesis and classification. J Urol 97:1–6, 1967.

3. ANOMALIES OF THE PROXIMAL TUBULE

Defects of Amino Acid Reabsorption

A. Congenital Cystinuria: Increased excretion of cystine results in the formation of cystine calculi in the urinary tract. Ornithine, arginine, and lysine are also excreted in abnormally large quantities. Nonopaque stones should be examined chemically to provide a specific diagnosis.

Maintain a high urine volume by giving a large fluid intake. Maintain the urine pH above 7.0 by giving sodium bicarbonate and sodium citrate plus acetazolamide (Diamox®) at bedtime to ensure an alkaline night urine. In refractory cases a low-methionine (cystine precursor) diet may be necessary. Penicillamine has proved useful in some cases.

B. Aminoaciduria: Many amino acids may be poorly absorbed, resulting in unusual losses. Failure to thrive and the presence of other tubular deficits suggests the diagnosis.

There is no treatment.

C. Hepatolenticular Degeneration: In this congenital familial disease, aminoaciduria is associated with cirrhosis of the liver and neurologic manifestations. Hepatomegaly, evidence of impaired liver function, spasticity, athetosis, emotional disturbances, and Kayser-Fleischer rings around the cornea constitute a unique syndrome. There is a decrease in synthesis of ceruloplasmin with a deficit of plasma ceruloplasmin and an increase in free copper which may be etiologically specific.

Give penicillamine to chelate and remove excess copper. Edathamil (Versenate®, EDTA) may also be used to remove copper.

Multiple Defects of Tubular Function (De Toni-Fanconi-Debre Syndrome)

Aminoaciduria, phosphaturia, glycosuria, and a variable degree of renal tubular acidosis characterize this syndrome. Osteomalacia is a prominent clinical feature; other clinical and laboratory manifestations are associated with specific tubular defects described separately above.

The proximal segment of the renal tubule is replaced by a thin tubular structure constituting the "swan neck" deformity. The proximal segment also is shortened to less than half the normal length.

Treatment consists of replacing cation deficits (especially potassium), correcting acidosis with bicarbonate or citrate, replacing phosphate loss with isotonic neutral phosphate (mono- and disodium salts) solution, and a liberal calcium intake. Vitamin D may be useful.

Defects of Phosphorus & Calcium Absorption

A. Vitamin D-Resistant Rickets: Excessive loss of phosphorus and calcium result in rickets or osteomalacia which respond poorly to vitamin D therapy. Treatment consists of giving large doses of vitamin D and calcium supplementation of the diet.

B. Pseudohypoparathyroidism: As a result of excessive reabsorption of phosphorus, hyperphosphatemia and hypocalcemia occur. Symptoms include muscle cramps, fatigue, weakness, tetany, and mental retardation. The signs are those of hypocalcemia; in addition, the patients are short, round-faced, and characteristically have short 4th and 5th metacarpal and metatarsal bones. The serum phosphorus is high, serum calcium low, and serum alkaline phosphatase normal. There is no response to parathyroid hormone.

Vitamin D therapy and calcium supplementation may prevent tetany.

Defects of Glucose Absorption (Renal Glycosuria)

This results from an abnormally low ability to reabsorb glucose, so that glycosuria is present when blood glucose levels are normal. Ketosis is not present. The glucose tolerance response is usually normal. In some instances, renal glycosuria may precede the onset of true diabetes mellitus.

There is no treatment for renal glycosuria.

Defects of Glucose & Phosphate Absorption (Glycosuric Rickets)

The symptoms and signs are those of rickets or osteomalacia, with weakness, pain, or discomfort of the legs and spine, and tetany. The bones become deformed, with bowing of the weight-bearing long bones, kyphoscoliosis, and, in children, signs of rickets. X-ray shows markedly decreased density of the bone, with pseudofracture lines and other deformities. Nephrocalcinosis may occur with excessive phosphaturia, and renal insufficiency may follow. Urinary calcium and phosphorus are increased and glycosuria is present. Serum glucose is normal, serum calcium is normal or low, serum phosphorus is low, and serum alkaline phosphatase is elevated.

Treatment consists of giving large doses of vitamin D and calcium supplementation of the diet.

4. ANOMALIES OF THE DISTAL TUBULE

Defects of Hydrogen Ion Secretion & Bicarbonate Reabsorption (Renal Tubular Acidosis)

Failure to secrete hydrogen ion and to form ammonium ion results in loss of "fixed base": sodium, potassium, and calcium. There is also a high rate of excretion of phosphate. Vomiting, poor growth, and symptoms and signs of chronic metabolic acidosis are accompanied by weakness due to potassium deficit and the bone discomfort due to osteomalacia. The urine is alkaline and contains larger than normal quantities of sodium, potassium, calcium, and phosphate. Nephrocalcinosis may be present. The blood chemical findings are those of metabolic acidosis (low HCO_3^- or CO_2) with hyperchloremia, low serum calcium and phosphorus, low serum potassium, and, occasionally, low serum sodium.

Treatment consists of replacing deficits and increasing the intake of sodium potassium, calcium, and phosphorus. Sodium and potassium should be given as bicarbonate or citrate. Additional vitamin D may be required.

Excess Potassium Secretion (Potassium "Wastage" Syndrome)

Excessive renal secretion or loss of potassium may occur in 4 situations: (1) Chronic renal insufficiency with diminished H^+ secretion. (2) Renal tubular acidosis and the De Toni-Fanconi syndrome, with cation loss resulting from diminished H^+ and NH_4^+ secretion. (3) Aldosteronism and hyperadrenocorticism. (4) Tubular secretion of potassium, the cause of which is yet unknown. Hypokalemia indicates that the deficit is severe. Muscle weakness, metabolic alkalosis, and polyuria with dilute urine are signs attributable to hypokalemia.

Treatment consists of correcting the primary disease and giving supplementary potassium.

Defects of Water Absorption (Renal Diabetes Insipidus)

Nephrogenic diabetes insipidus occurs more frequently in males. Unresponsiveness to antidiuretic hormone is the key to differentiation from pituitary diabetes insipidus.

Symptoms are related to an inability to reabsorb water with resultant polyuria and polydipsia. The urine volume approaches 12 liters/day, and osmolality and specific gravity are low. Mental retardation, atonic bladder, and hydronephrosis occur frequently.

Treatment consists primarily of an adequate water intake. Chlorothiazide may ameliorate the diabetes; the mechanism of action is unknown, but the drug may act by increasing isosmotic reabsorption in the proximal segment of the tubule.

5. UNSPECIFIED RENAL TUBULAR ABNORMALITIES

In **idiopathic hypercalciuria**, decreased reabsorption of calcium predisposes to the formation of renal calculi. Serum calcium and phosphorus are normal. Urine calcium excretion is high; urine phosphorus excretion is low.

See treatment of urinary stones containing calcium.

Efron, M.L.: Aminoaciduria. New England J Med 272:1058–1067, 1107–1113, 1965.

Leading article: Renal tubular acidosis. Lancet 1:92–95, 1961.

Morris, R.C.: Renal tubular acidosis: Mechanisms, classification and implications. New England J Med 281:1405–1413, 1969.

Perkoff, G.T.: Hereditary renal diseases. New England J Med 277:79–85, 129–138, 1967.

Relman, A.S., & N.G. Levinsky: Kidney disease: Acquired tubular disorders (with special reference to disturbances of concentrations and dilution and of acid-base regulation). Ann Rev Med 12:93–110, 1961.

Stanbury, J.B., Wyngaarden, J.B., & D.S. Fredrickson: *The Metabolic Basis of Inherited Disease,* 2nd ed. Blakiston, 1966.

Wilson, D.R., & E.R. Yendt: Treatment of the adult Fanconi syndrome with oral phosphate supplements and alkali. Am J Med 35:487–511, 1963.

6. CONGENITAL ANOMALIES

Renal Agenesis

Occasionally one kidney, usually the left, is congenitally absent. The remaining kidney is hypertrophied. Before performing a nephrectomy for any reason, it is mandatory to prove the patient has a second kidney.

Horseshoe Kidney

A band of renal tissue or of fibrous tissue may join the 2 kidneys. Associated abnormalities of the ureterocalyceal system, or hydronephrosis resulting from ureteral obstruction by aberrant vessels, predispose to pyelonephritis.

Ectopic Kidney

The kidney may occupy a site in the pelvis and the ureter may be shorter than normal. Infection is common in ectopic kidneys compromised by ureteral obstruction or urinary reflux.

Nephroptosis

Unusual mobility of the kidney permits it to move from its normal position to a lower one. The incidence of ureteral occlusion due to movement of a kidney is extremely low.

Megaloureter & Hydronephrosis

These anatomic abnormalities may occur congenitally but are more commonly the result of vesicoureteral urinary reflux.

Glenn, J.F.: Analysis of 51 patients with horseshoe kidney. New England J Med 261:684–687, 1959.

ANALGESIC NEPHROPATHY

Renal papillary necrosis has usually been associated with fulminating urinary tract infection in the presence of diabetes mellitus. Since 1953, however, increasing numbers of cases have been associated with long-term ingestion of phenacetin alone or in analgesic mixtures. The typical patient is a middle-aged woman with chronic and recurrent headaches or a patient with chronic arthritis who habitually consumes large amounts of analgesic mixtures containing phenacetin. The ensuing damage to the kidneys usually is detected late, after renal insufficiency has developed.

The kidney lesion is pathologically nonspecific, consisting of peritubular and perivascular inflammation with degenerative changes of the tubule cells (chronic interstitial nephritis). There are no glomerular changes. Renal papillary necrosis extending into the medulla may involve many papillae.

Hematuria is a common presenting complaint. Renal colic occurs when necrotic renal papillae slough away. Polyuria may be prominent. Signs of acidosis (hyperpnea), dehydration, and pallor of anemia are common. Infection is a frequent complication. The history of phenacetin ingestion may be concealed by the patient.

The urine usually is remarkable only for the presence of blood and small amounts of protein. Hemolytic anemia is usually evident. Elevated BUN and creatinine and the electrolyte changes characteristic of renal failure are typically present.

Urograms show typical cavities and ring shadows of areas of destruction of papillae.

Treatment consists of withholding analgesics containing phenacetin and aspirin. Renal failure and infection are treated as outlined elsewhere in this chapter.

INFECTIONS OF THE URINARY TRACT

Urinary tract infections are so common and so serious in long-term effects that meticulous attention must be paid to the details of diagnosis and treatment. Urinary tract infection is undoubtedly the commonest cause of chronic renal disease in both sexes; it is the commonest cause of "renal hypertension" in women and a frequent cause in men. Because the chronic form of the disease is associated with few symptoms, the diagnosis is often not established until signs of renal insufficiency or hypertension appear. Resistance to treatment is remarkable, and relapses are frequent and often associated with anatomic defects.

The following clinical classification (modified from Petersdorf) provides a useful approach to the patient:

(1) Acute infection, uncomplicated.
(2) Acute infection, complicated.
    (a) Anatomic defect not demonstrable.
    (b) Anatomic defect demonstrable.

(3) Asymptomatic bacteriuria.
(4) Chronic infection.

1. ACUTE INFECTION OF THE UPPER URINARY TRACT

Essentials of Diagnosis

- Sudden onset of chills and fever with urinary frequency and urgency and burning on urination; pain and tenderness in the costovertebral angle over the kidneys.
- Headache, prostration, nausea and vomiting.
- Urine contains pus (pyuria), few to many red cells, granular and white cell casts, small to moderate amounts of protein, bacteria.
- Leukocytosis, rapid sedimentation rate. Occasionally bacteremia.

General Considerations

Acute urinary tract infections may be confined to the bladder, but more often the infection involves the ureters and kidneys as well. In many cases, anatomic defects of the genitourinary tract produce obstruction or stasis which favor invasion and persistence of pathogenic organisms. The organisms most frequently found are the gram-negative bacilli, ie, *Escherichia coli, Enterobacter (Aerobacter) aerogenes,* Paracolon species, *Pseudomonas aeruginosa, Proteus vulgaris,* and salmonellae; and the gram-positive cocci, ie, streptococci (enterococci) and staphylococci. In acute urinary tract infections the causative organism is present in great numbers, ranging from 10,000 to hundreds of millions of bacteria per milliliter of urine.

Predisposing factors are of importance. In young people infection is much more frequently encountered in the female; in the older age groups, infection is more common in the male since urinary tract obstruction is more frequent. Pregnancy, diabetes mellitus, papillary necrosis, metabolic disorders with nephrolithiasis, obstructive uropathy, neurogenic bladder, and genitourinary instrumentation are all associated with a high incidence of urinary tract infection.

Pathologic examination shows inflammation of the bladder, ureters, and kidney pelvis, with edema, intense capillary congestion, patchy ulceration, and submucosal hemorrhage in the more severe cases. On section the kidney shows linear streaks of yellow, which represent purulent involvement of the tubules and interstitial tissues of the pyramids and medulla, often extending into the cortex. Microscopically, interstitial tissue suppuration with patchy necrosis and pus-filled tubules are prominent. Although the glomeruli are not directly involved, interstitial inflammation around the glomeruli may be intense.

Differential Diagnosis

Acute infection involving the upper urinary tract must be differentiated from other acute causes of abdominal pain as well as from basal pneumonia. Acute pancreatitis must also be considered. The presence of pus and bacteria in the urine will usually confirm the diagnosis.

Clinical Findings

A. Symptoms and Signs: Symptoms are those of acute infection, with chills, fever, prostration, and headache. Local urinary tract symptoms include urinary urgency and frequency, dysuria, tenesmus, pain and tenderness in the flanks over the kidneys, and backache. Nausea, vomiting, and occasionally diarrhea are common. There may be no signs of infection other than dysuria and frequency. Physical examination usually reveals little except tenderness over the kidneys and the signs of fever and prostration.

B. Laboratory Findings: The white count is usually 14,000–20,000/cu mm, with an increase of polymorphonuclear neutrophils (including band forms). The sedimentation rate is very rapid. The urine contains large numbers of polymorphonuclear leukocytes, granular and leukocyte casts, some red cells and epithelial cells, shreds of mucus, protein, and at times acetone.

Cultures of the urine reveal multitudes of bacteria; blood cultures are occasionally positive as well. Examination of the urine is extremely important, for only if the organism is identified can therapy be properly directed. A gram-stained smear of the sediment obtained from 5–10 ml of urine will show identifiable bacteria when these are present in concentrations of 10,000 or more per ml of urine. Urine cultures should be performed either on fresh catheterized specimens or on fresh midstream specimens after proper cleansing of the urethral meatus and, in the female, exclusion of labial and vaginal contamination. Percutaneous aspiration of urine from the bladder, using a sterile needle and syringe and strict aseptic technic, has the advantage of avoiding the hazards of catheterization but involves the more serious risk of puncture of the peritoneum or gut unless the procedure is performed carefully by or under the supervision of a physician skilled in the technic. The procedure is not indicated in known urinary tract infection and should not be attempted in any condition in which abdominal puncture may be dangerous or difficult. For accurate quantitative cultures, the urine must be cultured promptly; specimens permitted to remain at room temperature for more than 1 hour or in the refrigerator for longer than 24 hours are not suitable. Quantitative cultures should be done with 0.1 ml of undiluted urine and 0.1 ml of 1:100 dilution. Each colony on the plate inoculated with the undiluted urine represents 10 bacteria per ml; and each colony on the plate inoculated with the 1:100 dilution represents 1000 bacteria per ml. Higher dilutions may be cultured if counts over 100,000 are expected. If bacteria are seen on a gram-stained smear or if the quantitative culture exceeds ·10,000 organisms per ml of urine, the diagnosis of urinary tract infection is confirmed. Counts of 1000 or less can be considered to represent contamination; counts between 1000 and 10,000 are indeterminate, although urinary tract infection is unlikely in these instances.

Treatment

A. Specific Measures: Give specific antimicrobial drugs chosen on the basis of cultures and sensitivity tests. The sulfonamides, penicillins, nitrofurantoin, and the tetracyclines should be employed in doses sufficient to produce adequate levels in the renal tissues and urine. Chloramphenicol, the colistins, neomycin, and polymyxin should be reserved for cases refractory to other agents.

In the uncomplicated case of the initial attack of urinary tract infection in the female, treatment with the appropriate antibiotic for 10 days will usually produce a cure. Cultures should be repeated at 2 weeks and 3 months after therapy has ceased to prove the absence of infection.

In the case of recurrence or reinfection in females and in all cases of infection in males, complicating or predisposing anatomic defects or obstruction must be ruled out. When the acute phase has passed, diagnostic studies should be undertaken to demonstrate any anatomic or metabolic defect: x-ray of the abdomen, urograms, cystoscopy, ureteral urine culture, and cystograms and cystourethrograms to determine reflux of urine into the ureters; and appropriate tests for coexisting metabolic disease such as diabetes mellitus.

Anatomic abnormalities which cause obstruction, stasis, or reflux should be corrected if possible, for their persistence precludes permanent cure.

B. General Measures: Place the patient at bed rest on a regular diet as tolerated and force fluids to maintain a high urine output. Intravenous administration of fluids is often required. Give antipyretics and analgesics as indicated. Treat associated disease such as diabetes mellitus.

Prognosis

In the absence of anatomic defects of the urinary tract, appropriate antimicrobial therapy will usually result in cure. Recurrent or continued infection produces renal damage with ultimate development of renal insufficiency or hypertension.

See references under Chronic Infection of the Urinary Tract, below.

2. CHRONIC INFECTION OF THE URINARY TRACT

Essentials of Diagnosis

- Asymptomatic except for exacerbations of symptoms of acute urinary tract infection.

TABLE 15–1. Anti-infective agents for urinary tract infections.
(Modified after Petersdorf, R.: Hospital Practice 2:68, 1967.)

Organism	Acute Infection	Chronic Bacteriuria*	Bacteremia*
Escherichia coli	Sulfonamides, ampicillin, penicillin G, tetracyclines, nitrofurantoin, cephalosporins†	Ampicillin, penicillin G, cephalosporins,† nitrofurantoin, nalidixic acid	Ampicillin, cephalosporins,† kanamycin,‡§ gentamicin§
Enterobacter (Aerobacter)	Tetracyclines, nalidixic acid, chloramphenicol**	Tetracyclines, nalidixic acid	Kanamycin,‡§ gentamicin§
Klebsiella	Tetracyclines, nalidixic acid, cephalosporins,† chloramphenicol**	Tetracyclines, nalidixic acid, cephalosporins†	Cephalosporins,† kanamycin,‡§ gentamicin§
Proteus vulgaris and *P morganii*		Nitrofurantoin, tetracyclines, nalidixic acid, chloramphenicol**	Kanamycin,‡§ carbenicillin, gentamicin§
Proteus mirabilis	Ampicillin, penicillin G, cephalosporins†	Ampicillin, penicillin G, nitrofurantoin, cephalosporins,† nalidixic acid	Ampicillin, cephalosporins,†, kanamycin,‡§ gentamicin§
Pseudomonas		Tetracyclines, polymyxin B,‡ colistin‡	Polymyxin B,‡ colistin,‡ carbenicillin, gentamicin§
Enterococci	Ampicillin, tetracyclines	Ampicillin	Ampicillin

*Sensitivity tests required.
†Cephalosporins: oral, cephaloglycine and cephalexin; IM or IV, cephalothin and cephaloridine.
‡Nephrotoxic. Use cautiously in presence of impaired renal function.
§Eighth nerve toxicity. Use cautiously in presence of renal failure.
**To be used only if other agents fail and if sensitivity tests and clinical circumstances warrant.

- End stages of chronic infection are characterized by symptoms and signs of renal insufficiency, uremia, and hypertension.
- Urine may be unremarkable or may contain leukocytes, bacteria, and protein.

General Considerations

Chronic infection is often unsuspected unless a history of urinary tract infection or of unexplained and peculiar gastrointestinal symptoms is elicited. When hypertension is present the possibility of long-standing asymptomatic infection must always be entertained, since the disease is often unilateral and nephrectomy may be curative if the function of the other kidney is normal. Before renal insufficiency develops, proper treatment may delay or prevent the serious sequelae of continuing infection.

Because of variations in the degree of involvement, one kidney may be larger than the other. Severely damaged kidneys are greatly "contracted," and may consist mostly of scar tissue and remnants of renal tissue enclosed in a thickened capsule. Areas of chronic or acute interstitial inflammation may be present. Terminally the clinical features are indistinguishable from the end stage of glomerulonephritis or nephrosclerosis.

Clinical Findings

There are none unless clear-cut exacerbations of more acute urinary tract infection occur. The late manifestations are those of renal insufficiency or of hypertension.

Treatment

(See also the discussions of acute infection, uremia, and hypertension.)

Treatment of patients with chronic bacteriuria who have had bacteriologic relapses with upper urinary tract involvement must be vigorous and of extended duration. Often a 10- to 14-day course of therapy is inadequate. The drug used must be selected on the basis of culture and sensitivity tests, with preference for oral agents. Treatment should continue for 2–6 weeks. (All agents must be employed with caution in the presence of renal insufficiency.)

A thorough investigation is required to rule out obstruction, stone, anatomic defects, and neuromuscular defects. Urograms, cystoscopy, ureteral catheterization, cystograms, and voiding cystourethrography may be employed to delineate defects responsible for intractable infection. Surgical correction of anatomic abnormalities or relief of obstruction may improve the chances for cure.

Prognosis

Unless the infection is eradicated, one or both kidneys will be damaged so severely that irremediable hypertension or renal insufficiency will result. However, the course of the disease may be protracted over many years, and with careful management these patients may lead a reasonably comfortable life even when renal "reserve" is limited.

Allen, T.D.: Pathogenesis of urinary-tract infections in children. New England J Med 273:1472–1476, 1965.

Katz, Y.J., & S.R. Bourdo: Chronic pyelonephritis. Ann Rev Med 13:481–496, 1962.

Kleeman, C.R., Hewitt, W.L., & L.B. Guze: Pyelonephritis. Medicine 39:3–116, 1960.

Kunin, C.M., & R.C. McCormack: Prevention of catheter-induced urinary-tract infections. New England J Med 274:1155–1161, 1966.

Leadbetter, G.W., Jr.: Urinary tract infection and obstruction in children. Clin Pediat 5:377–384, 1966.

McCabe, W.R., & G.G. Jackson: Treatment of pyelonephritis. New England J Med 272:1037–1044, 1965.

Seneca, H., & P. Peer: Drug susceptibility of pathogens of urinary system: Changing patterns. Surgery 60:652–667, 1966.

Smith, D.R.: *General Urology,* 6th ed. Lange, 1969.

Smith, L.H., & W.J. Martin: Infections of the urinary tract. M Clin North America 50:1127–1136, 1966.

Turck, M., Anderson, K.N., & R.G. Petersdorf: Relapse and reinfection in chronic bacteriuria. New England J Med 275:70–73, 1966.

LOWER URINARY TRACT INFECTION

Because the urinary tract is a continuous duct with relatively ineffective separation of the ureterocalyceal system from the urinary bladder, it is hazardous to assume that an isolated infection of the bladder exists.

The principles of diagnosis and management of urinary tract infection stated above apply to the so-called lower urinary tract infections or cystitis also. Anatomic and neurogenic defects and metabolic diseases such as diabetes mellitus and those conducive to stone formation must be searched for and corrected. Cystitis with overt hematuria (hemorrhagic cystitis) requires hospital care, for bleeding may be severe. Cultures must be made and suitable antimicrobial agents employed.

It is important to remember that a urinary tract infection is not an infection in the urine alone but in the tissues of the urinary tract as well.

TUBERCULOSIS OF THE URINARY TRACT

Essentials of Diagnosis

- Early symptoms usually include burning on urination, frequency, and nocturia.
- Malaise, fatigability, fever, night sweats.
- Urine contains "pus without organisms" on a Gram or methylene blue stain, red cells, and usually protein.
- Culture or guinea pig inoculation confirms the presence of *Mycobacterium tuberculosis.*
- Urograms show "moth-eaten" appearance of calyces, abscess cavities, and varying degrees of kidney destruction.
- Cystoscopy may reveal ulcers and granulomas on the bladder wall. Biopsy may aid in diagnosis.

General Considerations

Hematogenous dissemination of tubercle bacilli from foci in the lung or lymph nodes is the usual source of tuberculosis of the kidney; rarely does the infection originate in the genital tract. The genital organs may become infected by hematogenous spread or secondary to kidney infection. The prostate, seminal vesicles, epididymides, and, rarely, the testes may be infected. The fallopian tubes are more frequently involved than the ovaries and uterus.

The kidney and ureter may show little gross change. Caseous nodules in the renal parenchyma and abscess formation with destruction of tissue and fibrosis often produce extensive damage. Calcification in the lesions is common. The ureter and calyces are thickened, and stenosis may occur with total destruction of functioning renal tissue above. The bladder shows mucosal inflammation and submucosal tubercles which become necrotic and form ulcers. Fibrosis of the bladder wall occurs late or upon healing. Tubercles with caseous necrosis and calcification are found in the genital organs. Microscopically, typical tubercles are found, and demonstration of the tubercle bacilli in the lesions is usually easily accomplished.

The search for tuberculosis elsewhere in the body must be complete whenever urinary tract tuberculosis is found.

Clinical Findings

A. Symptoms and Signs: Symptoms are not characteristic or specific. Manifestations of chronic infection with malaise, fever, fatigability, and night sweats may be present. Kidney and ureter infection is usually silent. Bladder infection produces frequency, burning on urination, nocturia, and, occasionally, tenesmus. If bleeding occurs with clot formation, ureteral or vesical colic may occur. Gross hematuria is fairly common. Genital involvement becomes apparent as enlargement of the epididymis occurs or as a sinus tract forms. Induration or nodularity of the prostate and thickening of the seminal vesicles indicate infection.

Examination may reveal only costovertebral angle tenderness and the alterations in the genital tract organs available to palpation.

B. Laboratory Findings: The urine contains "pus without bacteria," red cells, and usually protein. Culture for tubercle bacilli and guinea pig inoculation confirm the diagnosis. If renal damage is extensive, signs of renal insufficiency can be demonstrated: elevated BUN or NPN and serum electrolyte abnormalities characteristic of uremia. A mild anemia usually is present, and the sedimentation rate is rapid.

C. X-Ray and Cystoscopic Findings: Excretory urograms will reveal the moth-eaten appearance of the involved calyces or the obliteration of calyces, stenosis of calyces, abscess cavities, ureteral thickening and stenosis, and the nonfunctioning kidney (autonephrectomy). Calcification of involved tissues is common. Thorough cystoscopic examination is required to determine the extent of bladder wall infection and to provide biopsy material if needed. Culture of urine obtained from ureteral catheters will help establish whether one or both kidneys are affected.

Differential Diagnosis

The "sterile" pyuria of chronic pyelonephritis and chronic nonspecific urethritis and cystitis may mimic tuberculous infection. Culture should serve to distinguish tuberculosis from these.

Treatment

A. Medical Treatment: If renal infection is unilateral but gross necrosis is not evident, or if renal infection is bilateral, place the patient at bed rest and give antituberculosis therapy. Specific antimicrobial therapy includes 3 agents:

1. Aminosalicylic acid (PAS) as the sodium salt 3–4 times daily for a total dose of 12–15 gm or, alternatively, a single daily dose of 7 gm after a full meal. If sodium restriction is required, the calcium or potassium salt may be used.

2. Isoniazid (INH), 5–10 mg/kg orally daily. The average dose is about 300 mg/day. INH may be given as a single daily dose.

3. Streptomycin, 1 gm IM twice a week.

Toxicity is relatively common and the patient must be watched carefully for dermatitis and fever (PAS), peripheral neuritis (INH), and vertigo and deafness (streptomycin). INH-induced vitamin B_6 depletion which results in peripheral neuropathy may be prevented by giving pyridoxine, 50 mg twice daily.

Cycloserine, 250 mg orally twice daily, has recently been employed as a substitute for streptomycin. Ethambutol is an effective alternative drug in patients who cannot tolerate aminosalicylic acid.

In the presence of renal insufficiency, the dose of INH and streptomycin must be reduced.

B. Surgical Plus Medical Treatment: If renal infection is unilateral and the involved kidney is severely damaged, with areas of necrosis, or if stenosis of the calyces or ureter is present, combined medical treatment (as above) plus nephrectomy is indicated. If one kidney is severely involved by a caseous hydronephrosis or is bleeding severely, nephrectomy (and medical therapy) may be necessary even though the other kidney is infected.

Combined therapy may be required also for advanced genital organ or vesical tuberculosis.

Prognosis

The prognosis varies with the extent of renal involvement and damage to renal function. Antimicrobial therapy has improved the outlook remarkably. Anatomic defects resulting from scar and healing or from stenosis of the ureter with hydronephrosis may delay or preclude cure.

Vesical or genital tuberculosis responds less well than does uncomplicated renal infection.

Cohen, A.C.: *The Drug Treatment of Tuberculosis.* Thomas, 1966.

Gorgis, A.S., & J.K. Lattimer: The chemotherapy of genitourinary tuberculosis with regimens using cycloserine. J Urol 89:9–12, 1962.
Lattimer, J.K., & R.J. Kohen: Renal tuberculosis. Am J Med 17:533–539, 1954.
Mitchell, R.S.: Control of tuberculosis. New England J Med 276:842–848, 905–911, 1967.

PROSTATITIS

Acute

Acute prostatitis may represent an exacerbation of chronic prostatitis (perhaps due to instrumentation) or may occur as a result of hematogenous infection from a distant source or local extension of a urethral infection. Urinary tract infection and urinary retention often occur with acute prostatitis. The pathologic changes are those characteristic of infection and inflammation, occasionally with abscess formation.

The manifestations are those of infection and local inflammation. Characteristic symptoms are low-grade to high fever, low back or perineal pain, and urinary bladder irritability with dysuria, frequency, nocturia, urgency, and, at times, inability to void because of urethral obstruction. The physical finding of an exquisitely tender, swollen prostate gland confirms the diagnosis. Variable leukocytosis, pyuria, bacteriuria, and often a purulent urethral discharge are present. Smear and culture of the urethral discharge is required to identify the specific organism.

Acute prostatitis must be differentiated from urinary tract infection.

Antibiotics should be selected on the basis of cultures and sensitivity tests. Instrumentation of the urethra is contraindicated. Drainage of an abscess requires perineal exposure of the gland. Bed rest is essential. Analgesics, sitz baths, and bladder sedatives should be given as necessary for discomfort. A high fluid intake is helpful.

Acute prostatic infection is usually readily controlled with appropriate antibiotics. Inadequate treatment may result in a chronic residual infection.

Chronic

Chronic prostatitis may persist after an acute infection has subsided. The gland usually feels normal, but it may be firmer than normal as fibrosis takes the place of inflamed tissue. The ducts contain pus and the ductal mucosa degenerates. Seminal vesical inflammation and, in a few cases, epididymitis are present.

Although chronic prostatitis is usually asymptomatic, there may be complaints of fullness and pain in the perineum or low back. Urethral discharge may occur. Symptoms of cystitis, epididymitis, or partial urethral obstruction may be present. The prostate usually feels normal, but it may be enlarged and boggy, with indurated areas. Crepitation may be elicited on palpation if stones are present. The prostatic and seminal fluid will be purulent. The urethral discharge will reveal the offending bacterial organism or trichomonads. Careful examination of the prostatic secretion is important. Calcium stones of the prostate may be seen on x-ray.

Antibiotic therapy with appropriate agents should be employed, particularly to eradicate secondary cystitis. Prostatic massage may be helpful and should be repeated every 1–3 weeks. Vigorous therapy of epididymitis or complicating urinary tract infection is mandatory. Urethral obstruction, epididymitis, and urinary tract infection are serious complications. Otherwise, chronic prostatitis is not likely to be harmful, but eradication of infection should be attempted to prevent complications which, in turn, sustain chronic disease.

Gonder, M.J.: Prostatitis. S Clin North America 45:1449–1454, 1965.

URINARY STONES

Urinary stones and calcification in the kidney may be associated with metabolic disease, may be secondary to infection in the urinary tract, may occur in sponge kidney, tuberculosis of the kidney, or papillary necrosis, or may be idiopathic. The incidence of urinary tract calculus is higher in men.

NEPHROCALCINOSIS

Essentials of Diagnosis
- Asymptomatic, or symptoms of primary disease producing hypercalciuria.
- Physical signs of the primary disease.
- Anemia is common.
- Blood chemical findings of primary disease plus variable degrees of renal insufficiency.

General Considerations
Chronic hypercalciuria and hyperphosphaturia may result in precipitation of calcium salts in the renal parenchyma. The commonest causes are hyperparathyroidism, hypervitaminosis D (particularly with associated high-calcium intake), and excess calcium and alkali intake. Chronic pyelonephritis predisposes to nephrocalcinosis. Other causes include acute osteoporosis following immobilization, sarcoidosis, renal tubular acidosis, the De Toni-Fanconi syndrome, and destruction of bone by metastatic carcinoma.

Clinical Findings
The symptoms, signs, and laboratory findings are those of the primary disease. The diagnosis is usually established by x-ray demonstration of calcium deposits in the kidney, which appear as minute calcific densities with linear streaks in the region of the renal papillae. True renal stones may be present as well.

Differential Diagnosis
Differentiate from renal calculi, renal tuberculosis, and medullary sponge kidney.

Treatment
Specific treatment is directed at the primary disorder. Particular attention is directed to treatment of urinary tract infection and renal insufficiency. When renal tubular acidosis or the De Toni-Fanconi defect is present, it is essential to maintain a high fluid intake, to replace cation deficit, and to alkalinize the urine with sodium bicarbonate, 1–1.5 mEq/kg/day in 3 divided doses, or with Shohl's solution (hydrated crystalline sodium citrate, 98 gm, and citric acid, 140 gm, in 1000 ml water). One ml of Shohl's solution equals 1 mEq of bicarbonate. Give 50–150 ml/day in 3 divided doses. Potassium supplements may be required and can be given as 50% potassium citrate solution (4 ml 3 times daily provides approximately 50 mEq/day). Even with adequate treatment, the prognosis is poor.

McMillan, D.E., & R.B. Freeman: The milk-alkali syndrome: A study of the acute disorder with comments on the development of the chronic condition. Medicine 44:485–502, 1965.
Mortensen, J.D., & A.H. Baggenstoss: Nephrocalcinosis: A review. Am J Clin Path 24:45–63, 1954.
Mortensen, J.D., & J.L. Emmett: Nephrocalcinosis: A collective and clinicopathologic study. J Urol 71:398–406, 1954.
Rodriquez-Soriano, J., & C.M. Edelmann, Jr.: Renal tubular acidosis. Ann Rev Med 20:363–382, 1969.
Seldin, D.W., & I.O. Wilson: Renal tubular acidosis. In: Metabolic Basis of Inherited Disease, 2nd ed. McGraw-Hill, 1966.

RENAL STONE

Essentials of Diagnosis
- Often asymptomatic.
- Symptoms of obstruction of calyx or ureteropelvic junction, with flank pain and colic.
- Nausea, vomiting, abdominal distention.
- Hematuria.
- Chills and fever and bladder irritability if infection is present.

Etiology
A. **Excessive Excretion of Relatively Insoluble Urinary Constituents:**
  1. **Calcium—**
    a. With hypercalcemia and hypercalciuria—
      (1) Primary hyperparathyroidism produces increased excretion of calcium

and phosphate in the urine. Serum calcium is high and serum phosphorus low.

    (2) High vitamin D intake increases dietary calcium absorption, which increases the load of calcium excreted by the kidney.

    (3) Excessive intake of milk and alkali.

    (4) Prolonged immobilization (due to spinal cord injury, poliomyelitis, fractures).

    (5) Destructive bone disease from neoplasm or metabolic origin (Cushing's syndrome).

  b. With hypercalciuria but normal or low serum calcium—

    (1) Idiopathic hypercalciuria.

    (2) Renal tubular acidosis is associated with inability to conserve cations, including calcium.

  2. **Oxalate**—About half of urinary stones are composed of calcium oxalate.

    a. High oxalate intake (cabbage, spinach, tomatoes, rhubarb, chocolate).

    b. Congenital or familial oxaluria.

  3. **Cystine**—Hereditary cystinuria.

  4. **Uric acid**—

    a. Gout—Stone may form spontaneously or due to treatment with uricosuric agents.

    b. Therapy of neoplastic disease with agents which cause rapid tissue breakdown, resulting in increased excretion of uric acid.

    c. Myeloproliferative disease such as leukemia, myeloid metaplasia, polycythemia vera.

B. Physical Changes in the Urine:

  1. Increased concentration of urinary constituents when fluid intake is low.

  2. Urinary pH—Inorganic salts are ordinarily less soluble at high pH. Organic substances are least soluble at low pH.

C. Nucleus (Nidus) for Stone Formation:

  1. Organic material, particularly bits of necrotic tissue or blood clot, may serve as a nucleus for stone formation.

  2. Clumps of bacteria, particularly when infection is accompanied by stasis or obstruction.

D. Congenital or Acquired Deformities of the Kidneys:

  1. Sponge kidney.

  2. Horseshoe kidney.

  3. Local obstruction of calyceal system.

General Considerations

The location and size of the stone and the presence or absence of obstruction determine the changes which occur in the kidney and calcyceal system. The pathologic changes may be modified by ischemia due to pressure or by infection.

Clinical Findings

A. Symptoms and Signs: Often a stone trapped in a calyx or in the renal pelvis is asymptomatic. If a stone produces obstruction in a calyx or at the ureteropelvic junction, dull flank pain or even colic may occur. Hematuria and symptoms of accompanying infection may be present. Nausea and vomiting may suggest enteric disease. Flank tenderness and abdominal distention may be the only physical findings.

B. Laboratory Findings: Leukocytosis may be present if there is an infection. The urine may contain red cells, white cells, and protein; pus and bacteria occur with infection. Crystals in the urine may provide a clue to the type of stone, eg, uric acid or cystine. Chemical abnormalities in the blood and urine will confirm the diagnosis of the primary metabolic disease (eg, hyperparathyroidism, gout, cystinuria, renal tubular acidosis).

C. X-Ray Findings: The x-ray examination will reveal radiopaque stones, delineate kidney size, demonstrate bone lesions of parathyroid disease, gout, and metastatic neoplasm. Excretory and retrograde urograms help to delineate the site and degree of obstruction and to confirm the presence of nonopaque stones (uric acid, cystine).

Differential Diagnosis

Differentiate from acute pyelonephritis, renal tumor, renal tuberculosis, and infarction of the kidney.

Complications

Infection and hydronephrosis are complications which may destroy renal tissue.

Prevention of Further Stone Formation

Obtain a stone for analysis whenever possible.

Treat predisposing disease, eg, surgical removal of parathyroid tumor or hyperplastic parathyroid glands; treat gout, cystinuria, and renal tubular acidosis as indicated.

For calcium phosphate and calcium oxalate stones (excluding those associated with renal tubular acidosis), inorganic orthophosphate has proved useful. Give potassium acid phosphate (K-Phos®), 6 gm daily divided into 3–4 doses before meals and at bedtime. If gastrointestinal irritability results from the acid phosphate, give a mixture of monobasic and dibasic phosphate (Neutra-Phos®), available as a powder 2¼ oz of which is added to 1 gallon of warm water. The usual dose is 12–15 oz of solution per day, divided into 3–4 doses.

A high fluid intake throughout the 24 hours to produce 3–4 liters of urine a day is important. This program is aimed at prevention of new stone formation and must be maintained indefinitely. It may be used in hyperparathyroidism while awaiting surgical attack on the parathyroid.

Prevention of uric acid stones by inhibiting the formation of uric acid is now possible. A xanthine oxidase inhibitor, allopurinol, blocks the conversion of xanthine to uric acid, permitting the excretion of purine catabolic products such as xanthine, hypoxanthine, and uric acid, the solubilities of which are independent. Thus, in all situations in which urinary uric acid is increased, allopurinol is useful.

The usual adult dose of allopurinol (Zyloprim®) is 600 mg/day (300 mg every 12 hours). This will reduce elevated serum uric acid to normal levels and markedly reduce the excretion of uric acid. It is even effective in the presence of renal failure associated with gouty nephropathy. The drug is well tolerated and apparently produces no alteration of renal function. Treatment should be continued indefinitely in patients with gout (see Chapter 13) or myeloproliferative disorders. Allopurinol may be used in association with antileukemia and anticancer agents.

While the allopurinol effect is developing, treatment should include a high fluid intake and alkalinization of the urine with sodium bicarbonate, 10–12 gm/day in divided doses.

Cystine stone formation can be reduced by forcing fluids to produce a urine output of 3–4 liters/day and alkalinizing the urine with sodium bicarbonate, 10-12 gm daily, or sodium citrate, 50% solution, 4–8 ml 4 times daily or oftener. Urine pH should be maintained at 7.5 or higher, at which levels cystine solubility is greatly increased.

A low methionine diet may help, but protein deprivation must be avoided.

Patients with severe cystinuria may require penicillamine, which complexes cysteine and reduces the total excretion of cystine. There are many side-effects which appear to be dose related.

Treatment

Small stones may be passed. They do no harm if infection is not present. Larger stones may require surgical removal if obstruction is present or renal function threatened. Nephrectomy may be necessary.

Force fluids to maintain a dilute urine and restrict calcium intake.

Combat infection with appropriate antibiotics.

Prognosis

If obstruction can be prevented and infection eradicated, the prognosis is good.

URETERAL STONE

Essentials of Diagnosis

- Obstruction of ureter produces severe colic with radiation of pain to regions determined by position of the stone in the ureter.
- Gastrointestinal symptoms common.
- Urine usually contains fresh red cells.
- May be asymptomatic.
- Exacerbations of infection when obstruction occurs.

General Considerations

Ureteral stones are formed in the kidney but produce symptoms as they pass down the ureter.

Clinical Findings

A. Symptoms and Signs: The pain of ureteral colic is intense. The patient may be in mild shock, with cold, moist skin. There is marked tenderness in the costovertebral angle. Abdominal and back muscle spasm may be present. Referred areas of hyperesthesia may be demonstrated.

B. Laboratory Findings: As for renal stone.

C. X-Ray and Instrumental Examination: X-rays may show the stone lodged in the ureter or at the ureterovesical junction. Nonopaque stones can be demonstrated by excretory urograms, which reveal the site of obstruction and the dilated ureteropelvic system above it. Because of the danger of infection, cystoscopy and ureteral catheterization should be avoided unless retrograde urography is essential.

Differential Diagnosis

Differentiate from clots due to hemorrhage, from tumor, acute pyelonephritis, and acute cholecystitis.

Prevention

As for renal stone.

Treatment

A. Specific Measures: Most stones will pass spontaneously if spasm of the ureter is relieved and fluids are forced. Surgical removal by cystoscopy or cystotomy may be necessary if the stone is large or if infection is present which does not respond readily to treatment.

B. General Measures: Morphine or other opiates should be given in doses adequate to control pain. Morphine sulfate, 8 mg (or equivalent dosage of other drugs), may be given IV and repeated in 5–10 minutes if necessary. Thereafter, subcutaneous administration is usually adequate. Atropine sulfate, 0.8 mg subcut, or methantheline bromide (Banthine®), 0.1 gm IV, may be used as antispasmodics.

Prognosis

If obstruction and infection can be treated successfully, the outlook is excellent.

VESICAL STONE

Essentials of Diagnosis

- Bladder irritability with dysuria, urgency, and frequency.
- Interruption of urinary stream as stone occludes urethra.
- Hematuria.
- Pyuria.

General Considerations

Vesical stones occur most commonly when there is residual urine infected with urea-splitting organisms (eg, proteus, staphylococci). Thus, bladder stones are associated with urinary stasis due to bladder neck or urethral obstruction, diverticula, neurogenic bladder, and cystocele. Foreign bodies in the bladder act as foci for stone formation. Ulceration and bladder inflammation predispose to stone formation.

Most vesical stones are composed of calcium phosphate, calcium oxalate, or ammonium magnesium phosphate. Uric acid stones are common in the presence of an enlarged prostate and uninfected urine.

Clinical Findings

A. Symptoms and Signs: Symptoms of chronic urinary obstruction or stasis and infection are usually present. Dysuria, frequency and urgency, and interruption of the urinary stream (causing pain in the penis) when the stone occludes the urethra are common complaints. Physical findings include prostatic enlargement, evidence of distended (neurogenic) bladder, a cystocele. Occasionally the stone may be palpable.

B. Laboratory Findings: The urine usually shows signs of infection and contains red cells.

C. X-Ray and Cystoscopic Examination: X-ray examination shows the calcified stone, and urograms show the bladder abnormalities and upper urinary tract dilatation due to long-standing back pressure. Direct cystoscopic examination may be necessary for final diagnosis.

Differential Diagnosis

Differentiate from pedunculated vesical tumor.

Treatment

A. Specific Measures: Surgical removal of the stone is indicated, either by transurethral manipulation or cystotomy. Any prostatic or urethral obstruction must be eliminated.

B. General Measures: Give analgesics as required and treat infection with appropriate antibiotics. Anti-infective measures are usually of little value until stone is removed and obstruction is relieved.

Prognosis

If obstruction and infection can be prevented, the prognosis is excellent.

Earll, J.M., & F.O. Kolb: Treatment of cystinuria and cystine stone disease. Mod Treat 4:539–549, 1967.

Elliot, J.S.: Urinary calculus disease. S Clin North America 45:1393–1404, 1965.

Gershoff, S.N.: The formation of urinary stones. Metabolism 13:375–387, 1964.

Hockaday, T.D.R., & L.H. Smith, Jr.: Renal calculi. Disease-A-Month, November 1963.

Levinson, M.P., & J.F. Cooper: Urological findings in 58 surgically verified cases of parathyroid adenoma. J Urol 96:1–5, 1966.

Maurice, P.F., & P.H. Henneman: Medical aspects of renal stones. Medicine 40:315–346, 1961.

Silberman, H.R.: A new approach to the treatment of uric acid stones. Mod Treat 4:531–538, 1967.

Smith, L.H. (editor): Symposium on stones. Am J Med 45:649–783, 1968.

Thomas, W.C., Jr., & G.H. Miller, Jr.: Inorganic phosphate in the treatment of renal calculi. Mod Treat 4:494–504, 1967.

TUMORS OF THE GENITOURINARY TRACT

ADENOCARCINOMA OF KIDNEY
(Hypernephroma)

Essentials of Diagnosis

- Painless gross hematuria.
- Fever.
- Enlarged kidney may be palpable.
- Evidence of metastases.

General Considerations

The commonest malignant tumor of the kidney is adenocarcinoma, which occurs more frequently in males. This tumor metastasizes early to the lungs, liver, and long bones.

Adenocarcinoma of the kidney apparently arises from renal tubule cells or adenomas. It invades blood vessels early. Microscopically the cells resemble renal tubule cells arranged in cords and varying patterns.

Clinical Findings

A. Symptoms and Signs: Gross hematuria is the most frequent sign. Fever is often the only symptom. A flank mass may be palpable. Vena cava occlusion may produce characteristic patterns of collateral circulation and edema of the legs.

A hypernephroma may not produce classical symptoms of renal tumor. It may produce symptoms and signs suggesting a wide variety of diseases: fever of obscure origin, leukemoid reaction, refractory anemia, polycythemia, liver or biliary disease, hypercalcemia, peripheral neuropathy, and an abdominal mass of indeterminate origin.

B. Laboratory Findings: Polycythemia occasionally develops as a result of increased secretion of erythropoietin by the tumor. Anemia is more commonly found. Hematuria is almost always present. The erythrocyte sedimentation rate is rapid.

C. X-Ray Findings: X-ray examination may show an enlarged kidney. Metastatic lesions of bone and lung may be revealed. Excretory or retrograde urography (or both) must be employed to establish the presence of a renal tumor.

Differential Diagnosis

Differentiate from focal nephritis, hydronephrosis, polycystic kidneys, renal cyst, and renal tuberculosis.

Treatment

Nephrectomy is indicated if no metastases are present. Even when metastases are present, nephrectomy may be indicated if bleeding or pain is intractable.

X-ray irradiation of metastases may be of value, although the lesions are usually fairly radioresistant. Isolated single pulmonary metastases can occasionally be removed surgically. At present, chemotherapy is ineffective.

Prognosis

The course is variable. Some patients may not develop metastases for 10–15 years after removal of the primary tumor. About 25% of patients live more than 5 years.

Arner, D., & others: Renal adenocarcinoma: Morphology, grading of malignancy, prognosis. A study of 197 cases. Acta chir scandinav, Suppl 346, 1965.

Kiely, J.M.: Hypernephroma–the internist's tumor. M Clin North America 50:1067–1084, 1966.

Mims, M., & others: Nephrectomy for extensive renal cell carcinoma: 10-year evaluation. J Urol 95:10–15, 1966.

Pinals, R.S., & S.M. Krane: Medical aspects of renal carcinoma. Postgrad MJ 38:507–519, 1962.

Rubin, P. (editor): Cancer of the urogenital tract: Kidney. JAMA 204:219–233, 603–613, 981–990, 1968.

EMBRYOMA OF THE KIDNEY
(Wilms's Tumor)

Embryoma is a highly malignant mixed tumor which occurs almost exclusively in children under 6 years of age. It metastasizes early to the lungs, liver, and brain.

Weight loss and anorexia are the most common signs. Pain occurs rarely. The enlarged kidney is usually easily palpable. Metastases produce an enlarged liver. Hypertension is common. Anemia may be present. The urine is not remarkable. X-ray examination demonstrates the tumor and metastases in the lung. Excretory urograms and gastrointestinal examination help to determine the size of the tumor.

Wilms's tumor must be differentiated from hydronephrosis, polycystic kidney disease, and neuroblastoma of the adrenal medulla.

Treatment consists of nephrectomy followed by local irradiation and irradiation of metastases. Antitumor chemotherapy with dactinomycin (actinomycin D) increases the cure rate and is usually effective in controlling local recurrences and metastases.

Cure can be achieved if metastases have not occurred before nephrectomy.

Baert, L., Verduyn, H., & R. Vereecken: Wilms' tumor (nephroblastomas): Report of 57 histologically proved cases. J Urol 96:871–874, 1966.

Burgert, E.O., & O. Glidewell: Dactinomycin [actinomycin D] in Wilms' tumor. JAMA 199:464–468, 1967.

Fernbach, D.J., & D.T. Martyn: Role of dactinomycin in the improved survival of children with Wilms' tumor. JAMA 195:1005–1009, 1966.

Vaeth, I.M., & S.H. Levitt: Five-year results in the treatment of Wilms' tumor of children. J Urol 90:247–249, 1963.

TUMORS OF THE
RENAL PELVIS & URETER

Epithelial tumors of the renal pelvis and ureter are relatively rare. They are usually papillary and tend to metastasize along the urinary tract. Epidermoid tumors are highly malignant and metastasize early.

Painless hematuria is the most common complaint. Colic occurs with obstruction due to blood clot or tumor. Tenderness in the flank may be found. Anemia due to blood loss occurs. The urine contains red cells and clots; white cells and bacteria are present when infection is superimposed. Urography should reveal the filling defect in the pelvis or show obstruction and dilatation of the ureter. At cystoscopy, the bleeding from the involved ureter may be seen and satellite tumors identified. Exfoliative cytologic studies should be done.

Radical removal of the kidney, the involved ureter, and the periureteral portion of the bladder should be done unless metastases are extensive.

Irradiation of metastases is usually of little value.

The prognosis depends upon the type of tumor. With anaplastic neoplasms, death usually occurs within 2 years.

TUMORS OF THE BLADDER

Essentials of Diagnosis

- Hematuria.
- Suprapubic pain and bladder symptoms associated with infection.
- Visualization of tumor at cystoscopy.

General Considerations

Bladder tumors are second to prostatic tumors in frequency. At least 75% of bladder tumors occur in males over the age of 50. Tumors usually arise at the base of the bladder and involve ureteral orifices and the bladder neck. The common tumor is transitional in type; epidermoid tumors, adenocarcinomas, and sarcomas are rare. Metastases involve regional lymph nodes, bone, liver, and lungs.

Clinical Findings

A. Symptoms and Signs: Hematuria is the commonest symptom. Cystitis with frequency, urgency, and dysuria is a frequent complication. With encroachment on the bladder neck, the urinary stream is diminished. Suprapubic pain occurs as the tumor extends beyond the bladder. Obstruction of the ureters produces hydronephrosis, frequently accompanied by renal infection and in which case the signs of urinary tract infection may be present. Physical examination is not remarkable. The bladder tumor may be palpable on bimanual (abdominorectal or abdominovaginal) examination. Exfoliative cytology is often diagnostic.

B. Laboratory Findings: Anemia is common. The urine contains red cells, white cells, and bacteria. Exfoliative cytology is usually confirmatory.

C. X-Ray and Instrumental Examination: Excretory urography may reveal ureteral obstruction. Cystograms usually show the tumor. Cystoscopy and biopsy confirm the diagnosis.

Differential Diagnosis

Hematuria and pain can be produced by other tumors of the urinary tract, urinary calculi, renal tuberculosis, acute cystitis, or acute nephritis.

Treatment

A. Specific Measures: Transurethral resection may be adequate to remove local and superficial tumors. Cystectomy with ureterosigmoidostomy or another urinary diversion procedure is required for invasive tumors. Radiation therapy may be useful for more anaplastic tumors. Chemotherapy has not been effective.

B. General Measures: Urinary tract infection should be controlled with appropriate antibiotics. Anastomosis of ureters to an isolated loop of ileum or sigmoid colon, one end of which is brought to the skin to act as a conduit, is relatively free of renal complications and of alteration of body fluid electrolytes. Diversion of urine to the sigmoid colon often produces hyperchloremic acidosis and azotemia, which can be controlled only by frequently emptying the bowel and by meticulous control of electrolyte intake.

Prognosis

There is a tendency toward recurrence and increasing malignancy. With infiltrating carcinomas the outlook is poor even with radical resection.

Buschke, F., & G. Jack: Twenty-five years' experience with supervoltage therapy in the treatment of transitional cell carcinoma of the bladder. Am J Roentgenol 99:387–392, 1967.

Caldwell, W.L., Bagshaw, M.A., & H.S. Kaplan: Efficacy of linear accelerator x-ray therapy in cancer of bladder. J Urol 97:294–303, 1967.

Melamed, M.R., & others: Natural history and clinical behavior of in situ carcinoma of the human urinary bladder. Cancer 17:1533–1545, 1964.

Riches, E.: Surgery and radiotherapy in urology: The bladder. J Urol 90:339–350, 1963.

Rubin, P. (editor): Cancer of the urogenital tract: Bladder cancer. JAMA 206:1761–1776, 2719–2728, 1968; 207:341–352, 1131–1139, 1969.

BENIGN PROSTATIC HYPERPLASIA

Essentials of Diagnosis

- Prostatism: hesitancy and straining to initiate micturition, reduced force and caliber of the urinary stream, nocturia.
- Acute urinary retention.
- Enlarged prostate.
- Uremia follows prolonged obstruction.

General Considerations

Hyperplasia of the prostatic periurethral glands produces enlargement of the prostate and urethral obstruction.

Clinical Findings

A. Symptoms and Signs: The symptoms of prostatism increase in severity as the degree of urethral obstruction increases. On rectal examination, the prostate is usually found to be enlarged. Infection commonly occurs with stasis and retention of "residual urine." Hematuria may occur. Uremia may result from prolonged back pressure and severe bilateral hydronephrosis. Residual urine can be measured by postvoiding catheterization.

B. X-Ray and Cystoscopic Examination: Excretory urograms reveal the complications of back pressure: ureteral dilatation and hydronephrosis and postvoiding urinary retention. Cystoscopy will reveal the enlargement of the prostate and the secondary bladder wall changes such as trabeculation, diverticula, inflammation due to infection, and vesical stone.

Differential Diagnosis

Other causes of urethral obstruction include urethral stricture, vesical stone, bladder tumor, neurogenic bladder, or carcinoma of prostate.

Treatment

A. Specific Measures: Relieve acute urinary retention by catheterization. Maintain catheter drainage if the degree of obstruction is severe. Surgery is usually necessary. There are various indications for each of the 4 approaches: transurethral resection or prostatectomy by suprapubic, retropubic, and perineal procedures.

B. General Measures: Treat infection of the urinary tract with appropriate antibiotics.

Prognosis

Surgical resection will relieve symptoms. Surgical mortality is low.

Mad, P., & others: Human prostatic hyperplasia. Arch Path 79:270–283, 1965.

CARCINOMA OF THE PROSTATE

Essentials of Diagnosis

- Prostatism.
- Hard consistency of the prostate.

- Metastases to bone produce pain, particularly in the low back.
- Anemia. Elevated serum acid phosphatase with extension of the cancer beyond the prostatic capsule.

General Considerations

Cancer of the prostate is rare before the age of 60. It metastasizes early to the bones of the pelvis and locally may produce urethral obstruction with subsequent renal damage. The growth of the tumor is increased by androgens and inhibited by estrogens. The prostatic tissue is rich in acid phosphatase, and when cancer has extended beyond the prostate to the periprostatic tissue, or to bone, the serum acid phosphatase is increased; when bone metastases occur, the serum alkaline phosphatase is increased. The serum acid phosphatase concentration thus provides a good index of the extent and growth of the tumor, and serum alkaline phosphatase signifies its extension to bone.

Clinical Findings

A. Symptoms and Signs: Obstructive symptoms similar to those of benign prostatic hyperplasia are common. Rectal examination reveals a stone-hard prostate which is often nodular and fixed. Low back pain occurs with metastases to the bones of the pelvis and spine. Pathologic fractures may occur at the sites of metastases. Obstruction may produce renal damage and the symptoms and signs of renal insufficiency.

B. Laboratory Findings: Anemia may be extreme if bone marrow is replaced by tumor. The urine may show evidence of infection. Serum acid phosphatase is increased when metastases have occurred, and serum alkaline phosphatase may be elevated as new bone is formed at the site of metastases. Biopsy by transurethral resection or by needle aspiration through the perineum establishes the diagnosis.

C. X-Ray Findings: X-ray examination of the bones of the pelvis, spine, ribs, and skull will reveal the typical osteoblastic metastases. Excretory urograms delineate changes secondary to urethral obstruction and the back pressure of urine retention.

Differential Diagnosis

Differentiate from benign prostatic hyperplasia, urethral stricture, vesical stone, bladder tumor, and neurogenic bladder.

Treatment

Cure may be obtained before metastasis has occurred by radical resection of the prostate, including the seminal vesicles and a portion of the bladder neck. Palliative therapy includes transurethral resection to relieve obstruction. Antiandrogen therapy slows the rate of growth and extension of the cancer. Orchiectomy and diethylstilbestrol, 5 mg daily (or equivalent of another estrogen), or estrogen therapy alone, are often effective. Radiotherapy with the linear accelerator on radioactive cobalt has provided good remission. Irradiation of bone metastases may afford relief.

The effectiveness of therapy can be judged by clinical response and by periodic measurements of the serum acid and alkaline phosphatase.

Prognosis

Palliative therapy is often not effective for long. Most patients die within 3 years; a few survive for 5–10 years.

Bagshaw, M.A., & others: Linear accelerator supervoltage radiotherapy. VII. Carcinoma of the prostate. Radiology 85:121–129, 1965.

George, F.W., & others: Cobalt-60 telecurietherapy in the definitive treatment of carcinoma of the prostate: A preliminary report. J Urol 93:102–109, 1965.

Mellinger, G.T.: Carcinoma of the prostate. S Clin North America 45:1413–1426, 1965.

Scott, W.W.: An evaluation of endocrine therapy plus radical perineal prostatectomy in the treatment of advanced carcinoma of the prostate. J Urol 91:97–102, 1964.

Whitmore, W.F., Jr.: The rationale and results of ablative surgery for prostatic cancer. Cancer 16:1119–1132, 1963.

TUMORS OF THE TESTIS*

Essentials of Diagnosis

- Painless enlargement of the testes.
- Mass does not transilluminate.
- Evidence of metastases.

General Considerations

The incidence of testicular tumors is about 0.5% of all types of cancer in males. Tumors occur most frequently between the ages of 20 and 35 and are often malignant. Classification of tumors of the testes is based upon their origin from germinal components or from nongerminal cells. The most common are the germinal tumors: seminomas; embryonal tumors, including embryoma, choriocarcinoma, embryonal carcinoma, teratocarcinoma, and adult teratoma; and the gonadoblastomas of intersexes. Nongerminal tumors include those of interstitial cell, Sertoli cell, and stromal origin. Rarely, lymphomas, leukemias, plasmacytomas, and metastatic carcinoma may involve the testis.

Seminomas, the most common testicular tumors, tend to spread slowly via the lymphatics to the iliac and periaortic nodes and disseminate late. Embryonal tumors invade the spermatic cord and metastasize early, particularly to the lungs. Seminomas are usually radiosensitive; embryonal tumors are usually radioresistant. Chemotherapy may be helpful in choriocarcinoma.

Secretion of gonadotropic hormones occurs with only about 10% of tumors. The literature on tumor-hormonal relationships is limited and confusing.

Gynecomastia may be associated with testicular tumors. Interstitial cell tumors, which occur at any age

---

*See also discussion in Chapter 18.

and are rarely malignant, are occasionally associated with gynecomastia and with sexual precocity and virilization.

Clinical Findings

A. Symptoms and Signs: Painless enlargement of the testes is typical. The enlarged testis may produce a dragging inguinal pain. The tumor is usually symmetrical and firm, and pressure does not produce the typical testicular pain. The tumors do not transilluminate. Attachment to the scrotal skin is rare. Gynecomastia may be present. Virilization may occur in patients with Leydig cell tumors.

Metastases to regional lymph nodes and to the lung may be evident. Hydrocele may develop.

B. Laboratory Findings: Gonadotropins may be present in high concentrations in urine and plasma in cases of chorioepithelioma, and pregnancy tests are positive. 17-Ketosteroids are elevated in Leydig cell tumors. Estrogens may be elaborated in Sertoli cell tumors.

C. X-Ray Findings: Pulmonary metastases are demonstrated by chest films. Lymphangiography will reveal enlarged iliac and periaortic nodes. Displacement of ureters by enlarged lymph nodes can be demonstrated by urography.

Differential Diagnosis

Tuberculosis, syphilitic orchitis, hydrocele, spermatocele, and tumors or granulomas of the epididymis may produce similar local manifestations.

Treatment

The testicle should be removed and the lumbar and inguinal nodes examined. Radical resection of iliac and lumbar nodes is usually indicated except for seminoma, which is radiosensitive. Radiation is the treatment of choice following removal of the testis bearing a seminoma. Radiation is employed following radical surgery for other malignant tumors. Chemotherapy (Table 30—2) is effective against chorionic tumors (choriocarcinoma).

Prognosis

The presence of metastases or high gonadotropin secretion indicates a poor prognosis. Seminomas are least malignant, with 90% 5-year cures. Almost all patients with choriocarcinoma are dead within 2 years. Less than ½ of those with other tumors will live 5 years.

Collins, D.H., & R.C.B. Pugh: The pathology of testicular tumors. Brit J Urol 36(Suppl):1—111, 1966.

Dykhuizen, R.F., & others: The use of cobalt-60 telecurietherapy or x-ray therapy with and without lymphadenectomy in the treatment of testis germinal tumors: A 20 year comparative study. J Urol 100:321—328, 1968.

Hobson, B.M.: Male chorionic gonadotropin excretion. Acta endocrinol 49:337—348, 1965.

Jacobs, E.M.: Combination chemotherapy of metastatic testicular germinal cell tumors and soft part sarcomas. Cancer 25:324, 1970.

• • •

MANIFESTATIONS OF THE URINARY SYSTEM DUE TO PARASITIC DISEASES

Hemoglobinuria: Malaria (blackwater fever).
Hematuria: Schistosomiasis haematobium.
Cystitis: Schistosomiasis.
Funiculitis: Filariasis.
Elephantiasis: Filariasis.
Vesical polyps, carcinoma: Schistosomiasis haematobium.
Epididymitis: Filariasis.

• • •

General Bibliography

Addis, T.: *Glomerular Nephritis.* Macmillan, 1948.

Allen, A .C.: *The Kidney: Medical and Surgical Diseases.* Grune & Stratton, 1962.

Barger, A.C., & others: The renal circulation. New England J Med 284:482–490, 1971.

Barnett, H.L.: Paediatric nephrology: Scientific study of kidneys and their diseases in infants and children. Arch Dis Childhood 41:229–237, 1966.

Barry, K.G., & others: Acute uric acid nephropathy. Arch Int Med 111:452–459, 1963.

Becker, E.L. (editor): Symposium on treatment of renal disease. Mod Treat 1:13–121, 1964.

Benoit, F.L., & others: Goodpasture's syndrome: A clinico-pathologic entity. Am J Med 37:424–444, 1964.

Berman, L.B.: The art of urinalysis. GP 34:94–108, Nov 1966.

Black, D.A.K.: *Renal Disease,* 2nd ed. Oxford, 1967.

Gonick, H.C., & others: The renal lesion in gout. Ann Int Med 62:667–674, 1965.

Harrow, B.R.: Renal papillary necrosis: Critique of pathogenesis. J Urol 97:203–208, 1967.

Honey, G.E., Pryse-Davies, J., & D.M. Roberts: A survey of nephropathy in young diabetics. Quart J Med 31:473–483, 1962.

Lieberman, E., & others: Hemolytic-uremic syndrome. New England J Med 275:227–235, 1966.

Lindheimer, M.D., & others: The kidney in pregnancy. New England J Med 283:1095–1097, 1970.

Milne, M.D.: Genetic aspects of renal disease. Progr Med Genet 7:112–162, 1970.

Mostofi, F.K., & D.E. Smith (editors): *The Kidney.* Williams & Wilkins, 1966.

Pitts, R.F.: *Physiology of the Kidney and Body Fluids,* 2nd ed. Year Book, 1968.

Proceedings of the Fourth International Congress of Nephrology. Munksgaard, 1970.

Relman, A.S.: Renal acidosis and renal excretion of acid in health and disease. Advances Int Med 12:295–347, 1966.

Schreiner, G.E., & J.F. Maher: Toxic nephropathy. Am J Med 38:409–449, 1965.

Smith, D.R.: *General Urology,* 6th ed. Lange, 1969.

Smith, L.H., Jr. (editor): Symposium on stones. Am J Med 45:649–783, 1968.

Strauss, M.B., & L.G. Welt (editors): *Diseases of the Kidney.* Little, Brown, 1971.

Symposium on the kidney. Am J Med 36:641–777, 1964.

Symposium on renal disorders. P Clin North America 11:515–766, 1964.

Wallace, S.L., & D. Bernstein: The relationship between gout and the kidney. Review article. Metabolism 12:440–446, 1963.

Welt, L.G. (editor): Symposium on uremia. Am J Med 44:653–802, 1968.

Wesson, L.G., Jr.: *Physiology of the Human Kidney.* Grune & Stratton, 1969,

Woolf, L.I.: *Renal Tubular Dysfunction.* Thomas, 1966.

16 ...

Nervous System

Joseph G. Chusid

DISORDERS OF CONSCIOUSNESS

Disturbances of the sensorium may be associated with decreased motor activity (eg, stupor or coma) or increased motor activity (eg, excitement, delirium, mania). Sensorial disturbances may range from partial clouding to complete obliteration of consciousness. The pattern of reaction of these disorders depends upon the nature and intensity of the stimulus and the physical, mental, and emotional status of the patient. Causative factors include trauma, cerebrovascular accidents, drug and other poisonings, fever, metabolic disorders, meningitis, overwhelming infection, brain tumors, convulsive disorders, and cardiac decompensation.

STUPOR & COMA

Stupor ranges from partial to almost complete loss of consciousness. Coma is complete unconsciousness from which the patient cannot be aroused even by the most painful stimuli.

Etiology of Coma

Coma may be of intracranial or extracranial origin. Examples are given below.

A. Intracranial: Head injuries, cerebrovascular accidents, CNS infections, tumors, convulsive disorders, degenerative diseases, increased intracranial pressure.

B. Extracranial: Vascular (shock or hypotension, as with severe hemorrhage, myocardial infarction, arterial hypertension); metabolic (diabetic acidosis, hypoglycemia, uremia, hepatic coma, addisonian crisis, electrolyte imbalance); intoxications (alcohol, barbiturates, narcotics, bromides, analgesics, tranquilizers, carbon monoxide, heavy metals); miscellaneous (hyperthermia, hypothermia, electric shock, anaphylaxis, severe systemic infections).

Clinical Findings

A. History: Interrogate the patient during lucid intervals. Valuable information may also be obtained from the patient's friends, relatives, and attendants. Inquire specifically about the patient's occupation; previous physical, mental, or emotional illness; trauma, the use of alcohol and drugs, epilepsy, and hypertension.

B. Physical Examination: Place particular emphasis on vital signs, evidence of injury or intoxication, and neurologic abnormalities. Do not assume that sensory disturbances are due to alcoholic intoxication merely because an alcoholic breath is detected. Inspect the head and body carefully for evidence of injury. Discoloration of the skin behind the ear often is associated with skull fractures (Battle's sign).

Observe respiration, which may be deep and labored (suggesting diabetic acidosis) or of the Cheyne-Stokes type. Puffing out of one cheek with each expiration indicates paralysis of that side of the face.

Spontaneous movements may indicate which areas are normal parts or may represent the onset of focal motor convulsions.

Paralysis of extremities may be determined by lifting each extremity and allowing it to fall. In light coma the paralyzed limb will fall heavily, whereas a normal limb will gradually sink to the bed. Vigorous stimulation of the feet may cause a normal leg to react, where a paralyzed leg will not. Passive motion may disclose diminished tone of affected limbs in acute or recent flaccid hemiplegia.

Decerebrate rigidity or the presence of tonic neck reflexes suggests dysfunction at a brain stem level.

Check the eyes carefully. Hemianopsia may be demonstrable in stupor by failure of flinching on threatening hand gestures initiated from the hemianopsic side. Pupillary differences may be of vital diagnostic importance; an enlarged pupil is often present with ipsilateral subdural hematoma. Papilledema indicates elevated intracranial pressure and is a grave prognostic sign.

Oculomotor paralysis of one eye is often associated with a ruptured aneurysm of the anterior portion of the circle of Willis.

Pronounced nuchal rigidity usually signifies meningeal irritation (meningitis, subarachnoid bleeding) or herniation of the cerebellar tonsils due to intracranial tumor or vascular accident.

C. Laboratory Findings: Catheterize the patient if necessary and examine the urine especially for protein, blood, glucose, and acetone. Take hemoglobin, white blood count, differential count, and hematocrit. Draw blood for NPN, glucose, and blood ammonia when indicated (for diagnosis of uremia, diabetic coma, or hepatic coma). Lumbar puncture should be considered for comatose patients unless there are specific contraindications (eg, suspected posterior fossa lesions). CSF examination and culture may be helpful. Special studies may be indicated, eg, blood cultures and analysis of body fluids for evidence of toxins. Skull x-rays, EEG, echoencephalography, brain scan, cerebral angiography, and pneumography are valuable aids in brain tumor and subdural hematoma suspects. Order chest x-ray and other x-rays as indicated.

Treatment

A. Emergency Measures: The immediate objective is to maintain life until a specific diagnosis has been made and appropriate treatment can be started.

1. Maintain adequate ventilation—First determine the cause of any respiratory difficulty (eg, obstruction, pulmonary disease, depression of respiratory center, vascular collapse).

Keep airways open. Place the patient on his side or abdomen with his face to the side and his head well extended (**never** on his back or with the head flexed). If necessary, pull the tongue forward with fingers or forceps and maintain in an extended position (eg, by pharyngeal airways). Aspirate mucus, blood, and saliva from the mouth and nose with a lubricated soft rubber catheter. If no suction apparatus is available, use a 25–50 ml syringe. Endotracheal catheterization or tracheostomy may be necessary. (*Caution:* If the endotracheal tube remains in place for more than 2 hours, there is danger of laryngeal edema and further obstruction upon its removal.) The services of a trained anesthetist or otolaryngologist are desirable.

Artificial respiration may be administered if respirations have ceased or are failing. Closed chest cardiac massage may be necessary. (See Appendix.)

Oxygen may be administered by mask, catheter, or tent as indicated (see Chapter 6).

2. Shock—Institute immediate treatment if the patient is in shock or if shock is threatened (see chapter 1).

B. General Measures: The patient must be observed constantly. Place him in the "shock" position (unless contraindicated), and change body positions every 30–60 minutes to prevent hypostatic pneumonia and skin ulcerations. Catheterize the patient if coma persists for longer than 8–12 hours and the patient fails to void. If necessary, insert an indwelling catheter (with appropriate aseptic technic).

Provide proper fluid and nutrition with intravenous glucose, amino acids, and saline solutions for the first few days until the patient is able to take fluids by mouth. If the patient is comatose for more than 2–3 days, tube feedings should be employed.

Whenever possible, avoid sedation or other depressant medications until a specific diagnosis has been made. Sedation with paraldehyde, barbiturates, or tranquilizers may be necessary for mild restlessness in coma which is not due to barbiturate or other drug toxicity.

Intravenous urea: Increased intracranial pressure (eg, in brain tumor, head injury, brain swelling) may be reduced for 3–10 hours by intravenous administration of urea. Give urea as 30% sterile solution (in 10% invert sugar) in a dosage of about 1 gm/kg at a rate of about 60 drops/minute. Poor renal function or active intracranial bleeding are contraindications.

Corticosteroids: Parenteral corticosteroids may be used to treat cerebral edema associated with brain tumor, head injury, subarachnoid hemorrhage, x-ray irradiation, and other causes. Give dexamethasone, 8–40 mg/day IV or IM.

Hypertonic solutions (such as 30% fructose plus 15% mannitol in water) may be used to reduce increased intracranial pressure quickly.

C. Specific Measures: Treat specific causes, such as fevers, infections, and poisonings. In the absence of hypothermia or sedation, irreversible brain damage or brain death may be suspected when there is areflexia, loss of spontaneous respirations, fixed dilated pupils, motor and sensory paralysis, and an iso-electric (flat) EEG for 24 hours.

Barrett, R., Merritt, H.H., & A. Wolf: Depression of consciousness as a result of cerebral lesions. Res Publ A Nerv Ment Dis 65:241–276, 1967.

Becker, D.P., & others: An evaluation of cerebral death. Neurology 20:459–462, 1970.

A definition of irreversible coma. Special communication. JAMA 205:337–340, 1968.

Ingvar, D.H., & P. Sourander: Destruction of the reticular core of the brain stem. Arch Neurol 23:1–9, 1970.

Locke, S.: The neurological aspects of coma. S Clin North America 48:251–258, 1968.

Plum, F., & J. Posner: *The Diagnosis of Stupor and Coma.* Davis, 1966.

Silverman, D., & others: Cerebral death and the electroencephalogram. JAMA 209:1505–1511, 1969.

Silverman, D., & others: Irreversible coma associated with electrocerebral silence. Neurology 20:521–533, 1970.

NARCOLEPSY

Narcolepsy is a chronic clinical syndrome of unknown etiology characterized by recurrent episodes of uncontrollable desire to sleep. It is frequently associated with a transient loss of muscle tone (cataplexy), especially during emotional reactions (laughing, crying). Inability to move in the interval between sleep and arousal (sleep paralysis) and hallucinations at the onset of sleep (hypnagogic hallucinations) may also occur. The attacks of sleep may occur once or several times a day and may last minutes to hours. The sleep is similar to that of normal sleep, but is apt to occur at inappropriate times, such as during work or while walking or driving. Narcolepsy is about 4 times as frequent in males as in females.

Treatment

A. Amphetamine Sulfate (Benzedrine®): The average dose is 10–20 mg 3 times daily, but more may be required for some patients. The optimal dosage may be determined by starting with 10 mg each morning and increasing the dosage as necessary to control symptoms.

B. Dextroamphetamine Sulfate (Dexedrine®): Give 5 mg each morning initially and increase as necessary. Long-acting capsules (Dexedrine Spansules®) are available in 5, 10, and 15 mg doses.

C. Methylphenidate Hydrochloride (Ritalin®): Used in doses of 5–10 mg 3–4 times daily (or more if necessary).

D. Ephedrine Sulfate: Ephedrine is not as satisfactory as amphetamine but is helpful in many cases. The average dose is 25–50 mg 2–4 times daily.

Prognosis

Narcolepsy usually persists throughout life. Although the attacks of somnolence and sleep may be relieved by medical treatment, the cataplexy and attacks of muscular weakness which accompany emotional reactions (laughing, crying) are usually not affected by drug therapy.

Dement, W., Rechtschaffen, A., & G. Gulevich: The nature of narcoleptic sleep attack. Neurology 16:18, 1966.

Sours, J.A.: Narcolepsy and other disturbances in the sleep-waking rhythm. A study of 115 cases with review of the literature. J Nerv Ment Dis 137:526, 1963.

Yoss, R.E., & D.D. Daly: On the treatment of narcolepsy. M Clin North America 52:781–788, 1968.

SYNCOPE & VERTIGO

VASODEPRESSOR SYNCOPE
(Vasovagal Syncope, Simple Fainting, Benign Faint)

Vasodepressor syncope, the most common type, is usually characterized by a sudden fall in blood pressure and a slowing of the heart. The causative stimuli may be sensory (eg, sudden pain) or entirely emotional (eg, grief or bereavement). The patient is usually upright when the faint occurs; recumbency rapidly restores consciousness. In the early phase there may be motor weakness, epigastric distress, perspiration, restlessness, yawning, and sighing respirations. The patient may appear anxious, with a pale face and cold, moist extremities. After several minutes, lightheadedness, blurring of vision, and sudden loss of consciousness with decreased muscle tone may occur. If the patient remains erect, a brief but mild convulsion may follow. Syncope is believed to occur when the arterial pressure drops below 70 mm Hg systolic and is usually precipitated by fear, anxiety, or pain. Electroencephalographic changes occur after the onset of unconsciousness in a syncopal attack.

The patient should be placed in the recumbent position with his head lower than the rest of his body. Inhalation of aromatic spirits of ammonia may help revive the patient in a faint.

Ebert, E.V.: Syncope. Circulation 27:1148, 1963.

Ruetz, P.P., & others: Fainting: A review of its mechanism and a study in blood donors. Medicine 46:363–384, 1967.

Thomas, J.E., & E.D. Rooke: Fainting. Proc Staff Meet Mayo Clin 38:397–410, 1963.

Wayne, H.H.: Syncope. Physiological considerations and an analysis of the clinical characteristics in 570 patients. Am J Med 30:418–438, 1961.

ORTHOSTATIC HYPOTENSION
(Postural Hypotension)

Syncope may occur as the patient assumes an upright position. This type of syncope is characterized by repeated fainting attacks associated with a sudden drop in arterial blood pressure when the patient stands up. Recognized contributory factors are prolonged convalescence and recumbency, idiopathic disorders of postural reflexes, sympathectomy, peripheral venous stasis, chronic anxiety, and the use of antihypertensive drugs.

Treatment is directed toward the underlying cause when possible. Withdraw or reduce the dosage of hypotensive drugs. Caution the patient against rising too rapidly from the sitting or lying position. If abdominal ptosis is present, an abdominal belt may help. Elastic stockings may be of value. Vasoconstrictor drugs may be tried but usually do not help.

Ephedrine sulfate, up to 75 mg daily, may be useful. Fludrocortisone acetate has also been reported to be effective in daily doses of 0.1 mg or more.

Hughes, R.C., Cartledge, N.E.F., & P. Milac: Primary neurogenic orthostatic hypotension. J Neurol Neurosurg Psychiat 33:363–371, 1970.

Lewis, H.D., Jr., & M. Dunn: Orthostatic hypotension syndrome. Am Heart J 74:396–401, 1967.

Martin, J.B., Travis, R.H., & S. van den Noort: Centrally mediated orthostatic hypotension. Arch Neurol 19:163–173, 1968.

Roessman, U., van den Noort, S., & D.E. McFarland: Idiopathic orthostatic hypotension. Arch Neurol 24:403–511, 1971.

Thapedi, I.M., & others: Shy-Drager syndrome. Neurology 21:26–33, 1971.

Thomas, J.E., & A. Schirger: Orthostatic hypotension: Etiologic considerations, diagnosis and treatment. M Clin North America 52:809–816, 1968.

Thomas, J.E., & A. Schirger: Idiopathic orthostatic hypotension. Arch Neurol 22:289–294, 1970.

CAROTID SINUS SYNCOPE

Patients who suffer from attacks of carotid sinus syncope usually give a history of fainting associated with spells of dizziness between attacks. A definite relation between the attacks and sudden turning or raising of the head or the wearing of a tight collar may be elicited. The diagnosis is usually confirmed by reproducing an attack by firm pressure and massage over the carotid sinus for 10–20 seconds. *Caution:* Stimulate only one carotid sinus at a time. Care must be exercised in stimulating the sinuses in elderly patients. Cerebrovascular accidents have been precipitated by this maneuver.

Three types of carotid sinus syncope are known to occur: (1) The vagal type (most common) is most often seen in older persons. Carotid sinus pressure slows the heart rate. This response can be abolished by the injection of atropine sulfate, 1 mg IV. (2) The vasomotor or depressor type occurs more frequently in younger individuals. Carotid sinus pressure causes a fall in blood pressure which can be abolished by injection of 0.5 ml of epinephrine, 1:1000 solution, but is unaffected by atropine sulfate. (3) In the cerebral type carotid sinus pressure affects neither heart rate nor blood pressure, and neither epinephrine nor atropine affects the reflex. A direct cerebral effect is postulated.

Treatment

Correct all abnormalities whenever possible. Eliminate emotional problems and forbid the use of tight collars. In severe cases, denervation of the sinuses may be necessary. Local anesthesia of the carotid sinuses abolishes all types of carotid sinus syncope.

A. Vagal Type: Atropine sulfate, 0.4–0.6 mg 3–4 times daily (or more, if needed), will usually abolish attacks. Ephedrine sulfate, 25 mg, with phenobarbital, 15 mg 3–4 times daily, or amphetamine sulfate, 5–10 mg, may be used.

B. Vasomotor Type: Ephedrine and phenobarbital as above will usually prevent attacks.

C. Cerebral Type: Drugs are of no value.

Brodie, R.E., & R.S. Dow: Studies in carotid compression and carotid sinus sensitivity. Neurology 18:1047–1055, 1968.

Hutchinson, E.C., & J.P.P. Stock: The carotid sinus syndrome. Lancet 2:445–449, 1960.

Thomas, J.E.: Hyperactive carotid sinus reflex and carotid sinus syncope. Mayo Clin Proc 44:127, 1969.

SYNCOPE DUE TO CARDIOVASCULAR DISORDERS

Syncope due to cerebral anoxia resulting from a temporary fall in cardiac output may occur in Stokes-Adams syndrome, myocardial infarction, pulmonary embolism, and the onset of paroxysmal tachycardia; and occurs in certain other types of heart disease (eg,

aortic stenosis and tetralogy of Fallot). Syncope may occur with "cyanotic crisis" (low arterial oxygen saturation and low cardiac output).

Treatment consists of correcting the underlying abnormality.

Tufo, H.M., Ostfeld, H.M., & R. Shekelle: Central nervous system dysfunction following open heart surgery. JAMA 212:1333–1340, 1970.

Walter, P.F., Reid, S.D., Jr., & N.K. Wenger: Transient cerebral ischemia due to arrhythmia. Ann Int Med 72:471–474, 1970.

SYNCOPE DUE TO METABOLIC DISTURBANCES

In some types of syncope, impaired cerebral metabolism may be the most significant factor. These varieties include (1) anoxemia, as in patients with congenital heart disease; (2) severe chronic debilitating anemias; (3) hypoglycemia, as in labile diabetics after overexertion, or failure to eat after taking insulin; (4) acidosis, as in some patients with uncontrolled diabetes mellitus; (5) drug intoxication, as with barbiturates; (6) acute alcoholism; and (7) hyperventilation with associated respiratory alkalosis and tetany.

Treat the specific cause whenever possible. Consciousness may be restored in hyperventilation by rebreathing into a paper bag, breath-holding, or administration of 5–10% CO_2 with oxygen by mask. Recurrent attacks of hyperventilation syndrome suggest that psychiatric consultation should be considered.

Bell, W.E., Samaan, N.A., & D.S. Longnecker: Hypoglycemia due to organic hyperinsulinism in infancy. Arch Neurol 23:330–339, 1970.

Burton, R.A., & N.H. Raskin: Alimentary (postgastrectomy) hypoglycemia. Arch Neurol 23:14–18, 1970.

Gabrilove, J.L.: Neurologic and psychiatric manifestations in the classic endocrine syndromes. Res Publ A Nerv Ment Dis 63:419–441, 1966.

Merritt, H.H., & C.C. Hare (editors): *Metabolic and Toxic Diseases of the Nervous System.* Res Publ A Nerv Ment Dis, vol 33. Williams & Wilkins, 1953.

Senior, R.M., & others: The recognition and management of myxedema coma. JAMA 217:61–65, 1971.

SYNCOPE DUE TO IMPAIRED BRAIN CIRCULATION

Impairment of brain circulation may lead to syncopal attacks. Syncope associated with transient focal neurologic findings is encountered among elderly patients with arteriosclerotic cerebrovascular disease. Dizziness followed by syncope can occur following abrupt head movements in patients with recent head injuries. Lightheadedness, and occasionally syncope, may occur in migraine in association with diminished cranial arterial blood flow. A type of syncope associated with hypersensitivity of the carotid sinus may occur with profound fall in blood pressure and consequent impaired brain circulation. In some patients with brain tumors or vascular malformations, syncopal episodes sometimes occur which may be related to displacement, engorgement, or insufficiency of cranial circulation. (See Cerebrovascular Accidents, p 517.)

Fazekas, J.F.: Cerebrovascular consequences of hypertension. Therapeutic implications. Am J Cardiol 17:608–611, 1966.
Gray, F.D., & G.J. Horner: Survival following extreme hypoxemia. JAMA 211:1815–1817, 1970.
Lees, F., & S.M. Watkins: Loss of consciousness in migraine. Lancet 2:647–649, 1963.
Livingston, S.: Breath-holding spells in children. JAMA 212:2231–2236, 1970.

VERTIGO
(Dizziness)

The terms "vertigo" and "dizziness" are generally used to denote the subjective sensation of rotatory movement, either of the individual or his environment, and imply an inability to orient the body in relation to surrounding objects. Vertigo is found mainly in disease processes involving the labyrinths, the vestibular portion of the 8th cranial nerve, and their nuclei or connections. True vertigo is usually manifested by nystagmus, falling to one side, and abnormal reaction to tests of vestibular function. Among the more common causes are Ménière's syndrome; acute labyrinthitis; organic brain damage involving the vestibular nerve, its end organs or connections, or the cerebellum; and drug and chemical toxicity.

Treatment is based upon accurate diagnosis of the underlying disorder.

Caparosa, R.J.: Dizziness. Postgrad Med 40:661–665, 1966.
Hicks, J.J., Hicks, J.W., & H.N. Cooley: Ménière's disease. Arch Otolaryng 86:610–613, 1967.
Koenigsberger, M.B., & others: Benign paroxysmal vertigo of childhood. Neurology 20:1108–1114, 1970.
Saunders, W.H.: Vertigo: Ménière's disease and the differential diagnosis. Postgrad Med 34:449–454, 1963.
Schneider, R.C., Calhoun, H.D., & E.C. Crosby: Vertigo and rotational movement in cortical and subcortical lesions. J Neurol Sc 6:493–516, 1968.
Williams, D.J., & others: Vertigo. Proc Roy Soc Med 60:961–970, 1967.

MOTION SICKNESS

Motion sickness is an acute illness characterized by anorexia, nausea, dizziness, and vomiting. The principal factors in its etiology are visual, kinesthetic, and psychologic. Physiologically, the vestibular apparatus appears to be involved.

Prevention

Preventive measures are often effective. Attacks of motion sickness are difficult to treat successfully.

A. The antihistamines appear to be of benefit. Dimenhydrinate (Dramamine®) or diphenhydramine hydrochloride (Benadryl®), 50–100 mg 4 times daily, may be effective.

B. Meclizine hydrochloride (Bonine®), 50 mg every 6–12 hours as needed, is a long-acting effective agent.

C. Cyclizine hydrochloride (Marezine®) is effective in oral or IM doses of 50 mg every 4–6 hours as needed.

D. Parasympathetic depressants, alone or in combination with mild sedatives: scopolamine hydrobromide or atropine sulfate, 0.2–0.4 mg every 3–6 hours.

E. Mild Sedation: Phenobarbital, 15–30 mg every 3–6 hours, may help prevent attacks.

Chinn, H.I., & P.K. Smith: Motion sickness. Pharmacol Rev 7:33–82, 1955.
Ley, A., & others: Chronic and subacute labyrinthine disorders. A major causative agent in some neurological syndromes. J Nerv Ment Dis 147:91–100, 1968.

HEADACHE

HEADACHE DUE TO MENINGEAL INVOLVEMENT

This is the most severe type of headache. Salicylate analgesics are usually effective, but narcotics may be necessary if pain is severe. Lumbar puncture performed very cautiously sometimes relieves headache due to increased intracranial pressure (eg, subarachnoid hemorrhage). It is contraindicated for relief of increased pressure in posterior fossa tumors.

Lumbar puncture headaches are believed to be due to leakage of CSF from the puncture site, and are more likely to occur when a large-bore needle is used. If headache is mild upon arising, aspirin may suffice. Intrathecal injection of small quantities of sterile normal saline may afford relief in severe cases.

Elkins, A.H., & A.P. Friedman: Review of headache. New York J Med 67:255–262, 426–435, 552–559, 1967.
Friedman, A.P., & others: Classification of headache. Neurology 12:378–380, 1962.
MacNeal, P.S.: The patient with headache. Postgrad Med 42:249–255, 1967.
Symposium on headache: Its mechanism, diagnosis and management. Neurology 13:1–44, 1963.

MIGRAINE

Migraine is characterized by paroxysmal attacks of headache often preceded by psychologic or visual disturbances and sometimes followed by drowsiness. It is said to affect about 8% of the population. It is more frequent among women than men and occurs more commonly among persons with a background of inflexibility and shyness in childhood and with perfectionistic, rigid, resentful, and ambitious character traits in adult life. There is commonly a history of similar headaches in blood relations.

The headache of migraine is believed to result from vascular changes. An initial episode of cerebral, meningeal, and extracranial arterial vasoconstriction is believed to occur (accounting for the visual and other prodromal phenomena), followed by dilatation and distention of cranial vessels, especially of the external carotid artery. Increased amplitude of pulsation is said to determine the throbbing nature of the headache. Rigid, pipe-like vessels result from persistent dilatation, and the headache becomes a steady ache. A phase of muscle contraction, with pain, is believed to follow.

Migraine often begins in childhood; about half of migraine patients report their initial attack before the age of 15 years. Characteristically, the headache occurs in episodes associated with gastrointestinal or visual symptoms (nausea, vomiting, scintillating scotomas, photophobia, hemianopsia, blurred vision).

Prevention

Methysergide maleate (Sansert®) may be effective in preventing vascular headache. The average daily dose is 4–8 mg, preferably 2 mg with each meal. This drug is contraindicated in pregnancy, peripheral vascular disease, and arteriosclerosis. Retroperitoneal fibrosis may occur with this drug.

The use of sedatives, tranquilizers, antidepressants, and psychotherapy may help reduce the frequency of attacks.

Treatment

A. Treatment of Acute Attack:

1. Ergotamine tartrate (Gynergen®), 0.25–0.5 mg IM, will relieve headache within an hour in most cases. Administer the drug as early in the attack as possible. Do not repeat more often than once weekly. Oral or sublingual administration is less effective, and if the patient vomits it is impossible to know how much of the drug he has absorbed. The dosage is 4–5 mg sublingually or orally; continue with 2 mg every hour until headache has disappeared or until a total of 11 mg has been administered.

Toxicity: Do not administer ergotamine to patients in septic or infectious states or who have peripheral vascular or arteriosclerotic heart disease, or to pregnant women. A few patients complain of numbness and tingling of extremities and some muscle pains and tension.

2. Dihydroergotamine (DHE 45®), in doses of 1 mg IM or IV, may be substituted for ergotamine tartrate. Repeat in 1 hour if necessary.

3. Ergotamine with caffeine (Cafergot®) or atropine is sometimes more effective by the oral route alone and requires a smaller total dose. It is available as suppositories for rectal use if vomiting prevents oral administration.

4. Pressure on the external carotid artery or one of its branches early in the attack may abolish pain. Oxygen, 100%, by nasal mask may relieve the acute attack.

B. General Measures: Until the drug begins to relieve headache, have the patient at rest in a chair. After headache has been relieved, he should rest in bed for at least 2 hours in a quiet, darkened room without food or drink. This will promote relaxation and is necessary to prevent another attack from occurring immediately.

C. Aborting an Attack: When the patient feels an attack of migraine coming on he should seek relaxation in a warm bath and then rest in bed in a quiet, darkened room. The following drugs may help: Pentobarbital, 0.1 gm orally; ergotamine tartrate (Gynergen®), 3–4 mg sublingually; or even aspirin, with or without codeine.

Anthony, M., & J.W. Lance: Monoamine oxidase inhibition in the treatment of migraine. Arch Neurol 21:263–269, 1969.

Friedman, A.P.: The migraine syndrome. Bull New York Acad Med 44:45–62, 1968.

Slatter, K.H.: Some clinical and EEG findings in patients with migraine. Brain 91:85–98, 1968.

Whitty, C.W.M., & J.M. Hockaday: Migraine: A follow-up study of 92 patients. Brit MJ 1:735–736, 1968.

CLUSTER HEADACHES
(Histaminic [Horton's] Cephalalgia)

"Histaminic cephalalgia" (or cluster headaches) is characterized by a sudden onset of severe unilateral pain. The pain is of short duration and subsides abruptly but may recur several times daily. Associated signs include redness of the eye, lacrimation, rhinorrhea or stuffiness of the nostril, swelling of the temporal vessels on the affected side, and dilatation of the vessels of the pain area. The headache involves the orbital area, frequently radiating to the temple, nose, upper jaw, and neck. Typical attacks can be induced by injection of small quantities of histamine diphosphate. Attacks occur most frequently during sleep.

Treatment

Methysergide maleate (UML-491, Sansert®) may be effective in preventing vascular headache. The average daily dose is 4–8 mg, preferably 2 mg with each meal. This drug is contraindicated in pregnancy, peripheral vascular disease, and arteriosclerosis.

Although Horton initially recommended "desensitization" to histamine, these headaches are now treated as migraine variants. Because of the short duration of individual attacks and frequent spontaneous long remissions, evaluation of therapy is difficult.

Robinson, B.W.: Histaminic cephalgia. Medicine 37:161–180, 1958.
Ryan, R.E.: Histamine cephalgia. Eye Ear Nose Throat Monthly 44:61–65, 1965.
Stowell, A.: Physiologic mechanism and treatment of histaminic or petrosal neuralgia. Headache 9:187–194, 1970.

HEADACHES DUE TO MUSCULOSKELETAL INVOLVEMENT

Muscle contraction or spasm may be caused by disease of the muscle or adjacent structures or may be associated with excessive fatigue or emotional tension. The muscles attached to the occiput are most frequently involved and cause the characteristic "occipital" headache. There may also be a feeling of pressure or tightness or a band-like constriction around the head associated with emotional tension.

Tension headaches are by far the most commonly encountered of all types. However, since emotionally disturbed patients may have headaches due to other causes, a complete and adequate history and examination is always necessary.

Tension headaches seem to have no precise localization and usually do not conform to the distribution of cranial or peripheral nerves or roots. The headache is described as being dull, drawing, pressing, burning, or vague in character, and is usually occipital and supraorbital. Medications, including potent analgesics, may not give complete relief. Exacerbation of complaints and association with anxiety, worry, or other emotional upsets is not always obvious to the patient.

Treatment

Muscle spasm due to organic disease and bone or joint pain may be relieved by appropriate physical therapeutic measures. Analgesics are usually also of value. Specific therapy should be directed at the underlying disease.

For muscle tension headache rest, relaxation, and freedom from emotional stress are of primary importance. Heat to the involved muscles by means of hot towels, a heating pad, or a warm bath will help relieve the discomfort. Gentle massage of the muscles will usually also be of benefit. Drugs may be of value in acute cases, but prolonged use should be avoided. Phenobarbital, 15–30 mg 4 times daily, will temporarily relieve many headaches due to "nervous tension." Aspirin or sedatives plus tranquilizers may also be of benefit.

Dutton, C.B., & L.H. Riley: Cervical migraine. JAMA 47:141–148, 1969.
Rooke, E.D.: Benign exertional headache. M Clin North America 52:801–808, 1968.
Sam, J., & J.N. Plampin: Potent skeletal muscle relaxants. J Pharmaceut Sc 53:538–543, 1964.

CONVULSIVE DISORDERS (EPILEPSY)

Essentials of Diagnosis

- Abrupt onset of paroxysmal, transitory, recurrent alterations of brain function, usually accompanied by alterations in consciousness.
- Signs may vary from behavioral abnormalities to continuous prolonged motor convulsions.
- Primary brain disorder may be present.
- Family history of epilepsy may be present.

General Considerations

Convulsive disorders are characterized by abrupt transient symptoms of a motor, sensory, psychic, or autonomic nature, frequently associated with changes in consciousness. These changes are believed to be secondary to sudden transient alterations in brain function associated with excessive rapid electric discharges in the gray matter. Seizures are more apt to occur in a patient with organic brain disease than in one with a normal CNS. Symptomatic epilepsy may be produced by a variety of pathologic states and intoxications (eg, brain tumor, cerebrovascular accidents, head trauma, intracranial infections, uremia, hypoglycemia, hypocalcemia, and overhydration). In idiopathic epilepsy, morphologic changes may not be demonstrable. Individuals may inherit a convulsive tendency. The onset of idiopathic epilepsy is usually before the age of 30 years. Later age of onset suggests organic disease.

Some seizures tend to occur during sleep or following physical stimulation (eg, light or sound). In some patients emotional disturbances play a significant "trigger" role.

Clinical Findings

A. Classification of Seizures:

1. Grand mal (major epilepsy)—(Grand mal and petit mal may coexist.) A typical aura may herald a major seizure; it may be stereotyped for an individual, eg, an "odd" sensation in the epigastrium, memory phenomena, or a particular unpleasant taste or smell. The aura may consist of a motor phenomenon (eg, spasm of a limb, turning of the head and eyes) or a sensory aberration (eg, numbness). The patient may remember or actually "see" a scene or event from his past.

Consciousness is apt to be lost soon after the appearance of the aura; the subject may fall to the floor and emit a cry. The skeletal muscles then undergo strong tonic contractions; dyspnea and cyanosis may be present. Severe generalized clonic convulsive movements of the body begin a few seconds later, usually becoming less frequent as the attack persists. Frothing at the mouth, loss of bladder and bowel control, tongue biting, bruises, and contusions commonly occur at this time. A period of flaccid coma follows during which the pupils may be dilated, corneal and

TABLE 16–1. Drugs used in epilepsy.*

Drug	Average Daily Dose	Indications	Toxicity and Precautions
Diphenylhydantoin sodium (Dilantin®)	0.3–0.6 gm in divided doses	Safest drug for grand mal, some cases of psychomotor epilepsy. May accentuate petit mal.	Gum hypertrophy (dental hygiene); nervousness, rash, ataxia, drowsiness, nystagmus (reduce dosage).
Mephenytoin (Mesantoin®)	0.3–0.5 gm in divided doses	Grand mal, some cases of psychomotor epilepsy. Effective when grand mal and petit mal coexist.	Nervousness, ataxia, nystagmus (reduce dosage); pancytopenia (frequent blood counts); exfoliative dermatitis (stop drug if severe skin eruption develops).
Ethotoin (Peganone®)	2–3 gm in divided doses	Grand mal.	Dizziness, fatigue, skin rash (decrease dose or discontinue).
Trimethadione (Tridione®)	0.3–2 gm in divided doses	Petit mal.	Bone marrow depression, pancytopenia, exfoliative dermatitis (as above); photophobia (usually disappears; dark glasses); nephrosis (frequent urinalysis; discontinue if renal lesion develops).
Paramethadione (Paradione®)	0.3–2 gm in divided doses	Petit mal.	Toxic reactions said to be less than with trimethadione. Other remarks as for trimethadione.
Phenacemide (Phenurone®)	0.5–5 gm in divided doses	Psychomotor epilepsy.	Hepatitis (liver function tests at onset; follow urinary urobilinogen at regular intervals); benign proteinuria (stop drug; may continue if patient is having marked relief); dermatitis (stop drug); headache and personality changes (stop drug if severe).
Phenobarbital	0.1–0.4 gm in divided doses	One of the safest drugs for all epilepsies, especially as adjunct. May aggravate psychomotor seizures.	Toxic reactions rare. Drowsiness (decrease dosage); dermatitis (stop drug and resume later; if dermatitis recurs, stop drug entirely).
Mephobarbital (Mebaral®)	0.2–0.9 gm in divided doses	As for phenobarbital.	As for phenobarbital. Usually offers no advantage over phenobarbital and must be given in twice the dosage.
Metharbital (Gemonil®)	0.1–0.8 gm in divided doses	Grand mal. Especially effective in seizures associated with organic brain damage and in infantile myoclonic epilepsy.	Drowsiness (decrease dosage).
Primidone (Mysoline®)	0.5–2 gm in divided doses	Grand mal. Useful in conjunction with other drugs.	Drowsiness (decrease dosage); ataxia (decrease dosage or stop drug).
Bromides (potassium or sodium)	3–6 gm in divided doses	All epilepsies, especially as adjuncts. Rarely used now. Effective at times when all else fails.	Psychoses, mental dullness, acneiform rash (stop drug; may resume at lower dose).
Phensuximide (Milontin®)	0.5–2.5 gm in divided doses	Petit mal.	Nausea, ataxia, dizziness (reduce dosage or discontinue); hematuria (discontinue).
Methsuximide (Celontin®)	1.2 gm in divided doses	Petit mal, psychomotor epilepsy.	Ataxia, drowsiness (decrease dosage or discontinue).
Ethosuximide (Zarontin®)	750–1500 mg in divided doses	Petit mal.	Drowsiness, nausea, vomiting (decrease dosage or discontinue).

*Modified and reproduced, with permission, from J.G. Chusid: *Correlative Neuroanatomy & Functional Neurology*, 14th ed. Lange, 1970.

TABLE 16–1 (cont'd). Drugs used in epilepsy.

Drug	Average Daily Dose	Indications	Toxicity and Precautions
Acetazolamide (Diamox®)	1–3 gm in divided doses†	Grand mal, petit mal.	Drowsiness, paresthesias (reduce dosage).
Chlordiazepoxide (Librium®)	15–60 mg in divided doses	Mixed epilepsies. Useful in patients with behavior disorders; also in status epilepticus (by intravenous infusion).	Drowsiness, ataxia (decrease dosage or discontinue).
Diazepam (Valium®)	8–30 mg in divided doses		
Meprobamate (Equanil®, Miltown®)	1.2–2 gm in divided doses	Absence attacks, myoclonic seizures.	Drowsiness (decrease dosage or discontinue).
Dextroamphetamine sulfate (Dexedrine®)	20–50 mg in divided doses	Absence and akinetic attacks. Counteracts sleepiness. Useful in narcolepsy.	Anorexia, irritability, insomnia (decrease dosage or discontinue).
Methamphetamine (Desoxyn®)	2.5–10 mg in divided doses		

†Begin with 0.25 gm 3 times daily.

deep reflexes absent, and the Babinski reflex positive. The patient may remain confused and disoriented during the initial stage of recovery. A period of deep sleep often follows. Upon awakening, the patient may complain of sore muscles.

2. Petit mal (minor epilepsy)–(Petit mal and grand mal may coexist.) The so-called "petit mal triad" includes myoclonic jerks, akinetic seizures, and brief absences (blank spells) without associated falling and body convulsions. A specific 3/second spike and wave EEG pattern is present.

Petit mal epilepsy is more often encountered in children. There may be momentary or transient loss of consciousness, so fleeting or hidden in ordinary activity that neither the patient nor his associates are aware of it. Classic petit mal is characterized by a sudden vacant expression, cessation of motor activity, and loss of muscle tone. Consciousness and mental and physical activity return abruptly. As many as 100 attacks may occur daily.

3. Jacksonian epilepsy–This type of epilepsy consists of a focal convulsion during which consciousness is often retained. The seizure may be motor, sensory, or autonomic in type. The seizure commonly starts in part of a limb (eg, thumb or great toe) or face (eg, at the angle of the mouth) as a localized clonic spasm, and spreads in a more or less orderly fashion. For example, a seizure may pass from the hand along the upper extremity to involve the shoulder, trunk, thigh, and leg muscles.

Loss of consciousness is apt to occur when the seizure spreads to the opposite side and becomes generalized.

The seizure may remain confined to the site of origin, waxing and waning in intensity ("epilepsia partialis continua").

4. Psychomotor seizures–In this category are included most types of attacks which do not conform to the classical criteria of grand mal, jacksonian seizures, or petit mal. Automatisms, patterned movements, apparently purposeful movements, incoherent speech, turning of head and eyes, smacking of the lips, twisting and writhing movements of the extremities, clouding of consciousness, and amnesia commonly occur. Temporal lobe foci (spikes, sharp waves, or combinations of these) are frequently noted in the EEG, and striking accentuation of these abnormalities is often seen during light phases of sleep.

5. Status epilepticus–Recurrent severe seizures with short or no intervals between seizures are frequently of serious import. Patients who remain comatose are apt to become exhausted and hyperthermic, and may die.

6. Febrile convulsions–In the very young, convulsions may be associated with or precipitated by a febrile illness. A febrile convulsion is sometimes the initial convulsion of an epileptic child, and many of these children subsequently develop psychomotor seizures. Febrile convulsions are more common in children with a family history of epilepsy. Nonfebrile convulsions often occur in patients with a history of febrile convulsions.

7. Massive spasms–This type of seizure is most commonly encountered in the first 2 years of life, especially in children with evidence of motor and mental retardation. Sudden strong contraction of most of the body musculature occurs, often resulting in transient doubling up of the body and flexion-adduction of the limbs. A characteristic EEG pattern ("hypsarhythmia") is often present. A favorable response to treatment with corticotropin has been reported for some patients.

B. Laboratory Findings: EEG is the most important test in the study of epilepsy. In some cases provocative measures (eg, hyperventilation, sleep, drugs, photic stimulation) are of diagnostic value.

Skull x-rays, CSF studies, blood glucose and blood calcium determinations, pneumograms, brain scans, and cerebral angiograms may aid in determining the cause of convulsions.

Differential Diagnosis

In syncope there is an associated drop in blood pressure, the muscles are flaccid, there are no convulsive movements initially, and the attack subsides with increased brain blood flow in recumbency.

In hysteria there is usually no loss of consciousness, incontinence, tongue biting, or self-injury. The patient may be resistive, and the "convulsion" is erratic and atypical.

Narcolepsy is characterized by irreversible sleep attacks of brief duration, frequently associated with catalepsy (sudden loss of muscle tone with no loss of consciousness, precipitated by acute emotional disturbances such as fright or laughter).

Complications

Fractures and soft tissue injuries may occur during seizures. Mental and emotional changes, particularly in poorly controlled epileptics, sometimes occur. Behavioral or emotional components may mask an underlying convulsive disorder. Examples are disorientation, hallucinations, excitement, incoherent speech, erratic behavior, automatisms, mental dullness, and irritability.

Treatment

The objective of therapy is complete suppression of symptoms, though in many cases this is not possible. Epileptics may continue to receive anticonvulsant therapy throughout life. However, if seizures are entirely controlled for 3–5 years, the dosage may be slowly reduced (over a period of 1–2 years) and finally withdrawn to ascertain if seizures will recur.

The patient must be acquainted with his disease and encouraged to become a member of local branches of groups interested in the welfare of epileptics, such as the Epilepsy Association of America. Patients may receive information regarding research and treatment from these organizations.

Excellent books about epilepsy are W.G. Lennox: *Science and Seizures,* Harper, 1941; T.J. Putnam: *On Convulsive Seizures, A Manual for Patients.,* Lippincott, 1945; and F.A. Gibbs and F.W. Stamps: *Epilepsy Handbook,* Thomas, 1958.

Epileptic patients should avoid hazardous occupations and driving. It is important to maintain a regular program of activity to keep the patient in optimal physical condition but avoiding excessive fatigue. Forbid all alcohol. Treat emotional factors as indicated. Impress upon the patient the absolute necessity of faithful adherence to the drug regimen. An epilepsy identification card should be carried at all times.

Except in status epilepticus, no specific treatment is usually given during an attack except to protect the patient from injury. Anticonvulsant measures (see also Table 16–1) in the 4 principal types of epilepsy are as follows:

A. Grand Mal: *Caution:* Never withdraw anticonvulsant drugs suddenly.

1. Diphenylhydantoin sodium (Dilantin®) is the drug of choice. Give 0.1 gm after the evening meal for 3–7 days, increasing dosage by 0.1 gm daily every week until seizures are brought under control. If attacks are severe and frequent, it may be necessary to begin with 0.3 gm daily on the first visit. The average dose is 0.3–0.6 gm daily. After convulsive seizures are controlled, the dosage may be reduced if desired, but the dosage should immediately be raised again if symptoms return. A therapeutic level of serum diphenylhydantoin is believed to be 10–20 μg/ml (1–2 mg/100 ml).

2. Phenobarbital—If the patient is on maximum dosage of diphenylhydantoin and there is inadequate response, give phenobarbital in addition to diphenylhydantoin, increasing dosage as with diphenylhydantoin, while maintaining full dosage of diphenylhydantoin. Some clinicians prefer to begin with phenobarbital and maintain without diphenylhydantoin if possible. In many cases the 2 drugs used in combination are more effective than either drug used alone.

3. Mephenytoin (Mesantoin®)—If excessive gum hypertrophy results from the use of diphenylhydantoin, mephenytoin may be tried in its place. The dosage is the same. This drug may be effective where grand mal and petit mal exist. Do not change suddenly to mephenytoin, but gradually substitute for diphenylhydantoin. Combinations of both may prove more useful than the individual drugs.

4. Bromides, primidone (Mysoline®), mephobarbital (Mebaral®), or ethotoin (Peganone®) may be tried (Table 16–1).

B. Petit Mal: In very mild petit mal, if attacks are rare, treat only with phenobarbital.

For moderate and severe petit mal, the succinimides (ethosuximide [Zarontin®], methsuximide [Celontin®], and phensuximide [Milontin®]) and the diones (trimethadione [Tridione®] and paramethadione [Paradione®]) are highly effective. Unfortunately Tridione® is not an entirely safe drug since it causes bone marrow depression in some patients. *Caution:* Whenever this drug is used, perform a complete blood count once or twice a week for the first month, then every 2 weeks for 2–3 months, and monthly thereafter. Begin with 0.3 gm daily and increase the daily dose by 0.3 gm every 7 days until attacks are controlled. Do not give more than 2 gm daily.

If grand mal seizures occur also, trimethadione may aggravate this tendency; it may therefore be necessary to administer medication for grand mal seizures simultaneously, and in some cases to stop the trimethadione. Paramethadione (Paradione®) is said to be less toxic than trimethadione. It is almost equally effective in petit mal attacks, and may be effective where other drugs fail. Observe precautions as for trimethadione.

Phensuximide (Milontin®), phenobarbital, methsuximide (Celontin®), acetazolamide (Diamox®), or mephobarbital (Mebaral®) may prove useful (Table 16–1). Ethosuximide (Zarontin®) is very effective in petit mal.

C. Status Epilepticus: Amobarbital sodium (Amytal Sodium®), 0.5–1 gm IV, may be given. Intravenous phenobarbital sodium, 0.4–0.8 gm, injected slowly, may be used. Paraldehyde, 1–2 ml diluted in a triple volume of saline IV slowly, is an effective alternative. If the convulsion continues, repeat the intravenous dose **very slowly and cautiously**, or give 8–12 ml IM. Diphenylhydantoin sodium (Dilantin Sodium®) may be injected intravenously at a rate not exceeding 50 mg/minute. A total dosage of 150–250 mg may be required. General anesthesia may be used if all measures fail. Diphenylhydantoin sodium (Dilantin Sodium®), 250–500 mg IM daily, or phenobarbital sodium, 30–60 IM 4 times daily (**or both**), may be required until the patient is able to take medication orally. Diazepam (Valium®), 10 mg IV, is effective and may be repeated once or twice as necessary. Hypotension and respiratory depression may occur as side-effects.

D. Psychomotor Epilepsy: Patients must be watched and guarded to prevent injury to themselves or others. Diphenylhydantoin sodium (Dilantin®), with or without phenobarbital, as for grand mal epilepsy, is the treatment of choice. Phenacemide (Phenurone®) is also effective. Give initially 0.5 gm 3 times daily and increase (until symptoms are controlled) up to 5 gm daily in 3–5 equal doses. Mephenytoin (Mesantoin®), mephobarbital (Mebaral®), primidone (Mysoline®), acetazolamide (Diamox®), and methsuximide (Celontin®), alone or in combination with other drugs, are frequently useful.

Prognosis

In symptomatic epilepsy due to identifiable lesions, the outcome varies with the underlying disease. In idiopathic epilepsy, skillful use of anticonvulsant drugs causes significant improvement in the great majority of cases.

Carter, S., & A. Gold: Convulsions in children. New England J Med 278:315–316, 1968.

Coatsworth, J.J.: Studies on the clinical efficacy of marketed antiepileptic drugs. NINDS Monograph No. 12, 1971.

Falconer, M.A.: Genetic and related aetiological factors in temporal lobe epilepsy. Epilepsia 12:13–21, 1971.

Falconer, M.A., & D.C. Taylor: Surgical treatment of drug-resistant epilepsy due to mesial temporal sclerosis. Arch Neurol 19:353–361, 1968.

Frantzen, E., & others: A genetic study of febrile convulsions. Neurology 20:909–917, 1970.

Karnes, W.E.: Medical treatment for convulsive disorders. M Clin North America 52:959–976, 1968.

Livingston, S.: *Drug Therapy for Epilepsy.* Thomas, 1966.

Millichap, J.G., & F. Amyat: Treatment and prognosis of petit mal epilepsy. P Clin North America 14:905–920, 1967.

Nicol, C.F., Tutton, J.C., & B.H. Smith: Parenteral diazepam in status epilepticus. Neurology 19:332–344, 1969.

Rennie, L.E.: Management of epilepsy. GP 39:116–140, March 1969.

Robb, P.: Epilepsy: A review of basic and clinical research. NINDB Monograph No. 1, 1965.

Sawyer, G.T., Webster, D.D., & L.J. Schut: Treating uncontrolled seizures with diazepam. JAMA 203:913–918, 1968.

Schwartz, J.F.: Recent advances in treating epileptic children. Postgrad Med 44:107–115, 1968.

Symposium on post-traumatic epilepsy. Epilepsia 11:1–124, 1970.

Wallis, W., Kutt, H., & F. McDowell: Intravenous diphenylhydantoin in treatment of acute repetitive seizures. Neurology 18:513–525, 1968.

Waddington, M.W.: Angiographic changes in focal motor epilepsy. Neurology 20:879–888, 1970.

CONGENITAL CNS DEFECTS

SYRINGOMYELIA

Essentials of Diagnosis

- Loss of pain and temperature sense but preservation of other sensory function (painless burning or injury to hands).
- Weakness, hyporeflexia or areflexia, wasting of muscles at level of spinal cord involvement (usually upper limbs and hands).
- Hyperreflexia and spasticity at lower levels.

General Considerations

Syringomyelia is a disease of the spinal cord and brain stem of unknown cause, associated with gliosis and cavitation of the spinal cord and brain stem. The onset of symptoms is usually in the 3rd or 4th decade. Although the etiology is not known, a developmental defect has been inferred because other congenital defects are usually present also. A coincidence of syringomyelia and intramedullary tumors (gliomas, hemangiomas) has also been noted.

Clinical Findings

The characteristic clinical picture is that of muscular wasting and weakness, dissociation and loss of the pain-temperature sense, and signs of injury to the long tracts.

A. Symptoms and Signs: The most common form is cervical syringomyelia involving the cervical spinal cord. Loss of pain and temperature sensibility in the cervical and thoracic dermatomes in shawl-like distribution is characteristic. The following are variably present: painless burns of the fingers or forearms, atrophy of the small muscles of the hands (usually present), weakness and atrophy of the shoulder girdle muscles, Horner's syndrome, nystagmus, vasomotor and trophic changes of the upper extremities, absence of deep reflexes of the upper extremities, Charcot joints in affected limbs, spasticity and ataxia of the lower extremities, and neurogenic bladder.

Involvement of the lumbosacral spinal cord may also occur, with weakness and atrophy of the lower extremities and pelvic girdle, dissociated sensory loss in the lumbosacral area, bladder paralysis, and vasomotor and trophic disturbances of the lower extremities.

When the medulla oblongata of the brain stem is involved, the process may be referred to as syringobulbia. This is characterized by atrophy and fibrillation of the tongue, loss of pain and temperature sensibility in the face, and nystagmus. Dysphonia and respiratory stridor may occur.

B. Laboratory Findings: Myelography discloses the presence in many cases of partial or complete block in the zone of the syringomyelia. A characteristic deformity of the contrast column may be noted on the myelogram.

Differential Diagnosis

Spinal cord tumor gives a characteristic myelographic deformity, and is more apt to be associated with complete subarachnoid spinal block.

In multiple sclerosis the symptoms are intermittent and there are usually no associated trophic changes or scoliosis and no dissociation or loss of pain and temperature sensibility.

Amyotrophic lateral sclerosis is characterized by symmetric, widespread muscle wasting with no sensory loss, and fasciculations of muscle. In tabes dorsalis, serology is usually positive. Argyll Robertson pupils may be present, and the areas of cutaneous sensory deficit are smaller.

Platybasia and cervical spine anomalies show characteristic skull and cervical spine x-rays and characteristic myelograms.

Treatment

The treatment varies with the degree of clinical involvement and evidence of block on myelography. Laminectomy and decompression may be required, with needle aspiration or myelotomy through the posterior median fissure of the spinal cord in properly selected cases. Roentgen therapy of the affected area of the spinal cord has also been recommended, but the effects are poor.

Prognosis

Syringomyelia is slowly progressive over a period of many years. Severe incapacity may occur because of paralysis, muscular atrophies, and sensory defects. In spinal cases, intercurrent infections, especially of the bladder, commonly occur. In syringobulbia, death may occur in several months because of the destruction of vital medullary nuclei.

Love, J.G., & R.A. Olafson: Syringomyelia: A look at surgical therapy. J Neurosurg 24:714, 1966.

McIlroy, W.J., & J.C. Richardson: Syringomyelia: A clinical review of 75 cases. Canad MAJ 93:731–734, 1965.
Pitts, F.W., & R.A. Groff: Syringomyelia: Current status of surgical therapy. Surgery 56:806–809, 1964.

CERVICAL RIB (NAFFZIGER'S) SYNDROME
(Scalenus Anticus Syndrome)

The brachial plexus and subclavian artery may be compressed in the neck by a rudimentary cervical rib, fibrous band, first thoracic rib, or tight scalene muscle giving rise to sensory, motor, or vascular symptoms in one or both upper extremities. The onset of symptoms has been related by some to the loss of tone in shoulder girdle muscles with age or excessive trauma to these parts incurred by lifting or straining.

Clinical Findings

Cervical ribs, rudimentary or fully developed, are relatively common although frequently asymptomatic. Although they are often bilateral, cervical ribs may give rise to unilateral complaints. Prominence of the lower neck above the clavicle on one or both sides may be obvious on inspection. Pressure in this region will give rise to local pain as well as pain referred to the hand and arm. Pain and paresthesia, particularly in the ulnar portion of the hand and forearm, most commonly occur. Impaired perception of pain and light touch in the hand or forearm, and muscular weakness of small hand muscles, may also be present. Coldness and blueness of the hand and diminished pulsation in the radial and ulnar arteries may be noted. Horner's syndrome, resulting from damage to cervical sympathetics, has occurred. Adson's test or maneuver is usually positive on the affected side. The patient, seated with hands resting on thighs, takes a rapid deep inspiration, holds his breath, hyperextends his neck, and turns his head as far as possible first to one side and then the other. Obliteration of the pulse on one side is considered a positive test.

Treatment & Prognosis

The clinical course is variable. Frequent remissions or slow progression occur. Temporary relief may be obtained by wearing a sling support on the affected extremity. Rest in bed, traction on the neck, and the use of pillows to support the shoulders are also helpful. Surgical removal of cervical ribs, division of fibrous bands, or section of the scalenus anticus muscles may give permanent relief.

Frankel, S.A., & I. Hirata, Jr.: The scalenus anticus syndrome and competitive swimming. JAMA 215:1796–1798, 1971.
Moore, M., Jr.: Scalenus anticus syndrome. South MJ 59:954–959, 1966.
Neviaser, J.S.: Musculoskeletal disorders of the shoulder region causing cervicobrachial pain: Differential diagnosis and treatment. S Clin North America 43:1703–1714, 1963.
Schlesinger, E.B.: The thoracic outlet syndrome from a neurosurgical point of view. Clin Orthop 51:49–52, 1967.

VASCULAR DISEASES
OF THE CNS

CEREBROVASCULAR ACCIDENTS
(Strokes)

Essentials of Diagnosis

- Sudden onset of neurologic complaints varying from focal motor or hypesthesia and speech defects to profound coma.
- May be associated with vomiting, convulsions, or headaches.
- Nuchal rigidity frequently found.

General Considerations

Cerebrovascular accident or stroke is a focal neurologic disorder due to a pathologic process in a blood vessel. In most cases the onset is abrupt and evolution rapid, and symptoms reach a peak within seconds, minutes, or hours. Partial or complete recovery may occur over a period of hours to months.

Three basic processes account for most cerebrovascular accidents: thrombosis, embolism, and hemorrhage. Other infrequent causes include recurrent ischemic attacks, hypertensive encephalopathy, migrainous hemiplegia, and syncope.

Cerebrovascular accident is uncommon in persons under 40 years of age. The most frequent predisposing illnesses in cerebral thrombosis are cerebral arteriosclerosis, syphilis and other infections, dehydration, and trauma. Cerebral embolism may consist of small pieces of blood clot, tumor, or fat, or clumps of bacteria. Cerebral hemorrhage is usually caused by rupture of an arteriosclerotic cerebral vessel. Subarachnoid hemorrhage is usually due to rupture of a congenitally weak blood vessel or aneurysm.

Occlusion of a cerebral artery by thrombosis or embolism results in a cerebral infarction with its associated clinical effects. Other conditions may on occasion also produce cerebral infarction and thus may be confused with cerebral thrombosis or embolism. These include cerebral venous thrombosis, cerebral arteritis, systemic hypotension, reactions to cerebral angiography, and transient cerebral ischemia.

Transient cerebral ischemia may also occur without producing a cerebral infarction. Premonitory recurrent focal cerebral ischemic attacks may occur and are apt to be in a repetitive pattern in a given case. Attacks may last for 10 seconds to 1 hour, but the average duration is 2–10 minutes. As many as several hundred such attacks may occur.

Narrowing of the extracranial arteries (particularly the internal carotid artery at its origin in the neck and, in some cases, the intrathoracic arteries) by arteriosclerotic patches has been incriminated in a significant number of cases of transient cerebral ischemias and infarction.

Clinical Findings

A. Early Symptoms and Signs: Variable degrees and types occur. The onset may be violent, with the patient falling to the ground and lying inert like a person in deep sleep, with flushed face, stertorous or Cheyne-Stokes respirations, full and slow pulse, and one arm and leg usually flaccid. Death may occur in a few hours or days. Lesser grades of stroke may consist of slight derangement of speech, thought, motion, sensation, or vision. Consciousness need not be altered. Symptoms may last seconds to minutes or longer, and may persist indefinitely. Some degree of recovery is usual.

Premonitory symptoms may include headache, dizziness, drowsiness, and mental confusion. Focal premonitory symptoms are more likely to occur with thrombosis.

Generalized neurologic signs are most common with cerebral hemorrhage and include fever, headache, vomiting, convulsions, and coma. Nuchal rigidity is frequent with subarachnoid hemorrhage or intracerebral hemorrhage. Mental changes are commonly noted in the period following a stroke and may include confusion, disorientation, and memory defects. Specific focal signs and symptoms are apt to be associated with disorders of particular arteries:

1. **Middle cerebral artery**—Contralateral monoparesis or hemiparesis, numbness, tingling; dysphagia, homonymous hemianopia, scintillating scotomas.

2. **Anterior cerebral artery**—Weakness or numbness of the opposite leg; reflex incontinence.

3. **Posterior cerebral artery**—Hemianopia, scintillating scotomas, possibly blindness.

4. **Internal carotid artery**—Contralateral weakness, numbness, or dysphagia; mental confusion, poor memory, motor aphasia and personality changes; transient blindness or amblyopia, and decreased central retinal artery pressure (by ophthalmodynamometry) on the involved side.

5. **Vertebral and basilar arteries**—Dizziness; monoparesis, hemiparesis, or quadriparesis; bilateral numbness, staggering gait, ataxia, diplopia, dysphagia, dysarthria, blindness, deafness, confusion, or loss of memory and consciousness.

6. **Great vessels of aortic arch**—Diminished or absent pulsation in the common carotid, intermittent claudication, localized bruit and blood pressure differences in the 2 arms.

7. **Subclavian and innominate artery**—Occlusion of these vessels (subclavian steal syndrome) may cause collateral vertebral artery circulation on the involved side, resulting in retrograde flow and reduced blood supply to the brain, with dizzy spells and other cerebral symptoms.

B. Late Symptoms and Signs: usually resembling the acute manifestations and related to the location and degree of brain infarction or hemorrhage. Recovery is sometimes remarkably complete, so that altered brain function may be hardly demonstrable even with special tests (EEG, psychometrics, pneumoencephalography, etc). Generally, however, patients have lesser

TABLE 16—2. Diagnosis of cerebrovascular disorders.*

	Intracerebral Hemorrhage	Cerebral Thrombosis	Cerebral Embolism	Subarachnoid Hemorrhage	Vascular Malformation and Intracranial Bleeding
Onset	Generally during activity. Severe headache (if patient is able to report findings).	Prodromal episode of dizziness, aphasia, etc, often with improvement between attacks. Unrelated to activity.	Onset usually within seconds or minutes. No headache. Usually no prodrome. Unrelated to activity.	Sudden onset of severe headache unrelated to activity.	Sudden "stroke" in young patient. No headache. Unrelated to activity.
Course	Rapid hemiplegia and other phenomena over minutes to 1 hour.	Gradual progression over minutes to hours. Rapid improvement at times.	Rapid improvement may occur.	Variable; apt to be at worst in initial few days after onset.	Most critical period is usually in early stages.
History and related disorders	Suspect diagnosis especially if other hemorrhagic manifestations are present and in acute leukemia, aplastic anemia, thrombopenic purpura, and cirrhosis of the liver.	Evidence of arteriosclerosis, especially coronary, peripheral vessels, aorta. Associated disorders: diabetes mellitus, xanthomatosis.	Evidence of recent emboli: (1) other organs (spleen, kidneys, lungs), extremities, intestines; (2) several regions of brain in different cerebrovascular areas.	History of recurrent stiff neck, headaches, subarachnoid bleeding.	History of repeated subarachnoid hemorrhages, epilepsy.
Sensorium	Rapid progression to coma.	Relative preservation of consciousness.	Relative preservation of consciousness.	Relatively brief disturbance of consciousness.	Relatively brief disturbance of consciousness.
Neurologic examinations	Focal neurologic signs or special arterial syndromes; nuchal rigidity.	Focal neurologic signs or special arterial syndromes.	Focal neurologic signs or special arterial syndromes.	Focal neurologic signs frequently absent; nuchal rigidity, positive Kernig and Brudzinski signs.	Focal neurologic signs; cranial bruit.
Special findings	Hypertensive retinopathy, cardiac hypertrophy, and other evidences of hypertensive cerebrovascular disease may be present.	Evidence of arteriosclerotic cardiovascular disease frequently present.	Cardiac arrhythmias or infarction (source of emboli usually in the heart).	Subhyaloid (preretinal) hemorrhages.	Subhyaloid (preretinal) hemorrhages and retinal angioma.
Blood pressure	Arterial hypertension.	Arterial hypertension frequent.	Normotensive.	Arterial hypertension frequent.	Normotensive.
CSF	Grossly bloody.	Clear.	Clear.	Grossly bloody.	Grossly bloody.
Skull x-ray	Shift of pineal to opposite side.	Calcification of internal carotid artery siphon visible; shift of pineal to opposite side may occur.	Pineal apt to show little if any displacement.	Partial calcification of walls of aneurysm sometimes noted.	Characteristic calcifications · in skull x-rays may be present.
Cerebral angiography	Hemorrhagic area seen as avascular zone surrounded by stretched and displaced arteries and veins.	Arterial obstruction or narrowing of circle of Willis (internal carotid, etc).	Arterial obstruction of circle of Willis branches (internal carotid, etc).	Typical aneurysmal pattern in circle of Willis arteries (internal carotid, middle cerebral, anterior cerebral, etc).	Characteristic pattern showing cerebral arteriovenous malformation.

*Reproduced, with permission, from J.G. Chusid: *Correlative Neuroanatomy & Functional Neurology*, 14th ed. Lange, 1970.

degrees of their initial defects (eg, hemiparesis, numbness, aphasia, hemianopsia, impaired mentation). Paralyzed limbs and parts in this later stage usually show signs of upper motor neuron disease: spastic weak muscles with little muscle atrophy, hyperactive deep reflexes, diminished or absent superficial reflexes, and pathologic reflexes such as a positive Babinski's sign. The patient may remain disoriented or comatose for prolonged periods. Death is often due to pneumonia.

C. Laboratory Findings: Careful lumbar puncture will reveal bloody CSF, often under increased pressure, in cerebral or subarachnoid hemorrhage.

D. X-Ray Findings: Cerebral angiography is essential for the diagnosis of aneurysms and vascular malformations, and may show narrowing, occlusion, or other abnormality of extracranial as well as intracranial vessels. Skull x-rays may show a displaced pineal gland, or calcification within the vascular malformation or aneurysm. Arteriography should usually consist of a series of studies which include all 4 arteries to the brain. An aortic arch study may be done first, usually by means of a catheter inserted into the arch through the right axillary or brachial artery or through one of the femoral arteries, usually using the percutaneous method of catheterization.

E. Special Studies: The EEG is abnormal in most major cerebrovascular accidents and may be used serially to help follow the clinical course. ECG may establish the presence of "silent" recent myocardial infarct, which is a contributing factor in certain cerebral infarctions.

Differential Diagnosis

In brain tumor there is a progression of clinical findings, elevated CSF pressure and protein, and papilledema. Focal neurologic signs are common.

Patients with subdural hematoma may give a history of head trauma, and there may be visible evidence of head injury, a shift of the pineal gland on skull x-ray, and a characteristic angiogram.

Meningitis and encephalitis are differentiated on the basis of CSF changes (clouding; increased cells, protein, pressure; positive culture).

Hypertensive encephalopathy is associated with elevated blood pressure, and the episodes are frequently transient.

Multiple sclerosis shows diffuse neurologic findings, and the clinical course is characterized by remission and then progression.

Treatment

A. Acute Stage or Onset:

1. General measures—Place the patient at complete bed rest and handle him carefully to avoid injury. If he is agitated, give tranquilizers or sedatives as necessary. If he is unconscious or unable to swallow, maintain nutrition with tube feedings or by parenteral means; do not attempt to give feedings by mouth. Catheterization may be necessary if spontaneous voiding does not occur.

2. Lumbar puncture—If hemorrhage has occurred, lumbar puncture should be performed very cautiously.

3. Anticoagulant therapy— Maintenance on anticoagulant therapy (see Chapter 8) has been advocated for treatment and prevention of cerebral thrombosis or insufficiency of the carotid or vertebral-basilar system. However, recent studies by several groups suggest that anticoagulant therapy helps only a few individuals in any large series of patients with the clinical picture of stroke. The evidence is most promising for transient cerebral ischemia. The risk of hemorrhage, particularly in hypertensive patients, is great.

4. Surgery—Narrowing of the extracranial arteries (eg, internal carotid) as shown on angiography may be an indication for surgical correction. Surgery may restore a more normal blood flow to the brain, and improvement may result if the collateral flow has not been adequate. Surgery may provide some future protection to the brain from damage due to a progression of the arterial disease with further reduction of total blood flow, or from emboli to the brain originating in the areas of stenosis. Stenoses that narrow the lumen less than 50% are not significant and should be left alone; "prophylactic" surgery on stenotic vessels in patients with no CNS symptoms is seldom indicated.

Emergency surgery for acute stroke has been disappointing, and fatal postoperative bleeding into an area of infarcted brain is not infrequent. In most cases, particularly if the patient is in coma or semi-coma, arterial studies and surgery should probably be deferred until the condition has stabilized and the collateral circulation has become better established. Patients with intermittent symptoms or constant mild neurologic defects—or those who have recovered well from a major vascular insult—should be evaluated for surgery. Patients with complete hemiplegia who show no signs of recovery will probably not be benefited by an operation to improve the blood supply to the damaged brain. If the occlusion of the internal carotid artery is complete and is more than a few hours old, the vessel will probably be thrombosed beyond the cervical segment of the internal carotid artery. Surgery to reestablish flow through this vessel is often unsuccessful.

Although the occlusive lesions of the larger intrathoracic vessels lend themselves best to surgical therapy, the results are also quite satisfactory in the surgical treatment of the stenotic lesions of the proximal internal carotid artery. Stenosis of the smaller vertebral artery may also be treated successfully, but if carotid disease also exists it should be treated in preference to the vertebral stenosis. Surgery for complete occlusion of the internal carotid or vertebral arteries or for significant and persistent CNS changes yields poor results in most cases.

B. Stage of Recovery and Convalescence:* The rehabilitation of the patient with a stroke should be started early and should be intensive. The rehabilitation goals are: (1) achievement of mobility and ambulation, (2) achievement of self-care, (3) psychosocial adjustment to disability, and (4) prevention of

*Prepared by Gerald G. Hirschberg, MD.

secondary disability. Since stroke patients have various disabilities, the rehabilitation program has to be related to the functional loss. Rehabilitation of patients whose only disability is hemiplegia is relatively simple. The program can be divided into 4 phases: bed phase, standing phase, stair-climbing phase, and cane-walking phase.

1. Bed Phase—The bed phase starts on the second or third day after onset or as soon as the patient is conscious. The patient's bed should be of chair height and should have side rails and an overhead trapeze.

a. Exercises—Start with 10 minutes of exercise every 4 hours and increase gradually.

(1) With the uninvolved arm and leg, turn from back to side to abdomen and return.

(2) With the uninvolved hand on the trapeze, pull to a sitting position.

(3) Move sideways, upward, and downward in bed.

(4) Sit up on the edge of the bed, legs dangling; move along the edge of the bed with the aid of the good arm and leg.

b. Self care—Done with the uninvolved hand.

(1) Toilet activities—Wash face and hands, comb hair, shave.

(2) Feeding activities—At first in bed with the back rolled up; later, sitting on the edge of the bed.

2. Standing phase—This phase starts 3–5 days after the beginning of the bed phase.

a. Exercise—The patient is placed in an armchair with his unaffected side next to the foot of the bed, the vertical bar of the overhead frame in reach of his uninvolved hand, and the paralyzed arm in a sling. Each of the following exercises is done 10 times every 4 hours, holding on with the uninvolved hand:

(1) Rise to a standing position using the uninvolved leg. Sit back.

(2) Stand up. Perform a slight knee bend and straighten up. Repeat with gradually deeper knee bends. Sit down.

(3) Stand up. Go up on toes, come back down. Sit down.

b. Self care—Use the uninvolved hand.

(1) Toilet activities—Complete bath in bed.

(2) Dressing activities—Dress and undress except for shoes.

3. Stair-climbing phase—This phase starts 2–10 days after the beginning of the standing phase.

a. Exercise—The patient is placed in a chair facing the foot of a flight of stairs, his uninvolved arm next to the banister. The paralyzed arm is in a sling, and the paralyzed leg is braced if necessary.

(1) Pull to a standing position, holding to the banister; step up one step with the uninvolved leg, and then pull the paralyzed leg up to the same step. Continue for several steps.

(2) Step backward and down with the paralyzed leg and put the uninvolved leg down next to it.

b. Self care—Complete toilet, feeding, and dressing activities should be possible by this time.

c. Bracing—

(1) If the patient has a foot drop during stair climbing, he should wear a short-leg brace with a 90° posterior stop at the ankle.

(2) If the patient shows evidence of inversion of the foot, he should have a short-leg brace with a T-strap.

(3) If the paralyzed leg remains completely flail, a long-leg brace is needed.

4. Cane-walking phase—This phase starts as soon as the patient is able to walk up and down a whole flight of stairs without tiring. A cane is held with the uninvolved hand.

a. Slow gait—(For fearful patients or patients with poor balance.) Move the cane forward, place the uninvolved foot next to the cane, and move the paralyzed foot next to it.

b. Fast gait—Standing on the uninvolved leg, move the cane and the paralyzed leg forward simultaneously and put weight on them. Swing the uninvolved leg through in front of the cane and the paralyzed leg and put weight on it. Continue in this fashion.

C. Special Problems in Hemiplegic Patients:

1. Care of the paralyzed upper extremity—In most cases no useful function returns to the paralyzed upper extremity. The sling may be discarded when the shoulder muscles become spastic. With his uninvolved hand, the patient should move the paralyzed fingers, wrist, and elbow through the full range of motion twice a day. In order to move the paralyzed shoulder through the full range of motion, the patient may use an overhead pulley by means of which the paralyzed arm, tied at the wrist, can be pulled up with the uninvolved arm. Ninety percent of hemiplegics develop a painful shoulder due to trauma during initial care. Careful positioning in bed and the arm sling may prevent injury. Treatment of painful shoulder consists of analgesics, immobilization, and gentle range of motion exercises.

If only partial function returns to the paralyzed extremity, the patient should use it only to the extent to which it is helpful or expedient.

2. Treatment of aphasia—If aphasia occurs, speech therapy (daily in ½-hour periods) should be started as soon as possible. If sensory or receptive aphasia is present, the above program may be rendered extremely difficult since it is based on the ability of the patient to understand what is required of him.

3. Care of hemianopsia—(A minor problem.) If hemianopsia is present, the patient should be trained to turn his head to the hemianopsic side in order to bring his visual field in front of him.

4. Care of sphincters—Some hemiplegics are incontinent in the early phase. An indwelling catheter is rarely necessary. The patient should be reminded to empty his bladder voluntarily at hourly intervals. These intervals can be gradually increased.

5. Organic brain syndrome—Impaired mentation is an obstacle to the rehabilitation program. The confusion may be present at one time and absent at another, and advantage should be taken of the patient's lucid periods. The organic brain syndrome occurs more often in patients who have had several strokes. The patient's mental state improves considerably during an active rehabilitation program.

6. Medications—All CNS depressing drugs, even in small doses, may have a detrimental effect on the stroke patient. They may cause or aggravate confusion, aphasia, lack of balance, and incontinence. If used as hypotensive or anticonvulsive agents, they should be replaced if possible by nondepressive drugs (eg, chlorothiazide instead of reserpine). On the other hand, CNS stimulating drugs can help improve function in the confused and depressed patient. Dextroamphetamine (one long-acting dose daily, 10–15 mg) is particularly useful.

Prognosis

In cerebral thrombosis, the outcome is determined to a great extent by the location and extent of the infarct as well as the general condition of the patient. The greater the delay in improvement, the poorer the prognosis.

In cerebral embolism, the underlying condition and the presence of emboli in other organs are significant factors.

In intracerebral hemorrhage, the prognosis is poor, particularly in the presence of hypertension and arteriosclerosis.

If the patient survives the acute attack, the prognosis for life may be good. With active rehabilitation, many patients are able to walk and care for themselves. Return of useful function to the upper extremity occurs infrequently. The prognosis for functional recovery is poor in patients with severe residual organic mental syndrome or receptive aphasia.

Acheson, J., & E.C. Hutchison: The nature of "focal cerebral vascular disease." Quart J Med 60:15–23, 1971.

A classification and outline of cerebrovascular disease. Neurology 8:395–434, 1958.

Baker, R.N., Ramseyer, J.C., & W.S. Schwartz: Prognosis in patients with transient cerebral attacks. Neurology 18:1157–1166, 1968.

Baker, R.N., Schwartz, W.S., & A.S. Rose: Transient ischemic strokes: A report of a study of anticoagulant therapy. Neurology 16:841–847, 1966.

Bauer, R.B., & others: Joint study of extracranial occlusion. III. Progress report of controlled study of long-term survival in patients with and without operation. JAMA 208:509–518, 1969.

Blaisdell, W.F., & others: Joint study of extracranial arterial occlusion. IV. A review of surgical considerations. JAMA 209:1889–1895, 1969.

Bradshaw, P., & E. Casey: Outcome of medically treated stroke associated with stenosis or occlusion of the internal carotid artery. Brit MJ 1:201–204, 1967.

Browne, T.R., & D.C. Poskanzer: Treatment of strokes. New England J Med 281:594–602, 650–657, 1969.

Fields, W.S., & others: Joint study of extracranial occlusions. V. Progress report of prognosis. JAMA 211:1993–2003, 1970.

Gurdjian, E.S., Darmody, W.R., & L.M. Thomas: Recurrent strokes due to occlusive disease of extracranial vessels. Arch Neurol 21:447–455, 1969.

Hirschberg, G.G.: The use of stand-up and step-up exercises in rehabilitation. Clin Orthop 12:30–46, 1958.

Hirschberg, G.G., Bard, G., & K. Robertson: Technics of rehabilitation of hemiplegic patients. Am J Med 35:536–545, 1963.

Hirschberg, G.G., Lewis, L., & D. Thomas: *Rehabilitation: A Manual of the Care of the Disabled and Elderly.* Lippincott, 1964.

Javid, H., & O.C. Julian: Prevention of stroke by carotid and vertebral surgery. M Clin North America 51:113–122, 1967.

Lhermitte, F., Gautier, J.C., & C. Derouesne: Nature of occlusions of the middle cerebral artery. Neurology 20:82–88, 1970.

Locksley, H.B.: Hemorrhagic strokes: Principal causes, natural history, and treatment. M Clin North America 52:1193–1212, 1968.

Louis, S., & F. McDowell: Stroke in young adults. Ann Int Med 66:932–938, 1967.

Marshall, J.: The differential diagnosis of "little strokes." Postgrad MJ 44:543–548, 1968.

McHenry, L.C., Jr., & M.E. Jaffe: Cerebrovascular disease. Part II. Management. GP 37:98–106, April 1968.

Millikan, C.H. (editor): *Cerebrovascular Disease.* Res Publ A Nerv Ment Dis, vol 61. Williams & Wilkins, 1966.

Moore, W.S., & A.D. Hall: Ulcerated atheroma of the carotid artery: A cause of transient cerebral ischemia. Am J Surg 116:237–242, 1968.

Norris, J.W., Elsen, A.A., & C.L. Branch: Problems in cerebellar hemorrhage and infarction. Neurology 19:1043–1048, 1969.

Santschi, D.R., & others: The subclavian steal syndrome: Clinical and angiographic considerations in 74 cases in adults. J Thoracic Cardiovas Surg 51:103, 1966.

Schoenberg, B.S., & others: Strokes in women of childbearing age. Neurology 20:181–189, 1970.

Waltz, AG: Studies of the cerebral circulation: What have they taught us about strokes? Proc Mayo Clin 46:268–274, 1971.

Yashon, D.: Strokes: Emergency detection and management. Postgrad Med 41:171–177, 1967.

INTRACRANIAL ANEURYSM
(Subarachnoid Hemorrhage)

Essentials of Diagnosis

Before Rupture:
- Headache on effort.
- Disorder of cranial nerves II, III, and V.
- Cranial bruit.
- Often asymptomatic.

After Rupture:
- Sudden onset of severe headache without apparent cause.
- Only brief disturbance of consciousness.
- Nuchal rigidity.
- Bloody CSF.

General Considerations

Intracranial aneurysms vary in size from 5–6 mm to 10 cm in diameter, and individual aneurysms may vary in size from time to time. Larger aneurysms may erode the bones of the skull and sella turcica and compress adjacent cerebral tissue and cranial nerves. Most are located near the basilar surface of the skull, and almost ½ arise from the internal carotid or middle cerebral arteries. They usually occur singly. A coincidence of congenital intracranial aneurysms and polycystic kidneys and coarctation of the aorta has been noted. Saccular aneurysms are rare in childhood; their peak incidence is between 35 and 65 years of age.

Fusiform dilatation of the basilar arteries or the terminal portions of the internal carotids may occur as a consequence of diffuse arteriosclerotic changes. Miliary, saccular aneurysms frequently occur near the bifurcation of a vessel in the circle of Willis and are associated with congenital abnormalities of the muscularis. A mycotic aneurysm, the result of an arteritis produced by bacterial emboli, is relatively infrequent. Larger aneurysms may be partially or completely clot-filled; occasionally they are calcified.

Clinical Findings

A. **Symptoms and Signs**: Prior to rupture, aneurysms may be asymptomatic or may cause symptoms depending upon their location and size. Headache on effort and symptoms of involvement of cranial nerves II, III, and V may be present. A bruit is sometimes heard over the affected site.

Following rupture, the symptoms are those of acute subarachnoid hemorrhage. Recurrent unilateral headaches which clinically resemble those of migraine sometimes occur. Convulsions due to cortical irritation by blood may occur; blood pressure is often elevated.

B. **X-Ray Findings**: By use of carotid or vertebral arterial angiography, an aneurysm may be demonstrated on x-ray.

Differential Diagnosis

Differentiate from intracranial tumor or other causes of sudden intracranial hemorrhage.

Treatment & Prognosis

In most cases the patient survives the first attack of hemorrhage, but recurrence of bleeding is likely. Because of the high mortality rate associated with spontaneous subarachnoid bleeding and the probability of recurrence of subarachnoid hemorrhage, intracranial aneurysms are considered a serious pathologic entity. The choice of surgical as opposed to medical treatment rests upon many circumstances, including the size and location of the aneurysm, the clinical status of the patient, the skill and experience of the surgeon, and the current enthusiasm for a particular therapeutic regimen. Various surgical procedures, including "trapping" the aneurysm with clips on either side, clipping the neck of the sac, and packing muscle around the aneurysm, have been successful in some cases.

Bailey, W.L., & J.D. Loeser: Intracranial aneurysms. JAMA 216:1993–1996, 1971.

Crompton, M.R.: The pathogenesis of cerebral aneurysms. Brain 89:797–814, 1966.

Du Boulay, G.H.: The natural history of intracranial aneurysms. Am Heart J 73:723–729, 1967.

Jamieson, K.G.: Aneurysms of the vertebrobasilar system: Further experience with nine cases. J Neurosurg 28:544–555, 1968.

McKissock, W., Richardson, A., & L. Walsh: Communicating aneurysms: A trial of conservative and surgical treatment. Lancet 1:873–876, 1965.

Nishioka, H.: Evaluation of the conservative management of ruptured intracranial aneurysms. J Neurosurg 25:574–592, 1966.

Raskind, R., & A. Doria: Long-term follow-up of intracranial aneurysms treated by cervical carotid ligation. Angiology 19:326–332, 1968.

Richardson, A.: Subarachnoid hemorrhage. Brit MJ 4:89–91, 1969.

Sahs, A.L., & others: *Intracranial Aneurysms and Subarachnoid Hemorrhage: A Cooperative Study.* Lippincott, 1969.

Skultety, F.M., & H. Nishioka: The results of intracranial surgery in the treatment of aneurysms. J Neurosurg 25:683–705, 1966.

Sundt, T.M.: Intracranial aneurysms and subarachnoid hemorrhage: A subject review for the clinician. Mayo Clin Proc 45:455–466, 1970.

Thomas, J.E., & T.J. Reagan: Nonhemorrhagic complications of intracranial aneurysms of the internal carotid artery. Neurology 20:1043–1052, 1970.

Uihlein, A., Thomas, R.L., & J. Cleary: Aneurysms of anterior communicating artery complex. Mayo Clin Proc 42:73–87, 1967.

Zingesser, L.H., & others: On the significance of spasm associated with rupture of a cerebral aneurysm. Arch Neurol 18:520–528, 1968.

CEREBRAL ANGIOMA

Subarachnoid hemorrhage from a cerebral angioma may bear a close clinical resemblance to a ruptured intracranial aneurysm. This type of angioma may vary from a small (2–3 mm) blemish in the cortex to large masses of tortuous channels (arteriovenous shunt), and may be designated as capillary, venous, or arterial (although the vessels are all abnormal). Clinically, cerebral angiomas are often associated with seizures which usually start in youth and are focal in nature. The patient may be aware of a pulsating mass in the head, and a bruit may be audible. Roentgenograms may show crescentic linear calcifications in the vessel walls.

The prognosis for ruptured angioma is generally believed to be better than for rupture of an aneurysm of the circle of Willis, and depends upon the size and site of the lesion. Surgical removal, when feasible, is performed at most centers; however, since a severe neurologic deficit may follow surgery, particularly if the dominant cerebral hemisphere is involved, the choice of operative versus nonoperative treatment often presents the clinician with a thereapeutic dilemma.

Berry, R.C., Alpers, B.J., & J.C. White: The site, structure and frequency of intracranial aneurysms, angiomas and arteriovenous malformations. Res Publ A Nerv Ment Dis 61:40–72, 1966.

Henderson, W.R., & R.D.L. Gomez: Natural history of cerebral angiomas. Brit MJ 1:571–574, 1967.

McCormick, W.F., Hardman, J.M., & T.R. Boulten: Vascular malformations ("angiomas") of the brain with special reference to those occurring in the posterior fossa. J Neurosurg 28:241–251, 1968.

Pool, J.L.: Excision of cerebral arteriovenous malformations. J Neurosurg 29:312, 1968.

Schatz, S., & H. Botterell: The natural history of arteriovenous malformations. Res Publ A Nerv Ment Dis 61:180–187, 1966.

BRAIN ABSCESS

Essentials of Diagnosis

- A history of preceding infection (eg, otitis media, mastoiditis, bronchiectasis, septicemia) is often present.
- Progressive or focal neurologic features.
- Evidence of increased intracranial pressure may be present.

General Considerations

Localized suppurations may occur within the brain as in other portions of the body. Following acute purulent infection, pus in brain tissue may be free or encapsulated. Abscesses vary in size from microscopic to an area covering most of a cerebral hemisphere.

Brain abscess is usually caused by staphylococci or pneumococci, although any of the common pyogenic bacteria may be found. The organism may gain access to the brain by direct extension from otitis media, mastoiditis, sinusitis, and infected head injuries, or, more rarely, via the blood stream from distant sources, such as lung infections and bacteremias.

Abscesses occurring by extension from infections of the middle ear or mastoid are usually located within the temporal lobe or cerebellum. Abscesses occurring by extension from the paranasal sinuses usually occur in the frontal lobe. Abscesses following bacteremia are apt to be multiple. Metastatic abscesses are commonly secondary to suppurative pulmonary infections.

Clinical Findings

A. Symptoms and Signs: A history or evidence of preceding infection is usually present. Otitis media, mastoiditis, sinusitis, bronchiectasis, or pneumonia is frequently present. Focalizing manifestations may occur, producing visual field defects, motor and other sensory changes, aphasia, and cranial nerve palsies similar to those caused by any other intracranial mass.

Signs of increased intracranial pressure may occur, such as papilledema, headache, and slowed pulse and respirations. Mild meningeal signs may be present, such as a mild rigidity of the neck and a positive Kernig sign. Somnolence and slowing of the mental processes are common. The temperature is mildly elevated and rarely exceeds 102° F (39° C) if complications such as meningitis do not occur.

B. Laboratory Findings: EEG, brain scan, air ventriculography, pneumoencephalography, or cerebral angiography is frequently necessary to determine the site of abscess.

C. Special Examinations: Brain abscesses may be located at operation with the use of needle aspiration.

Differential Diagnosis

Brain abscesses may be confused with other clinical entities such as brain tumors, leptomeningitis, or encephalitis. In brain tumor, a history or evidence of preceding infection is usually absent and the CSF cell count is usually normal. Leptomeningitis can usually be differentiated by means of a positive culture of the CSF. Acute fulminating leptomeningitis is easily distinguished clinically from brain abscess; mild leptomeningitis, such as tuberculous and syphilitic leptomeningitis, may be clinically indistinguishable. Encephalitis usually fails to exhibit the focalizing signs of brain abscess and usually provokes more profound and severe changes in the sensorium and personality.

Treatment & Prognosis

Treatment consists of operative drainage of pus. Surgery is usually delayed until the abscess is firmly encapsulated. If the abscess is well encapsulated and if it is practicable to do so, excision in toto is sometimes performed. Marsupialization of the cavity, packing of the cavity, and various types of incision and drainage are commonly employed. After surgical drainage has been instituted, irrigations of the abscess cavity with antibiotic solutions are helpful. Treatment of the original focus of infection, such as a chronic mastoiditis, is sometimes necessary before a brain abscess will heal completely.

The use of chemotherapy has greatly improved the outlook for brain abscess. It has even been maintained that the formation of brain abscesses—eg, in debilitated patients with pyogenic infections elsewhere—can be aborted with the use of appropriate antibiotic and sulfonamide drugs. Without treatment, brain abscess is usually fatal.

Gotten, N., & J. Howser: Brain abscess. A study of ninety-four cases. Pacific Med Surg 73:51–53, 1965.

Liske, E., & N.J. Weikers: Changing aspects of brain abscesses: Review of cases in Wisconsin 1940 through 1962. Neurology 14:294–300, 1964.

Loeser, E., Jr., & L. Scheinberg: Brain abscess. A review of ninety-nine cases. Neurology 7:601, 1957.

Tarkkanen, J., & A. Kohonen: Otogenic brain abscesses. Arch Otolaryng 91:91–93, 1970.

Victor, M., & B.Q. Banker: Brain abscess. M Clin North America 47:1355–1370, 1963.

TRAUMATIC DISEASES OF THE CNS

HEAD INJURY

Emergency Evaluation

Any patient who gives a history of head injury followed by unconsciousness, and any unconscious patient who may have sustained a head injury, should receive careful neurologic evaluation. Particular effort should be made to detect focal or progressive neurologic changes. Skull x-rays should be taken as soon as possible.

The following are the most important features of the examination:

(1) **State of consciousness**—The depth and duration of unconsciousness usually reflect the degree of trauma. However, an initially alert and well-oriented patient may become drowsy, stuporous, and comatose as a result of progressive intracranial hemorrhage. During the first 24–48 hours it may be necessary to awaken the patient hourly to evaluate his degree of orientation, alertness, and general response to stimulation. *Caution:* Do not discharge the patient to home care unless it is certain that a responsible person will be on hand to awaken him from "sleep" every hour and to summon aid if he cannot be completely aroused.

(2) **Vital signs**—Temperature, pulse, respirations, and blood pressure should be observed at intervals of ½–12 hours, depending upon the extent of injury.

(3) **Paralysis**—In the stuporous or unconscious patient, paralysis can be demonstrated only by careful examination. Loss of strength and motion, although of minimal grade, may indicate intracranial hemorrhage.

(4) **Ocular signs**—The pupils should be observed regularly along with the vital signs. A fixed dilated pupil often means an ipsilateral epidural or subdural hemorrhage or ipsilateral brain damage. Ophthalmoscopic examination may reveal evidence of papilledema (due to intracranial pressure) or retinal hemorrhage.

(5) **Convulsions**—Convulsions are apt to occur soon after a head injury; focal (jacksonian) convulsions suggest an irritative lesion of the contralateral cerebral hemisphere. Cerebral contusion and laceration, often in association with epidural, subdural, or intracranial hemorrhage causes focal convulsions.

(6) **Nuchal rigidity**—Although nuchal rigidity may result from the subarachnoid bleeding often associated with head injuries, cervical spine injury must be ruled out by appropriate x-ray and clinical examinations.

(7) **Bleeding from the ear**—Otorrhagia suggests basilar fracture through the petrous pyramid of the temporal bone, but it may also occur as a result of traumatic rupture of the tympanic membrane or laceration of the mucous membranes without perforation of the drum.

General Considerations

Craniocerebral injuries are frequently classified on the basis of the nature of the injury to the skull, although the prognosis for recovery depends primarily upon the nature and severity of the damage to the brain.

Closed head injuries are those in which there is no injury to the skull or in which the skull injury is limited to simple undisplaced fracture of the skull. They may be considered clinically as mild, moderate, or severe. Mild head injuries are characterized by brief loss of consciousness (seconds to minutes) without demonstrable neurologic changes (usually the same as cerebral concussion). CSF findings are usually normal. Retrograde amnesia may be present. Moderate head injuries are characterized by longer periods of unconsciousness, frequently with abnormal neurologic signs, and are often associated with cerebral edema and contusion. Severe head injuries cause prolonged unconsciousness and abnormal neurologic signs and are usually associated with cerebral contusion and laceration.

Open head injuries include scalp lacerations, compound fractures of the skull, and various degrees of cerebral destruction. If fragmentation of bone occurs, there will be extensive associated contusion and laceration of the brain. Consciousness may not be impaired at first, although depression of consciousness may occur later if progressive intracranial bleeding or edema occurs. Scalp lacerations should be sutured immediately unless they overlie a depressed fracture or penetrating wound of the skull, in which case the skin wound is treated in conjunction with the fracture in the operating room.

Fractures may be simple or compound, and linear (with no displacement of fragments), comminuted, or depressed.

Cerebral edema may follow head injury. Clinically, there is considerable variation in the severity of the findings. Localizing signs such as convulsions, hemiplegia, and aphasia are not uncommon. CSF pressure is usually slightly increased. At operation, the brain looks very pale and swollen.

Contusion or bruising of the brain at or directly contralateral to the zone of impact (contrecoup injury) may be limited to the superficial cortex, or associated hemorrhage into the underlying brain may also occur. Contusions frequently occur along the base of the posterior frontal lobes and the adjacent temporal lobe tips. Brain contusion is often clinically indistinguishable from concussion or laceration of the brain.

Brain laceration (a tear in the substance of the brain) usually occurs at the point of application of great force to the head or directly opposite (contrecoup effect). Lacerations involving the base of the brain usually cause death in a short time. Focal neurologic signs may persist after the acute episode has subsided. Associated subarachnoid or intracerebral hemorrhage is usually present, and the CSF is bloody. Brain laceration (or contusion) may occur with no injury (or minimal injury) to the skull. The frontal and temporal lobes are common sites. Minor injuries may cause tearing of the brain and meninges and extensive hemorrhagic necrosis of the cortex and subcortical white matter. Associated hemorrhage of the basal ganglia and brain stem may also occur. Laceration of arachnoidal vessels may result in subarachnoid bleeding or the formation of subdural hematoma. Tearing of the middle meningeal artery or the dural sinuses or veins may be followed by bleeding into the extradural spaces.

Clinical Findings

A. Symptoms and Signs: Transient loss of consciousness lasting seconds to minutes occurs classically with concussion of the brain. In coma which lasts for several hours or days there is a likelihood of edema or of contusion and laceration of the brain. The period of coma depends upon the extent and site of injury; in severe cases it may last for several hours, days, or weeks.

After the patient recovers consciousness, symptoms and signs are related to the severity and nature of associated brain injury. With mild concussion, the patient may be normal within a few minutes; with laceration or contusion of the brain, mental confusion is apt to be present. Hemiplegia, aphasia, cranial nerve paralysis, and other focal neurologic signs may also be noted depending upon the nature and extent of the brain injury. The ipsilateral pupil is often dilated in dural hemorrhage.

In the recovery phase and for months thereafter there may be complaints of headache, dizziness, and personality changes ("post-traumatic cerebral syndrome").

Loss of memory for the period immediately after recovery of consciousness post-traumatic amnesia) and for the period immediately preceding the injury (pretraumatic or retrograde amnesia) may occur and is often related to the extent of brain damage.

If the patient remains unconscious, diagnosis of a progressive intracranial hemorrhagic lesion is difficult. Vital signs (pulse rate, respirations, blood pressure) may change, although these are not reliable. In case of deepening or unusually prolonged coma, exploratory trephination is indicated; cerebral angiography may show pathognomonic features of subdural, epidural, or intracerebral hemorrhage. Prolonged unconsciousness is believed to indicate severe damage to the brain stem, usually due to secondary hemorrhage or compression of the brain stem.

B. Laboratory Findings:

1. Lumbar puncture may establish the presence of subarachnoid hemorrhage and establish a base-line appearance and pressure of the CSF. CSF is frequently normal in all respects in brain concussion or cerebral edema. With contusion or laceration of the brain, bloody CSF under increased pressure may be found.

2. Skull x-rays should be taken as soon as the patient's physical condition permits. Cerebral angiography may help demonstrate subdural or intracerebral hematoma. A pneumogram often is useful in demonstrating ventricular distortion, shift, or dilatation following head injury.

3. EEG and brain scans may be of diagnostic and prognostic aid in selected cases.

Differential Diagnosis

The history of a blow to the head makes the etiology of the unconsciousness evident; however, especially where a history of trauma is lacking, it is necessary to differentiate head injury from other causes of unconsciousness such as diabetic, hepatic, or alcoholic coma, cerebrovascular accident, and epilepsy (where trauma to the head may actually occur during the attack).

Differentiate the neurologic findings following head injury from those caused by epidural hematoma, subdural hematoma, brain tumor, etc.

Complications & Sequelae

The complications of head injuries include vascular lesions (hemorrhage, thrombosis, aneurysm formation), infections (meningitis, abscess, osteomyelitis), rhinorrhea and otorrhea, pneumatocele, leptomeningeal cysts, cranial nerve injuries, and focal brain lesions. The sequelae include convulsive seizures, psychoses, mental disturbances, and the post-traumatic cerebral syndrome.

A. Subarachnoid Hemorrhage: Bleeding into the subarachnoid space is often associated with other types of brain injury and is relatively common in traumatized patients who have been unconscious for 1 hour or more. The clinical and diagnostic features of traumatic and spontaneous subarachnoid hemorrhage are similar. Painful stiffness of the neck and the presence of fresh blood in the CSF are the usual findings.

B. Subdural Hematoma: Acute subdural hematoma may occur after a head injury in association with contusion or laceration of the brain. In such cases, especially when the subdural hematoma is not massive, the patient's clinical course may be unaffected by evacuation of the subdural hematoma. In chronic subdural hematomas, particularly when a history of head injury is not obtained, the clinical course may be variable or suggestive of an intracranial mass.

In infants, the diagnosis may be readily established by direct needle aspiration of the subdural space at the lateral margin of the open anterior fontanelle (subdural tap). In others, the cerebral angiogram remains the single most reliable diagnostic test, since a highly specific angiographic pattern is usually found. However, changes suggestive of subdural hematoma may also be noted in skull x-ray (shift of pineal), pneumogram (shift and distortion of ventricle), and electroencephalogram (focal low amplitude or slow waves).

C. Extradural Hemorrhage: Extradural hemorrhage classically follows traumatic rupture of the middle meningeal artery or vein, and may be difficult to detect early. A blow on the temporal area, with dazing or transient loss of consciousness and apparent quick return to normal, usually occurs. A "lucid interval," lasting as long as a day or more in extreme cases, customarily follows; during this time the patient develops signs of increased intracranial pressure. This is caused by the continued steady accumulation of blood in the extradural space from the bleeding middle meningeal vessel.

Trephining of the skull is frequently necessary to make the diagnosis. Blood may then be evacuated through the trephine openings.

A fracture which by x-ray is found to cross the middle meningeal groove should raise the suspicion that this syndrome may be present.

D. Intracerebral Hemorrhage: A large subcortical hematoma may develop, but the most common findings are multiple small intracerebral hemorrhages near the contused area. The angiographic pattern is characteristic.

E. Rhinorrhea and Otorrhea: Rhinorrhea (leakage of CSF from the nose) may follow fracture of the frontal bone with associated tearing of the dura mater and arachnoid. Erect posture, straining, and coughing usually cause an increase in the flow of fluid. Replacement of lost fluid by air entering the cranial vault through the same (or a similar) pathway may give rise to an aerocele. Otorrhea (leakage of CSF from the ear) is usually of serious prognostic importance since it is caused by injuries to the more vital areas of the base of the brain.

Infection and meningitis are potential hazards in both instances and may be prevented by the early use of prophylactic antibiotic therapy. In the case of rhinorrhea, surgical repair of the dural tear may be necessary to stop the flow of CSF and to close off a potential route of infection.

F. Cranial Nerve Paralysis: Injury to the cranial nerves may occur. Commonly affected nerves are the olfactory (anosmia), facial (paralysis), auditory (tinnitus and deafness), and optic (atrophy).

G. Post-Traumatic Syndrome: The post-traumatic syndrome is more common after serious head injuries, but severe symptoms may be produced by relatively minor injuries. Headache, giddiness, easy fatigability, memory defects, and impaired ability to concentrate are common complaints. Personality changes are not uncommon. Changes of posture, exposure to sunlight or heat, exercise, and alcohol ingestion are apt to make the symptoms worse.

On pathologic examination the brain may appear normal or may show severe cortical atrophy and ventricular dilatation.

H. Post-Traumatic Epilepsy: The exact incidence of seizures following head injuries is not known. In general, the more severe the injury, the greater the possibility of seizures. EEG studies are important in establishing the diagnosis.

I. Other Complications of Head Injuries:

1. Increased intracranial pressure may be manifested by changes in the level of consciousness, headache, restlessness, unequal pupils, a slowly falling respiratory rate, a falling pulse rate, a slowly rising blood pressure, papilledema, hemiparesis, and elevated CSF pressure. Intracranial bleeding (subdural, epidural, or intracerebral) must be ruled out.

2. Wound infection or osteomyelitis may be prevented by prophylactic antibiotic therapy in patients with compound or depressed fractures of the skull, rhinorrhea, otorrhea, or extensive scalp lacerations, and by meticulous aseptic technic for all dressings.

3. Pulmonary infections or atelectasis may be prevented or treated by the proper use of suction, positioning on the side, or, if necessary, intubation or tracheostomy.

4. Hyperthermia may result from injury to the hypothalamus or brain stem, local or general infection, or marked dehydration.

5. Shock may occur in patients with head injuries complicated by other severe injuries to the trunk and extremities, and must be treated at once.

Treatment

A. Emergency Measures:

1. Treat shock if present; parenterally administered fluids and blood may be required (see chapter 1).

2. Maintenance of an adequate airway and pulmonary ventilation is vital. The patient should be placed prone, with head turned to one side to facilitate drainage of secretions from the mouth and keep the tongue from obstructing the pharynx. Endotracheal intubation or tracheostomy may be necessary to maintain an open airway. Give oxygen if necessary.

B. General Measures:

1. During the acute or initial phases, restlessness may be a disturbing factor. Special nursing care and sedatives may be required. Avoid morphine because of its medullary depressant effects. Catheterization of a full bladder may ameliorate restlessness.

2. Antibiotic treatment is always indicated if there is active bleeding or discharge from the nose or ears. Give procaine penicillin G, 600,000 units twice daily, or broad-spectrum antibiotics, until the danger of infection is past.

3. Continued careful observation is essential.

Course & Prognosis

Prognosis and course are related to the severity and site of cranial injury. With simple concussion recovery is usually rapid. With laceration of the brain, mortality may be 40–50%.

Subdural or epidural hematoma ordinarily requires prompt surgical evacuation in order to prevent death or serious neurologic complications.

In general, residual symptoms and signs in patients with head trauma are likely to be more extensive and incapacitating in those with the more severe types of brain injury. It is not uncommon, however, for patients to remain symptomatic (headache, dizziness, impaired memory, personality changes) even though neurologic diagnostic studies are negative.

Predictions regarding the clinical outcome are more accurate when made 6–12 months after the injury or when the clinical status of the patient has stabilized. Great variations occur in individual cases. A patient in whom subdural hematoma has been successfully removed may recover completely. On the other hand, many patients continue to have severe complaints after an apparently trivial head injury. A complicating factor in many cases is the role played by the "secondary gain" for the patient via lawsuits, insurance, and other types of compensation.

De Jesus, P.V., Jr., & C.M. Poser: Subdural hematomas: A clinicopathologic study of 100 cases. Postgrad Med 44:172–181, 1968.

Evans, J.P.: Acute trauma to the head: Fundamentals of management. Postgrad Med 39:27–30, 1966.

Evans, J.P.: Advances in the understanding and treatment of head injury. Canad MAJ 95:1337–1348, 1966.

Jellinger, K., & F. Seitelberger: Protracted post-traumatic encephalopathy: Pathology, pathogenesis and clinical implications. J Neurol Sc 10:57–94, 1970.

Lewin, W.: Severe head injuries. Proc Roy Soc Med 60:1208–1211, 1967.

Mannarino, E., & R.L. McLaurin: Management of head injuries. Surg Clin 48:723–736, 1968.

Smith, S.W.: Subdural hematomas in adults. Postgrad Med 42:59–71, 1967.

Taylor, A.R.: Post-concussional sequelae. Brit MJ 3:62–70, 1967.

Walker, A.E., & others: Life expectancy of head injured men with and without epilepsy. Arch Neurol 29:95–101, 1971.

HERNIATION OF INTERVERTEBRAL DISK

Essentials of Diagnosis

Lumbosacral Disk

- Back pain aggravated by motion, and pain radiating down the back of the leg and aggravated by coughing or straining.
- Weakness of muscles, decreased sensation, hyporeflexia of leg and foot.
- Sciatic nerve painful to pressure and stretch (straight-leg raising).
- CSF protein may be elevated; myelograms reveal characteristic defect.

Cervical Disk

- Paroxysmal pains and paresthesias from back of neck radiating into the arms and fingers, usually in distribution of C6, C7, or C8; accentuated by coughing, sneezing, straining.
- Restricted mobility of neck; cervical muscle spasm.
- Paresthesias and pains in fingers, diminished biceps or triceps jerk, weakness or atrophy of forearm and hand muscles.
- Narrowing of vertebral interspace on x-ray; characteristic filling defect or deformity on myelogram.

General Considerations

In most cases rupture or herniation of an intervertebral disk is caused by trauma. Sudden straining with the back in an "odd" position and lifting in the trunk-flexed posture are commonly recognized precipitating causes. The defect may occur immediately after an injury or following an interval of months to years.

The lumbosacral intervertebral disks (L5–S1 or L4–L5) are most commonly affected, producing the clinical picture of sciatica. Herniation occasionally occurs in the cervical region (characterized by cervical radicular complaints); rarely in the thoracic region.

Clinical Findings

A. Symptoms and Signs: These usually depend upon the location and size of the herniated or extruded disk material. Compression of a nerve root by a disk may be confined to a single nerve root; however, several roots may be compressed (eg, cauda equina by disk at L5–S1). Larger cervical and thoracic lesions may even compress the spinal cord and produce symptoms commonly associated with tumors.

1. Lumbosacral disk–In the great majority (over 90%), rupture of the disk occurs at the level of the 4th or 5th lumbar interspace. This is characterized by straightening of the normal lumbar curve, scoliosis toward the side opposite the sciatic pain, limitation of motion of the lumbar spine, impaired straight-leg raising on the painful side, tenderness to palpation in the sciatic notch and along the course of the sciatic nerve, mild weakness of the foot or great toe extensors, impaired perception of pain and touch over the dorsum of the foot and leg (in L5 or S1 distribution), decreased or absent ankle jerk, and radiation of pain along the course of the sciatic nerve to the calf or ankle on coughing, sneezing, or straining.

2. Cervical disk herniation (5–10% of herniated disks)–The cervical disks most commonly involved are between C5–C6 and C6–C7. Paresthesias and pain occur in the upper extremities (hands, forearms, and arms) in the affected cervical root distribution (C6 or C7). Slight weakness and atrophy of the biceps or triceps may be present, with diminution of biceps or triceps jerk. The mobility of the neck is restricted with accentuation of radicular and neck pains by neck motion, coughing, sneezing, or straining. Long tract signs (extensor plantar response, sensory or motor impairment of lower levels, etc) occasionally occur, indicating compression of the spinal cord by the disk.

B. Laboratory Findings: CSF protein may be elevated, and complete or partial CSF block is occasionally demonstrated.

C. X-Ray Findings: Spine x-rays may show loss of normal curvature, scoliosis, and narrowing of the intervertebral disk. A characteristic roentgenologic defect in the subarachnoid space is usually produced by a herniated disk and is readily demonstrable by myelography. Electromyography (EMG) may be of value in localizing the site of a ruptured disk if characteristic denervation potentials can be demonstrated in muscles of a particular root distribution.

Differential Diagnosis

In tumors of the spinal cord the course is progressive, CSF protein is elevated, partial or complete spinal subarachnoid block is present, and the myelographic pattern is distinctive.

In arthritis neurologic findings are usually minimal or absent, and the myelogram is usually negative.

Spinal column anomalies show characteristic x-ray findings, CSF findings are negative, and myelographic changes are dissimilar or absent.

Treatment

A. General Measures:

1. Lumbosacral disk—In the acute phase, bed rest, heat applied locally to the back, salicylate analgesics, and the use of a bed board under the mattress are indicated. Traction to the lower extremities is frequently beneficial. The avoidance of severe physical effort and strain is essential to minimize recurrence of symptoms after the initial episode. Low back belts, braces, or supports may be beneficial. It is important to instruct the patient in the proper methods of bending, lifting (with knees flexed), and carrying (with the object held close to the body).

2. Cervical disk—In acute exacerbations of herniated cervical disks, bed rest with cervical halter traction is indicated. In subacute or mild episodes, intermittent cervical halter traction with various devices may be employed on an outpatient basis or at home. The use of a light collar may be helpful. Local application of heat, diathermy, and similar measures may be of temporary value.

B. Surgical Measures: If the response to conservative measures is poor or recurrences are disabling, diskectomy is indicated.

Prognosis

Conservative management with or without traction may bring about improvement to the point of "practical" recovery. Relief of pain usually follows removal of the damaged disk. Reversal of motor dysfunction, muscle atrophy, and skin sensory changes may occur.

Crandall, P.H., & U. Batzdorff: Cervical spondylotic myelopathy. J Neurosurg 25:57–66, 1966.

Epstein, J.A., & others: Herniated disks of the lumbar spine. JAMA 202:187–190, 1967.

Jacobs, B., Krueger, E.G., & D.M. Levy: Cervical spondylosis with radiculopathy. JAMA 211:2135–2139, 1970.

Kahn, E.A., & A.B. Rossier: Acute injuries of the cervical spine. Postgrad Med 39:37–44, 1966.

Levine, R.A., & others: Cervical spondyloses and dyskinesias. Neurology 20:1194–1200, 1970.

Petrie, J.G.: Conservative management of lumbar disk protrusion. Postgrad Med 38:654–657, 1965.

Raaf, J.: Some observations regarding 905 patients operated upon for protruded lumbar intervertebral disk. Am J Surg 97:388–399, 1959.

Symon, L., & P. Lavender: The surgical treatment of cervical spondylotic myelopathy. Neurology 17:117–127, 1967.

Wilkinson, H.A., LeMay, M.L., & E.J. Ferris: Clinical-radiographic correlations in cervical spondylosis. J Neurosurg 30:213–218, 1969.

INTRACRANIAL TUMORS

Essentials of Diagnosis

- Headache, personality changes, vomiting.
- Focal neurologic changes, often progressive.
- Increased CSF pressure, papilledema evidence of space-occupying lesion demonstrable on special examination (EEG, angiogram, pneumogram, cerebroscintigram, echoencephalogram).

General Considerations

Intracranial tumors account for many admissions to the average neurologic service. Metastatic tumors to the brain arise principally from the lung, breast, gastrointestinal tract, and thyroid. Less frequently, sarcoma, hypernephroma, melanoblastoma, and retinal tumors are the primary sources.

Primary intracranial tumors are unlike the carcinomas and sarcomas found outside the brain in that they rarely metastasize outside the CNS. They may be of congenital origin, eg, dermoids, teratomas, craniopharyngiomas; mesodermal origin, eg, meningiomas, neurinomas, angiomas, and hemangioblastomas; pituitary origin, eg, chromophobe tumors and chromophil tumors; or ectodermal origin, eg, the gliomas.

Gliomas account for 40–50% of intracranial tumors in some series. Depending upon the principal cell types and morphology, gliomas are subclassified into various types (eg, glioblastoma multiforme, astrocytoma, medulloblastoma, astroblastoma, ependymoma, oligodendroglioma). The majority of tumors of the brain in children arise from the cerebellum (medulloblastoma and astrocytoma). In adults, tumors of the cerebral hemispheres are common, particularly astrocytoma and glioblastoma multiforme. Gliomas of the brain in adults are most commonly encountered in the 40–50 year age group.

Clinical Findings

A. Symptoms and Signs: These are commonly divided into manifestations caused by the intracranial mass (headache, vomiting, papilledema) and those resulting from interference with local brain function. Focal neurologic changes frequently reflect the location of the tumor:

1. Frontal lobe tumor—These tend to produce a disturbed mental state with defective memory, impaired judgment, irritability, mood changes, and facetiousness. Convulsive seizures may occur, as well as loss of speech in left-sided (dominant hemisphere) tumor. Anosmia may occur with tumors at the base of the frontal lobe.

2. Parietal lobe tumor—Sensory and motor abnormalities are common. Motor or sensory focal seizures, contralateral hemiparesis, hyperreflexia, impaired sensory perception, astereognosis, and a positive Babinski toe sign may be present. With a left parietal lobe tumor aphasic components may be demonstrable.

3. **Occipital lobe tumor**—Visual alterations and seizures preceded by an aura of lights and visual hallucinations are characteristic. Contralateral homonymous hemianopsia, frequently with sparing of the macular area, often occurs. Headache and papilledema may be found.

4. **Temporal lobe tumor**—Convulsive seizures of the psychomotor type are commonly present, as is aphasia also if the dominant (left) cerebral hemisphere is involved. A contralateral homonymous visual field defect may be demonstrated.

5. **Cerebellar tumor**—This is characterized by disturbances of equilibrium and coordination, and early development of increased intracranial pressure and papilledema.

B. X-Ray Findings: Skull x-rays, lumbar puncture, pneumograms, electroencephalography, echoencephalogram, cerebroscintigram, and angiography may aid in diagnosis and localization of an intracranial mass. Chest x-ray, gastrointestinal series, urograms, and other studies may be necessary to determine the primary site of a metastatic brain tumor.

Differential Diagnosis

Differentiate from other disorders which cause increased intracranial pressure or appear to be due to progressive cerebral lesions, eg, intracranial abscess, arachnoiditis, aneurysm, subdural hematoma, and neurosyphilis; and from epilepsy and cerebrovascular accident.

Treatment

A. General Measures: Intravenous urea, 30% in 10% invert sugar, will reduce increased intracranial pressure for periods of a few hours and gives welcome relief in the operative and early postoperative phases of treatment. Parenteral corticosteroids may be used to reduce cerebral edema in the preoperative and early postoperative phase. Give dexamethasone, 8–40 mg/day IV or IM. Symptomatic therapy, including the use of analgesics, anticonvulsants, and sedatives as required, is essentially the same as for patients with similar complaints not associated with brain tumors.

B. Specific Measures: In general, treatment consists of surgical removal of the tumor, although gratifying results may be achieved in a small number of selected patients with intensive radiation. Pituitary tumors may be "cured" with x-ray treatment. Medulloblastoma of the cerebellum in children is highly sensitive to an initial course of irradiation, but recurrence is the rule. Radical excision and hemispherectomy is occasionally successful in selected cases.

Prognosis

The outcome in any particular case depends upon the type, size, and location of the tumor. Early diagnosis and proper surgical treatment may be curative in benign tumors (meningiomas, neurinomas) as well as in certain gliomas (especially in frontal and occipital locations).

For the majority of patients with malignant brain tumors, the prognosis is poor.

Bucy, P.C., & P.W. Thieman: Astrocytomas of the cerebellum. Arch Neurol 18:14–19, 1968.

Faust, D.S., & others: Radiation therapy in the management of medulloblastoma. Neurology 20:519–522, 1970.

Fessard, C.: Cerebral tumors in infancy. Am J Dis Child 115:302–308, 1968.

Geissinger, J.D., & P.C. Bucy: Astrocytomas of the cerebellum in children. Arch Neurol 24:125–136, 1971.

Jelsma, R., & P.C. Bucy: Glioblastoma multiforme. Arch Neurol 20:161–171, 1969.

Jelsma, R., & P.C. Bucy: The treatment of glioblastoma multiforme. J Neurosurg 27:388–400, 1967.

Netsky, M.G., & J.M. Watson: The natural history of intracranial neoplasms. Ann Int Med 45:275–284, 1956.

Potts, D.G.: Brain tumors: Radiologic localization and diagnosis. Radiol Clin North America 3:511–528, 1965.

Wilson, C.B., & H.A. Norell, Jr.: Secondary tumors of the brain. Dis Nerv System 28:433–440, 1967.

DEGENERATIVE DISORDERS OF THE CNS

MULTIPLE SCLEROSIS
(Disseminated Sclerosis)

Essentials of Diagnosis

- Sudden, transient motor and sensory disturbances; impaired vision.
- Diffuse neurologic signs, with remissions and exacerbations.
- Euphoria (late).
- Onset in early adult life.
- Abnormal colloidal gold curve; increased gamma globulin in CSF.

General Considerations

Multiple sclerosis is characterized by the onset in early adult life of progressive diffuse neurologic disturbances, with irregular fluctuating periods of exacerbation and apparent improvement or quiescence. The etiology is not known; a wide variety of degenerative, toxic, and inflammatory agents and deficiency states have been implicated in various theories of pathogenesis.

Irregular gray patches of degeneration occur in the brain and spinal cord with a predilection for the white matter, varying in size from a few millimeters to several centimeters.

Clinical Findings

A. Symptoms and Signs: The initial attack and subsequent relapses may occur following acute infections, trauma, vaccination, serum injections, pregnancy, or types of somatic stress.

Signs of multiple involvement of the CNS may include slurred speech, intention tremor, nystagmus, retrobulbar neuritis, incontinence, spastic paralysis, pallor of the temporal halves of the optic disks, increased deep tendon reflexes, and bilateral extensor plantar responses. Late in the course of the disease the mental state is characterized by euphoria with little insight into condition or disability. Excited and even maniacal states may occur.

The illness, therefore, is characterized by the fact that (1) the neurologic lesions are widespread and cannot be explained on a single anatomic basis, and (2) the signs and symptoms are subject to repeated exacerbations and remissions.

B. Laboratory Findings: The CSF may show a "first zone" or "second zone" colloidal gold curve. CSF gamma globulin is likely to be increased. No pathologic alterations in CSF may be noted in some patients.

Differential Diagnosis

Neurosyphilis is classically characterized by Argyll Robertson pupils and positive blood and CSF serology. Posterolateral sclerosis is usually associated with pernicious anemia and achylia, and signs of a posterior and lateral column disorder. Cerebral tumors cause progressive clinical findings, a distinctive EEG, characteristic pneumograms and cerebral angiograms, increased CSF pressure and protein, and a pineal shift in skull x-rays. Friedreich's ataxia is manifested by scoliosis, club foot, absent deep reflexes, and a positive family history. Platybasia, Arnold-Chiari malformation, and cervical spine malformation are differentiated on the basis of skull and cervical x-rays, partial subarachnoid spinal block, and positive myelograms. Tumors of the posterior fossa cause papilledema, increased CSF pressure, and characteristic ventriculograms and vertebral angiograms.

Complications

The hazards of chronic invalidism usually increase the longer the patient survives. The immediate cause of death is usually some intercurrent disease. Infections of the bladder and kidney are common.

Treatment

A. Medical Treatment: There is no specific treatment. Corticosteroids and vasodilators (inhalations of 5–10% CO_2, histamine infusions, amyl nitrite inhalations) have been advocated for treatment of acute relapses, but the results are poor. Therapeutic claims have also been made for tolbutamide, isoniazid, vitamin B_{12}, procaine, blood transfusions, and fat-free diets, but their value has not been established.

B. General Measures: Adequate sleep at night and rest in the afternoon have been found to make patients more comfortable. Avoid sudden changes in temperature (external or internal). Heat makes these patients much worse; cold often improves them temporarily.

Rehabilitation, physical therapy, and psychotherapy are indicated in an attempt to encourage the patient to live with his disability and make the most of whatever assets he still retains.

Prognosis

The course is varied and unpredictable. In almost all cases there is a remission of the initial symptoms; but with each recurrence of a symptom the chances of remission decrease. Early remissions may be remarkably complete; later in the course of the disease remissions tend to be partial. Remissions may last several months to years.

A clinical course of 10–20 years is not uncommon. In one large series, the average survival after onset of symptoms was estimated at 27 years.

Adams, J.M., & others: Measles antibodies in patients with multiple sclerosis and with other neurological and non-neurological diseases. Neurology 20:1039–1042, 1970.

Alter, M., & J. Speer: Clinical evaluation of possible etiologic factors in multiple sclerosis. Neurology 18:109–116, 1968.

Antonovsky, A., & others: Reappraisal of possible etiologic factors in multiple sclerosis. Am J Pub Health 58:836–848, 1968.

Dean, G.: The multiple sclerosis problem. Sc Am 223:40–46, 1970.

Hyland, H.H.: Prognosis and treatment of multiple sclerosis: With comments on other demyelinating disease. Postgrad Med 37:241–248, 1965.

Ivers, R.R., & N.P. Goldstein: Multiple sclerosis: A current appraisal of symptoms and signs. Proc Staff Meet Mayo Clin 38:457–466, 1963.

Kolar, O.J., Ross, A.T., & J.C. Herman: Serum and cerebrospinal fluid immunoglobulins in multiple sclerosis. Neurology 20:1052–1062, 1970.

Kurtzke, J., & others: Studies on natural history of multiple sclerosis. Acta neurol scandinav 44:467–494, 1968.

MacKay, R.P., & N.C. Myrianthopolous: Multiple sclerosis in twins and their relatives. Arch Neurol 15:449, 1966.

Merritt, H.H.: Multiple sclerosis. Med World News 11:29–39, 1970.

Rose, A.S., & others: Cooperative study in the evaluation of therapy in multiple sclerosis: ACTH vs placebo. Neurology 20 (part 2):1–59, 1970.

Schapira, K., & others: Marriage, pregnancy and multiple sclerosis. Brain 89:419–428, 1966.

Scheinberg, L.C., & others: Research in demyelinating diseases. Ann New York Acad Sc 122:1, 1965.

Schneck, S., & H.N. Claman: CSF immunoglobulins in multiple sclerosis and other neurological diseases. Arch Neurol 20:132–139, 1969.

Schumacher, G.: Demyelinating diseases. New England J Med 262:969–975, 1019–1022, 1069–1075, 1119–1126, 1960.

Swank, R.L.: Multiple sclerosis: Twenty years on low fat diet. Arch Neurol 23:460–475, 1970.

Veterans Administration Multiple Sclerosis Group: Five year follow-up study on multiple sclerosis. Arch Neurol 11:583–592, 1964.

PARKINSONISM
(Paralysis Agitans)

Essentials of Diagnosis

- "Pill-rolling" tremor maximal at rest, with fixed facial expression.
- Slow, shuffling, often festinating gait.
- Diminished motor power, rigidity of limb muscles upon passive motion (lead pipe or cogwheel).
- Insidious onset in 50's and 60's with slow progression.

General Considerations

Paralysis agitans is characterized by involuntary tremors, diminished motor power, and rigidity; the mental faculties are not affected. Onset is usually in the 50's and 60's. In most cases, a specific etiology cannot be established. The disease occurs as a complication of epidemic encephalitis, and has been known to occur in vascular disorders, neurosyphilis, and following head trauma. Reversible extrapyramidal reactions, including paralysis agitans, with gait and postural abnormalities, rigidity, tremor, salivation, and similar symptoms, may follow the use of tranquilizers such as the phenothiazines. In many cases, however, a precipitating cause is not known, and these are attributed to degeneration of the cells and tracts of the striate bodies, globus pallidus, and substantia nigra.

Clinical Findings

The onset is insidious, with increasing rigidity or tremor (or both). The rate of progression may be slow. The facial expression may be fixed or less mobile than normal; smiling spreads and disappears slowly. The body movements generally become slower. There may be gradually increasing rigidity with diminished swaying of the arms in walking. The legs may begin to feel stiff and heavy, and excessive effort may be required to lift them from the ground in walking. A stooping posture is common, with the arms at the sides, elbows slightly flexed, and fingers abducted. Intermittent tremor (about 2–6/second) occurs which is worse when the limb is at rest. Tremors frequently are of the pill-rolling type, involving the thumb, index finger, or wrist, and are sometimes associated with a to-and-fro tremor of the head. Emotional disturbances and fatigue are apt to aggravate the tremor.

The limb muscles on passive motion are rigid (lead-pipe or cogwheel). There may be difficulty in getting out of a chair, so that several efforts or attempts to rise are made. Turning is difficult, even when standing or in bed. Movements such as adjusting a tie, buttoning the coat, and brushing the hair ultimately become impossible without assistance. Some patients have a tendency to break into a run or trot (festination gait). The voice tends to become weak, low in volume, and monotonous Oculogyric crises may occur.

Differential Diagnosis

A. Tremor: Senile tremor is finer and more rapid, and not associated with muscular weakness or rigidity. Hysterical tremor is inconstant, increases when attention is called to the affected part, and decreases when the attention is distracted. Other hysterical symptoms are present also. Familial tremor begins early in life, is increased by voluntary motion, and may remain constant throughout life without other nervous abnormalities. The tremors of hyperthyroidism, toxic tremors (delirium tremens), and those seen in early general paralysis of syphilis are not difficult to distinguish from those of paralysis agitans.

B. Rigidity: In catatonia a fixed, rigid attitude is maintained for long periods and there are associated mental changes. The spasticity which occurs in pyramidal tract disease affects selected muscles, and is greatest at the beginning of passive motion and less as motion proceeds. In multiple arthritis there is a history of pain and evidence of a joint and not a muscle disorder.

Treatment

A. Medical Measures: (See Table 16–3.) Treatment is mainly symptomatic.

1. A number of drugs have been found to be effective in alleviating the symptoms of parkinsonism. These drugs are usually used in combination to obtain the optimal therapeutic result. Combinations such as trihexyphenidyl (Artane®) and diphenhydramine (Benadryl®) 3 times daily may be used initially. *Caution:* Do not stop drugs abruptly when changing to new ones. The dosage of the new drug should be increased as the other drug is gradually withdrawn.

2. Newer drugs—

a. Levodopa (Dopar®, Larodopa®) is effective against the akinesia and rigidity of parkinsonism and, to a lesser extent, tremor. Capsules (250 mg) are given 3–4 times daily and increased to tolerance over several weeks or until significant effects are noted. Maximum daily dosage ranges from 4–8 gm. Side-effects—including nausea, vomiting, postural hypotension, cardiac dysrhythmia, and choreiform movements—may respond to adjustment of dosage.

b. Amantadine hydrochloride (Symmetrel®)— This antiviral agent for A_2 (Asian) influenza may be effective against akinesia, rigidity, and tremor of parkinsonism. The daily dosage is 200 mg (100 mg twice daily). Side-effects may be controlled by adjusting the dosage or concomitant medication and include insomnia, jitteriness, abdominal distress, dizziness, depression, confusion, hallucinations, and livedo reticularis.

B. Surgical Measures: In carefully selected patients, surgical destruction of portions of the globus pallidus or the ventrolateral nucleus of the thalamus has proved highly beneficial.

C. General Measures: Physical therapy should include massage, stretching of muscles, and active exercise when possible. The patient should be taught to exercise daily the muscles most severely affected, especially those of the hands, fingers, wrists, elbows, knees, and neck.

TABLE 16–3. Antiparkinsonism drugs.*

| Drug | Chief Effect On | | | | Dosage | Precautions and Remarks |
	Tremor	Rigidity and Spasms	Akinesia (Weakness)	Oculogyric Crisis		
Trihexyphenidyl (Artane®)		•	•	•	1–5 mg 3 times daily, starting at low dosage and slowly increasing. For oculogyric crisis, use 10 mg 3 times daily.	May precipitate acute glaucoma in elderly persons and contraindicated in patients with glaucoma. Blurred vision, dryness of mouth, vertigo, and tachycardia are early toxic symptoms; late symptoms are vomiting, dizziness, mental confusion, and hallucinations. The synthetic drugs are apt to cause more dizziness than the natural alkaloids and are somewhat less potent parasympatholytics.
Biperiden (Akineton®)		•		•	2 mg 3–4 times daily.	
Procyclidine (Kemadrin®)		•			2.5–5 mg 3 times daily after meals.	
Cycrimine (Pagitane®)		•	•	•	1.25–5 mg 3–4 times daily. Dosage may be gradually increased up to the limits of tolerance.	Useful when effects of trihexyphenidyl wear off. Other remarks as for atropine.
Benztropine methanesulfonate (Cogentin®)	•	•			0.5 mg 1–2 times daily, increasing by 0.5 mg at intervals of several days to 5 mg daily or toxicity. Often most effective as single dose at bedtime.	Side-effects similar to those of atropine. Best effect by combining with trihexyphenidyl or dextroamphetamine.
Diphenhydramine (Benadryl®)	•				50 mg 2–4 times daily.	Reduce dosage if transient drowsiness occurs.
Orphenadrine (Disipal®)	•	•			50 mg 3–5 times daily.	
Chlorphenoxamine (Phenoxene®)		•			50 mg 3–4 times daily.	Valuable adjunct to other drugs.
Ethopropazine (Parsidol®, Lysovane®)	•	•			25–30 mg 4 times daily.	May be used in conjunction with other antispasmodic drugs. Drug is related to chlorpromazine; precautions as for this class of drugs.
Dextroamphetamine sulfate (Dexedrine®)			•		5 mg morning or noon.	CNS stimulant to be used with caution in cardiac patients.
Levodopa (Larodopa®, Dopar®)	•	•	•		250 mg 3 times daily. Increase to tolerance (4–8 gm daily).	Nausea, vomiting, postural hypotension, choreiform movements.
Amantadine (Symmetrel®)	•	•	•		100 mg twice daily.	Jitteriness, insomnia, depression, confusion, hallucinations.

*Modified and reproduced from Chusid: *Correlative Neuroanatomy & Functional Neurology,* 14th ed. Lange, 1970.

Reassurance and psychologic support are of decided value, stressing the positive aspects of the disease: (1) symptomatic relief with drugs, (2) no impairment of mental faculties, (3) slow progression over many years, and (4) active research and the hope of therapeutic breakthroughs.

Avoid barbiturates. Permit moderate use of alcohol to relax tension. Nonbarbiturate sedatives (eg, meprobamate, not phenothiazines) may be of value.

Prognosis

The disease is usually slowly progressive; the patient may live for many years.

With increased disability, patients are apt to become depressed, anxious, and emotionally disturbed.

Treatment with drugs may produce amelioration of complaints. In selected patients, operative treatment (pallidotomy, thalamotomy) may produce significant improvement of tremor and rigidity. The effect of long-term therapy with newer drugs such as levodopa and amantadine is under current study.

Barbeau, A.: L-dopa therapy in Parkinson's disease: A critical review of 9 years' experience. Canad MAJ 101:59–86, 1969.

Calne, D.B., & others: L-dopa in idiopathic parkinsonism. Lancet 2:973–976, 1969.

Celesia, J.J., & A.N. Barr: Psychoses and other psychiatric manifestations of levodopa therapy. Arch Neurol 23:193–200, 1970.

Cotzias, G.C., Papasvilliou, P.S., & R. Gellene: Modification of parkinsonism: Chronic treatment with L-dopa. New England J Med 280:337–345, 1969.

Hofmann, W.W., & R.L. Ryan: A controlled study of L-dopa in Parkinson's disease. California Med 112:9–14, Feb, 1970.

Klawans, H.L., Jr.: The pharmacology of parkinsonism. Dis Nerv System 29:805–816, 1968.

Martin, W.E.: Adverse reactions during treatment of Parkinson's disease with levodopa. JAMA 216:1979–1983, 1971.

McDowell, F., & others: Treatment of Parkinson's syndrome with dihydroxyphenylalanine (levodopa). Ann Int Med 72:29–35, 1970.

Pharmacologic and clinical experiences with levodopa: A symposium. Neurology 20 (part 2):1–65, 1970.

Pollock, M., & R.W. Hornabrook: The prevalence, natural history and dementia of Parkinson's disease. Brain 89:429–448, 1966.

Schwab, R.S., & others: Amantadine in the treatment of Parkinson's disease. JAMA 208:1168–1170, 1969.

Wilkins, R.H., & I.A. Brody: Parkinson's syndrome. Arch Neurol 20:440–445, 1969.

Yahr, M.D., & others: Treatment of parkinsonism with levodopa. Arch Neurol 21:343–355, 1969.

HEPATOLENTICULAR DEGENERATION
(Wilson's Disease)

Wilson's disease is a familial disorder characterized by clinical findings of basal ganglia disease and accompanied by cirrhosis of the liver and usually a greenish-brown corneal pigmentation (Kayser-Fleischer ring). A metabolic disturbance has been implicated because of the increased excretion of copper and amino acids in the urine and the decrease in ceruloplasmin of serum. The cerebellum, cerebral cortex, and other parts of the nervous system may also be affected. The onset of symptoms is insidious, usually between the ages of 11 and 25 years.

Tremors and rigidity are the commonest early symptoms. Tremors are apt to be of the intention or alternating type; bizarre "wing-beating" of the upper extremities is accentuated by extension of these parts. The rigidity resembles paralysis agitans.

Dimercaprol (BAL) has been reported to be effective in removing the excessive copper and presumably impeding the progress of the disease. The clinically useful dose is 2.5 mg/kg IM twice daily in courses of 10–12 days every other month. Penicillamine (Cuprimine®) is an effective chelating agent suitable for oral administration, and may far surpass the effect of BAL in increasing excretion of copper. Some of the specific manifestations may be palliated by symptomatic therapy.

The course is progressive, with partial remissions and exacerbations until death occurs (usually within 10 years). The full effect of dimercaprol or penicillamine therapy on the course or longevity has not as yet been determined.

Denny-Brown, D.: Hepatolenticular degeneration (Wilson's disease): Two different components. New England J Med 270:1149–1156, 1964.

Goldstein, N.P., & others: Wilson's disease (hepatolenticular degeneration). Arch Neurol 24:391–401, 1971.

Richmond, J., & others: Hepatolenticular degeneration (Wilson's disease) treated by penicillamine. Brain 87:619–638, 1964.

Sternlieb, I., & I.H. Scheinberg: Prevention of Wilson's disease in asymptomatic patients. New England J Med 278:352–359, 1968.

Sternlieb, I., & I.H. Scheinberg: The diagnosis of Wilson's disease in asymptomatic patients. JAMA 183:747–751, 1963.

Sternlieb, I., & I.H. Scheinberg: Pencillamine therapy for hepatolenticular degeneration. JAMA 189:784, 1964.

CHRONIC PROGRESSIVE (HUNTINGTON'S) CHOREA

Huntington's chorea is a hereditary disease of the basal ganglia and cortex, characterized by the onset in adult life of choreiform movements and mental deterioration. Many cases in America have been traced to 2 brothers who emigrated to Long Island from England. The movements are abrupt and jerky, though less rapid and lightning-like than those of Sydenham's chorea. Any somatic musculature may be involved. The disease is chronically progressive and usually leads to death in about 15 years.

Treatment is symptomatic. Tranquilizers such as reserpine, phenothiazines, or haloperidol are helpful in management.

Bird, M.T., & G.W. Paulson: The rigid form of Huntington's chorea. Neurology 21:271–277, 1971.

Byers, R.K., & J.A. Dodge: Huntington's chorea in children: Report of four cases. Neurology 17:587–596, 1967.

Gath, J., & B. Vinje: Pneumoencephalographic findings in Huntington's chorea. Neurology 18:991–996, 1968.

Goodman, R.M., & others: Huntington's chorea: Multidisciplinary study of kindred. Arch Neurol 15:345–355, 1966.

Hansotia, P., Cleeland, C.S., & R.W.M. Chun: Juvenile Huntington's chorea. Neurology 18:217–224, 1968.

Myrianthopoulos, N.: Huntington's chorea. J Med Genetics 3:298, 1966.

Symposium on Huntington's chorea. Proc Staff Meet Mayo Clin 30:349–370, 1955.

SYDENHAM'S CHOREA
(St. Vitus' Dance)

Essentials of Diagnosis

- Quick, jerky, involuntary, irregular movements of the face, trunk, and extremities.
- Gait and speech often markedly impaired.
- Irritability, restlessness, and emotional instability.
- Mild muscular weakness, hypotonia.
- Associated rheumatic fever or residuals.

General Considerations

Sydenham's chorea is seen mostly in young persons and is characterized by involuntary irregular movements, incoordination of voluntary movements, mild muscle weakness, and emotional disturbance. The disorder is usually (but not always) associated with rheumatic fever and is considered to be one of its sequels; other clinical evidence of rheumatic fever is apt to be present.

Clinical Findings

The patient becomes irritable, excitable, restless, and sleepless. Grimacing, clumsy movements, and stumbling frequently occur. Involuntary dysrhythmic movements of the face, trunk, and extremities occur with varying severity. These are sudden, quick, short, and jerky. Gait and speech may be affected. Voluntary movement and excitement may aggravate the involuntary movements. Affected limbs may be weak and hypotonic.

Clinical evidence of rheumatic fever or rheumatic heart disease is often present, the latter sometimes evident only late in the course of the disease.

Differential Diagnosis

Distinguish from tics or habit spasms, which are usually manifested as facial grimacing with blinking, smacking of lips, and clicking noises, and in which there is no difficulty in articulation, no associated muscle weakness, and no evidence of rheumatic fever; and from Huntington's chorea, which is a progressive hereditary disease of adult life characterized by chorea and mental deterioration and usually leads to death in about 15 years.

Treatment

Corticosteroids and corticotropin may shorten the course and suppress the rheumatic manifestations. Sedatives (such as phenobarbital) or tranquilizers (such as phenothiazines or haloperidol) are helpful in suppressing the involuntary movements of chorea.

Prognosis

The acute phase of chorea usually runs a limited course, with maximum symptoms 2–3 weeks after onset. Gradual recovery occurs in about 2–3 months.

Aron, A.M., Freeman, J.M., & S. Carter: The natural history of Sydenham's chorea. Am J Med 38:83, 1965.

Kurland, H.D.: Symptomatic control of Sydenham's chorea. Internat J Neuropsychiat 1:152–157, 1965.

Tierney, R.C., & others: Treatment of Sydenham's chorea. Am J Dis Child 109:408–412, 1965.

COMBINED SYSTEM DISEASE
(Posterolateral Sclerosis)

Essentials of Diagnosis

- Numbness, "pins and needles," tenderness, weakness, feeling of heaviness of toes, feet, fingers, and hands.
- Stocking and glove distribution of sensory loss; extensor plantar response, hyperreflexia, flexor spasms; flaccid paralysis and hyporeflexia less often; loss of position and vibratory sense.
- Memory defects or psychotic states.
- Associated blood and gastric findings of pernicious anemia.

General Considerations

Posterolateral sclerosis is a progressive degeneration of the posterior and lateral columns of the spinal cord, sometimes with degeneration of the peripheral nerves. The middle and older age groups are most often affected.

Although posterolateral sclerosis is usually associated with pernicious anemia, its severity does not necessarily parallel the degree of anemia, which suggests that the causes of spinal cord and blood changes may not be the same. Degeneration of the spinal cord may develop before clinical manifestations of pernicious anemia.

Clinical Findings

Tingling, numbness, and "pins and needles" sensations in the toes and feet and later in the fingers are the first symptoms. Sensations of swelling, coldness, and wetness of the feet may occur. Weakness of the legs, fatigue, a feeling of heaviness in the feet, and unsteady gait are common. Dyspnea on exertion with recurrent episodes of dizziness may be produced by the anemia; gastric distress may result from achlorhydria.

In the **flaccid** type the involvement is principally of the peripheral nerves, manifested as follows: weakness of the lower extremities (especially of the distal segments), tenderness of the soles and calf muscles, stocking distribution impairment of touch sensibility in the lower extremities up to knee level, loss of appreciation of vibratory sensation, ataxia, a positive Romberg sign, depression or absence of knee and ankle jerks, and extensor plantar responses. In the **spastic** type spinal cord signs, especially of the lateral columns, predominate: increased deep tendon reflexes, clonus and hypertonicity of muscles, and flexor spasms with progressive weakness. Paraplegia in flexion may follow. When sensory losses become more severe, loss of sphincter control and decubiti may occur.

Mental symptoms may also be present, even early in the disease. Apathy, mental dullness, hypomania, paranoid states, hallucinations, disorientation, and memory defects have been reported.

Laboratory findings are as for pernicious anemia.

Differential Diagnosis

The presence of macrocytic anemia and achlorhydria usually makes the diagnosis more certain, but it may be necessary to distinguish from the familial ataxias, tabes dorsalis, multiple sclerosis, myelitis, and spinal compression by tumor.

Treatment

Treat as for pernicious anemia.

Prognosis

With adequate treatment of pernicious anemia, improvement, especially of peripheral nerve involvement, may occur. Little improvement can be expected when the spinal cord is severely affected.

Paresthesias and sensory changes may persist even in those treated intensively, early, and fully.

The prognosis is worse in patients over 60 years of age.

Robertson, D.M., Dinsdale, H.B., & R.J. Campbell: Subacute combined degeneration of the spinal cord. Arch Neurol 24:203–210, 1971.

Weir, D.G., & P.B.B. Gatenby: Subacute combined degeneration of the cord after partial gastrectomy. Brit MJ 2:1175–1176, 1963.

See also references under Multiple Sclerosis.

DISORDERS OF CRANIAL NERVES

TRIGEMINAL (TRIFACIAL) NEURALGIA
(Tic Douloureux)

Trigeminal neuralgia is characterized by a sudden attack of excruciating pain of short duration along the distribution of the 5th cranial nerve. The attack is often precipitated by stimulation (usually mild) of a "trigger zone" in the area of the pain, and is characterized by recurrent paroxysms of sharp, stabbing pains in the distribution of one or more branches of the nerve. The onset is usually in middle or late life, and the incidence is higher in women. The pain may be described as searing or burning, occurring in lightning-like jabs, lasting only 1–2 minutes or as long as 15 minutes. The frequency of attacks varies from many times daily to several times a month or a year. The patient often tries to immobilize his face during conversation, or attempts to swallow food without chewing in order not to irritate the trigger zone.

Treatment

A. Medical Treatment: Medical treatment includes the following:

1. Carbamazepine (Tegretol®)—This tricyclic drug is remarkably effective in relieving and preventing the pain of trigeminal neuralgia. The dose may vary from 0.2–2 gm/day. Observe carefully for evidence of serious hematologic and cutaneous reactions.

2. Anticonvulsants, eg, diphenylhydantoin sodium (Dilantin®), 0.1 gm 4 times daily, may be beneficial in some cases.

3. Massive doses of vitamin B_{12} (1 mg IM daily for 10 days) have been reported to relieve the severe pain.

4. Alcohol injection of the ganglion or the branches of the trigeminal nerve may produce analgesia and relief from pain for several months or years. Repeated injections may be required at later intervals.

B. Surgical Measures: Surgery may be required if medical treatment gives no relief.

Prognosis

In most cases the paroxysms of pain are present for several weeks or months. Remissions may last from a few days to as long as several months or years. As patients become older, remissions tend to become shorter.

Amols, W.: A new drug for trigeminal neuralgia (clinical experience with carbamazepine in large series of patients over two years). Tr Am Neurol A 91:163, 1966.

Blom, S.: Tic douloureux treated with new anticonvulsant. Arch Neurol 9:285–290, 1963.

Dalessio, D.J.: Medical treatment of tic douloureux. J Chronic Dis 19:1043–1048, 1966.

Fager, C.A.: Trigeminal neuralgia. Geriatrics 20:475–480, 1965.

Graham, J.G., & K.J. Zilkha: Treatment of trigeminal neuralgia with carbamazepine: A follow-up study. Brit MJ 1:210, 1966.

Henderson, W.R.: Trigeminal neuralgia: The pain and its treatment. Brit MJ 1:7–14, 1967.

Iannone, A., Baker, A.B., & F. Morrell: Dilantin in the treatment of trigeminal neuralgia. Neurology 8:126–128, 1958.

Kerr, F.W.L.: The etiology of trigeminal neuralgia. Arch Neurol 8:15–26, 1963.

Killian, J.M., & G.H. Fromm: Carbamazepine in the treatment of neuralgia. Arch Neurol 19:129–136, 1968.

King, R.B.: Management of tic douloureux. Postgrad Med 40:684–688, 1966.

Rockliffe, B.W., & E.H. Davis: Controlled sequential trials of carbamazepine in trigeminal neuralgia. Arch Neurol 15:129–136, 1966.

Rushton, J.G.: Medical treatment of trigeminal neuralgia: With a note on the results of alcohol injection. M Clin North America 52:797–800, 1968.

BELL'S PALSY
(Peripheral Facial Paralysis)

Bell's palsy is a paralysis of the muscles of one side of the face, sometimes precipitated by exposure, chill, or trauma. It may occur at any age, but is slightly more common in the age group from 20 to 50.

Assure the patient that recovery usually occurs in 2–8 weeks (or up to 1–2 years in older patients). Keep the face warm and avoid further exposure, especially to wind and dust. Protect the eye with a patch if necessary. Support the face with tape or wire anchored at the angle of the mouth and looped about the ear. Electric stimulation (every other day after the 14th day) may be used to help prevent muscle atrophy. Gentle upward massage of the involved muscles for 5–10 minutes 2–3 times daily may help to maintain muscle tone. Heat from an infra-red lamp may hasten recovery.

In the vast majority of cases partial or complete recovery occurs. When recovery is partial, contractures may develop on the paralyzed side. Recurrence on the same or the opposite side is occasionally reported.

Hauser, W.A., & others: Incidence and prognosis of Bell's palsy in the population of Rochester, Minn. Proc Mayo Clin 46:258–265, 1971.

Langworth, E.P., & D. Taverner: The prognosis in facial palsy. Brain 86:465–480, 1963.

Leibowitz, U.: Bell's palsy: Two disease entities? Neurology 16:1105–1109, 1966.

Miller, H.: Facial paralysis. Brit MJ 3:815–818, 1967.

Wilkins, R.H., & I.A. Brody: Bell's palsy and Bell's phenomenon. Arch Neurol 21:661–669, 1969.

Winokur, S.: Bell's palsy: Prognosis and treatment. South MJ 56:959–961, 1963.

Zohn, D.A., & C.J. Duke: Bell's palsy: Management based on prognosis. GP 36:98–103, Oct 1967.

DISORDERS OF
PERIPHERAL NERVES

POLYNEURITIS
(Multiple Neuritis, Peripheral Neuritis, Peripheral Neuropathy)

Essentials of Diagnosis
- Slowly progressive muscular weakness, paresthesias, tenderness, and pain, mostly of distal portions of extremities.
- Stocking and glove hypesthesia or anesthesia, especially for vibratory sense.
- Hyporeflexia or areflexia.
- Muscular wasting of affected parts.

General Considerations
Polyneuritis is a syndrome characterized by widespread sensory and motor disturbances of peripheral nerves. It may appear at any age, although it is most common in young or middle-aged adults, especially in men. In most cases a noninflammatory degeneration of the peripheral nerves is present.

Polyneuritis may be caused by (1) chronic intoxications (eg, alcohol, carbon disulfide, benzene, phosphorus, sulfonamides); (2) infections (eg, meningitis, diphtheria, syphilis, tuberculosis, pneumonia, Guillain-Barré syndrome, mumps); (3) metabolic causes (eg, diabetes mellitus, gout, pregnancy, rheumatism, porphyria, polyarteritis nodosa, lupus erythematosus); (4) nutritional causes (eg, beriberi, vitamin deficiencies, cachectic states); and (5) malignancies.

Clinical Findings
Symptoms usually develop slowly over a period of weeks. Notable exceptions with rapid onset may occur in infections plus alcoholic polyneuritis. Pains, tenderness, paresthesias, weakness and fatigability, and sensory impairment may be present. The pains may be mild or, occasionally, burning and sharp. Muscular weakness is usually greatest in the distal portions of the extremities. Impaired sensory perception, especially of vibration, is frequent; in alcoholic and arsenical polyneuritis, severe and extensive sensory defects may occur. The cutaneous sensory defect may consist of hypesthesia or anesthesia in an irregular stocking or glove distribution.

Tendon reflexes are usually depressed or absent. With paralyzed toes, the plantar response may be absent; with weak abdominal muscles, abdominal skin reflexes may be diminished or absent. Flaccid weakness and muscular atrophy of affected parts may occur, especially in the distal portions of the extremities. Foot drop with associated steppage gait may result.

Trophic changes of the skin of the extremities are manifested by a glossy red skin and impairment of the sweating mechanism. Muscles and nerves may be tender and hypersensitive to pressure and palpation.

Differential Diagnosis

Differentiate from neuritis involving only a single nerve and its distribution; tabes dorsalis, which is not associated with muscular atrophy or nerve tenderness; acute anterior poliomyelitis, with systemic as well as neurologic manifestations; and myositis, in which there is no nerve involvement and usually no sensory or reflex changes.

Treatment

A. Specific Measures: Remove from exposure to toxic agents (eg, alcohol, lead). In lead polyneuritis, calcium disodium edetate (Versenate®) may be beneficial. In arsenical polyneuritis, give dimercaprol (BAL).

Give a high caloric diet with liberal use of vitamins, especially B complex. The entire B complex can be administered with thiamine hydrochloride, 15 mg 3–4 times daily orally or parenterally.

B. General Measures: Place the patient at bed rest and forbid use of the affected limb. If a lower extremity is affected, keep a cradle over the foot of the bed to prevent pressure of bed covers. Give analgesics as necessary to control pain. After pain has subsided, massage and passive motion may be of value. Encourage active motion at the same time. Prevent contractures by means of splints and passive stretching.

Prognosis

In most forms of polyneuritis, recovery may occur once the cause has been corrected. In some cases the disorder progresses for weeks, remains stationary, for a time, and goes on to slow recovery in 6–12 months. Objective sensory changes usually disappear first, and paralyses later; dysesthesias may persist during recovery.

Dyck, P.J.: Peripheral neuropathy: Changing concepts, differential diagnosis, and classification. M Clin North America 52:895–908, 1968.

Gamstorp, I.: Polyneuropathy in childhood. Acta paediat scandinav 57:230–238, 1968.

Gibberd, F.B.: Ophthalmoplegia in acute polyneuritis. Arch Neurol 23:161–165, 1970.

Low, N.L., & others: Polyneuritis in children. Pediatrics 22:972–990, 1958.

Matthews, W.B., Howell, D.A., & R.C. Hughes: Relapsing corticosteroid-dependent polyneuritis. J Neurol Neurosurg Psychiat 33:330–337, 1970.

Pleasure, D.E., Lovelace, R.E., & R.C. Duvoisin: The prognosis of acute polyneuritis. Neurology 18:1143–1148, 1968.

Watters, G.V., & C.F. Barlow: Acute and subacute neuropathies. P Clin North America 14:997–1008, 1967.

Wederholt, W.C., Mulder, D.W., & E.H. Lambert: Polyradiculoneuropathy. Proc Staff Meet Mayo Clin 39:427–451, 1964.

Wisniewski, H., & others: Landry-Guillain-Barré syndrome. Arch Neurol 21:269–277, 1969.

PERIPHERAL NERVE INJURIES

Peripheral nerve injuries, ranging from simple contusions causing temporary dysfunction to complete anatomic section causing total cessation of function, may occur with lacerations, bone fractures, crushing injuries, or penetrating wounds. In the acute early phase, associated tissue damage, pain, and other circumstances may interfere with tests of motor or sensory function. Tinel's sign (a tingling sensation in the distribution of an affected nerve) may be elicited after the acute phase by percussion of the nerve or adjacent areas. In some old nerve injuries, trophic changes affecting the nails and skin, as well as painless skin ulcers, may be noted. Electrodiagnostic tests may be helpful in assessing the degree and nature of the neural deficit.

Treatment depends upon many factors, including the time and type of nerve injury, associated defects, and the general condition of the patient. When possible, end-to-end anastomosis of acutely severed nerves should be attempted. In old nerve injuries, good results are possible as long as 1–2 years after injury, when lysis of a scar, resection of a neuroma, nerve transplants, and other surgical procedures may be attempted.

Adler, J.B., & R.L. Patterson, Jr.: Erb's palsy. Long term results of treatment in eighty-eight cases. J Bone Joint Surg 49A: 1052–1064, 1967.

Baker, A.G., & F.G. Winegarner: Causalgia. Am J Surg 117:690–694, 1969.

Cracchiolo, A., III, & L. Marmor: Peripheral entrapment neuropathies. JAMA 204:431–434, 1968.

Davis, R.A.: Management of peripheral nerve injuries. Postgrad Med 38:509–514, 1965.

De Takats, G.: Sympathetic reflex dystrophy. M Clin North America 49:117–130, 1965.

Edshage, S.: Peripheral nerve injuries: Diagnosis and treatment. New England J Med 278:1431–1435,1968.

Lynch, A.C., & P.R. Lipscomb: The carpal tunnel syndrome and Colles' fractures. JAMA 185:363–367, 1963.

Sakellarides, H.: A followup study of 172 peripheral nerve injuries in the upper extremity in civilians. J Bone Joint Surg 44A:140–148, 1962.

NEUROMUSCULAR DISORDERS

The neuromuscular disorders include a number of chronic diseases which are characterized by a progressive weakness and atrophy of certain groups of muscles. It is important to differentiate atrophies from dystrophies: Muscular **atrophies** result from a neural lesion, involving either the cell body or axon of the lower motor neuron; muscular **dystrophies** result from primary disease of the muscle itself.

TABLE 16–4. Differential diagnosis of atrophies and dystrophies.

Atrophies	Dystrophies
Generally occur late in life	Usually occur in childhood
Affect distal muscle groups, eg, the small muscles of the hand	Affect the proximal muscle groups, eg, the hip and shoulder girdle
Show fasciculations	No fasciculations
May show spastic phenomena	No spastic phenomena
No familial incidence	Generally familial

Adams, G.M., Eaton, L.M., & G.M. Shy (editors): *Neuromuscular Disorders.* Res Publ A Nerv Ment Dis, vol 38. Williams & Wilkins, 1960.

Aird, R.B.: Disorders of the peripheral motor system. Postgrad Med 40:578–585, 1966.

Engel, W.K.: Muscle biopsies in neuromuscular disease. P Clin North America 14:963–996, 1967.

Lambert, E.H.: Electrodiagnosis of neuromuscular disease. Pediatrics 34:599–600, 1964.

Walton, J.N.: Diseases of muscle. Abstr World Med 40:1–12, 81–94, 1966.

PROGRESSIVE MUSCULAR ATROPHIES
(Motor Neuron Disease)

The progressive muscular atrophies are due to nuclear involvement of the lower motor neuron by progressive lesions. Since the causative agent is usually not known, the classification has been based upon the level of involvement rather than upon etiology. There is no effective treatment.

Aran-Duchenne Atrophy (Myelopathic Muscular Atrophy)

This is the adult form of progressive spinal muscular atrophy. It is a rare disorder of middle age, starting in the small hand muscles with atrophy and fibrillations and slowly extending to involve the arm, shoulder, and trunk muscles. A degenerative lesion is found in the cervical gray matter of the cord. It may occur as the first stage of an amyotrophic lateral sclerosis (see below).

Werdnig-Hoffman Paralysis

This is a hereditary form of progressive spinal muscular atrophy occurring in children, starting in the pelvic girdle and thighs and spreading to the extremities. Associated adiposity may produce a pseudohypertrophy.

True Bulbar Palsy

This type is caused by a nuclear involvement of the last 4 or 5 cranial nerves and characterized by twitchings and atrophy of the tongue, palate, and larynx, drooling, dysarthria, dysphagia, and finally respiratory paralysis. True bulbar palsy is usually a manifestation of amyotrophic lateral sclerosis.

Amyotrophic Lateral Sclerosis

This is a combined upper and lower motor neuron lesion which may involve either the spinal or bulbar level, or both. It is a chronic progressive disease of unknown etiology associated with fibrillation and atrophy of the somatic musculature. It is predominantly a disease of middle life, with onset usually between the ages of 40 and 60 years. Degeneration of the motor cells of the spinal cord and brain stem and, to a lesser extent, of the motor cortex may occur, with secondary degeneration of the lateral and ventral portions of the spinal cord. There may be spastic weakness of the trunk and extremities, with associated hyperactive deep reflexes and extensor plantar responses. If the fibers of the bulbar nuclei become involved, pseudobulbar or bulbar paralysis may appear. The initial symptom is often weakness and wasting of the extremities (usually the upper extremities). The course is progressively downhill without remission. The average duration of life from the appearance of the first symptoms is about 3 years.

Neural Form of Peroneal Muscular Atrophy:
Charcot-Marie-Tooth Disease

This relatively rare disease is characterized by clubbing of the feet and muscular wasting which begins in the legs and later involves the muscles of the distal portions of the thighs and upper extremities. Atrophy of the leg muscles gives a characteristic "stork-leg" appearance; atrophy usually starts in the intrinsic muscles of the feet and in the peroneal muscles. The onset of symptoms is usually before 20 years of age, but is sometimes delayed until 40 or 50 years. Objective loss of sensation occasionally occurs.

Boman, K., & T. Mewman: Prognosis of amyotrophic lateral sclerosis. Acta neurol scandinav 43:489–498, 1967.

Brown, J.C., & R.M.H. Kater: Pancreatic function in patients with amyotrophic lateral sclerosis. Neurology 19:185–189, 1969.

Brownell, B., Oppenheimer, D.R., & J.T. Hughes: The central nervous system in motor neuron disease. J Neurol Neurosurg Psychiat 33:338–357, 1970.

Currier, R.D., & A.F. Haerer: Amyotrophic lateral sclerosis and metallic toxins. Arch Envir Health 17:712–719, 1968.

Eaton, L.M., & others: Symposium: Amyotrophic lateral sclerosis. Proc Staff Meet Mayo Clin 32:425–462, 1957.

Mackay, R.P.: Course and prognosis in amyotrophic lateral sclerosis. Arch Neurol 8:117–128, 1963.

Metcalf, C.W., & A. Hirano: Amyotrophic lateral sclerosis. Arch Neurol 24:518–524, 1971.

Pearce, J., & D.G.F. Harriman: Chronic spinal muscular atrophy. J Neurol Neurosurg Psychiat 29:509–520, 1966.

Schwartz, A.R.: Charcot-Marie-Tooth disease. Arch Neurol 9:623–634, 1963.

Störtebecker, P., & others: Vascular and metabolic studies of amyotrophic lateral sclerosis. Neurology 20:1157–1161, 1970.

PROGRESSIVE MUSCULAR DYSTROPHY

Essentials of Diagnosis

- Onset usually in childhood or at puberty of weakness of the proximal musculature of the extremities.
- Waddling gait and "climbing up" on body to attain upright position.
- Contractures, scoliosis, lordosis, diminished deep tendon reflexes.
- Involved muscle hypertrophic or atrophic.
- Heredofamilial trend.

General Considerations

The most common of the muscular diseases is progressive muscular dystrophy. Three principal types are recognized, depending upon the site of initial muscular involvement and the distribution of apparent hypertrophy and atrophy. In the pseudohypertrophic type (Duchenne), there is enlargement of the calves and sometimes the thighs. In the facioscapulohumeral type (Landouzy-Déjerine), the face and shoulder girdle are involved early. In the limb-girdle type (Erb), the shoulder and pelvic girdle are involved.

The cause is not known. A heredofamilial trend is usually noted. Various types of inheritance may occur: simple dominant, simple recessive, or X-linked recessive.

Clinical Findings

A. Symptoms and Signs:

1. Pseudohypertrophic type (Duchenne)—This type occurs in early youth and is characterized by bulky calf and forearm muscles, which, however, are quite soft as a result of infiltration by fat and fibrous tissue; and progressive atrophy and weakness of the thigh, hip, and back muscles and shoulder girdle. It usually occurs in males and rarely in females, with onset in the first 3 years of life. It is considered to be X-linked and recessive, with a high mutation rate (rarely, autosomal recessive). Symmetric early involvement of the pelvic girdle muscles and, later, of the shoulder girdle muscles occurs. In about 80% of cases there is pseudohypertrophy, particularly of the calf muscles but sometimes of the quadriceps and deltoids. Steady and rapid progression usually leads to inability to walk within 10 years. The gait becomes waddling, and there is difficulty in going up or down stairs. In rising from a recumbent position the patient does so laboriously by "climbing up upon himself." When an effort is made to lift the patient by his armpits, the loose shoulder girdle permits his head to slip through the examiner's hands. Lordosis frequently develops from the weakness of the trunk muscles. Late in the disease the patient becomes too weak to move or support himself. Progressive deformity with muscular contractures, skeletal distortion, and atrophy results. Death from inanition, respiratory infection, or cardiac failure usually occurred in the second decade of life in the past; but with current antibiotic, supportive, and intensive care, patients often reach the middle years of life.

2. Facioscapulohumeral type (Landouzy-Déjerine)—Atrophy begins early in life and affects the muscles of the face, shoulder girdle, and upper arms; the muscles of the forearms are not involved. It occurs in either sex, with onset at any age from childhood until late adult life. It is transmitted usually as an autosomal dominant, occasionally with sex limitation. Abortive cases are common. Initially, the face and shoulder girdle muscles are involved and later the pelvic girdle muscles. Muscular pseudohypertrophy, contractions, and skeletal deformity are the rule. The characteristic facial involvement, with drooping of the eyelids, is known as "myopathic facies" and the thickened overhanging lip as "tapir lip." The weakened shoulder girdle causes "winging" of the scapula. The absence of forearm involvement gives a "Popeye the sailor" appearance. The disease progresses insidiously with prolonged periods of apparent arrest, and most patients survive and remain active to a normal age.

3. Limb-girdle type (Erb)—This form of muscular dystrophy involves the shoulder and pelvic girdles. The face is not affected. It occurs in either sex, with onset usually in the second or third decade but occasionally late in the first decade or in middle life. It is usually transmitted as an autosomal recessive characteristic. Primary involvement of either shoulder girdle or pelvic girdle muscle is noted, with spread to the other after a variable period. Muscular pseudohypertrophy occurs uncommonly. Abortive or static cases are uncommon. Variable severity and rate of progression may occur, but severe disability usually is present 20 years after onset. Muscular contractions and skeletal deformity come on late in the course of the disease. Most patients become severely disabled in middle life, and the life span is shortened.

B. Laboratory Findings: Biopsy of muscle may show typical degenerative changes. EMG may show changes characteristic of myopathy. Serum enzymes (creatine phosphokinase, transaminases, aldolase) may be elevated.

Differential Diagnosis

Progressive muscular atrophy develops later in life, beginning distally in the small muscles of the hand. Muscular fibrillation is present.

Dystrophic myotonia involves the sternomastoids, which are rarely affected in other dystrophies, and there is associated myotonia.

Progressive hypertrophic polyneuritis is characterized by distal involvement, sensory changes, and a thickened nerve.

Complications & Sequelae

Contractures commonly occur in the advanced stages. Pes equinus is due to calf muscle contracture.

Respiratory complications, such as pneumonia, are apt to occur. There may be clinical or laboratory evidence of cardiac disease, probably due to intrinsic dystrophy of the myocardium.

Treatment

Supportive measures, physical therapy, and orthopedic devices may give some help and comfort.

Prognosis

The disease is usually progressive and greatly resistant to medical therapy. Patients may continue to show progression for 20–30 years. Patients become progressively weaker, ultimately being confined to chairs or beds.

Dowben, R.M., & others: Polymyositis and other diseases resembling muscular dystrophy. Arch Int Med 115:584–594, 1965.

Engel, A.G.: Ultrastructural reactions in muscle disease. M Clin North America 52:909–932, 1968.

Jackson, C.E., & D.A. Strehler: Limb-girdle muscular dystrophy: Clinical manifestations and detection of preclinical disease. Pediatrics 41:495–502, 1968.

Magora, A., & H. Lauberman: Ocular myopathy. Arch Neurol 20:1–8, 1969.

Patel, A.N., Razzack, Z.A., & D.K. Dastur: Disuse atrophy of human skeletal muscle. Arch Neurol 20:413–421, 1969.

Pearson, C.M., & others: Skeletal muscle. Basic and clinical aspects and illustrative new diseases. Ann Int Med 67:614–650, 1967.

Penn, A.S., Lisak, R.P., & L.P. Rowland: Muscular dystrophy in young girls. Neurology 20:147–159, 1970.

Swaiman, K.F.: Chemical laboratory studies in muscular disease. Postgrad Med 41:144–147, 1967.

Vignos, P.J., Jr.: Diagnosis of progressive muscular dystrophy. J Bone Joint Surg 49A:1212–1220, 1967.

Zundel, W.S., & F.H. Tyler: The muscular dystrophies. New England J Med 273:537–543, 1965.

MYASTHENIA GRAVIS

Essentials of Diagnosis

- Weakness of the bulbar-innervated musculature, progressing as muscles are used (fatigue).
- Ptosis of lids, diplopia, facial weakness; weakness in chewing, swallowing, and speaking.
- Positive neostigmine (Prostigmin®) and edrophonium chloride (Tensilon®) tests.

General Considerations

This disorder, characterized by marked weakness and fatigability of muscles, is believed to affect the motor apparatus at the myoneural junction. Although almost any muscle in the body may be affected, the disease shows a special affinity for muscles innervated by the bulbar nuclei (face, lips, eyes, tongue, throat, and neck). The cause is essentially unknown, although some investigators consider myasthenia gravis to be a metabolic disorder. Dysfunction at the myoneural junction with unusually rapid splitting and inactivation of acetylcholine has been inferred from chemical and biologic studies.

Pathologic examination has failed to demonstrate consistent specific changes in the CNS, peripheral nerves, or muscles. Abnormalities of the thymus gland, including enlargement and tumor formation, have been described in some patients. It has been suggested that myasthenia gravis is an autoimmune disease since multiple auto-antibodies (including antiskeletal muscle antibody) have been found in the sera of patients with this disorder.

Clinical Findings

A. Symptoms and Signs: There is usually pronounced fatigability of muscles, with consequent weakness and paralysis. The muscles innervated by the bulbar nuclei are especially susceptible. Weakness of the extraocular muscles results in diplopia and strabismus. Ptosis of the eyelids may become most apparent late in the day. Speech and swallowing difficulties may be recognized after prolonged exercise of these functions. Difficulty in the use of the tongue and a high-pitched, nasal voice may be present. A snarling, nasal ("myasthenic") smile may be evident.

Women are more often affected than men, and the disease appears most commonly between 20 and 30 years of age.

Other somatic musculature may also be affected, resulting in generalized weakness. Fatigability of the deep tendon reflexes, with increasing diminution in response on repeated tendon tapping, is sometimes demonstrable. After a short rest, a single stimulus may then produce a strong muscle contraction. The Jolly reaction refers to the unusual fatigability of muscle upon repeated electric response, with pronounced capacity to recover after a short rest.

B. Diagnostic Tests:

1. Neostigmine (Prostigmin®) test—Prompt relief of symptoms (appearing within 10–15 minutes and lasting up to 4 hours) follows the subcutaneous injection of neostigmine methylsulfate, 1.5 mg, in most cases of myasthenia gravis. Atropine sulfate, 0.6 mg, is administered simultaneously to counteract side reactions. Observations are made 30 minutes later. If dysphagia is present, the response to neostigmine may be readily observed fluoroscopically as the patient swallows a thin barium paste.

2. Edrophonium (Tensilon®)—Edrophonium is a quaternary ammonium salt which exerts a direct stimulant effect on the neuromuscular junction. Intravenous injection of 10 mg edrophonium may relieve weakness within 20–30 seconds. Intramuscular injection of 25–50 mg may produce improvement lasting for several hours. Intravenous injection of 2–3 mg may be used as a test dose to distinguish myasthenic crisis (which improves) from overtreatment intoxication (no change) in myasthenic patients under treatment.

Treatment

A. Emergency Treatment: Sudden inability to swallow or respiratory crises may occur at any time. The patient should always carry 2 ampules of 0.5 mg of neostigmine methylsulfate (Prostigmin®), to be given immediately subcut or IM if severe symptoms develop. He should be placed under medical care at once; if additional neostigmine is needed, 1 mg may be given parenterally 2–3 times in 1 hour until an adequate response is obtained.

Progressively and potentially fatal weakness of the muscles of respiration may occur in spite of the administration of increasingly large amounts of neostigmine. A tracheostomy set, oxygen equipment, suction apparatus, and respirator should be available. After tracheostomy is performed, place the patient in a respirator and give oxygen as needed. Withhold neostigmine. Maintain fluid and electrolyte balance during the period of artificial respiration. After a few days, it is usually possible to gradually decrease the time spent in the respirator. In patients who survive the crisis remissions may occur, in some instances lasting for several years.

B. General Measures: Acquaint the patient with his disease, using simple lay terms. Maintain good nutrition and health.

C. Specific Measures:

1. Neostigmine bromide, 15 mg orally 4 times a day and increase (up to 180 mg/day) as required to give relief.

2. Pyridostigmine bromide (Mestinon®), an analogue of neostigmine, is at times more effective in treatment of bulbar muscle weakness. Give 0.6–1.5 gm daily at intervals spaced to provide maximal relief. Long-acting tablets (Mestinon Timespan®), 180 mg each, are especially useful at bedtime.

3. Ambenonium chloride (Mytelase®) may act twice as long as neostigmine and has fewer side-effects. Start with 5 mg 3 times daily and increase as necessary to give relief. The average dose is 5–25 mg 4 times daily.

4. Edrophonium chloride (Tensilon®) may relieve myasthenic weakness. Ten mg IV give relief in 20–30 seconds; 25–50 mg IM give improvement lasting for hours. Two to 3 mg IV may be used as a test dose for patients under treatment to distinguish between myasthenic crisis (improves) and overtreatment (no change).

5. Ephedrine sulfate, 12 mg with each dose of neostigmine, often enhances the action of neostigmine.

6. Potassium has also been found to be of value to supplement neostigmine, but it must be given in nearly toxic doses: 4–6 gm potassium chloride.

7. Side-effects of treatment with anticholinesterase drugs (eg, abdominal cramps, nausea and vomiting) may be ameliorated or prevented by adding atropine or atropine-like drugs to the therapeutic regimen as necessary.

8. Galanthamine and lycoramine compounds increase muscle contraction and inhibit cholinesterase. They are now under study and show promise as effective agents for the treatment of myasthenia gravis.

D. X-Ray Therapy: Patients who do not respond satisfactorily to oral medications may be given x-ray therapy (3000 r) to the thymus in 10–12 divided doses. Partial remission occurs in about ½ of patients so treated.

E. Surgical Measures: Thymectomy has been recommended for women under 40 years of age who have responded poorly to other measures. Complete remissions occur in about 1/3 and partial remission in another 1/3. The results in men are uncertain.

F. Thymoma: For thymoma the recommended treatment is thymectomy following a 3000 r course of x-ray therapy to the thymus over a period of 3–6 weeks.

Management of Newborn Infants of Myasthenic Mothers

Immediately after delivery, children of patients with myasthenia gravis may have severe signs of the disease. Immediate treatment with neostigmine is necessary to preserve life. After a few days the symptoms may disappear, and the child thereafter usually does not suffer from myasthenia.

Prognosis

Spontaneous remissions occur frequently, but relapse is the rule. Pregnancy usually produces amelioration, although exacerbations may also occur at this time.

Myasthenic crisis, with sudden death from apparent respiratory failure, may occur. Survival of crisis may be followed by a remission. Overtreatment with neostigmine may produce muscle weakness simulating myasthenic crisis.

In myasthenic crisis the mortality may be reduced by withdrawing anticholinesterase medications for about 72 hours after onset of respiratory difficulty or arrest and instituting early tracheostomy with positive pressure respiration using a cuffed tracheostomy tube.

According to some studies, the most critical period is the 2 years following onset.

Herman, M.N.: Familial myasthenia gravis. Arch Neurol 20:140–146, 1969.

Kirschner, P.A., & others: Studies in myasthenia gravis: Transcervical total thymectomy. JAMA 209:906–910, 1969.

Kreel, I., & others: Role of thymectomy in the management of myasthenia gravis. Ann Surg 165:111–117, 1967.

Namba, T., Sato, T., & D. Grob: Myasthenia gravis. Arch Neurol 17:637–644, 1967.

Namba, T., & others: Familial myasthenia gravis. Arch Neurol 24:49–60, 1971.

Osserman, K.E.: Thymectomy for myasthenia gravis. Ann Int Med 69:398–399, 1968.

Osserman, K.E.: Myasthenia gravis. Ann New York Acad Sc 135:5, 1966.

Osterhius, H.J.G.H., Bethlem, J., & T.E.W. Feltkamp: Muscle pathology, thymoma, and immunological abnormalities in patients with myasthenia gravis. J Neurol Neurosurg Psychiat 31:460–463, 1968.

Perlo, V.P., & others: Myasthenia gravis: Evaluation of treatment in 1355 patients. Neurology 16:431, 1966.

Shapiro, S.M., Namba, T., & D. Grob: Corticotropin therapy and thymectomy in management of myasthenia gravis. Arch Neurol 24:65–72, 1971.

Simpson, J.F., Westerberg, M.R., & K.R. Magee: Myasthenia gravis: An analysis of 295 cases. Acta neurol scandinav 42(Suppl 23):1–27, 1966.

MYOTONIA CONGENITA
(Thomsen's Disease)

Myotonia congenita is a rare heredofamilial disorder characterized by localized or generalized myotonia. Hypertrophy and hypertonicity of the muscles may occur, rendering them rigid and unyielding. The disease has occurred in 5 successive generations in the family of Dr. Thomsen, who first described it. Although it usually is not serious, the increased muscle stiffness makes it difficult for its victims to enjoy physical activity. Some have periodic attacks of generalized muscular spasm. Typically the disorder is present from birth and there is stiffness and difficulty in relaxation of the entire voluntary musculature. Stiffness is usually accentuated by cold and relieved by exercise, and generalized muscular hypertrophy is common. It is inherited usually as an autosomal dominant characteristic. Quinine has been used successfully in relieving hypertonicity. **Myotonia acquisita** is a form of Thomsen's disease which has its onset late in life.

MYOTONIA ATROPHICA
(Dystrophia Myotonica; Steinert's Disease)

Myotonia atrophica is a rare heredodegenerative disease of adult life which appears to be a mixture of Thomsen's disease and muscular dystrophy. There is hypertonicity of some muscles, usually of the tongue and the fist-making muscles of the hand, together with atrophy and weakness of the face, jaw muscles, peronei, and others. In both myotonia congenita and myotonia atrophica the patient characteristically grasps an object and then is unable to release his grip immediately. Myotonia, muscle atrophy (especially of face and neck), cataracts, early baldness, testicular atrophy, and evidence of dysfunction of other endocrine glands usually occur. Serum gamma globulin concentration is frequently reduced in myotonic dystrophy (IgG or $7S_\gamma$ fraction of immunoglobulins) due to increased catabolism of this protein.

Paramyotonia congenita is a relatively rare disorder characterized by myotonia which increases in the presence of cold, intermittent flaccid paresis which is not necessarily dependent upon cold or myotonia, and a hereditary pattern dependent upon a single autosomal dominant gene. It has been suggested that paramyotonia congenita is identical with or closely related to hyperkalemic periodic paralysis.

FAMILIAL PERIODIC PARALYSIS

This is a rare disorder in which the victim undergoes periodic attacks of flaccid paralysis lasting from a few minutes to several hours. Between attacks he is apparently normal. A severe attack may cause death from respiratory paralysis. A "cadaveric" electric reaction accompanies the attack. Decrease in serum potassium and serum phosphate is associated. Treatment includes oral administration of potassium salts. Attacks in susceptible individuals may be produced by injection of hypertonic glucose, insulin, desoxycorticosterone, or epinephrine, or by water diuresis or excess sodium intake.

During attacks the muscle potassium and sodium are not significantly elevated and the muscle becomes electrically unexcitable. Membrane potentials recorded by microelectrodes within the muscle cell do not disclose hyperpolarization. During attacks increased fluid may be noted in large vacuoles within the endoplasmic reticulum of muscle cells. Accumulation of abnormal glycogen breakdown products in these vacuoles may cause the influx of electrolytes and water into muscle cells to preserve ion balance.

Treatment is with potassium chloride, 5–10 gm orally when diagnosis has been made and then 5 gm 2–4 times daily during acute episodes as needed to prevent weakness or paralysis. In respiratory paralysis, give a prepared solution containing 1 gm potassium chloride in 50–60 ml distilled water very slowly IV. *Caution:* This is a dangerous procedure.

Patients with this disease should avoid high-carbohydrate foods. Routine administration of potassium chloride enteric-coated tablets, 8–12 gm 3 times daily, prevents attacks.

Recently acetazolamide (Diamox®) 250–750 mg daily has been reported to be effective in preventing attacks.

With adequate treatment, the prognosis is excellent. Death may result from respiratory paralysis, but this rare.

Adynamia episodica hereditaria, described by Gamstorp, is a disorder in which an increase in serum potassium accompanies paralytic attacks. Muscle weakness may be provoked in these patients by administration of potassium chloride or by rest after physical exertion. Onset is usually in the first decade. Attacks occur during rest after physical exertion. Mild paresthesias of the limbs usually precede attacks, and if exercise is begun at this stage paralysis may be aborted.

Brooks, J.E.: Hyperkalemic periodic paralysis. Arch Neurol 20:13–18, 1969.

Coppen, A.J., & E.H. Reynolds: Electrolyte and water distribution in familial hypokalemic periodic paralysis. J Neurol Neurosurg Psychiat 29:107, 1966.

Dyken, M., Zeman, W., & T. Rusche: Hypokalemic periodic paralysis. Neurology 19:691–700, 1969.

Griggs, R.C., Engel, K.W., & J.S. Resnick: Acetazolamide treatment of hypokalemic periodic paralysis. Ann Int Med 73:39–48, 1970.

Macdonald, R.D., Rewcastle, N.B., & J.G. Humphrey: The myopathy of hyperkalemic periodic paralysis. Arch Neurol 19:274–283, 1968.

Pearson, C.M.: The periodic paralyses: Differential features and pathological observations in permanent myopathic weakness. Brain 87:341–354, 1964.

STIFF-MAN SYNDROME

This is a rare syndrome of tonic muscle rigidity of unknown origin. There are no characteristic histologic changes in muscle. The disorder usually begins with episodic aching and tightness of the axial musculature which over a period of weeks or months becomes constant and spreads to the extremities. Ultimately there is a tight, board-like hardness of most of the limb, trunk, and neck muscles which interferes with voluntary movement. Sudden stimuli may precipitate intensely painful paroxysms of muscle spasm which may last for several minutes. Skeletal abnormalities, including subluxation and spontaneous fractures, are not uncommon. Electromyography reveals persistent tonic contraction, even at rest. Myoneural blocking agents (eg, succinylcholine) and peripheral nerve block abolish the pain and tonicity. Diazepam (Valium®) has been used successfully in a few cases. Most victims of this disorder become bedridden invalids.

Gordon, E.E., Januszko, D.M., & L. Kaufman: A critical survey of stiff-man syndrome. Am J Med 42:582–599, 1967.

Kasparek, S., & S. Zibrowski: Stiff-man syndrome and encephalomyelitis. Arch Neurol 24:22–30, 1971.

• • •

MANIFESTATIONS INVOLVING THE NERVOUS SYSTEM DUE TO PARASITIC DISEASES

Parasitic diseases of the nervous system may be manifest in various ways including the following:

(1) Cysts, granulomas, calcifications: Echinococcosis, cysticercosis, schistosomiasis, paragonomiasis, toxoplasmosis.

(2) Hydrocephalus or microcephalus: Toxoplasmosis, cysticercosis.

(3) Encephalitis: Malaria, cysticercosis, paragonomiasis, toxoplasmosis, trichinosis, angiostrongyliasis.

(4) Convulsive disorders: Malaria, cysticercosis, paragonomiasis, taeniasis, hymenolepiasis.

• • •

General Bibliography

Baker, A.B.: *Clinical Neurology,* 2nd ed. Hoeber, 1962.

Brain, R., & J.N. Walton: *Diseases of the Nervous System,* 7th ed. Oxford, 1969.

Chusid, J.G.: *Correlative Neuroanatomy and Functional Neurology,* 14th ed. Lange, 1970.

De Jong, R.N., & O. Sugar: *Yearbook of Neurology and Neurosurgery.* Year Book, 1971.

Farmer, T.W. (editor): *Pediatric Neurology.* Hoeber, 1964.

Ford, F.R.: *Diseases of the Nervous System in Infants, Childhood and Adolescence,* 5th ed. Thomas, 1966.

Grinker, R.C., & A.L. Sahs: *Neurology,* 6th ed. Thomas, 1966.

Merritt, H.H.: *A Textbook of Neurology,* 4th ed. Lea & Febiger, 1967.

Spiegel, E.A. (editor): *Progress in Neurology and Psychiatry: An Annual Review.* Grune & Stratton, 1970.

Walsh, F.M.R.: *Diseases of the Nervous System,* 10th ed. Williams & Wilkins, 1963.

Wechsler, I.S.: *A Textbook of Clinical Neurology,* 9th ed. Saunders, 1963.

Wilson, S.A.K.: *Neurology,* 2nd ed. Williams & Wilkins, 1955.

17...

Psychiatric Disorders

Harry K. Elkins

GENERAL PRINCIPLES OF PSYCHIATRIC DIAGNOSIS & MANAGEMENT

For many emotional difficulties experienced by patients, formal psychiatric diagnosis is not possible and specialized psychiatric treatment is not necessary. Almost all persons occasionally experience varying degrees of emotional discomfort which do not incapacitate or markedly contribute to maladjustment. In general, these feelings of discomfort may be attributed to situational factors, finances, personal status, and feelings of worth and affection about oneself or others. Special "problems" of childhood, adolescence, middle age, and old age occur, and variations in general health—including the hormonal stresses of menstruation—are apt to evoke tension, depression, withdrawal, or inappropriate emotional responses. Most of these emotional discomforts tend to pass readily and help strengthen the individual to handle the normal anxieties of living. It is only when feelings and behavior get out of hand or impair adjustment that they should be considered psychiatric problems. The physician who concerns himself with the emotional problems of his patients is practicing the art of medicine, which is as inseparable from the science of medicine as psyche is from soma. This means that the emotional component present in any physical illness must be handled with due care and consideration. The very presence of the physician offers reassurance, security, and hope; and what the physician does or says is often less important than how he does or says it. The "bedside manner" is not mere fiction; it cannot be affected or readily learned, but reflects the physician's own concern for his patient's total welfare. For example, the prescription of a placebo or "TLC" (tender loving care), the use of firm guidance or persuasion, admonition and direct advice, and sometimes "just listening" are all aspects of informal psychiatric treatment.

Conference on normal behavior. Arch Gen Psychiat 17:257–330, 1967.

Lowinger, P., & S. Dobie: What makes the placebo work? Arch Gen Psychiat 20:84–88, 1969.

Stein, L.I.: The doctor-nurse game. Arch Gen Psychiat 16:699–703, 1967.

EMOTIONAL FACTORS SECONDARY TO PHYSICAL ILLNESS

In many instances physical illness may increase or help precipitate emotional difficulties; and emotional difficulties may themselves augment or precipitate physical dysfunction or pain. A vicious cycle or "closed circuit" may thus be set up so that the patient eventually loses the ability to function both physically and emotionally.

Anxiety and depression commonly accompany physical illness. Both are discussed in greater detail below, but since the alleviation of anxiety and depression is often important in the treatment of physical illness it is well to keep the following in mind: (1) Many patients who would ordinarily relieve normal tension through work, play, and other activities become unusually depressed when deprived of physical outlets because of illness. (2) Physical illness often evokes feelings in the patient of helplessness and dependency. (3) A physical incapacity may be used unconsciously as an opportunity for secondary gain in the form of attention, love, special consideration, or pity. (4) A physical illness may be regarded by the patient (sometimes unconsciously) as deserved punishment for thoughts, feelings, or behavior about which he feels guilty. (5) Overly conscientious and guilt-ridden persons often experience depression and anxiety when their physical illness prevents them from carrying out their strongly felt obligations, especially to their spouse, children, or job, or when they feel that the expense of their illness or hospitalization is an economic burden out of proportion to their worth.

Feigning or exaggeration of physical illness may also be used consciously, as in malingering, for the purpose of avoiding responsibility or financial gain. In such cases anxiety and depression are not prominent features, and the tension present is more apt to be due to the malingerer's fears that his dishonesty will be exposed. He usually responds with anger when confronted with his failure to get well.

Baker, A.A.: Psychiatric Disorders in Obstetrics. Davis, 1967.

Barry, M.J., Jr.: Non-neurotic neurotics. Postgrad Med 43:87–95, 1968.

Waggoner, R.W., & R.W. Waggoner, Jr.: Somatic concomitants of depression. South MJ 62:285–289, 1969.

ANXIETY & DEPRESSION

Anxiety and depression are not only often present as secondary factors in many physical illnesses but are also the primary symptoms in most psychiatric illnesses. They frequently exist together and are apt to be so disabling that treatment is often focused directly on the alleviation of these symptoms. Some understanding of the nature of anxiety and depression is necessary for every physician.

Anxiety

Anxiety, as the term is used in psychiatry, is fear in the absence of an external threat. It is often precipitated, however, by apparently irrelevant situations in the environment, eg, being alone or being in a group, talking to certain persons, crossing a bridge, or the necessity for writing a letter, signing a check, or standing in front of a group to talk. It is sensed as an inner uneasiness, and may be brief and self-limited; sometimes felt as intense dread and alarm; or may assume panic proportions. Anxiety may be related to specific circumstances or objects (as a phobia); a specific body part or organ system (as in some forms of conversion hysteria or psychophysiologic disorders); may be so vaguely fixed that the patient can only say, "I don't know why I feel so upset" (as in anxiety neurosis); may be the most outstanding early symptom of psychotic break with reality (as in schizophrenic disorders); and may be accompanied by asocial or hostile behavior (as in the sociopathic and character disorders). The patient may attempt to narcotize his anxiety with alcohol or other addicting substances, or may seek relief from anxiety through increased time and effort at work or hobbies, involvement in social activities, or in verbosity with others.

Somatic complaints commonly associated with a "free-floating" type of anxiety include palpitations, tachycardia, gastrointestinal spasms, diarrhea, constipation, muscle spasms, tremors, sweats, constrictions in the throat or other parts of the body, insomnia, and headache.

Restlessness, emotional discomfort even when alone, irritability, and difficulty in relationships with others are usually present.

The basic reasons for anxiety are not completely understood, but it is believed that anxiety symptoms are directly related to feelings of insecurity and the feeling of an inner threat to life itself. Acute anxiety is often described by patients as a feeling of "loss of control" or "going to die." In some cases intensely hostile feelings at an unconscious level appear to be the cause of anxiety.

Lader, M.H.: Physical and physiologic aspects of anxiety and depression. Brit J Clin Pract 24:55–59, 1970.
Lesse, S.: *Anxiety: Its Components, Development and Treatment.* Grune & Stratton, 1970.

Depression

Depression is a feeling of sadness, dejection, or despondency. Like anxiety, it may be present in many emotional disorders and may also occur as a more or less normal reaction, eg, whenever an important loss is sustained. Depression is normally encountered following the death of a loved one, following romantic disappointments, during the climacteric if physical, business, or sexual activity is interfered with, at retirement for some individuals, and during illness and incapacitation. The loss may be of a material nature or may consist of a reduction in status, or enforced separation from another person with whose life the patient's own is closely identified (eg, a son or daughter going away to college). A more complete discussion of depression as it occurs in specific psychiatric illnesses is found under Psychoneurotic Disorders.

The practitioner commonly must deal with depression as a secondary factor after surgery or childbirth, when prolonged bed rest or dietary restrictions are necessary, and in association with physical disability.

The symptoms of depression include mood changes, insomnia, mild apathy, lessened interest in the environment, loss of motivation, and suicidal thoughts or frank attempts to commit suicide. The extent to which even a mild physical illness may evoke a sense of failure depends greatly on the early circumstances of the patient's life as well as current factors. In evaluating a patient's depressed response to an illness the physician should consider (1) how that patient has reacted in the past under similar circumstances, and (2) the patient's current life situation (including family, financial, and other personal factors).

Blinder, M.G.: Differential diagnosis and treatment of depressive disorders. JAMA 195:8–12, 1966.
Cole, J.O.: Psychopharmacology: The picture is not entirely rosy. Am J Psychiat 127:224–225, 1970.
Rosenthal, S.H.: Recognition of depression. Geriatrics 23:111–115, 1968.

THE COMBINED MEDICAL & PSYCHIATRIC EXAMINATION

Psychiatric diagnoses must be based upon positive psychiatric findings and not simply the exclusion of organic findings. For this reason, the combined medical and psychiatric examination is of great importance in the evaluation of a patient with a suspected psychiatric disorder. Furthermore, a thorough history and examination may have considerable therapeutic as well as diagnostic value.

The interview should be conducted in a comfortable, quiet room without noise or interruption. After inquiring about the presenting complaint, the physician should permit the patient to tell his own story in his own way. The most appropriate attitude is one of noncritical patience and concern. The interview is best made when the physician can indicate his personal interest in the patient without conveying his own judgmental values or his own undue alarm or voyeuristic interest in whatever the patient tells him. It is best to remain clinical but not coldly clinical. Not only the content but also the manner in which the patient communicates are important clues in understanding the patient. Unnecessary direct questioning and interpretative comment should be avoided. In most cases it is wiser to avoid writing while the patient is giving his history, especially those portions of the history which he may consider to be personal or confidential. Attempt to develop a retentive memory and write down or dictate pertinent information as soon as possible, but preferably not in the patient's presence.

It is important to determine the patient's real reason for seeking medical assistance. The presenting complaint may not be the real reason, or the appointment may have been made at the insistence of the spouse or other relative. Allow the patient complete freedom in developing his history and feelings. If he should pause, encourage him to continue by an appropriate word, expression, or gesture.

A relaxed examination of this sort will frequently elicit pertinent information which would not have been drawn out by direct questioning. It also helps to establish a comfortable doctor-patient relationship which will be useful in further treatment. If the patient resists giving information on questioning in a certain area it is best to postpone further discussion of that topic until the relationship is more firmly established. Long, rambling discussions may be controlled by subtly interjecting questions about the patient's illness or his reaction to it. Less pertinent questions can be asked and bits of information pieced together at subsequent visits.

It is not necessary at this point that the physician "do" something in order to effect treatment; it is frequently sufficient that he listen attentively. The patient's use of particular words and expressions may help to identify the recurrent theme of his feelings. The patient will generally convey his conscious as well as his unconscious feelings, the latter often hidden behind strong defenses such as rationalization or projection. His feelings may be revealed not only with words but with many nonverbal clues as well: gestures, tones of voice, significant omissions, parrying of direct questions, and sudden shifts of subject matter as he breaks off a description of his headaches, for example, to mention an impending visit from his parents. Apparently inconsequential and irrelevant matter may be recognized by the physician as a deliberate or unconscious attempt to divert discussion from a painful area. In all this the physician's objective can be stated quite simply: It is to understand his patient's feelings so that he may help the patient understand and accept himself. Whatever change the patient may make in his external life situation should come primarily because of emotional changes the patient is able to make within himself.

An adequate psychiatric examination frequently requires additional interviews with intimate family members, especially the spouse or the parents of minors. The objective observations of these persons who live with or know the patient intimately can be very helpful to the examiner, but it is often most difficult for close family members or friends to offer truly objective information. The emotional reactions of close relatives and friends must be carefully assessed since in many cases close relatives (especially the spouse or parent) are unwitting participants in the patient's emotional reactions. The examiner will often become aware of an interaction, a kind of interpersonal "game," which involves the patient with those who are emotionally close to him (eg, the spouse). In such cases the focus in treatment may have to be placed on the nature of and reasons for this "game," and treatment may have to include to some degree the involved person (eg, the spouse or the parents of a minor).

At times it may be convenient or necessary to postpone the conventional medical history (eg, past medical history and system review) to a later visit. Unless the patient is severely ill, the physical examination and other diagnostic studies may also profitably be postponed until the patient is reasonably at ease. The medical examination must be performed in such a way as to assure the patient that he is being well taken care of and that the physician takes his complaints seriously. However, elaborate and expensive x-ray, laboratory, or other diagnostic studies for the purpose of mere reassurance of the patient are not warranted.

Gray, M.: Principles of the comprehensive examination. Arch Gen Psychiat 10:370–381, 1964.
Mannino, F.V., & H.W. Wylie, Jr.: Evaluation of the physical examination as part of psychiatric clinic intake practice. Am J Psychiat 122:175–179, 1965.

THE PSYCHIATRIC INTERVIEW

If it appears that the patient's problems are largely psychogenic, it is desirable to expand the history and examination to elicit further information of psychiatric interest.

As noted above, the psychiatric interview is much more than a mere compilation of facts, feelings, and an assessment of the patient's reactions to the interviewer. Since the examination itself most often has an effect on the patient which will be therapeutic or nontherapeutic to his emotional state, it is wise to elicit information in such a manner that information-gathering as such does not become a forced issue. Questions should be posed simply and tactfully, and more than one session may be necessary.

Routine Diagnostic Procedure

The following areas in the patient's life should be explored, some more and some less extensively than others depending upon the patient's condition and the nature of the problem.

A. **Family History of Psychiatric Illness.**

B. **Environmental Factors During Development:** Early childhood training and experiences, family and social relationships, important friendships, scholastic record, desires and interests, sex experiences and attitudes, vocational training and experience, personal ambitions, religious attitudes.

Certain childhood traits, especially when several are present, are highly suggestive of neurotic problems: strong fears (eg, of animals, high places, closed places, dark), nailbiting, temper tantrums, bedwetting, sleepwalking, stammering, nightmares and night terrors, dizziness, fainting, convulsions, tics, and sulking. Also to be considered are difficulties in adjusting with peers, failure to accept authority, clinging over-dependency, and overtly aggressive behavior. During childhood, many of these symptoms are reactions to attitudes within the family—especially of parents and siblings—which the child senses as rejecting, severe, or deprecatory or which do not allow for self-sufficiency and self-expression. Anxiety within one of the parents and domestic tensions of all sorts are frequently sensed by children and expressed in a wide variety of somatic or behavioral difficulties.

C. Precipitating Factors: Most important are romantic or sexual difficulties, domestic and occupational problems, financial reverses, anxiety over health, upheavals in way of living, deaths in the family, and overwork and fatigue. Attempt to find out from the patient (or his family) what his feelings and modes of reaction during previous occasions of stress have been, ie, whether he tended to become withdrawn, angry, act out his feelings, or "somaticize" them and become physically ill.

D. Mental Status:

1. Appearance and behavior: Eg, tone of voice, gestures, tics, physical activity, peculiar habits.

2. Attitude toward interview: Degree of cooperation. Is the patient silly, provocative, hostile, guarded? How does he relate to interviewer?

3. Emotional status: Eg, flat, dulled, apathetic, confused, tense, depressed, elated, acutely anxious or panicky. Are the emotions expressed appropriate to the interview situation?

4. Content: Is the patient talking about things which seem to be pertinent, sequential, and logical? Is the content inconsequential and immaterial? Does it suggest fear, suspicion, frank paranoia, anger? Try to detect any underlying theme, eg, self-pity or suggestion of feeling cheated, hurt, or omnipotent.

5. Special preoccupations: Eg, body concern, obsessions, guilt, fear of sleep or dying, lack of self-confidence, sexual fears, delusions, hallucinations, mystical experiences, fantasies, day or night dreams.

6. Defense mechanisms: Eg, projection, denial, rationalization.

7. Orientation and memory: Is the patient able to perceive his environment clearly? (Time, place, other persons, himself.) Are there gaps or deficits in memory for recent or remote events?

8. Intellectual capacity and current intellectual functioning: Attempt to estimate this by presenting simple problems in arithmetic and asking simple questions about history and current events.

9. Thought processes: Is the patient's thinking process clear, or is it fragmented to a degree that he does not "make sense," as in schizophrenic disorders? Does the patient merely misinterpret the thoughts and behavior of others, or has he constructed a thinking system of his own? Test abstract reasoning, eg, by requiring interpretation of proverbs.

10. Competence: Is the patient competent to care for himself, handle money, be responsible for others?

11. Insight: To what degree does the patient recognize he has problems, what they are due to, and how he can be helped? Will he accept treatment or help from others?

Redlich, F.C., & D.X. Freedman: *The Theory and Practice of Psychiatry.* Basic Books, 1966.

Special Diagnostic Aids

In addition to the psychiatric evaluation approached by means of the interview, several additional diagnostic procedures may be useful. These should be performed and interpreted by specialists in their respective fields.

A. Electroencephalographic Studies (EEG): Useful in helping to differentiate organic from functional types of disorders, identifying convulsive seizure problems, etc.

B. Psychometric Testing: Useful in helping to differentiate organic from psychogenic disorders, measuring intelligence and special abilities, and in gaining information about the patient's personality, feelings, and psychic problems.

1. Objective tests—These provide a quantitative evaluation of personality traits or abilities as compared with established norms.

a. Intelligence tests (eg, Wechsler-Bellevue, Stanford-Binet).

b. Minnesota Multiphasic Personality Inventory (describes 9 levels of personality categories: hypochondriasis, depression, hysteria, masculinity-femininity, schizophrenia, etc).

c. Vocational aptitude and interest tests.

2. Projective tests—These attempt to evaluate the patient's feelings through his responses to stimuli which may be variously interpreted. Many such tests have been devised. Two of the more commonly used tests are the Rorschach test (inkblots used as stimuli) and the Thematic Apperception Test (TAT; unstructured or ambiguous pictures used as stimuli).

Psychologic testing is indicated in the following circumstances:

(1) For children:

(a) Wherever a question of mental retardation is present.

(b) To determine IQ, scholastic deficiencies, and "grade age."

(c) For adoption purposes or when commitment or sterilization is contemplated.

(d) As an adjunct (along with EEG studies) to the physical examination and history to help identify or rule out a possible organic cause of certain behavior

**Standard Classification (Modified) of the American Psychiatric Association
(Effective July 1, 1968) (See p 550.)**

I.   **Mental Retardation**
Borderline
Mild
Moderate
Severe
Profound
Unspecified

With each: Following or associated with—
Infection or intoxication
Trauma or physical agent
Disorders of metabolism, growth, or
nutrition
Gross brain disease (postnatal)
Unknown prenatal influence
Chromosomal abnormality
Prematurity
Major psychiatric disorder
Psychosocial (environmental) deprivation
Other condition

II. **Organic Brain Syndromes**
A. **Psychotic Organic Brain Syndromes:**
1. **Senile and presenile dementia—**
Senile dementia
Presenile dementia
2. **Alcoholic psychosis—**
Delirium tremens
Korsakoff's psychosis
Other alcoholic hallucinosis
Alcohol paranoid state
Acute alcoholic intoxication
Alcoholic deterioration
Pathologic intoxication
Other alcoholic psychosis
3. **Psychosis associated with intracranial
infection—**
General paralysis
Syphilis of CNS
Epidemic encephalitis
Other and unspecified encephalitis
Other intracranial infection
4. **Psychosis associated with other cerebral
condition—**
Cerebral arteriosclerosis
Other cerebrovascular disturbance
Epilepsy
Intracranial neoplasm
Degenerative disease of the CNS
Brain trauma
Other cerebral condition
5. **Psychosis associated with other physical
condition—**
Endocrine disorder
Metabolic and nutritional disorder
Systemic infection

Drug or poison intoxication (other
than alcohol)
Childbirth
Other and unspecified physical
condition

B. **Nonpsychotic Organic Brain Syndromes:**
Intracranial infection
Alcohol (simple drunkenness)
Other drug, poison, or systemic intoxication
Brain trauma
Circulatory disturbance
Epilepsy
Disturbance of metabolism, growth, or
nutrition
Senile or presenile brain disease
Intracranial neoplasm
Degenerative disease of the CNS
Other physical condition

III. **Psychoses Not Attributed to Physical
Conditions Listed Previously**
A. **Schizophrenia:**
Simple
Hebephrenic
Catatonic
Catatonic type, excited
Catatonic type, withdrawn
Paranoid
Acute schizophrenic episode
Latent
Residual
Schizo-affective
Schizo-affective, excited
Schizo-affective, depressed
Childhood
Chronic undifferentiated
Other schizophrenia

B. **Major Affective Disorders:**
Involutional melancholia
Manic-depressive illness, manic
Manic-depressive illness, depressed
Manic-depressive illness, circular
Manic-depressive, circular, manic
Manic-depressive, circular, depressed
Other major affective disorder

C. **Paranoid States:**
Paranoia
Involutional paranoid state
Other paranoid state

D. **Other Psychoses:**
Psychotic depressive reaction

IV. **Neuroses**
  Anxiety
  Hysterical
    Hysterical, conversion type
    Hysterical, dissociative type
  Phobic
  Obsessive-compulsive
  Depressive
  Neurasthenic
  Depersonalization
  Hypochondriacal
  Other neurosis

V. **Personality Disorders and Certain Other Nonpsychotic Mental Disorders**
  A. **Personality Disorders:**
    Paranoid
    Cyclothymic
    Schizoid
    Explosive
    Obsessive-compulsive
    Hysterical
    Asthenic
    Antisocial
    Passive-aggressive
    Inadequate
    Other specified types

  B. **Sexual Deviation:**
    Homosexuality
    Fetishism
    Pedophilia
    Transvestitism
    Exhibitionism
    Voyeurism
    Sadism
    Masochism
    Other sexual deviation

  C. **Alcoholism:**
    Episodic excessive drinking
    Habitual excessive drinking
    Alcohol addiction
    Other alcoholism

  D. **Drug Dependence:**
    Opium, opium alkaloids and their derivatives
    Synthetic analgesics with morphine-like effects
    Barbiturates
    Other hypnotics and sedatives or "tranquilizers"
    Cocaine
    Cannabis sativa (hashish, marihuana)

Other psycho-stimulants
Hallucinogens
Other drug dependence

VI. **Psychophysiologic Disorders**
  Skin
  Musculoskeletal
  Respiratory
  Cardiovascular
  Hemic and lymphatic
  Gastrointestinal
  Genitourinary
  Endocrine
  Organ of special sense
  Other type

VII. **Special Symptoms**
  Speech disturbance
  Specific learning disturbance
  Tic
  Other psychomotor disorder
  Disorders of sleep
  Feeding disturbance
  Enuresis
  Encopresis
  Cephalalgia
  Other special symptom

VIII. **Transient Situational Disturbances**
  Adjustment reaction of infancy
  Adjustment reaction of childhood
  Adjustment reaction of adolescence
  Adjustment reaction of adult life
  Adjustment reaction of late life

IX. **Behavior Disorders of Childhood and Adolescence**
  Hyperkinetic reaction
  Withdrawing reaction
  Overanxious reaction
  Runaway reaction
  Unsocialized aggressive reaction
  Group delinquent reaction
  Other reaction

X. **Conditions Without Manifest Psychiatric Disorder and Nonspecific Conditions**
  Social Maladjustment Without Manifest Psychiatric Disorder:
    Marital maladjustment
    Social maladjustment
    Occupational maladjustment
    Dyssocial behavior
    Other social maladjustment

problems. (Psychologic tests are not very useful for this purpose in children under 9 years of age.)

(2) For adults:

(a) As an adjunct to psychiatric diagnosis. They may be especially useful in helping to differentiate organic from nonorganic problems, and are also helpful in ascertaining the presence and degree of schizophrenic thinking.

(b) To help determine psychodynamics, the depth of psychiatric treatment indicated, and the suitability of psychoanalysis.

(c) To estimate the validity of unusual mental phenomena (eg, some apparently delusional or paranoid material may be real).

(d) For vocational guidance, identification of aptitudes, skills, and interests.

McReynolds, P. (editor): *Advances in Psychological Assessment.* Science & Behavior Books, 1968.

PSYCHOGENIC vs ORGANIC ETIOLOGY

Since psychiatric disorders may have somatic manifestations and since organic disease may have psychic manifestations, the differentiation of psychogenic ("functional") from organic disorders may be difficult. The difficulty stems in part from the patient's reluctance to admit that his illness, which may indeed be disabling, is "imaginary" or of an emotional nature; and the clinician's natural reluctance to ascribe an illness to psychogenic factors solely on the basis of absence of organic findings even when psychic features are evident. The problem is further complicated by the fact that the initial phase of certain serious organic disorders may be insidious and occult, and objective medical findings may be equivocal or absent.

The following may be helpful in differentiating psychogenic illnesses from those of organic origin: (See also Table 17–1.)

(1) A history of anxiety or unusual behavior since childhood or at adolescence.

(2) Multiplicity of symptoms involving many organ systems.

(3) Preoccupation with bodily functions and morbid fear of disease.

(4) Bizarre symptoms (unusual location, character, and severity) and atypical response to treatment.

(5) History of "physician-shopping" and failure to follow through any recommended treatment.

(6) Absence of objective medical findings, or symptoms out of proportion to medical findings.

(7) Absence of concern or anxiety in the face of apparent disability (eg, "paralysis").

(8) Onset or aggravation of symptoms coincident with anxiety or stress situations.

(9) Secondary gain considerations (eg, attempts to utilize "illness" unconsciously or consciously to attract attention, obtain sympathy, evade responsibility, or collect insurance).

(10) Dependence upon a variety of medications, including alcohol, to relieve distress.

(11) Symptoms which appear to be precipitated by or increase in severity with specific situations or persons: Eg, somatic symptoms before or after intercourse; following telephone calls from parents, children, or substitute figures; in certain social or business contacts.

Dasberg, H., & M. Assabel: Somatic manifestations of psychotic depression. Dis Nerv System 29:399–404, 1968.

Gross, M.D.: Marital stress and psychosomatic disorders. Med Aspects Human Sexuality 3:22–32, Jan 1969.

PSYCHIATRIC CLASSIFICATION

In the actual practice of psychotherapy diagnostic labels are often set aside completely in favor of understanding the patient in dynamic terms, ie, the underlying patterns of emotional reaction to stress and the current precipitating and situational factors in the patient's life. As long as the physician maintains a neutral attitude and helps the patient deal with immediate problems with sympathetic understanding, a great deal of benefit can be obtained, for example, from simple ventilating sessions.

However, for the purposes of formal professional communication specific diagnoses are often desirable and necessary, and numerous attempts have been made to organize the psychiatric disorders into a single classification system which would include both etiologic and descriptive information as well as give some indication of psychodynamics, ie, what is "going on" in the patient's emotional life and what his mode of reaction to stress is likely to be. Other important considerations in any system of classification involve the question of the principal mechanisms of defense which the patient uses (eg, denial, repression, projection) as well as the stage of personality development to which his emotions and behavior reactions have apparently regressed. So much overlapping of symptoms, dynamics, and etiology occurs that it is impossible at present to evolve an ideal system of classification. Most psychiatrists in the United States, however, for administrative and legal purposes, report their observations in terms of the Standard Classification of the American Psychiatric Association.

On July 1, 1968, the new psychiatric system of classification—*Diagnostic and Statistical Manual (DSM II)*—was adopted by the American Psychiatric Association (see pp 548–549). It is now in use in the USA, and it is more closely similar than before to the *International Classification of Diseases (ICD-8)*, although some differences still exist. *DSM II* differs from *DSM I*, which had been in use since 1952, in the following ways:

(1) Additional diagnoses: Over 50 new diagnoses have been added, usually by further subdividing older

categories. For example, hysterical neurosis is now divided into a conversion type and a dissociated type. Alcoholism, sexual deviation, and drug dependence may now be classified as several different specific types. Behavior disorders of childhood and adolescence now offer 7 possible types, and such new diagnostic labels as marital maladjustment and occupational maladjustment have been introduced. Three new personality disorders are included: explosive personality, hysterical personality, and asthenic personality.

(2) The term "reaction" has been eliminated from many diagnostic labels, eg, "schizophrenic reaction" is now simply "schizophrenia." The same is true for such previous designations as psychoneurotic reaction, psychophysiologic reaction, affective reaction, and paranoid reaction. The term "reaction" is retained in psychotic depressive reaction, transient situational disturbances, and a new group designated behavior disorders of childhood and adolescence.

(3) The recording of multiple psychiatric diagnoses is encouraged—eg, alcoholism, which previously would not be listed as a separate diagnosis if it were viewed as associated with an underlying disorder, may now be listed along with any other associated disorder. Similarly, whenever organic brain syndrome or mental retardation is caused by a specific physical condition, both the underlying physical condition and the organic brain syndrome should be recorded as separate diagnoses.

(4) There are also some changes in the exact definitions of the psychiatric disorders themselves.

Jackson, B.: The revised diagnostic and statistical manual of the American Psychiatric Association. Am J Psychiat 127:65–73, 1970.

Small, I.F., & others: Organic cognates of acute psychiatric illness. Am J Psychiat 122:790–797, 1966.

Spitzer, R.L., & P.T. Wilson: A guide to the American Psychiatric Association's new diagnostic nomenclature. Am J Psychiat 124:1619–1629, 1968. Also obtainable as a reprint (for 25 cents) from Publications Services Division, American Psychiatric Association, 1700 18th St, NW, Washington, DC.

THE PHYSICIAN AS GENERAL COUNSELOR

A variety of terms are currently in use to denote a broad range of relationship-type therapy. The term counseling is frequently used for the types of guidance, education, and clarification frequently offered by physicians, ministers, social workers, marriage counselors, and psychologists. The terms "psychotherapy" and "psychoanalysis" are more correctly applied to treatment which attempts to permanently alter recurrent or lifelong patterns of feelings and behavior. In successful psychoanalysis it is necessary to establish a prolonged and rather special kind of emotional relationship (called "transference") between the patient and his therapist, in which the feelings and events in the patient's life are dealt with in depth rather than completely restricted to current life situations.

It would be an error, however, to infer that "depth" therapy is superior to counseling or that it is necessarily the treatment of choice in many cases. "Transference"—or the fixing of emotions onto the therapist—is not exclusive to psychoanalysis and usually takes place in any type of psychotherapy. Referral to many different kinds of special counselors is often more practical and may be preferred by the patient, eg, for many child guidance and marital problems.

In the practice of medicine a great deal of general counseling is inevitably done by the physician. He is frequently called upon to provide emotional support and give advice about such matters as childbirth and child-rearing, adolescent adjustment, sexual and marital problems, and even personal and business frustrations and the difficulties of adjusting one's inner desires to the real world. A healthy personal philosophy, a thorough knowledge of the patient as a person and of his family and background, and plain common sense will enable the physician to assist most patients to work out their own solutions to these problems. Along with the clergyman, the physician can be of great help to his patients during times of stress, and can thus help to prevent many severe psychiatric disorders. In each case consideration of the patient's total life situation, his past psychic experiences, and his mode of relating to others are important.

The physician must also bear in mind that a disturbed patient's feelings and behavior, although they may be troublesome to the patient and to others, are due to causes, often obscure, which are beyond the patient's control. Exhortations to exert "will power" or to "snap out of it" are generally futile and may be harmful.

Many of the emotional reactions in the adult which the physician must understand and treat represent regressions to childish or infantile patterns of thought, feelings, and behavior which often seem inappropriate or bizarre. Unfortunately, intellectual understanding alone does not necessarily help the patient unless it is backed up by or incorporated into his emotional life and his behavior.

Counseling of Families

In many child-parent and husband-wife problems the difficulties lie in the failure of one or both parties to fulfill the other's emotional expectations. Emotional problems of dependency or control may be acted out by one party upon the other. In some cases each party becomes sensitized and reacts to the behavior of the other in such a way that mutually destructive behavior results. In these cases the physician faces the difficult task of dealing with 2 or more individuals and their feelings and responses to each other. It may be possible to educate the individuals so that each can recognize the "game" both are unconsciously playing and at least understand why discord results.

The more skillful and intrepid practitioner may attempt to counsel both partners, separately and together; and some psychiatric specialists in this field will counsel the entire family as a group ("family therapy"). In some cases it might be better to recommend that another therapist treat one of the parties so that a "triangular" situation can be avoided. Whatever counsel is offered should be stated in positive terms which are ego-strengthening rather than in negative or critical phrases. Emphasis should be placed on the strengths which already exist rather than on personality weaknesses.

Ackerman, N.W.: *Treating the Troubled Family*. Basic Books, 1968.
Bakwin, H.: Learning problems and school phobia. P Clin North America 12:995–1014, 1965.
Berne, E.: *Games People Play*. Grove Press, 1964.
Busse, E.W.: Geriatrics today: An overview. Am J Psychiat 123:1226–1233, 1967.
Haley, J., & L. Hoffman: *Techniques of Family Therapy*. Basic Books, 1968.
Lederer, W.J., & D.D. Jackson: *The Mirages of Marriage*. Norton, 1968.
Normal adolescence. GAP Report No. 68, vol 6. Group for the Advancement of Psychiatry, 1968.
Sherein, L., & W.E. Overstreet: Therapeutic abortion: Attitudes and practices of California physicians. California Med 105:337–339, 1966.
Symonds, M.: The management of the troubled child at home. Am J Psychoanal 29:18–21, 1970.
Usdin, G.L. (editor): *Adolescence: Care and Counseling*. Lippincott, 1967.

Transference & Countertransference

The person with emotional problems may be expected to feel and act toward his physician not only as he would toward a professional person from whom he expects help but also in a pattern characteristic of his emotional relationships with key persons in his earlier life. This is especially true if the patient's contacts with the physician are prolonged and close. The process whereby such feelings are projected upon the physician is known as "transference." A patient may thus come to feel (unconsciously) toward his physician as he once felt or currently feels toward a parent, sibling, spouse, or other figure who is or has been emotionally important to him.

In most professional situations involving the emotional management of his patients the medical practitioner may expect to move with ease and effectiveness depending upon his interest in and knowledge of the field, his personal ability and desire to be of service, and the time available. However, the physician must remember that it is his interest, knowledge, and skill, but not his personal involvement that are the basis of sound medical treatment. Since the physician also has his own emotional needs, both current and past, he may unconsciously assume certain attitudes toward the patient (eg, attempting to correct, teach, punish, rescue, or feel close to him) which serve his own emotional needs (countertransference). These feelings may seriously interfere with treatment. Unless the physician is aware of the ways in which he may possibly be emotionally "using" the patient for his own needs, he would do well to refer the patient to someone else for help. Referral should not be postponed for fear of offending the patient or his family, because of a misconception of the cost and nature of psychiatric help, or because of the physician's unwillingness to admit failure.

MANAGEMENT OF SITUATIONAL DISORDERS

In addition to permitting the patient to "tell his troubles" (emotional catharsis), the practicing physician can deal with many problems due to environmental maladjustments in the following ways:

(1) Determine the patient's reasons for reacting to his situation in emotionally disturbed ways. If the patient is assisted in facing his problems objectively, an altered philosophy or change in attitude may make his situation more tolerable.

(2) Help the patient to correct or alleviate situational factors. Utilize religious, legal, social service, or welfare agencies as indicated. The patient's family or associates can be approached (with the patient's consent) to obtain additional information and can often be persuaded to make favorable changes in the patient's environment. Encourage him to "change those things which can be changed, learn to accept those he cannot change, and be able to know the difference." Assistance often includes helping the patient come to his own conclusions regarding changes in environment, marital status, or occupational status; but drastic changes of this sort are often impossible and may complicate rather than simplify the patient's problems. Help the patient to find his own solution, but do not attempt to make decisions for him.

(3) Utilize sublimating (diverting) technics. Encourage the patient to develop other interests and skills (eg, sports, hobbies), particularly when he has excessive time for self-preoccupation. At times it is helpful for the patient to offer services to others. This is both an opportunity for unselfish expression and a means of obtaining approbation.

(4) Adopt a kindly attitude. Reassurance, suggestion, persuasion, and even admonition may be useful as the case demands. Avoid reproaching or arguing with the patient.

Garner, H.H.: Brief psychotherapy. Internat J Neuropsychiat 1:616–622, 1966.
Lion, J.R., & others: Violent patients in the emergency room. Am J Psychiat 125:1706–1711, 1969.
Mattsson, A., & others: Child psychiatric emergencies: Clinical characteristics and follow-up results. Arch Gen Psychiat 17:584–592, 1967.
Medlicott, R.W.: Brief psychotic episodes (temporary insanity). New Zealand MJ 65:966–972, 1966.
Wayne, G.J., & R.R. Koegler (editors): *Emergency Psychiatry and Brief Therapy*. Little, Brown, 1966.

MANAGEMENT OF DEEP-SEATED NEUROSES

Reeducation or reorientation technics are best left to the psychiatrist. If psychiatric help is not available, symptomatic and supportive medical measures, including the occasional use of tranquilizing medication during acute episodes, deserve the greatest consideration.

Precautions

(1) Avoid brutally confronting the patient with possible causal factors of neurotic symptoms.

(2) Avoid premature interpretation of psychiatric data.

(3) Avoid anger toward the patient because of failure of improvement.

(4) Avoid aggressive psychotherapy during the acute or symptomatic phase of the patient's disease.

(5) Do not tear down or destroy useful defenses. Focus only on those defenses which are ultimately detrimental.

SLEEP DISTURBANCES*

Normal sleep requires not only an absence of physical pain and psychic distress but also physical and psychologic energy depletion. Patterns of sleep and the amounts of sleep needed to provide adequate physical and mental refreshment vary considerably depending upon age, individual habit patterns, and hours of work routine.

Disturbed sleep is a frequent complaint and may be a symptom of emotional disorder (especially depression). Inquiry into the pattern of sleep disturbance may be helpful in determining the cause or causes.

Insomnia & Restlessness

Insomnia (difficulty in falling asleep) and restless, fitful sleep (reported by the patient as "poor sleep") are the most common complaints relating to sleep. They are usually due to one or more of the following factors: (1) Extraneous physical distraction (noise, light, uncomfortable bed). (2) Emotional tension centering around health, finances, family problems, interpersonal relationships, sexual tension, marked preoccupation with self. (3) Guilt feelings, fear of assault while asleep, or fears of dying while asleep. (4) An established habit pattern of dependency upon a particular person or a sedative-hypnotic drug to induce sleep and the unavailability of that person or drug.

Any of these areas can be further explored by the physician as indicated. Insomnia and restless, fitful sleep and early awakening, often with a sense of anxiety and uneasiness, is a common symptom in reactive

*Narcolepsy is discussed in Chapter 16.

and involutional type depressions. It is frequently one of the earliest indications of depression.

Other types of disturbed sleep patterns include those in which the patient seeks sleep repetitively during the daytime, retires earlier than physiologically necessary, or tends to stay in bed longer than physical need requires.

Such symptoms require psychiatric evaluation along the themes of escape from reality and responsibility, depression, and possible identification with a deceased person.

Treatment, after ruling out extraneous factors which disturb sleep, consists principally of ventilation of specific causes of tension, fears, and guilt. Discontinue sedative-hypnotic drugs where drug dependency exists. Substitute temporary anti-anxiety drugs at evening as a substitute for barbiturates and other sedative-hypnotics if necessary.

Temporary use of a sedative-hypnotic drug along with reassurance may help break a pattern of wakefulness and help reestablish a normal sleep pattern.

In some cases, simple measures such as a warm bath at bedtime, an evening snack, or reading in bed will promote natural sleep. Healthful daytime habits—physical, mental, and emotional—should be encouraged.

Kales, A., & others: Hypnotic drug abuse: Clinical and experimental aspects. Med Counterpoint 3:13–23, April 1971.
Webb, W.B., & H.W. Agnew, Jr.: Sleep stage characteristics of long and short sleepers. Science 168:146–147, 1970.

PSYCHIATRIC REFERRAL

Evaluation of Patients to be Referred

Many neurotic as well as psychotic patients may be helped considerably by the physician who is interested in emotional problems and is willing to devote the time and has the necessary training and ability. As a matter of fact, such patients constitute a significant portion of the practice of most physicians. However, when the cause of the patient's symptoms remains obscure or when symptoms are disabling or persistent in spite of the common sense insights, counseling, and medical treatment which the physician can provide, some type of psychiatric intervention should be sought.

Psychiatric referral should be considered in the following circumstances:

(1) Whenever it is feared that the patient may harm himself or others.

(2) When anxiety and depression do not readily respond to informal psychotherapy and medical treatment.

(3) When disturbances in mood, thinking, or behavior are prolonged, out of proportion to apparent cause, or so acutely bizarre as to suggest significant psychiatric disturbance.

(4) When paranoid thinking or behavior is present.

(5) When physical dysfunction or pain is present for which no organic basis can be discovered.

(6) When specific phobias (irrational fears) or compulsions tend to cripple the patient or limit his effectiveness in any area of adjustment.

(7) When sexual aberrations or impotence and frigidity are present.

(8) When drug or, in many cases, alcohol addiction is present.

(9) For those cases of marital discord and child or adolescent behavior disorders which are more severe than normal.

Schorer, C.E., & others: Improvement without treatment. Dis Nerv System 29:100–104, 1968.

Schwab, J.J., & J. Brown: Uses and abuses of psychiatric consultation. JAMA 205:65–68, 1968.

Visher, J.S.: Trends in psychiatric treatment: A report of a private psychiatric practice. Am J Psychiat 125:959–963, 1969.

Preparing the Patient for Referral

When the clinician feels that psychiatric referral is necessary, he should explain the need carefully and tactfully, in a matter of fact manner, without apology and without misrepresentation. If the patient has psychosomatic complaints the physician must explain their possible emotional origin as well as he can, showing at the same time that he understands that the pain or disability is just as severe and just as "real" as if it were due to organic disease.

It may be necessary to enlist the support of the patient's relatives or friends, particularly if the patient lacks insight or if he shows considerable resistance to psychiatric referral.

After referral, the physician's continued interest in and contact with his patient—at least until rapport with the psychiatrist has been established—may contribute greatly to the success of psychotherapy. In most instances the referring physician makes the initial contact for the patient. At times the patient may select from 2 or more psychiatrists suggested by the physician. In either case some degree of verbal or written communication between the referring physician and the psychiatrist may be expected.

The procedure for commitment of disturbed patients who are not able or willing to accept voluntary hospital treatment is discussed under Psychotic Disorders.

Other Types of Referral Resources

In most large cities in the USA a variety of referral resources are available for the physician or counselor dealing with certain types of problems, eg, marital and child behavior difficulties. The Family Service Association is available in most US cities with populations over 30,000. The Catholic Church and some other churches also support special counseling services with trained counselors for the purpose of psychiatric type help for various family problems. Within the past decade there has been a marked increase in the numbers of professionally qualified psychiatric social workers and psychologists to provide counseling services on a private fee basis. Many of these persons work under medical direction, and some without it. Referrals to any of these resources may be made with impunity so long as the referring physician has assured himself that medical and organic factors are well understood by the agency or individual counselor to whom the client is being referred and that such problems remain under the treatment of a physician.

Many of these counseling agencies and some privately operating counselors use group therapy, in which a small group of clients with similar problems (sometimes with mixed kinds of problems) meet periodically for professionally directed self-help. The varieties of group therapy are multitudinous: couples who are having marriage difficulties may meet together as a group, or the wives or husbands may meet separately, to share their experiences and learn from each other; parents of problem children, adolescents with behavior problems, child-parent groups, and mothers of schizophrenic children are other typical classes of patients who have benefited from the group therapy approach.

In general, it is wise if the referring physician knows the resources available in his own community and something about the professional qualifications and personality of the person to whom he refers his troubled patients.

Coleman, J.V.: Aims and conduct of psychotherapy. Arch Gen Psychiat 18:1–6, 1968.

Schwab, J.J.: Psychiatric consultations with medical patients. South MJ 59:277–280, 1966.

SPECIAL PSYCHIATRIC TREATMENT

The variety of schools of psychiatric theory which exist, along with a common notion that all psychiatric treatment is necessarily expensive, has led to some erroneous ideas regarding the usual methods of psychiatric practice. Many psychiatric problems require only short-term intervention and the cost is not prohibitive. No particular psychiatric school of thought has been shown on statistical or clinical grounds to give superior results, and most psychiatrists will use a number of technics, procedures, and medications along with the special kind of verbal relationship known as psychotherapy.

In many cases the patient's attitude toward the "stigma" often felt to be associated with psychiatric illness must be adroitly manipulated by the physician before referral can be accomplished. Unfortunately, many physicians have themselves not yet come to terms with the concept of the psychiatrist's role in the total health care of persons who are not strikingly "deranged." Knowledgeable physicians in their own local communities will combat these unconstructive attitudes so that the undoubted benefits of psychiatric services can be made available to a wider segment of the patient population as a preventive mental health measure.

The USA today is in an era of active psychotherapies. To some degree, much as the church as an institution has become more activist on social, cultural, and political issues, psychiatry has taken a more direct and active role in treatment of the patient. The impact of behavior therapy, role-playing, and a variety of "family" and group therapies (including "marathon" groups which may go on continuously day and night) has greatly altered the earlier model of "the patient on the couch." Such terms as "crisis intervention," "confrontation," and "gut level" (the latter taken from Synanon) have come into psychiatric literature and practice.

Many psychotherapists have come to the conclusion that insight and catharsis alone have severe limitations in that the patient who is helped to know all about himself may still be essentially unchanged. The view that symptoms as such should be regarded as the illness is gaining credence, and that it is unnecessary or futile to seek relief of symptoms in their origins in the patient's earlier life. Removal or alleviation of the patient's symptoms lessens his distress and is in itself a change toward health. In psychiatric practice, this implies less concern about instincts and more focus on the object of the patient's instincts. Sex becomes less important than love in the wide sense of the word, and treatment deals more directly with the patient's relationships or the "game" he plays.

The use of appropriate medication or physical procedures is not necessarily contrary to psychiatric principles. Any approach which helps to modify symptoms, increase comfort, allay nontherapeutic anxiety, and prevent destructive behavior may be used. However, whatever procedures or medications are used are only adjunctive to the vital psychotherapeutic patient-doctor relationship.

Brill, N.Q.: Results of psychotherapy. California Med 104:249–253, 1966.

Enelow, A.J., & M. Wexler: *Psychiatry in the Practice of Medicine.* Oxford, 1966.

Flinn, D.E.: New methods of psychiatric treatment. California Med 115:88–95, July 1971.

Grinker, R.R.: Research in a behavioural science. Canad Psychiat AJ 15:567–576, 1970.

Kelman, H.: What is technique? Am J Psychoanal 29:157–167, 1969.

Lewis, J.M.: Changing moral concepts. South MJ 62:290–294, 1969.

Marks, I.: The future of psychotherapies. Brit J Psychiat 118:69–72, 1971.

Pande, S.K.: Mystique of "western" psychotherapy: Eastern interpretation. J Nerve Ment Dis 146:425–432, 1968.

Voth, H.M.: Choice of illness and defense: A clinical study. Comprehensive Psychiat 11:295–304, 1970.

Yalom, I.D., & M.A. Lieberman: A study of encounter group casualties. Arch Gen Psychiat 25:16–30, 1971.

Hospital Milieu Treatment (The Therapeutic Community)

Within the past decade especially, in the USA and Great Britain, there has been an increased emphasis on hospital or outpatient treatment of small groups of psychiatric patients in a professionally guided environment where patients are able to express, share, and help correct their own and each others' emotional reactions. The recent tendency to incorporate psychiatric wards into the general hospital setting, the advent of useful psychotropic drugs, and the increased availability of skilled professional persons (psychiatrists and psychiatrically trained nurses, aides, psychologists, social workers, occupational and recreational therapists) have brought about a major change in psychiatric treatment.

Almost all categories of patients, except those who are grossly disturbed or destructive, are suitable for treatment in such a therapeutic community. Some of the principles involved in such treatment are as follows:

(1) The residual healthy aspects of the patient's personality are given every opportunity for expression and growth, eg, through patient self-government, occupational, work, and recreation programs.

(2) Group therapy sessions are held regularly (usually once a day) in which ventilation, group discussion, and mutual correction of feelings and behavior may develop. The connection between current problems with prehospital problems is made wherever possible. The group is under the supervision of a trained person, usually a psychiatrist or psychologist.

(3) Both male and female patients may be treated in the same setting and share common eating and activity facilities. Healthy mixing between patients is encouraged and considerable freedom within the ward and for outside ward passes is allowed for those patients able to accept the responsibility involved.

(4) Family and community contacts are fostered so that the patient will not become separated or alienated from normal life. In many cases family members are brought into group discussions with the patient or in special "family groups" in order to convey understanding and correct their misconceptions of psychiatric illness and to change the family's reactions to the ill person.

(5) The use of electroconvulsive treatment is kept to a minimum, and medication is provided only to allay symptoms. Emphasis is placed on self-recognition of problems and is enhanced by the patient's understanding and acceptance of other people's emotional difficulties.

(6) Post-hospital insight treatment may continue in an outpatient setting between the patient and his psychiatrist or in outpatient groups.

Jones, M.: Therapeutic community practice. Am J Psychiat 122:1275–1279, 1966.

Mannucci, M., & M.R. Kaufman: The psychiatric inpatient unit in a general hospital: A functional analysis. Am J Psychiat 122:1329–1343, 1966.

Melzoff, J.: *The Day Treatment Center.* Thomas, 1966.

Moore, R.A., & R.A. Henry: Trials and tribulations in establishing a community hospital psychiatric unit. Am J Psychiat 125:186–191, 1968.

COMMUNITY PSYCHIATRY

As a corollary to the trend in the USA to treat patients on an ambulatory basis rather than by hospitalization, some important changes have taken place in the large state mental hospitals as well as in the community.

Prolonged confinement in a mental hospital sometimes results in the patient's adaptation to his hospital environment so that his ability to adjust in society eventually lessens or deteriorates. For this reason, the current tendency is to provide brief hospitalization only in order to help manage acute problems of maladjustment. Early release from hospital and continued management in the community are aimed for. All community resources are enlisted: psychiatric help (individual or group therapies), supervised medications (tranquilizers, antidepressants, anticonvulsants, etc), job and recreational assistance, welfare and legal assistance when necessary, and counseling for families to help the ambulatory patient adjust in the home. A vast network of community mental health services is gradually developing which will serve such persons. As a result, many of the large mental hospitals which had become reservoirs for chronic patients are now better able to focus on brief treatment for acute phases of mental illness.

The dimensions of community psychiatry. GAP Report No. 69, vol 6. Group for the Advancement of Psychiatry, 1968.
La Burt, H.A., & others: The state hospital and community psychiatry. Dis Nerv System 29:556–558, 1968.
Lamb, H.R.: Release of chronic psychiatric patients into the community. Arch Gen Psychiat 19:38–44, 1968.

Common Adjunctive Psychiatric Technics

In addition to the verbal psychotherapeutic relationship and hospital milieu treatment, the most commonly used technics of the psychiatrist include the following:

A. **Somatic Procedures:**

1. Electroconvulsive (ECT) and insulin therapy.

2. Narcoanalysis and narcosynthesis (amobarbital [Amytal®] and thiopental [Pentothal®] interview).

3. CO_2 and sleep therapy (neither of these have gained wide acceptance in the USA).

4. Psychosurgery (lobotomy, prefrontal lobotomy, thalamectomy). These are rarely indicated.

5. Physical therapies (hydrotherapy, cold pack, continuous tub, special exercises, muscle relaxation, heat, massage).

B. **Hypnotherapy:** In the hands of (or under the supervison of) a qualified psychiatrist, hypnotherapy has special value in selected cases.

Within the past few years there has been renewed interest in hypnotism. Although it currently has a number of enthusiastic adherents, it is generally recognized that hypnotism at best may be used to strengthen and underscore an important step forward in psychotherapy. It may give symptomatic relief (which may be tremendously important), but it is not curative of any underlying psychic problem. Its effectiveness is not limited to any one diagnostic category and hence it is not specific to any one type of illness or symptom.

C. **Medications:** (See also Psychotropic Drugs.) Almost any type of medication may be used for psychotherapeutic purposes. Not only the medication itself but the route selected, oral or intramuscular, may be selected for psychotherapeutic reasons.

1. Sedatives, hypnotics, tranquilizing drugs.

2. Antidepressants.

3. All current evidence indicates that lysergic acid diethylamide (LSD) and associated hallucinogenic drugs (see further discussion on p 571) have no place at present in the routine treatment of psychiatric patients, although some investigators have reported good results with neurotic and alcoholic patients.

The American Psychiatric Association has taken the position regarding LSD that, "While neither laboratory nor clinical findings have yet adequately established the therapeutic usefulness of the drug, they have elicited sufficient information to justify continuing research into its possible values. The Association is confident that when conducted by qualified investigators such research has been and will continue to be carried out with a degree of safety comparable to that of many other drugs."

D. **Work therapy,** educational and recreational guidance, and advice concerning diet, sleep, rest, and sex activities may be important adjuncts in psychiatric treatment.

Conn, J.H.: Hypnosis in general practice. Med Opin Rev 5:120–129, June 1969.
Dalai, A.S.: An empirical approach to hypnosis. Arch Gen Psychiat 15:151–157, 1966.
Ewalt, J.R., & P.L. Ewalt: History of the community psychiatry movement. Am J Psychiat 126:43–52, 1969.
Kolb, L.C.: Community mental health centers: Some issues in their transition from concept to reality. Hosp Community Psychiat 19:335–340, 1968.

Psychotherapy

Most practicing psychiatrists today tend to take a holistic approach toward treatment, ie, the patient is viewed in his "totality" as "a whole person." Biologic, psychologic, cultural, economic, and family factors are all interwoven in the complex network which determines an individual's particular response to life. Each individual has his own degree of ability to handle emotional stress, and this ability may vary considerably from time to time in the patient's life. Stress varies also, and what may act as a negative force upon one person may act as a constructive challenge to another. Early conditioning and learned behavior frequently seem to determine how any given individual will react to the emotional impact of stress. There are a limited number of ways in which people are able to react to stress. One person may respond by withdrawal and depression; another may become hyperactive; a third may resort to alcohol or other drugs; another by developing somatic symptoms; and still another by acting out his tension through unusual sexual activity, gambling, or compulsive work. No person consciously determines just how he will attempt to adapt to emotional stress, but it is important that self-destructive, painful, negating, or disabling symptoms be replaced by constructive and life-fulfilling feelings and behavior. The psychiatrist's main task is to help the patient free himself from himself so that both physical and emotional health can be realized.

The psychotherapeutic relationship is developed differently with each therapist and for each patient. The general purpose, no matter what steps are taken first, is to provide a feeling of well-being, encourage insight, redirect harmful attitudes, and foster emotional growth. The psychiatrist does these things in various ways.

A. Psychiatrist's Attitude: His sincere interest in and intelligent understanding of the patient's emotional state is an immediate source of support. The first general rule in treatment is that the patient should not feel alone with his problem.

B. Ventilation by the Patient: For many patients the act of ventilating their feelings in the presence of an understanding physician is sufficient treatment in itself. The patient feels he has relieved himself of emotional pressure and that he still is accepted without censure.

C. Abreaction: In many cases the patient's feelings are so strong that they also must be relieved by actual expression in the presence of an accepting person. Great relief may be obtained if the patient can also express his pent-up feelings through an outburst of tears, anger, or a show of frustration or sorrow.

D. Shift of Emphasis: Patients will often be unaware of the real source of their feelings and tend to place emphasis on the wrong persons or areas of their lives. Thus a wife may show considerable feeling about the manner in which her husband treats her without being aware that the husband represents other persons who have frustrated, ignored, rejected, pampered, placated her, etc, in the past, eg, parents, siblings, or other key persons. Such feelings are usually out of proportion to the facts and quite frequently the patient seeks out, sets up, and precipitates reactions in others in order to fulfill his own unconscious feelings. The psychiatrist, when he has sufficient clues to these possibilities, will help the patient shift emphasis onto those areas of his life and those relationships in which the patient's feelings originated. The psychiatrist must help the patient to recognize how he projects old patterns and unresolved feelings onto those persons currently involved in his life, eg, spouse, children, employer, or society in general.

E. Interpretation and Insight: Feelings should be correlated with pertinent life situations, so that a coherent pattern of repetitive situations and responses becomes discernible to the patient.

F. Reassurance, Support, Direction, and Persuasion: These technics may be used whenever necessary to protect the patient, reduce unnecessary anxiety, and guide the patient toward an acceptance of himself.

G. The Transference Mechanism: The patient should ultimately recognize that he may tend to react emotionally to his psychiatrist in much the same way he has reacted to other important persons in his past. The ultimate "working out" or resolution of this transference of feelings is one of the important aspects of analytically oriented psychotherapy, including psychoanalysis.

Coleman, J.V.: Aims and conduct of psychotherapy. Arch Gen Psychiat 18:1–6, 1968.
Jackson, D.D., & J. Haley: Transference revisited. J Nerv Ment Dis 137:363–371, 1963.
Ornstein, P.H.: What is and what is not psychotherapy? Dis Nerv System 29:118–123, 1968.
Wolberg, L.R.: *The Technique of Psychotherapy*, 2nd ed. Grune & Stratton, 1967.

Psychoanalytic Treatment

Psychoanalysis is useful for many of the psychoneurotic disorders. It is probably less effective for personality disorders, and is of questionable value in sociopathic disturbances and the psychoses. Not all patients, however, even in the psychoneurotic group, are suitable candidates for formal psychoanalysis. Psychoanalysis is a demanding therapeutic venture which places heavy burdens on the patient's time (and purse) and in a sense his talents and intellectual resources also. Only a person who is capable of making creative leaps between obscure emotional relationships will benefit from depth analysis. This implies the necessity for critical introspection, a willingness to read and learn, and a strong motivation for improvement. Psychoanalytic treatment usually requires frequent sessions over a period of more than 1–2 years.

Psychoanalytic treatment will vary to some degree depending upon the personalities of the analyst and the patient. The use of free association to uncover unconscious feelings, including those expressed in dreams, is one of the important technics used in psychoanalysis. The development of a "transference neurosis," in which the patient reacts as though the therapist were the significant person (or persons) in the patient's earlier life, and the ultimate resolution of this transference neurosis, is one of its special features.

Much of the point of view and many of the technics of psychoanalysis have been absorbed into the practice of general psychotherapy. Various schools of psychoanalytic theory which previously focused on the importance of "sexual" factors and instincts as opposed to interpersonal or cultural factors have given way to a recognition that in actual treatment all forces and aspects of the patient's life—instinctual, interpersonal, cultural, and social—must be considered.

Marmor, J.: Current status of psychoanalysis in American psychiatry. Am J Psychiat 125:679–680, 1968.

THE PSYCHONEUROTIC DISORDERS

ANXIETY
(Anxiety Neurosis, Anxiety State, Anxiety Reaction)

Essentials of Diagnosis

- Acute attacks of increased anxiety, tension, and feelings of impending doom, often associated with various somatic symptoms, eg, chest tightness, breathlessness, choking, sweating, and palpitation.
- Physical findings of widespread autonomic excitation.
- Often no evident external cause for anxiety attack.
- Between attacks: fatigue, weakness, nervousness, headache, and irritability.

General Considerations

The anxiety state is characterized by a subjective feeling of apprehension or tension, usually unrelated to appropriate external stimuli, and by the objective psychic reaction (autonomic excitation) of fear. Acute anxiety attacks usually last from a few minutes to hours, but the chronic anxiety state may last for months to years interspersed with acute attacks.

The anxiety state may occur as an isolated psychiatric illness or may be a prominent component of many other psychiatric illnesses such as depression, schizophrenia, and hysteria.

The basic nature of anxiety is not known, but it is felt that anxiety represents a response to danger which is felt internally and is frequently symbolic. In many cases the patient's fear of the consequences of his own anger, which he may not be consciously aware of, appears to be the basis of his anxiety.

Clinical Findings

The acute attack usually begins with a sudden onset of fear accompanied by restlessness, increased tension, tightness of the chest, breathlessness, palpitation, sweating, flushing, tightness in the throat, and trembling. Hyperventilation is usually marked, and the alkalosis which results from the blowing off of CO_2 results in tingling of the fingers, toes, and perioral area which may progress to tetany. The patient has an impression of "impending doom." The attack lasts from a few minutes to hours and is usually followed by weakness and exhaustion lasting hours to days. Between attacks the patient's condition may vary from entirely well to nervous, tired, and concerned about the possibility of a new attack. Attacks may occur rarely or in rapid sequence up to several per day.

In chronic anxiety the complaints are usually those of nervousness, irritability, restlessness, headache, insomnia, and fatigue.

Physical examination may reveal excessive perspiration of the hands or axillas, mild tachycardia, signs of tetany, and tremors. Routine laboratory analyses are normal. Functional hypoglycemia may be present.

Differential Diagnosis

Individual symptoms and signs of anxiety may suggest similar manifestations of other diseases such as angina pectoris (chest and arm pain), thyrotoxicosis (nervousness, sweating), pheochromocytoma (hypoglycemia), bronchial asthma or heart failure (shortness of breath), and the menopausal syndrome (sweating, flushing, palpitations).

Treatment & Prognosis

A complete medical investigation will assist the physician in reassuring the patient that no organic disease is present. It may be necessary to see the patient on subsequent visits for further reassurance. Instruction regarding the voluntary control of hyperventilation (holding the breath or rebreathing in a paper bag) and the use of mild sedatives will usually be sufficient supportive care in the majority of cases.

For more resistant cases, treatment is aimed along 2 lines: those measures taken primarily to relieve anxiety symptomatically, and those taken to uncover, understand, and resolve the basic reasons for the anxiety.

Symptomatic measures for the relief of anxiety are the various drug therapies, physical therapy, hydrotherapy, occupational therapy, and attempts to channel anxiety into useful, creative, and productive areas such as work, volunteer services, and hobbies.

The use of tranquilizing medications, especially the phenothiazines and meprobamate, is in vogue at present, but the dangers of toxicity as well as a tendency toward habituation in some patients cannot be overlooked. Tranquilizing medications should be employed only in conjunction with efforts to relieve stress and provide support in the usual ways. Acute anxiety and panic states may require parenteral phenothiazines, eg, promazine or chlorpromazine, or the barbiturates.

Basic character changes can be brought about only by means of long-term psychotherapy, including psychoanalysis.

Andresen, A.F.R., Jr.: A practical approach to anxiety reactions. New York J Med 63:1144–1147, 1963.

Bennett, A.E.: Anxiety as a symptom of mental illness. GP 27:101–106, May 1963.

Braceland, F.J.: Drugs effective in emotional disorders. Postgrad Med 35:237–242, 1964.

Knoff, W.: A history of the concept of neurosis, with a memoir of William Cullen. Am J Psychiat 127:80–84, 1970.

HYSTERIA
(Dissociative Reactions, Conversion Reactions, Conversion Hysteria)

Essentials of Diagnosis

- Usually in patients with immature, histrionic, unsophisticated personalities, often under great stress, eg, frequently noted in wartime among military personnel facing hazardous assignments.
- Indifference of the patient to his behavior or to the loss of function of the affected part.
- In conversion hysteria there is no correlation between symptoms and anatomic nerve distribution.
- Usually a history of poor sexual adjustment and the existence of troubling phobias.

General Considerations

The dissociative reactions and the conversion reactions are disorders in which a segment of the patient's behavior or motor function is split off or isolated from the rest of his personality. The split, however, is partial rather than complete fragmentation, as in the case of the schizophrenic reaction, and in general the personality remains intact. The isolated bit of behavior or motor loss is often expressed in a fashion which is bizarre or dramatic.

In the dissociative reaction the isolated phenomenon occurs in the behavior of the patient, eg, as in the fugue state or amnesia. Rarely, a complete depersonalization or dual personality may occur, as in the well-known story of Dr. Jekyll and Mr. Hyde.

In the conversion reaction the isolated disturbance occurs in the motor function of the patient, eg, hysterical paralysis of a limb, psychic blindness or mutism, and hysterical convulsive seizures.

In both reactions the isolated symptom is due to highly charged anxiety surrounding some incident or set of circumstances in the patient's current or past life which has been completely repressed. The symptom itself or the organ selected for dysfunction has symbolic meaning. The paralyzed part may prevent the patient from action which he unconsciously does not want to perform, and also symbolizes sexual organs and acts or hostile objects which frighten him. For example, the paralyzed hand or leg or the blind eye represents a sexual idea which the patient has repressed (phallus, masturbation, watching coitus, etc).

Differentiation of the dissociative and conversion reactions from organic disease and psychosomatic illness is shown in Table 17–1. It may be quite difficult to differentiate conversion hysteria from malingering. Continued observation will often reveal the lowering of the defenses of the malingerer when he feels he is not being observed.

Clinical Findings

The hysterical patient is usually melodramatic, impulsive, immature, egocentric, and highly suggesti-

ble. The specific infirmity reflects his own lay misconception of the apparent illness: the entire limb is paralyzed rather than a specific muscle group; anesthesia does not follow nerve pathways but occurs in stocking or glove distribution; and amnesia is usually restricted to a circumscribed series of events. Of greatest importance, however, is the patient's lack of concern about his infirmity (*la belle indifférence*).

When these patients have hysterical convulsive seizures they remain conscious, do not injure themselves, and are not incontinent of urine or feces. Hysterical motor tics involve coordinated groups of muscles and differ from organic tics. In the hysterically paralyzed limb vasomotor disturbances may occur; the limb may be blue and cold, and dermographia may be present.

Treatment & Prognosis

In some cases of conversion reaction or dissociative reaction, removing the patient from a threatening situation will completely relieve symptoms. This is as true for ordinary life situations as it is during combat situations, where conversion disorders are more frequently found.

Disappearance of symptoms such as hysterical paralysis, blindness, aphonia, and anesthesia may sometimes follow strong authoritative suggestion with or without hypnosis. Permanent cures are difficult to achieve in this way, and for many patients only limited benefits may be expected from long-term directive psychotherapy.

Halleck, S.L.: Hysterical personality traits. Arch Gen Psychiat 16:750–757, 1967.

Knoff, W.F.: Four thousand years of hysteria. Comprehensive Psychiat 12:156–163, 1971.

Stevens, H.: Conversion hysteria: Neurologic emergency. Mayo Clin Proc 43:54–64, 1968.

Woodruff, R.A., Clayton, P.J., & S.B. Guze: Hysteria. JAMA 215:425–428, 1971.

PHOBIC NEUROSIS
(Phobic Reactions)

A phobia is an intense dread, fear, or panic fixated upon a specific idea or thing. Many specific phobias have been described. Some of the more common ones are fear of high places, enclosed places, open spaces, cancer; dirt, filth, or feces; cats, death and dead bodies, darkness, crowds, and sharp objects. The particular thing, circumstance, or abstraction which provokes the reaction is a symbol of the fear of something else in the patient's unconscious life. For example, the patient who becomes anxious in enclosed places may in this way be expressing his aversion to being "trapped" in an unsatisfactory life situation (job, marriage, etc) or his resentment of parental control in childhood. Fears of cancer, dirt, and death may represent unconscious hostile feelings toward specific persons or situations in his past or present life, or the patient's fear that he is indeed "dirty," "doomed," or "deserves to die."

Treatment

Any insight which the patient may acquire regarding the symbolic or unconscious meaning of his feared object can often be useful. Persuasive technics and building up the patient's self-confidence so that he can gradually desensitize himself to his phobia are useful in a few cases; hypnosis has also been reported as "curative." Most cases, however, require total character reorganization through prolonged psychotherapy. When the patient is not motivated for insight psychotherapy, little more can be offered than persuasion, reconditioning, and gradual desensitization.

Kahn, J.H.: School phobia. Acta paedopsychiat 35:4–10, 1968.
Levin, S.: Occurrence of phobias in states of depression. Bull Philadelphia A Psychoanal 19:65–75, 1969.
Watson, J.P., & R. Gaind: Prolonged exposure: A rapid treatment for phobias. Brit MJ 1:13–15, 1971.

OBSESSIVE-COMPULSIVE NEUROSIS

Essentials of Diagnosis

- Repetitive uncontrollable thoughts (obsessions) and acts (compulsions).
- The thoughts and acts are usually recognized as illogical, and may be repulsive to the patient.
- The patient is usually a meticulous, guilt-ridden, intelligent, insecure person.
- Tics are often a prominent manifestation of obsessive-compulsive reaction in children.

General Considerations

The obsessive-compulsive reaction is a disorder in which constantly recurring thoughts or acts intrude upon otherwise normal thinking or behavior. The intrusive thought or action is alien to the situation and the patient feels a compelling need to think about the specific thought or perform the specific act in order to relieve his anxiety. It is believed that this type of reaction is the result of rigid discipline in childhood with undue stress on neatness, cleanliness, punctuality, and memory (ie, attempts to make the child conform to adult standards of behavior). In its mildest form this type of repetitive action or thought is universal, eg, the persistent recurrence of a musical theme or a group of words, and is not considered pathologic. Only when these traits become exaggerated to the point of intruding upon the normal life of the individual and making him subservient to them are they considered abnormal.

Obsessive-compulsive reactions may occur in any age group—rarely, however, before the age of 6 years.

Clinical Findings

The obsessive-compulsive patient is usually highly intelligent, sociable, agreeable, pleasant, precise, oversensitive, shy, and self-conscious, and feels inadequate and insecure. His life is one of order and regularity. The obsessions and compulsions, however, are quite distressing. The patient realizes that they are illogical, but he feels anxious until he performs the compulsive act, and performing it relieves his tension. His obsessions may interrupt his thought so frequently that he is incapable of productive thinking. The obsessions may be thoroughly distasteful to the patient, eg, "indecent" thoughts, or thoughts about injuring another person. Repetitive handwashing, special rituals performed before sexual activity or sleep can be initiated, and various "magic" words or acts which must be routinely performed are a few examples of compulsive behavior.

The obsessive-compulsive state is frequently accompanied by restlessness, irritability, tension, weakness, and fatigue as a result of the struggle to resist awareness of obsessive thoughts or the impulse to compulsive behavior.

Differential Diagnosis

Compulsions and obsessions may also occur in paranoia, schizophrenia, and manic-depressive reactions, but in these conditions there is no recognition by the patient that his behavior or thoughts are absurd.

Treatment & Prognosis

Treatment is usually very difficult and must be undertaken by a psychiatrist. In adolescents and young adults some relief may be achieved by a psychoanalytic type of therapy. Often the patient will obtain some relief by discussing his symptoms with the physician.

One of the most important things the physician can do is to point out that the symptoms are not due to supernatural forces but follow the laws of cause and effect. Only by understanding the relationship between events in his past life and his present feelings and the compulsive acts or obsessive thoughts can the patient free himself from them.

Even with treatment there is a tendency toward exacerbations and remissions, which in itself makes evaluation of therapy difficult.

Goodwin, D.W., & others: Follow-up studies in obsessional neurosis. Arch Gen Psychiat 20:182–187, 1969.
Salzman, L.: The Obsessive Personality. Science House, 1968.
Salzman, L.: Therapy of obsessional states. Am J Psychiat 122:1139–1146, 1966.

DEPRESSION
(Depressive Reactions, Psychoneurotic Types)

Depression is a mood of sadness, dejection, or despair. The intensity and duration of this mood varies considerably depending upon the personality background, the precipitating factors, and the current life situation of the patient. In many cases a patient's presenting symptom may be a mask or substitute for depression, eg, some cases of menstrual difficulty, chronic tiredness, obesity, underweight problems, or prolonged and accentuated reaction to any mild illness. The alert physician will tend to evaluate the patient's mood and personal history in order to detect those persons whose underlying illness is actually a depression.

Depression may occur at any time from childhood to old age, but is most common during adolescence, during pregnancy and immediately following childbirth, following separation, divorce, or death of a close person, at the climacteric (in both men and women), and in old age. In many instances a feeling of "going it alone" is present.

Frequent findings are those of a general pessimistic attitude, feelings of hopelessness and failure, apathy, fatigue, loss of interest in the environment, sleep disturbances, loss of appetite and weight, diminution of sexual interest, and vague somatic complaints. Difficulties in concentration and reduced psychomotor activity are present, and the patient frequently "looks unhappy" although he may assume a feigned cheerfulness.

Classification

A. Primary Depression:

1. Psychoneurotic types—

a. Grief reactions or acute situational reactions— These are often self-limiting, and occur in response to recent loss or frustration.

b. Reactive or neurotic depressions—These may be precipitated by circumstances in the immediate environment, but the depressive response is often out of proportion to its cause and is augmented by earlier loss or feelings of self-deprecation.

2. Psychotic types—

a. Manic-depressive reactions—Many of these may not reach total psychotic proportions but are exaggerations of a basic cyclothymic personality with profound mood swings.

b. Involutional depressive states (involutional melancholia).

B. Secondary Depressions:

1. Psychoneurotic types—Associated with various physical illnesses or incapacity.

2. Psychotic types—

a. Associated with toxic states (eg, alcoholism).

b. Associated with organic brain disease.

c. Associated with schizophrenia—In some cases depression may be the outstanding symptom preceding or accompanying a schizophrenic reaction.

Diagnosis of Primary Depressions

A. Grief Reactions (Acute Situational Reactions): Loss is usually experienced through the death of, separation from, or rejection by a person with whose life the patient's own has been closely identified. Career

disappointments may also result in this type of depressive response. Denial of the emotional impact of the loss through expressions of hostility and general irritability may be present. Sleep, appetite, and sexual disturbances are common but generally mild, and suicide is not a prominent risk.

B. Reactive Depressions (Neurotic Depressive Reactions): Precipitating factors are not always readily discernible, or may seem to be too minor to account for the profound or prolonged reaction which results. There is usually a long history of neurotic symptoms in which anxiety has been the outstanding component. In many cases it appears that a disappointment or failure acts merely to open the door to existing unconscious feelings of rejection and failure. The symptoms and signs of acute situational depression are also present in the reactive depression. Sleep disturbances with troublesome dreams are common since these patients usually have had unconscious negative images of themselves for a long time. Many patients may be able to fall asleep readily but awaken during the night (sometimes in the early morning hours), with anxiety to the point of agitation. Diurnal variation in mood is also frequently found, some patients finding themselves depressed only later in the day. Crying spells, especially in women, and a deep sense of guilt and helplessness mark the course of many neurotic depressions.

Good contact with reality is maintained, and although work function is impaired these persons are generally able to continue their daily routine.

Treatment

The physician may empathize with but not sympathize with the patient. The difference lies in giving support and understanding without giving the patient further reason to feel sorry for himself. Psychotherapy is provided for the purpose of encouraging insight into early as well as present causes of the patient's negative self-image. Ventilation and abreaction of feelings should be encouraged. Creative and productive pursuits should be recommended to assist the patient to adopt a more positive attitude toward his personal value. The patient should be strongly supported and encouraged to handle current and future life situations with increasing self-sufficiency. Specific advice should be given on how to make creative readjustments at work and at home.

Primary depressions are usually self-limiting. Antidepressant drugs and other medications as indicated should be given to ensure sufficient sleep and to reduce anxiety during the day.

Psychotherapeutic referral is indicated if suitable readjustment seems to be impossible for those patients whose anxiety becomes overwhelming.

Treatment of secondary types of depression consists of general psychotherapeutic support and antidepressant medications along with specific attention to the primary illness.

Patients with prolonged and disabling depressions who do not respond to the kinds of treatment described above may be suitable candidates for ECT (see p 581).

The treatment of involutional depressive states and manic-depressive reactions is discussed on pp 583 and 584.

Blinder, M.G.: Differential diagnosis and treatment of depressive disorders. JAMA 195:8–12, 1966.

Lesse, S.: Masked depression: A diagnostic and therapeutic problem. Dis Nerv System 29:169–173, 1968.

Paykel, E.S.: Classification of depressed patients: A cluster analysis derived grouping. Brit J Psychiat 118:275–287, 1971.

Rickels, K., & others: Amitriptyline and trimipramine in neurotic depressed outpatients. Am J Psychiat 127:208–218, 1970.

POSTPARTUM DEPRESSION

The postpartum period is complicated for some women by feelings of depression and despair about the role of being a mother and by fears of inability to handle the increased responsibility for another person's welfare. Rumination and a feeling of being trapped, with resentment toward the baby and the husband, can make this a difficult time—especially for a woman with a passive-dependent personality structure or one who feels that marriage and motherhood have frustrated her desires for other types of fulfillment in life.

The course of the prenatal period is no direct indication of the degree of depression and anxiety which may occur after delivery since much depends on what "being a mother" may mean to some women. For example, if it implies, "Now I am tied down, prevented from the satisfaction of other desires and the pursuit of other goals"; if it evokes unpleasant memories of personal relationships with her own mother; or if the patient feels she should have presented her husband with a son instead of a daughter, she is apt to respond with a varied emotional picture in which depression is the outstanding feature. The woman who is dependent or emotionally immature is especially prone to be overwhelmed with anxiety about becoming a mother if she still feels like a child herself.

Strangely enough, psychotic reactions are more common among multiparas. Because motherhood often represents the necessity for making decisions for another human being, the incidence of postpartum depression is greater among passive-dependent women, who feel unconsciously inadequate about themselves and lack strong key persons to whom they can turn for emotional support.

The treatment of postpartum depression may require considerable attention by the physician as well as his support as a substitute parental figure. Profound or prolonged postpartum depression is an urgent indication for psychiatric consultation, especially when anxiety is acute or psychotic elements are present. In occasional cases postpartum depression may assume the proportions of a full-blown manic-depressive or schizophrenic reaction, in which case ECT is generally effective.

Patt, S.L., Rappaport, R.G., & P. Barglow: Follow-up of therapeutic abortion. Arch Gen Psychiat 20:408–414, 1969.

Yalom, I.D.: "Postpartum blues" syndrome. Arch Gen Psychiat 18:16–27, 1968.

SUICIDE

Suicide is a major public health problem throughout the world and is one of the 10 leading causes of death in the USA. Early recognition of suicidal tendencies, careful evaluation of depressive tendencies, and prompt preventive measures are necessary if the suicide rate is to be reduced.

Depressed patients must always be regarded as potentially suicidal, but certain attitudes and responses of the patient may assist the doctor in determining the relative probability of suicide.

Recognition of Suicidal Tendencies

(1) Elicit a history and search for physical evidence of previous attempts (eg, wrist or neck scars, mouth or esophageal scarring and strictures from ingestion of corrosive poisons). Distinguish serious attempts which have failed from superficial gestures (benign attempts). Both are important since a superficial gesture may end in suicide by "mistake." A history of suicide among family members, especially such key persons as a parent or older sibling, is often associated with suicidal tendencies.

(2) Expressions of Death Wishes or Suicidal Intentions: The discovery by the family of informal wills or bequests of property is a strong clue. One-third of suicides announce their intention. It is impossible to generalize that, "Those who talk about suicide never do so," or that, "Those who deny the intention of suicide are the ones to watch out for." A patient who feels that he "deserves to die" or that "life holds no hope" is more liable to commit suicide; these patients may think of suicide but carefully conceal their intentions.

(3) Evidences of mental depression of any type, unexplained fatigue and weakness, bizarre somatic delusions, apprehension, self-deprecation; self-accusation and a pathologic sense of guilt; lack of interest in family, sexual activity, work, and friends; anorexia, weight loss, and constipation; insomnia; recent personal failure, grief, or tragedy; disappointment, especially in love affairs; and loss of self-esteem during adolescence, following divorce, or discovery of a spouse's infidelity. In many cases a minor or casual incident seems to trigger the unconscious thought of suicide which has been building up for a prolonged period.

(4) If a patient remains depressed in spite of a physician's help, the chances of suicide are increased. Caution must be observed since at times a lessening of the depression may indicate that the patient has made the decision to commit suicide; he has a feeling of relief since he knows his "problems will soon be over."

(5) Be alert for the "cry for help" which is often a vague, disguised, or completely masked message to the physician, a friend, or family member that the patient wants his suicide prevented by outside intervention. The "final phone call" or a departing statement as the patient leaves hospital, home, or the physician's office may sometimes carry the message, "Stop me, now."

(6) A patient who has withdrawn from routine living is a poor suicidal risk. The patient who, even with effort, continues his normal daily contacts and work is generally not so liable to be suicidal.

(7) An increase in neurotic symptoms, which serve as defense mechanisms, usually indicates that the patient is less likely to commit suicide.

"Equivocal" Suicide

Many cases of "accidental death" appear to be disguised or unconscious types of suicide. Thus, reaching for the wrong bottle on the shelf, accidentally discharging a firearm while examining or playing with it, and some automobile accidents appear to be unconscious suicidal acts which could not be consciously performed.

Prevention of Suicide

Prompt psychiatric consultation is indicated for any seriously depressed patient in order to evaluate the risk of suicide. Hospitalization should be sought so that the patient may be protected from himself and appropriate treatment instituted: antidepressant medications, sedatives for sleep, psychotherapy (individual or group), activity therapy, and ECT if necessary. One must avoid premature discharge from the hospital of suicidal patients who seem to recover almost too rapidly or with a bland affect which may merely disguise their decision to attempt suicide again. Psychiatric observation and treatment should be continued following discharge until the physician is reasonably satisfied that the danger of suicide is past. Sedative or hypnotic drugs should be given with caution and in small amounts, since some medications may intensify depression and they may also be hoarded for suicidal purpose. If sedatives are requested for sleep they may often be placed in the custody of another member of the family. One must keep in mind also that for the depressed person who tends to use alcohol injudiciously the additive depressant effects of many medications (especially the barbiturates) and alcohol may be lethal.

Birtchnell, J., & J. Alarcon: The motivation and emotional state of 91 cases of attempted suicide. Brit J M Psychol 44:45–52, 1971.

Noyes, R., Jr.: Shall we prevent suicide? Comprehensive Psychiat 11:361–370, 1970.

Philip, A.D.: Traits, attitudes and symptoms in group of attempted suicides. Brit J Psychiat 116:475–482, 1970.

Pokorny, A.D.: A follow-up study of 618 suicidal patients. Am J Psychiat 122:1109–1116, 1966.

Ross, M.: Suicide among college students. Am J Psychiat 126:220–225, 1969.

Schrut, A., & T. Michels: Adolescent girls who attempt suicide: Comments on treatment. Am J Psychother 23:243–251, 1969.

PERSONALITY & PERSONALITY TRAIT DISORDERS (CHARACTER DISORDERS)

Persons with character disorders have a life-long history of behavioral difficulties which generally consist of poor judgment, impulsive or irrational behavior, and poor social compatibility. They usually have little anxiety about their actions. The principal types of character disorders are the inadequate personality, schizoid personality, cyclothymic personality, emotionally unstable personality, passive-aggressive personality, paranoid personality, and compulsive personality.

The conflict for these persons is not felt as anxiety within themselves, as is true with most other psychiatric disorders, but is experienced rather as a conflict between the individual and his environment. These persons do not generally consider themselves sick, and they usually seek help only when their personal inadequacies have brought them into difficulties with others, eg, their families, co-workers, or neighbors; their usual reason for coming to a physician is to be extricated from their difficulties. They are frequently brought to the physician by the marital partner or a parent to be "changed."

In most personality trait disorders, supportive counseling and advice regarding specific difficulties are all that can be offered by the physician. Medications are of little or no value. Persuasion, guidance, and insight therapy are generally ineffective; but in selected cases, where sufficient anxiety about behavior is present, some benefits may be derived from prolonged psychotherapy.

Chamberlin, C.R., Jr.: The psychiatrist in the juvenile court. Bull Menninger Clin 29:37–44, 1965.

Miller, M.H.: Time and the character disorder. J Nerv Ment Dis 138:535–540, 1964.

PASSIVE & AGGRESSIVE PERSONALITIES

The passive personality, the aggressive personality, and the passive-aggressive personality are among the more commonly encountered types of character disorder.

(1) **The passive personality:** During infancy and childhood considerable emotional and physical depen-

dency upon parental figures may be expected. There are norms, however, even during this period of expected dependency; and the child who is over-clinging or is so passive that he must obtain tacit permission or approval for every minor decision may be considered to have emotional problems. In some children it appears that overprotection or rejection (or alternations of both attitudes) conditions them to a lifelong expectation of being helped or cared for. Covertly, however, they may resent or reject the protecting person. Passive-dependent persons often attach themselves to stronger persons (in marriage, at work, in social contacts) but continue to react with unconscious anger toward the substitute parental figure and develop increased feelings of inadequacy about themselves. Depression is a frequent symptom when they eventually discover that they have failed to fulfill themselves as mature persons.

(2) **The aggressive personality:** During early adolescence one may normally expect to find occasional aggressive and hostile behavior aimed toward specific authority figures (parents, school, or police) or toward the existing social order. To some degree, such behavior represents normal development as the adolescent attempts to break away from dependency and controls in order to develop self-sufficiency. To the extent, however, that resentment and aggression toward authority figures and necessary social control are out of proportion to normal accepted behavior or continues into adult life, it may be considered pathologic. In the pathologic type of aggressive personality, the individual is repetitively or consistently unable to make flexible adjustments to marriage, work, or society.

(3) **The passive-aggressive personality:** This type shows alternations or combinations of the 2 patterns of behavior.

Guidance and maintenance of firm boundaries to control acting-out tendencies are necessary for all of the character disorders, especially the passive and aggressive types. As in the case of the other character disorders, psychotherapy (especially psychoanalysis) is of some value when anxiety is present.

Small, I.F., & others: Passive aggressive personality disorder: A search for a syndrome. Am J Psychiat 126:973–983, 1970.

THE COMPULSIVE PERSONALITY

The obsessive-compulsive reactions as a specific psychiatric diagnosis (see p 560) should be distinguished from other types of compulsive behavior such as a compulsive need for neatness and order or compulsive eating, smoking, talking, drinking, or masturbation. Such individuals are more properly designated as compulsive personalities with anxiety. Anxiety is relieved by performing the compulsive act, but the anxi-

ety is usually related to a specific situation about which the patient is aware. These acts are also more suitably related to the general situation in which they are performed and hence do not seem illogical to the patient, whereas in the obsessive-compulsive reaction the thought or act is completely alien to whatever the patient is doing, thinking, or feeling at the time.

The compulsive personality may be subject to a wide variety of functional disorders. Certain diseases (eg, migraine, idiopathic ulcerative colitis) occur with increased frequency in patients with compulsive personalities.

Treatment consists of simple psychotherapy designed to relieve anxiety. Tranquilizing medication and environmental changes are of value only in relieving the accompanying anxiety.

NONPSYCHOTIC PARANOID PERSONALITIES

Paranoid disorders range from simple paranoid personalities ("cranks," habitual litigants, espousers of various odd causes) to the truly psychotic paranoid (one of the subtypes of schizophrenia). It is important to ascertain the degree of affect in the paranoid person and to assess the possibility of his acting out his paranoid ideas. This is not always easy to do, but, in general, persons with more fragmented personality (those who are more truly psychotic) or have developed fixed or closed delusional systems should be considered potentially dangerous to others.

Nonpsychotic paranoid personalities frequently give a lifelong history of sensitivity, rigid ideas, and dedication to unpopular causes. Strong suspicions of others may also occur as a temporary response out of proportion to the extent of personal insult or rejection which the individual has actually endured. One may also observe many individuals from deprived backgrounds who, because of physical differences or economic, social, or cultural reasons, feel discriminated against and develop paranoid responses.

In both the psychotic and nonpsychotic types, intelligence is preserved but logical thinking is based on illogical premises. The patient is oversensitive to the attitudes of others, and reacts with wounded pride, withdrawal, or sometimes with verbal assault to attempts to convince him that he has misinterpreted the facts.

The simple paranoid personality may, with some tolerance on the part of his associates, function quite harmlessly in society. Psychotic paranoid individuals should be evaluated by a psychiatrist. Hospitalization and treatment with psychotherapy, tranquilizing drugs, and ECT are effective in some cases.

Schwartz, D.A.: A re-view of the "paranoid" concept. Arch Gen Psychiat 8:349–361, 1963.

Swanson, D.W., & others: *The Paranoid.* Little, Brown, 1970.

ANTISOCIAL PERSONALITY (SOCIOPATHIC PERSONALITY DISTURBANCES, PSYCHOPATHIC DISORDERS)

In general, patients with these disorders have basic feelings of insecurity and inadequacy and act out their feelings in asocial or antisocial patterns. Behavior is impulsive, without regard for the feelings or welfare of others; and the pattern usually begins in childhood and lasts throughout life, with disastrous consequences in marriage and interpersonal relationships and frequent encounters with law-enforcement agencies. Feelings of guilt are usually not present, and the patient often presents a surface glibness and deceptive facade which conceal his egocentric and narcissistic personality.

The potential antisocial personality is often an egocentric child who has frequent temper tantrums, lies with considerable facility, and seems unable to relate closely with anyone. Overt cruelty to animals or small children is occasionally seen but is not necessarily present. During adolescence he may show an inordinate interest in sexual matters, may be shy, is often in conflict with parental and community authority, and may exhibit a variety of impulsive emotional reactions which are out of proportion to precipitating factors. Failure to identify with mature persons during early life (sometimes because of separation from or rejection by a parent) is thought to be an important etiologic factor. During adolescence there is a tendency to seek out similarly lost or uncertain personalities and to establish ties and identifications with them which are frequently loose or superficial but serve to promote the individual's physical or emotional comfort. By adulthood, especially in a free society which offers a wide range of possible behavior, his narcissistic acting out becomes more damaging to others, with unhappy marriages, wild business schemes, sexual perversions, gambling, and attempts to anesthetize hurts, resentments, and loneliness with alcohol and addictive drugs.

It is well to remember that in some cases antisocial behavior overlies a more basic psychosis or occurs as the result of brain damage. Psychometric and neurologic investigations, including EEG studies, are frequently of value.

Most antisocial personalities respond poorly to formal psychotherapy. As a rule they seek help only when they are in difficulties with the law or when their egocentric needs are threatened. They then seek only extrication from their distress and tend to project their difficulties onto the outside world. Insight with feeling is difficult for them to attain.

In many circumstances the best that can be offered the antisocial personality is to provide structured situations with adequate disciplinary control in an attempt to limit the damage which he can do to himself or others: summer camps and special schools for young people; vocational training, prescribed work, probation and legal restraints for the adult.

Donnelly, J.: Aspects of the psychodynamics of the psychopath. Am J Psychiat 120:1149–1154, 1964.

MacDonald, J.M.: The prompt diagnosis of psychopathic personality. Am J Psychiat 122:45–50, 1966.

Mathis, J.L., & M. Collins: Mandatory group therapy for exhibitionists. Am J Psychiat 126:1162–1167, 1970.

McGarry, A.L.: Psychiatry and the dangerous offender. New England J Med 272:684–685, 1965.

SEXUAL DEVIATIONS

In the broadest sense, the terms "sexual deviation" and "perversion" refer to those types of sexual behavior which provide an individual with his major sexual gratification outside the normal act of coitus. Almost any kind of sexual behavior, however, may accompany normal coitus, in which case such behavior may be considered nonpathologic. Covert interest in the unusual aspects of sexuality is present to some degree in most persons.

Sexual deviations and perversions are found in both sexes, but are more common among men. Common types include overt homosexuality, pedophilia (sexual assault upon or activity with children), fetishism (sexual fixation on parts of the body, eg, hair, or on an article of clothing, eg, a shoe or corset), transvestism (gratification gained through wearing the clothing of the opposite sex), exhibitionism, voyeurism (peeping Toms), and sadomasochism (gratification obtained through inflicting or experiencing pain).

Many degrees of deviation and perversion exist. For example, it is possible for an individual to marry and beget and rear children and also to carry on an active homosexual relationship outside of marriage. Other persons who would not ordinarily engage in homosexual activities may actively do so during periods of prolonged isolation from the opposite sex while in prison, remote military camps, or boarding schools. The extent to which such behavior may be considered pathologic depends greatly on the persistence, repetition, and nature of the physical contact beyond the puberal years. Casual "crushes" on persons of the same sex are considered more or less normal during puberty or early adolescence. Considerable difference in point of view exists today about whether the homosexual is indeed "sick" in any useful sense of the word. What may be called The Establishment as represented by social mores, most existing laws, and psychiatric theory is most apt to take the view that homosexuality is a complex pathologic entity no matter whether the homosexual is "born that way, acquires it, or has it thrust upon him." Increasingly vocal arguments often presented by homosexuals as well as by some social, religious, and medical groups deny that any psychopathology exists in homosexuality and point out that the only difficulty is in the inability of organized society to accept the idea of anything other than heterosexuality as "normal." The difference in point of view may be largely semantic. The fact remains that most homosexual persons have considerable emotional and adjustment problems in society as it currently exists.

For practical reasons all cases of chronic or repetitive sexual deviation and perversion present a severe underlying psychic disturbance. The origin appears to be in childhood. Few cases, if any, are due to hormonal imbalance.

Sexual Perversion & the Law

For legal reasons the physician must often distinguish 2 different categories of these disorders: those which represent actual threats to other persons or to public welfare, and those which are merely distasteful or annoying or which arouse public anxiety. In the first group are those acts which are carried out in public places, are performed with or upon a minor, or which involve coercion or violence. In the latter group are included many acts of voyeurism or exhibitionism, which are usually considered to have little more than annoyance value. The distinction is not always easy to make, however, since a child or impressionable person may be psychologically damaged by the act of an exhibitionist.

The physician called upon to evaluate problems involving sexual deviations must be aware that some minors may actually indicate readiness for or overtly invite sexual acts from an adult. Under the law, however, the responsibility rests upon the adult.

In many cases which involve two or more adults there is no clear evidence about which is the offender and which the victim, and some degree of willing participation on the part of both is the rule.

Acts of perversion are sometimes carried out while under the influence of alcohol or other drugs by individuals who would not otherwise act upon such impulses. In some cases the sexual problem may be complicated by the problem of drug addiction.

In recent years, both in England and in many states in the USA, the laws have changed considerably, so that unharmful sexual acts of any kind between mutually consenting adults in private are regarded as purely personal and nonlegal matters. The establishment of psychiatric rehabilitation programs in state prisons and special treatment centers for sexual offenders represents efforts by society to help as well as isolate those whose sexual aberrations constitute a threat to the community.

Treatment

All perversions are most difficult to modify with any known form of treatment; the restraining actions of the law and community sanction remain the most effective deterrents. A few reports have recently appeared in the medical literature of homosexuals who have successfully become heterosexual through group therapy. Treatment with hormones is generally futile.

Sexual deviates rarely seek help for their sexual problems since they do not wish to be deprived of opportunities for gratification. They may be brought to the physician through external pressures (family or the courts), or they may seek psychiatric help for emotional problems which are peripheral to their sexual difficulty, eg, jealousy, hostility, or depression when jilted by a partner. Some help for these secondary emotional problems can and should be given, but basic change rarely is possible through psychotherapy.

With some adolescents who have only recently been introduced to perverse behavior or who fear that they may develop homosexual patterns, the prognosis is not entirely unfavorable. Prolonged psychotherapy and counseling may be effective.

Auerback, A.: Understanding sexual deviations. Postgrad Med 43:125–133, 169–178, 1968.
Kaplan, E.A.: Homosexuality: A search for the ego-ideal. Arch Gen Psychiat 15:355–358, 1967.
Kremer, M.W., & A.H. Rifkin: The early development of homosexuality: A study of adolescent lesbians. Am J Psychiat 126:91–96, 1969.
Stoller, R.J.: It's only a phase: Femininity in boys. JAMA 201:314–315, 1967.

CONFLICT, AGGRESSION, & VIOLENCE

The frequency and extent of violence on the world scene today and the various ways it is manifested—on the street as individual crime, between groups, against the "Establishment," in war, and in reporting the presentation of these conflicts through mass media, art, and the theater—leads to the question whether such violence represents merely the symptoms of sick individuals or of a "sick society." It is probably evidence of both. Value systems and behavior are undoubtedly in great flux, and vast social changes are rapidly taking place.

Conflict, aggression, and violence must be viewed from the vantage points of individual psychology, group psychology, and social psychology. It is often difficult to ascertain to what extent individual aggression expressed against a group or social level represents conflicts within the individual himself. Most persons seek identifications through group affiliation. Traditionally, these affiliations are along the lines of economic, social, cultural, religious, and family identifications.

The proliferation of new social, cultural, religious, and other groups on the social scene today, with the intense polarization and conflict which are current, suggest many interpretations, especially when aggression and violence become manifest.

In many instances an individual aligned with a group participates in violence because of personal psychopathology. Many acts of aggression and violence are performed by individuals suffering from psychoses, persons with manic personalities or paranoid traits, those under the influence of mind-altering drugs, or those with organic brain damage. These represent clearcut cases in which intrapsychic pathology may be discerned.

Many other persons who become involved in acts of physical aggression have more subtle types of psychologic problems which find expression in group action: those with severe oedipal problems and immature responses to authority, those with unresolved sibling rivalries, those seeking identification out of desperation because of deep feelings of inadequacy, and those with an unconscious drive toward self-destruction or a need to prove themselves acceptable to a peer group. Any of these psychiatric difficulties readily enable one to act out in group aggression. Strong early conditioning toward prejudices, as well as economic and cultural deprivation, are potent forces toward building a reservoir of anger, resentment, and overt hate.

Acts of violence—as well as acts of love, compassion, jealousy, fear, etc—have some basis in the psychologic makeup of every individual. Questions about whether group action was aimed toward an ultimate social good and "what group did what to whom" are of another order and are often answered in a judgmental manner.

Studies in the field of group psychology and social psychology have been useful in describing how physical proximity to violence can involve a nonparticipant in group participation, what personality types are more prone to translate feelings of resentment and deprivation into aggressive action, and what are the various phases a group moves through when conflict grows into violent action.

Feshbach, S.: Dynamics and morality of violence and aggression: Some psychological considerations. Am Psychol 26:281–290, 1971.

Heller, M.S., & S. Polsky: Television violence. Arch Gen Psychiat 24:279–285, 1971.

Martins, C.: Poverty and mental health. Canad Psychiat AJ 15:159–165, 1970.

Silver, L.B., & others: Does violence breed violence? Am J Psychiat 126:404–407, 1969.

Solomon, P., & S.T. Kleeman: Medical aspects of violence. California Med 114:19–24, May 1971.

Symonds, A.: The psychology of the female liberation movement. Med Aspects Human Sexuality 5:24–33, April 1971.

DRUG ABUSE & DRUG DEPENDENCE

Multiple factors are involved in the phenomenon of drug abuse, which has spread in recent years from small special cultural loci to what has been termed "endemic and epidemic proportion." Only the medical factors involved will be dealt with here, but the importance of the various social, legal, economic, cultural, ethical, and religious aspects of drug abuse should be evident.

The drugs under consideration here are those that alter mood, thinking, or behavior, induce sleep, act as stimulants or sedatives, or provide a psychotomimetic experience of delusions, hallucinations, depersonalization, and time and sensory distortions. Some of these drugs have value in medical treatment, but many have no accepted pharmacologic value. The medically accepted drugs may be said to be misused ("drug misuse") insofar as they are frequently overprescribed, too readily prescribed, or prescribed for the wrong reasons.

Any psychotropic drug is abused ("drug abuse") if it is obtained illegally (black market), is self-prescribed, or is used for other than valid medical reasons.

Drug dependence is a general term to indicate a state of psychologic or physical dependence on a drug. The development of drug dependence requires not only the drug itself but also an individual who is prone to develop dependent responses to the drug experience and the time, place, circumstances, and cultural milieu in which the drug is used.

Psychologic dependence indicates an emotional need, compulsion, or desire to continue taking a drug despite its effects or consequences. Withdrawal produces tension, anxiety, depression, restlessness, irritability, insomnia, and personality changes. The term **habituation** implies the occurrence of these psychologic symptoms on withdrawal but without physical withdrawal phenomena.

Physical dependence signifies that, in addition to some of the psychologic symptoms arising from withdrawal of a drug, physical disturbances also occur—muscle spasm and twitching, gastrointestinal disturbances, palpitations, sweats, hot and cold flashes, and convulsive seizures, sometimes accompanied by delirium or by manic or psychotic episodes. The term **addiction** implies the presence of these physical phenomena on withdrawal.

Tolerance signifies that a drug has a declining effect on the user, so that the dose must be increased to obtain the desired or necessary effect. **Cross-tolerance** occurs when the use of one drug creates tolerance to another drug in the same pharmacologic class.

The term **idiosyncratic response** implies that the effects of the drug differ in different people or at different times in the same person. It may depend on the setting and mood in which the drug is taken.

The practicing physician is apt to be involved in problems arising from drug dependence in several ways:

(1) Injudicious or overprescribing of any drug to any patient may contribute to a problem of drug dependence. "Open-end" prescription writing is a common error. It must also be kept in mind that patients may share their prescribed drugs with other persons who are not under medical supervision.

(2) Some patients obtain prescribed drugs from more than one physician. It thus becomes difficult for the physician to know how much of any given drug and what other drugs his patient is using. Mixtures of drugs and the total quantities used complicate the entire problem of drug dependence.

(3) The problems of acute drug toxicity as well as the psychologic and physical phenomena of withdrawal require a high level of suspicion and early diagnosis and treatment.

(4) The legal aspects of drug abuse are such that the physician must often deal with law officers, other officials, or family members who inquire about the drug abuse of patients under his care.

(5) Patients under a physician's care for many other types of medical problems (eg, accidents, hepatitis, malnutrition, pregnancy, psychiatric conditions) may unexpectedly prove to have an additional and potentially serious problem of drug dependence.

(6) The federal laws regarding the use of many abused drugs have been changed quite recently in the USA. Most of the sedative-hypnotics and the stimulants as well as a number of other drugs not in these categories require a specially issued BNDD (Bureau of Narcotics & Dangerous Drugs) number to accompany any legal prescription. Any physician now prescribing these drugs (eg, amphetamines used in weight reduction) must obtain his BNDD number from the Federal Bureau of Narcotics.

General Aspects of Treatment of Drug Dependence

A. Treatment of Acute Toxicity: Exact identification of the chemical agent taken is often difficult. The patient's confused or unreliable account is one factor, although a responsible companion may be of help. The wide differences in purity and strength and the existence of drug mixtures, which are common in black market drugs, present a further difficulty.

Laboratory tests may be of great value in determining barbiturate, alcohol, or narcotics levels, but no such tests are available for detecting exposure to the hallucinogens and marihuana.

The examiner should search for needle tracks along the veins in the arms and wrists and for evidence of diseases (principally hepatitis) which may result from the use of contaminated needles.

The objectives of treatment of acute drug toxicity are to preserve vital functions, restore and maintain body fluid balance, and eliminate or neutralize the effects of the drugs. Emesis and gastric lavage are important when a drug has been recently ingested, but care must be taken to prevent aspiration of regurgitated fluids. Anxiety and hyperactivity must be dealt with, especially in acute reactions to hallucinogens.

B. Treatment of Withdrawal: Both psychologic and physical symptoms may be present. In the case of narcotic, barbiturate, and alcohol addiction, physical distress during withdrawal may be great, including the likelihood of convulsive seizures and other physical complications. Substitute drugs are usually necessary in order to accomplish an uneventful withdrawal. Most drug abusers will try to continue their drug long past withdrawal need, even in small allotted doses. Drug abusers may readily become dependent upon any drug provided them.

A firm position taken by the physician and considerable psychologic support, including education of

and firm support by key family members, are important to accomplish safe and satisfactory withdrawal.

C. Long-Term Treatment: Almost all patients with drug dependence have personality or situational problems that should be reviewed by a psychiatrist or social worker. These patients have generally had many problems before they started using drugs, and their difficulties are further complicated by the results of drug use. In the long-term treatment of hallucinogen users, the "flashback" or recurrence of a trip long after the last dose may be a chronic recurring problem.

A few broad categories of drug users can be delineated: adolescents and young adults who experiment with marihuana, the hallucinogens, and amphetamines; special cultural and minority groups, including a large segment of "white middle class" adolescents and young adults who have become addicted to narcotics; certain professional groups for whom barbiturates, narcotics, and amphetamines are more readily obtainable; and lonely, depressed, and isolated persons.

Psychiatric evaluation for possible long-term treatment is indicated for all individuals who abuse any drug. Cultural, social, economic, and situational factors must all be considered. Total and permanent abstinence from the specific drug used, as well as from any substitute drug, is the ideal goal, but in many cases this cannot be attained without major reconstitution of the patient's life.

Blaine, G.B., Jr.: Why intelligent young people take drugs. J Iowa Med Soc 59:37–42, 1969.

Cohen, M., & D.F. Klein: Drug abuse in a young psychiatric population. Am J Orthopsychiat 40:448–455, 1970.

Diagnosis and management of reactions to drug abuse. Med Lett Drugs Ther 12:65–68, 1970.

Edwards, G.: Place of treatment professions in society's response to chemical abuse. Brit MJ 2:195–199, 1970.

Louria, D.B.: Medical complications of pleasure-giving drugs. Arch Int Med 123:82–87, 1969.

Mizner, G.L., Barter, J.T., & P.H. Werme: Patterns of drug use among college students: A preliminary report. Am J Psychiat 127:15–24, 1970.

Ungerleider, J.T., & H.L. Bowen: Drug abuse and the schools. Am J Psychiat 125:1691–1697, 1969.

Wikler, A.: Some implications of conditioning theory for problems of drug abuse. Behav Sc 16:92–96, 1971.

DEPENDENCE ON BARBITURATES & OTHER SEDATIVE-HYPNOTICS

Both psychologic and physical dependence occur with these drugs. The short-acting barbiturates (eg, secobarbital, amobarbital, pentobarbital) are the most commonly used drugs that result in physical dependence (addiction). Since tolerance readily occurs, they may be taken in total daily doses of 2 gm/day or more. This is the most commonly used group of drugs taken with suicidal intent.

Other commonly encountered addictive sedative-hypnotics are glutethimide (Doriden®), meprobamate

(Equanil®, Miltown®), chlordiazepoxide (Librium®), diazepam (Valium®), and chloral hydrate.

Acute Toxicity

Symptoms include confusion, slurred speech, yawning, somnolence, amnesia, ataxia, coma, and shock. The pupils are normal. Blood pressure, respiration, and tendon reflexes are all depressed.

Treatment is discussed in Chapter 28.

Withdrawal

Symptoms include restlessness, insomnia, tremors, convulsions (at times fatal), and acute brain syndrome with disorientation and delirium.

Depending upon the total daily dose prior to withdrawal, cautious daily reduction of dosage should be accomplished over a period of 1–3 weeks. Give pentobarbital, 200 mg orally (or, if necessary, parenterally), and evaluate the sensorium in 1 hour. The nontolerant patient will be somnolent but arousable. At the other extreme, patients tolerant to 900 mg/day or more will show no signs of intoxication with a test dose of 200 mg.

Diphenylhydantoin (Dilantin®) does not prevent the convulsions of barbiturate withdrawal unless the patient is also an epileptic, in which case it may be necessary to use diphenylhydantoin in addition to the barbiturates.

Long-Term Management

All patients should receive psychiatric review. Many of these people have severe problems of emotional dependency. Many have family or marital problems which are "sedated" by the use of drugs; others have become dependent on sedative-hypnotics as a substitute for (or in combination with) dependence on alcohol. Almost any kind of situational or personality problem may underlie dependence on the sedative-hypnotic group, and each case must be individually evaluated. Careful attention should be given to those persons who have used these drugs with either conscious or unconscious suicidal intent.

Smith, D.E.: Phenobarbital technique for the treatment of barbiturate dependence. Arch Gen Psychiat 24:56–60, 1971.

DEPENDENCE ON STIMULANT DRUGS

This group of drugs includes the amphetamines (Benzedrine®, Dexedrine®, Methedrine®), phenmetrazine (Preludin®), and cocaine, frequently augmented by or adulterated with anticholinergic drugs (atropine, scopolamine, belladonna) and antihistamines. The stimulants are capable of increasing the availability of norepinephrine at nerve cell connections and hence act to increase alertness, speed cardiac action, and elevate mood. Their use is now in greater vogue in the USA than the use of LSD, which seems to be losing its popularity among drug-using cultures. It should be kept in mind, however, that not all persons dependent on this (or any other) group of drugs necessarily belong to or identify with a "drug culture" group. Addiction to stimulants is known among solitary users, some of them persons whose occupations make the drugs easily available (eg, physicians, nurses).

The stimulants provide a transient sense of well-being, alertness, and relief from fatigue. In larger doses (since tolerance readily occurs)—and especially when taken by the parenteral route—the results include tremor, tension, shakes, muscle pains, and sometimes collapse and death. Liver and brain damage are known to occur following large doses.

The amphetamine group of drugs is physically addicting since physical symptoms occur in withdrawal in chronic high-dose users. Psychologic effects include irritability and paranoid reactions, volubility, hyperactive behavior, and general deterioration in personal relationships and adjustment to society.

Tolerance to the amphetamines develops rapidly, and consistent users increase the dose so that 50–100 mg/day is not an uncommon dose.

In order to experience the "rush" that some users desire, enormous intravenous doses may be injected.

Prolonged heavy use of amphetamines can serve to prevent orgasm in the male, with impaired ability to attain an erection. Complete impotence is apt to occur later. Both failure of orgasm and failure of erection are reversible after a period of abstinence from amphetamines if serious depression is not present.

Acute Toxicity

Symptoms include excitement, exhilaration, confusion, insomnia, anorexia, improved psychomotor performance, clouded sensorium, disorientation, amnesia, and visual hallucinations. Signs include dilated pupils, tachycardia, hypertension, muscle tremors, and dry mouth, skin, and mucosa. Fever and respiratory collapse may occur.

Treatment of acute toxicity consists of support of vital functions (cardiovascular and respiratory). Anxiety, restlessness, or panic can be controlled with chlorpromazine (Thorazine®), 50 mg orally or IM, or other antipsychotic agents. The presence of a calm, accepting person to help "talk the patient down" in a quiet setting is often most useful.

Withdrawal

Withdrawal problems are usually minimal except in chronic high-dose users. Sedatives and anti-anxiety (or antipsychotic) agents may be used for restlessness and tension.

Long-Term Management

All patients should have psychiatric evaluation and follow-up.

Since many of the young persons who become dependent on this group of drugs belong to special cultures and groups, it is important that the patient not return to that way of life in the same role as a user. Some of these individuals are able to sustain abstinence by becoming instructors, proselytizers, and indigenous workers in helping other victims overcome their addictions.

Ellinwood, E.H., Jr.: Assault and homicide with amphetamine abuse. Am J Psychiat 127:1170–1175, 1971.
Watkins, C.: Use of amphetamines by medical students. South MJ 63:923–928, 1970.

DEPENDENCE ON NARCOTICS
(Opium Derivatives & Synthetic Analgesics)

This group includes opium and its derivatives (morphine, codeine, heroin), synthetic drugs with morphine-like action, and such commonly used preparations as antidiarrheal drugs (paregoric) and cough syrups which contain narcotics. All of them are addictive, and tolerance develops rapidly, so that enormous doses may be taken.

Heroin is the most widely abused narcotic and accounts for 90% of the narcotic addiction problem in the USA. It is one example of a drug habit previously confined to special cultural and social groups which has spread to endemic proportions in the past several years.

The heroin addict, more so than any other addict, centers his life around his addiction. His constant preoccupation is how to obtain his next "fix." All other desires, including sexual desires, are subordinated to his need for heroin. Without ample funds and a secure "connection," the addict is driven to theft, peddling and pushing drugs, prostitution, and pandering to meet his financial need.

The signs and symptoms of recent heroin use are contracted pupils, flushing, drowsiness, and sniffling. Chronic users often present with poor nutrition, hepatitis, skin abscesses and infections, needle marks (arms and thighs), and a general state of personal neglect. Venereal disease, tuberculosis, bacterial endocarditis, and pneumonia should not be overlooked. Evidence of recent use may be established by detection of heroin in the urine.

Overdosages by the user inadvertently occur and may result in pulmonary edema, collapse, and rapid death.

Acute Toxicity

Manifestations include fixed pinpoint pupils, evidence of needle marks, depressed blood pressure and respiration, coma, and shock (see Chapter 28).

The patient must be treated in a hospital. Maintain respiratory and renal function and treat shock with plasma expanders and pressor drugs (see Chapter 2). Depressed respiration may be treated by administration of nalorphine (Nalline®), 5–10 mg IV as necessary.

Withdrawal

Because of the physical phenomena that attend withdrawal from narcotics, the narcotic addict presents special problems. Hospitalization is almost always necessary in order to obtain a structured life environment and protection from availability of drugs. Withdrawal symptoms appear within 4–16 hours after the last dose and include yawning, tremors, sweats, lacrimation, vomiting, muscle spasms, abdominal pain, diarrhea, and convulsions. Delusions, hallucinations, and panic are fairly frequent.

The synthetic analgesic methadone (Dolophine®) is most frequently used to alleviate the symptoms of withdrawal from morphine, heroin, and related narcotics. The usual dose is 2.5 mg orally (also IM or subcutaneously) every 4 hours as needed. Doses of 40–60 mg for the first day are usual. When given orally, the dosage may be as high as 20 mg at one time if necessary, but parenteral doses should not exceed 10 mg. The dosage is rapidly reduced by 5–10 mg/day— enough to keep the patient comfortable. In most cases, withdrawal may be accomplished within 1 week.

"Cold turkey" (ie, withdrawal without substitute medication) is generally not possible for long-time addicts who have built up considerable tolerance to their drug. However, this method of withdrawal has many proponents among former addicts who maintain that it is the only way a permanent cure of narcotic addiction is possible.

Long-Term Management

The recurrence of craving or psychologic need for the narcotic group of drugs and the persistence of physical symptoms from withdrawal are especially intense. Prolonged hospitalization or supervised environmental care with total rehabilitation efforts is necessary in many cases.

Many other cases, especially those whose addiction is of short duration or those who have not developed an excessive degree of tolerance, may be treated on an outpatient basis by the daily administration of methadone in an officially designated Methadone Maintenance Clinic. Such clinics have been established in a number of urban centers in the USA, and there are usually waiting lists of addicts who desire this kind of help. Some differences exist in their methods of operation. Some programs provide daily methadone only in amounts sufficient to keep the addict comfortable and relieve him of his craving for narcotics; others provide larger doses to block the addict's capacity to achieve a "glow" from heroin. Most programs require daily attendance at the clinic to receive an allotted dose of methadone and to have a urine sample tested to make sure that other narcotics are not being used. After a 3-month "clean" period, the patient is given a supply of methadone for weekends. Eventually, he is required to come to the clinic only twice a week.

Many patients so treated are enabled after several months of methadone maintenance to give up their need for methadone itself; many others, it appears, continue to be dependent on their substitute drug, methadone.

Opponents of methadone treatment question whether substitution of one addictive agent for another is a valid therapeutic result. Its proponents point out that some patients are relieved of their necessity to support an illegal narcotic addiction through crime; that the cost of methadone is but a few cents a day; and that many addicts are thus enabled to reconstitute their lives and live without either illegal narcotic substances or methadone.

The adherents of the abrupt withdrawal and total abstinence ("cold turkey") method feel that no substitute drug is useful in the long run. The Synanon group urges a prolonged relearning approach in which the addict is allowed to work his way up from a demeaned status to one of privilege through accepted group membership and by proving himself worthy through his freedom from drug use. Many variations on the Synanon theme exist, most of them supported and supervised by abstinent former addicts.

Bates, R.C.: Thumbs down on the methadone thing. Med Economics, 138–151, June 1971.

Kramer, J.C.: Methadone maintenance for opiate dependence. California Med 113:6–11, Dec 1970.

Ramer, B.S., & J. Langan: Is methadone enough? The use of ancillary treatment during methadone maintenance. Am J Psychiat 127:1040–1044, 1971.

DEPENDENCE ON HALLUCINOGENS

None of the drugs in this group have accepted value in medical treatment and thus are always obtained through illegal sources. They have been variously known as hallucinogens, psychotomimetics, psychedelics, and "mind expanders," since they have the effect of producing distortion of senses: hallucinations, delusions, dream-like states, distortions in time, and feelings of depersonalization. Emotional reactions vary from euphoria, ecstasy, or fantasy to depression, and from minor anxiety to acute panic and manic psychotic behavior. The experience is commonly known as the "trip," and, depending upon the net effect on the user, is often termed a "good trip" or a "bad trip."

The principal drugs in this group are lysergic acid diethylamide (LSD), obtained from ergot or synthetically produced; mescaline, obtained from mushrooms but also synthetically produced; and bufotenine, obtained from various seeds. A number of other potent but less commonly used hallucinogens exist.

Marihuana (see below) is also capable of producing hallucinogenic effects but is probably the least potent of this group and the most commonly used.

LSD and mescaline have been used experimentally for a number of disorders: chronic neuroses, alcoholism, psychoses, and the intractable pain of terminal malignancy. At present there is no evidence that these drugs have any value in medical practice.

The kind and extent of the reaction vary with the amount taken, the strength and purity of the drug, the personality of the individual, and the conditions ("setting") under which the drug is taken. As in the case of most black market drugs, mixtures with other drugs often occur. Furthermore, the strength or potency of different batches of drugs is so variable that the experience of one trip is apt to be vastly different from another.

Self-injury, suicide, and murder have all been known to occur under the influence of the hallucinogens. Their chronic use may cause major permanent personality changes which suggest organic brain damage. Decrease in memory and attention span, difficulty in abstract thinking, and mental confusion are not unusual. Not all of these changes are always reversible after discontinuance of the drug. There are also reported changes in the chromosomes of chronic users, and the question whether congenital malformations may occur in the offspring of LSD users is not resolved at this date.

Acute Toxicity

Physical effects include slight dilatation of the pupils, mild increase in heartbeat, and rise in systolic and diastolic blood pressures. The deep tendon reflexes are hyperactive. There may be an increase in the blood glucose level. Both the central and autonomic nervous systems are affected, so that increased stimulation of voluntary and involuntary organs may occur. Sensory distortions, hallucinations, and delusions are common, sometimes with fervid religious or paranoid features. Acute anxiety increasing to panic and delirium are not unusual in severe toxic states.

In the management of "bad trips," acute anxiety, apprehension, panic, and delusionary ideas are generally the most frequent therapeutic problems. The patient must be protected from behavior dangerous to himself or others. An attempt should be made to establish contact by verbal reassurance and a calm attitude in a neutral setting. This may be all that is necessary to allay apprehension and panic, but the "talking down" period may take several hours.

The use of medications (phenothiazines or sedatives) will help allay panic and provide better opportunity for reassurance and verbal contact. The usual procedure is to give chlorpromazine (Thorazine®), 25–50 mg orally or IM, or chlordiazepoxide (Librium®), 100 mg IM, every 4 hours as necessary. Paraldehyde, diazepam (Valium®), or short-acting barbiturates are also useful.

If the patient has taken anticholinergic agents, his symptoms may be exacerbated by the phenothiazines. Watch for hypotension when giving intramuscular phenothiazines.

If panic and delusions have not subsided and if contact with reality has not been made within 24 hours, suspect an underlying or resultant psychotic process. Psychiatric hospitalization and observation are then required.

Long-Term Management

As with all other kinds of drug dependency, each case requires overall evaluation of the psychiatric, socioeconomic, and situational factors which may be present. Except for those cases which result in persistent psychotic features, there is little evidence that long-term psychiatric treatment has much value.

General counseling, especially for younger persons, may be of considerable value. One large group of hallucinogen experimenters consists of young persons of high-school and college age who are seeking ways of feeling "turned on." Some use these drugs as a means of identifying with a group, seeking controls, expressing resentments or desire for intimacy with parents and authority, or merely "testing limits." For all of these patients, counseling and education about drugs can be most useful. Some of the young hallucinogen users, if not counseled, educated, or interrupted in their use of hallucinogens, are apt to continue a pattern of experimenting with drugs and proceed to the use of amphetamines, barbiturates, or narcotics.

Phenothiazines or sedatives discussed above in the sections on acute toxicity will help to alleviate "flashback" symptoms.

Barter, J.T., & M. Reite: Crime and LSD: The insanity plea. Am J Psychiat 126:531–537, 1969.

McGlothlin, W.H., Sparkes, R.S., & D.O. Arnold: Effect of LSD on human pregnancy. JAMA 212:1483–1487, 1970.

Taylor, R.I., Maurer, J.I., & J.R. Tenklenberg: Management of "bad trips" in an evolving drug scene. JAMA 213:422–425, 1970.

DEPENDENCE ON MARIHUANA

Pharmacologically, marihuana may act as a sedative, stimulant, tranquilizer, or hallucinogen. It is the hallucinogenic symptoms that are most apt to bring the marihuana user to medical attention. The usual symptoms which require medical management are those of time and sensory distortions, delusions, confusion, and feelings of depersonalization.

Marihuana is obtained from the leaves and flowering tops of the hemp plant (*Cannabis sativa*), which grows wild in the USA and many parts of the world. Many other varieties, some of them with more potent effects, are found in the Middle East (hashish, bhang, etc) and elsewhere. The active ingredient is tetrahydrocannabinol (THC), and the drug is generally taken by smoking "joints" or rolled cigarettes.

Although marihuana is not physically addicting, it does cause a bona fide dependence with psychologic need in many cases. Marihuana smoking does not necessarily progress to the use of other drugs, although

there is evidence that "dependency breeds further dependency" and that a marihuana user with a dependent personality may develop other drug dependencies more easily than other people who experiment with the drug.

The symptoms and signs of marihuana toxicity are red conjunctivas, restless or lethargic behavior, and distortions of perceptions and body image. The pupils are not affected. Unfortunately, no laboratory tests are available to detect marihuana in body fluids.

The only treatment usually required for acute symptoms is abstinence from marihuana. If restlessness and delusional or other hallucinogenic symptoms are present, the administration of phenothiazines or sedatives in small to moderate doses is generally sufficient. There are no marked withdrawal symptoms.

Again, each case must be individually evaluated with special attention to possible underlying psychologic problems which may require psychiatric treatment or counseling. Abstinence is the best long-term treatment.

Bialos, D.S.: Adverse marijuana reactions. Am J Psychiat 127:819–823, 1970.

Kolensky, H., & W.T. Moore: Effects of marijuana on adolescents and young adults. JAMA 216:486–492, 1971.

Lieberman, C.M., & B.W. Lieberman: Marihuana: A medical review. New England J Med 284:88–91, 1971.

Marijuana and Health: A Report to the Congress. National Institute of Mental Health, 1971. [Summary published in Am J Psychiat 128:189–193, 1971.]

McGlothlin, W.H., & others: Marijuana use among adults. Psychiatry 33:433–443, 1970.

Waskow, I.E., & others: Psychological effects of tetrahydrocannabinol. Arch Gen Psychiat 22:97–107, 1970.

DRUG DEPENDENCE DUE TO IATROGENIC CAUSES

The frequency with which physicians may prescribe large amounts of medications of all types has led to a current situation which may well be termed an iatrogenic drug dependence problem.

Most of the drugs in this class are anti-anxiety or sedative-hypnotic preparations which have been provided for situational tension, sleeplessness, and emotional problems of all sorts. The tension never seems to subside or be resolved, and countless persons have learned to live on their quota of pills or obtain over-the-counter preparations for their anxiety, insomnia, and depression.

It is difficult to assess to what extent many of these substances cause physical or psychologic dependency. Voluntary withdrawal and cessation are almost impossible for some persons because of basic dependency problems and the overall circumstances of their lives.

Treatment consists of persuading the patient to give up all such medications (prescribed and nonprescribed) and strengthening his inner emotional resources so that he can cope with life's difficulties. Often this is not possible.

Each patient must be individually assessed, and each physician will have to assess his own reasons for creating or participating in any iatrogenically imposed drug dependence.

The symptoms of withdrawal in these cases are usually increased anxiety, tension, insomnia, depression, apathy, restlessness, or turning to some other substance to replace the loss of the drug: food, alcohol, tobacco, pills of any sort, etc. The physician may find himself in the uneasy situation of providing as useful a balance as he can for the patient, restricting the prescribed medication whenever possible or refusing it completely.

ALCOHOLISM
(Problem Drinking & Alcohol Addiction)

Essentials of Diagnosis

- Repetitive or chronic use of alcohol in any form to solve personal problems.
- Continuing problems in any area of life that are related to the use of alcohol: economic, social, family relationships, physical well-being, or self-deprecation.
- Usually marked emotional difficulties such as depression, insecurity, feelings of inadequacy, and need for control over others.
- Alcohol use, even in small quantity, allows expression of emotions otherwise repressed.
- In the addictive phase, there is a loss of control, so that ethyl alcohol in any form or any amount initiates a cycle of uncontrolled drinking.

General Considerations

Alcoholism is a syndrome consisting of 2 phases: problem drinking and alcohol addiction. Problem drinking is the chronic or repetitive use of alcohol to alleviate tension or help solve other emotional problems. Alcohol addiction is a true addiction similar to that which occurs following repeated use of narcotics. Problem drinking usually progresses to addiction. Both phases should be treated as aspects of a single illness, which must be considered chronic and progressive as long as the use of alcohol continues.

The acute intoxicated state (drunkenness) and the postintoxicated state (hangover) may occur in either the problem drinker, the true alcohol addict, or in any person who drinks a sufficient amount of alcohol. Neither the problem drinker nor the alcohol addict can be diagnosed upon the basis of drunkenness alone since the drinking patterns and amounts consumed may be such that obvious drunkenness is not always attained. Until recently, most physicians have considered medical treatment to be appropriate only for the acute

intoxicated state, hangover, specific complications of chronic use of alcohol such as delirium tremens, and for the many physical complications which result from chronic use, eg, cirrhosis of the liver, cardiac disorders, neuropathies, and gastrointestinal ulcers. The current tendency, however, is to regard alcoholism as a disease entity, and many approaches to treatment have been devised.

The causes of alcoholism are varied and include psychic, cultural, and perhaps physiologic factors. Certain cultural groups (eg, those of northern and central Europe and native American Indians) seem to be more prone to alcoholism than others. Proneness involves cultural factors rather than purely physiologic factors.

Most persons who develop a dependence upon alcohol have long-standing problems of anxiety, depression, and feelings of dissatisfaction with life and personal inadequacy. A few alcoholics have basic psychotic problems and use alcohol to alleviate the extreme panic which occurs when they fear an approaching loss of contact with reality.

Alcoholics are prone to transfer their dependence on alcohol to other substances, especially the tranquilizers, barbiturates, paraldehyde, and amphetamines. The combination of alcohol with any of these substances imposes an additional hazard to health.

Diagnosis

The diagnosis of alcoholism is often missed by the physician since its protean manifestations must be sought in the often closely guarded emotional and adjustment areas of the patient's life and since the physical effects of persistent drinking do not become apparent until many years have passed. Physical examination of the problem drinker and the early alcohol addict usually reveals nothing abnormal.

The alcoholic person is naturally reluctant to talk about his reliance upon alcohol and in many cases is not even aware that he has a drinking problem. He may deny or minimize the extent or ways in which he uses alcohol when directly questioned. The spouse may tend to shield the patient from exposure, but in most cases the wife or husband is well aware of the difficulty and is deeply concerned about it.

Alcoholism affects both sexes. Most cases go unidentified for several years until one or more crises arise in the alcoholic's life. Overt evidence of alcoholism appears most commonly in the age group from 35–50.

No economic, social, or ethnic group is immune, and it has been estimated that about 8–9 million persons in the USA are alcoholics. Fewer than 10% of alcoholics are on "skid row" (living a minimal socioeconomic existence), and the ratio of men to women alcoholics in the USA is 5:1.

The form in which alcohol is used (beer, wine, distilled spirits, etc) does not alter the ultimate diagnosis of alcoholism, nor does the frequency of use and the pattern of drinking. Some alcoholics drink daily, some only after a particular hour of the day, on weekends, paydays, or on occasional binges. Some prefer to

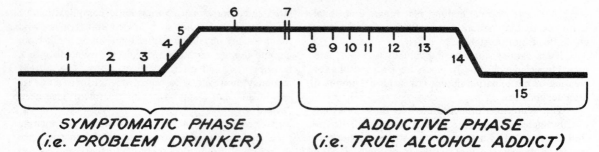

SYMPTOMATIC PHASE
(i.e. PROBLEM DRINKER)

ADDICTIVE PHASE
(i.e. TRUE ALCOHOL ADDICT)

FIG 17–1. The progression of problem drinking to alcohol addiction (modified from Jellinek).

1. Increase in frequency of alcohol use.
2. Begins to move in those groups where alcohol is part of "social communication."
3. Sneaking drinks.
4. Gulping drinks.
5. Increase in tolerance to alcohol: needs more for same effect.
6. Occurrence of blackouts, ie, brief periods of amnesia while under influence of alcohol.
7. Physiologic-psychologic change occurs: One drink leads to another. Compulsive need for alcohol. Changes in feelings occur after first drink, leading to sensitivity about reference to drinking, suspicions, resentments. This is a **point of no**

return; the ability to drink socially is never regained, and total and permanent abstinence is necessary.
8. Drinking in the morning ("eye-openers").
9. Prolonged bouts of drinking ("binges").
10. Belligerent and grandiose behavior.
11. Geographical cures, ie, patient moves from town to town, changes jobs, marriages, living habits, in each case "swearing off" to start life all over in another pattern.
12. Hiding and hoarding of alcohol supply.
13. Paranoid ideas.
14. Decrease in tolerance to alcohol.
15. Physiologic changes with pathology in liver, cardiovascular system, central and peripheral neuropathies.

drink alone or with friends in bars; others drink clandestinely, hiding the bottle from others in the family. Alcoholics who claim "social drinking only" can usually be shown, upon close inspection, to be drinking more than others in their social group.

The most appropriate attitude for the physician is neither to condemn nor to condone the drinking. Frank discussion of the patient's dependence on alcohol is important, and the physician may have to take the initiative in this since many alcoholics prefer to evade the issue of the importance of alcohol in their lives.

General Principles of Treatment

No matter what form of treatment is used, the most practical goal for the alcoholic is total and permanent abstinence. Almost all aspects of his physical and emotional health depend upon achieving this goal. Neither total nor permanent abstinence may be expected for many alcoholics, but even partial gains are important since they help arrest the progression of alcoholism and help set the stage for more complete success at a later time.

The following general guides should be observed in treatment:

(1) Use medications and hospitalization sparingly, and only when necessary to interrupt acute binge drinking, for difficult withdrawal symptoms, severe depression, or other serious complications.

(2) Treat all physical difficulties directly or indirectly related to alcoholism.

(3) Provide the patient and his family with clear information regarding the diagnosis, nature, and prognosis of his illness.

(4) Counseling should be provided for both the alcoholic and the spouse or other involved pertinent person (parent, sibling, employer, friend) insofar as such confidentiality is agreed on by the patient. It may be given by a physician, clergyman, or psychiatrist, or by abstinent alcoholics. A combination of counselors with different backgrounds is sometimes more useful than one counselor only, but all counselors must be of common opinion and must avoid confusing the patient with conflicting advice.

(5) Refer the alcoholic whenever possible to Alcoholics Anonymous (AA) and the spouse to Alanon (an organization for the relatives of alcoholics).

(6) Special medications such as disulfiram (Antabuse®) and special procedures such as conditioned reflex treatment will be beneficial for selected patients.

Complications During Acute Toxic & Withdrawal
Periods

The acute brain syndrome which ensues from alcohol toxicity gives rise to complications which require special consideration: alcoholic hallucinosis, delirium tremens, convulsive seizures, alcoholic "blackout," and alcoholic hypoglycemia. The first 3 of these conditions may occur during the period of alcohol intake or not until 7–10 days after cessation of alcohol; the alcoholic "blackout" occurs only during active alcohol intake.

A. Alcoholic Hallucinosis: This is the most common of the acute complications. The symptoms resemble those of an acute psychotic episode with delusions and hallucinations (frequently auditory) with strong paranoid content. Sensory distortions, disorientation, and panic are usually present.

Alcoholic hallucinosis in lay parlance (especially among alcoholics who have experienced this condition) is often erroneously equated with delirium tremens (see below).

The treatment of alcoholic hallucinosis consists of cessation of alcohol intake, phenothiazines given intramuscularly, a reassuring protective environment, and various other measures discussed below in the section on acute alcohol toxicity.

B. Delirium Tremens: An acute toxic psychosis with physical manifestations may occur during a bout of excessive drinking or 7–10 days following cessation of alcohol intake. It is a fulminating delirium, and although the same symptoms of alcoholic hallucinosis (with which it is frequently confused) commonly precede a bona fide episode of delirium tremens, the latter condition presents a much more serious problem of medical management.

The delirium is usually preceded by restlessness, disturbed sleep, and irritability following a recent binge. Symptoms include clouded consciousness, confusion, epileptiform seizures, maniacal destructive behavior, and terrifying hallucinations (frequently of distorted moving animals and figures). Panic is intense, and fever, sweating, and increase in blood pressure and cardiac rate accompany the physical frenzy, which may culminate in prostration and death.

Delirium tremens is most apt to occur in middle-aged males with a long (several years) history of heavy drinking who have previously experienced episodes of alcoholic hallucinosis and who have severe underlying psychopathologic disorders. There is considerable evidence that the delirium is precipitated by cessation of alcohol intake and the subsequent fall in blood alcohol level. The drop in blood magnesium level and its role in delirium tremens is not completely resolved, but magnesium has been reportedly used successfully in the management of this condition.

Treatment consists of hospitalization and protection of the patient from physical injury to himself or others. Restraints may be necessary during the height of maniacal behavior.

Tranquilizing and sedating drugs are necessary: phenothiazines intramuscularly as described below in the section on acute alcohol toxicity as well as barbiturates given intramuscularly or intravenously if necessary to control the hyperactivity.

In order to prevent the blood alcohol level from dropping too precipitously, some clinicians believe that it is necessary to give alcoholic beverage in diminishing amounts. Paraldehyde may be given in such cases since its chemical effects are quite similar to those of alcohol. Give thiamine and multiple vitamin preparations intramuscularly. Diphenylhydantoin (Dilantin®) is given orally.

C. Convulsive Seizures: Grand mal seizures are fairly common during an acute bout of drinking, especially in persons prone to have seizures, and may be precipitated by minimal amounts of alcohol. Convulsions occur more frequently during the withdrawal phase, and the general principles of withdrawal treatment (see above) should be observed.

In general, diphenylhydantoin (Dilantin®) should be given to any patient in whom convulsive seizures are anticipated.

D. Alcoholic Blackouts: This condition is experienced as a well demarcated span of amnesia during a drinking bout and is not necessarily associated with profound drunkenness. In some cases, minimal amounts of alcohol have been used. The amnesia may be partial or total for a period of 2–24 hours. Upon recovery (after cessation of alcohol intake), there is no memory deficit for events preceding or subsequent to the amnesic period. The physiologic mechanism is not completely understood, but it is believed to be related to constriction of the cerebral vessels.

E. Alcoholic Hypoglycemia: Alcohol is a potent hypoglycemic agent, particularly in chronic alcoholism, malnutrition, decompensated diabetes, thyrotoxicosis, and hypoadrenocorticalism. The hypoglycemia may become evident 5–10 hours after cessation of drinking, especially if the patient has not been eating. Lethargy, hypothermia, stupor, and coma may occur without localizing neurologic findings. Blood glucose levels may be very low ($<$ 10 mg/100 ml).

Treatment consists of immediate administration of glucose orally or intravenously. Abstinence from alcohol is essential to prevent further episodes. Diagnostic studies should be performed to exclude the possibility of specific endocrinopathy.

Complications of Chronic Alcoholism

A. Psychosocial Complications: The earliest complications, subtle at first but more evident as time goes on, are noted in the patient's personal relationships with family members. Absences from work and impaired effectiveness at work may be successfully camouflaged for an extended period but eventually come out in the open.

The effects within the marriage are profound. The spouse denies or helps cover up for the partner's drinking habit and is in the uneasy position of enduring family problems alone or reacting with depression, resentment, confusion, or various methods of escaping the marriage. Many such distraught spouses eventually seek psychiatric help. Many seek divorce as the only way out of an apparently hopeless situation.

The alcoholic experiences recurring episodes of remorse, guilt, ineffectual behavior, depression, and desperate attempts to run from his problems. Most alcoholics seem to have an ambivalent attitude toward life. Their personal lives are seriously impaired by drinking, and the physical complications of chronic alcoholism statistically shorten their lives.

B. Physical Complications: Alcohol can cause extensive physical damage to almost every portion of the human body. It acts as a direct toxin to all body tissues and predisposes to malnutrition and increased hazards of infection and trauma.

The well known effects of alcohol on the liver, stomach, and pancreas are discussed in Chapter 10. Effects on certain other organ systems are discussed elsewhere in the book.

General physical debilitation with increased susceptibility to pneumonia and tuberculosis are special problems among homeless or skid row alcoholics, and the reactivation of tuberculosis in arrested cases presents a special public health problem.

The nervous system is particularly susceptible to the pathologic effects of alcohol. The functional psychiatric syndromes due to alcohol are described above. Actual nerve damage may be of several types but is essentially due to vitamin deficiency—especially thiamine deficiency—which apparently cannot be properly utilized by nerve cell tissue in alcoholics. Some of the vitamin deficiency is undoubtedly also due to the generally poor nutritional state of many alcoholics.

1. Alcoholic neuritis (peripheral neuropathy)— The first symptoms are sharp burning pains in the distal extremities, especially the feet. Deep muscle tenderness with numbness, tingling, and superficial hyperesthesias follow. The lower extremities are more frequently affected than the upper extremities, and the condition is usually bilateral. The peroneal, tibial, and radial nerves are most often involved, with resultant muscle weakening, wasting, and paralysis. Coarse tremors, foot drop, and wrist drop ultimately develop unless drinking is totally stopped and replenishment with vitamins and improved general nutrition are able to halt the degenerative process.

Pathologic nerve cell changes in the frontal lobes occur on the same vitamin-nutritional basis as that which causes the peripheral neuropathy. The degenerative process in frontal lobe cells results in loss of higher levels of intellectual capability, memory defects, and impaired judgment and capacity for abstract thinking.

2. Korsakoff's syndrome (psychosis)—This type of chronic brain syndrome is one of the less common complications of long-term heavy alcoholism. It may also result from other toxic conditions and from cerebral atherosclerosis. When it does occur, it most frequently follows an episode of delirium tremens.

The characteristic change is that of memory loss for recent events with little or no impairment of remote memory. The patient has a euphoric and expansive mood and fills his memory loss for recent events with delusional ideas (confabulation), usually reports of absurd grandeur. Disorientation of time, place, and person occurs. Other symptoms may include peripheral neuritides, ocular palsies, and nystagmus. Acute symptoms last for several days (usually after delirium tremens), with residual permanent memory defects and emotional and intellectual deterioration.

The acute condition is treated with large doses of thiamine given orally or intravenously and perhaps niacin, but the permanent damage to the brain does not respond to any type of treatment.

3. Wernicke's encephalopathy (disease)—This chronic brain syndrome associated with long-term heavy use of alcohol is infrequently seen. It is probably due to thiamine and niacin deficiency and results in degeneration in the basal ganglia.

Many clinicians now consider Wernicke's encephalopathy to be synonymous with or merely a different phase of Korsakoff's psychosis—hence the term Wernicke-Korsakoff psychosis.

The onset may be acute or gradual, with nausea, vomiting, diplopia, and sleep disturbance. Symptoms include nystagmus, complete or partial ophthalmoplegia, rigidity of extremities, and abnormal body posture and movements.

Treatment during the acute phase consists of giving large doses of thiamine orally and intravenously and perhaps niacin. Symptoms may disappear after several weeks of adequate nutrition and abstinence, but will recur if drinking is resumed. Permanent deficits usually remain.

ACUTE ALCOHOL TOXICITY

Acute alcoholic intoxication is characterized by a history of recent (past 24–48 hours) alcohol intake, alcohol odor on breath (not invariably present), slurred speech, staggering gait, and lack of motor coordination. A wide range of psychologic reactions are possible: anxiety and remorse, variable mood ranging from depressed and apathetic to euphoric and manic, behavioral responses varying from lethargic to hyperactive and assaultive, and thought disorders varying from confused to paranoid. Sensory distortions are fairly frequent, with delusions and hallucinations (acute alcoholic hallucinosis). The blood alcohol level is often over 150 mg/100 ml, which in most jurisdictions is well above the legal definition of drunkenness.

Other medical conditions may be masked by the alcoholic picture, eg, diabetic coma and injuries of all sorts, including intracranial trauma.

It is important to detect exposure to other drugs along with alcohol—notably barbiturates.

In severe cases, cardiac and respiratory arrest, coma, shock, and death may occur.

Treatment of Acute Alcoholism

Examine for possible trauma such as head injury, fractures, lacerations, bruises, and pulmonary and abdominal emergencies. Rule out diabetic crisis. Protect vital functions (cardiac and respiratory).

Phenothiazines given intramuscularly will quickly reduce panic and craving for the next drink in most cases. Give chlorpromazine (Thorazine®), 100 mg IM every 4–6 hours, or promazine (Sparine®), 75 mg IM every 4–6 hours (watch for hypotensive effect).

Oral phenothiazines are of little value in acute panic and craving. If alcohol is available to the patient, he will prefer alcohol over any other substance to relieve his distress.

Chloral hydrate, 0.5–1 gm orally (or by rectal suppository) every 4 hours, may be used as a substitute for intramuscular phenothiazines to relieve panic and craving.

Paraldehyde, although it continues to be used frequently and effectively, is inferior to intramuscular phenothiazines except in patients who are hospitalized under nursing care and those who are apt to develop delirium tremens.

Barbiturates and other sedative-hypnotic drugs are contraindicated in acute alcoholism.

If hospitalization is not feasible, provide a "sitter" after giving phenothiazines intramuscularly to reassure the patient and provide supervision during withdrawal.

Stress the need for immediate abstinence (not necessarily permanent abstinence, which no patient can honestly promise) for at least 24 hours.

"Tapering off" is generally not recommended, although many alcohol abusers have adapted themselves to this routine.

The following drugs are useful during the acute phase and should be continued for several days into the withdrawal phase: (1) Vitamin B complex preparations should be given orally as soon as possible. (2) Diphenylhydantoin (Dilantin®), 0.1 gm 3 times daily for 7–10 days, if there is a history of epilepsy. (3) Antacids may be started early and continued into withdrawal as necessary to relieve gastritis.

Intravenous fluids should be used only if dehydration is present and the patient is unable to take liquids orally after 12–24 hours.

Treatment of Withdrawal

Both physical and psychologic symptoms are present during withdrawal. The most common symptoms are sweating, tremors, "shakes," headache, gastritis, tension, restlessness, remorse, and depression.

The physical and psychologic distress experienced by many alcoholics during withdrawal, unless adequately relieved by medication, usually results in a continued "craving" for another drink. Further drinking abates distress at least temporarily. If withdrawal is to be accomplished satisfactorily, craving must be interrupted and continued total abstinence from alcohol in any form (even in minimal amounts) must be maintained.

Patients with hallucinations (alcoholic hallucinosis), overt paranoid ideation, potential convulsive seizures, and delirium tremens are best managed in a hospital. The supervised use of diminishing amounts of oral or intramuscular phenothiazines or oral chloral hydrate or paraldehyde should be continued until "craving" has ceased. Continue to give vitamin preparations as well as diphenylhydantoin in patients with a history of convulsions. Give antacids as necessary for continued gastric distress, vomiting, or nausea. Promote intake of food and fluids. Candy seems to be especially useful. Insomnia may be handled by the use of nonbarbiturate sedatives (eg, glutethimide [Doriden®], 0.5–1 gm orally), or phenothiazines such as thioridazine (Mellaril®), 50–75 mg orally, at bedtime. Refer the patient to AA as soon as he is ambulatory and whenever feasible or appropriate. Daily review of the patient's progress is important.

Long-Term Treatment of Alcoholism

Although total and permanent abstinence is the ideal goal of treatment, it is not attainable in many cases. Other goals are improved physical health, better social and economic adjustment, lessening of psychologic problems (tension, depression, overt psychosis), improved family relationships, and an increase in confidence and social adequacy without dependence on alcohol or other drugs.

Even if total abstinence is attained, "slips" are to be expected in many cases—usually precipitated by periods of emotional or situational stress.

Many abstinent alcoholics, especially during the early months or years of abstinence, experience episodes of feeling "dry drunk" in which they are beset by anxiety, fear of drinking again, confusion, and uneasiness.

Each case must be assessed on an individual basis to determine whether psychiatric intervention, other appropriate directive therapy, or temporary use of sedatives or other medication is warranted. Persons who have previously done well by affiliation with AA and have "slipped away" may often be redirected to that organization. Others may need brief psychiatric support, marriage counseling, changes in their life situation, or extensive psychiatric help.

A. Alcoholics Anonymous: Alcoholics Anonymous (AA) is probably the most widely known, the simplest, and the most practical method of achieving abstinence for most alcoholics. AA is most effective when the patient also seeks some form of personal psychotherapy or counseling. AA chapters exist in almost every city and close to almost every small community in the USA. The sincere desire to become abstinent is the only qualification necessary, and a phone call to an AA member is all that is required. Contact should be made by the drinker himself, but the physician may be useful in introducing the idea to his patient and acting as liaison with an AA member who is willing to help.

AA is effective for several reasons: the spiritual nature of the organization, the understanding support of other alcoholics, the freedom to ventilate in the presence of other alcoholics, and the constant reminder through regular meetings that abstinence must be maintained on a daily or even an hourly basis.

B. Religious Conversion, Self-Conversion, Etc: No reliable information is available about the number of alcoholics who have become abstinent without benefit of any formal or outside help. Undoubtedly many persons meet some crisis in their personal lives which serves to turn them away from alcohol ("swearing off"). Some of these take place as a "personal conversion" or spiritual transformation without benefit of religious persuasion. Others occur through the active intervention of a particular personal or religious philosophy with or without a powerful emotional component.

C. Conditioned Reflex Treatment: Aversion therapy is sometimes successful in patients willing to accept this form of treatment. The procedure consists of the use of apomorphine or emetine to produce extreme nausea and vomiting at the moment of exposure (smell or ingestion) to alcohol. Periodic reinforcement is necessary until the reflex is firmly fixed or the patient is able to remain abstinent voluntarily.

D. Disulfiram (Antabuse®): Disulfiram may be a useful adjunct in achieving abstinence for the patient who is willing to accept this method of self-imposed control. Disulfiram should not be given without medical evaluation and without some type of ongoing general program of supervised help, counseling, or rehabilitative effort.

Disulfiram does not diminish or destroy the patient's desire to drink but merely acts as a deterrent to drinking insofar as the patient recognizes that combining alcohol with this drug will result in disagreeable or devastating physical symptoms. Administration by anyone other than the patient himself is rarely effective, and then only when the patient accepts the person who administers the drug as a helpful person rather than a controlling one.

The effects of combining disulfiram with alcohol in minimal quantities are flushing, profuse sweating, precordial pain, marked palpitations, gastrointestinal spasms, and a feeling of impending death. These effects must be carefully explained to the patient before he decides whether to use the drug or not. The drug cannot be given unless the patient has been totally abstinent for 72 hours, and he cannot drink safely until 72 hours after taking it. The usual dosage is 1 gm daily for 4 days and 0.5 gm daily for several months or until the patient feels secure in his abstinence.

A test of the effects of disulfiram when combined with alcohol is often useful in demonstrating initially to the patient what will happen if he drinks, but it is not necessary to perform such a test on a patient who is fully cooperative.

Patients with cardiac disease, severe liver damage, diabetes mellitus, and pulmonary disease should not be given disulfiram.

A variety of mild side-effects are reported by some patients, but few are serious enough to warrant discontinuation of the drug. Reported side-effects include dizziness, "bad taste in the mouth," gastrointestinal complaints, and weakness, and are generally believed to be the psychic results of withdrawal from alcohol rather than the physiologic effects of disulfiram.

All patients taking disulfiram should receive periodic follow-up interviews and examinations.

Arky, R.A.: States of unconsciousness associated with alcohol. S Clin North America 48:403–413, 1968.

Gessner, P.K.: Diphenylhydantoin and alcoholic withdrawal. JAMA 216:887, 1971.

Goodwin, D.W., Crane, J.B., & S.B. Guze: Alcoholic "blackouts": A review and clinical study of 100 alcoholics. Am J Psychiat 126:191–198, 1969.

Jellinek, E.M.: *The Disease Concept of Alcoholism.* Hillhouse Press, 1960.

Khoury, N.J.: When alcoholics stop drinking. Postgrad Med 43:119–129, 1968.

Kissin, B., & M.M. Gross: Drug therapy in alcoholism. Am J Psychiat 125:31–41, 1968.

Riston, B.: Personality and prognosis in alcoholism. Brit J Psychiat 118:79–82, 1971.

PSYCHOPHYSIOLOGIC DISORDERS (PSYCHOSOMATIC DISORDERS)

Commonly encountered psychosomatic disorders are as follows:

(1) Circulatory system: Essential hypertension, neurocirculatory asthenia, many arrhythmias.

(2) Skin: Neurodermatitis, alopecia, angioneurotic edema, urticaria, pruritus in erogenous zones.

(3) Respiratory system: Bronchial asthma.

(4) Digestive tract: Cardiospasm, anorexia nervosa, peptic ulcer, regional ileitis, mucous colitis, nonspecific ulcerative colitis, nervous vomiting.

(5) Glandular (anterior pituitary, thyroid, pancreatic glands): Many cases of obesity as well as inability to gain weight.

(6) Nervous system: Migraine.

(7) Genitourinary system: Enuresis, vaginismus, frigidity and impotence.

(8) Musculoskeletal system: Arthritis and backache.

Considerable confusion exists about the varying interpretations of some of the terms used to describe or explain the relationship between psychologic factors and bodily dysfunction. The following terms are most commonly used:

Psychogenic (functional) illness is a general term used to denote symptoms in which no morphologic change takes place. Many cases of muscular, cardiac, and abdominal spasm, dyspareunia, headache, and bowel and urinary irregularities (to list but a few) represent conditions due primarily to emotional causes. Tension and depression usually underlie these symptoms, which may be mixed with a strong bid for emotional dependency.

The term **psychogenic factor** signifies that emotional problems accentuate or aggravate pathologic processes. Thus, in some persons, the excessive pain and dysfunction of a bruised thumb or a prolonged postoperative recuperation period may be due to unconscious emotional factors. It is estimated that fully 50% of symptoms seen in general practice are purely psychogenic (functional) or have a large psychogenic factor.

Psychophysiologic disorder is a term which has now largely supplanted the term "psychosomatic illness." These conditions represent organic dysfunction with morphologic changes in which psychologic factors have played an important role. The autonomic nervous

TABLE 17−1. Differentiation of organic and psychosomatic disorders from conversion reactions.

Organic and Psychosomatic Disorders	Conversion Reactions
(1) Involvement of organs and viscera under autonomic nervous system control	(1) Involvement of parts under voluntary control
(2) Anxiety is not alleviated by the symptoms	(2) Anxiety is alleviated by the symptoms
(3) Symptoms primarily physiologic, eg, essential hypertension, peptic ulcer	(3) Symptoms primarily symbolic, eg, "paralysis"
(4) The physiologic changes may threaten life	(4) The symptoms do not threaten life

system is most often involved, and, although the mechanisms are not fully understood, it appears that organs and viscera under autonomic control are affected by vascular, nerve, and hormonal changes due to emotions. The net result is pathologic change in the organ itself (eg, peptic ulcer, asthma, some cases of arthritis). Psychophysiologic disorders are not uncommon. Almost any organ system may be affected, but the skin, the respiratory system, the heart, and the gastrointestinal tract are most commonly involved. The underlying anxiety is not relieved by psychophysiologic disorders—ie, the symptom does not "take the place" of the emotional cause, as it may do in some of thy hysterical neuroses.

Psychoneurotic conversion disorders (not common nowadays) were known in past terminology as **hysteria** and are characterized by dysfunction of an anatomic part: loss of voice, blindness, motor paralysis of a limb, etc. Anxiety is relieved totally or in large part in such cases.

Anxiety may in some persons be expressed by somatic fixation on any one of the visceral organs, as in many cases of peptic ulcer, essential hypertension, and neurodermatitis. Physiologic dysfunction and organic changes usually occur in the affected organ. Feelings of depression, rejection, anger, guilt, shame, power strivings, etc usually accompany somatization.

Earlier investigation in the field of psychosomatic disorders suggested that specific types of personalities were more prone to develop specific types of physical illness. Thus, essential hypertension has often been equated with the intense and driven type of personality, peptic ulcer with the worrier, bronchial asthma with the crying of the child, etc. These generalities have not been authenticated, and it is not known why in some persons certain organs or physiologic systems are selected for the somatic expression of their anxiety.

It is often difficult to determine to what degree physiologic changes are due directly to emotional factors and to what extent they are due to special habits and patterns in the patient's life, eg, the dietary insult which often accompanies peptic ulcer.

Treatment

Many patients with psychosomatic illnesses need help with their emotional problems along with medical management of their physical difficulty. Some may be suffering from specific anxieties which tend to intensify the illness even when they are not the direct and only cause of it. Others need considerable reorientation of their lives in order to reduce general stress as well as the specific feelings which have found expression through physiologic dysfunction. Medical treatment consists of relieving symptoms as well as giving definitive treatment, and psychiatric efforts should be aimed at relieving psychogenic factors insofar as the latter is possible. For still other patients it appears that their somatic difficulty is the only possible manner in which the body can adapt itself to a given life situation. Psychiatric intervention in such cases accomplishes little and may in unusual cases provoke or evoke profound emotional disruption. Each case must be individually evaluated, and it sometimes appears to be wiser to allow the patient to live as well as he can with his physical disability. Although psychotherapy may be of considerable value, it will not bring about physiologic changes.

Hickam, J.B., Cargill, W.H., & A. Golden: Cardiovascular reactions to emotional stimuli. Arch Int Med 127:597−605, 1971.

Lipowski, Z.J.: New perspectives in psychosomatic medicine. Canad Psychiat AJ 15:515−525, 1970.

Looff, D.H.: Psychophysiologic and conversion reactions in children. J Am Acad Child Psychiat 9:318−331, 1970.

Morton, J.H.: Obesity and psychosomatic problems. Psychosomatics 7:175−181, 1966.

NEUROCIRCULATORY ASTHENIA
(Effort Syndrome)

Neurocirculatory asthenia is a chronic disorder of young adults which is considered to be a psychiatric disorder; it is characterized by 4 cardinal symptoms: dyspnea on effort, palpitations, left chest pain, and easy fatigability. The symptoms are often more closely related to the emotional connotations of effort than to the effort itself. Examination reveals no clinical findings of heart disease, although tachycardia is often present.

Treatment

A. Psychotherapy and Reassurance: The medical examination and the manner of handling the patient have important therapeutic value. The medical examination should be thorough. The patient should be assured that no organic disorder exists. Further and more intensive psychotherapy may be of value.

B. General Measures: Treat hyperventilation; an acute attack may be aborted by the administration of 5% carbon dioxide, rebreathing in a bag, or by "holding the breath." Do not give ammonium chloride. It does not relieve symptoms and may precipitate acidosis, inasmuch as fixed base has been lost in compensating for the alkalosis.

Good hygiene with moderation in all activities, a well balanced diet, and progressive increase in exercise under supervision and with encouragement are important.

Prognosis

The prognosis for survival is good but is often discouragingly poor for relief of symptoms.

SEXUAL PROBLEMS

Transient impotence in the male and frigidity in the female are common experiences and do not necessarily imply physical or psychologic disorder. The temporary reduction of sexual desire or ability in either sex is often related to mild degrees of anxiety, depression, preoccupation, or fatigue associated with the ordinary problems of living.

Chronic impotence (or frigidity), on the other hand, is due either to physical or psychologic reasons. Psychologic problems account for at least 90% of cases of impotence, and the remainder are due to physical factors. Physical factors should be ruled out first and include acute or chronic debilitating illness, alcoholism or drug addiction, diabetes, CNS disease such as multiple sclerosis and transverse myelitis, hypogonadism, and certain urologic conditions such as tight frenulum, inguinal hernia, hydrocele, etc. It is estimated that the incidence of impotence in men over age 65 is 50%, but even in these cases ebbing male hormone is not the sole cause and psychologic factors are usually involved.

Psychologic reasons for chronic impotence usually include one or more of the following:

(1) Underlying guilt and anxiety, either about the sexual act itself, about the partner (as in cases of infidelity), or about other matters in one's life which do not allow for complete ease of mind.

(2) Resentments and hostilities toward the partner. The often casual and covert belittling by the female partner may reduce many a sensitive male to sexual impotence. Remarks and attitudes which leave some males with feelings of inadequacy (not necessarily with reference solely to sexual matters) are of crucial importance. In such cases, counseling with the wife, either alone, with the husband, and sometimes in marital group therapy, can be helpful. Some wives may need individual psychiatric help for their unconscious "castrating" tendencies.

(3) In some males the hesitancy to assume responsibility for and commitment to marriage and children may be responsible for impotence.

(4) Covert homosexuality, unconscious emotional ties to the mother or to older women, and problems of deep dependency are sometimes at fault.

Frigidity in the female may range from outright rejection of the sexual act to those cases in which anxiety, vaginal spasm, and pain are experienced or those in which no pleasure is derived but the female accepts intercourse with resignation as a duty. In other cases, some pleasure and emotional reassurance may be obtained but without full climax.

Many of the reasons noted above for impotence in the male apply equally well to frigidity in the female. Anxiety, guilt, ignorance about sexual matters, fears of becoming pregnant, unconscious feelings of resentment toward the partner, a fear of being trapped or controlled, and feelings of being used as a sexual object rather than being protected and cherished by the partner are all important in causing frigidity. Some of these cases will require special counseling or psychiatric help in which both partners should be involved.

Whereas frigidity and impotence represent the inability to obtain physical and emotional satisfaction from intercourse, there are some individuals who have an overwhelming drive to participate in sexual acts. The uncontrollable and morbid desire for sex (satyriasis in the male, nymphomania in the female) has no endocrinologic or other physiologic basis. These persons sometimes represent individuals who have great need to deny basic feelings of inadequacy (they "protest too much"). Some are psychologically arrested at an adolescent phase when such sexual prowess is held in special esteem in our society. Others have discovered that sexual expression alleviates anxiety, much as one might take refuge from anxiety in work, drugs, verbosity, alcohol, etc, and some look upon sexual intercourse as a "getting" rather than a "giving" relationship. These persons rarely seek help on their own inclination but only when brought by a distraught family, when in difficulty with the law, or when their Don Juanism entangles them in a complicated predicament. Psychotherapy is sometimes helpful.

Greenson, R.R.: On sexual apathy in the male. California Med 108:275–279, 1968.

Kaye, H.E., & others: Homosexuality in women. Arch Gen Psychiat 17:626–634, 1967.

Stoller, R.J.: Pornography and perversion. Arch Gen Psychiat 22:490–499, 1970.

Willis, S.E.: *Understanding and Counseling the Male Homosexual.* Little, Brown, 1967.

THE PSYCHOTIC DISORDERS

The psychoses may be classified as those of psychogenic origin and those due to toxic or organic causes. The former consist of involutional psychosis (involutional melancholia), manic-depressive psychosis, psychotic depression, and schizophrenia. The toxic and organic psychoses are caused by temporary or permanent physical and chemical changes in brain cell function.

The principal difference between the psychoneurotic disorders and the psychoses is that in the former the personality remains essentially intact, whereas in the psychotic disorders an almost total personality change occurs. The differences are qualitative rather than quantitative, and some of the psychoneuroses may be more severe and may have a poorer prognosis than some psychoses.

It has been said that the neurotic builds a house of fantasy but continues to live in the real world, whereas the psychotic withdraws from reality and lives in his house of fantasy. The psychotic patient, probably because of the anxiety he experiences in his private house, constructs, on the basis of his emotions, his own laws of relating to people and interpreting his world. The bizarre behavior, inappropriate moods, and the thinking disorder so characteristic of the schizophrenic apparently have meaning to the patient on the basis of the symbolism and the "laws" or points of reference which he establishes for himself.

Personality transformation in the psychoses occurs in 3 areas: (1) A predominantly symbolic transformation, in which the patient communicates by means of words and concepts which are apparently unrelated to his true feelings but in fact are substitutes for them—as in schizophrenia; (2) a predominantly affective transformation, in which the patient responds to internal stress with exaggerated mood changes—as in the psychotic depressions and manic-depressive psychoses; and (3) a predominantly cognitive transformation, in which the patient loses the ability to recognize and identify familiar objects and people—as in the psychoses due to toxic and organic causes.

A variety of physical and physiologic changes have been described in some of the psychoses (eg, in the blood, urine, brain, and skin), but at this stage of medical knowledge it is not known to what extent these changes are clues to etiology or are the result of the psychotic's altered way of life.

The principal forms of therapy currently available for the treatment of the psychoses are as follows: (1) Electroconvulsive (ECT, EST) and insulin shock therapy. (2) Hydrotherapies and physical therapies during periods of acute disturbance. (3) Psychopharmacologic agents, especially tranquilizing and antidepressant medications which help the patient become more amenable to psychotherapy. (4) Hospital milieu therapy, which includes group psychotherapy, re-education programs, occupational therapy, socialization, music therapy, work therapy, and various guided or sheltered reorientation programs.

Some unique forms of individual and group psychotherapy have been reported for the psychoses, but their success depends largely on the selection of patients and the personality of the therapist.

Psychosurgery is not generally used.

Hollister, L.E.: Choice of antipsychotic drugs. Am J Psychiat 127:186—190, 1970.

Levy, N.J.: Therapy of psychotic patients in office practice. Am J Psychiat 29:23—33, 1969.

Electroconvulsive Therapy (ECT)

This type of treatment consists of producing a convulsive seizure by means of a small controlled electric current through electrodes placed on the patient's temples. ECT is used for many types of depression and for some types of schizophrenia. Flurothyl (Indoklon®), a cortical stimulant which may be given as a gas by inhalation or by the intravenous route, has also been used to produce convulsive seizures.

The number of convulsive seizures given and the intervals between shocks vary considerably depending upon the nature of the psychiatric illness and certain other factors such as the patient's physical condition and previous response to ECT. It is not known precisely why convulsive therapy works, but the therapeutic value resides in the convulsion itself rather than in the electric current. Theories of its value range from explanations based on purely organic reasoning to purely psychologic ones. For example, it has been argued that the convulsion may cause chemical changes in the brain cells, that it may help to muster all of the vital forces of the patient for survival, or that it may fulfill the patient's fantasies of death and rebirth. Inasmuch as all patients experience temporary loss of memory following ECT, it is also possible that the temporary memory loss may be a major factor in improvement.

The main purpose of ECT is to restore the patient's contact with reality. In all cases, follow-up psychotherapy is indispensable.

This type of treatment should be given by a psychiatrist skilled in the procedure. A hospital setting is best but is not mandatory.

A. Types of Psychiatric Illnesses Which Respond to ECT:

1. Involutional melancholia (all moderately severe and severe cases)—ECT is especially effective for these patients and is the treatment of choice. Improvement usually occurs after 4—6 applications given at intervals of a few days. Up to 12—20 applications are usually given to ensure improvement. Patients whose depressions have a paranoid component do not respond as well as others.

2. Manic-depressive psychosis—ECT may be used for both the depressed and the manic phase. Four to 6 applications usually produce a return to normal mood and better contact with reality. Twelve to 20 further applications are given to sustain improvement. During an acute manic episode daily applications may be necessary.

3. Postpartum psychosis—Twelve to 20 applications generally produce marked improvement except when schizophrenic elements are present and especially if there is a history of benign schizophrenic symptoms.

4. Senile depression—A few applications are frequently successful and should be given in almost all cases of severe senile depression unless significant organic brain changes are quite evident.

5. Psychotic depression–ECT is the treatment of choice. Usually 12–20 applications are necessary. Follow-up ECT may be necessary to sustain the patient's contact with reality.

6. Severe psychoneurotic depression–Patients with or without agitation who do not respond to drugs and psychotherapy should be seriously considered for ECT. No precise rules can be laid down for the selection of these patients, but the current tendency is to defer ECT for neurotic types of depression in patients who have shown some response, no matter how slight, to any other kind of treatment. The following should be considered:

a. Length of time in psychotherapy and whether or not any improvement has occurred.

b. Whether or not a favorable response has occurred with antidepressant drugs or other medication.

c. Whether or not environmental manipulation, changes in work or residence, vacations, or changes in the attitudes of people in the immediate environment have been effective.

d. How long the patient has been completely unable to continue his usual occupation or how long he has shown complete lack of interest in his environment or in prescribed forms of activity (occupational and recreational therapies).

7. Many types of schizophrenia–ECT is generally useful for most of the acutely disturbed periods of this illness. The catatonic schizophrenic generally responds quite well, but the other types of schizophrenia are less amenable to ECT. Simple and hebephrenic types of schizophrenia tend to respond poorly. Up to 30–40 applications (over a period of weeks or months) are commonly used.

B. Psychiatric Contraindications to ECT: ECT is not indicated for psychiatric illnesses other than those listed above. It should not be used for the psychoneuroses other than prolonged severe depression which does not respond to psychotherapy and medication, nor for the sociopathic and personality disorders, psychophysiologic disorders, and addictions.

C. Safety of ECT: Patients with coronary disease and severe cardiac decompensation for whom ECT is contemplated must be carefully evaluated with due consideration for the risks of treatment as opposed to the necessity for treatment. In general, however, most of the medical conditions previously believed to be contraindications to ECT have been found to respond with complete safety to this form of therapy. Examples are as follows:

1. Old age–ECT may be given safely to elderly and senile persons.

2. Hypertension–There is now general agreement that hypertensives react well to ECT and that the treatment may be effective in lowering blood pressure.

3. Pulmonary tuberculosis–No contraindications to ECT.

4. Pregnancy–ECT may be given practically up to full term without causing rupture of membranes, uterine contractions, or injury to the fetus.

5. Peptic ulcer with a history of bleeding–No contraindication to ECT, especially when the patient is properly prepared with muscle relaxants.

6. Compensated nonacute cardiovascular disease–No contraindication to ECT.

7. Patients with a history of recent fracture or with bone disease may be given ECT when properly prepared with muscle relaxants.

D. Mishaps Due to ECT: Accidents are uncommon with proper selection of patients and appropriate premedication (usually one of the barbiturates and muscle relaxants). Those accidents which do occur are usually fractures or dislocations of the lower and middle spine, the upper extremities (including the clavicle), and sometimes the mandible. Other complications are rare.

In all cases ECT causes a temporary complete loss of memory (in all spheres, both recent and remote events) which may last for several weeks. Memory gradually returns, however, and there is no impairment of intellectual ability. During follow-up psychotherapy it is frequently necessary to reassure the patient that memory will return intact.

Malmquist, C.P., & J.H. Matthews: Electroshock therapy in high-risk patients. Am J Psychiat 122:1265–1269, 1966.

Insulin Therapy

Insulin therapy may be given in 2 forms: in subcoma doses or in full doses to achieve coma (insulin shock). Neither type is in wide use at the present time in the USA since the psychopharmacologic agents and ECT are of such broad value. Subcoma insulin continues to be used at some psychiatric centers, however, in the treatment of prolonged intensive anxiety. The use of insulin shock is considered to be of value for some of the psychoses which do not respond to ECT and drugs. In the latter cases insulin shock is sometimes given in conjunction with ECT as a combined treatment.

Detention & Commitment of Disturbed Persons

Detention of emotionally disturbed persons, even for an hour, must have legal sanction. In actual practice most law enforcement officers, upon a physician's request, will detain persons who seem to be intoxicated, drugged, seriously confused, suicidal, homicidal, or otherwise mentally ill pending possible commitment procedures. The usual procedure for commitment in most states of the USA is as follows:

(1) A member of the patient's immediate family requests the district attorney (or comparable legal officer) to initiate commitment procedures. The family attorney may be called upon to assist with the arrangement. A physician's written opinion that the patient is disturbed and needs hospitalization and will not or cannot accept it voluntarily because of his disturbed condition usually accompanies this request. A public health commitment may also be sought in special circumstances upon the request of 2 physicians.

(2) Law enforcement officers escort the patient to a hospital, where psychiatric evaluation and recommendations are made within a few days.

(3) A judge rules on the mental competency of the patient and the advisability of commitment, basing his decision on the recommendations submitted by the hospital psychiatrists and psychologists. The patient may demand a jury "sanity" trial at this point.

(4) The patient's civil rights are suspended if he is judged incompetent.

(5) The court may appoint a guardian of the patient's person, of his property only, or of both.

(6) Upon release from the hospital the patient may petition for restitution of his civil rights and release from guardianship.

Commitment procedures should be initiated by the family and not the physician. After commitment is initiated the physician may safely offer his professional opinion about the patient's mental and emotional condition.

He should retain notes of his examination for future reference.

Robey, A.: Criteria for competency to stand trial. Am J Psychiat 122:616–623, 1965.

INVOLUTIONAL MELANCHOLIA
(Involutional Psychotic Reaction, Involutional Paranoid Reaction)

Essentials of Diagnosis

- Onset between ages 40–55 (women); ages 50–65 (men).
- Withdrawal of interest in environment; including interest in people, work, food, and sex.
- Sleep disturbances, particularly difficulty in falling asleep and early awakening.
- Some cases show only paranoid features.
- Unusual somatic concern with feelings of worthlessness and failure.
- Considerable agitation is usually present.
- Higher incidence among women.

General Considerations

The involutional psychotic reaction is generally a severe depression, although in some cases the agitated or paranoid features are predominant. It occurs during or after the climacteric in both men and women, although women are more frequently affected. In earlier stages of this illness the psychotic features may be minimal or entirely lacking.

During and following the climacteric many persons are unable to recognize and accept the inevitable decline in their physical, sexual, and working abilities and the fact that they can no longer compete successfully with younger and stronger persons. The degree of depression which may occur and the extent of associ-

ated mental, mood, and behavioral changes vary considerably. Without treatment this type of depression tends to run a chronic worsening course, and suicide is a constant risk. Medical intervention of some sort is always indicated.

The premorbid personality: The typical person who develops involutional melancholia is the overly-conscientious, compulsive person who feels he has sought little for himself, tending to devote his efforts to others (family, employees, society at large) whose acceptance he has unconsciously sought. During the climacteric such a person may come to feel he has deluded himself and wasted his energies, and that his chances for personal fulfillment are now lost. Such a patient may be deeply angry at himself for thus failing to realize his earlier ambitions. Precipitating factors are not always evident but may sometimes be obvious, eg, the marriage of a son or daughter, reduction of income, or enforced retirement.

Clinical Findings

Depression is usually intense, and is marked by considerable anxiety and agitation. Profound sleep disturbances and loss of appetite and weight occur. Sexual interest is reduced or absent, often to the point of impotence or frigidity. Somatic concern is common, sometimes with delusional paranoid ideas regarding certain organs or parts of the body. Vasomotor instability, characterized by hot flushes, sweats, headaches, and general apathy, is a frequent feature.

Frenzied activity with vicarious aggressions, including unusual sexual interests and behavior, sometimes results and represents attempts to deny or fight against the curtailment of abilities.

Differential Diagnosis

The involutional psychotic reaction may sometimes be confused with a severe reactive type depression, manic-depressive psychosis, or an acute schizophrenic reaction. The premorbid personality of the involutional psychotic, however, will help in making the distinction. A history of disturbed behavior is generally present in the patient who develops a manic-depressive or schizophrenic type disorder in this age group whereas the premorbid adjustment of the involutional psychotic is usually excellent. In some cases of severe or prolonged reactive depression the evidence of a "loss" in the patient's life may not be recognizable, so that it may be difficult to make a distinction between the reactive depression and a mild involutional (psychotic) depression.

Treatment

A. Mild Cases: Mild cases may be treated at home or in a nursing home if adequate and constant supervision is possible. Treatment may begin with complete bed rest for a few weeks. Food intake must often be encouraged by assisting the patient in eating, and insomnia treated symptomatically with barbiturates. Small doses of insulin are sometimes useful to encourage appetite. Tonics and vitamins are generally of no value, and forced (tube) feeding may be necessary. Simple reassurance and persuasion may be of the greatest value. Endocrine therapy may produce dramatic results, especially when the predominant symptoms are those of vasomotor instability. In most cases, however, the psychosis is based on factors more complicated than endocrine deficiency.

B. Severe Cases: For more acutely disturbed patients, ie, those in whom agitation and paranoid or suicidal tendencies are present, hospitalization is mandatory. Antidepressant medications are not generally useful, but the use of phenothiazines (eg, chlorpromazine up to 600 mg/day) may be useful in controlling agitation. ECT is the most effective treatment, and the results are usually dramatic. For some cases of involutional melancholia, periodic follow-up applications of ECT (eg, once monthly or less frequently) may be necessary.

C. Follow-Up Treatment: Psychotherapy is indicated after ECT. The objective is to guide the patient toward insight and readjustment on a realistic level; to prevent the development of the egocentric, bigoted attitudes which some patients cling to in an attempt to bolster their self-esteem; and to prevent the patient from sinking into an attitude of apathy, feelings of inferiority, and defeat.

The patient should be urged to develop new and creative interests which involve close association with other people.

Enelow, A.J.: Drug treatment of psychotic patients in general medical practice. California Med 102:1−4, 1965.

MANIC-DEPRESSIVE PSYCHOSIS

Essentials of Diagnosis

- First episode occurs most frequently in young adults.
- Marked mood swings with phases either of increased psychomotor activity (mania) or decreased psychomotor activity (depression); or alternations or combinations of both.
- Phases are extremely variable in severity, duration, and frequency.
- Impairment of intellectual capacities is usually not evident during remissions.

General Considerations

Although the term manic-depressive psychosis is most often used to signify psychotic states in which depression or elation and excitement are present, less pronounced forms of manic-depressive illness are quite common. The depression may be precipitated by real or symbolic circumstances which suggest loss to the patient. Most of these persons are cyclothymic personalities and have tended to respond throughout life with exaggerated mood swings. There is some evidence that hereditary, familial, and cultural factors may predispose to this disorder.

The manic and depressed phases of this illness represent mood changes during which the individual alternately feels himself worthless and full of self-blame (during the depressed phase) and omnipotent (during the manic phase).

Clinical Findings

Almost any combination of the manic and depressive phases may occur. In atypical cases, manic and depressive features may be present simultaneously (eg, agitated depression).

A. Depressed Phase: Along with other signs of depression there are characteristically a number of physiologic components: dry mouth, constipation, and sometimes blurring of vision. Appetite is poor, with concomitant weight loss, during the depressed period. The patient frequently complains that he would like to cry but is often not able to do so. Somatic complaints referable to the head and abdomen are quite common.

In almost all cases psychomotor retardation is present; the patient sits quietly, incapable of reacting to his environment, from which he may feel estranged.

One or more attacks may be experienced throughout the patient's life, with a tendency for recurrence of minor or major attacks. To a considerable extent the depressed period (as well as the elated period) is self-limiting after a period of several months. Suicide is a serious possibility during the depressed state, and most manic-depressive patients should be in a hospital under psychiatric supervision during either of the extreme periods.

B. Manic Phase: The manic phase is characterized by an extreme increase in psychomotor activity, with rapidity of speech, flights of ideas, silly behavior, distractability, excitement, and meaningless physical movements (eg, restless pacing, running, jumping, hitting walls, pounding doors, howling, tearing up clothing, and breaking furniture). In milder cases (hypomania) the patient is not disoriented, psychomotor activity is less marked, and there is no clouding of consciousness. In so-called acute mania the psychomotor activity is so marked that extreme physical exhaustion results, disorientation occurs, and consciousness is almost completely lacking.

Differential Diagnosis

Differentiation from the catatonic type of schizophrenia or simple schizophrenia with secondary depression is not always easy in markedly depressed patients, but the absence of bizarre behavior and paranoid ideation is useful in making the differentiation.

Treatment

These patients should be under the care of a psychiatrist. Hospitalization is necessary for the treatment of acute episodes in order to protect the patient as well as others. ECT is effective in shortening the depressed phase as well as the manic phase, although its effect on the ultimate prognosis of manic-depressive psychosis is questionable.

Good nursing care is essential. Tube feeding may be necessary.

Psychotherapy and medications (especially tranquilizing or antidepressant drugs) after acute episodes may be used as an adjunct to ECT.

The antidepressant drugs have been of value in the treatment of some of the psychotic depressive reactions, but their long-range effectiveness and toxicity remain uncertain.

Treatment of the manic phase is directed toward protecting the patient as well as others. Sedative-hypnotic and tranquilizing drugs may be administered orally or parenterally to control physical agitation. ECT is often necessary to control severely excited and elated phases of this illness.

Lithium carbonate may be of value in the treatment of manic episodes in manic-depressive psychosis. It frequently calms the manic patient and controls manic symptoms within a few days, often regardless of the length and severity of the episode. Unlike tranquilizing and sedative drugs, lithium apparently acts directly on the aberrant mood and allows the patient to participate in adjunctive therapies and activities.

Optimal response can usually be established on 600 mg of lithium carbonate 3 times daily until serum lithium levels of 0.5–1.5 mEq/liter is reached, after which a dosage of 300 mg 3 times daily can be given to maintain a level of 0.5–1 mEq/liter. Laboratory determination should be made daily until a stable blood lithium level is attained and then rechecked twice weekly.

The use of lithium is contraindicated in patients with cardiovascular or renal disease or organic brain damage. Insufficient data are at present available to determine the hazards during pregnancy.

During administration of lithium, it is important to maintain a normal diet, including adequate salt and fluid intake.

Adverse reactions are seldom encountered at serum lithium levels below 1.5 mEq/liter; when they occur, they usually consist of fine hand tremors, polyuria, thirst, nausea, diarrhea, vomiting, drowsiness, muscle weakness, ataxia, and blurred vision. No specific treatment for lithium toxicity is known other than to withdraw (or reduce) the drug. In mild intoxication, 5–10 gm of sodium chloride orally (above the amount provided by the diet) promotes slow excretion of lithium. Rapid osmotic diuresis by means of intravenous urea or mannitol—or hemodialysis—may be necessary for severe lithium toxicity. It is mandatory to obtain frequent and accurate blood lithium level determinations.

Prognosis

The course is highly variable. Acute episodes may vary in duration from a few days to many years. Recovery from single episodes usually occurs, with or without treatment, although recurrences may be expected in about 50% of cases. If the onset is in early life, the prognosis appears to be less favorable.

Baldessarini, R.J., & J.H. Stephens: Lithium carbonate for affective disorders. Arch Gen Psychiat 22:72–77, 1970.

Food and Drug Administration: Lithium carbonate. Ann Int Med 73:291–293, 1970.

Gershon, S.: Lithium in mania. Clin Pharmacol Therap 11:168–187, 1970.

Goodwin, F.K., Murphy, D.L., & W.F. Bunney, Jr.: Lithium carbonate treatment in depression and mania. Arch Gen Psychiat 21:486–496, 1969.

Janowsky, D.S., Leff, M., & R.S. Epstein: Playing the manic game. Arch Gen Psychiat 22:252–261, 1970.

Lipkin, K.M., Dyrud, J., & G.G. Meyer: The many faces of mania. Arch Gen Psychiat 22:262–267, 1970.

Shull, W.K., & J.D. Sapira: Critique of studies of lithium salts in the treatment of mania. Am J Psychiat 127:218–222, 1970.

Straker, M.: Clinical experience with lithium carbonate. Canad Psychiat AJ 15:21–27, 1970.

Vincent, M.O., & C.F. Story: The disappearing manic-depressive. Canad Psychiat AJ 15:475–483, 1970.

PSYCHOTIC DEPRESSIVE REACTION

The psychotic depressive reactions are severe depressions in which contact with reality is lost and total withdrawal into a delusional state occurs. The illness resembles the depressed phase of manic-depressive psychosis except that it may occur at any age.

The clinical findings of psychotic depression include intractable insomnia; delusions and hallucinations in which parts of the body may be conceived as dead, rotting, or alien to the patient; and severe depression, with refusal to take food and ruminations about suicide. In some cases of psychotic depression the general psychomotor retardation is combined with severe agitation.

Psychotic depression is sometimes difficult to differentiate from neurotic (reactive) depressions, manic-depressive psychosis, and involutional psychosis. In reactive depression contact with reality is not lost and there are no hypochondriacal characteristics, no delusions or hallucinations, and no severe psychomotor retardation. In manic-depressive psychosis the life history usually shows mood swings or alternations. In involutional psychosis the clinical findings may be quite similar, but the latter occurs only in the middle or later years of life.

Treatment should be by a psychiatrist and is similar to that for manic-depressive psychosis and involutional melancholia—especially the use of ECT.

After the acute psychotic symptoms have subsided following ECT, psychotherapy, with guidance and direction in reorienting the patient's life, is usually necessary.

SCHIZOPHRENIA
(Schizophrenic Reactions, Formerly Known as Dementia Praecox)

Essentials of Diagnosis
- Usually a slowly progressive (but may be rapid) withdrawal from reality.
- Inappropriate responses in thinking, speech, and behavior.
- Alternations of mood—flat, euphoric, withdrawn, or depressed—without apparent relationship to circumstances.
- Speech and behavior become irrelevant (circumstantial) or irrational and delusional.

Frequent Additional Signs
- Depersonalization, in which the patient behaves as if he were a detached observer of his own actions, is a common finding.
- Delusions of grandeur or persecution are often present.
- Religious or sexual preoccupations are common.
- Logical reasoning becomes impossible.
- Flights of ideas and incoherence take the place of thought.
- Mentation and speech become blocked in emotionally charged situations.
- Auditory hallucinations, stereotyped activity, and ritualistic behavior are common.
- Disturbances of consciousness, memory, and orientation are often present.

General Considerations
Schizophrenia in any of its forms is one of the most common types of emotional disorder. Over 50% of mental hospital beds are occupied by patients with this illness. The onset may be at any age, but usually occurs during late adolescence and early adulthood. Schizophrenia is characterized by severe disruption in the usual logical connection of thoughts. The patient's thoughts are dissociated from his feelings, and a separation thus occurs between the patient and reality. Mood and behavioral changes occur, and various degrees of disintegration of the personality. Some authorities maintain that this illness is a syndrome or group of disorders ("the schizophrenias"). All patients in the "group," however, have certain common characteristics which would seem to justify classifying them together as suffering from a common entity called the schizophrenic reaction.

Four main types have been described, although others have been described and may be recorded. All types seem to be essentially one and the same illness, and considerable fluidity between types occurs.

(1) Simple type: Characterized by a gradual withdrawal from reality, apathy, inappropriate moods and behavior, irritability out of proportion to the stress, and slow mental and intellectual deterioration. Delusions and hallucinations are rare.

(2) Paranoid type: Suspiciousness rapidly progresses to active auditory and visual hallucinations of a persecutory nature. The delusions frequently involve those elements in the patient's culture which symbolize power or magic to him, eg, electricity, religion, TV, atomic energy, with elaborate rationalizations by the patient. Food may be refused on the grounds that it is poisoned. Acts of violence and murder may be carried out against those suspected of persecuting the patient.

(3) Catatonic type: Fluctuating episodes of stupor and excitement occur. During the stuporous or negative phase the patient may assume bizarre body postures, including that of waxy flexibility, or may stare for hours into space listening to condemnatory or commanding voices. The delusion of being God or Christ or having supernatural powers is not uncommon.

(4) Hebephrenic type: Bizarre mannerisms, incoherent speech, and silly and grotesque behavior with hysterical laughing and crying may be present. There is some evidence that the hebephrenic type is a further deterioration of the paranoid type, and it is less common now that enlightened hospital care has tended to prevent deterioration.

There is some evidence that any of the 4 types may be expressed clinically in either of the 2 following ways: reactive schizophrenia, in which the patient's illness is his unique response to extraordinary stress and which tends to be short-lived or recurrent, with periods of relatively adequate adjustment between reactions; and "process" or malignant schizophrenia, which begins fairly early in life, follows a more chronic course, and becomes a distinct way of life. In the latter type prolonged hospitalization or special foster home care is often necessary.

Etiology
The causes of the schizophrenic reaction are still unclear and are probably multiple. A genetic potential or susceptibility may exist; frustrations and deprivations, especially those which occur during the early years of life, seem crucial; later childhood conditioning (eg, rejection through separation of the parents) augments a tendency to "turn inward"; later environmental factors, usually resulting in poor personal relationships, may propel a predisposed individual into a schizophrenic type of reaction. In either case, the psychic trauma or insult has occurred over a prolonged period during early life and there is some evidence that some families may unconsciously "select" one member of the family to act as the "scapegoat" or target of their own anxieties and hostile feelings, thereby providing the milieu for the schizophrenic reaction.

Onset & Course
A. Acute Onset: The schizophrenic reaction may manifest itself at any age as a sudden break with reality. Excitement, inappropriate affect, irrelevant babbling and weird gesturing, and suicidal, homicidal, or maniacal behavior may be present. The duration may be relatively brief (if prompt treatment is given), or the disease may progress to a chronic or recurrent form.

B. Slow Onset: Slowly progressive deterioration, usually during late adolescence or early adulthood, is more common than acute onset. Inasmuch as premorbid signs are usually evident, it is important that the physician be able to recognize the harbingers of the schizophrenic break with reality. The "odd" individual who is out of harmony with himself and the world is most suspect. The brooding post-adolescent; persons who indulge types of thinking which involve an unusual fantasy life, sexual preoccupation, philosophic speculations and quests for the mystical or absolute; the antisocial, critical, stubborn, and inflexible person who finds no direct satisfaction in life all are predisposed to this disorder.

Treatment

Treatment depends upon the stage of the illness, the depth of regression, the degree of grasp upon reality that remains, the motivation of the patient for treatment, the response to medication and ECT, and the ability of the patient to establish a relationship with a therapist.

A. Less Severe Cases: Mild forms of this psychosis which seem to be precipitated by overwhelming external stress may sometimes be treated by environmental manipulation. At best, changes in the external circumstances of the patient's life can be helpful in returning him to his prepsychotic level of adjustment. Tranquilizing medication is indicated, often in massive doses if anxiety is intense. Among the more useful psychopharmacologic agents are the phenothiazines and meprobamate. Trifluoperazine (Stelazine®) (up to 20 mg/day) is particularly recommended for the more withdrawn type of patient; and chlorpromazine (up to 600 mg/day) for those with agitated features.

Many "recovered" schizophrenics will have occasional recurrences of mild psychotic symptoms in response to stress. For these patients supportive psychotherapy with tranquilizing medications tends to prevent the illness from becoming more severe.

In all milder forms of schizophrenia some type of continued relationship therapy is indicated. Psychotherapy takes the form of simple reality testing, reassurance, guidance, and insights within the limits of the patient's ability to understand his feelings and the meaning of his symptoms. Anxiety must be kept to a minimum, and a positive relationship with the therapist must be maintained.

Depending upon the patient's ability to form emotional ties with objects or persons outside himself, therapy may be through individual or group sessions. Verbal, occupational, and activity forms of therapy may be used, and should be carried out by persons who are skilled in working with such patients.

Routines of work and daily living will enable many patients to overcome some of their personality defect.

B. Severe Acute Cases: Acute and severely disturbed schizophrenic reactions call for immediate hospital care. Hydrotherapy (continuous tubs, cold packs) and the use of sedation, often by parenteral routes, are indicated. The barbiturates and many of the phenothiazines may be used, as well as chloral hydrate orally or intramuscularly.

ECT is strongly indicated for most of the acutely disturbed forms of the disease which do not promptly respond to psychiatric hospital milieu treatment no matter whether the predominant symptoms are those of excitement or withdrawal, and is the most suitable type of treatment for all acute stages of this illness.

C. Treatment During Partial Remission: Well-supervised self-care programs of work and play are necessary. Re-educative procedures of all kinds are best undertaken in a hospital setting along with individual and group forms of psychotherapy.

D. Chronic Forms of Schizophrenia: The majority of psychiatric hospital beds in this country are occupied by patients with chronic schizophrenia, which is the end result of personality deterioration. Many of these patients, depending upon the quality of hospital treatment, are capable of partial readjustment in a closely structured situation in the hospital or in foster homes. ECT during periods of overt psychotic disturbance or withdrawal and the judicious use of psychopharmacologic agents, along with routine physical evaluation and daily life supervision, are indicated. Individual and group psychotherapy are also useful in maintaining reasonable adaptation and preventing further regression.

E. Psychotherapy With Schizophrenic Patients: Aside from the supportive forms of psychotherapy, a variety of unique forms of symbolic, analytic, interpretative, and directive psychotherapy have been described (eg, by John Rosen, Frieda Fromm-Reichman). The results obtained seem to be due to careful selection of patients and the individualized technics and personality of the therapist. There is no doubt that all patients who have benefited from these forms of psychotherapy have received the benefit of extensive and highly personalized relationships with the therapist during frequent long sessions for many months or years.

Prognosis

The course in the benign type is variable. Some patients recover fairly promptly and are able to return to their premorbid level of adjustment. Many cases "heal with scarring of the personality" so that, despite their recovery, they still give the impression of being odd persons. Others progress to a more or less chronic course; with enlightened hospital treatment, they have less tendency now than formerly to deteriorate to such a degree that they cannot take care of such basic needs as feeding and dressing themselves; many patients are able to do simple productive work with minimal supervision.

Many acutely disturbed patients recover readily and, with follow-up psychotherapeutic help, are able to readjust adequately although the possibility of recurrences remains.

Follow-up Treatment for Psychotic Patients

Without exception, persons who have recovered from a psychotic illness (schizophrenic, manic-depressive, or other) will profit considerably from some type of follow-up psychiatric help. This is especially true if ECT has been used. Special attention must be given to the temporary memory loss which generally follows convulsive treatment. But with or without the use of ECT, postpsychotic patients will need help for some of the following aspects of their illness:

(1) Loss of confidence and self-esteem following hospitalization and psychosis.

(2) Readjusting personal relationships and reestablishing social and economic aspects of their lives.

(3) Clarifying some of the problems which precipitated their psychosis.

(4) Strengthening the personality to prevent psychiatric problems in the future.

Follow-up treatment may proceed along one or more of several lines:

(1) Individual psychiatric sessions for a prolonged period.

(2) Group therapy, often undertaken with other posthospital patients. (May be used in addition to individual sessions.)

(3) Follow-up medications, especially the use of tranquilizing and antidepressant drugs. (*Caution:* Prolonged use of these medications without routine medical and psychiatric evaluation and personal relationship therapy is never warranted.)

Bender, L.: The life course of schizophrenic children. Biol Psychiat 2:165–172, 1970.

Bleuler, M.: Some results of research in schizophrenia. Behav Sc 15:211–218, 1970.

Bruck, H.: Psychotherapy with schizophrenics. Arch Gen Psychiat 14:346–351, 1966.

Grinspoon, L., & others: Psychotherapy and pharmacology in chronic schizophrenia. Am J Psychiat 124:1645–1652, 1968.

May, P.R.A.: *Treatment of Schizophrenia: A Comparative Study of Five Treatment Methods.* Science House, 1968.

Rubins, J.L.: A holistic approach to the psychoses. I. The affective psychoses. Am J Psychoanal 28:139–153, 1968.

Warnes, H.: Suicide in schizophrenics. Dis Nerv System 29 (Suppl):35–40, 1968.

TOXIC & ORGANIC PSYCHOSES

This group of psychoses are due to actual physical or chemical change in brain cell tissue. They are classified on the clinical basis of their course as either (1) acute brain syndrome or (2) chronic brain syndrome.

ACUTE BRAIN SYNDROME

Acute brain syndrome is the term given to a group of disorders of perception and interpretation associated with delirium. The causes are varied and include intoxication with drugs, metabolic diseases, pellagra, dehydration, systemic infection with high fever, intracranial infections, and head injury. The principal clinical findings are confusion, disorientation, and delirium, often more severe at night. Without treatment, these symptoms will progress to extreme confusion, disorientation, hallucinations (mainly visual), marked restlessness and excitement, and defects in memory and retention. The severity of symptoms fluctuates markedly. In extreme cases there may even be sudden attempts at homicide or suicide. Laboratory findings are important in determining the cause of the delirium, eg, elevated blood bromide or alcohol levels, urinary barbiturate levels, and BUN.

Treatment

Specific causes of delirium should be determined and treated (eg, treat congestive heart failure, hepatic coma, uremia).

A. Protect From Physical Injury: Hospitalize the patient and use the safest room available. Windows should be covered with heavy locked screens if possible. Remove potentially hazardous furnishings except for a low bed with side rails. Avoid mechanical restraints whenever possible, except for specific medical or surgical reasons. Use "chemical" restraints (see below).

B. Provide Support and Reassurance: Recognize the patient's actions as those of a confused and sick person. Help him to understand what is happening and why he is in his particular situation. Do not misrepresent the facts. Explain diagnostic and therapeutic procedures when necessary. Recruit the aid of the patient's relatives and friends, since, as familiar figures, they may allay his apprehension. (However, some patients frequently become disturbed under these circumstances.) Constant nursing attendance is necessary. Give special attention to vital signs (pulse, respiration, and blood pressure).

C. Sedative-Hypnotic Drugs and Tranquilizers: (*Caution:* Avoid overdosage. Observe patient carefully for the effect of these agents in the course of the delirium. Take into consideration the potentiating effect of combinations of the sedative and tranquilizer drugs. See Tables 17–3 and 17–4.)

1. Chlorpromazine (Thorazine®) or thioridazine (Mellaril®), 50–100 mg orally or IM, may be given every 2–3 hours as indicated. The phenothiazines are not effective in treating sedative withdrawal reactions or for the control of convulsions.

2. Paraldehyde is useful in delirium (including delirium tremens). The dose is 5–15 ml in milk or fruit juice orally, 5–10 ml deeply into the buttocks IM, or 15–30 ml in vegetable oil (1:2 dilution) rectally. The oral route is preferred unless the patient is unable to swallow.

3. Chloral hydrate may be given instead of paraldehyde. The dosage is 0.5–1 gm orally in a flavored 25% solution or in capsules (Noctec®).

4. Barbiturates may be useful in the treatment of delirium due to withdrawal of sedative-hypnotic drugs of the alcohol-barbiturate group and for the control of convulsions. In general, they are not well tolerated by elderly or debilitated patients. Give pentobarbital sodium, 100–200 mg orally or IM every 1–2 hours only as needed, with gradual reduction every 6 hours until the drug can be safely discontinued.

5. Chlordiazepoxide (Librium®), 50–100 mg, or diazepam (Valium®), 10 mg, may be given IM. Switch to oral sedative doses of chlordiazepoxide, 10–25 mg, or diazepam, 5–10 mg, 2–4 times daily.

6. Diphenylhydantoin (Dilantin®), 200–300 mg daily, may be given for convulsions. This drug is not effective in sedative withdrawal reactions.

D. Nutrition and Hydration: Unless there is a specific indication for restricting fluid intake, a normal state of hydration must be maintained. This is especially true in the presence of fever. The total daily fluid intake should be 5–6 liters. For delirium tremens of alcoholism, several liters of 5–10% glucose solution containing 100 mg of thiamine hydrochloride and 100 mg of nicotinic acid may be given daily. Attempt to maintain nutrition. Small, frequent feedings are tolerated best. Nicotinamide, 200 mg orally twice daily, may be a valuable supplement.

E. Psychiatric Care: If the measures outlined above do not suffice, consider transfer to a psychiatric facility.

CHRONIC BRAIN SYNDROME

Chronic brain syndrome is usually an irreversible impairment of cerebral function resulting from brain damage or atrophy due to any cause (most commonly cerebral arteriosclerosis), beginning usually between the ages of 50 and 60. It is manifested by general coarsening of the personality with loss of adaptability and decrease of mental function. The patient becomes crude and slovenly, irritable, confused, and stubborn. Somatic complaints are often present, and depression and suicidal attempts are frequently reported. Specific laboratory and x-ray examinations may reveal the underlying cause. EEG findings are frequently abnormal.

Psychologic testing is frequently helpful in differentiating organic from psychogenic disorders.

Treatment

In addition to specific therapy of the underlying disease when possible, treatment is primarily symptomatic and supportive. Most cases are progressive and irreversible, and custodial care in an institution is usually necessary. Pleasant, friendly surroundings and continued usefulness within the limits of the patient's ability are important therapeutic considerations. The family should be encouraged to cooperate with the long-term treatment program; this may in fact be the single most important aspect of therapy.

Agitation may be controlled with promazine (Sparine®) or related drugs, and night confusion minimized by having the room lighted.

Cramond, W.A.: Organic psychosis. Brit MJ 4:561–564, 1968.

Epstein, L.J., & A. Simon: Organic brain syndrome in elderly persons. Geriatrics 22:145–150, 1967.

Goldfarb, A.I.: Psychiatry in geriatrics. M Clin North America 51:1515–1527, 1967.

Tucker, W.I.: Acute toxic psychosis. M Clin North America 53:275–279, 1969.

Twerski, A.J.: When to hospitalize the alcoholic. Hosp Practice 4:47–55, 1969.

Wolfe, S.M., & M. Victor: The relationship of hypomagnesemia and alkalosis to alcohol withdrawal symptoms. Ann New York Acad Sc 162:973–984, 1969.

•　•　•

MENTAL DEFICIENCY
(Mental Retardation)

Previous concepts of mental deficiency in terms of diagnostic entities based upon clinical impressions and empiric observations have fortunately been discarded. The terms "moron," "imbecile," and "idiot" no longer serve a useful purpose and can actually be misleading. Mental deficiency is now classified according to cause (eg, hereditary, familial, or secondary to organic disease); and degrees of deficiency are expressed as "borderline," "mild," "moderate," or "severe" according to the results of psychometric tests.

Psychometric tests should measure both the verbal IQ and the performance IQ as well as the so-called full-scale IQ. Discrepancies between the verbal IQ and the performance IQ are frequently reported. In borderline cases (IQ 75–85) it is essential to perform a battery of psychologic tests or to repeat certain tests in order to determine the validity of the results. Special attention must be paid to factors which may influence the validity of psychometric tests (eg, educational limitations, language handicaps, defective vision or hearing, or marked anxiety or apprehension during the examination).

The social adjustment of a mentally defective person is usually more difficult than that of the normal person, and much depends upon early recognition of the problem, understanding, and skillful social and vocational guidance. It is not uncommon for a maladjusted mentally retarded person to develop neurotic, sociopathic, or psychotic reaction mechanisms.

Many mentally retarded patients can learn to occupy a useful, productive, and acceptable place in society. Important aspects of the assistance program are a protective environment; vocational training programs within the physical and mental capacity of the retarded person; understanding and accepting parents, friends, teachers, and physicians; and community facilities as indicated.

Bolian, G.C.: The child psychiatrist and the mental retardation "team." Arch Gen Psychiat 18:360–366, 1968.

Bortner, M. (editor): *Evaluation and Education of Children With Brain Damage.* Thomas, 1967.

Jervis, G.A. (editor): *Mental Retardation: A Symposium From the Joseph P. Kennedy Foundation.* Thomas, 1967.

Menolascino, F.J.: The facade of mental retardation: Its challenge to child psychiatry. Am J Psychiat 122:1227–1235, 1966.

PSYCHOTROPIC DRUGS

The great number and variety of drugs which have become available for psychiatric use in the past 2 decades, their reputed values, and their reported side-effects and adverse reactions may be confusing to the physician who has not had extensive experience with their clinical use.

The clinician must ultimately decide for himself which drugs are most useful for certain symptoms and to what extent he will use drugs to control or modify his patients' emotional problems. At best, these drugs are merely adjuncts to psychiatric treatment.

The advantages of the psychotropic drugs are that they relieve symptoms, making many patients more amenable to psychotherapy; keep patients ambulatory and out of hospitals; and reduce the need for other somatic therapies such as electroshock and restraints. The disadvantages are that they tend to create dependencies and habituation and represent a possible method of suicide in high-risk patients. Relief of symptoms may also relieve the patient of the more difficult but more important task of facing problems and solving them. Many effects of these drugs are subjective—ie, patients will react differently depending upon individual factors and individual settings in which the drug was given. There are many side-effects and

TABLE 17–2. Recognition of acute intoxication by psychotropic drugs. (Manifestations vary depending upon the individual, purity of drug, drug combinations, dosage, routes of administration, and duration of use.)

	Hallucinogens[1]	Cannabis (Marihuana)[2]	Narcotics[3]	Sedative-Hypnotics[4]	CNS Stimulants[5]
Physical signs					
Pupils	Dilated, react to light	Normal	Pinpoint, fixed	Normal	Dilated, react to light
Conjunctivas		Reddened			
Skin	Flushing, sweating, gooseflesh		Flushing, needle marks (IV)		Sweating, needle marks (IV)
Mouth		"Burnt leaves" odor	Yawning	Yawning	Dry
Respiration	Increased		Decreased, pulmonary edema (IV)	Decreased	Increased, shallow
Pulse rate	Increased	Increased	Decreased		Increased
Blood pressure	Increased	Postural hypotension	Decreased	Decreased	Increased
Deep reflexes	Hyperactive			Hypoactive	Hyperactive
Speech				Slurred	
Coordination				Incoordination, ataxia	
Psychiatric symptoms					
Mood	Range from ecstasy to panic	Euphoria	Euphoria, drowsiness	Excitement → somnolence → coma	Tense and jittery
Sensorium	Often clear		Usually dulled	Confusion	Clear (mild); confusion (severe)
Sensory perception	Distorted	Distorted			
Memory		Mild transient loss		Impaired	
Hallucinations	Any type (often kaleidoscopic)	Rare, any type			
Delusions	Variable, dose-connected	Paranoid, dose-connected			
Laboratory findings	Hyperglycemia (occasionally)		Drug detected in urine	Drug detected in blood and urine	

[1] **Hallucinogens:** LSD, mescaline, psilocybin, STP, DMT.
[2] **Cannabis:** Marihuana, hashish, THC.
[3] **Narcotics:** Opium, heroin, morphine, methadone, meperidine.
[4] **Sedative-hypnotics:** Barbiturates, chloral hydrate, meprobamate, glutethimide, chlordiazepoxide, diazepam.
[5] **CNS stimulants:** Amphetamines, cocaine.

TABLE 17–3. Commonly used sedative-hypnotic agents.

	Oral Doses		
	Single Dose as Sedative	Single Dose as Hypnotic	Comments
Barbiturates			
Phenobarbital	15–30 mg	100–150 mg	Also available for parenteral use as phenobarbital sodium. The dosage is 100–300 mg IM or IV.
Amobarbital (Amytal®)	15–30 mg	100–300 mg	Also available for parenteral use.
Pentobarbital (Nembutal®)	30 mg	100–200 mg	Also available for parenteral use.
Secobarbital (Seconal®)	30 mg	100–200 mg	Also available for parenteral use.
Sodium butabarbital (Butisol Sodium®)	8–60 mg	50–100 mg	
Nonbarbiturates			
Chloral hydrate		0.5–1.5 gm	Contraindicated in severe hepatic or renal dysfunction.
Ethchlorvynol (Placidyl®)	100–200 mg	0.5–1.0 gm	
Flurazepam (Dalmane®)	15 mg	15–30 mg	Less risk of hangover effect and lethal overdosage.
Glutethimide (Doriden®)	250 mg	0.5–1.0 gm	
Methaqualone (Quaalude®)	75 mg	150–400 mg	
Methyprylon (Noludar®)	50–100 mg	200–300 mg	
Paraldehyde	10–30 ml	10–30 ml	

adverse reactions, some of them severe; and a number of combinations which must be avoided. (On the other hand, there are combinations—not fixed combinations—which are useful.)

The extent to which patients have become truly dependent upon these drugs can only be estimated. However, it is probable that the ready availability of pharmacologic palliation to large numbers of anxious, dependent, and demanding patients has yielded an immense crop of dependent pill-users. Many of these patients can be abruptly cut off from their supply without ill effect. Others require gradual withdrawal, substitution with a less habituating drug, and a great deal of psychologic support and help.

Four general classes of psychotropic drugs most commonly used in clinical practice will be discussed: (1) sedatives and hypnotics, (2) anti-anxiety agents, (3) antipsychotic agents, and (4) antidepressants. Lithium carbonate as an antipsychotic agent will be discussed separately. Grouping the drugs into these 4 categories is for clinical purposes and tends to cross pharmacologic classifications.

SEDATIVES & HYPNOTICS
(See Table 17–3.)

Insofar as reduction of restlessness and tension can be attained without lowering sensory perception and alertness to unsafe levels, these drugs are useful in helping many patients to regain self-confidence and a sense of control over themselves and their environment. When given in large doses to facilitate restful sleep, they enable many individuals to cope more effectively with their tensions and problems on the next day. Although sedatives have no analgesic value, they do help to alleviate the anxiety which is often associated with pain.

The smallest dose necessary to accomplish these objectives should be used. Excessive doses cause undesirable side-effects, and prolonged use of large doses results in psychic and physical dependency. Open prescriptions must be avoided, and large amounts must be cautiously provided. The sedatives and hypnotics are the most frequently traded, given, and shared drugs by those who have them—sometimes with unfortunate results.

Clinical Uses
In small doses, these drugs are used as sedatives to reduce restlessness and emotional tension; in larger doses, to induce sleep.

Adverse Reactions
Excessive doses cause drowsiness, lethargy, and hangover.

Less common reactions include skin eruptions, urticaria, angioneurotic edema, and gastrointestinal complaints. In some cases, especially in very young or elderly patients, a paradoxical reaction of restlessness and excitement may occur.

Withdrawal symptoms include anxiety, tremor, convulsions, and hyperexcitability.

Ataxia and disinhibition (similar to the effects of alcohol) are to be expected with large doses when not used for the purpose of inducing sleep.

Very large doses can cause coma and death. One of the more common factors in suicide or "death due to accidental overdosage" is the additive depressant effect of small amounts of barbiturates combined with moderate amounts of alcohol.

Precautions

Habituation is frequent when these drugs are used over long periods in dosages above the prescribed level. Prescriptions should be for limited doses, and patients should be followed to ensure against habituation or misuse. Use with special care in combination with other central depressants, including alcohol.

ANTI-ANXIETY AGENTS
(See Table 17–4.)

These drugs have sometimes been called "minor tranquilizers" to distinguish them from the antipsychotic agents ("major tranquilizers"). The 2 groups are used for quite different purposes.

Anti-anxiety agents, as the name implies, are directed toward the symptom of anxiety as such; the antipsychotic agents are directed toward the various affective, behavioral, and thought disorders which are characteristic of psychosis.

Pharmacologically, many of the drugs in the anti-anxiety group are CNS depressants and are sedatives to that extent, but even in large doses they are much less likely than the sedative-hypnotics to be soporific or to cause clouding of sensory perception and loss of consciousness.

Clinical Uses

These drugs help control mild to moderate emotional tension during periods of stress (situational anxiety) and the anxiety that occurs as part of the symptomatology of various neuroses. Large oral or parenteral doses are useful in controlling psychotic hyperactivity, for patients in withdrawal from alcohol, and in handling the confusion, hallucinations, and disorientation of toxic psychosis. (*Note:* The anti-anxiety agents will not alter the course of severe psychotic illness but will help control acute tension, panic, and hyperexcitability in some severe psychotic patients.)

Adverse Reactions

Drowsiness and ataxia are most common adverse reactions. (Caution is required in administering these drugs to patients who need mental alertness at their work, driving a car, etc.) Other adverse effects include dryness of the mouth, gastrointestinal discomfort, nausea, and skin rashes. A paradoxical reaction with increase of anxiety and hyperexcitability is infrequently reported.

Precautions

These drugs are often inappropriately used to counteract the anxiety associated with normal everyday stress situations. They should be prescribed for limited reasons, in limited amounts, and for limited periods of time, especially for patients dependent on alcohol or other medications. It is best to start with small doses and increase as necessary.

ANTIPSYCHOTIC AGENTS
(See Table 17–5.)

Sometimes known as the "major tranquilizers," these drugs have the ability to decrease aggressive disorganized behavior and disturbed thinking as well as to alter the course of psychotic reactions. The reduction of patient populations in large state hospitals over the last decade has been due largely to these drugs. Because large doses do not produce unconsciousness or depress vital centers, they may be given with less risk than is the case with the sedative-hypnotic and the anti-anxiety groups of drugs. Furthermore, there is less likelihood of developing physical or psychologic dependence with these drugs.

Most of the drugs in this group are phenothiazines. Some are available in liquid form or as timed-release capsules. Some may be given parenterally. The various choices provide considerable flexibility in their use, and the response after intramuscular or intravenous injection is immediate. The combination of some antipsychotic agents appears to be particularly useful in cases where there is little response to either drug when used alone. An example of such a combination is chlorpromazine (Thorazine®) plus trifluoperazine (Stelazine®).

Clinical Uses

The principal use of this group of drugs is in the treatment of the psychoses: acute and chronic schizophrenia, the manic phase of manic-depressive psycho-

TABLE 17–4. Commonly used anti-anxiety agents.

	Oral Doses	
	As Single Dose	Maximum Daily Oral Dose Recommended
Act also as muscle relaxants		
Chlordiazepoxide (Librium®)*†	5–25 mg	50 mg
Diazepam (Valium®)*	2–10 mg	30 mg
Meprobamate (Equanil®, Miltown®)*	400 mg	1200 mg
Oxazepam (Serax®)*	10–30 mg	30 mg
Phenaglycodol (Ultran®)	300 mg	1200 mg
Also have antihistaminic, antiemetic, and anticholinergic effects		
Hydroxyzine hydrochloride (Atarax®)	25–100 mg	300 mg
Hydroxyzine pamoate (Vistaril®)	25–100 mg	300 mg
Also relieves depression		
Doxepin (Sinequan®)	25–50 mg	300 mg

*Long-term use, especially in higher doses, may create physical dependency with withdrawal symptoms, including convulsions.
†Available for parenteral use for alcohol withdrawal: 50–100 mg IM or IV.

TABLE 17—5. Commonly used antipsychotic agents.

	Usual Oral Doses	Comments
Phenothiazines		
Chlorpromazine (Thorazine®)	25—50 mg 4 times daily	In hospitalized psychotics, the total daily dose may exceed 800 mg/day.
Thioridazine (Mellaril®)	25—50 mg 4 times daily	
Promazine (Sparine®)	50—200 mg 4 times daily	Useful by intramuscular route in alcohol withdrawal but has considerable hypotensive effect.
Trifluoperazine (Stelazine®)	1—5 mg 3 times daily	Larger doses (up to 40 mg/day) may be considered in some cases.
Perphenazine (Trilafon®)	2—8 mg 3 times daily	
Fluphenazine (Prolixin®)	2.5—10 mg daily in divided doses	
Prochlorperazine (Compazine®)	30—150 mg daily in divided doses	
Mesoridazine (Serentil®)	50—400 mg daily in divided doses	
Nonphenothiazines		
Chlorprothixene (Taractan®)	30—600 mg daily in divided doses	
Thiothixene (Navane®)	6—60 mg daily in divided doses	
Haloperidol (Haldol®)	2—6 mg daily in divided doses	

sis, and involutional, senile, and toxic psychoses. They are used (often parenterally) as emergency treatment to reduce panic, fear, and hostility in acute psychotic episodes, including those due to drugs and alcohol, and in the amelioration of combative, hostile, aggressive, and withdrawn behavior of hospital psychotics in order to make discharge possible. Small doses are given to suppress anxiety and tension in neurotic patients, but in general these drugs are poorly tolerated by neurotic patients.

Other uses include alleviation of emotional instability and "odd" behavior in chronic brain syndrome or senile psychoses. These drugs are often effective in relief of depression, especially when anxiety is a concomitant factor.

Adverse Reactions

Dry mouth, constipation, mydriasis, failure to accommodate for near vision, tachycardia, postural hypotension, and vascular hypotension are fairly common. Photosensitivity occurs occasionally. More severe extrapyramidal effects with higher doses are mask-like facies, parkinsonism, dystonia, and oculogyric crises. Severe agranulocytosis may occur.

Precautions

These drugs are not effective as anti-anxiety agents in neuroses. They must be used cautiously with patients under the influence of alcohol and barbiturates.

When given in high doses or when symptoms of parkinsonism appear, give antiparkinsonism drugs (see Chapter 16).

Watch for sore throat, weakness, or fever, which may be signs of a sensitivity or hematologic reaction.

Watch for falls in blood pressure and syncope in unattended patients.

LITHIUM CARBONATE
(Eskalith®, Lithane®, Lithonate®)

This drug has been found to be useful in treating the manic phases of manic-depressive illness. It is prepared in 300 mg capsules. The usual dose for adults is 600 mg 3 times daily for a total of 1800 mg daily for the first 4 days or until the blood lithium level reaches no more than 2 mEq/liter. Thereafter, the dosage should be reduced until the lithium blood level reaches 0.5 mEq/liter and maintained at that level for several weeks following the disappearance of manic symptoms. One or 2 capsules (300—600 mg) of lithium carbonate per day will usually maintain the desired level.

Throughout the administration of this drug, it is important to obtain regular lithium blood level readings (usually 2—3 times weekly) so that the level never rises above 2 mEq/liter.

Lithium should not be used if there is evidence of hepatic or hematologic disease.

ANTIDEPRESSANT DRUGS
(See Table 17—6.)

Three chemically different groups of drugs have been found useful in alleviating various types of depression: (1) tricyclic compounds, (2) monoamine oxidase inhibitors, and (3) psychomotor stimulants.

The amphetamines, which are CNS stimulants, were frequently used in the past as antidepressant agents; they are rapidly losing place in psychiatric treatment, although they may still be useful in selected cases (eg, narcolepsy). They are readily abused and may become habituating. The newer types of antide-

TABLE 17–6. Commonly used antidepressant agents.

	Usual Oral Dose	Comments
Tricyclic compounds		
Imipramine (Tofranil®)	30–150 mg daily in divided doses	May be increased up to 300 mg/day.
Amitriptyline (Elavil®)	75 mg daily in divided doses	Hospitalized patients may be given up to 300 mg/day.
Desipramine (Norpramin®, Pertofrane®)	75–150 mg daily in divided doses	
Doxepin (Sinequan®)	25–150 mg daily in divided doses	May be increased up to 300 mg/day.
Nortriptyline (Aventyl®)	20–40 mg daily in divided doses	May be increased up to 100 mg/day.
Protriptyline (Vivactil®)	10–60 mg daily in divided doses	
Monoamine oxidase inhibitors		
Isocarboxazid (Marplan®)	30 mg daily in divided doses	Maintenance on 10–20 mg/day or less.
Phenelzine (Nardil®)	15–75 mg daily in divided doses	Maintenance on 15 mg/day or less.
Tranylcypromine (Parnate®)	20 mg daily in divided doses	
Psychomotor stimulants		
Methylphenidate (Ritalin®)	Adults: 10 mg 3 times daily Children: 5 mg twice daily with gradual increase up to 50 mg/day	
Amphetamines (Not recommended for psychiatric use.)	5–50 mg daily in divided doses	

pressant agents have largely superseded the amphetamines in psychiatric use.

None of the 3 chemically different groups of antidepressants to be discussed here are as specific for depression as are the phenothiazine antipsychotic agents in treating the psychoses. Although these drugs may offer dramatic relief from depression in selected cases, they have serious limitations in the treatment of depression.

Depression often appears as a primary psychiatric symptom, frequently endogenous or reactive in origin. However, it is often so closely allied with anxiety that both symptoms must be managed as a single entity. It is thus not surprising that the antidepressant agents may be combined with the phenothiazine antipsychotic drugs with good results in many cases. Furthermore, there are cases in which the phenothiazine antipsychotic agents alone may prove to be more effective for depression than the use of an antidepressant. In short, if tension can be alleviated, some depressions can be resolved.

The antidepressants should be employed only for the more intractable forms of depression and not for the far more common cases of depressions that are self-limiting or situational in nature.

Clinical Uses

The antidepressants may be used alone or in combination with the phenothiazine antipsychotic agents in the treatment of severe, disabling, otherwise intractable cases of depression or in cases where the depression seems to have borderline or frankly psychotic features. They may be used as a trial of effectiveness for depression before giving EST.

The use of the psychomotor stimulant methylphenidate (Ritalin®) or the amphetamines is mentioned here only to acknowledge their acceptance in treating hyperactivity, aggressiveness, and poor school performance in hyperactive children. Paradoxically, the use of a psychomotor stimulant is of symptomatic value in reducing hyperactivity in children, enabling them to learn and achieve other social benefits.

Adverse Effects

The tricyclic group of antidepressants should not be given simultaneously or within 3 weeks after any of the monoamine oxidase inhibitor group, and vice versa; severe adverse reactions (including some deaths) have been reported.

Severe hypertensive reactions (including deaths) have been reported from the use of the monoamine oxidase inhibitor group and the ingestion of enzymes present in some cheeses and alcoholic beverages.

Dry mouth is the most frequent side-effect of the tricyclic group. This often disappears after a few days and can generally be relieved by drinking more water.

As in the case of the phenothiazine antipsychotic agents, hypotension and blurred vision are not uncommon. When this happens, reduce the dosage or stop the drug or provide antiparkinsonism medication (see Chapter 16).

A wide variety of less common adverse reactions may occur—some of them quite severe.

Limitations

The tricyclic and monoamine oxidase inhibitor groups of drugs are not immediately effective; 2–3 weeks are usually necessary before any benefits are discernible. If no benefit is noted after 2 weeks, the dosage should be raised from regular initial dosage to maximum level.

Although the antidepressants may be quite effective for many depressions, they do not by themselves alter the course of schizophrenia. Some reports indicate a worsening of thought disorders after their use.

American Medical Association Drug Evaluation Manual, 1st ed. American Medical Association, 1971.

Hollister, L.E.: Choice of antipsychotic drugs. Am J Psychiat 127:186–190, 1970.

Physician's Desk Reference to Pharmaceutical Specialties and Biologicals [PDR]. Medical Economics, Inc. [Annual.]

Schnee, J.: Pharmacological and dynamic factors in psychotropic drug therapy. Am J Psychoanal 30:169–176, 1970.

Winston, F.: Combined antidepressant therapy. Brit J Psychiat 118:301–304, 1971.

• • •

General Bibliography

Alcoholics Anonymous: The Story of How Many Thousands Have Recovered From Alcoholism, 7th printing. Cornwall, 1965.

Becker, E.: *The Revolution in Psychiatry.* Macmillan, 1964.

Bromberg, W.: Is punishment dead? Am J Psychiat 127:245–248, 1970.

Elkins, H.K.: Psychiatry. Chap 20 in *Current Medical References,* 6th ed., Chatton, M.J., & P.J. Sanazaro (editors). Lange, 1970.

English, O.S., & S.M. Finch: *Introduction to Psychiatry.* Norton, 1964.

Ewalt, J.R., & D.L. Farnsworth: *Textbook of Psychiatry.* McGraw-Hill, 1963.

Hollister, L.: Psychopharmacological drugs. JAMA 196:411–413, 1966.

Kaufman, M.R. (editor): *The Psychiatric Unit in a General Hospital.* International Universities, 1966.

McGarry, A.L.: The fate of psychotic offenders returned for trial. Am J Psychiat 127:1181–1184, 1971.

Menninger, K.: The future of criminal law. Reflections 3:40–51, 1968.

Redlich, F.C., & D.X. Freedman: *The Theory and Practice of Psychiatry.* Basic Books, 1966.

Robey, A., & W.J. Bogard: The compleat forensic psychiatrist. Am J Psychiat 126:519–525, 1969.

Robitscher, J.B.: *Pursuit of Agreement: Psychiatry and the Law.* Lippincott, 1966.

Searles, H.F.: *Collected Papers on Schizophrenia and Related Subjects.* International Universities, 1966.

Shaw, C.R.: *Psychiatric Disorders of Childhood.* Appleton-Century-Crofts, 1966.

Solomon, P., & B.C. Glueck, Jr. (editors): *Recent Research on Schizophrenia.* Am Psychiat Assoc Publ, 1966.

Solomon, P., & V.D. Patch: *Handbook of Psychiatry* 2nd ed. Lange, 1971.

Weihofen, H., & G.L. Usdin: Who is competent to make a will? Ment Hyg 54:34–43, 1970.

Wolberg, L.R.: *Psychotherapy and the Behavioral Sciences.* Grune & Stratton, 1966.

18 . . .

Endocrine Disorders

Felix O. Kolb

The Difficulties of Diagnosis of Endocrine Diseases

The diagnosis of endocrine disorders is complicated by the following factors peculiar to these organs:

A. Interrelationships of the Endocrine Glands: Because the endocrine glands are so closely interrelated, the presenting symptoms and signs of any endocrine disorder may represent a secondary disturbance in another gland or even in more than one gland. The diagnostic clue may therefore be in an organ which is secondarily affected by hypofunction or hyperfunction of the gland in question. For example, amenorrhea may be due to an abnormality of the pituitary or adrenal gland rather than due to a primary ovarian lesion.

B. Homeostatic (Compensatory) Mechanisms: A well-balanced system of homeostasis often disguises the existence of pathologic changes in the pituitary, which is inhibited by rising levels of secretions of the "target" glands.

C. Size of Lesion vs Magnitude of Effect: The metabolic effect of an endocrine disturbance is not necessarily proportionate to the size of the lesion. A small tumor may cause extensive disturbance, whereas a striking enlargement may have no pathologic significance except as a space-occupying lesion.

D. Physiologic vs Pathologic States: The line between a physiologic aberration and a pathologic state may be quite tenuous (eg, physiologic growth spurt vs gigantism). The "target" organ may be unduly sensitive or resistant to usual amounts of hormonal secretion. Many hormones appear to act on target organs by stimulation of cyclic AMP formation; some may act through stimulation of prostaglandins.

E. Deficiencies of Knowledge: Some of the endocrine glands are activated by ill-defined neurohumoral factors presumably located in the hypothalamus. The diagnosis of disturbances along the pathway of this mechanism is largely beyond the reach of present-day medicine. The recently reported synthesis of TSH and LH releasing factors shows promise of future application to diagnosis and treatment.

F. Multiple and Nonendocrine Involvement: The increasing number of recognized syndromes of multiple endocrine tumors and autoimmune deficiencies (often familial) and the endocrinopathies associated with nonendocrine gland cancers has complicated the problem of diagnosis.

G. Difficulties of Laboratory Diagnosis: Direct chemical and immunoassays of various hormones in blood and urine are being developed in increasing numbers, but until they are perfected, less costly, and more generally available for clinical use, bedside observation and sensitive indirect diagnostic procedures are still required to establish the proper diagnosis of most endocrine disorders. Radiologic diagnosis of endocrine tumors has made rapid progress (see Steinbach reference, below).

Bower, B.F., & G.S. Gordan: Hormonal effects of nonendocrine tumors. Ann Rev Med 16:83–118, 1965.

Butcher, R.W.: Role of cyclic AMP in hormone actions. New England J Med 279:1378–1384, 1968.

Catt, K.J.: ABC of endocrinology. I. Hormones in general. Lancet 1:763, 1970.

Johnson, G.J., & others: Kindred with multiple endocrine adenomatosis. New England J Med 277:1379–1385, 1967.

Katz, F.H.: Laboratory aids in the diagnosis of endocrine disorders. M Clin North America 53:79–96, 1969.

Lawrence, A.M.: Immunoassays in the diagnosis of endocrine disorders. S Clin North America 49:3–10, 1969.

Liddle, G.W., & others: Clinical and laboratory studies of ectopic humoral syndromes. Recent Progr Hormone Res 25:283, 1969.

Martini, L., & W.F. Ganong (editors): *Neuroendocrinology.* 2 vols. Academic Press, 1966, 1967.

Ranninger, K.: The radiologic diagnosis of tumors of the endocrine glands. S Clin North America 49:11–26, 1969.

Steinbach, H.L., & H. Minagi: *The Endocrines: Atlas of Tumor Radiology.* Year Book, 1969.

Symposium: Autoimmunity in endocrine disease. Proc Roy Soc Med 61:271–280, 1968.

Weichert, R.F., III: The neural ectodermal origin of the peptide-secreting endocrine glands. Am J Med 49:232–241, 1970.

NONSPECIFIC MANIFESTATIONS

Delayed Growth

Growth delays due to endocrine and metabolic disorders are at times difficult to distinguish from familial or genetic dwarfism. Often there is an association with delayed genital development. Rule out bone diseases and nutritional, metabolic, and renal disorders which delay growth. Look for associated stigmas such as polydactylia and webbing. Plotting of the growth rate will demonstrate whether growth has been delayed since birth or only during a specific period in childhood. Hypothyroidism must be excluded, as it is at times subtle and can be diagnosed only by sensitive tests of thyroid function or by a trial of thyroid therapy. Epiphyseal dysgenesis (stippling) may be the telltale sign of juvenile hypothyroidism. The differentiation of hypopituitarism from delayed adolescence will usually become apparent in adult life. Dwarfing due to isolated lack of pituitary growth hormone has recently been described. Dwarfing is also seen with gonadal dysgenesis in Turner's syndrome and with pseudohypoparathyroidism. A rapid growth spurt with eventual short stature is typical of sexual precocity and of the adrenogenital syndromes. (*Note:* In any problem of growth delay, obtain an accurate determination of bone age and an x-ray of the sella turcica, and measure the skeletal proportions carefully.)

Excessive Growth

Excessive growth may be a familial or racial characteristic or a physiologic event (eg, the growth spurt of puberty) as well as a sign of endocrine disease. If precocious genital development occurs, consider true precocity due to pituitary or hypothalamic disorders, or pseudoprecocious puberty due to excess of adrenal, ovarian, or testicular hormones (often due to tumors). These patients, if not treated rapidly, will eventually be of short stature as a result of premature closure of their epiphyses. Pituitary eosinophilic tumors are rare before puberty; thereafter, they cause pituitary gigantism associated with enlargement of the sella turcica and visual field defects. After closure of the epiphyses acromegalic gigantism will result. A few cases of nonpituitary "cerebral gigantism" have been described. Eunuchoid individuals tend to grow taller, with span exceeding height. Diabetic children are often tall.

Obesity

Although obesity is a common presenting "endocrine" complaint, most cases are due to constitutional factors and excessive food intake. A sudden onset of massive obesity associated with lethargy or polyuria suggests a hypothalamic lesion (rare). While most cases of extreme obesity are associated with delayed puberty, slight excesses of food intake may lead to precocity. Hypothyroidism is usually *not* associated with marked obesity. In Cushing's disease or syndrome, there is moderate obesity with a characteristic "buffalo hump" and trunk obesity with thin extremities. Striae are common with any type of obesity. They are more often purplish in Cushing's syndrome. Amenorrhea, hypertension, and glycosuria or a diabetic glucose tolerance curve are commonly associated with obesity, and may improve after adequate weight loss. Islet cell adenomas are usually associated with obesity, but these are quite rare. In most instances the obese patient requires increased activity, reduction in caloric intake, and, at times, psychotherapy.

Wasting & Weakness

Pituitary cachexia (Simmonds' disease) is quite rare. Always rule out nonendocrine causes and consider anorexia nervosa and dietary fanaticism before looking for endocrine disturbances. Consider the possibility of diabetes mellitus, thyrotoxicosis, pheochromocytoma, and Addison's disease if weight loss is progressive.

Abnormal Skin Pigmentation or Color

First consider normal individual, familial, and racial variations. Hyperpigmentation may coexist with depigmentation (vitiligo) in Addison's disease, which must be ruled out by standard tests. Search carefully for pigmentary spots on mucous membranes, gums, and nipples. Differentiate Addison's disease from sprue, hemochromatosis, and argyria. Pregnancy and thyrotoxicosis are at times associated with spotty brown pigmentation, especially over the face (chloasma). A similar type of pigmentation has been seen occasionally with oral contraceptive administration. Other drugs (eg, diethylstilbestrol) will cause localized brown-black pigmentation over the nipples. Brown pigment spots with a ragged border are typical of Albright's syndrome (associated with fibrous dysplasia and precocious sexual development in the female); smooth pigmented nevi are seen in neurofibromatosis. Acanthosis nigricans may be associated with acromegaly and other endocrine tumors. Patients with Cushing's disease usually have a ruddy complexion. Hyperpigmentation, especially after adrenalectomy, suggests a pituitary tumor or, more rarely, an extra-adrenal cancer. Malar flush is characteristic of primary myxedema. The hypogonadal or hypopituitary patient has a sallow, waxy, and at times yellowish or "fawn" color, and is unable to tan on exposure to sunlight.

Hirsutism

Marked normal variations in the amount of body hair occur on a racial, familial, or genetic nonendocrine basis. Hirsutism, however, is one of the major presenting complaints of women and may be the first sign of a serious neoplastic disease; if so, it is rarely completely reversible even if the tumor is removed. Hirsutism is of greater significance if it occurs other than at puberty, with pregnancy, or at the menopause, if it is associated with other features of virilization, such as voice changes, balding, or enlargement of the clitoris, and if the onset is sudden. Always investigate the patient's adrenal status and rule out tumor and hyperplasia. Ovarian causes include polycystic ovaries (Stein-Leventhal syndrome), hilar cell tumors, arrhenoblastoma, and theca cell luteinization. As a minimum screening procedure, a urinary 17-ketosteroid determination should be obtained; but the more specific testosterone determinations, though not generally available, are of greater diagnostic value. It is important to make certain that the patient has not received androgenic medication or certain drugs (eg, diphenylhydantoin).

Change in Appetite

Polyphagia (associated with polydipsia and polyuria) is classically found in uncontrolled diabetes mellitus. However, excessive eating is usually not an endocrine problem but a compulsive personality trait. Only rarely is it due to a hypothalamic lesion, in which case it is associated with somnolence and other signs of the hypothalamic disease (Fröhlich's syndrome). Excessive appetite with weight loss is observed in thyrotoxicosis; polyphagia with weight gain may indicate acromegaly or hypoglycemia due to an islet cell adenoma.

Anorexia and nausea associated with weight loss and diarrhea may occur at the onset of addisonian crisis or uncontrolled diabetic acidosis. Anorexia and nausea with constipation are found with any state of hypercalcemia, eg, hyperparathyroidism, and may be indistinguishable from the same symptoms occurring in peptic ulcer (which may coexist with hyperparathyroidism).

Polyuria & Polydipsia

Polyuria, commonly associated with polydipsia, is usually of nonendocrine etiology, due to a habit of drinking excessive water (psychogenic). However, if it is severe and of sudden onset it suggests diabetes mellitus or diabetes insipidus. Diabetes insipidus may develop insidiously or may appear suddenly after head trauma or brain surgery. Always attempt to rule out an organic lesion in or about the posterior pituitary-supraoptic tract. In children one must consider nephrogenic diabetes insipidus and eosinophilic granuloma.

A urine specific gravity over 1.016 virtually rules out diabetes insipidus.

Polyuria and polydipsia are frequently seen in any state of hypercalcemia, such as hyperparathyroidism, and are also part of the syndrome of primary hyperaldosteronism, in which they are typically nocturnal. Polyuria may occur in renal tubular disorders, such as renal tubular acidosis and Fanconi's syndrome.

Gynecomastia

Enlargement of one or both breasts, usually painless and of rapid onset, is a common finding in adolescent boys. It may also be seen in old men. It is often transient and of little significance. One must differentiate between true glandular enlargement and simple fat pads or ballooning of the areolar tissue. Any painless hard lump, especially if unilateral, may be carcinoma.

True gynecomastia is found in many endocrine and nonendocrine disorders, eg, thyrotoxicosis, liver disease, paraplegia, and adrenal tumors. If associated with small testicles and lack of sperm, it may be part of Klinefelter's syndrome. Obtain a buccal smear, which may indicate a positive chromatin nuclear pattern.

Breast enlargement and tenderness may be due to estrogen therapy, but also occur after the administration of androgens, especially to eunuchoid patients.

Gynecomastia may be the presenting sign of serious testicular tumors, such as choriocarcinoma, which may be too small to be palpable yet may metastasize widely. It may occur in bronchogenic carcinomas which produce gonadotropic hormones. It has been observed after hemodialysis.

Breast enlargements may be transitory or may persist even after the cause (eg, exogenous estrogen) is removed; plastic surgical removal is often necessary for cosmetic reasons.

Abnormal Lactation

Lactation is a physiologic phenomenon when seen in the newborn ("witch's milk"); it may occur before menstruation or may persist for prolonged periods after recent delivery, and is part of the syndrome of pseudocyesis. It is frequently present in both sexes in acromegaly and, more rarely, in thyrotoxicosis and myxedema. In some patients with amenorrhea with or without small chromophobe adenomas of the pituitary (eg, Chiari-Frommel syndrome), lactation may be so profuse that it is distressing to the patient. It may occur after pituitary stalk section, after thoracoplasty, or even after hysterectomy. Abnormal lactation occurs rarely with estrogen-secreting adrenal tumors and quite rarely with corpus luteum cysts and chorio-epithelioma. Some drugs (eg, chlorpromazine) may produce lactation.

Precocious Puberty (in Both Sexes)

Precocious puberty is often a familial trait, but it may indicate serious organic disease. One must differentiate true precocity from pseudoprecocity. At times there is only premature breast development ("thelarche") or only premature appearance of pubic and axillary hair ("adrenarche") with normal subsequent menarche. Hypothalamic lesions, encephalitis, and certain tumors (eg, hamartoma of the tuber cinereum) may cause true sexual precocity. The same is found in girls who have associated fibrous dysplasia of bone and pigment spots (Albright's syndrome). Adrenal hyperplasia or tumor and gonadal tumors usually cause pseudoprecocious puberty with virilization or feminization. Hepatomas may rarely cause isosexual precocity. Reversible precocity with lactation and pituitary enlargement may be seen in juvenile hypothyroidism. The cause must be detected early since almost all children with precocious puberty will eventually be short or even dwarfed as a result of premature closure of the epiphyses, and because many of the responsible tumors are potentially malignant.

Sexual Infantilism & Delayed Puberty

It is often difficult to differentiate between simple functional delay of puberty (often a familial trait) and organic causes for such delays. Any type of gonadal or genetic defect may manifest itself primarily by failure of normal sexual development. Many patients grow to eunuchoid proportions, with span exceeding height. Consider hypothalamic lesions, craniopharyngioma, pituitary tumors, and defective testes or ovaries, and look for associated stigmas (webbed neck of Turner's syndrome, gynecomastia of Klinefelter's syndrome). Pituitary gonadotropin and urinary steroid excretion studies may help classify these disorders. Determine chromatin sex pattern on a buccal smear or by chromosomal analysis.

Lack of Potency & Libido in Males

Almost all cases are psychogenic in origin and are not helped by hormone therapy. Occasionally, however, lessening of sex desire or impairment of function may be the presenting sign of pituitary adenoma, Addison's disease, or testicular damage. The earlier in life the deficiency makes its appearance, the more pronounced is loss of libido associated with genital hypoplasia. Diabetes mellitus (especially with neuropathy) and thyrotoxicosis may first become manifest with this complaint. Chronic alcoholism, use of sedative and hypnotic drugs, and, occasionally, CNS lesions may be responsible. Be sure to rule out estrogenic or feminizing tumors of the testis or adrenal and search for other signs of feminization, such as gynecomastia. Most patients will require psychotherapy.

Cryptorchism

Failure of descent of the testes is often of great concern to parents, but it is not usually a medical problem since the testes, if present, will descend spontaneously at or shortly after puberty. They may descend after application of heat to the scrotum, as in a warm bath, which demonstrates that they are present and will later descend normally through an unimpeded passageway.

There is no agreement about when hormonal therapy should be instituted. If the testes are present, gonadotropic hormone will bring them down unless a hernia or blockage of the passageway prevents their descent. If there is doubt about whether the testes are present or not, determine urinary gonadotropin levels and obtain a buccal smear to determine the sex chromatin pattern.

Early surgical repair is advisable because intra-abdominal testes may later fail to produce sperm normally and because the incidence of malignancy in intra-abdominal testes is high. Cryptorchism may be associated with hypogonadism or may be part of pseudohermaphroditism.

Bone & Joint Pains & Pathologic Fractures

If the onset is at an early age and if there is a family history of similar disorders, consider osteogenesis imperfecta (look for blue scleras). Bowing of the bone and pseudofractures suggest rickets or osteomalacia, due either to intestinal or, more commonly, renal tubular disorders. If bone pain, bone cysts, and fractures are associated with renal stones, consider hyperparathyroidism. Back pain with involvement of the spine suggests osteoporosis, especially when it occurs after the menopause. Aches and pains in the extremities are suggestive of rickets or osteomalacia. Rule out metastatic tumors, multiple myeloma, and Paget's disease in elderly patients. Differentiate metabolic from nonmetabolic bone disorders. In doubtful cases, bone biopsy is indicated.

Renal Colic, Gravel & Stone Formation

A metabolic cause must be sought for recurrent stone formation and for kidney stones in children. If there is a family history, cystinuria and uric acid stones must be considered, or renal tubular acidosis with nephrocalcinosis. About 5% of stones are due to hyperparathyroidism, which must be ruled out in every instance of calcium stones. Look for bone disease, especially subperiosteal resorption of the bones of the fingers. Look also for signs of osteomalacia associated with excessive renal loss of calcium. Vitamin D intoxication, sarcoidosis, and excessive intake of milk and alkali must be considered. Any rapid bone breakdown may give rise to renal calcium stones, eg, in Paget's disease. Uric acid stones may occur in patients with gouty arthritis, but often they occur simply because the urinary pH is very acid; they occur also after any type of intensive therapy for leukemia or polycythemia. Primary hyperoxaluria is a rare cause of severe renal calcification and may be associated with deposition of oxalate in soft tissues (oxalosis). At times stones form in a structurally abnormal kidney (eg, medullary sponge kidney). Metabolic causes of renal stones must be corrected early before renal damage due to infection and obstruction occurs, since this may not be reversed upon removal of the initiating factor. The key to proper diagnosis is a careful stone analysis.

Tetany & Muscle Cramps

Mild tetany with paresthesias and muscle cramps is usually due to hyperventilation with alkalosis resulting from an anxiety state. If tetany occurs in children, rule out idiopathic hypoparathyroidism or pseudohypoparathyroidism. Look for calcification in the lens, poor teeth, and x-ray evidence of basal ganglia calcification. Consider latent hypoparathyroidism in the post-thyroidectomy patient. Tetany may be the presenting complaint of osteomalacia or rickets or of acute pancreatitis. Neonatal tetany is probably due to the high phosphate content of milk and relative hypoparathyroidism. A similar mechanism has been considered responsible for leg cramps during pregnancy. Neonatal tetany may rarely indicate maternal hyperparathyroidism. Severe hypocalcemic tetany will occasionally produce convulsions and must be differentiated from "idiopathic" epilepsy. Classical signs of tetany are Chvostek's sign and Trousseau's phenomenon. If associated with hypertension and polyuria, consider primary hyperaldosteronism. Leg cramps may occur in some diabetic patients. Magnesium deficiency must be considered in tetany unresponsive to calcium.

Mental Changes

Disturbances of mentation are often subtle and may be difficult to recognize, but they may be important indications of underlying endocrine disorders. Nervousness and excitability are characteristic of hyperthyroidism, pheochromocytoma, and hypoparathyroidism. Convulsions with abnormal EEG findings may occur in hypocalcemic tetany or in hypoglycemia, either spontaneously or induced by insulin. Islet cell tumors may cause sudden loss of consciousness, somnolence and prolonged lethargy, or coma. Diabetic acidosis may progress gradually into coma. Hypercalcemia leads to somnolence and lethargy, with marked weakness. Mental confusion may occur in hypopituitarism or Addison's disease or in long-standing myxedema. Mental deterioration is the rule in long-standing and untreated hypoparathyroidism and hypothyroidism (cretinism). Insomnia and psychosis are part of Cushing's syndrome, either spontaneous or induced. Early detection may prevent permanent brain damage. Mental deficiency may be associated with abnormal excretion of amino acids in the urine (eg, phenylketonuria) and with chromosomal abnormalities.

DISEASES OF
THE PITUITARY GLAND

PANHYPOPITUITARISM
& HYPOPITUITARY CACHEXIA
(Simmonds' Disease)

Essentials of Diagnosis

- Sexual dysfunction; weakness; lack of resistance to stress, cold, and fasting; axillary and pubic hair loss.
- Low blood pressure; may have visual field defects.
- All low: BMR, PBI, ^{131}I uptake, FSH, urinary 17-ketosteroids and corticosteroids, growth hormone.
- X-ray may reveal sellar lesion.

General Considerations

Hypopituitarism is a relatively rare disorder in which inactivity of the pituitary gland leads to insufficiency of the target organs. All or several of the tropic hormones may be involved. Isolated defects, eg, of the gonadotropins, are not rare. There is also great variation in the severity of the lesions, from those merely involving pathways (hypothalamic lesions) to almost complete destruction of the gland itself. The etiology of this disorder includes circulatory collapse due to hemorrhage following delivery and subsequent pituitary necrosis (Sheehan's syndrome), granulomas, hemochromatosis, cysts and tumors (Rathke's pouch cyst, chromophobe adenoma), surgical hypophysectomy, and functional hypopituitarism as seen in starvation and severe anemia. True pituitary cachexia (Simmonds' disease) is quite rare.

The pituitary tumor may be part of the syndrome of multiple endocrine adenomatosis. Isolated or partial deficiencies of anterior pituitary hormones may occur and may be detected by refined technics.

Clinical Findings

These vary with the degree of pituitary destruction, and are related to the lack of hormones from the "target" endocrine glands.

A. Symptoms and Signs: Weakness, lack of resistance to cold, to infections, and to fasting, and sexual dysfunction (lack of development of primary and secondary sex characteristics, or regression of function) are the most common symptoms. In expanding lesions of the sella, interference with the visual tracts may produce loss of temporal vision, whereas a craniopharyngioma may cause blindness. Short stature is the rule if the onset is during the growth period.

In both sexes there is sparseness or loss of axillary and pubic hair, and there may be thinning of the eyebrows and of the head hair, which is often silky.

The skin is almost always dry, with lack of sweating, has a peculiar pallor, and is sallow ("fawn"-colored). Pigmentation is lacking even after exposure to sunlight. Fine wrinkles are seen, and the facies present a "sleepy appearance."

The heart is small and the blood pressure low. Orthostatic hypotension is often present. Cerebrovascular symptoms may be present. Abnormal lactation may occur.

B. Laboratory Findings: The fasting blood sugar is usually low with a flat glucose tolerance curve. The insulin tolerance test (use only 0.05 units/kg IV) shows insulin sensitivity and is dangerous in these patients since severe reactions may occur. The BMR is usually low. The PBI level is low normal. Radioactive iodine uptake is low, with a rise following TSH (this does not occur in primary myxedema). Urinary 17-ketosteroids and corticosteroids are low, but rise slowly after corticotropin administration (this does not occur in primary Addison's disease). Both TSH and corticotropin may have to be given for several days. The metyrapone (Metopirone®) test has been used to demonstrate limited pituitary reserve. Urinary gonadotropins (FSH) are very low, usually less than 3 mouse units/24 hours. Anemia is common. Direct assay of growth hormone levels in blood by immunochemical methods, when available, shows low levels with little response to insulin hypoglycemia or to arginine infusion (see Merimee reference, below). ACTH, TSH, LH, and FSH levels are low.

C. X-Ray Findings: X-rays of skull may show a lesion in or above the sella. In growing children one may find delay in bone age.

D. Eye Examination: Visual field defects may be present.

Differential Diagnosis

The most difficult problem is differentiation from anorexia nervosa, which may simulate hypopituitarism. In fact, severe malnutrition may give rise to functional hypopituitarism. By and large, cachexia is far more common in anorexia nervosa, and loss of axillary and pubic hair is rare; at times mild facial and body hirsutism is seen in anorexia nervosa. The 17-ketosteroids are low normal or not as low as in hypopituitarism, and may respond rapidly to corticotropin stimulation, and the urinary gonadotropins are usually present at levels of 3 mouse units/24 hours. Recently, direct pituitary growth hormone assays have shown high levels in anorexia nervosa and very low levels in hypopituitarism. The response to diet and psychotherapy at times settles the diagnosis.

Primary Addison's disease and primary myxedema are at times difficult to differentiate from pituitary insufficiency, but the response to corticotropin and TSH often helps. Direct radioimmune assay of ACTH and TSH, if available, is a more direct diagnostic method.

The enlargement of the sella may require pneumoencephalograms to rule out the "empty sella syndrome," where minimal or few endocrine abnormalities are present and radiation is contraindicated (see Caplan reference, below).

At times hypopituitarism may masquerade as "nephrosis" or as "pernicious anemia."

The severe hypoglycemia after fasting may cause confusion with hyperinsulinism.

The mental changes of hypopituitarism may be mistaken for a primary psychosis.

Complications

In addition to those of the primary lesion (eg, tumor), complications may develop at any time as a result of the patient's inability to cope with minor stressful situations. This may lead to high fever, shock, coma, and death. Sensitivity to thyroid may precipitate an adrenal crisis when thyroid is administered. Corticosteroids may cause psychosis.

Treatment

The pituitary lesion, if a tumor, is treated by surgical removal, x-ray irradiation, or both. Endocrine substitution therapy must be used before, during, and almost always permanently after such procedures.

With the exception of corticotropin, there is no readily available effective pituitary replacement preparation; therapy must therefore be aimed at correcting the end-organ deficiencies. This must be continued throughout life. Almost complete replacement therapy can be carried out with corticosteroids, thyroid, and sex steroids.

A. Corticosteroids: Give hydrocortisone, 20–30 mg orally daily in divided doses. Since edema is common with corticosteroid treatment, prednisolone or dexamethasone (Decadron®) is often preferable. Give prednisolone, 5–7.5 mg orally daily in divided doses, or dexamethasone, 0.5–1 mg orally daily in divided doses. Additional amounts of rapid-acting corticosteroids must be given during states of stress, eg, during infection or in preparation for surgery.

B. Thyroid: Thyroid (and insulin) should rarely, if ever, be used in panhypopituitarism unless the patient is receiving corticosteroids. Because of lack of adrenal function, patients are exceedingly sensitive to these drugs. For this reason one should exercise special care in differentiating primary myxedema from hypopituitarism—often a difficult problem.

Begin with small doses of thyroid, eg, 15–30 mg (¼–½ gr) daily, and gradually increase to tolerance: 60–120 mg (1–2 gr) is usually adequate. L-Thyroxine, 0.1–0.3 mg daily, may be preferred.

C. Sex Hormones:

1. Testosterone or one of the newer anabolic steroids may be used in males and at times also in females, primarily for their tissue building (protein anabolic) effect. For males give one of the longer-acting parenteral testosterone preparations every 3–4 weeks; or methyltestosterone, 10–20 mg orally daily. In females the dosage of these drugs is ½ that for males. If signs of virilizing action appear in the female, the drug should be withdrawn and they will lessen. They do not usually occur if the dose of methyltestosterone is kept under 300 mg/month. Fluoxymesterone may be given in doses of 2–10 mg orally daily.

2. Estrogens are useful in the female for their mild anabolic effect, their effect on secondary sex characteristics, and their possible neutralizing effect on androgens. Give diethylstilbestrol, 0.5–1 mg daily orally; ethinyl estradiol, 0.02–0.05 mg daily orally; or conjugated estrogenic substances (eg, Premarin®), 0.625–1.25 mg daily orally. Omit treatment for one week each month.

3. Chorionic gonadotropic hormone (APL®) in combination with human pituitary FSH or postmenopausal urinary gonadotropin may be used in an attempt to produce fertility.

Note: Sex hormones, especially estrogens, should be employed cautiously in young patients with panhypopituitarism or the epiphyses will close before maximum growth is achieved. Most androgens, with the possible exception of fluoxymesterone, also share this property—especially when given in large doses.

D. Human Growth Hormone: This hormone is by far the most effective agent for increasing height, but it is available for only a few patients. Human placental lactogen is under investigation as a pituitary growth hormone substitute. A better understanding of growth hormone releasing factors may offer alternative forms of treatment in the future (see Van der Laan reference, below).

Prognosis

This depends on the primary cause. If it is due to postpartum necrosis (Sheehan's syndrome), partial or even complete recovery may occur. Functional hypopituitarism due to starvation and similar causes may also be corrected.

If the gland has become permanently destroyed the problem is to replace target hormones, since replacement with pituitary tropic hormones is not yet feasible. It is possible to prolong life if states of stress such as starvation, infection, or trauma are treated with prompt and adequate replacement therapy. If the onset of the disease is in childhood, the patient's ultimate height will be subnormal unless human growth hormone is used. Surgical procedures, eg, hypophysectomy to preserve vision in chromophobe adenomas, have become safer since the advent of corticosteroids.

Brasel, J.A., & others: An evaluation of 75 patients with hypopituitarism beginning in childhood. Am J Med 38:484–498, 1965.

Brown, J., & others: Purified human pituitary hormones: Treatment of pituitary insufficiency. Ann Int Med 66:594, 1967.

Caplan, R.H., & G.D. Dobben: Endocrine studies in patients with "empty sella syndrome." Arch Int Med 123:611–619, 1969.

Catt, K.C.: ABC of endocrinology. II. Pituitary function. Lancet 1:827, 1970.

Espinosa, R.E., & R.V. Randall: Early symptoms and signs of chromophobe adenoma. M Clin North America 52:827–834, 1968.

Friesen, H., & E.B. Astwood: Hormones of the anterior pituitary body. New England J Med 272:1216–1223, 1272–1277, 1328–1335, 1965.

Gemzell, C., & P. Roos: Pregnancies following treatment with human gonadotropins. Am J Obst Gynec 94:490–496, 1966.

Goodman, H.G., & others: Growth and growth hormone. New England J Med 278:57, 1968.

Grumbach, M.M.: Growth hormone and growth. Pediatrics 37:245–248, 1966.

Guillemin, R.: The adenohypophysis and its hypothalamic control. Ann Rev Physiol 29:313, 1967.

Henneman, P.H.: Human growth hormone and hypopituitarism. JAMA 205:828–836, 1968.

Merimee, T.J., & others: Plasma growth hormone after arginine infusion. New England J Med 276:434–438, 1967.

Moe, P.J.: Hypopituitary dwarfism. The importance of early therapy. Acta paediat scandinav 57:300–304, 1968.

Odell, W.D.: Isolated deficiencies of anterior pituitary hormones. JAMA 197:1006, 1966.

Peake, G.T., & W.H. Daughaday: Disturbances of pituitary function in central nervous system disease. M Clin North America 52:357–370, 1968.

Seidensticker, J.F., & M. Tzagournis: Anorexia nervosa—clinical features and long-term follow-up. J Chronic Dis 21:361–368, 1968.

Sheehan, H.L., & J.C. Davis: Pituitary necrosis. Brit M Bull 24:59–70, 1968.

Sheline, G.E., Boldrey, E.B., & T.L. Phillips: Chromophobe adenomas of the pituitary gland. Am J Roentgenol 92:160, 1964.

Sonenberg, M. (editor): Growth hormone. Ann New York Acad Sc 148:289, 1968.

Stocks, A.E., & F.I.R. Martin: Pituitary in haemochromatosis. Am J Med 45:839–845, 1968.

Van der Laan, W.P.: Changing concepts in the control of growth hormone secretion in man. California Med 115:38–46, Aug 1971.

HYPERPITUITARISM
(Eosinophilic Adenoma of the Anterior Pituitary)
GIGANTISM & ACROMEGALY

Essentials of Diagnosis

- Excessive growth of hands (increased glove size), feet (increased shoe size), jaw (protrusion of lower jaw), and internal organs; or gigantism before closure of epiphyses.
- Amenorrhea, headaches, visual field loss, sweating, weakness.
- Elevated serum inorganic phosphorus and BMR; PBI normal; glycosuria.
- Elevated serum growth hormone with failure to suppress after glucose.
- X-Ray: Sellar enlargement and terminal phalangeal "tufting." Increased heel pad.

General Considerations

An excessive amount of growth hormone, presumably due to overactivity of the eosinophilic portion of the anterior lobe of the pituitary, is most often produced by a benign adenoma. The tumor may be small or, rarely, located within the sinuses rather than within the sella. The disease may be associated with adenomas elsewhere, such as in the parathyroids or pancreas. Carcinoid tumors may be associated with acromegaly. If the onset is before closure of the epiphyses, gigantism will result. If the epiphyses have already closed at onset, only overgrowth of soft tissues and terminal skeletal structures (acromegaly) results. At times the disease is transient ("fugitive acromegaly").

Clinical Findings

A. Symptoms and Signs: Crowding of other hormone-producing cells, especially those concerned with gonadotropic hormones, causes amenorrhea and loss of libido. Production of excessive growth hormone causes doughy enlargement of the hands with spade-like fingers, large feet, jaw, face, tongue, and internal organs, wide spacing of the teeth, and an oily, tough, "furrowed" skin with multiple fleshy tumors (mollusca). Hoarse voice is common. At times, acanthosis nigricans is present. Pressure of the pituitary tumor causes headache, bitemporal hemianopsia, lethargy, and diplopia. In long-standing cases secondary hormonal changes take place, including diabetes mellitus, goiter, and abnormal lactation. Less commonly, these may be the presenting picture in acromegaly. Excessive sweating may be the most reliable sign of activity of the disease.

B. Laboratory Findings: Serum inorganic phosphorus may be elevated (over 4.5 mg/100 ml) during the active phase of acromegaly. The urinary FSH level is usually low, but it may be normal or even high. Glycosuria and hyperglycemia may be present, and there is resistance to the administration of insulin. Hypercalciuria is common. The BMR may be elevated. The PBI may be normal and may not fall after antithyroid medication. 17-Ketosteroids and hydroxycorticosteroids may be high or low, depending upon the stage of the disease. Immunologic assay for growth hormone in blood, if available, shows high levels in the active phase of the disease; administration of glucose, unlike in normal individuals, fails to suppress the serum level.

C. X-Ray Findings: X-ray of the skull may show a large sella with destroyed clinoids, but a sella of usual size does not rule out the diagnosis. The frontal sinuses may be large. One may also demonstrate thickening of the skull and long bones, with typical overgrowth of vertebral bodies and severe spur formation. Dorsal kyphosis is common. Typical "tufting" of the terminal phalanges of the fingers and toes may be demonstrated. A lateral view of the feet demonstrates increased thickness of the heel pad.

D. Eye Examination: Visual field examination may show bitemporal hemianopsia.

Differential Diagnosis

Hyperpituitarism is to be considered if there is rapid growth or resumption of growth once stopped (eg, change in shoe size or ring size). Suspect the diagnosis also in unexplained amenorrhea, insulin-resistant diabetes mellitus, or goiter with elevated BMR which does not respond to antithyroid drugs. Physiologic spurts of growth and increase in tissue size from exercise, weight gain, or from certain occupations enter into the differential diagnosis. The syndrome of cerebral gigantism with mental retardation and ventricular dilatation but normal growth hormone levels resembles acromegalic gigantism. Myxedema and, rarely, pachydermoperiostitis may resemble acromegaly. Serial photographs are of help in differentiating familial nonendocrine gigantism and facial enlargement.

Complications

Complications include pressure of the tumor on surrounding structures, rupture of the tumor into the brain or sinuses, the complications of diabetes, cardiac enlargement, and cardiac failure. The carpal tunnel syndrome, due to compression of the median nerve at the wrist, may cause disability of the hand. Cord compression due to large intervertebral disks may be seen.

Treatment

The treatment of choice of active tumors without visual field loss used to be pituitary irradiation, with or without the use of sex hormones. If visual fields are markedly reduced, x-ray therapy may be hazardous and surgery is the treatment of choice. The recent finding that conventional x-ray treatment causes a slow fall in growth hormone level favors heavy particle irradiation or surgical hypophysectomy in the future. The simpler cryohypophysectomy has been shown to be an effective and safe procedure. Periodic reassessment of pituitary function after these procedures is advisable. In the "burnt out" case, hormonal replacement as for hypopituitarism is required. Medical treatment of active acromegaly with progesterone and chlorpromazine must be considered experimental and requires long-term evaluation.

Prognosis

Prognosis depends upon the age at onset and, more particularly, the age at which therapy is begun. Menstrual function may be restored. Severe headaches may persist even after treatment. Secondary tissue and skeletal changes do not respond completely to removal of the tumor. The diabetes may be permanent in spite of adequate pituitary ablation. The patient may succumb to the cardiovascular complications. The tumor may "burn out," causing symptoms of hypopituitarism.

Adams, J.E., & others: Transsphenoidal cryohypophysectomy in acromegaly: Clinical and endocrinological evaluation. J Neurosurg 28:100–104, 1968.

Catt, K.J.: ABC of endocrinology. III. Growth hormone. Lancet 1:933, 1970.

Earll, J.M., & others: Glucose suppression of serum growth hormone in the diagnosis of acromegaly. JAMA 201:628, 1967.

Fraser, R., & A.D. Wright: Standard procedures for assessing hypersecretion or secretory capacity for human growth hormone, using the radioimmunoassay. Postgrad MJ 44:53–57, 1968.

Kjellberg, R.N., & others: Proton-beam therapy in acromegaly. New England J Med 278:689–694, 1968.

Kolodny, H.D., & others: Acromegaly treated with chlorpromazine. New England J Med 284:819–822, 1971.

Kozak, G.P., & others: Acromegaly pre- and postpituitary irradiation. Metabolism 15:290–303, 1966.

Lawrence, A.M., & H. Kirstens: Progestins in the medical management of active acromegaly. J Clin Endocrinol 30:646, 1970.

Lopis, S., Rubenstein, A.H., & A.D. Wright: Measurement of serum growth hormone and insulin in gigantism. J Clin Endocrinol 28:393–398, 1968.

McMillan, D.E., & others: Evaluation of clinical activity of acromegaly by observation of the diurnal variation of serum inorganic phosphate. Metabolism 17:966–976, 1968.

Roth, J., & others: Acromegaly and other disorders of growth hormone secretion. Ann Int Med 66:760, 1967.

Stephenson, J.N., & others: Cerebral gigantism. Pediatrics 41:130–138, 1968.

Taylor, A.L., & others: Pituitary apoplexy in acromegaly. J Clin Endocrinol 28:1784–1792, 1968.

Wright, A.D., & others: Mortality in acromegaly. Quart J Med 39:1, 1970.

DIABETES INSIPIDUS

Essentials of Diagnosis

- Polydipsia (4–40 liters/day); excessive polyuria.
- Urine sp gr < 1.006.
- Inability to concentrate urine on fluid restriction. Hyperosmolarity of plasma.
- Vasopressin reduces urine output.

General Considerations

Diabetes insipidus is an uncommon disease of young adults (particularly males) which is characterized by an increase in thirst and the passage of large quantities of urine of a low specific gravity. The urine is otherwise normal. The disease may occur acutely, eg, after head trauma or surgical procedures near the pituitary region, or may be chronic and insidious in onset. It is due to insufficiency of the posterior pituitary or impaired function of the supraoptic pathways which regulate water metabolism. More rarely, it is due to unresponsiveness of the kidney to vasopressin (Pitressin®) (nephrogenic diabetes insipidus).

The causes may be classified as follows:

A. Due to Deficiency of Vasopressin:

1. Primary diabetes insipidus, due to a defect inherent in the gland itself (where no organic lesion is demonstrable), may be familial, occurring as a dominant trait; or, more commonly, sporadic or "idiopathic."

2. Secondary diabetes insipidus is due to destruction of the functional unit by trauma, infection (eg, encephalitis, tuberculosis, syphilis), primary tumor or metastatic tumors from the breast or lung (common), vascular accidents (rare), and xanthomatosis (eosinophilic granuloma of Hand-Schüller-Christian disease).

B. "Nephrogenic" Diabetes Insipidus: This disorder is due to a defect in the kidney tubules which interferes with water reabsorption and occurs as a sex-linked, recessive trait. Patients with this type of the disease are the so-called "water babies." At times this type is acquired, eg, after pyelonephritis, potassium depletion, or amyloidosis. The disease is unresponsive to vasopressin.

Clinical Findings

A. Symptoms and Signs: The outstanding signs and symptoms of the disease are intense thirst, especially with a craving for ice water, and polyuria, the volume of ingested fluid varying from 4–40 liters daily, with correspondingly large urine volumes. Restriction of fluids causes marked weight loss, dehydration, headache, irritability, fatigue, muscular pains, hypothermia, and tachycardia.

B. Laboratory Findings: A polyuria of over 6 liters/day with a specific gravity below 1.006 is highly suggestive of diabetes insipidus, and a specific gravity of 1.015 or higher after fluid restriction rules out the disease. Special tests have been devised to distinguish true diabetes insipidus from psychogenic diabetes insipidus (Hickey-Hare and Carter-Robbins tests). The latter will respond (with reduction in urine flow and increase in urinary specific gravity) to administration of hypertonic (3%) saline solution; true diabetes insipidus does not. Although a positive response tends to rule out true diabetes insipidus, a negative result must be followed by careful prolonged dehydration and measurement of both urine and plasma osmolality and body weight under hospital conditions. Failure to respond to vasopressin (Pitressin®) indicates "nephrogenic" diabetes insipidus if the serum calcium and potassium levels are normal.

If true primary diabetes insipidus seems likely on the basis of these tests, search for a possible brain lesion with x-rays of the skull, visual field tests, and encephalograms. Search also for associated bone lesions of xanthomatosis and obtain biopsy for confirmation. Look for a primary tumor in the lung or breast. In nephrogenic diabetes insipidus, rule out pyelonephritis or hydronephrosis.

Differential Diagnosis

The most important differentiation is from the "psychogenic" water habit (see above). Polydipsia and polyuria may also be seen in diabetes mellitus, chronic nephritis, hypokalemia (eg, in primary hyperaldosteronism), and in hypercalcemic states such as hyperparathyroidism. The low fixed specific gravity of the urine in chronic nephritis does not rise after administration of vasopressin. On the other hand, in spite of the inability of patients with diabetes insipidus to concentrate urine, other tests of renal function yield essentially normal results (the NPN may even be below normal).

Complications

If water is not readily available the excessive output of urine will lead to severe dehydration, which rarely proceeds to a state of vasomotor collapse and shock. Insomnia and dysphagia may occur. All the complications of the primary disease may eventually become evident.

Treatment

A. Specific Measures: Vasopressin tannate (Pitressin Tannate®), 0.5–1 ml in oil IM, is the standard treatment. It is effective for 24–72 hours. It is usually best to administer the drug in the evening so that maximal results can be obtained during sleep. Patients learn to administer the drug themselves, and the dosage is adjusted as necessary. Warn the patient to shake well before filling the syringe. Posterior pituitary snuff inhaled 2–3 times a day may be used and is the most economical form of treatment, but it may be quite irritating and absorption is uncertain. The dose varies from 30–60 mg. Aqueous vasopressin injection is rarely used in continuous treatment because of its short duration of action (1–4 hours). An occasional patient is allergic to animal vasopressin; a synthetic substitute, lysine-8 vasopressin, is available as a nasal spray (lypressin [Diapid®]). This form of treatment may be preferred by patients with mild disease. It is free of local side-effects, and water intoxication, which is not unusual with vasopressin tannate in oil, does not occur.

B. Other Measures: Mild cases (or vasopressin-resistant cases) require no treatment other than adequate fluid intake. Hydrochlorothiazide (Hydrodiuril®), 50–100 mg/day (with KCl), is of some help in reducing the urine volume of true or nephrogenic diabetes insipidus. Chlorpropamide (Diabinese®) has been found to be an effective antidiuretic and may be tried in mild cases or to potentiate the action of vasopressin. After an initial dose of 250 mg twice daily, many patients can be maintained on 125–250 mg daily. Side-effects include nausea, skin allergy, hypoglycemia, and a disulfiram-like reaction to alcohol. Phenformin (DBI) is a less effective antidiuretic agent in doses of 50 mg once or twice daily. Solute restriction may be of additional help. Psychotherapy is required for most patients with compulsive water drinking.

C. X-Ray Therapy: This may be used in the treatment of some cases due to tumor (eg, eosinophilic granuloma).

Prognosis

Diabetes insipidus may be latent, especially if there is associated lack of anterior pituitary function;

and may be transient, eg, following head trauma. The ultimate prognosis is essentially that of the underlying disorder. Since many cases are associated with organic brain disease, the prognosis is often poor. Surgical correction of the primary brain lesion rarely alters the diabetes insipidus.

If the disease is due to an eosinophilic granuloma of the skull, temporary amelioration or even complete cure may be effected with x-ray therapy.

The prognosis of the "nephrogenic" type is only fair since intercurrent infections are common, especially in infants affected with the disease. The acquired forms of this type may be reversible—eg, if urinary tract infection or obstruction is alleviated.

Abelson, H.: Nephrogenic diabetes insipidus. Pediat Res 2:271–282, 1968.

Cushard, W.G., & others: Oral therapy of diabetes insipidus with chlorpropamide. California Med 115:1–5, August 1971.

DeWardener, H.E.: Polyuria. J Chronic Dis 11:199, 1960.

Ettinger, B., & P.H. Forsham: Mechanism of chlorpropamide antidiuresis in diabetes insipidus. J Clin Endocrinol 31:552–555, 1970.

Mimica, N., Wegienka, L.C., & P.H. Forsham: Lypressin nasal spray. JAMA 203:802–803, 1968.

Reforzo-Membrives, J., & others: Antidiuretic effect of 1–propyl-3-p-chlorobenzene-sulfonylurea (Chlorpropamide®). J Clin Endocrinol 28:332–336, 1968.

Schwartz, I.L., & W.B. Schwartz: Symposium on antidiuretic hormones. Am J Med 42:651, 1967.

Utiger, R.D.: Disorders of antidiuretic hormone secretion. M Clin North America 52:381–392, 1968.

Webster, B., & J. Bain: Antidiuretic effect and complications of chlorpropamide therapy in diabetes insipidus. J Clin Endocrinol 30:215, 1970.

INAPPROPRIATE SECRETION OF ANTIDIURETIC HORMONE

This syndrome, which is essentially water intoxication, consists of irritability, lethargy, confusion, and seizures. It may lead to coma and death if not recognized. Manifestations include hyponatremia and hypoosmolarity of the serum, continued renal excretion of sodium, formation of hyperosmolar urine, and expanded fluid volume. Adrenal and renal function are usually normal. It is most commonly caused by oat cell bronchogenic carcinoma, but may also be present in pulmonary tuberculosis, porphyria, myxedema, and CNS disorders. It may be induced by chlorpropamide.

Treatment is best accomplished by water restriction, which succeeds if the syndrome is recognized early. A search for the primary cause of the disorder must also be undertaken. Prognosis is usually poor because of the advanced stage of the syndrome at the time of recognition and the serious primary disorder causing it.

Bartter, F.L., & W.B. Schwartz: The syndrome of inappropriate secretion of antidiuretic hormone. Am J Med 42:790, 1967.

Ivy, H.K.: The syndrome of inappropriate secretion of antidiuretic hormone. M Clin North America 52:817–826, 1968.

Nolph, K.D., & R.W. Schrier: Sodium, potassium and water metabolism in the syndrome of inappropriate antidiuretic hormone secretion. Am J Med 49:534–545, 1970.

Vorherr, H., & others: Antidiuretic principle in malignant tumor extracts from patients with inappropriate ADH syndrome. J Clin Endocrinol 28:162–168, 1968.

Weissman, P.N., Shenkman, L., & R.I. Gregerman: Chlorpropamide hyponatremia: Drug-induced inappropriate ADH activity. New England J Med 284:65–71, 1971.

Wessler, S., & L.V. Avioli: Inappropriate antidiuretic hormone. JAMA 205:349–355, 1968.

DISEASES OF THE THYROID GLAND

Thyroid hormone affects cellular oxidative processes throughout the body. It is normally elaborated within the follicles of the gland by a combination of inorganic iodine, which is trapped by the gland under the influence of pituitary TSH, and tyrosine, forming monoiodotyrosine and diiodotyrosine, which further combine to form thyroxine and triiodothyronine (T_3), the principal hormones of the gland. The "storage" form of the hormone is thyroglobulin, a combination of thyroxine and thyroid globulin, and it is in this colloidal form that the hormone is found within the follicles.

Under the influence of TSH, the active hormones are released from the gland as the need arises. Circulating thyroxine is bound to plasma proteins, primarily thyroxine-binding globulins, and prealbumin. They can be measured as "protein-bound" iodine (PBI), the normal levels ranging from 4–8 μg/100 ml. High levels of estrogen (eg, in pregnancy or in women taking oral contraceptives) increase the thyroxine-binding globulin levels and thus also the PBI. The binding can be inhibited by certain compounds, eg, diphenylhydantoin and aspirin, which lower the PBI. The free (unbound) levels of circulating hormones regulate TSH release. Recently, the hypothalamic TSH-releasing factor (TRF), a tripeptide, has been isolated and synthesized.

The requirements for iodine are minimal (about 20–200 μg/day), but if a true deficiency arises or if the demand for iodine is increased (eg, during puberty), hormone production will be insufficient and circulating levels will be low. This leads to increase in pituitary TSH output, and hyperplasia of the thyroid gland follows.

Thyroid disorders may occur with or without diffuse or nodular enlargement of the gland (goiter). Symptoms may be due to pressure alone or to hyperfunction or hypofunction.

Since thyroid hormone affects all vital processes of the body, the time of onset of a deficiency state is most important in mental and physical development. Prolonged insufficiency which is present since infancy (cretinism) causes irreversible changes. Milder degrees of hypofunction, especially in adults, may go unrecognized or may masquerade as symptoms of disease of another system, eg, menorrhagia. Diagnosis will then depend to a large extent upon laboratory aids.

In any age group, whenever an isolated thyroid nodule is felt which is not associated with hyperfunction or hypofunction—and especially if there is any change in size of the nodule—the possibility of neoplasm must be considered.

Catt, K.J.: ABC of endocrinology. VI. The thyroid gland. Lancet 1:1383, 1970.

Means, J.H., De Groot, L.J., & J.B. Stanbury: *The Thyroid and Its Disorders.* McGraw-Hill, 1963.

Pittman, J.A. (editor): Treatment of thyroid disease. Mod Treat 6:441–549, 1969.

Selenkow, H.A., & F. Hoffman (editors): *Diagnosis and Treatment of Common Thyroid Diseases.* Excerpta Medica, International Congress Series No. 227, 1971.

Werner, S.C., & J.A. Nauman: The thyroid. Ann Rev Physiol 30:213, 1968.

TESTS OF THYROID FUNCTION

Basal Metabolic Rate (BMR). (With or without sedation. Rarely used today.)

Normal: ± 20%.

A. Elevated:

1. Markedly elevated—Hyperthyroidism, polycythemia, leukemia, pheochromocytoma.

2. Moderately elevated—Hyperthyroidism, anemia, congestive heart failure, Paget's disease, gigantism and acromegaly, malignancy, pregnancy, drugs (eg, caffeine).

3. Slightly elevated—Febrile illnesses (7% per degree F above normal), anxiety.

B. Low: Myxedema (−30% to −60%). Low rates are also found in panhypopituitarism, Addison's disease, anorexia nervosa, chronic debility, starvation, and also at times in nephrosis.

Protein-Bound Iodine (PBI, "Hormonal Iodine")

Normal: 4–8 μg/100 ml serum.

A. Elevated: In hyperthyroidism, thyroiditis, and due to administration of iodides, desiccated thyroid, or

TABLE 18–1. Usual test results in thyroid & other disorders.*

Condition	BMR	^{131}I Uptake	PBI	T_3 Test	Other Useful Tests
Diffuse toxic goiter	H	H	H	H	Suppression test negative
Toxic nodular goiter	H	H or N	H	H	Suppression test negative
Pregnancy	H	H	H	L	Suppression test normal
T_4 toxic factitia	H	L	H	H	
T_3 toxic factitia	H	L	L	H	
TSH injection	H	H	H	H	
Primary hypothyroidism	L	L	L	L	TSH test negative
Pituitary hypothyroidism	L	L	L	L	TSH test positive
Subacute thyroiditis	H or N	L	H	H or N	TSH test negative; antibody test positive
Hashimoto's thyroiditis	H or L	N or H	N or L	H or N	Perchlorate and antibody tests positive
Riedel's struma (early)	N	N	N	N	
Riedel's struma (late)	L	L	L	L	TSH test negative
Thyroid cancer	N	N	N	N	TSH and suppression tests normal
Nontoxic goiter	N	N or H	N or L	N	Suppression test usually normal
Goitrous cretinism	L	H	L	L	Perchlorate test may be positive
"Hot" nodule in euthyroidism	N	H	N	N	Scintigram, suppression test negative
Antithyroid treatment	H, N, L	L	H, N, L	H, N, L	
Post-methimazole rebound	N	H	N	N	
Cirrhosis	N	N or H	L, N, H	N or H	
Uremia	N	L, N, H	N	N	
Mercurial (diuretic)	N	N	L	N	
Iodide compounds	N	L	H	N	
Antiovulatory drugs or hyperestrogenic states	N	N	H	L	

*Modified and reproduced, with permission, from Williams: *Textbook of Endocrinology*, 4th ed. Saunders, 1968. N = Normal; H = High; L = Low.

TABLE 18−2. Effect of common drugs on 3 thyroid tests.*

Drug	Duration of Interference	Effect on Test Values		
		PBI	^{131}I	T₃
Adrenocortical steroids and corticotropin	Rare interference for 3−7 days following a dose exceeding 100 mg/day of cortisone equivalents	Decr	Decr	None
Anticoagulants (coumarin derivatives)		None	None	Incr
Antithyroid drugs (thioureas, thiocyanates, perchlorates)		Decr	Decr	Decr (thioureas only)
Antituberculosis drugs		None	Decr	None
Cobalt		None	Decr	None
Diphenylhydantoin sodium	Exceeding 1 week	Decr	None	Incr
All estrogens, including oral contraceptives		Incr	None	Decr
Gold salts		Incr	None	None
Iodine-containing agents Topical iodine (antiseptics, iodoform gauze, suntan lotion, ointments, iodo-chlorhydroxyquin suppositories)		Incr	None	None
Inorganic iodides (cough syrup in large doses, NaCl substi-tutes, asthma medicine, amebicides, some penicillin preparations, some vitamin tablets)	Up to 10 weeks following dose of 125−600 µg/day; up to 4 months following dose ex-ceeding 3000 µg/day	Incr	Decr	None
Organic iodinated compounds Short life: Most IV radio-contrast media (eg, iodo-pyracet, iopanoic acid)	3−8 days	Incr	Decr	Incr (ipodate only)
Intermediate life: Most common gallbladder con-trast media (eg, iodo-alphionic acid)	6−12 weeks			
Long life (eg, ethyl iodo-phenylundecylate, Lipiodol®)	Years			
Mercurials		Decr	None	None
Perphenazine		Incr	None	None
Phenylbutazone		None	Decr	Incr
Resorcinol		None	Decr	None
Salicylates (large doses)		Decr	None	Incr
Testosterone		Decr	None	Incr
Thyroid hormone drugs Levothyroxine		Incr	Decr	Incr
Liothyronine		Decr	Decr	Incr
Thyroglobulin		Incr	Decr	Incr
Thyroid-stimulating hormone (TSH)		None	Incr	None

*Reproduced, with permission, from S. Borushek: Consultant, March 1967.

thyroxine. Inorganic iodides increase levels for up to 3 weeks; organic iodides (eg, in urograms, cholecysto-grams) for 6 months or longer; oil-soluble organic iodides (eg, Lipiodol®) for months to years. Pregnancy and Enovid® or similar preparations raise the PBI due to increased thyroxine-binding protein.

B. Low: Hypothyroidism. Falsely low levels may be due to mercurial diuretics (low for 3−7 days), uri-nary loss of protein (eg, in nephrosis), or T₃ (Cyto-mel®) administration.

The **BEI (butanol-extractable iodine) test** roughly parallels the PBI and is not affected by inorganic iodides. It is, however, raised by organic iodides. Nor-mal: 3−7 µg/100 ml.

A large discrepancy between the PBI and BEI sug-gests the presence of abnormal iodoproteins, as seen in certain types of goiter.

Thyroxine-iodine by column chromatography and T_4 by binding displacement (T_4D or TT_4; not generally available) are more direct measures of circulating T_4. Normal range: $3-7.5$ $\mu g/100$ ml.

"Free" thyroxine determination measures the metabolically effective fraction of circulating T_4. Normal range: $1.4-3.5$ ng/100 ml.

Radioiodine (^{131}I) Uptake of Thyroid Gland

Normal: $10-40\%$ in 24 hours.

A. Elevated: Thyrotoxicosis, hypofunctioning large goiter, iodine lack.

B. Low: Administration of iodides (similar to factors raising the PBI), T_4, antithyroid drugs, thyroiditis, myxedema, hypothyroidism.

A scintigram over the gland outlines areas of increased and decreased activity. If the uptake of ^{131}I is blocked, technetium may be used to obtain a scintigram. Suppression of uptake after administration of 75 μg of T_3 daily for several days will determine if the area in the gland is autonomous or TSH-dependent. Administration of TSH for 2 or more days, with increase in ^{131}I uptake over low control levels, indicates the presence of thyroid tissue, and hence shows that low uptake was due to lack of TSH.

Radioactive T_3 Uptake of Red Cells or Resin

Normal (varies with methods): Red cells—males, $12-19\%$; females, $13-20\%$. Resin—males, $25-35\%$; females, $24-34\%$.

This test is not dependent upon exogenous organic or inorganic iodides. It is an indirect measure of thryoxine-binding protein which is of value in certain patients, eg, in pregnancy when the PBI is falsely high due to increased thyroxine-binding while T_3 uptake is low. In general, T_3 uptake parallels the PBI except in the rare euthyroid patient with deficient thyroxine-binding protein, where the PBI is low but the T_3 uptake normal or high. A combination of this test and the PBI may be of greater value. (See Clark reference, below.) The **free thyroxine index** is a measurement of the product of T_4 and resin T_3 uptake. This corrects for abnormalities of thyroxine binding. Normal: $0.75-2.6$. (See Anderson reference, below).

The more direct tests are subject to technical variables. They should be used when the more standard tests do not give decisive information, since many drugs cause interference with these thyroid tests (Table 18–2).

Serum Cholesterol

Normal: $150-280$ mg/100 ml.

A. Relatively Elevated: Myxedema. Hypothyroidism.

B. Relatively Low: Thyrotoxicosis (occasionally).

This test is nonspecific, as many factors may influence cholesterol level.

The absolute level is less significant than the change after institution of therapy.

Achilles Tendon Reflex (Photomotograph)

The relaxation time is often prolonged in hypothyroidism, but also in pregnancy, diabetes, etc. It is rapid in hyperthyroidism. The test may be of value in following response to therapy. Normal range: $240-380$ msec.

Serologic Tests

Antibodies against several thyroid constituents may be found in the sera of patients with various types of thyroiditis (especially Hashimoto's disease) and, at times, in adenomatous goiters, in myxedema, and, rarely, in Graves' disease and thyroid carcinoma.

Miscellaneous Tests

More sophisticated tests may at times be performed. Many are still mainly research tools. Among them are the thyroid-binding globulin test and assay of thyroid stimulating hormone (TSH) or long-acting thyroid stimulator (LATS) in serum.

Anderson, B.G.: Free thyroxine in serum and thyroid function. JAMA 203:577–582, 1968.

Beall, G.N., & D.H. Solomon: LATS and thyroid autoantibodies. Clin Exper Immunol 3:615–620, 1968.

Brown, D.M.: Serum measurements of thyroid function. Postgrad Med 44:37–58, 1968.

Burke, G.: The thyrotrophin stimulation test. Ann Int Med 69:1127–1139, 1968.

Clark, E., & D.B. Horn: Assessment of thyroid function by the combined use of the serum protein-bound iodine and the resin uptake of ^{131}I-triiodothyronine. J Clin Endocrinol 25:39–45, 1965.

Dodds, W.J., & M.R. Powell: Thyroid scanning with technetium 99m pertechnetate. Radiology 91:27–31, 1968.

Howorth, P.J.N., & N.F. MacLagan: Clinical application of serum total-thyroxine estimation, resin uptake, and free-thyroxine index. Lancet 1:224–227, 1969.

Nakajima, H., & others: A new and simple method for the determination of thyroxine in serum. J Clin Endocrinol 26:99–103, 1966.

Nuki, G., & R.I.S. Bayliss: The Achilles tendon reflex as an index of thyroid function. Postgrad MJ 44:97–101, 1968.

Thoma, G.E., & W.F. Leightner: Dynamic clinical laboratory tests of thyroid functions. M Clin North America 52:463, 1968.

Thomson, J.A., & others: Evaluation of discordant laboratory data in patients with thyroid disorders. J Clin Path 21:511–517, 1968.

Utiger, R.D.: Thyrotrophin radioimmunoassay: Another test of thyroid function. (Editorial.) Ann Int Med 74:627–628, 1971.

SIMPLE GOITER

Essentials of Diagnosis

- Enlarged thyroid gland in a patient living in an endemic area.
- No symptoms except those associated with compression by large gland.

- BMR, PBI, serum cholesterol normal; radioactive iodine uptake normal or elevated.

General Considerations

Simple goiter is due to iodine lack, and occurs most commonly in endemic areas away from the seacoast. Relative insufficiency of the iodine leads to functional overactivity and hyperplasia of the gland, which becomes filled with colloid poor in iodine. If the deficiency is corrected, the enlargement may subside. In long-standing cases, the goiter persists. Simple goiter may occur transiently when there is greater demand for thyroid hormone, eg, with the onset of puberty or during pregnancy. Rarely, goiter may occur in spite of adequate iodine intake when there is interference with formation of thyroid hormones, eg, due to excess intake of certain goitrogenic vegetables (rutabagas, turnips), exposure to thiocyanate, or congenital lack of certain enzyme systems. Goiter is more readily preventable than cured, and is less common since the introduction of iodized salt.

Clinical Findings

A. Symptoms and Signs: The gland is visibly enlarged and palpable. There may be no symptoms, or symptoms may occur as a result of compression of the structures in the neck or chest: wheezing, dysphagia, respiratory embarrassment. (*Note:* Recurrent laryngeal compression is rare.) There may be associated congenital deafness and disorders of taste.

B. Laboratory Findings: The BMR, PBI, T_4, and serum cholesterol are usually normal. The radioiodine uptake of the gland may be normal or high. Radioactive uptakes over nodules show them to be low in activity (in contrast to toxic nodular goiters).

With special technics it is possible to demonstrate enzymatic defects in thyroid hormone production or abnormal circulating compounds in a considerable number of patients with goiters, especially the familial types. Thyroid auto-antibodies may also be demonstrated.

Differential Diagnosis

It may be difficult to differentiate simple goiter from toxic diffuse or nodular goiter, especially in a patient with a great many nervous symptoms. A history of residence in an endemic area, a family history of goiter, or onset during stressful periods of life (eg, puberty or pregnancy) will often help. If nodular, and especially if only a single nodule is present, neoplasm must be considered.

Prevention

With a dietary intake of 100–200 μg of iodine daily, simple goiter should not occur. During times of stress (puberty, pregnancy, and lactation), the upper limits of this dose may be necessary. This amount is provided in 1–2 gm of iodized salt daily. Iodinated oil has recently been introduced in certain areas of the world as a prophylactic agent for goiter.

Treatment

A. Specific Measures:

1. Thyroid–Thyroid, 60–120 mg (1–2 gr) or more, or levothyroxine, 0.2 mg or more, especially if the goiter is multinodular, appears to be of value in about half of cases. An excellent guide to therapy is the PBI, which should be maintained in the high normal range (6–7 mg/100 ml). (*Note:* Misleading high blood iodine values may follow the use of iodized salt or diagnostic or therapeutic iodine-containing drugs. This may be circumvented by measuring the T_4 by displacement [TT_4]).

2. Iodine therapy (early)–If the enlargement is discovered early, it may disappear completely with adequate iodine administration. Five drops daily of saturated solution of potassium iodide or strong iodine solution (Lugol's solution) in ½ glass water is sufficient. Continue therapy until the gland returns to normal size, and then place the patient on a maintenance dosage or use iodized table salt. Iodized oil injections may be preferable.

3. Iodine therapy (late)–If the enlargement is of long standing iodine therapy as above may be used, but significant regression in the size of the gland should not be expected. **Note:** Thyroid treatment is preferable in most patients with simple goiter.

B. Indications for Surgery:

1. Signs of pressure–If signs of local pressure are present, the gland should be removed surgically.

2. Potential malignancy–Surgery should be considered for any thyroid gland with a single nodule, for the chances of a single nodule being malignant are quite high. This is particularly true in younger people and in any case when there is no decrease in size or abnormal growth in spite of thyroid therapy after a period of 3–6 months.

Prognosis

Simple goiter may disappear spontaneously or may become large, causing compression of vital structures. Multinodular goiters of long standing, especially in people over 50 years of age, may become toxic. Whether they ever become malignant is not established.

Astwood, E.B., Cassidy, C.E., & G.D. Aurbach: Treatment of goiter and thyroid nodules with thyroid. JAMA 174:459–464, 1960.

Butterfield, I.H.: Correction of iodine deficiency in New Guinea natives by iodized oil injection. Lancet 2:767, 1965.

Veith, F.J., & others: The nodular thyroid gland and cancer: A practical approach to the problem. New England J Med 270:431–435, 1964.

Welch, C.E.: Therapy for multinodular goiter. JAMA 195:339–341, 1966.

Zacharewicz, F.A.: Management of single and multinodular goiter. M Clin North America 52:409–416, 1968.

HYPOTHYROIDISM

In view of the profound influence exerted on all tissues of the body by thyroid hormone, lack of the hormone may affect virtually all body functions. The degree of severity ranges from mild and unrecognized hypothyroid states to striking myxedema.

A state of hypothyroidism may be due to primary disease of the thyroid gland itself, or lack of pituitary TSH. A true end-organ insensitivity to normal amounts of circulating hormone has been postulated but is rarely observed. Although gross forms of hypothyroidism, ie, myxedema and cretinism, are readily recognized on clinical grounds alone, the far more common mild forms often escape detection without adequate laboratory facilities.

1. CRETINISM & JUVENILE HYPOTHYROIDISM

Essentials of Diagnosis

- Dwarfism, mental retardation, dry, yellow, cold skin, "pot belly" with umbilical hernia.
- PBI and T_4 low; serum cholesterol elevated.
- Delayed bone age; "stippling" of epiphyses.

General Considerations

The causes of cretinism and juvenile hypothyroidism are as follows (after Wilkins):

A. Congenital (Cretinism):

1. Thyroid gland absent or rudimentary (embryonic defect; most cases of sporadic cretinism).

2. Thyroid gland present but defective in hormone secretion; goitrous or secondarily atrophied. Due to extrinsic factor (deficient iodine, goitrogenic substances?; most cases of endemic cretinism); or due to maternal factors (some cases of congenital goiter). Many cases are familial.

B. Acquired (Juvenile Hypothyroidism): Atrophy of the gland or defective function may be due to unknown causes, thyroiditis, or operative removal (lingual thyroid or toxic goiter), or secondary to pituitary deficiency.

Clinical Findings

A. Symptoms and Signs: All degrees of dwarfism may be seen, with delayed skeletal maturation, apathy, physical and mental torpor, dry skin with coarse, dry, brittle hair, constipation, slow teething, poor appetite, large tongue, "pot belly" with umbilical hernia, deep voice, cold extremities and cold sensitivity, and true myxedema of subcutaneous and other tissues. A yellow, carotenemic skin is not infrequent. The thyroid gland is usually not palpable, but a large goiter may be present which may be diffuse or nodular. Sexual development is retarded but maturation eventually occurs. Menometrorrhagia or amenorrhea may be seen in older girls. Rarely, sexual precocity and galactorrhea with pituitary enlargement may occur. Deafness is occasionally associated with goiters. Nephrocalcinosis is a rare finding in cretinism.

B. Laboratory Findings: The BMR is probably the least reliable (in infants and children) and the TT_4 the most reliable index of thyroid activity; the latter (not generally available) is usually under 3 $\mu g/100$ ml. Serum cholesterol is elevated. Radioactive iodine uptake is very low in athyroid individuals, but it may be high in goitrous cretins although the iodine is not bound in the gland and is released. By special technics, abnormal circulating iodine compounds and enzymatic defects in thyroid hormone production and release are demonstrable in some patients. Others show circulating autoantibodies to thyroid constituents.

C. X-Ray Findings: Delayed skeletal maturation is a constant finding, often with "stippling" of the epiphyses (especially of the femoral head), with flattening; widening of the cortices of the long bones, absence of the cranial sinuses, and delayed dentition may also be noted.

Differential Diagnosis

It is of practical interest to differentiate primary hypothyroidism from pituitary failure because in the latter instance a search for a pituitary lesion must be undertaken. Treatment with thyroid hormone must be instituted cautiously when hypothyroidism is secondary to pituitary failure since it may precipitate adrenal crisis. Radioiodine uptake studies before and after exogenous TSH administration will often show whether a gland is present or not. True myxedema and hypercholesterolemia are less common with hypopituitarism. Cretinism is most often confused with Down's syndrome, although retarded skeletal development is rare in mongoloid infants. Macroglossia may be due to tumor, eg, lymphangioma. The dry skin of ichthyosis may be misleading. All causes of stunted growth and skeletal development (see above) must be considered as well. Rather than risk the development of full-blown cretinism in the questionable case, a trial of thyroid therapy is reasonable.

Treatment

See Myxedema, below.

Prognosis

The progress and outcome of the disease depend largely upon the duration of thyroid deficiency and the adequacy and persistence of treatment. Since mental development is at stake, it is of utmost importance to start treatment early.

The prognosis for full mental and physical maturation is much better if the onset is later in life. Congenital cretins almost never attain full mental development. Skeletal and sexual maturation, though often retarded, do take place normally under continued thyroid therapy.

By and large, the response to thyroid therapy is gratifying but therapy usually must be maintained throughout life.

De Groot, L.J.: Current views on formation of thyroid hormones. New England J Med 272:243–249, 297–303, 355–361, 1965.

Stanbury, J.B., Wyngaarden, J.B., & D.S. Fredrickson: Familial goiter. Chap 10 in: *Metabolic Basis of Inherited Disease,* 2nd ed. McGraw-Hill, 1966.

2. ADULT HYPOTHYROIDISM & MYXEDEMA

Essentials of Diagnosis

- Weakness, fatigue, cold intolerance, constipation, menorrhagia, hoarseness.
- Dry, cold, yellow, puffy skin; scant eyebrows, thick tongue, "water bottle" heart, bradycardia, delayed return of deep tendon reflexes.
- All low: PBI, T_4, BMR, radioiodine uptake.
- Anemia.

General Considerations

Primary thyroid deficiency is much more common than secondary hypofunction due to pituitary insufficiency. Primary myxedema occurs after total thyroidectomy, eradication of thyroid by radioactive iodine, ingestion of goitrogens (eg, thiocyanates, rutabagas), or chronic thyroiditis. Most cases, however, are due to atrophy of the gland from unknown causes, possibly an autoimmune mechanism. This may also involve other endocrine glands, eg, adrenals, in the same patient (Schmidt's syndrome).

Secondary hypothyroidism may follow destructive lesions of the pituitary gland, eg, chromophobe adenoma or postpartum necrosis (Sheehan's syndrome). It is usually manifested by associated disorders of the adrenals and gonads. Since thyroid hormone is necessary for all glandular functions, primary myxedema may lead to secondary hypofunction of the pituitary, adrenals, and other glands, making diagnosis difficult.

Clinical Findings

These may vary from the rather rare full-blown myxedema to mild states of hypothyroidism, which are far more common and may escape detection unless a high index of suspicion is maintained.

A. Symptoms and Signs:

1. Early—The principal symptoms are weakness, fatigue, cold intolerance, lethargy, dryness of skin, headache, and menorrhagia. Nervousness is a common finding. Physical findings may be few or absent. Outstanding are thin, brittle nails; thinning of hair, which may be coarse; and pallor, with poor turgor of the mucosa. Delayed return of deep tendon reflexes is often found.

2. Late—The principal symptoms are slow speech, absence of sweating, weight gain, constipation, peripheral edema, pallor, hoarseness, aches and pains, dyspnea, anginal pain, deafness, and amenorrhea. Physical findings include puffiness of the face and eyelids, typical "malar flush," thinning of the outer halves of the eyebrows, thickening of the tongue, hard pitting edema, and effusions into the pleural, peritoneal, and pericardial cavities. Cardiac enlargement ("myxedema heart") is often due to pericardial effusion. The heart rate is slow; the blood pressure is more often normal than low, and even hypertension may be found which reverses with treatment. (*Note:* Obesity is not a common feature of hypothyroidism.)

B. Laboratory Findings: A BMR below 30% is suggestive, especially in the nonobese patient. The PBI is under 3.5 μg/100 ml. Radioiodine uptake is decreased (below 10% in 24 hours), but this test is not always reliable. The radioactive T_3 uptake of red cells or resin is low. Plasma cholesterol is elevated in primary and, less commonly, in secondary hypothyroidism (fall on thyroid therapy is a sensitive index). Macrocytic anemia may be present. Increase in ^{131}I uptake and PBI after administration of 10–20 units of thyrotropic hormone (given for several days) suggests secondary hypothyroidism rather than primary myxedema. 17-Ketosteroids may be very low.

Differential Diagnosis

Mild hypothyroidism must be considered in all states of neurasthenia, menstrual disorders without grossly demonstrable pelvic disease, unexplained weight gain, and anemia. Myxedema enters into the differential diagnosis of unexplained heart failure which does not respond to digitalis or diuretics, "idiopathic" hyperlipemia, and unexplained ascites. The protein content of myxedematous effusions is high. The thick tongue may be confused with that seen in primary amyloidosis. Pernicious anemia may be suggested by the pallor and the macrocytic type of anemia seen in myxedema. Some cases of primary psychosis and cerebral arteriosclerosis or even brain tumors must be differentiated from profound myxedema. (*Note:* The CSF proteins may be elevated in myxedema.) If laboratory tests are not convincing, response to cautious thyroid administration may establish the true nature of the disorder.

Complications

Complications are mostly cardiac in nature, occurring as a result of advanced coronary artery disease and congestive failure, which may be precipitated by too vigorous thyroid therapy. There is an increased susceptibility to infection. Organic psychoses with paranoid delusions may occur ("myxedema madness"). Rarely, adrenal crisis may be precipitated by thyroid therapy of pituitary myxedema. Hypothyroidism is an accepted cause of infertility, which often responds to thyroid medication.

Caution: Myxedematous patients are unusually sensitive to opiates and may die from average doses.

Refractory hyponatremia may be seen in severe myxedema, probably due to inappropriate secretion of antidiuretic hormone.

Treatment

A. Specific Therapy: Thyroid or a synthetic preparation is used. The initial dosage varies with the severity of the hypothyroidism.

1. *Caution*—When treating patients with severe myxedema or myxedema heart disease, or elderly patients with hypothyroidism with other associated heart disease, begin with small doses of thyroid, 8—15 mg (1/8—1/4 gr) daily for 1 week, and increase the dose every week by 15 mg (1/4 gr) daily up to a total of 100—200 mg (1½—3 gr) daily. This dosage should be continued until signs of hypothyroidism have vanished or toxic symptoms appear, and the dosage then stabilized to maintain the BMR or PBI at normal or just below the level of toxicity (see Hyperthyroidism, below).

2. Patients with early hypothyroidism may be started with larger doses, 30 mg (½ gr) daily, increasing by 30 mg (½ gr) every week to the limit of tolerance.

3. Maintenance—Each patient's dose must be adjusted to obtain the optimal effect. Most patients require 60—200 mg (1—3 gr) daily for maintenance. Optimal dosage can be estimated by following the PBI or BMR, but clinical judgment is often the best guide.

4. Levothyroxine sodium (Synthroid®, Letter®), 0.1—0.3 mg/day, is as good as thyroid. Its action is more predictable than that of crude thyroid.

5. When a rapid response is necessary, sodium liothyronine (T_3, Cytomel®) may be employed. Begin with very low doses because of its speed of action. Begin with 5 µg and increase slowly (see p 677); *Note:* The PBI cannot be used as a guide to T_3 therapy.

6. Mixtures of T_4 and T_3 in a ratio of 4:1—liotrix (Euthroid®, Thyrolar®)—have been introduced as complete replacement therapy (see Selenkow and Smith references, below).

7. Myxedema coma is a medical emergency with a high mortality rate. Triiodothyronine, 10—25 µg or more given by stomach tube or parenterally every 8 hours, or Synthroid® injection, 200—400 µg IV as a single injection and repeated once in a dose of 100—200 µg in 24 hours, with the addition of hydrocortisone, 100 mg every 8 hours, may be lifesaving. The patient must not be warmed, and adequate pulmonary ventilation must be provided.

8. Sodium dextrothyroxine (Choloxin®) may be used in cardiac hypothyroid patients who cannot tolerate other thyroid medications.

B. Needless Use of Thyroid:

1. Questionable diagnosis—If a patient can tolerate above 200 mg (3 gr) daily of thyroid, the diagnosis of hypothyroidism should be questioned even though some hypothyroid patients require this or larger amounts. Normal individuals and obese and other nonhypothyroid individuals can often tolerate doses up to 300—500 mg (4½—7½ gr) daily without changes in BMR or development of toxic symptoms.

2. Nonspecific use of thyroid—The use of thyroid medication as nonspecific stimulating therapy is mentioned only to be condemned. It has been shown that the doses usually employed (100—200 mg) merely suppress the activity of the patient's own gland.

"Metabolic insufficiency" is a questionable entity. The empiric use of thyroid medication in cases of amenorrhea or infertility warrants further consideration.

Prognosis

The patient may succumb to the complications of the disease if treatment is withheld too long, eg, myxedema coma. With early treatment, striking transformations take place both in appearance and mental function. Return to a normal state is possible, but relapses will occur if treatment is interrupted. On the whole, response to thyroid treatment is most satisfactory in true hypothyroidism, and complete rehabilitation of the patient is possible if treatment is adequate and maintained indefinitely.

Bakke, J.: Treatment of hypothyroidism with synthetic hormones. Northwest Med 68:651, 1969.

Becker, C.E.: Coma in myxedema. California Med 110:61—69, 1969.

Carpenter, C.C.J., & others: Schmidt's syndrome (thyroid and adrenal insufficiency). Medicine 43:153, 1964.

Green, W.L.: Guidelines for the treatment of myxedema. M Clin North America 52:431—450, 1968.

Rosenberg, I.N.: Hypothyroidism and coma. S Clin North America 48:353—360, 1968.

Selenkow, H., & M.S. Wool: A new synthetic thyroid hormone combination for clinical therapy. Ann Int Med 67:90, 1967.

Smith, R.N., & others: Controlled clinical trial of combined triiodothyronine and thyroxine in the treatment of hypothyroidism. Lancet 2:145, 1970.

HYPERTHYROIDISM
(Thyrotoxicosis)

Essentials of Diagnosis

- Weakness, sweating, weight loss, nervousness, loose bowel movements, heat intolerance.
- Tachycardia; warm, thin, soft, moist skin; exophthalmos; stare, tremor.
- Goiter, bruit.
- BMR, PBI, T_4, radio-T_3 red cell uptakes, and radioiodine uptake elevated. Failure of suppression by T_3 administration.

General Considerations

Thyrotoxicosis is one of the most common endocrine disorders. Its highest incidence is in women between the ages of 20 and 40. When associated with ocular signs or ocular disturbances and a diffuse goiter, it is called Graves' disease. This term, however, is commonly used to mean all forms of hyperthyroidism. Instead of a diffuse goiter, there may be a nodular toxic goiter, or all the metabolic features of thyrotoxicosis may be present without visible or palpable thyroid enlargement. The latter form is quite common in the elderly patient, who may even lack some of the hypermetabolic signs ("apathetic Graves' disease") but may present with a refractory cardiac illness. Lastly, a poorly understood syndrome of marked eye signs, often without hypermetabolism, may precede, accompany, or follow treatment of thyrotoxicosis, and has been termed hyperexophthalmic Graves' disease, exophthalmic ophthalmoplegia, and malignant (progressive) exophthalmos. It has been recently associated with the findings of high levels of long-acting thyroid stimulator (LATS), a 7S gamma globulin of extrapituitary origin, although this factor may not be causally related to the disease.

Clinical Findings

A. Symptoms and Signs: (See Table 18–3.) Restlessness, nervousness, irritability; easy fatigability, especially toward the latter part of the day; and unexplained weight loss in spite of ravenous appetite are often the early features. There is usually excessive sweating and heat intolerance, quick movements with incoordination varying from fine tremulousness to gross tremor. Less commonly, the patient's primary complaint is difficulty in focusing his eyes, pressure from the goiter, diarrhea, or rapid, irregular heart action.

TABLE 18–3. Incidence of symptoms and signs observed in 247 patients with thyrotoxicosis.*

Symptoms	Percent
Nervousness	99
Hyperhidrosis	91
Hypersensitivity to heat	89
Palpitation	89
Fatigue	88
Weight loss	85
Tachycardia	82
Dyspnea	75
Weakness	70
Hyperorexia	65
Eye complaints	54
Swelling of legs	35
Hyperdefecation (without diarrhea)	33
Diarrhea	23
Anorexia	9
Constipation	4
Weight gain	2
Signs	**Percent**
Tachycardia	100
Goiter	100
Skin changes	97
Bruit over thyroid	77
Eye signs	71
Atrial fibrillation	10
Splenomegaly	10
Gynecomastia	10
Liver palms	8

*Modified and reproduced, with permission, from Williams: *Textbook of Endocrinology,* 4th ed. Saunders, 1968.

The patient is quick in all motions, including speech. The skin is warm and moist and the hands tremble. A diffuse or nodular goiter may be seen or felt with a thrill or bruit over it. The eyes appear bright, there may be a stare, at times periorbital edema, and commonly lid lag, lack of accommodation, exophthalmos, and even diplopia. The hair and skin are thin and of silky texture. At times there is increased pigmentation of the skin, but vitiligo may also occur. Spider angiomas are common. Cardiovascular manifestations vary from tachycardia, especially during sleep, to paroxysmal atrial fibrillation and congestive failure of the "high-output" type. At times a harsh pulmonary systolic murmur is heard (Means' murmur). Lymphadenopathy and splenomegaly may be present. Wasting of muscle and bone (osteoporosis) are common features, especially in long-standing thyrotoxicosis. Rarely one finds nausea, vomiting, and even fever and jaundice (in which case the prognosis is poor). Mental changes are common, varying from mild exhilaration to delirium and exhaustion progressing to severe depression.

Associated with severe or malignant exophthalmos is at times a localized, bilateral, hard, nonpitting, symmetric swelling ("pretibial myxedema") over the tibia and dorsum of the feet (dermopathy). At times there is clubbing and swelling of the fingers (acropachy). It often subsides spontaneously.

Thyroid "storm," rarely seen today, is an extreme form of thyrotoxicosis, which may occur after iodine refractoriness or thyroid surgery and is manifested by marked delirium, severe tachycardia, vomiting, diarrhea, and dehydration, and often very high fever. The mortality is high.

B. Laboratory Findings: The BMR is elevated, the PBI and T_4 are over 8 μg/100 ml, and radioiodine and radio-T_3 red cell or resin uptakes are increased. The radioiodine uptake cannot be suppressed by T_3 administration (see p 608). In toxic nodular goiter, a high radioiodine uptake in the nodule may be diagnostic if combined with elevated BMR and PBI. Serum cholesterol determinations are low (variable). Postprandial glycosuria is occasionally found. Urinary creatinine is increased. Lymphocytosis is common. Urinary and, at times, serum calcium are elevated. Low levels of TSH—and, less consistently, an elevated LATS (long-acting thyroid stimulator) level of unknown source—may be present in the serum or urine, but these tests are not generally available.

C. X-Ray Findings: Barium swallow may demonstrate low or intrathoracic goiter. Skeletal changes include diffuse demineralization or, at times, resorptive changes (osteitis). Hypertrophic osteoarthropathy with proliferation of periosteal bone may be present, especially in the hands (acropachy).

D. ECG Findings: ECG may show tachycardia, atrial fibrillation, and P and T wave changes.

Differential Diagnosis

The most difficult differentiation is between hyperthyroidism and anxiety neurosis, especially in the menopause. Acute or subacute thyroiditis may present with toxic symptoms; the gland is usually quite tender, and the thyroid antibody test may be positive (BMR is high, PBI may be elevated, but radioiodine uptake is very low). Exogenous thyroid administration will present the same laboratory features as thyroiditis. A rare chorionic or pituitary tumor may produce the picture of thyrotoxicosis. A hypermetabolic state due mainly to overproduction of T_3 has recently been described ("T_3 thyrotoxicosis"; see Sterling reference, below). The T_4 is normal or low. The radioiodine uptake is normal or elevated but fails to be suppressed by T_3 administration.

Some states of hypermetabolism without thyrotoxicosis, notably severe anemia, leukemia, polycythemia, and malignancy, rarely cause confusion. Pheochromocytoma and acromegaly, however, may be associated with high BMR, with enlargement of the thyroid gland and profuse sweating, and make differentiation difficult.

Cardiac disease (eg, atrial fibrillation, failure) refractory to treatment with digitalis, quinidine, or diuretics suggests underlying hyperthyroidism. Other causes of ophthalmoplegia (eg, myasthenia gravis) and exophthalmos (eg, orbital tumor) must be considered. Thyrotoxicosis must also be considered in the differential diagnosis of muscle wasting diseases and diffuse bone atrophy. Hypercalciuria and bone demineralization may resemble hyperparathyroidism. The 2 diseases may be present in the same patient. Diabetes mellitus and Addison's disease may coexist with thyrotoxicosis.

Complications

The ocular and cardiac complications of long-standing thyrotoxicosis are most serious. Severe malnutrition and wasting with cachexia may become irreversible. If jaundice is present, the mortality increases. Periodic paralysis may complicate thyrotoxicosis. Thyroid "storm" (see p 616) is rarely seen but may be fatal. Malignancy rarely accompanies toxic goiter. Complications of treatment for goiter include drug reactions following iodine and thiouracil treatment, hypoparathyroidism and laryngeal palsy from surgical treatment, and progressive exophthalmos. The exophthalmos may progress despite adequate therapy to the point of corneal ulceration and destruction of the globe unless orbital decompression is done. Hypercalcemia and nephrocalcinosis may occur.

Treatment

Treatment is aimed at halting excessive secretion of the thyroid hormone. Several methods are available; the method of choice is still being debated and varies with different patients. The most widely accepted method, however, is subtotal removal after adequate preparation. (*Note:* In this discussion, the term BMR is used in a clinical sense, since laboratory determination of PBI, T_4, T_3 uptake, etc have virtually replaced spirometry.)

A. Subtotal Thyroidectomy: Adequate preparation is of the utmost importance. One or 2 drugs are generally necessary for adequate preparation: one of the thiouracil group of drugs alone, or a thiouracil plus iodine.

1. Thiouracil and similar drugs—Several thiouracil drugs or similar derivatives are available: propylthiouracil, methimazole, and one containing iodine in the molecule, iothiouracil (Itrumil®). The modes of action of the first 2 are probably identical; the mode of action of iothiouracil is still not entirely clear, and this drug is of questionable value.

(1) Propylthiouracil has been most widely used and appears to be the least toxic. It is the thiouracil preparation of choice. When given in adequate dosage, propylthiouracil prevents the thyroid gland from transforming inorganic iodine into its organic (hormonal) form. This effect is rapid (within a few hours) and continues as long as the drug is given. As the level of circulating hormone falls, TSH elaboration rises. The BMR invariably falls, the rate of fall depending upon the total quantity of previously manufactured PBI available from the gland or in the circulating blood. (More PBI is present if iodine has been given previously.) The average time required for the BMR to return to normal is about 4–8 weeks. If the drug is continued, the BMR will continue to fall until the patient becomes myxedematous.

Propylthiouracil appears to be an ideal drug except for 2 disadvantages: the danger of toxic reactions (especially granulocytopenia) and interference with surgery. Toxic reactions to propylthiouracil are rare, however, and could be anticipated if the patient were examined weekly and a weekly or a biweekly blood count taken, but this is rarely feasible. In practice, patients are instructed to watch for fever, sore throat, or rash and to notify their physicians immediately if any of these occurs so that blood count and examination can be performed. If the white count falls below 4500 or if less than 45% granulocytes are present, therapy should be discontinued. Other rare reactions are drug fever, rash, and jaundice. The second objection is of a technical nature; since the gland may remain hyperplastic and vascular, surgical removal is more difficult. For this reason, combined therapy, using propylthiouracil and iodine, is the method of choice in preparing patients for thyroidectomy (see below).

Preparation is usually continued and surgery deferred until the BMR, PBI, T_4 etc are normal. There is no need to rush surgery and no danger of "escape" as with iodine. In severe cases, 100–200 mg 4 times daily (spaced as close to every 6 hours as possible) is generally adequate. Larger doses (eg, for patients with very large glands) are occasionally necessary. In milder cases, 100 mg 3 times daily are sufficient, although the larger doses are not more harmful.

(2) Methimazole (Tapazole®)—The action of this drug is similar to that of the thiouracils. The average dose is 10–15 mg every 8 hours. The smaller dosage is no guarantee against toxic reactions, especially skin rash, which are more common with this drug than with the thiouracils.

2. Iodine—Iodine is given in daily dosages of 5–10 drops of strong iodine solution (Lugol's solution) or saturated solution of potassium iodide with nonspecific therapy (see below) until the BMR has dropped toward normal, the signs and symptoms have become less marked, and the patient has begun to gain weight. The disadvantages of preparation with iodine are that (1) a few patients may not respond, especially those who have received iodine recently; (2) sensitivity to iodides may be present; (3) if there is too long a wait before surgery, the gland may "escape" and the patient develops a more severe hyperthyroidism than before; and (4) it is generally impossible to reduce the BMR to normal with iodine alone.

3. Combined propylthiouracil-iodine therapy– The advantage of this method is that one obtains the complete inhibition of thyroid secretion with the involuting effect of iodine. This can be done in 2 ways:

(1) Propylthiouracil followed by iodine–This appears at present to be the method of choice. Begin therapy with propylthiouracil; about 10–21 days before surgery is contemplated (when all thyroid tests have returned to normal or low normal range), begin the iodine and *continue* for 1 week after surgery.

(2) Concomitant administration of the 2 drugs from the start in dosages as for the individual drugs, ie, 100–200 mg propylthiouracil 4 times daily and strong iodine solution, 10–15 drops daily. This method is less commonly used and less desirable than sequential administration (outlined above).

B. Continuous Propylthiouracil Therapy (Medical Treatment): Control of hyperthyroidism with propylthiouracil alone, without surgery, is advocated by some. The advantage is that it avoids the risks and postoperative complications of surgery, eg, myxedema, hypoparathyroidism. The disadvantage is the remote possibility of toxic reactions plus the necessity of watching the patient carefully for signs of hypothyroidism. Since the advent of propylthiouracil, it appears that the incidence of toxic reactions is slight.

Begin with 100–200 mg every 6–8 hours and continue until the BMR, PBI, T_4, etc are normal and all signs and symptoms of the disease have subsided; then place the patient on a maintenance dose of 50–150 mg daily, observing the thyroid function tests periodically to avoid hypothyroidism.

An alternative method is to continue with doses of 50–200 mg every 6–8 hours until the patient becomes hypothyroid and then maintain BMR or PBI at normal with thyroid hormone. (This may be the preferred treatment of exophthalmic goiter.)

The duration of therapy and the recurrence rate with nonsurgical therapy have not been completely worked out. At present it would seem that of the patients kept on propylthiouracil between 6 and 18 months (the dosage slowly decreased), about 50–70% will have no recurrence. Increasing the duration of therapy to about 2 years or more does not increase the "cure" rate.

C. Continuous Iodine Therapy: In the past this method was used in selected cases of mild hyperthyroidism with fair results; however, because of the danger of "escape" and because propylthiouracil is a better drug, iodine should be used only for preoperative

preparation. *Note:* Iodide administration to patients rendered euthyroid after treatment of toxic goiter may induce myxedema.

D. Radioactive Iodine (^{131}I): The administration of radioiodine has proved to be an excellent method for destruction of over-functioning thyroid tissue. The rationale of treatment is that the radioiodine, being concentrated in the thyroid, will destroy the cells that concentrate it. Because special technics are necessary to measure and handle radioiodine, the method is still generally limited to use in medical centers. The only objections to date to radioiodine therapy are the possibility of carcinogenesis and the possibility that an early carcinoma which might be removed surgically may remain undetected. For these reasons, the use of radioiodine should generally be limited to older age groups (40 or above); however, the age level is not absolute, and some children are best treated with radioiodine. *Do not use this drug in pregnant women.* A high incidence of hypothyroidism several years after this form of treatment has recently been recognized. Prolonged follow-up is therefore mandatory. There is a greater tendency toward higher-dosage radioiodine ablation of the toxic gland, with subsequent replacement therapy with thyroid hormone.

E. General Measures:

1. The patient with hyperthyroidism should be at bed rest, especially in severe cases and in preparation for surgery. Mild cases may be treated with propylthiouracil or radioiodine on an ambulatory basis. However, early bed rest hastens recovery.

2. Diet should be high in calories, proteins, and vitamins. Hyperthyroid patients consume great quantities of food, are generally in negative nitrogen balance, and need the excess foods and vitamins because of their increased metabolic needs. Supplemental vitamin B complex should be given.

3. Sedation–When first seen, these patients are often very nervous. Sedation is always helpful, and large doses, eg, phenobarbital, 30 mg (½ gr) 3–6 times daily, may be necessary. Since many signs resemble the effects of catecholamines, sympathetic blocking agents (reserpine, guanethidine, propranolol) have been recommended. Their use is controversial and should probably be restricted to states of extreme excitability, eg, thyrotoxic storm (see below).

4. Testosterone propionate, 25–50 mg IM daily or 2–3 times/week, has been shown to be of value in restoring positive nitrogen balance, especially in debilitated patients. Do not use methyltestosterone, as this aggravates the creatinuria.

F. Treatment of Complications:

1. Exophthalmos–The exact cause of exophthalmos in hyperthyroidism is still not known. Although it may be due to excessive secretion of a hormone (EPS) which is different from TSH or from LATS (long-acting thyroid stimulator), the evidence is still inconclusive. It has been shown that exophthalmos is due to edema and later cellular infiltration of the retrobulbar tissues. Removing the thyroid secretion (extirpation or administration of propylthiouracil) does not necessarily help this condition and may possibly even aggravate it, leading to malignant exophthalmos. It has been suggested that this is because the thyroid secretion exerts an inhibitory effect on the anterior pituitary, and removal of the gland allows the anterior pituitary to secrete more hormones and aggravate the condition. Therefore, it would seem rational to treat exophthalmos by giving thyroid orally. However, it is questionable whether such therapy is of use in exophthalmos.

(1) Thyroid—Immediately after surgery, or after the BMR, PBI, T_4, etc have returned to normal with propylthiouracil therapy, begin giving thyroid, 100–200 mg daily, or levothyroxine sodium (Synthroid®), 0.1–0.3 mg daily. Give a dosage which is adequate to maintain the PBI at about 7–9 mg/100 ml. Although it is not always effective, this therapy should be used whenever there is a tendency for progression of the exophthalmos.

(2) Dark glasses, protection from dust, eye shields, tarsorrhaphy, and other measures may be necessary to protect the eyes. Ophthalmologic consultation should be requested.

(3) Corticotropin (ACTH) or corticosteroids in large doses have proved helpful in some cases. They act by reducing the inflammatory reaction in the periorbital tissues. They may also reduce the level of LATS.

(4) Estrogen treatment has been used with some benefit, especially in the postmenopausal age group.

(5) Surgery for malignant exophthalmos—Every patient with exophthalmos should be measured periodically with an exophthalmometer; do not rely upon clinical judgment to determine whether or not exophthalmos is present or progressing. In severe progressive cases, where corneal edema or ulceration, limitation of extraocular muscle movements, and failing vision occur, orbital decompression is necessary to save the eyesight.

(6) There have been a few encouraging reports on the use of pituitary stalk section or even hypophysectomy with yttrium in severe malignant exophthalmos; however, since EPS and LATS are probably extrapituitary in origin, the rationale of such procedures is questionable. Orbital irradiation may be helpful.

2. **Cardiac complications**—A number of cardiac complications are at times associated with hyperthyroidism.

(1) Some degree of tachycardia is almost always found if normal rhythm is present in thyrotoxicosis. This requires only the treatment of the thyrotoxicosis. Reserpine is at times helpful. Phentolamine (Regitine®), guanethidine (Ismelin®), or propranolol (Inderal®) may be preferable drugs.

(2) Congestive failure tends to occur in long-standing thyrotoxicosis, especially in the older age groups. Treatment is the same as for congestive failure due to any cause. Digitalis seems to be effective in congestive failure associated with thyrotoxicosis.

(3) Atrial fibrillation may occur in association with thyrotoxicosis. Treat as any other atrial fibrillation, but do not try to convert the atrial fibrillation in a toxic patient. Most cases will revert to normal

rhythm soon after toxicity is removed. However, if fibrillation remains for 2 weeks after surgery or for 2–4 weeks after BMR or PBI, T_4, etc have returned to normal with propylthiouracil therapy, and if no contraindications are present, one should consider using quinidine to convert to a normal rhythm.

3. **"Crisis" or "storm"**—Fortunately, this condition is rare with modern therapy. It occurs now mainly in patients inadequately prepared with propylthiouracil and iodine, immediately after subtotal thyroidectomy. It can occur spontaneously or after any sudden stress in an untreated patient with thyrotoxicosis. It is characterized by high fever, tachycardia, CNS irritability, and delirium. The cause is uncertain, but absolute or relative adrenocortical insufficiency may be important. Large doses of corticotropin (ACTH) or the corticosteroids may be lifesaving. Sodium iodide, 1–2 gm IV and repeated every 12–24 hours, has also been advocated. Large doses of reserpine or guanethidine, or propranolol intravenously, may be of value. General measures consist of cold packs and sedation.

Prognosis

Thyrotoxicosis is a cyclic disease and may subside spontaneously. More commonly, however, it progresses, especially with recurrent psychic trauma, pregnancy, and other types of stress. The ocular, cardiac, and psychic complications often are more serious than the chronic wasting of tissues and may become irreversible even after treatment. Progressive exophthalmos is perhaps more common after surgical than after "medical" thyroidectomy. Hypoparathyroidism and vocal cord palsy are usually permanent after surgical thyroidectomy. With any form of therapy, recurrence rates are about 30%, especially if thyrotoxicosis is diffuse. With adequate treatment and long-term follow-up, the results are good. It is perhaps wiser to speak of induced remission rather than cure. Post-treatment hypothyroidism is common. It may occur several years after radioactive iodine therapy.

Patients with jaundice and fever have a less favorable prognosis. Periorbital swelling and chemosis often precede serious and progressive malignant exophthalmos leading to blindness, and must be watched carefully.

Although it is rare, thyroid storm has the worst prognosis. It is best avoided by careful preoperative preparation of the patient rather than treated once it appears.

Braverman, L.E., Woeber, K.A., & S.H. Ingbar: Induction of myxedema by iodide in patients euthyroid after treatment of toxic goiter. New England J Med 281:816–821, 1969.

Brown, J., & others: Adrenal steroid therapy of severe infiltrative ophthalmopathy of Graves' disease. Am J Med 34:786, 1963.

Das, G., & M. Krieger: Treatment of thyrotoxic storm with intravenous administration of propranolol. Ann Int Med 70:985, 1969.

Dillon, P.T., & others: Reserpine in thyrotoxic crisis. New England J Med 283:1020–1023, 1970.

Green, M., & G.M. Wilson: Thyrotoxicosis treated by surgery or iodine-131. With special reference to development of hypothyroidism. Brit MJ 1:1005–1009, 1964.

Hadden, D.R., & others: Propranolol and iodine-131 in the management of thyrotoxicosis. Lancet 2:852–853, 1968.

Hamburger, J., & S. Paul: When and how to use higher ^{131}I doses for hyperthyroidism. New England J Med 279:1361, 1968.

Hamilton, C.R., Jr., Adams, L.C., & F. Maloof: Hyperthyroidism due to thyrotropin-producing pituitary chromophobe adenoma. New England J Med 283:1077–1080, 1970.

Hayek, A., Chapman E.M., & J.D. Crawford: Long-term results of ^{131}I treatment of thyrotoxicosis in children. New England J Med 283:949–953, 1970.

Hershman, J.M., & H.P. Higgins: Hydatidiform mole: A cause of clinical hyperthyroidism. New England J Med 284:573–577, 1971.

Hetzel, B.S.: The aetiology and pathogenesis of hyperthyroidism. Postgrad MJ 44:363–376, 1968.

Ingbar, S.H.: Thyrotoxic storm. New England J Med 274:1252, 1966.

Kriss, J.P.: The long-acting thyroid stimulator. California Med 109:202, 1968.

McKenzie, J.M.: Humoral factors in the pathogenesis of Graves' disease. Physiol Rev 48:252, 1968.

Ochi, Y., & L.J. De Groot: Current concepts: Long acting thyroid stimulator of Graves' disease. New England J Med 278:718–720, 1968.

Resnick, J.S., Dorman, J.D., & W.K. Engel: Thyrotoxic periodic paralysis. Am J Med.47:831–836, 1969.

Solomon, D.H., & others: Hyperthyroidism. Ann Int Med 69:1015–1036, 1968.

Sterling, K., & others: T_3 thyrotoxicosis. JAMA 213:571–575, 1970.

CARCINOMA OF THYROID GLAND

Essentials of Diagnosis

- Painless swelling in region of thyroid, or thyroid nodule not responding to suppression.
- Normal thyroid function tests.
- Past history of irradiation to neck, goiter, or thyroiditis.

General Considerations

Although carcinoma of the thyroid is rarely associated with functional abnormalities, it enters into the differential diagnosis of all types of thyroid lesions. Recent evidence suggests that it may be the end result of long-standing overstimulation of the thyroid gland by pituitary TSH, especially in certain types of goiter and thyroiditis. It is common in all age groups, but especially in patients who have received irradiation therapy to the neck structures (eg, thymus gland). The cell type determines to a large extent the type of therapy required and the prognosis for survival.

Clinical Findings

A. Symptoms and Signs: The principal signs of thyroid cancer is a painless nodule, a hard nodule in an enlarged thyroid gland, so-called lateral aberrant thyroid tissue, or palpable lymph nodes with thyroid enlargement. Signs of pressure or invasion of the neck structures are present in anaplastic or longstanding tumors. A rare patient with medullary carcinoma may present with hypocalcemic tetany due to thyrocalcitonin excess.

B. Laboratory Findings: With very few exceptions all thyroid function tests are normal unless the disease is associated with thyroiditis. The scintigram shows a "cold nodule" which cannot be suppressed readily with T_3 or T_4. Serum autoantibodies are sometimes found. Hypocalcemia may be present in medullary carcinoma.

C. X-Ray Findings: Extensive bone and soft tissue metastases (some of which may take up radioiodine) may be demonstrable.

Differential Diagnosis

Since nonmalignant enlargements of the thyroid gland are far more common than carcinoma, it is at times most difficult to establish the diagnosis except by biopsy (which should be an open biopsy rather than needle biopsy). The incidence of malignancy is much greater in single than in multinodular lesions, and far greater in nonfunctioning than in functioning nodules. The T_3 suppression test is of some value in differentiating benign from autonomous lesions. The differentiation from chronic thyroiditis is at times most difficult, and the 2 lesions may occur together. Any nonfunctioning lesion in the region of the thyroid which does not decrease in size on thyroid therapy or increases rapidly must be considered carcinoma until proved otherwise.

Complications

The complications vary with the type of carcinoma. Papillary tumors invade local structures, such as lymph nodes; follicular tumors metastasize through the blood stream; anaplastic carcinomas invade local structures, causing constriction and nerve palsies, as well as leading to widespread metastases. The complications of radical neck surgery often include permanent hypoparathyroidism, vocal cord palsy, and myxedema.

Medullary carcinoma may be associated with pheochromocytoma and hyperparathyroidism (Sipple's syndrome). Elevated calcitonin levels have been demonstrated in this tumor, although hypocalcemia rarely occurs.

Treatment

Surgical removal, if possible, is the treatment of choice for most thyroid carcinomas. Papillary tumors may respond to thyroid suppressive treatment, which may also be of value in other types, eg, medullary carcinoma (especially after most of the functioning gland has been removed). Some follicular tumors have been treated with radioiodine; metastases may take up radioactive iodine after thyroidectomy or iodide depletion. External irradiation may be useful for local as well as distant metastases. Postoperative myxedema

TABLE 18–4. Some characteristics of thyroid cancer.

	Papillary	Follicular	Amyloidic Solid	Anaplastic
Incidence*(%)	61	18	6	15
Average age*	42	50	50	57
Females*(%)	70	72	56	56
Deaths due to thyroid cancer*†(%)	6	24	33	98
Invasion: Juxtanodal	+++++	+	++++++	+++
Blood vessels	+	+++	+++	+++++
Distant sites	+	+++	++	++++
Resemblance to thyroid	+	+++	+	±
^{131}I uptake	+	++++	+	0
Degree of malignancy	+	++ to +++	+++	++++++++

*Data based upon 885 cases analyzed by Woolner & others; figures have been rounded to the nearest digit. (Reproduced, with permission, from Williams: *Textbook of Endocrinology,* 4th ed. Saunders, 1968.)

†Some patients have been followed up to 32 years after diagnosis.

and hypoparathyroidism must be treated in the usual manner.

Prognosis

The prognosis is apparently directly related to the cell type. The anaplastic carcinomas advance rapidly in spite of early diagnosis and treatment; while papillary tumors, in spite of frequent bouts of recurrence, are almost never fatal. In general, the prognosis is less favorable in elderly patients.

Cline, R.E., & W.W. Shingleton: Long-term results in the treatment of carcinoma of the thyroid. Am J Surg 115:545–551, 1968.

Cunliffe, W.J., & others: A calcitonin-secreting medullary thyroid carcinoma associated with mucosa neuromas, marfanoid features, myopathy, and pigmentation. Am J Med 48:120–126, 1970.

Jackson, I.M.D., & J.A. Thomson: The relationship of carcinoma to the single thyroid nodule. Brit J Surg 54:1007–1009, 1967.

Lindsay, S.: *Carcinoma of the Thyroid Gland.* Thomas, 1960.

Lindsay, S., & I.L. Chaikoff: The effects of irradiation on the thyroid gland with particular reference to the induction of thyroid neoplasm: A review. Cancer Res 24:1099–1107, 1964.

Medina, R.G., & D.W. Elliott: Thyroid carcinoma. Arch Surg 97:239–245, 1968.

Sarosi, G., & R.P. Doe: Familial occurrence of parathyroid adenomas, pheochromocytoma, and medullary carcinoma of thyroid with amyloid stroma (Sipple's syndrome). Ann Int Med 68:1305, 1968.

Tashjian, A.H., & K.E.W. Melvin: Medullary carcinoma of the thyroid gland: Studies of thyrocalcitonin in plasma and tumor extracts. New England J Med 279:279–283, 1968.

Taylor, S.: Thyroid carcinoma and its treatment. Postgrad MJ 44:404–410, 1968.

Vander, J.B., Gaston, E.A., & T.R. Dawber: The significance of nontoxic thyroid nodules. Ann Int Med 69:537–540, 1968.

Williams, E.D.: Medullary carcinoma of the thyroid. J Clin Path 20:395–398, 1967.

THYROIDITIS

Essentials of Diagnosis

- Painful swelling of thyroid gland, causing pressure symptoms in acute and subacute forms and painless enlargement in chronic forms.
- Thyroid function tests variable; discrepancy in PBI and radioiodine uptake common.
- Serologic autoantibody tests often positive.

General Considerations

Thyroiditis has been more frequently diagnosed in recent years since special serologic tests for thyroid auto-antibodies became available. This heterogeneous group can be divided into 2 groups.

Clinical Findings

A. Symptoms and Signs:

1. Thyroiditis due to specific causes (pyogenic infections, tuberculosis, syphilis)—A rare disorder causing severe pain, tenderness, redness, and fluctuation in the region of the thyroid gland.

2. Nonspecific (?autoimmune) thyroiditis—

a. Acute or subacute nonsuppurative thyroiditis (De Quervain's thyroiditis, granulomatous thyroiditis, giant cell thyroiditis, giant follicular thyroiditis)—An acutely painful enlargement of the thyroid gland, with dysphagia. The pain radiates into the ears. The manifestations may persist for several weeks and may be associated with signs of thyrotoxicosis and malaise. Middle-aged women are most commonly affected. Viral infection (perhaps mumps) has been suggested as the cause.

b. Hashimoto's thyroiditis (struma lymphomatosa, lymphadenoid goiter, chronic lymphocytic thyroiditis)—This is the most common form of thyroiditis, and is seen principally in middle-aged women. Onset of enlargement of the thyroid gland is insidious, with few pressure symptoms. Signs of thyroid dysfunction seldom appear, but in a few cases the disease may progress to myxedema. The gland may show marked enlargement.

c. Riedel's thyroiditis (chronic fibrous thyroiditis, Riedel's struma, woody thyroiditis, ligneous thyroiditis, invasive thyroiditis)—This is the rarest form of thyroiditis and is found only in middle-aged women. Enlargement is often asymmetric; the gland is stone hard and adherent to the neck structures, causing signs of compression and invasion, including dysphagia, dyspnea, and hoarseness.

B. Laboratory Findings: BMR may be elevated in the early stages of acute and subacute thyroiditis, and may be very low in the late stages of chronic thyroiditis. The PBI, T_4, and T_3 uptake of red cells or resin is usually elevated in acute and subacute thyroiditis and normal or low in the chronic forms. Radioiodine uptake is characteristically very low in subacute thyroiditis; it may be high in chronic thyroiditis with enlargement of the gland, and low in Riedel's struma. The TSH stimulation test shows lack of response in most forms of thyroiditis. Leukocytosis, elevation of the sedimentation rate, and increase in serum globulins are common in acute and subacute forms. Thyroid autoantibodies are most commonly demonstrable in Hashimoto's thyroiditis but are also found in the other types.

Complications

In the suppurative forms of thyroiditis any of the complications of infection may occur; the subacute and chronic forms of the disease are complicated by the effects of pressure on the neck structures: inanition, dyspnea, and, in Riedel's struma, vocal cord palsy. Many patients remain permanently myxedematous when the disease process subsides. Carcinoma may be associated with chronic thyroiditis and must be considered in the diagnosis of uneven painless enlargements which continue in spite of treatment. Chronic thyroiditis may be associated with Addison's disease (Schmidt's syndrome), various collagen diseases, cirrhosis, and gonadal dysgenesis.

Differential Diagnosis

Thyroiditis must be considered in the differential diagnosis of all types of goiters, especially if enlargement is rapid. In the acute or subacute stages it may simulate thyrotoxicosis, and only a careful evaluation of several of the laboratory findings will point to the correct diagnosis. The very low radioiodine uptake in subacute thyroiditis with elevated PBI and a very rapid sedimentation rate is of the greatest help. Chronic thyroiditis, especially if the enlargement is uneven and if there is pressure and invasion of surrounding structures, may resemble carcinoma, and both disorders may be present in the same gland. The subacute and suppurative forms of thyroiditis may resemble any infectious process in or near the neck structures; and the presence of malaise, leukocytosis, and a high sedimentation rate is confusing. The thyroid auto-antibody tests have been of great help in the diagnosis of chronic thyroiditis, but the tests are not specific and may also be positive in patients with goiters, carcinoma, and occasionally even in thyrotoxicosis. Biopsy may be required at times to establish the diagnosis.

Treatment

A. Suppurative Thyroiditis: Antibiotics, and surgical drainage when fluctuation is marked.

B. Subacute Thyroiditis: All treatment is empiric, and must be maintained for several weeks since the recurrence rate is high. Corticotropin or corticosteroid treatment is often helpful, especially in the early stages. Salicylates in large doses (6–8 gm/day) may be given for pain. Desiccated thyroid, 120–200 mg (2–3 gr), or thyroxine, 0.2–0.3 mg, may be helpful in shrinking the size of the gland after toxic symptoms have subsided. Low-dosage x-ray therapy (600–1200 r) is at times required if other measures fail. Propylthiouracil, 100–200 mg every 8 hours, or methimazole, 20–40 mg every 8 hours, may decrease tenderness.

Surgery is rarely required; splitting of the isthmus to relieve pressure and biopsy is the procedure of choice.

C. Hashimoto's Thyroiditis: Thyroid, thyroxine, or triiodothyronine in full doses may reduce the size of the gland markedly; since the disease will often progress to myxedema, this treatment probably should be continued indefinitely. Corticosteroid treatment often reduces the gland rapidly (this may be of diagnostic help). X-ray therapy, propylthiouracil, and partial thyroidectomy are rarely required.

D. Riedel's struma often requires partial thyroidectomy to relieve pressure; adhesions to surrounding structures make this a difficult operation.

Prognosis

The course of this group of diseases is quite variable. Spontaneous remissions and exacerbations are common in the subacute form, and therapy is nonspecific. The disease process may smolder for weeks. Thyrotoxicosis may occur. The chronic form may be part of a systemic collagen disease (eg, lupus erythematosus, Sjögren's syndrome) with all of the complications of that disease. Recurrent subacute and, more often, chronic thyroiditis lead to permanent destruction of the thyroid gland in a large number of patients and to myxedema. Continuous thyroid replacement therapy, by suppressing TSH, may shrink the gland. It has also been suggested that this may lessen the tendency of malignant transformation in chronic thyroiditis.

Colcock, B.P., & O. Pena: Diagnosis and treatment of thyroiditis. Postgrad Med 44:83–92, 1968.

Doniach, D.: Thyroid autoimmune disease. J Clin Path 20:385–390, 1967.

Greene, J.N.: Subacute thyroiditis. Am J Med 51:97–108, 1971.

Hall, R., & J.B. Stanbury: Familial studies of autoimmune thyroiditis. Clin Exper Immunol 2:719–726, 1967.

Thomas, W.C., Jr., & others: Clinical studies in thyroiditis. Ann Int Med 63:808–818, 1965.

Williams, E.D., Engel, E., & A.P. Forbes: Thyroiditis and gonadal dysgenesis. New England J Med 270:805–809, 1964.

THE PARATHYROIDS

HYPOPARATHYROIDISM & PSEUDOHYPOPARATHYROIDISM

Essentials of Diagnosis

- Tetany, carpopedal spasms, stridor and wheezing, muscle and abdominal cramps, urinary frequency, personality changes, mental torpor.
- Cataracts; positive Chvostek's sign and Trousseau's phenomenon; defective nails and teeth.
- Serum calcium low; serum phosphate high; alkaline phosphatase normal; urine calcium (Sulkowitch) negative.
- Basal ganglia calcification on x-ray of skull.

General Considerations

A deficiency of parathyroid hormone is most commonly seen following thyroidectomy or, more rarely, following surgery for parathyroid tumor. Very rarely it follows x-ray irradiation to the neck or massive radioactive iodine administration for cancer of the thyroid. Partial hypoparathyroidism is now recognized in a significant number of patients following thyroidectomy.

Transient hypoparathyroidism may be seen in the neonatal period, presumably due to a relative underactivity of the parathyroid; or to extraordinary demands on the parathyroids by the intake of cow's milk containing a great deal of phosphate. A similar mechanism may operate in the tetany of pregnancy.

Neonatal tetany may be a manifestation of maternal hyperparathyroidism.

Idiopathic hypoparathyroidism, often associated with candidiasis, may be familial and may be associated with Addison's disease. Pseudohypoparathyroidism is a genetic defect associated with short stature, round face, obesity, short metacarpals, hypertension, and ectopic bone formation. The parathyroids are present and often hyperplastic, but the renal tubules do not respond to the hormone.

Clinical Findings

A. Symptoms and Signs: Acute hypoparathyroidism causes tetany, with muscle cramps, irritability, carpopedal spasm, and convulsions; stridor, wheezing, dyspnea; photophobia and diplopia; abdominal cramps, and urinary frequency. Symptoms of the chronic disease are lethargy, personality changes, anxiety state, blurring of vision due to cataracts, and mental retardation.

Chvostek's sign (facial contraction on tapping the facial nerve near the angle of the jaw) is positive and Trousseau's phenomenon (carpopedal spasm after application of a cuff) is present. Cataracts may occur; the nails may be thin and brittle; the skin dry and scaly, at times with fungus infection (candidiasis) and loss of hair (eyebrows); and deep reflexes may be hyperactive. In pseudohypoparathyroidism the fingers and toes are short, with absence of the knuckles of the 4th and 5th fingers on making a fist; ectopic soft tissue calcification may be seen and felt. Choking of the optic disks is rarely found. Teeth may be defective if the onset of the disease occurs in childhood.

B. Laboratory Findings: Serum calcium is low, serum phosphate high, urinary phosphate low (TRP above 95%), urinary calcium low to absent (negative Sulkowitch test), and alkaline phosphatase normal. Alkaline phosphatase may be elevated in pseudohypoparathyroidism. NPN is normal.

C. X-Ray Findings: X-rays of the skull may show basal ganglia calcifications; the bones may be denser than normal (in pseudohypoparathyroidism short metacarpals and ectopic bone may be seen, and bones may be demineralized).

D. Other Examinations: Slit lamp examination may show early cataract formation. EEG shows generalized dysrhythmia (partially reversible). ECG may show prolonged Q–T intervals.

Complications

Acute tetany with stridor, especially if associated with vocal cord palsy, may lead to respiratory obstruction requiring tracheostomy. Severe hypocalcemia may lead to cardiac dilatation and failure. The complications of chronic hypoparathyroidism depend largely upon the duration of the disease and the age at onset. If it starts early in childhood, there may be stunting of growth, malformation of the teeth, and retardation of mental development. There may be associated sprue syndrome, pernicious anemia, and Addison's disease, probably on the basis of an autoimmune mechanism. In pseudohypoparathyroidism, hypothyroidism due to deficiency of thyrotropin is often found. In longstanding cases, cataract formation and calcification in the basal ganglia are seen. Permanent brain damage with convulsions or with psychosis may lead to admission to mental institutions. In addition, there may be complications of overtreatment with calcium and vitamin D, with renal impairment and calcinosis.

Differential Diagnosis

The symptoms of hypocalcemic tetany are most commonly confused with or mistaken for tetany due to metabolic or respiratory alkalosis, in which the serum calcium is normal. Symptoms of anxiety are common in both instances, and fainting is not uncommon in the hyperventilation syndrome. The typical blood and urine findings should differentiate the 2 disorders. This holds true also for less common causes of hypocalcemic tetany, such as rickets and osteomalacia in the early stages. In this condition the serum phosphate is invariably low or low normal; rarely high. Confusion might arise with the tetany due to chronic renal failure, in which retention of phosphorus will produce a high serum phosphorus with low serum calcium, but the differentiation should be obvious on clinical grounds (eg, uremia, azotemia).

In primary hyperaldosteronism with tetany (due to alkalosis) there is associated hypertension and hypokalemia with inability to concentrate the urine. Hypomagnesemia must be considered if tetany fails to respond to calcium.

The physical signs of pseudohypoparathyroidism without the abnormal blood chemical findings are seen in certain dysplasias ("pseudopseudohypoparathyroidism").

In order to differentiate true hypoparathyroidism, which responds to parathyroid extract, from pseudohypoparathyroidism, which does not respond, the Ellsworth-Howard test (phosphaturia after administration of 200 units of parathormone IV) has to be performed. The parathormone resistance has been demonstrated to be due to failure of activation of renal adenyl cyclase with defective excretion of cyclic AMP. Recently, high levels of calcitonin have been demonstrated in thyroid tissue of patients with pseudohypoparathyroidism, but thyroidectomy is of little help. Medullary carcinoma of the thyroid may also be associated with hypocalcemia due to excess calcitonin.

At times hypoparathyroidism is misdiagnosed as brain tumor (on the basis of brain calcifications, convulsions, choked disks) or, more rarely, as "asthma" (on the basis of stridor and dyspnea). Other causes of cataracts and basal ganglia calcification also enter into the differential diagnosis.

Treatment

A. Emergency Treatment for Acute Attack (Hypoparathyroid Tetany): This usually occurs after surgery and requires immediate treatment. *Note:* Be sure an adequate airway is present.

1. Calcium chloride, 5–10 ml of 10% solution IV slowly until tetany ceases, or calcium gluconate, 10–20 ml of 10% solution IV, may be given. Ten to 50 ml of either solution may be added to 1 liter of 5% glucose in water or saline and administered by slow IV drip. The rate should be so adjusted that hourly determination of urinary calcium by means of the Sulkowitch test will be positive. *Note:* Do not treat tetany too vigorously, or irreversible tissue calcification will occur.

2. Calcium salts should be given orally as soon as possible to supply 1–2 gm of calcium daily: calcium gluconate, 8 gm 3 times daily; calcium lactate, 4–8 gm 3 times daily (some patients prefer tablet form); or calcium chloride, 2–4 gm 3 times daily (as 30% solution). OsCal®, a preparation of calcium carbonate containing 250 mg calcium, is well tolerated. Dosage is 4–8 tablets/day.

3. Dihydrotachysterol (Hytakerol®) and calciferol–Give either compound as soon as oral calcium is begun. Begin with 4–10 ml of oily solution of dihydrotachysterol (1.25 mg/ml) orally daily for 2–4 days, reduce dose to 1–2 ml daily for 1–3 weeks, and then determine maintenance requirements. The action of dihydrotachysterol is irregular, and the drug is expensive. Pure crystalline preparations (eg, Digratyl®) in tablets of 0.2 mg are now available. The initial dose is 0.8–2.4 mg daily for several days. Calciferol, 80–160 thousand units (2–4 mg) daily, is just as effective (though its effects are slower in onset) and probably should be used in the majority of patients.

4. Parathyroid injection, 50–100 units IM or subcut 3–5 times daily as necessary to prevent tetany–Do not use parathyroid hormone for over 1 week. Use only as long as absolutely necessary. Actually, parathormone is rarely ever used; it is not very practical and usually not necessary.

B. Maintenance Treatment:

1. High-calcium, low-phosphate diet (omit milk and cheese).

2. Calcium salts (as above except chloride) are continued.

3. Dihydrotachysterol (Hytakerol®), 0.5–1 ml daily to maintain blood calcium at normal level. (*Caution:* The usual preparation [AT 10] is not always reliable. See above.) Tablets of 0.2 mg are available. The dose is 0.2–1.8 mg weekly.

4. Calciferol, 40–200 thousand units (1–5 mg) daily. In some cases up to 7 or 8 mg of calciferol daily may be needed. Its action is probably similar to that of dihydrotachysterol, and it can certainly be substituted adequately clinically. The initial action of vitamin D appears to be slower. However, the cost to the patient is less than with dihydrotachysterol, and the margin of safety is probably greater. It accumulates in the body over prolonged periods. *Note:* Corticosteroids and sodium phytate (Rencal®) are effective antidotes in vitamin D intoxication.

5. Aluminum hydroxide gels may be employed to help lower the serum phosphate level in the initial stages of treatment.

6. Diphenylhydantoin and phenobarbital have recently been shown to control overt and latent tetany without alteration in calcium levels. They may be used as adjuncts in the management of refractory patients.

Caution: Phenothiazine drugs should be administered with caution in hypoparathyroid patients since they may precipitate dystonic reactions.

Prognosis

The outlook is fair if prompt diagnosis is made and treatment instituted. Some changes (eg, in the EEG) are reversible, but the cataracts and brain calcifications are permanent. They may be in part genetically determined and not related to hypocalcemia per se. Although treatment of the immediate acute attack is simple and effective, long-term therapy is tedious and expensive since a good preparation of parathormone is not available. Adequate control by a fairly intelligent patient is required to avoid undertreatment or overtreatment. Periodic blood chemical evaluation is required since sudden changes in blood levels may call for modification of the treatment schedule. (*Note:* The urinary calcium [Sulkowitch test] is of little value since hypercalciuria, regardless of blood calcium level, may occur with prolonged vitamin D therapy. Sudden appearance of hypercalcemia, especially in children, may be due to associated Addison's disease.)

Unrecognized or late cases may find their way into mental institutions.

Blizzard, R.M., & others: The incidence of parathyroid and other antibodies in the sera of patients with idiopathic hypoparathyroidism. Clin Exper Immunol 1:119–128, 1966.

Bronsky, D., Kiamko, R.T., & S.S. Waldstein: Familial idiopathic hypoparathyroidism. J Clin Endocrinol 28:61–65, 1968.

Chase, L.R., & others: Pseudohypoparathyroidism: Defective excretion of 3′,5′-AMP in response to parathyroid hormone. J Clin Invest 48:1832–1844, 1969.

Fonseca, O.A., & J.R. Calverley: Neurological manifestations of hypoparathyroidism. Arch Int Med 120:202, 1967.

Harrison, H.E., & others: Comparison between crystalline dihydrotachysterol and calciferol in patients requiring pharmacologic vitamin D therapy. New England J Med 276:894, 1967.

Hung, W., Migeon, C.F., & R.H. Parrott: A possible autoimmune basis for Addison's disease in three siblings, one with idiopathic hypoparathyroidism, pernicious anemia and superficial moniliasis. New England J Med 269:658–663, 1963.

Ireland, A.W., & others: The calciferol requirements of patients with surgical hypoparathyroidism. Ann Int Med 69:81, 1968.

King, L.R., & others: Serum calcium homeostasis following thyroid surgery as measured by EDTA infusion. J Clin Endocrinol 25:577–584, 1965.

Kleeman, C.R., & others: The clinical physiology of calcium homeostasis, parathyroid hormone, and calcitonin. California Med 114:16–43, March 1971; 114:19–30, April 1971.

Kolb, F.O., & others: Primary hypoparathyroidism, Addison's disease and ovarian failure. Page 116 in: *Reproductive Endocrinology*. W.J. Irvine (editor). Livingstone, 1970.

Lee, J.B., & others: Parathyroid hormone and thyrocalcitonin in familial pseudohypoparathyroidism. New England J Med 279:1179–1184, 1968.

Mizrahi, A., & others: Neonatal hypocalcemia: Its causes and treatment. New England J Med 278:1163, 1968.

O'Malley, B.W., & P.O. Kohler: Hypoparathyroidism. Postgrad Med 44:71–79, 182–190, 1968.

Schaaf, M., & C.A. Payne: Dystonic reactions to prochlorperazine in hypoparathyroidism. New England J Med 275:991, 1966.

Schaaf, M., & C.A. Payne: Effect of diphenylhydantoin and phenobarbital on overt and latent tetany. New England J Med 274:1228, 1966.

Suh, S.M., & others: Pseudohypoparathyroidism: No improvement following total thyroidectomy. J Clin Endocrinol 29:429–439, 1969.

Zisman, E., & others: Studies in pseudohypoparathyroidism. Two new cases with a probably selective deficiency of thyrotropin. Am J Med 46:464–471, 1969.

HYPERPARATHYROIDISM

Essentials of Diagnosis

- Renal stones, nephrocalcinosis, polyuria, polydipsia, hypertension, uremia, intractable peptic ulcer, constipation.
- Bone pain, cystic lesions, and, rarely, pathologic fractures.

TABLE 18–5. Principal findings in the various parathyroid syndromes.*

Syndrome	Low Serum Ca With High Serum P	Serum Alkaline Phosphatase	Cataracts; Calcification of Basal Ganglia	Microdactylia; Ectopic Bone	Subperiosteal Resorption (Osteitis)	Parathyroid Hyperplasia	Ellsworth-Howard Test†
Hypoparathyroidism	+	Normal	+	0	0	0	+
Pseudohypoparathyroidism	+	Normal	+	+	0	+	0
Pseudopseudohypoparathyroidism	0	Normal	0	+	0	0	+
Secondary (renal) hyperparathyroidism	+ (NPN↑)	↑	0	0	+	+	±
Pseudohypoparathyroidism with secondary hyperparathyroidism	+ (NPN normal)	↑	±	+	+	+	0

*Reproduced, with permission, from Kolb, F.O., & H.L. Steinbach: Pseudohypoparathyroidism with secondary hyperparathyroidism and osteitis fibrosa. J Clin Endocrinol 22:68, 1962.

†Responsiveness to parathyroid hormone.

- Serum and urine calcium elevated; urine phosphate high with low to normal serum phosphate; alkaline phosphatase normal to elevated.
- "Band keratopathy" on slit lamp examination of eye.
- X-ray: subperiosteal resorption, loss of lamina dura of teeth, renal parenchymal calcification or stones, bone cysts.

General Considerations

While primary hyperparathyroidism is a relatively rare disease, it is potentially curable if detected early. Recent surveys suggest that hyperfunction of the parathyroids, often as asymptomatic hypercalcemia, may be present in 0.1% of patients examined. (*Note:* It should always be suspected in obscure bone and renal disease, especially if calculi or nephrocalcinosis are present.) At least 5% of renal stones are associated with this disease.

About 90% of cases of primary hyperparathyroidism are caused by a single adenoma (or, in rare cases, 2 adenomas); 8% are caused by primary hypertrophy and hyperplasia of all 4 glands; and 2% are caused by carcinoma of one gland. Multiple adenomas, often familial, of the pancreas and pituitary, thyroid, and adrenal glands may be associated with primary hyperparathyroidism due to tumor or, more commonly, due to hyperplasia of the parathyroids.

Secondary hyperparathyroidism is almost always associated with hyperplasia of all 4 glands, but on rare occasions an autonomous tumor may arise in hyperplastic glands ("tertiary hyperparathyroidism"). It is most commonly seen in chronic renal disease, but is also found in rickets, osteomalacia, and acromegaly.

Hyperparathyroidism causes excessive excretion of calcium and phosphate by the kidneys; this produces eventually either diffuse parenchymal calcification (nephrocalcinosis) or calculus formation within the urinary tract (the 2 types rarely coexist). If the excessive demands for calcium are met by dietary intake, the bones may not become drained (most common type in the USA). If calcium intake is not adequate, bone disease may occur. Factors other than the calcium intake probably determine whether bone disease will be present in hyperparathyroidism. This may show either diffuse demineralization, pathologic fractures, or cystic bone lesions throughout the skeleton ("osteitis fibrosa cystica").

Clinical Findings

A. Symptoms and Signs: The manifestations of hyperparathyroidism may be divided into those referable to (1) skeletal involvement, (2) renal and urinary tract damage, and (3) hypercalcemia per se. Since the adenomas are small and deeply located, only about 5% of cases of adenoma can be demonstrated by barium swallow displacing the esophagus or by palpation of a mass in the neck. It may be associated with a thyroid adenoma or carcinoma. (*Note:* Some patients have surprisingly few symptoms and the tumors are discovered accidentally by blood chemical findings.)

1. Skeletal manifestations—These may vary from simple back pain, joint pains, painful shins, and similar complaints, to actual pathologic fractures of the spine, ribs, or long bones, with loss of height and progressive kyphosis. At times an epulis of the jaw (actually a "brown tumor") may be the telltale sign of osteitis fibrosa. "Clubbing" of the fingers due to fracture and telescoping of the tips occur more rarely.

2. Urinary tract manifestations—Polyuria and polydipsia occur early in the disease. Sand, gravel, or stones containing calcium oxalate or phosphate may be passed in the urine. Secondary infection and obstruction may cause nephrocalcinosis and renal damage, leading eventually to uremia.

3. Manifestations of hypercalcemia—Thirst, nausea, anorexia, and vomiting are outstanding symptoms. Often one finds a past history of peptic ulcer, with obstruction or even hemorrhage. There may be stubborn constipation, asthenia, anemia, and weight loss. Hypertension is commonly found. Depression and psychosis may occur. Of unusual interest is hypermotility of joints. The fingernails and toenails may be unusually strong and thick. Calcium may precipitate in the eyes ("band keratopathy"). In secondary (renal) hyperparathyroidism, calcium also precipitates in the soft tissues, especially around the joints. Recurrent pancreatitis occurs in some patients.

B. Laboratory Findings: Serum calcium is usually high (adjust for serum protein); the serum phosphate is low or normal; the urinary calcium is often high; there is an excessive loss of phosphate in the urine in the presence of low to low normal serum phosphate (low tubular reabsorption of phosphate; TRP below 80–90%); the alkaline phosphatase is elevated only if bone disease is present (in about 25% of cases). The plasma chloride level is slightly elevated. (In secondary hyperparathyroidism the serum phosphate is high as a result of renal retention, and the calcium is usually low or normal.) Radioimmune assays for parathormone will be available in the near future.

Note: A great number of special tests have been devised to demonstrate abnormal phosphate dynamics in primary hyperparathyroidism. None of these are as consistently reliable as several accurately performed serum calcium determinations, which demonstrate hypercalcemia for which no other cause can be detected. (See Strott reference.) Control of the dietary phosphate is important since high phosphate intake may normalize borderline high serum calcium levels.

C. X-Ray Findings: X-ray rarely demonstrates the tumor on barium swallow; at times, special angiography may demonstrate it. If bone disease is present, one may see diffuse demineralization; subperiosteal resorption of bone (especially in the radial aspects of the fingers); and often loss of the lamina dura of the teeth. There may be cysts throughout the skeleton, mottling of the skull ("salt and pepper appearance"), or pathologic fractures. Articular cartilage calcification is commonly found. One may find diffuse stippled calcifications in the region of the kidneys (nephrocalcinosis) or calculi in the urinary tract. Soft tissue calcifications

TABLE 18–6. Most common laboratory findings in diseases associated with hypercalcemia.*

	Serum Phosphorus	Serum Alkaline Phosphatase	Blood Urea Nitrogen	Plasma Protein	Urinary Calcium	Renal Phosphorus Clearance	Renal Tubular Reabsorption of Phosphorus	Response to Steroids	Miscellaneous Findings
Malignant tumors Osteolytic metastases	N	N	N	N	↑	N	N	Usually	Visualization of localized bone lesion on x-ray study.
Secretion of parathyroid hormone-like substance	↓ or N	N or ↑	N	N	↑	N or ↑	↓ or N	Sometimes	
Multiple myeloma	N or ↑	N or ↑	↑	↑ (M protein)	↑	N	↓	Usually	Bone marrow abnormality; Bence Jones protein in urine.
Lymphoma or leukemia	N or ↑	N	N or ↑	N or ↑	N or ↑	N	↓ or N	Yes	Bone marrow abnormality.
Hyperparathyroidism†	↓ or N	N or ↑	N	N	N or ↑	↑	↓	Rarely	Abnormality on x-ray study of chest; liver disease; lymph node biopsy positive; elevated sedimentation rate.
Sarcoid	N	N or ↑	N	N (globulin) ↑	↑	↑	↓	Yes	
Vitamin D intoxication	↑	N or ↑	↑	N	↑	↑	↑	Yes	History positive.
Milk-alkali syndrome	N	N	↑	N	N	N	↓ or N	Yes	Alkalosis; rapid improvement after withdrawal of milk and alkali; band keratopathy, calcinosis.
Hyperthyroidism	N	N	N	N	N	N	N	Sometimes	Protein-bound iodine and ^{131}I uptake abnormal.
Acute bone atrophy (immobilization)									
Paraplegia	N	N	N	N	↑	N	N	No	
Fracture	N	↑	N	N	↑	N	N	No	
Paget's disease of bone	N	↑↑	N	N	↑	N	N	No	
Adrenal insufficiency	N	N	N or ↑	N or ↑	N	N	↓ or N	Yes	Hyperkalemia, hypotension, etc.
Idiopathic hypercalcemia of infancy	N or ↑	N	↑	N or ↑	N	N	↓ or N	Yes	Characteristic elfin facies; deafness.
(Effects of renal insufficiency)	↑	–	↑	–	↓	↓	↓	–	

*Reproduced, with permission, from Goldsmith, R.S.: Differential diagnosis of hypercalcemia. New England J Med 274:676, 1966.

†Hyperparathyroidism secondary to phosphorus retention in renal insufficiency is probably not associated with hypercalcemia unless glands become autonomous or form adenoma.

around the joints and in the blood vessels may be seen in renal osteitis.

D. Other Examinations: ECG may show a shortened Q–T interval. Slit lamp examination of the eye may show corneal calcification ("band keratopathy").

The localization of parathyroid tumors by selenomethionine scanning, in vivo parathyroid staining, and selective radioimmune assay via venous catheter are largely experimental.

Complications

Although the striking complications are those associated with skeletal damage (eg, pathologic fractures), the serious ones are those referable to renal damage. Urinary tract infection due to stone and obstruction may lead to renal failure and uremia. If the serum calcium level rises rapidly (eg, due to dehydration or salt restriction), "parathyroid poisoning" may occur, with acute renal failure and rapid precipitation of calcium throughout the soft tissues (hyperhyperparathyroidism). Peptic ulcer and pancreatitis may be intractable before surgery. Pancreatic islet cell adenoma with hypoglycemia may be associated, or ulcerogenic pancreatic tumor may coexist. Hypertension is frequently found. There may be associated hyperthyroidism or thyroid carcinoma. There is also an increased incidence of hyperuricemia and gouty arthritis.

Differential Diagnosis (See Table 18–6.)

If chemical determinations are reliable, the combination of high calcium and low phosphate in the serum, high urinary phosphate and calcium, and normal or high alkaline phosphatase is almost pathognomonic of hyperparathyroidism. Only rarely has this combination been seen in multiple myeloma, metastatic cancer (kidney, bladder, thyroid), and hyperthyroidism. If renal damage is present, the typical picture may be obscured, ie, the serum phosphate may not be low. Other causes of hypercalcemia (eg, sarcoidosis, vitamin D intoxication) will respond to the administration of cortisone (cortisone test), which usually does not affect the hypercalcemia of primary hyperparathyroidism. Chlorothiazides may raise the serum calcium level. If bone disease is present, the typical subperiosteal resorption may differentiate osteitis fibrosa from nonmetabolic bone disease and from osteoporosis. Bone biopsy may at times settle the diagnosis.

Recently, nonmetastasizing carcinomas (eg, of the lung, kidney, or ovary) have been described with blood chemical changes identical with those seen in hyperparathyroidism; these changes are often reversible upon removal of these tumors, which appear to produce a parathyroid-like hormone. (See Lafferty reference, below.)

Treatment

A. Surgical Measures: If a parathyroid tumor, the usual cause, is found, it should be removed surgically. The surgeon must be aware that multiple tumors may be present; the tumor may be in an ectopic site, eg, the mediastinum. Hyperplasia of all glands requires removal of 3 glands and subtotal resection of the 4th

before cure is assured. *Caution:* After surgery the patient may in the course of several hours or days develop tetany (usually transient) as a result of rapid fall of blood calcium even though the calcium level may fall only to the normal or low normal range. *Caution:* Be certain that an adequate airway is present.

Therapy is as for hypoparathyroid tetany (see p 621). Prolonged hypocalcemia due to recalcification of the "hungry" skeleton may require large amounts of calcium and vitamin D. Additional magnesium salts may have to be given postoperatively.

B. Fluids: A large fluid intake is necessary so that a diluted urine will be excreted to minimize the formation of calcium phosphate renal stones.

C. Treatment of Hypercalcemia: Force fluids both orally and parenterally (sodium chloride given IV is most helpful); mobilize the patient; reduce calcium intake; and add extra phosphate or give sodium phytate (Rencal®), 3 gm 3 times daily orally, or sodium sulfate. Cortisone therapy is usually not effective in this type of hypercalcemia. Sodium sulfate and sodium and potassium phosphate as slow IV infusions have been used successfully in patients with hypercalcemia but must be used with caution. Furosemide or ethacrynic acid may be helpful. If renal function is impaired, hemodialysis may be lifesaving if only for a short time. Mithramycin may reduce the hypercalcemia due to malignancy, but this drug is quite toxic. The recently discovered hormone calcitonin (thyrocalcitonin), which lowers serum calcium, has been used experimentally in the treatment of hypercalcemia, but its value is uncertain. (*Note:* The patient with hypercalcemia is very sensitive to the toxic effects of digitalis.)

Prognosis

The disease is usually a chronic progressive one unless treated successfully by surgical removal. There are at times unexplained exacerbations and partial remissions. Completely asymptomatic patients with mild hypercalcemia may be watched by serial calcium determinations, and placed on a high fluid and phosphate intake to prevent renal stones.

Spontaneous cure due to necrosis of the tumor has been reported but is exceedingly rare. The prognosis is directly related to the degree of renal impairment. The bones, in spite of severe cyst formation, deformity, and fracture, will heal completely if a tumor is successfully removed. Once significant renal damage has occurred, however, it progresses even after removal of an adenoma, and life expectancy is materially reduced. Secondary hyperparathyroidism not infrequently results due to irreversible renal impairment. In carcinoma of the parathyroid (rare), the prognosis is often hopeless. The presence of pancreatitis increases the mortality. If hypercalcemia is severe, the patient may suddenly die in cardiac arrest or may develop irreversible acute renal failure. However, early diagnosis and cure of this disease in an increasing number of patients has led to dramatic metabolic changes and cessation of recurrent renal stones, the most consistent presenting symptom.

Aurbach, G.D., & others: Polypeptide hormones and calcium metabolism. Ann Int Med 70:1243, 1969.

Avioli, L.V.: The diagnosis of primary hyperparathyroidism. M Clin North America 52:451–462, 1968.

Ballard, H.S., Frame, B., & R.J. Hartsock: Familial multiple endocrine adenoma-peptic ulcer complex. Medicine 43:481, 1964.

Barnes, B.A., & O. Cope: Carcinoma of the parathyroid glands. JAMA 178:556–559, 1961.

Boonstra, C.E., & C.E. Jackson: Hyperparathyroidism detected by routine serum calcium analysis. Ann Int Med 63:468, 1965.

Carey, R.W., & others: Massive extraskeletal calcification during phosphate treatment of hypercalcemia. Arch Int Med 122:150, 1968.

Chakmakjian, Z.H., & J.E. Bethune: Sodium sulfate treatment of hypercalcemia. New England J Med 275:862, 1966.

Davies, D.R., Dent, C.E., & L. Watson: Tertiary hyperparathyroidism. Brit MJ 3:395–399, 1968.

Dent, C.E.: Some problems of hyperparathyroidism. Brit MJ 2:1419–1425, 1495–1500, 1962.

Dent, C.E., & L. Watson: The hydrocortisone test in primary and tertiary hyperparathyroidism. Lancet 2:662–663, 1968.

Dodds, W.J., & H.L. Steinbach: Primary hyperparathyroidism and articular cartilage calcification. Am J Roentgenol 104:884–892, 1968.

Egdahl, R.H., Canterbury, J.M., & E. Reiss: Measurement of circulating parathyroid hormone concentration before and after parathyroid surgery for adenoma or hyperplasia. Ann Surg 168:714–719, 1968.

Eisenberg, E.: Effects of varying phosphate intake in primary hyperparathyroidism. J Clin Endocrinol 28:651–660, 1968.

Forscher, B.K., & C.D. Arnaud (editors): F.R. Keating, Jr. Memorial Symposium: Hyperparathyroidism, 1970. Am J Med 50:557–700, 1971.

Foster, G.V.: Calcitonin (thyrocalcitonin). New England J Med 279:349, 1968.

Garrow, J.S., & R. Smith: The detection of parathyroid tumours by selenomethionine scanning. Brit J Radiol 41:307–311, 1968.

Goldsmith, R.S., & S.H. Ingbar: Inorganic phosphate treatment of hypercalcemia of diverse etiologies. New England J Med 274:21, 1966.

Gordan, G.S.: Recent progress in calcium metabolism: Clinical application. California Med 114:28–43, May 1971.

Holmes, E.C., & others: Parathyroid carcinoma: Collective review. Ann Surg 169:631–640, 1969.

Keating, F.R., Jr.: The clinical problem of primary hyperparathyroidism. M Clin North America 54:511, 1970.

Lafferty, F.W.: Pseudohyperparathyroidism. Medicine 45:247, 1966.

Lloyd, H.M.: Primary hyperparathyroidism: An analysis of the role of the parathyroid tumor. Medicine 47:53–72, 1968.

Massry, S.G., & others: Inorganic phosphate treatment of hypercalcemia. Arch Int Med 121:307–312, 1968.

Owens, M.P., Sorock, M.L., & E.M. Brown: The clinical application of in vivo parathyroid staining. Surgery 64:1049–1052, 1968.

Petersen, P.: Psychiatric disorders in primary hyperparathyroidism. J Clin Endocrinol 28:1491–1495, 1968.

Rienhoff, W.F., & others: The surgical treatment of hyperparathyroidism. Ann Surg 168:1061–1074, 1968.

Shackney, S.: Precipitous fall in serum calcium, hypotension, and acute renal failure after intravenous phosphate therapy for hypercalcemia. Ann Int Med 66:906, 1967.

Steinbach, H.L., & others: Primary hyperparathyroidism: A correlation of roentgen, clinical, and pathologic features. Am J Roentgenol 86:329–343, 1961.

Strott, C.A., & C.A. Nugent: Laboratory tests in the diagnosis of hyperparathyroidism in hypercalcemic patients. Ann Int Med 68:188, 1968.

Suki, W.N., & others: Acute treatment of hypercalcemia with furosemide. New England J Med 283:836–840, 1970.

Yendt, E.R., & R.J.A. Gagne: Detection of primary hyperparathyroidism, with special reference to its occurrence in hypercalciuric females with "normal" or borderline serum calcium. Canad MAJ 98:331–336, 1968.

METABOLIC BONE DISEASE

OSTEOMALACIA & RICKETS

Essentials of Diagnosis

- Muscular weakness, listlessness.
- Aching and "bowing" of bones.
- Serum calcium low to normal; serum phosphate low; alkaline phosphatase elevated.
- "Pseudofractures" and "washed out" bone on x-ray.

General Considerations

Osteomalacia is the adult form of rickets. It is a condition resulting from a calcium and phosphorus deficiency in the bone. It may be caused by insufficient absorption from the intestine, due either to a lack of calcium alone, or a lack of or resistance to the action of vitamin D. In adults, this form of osteomalacia is almost always found in association with disorders of fat absorption (diarrhea, sprue, pancreatitis, gastrectomy). The other more common variety of osteomalacia is found in association with renal calcium or phosphorus losses ("vitamin D-resistant rickets"). This is often a familial disorder. It is found in tubular disorders, either tubular "leaks" of phosphate and calcium due to failure of reabsorption, or due to excessive losses associated with tubular acidosis (calcium dissolved out of the bone to spare sodium or potassium, or both). There may be associated glycosuria and aminoaciduria (Fanconi's syndrome). Osteomalacia due to chronic phosphate depletion from prolonged use of aluminum hydroxide gels has been described (see Lotz reference, below).

Almost all forms of osteomalacia are associated with compensatory, secondary hyperparathyroidism, set off by the low calcium level. It is for this reason that most patients will show only slightly low serum calcium levels (compensated osteomalacia). In chronic uremic states a mixed picture of osteomalacia and secondary hyperparathyroidism is seen ("renal osteodystrophy"). Resistance to the action of vitamin D due to failure of its conversion to the biologically active form, 25-hydroxycholecalciferol, has recently been demonstrated.

TABLE 18–7. Summary of chemical findings in metabolic and nonmetabolic bone disease.*

Disease	Serum Calcium (mg/100 ml)	Serum Phosphorus (mg/100 ml)	Serum Alkaline Phosphatase (Bodansky Units)	Urinary Calcium† (mg/24 hours)
Normal adult	9–11	3–4.5	2–4.5	50–175
Metabolic				
Osteoporosis	Normal, rarely high	Normal	Normal	Normal or high
Osteomalacia	Low or normal	Low	High	Low if absorptive defect, high if renal defect.
Osteitis fibrosa cystica				
Primary hyperparathy-roidism	High	Low	High	High
Secondary hyperparathy-roidism	Low or normal	High	High	Low, normal, or high
Nonmetabolic				
Paget's disease	Normal or high	Normal	High	Normal or high
Multiple myeloma	Normal or high	Normal (rarely high or low)	Normal or high	Normal or high
Metastatic malignancy	Normal or high	Normal (or rarely low)	Normal or high	Normal or high
Fibrous dysplasia, neurofi-bromatosis, xanthomatosis	Normal	Normal	Normal	Normal

*Reproduced, with permission, from Kolb, F.O.: Metabolic diseases of bone in the adult. Kaiser Foundation Medical Bulletin 4:351, 1956.

†Urinary calcium on a diet free of milk and cheese and their products. Instead of a quantitative test, spot checks with Sulkowitch reagent are informative. (Use equal amounts, about 5 ml each of urine and reagent.) Normal patients have 1–2+ urine test depending upon urine volume. Read as follows: 0 = no cloud; 1+ = faint cloud after several seconds; 2+ = faint cloud appearing immediately; 3+ = dense cloud without flocculation; 4+ = heavy flocculation.

A special form of osteomalacia is the so-called Milkman's syndrome, an x-ray diagnosis of multiple, bilaterally symmetric pseudofractures which may represent the shadows of calluses near arterial blood vessels traversing and eroding the soft skeleton. Rickets, which is the counterpart of osteomalacia in the growing child, shows additional features, especially around the epiphyses, which are widened and "motheaten" on x-ray. There is also beading of the ribs, Harrison's groove, bowlegs, and disturbances in growth.

In contrast to osteoporosis, where fractures are more common, osteomalacia is more often associated with bowing of bones.

Clinical Findings

A. Symptoms and Signs: Manifestations are variable, ranging from almost none in mild cases to marked muscular weakness and listlessness in advanced cases. There is usually mild aching of the bones, especially of long bones and ribs, and a tendency to bowing. In the very early and acute osteomalacias a rapidly falling calcium level may be associated with clinical tetany, although this is rare. As compensation takes place, tetanic features are absent. In states of deficient absorption, other features of the sprue syndrome, such as glossy tongue or anemia, may be present. A low potassium syndrome with muscular weakness and paralysis may be present with renal tubular disorders.

B. Laboratory Findings: Serum calcium is low or normal, but never high. Serum phosphate is low (may be normal in early stages). The alkaline phosphatase is elevated except in the early phase. Urinary calcium and phosphate are usually low in absorption disorders and high in renal lesions. The intravenous calcium infusion test demonstrates avidity of bone for calcium (80–90% retained) in osteomalacia due to malabsorption. Laboratory findings of the primary steatorrhea or renal disease may be present. In renal tubular acidosis the serum CO_2 is low and the serum chloride level is elevated; the serum potassium may be very low; the urinary pH is fixed near the alkaline side. Glycosuria and aminoaciduria are found in the Fanconi syndrome.

C. X-Ray Findings: Involvement of the pelvis and long bones, with demineralization and bowing; less often, the spine and skull are involved as well. Fractures are rare except for "pseudofractures."

Differential Diagnosis (See Table 18–6.)

It is most important to recognize osteomalacia and consider it in the differential diagnosis of bone disease since it is a potentially curable disease. The childhood forms may be mistaken for osteogenesis imperfecta or other nonmetabolic bone disorders.

The acute forms must be differentiated from other forms of tetany. The long-standing disease enters into the differential diagnosis of any metabolic or generalized nonmetabolic bone disease (see Table 18–7). The pseudofracture is often the only outstanding sign of latent osteomalacia. Osteoporosis may exist as well, and may obscure the osteomalacia. At times the diagnosis is confirmed by a rise and subsequent fall of the serum alkaline phosphatase after treatment with vitamin D and calcium. Renal tubular acidosis is a cause of nephrocalcinosis, and must be considered in the differential diagnosis of kidney calcifications with bone disease, such as hyperparathyroidism. The joint aches and pains may be mistaken for some form of arthritis. The cachexia suggests malignancy. Bone biopsy (eg, of the rib) with tetracycline labeling or microradiography may establish the diagnosis of latent osteomalacia.

Treatment

A. Specific Measures:

1. Rickets—Vitamin D, even in small doses, is specific; 2000–5000 units daily are adequate unless resistance to vitamin D is present.

2. Adult osteomalacia and Milkman's syndrome—Vitamin D is specific, but very large doses are necessary to overcome the resistance to its calcium absorptive action and to prevent renal loss of phosphate. Give until an effect is noted on the blood calcium. The usual dose is 25–100 thousand units daily. Doses up to 300,000 units or more daily may be necessary, but if the doses are over 100,000 daily, they must be used cautiously with periodic determinations of serum and urine calcium; the serum phosphate may remain low.

3. Pancreatic insufficiency—Adequate replacement therapy with pancreatic enzyme is of paramount importance; high calcium intake and vitamin K are also of value.

4. Sprue syndrome—Folic acid and vitamin B_{12} appear to be of value. A gluten-free diet should be used in patients with gluten sensitivity.

5. Some rare forms of renal disease—Treatment is aimed at the altered renal physiology, eg, alkali therapy in renal tubular acidosis, potassium replacement, etc.

B. General Measures: High-calcium diet and calcium gluconate or calcium lactate, 4–20 gm daily. A high-phosphate diet or phosphate salts may be of value in certain types of renal rickets.

Prognosis

The prognosis is usually excellent in the absorptive disorders if diagnosed early. This does not hold for certain of the vitamin D-resistant forms of osteomalacia or rickets or for Fanconi's disease, which respond slowly or not at all unless huge amounts of vitamin D are given. Hypercalcemia may occur as a complication of therapy. In severely refractory cases, parathyroidectomy has improved the prognosis. In the renal forms, the ultimate prognosis is that of the basic kidney disease. Respiratory paralysis due to hypokalemia may prove fatal.

Albright, F., & others: Osteomalacia and late rickets. Medicine 25:399–479, 1946.

Arnstein, A.R., & others: Recent progress in osteomalacia and rickets. Ann Int Med 67:1296, 1967.

Dent, C.E.: Rickets (and osteomalacia): Nutritional and metabolic (1919–69). Proc Roy Soc Med 63:27, 1970.

Eddy, R.L.: Metabolic bone disease after gastrectomy. Am J Med 50:442–449, 1971.

Lotz, M., Zisman, E., & F.C. Bartter: Phosphorus-depletion syndrome in man. New England J Med 278:409–415, 1968.

Riggs, B.L., & others: Parathyroidectomy in vitamin-D-resistant hypophosphatemic osteomalacia. New England J Med 281:762–766, 1969.

Stanbury, S.W.: The treatment of renal osteodystrophy. Ann Int Med 65:1133, 1966.

Steinbach, H.L., & M. Noetzli: Roentgen appearance of the skeleton in osteomalacia and rickets. Am J Roentgenol 91:955–972, 1964.

Stickler, G.B., & others: Vitamin D-resistant rickets: Clinical experience with 41 typical familial hypophosphatemic patients and 2 atypical nonfamilial cases. Mayo Clin Proc 45:197, 1970.

Williams, T.F.: Pathogenesis of familial vitamin D-resistant rickets. Ann Int Med 68:706–707, 1968.

Wilson, D.R., & others: Studies in hypophosphatemic vitamin D-refractory osteomalacia in adults. Medicine 44:99–134, 1965.

OSTEOPOROSIS
(Osteopenia)

Essentials of Diagnosis

- Asymptomatic to severe backache.
- Spontaneous fractures and collapse of vertebrae without spinal cord compression, often discovered "accidentally" on x-ray; loss of height.
- Calcium, phosphorus, and alkaline phosphatase normal.
- Demineralization of spine and pelvis.

General Considerations

Osteoporosis is the most commonly seen metabolic bone disease in the USA. The classical explanation is that osteoporosis is due to a lack of bone matrix, which leads to thinning of the skeleton and decrease in precipitation of lime salts. Inadequate calcium absorption may be another defect, so that osteoporosis may actually resemble osteomalacia. Excessive bone resorption is an additional factor. The term "osteopenia" describes this disorder more accurately. There is a physiologic progressive loss of bone with advancing age, most evident in white females.

Etiology

A. Principal Causes:

1. Lack of activity, eg, immobilization as in paraplegia or rheumatoid arthritis. (Osteoblasts depend upon strains and stresses for proper function.)

2. Lack of estrogens ("postmenopausal osteoporosis"). (Females are deprived of estrogens relatively

early in life. About 30% of women over 60 years of age have clinical osteoporosis. Some degree of osteoporosis is almost always present in senility.)

3. More recently a chronic low intake of calcium has been suggested as of etiologic importance. However, the evidence for this is still not conclusive.

4. Intestinal lactase deficiency may be an important factor in elderly patients with osteoporosis. (See Birge reference.)

B. Less Common Causes:

1. Developmental disturbances (eg, osteogenesis imperfecta).

2. Nutritional disturbances (eg, protein starvation and ascorbic acid deficiency).

3. Chronic calcium depletion is claimed by some investigators to cause osteoporosis.

4. Endocrine diseases—Lack of androgens (eunuchoidism, senility in men). hypopituitarism (causes secondary gonadal failure), acromegaly (cause unknown; possibly due to hypogonadism), thyrotoxicosis (not constant; causes excessive catabolism of protein tissue), excessive exogenous or endogenous ACTH or corticosteroids causing catabolism of bone (eg, Cushing's disease), and long-standing uncontrolled diabetes mellitus (rare).

5. Bone marrow disorders—The presence of abnormal cells in the bone marrow, such as in myeloma or leukemia, may prevent osteoblastic activity and cause osteoporosis. This is in addition to the active replacement of the marrow with tumor cells.

6. Prolonged use of heparin may lead to osteoporosis.

7. Idiopathic osteoporosis—The cause is undetermined. It is most common in young men and women but occasionally occurs in older people, and does not respond well to therapy.

Clinical Findings

A. Symptoms and Signs: Osteoporosis may first be discovered accidentally on x-ray examination, or may present as backache of varying degrees of severity. On other occasions it presents as a spontaneous fracture or collapse of a vertebra.

B. Laboratory Findings: Serum calcium, phosphate, and alkaline phosphatase are normal. The alkaline phosphatase may be slightly elevated in osteogenesis imperfecta and also in other forms of osteoporosis if there has been a recent fracture. Urinary calcium is high early, normal in chronic forms.

C. X-Ray Findings: X-ray shows compression of vertebrae. The principal areas of demineralization are the spine and pelvis; demineralization is less marked in the skull and extremities. The lamina dura is preserved. Kidney stones may be seen in acute osteoporosis.

Differential Diagnosis (See Table 18—6.)

It is important not to confuse this condition with other metabolic bone diseases, especially osteomalacia and hyperparathyroidism; or with myeloma and metastatic bone disease, especially of the breast and uterus, since estrogen therapy may aggravate them (see Table

18—7). Bone biopsy may be required, since these conditions may coexist in the postmenopausal patient.

A rare case of hypophosphatasia may appear as "osteoporosis."

Treatment

A. Specific Measures: Specific treatment varies with the cause; but combined hormone therapy is usually employed, although its effectiveness has not been proved.

1. Postclimacteric (mostly in females)—Estrogens may be of value in stimulating osteoblasts. Before beginning estrogen therapy in a postmenopausal woman, perform a careful pelvic examination to rule out neoplasm or other abnormality and warn the patient or a relative that vaginal bleeding may occur. Administer estrogen daily except for the first 5—7 calendar days of each month and then repeat the cycle. Any of the following may be used: (1) Diethylstilbestrol, 0.5—2 mg orally daily as tolerated (may produce nausea). (2) Ethinyl estradiol, 0.02—0.05 mg orally daily as tolerated. (3) Estrone sulfate and conjugated estrogenic substances (Premarin®, Amnestrogen®, etc) are well tolerated and widely used. The dosage is 1.25—2.5 mg orally daily. The long-acting injectable estrogen preparations may be more reliable.

Testosterone may be used in addition to estrogen for its protein anabolic effect and hence its tendency to lay down bone matrix. Give methyltestosterone, 5—10 mg orally daily. Avoid overdosage in females since excessive use may cause the appearance of male secondary sex characteristics. While some of these regress if therapy is stopped, others (eg, hoarseness, hirsutism) may persist. Some of the newer anabolic agents, eg, estradiol valerate and testosterone enanthate (Deladumone®), norethandrolone (Nilevar®), or methandrostenolone (Dianabol®), may be used (see p 685).

2. Old age and idiopathic—As for postclimacteric; both testosterone and estrogens should be used in both males and females. Use with caution in very old people.

3. Patients with malnutrition—Adequate diet is of great importance. However, hormones may be used as above if response to diet alone is poor.

4. Cushing's disease—See p 636.

5. Sodium fluoride has recently been tried in refractory osteoporotic patients but it must be considered still an experimental procedure.

6. Phosphate supplements may be of value in certain types of osteoporosis (eg, after fractures, myeloma).

7. Intravenous infusions of calcium have been advocated recently for refractory osteoporosis. This must be considered an experimental procedure and may act by stimulating calcitonin.

8. Calcitonin therapy of osteoporosis is under investigation.

B. General Measures: The diet should be high in protein and adequate in calcium (milk and milk products are desirable). Increased calcium intake by use of supplementary calcium salts (eg, calcium lactate), up to 1–2 gm calcium per day, may be warranted. Patients should be kept active; bedridden patients should be given active or passive exercises. The spine must be adequately supported (eg, with a Taylor brace), but rigid or excessive immobilization must be avoided.

Prognosis

With proper and prolonged therapy the prognosis is good for postclimacteric osteoporosis. Spinal involvement is not reversible on x-ray, but progression of the disease is often halted. In general, osteoporosis is a crippling rather than a killing disease, and the prognosis is essentially that of the underlying disorder (eg, Cushing's disease). The idiopathic variety does not respond appreciably to any form of therapy. Careful periodic records of patient's height will indicate if the disease process has become stabilized.

Albright, F., & E.C. Reifenstein: *The Parathyroid Glands and Metabolic Bone Disease.* Williams & Wilkins, 1948.

Birge, S.J., & others: Osteoporosis, intestinal lactase deficiency and low dietary calcium intake. New England J Med 276:445, 1967.

Dent, C.E., & M. Friedman: Idiopathic juvenile osteoporosis. Quart J Med (New Series) 34:177, 1965.

Goldsmith, R.S., & others: Effect of phosphate supplements in patients with fractures. Lancet 1:687, 1967.

Griffith, G.C., & others: Heparin osteoporosis. JAMA 193:91, 1965.

Harris, W.H., & R.P. Heaney: Skeletal renewal and metabolic bone disease. New England J Med 280:3–202, 253–259, 303–311, 1969.

Heaney, R.P.: A unified concept of osteoporosis (editorial). Am J Med 39:877, 1965.

Henneman, P.H., & S. Wallach: The use of androgens and estrogens and their metabolic effects. Symposium: A review of the prolonged use of estrogens and androgens in postmenopausal and senile osteoporosis. Arch Int Med 100:715–723, 1957.

Jowsey, J., & others: Some results of the effects of fluoride on bone tissue in osteoporosis. J Clin Endocrinol 28:869, 1968.

Jowsey, J., & others: The treatment of osteoporosis with calcium infusions: Evaluation of bone biopsies. Am J Med 47:17, 1969.

Lutwak, L., & G.D. Whedon: Osteoporosis. Disease-A-Month. Year Book, April 1963.

Nordin, B.E.C., MacGregor, J., & D.A. Smith: The incidence of osteoporosis in normal women: Its relation to age and the menopause. Quart J Med 35:25–38, 1968.

Pak, C.Y., & others: The treatment of osteoporosis with calcium infusions: Clinical studies. Am J Med 47:7, 1969.

Raisz, L.G.: Physiologic and pharmacologic regulation of bone resorption. New England J Med 282:909. 1970.

Spencer, H., & others: Absorption of calcium in osteoporosis. Am J Med 37:223–234, 1964.

Steinbach, H.L.: The roentgen appearance of osteoporosis. Radiol Clin North America 2:191–208, 1964.

Villanueva, A.E., & others: Cortical bone dynamics measured by means of tetracycline labeling in 21 cases of osteoporosis. J Lab Clin Invest 68:599, 1966.

NONMETABOLIC BONE DISEASE
(See Table 18–7.)

POLYOSTOTIC FIBROUS DYSPLASIA
(Osteitis Fibrosa Disseminata)

Essentials of Diagnosis

- Painless swelling of involved bone or fracture with minimal trauma; brown skin pigmentation with ragged borders may be present.
- Bone cysts or hyperostotic lesions; usually multiple, but occasionally single, in segmental distribution.
- Precocious puberty may occur in females.
- Serum calcium and phosphate normal; alkaline phosphatase sometimes elevated.

General Considerations

Polyostotic fibrous dysplasia is a rare disease which is frequently mistaken for osteitis fibrosa generalisata due to hyperparathyroidism since both are manifested by bone cysts and fractures. Polyostotic fibrous dysplasia is not a metabolic disorder of bone but a congenital dysplasia in which bone and cartilage do not form but remain as fibrous tissue.

Polyostotic fibrous dysplasia which is associated with "brown spots" with ragged margins and with true precocious puberty in the female is called Albright's syndrome. Hyperthyroidism and acromegaly may be present also.

Clinical Findings

A. Symptoms and Signs: The manifestations are painless swelling of the involved bone (usually the skull, upper end of femur, tibia, metartarsals, metacarpals, phalanges, ribs, and pelvis), either singly or in multiple distribution, with cysts or hyperostotic lesions and at times with brown pigmentation of the overlying skin. Involvement is segmental and may be unilateral. True sexual precocity may occur in females, with early development of secondary sex characteristics and rapid skeletal growth.

B. Laboratory Findings: Calcium and phosphorus are normal; the alkaline phosphatase may be elevated.

C. X-Ray Findings: X-rays reveal rarefaction and expansion of the affected bones or hyperostosis (especially of base of the skull). Fractures and deformities may also be visible.

Differential Diagnosis (See Table 18–6.)

The bone cysts and fractures should by their distribution and skin pigmentation be distinguished from those of hyperparathyroidism and neurofibromatosis. All other types of bone cyst and tumor must be considered also. The hyperostotic lesions of the skull must be distinguished from those of Paget's disease. Biopsy of bone may be required to settle the diagnosis.

Complications

Shortening of the extremity or deformity (eg, shepherd's crook deformity of femur) may follow extensive involvement of bone. The involvement of the orbit may cause proptosis or even blindness.

Treatment

There is no treatment except for surgical correction of deformities, eg, fractures, expanding cyst in the orbit. Calcitonin has been used in active disease, but the results are not conclusive.

Prognosis

Most lesions heal and the progression is slow. Since precocity is of the isosexual type, girls are susceptible to early pregnancy. They will ultimately be of short stature. On rare occasions sarcomatous transformation of bone occurs.

Bell, N.H., & others: Effect of calcitonin in Paget's disease and polyostotic fibrous dysplasia. J Clin Endocrinol 31:283–291, 1970.

Benedict, P.: Endocrine features in Albright's syndrome (fibrous dysplasia of bone). Metabolism 11:30–45, 1962.

Benedict, P.H., & others: Melanotic macules in Albright's syndrome and in neurofibromatosis. JAMA 205:618–626, 1968.

Buker, R.H., Hughes, F.A., Jr., & J.D. Mashburn: Polyostotic fibrous dysplasia (Albright's syndrome). J Thoracic Cardiovas Surg 49:241–246, 1965.

Schwartz, D.T., & M. Alpert: The malignant transformation of fibrous dysplasia. Am J M Sc 247:1, 1964.

PAGET'S DISEASE
(Osteitis Deformans)

Essentials of Diagnosis

- Often asymptomatic. Bone pain may be the first symptom.
- Kyphosis, bowed tibias, large head, waddling gait, and frequent fractures which vary with location of process.
- Serum calcium and phosphate normal; alkaline phosphatase elevated.
- Dense, expanded bones on x-ray.

General Considerations

Paget's disease is a nonmetabolic bone disease of unknown etiology which causes excessive bone destruction and repair, with associated deformities since the repair takes place in an unorganized fashion. Up to 3% of persons over age 50 will show isolated lesions, but clinically important disease is much less common.

Clinical Findings

A. Symptoms and Signs: Often mild or asymptomatic. Deep "bone pain" is usually the first symptom. The bones become soft, leading to bowed tibias, kyphosis, and frequent fractures with slight trauma.

The head becomes large, and headaches are a prominent symptom. Increased vascularity over the involved bones causes increased warmth.

B. Laboratory Findings: The blood calcium and phosphorus are normal, but the alkaline phosphatase is markedly elevated. Urinary hydroxyproline may be elevated.

C. X-Ray Findings: On x-ray the involved bones are expanded and denser than normal. Multiple fissure fractures may be seen in the long bones. The initial lesion may be destructive and radiolucent, especially in the skull ("osteoporosis circumscripta").

Differential Diagnosis

Differentiate from primary bone lesions such as osteogenic sarcoma or multiple myeloma, and secondary bone lesions such as metastatic carcinoma and osteitis fibrosa cystica. If serum calcium is elevated, hyperparathyroidism may be present in some patients as well.

Complications

Fractures are frequent and occur with minimal trauma. If immobilization takes place and there is an excessive calcium intake, hypercalcemia and kidney stones may develop. Bony overgrowth may impinge on vital structures, especially nerves, causing deafness and blindness. Long-standing cases may progress to osteosarcoma. The increased vascularity, acting as multiple arteriovenous fistulas, may give rise to high-output cardiac failure.

Treatment

Supply a high-protein diet with adequate vitamin C intake. A high-calcium intake is desirable also unless the patient is immobilized, in which case calcium must be restricted. Vitamin D, 50,000 units 3 times a week, is helpful in some patients. Anabolic hormones, eg, estradiol valerate and testosterone enanthate (Deladumone®), 1–3 ml/month, should be given as for osteoporosis. Corticosteroid treatment relieves pain but aggravates coexisting osteoporosis. Salicylates in large doses have recently been claimed to be useful in combating pain and reducing hypercalciuria. Sodium fluoride has also been tried in refractory cases (see Osteoporosis). Phosphate therapy may be helpful. Thyrocalcitonin and mithramycin are under investigation for the treatment of symptomatic and progressive disease.

Prognosis

The prognosis of the mild form is good, but sarcomatous changes (in 1–3%) or renal complications secondary to hypercalciuria (in 10%) alter the prognosis unfavorably. In general, the prognosis is worse the earlier in life the disease starts. Fractures usually heal well. In the severe forms, marked deformity, intractable pain, and cardiac failure are found.

Avioli, L.V., & M. Berman: Role of magnesium metabolism and the effects of fluoride therapy in Paget's disease of bone. J Clin Endocrinol 28:700–710, 1968.

Barry, H.C.: *Paget's Disease of Bone.* Livingstone, 1969.

Bijvoet, O.L.M., Van der Sluys Veer, J., & A.P. Jansen: Effects of calcitonin on patients with Paget's disease, thyrotoxicosis, or hypercalcaemia. Lancet 1:876–880, 1968.

De Deuxchaisnes, C.N., & S.M. Krane: Paget's disease of bone: Clinical and metabolic observations. Medicine 43:233–266, 1964.

Evens, R.G., & F.C. Bartter: The hereditary aspects of Paget's disease. JAMA 205:900–902, 1968.

Haddad, J.G., & others: Effects of prolonged thyrocalcitonin administration in Paget's disease of bone. New England J Med 283:549–555, 1970.

Harris, E.D., & S.M. Krane: Paget's disease of bone. Bull Rheumat Dis 18:506, 1968.

Kolb, F.O.: Paget's disease. California Med 91:245–250, 1959.

Ryan, W.G., & others: Effects of mithramycin on Paget's disease of bone. Ann Int Med 70:549, 1969.

Steinbach, H.L., & W.J. Dodds: Clinical radiology of Paget's disease. Clin Orthopaed Related Res 57:277–298, 1968.

DISEASES OF THE ADRENAL CORTEX

Total destruction of both adrenal cortices is not compatible with human life. The cortex regulates a variety of metabolic processes by means of secretion of some 30 steroid hormones.

The stimulus for release of steroid hormones from the adrenal cortex—with the possible exception of aldosterone—appears to be adrenocorticotropic hormone (ACTH) from the anterior pituitary which, in turn, is under the control of the hypothalamic corticotropin-releasing factor. The plasma free cortisol level regulates ACTH secretion. Aldosterone secretion, in contrast, is principally controlled by volume receptors, angiotensin II, and, possibly, the potassium concentration. Clinical syndromes of adrenal insufficiency or excess may thus be due to primary lesions of the adrenal glands themselves or may be secondary to pituitary disorders. Although the differentiation is often important from the diagnostic standpoint, treatment is usually directed toward the cortical disorder itself, whether primary or secondary. Many of the steroids isolated from the adrenal cortex are not active, and some have more than one action. Transcortin, a globulin, avidly binds cortisol and thus inactivates it. Estrogens increase transcortin levels. An active equilibrium exists between bound and free unbound cortisol. In general, the adrenocortical hormones have 3 types of activity:

(1) **Anabolic (sex steroids):** Androsterone and related steroids are protein builders and are also virilizing and androgenic, and represent the principal source of androgens in the female. This group also includes adrenal estrogens and progesterone-like steroids, but these are of lesser clinical importance.

(2) **Antianabolic or catabolic (glucocorticoids):** Cortisol, corticosterone, cortisone, and related steroids, the "stress hormones" of the adrenal cortex, are vital for survival. They are glycostatic, and cause gluconeogenesis from protein. They also play a role in potassium and water diuresis. Increased production or administration of large doses causes increased fat deposition in special sites (face, buffalo hump), raises blood pressure, and causes eosinopenia and lymphopenia.

(3) **Electrolyte-regulating (mineralocorticoids):** The principal hormone in this group is aldosterone. Its primary role is in retaining sodium and excreting potassium and thus "regulating" the extracellular fluid compartment and the blood pressure. It has minor effects on carbohydrate metabolism.

Most of the clinical features of both adrenal insufficiency and excess can be explained on the basis of the above types of activity. Since mixed pictures occur, however, and since excess of one type of activity may coexist with deficiency of another (eg, congenital adrenal virilism), exact physiologic correlation is difficult. Some phenomena, eg, the pigmentation of adrenal insufficiency, are not yet fully explained, and may be due to a pituitary intermedin or ACTH excess.

Bransome, E.D., Jr.: Adrenal cortex. Ann Rev Physiol 30:171, 1968.

Catt, K.J.: ABC of endocrinology. V. Adrenal cortex. Lancet 1:1275, 1970.

Eisenstein, A. (editor): *The Adrenal Cortex.* Little, Brown, 1967.

Forsham, P.H.: The adrenals. Chap 5 in: *Textbook of Endocrinology,* 4th ed. R.H. Williams (editor). Saunders, 1968.

Nelson, D.H. (editor): Treatment of adrenal disorders. Mod Treat 3:1327–1434, 1966.

Smilo, R.P., & P.H. Forsham: Diagnostic approach to hypofunction and hyperfunction of the adrenal cortex. Postgrad Med 45:146, 1969.

ADRENAL CORTICAL HYPOFUNCTION
(Adrenocortical Insufficiency)

1. ACUTE ADRENAL INSUFFICIENCY
(Adrenal Crisis)

Essentials of Diagnosis

- Onset of weakness, abdominal pain, high fever, confusion, nausea, vomiting, and diarrhea, with infection, or adrenal destruction, or cortisone withdrawal.
- Low blood pressure, dehydration, and increased skin pigmentation.
- Serum sodium low, serum potassium high, blood and urine corticosteroids low.
- Eosinophilia, elevated NPN.

General Considerations

Acute adrenal insufficiency is a true medical emergency caused by sudden marked deprivation or insufficient supply of adrenocortical hormones. Crisis may occur in the course of chronic insufficiency in a known addisonian patient out of control, or it may be the presenting manifestation of adrenal insufficiency. It may be a temporary exhaustion or may go on to permanent insufficiency. Acute crisis is more commonly seen in diseases of the cortex itself than in disorders of the pituitary gland causing secondary adrenocortical hypofunction.

Adrenal crisis may occur in the following situations: (1) Following stress, eg, trauma, surgery, infection, or prolonged fasting in a patient with latent insufficiency. (2) Following sudden withdrawal of adrenocortical hormone after replacement in a patient with chronic insufficiency or in a patient with normal adrenals but with temporary insufficiency due to suppression. (3) Following bilateral adrenalectomy or removal of a functioning adrenal tumor which had suppressed the other adrenal. (4) Following sudden destruction of the pituitary gland (pituitary necrosis), or when thyroid or insulin are given to a patient with panhypopituitarism. (5) Following injury to both adrenals by trauma, hemorrhage, thrombosis, infection, or, rarely, metastatic carcinoma. In overwhelming sepsis (principally meningococcemia), massive bilateral adrenal hemorrhage may occur (Waterhouse-Friderichsen syndrome).

Clinical Findings

A. Symptoms and Signs: The patient complains of headache, lassitude, nausea and vomiting, and often diarrhea. Costovertebral angle pain and tenderness (Rogoff's sign) and confusion or coma may be present. Fever may be 40.6° C (105° F) or more. The blood pressure is low. Other signs include cyanosis, petechiae (especially with meningococcemia), dehydration, abnormal skin pigmentation with sparse axillary hair, and lymphadenopathy.

B. Laboratory Findings: A normal or high eosinophil count (200 or above) in the presence of severe stress due to trauma, infection, and other mechanisms is strongly suggestive of adrenal failure. The blood glucose and serum sodium levels are low. Serum potassium and NPN are high. Blood culture may be positive (usually meningococci). Urinary and blood cortisol levels are very low.

C. ECG Findings: ECG shows decreased voltage.

Differential Diagnosis

This condition must be differentiated from other causes of coma and confusion, such as diabetic coma, cerebrovascular accident, and acute poisoning, and from other causes of high fever. Eosinophilia, which is usually absent in other emergencies, helps in the differentiation. (*Note:* If the diagnosis is suspected, treat with corticosteroids *immediately* while awaiting the results of laboratory tests.)

Complications

Any of the progressive complications of the initiating disease may occur. The complications of treatment or those occurring during the course of treatment are discussed below.

When treatment is instituted, certain complications may be observed. Hyperpyrexia, loss of consciousness, generalized edema with hypertension, and flaccid paralysis due to low potassium has followed excessive use of intravenous fluids and corticosteroids. Psychotic reactions may occur with cortisone therapy.

Treatment

The patient must be treated vigorously and observed constantly until well out of danger. (*Note:* It is better to overtreat rather than to undertreat.)

A. Severe Crisis:

1. Emergency treatment—Institute appropriate antishock measures (see Chapter 1), especially intravenous fluids and plasma, vasopressor drugs, and oxygen. Do not give narcotics or sedatives.

Give sulfadiazine or other indicated anti-infective agents as for meningococcal meningitis and hydrocortisone phosphate or hydrocortisone sodium succinate (Solu-Cortef®), 100 mg IM or IV immediately and repeat 50 mg every 6 hours for the first day. Give the same amount every 8 hours on the second day and then gradually reduce the dosage every 8 hours.

If hydrocortisone hemisuccinate or prednisolone phosphate is not available, give cortisone acetate, 10–25 mg IM in 4 different sites (to a total of 40–100 mg), following with single injections of cortisone, 25–50 mg IM every 6 hours, and gradually lengthen the intervals of administration to 25 mg every 8 hours.

If parenteral hydrocortisone, prednisolone, or cortisone is not available, or if the patient is unresponsive, give aqueous adrenocortical extract, 25–50 ml IV immediately and follow with 100–200 ml in 1 liter of saline-dextrose as an IV infusion.

2. Convalescent treatment—When the patient is able to take food by mouth, give oral cortisone, 12.5–25 mg every 6 hours, and reduce dosage to maintenance levels as needed.

B. Moderate Crisis: If the patient's physical condition does not appear to be critical and is not associated with a significant degree of shock, the treatment outlined above may be modified by appropriate reduction in dosage. However, it is generally best to overtreat the patient in moderate crisis during the first 24 hours rather than risk undertreatment.

C. Complications During Treatment: Excessive use of intravenous fluids and corticosteroids may cause high fever, loss of consciousness, generalized edema with hypertension, flaccid paralysis due to potassium depletion, and psychotic reactions.

1. Overhydration, usually due to sodium retention, may result in cerebral edema (with unconsciousness or convulsions) or pulmonary edema. Withhold sodium and fluids temporarily and treat for these conditions.

2. Hypokalemia—Flaccid paralysis, with low serum potassium, usually occurring on the 2nd to 4th days of treatment, may be treated with potassium salts.

3. Hyperpyrexia is rare with present treatment methods.

4. For other complications of adrenal steroid therapy (eg, psychotic reactions), see p 680.

Prognosis

Before replacement therapy and antibiotics became available, acute adrenal crisis was often rapidly fatal. Even today, if treatment is not early and vigorous, death occurs in several hours. Once the crisis has passed, the patient must be observed carefully to assess the degree of permanent adrenal insufficiency.

Frawley, T.F.: Treatment of adrenal insufficiency states including Addison's disease. Mod Treat 3:1328, 1966.

2. CHRONIC ADRENOCORTICAL INSUFFICIENCY
(Addison's Disease)

Essentials of Diagnosis

- Weakness, easy fatigability, anorexia; frequent episodes of nausea, vomiting, and diarrhea.
- Sparse axillary hair; increased skin pigmentation of creases. pressure areas, and nipples.
- Hypotension, small heart.
- Serum sodium and chloride and urinary 17-ketosteroids and 17-hydroxycorticosteroids are low. Serum potassium and NPN are elevated. Eosinophilia and lymphocytosis are present.
- Plasma cortisol levels are low to absent and fail to rise after administration of corticotropin.

General Considerations

Addisonism was a rare disease before the advent of adrenal surgery for cancer, hypertension, and other disorders. It is characterized by chronic deficiency of hormones concerned with glycostasis and with mineral metabolism, and causes unexplained and often striking skin pigmentation. Electrolyte deficiencies may be the dominant manifestation, and may even be associated with excess of adrenal androgens (see Adrenogenital Syndrome). If chronic adrenal insufficiency is secondary to pituitary failure (atrophy, necrosis, tumor), lack of glycostasis is more commonly seen than electrolyte deficiencies, and skin pigmentary changes are not encountered. Recently, a rare syndrome of isolated aldosterone lack has been described with persistent hyperkalemia, periodic paralysis, salt wasting, and acidosis.

Tuberculosis accounts today for less than half of cases, and in this form the electrolyte deficiencies are more striking. Idiopathic atrophy accounts for most of the other cases, and in this group hypoglycemia is more striking than the electrolyte changes. There may be associated thyroiditis, hypoparathyroidism, hypogonadism, and candidiasis. An autoimmune mechanism has been postulated for these and other causes of idiopathic atrophy.

Rare causes include metastatic carcinoma (especially of the breast or lung), coccidioidomycosis of the adrenal gland, syphilitic gummas, scleroderma, amyloid disease, and hemochromatosis.

Clinical Findings

A. Symptoms and Signs: The symptoms are weakness and fatigability, anorexia, nausea and vomiting, diarrhea, nervous and mental irritability, and faintness, especially after missing meals. Pigmentary changes consist of diffuse tanning over nonexposed as well as exposed parts or multiple freckles; or accentuation of pigment over pressure points and over the nipples, buttocks, perineum, and recent scars. Black freckles may appear on the mucous membranes of tongue. Seven to 15% of patients have associated vitiligo.

Other findings include hypotension with small heart, hyperplasia of lymphoid tissues, stiffness of the cartilages of the ear (Thorn's sign), scant to absent axillary and pubic hair (especially in females), absence of sweating, severe dental caries, and at times costovertebral angle tenderness.

B. Laboratory Findings: The white count shows moderate neutropenia (about 5000/cu mm), lymphocytosis (35–50%), and a total eosinophil count over 300/cu mm. Hemoconcentration is present. Serum sodium and chloride are low; serum potassium and NPN are elevated. Urinary 17-ketosteroid and 17–hydroxycorticosteroid excretion is low. The fasting blood glucose level and BMR are low.

Low blood corticosteroids (less than 8 μg/100 ml) are diagnostic.

Adrenal calcification on x-ray may be found in about 10% of cases.

C. Special Tests:

1. The **4-hour corticotropin** (Thorn) test (rarely used) is confirmatory if total blood eosinophils fail to fall by at least 50% within 4 hours following the administration of 40 units of corticotropin IM.

2. The **8-hour intravenous corticotropin** test is the most specific and reliable diagnostic test. It consists of giving 25 units of corticotropin or 0.25 mg of the synthetic cosyntropin (Cortrosyn®) in 1000 ml of physiologic saline by IV infusion; in primary Addison's disease the 24-hour urine 17-ketosteroid and 17-hydroxycorticosteroid values fail to rise; in adrenal insufficiency secondary to pituitary insufficiency or in patients who have had suppressive corticosteroid therapy, there is a slow, abnormal rise of 17-ketosteroid and 17-hydroxycorticosteroid levels, at times only after several days of stimulation. (*Note:* The patient suspected of having Addison's disease can be protected from untoward reactions to ACTH by the administration of 0.1–0.2 mg of 9a-fluorocortisol or 0.5 mg of dexamethasone without materially altering the urinary steroid levels.) A more rapid test is the **plasma cortisol response to ACTH.** Plasma cortisol samples are obtained in the basal state and 30 minutes after IM injection of 25 units of corticotropin or 0.25 mg of cosyn-

tropin (Cortrosyn®). If the plasma cortisol does not rise by at least 10 µg/100 ml, the diagnosis of Addison's disease is likely.

3. A simpler, less specific but rapid test for adrenocortical insufficiency (Perlmutter) is based on simultaneous determination of sodium levels in blood and urine and demonstrates sodium wasting, which is reversible by DOCA administration in Addison's disease but not in salt-losing nephritis.

4. Water excretion tests (Robinson-Kepler-Power or Soffer modification) demonstrate delayed water diuresis.

5. Other tolerance tests are *dangerous and rarely used:* Cutler-Power-Wilder test, prolonged fasting, glucose and insulin tolerance test.

6. Autoimmune antibodies to adrenal tissue may be found in idiopathic adrenal atrophy.

7. Plasma ACTH levels are high in primary adrenal insufficiency.

D. ECG Findings: The ECG shows low voltage and prolonged P–R and Q–T intervals.

E. EEG Findings: Slowing of electric discharge (reversed by cortisone but not by deoxycorticosterone).

Differential Diagnosis

Differentiate from anorexia nervosa, sprue syndrome, and malignant tumors. Weakness must be differentiated from that due to hyperparathyroidism, hyperthyroid myopathy, and myasthenia gravis; skin pigmentation from that of primary skin diseases, argyria, and hemochromatosis. The serum electrolyte abnormalities may resemble those of salt-losing nephritis and low-sodium states with chronic pulmonary disease.

Complications

Any of the complications of the underlying disease (eg, tuberculosis) are more likely to occur, and the patient is susceptible to intercurrent infections which may precipitate crisis. Diabetes mellitus and, rarely, thyrotoxicosis may be associated. Hypercalcemia is most apt to occur in children, especially when the adrenocortical level is suddenly reduced.

The dangers of overzealous treatment as well as inadequate replacement must be guarded against. Psychoses, gastric irritation, and low-potassium syndrome may occur with corticosteroid treatment. Corticosteroid treatment may impair the patient's resistance to tuberculosis, which may spread. Excessive deoxycorticosterone administration is rare today, but formerly led to hypertension, edema, anasarca, muscular weakness and tendon contractures.

Treatment

A. Specific Therapy:

1. Cortisone and hydrocortisone are the drugs of choice. Most addisonian patients are well maintained on 12.5–37.5 mg of cortisone or 10–40 mg of hydrocortisone orally daily in 3–4 divided doses. On this dosage most of the metabolic abnormalities are corrected. Many patients, however, do not obtain suffi-

cient salt-retaining effect from these drugs, and require deoxycorticosterone or fludrocortisone supplementation or extra dietary salt.

2. Fludrocortisone acetate has a potent sodium-retention effect. The dosage is 0.1–0.25 mg orally daily or every other day.

3. Deoxycorticosterone acetate controls electrolyte balance and has no other significant metabolic effect. It may be given intramuscularly initially, but this is rarely necessary. The usual dose is 1–4 mg IM daily. When the response is adequate, give buccally, 1 tablet (2 mg) daily or at most 1 tablet (2 mg) twice daily. The tablet is placed between cheek and teeth and allowed to dissolve.

Deoxycorticosterone trimethylacetate, 25–75 mg IM once monthly, may be used instead; deoxycorticosterone trimethylacetate (25 mg) IM once monthly = about 1 mg deoxycorticosterone acetate in oil per day.

Caution: Whenever using deoxycorticosterone acetate or fludrocortisone, avoid overdosage. Do not place the patient on a low-potassium diet when giving these drugs, for he may develop potassium deficiency.

4. Sodium chloride in large doses (5–20 gm daily) may be used to supplement cortisone therapy instead of deoxycorticosterone acetate or if deoxycorticosterone acetate or fludrocortisone is not available.

B. General Measures: Give a high-carbohydrate, high-protein diet. Frequent small feedings tend to be better tolerated than 3 large ones. Prevent exposure to infection and treat all infections immediately and vigorously. Methyltestosterone, 10–20 mg daily orally, testosterone propionate in oil, 10–25 mg IM 3 times weekly, or testosterone cyclopentylpropionate (Depo-Testosterone®) or testosterone enanthate (Delatestryl®), 200–400 mg/month, is often helpful for its protein anabolic effect and for the nonspecific feeling of well-being it induces in the debilitated patient. In female patients, smaller amounts (eg, 5 mg of methyltestosterone or 2 mg of fluoxymesterone daily) are adequate.

C. Treatment of Complications: Treat spread of tuberculosis (especially renal tuberculosis) and intercurrent infections with appropriate measures. The treatment of complications due to inadequate dosage or overdosage of corticosteroids consists of adjusting the dosage or in some cases discontinuing therapy for a short time.

Criteria of Adequate Therapy & Overdosage

A. Adequate Therapy:

1. Return of blood pressure to normal (may require up to 3–4 months).

2. Maintenance of normal fasting blood glucose level.

3. Return of serum electrolytes to normal levels.

4. Weight gain (usually due to fluid).

5. Improvement of appetite and strength.

6. Increase in size of heart to normal.

B. Overdosage: Excessive administration of cortisone or deoxycortisterone acetate must be avoided, especially in patients with cardiac or renal complications.

1. Signs and symptoms of cortisone overdosage are discussed on p 681.

2. Development of dependent edema, or excessive weight gain.

3. Development of hypertension.

4. Increase of diameter of heart above normal.

5. Development of signs of potassium deficiency (weakness followed by loss of muscle power and finally paralysis), especially if the patient is on a low-potassium diet.

Prognosis

With adequate replacement therapy the life expectancy of patients with Addison's disease is markedly prolonged. Active tuberculosis may respond to specific chemotherapy. Withdrawal of treatment or increased demands due to trauma, surgery, or other types of stress may precipitate crisis with a sudden fatal outcome. Pregnancy may be followed by marked exacerbation of the disease. Psychotic reactions may interfere with management.

The ultimate prognosis depends largely upon the intelligence of the patient and the availability of medical supervision. A fully active life is now possible for the majority of patients.

Cope, C.L., & D. Mattingly: Some recent advances in adrenal diagnosis. Postgrad MJ 44:23–25, 1968.

Eisenstein, A.B.: Addison's disease: Etiology and relationship to other endocrine disorders. M Clin North America 52:327–338, 1968.

Irvine, W.J.: Clinical and immunological associations in adrenal disorders. Proc Roy Soc Med 61:271–274, 1968.

Mason, A.S., & others: Epidemiological and clinical picture of Addison's disease. Lancet 2:744–747, 1968.

Nelson, D.H.: Treatment of adrenal insufficiency. GP 29:134, March 1964.

O'Donnell, W.M.: Changing pathogenesis of Addison's disease. Arch Int Med 36:266, 1965.

Posner, J.B., & D.R. Jacobs: Isolated analdosteronism. I. Clinical entity, with manifestations of persistent hyperkalemia, periodic paralysis, salt-losing tendency, and acidosis. Metabolism 13:513–521, 1964.

ADRENOCORTICAL OVERACTIVITY

Overactivity of the adrenal secretions is caused either by bilateral hyperplasia or by adenoma or, more rarely, carcinoma of one adrenal. The clinical picture will vary with the type of secretion produced, but in general 3 clinical disorders can be differentiated: (1) Cushing's syndrome, in which the glucocorticoids predominate; (2) the adrenogenital syndrome, in which the adrenal androgens predominate (feminizing tumors are rare); and (3) aldosteronism, with electrolyte changes. The clinical picture is most apt to be mixed in cases of malignant tumor and in bilateral hyperplasia. All syndromes of adrenal overactivity are far more common in females than in males.

1. CUSHING'S SYNDROME
(Adrenocortical Hyperfunction)
& CUSHING'S DISEASE
(Pituitary Basophilism)

Essentials of Diagnosis

- Buffalo obesity, easy bruisability, psychosis, hirsutism, purple striae, and acne associated with impotence or amenorrhea.
- Osteoporosis, hypertension, glycosuria.
- Elevated 17-hydroxycorticosteroids, low serum potassium and chloride, low total eosinophils, and lymphopenia.
- Special x-ray studies may reveal a tumor or hyperplasia of the adrenals.

General Considerations

This disorder is due to an excess of cortisone-like substances elaborated by the adrenal cortex. The adrenal cortex is almost always involved, either by hyperplasia or by adenoma or carcinoma; but a basophilic pituitary adenoma may be the primary lesion.

Hyperplasia of both adrenal cortices is the most common form (80%). Occult small pituitary adenomas are present in a significant number of these patients. Adenoma of one adrenal (single adenoma) is the next most common form (15%), and this type often constitutes the clearest form of Cushing's syndrome. The opposite adrenal is atrophic.

Carcinoma of the adrenal (5%) is always unilateral and often metastasizes late. A mixed picture with virilization is often present. The opposite adrenal is atrophic.

Adrenal rest tumors in the ovary rarely cause Cushing's syndrome; they are more commonly associated with virilizing syndromes.

Carcinoma of the anterior pituitary is a most unusual cause of Cushing's disease.

Administration of corticotropin causes adrenal hyperplasia; administration of cortisone causes adrenal atrophy associated with most features of Cushing's syndrome. These effects are reversible when medication is withdrawn.

Most rarely, certain extra-adrenal malignant tumors (eg, bronchogenic oat cell carcinoma) have been reported to produce severe Cushing's syndrome with bilateral adrenal hyperplasia. Severe hypokalemia and hyperpigmentation are commonly found in this group.

Clinical Findings

A. Symptoms and Signs: Cushing's syndrome or disease causes "moon face" and "buffalo hump," obesity with protuberant abdomen, and thin extremities; a plethoric appearance; oligomenorrhea or amenorrhea (or impotence in the male); weakness, backache, headache; hypertension; mild acne and superficial skin infections; chloasma-like pigmentation (especially on the face), hirsutism (mostly of the lanugo hair over the face and upper trunk, arms, and legs), purple striae (especially around the thighs, breasts, and abdomen), and easy bruisability (eg, hematoma formation following venipuncture). Patients with Cushing's disease or syndrome are less prone than normal people to develop "colds" or allergic disorders. Mental symptoms may range from increased lability of mood to frank psychosis.

B. Laboratory Findings: Glucose tolerance is low, often with glycosuria. The patient is resistant to the action of insulin. Urinary 17-hydroxycorticosteroids and blood corticosteroids are high (the latter over 20 μg/100 ml). (*Note:* In patients receiving estrogens—eg, contraceptive pills—the plasma cortisol levels are elevated due to increase in cortisol-binding globulin.) The usual diurnal variation in plasma cortisol levels is absent in Cushing's syndrome. Urinary 17-ketosteroids are often low or normal in Cushing's syndrome due to adenoma; normal or high if the disorder is due to hyperplasia; and very high if due to carcinoma. Total eosinophils are low (under 50/cu mm), lymphocytes are under 20%, and red and white blood cell counts are elevated. Serum CO_2 is high and serum chloride and potassium are low in some cases, especially those associated with malignant tumors.

C. X-Ray Findings: Osteoporosis of the skull, spine, and ribs is common. Nephrolithiasis may be seen. Intravenous urograms or retroperitoneal pneumograms may demonstrate a tumor of the adrenal or bilateral enlargement. X-ray of the sella is usually not helpful since basophilic adenomas are very small, but serial x-rays may demonstrate progressive enlargement (especially after adrenalectomy).

Adrenal phlebography may demonstrate small adrenal tumors.

D. ECG Findings: ECG may show characteristic signs of hypertension and hypokalemia.

E. Special Tests: (*Note:* Exceptions to the following rules are occasionally seen.)

1. ACTH stimulation test—The administration of ACTH causes marked hypersecretion of urinary 17-ketosteroids and 17-hydroxycorticosteroids in Cushing's disease or syndrome due to hyperplasia and often also in cases due to adenoma but does not stimulate secretion in cases due to carcinoma.

2. Cortisone suppression test—Administration of fludrocortisone or its derivatives in large doses (eg, dexamethasone, 2 mg every 6 hours for 2–3 days) suppresses the activity of hyperplastic adrenals but has no effect on adrenal hyperactivity due to adenoma or carcinoma. A small dose of dexamethasone (0.5 mg every 6 hours for 2–3 days) will suppress normal adrenals but fails to suppress hyperplastic adrenals. A rapid screening test for Cushing's syndrome is the administration of 1 mg of dexamethasone at 11:00 p.m. with measurement of the plasma hydroxycorticosteroids the following morning (see Pavlatos reference, below). Patients under stress or those receiving chronic drug therapy (eg, diphenylhydantoin) may not respond with normal suppression.

3. Metyrapone (Metopirone®) stimulation test—Failure of corticosteroids to rise after a 4-hour infusion or after an oral dose of 500 mg every hour for 5 doses favors neoplasm rather than hyperplasia.

4. Direct assay of plasma ACTH—This test is not generally available. ACTH is detectable in the plasma in bilateral adrenal hyperplasia but not in adrenal tumors. It is markedly elevated in ectopic tumors producing Cushing's syndrome. (See Sparks reference, below).

5. The urinary free cortisol test—This test (not generally available) is most specific for the diagnosis of Cushing's syndrome since, unlike the 17-hydroxycorticosteroids, free cortisol is not affected by drugs, obesity, stress, etc. (See Mattingly reference, below.)

Differential Diagnosis

The most difficult problem is differentiating true Cushing's syndrome from obesity associated with diabetes mellitus, especially if there are hirsutism and amenorrhea. The distribution of the fat, the virtual absence of virilization, and the laboratory studies often help, but are not infallible. Cushing's syndrome must be differentiated from the adrenogenital syndrome (see below), since the latter may be amenable to medical treatment unless it is caused by tumor. The 2 diseases may coexist. An elderly woman with osteoporosis, diabetes, and mild hirsutism may present a difficult problem in differentiation. Exogenous administration of corticosteroids must be kept in mind.

In rare cases the outstanding manifestation of Cushing's disease or syndrome may be only diabetes, osteoporosis, hypertension, or psychosis. Adrenal disease must be ruled out in patients with these disorders, especially in insulin-resistant diabetes mellitus, since early treatment may be curative.

Complications

The patient may suffer from any of the complications of hypertension, including congestive failure, cerebrovascular accidents, and coronary attacks, or of diabetes. Susceptibility to infections, especially of the skin and urinary tract, is increased. Compression fractures of the osteoporotic spine may cause marked disability. Renal colic may occur. Intractable gastric ulcer may be present. Most serious, perhaps, are the psychotic complications not infrequently observed in this disease. After adrenalectomy, hypercalcemia and pancreatitis may complicate the recovery. Pituitary enlargement (due to chromophobe adenomas) and deepening skin pigmentation have been observed following adrenalectomy for hyperplasia, causing cranial nerve palsies.

Treatment

A. Specific Measures:

1. Surgical removal of the tumor or total (preferred) or subtotal resection of both adrenals (in the case of diffuse bilateral hyperplasia) is the present treatment of choice. Adequate preoperative medication and care are of utmost importance. The patient should receive all general measures listed below, plus adequate hormonal supplementation.

If bilateral adrenalectomy is contemplated, give high doses of the cortisones, eg, cortisone acetate,

100–300 mg IM, or, preferably, 100–300 mg of Solu-Cortef® in divided doses IM or IV, on the day of surgery; continue the IM dosage for 1–2 days after surgery, then gradually decrease the dose and maintain on oral hydrocortisone as for Addison's disease. Because of the danger of precipitating heart failure, care must be taken to avoid excessive fluids and sodium.

In cases of unilateral tumor, the patient is prepared as for total adrenalectomy. After surgery, cortisol as well as corticotropin may be given to stimulate the atrophic gland. Treatment with cortisol may have to be continued for weeks since the gland may be slow to recover function.

2. X-ray therapy to the pituitary (either alone, or following unilateral adrenalectomy) may be of value in selected cases of hyperplasia. It may be tried initially; if not successful, total adrenalectomy must be performed. Partial destruction of the pituitary by other means (proton beam, yttrium implant, cryotherapy) has been attempted. Surgical hypophysectomy may be required for large chromophobe adenomas.

3. Removal of an extra-adrenal malignant tumor producing Cushing's syndrome is rarely feasible but may induce a temporary remission.

4. Chemical treatment by means of adrenocortical inhibitors has been largely unsuccessful. The least toxic of these, o,p'DDD, has limited use in inoperable carcinomas. (See Temple reference, below.) Metyrapone (Metopirone®) and aminoglutethimide (Elipten®) have been used to reduce adrenocortical overactivity, but the results are erratic.

B. General Measures: A high-protein diet should be given, although dietary attempts to correct the negative nitrogen balance are never successful. Testosterone or one of the newer anabolic agents may be of value in reversing the negative nitrogen balance. Potassium chloride administration may replace losses before and after surgery.

Insulin is usually of little value in controlling the glycosuria and hyperglycemia, and is usually unnecessary as the diabetes is quite mild.

Prognosis

This is a chronic disease which is subject to cyclic exacerbations (especially with pregnancy) and spontaneous remissions; it is a serious and often fatal disease unless discovered and treated early. A rather rapid course suggests a malignant tumor, but these may be dormant for years.

The best prognosis for eventual recovery is for patients in whom a benign adenoma has been removed and who have survived the postadrenalectomy state of adrenal insufficiency. A small number of patients with bilateral hyperplasia may respond to pituitary irradiation alone or combined with subtotal adrenalectomy.

Complete adrenalectomy necessitates chronic replacement therapy, which is feasible today.

Malignant extra-adrenal tumors are usually rapidly fatal, even after such drastic attempts at treatment as total adrenalectomy.

Cope, C., Isard, H.J., & W.E. Wesolowski: Selective adrenal phlebography. Radiology 90:1105–1112, 1968.

Egdahl, R.H.: Surgery of the adrenal. New England J Med 278:939–949, 1968.

Freeark, R.J., & S.S. Waldstein: Present status of the diagnosis and treatment of Cushing's syndrome. S Clin North America 49:179–190, 1969.

Friedman, M., Marshall-Jones, P., & E.J. Ross: Cushing's syndrome: Adrenocortical hyperactivity secondary to neoplasms arising outside the pituitary-adrenal system. Quart J Med 35:193–214, 1966.

Glenn, F., & H. Mannix, Jr.: Diagnosis and prognosis of Cushing's syndrome. Surg Gynec Obst 126:765–776, 1968.

Hunder, G.G.: Pathogenesis of Cushing's disease. Mayo Clin Proc 41:29–39, 1966.

Hutter, A.M., Jr., & D.E. Kayhoe: Adrenal cortical carcinoma. Clinical features of 138 patients. Am J Med 41:572–580, 1966.

Jubiz, W., & others: Effect of diphenylhydantoin on metabolism of dexamethasone. New England J Med 283:11–14, 1970.

Liddle, G.W.: Tests of pituitary adrenal suppressibility in the diagnosis of Cushing's syndrome. J Clin Endocrinol 20:1539–1560, 1960.

Liddle, G.W., & A.M. Shute: The evolution of Cushing's syndrome. Advances Int Med 15:41, 1969.

Mattingly, D., & C. Tyler: Simple screening test for Cushing's syndrome. Brit MJ 4:394, 1967.

Minagi, H., & H.L. Steinbach: Roentgen aspects of pituitary tumors manifested after bilateral adrenalectomy for Cushing's syndrome. Radiology 90:276–280, 1968.

Nelson, D.H., & others: ACTH-producing pituitary tumors following adrenalectomy for Cushing's syndrome. Ann Int Med 52:560, 1960.

Nichols, T., Nugent, C.A., & F.H. Tyler: Steroid laboratory tests in the diagnosis of Cushing's syndrome. Am J Med 45:116–128, 1968.

Orth, D.N., & G.W. Liddle: Results of treatment in 108 patients with Cushing's syndrome. New England J Med 285:243–247, 1971.

Pavlatos, F.Ch., Smilo, R.P., & P.H. Forsham: Screening test for Cushing's syndrome. JAMA 193:720–723, 1965.

Rovit, R.L., & T.D. Duane: Cushing's syndrome and pituitary tumors. Pathophysiology and ocular manifestations of ACTH-secreting pituitary adenomas. Am J Med 46:416–427, 1969.

Sawin, C.T.: Measurement of plasma cortisol in the diagnosis of Cushing's syndrome. Ann Int Med 68:624, 1968.

Scott, H.W., & others: Cushing's syndrome due to adrenocortical tumor: Eleven-year review of 15 patients. Ann Surg 162:505, 1965.

Sparks, L., & others: Experience with a rapid oral metyrapone test and the plasma ACTH content in determining the cause of Cushing's syndrome. Metabolism 18:175, 1969.

Temple, T.E., Jr., & others: Cushing's disease: Correction of hypercortisolism by o,p'DDD. New England J Med 281:801–805, 1969.

2. THE ADRENOGENITAL SYNDROME: PREPUBERAL

Essentials of Diagnosis

- Abnormal urogenital development noted at birth or precocious development early in life. Often familial.
- Enlarged clitoris or phallus, hirsutism, short stature, excessive muscular development, acne, seborrhea.
- 17-Ketosteroids elevated, FSH absent to low, pregnanetriol elevated.

General Considerations

This disorder is produced by androgenic excess, due either to adrenal hyperplasia (often familial) or adrenal tumors, and manifests its virilizing effects by interfering with the normal sexual development of the fetus, infant, or child. The congenital form of the adrenogenital syndrome is due to hyperplasia; the childhood form, occurring after normal intrauterine development, may be due either to tumor or to hyperplasia. Congenital adrenocortical hyperplasia is rare, often familial, much more common in females, and often associated with an addisonian-like state in male infants. Rarely, congenital virilization is caused by testosterone or progesterone administration to the pregnant mother. Gynecomastia may be the presenting complaint of a feminizing adrenocortical tumor.

Clinical Findings

A. Symptoms and Signs:

1. Congenital adrenocortical hyperplasia—In females, pseudohermaphroditism, enlargement of the clitoris, urogenital sinus formation, and, later, hirsutism are found; in males, phallic enlargement (macrogenitosomia praecox), precocious virilization, and (in infants) an addisonian-like state which may be confused with pyloric stenosis, characterized by nausea and vomiting, dehydration, and electrolyte deficiencies.

2. Adrenogenital syndrome in children—Somatic growth is accelerated; bone age is accelerated with early epiphyseal closure and eventual short stature. Other findings include excessive muscular development ("infant Hercules"), precocious virilization, and in some cases acne and seborrhea. With tumors some clinical features of Cushing's disease may be present. Hypertension may occur.

B. Laboratory Findings: Bone age is advanced on x-ray examination; 17-ketosteroids are elevated for the age. Intravenous urograms or retroperitoneal oxygen studies may demonstrate adrenal pathology. FSH is absent or very low. ACTH stimulation tests and cortisone suppression tests help distinguish normal, hyperplastic, and neoplastic adrenals. Urinary pregnanetriol excretion is elevated in congenital adrenal hyperplasia and in carcinomas.

Differential Diagnosis

A. In Either Sex: Distinguish from Cushing's syndrome (Table 18–8).

TABLE 18–8. Differentiation of adrenogenital syndrome and Cushing's syndrome.

	Adrenogenital Syndrome	Cushing's Syndrome
Hirsutism	+++	+
Virilism	+++	0
Growth rate	++	*
Muscles	+++	Decr
17-Ketosteroids	+++	+
17-Hydroxy-corticosteroids	N or decr	+++
Pregnanetriol	++	0

*Retarded in children.

B. In Males: Differentiate from true isosexual precocity, either constitutional or due to hypothalamic or pineal lesions. In this situation the FSH test is positive and the 17-ketosteroids normal or only slightly elevated; the testes are larger than the testes of the adrenogenital boy, and spermatogenesis may occur. The other important condition causing pseudosexual precocity is unilateral or bilateral interstitial tumor of the testis. These are usually palpable within the scrotum. 17-Ketosteroid excretion is not as high in interstitial tumor as in adrenal tumor.

C. In Females: The most important differentiation is from genetic intersexuality (true hermaphrodite with testes, ovotestes, or ovaries). 17-Ketosteroid excretion is normal in intersex, and the chromosomal count on a buccal or vaginal smear helps to establish the diagnosis. Premature appearance of pubic hair may cause confusion, but other stigmas of virilization are not present. Since arrhenoblastomas of the ovary do not occur before puberty, they should not cause confusion.

Treatment

Treatment is discussed with the treatment of Adrenogenital Syndrome and Virilizing Diseases of Women, below.

Prognosis

Males with congenital adrenal hyperplasia, even when treated intensively, often die in infancy of severe fluid and electrolyte loss. Some tumors are malignant and often fatal, but early removal will cause regression of virilization. The use of cortisone in bilateral hyperplasia has been most effective in suppressing adrenal virilization and restoring a normal state with breast development, menses, etc in girls and spermatogenesis in males. The ultimate prognosis for patients who receive cortisone is not yet known, but in some cases remissions have been sustained for several years even though cortisone is discontinued. Normal pregnancy has occurred after long-term cortisone therapy.

Bongiovanni, A.M., & A.W. Root: The adrenogenital syndrome. New England J Med 268:1283–1289, 1342–1351, 1391–1399, 1963.

Gabrilove, J.L.: Feminizing adrenocortical tumors in the male: A review of 52 cases. Medicine 44:37–80, 1965.

Kenny, F.M., & others: Virilizing tumors of the adrenal cortex. Am J Dis Child 115:445–458, 1968.

Migeon, C.J.: Treatment of congenital adrenal hyperplasia. Mod Treat 3:1348, 1966.

New, M.I.: Congenital adrenal hyperplasia. Symposium on recent clinical advances. P Clin North America 15:395–408, 1968.

Rappaport, R., Cornu, G., & P. Royer: Statural growth in congenital adrenal hyperplasia treated with hydrocortisone. J Pediat 73:760–766, 1968.

3. ADRENOGENITAL SYNDROME & VIRILIZING DISEASES OF WOMEN

Essentials of Diagnosis

- Menstrual disorders and hirsutism.
- Regression or reversal of primary and secondary sex characteristics with balding, hoarse voice, acne, and enlargement of the clitoris.
- Occasionally a palpable pelvic tumor.
- 17-Ketosteroids elevated in adrenal disorders, variable in others.
- Urinary and plasma testosterone elevated.

General Considerations

The diagnosis of virilizing disorders in adult females is more difficult since other sources of abnormal androgens exist, principally the ovaries. There is no interference with formation of the female genital tract or secondary sex characteristics, but rather a regression or sex reversal of varying degree. Although the diagnosis is readily apparent in a complete state of the virilizing syndrome (eg, the adult form of the congenital adrenogenital syndrome), the milder forms, presenting primarily with defeminization or merely excessive hirsutism, may be caused by equally serious adrenal and ovarian disorders such as tumors. A sudden change in amount of hair (other than at puberty, pregnancy, or menopause) is of greater importance than hirsutism which has been present throughout life.

Besides adrenal hyperplasia and tumors, adult female virilization may be caused by the following disorders:

(1) **Ovarian disorders:** Arrhenoblastoma, Stein-Leventhal syndrome (large, polycystic ovaries, most common), theca luteinization (thecosis ovarii), hilar cell tumor or hyperplasia, adrenal cell rests, dysgerminoma (rare).

(2) **Hypothalamic-pituitary disorders:** Acromegaly (eosinophilic adenoma), hyperostosis frontalis (Stewart Morgagni-Morel syndrome).

(3) **Placental causes:** Pregnancy, chorio-epithelioma.

(4) **Miscellaneous causes:** True hermaphroditism, thymic tumors, drugs (eg, testosterone).

Clinical Findings

A. Symptoms and Signs: Symptoms include scant menstrual periods or amenorrhea, acne and roughening of the skin, odorous perspiration, and hoarseness or deepening of voice. Hirsutism is present over the face, body, and extremities, with thinning or balding of head hair. Musculature is increased and feminine contours are lost. The breasts and genitalia are atrophied, the clitoris and "Adam's apple" enlarged. A tumor may rarely be palpable on pelvic examination (arrhenoblastoma, polycystic ovaries).

B. Laboratory Findings: Urinary 17-ketosteroid determination is the most important single test in the diagnosis of adrenogenital syndrome. It helps differentiate constitutional hirsutism from adrenal disorders, in which the 17-ketosteroids are significantly elevated. Very high levels favor a diagnosis of adrenal tumor. In arrhenoblastoma or Stein-Leventhal syndrome, 17-ketosteroids may be normal or moderately elevated. The ACTH stimulation test and the cortisone suppression test may distinguish between adrenal tumors, adrenal hyperplasia, and ovarian lesions. Elevated pregnanetriol levels suggest an adrenal lesion.

True assay of androgens (eg, testosterone) in the blood and urine has recently become possible, but the tests are not yet available for general use.

C. X-Ray Findings: Intravenous urograms or retroperitoneal pneumograms may reveal an adrenal tumor. Gynecography may show large ovaries.

Differential Diagnosis

Since hirsutism may be the only sign of adrenal tumor, all of the disorders characterized by excessive hair have to be considered in the differential diagnosis. From the practical standpoint, however, the diagnosis commonly depends upon whether one is dealing simply with racial, familial, or idiopathic hirsutism, where an unusual end-organ sensitivity to endogenous male hormone exists; or whether excessive amounts of male hormone are being produced. In general, if not only hirsutism but also enlargement of the clitoris and deepening of the voice are present (or loss of head hair), and if the onset is rapid, one can assume that a tumor of the adrenal or ovary is present. In these circumstances exploratory operation is mandatory in spite of equivocal laboratory and physical findings. Although virilization is not the rule with Cushing's syndrome, a mixed picture is at times seen in malignant adrenal tumors and, more rarely, in hyperplasia.

Complications

Aside from the known high incidence of malignancy in tumors causing virilization, the interference with femininity and consequent sterility may be irreversible. Diabetes and obesity may be complicating features. At times mental disorders accompany states of defeminization.

Treatment

When tumor is present, surgical removal is the treatment of choice. In some cases of adrenal hyperplasia, especially in infancy, there may be associated manifestations of hypoadrenocorticism (eg, excessive salt and water loss and failure to maintain a fasting blood sugar). This condition is apparently due to a congenital absence of hydroxylating enzymes of the adrenals. The "androgenic" compounds formed have no cortisol activity and are unable to suppress endogenous ACTH; hence the continued adrenal stimulation and large glands. Treatment with corticosteroids has proved valuable in reducing the activity of the glands (apparently by suppressing endogenous ACTH) and in supplying exogenously needed corticosteroids. In adults the drugs of choice appear to be prednisone or prednisolone, 5–25 mg daily orally, or dexamethasone, 0.5–1.5 mg daily orally, in divided doses; use the smallest dose which keeps the 17-ketosteroid, pregnanetriol, and testosterone levels within the normal range.

The response of congenital adrenal hyperplasia to long-term corticosteroid therapy is gratifying, with lessening of virilization and hirsutism, and eventually normal cyclic menstruation. Plastic repair (removal of the clitoris and repair of a urogenital sinus) is required. Corticosteroid therapy of milder forms of virilization (eg, simple hirsutism) is less successful. Estrogen therapy may be of some value, but must be used in large dosage.

Prognosis

The outlook is favorable if a malignant tumor is removed early, since metastasis often occurs late. Wedge resection of polycystic ovaries may restore fertility. Cortisone therapy may be of help in hyperplastic lesions.

The ultimate fate of the virilized woman depends not only upon the underlying cause (ie, tumor or hyperplasia), but more particularly upon the age at onset of the virilizing influence and its duration. If virilization is of long standing, restoration of normal femininity or loss of hirsutism is unlikely even though the causative lesion is successfully removed.

Note: Most cases of simple hirsutism in females are due not to endocrine disease but to hereditary or racial factors and cannot be treated effectively with systemic medications or surgery. Epilation, preferably by electrolysis, is the treatment of choice.

Deller, J.J., & others: Testosterone metabolism in idiopathic hirsutism. Ann Int Med 63:369, 1965.

Forbes, A.P.: Current concepts: Hypertrichosis. New England J Med 273:602–603, 646–647, 1965.

Greenblatt, R.: *The Hirsute Female.* Thomas, 1963.

Jacobs, J.P.: Hirsutism and benign androgenic hyperplasia of the adrenals. Am J Obst Gynec 101:37–42, 1968.

Lipsett, M.B., & others: Physiological basis of disorders of androgen metabolism. Ann Int Med 68:1327, 1968.

Mahesh, V.B., Greenblatt, R.B., & R.F. Coniff: Urinary steroid excretion before and after dexamethasone administration and steroid content of adrenal tissue and venous blood in virilizing adrenal tumors. Am J Obst Gynec 100:1043–1054, 1968.

Muller, S.A.: Hirsutism. Am J Med 46:803, 1969.

Nichols, T., & others: Glucocorticoid suppression of urinary testosterone excretion in patients with idiopathic hirsutism. J Clin Endocrinol 26:79, 1966.

Prunty, F.T.: Review: Hirsutism, virilism and apparent virilism and their gonadal relationship. J Endocrinol 38:85–103, 203–227, 1967.

PRIMARY ALDOSTERONISM

Essentials of Diagnosis

- Hypertension, polyuria, polydipsia, muscular weakness, tetany.
- Hypokalemia, hypernatremia, alkalosis, renal damage.
- Elevated urinary aldosterone level and low plasma renin level.
- Tumors usually too small to be visualized by x-ray.

General Considerations

Primary aldosteronism is a relatively rare disorder caused by aldosterone excess. Conn suggested that it may be a common cause of hypertension (20%), but other investigators feel that it accounts for less than 5% of cases. It is more common in females, and is most often caused by small adrenocortical adenomas (although it is at times found with adrenocortical hyperplasia and very rarely with adrenocortical carcinoma or normal-sized adrenals). Edema is rarely seen in primary aldosteronism, but secondary aldosteronism is often found in edematous states such as cardiac failure and hepatic cirrhosis. Since sodium restriction stimulates aldosterone production, low-sodium diets or diuretic agents must be discontinued before the diagnosis can be confirmed with chemical tests.

Clinical Findings

A. Symptoms and Signs: Hypertension (usually benign), muscular weakness (at times with paralysis simulating periodic paralysis), paresthesia with frank tetanic manifestations, headache, polyuria (especially nocturnal), and polydipsia are the outstanding complaints. Edema is rarely present.

B. Laboratory Findings: Low serum potassium, hypernatremia, and alkalosis are pathognomonic of primary aldosteronism, but at times the potassium level is normal. Various degrees of renal damage are manifested by proteinuria, alkaline urine, nephrocalcinosis, and low urine specific gravity unresponsive to vasopressin. If spironolactone (Aldactone®), 50–75 mg 4 times daily for 5–8 days, restores serum potassium to normal, suspect hyperaldosteronism. Urinary aldosterone levels are markedly elevated and plasma renin levels are low, but these tests are not generally available.

A diabetic glucose tolerance curve may be seen.

There is resistance to the administration of deoxycorticosterone acetate (20 mg/day for 3 days) with failure to retain fluid and to suppress elevated aldosterone levels.

C. ECG Findings: ECG changes are due to prolonged hypertension and hypokalemia.

D. X-Ray Findings: Cardiac hypertrophy due to hypertension is the only x-ray finding. The tumors are usually too small to be visualized, except by adrenal phlebography.

E. Other Findings: The plasma volume is increased 30–50% above normal.

Differential Diagnosis

This important reversible cause of hypertension must be considered in the differential diagnosis in any patient who shows muscular weakness and tetanic manifestations; and in the differential diagnosis of periodic paralysis, potassium- and sodium-losing nephritis, nephrogenic diabetes insipidus, and hypercalcemia and hypokalemia (be certain the patient has not been receiving diuretic agents). Excessive ingestion of licorice or laxatives may simulate aldosteronism. The oral contraceptives may raise aldosterone secretion in some patients. Unilateral renal vascular disease producing secondary hyperaldosteronism with severe hypertension must be ruled out. The angiotensin II infusion test, which shows reduced vascular response in this disorder, may be helpful in the differential diagnosis. Plasma renin activity is low in primary aldosteronism and elevated in renal vascular disease. Excessive secretion of deoxycortisol and compound B may produce a similar clinical picture. (See Biglieri reference, below.) A rare cause of secondary hyperaldosteronism is due to juxtaglomerular cell hyperplasia (Bartter's syndrome).

Complications

All of the complications of chronic hypertension are encountered in primary aldosteronism. Progressive renal damage is less reversible than hypertension. The incidence of pyelonephritis and nephrocalcinosis is high.

Treatment

The specific treatment for primary aldosteronism is surgical removal of adenomas or subtotal or total resection of hyperplastic glands.

An occasional patient responds to dexamethasone suppression.

Secondary aldosteronism may be treated with the chemical aldosterone antagonist spironolactone (Aldactone®), or may respond to unilateral renal artery surgery or nephrectomy.

Prognosis

The hypertension is reversible in about 2/3 of cases, but persists or returns in spite of surgery in the remainder. The renal disease is partially reversible, but once pyelonephritis is established it may continue along its natural course.

Prognosis is much improved by early diagnosis.

Biglieri, E.G., & others: Hypermineralocorticoidism. Am J Med 45:170, 1968.

Cannon, P.J., & others: Juxtaglomerular cell hyperplasia and secondary hyperaldosteronism (Bartter's syndrome): A re-evaluation of the pathophysiology. Medicine 47:107–132, 1968.

Conn, J.W., & others: Normokalemic primary aldosteronism. JAMA 195:21-26, 1966.

Conn, J.W., Rovner, D.R., & E.L. Cohen: Licorice-induced pseudoaldosteronism. JAMA 205:492–496, 1968.

Conn, J.W., & others: Preoperative diagnosis of primary aldosteronism. Arch Int Med 123:113–123, 1969.

Ehrlich, E.N.: Aldosterone, the adrenal cortex, and hypertension. Ann Rev Med 19:373–398, 1968.

George, J.M., & others: The syndrome of primary aldosteronism. Am J Med 48:343–356, 1970.

Jose, A., & N.M. Kaplan: Plasma renin activity in the diagnosis of primary aldosteronism. Arch Int Med 123:141–146, 1969.

Kaplan, N.: Hypokalemia in the hypertensive patient, with observations on the incidence of primary aldosteronism. Ann Int Med 66:1079, 1967.

Priestley, J.T., & others: Primary aldosteronism: Surgical management and pathologic findings. Mayo Clin Proc 43:761–775, 1968.

Sutherland, D.J.A., & others: Hypertension, increased aldosterone secretion and low plasma renin activity relieved by dexamethasone. Canad MAJ 95:1109, 1966.

Weinberger, M.H., & others: Hypertension induced by oral contraceptives containing estrogen and gestagen. Ann Int Med 71:891, 1969.

DISEASES OF THE ADRENAL MEDULLA

PHEOCHROMOCYTOMA

Essentials of Diagnosis

- "Spells" or "attacks" of headache, visual blurring, severe sweats, vasomotor changes in a young adult, weight loss.
- Hypertension, often paroxysmal ("spells") but frequently sustained.
- Postural tachycardia and hypotension; cardiac enlargement.
- Elevated BMR with normal PBI; glycosuria, negative cold pressor test; positive provocative (histamine) and blocking agent tests (phentolamine).
- Elevated urinary catecholamines or their metabolites.

General Considerations

A not uncommon disease characterized by paroxysmal or sustained hypertension due to a tumor of pheochrome tissue, most commonly located in either or both adrenals (90%) or anywhere along the sympathetic nervous chain, and rarely in such aberrant locations as the thorax, bladder, or brain. About 10% of patients have multiple tumors, and these have a familial tendency. A small percentage becomes malignant and may show functioning metastases. Pheochrome tumors are associated with neurofibromatosis in about 5% of cases (often familial). There may be associated medullary carcinomas of the thyroid, parathyroid adenomas, and neuromas. The tumors, which are more commonly located on the right side, may vary in size and are rarely large enough to be palpable. They contain varying proportions of epinephrine and norepinephrine, with the latter usually predominating (50–90%). Norepinephrine-producing tumors are more likely to cause sustained hypertension; the paroxysmal variety is more common with epinephrine. Pregnancy or trauma is frequently the precipitating event in this disease, which is most common in women between the ages of 20 and 40.

Clinical Findings

A. Symptoms and Signs: Pheochromocytoma is manifested by attacks of severe headache, palpitation or tachycardia, profuse sweating, vasomotor changes (including pallor or flushing of the face or extremities), precordial or abdominal pain, nausea and vomiting, visual disturbances (including blurring or blindness), aphasia and loss of consciousness (rarely), increasing nervousness and irritability, increased appetite, dyspnea, angina, and loss of weight. Physical findings include hypertension, either in attacks or sustained, with cardiac enlargement; postural tachycardia (change of more than 20 beats/minute) and postural hypotension; mild elevation of basal body temperature; abdominal or flank tumor (in about 5%); and, rarely, transient swelling of the thyroid. Retinal hemorrhage or papilledema occurs occasionally.

B. Laboratory Findings: The cold pressor response is negative (blood pressure fall, or a rise of less than 20/15); BMR is elevated; PBI is normal; and glycosuria or hyperglycemia (or both) may be present. An attack of hypertension may in rare cases be produced by massage of either flank.

C. Special Tests:

1. Provocative test (for use during the normotensive phase)—The histamine test is positive if administration of histamine causes release of medullary hormone and consequent rise in blood pressure. *Caution:* Phentolamine (Regitine®) should be on hand in case blood pressure rise is excessive. (Tyramine and glucagon have recently been advocated as safer provocative tests.)

2. Blocking agent test (for use during the hypertensive phase)—Administration of phentolamine (Regitine®), 5 mg rapidly IV, blocks medullary hormone and causes a fall of blood pressure. (*Note:* The patient should not receive sedatives or antihypertensive drugs for at least 24 hours prior to the test.)

3. Assay of urinary catecholamines on a 24-hour urine specimen—and the simpler test for 3-methoxy-4-hydroxymandelic acid (vanillylmandelic acid, VMA)—are now generally available. The levels of these urinary constituents will be elevated in all cases of sustained and most cases of paroxysmal hypertension due to pheochromocytoma.

4. The most reliable test for pheochromocytoma associated with paroxysmal hypertension is direct **assay of epinephrine and norepinephrine** in the blood and urine during or following an attack. High epinephrine levels favor tumor localization within the adrenal gland. Proper collection of specimens is essential.

5. X-ray visualization of the tumor by intravenous urogram, retroperitoneal oxygen study, or arteriogram is often successful.

Differential Diagnosis

Pheochromocytoma should always be suspected in any patient with labile hypertension, especially if some of the other features such as elevated BMR or glycosuria are present in a young person. Because of such symptoms as tachycardia, tremor, palpitation, and high BMR, pheochromocytoma is often confused with thyrotoxicosis. About 10% are mistakenly treated as diabetes mellitus because of the glycosuria. Pheochromocytoma may also be misdiagnosed as essential hypertension, glomerulonephritis or other renal lesions, toxemia of pregnancy, eclampsia, and psychoneurosis. It rarely masquerades as gastrointestinal hemorrhage and abdominal disorders of an emergency nature. Serotonin tumors may present a similar clinical picture but are quite rare. Conversely, the presence of an abdominal tumor such as aortic aneurysm or renal cyst in a patient with a falsely positive phentolamine test for pheochromocytoma has led to an erroneous diagnosis. Although false-positive tests are not uncommon with pharmacologic agents and may lead to unnecessary explorations, the occasional false-negative test may permit a potentially curable fatal disease to go unrecognized. The availability of urinary catecholamine determination has made the diagnosis much more accurate.

Complications

All of the complications of severe hypertension may be encountered. Hypertensive crises with sudden blindness or cerebrovascular accidents are not uncommon. These may be precipitated by sudden movement, by manipulation during or after pregnancy, by emotional stress or trauma, or during surgical removal of the tumor.

After removal of the tumor, a state of severe hypotension and shock (resistant to epinephrine and norepinephrine) may ensue with precipitation of renal failure or myocardial infarction. These complications can be avoided by judicious preoperative and operative use of catecholamine blocking agents such as phentolamine and by the use of blood or plasma to restore blood volume. Hypotension and shock may occur from spontaneous infarction of the tumor.

On rare occasions a patient dies as a result of the complications of diagnostic tests or during surgery.

Some patients have associated thyroid carcinomas or hyperparathyroidism.

Treatment

Surgical removal of the tumor or tumors is the treatment of choice. This may require exploration of the entire sympathetic chain as well as both adrenals. Administration of phentolamine and blood or plasma before and during surgery and postoperative maintenance with norepinephrine and cortisone have made this type of surgery a great deal safer in recent years. Propranolol (Inderal®) is of value in controlling arrhythmias.

Since there may be multiple tumors, it is essential to recheck urinary catecholamine levels postoperatively.

Long-term treatment with phentolamine is not successful. Recently, oral phenoxybenzamine (Dibenzyline®) has been successfully used as chronic treatment in inoperable carcinoma and preoperatively in severely ill patients.

Prognosis

The prognosis depends entirely upon how early the diagnosis is made. If the tumor is successfully removed before irreparable damage to the cardiovascular system has occurred, a complete cure is usually achieved. Complete cure (or improvement) may follow removal of a tumor which has been present for many years. Rarely, hypertension persists or returns in spite of successful surgery. Only a small percentage of tumors are malignant.

Before the advent of blocking agents the surgical mortality was as high as 30%, but this is rapidly being reduced.

If after removal of a tumor a satisfactory fall of blood pressure does not occur, always consider the presence of another tumor.

It has been estimated that in the USA alone about 800 deaths a year are due to unrecognized pheochromocytoma.

Batsakis, J.G., & others: Pheochromocytoma of the bladder. Arch Surg 96:254–258, 1968.

Engelman, K., & A. Sjoerdsma: Chronic medical therapy for pheochromocytoma: A report of four cases. Ann Int Med 61:229–241, 1964.

Engelman, K., & others: Further evaluation of the tyramine test for pheochromocytoma. New England J Med 278:705–708, 1968.

Goldfien, A.: Pheochromocytoma: Diagnosis and anesthetic and surgical management. Anesthesiology 24:462–471, 1963.

Harrison, T.S., Bartlett, J.D., Jr., & J.F. Seaton: Current evaluation and management of pheochromocytoma. Ann Surg 168:701–713, 1968.

Lawrence, A.M.: Glucagon provocative test for pheochromocytoma. Ann Int Med 66:1091, 1967.

Melmon, K.: Catecholamines and the adrenal medulla. Pages 379–403 in: Williams, R.H. (editor): Textbook of Endocrinology, 4th ed. Saunders, 1968.

Rossi, P., Young, I.S., & W.F. Panke: Arteriography in pheochromocytoma. JAMA 205:547–553, 1968.

Sarosi, G., & R.P. Doe: Familial occurrence of parathyroid adenomas, pheochromocytoma, and medullary carcinoma of the thyroid with amyloid stroma (Sipple's syndrome). Ann Int Med 68:1305, 1968.

Schimke, R.N., & others: Pheochromocytoma, medullary thyroid carcinoma and multiple neuromas. New England J Med 279:1–6, 1968.

Sheps, S.G., & F.T. Maher: Tests in diagnosis of pheochromocytoma. JAMA 205:895–899, 1968.

Sjoerdsma, A., & others: Pheochromocytoma: Current concepts of diagnosis and treatment. Ann Int Med 65:1302, 1966.

Wurtman, R.J.: Catecholamines. New England J Med 273:637–646, 693–700, 746–753, 1965.

DISEASES OF THE PANCREATIC ISLET CELLS

DIABETES MELLITUS

Essentials of Diagnosis

- Glucose found in urine on routine testing.
- Polyuria, polydipsia, polyphagia, weight loss, somnolence, pruritus, paresthesias.
- Retinal microaneurysms and vitreous hemorrhages, skin infections, premature atherosclerosis with angina and claudication, peripheral neuritis.
- Hyperglycemia, decreased glucose tolerance, hypercholesterolemia.

General Considerations

Diabetes mellitus is probably the most important of all endocrine diseases. Over 4% of females and 2% of males in the USA are or will eventually become diabetic. Up to 20 million carriers of the trait are estimated. The disease affects all age groups, and the incidence in children under fifteen is 4/10,000. The exact cause of diabetes mellitus is not known, but the major metabolic defects may be corrected by the administration of insulin.

Most of the metabolic abnormalities in diabetes can be traced to the inability of the organism to metabolize glucose properly, which in turn places an undue stress on protein and fat catabolism for the availability of energy. Insulin is concerned not only with the utilization of glucose, but also with its active transfer across cell membranes and its storage as glycogen in the liver; if insulin is lacking, the capacity of the organism to store glycogen is impaired. Insulin is also important in lipogenesis.

There is good evidence that there are 2 different types of diabetes: (1) true deficiency of pancreatic islets ("insulopenia"), commonly found in "juvenile diabetes"; and (2) imbalance of the other regulatory hormones or insulin antagonists or production of insulin antibodies, which tends to increase the blood glucose. This is more often seen in "maturity onset" diabetes—especially in the obese—but there is no clearcut differentiation between the 2 types (see Rosenbloom reference, below). A rare type of insulin-resistant diabetes is associated with absence of subcutaneous fat and cirrhosis (lipoatrophic diabetes). Certain drugs, eg, the benzothiadiazines, may induce a diabetic state, possibly through their depleting action on potassium. A similar mechanism may be responsible for the abnormal glucose tolerance in hyperaldosteronism. An unusual rare form of diabetes due to a pancreatic tumor producing excessive amounts of glucagon has recently been described. Inappropriate secretion of glucagon has been demonstrated recently in diabetics (see Müller reference, below).

Prolonged hyperglycemia in diabetes with underutilization of glucose will lead to increased protein and fat catabolism. Prolonged hyperglycemia and hyperlipemia may lead to premature vascular degeneration, with coronary and peripheral atherosclerosis. A peculiar type of renal disease, intercapillary glomerulosclerosis (Kimmelstiel-Wilson disease), and retinal degeneration with microaneurysms and eventual retinitis proliferans are typical of diabetes and may not be related to either the severity or the excellence of control of hyperglycemia. Recent evidence suggests that the abnormality of small blood vessels (microangiopathy) may precede the onset of clinical diabetes and may be a widespread genetic defect. Additional pathologic changes noted are neuropathy, severe nephrosclerosis or chronic pyelonephritis, and, more rarely, papillary renal necrosis. The incidence of infections is markedly enhanced.

Early detection and treatment has in part forestalled some but not all of the serious and fatal complications of diabetes. By and large, the life expectancy of the adult diabetic who is well controlled and does not undergo repeated episodes of coma or insulin shock is about the same as that of a normal person of the same age. The outlook for the juvenile diabetic is not so favorable.

There is a well-known hereditary predisposition to diabetes and the greater incidence in the obese is demonstrated by insurance statistics. The fetal mortality rate is much higher in diabetic women than in normal women. Trauma, infections, and emotional stress often precipitate the disease in susceptible persons. The onset of diabetes may be preceded by functional hyperinsulinism.

The American Diabetes Association classification of diabetes according to the degrees of abnormalities of carbohydrate metabolism includes the following (in order of decreasing severity): (1) **Overt diabetes mellitus:** With fasting hyperglycemia and symptoms, often with ketoacidosis. (2) **Chemical or latent diabetes:** Usually asymptomatic, with postprandial hyperglycemia. (3) **Suspected diabetes ("stress hyperglycemia"):** Temporary hyperglycemia, with symptoms only during stress, eg, pregnancy, obesity, trauma, infection. (4) **Prediabetes:** Asymptomatic, but suspected by virtue of a strong family history. Progression or regression from one stage to the other may never occur, may proceed slowly over many years, or may occur rapidly. The type of treatment outlined below is directly related to the degree of severity and type of diabetes. (See Hawmi reference, below.)

Clinical Findings

A. Symptoms: Polyuria and excessive thirst may go unnoticed for years. Nocturia and enuresis may occur in juvenile diabetics. Increased appetite and loss of weight are common in children but rare in adults. Pruritus (especially of the vulvar and anal mucous membranes) is usually present. Premature perialveolar resorption with loosening of the teeth, asthenia, somnolence, paresthesias, impotence, painless parotitis, and cyclic edema may occur. A history of very large babies with polyhydramnios may be of importance.

B. Signs:

1. Ocular manifestations—Refractive changes, premature cataracts, retinopathy with microaneurysms, vitreous and retinal hemorrhage, optic neuritis.

2. Skin manifestations—Mycotic infections (candidiasis, perlèche), carotenemia (xanthosis), xanthomatous tumors (rare), boils or carbuncles (common).

3. Cardiovascular-renal manifestations—Atherosclerosis manifested by premature coronary atherosclerosis, nonhealing ischemic leg ulcer with gangrene, edema, heart failure.

4. Neurologic manifestations—Peripheral neuritis, areflexia, loss of vibration sense, neurogenic bladder, nocturnal diarrhea.

C. Laboratory Findings: Although none of the tests described below are pathognomonic of diabetes, the diagnosis rests on laboratory determinations because the clinical features of the disease are so variable. The principal laboratory signs of diabetes are glycosuria, hyperglycemia, decreased glucose tolerance, and elevated serum cholesterol.

1. Glycosuria—The presence of reducing substances identified as glucose in the urine is excellent presumptive evidence of diabetes. Reducing substances in the urine may be identified with any of the following tests: (1) Benedict's qualitative test: Add 8 drops of urine to 5 ml of Benedict's qualitative solution and bring to a boil. Responses vary from blue (negative) to brick red (4+). (2) Clinitest® tablets placed in a test tube with 5 drops of urine and 10 drops of water show reducing substance by means of color reactions as observed with Benedict's test. The tablets must be fresh. (3) Clinistix® and Tes-Tape® are impregnated papers which identify glucose in the urine by means of specific color reactions. The readings with these are more sensitive and erratic than the above, and semiquantitative results are not as reliable for control (see below).

2. Hyperglycemia—Determine the fasting blood glucose and postprandial glucose levels (before and 2 hours after a meal containing 50–100 gm of carbohydrate). An initial fasting blood glucose of 200 mg/100 ml or more is almost conclusive evidence of diabetes; a fasting blood glucose above 140 mg/100 ml with a high postprandial blood glucose is very strong evidence of diabetes. Dextrostix® is a simple screening device for hyperglycemia, but it requires experience and is not a substitute for quantitative methods.

3. Glucose tolerance tests—Since a normal fasting blood glucose level does not rule out diabetes, and since the postprandial blood glucose is occasionally elevated in other disorders (eg, liver disease), glucose tolerance tests are performed. This is also true in borderline cases, ie, when the fasting blood glucose levels are between 100 and 140 mg/100 ml. (*Note:* It is not necessary and it may be harmful to perform a glucose tolerance test in a patient whose initial fasting blood glucose level is over 200 mg/100 ml.) If the test is performed, be certain the patient has had a high-carbohydrate intake for 48–72 hours before the test, since carbohydrate restriction decreases tolerance.

a. **Standard glucose tolerance test**—Take an initial blood sample from a fasting patient, have him empty his bladder, and give 100 gm of glucose in 300 ml of water or 75 gm of Glucola® orally. Obtain samples of blood and urine for glucose determinations ½ hour, 1 hour, 2 hours, and 3 hours later. In normal people the fasting and 2-hour blood samples will contain less than 120 mg/100 ml of glucose and the ½-hour specimen will contain less than 180 mg/100 ml (Folin-Wu). The 1-hour and 2-hour blood specimens in conjunction with the other specimens are of value in interpreting the severity of diabetes or detecting other causes of hyperglycemia in the event that tolerance is shown to be decreased. The urine samples are taken so that the threshold for glucose can be correlated with the blood findings to fortify the diagnosis. In addition to the standard 3-hour glucose tolerance test there are several modifications, eg, a 1-hour, 2-dose test, and intravenous tests. Prolongation of the test to 5–6 hours may demonstrate delayed hypoglycemia.

b. **Insulin tolerance test**—This test is of greatest value in differentiating insulin-sensitive diabetes from "insulin-resistant" forms such as may occur in acromegaly and Cushing's disease. It is performed as follows: Give 0.1 unit of crystalline zinc insulin per kg ideal body weight IV. Determine the blood glucose levels immediately and at 20, 30, 45, 90, and 120 minutes. Normal sensitivity to insulin will cause the blood glucose level to fall to half its initial value, or below 50 mg/100 ml in 20–30 minutes, with return to normal levels in 90–120 minutes.

c. **Orinase® tolerance test**—This test of "insulin reserve" is of value in assessing insulin production when the diagnosis of diabetes is questionable, eg, in the prediabetic state. Give 1 gm of sodium tolbutamide (Orinase®) IV in 20 ml of physiologic saline solution. Failure of the normal fasting blood glucose level to fall by 30% within 30 minutes indicates limited insulin production. This is seen in the prediabetic state as well as in the diabetic.

d. **Cortisone test**—Decreased glucose tolerance following a short course of cortisone therapy is considered by some authors to be evidence of the prediabetic state.

4. **Serum cholesterol** is often increased in diabetes, especially if poorly controlled.

5. **Direct measurements of circulating insulin** have recently demonstrated normal or high levels in the adult type of diabetes, especially after a glucose load, and low or absent levels in the juvenile type.

6. **Insulin autoantibodies** have been demonstrated in high titers in patients with insulin resistance.

D. X-Ray Findings: A plain film of the abdomen may show evidence of calcification of the pelvic blood vessels. This is an especially unfavorable sign in a young patient.

E. Other Findings: Biopsy of the skin or muscle has demonstrated microangiopathy in most diabetics and even in the prediabetic state.

Differential Diagnosis

Ten to 15% of patients whose routine urinalyses show glycosuria do not have diabetes mellitus. These positive reactions are due to urine sugars other than glucose, urine constituents which are not sugars but which give positive reactions, and benign nondiabetic glycosuria (the most common problem in diagnosis). Fructosuria, pentosuria, and galactosuria are usually asymptomatic, but can be identified with special tests. Salicylates, alkaptones, amino acids, and other substances in the urine may also give false-positive reactions to Benedict's test, but the use of Tes-Tape®, which is specific for glucose, will eliminate this source of confusion. Benign nondiabetic glycosuria may occur in renal glycosuria, ie, overflow of glucose at normal blood glucose levels as a result of a tubular defect, often familial and rarely associated with other tubular defects such as the De Toni-Fanconi syndrome. It may occur during pregnancy. Alimentary hyperglycemia and glycosuria may occur in states of rapid absorption or poor storage capacity, eg, dumping syndrome, starvation, or liver disease. They can be ruled out by observation of the glucose tolerance curve.

Transient emotional or stress glycosuria is attributable to epinephrine or to adrenal stress hormones. True diabetes mellitus develops eventually in about 10% of these patients, or the 2 types may coexist when the patient is first seen. A physiologic decrease of glucose tolerance with advancing age must also be considered.

Also to be differentiated is the insulin-resistant diabetes seen in acromegaly and Cushing's syndrome and the glycosuria which is present in thyrotoxicosis and pheochromocytoma.

If diabetes is associated with hypogonadism, consider hemochromatosis. Addison's disease and thyrotoxicosis may be associated with diabetes.

Complications

A. Acute Complications:

1. Diabetic ketosis, acidosis, and coma (see p 657).

2. Insulin reactions (actually a complication of therapy) usually occur when there is a sudden change in insulin requirement. The principal symptoms are weakness, hunger, irritability, tremor, and coma or convulsions (or both), all of which are promptly relieved by giving glucose. In addition, and especially with protamine zinc insulin, confusion or even psychotic reactions are not uncommon. Prolonged hypoglycemia after tolbutamide is occasionally seen, but is quite rare compared with insulin. If the diagnosis of insulin reaction is in doubt, a therapeutic trial of glu-

cose is indicated. Diabetics should carry proper identification.

3. Insulin allergy—Hives or painful lumps at the site of injection.

B. Chronic Complications: Certain complications, notably infections (eg, around the toenails) and degenerative vascular diseases, occur more frequently among people with diabetes than in the general population. The following disorders may appear in longstanding diabetes:

1. Premature arteriosclerosis with leg claudication, trophic ulcer, angina.

2. Neuropathy, varying from paresthesias to actual muscular atrophy. Neuropathy is also the cause of nocturnal diarrhea and bladder atony. Absence of sweating and orthostatic hypotension may be seen.

3. Ocular disorders ranging from premature cataracts, microaneurysms, and vitreous hemorrhage to retinitis proliferans and blindness.

4. Intercapillary glomerulosclerosis (Kimmelstiel-Wilson disease) with associated hypertension, proteinuria, and edema.

5. Pyelonephritis (common) and papillary necrosis (rare).

6. Chronic pyogenic infections of the skin.

7. Xanthomas (only in long-standing uncontrolled cases).

8. An unusual skin lesion, necrobiosis lipoidica diabeticorum, may appear in the diabetic patient, as well as fat atrophy and hypertrophy at the sites of insulin injections.

9. The incidence of tuberculosis in the diabetic is higher than in the general population.

10. Insulin resistance—For unexplained reasons the insulin required may suddenly (at times temporarily) increase tremendously.

Treatment*

The treatment of diabetes mellitus requires a thorough understanding of the action of insulin and the various types of insulin and oral hypoglycemic agents available, dietary concepts, the influence of exercise, the complications of the disease and the complications which may arise as a result of its treatment.

While milder forms may require only dietary limitations with or without oral hypoglycemic agents, severe forms of diabetes with ketoacidosis have to be managed with insulin on a temporary or, most often, a permanent basis.

A. Insulin: Insulin is given to enhance carbohydrate utilization. This is measured clinically by noting the lowering of the blood glucose or the lessening or disappearance of glycosuria.

Three principal types of insulin are available: short-acting, long-acting, and intermediate-acting. Short-acting insulin (crystalline zinc insulin) is useful mainly in controlling postprandial blood sugar elevations, in the treatment of diabetic coma, and when the insulin requirement is changing rapidly (eg, postoperatively). Long-acting insulins are useful for con-

trolling the milder hyperglycemia which is present during the remainder of the time between meals. The 2 forms available are protamine zinc insulin (PZI) and ultra-lente insulin, which is similar in effect to PZI (although its effect may be prolonged to 48—72 hours). Intermediate-acting insulin is available in several forms: **(1) Isophane insulin (NPH),** a stable "mixture" with properties much like a 2:1 mixture of crystalline zinc and PZI insulin, has tended to replace PZI in the management of most diabetic patients. It may also be "tailored to fit the patient" by the addition of appropriate amounts of regular insulin. **(2) Lente insulin,** a mixture of 30% semi-lente and 70% ultra-lente, is made by the action of zinc on insulin under special conditions (protamine-free and phosphate-free). Its action is almost identical with that of NPH insulin. **(3) Globin zinc insulin** is similar in action to a 2:1 insulin mixture except that its duration of effect is not so prolonged. It is useful in many diabetic patients, but it cannot be mixed with short-acting insulin. **(4) Semi-lente insulin** has the shortest action of all the intermediate insulins.

Insulin mixtures: Intermediate insulin may be prepared by mixing a short-acting or intermediate (commercial) and a long-acting insulin (add last) in the same syringe. This gives a balance between the immediate and the prolonged effects; by modifying the mixtures, one can "tailor" the insulin requirements to individual needs. The mixtures usually employed are 2:1 and 3:1 (crystalline zinc:PZI) or 2:1 and 3:1 (NPH:crystalline). Crystalline insulin must always be drawn into the syringe before the PZI (because of the protamine excess in PZI), and the same concentration per ml of crystalline insulin and PZI must be used. The general effect of crystalline zinc:PZI mixtures is as follows: 1:1 gives essentially the same effect as PZI alone and there is little point to this mixture; 2:1 gives an intermediate daytime-nighttime effect; and 3:1 gives a greater daytime effect. (*Note:* Lente insulin should be mixed only with semi-lente, ultra-lente, or regular insulin.)

Tailored insulin mixtures are used as follows: (1) If glycosuria occurs in all urines, increase total insulin mixtures. (2) If glycosuria occurs in urines voided before lunch and dinner (daytime glycosuria), increase the proportion of crystalline zinc insulin in the mixture. (3) If glycosuria occurs in urines voided before bedtime and before breakfast (nighttime glycosuria), increase the proportion of PZI mixture. For best control, division of insulin (NPH or lente) into 2 doses, 3/4 at breakfast and 1/4 at dinner, is advisable.

Commercial insulin preparations come in various strengths (units/ml), usually in 10 ml vials. Most of them are prepared in U40 and U80 forms. Crystalline zinc insulin is also available as U100 and U500.

Administration of insulin: Because the large number of insulin preparations available may cause confusion regarding dosage, it is recommended that the patient be placed on one type of insulin so that he can become familiar with it. Prescribe an insulin of such strength that the volume per injection is kept at

*See also Steps in the Management of the Diabetic Patient, p 653.

**Instructions in the Care of the Feet
for Persons With Diabetes Mellitus or Vascular Disturbances**

Hygiene of the Feet

(1) Wash feet daily with mild soap and luke-warm water. Dry thoroughly between the toes by pressure. Do not rub vigorously, as this is apt to break the delicate skin.

(2) When feet are thoroughly dry, rub well with vegetable oil to keep them soft, prevent excess friction, remove scales, and prevent dryness. Care must be taken to prevent foot tenderness.

(3) If the feet become too soft and tender, rub them with alcohol about once a week.

(4) When rubbing the feet, always rub upward from the tips of the toes. If varicose veins are present, massage the feet very gently; never massage the legs.

(5) If the toenails are brittle and dry, soften them by soaking for ½ hour each night in lukewarm water containing 1 tbsp of powdered sodium borate (borax) per quart. Follow this by rubbing around the nails with vegetable oil. Clean around the nails with an orangewood stick. If the nails become too long, file them with an emery board. File them straight across, and no shorter than the underlying soft tissues of the toe. Never cut the corners of the nails. (If the patient goes to a podiatrist for this attention, he should tell him that he has diabetes.)

(6) Wear low-heeled shoes of soft leather which fit the shape of the feet correctly. The shoes should have wide toes that will cause no pressure, fit close in the arch, and grip the heels snugly. Wear new shoes ½ hour only on the first day and increase by 1 hour each day following. Wear thick, warm, loose stockings.

Treatment of Corns and Calluses

(1) Corns and calluses are due to friction and pressure, most often from improperly fitted shoes and stockings. Wear shoes that fit properly and cause no friction or pressure.

(2) To remove excess calluses or corns, soak the feet in lukewarm (not hot) water, using a mild soap, for about 10 minutes, and then rub off the excess tissue with a towel or file. Do not tear it off. Under no circumstances must the skin become irritated.

(3) Do not cut corns or calluses. If they need attention it is safer to see a podiatrist.

(4) Prevent callus formation under the ball of the foot (a) by exercises, such as curling and stretching the toes several times a day; (b) by finishing each step on the toes and not on the ball of the foot; and (c) by wearing shoes that are not too short and that do not have high heels.

Aids in Treatment of Imperfect Circulation (Cold Feet)

(1) Never use tobacco in any form. Tobacco contracts blood vessels and so reduces circulation.

(2) Keep warm. Wear warm stockings and other clothing. Cold contracts blood vessels and reduces circulation.

(3) Do not wear circular garters, which compress blood vessels and reduce blood flow.

(4) Do not sit with the legs crossed. This may compress the leg arteries and shut off the blood supply to the feet.

(5) If the weight of the bedclothes is uncomfortable, place a pillow under the covers at the foot of the bed.

(6) Do not apply any medication to the feet without directions from a physician. Some medicines are too strong for feet with poor circulation.

(7) Do not apply heat in the form of hot water, hot water bottles, or heating pads without a physician's consent. Even moderate heat can injure the skin if circulation is poor.

(8) If the feet are moist or the patient has a tendency to develop athlete's foot, a prophylactic dusting powder should be used on the feet and in shoes and stockings daily. Change shoes and stockings at least daily or oftener.

(9) Exercises to increase circulation should be prescribed by a physician.

Treatment of Abrasions of the Skin

(1) Proper first-aid treatment is of the utmost importance even in apparently minor injuries. Consult a physician immediately for any redness, blistering, pain, or swelling. Any break in the skin may become ulcerous or gangrenous unless properly treated by a physician.

(2) Dermatophytosis (athlete's foot), which begins with peeling and itching between the toes or discoloration or thickening of the toenails, should be treated immediately by a physician or podiatrist.

(3) Avoid strong irritating antiseptics such as tincture of iodine.

(4) As soon as possible after any injury, cover the area with sterile gauze. Sterile gauze in sealed packets may be purchased at drug stores.

(5) Elevate and, as much as possible until recovery, avoid using the foot.

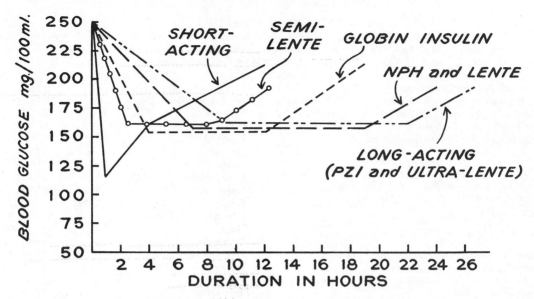

FIG 18–1. Extent and duration of action of various types of insulin (in a fasting diabetic).

0.25–0.5 ml. About 80% of patients are able to use U40 insulins.

Syringes are calibrated in units (U) rather than ml. If syringes with 2 calibrations (U20–U40 or U40–U80) are used, it is important that the patient should understand which scale he is using. It is preferable, however, to use a syringe with one calibration only. Special syringes are available for blind diabetic patients.

Insulin is usually administered subcutaneously. The site of injection is generally the anterior thigh, but insulin may also be given in the lateral thigh, in the arms or anterior abdomen, or, in unusual circumstances, subcutaneously in other parts of the body. It is important that the sites be rotated so that the same site is not injected more often than once every 2–3 weeks. Crystalline zinc insulin may be administered intravenously to patients who have been taking insulin without allergic reactions. (*Note:* Do not give PZI, NPH, or lente insulin intravenously.)

B. Diet: (See Tables 18–9 and 18–10.) The diet for each individual is based upon normal nutritional needs expressed in terms of total caloric requirement and a ratio of this in grams of carbohydrate, protein, and fat.

Distribution of the diet through the day depends upon the type of control used: insulin, oral hypoglycemic agents, or diet alone. The type of insulin used and its pattern of absorption and activity peaks influence the pattern of food intake. For short-acting insulins, foods are fairly evenly divided into meals given shortly after required injections. For medium-acting insulins (NPH, lente, globin), foods are divided into regular meals with a mid-afternoon and evening snack. For long-acting insulins (PZI, ultra-lente insulin), foods are divided to give a larger evening meal and bedtime snack. If mixtures of insulin are given, a larger breakfast may be given with mid-afternoon and bedtime snacks provided.

An even distribution of the diet is made when oral hypoglycemic agents are administered. Likewise, if only dietary control is used, there should be a fairly consistent balance of meals through the day, avoiding a load of glucose at any one point.

1. Caloric needs–Calorie specifications are based on ideal weight with allowances for age, physical activity, growth, and state of health. If the individual is obese, calories should be reduced to allow gradual weight loss; if underweight or growing, calories need to be increased to suit these needs.

2. Carbohydrates–As a general rule, the carbohydrate allowance in grams is about 40% of the total caloric requirement. It is inadvisable to allow less than 100 gm carbohydrate per day since the diet is unappealing and might result in ketosis. Amounts over 300 gm/day may be too much for metabolic capacity and may result in glucose loss in the urine. Slowly absorbed carbohydrate foods are suggested rather than concentrated types such as sugars.

3. Protein–Recommended allowances for protein should be made according to normal age group requirement, ie, children below 3 years of age require 2.5 gm protein per kg body weight; older children require 2 gm/kg/day; and healthy adults require 1 gm/kg/day. The amount of protein required (in grams) is generally ½ the carbohydrate content, or 20% of total calories.

4. Fat–The fat content of the diabetic diet is about ½ (in grams) the carbohydrate content (in grams) per day, or about 40% of the total calories. Animal fats and high-cholesterol foods should be restricted, and fish and poultry should be recommended. Polyunsaturated rather than saturated fats are recommended.

C. Oral Hypoglycemic Agents: These agents are of 2 types: (1) the sulfonylurea group of drugs (useful primarily in the older diabetic with a mild form of the disease); and (2) the biguanide group of drugs (which

TABLE 18–9. Diabetic diet.

(Adapted from the following sources: *You and Your Diabetes*. Diabetes Teaching Program, University Hospitals, Cleveland, 1970; Prater, B.M., & others: *Food and You*. University of Utah Medical Center, 1970; Cole, H.S., & others: Diet therapy of diabetes mellitus. M Clin North America 54:1577–1587, 1970.)

The diabetic diet is calculated to furnish basic nutritional needs but must be individualized according to physical activity, growth, and state of health. Foods are grouped according to the "basic four" with the addition of a fat group. The food groups are also referred to as exchanges or choices.

Milk Group

Each portion contains approximately
    12 gm carbohydrate
    8 gm protein
    9 gm fat
    165 Calories

Milk, whole (homogenized, pasteurized) – 1 cup (8 oz)
    Low fat (2%) – 1 cup + 1 fat portion
    Nonfat (skimmed or buttermilk) – 1 cup + 1 fat portion
    Evaporated – ½ cup
    Powdered nonfat – ¼ cup + 2 fat portions

Meat, Eggs, and Cheese Group

Each portion contains approximately
    7 gm protein
    5 gm fat
    Little or no carbohydrate
    73 Calories

Meat, fish, and poultry, cooked edible* – 1 oz
    Beef, ham, lamb, pork, veal
    Fish, chicken, turkey
    Cold cuts (1 slice), frankfurter (1 medium)
    Liver and organ meats
Egg – 1
Cheese (American, cheddar, Swiss) – 1 oz
Cottage cheese – 2 oz (¼ cup)

Fruit and Vegetable Group

Fruits: Unsugared, fresh, frozen, canned (water or juice pack), or juices

Each portion contains approximately
    15 gm carbohydrate
    1 gm protein
    No fat
    64 Calories

Apple	1 medium
Applesauce	1 cup
Apricots, fresh or dried (whole)	4 medium
Apricots, canned	1 cup
Banana	1 small
Berries (blackberry, blueberry, boysenberry, raspberry), fresh or canned	1 cup
Cantaloupe†	½ medium
Cherries, fresh	20
Cherries, canned	1 cup
Dates	2 medium
Fruit cocktail, canned	1 cup
Figs, dried	1 medium
Grapes, purple, American	22
Grapes, green seedless	35

Grapefruit†	½ medium
Honeydew melon†	¼ medium
Nectarines	2 medium
Oranges†	1 medium
Papaya†	½ medium
Persimmon	½ medium
Peach, fresh	1 large
Peach, canned	1 cup
Pear, fresh	½ large
Pear, canned	1 cup
Pineapple, fresh or canned	1 cup
Plums	3 medium
Pomegranates	1 medium
Prunes, dried or stewed	3 medium
Raisins	2 tbsp
Strawberries, fresh†	1 cup
Tangerines†	1 large
Watermelon	1 slice (1 inch thick or 1 cup diced)

Fruit juices: Unsugared, fresh, frozen or canned: ½ cup (4 oz) per portion

Each portion contains approximately
    15 gm carbohydrate
    Little or no protein
    No fat
    60 Calories

Apple	Lemon†
Apricot	Orange†
Cranberry	Pineapple
Grapefruit†	Prune
Grapefruit-orange†	Tangerine
Grape	

Vegetables, group A: Raw or cooked fresh, frozen, or canned: ½ cup per portion or as noted; limited to not more than 3 per meal

Each portion contains approximately
    4 gm carbohydrate
    Little or no protein
    Little or no fat
    16 Calories

Asparagus	Green peppers† (1 shell)
Broccoli‡	Pickles, dill or sour (large)
Brussels sprouts‡	
Cabbage†	Pickles, sweet (1 medium)
Catsup and chili sauce (1 tbsp)	Pimiento (2 medium)
Cauliflower	Radishes (10 small)
Celery	Rhubarb
Cucumber (½ medium)	Sauerkraut
Egg plant	Spinach‡
Greens:‡ Beet, chard, mustard, kale, dandelion, turnip	Summer squash
	Turnips
Lettuce and salad greens	Tomato†
Mushrooms	Tomato juice†
Okra	Vegetable juice

TABLE 18-9 (cont'd). Diabetic diet.

Vegetables, group B: Raw, or cooked fresh, frozen, canned: ½ cup per portion or as noted

Each portion contains approximately
14 gm carbohydrate
3 gm protein
Little or no fat
68 Calories

Artichoke (1 medium)	Peas
Beans, green, lima, or dried	Potatoes, white mashed
Beets	or 1 small
Carrots‡	Pumpkin‡
Corn (5 inch ear)	Squash, winter (yellow)‡
Onions	Sweet potatoes (½ cup)‡
Parsnips	Yams (½ cup)‡

Bread and Cereal Group

Each portion contains approximately
15 gm carbohydrate
2 gm protein
Little or no fat
68 Calories

Bread, enriched white, whole grain, pumpernickel, raisin (slice)	1
Biscuit (2 inch diameter)	1
Cornbread (2 inch square)	1
Buns or rolls, hamburger, hot dog, dinner	1
Muffin	1
Pancake (4 inch diameter)	1
Waffle (5½ inch diameter)	½
Tortilla (6 inch diameter)	1
Crackers	
Animal	8
Arrowroot	4
Graham (squares)	2
Oyster	20
Ry-Krisp®	3
Saltines	5
Ritz®	7
Triscuits®	5
Wheat Thins®	12
Zwieback	3
Cereals (ready to eat, without sugar)	
Flake types, Kix®, Cheerios®, Krispies®	¾ cup
Puffed types, Special K®	1 cup
Shredded wheat	1 biscuit
Cereals (cooked)	
All kinds, unsugared	½ cup
Pastes (cooked)	
Macaroni, spaghetti, noodles,	½ cup
Rice, brown (instant), white	½ cup

Other starches

Bread crumbs, dry	¼ cup
Cake, angel, sponge (small piece—1/16 of 9 inch cake)	1
Cornstarch	2 tbsp
Cracker meal	1/6 cup
Ice cream cone, plain (cone only— no ice cream)	1
Ice cream, plain (subtract 2 fat portions)	½ cup (1 scoop)
Iced milk, plain (no nuts, ripples, candy, or marshmallows)	½ cup (1 scoop)
Popcorn, popped	1½ cups
Sherbet	1/3 cup
Wheat flour	3 tbsp

Fats and Oils Group

Each portion contains approximately
Little or no carbohydrate
Little or no protein
5 gm fat
45 Calories

Avocado	1/8 small
Bacon, crisp	1 slice
Butter, margarine	1 tsp
Cream	
Table, half and half, sour, whipped	2 tbsp
Heavy	1 tbsp
Cream cheese	1 tbsp
Mayonnaise	1 tsp
Nuts	6 small
Oils (vegetable or cooking)	1 tsp
Olives	5 small
Peanut butter	1 tsp
Salad dressings (bleu cheese, French, Italian, thousand island)	2 tsp
Shortenings	1 tsp

Free Food Group

Need not be measured. May be taken in unlimited amounts.

Broth (clear), bouillon, consommé	Herbs, spices
	Meat tenderizers
Coffee (black), tea, Postum®, Sanka®	Salt, seasoning salts
	Soft drinks (low calorie, artificially sweetened)
Cranberries (without sugar)	
Flavorings (vanilla, etc)	Sweeteners (artificial, sugar substitutes)
Garlic, mint, parsley, chives	
Gelatin (plain, unsweetened)	Vinegar

*In cooking, meat loses about 1 oz for every 4 oz raw meat; ¼ lb or 4 oz raw meat yields 3 oz cooked; 1/3 lb or 5 oz yields 4 oz cooked.
†Good sources of vitamin C.
‡Good sources of vitamin A.

TABLE 18–10. Diabetic diet: Daily food intake according to caloric levels.

Total calories	1000	1200	1500	1800	2000	2500	3000
Carbohydrate (gm)	104	136	155	175	208	258	288
Protein (gm)	57	65	70	83	91	116	140
Fat (gm)	40	45	65	85	90	111	150
Portions to use daily*							
Fruit	3	4	4	4	5	6	7
Breads or cereals	1½	2	3	4	4½	6	7
Milk, whole	—	—	—	2	2	3	3
Milk, nonfat	2	2	2	—	—	—	—
Vegetable, group A	3	4	3	4	3	3	3
Vegetable, group B	—	—	1	1	2	2	2
Meat, eggs, cheese	5	6	6	7	8	10	13
Fats and oils	3	3	7	6	6	6	11
Distribution in Meals							
Morning							
Fruit	1	1	1	1	1	2	2
Breads or cereals	½	1	1	1	1	2	2
Milk, whole	—	—	—	1	1	1	1
Milk, nonfat	½	½	1	—	—	—	—
Vegetable, group A	—	—	—	—	—	—	—
Vegetable, group B	—	—	—	—	—	—	—
Meat, eggs, cheese	1	1	1	1	2	2	2
Fats and oils	1	1	1	1	1	2	2
Noon							
Fruit	1	1	1	1	2	2	2
Breads or cereals	1	1	2	2	2	2	2
Milk, whole	—	—	—	1	1	1	1
Milk, nonfat	1	1	½	—	—	—	—
Vegetable, group A	1	1	1	2	1	1	1
Vegetable, group B	—	—	—	—	—	—	—
Meat, eggs, cheese	1	2	2	3	2	3	4
Fats and oils	1	1	3	2	2	2	4
Evening							
Fruit	1	2	2	2	1	2	2
Breads or cereals	—	—	—	1	1	1	1
Milk, whole	—	—	—	—	—	—	—
Milk, nonfat	½	½	½	—	—	—	—
Vegetable, group A	2	2	2	2	2	2	2
Vegetable, group B	—	—	1	1	2	2	2
Meat, eggs, cheese	3	3	3	3	3	4	4
Fats and oils	1	1	3	3	3	2	4
Snacks†							
Fruit	—	—	—	—	1	1	1
Breads or cereals	—	—	—	—	½	1	2
Milk, whole	—	—	—	—	—	1	1
Milk, nonfat	—	—	—	—	—	—	—
Vegetable, group A	—	—	—	—	—	—	—
Vegetable, group B	—	—	—	—	—	—	—
Meat, eggs, cheese	—	—	—	—	1	1	3
Fats and oils	—	—	—	—	—	—	3

*Portions are defined in Table 18–9.
†Between-meal snacks may be taken from preceding meal plan unless calculated as part of daily intake.

are effective in reducing blood sugar in almost all diabetics).

In substituting one of the oral agents for insulin in a patient who has been taking insulin, it is well to remember that insulin can be discontinued abruptly only in those patients who do not develop ketosis without insulin. In patients who do develop ketosis, it is advisable to decrease the insulin dosage slowly, adding the oral agents at first in small doses and gradually increasing the dosage, and observing the patient closely for side reactions.

1. Sulfonylurea drugs—**Tolbutamide** (Orinase®), **chloropropamide** (Diabinese®), **acetohexamide** (Dymelor®), and **tolazamide** (Tolinase®) are sulfonamide derivatives, although they have no antibacterial properties. Their apparent mode of action is to stimulate the production of insulin by the beta cells of a pancreas which would not otherwise produce adequate amounts. They do not potentiate the action of insulin and are of no value unless the pancreas is capable of secreting insulin. Therefore, these drugs are of limited use (and should rarely be tried) in severe diabetes (eg, juvenile-onset) or in those diabetic patients who tend to develop ketosis easily. Their principal area of usefulness is in the older patient with a mild degree of diabetes which cannot be controlled by diet alone ("relatively mild adult," "maturity-onset," "nonketotic" types).

Tolbutamide is supplied in tablets of 0.5 gm. Give an initial dose of 3 gm daily in divided doses and decrease rapidly to the minimal effective dose. The average maintenance dose is 0.5–1.5 gm daily. Toxic reactions are rare; skin rashes and gastrointestinal distress occur only occasionally. Prolonged hypoglycemia has been reported on rare occasions, especially if hepatic or renal disease is present.

Chlorpropamide is supplied in tablets of 250 mg and 100 mg. This drug has a greater duration of action than tolbutamide (up to 3–5 days). *Always start patients on 0.25 gm daily.* The average maintenance dosage is 0.25 gm as a single dose with breakfast; rarely, 750 mg daily may be required *(maximum dose)*. Toxic reactions are more frequent than with tolbutamide, and jaundice has been reported. Chlorpropamide is excreted by the kidneys and is contraindicated in renal insufficiency.

Acetohexamide is supplied in tablets of 500 mg. Its duration of action is intermediate between that of tolbutamide and chlorpropamide. The usual dosage is 0.5–1.5 gm/day. Side reactions are the same as those of other drugs.

Tolazamide is supplied in tablets of 100 mg and 250 mg. It is about 10 times as potent as tolbutamide; longer acting and more potent than acetohexamide; and about as potent but not as long-acting as chlorpropamide. It may be more effective if used in combination with phenformin. The usual dose is 100–250 mg each morning. Side-effects are similar to those of other oral hypoglycemic drugs, but hypoglycemia is more common.

Note: The effects of barbiturates and other sedatives and hypnotics may be prolonged when these agents are used. Phenylbutazone, oxyphenbutazone, probenecid, salicylates, the bacteriostatic sulfonamides, the MAO inhibitors, and, possibly, alcohol may potentiate their action, and prolonged hypoglycemia may result. (See also Warning, p 656.)

2. Biguanides—**Phenformin** (DBI®), supplied in tablets of 25 mg, exerts a hypoglycemic action either in the absence or presence of insulin. Its mode of action is not known, but phenformin appears to inhibit gluconeogenesis from protein and possibly increases anaerobic glycolysis. It is not known whether these reactions are harmful. The drug may be of use in "juvenile" diabetes, to lower insulin requirements or help stabilize brittle diabetics. It can be combined with the sulfonylureas. It may be the drug of choice in the obese diabetic. The chief side reactions are gastrointestinal disturbances with higher effective doses. The introduction of long-acting capsules of phenformin (DBI-TD®), 25 and 50 mg, has lessened this tendency and improved control. The usual starting dose is 50–150 mg daily in divided doses. A dose of 150 mg/day should rarely be exceeded, since side-effects increase rapidly beyond this level. (*Note:* Ketonemia and acidosis may be aggravated by phenformin, and additional insulin must be given if this occurs.)

D. Other Factors Influencing Diabetes:

1. **Exercise**—Exercise enhances the oxidation of sugar; hence it diminishes the need for insulin. Therefore, exercise in moderation is beneficial. However, patients taking insulin should be cautioned against strenuous exercise without fortifying themselves previously with extra carbohydrate. (It is not uncommon to have a hypoglycemic reaction after a set of tennis.) When regulating a patient, have him perform approximately the same amount of exercise as will be required during his normal activities. This is true also of hospital-regulated diabetics.

2. **Complicating factors**—Many factors adversely affect the course of diabetes by altering the absorption of glucose, by interfering with carbohydrate oxidation, or by causing excessive carbohydrate formation. The most important of these factors are infections, especially pyogenic infections with fever and toxemia. Any infection is serious in a diabetic patient because it completely upsets the equilibrium established by therapy, increases the need for insulin, and is one of the most common precipitating causes of ketosis and acidosis. Infections should therefore be avoided whenever possible; when they occur, they must be treated promptly and vigorously. During severe infections it is generally advisable to discontinue PZI and NPH insulin and to begin therapy in divided doses 3–6 times daily with crystalline zinc insulin as needed to cover postprandial glycosuria.

Thiazide drugs may aggravate the diabetic state, possibly because they result in potassium depletion. Corticosteroid administration raises the insulin requirement of most diabetics.

3. **General factors**—Patients with diabetes should live as nearly normal hygienic lives as possible. They should be assured of adequate rest, should be able to eat at home if possible, and should engage in an occupation requiring at least moderate exercise but must avoid strenuous occupations; of greatest importance, they should avoid obesity and have a good general knowledge of diabetes. Psychologic factors are of great importance in the outlook of the patient and his adjustment to a life which imposes certain limitations on activity, dietary habits, etc. Some patients react with a compulsively strict control of diet and sugar levels, while others display a self-destructive neglect of their illness.

Steps in the Management of the Diabetic Patient

There are many adequate methods for managing diabetes. The following is a plan used by many authors which is felt to be both practical and physiologically sound.

A. Diagnostic Examination:

1. Complete history and physical examination for diagnosis and to rule out the presence of coexisting or complicating disease.

2. Urinalysis for qualitative glucose on a morning fasting urine specimen and on specimens collected 2–3 hours after each meal. If glucose is present, check for acetone and diacetic acid.

3. Blood glucose examination—Fasting and 2-hour postprandial levels are determined or, if necessary, a glucose tolerance test performed. In elderly patients or in the presence of renal disease, it is advisable to perform a glucose tolerance test with simultaneous urine glucose to determine the approximate renal threshold. If this is very high (over 160–180 mg/100 ml), it may be necessary to use blood glucose levels rather than the glycosuria as a check on adequacy of therapy.

B. Calculation and Arrangement of Diet: See p 649 and Tables 18–9 and 18–10.

C. Trial of Sulfonylureas: (See above.) This is indicated in maturity-onset diabetes or possibly in very early, mild juvenile diabetes. Phenformin may be preferable in obese adult diabetics. Combinations of these agents may stabilize the diabetic state. If this is not successful, and especially if the patient is ketosis-prone, start insulin therapy as outlined below.

D. Insulin Therapy: Determination of insulin requirements:

1. Determine amount of glycosuria. Have the patient eat his diabetic diet for 1 day, preferably without change in activity. For the next 24 hours he is to collect and label fractional urines as follows: (Patient voids just before breakfast and discards this specimen.) Urine No. 1, all urine voided from breakfast to just before lunch. This is pooled and a few drops taken for qualitative sugar. The remainder is saved. Urine No. 2, all urine from lunch to just before dinner. Pool and save as above. Urine No. 3, all urine from dinner to just before retiring. Pool and save as above. Urine No. 4, all urine from retiring to just before breakfast. Pool and save as above. A few drops of each urine fraction are analyzed qualitatively for glucose. The remainder may be pooled for the daily total quantitative glucose determination (optional).

2. One may calculate the approximate insulin requirements from quantitative urine sugar determinations, since, roughly, 1 unit of insulin will "cover" 2 gm of glucose, but this is usually misleading. More commonly, therefore, one starts with 10–20 units daily and increases the amount every few days according to the spot and fractional urine reductions.

The 24-hour insulin requirement is generally given as NPH or lente, or as a mixture in a single dose ½ hour before breakfast. The usual mixtures are 2:1 or 3:1 (crystalline zinc:PZI) or NPH:crystalline mixture. In severe or complicated diabetes, because the patient needs insulin immediately, this method of determining the requirement cannot be used. Furthermore, in certain elderly patients or those with renal disease who have a high renal threshold for glucose, this method will be without value. These patients must be controlled by the determination of the blood glucose levels while fasting and 1 hour after meals. In these cases, begin with small doses of long-acting insulin (5–10 units/day) and increase as indicated by tests.

3. Adjustment of insulin dosage and mixture—The patient continues to collect his urine fractions as outlined above, and the dosage and composition of the insulin mixture is determined each morning after completing the qualitative glucose analysis for the previous day. Quantitative glucose determinations are usually not necessary after the first day but may be used from time to time to assess adequacy of control. The amount and time of glycosuria on the preceding day determine the readjustment to be made. (*Note:* Clinitest® determination is more reliable than Tes-Tape® or Clinistix® for regulation of insulin dosage.) The glycosuria at any time should be kept at a minimum, ie, no greater than green reduction (or +) with enzymatic test paper methods in any specimen. In general, especially with longer-acting insulins, changes should not be made frequently simply because marked insulin reactions occasionally occur.

(1) If all specimens are green, no adjustment of dosage or composition of insulin is necessary.

(2) If glycosuria (greater than green reduction) occurs after breakfast or after the noon meal, the proportion of crystalline zinc insulin in the mixture is increased.

(3) If glycosuria occurs in the afternoon, after the evening meal, or before breakfast, the proportion of protamine zinc insulin in the mixture is increased; or it may be preferable to give a second smaller dose of NPH insulin at bedtime. Many diabetics are best controlled by giving ¾ of the daily dose of NPH or lente insulin before breakfast, and ¼ before supper.

(4) If glycosuria occurs in all specimens, both crystalline zinc and protamine zinc insulins must be given in higher dosages. An occasional labile diabetic may be controlled only by giving multiple injections of regular insulin. The combination of insulin with the oral hypoglycemic agents should be tried.

sliding Scale

(5) The amount of insulin which should be added will vary with each patient. A very rough guide ("rainbow scale") is as follows: green reduction (or +), 0–5 units; yellow reduction (or ++), add up to 5 units; orange reduction (or +++), add 5–10 units; brick-red reduction (or ++++), add 10–15 units.

(6) If there is no glycosuria (specimen remains blue), the patient should be questioned for evidence of hypoglycemia and each urine voided should be examined. Adjustment of dosage must be made in accordance with the findings.

4. Readjustment of the size of feedings—If variations of the insulin dosage and composition do not maintain the glycosuria at a minimum for a given period, the dietary intake for the preceding meal should be decreased and the intake for other meals increased a similar amount.

E. Follow-Up of Patient: After the patient has been adequately controlled, he should be seen at regular intervals.

1. Hypoglycemic reactions—Carefully question the patient about the occurrence of any hypoglycemic reactions. If these occur, reduce the insulin dosage or oral hypoglycemic agents according to the time of day the reactions take place.

2. Examine the urine—If all urine is entirely free of glucose, the patient is controlled (if the renal threshold is normal). However, if all urines are blue early in therapy, be careful of hypoglycemic reactions since the patient's tolerance will improve under therapy. There is no contraindication to having some green reductions. If there is marked glycosuria in any urine, the insulin dosage or oral therapy is adjusted accordingly.

3. Weigh the patient to be sure that the weight is increasing, decreasing, or remaining stationary, as desired. If not, alter the diet accordingly.

4. Draw blood for fasting blood glucose test to determine whether fasting hyperglycemia is being adequately controlled. Record the 3:00 p.m. blood glucose level as a check on postprandial hyperglycemia. (This need not be done on every visit; in fact, it can be done quite infrequently once the patient's control is stabilized.)

5. Criteria for adequate control—(1) The glycosuria in 24 hours should not exceed 5% of the total carbohydrate intake. (2) The majority of blood glucose levels should be no more than 130 mg/100 ml before meals. (3) The urines should be free from ketone bodies. (4) The serum cholesterol should be below 250 mg/100 ml.

Complications of Insulin Therapy

A. Hypoglycemia: Hypoglycemia is the most common complication of insulin therapy. It usually occurs when the patient fails to eat or engages in too strenuous exercise. It is manifested by weakness, hunger, sweating, irritability, faintness, and tremors and convulsions, all of which are relieved promptly by the administration of glucose. If a diabetic patient is seen while unconscious, and if a diagnosis of coma or insulin reaction is impossible or in doubt, give 50% glucose IV. This will definitely overcome the insulin reaction and will not generally harm the patient in diabetic acidosis.

Because of the danger of insulin reaction, the diabetic patient should carry several lumps of sugar or glucose lozenges at all times. If he feels the onset of a reaction, he should take some sugar. It may be advisable to have every diabetic patient carry a glucagon ampule (1 mg) (with diluent), to be injected if he is found unconscious.

I Am a Diabetic and Take Insulin

If I am behaving peculiarly but am conscious and able to swallow, give me sugar or hard candy or orange juice slowly. If I am unconscious, call an ambulance immediately, take me to a physician or a hospital, and notify my physician. *I am not intoxicated.*

My name _____

Address _____

Telephone _____

Physician's name _____

Physician's address _____

Telephone _____

Every diabetic should carry an identification bracelet or tag and a card with information (see box).

Treatment: If the patient is conscious and able to swallow (mild hypoglycemia), sugar, glucose, or orange juice may be given. If the patient is unconscious (moderate to severe hypoglycemia), one of 4 methods may be used: (*Caution:* Do not attempt to feed glucose to an unconscious patient.)

(1) Intravenous glucose (treatment of choice): Give 20–50 ml of 50% glucose IV slowly. As soon as consciousness returns, oral feedings may begin.

(2) Glucagon: One mg IV will restore the blood glucose to normal if the hepatic glycogen reserve is adequate. This drug does not cause the autonomic side-effects which occur with epinephrine. The solution is not stable.

(3) Epinephrine: If the patient is well-nourished, and especially if he has been using short-acting insulin and the liver is not depleted of glycogen, epinephrine, 0.5–1 ml of 1:1000 solution subcut, may cause return of consciousness so that food may be taken by mouth.

(4) Rectal feeding: If the patient is unconscious and intravenous glucose is not available (and if epinephrine is either not available or not feasible or successful), glucose by rectum may be lifesaving. Add 2 tbsp of syrup or honey to a pint of warm water and give slowly by rectum.

When patients taking protamine zinc insulin develop reactions, they should be carefully watched for the possibility of relapse. High-protein foods such as milk should be given in addition to carbohydrate.

B. Allergic Reactions: Fortunately, allergic reactions to insulin are very rare, and most are localized. Patients who develop reactions are usually sensitive to pork pancreas, from which about 60% of commercial insulin is made (the other 40% is from beef pancreas). These patients should be given pure beef insulin preparation ("special insulin"), which is supplied in 10 ml vials containing 40 units/ml. If this does not prevent reactions, desensitization measures should be tried.

C. Lipoatrophy: This rare complication consists of atrophy of subcutaneous fat at the sites of insulin injection. It may be due to improper rotation of injection sites, but some cases occur in spite of careful therapy. These patients should use U80 or U100 insulin, rotate injection sites, and inject only on body areas which are clothed at all times.

Prognosis

Although diabetes is still an unpredictable disease, since the advent of insulin and antibiotics the life expectancy of the adult diabetic is about the same as that of other people. The ultimate outcome depends in part upon the duration of the illness (juvenile diabetics fare worse than adults) and the adequacy of treatment. The greater the number of episodes of coma and insulin reactions, the worse seems to be the generalized vascular degeneration, especially of the peripheral arteries and the coronary arteries. Other factors than strict control seem to be responsible for the progression of retinal and renal changes. Strict attention to hygiene, periodic x-rays of the chest, and vigorous treatment of minor infections often will forestall major complications.

The juvenile diabetic often shows marked lability of control; this, together with emotional factors, makes him more liable to complications.

Pregnancy and the menopause seem to increase the severity of diabetes, and diabetes is associated with a greater incidence of toxemia, edema, and prolonged gestation with large babies and hydramnios. The fetal mortality is increased markedly. Strict supervision during pregnancy and early termination of pregnancy have reduced these hazards.

Special attention is also required when the diabetic patient has to undergo surgery (see below).

The insulin requirement, once established, may vary from time to time. Sudden unexplained and temporary periods of marked insulin resistance, requiring extremely large amounts of insulin, may make management difficult. Insulin auto-antibodies have been demonstrated in these patients. Corticosteroid administration has been of some help in reversing insulin resistance. Likewise, increased sensitivity to insulin, with periods of hypoglycemia, especially in the sleeping hours, may aggravate the vascular degeneration and may lead to permanent mental changes.

It is always wise to make sure that the patient presenting himself as a diabetic actually has diabetes and that he does not have a potentially curable disease such as acromegaly, pheochromocytoma, thyrotoxicosis, or Cushing's disease in a subtle form. If detected early, before permanent damage to the pancreas has taken place, the diabetic state in these disorders will improve with cure of the primary disease. Likewise, should a sudden change in insulin sensitivity take place, one must consider associated lesions of the adrenal or pituitary.

In general it can be stated that the ultimate prognosis of the diabetic is directly related to his intelligence and motivation and to his personal understanding of his disease and its potential complications. Some complications, however, notably the retinal and renal complications, may progress relentlessly in spite of the best treatment, which raises some doubts as to the ultimate benefit of even rigid diabetic control. There is increasing evidence, however, that strict control of hyperglycemia by multiple doses of insulin may lessen the excessive production of mucopolysaccharides leading to microangiopathy. The results of pituitary surgery or irradiation, diets very low in fat, or of estrogen therapy in hopeless cases with vascular complications (eg, blindness) are controversial. Photocoagulation may forestall retinal detachment in patients with diabetic retinopathy who are showing active hemorrhages.

The use of the oral antidiabetic agents in the potential diabetic or in the prediabetic state is now under investigation to see if they can materially alter the ultimate prognosis of diabetes mellitus and its complications.

Warning: A recent study* shows *no evidence* that, in diabetics with adult onset stable disease, therapy with a fixed dose of one such agent (tolbutamide) and diet is more effective in prolonging life than diet alone. The study also suggests that such a regimen may be less effective insofar as cardiovascular mortality is concerned than diet alone or than diet and insulin combined. Pending confirmation of these findings, the Food & Drug Administration recommends that the use of tolbutamide (Orinase®) and other sulfonylurea type agents—acetohexamide (Dymelor®), chlorpropamide (Diabinese®), and tolazamide (Tolinase®)—should be limited to those patients with symptomatic adult onset nonketotic diabetes mellitus which cannot be adequately controlled by diet or weight loss alone and in whom the addition of insulin is impractical or unacceptable. The oral hypoglycemic agents are not recommended in the treatment of chemical or latent diabetes, in suspected diabetes, or in prediabetes, and they are *contraindicated* in patients with ketoacidosis.

Strict avoidance of obesity—or weight reduction in obese potential diabetics—is probably the single most effective means of prevention and treatment.

Diabetics should not marry each other, since their children will all eventually develop diabetes. Ideally, an individual with a strong family history of diabetes should not marry into a similar family.

Alexander, R.W.: Diabetes mellitus: Current criteria for laboratory diagnosis. California Med 110:107—113, 1969.

Beaser, S.B.: Regulating severe adult diabetes with oral antidiabetics. Postgrad Med 44:150—161, 1968.

Boshell, B.R., & others: Insulin resistance. Response to insulin from various animal sources, including human. Diabetes 13:144—152, 1964.

*The University Group Diabetes Program. Diabetes 19, Suppl. 2, 1970. This report will require confirmation by further studies, but strict control of diet appears to be as important as the oral agents in many adult diabetics. A "fixed dose" program on any oral agent should be avoided.

Bressler, R. (editor): Symposium on diabetes mellitus. Arch Int Med 123:219—323, 1969.

Brown, J., & others: Diabetes mellitus: Current concepts and vascular lesions (renal and retinal). Ann Int Med 68:634—661, 1968.

Caird, F.I., Burditt, A.F., & G.J.Draper: Diabetic retinopathy. A further study of prognosis for vision. Diabetes 17:121—123, 1968.

Danowski, T.S. (editor): *Diabetes Mellitus: Diagnosis and Treatment.* American Diabetes Association, 1964.

Danowski, T.S., & others: Pituitary ablation, insulin dosage, and course of diabetic retinopathy. Metabolism 17:953—965, 1968.

Davidoff, F.F.: Oral hypoglycemic agents and the mechanism of diabetes mellitus. New England J Med 278:148—154, 1968.

Deckert, T., & others: Prognosis of proliferative retinopathy in juvenile diabetics. Diabetes 16:728, 1967.

Greenberg, B., Weihl, C., & G. Hug: Chlorpropamide poisoning. Pediatrics 41:145—146, 1968.

Grodsky, G.M.: Insulin and the pancreas. Vitamins Hormones 28:37—101, 1970.

Hadden, D.R., & J.A. Weaver: Oral hypoglycaemic agents. Practitioner 200:129—136, 1968.

Hawmi, G.J., & T.S. Danowski (editors): *Diabetes Mellitus: Diagnosis and Treatment.* Vol 2. American Diabetes Association, 1967.

Ibrahim, M., & A. Mottaleb: Comparative efficacy of oral hypoglycaemic agents in diabetes mellitus. Practitioner 199:669—672, 1967.

Karam, J.H.: Insulin secretion in obesity: Pseudodiabetes? Am J Clin Nutr 21:1445, 1968.

Keen, H., & R.J. Jarrett: Current surveys: The uses of biguanides in diabetes mellitus. Postgrad MJ 44:466—467, 1968.

Kipnis, D.M.: Insulin secretion in diabetes mellitus. Ann Int Med 69:891, 1968.

Lampe, W.T.: Hypoglycemia due to acetohexamide. Arch Int Med 120:239, 1967.

Luft, R.: Some considerations on the pathogenesis of diabetes mellitus. New England J Med 279:1086—1092, 1968.

Lukens, F.D.W.: The rediscovery of regular insulin. New England J Med 272:130, 1965.

Marble, A.: Angiopathy in diabetes: An unsolved problem. Diabetes 16:825—838, 1967.

Müller, W.A., & others: Abnormal alpha-cell function in diabetes: Response to carbohydrate and protein. New England J Med 283:109—115, 1970.

Raff, M.C., & A.K. Asbury: Ischemic mononeuropathy and mononeuropathy multiplex in diabetes mellitus. New England J Med 279:17—21, 1968.

Rhodes, E.L.: Dermatological problems in the diabetic patient. Geriatrics 23:132—136, 1968.

Robertson, W.B.: Diabetes, hypertension and atherosclerosis. Postgrad MJ 44:939—943, 1968.

Rosenbloom, A.L.: Insulin responses of children with chemical diabetes mellitus. New England J Med 282:1228—1231, 1970.

Shipp, J.C., & others: Insulin resistance: Clinical features, natural course and effects of adrenal steroid treatment. Medicine 44:165, 1965.

Soelder, J.S.: Diagnosis and treatment of diabetes mellitus: Recent concepts—chemical diabetes. Postgrad Med 43:76—86, 1968.

Steiner, D.F.: Proinsulin and the biosynthesis of insulin. New England J Med 280:1106—1112, 1969.

Triglycerides FFA utilized for energy
$$R-C-C-\overset{O}{C}-OH \rightarrow R-\overset{O}{C}-OH$$

Weil, W.B., Jr.: Current concepts: Juvenile diabetes mellitus. New England J Med 278:829–830, 1968.

West, K.M.: Laboratory diagnosis of diabetes. Arch Int Med 117:187–191, 1966.

DIABETIC KETOSIS, ACIDOSIS, & COMA

Essentials of Diagnosis

- Nausea, vomiting, excessive thirst, "fruity" breath odor, hyperpnea, fever, and increasing somnolence.
- History of diabetes, with poor control.
- Soft eyeballs; warm, dry skin; rapid, thready pulse; low blood pressure.
- Hyperglycemia and glycosuria; positive urine and plasma acetone; low serum CO_2; high NPN, lipemia, and cholesterolemia.

General Considerations

The transition from ketosis to coma may be subtle and progressive, and may escape detection. Certain factors, especially infection, vomiting, and diarrhea, may suddenly precipitate coma. This is more prone to occur in juvenile diabetics.

Clinical Findings

A. Symptoms and Signs: Although the symptoms of ketosis are few, there may be mild nausea, excessive thirst, or malaise, which may progress to those of acidosis with vomiting, drowsiness, hyperpnea, and fever. Abdominal pains and diarrhea, at times with a rigid abdomen, may be present. The typical "fruity" odor of acetone may be detected on the breath. On physical examination the skin and mucosa are dry, the eyeballs soft, and the blood pressure low, with a rapid and thready pulse and deep breathing (Kussmaul type). This may progress to loss of consciousness or coma.

B. Laboratory Findings: 4+ acetone and sugar in the urine, positive urinary diacetic acid, elevated blood glucose, low serum CO_2; serum potassium usually elevated, serum sodium and chloride low. Plasma acetone is positive. The NPN is elevated. Lipemia is present.

Differential Diagnosis

The diagnosis is at times difficult without a history or laboratory data. In most cases in a known diabetic it is possible to decide whether loss of consciousness is due to coma or excess insulin on clinical grounds alone. While awaiting laboratory data, it is always safe to administer intravenous glucose immediately; if no response occurs, coma is not due to insulin excess. Two types of nonketotic diabetic coma must be considered as well: (1) lactic acidosis, often with phenformin therapy; and (2) hyperglycemic-hyperosmolar coma, with severe dehydration and cerebral manifestations. An abdominal emergency or cerebrovascular accident may cause confusion, and its coexistence with coma cannot be ruled out readily. Once coma and acidosis are controlled, the situation usually becomes clarified. Rarely, toxic reactions to drugs (eg, salicylates) may be confusing, especially if a positive reaction for urine glucose or ketone is present. Lack of response to treatment is the important clue in these cases.

Treatment

A. Diabetic Ketosis Without Acidosis: The patient should be hospitalized for regulation if ketosis is severe. Treat any infection which may aggravate the disordered metabolism. Arrange the diet to consist of 3 equal feedings plus interval feedings between each meal and in the evening. If ketosis is severe, use only short-acting insulins. Give insulin to cover each meal as necessary until the urine is free of ketone bodies. Then reduce the insulin dosage slowly as tolerance to carbohydrate improves. If ketosis is not severe, treat and regulate as for uncomplicated diabetes.

When ketonuria has cleared, the patient is managed as for uncomplicated diabetes according to the severity of his disease.

B. Diabetic Acidosis and Coma: (For emergency management, see below.) The principles of therapy are the same whether the patient is precomatose or in coma. It is imperative that a patient with acidosis be hospitalized and treated as a medical emergency. Each case must be individualized. Insulin in large amounts is necessary to bring about a return to normal metabolism. Use short-acting insulin. (*Note:* Never treat patients in coma with PZI, NPH, or lente insulin.) The first dose of insulin should be 100–200 units; one-half should be given intravenously and the other half subcutaneously. Insulin may also be added to intravenous fluids. Because of the mode of action of insulin, there is no need to repeat sooner than in 1–2 hours. The dose may then be repeated subcutaneously or intravenously, giving 50–75 units every 1–2 hours as needed until the ketonuria begins to disappear. If shock is present, the insulin should be given intravenously, because of the unreliable absorption during shock of material given subcutaneously.

In diabetic acidosis one is treating the ketosis and acidosis and not the hyperglycemia and glycosuria. Although the patient with acidosis may have a high blood glucose level, the total available carbohydrate stores may actually be very low. Therefore, since it is necessary to have an adequate glucose supply upon which insulin can act in overcoming acidosis, these patients should be given glucose when the blood glucose level has begun to fall rapidly. It has been shown that ketosis can be reduced by giving large amounts of glucose to diabetic patients who are deprived of insulin. Glucose must not be given in hyperosmolar coma. The sooner the normal metabolic pathways are reestablished, the sooner excess fat oxidation ceases and ketonemia is overcome. In addition, it is possible to precipitate a hypoglycemic reaction in a patient with low glucose reserves before the ketosis is brought under control.

Fluids must be given to replace those lost by diuresis and vomiting. These are usually best given intravenously. Water is very important. These patients are almost always hyperosmotic, and the initial fluids should be hypotonic (0.45% saline).

Adequate sodium chloride is very important. This replaces fixed base in the extracellular fluid and so helps in overcoming the acidosis. As a result of ketosis the loss of sodium chloride from the body may be as high as 30 gm (50% of average total body sodium) in 24–48 hours. In the mild case, sodium chloride must be replaced; sodium chloride solution with glucose is usually adequate fluid therapy in mild to moderate acidosis.

As the ketone bodies are excreted or oxidized, CO_2 is returned which replaces the disappearing ketones and the CO_2 combining power returns to normal. However, in patients with severe uncomplicated metabolic acidosis, it is advisable to administer more rapidly available HCO_3^- and fixed base. This may be given intravenously as sodium bicarbonate, 3.75 gm (44 mEq) in 50 ml, or diluted (1.5% $NaHCO_3$ [7.5 gm $NaHCO_3$/500 ml water or 5% dextrose in water]), or as M/6 sodium lactate. Lactate must not be given in lactic acidosis or when the patient is hypoxic or in shock.

During the period of acidosis, potassium is lost from the cells. As sodium is administered (as sodium chloride, sodium bicarbonate, or sodium lactate) and glucose is metabolized and stored, the potassium which has entered the extracellular fluid migrates rapidly intracellularly or is washed out with the fluid through the kidneys. When this occurs there may be a temporary and dangerous extracellular potassium deficiency, with weakness, respiratory distress, and, at times, cardiac arrest. Solutions containing potassium must be given to correct this, and generally when intravenous glucose becomes indicated potassium may be added to the infusion mixture. It must be used with extreme caution and *slowly,* especially in the absence of adequate urinary output. The level may roughly be checked with the ECG.

1. **Emergency measures**—The following outline of therapy may be employed in the average patient in diabetic coma; however, each case must be individualized and therapy modified as necessary according to the needs of the patient:

a. Hospitalize the patient and keep him warm, but avoid excessive warmth. Do not give barbiturates or narcotics.

b. If he is in shock, treat with intravenous plasma and other antishock measures (see p 3).

c. Draw blood for CO_2 combining power and blood glucose, and for serum sodium, potassium, and chloride if these tests can be performed. Determine the degree of ketonemia with Acetabs® on undiluted and diluted plasma.

d. Give insulin at once. Through the same needle used for drawing blood, give 50–100 units of crystalline insulin IV immediately, as well as a like amount subcut. Repeat insulin, giving 50–75 units subcut every 1–2 hours until there is a rapid diminution in blood or urine glucose. A rough guide to dosage is as follows:

(1) By blood glucose: 100 units subcut or IV every 1–2 hours for every 100 mg/100 ml rise of blood glucose above 200 mg/100 ml.

(2) By plasma ketones: If 4+ in dilution 0, give 25 units; if 4+ in dilution 2 ×, give 50 units; if 4+ in dilution 4 ×, give 100 units; if 4+ in dilution 8 ×, give 200 units.

e. Catheterize the patient. An indwelling catheter may be left in place; allow this to drain continuously. Examine urine every hour for ketone bodies and sugar.

f. Fluids, electrolytes, and glucose—Begin an intravenous infusion of 0.45% saline solution. A clysis of saline, intravenous sodium bicarbonate or M/6 sodium lactate, or other indicated solutions may be started at the same time. When the urine glucose has changed to olive or green reduction, change intravenous fluids to 5% glucose in saline, to which is added 0.5–1 unit of insulin/gm of glucose (25–50 units insulin/liter) and 20 mEq potassium and possibly phosphate. The urine should contain glucose at all times to avoid hypoglycemic reactions.

As soon as reports come from the laboratory, if CO_2 combining power is below 5 mEq/liter (10 vol %), administer sodium lactate (M/6) or, preferably, sodium bicarbonate intravenously immediately. (To administer sodium bicarbonate intravenously, add one or two 50 ml ampules containing 3.75 gm sodium bicarbonate [44 mEq] to 1000 ml water or 5% dextrose in water, and give 1000–3000 ml.)

Gastric lavage may be performed with or without the introduction of 200 ml of physiologic saline or 5% sodium bicarbonate.

As long as the patient is unconscious, administer 5% glucose in saline or other salt solution as indicated (about 60 drops/minute).

As soon as the patient is conscious and able to swallow, give fruit juice (200 ml of orange juice with 1 tbsp of honey, syrup, or glucose) and bouillon every 3–4 hours until ketonuria has disappeared. Stop intravenous glucose and fluids.

2. **Follow-up care**—

a. Potassium deficiency—After 4–8 hours of administration of intravenous fluids, watch the patient carefully for potassium deficiency (eg, weakness, respiratory distress) and check the ECG. Give solutions containing potassium, preferably as buffered potassium phosphate 40 mEq/liter over a period of 3–4 hours, as indicated. It may be advisable to begin administration of potassium as soon as the coma treatment is begun, but this is still not settled. When the patient is able to swallow, give supplementary potassium salts by mouth (the safest route).

b. Oral feedings and fluids—If ketonuria is disappearing or is rapidly improving (usually in 24–48 hours) and the patient is conscious, give small frequent feedings of liquid and semiliquid foods containing 50–75 gm glucose and protein (eg, as milk) every 3–4 hours day and night and cover with 25–35 units of crystalline zinc insulin every 4 hours; force fluids by mouth; and examine the urine for sugar and ketone bodies every 3–4 hours.

c. Regular diet—After 24—48 hours, if the patient shows steady improvement, place on a regular diabetic diet and begin regulation with NPH or lente insulin, 20—50 units/day, and additional amounts of crystalline insulin as outlined above.

Prognosis

Prognosis depends largely upon the duration of coma, the age of the patient, the severity of unconsciousness, and the principal cause of coma (eg, infection). Sudden death associated with cerebral edema may occur after initial improvement. In spite of apparently good treatment the mortality remains around 3%.

Addis, G.J., Thomson, W.S.T., & J.D. Welch: Bicarbonate therapy in diabetic acidosis. Lancet 2:223—224, 1964.

Arky, R.A., & D. Hurwitz: The therapy of diabetic ketoacidosis. New England J Med 274:1135, 1966.

Johnson, R.D.: Management of diabetic ketoacidosis. Postgrad Med 39:246—255, 1966.

Johnson, R.D., & others: Mechanisms and management of hyperosmolar coma without ketoacidosis in the diabetic. Diabetes 18:111, 1969.

Kolodny, H.D., & L. Sherman: Hyperglycemia nonketotic coma. JAMA 203:461—463, 1968.

Martin, A.: Hyperosmolar non-keto-acidotic diabetic coma. A report of three cases and review of the literature. Postgrad MJ 44:218—222, 1968.

Smith, K., & H.E. Martin: Response of diabetic coma to various insulin dosages. Diabetes 3:287—295, 1964.

Steinberg, T., King, C., & G. Gwinup: Simplified treatment of diabetic ketoacidosis. GP 38:91—97, Aug 1968.

THE DIABETIC PATIENT & SURGERY

Surgery in the diabetic patient is little more hazardous than the same procedure performed on a nondiabetic patient. However, certain problems are peculiar to the diabetic patient, and these naturally vary with the severity of the disease and the urgency of the operation. A patient who is controlled on oral antidiabetic agents will usually require additional insulin because of the tendency to acidosis.

Emergency Surgery

A. For Nontraumatic Conditions: Diabetics who require emergency surgery for nontraumatic disorders are usually in a state of ketosis with or without acidosis and require immediate treatment of their diabetes. They should be treated as patients with acidosis or coma (the latter if a general anesthesia is to be used). The general program should be as follows:

1. Draw blood for CO_2 combining power and blood glucose; also for serum sodium, potassium, and chloride if possible.

2. Begin a slow intravenous infusion of 5% glucose in physiologic saline (not over 70 drops/minute) and continue the infusion throughout the surgical procedure. One unit of insulin/2 gm of glucose may be added to the infusion (25 units for each liter of 5% glucose).

3. Give 50 units of short-acting insulin IV if ketosis is present.

4. Continue therapy postoperatively as for diabetic coma until oral feeding can be given and ketosis and hyperglycemia are controlled.

B. For Traumatic Disorders Requiring Surgery: Although increased carbohydrate tolerance may develop rapidly as a result of trauma, the principal danger in a treated diabetic who is injured is the possibility of having a severe hypoglycemic reaction because he fails to eat. Therefore, if the patient is conscious, give sweetened orange juice or candy by mouth; if surgery is necessary, give 5% glucose IV in water or saline slowly. One may add to the infusion 1 unit of insulin for each 2—3 gm of glucose; however, the need is not for insulin so much as for glucose to avoid hypoglycemia. After surgery, treat according to the severity of the disease.

Elective Surgery

A. Initial Hospital Measures: The patient should enter the hospital several days before surgery. Discontinue long-acting insulin. The diabetes should be brought under optimal control with crystalline zinc insulin. Ketosis should be absent.

B. During and After Surgery:

1. No food or insulin should be administered on the morning of surgery.

2. Management during surgery—

a. If the patient's diabetes is mild and has been properly controlled, if he does not tend to develop ketosis, and if the surgery is not too extensive, he may be operated on without intravenous glucose or insulin.

b. If the patient's diabetes is moderate or severe or if extensive surgery must be performed, begin an infusion of 5% glucose in saline or water to which has been added 1 unit of crystalline insulin/2 gm of glucose. Continue the infusion throughout the operation. Give the infusion at a rate of about 60—70 drops/minute. Additional amounts of subcutaneous insulin may be required if ketonemia is excessive.

3. After surgery the patient should receive small frequent feedings (50—75 gm of carbohydrate) every 3—4 hours covered with 15—25 units of crystalline zinc insulin subcut before the meal. These small feedings are continued until normal nutrition can be re-established.

4. If gastrointestinal surgery has been performed and the patient cannot take food by mouth, nutrition must be maintained by parenteral methods; one may give 1 liter of 5% glucose in 5% amino acid solution IV slowly over a period of 4 hours. This should be covered with 15—40 units of crystalline zinc insulin subcut before beginning the infusion. Three liters per day is an average requirement. This therapy may be continued until oral nutrition can be resumed.

The principles of management of a pregnant diabetic during delivery are essentially the same as for elective surgery. Since many diabetic pregnancies persist beyond the expected term and since the infants are often large, termination of pregnancy at about 36 weeks, preferably by cesarian section, is recommended.

Boronow, R.C., & T.W. McElin: Diabetes in pregnancy. Am J Obst Gynec 91:1022–1028, 1965.

Hughes, E.C.: Diabetes and pregnancy. Postgrad Med 42:487–492, 1967.

Podolsky, S.: Special needs of the diabetic undergoing surgery. Postgrad Med 45:128–137, 1969.

THE HYPOGLYCEMIC STATES
(See Table 18–11.)

1. ORGANIC HYPERINSULINISM

Essentials of Diagnosis
- Sudden hunger and weakness, with sweating, pallor, paresthesias, and personality changes.
- Tremor, paralysis, convulsions.
- Low fasting blood glucose with attacks and prompt response to administration of glucose.

General Considerations
Organic hyperinsulinism in the adult is most commonly due to an adenoma of the islets of Langerhans; at times these may be multiple and small and may escape detection. A few become malignant with functional metastases. More rarely, and almost always only in children, there is primary hypertrophy and hyperplasia of all islets rather than a single adenoma. Adenomas may be familial, and may be associated with adenomas of the parathyroids and of the pituitary. In rare instances tumors in organs other than the pancreas may produce a picture indistinguishable from that of the insulinomas.

The signs and symptoms are those of acute and chronic hypoglycemia; the disease may progress to permanent and irreversible brain damage. Although the adenoma is more commonly located in the tail and body, the head of the pancreas may also be the site.

TABLE 18–11. Differential diagnosis of hypoglycemic states.*

Condition	Fasting Blood Sugar	5-Hour Glucose Tolerance Test	3-Hour Intravenous Tolbutamide Tolerance Test	Leucine Tolerance Test	48- to 72-Hour Fast With Exercise	Rise of Blood Sugar After Glucagon or Epinephrine Tolerance Tests
Islet cell tumor	Normal or low	Normal or diabetic	Sustained hypoglycemia	Normal or sustained hypoglycemia	Hypoglycemia	Normal
Extrapancreatic tumors	Normal or low	Normal or diabetic	Normal	Normal	Hypoglycemia	Normal
Liver disease	Normal or low	Diabetic	Normal or diabetic	Normal	Hypoglycemia	Abnormal
Malnutrition	Low	Diabetic	Normal or diabetic	Normal	Hypoglycemia	Abnormal
Hypopituitarism and hypoadrenalism	Normal or low	Normal	May have excessive drop in first hour but returns toward normal by 2–3 hours	Normal	Normal or hypoglycemia	Normal
Reactive (functional) hypoglycemia	Normal	Normal or low at 2 hours with hypoglycemia between 1½ and 4 hours	Normal (may show early marked drop)	Normal	Normal	Normal
Early diabetes mellitus	Normal	Diabetic during first 2 hours with hypoglycemia between 3rd and 5th hours	Diabetic	Normal	Normal	Normal
In children Prematurity	Low	Diabetic	Diabetic	Normal	Hypoglycemia	Abnormal
Leucine sensitivity	Normal or low	Normal	Normal	Significant hypoglycemia	Normal blood sugar	Normal
Glycogen storage disease	Low	Diabetic	Diabetic	Normal	Hypoglycemia	Abnormal

*Modified after Boshell, B.R.: Treatment of hypoglycemia. Mod Treat 3:337, 1966.

Clinical Findings

Whipple's triad consists of (1) a history of attacks of hunger, weakness, sweating, and paresthesias coming on during the fasting state; (2) a fasting blood glucose level of 40 mg/100 ml or less during attacks; and (3) immediate recovery upon administration of glucose. There is a history of previous good health but an intolerance to exercise in the fasting state.

A. Symptoms and Signs: Premonitory manifestations (mostly vasomotor) may include sudden hunger and weakness, especially in the fasting state; headache or faintness, vertigo, sweating, paresthesias of the face, lips, or tongue, visual disturbances, and tremors or palpitation. CNS changes may appear, including vomiting, diplopia, and ataxia, and hypalgesias, aphasia, twitchings and rigor, paralysis, convulsions, or coma. Personality and mental changes vary from anxiety or exhilaration to severe psychotic states, often mistaken for alcoholism or catatonia. Patients with long-standing hyperinsulinism are obese as a result of chronic high-carbohydrate intake.

B. Laboratory Findings: The fasting blood glucose is low, and the glucose tolerance curve is low or may have a sharp fall to low levels in 2–5 hours, with no spontaneous return to normal. These findings are not of great diagnostic value except to differentiate organic hyperinsulinism from functional hyperinsulinism.

Insulin tolerance is variable, and the patient may show resistance to insulin; whereas in adrenal and pituitary insufficiency the patient is sensitive to insulin. Epinephrine causes a variable rise in blood glucose which does not occur in severe liver disease.

C. Special Tests:

1. Prolonged fasting–The patient receives no food and only water or black coffee with saccharin for up to 72 hours. During this time he exercises mildly. In almost all patients with islet cell adenoma on this regimen the blood glucose will fall to below 30 mg/100 ml and the symptoms of hypoglycemia will be produced.

2. Orinase® tolerance test–One gm of sodium tolbutamide (Orinase®) is injected *slowly* IV in 20 ml of physiologic saline solution, or 3 gm of tolbutamide plus 3 gm sodium bicarbonate are given orally. In patients with islet cell adenoma the blood glucose usually falls to 50–80% of the fasting level in 30 minutes and remains low for several hours; whereas in nonorganic or functional hyperinsulinism the blood glucose level falls to hypoglycemic levels and then rises to normal levels in 1–2 hours. This rapid screening test is not without danger, and at times must be interrupted by the administration of intravenous glucose to prevent severe convulsions and coma. While atypical curves are noted in some patients with islet cell adenomas, an entirely normal response would be against this diagnosis.

3. The leucine and glucagon response tests are not of great additional diagnostic value.

4. Assay of insulin, either by bioassay or immunoassay, has not shown consistent elevations in insulinomas. Excessive rise after tolbutamide or glucagon may be of greater diagnostic value (see Marks reference, below). Increased levels of proinsulin have recently been found in patients with insulinomas.

Differential Diagnosis (See Table 18–11.)

The most important differentiation is that between organic and functional hyperinsulinism. The latter is not progressive in severity, occurs more frequently under emotional tension, and is not precipitated by fasting or exercise. Other disorders which must be distinguished as rarer causes of hypoglycemia are liver disease, malnutrition, strenuous exercise, renal glycosuria, epilepsy and brain tumor, acute and chronic alcoholism, cerebrovascular accident, and bizarre neuromuscular disorders. Addison's disease, myxedema, and partial or complete hypopituitarism may be associated with severe hypoglycemia. (*Note:* Always make sure that the patient has not been taking insulin or oral hypoglycemic agents.) In children, differentiate from galactosemia, Von Gierke's disease, and hypoglycemosis associated with leucine sensitivity. In adults, large retroperitoneal sarcomas and other extrapancreatic tumors may give rise to a clinical picture similar to that of hyperinsulinism. Spontaneous hypoglycemia may at times precede the onset of diabetes mellitus.

Complications

Complications become more important the longer hypoglycemia persists. Retinal and cerebrovascular hemorrhages may occur. Coronary insufficiency and paroxysmal tachycardia may be precipitated by hypoglycemia. Repeated attacks may lead to progressive neuropathy and myelopathy with irreversible damage, causing foot drop, muscle atrophy, and pyramidal signs. Permanent personality changes and even mental defects secondary to hydrocephalus have been observed; these changes may occur even after successful surgical treatment. After surgery, transient or even permanent diabetes mellitus may occur; if too much pancreatic tissue has had to be removed, pancreatic insufficiency may ensue. Fistulas from the pancreas to the skin are not rare. If symptoms recur after an adenoma has been removed, multiple adenomas must be considered.

In any case of organic hyperinsulinism it must be remembered that parathyroid and pituitary adenomas are at times associated with islet cell adenomas, and that gastric ulceration is frequently present as well. This syndrome may be familial (syndrome of multiple endocrine adenomatosis).

Treatment

A. Emergency Treatment: Treat as for hypoglycemic reaction due to insulin overdosage (see p 654).

B. Other Measures:

1. Drug therapy–The administration of **corticotropin (ACTH) or the corticosteroids** (for their hyperglycemic effect) has been shown to be of considerable benefit in the management of some children suffering from this condition. In adults, these drugs have not

been as effective. Recently, success in the management of inoperable hyperinsulinism has been reported with **diazoxide**, a benzothiadiazine compound, and with **zinc glucagon**.

    2. Diet—Dietary management is of great value in the management of functional hypoglycemia but will usually fail in organic hyperinsulinism and in severe liver failure (hepatogenic hypoglycemia). However, a diet should be tried. The diet is low in carbohydrates in order to avoid stimulation of the pancreas to elaborate insulin. Rapidly utilized carbohydrates are replaced by slow-acting ones (eg, 3 and 7% vegetables, 10–15% fruits, and bananas). Protein is an important source of slowly liberated carbohydrate which apparently has less stimulating effect on the pancreas and is useful in supplying added calories. In some patients proteins may lead to increased release of insulin and thus aggravate hypoglycemia.

    The diet is best divided into 6 or more meals a day. It may be necessary to feed the patient at regular intervals throughout the 24-hour period. If the hypoglycemia is as severe as this, it is advisable not to prolong medical therapy but to prepare the patient properly for surgery.

    3. Sedation—Phenobarbital, 15–30 mg 4 times daily, may be valuable in reducing neuromuscular irritability.

    4. Restriction of physical activity—Exercise increases the utilization of glucose, thereby exaggerating the effect of excess insulin. If exercise is unavoidable, such activity should be preceded by supplementary carbohydrates.

    5. Identification card—Patient should carry a bracelet or card similar to that used by a diabetic (see p 655).

    6. Emergency carbohydrates—The patient should carry a small supply of rapidly available carbohydrate (candy, lumps of sugar) at all times. He is to avoid taking these except when definitely indicated.

    C. Surgery: Complete excision of hyperplastic or adenomatous islet tissue is indicated when this is found to be the cause. At times total pancreatectomy is required. The tumors may be in ectopic sites.

Prognosis

    If organic hyperinsulinism is diagnosed early and cured surgically, complete recovery is likely. Medical therapy with corticotropin or corticosteroid is not very effective in long-term treatment but has been used successfully in children (in whom the disease may be transient), in the preoperative phase, and in rare cases when tumors cannot be located or surgery is refused. Diazoxide is more effective in long-term management of inoperable hypoglycemia but has distressing side-effects, including edema and hypertrichosis. Brain damage usually is not reversible in spite of removal of the tumor. Operation may cure the patient even if the tumor has been present for several years, since the incidence of malignancy is low and metastases occur late. The prognosis is worse in children and in the elderly, who are ill-equipped to handle sudden changes in glucose.

2. FUNCTIONAL HYPERINSULINISM

    Functional hyperinsulinism, also called "reactive," "spontaneous," "neurogenic," and "idiopathic" hypoglycemia, is by far the most common cause of hypoglycemia. In most instances, functional hypoglycemia is considered to be due to an excess of insulin, although the mechanism of its increased production cannot always be established.

    Extreme degrees of hypoglycemia seldom occur as a result of functional hypoglycemia, and, rather than the progressive severity which characterizes organic hypoglycemic states, the disorder remains fairly static. (See Table 18–11.) Individuals with functional hypoglycemia are frequently emotionally unstable and are anxious and tense. They often show evidences of autonomic nervous system dysfunction such as neuro-circulatory asthenia and excessive perspiration. Symptoms attributable to hypoglycemia may occur in these individuals when blood sugar levels are elevated, normal, or low; at times, moderately low blood sugar levels produce no symptoms. These findings tend to implicate dysfunction of the autonomic nervous system as the underlying cause of symptoms or as a factor in producing hypoglycemia.

    Functional hypoglycemia is considered to be one of the early manifestations of diabetes mellitus if in the glucose tolerance test the initial hyperglycemic phase, characteristic of diabetes, is followed by a delayed hypoglycemic phase. Some investigators report the development of diabetes in a high percentage of such cases, but this finding has not been generally confirmed.

    Alimentary hypoglycemia, another form of functional hypoglycemia, occurs when there is a rapid delivery of ingested carbohydrate into the small bowel followed by rapid glucose absorption. This is seen most often in patients after gastrointestinal surgery, particularly after gastrectomy ("dumping syndrome"). The mechanism of alimentary hypoglycemia is excessive insulin release by gut factors from the pancreas resulting from the stimulus of pronounced hyperglycemia. Typically, the symptoms occur 1–2 hours after eating (see Karam reference, below).

Treatment

    The objective of treatment of functional hypoglycemia is relief of symptoms. This involves (1) psychologic management, (2) dietary management, and (3) drugs.

    A frank discussion with the patient about the relationship of blood sugar and the autonomic nervous system will often suffice. The importance of avoiding emotional stress and resumption of regular habits of eating, working, exercising, and sleeping should be stressed. Frequent feedings of a diet high in protein and low in rapidly absorbable carbohydrates is helpful, although some patients insist on taking candy, sugar, etc at the onset of slight symptoms because they give rapid relief. An occasional patient may feel worse on

high-protein diets since they may cause excessive release of insulin. The frequency of feedings rather than
the composition of the diet may be of greater importance.

Anticholinergic drugs may be helpful, especially
in cases of alimentary hypoglycemia. Mild sedatives or
tranquilizers are often helpful, although some patients
respond better to adrenergic drugs such as dextroamphetamine with or without amobarbital (Dex-
amyl®). The administration of oral hypoglycemic
agents, such as tolbutamide, in small doses prior to
meals has been advocated by some in the hypoglycemia preceding the onset of overt diabetes. It is
thought that this would release insulin more rapidly,
thus avoiding delayed hypoglycemia. Results with
this form of treatment are not universally successful.

Prognosis

The immediate response to a rigid, well outlined
program is usually good in the cooperative patient.
Long-term results depend on continued effort and
interest on the part of both patient and physician. The
response is perhaps best in alimentary hypoglycemia.

It is common for the patient to disregard dietary
and other measures once symptoms improve, with subsequent recurrence.

Patients with delayed hypoglycemia must be
watched for the development of overt clinical diabetes.
A rare patient with severe reactive hypoglycemia may
eventually prove to have an islet cell adenoma.

Baker, R.J.: Newer considerations in the diagnosis and management of fasting hypoglycemia. S Clin North America
49:191, 1969.

Blackard, W.G.: Hypoglycemia in the adult patient. Clin Med
75:29–34, 1968.

Boshell, B.R. (editor): Treatment of hypoglycemia. Mod Treat
3:329–426, 1966.

DeMoura, M.C., & others: Clinical alcohol hypoglycemia. Ann
Int Med 66:893, 1967.

Faludi, G., Bendersky, G., & P. Gerber: Functional hypoglycemia in early latent diabetes. Ann New York Acad Sc
148:868–874, 1968.

Field, J.B., & A. Dekaban: Clinical and physiologic aspects of
hypoglycemia. Postgrad Med 38:23–29, 1965.

Frawley, T.F., & S. Pensuwan: Hypoglycemia: Tolbutamide and
leucine tests in insulinoma. M Clin North America
52:283–294, 1968.

Gutman, R.A., & others: Circulating proinsulin-like material in
functioning insulinomas. New England J Med
284:1003–1008, 1971.

Karam, J.: Reactive hypoglycemia: Mechanisms and management. Medical Staff Conference. California Med
114:64–70, May 1971.

Laroche, G.P., & others: Hyperinsulinism. Arch Surg
96:763–772, 1968.

Levin, M.E.: Endocrine syndromes associated with pancreatic
islet cell tumors. M Clin North America 52:295–312,
1968.

Marks, V., & E. Samols: Glucagon test for insulinoma: A chemical study in 25 cases. J Clin Path 21:346–352, 1968.

Nissan, S. Bar-Maor, A., & E. Shafrir: Hypoglycemia associated
with extrapancreatic tumors. New England J Med
278:177–182, 1968.

Roth, H., & others: Zinc glucagon in the management of refractory hypoglycemia due to insulin producing tumors. New
England J Med 274:493, 1966.

Silverstein, M.N., & others: Hypoglycemia associated with neoplasia. Am J Med 36:415, 1964.

Smith, H.M. (consulting editor): Diazoxide and the treatment of
hypoglycemia. Ann New York Acad Sc 150:193–464,
1968.

Wermer, P.: Endocrine adenomatosis and peptic ulcer in a large
kindred. Am J Med 35:205, 1963.

Whelton, M.J., & others: Factitious hypoglycemia in a diabetic:
Metabolic studies and diagnosis with radioactive isotopes.
Metabolism 17:923, 1968.

DISEASES OF THE TESTES*

MALE HYPOGONADISM

Male hypogonadism may be classified according
to time of onset, ie, prepuberal, puberal (Klinefelter's
syndrome), or postpuberal. Eunuchism implies complete failure of gonadal development; eunuchoidism
implies only partial deficiency.

The etiologic diagnosis of hypogonadism (eg, primary or secondary) is usually based on laboratory tests
(Table 18–12).

1. PREPUBERAL HYPOGONADISM

The diagnosis of hypogonadism cannot usually be
made in boys under the age of 17 or 18, since it is
difficult to differentiate from "physiologic" delay of
puberty.

Prepuberal hypogonadism is most commonly due
to a specific gonadotropic deficiency of the pituitary.
It may be familial and associated with anosmia. It may
also occur as a result of destructive lesions near the
pituitary region (eg, suprasellar cyst) or, more rarely,
as a result of destruction or malformation of the testes
themselves (prepuberal castration).

In cases associated with a complete pituitary
defect, the patient is of short stature or fails to grow
and mature. Otherwise the patient is strikingly tall due
to overgrowth of the long bones. The external genitalia
are underdeveloped, the voice is high-pitched, the
beard does not grow, and the patient lacks libido and
potency and is unable to tan. In adult life he presents a
youthful appearance, with obesity (often in girdle distribution), disproportionately long extremities (span
exceeds height), lack of temporal recession of the hairline, and a small Adam's apple. Gynecomastia is occa-

---

*See also Tumors of the Testis in Chapter 15.

TABLE 18–12. Laboratory tests in diagnosis of hypogonadism.

Type of Hypogonadism	Urinary Gonadotropins	Urinary 17-Ketosteroids
Primary testicular failure	"Hypergonadotropic"	
Complete (eg, castration)	Elevated	Low or normal
Partial–		
Leydig cell failure only	Moderately elevated	Low or normal
Seminiferous tubule failure (eg, Klinefelter's syndrome)	Elevated	Normal or low
Secondary to pituitary failure	"Hypogonadotropic"	
Complete: Panhypopituitarism	Very low	Very low
Partial: Isolated lack of FSH	Very low	Low
Secondary to miscellaneous factors		
Starvation, anorexia, severe hypothyroidism, etc	Low or low normal	Low to normal

sionally seen (but apparent gynecomastia may be merely fat). The skin is fine-grained, wrinkled, and sallow, especially on the face. The penis is small and the prostate undeveloped. Pubic and axillary hair are scant. The testes may be absent from the scrotum (cryptorchism) or very small. Spermatogenesis does not occur.

Bone age is retarded. Skull x-rays may show a lesion of the sella or above the sella (eg, craniopharyngioma). Anemia may be present. Urinary 17-ketosteroids are low or normal in testicular failure; very low or absent in primary pituitary failure. Urinary FSH is absent in primary pituitary failure, elevated in castration or testicular failure. Plasma testosterone and serum luteinizing hormone (LH) measurements are more specific than urinary 17-ketosteroids and "FSH" levels respectively, but these tests are not generally available.

Determination of the genetic chromosomal type may reveal anomalies, eg, hermaphroditism.

The response to chorionic gonadotropin injections in cases due to pituitary failure will be maturation, rise of urinary 17-ketosteroids, and occasionally descent of cryptorchid testes. (In primary testicular failure, no such response occurs.) Testicular biopsy shows immature tubules and Leydig cells in hypopituitary patients.

Adequate testosterone therapy can make these individuals into apparently normal males except that they usually cannot produce sperm. In order to produce spermatogenesis, a combination of an FSH preparation, eg, human menopausal gonadotropin (Pergonal®), with human chorionic gonadotropin (eg, APL®) is required. This treatment is expensive and is not generally available. Patients with prepuberal hypogonadism must be placed on testosterone and maintained for life on adequate doses. Long-acting testosterone preparations, 200–300 mg IM every 2–4 weeks, may be employed. An alternative method, oral administration of other androgens, entails all the difficulties of prolonged oral administration. Dosage varies with different patients, but 10–25 mg of methyltestosterone daily orally is usually adequate to cause and maintain maturation and virilization. There is no great advantage of buccal over oral administration.

Howard, R.P., & others: Testicular deficiency: A clinical and pathologic study. J Clin Endocrinol 10:121–186, 1950.

Johnson, S.G.: A study of human testicular function by the use of human menopausal gonadotrophin and human chorionic gonadotrophin in male hypogonadotrophic eunuchoidism and infantilism. Acta endocrinol 53:315, 1966.

Paulsen, C.A.: The testes. Chap 6 *in:* Williams, R.H. (editor): *Textbook of Endocrinology,* 4th ed. Saunders, 1968.

Sparkes, R.S., Simpson, R.W., & C.A. Paulsen: Familial hypogonadotropic hypogonadism with anosmia. Arch Int Med 121:534–538, 1968.

2. PUBERAL HYPOGONADISM
(Klinefelter's Syndrome)

The outstanding example of this group of diseases is the so-called Klinefelter's syndrome (puberal seminiferous tubule failure). It is a genetic disorder which is recognized at or shortly after puberty. It is at times familial. A similar acquired syndrome has been ascribed to infection. Most commonly there is only failure of the tubules and lack of the testicular estrogenlike hormone, with permanent sterility. The secretory function of the Leydig cells ranges from normal to definite failure. Study of the chromosomal pattern shows that the majority of these patients are "chromatin positive." A variant of the syndrome has been reported in hypogonadal males with hypospadias and a "negative" chromatin pattern (Reifenstein's syndrome).

The clinical findings are swelling of the breasts (gynecomastia), sterility, lack of libido and potency (rare), and at times lack of development of body hair, and female escutcheon. Skeleton and muscular development are usually normal. There may be associated mental retardation. The testes are usually small, but are larger than in prepuberal hypogonadism. The penis and prostate are usually normal. The ejaculate usually contains no spermatozoa, although an occasional case with spermatogenesis in a mosaic variant has been described. Urinary 17-ketosteroids are low normal or normal. Urinary FSH is elevated (a most significant finding). Testicular biopsy shows sclerosis of the tubules, nests of Leydig cells, and no spermatozoa. The sex chromatin count is most commonly XXY (rarely, XXXY or "mosaic"), with a chromatin-positive buccal smear. Bone age may be delayed.

All causes of gynecomastia must be differentiated from Klinefelter's syndrome, including simple gynecomastia of puberty, liver disorders, chorio-epithelioma, estrogen-producing tumors, and obesity with small genitalia. The urinary FSH and the testicular biopsy will settle the diagnosis.

A similar picture is at times associated with myotonia dystrophica.

No treatment is necessary unless lack of potency is a problem, in which case testosterone should be given as for prepuberal hypogonadism. If gynecomastia is disfiguring, plastic surgical removal is indicated.

Becker, K.L., & others: Klinefelter's syndrome: Clinical and laboratory findings in 50 patients. Arch Int Med 118:314, 1966.

Bowen, P., & others: Hereditary male pseudohermaphroditism with hypogonadism, hypospadias, and gynecomastia (Reifenstein's syndrome). Ann Int Med 62:252–270. 1965.

Jones, H.W., Jr., & P.A. Zourlas: Clinical, histologic, and cytogenetic findings in male hermaphroditism. I. Male hermaphroditism with ambiguous or predominantly masculine external genitalia. Obst Gynec 25:597–606, 1965.

Kvale, J.N., & J.R. Fishman: Psychosocial aspects of Klinefelter's syndrome. JAMA 193:567–572, 1965.

Wershub, L.P.: Hypogonadism in the male. Fertil Steril 15:9–14, 1964.

3. POSTPUBERAL HYPOGONADISM

Any pituitary lesion (eg, tumor, infection, necrosis) may lead to lack of gonadotropin; often hypogonadism is an early sign. The testes may be damaged by trauma, x-ray irradiation, infection, or in other ways. States of malnutrition, anemia, and similar disorders may lead to functional gonadal underactivity. The male climacteric, although a somewhat disputed syndrome, probably does exist; it makes its appearance about 20 years later than the female menopause.

The symptoms are varying degrees of loss of libido and potency; retardation of hair growth, especially of the face; vasomotor symptoms (flushing, dizziness, chills); lack of aggressiveness and interest; sterility; and muscular aches and back pain. Atrophy or hypoplasia of external genitalia and prostate is rare. The skin of the face is thin, finely wrinkled, and "fawn-colored," and the beard is scant. Hair is absent on the antitragus of the ear (Hamilton's sign). Girdle type obesity and kyphosis of the spine are present.

Urinary 17-ketosteroids are low. Urinary and plasma testosterone levels are low. Urinary FSH may be normal, but is low in cases due to pituitary lesions and elevated in true testicular failure. The sperm count is low or spermatozoa may be absent. Bone age is usually normal, but the skeleton may show "epiphysitis," especially of the vertebral column (Scheuermann's disease), and osteoporosis.

True adult hypogonadism must be differentiated from the far more commonly seen psychogenic lack of libido and potency. Confusion may also arise in men who are obese and have a sparse beard and small genitalia, but normal sperm counts and urinary FSH ("fertile eunuchs"). These patients may represent examples of end-organ unresponsiveness or isolated lack of luteinizing hormone.

Oral methyltestosterone or fluoxymesterone is highly effective. The dosage necessary to control symptoms and to aid in overcoming the protein loss and debility of age is often as low as 5–20 mg daily. This dose may be used for a short period of time to control symptoms or may be continued indefinitely for control of symptoms and for its protein anabolic effect. The use of the long-acting testosterones by injection may be more practical for prolonged treatment. Treatment of long-standing hypogonadism with androgens may precipitate anxiety and acute emotional problems which often require concomitant psychotherapy. (See Huffer reference.)

• • •

Prognosis of Hypogonadism

If hypogonadism is due to a pituitary lesion, the prognosis is that of the primary disease (eg, tumor, necrosis). The prognosis for restoration of virility is good if testosterone is given. The sooner administration is started, the fewer stigmas of eunuchoidism remain (unless therapy is discontinued).

The prognosis for fertility is usually not good. It is only feasible in the instances where the testicular elements are present but are unstimulated due to lack of pituitary tropic hormones. This therapy may become practical with the availability of gonadotropin from postmenopausal urine (human menopausal gonadotropins [HMG] ; Pergonal®).

Minor forms of hypogonadism may be corrected by proper nutrition, by the use of thyroid hormone, and by general hygienic measures.

Cryptorchism should be corrected surgically early, since the incidence of malignant testicular tumors is higher in ectopic testicles and the chance of ultimate fertility is lessened in long-standing cases.

Albert, A., & R.N. Andersen: Large-scale chromatographic separation of male urinary follicle-stimulating and luteinizing hormones. Mayo Clin Proc 43:177–190, 1968.

Crooke, A.C., Davies, A.G., & R. Morris: Treatment of eunuchoidal men with human chorionic gonadotrophin and follicle-stimulating hormone. J Endocrinol 42:441–451, 1968.

Faiman, C., & others: "Fertile eunuch" syndrome: Demonstration of isolated luteinizing hormone deficiency by radioimmunoassay technique. Mayo Clin Proc 43:661–667, 1968.

Gross, R.E., & R.L. Replogle: Treatment of the undescended testis: Opinions gained from 1,767 operations. Postgrad Med 34:266–270, 1963.

Huffer, V., & others: Psychologic studies of adult male patients with sexual infantilism before and after androgen therapy. Ann Int Med 61:255–258, 1964.

Money, J.: Problems in sexual development, endocrinologic and psychologic aspects. New York J Med 63:2348–2354, 1963.

Volpé, R.: Drugs for hypogonadism. Canad MAJ 90:1081, 1964.

MALE HYPERGONADISM & TESTICULAR TUMORS

In adults, almost all lesions causing male hypergonadism are functioning testicular tumors, which quite frequently are malignant. In children, male hypergonadism may take the form of true precocious puberty, due to pituitary or hypothalamic lesions; or pseudoprecocious puberty, due to lesions of the testes or adrenal glands.

1. PREPUBERAL HYPERGONADISM

The symptoms and signs are premature growth of pubic and axillary hair, beard, and external genitalia and excessive muscular development. In true precocity due to pituitary or hypothalamic lesions the testicles enlarge as well and spermatogenesis occurs. In adrenal virilization or testicular tumor there is testicular atrophy, with or without palpable nodules; spermatogenesis does not take place. In childhood, interstitial cell tumors are the principal testicular tumors to be considered. Bilateral interstitial cell nodules are also seen with adrenal hyperplasia. Cases of hepatoma with true isosexual precocity have been reported.

If the cause of precocity is "constitutional," it is usually a harmless disorder, although the sex activities of these children must be controlled to prevent socially undesirable conceptions. If precocity is due to hypothalamic or pituitary lesions, the prognosis is poor since most of these tumors are not removable. Adrenal tumors and testicular tumors are often malignant.

Most patients with this syndrome who survive into adulthood will be short as a result of premature maturation and closure of their epiphyses.

Treatment

In cases where the tumor is accessible, surgical removal is the treatment of choice. Bilateral adrenal hyperplasia which causes pseudoprecocious puberty can be successfully treated with cortisone, and normal development and spermatogenesis will occur following

TABLE 18–13. Sexual precocity along isosexual pattern.

Types and Causes	Characteristics
Neurogenic: Brain tumor Encephalitis Congenital defect with hypothalamic involvement **Pituitary:** Idiopathic activation, "constitutional" type	Testes mature normally; spermatogenesis occurs; secondary characteristics normal; sex hormones excreted in normal adult amounts.
Gonadal: Interstitial cell tumor of testis	Tumor in one gonad, the other gonad immature or atrophic; spermatogenesis does not occur; sex hormones excreted in excessive amounts.
Adrenal: Embryonic hyperplasia or tumor	Testes usually small and immature, occasionally containing aberrant adrenal tissue; no spermatogenesis; often results in adrenocortical insufficiency in males.

treatment. The use of progesterone preparations (eg, Depo-Provera®) in the treatment of sexual precocity is under investigation.

Hahn, H.B., Jr., Hayles, A.B., & A. Albert: Medroxyprogesterone and constitutional precocious puberty. Proc Staff Meet Mayo Clin 39:182–190, 1964.

Jolly, H.: *Sexual Precocity.* Thomas, 1955.

Schoen, E.: Treatment of idiopathic precocious puberty in boys. J Clin Endocrinol 26:363, 1966.

Sigurjonsdottir, T.J., & A.B. Hayles: Precocious puberty. Am J Dis Child 115:309–321, 1968.

Wilkins, L.: Variations in pattern of adolescent development. Chap 10 in: *The Diagnosis and Treatment of Endocrine Disorders in Childhood and Adolescence,* 3rd ed. Thomas, 1965.

2. NEOPLASMS OF THE TESTES IN ADULTS
(Postpuberal Hypergonadism)

Many or most testicular neoplasms are functioning (ie, productive of androgenic or estrogenic hormones), and the majority are highly malignant (see Table 18–14). They are at times quite small, and are clinically recognized because of their hormonal effects or because of the presence of metastases. In general, once hormonal manifestations have become pronounced, cure by surgical removal is very unlikely. Some tumors are bilateral, eg, interstitial cell tumors. Often a mixed picture is present. Gonadotropin-

TABLE 18-14. Characteristics of testicular tumors.*

Tumor and Hormone	Clinical Manifestations
Seminoma: Elevation of urinary FSH	Onset usually at age 30–50. Tumor radiosensitive. No endocrinologic manifestations.
Teratoma: No hormone elaborated except in mixed tumors	May occur in childhood also. No endocrinologic manifestations unless the tumor is of a mixed type. Tumor radioresistant, invasive.
Chorio-epithelioma: Chorionic gonadotropin elevated. Pregnancy test positive.	Rare. Gynecomastia. Tumor rapidly invasive and metastasizing, radioresistant. Leydig cells overactive due to stimulation by tumor.
Leydig cell: 17-Ketosteroids elevated	Very rare. Occurs at any age and causes virilization. At times bilateral, often multiple.
Sertoli cell and tubular adenoma of Pick: May elaborate estrogens	Benign tumors, probably developmental rests. Associated with congenital anomalies of genital tract. Rarely feminizing.

*Dean, A.L.: The treatment of testes tumors. J Urol 76:439–446, 1956.

secreting bronchogenic carcinomas have been recently described (see Faiman reference, below).

The incidence of malignancy in cryptorchism is high.

Treatment

If the diagnosis is made early, surgical removal may be curative; radiotherapy is feasible as a palliative measure in radiosensitive types. Chemotherapy may control the growth of chorio-epitheliomas.

Bagshawe, K.D.: *Choriocarcinoma*. Arnold, 1969.

Faiman, C., & others: Gonadotropin secretion from a bronchogenic carcinoma. New England J Med 277:1395–1398, 1967.

MacKenzie, A.R.: Chemotherapy of metastatic testis cancer. Cancer 19:1369, 1966.

Patton, J.F., & others: Diagnosis and treatment of testicular tumors. Am J Surg 99:525, 1960.

Wegienka, L., & F.O. Kolb: Hormonal studies of a benign interstitial tumour of the testis producing androstenedione and testosterone. Acta endocrinol 56:481, 1967.

DISEASES OF THE OVARIES*

I. FEMALE HYPOGONADISM

The outstanding symptom of female hypogonadism is amenorrhea (see below). Partial deficiencies, principally corpus luteum failure, may occur which do not always cause amenorrhea but more often produce anovulatory periods or metrorrhagia.

Estrogenic failure has far-reaching effects, especially if it begins early in life (eg, Turner's syndrome).

Primary pituitary disorders are much less common causes of hypogonadism in the female than primary ovarian disorders, and are almost always associated with other signs of pituitary failure.

Ovarian failure starting in early life will lead to delayed closure of the epiphyses and retarded bone age, often resulting in tall stature with long extremities. On the other hand, in ovarian agenesis, dwarfism is the rule (see below). In adult ovarian failure, changes are more subtle, with some regression of secondary sex characteristics. In estrogenic deficiency of long standing in any age group, osteoporosis, especially of the spine, is almost always found since estrogen is a potent stimulus of osteoblasts.

A relatively rare form of ovarian failure is seen in states of androgenic excess, usually derived from the adrenal cortex, when estrogens, though present in the body, are suppressed by the presence of large amounts of androgens (see Virilizing Disorders of the Ovary).

AMENORRHEA

Since regular menstruation depends upon normal function of the entire physiologic axis extending from the hypothalamus and pituitary to the ovary and the uterine lining, it is not surprising that menstrual disorders are among the most common presenting complaints of endocrine disease in women. Correct diagnosis depends upon proper evaluation of each component of the axis, and nonendocrine factors must also be considered.

If menstruation is defined as shedding of endometrium which has been stimulated by estrogen or by estrogen and progesterone which are subsequently withdrawn, it is obvious that amenorrhea can occur

*General references: (1) Richardson, G.S.: Ovarian physiology. New England J Med 274:1008–1015, 1064–1075, 1121–1134, 1183–1194, 1966. (2) Lang, W.R. (editor): Pediatric and adolescent gynecology. Ann New York Acad Sc 142:549–834, 1967. (3) Swerdloff, R.S., & W.D. Odell: Gonadotropins: Present concepts in the human. California Med 109:467–485, 1968. (4) Catt, K.J.: ABC of endocrinology. IV. Reproductive endocrinology. Lancet 1:1097, 1970.

either when hormones are deficient or lacking (the hypohormonal or ahormonal type) or when these hormones, though present in adequate amounts, are never withdrawn (the continuous hormonal type).

Primary amenorrhea implies that menses have never been established. This diagnosis is not usually made before the age of about 18. Secondary amenorrhea means that menses once established have ceased (temporarily or permanently).

The most common type of hypohormonal amenorrhea is the menopause, or physiologic failure of ovarian function. The most common example of continuous hormonal amenorrhea is that due to pregnancy, when cyclic withdrawal is prevented by the placental secretions. These 2 conditions should always be considered before extensive diagnostic studies are undertaken.

The principal diagnostic aids which are used in the study of amenorrhea are as follows: (1) vaginal smear for estrogen effect; (2) endometrial biopsy; (3) "medical D and C" (see below); (4) BBT determination; (5) urine determinations of 17-ketosteroids, FSH, and pregnanediol; (6) culdoscopy and gynecography; (7) chromosomal studies (eg, buccal or vaginal smear); (8) pelvic exploratory operation and gonadal biopsy; (9) radioimmune assays of FSH and LH will soon be generally available for specific diagnosis of certain types of amenorrhea; and (10) plasma testosterone assay.

Albert A.: Bioassay and radioimmunoassay of human gonadotropins. J Clin Endocrinol 28:1683–1689, 1968.

Dewhurst, C.J.: Amenorrhea. Brit MJ 1:711–713, 1971.

Saxena, B.B., & others: Radioimmunoassay of human follicle stimulating and luteinizing hormones in plasma. J Clin Endocrinol 28:519–534, 1968.

Tamm, J. (editor): *Testosterone*. Thieme, 1968.

1. PRIMARY AMENORRHEA

Most cases of primary amenorrhea are of the hypohormonal or ahormonal type. Exact diagnosis is essential to rule out organic lesion along the hypothalamic-pituitary-gonadal axis. The chromosomal sex pattern must be determined in all cases. Pelvic exploration is often required to establish the diagnosis.

The causes are as follows:

(1) Hypothalamic causes: Constitutional delay in onset, debility, serious organic illness.

(2) Pituitary causes (with low or absent urinary FSH): Suprasellar cyst, pituitary tumors (eosinophilic adenomas, chromophobe adenomas, basophilic adenomas), isolated lack of pituitary gonadotropins.

(3) Ovarian causes (with high urinary FSH): Ovarian agenesis (Turner's syndrome), destruction of ovaries (eg, due to infection or, possibly, autoimmunity), "premenarchal menopause."

(4) Uterine causes (usually with normal urinary FSH): Malformations, imperforate hymen, hermaphroditism, unresponsive or atrophic endometrium.

(5) Miscellaneous causes: Adrenal virilism, ie, pseudohermaphroditism (with high urinary 17-ketosteroid and pregnanetriol levels), various androgenic tumors. Testicular feminization (with inguinal gonads and blind vagina). (See Simmer reference, below.)

Treatment

Treatment is similar to that of secondary amenorrhea (see below). The underlying organic cause should first be corrected if possible. An abnormal gonad is usually removed surgically, since the incidence of gonadal neoplasm is high. Plastic repair of the vaginal tract is often required. If secondary sex characteristics have not developed, estrogens alone may be of value.

2. SECONDARY AMENORRHEA

Temporary cessation of menses is extremely common and does not require extensive endocrine investigation. In the childbearing age, pregnancy must be ruled out. In women beyond the childbearing age, menopause should be considered first. States of emotional stress, malnutrition, anemia, and similar disorders may be associated with temporary amenorrhea and correction of the primary disorder will usually also reestablish menses. Some women fail to menstruate regularly for prolonged intervals after stopping oral contraceptive pills. Lactation may be associated with amenorrhea, either physiologically or for abnormally prolonged periods after delivery (Chiari-Frommel syndrome).

By the use of the "medical D and C" (see p 687), ie, the administration of progesterone with subsequent withdrawal, these amenorrheas can be arbitrarily divided into amenorrhea with negative D and C, and amenorrhea with positive D and C. The former (with the exception of pregnancy) show an atrophic or hypoestrin type of endometrium; the latter show an endometrium of the proliferative type but lacking progesterone.

(1) Secondary amenorrhea with negative medical D and C may be due to the following causes: Pregnancy (pregnancy tests positive), menopause (urinary FSH elevated), pituitary tumor, pituitary infarction (Sheehan's syndrome), virilizing syndromes such as arrhenoblastoma; Cushing's disease; Addison's disease, and miscellaneous causes such as anorexia nervosa, profound myxedema, irradiation of the uterine lining, and hysterectomy.

(2) Secondary amenorrhea with positive medical D and C may be due to the following causes: metropathia hemorrhagica, Stein-Leventhal syndrome, estrogen medication, estrogenic tumors, ie, granulosa cell tumors (rare), hyperthyroidism, and perhaps liver disease.

Some degree of overlap in these 2 groups is sometimes found.

Treatment

The aim of therapy is not only to reestablish menses (although this is valuable for psychologic reasons) but also to attempt to establish the etiology (eg, pituitary tumor) of the amenorrhea and to restore reproductive function.

Treatment depends upon the underlying disease. It is not necessary to treat all cases, especially temporary amenorrhea or irregular menses in unmarried girls or women. These cases usually are corrected spontaneously after marriage or first pregnancy.

In patients whose response to progesterone is normal, the administration of this hormone during the last 10–14 days of each month, orally or parenterally (see p 687), will correct the amenorrhea.

In patients who are unresponsive to progesterone and whose urinary gonadotropin levels are low, treatment of a pituitary lesion may restore menstruation; gonadotropins would appear to be of value, and human pituitary FSH has been used with some success experimentally. This, or FSH from postmenopausal urine in combination with APL®, has given good results in secondary amenorrhea. Clomiphene citrate (Clomid®) has been extensively and often successfully tried for the treatment of these patients. However, in current clinical practice, estrogen alone or in combination with progesterone is more commonly used. If urinary gonadotropins are high, gonadotropins are of no value; treat with estrogens alone or with estrogens and progesterone. Corticosteroids may restore menstruation in certain virilizing disorders. Wedge resection of the ovaries often restores regular menstruation in the Stein-Leventhal syndrome.

General measures include dietary management as required to correct overweight or underweight; psychotherapy in cases due to emotional disturbance; and correction of anemia and any other metabolic abnormality which may be present (eg, mild hypothyroidism).

endometrial biopsy show mild hypoestrin effects. The response to progesterone (medical D and C) is variable. The endometrium responds to cyclic administration of estrogens.

Menses often return spontaneously or after several induced "cycles." Psychotherapy is of the greatest value. Clomiphene citrate (Clomid®) may be tried to reestablish menses. If amenorrhea persists, signs of severe estrogen deficiency will appear and must be treated.

It is most important to recognize this syndrome and not to mistake it for an organic type of amenorrhea with a very different prognosis.

Crooke, A.C., & A.D. Tsapoulis: Comparison of clomiphene and follicle-stimulating hormone for treatment of anovulation. J Endocrinol 41:ii–iii, May 1968.

Ferriman, D., Purdie, A.W., & M. Corns: Factors affecting the response to clomiphene therapy. J Endocrinol 41:i–ii, May 1968.

Gemzell, C.: Human pituitary gonadotropins in the treatment of sterility. Fertil Steril 17:149–159, 1966.

Goldfarb, A.F. (editor): *Advances in the Treatment of Menstrual Dysfunctions.* Lea & Febiger, 1964.

Kempers, R.D., & others: Induction of ovulation with clomiphene citrate. Obst Gynec 30:699, 1967.

Pernoll, M.F.: Diagnosis and treatment of galactorrhea. Postgrad Med 49:76–82, 1971.

Rosenberg, E., & T.T. Nwe: Induction of ovulation with human postmenopausal gonadotropin: Experience with 23 patients. Fertil Steril 19:197–205, 1968.

Simmer, H.H., & others: *Testicular Feminization.* Thomas, 1965.

Taymor, M.L.: Gonadotropin therapy. JAMA 203:362–364, 1968.

Vande Wiele, R.L., & R. Nuran: The use of human menopausal and chorionic gonadotropins in patients with infertility due to ovulatory failure. Am J Obst Gynec 93:632–640, 1965.

3. HYPOTHALAMIC AMENORRHEA

Secondary hypothalamic amenorrhea, due to emotional or psychogenic causes is far more common in young women than amenorrhea due to organic causes (except for pregnancy). It is probably mediated by a hypothalamic block of the release of pituitary gonadotropic hormones, especially LH. Pituitary FSH is still produced and is found in normal or low levels in the urine. Since some LH is necessary in the production of estrogen as well as FSH, a state of hypoestrinism with an atrophic endometrium will eventually result. Galactorrhea may be associated with amenorrhea (see Pernoll reference, below).

A history of psychic trauma just preceding the onset of amenorrhea can usually be obtained. The urinary FSH level is normal or low normal, and the 17-ketosteroid level is low normal. Vaginal smear and

TURNER'S SYNDROME
(Primary Ovarian Agenesis, Gonadal Dysgenesis)

Turner's syndrome is a rather rare disorder due to congenital absence of the ovaries and associated with dwarfism and other anomalies. Evidence suggests that in most instances patients with this syndrome lack one of the 2 X chromosomes. A rarer variant shows androgenic tissue in the gonadal remnant with mild virilization.

The principal features include congenital ovarian failure; genital hypoplasia with infantile uterus, vagina, and breasts and primary amenorrhea; scant axillary and pubic hair; short stature, usually between 122–142 cm (48–56 inches); increased carrying angle of arms; webbing of neck (quite common); eye disorders; stocky "shield" chest; cardiovascular disorders, especially coarctation of the aorta, congenital valve defects; os-

teoporosis and other skeletal anomalies (short metacarpals, exostosis of tibia, etc) with increasing age; and
prematurely senile appearance. Nevi are common.
Idiopathic edema is seen in infants. There is an increased incidence of autoimmune thyroiditis and diabetes.

Urinary FSH is high, and 17-ketosteroids are low.
Bone age is retarded. The chromatin sex pattern most
often shows a "negative" buccal smear and XO chromosomal pattern.

Exploratory operation shows a "streak ovary"
and, at times, islands of interstitial cells.

The principal disorder to be differentiated is
pituitary dwarfism. In this disorder the urinary FSH is
low or absent and other signs of pituitary failure are
present. The axillary and pubic hair is absent in pituitary dwarfs; although it is scant in Turner's syndrome,
it increases with estrogen administration. Other forms
of constitutional dwarfism, such as Laurence-Moon-
Biedl syndrome, are ruled out by the urinary FSH and
lack of stigmas such as polydactylia, and the presence
of retinitis pigmentosa and other signs of the disease.
The short stature and occasional metacarpal deformities may resemble pseudohypoparathyroidism, but
these patients menstruate normally.

With the administration of estrogens some increase in height can be achieved, but this is almost
never enough to increase stature significantly; androgens may also promote growth. Some cases respond to
pituitary growth hormone.

If untreated, growth will eventually cease since
the epiphyses will close spontaneously (though late).
The administration of estrogen will develop the breasts
and uterus and lead to anovulatory menses upon cyclic
withdrawal. Fertility can never be achieved.

The associated congenital cardiovascular anomalies may cause early death or may require surgical correction (eg, coarctation). Webbing of the neck can be
corrected by plastic surgery.

Several variants of this syndrome with different
chromosomal patterns have been recently described.
"Pure gonadal dysgenesis" has only "streak" gonads
without other associated skeletal anomalies. "Mixed"
or "atypical" gonadal dysgenesis, a form of hermaphroditism, has a "streak" gonad on one side and an
abnormal gonad, prone to neoplasm, on the other side,
making prophylactic removal a reasonable procedure.

Dmowski, W.P., & R.B. Greenblatt: Ambiguous external genitalia in the newborn and prepubescent child. JAMA
212:308–311, 1970.
Donaldson, C.L., & others: Growth hormone studies in Turner's
syndrome. J Clin Endocrinol 28:383–385, 1968.
Doniach, D., Roitt, I.M., & P.E. Polani: Thyroid antibodies and
sex-chromosome anomalies. Proc Roy Soc Med
61:278–280, 1968.
Goldberg, M.B., & A.L. Scully: Gonadal malignancy in gonadal
dysgenesis: Papillary pseudomucinous cystadenocar-
cinoma in a patient with Turner's syndrome. J Clin Endocrinol 27:341, 1967.
Goldberg, M.B., & others: Gonadal dysgenesis in phenotypic
female subjects: A review of eighty-seven cases with
cytogenetic studies in fifty-three. Am J Med 45:529–543,
1968.
Judd, H.L., & others: Pure gonadal dysgenesis with progressive
hirsutism: Demonstration of testosterone production by
gonadal streaks. New England J Med 282:881, 1970.
Morishima, A., & M.M. Grumbach: The interrelationship of sex
chromosome constitution and phenotype in the syndrome
of gonadal dysgenesis and its variants. Ann New York
Acad Sc 155:695–715, 1968.
Preger, L., & others: Roentgenographic abnormalities in phenotypic females with gonadal dysgenesis. Am J Roentgenol
104:899, 1968.
Sohval, A.R.: The syndrome of pure gonadal dysgenesis. Am J
Med 38:615–625, 1965.
Sohval, A.R.: Hermaphroditism with "atypical" or "mixed"
gonadal dysgenesis. Relationship to gonadal neoplasm.
Am J Med 36:281–292, 1964.

MENOPAUSAL SYNDROME

Essentials of Diagnosis

- Menstrual irregularities associated with hot
  flushes and personality changes.
- Age 45–55 years (unless due to surgery or
  irradiation).
- Hypoestrin vaginal smear, urinary FSH elevated; osteoporosis in later years.

General Considerations

The term menopause refers to the permanent or
final cessation of menstrual function either as a normal
physiologic event or as a result of surgery or ovarian
irradiation. In a broader sense the "menopausal
syndrome" includes all of the sequelae of permanent
cessation of ovarian function, of which the absence of
menstruation is only a part.

The majority of women go through physiologic
menopause at about 45–50 years of age, but premature ovarian failure may occur before the age of 30.
Early menopause is more common in women who have
had an infection or surgical disorder of the genital
tract.

The time of onset of the menopause is often a
familial trait. Rarely, premature ovarian failure may be
part of generalized polyendocrine insufficiency, presumably on an autoimmune basis. (See Irvine and
Golonka references, below.)

The surgical or x-ray menopause differs from the
natural menopause in its more abrupt onset and the
greater severity of manifestations.

The earlier ovarian failure takes place, the more
severe are the effects on certain structures, principally
the skeleton.

The clinical diagnosis of the menopause is at
times difficult, since psychologic factors often over-
shadow symptoms due to hormonal deficiency. It is
also of interest that many women never show any evidence of the menopause, whereas others suffer severely
and may even develop psychoses.

Treatment must be directed at the immediate symptoms, but at times—and especially if postmenopausal osteoporosis is present—it must be maintained for prolonged periods.

Although reproductive function ceases, sexual activity past the menopause is not impaired unless psychic factors and misinformation produce an emotional block.

Clinical Findings

A. Symptoms and Signs: Amenorrhea is frequently preceded by menometrorrhagia or oligomenorrhea. Hot flushes are often severe, lasting only a few minutes but recurring frequently. The patient complains of feelings of tension, especially fullness in the head. Weight gain and nervous instability with depression, exhilaration, or lassitude are often present. Various aches and "rheumatic pains" commonly occur. Sexual changes include dyspareunia, loss of libido, or in some cases increased sexual interest. The breasts may be painful. Bladder irritation is common.

There are very few objective findings. Mild hypertension, mild hirsutism, tenderness over the spine, and dry skin with coarsening of the hair may occur.

B. Laboratory Findings: A hypoestrin type vaginal smear and an elevated urinary FSH level (80 mouse units or above) are the only laboratory findings, but they may be quite delayed in their appearance.

C. X-Ray Findings: X-ray may show osteoporosis of the spine in later years.

Differential Diagnosis

Since most of the manifestations of the menopausal syndrome are purely subjective, it is often difficult to make an exact diagnosis unless a trial of estrogenic (or androgenic) therapy gives striking relief. The most difficult differentiation is from anxiety states with features of reactive depression. Pheochromocytoma and hyperthyroidism must also be considered. A variety of causes of back pain, including osteoarthritis and rheumatoid arthritis, may be considered in the differentiation from pain due to osteoporosis and menopausal arthralgia. In hypothyroidism menstrual irregularities, emotional changes, and aches and pains are also common. One must make certain that ovarian or uterine neoplasm is not the cause of the menstrual irregularity and back pains.

Complications

The serious complications of the menopause are psychosis and, in long-standing cases, osteoporosis. Diabetes mellitus may appear with the menopause. Senile vaginitis may also occur. The postmenopausal patient is more susceptible to degenerative cardiovascular disease and gout.

Treatment

A. Natural Menopause:

1. Physiologic aspects (estrogen therapy)—If cycles are very irregular and the patient suffers from menopausal symptoms, begin estrogens about 5 days after the onset of the last menstrual period and continue in a cyclic fashion. Give ethinyl estradiol, 0.05 mg, diethylstilbestrol, 0.5–1 mg, or estrone sulfate, 1.25 mg by mouth daily except for the first 5 days of each month. This is simple for patients to remember. In the younger patient who still has an occasional menstrual period, the use of the anovulatory agents may be the preferred treatment and also affords protection against unwanted pregnancies. An occasional patient is even intolerant to physiologic doses of estrogens, responding with painful breasts, fluid retention, etc. Reducing the dosage and the use of diuretics, vitamin B complex, and other measures may be helpful. If spotting or "breakthrough" bleeding occurs, cyclic progesterone therapy may be required. The use of androgens is usually not advisable because of undesirable side-effects (eg, hirsutism, voice changes).

If the patient has become amenorrheal, there is no reason to give estrogens in doses large enough to reinstitute menses but only to control symptoms. This is not always possible.

The duration of therapy has not been standardized and must be adjusted to the individual case. Three months to 1 year usually suffices, but in some cases therapy may have to be continued over prolonged periods.

Because of the anabolic effect of estrogens and because of their known beneficial effects on bone metabolism and on blood vessels, estrogen therapy has been recommended for life for women beyond the menopause. The advisability of this practice remains unsettled. If a patient is on long-term estrogen therapy she should keep an accurate record of her dosage schedule and bleeding. Uterine myomas may increase in size, and endometrial hyperplasia may occur. Whenever bleeding occurs that is not on schedule (during the withdrawal phase), tumor should be suspected. (*Note:* Breast and pelvic examination and vaginal cytologic examination for pelvic malignancy should be done routinely once or twice a year.)

2. Psychologic aspects—Many of the symptoms of the menopause are undoubtedly psychologic. The most common symptom is anxiety; more severe emotional disorders may occur. The most serious is involutional psychotic reaction or involutional melancholia; sedative drugs or psychic energizers (eg, Ritalin®, Niamid®, Valium®) may be of value (see Chapter 17). Simple explanation and reassurance that their lives need not be changed because of the menopause are adequate in most patients. In more severe cases the aid of a psychiatrist may be necessary.

B. Surgical and X-Ray Menopause: These cases differ from the natural menopause only in the abruptness and severity of the symptoms. It is advisable to help these patients live as normal lives as possible by permanent hormonal replacement therapy. If normal periods cannot be reinstituted but the patient understands that her sexual function will continue unchanged, she usually makes a suitable adjustment. Estrogen therapy is as for natural menopause (see above).

C. **Treatment of Complications:**

1. **Osteoporosis** is discussed on p 628.

2. **Senile vaginitis**—Give oral diethylstilbestrol or other estrogens daily. Diethylstilbestrol vaginal suppositories containing 1 mg may be used daily for 10–14 days while continuing oral diethylstilbestrol. Dienestrol vaginal cream is often helpful.

Prognosis

Most women pass through the menopause without requiring extensive therapy. A short course of estrogen therapy may alleviate their symptoms. Others, however, require prolonged and intensive therapy. The average duration of symptoms is 2–3 years.

Some patients show severe depression (involutional melancholia or psychotic reaction; see Chapter 17) and even suicidal tendencies.

Consideration has recently been given to long-term replacement therapy with estrogen of postmenopausal females in an attempt to prevent cardiovascular degeneration, osteoporosis, etc. Such a program must be carefully supervised since latent neoplasms of breast and uterus may be stimulated by long-term estrogen therapy.

Cohen, E.J. (editor): Treatment of menopausal problems. Mod Treat 5:543,1968.

Davis, M.E., Strandjord, N.M., & L.H. Lanzl: Estrogens and the aging process. JAMA 196:219–224, 1966.

Golonka, J.E., & A.D. Goodman: Coexistence of primary ovarian insufficiency, primary adrenocortical insufficiency and idiopathic hypoparathyroidism. J Clin Endocrinol 28:79–82, 1968.

Irvine, W.J., & others: Immunologic aspects of premature ovarian failure associated with idiopathic Addison's disease. Lancet 2:883, 1968.

Keettel, W.C., & J.T. Bradbury: Premature ovarian failure, permanent and temporary. Am J Obst Gynec 89:83–96, 1964.

Meena, H.E., Bunker, M.L., & S. Meena: Loss of compact bone due to menopause. Obst Gynec 26:333–343, 1965.

Rogers, J.: Estrogens in menopause and postmenopause. New England J Med 280:364–367, 1969.

II. FEMALE HYPERGONADISM

Excesses of ovarian hormones are often encountered during the normal reproductive life of women, and most frequently give rise to irregular or excessive menstrual bleeding and, more rarely, to amenorrhea. Excesses before the age of puberty or after the menopause, however, should be thoroughly investigated since the possibility of malignant lesions is great. Estrogenic excess is more common than progesterone excess, which is seen in pregnancy and in chorioepithelioma. Other extra-ovarian sources of estrogens are malignant tumors of the adrenals, which secrete abnormal amounts of estrogens. Since these tumors usually produce excesses of androgens as well, their hyperestrogenic effects are rarely detectable clinically in the female.

Another cause of hyperestrogenism is the ingestion or other use of hormones (eg, in face creams).

PREPUBERAL FEMALE HYPERGONADISM

It is important to differentiate organic lesions of the pituitary-hypothalamic region, which cause true precocious puberty in females, from pseudoprecocity due to granulosa cell tumors and choriocarcinoma. Constitutional true sexual precocity may be partial, consisting only of precocious breast development and early growth of pubic hair, or it may be associated with premature menarche as well. It is often familial. Albright's syndrome causes true precocity with fibrous dysplasia of bone (osteitis fibrosa disseminata) and pigmentary changes of the skin (see Chapter 3).

Granulosa cell tumors of the ovary cause uterine bleeding by virtue of their estrogenic secretions, but they do not cause ovulation and these girls are not fertile. The same is usually true of choriocarcinoma. Both of these tumors are highly malignant.

Simple follicle cysts of the ovary, at times easily palpable, may cause precocity.

Pseudoprecocious puberty may also be caused by ingestion of estrogens. Thiazolsulfone (Promizole®) occasionally causes early growth of pubic hair.

The significance of the differentiation between true and pseudoprecocious puberty is that in true precocity ovulatory cycles may occur and the patient must be protected from pregnancy. The most useful guide to the differentiation is the urinary FSH determination. Urinary FSH is not present in girls before the age of puberty, even in pseudoprecocious puberty; whereas girls with true precocious puberty may secrete 5–10 mouse units/day.

The diagnosis of either true or pseudoprecocious puberty is important because many cases are due to tumors which must be found and removed if possible. Unfortunately, most estrogen-secreting tumors are highly malignant, and tumors of the third ventricle and other lesions near the hypothalamus are quite difficult to remove.

Precocious development of breasts and early onset of menses may cause psychic disturbances, which may be severe. Short stature in adult life is the rule since bone age is advanced and the epiphyses close prematurely. As adults these patients may suffer a great deal from excessive menstrual bleeding, which may cause anemia unless it is checked. Cystic mastitis is a chronic problem, and the incidence of uterine adenofibromas is high. It is not definitely known whether long-standing hyperestrinism causes a higher incidence of breast and genital tract cancer, but it may be a significant aggravating factor.

The only treatment is surgical removal of tumors, but most are malignant and metastasize early. The prognosis for simple constitutional precocity is not so unfavorable, although these girls must be watched to prevent pregnancy. Recent reports on the use of progesterone (Depo-Provera®) are encouraging but response is variable (see Rifkind reference, below).

Benedict, P.H.: Sex precocity and polyostotic fibrous dysplasia. Am J Dis Child 111:426–429, 1966.

Eberlein, W.R., & others: Ovarian tumors and cysts associated with sexual precocity: Report of 3 cases and review of literature. J Pediat 57:484–497, 1960.

Hahn, H.B., Jr., Hayles, A.B., & A. Albert: Medroxyprogesterone and constitutional precocious puberty. Proc Staff Meet Mayo Clin 39:182–190, 1964.

Rifkind, A.B., & others: Suppression of urinary excretion of luteinizing hormone (LH) and follicle stimulating hormone (FSH) by medroxyprogesterone acetate. J Clin Endocrinol 29:506, 1969.

Sigurjonsdottir, T.J., & A.B. Hayles: Precocious puberty. Am J Dis Child 115:309, 1968.

Steiner, M.M., & S.A. Hadawi: Sexual precocity. Am J Dis Child 108:28, 1964.

ADULT FEMALE HYPERGONADISM

Adult female hypergonadism may be due to estrogenic excess alone or to combined excess of estrogen and progesterone. Estrogenic excess is characterized by menorrhagia or, rarely, amenorrhea. The vaginal smear shows estrogenic excess. Lack of ovulation is demonstrated by the absence of BBT rise. Sterility is the rule. The medical D & C is positive, ie, bleeding starts after a short course of progesterone. Endometrial biopsy shows a proliferative endometrium. The urinary FSH level is low.

Adult female hyperestrogenism may be caused by (1) states in which ovulation does not occur, leading to "metropathia hemorrhagica" or dysfunctional uterine bleeding; (2) liver disease, which interferes with the catabolism of estrogens; (3) drug administration (eg, estrogen creams or tablets); (4) granulosa cell and theca cell tumors (both types are usually present); and (5) Stein-Leventhal syndrome (see below).

Estrogen and progesterone excess often causes amenorrhea without other evidence of hypogonadism. Excess of both hormones may be due to (1) pregnancy, (2) chorio-epithelioma or teratoma, (3) luteoma, or (4) malignant adrenal tumors (possibly). The medical D and C is negative. Pregnanediol is found in the urine. Secretory endometrium is demonstrated on biopsy. The urinary FSH level (actually chorionic gonadotropin) may be high, and pregnancy tests may be positive.

Treatment depends upon the cause. Cyclic administration of progesterone, wedge resection of the ovary, or surgical removal of functioning tumors at times restores normal cyclic ovarian function. Recent reports of treatment of functional anovulation with human pituitary FSH and clomiphene are encouraging.

TABLE 18–15. Hormones elaborated by actively secreting ovarian tumors.

Type	Secretion
Feminizing	
Granulosa	Estrogen +++
Theca cell	Estrogen ++
Luteoma?	Estrogen + and/or progesterone
Virilizing*	
Arrhenoblastoma	Androgen +++
Adrenal rest (lipoid cell)	Androgen ++ and corticosteroids
Hilus cell	Androgen +++
Miscellaneous	
Choriocarcinoma	Gonadotropins ++++ and estrogens; ?TSH
Dysgerminoma*	Gonadotropins + and androgens?
Gynandroblastoma	Androgens ++ and estrogens +++
Struma ovarii	Thyroxine +

*Most women have complete amenorrhea with negative medical D & C since the endometrium is atrophic.

The prognosis is that of the underlying disease. Treatment with progesterone alone or with estrogen in cyclic fashion is usually quite effective in temporary disorders of ovulation. Stubborn anovulation may persist, however, after cessation of therapy.

Bagshawe, K.D.: *Choriocarcinoma.* Arnold, 1969.

DeCosta, E.J.: Ovarian tumors with endocrine activity and related problems. S Clin North America 49:105–120, 1969.

Fontana, A.L., & A.J. Simpson: Arrhenoblastoma: Review of the literature and report of a case. Obst Gynec 23:730–734, 1964.

Fox, H.: Ovarian tumors. Histogenesis and systemic effects. California Med 109:295, 1968.

Morris, J.Mc.L., & R.E. Scully: *Endocrine Pathology of the Ovary.* Mosby, 1958.

VIRILIZING DISORDERS OF THE OVARY
(See also under Adrenal.)

Stein-Leventhal Syndrome

Stein-Leventhal syndrome occurs only in young women. It is characterized by bilaterally enlarged polycystic ovaries, mild hirsutism, obesity, and oligomenorrhea or amenorrhea. Urinary FSH is normal, the medical D & C produces withdrawal bleeding, estrogen is present, and the urinary 17-ketosteroids are present in high normal amounts. The hirsutism has been shown to be related to abnormal production of testosterone and related compounds by the ovaries and possibly also by the adrenals. Hereditary factors may be involved. Pelvic pneumography is most helpful in demonstrating bilateral enlargement of the ovaries. At operation the enlarged ovaries are found to have many follicles on the surface and are surrounded by a thick capsule ("oyster ovaries").

Wedge resection often restores ovulatory periods and fertility, but hirsutism is not helped by this procedure unless large doses of estrogens are also used. Corticosteroids may be of value. Recently, ovulation followed by pregnancy has been produced by human pituitary FSH and also by clomiphene. There is danger of rapid enlargement of the ovaries due to cyst formation and rupture if the dosage is not carefully controlled. Multiple pregnancies may occur.

Diffuse Theca Luteinization

This disorder is similar to the Stein-Leventhal syndrome, but many follicles are not found in the ovaries. Hirsutism and often more marked virilization are associated with amenorrhea.

Excessive testosterone and androstenedione production has been demonstrated recently in ovarian slices removed surgically and also in blood and urine in these patients, which may explain the virilization.

There is a greater incidence of endometrial carcinoma in these patients, possibly related to continued estrogen stimulation.

Bardin, C.W., Hembree, W.C., & M.B. Lipsett: Suppression of testosterone and androstenedione production rates with dexamethasone in women with idiopathic hirsutism and polycystic ovaries. J Clin Endocrinol 28:1300–1306, 1968.

Cooper, H.E., & others: Hereditary factors in the Stein-Leventhal syndrome. Am J Obst Gynec 100:371–387, 1968.

Deller, J.J., & others: Testosterone metabolism in idiopathic hirsutism. Ann Int Med 63:369, 1965.

Greenblatt, R.B.: *The Hirsute Female.* Thomas, 1963.

Jeffcoate, T.N.A.: The androgenic ovary, with special reference to the Stein-Leventhal syndrome. Am J Obst Gynec 88:143–156, 1964.

Lipsett, M.B., & others: Physiologic basis of disorders of androgen metabolism. Ann Int Med 68:1327–1344, 1968.

Sherins, R., & R. Horton: Hirsutism and virilization. California Med 106:87, 1967.

Sherman, R.P.: The enigmatic polycystic ovary. Obst Gynec Surg 21:1, 1966.

Thomas, J.P.: Adrenocortical function in Stein-Leventhal syndrome. J Clin Endocrinol 28:1781–1783, 1968.

HORMONES & HORMONE-LIKE AGENTS

ANTERIOR PITUITARY HORMONES

All of the anterior pituitary hormones are protein substances and must therefore be administered paren-terally to be effective; if taken by mouth, they are digested by the digestive enzymes. In general, with the exception of the growth and lactogenic hormones, whose effects are not mediated directly through other glands, the anterior pituitary hormones appear to have a regulatory function on the other glands of internal secretion. The anterior pituitary in turn is regulated to a great extent by hypothalamic-pituitary humoral "releasing factors."

Several of these hormones have been prepared in "pure" or "almost pure" form: adrenocorticotropin (ACTH, corticotropin), growth, lactogenic (luteotropic), follicle-stimulating (FSH), interstitial cell-stimulating (luteinizing), and thyroid-stimulating (TSH) hormones. There may be other factors in the anterior pituitary, but they have not yet been fully identified. Of the pure preparations, only corticotropin and thyrotropin are at present commercially available. The TSH and LH releasing factors have been isolated recently.

Corticotropin (ACTH)

Corticotropin has been shown to have remarkable effects in arresting many disease processes which are not satisfactorily influenced by other therapeutic agents. Its effect is entirely mediated by the stimulation of the adrenal cortex. Corticotropin is a protein of small molecular size, and certain peptides derived from it have been found to have similar and as marked physiologic effects as the hormone itself.

A. Metabolic Effects in Humans: ACTH in adequate doses in normal human beings produces the following metabolic effects: increased excretion of nitrogen, potassium, and phosphorus; retention of sodium and secondary retention of water; elevation of fasting blood glucose and diabetic glucose tolerance curve; and increased urinary excretion of uric acid, calcium, 17-ketosteroids, and corticosteroids; fall of circulating eosinophils and lymphocytes; and elevation of polymorphonuclear neutrophils.

B. Clinical Effects, Uses, and Dosages: See p 680.

Pituitary Growth Hormone (PGH)

"Pure" PGH has been employed in normal humans, pituitary dwarfs, and panhypopituitary individuals. Only the material prepared from human and possibly monkey pituitary glands has metabolic and growth promoting effect on humans. Because the amount of these materials produced is very small, they are available for experimental purposes only. The older crude growth hormone preparations have been of no benefit under controlled experimental conditions.

Lactogenic (Luteotropic) Hormone

This hormone has not been employed extensively in human research. Its presence is necessary for the initiation and apparently for the continuation of lactation in breasts which have been prepared for lactation by estrogen and progesterone during pregnancy. Recently, there have been reports of a "growth hormone-like activity" in humans with the use of ovine prolactin.

TABLE 18–16. Anterior pituitary hormones. Preparations available.

Name	Action	Average Dose
Vasopressin tannate (Pitressin Tannate®)	Antidiuretic; pressor	0.3-1 ml IM every 12–72 hours
Vasopressin injection (Pitressin®)		0.25–0.5 ml IM every 3–4 hours
Posterior pituitary powder (snuff)		5–20 mg 3–4 times daily
Lypressin (Diapid®)	Antidiuretic	1–2 sprays in each nostril daily
Oxytocin injection (Pitocin®), synthetic oxytocin (Syntocinon®)	Oxytocic	1 ml dissolved in 1 liter saline; give by continuous IV drip

Follicle-Stimulating Hormone (FSH)

FSH has different actions in male and female. In the female FSH stimulates the development of ovarian follicles. Human FSH combined with chorionic gonadotropin has produced ovulation in patients with amenorrhea. In the male it stimulates the germinal epithelium of the testis to produce spermatozoa. It apparently has no effect on the Leydig cells, hence does not influence testosterone secretion. Human pituitary FSH and FSH from the urine of menopausal women (Pergonal®), followed by chorionic gonadotropin, have been used in patients with amenorrhea to induce ovulation. Clomiphene citrate (Clomid®), a synthetic analogue of the nonsteroidal estrogen chlorotrianisene (TACE®), has been almost equally effective in inducing ovulation.

Interstitial Cell Stimulating Hormone (ICSH; Luteinizing Hormone)

In the female, ICSH apparently has a dual action, ie, it stimulates the growth of theca lutein cells and transforms the mature follicles into corpora lutea. In the male it stimulates the Leydig cells of the testis to secrete testosterone, and possibly also estrogen.

There is no good commercial pituitary ICSH. Chorionic gonadotropins, which have a similar action, are used clinically.

Thyroid-Stimulating Hormone (TSH, Thyrotropin, Thytropar®)

TSH is exceedingly efficient in stimulating the thyroid gland. It has limited clinical usefulness at present; its principal uses are to differentiate pituitary hypothyroidism from primary hypothyroidism or from low radioiodine uptake due to exogenous thyroid hormone or iodine. It has also been used in an attempt to "stimulate" metastatic thyroid cancer to take up radioiodine for therapeutic purposes.

Thyrotropin (available as Thytropar®) has been advocated for the treatment of thyroiditis, but its place in the management of this disease is still open to question.

The dosage is 5–10 units IM every 12 or 24 hours for 1–3 days. Repeat radioiodine uptake or PBI. If uptake or PBI is increased, primary hypothyroidism is not present.

POSTERIOR PITUITARY HORMONES

The posterior pituitary hormones are polypeptides composed of 8 amino acids. Their exact chemical structures have been determined and they have recently been synthesized. Like the anterior pituitary hormones they are effective only when administered parenterally, but they can also be absorbed through the nasal mucous membranes (as snuff). They exert 3 actions: They (1) raise blood pressure (pressor action); (2) cause fluid retention without osmotically equivalent sodium retention (antidiuretic action); and (3) cause uterine contractions (oxytocic action).

To date, the antidiuretic and pressor principles have not been fully separated; they may be identical. The oxytocic factor may likewise have some pressor effect.

Clinical Indications

A. Pressor-Antidiuretic: The pressor and antidiuretic principle is used primarily for the treatment of diabetes insipidus and to prevent and control abdominal distention.

B. Obstetric Use: Oxytocin is employed in obstetrics for induction of uterine contractions.

PITUITARY-LIKE HORMONES ELABORATED BY THE PLACENTA

The most important of the pituitary-like hormones elaborated by the placenta is referred to as "chorionic gonadotropin." Its physiologic action is almost identical with that of ICSH (see above). It has been shown that this hormone apparently functions only if an intact anterior pituitary gland is present. It is of little value by itself in inducing spermatogenesis or ovulation or maintaining a functional corpus luteum, but it may be effective for these purposes if preceded by pituitary FSH. Many of its alleged effects have been due to the presence of FSH, whose action the presence of chorionic gonadotropin may potentiate.

Placental lactogen (prolactin) is under investigation as a substitute for pituitary growth hormone.

Clinical Indications

In the male, chorionic gonadotropin may induce descent of cryptorchid testes in selected cases and is useful in some types of hypogonadism (although testosterone is generally preferred). In the female, chorionic gonadotropin may aid in inducing ovulation and maintaining corpus luteum in a few selected cases of sterility (if adequate FSH is present). The use of chorionic gonadotropin in the treatment of obesity has no rational basis.

Preparations Available

A. Chorionic gonadotropin, derived from the urine of pregnant women, is available commercially under a variety of trade names (eg, APL®, Follutein®).

B. Equine gonadotropins, derived from the serum of pregnant mares, are also available commercially. This preparation is a mixture of FSH and ICSH. It is not generally recommended because of its marked sensitizing effect and because antihormones are produced by protracted use. Only short courses should be employed.

Average Doses

The usual doses are 200–1000 units IM every day or every other day.

THYROID HORMONE

The active principles of the thyroid gland appear to be the iodine-containing amino acids, thyroxine (T_4) and triiodothyronine (T_3). Thyroid hormones act as a general cellular metabolic stimulant with resultant increased oxygen consumption (ie, increased metabolic rate). Their exact mode of action is not known.

Method of Administration

Thyroid hormone, either in the form of thyroglobulin (desiccated thyroid), T_4, or T_3, is effective when taken orally. There is a marked difference in rates of metabolic responses between T_3 and thyroid or T_4. In the case of T_4, little effect is noted after a single dose for about 24 hours, and the maximal effect is not reached for several days. After the medication is stopped there is a slow loss of the effect, depending upon the initial BMR and the level reached during thyroid medication. In general, at least 3–6 weeks must elapse after thyroid medication has been discontinued before one can be reasonably certain that the effects have been dissipated. In the case of T_3, the

peak effect is reached in 12–24 hours and the effect is over in about 6–14 days or less.

The dextrorotatory isomers of T_4 and T_3 have recently become available. They exert a less marked "metabolic" effect in the same dosages in which T_4 and T_3 are given. They have been advocated primarily as cholesterol-lowering agents. Other analogues—in which such compounds as proprionic or acetic acid are substituted for the alanine side chain or in which fewer iodine atoms are incorporated into the molecule—have also been studied.

Clinical Indications

Thyroid hormone is indicated only in thyroid deficiency states. It is not effective and not indicated as a general metabolic stimulant. It has been shown that patients with thyroid deficiencies rarely require over 0.2 gm (3 gr) of desiccated thyroid daily. Patients without deficiency states can easily tolerate 0.3–0.5 gm (5–7½ gr) or more daily without any effect on BMR, although the radioiodine uptake is suppressed. A good general rule is that if a patient requires over 2–3 gr of thyroid daily, his need for thyroid medication should be carefully evaluated.

Preparations & Dosages

A. Desiccated Thyroid: This is a good compound for thyroid replacement. The chief difficulty is that the official assay is for iodine content, which may or may not represent active thyroid hormone so that there may be variations in metabolic effect. Pure beef thyroid (Thyrar®) is available. Proloid® is more stable in hormonal content. There is no evidence that any of the commercial preparations which contain more or less iodine than the official preparation are any less "toxic." Replacement therapy may be periodically appraised with PBI determinations, but this may not be reliable because of variable iodine content. The dose is 65–200 mg (1–3 gr) daily.

B. Sodium Levothyroxine (T_4, Synthroid®, Letter®, Levoid®, Titroid®): An excellent compound for thyroid replacement. The principal advantage of this compound over desiccated thyroid is its assured constant potency. Because it is about 600 times as potent as thyroid, small changes in dose may lead to toxic levels. Dosage may be appraised by periodic PBI or T_4 determinations, which are raised to a higher level by T_4 than by desiccated thyroid. 0.1 mg is equivalent to 60 mg (1 gr) of desiccated thyroid. The average dose is 0.1–0.3 mg daily.

TABLE 18–17. Equivalency of thyroid preparations.

Desiccated Thyroid	Approximate Equivalent In		
	Sodium Levothyroxine (Letter®, Synthroid®, etc)	Sodium Liothyronine (Cytomel®, Trionine®)	Liotrix (Euthroid®, Thyrolar®)
30 mg	0.05 mg	12.5 µg	½
65 mg	0.1 mg	25 µg	1
130 mg	0.2 mg	50 µg	2
200 mg	0.3 mg	75 µg	3

C. Synthroid® Injection: 10 ml vial containing 500 μg lyophilized active substance with 10 mg of mannitol. Dilute with 5 ml of sodium chloride just prior to use. For intravenous use in myxedema coma. **Dosage:** 200–400 μg IV on the first day; 100–200 μg IV on the second day.

D. Sodium Liothyronine (T₃, Cytomel®, Trionine®): This preparation has a more rapid action and disappearance of effect than thyroid or thyroxine, and is 3–4 times as calorigenic as T₄. Its disadvantage is that the PBI cannot be used to determine dosage when this drug is used in replacement therapy. The average maintenance dose is 0.05–0.075 mg daily in divided doses. Available as 5 μg, 25 μg, and 50 μg tablets.

E. Liotrix (Euthroid®, Thyrolar®): Liotrix, a mixture of T₄ and T₃ in a ratio of 4:1, is now commercially available as replacement therapy. It is available in 4 potencies (see Table 18–17). It closely simulates the effects of endogenous thyroid secretion and its uniform potency should make response predictable. The PBI can be used to follow therapy.

F. Sodium Dextrothyroxine (Choloxin®): Available in 2 mg and 4 mg tablets as a cholesterol-lowering agent. It may also be used as replacement therapy for hypothyroidism in patients with cardiac disease who cannot tolerate other thyroid medications.

PARATHYROID HORMONE

Parathyroid hormone is a protein substance derived from parathyroid glands. It is only effective when given parenterally.

Parathyroid hormone has a major effect on calcium and phosphorus and hence bone metabolism. Its effect is to cause an increased renal excretion of phosphorus and a direct decalcification of bone through stimulation of the osteoclasts, leading to mobilization of calcium and phosphorus from bone.

Because of the high cost and general unavailability of parathyroid hormone, 2 other preparations are employed in its place. They are dihydrotachysterol (AT 10) and vitamin D. Both of these are sterols and are effective by mouth. Although at first AT 10 was the preparation of choice, it now appears that vitamin D, which is less expensive, is almost equally effective and more predictable in its action.

Clinical Indications

Parathyroid hormone is indicated only in acute postsurgical hypoparathyroid tetany (after accidental removal of the parathyroid glands) and for special tests (see Ellsworth-Howard test).

Preparations Available for Treatment of Hypoparathyroidism

A. Parathyroid Injection: The average dose is 50–100 units (0.5–1 ml) in aqueous solution 3–5 times daily IM as indicated.

B. Dihydrotachysterol (Hytakerol®, Digratyl®): For dosage, see Hypoparathyroidism.

C. Calciferol (Vitamin D₂): This preparation has a potency of 40,000 units/mg. The dosage is 1–5 mg daily.

ADRENOCORTICAL HORMONES

The hormones of the adrenal cortex are all steroids. To date over 30 different steroids have been isolated and identified from animal adrenal glands or adrenal venous blood. Only a few of these have demonstrable metabolic effects.

The question has been raised whether all the steroids apparently isolated from the adrenal cortex are in fact naturally-occurring or whether they are artifacts produced in the chemical laboratory. Isolation of hormones from blood obtained by catheterization of renal veins shows that about 90% of the hormones of the adrenal cortex are 11,17-hydroxycorticosterone (compound F) and about 10% corticosterone (compound B). In general it may be stated that the best demonstration of the effects of adrenocortical hormone or hormones is that seen following corticotropin (ACTH) administration (see below).

Aldosterone has been isolated from adrenals. This hormone appears to have only sodium- and water-retaining and potassium-losing effects. It is about 20 times as potent as deoxycorticosterone.

Hormones with estrogenic and androgenic effects have also been isolated.

Clinical Effects and Indications

A. Deoxycorticosterone Acetate (DOCA®): The only significant metabolic effects of this hormone are sodium and water retention and increased urinary potassium excretion. In this respect it is about 20 times as potent as cortisone. It has little effect on carbohydrate or protein metabolism.

B. Cortisone Acetate: The principal metabolic effects of cortisone include retention of some sodium and water; increased excretion of nitrogen, potassium, and phosphorus; increased blood glucose and ability to maintain blood glucose levels during fasting in addisonian patients; and return of the EEG pattern to normal in addisonian patients. One of the most important effects is the adrenocortical atrophy which results with prolonged use; this is probably due to endogenous ACTH inhibition and may interfere with the "normal" response of the pituitary-adrenal axis to stress.

For clinical effects and use, see below.

C. Hydrocortisone: This compound is available for oral, intravenous, and local (eg, intra-articular) use. Its actions are similar to those of cortisone and its metabolic effects appear to be identical. It is somewhat more potent than cortisone on a weight basis. Hydrocortisone (Hydrocortone® Phosphate) and hydrocortisone sodium succinate (Solu-Cortef®) are also available for intravenous or intramuscular use.

TABLE 18−18. Corticotropin (ACTH) and the corticosteroids.

Preparation	Daily Dosage	Remarks	Potency/mg† Compared to Hydrocortisone
Corticotropin (ACTH)* Lyophilized powder	5−200 U	**IV**: Administer in any intravenous fluid by slow drip. For greater effect, give intravenously during entire 24-hour period. May use also for 8−12 hours. Maximal effect obtained by intravenous use of 15−40 U.	
Solution	5−200 U	**Subcut or IM**: Administer in saline every 6 hours. By this route long-acting preparations are usually used (see below). Give 40−200 U.	
Repository injection (gel)	10−200 U	**IM or subcut**: Longer acting than the powder or solution. For maximum effect give every 12 hours. May be used once daily in some patients.	
Cortrophin-Zinc®	10−100 U	**IM or subcut**: Duration of action 24 hours.	
Oral Corticosteroids: Cortisone acetate (Cortone®, Cortogen®)	25−200 mg or more	For maximum effect use every 6 hours or 4 times daily. Rarely used clinically now (sodium retention and potassium excretion) except in Addison's disease.	4/5
Hydrocortisone (Cortef®, Cortril®, Hydrocortone®)	20−200 mg or more	As for cortisone, above.	1
Prednisone (Meticorten®, Deltasone®, Deltra®, Paracort®) **and** Prednisolone (Meticortelone®, Delta-Cortef®, Hydeltra®, Paracortol®, Prednis®, Sterane®, Sterolone®)	5−20 mg or more (avg, 10−20)	Δ1-Derivative of cortisone and hydrocortisone. Drug of choice; has no significant sodium-retaining effect. Give every 6 hours or 4 times daily. Good economical drugs.	4−5
Meprednisone (Betapar®)	4−40 mg (avg, 8−16)	About 20% more potent than prednisone. Available as 4 mg tablet. Less sodium retention and lower cost than prednisone.	5−6
Methylprednisolone (Medrol®)	4−40 mg (avg, 8−16)	About 15−25% more potent than prednisone. 16 mg tablets available for alternate day therapy.	5−6
Triamcinolone (Aristocort®, Kenacort®)	4−40 mg (avg, 8−16)	About the same as methylprednisolone. May produce bizarre effects, eg, nausea, weight loss, dizziness, and vague "toxic" symptoms.	5−6
Dexamethasone (Decadron®, Deronil®, Gammacorten® Hexadrol®, Dexameth®)	0.5−10 mg (avg, 1.5−3)	0.75 mg dexamethasone = 5 mg prednisolone. May cause sodium retention, especially at higher levels. No reduction of other side reactions. No advantages over prednisolone.	25−35
Betamethasone (Celestone®)	0.6−6 mg (avg, 1.2−2.4)	0.6 mg betamethasone = 5 mg prednisolone. No advantage over prednisolone.	33
Paramethasone (Haldrone®)	2−20 mg (avg, 4−8)	2 mg paramethasone = 5 mg prednisolone. No advantage over prednisolone.	10−12
Fluprednisolone (Alphadrol®)	1.5−15 mg (avg, 3−5)	1.5 mg fluprednisolone = 5 mg prednisolone. No advantage over prednisolone.	12−15
Fludrocortisone (Florinef®, F-Cortef®, Alflorone®)	0.1−0.3 mg	Used almost entirely in Addison's disease. Potent sodium-retaining effect. Supplements hydrocortisone in Addison's disease. May be useful also as diagnostic tool in adrenal hyperplasia.	20

*Cosyntropin (Cortrosyn®), a synthetic corticotropin, is now available. It is used primarily for tests of adrenal function or in patients allergic to animal ACTH. 0.25 mg is equivalent to 25 units of corticotropin.

†To convert to equivalent hydrocortisone dosage, multiply by the potency factor shown. *Note:* If this is greater than 20, the physiologic limits are exceeded.

TABLE 18–18 (cont'd). Corticotropin (ACTH) and the corticosteroids.

Preparation	Daily Dosage	Remarks
Parenteral Corticosteroids: (1) For IV use only:		
Hydrocortisone IV infusion concentrate	100–200 mg	Most reliable emergency drug in absolute or relative adrenal failure. **Caution:** Must dissolve in at least 500 ml solution.
Parenteral Corticosteroids: (2) For IV or IM use: (Highly soluble. Rapid action and rapid excretion.)		
Hydrocortisone sodium succinate (Solu-Cortef®), hydrocortisone 21-phosphate	100–200 mg	Dissolve 1–10 ml or more of solution. May administer in small volume or intravenous fluids. Water-soluble. For emergency use. Active intravenously or intramuscularly. Intramuscular dose must be given every 6 hours for maximum effect.
Prednisolone sodium succinate (Meticortelone Soluble®)	50–100 mg	As for hydrocortisone sodium succinate, above, but not used in adrenal insufficiency. Indicated when corticosteroids can not be taken orally.
Dexamethasone-21-phosphate (Decadron® phosphate injection)	8–40 mg	As for prednisolone sodium succinate, above.
Prednisolone-21-phosphate (Hydeltrasol®)	40–100 mg	As for prednisolone sodium succinate, above.
Methylprednisolone sodium succinate (Solu-Medrol®)	40–120 mg	As for prednisolone sodium succinate, above. Also advocated as retention enemas in ulcerative colitis. Available as 40 mg, 125 mg, 500 mg, and 1000 mg vials with diluent.
Parenteral Corticosteroids: (3) For IM systemic use: (Insoluble. Slowly absorbed and excreted.)		
Cortisone acetate, aqueous suspension	25–200 mg	Intramuscularly only in doses every 12–24 hours. Used as long-acting parenteral corticosteroid, mainly in adrenal insufficiency.
Methylprednisolone acetate	10–80 mg	As hydrocortisone. May be used systemically for anti-inflammatory effect. (Dosage 40–180 mg in single dose.)
Triamcinolone acetonide (Kenalog®)	40–80 mg	Intramuscular (40 mg/ml) every 2–4 weeks.

Parenteral Corticosteroids: (4) For local use only (intrasynovial, soft tissue): Very insoluble. Many preparations available. (1) Hydrocortisone acetate, 25 mg/ml; (2) hycrocortisone tertiary butyl acetate (Hydrocortone®, TBA) 5 ml vials, 25 mg/ml); (3) prednisolone acetate aqueous suspension (Meticortelone®) (5 ml vials, 25 mg/ml); (4) prednisolone tertiary butyl acetate (Hydeltra®, TBA) (5 ml vials, 20 mg/ml); (5) triamcinolone acetonide (Kenalog®), parenteral (5 ml vials, 10 mg/ml); (6) Celestone Solu-span® (betamethasone acetate and betamethasone disodium phosphate) (6 mg/ml as sterile aqueous suspension for intramuscular, intrabursal, intra-articular, or intralesional injection), has both local and systemic effects of corticosteroids. (Dosage: 1–2 ml 1–2 times weekly.)

Local Corticosteroids: Almost all of the above steroids, plus others (eg, flurandrenolone [Cordran®], fluocinolone acetonide [Synalar®], flumethasone pivalate [Locorten®]), have been incorporated into various vehicles for local application to the skin, eyes, or mucous membranes. They are effective anti-inflammatory agents when so used. At present there appears to be little to choose among them, but marked differences in potency are observed (see Table 18–19).

D. Cortisone and Hydrocortisone Analogues: Many modifications have been made in the cortisone-hydrocortisone molecule to decrease side reactions in relationship to therapeutic effect. The only beneficial effects of these modifications have been to decrease the sodium-retaining and potassium-losing effects of the compounds. All of these preparations are more potent on a weight basis than their parent compounds.

E. Fludrocortisone Acetate (Alflorone®, Florinef®, F-Cortef®) and Fluprednisolone: These potent anti-inflammatory drugs have been found useful in Addison's disease and also in dermatologic disorders. They have powerful sodium-retaining effects. Except in Addison's disease, they must be used locally only; and even with local use their absorption may cause excessive sodium retention.

F. Whole Cortical Extract: A water-soluble extract of the adrenal gland. Although its steroid content (if any) and mode of action are poorly understood, this agent appears to be of value only for an occasional patient who fails to respond to cortisone in the emergency management of adrenal crisis.

Preparations Available

A. Deoxycorticosterone Acetate (DOCA®) or Deoxycorticosterone Trimethylacetate: Used only for supplementary maintenance in Addison's disease.

1. Buccal tablets—DOCA® is ineffective when swallowed. The dosage is ½–2 tablets daily dissolved in the buccal gutter. The drug is almost equally effective in a given dose as when injected.

2. Solution in sesame oil—The dosage is 1–3 mg IM daily for maintenance.

3. Pellets—The dosage is one 75 mg pellet for each mg of DOCA® required by injection, up to 3 mg/day. If requirements by injection exceed 3 mg, one additional pellet should be implanted (eg, for a requirement of 5 mg/day by injection, implant 6 pellets). The duration of action is 6–8 months.

4. Deoxycorticosterone trimethylacetate (Percorten Pivalate®)—The most practical preparation, 25–75 mg IM once a month.

B. Adrenal Cortex Extract: (Rarely used.) May be administered intramuscularly, subcutaneously, or intravenously in treatment of addisonian crisis. The dosage is 20–100 ml or more daily as indicated.

C. Lipo-Adrenal Cortex, Sterile Solution: (Rarely used.) Administered intramuscularly only. The dosage is 5 ml IM daily during crisis in addition to aqueous adrenal cortical extract; 1–2 ml daily for maintenance.

D. Cortisone (Compound E): See Table 18–18.

E. Hydrocortisone (Compound F): See Table 18–18.

F. Fludrocortisone: See Table 18–18.

G. Prednisone, Prednisolone, and Related Compounds: See Table 18–18.

H. Aldosterone Antagonist: Spironolactone (Aldactone®, 25 mg tablets), for states of excessive aldosterone production and edema.

I. Hydrocortisone Inhibitor: Metyrapone (Metopirone®, 250 mg tablets or 10 ml ampules of metyrapone ditartrate) for testing of pituitary-adrenal function.

CLINICAL USE OF CORTICOTROPIN (ACTH) & THE CORTICOSTEROIDS

Both pituitary adrenocorticotropin (ACTH), acting by adrenal stimulation, and the C-11-oxygenated adrenal steroids (corticosteroids) have been shown to have profound modifying effects on many disease processes. These effects cannot be explained at present on the basis of the known metabolic and immunologic activities of these compounds.

These agents do not appear to "cure." Their action appears to be a modification of cellular activity or permeability so that "toxins" no longer can affect the cell. When the drug is discontinued, the disease may rapidly recur.

No other hormones or combinations of agents that are available commercially today have the same effects as these substances.

In general these agents are interchangeable, but occasionally a patient will be responsive to one and not to another. Both cause varying degrees of pituitary suppression, while the corticosteroids lead to adrenal atrophy after prolonged use as well. They should not be stopped suddenly, and during periods of stress (eg, surgery, trauma) additional amounts of rapidly acting steroids must be provided. Some patients become dependent on corticosteroids, and withdrawal is difficult.

Toxicity & Side Reactions

These agents are potentially very dangerous, but with proper precautions most of these dangers can be avoided. (See below.)

A. Hyperglycemia and glycosuria (diabetogenic effect) is of major significance in the early or potential diabetic.

TABLE 18–19. Systemic vs topical activity of corticosteroids. (Hydrocortisone = 1 in potency.)

	Systemic Activity	Topical Activity
Prednisolone	4–5	1–2
Fluprednisolone	8–10	10
Triamcinolone	5	1
Triamcinolone acetonide	5	40
Dexamethasone	30	10
Betamethasone	30	5–10
Betamethasone valerate		50–150
Methylprednisolone	5	5
Fluocinolone acetonide		40–100
Flurandrenolone acetonide		20–50
Fluorometholone	1–2	40

B. Marked retention of sodium and water, with subsequent edema, increased blood volume, and hypertension is minimized by the use of the newer agents.

C. Negative nitrogen and calcium balance may occur, with loss of body protein and consequent osteoporosis.

D. Potassium loss may lead to hypokalemic alkalosis.

E. Hirsutism and acne are especially disagreeable in females. Amenorrhea may occur.

F. Cushing's features or facies may develop with prolonged administration.

G. Peptic ulcer may be produced or aggravated.

H. Resistance to infectious agents is lowered.

Technics Employed to Correct or Minimize Dangers

(1) Always reduce the dosage as soon as consistent with the clinical response. Intermittent alternate-day use may be a preferable and safer method of treatment.

(2) During the first 2 weeks of therapy, blood pressure and weight should be carefully observed. Take an initial complete blood count and sedimentation rate and repeat as indicated. Determine the urine glucose; if reducing substances are found in the urine, determine fasting blood glucose. Serum potassium, CO_2, and chloride should be checked occasionally if large doses of these hormones are to be given over a period of more than several days. Eosinophil count or measurement of urinary steroid excretion is indicated if any question of lack of adrenal response to corticotropin arises.

(3) All patients should be on high-protein diets (100 gm or more of protein daily) with adequate calcium intake.

(4) If edema develops, place the patient on a low-sodium diet (200–400 mg of sodium daily). Diuretics may be employed when strict sodium restriction is impossible.

(5) Potassium chloride, as enteric-coated tablets or in solution, 3–15 gm daily in divided doses, should be administered if prolonged use or high dosage is employed.

(6) In cases of long-continued administration, anabolic preparations (see p 685) may be used to counteract the negative protein, calcium, and potassium balance. Unfortunately, the distressing osteoporosis cannot be prevented. Sodium fluoride may aid in new bone formation. (See Cass reference, below.)

(7) Do not stop either ACTH or corticosteroids abruptly since sudden withdrawal may cause a severe "rebound" of the disease process or a malignant necrotizing vasculitis. Also remember that cortisone (or hydrocortisone) causes atrophy of the adrenal cortex, probably through endogenous ACTH inhibition; sudden withdrawal may lead to symptoms of Addison's disease.

(8) When treating mild disorders, give corticosteroids during the daytime only since this causes less suppression of endogenous ACTH. When discontinuing therapy, withdraw the evening dose first.

Contraindications & Special Precautions

A. Stress in Patients Receiving Maintenance Corticosteroids: Patients receiving corticosteroids, especially the oral preparation (or even ACTH), must be carefully watched because suppression of endogenous ACTH interferes with the normal response to stressful situations (eg, surgery or infections). Patients should be warned of this danger, and probably should carry identification cards showing what drug they are taking, the dosage, and the reason for taking it. Whenever such a situation occurs or is about to occur, the dosage of cortisone or hydrocortisone should be increased or parenteral corticosteroids given (or both). If oral cortisone or hydrocortisone can be administered, it must be administered in larger doses at least every 6 hours.

B. Heart Disease: These agents should be used with caution in patients with a damaged myocardium. The increase in extracellular fluid may lead to cardiac decompensation. Always begin with small doses and place the patient on a low-sodium diet.

C. Severe Renal Disease: With the exception of nephrosis, these drugs are probably contraindicated or should be used with extreme caution in patients with major renal damage associated with edema or oliguria.

D. Predisposition to Psychosis: These drugs cause a sense of well-being and euphoria in most persons, but in patients who are predisposed to psychosis an acute psychotic reaction may occur. (Insomnia may be the presenting symptom in impending psychosis.) In these cases the drug should be stopped or the dosage reduced, and the patient should be carefully observed and protected. Persons have committed suicide under the influence of these drugs.

E. Effect on Thyroid: When given for prolonged periods, these drugs may depress thyroid function.

F. Effect on Peptic Ulcer: Active peptic ulcer is a contraindication to the use of these drugs because of the danger of perforation or hemorrhage. These agents also tend to activate ulcers, and should be used only in emergency situations or with optimal anti-ulcer therapy in patients who have a history of peptic ulcer. Acute pancreatitis has been reported as well.

G. Tuberculosis: Active or recently healed tuberculosis is a contraindication to the use of these drugs unless intensive antituberculosis therapy is also carried out. A chest x-ray should be taken before and periodically during treatment with corticosteroids.

H. Infectious Diseases: Because these drugs tend to lower resistance and therefore to promote dissemination of infections, they must be used with extreme caution, even when appropriate antibiotics are being given, in any acute or chronic infection.

I. Bleeding Tendency: A bleeding tendency (eg, ecchymoses) has been reported as a side reaction in patients receiving the newer substituted hormones. Thrombosis may occur, especially on sudden withdrawal or too rapid reduction of dosage.

J. Myopathy: A peculiar steroid myopathy has been reported, especially with the substituted steroids.

K. Fatty Liver: Fatty liver and fat embolism may occur.

L. Ocular Contraindications: These agents apparently stimulate the activity of herpes simplex virus and so are contraindicated for local use in herpes simplex keratitis. Local use in the eye is often complicated by fungal infections of the cornea. Cataract formation has been reported in patients with rheumatoid disorders who are receiving corticosteroids. Increased intraocular pressure and pseudotumor cerebri may occur.

M. Diagnostic Errors: Administration of these drugs may interfere with certain immune mechanisms which are of diagnostic value, eg, in skin tests and agglutination tests; they produce leukocytosis and lymphopenia, which may be confusing. The potent substituted corticosteroids (eg, dexamethasone) will suppress the urinary ketosteroids and hydroxycorticosteroid values. The signs and symptoms of infection may be masked by corticosteroid therapy. These drugs may also interfere with normal pain perception (eg, joint pain), which may lead to Charcot-like disintegration of the weight-bearing joints after local or systemic corticosteroid therapy.

Ackerman, G.L., & C.M. Nolan: Adrenocortical responsiveness after alternate-day corticosteroid therapy. New England J Med 278:405–408, 1968.

Amatruda, T.T., Jr., Hurst, M.M., & N.N. D'Esopo: Certain endocrine and metabolic facets of the steroid withdrawal syndrome. J Clin Endocrinol 25:1207–1217, 1965.

Cass, R.M., & others: New bone formation in osteoporosis following treatment with sodium fluoride. Arch Int Med 118:111, 1966.

Jacobsen, M.E.: The rationale of alternate-day corticosteroid therapy. Postgrad Med 49:181, 1971.

London, D.R.: The corticosteroids. Practitioner 100:113–120, 1968.

Martin, M.M., & others: Intermittent steroid therapy. New England J Med 279:274, 1968.

Rabhan, N.B.: Pituitary-adrenal suppression and Cushing's syndrome after intermittent dexamethasone therapy. Ann Int Med 69:1141–1148, 1968.

Thorn, G.W.: Clinical considerations in the use of corticosteroids. New England J Med 274:775–781, 1966.

Treadwell, B.L., & others: Side-effects of long-term treatment with corticosteroids and corticotrophin. Lancet 1:1121–1123, 1964.

ADRENAL MEDULLARY HORMONES

The adrenal medulla contains 2 closely related hormones, epinephrine (about 80%) and norepineph-rine (about 20%). They have different actions, as outlined below.

Since epinephrine may be synthetic or derived from natural sources (usually the latter) and thus contaminated with norepinephrine, the reason for some of the apparently paradoxic physiologic effects of the present preparation becomes clearer.

Epinephrine causes an immediate elevation of blood glucose by inducing glycogenolysis in liver and muscle.

Epinephrine

A. Clinical Uses: Epinephrine is used in a great many clinical conditions, including the following: allergic conditions (eg, bronchial asthma, urticaria, angioneurotic edema); for control of superficial bleeding, especially from mucous membranes; with local anesthetics to slow down absorption; rarely in cardiovascular disorders (eg, Stokes-Adams syndrome, cardiac arrest); and in tests of hepatic glycogen storage.

B. Preparations Available:

1. Epinephrine injection is usually administered subcutaneously but may be given intramuscularly and even intravenously if diluted in 1 liter of solution. The dosage is 0.2–1 ml of 1:1000 solution as indicated.

2. Epinephrine inhalation, 1:100, for inhalation only.

3. Epinephrine in oil injection, 1:500, administered only intramuscularly. The usual dose is 0.2–1 ml.

Levarterenol (Norepinephrine)

A. Clinical Indications: Levarterenol is used almost exclusively for its vasopressor effect in acute hypotensive states (surgical and nonsurgical shock, central vasomotor depression, and hemorrhage; see chapter 1), and in the postoperative management of pheochromocytoma.

B. Preparations Available: Levarterenol bitartrate (Levophed®), 0.2% solution containing 1 mg free base/ml (1:1000) in ampules containing 4 ml.

C. Mode of Administration: Add 4–16 ml of levarterenol (or occasionally more) to 1 liter of any isotonic solution and give intravenously through a Murphy drip bulb. Determine response and then maintain flow at a rate calculated to maintain blood pressure (usual rate, 0.5–1 ml/min). (*Note:* Levarterenol is a very potent drug, and great care must be employed in its use. Do not allow the solution to infiltrate the tissues or slough may result.)

TABLE 18–20. Effects of epinephrine and norepinephrine.

	Blood Vessels	Cardiac Output	Blood Pressure	Blood Glucose
Epinephrine	Vasodilatation (overall) usually	Increased	Elevated (?)	Elevated
Norepinephrine (levarterenol)	Vasoconstriction (overall)*	No effect	Elevated	Elevated 1/8 that of epinephrine

*Vasodilator of coronary arteries.

TABLE 18–21. Characteristics of commercially available insulins.

Type	Appearance	Onset of Action	Duration (Hours)	Buffer	Proteins
Regular crystalline	Clear	Rapid	5–7	None	None
Semi-lente	Turbid	Rapid	12–16	Acetate	None
Globin	Clear	Intermediate	18–24	None	Globin
NPH	Turbid	Intermediate	24–28	Phosphate	Protamine
Lente	Turbid	Intermediate	24–28	Acetate	None
Protamine zinc	Turbid	Prolonged	36+	Phosphate	Protamine
Ultra-lente	Turbid	Prolonged	36+	Acetate	None

D. Levarterenol Antagonist: Give phentolamine (Regitine®), 5 mg IV, for the diagnosis of pheochromocytoma, and larger amounts IM or orally for the preoperative and operative management of pheochromocytoma.

E. Angiotensin Amide (Hypertensin®): This octapeptide apparently plays a role in normal blood pressure regulation. It is a potent vasopressor. It may be of use in some cases which are refractory to levarterenol.

HORMONES & HORMONE-LIKE AGENTS AFFECTING BLOOD SUGAR

1. HYPOGLYCEMIC AGENTS

These preparations are discussed in detail above. Tables 18–21 and 18–22 summarize the available compounds and their average doses.

Insulin Preparations

All preparations are combined with zinc and are available as 40 and 80 units/ml (U40, U80). Regular insulin is also supplied as 100 and 500 units/ml for the treatment of coma and insulin resistance.

While the standard preparations of insulin are made from a mixture of beef and pork insulin, pure beef insulin, labeled "special," and pure pork insulin, labeled "pork," are available. The latter has a lesser tendency to antibody formation, since it is more like human insulin. Beef insulins are used in patients allergic to pork or who avoid pork for religious reasons.

Oral Hypoglycemic Agents

The oral hypoglycemic agents are summarized in Table 18–22.

Tolbutamide (Orinase®) Diagnostic

Available as 1 gm powder in vial with 20 ml diluent for intravenous use in the diagnosis of islet cell adenomas and mild diabetes.

TABLE 18–22. Oral hypoglycemic agents.

	Market Unit (mg)	Usual Times Given Daily	Usual Daily Dose (mg)	Duration of Action (Hours)
Sulfonylurea compounds				
Tolbutamide (Orinase®)	500	2	500–2000	6–12
Chlorpropamide (Diabinese®)	100, 250	1	250–500	Up to 60
Acetohexamide (Dymelor®)	250, 500	1 or 2	250–1500	12–24
Tolazamide (Tolinase®)	100, 250	1 or 2	250–500	12–24
Biguanide compounds				
Phenformin (DBI®)	25	2–4	50–150	4–6
Phenformin, timed disintegration (DBI-TD®)	50*	1 or 2	50–150	8–12

*Capsule. All other preparations are marketed as tablets.

2. HYPERGLYCEMIC AGENTS

Glucagon

Glucagon for injection USP is a crystalline polypeptide extracted from the pancreas. It is available as a lyophilized powder, 1 mg with 1 ml diluting solution or 10 mg with 10 ml diluting solution, for intramuscular or intravenous emergency use in hypoglycemic states (eg, insulin reactions). A preparation of zinc glucagon will become available for the treatment of chronic hypoglycemia.

Diazoxide (Hyperstat®)

Diazoxide, a thiazide compound, has been used successfully in chronic hypoglycemic states. It is still an experimental compound with significant side-effects, including edema, hyperuricemia, and hypertrichosis.

MALE SEX HORMONE
(Testosterone)

Of the many steroid hormones which have been isolated from the testis, the most potent androgen is testosterone. It is believed, therefore, that testosterone is "the male sex hormone." Testosterone is responsible for the development of secondary sex characteristics in the male (ie, facial hair, deep voice, development of penis, prostate, and seminal vesicles). Administration of testosterone to the female causes development of male secondary sex characteristics. In the female, the adverse androgenic effects can only be partially overcome by the simultaneous administration of estrogens.

Perhaps of greater importance than its androgenic effect is the protein anabolic (tissue building) effect of testosterone. Testosterone also has mild sodium-, chloride-, and water-retaining effects. It should be used with caution in children to prevent premature closure of the epiphyses.

Free testosterone and testosterone propionate are not effective when swallowed. The only way to administer these agents effectively is parenterally, by intramuscular injection or as implanted pellets. Testosterone preparations which do not occur naturally, eg, methyltestosterone, are effective when swallowed. Methyltestosterone in humans induces a marked creatinuria and has apparently produced jaundice after prolonged administration; otherwise, however, its metabolic and androgenic effects are similar to those of testosterone and testosterone propionate. Testosterone and testosterone propionate, when injected, are partially (about 30–50%) excreted as 17-ketosteroids in the urine. Methyltestosterone is not excreted as 17-ketosteroid. In fact, its administration will result in diminished urinary 17-ketosteroids due to diminished endogenous testosterone production.

Clinical Indications

Testosterone may be indicated in any debilitating disease or in states of delayed growth and development (in both sexes) for its protein anabolic function. It may be of value in certain refractory anemias. In addition, there are certain uses specific to each sex.

A. Males: Testosterone is used as replacement therapy in failure of endogenous testosterone secretion (eg, eunuchoidism, male climacteric). Its use in impotence, angina pectoris, homosexuality, gynecomastia, and benign prostatic hypertrophy is without benefit.

B. Females: Testosterone is used in women for functional uterine bleeding, endometriosis, dysmenorrhea, premenstrual tension, advanced breast carcinoma, chronic cystic mastitis, and suppression of lactation. The virilizing effects limit the total amount that can be used. While 150–300 mg of testosterone per month are said to be a safe dose, smaller doses may virilize a susceptible patient.

Preparations & Dosages

A. Testosterone (Free): The most common method of administration is in aqueous solution intramuscularly; the dosage is similar to that of testosterone propionate in oil (below). Pellets (rarely used now) may be implanted subcutaneously; the dosage is 4–8 pellets (containing 75 mg each) over 3–4 months.

B. Testosterone Propionate in Oil (Perandren Propionate®, Oreton Propionate®): The dosage is 10–100 mg IM every 2–3 days.

C. Testosterone Cypionate in Oil (Depo-Testosterone®): The duration of action is 2–5 times or more that of testosterone propionate. The dosage is 100–200 mg weekly to 500 mg monthly in a single dose.

D. Testosterone Enanthate in Oil (Delatestryl®): The duration of action is comparable to that of testosterone cypionate. The average dose is 200–400 mg IM every 3–4 weeks.

E. Testosterone Phenylacetate (Perandren Phenylacetate®): This microcrystalline aqueous suspension for intramuscular use has a prolonged action similar to Depo–Testosterone®. It is supplied as 10 ml vials of 50 mg/ml. The average dose is 50–200 mg every 3–5 weeks. It is contraindicated in persons with known sensitivity to procaine.

F. Methyltestosterone (Metandren®, Oreton Methyl®): Available as tablets of 10 and 25 mg or as linguets of 5 and 10 mg. The dosage is 5–25 mg daily. (*Note:* Do not use methyltestosterone in the treatment of thyrotoxicosis, acromegaly and gigantism, or liver disease.)

G. Fluoxymesterone (Halotestin®, Ora-Testryl®, Ultandren®): This drug is a fluoro derivative of methyltestosterone. It is about 2.5 times as potent as the parent drug. Its toxicity is similar to that of methyltestosterone. It has less effect than other preparations on epiphysial closure and is therefore the drug of first choice in children, but it must be used cautiously. The dosage is 2–10 mg orally daily.

H. Anabolic Hormones: Several new drugs have been introduced whose relative protein anabolic effects (vs their androgenic effects) are claimed to be greater than those of the other testosterone preparations listed above. These claims have yet to be fully evaluated. Most of them appear to induce BSP retention, and they may have other as yet unrecognized side-effects.

1. Norethandrolone (Nilevar®) is given in dosages of 30–50 mg daily orally.

2. Stanolone (Neodrol®)—The dosage is 50–150 mg IM once or twice a week.

3. Methandrostenolone (Dianabol®)—This drug has a definite androgenic effect in some women at doses of 10–15 mg/day orally, and may cause BSP retention by the liver after prolonged use. The average dose is 5 mg/day.

4. Nandrolone phenylpropionate (Durabolin®)—The dosage is 25 mg/week or 50–100 mg every 2 weeks IM or subcut. Skin reactions may occur in some patients.

5. Oxymetholone (Anadrol®, Adroyd®)—The dosage is 2.5 mg orally three times daily.

6. Stanozolol (Winstrol®), 1–2 mg three times daily orally.

7. Ethylestrenol (Maxibolin®)—4–8 mg daily as tablets or elixir.

8. Methylandrostenediol (Stenediol®)—Tablets and linguets of 10 and 25 mg or suspension of 25 and 50 mg/ml, 10 ml.

Choice of Preparations

In view of the great number of preparations available, it may be difficult to decide which one to use. The physician should choose those preparations which are most economical to the patient and still are effective. The use of short-acting testosterone preparations by repeated injections should be reserved only for those very few conditions in which the patient must be under close observation (preferably in a hospital) or when the dose must be very exact (ie, research). The preparations of choice when both androgenic and anabolic effects are desired are either methyltestosterone orally or one of the longer-acting testosterones intramuscularly or subcutaneously. If less androgenicity is desirable one of the newer anabolic agents should be considered, although much more experience will be needed before their true effectiveness has been determined.

Caution: Men receiving testosterone should be observed carefully for prostatic cancer. The virilizing effect of testosterone in women and children may become permanent even after withdrawal of testosterone.

Wynn, V.: The anabolic steroids. Practitioner 200:509–518, 1968.

ESTROGENS

Estrogens control proliferation of endometrium, changes in vaginal cells (cornification and lowering of vaginal pH below 4.0), and ductal proliferation of breasts. They stimulate osteoblastic activity and have a slight protein anabolic effect and a moderate calcium-, sodium-, and water-retaining effect. They may also have a cholesterol-lowering effect.

Clinical Indications

Estrogens are useful in both men and women for their effect on osteoblasts in the treatment of osteoporosis. In women, estrogen is used as replacement therapy in cases of ovarian failure (eg, menopause). In men, it is used as an adjunct in the treatment of carcinoma of the prostate.

Preparations & Dosages

Many substances have estrogenic activity, including some nonsteroids (eg, diethylstilbestrol, dienestrol, hexestrol). However, only some of the steroids are useful clinically. There is no evidence that any of the estrogens are less "toxic" than others. Toxicity (eg, nausea and vomiting) is usually due to overdosage. Most of the estrogens exert profound physiologic effects in very small doses, and their therapeutic and toxic dosages are quite similar. The physician should familiarize himself with the use of one or 2 preparations and resist the tendency to try out new ones.

There is little need at present to administer estrogens by any but the oral route; absorption in the gastrointestinal tract seems to be complete, and there is no evidence that nausea and vomiting can be minimized by parenteral administration. There is likewise no evidence that the "naturally-occurring" estrogens are any more effective than the synthetic ones, although they may be better tolerated.

Although estrogens apparently play a role in mammary tumors of animals, there is no evidence that they are carcinogenic in humans. Even so, it is advisable to perform periodic breast examinations and Papanicolaou smears in patients receiving prolonged estrogen therapy. Cyclic administration is always preferable when estrogens must be given over long periods.

A. Nonsteroid Estrogens:

1. Diethylstilbestrol—A synthetic nonsteroid estrogen; an excellent preparation, and the cheapest available. The dosage is 0.5–1 mg daily orally.

2. Hexestrol, dienestrol, benzestrol, chlorotrianisene (TACE®), methallenestril (Vallestril®)—These preparations have no advantage over diethylstilbestrol, and are more expensive.

3. Diethylstilbestrol diphosphate (Stilphostrol®)—For treatment of prostatic carcinoma; well tolerated in large doses. Dosage is 1 tablet (50 mg) 3 times daily to 4 or more tablets 3 times daily, depending on tolerance.

TABLE 18–23. Oral antifertility drugs available in the USA.

Trade Name	mg	Estrogen	mg	Progestogen
Combination products				
Enovid®	0.075	Mestranol	5	Norethynodrel
	0.1	Mestranol	2.5	Norethynodrel (Enovid-E®)
	0.15	Mestranol	9.85	Norethynodrel
Norinyl®	0.05	Mestranol	1	Norethindrone
Noriday®: 21 tablets of Norinyl® 1 plus 7 inert tablets.				
Norinyl 1+80®	0.08	Mestranol	1	Norethindrone
	0.1	Mestranol	2	Norethindrone
Norlestrin® and Norlestrin® 28	0.05	Ethinyl estradiol	1	Norethindrone acetate
	0.05	Ethinyl estradiol	2.5	Norethindrone acetate
Ortho-Novum®	0.05	Mestranol	1	Norethindrone
	0.06	Mestranol	10	Norethindrone
Ortho-Novum 1/50®□21 or 20	0.05	Mestranol	1	Norethindrone
Ortho-Novum 1/80®□21	0.08	Mestranol	1	Norethindrone
	0.1	Mestranol	2	Norethindrone
Demulen®	0.05	Ethinyl estradiol	1	Ethynodiol diacetate
Ovulen® and Ovulen-21®	0.1	Mestranol	1	Ethynodiol diacetate
Ovral®	0.05	Ethinyl estradiol	0.25	D-Norgestrel
Sequential products				
Oracon®	0.1	Ethinyl estradiol	25	Dimethisterone
Ortho-Novum SQ®	0.08	Mestranol	2	Norethindrone
Norquen®	0.08	Mestranol	2	Norethindrone

TABLE 18–24. Endocrine properties of oral progestogens (currently in clinical use in the USA).*

	Progesta-tional	Estrogenic	Androgenic	Anabolic	Anti-estrogenic	Pregnancy Maintenance
Norethynodrel	+	+	0	0	0	0
Norethindrone	+	0	+	+	+	0
Norethindrone acetate	+	0	+	+	n.d.	0
Dimethisterone	+	0	0	0	n.d.	0
Hydroxyprogesterone caproate (Delalutin®)	+	0	0	0	n.d.	+
Medroxyprogesterone acetate (Provera®)	+	0	n.d.	n.d.	+	+
Chlormadinone acetate	+	0	n.d.	n.d.	+	+
Ethynodiol diacetate	+	+	+	0	+	0
Dydrogesterone (Duphaston®, Gynorest®)	+	0	0	0	0	+
Ethisterone	+	0	+	n.d.	n.d.	0

n.d. = No information available.
*Modified after Greenblatt, R.B.: Medical Science, May 1967.

B. Steroidal Estrogens for Oral Use:

1. Ethinyl estradiol (Estinyl®, Feminone®, etc)–An excellent synthetic estrogen. The dosage is 0.02–0.05 mg daily orally.

2. Conjugated estrogenic substances (estrone sulfate) (eg, Premarin®, Amnestrogen®, Menest®, Evex®)–A "natural" estrogen which is well tolerated. The dosage is 0.6–2.5 mg daily orally.

3. Piperazine estrone citrate (Sulestrex®)–Tablets of 1.5 mg. The dose is 0.75–1.5 mg/day.

4. Hormonin®–Hormonin # 1® is a mixture of 0.135 mg estriol, 0.3 mg estradiol, and 0.7 mg estrone per tablet. Hormonin # 2® contains double these amounts. The dosage is 1–2 tablets of # 1 or 1 tablet of # 2.

C. Estrogens for Injection:

1. Estrone (Theelin®)–Little used at present; the conjugated estrogens listed above are preferred. The dosage is 1 mg 2–3 times weekly or 1000 units daily IM.

2. Estradiol valerate in sesame oil (Delestrogen®)–A long-acting estrogen. The dosage is 10–20 mg IM every 2–3 weeks.

3. Estradiol benzoate injection in oil (Progynon® and others)–The dosage is 0.5–1 mg every other day IM.

4. Estradiol dipropionate injection (Ovocyclin® and others)–This preparation has a slightly longer duration of effect than estradiol benzoate. The dosage is 2–5 mg IM 1–2 times weekly.

5. Conjugated estrogenic substances (estrone sulfate), 2.5 mg daily IM. Premarin® IV (20 mg) is a rapid-acting preparation which is given to stop bleeding in menorrhagia.

6. Diethylstilbestrol diphosphate (Stilphostrol®), 5 ml ampule containing 0.25 gm, for intravenous use in prostatic carcinoma.

PROGESTINS
(Gestagens)

Up to the present time progesterone has had a limited use in clinical medicine. Recently a number of new compounds with progestational activity have been introduced. However, these new compounds also have other actions which are summarized below.

Progesterone leads to the secretory phase of endometrium. In the absence of estrogens it does not have any significant effect on the uterus, ie, the uterus must be stimulated (proliferated) by estrogens before progesterone can act. Progesterone also causes acinar proliferation of breasts.

Clinical Indications

A. Menstrual Irregularities: Progesterone may be used with estrogens to maintain more "normal" cyclic menstrual function in women who otherwise do not menstruate.

B. "Medical D & C": Progesterone is used to produce the so-called "medical dilatation and currettage," which is actually a test of adequacy of endogenous estrogen production. If withdrawal bleeding does not occur, it may also indicate that the patient is pregnant. The test may be performed in one of 3 ways.

1. Give 10 mg of progesterone IM daily for 5 days. If menstrual bleeding occurs within 2–5 days after stopping, endogenous estrogen production is adequate.

2. Give 20 mg of norethindrone (Norlutin®) or medroxyprogesterone (Provera®) orally daily for 4–5 days. If menstrual bleeding occurs within 2–3 days, endogenous estrogen production is adequate.

3. Give 250–375 mg of hydroxyprogesterone caproate (Delalutin®) IM once. If menstrual bleeding occurs within 10–16 days, endogenous estrogen production is adequate.

C. Obstetric Use: The progestins are used in large doses in some cases of habitual or threatened abortion, eg, hydroxyprogesterone caproate (Delalutin®), 500 mg/week IM.

D. Use as Contraceptive: Some of the newer agents are being used effectively as contraceptives; they act by preventing ovulation. These drugs consist of progestational agents combined with various estrogens. They are usually given daily beginning on the 5th day after onset of menses and continued for 20 days; then resumed on the 5th day of the cycle, etc. If breakthrough bleeding occurs, the dose may have to be increased. These agents are contraindicated in women with a history of thromboembolism, preexisting genital or breast cancer, liver disease, or cerebrovascular accident.

The principal drugs (and usual dosages) employed for this purpose at present are given in Table 18–23.

The introduction of sequential therapy may provide effective contraception with fewer side-effects. The sequential contraceptives may also provide good estrogen replacement for women near and past the menopause, thus preventing premature osteoporosis, etc.

E. In endometriosis the progestins, at times combined with estrogens, are used continuously in large dosage to induce a state of pseudopregnancy.

F. Precocious Puberty: The progestins have been used recently in children with precocious puberty.

Preparations & Dosages

A. True Progestational Hormones:

1. Progesterone, 5–10 mg daily IM, or 100–200 mg daily orally or IM (for threatened or habitual abortion).

2. Hydroxyprogesterone caproate (Delalutin®), 125–250 mg IM every 2 weeks.

3. Ethisterone, 60–100 mg daily orally.

4. Medroxyprogesterone (Provera®), 10–30 mg/day orally, or 100 mg IM every 2 weeks (for endometriosis only).

B. Hormones With Progestational (and Other) Activity: See Table 18–24.

Side-Effects of Progesterone & Progesterone Plus Estrogen Treatment

Prolonged progesterone plus estrogen therapy may cause abdominal distention, weight gain, nausea, acne, skin pigmentation, masculinization of a female fetus, and decidual casts ("pseudomalignant changes") of the endometrium. Some of these side-effects may be prevented by lower dosage or sequential therapy (see above). Prolonged amenorrhea after stopping these drugs may occur.

The following adverse reactions have been observed in varying incidence in patients receiving oral contraceptives:

Nausea
Vomiting
Gastrointestinal symptoms
Breakthrough bleeding
Spotting
Change in menstrual flow
Amenorrhea
Edema
Chloasma
Breast changes: tenderness, enlargement, secretion
Loss of scalp hair
Change in weight (increase or decrease)
Changes in cervical erosion and cervical secretions
Suppression of lactation when given immediately postpartum
Cholestatic jaundice
Erythema multiforme
Erythema nodosum
Hemorrhagic eruption
Migraine
Rash (allergic)
Itching
Rise in blood pressure in susceptible individuals (see Weinberger reference, below)
Mental depression

The following occurrences have been observed in users of oral contraceptives; a cause and effect relationship has not been established:

Thrombophlebitis
Pulmonary embolism
Neuro-ocular lesions
Carcinogenic potential (see Hertz reference, below)

The following laboratory results may be altered by the use of oral contraceptives:

Bromsulphalein® (BSP) retention and results of other hepatic function tests: increased
Coagulation tests: increase in prothrombin, factors VII, VIII, IX, and X
Thyroid function: increase in protein-bound iodine (PBI), butanol extractable iodine (BEI) and T_4, and decrease in T_3 resin uptake values (radioiodine uptake not affected)
Metyrapone test
Pregnanediol determinations
Glucose tolerance test

Drill, V.: *Oral Contraceptives*. McGraw-Hill, 1966.

Garcia, C.R., & G. Pincus: Clinical considerations of oral hormonal control of human fertility. Clin Obst Gynec 7:844, 1964.

Hertz, R.: Experimental and clinical aspects of the carcinogenic potential of steroid contraceptives. Internat J Fertil 13:273–286, 1968.

Kallman, S.M.: Effects of oral contraceptives. Ann Rev Pharmacol 9:363–378, 1969.

Lauritzen, C.: On endocrine effects of oral contraceptives. Acta endocrinol (Suppl)124:87–100, 1967.

Mestman, J.H., Anderson, G.V., & D.H. Nelson: Adrenal-pituitary responsiveness during therapy with an oral contraceptive. Obst Gynec 31:378–386, 1968.

Salhanick, H.A., & others (editors): *Metabolic Effects of Gonadal Hormones and Contraceptive Steroids*. Plenum Press, 1969.

Weinberger, M.H., & others: Hypertension induced by oral contraceptives containing estrogen and gestagen. Ann Int Med 71:891, 1969.

MISCELLANEOUS OVARIAN HORMONES

Various other hormones of the ovary have been described. Two which have a relaxant effect on the uterus have been prepared for clinical use. They may be identical. The exact place of these drugs in clinical therapy has not yet been established.

Relaxin (Releasin®, Cervilaxin®)

For premature labor or threatened abortion. Dosage varies with indications.

Lututrin (Lutrexin®)

Possibly useful in dysmenorrhea, threatened abortion, and premature labor. Dosage varies with indications.

●   ●   ●

General Bibliography

Albright, F., & E.C. Reifenstein: *The Parathyroid Glands and Metabolic Bone Disease.* Williams & Wilkins, 1948.

Astwood, E.B.: *Clinical Endocrinology I.* Grune & Stratton, 1960.

Astwood, E.B., & C.E. Cassidy (editors): *Clinical Endocrinology II.* Grune & Stratton, 1966.

Bloodworth, J.M.B., Jr (editor): *Endocrine Pathology.* Williams & Wilkins, 1969.

Bondy, P.K. (editor): *Duncan's Diseases of Metabolism,* 6th ed. Saunders, 1969.

Boshell, B.R.: *Treatment of Hypoglycemia.* Modern Treatment. Harper & Row, 1966.

Danowski, T.S. (editor): *Diabetes Mellitus: Diagnosis and Treatment.* American Diabetes Association, 1964.

Danowski, T.S.: *Outline of Endocrine Gland Syndromes,* 2nd ed. Williams & Wilkins, 1968.

Danowski, T.S.: *Clinical Endocrinology,* vols 1—4. Williams & Wilkins, 1962.

Dorfman, R.I., & F. Ungar: *Metabolism of Steroid Hormones.* Academic Press, 1965.

Eisenstein, B. (editor): *The Adrenal Cortex.* Little, Brown, 1967.

Federman, D.D.: *Abnormal Sexual Development.* Saunders, 1967.

Frawley, T.F. (editor): *Treatment of Diabetes Mellitus.* Modern Treatment. Harper & Row, 1965.

Frost, H.M.: *Bone Dynamics in Osteoporosis and Osteomalacia.* Thomas, 1966.

Gaillard, P.J., & others (editors): *The Parathyroid Glands.* Univ of Chicago Press, 1965.

Ganong, W.F., & L. Martini: *Frontiers in Neuroendocrinology.* Oxford, 1969.

Gardiner-Hill, H. (editor): *Modern Trends in Endocrinology.* Appleton-Century-Crofts, 1967.

Gardner, L.I. (editor): *Endocrine and Genetic Diseases of Childhood.* Saunders, 1969.

Gold, J. (editor): *Textbook of Gynecologic Endocrinology.* Hoeber, 1968.

Gordan, G.S. (editor): *Treatment of Calcium Disorders.* Modern Treatment. Harper & Row, 1970.

Greenblatt, R.B. (editor): *Ovulation.* Lippincott, 1966.

Harris, G.W., & B.T. Donovan: *The Pituitary Gland.* 3 vols. Butterworth, 1966.

Harris, W.H., & R.P. Heaney: *Skeletal Renewal and Metabolic Bone Disease.* Little, Brown, 1970.

Hawmi, G.J., & T.S. Danowski (editors): *Diabetes Mellitus: Diagnosis and Treatment.* Vol 2. American Diabetes Association, 1967.

Irvine, W.J. (editor): *Reproductive Endocrinology.* Livingstone, 1970.

Jackson, W.P.U.: *Calcium Metabolism and Bone Disease.* Williams & Wilkins, 1967.

Joslin, E.P., & others: *The Treatment of Diabetes Mellitus,* 9th ed. Lea & Febiger, 1952.

Loraine, J.A., & E.T. Bell: *Fertility and Contraception in the Human Female.* Williams & Wilkins, 1968.

McKusick, V.A.: *Heritable Disorders of Connective Tissue,* 3rd ed. Mosby, 1966.

McLean, F., & M. Urist: *Bone: Fundamentals of the Physiology of Skeletal Tissue,* 3rd ed. Univ of Chicago Press, 1968.

Money, J.: *Sex Errors of the Body.* Johns Hopkins Press, 1968.

Netter, F.H.: *Endocrine System and Selected Metabolic Diseases.* Ciba Collection of Medical Illustrations, vol 4. P.H. Forsham (editor). Ciba, 1965.

Nordin, B.E.C., & D.A. Smith: *Diagnostic Procedures in Disorders of Calcium Metabolism.* Little, Brown, 1965.

Oakley, W.G., Pyke, D.A., & K.W. Taylor: *Clinical Diabetes and Its Biochemical Basis.* Blackwell, 1968.

Odell, W.D., & D.L. Moyer: *Physiology of Reproduction.* Mosby, 1971.

Pincus, G. (editor): *Recent Progress in Hormone Research,* Vols 18—25. Academic, 1962—1968.

Pitt-Rivers, R., & W.R. Trotter (editors): *The Thyroid Gland.* Butterworth, 1964.

Pittman, J.A. (editor): Treatment of thyroid disease. Mod Treat 6:441—549, 1969.

Randall, R.V. (editor): *Treatment of Pituitary Disorders.* Modern Treatment. Harper & Row, 1966.

Richardson, G.S.: *Ovarian Physiology.* Little, Brown, 1968.

Sawin, C.T.: *The Hormones: Endocrine Physiology.* Little, Brown, 1969.

Stanbury, J.B., Wyngaarden, J.B., & D.S. Fredrickson: *The Metabolic Basis of Inherited Disease,* 2nd ed. McGraw-Hill, 1966.

Taylor, S., & G. Foster (editors): *Calcitonin.* Springer, 1970.

Waife, S.O. (editor): *Diabetes Mellitus,* 7th ed. Eli Lilly, 1967.

Walker, N.E.: *Basic Endocrine Pathology.* Year Book, 1971.

Weller, C. (editor): *The New Management of Stable Adult Diabetes.* Thomas, 1969.

Werner, S.C.: *The Thyroid: A Fundamental and Clinical Text,* 3rd ed. Hoeber, 1971.

Wilkins, L.: *The Diagnosis and Treatment of Endocrine Disorders in Childhood and Adolescence,* 3rd ed. Thomas, 1965.

Williams, R.H. (editor): *Textbook of Endocrinology,* 4th ed. Saunders, 1968.

Year Book of Endocrinology (1965—66, 1966—67, 1967—68, 1968—69, 1970—71). Schwartz, T.B. (editor). Year Book, 1966, 1967, 1968, 1969, 1970, 1971.

19 . . .
Nutrition; Nutritional &
Metabolic Disorders

Milton J. Chatton & Phyllis Ullman

Human nutrition in the broad sense involves much more than the traditional concepts derived from the study of nutritional deficiencies. Malnutrition can result from dietary excess or imbalance as well as from deficiency, and may have subtle as well as gross effects. It may be a reflection of biochemical alterations at every level of human nutrition, ranging from variations in the composition of foods through the entire process of ingestion, digestion, absorption, and ultimate utilization by the body at the molecular level. Malnutrition may occur as a result of metabolic requirements which are altered by heredity or disease. Recent data indicate that racial and cultural groups differ greatly not only in their appetite for certain foods but also in their ability to benefit nutritionally from certain foods, notably dairy products.

Normal human nutrition presupposes the availability of nutrients (proteins, carbohydrates, fats, vitamins, and minerals) adequate to meet the qualitative and quantitative metabolic needs of the body under varying conditions such as growth, development, physical activity, pregnancy and lactation, environmental stress, and illness. Optimal conditions of nutrition unfortunately do not prevail for millions of underprivileged people throughout the world. The world food supply, never evenly distributed in human history for reasons of economics, improvidence, drought, pestilence, ignorance, natural disaster, and conflict, is increasingly threatened by environmental contamination and by a dangerously burgeoning population. Nutritional deficiencies due to inadequate food supplies may markedly impair the intellectual and physical development and well-being of countless millions who are spared death by actual starvation.

Even if there were an unlimited food supply throughout the world, there would undoubtedly be nutritional problems in otherwise healthy populations arising from defective production, processing, storage, distribution, preservation, contamination, preparation, and serving of foods.

A well-balanced diet (USA) usually consists of 6 basic categories of foods: (1) breads and cereals, (2) vegetables and fruits, (3) meats, (4) dairy products, (5) fats and oils, and (6) sugars (Table 19–1). This diet may be altered by choice or circumstance yet remain nutritionally adequate if the correct combinations and quantity of natural foodstuffs are ingested. Unfortunately, through poverty, ignorance of food selection and preparation, dietary faddism, and confusion regarding the nutritive value of processed foods (eg, frozen foods, dehydrated foods, breakfast cereals, TV dinners), caloric requirements may be met or exceeded without meeting total nutritional needs.

The criteria for determining the nutritional adequacy of foods, therefore, are subject to reappraisal and challenge. The quantity and quality of proteins, fats, carbohydrates, minerals, and vitamins may vary not only with the class of foodstuff but with the specific type and source of food. Furthermore, the roles of food combinations, processed foods, new or unknown micronutrients, and food-drug combinations are receiving deserved attention.

The "biologic value" of the protein contained in various foods depends upon its essential amino acid content. For example, dairy products and eggs contain all of the amino acids and are of high biologic value; meat, poultry, fish, and potatoes have somewhat less biologic value; and cereals, breads, and most root vegetables have only fair biologic value. Proper combination of foods which have only fair protein value, however, may result in apparently adequate protein nutrition. The ability to metabolize specific amino acids may be altered in certain hereditary disorders of protein metabolism.

Qualitative differences in the type of fat in foods may be of importance in nutrition. Comparison of the relatively high content of saturated fats in coconut oil and hydrogenated or solid vegetable shortenings with the high content of polyunsaturated fats in safflower oil and certain other unsaturated vegetable oils provides an example of qualitative difference in fats which has had a significant application to the dietary prevention and treatment of certain types of hyperlipidemia. Genetic factors play a large role in determining the ability to metabolize fat in several clinical disorders.

Diabetes mellitus is the best known disorder of carbohydrate metabolism in which it is important to control the quantity and quality of dietary carbohydrates. The relationship of sugar to dental caries is reasonably well established. Disaccharide intolerance is a readily treatable form of malabsorption syndrome. Galactosemia and numerous other hereditary disorders of carbohydrate metabolism exist.

It is only a relatively recent concept that there may be a considerable variation in the requirement of vitamins for hereditary and acquired reasons. Both markedly decreased and increased physiologic requirements have been described. Periodically, however,

TABLE 19–1. Basic food groups: The daily food guide.

Food	Nutrients Provided	Recommended Daily Amounts
Breads and cereals, enriched white or whole grain	Carbohydrate Protein Vitamin B complex	Four or more servings. One serving equals: —1 slice bread —1 oz (1 cup) cereal, ready-to-eat, flake, or puffed —1/2 to 3/4 cup cooked cereal —1/2 to 3/4 cup cooked pastes (macaroni, spaghetti, noodles) —5 saltines, 2 Graham crackers
Fruits and vegetables	Carbohydrate Protein Vitamins A, B complex, C Minerals (iron, calcium, phosphorus, potassium, sodium, and trace elements)	Four or more servings, at least one to be citrus or tomato daily and one to be dark green or deep yellow. One serving equals 1/2 cup vegetable or fruit, one medium orange, apple, or potato, or 1/2 cup (4 oz) juice
Meats (beef, lamb, pork, veal, poultry, game, fish) and eggs	Protein Iron Trace elements Vitamin B complex	Two or more servings. One serving equals: —3 oz cooked, lean, boneless meat or fish (1/4 lb raw) —1/4 chicken or 1/2 cup cooked meat —2 eggs —1 cup cooked dry beans or peas —4 tbsp peanut butter —1/2 cup cottage cheese
Milk and dairy products: Cheese, ice cream, and any product made with milk (whole, low-fat, or nonfat)	Protein Calcium Riboflavin Vitamin A	Adults: 1–2 cups (8–16 oz) Teenagers: 4 or more cups Children 9–12: 3 or more cups Children under 9: 2–3 cups Pregnant women: 3 or more cups Lactating women: 4 or more cups One serving equals 1 oz cheese, 1/2 cup cottage cheese, 1/2 cup ice cream
Fats and oils: Butter, margarine, cream, oils, salad dressings, avocado, nuts	Fat Vitamins A, D, E	6–12 tsp or more depending upon caloric requirements. At least 1 tbsp oil or margarine daily. One serving equals 2 tbsp cream, 1/8 avocado, 6 small nuts
Sugars, syrups, honey, jellies, etc	Carbohydrate	As needed for caloric requirements

there have been proposals to utilize the pharmacologic (rather than physiologic) effect of massive doses of vitamins to prevent or treat clinical disorders which are poorly understood or for which no satisfactory treatment is available. There is certainly no objection to performing carefully controlled studies of such hypotheses if it is recognized that large pharmacologic dosages of some vitamins (eg, vitamins A, D, and K) are decidedly toxic to man.

Although the roles of iron, cobalt, iodine, and fluoride are well recognized, the roles of zinc, copper, chromium, selenium, and manganese in human nutrition are poorly understood. Even more obscure are the metabolic functions of cadmium, strontium, nickel, and molybdenum, which have been the subject of nutritional studies in lower animals. Zinc deficiency has been reported to be associated with dwarfism and hypogonadism. Copper deficiency may result in

anemia. Relative or absolute deficiency of chromium may be related to certain forms of maturity-onset diabetes. Unfortunately, it is difficult to establish firm cause and effect relationships of micronutrient deficiency and human disease on the basis of short-term studies.

The interaction of drugs and dietary factors was perhaps first recognized in the case of chronic alcoholism and vitamin B complex deficiency. Hypomagnesemia has been described in the psychiatric syndromes due to alcoholism. Folate deficiency may be caused by chronic use of oral contraceptives and anticonvulsants. The corticosteroids are known to deplete muscle protein, lower glucose tolerance, and induce osteoporosis. Vitamin K deficiency can be caused by oral antibiotics, especially if the diet is inadequate. It should also be mentioned that certain nutrients can either decrease the effectiveness of drugs (eg, pyridoxine reverses the antiparkinsonism effect of levodopa) or can markedly enhance the toxicity (eg, tyramine-containing substances such as cheese, beer, and red wine can induce hypertensive crises in patients receiving monoamine oxidase inhibitors).

Given an abundant supply of nutritionally adequate food available to all, there remain many factors which can result in malnutrition. Examples are given below.

(1) Failure to take the proper quantity and quality of foods to meet individual requirements:
  (a) Psychologic (anorexia nervosa, mental depression, psychosis, individual food eccentricities).
  (b) Psychosocial (dietary fads, "crash diets," reliance on snack foods).
  (c) Cultural (regional or national food habits).
  (d) Educational (ignorance of dietary essentials).
  (e) Inability to obtain, prepare, and serve foods to self (elderly or physically handicapped patients).
  (f) Chronic alcoholism and drug addiction.
  (g) Iatrogenic (protracted use of unbalanced, restrictive, or inadequate therapeutic diets, or use of certain therapeutic drugs).
  (h) Anorexiant drugs (amphetamines).

(2) Inadequate intake of food because of gastrointestinal disorders:
  (a) Anorexia following major surgery, especially gastrointestinal surgery.
  (b) Loss of sense of taste or smell.
  (c) Difficulty or inability to swallow food (neurologic or obstructive lesions).
  (d) Pain on ingestion of food (oral, esophageal, or gastric lesions).
  (e) Chronic nausea and vomiting due to any cause.
  (f) Postgastrectomy dumping syndrome.
  (g) Afferent loop (postgastrectomy) pain or vomiting.

(3) Defective absorption or utilization of food because of gastrointestinal disorders:
  (a) Chronic diarrhea due to any cause.
  (b) Malabsorption syndromes (postgastrectomy; postsurgical short bowel, with loss of mucosal surface and bile salt depletion; hepatic insufficiency, pancreatic insufficiency, tropical and nontropical sprue, lactase deficiency).
  (c) Protein-losing enteropathy.

  (d) Intestinal parasitism.
(4) Increased need for food:
  (a) Increased physical activity (heavy labor or exercise).
  (b) Chronic febrile states.
  (c) Increased metabolism (hyperthyroidism, ACTH overproduction due to physical stress).
  (d) Abnormal excretion (renal impairment).
(5) Impaired metabolism of nutrients:
  (a) Hereditary biochemical disorders ("inborn errors of metabolism").
  (b) Acquired biochemical disorders (liver damage, drugs).
(6) Interaction of drugs and nutrients.

The human diet, therefore, must meet the caloric needs (Table 19–2) and the quantitative and qualitative nutrient requirements of the individual based upon age, weight, physical activity, pregnancy, lactation, and state of health. Special therapeutic diets may be necessary to correct acquired or hereditary nutritional and metabolic abnormalities. In certain instances when patients are unable to take food by mouth, tube feedings or intravenous hyperalimentation may be necessary.

Arena, J.M.: Contamination of the ideal food. Nutr Today 5:2–8, 1970.

Balsley M., Brink, M.F., & E.W. Speckmann: Nutrition in disease and stress. Geriatrics 26:87–93, 1971.

Council on Foods and Nutrition, AMA: Malnutrition and hunger in the United States. JAMA 213:272–275, 1970.

Fox, M.R.S.: The essential trace elements. FDA Papers 5:8–14, 1971.

French, A.B., Cook, H.B., & H.M. Pollard: Nutritional problems after gastrointestinal surgery. M Clin North America 53:1389–1402, 1969.

Harwood, A.: The hot-cold theory of disease: Implications for treatment of Puerto Rican patients. JAMA 216:1153–1158, 1971.

Henkin, R.I.: Idiopathic hypogeusia with dysgeusia, hyposmia and dysosmia: A new syndrome. JAMA 217:434–440, 1971.

Kallen, D.J.: Nutrition and society. JAMA 215:94–100, 1971.

Krumdiek, C.L.: The rural-to-urban malnutrition gradient: A key factor in the pathogenesis of urban slums. JAMA 215:1652–1654, 1971.

McCracken, R.D.: Adult lactose intolerance. Editorial. JAMA 213:2257–2260, 1970.

TABLE 19–2. General approximations for daily adult basal and activity energy needs.

	Men (70 kg) (Calories)	Women (58 kg) (Calories)
Basal energy needs (avg = 1 Cal/kg/hour)	70 × 24 = 1680	58 × 24 = 1390
Activity energy needs		
Very sedentary (plus 20% basal)	1680 + 340 = 2020	1390 + 280 = 1670
Sedentary (plus 30% basal)	1680 + 500 = 2180	1390 + 420 = 1810
Moderately active (plus 40% basal)	1680 + 670 = 2350	1390 + 560 = 1950
Very active (plus 50% basal)	1680 + 840 = 2520	1390 + 700 = 2090

Manier, J.W.: Diet in gastrointestinal disease. M Clin North America 54:1357–1365, 1970.

Mayer, J.: Report from the White House Conference [Nutrition] . Nutr News 33:5–10, 1970.

Sandstead, H.H., & others: Current concepts on trace minerals: Clinical considerations. M Clin North America 54:1355–1613, 1970.

Scrimshaw, N.S.: Synergism of malnutrition and infection: Evidence from field studies in Guatemala. JAMA 212:1685–1691, 1970.

Zee, P., Walters, T., & C. Mitchell: Nutrition and poverty in preschool children. A nutritional survey of preschool children from impoverished black families, Memphis. JAMA 213:739–742, 1970.

THERAPEUTIC DIETS

Special diet therapy should be based upon sound, reasonable, and scientific evidence rather than upon myth, tradition, or propaganda. In no aspect of medical therapeutics is there more bias, emotionalism, and inconclusive evidence than in the use of many of the so-called special diets.

There is little evidence to support the value of many classical or traditional diets (eg, Sippy diet for peptic ulcer, low purine diet for gout, low residue diet for ulcerative colitis). There is nothing to substantiate the extravagant claims made for most of the innumerable special diets proposed for the treatment of obesity, and in many instances these diets are nutritionally inadequate. It is not possible to comment individually on the numerous dietary fads which periodically sweep the USA except to state that they are regrettable.

On the other hand, there is good clinical and experimental evidence to support the use of special diets for many conditions: low sodium diet for congestive heart failure and arterial hypertension, high potassium diet as an adjunct to corticosteroid therapy, gluten elimination diet in nontropical sprue, disaccharide elimination in disaccharidase deficiency, lactose elimination in lactase deficiency, nutritionally well-balanced and low calorie diet for obesity, and the controlled carbohydrate diet for diabetes mellitus. Not quite so clearly advantageous are the fat and carbohydrate restrictions in the prevention or treatment of hyperlipidemia. Allergy to certain foods may be very marked in some individuals, and in such instances special nonallergenic diets may be of great value. In many instances, however, such "allergies" may be more readily related to psychosocial factors.

Potassium Content of Foods

A high intake is recommended when certain diuretic agents are administered.

A. High Content: (300–500 mg or 7.6–12.5 mEq per average serving.) All-Bran, milk of all kinds, yogurt, apricots (fresh and dried), avocados, bananas, dates, melons (casaba and honeydew), oranges (medium to large), peaches (dried), persimmons, raisins, prune juice, cooked chicken, beef, lamb, liver, ham, pork, veal, fish of all kinds, peanuts, pecan halves, artichokes (globe type), cooked dried white or red beans or black-eyed peas, lima beans, beet greens, raw carrots, celery, mushrooms, cooked chard, parsnips, white potatoes, radishes, cooked spinach, sweet potatoes, and raw tomatoes.

B. Medium High Content: (150–300 mg or 3.8–7.6 mEq per average serving.) Fresh and canned peaches, orange juice, canteloupe, nectarines, plums, watermelon, fresh and cooked asparagus, cabbage, cauliflower, greens, corn, eggplant, onions, rutabagas, squash of all kinds, tomato juice, turnips, shellfish, cured meats such as corned and dried beef, sausage and luncheon meats, and desserts containing dried raisins and nuts.

C. Low Content: (50–150 mg or 1.25–3.8 mEq per average serving.) Cooked green and wax beans, beets, peas, broccoli, brussels sprouts, carrots, corn, eggplant, mixed vegetables, onions, green peppers, raw lettuce and salad greens, berries of all kinds, bread of all kinds, rolls, buns, hot breads, cheeses of all kinds, cereals (cooked or dry prepared), eggs, canned soups, candies, desserts, and wines.

D. Little or No Content: (Less than 50 mg or 1.25 mEq per average serving.) Beverages such as coffee, beer, gin, rum, vodka, whisky, tea; hard sugar candies, butter, margarine, oils, and shortenings.

Sodium Content of Foods

A. High Content: (125–1000 mg and over, or 5.4–43.5 mEq per average serving.) Cheese of all kinds, soda and graham crackers, condiments, relishes and sauces (soy, Worcestershire, ketchup, chili, barbecue), pickles, olives, cured and canned meats, fish, poultry, commercially prepared desserts, foods made with baking powder or baking soda, buttermilk, sauerkraut, tomato juice, celery, potato chips, snack foods, pretzels, frozen meals or dinners, canned vegetables, canned soups, prepared cereals, frozen peas and lima beans.

B. Medium High Content: (50–125 mg or 2.2–4.3 mEq per average serving.) Commercial breads, butter, margarine, fresh fish and shellfish, milk, fresh meats, poultry, eggs, fresh vegetables, chocolate candies, ice cream, iced milk, sherbet, angel food cake, sponge cake, artichokes, beet greens, turnips, spinach, celery, carrots, beets, chard, and kale.

C. Low Content: (Less than 50 mg or 2.2 mEq per average serving.) All fruits (fresh, frozen, canned, dried), fruit juices, jellies, jams, syrups, honey, sugar (both white and brown), soybean curd, unsalted nuts, hard sugar candies, coffee, oil, tea, sweet or salt-free butter or margarine, herbs, plain gelatin, most fresh vegetables, puffed rice, puffed wheat, shredded wheat, Sugar Pops®, nonenriched or quick-cooking cereals such as oatmeal, rolled wheat, cracked wheat, farina, cornmeal, grits, rice, Ralston®, Wheatena®, or Wheathearts®.

Low Fat Diet (50–60 gm/day)

Fat and fiber tolerances appear to be very individualized, and no clearcut rationale for any food

TABLE 19–3. Nutrient content of foods.*

Food	Average Serving	Protein (gm)	Fat (gm)	Carbo-hydrate (gm)	Calories
Fruits A (unsugared)					
Apples, apricots, berries, grape-fruit, lemons, limes, melons, or-anges, peaches, pears, pineapple, tangerines	1/2 cup or 4 oz	0	0	12–15	50–75
Fruits B (unsugared)					
Bananas, fresh figs, grapes, plums	1/2 cup	0	0	20	80
Dried fruit (prunes, apricots, peaches, dates)	1/4 cup				
Vegetables A					
Asparagus, broccoli, brussels sprouts, cabbage, cauliflower, celery, cucumber, eggplant, greens (beet, chard, collard, dandelion, kale, mustard, poke, spinach, tur-nip), lettuce, mushrooms, okra, parsley, green pepper, radishes, rhubarb, sauerkraut, stringbeans, wax beans, summer squash, to-matoes, watercress	1/2 cup	1–2	0	3–5	16–20
Vegetables B					
Beets, carrots, artichokes, green peas, onions, pumpkin, rutabagas, turnips, winter or yellow squash	1/2 cup	2	0	7–9	35–45
Breads (enriched white or whole grain)					
Bread, cornbread	1 slice	2	1	12–14	65–73
Muffins, biscuits, dinner rolls, hamburger or frankfurter buns, pancakes	1				
Waffles	1/2				
Cereals					
Cooked	2/3 cup	2	1	14	65
Dry flaked type	2/3 cup				
Dry puffed type	1 cup				
Shredded wheat	1 biscuit				
Crackers					
Soda or Graham	2 squares	2	1	10	55
Melba toast	4 pieces				
Saltines or Ritz®	6				
Ry-Krisp®	2				
Oyster	20 (1/2 cup)				
Starches					
Cooked macaroni, noodles, spa-ghetti, or rice	1/2 cup	3	1	20	100
Corn	1/2 cup or 1 ear	3	1	16–20	85–100
Peas (fresh or frozen)	1/2 cup	4.5		10	58
Potatoes					
Cooked	1 small	3		20	100
Chips	10 (or 1 oz bag)	1	8	10	115
Mashed	1/2 cup	2	4	12	92
Sweet or yams	1/4 cup				
Popcorn (without butter)	1 cup	1		5	25

*From: *Nutritive Value of Foods.* Home & Garden Bulletin No. 72 (revised). US Department of Agriculture, 1970.

TABLE 19–3 (cont'd). Nutrient content of foods.

Food	Average Serving	Protein (gm)	Fat (gm)	Carbohydrate (gm)	Calories
Soup (canned, undiluted)					
Vegetable or cream style (average)	1/2 cup	3	3–5	10–15	70–120
Milk					
Whole (homogenized)	1 cup (8 oz)	8	10	12	170
Low-fat (2%)	1 cup	8	5	12	125
Nonfat, skimmed, or buttermilk	1 cup	8	0	12	80
Evaporated whole	1/2 cup	8	10	12	170
Powdered skimmed, dry	1/4 cup	8	0	12	80
Yogurt, plain, low-fat	1 cup (8 oz)	8	4	13	125
Meat (medium fat, cooked)					
Beef, ham, lamb, pork, veal	1 oz	7	5	0	73
Liver	1 oz	7	0	0	28
Sausage (pork)	1 oz (2 links)	7	15	0	165
Luncheon (cold cuts)	1 oz	7	10	0	120
Frankfurters (8–9/lb)	1	7	10	0	120
Poultry (cooked)					
Chicken, duck, goose, turkey	1 oz	7	2–5	0	50–75
Fish					
Fin type (cooked)	1 oz	7	2–5	0	50–75
Shellfish					
Clams	5 small	7	0	0	28
Lobster	1 small tail	7	0	0	28
Oysters	5 medium	7	0	2	56
Scallops (12/lb)	1 large	7	0	0	28
Shrimp	5 small	7	0	0	28
Eggs	1	6	6	0	78
Cheese					
American, cheddar, Swiss, blue, processed	1 oz	7	9	1	115
Cheese spreads	1 oz	5	6	2	80
Cottage cheese (creamed)	1/2 cup	16	5	3	130
Cream cheese	1 oz	2	10	0	98
Nuts					
Peanuts (shelled, whole)	25 (1 oz)	8	15	6	190
Peanut butter	1 tbsp (1–2 oz)	4	8	3	95
Almonds, cashews, walnuts	1 oz (8–10 nuts)	5	15	6	180
Pecans	1 oz	2	17	3	190
Fats					
Avocado (4 inch diameter)	1/8	0	4	0	36
Bacon (crisp)	1 strip	2	4	0	45
Butter or margarine	1 tsp or 1/8 inch cut (cube)	0	4	0	36
Cooking fats (shortenings)	1 tsp	0	4	0	36
Cream					
Half and half	2 tbsp	2	4	2	52
Sour	2 tbsp	0	4	2	40
Whipped	1 tbsp	0	5	1	50
Whipped topping (with sugar)	2 tbsp	0	2	2	22
Mayonnaise	1 tsp	0	4	0	36
Salad oils	1 tsp	0	4	0	36
Olives (black or green)	3 medium	0	4	0	36

Table 19–4. Food sources of vitamins.*

Vitamin	Recommended Allowances	Food Sources
Vitamin A activity	Adults: 5000 IU/day Pregnant and lactating women: 6000–8000 IU/day	Milk, butter, oils, fortified margarines, carotene precursors, carrots, sweet potatoes, apricots, spinach, leafy green vegetables
Vitamin B_1 (thiamine)	1.2–1.4 mg/day	Enriched white and whole grain breads and cereals, liver, meat, egg yolk, yeast, legumes
Vitamin B_2 (riboflavin)	1.5–1.7 mg/day	Milk, meat, liver, eggs, enriched white and whole grain breads and cereals, yeast
Niacin equivalents	13–18 mg/day	Enriched white and whole grain breads and cereals, liver, meat, bran, yeast
Vitamin B_6 (pyridoxine)	2 mg/day	Bananas, whole grain cereals, chicken, legumes, egg yolk, most dark green leafy vegetables, most fish and shellfish, meats, organ meats, nuts, peanut butter, potatoes, sweet potatoes, prunes, raisins, yeast
Vitamin B_{12} (cyanocobalamin)	5 μg/day	Present in foods of animal origin only: liver, kidney, meats, milk, most cheeses, most fish, shellfish, eggs
Folic acid (folacin)	0.4 mg/day	Green leafy vegetables, yeast, organ meats, liver, kidney
Vitamin C (ascorbic acid)	55–60 mg/day	Citrus fruits, tomatoes, parsley, green pepper, radishes; green leafy raw vegetables; melons
Vitamin D	400 IU/day	Butter, fortified margarines and milk, fish liver oils, salt water fish, liver, egg yolk
Vitamin E activity	25–30 IU/day	Vegetable oils, margarines, salad dressings, whole grain cereals, nuts

*From: *Recommended Dietary Allowances,* 7th ed. National Academy of Sciences, 1968; and *Nutritive Value of Foods.* Home & Garden Bulletin No. 72 (revised). US Department of Agriculture, 1970.

restriction has been verified. However, the following foods may relieve indigestion or flatulence.

A. Protein: Normal amounts of lean meats, fish, and poultry (with all visible fat removed), eggs as tolerated, low fat or nonfat milk, yogurt, buttermilk, cottage cheese and mild cheddar cheeses, fat-free meat stock, bouillon, or broth.

B. Fats: One to 2 tbsp may be tolerated but may be decreased if weight control is desired. Use butter, margarine, mayonnaise, and oils. Avoid cooking any food in fat.

C. Carbohydrates: Enriched or whole grain breads and cereals; fresh, cooked, canned, or juices of all fruits and most vegetables; soft desserts or those made without added fat.

Avoid or limit intake (according to individual tolerances) of cooked or raw brussels sprouts, broccoli, cauliflower, cabbage, onions, turnips, green peppers, lettuce, radishes, dried peas and beans, nuts, fresh melons, raw apples, chocolate, pastries, and any fried food. Spicy, peppery, and highly seasoned foods may cause discomfort.

D. Beverages: Coffee, tea, fruit juices, carbonated beverages, and decaffeinated beverages may be given. Wine, beer, and alcohol are to be avoided.

Note: Foods should be given in 6 or more small feedings throughout the day.

Low Protein Diet (40–50 gm/day)

A. Protein: Two oz meat, fish, or poultry; 1 cup milk; 1 egg or 1 oz cheese.

B. Carbohydrates: Fruits and juices as desired; cooked and raw vegetables as desired. Three servings of breads and cereals. One serving of potatoes, corn, etc. One serving of dessert. Sugar, hard candies, syrup, or honey as desired.

C. Fats: Butter, margarine, oils, and salad dressings as desired.

D. Salt: Restrict as indicated.

Note: Small, frequent feedings are recommended, with juices and fruits for between-meal snacks.

Low Carbohydrate Diet (100–150 gm/day)

A. Protein: Meat, fish, poultry, cheese, or nuts as desired.

B. Carbohydrates: Breads and cereals, not over 3 servings/day. Unsugared fruits and juices, not over 3 servings/day. Vegetables (raw or cooked), 3–6 servings/day. Starches such as potatoes, rice, or corn, 1 serving/day. No desserts containing sugar; artificially sweetened desserts or beverages in moderation.

C. Fats: Butter, margarine, oils, and salad dressings as desired.

Note: It is recommended that a higher protein intake be taken earlier in the day, with small, frequent feedings of cheese, nuts, etc throughout the day.

High Calorie, High Protein, High Vitamin Diet

Increase caloric value to 25–50% above normal. Increase protein to 90–100 gm/day for adults. Select foods high in vitamin content, especially vitamin B

TABLE 19–5. Food sources of minerals.*

Mineral	Recommended Allowances	Food Sources
Calcium	Adults: 0.8 gm/day Pregnant or lactating women: 1.2–1.3 gm/day	Milk (1 gm calcium/quart), milk products, cheeses, leafy green vegetables
Phosphorus	Adults: 0.8 gm/day Pregnant or lactating women: 1.2–1.3 gm/day	Milk, whole grain cereals, cheeses, legumes, eggs, meat, peanut butter, nuts, liver
Iron	Women: 15 mg Men: 10 mg	Liver, meat, legumes, whole or enriched grains, potatoes, egg yolk, green vegetables, dried fruits
Sodium	100–300 mEq/day or 2.5–7 gm/day	Table salt, seafoods, milk, vegetables, prepared foods
Potassium	50–150 mEq/day or 2–6 gm/day	Meats, cereals, vegetables, legumes, fruits (particularly dried), cream of tartar
Copper	1–2 mg/day	Liver, egg yolk, nuts, legumes, bran, oatmeal
Magnesium	350–400 mg/day	Bananas, whole grain cereals, legumes, milk, nuts, most dark green leafy vegetables
Iodine	0.1–0.15 mg/day	Iodized salt, seafoods, vegetables grown in iodine-rich soil
Chlorine	0.5 gm/day	Table salt, seafoods, animal products
Sulfur	Adequate if protein intake is adequate	Protein foods: meats, fish, poultry, eggs, cheeses, milk
Trace minerals (chromium, cobalt, manganese, molybdenum, selenium, zinc)	Minute traces	Leafy green vegetables, whole grains, fruits, legumes, meats, seafoods, organ meats

*From: *Recommended Dietary Allowances,* 7th ed. National Academy of Sciences, 1968; and *Nutritive Value of Foods.* Home & Garden Bulletin No. 72 (revised). US Department of Agriculture, 1970.

complex. Provide foods in small, frequent feedings (6–8 times/day). Add sugars and fats as tolerated.

A. Protein:

1. Milk–Up to 1 quart/day, as beverage or in or on foods.

2. Eggs–One or more, prepared in any way or added to other foods.

3. Cheeses–All kinds, as meat substitutes, added to sauces or dishes, or as between-meal snacks.

4. Meats, fish, poultry–Two to 3 portions/day (2–3 oz/serving), simply prepared by broiling, roasting, or stewing, or with cream or cheese sauces.

B. Fats: Two to 3 tbsp/day of butter, cream, margarine, mayonnaise, or oils.

C. Carbohydrates:

1. Bread and cereals–Four to 8 servings of any kind, but preferably whole grain or enriched white.

2. Fruits and fruit juices–Four to 6 servings (with added sugar) of any kind, fresh, cooked, or canned.

3. Vegetables–

a. Fresh or raw–Small portions 1–2 times/day with mayonnaise or dressings.

b. Cooked–One or 2 portions/day of green, white, red, or yellow vegetables.

4. Starches–One to 2 servings as potatoes, rice, etc, with added sauces, butter, gravies, or cream or cheese sauces.

5. Soups–Cream style or thick soups as desired.

6. Ice cream, sherbet, custard, pudding, plain cake, fruit dessert, gelatin, or cookies–One to 2 (or more) servings. Brown, white, or maple sugars; jellies, honey, syrups, 2–4 tbsp (or more).

7. Beverages–Coffee and tea in moderation; decaffeinated beverages, Postum®, cocoa, eggnog, milk shakes, sweetened carbonated beverages, and fruit juices as desired. Wines and alcohol with discretion. Other milk-containing supplementary foods such as Metrecal®, Meritene®, Nutrament®, or Sustagen® can be used for meals or between-meal snacks.

Bland Diet

A. "Classical" or Traditional:

1. Protein–Adequate amounts of lean meats, fish, poultry, eggs, cottage cheese, and milk.

2. Fats–Moderate amounts of butter, margarine, cream, and cream cheese (to suppress gastric secretion and motility). Polyunsaturated fats (soft margarines) are recommended in place of saturated types.

3. Carbohydrates–Only potatoes (white or sweet) and applesauce allowed during acute phase.

4. Other foods–Restrict gastric secretagogues and irritants such as alcohol and caffeine (coffee, tea, cocoa, and cola beverages). Chili powder, nutmeg, mustard seeds, cloves, and black pepper should be avoided.

B. Liberal:

1. Protein and fat—As in classical bland diet.

2. Carbohydrates—Fruits, vegetables, and those foods that can be properly chewed and mixed with saliva may be added. Puréed or strained foods are recommended only when dentition is poor.

3. Other foods—Continue restriction of black pepper and control of alcohol, coffee, tea, and cocoa intake.

Note: Meals should be frequent and slowly eaten, with size varied according to individual needs and tolerances.

Minimum Residue Diet

Indication: Preoperatively, to clear the operative site of any fecal residue; postoperatively, to reduce irritation.

A. Protein: Ground or tender beef, chicken, fish, lamb, liver, veal, crisp bacon, eggs. Avoid milk, milk products, cheeses of all kinds.

B. Carbohydrate: Soda crackers, French bread, melba toast, refined cereals, rice, strained oatmeal, cornflakes, puffed rice, plain cakes and cookies; macaroni, noodles, spaghetti, gelatin desserts, water ices, strained fruit juices, hard candies, marshmallows, sugar, syrup, honey, carbonated beverages, tomato juice.

C. Fat: Butter, margarine, mayonaise.

D. Other Foods: Beverages such as coffee, tea, Sanka®, Postum®; salt, vinegar, gravies, spices, and herbs in moderation.

Low Residue Diet

A. Protein: Without restriction.

B. Fats: Without restriction.

C. Carbohydrates: Soft vegetables and fruits according to dentition and site of strictures. Omit residue from corn, fruit peel or skin, fibrous vegetables, and whole grain or bran cereals.

Low Carbohydrate, High Protein, High Fat Diet

Diet may be inadequate in calcium and ascorbic acid.

A. Protein: Meats, fish, poultry, eggs, cheese for meals and between-meal snacks.

B. Fat: Increased use of butter, margarine, mayonnaise, oils, whipping cream, sour cream, cream cheese, and peanut butter (if tolerated).

C. Carbohydrate: Unsugared fresh, frozen, or canned fruits (no juices), fresh, frozen, or canned vegetables, breads, cereals, and starches. Desserts made with sugar substitutes.

Disaccharide Intolerance Diet (Low Lactose, Sucrose, Maltose, Galactose)

Indication: Those conditions which have been determined to be due to deficiencies of one or more enzymes such as lactase, invertase or sucrase, maltase and isomaltase, and galactase.

In infants, a nonlactose mixture of amino acids such as Nutramigen®, a protein hydrolysate, or one of the soybean formulas may be given. In adults, omit all forms of milk, cheese, ice cream, frozen desserts containing milk, milk drinks, white breads and crackers, biscuits, muffins, cream soups, creamed dishes, desserts and prepared foods containing milk, some salad dressings, some cold or luncheon meat products, cream substitutes, candies, some health and geriatric products, and some medications which may use lactose as a bulking agent, filler, or excipient.

Sucrase or invertase deficiency requires the omission of granulated sugar (cane or beet), syrups, jellies, molasses, cakes, cookies, puddings and candies, sorghum, pineapple, carrots, apricots, bananas, dates, melons, oranges, and peas. Some medications such as antibiotic syrups may also contain sucrose.

Isomaltase deficiency may occur in conjunction with invertase deficiency. Germinating cereals, malt, and probably wheat and potatoes should be restricted. Sucrose and foods containing sucrose should also be avoided.

A rare disorder, glucose-galactose malabsorption, requires omission of all sources of sucrose, starch, and lactose. Special formulas and diets need to be devised.

Low Gluten Diet

Eliminates gluten-containing foods such as wheat, oats, rye, barley, and buckwheat.

A. Protein: Meats, fish, poultry, eggs, cheese, and milk as desired. Substitutes such as beans, peas, or nuts may be taken as tolerated.

B. Fat: Butter, margarine, oils, salad dressings, and cream as desired or tolerated.

C. Carbohydrate: Fruits, vegetables, and sugars as desired; desserts such as gelatins, iced milk, and sherbet; cakes, cookies, puddings, or pastries made with corn, rice, potato, or soya starches or flours. (Most commercial or prepared mixes contain flours that should be omitted from this diet.) Breads made from wheat starch or special baking mixes such as Paygel®, Resource®, or those made with corn, rice, potato, soya, or lima bean starches or flours. Cereals: rice, corn, cornflakes, Rice Krispies®, corn meal.

D. Other Foods: Condiments, salt, vinegar, spices, and herbs as desired or tolerated.

Low Calcium Diet (500—700 mg calcium, 1000—1200 mg phosphorus)

A. Protein:

1. Meat, fish, or poultry. Only 4 oz cooked per day.

2. Eggs—One per day; egg whites as desired.

3. Milk—1 cup (½ pint)/day; may use diluted whipping cream as milk substitute.

4. Cheese—Cottage cheese, only 2 oz/day.

Avoid organ meats such as brains, heart, liver, kidney, sweetbreads; sardines, fish roe; game such as pheasant, rabbit, deer; cheddar or other cheeses, milk-containing foods.

B. Fat: Whipping cream, butter, margarine, salad dressings, and oils as desired.

C. Carbohydrate:

1. Fruits—3 to 5 servings daily, including citrus.

2. Vegetables, raw—Salads as desired (see Avoid list).

3. Vegetables, cooked—2 or 3 servings (see Avoid list).

4. Starches—Potatoes and corn, 1 or more servings (see Avoid list).

5. Breads, cereals, and pastes—Enriched white breads, rolls, crackers (see Avoid list), nonenriched farina, cornflakes, corn meal, hominy grits, rice, Rice Krispies®, puffed rice, macaroni, spaghetti, noodles.

6. Desserts—Fruit pies, fruit ices, fruit gelatin, puddings made with allowed milk and egg, angel food cake, meringues, shortbreads (see Avoid list), sugar, jellies, honey, sweetened beverages (colas, ginger ale, etc).

Avoid rhubarb, beet greens, chard, collards, mustard greens, spinach, turnip greens, dried beans, peas, lentils, soybeans; whole grain breads, cereals, and crackers; rye bread and all breads made with self-rising flour; oatmeal, brown and wild rice, bran, bran flakes, wheat germ, and any dry cereal not listed above; any milk-containing dessert except as allowed; nuts, peanut butter, chocolate, and cocoa; condiments having a calcium or phosphate base.

Low Purine Diet

Rigid purine restriction does not significantly reduce the level of serum uric acid, and much better control of hyperuricemia is accomplished with medication. It may occasionally be advisable to limit high purine foods such as organ meats, anchovies, sardines, and dried beans and peas, but the normal well-balanced dietary pattern has been found suitable for most patients. Weight control is recommended, and the patient should be placed upon a decreased caloric diet for gradual weight reduction.

High Calcium Diet

Indication: For conditions requiring the intake of over 1 gm calcium per day.

The normal well-balanced diet furnishes 800—1000 mg calcium per day, mostly from milk and cheese. Increasing milk consumption to over 1 quart per day will provide 1150 mg calcium or more. Other foods which will add to the total calcium intake are cheeses, particularly cheddar or American types; leafy green vegetables such as "greens" (dandelion, beet, mustard and turnip, kale), cabbage, broccoli, and brussels sprouts; dried beans and peas, nuts, and milk-containing desserts.

If milk is not well tolerated, calcium gluconate or lactate, 1—2 gm daily, may be used as a supplement.

Low Phosphorus Diet

Indication: When less than 1 gm phosphorus per day is required.

A. Protein:

1. Meats—5—6 oz/day of beef, lamb, veal, pork, rabbit, and poultry. Fish and shellfish are to be avoided, as are cured meats such as ham, bacon, sausage, chipped beef, and organ meats such as liver, brains, kidneys, and sweetbreads.

2. Eggs—Limited to 1 per day.

3. Milk—Limited to 1 cup per day or 3 tbsp powdered. Cheese is allowed in very small amounts.

B. Fat: Butter, margarine, oils, shortenings, and salad dressings.

C. Carbohydrate:

1. Fruits and juices, except as dried fruits.

2. Vegetables (limited to 2 servings daily)—Asparagus, carrots, beets, green beans, squash, lettuce, turnips, tomatoes, celery, peas, onions, cucumber, corn, cabbage, spinach, broccoli, cauliflower, brussels sprouts, artichokes.

3. Desserts—Pie, cookies, cakes, gelatin, angel food cake, sherbet, puddings made with juices or milk allowance, sugars, jellies, and jams as desired.

4. Breads (white only)—French, hard rolls, soda crackers, rusks.

5. Cereals and pastes—Cream of wheat, rice, corn meal, cornflakes, macaroni, spaghetti, noodles.

D. Other Foods: Coffee, tea, Sanka®, Postum®, carbonated sweetened beverages; salt, spices, vinegar, and herbs.

Diets for Glucose Tolerance Tests

A. 100 gm Carbohydrate Breakfast: Orange juice, 6 oz; cooked or dry, prepared cereal, 1 cup; sugar, 2 tsp; milk, ½ cup; bread or toast, 2 slices; margarine or butter, as desired; jelly or honey, 1 tbsp; coffee or tea as desired with 1 tsp sugar.

B. 250 gm Carbohydrate Diet for 5 Days Prior to Test:

1. Morning—Fruit or juice, 1 cup; cereal, 1 cup, or bread, 2 slices; sugar, jelly, or honey, 1 tbsp; milk, ½ cup; egg or bacon, as desired; tea or coffee, as desired.

2. Mid-morning—Sweetened carbonated beverage, 1 (6 oz) bottle, or 1 cup fruit juice.

3. Noon—Sandwich made with bread (2 slices) or 1 bun: hamburger, meat, tuna, eggs, cheese, peanut butter, as desired; condiments as desired; milk, 1 glass; ice cream, 1 scoop, or 1 dish (½ cup) cornstarch pudding; tea or coffee as desired.

4. Mid-afternoon—Sweetened carbonated beverage, 1 (6 oz) bottle, or 1 small candy bar.

5. Evening—Meat, fish, poultry, eggs, or cheese, as desired; potato, rice, corn, beans, or paste, 1 serving or ½ cup; cooked vegetable, 1 or 2 servings; butter or margarine, as desired; salad with dressing, as desired; bread, 1 slice, or 1 biscuit; dessert, 1/6 fruit pie or 1 cupcake or 1 large scoop ice cream or sherbet; tea or coffee, as desired.

Calcium Test Diet (200 mg calcium, 700 mg phosphorus)

Indication: For diagnosis of hypercalciuria, to be followed for 3 days; in treatment of acute hypercalcemia.

A. Morning: Orange or grapefruit juice, ½ cup; cornflakes or Rice Krispies®, 3/4 cup; 5 soda crackers or sourdough French bread, 1–2 slices; butter, 3–4 tsp; bacon, 3 strips; sugar and jelly, as desired; coffee or tea made with distilled water.

B. Noon: Broiled, baked, or boiled beef, lamb, veal, or chicken, 3 oz; potato, boiled or baked, ½ cup, with butter, 1–2 tsp; tomato, raw, canned, or juice, 1 small or ½ cup; 5 soda crackers or 1–2 slices of sourdough French bread; butter, 3 tsp; applesauce, ½ cup; coffee or tea made with distilled water.

C. Evening: Broiled, baked, or boiled beef, lamb, veal, or chicken, 3 oz; rice, cooked, ½ cup; corn, fresh, frozen, or canned, ½ cup; 5 soda crackers or 1–2 slices of sourdough French bread; butter, 5 tsp; sugar and jelly, as desired; applesauce, ½ cup, or banana, 1 small, or 1 peach, fresh or canned; coffee or tea made with distilled water.

D. Between Meals: Distilled water, hard sugar candies, carbonated sweetened beverages.

Avoid all dairy products except butter, including that incorporated in all prepared foods.

TUBE FEEDINGS

There are 2 general types of tube feedings: (1) blended, strained preparations made from common foods, and (2) those with a milk base to which other foods may be added. Commercial preparations are also available.

Tube feedings are employed when the patient is unable or unwilling to take food by mouth. Feedings may be administered through a pliable polyethylene tube passed intranasally. In some circumstances, a gastrostomy is necessary.

The tube feeding should supply the patient's requirements for carbohydrate, protein, fat, electrolytes, and water. It must be fluid enough to pass through the tube without clogging. The feeding should be as close to the osmolarity of blood plasma as possible.

For a person of normal weight, the estimated nutritional need is 15 Calories/lb. However, metabolic response to surgery may necessitate an increase in caloric intake. Protein should make up about 20% of the calories. Carbohydrates (along with electrolytes) give the tube feeding its osmolarity and should be limited to 35–40% of the calories. Fat will provide 30–45% of calories. A suitable concentration is 1 Calorie/ml. A normal adult requires about 2.5 liters of water in 24 hours.

Tube feedings may serve as excellent media for the growth of bacteria and must be refrigerated and not held over 24 hours. To prevent the tube from clogging, each feeding should be followed with a small quantity of water. Measured volumes (150–200 ml) can be given every 2–4 hours.

Caution: (1) Begin with more dilute material and administer slowly. (2) The best rate is usually 3 liters per 24 hours. (3) Most patients tolerate feedings best when not over 200 ml are given at a time. (4) If foods must be given rapidly, warm to body temperature. (5) If gastric distention is suspected, aspirate with a gastric tube. (6) Use with care in comatose patients to prevent aspiration. (7) If diarrhea occurs, the addition of ½ oz fluid pectin (Certo®) to 1 quart of feeding may be beneficial.

Blenderized (Blended) Tube Feeding Formula

The following formula supplies 1 Calorie/ml in a volume of 2500 ml. The nutrient contents are as follows: Protein, 20% or 123 gm; fat, 45% or 123 gm; carbohydrate, 35% or 226 gm; calcium, 1312 mg; phosphorus, 1518 mg; iron, 24 mg; vitamin A, 7582 IU; thiamine, 2.675 mg; riboflavin, 3.746 mg; niacin, 27.91 mg; ascorbic acid, 163 mg; sodium, 2557 mg; potassium, 4159 mg.

Strained oatmeal	10 gm
Dextri-Maltose®	50 gm
Instant nonfat dry milk	50 gm
Strained liver	20 gm
Strained beef	568 gm
Strained applesauce	402 gm
Strained green beans	484 gm
Oil	85 ml
Orange juice	200 ml
Milk, homogenized	300 ml
Water	500 ml

Milk Base Tube Feeding Formula

The following formula supplies 1.4 Calorie/ml in a volume of 1500 ml. The nutrient contents are as follows: Protein, 100 gm; fat, 110 gm; carbohydrate, 190 gm; sodium, 3565 mg; potassium, 3900 mg. *Note:* This formula is inadequate in iron.

Homogenized milk	800 ml
Half and half	600 ml
Eggnog powder	100 gm
Instant nonfat dry milk	90 gm
Salt	5.5 gm
*Vitamin preparation	5 ml
Water to 1500 ml	

It has been recommended that pasteurized powdered egg or eggnog powder be substituted for raw egg because of the possibility of salmonella infection. One tbsp (15 gm) powdered egg is equivalent to one egg. Various eggnog powders are available commercially.

INTRAVENOUS HYPERALIMENTATION

When it is not possible to provide adequate nourishment by the normal alimentary route, it may now be possible to meet nutritional needs for extended

*Vitamin supplement contains 2 mg thiamine, 3 mg riboflavin, 30 mg niacin, and 100 mg ascorbic acid.

periods exclusively by intravenous alimentation. This has proved to be effective and even lifesaving in patients with conditions such as severe alimentary disturbances (eg, inflammatory intestinal disease, massive resection, pancreatic and enterocutaneous fistulas), extensive trauma or burns, or overwhelming infections.

The basic nutrient solution for the average adult consists of 20–25% dextrose, 5% fibrin hydrolysate, 40–50 mEq sodium chloride, 30–40 mEq potassium chloride, and 4–5 mEq magnesium sulfate. Vitamin requirements are added to the solution daily. When intravenous feedings are prolonged for more than 1 month, trace elements may be required.

With careful skin preparation and sterile technic, a catheter is introduced via a subclavian vein and the nutrient solution may be infused into the superior vena cava for long periods if necessary. Patients can be maintained in positive nitrogen balance, with weight gain and clinical improvement over periods up to several months, tiding them over until such time as definitive treatment of the primary medical or surgical problem can be carried out. Clinical application of this new method of nutrition will probably be expanded into practically every medical specialty.

Dudrick, S.J., & J.E. Rhoads: New horizons in intravenous feeding. JAMA 215:939–949, 1971.

Dudrick, S.J., Long, J.M., & E. Steiger: Intravenous hyperalimentation. M Clin North America 54:577–589, 1970.

VITAMINS & VITAMIN DISORDERS

In illness there may be considerable variation in the body's requirements for vitamins, depending upon age, activity, diet, metabolic rate, and other factors affecting vitamin absorption, utilization, and excretion. Vitamin deficiencies are almost always multiple, although a particular symptom complex may predominate.

Early signs of vitamin deficiency are usually nonspecific, vague, and mild and are easily misinterpreted or missed entirely.

The "crude" sources containing multiple vitamins are often more effective in therapy than the pure or synthetic preparations; as a rule, only during the more severe phases and in instances of "specific" deficiencies is it necessary to use "pure" vitamins. The use of a "pure" vitamin in the face of a true multiple vitamin deficiency may aggravate rather than alleviate the condition. The treatment of vitamin deficiencies consists of giving an adequate, balanced, high-protein, high-vitamin diet with vitamin supplementation as indicated. In general, it is wise to use vitamins therapeutically in 5–10 times the amounts required for daily maintenance.

Vitamin dependencies, which are of hereditary origin, should be distinguished from the acquired vitamin deficiencies. Almost a dozen vitamin-dependent genetic diseases, involving 6 different vitamins (thiamine, nicotinamide, pyridoxine, vitamin B_{12}, and vitamin D) have been described. The vitamin dependencies do not respond to physiologic replacement therapy but only to large, pharmacologic doses of the needed vitamin. At the other extreme, in the case of at least one vitamin (vitamin D), patients may react adversely to doses below the recommended prophylactic requirement.

Large doses of some vitamins are toxic and may cause illness, particularly when continued for long periods.

Graham, G.G. (editor): Johns Hopkins conjoint clinic on vitamins. J Chronic Dis 19:1067–1081, 1966.

Rosenberg, L.E.: Vitamin-dependent genetic disease. Hospital Pract 5:59–66, 1970.

FAT-SOLUBLE VITAMINS

1. VITAMIN A

Vitamin A is an alcohol of high molecular weight which is stored in the liver. Much of it is derived from conversion of beta-carotene in foods to vitamin A, mainly by the mucosa of the small intestine. It is necessary for normal function and structure of all epithelial cells and for the synthesis of visual purple in the retinal rods (hence for vision in dim light). Carotene only is present in leafy green and yellow fruits and vegetables; vitamin A and, at times, carotene are present in whole milk, butter, eggs, fish, and liver oil. The recommended daily allowances for adults are 5000 IU (or USP units); during pregnancy and lactation, 6000–8000 IU.

Hypovitaminosis A

A. Clinical Findings: Mild or early manifestations consist of dryness of the skin, night blindness, and follicular hyperkeratosis. Severe or late manifestations are xerophthalmia, atrophy and keratinization of the skin, and keratomalacia.

B. Tests for Deficiency: Dark adaptation is impaired. A low serum value (below 20 μg/100 ml) of vitamin A may be helpful but is not diagnostic. A therapeutic test with 25,000–75,000 IU daily for 4 weeks may be helpful.

C. Treatment: Give oleovitamin A, 15–25 thousand units once or twice daily. If an absorption defect is present, it may be necessary to administer bile salts with the vitamin A or to give the same dosage in oil intramuscularly (50,000 units/ml in sesame oil). Skin lesions or profound malnutrition (eg, kwashiorkor) may require more treatment.

Hypervitaminosis A

This disorder is rare in adults. It may occur in children as a result of excessive ingestion of vitamin A preparations. The minimal toxic adult dose is about 75–100 thousand units daily for 6 months.

A. Clinical Findings: Anorexia, loss of weight, hair loss, hyperostosis and periosteal elevation of bone, hepatomegaly, splenomegaly, anemia, skin rash, and CNS manifestations.

B. Tests of Excess: Serum levels of vitamin A over 400 μg/100 ml are found.

C. Treatment: Withdraw the medicinal source.

Pereira, S.M., & others: Vitamin A therapy in children with kwashiorkor. Am J Clin Nutr 20:297–304, 1967.

Roels, O.A.: Vitamin A physiology. JAMA 214:1097–1102, 1970.

2. VITAMIN D

The vitamins D are sterols formed by ultraviolet irradiation of plant sterol precursors. This irradiation usually takes place in the skin of man. They cause increased calcium absorption from the intestine, mobilization of bone, and urinary phosphorus excretion. They are present in fish livers; their precursors are widely distributed in plants. The daily allowances for adults are not known. For children and for some women during pregnancy and lactation, 400 units are recommended.

There is a complete spectrum of varying responsiveness to vitamin D. Some patients may require more than 50 times the therapeutic dose to correct manifestations of vitamin deficiency (eg, vitamin D resistant rickets), whereas other patients are hyperreactive to doses below the recommended requirement. The latter may be due to a genetic trait or to disorders associated with hypercalcemia or hyperphosphatemia.

Hypovitaminosis D

Hypovitaminosis D is usually due to inadequate dietary intake, lack of sunlight, or an absorption defect (eg, pancreatitis, sprue).

A. Clinical Findings: Deficiency of vitamin D leads to osteomalacia in children (rickets). Some cases of adult osteomalacia appear to be associated with increased requirements of vitamin D.

B. Tests for Deficiency: Serum calcium and phosphorus may be normal or decreased and serum alkaline phosphatase is generally increased. The urinary calcium is usually low.

C. Treatment: See Osteomalacia.

Hypervitaminosis D

This disorder is usually caused by prolonged ingestion of 5–150 thousand units daily.

A. Clinical Findings: The manifestations of hypercalcemia are present and may progress to renal damage and metastatic calcification.

B. Tests of Excess: Serum calcium elevation (over 11.5 mg/100 ml) occurs if large doses of vitamin D are taken. (Always consider other causes of hypercalcemia.)

C. Treatment: Withdraw the medicinal source. Complete recovery will occur if overtreatment is discontinued in time. Corticosteroids or sodium phytate (Rencal®) reverses hypercalciuria due to vitamin D intoxication.

Arnstein, A.R., Frame, B., & H.M. Frost: Recent progress in osteomalacia and rickets. Ann Int Med 67:1296–1330, 1967.

De Luca, H.F.: Current concepts: Vitamin D. New England J Med 281:1103–1104, 1969.

Seelig, M.S.: Hyper-reactivity to vitamin D. Med Counterpoint 2:28–49, 1970.

3. VITAMIN K

The vitamins K are chemical compounds which are necessary for prothrombin synthesis by the liver and so are important in the blood coagulation mechanism. They are widely distributed in green leaves of plants, egg yolk, and soybeans. They are also synthesized by microorganisms in the intestines. The daily allowances are not known.

Hypovitaminosis K

Hypovitaminosis K may result from liver disease which interferes with synthesis of prothrombin, inadequate bile supply with poor absorption, or ingestion of drugs which depress prothrombin synthesis (eg, coumarins, salicylates).

A. Clinical Findings: Bleeding.

B. Tests for Deficiency: Prolonged prothrombin time.

C. Treatment: See Liver Disease, Bishydroxycoumarin Poisoning, and Hemorrhagic Disease of the Newborn.

Hypervitaminosis K

Large doses of water-soluble vitamin K to infants, particularly premature infants, may cause hemolytic anemia, hyperbilirubinemia, hepatomegaly, and even death.

Goldsmith, G.A.: Diet advice to the healthy patient. M Clin North America 48:1124, 1964.

4. VITAMIN E
(Tocopherol)

Vitamin E is a natural antioxidant which plays a role in the normal physiology of animals and possibly also of man, although its exact role in man is unknown. It is relatively nontoxic. Anemia allegedly due to vitamin E deficiency has been reported in children, especially premature infants being given certain commercial formulas. Recommended daily allowances for adults are 30 IU for males and 25 IU for females, with 30 IU during pregnancy and lactation.

Richie, J.H., & others: Edema and hemolytic anemia in premature infants: Vitamin E deficiency. New England J Med 279:1185–1190, 1968.

Roels, O.A.: Present knowledge of vitamin E. Nutr Rev 25:33–37, 1967.

WATER-SOLUBLE VITAMINS: VITAMIN B COMPLEX

The members of the vitamin B complex are intimately associated in occurrences as well as in function. As a result of this close interrelationship, it is doubtful that a deficiency of a single B vitamin ever exists except under experimental conditions. Deficiency of a single member of the B complex would probably lead to impaired metabolism of the others. Hence, although certain clinical features may predominate in the absence of a single member of the complex, this does not mean that the deficiency can be entirely corrected by replacing that factor alone. Therefore, "specific therapy" always consists of providing adequate dietary or parenteral sources of all members of the B complex.

1. VITAMIN B₁
(Thiamine Hydrochloride)

Vitamin B_1 is the coenzyme for decarboxylation of alpha-keto acids (eg, pyruvic and alpha-ketoglutaric acid). It is important, therefore, for normal carbohydrate oxidation. Dietary sources are liver, lean pork, kidney, and whole grain cereals. Steaming or exposure to moist heat reduces the thiamine content of foods. The daily dietary allowances are about 0.5 mg/1000 Calories (average, 1–1.7 mg/day).

Hypovitaminosis B_1 (Beriberi)
Hypovitaminosis B_1 results from an inadequate intake due usually to idiosyncrasies of diet or excessive cooking or processing of foods. The increased need for vitamin B_1 during fever, high carbohydrate intake, alcoholism, or thyrotoxicosis may lead to a deficiency.
A. Clinical Findings: Mild or early manifestations consist of vague multiple complaints suggestive of neurasthenia, and include anorexia, formication and muscle cramps, calf tenderness, paresthesias, and hyperactivity followed later by hypoactivity of knee and ankle jerks.
Severe or late manifestations (beriberi) are anorexia, polyneuritis, serous effusions, subcutaneous edema, paralyses (particularly in the extremities), and cardiac insufficiency manifested by tachycardia, dyspnea, edema, and normal or decreased circulation time, elevated venous pressure, and nonspecific ECG changes.

A particularly virulent form of beriberi heart disease, probably associated with metabolic acidosis, is referred to as Shoshin beriberi in the Orient.
B. Treatment: Give thiamine hydrochloride, 20–50 mg orally, IV, or IM daily in divided doses for 2 weeks, and then 10 mg daily orally. An alternative is to give dried yeast tablets (brewer's yeast), 30 gm 3 times daily. A well balanced diet of 2500–4500 Calories/day should be given when tolerated.

Jeffrey, F.E., & W.H. Abelman: Recovery from proved Shoshin beriberi. Am J Med 50:123–128, 1971.

Tomasulo, P.A., Kater, R.M.H., & F.L. Iber: Impairment of thiamine absorption in alcoholism. Am J Clin Nutr 21:1341–1344, 1968.

Wuest, H.M. (editor): Unsolved problems of thiamine. Ann New York Acad Sc 98:385–613, 1962.

2. VITAMIN B₂
(Riboflavin)

Riboflavin serves as coenzyme for hydrogen transfer. It is present in milk and milk products, leafy green vegetables, and liver. The daily dietary allowances for adults are 1.5–1.7 mg; in pregnancy and lactation, 1.8–2 mg.

Hypovitaminosis B_2 (Ariboflavinosis)
The etiologic factors in ariboflavinosis are similar to those of thiamine deficiency, but inadequate intake of milk is important. The manifestations of deficiency are highly variable and usually occur along with those of thiamine and niacin deficiency, but may occur earlier.
A. Clinical Findings: Mild or early manifestations are oral pallor, superficial fissuring at the angles of the mouth, conjunctivitis and photophobia, lack of vigor, malaise, weakness, and weight loss. Severe or late manifestations consist of cheilosis (fissuring at the angles of the mouth), fissuring of the nares, magenta tongue, moderate edema, anemia, dysphagia, corneal vascularization and circumcorneal injection, and seborrheic dermatitis.
B. Treatment: Give riboflavin, 40–50 mg IV, IM, or orally daily until all symptoms have cleared. An alternative is to give dried yeast tablets (brewer's yeast), 30 gm 3 times daily. A well balanced diet consisting of 2500–4500 Calories/day should be given when tolerated.

Horwitt, M.K.: Nutritional requirements of man, with special reference to riboflavin. Am J Clin Nutr 18:458–466, 1966.

Rivlin, R.S.: Riboflavin metabolism. New England J Med 283:463–472, 1970.

3. NICOTINIC ACID (Niacin) & NICOTINAMIDE (Niacinamide)

Niacin and niacinamide function in important enzyme systems concerned with reversible oxidation and reduction. They are present in liver, yeast, meat, whole-grain cereals, and peanuts. Nicotinic acid may be synthesized in the body from tryptophan. Therefore, a high-protein diet virtually assures adequate nicotinic acid. Sixty mg of tryptophan are needed to substitute for 1 mg of nicotinic acid.

The daily allowances for adults are 10–18 mg; for adolescents, 15–20 mg. Niacin may be used therapeutically as a vasodilating agent for headaches, myalgias, neurologic disorders, and edema of the labyrinth (100 mg or more daily in divided doses). Niacinamide does not possess this vasodilating effect.

Pellagra

The etiologic factors in deficiency of these components of the B complex are similar to those of thiamine deficiency. Niacin deficiency is the principal but not the only dietary defect in pellagra; low tryptophan content of some foods also plays a role.

A. Clinical Findings: Mild or early manifestations consist of multiple vague complaints, a reddened, roughened skin, and redness and hypertrophy of the papillae of the tongue. Severe or late manifestations are marked roughening of the skin when exposed to light and friction, diarrhea, abdominal distention, scarlet red tongue with atrophy of papillae, stomatitis, depression, mental dullness, rigidity, and peculiar sucking reactions.

B. Treatment: Give nicotinamide (niacinamide), 50–500 mg IV, IM, or orally daily until symptoms subside. Nicotinic acid (niacin) is less often used because of its vasodilating effect; the dosage is similar. Give therapeutic doses of thiamine, riboflavin, and pyridoxine also. An alternative is to give dried yeast tablets (brewer's yeast), 30 gm 3 times daily.

A well balanced diet consisting of 2500–4500 Calories/day and ample proteins should be given when tolerated. Dementia may require constant supervision.

Nicotinic Acid Poisoning

Large oral doses of nicotinic acid may cause flushing and burning of the skin and dizziness, but are usually not harmful. After intravenous administration hypotension may be severe. Anaphylaxis occurs rarely.

Prinsloo, J.G., & others: Protein nutrition status in childhood pellagra: Evaluation of nicotinic acid status and creatinine excretion. Am J Clin Nutr 21:98–106, 1968.

Stokstad, E.L.R.: The biochemistry of the water soluble vitamins. Ann Rev Biochem 31:451–490, 1962.

WATER-SOLUBLE VITAMINS: VITAMIN C (Ascorbic Acid)

Vitamin C is concerned with the formation and maintenance of intercellular supporting structures (dentine, cartilage, collagen, bone matrix). Its biochemical action is not known. Dietary sources include citrus fruits, tomatoes, paprika, bell peppers, and all leafy green vegetables. The ascorbic acid content of foods is markedly decreased by cooking, mincing, air contact, alkalies, and contact with copper utensils. The US recommended allowances for adults are 55–60 mg daily.

Ascorbic acid has been used in the treatment of certain poisonings in doses of 0.5 gm or more, but proof of its value is lacking. It is used in dosages up to 200 mg daily orally to promote healing of wounds or ulcers or during recovery from protracted disease (eg, tuberculosis). Pharmacologic megadosages have been recently recommended for the prevention of the common cold. Only well controlled clinical studies on large population groups can help clear the confusion that has been created by the therapeutic claims.

Hypovitaminosis C (Scurvy)

Scurvy is usually due to inadequate intake of vitamin C, but may occur with increased metabolic needs.

A. Clinical Findings: Mild or early manifestations are edema and hemorrhage of the gingivae, porosity of dentine, and hyperkeratotic hair follicles. Severe or late manifestations consist of severe muscle changes, swelling of the joints, rarefaction of bone, a marked bleeding tendency, extravasation of blood into fascial layers, anemia, loosening or loss of the teeth, and poor wound healing.

B. Tests for Deficiency: Capillary resistance is reduced, and x-rays of the long bones may show typical changes. Epiphyseal changes in children are pathognomonic. There is also a lowering of serum or white cell ascorbic acid levels.

C. Treatment: Give sodium ascorbate injection, 100–500 mg IM, or ascorbic acid, 100–500 mg orally daily, as long as deficiency persists.

King, C.G.: Present knowledge of ascorbic acid. Nutr Rev 26:33–35, 1968.

OTHER VITAMINS

Many other vitamins have been described. Some are important in human nutrition and disease; most play an unknown role.

Pyridoxine Hydrochloride

Pyridoxine may be important in transamination and decarboxylation of proteins. Recommended daily allowance for adults is about 2 mg/day. It may relieve nervous symptoms and weakness in pellagrins when niacin fails and may relieve glossitis and cheilosis when riboflavin fails. Its role (if any) in human atherosclerosis is uncertain. The therapeutic dosage is 10–50 mg IV or IM daily with other factors of the B complex.

Johansson, S., & others: Studies on the metabolism of labelled pyridoxine in man. Am J Clin Nutr 18:185–196, 1966.

Folic Acid

Folic acid seems to be essential for the metabolism of cell nuclear materials. It is effective in the treatment of certain macrocytic anemias. Recommended daily allowance for adults is 0.4 mg daily. In pregnancy this is increased to 0.8 mg and in lactation to 0.5 mg.

Body reserves of folate may be rapidly depleted in chronic alcoholism. Folate deficiency has been described in patients taking oral contraceptives and anticonvulsant drugs.

Eichner, E.R., Pierce, H.I., & R.S. Hillman: Folate balance in dietary induced megaloblastic anemia. New England J Med 284:933–938, 1971.
Herbert, V.: Nutritional requirements for vitamin B_{12} and folic acid. Am J Clin Nutr 21:743–752, 1968.
Streiff, R.R.: Folate deficiency and oral contraceptives. JAMA 214:105–108, 1970.

Cyanocobalamin (Vitamin B_{12})

Vitamin B_{12} is a phosphorus- and cobalt-containing material isolated from purified liver extract; it is the effective principle (extrinsic factor) which is lacking in pernicious anemia. Recommended daily allowance for adults is 5–6 μg/day.

Chanarin, I.: Pernicious anemia and other vitamin B_{12} deficiency states. Abstr World Med 44:73–85, 1970.
Herbert, V., & others: Symposium on vitamin B_{12} and folate. Am J Med 48:539–617, 1970.

•   •   •

OBESITY

Obesity is a complex disorder which may be defined as an increase in weight of over 10% above "normal," due to generalized deposition of fat in the body. "Normal" weight is difficult to determine; clinically, however, the standard age, height, and weight tables are ordinarily used for practical purposes, although they are not always reliable. Body build, musculature, familial tendencies, and socioeconomic factors must be taken into consideration. Social factors have a marked influence on the prevalence of obesity, and situational determinants have a great effect on the eating habits of obese persons. The measurement of skinfold thickness (triceps fat fold) has been reported to be a reliable method identifying obesity among individuals in the medium range of body size.

From a metabolic point of view, all obesity has a common cause: intake of more calories than are required for energy metabolism. The reasons for differences in the food intake energy utilizations of various individuals, which make it possible for one person to utilize his calories more "efficiently" than another, are not always known. Many clinicians feel that the metabolic changes in obesity are a result of obesity rather than a cause of it. Obese patients have been found to have an increased number of fat cells as well as increased size of fat cells. Weight reduction in obese patients may decrease the size of fat cells, but the total number remains constant.

Although most cases of obesity are due to simple overeating resulting from emotional, familial, metabolic, and genetic factors, a few endocrine and metabolic disorders lead to specific types of obesity (eg, Cushing's syndrome and hypothalamic lesions). Compulsive overeating is similar in some respects to the addiction to tobacco or alcohol. It is particularly difficult to explain the phenomena of fluid retention and fat mobilization and storage.

Hypothyroidism is rarely associated with obesity.

The association of obesity with increased morbidity and mortality is well known. Hypertension, diabetes mellitus, gallbladder disease, gout, and possibly coronary atherosclerosis are frequently associated with obesity. Obesity presents special hazards in pregnancy and in surgical patients. The psychologic and cosmetic implications of obesity are also significant factors. An extreme manifestation of massive obesity is the cardiopulmonary failure described as the Pickwickian syndrome.

Treatment

"Specific" weight-reducing chemical agents and hormones, singly or in combination, are either ineffective or hazardous and have no place in the treatment of obesity. Juvenile onset obesity is often very difficult to treat, possibly due to some ill-defined metabolic disorder, and it is important to institute a therapeutic program as early as possible.

A. Diet: Diet is the most important factor in the management of obesity. Diets which claim to offer easy weight reduction by reliance on certain "special" foods or unusual combinations of foods are not only invalid but may actually be harmful. There are a number of points to consider:

1. Calories—In order to lose weight it is necessary to decrease the intake to below the caloric requirements of the individual. One can determine a very approximate average daily weight loss with a given diet by the following formula:

$$\frac{\text{Approximate Daily Caloric Requirements} - \text{Number of Calories in Diet}}{3500}$$

$$= \text{Weight Loss in lb/Day}$$

The number of calories per day to prescribe for a patient varies with age, occupation, temperament, and

TABLE 19–6. Low-calorie diets: Foods to be distributed into regular meals during the day.*

	800 Calories	1000 Calories	1200 Calories	1500 Calories
Breads, enriched white or whole grain†	1/2 slice	1 slice	2 slices	3 slices
Fruit, unsugared (1/2 cup)	3 servings	3 servings	3 servings	3 servings
Eggs, any way but fried	One	One	One	One
Fats and oils, butter, margarine, may-onnaise, or oil	None	3 tsp	5 tsp	6 tsp
Milk (nonfat, skimmed, or buttermilk)	2 cups	2 cups	2 cups	2 cups
Meat, fish, or poultry, any way but fried‡	4 oz	5 oz	6 oz	6 oz
Vegetables, raw (salads) (1 serving = 1/2 cup)	2 servings	2 servings	2 servings	2 servings
Vegetables, cooked, green, yellow, or soup (1 serving = 1/2 cup)	2 servings	2 servings	3 servings	3 servings
Starch, potato, etc	None	None	None	1 serving
Artificial sweeteners	As desired	As desired	As desired	As desired

*See also Table 19–3.
†May substitute 1/2 cup cooked cereal or 1 cup dry prepared cereal for 1 slice bread.
‡May substitute 1/2 cup cottage cheese or 3 slices (3 oz) cheddar type cheese for 3 oz meat.

the urgency of the need for weight reduction. A daily caloric intake of 800–1200 Calories is satisfactory for a reducing diet.

There is no evidence that supervised rapid weight loss is physically harmful. However, all diets should attempt to maintain nitrogen balance, although this is not always possible. In these markedly restricted diets, ketonuria may appear; it is usually very slight after the first few days, however, and acidosis has never been observed. In addition, since the patients realize they are on a "diet," they often will adhere more willingly when they show rapid weight loss than when the results seem to be slow in appearing.

2. Proteins–A protein intake of at least 1 gm/kg should be maintained. If it is necessary to add protein to the low-calorie diet, protein hydrolysate or casein (free of carbohydrate and fat) can be used.

3. Carbohydrate and fat–To keep the calories and ketosis down, fats must be decreased. After the protein requirements have been met, the remaining calories may be supplied as half carbohydrate and half fat.

4. Vitamins and minerals–Most reducing diets are likely to be deficient in vitamins but adequate in minerals. Therefore, vitamins should be used to supply the average daily maintenance requirements during the time of weight reduction.

5. Sodium restriction–It has been shown that a normal person on a salt-free diet will lose from 2–3 kg; this reduction is temporary, and the weight will return when salt is added to the diet. The same is true of the obese patient, and, although an apparently dramatic effect can be obtained with salt-free diets, it is of no permanent value.

6. Starvation regimen–Total starvation has again been advocated as a weight reduction regimen. Although rapid loss of weight can be achieved by this means, the method may be quite hazardous and must be carried out in a hospital setting with strict super-

vision. Several deaths have occurred. Total starvation results largely in breakdown of fat, but it may also lead to excessive protein breakdown, fainting due to decrease in extracellular fluid volume because of sodium loss, and other unphysiologic results. Massive weight reduction can result in severe hepatic impairment or even fatal hepatic necrosis. Periodic total fasting to the point of producing ketonemia has seemed to cause accelerated weight loss in patients who fail to lose significantly on 1000 Calorie diets. This accelerated weight loss is spurious, however, and represents fluid loss due to ketonuria.

7. Shunt operation–Jejuno-ileal shunt has been performed on selected patients whose marked obesity was considered to be a hazard to health. The procedure provides permanent weight reduction and alleviates many of the physiologic abnormalities associated with obesity, but the operation is still considered to be investigative. Patients must be observed carefully for intestinal malabsorption, and the long-term effects are uncertain. Severe arthropathy and, more importantly, hepatic cirrhosis may occur.

B. Medication:

1. Appetite suppressants (anorexigenic drugs)–Amphetamine sulfate (Benzedrine®) and dextroamphetamine sulfate (Dexedrine®) may be of temporary value in aiding selected patients on reducing regimens by decreasing the appetite and giving a sense of well-being. Because of their relative inefficacy on a long-term basis and because of the hazard of habituation, there has been a marked trend away from the use of these and related anorexiant drugs.

2. Drugs to speed up metabolism–*Note:* There is no satisfactory drug to speed up metabolism. Thyroid has little or no place in the management of obesity. The low BMR associated with obesity is merely due to the fact that BMR is a measurement of oxygen consumption in terms of body surface area. The body

TABLE 19–7. Caloric values of common "snack" foods.*

	Amount or Average Serving	Calorie Count
Sandwiches		
Hamburger on bun	3 inch patty	500
Peanut butter	2 tsp	370
Cheese	1½ oz	400
Ham	1½ oz	350
Beverages		
Carbonated drinks, soda, root beer, etc	6 oz glass	80
Cola beverages	12 oz glass (Pepsi)	150
Club soda	8 oz glass	5
Chocolate malted milk	10 oz glass (1¾ cups)	450
Ginger ale	6 oz glass	60
Tea or coffee, no cream or sugar	1 cup	0
Tea or coffee, with 2 tbsp cream and 2 tsp sugar	1 cup	90
Alcoholic Drinks		
Ale	8 oz glass	130
Beer	8 oz glass	110
Highball (with ginger ale—ladies' style)	8 oz glass	140
Manhattan	Average	175
Martini	Average	160
Oldfashioned	Average	150
Sherry	2 oz glass	60
Scotch, bourbon, rye	1 oz jigger	80
Fruits		
Apple	One 3-inch	90
Banana	One 6-inch	100
Grapes	30 medium	75
Orange	One 2¾-inch	80
Pear	One	100
Salted Nuts		
Almonds	10	130
Cashews	10	60
Peanuts	10	60
Pecans	10 halves	150
Candies		
Chocolate bars		
Plain	1 bar (1¼ oz)	190
With nuts	1 bar	275
Chocolate covered bar	1 bar	250
Chocolate cream, bonbon, fudge	1 piece 1 inch square	90
Caramels, plain	1 piece ¾ inch cube	35
Chocolate nut caramels	1 piece	60
Desserts		
Pie: Fruit—Apple, etc	1/6 pie	560
Custard	1/6 pie	360
Lemon meringue	1/6 pie	470
Pumpkin pie with whipped cream	1/6 pie	460
Cake: Iced layer—2 layers white cake	1 serving	345
Fruit—thin slice (¼ inch)	1 serving	125
Sweets		
Ice cream		
Vanilla	1/2 cup	195
Chocolate and other flavors	1/2 cup	200
Milk sherbet	1/2 cup	120
Sundaes, small chocolate nut with whipped cream	Average	400
Ice cream sodas, chocolate	10 oz glass	270
Late Snacks		
Cold potato	½ medium	65
Chicken leg	1 average	88
Milk	7 oz glass	140
Mouthful of roast	½ × 2 × 3 inches	130
Piece of cheese	¼ × 2 × 3 inches	120
Left-over beans	½ cup	105
Brownie	¾ × 1¾ × 2¼ inches	300
Cream puff	4 inch diameter	450

*Modified and reprinted by permission of Smith, Kline, & French Laboratories.

surface area of obese patients is increased, but the increase is due to a relatively poor oxygen consumer (fatty tissue) rather than the other more active tissues, and so an apparently low BMR results. Actually, the basal caloric requirements of an obese person are greater than they would be if the same person were of normal weight, for fat tissues have a definite but slow metabolism. It has been shown that obese people with low BMR's can tolerate 0.2 gm or more of thyroid per day without change in BMR. Prolonged administration of thyroid may suppress the patient's normal thyroid secretion.

C. Exercise: Although exercise increases the energy output, extreme exercise is necessary to significantly alter weight. Playing 18 holes of golf, for instance, raises the total caloric requirements only by about 100–150 Calories. However, general increase in activity is an important factor in long-range weight maintenance.

D. Psychologic Factors: Overeating is largely a matter of habit and may be associated with psychologic problems. Psychotherapy, however, is seldom of lasting value in weight reduction. Whatever the cause, the patient must be retrained in his eating habits and educated to understand that once his weight is normal he can easily become obese again by eating more than necessary. Self-help groups of obese patients (similar to AA for alcoholics) are effective for some patients.

Note: Sudden weight reduction in emotionally unstable persons may have severe psychic consequences, eg, anorexia nervosa, psychotic reactions.

Bortz, W.M.: Metabolic consequences of obesity. Ann Int Med 71:833–843, 1969.

Bray, G.A.: The myth of diet in the management of obesity. Am J Clin Nutr 23:1141–1148, 1970.

Bray, G.A.: Measurement of subcutaneous fat cells from obese patients. Ann Int Med 73:565–569, 1970.

Cahill, G.F., Jr.: Starvation in man. New England J Med 282:668–675, 1970.

Drenick, E.J., Simmons, F., & J.F. Murphy: Effect on hepatic morphology of treatment of obesity by fasting, reducing diets and small-bowel bypass. New England J Med 282:829–834, 1970.

Edison, G.R.: Amphetamines: A dangerous illusion. Ann Int Med 74:605–610, 1971.

MacGregor, M.I., Block, A.J., & W.C. Ball, Jr.: Serious complications and sudden death in the Pickwickian syndrome. Johns Hopkins Med J 126:279–295, 1970.

Mayer, J.: Some aspects of the problem of regulation of food intake and obesity. New England J Med 274:610–616, 662–673, 722–731, 1966.

Payne, J.H., & L.T. De Wind: Surgical treatment of obesity. Am J Surg 118:141–147, 1969.

Penick, S.B., & A.J. Stunkard: Newer concepts of obesity. M Clin North America 54:745–754, 1970.

Roberts, H.J.: Overlooked dangers of weight reduction. Med Counterpoint 2:14–20, Sept 1970.

Ruffer, W.A.: Two simple indexes for identifying obesity compared. J Am Diet A 57:326–330, 1970.

Runcie, J., & T.J. Thomson: Prolonged starvation: A dangerous procedure. Brit MJ 3:432–435, 1970.

The treatment of obesity. Med Let Drugs Ther 13:61–63, 1971.

PROTEIN & CALORIE MALNUTRITION

Protein and calorie malnutrition occurs in a clinical continuum ranging from inadequate proteins with adequate calories (kwashiorkor) to inadequate proteins and calories (marasmus). These conditions constitute the most important problems in the nutrition of young children throughout the world.

Kwashiorkor

Kwashiorkor is a nutritional deficiency syndrome which usually occurs in weanling infants (usually 2 years of age or older) at the birth of a sibling but may occur in children of any age, and even in adults. It is attributed primarily to inadequate intake of proteins or perhaps of specific essential amino acids with adequate calories, but mineral and vitamin deficiencies may also play a role. It is prevalent in underprivileged sections of Africa, Asia, southern Europe, and Central and South America, in areas where the protein content of the diet is deficient in amount or of poor quality (vegetable protein). The condition may be precipitated by tropical infections, diarrhea, and extreme heat, which aggravate the nutritional deficiency by curtailing the intake, decreasing the absorption, and increasing the demand. The liver shows the most marked pathologic changes: hepatic enlargement and fatty infiltration which may progress to a condition resembling portal cirrhosis. There is also atrophy of the pancreatic acini with loss of granules followed by fibrosis.

Kwashiorkor is characterized clinically by growth failure, irritability and apathy, skin changes (rash, desquamation, hyperpigmentation or depigmentation, ulceration), cheilosis, stomatitis, conjunctivitis, sparse or depigmented hair, anorexia, vomiting, diarrhea, hepatomegaly, muscular wasting, and edema. Blood changes include anemia, hypoalbuminemia, hyperglobulinemia, and low levels of urea, potassium, cholesterol, alkaline phosphatase, amylase, and lipase.

Prevention of the disease is a combined public health and socioeconomic problem and, in cases where personal or cultural food preferences prejudice the protein intake, a psychologic and educational problem.

Treatment consists of supplying an adequate intake of protein (3–4 gm/kg) of high biologic value (eg, milk, eggs, meat, soybeans). Patient and regular administration of skimmed or whole milk will often result in rather prompt recovery if the condition is not too far advanced. If oral feeding is a problem, tube feeding may be necessary. Vitamin supplements may be indicated. Intramuscular injection of the water-soluble palmitate has been recommended in severe vitamin A deficiency. Patients who are dehydrated due to vomiting or diarrhea, especially when critically ill, require appropriate oral or parenteral fluid and electrolyte replacement. Concomitant infections require simultaneous treatment. Whole blood or plasma transfusions may be necessary. During the recovery phase, attention should be paid to total calories as well as high-protein intake.

Kwashiorkor syndromes occur in all degrees of severity, and the rate of recovery with proper treatment will vary accordingly. Without treatment, the mortality rate in advanced or complicated cases is very high.

Marasmus

Marasmus, or total starvation, is characterized by retarded growth, atrophy of tissues, no edema, and skin changes as in kwashiorkor. Subcutaneous fat, however, is minimal or absent. The condition may be caused not only by unavailability of food but also by such factors as prematurity, diarrhea, cystic fibrosis, and mental retardation. Treatment is similar to that for kwashiorkor. *Caution:* Initial feedings of the starving patient should be slow and increased gradually; large quantities of food should be avoided. There must be an adequate intake of calories as well as protein.

Ashworth, A., & others: Calorie requirements of children recovering from protein-calorie malnutrition. Lancet 2:600–603, 1968.

Garrow, J.S.: Protein requirements in health and disease. Practitioner 201:283–291, 1968.

Scrimshaw, N.S., & M. Behar: Malnutrition in underdeveloped countries. New England J Med 272:137–143, 1965.

HEREDITARY
METABOLIC DISEASES

Garrod's original description of 4 inborn errors of metabolism in 1908 was regarded with interest, but these disorders were largely considered to be rare medical curiosities of little clinical importance. The several hundred hereditary metabolic disorders about which we now have at least some knowledge include common and uncommon, benign and serious diseases, metabolic disturbances involving almost every class of biochemical substance, and diseases of all organs and tissues of the body. Newly recognized metabolic disorders are being reported at a rapid rate (see also Chapter 29), and this information has contributed greatly to the molecular biology of humans and animals.

Information about metabolic abnormalities is not only of importance in furthering our understanding of hitherto obscure disease processes, but is fundamental to a proper therapeutic approach to them. Old concepts of hereditary transmission of physical traits simply as dominant or recessive have had to be modified to explain the "asymptomatic carriers" of hereditary traits. Biochemical studies on relatives of patients with hereditary metabolic disorders may reveal deficiencies not clinically manifest. Recognition of the heterozygote carrier may be of extreme value from a eugenic point of view (in preventing potentially incompatible matings) and from the standpoint of the health of the individual (eg, in suggesting special dietary control, appropriate medication, and avoidance of drug idiosyncrasies).

Determination of the genetic basis of metabolic disorders is made by a careful family history and appropriate biochemical studies on the patient and on available relatives. Biochemical studies may include the determination of essential blood constituents, abnormal protein molecules, specific enzymes, abnormal metabolites, electrolytes, renal transport mechanisms, and tolerance or restriction tests with food or chemicals.

Several of the hereditary metabolic disorders (eg, diabetes mellitus, gout) as they relate to specific organ systems are discussed in other sections of this book. Some examples of other metabolic disorders that are well-known or of unusual interest are included in this chapter. (See also Chapter 29.)

DEFICIENCY OF PLASMA
PROTEIN FRACTIONS

Agammaglobulinemia & Hypoglobulinemia

Congenital agammaglobulinemia is a rare X-linked recessive hereditary disorder due to deficiency or absence of gamma globulin. It occurs only in males and is manifest clinically by recurrent bacterial infections. The response to viral infections is usually normal. Immunologic responses (eg, blood typing, immunization) fail to occur. The diagnosis is confirmed by demonstration of marked deficiency or absence of gamma globulin by electrophoretic or immunologic methods. (See Table 19–8.)

Treatment consists of monthly lifetime IM injections of 0.1 gm/kg of human gamma globulin, early recognition of bacterial infections, and treatment at the time of infection with gamma globulin and appropriate anti-infective agents.

Secondary agammaglobulinemia (preferably referred to as hypoglobulinemia) occurs most commonly in older children or adults. It is usually secondary to one of the following diseases: (1) diseases associated with hypoproteinemia (eg, liver disease, nephrosis, malnutrition, congenital panhypoproteinemia, transient dysproteinemia); or (2) neoplastic diseases (eg, multiple myeloma, lymphoma, lymphatic leukemia). It usually manifests itself by recurrent infections, but immunologic response is usually present. Although the gamma globulins are decreased, they rarely fall to the very low or disappearance levels characteristic of primary agammaglobulinemia.

Treatment is directed at the primary disease, and gamma globulins are given as for primary agammaglobulinemia. Do not use antibiotics prophylactically, but treat infections with appropriate antibiotics as they occur.

The gamma globulins. New England J Med 275:480–486, 536–542, 591–596, 652–658, 709–715, 769–775, 826–831, 1966.

TABLE 19–8. Characteristics of immunoglobulins.*

Immuno-globulin	Sedimen-tation Constant	Molecular Weight	Crosses Placenta	Elicit PCA†	Percent Carbohy-drate	Examples	Average Serum Concentration (mg/100 ml)
IgG	7 S	150,000	Yes	Yes	2.5	Many antibodies to bacteria, viruses, toxins, especially late in antibody response.	1000–1500
IgM	19 S	900,000	No	No	5–10	Many early antibodies to infectious agents and other antigens.	60–180
IgA	7 S or 11 S	170,000 or 380,000	No	No	5–10	Isohemagglutinins; antibody in external secretions: 2 mol of 7 S IgA linked by "secretory" piece of molecular weight 60,000.	100–400
IgD	7 S	150,000	No	No	?	Antibody activity not established.	3–5
IgE	8 S	200,000	No ?	No	10	Skin-sensitizing antibody in allergy; reagin.	0.1

*Reproduced, with permission, from Jawetz, E., Melnick, J.L., & E.A. Adelberg: *Review of Medical Microbiology,* 9th ed. Lange, 1970.
†Passive cutaneous anaphylaxis.

ABNORMALITY OF MOLECULAR STRUCTURE

Methemoglobinemia

Congenital methemoglobinemia is caused either by a deficiency in the specific enzyme, erythrocyte nucleotide diaphorase, required in conversion of methemoglobin to hemoglobin, or by the presence of an abnormal hemoglobin M. Clinically, it is manifested by a persistent gray cyanosis not associated with cardiac or respiratory abnormality, and by easy fatigability, dyspnea, tachycardia, and dizziness with exertion. The venous blood is brown; the oxygen capacity of arterial blood is reduced, and excessive amounts of methemoglobin are present in the blood.

Continuous administration of methylene blue by mouth, 240 mg daily, will relieve the symptoms and cyanosis in some cases. The prognosis for life is good.

Fialkow, P.J., & others: Mental retardation in methemoglobinemia due to diaphorase deficiency. New England J Med 273:840–845, 1965.

DISORDERS OF AMINO ACID METABOLISM

Albinism

Albinism is a congenital disorder associated with the absence of tyrosinase in the melanocytes and mani-fest clinically by the absence of pigment in the skin, hair, and eyes. The skin and hair are white, the irides reddish, and the pupils are red. Photophobia, nystagmus, and defective vision may occur.

There is no specific treatment.

Ghadini, H.: Diagnosis of inborn errors of amino acid metabolism. Am J Dis Child 114:433–439, 1967.

Alkaptonuria

Alkaptonuria is a rare metabolic disorder inherited as a recessive trait. It is due to absence from the liver of an enzyme, homogentisate oxidase, which is necessary for the oxidation of homogentisic acid. Absence of the enzyme permits homogentisic acid to be excreted unmetabolized in the urine. Diapers or clothing may be stained with homogentisic acid in the urine. Staining of the cartilage of the nose and ears (ochronosis) may occur in older patients, and ochronosis sometimes causes cartilaginous degeneration of joints and severe arthritis. The urine test for homogentisic acid (with dilute ferric chloride solution) produces a transient deep blue color.

No specific treatment is available.

Brown, N.K., & E.A. Smuckler: Alkaptonuria and Gilbert's syndrome. Am J Med 48:759–765, 1970.

Phenylketonuria (Phenylpyruvic Oligophrenia, PKU)

Phenylketonuria is a not uncommon metabolic disorder inherited as a recessive trait. It is due to absence of an enzyme, phenylalanine hydroxylase, which is capable of converting phenylalanine to tyrosine. Phenylalanine accumulates in the blood and the deamination product, phenylpyruvic acid, is excreted in the urine. If untreated, mental retardation and schizoid changes almost invariably occur, frequently to a marked degree. Patients are most often blue-eyed blonds and, because of pigmentary defects, are predisposed to photosensitivity and eczema. Physical development is usually normal. There may be signs of extrapyramidal involvement, with tremor, ataxia, and hypertonicity in 2/3 of cases. Perspiration is usually excessive. Convulsions may occur. Pneumoencephalography may show frontal lobe atrophy. Phenylpyruvic acid may be demonstrated in the urine if a dark green color results when dilute ferric chloride is added to acidified urine. Elevated serum phenylalanine levels (> 20 mg/100 ml) are more definitive, but not every newborn infant with phenylalaninemia has PKU because phenylalaninemia may be transient in nature and may also be found in other, unrelated diseases. Blood phenylalanine may be increased in the absence of positive urine findings.

Since present evidence suggests a positive correlation between biochemical findings of untreated (or delayed treatment of) PKU and mental retardation, early further evaluation by a specialist is necessary to either confirm or disprove the diagnosis. Expert dietary treatment is necessary to maintain normal phenylalanine levels (3–7 mg/100 ml) without causing phenylalanine depletion and otherwise seriously disturbing the nutritional status of the infant. Although a carefully regulated low-phenylalanine diet should be started in the first few weeks of life to prevent mental retardation, in more established cases such a diet may occasionally arrest or improve the condition. Patients with PKU who have not received dietary therapy are rarely normal mentally. Routine testing of newborn infants for PKU is common; large-scale detection programs have been established in many areas of the USA.

Berman, J.L.: Phenylketonuria. Family Physician 3:432–435, 1970.

Holm, V.A., Deering, W.M., & R.L. Penn: Some factors influencing the development of a voluntary PKU screening program. JAMA 212:1835–1842, 1970.

Levy, H.L., & others: Screening the "normal" population in Massachusetts for phenylketonuria. New England J Med 282:1455–1458, 1970.

Maple Syrup Urine Disease

Maple syrup urine disease is a recessive familial disorder caused by the absence of amino acid decarboxylase and resulting in a disorder of metabolism of essential branched-chain amino acids. Symptoms usually appear in the first week of life and consist of spasticity, opisthotonos, irregular respirations, and feeding difficulties. The disease may remain dormant until late childhood and may become apparent due to an episode of infection or trauma. A variant of maple syrup urine disease with intermittent branched-chain ketonuria has been described. The relationship

between the CNS changes and the amino acid anomaly is not clear. The urine has a maple sugar odor and gives a characteristic positive ferric chloride reaction, as in phenylketonuria. It is possible to detect a heterozygous carrier by means of a leucine "loading" test.

If the disease is detected early, a diet low in branched-chain amino acids (leucine, isoleucine, and valine) may prevent brain damage. A new variant of the disease has been described which responds to thiamine chloride, 10 mg daily. If detected after severe CNS damage has occurred, death occurs within weeks or months.

Schulman, J.D., & others: A new variant of maple syrup urine disease (branched chain ketoaciduria): Clinical and biochemical evaluation. Am J Med 49:118–124, 1970.

Scriver, C.R., & others: Thiamine-responsive maple syrup urine disease. Lancet 2:310–312, 1971.

Snyderman, S.E., & others: Maple syrup urine disease, with particular reference to dietotherapy. Pediatrics 34:454–472, 1964.

Cystinuria

Cystinuria is a hereditary metabolic disorder due to a defective renal transport mechanism for dibasic amino acids. Because of impaired renal tubular reabsorption of cystine, lysine, arginine, and ornithine, these dibasic amino acids are excreted in the urine. Since cystine is relatively insoluble in neutral or acid solution, urinary calculi of almost pure cystine are common.

Treatment is aimed at preventing stone formation by increasing the fluid intake and alkalinizing the urine. In severe cystinuria it may be necessary to control urinary excretion of cystine by administration of a low-methionine (and low-cystine) diet. Prolonged therapy with D-penicillamine is reported to result in a dramatic reduction in total cystine with decrease in size, and actual dissolution, of cystine stones. Administration for an indefinite time is required. Its use, however, should not replace conventional therapy.

Farris, B.L., & F.O. Kolb: Factors involved in crystal formation in cystinuria. JAMA 205:846–848, 1968.

Stokes, G.S., & others: New agent in the treatment of cystinuria: N-acetyl-D- penicillamine. Brit MJ 1:284–288, 1968.

Homocystinuria

Homocystinuria is a rare hereditary disorder of amino acid metabolism. It is believed to be due to a deficiency of the enzyme cystathionine synthetase in the liver, with resultant deficiency of cysteine in the neonatal period, when the need for cysteine is great. The disorder is characterized clinically by frequent occurrence of mental retardation, dislocation of the lenses, sparse blond hair, long thin extremities with genu valgum, tendency to arterial and venous thromboses, and emotional disturbances. Plasma homocystine and methionine levels are elevated. Urinary excretion of homocystine is increased, and the urine shows a characteristic magenta color on the nitroprusside test. There are, usually, abnormal EEG findings.

There is no known treatment. A trial of low-methionine diet with cystine supplementation may be warranted.

Hambraeus, L., Wranne, L., & R. Lorentsson: Biochemical and therapeutic studies in cases of homocystinuria. Clin Sc 35:457–466, 1968.

Fanconi's Syndrome

Fanconi's syndrome is a hereditary metabolic disorder, presumably of multiple causes and associated with multiple defects of the renal transport mechanisms. It is manifested clinically by emaciation, dwarfism, renal rickets or osteomalacia (resistant to vitamin D in the usual doses), dehydration, hypophosphatemia, spontaneous fractures, polyuria, aminoaciduria, proteinuria, and glycosuria. The disorder may not become evident until adult life and should be suspected in any case of spontaneous fracture, glycosuria, and aminoaciduria.

Treatment, which is usually ineffective, consists of giving large doses of vitamin D, alkalinization of the urine with sodium or potassium bicarbonate, and adequate hydration. Patients usually die of renal failure.

Efron, M.L.: Aminoaciduria. New England J Med 272:1058–1067, 1107–1114, 1965.

Hartnup's Disease (H Disease)

Hartnup's disease is a rare genetic defect in the renal transport mechanism for tryptophan. Clinical findings consist of dermatitis, cerebellar ataxia, mental retardation, renal aminoaciduria, and increased excretion of indole and indican compounds.

Treatment consists of hydration to prevent the formation of renal calculi. Dietary protein restriction and treatment with niacinamide are of questionable value.

Halvorsen, K., & S. Halvorsen: Hartnup's disease. Pediatrics 31:29–38, 1963.

Leucine Sensitivity Disease

Leucine sensitivity disease is a genetic metabolic disorder characterized by abnormal hypoglycemia and is due to leucine sensitivity. Clinically it is manifest as hypoglycemia, flushing, sweating, and convulsions. It is important to consider leucine sensitivity in infants with hypoglycemia. Sensitivity to the hypoglycemic effects of leucine may also occur in insulinoma and so-called idiopathic hypoglycemia. Intravenous leucine may cause a slight fall in blood sugar in healthy subjects.

No specific treatment is available.

Fajan, S.S.: Current concepts: Leucine-induced hypoglycemia. New England J Med 272:1224–1227, 1965.

DISORDERS OF CARBOHYDRATE METABOLISM

Fructosuria

Fructosuria is an inborn error of metabolism which is probably due to a deficiency of the enzyme fructokinase, resulting in elevated blood levels of fructose and excretion of fructose in the urine. There are no clinical manifestations, and no treatment is necessary. However, if the diet contains large quantities of foods rich in fructose and sucrose, a considerable proportion of dietary carbohydrate may be lost.

Froesch, E.R., & others: Heriditary fructose intolerance: An inborn defect of hepatic fructose-1-phosphate splitting aldolase. Am J Med 34:151–165, 1963.

Fructosemia

Hereditary fructose intolerance is a rare inborn error of carbohydrate metabolism due to a deficiency of fructose-1:6-diphosphate aldolase. Fructose ingestion causes fructosemia, resulting in clinical hypoglycemia. The disorder is usually mild but can occasionally be severe (eg, Fanconi's syndrome). Treatment consists of withholding fructose from the diet and supportive measures as needed.

Levin, B., & others: Fructosaemia. Am J Med 45:826–838, 1968.

Galactosemia

Galactosemia is an inborn error of metabolism which is due to a deficiency of the enzyme galactose-1-phosphate uridyl transferase. This enzyme is necessary for the conversion of galactose to glucose. Clinically the disorder becomes manifest soon after birth by feeding problems, vomiting, diarrhea, abdominal distention, hepatomegaly, jaundice, ascites, cataracts, mental retardation, and elevated blood and urine galactose levels. Transferase deficiency can be- detected at birth by the enzyme fluorescence spot test on umbilical cord specimens.

Exclusion from the diet of milk and all foods containing galactose and lactose for the first 3 years of life will prevent the above manifestations if instituted immediately and will bring about improvement in those patients in whom symptoms and signs have already appeared.

Shih, V.E.: Galactosemia screening of newborn infants in Massachusetts. New England J Med 284:753–757, 1971.

Von Gierke's Disease

Von Gierke's disease is a rare inborn error of metabolism characterized by the excessive deposition of glycogen in the liver and kidney, secondary to a deficiency of the enzyme glucose-6-phosphatase, which is required for the degradation of glycogen to glucose. The disorder becomes manifest in infancy or early childhood by easy fatigability, hepatomegaly (glycogen deposition), and hypoglycemia and ketosis (unavailability of glucose) with resulting shock and convulsions. The serum glucose does not respond to the epinephrine test.

Treatment is directed toward improvement of nutrition and correction of the hypoglycemia by frequent feedings. Corticotropin or the corticosteroids may be of some value. Death usually occurs in infancy or childhood, but if the patient survives this period the symptoms usually improve as the child grows older.

Hsia, D.Y-Y.: The diagnosis and management of the glycogen storage diseases. Am J Clin Path 50:44–51, 1968.

DISTURBANCES OF LIPID METABOLISM

Gaucher's Disease

Gaucher's disease is a familial disorder of excess storage of a glucocerebroside in the reticuloendothelial cells. It is apparently due to an enzymatic deficiency. Proliferation of these abnormal cells causes progressive hepatomegaly, splenomegaly, and skeletal lesions, with bone fracture at the site of the lesions. The disease may have its onset at any age, although onset is usually in childhood. Anemia, jaundice, thrombocytopenia, and at times neurologic lesions may also be present. The course of the disease is variable. In children it usually progresses rapidly, resulting in death in a few months; in older adults, it progresses so slowly that the patient often dies of intercurrent disease.

Treatment is supportive. Splenectomy is indicated only when hypersplenism occurs.

Groen, J.J.: Gaucher's disease. Arch Int Med 113:543–549, 1964.
O'Brien, J.S.: Ganglioside storage diseases. New England J Med 284:893–896, 1971.
Yatsu, F.M.: Sphingolipidoses. California Med 114:1–6, April 1971.

Lipogranulomatosis

Lipogranulomatosis is a congenital disorder of lipid metabolism due to excessive storage of lipoglycoprotein in the subcutaneous and periarticular tissues. It becomes manifest shortly after birth by sensitivity and swelling of the extremities and a hoarse, weak cry. There is a progressively severe generalized involvement of the joints associated with subcutaneous and periarticular nodules. Fixation of the laryngeal cartilage results in dysphonia, and pulmonary infiltration produces dyspnea. Fever is variable.

There is no known effective treatment.

Niemann-Pick Disease (Sphingomyelin Lipidosis)

Niemann-Pick disease is a rare, genetically determined, recessive disorder characterized by the excessive storage of phospholipids, especially sphingomyelin, in the reticuloendothelial system. Manifestations occur early in infancy and consist primarily of hepatosplenomegaly and CNS involvement, with mental retardation and convulsions. Other symptoms and signs include diffuse pulmonary infiltrations, cutaneous lesions, a cherry-red macular spot, gastrointestinal bleeding, lymph node enlargement, thrombocytopenia, anemia, and foam cells in hepatic or marrow biopsies.

Treatment is supportive. Death usually occurs during childhood.

Familial Essential Xanthomatosis

Familial essential xanthomatosis is a genetically determined dominant disorder characterized by the excessive storage of cholesterol and its esters in the reticuloendothelial system. Cholesterol is deposited in the skin (xanthoma tuberosum et planum), blood vessels, eyelids (xanthelasma), endocardium, and tendons. Premature arteriosclerosis and myocardial infarctions are common. The total and esterified serum cholesterol is elevated.

Treatment consists of the use of polyunsaturated fats in the diet and possibly the use of the various commercially available oral cholesterol-lowering agents. Surgical removal of deposits may be required when they interfere with function or for cosmetic reasons (xanthelasma).

Thannhauser, S.J.: *Lipidoses: Diseases of the Intracellular Lipid Metabolism,* 3rd ed. Grune & Stratton, 1958.

DISORDERS OF PORPHYRIN METABOLISM

The porphyrins are cyclic compounds containing 4 pyrrole rings which are the precursors of hemoglobin and of other important enzymes and pigments. Heme is the complex of iron and porphyrin which unites with the protein, globin, to form hemoglobin. Disorders of porphyrin metabolism, which may be hereditary or acquired, are due to disturbances in the anabolic sequence of porphyrin metabolism. There has been considerable progress recently in elucidating the nature of the metabolic changes. Several porphyric syndromes are recognized: (1) hereditary porphyrias, either hepatic (hepatogenic) or erythropoietic (congenital); and (2) acquired porphyrinurias.

Hepatic Porphyrias

The hepatic porphyrias are autosomal dominant hereditary disorders characterized by excessive production of porphyrins and related compounds by the liver. They become clinically and biochemically manifest only after puberty. Mixed or combined hepatic porphyrias may occur. The porphyric trait, as manifested biochemically, may exist in completely asymptomatic individuals.

A. Acute, Intermittent Porphyria: This is the most common type of porphyria. It is characterized by attacks of gastrointestinal symptoms (abdominal colic, vomiting, and constipation), CNS symptoms (flaccid paralysis, peripheral neuritis, psychic disturbances, and convulsions), and sinus tachycardia. Photosensitivity does not occur. Blood volume decreases by about 20% during attacks. The urine, which contains porphobilinogen, is often colorless when freshly voided, but may darken on standing or when exposed to ultraviolet light. The modified Ehrlich test of the urine (Watson-Schwartz test) is positive. Type III coproporphyrin and uroporphyrin may be excreted in the urine in large quantities. Acute attacks may be precipitated by barbiturates, alcohols, and many other chemicals, as well as by menses, pregnancy (postpartum), infections, and psychic trauma.

Treatment is nonspecific. Phenothiazine drugs. given early in the attack may lessen the severity of symptoms. All other drugs or toxins (especially barbiturates and alcohol) must be avoided.

The overall mortality rate is 15–20%. Death usually occurs as a result of motor paralysis during an acute attack. Most patients, however, survive acute attacks, and the prognosis for life is much better than was formerly believed.

B. Porphyria Cutanea Tarda: This type occurs most commonly in middle-aged persons. Although it is usually hereditary, it may occur secondary to other liver disorders. There is varying photosensitivity of the skin, resulting in eczema, vesicles, and bullae. The hepatic content of porphyrin is greatly increased, and liver function is impaired. Mild jaundice may be present. There is no porphobilinogen in the urine, but there is an abnormally high excretion of uroporphyrin and coproporphyrin.

Treatment consists of protection of skin from strong light and complete abstinence from alcohol. Phlebotomy, with removal of 2500–8500 ml of blood over a period of 3–9 months, has been reported to markedly reduce uroporphyrin excretion associated with a clinical remission in all patients. Recent studies have reported the successful control of symptoms and reduction in urinary excretion of porphyrins and their precursors with daily doses of 100 mg of water-soluble vitamin E orally.

Erythropoietic Porphyria

This is a rare, inherited disorder transmitted as an autosomal recessive trait. It is usually evident from birth and is due to an abnormality of developing normoblasts in the bone marrow which causes increased production of porphyrin. It is characterized by red urine, pink teeth which fluoresce with ultraviolet light, cutaneous photosensitivity with resultant vesicles, bullae, and scarring and pigmentation of the skin, hepatosplenomegaly, and anemia. Porphobilinogen is absent from the urine, but there are large amounts of type I coproporphyrin and uroporphyrin in the feces and urine.

Congenital erythropoietic porphyria must be differentiated from the more recently described erythropoietic protoporphyria. In the latter condition, vesicles and bullae and anemia are rare, and protoporphyrins are increased in the plasma and feces.

Treatment consists of protection against sunlight and ultraviolet light. Oral beta-carotene has been reported to provide some degree of protection against photosensitivity to sunlight and artificial light. Splenectomy may sometimes be of value when hemolysis is present.

Acquired (Secondary) Porphyrinurias

Secondary or "symptomatic" porphyrinurias (coproporphyrinurias) may follow poisoning with lead or other heavy metals and many other organic and inorganic poisons. They may also occur in the hemolytic and pernicious anemias, parenchymal liver disease, obstructive jaundice, the collagen diseases, and CNS disorders.

Bloomer, J.R., & others: Blood volume and bilirubin production in acute intermittent porphyria. New England J Med 284:17–20, 1971.

Epstein, J.H., & A.G. Redeker: Porphyria cutanea tarda: A study of the effect of phlebotomy. New England J Med 279:1301–1304, 1968.

Mathews-Roth, M.M., & others: Beta-carotene as a photoprotective agent in erythropoietic protoporphyria. New England J Med 282:1231–1234, 1970.

Nair, P.P., & others: The effect of vitamin E on porphyrin metabolism in man. Arch Int Med 128:411–415, 1971.

OTHER METABOLIC DISORDERS

Cystic Fibrosis (Mucoviscidosis)

Pancreatic cystic fibrosis is a recessive inherited disease causing dysfunction of the exocrine glands of the pancreas, respiratory system, and sweat glands. It usually begins in infancy, and is manifested by steatorrhea, malnutrition, repeated pulmonary infections, bronchitis, viscid sputum, and excessive sodium and chloride loss in the sweat (leading often to heat exhaustion in hot weather or during febrile episodes). Pancreatic enzymes are present in decreased amounts in the stools.

Treatment consists of a high-protein diet, moderate fat restriction, high doses of vitamins, especially vitamin A, and pancreatin to aid digestion. Both physical and chemical means should be used to decrease viscosity of pulmonary secretions and help in their removal, and to provide for adequate ventilation of the lungs. Infections (especially respiratory infections) should be guarded against and treated promptly with antibiotics when they occur.

The disease is not curable, but since its recognition as a disease is only recent, long-term survival figures are not available.

White, H., & W.F. Rowley: Cystic fibrosis of the pancreas. P Clin North America 11:139–169, 1964.

Zelkowitz, P.S., & S.T. Giammona: Cystic fibrosis: Pulmonary studies in children, adolescents and young adults. Am J Dis Child 117:543–547, 1969.

Primary Hyperoxaluria (Oxalosis)

Primary hyperoxaluria is a rare hereditary metabolic disease characterized by a continuously high urinary excretion of oxalate (unrelated to dietary intake of oxalate). It is probably related to a defect in the transamination of glyoxalate. Clinically it is manifested by progressive bilateral calcium oxalate urolithiasis, nephrocalcinosis, and recurrent urinary tract infections. Death usually occurs early as a result of renal failure or hypertension.

There is no specific treatment, although a low-oxalate diet and hydration to increase solubility may be of some help. Calcium carbimide, 1 mg/kg orally daily used carefully over a prolonged period, has had a limited successful trial and warrants further study.

Solomon, C.C., Goodman, S.L., & C.M. Riley: Calcium carbamide in the treatment of primary hyperoxaluria. New England J Med 276:207–210, 1967.

Marfan's Syndrome

Marfan's syndrome is an autosomal dominant hereditary disorder of connective tissue, the basic metabolic defect of which remains unknown. The disease involves primarily the skeletal system, the cardiovascular system, and the eyes, but there are many other clinical manifestations. These patients are tall and thin. The extremities are long in relation to the trunk: The hands are spider-like (arachnodactyly), with thin, tapered, webbed fingers. Pes planus, pes cavus, and hammer toes may be present. "Tower skull" (long, narrow, and pointed head) and a high palatal arch are common findings. Winging of the scapulas and pigeon or funnel chest may occur. Dislocation of the lens (ectopia lentis), myopia, detached retinas, and other ocular abnormalities may be present. Cardiovascular deformities may include dilatation of the aorta and pulmonic arteries, with resultant valvular insufficiency, dissecting aneurysm, and occasionally atrial septal defect. Serum mucoproteins are low, and urinary excretion of hydroxyproline is increased. Mild, incomplete (atypical) forms of the disease may exist.

Treatment is directed toward cardiovascular complications and is otherwise merely symptomatic and supportive.

Mortality during infancy is high. Death is usually due to cardiac complications.

McKusick, V.A.: *Heritable Disorders of Connective Tissue,* 3rd ed. Mosby, 1966.

·   ·   ·

AMYLOIDOSIS

Amyloidosis is a poorly understood disorder of protein metabolism which usually occurs secondary to chronic suppurative disease but which may also occur as the so-called "primary" type in patients without apparent preexisting disease. The onset is insidious, and the clinical manifestations may vary widely depending upon the organs or tissues in which the peculiar homogeneous, amorphous, proteinaceous amyloid substance is deposited. There appears to be some relationship between amyloidosis and the various other diseases associated with abnormalities of the serum globulin (eg, multiple myeloma).

Four clinical types of amyloidosis have been described:

(1) **Primary systemic amyloidosis,** a rare disorder, occurs in patients without known preexisting disease. Amyloid is deposited chiefly in mesenchymal tissues, with resultant involvement of many organs. It is characterized by weakness, weight loss. purpura, macroglossia, lymphadenopathy, hepatosplenomegaly, congestive heart failure, nephrotic syndrome, and abnormality of serum proteins.

(2) **Amyloidosis associated with multiple myeloma** may be a variation of the primary systemic type, but the relationship is uncertain.

(3) **Primary localized (tumor-forming) amyloidosis** is a rare disorder involving the upper respiratory tract (eg, the larynx), again in the absence of preexisting disease and without evidence of amyloidosis in other tissues.

(4) **Secondary amyloidosis,** the most common type, is associated with chronic debilitating and suppurative disorders. Amyloid is deposited widely in parenchymatous organs. (The liver, spleen, kidneys, and adrenal glands are most frequently involved.) Tuberculosis is the most common predisposing cause, but the condition may also follow rheumatoid arthritis, ulcerative colitis, chronic osteomyelitis, and other chronic wasting and suppurative disorders.

The diagnosis of amyloidosis is based first on a suspicion that it may be present, since clinical manifestations may be varied and atypical. Preexisting long-standing infection or debilitating illness should suggest the possibility of its existence. Microscopic examination of biopsy or surgical specimens after suitable staining procedures is diagnostic. Intravenous injection of Congo red in patients with systemic amyloidosis results in a 90–100% disappearance of the dye within 1 hour (normally, less than 40% is removed).

Treatment of localized amyloid "tumors" is by surgical excision. There is no effective treatment of systemic amyloidosis, and death usually occurs within 1–3 years. Variable effectiveness of corticosteroids has been reported. Treatment of infection may cause a temporary remission of the disease. Early and adequate treatment of pyogenic infections will probably prevent much secondary amyloidosis. Since the advent of antibiotic and other anti-infective drugs for the treatment of infection, the incidence of amyloidosis is expected to decline.

Barth, R.F., & others: Amyloid coronary artery disease, primary systemic amyloidosis and paraproteinemia. Arch Int Med 126:627–630, 1970.

Barth, W.F., & others: Primary amyloidosis: Clinical, immuno-chemical and immunoglobulin metabolism studies in fifteen patients. Am J Med 47:259–273, 1969.

Lowenstein, J., & G. Gallo: Remission of the nephrotic syndrome in renal amyloidosis. New England J Med 282:128–132, 1970.

Mahloridji, M.: The genetic amyloidosis to hereditary neuropathic amyloidosis type 2. Medicine 48:1–37, 1969.

RETICULOENDOTHELIOSES
(Histiocytosis X)

The reticuloendotheliosis include several so-called distinct clinical diseases: eosinophilic granuloma, Hand-Schüller-Christian disease, and Letterer-Siwe disease. There is some feeling, however, that because the pathologic findings are similar and because some transitional cases have been reported, these clinical syndromes may actually represent different phases or stages of the same disease.

The reticuloendotheliosis are not familial, and their etiology has not been determined.

Eosinophilic Granuloma

Eosinophilic granuloma is a relatively benign disorder of the reticuloendothelial system which usually occurs in children but may occur at any age. The characteristic skeletal lesions, which begin in the marrow, show proliferation of eosinophils and histiocytes. Eventually the lesion erodes the bony cortex, causing an enlargement in the area of involvement. The lesions may be solitary or multiple, and usually occur in the skull and in the bones of the trunk and proximal portions of the extremities. The granulomas may be quite painful and pathologic fractures may occur. Fever, leukocytosis, eosinophilia, skin lesions, lymphadenopathy, and pleurisy or interstitial pulmonary infiltrations occasionally occur. X-rays show rounded areas of bony rarefaction, often punched-out. The diagnosis is established by biopsy.

Treatment, consisting of curettement, excision, or x-ray therapy, is quite successful.

Letterer-Siwe Disease

Letterer-Siwe disease is usually a rapidly progressive and fatal disorder of the reticuloendothelial system which occurs most frequently in infancy or early childhood and, rarely, in young adults. The pathologic lesions consist of widespread proliferation of histiocytes which may involve bone, but, to a much greater extent than eosinophilic granuloma, involves the skin, lymph nodes, and viscera as well. Clinical manifestations include fever, anemia, hemorrhagic tendency, lymphadenopathy, hepatosplenomegaly, and skeletal and variable cutaneous lesions. The diagnosis is made by biopsy of bone marrow or lymph nodes, which show characteristic nonlipid-containing histiocytes.

Treatment is symptomatic and supportive. Antibiotics may be required for the treatment of secondary infection. Corticosteroids have not been of value. X-rays may halt the progress of bone lesions.

Hand-Schüller-Christian Disease (Cranial Xanthomatosis)

Hand-Schüller-Christian disease is a chronic disorder of the reticuloendothelial system characterized by lipoid cell hyperplasia and proliferation of histiocytes. The onset is in early childhood. Classical clinical features include unilateral or bilateral exophthalmos, softened areas of the skull and other membranous bones, and diabetes insipidus. Otitis media is a common presenting complaint. Multiple small cutaneous plaques may appear on the skin, often resembling seborrheic dermatitis. Lymphadenopathy, hepatosplenomegaly, and anemia often occur. Blood cholesterol levels are often normal. Bony defects in the skull and flat bones are readily seen on x-ray.

No specific treatment is available, although low-fat diets have been recommended. Corticosteroids may occasionally modify the course of the illness. The course is chronic and relatively benign unless there is extensive involvement of vital organs. X-ray therapy may be of value in the treatment of specific local lesions.

Dargeon, H.W.: Considerations in the treatment of reticuloendotheliosis. Am J Roentgenol 93:521–536, 1965.

• • •

General References: Diet Therapy

American Dietetic Association: Position Paper on Bland Diet in the Treatment of Chronic Duodenal Ulcer Disease. J Am Diet Assoc 59:44–45, 1971.

American Heart Association: *Sodium Restricted Diets* (1969); *The Way to a Man's Heart: Fat-Controlled, Low Cholesterol, Meal Plan to Reduce Risk of Heart Attack* (1970); *Planning Fat Controlled Meals for 1200 and 1800 Calories* (1968).

Church, C.F., & H.N. Church: *Food Values of Portions Commonly Used,* 11th ed. Lippincott, 1970.

Davidson, S., & R. Passmore: *Human Nutrition and Dietics,* 3rd ed. Williams & Wilkins, 1966.

Food & Nutrition Board, National Academy of Sciences–National Research Council: *Recommended Dietary Allowances,* 7th ed. Publication 1694. Washington, DC, 1968.

Fredrickson, D., & R.I. Levy: *Dietary Management of Hyperlipoproteinemia.* National Heart and Lung Institute, 1970.

Goodhart, R.S., & M.G. Wohl: *Manual of Clinical Nutrition.* Lea & Febiger, 1964.

Halpern, S.L. (editor): Symposium on current concepts in clinical nutrition. M Clin North America 54:1355–1613, 1970.

Institute of Home Economics, Agricultural Research Service: *Nutritive Value of Foods.* US Government Printing Office, 1960.

Kaiser, C.M.: *Nutritional Care of Patients Receiving Tube Feedings: Individual Study Kit Program.* American Dietetic Association, 1969.

Krause, M.V.: *Food Nutrition and Diet Therapy,* 4th ed. Saunders, 1966.

Levy, R.I., & D.S. Fredrickson: Diagnosis and management of hyperlipoproteinemia. Am J Cardiol 22:576–583, 1968.

Leverton, R.M., & G.V. Odell: *Nutritive Value of Cooked Meat.* Oklahoma Agricultural Experimental Station MP 49, 1958.

Mitchell, H., & others: *Cooper's Nutrition in Health and Disease,* 15th ed. Lippincott, 1968.

National Research Council: *Sodium Restricted Diets.* Publication 325, 1954.

O'Dell, A.: Ulcer dietotherapy: Past and present. J Am Diet A 58:447–450, 1971.

Ohlson, M.A.: *Handbook of Experimental and Therapeutic Diets.* Burgess, 1962.

Rowe, A.H.: *Elimination Diets and the Patient's Allergies: A Handbook of Allergy.* Lea & Febiger, 1941.

Rowe, A.H., & A.H. Rowe, Jr.: *Bronchial Asthma: Its Diagnosis and Treatment.* Thomas, 1963.

Turner, D.: *Handbook of Diet Therapy.* Univ of Chicago Press, 1965.

Watt, B.K., & A.L. Merrill: *Composition of Foods–Raw, Processed, Prepared.* Rev ed. US Dept of Agriculture Handbook No. 8, 1963.

Williams, S.R.: *Nutrition and Diet Therapy.* Univ of Chicago Press, 1970.

Wohl, M.G., & R.S. Goodhart: *Modern Nutrition in Health and Disease,* 4th ed. Lea & Febiger, 1968.

Year Book of Agriculture: *Food.* US Dept of Agriculture, 1959.

General References: Nutritional & Metabolic Disorders

Brady, R.O.: The sphingolipidoses. New England J Med 275:312–317, 1966.

Crouch, W.H., & C.M. Evanhoe: Inborn errors of metabolism. P Clin North America 14:269–282, 1967.

Davidson, S., & R. Passmore: *Human Nutrition and Dietetics,* 4th ed. Williams & Wilkins, 1969.

Duncan, G.G. (editor): *Diseases of Metabolism,* 6th ed. Saunders, 1969.

Food and Nutrition Board, National Academy of Sciences-National Research Council: *Recommended Dietary Allowances,* 7th ed. Publication 1146, Washington, DC, 1968.

Garrod, A.E. (with Supplement by H. Harris): *Garrod's Inborn Errors of Metabolism.* Oxford, 1963.

Halpern, S.L. (editor): Symposium on recent advances in applied nutrition. M Clin North America 48:1111–1269, 1964.

Hsia, D.Y-Y.: *Human Development Genetics.* Year Book, 1968.

Hsia, D.Y-Y.: *Inborn Errors of Metabolism.* Year Book, 1966.

Hsia, D.Y-Y.: *Lectures in Medical Genetics.* Year Book, 1966.

Jolliffe, N.: *Clinical Nutrition,* 2nd ed. Hoeber, 1962.

Littlefield, J.W.: The expression of genetic information. New England J Med 268:873–881, 1963.

McHenry, E.W.: *Basic Nutrition,* rev ed. Lippincott, 1963.

McKusick, V.A.: *Heritable Disorders of Connective Tissue,* 3rd ed. Mosby, 1966.

McKusick, V.A.: *Medical Genetics 1961–1963.* Pergamon, 1966.

Penrose, L.S.: *Outline of Human Genetics.* Wiley, 1959.

Reed, S.C.: *Counseling in Medical Genetics,* 2nd ed. Saunders, 1963.

Stanbury, J.B., & others: *The Metabolic Basis of Inherited Disease,* 2nd ed. Blakiston, 1966.

Wolff, O.H., & others: Recent developments in the management and prognosis of some inborn errors of metabolism. Proc Roy Soc Med 60:1147–1158, 1967.

20...

Infectious Diseases: Viral & Rickettsial

Henry B. Bruyn, J. Ralph Audy, & Ernest Jawetz

VIRAL DISEASES

RUBEOLA
(Measles)

Essentials of Diagnosis

- Prodrome of fever, coryza, cough, conjunctivitis, photophobia, Koplik's spots.
- Rash: brick-red, irregular, maculopapular; onset 4 days after onset of prodrome; face to trunk to extremities.
- Leukopenia.
- Exposure 14 days before rash.

General Considerations

Measles is a systemic viral infection transmitted by inhalation of infective droplets. Its highest age incidence is in young children. One attack confers permanent immunity. Communicability is greatest during the pre-eruptive stage, but continues as long as the rash remains.

Clinical Findings

A. Symptoms and Signs: Fever is often as high as 40–40.6° C (104–105° F). It persists through the prodrome and rash (about 7 days), but may remit briefly at the onset of rash. Malaise may be marked. Coryza resembles that seen with upper respiratory infections (nasal obstruction, sneezing, and sore throat). Cough is persistent and nonproductive, and arouses the suspicion of pneumonia. There is conjunctivitis, with redness, swelling, photophobia, and discharge.

Koplik's spots are pathognomonic of measles. They appear about 2 days before the rash and last 1–4 days as tiny "table salt crystals" on the dull red mucous membranes of the cheeks and often on inner conjunctival folds and vaginal mucous membranes. The pharynx is red, and a yellowish exudate may appear on the tonsils. The tongue is coated in the center; the tip and margins are red. Moderate generalized lymphadenopathy is common. Splenomegaly occurs occasionally.

The rash usually appears first on the face and behind the ears 4 days after the onset of symptoms.

The initial lesions are pinhead-sized papules which coalesce to form the brick-red, irregular, blotchy maculopapular rash which may further coalesce in severe cases to form an almost uniform erythema on some areas of the body. By the second day the rash begins to coalesce on the face as it appears on the trunk. On the third day the rash is confluent on the trunk and begins to appear on the extremities. The rash begins to fade on the face on the third and thereafter fades in the order of its appearance. Hyperpigmentation remains in fair-skinned individuals and severe cases. Slight desquamation may follow.

The early rash resembles drug reaction or other exanthematous diseases.

B. Laboratory Findings: Leukopenia is usually present unless secondary bacterial complications exist. Febrile proteinuria is present.

Complications

Secondary bacterial infections are common. Streptococcal, staphylococcal, pneumococcal, and other infections should be suspected if fever persists after the rash has disappeared or if leukocytosis occurs.

Catarrhal otitis media occurs in many cases and is of little importance. Purulent otitis media is manifested by fever, earache, and bulging eardrums.

Bronchial pneumonia is the cause of most deaths due to measles. It may be due to measles virus or secondary bacterial invaders. Fever, tachypnea, medium or fine rales, or signs of consolidation are important diagnostically.

Cervical adenitis is usually due to secondary bacterial infection.

Mild laryngitis with hoarseness, croupy cough, and stridor may be due to measles virus; if severe, it is due to secondary infection and may result in obstruction.

Postmeasles encephalitis occurs with varying frequency in different epidemics. It usually appears after the height of the rash or during convalescence, and occasionally occurs before the eruption.

Prevention*

Attenuated live virus vaccine is available and

---

*Most vaccines are made in chick embryo cells, and there is no good evidence of egg allergy. Canine cell vaccine is also available.

effective and should be used for children with no history of measles at (or as soon as possible after) 9 months of age. For children exposed to measles who have not been protected by active immunization, gamma globulin may be given shortly after exposure in a dose of 0.1 ml/lb body weight (for protection) or 0.02 ml/lb for modification. (See Immunization Schedules in Appendix.)

Live attenuated vaccine produces a febrile illness in 10% of cases and a modified rash in 5%, but results in immunity equivalent to natural infection in 99%. If measles immune globulin is given simultaneously, the reaction rate is lower and antibody rates are only slightly less. Killed virus vaccine is not recommended.

Treatment

A. General Measures: Isolate the patient for the week following onset of rash and keep at bed rest until afebrile. Give aspirin, saline eye sponges, vasoconstrictor nose drops, and a sedative cough mixture as necessary.

B. Treatment of Complications: Secondary bacterial infections of the middle ear, throat, larynx, or lungs are treated with appropriate anti-infective drugs. Postmeasles encephalitis may only be treated symptomatically, ie, lumbar puncture for relief of headache, and anticonvulsants.

Prognosis

The mortality rate of measles in the USA is 0.2%, but it may be as high as 10% in underdeveloped areas. Deaths are due principally to encephalitis (15% mortality) and bacterial pneumonia.

Advisory Committee on Immunization Practices, US Public Health Service: Measles vaccines. Ann Int Med 67:1055–1058, 1967.

Dandoy, S.: Measles epidemiology and vaccine use in Los Angeles County, 1963 and 1966. Pub Health Rep 82:659–666, 1967.

EXANTHEM SUBITUM
(Roseola Infantum)

Exanthem subitum is a communicable viral disease, principally of infants and young children. Fever begins suddenly, often accompanied by mild leukocytosis and suboccipital adenopathy, lasts 1–5 days (usually 3), and falls by crisis. A pink rubelliform rash, predominantly on the trunk, appears after the fever has subsided. During this stage the white count shows leukopenia and lymphocytosis.

Treatment is symptomatic only, eg, aspirin and tepid sponges for high fever.

The prognosis is uniformly good. Febrile convulsions may occur.

Clemens, H.H.: Exanthem subitum (roseola infantum). J Pediat 26:66–77, 1945.

RUBELLA
(German Measles)

Essentials of Diagnosis

- No prodrome; mild symptoms (fever, malaise, coryza) coinciding with eruption.
- Posterior cervical and postauricular lymphadenopathy.
- Fine maculopapular rash of 3 days' duration; face to trunk to extremities.
- Leukopenia.
- Exposure 14–21 days previously.

General Considerations

Rubella is a systemic viral disease transmitted by inhalations of infective droplets. It attacks principally older children and young adults. It is not as communicable as measles. One attack usually confers permanent immunity. The incubation period is 14–21 days (average 16). The disease is transmissible as long as 1 week before the rash appears.

Rubella often occurs without rash, with only fever and lymphadenopathy. It thus resembles infectious mononucleosis, and the distinction can only be made by serologic tests. The rash of rubella resembles a drug reaction, and on the third day may resemble scarlet fever.

Clinical Findings

A. Symptoms and Signs: Fever and malaise, usually mild, accompanied by tender suboccipital adenitis, may precede the eruption by as long as a week. Mild coryza may be present. Joint pain (polyarthritis) occurs in about 25% of adult cases. These symptoms usually subside in less than 7 days.

Posterior cervical and postauricular lymphadenopathy is very common. Erythema of the palate and throat, sometimes blotchy, may be noted. A fine, pink maculopapular rash appears on the face, trunk, and extremities in rapid progression (2–3 days) and fades quickly, usually lasting 1 day in each area. Rubella without rash may be at least as common as the exanthematous disease. Diagnosis depends on epidemiologic evidence of the disease in the community and occurrence of a mildly febrile generalized lymphadenopathy.

B. Laboratory Findings: Leukopenia may be present early and may be followed by an increase in plasma cells. Virus isolation and serologic tests of immunity are available. A rapid rubella virus hemagglutination-inhibition test and a fluorescent antibody test have been recently introduced.

Complications

Fetal abnormalities constitute a serious threat in rubella occurring during the first trimester of pregnancy and may produce the "rubella syndrome," a chronic congenital infection characterized by prolonged virus excretion, thrombocytopenia, cardiac lesions, hepatosplenomegaly, cataracts, prematurity, and other anomalies.

TABLE 20–1. Diagnostic features of some acute exanthems.*

Disease	Prodromal Signs and Symptoms	Nature of Eruption	Other Diagnostic Features	Laboratory Tests
Measles (rubeola)	3–4 days of fever, coryza, conjunctivitis and cough.	Maculopapular, brick-red; begins on head and neck; spreads downward. In 5–6 days rash brownish, desquamating.	Koplik's spots on buccal mucosa.	White blood count low; specialized complement fixation and virus neutralization in tissue culture.
German measles (rubella)	Little or no prodrome.	Maculopapular, pink; begins on head and neck, spreads downward, fades in 3 days. No desquamation.	Lymphadenopathy, postauricular or occipital.	White blood count normal or low. Serologic tests for immunity.
Chickenpox (varicella)	0–1 day of fever, anorexia, headache.	Rapid evolution of macules to papules, vesicles, crusts; all stages simultaneously present; lesions superficial, distribution centripetal.	Lesions on scalp and mucous membranes.	Specialized complement fixation and virus neutralization in tissue culture.
Smallpox (variola)	3 days of fever, severe headache, malaise, chills.	Slow evolution of macules to papules, vesicles, pustules, crusts; all lesions in any area in same stage; lesions deep-seated, distribution centrifugal.		Virus isolation. Serologic tests for immunity.
Scarlet fever	½–2 days of malaise, sore throat, fever, vomiting.	Generalized, punctate, red; prominent on neck, in axilla, groin, skinfolds; circumoral pallor; fine desquamation involves hands and feet.	Strawberry tongue, exudative tonsillitis.	Group A hemolytic streptococci cultures from throat; antistreptolysin O titer rise.
Exanthem subitum	3–4 days of high fever.	As fever falls by crisis, pink maculopapules appear on chest and trunk; fade in 1–3 days.		White blood count low.
Erythema infectiosum	None. Usually in epidemics.	Red, flushed cheeks; circumoral pallor; maculopapules on extremities.	"Slapped face" appearance.	White blood count normal.
Meningococcemia	Hours of fever, vomiting.	Maculopapules, petechiae.	Meningeal signs.	Cultures of blood, CSF. High white blood count.
Rocky Mt spotted fever	3–4 days of fever, chills, severe headaches.	Maculopapules, petechiae, distribution centrifugal.	History of tick bite.	Agglutination (OX19, OX2), complement fixation.
Typhus fevers	3–4 days of fever, chills, severe headaches.	Maculopapules, petechiae, distribution centripetal.	Endemic area, lice.	Agglutination (OX19), complement fixation.
Infectious mononucleosis	Fever, adenopathy, sore throat.	Maculopapular rash resembling rubella, rarely papulovesicular.	Splenomegaly.	Atypical lymphs in blood smears; heterophil agglutination.
Enterovirus infections	1–2 days of fever, malaise.	Maculopapular rash resembling rubella, rarely papulovesicular or petechial.	Aseptic meningitis.	Virus isolation from stool or CSF; complement fixation titer rise.
Drug eruptions	Occasionally fever.	Maculopapular rash resembling rubella, rarely papulovesicular.		Eosinophilia.
Eczema herpeticum	None.	Vesiculopustular lesions in area of eczema.		Herpes simplex virus isolated on tissue culture; complement fixation.

*Courtesy of Ernest Jawetz, MD.

The incidence of malformations in the infant, summarizing reported studies, is 35% in the first month, 25% in the second month, 10% in the third month, and 4% in the fourth month. The incidence of malformation following rubella in the fifth month and thereafter is extremely low.

Prevention

The availability of rapid laboratory tests for rubella antibody shows promise that the decision for therapeutic abortion can be based on the demonstration of absent antibodies in the exposed woman.

Live attenuated rubella virus vaccine is now commercially available and is highly effective. It should certainly be given to all girls before the menarche, and probably to all boys as well. The presence of a pregnant woman in the immediate family would contraindicate the use of the vaccine. Before giving the vaccine to an adult woman, it is advised that the presence or absence of pregnancy be determined, that the presence or absence of antibodies against rubella be determined, and that birth control be practiced for at least 3 months after the use of the vaccine.

Treatment

Give aspirin as required for symptomatic relief. Encephalitis and thrombocytopenic purpura can only be treated symptomatically.

Prognosis

The illness is usually mild and rarely lasts longer than 3–4 days.

Heggie, A.D.: Rubella: Current concepts in epidemiology and teratology. P Clin North America 13:251–266, 1966.

Miller, C.H., & others: Prevention of rubella with γ-globulin. JAMA 201:560–561, 1967.

Sever, J.L., & others: Rubella antibody determinations. Pediatrics 40:789–797, 1967.

Stewart, G.L., & others: Rubella-virus hemagglutination-inhibition test. New England J Med 276:554–557, 1967.

CYTOMEGALOVIRUS DISEASE

Cytomegalovirus disease, once thought to be a rare type of congenital infection which was usually fatal, is now recognized as the cause of several types of disease of which the congenital variety is perhaps the least common.

Cytomegalovirus is isolated easily from the urine and body tissues of acutely ill patients. It can also be isolated from the urine for many months after the acute illness or, in congenital cases, after birth. Characteristic large inclusion bodies are present in the epithelial cells found in the urinary sediment.

Clinical Findings

A. Congenital Disease: Rapid onset of jaundice occurs shortly after birth, with hepatosplenomegaly, purpura, hematuria, and signs of encephalitis. Laboratory findings include thrombocytopenia, erythroblastosis, bilirubinemia, and marked lymphocytosis. Downey type abnormal lymphocytes are present in large numbers. Sequelae include intracranial calcifications, microcephaly, mental retardation, convulsive state, and optic atrophy. Although many infections are subclinical, the prognosis is poor in clinical disease.

B. Acute Acquired Cytomegalovirus Disease: The clinical picture is similar to that of infectious mononucleosis, with sudden onset of fever, malaise, joint pains, and myalgia. Pharyngitis is minimal, and respiratory symptoms are absent. Lymphadenopathy is generalized. The liver is enlarged and often slightly tender. Laboratory findings include the hematologic picture of mononucleosis as well as bilirubinemia. Heterophil antibody does not appear. This infection is common following massive transfusions in organ transplant surgery.

Treatment

There is no specific treatment. Control fever, pain, and convulsions with appropriate drugs. Corticosteroids have been reported to produce amelioration of symptoms and are of particular value for congenital disease, where the prognosis is so poor.

Carlström, G., & others: Acquired cytomegalovirus infection. Brit MJ 2:521–524, 1968.

Stern, H.: Isolation of cytomegalovirus and clinical manifestations of infection at different ages. Brit MJ 1:665–669, 1968.

VARICELLA
(Chickenpox)

Essentials of Diagnosis

- Mild symptoms (fever, malaise) just preceding or simultaneous with eruption.
- Rash: pruritic, centripetal, papular, changing to vesicular, pustular, and finally crusting.
- Leukopenia.
- Exposure 14–20 days previously.

General Considerations

Varicella is a viral disease spread by inhalations of infective droplets or crusts. Most cases occur in children. One attack confers permanent immunity. The virus is identical to that of herpes zoster. The incubation period is 10–20 days (average 14 days).

Clinical Findings

A. Symptoms and Signs: Fever and malaise are usually mild in children, more severe in adults. Itching is characteristic of the eruption. Vesicular lesions, quickly rupturing to form small ulcers, may appear first in the oropharynx. The rash is most prominent on the face, scalp, and trunk, but to a lesser extent commonly involves the extremities (centripetal). Maculopapules are succeeded in a few hours by vesicles which quickly become pustular and eventually form crusts. New lesions may erupt for 1–5 days (usually 3 days), so that all stages of the eruption are generally present simultaneously. The crusts usually slough in 7–14 days. The vesicles and pustules are superficial, elliptical, and have slightly serrated borders.

The distribution and recurrent eruption of varicella distinguishes it from herpes zoster and smallpox.

B. Laboratory Findings: Leukopenia is commonly present. Multinucleated giant cells may be found in scrapings of the base of the vesicles. Virus isolation is possible.

Complications

Secondary bacterial infection of the lesions is common and may produce a pitted scar. Cellulitis, erysipelas, or surgical scarlet fever may occur.

Pneumonia may be due to varicella virus or secondary bacterial infection.

Encephalitis may follow the eruption.

Death may occur in patients receiving corticosteroid therapy.

Prevention

Temporary passive protection irregularly follows intramuscular administration of 20 ml of convalescent serum, but this is rarely warranted. Zoster hyperimmune globulin has been shown to be highly effective in prevention, although at the present time this material is available only from very limited resources.

Treatment

A. General Measures: Isolate the patient until primary crusts have disappeared, and keep at bed rest until afebrile. Keep the skin clean by means of frequent tub baths or showers when afebrile. pHisoHex® is preferable to soap to reduce the incidence of secondary bacterial infection. Calamine lotion locally and antihistaminics orally may relieve the pruritus.

B. Treatment of Complications: Secondary bacterial infection of local lesions may be treated with bacitracin or tyrothricin ointment; if extensive, penicillin intramuscularly may be given. Postvaricella encephalitis and varicella pneumonia are treated symptomatically. Corticosteroids have been reported to have a beneficial effect. Bacterial pneumonia is treated with appropriate antibiotics.

Prognosis

The total duration from onset of symptoms to the disappearance of crusts rarely exceeds 2 weeks. Fatalities are rare.

Brunell, P.A., & others: Prevention of varicella by zoster immune globulin. New England J Med 280:1191–1194, 1969.

Sargent, E.N., Carson, M.J., & E.D. Reilly: Varicella pneumonia: A report of twenty cases, with postmortem examination in six. California Med 107:141–148, 1967.

VARIOLA
(Smallpox, Variola Major)

Essentials of Diagnosis

- Severe symptoms (headache, nausea, fever, prostration) precede eruption by 2–4 days.
- Centrifugal macular rash, changing to papular, vesicular, and pustular; and finally crusting and occasionally hemorrhagic eruptions of similar stage in any given area.
- Leukopenia early; leukocytosis late.
- Exposure 7–21 days previously (usually 10–14 days).

General Considerations

Smallpox is a highly contagious viral disease transmitted by droplets or by contact with infected crusts. All ages are susceptible, depending upon the interval since vaccination. Previous effective vaccination prevents or modifies the disease (varioloid). Variola major is more virulent than variola minor (alastrim). The incubation period is 7–21 days (average 12 days).

Clinical Findings

A. Symptoms and Signs: Fever, usually 38.9–40.6° C (102–105° F) appears 2–4 days before the eruption and may abate temporarily at the beginning of eruption to increase again during the stage of pustule formation. Malaise and prostration are usually marked. Headache and low backache are characteristically severe. Nausea and vomiting, dizziness, and constipation may occur.

Erythematous, hemorrhagic, or morbilliform rashes occasionally occur during the prodromal illness. The rash appears first on the face and scalp, then on the wrists, hands, neck, back, chest, arms, legs, and feet. New lesions appear for 2–3 days. Pink macules rapidly become papules, which become vesicles in about 3 days. On about the 6th day of eruption, the vesicles become pustules; these in turn become crusts on the 11th or 12th day. Marked edema and oozing may occur during the stage of pustule formation. The crusts may persist for a week or longer, especially on the palms and soles. The individual lesions are round and deeply set in the skin, giving a shotty sensation upon palpation. The distribution of the lesions, even in mild cases, is centrifugal, with lesions densest on the face and distal portions of the extremities. In milder cases the lesions are discrete; in severe cases they may be confluent. The lesions in any given area tend to be of a similar stage of evolution.

Lesions on the mucous membranes may precede the exanthem by a short interval.

The initial eruption may be hemorrhagic and accompanied by hemorrhage from mucous membranes. This type is invariably fatal. Delayed hemorrhage (less often fatal) may occur into the vesicles or pustules.

B. Laboratory Findings: Leukopenia may occur during the early stages, succeeded by leukocytosis during the stage of pustule formation. Proteinuria is common. The rabbit eye test of Paul is positive if vesicular and necrotizing lesions appear on a rabbit cornea 36–48 hours after scarification with a needle dipped in vesicular or pustular fluid.

Chick embryo inoculation is positive if a pock appears on chick chorio-allantois inoculated with blood or fluid from lesion.

Complement fixation and flocculation tests with pock material and specific immune sera are available.

Complement-fixing and chicken erythrocyte agglutination inhibiting antibodies appear during or after the second week of the disease.

The fluorescent antibody technic may be used for prompt identification of inclusion bodies in material from a pock.

Immediate identification of a virulent antigen by gel diffusion of vesicle material against hyperimmune specific serum is possible if laboratory facilities are available.

Differential Diagnosis

The pre-eruptive stage may be mistaken for an acute respiratory infection; the eruptive stage may be mistaken for chickenpox. The rash must be distinguished from that of rickettsialpox, syphilis, measles, Kaposi's varicelliform eruption, and drug sensitivity.

Complications

Secondary infection of the lesions is the rule. Residual pitting is common. Erysipelas, surgical scarlet fever, or gangrene may occur. Septicemia, often streptococcal, may occur. Respiratory obstruction may occur due to laryngeal lesions.

Prevention

Vaccination (see Vaccinia, below). Methisazone (Marboran®) promises to be an effective chemoprophylactic agent in variola in exposed persons. The dosage is 2–4 gm daily orally (100 mg/kg/day) for 2 days beginning 1–2 days after exposure.

Treatment

A. General Measures: Penicillin has a generally favorable effect by controlling secondary bacterial invaders during pustulation.

B. Local Measures: Early in the disease, provide good oral hygiene and apply petrolatum or mineral oil swabs to the nares. Gentle cleansing of the skin is advisable. If lesions are confluent and suppurating, treat as pyoderma. Treat itching with antipruritic lotions; restraints and sedation may be necessary.

C. Treatment of Complications: Treat as indicated for secondary infections; otherwise, treatment is symptomatic.

Prognosis

The crusts usually disappear after 3 weeks. The severity of the illness and mortality depend upon the strain of virus: variola minor, 1%; variola major, 20%. Modified smallpox is rarely fatal.

Kempe, C.H., & A.S. Benenson: Smallpox immunization in the US. JAMA 194:161–166, 1965.

Neff, J.M., & others: Complications of smallpox vaccination. New England J Med 276:125–131, 1967.

Quie, P.G., & J.M. Matsen: Treatment of smallpox and complications of smallpox vaccination. GP 36:130–170, Oct 1967.

Rao, A.R., McFadzean, L.A., & K. Kamalakshi: An isothiazole thiosemicarbazone [methisazone; Marboran®] in the treatment of variola major in man. Lancet 1:1068–1072, 1966.

VACCINIA

Vaccinia is the cutaneous and sometimes general reaction which occurs following the introduction of vaccinia virus in the course of immunization against smallpox. In normal circumstances it consists of a single local lesion at the site of inoculation which undergoes a characteristic evolution depending upon the state of immunity of the patient.

When no local reaction occurs following inoculation, either the vaccine or the technic is at fault. This is not due to immunity.

Types of Vaccinia

A. Primary Vaccinia: In nonimmune inoculated patients a papule will appear on the 3rd or 4th day, followed on the next day by an umbilicated vesicle which, in the course of 3–4 days, is surrounded by an erythematous area as pustulation occurs; the area of erythema is greatest between the 8th and 12th days after vaccination. The pustule dries to form a crust by about the 12th day. The crust detaches in the ensuing week to leave the characteristic pitted vaccination scar.

Fever and malaise may appear on about the 6th day and persist for 1–2 days. Axillary adenopathy may be present. Viremia occurs regularly; and the virus may be isolated from throat secretions.

B. Accelerated (Vaccinoid) Reaction: In subjects with partial immunity, the course of vaccinia is accelerated and less severe. A papule appears, usually within 24 hours, at the site of the vaccination. Vesiculation appears earlier than in the primary reaction, and erythema is considerably less. The height of the erythematous reaction is reached between the 4th and the 7th days. Systemic manifestations are usually mild.

C. Immediate (Allergic) Reaction: This reaction may indicate no more than sensitivity to viral protein from previous primary vaccination or from disease. It is seen in the fully immune individual. However, it may also be elicited by deteriorated (dead) vaccine or poor technic in individuals who have lost their immunity but have retained their viral sensitivity. This reaction does not necessarily mean, therefore, that the subject is immune. When it occurs, the procedure should be repeated at least once with known potent vaccine and careful technic to ensure successful vaccination. The immediate or allergic reaction is characterized by the occurrence of a papule or perhaps a small area of redness within the first 24 hours following vaccination. It may be very slight, and the height of the erythematous reaction may be passed within 3 days. (See Immunization Schedules in Appendix.)

Complications

Autoinoculation may result in one or more satellite lesions around the vaccination site or distant lesions elsewhere (including the conjunctivas).

Generalized vaccinoid lesions may occur a few days after vaccination.

Eczema vaccinatum occurs in persons with generalized dermatoses who themselves are vaccinated or who are exposed to someone with vaccinia. The eruption becomes generalized, particularly in the area of dermatosis; it is associated with high fever and the manifestations of severe systemic disease, and may be fatal. It must be distinguished from generalized herpes simplex infection in persons with dermatoses (Kaposi's varicelliform eruption). An attenuated vaccine appears to result in a lower incidence of eczema vaccinatum.

In persons with agammaglobulinemia or with a defect of delayed (tuberculin type) immunity, the lesion of vaccinia may proceed to a fatal outcome.

Secondary infection of the lesion due to streptococcal, staphylococcal, or, rarely, *Clostridium tetani* may occur.

Postvaccinal scarlatiniform or rubelliform rash, erythema multiforme, and gangrene of lesions may occur.

Postvaccinal encephalitis, manifested by sensory alterations, meningeal irritation, and abnormal neurologic findings, occurs extremely rarely and usually 10–14 days after vaccination. Death may occur. Residua are not common.

Treatment

No treatment nor dressing is required for uncomplicated vaccinia. Secondary infection may be treated with hot compresses and antibiotic ointment or systemic chemotherapy. Generalized vaccinia and eczema vaccinatum should be treated with vaccinia immune globulin, 1 ml/kg IM. No specific treatment is available for postvaccinal encephalitis.

Methisazone (Marboran®) promises to be effective in some cases of progressive vaccinia.

Brainerd, H., Hanna, L., & E. Jawetz: Methisazone in progressive vaccinia. New England J Med 276:620–622, 1967.

Kempe, C.H., & A.S. Benenson: Smallpox and vaccinia. P Clin North America 2:19–32, 1955.

EPIDEMIC PAROTITIS
(Mumps)

Essentials of Diagnosis

- Painful, swollen salivary glands, usually parotid.
- Orchitis, meningoencephalitis, pancreatitis; CSF lymphocytic pleocytosis in meningoencephalitis.
- Exposure 14–21 days previously.

General Considerations

Mumps is a viral disease spread by respiratory droplets which usually produces inflammation of the salivary glands and, less commonly, orchitis, meningoencephalitis, pancreatitis, and oophoritis. Most patients are children. The incubation period is 14–21 days (average 18 days). Infectivity precedes the symptoms by about 1 day, is maximal for 3 days, and then declines until the swelling has disappeared.

Clinical Findings

A. Symptoms and Signs: Fever and malaise are variable but are often minimal in young children. High fever usually accompanies orchitis or meningoencephalitis. Pain and swelling of one or both (75%) of the parotid or other salivary glands occurs, usually in succession 1–3 days apart. Occasionally one gland subsides completely (usually in 7 days or less) before others become involved. Pain and swelling of the testicle (orchitis) occurs in 25% of adult males with mumps. Headache and lethargy suggest meningoencephalitis. Upper abdominal pain, nausea, and vomiting suggest pancreatitis. Lower abdominal pain in females suggests oophoritis.

Parotid swelling is the commonest physical finding. Tenderness is usually present. Edema is occasionally marked. Swelling and tenderness of the submaxillary and sublingual glands is variable. The orifice of Stensen's duct may be reddened and swollen. Neck stiffness and other signs of meningeal irritation are commonly present in meningoencephalitis. Testicular swelling and tenderness (unilateral in 75%) denote orchitis. Epigastric tenderness may be observed in pancreatitis. Lower abdominal tenderness and ovarian enlargement may be noted in mumps oophoritis, but the diagnosis is often difficult. Salivary gland involvement must be differentiated from lymph gland involvement in the anterior cervical space. Mumps meningoencephalitis must be distinguished from the less common types of aseptic meningitis.

B. Laboratory Findings: Relative lymphocytosis may be present, although the blood picture is not of great diagnostic assistance. Serum amylase is commonly elevated with or without pancreatitis. Lymphocytic pleocytosis of the CSF is present in meningoencephalitis, which may be asymptomatic. Complement-fixing and chick cell agglutination inhibiting antibodies appear about 2 weeks after the onset of the disease.

Complications

The "complications" of mumps are simply other manifestations of the disease less common than inflammation of the salivary glands. These usually follow the parotitis but may precede it or occur without salivary gland involvement: meningoencephalitis (30%), orchitis (25% of adult males), pancreatitis, oophoritis, thyroiditis, neuritis, and myocarditis.

Prevention

Mumps live virus vaccine is highly effective and safe and is recommended for all susceptible individuals over 1 year of age. Exceptions include individuals with febrile illness, marked hypersensitivity to egg protein, leukemia, other generalized malignancies, altered resistance from therapy, and pregnancy.

Treatment

A. General Measures: Isolate the patient until swelling subsides and keep at bed rest during the febrile period. Give aspirin or codeine for analgesia as required, and alkaline aromatic solution mouth washes.

B. Treatment of Complications:

1. Meningoencephalitis (may be asymptomatic)—Give analgesics as necessary, and do lumbar puncture if necessary to reduce headache. If symptoms are very severe, hydrocortisone as for orchitis may be used.

2. Orchitis—Suspend the scrotum in a suspensory or toweling "bridge" and apply ice bags. Incision of the tunica may be necessary in severe cases. Give codeine or morphine as necessary for pain. Pain can also be relieved by injection of the spermatic cord at the external inguinal ring with 10–20 ml of 1% procaine solution. The inflammatory reaction may be reduced with hydrocortisone sodium succinate, 100 mg IV, followed by 20 mg orally every 6 hours for 2–3 days.

3. Pancreatitis—Symptomatic relief only, and parenteral fluids if necessary.

4. Oophoritis—Symptomatic treatment only.

Prognosis

The entire course of the infection rarely exceeds 2 weeks. Fatalities (due to encephalitis) are very rare.

Davidson, W.L., & others: Live attenuated mumps virus vaccine. JAMA 201:995–998, 1967.

Habel, K., & J.P. Utz: Mumps. P Clin North America 7:979–988, 1960.

Mumps vaccine. Recommendations of the PHS Advisory Committee on Immunization Practices. Clin Pediat 7:156–157, 1968.

POLIOMYELITIS

Essentials of Diagnosis

- Muscle weakness, headache, stiff neck, fever, nausea, vomiting, sore throat.
- Lower motor neuron lesion (flaccid paralysis) with decreased deep tendon reflexes and muscle wasting.
- CSF shows excess cells. Lymphocytes predominate; rarely more than 500/cu mm.

General Considerations

Poliomyelitis virus is present in throat washings and stools, and infection probably can be acquired by the respiratory droplet route or by ingestion. The incidence of the disease has been sharply reduced since the introduction of effective vaccine. In less than a decade poliomyelitis has become a rare disease, except in so-called underdeveloped areas.

Three antigenically distinct types of poliomyelitis virus (I, II, and III) are recognized, with no cross-immunity between them.

The incubation period is 5–35 days (usually 7–14 days). Infectivity is maximal during the first week, but excretion of virus in the stools may continue for several weeks. The family or other contacts of diagnosed cases may be "transient carriers" and excrete virus in the absence of symptoms or during the abortive type of infection.

Clinical Findings

A. Symptoms and Signs:

1. Abortive poliomyelitis—The symptoms are fever, headache, vomiting, diarrhea, constipation, and sore throat.

2. Nonparalytic poliomyelitis—Headache, neck, back, and extremity pain; fever, vomiting, abdominal pain, lethargy, and irritability are present. Muscle spasm—spontaneous shortening of the muscle or hyperactive stretch reflex with limitation of extension by pain and contraction—is always present in the extensors of the neck and back, usually present in the hamstring muscles, and variably present in other muscles. Resistance to flexion of the neck is noted after a varying range of free flexion. The patient assumes the "tripod" position upon sitting up, which he usually does by "rolling" to avoid flexing the back. Straight-leg raising is less than 90°. Spasm may be observed when the patient is at rest or may be elicited by putting each muscle through the maximum range of motion. The muscle may be tender to palpation.

3. Paralytic poliomyelitis—Paralysis may occur at any time during the febrile period. In addition to the symptoms of nonparalytic poliomyelitis, tremors and muscle weakness appear. Paresthesias and urinary retention are noted occasionally. Constipation and abdominal distention (ileus) are common. Paralytic poliomyelitis may be divided into 2 forms which may coexist: (1) spinal poliomyelitis, with weakness of the muscles supplied by the spinal nerves; and (2) bulbar poliomyelitis, with weakness of the muscles supplied by the cranial nerves and variable "encephalitis" symptoms. Bulbar symptoms include diplopia (uncommon), weakness of mastication, facial weakness, dysphagia, dysphonia, nasal voice, regurgitation of fluids through the nose, weakness of the sternocleidomastoid and trapezius muscles, difficulty in chewing, and inability to swallow or expel saliva and respiratory tract secretions. The most life-threatening aspect of bulbar poliomyelitis is respiratory paralysis.

Paralysis of the neck flexors is manifested by "neck drop" on lifting the shoulders from the bed. Paralysis of the shoulder girdle often precedes inter-costal and diaphragmatic paralysis. Partial paralysis of the rectus abdomini is manifested by deviation of the umbilicus on active flexion of the neck. Weakness of the intercostal muscles and diaphragm is demonstrated by diminished chest expansion, "rocking horse" respiration with paradoxic movement of the diaphragm, use of accessory muscles, and decreased vital capacity. Cyanosis and stridor may appear later due to hypoxia. Paralysis may quickly become maximal or may progress over a period of several days until the temperature becomes normal.

Deep tendon reflexes are diminished or lost, often asymmetrically, in areas of involvement.

In bulbar poliomyelitis there may be strabismus (rare), facial asymmetry, deviation of jaw on opening, loss of gag reflex, loss of movement of palate and pharyngeal muscles, pooling of secretions in the oropharynx, deviation of tongue, and loss of move-ment of the vocal cords. In bulbar respiratory involve-ment the respirations are dysrhythmic (varying in rate, rhythm, and depth). The patient can usually take deep breaths on command.

Lethargy or coma may be due to encephalitis or hypoxia. Such disturbances of consciousness are most often due to hypoventilation.

Hypertension, hypotension, and tachycardia may occur. Convulsions are rare.

B. Laboratory Findings: The white count is not characteristic. The sedimentation rate may be normal or mildly elevated. CSF pressure is normal or slightly increased; protein normal or slightly increased; glucose not decreased; cells usually less than 500/cu mm (pre-dominantly lymphocytes; polymorphonuclears may be elevated at first). CSF is normal in 5% of patients. The virus may be recovered from throat washings (early) and stools (early and late). Neutralizing and comple-ment-fixing antibodies appear during or after the second week.

Differential Diagnosis

Abortive poliomyelitis may simulate acute respi-ratory infection or gastroenteritis, and is usually not dangerous. Nonparalytic poliomyelitis is difficult to distinguish from other aseptic meningitides (encephali-tis, mumps, Coxsackie virus infection, choriomeningi-tis), meningismus, and granulomatous meningitis. Paralytic poliomyelitis may be mimicked by hysteria, especially during outbreaks; hysterical paralysis may also occur with viral meningitis or other CNS disorders. Paralysis simulating or identical with that due to polio-myelitis is now being observed in infections due to other enteric neurotropic viruses and in Guillain-Barré syndrome.

Complications

Urinary tract infection, atelectasis, pneumonia, myocarditis, and pulmonary edema may occur. Late complications include skeletal and soft tissue defor-mities, cor pulmonale, osteoporosis, urolithiasis, and chronic colonic distention.

Prevention

Note: Specific immunization schedules are given in the Appendix.

Although both inactivated poliomyelitis vaccine (IPV, Salk) and oral vaccine (live virus, Sabin) are licensed by the Food & Drug Administration for use in immunization, the effectiveness and duration of immunity following the live virus preparation is such that it is the preparation of choice. It also has the advantage of being administered orally.

For information concerning dosage forms, stor-age, methods of administration, and use in mass vac-cination programs, reference should be made to the brochures provided by pharmaceutical manufacturers or to public health agencies.

Because poliomyelitis is indistinguishable from other viral infections of the nervous system (see Cox-sackie- and Echovirus Infections), symptoms of men-ingeal irritation warrant a regimen of rest and close observation, especially during the febrile period.

Treatment

A. Early Phase: The patient should avoid travel, activity, and psychic stress, and should be spared unnecessary examinations. Perform a brief and cursory muscle check not more than once daily in acute cases. Muscle examination should not require vigorous mus-cular activity on the part of the patient. Maintain com-fortable but changing positions in a "polio bed": firm mattress, foot board, sponge rubber pads or rolls, sand-bags, and light splints. Give aspirin or aspirin combined with amphetamine and phenobarbital for pain and anxiety. Do not give opiates and barbiturates in seda-tive doses. Tranquilizers should be used with caution.

Hot wool packs (Kenny) or hydrocollator pads may be applied to the extremities or other areas for the relief of pain during the febrile period, but com-plete body packs should be used only when the patient is afebrile. Change of position, extremity packs, and analgesic drugs usually suffice to control muscle spasm. Depot forms of tubocurarine may be used with cau-tion.

Dehydration and intestinal hypoactivity often lead to fecal impaction. Examine the patient frequent-ly and give sufficient fluids to prevent this. Use enemas and neostigmine intramuscularly if necessary.

Bladder weakness may occur with paralysis involving any muscle group, most commonly with paraplegia. If this happens, insert a Foley catheter with great aseptic care and connect it with a gravity bottle by means of a sterile clear plastic tube. Change the catheter every 5 days and remove it as soon as possible. Do not attempt chemoprophylaxis with antimicrobials. Treat specific urinary infection after removal of the catheter (or if fever and rigor occur), and only after identification of the organism and sensitivity tests.

During the early phase and as long as the patient is bedfast, give a neutral ash diet with a maximum of 0.5 gm calcium content daily (no milk or milk products), and maintain fluid intake to ensure an adequate daily output of low specific gravity urine (1.5–2 liters/day for adults). If nasogastric feedings are necessary, use liquid meat baby foods, juices, low-calcium soybean milk substitutes, lactose, and vitamins.

B. Severe Cases:

1. Mobilization of personnel and equipment— Symptoms of grave poliomyelitis (or of respiratory muscle paralysis in Guillain-Barré syndrome, or respiratory depression due to drugs or poisons or due to botulism) require emergency mobilization of a medical-surgical team and basic equipment: tank respirator, preferably with a positive pressure attachment; tracheostomy surgical set; intravenous set (with polyethylene catheter and cut-down instruments); and aspirating pump.

2. Tracheostomy, artificial respiration, long-term ventilatory assistance—See Chapter 6. In patients with respiratory dysrhythmia (central paralysis), utilize combined endotracheal positive pressure synchronously with the tank to maintain adequate tidal volume. In desperate cases, give tubocurarine chloride, 0.2–0.4 mg/kg every 8–12 hours, to induce relaxation of respiratory muscles.

For sleep use relatively nondepressant sedatives such as antihistamines. Do not give barbiturates.

For treatment or (rarely) chemoprophylaxis of respiratory tract infections, use penicillin (preferably) or erythromycin. Avoid prolonged use of broad-spectrum antibiotics to prevent the development of resistant urinary and respiratory tract infections.

Maintain tidal air required for patient's respiratory rate and weight. (See E.P. Radford, Jr., & others: Clinical use of a nomogram to estimate proper ventilation during artificial respiration. New England J Med 251:877, 1954.) Avoid respiratory alkalosis by control of tidal air and appropriate arterial blood-alveolar air monitoring, especially alveolar or arterial P_{CO_2}.

C. Convalescence and Rehabilitation: The principles are to prevent deformity, avoid exercise during the febrile period, and mobilize early; give range of motion exercise and change position frequently during the febrile period; provide early active exercise under skilled direction as soon as feasible. Early bracing and splinting for therapeutic purposes are required to activate the therapy program. *Note:* All available physical and occupational therapy services, individual and group psychology, social services, and the cooperation of all medical specialities may be required in the rehabilitation process.

D. Treatment of Complications:

1. Gastric distention—Relieve by nasogastric intubation and aspiration; replace lost electrolytes by the intravenous route.

2. Gastric hemorrhage (uncommon, but may be fatal)—Give whole blood transfusions if bleeding occurs or a perforated Curling's ulcer is suspected. Surgery should be undertaken under positive-pressure respiration if perforation is proved.

3. Bladder atony and infection—See above.

4. Ileus and impaction—See above.

5. Atelectasis—Prevent by aerosolization of the air stream, preferably with aerosol saturated with water vapor at body temperature or supersaturated by means of mist produced by ultrasound; periodic deep breathing by increasing tank pressure briefly, or by special vacuum attachment; change of position; and prevention of respiratory infection, as well as good tracheobronchial toilet. If atelectasis occurs, treat with positive-pressure aerosol therapy, bronchial dilators, and wetting agents. Bronchoscopy is usually ineffective unless inspissated secretions are present.

6. Mental changes—Psychosis (usually short-lived), with confusion, disorientation, and hallucinations or delusions occurs in a small percentage of cases. Early psychic disturbances usually indicate hypoxia. Postacute depression is common in severe disease. It subsides in 6–8 weeks with supportive psychologic care and can often be prevented by meticulous care to prevent psychic trauma.

7. Pregnancy—Pregnant women, unless immunized, are susceptible to poliomyelitis and often develop severe disease. Expectant care should be attempted until term. At or near term carry the patient with respiratory muscle weakness through labor in a tank respirator and deliver on an open respirator under positive-pressure respiration with local block or do cesarean section. The mortality rate is negligible with a well-coordinated respiratory and obstetric program. Early in pregnancy, spontaneous abortion may occur or surgical abortion may be necessary. Try to avoid surgical abortion until the end of the febrile period.

Prognosis

Paralysis may occur or progress during the febrile period (3–10 days). Diffuse mild weakness is more favorable for functional recovery than severe weakness of a few important muscles. Bulbar poliomyelitis (10–20%) is the most serious. The overall mortality rate is 5–10%.

Hirschberg, G.G., Lewis, L., & D. Thomas: *Rehabilitation: A Manual for the Care of the Disabled and Elderly.* Lippincott, 1964.

Lepow, M.L., Nankervis, G.A., & F.C. Robbins: Immunity after oral poliomyelitis vaccination. JAMA 202:27–31, 1967.

ENCEPHALITIS

Essentials of Diagnosis

- Fever, malaise, stiff neck, sore throat, and nausea and vomiting, progressing to stupor, coma, and convulsions.

- Signs of an upper motor neuron lesion (exaggerated deep tendon reflexes, absent superficial reflexes, pathologic reflexes, spastic paralysis).
- CSF protein and pressure often increased, with lymphocytic pleocytosis.

General Considerations

Infectious encephalitis results from direct invasion of brain tissue by an infectious agent (Table 20–2). Evidence of a chronic viral encephalitis has been demonstrated in western equine encephalitis and in Japanese B encephalitis. Chronic, continuing viral activity might be extremely important in explaining some of the serious and slowly developing sequelae of infectious encephalitis in children.

Parainfectious encephalitis, as the name implies, is associated with an infection but is not due to direct invasion of the nervous system by the infecting agent. These cases are of 2 basic types: (1) those probably due to an antigen-antibody reaction associated with a systemic infection, and (2) those due to the direct effect of a toxin which is the byproduct of bacterial or viral proliferation in a systemic infection (Table 20–3). Postvaccinal encephalitis is included in this category because it is clearly related to an infectious agent and because the pathologic process is similar to encephalopathy that follows or accompanies an acute infection such as rubeola or varicella. The encephalopathy that follows inoculation of killed pertussis vaccine is unique in that the pathologic process is entirely similar to that associated with a systemic infection.

Clinical Findings

A. Symptoms and Signs: The symptoms are fever, malaise, sore throat, nausea and vomiting, lethargy, stupor, coma, and convulsions. Signs include stiff neck, signs of meningeal irritation, tremors, convulsions, cranial nerve palsies, paralysis of extremities, exaggerated deep reflexes, absent superficial reflexes, and pathologic reflexes.

B. Laboratory Findings: The white count is variable. CSF pressure and protein content are often increased; glucose is normal; lymphocytic pleocytosis may be present (polymorphonuclears may predominate early in some forms). Blood from patients can cause encephalitis when inoculated into mice. Serologic tests of blood may be diagnostic in a few specific types of encephalitis.

Differential Diagnosis

Mild forms of encephalitis must be differentiated from aseptic meningitis, lymphocytic choriomeningitis, and nonparalytic poliomyelitis; severe forms from cerebrovascular accidents, brain tumors, and brain abscess.

Complications

Bronchial pneumonia, urinary retention and infection, and decubitus ulcers may occur. Late sequelae are mental deterioration, parkinsonis, and epilepsy.

Treatment

Although specific therapy for the majority of etiologic entities is not available, a variety of treatment measures and procedures are necessary and may contribute significantly to a more successful outcome. Such measures include reduction of intracranial pressure by the use of mannitol or a urea-invert sugar preparation, the control of convulsions, maintenance of the airway, administration of oxygen, and attention to adequate nutrition during periods of prolonged coma. After 72 hours of conventional intravenous nutrition, it is probable that a nasogastric tube will have to be installed and intestinal feedings begun.

TABLE 20–2. Infectious encephalitis in the USA.

Arthropod-borne
  Western equine encephalitis
  St. Louis encephalitis
  Eastern equine encephalitis
Enterovirus
  ECHO
  Coxsackie
  Polio
Myxovirus
  Mumps
Miscellaneous viruses
  Herpes simplex
  Lymphocytic choriomeningitis
  Rabies
Other agents
  Torulosis (cryptococcosis)
  Toxoplasmosis
  Mycoplasma pneumoniae (?)

TABLE 20–3. Parainfectious encephalitis.

Antigen-antibody type
  Accompanying or following:
    Rubeola
    Varicella
    Rubella
    Infectious mononucleosis
    Herpes zoster (?)
    Roseola infantum (?)
  Following:
    Vaccinia inoculation
    Pertussis vaccine
    Rabies vaccine
    Yellow fever vaccine
Toxic type
  Influenza
  Shigellosis
  Salmonellosis
  Scarlet fever

Prevention or early treatment of decubiti, pneumonia, and urinary tract infections is important. Give anticonvulsants as needed.

Prognosis

It should always be guarded, especially in younger children. Sequelae may become apparent late in the convalescence of what appears to be a successful recovery.

Brown, E.H.: Virus meningitis. Postgrad MJ 43:418–421, 1967.

Klemola, E., & others: Studies on viral encephalitis. Acta med scandinav 177:707–716, 1965.

Riggs, S., Smith, D.L., & C.A. Phillips: St. Louis encephalitis in adults, Houston, 1964. JAMA 193:284–288, 1965.

Wilkins, R.H., & I. A. Brody: Encephalitis lethargica. Arch Neurol 18:324, 1968.

LYMPHOCYTIC CHORIOMENINGITIS

Essentials of Diagnosis

- "Influenza-like" prodrome of fever, chills, malaise, and cough, followed by meningitis with associated stiff neck.
- Kernig's sign, headache, nausea, vomiting, and lethargy.
- CSF: slight increase of protein, lymphocytic pleocytosis (500–1000/cu mm).
- Complement-fixing antibodies within 2 weeks.

General Considerations

Lymphocytic choriomeningitis is a viral infection of the CNS. The reservoir of infection is the infected house mouse, although naturally infected guinea pigs, monkeys, dogs, and swine have been observed. The virus escapes from the infected animal by means of oronasal secretions, urine, and feces, with transmission to man probably through contaminated food and dust. The incubation period is not definitely known, but is probably 8–13 days to the appearance of systemic manifestations and 15–21 days to the appearance of meningeal symptoms. The disease is not communicable from man to man. Complications are rare.

This disease has not been identified west of the Rocky Mountains. It is principally confined to the eastern seaboard and northeastern states.

Clinical Findings

A. Symptoms and Signs: The prodromal illness is characterized by fever, chills, headache, myalgia, cough, and vomiting; the meningeal phase by headache, nausea and vomiting, and lethargy. Signs of pneumonia are occasionally present during the prodromal phase. During the meningeal phase there may be neck and back stiffness and a positive Kernig sign (meningeal irritation). Severe meningoencephalitis may disturb deep tendon reflexes and may cause paralysis and anesthesia of the skin.

The prodrome may terminate in complete recovery, or meningeal symptoms may appear after a few days of remission.

B. Laboratory Findings: Leukocytosis may be present. CSF lymphocytic pleocytosis (total count is often 500–3000/cu mm) may occur, with slight increase in protein and normal glucose. Complement-fixing antibodies appear during or after the second week. The virus may be recovered from the blood and CSF by mouse inoculation.

Differential Diagnosis

The influenza-like prodrome and latent period before the development of the meningitis helps distinguish this from other aseptic meningitides, meningismus, and bacterial and granulomatous meningitis. A history of exposure to mice is an important diagnostic clue.

Treatment

Treat as for encephalitis.

Prognosis

Fatality is rare. The illness usually lasts 1–2 weeks, although convalescence may be prolonged.

Maurer, F.D.: Lymphocytic choriomeningitis. J Nat Cancer Inst 20:867–870, 1958.

DENGUE
(Breakbone Fever, Dandy Fever)

Essentials of Diagnosis

- Sudden onset of high fever, chills, severe aching, headache, sore throat, prostration, and depression.
- Biphasic fever curve: initial phase, 3–4 days; remission, few hours to 2 days; second phase, 1–2 days.
- Rash: maculopapular, scarlatiniform, morbilliform, or petechial; on extremities to torso, occurring during remission or second phase.
- Leukopenia.

General Considerations

Dengue is a viral disease transmitted by the bite of the Aedes mosquito. It is a clinical entity which may be caused by one of several viruses, eg, dengue 1 or 2 or West Nile fever virus. It occurs only in the active mosquito season (warm weather). The incubation period is 3–15 days (usually 5–8 days).

Clinical Findings

A. Symptoms and Signs: Dengue begins with a sudden onset of high fever, chilliness, and severe aching ("breakbone") of the head, back, and extremities, accompanied by sore throat, prostration, and depression. There may be conjunctival redness, and flushing or blotching of the skin. The initial febrile phase lasts 3–4 days, typically but not inevitably followed by a remission of a few hours to 2 days. The skin eruption appears in 80% of cases during the remission or during the second febrile phase, which lasts 1–2 days and is accompanied by similar but usually milder symptoms than in the first phase. The rash may be scarlatiniform, morbilliform, maculopapular, or petechial. It appears first on the dorsum of the hands and feet and spreads to the arms, legs, trunk, and neck but rarely to the face. The rash lasts 2 hours to several days and may be followed by desquamation. Petechial rashes and even internal hemorrhages may occur in a high proportion of cases (mosquito-borne hemorrhagic fever) from Taiwan to Malaysia.

Before the rash appears, it is difficult to distinguish dengue from malaria, yellow fever, or influenza. With the appearance of the eruption, which resembles rubella, the diagnosis is usually clear.

B. Laboratory Findings: Leukopenia is characteristic.

Complications

Depression, pneumonia, iritis, orchitis, and oophoritis are rare complications.

Prevention

Available prophylactic measures include control of mosquitoes by screening and DDT. An effective vaccine has been developed but has not been produced commercially.

Treatment

Give salicylates as required for discomfort. Permit gradual restoration of activity during prolonged convalescence.

Prognosis

Fatality is rare. Convalescence is slow.

Halstead, S.B.: Dengue and hemorrhagic fevers of southeast Asia. Yale J Biol Med 37:434–454, 1965.

Symposium on mosquito-borne haemorrhagic fevers in southeast Asia and western Pacific: Haemorrhagic fevers. Bull World Health Organ 35:1–94, 1966.

COLORADO TICK FEVER

Essentials of Diagnosis

- Fever, chills, myalgia, headache, prostration.
- Leukopenia.
- Second attack of fever after remission lasting 2–3 days.
- Onset 3–6 days following tick bite.

General Considerations

Colorado tick fever is an acute viral infection transmitted by *Dermacentor andersoni* bites. The disease is limited to the western USA and is most prevalent during the tick season (March to July). The incubation period is 3–6 days.

Clinical Findings

A. Symptoms and Signs: The onset of fever (to 102–105° F) is abrupt, sometimes with chills. Severe myalgia, headache, photophobia, anorexia, nausea and vomiting, and generalized weakness are prominent symptoms. There are no abnormal physical findings. Fever continues for 3 days, followed by a remission of 2–3 days and then by a full recrudescence lasting 3–4 days. In an occasional case there may be 1 or 3 bouts of fever.

Influenza, Rocky Mountain spotted fever, and other acute leukopenic fevers must be differentiated.

B. Laboratory Findings: Leukopenia (2000–3000/cu mm) with a shift to the left occurs. Viremia may be demonstrated by inoculation of blood into hamsters or suckling mice. Complement-fixing antibodies appear during the third week after onset.

Complications

Aseptic meningitis or encephalitis occurs rarely. Asthenia may follow.

Treatment

No specific treatment is available. Aspirin or codeine may be given for pain.

Prognosis

The disease is self-limited and almost invariably benign.

Eklund, C.M., Kohls, G.M., & J.M. Brennan: Distribution of Colorado tick fever and virus-carrying ticks. JAMA 157:335–337, 1955.

RABIES

Essentials of Diagnosis

- Paresthesia, hydrophobia, aerophobia, rage alternating with calm.
- Convulsions, paralysis, thick tenacious saliva.
- History of animal bite.

General Considerations

Rabies is a viral disease of animals and man, transmitted by infected saliva which gains entry into the body by a bite or an open wound. In the USA, rabies in man is usually due to the bite of an infected dog, although cats, wolves, skunks, bats, and other warm-blooded animals may be the source of infection. There is no specific climatic, geographic, or racial incidence. The incubation period may range from 10 days to 2 years, but is usually 3–7 weeks. The virus travels in the nerves to the brain, multiplies there, and then migrates along the efferent nerves to the salivary glands.

Clinical Findings

A. Symptoms and Signs: There is usually a history of animal bite. Pain appears at the site of the bite, followed by tingling. The skin is quite sensitive to changes of temperature, especially air currents. Periods of rage alternate with calm intervals. Attempts at drinking cause extremely painful laryngeal spasm so that the patient finally refuses to drink (hydrophobia). The patient is restless, and behaves in a peculiar manner. There is muscle spasm, laryngospasm, and extreme excitability. Convulsions occur, and blowing on the back of the patient's neck will often precipitate a convulsion. Large amounts of thick tenacious saliva are present.

B. Laboratory Findings: Biting animals who are apparently well should be kept under observation. Sick or dead animals should be examined for rabies. The diagnosis of rabies in the brain of a rabid animal may be made rapidly by the fluorescent antibody technic. The animal's brain should be examined for characteristic Negri bodies by immunofluorescence if possible.

Differential Diagnosis

Fear of the disease may result in a hysterical state which may closely simulate rabies. Muscle spasm may cause confusion with tetanus.

Treatment

Treatment consists of absolute quiet and freedom from stimulation; use sedation, as in tetanus, for preventing convulsions. No specific measures are available.

Prevention

If possible, the animal should be isolated and kept under observation for 7 days. If the animal remains healthy, one can assume that the bitten individual does not have rabies. The wound should be thoroughly washed with green soap.

After a positive diagnosis of rabies or after a bite by a suspected animal if the animal cannot be observed or if the bite is on the head, give rabies vaccine. Use Semple type nerve tissue vaccine for the first 7 consecutive daily doses. Use duck embryo vaccine for the remaining consecutive daily doses and for 2 follow-up booster doses 10 days and 20 days after the last consecutive dose. Rabies hyperimmune serum should be administered in addition to vaccine in any case where the examining physician considers the animal very likely to be rabid or certainly rabid.

Prognosis

Once the symptoms have appeared, death almost inevitably occurs after 2–3 days as a result of cardiac or respiratory failure or generalized paralysis.

Advisory Committee on Immunization Practices, US Public Health Service: Rabies prophylaxis. Am Int Med 67:159–163, 1967.

Jones, R.C.: Rabies: Present attitudes. Postgrad Med 43:141–151, 1968.

Karliner, J.S., & G.S. Belaval: Reaction after antirabies serum. JAMA 193:359–362, 1965.

Rabies. Leading article. Brit MJ 1:1565, 1965.

Rabies in man and animals. WHO Chronicle 20:115–121, 1966.

YELLOW FEVER

Essentials of Diagnosis

- Sudden onset of severe headache, aching in legs, and tachycardia. Later, bradycardia, hypotension, jaundice, hemorrhagic tendency ("coffee-ground" vomitus).
- Proteinuria, leukopenia, bilirubinemia, bilirubinuria.
- Endemic area.

General Considerations

Yellow fever is a viral infection transmitted by the Aedes and jungle mosquitoes. It is endemic to Africa and South America (tropical or subtropical), but epidemics have extended far into the temperate zone during warm seasons. The mosquito transmits the infection by first biting an individual having the disease and then biting a susceptible individual after the virus has multiplied within the mosquito's body. The incubation period in man is 3–6 days.

Clinical Findings

A. Symptoms and Signs:

1. Mild form—Symptoms are malaise, headache, fever, retro-orbital pain, nausea and vomiting, and photophobia. Bradycardia may be present.

2. Severe form—Symptoms are as for the mild form with sudden onset, severe pains throughout the body, extreme prostration, bleeding into the skin and from the mucous membranes ("coffee-ground" vomitus), oliguria, and jaundice. Signs include tachycardia, erythematous face, and conjunctival redness during the congestive phase; followed by a period of calm (on about the third day), with a normal temperature and bradycardia; and then a toxemic stage, with return of fever, bradycardia, hypotension, jaundice, hemorrhages (gastrointestinal tract, bladder, nose, mouth, subcutaneous), and later delirium. The short course and mildness of the icterus distinguish yellow fever from leptospirosis. The mild form is difficult to distinguish from infectious hepatitis.

B. Laboratory Findings: Leukopenia occurs, although it may not be present at the onset. Proteinuria is present, sometimes as high as 5–6 gm/liter, and disappears completely with recovery. With jaundice there is bilirubinuria and bilirubinemia. The virus may be isolated from the blood by intracerebral mouse inoculation (first 3 days). Antibodies appear during and after the second week.

Differential Diagnosis

It may be difficult to distinguish yellow fever from leptospirosis and other jaundices on clinical evidence alone, although the short course and mildness of the jaundice in yellow fever allow for some differentiation.

Prevention

Transmission is prevented through mosquito control. Live virus vaccine is highly effective. (See Immunization, p 905.)

Treatment

Treatment consists of giving a liquid diet, limiting food to high-carbohydrate, high-protein liquids as tolerated; intravenous glucose and saline as required; analgesics and sedatives as required; and saline enemas for obstipation.

Prognosis

Mortality is high in the severe form, with death occurring most commonly from the 6th to the 9th day. In survivors the temperature returns to normal by the 7th to 8th day. The prognosis in any individual case should be guarded at the onset, since sudden changes for the worse are not uncommon. Hiccup, copious black vomitus, melena, and anuria are unfavorable signs.

Burnet, F.M.: Yellow fever. Chap 25, pp 331–337, in: *Natural History of Infectious Disease,* 3rd ed. Cambridge, 1933.
Draper, C.C.: A yellow fever vaccine free from avian leucosis viruses. J Hyg 65:505–513, 1967.

INFLUENZA

Essentials of Diagnosis

- Abrupt onset with fever, chills, malaise, cough, coryza, and muscle aches.
- Aching, fever, and prostration out of proportion to catarrhal symptoms.
- Leukopenia.

General Considerations

Influenza is transmitted by the respiratory route. While sporadic cases occur, epidemics and pandemics appear at varying intervals, usually in the fall or winter. The 3 antigenic types (A, B, and C) produce clinically indistinguishable infections. The incubation period is 1–4 days.

It is difficult to diagnose influenza in the absence of a classic epidemic. It resembles many other mild febrile illnesses, but always will be accompanied by a cough. The sudden onset, often within minutes, is also characteristic.

Clinical Findings

A. Symptoms and Signs: The onset is usually abrupt, with fever, chills, malaise, muscular aching, substernal soreness, headache, nasal stuffiness, and occasionally nausea. In severe infections the patient may be prostrated. Fever lasts 1–7 days (usually 3–5). Coryza, nonproductive cough, and sore throat are present. Signs include mild pharyngeal injection, flushed face, and conjunctival redness.

B. Laboratory Findings: Leukopenia is common. Proteinuria (due to fever) may be present. The virus may be isolated from the throat washings by inoculation of chick embryo. Complement fixing and chick cell hemagglutination-inhibiting antibodies appear during or after the second week.

Complications

Influenza causes necrosis of the respiratory epithelium which predisposes to secondary bacterial infections. The most frequent complications are acute sinusitis, otitis media, purulent bronchitis and bronchiolitis, bronchiectasis, and pneumonia.

Pneumonia is commonly due to bacterial infection with pneumococci or staphylococci and very rarely to the influenza virus itself.

The circulatory system is not usually involved, but pericarditis, myocarditis, and thrombophlebitis sometimes occur.

Prevention

Polyvalent influenza virus vaccine, 1 ml subcut, or 0.1–0.2 ml intradermally, given twice (1–2 weeks apart), exerts moderate temporary protection. Immunity lasts a few months to 1 year. Amantadine hydrochloride (Symmetrel®), 200 mg orally daily, may reduce the incidence of infection in individuals exposed to influenza A_2 (Asian influenza) if begun immediately and continued for 10 days. The drug does not prevent other viral diseases.

Treatment

Bed rest to reduce complications is the most important consideration. Analgesics and a sedative cough mixture may be used. Antibiotics should be reserved for treatment of bacterial complications.

Prognosis

The duration of the uncomplicated illness is 1–7 days, and the prognosis is excellent. Purulent bronchiolitis and bronchiectasis may result in chronic pulmonary disease and fibrosis which persist throughout life. Most fatalities are due to bacterial pneumonia. In recent epidemics mortality has been low except in debilitated persons, especially those with severe heart disease.

If the fever persists more than 4 days, cough becomes productive, or the white count rises above 12,000/cu mm, secondary bacterial infection should be ruled out or verified and treated.

Advisory Committee on Immunization Practices, US Public Health Service: Influenza immunization. Ann Int Med 67:852–855, 1967.
Stuart-Harris, C.H.: Influenza and its complications. Brit MJ 1:217–218, 1966.

Togo, Y., Hornick, R.B., & A.T. Dawkins, Jr.: Studies on induced influenza in man. I. Prophylactic efficacy of
amantadine hydrochloride. JAMA 203:1089–1094, 1968.

Wendell, H.A., Synder, M.T., & S. Pell: Trial of amantadine in
epidemic influenza. Clin Pharmacol Therap 7:38–43,
1966.

CAT-SCRATCH FEVER

Essentials of Diagnosis

- A primary infected ulcer or papule-pustule at site of inoculation (30% of cases).
- Regional lymphadenopathy which often suppurates.
- History of scratch by cat at involved area.
- Positive intradermal test.

General Considerations

Cat-scratch fever is an acute infectious disease of unknown cause. It was formerly assumed to be due to a virus but may be due to the agent of psittacosis and lymphogranuloma venereum. It is transmitted by healthy cats, principally by scratching, although cases have been reported to follow skin pricks by a splinter or thorn. The disease is worldwide in distribution, and appears to be quite common. Children are affected more often than adults.

Clinical Findings

A. Symptoms and Signs: A few days after the scratch, about 1/3 of cases develop a primary lesion at the site of inoculation. This primary lesion appears as an infected, scabbed ulcer or a papule with a central vesicle or pustule. One to 3 weeks later, symptoms of generalized infection appear (fever, malaise, headache) and the regional lymph nodes become enlarged without evidence of lymphangitis. The nodes may be tender and fixed, with overlying inflammation; or nontender, discrete, and without evidence of surrounding inflammation. Suppuration may occur with the discharge of sterile pus.

Lymph node enlargement must be differentiated from that of lymphoma, tuberculosis, lymphogranuloma venereum, and acute bacterial infection.

B. Laboratory Findings: The sedimentation rate is elevated, the white count is usually normal, and the pus from the nodes is sterile. Intradermal skin testing with antigen prepared from lymph node pus is positive (tuberculin-like reaction) in the majority of cases.

Complications

Encephalitis occurs rarely. Macular or papular rashes and erythema nodosum are occasionally seen.

Treatment

There is no specific treatment. Presently available antimicrobial drugs have been shown to be ineffective. Surgical removal of a large node or aspiration of liquid contents usually produces an amelioration of symptoms and fever.

Prognosis

The disease is benign and self-limiting. Symptoms may continue for 5 days to 2 weeks.

Margileth, A.M.: Cat scratch disease: Non-bacterial regional
lymphadenitis, the study of 145 patients and a review of
the literature. Pediatrics 42:803–809, 1968.

INFECTIOUS MONONUCLEOSIS

Essentials of Diagnosis

- Fever, sore throat, malaise, lymphadenopathy.
- Frequently splenomegaly, occasionally maculopapular rash.
- Positive sheep cell agglutinins (over 1:100); lymphocytosis with abnormal lymphocytes.
- Hepatitis frequent, and occasionally myocarditis, neuritis, encephalitis.

General Considerations

Infectious mononucleosis is an acute infectious disease probably due to a virus closely related to or identical with the Epstein-Barr virus first isolated from cases of lymphoma in West Africa. It is universal in distribution and may occur at any age, but usually occurs in people between ages 10 and 35. It may occur both in an epidemic form or as sporadic cases. Its mode of transmission is unknown, but the agent presumably is airborne. The incubation period is probably 5–15 days.

Clinical Findings

A. Symptoms and Signs: Symptomatology is varied, but the typical case is represented by fever; discrete, nonsuppurative, slightly painful, moderately enlarged lymph nodes, especially those of the posterior cervical chain; and, in approximately ½ of cases, splenomegaly. Sore throat is often present, and toxic symptoms (malaise, anorexia, and myalgia) occur frequently in the early phase of the illness. A macular to maculopapular or occasionally petechial rash occurs in less than 50% of cases. Exudative pharyngitis, tonsillitis, or gingivitis may also occur.

A common manifestation of infectious mononucleosis is hepatitis with hepatomegaly, nausea, anorexia, and jaundice; CNS involvement with headache, neck stiffness, photophobia, pains of neuritis, and occasionally even Guillain-Barré syndrome; pulmonary involvement with chest pain, dyspnea, and cough, and myocardial involvement with tachycardia and arrhythmias.

The varying symptoms of infectious mononucleosis raise difficult differential diagnostic problems. The sore throat, hepatitis, rash, and lymphadenopathy all represent difficulties in differentiation.

B. Laboratory Findings: Initially there is a granulocytopenia followed within 1 week by a lymphocytic leukocytosis. Many of these lymphocytes are larger than normal adult lymphocytes, stain more darkly, and frequently show vacuolization of the cytoplasm and nucleus.

The heterophil test (sheep cell agglutination test) is usually positive but may not become positive until late in the course of the disease (4th week) or may be positive only transiently. A titer over 1:100 is significant. The STS is falsely positive in less than 10% of cases.

In CNS involvement the CSF may show increase of pressure, abnormal lymphocytes, and protein.

With myocardial involvement the ECG may show abnormal T waves and prolonged P–R intervals.

Liver function tests are commonly abnormal.

Complications

These usually consist of secondary throat infections, often streptococcal, and (rarely) rupture of the spleen or hypersplenism.

Treatment

A. General Measures: Place the patient at bed rest until afebrile and give symptomatic treatment with aspirin, codeine, and hot saline or 30% glucose throat irrigations or gargles 3 or 4 times daily. In severely ill patients, symptomatic relief can be obtained through a short course of corticosteroids. Diagnosis must be well established.

B. Treatment of Complications: Hepatitis, myocarditis, or encephalitis are treated symptomatically. Rupture of the spleen requires emergency splenectomy. Frequent vigorous palpation of the spleen is unwise.

Prognosis

In the uncomplicated case the fever disappears in 10 days, the lymphadenopathy and splenomegaly in 4 weeks. In some cases the illness may linger for 2–3 months.

Death is uncommon; when it does occur it is usually due to splenic rupture or hypersplenic phenomena (severe hemolytic anemia, thrombocytopenia purpura, or encephalitis).

There are usually no sequelae.

Davidson, R.J.L.: New slide test for infectious mononucleosis. J Clin Path 20:643–646, 1967.

Gordon, M.P.: Corticosteroid treatment of infectious mononucleosis in a military population. Mil Med 133:303–305, 1968.

Niederman, J.C., McCollum, R.W., & W. Henleg: Infectious mononucleosis: Clinical manifestations in relation to E-B virus antibodies. JAMA 203:139–143, 1968.

Porter, E.E., Wimberly, I., & M. Benyesh-Melnick: Prevalence of antibodies to E-B virus and other herpesviruses. JAMA 208:1675–1679, 1969.

EPIDEMIC NEUROMYASTHENIA

This is a prolonged and variable syndrome consisting of headache, nausea and vomiting, diarrhea, myalgia, depression, disturbances of mentation, transient muscle weakness, and nuchal rigidity without other abnormal physical findings or CSF pleocytosis. It may occur in epidemics. Treatment is symptomatic.

COXSACKIEVIRUS INFECTIONS

Coxsackievirus infections cause several clinical syndromes. As with other enteroviruses, infections are most common during the summer. Two groups, A and B, are defined by their differing behavior after injection into suckling mice. There are 31 serotypes, but many of these have not been shown to cause disease.

Clinical Findings

A. Symptoms and Signs: The 6 clinical syndromes associated with coxsackievirus infection may be described briefly as follows:

1. Summer grippe (Coxsackie A and B)—A febrile illness, principally of children, which lasts 1–4 days; minor symptoms and respiratory tract infection are often present.

2. Herpangina (Coxsackie A2, 4, 5, 6, 7, 10)—Sudden onset of fever, which may be as high as 40.6° C (105° F), sometimes with febrile convulsions; headache, myalgia, vomiting; and sore throat, characterized early by petechiae or papules which become shallow ulcers in about 3 days and then heal.

3. Epidemic pleurodynia (Coxsackie B1, 2, 3, 4, 5)—Sudden onset of recurrent pain in the area of diaphragmatic attachment (lower chest or upper abdomen); fever is often present during attacks of pain; headache, sore throat, malaise, nausea; tenderness, hyperesthesia, and muscle swelling of the involved area; orchitis, pleurisy, and aseptic meningitis may occur. Relapse may occur after recovery.

4. Aseptic meningitis (Coxsackie A2, 4, 7, 9, 10, 16; B viruses)—Fever, headache, nausea, vomiting, stiff neck, drowsiness, CSF lymphocytosis without chemical abnormalities; rarely, muscle paralysis. See also Viral Meningitis.

5. Acute nonspecific pericarditis (Coxsackie B5)—Sudden onset of anterior chest pain, often worse with inspiration and in the supine position; fever, myalgia, headache; pericardial friction rub appears early; pericardial effusion with paradoxic pulse, increased venous pressure, increase in heart size may appear; ECG and x-ray evidence of pericarditis often present. One or more relapses may occur.

6. Myocarditis neonatorum (Coxsackie B3, 4)—Heart failure in the neonatal period may be the result of congenital heart disease due to maternal infection. Adult heart disease may be caused by coxsackievirus group B.

B. Laboratory Findings: Routine laboratory studies show no characteristic abnormalities. Neutralizing antibodies appear during convalescence. The virus may be isolated from throat washings or stools inoculated into suckling mice.

Treatment & Prognosis

Treatment is symptomatic. With the exception of myocarditis, all of the syndromes caused by coxsackieviruses are benign and self-limited.

Brown, G.C., & T.N. Evans: Coxsackie virus and congenital heart disease. JAMA 199:183–187, 1967.

Novack, A., & others: A community-wide coxsackievirus A9 outbreak. JAMA 202:862–866, 1967.

ECHOVIRUS INFECTIONS

Echoviruses are enteroviruses which produce several clinical syndromes, particularly in children. Infection is most common during the summer.

Twenty serotypes have been demonstrated. Types 4, 6, and 9 cause aseptic meningitis, which may be associated with rubelliform rash. Types 9 and 16 cause an exanthematous illness (Boston exanthem) characterized by a sudden onset of fever, nausea, and sore throat, and a rubelliform rash over the face and trunk which persists 1–10 days. Orchitis may occur. Type 18 causes epidemic diarrhea, characterized by a sudden onset of fever and diarrhea in infants. Types 18 and 20 cause common respiratory disease (see Chapter 5). There are no characteristic laboratory abnormalities.

Treatment is symptomatic and the prognosis is excellent. Paralysis has occurred in aseptic meningitis due to echovirus infection, but very rarely.

ADENOVIRUS INFECTIONS

Adenoviruses (there are at least 18 antigenic types) produce a variety of clinical syndromes. These infections are self-limited, and most common among military recruits, although sporadic cases occur in civilian populations. The incubation period is 4–9 days.

There are 4 clinical types of adenovirus infection:

(1) The common cold: Many infections produce rhinitis, pharyngitis, and mild malaise without fever indistinguishable from the symptoms and signs of other infections which produce the common cold syndrome.

(2) Acute undifferentiated respiratory disease, nonstreptococcal exudative pharyngitis: Fever lasts 2–12 days (usually 5 days), accompanied by malaise and myalgia. Sore throat is often manifested by diffuse injection, a patchy exudate, and cervical lymphadenopathy. Cough is sometimes accompanied by rales and

x-ray evidence of pneumonitis (primary atypical pneumonia). Conjunctivitis is often present.

(3) Pharyngoconjunctival fever: Fever and malaise, conjunctivitis (often unilateral), and mild pharyngitis.

(4) Epidemic keratoconjunctivitis (shipyard eye): Unilateral conjunctival redness, mild pain, and tearing, with a large preauricular lymph node. Caused by adenovirus type 8.

(5) Acute hemorrhagic cystitis in children.

A polyvalent vaccine is not available for general use. A vaccine containing live attenuated type 4 has been used experimentally.

Treatment is symptomatic.

Evans, A.S.: Adenovirus infections in children and young adults: With comments on vaccination. New England J Med 259:464–468, 1958.

Numazaki, Y., & others: Acute hemorrhagic cystitis in children. New England J Med 278:700–704, 1968.

Van der Veen, J.: The role of adenoviruses in respiratory disease. Am Rev Resp Dis 88:167–180, 1963.

MISCELLANEOUS VIRAL UPPER RESPIRATORY INFECTIONS

Newer tissue culture technics have led to the association of several viruses with the syndrome of the common cold. The incidence of infection with rhinoviruses, parainfluenza viruses, reoviruses, and respiratory syncytial viruses is not clear, but it is evident that they may produce the classic familiar syndrome characterized by nasal obstruction and discharge, sneezing, sore throat, and variable degrees of hoarseness, cough, and malaise. Fever is usually lacking except in children. Immunity probably is short-lived. Secondary bacterial infection may result in otitis media or sinusitis, especially in children.

Treatment

(1) Aspirin, 0.6 gm every 4 hours.

(2) Phenylephrine (Neo-Synephrine®), 0.25% solution, as nose drops 4 times daily. Adults may use dextroamphetamine inhaler.

(3) Sedative cough mixture as necessary.

(4) Antimicrobial agents have no place in the management of the common cold unless secondary bacterial infection is definitely present. Antihistaminics are of value only in allergic or vasomotor rhinitis.

Gwaltney, J.M., Jr., & others: Rhinovirus infections in an industrial population. New England J Med 275:1261–1268, 1966.

Parrott, R.H.: Viral respiratory tract illness in children. Bull New York Acad Med 39:629–648, 1963.

Portonoy, B.: Pediatric virology. California Med 102:431–445, 1965.

RICKETTSIAL DISEASES
(RICKETTSIOSES)

The rickettsioses are a group of febrile diseases caused by infection with rickettsiae. Rickettsiae are obligate intracellular bacteria most of which (except coxiella of Q fever) are parasites of arthropods. In arthropods, rickettsiae grow in the cells lining the gut, often without harming the host. Human infection results either from the bite of the specific arthropod or from respiratory tract contamination with its feces. In humans, rickettsiae grow principally in endothelial cells of small blood vessels, producing necrosis of cells, thrombosis of vessels, skin rashes, and organ dysfunctions.

Different rickettsiae and their vectors are endemic in different parts of the world, but 2 or more types may coexist in the same geographic area. The clinical picture is variable but usually includes a prodromal stage followed by fever, rash, and prostration. Laboratory diagnosis relies heavily on the nonspecific development of agglutinating antibodies to certain proteus strains (Weil-Felix reaction) and of specific complement-fixing antibodies. Isolation of the organism from the patient is cumbersome and difficult, and is successful only in specialized laboratories.

Prevention & Treatment

Preventive measures are directed at control of the vector, specific immunization when available, and (occasionally) drug chemoprophylaxis. All rickettsiae can be inhibited by tetracyclines or chloramphenicol. All clinical infections respond in some degree to treatment with these drugs. Treatment usually consists of giving either chloramphenicol or tetracycline hydrochloride, 0.5 gm orally every 3–6 hours for 4–10 days (50 mg/kg/day). In seriously ill patients, initial treatment may consist of 1 gm tetracycline hydrochloride or chloramphenicol IV. Supportive measures may include parenteral fluids, sedation, oxygen, and skin care. The vector (louse, tick, mite) must be removed from patients by appropriate measures.

Gear, J.H.: Rickettsial vaccines. Brit M Bull 25:171–174, 1969.

EPIDEMIC LOUSE-BORNE TYPHUS

Essentials of Diagnosis

- Prodrome of malaise and headache followed by abrupt chills and fever.
- Severe, intractable headaches, prostration, persisting high fever.
- Maculopapular rash appears on the 4th–7th day on the trunk and in the axillas, spreading to the rest of body but sparing the face, palms, and soles.
- Laboratory confirmation by proteus OX-19 agglutination and specific complement fixation tests.

General Considerations

Epidemic louse-borne typhus is due to infection with *Rickettsia prowazeki*, a parasite of the body louse, which ultimately kills the louse. Transmission is greatly favored by crowded living conditions, famine, war, or any circumstances that predispose to heavy infestation with lice. When the louse sucks the blood of a person infected with *R prowazeki*, the organism becomes established in the gut of the louse and grows there. When the louse is transmitted to another person (through contact or clothing) and has a blood meal, it defecates simultaneously and the infected feces are rubbed into the itching bite wound. Dry, infectious louse feces may also enter respiratory tract mucous membranes and result in human infection. A deloused and bathed typhus patient is no longer infectious for other humans.

In a person who recovers from clinical or subclinical typhus infection, *R prowazeki* may survive in lymphoid tissues for many years. At times such a person may have recrudescence of disease without exogenous exposure to lice or to the infectious agent. Such a recrudescence (Brill's disease) can serve as a source of infection for lice.

Clinical Findings

A. Symptoms and Signs: Prodromal malaise, cough, headache, and chest pain begin after an incubation period of 10–14 days. There is then an abrupt onset of chills, high fever, and prostration, with "influenzal symptoms" progressing to delirium and stupor. The headache is intractably severe, and the fever is unremitting for many days.

Other findings consist of conjunctivitis, flushed face, rales at the lung bases, and often splenomegaly. A macular rash (which soon becomes papular) appears first in the axillas and then over the trunk, spreading to the extremities but rarely involving the face, palms, or soles. In severely ill patients, the rash becomes hemorrhagic and hypotension becomes marked. There may be renal insufficiency, stupor, and delirium. In spontaneous recovery, improvement begins 13–16 days after onset with rapid drop of fever.

B. Laboratory Findings: The white blood count is variable. Proteinuria and hematuria occur commonly. Serum obtained 5–12 days after onset of symptoms usually shows agglutinating antibodies for proteus OX-19 (rarely also OX-2)–*R prowazeki* shares antigens with these proteus strains–and specific complement-fixing antibodies with *R prowazeki* antigens. A titer rise is most significant. In primary rickettsial infection, early antibodies are IgM; in recrudescence (Brill's disease), early antibodies are predominantly IgG and the Weil-Felix test is negative.

C. X-Ray Findings: X-rays of the chest may show patchy consolidation.

Differential Diagnosis

The prodromal symptoms and the early febrile stage are not specific enough to permit diagnosis in nonepidemic situations. The rash is usually sufficiently distinctive for diagnosis, but it may be missing in 5—10% of cases and may be difficult to observe in dark-skinned persons. A variety of other acute febrile diseases may have to be considered.

Brill's disease (recrudescent epidemic typhus) has a more gradual onset than primary *R prowazeki* infection, fever and rash are of shorter duration, and the disease is milder and rarely fatal.

Complications

Pneumonia, vasculitis with major vessel obstruction and gangrene, circulatory collapse, myocarditis, and uremia may occur.

Prevention

Prevention consists of louse control with DDT and other insecticides, particularly by applying chemicals to clothing or treating it with heat, and frequent bathing. Immunization with vaccines consisting of inactivated egg-grown *R prowazeki* gives good protection against severe disease but does not prevent infection or mild disease. The usual method is to give 2 injections of 0.5 ml IM 4—6 weeks apart. A booster injection is desirable prior to heavy exposure. Live, attenuated strain vaccine is under investigation.

Treatment

See above.

Prognosis

The prognosis depends greatly upon age and immunization status. In children under age 10, the disease is usually mild. The mortality is 10% in the 2nd and 3rd decades, but may reach 60% in the 6th decade. Active immunization usually changes a potentially serious disease into a relatively mild one, with low or no mortality.

Murray, E.S., & others: Differentiation of 19S and 7S complement-fixing antibodies in primary versus recrudescent typhus. Proc Soc Exper Biol Med 119:291—295, 1965.

ENDEMIC FLEA-BORNE TYPHUS
(Murine Typhus)

Rickettsia mooseri (R typhi), a parasite of rats, is transmitted from rat to rat through the rat flea (rarely, the rat louse). Man acquires the infection when bitten by an infected flea, which releases infected feces while sucking blood.

Flea typhus resembles Brill's disease (recrudescent epidemic typhus) in that it has a gradual onset and the fever and rash are of shorter duration (6—13 days) and the symptoms less severe than in louse-borne typhus. The rash is maculopapular, concentrated on the trunk, and fades fairly rapidly. Even without antibiotic treatment, flea typhus is a mild disease. Pneumonia or gangrene is rare. Fatalities are rare and limited to the elderly.

Complement-fixing antibodies can be detected in the patient's serum with specific *R mooseri* antigens. The Weil-Felix test reveals agglutinating antibodies for proteus OX-19 in rising titer.

Preventive measures are directed at control of rats and their ectoparasites. Insecticides are first applied to rat runs, nests, and colonies, and the rats are then poisoned or trapped. Finally, buildings must be rat proofed. Antibiotic treatment (see p 815) need not be intensive because of the mildness of the natural disease. An experimental vaccine was fairly effective, but it is not commercially available now.

SPOTTED FEVERS
(Tick Typhus)

Tick-borne rickettsial infections occur in many different regions of the world and have been given regional or local names, eg, Rocky Mountain spotted fever in North America, Queensland tick typhus in Australia, boutonneuse fever in Africa. The etiologic agents are all antigenically related to *Rickettsia rickettsi,* and all are transmitted by hard (ixodid) ticks and have cycles in nature which involve dogs, rodents, or other animals. Rickettsiae are often transmitted from one generation of ticks to the next (transovarian transmission) without passage through a vertebrate host. Patients infected with spotted fevers usually develop antibodies to proteus OX-19 and OX-2 in low titer, in addition to rickettsial complement-fixing antibodies.

Control of spotted fevers involves prevention of tick bites, specific immunization when available, and antibiotic treatment of patients.

1. ROCKY MOUNTAIN SPOTTED FEVER

Essentials of Diagnosis

- History of possible exposure to tick bite in endemic area.
- "Influenzal" prodrome followed by chills, fever, severe headache, widespread aches and pains, restlessness, and prostration—occasionally, delirium and coma.
- Red macular rash appears between the 2nd and 6th days of fever, first on the wrists and ankles and spreading centrally; it may become petechial.
- Proteus OX-19 and OX-2 agglutinins appear, as well as specific complement-fixing antibodies.

General Considerations

The etiologic agent, *Rickettsia rickettsi,* is transmitted to man by the bite of the wood tick, *Dermacentor andersoni,* in western USA and by the bite of the dog tick, *Dermacentor variabilis,* in eastern USA. Other hard ticks transmit the rickettsia in the southern USA and in Central and South America and are responsible for transmitting it among rodents, dogs, porcupines, and other animals in nature. Most human cases occur in late spring and summer.

Clinical Findings

A. Symptoms and Signs: Three to 10 days after the bite of an infectious tick there is anorexia, malaise, nausea, headache, and sore throat. This progresses with chills, fever, aches in bones, joints, and muscles, abdominal pain, nausea and vomiting, restlessness, insomnia, and irritability. Delirium, lethargy, stupor, and coma may appear. The face is flushed and the conjunctivas injected. Between days 2 and 6 of fever, a rash appears first on the wrists and ankles, spreading centrally to the arms, legs, and trunk. The rash is initially small, red, and macular but becomes larger and petechial. It spreads for 2–3 days. In some cases there is splenomegaly, hepatomegaly, jaundice, gangrene, myocarditis, or uremia.

B. Laboratory Findings: Leukocytosis, proteinuria, and hematuria are common. Rickettsiae can sometimes be isolated in special laboratories from blood obtained in the first few days of illness. A rise in antibody titer during the second week of illness can be detected by specific complement fixation tests or by the Weil-Felix agglutination test with proteus OX-19 and OX-2.

Differential Diagnosis

The early signs and symptoms of Rocky Mountain spotted fever are shared with many other infections. The rash may be confused with that of measles, typhoid, or meningococcemia. The suspicion of the latter requires blood cultures and CSF examination.

Prevention

Protective clothing, tick-repellent chemicals, and the removal of ticks at frequent intervals are helpful. A vaccine of inactivated *R rickettsi* grown in eggs given IM 3 times at intervals of 1 week offers moderate protection.

Treatment & Prognosis

In mild, untreated cases, fever subsides at the end of the second week. The response to chloramphenicol or tetracycline (see pp 821 and 822) is prompt if the drugs are started early.

The mortality rate from Rocky Mountain spotted fever varies strikingly with age. In untreated, middle-aged adults it may be 70%; in children, less than 20%.

Hand, W.L., & others: Rocky Mountain spotted fever: A vascular disease. Arch Int Med 125:879–882, 1970.
Hazard, G.W., & others: Rocky Mountain spotted fever in eastern U.S. New England J Med 280:57–62, 1969.

2. OTHER SPOTTED FEVERS

Tick-borne rickettsial infections in Africa, Asia, and Australia may resemble Rocky Mountain spotted fever but cover a wide spectrum from very mild to very severe. In many cases, a local lesion develops at the site of the tick bite (eschar), often with painful enlargement of the regional lymph nodes.

RICKETTSIALPOX

Rickettsia akari is a parasite of mice, transmitted by mites *(Allodermanyssus sanguineus).* Upon close contact of mice with men, infected mites may transmit the disease to humans. Rickettsialpox has an incubation period of 7–12 days. The onset is sudden, with chills, fever, headache, photophobia, and disseminated aches and pains. The primary lesion is a red papule which vesicates and becomes a black eschar. Two to 4 days after onset of symptoms, a widespread papular eruption appears which becomes vesicular and forms crusts which are shed in about 10 days. Early lesions may resemble those of chickenpox or even smallpox.

Leukopenia and a rise in antibody titer with rickettsial antigen in complement fixation tests are often present. However, the Weil-Felix test is negative.

Treatment with tetracycline produces rapid improvement, but even without treatment the disease is fairly mild and self-limited. Control requires the elimination of mice from human habitations after insecticide has been applied to suppress the mite vectors.

Lackman, D.B.: A review of information on rickettsialpox in the United States. Clin Pediat 2:296–301, 1963.

SCRUB TYPHUS
(Tsutsugamushi Disease)

Essentials of Diagnosis

- Exposure to mites in endemic area of Southeast Asia and Japan.
- Black eschar at site of bite, with enlarged, tender regional lymph nodes and generalized adenopathy.
- Conjunctivitis and a short-lived macular rash.
- Frequent pneumonitis, encephalitis, and cardiac failure.
- Weil-Felix test positive, with antibody titer rise to proteus OXK.

General Considerations

Scrub typhus is caused by *Rickettsia tsutsugamushi (R orientalis),* which is principally a parasite of rodents transmitted by mites. The infectious agent can be transmitted from one generation of mites to the next (transovarian transmission) without a vertebrate host. The mites may spend much of their life cycle on vegetation but require a blood meal to complete maturation. At that point, humans coming in contact with infested vegetation are bitten by mite larvae and are infected.

Clinical Findings

A. Symptoms and Signs: After an incubation period of 1–3 weeks, there is a nonspecific prodrome with malaise, chills, severe headache, and backache. At the site of the mite bite a papule develops which vesicates and forms a flat black eschar. The regional draining lymph nodes are enlarged and tender, and there may be generalized adenopathy. Fever rises gradually, and a generalized macular rash appears at the end of the first week of fever. The rash is most marked on the trunk, and may be fleeting or may last for a week. Pneumonitis, encephalitis, and cardiac failure may occur during the second week of fever. The patient appears obtunded, confused, and out of contact with his environment.

B. Laboratory Findings: Blood obtained during the first few days of illness may permit isolation of the rickettsia by mouse inoculation in specialized laboratories. The Weil-Felix test usually shows a rising titer to proteus OXK during the second week of illness. The complement fixation test is often unsatisfactory.

Differential Diagnosis

Leptospirosis, typhoid, dengue, malaria, and other rickettsial infections may have to be considered. When the rash is fleeting and the eschar not evident, laboratory results are the best guide to diagnosis.

Prevention

Efforts must be made in endemic areas to minimize contact between humans and infected mites. Repeated application of long-acting miticides can make endemic areas safe. When this is not possible, insect repellents on clothing and skin provide some protection. For short exposure, chemoprophylaxis with chloramphenicol can prevent the disease but permits infection. No effective vaccines are available at present.

Treatment & Prognosis

Without treatment, fever may subside spontaneously after 2 weeks but the mortality rate may be 10–40%. Early treatment with chloramphenicol or tetracyclines can virtually eliminate deaths.

Elsom, K.A., & others: Scrub typhus: A follow-up study. Ann Int Med 55:784–795, 1961.

TRENCH FEVER

Trench fever is a self-limited, louse-borne relapsing febrile disease caused by *Rickettsia quintana*. This organism grows extracellularly in the louse intestine and is excreted in feces. Humans are infected when infected louse feces enter defects in skin. No animal reservoir except humans has been demonstrated.

This disease has occurred in epidemic forms during wars in louse-infested troups and civilians, and in endemic form in Central America. Onset is abrupt, with fever lasting 3–5 days, often followed by relapses. The patient becomes weak and complains of severe pain behind the eyes and in the back and legs. Lymphadenopathy and splenomegaly may appear, as well as a transient maculopapular rash. Subclinical infection is frequent, and a carrier state may occur. The differential diagnosis includes dengue, leptospirosis, malaria, relapsing fever, and typhus fever.

R quintana is the only rickettsia which has been grown on artificial media without living cells. The organism can be cultivated on blood agar in 10% fresh blood, and has been recovered from blood cultures of patients. In volunteers, such agar-grown rickettsiae caused typical disease. The Weil-Felix test is negative, but specific complement fixation tests are being developed.

The illness is self-limited and recovery regularly occurs without treatment.

Varela, G., & others: Trench fever: Propagation of *R quintana* on cell-free medium from blood of patients. Am J Trop Med 18:707–713, 1969.

Q FEVER

Essentials of Diagnosis

- An acute or chronic febrile illness with severe headache, cough, prostration, and abdominal pain.
- Marked pulmonary infiltration on chest films in the presence of relatively slight signs and symptoms.

General Considerations

Coxiella burneti is unique among rickettsiae in that it is usually not transmitted to humans by arthropods but by inhalation of infectious aerosols or ingestion of infected milk. It is a parasite of cattle, sheep, and goats, in which it produces mild or subclinical infection. It is excreted by cows and goats principally through the milk and placenta and from sheep through feces, placenta, and milk. Dry feces and milk, dust contaminated with them, and the tissues of these animals contain large numbers of infectious organisms which are spread by the airborne route. Inhalation of contaminated dust is the main source of human infection. Coxiella in milk is relatively resistant to pasteurization, and infection may occur through drinking infected milk. Spread from one human to another does not occur with significant frequency even in the presence of florid pneumonitis.

Clinical Findings

A. Symptoms and Signs: After an incubation period of 1–3 weeks, a febrile illness develops with headache, prostration, and muscle pains, occasionally with a nonproductive cough, abdominal pains, or jaundice. Physical signs of pneumonitis are slight. True endocarditis occurs very rarely. The clinical course may be acute or chronic and relapsing.

B. Laboratory Findings: Laboratory examination often shows leukopenia and a diagnostic rise in specific complement-fixing antibodies to coxiella. The Weil-Felix test is negative. Liver function tests occasionally reveal hepatitis. Special laboratories may attempt isolation of the organism from blood.

C. X-Ray Examination: Chest x-ray shows marked pulmonary infiltration.

Differential Diagnosis

Primary atypical pneumonia, viral hepatitis, brucellosis, tuberculosis, psittacosis, and other animal-borne diseases must be considered. The history of exposure to animals or animal dusts or animal tissues (eg, in slaughterhouses) should lead to appropriate specific serologic tests.

Prevention

Prevention must be based on detection of the infection in livestock, reduction of contact with infected animals or dusts contaminated by them, special care during contact with placental tissues, and effective pasteurization of milk.

Treatment & Prognosis

Treatment with tetracyclines can suppress symptoms and shorten the clinical course but does not always eradicate the infection. Even in untreated patients, the mortality rate is negligible.

Grist, N.R.: Q fever endocarditis. Am Heart J 75:846–851, 1968.

Schachter, J., & others: Potential danger of Q fever in a university hospital. J Infect Dis 123:301–303, 1971.

●   ●   ●

General Bibliography

Antiviral chemotherapy. Med Lett Drugs Therap 13:77–79, 1971.

Grist, N.R.: *Diagnostic Methods in Clinical Virology.* Davis, 1966.

Hilleman, M.R.: Advances in control of viral infections by nonspecific measures and by vaccines, with special reference to live mumps and rubella virus vaccines. Clin Pharmacol Therap 7:752–762, 1966.

Horsfall, F.L., & I. Tamm: *Rivers' Viral and Rickettsial Infections of Man,* 4th ed. Lippincott, 1965.

Jawetz, E., Melnick, J.L., & E.A. Adelberg: *Review of Medical Microbiology,* 9th ed. Lange, 1970.

Sweeney, F.J. (editor): Symposium on what's new in infectious diseases: Prevention and immunization. M Clin North America 51:579–846, 1967.

21...

Infectious Diseases: Bacterial

Henry B. Bruyn, Rees B. Rees, Jr., & Ernest Jawetz

STREPTOCOCCAL INFECTION OF THE UPPER RESPIRATORY TRACT; STREPTOCOCCAL PHARYNGITIS; SCARLET FEVER

Essentials of Diagnosis

- Abrupt onset of fever, malaise, sore throat, vomiting.
- Throat red, edematous, with patchy or follicular exudate.
- Finely papular erythematous rash appears promptly, especially in the axilla and groin.
- Diagnosis confirmed by throat culture.

General Considerations

Streptococcal respiratory infections are caused by Lancefield group A beta-hemolytic streptococci. Transmission is primarily via respiratory droplets from patients with active disease or asymptomatic carriers. Scarlet fever occurs when the streptococcal strain is able to elaborate an erythrogenic toxin and in patients who are susceptible to the action of the toxin, and thus differs from streptococcal pharyngitis only by the appearance of a rash, with strawberry tongue and other manifestations. The incubation period of streptococcal infection is 1–7 days.

Clinical Findings

A. Symptoms and Signs: Fever usually appears abruptly, accompanied by chills, or, in children, by convulsions. Malaise, arthralgia, nausea and vomiting, and abdominal pains may occur and may be very severe. The throat is usually extremely sore and painful.

The local pharyngeal lesions are identical in streptococcal pharyngitis and scarlet fever. There is marked erythema and moderate edema of the pharynx, with enlargement of the tonsils if they are present. A patchy or follicular purulent exudate which is easily removed is present on the tonsils, often on the posterior pharynx, and occasionally on the soft palate. The anterior cervical lymph nodes are tender and enlarged, and there is usually a slight generalized lymphadenopathy.

With the toxic manifestations (scarlet fever) the skin is diffusely erythematous with a punctate rash caused by enlarged skin papillae which are more deeply red than the surrounding skin. The rash is most intense in the axillas and groin and on the lateral trunk wall, the flexor surfaces of the arms, and the dorsum of the feet. It blanches on pressure. The extensor surfaces of the arms are usually spared. The skin folds are hyperpigmented and will not blanch on pressure. Small petechial hemorrhages may appear in the skin. The rash usually fades in 2–5 days and may be followed by a desquamation which begins with "pinholes" over the skin papillae. The face is usually flushed (with circumoral pallor) but is not involved by the rash. An enanthem—also due to the erythrogenic toxin—appears as a stippling of the soft palate analogous to the skin rash. The "strawberry tongue" begins to develop on the 1st day of exanthem. The tongue is heavily coated; prominent papillae are visible. The coat disappears at the tip and lateral margins on the 2nd day; on the 3rd day it is 1/2–2/3 gone; and on the 4th day the tongue is smooth and bright red, with enlarged papillae.

B. Laboratory Findings: Leukocytosis is present early; eosinophilia may appear during convalescence. The urine may show proteinuria, cylindruria, and hematuria. The sedimentation rate is elevated and returns to normal during the second week in uncomplicated cases. The antistreptolysin O titer rises during convalescence. Beta-hemolytic streptococci are usually cultured from the throat.

Complications

The common bacterial complications include rhinitis, sinusitis, and otitis media. Less often, there is mastoiditis, suppurative cervical lymphadenitis, pneumonia and empyema (rare), suppurative arthritis, and meningitis. Rheumatic fever may occur after the second week; acute glomerulonephritis (with nephritogenic strains of streptococci) may occur 1–4 weeks after the onset of streptococcal pharyngitis.

Differential Diagnosis

Streptococcal pharyngitis may greatly resemble the following: (1) Viral pharyngitis, caused by adenoviruses, coxsackieviruses, herpesviruses, and others. (2) Diphtheria, in which the throat is less red and the pseudomembrane is confluent. (3) Vincent's angina, with shallow ulcers usually involving the mouth. (4) Infectious mononucleosis, with more marked adenopathy, splenomegaly, abnormal lymphocytes, and a positive heterophil test. (5) Candidiasis, usually with dead-white patches of exudate and little erythema.

The rash of scarlet fever must be differentiated from the following: (1) Measles, distinguished by Koplik's spots and leukopenia. (2) Rubella, in which the fading rash may simulate scarlet fever; facial involvement is uncommon in scarlet fever. (3) Echovirus infections. (4) Other erythemas (solar, febrile), usually differentiated on the basis of the history. (5) Prodromal rashes in varicella and variola (rare). (6) Drug rashes.

Prevention

Sulfonamides, 0.5 gm twice daily, penicillin G, 250,000 units by mouth twice daily, or benzathine penicillin, 1,200,000 units IM once a month, reduce the incidence of streptococcal infection. These should be reserved for persons with rheumatic lesions to prevent recurrence of rheumatic fever.

Treatment

A. Specific Measures:

1. Benzathine penicillin G, 2.4 million units in a single dose, or procaine penicillin G, 300,000 units daily IM for 10 days. Oral penicillin G, 400,000 units, or phenethicillin (Syncillin®), 250 mg every 6 hours for 10 days. Penicillin by lozenges is worthless.

2. Erythromycin, 0.2–0.5 gm every 6 hours for 10 days, may be given to patients hypersensitive to penicillin.

3. Cephalothin (Keflin®), 1.5 gm IM every 6 hours, may be used in severely ill patients who are sensitive to penicillin.

B. General Measures:
Place the patient at bed rest until he is afebrile and the sedimentation rate is normal. Modify the diet as necessary for sore throat. Hot saline or 30% glucose gargles or throat irrigations 3 or 4 times daily may be used for relief of sore throat. Give aspirin or codeine as necessary for symptomatic relief.

C. Treatment of Complications:
Bacterial complications can usually be treated effectively with penicillin. Rheumatic fever may be prevented by early vigorous treatment of the infection with penicillin. Acute hemorrhagic glomerulonephritis is discussed in chapter 16.

D. Treatment of Carriers:
300,000 units of procaine penicillin G daily IM for 10 days, or benzathine penicillin G, 1,200,000 units IM, usually abolishes the carrier state.

Prognosis

In untreated, uncomplicated cases, fever persists 3–7 days and the rash begins to fade after 3–5 days. The course is shortened and complications minimized by early active treatment. Mortality is negligible.

Disney, F.A.: Office diagnosis of streptococcal infections. New York State J Med 68:1699–1701, 1968.

Feingold, D.S., Stagg, N.L., & L.J. Kunz: Extrarespiratory streptococcal infections. New England J Med 275:356–361, 1966.

DIPHTHERIA

Essentials of Diagnosis

- Gray, homogeneous, tenacious pseudomembrane at portal of entry.
- Sore throat, nasal discharge, hoarseness, malaise, fever.
- Myocarditis, neuritis.
- Culture confirms diagnosis.

General Considerations

Diphtheria is an acute contagious infection, caused by *Corynebacterium diphtheriae,* which usually attacks the respiratory tract but may involve any mucous membrane or skin wound. The organism usually gains entry through the respiratory tract, and is spread chiefly by respiratory secretions from patients with active disease or healthy carriers. The incubation period is 2–7 days. Myocarditis and late neuritis caused by an exotoxin are also characteristic of the infection.

Clinical Findings

A. Symptoms and Signs:
Characteristically there is a homogeneous, tenacious gray membrane growing rapidly from the tonsil onto the pillars and pharyngeal walls, surrounded by a very narrow zone of erythema and a more extensive zone of edema. The pharyngitis is relatively painless during the earliest stages. Early manifestations are mild sore throat, fever, and malaise, rapidly followed by severe signs of toxemia and prostration. The membrane may grow into the larynx and trachea, producing respiratory obstruction. Associated edema of the pharynx may add to the respiratory embarrassment.

If myocarditis develops it will be manifested by a rapid thready pulse, indistinct heart sounds, cardiac arrhythmia, and, finally, cardiac decompensation with falling blood pressure, hepatic congestion, and associated nausea and vomiting.

With toxic neuritis the cranial nerves are involved first, causing nasal speech, regurgitation of food through the nose, diplopia, strabismus, and inability to swallow, resulting in pooling of saliva and respiratory secretions. The neuritis may progress to involve the intercostal muscles and those of the extremities. Sensory manifestations are much less prominent than motor weakness.

B. Laboratory Findings:
The urine usually shows protein due to toxic nephritis. Polymorphonuclear leukocytosis is present. Bacterial culture will confirm the diagnosis. Throat smears are often unreliable. Albuminocytologic dissociation of the CSF is noted in postdiphtheritic neuritis.

C. ECG Findings:
In myocarditis the ECG may show an arrhythmia, P–R prolongation, heart block, and inversion of the T waves.

Differential Diagnosis

Diphtheria must be differentiated from streptococcal pharyngitis with its extremely red, very sore, and edematous features, and from infectious mononucleosis with its white, easily removed membrane. A presumptive diagnosis of diphtheria must be made on clinical grounds without waiting for laboratory verification since treatment is emergent.

Complications

Acute otitis media or bronchial pneumonia may occur.

Prevention

A. Children: Give 3 IM injections (0.5 ml each) of diphtheria toxoid (alum-precipitated or aluminum hydroxide-adsorbed) at 2 months, 3 months, and 4 months of age. Diphtheria immunization may be combined with tetanus and pertussis immunization (DPT). Give 0.5 IM as recall injection at 1 year of age, then at 3 years after primary course, and at 7 years after primary course, and then every 10 years.

B. Adults: Adults tend to react severely to the usual or pediatric diphtheria toxoids. Hence, the product of choice is adsorbed diphtheria toxoid (for adult use). This is administered in 3 doses of 0.5–1 ml subcut 4–6 weeks apart, with a third dose approximately 12 months after the second. (See Immunization Schedules in Appendix.)

Treatment

A. Specific Measures:

1. Diphtheria antitoxin must be given in all cases when diphtheria cannot be excluded by simple clinical examination. The intravenous route is preferable in all but the mildest cases or in patients who are sensitive to horse serum. Conjunctival and skin tests for serum sensitivity should be done in all cases, and desensitization carried out if necessary. The dose varies with the duration of the disease, the location of the lesion, and the size of the patient. A single dose should suffice.

2. Procaine penicillin, 300,000 units IM daily, accelerates slightly the disappearance of the organism from the throat and acts against secondary streptococcal invaders; it does not alter the course of the disease itself.

B. General Measures: Place the patient at absolute bed rest for at least 3 weeks and until the ECG is

TABLE 21–1. Diphtheria antitoxin dosage schedule.

Location	Child	Adult
Anterior nasal	5,000 units	10,000 units
Mild pharyngeal	10,000 units	20,000 units
Moderate pharyngeal	20,000 units	40,000 units
Severe pharyngeal and nasopharyngeal	40,000 units	80,000 units
Laryngeal	10,000 units	20,000 units
Any 2 sites or late cases	40,000 units	80,000 units

normal. Give a liquid to soft diet as tolerated, hot saline or 30% glucose throat irrigations 3–4 times daily, and aspirin or codeine as required for relief of pain.

C. Special Problems:

1. **Myocarditis**—No definitive treatment is known. Oxygen by tent or mask may be needed. Hypertonic glucose solution, 100 ml of 20% solution daily, may be of value. Digitalis and quinidine should be reserved for arrhythmias with rapid ventricular rate. It may be necessary to treat the patient for shock (see Chapter 1).

2. **Neuritis**—Nasal feeding should be attempted if paralysis of deglutition is present. Tracheostomy and the use of a mechanical respirator may be necessary. Corrective splinting and physical therapy may be of value.

3. **Respiratory tract obstruction**—Croupy cough, stridor, and dyspnea suggest laryngeal obstruction. Suction of membrane and secretions under direct laryngoscopy may help. Intubation or tracheostomy should be performed before the appearance of cyanosis if the distress increases.

4. A chronic skin ulceration due to *C diphtheriae* occurs particularly in warm, humid climates and can be followed by the complications of myocarditis and neuritis. Treatment is required as for pharyngeal disease.

D. Treatment of Complications: Acute otitis media and bronchial pneumonia are discussed in Chapters 5 and 6, respectively.

E. Treatment of Carriers: Penicillin has little effect on the carrier state.

Prognosis

The mortality rate varies between 10 and 30%; it is higher in older persons and when treatment has been delayed. Myocarditis which appears early is often fatal. Disturbances of conduction or the appearance of an arrhythmia implies a poor prognosis. Neuritis is rarely fatal unless respiratory muscle paralysis occurs. Myocarditis and neuritis will subside slowly but completely if the patient survives.

AMA Council on Drugs: Immunologic agents. Pages 643–646 in: *AMA Drug Evaluations.* American Medical Association, 1971.

Burch G.E., & others: Diphtheritic myocarditis. Am J Cardiol 21:261–268, 1968.

McCloskey, R.V. Green, M., & S.E.M. Richards: The 1970 epidemic of diphtheria in San Antonio. Ann Int Med 75:495–503, 1971.

National Communicable Disease Center: *Diphtheria Surveillance: Annual Diphtheria Summary–1967.* Report No. 9. US Public Health Service, 1969.

PERTUSSIS
(Whooping Cough)

Essentials of Diagnosis

- Paroxysmal cough ending in a high-pitched inspiratory "whoop."

- Two-week prodromal catarrhal stage of malaise, cough, coryza, and anorexia.
- Predominantly in infants under 2 years of age.
- Absolute lymphocytosis.
- Culture confirms diagnosis.

General Considerations

Pertussis is an acute, highly communicable infection of the respiratory tract caused by *Bordetella (Hemophilus) pertussis.* It is transmitted by respiratory droplets from infected individuals. The incubation period is 7–14 days. Infectivity is greatest early in the disease and decreases until the organisms disappear from the nasopharynx (after about 1 month). Infants are most commonly infected; ½ of all cases occur before 2 years of age.

Clinical Findings

A. Symptoms and Signs: Physical findings are minimal or absent. Fever, if present, is low-grade. Although atypical cases lasting only a few days to a week have been described, the symptoms of classical pertussis last about 6 weeks and are divided into 3 consecutive stages:

1. Catarrhal stage—The onset is insidious, with lacrimation, sneezing, coryza, anorexia, malaise, and a hacking night cough which tends to become diurnal.

2. Paroxysmal stage—This follows the beginning of the catarrhal stage by 10–14 days, and is characterized by rapid consecutive coughs usually followed by a deep hurried inspiration (whoop). Paroxysms may involve 5–15 coughs before a breath is taken, and may occur up to 50 times in 24 hours. Psychic stimuli such as fright or anger, crying, sneezing, inhalation of irritants, and overdistention of the stomach may produce the paroxysms. The cough is productive of copious amounts of thick mucus. Vomiting is common during the paroxysms.

3. Convalescent stage—This stage usually begins 4 weeks after the onset of the illness, and is manifested by a decrease in the frequency and severity of paroxysms of cough.

B. Laboratory Findings: The white count is usually 15,000–20,000/cu mm (rarely, to 50,000), 60–80% lymphocytes. Culture and identification of the causative organism by cough plate or nasopharyngeal swab is possible in 70% of cases.

Differential Diagnosis

Pertussis must be differentiated from aspiration of a foreign body in the child, or virus pneumonia, influenza, and acute bronchitis in the older individual. The lymphocytosis may suggest acute leukemia.

Complications

Asphyxia, the most common complication, occurs most frequently in infants and may lead to convulsions and brain damage. The increased intracranial pressure during a paroxysm may also lead to brain damage by causing cerebral hemorrhage. Pneumonia, atelectasis, interstitial and subcutaneous emphysema, and pneumothorax may occur as a result of damaged respiratory mucosa, inspissated mucus, or increased intrathoracic pressure.

Prevention

Passive prophylaxis of exposed susceptibles by the injection of 20 ml of hyperimmune serum or 2.5 ml of hyperimmune gamma globulin IM is of doubtful value.

Active immunity may be produced with pertussis vaccine given alone or in combination with diphtheria and tetanus toxoids (DPT). The latter method is preferred. (See p 904.)

Treatment

A. Specific Measures:

1. Antibiotics—Give one of the following: (1) Ampicillin, 150 mg/kg/day. (2) Erythromycin, 50 mg/kg/day orally. Antibiotics are of doubtful value at the paroxysmal coughing stage.

2. Hyperimmune gamma globulin, 10 ml IM, appears to hasten recovery, prevent complications, and reduce mortality.

B. General Measures:

1. Nutrition—Frequent small feedings may be necessary. Re-feed if vomiting occurs shortly after a meal. A high-caloric formula by gavage tube may be required in infants who refuse to eat. Parenteral fluids may be used to ensure adequate fluid intake in severe cases.

2. Cough—Sedative and expectorant cough mixtures are of slight benefit. Atropinization to the point of facial flushing with increasing doses of tincture of belladonna every 4 hours, starting with 1 drop, is occasionally helpful. Ether in oil by rectum may be used in severe cases.

C. Treatment of Complications: Pneumonia, usually due to secondary invaders, should be treated with penicillin, ampicillin, cephalothin, or cephaloridine, depending upon specific bacteriologic diagnosis. Oxygen is often required.

Convulsions may require sedation, 100% oxygen inhalation, and lumbar puncture.

Prognosis

In children under 1 year of age the mortality rate until recently was over 20%; this rate has been reduced to 1–2% with antibacterial therapy. Bronchiectasis is a fairly common sequel.

Brooksaler, F., & J.D. Nelson: Pertussis. Am J Dis Child 114:389–396, 1967.

Kaufman, S., & H.B. Bruyn: Pertussis: A clinical study. Am J Dis Child 99:417–422, 1960.

Preston, N.W.: Effectiveness of pertussis vaccines. Brit MJ 2:11–12, 1965.

INFECTIONS OF THE CNS

Infections of the CNS can be caused by almost any infectious agent, but most commonly are due to pyogenic bacteria, mycobacteria, fungi, spirochetes, and viruses. Certain symptoms and signs are more or less common to all types of CNS infection: headache, fever, sensorial disturbances, neck and back stiffnes, positive Kernig's and Brudzinski's signs, and CSF abnormalities. In patients presenting with these manifestations the possibility of CNS infection must be considered and, when possible, the specific cause established by means of a careful history and physical examination as well as study of the CSF and other appropriate laboratory procedures.

CNS infections must not be confused with meningismus, which consists of the signs of meningeal irritation in the absence of meningeal inflammation. Meningismus occurs with certain febrile diseases such as streptococcal pharyngitis, pneumonia, and bacterial enteritis in children.

Etiologic Classification

CNS infections can be divided into 3 broad categories which usually can be readily distinguished from each other by CSF examination as the first step toward etiologic diagnosis (see Table 21–2).

A. Purulent Meningitis: Eg, due to infection with meningococci (40% of cases), pneumococci, streptococci, *Hemophilus influenzae,* staphylococci, and other pyogenic organisms.

B. Granulomatous Meningitis: Eg, due to *Mycobacterium tuberculosis;* coccidioides, cryptococcus, histoplasma, and other fungi; or *Treponema pallidum* (meningovascular syphilis).

C. Viral Meningitis: Eg, due to the viruses of the following diseases: poliomyelitis, arthropodborne encephalitis, lymphocytic choriomeningitis, mumps, rabies, infectious mononucleosis, herpes simplex, and to coxsackie virus or echovirus infection.

The aseptic meningitis syndrome is of diverse etiology and presents the clinical and CSF findings of viral meningitis in the absence of the specific clinical phenomena diagnostic of a particular disease, eg, lower motor neuron paralysis in poliomyelitis, salivary gland involvement in mumps, or marked sensorial disturbance in encephalitis. Among the important causes of the aseptic meningitis syndrome are nonparalytic poliomyelitis, mumps, leptospirosis, and Coxsackie and ECHO viral infections.

Laboratory Diagnosis

Clinical descriptions of the various forms of CNS infections will be found elsewhere in the book. Although a history of exposure to disease or vectors, the presence of infections outside the CNS, rashes, neurologic abnormalities, blood culture, skin tests, serologic tests, and other clues are important in differential diagnosis, examination of the CSF is the single most useful tool in the diagnosis of CNS infections.

Groover, R.V., Sutherland, J.M., & B.H. Landing: Purulent meningitis of newborn infants: Eleven-year experience in the antibiotic era. New England J Med 264:1115–1121, 1961.

Rose, F.C., & J. Condon: The diagnosis of pyogenic meningitis. Postgrad MJ 43:376–378, 1967.

Swartz, M.N., & P.R. Dodge: Bacterial meningitis: A review of selected aspects. New England J Med 272:725–730, 779–786, 842–848, 898–902, 1965.

Wellman, W.E.: Bacterial meningitis. Postgrad Med 42:7–13, 1967.

1. MENINGOCOCCAL MENINGITIS

Essentials of Diagnosis

- Fever, headache, vomiting, confusion, delirium, convulsions.
- Petechial rash of skin and mucous membranes.
- Neck and back stiffness with positive Kernig's and Brudzinski's signs.
- Purulent spinal fluid with gram-negative intracellular and extracellular organisms.
- Culture of CSF, blood, or petechial aspiration confirms the diagnosis.

General Considerations

Meningococcal meningitis is caused by *Neisseria meningitidis* and results from a bacteremia originating

---

TABLE 21–2. Typical CSF findings in various CNS diseases.

Type of Infection	Cells/ cu mm	Cell Type*	Pressure	Protein (mg/100 ml)	Glucose (mg/100 ml)
Purulent meningitis	>1000	PMN	++++	>100	<40
Granulomatous meningitis	<1000	L†	+++	>100	<40
Viral infection	<1000	L†	N to +	<100	>40
"Neighborhood" reaction‡	Variable	Variable	Variable	Variable	>40

*PMN = polymorphonuclear neutrophil; L = lymphocyte.

†PMN's may predominate early.

‡May occur in mastoiditis, sinusitis, brain abscess, brain tumor, epidural abscess.

in a nasopharyngeal focus localizing in the meninges. The infection is spread by respiratory droplets from persons with mild upper respiratory meningococcal infections, mainly healthy carriers (a 30–80% carrier incidence has been observed during epidemics). The meningococcemia may not be clinically evident, or may be fulminating and rapidly fatal with little or no evidence of meningitis. The meningococcemia may also be associated with adrenal hemorrhage (Waterhouse-Friderichsen syndrome). The incubation period is 3–7 days, with infectivity occasionally present for several days before the appearance of the meningitis.

Clinical Findings

A. Symptoms and Signs: High fever, chills, and headache; back, abdominal, and extremity pains; and nausea and vomiting are present. In severe cases rapidly developing confusion, delirium, and coma occur. Convulsive twitchings or frank convulsions may also be present.

Nuchal and back rigidity are present, with positive Kernig's and Brudzinski's signs. A petechial rash is found in most cases. Petechiae may vary from pinhead-sized to large ecchymoses or even areas of skin gangrene which may later slough if the patient survives. These petechiae are found in any part of the skin, mucous membranes, or the conjunctivas, but never in the nail beds, and they usually fade in 3–4 days. The increased intracranial pressure will cause the anterior fontanel to bulge (if not closed) and may produce Cheyne-Stokes or Biot's respiration.

B. Laboratory Findings: Leukocytosis is usually marked and occurs very early in the course of the disease. The urine may contain protein, casts, and red cells. Lumbar puncture reveals a cloudy to frankly purulent CSF, with elevated pressure, increased protein, and decreased glucose and chloride content. The fluid usually contains more than 1000 cells/cu mm, with polymorphonuclear cells predominating and containing gram-negative intracellular cocci. The absence of organisms in a gram-stained smear of the CSF sediment does not rule out the diagnosis but in fact favors meningococcal etiology in a purulent meningitis. The organism is usually demonstrated by smear or culture of the CSF, oropharynx, blood, or aspirated petechiae.

Differential Diagnosis

Meningococcal meningitis must be differentiated from other meningitides. In small infants the clinical manifestations of meningeal infection may be erroneously diagnosed as upper respiratory infection or other acute infections.

Complications

Arthritis, cranial nerve damage (especially the 8th nerve, with resulting deafness), internal hydrocephalus, and iritis may occur as complications. Myocarditis, nephritis, and intravascular coagulation may occur in severe cases.

Prevention

The carrier rate of the organism varies from 20–100% in epidemics. Reduction of the carrier rate by mass use of sulfonamides—either sulfadiazine or sulfisoxazole, 2–4 gm in 2–4 doses daily for 5 days—can be effective only if the epidemic strain is sensitive to sulfonamides. Penicillin treatment of carriers or exposed individuals in the family or in a hospital is usually not indicated. Full therapeutic doses of penicillin as described below are necessary to assure success, and smaller doses will not effectively clear the carrier state.

Rifampin is reported to be effective in clearing the carrier state in 90–95% of carriers. This drug should be administered once daily for 4 consecutive days. The dose for adults is 600 mg orally in a single daily dose; for children, the dosage is 10–20 mg/kg orally, not to exceed 600 mg/day.

Treatment

A. Specific Measures: If there is a high degree of suspicion, prompt antibacterial treatment is necessary, ie, before the laboratory studies are completed.

1. Penicillin—Give aqueous penicillin, 20 million units IV immediately, pending the results of culture, followed by 20 million units IV daily for at least 6 days. Ampicillin, 4–8 gm daily IV, may be used. There is cross-sensitivity to penicillin.

2. Chloramphenicol—2–4 gm IV daily for 7 days can be used in penicillin-sensitive individuals.

3. Tetracyclines, erythromycin, and sulfonamides are alternative drugs.

Antibacterial therapy should be continued until the patient has been afebrile, alert, and eating well for at least 3 days.

B. General Measures: Give paraldehyde, sodium amobarbital (intravenously), or morphine sulfate as necessary for restlessness, and restraints, if necessary, for marked restlessness. Fluid intake should be at least 3 liters daily and should be sufficient to maintain a urinary output of at least 1000–1500 ml. Replace fluid lost by vomiting and give parenterally if necessary. If the patient is comatose more than 3 days, give feedings (and medication) by stomach tube. Repeat lumbar puncture if evidence of increased intracranial pressure persists or to check the response to therapy by CSF glucose level. For treatment of septic shock, see Chapter 1.

Prognosis

The overall mortality of meningococcal meningitis is 10%. Young healthy individuals and those who retain consciousness usually survive.

Artenstein, M.S., & R. Gold: Current status of prophylaxis of meningococcal disease. Mil Med 135:735–739, 1970.

Baird, G.D.: Meningococcal meningitis. GP 36:95–100, Sept 1967.

Greenfield, S., & H.A. Feldman: Familial carriers and meningococcal meningitis. New England J Med 277:497–502, 1967.

Jensen, W.L.: Treatment of acute meningococcal infections with penicillin G. Arch Int Med 122:322–325, 1968.

Leedom, J.M., & others: Importance of sulfadiazine resistance in meningococcal disease in civilians. New England J Med 273:1395–1401, 1965.

Wolf, R.E., & C.A. Birbara: Meningococcal infections at an army training center. Am J Med 44:243–255, 1968.

2. PNEUMOCOCCAL, STREPTOCOCCAL, & STAPHYLOCOCCAL MENINGITIS

The symptoms are similar to those of meningococcal meningitis, but a preceding infection is usually present and a focus is often demonstrable in the lungs (pneumococcal), the middle ear, or sinuses. The CSF must be cultured and examined to determine the causative agent.

Specific treatment of pneumococcal and streptococcal meningitis consists of aqueous penicillin, 1 million units IM every 2 hours or by continuous IV drip. In severe cases it may also be necessary to give 20,000 units of penicillin in 10 ml of physiologic saline once daily intrathecally until the CSF glucose is normal. Treat staphylococcal meningitis with sodium oxacillin (Prostaphlin®), 6–12 gm IM daily, or methicillin (Staphcillin®), 10–12 gm daily IV or IM. Nafcillin and cloxacillin may also be used. If the staphylococcus is sensitive to penicillin G, treat as pneumococcal meningitis. Treatment should be continued for 2–4 weeks.

With adequate and at times very large doses of antibiotics, the mortality rate is strikingly reduced. Staphylococcal meningitis carries the gravest prognosis.

Weiss, W., & others: Prognostic factors in pneumococcal meningitis. Arch Int Med 120:517–524, 1967.

3. TUBERCULOUS MENINGITIS

Essentials of Diagnosis

- Gradual onset of listlessness, irritability, and anorexia.
- Headache, vomiting, coma, convulsions; neck and back rigidity.
- Tuberculous focus usually evident elsewhere.
- Usually in children below 5 years of age.
- CSF with web and pellicle showing organisms by smear or culture.

General Considerations

Tuberculous meningitis is caused by meningeal spread of the tubercle bacilli from a gross or microscopic focus usually in the lungs or the peritracheal, peribronchial, or mesenteric lymph nodes, or as a result of miliary spread. Its greatest incidence is in children between the ages of 1 and 5 years.

Clinical Findings

A. Symptoms and Signs: The onset is usually gradual, with listlessness, irritability, anorexia, and fever, followed by headache, vomiting, night cries, convulsions, and coma. In older patients headache and behavioral changes are prominent early symptoms.

Nuchal rigidity, opisthotonos, and paralysis occur as the meningitis progresses. Paralysis of the extraocular muscles is common. Ophthalmoscopic examination may reveal choroid tubercles. General physical examination may reveal evidence of tuberculosis elsewhere. The tuberculin skin test may be negative in miliary tuberculosis.

B. Laboratory Findings: The CSF is frequently xanthochromic, with increased pressure and 50–500 cells/cu mm (early, polymorphonuclear neutrophils; later, lymphocytic), decreased glucose, and decreased chloride content. On standing the CSF may form a web and pellicle from which organisms may be demonstrated by smear, culture, or guinea pig inoculation. Moderate leukocytosis is common. Chest x-ray often reveals a tuberculous focus.

Differential Diagnosis

Tuberculous meningitis may be confused with any other meningitis, but the gradual onset and evidence of tuberculosis elsewhere usually help to clarify the diagnosis.

Complications

After recovery there may be residual brain damage resulting in motor paralysis, convulsive states, mental impairment, and abnormal behavior. The incidence of these complications increases the longer therapy is withheld. Ataxia and deafness are most often due to streptomycin therapy.

Treatment

A. Specific Measures: Give streptomycin, 1 gm IM daily for 14 days and then twice weekly for 6–12 months. In addition to streptomycin, give isoniazid, 10 mg/kg/day in 2–4 doses for 1–2 years; and either aminosalicylic acid (or its salts), 8–12 gm daily in divided doses after meals for 1–2 years, or ethambutol, 15–25 mg/kg in a single dose daily for 1–2 years. Optic or peripheral neuritis caused by isoniazid may be prevented by giving 50–100 mg pyridoxine daily. For the first few weeks, corticosteroids in full therapeutic doses (eg, 80 mg prednisone, or equivalent, daily) should also be used.

B. General Measures: Treat symptoms as they arise and maintain good nutrition and adequate fluid intake. Treat hyponatremia due to inappropriate ADH secretion which may be present.

Prognosis

The natural course of the disease is death within 6–8 weeks. When it is diagnosed and treated early the recovery rate is up to 90%; if treatment is not instituted until the disease has reached the late stage, the recovery rate is 25–30%.

Tahernia, A.C.: Tuberculous meningitis. Modern diagnosis, treatment and prognosis, as exemplified in 38 cases in southern Iran. Clin Pediat 6:173–177, 1967.

HEMOPHILUS INFLUENZAE MENINGITIS

Hemophilus influenzae meningitis occurs most frequently in children under 10 years of age.

Nothing about the onset, symptoms, or signs distinguishes this illness from other purulent meningitides. It may exist for several days as an apparent respiratory infection; however, headache, irritability, fever, malaise, vomiting, unexplained leukocytosis, and some nuchal and back rigidity should suggest meningitis. Lumbar puncture will reveal the gram-negative pleomorphic rods in the purulent spinal fluid smear or culture. A capsule-swelling test can be performed on any organisms found if antiserum is available. Culture confirms the diagnosis.

Differential Diagnosis

It is impossible to distinguish *Hemophilus influenzae* meningitis from other purulent meningitides on the basis of symptoms and signs, but the discovery and identification of the specific organism in the CSF makes exact diagnosis possible.

Treatment

A. **Specific Measures:** The treatment of choice is with sodium ampicillin (adults, 10–20 gm/day; children, 100–200 mg/kg/day). Give IV in 4–6 doses instilled into an already started intravenous drip. Alternative treatment is streptomycin (adults, 1 gm; children, 250 mg) IM every 6 hours for 1 week, and streptomycin, 25 mg in 10 ml of physiologic saline solution intrathecally daily until the CSF glucose is normal. Give also sulfadiazine, 150 mg/kg/day, with adequate fluids to prevent crystal formation. Tetracycline drugs, 0.5 gm every 6 hours, are of value.

Chloramphenicol, 50 mg/kg/day in children or 5 gm/day in adults continued for 7 days is another alternative.

B. **General Measures:** Treat symptoms as they arise and maintain good nutrition and adequate fluid intake.

Prognosis

Prompt treatment is required to prevent death or permanent CNS damage. Before the advent of chemotherapeutic agents the mortality rate was virtually 100%.

Shaw, E.B., & H.B. Bruyn: Streptomycin in therapy of *Hemophilus influenzae* meningitis. J Pediat 56:253–258, 1960.

SALMONELLOSIS

Salmonellosis includes infection by any of approximately 900 serotypes of salmonellae. Three general clinical patterns are recognized: (1) typhoid fever, most commonly due to *Salmonella typhi;* (2) acute gastroenteritis, caused by *S typhimurium* and many other types; and (3) the "septicopyemia" type, characterized by bacteremia and focal lesions and most commonly caused by *S choleraesuis.* Any serotype may cause any of these clinical patterns. All are transmitted by ingestion of the organism in contaminated food or fluid.

1. TYPHOID FEVER

Essentials of Diagnosis

- Gradual onset of malaise, headache, sore throat, cough, and finally "peasoup" diarrhea or constipation.
- Slow (stepladder) rise of fever to maximum and then slow return to normal.
- Rose spots, relative bradycardia, splenomegaly, and abdominal distention and tenderness.
- Leukopenia: positive blood, stool, and urine culture.
- Elevated or rising specific (Widal) agglutination titers.

General Considerations

Typhoid fever is caused by the gram-negative rod *Salmonella typhi,* which enters the patient via the gastrointestinal tract where it penetrates the intestinal wall and produces inflammation of the mesenteric lymph nodes and the spleen. As the defense mechanism of the host is overwhelmed, bacteremia occurs, and the infection eventually localizes principally in the lymphoid tissue of the small intestine (particularly within the 2 feet of the ileocecal valve). These Peyer's patches become inflamed and finally may ulcerate. Ulceration and sloughing reach a maximum during the third week of the disease. Occasionally the organism may localize in the lung, gallbladder, kidney, or CNS with resulting inflammation. Infection is transmitted by eating or drinking contaminated food or liquid. Most infections are transmitted by chronic carriers with a persistent gallbladder or urinary tract focus. The incubation period is 5–14 days.

Clinical Findings

A. **Symptoms and Signs:** In most instances the onset is insidious; less commonly, but especially in children, the onset may be abrupt, with chills and a sharp rise in temperature. The course of classical untreated typhoid fever can be divided into 3 stages:

1. **The prodromal stage**—During the period of invasion the patient gradually begins to feel unwell.

Increasing malaise, headache, cough, general body aching, sore throat, and epistaxis are common. Frequently (but not invariably) there are symptoms referable to the gastrointestinal tract, including abdominal pain, constipation or diarrhea, and vomiting. During this period the fever ascends in a stepladder fashion, the maximum temperature on each day being slightly higher than the preceding day. In the evening the temperature is generally higher than in the morning.

2. The fastigium—After about 7–10 days the fever stabilizes, varying less than 2° F during the day, and the patient becomes quite sick. Symptoms referable to the intestinal tract ("pea-soup" diarrhea or severe constipation, or marked abdominal distention) are common. Severe cases enter what is known as the typhoid state, in which the patient lies motionless and unresponsive, with eyes half-shut, appearing wasted and exhausted. He can usually be aroused to carry out simple commands.

3. The stage of defervescence—If the patient survives the severe toxemia of the second stage of the disease, or does not die of complications, his condition gradually improves. The fever declines in a "mirror image" of the onset, usually requiring 7–10 days to reach normal. The patient gradually becomes more alert and his abdominal symptoms disappear. During this stage recrudescence or relapse may occur as late as 1–2 weeks after the temperature has returned to normal. This relapse is usually milder than the original infection; however, occasionally all of the phenomena seen during the fastigium will be duplicated.

During the early prodromal period physical findings are slight or absent. Later, splenomegaly, abdominal distention and tenderness, relative bradycardia, dicrotic pulse, and occasionally meningismus, systolic murmur, and gallop rhythm appear. The rash (rose spots) commonly appears during the second week of the disease and may continue to erupt in crops until the period of convalescence. The individual spot is a pink papule 2–3 mm in diameter which fades on pressure. The papules are found principally on the trunk, and there are rarely more than 12. Each spot fades over a period of 3–4 days.

B. Laboratory Findings: Blood cultures may be positive as early as the first week and remain positive for a variable period thereafter (usually as long as the rose spots are present). Stools are positive for the organism after the first week of the disease; the urine may be positive at any time after the first week, although the organism is less frequently found in the urine than in the stool.

During the second week of the disease, antibodies begin to appear in the blood and continue to rise in titer until about the end of the third week (Widal test). If an anamnestic response to other infectious diseases or recent vaccination is ruled out, an O (somatic) antibody titer of 1–60 is presumptively diagnostic; a rising titer (as demonstrated by 2 specimens taken approximately a week apart) is almost completely diagnostic.

Moderate anemia is almost always seen during the height of infection. Leukopenia is the rule. Proteinuria is common.

Differential Diagnosis

Typhoid fever must be distinguished from other prolonged fevers associated with normal or depressed white count. Examples include tuberculosis, virus pneumonia, psittacosis, bacterial endocarditis, brucellosis, and Q fever.

Complications

Complications occur in about 30% of untreated cases and account for ¾ of all deaths. Intestinal hemorrhage is most likely to occur during the third week and is manifest by a sudden drop in temperature, rise in pulse, and signs of shock followed by dark or fresh blood in the stool. Intestinal perforation is most likely to occur during the third week. Sudden rigor, drop in temperature, and increase in pulse rate, accompanied by abdominal pain and tenderness, may be noted. Less frequent complications include urinary retention, pneumonia, thrombophlebitis, myocarditis, psychosis, cholecystitis, nephritis, spondylitis (typhoid spine), and meningitis.

Prevention

Typhoid vaccine is administered in 2 injections of 0.5 ml each, subcut, not less than 4 weeks apart. Normally, revaccinate twice only, with a single injection of 0.5 ml intracut administered at 4-year intervals. (See Immunization Schedules in Appendix.)

Environmental hygiene and sanitation must be well maintained, with particular attention to the protection of food and water and to waste disposal. Special measures may be required in the presence of an epidemic.

Carriers must be rigidly controlled and not permitted to be food handlers.

Treatment

A. Specific Measures: Give chloramphenicol (Chloromycetin®), 1 gm orally every 6 hours until fever disappears, and then 0.5 gm every 6 hours. (With children, give 50 mg/kg/day followed by 25 mg/kg/day when afebrile.) Continue treatment for 2 weeks. Hydrocortisone, 100 mg IV every 8 hours, may be used temporarily in severely toxic patients. Complete blood count should be obtained every 5 days to detect chloramphenicol toxicity. Ampicillin is also effective, but probably less so than chloramphenicol.

B. General Measures: Prevent decubiti by careful bathing, skin massage, and use of rubber "doughnuts" over pressure areas. Careful oral hygiene is important.

Give a high-caloric, low-residue diet (approximately 3600–4800 Calories/day). Complete vitamin supplementation must be used. The Coleman diet (about 1500 Calories/liter) consists of lactose, 400 gm; cream, 800 ml; and milk, 2800 ml. The casein hydrolysate formula (about 1050 Calories/liter) consists of casein hydrolysate, 125 gm; and milk, 1 liter.

Parenteral glucose solution may be necessary to supplement fluid intake and maintain urine output. Abdominal distention may be relieved by gentle colonic flushes and abdominal stupes. Vasopressin and neostigmine must be used with great caution because of the danger of perforation.

Diarrhea may be controlled with paregoric or other intestinal antispasmotics.

The patient must be strictly isolated and his excreta sterilized until negative stool cultures have been obtained.

C. Treatment of Complications: Secondary pneumonia may be treated with antibiotics or sulfonamides, depending on the etiologic agent.

Transfusions should be given as required for hemorrhage. If perforation occurs, immediate surgery is required; anticipate and treat shock (see Chapter 1) before it is manifest.

D. Treatment of Carriers: Chemotherapy is usually ineffective in abolishing the carrier state, although ampicillin is sometimes effective.

Prognosis

The mortality rate of typhoid fever is about 2% in treated cases. Elderly or debilitated persons are likely to do poorly. In children the course is milder.

With complications the prognosis is poor. Relapses occur in up to 15% of cases. A residual carrier state frequently persists in spite of chemotherapy.

2. SALMONELLA GASTROENTERITIS

The salmonella strains other than *Salmonella typhi* were formerly referred to as "paratyphoid organisms." They are serotyped into groups A, B, C; *Salmonella typhi,* the cause of typhoid fever, is in group D.

By far the most common form of salmonellosis is acute gastroenteritis. The commonest causative serotypes are *S typhimurium, S derby, S heidelberg, S infantis, S newport,* and *S enteritidis.* The incubation period is 8–48 hours after ingestion of contaminated food or liquid.

Symptoms and signs consist of fever, often with chills, nausea and vomiting, cramping abdominal pain, and diarrhea, sometimes bloody. The course is 3–5 days. Differentiation must be made from viral gastroenteritis, food poisoning, shigellosis, amebic dysentery, acute ulcerative colitis, and acute surgical conditions of the abdomen. Leukocytosis is usually absent. The organisms can be cultured from the stools, and occasionally the blood.

Partial or complete restriction of food may be necessary. Correction of fluid and electrolyte depletion by parenteral fluids is usually necessary. Paregoric or other antispasmodic agents may be used.

The place of chloramphenicol or ampicillin therapy is unclear, but chemotherapy is indicated only in severely ill patients.

3. SEPTICOPYEMIC SALMONELLOSIS

Rarely, salmonella infection may be manifested by prolonged or recurrent fever accompanied by bacteremia and by localization and abscess formation in one or more sites—such as the bones, joints, pleura, pericardium, endocardium, meninges, and lungs. Treatment is as for typhoid fever and should include drainage of accessible lesions.

Advisory Committee on Immunization Practices of the USPHS: Immunization against typhoid. Ann Int Med 65:1300–1301, 1966.

Hornick, R.B., & others: Typhoid fever vaccine—yes or no? M Clin North America 51:617–624, 1967.

McFadzean, A.J.S., & G.B. Ong: Intrahepatic typhoid carriers. Brit MJ 1:1567–1571, 1966.

Prost, E., & H. Riemann: Food-borne salmonellosis. Ann Rev Microbiol 21:495–528, 1967.

Robertson, R.P., Wahab, M.F.A., & F.O Raasch: Evaluation of chloramphenicol and ampicillin in salmonella enteric fever. New England J Med 278:171–176, 1968.

Rowland, H.A.K.: Typhoid immunization. Practitioner 195:312–316, 1965.

Simon, H.J., & R.C. Miller: Ampicillin in the treatment of chronic typhoid carriers: Report on 15 treated cases and a review of the literature. New England J Med 274:807–815, 1966.

Smith, D.H.: Salmonella with transferable drug resistance. New England J Med 275:625–629, 1966.

Taylor, J.: Salmonella food poisoning. Practitioner 195:12–17, 1965.

Wilder, A.N., & R.A. MacCready: Isolation of salmonella from poultry. New England J Med 274:1453–1460, 1966.

BRUCELLOSIS

Essentials of Diagnosis

- Vague complaints of easy fatigability, headache, arthralgia, anorexia, sweating, and irritability, all of insidious onset.
- Intermittent fever especially noted at night may become chronic and undulant.
- Cervical-axillary lymphadenopathy, splenomegaly.
- Lymphocytosis, positive blood culture, elevated agglutination and complement fixation titer.

General Considerations

The infection is caused by any of 3 species of Brucella organisms: *Brucella abortus* (cattle), *B suis* (hogs), and *B melitensis* (goats). Transmission to man is by direct contact with excretions and secretions of infected animals. The organism gains entry into man through minor skin abrasions or ingestion of raw contaminated milk or milk products. Human-to-human transmission is rare. The disease is mainly occupational among meat handlers, farmers, and veterinarians. The incubation period varies from 5–20 days, although the time between exposure and overt disease may extend up to several months. The disorder may become chronic and persist for years.

Clinical Findings

A. Symptoms and Signs: The onset may be acute, with fever, chills, and sweats similar to those seen in any acute febrile illness, but in most instances the disease begins so insidiously that it may be weeks before the patient presents himself to the physician with vague symptoms—often of weakness and exhaustion upon minimal activity. Symptoms also include headache, abdominal pains with anorexia and constipation, and arthralgia, sometimes associated with periarticular swelling but not local heat. The fever may be septic, sustained, undulating, low-grade, or even absent, but is more often of the intermittent type preceded by a feeling of chilliness, rising during the evening hours, and falling with a sweat (night sweat) in the early morning hours. In the chronic form it may assume an undulant nature, with periods of relatively absent fever between acute attacks. In the chronic form the above symptoms plus emotional instability and irritability and weight loss may persist for years, either on a continuous or intermittent basis.

Physical findings are minimal. Half of cases have peripheral lymph node enlargement and splenomegaly; hepatomegaly is less common.

B. Laboratory Findings: The white count is usually normal to low, with a relative or absolute lymphocytosis. The organism can be recovered from the blood, CSF, urine, and tissues early in the infection; later, this may be difficult, and an agglutination titer greater than 1:100 (and especially a rising titer) is usually used as laboratory verification of the disease. The intradermal skin test is of no value in diagnosing active disease and may confuse the agglutination titers.

Differential Diagnosis

Brucellosis must be differentiated from an acute febrile disease, especially tularemia, Q fever, and typhoid fever. Its chronic form resembles Hodgkin's disease, tuberculosis, and malaria. The chronic form is also often confused with psychoneurosis.

Complications

The most frequent complications are bone and joint lesions such as spondylitis and suppurative arthritis, usually of a single joint; subacute bacterial endocarditis, encephalitis, and meningitis. Less common complications are pneumonitis with pleural effusion, hepatitis, and cholecystitis. Abortion in humans is no more common with this disease than with any other acute bacterial disease during pregnancy.

Prevention

Preventive measures consist of destruction of infected dairy animals and immunization of susceptible animals, and pasteurization of all milk and milk products.

Treatment

A. Specific Treatment: (1) A combination of streptomycin, 1 gm IM daily, and one of the tetra-cycline drugs, 2 gm orally daily for 21 days, is the treatment of choice. (2) Tetracyclines alone in the same dosage are also effective. (3) Erythromycin is an alternative drug, but is less effective.

B. General Measures: Place the patient at bed rest during the acute febrile stage and maintain adequate nutrition.

Prognosis

In a few cases brucellosis may remain active for many years as an intermittent illness, but about 75% recover completely within 3—6 months and fewer than 20% have residual disease after 1 year. Treatment has considerably shortened the natural course of the disease.

Brucellosis is rarely fatal either in the acute or the chronic form. Residual psychoneurosis is common in recovered patients.

Martin, W.J.: The present status of streptomycin in antimicrobial therapy. M Clin North America 54:1161—1172, 1970.

Rizzo-Naudi, J., Griscti-Soler, N., & W. Ganado: Human brucellosis: An evaluation of antibiotics in the treatment of brucellosis. Postgrad MJ 43:520—526, 1967.

GAS GANGRENE

Essentials of Diagnosis

- Sudden onset of pain and edema in area of wound contamination.
- Brown to blood-tinged watery exudate, with skin discoloration of surrounding area.
- Gas demonstrated in the tissue by palpation or x-ray.
- Organisms demonstrated on culture or smear of exudate.

General Considerations

Gas gangrene is an infection caused by any of several anaerobic gram-positive bacilli which gain entry into the tissue by dirt or fecal contamination of wounds, usually those containing devitalized tissue. The puerperal tract may be infected. The organism grows only in anaerobic conditions, producing toxins which spread into and destroy the surrounding tissues and thus create increasing areas of reduced oxygen tension into which the organism may advance. In the process gas is produced. It is probable that the entire infection is a local reaction, although the possibility of toxins invading the blood and affecting distant vital centers has been postulated. The incubation period is 6 hours to 3 days after injury.

Clinical Findings

A. Symptoms and Signs: The onset is usually sudden, with rapidly increasing pain in the affected area accompanied by a fall in blood pressure, and tachycardia. The temperature may be elevated, but not proportionate to the severity of the inflammation. In the last stages of the disease severe prostration, stupor, delirium, and coma occur.

The wound becomes swollen, and the surrounding skin is pale as a result of fluid accumulation beneath it. This is followed by a discharge of a brown to blood-tinged, serous, foul-smelling fluid from the wound. As the disease advances the surrounding tissue changes from pale to dusky to finally become deeply discolored with coalescent red, fluid-filled vesicles. Gas may be palpable in the tissues. In clostridial septicemia, hemolysis and jaundice are common, often complicated by acute renal failure.

B. Laboratory Findings: Gas gangrene is a clinical rather than a bacteriologic diagnosis, although culture of the exudate confirms the diagnosis and stained smear of the exudate showing the typical gram-positive rods is a valuable clue to the diagnosis.

C. X-Ray Findings: X-ray may show gas in the soft tissues spreading along fascial planes.

Differential Diagnosis

Other types of infection can cause gas formation in the tissue, eg, aerobacter and escherichia infections. These organisms produce much more gas than clostridia. Clostridia may produce serious puerperal infection.

Treatment

A. Specific Measures: Give penicillin, 1,000,000 units IM every 3 hours. Polyvalent gas gangrene antitoxin, 20,000 units IV, may be given and repeated every 6–8 hours, although its value is doubtful.

B. Surgical Measures: Adequate surgical debridement and exposure of infected areas. Hyperbaric oxygen therapy, if available, may be beneficial when used in conjunction with other measures.

Prognosis

Without treatment the disease is invariably fatal.

Grossman, M., & W. Silen: Serious posttraumatic infections: With special reference to gas gangrene, tetanus and necrotizing fasciitis. Postgrad Med 32:110–118, 1962.
Hitchcock, C.R., Haglin, J.J., & O. Arnar: Treatment of clostridial infections with hyperbaric oxygen. Surgery 62:759–769, 1967.

ANTHRAX

Anthrax is a disease of sheep, cattle, horses, goats, and mules caused by *Bacillus anthracis,* a gram-positive spore forming bacillus which is transmissible to man by entry through broken skin or mucous membranes or, less commonly, by inhalation. Human infection is rare. It is most common in farmers, veterinarians, and tannery and wool workers. Several clinical forms have been observed.

Clinical Findings

A. Symptoms and Signs:

1. Cutaneous anthrax ("malignant pustule")—An erythematous patch appears on an exposed area of skin, and becomes papular and then vesicular, with a firm purple to black center. The area around the lesion is swollen or edematous, consisting of a dense ring surmounted by vesicles. The center of the lesion finally forms a necrotic eschar and sloughs. Regional adenopathy; variable fever, malaise, headache; and variable nausea and vomiting are present. Septicemic spread may occur after the eschar sloughs, at times manifested by shock, cyanosis, sweating, and collapse. Cerebral hemorrhage may occur.

2. Malignant edema—This form of the disease is characterized by fever, malaise, and rapidly spreading edema of the skin or mucous membranes followed by sloughing and gangrene.

3. Pulmonary anthrax ("woolsorter's disease")—Characterized by fever, malaise, headache, dyspnea, cough; congestion of the nose, throat, and larynx; and auscultatory or x-ray signs of pneumonia.

B. Laboratory Findings: The white count may be elevated or low. Sputum or blood culture may be positive for *Bacillus anthracis.* Smears of skin lesions show gram-positive rods.

Treatment

Give penicillin G, 10 million units IV daily; or a tetracycline, 0.5 gm orally every 6 hours, in mild, localized cases.

Prognosis

The prognosis is excellent in the cutaneous form of the disease if treatment is given early. Malignant edema and pulmonary anthrax have a grave prognosis. Bacteremia is a very unfavorable sign.

Gold, H.: Treatment of anthrax. Fed Proc 26:1563–1568, 1967.

TETANUS

Essentials of Diagnosis

- Jaw stiffness followed by spasms of jaw muscles (trismus).
- Stiffness of the neck and other muscles, dysphagia, irritability, hyperreflexia.
- Finally, painful convulsions precipitated by minimal stimuli.
- History of wound and possible contamination.

General Considerations

Tetanus is an acute CNS intoxication caused by fixation in the CNS of a toxin elaborated by the slender, sporeforming, gram-positive, anaerobic bacillus, *Clostridium tetani.* The organism is found mainly in the soil and in the feces of animals and humans, and enters the body by wound contamination. Although puncture wounds or purulent necrotic lesions are usually contaminated, because the organism is universal in distribution even the most trivial and relatively clean wound may be inoculated.

The exotoxin acts on the motor nerve end plates and anterior horn cells of the spinal cord and brain stem. Once the exotoxin is fixed in the tissue it is doubtful if it can be neutralized. The question of whether the toxin enters the CNS via the blood stream or through motor nerves is still unsettled. The incubation period is 5 days to 15 weeks.

Clinical Findings

A. Symptoms and Signs: Occasionally the first symptom is pain and tingling at the site of inoculation followed by spasticity of the group of muscles nearby. This may constitute the entire disease, especially in those individuals treated with inadequate prophylactic doses of antitoxin. More frequently, however, the presenting symptoms are stiffness of the jaw, neck stiffness, dysphagia, and irritability. Hyperreflexia develops later, with spasms of the jaw muscles (trismus) or facial muscles, and rigidity and spasm of the muscles of the abdomen, neck, and back. Painful tonic convulsions precipitated by minor stimuli are common. Although the patient is awake and alert during the entire course of the illness, during convulsions the glottis and respiratory muscles go into spasm so that the patient is unable to breathe and cyanosis and asphyxia may ensue. The temperature is only slightly elevated.

B. Laboratory Findings: The diagnosis of tetanus is made clinically. There is usually a polymorphonuclear leukocytosis.

Differential Diagnosis

Tetanus must be differentiated from other types of acute CNS infection. The trismus must be differentiated from that occasionally occurring with the use of drugs such as Atarax® or Thorazine®.

Complications

Malnutrition may occur as a result of dysphagia. Urinary retention and constipation may result from spasm of the sphincters. Respiratory arrest and cardiac failure may occur.

Prevention

Active immunization with tetanus toxoid should be universal. Give 2 injections of 0.5 ml IM, 4–8 weeks apart, with a third approximately 12 months after the second. A booster dose should be administered at the time of injury. To maintain effective protection against tetanus from obscure or trivial injuries, a booster or recall dose of toxoid every 10 years is desirable. (See p 904.)

For soil-contaminated wounds in nonimmunized individuals—especially puncture wounds, compound fractures, and powder burns and for patients sensitive to horse serum—give tetanus immune globulin (human) (Hyper-Tet®), 250 units IM, if available. Otherwise give tetanus antitoxin, 6000 units IM. Do not give inadequate doses. Follow with active immunization program, using toxoid.

Adequate debridement of wounds is one of the most important preventive measures. In suspect cases, benzathine penicillin, 1.2 million units IM, may be a reasonable preventive measure.

Treatment

A. Specific Measures: If available, give tetanus immune globulin (human) (Hyper-Tet®), 5000 units IM; this antitoxin does not cause sensitivity reactions. Otherwise give tetanus antitoxin, 100,000 units IV, after testing for horse serum sensitivity. The value of antitoxin treatment has recently been questioned.

B. General Measures: Place the patient at bed rest and minimize stimulation. Sedation and anticonvulsant therapy are essential. Experience from India and other areas of high incidence appears to indicate that most convulsions can be eliminated by treatment with chlorpromazine (50–100 mg 4 times daily) combined with a sedative (amobarbital, phenobarbital, or meprobamate). Diazepam (Valium®) has been reported to be of value in relieving muscle spasm, especially when used in combination with other sedative and anticonvulsant drugs. Mild cases of tetanus can be controlled with only one or the other. Only rarely is general curarization required. Other anticonvulsant regimens which have been recommended are as follows: (1) Tribromoethanol, 15–25 mg/kg rectally every 1–4 hours as needed. (2) Amobarbital sodium, 5 mg/kg IM as needed. (3) Paraldehyde, 4–8 ml IV (2–5% solution) may be combined with barbiturates. Penicillin is of value but should not be substituted for antitoxin.

Give intravenous fluids as required. Tracheostomy may be required for laryngeal spasm. Assisted respiration is required in conjunction with curarization. Hyperbaric oxygen therapy is reported to be of doubtful value.

Prognosis

The mortality rate is higher in very small children and very old people, with shorter incubation periods, with shorter intervals between onset of symptoms and the first convulsion, and with delay in treatment. If trismus develops early, the prognosis is grave. The overall mortality is about 40%. Contaminated lesions about the head and face are more dangerous than wounds on other parts of the body.

If the patient lives, recovery is complete.

Adams, E.B., & others: Usefulness of intermittent positive-pressure respiration in the treatment of tetanus. Lancet 2:1176–1181, 1966.

Edsall, G., & others: Excessive use of tetanus toxoid boosters. JAMA 202:17–19, 1967.

Femi-Pearsö, D.: Experience with diazepam (Valium®) in tetanus. Brit MJ 2:862–865, 1966.

International Conference on Tetanus: Prevention of tetanus. Ann Int Med 65:1079–1080, 1966.

Levine, L., & others: Active-passive tetanus immunization: Choice of toxoid, dose of tetanus immune globulin and timing of injections. New England J Med 274:186–189, 1966.

Nyhan, W.L., & others: Tetanus. California Med 115:24–33, Oct 1971.

Robles, N.L., Walske, B.R., & A.R. Tella: Tetanus prophylaxis and therapy. S Clin North America 48:799–806, 1968.

Steigman, A.J.: Abuse of tetanus toxoid. J Pediat 72:749–750, 1968.

Vaishnava, H., & others: A controlled trial of antiserum in the treatment of tetanus. Lancet 2:1371–1373, 1966.

BOTULISM

Essentials of Diagnosis

- Sudden onset of cranial nerve paralysis heralded by ocular involvement (especially diplopia).
- History of ingestion of home-canned food or finding the toxin in suspected food.

General Considerations

Botulism is a food poisoning caused by ingestion of preformed toxin of *Clostridium botulinum.* It is characterized by involvement of the CNS, especially of the bulbar region. The toxin interferes with the release of acetylcholine by the nerve tissue. In the USA most cases follow ingestion of improperly prepared home-canned foods, especially vegetables and meats. The toxin is heat-labile and is destroyed by proper cooking of foods.

Clinical Findings

A. Symptoms and Signs: Symptoms appear abruptly 18–36 hours after the ingestion of the toxin, and are usually ushered in by visual disturbances (diplopia, loss of powers of accommodation, and reduced visual acuity). This is followed by involvement of the bulbar cranial nerves, causing dysphagia, dysphonia, nasal regurgitation, and vomiting. The muscles of the extremities become weak, and vertigo is common. The sensorium remains clear. The temperature is normal unless intercurrent infection occurs.

B. Laboratory Findings: The blood, urine, and CSF findings are normal. All suspected food should be collected and examined for the causative toxin by injection into mice. Toxin may be demonstrated in blood.

Differential Diagnosis

Botulism must be differentiated from bulbar poliomyelitis, myasthenia gravis, and infectious neuronitis.

Complications

Difficulty in swallowing often causes aspiration pneumonia. Respiratory paralysis may lead to death.

Prevention

All canned foods must be sterilized. Home-canned foods must be boiled for 10–20 minutes before they are eaten. Cans with bulging lids or jars with leaking rings should be destroyed.

Treatment

A. Specific Measures: Botulinus antitoxin (types A, B, and E), 10,000–50,000 units IM as soon as possible.

B. General Measures:

1. Absolute rest with foot of bed elevated to promote drainage from respiratory tract.

2. Aspiration of respiratory tract frequently. Tracheostomy may be required.

3. Oxygen by mask or catheter as indicated.

4. Respirator as required for respiratory paralysis.

5. Intravenous fluids as necessary.

6. Treat complicating pneumonia with antibiotics.

Prognosis

The mortality rate of botulism is 60%; death occurs in 20 hours to 10 days. If the patient survives, there are usually no sequelae, although residual motor weakness may persist for months.

Koenig, M.G., & others: Type B botulism in man. Am J Med 42:208–219, 1967.

Lamanna, C., & C.J. Carr: The botulinal, tetanal and enterostaphylococcal toxins: A review. Clin Pharmacol Therap 8:286–332, 1967.

TULAREMIA

Essentials of Diagnosis

- Sudden onset of fever, chills, nausea, vomiting, and prostration.
- Papule progressing to pustule to clean ulcer at the site of inoculation.
- Regional lymph node enlargement and suppuration.
- History of contact with contaminated wild animals, especially rabbits.
- Diagnosis confirmed by culture of ulcer, lymph node drainage, or blood.

General Considerations

Tularemia is caused by the gram-negative organism *Francisella (Pasteurella) tularensis.* The infection is acquired by man from infected animals by ingestion of the contaminated meat, contamination of the skin (even unbroken skin), or by bites of insects which have bitten the infected animal. Most cases are traceable to infected wild rabbits or other rodents. The lesions consist of areas of focal necrosis scattered throughout the body. The incubation period is 2–10 days.

Clinical Findings

A. Symptoms and Signs: There is a sudden onset of fever, chills, headache, nausea, vomiting, sweats, and severe weakness, followed within 1–2 days by the formation of a papule or papules at the site of inoculation (ulceroglandular form). The papule soon becomes a pustule and finally ulcerates to produce a clean crater. The regional lymph nodes become enlarged, and may ulcerate and drain profusely. An atypical pneumonia with pleurisy (pneumopleuritic form) or a typhoid-like state (typhoidal form), or a combination of both types of involvement, frequently develops within 4–5 days. A nonspecific roseola-like rash may appear at any time. The spleen is frequently enlarged, and a perisplenitis may develop. If the site of inoculation is the eye, conjunctivitis and preauricular adenitis result.

B. Laboratory Findings: A relative or absolute polymorphonuclear leukocytosis is present. After the 3rd day the intradermal skin test is positive, and after the 10th day the agglutination test is positive. The organism may be recovered and cultured from the blood, lymph node drainage, the skin ulcer, or the nasopharynx.

Differential Diagnosis

Tularemia must be differentiated from meningococcemia, rickettsial infections, atypical pneumonia, psittacosis, typhoid fever, infectious mononucleosis, and cat scratch disease. The prolonged fever resembles that of brucellosis.

Complications

Pericarditis, lung abscess, and meningitis due to tularemia have been reported on rare occasions. Pneumonia, meningitis, and peritonitis account for most tularemic deaths.

Treatment

Treatment, in addition to giving symptomatic and supportive measures as required, consists of giving one of the following: (1) tetracycline drugs, 0.5 gm every 6 hours orally for 5–10 days; (2) streptomycin, 2 gm IM daily in divided doses every 6 hours for 5–10 days; or (3) chloramphenicol (Chloromycetin®), 0.5 gm orally every 6 hours for 5–10 days.

Prognosis

The mortality rate of untreated tularemia is 5%, but of tularemic pneumonia 30%. Death may occur within 4 days to 9 months after the onset. In untreated cases the duration of fever is 3–4 weeks, adenopathy 3–4 months, and the disease itself 5–6 months. Early chemotherapy has virtually eliminated fatalities.

Assal, N., Blenden, D.C., & E.R. Price: Epidemiologic study of human tularemia reported in Missouri, 1949–65. Pub Health Rep 82:627–632, 1967.

PLAGUE

Essentials of Diagnosis

- Sudden onset of chills, fever, malaise, muscular pains, and prostration.
- Regional lymphangitis and adenitis with, finally, suppuration of the nodes.
- Septicemia and pneumonitis may occur.
- History of contact with human cases or infected animals (southwest USA).
- Confirmation by culture or animal inoculation.

General Considerations

Plague is an acute epidemic infection caused by the gram-negative bacillus, *Yersinia (Pasteurella) pestis,* which is usually transmitted to man by rodent fleas when the fleas go from dying animal vector to human hosts. Transmission is by deposition of contaminated feces on excoriated skin or regurgitation of contaminated blood at the time of feeding. The pneumonic form of the disease is transmitted from man to man by inhalation of infected droplets. Cases are occurring in southwest USA from contact with infected rodents. The infection spreads via the lymphatics to the lymph nodes, and may finally become generalized (septicemic) to involve the brain, liver, lungs, and spleen with focal areas of suppuration and necrosis. Carriers of pharyngeal plague have for the first time been identified in Vietnam. The incubation period is 2–10 days.

Clinical Findings

A. Symptoms and Signs: The onset is usually acute, with high, intermittent fever, chills, headache, vomiting, generalized muscular pains, and mental abnormalities ranging from mental dullness to acute mania. The patient exhibits marked anxiety and fear. In the pneumonic form there is also tachypnea, productive cough, and finally cyanosis and blood-tinged sputum. Meningitis may develop.

A pustule at the site of inoculation is uncommonly found, but the signs of a spreading lymphangitis are usually evident. Red, tender, and finally suppurative lymph node involvement (buboes) appear on about the second day. In the severe form of the disease, with septicemia, the characteristic purpuric spots (black plague) appear on the third day. The spleen is often palpable.

B. Laboratory Findings: The organism may be identified on a methylene blue, Gram, or immunofluorescent stain of material obtained from the buboes or the bloody sputum. Confirmation is obtained by bacterial culture or animal inoculation of bubo aspirate, blood, or sputum. The x-ray in the pneumonic form shows pulmonary infiltrations. The leukocyte count is usually greatly elevated.

Differential Diagnosis

The adenitis of plague must be distinguished from the adenitis of streptococcal and staphylococcal infec-

tion, infectious mononucleosis, syphilis, lymphogranuloma venereum, tularemia, and cat scratch fever; the
septicemic form may be confused with other types of
sepsis, tularemia, typhus, typhoid fever, and malaria.
The pneumonic form must be distinguished from viral
pneumonitis, psittacosis, and bacterial bronchial pneumonia.

Complications

Pneumonic plague may occur as a complication of
bubonic plague or may exist as a primary form in the
case of droplet infections from human contacts. Most
complications are secondary to bacterial invasion of
the draining buboes or of the lung.

Prevention

Rodent and flea control measures and strict isolation of patients are of paramount importance.

Drug prophylaxis may be indicated, using tetracyclines or sulfonamides for those exposed briefly to
definite risks of infection, especially to pneumonic
plague.

Plague vaccine is administered in a basic series of
3 subcutaneous or intramuscular injections: the first,
0.5 ml; the second, 1 ml administered 4–6 weeks later;
and the third, 0.5 ml 4–6 months after the second.
Booster doses of 0.5 ml each at intervals of 4–6
months thereafter are indicated if opportunity for
infection continues.

Treatment

Treat as early as possible with streptomycin, 4 gm
daily IM in divided doses; and tetracycline drugs, 0.5
gm every 4 hours orally, or 2 gm/24 hours IV. Give
symptomatic and supportive measures as needed.

Prognosis

The disease usually runs its course in 3–6 days.
The prognosis is extremely variable due to the marked
range of severity of the illness; however, the mortality
rate in untreated cases probably ranges from 25–75%.
The septicemic and pneumonic forms are almost invariably fatal if untreated. Chemotherapy has markedly
improved the outlook for survival.

Finegold, M.J.: Pathogenesis of plague. Am J Med 45:549–554,
    1968.
Marshall, J.D., Jr., & others: Plague in Vietnam 1965–1966.
    Am J Epidem 86:603–616, 1967.
Pan-American Health Organization: Plague in the Americas.
    Science Publication No. 115. Washington DC, 1965.
Reed, W.P., & others: Bubonic plague in southwestern U.S.
    Medicine 49:465–486, 1970.

CHOLERA

Essentials of Diagnosis

- Sudden onset of severe, voluminous, frequent diarrhea.

- Vomiting without antecedent nausea.
- Diarrhea and vomitus are gray, turbid, and
  watery (rice water), with little or no blood
  or pus.
- Marked dehydration and electrolyte imbalance; uremia and shock often present.
- History of being in an endemic area or contact with an infected individual.
- Positive stool cultures confirmed by agglutination by specific sera.

General Considerations

Cholera is an acute (diarrheal) disease caused by
Vibrio cholerae. Since the late 1950s a new pandemic
caused more by biotype El Tor than classical *V cholerae* has been spreading across the world. The infection
is spread by the ingestion of food or drink contaminated by feces from cases or carriers. The organism
may multiply in water for as long as 3–20 days. Since
warm weather is necessary for survival of the organism
in the feces or water, the infection is usually found in
warm countries. The agent primarily localizes in the
ileum; the disease is due to a powerful toxin liberated
on disintegration of the organism which induces hypersecretion of fluid and electrolytes in the gut. The
incubation period is 1–5 days. Persistent carriers of *V
cholerae* are rare. However, the El Tor vibrio can establish itself in the gallbladder, and carrier states have
been reported for up to 4–5 months in convalescents.

Clinical Findings

A. Symptoms and Signs: Although mild cases
occur, the typical case begins with a sudden onset of
voluminous, frequent, watery stools that soon lose all
fecal appearance and become grayish and turbid (rice
water), with degenerated epithelium and mucus but
with little or no blood or pus. The stool volume may
reach 15 liters in 24 hours. Vomiting may become
severe, and soon the individual is unable to retain food
or drink and becomes markedly dehydrated, with dry
skin, cyanosis, sunken eyes, hypotension, and subnormal temperature. Severe muscle cramps may occur, the
urine volume diminishes, and uremia supervenes.

B. Laboratory Findings: Routine blood studies
show marked dehydration. Very high hemoglobin
values (up to 20 gm/100 ml) and a white count up to
25,000/cu mm may be found. The CO_2 combining
power reveals acidosis, and the nonprotein nitrogen
may be elevated. The diagnosis is confirmed by isolation of the organism from the stool and identification
by agglutination reactions.

Differential Diagnosis

Cholera must be distinguished from other causes
of diarrhea, dehydration, and shock. Mild cases of
cholera are probably misdiagnosed as simple diarrhea
or food poisoning. Misdiagnoses are facilitated in
nonendemic areas by confusion of identification when
using routine media and methods; and antisera, which
are diagnostically reliable, are rarely stocked.

Prevention

Cholera vaccine is given in 2 injections of 0.5 and 1 ml, subcut or IM, not less than 4 weeks apart. Reimmunize with 0.5 ml every 4–6 months when cholera is a hazard. El Tor vibrios should be included in the vaccine. (See p 905.)

Isolation of cases and decontamination of excreta are important. In endemic areas all water, milk, and potentially contaminated utensils and foods must be boiled, other food avoided, and protective screening against flies must be used.

Treatment

Water and electrolytes lost in evacuations must be replaced intravenously as rapidly as possible and acidosis corrected. One liter of isotonic saline and isotonic sodium lactate (or bicarbonate) in a 2:1 ratio should be given in 10–15 minutes. A second liter should be given in the next 30–45 minutes. Subsequent replacement is determined by estimates of fluid loss based on plasma specific gravity determinations or clinical observations, particularly blood pressure and urinary output. For every 0.001 increase in plasma specific gravity above 1.025, the patient requires 4 ml/kg of fluid. When acidosis has been corrected, physiologic saline with 5% glucose may be substituted. Most patients require replacement of 5–10 liters in the first 24 hours, but some require up to 20 liters. Potassium replacement is necessary in severe cases but should be started only after the patient is rehydrated and has adequate urinary output. Oral administration is preferable (up to 10 gm of KCl in 24 hours). Oral fluid containing glucose should be started as soon as possible. Tetracycline (500 mg orally every 6 hours for 48 hours) shortens the course of the illness and reduces the time of *V cholerae* excretion.

Prognosis

The untreated disease lasts 3–5 days. The prognosis depends largely upon the previous health of the patient and the adequacy of treatment. The mortality rate in untreated cases averages about 50% (range, 15% to 90%); with prompt treatment the rate may be reduced to less than 3%.

Lindenbaum, J., & others: Antibiotic therapy of cholera. Bull WHO 36:871-883, 1967.

Phillips, R.A.: Asiatic cholera. Am Rev Med 19:69–80, 1968.

Sinha, R., & others: Cholera carrier studies in Calcutta in 1966–67. Bull WHO 37:89–100, 1967.

WHO Expert Committee on Cholera: Second Report. WHO Technical report Series No. 352, 1967.

LEPROSY

Essentials of Diagnosis

- Pale, anesthetic macular, or nodular and erythematous skin lesions.
- Superficial nerve thickening with associated sensory changes.
- History of residence in endemic area.
- Acid-fast bacilli in skin lesions or nasal scrapings, or characteristic histologic nerve changes.

General Considerations

Leprosy is a mildly contagious chronic infectious disease caused by the acid-fast rod *Mycobacterium leprae*. The mode of transmission is unknown, and attempts to infect human volunteers have been unsuccessful. Susceptibility to leprosy may involve a hereditary factor.

Clinical Findings

The onset of leprosy is insidious. The lesions involve the cooler tissues of the body: skin, superficial nerves, nose, pharynx, larynx, eyes, and testicles. The skin lesions may occur as pale, anesthetic macular lesions 1–10 cm in diameter; diffuse or discrete erythematous, infiltrated nodules 1–5 cm in diameter; or a diffuse skin infiltration. Neurologic disturbances are manifest by nerve infiltration and thickening, with resultant anesthesia, neuritis, paresthesia, trophic ulcers, and bone reabsorption and shortening of digits. The disfiguration due to the skin infiltration and nerve involvement in untreated cases may be extreme.

The disease is divided clinically and by laboratory tests into 2 distinct types: lepromatous and tuberculoid. In the lepromatous type the course is progressive and malign, with nodular skin lesions; slow, symmetric nerve involvement; abundant acid-fast bacilli in the skin lesions, and a negative lepromin skin test. In the tuberculoid type the course is benign and nonprogressive, with macular skin lesions, severe asymmetric nerve involvement of sudden onset with few bacilli present in the lesions, and a positive lepromin skin test. In the lepromatous type an acute febrile episode with evanescent skin lesions may occur and last for weeks. Eye involvement (keratitis and iridocyclitis), nasal ulcers, and epistaxis may occur in both types but are most common in the lepromatous type.

Anemia and lymphadenopathy may also occur.

Laboratory confirmation of leprosy requires the demonstration of acid-fast bacilli in scrapings from involved skin or the nasal septum. Biopsy of an involved, thickened nerve also gives a typical histologic picture.

Differential Diagnosis

The skin lesions of leprosy need to be distinguished often from those of lupus erythematosus, sarcoidosis, syphilis, erythema nodosum, erythema multiforme, and vitiligo; nerve involvement, sensory dissociation, and resulting deformity may require differentiation from syringomyelia and scleroderma.

Complications

Intercurrent tuberculosis is common in the lepromatous type. Amyloidosis may occur with longstanding disease.

Treatment

Drugs should be given cautiously, with slowly increasing doses, and must be withheld when they show signs of producing an induced exacerbation with leprotic fever; progressive anemia with or without leukopenia; severe gastrointestinal symptoms, allergic dermatitis, hepatitis, or mental disturbances; or erythema nodosum. It is important, therefore, to observe temperature, blood counts, and biopsy changes in lesions at regular intervals. The duration of treatment must be guided by progress, preferably as judged by biopsy. Treatment must be continued for several years or indefinitely because recrudescence may occur after cessation of therapy.

A. Dapsone (Avlosulfon®, DDS) is given orally to a maximum of 600 mg a week for adults in divided doses. Start with 25 mg twice weekly and increase to the maximum by 50 mg increments every 2 weeks, by which time the dose of 600 mg weekly may be spread in daily or other fractions. Children tolerate all the sulfones well in doses proportionate to age (eg, 300 mg/week for a child of 12). If the lepra reaction occurs, stop treatment until recovery is complete and then start again at the beginning or change to another sulfone. All sulfones apparently act in the body in the same way as DDS, but some produce fewer reactions.

B. Solapsone (Sulphetrone®), a complex substituted derivative of DDS, is given initially in a dosage of 0.5 gm 3 times daily orally. The dose is then gradually increased until a total daily dose of 6–10 gm is reached.

C. Diphenylthiourea (DPT) is given orally in divided doses, beginning with 250 mg/day and increasing to a maximum of 2 gm/day. This drug is indicated if intolerance develops to the above drugs. It may be continued for about 3 years before resistance develops.

D. Sulfoxone sodium (Diasone®) is given orally, 300 mg daily Monday through Friday for 1 week and 600 mg daily Monday through Friday thereafter.

E. Thalidomide, 100 mg 4 times daily orally, is a valuable adjunct (in addition to antileprosy drugs) in the management of the erythema nodosum of lepromatous leprosy. Corticosteroids are somewhat less effective and carry a somewhat greater risk of complications.

F. Rifampin is being actively investigated as an antileprosy drug in combination with a sulfone.

G. Surgical care of the extremities (hands and feet) requires careful consideration.

H. BCG vaccination is being studied and shows promise as a means of immunizing children. Both dapsone and BCG are being tested for their prophylactic value for family contacts of patients with lepromatous leprosy.

Prognosis

Untreated lepromatous leprosy is progressive and fatal in 10–20 years. In the tuberculoid type spontaneous recovery usually occurs in 1–3 years; it may, however, produce crippling deformities.

With treatment the lepromatous type regresses slowly (over a period of 3–8 years), and recovery from the tuberculoid type is more rapid. Recrudescences are always possible and it may be safe to assume that the bacilli are never eradicated. Deformities persist, however, after complete recovery, and may markedly interfere with function and appearance.

Beiguelman, B.: Leprosy and genetics. Bull WHO 37:461–476, 1967.

Browne, S.G.: The drug treatment of leprosy. Tr Roy Soc Trop Med Hyg 61:265–271, 1967.

Fasal, P., Fasal, E., & L. Levy: Leprosy prophylaxis. JAMA 199:905–908, 1967.

Hastings, R.C., & others: Thalidomide in the treatment of erythema nodosum leprosum. Clin Pharmacol Therap 11:481–487, 1970.

Symposium on leprosy. Tr Roy Soc Trop Med Hyg 61:581–607, 1967.

Warren, A.G.: A preliminary report on the use of B663 in the treatment of Chinese leprosy patients with chronic reaction. Leprosy Rev 39:61–66, 1968.

CHANCROID

Chancroid is an acute, localized, often autoinoculable venereal disease caused by the fine, short, gram-negative bacillus, *Hemophilus ducreyi*. Infection occurs by contact during intercourse, although nonvenereal inoculation has occurred in medical personnel through contact with chancroid patients. The incubation period is 3–5 days.

The initial lesion at the site of inoculation is a macule or vesicopustule which soon breaks down to form a sharply circumscribed, tender ulcer with a necrotic base, surrounding erythema and undermined edges. Multiple lesions may develop by auto-inoculation. In over half of cases inguinal adenitis develops 10–20 days after disappearance of the primary lesion. The adenitis is usually unilateral and consists of tender fused nodes of moderate size with overlying erythema. The node mass softens, becomes fluctuant, and may rupture spontaneously. With lymph node involvement fever, chills, and malaise may occur.

Culture of serous fluid from the lesion in 10 ml of the patient's blood (inactivated at 56° C for 30 minutes) at 35° C gives typical "school of fish" chains of *H ducreyi* in 48 hours. The chancroid skin test (of limited value) usually becomes positive 8–25 days after the appearance of the primary lesion and probably remains positive for life. Because 12–15% of primary lesions represent mixed syphilis-chancroid infection, dark-field examination should be done on all chancroid lesions.

Balanitis, phimosis, and paraphimosis are frequent complications. Infection of the ulcer with fusiform-spirochete organisms is not uncommon. A serpiginous type which spreads to the groin and thighs may occur.

Sulfonamides and tetracyclines are equally effective. Give sulfisoxazole (Gantrisin®), 1 gm 4 times daily for 1 week; or one of the tetracyclines, 0.5 gm every 6 hours for 5—7 days. Careful cleansing of ulcerations with soap and water twice daily (after the diagnosis has been made) is the only local treatment usually required. When the lesions fail to heal promptly, soaks or compresses of 1:10,000 potassium permanganate solution may be necessary. Fluctuant buboes may be aspirated with a large (No. 16) needle as indicated. Warm compresses or a hot-water bottle may be applied to the groin for comfort and to hasten fluctuation or regression of buboes.

Chancroid usually responds well to treatment. Even without treatment it usually is self-limited, although the serpiginous type may persist for years.

Borcherdt, K., & A.W. Hoke: Simplified laboratory technique for diagnosis of chancroid. Arch Dermat 102:188—192, 1970.

Kerber, R.E., & others: Treatment of chancroid. Arch Dermat 100:604—607, 1969.

GONORRHEA

Essentials of Diagnosis

- Purulent urethral discharge with meatal irritation and burning occurs 4—10 days after exposure.
- Other urogenital structures are frequently involved later (prostate, Bartholin's and Skene's glands, vagina, cervix, uterus, and tubes).
- Pelvic peritonitis occurs occasionally in females (pelvic inflammatory disease or "PID").
- Systemic involvement is possible (arthritis, pleuritis, myositis, meningitis, endocarditis).
- Gram-negative intracellular diplococci may be seen on a smear of exudate (and should be cultured) from the cervix, urethra, rectum, and any inflammatory exudate.

General Considerations

Gonorrhea is an infectious disease caused by the gram-negative intracellular diplococcus, *Neisseria gonorrhoeae*. Infection usually involves the mucous membranes of the genitourinary tract and is most frequently acquired in adults by sexual intercourse. Infection may also occur by contact with contaminated material, eg, instruments, washcloths, and bath water, especially in female infants and prepuberal children. The organism is destroyed promptly on drying or at temperatures over 41.1° C (106° F), but it may remain viable for days in a moist environment and especially if refrigerated. The incubation period is 4—10 days. The disease is epidemic at present.

Clinical Findings

A. Symptoms and Signs:

1. Men—Acute anterior urethritis is usually the first manifestation. There is a scant serous to milky urethral discharge associated with an inflamed meatal orifice and meatal burning, especially on urination. The entire urethra then becomes inflamed; the discharge thickens and becomes yellow and more profuse, and may be blood-tinged (see also Complications, below).

2. Women—Infection often is asymptomatic, but there is usually a purulent urethral discharge, in many cases evident only on "milking" the urethra. Dysuria, frequency, urgency, and nocturia occur, especially in first infections. The meatus may be red and swollen. Vaginitis, cervicitis, and inflammation of Bartholin's and Skene's glands are common.

3. Infants and prepuberal children—In children the same symptoms and signs are present but the onset is more acute, the course is more rapid, and the effects of the disease are more severe.

B. Laboratory Findings: Typical gram-negative intracellular diplococci are usually found in a thin smear of the urethral discharge of men and, much less frequently, in material obtained from the cervix or from Bartholin's or Skene's glands in women. A 2-glass urinary test may be of aid, since in very few other disorders is the first glass cloudy and the second glass clear. The spun sediment of the first glass may be used for identifying the organism when urethral discharge is scanty or absent. The organism may also be grown and identified on chocolate agar at reduced oxygen tension. If the disease is asymptomatic in women suspected of having gonorrhea, the only reliable method of establishing a diagnosis may be by culture of endocervical material. A complement fixation test may be positive several weeks after initial infection, but this test is not reliable and is rarely used. The fluorescent antibody test may be performed directly on the exudate on a slide or on a culture slant.

Differential Diagnosis

Distinguish from nonspecific urethritis and prostatitis, trichomonas and candida infections, other causes of peritonitis, and other specific causes of urethritis, acute cystitis, arthritis, meningitis, endocarditis, and pleuritis.

Complications

In men, direct extension of the infection into the posterior urethra, prostate, and epididymis may occur in neglected infections and with inadequate treatment. Trigonitis may occur, but cystitis is rare. Stricture of the urethra may also accompany gonorrhea. A refractory urethritis and prostatitis may persist after apparent bacteriologic "cure."

In women, local complications include Bartholin's gland abscess and chronic infection of Skene's glands. There may be extension of the infection into the endocervix, uterus, and tubes and into the surrounding pelvic structures, causing fever, chills, lower abdominal pains, and findings similar to those of acute appendicitis. Sterility due to scarring of the tubes may result.

In either sex systemic complications may occur as a result of septicemic spread, causing arthritis, myositis, pleuritis, meningitis, and endocarditis; other than arthritis, these complications are uncommon. Arthritis usually involves several joints at first but ultimately only one or 2, and often is associated with iritis or iridocyclitis. Gonococcal proctitis may occur in either sex. Gonococcal conjunctivitis or endophthalmitis may occur. With hematogenous spread of organisms, there may be pustular skin lesions (rare).

Prevention

The only way gonorrhea can be prevented is by educating every generation to recognize the dangers of promiscuous sexual behavior with unknown or doubtfully responsible partners. Few or no cases occur among faithful marriage partners if premarital counseling and examinations have been adequate. It is the duty of every physician who deals with young people to play an appropriate role in the control or eradication of what has become one of the most common reportable infectious diseases in the USA and many other parts of the world.

Complete abstinence by young people before marriage is no longer a reasonable expectation except in those instances where parental control or religious influences continue to be stronger than the temptations offered by the changing attitudes toward such matters that are a feature of modern life. Physician counseling and sex education can be used effectively to reduce the infection rate. The contacts of patients presenting for treatment should be sought out and treated whenever possible.

Wearing condoms may be of some value. In the case of known exposure with a partner who has gonorrhea, a full dose of penicillin as specified in the section on treatment will prevent development of the disease.

Treatment

Penicillin, tetracyclines, ampicillin, and erythromycin are all effective, although penicillin is usually the drug of choice. Relative drug resistance, which apparently varies in various parts of the world, now requires much higher doses than a few years ago. Streptomycin and sulfonamides are no longer effective.

A. Acute or Chronic Uncomplicated Urethritis (Male or Female): *Note:* Local treatment (irrigations, manipulations, and instillations) is contraindicated.

1. Penicillin therapy—Several effective technics are available. Always draw a preliminary blood specimen for STS and examine the patient for evidence of syphilis. Give procaine penicillin G, 2.4 million units IM in each buttock for women (cure rate, 86–96%) and 2.4 million units in one dose for men (98% cures). Probenecid, 1 gm orally one hour before penicillin injection, may enhance effectiveness. In some instances, procaine penicillin G, 4.8 million units IM daily for 5 days, has been recommended for women with acute gonorrhea.

2. Alternative therapy—If the patient is allergic to penicillin or if local experience shows relative penicillin resistance, give tetracycline or erythromycin, 2 gm orally immediately and then 0.5 gm every 6 hours for 5–7 days. A single oral dose of 3.5 gm ampicillin, with preliminary probenecid 1 gm orally, has been reported

to effect a high cure rate in men with acute gonorrhea and in women with asymptomatic gonorrhea. If coincidental exposure to syphilis is suspected, treat as for early syphilis (see Chapter 22).

3. Follow-up—Examine the patient once a week for at least 3 weeks for evidence of urethral discharge, chancre, or rash. Culture any inflammatory exudate in a week, and again in 2 weeks, on Peizer or Thayer-Martin medium. Avoid prostatic massage, urethral swabs, or instrumentation as a means of obtaining material for examination in acute cases. Take a blood sample for STS and examine for clinical evidence of syphilis at the end of the third week and again at 3, 6, 12, and 24 months.

4. Retreatment of penicillin failures—(Suspect other etiology.) If any of the weekly examinations shows bacteriologic evidence of persistent gonorrheal infection, increase penicillin treatment as above. If urologic complications can be reasonably excluded, give increased doses of penicillin or give tetracyclines, 2 gm orally immediately and then 0.5 gm every 6 hours for 7 days. Other drugs may be necessary, such as (1) doxycycline, 200 mg orally at once and 100 mg every 12 hours for 5 days, preferably on an empty stomach; (2) cephaloridine (Loridine®), 500 mg IM 3 or 4 times daily (to a maximum of 1 gm) (less in patients with impaired renal function because of possible tubular necrosis); or spectinomycin (Trobicin®), 2 gm (males) or 4 gm (females) as a single dose IM.

5. Persistent failures—"Treatment failures" are often reinfections; this is due in part to the fact that the public has come to believe that penicillin has removed the danger from gonorrheal infection. Promiscuous patients must be warned against this error.

B. Acute and Chronic Prostatitis: Treat as above. Hot sitz baths and alkalinization of the urine may provide symptomatic relief.

C. Acute Epididymitis: Treat as above and give bed rest, cold compresses to scrotal region, analgesics as necessary, and a scrotal supporter for the ambulatory phase of convalescence.

D. Pelvic Inflammatory Disease (Acute Gonococcal Salpingitis):

1. Acute—Place the patient at absolute bed rest, and withhold douches and unnecessary manipulation during the acute phase. Examine carefully for clinical evidence of syphilis, and draw blood for STS. Give procaine penicillin G, 4.8 million units IM daily for 7 days. If fever and other symptoms disappear, keep the patient at bed rest until white count and sedimentation rate become normal (may take a month or more). Observe her during and following the next menstrual period for pain and changes in pelvic examination. If she remains well, discharge her to home care on the convalescent program outlined below.

If symptoms, fever, leukocytosis, increased sedimentation rate persist or if the vaginal smear remains positive—or if symptoms and signs recur at the time of menses—administer a second course of the above large dosage of penicillin.

If the patient fails to respond to 2 courses of penicillin therapy, give one of the tetracyclines, 2 gm orally immediately and then 0.5 gm at 6-hour intervals for 7 days.

After the patient is discharged from the hospital she should lead a sedentary life for at least 6 weeks and should abstain from sexual intercourse until signs and symptoms have completely cleared (usually takes about 6–8 weeks). Prescribe prolonged douches of warm tap water, using 1–2 gallons and administering slowly and gently (in the bathtub) over a 15–20 minute period once or twice daily.

2. Subacute (or acute exacerbation of chronic form)—Prescribe absolute bed rest until the signs and symptoms have cleared, and prolonged douching as above. Penicillin (as above) is much less effective in this phase of the disease, but a trial of therapy is warranted.

3. Chronic (gonococcal salpingitis)—Prescribe bed rest during acute exacerbations. Penicillin and other antibiotics are usually ineffective but should be tried. A course of pelvic diathermy treatments may be of value. Surgical procedures (upon a gynecologist's advice) may be indicated, but are not uniformly satisfactory.

E. Gonococcal Ophthalmia Neonatorum: Give crystalline penicillin in aqueous solution, 2 drops in each eye every 5 minutes for 30 minutes, then less often. Give aqueous penicillin G, 50,000 units/kg IM for 5 days.

Prognosis

Gonorrhea responds well to chemotherapy, but late manifestations of the disease (salpingitis, epididymitis, urethral stricture, and Bartholin's gland abscess) cause damage (sterility, upper urinary tract dilatation, and persistent sterile abscess) which requires separate treatment and correction.

Women should have 2 negative cultures a week apart on Thayer-Martin medium before being pronounced cured.

Follow-up serologic tests are indicated in all cases of gonorrhea because about 2% of patients acquire syphilis at the same exposure.

Brown, R.C.: The prevalence of infectious syphilis in patients with acute gonorrhea. South MJ 61:98–100, 1968.

Cave, V.G.: Gonorrhea: The perilous complacency. Drug Therapy 1:8–19, 1971.

Charles, A.G., & others: Asymptomatic gonorrhea in prenatal patients. Am J Obst Gynec 108:595–599, 1970.

Editorial: Treatment of gonorrhea. Brit MJ 1:398–399, 1968.

Fletcher, A., & R.R. Landes: Treatment of gonorrhea today. Med Aspects Human Sexuality 4:50–61, Aug 1970.

Fischnaller, J.E., & others: Kanamycin and acute gonorrheal urethritis. JAMA 203: 909–912, 1968.

Johnson, D.W., & others: Single-dose antibiotic treatment of asymptomatic gonorrhea in hospitalized women. New England J Med 283:1–6, 1970.

Kvale, P.A., & others: Single oral dose ampicillin-probenecid treatment of gonorrhea in the male. JAMA 215:1449–1453, 1971.

Recommended Treatment Schedules for Gonorrhea. National Communicable Disease Center, USPHS, Atlanta, 1970.

GRANULOMA INGUINALE

Granuloma inguinale is a chronic, relapsing, granulomatous anogenital infection due to *Donovania granulomatis,* which is auto-inoculable but only slightly contagious. In the USA it occurs predominantly in blacks. *D granulomatis,* a pleomorphic rod 1–2 μm long, occurs intracellularly, singly or in clusters, and is difficult to find. The pathognomonic cell, found in tissue scrapings or secretions, is large (25–90 μm) and contains intracytoplasmic cysts filled with bodies (Donovan bodies) which stain deeply with Wright's stain.

The incubation period is 8–12 weeks.

The onset is insidious. The lesions tend to be singular, on the skin or mucous membranes of the genitalia or perineal area. They are relatively painless infiltrated nodules which soon slough. A shallow, sharply demarcated ulcer forms, with a beefy red. friable base of granulation tissue. The lesion spreads by contiguity. The advancing border has a characteristic rolled edge of granulation tissue. Large ulcerations which advance up onto the lower abdomen and thighs are not uncommon. Scar formation and healing may occur along one border while the opposite border advances. The process may become indolent and stationary.

The characteristic Donovan bodies are found in scrapings from the ulcer base or on histologic sections. The microorganism may also be cultured on special media. A complement fixation test has been developed but is not widely available for clinical use.

Superinfection with spirochete-fusiform organisms is not uncommon. The ulcer then becomes purulent, painful, foul-smelling, and extremely difficult to treat. Other venereal diseases may coexist. Rare complications include superimposed malignancy and secondary elephantoid swelling of the genitalia.

Tetracyclines and chloramphenicol *(caution)* are both effective in doses of 1 gm daily for 1–2 weeks. Streptomycin is also effective but is more toxic. The dose is 1 gm IM daily until the lesion is healed (10 or more days).

With antimicrobial therapy, most cases can be cured. In resistant or untreated cases massive extension of the lesion may occur, with resulting anemia, cachexia, and death.

Lal, S., & others: Epidemiological and clinical features in 165 cases of granuloma inguinale. Brit J Ven Dis 46:461–463, 1970.

Thew, M.A., & others: Ampicillin in the treatment of granuloma inguinale. JAMA 210:866–867, 1969.

BARTONELLOSIS
(Oroya Fever, Carrión's Disease)

Bartonellosis, an acute or chronic infection which occurs in the high Andean valleys of Colombia, Ecuador, and Peru, is caused by a gram-negative, very pleomorphic organism (*Bartonella bacilliformis*) which is transmitted to man by the bite of Phlebotomus. The organism is parasitic in man in red cells and cells of the reticuloendothelial system. The initial stage (Oroya fever) exhibits intermittent or remittent fever, malaise, headache, and bone and joint pains. The disease becomes more apparent with the rapid progression of severe megaloblastic anemia, hemorrhagic lymph nodes, and hepatosplenomegaly. Masses of organisms fill the cytoplasm of vascular endothelial cells, resulting in occlusion and thrombosis. In favorable cases Oroya fever lasts 2–6 weeks and subsides. In those who survive, the eruptive stage of the disease (verruga peruana) commonly begins 2–8 weeks later. Verruga may also appear in the apparent absence of Oroya fever, possibly because of a mild, subclinical first stage. Multiple miliary and nodular hemangiomas appear in crops, particularly on the face and limbs. The lesions bleed easily, sometimes ulcerate, usually persist for 1–12 months, finally heal without scar formation, and produce little systemic reaction. In early Oroya fever, the organisms are best demonstrated by blood culture. Later, Bartonella organisms appear in red cells in large numbers. The severe macrocytic, usually hypochromic anemia (hemoglobin as low as 3–5 gm) of Oroya fever is accompanied by slight jaundice, marked reticulocytosis, and numerous megaloblasts and normoblasts. In verrugous lesions the organisms may be demonstrated in endothelial cells.

Chloramphenicol, penicillin, streptomycin, or tetracyclines in large doses have been effective in overcoming the infection and reducing the mortality rate. Transfusion may be necessary if the anemia is severe.

BEDSONIA (CHLAMYDIA) INFECTIONS

LYMPHOGRANULOMA VENEREUM
(Lymphopathia Venereum)

Essentials of Diagnosis

- Evanescent vesicular or ulcerative genital lesion.
- Lymph node enlargement, softening, and suppuration, with draining sinuses.
- Proctitis and rectal stricture in females or homosexual males.
- Systemic, joint, eye, and CNS involvement may occur.
- Positive Frei skin test and complement fixation test.
- Elevated serum globulin.

General Considerations

Lymphogranuloma venereum is an acute and chronic contagious venereal disease caused by an organism of the psittacosis-LGV-trachoma (chlamydia) group. After the genital lesion disappears, the infection spreads to lymph channels and lymph nodes of the genital and rectal areas. The disease is acquired during intercourse or through contact with contaminated exudate from active lesions. The incubation period is 5–21 days. Inapparent infections and latent disease (as shown by skin testing) are not uncommon in promiscuous individuals.

Clinical Findings

A. Symptoms and Signs: In males, the initial vesicular or ulcerative lesion (on the external genitalia) is evanescent and often goes unnoticed. Inguinal buboes appear 1–4 weeks after exposure, are often bilateral, and have a tendency to fuse, soften, and break down to form multiple draining sinuses with extensive scarring. Proctoscopic examination is important for diagnosis and in evaluating therapy. In the female the genital lymph drainage is to the perirectal glands. Early anorectal manifestations are proctitis with tenesmus and bloody purulent discharge; late manifestations are chronic cicatrizing inflammation of the rectal and perirectal tissue. These changes lead to obstipation and rectal stricture, and, occasionally, rectovaginal and perianal fistulas. They are also seen in homosexual males.

Systemic invasion may occur, causing fever, arthralgia, arthritis, a skin eruption, conjunctivitis, and iritis. Nervous system invasion causes headache and meningeal irritation.

B. Laboratory Findings: The intradermal skin test (Frei test) and the complement fixation test are positive, but cross-reaction with the organism of psittacosis and other chlamydiae takes place. Because both tests remain positive throughout life, a positive reaction may reflect an old (healed) infection; however, high complement fixation titers usually imply current infection.

The serum globulin is often greatly elevated, with an inversion of the albumin-globulin ratio. A low-titer false-positive test for syphilis may be present.

Differential Diagnosis

The early lesion of lymphogranuloma venereum must be differentiated from the lesions of syphilis, herpes progenitalis, and chancroid; lymph node involvement must be distinguished from that due to lymphoma, tularemia, tuberculosis, plague, and neoplasm; rectal stricture must be differentiated from that due to neoplasm and ulcerative colitis.

Complications

Lymphatic involvement and blocking may cause marked disfiguration of the external genitalia (elephantiasis) as well as extensive scarring. Rectal stricture resists treatment and may require colostomy.

Treatment

A. Specific Therapy: The tetracyclines or chloramphenicol (Chloromycetin®) *(caution)*, 0.25−1 gm orally 4 times daily for 10−20 days, are the antibiotics of choice. Sulfadiazine, 1 gm 3 times daily for 2−3 weeks or longer, has little effect on the chlamydial infection but reduces bacterial complications.

B. Local and General Measures: Place the patient at bed rest, apply warm compresses to buboes, and give analgesics as necessary. Aspirate fluctuant nodes under aseptic conditions (see below). *Note:* Incision and drainage are to be avoided (to prevent lymphatic obstructions). Extensive plastic operations may be necessary in the chronic anorectal form of the disease. Rectal strictures should be treated by prolonged gentle dilatation, although in extreme cases this may be impossible and colon shunting procedures may be necessary.

Prognosis

Prompt early treatment will cure the disorder and prevent late complications; the longer treatment is delayed the more difficult it is to eradicate the infection and to reverse the pathologic changes. There may be a higher incidence of rectal carcinoma in persons with anorectal lymphogranuloma venereum.

Jawetz, E.: Chemotherapy of chlamydial infections. Advances Pharmacol 7:253−282, 1969.

Lassus, A., & others: Autoimmune serum factors and IgA elevation in lymphogranuloma venereum. Ann Clin Res (Helsinki) 2:51−56, 1970.

Management of Chancroid, Granuloma Inguinale, and Lymphogranuloma Venereum in General Practice. USPHS Publication No. 255. US Government Printing Office, Washington, DC, 1968.

PSITTACOSIS
(Ornithosis)

Essentials of Diagnosis

- Fever, chills, malaise, prostration; cough, epistaxis; occasionally, rose spots and splenomegaly.
- Slightly delayed appearance of signs of pneumonitis.
- Isolation of bedsonia or rising titer of complement-fixing antibodies.
- Contact with infected bird (psittacine, pigeons, many others) 7−15 days previously.

General Considerations

Psittacosis is due to a member of the psittacosis-LGV-trachoma (bedsonia-chlamydia) group acquired from contact with birds (parrots, parakeets, pigeons, chickens, ducks, and many others). Human-to-human spread is rare. The incubation period is 7−15 days.

Clinical Findings

A. Symptoms and Signs: The onset is usually rapid, with fever, chills, headache, backache, malaise, myalgia, epistaxis, dry cough, and prostration. Signs include those of pneumonitis, alteration of percussion note and breath sounds, and rales. Pulmonary findings may be absent early. Rose spots, splenomegaly, and meningismus are occasionally seen. Delirium, constipation or diarrhea, and abdominal distress may occur. Dyspnea and cyanosis may occur later.

B. Laboratory Findings: The white count is normal or decreased, often with a shift to the left. Proteinuria is frequently present. The organism may be isolated from the blood and sputum by mouse inoculation. Complement-fixing antibodies appear during or after the second week. The rise in titer may be minimized or delayed by early chemotherapy.

C. X-Ray Findings: The x-ray findings in psittacosis are those of central pneumonia which later becomes widespread or migratory. Psittacosis is indistinguishable from viral pneumonias by x-ray.

Differential Diagnosis

This disease can be differentiated from acute viral, mycoplasmal, or rickettsial pneumonias only by the history of contact with potentially infected birds. Rose spots and leukopenia suggest typhoid fever.

Complications

Myocarditis, secondary bacterial pneumonia.

Treatment

Treatment consists of giving a tetracycline drug or chloramphenicol, 0.5 gm every 6 hours orally or 0.5 gm IV every 12 hours for 10−14 days. Give oxygen and sedation as required.

Prognosis

Psittacosis may vary from a mild respiratory infection (especially in children) to a severe, protracted illness unless treated. Mortality with treatment is very low.

Brainerd, H.: Q fever and psittacosis. P Clin North America 3:68−72, 1955.

Schaffner, W., & others: The clinical spectrum of endemic psittacosis. Arch Int Med 119:433−443, 1966.

• • •

General Bibliography

Austrian, R.: The role of microbiological laboratory in the management of bacterial infections. M Clin North America 50:1419–1432, 1966.

The choice of systemic antimicrobial drugs. Med Lett Drugs Ther 13:37–44, 1971.

Conn, H.F. (editor): Symposium on efficacy of antibiotic and antifungal agents. M Clin North America 54:1075–1350, 1970.

Dubos, R.J., & J.G. Hirsch (editors): *Bacterial and Mycotic Infections of Man,* 4th ed. Lippincott, 1965.

Feingold, D.S.: Antimicrobial chemotherapeutic agents: The nature of their action and selective toxicity. New England J Med 269:900–907, 957–964, 1963.

Horsfall, F.L., & I. Tamm (editors): *Rivers' Viral and Rickettsial Infections of Man,* 4th ed. Lippincott, 1965.

Jawetz, E.: Chemotherapy of chlamydial infections. Advances Pharmacol 7:253–282, 1969.

Jawetz, E., Melnick, J.L., & E.A. Adelberg: *Review of Medical Microbiology,* 9th ed. Lange, 1970.

Krugman, S., & R. Ward: *Infectious Diseases of Children.* Mosby, 1958.

Kunin, C.M.: A guide to the use of antibiotics in patients with renal disease. Ann Int Med 67:151–158, 1967.

Merigan, T.C., & others: Infections. Chap 23, pp 439–498, in: *Current Medical References,* 6th ed. Chatton, M.J., & P.J. Sanazaro (editors). Lange, 1970.

Stimson, P.M., & H.L. Hodges: *A Manual of Common Contagious Diseases,* 5th ed. Lippincott, 1959.

Sweeney, F.J., Jr.: Therapy of infections caused by gram-negative bacilli. M Clin North America 49:1391–1402, 1965.

Top, F.H.: *Communicable and Infectious Diseases,* 5th ed. Mosby, 1964.

22 . . .

Infectious Diseases: Spirochetal

Rees B. Rees, Jr., J. Ralph Audy, & Henry B. Bruyn

SYPHILIS

Syphilis is an acute or chronic, contagious granulomatous infection due to *Treponema pallidum,* a spirochetal organism which can infect any tissue or organ of the body. Since almost any disease may be mimicked by syphilis in one of its 3 clinical stages (primary, secondary, and tertiary), it is referred to as the "great imitator." Although infection usually occurs during sexual intercourse (entry into the body is gained through minor skin or mucosal genital lesions), transfer of organisms by infected blood and plasma and passage from the mother to the fetus through the placenta (congenital syphilis) is possible. Extragenital infection (tongue, breast, finger) may also occur. The organism cannot survive outside of body tissues and fluids, and infection other than through direct personal contact or through blood products is rare.

Formerly, penicillin therapy greatly reduced the incidence of syphilis, but the disease is again a major public health problem. Restrictive attitudes toward adequate education on venereal disease must be abandoned, and early case-finding must be accelerated.

Initial infections, except for grossly visible lesions, are usually associated with little or no tissue reaction, damage, or disability; late syphilis is associated with vasculitis, necrosis, tissue destruction, scar formation, and permanent damage and disability.

The natural history of acquired syphilis is usually divided into 2 stages: early, meaning primary and secondary syphilis, including relapsing forms; and late, including CNS, cardiovascular, ocular, and benign cutaneous, visceral, and osseous forms. A symptom-free but insidiously destructive latent form may divide the two. Congenital syphilis is considered separately.

The discussion of specific stages and types of syphilis begins on p 767.

Laboratory Diagnosis

A. Serologic Tests for Syphilis (STS):

1. Nontreponemal antigen tests—Nontreponemal antigen tests are commonly employed to measure the antibody complex (reagin) to *T pallidum* which appears in the serum of syphilitic patients. They are of 2 types: (1) flocculation (VDRL, Hinton) and (2) complement fixation (Kolmer, Wasserman). Quantitative expression of the reactivity of the serum, based upon titration of geometrically progressive dilutions of serum, may be very valuable in establishing the diagnosis and in evaluating the efficacy of treatment. The VDRL test usually becomes positive 4–6 weeks after infection, or 1–3 weeks after the appearance of the primary lesion. The VDRL titer is usually high in secondary syphilis and tends to be lower or even negative in late forms of syphilis, although this is highly variable. In tabes, for example, the reaction may be negative in 25–50% of cases, whereas in late visceral syphilis very high VDRL titers may be obtained. A falling titer in treated early syphilis or a falling or stable titer in latent or late syphilis indicates satisfactory therapeutic progress. Serologic tests are not completely specific, and must be closely correlated with the history, physical findings, and other laboratory tests. Biologic "false-positive" serologic reactions are encountered in a wide variety of disorders such as the collagen diseases, infectious mononucleosis, malaria, many febrile diseases, leprosy, and nonsyphilitic spirochetal infections; some individuals, especially aged persons (> 70), may for no apparent reason have a positive VDRL. False-positive reactions are usually of low titer and transient, but there is considerable variation.

2. Treponemal antibody test; fluorescent treponemal antibody-absorption (FTA-ABS) test—This recently introduced serologic test for syphilis is as specific as (and much more sensitive than) the *Treponema pallidum* immobilization (TPI) test. It is of value in determining whether a positive routine STS is a "false positive" or is indicative of syphilitic disease. It is also of value when there is clinical evidence of syphilis but the routine STS is negative. The test is widely available. It becomes positive later than the STS and remains positive longer and in a higher percentage of successfully treated patients. False-positive FTA-ABS tests have been reported in pregnancy, in systemic lupus erythematosus, and in disorders associated with abnormal globulins.

Final decision about the significance of STS, when either positive or negative, must be based upon a total clinical appraisal.

B. Dark-field Examination: In early syphilis, *T pallidum* may be demonstrated by dark-field examination of the serum from lesions or of material aspirated from regional lymph nodes. The dark-field examination requires experience and care in the proper collection of specimens and identification of spirochetes.

Repeated examinations may be necessary. The spirochete is usually not found in any of the late syphilitic lesions by this technic.

An immunofluorescent staining, ultraviolet microscopy technic for demonstrating *T pallidum* in smears of fluid taken from early syphilitic lesions is now available in many health departments and medical center laboratories. Although this method holds promise because of convenience to physicians without easy access to dark-field microscopy, it may still be regarded primarily as a research tool.

C. Spinal Fluid Examination: The CSF findings in neurosyphilis usually consist of elevation of total protein (> 40 mg/100 ml), increase in the cell count, and a positive reagin test (STS). Biologic false-positive reagin tests rarely occur in the CSF. Improvement of the CSF findings is of great prognostic value. A positive CSF in the absence of CNS symptoms (asymptomatic neurosyphilis) indicates the need for active penicillin treatment. In a small percentage of cases of CNS syphilis, the CSF may be negative.

Prevention

Prophylactic advice should be given, but avoidance of illicit sexual contact is the surest of all prophylactic methods. Such advice is usually futile.

A. Mechanical: The standard rubber condom is effective but protects covered parts only. The exposed parts should be washed with soap and water as soon after contact as possible. This applies to both sexes.

B. Antibiotic: If there is known exposure to infectious syphilis, abortive penicillin therapy may be used. Give 2–4 million units of repository penicillin IM in one dose. Epidemiologic treatment in full dosage of all contacts has been advocated, balancing the known risk of individual penicillin reactions against the benefit to community health.

C. Vaccine: An effective vaccine against syphilis is not yet available.

Treatment

A. Specific Measures: Carefully evaluate the physical status of the patient before beginning specific therapy.

1. Penicillin, as benzathine penicillin G (Bicillin®) or procaine penicillin G with 2% aluminum monostearate (PAM), is the drug of choice for all forms of syphilis and other spirochetal infections. It is highly effective in early infections and variably effective in the late stages of syphilis. The recommended treatment schedules are included in the discussion of the various forms of syphilis. See stage of disease for dosage.

2. Other antibiotic therapy—Oral tetracycline compounds and erythromycin are effective in the treatment of syphilis but are not recommended unless patients are sensitive to penicillin or have relapses following one or more courses of penicillin. Tetracycline, 30–40 gm, or erythromycin, 30–40 gm, is given over a period of 10–15 days. Since experience with these antibiotics in the treatment of syphilis is limited, careful follow-up is necessary.

B. Local Measures (Mucocutaneous Lesions): Local treatment is usually not necessary. No local antiseptics or other chemicals should be applied to a suspected syphilitic lesion until repeated dark-field examinations have been made. If, after the diagnosis has been established, the lesion should become secondarily infected, it may be treated as for any pyogenic ulceration. (This in addition to systemic antisyphilitic treatment.)

C. Public Health Measures: Uncooperative and sexually promiscuous patients with infectious syphilis should be somehow isolated or quarantined until rendered noninfectious by preliminary therapy. Attempt to identify all possible contacts. Report all cases of syphilis to the appropriate public health agency.

Complications of Specific Therapy

The Jarisch-Herxheimer reaction is ascribed to the massive destruction of spirochetes by specific treatment and is manifested by fever and aggravation of the existing clinical picture and of the lesion itself. It is most likely to occur in early syphilis. Treatment is not discontinued unless the symptoms become severe or threaten to be fatal or in the presence of syphilitic laryngitis, auditory neuritis, or labyrinthitis, where such a reaction may cause irreversible damage. This reaction may be prevented or modified by simultaneous administration of corticosteroids. The reaction usually begins within the first 24 hours and usually subsides spontaneously within the next 24 hours without any treatment.

Follow-Up

Patients who receive adequate treatment for early syphilis should be followed clinically and with periodic quantitative VDRL tests for at least 1 year. Patients with all other types of syphilis should be under similar observation for 2 or more years.

Adequate treatment of early syphilis followed by 1–2 years of observation (as above), although not foolproof against transmission to the marital partner, is a reasonable safeguard. Husband and wife should be instructed to have careful follow-up, including early prenatal care.

Course & Prognosis

Primary and secondary syphilis are self-limiting infections which resolve with little to no residua. Late syphilis may be highly destructive and permanently disabling, and may lead to death. With treatment the STS will usually return to negative in early syphilis (primary and secondary). In late latent and late syphilis, serofastness is not uncommon, even after adequate treatment. In broad terms, if no treatment is given, about one-third of people infected with syphilis will undergo spontaneous cure, about one-third will remain in the latent phase throughout life, and about one-third will develop serious late lesions.

Buchanan, C.S., & J.R. Haserick: FTA-ABS test in pregnancy. Arch Dermat 102:322–325, 1970.

Fiumara, N.J.: Syphilis resurgent: Reminders on recognition and drug therapy. Drug Therapy 1:47–49, 1971.

Knox, J.M.: A vaccine for syphilis. Dermat Digest 8:17–20, 1969.

Newcomer, V.D.: Venereal disease among adolescents. Cutis 7:169–174, 1971.

Smith, J.L., & C.W. Israel: Spirochetes in late seronegative syphilis. JAMA 1:980–984, 1967.

Sparling, P.F.: Diagnosis and treatment of syphilis. New England J Med 284:642–653, 1971.

Syphilis: A Synopsis. Public Health Services Publication No. 1660, Jan 1968. 133 pp. US Government Printing Office, Washington, D.C.

Tuffanelli, D.L.: False-positive reactions for syphilis. Arch Dermat 98:606–611, 1968.

Tuffanelli, D.L., & others: Fluorescent treponemal antibody-absorption tests. New England J Med 276:258–261, 1967.

Samenius, B.: Primary syphilis of the anorectal region. Dis Colon Rectum 11:462–466, 1968.

Wright, D.J.M.: New antibody in early syphilis. Lancet 1:740–743, 1970.

STAGES & TYPES OF SYPHILIS

1. PRIMARY SYPHILIS

This is the stage of invasion and may pass unrecognized. A history of contact with an infected individual 1–8 weeks previously may be obtained. The typical lesion is the chancre at the site or sites of inoculation, most frequently located on the penis, labia, or cervix or anorectal region. The chancre starts as a small erosion 10–90 days (average 3–4 weeks) after inoculation which rapidly develops into a painless superficial ulcer with enlargement of regional lymph nodes, which are rubbery, discrete, and nontender. Secondary infection of the ulcer is not uncommon and may lead to pain. Healing occurs without treatment, but a scar may form, especially with secondary infection. The typical hunterian chancre is a firm eroded plaque 1–3 cm in diameter.

The blood STS is usually positive 1–2 weeks after the primary lesion is noted; rising quantitative titers are especially significant since a positive STS may otherwise represent previous infection. The chancre will show organisms in over 95% of cases on repeated dark-field examination. The spinal fluid is normal at this stage.

The syphilitic chancre may be confused with chancroid, tularemia, or neoplasm. Any lesion on the genitalia should be considered as a possible primary syphilitic lesion.

Treatment

Give benzathine penicillin G (Bicillin®), 1.2 million units in each buttock for a total dose of 2.4 million units; or procaine penicillin with aluminum monostearate in oil (PAM): first dose, 2.4 million units intragluteally, then 1.2 million units IM every other day to a total of 4.8 million units; or procaine penicillin G, 600,000 units daily IM for 8–10 consecutive days.

2. SECONDARY SYPHILIS

The secondary stage of syphilis is the period of dissemination, 7–10 weeks after exposure (2–3 weeks after appearance of the chancre). Systemic involvement with fever and generalized lymphadenopathy is often manifest. Almost any tissue of the body may be temporarily invaded and affected, but the most common manifestations are skin and mucosal lesions. The skin lesions are nonpruritic, macular, papular, pustular, or follicular (or combinations of any of these types), although the maculopapular rash is the most common. The skin lesions usually are generalized; involvement of the palms and soles may be especially suspicious, since these areas are less commonly involved in other types of rashes. Annular lesions simulating ringworm are observed in Negroes. Mucous membrane lesions range from ulcers and papules of the lips, mouth, throat, genitalia, and anus ("mucous patches") to a diffuse redness of the pharynx. Both skin and mucous membrane lesions are highly infectious at this stage. Specific lesions, **condylomata lata**, are fused papules on the moist areas of the skin and mucous membranes.

Meningeal, hepatic, renal, bone, and joint invasion and inflammation with resulting cranial nerve palsies, jaundice, nephrotic syndrome, and periostitis may occur. Alopecia (moth-eaten appearance), iritis, and iridocyclitis may also occur. A transient myocarditis manifested by temporary ECG changes has been noted.

Blood STS is positive in almost all cases. The cutaneous and mucous membrane lesions may show *Treponema pallidum* on dark-field examination. There is usually a transient CSF involvement, with pleocytosis and elevated protein, although only 5% of cases have positive CSF serologic reactions. A transient proteinuria with waxy casts is seen in mild renal involvement. Blood and urine tests may be positive for bile in hepatic involvement. Subperiosteal osteoporosis may be observed (rarely) on x-ray examination in cases of bone involvement.

The skin lesions may be confused with the infectious exanthems, pityriasis rosea, and drug eruptions. The visceral lesions may suggest nephritis or hepatitis due to other causes. The diffusely red throat may mimic other forms of pharyngitis.

Treatment is as for primary adult syphilis.

3. RELAPSING SYPHILIS

After inadequate or inappropriate therapy, secondary syphilis may relapse (often between the 3rd and

9th post-treatment months). These relapses may be only serologic, with no clinical manifestations, or clinical, with recurrence (or first appearance) of any of the findings noted under secondary syphilis, above: skin and mucous membrane, neurologic, ocular, bone, or visceral (although visceral relapse involving the liver has not yet been reported following penicillin therapy). Unlike the usual asymptomatic neurologic involvement of secondary syphilis, neurologic relapses may be fulminating, leading to death. It is important, however, to distinguish serologic relapse from the STS change from negative to positive that occurs despite penicillin therapy because of serologic lag, or that which occurs with intercurrent infections (biologic false-positive).

Treatment is as for primary adult syphilis.

4. LATENT ("HIDDEN") SYPHILIS

Latent syphilis is the clinically quiescent phase during the interval between disappearance of secondary lesions and before the appearance of tertiary symptoms. There are no clinical manifestations, and the only significant laboratory finding is a positive blood STS. To diagnose latent syphilis the CSF must be entirely negative, x-ray and physical examination must show no evidence of cardiovascular involvement, and false-positive tests for syphilis must be ruled out. The latent phase may last from months to a lifetime. Since the individual is potentially infectious only during the first 2–4 years of latent syphilis, this phase is divided into potentially infectious early latent (first 4 years) and noninfectious late latent (after 4 years).

It is important to differentiate latent syphilis from false-positive blood tests due to clerical errors, acute fevers, yaws, infectious mononucleosis, malaria, leprosy, leishmaniasis, smallpox vaccination, lymphogranuloma venereum, systemic lupus erythematosus, and other collagen diseases.

Give benzathine penicillin G, a total of 6–9 million units in doses of 3 million units at 7-day intervals; or a total of 6–9 million units of procaine penicillin G with aluminum stearate suspension (in doses of 1.2 million units IM at 3-day intervals); or aqueous procaine penicillin G, 6–9 million units in doses of 600,000 units daily. Only a small percentage of blood STS will be appreciably altered by treatment with penicillin. The treatment of this stage of the disease is intended to prevent the late sequelae.

Pereyra, A.J., & R.L. Voller: A graphic guide for clinical management of latent syphilis. California Med 112:13–18, May 1970.

5. LATE (TERTIARY) SYPHILIS

This stage may occur at any time after secondary syphilis, even after years of latency. Late lesions prob-

ably represent an allergic reaction of the tissue to the organism and are usually divided into 2 types: (1) A gummatous reaction with a relatively sudden onset, and (2) diffuse inflammation of a more insidious onset which characteristically involves the CNS and large arteries. Nodular, nodulo-ulcerative, or gummatous lesions may appear on the skin; gummas may involve any area of the body; there may be evidence of aortic aneurysm, aortic insufficiency, or aortitis; or diffuse or localized CNS involvement may occur.

Late syphilis must be differentiated from neoplasms of the skin, liver, lung, stomach, or brain; other forms of meningitis; and primary neurologic lesions.

Treat as for latent syphilis. Reversal of positive STS does not usually occur. A second course of penicillin therapy may be given if necessary.

There is no known method for eradicating the treponeme from man in the late stages of syphilis.

Although almost any tissue and organ may be involved in late syphilis, the following are the most common types of involvement. (Spirochetes may be found in the eye, in CSF, and elsewhere in "adequately" treated syphilis.)

Skin

Cutaneous lesions of syphilis are of 2 varieties:

A. Nodular or Nodulo-ulcerative Lesions: Multiple, flat, circumscribed, indurated, copper-colored lesions varying from 0.5–3 cm in diameter and covered with scales (syphiloderm). These lesions eventually ulcerate (nodulo-ulcerative) or resolve by forming atrophic, pigmented scars.

B. Solitary Gummas: These start as painless, freely movable subcutaneous nodules which enlarge, attach to the overlying skin, eventually ulcerate, and present a gummy ulcerated base. Healing is by scarring, which often produces extensive disfiguring and distorting lesions of the face, scalp, forehead, and extremities.

Mucous Membranes

Late lesions of the mucous membranes are nodular gummas or leukoplakia, highly destructive to the involved tissue.

Skeletal

Bone lesions are destructive, causing periostitis, osteitis, and arthritis with little or no associated redness or swelling but often marked myalgia and myositis of the neighboring muscles. The pain is especially severe at night.

Eyes

Late ocular lesions are gummatous iritis, chorioretinitis, optic atrophy, and cranial nerve palsies, in addition to the lesions of CNS syphilis.

Respiratory System

Respiratory involvement by late syphilis is caused by gummatous infiltrates into the larynx, trachea, and pulmonary parenchyma, producing discrete pulmonary infiltrates. There may be hoarseness, respiratory distress, and wheezing secondary to the gummatous lesion itself or to subsequent stenosis occurring with healing.

Gastrointestinal

Gummas involving the liver produce the usually benign, asymptomatic **hepar lobatum**. Infiltration into the stomach wall causes "leather bottle" stomach with epigastric distress, inability to eat large meals, regurgitation, belching, and weight loss. Occasionally a picture not unlike Laennec's cirrhosis is produced by liver involvement.

Grave Medical Complications

Of greatest importance, however, are the late lesions involving the cardiovascular and central nervous systems, since these are often progressive, disabling, and life-threatening. Cardiovascular and CNS involvement represent 10% and 20%, respectively, of all late lesions. Cardiovascular lesions not infrequently accompany CNS lesions.

Cardiovascular (See also p 213.)

Cardiovascular lesions (about 10% of late syphilitic lesions) are often progressive, disabling, and life-threatening. CNS lesions are often present also. Involvement usually starts as an arteritis in the supracardiac portion of the aorta and progresses to cause one or more of the following: (1) Narrowing of the coronary ostia with resulting decreased coronary circulation, angina, cardiac insufficiency, and acute myocardial infarction. (2) Scarring of the aortic valves, producing aortic insufficiency with its water-hammer pulse, aortic diastolic murmur, frequently aortic systolic murmur, cardiac hypertrophy, and eventually cardiac insufficiency. (3) Weakness of the aorta wall, with saccular aneurysm formation and associated pressure symptoms of dysphagia, hoarseness, brassy cough, back pain (vertebral erosion), and, not too infrequently, rupture of the aneurysm either into one of the bronchi or externally. Repeated attacks of respiratory infection are common as a result of pressure on the trachea and bronchi.

Treatment of cardiac problems requires first consideration. Then give a total of 6–9 million units of penicillin G as for latent syphilis.

Neurosyphilis

Neurosyphilis (20% of late syphilitic lesions; often present with cardiovascular syphilis) is, like cardiovascular syphilis, a progressive, disabling, and life-threatening complication. There are 4 clinical types:

(1) Asymptomatic neurosyphilis: This form is characterized by spinal fluid abnormalities (positive CSF, STS, increased cell count, occasionally increased protein) without symptoms or signs of neurologic involvement.

(2) Meningovascular syphilis: This form is characterized by meningeal involvement or changes in the vascular structures of the brain (or both), producing symptoms of low-grade meningitis (headache, irritability); cranial nerve palsies (basilar meningitis); unequal

reflexes; irregular pupils with poor light and accommodation reflexes; and, when large vessels are involved, cerebrovascular accidents. The symptoms of acute meningitis are rare in late syphilis.

(3) Tabes dorsalis: This type of neurosyphilis is a chronic progressive degeneration of the parenchyma of the posterior columns of the spinal cord and of the posterior sensory ganglia and nerve roots. The symptoms and signs are those of impairment of proprioception and vibration, Argyll Robertson pupils (which react poorly to light but well to accommodation), and muscular hypotonia and hyporeflexia. Impairment of proprioception results in a wide-based gait and inability to walk in the dark. Paresthesias vary from analgesia (eg, absence of pain sensation on squeezing the testicles) to sharp recurrent pains in the muscles of the leg, described as "shooting" from the skin to the bone (shooting or lightning pains). Crises are also common in tabes: gastric crises, consisting of sharp abdominal pains with nausea and vomiting (simulating an acute abdomen); laryngeal crises, with paroxysmal cough and dyspnea; urethral crises, with painful bladder spasms; and rectal and anal crises. Crises may begin suddenly, last for hours to days, and cease abruptly. Neurogenic bladder with overflow incontinence is also seen. Trophic, painless ulcers may occur over pressure points on the feet. Joint damage may occur as a result of lack of sensory innervation (Charcot joint).

(4) Paresis: This is a generalized involvement of the cerebral cortex. The onset of clinical manifestations is insidious. There is usually a decrease in concentrating power, memory loss, dysarthria, tremor of the fingers and lips, irritability, and mild headaches. Most striking is the change of personality; the patient becomes slovenly, irresponsible, confused, and psychotic. Combinations of the various forms of neurosyphilis (especially tabes and paresis) are not uncommon.

Special considerations in treatment of neurosyphilis: The most important consideration is to prevent neurosyphilis by early diagnosis and adequate treatment and follow-up of early syphilis. Examination of all syphilitic patients for evidence of nervous system involvement must be a regular part of the follow-up examination. The pre-treatment clinical and laboratory evaluation should include detailed neurologic, ocular, and psychiatric examinations and a CSF examination. The high rate of coexistence of cardiovascular and CNS syphilis should be considered.

Give procaine penicillin G, 600,000 units IM daily to a total of 12 million units.

All patients must have a spinal fluid examination at 3-month intervals for the first year and every 6 months for the second year following completion of antisyphilis therapy. The adequacy of response is at times difficult to evaluate (especially during a short period of observation), but it may be gauged by clinical improvement and effective and persistent reversal of CSF changes. A second course of penicillin therapy may be given if necessary.

Aho, K., & others: Late complications of syphilis. Acta dermat 49:336–342, 1969.

Joffe, R., & others: Changing clinical picture of neurosyphilis: Report of seven unusual cases. Brit MJ 1:211–212, 1968.

Prewitt, T.A.: Syphilitic aortic insufficiency: Its increased incidence in the elderly. JAMA 211:637–639, 1970.

Smith, J.L.: Recent observations on the treatment of late ocular syphilis and neurosyphilis. Tr Am Acad Ophth 73:1113–1132, 1969.

6. PRENATAL SYPHILIS

Expectant mothers who have syphilis must be convinced of the urgent necessity for therapy. It is the physicians's responsibility to make certain that appropriate treatment is carried out immediately. Penicillin dosage schedules as advised for primary and secondary syphilis are satisfactory. When therapy is instituted after the 7th month in women with untreated early syphilis, larger doses of penicillin are advised.

Penicillin is curative in more than 90% of cases even when syphilis is discovered in the last trimester of pregnancy.

Follow-up must consist of monthly physical examinations and quantitative blood STS until delivery and for a month after delivery. If there is any clinical evidence of relapse, a failure of fall of blood STS titer, or a rise of STS titer, treatment should be repeated. The STS cannot always be converted to negative in mothers with late latent syphilis. In case of previously untreated or inadequately treated early latent syphilis, if the original STS titer does not significantly decline within 3 months after treatment, retreatment is advisable.

The infant should be examined for the stigmas of syphilis at birth and again at intervals of 2 or 3 weeks for 4–6 months. If the maternal blood is positive, a positive cord blood STS is of no diagnostic value. However, if the infant's blood is followed serially by quantitative blood STS at 2-week intervals for 4 months, a sustained or rising STS titer would indicate a diagnosis of congenital syphilis and a need for treatment.

Serum levels of IgM are frequently elevated in the cord blood of the infected neonate, and a rise in IgM may occur before the disease is clinically manifest. A recent modification of the FTA-ABS test utilizing fluorescein-labeled antihuman IgM is stated to be more specific than determination of IgM alone.

Mamunes, P., & others: Early diagnosis of neonatal congenital syphilis: Elevation of a gamma M-fluorescent treponemal antibody test. Am J Dis Child 120:17–21, 1970.

CONGENITAL SYPHILIS

The clinical manifestations of congenital syphilis are quite similar to those of the acquired form except for the rather indefinite clinical course and the absence of primary lesions. There is usually a family history of syphilis. Skin and mucous membrane lesions are present at birth or in early infancy. Characteristic later stigmas of congenital syphilis include interstitial keratitis, Hutchinson's teeth, 8th nerve deafness (Hutchinson's triad), saddle nose, rhagades, saber shins and other bone changes, and mental retardation. The STS is usually strongly positive at birth but gradually becomes negative over a period of years. IgM is usually elevated. Any of the tertiary sequelae of the adult disease (CNS, visceral, or cardiovascular) may occur.

Early congenital syphilis ($<$ 2 years of age) is treated with 50,000 units of benzathine penicillin G/kg as a single injection; or a total of 100,000 units PAM/kg IM, given at 2–3 day intervals in divided doses. The treatment of late congenital syphilis is as for late latent syphilis. Neurosyphilis of congenital origin should be treated as the acquired form.

Coblentz, D.R., & others: Roentgenographic diagnosis of congenital syphilis in the newborn. JAMA 212:1061–1064, 1970.

Robinson, R.C.V.: Congenital syphilis. Arch Dermat 99:599–610, 1969.

OTHER TREPONEMATOSES*

ENDEMIC SYPHILIS
(Bejel, Skerljevo, etc)

Endemic syphilis is an acute and chronic infection caused by an organism morphologically indistinguishable from *Treponema pallidum*; it is distinguished from sporadic syphilis by its occurrence in children of crowded, poor households in particular localities, by virtual absence of primary lesions, and the predilection of secondary lesions for oral and nasopharyngeal mucosa as well (in places) as the soles (plantar hyperkeratosis). It is distinguished from yaws by its occurrence in areas in which yaws is not endemic and by the absence of primary lesions and the presence of buccal lesions. It may be confused with angular stomatitis due to vitamin deficiency. It has been reported in a number of countries including Latin America, often with local names: bejel in Syria and Iraq; skerljevo in Bosnia; dichuchwa, njovera, and siti in Africa. Each has local distinctive characters.

*Turner, L.H.: Notes on the treponematoses with an illustrated account of yaws. Bull No. 9 Inst Med Res Malaya, 1959.

Secondary oral lesions are the most common manifestations. Generalized lymphadenopathy and secondary and tertiary bone lesions are common in bejel. Secondary lesions tend to heal in about a year.

Laboratory findings and treatment are the same as for primary syphilis.

Beerman, H., & others: Syphilis. Review of the recent literature, 1959–60. Arch Int Med 107:121–140, 1961.

PINTA

Pinta is a nonvenereal spirochetal infection caused by *Treponema carateum*. It occurs endemically in rural areas of Latin America, especially in Mexico, Colombia, and Cuba; the Philippines, and some areas of the Pacific. A nonulcerative, erythematous primary papule spreads slowly into a papulosquamous plaque showing a variety of color changes (slate, lilac, black). Secondary lesions resemble the primary one and appear within a year after it. These appear successively, new lesions together with older ones; and are commonest on the extremities but may cover most of the body. Mild local lymphadenopathy is common. There is later atrophy and depigmentation. Some cases show pigment changes and atrophic patches on the soles and palms, with or without hyperkeratosis, which are indistinguishable from "crab yaws."

Diagnosis and treatment are the same as for primary syphilis.

YAWS
(Frambesia)

Yaws is a contagious disease largely limited to tropical regions which is produced by *Treponema pertenue*. It is characterized by granulomatous lesions of the skin, mucous membranes, and bone. Yaws is rarely fatal, although if untreated it may lead to chronic disability and disfigurement. Yaws is acquired by direct nonvenereal contact. The disease is usually acquired in childhood, although it may occur at any age. The "mother yaw," a painless papule which later ulcerates, appears 3–4 weeks after exposure. There is usually associated regional lymphadenopathy. Six to 12 weeks later, similar secondary lesions appear and last for several months or years. Late gummatous lesions may follow, with associated tissue destruction and alteration involving large areas of skin and subcutaneous tissues. The late effects of yaws, with bone change, shortening of digits, and contractions, may be confused with similar changes occurring in leprosy. CNS, cardiac, or other visceral involvement is rare. STS (eg, VDRL), TPI, and FTA-ABS are positive, and the spirochetes may be demonstrated by dark-field examination or immunofluorescence.

Cleanliness of lesions is most important in treatment. Specific measures consist of giving one of the following: (1) penicillin procaine, 300,000 units IM daily for 7–10 days; or (2) one of the tetracyclines, 0.5 gm every 6 hours for 10 days.

Fry, L., & P. Rodin: Early yaws. Brit J Ven Dis 42:28–30, 1966.

MISCELLANEOUS SPIROCHETAL DISEASES

RELAPSING FEVER

Relapsing fever is the name of a group of clinically similar acute infectious diseases caused by several different species of spirochetes of the genus Borrelia. The disease is transmitted to man by insect vectors (head and body lice and ticks). The insect is infected by feeding on human acute cases (lice) or the animal reservoir (ticks), and transmits the disease to humans when insect feces or crushed insects are rubbed into the bite puncture wound, excoriated areas of skin, or the eyes. The disease is endemic in various parts of the world, including western USA. The incubation period is 2–15 days (average about 7 days).

Clinical Findings

A. Symptoms and Signs: The disease is characterized by relapses occurring at intervals of 1–2 weeks after the preceding episode with an interim asymptomatic period. The relapses duplicate the initial attack but become progressively less severe. Recovery occurs after 2–10 relapses.

The attack is of sudden onset with fever, chills, tachycardia, nausea and vomiting, myalgia, arthralgia, bronchitis, and a dry, nonproductive cough. Hepatomegaly and splenomegaly appear later. Jaundice may be present. An erythematous rash appears early in the course of the disease over the trunk and extremities, followed later by rose-colored spots in the same area. Petechiae may also be present. In severe cases neurologic and psychic manifestations are present. After 3–10 days the fever falls by crisis. Jaundice, iritis, conjunctivitis, cranial nerve lesions, and uterine hemorrhage are more common in the relapses.

B. Laboratory Findings: During the acute episodes the urine shows protein, casts, and occasionally erythrocytes; the blood shows a marked polymorphonuclear leukocytosis and in about one-fourth of cases, a false-positive STS. During the paroxysm spirochetes may be found in the patient's blood on dark-field examination of a blood smear stained with Wright's or Giemsa's stain; or the blood may be injected into a rat and the spirochetes found 3–5 days later in the tail blood. The Weil-Felix test may be positive in a titer of 1:80 or more.

Differential Diagnosis

The late manifestations of relapsing fever may be confused with malaria, leptospirosis, dengue, yellow fever, and typhus.

Treatment

Treat either with (1) tetracycline drugs, 0.5 gm every 6 hours orally for 7 days; or (2) procaine penicillin G, 600,000 units IM daily for 10 days.

Prognosis

The overall mortality rate is usually about 5%. Fatalities are most common in the old, debilitated, or very young patients. With treatment the initial attack is shortened and relapses largely prevented.

Southern, P.M., & J.P. Sanford: Relapsing fever. Medicine 48:129–170, 1969.

RAT-BITE FEVER
(Spirillary Rat-Bite Fever, Sodoku)

Rat-bite fever is an acute infectious disease caused by the *Spirillum minus* and transmitted to man by the bite of a rat. The organism gains entry into the rat's oral cavity from the drainage of a primary eye infection. The incubation period is 5–28 days.

Clinical Findings

A. Symptoms and Signs: The original rat bite, unless infected, heals promptly, only to be followed after the incubation period by a flare-up of the original site. The area of the rat bite then becomes swollen, indurated, and painful, assumes a dusky purplish hue, and may ulcerate. Regional lymphangitis and lymphadenitis, fever, chills, malaise, myalgia, arthralgia, and headache are present. Splenomegaly may occur. A dusky-red, sparse maculopapular rash appears on the trunk and extremities.

After a few days both the local and systemic symptoms subside, only to reappear again in a few days. This relapsing pattern of fever of 24–48 hours alternating with an equal afebrile period becomes established and may persist for weeks. The local and systemic findings, however (including the rash), usually recur only during the first few relapses.

B. Laboratory Findings: Leukocytosis is often present, and a blood STS may be falsely positive. The organism may be identified in dark-field examination of the ulcer exudate or aspirated lymph node material or by animal inoculation of exudate or blood. The organism cannot be cultured in artificial media.

Differential Diagnosis

Rat-bite fever must be distinguished from the rat-bite–induced episodic fever, lymphadenitis, and rash

of streptobacillary fever. In the latter the presence of septic nonmigratory polyarthritis, a specific agglutination titer, and the isolation of the causative organism differentiates the disorder from spirillary rat-bite fever. Rat-bite fever may also be distinguished from tularemia and relapsing fever by identification of the causative organism.

Treatment

Treat with procaine penicillin G, 300,000 units IM every 12 hours; or tetracycline drugs, 0.5 gm every 6 hours for 7 days. Give supportive and symptomatic measures as indicated.

Prognosis

The reported mortality rate is about 10%, but this should be markedly reduced by prompt diagnosis and treatment.

Schwartzman, G., & others: Repeated recovery of a spirillum by blood culture from 1200 children with prolonged and recurrent fevers. Pediatrics 8:227, 1951.

LEPTOSPIROSIS
(Including Weil's Disease)

Essentials of Diagnosis

- Sudden onset of fever, chills, headache, muscle pains and tenderness, photophobia, and conjunctival redness.
- Hepatitis, nephritis, meningitis, pneumonitis, iridocyclitis, and skin rash may occur.
- Proteinuria, leukocytosis.
- Organism identified by smear, animal inoculation, culture, and rising agglutination titer.

General Considerations

Leptospirosis is an acute infection caused by any of several Leptospira species. The 3 most common species and their reservoirs of infection are: *Lept icterohaemorrhagiae* of rats, *Lept canicola* of dogs, and *Lept pomona* of cattle and swine. Several other species, some as yet unidentified serologically, can also cause the disease, but *Lept icterohaemorrhagiae* causes the most severe illness. The disease is world-wide in distribution, and the incidence is higher than usually supposed. The parasite is transmitted to man by the ingestion of food and drink contaminated by the urine of the reservoir animal. The organism may also enter through minor skin lesions and probably the conjunctivas also; and many infections have followed bathing in contaminated pools or streams. The disease is an occupational hazard among sewer workers, rice-planters, and farmers. The incubation period is 5–13 days.

Clinical Findings

A. Symptoms and Signs: There is a sudden onset of fever to 38.9–40° C (102–104° F), chills, abdominal pains, vomiting, and myalgia especially of the calf muscles. Extremely severe headache is usually present. The conjunctivas are markedly reddened. The liver may be palpable, and in about 50% of cases (most commonly in *Lept icterohaemorrhagiae* infections) jaundice is present on about the 5th day and may be associated with nephritis. Splenomegaly is uncommon except in pretibial fever. Capillary hemorrhages and purpuric skin lesions may also appear. Meningeal irritation and associated findings may occur. In pretibial fever patchy erythema occurs on the skin of the lower leg and may be generalized.

Leptospirosis with jaundice must be distinguished from hepatitis, yellow fever, and relapsing fever.

B. Laboratory Findings: The leukocyte count may be normal or as high as 50,000/cu mm, with neutrophils predominating. The urine may contain bile, protein, casts, and red cells. Oliguria is not uncommon, and in severe cases uremia may occur. In cases with meningeal involvement, organisms may be found in the CSF. The organism may be identified by dark-field examination of the patient's blood (during the first 10 days), by guinea pig inoculation, or by culture on Korthof's medium. The organism may also be isolated from the urine from the 10th day to the 6th week. Specific agglutination titers develop after 7 days and may persist at high levels for many years.

Complications

Myocarditis, aseptic meningitis, renal failure, and massive hemorrhage are not common but are the usual cause of death. Iridocyclitis may occur.

Treatment

Treat as early as possible (and continue treatment for 6 days) with tetracyclines, 0.5 gm every 6 hours; or penicllin, 600,000 units IM every 3 hours for 1 day and then every 6 hours. Observe for evidences of renal failure and treat as necessary. The value of antimicrobial therapy has been questioned.

Prognosis

Without jaundice the disease is almost never fatal. With jaundice the mortality rate is about 15%. Death occurs from extreme toxemia or one of the above complications.

Hubbert, W.T., & G.L. Humphrey: Epidemiology of leptospirosis in California: A cause of aseptic meningitis. California Med 108:113–117, 1968.

Lawson, J.H., & S.W. Michna: Canicola fever in man and animals. Brit MJ 2:336–340, 1966.

Sitpriya, V., & H. Evans: The kidney in human leptospirosis. Am J Med 49:780–788, 1970.

Sundharagiati, B., Harinasuta, C., & U. Photha: Human leptospirosis in Thailand. Tr Roy Soc Trop Med Hyg 60:361–365, 1966.

● ● ●

General Bibliography

Merigan, T.C.: Venereal diseases. Chap 23, pp 486–489, in: *Current Medical References,* 6th ed. Chatton, M.J., & P.J. Sanazaro (editors). Lange, 1970.

Top, F.H.: *Communicable and Infectious Diseases,* 5th ed. Mosby, 1964.

Youmans, J.D. (editor): Symposium on syphilis and other venereal diseases. M Clin North America 48:571–824, 1964.

23 . . .

Infectious Diseases: Protozoal

J. Ralph Audy, Frederick L. Dunn, & Robert S. Goldsmith

AMEBIASIS

Essentials of Diagnosis

- Recurrent bouts of diarrhea, sometimes alternating with constipation.
- Semi-fluid stools containing no pus and only flecks of blood-stained mucus.
- In fulminant cases, bloody exudates and prostration.
- Tenderness and enlargement of the liver is frequent.
- Liver abscess, often without obvious association with dysentery.
- Amebas demonstrable in stools or abscess aspirate. Cysts in stools in quiescent infections. Hematophagous amebas in stools are diagnostic.

General Considerations

Amebiasis is an infection with protean clinical manifestations, almost worldwide in distribution, caused by the protozoon *Entamoeba histolytica*. The difficulties of diagnosis and treatment are often increased by the following: variations in invasive pathogenicity of strains of the potentially pathogenic organism *E histolytica;* by the apparent synergistic effect of various coexistent bacterial and, at times, helminthic or even viral intestinal infections; by momentary variations in resistance or susceptibility of the infected person; by regional and cultural variations in the clinical picture; by continued treatment with amebicides of various chronic (often iatrogenic) disorders misdiagnosed as amebiasis; by laboratory misdiagnoses of the ameba, which closely resembles certain innocent forms; and by misinterpretation of laboratory identifications which cannot reliably distinguish invasive from noninvasive forms but can only attempt taxonomic labels.

Supposedly nonpathogenic amebas such as *Dientamoeba fragilis* may occasionally cause symptoms and cannot be ignored.

Potentially pathogenic amebas may (1) live in the bowel as harmless commensals (asymptomatic amebiasis of carrier state—although some workers insist that they always cause minute lesions)—or, in particular circumstances, they may (2) invade the large bowel wall, causing amebic dysentery, or other viscera (metastatic infection), most commonly the liver (liver abscess). In other words, amebiasis may be asymptomatic, intestinal, or extra-intestinal. Asymptomatic amebiasis frequently evokes undue alarm; intestinal amebiasis is often misdiagnosed, or it relapses following inadequate treatment; liver abscess may be misdiagnosed until it is far advanced.

Amebic dysentery may occur in epidemics, and is a risk to newcomers in areas where sanitary facilities are poor. It is often a special problem in institutions, eg, orphanages. It is most common in the 2nd to 4th decades of life.

A bacteriophagous "small race" that might be *E hartmanni* is believed to be generally harmless, unlike the potentially hematophagous and pathogenic "large race." The life cycle of the ameba consists of 2 completely distinct stages (with some intermediary phases): (1) a cyst (infective) stage, which occurs only in the intestinal lumen and stools; (2) a motile ameba or trophozoite normally living as a commensal in the colon but producing lesions after activation to an invasive phase by, for example, coincident synergistic bacterial or possibly other bowel infections, diet, alterations in the host's physiologic state, or combinations of these factors. A particular strain of infecting ameba may or may not be especially liable to these processes of activation; ie, strains differ in potential virulence, the small strains being relatively innocent and therefore even more readily confused with the similar but nonpathogenic small species *E hartmanni*. It is believed that active invasiveness with hematophagy is usually due to relatively large ("large race") trophozoites, which apparently do not readily encyst; and that such trophozoites might develop from medium-sized as well as fairly large cysts.

Cysts gain entry to man in food and drink contaminated by feces. Trophozoites excyst from each cyst, probably in the region of the ileocecal valve. They may multiply and live commensally, cysts being passed at irregular intervals. The greatest densities of organisms are at the sites of greatest fecal stasis, ie, the cecum, descending colon, sigmoid, and rectum. During an invasive phase, the trophozoites penetrate the mucosa to produce flask-shaped microabscesses which, by enlargement and coalescence, may produce shallow, undermined ulcers with ragged edges covered by a loose yellow exudate. In fulminating cases the ulceration may be extensive and the bowel quite friable. There is little inflammation, and therefore relatively little fibrosis following healing.

During acute or chronic dysentery, and sometimes with only slight bowel disturbance, there is frequently some degree of liver tenderness and hepatomegaly. This may be nonspecific, but it is believed that some cases are due either to multiple portal amebic emboli or to aborting abscesses. Trophozoites may, however, remain active and multiply, producing a necrotic noninflammatory abscess. This may follow a subclinical intestinal infection. The incidence of liver abscess is not related to the severity of preceding amebic dysentery, and only about 1/3 of patients give a history of amebic dysentery.

An ameboma (amebic granuloma) is a tumor in the colon, usually in the cecum or sigmoid, caused by local exuberance of granulation tissue or fibrosis, and sometimes by abscess. The same pathologic process may give rise to stricture, most evident in the rectum. As with liver abscess, amebomas and strictures may have no reliable association with active amebic dysentery. Differentiation from carcinoma is important.

Asymptomatic infection (cyst-passers, carrier state) is fairly common. Five to 10% of people in the USA (mostly in the South) and 50% or more of people in endemic areas with poor sanitation may be carriers. Cyst-passers may be convalescents or may have no known relevant history of amebiasis. In some localities many of the cyst-passers may be carrying small races of *E histolytica* of negligible virulence. Confusion with cysts of the nonpathogenic species or subspecies hartmanni is common.

Clinical Findings

A. Symptoms and Signs: The onset is seldom abrupt. (An abrupt onset in amebiasis may signify a concurrent shigella infection or dietary indiscretion.) Increasingly severe diarrhea or moderate dysentery develops over a period of several days, associated with lower abdominal pain or discomfort and tenesmus. The patient is ambulatory, and there is characteristically no anorexia and no sign of toxicosis. The stools (5–10 a day except in fulminating cases, when there may be 50) are brown, semi-fluid, and have a characteristic foul smell, with flecks of blood-stained mucus and, in severe cases, blood and copious mucus. Fever is irregular and slight.

The acute attack usually subsides spontaneously. Remissions and recurrence follow, sometimes with various abdominal symptoms during remission, leading eventually to severe debility and prostration. Loss of weight becomes notable. Recurrences may be precipitated by emotional stress, alcoholic excess, or fatigue. Trophozoites are characteristically present in the dysenteric stools; cysts alone are present intermittently during remissions. Amebic ulceration may occur without diarrhea, and severe dysentery may occur in the absence of detectable amebas in the stools.

B. Laboratory Findings: When diarrhea or dysentery is present, the trophozoites may be identified in fresh stools or in tissues obtained from the edges of ulcers at the time of endoscopy. Trophozoites can be found and identified only in fresh stools or stools immediately preserved. Trophozoites are not found in formed stools. If possible, fresh stools should be rushed to the laboratory, and care should be taken to include samples of exudate plus specimens preserved in PVA (polyvinyl-alcohol) fixative and, if possible, also in MIF (merthiolate-iodine-formalin) preservative. The trophozoites are large, with a characteristic flowing motility in the warm fresh stool. A few of them will contain ingested red cells (smaller in diameter than free red cells because they are globular in the ameba), and this is pathognomonic provided the trophozoite is not confused with the occasional macrophage also containing red cells. Cysts (in formed stools) and trophozoites must be distinguished from the closely similar *E coli, E hartmanni,* and (occasionally) *E polecki,* as well as from *Iodamoeba bütschlii, Dientamoeba fragilis* (an occasional cause of intestinal disturbance), and *Endolimax nana.* The diagnosis must be positive, and this demands a great deal of skill and experience. In the stool, leukocytes and macrophages are relatively scarce (in contrast to bacillary dysentery) unless there is concomitant bacillary infection, as may be found with varying frequency according to locality. Charcot-Leyden crystals may be present. The white count is elevated during the acute attack, and often with hepatic abscess, but there is no eosinophilia.

With liver abscess, material for examination may be obtained by aspiration, although the central markedly necrotic material is usually free from organisms. The appearance is normally characteristic and has been described as resembling "anchovy paste." Divide the aspirated material into a succession of 20–30 ml samples as it is taken, so that the last sample only may be examined. Avoid sending only one large sample to the laboratory.

A complement fixation test is often positive in cases of hepatic involvement.

An intradermal reaction has been described, but experience has been limited.

Endoscopy may reveal the ulcerative lesions, with intact intervening mucosa. It is very valuable in experienced hands, and should be adopted as a routine.

Differential Diagnosis

Under sanitary conditions in temperate zones, amebic diarrhea (dysentery) must be distinguished from ulcerative colitis and acute nonspecific colitis (by endoscopy and stool examination); in tropical areas or under insanitary conditions, it must be distinguished from bacillary dysentery, in which there is a more acute onset with watery, purulent, bloody stools. At times amebic dysentery must be distinguished also from appendicitis, schistosomiasis, balantidiasis, cholecystitis, regional enteritis, and tuberculous enterocolitis. These may be recognized by the sigmoidoscopic and barium enema findings and the identification of a specific organism.

Complications

Liver abscess is the most common complication of intestinal infection. Amebas from the intestine may rarely travel to and infect the lungs, brain, or skin. A diffuse hepatitis which clears up on treatment with emetine or chloroquine is not infrequent. Perforation of the bowel may also occasionally take place, and an untreated hepatic abscess may perforate into the adjacent pleural space to produce an effusion and a pneumonitis. The bowel wall in amebic dysentery is quite friable, and surgery is contraindicated. Amebomas usually resolve completely with little residual fibrosis.

Treatment

Bed rest is recommended for all patients with frank symptoms and is imperative for any patient receiving emetine (see below). A high-protein, high-calorie, low-carbohydrate diet should be given as soon as practicable. It can usually be started immediately treatment is instituted. If anemia is present, iron therapy (see Chapter 9) should be given.

A. Intestinal Amebiasis; Acute or Chronic Amebic Dysentery:

1. Specific drugs and combined therapy—The drugs used in the treatment of amebiasis are of 3 distinct types, acting respectively against intestinal amebas, associated pathogenic intestinal bacteria, and metastatic (tissue) amebas. Most intestinal amebicides cannot reliably cure acute dysentery without fear of relapse if used alone. Therefore, current procedure is to combine intestinal amebicides with antibiotics aimed at the associated bacteria. (Acute attacks sometimes clear up with antibiotics alone, but may then relapse.)

Recommended specific intestinal amebicides are listed below. Emetine (see under Hepatic Amebiasis, below) requires intramuscular injection and bed rest, but synthetic dehydroemetine (DHE), also given intramuscularly, is less toxic and a promising substitute. Further comparative trials are needed. Emetine and dehydroemetine are essentially tissue amebicides like chloroquine and, therefore, are indicated for hepatic abscess but will not alone reliably cure dysentery. Nevertheless, presumably because amebas are also then in the intestinal tissues, emetine or DHE should be given briefly to ameliorate severe acute dysentery before going on to treat with intestinal amebicides.

Combinations of drugs which may be recommended for dysentery are, for milder cases, iodochlorhydroxyquin (or diiodohydroxyquin) plus chloroquine followed by an arsenical. If a second course of treatment is required, add oxytetracycline. For severe cases, start with emetine or DHE for the shortest time required to abate severe symptoms.

The patient must be closely observed for toxic reactions, especially when taking carbarsone, glycobiarsol, emetine, or DHE.

a. Iodochlorhydroxyquin (Vioform®), 0.25 gm 3 times daily orally for 10 days. Contraindicated in renal and possibly hepatic disease not due to amebiasis, but toxic effects (indigestion, diarrhea) are uncommon. An alternative but similar drug is diiodohydroxyquin (Diodoquin®), 650 mg 3 times daily for 21 days.

b. Carbarsone, 0.25 gm 3 times daily orally for 7–10 days; or glycobiarsol (Milibis®), 0.5 gm twice daily for 10 days. These arsenicals are contraindicated

in hepatic disease. Inspect daily for toxic symptoms (fever, abdominal discomfort or pain, nausea and vomiting, diarrhea, dermatitis), and discontinue at once if toxic effects are suspected. Severe reactions may be counteracted with dimercaprol (BAL).

c. Antibiotics are used for acute amebic dysentery, combined with a direct-acting amebicide. Use oxytetracycline (Terramycin®), 0.25 gm 3 times daily orally for 4–7 days. Fumagillin (Fumidil®), 30–60 mg orally daily for 10 days, is regarded as directly amebicidal; so also is paromomycin (Humatin®).

d. Emetine bismuth iodide (EBI®), enteric-coated, 0.2 gm daily for 12 days, preferably after the evening meal and with sedation for the first few days to minimize nausea. This also controls extra-intestinal amebiasis to a considerable extent.

e. Diloxanide (Entamide®) furoate, 500 mg 3 times daily for 10 days, especially in chronic intestinal amebiasis and for mass therapy.

f. Metronidazole (Flagyl®) in high doses—750 mg orally 3 times daily for 5 days—is very effective for acute dysentery and hepatic abscess. The usefulness of the drug for mild intestinal infections requires further clinical trials. Although approved for the treatment of trichomoniasis in the USA, the drug has not been approved by FDA for use against *E histolytica.*

2. Evaluation of therapy—Every patient must be followed for about 2 weeks after treatment and the stools examined for 6 successive days, or better still, at intervals of a few days. If stools are positive, re-examine the patient completely, check carefully for possible reinfection in his home or at work, and treat with a specific amebicide, possibly combined with erythromycin. If stools are negative, check by sigmoidoscopy and give no further treatment. Re-examine stools daily for 3–6 consecutive days after 3 months, and again after another 6 months or whenever symptoms appear. It is advisable to repeat sigmoidoscopy.

B. Hepatic Amebiasis:

1. Measures for hepatitis—

a. Chloroquine phosphate (Aralen®) is the drug of choice in hepatic amebiasis. Give 0.5 gm (or 0.3 gm of the base) twice daily for 2 days, followed by 250 mg twice daily for 26 days.

b. General supportive measures should be instituted as for infectious hepatitis. A 2-week rest period may be followed by a repeat course of treatment with chloroquine or emetine, with or without erythromycin as indicated.

c. Follow all cases at intervals as for intestinal amebiasis, with special attention to general health, appetite, gain in weight, and liver function.

2. Measures for liver abscess—

a. Treat with emetine plus chloroquine and diiodohydroxyquin or metronidazole. The emetine dosage is 1 mg/kg body weight (maximum, 65 mg) IM or subcut for 10 days. The chloroquine dosage is 500 mg orally (salt) twice daily for 2 days and then 250 mg twice daily for 26 days. The metronidazole dosage is 750 mg orally 3 times daily for 5 days. Metronidazole is not approved by FDA for this indication in the USA.

b. Localize the abscess as accurately as possible (x-rays often help), and drain it by aspiration under strict aseptic conditions. Repeat aspiration if necessary. Open drainage must be avoided unless the abscess is secondarily infected, in which case proceed as described below. Repeat drug therapy.

c. Secondarily infected abscess—Aspirated material contains pus and organisms. Identify the organisms by culture and determine antibiotic sensitivity. Treat with a full course of chloroquine and emetine combined with tetracycline or another indicated antibiotic. Consider open drainage and irrigations with antibiotic solution. Be on guard against involvement of the right chest and possible perforation through the diaphragm.

C. Amebiasis of Skin and Other Organs: For amebiasis of all internal organs, treat with emetine as for hepatic amebiasis. Chloroquine does not concentrate adequately in tissues other than the liver. In some countries (eg, Mexico), cutaneous amebiasis is much more common than has been suspected, and cases are probably being misdiagnosed. Amebiasis should be suspected in all eroding ulcerations in the perineal, anal, or genital region (especially in children with diarrhea and diapers) and around fistulas in the abdominal wall. The diagnosis may be confirmed by biopsy of the ulcer wall. Treat with emetine, but not chloroquine, which is not concentrated in the skin.

D. Asymptomatic Amebiasis ("Carrier State"):

1. Avoid overtreatment, follow with repeated stool examinations (as for amebic dysentery), and investigate possible sources of reinfection after therapy.

2. Iodochlorhydroxyquin (Vioform®), 0.25 gm 3 times daily orally for 10 days; or diiodohydroxyquin (Diodoquin®), 650 mg 3 times daily for 21 days; or diloxanide furoate, 0.5 gm 3 times daily for 10 days.

3. The cyst-passer must be considered wholly within the context of his surroundings, his similarities to and differences from the population in contact, and the prevailing endemicity of amebic dysentery. Thus, he may sometimes require continued surveillance and treatment or—for example, in most parts of the USA— he may at times be safely ignored. It is very important to avoid, if possible, the disturbing psychologic effects of awareness of passing cysts and being a potentially dangerous or ill person.

4. Some clinicians recommend a course of chloroquine (as for hepatic amebiasis) as a precaution against the possibility of accompanying early extra-intestinal infection. Others prefer to withhold such therapy until clinical indications for it are clear. The latter course seems more rational. The passage of small cysts (from *E hartmanni* or *E histolytica hartmanni*) is commonly regarded as not requiring therapy.

E. Follow-Up Care: A complete follow-up examination consists of sigmoidoscopy and study of 6 successive stools (at least one following a saline purge), daily or at intervals of a few days. The examination should be repeated within 1 year and specific treatment given only if amebas are demonstrated. Consider the possibility of secondary infection, irritation of

bowel by chemotherapy or over-treatment, and psychoneurosis in all patients in whom symptoms persist or recur without demonstration of amebas. The manner in which follow-up is conducted must not lead the patient to believe that he is "not cured."

Prognosis

The mortality rate from untreated amebic dysentery may reach 20–40%, with the highest incidence in the debilitated patient and in chronic recurrent cases. This incidence is reduced to 1–5% in treated cases. Amebiasis affecting the liver varies greatly in its mortality rate, depending upon the extent of the involvement, the number of abscesses, their accessibility to drainage, and the presence of secondary infections of the abscess.

Grigsby, W.P.: Surgical treatment of amebiasis. Surg Gynec Obst 128:609–627, 1969.

Kean, B.H., & C.L. Malloch: The neglected ameba: *Dientamoeba fragilis.* A report of 100 "pure" infections. Am J Digest Dis 11:735–746, 1966.

Lister, G.D.: Delayed myocardial intoxication following the administration of dehydroemetine hydrochloride. J Trop Med 71:219–223, 1968.

Maddison, S.E., & others: Comparison of intradermal and serologic tests for diagnosis of amebiasis. Am J Trop Med 17:540–547, 1968.

Miller, M.J., & F. Scott: The intradermal reaction in amebiasis. Canad MAJ 103:253–257, 1970.

Powell, S.J.: Drug therapy of amoebiasis. Bull WHO 40:953–956, 1969.

Powell, S.J., & others: Further trials of metronidazole in amoebic dysentery and amoebic liver abscess. Ann Trop Med 61:511–514, 1967.

Rab, S.M., & others: Amoebic liver abscess. Some unique presentations. Am J Med 43:811–816, 1967.

Turner, J.A., & others: Amebiasis: A symposium. California Med 114:44–55, March 1971.

Woodruff, A.W., & J.S. Bell: Amoebiasis: The evaluation of amoebicides. Tr Roy Soc Trop Med Hyg 61:435–440, 1967.

WHO Expert Committee: *Amoebiasis.* WHO Technical Report Series No. 421. World Health Organization, 1969.

AMEBIC MENINGOENCEPHALITIS
(Naegleria Infection)

A free-living amebic organism recently identified as *Naegleria gruberi* has been the causative agent of more than 30 cases of acute purulent meningoencephalitis in Australia, the USA, and Czechoslovakia in recent years. Many patients have given a history of swimming in pools or fresh water lakes. The disease has been uniformly fatal; no successful chemotherapy has yet been devised.

Carter, R.F.: Primary amoebic meningo-encephalitis: Clinical, pathological and epidemiological features of six fatal cases. J Path Bact 96:1–26, 1968.

MALARIA

Essentials of Diagnosis

- Paroxysms (often periodic) of chills, fever, and sweating.
- Splenomegaly, anemia, leukopenia.
- Delirium, coma, convulsions, gastrointestinal disorders, and jaundice.
- Characteristic parasites in erythrocytes, identified in thick or thin blood films.

General Considerations

Four species of ameboid protozoan parasites of the genus plasmodium are responsible for human malaria. Today the infection is generally limited to the tropics and subtropics, but over 3000 imported cases occurred in the USA in 1967. Temperate zone malaria is usually unstable and relatively easy to control or eradicate; tropical malaria is often more stable. In the tropics malaria generally disappears at altitudes above 6000 feet. The most common parasites, *P vivax* and *P falciparum,* are found throughout the malaria belt. *P malariae* is also broadly distributed but less common. The 4th parasite, *P ovale,* is rare, but in West Africa it seems to replace *P vivax.* Artificial transmission by blood transfusion is increasingly important (exclude all Vietnam veterans for 2 or more years), but in nature infection takes place through the bite of an infected female Anopheles mosquito. The mosquito is the host during the sexual phase of the life cycle; man is the host for the asexual developmental stages. After an infective bite the first stage of development in man takes place in the liver. Parasites escape from the liver into the blood stream 5½–11 days later. Erythrocytes are invaded, the parasites multiply, and 48 hours later (or 72 in the case of *P malariae*) the red cells rupture, releasing a new crop of parasites. This cycle of invasion, multiplication, and red cell rupture may be repeated many times. Symptoms do not appear until several of these erythrocytic cycles have been completed. The incubation period varies considerably, depending upon the species and strain of parasite, the intensity of the infection, and the immune status of the host. For *P vivax* and *P falciparum* it is usually 10–15 days, but it may be much longer (in some cases even months). The *P malariae* incubation period averages about 28 days. *P falciparum* multiplication is confined to the red cells after the first cycle in liver cells (the pre-erythrocytic stage). Thus any treatment which eliminates falciparum parasites from the blood stream will cure the infection. Without treatment the infection will terminate spontaneously in less than 2–3 years (usually 6–8 months). The other 3 species continue to multiply in liver cells long after the initial blood stream invasion. This exoerythrocytic cycle of multiplication coexists with the erythrocytic cycle, and may persist after parasites have apparently disappeared from the blood stream. Successful cure of *P vivax, P ovale,* and *P malariae* infections requires treatment aimed not only at parasites in red cells but also at those in the liver. Vivax and ovale infections may persist without treatment for as long as 5 years; *P malariae* infections which lasted for 40 years have been recorded.

Clinical Findings

A. Symptoms and Signs: The paroxysms of malaria are closely related to events in the blood stream. The chill, lasting from 15 minutes to an hour, begins as a generation of parasites ruptures their host red cells and escapes into the blood. Nausea, vomiting, and headache are common at this time. The succeeding hot stage, lasting several hours, is accompanied by a spiking fever, sometimes reaching 40° C (104° F) or higher. During this stage the parasites presumably invade new red cells. The third or sweating stage concludes the episode. The fever subsides and the patient frequently falls asleep to awake feeling relatively well. In vivax (benign tertian malaria), ovale, and falciparum (malignant tertian malaria) infections, red cells are ruptured and paroxysms occur every 48 hours. In malariae infections (quartan malaria) the cycle takes 72 hours. In the early stages of infection the cycles are frequently asynchronous and the fever patterns irregular. As the disease progresses, splenomegaly and, to a lesser extent, hepatomegaly appear. *P falciparum* infection is more serious than the others because of the high frequency of severe or fatal complications with which it is associated.

B. Laboratory Findings: The thick blood film, stained with Giemsa's stain or other Romanowsky stains, is the mainstay of malaria diagnosis. The thin film is used primarily for species differentiation after the presence of an infection is detected on a thick film. In all but falciparum infections the number of red cells infected seldom exceeds 2% of the total cells. Very high red cell infection rates may occur with falciparum infection (20–30% or more). For this reason anemia is frequently much more severe in falciparum malaria. The anemia is normocytic, with poikilocytosis and anisocytosis. During paroxysms there may be transient leukocytosis; leukopenia develops subsequently, with a relative increase in large mononuclear cells. During attacks hepatic function tests often become abnormal, but the tests revert to normal with treatment or spontaneous recovery. Hemolytic jaundice may develop in severe infections.

There are no specific blood chemical findings. In *P malariae* infections a form of nephrosis, with protein and casts in the urine, sometimes occurs in children. Severe falciparum infections may cause renal damage.

Differential Diagnosis

Uncomplicated malaria, particularly when modified by partial immunity, must be distinguished from a variety of other causes of fever, splenomegaly, anemia, or hepatomegaly. Some diseases often considered in the diagnosis of malaria in the tropics include genitourinary tract infections, typhoid fever, infectious hepatitis, dengue, kala-azar, influenza, amebic liver abscess, leptospirosis, and relapsing fever. Examination of blood films is essential to differentiate atypical malaria from some of the above.

Complications

Serious complications of malaria occur primarily in falciparum infections, particularly in those persons who have experienced repeated attacks with inadequate treatment. These complications, jointly referred to as pernicious malaria, include cerebral malaria with headache, convulsions, delirium, and coma; hyperpyrexia, closely resembling heat hyperpyrexia; gastrointestinal disorders resembling cholera or acute bacillary dysentery; and algid malaria, which in certain respects resembles acute adrenal insufficiency. Blackwater fever must be considered apart from other falciparum complications. This acute intravascular hemolytic condition develops in patients with long-standing falciparum infections and a history of irregular quinine dosage. The principal findings are profound anemia, jaundice, fever, and hemoglobinuria. The mortality rate may be as high as 30%, primarily due to anuria and uremia.

Treatment

A. Specific Measures:

1. Chloroquine–An effective agent against all but resistant forms of malaria, and the treatment of choice for these during the acute attack. It will terminate *P falciparum* infections, and prevents relapses of vivax malaria when administered in conjunction with primaquine. Although capable of causing ocular toxicity when used in large doses for prolonged periods, chloroquine causes few toxic symptoms when used in the doses given below. Mild headache, pruritus, anorexia, blurring of vision, malaise, and urticaria may occur. If symptoms become severe, stop the drug and give ammonium chloride, 4 gm initially and 1 gm every 4 hours; acidification promotes excretion of the drug.

a. Therapeutic dosage schedule–Give chloroquine phosphate (Aralen®), 1 gm as initial dose, 0.5 gm (salt) in 6 hours, and 0.5 gm daily for the next 2 days. In an emergency, give chloroquine hydrochloride, 0.2 gm of base IM (0.1 gm in each buttock), repeated in 6 hours if necessary, and follow with oral therapy as soon as possible. It is not necessary to administer this drug intravenously since an effective blood level is rapidly attained by the intramuscular route.

b. Suppressive dosage–Chloroquine phosphate, 0.5 gm weekly, taken on the same day each week. Continue for 8–12 weeks after leaving the endemic area.

2. Amodiaquin dihydrochloride (Camoquin®) is a congener of chloroquine.

a. Therapeutic dosage schedule–Give 0.2 gm (base) every 6 hours for 3 doses, then 0.2 gm twice daily for 2 days.

b. Suppressive dosage–0.4 gm (base) once weekly.

3. Quinine–If none of the more effective and less toxic newer agents are available, quinine is still a useful drug in arresting the acute attack of all types of malaria. Quinine in the following dosages may cause

"cinchonism" (tinnitus, vertigo, deafness, headache, and visual disturbances) in some individuals. The possibility of blackwater fever arising during or at the cessation of therapy appears to be higher in quinine-treated cases.

a. Therapeutic dosage schedule–Give quinine sulfate, 0.65 gm 3 times daily orally for 7–10 days; or quinine dihydrochloride, 0.65 gm in physiologic saline, glucose-saline mixture, or plasma. *Caution:* Inject intravenously by drip (over at least 30 minutes); repeat in 6 hours if necessary; and give no more than 3 injections in 24 hours. Quinine hydrochloride may also be administered by intravenous drip at the rate of 2 gm in 24 hours. Follow with oral therapy as soon as possible.

b. Suppressive dosage–Quinine sulfate, 0.3–0.65 gm daily while in endemic area.

4. Proguanil hydrochloride (Paludrine®) is used for chemosuppression of all forms of malaria. Give 0.1 gm daily or, for partially immune subjects, 0.3 gm once weekly.

5. Pyrimethamine (Daraprim®), although not recommended for the treatment of acute clinical malaria, is an effective agent for suppressive treatment. Suppressive cure is achieved against *P falciparum* infection and sometimes against *P vivax*. Toxicity is very low at the recommended dosage. Give 25 mg weekly on the same day of each week. For children give 12.5 mg weekly (may be dissolved in syrup).

6. Primaquine phosphate–This drug has been shown to be the most effective agent against the tissue forms of *P vivax*, *P malariae*, and *P ovale*. It is employed to eliminate tissue parasites rather than to treat the clinical attack. It will prevent relapses in most cases. The patient must be observed carefully. Severe hemolytic reactions occur in some individuals, especially Negroes, whose red blood cells are deficient in G6PD. Therefore, test for G6PD deficiency before initiating therapy and watch for fall of hemoglobin or reduction in red count.

Dosage for the prevention of relapse is 26 mg (salt) daily in single or divided doses for 14 days. Treatment must be reinforced by standard treatment with chloroquine phosphate or amodiaquin if given during an acute attack.

Some authorities recommend the use of primaquine as a suppressive, combined with chloroquine, in endemic areas. Seventy-eight mg (base) may be taken weekly and continued for 8–12 weeks after leaving the endemic area.

Note: Strains of *P falciparum* resistant to chloroquine and often to many of the other antimalarials have been recorded from Southeast Asia and Latin America. It is necessary to be on the alert for a wider occurrence of resistant strains. Several thousand military (and civilian) *P falciparum* cases in South Vietnam have required quinine therapy, and some of these infections have been refractory to quinine. In chloroquine-resistant cases, combine pyrimethamine, 25 mg orally twice daily for 3 days, and either sulfadiazine, 500 mg orally 4 times daily for 5 days, or dapsone, 25 mg orally daily for 28 days, with quinine, 650 mg orally 3 times daily for 14 days. Deaths have occurred despite intensive chemotherapy. Agranulocytosis and death may complicate dapsone therapy. Malaria must be suspected in persons with acute febrile illness who have traveled in Southeast Asia.

B. General Measures: The nonspecific treatment of malaria is no different from that of any other acute febrile illness.

Prognosis

The uncomplicated and untreated primary attack of vivax, ovale, or falciparum malaria usually lasts 2–4 weeks; that of malariae averages about twice as long (4–8 weeks). Each type of infection may subsequently relapse (once or many times) before the infection terminates spontaneously. Poorly treated or untreated falciparum malaria carries a less favorable prognosis than infections due to the other species because of the tendency to serious complications. When such complications as cerebral malaria and blackwater fever develop, the prognosis is often poor even with treatment. With modern antimalarials the prognosis is good for most malaria infections, even with complications.

Bruce-Chwatt, L.J.: Malaria: Clinical trials of antimalarial drugs. Tr Roy Soc Trop Med Hyg 61:412–426, 1967.

Clyde, D.F., & others: Prophylactic and sporontocidal treatment of chloroquine-resistant *Plasmodium falciparum* from Vietnam. Am J Trop Med 20:1–5, 1971.

Garnham, P.C.C.: *Malaria Parasites and Other Haemosporidia.* Blackwell, 1966.

Hiser, W.H., & others: *Plasmodium vivax* from Vietnam. Response to chloroquine-primaquine. Am J Trop Med 20:402–404, 1971.

Jacob, H.S., & H.H. Jandl: Screening tests for glucose-6-phosphate dehydrogenase deficiency. New England J Med 274:1162–1167, 1966.

Neva, F.A.: Malaria: Recent progress and problems. New England J Med 277:1241–1252, 1967.

Ognibene, A.J.: Agranulocytosis due to dapsone. Ann Int Med 72:521–524, 1970.

Powell, R.D., & W.D. Tigertt: Drug resistance of parasites causing human malaria. Ann Rev Med 19:81–102, 1968.

SIMIAN MALARIA IN MAN

Recent work has demonstrated that *Plasmodium knowlesi* of Malaysian macaque monkeys can be transmitted to man in nature; thus a 5th species of plasmodium has been added to those known to cause malaria in man. *P brasilianum* of South and Central American monkeys is morphologically similar to *P malariae* and transmissible to man experimentally. *P cynomolgi* of Southeast Asian macaques is also readily transmissible to man in the laboratory. A naturally acquired *P cynomolgi* infection in man could be mistaken for *P vivax*.

Chin, W., & others: A naturally acquired quotidian-type malaria in man transferable to monkeys. Science 149:865, 1965.

Coatney, G.R.: Simian malarias in man: Facts, implications, and predictions. Am J Trop Med 17:147–155, 1968.

BURKITT'S TUMOR
(Burkitt's Lymphoma)

Burkitt's lymphoma is included here because recent studies show that it seems to be particularly caused by certain viruses (a herpesvirus or a reovirus; perhaps it is also the agent of infectious mononucleosis) imposed on an abnormal lymphatic-reticuloendothelial system in "big-spleen" disease caused by holoendemic malaria. It is locally quite common in tropical Africa and New Guinea but can occur anywhere, the viruses presumably being only rarely oncogenic in normal subjects. The tumor is most common in children, the youngest being most likely to develop characteristic jaw lesions; otherwise, tumors develop retroperitoneally (causing flaccid paraplegia), in the abdominal viscera or ovaries. There may be massive bilateral breast involvement in adolescents and young adult females. The meninges, brain, and cranial nerves may be involved. Tumors are peculiarly multiple and bilateral, and develop very rapidly. Diagnosis is confirmed histologically by biopsy. Response to treatment by methotrexate, cyclophosphamide, vincristine, and other antimetabolites is good except for lesions protected by the blood-brain barrier, in which case the prognosis is always bad. Spontaneous remissions have been recorded.

Burkitt, D.P.: Etiology of Burkitt's lymphoma—an alternative hypothesis to a vectored virus. J Nat Cancer Inst 42:19–28, 1969.

Wright, D.H.: Burkitt's tumor and childhood lymphosarcoma. Clin Pediat 6:116–122, 1967.

AFRICAN TRYPANOSOMIASIS
(Sleeping Sickness)

Essentials of Diagnosis

- Inconspicuous local inflammatory reaction (trypanosomal chancre).
- Irregular fever, tachycardia, lymphadenitis, splenomegaly, transient rashes.
- Prolonged course (Gambian trypanosomiasis): Personality changes, headache, apathy, somnolence, tremors, speech and gait disturbances, anorexia, malnutrition, coma.
- Rapid course (Rhodesian trypanosomiasis): Findings as above, but lymph nodes less often enlarged.
- Death may occur before signs of CNS involvement appear.

- Trypanosomes in thick blood films or lymph node aspirates (early stages); CSF with trypanosomes, increased cells and protein (late stages).

General Considerations

Rhodesian and Gambian trypanosomiasis are caused by 2 morphologically similar protozoan parasites, *Trypanosoma rhodesiense* and *T gambiense,* found only as the mature trypanosome form in the blood stream, lymph nodes, myocardium, CSF, and brain. The disease occurs focally throughout tropical Africa. Both trypanosomes are transmitted by the bites of tsetse flies (*Glossina sp*).

Clinical Findings

A. Symptoms and Signs: The trypanosomal chancre, a local inflammatory reaction which appears about 48 hours after the tsetse fly bite, is the first sign of infection. Many patients give no history of such a reaction; in others the lesions are painful or pruritic and persist up to 3 weeks. The second stage, invasion of the blood stream and reticuloendothelial system, usually begins several weeks later. Symptoms may appear at once, particularly in rhodesiense infections, or after several years. An irregular fever pattern with persistent tachycardia is characteristic. Transient rashes, often circinate, and scattered areas of firm edema may appear. There may be delayed sensation to pain with deep hyperesthesia. The spleen is usually enlarged. Enlarged, rubbery, and painless lymph nodes, particularly those of the posterior cervical group (Winterbottom's sign) are commonly found in gambiense infection; lymph nodes are not often enlarged in rhodesiense infection. Signs of myocardial involvement appear early in Rhodesian trypanosomiasis. The patient may succumb to myocarditis before signs of CNS invasion appear. Manifestations of the final CNS stage appear within a few weeks or months of onset in rhodesiense infection. Gambian sleeping sickness differs from the acute and virulent Rhodesian form in that it develops more insidiously, starting 6 months to several years from onset. Personality changes, apathy, and headaches are among the early findings. Tremors, disturbances of speech and gait, mania, somnolence, and anorexia appear late. The patient becomes severely emaciated, and finally comatose. Death often results from secondary infection.

B. Laboratory Findings: Lymph node puncture and examination of fresh and stained aspirates is the method of choice for finding *T gambiense* prior to invasion of the CNS. In early rhodesiense infections blood films will usually reveal a few trypanosomes. In advanced cases lumbar puncture is necessary for diagnosis. The CSF, which is clear, colorless, and under normal pressure, shows increased cells (lymphocytes) and elevated protein. Trypanosomes may be demonstrated in the centrifuged CSF specimen. Serologic tests are of little value in diagnosis.

Other laboratory findings include microcytic anemia, increased sedimentation rate, increased serum globulin, and reduced total serum protein.

Differential Diagnosis

Trypanosomiasis may be mistaken for a variety of other diseases, including malaria, kala-azar, cerebral tumors, encephalitis, and cerebral syphilis. Serologic tests for syphilis may be falsely positive in trypanosomiasis. Malaria, suggested by fever and splenomegaly, may be ruled out by blood examinations; kala-azar, considered because of irregular fever, anemia, splenomegaly, and lymphadenitis, can usually be ruled out clinically without resorting to spleen or marrow puncture. Other CNS conditions are differentiated by neurologic examination and lumbar puncture findings.

Prevention

Excretion of pentamidine isethionate and suramin sodium (see below) from the body is slow. Either drug will prevent infection for a considerable time after injection. A single injection of 0.3–0.7 gm of suramin (IM or IV) will give protection for 6–12 weeks. One IM injection of pentamidine (3 mg/kg) will protect against rhodesiense infection for 2 months and against gambiense infection for 3–6 months.

Treatment

A. Specific Measures:

1. Suramin sodium (Naphuride®, Antrypol®) is the drug of choice in the early stages of trypanosomiasis before the CNS is invaded. This organic urea compound is administered intravenously in freshly prepared 10% solution in distilled water. Start treatment with a test dose of 100 mg. For adults, continue with 1 gm doses at 5–7 day intervals to a total of 10 gm. Because of occasional renal toxicity, frequent urinalyses are essential during therapy. Dermatitis and gastrointestinal disturbances are also reported. The drug is contraindicated in renal disease.

2. Pentamidine isethionate (Lomidine®) is a somewhat less effective alternative to suramin in treating early trypanosomiasis. It is administered as a 2% solution intramuscularly. The drug may induce a sudden fall in blood pressure or hypoglycemia if given intravenously. It is contraindicated in renal disease. Administer in doses of 4 mg/kg daily or every other day for 10–15 injections.

3. Tryparsamide, a pentavalent arsenical, has long been used in the treatment of gambiense infections of the CNS. It is much less effective against rhodesiense meningoencephalitis. The drug may cause dermatitis or optic atrophy. Discontinue treatment if eye pain, excessive lacrimation, or photophobia develops. Administer intravenously in a 20% solution in water. The dosage is 20–40 mg/kg, given at weekly intervals to a total course of 10–12 injections. The usual initial dose for adults is 1–1.5 gm; subsequent doses, 2–3 gm. Repeat the course if necessary after a rest period of at least 1 month. A course of suramin or pentamidine should be given simultaneously to remove any parasites remaining in the blood or lymph nodes.

4. Melarsoprol (Mel B®; melarsen oxide/BAL) is effective for the treatment of gambiense and rhodesiense infections of the CNS, but undesirable drug effects are not uncommon. A second course may be given for a relapse, but resistance develops rapidly. Melarsoprol must be given intravenously in 5% solution in propylene glycol. A recently introduced derivative, Mel W®, is water-soluble and may be given intramuscularly or subcutaneously. It is necessary to use either suramin sodium or pentamide isethionate in conjunction with melarsoprol to remove trypanosomes from the blood and lymph nodes. A recommended schedule is 3.6 mg/kg daily for 4 consecutive days, a rest of 7 days, and then a second series of 4 daily doses.

B. General Measures: Good nursing care, treatment of anemia and concurrent infections, and correction of malnutrition are essentials in the management of patients with advanced African trypanosomiasis.

Prognosis

Without treatment, 25–50% of gambiense infections and over 50% of rhodesiense infections are fatal. With treatment, 5–15% of gambiense infections and up to 50% of rhodesiense infections are fatal. Prognosis is considerably more favorable if treatment is started before invasion of the CNS occurs.

Duggan, A.J.: An approach to clinical problems of Gambian sleeping sickness. J Trop Med 62:268–274, 1959.

Editorial: The early signs of trypanosomiasis. Central Africa J Med 12:54, 1966.

Robertson, D.H.H.: The treatment of sleeping sickness (mainly due to *Trypanosoma rhodesiense*) with melarsoprol. Tr Roy Soc Trop Med Hyg 57:176–183, 1963.

AMERICAN TRYPANOSOMIASIS
(Chagas' Disease)

Essentials of Diagnosis

- Unilateral palpebral and facial edema and conjunctivitis (Romaña's sign).
- Hard, edematous, red, and painful cutaneous nodule (chagoma).
- Intermittent fever, lymphadenitis, hepatomegaly, signs and symptoms of acute or chronic myocarditis or meningoencephalitis.
- Demonstration of trypanosomes in blood smears or by culture, animal inoculation, or complement fixation test.

General Considerations

Chagas' disease is caused by *Trypanosoma cruzi*, a protozoan parasite of the blood and tissues of man and many other vertebrates. *T cruzi* is found in wild animals from southern South America to northern Mexico, Texas, and the southwestern USA. Human infection is less widespread. Many species of reduviid bugs (cone-nosed or kissing bugs) transmit the infection, which results from rubbing infected bug feces, passed during feeding, into the bite wound. In the vertebrate host the trypanosomes first multiply close to the point of entry, assuming a leishmanial form at one stage of their development. They then enter the blood stream and later the heart, brain, and other tissues. Further multiplication causes cellular destruction, inflammation, and fibrosis. In these tissues the parasites again assume a leishmanial form during part of each developmental cycle.

Clinical Findings

A. Symptoms and Signs: The earliest finding in the acute infection is either the chagoma or Romaña's sign. In heavily endemic areas initial infection commonly occurs in childhood. The acute form of the disease may be fatal, particularly in infants and young children. In addition to intermittent fever, local lymphadenitis, and hepatomegaly, there may be splenomegaly, psychologic changes, focal neurologic symptoms, convulsions, tachycardia, cardiac enlargement, arrhythmias, and cardiac failure. Myocardial damage dominates the chronic form of the disease; cases are seen with all types and stages of cardiac disorder. Symptomatic chronic CNS infection is rare; also uncommon are megacolon and megaesophagus, caused by damage to nerve plexuses in the bowel or esophageal wall.

B. Laboratory Findings: Trypanosomes are not usually found in large numbers in the blood except in the early stages of the acute infection. *T rangeli,* a nonpathogenic blood trypanosome also found in man in Central America and northern South America, must not be mistaken for *T cruzi.* In the acute stage trypanosomes may also be found in lymph node aspirates. Blood, or material from lymph nodes, marrow, or spleen, may be cultured on NNN medium or inoculated into laboratory mice or rats. In chronic infections xenodiagnosis, which consists of permitting uninfected reduviids to feed on the patient and then examining them for trypanosomal infection, often establishes the diagnosis. The Machado complement fixation test is of presumptive diagnostic value when positive; it should be used in conjunction with other diagnostic methods.

Differential Diagnosis

The early acute infection, with Romaña's sign, might be confused with trichinosis, but palpebral and facial edema is unilateral, not bilateral, and there is no eosinophilia. The chagoma may be mistaken for any of a variety of tropical skin lesions. Kala-azar resembles Chagas' disease in some respects (intermittent fever, hepatomegaly, splenomegaly), but in the former the spleen is much larger, there are no CNS symptoms, and cardiac symptoms usually appear only after anemia becomes severe. Chronic infection in adults, usually myocardial, is not clinically characteristic. Differentiation from other causes of chronic cardiac disease depends upon positive animal inoculation tests, complement fixation tests, or other laboratory procedures.

Treatment

No effective drug is available. Treatment is symptomatic and supportive.

Prognosis

Acute infections in infants and young children are often fatal, particularly when the CNS is involved. Adults with chronic cardiac infections also may ultimately succumb to the disease. Mortality rates are not known because infections are often asymptomatic and unrecognized. Other infections, particularly malaria, may seriously complicate the disease.

Laranja, F.S., & others: Chagas' disease: A clinical, epidemiologic, and pathologic study. Circulation 14:1035–1060, 1956.

LEISHMANIASIS

The 3 types of leishmaniasis are due to 3 species of protozoa related to the trypanosomes and transmitted by sandflies (*Phlebotomus sp*), in which they undergo cyclic development, from animal reservoirs (dogs and rodents). Visceral leishmaniasis (kala-azar) is due to *Leishmania donovani;* cutaneous leishmaniasis (oriental sore) is due to *L tropica;* and mucocutaneous or naso-oral leishmaniasis (espundia) is due to *L braziliensis.*

Cahill, K.M.: The human Trypanosomatidae. III. Leishmaniasis: Kala-azar. New York J Med 63:3405–3409, 1963.
Manson-Bahr, P.E.C., & B.A. Southgate: Recent research on kala-azar in East Africa. J Trop Med 67:79–84, 1964.
Summary of Recent Abstracts. V. Leishmaniasis. Trop Dis Bull 63:609–618, 1966.

1. VISCERAL LEISHMANIASIS
(Kala-Azar)

Essentials of Diagnosis

- Irregular fever, insidious and chronic; onset may be acute.
- Progressive and marked splenomegaly and hepatomegaly.
- Progressive anemia, leukopenia, and wasting.
- Progressive darkening of skin, especially on forehead and hands.
- Leishman-Donovan bodies demonstrable in splenic and sternal puncture smears.
- Nonspecific complement fixation test positive frequently and early.

General Considerations

Kala-azar is widespread geographically wherever sandfly vectors are found. In each locale the disease has its own peculiar clinical and epidemiologic features. It occurs in the Mediterranean littoral, equatorial Africa, Ethiopia, eastern India, central Asia and China, and South America. Although man is the major reservoir, animal reservoirs such as the dog are important. The incubation period varies from weeks to months. The parasites exist in one form in the body, as oval Leishman-Donovan bodies which parasitize reticuloendothelial cells and lead to their proliferation. They are easily detected in the spleen, liver, and bone marrow, and may be found in blood.

Clinical Findings

A. Symptoms and Signs: The fever is generally mild and is not usually associated with prostration. The characteristic double daily remission may escape detection. The spleen usually enlarges much more than the liver and may be palpable by the second month. Enlargement is painless, steady, and rapid, usually in waves with bouts of fever. At first doughy, the spleen finally becomes large and hard. Wasting occurs without anorexia.

Post-kala-azar dermal leishmaniasis may appear 1–2 years after apparent cure, especially in India but also in the Sudan and China. This may simulate leprosy as multiple hypopigmented macules or nodules which develop on pre-existing lesions. There may even be a degree of leontiasis. They take the form of erythematous patches, often on the face.

B. Laboratory Findings: There is usually progressive gross leukopenia (seldom over 3000/cu mm after the first 1–2 months), with relative or (usually) absolute monocytosis. Nevertheless, an occasional leukocytosis, due to concurrent sepsis, may be confusing. Diagnosis must always be confirmed by demonstrating Leishman-Donovan bodies in blood, sternal marrow, liver, or spleen. Blood culture is highly successful, and a nonspecific complement fixation test has been devised which is often positive in the first month but is meaningless in the presence of chronic pulmonary tuberculosis. Diagnosis may be supported by a positive formol-gel test, in which a drop of commercial formalin in 1 ml of serum produces opacity in 2 hours.

Differential Diagnosis

Kala-azar which is of subacute or acute onset resembles enteric fever (but there is no toxemia and Widal's test is negative) or malaria (in which case response to antimalarial therapy may aid the diagnosis, since concomitant malaria parasites may be present in the blood in kala-azar). Many patients present with abdominal enlargement, weakness, and wasting; these patients have irregular fevers and the spleen and liver are palpable, which differentiates this disease from brucellosis. Characteristic double (rarely triple) daily remissions (evening and morning) occur early.

Chronic cases may also be confused with infectious mononucleosis, leukemia, anemias due to other causes, and tuberculosis. Post-kala-azar dermatitis may resemble leprosy.

Treatment

General treatment must include a diet rich in protein and vitamins. Specific treatment is primarily with pentavalent antimonials, to which cases from India respond best whereas those from the Sudan are most resistant. Children tolerate antimonials well. In all cases resistance to antimonials can develop with inadequate dosage. In addition to antimonials, aromatic diamidines (see below) are powerful agents. They should be preceded by injection of epinephrine or an antihistaminic to minimize reactions. They are less effective for post-kala-azar dermal lesions. Fresh solutions only should be given and ampules stored away from heat. Intravenous injection must be given slowly.

(1) Antimony sodium gluconate (Pentostam®, Solustibosan®, Stibinol®), 0.2 gm followed by 0.3 gm daily as 5% solution IV for patients weighing over 30 kg. Continue treatment for 6–15 days.

(2) Stilbamidine isethionate is used only in antimony-resistant cases and must be given with great care because it is unstable and may produce immediate reactions or delayed trigeminal hyperesthesia. The initial adult dose is 25 mg IV daily, increasing by 10–20 mg daily to 2 mg/kg daily. The most that should be given is about 10 injections or a total of about 15 mg/kg.

(3) Ethylstibamine (Neostibosan®), 0.2 gm initially IV, then 0.3 gm IV daily or every 2 days for 16 doses.

(4) Urea stibamine (carbostibamide), IV in 10 ml water daily, in doses of 0.05, 0.1, 0.15, and subsequently 0.2 gm for about 15 days.

(5) Pentamidine isethionate (Lomidine®), 2–4 mg/kg IV, or preferably IM, daily or on alternate days, up to 15 injections.

Prognosis

Therapy is effective but there may be relapses. Keep the patient under observation for at least 6 months. The spleen, blood picture, and body weight should return to normal. Splenectomy before repetition of a course of treatment may be advisable in refractory cases.

See references above.

2. CUTANEOUS LEISHMANIASIS
(Oriental Sore)

Cutaneous swellings follow the bites of sandflies infected with *Leishmania tropica* after an interval of weeks or even years. Oriental sore is widespread in distribution, including Latin America. The swellings may ulcerate and discharge pus, or they may remain dry. Dry and moist forms are caused by locally distinct leishmanias.

Lesions tend to heal spontaneously, but secondary infection may lead to gross extension. Moist ulcerated lesions are covered with a scab and exude purulent material as a result of secondary infection.

Leishmanias cannot be detected in purulent discharge but may be seen in scrapings from the cleaned edge. Needle biopsy material from the edge can be cultured in NNN medium.

Single lesions may be cleaned, curetted, covered, and left to heal. Antibiotics may be required for secondary infection. Ethylstibamine (Neostibosan®) as for visceral leishmaniasis is effective.

Cahill, K.M.: The human Trypanosomatidae. IV. Cutaneous and mucocutaneous leishmaniasis. New York J Med 63:3549–3553, 1963.

Kurban, A.K., & others: Histopathology of cutaneous leishmaniasis. Arch Dermat 93:396–401, 1966.

Walton, B.C., & others: Treatment of American cutaneous leishmaniasis with cycloguanil pamoate. Am J Trop Med 17:814–818, 1968.

3. MUCOCUTANEOUS (NASO-ORAL) LEISHMANIASIS
(Espundia)

Espundia is a chronic infection, caused by *L braziliensis,* which occurs principally in Brazil, Paraguay, and Peru. It is characterized by cutaneous and naso-oral involvement, either by direct extension or, more often, metastatically. The initial lesions on exposed skin, often the ears, take more varied forms than is usual with oriental sore. Naso-oral involvement may follow healing of lesions, even after a considerable interval, or may develop simultaneously. The anterior part of the cartilaginous septum is commonly involved, and there may be gross and hideous erosion, including bone. Regional lymphadenitis is common. Leishman-Donovan bodies may be found in aspirated tissue-juice, and leishmanias may be cultured. If an injection of a suspension of killed leptomonads produces a fully developed papule in 2 days which disappears after a week (positive Montenegro's test), the diagnosis is fairly certain. A negative Montenegro's test is meaningless.

Specific treatment may be combined, if necessary, with local or systemic antibiotics or sulfonamides. Give antimony sodium gluconate (Pentostam®, Solustibosam®, Stibinol®), 600 mg IM or IV daily for 6–10 days; or amphotericin B, 0.25–1 mg/kg, by slow infusion daily or every 2 days for up to 8 weeks. Single doses containing 350 mg base of cycloguanil pamoate IM are not producing uniformly good results. Ethylstibamine (Neostibosan®) may be given as for visceral leishmaniasis. Pyrimethamine (Daraprim®) appears to be a promising alternative drug in the treatment of espundia.

See references above.

GIARDIASIS
(Lambliasis)

Giardia lamblia is a cosmopolitan intestinal flagellate protozoon which normally lives in the duodenum or jejunum and is usually of low pathogenicity or non-pathogenic for man. Cysts may be found in large numbers in the stools of asymptomatic persons. In some people, however, heavy giardia infection seems to cause irritation of the upper small bowel with resultant acute or chronic diarrhea (often alternating with constipation), mild abdominal cramps, flatulence, abdominal distention, and tenderness. The bile ducts and gallbladder may be invaded, causing a mild cholecystitis. Possible coincident giardiasis should be sought in troublesome dyspepsias, peptic ulcers, or pylorospasm. The distinctive cysts may be found in formed stools, and cysts and trophozoites may be found in liquid stools.

Treatment with quinacrine hydrochloride (Atabrine®), 0.1 gm orally 3 times daily for 5 days, will result in a 90% cure rate. The treatment may be repeated if necessary, or give metronidazole (Flagyl®), 0.25 gm 3 times daily for 10 days.

Hoskins, L.C., & others: Clinical giardiasis and intestinal malabsorption. Gastroenterology 53:265–279, 1967.

Yardley, J.H., & T.M. Bayless: Giardiasis. Gastroenterology 52:301–304, 1967.

BALANTIDIASIS

Balantidium coli is a large ciliated intestinal protozoon found throughout the world, particularly in the tropics. Infection results from ingestion of viable cysts from formed stools of humans or swine, the reservoir hosts. In the new host the cyst wall dissolves and the trophozoite may invade the mucosa and submucosa of the large bowel and terminal ileum, causing abscesses and irregularly rounded ulcerations. Many cases are asymptomatic. Chronic recurrent diarrhea, alternating with constipation, is the most common clinical manifestation, but attacks of severe dysentery with bloody mucoid stools, tenesmus, and colic may occur intermittently. Diagnosis is made by finding trophozoites in liquid stools and cysts in formed stools. The treatment of choice is oxytetracycline (Terramycin®) or related antibiotic, 1 gm daily in 4 divided doses for 4–5 days. Carbarsone, diiodohydroxyquin (Diodoquin®), iodochlorhydroxyquin (Vioform®), and acetarsone (Stovarsol®) have each been effective in a few patients. Asymptomatic infections may terminate spontaneously. In properly treated mild to moderate symptomatic cases the prognosis is good, but severe infections are sometimes fatal despite treatment.

Arean, V.M.: Balantidiasis. A review and report of cases. Am J Path 32:1089–1115, 1956.

TOXOPLASMOSIS

The protozoan parasite *Toxoplasma gondii* is found throughout the world in man and in many species of animals. Domestic cats have been incriminated in the transmission of the organism to man. The organism lives both intracellularly and extracellularly in the reticuloendothelial system, parenchymal cells, and exudates. Symptomatic infection is rare in adults; the active infection is most often encountered in the newborn, who acquire their infection in utero. Infants and young children may have hydrocephaly or microcephaly, psychomotor disturbances, cerebral calcifications, and chorioretinitis. In acquired infections of adults there may be fever, malaise, arthralgia, maculopapular rash and lymphadenopathy, conjunctivitis, and myocarditis. Toxoplasma organisms may be directly identified in smears of blood, bone marrow, CSF, or exudates. Inoculation into laboratory animals or serologic tests, including the Sabin-Feldman dye test (titers above 1:512), the indirect fluorescent antibody test, complement fixation tests, and neutralization tests are often necessary for diagnosis. The skin test is primarily a survey tool and is of little diagnostic value.

Acute infections may be treated with pyrimethamine (Daraprim®), 25–50 mg daily for 1 month, plus trisulfapyrimidines, 1 gm 4 times daily for 1 month. The course of infection should be followed during and after treatment by repeated Sabin-Feldman and complement fixation tests.

The congenital disease is often fatal, and if the infant survives the acute infection he is likely to be handicapped by serious residual CNS and ocular lesions. The acquired disease is usually asymptomatic or mild, but acute infection in adults may be fatal.

Feldman, H.A.: Toxoplasmosis. New England J Med 279:1370–1375, 1431–1437, 1968.

COCCIDIOSIS
(Isosporosis)

Two cosmopolitan intestinal species of coccidia, *Isospora belli* and *I hominis*, are found in man. The infection is usually sporadic, and is most common in the tropics and subtropics, although it has been reported in the USA. Infections result from the ingestion of viable cysts, and it is probable that the protozoa multiply in the intestinal mucosa. Many cases may be asymptomatic. About 1 week after ingestion of viable cysts, mild fever, lassitude, and malaise may appear, followed by mild diarrhea and vague abdominal discomfort. The infection is self-limited and symptoms usually subside within 1–2 weeks. Stool concentration technics are usually necessary to find the immature oocysts of *I belli* or the mature sporocysts of *I hominis*. Bed rest and a bland diet for a few days is the only treatment necessary.

Faust, E.C., & others: Human isosporosis in the western hemisphere. Am J Trop Med 10:343–349, 1961.

PNEUMOCYSTIS PNEUMONIA

Pneumocystis infection must be considered in the diagnosis of interstitial pneumonias in infants or in those whose resistance has been lowered. *P carinii* is a protozoon of uncertain relationships normally infecting various animals. Infections in the lungs are usually latent but occasionally produce an interstitial plasma cell pneumonitis in man and at least in household rodents also. The incubation period is 3–8 weeks. Those most liable to pneumonitis are premature or marasmic infants, children and adults receiving corticosteroids, cytotoxic drugs, or antibiotics over extended periods; or those suffering from agammaglobulinemia or leukemia. Outbreaks may occur in nurseries. The pneumonitis lasts for 1–4 weeks. Patients are characteristically poor risks, and the mortality is high (up to 50%). Physical signs are relatively slight. X-rays show the interstitial pneumonia. Cysts with 8 nuclei may be found in large numbers in the foamy contents of alveoli and bronchioles and among the infiltrating eosinophils and plasma cells, but can only rarely be detected in sputum or tracheal swabs.

Lung puncture biopsy has been reported to be successful. Treat with pentamidine isethionate (Lomidine®), 4 mg/kg IM daily for 12–14 days. Attention must be given to whatever is lowering the resistance of the subject, eg, give transfusions, stop corticosteroids.

Rykind, D., & others: Transplantation pneumonia. JAMA 189:808–812, 1964.

White, W.F., Saxton, H.M., & I.M.P. Dawson: Pneumocystis pneumonia. Report of three cases in adults and one in a child; with a discussion of the radiological appearance and predisposing factors. Brit MJ 2:1327–1337, 1961.

●   ●   ●

General Bibliography

Adams, A.R.D., & B.G. Maegraith: *Clinical Tropical Diseases,* 4th ed. Blackwell, 1966.

Chandler, A.C., & C.P. Read: *Introduction to Parasitology,* 10th ed. Wiley, 1961.

Chernin, E.: Trichomoniasis, toxoplasmosis. Chap 32, pp 567–589, in: *Preventive Medicine.* Clark, D.W., & B. MacMahon (editors). Little, Brown, 1967.

Faust, E.C., Russell, P.F., & R.C. Jung: *Craig and Faust's Clinical Parasitology,* 8th ed. Lea & Febiger, 1970.

Hunter, G.W., III, Frye, W.W., & J.C. Swartzwelder: *A Manual of Tropical Medicine,* 4th ed. Saunders, 1966.

Parasitic Disease Drug Service, National Communicable Disease Center. *See:* Public Health Reports 84:541, 1969.

Russell, P.F., & others: *Practical Malariology,* 2nd ed. Oxford, 1963.

Woodruff, A.W.: Advances in treatment of tropical diseases. Practitioner 201:638–645, 1968.

24...

Infectious Diseases: Metazoal

Frederick L. Dunn, J. Ralph Audy, & Robert S. Goldsmith

TREMATODE (FLUKE) INFECTIONS

SCHISTOSOMIASIS
(Bilharziasis)

Essentials of Diagnosis

- Transient pruritic petechiae on skin recently exposed to fresh water.
- Fever, malaise, nausea, urticaria, and eosinophilia.
- Either (1) diarrhea, dysentery, abdominal pain, anorexia, weight loss, splenomegaly, and ascites; or (2) terminal hematuria, urinary frequency, urethral and bladder pain.

General Considerations

Three blood flukes or trematodes are responsible for this worldwide complex of diseases. *Schistosoma mansoni,* the cause of intestinal schistosomiasis, is widespread in Egypt and is common locally in tropical Africa, eastern South America, and the Caribbean (including Puerto Rico). Vesical or urinary schistosomiasis, caused by *S haematobium,* is common in Egypt and in Africa and parts of the Middle East. Asiatic intestinal schistosomiasis, due to *S japonicum* infection, is important in China, Japan, and the Philippines. Various species of snails, the intermediate hosts, are infected by larvae hatched from eggs reaching fresh water in feces or urine. After development infective larvae (cercariae) leave the snails and penetrate human skin or mucous membranes which come in contact with water. Immature *S mansoni* migrate to branches of the inferior mesenteric veins in the large bowel wall. Here the adults mature, mate, and deposit eggs. Many eggs reach the bowel lumen and are passed in the feces; others lodge in the bowel wall and induce inflammation, fibrosis, ulceration, and granuloma, papilloma, or polyp formation. Eggs may be carried to the liver, where similar changes occur, provoking periportal cirrhosis. Diffuse hepatic cirrhosis in advanced cases is probably due to associated nutritional deficiency. Portal hypertension results in splenomegaly and ascites. Eggs may lodge ectopically in the lungs, spinal cord, or other tissues.

S japonicum adults lie in branches of the superior and inferior mesenteric veins in the small and large bowel walls. Eggs are passed in the stool or lodge in the bowel wall, provoking changes similar to those noted above. Because greater numbers of eggs are produced by *S japonicum,* the resulting disease is more extensive and severe. Eggs are frequently carried to the liver and occasionally to the CNS. Cirrhosis and portal hypertension are common as the immature flukes migrate through the blood vessels of various organs.

The adult *S haematobium* matures in the venous plexuses of the bladder, prostate, and uterus. Eggs are passed in the urine or retained in the tissues, particularly the bladder wall and the female genital organs. In addition to fibrosis, ulceration, and granuloma and papilloma formation, there is often bladder wall calcification, chronic cystitis, pyelitis, or pyelonephritis. Bladder cancer is common in advanced cases in Egypt.

Clinical Findings

A. Symptoms and Signs: The first sign of infection, an itchy petechial rash at sites of penetration of cercariae, lasts no more than 2–3 days. A second clinical stage occurs 4–5 weeks later as the immature flukes migrate through the blood vessels of various organs. Symptoms at this time are primarily allergic and vary greatly in severity. In addition to fever, urticaria, malaise, and respiratory symptoms, the liver and spleen may be temporarily enlarged. The patient again becomes asymptomatic in 2–8 weeks. The final clinical stage begins 6 months to several years after infection as lesions develop around eggs imbedded in the tissues. The course and severity of the disease depend upon the number of adult worms present, the number of eggs produced, and the sites of the lesions they provoke. Diarrhea, dysentery, and abdominal pain are common in the early stages of intestinal infections. Anorexia, weight loss, polypoid intestinal tumors, and signs of portal hypertension and hepatic insufficiency appear as the disease progresses. Death commonly results from intercurrent infection. The symptoms of urinary tract disease (particularly terminal hematuria, frequency, and pain) depend upon the extent of the pathologic changes described above. Ureteral and renal damage may result in fatal uremia, or the patient may die of bladder carcinoma many years after first being infected. Advanced schistosomiasis usually develops only after repeated reinfections.

B. Laboratory Findings: Eosinophilia is common during the migrations of the immature flukes, but the count usually returns to normal later. Diagnosis depends upon detection of eggs in urine or feces, on biopsy technics, or on serologic and skin tests. In urine eggs are found most easily by examining the terminal drops, preferably after the patient has exercised, or the sediment of a 24-hour urine collection. Eosinophils in the urine should not be mistaken for pus cells. Eggs may be found in stool specimens by direct examination, but some form of concentration is usually necessary and repeated examinations are often needed to find eggs in light infections. *S mansoni* infections are often diagnosed by rectal biopsy; biopsy through a cystoscope may confirm the diagnosis of urinary schistosomiasis. The complement fixation test becomes positive a few weeks after infection occurs and may remain so for several years. Few infected persons give negative reactions. The intradermal test is less valuable for clinical purposes.

Differential Diagnosis

Schistosomiasis mansoni should be considered in all unresponsive gastrointestinal disorders in persons who have been in endemic areas. Early intestinal schistosomiasis may be mistaken for amebiasis, bacillary dysentery, or other causes of diarrhea and dysentery. Later the various causes of portal hypertension or of bowel papillomas and polyps must be considered. Vesical schistosomiasis must be differentiated from other causes of hematuria, prostatic disease, genitourinary tract malignancies, and bacterial infections of the urinary tract.

Complications

Among the many complications of these diseases are transverse myelitis (*S mansoni* eggs in the spinal cord), seizures, optic neuritis, paralysis, mental disorders (*S japonicum* eggs in the brain), liver failure (*S mansoni, S japonicum*), ruptured esophageal varices due to portal hypertension, uremia and bladder neoplasms (*S haematobium*), and chronic pulmonary disease (periarteritis and endarteritis, primarily due to *S mansoni* eggs).

Treatment

A. General Measures: For patients with long-standing schistosomiasis and nonreversible lesions, supportive measures, improvements in diet, and corrective surgical procedures are usually more important than specific chemotherapy. Such therapy may even be dangerous in cases with hepatic insufficiency. At best, drugs prevent further progression and the development of complications. Surgical measures include removal of papillomas, polyps, and early carcinoma; splenectomy, portal shunt operations, craniotomy, and other neurosurgical procedures.

B. Specific Measures: In less advanced disease drug therapy often causes clinical and parasitologic cure, ie, relief of symptoms and shrinking or elimination of bladder and bowel ulcerations and granulomas. Periodic laboratory follow-up is essential for at least 6 months.

1. **Antimony potassium (or sodium) tartrate** is an inexpensive and effective but highly toxic drug. The patient must be at bed rest during treatment. Start with 30 mg in a 1–2% solution in 5% glucose or normal saline. Administer slowly intravenously with care to avoid leakage (to prevent tissue sloughing). On the 3rd day increase the dose to 60 mg; on the 5th day to 90 mg; and on the 7th day to 120 mg. On the 9th day and alternate days thereafter, give 140 mg.

A total of 1.8 gm is usually adequate for *S haematobium* infections; for both forms of intestinal schistosomiasis, use a total dose of 2.4 gm.

"Slow treatment" with this or with stibophen (Fuadin®), giving 1 full dose of an antimonial* every week for 12–16 weeks, has much to recommend it, especially for heavy infections in an early stage of advance.

Common side-effects include nausea, vomiting, diarrhea, abdominal pain, syncope, tachycardia, dyspnea, paroxysmal coughing, and erythematous rashes. More severe toxic effects include exfoliative dermatitis, toxic liver necrosis, and toxic myocarditis. Cardiac, pulmonary, renal, hepatic, CNS, and febrile diseases are contraindications; but treatment in the presence of schistosomal hepatitis may be practicable if prednisone is simultaneously administered.

2. **Stibophen (Fuadin®)** is less effective but far less toxic than antimony potassium tartrate. Only pulmonary and renal disease contraindicate its use. It may be given intramuscularly, an advantage with children and debilitated patients. It is supplied in 5 ml ampules of a 6.3% solution. Use 1.5 ml for a test dose, then 4 ml IM every weekday (5 days/week) to a total of 40 ml. After 1–2 weeks, the course should be repeated. Fuadin® is often effective in *S mansoni* infections and urinary schistosomiasis and occasionally effective in *S japonicum* infections using 8–10 ml daily for 10 days.

3. **Sodium antimony dimercaptosuccinate (Astiban®)** is an intramuscular preparation given in a course of 5 injections over a period of 2½–5 weeks. The average total dose for adults in recent trials was 40 mg/kg body weight. The drug is apparently as effective as stibophen (Fuadin®) in both *S mansoni* and *S haematobium* infections. Numerous side-effects include nausea, vomiting, headache, pruritus, and rashes. The short, convenient course outweighs these effects; Astiban® is suitable for outpatient use.

4. **Lucanthone hydrochloride (Miracil D®, Nilodin®)** is administered orally and is thus suitable for mass treatment, but only for children under 16. Numerous side-effects include anorexia, nausea, vomiting, dizziness, vertigo, tremors, insomnia, and muscular weakness. Cardiac and renal diseases are contraindications. The dosage is 15 mg/kg body weight/day divided into 3 doses and given for 7 days. The drug provides symptomatic relief in *S haematobium* and *S mansoni* infections and is often curative. It is of little value against *S japonicum*.

5. **Hycanthone (Etrenol®)**, the hydroxymethyl derivative of lucanthone, is undergoing clinical evaluation for the treatment of schistosomiasis.

6. **Niridazole (Ambilhar®)**, a nitrothiazole derivative, is reported to be effective in treating *S mansoni*

and *S haematobium* infections. Action against *S japonicum* has not been sufficiently investigated. (See also Amebiasis in Chapter 23.) Adult schistosomes are killed by the drug, which is relatively well tolerated and perhaps suitable for mass therapy. High cure rates have been achieved on oral doses of 25 mg/kg daily in 2 divided doses for 7 days. Drug side-effects include occasional nausea, vomiting, anorexia, headache, T wave depression, and possible temporary suppression of spermatogenesis. Deep brown coloration of the urine disappears after treatment. Effects due to destruction of worms and release of foreign proteins may appear after 3–4 days of therapy: tiredness, CNS excitability (rare), convulsions (very rare). The manufacturers note that Ambilhar® should not be given together with isoniazid.

7. Surgical filtering of *S mansoni* adults from the portal system should be considered whenever splenectomy is contemplated. A single dose of tartar emetic allows most worms to be washed back into the portal venous system, whence they are filtered by tapping the portal vein via the splenic and returning filtered blood to the saphenous vein. Thousands of worms have been removed in this way from a single case.

Prognosis

With treatment the prognosis is good in early and light infections if reinfection does not occur. In advanced disease with extensive involvement of the intestines, liver, bladder, or other organs, the outlook is poor even with treatment.

Clark,W.D.: Acute schistosomiasis in 10 boys. Ann Int Med 73:379–385, 1970.

Goldsmith, E.I., & others: Surgical recovery of schistosomes from the portal blood: Treatment of the parasitization in man. JAMA 199:235–240, 1967.

Jordan, P.: Chemotherapy of schistosomiasis. Bull New York Acad Med 44:245–258, 1968.

Lehman, J.S., & others: Hydronephrosis, bacteriuria, and maximal urine concentration in urinary schistosomiasis. Ann Int Med 75:49–55, 1971.

McMahon, J.E.: A study of some clinico-pathological manifestations in *Schistosoma mansoni* infections in Tanzania. Ann Trop Med 61:302–309, 1967.

Oliver-González, J.: Our knowledge of immunity to schistosomiasis. Am J Trop Med 16:565–567, 1967.

Wright, W.H.: Schistosomiasis as a world problem. Bull New York Acad Med 44:301–312, 1968.

FASCIOLOPSIASIS

The large intestinal fluke, *Fasciolopsis buski,* is a common parasite of man and pigs in China, Formosa, Indochina, Assam, and Bengal. When eggs shed in stools reach water they hatch to produce free-swimming larvae which penetrate and develop in the flesh of snails. Cercariae escape from the snails and encyst on various water plants. Man is infected by eating these infected plants, usually water chestnuts or caltrops, uncooked. Adult flukes, mature in about 3 months, live in the small intestine attached to the mucosa or buried in mucous secretions.

After an incubation period of several months, manifestations of gastrointestinal irritation appear in all but light infections. Symptoms in severe infections include cramping epigastric and hypogastric pains, diarrhea, intermittent constipation, anorexia, and nausea. Ascites and edema, particularly of the face, may occur later, apparently as a result of absorption of toxic metabolic products of the worms. Death may result from cachexia or intercurrent infection.

Leukocytosis with moderate eosinophilia is common. The diagnosis depends upon discovery of eggs, or occasionally flukes, in the stools.

Crystalline hexylresorcinol (Crystoids Anthelmintic®, Caprokol®) is the most effective drug. For adults give 1 gm orally in 0.1–0.2 gm capsules on an empty stomach in the morning. For children, give 0.1 gm/year of age to age 10. A light supper and prepurgation on the previous evening with sodium sulfate is desirable. Two hours after administration, repeat purgation with sodium sulfate. Repeat treatment in 3–4 days. Two courses are usually sufficient; occasionally 3 or more courses may be necessary. For somewhat greater effectiveness administer the drug transduodenally, 1 gm in 20 ml of water.

Tetrachloroethylene may be used if hexylresorcinol is not effective or not available. Administer as for hookworm disease. Alternatively, stilbazium iodide (Monopar®) may be given as for strongyloidiasis.

Heavy infections with severe toxemia may be fatal, particularly in children, in spite of treatment to remove the flukes. In all other cases, with treatment, the prognosis is good.

McCoy, O.R., & T.C. Chu: *Fasciolopsis buski* infection among school children in Shaohsing, and treatment with hexylresorcinol. Chinese MJ 51:937–944, 1937.

FASCIOLIASIS

Infection by *Fasciola hepatica,* the sheep liver fluke, results from ingestion of metacercariae on watercress or other aquatic vegetables. It is prevalent in sheep-raising countries, especially in Latin America and the Mediterranean littoral. Light infections may be asymptomatic; heavy infections may present as biliary colic with hepatitis. The adult flukes in the liver may be extremely destructive.

Diagnosis is made by detecting eggs (which resemble those of fasciolopsis) in the feces.

Fascioliasis may be treated with emetine hydrochloride, giving 1 mg/kg body weight IM up to a maximum of 65 mg daily for 7 days. Complete recovery is slow even if all flukes are killed. Bithionol (Bitin®) may also be given as for paragonimiasis.

Yoshida, Y., & others: Two cases of human infection with Fasciola sp and the treatment with bithionol. Jap J Parasitol 11:411–420, 1962.

CLONORCHIASIS

Infection by *Clonorchis sinensis,* the liver fluke, is endemic in parts of Japan, Korea, China, Formosa, and Indochina. Imported cases are seen in the USA. Certain snails are infected as they ingest eggs shed into water in human or animal feces. Larval forms escape from the snails, penetrate the flesh of various fresh water fish, and encyst. Human infection results from eating such fish, either raw or undercooked. In man the ingested parasites excyst in the duodenum and ascend the bile ducts into the bile capillaries where they lodge and mature. The adults remain in the liver throughout their lives, shedding eggs in the bile. Biliary epithelial hyperplasia and fibrosis develop around the worms. In heavy infections eggs may lodge in the liver parenchyma, causing granulomatous reactions.

Most patients harbor few worms and remain permanently free of symptoms from the time of infection. In some cases, with heavy infection, immature flukes migrating into the biliary capillaries may cause malaise, fever, liver tenderness, and jaundice. These symptoms are transient. With heavy infection symptoms later reappear after the flukes have matured. Progressive liver enlargement, tenderness, and right upper quadrant pain are the common findings. Vague abdominal symptoms, diarrhea, weakness, weight loss, jaundice, tachycardia, and a variety of other findings have been attributed to advanced clonorchiasis.

During the stage of invasion by the immature flukes there is often eosinophilia of 10–40%; later the count usually falls to normal. In advanced disease liver function tests will indicate parenchymal damage; the first test to become abnormal as the disease progresses is usually that for urine urobilinogen. Eggs may be found for diagnosis in the stools or duodenal aspirates.

Although there is no satisfactory specific drug and treatment is primarily symptomatic and supportive, prolonged administration of chloroquine phosphate should be tried. Although it apparently does not kill the flukes, it often reduces or stops the egg output, and may provide symptomatic relief. The adult dosage is 250 mg of the base orally 3 times daily for 6 weeks or as long as it is tolerated. Side reactions (nausea, anorexia, headache, pruritus, dizziness) in the first 2 weeks of therapy are common and may require temporary reduction of dosage; later these symptoms usually subside.

Emetine has been recommended, and a course (as for amebiasis) may be combined with chloroquine treatment.

Clonorchiasis is rarely a fatal disease in itself, but patients with advanced infections and impaired liver function may succumb more readily to other diseases. The prognosis is good for light to moderate infections.

Chung, H.-L., & others: Hexachloroparaxylol in treatment of clonorchiasis sinensis in animals and man. Chinese MJ 84:232–247, 1965.

Ehrenworth, L., & R.A. Daniels: Clonorchiasis sinensis. Clinical manifestations and diagnosis. Ann Int Med 49:419–427, 1958.

PARAGONIMIASIS

Paragonimus westermanii, the lung fluke, commonly infects man throughout the Far East, and locally in West Africa and northern South America. Other mammals may serve as alternate hosts for the adult flukes. Eggs reaching water, either in sputum or feces, hatch in 3–6 weeks. The miracidia penetrate snails and develop, and the emergent cercariae encyst in the tissues of crabs and crayfish. When these crustaceans are eaten raw—or, more usually, when crabs are crushed for extraction and wooden vessels or children's fingers are contaminated by metacercariae and later ingested—immature flukes excyst in the small intestine and penetrate into the peritoneal cavity. Most migrate through the diaphragm and enter the peripheral lung parenchyma; some may lodge in the peritoneum, the intestinal wall, the liver, or other tissues, but usually fail to mature. Rarely they may migrate to the brain or spinal cord. A capsule of fibrous and inflammatory tissue forms around the parasite as it matures. Later the capsule swells and ruptures into a bronchiole. Fluid containing eggs, blood, and inflammatory cells is released and expectorated in the sputum.

The infection is asymptomatic until the flukes mature and begin producing eggs. The insidious onset is marked by low-grade fever, cough, or hemoptysis. The cough is dry at first; later it becomes productive of viscous sputum, rusty or blood-flecked. Pleuritic chest pain is common. The condition is chronic and slowly progressive. Dyspnea, signs of bronchitis and bronchiectasis, weakness, malaise, and weight loss are apparent in heavy infections. Many patients with light infections do not appear seriously ill. Parasites in the peritoneal cavity or intestinal wall may cause abdominal pain, diarrhea, or dysentery. Those in the CNS, depending upon their location, may give rise to seizures, palsies, or meningoencephalitis.

Slight leukocytosis and eosinophilia are common. The sputum may contain eosinophils and Charcot-Leyden crystals in addition to blood and eggs. Eggs are more readily demonstrated by examining smears of centrifuged sodium hydroxide-treated sputum sediment. Eggs are also found in stool specimens, particularly after concentration. Skin and complement fixation tests are used as aids in diagnosis in some Far Eastern countries.

Bithionol (Bitin®), 40 mg/kg body weight, should be given on alternate days for 10–15 doses (20–30 days). Full courses of emetine, intramuscularly, followed by chloroquine, have been recommended in the past, but bithionol is now the drug of choice. Side-effects of bithionol, usually mild, are principally gastrointestinal irritation (diarrhea, nausea). Otherwise, treatment is symptomatic and supportive. Antibiotics may be necessary to control secondary pulmonary infection.

Barring reinfection, light to moderate infections subside spontaneously in 6–7 years and require little treatment. Heavy infections may be progressive for years, even without reinfection, and may be eventually fatal, particularly if there is concurrent tuberculosis. The prognosis is unfavorable for the less common CNS infections.

Harter, D.H., & S.I. Morse: Pulmonary paragonimiasis: Report of a case. Ann Int Med 51:1104–1109, 1959.

Yokogawa, M., & others: Chemotherapy of paragonimiasis with bithionol. Am J Trop Med 12:859–869, 1963.

CESTODE INFECTIONS

TAPEWORM INFECTIONS
(See Also Echinococcosis)

Essentials of Diagnosis

- Finding of segments in clothing or bedding.
- Most infections asymptomatic; occasionally diarrhea or vague abdominal pains.
- Characteristic eggs or segments in the stool.
- Rarely (in cysticercosis), seizures, mental deterioration, signs and symptoms of internal hydrocephalus.

General Considerations

A number of species of adult tapeworms have been recorded as human parasites, but only 6 infect man frequently. *Taenia saginata,* the beef tapeworm, and *T solium,* the pork tapeworm, are cosmopolitan and common. The fish tapeworm, *Diphyllobothrium latum,* is most often found in northern Europe, Japan, and the Great Lakes region of the USA. The dwarf tapeworms, *Hymenolepis nana* and *H diminuta,* are cosmopolitan throughout the tropics and subtropics. The dog tapeworm, *Dipylidium caninum,* is occasionally reported in children in Europe and North America.

The adult tapeworm consists of a head (scolex), which is a simple attachment organ, a neck, and a chain of individual segments (proglottids). While *H nana* adults are rarely more than 2.5–5 cm (1–2 inches) long, beef, pork, and fish tapeworms often exceed 10 feet in length. Gravid segments detach themselves from the chain and escape from the host intact, or rupture, releasing eggs in the feces. In the case of *T saginata,* the most common tapeworm found in man in the USA, eggs are expelled from the segments after they pass from the host. The eggs hatch when ingested by cattle, releasing embryos which encyst in muscles as cysticerci. Man is infected by eating undercooked beef

containing viable cysticerci. In the human intestine the cysticercus develops into an adult worm.

The life cycle of *T solium* is similar except that the pig is the normal host of the larval stage. Man may be infected by the larval pork tapeworm, however, if he accidentally ingests *T solium* eggs. As in the pig, the larvae find their way to many parts of the body and encyst as cysticerci. Only those lodging in the brain ordinarily produce symptoms (cerebral cysticercosis).

The intermediate hosts of the fish tapeworm are various species of fresh water crustaceans and fish. Eggs passed in human feces are taken up by crustaceans which are in turn eaten by fish. Human infection results from eating raw or poorly cooked fish.

The *H nana* life cycle is unusual in that both larval and adult stages of the worms are found in the human intestine. Adult worms expel eggs in the intestinal lumen. Newly hatched larvae invade the mucosa, where they develop for a time before returning to the lumen to mature. *H nana,* requiring no intermediate host, can be transmitted directly from man to man. A similar dwarf tapeworm, *H diminuta,* is a common parasite of rodents. Many arthropods, such as rat fleas, beetles, and cockroaches, serve as intermediate hosts. Man is infected by accidentally swallowing the infected arthropods, usually in cereals or stored products. Multiple dwarf tapeworm infections are the rule, whereas man rarely harbors more than one or 2 of the larger adult tapeworms.

Dipylidium caninum infections generally occur in young children living in close association with infected dogs or cats. Transmission results from swallowing the infected intermediate hosts, fleas or lice.

Spargana, or larval stages of certain tapeworms in frogs, reptiles, birds, and some mammals, may produce a variety of clinical conditions (sparganosis) ranging from local tender swellings (eg, eye) to a form of cutaneous larva migrans. One form is proliferating, invading all soft tissues. Infections are acquired from frog or other meat poultices, eating the raw flesh of small animals, or ingesting infected copepods in water. The diagnosis is usually made after surgical removal, but local physicians will make early diagnoses. Infections in animals are widespread; in humans more local, depending upon individual habits.

Clinical Findings

A. Symptoms and Signs: Adult tapeworms in the human intestine ordinarily cause no symptoms. Occasionally weight loss or vague abdominal complaints may be associated with heavy infections or large worms. Heavy infections with *H nana* may, however, cause diarrhea, abdominal pain, anorexia, weight loss, and nervous disturbances, particularly in children. In 1–2% of those harboring the fish tapeworm, a macrocytic anemia of considerable severity may be found. The anemia may be accompanied by glossitis, lethargy, and signs of nerve damage. In cysticercosis most larval tapeworms lodge in muscles or connective tissues where they remain silent and eventually calcify; in the brain, however, they may cause a wide variety of manifestations. Epileptic seizures, mental deterioration, personality disturbances, and internal hydrocephalus with headache, giddiness, papilledema, and nerve palsies are among the more common consequences of brain involvement.

B. Laboratory Findings: Infection by a beef tapeworm is often discovered by the patient when he finds one or more segments in his clothing or bedding. To determine the species of worm such segments must be flattened between glass slides and examined microscopically. Most tapeworm infections are detected by laboratory examination of stool specimens for eggs and segments. In cysticercosis x-rays often reveal calcified cysticerci in muscles, but those in the CNS rarely calcify and cannot be seen radiologically. When cysticerci lodge in the 4th ventricle the CSF pressure may be abnormal, and the fluid may show increased numbers of mononuclear cells and tapeworm scolices. Skin and complement fixation tests are also available as aids in diagnosis of cysticercosis.

When fish tapeworm macrocytic anemia is discovered, the marrow will be found to be megaloblastic, and hydrochloric acid is usually present in the stomach. This anemia is attributed to the affinity of the worm for dietary vitamin B_{12}.

Differential Diagnosis

Since most tapeworm infections are asymptomatic, a differential diagnosis need rarely be considered. When vague abdominal complaints and weight loss are present stool examinations are essential to rule out other forms of intestinal parasitism and primary gastrointestinal disorders. Fish tapeworm anemia may mimic pernicious anemia, but the presence of gastric hydrochloric acid and positive stool examinations will establish the diagnosis.

Complications

Pork tapeworm infection may be complicated by cysticercosis if the patient unwittingly contaminates his hands with eggs and transfers them to his mouth. For such a patient vomiting is also a hazard in that eggs may be propelled up the small intestine into the stomach, where they may hatch. The macrocytic anemia occasionally associated with *D latum* infection also constitutes a potentially serious complication.

Treatment

A. Specific Measures:

1. Niclosamide (Yomesan®) is the drug of choice for all tapeworms except *T solium*. Give 4 tablets (2 gm) thoroughly chewed as a single dose for *T saginata* and *D latum,* and daily for 5−7 days for *H nana.* Niclosamide rarely has side-effects and can be given to outpatients without prior or posttreatment purges.

2. Quinacrine hydrochloride (Atabrine®) is the drug of choice for *T solium* and effective for others, but care should be taken to avoid vomiting (some possibility of subsequent cysticercosis). On the day preceding treatment the patient should have only a liquid diet, with nothing but water or milkless tea or coffee for supper. On the evening before treatment, give a saline purge or a soapsuds enema. On the morning of treatment, withhold breakfast and confine the patient to bed. Give chlorpromazine (Thorazine®), phenobarbital, or a similar sedative to prevent vomiting. One hour later, give quinacrine in the range of 0.5 gm for children weighing 40−75 lb; to 1 gm for adults or children weighing over 100 lb. The dose may be divided to reduce the risk of vomiting, but all of it must be given within about 30 minutes. Administer quinacrine by duodenal tube if the patient persistently regurgitates the drug.

Two hours later (2 hours after the last dose, if divided doses are given), repeat the saline purge. No food should be permitted until the bowels move copiously.

Cure depends upon death or evacuation of the head (scolex). Evacuations should be collected in a basin of warm water, and toilet paper must be disposed of separately to allow search for the head and proglottids. Quinacrine absorbed by the head fluoresces under ultraviolet radiation (Wood's light, as used for ringworm). If no head is found, continue to examine the stools for eggs or proglottids once a month for 6 months. Repeat treatment if stools become positive.

3. Hexylresorcinol—Give 1 gm in 20 ml water by duodenal tube. Follow in 2 hours with a sodium or magnesium sulfate purge. Examine stools for the head of the worm. Crystoids Anthelmintic® as administered in ascariasis is the drug of choice for the treatment of light infections with *Hymenolepis nana* (dwarf tapeworm). For heavy infections use quinacrine hydrochloride as for treatment of *Taenia saginata* infections.

4. Dichlorophen, 6 gm as a single dose, should be used if quinacrine fails.

5. Bithionol (Bitin®), 50−70 mg/kg body weight in a single dose, should be given if other treatment fails (see Paragonimiasis, above).

6. Aspidium oleoresin—Use of this drug, which is toxic and frequently contraindicated, is no longer justified for helminths that cause relatively little trouble and are amenable to the newer drugs.

B. General Measures: Hospitalization is recommended for the treatment of persons with tapeworm infection. The success of treatment depends upon the cooperation of the patient, the physician, and the laboratory personnel. Proper pretreatment preparation of the patient and adequate postpurgation examination of stools for the head of the tapeworm are necessary. The stools should be examined after 6 months.

Prognosis

Because the prognosis is often poor in cerebral cysticercosis, the eradication of a *T solium* infection is a matter of much greater urgency than that of the other tapeworm infections, which are usually benign. With careful treatment adult tapeworms can be eliminated safely and with minimal discomfort to the patient.

Afshar, A.: Cysticercosis in Iran. Ann Trop Med 61:101−103, 1967.

Jopling, W.H., & A.W. Woodruff: Treatment of tapeworm infections in man. Brit MJ 2:542−544, 1959.

ECHINOCOCCOSIS
(Hydatid Disease)

Essentials of Diagnosis

- Cystic tumor of liver, lung, or, rarely, bone, brain, or other organs.
- Allergic manifestations, including urticaria, asthma, pruritus.
- Eosinophilia (5–50%).
- History of close association with dogs in an endemic area.
- Positive complement fixation and skin tests.
- Positive x-ray findings are frequently found.

General Considerations

Human echinococcosis results from parasitism by the larval stage of the small tapeworm, *Echinococcus granulosus.* This tapeworm is found in various hosts throughout the world, but the areas of heaviest human infection are those where sheep are raised, notably South America, Greece, and other Mediterranean countries. In North America echinococcosis occurs sporadically, but it is a problem only in Alaska and northwestern Canada, where Indians and Eskimos are occasionally infected. The definitive host of the adult worm is usually the domestic dog; other canines, including wolves, foxes, and jackals are locally important hosts. The sheep is the common host for the larval worm, but cattle, hogs, and, in northwestern North America, caribou and moose may also be infected. Man acquires the infection by ingesting eggs transferred from hand to mouth. The source of eggs is usually the fur of infected dogs. Once swallowed, the eggs liberate embryos which invade the blood stream through the intestinal wall and are carried to the liver. Most larvae are trapped and encyst (as hydatid cysts) in the liver; some may reach the lung, where they develop into pulmonary hydatids; only rarely do larvae reach the brain, bones, skeletal muscles, kidneys, or spleen.

Hydatid cysts are normally unilocular. Multilocular or alveolar cysts are due to infection by *E multilocularis,* mostly in Europe but also in Latin America and Australasia; it might be encountered in man in Alaska. Man typically is infected from soil or berries, etc, contaminated by eggs from fox feces. Slow growth in the liver provokes intrahepatic portal hypertension with hepatomegaly and no fever. The diagnosis is usually made at autopsy.

Clinical Findings

A. Symptoms and Signs: A liver cyst often remains silent for 5–10 years until it becomes large enough to be palpable or visible as an abdominal swelling. Such cysts rarely produce pressure effects, and cause no symptoms unless they begin to leak or are ruptured. When fluid and hydatid sand does escape from a cyst, pruritus, urticaria, asthma, and other allergic manifestations may appear and the eosinophil count rises. Jaundice and biliary colic with urticaria are a characteristic triad. If the cyst ruptures suddenly,

anaphylaxis and even sudden death may occur, or metastases will follow. Pulmonary cysts cause no symptoms (unless leaking occurs) until they become large enough to obstruct the bronchi, causing segmental collapse, or to erode into a bronchus and rupture. Cysts in the brain, symptomatic at a much earlier stage, may cause seizures or symptoms of increased intracranial pressure.

B. Laboratory Findings: When clinical findings, history, and x-ray point to hydatid cyst, the diagnosis can be confirmed with the Casoni intracutaneous test, positive in about 86% of cases, and the complement fixation test, positive in about 90% of cases. The eosinophil count is usually about 5–20% in asymptomatic cases, but it may go as high as 50% when allergic symptoms are present. Diagnosis may occasionally be made by examination of hydatid sand coughed up from a ruptured pulmonary cyst. Because of the danger of leakage or rupture, diagnostic aspiration of suspected hydatid cysts should never be undertaken. The final diagnosis is often made only by examination of cyst contents after surgical removal.

Differential Diagnosis

Hydatid cysts in any site may be mistaken for a variety of malignant and nonmalignant tumors or for abscesses, both bacterial and amebic. In the lung a cyst may be confused with an advanced tubercular lesion. Syphilis may also be confused with echinococcosis. Allergic symptoms arising from cyst leakage may resemble those associated with many other diseases.

Complications

Sudden rupture of a cyst leading to anaphylaxis and sometimes death is the most important complication of echinococcosis. If the patient survives the rupture he still faces the danger of multiple secondary cyst infections arising from seeding of daughter cysts. Segmental lung collapse, secondary infections of cysts, secondary effects of increased intracranial pressure, and severe renal damage due to kidney cysts are other potential complications.

Treatment

The only definitive treatment is surgical removal of the intact cysts, preferably preceded by inoculation into the cyst of hydrogen peroxide, Lugol's iodine, glycerine, or formalin. Often, however, the presence of a cyst is only recognized when it begins to leak or when it ruptures. Such an event calls for vigorous treatment of allergic symptoms or emergency management of anaphylactic shock. There is no treatment for alveolar cysts in the liver.

Bunamidine derivatives have been reported to be effective (see Nature 206:408–409, 1965) and should be tested further.

Prognosis

Patients may live for years with relatively large hydatid cysts before their condition is diagnosed. Liver and lung cysts often can be removed surgically without great difficulty, but for cysts in sites less accessible to surgery the prognosis is less favorable. The prognosis is always grave in secondary echinococcosis and with alveolar cysts. About 15% of patients with echinococcosis may eventually die because of the disease or its complications.

Bonakdarpour, A.: Echinococcocus disease: A report of 112 cases from Iran and a review of all cases from the United States. Am J Roentgenol 99:660–667, 1967.

Hutchison, W. F.: Serodiagnosis of echinococcus infection. Am J Trop Med 17:752–755, 1968.

Taiana, J.A.: Thoracic hydatid echinococcosis: Diagnosis and treatment. Dis Chest 49:8–14, 1966.

Webster, G.A., & T.W.M. Cameron: Epidemiology and diagnosis of echinococcosis in Canada. Canad MAJ 96:600–607, 1967.

Williams, J.F., Adaros, H.L., & A. Trejos: Current prevalence and distribution of hydatidosis with special reference to the Americas. Am J Trop Med 20:224–236, 1971.

Wilson, J.F., Diddams, A.C., & R.L. Rausch: Cystic hydatid disease in Alaska. A review of 101 autochthonous cases of *Echinococcus granulosus* infection. Am Rev Resp Dis 98:1–15, 1968.

NEMATODE (ROUNDWORM) INFECTIONS

TRICHINOSIS
(Trichiniasis)

Essentials of Diagnosis

- Muscle pains and tenderness, fever, periorbital edema, and splinter hemorrhages.
- Nausea, vomiting, cramps, and diarrhea.
- History of ingestion of raw or improperly cooked pork.
- Eosinophilia (as high as 75%).
- Positive skin test, muscle biopsy, and serologic tests.

General Considerations

Trichinosis is an acute infection caused by the roundworm, *Trichinella spiralis*. Although cosmopolitan in distribution, for dietary reasons this parasite is a greater problem in many temperate areas than in the tropics. It is a common parasite of garbage-fed hogs in the USA, and autopsy figures suggest that 10–20% of the human population have been infected at one time or another. Man acquires the infection by eating encysted larvae in raw or undercooked pork, bear, or walrus. In the stomach and duodenum the larvae emerge and rapidly mature. Mating takes place and the female worms burrow into the small intestinal mucosa, producing gastrointestinal symptoms which may be mild or severe depending upon their numbers. The females discharge larvae which migrate in the blood stream to many parts of the body. Larvae reaching striated muscle encyst and remain viable for several years. Calcification of the cysts usually begins within a year. The larvae which do not reach muscle are eventually destroyed. Adult worms and larvae are only rarely found in the stool.

Clinical Findings

A. Symptoms and Signs: The clinical picture varies considerably in severity depending upon the number of larvae disseminated, the tissues invaded, and the general health of the patient; thus the acute disease may be mild or fatal. Gastrointestinal symptoms, if any, usually occur within 2–3 days after eating infected pork. These irritative symptoms are followed a few days later by manifestations of larval migration and muscle invasion including fever, chills, muscle pains and tenderness, difficulty in swallowing and speaking, splinter hemorrhages, periorbital edema, edema of other dependent parts, urticaria, conjunctival and retinal hemorrhages, and photophobia. Still later, inflammatory reactions around larvae that have failed to reach striated muscle may produce meningitis, encephalitis, myocarditis, pneumonitis, and peripheral and cranial nerve disorders. If the patient survives, the fever usually subsides and recovery begins in the 4th week after onset of symptoms. Vague muscle pains and malaise may persist for several more months.

B. Laboratory Findings: Eosinophilia appears in the 2nd week after onset of symptoms, rises to a maximum of 20–75% in the 3rd or 4th week, and then slowly declines to normal. A delayed reaction to the trichinella skin test (noted only after 12–24 hours) occurs early in the disease (4th to 7th days), while an immediate reaction to the test (noted after 5 minutes) usually occurs from the 3rd week on. The skin test may remain positive up to 7 years after recovery. Precipitation and complement fixation tests become positive in the 2nd or 3rd week of the disease. The precipitation test may remain positive up to 2 years, the complement fixation test up to 9 months. Stool examinations rarely reveal either adult worms or larvae, but encysted larvae may be demonstrated by muscle biopsy (deltoid, biceps, gastrocnemium) in the 3rd to 4th weeks. Chest x-rays during the acute phase may show disseminated or localized infiltrates.

Differential Diagnosis

Mild cases and those with atypical symptoms are often difficult to diagnose. Because of its protean manifestations, trichinosis may resemble many other diseases. (A list of at least 50 such diseases has been compiled.) Moderate to severe infections with some or all of the most typical signs and symptoms can, however, usually be diagnosed readily. There are often several patients with similar symptomatology at the same time, and this is often the clue that leads to the diagnosis. A latex flocculation test is convenient for occasional use in laboratories.

Complications

Among the more important complications are secondary bacterial pneumonia, cerebral involvement, pulmonary embolism, and cardiac failure.

Treatment

Treatment is supportive and symptomatic. Severe acute cases require hospitalization and excellent nursing care. Corticotropin (ACTH) and the corticosteroids provide effective relief for the acute symptoms. A reduction of the eosinophil count, disappearance of fever and splinter hemorrhages, and a general improvement in the clinical state of the patient are guides which should be employed to determine the efficacy of treatment. In the acute stage, treat with relatively large doses of either drug for the first 24—48 hours. In the subacute stage, therapy may have to be continued for several days or weeks to prevent recurrence. Give in reduced dosage sufficient to keep symptoms under control. Thiabendazole (Thibenzole®, Mintezol®) has been used with reported success to decrease the severity of symptoms in acute trichinosis. Further trials are recommended. An oral dosage of 25 mg/kg body weight twice daily may be given for 2—4 days. Side-effects may occur (see Strongyloidiasis, below.) Successful therapy with a combination of thiabendazole and pyrvinium pamoate has also been reported.

Prognosis

The mortality rate for clinical trichinosis in the USA is probably about 5%. Death may occur in 2—3 weeks in overwhelming infections; more often it occurs in 4—8 weeks from a major complication such as cardiac failure or pneumonia.

Gray, D.F., Morse, B.S., & W.F. Phillips: Trichinosis with neurological and cardiac involvement. Ann Int Med 57:230—234, 1962.

Schoenfeld, M.R., & G.T. Edis: Trichinosis and glomerulonephritis. Arch Path 84:625—626, 1967.

Zimmerman, W.J., Steele, J.H., & I.G. Kagan: The changing status of trichiniasis in the US population. Pub Health Rep 83:957—966, 1968.

TRICHURIASIS
(Trichocephaliasis)

Essentials of Diagnosis

- Most infections are silent; heavy infections may cause abdominal pain, distention, flatulence, and diarrhea.
- Characteristic barrel-shaped eggs in the stool.

General Considerations

Trichuris trichiura is a common intestinal parasite of man throughout the world, particularly in the subtropics and tropics. The small slender worms, often called whipworms, attach themselves to the mucosa of the large intestine, particularly the cecum. The worms cause symptoms only when present in very large numbers. Eggs passed in the feces require 2—4 weeks for larval development after reaching the soil before becoming infective. New infections are acquired by direct ingestion of infective eggs.

Clinical Findings

A. Symptoms and Signs: Light to moderate infections rarely cause symptoms. Heavy to massive infections may be accompanied by a variety of symptoms arising from irritation of the mucosa. Among the most common of these are abdominal pain, tenesmus, diarrhea, distention, flatulence, nausea, vomiting, and weight loss. Heavy infections are most often found in malnourished young children. Bowel perforation with peritonitis and rectal prolapse may occur.

B. Laboratory Findings: Detection of whipworm eggs in the stool is usually essential for diagnosis. Eosinophilia (5—20%) is common with all but light infections, and hypochromic anemia has been attributed to heavy infection when there is erosion and sloughing of the mucosa.

Treatment

Asymptomatic light or moderate infections may be left untreated. For other infections, give 500 ml of 0.1% hexylresorcinol as an enema to be retained for 1 hour. This may be followed by thiabendazole, 25 mg/kg (maximum, 1.5 gm) orally twice daily for 2 days. Dithiazanine iodide (Abminthic®) was effective but too toxic and has been withdrawn from the market in the USA.

Khandaker, R.K., Kabir, A.M.F., & A. Hoque: Incidence and contribution of *Trichuris trichiura* infestation in gastrointestinal disorders. J Trop Med 71:176—177, 1968.

Vilela, M. de P., Zucas, A.W., & J. Iglesias: The therapy of trichuriasis with a combination of thiabendazole and pyrvinium pamoate. J New Drugs 5:86—89, 1965.

ASCARIASIS

Essentials of Diagnosis

- Pneumonitis with fever, cough, hemoptysis, urticaria, and accompanying eosinophilia.
- Vague abdominal discomfort and colic.
- Inflammatory reactions in organs and tissues invaded by wandering adult worms.
- Characteristic ova in the stool; larvae in the sputum.

General Considerations

Ascaris lumbricoides, a large intestinal roundworm, is the most common of the intestinal helminths of man. It is cosmopolitan in distribution, although it flourishes best in warm, humid climates. In temperate regions it is generally associated with low standards of personal hygiene. The adult worms live in the small intestine. After fertilization, the female produces enormous numbers of characteristic eggs which are carried out to the soil in feces. Under suitable conditions the eggs become infective, containing an active larva, in 2–3 weeks. Man is infected by ingestion of the mature eggs in fecally contaminated food and drink. The eggs hatch in the small intestine, releasing motile larvae which penetrate the wall of the small intestine and reach the right heart via the mesenteric venules and lymphatics. From the heart they move to the lung, burrow through the alveolar walls, and migrate up the bronchial tree into the pharynx, down the esophagus, and back to the small intestine. The larvae mature and female egg production begins about 60–75 days after ingestion of the infective eggs. The large adult worms, 20–40 cm long, may live for a year or more.

Clinical Findings

A. Symptoms and Signs: No symptoms arise from the early migration of the larvae after hatching. In the lung, however, they damage capillary and alveolar walls as they force their way through. Considerable hemorrhage may result from this trauma, and accumulations of leukocytes and serous exudates in and around the airspaces may lead to consolidation. Pneumonitis occasionally develops with heavy infections. Symptoms and signs include fever, cough, hemoptysis, rale , and other evidences of lobular involvement. Eosinophilia is usual at this stage, and urticaria is not uncommon. After passage through the lungs it is believed that the larvae may go astray, lodging in the brain, kidney, eye, spinal cord, or skin. Many bizarre symptoms may result from such invasions.

Small numbers of adult worms in the intestine usually produce no symptoms. With heavy infection vague abdominal discomfort and colic may occur, particularly in children. Ascaris infection in childhood can lead to marked nutritional impairment when a high parasite load is associated with a low protein intake. Intact worms are occasionally passed. Mild allergic manifestations, particularly urticaria and eosinophilia, may persist during the intestinal phase. When the infection is heavy, and particularly if the worms are aroused by dietary indiscretion or certain oral medications, wandering may occur. Adult worms may be coughed up, vomited, or passed out through the nose. They may also force themselves into the common bile duct, the pancreatic duct, the appendix, diverticula, and other sites. Mechanical blockage and inflammation usually result. With very heavy infestations masses of worms may cause intestinal obstruction and even bowel perforation, eg, during typhoid fever. It is important that ascaris infections be cured prior to bowel surgery because the worms have been known to break open suture lines postoperatively.

B. Laboratory Findings: The diagnosis usually depends upon finding the characteristic eggs in stool specimens. Occasionally a spontaneously passed adult worm reveals a previously unsuspected infection. There are no characteristic alterations of the blood picture during the intestinal phase. Skin tests are of no value in diagnosis. During the pulmonary phase there may be eosinophilia, and larvae may occasionally be found in the sputum.

Differential Diagnosis

Ascariasis must be differentiated from allergic disorders such as urticaria, Löffler's syndrome, and asthma. The pneumonitis associated with ascariasis is similar to other types of pneumonitis, especially that occurring with hookworm or strongyloides infection. Ascaris-induced pancreatitis, appendicitis, diverticulitis, etc must be differentiated from other causes of inflammation of these tissues.

Complications & Sequelae

Bacterial pneumonia may be superimposed upon pneumonitis resulting from larval migration. During the migratory stage allergic manifestations may be severe.

Treatment

Reports suggest that intragastric and intrarectal oxygen reduce worm hypermotility.

Ascaris and hookworm infections often go together. Treat for ascaris first and then for hookworm – bephenium for ancylostoma; tetrachloroethylene for necator (see below).

A. Piperazine: Piperazine is the drug of choice. Many brands of syrups and tablets of piperazine citrate or phosphate are available. They occasionally cause headache, dizziness, and visual disturbances. Usually each ml of syrup contains the equivalent of 100 mg piperazine hexahydrate; tablets usually contain 250 or 500 mg. The following daily doses may be given at any time and without special diet or purgation. If necessary, repeat after 1 week.

Up to 30 lb	1 gm	
30–50 lb	2 gm	Once daily for 2
50–100 lb	3 gm	consecutive days
Over 100 lb	3.5 gm	

B. Thiabendazole: This is as effective as piperazine, but side-effects are probably more frequent. Give 25 mg/kg body weight orally twice daily for 2 days. See Strongyloidiasis, below.

C. Hexylresorcinol: Especially for heavy infestations, reduce the diet on the day before treatment and allow a very light meal in the evening; then give no food until at least 5 hours after taking the hexylresorcinol. Alcohol is contraindicated before and during treatment. Hexylresorcinol, 5 hard gelatin capsules (crystoids), 0.2 gm (total 1 gm), is given in the morning on an empty stomach. These are to be swallowed whole, not chewed. Doses for children: Under 6 years of age, 0.4 gm; 6–8 years, 0.6 gm; 8–12 years, 0.8 gm. Two hours later give 30 gm sodium sulfate in water to remove the worms from the bowel. Repeat 2 hours later if necessary for purgation. Stool examination should be made 1 week later on 3 successive days to determine efficacy of treatment. Treatment may be repeated in 3 days if necessary.

D. Diethylcarbamazine Citrate (Hetrazan®): Give 3–6 mg/kg body weight orally 3 times daily for 7–11 days. A syrup preparation containing Hetrazan® powder in a concentration of 30 mg/ml is recommended for small children. Administer 12 mg/kg body weight once a day for 4 days or 6–10 mg/kg body weight 3 times daily for 7–10 days. When Hetrazan® is used for eradication of *Ascaris lumbricoides,* pretreatment fasting and posttreatment purgation are not necessary.

E. Pyrantal pamoate (Combantrin®) in a single oral dose of 10 mg/kg body weight has recently been reported to achieve a 100% cure rate in 10 days and is felt to be superior to piperazine. Experience with this drug has been limited.

F. Tetramisole (Decaris®): This new drug, now undergoing clinical investigation, is reported to be highly effective as a single oral dose of 2.5 mg/kg.

Prognosis

A heavy infection is usually not dangerous as long as the adult worms stay in their normal habitat, but the long list of major complications caused by wandering adults, plus the possibility of intestinal obstruction, requires that such infections be treated as soon as they are recognized.

Bell, W.J., & S. Nassif: Comparison of pyrantal pamoate and piperazine phosphate in the treatment of ascariasis. Am J Trop Med 20:584–588, 1971.

Sommers, H.M.: Intestinal nematode infestations and their laboratory diagnosis. Clin Pediat 4:515–522, 1965.

Tripathy, K., & others: Effects of ascaris infections on human nutrition. Am J Trop Med 20:212–218, 1971.

STRONGYLOIDIASIS

Essentials of Diagnosis

- Pruritic dermatitis at sites of penetration of larvae.
- Malaise, cough, urticaria.
- Colicky abdominal pain, flatulence, diarrhea alternating with constipation.
- Eosinophilia; characteristic larvae in fresh stool specimens.

General Considerations

Strongyloidiasis is caused by the roundworm, *Strongyloides stercoralis.* It is common in tropical and subtropical areas throughout the world. In the USA it is prevalent in the southeastern states. The adult female worm burrows into the mucosa of the intestinal villi and lays eggs within the tissues. The duodenum and jejunum are most heavily infected. The eggs develop into rhabditiform larvae which are passed in the feces. The free-living rhabditiform larvae then develop into infective filariform larvae. These larvae penetrate the skin of the next victim, enter the blood stream, and are carried to the lungs where they escape from capillaries into alveoli and ascend the bronchial tree to the glottis. The larvae are then swallowed and carried to the small intestine, where maturation to the adult stage takes place. The time from skin penetration to egg laying by the mature adult is about 4 weeks. The life span of the adult worm may be as much as 5 years.

Auto-infection may occur if the rhabditiform larvae are retained in constipated feces or if there is fecal contamination of the perianal region. Such infection may also occur in the presence of diarrhea. Auto-infection is responsible for the persistence of strongyloidiasis in persons who have left endemic areas.

Clinical Findings

A. Symptoms and Signs: The clinical picture is not distinctive; diagnosis depends upon laboratory demonstration of larvae in the feces. At the points of entry of larvae into the skin there may be erythema and a fine papular, intensely pruritic eruption. Papules may develop into vesicles, coalesce, and discharge serous fluid, or they may become hemorrhagic. Malaise and fever may occur with the dermatitis in severe cases. Vague signs and symptoms during the migratory stage may include malaise, anorexia, fever, and cough. Urticaria is not uncommon. Secondary bacterial pneumonia may be initiated by a heavy larval migration through the lungs. An asymptomatic period of a few weeks usually precedes the gastrointestinal symptoms, of which the most common is localized or diffuse colicky abdominal pain. Diarrhea is common, often alternating with constipation or periods of normal bowel activity. With heavy infection, diarrhea may be persistent and accompanied by lassitude, nausea, vomiting, flatulence, weight loss, and debilitation.

A hyperinfection syndrome with strongyloides has been described as a complication during the course of treatment for other serious diseases.

B. Laboratory Findings: During the stage of larval migration there is eosinophilia of 10–50% as well as leukocytosis up to 20,000/cu mm. In the intestinal phase eosinophilia may range from normal to 10%, but the white count is usually normal except in severe acute infections. A mild anemia may be present in this phase. The diagnosis is based on finding the characteristic rhabditiform larvae in a fresh stool specimen. Eggs are rarely found in the stool even in the case of severe diarrhea. Duodenal intubation may be required to establish the diagnosis when larvae are not found in the stools. Duodenal contents are examined directly or after concentration. Larvae are occasionally found in the sputum or urine. Fecal cultivation may produce larvae or free-living adults after about 48 hours. Serologic and intradermal tests are not of diagnostic value.

Differential Diagnosis

Because of the varied signs and symptoms at different stages of the infection, diagnosis may be difficult. During the stage of skin invasion, hookworm ground itch and creeping eruption due to *Ancylostoma braziliense* are the conditions which most closely resemble strongyloides ground itch, particularly because of the ankle-foot distribution of the skin lesions. During the later stages of the infection many causes of transient pneumonitis, urticaria, and gastrointestinal symptoms may have to be considered. Sputum and stool examinations for parasites will help to rule out other helminthic infections (suggested by the presence of eosinophilia).

Complications

Larval migration through the lungs may initiate a secondary bacterial pneumonia. Hepatitis, cholecystitis, myocarditis, paralytic ileus, and meningitis may occur with massive infections. Associated hookworm or ascaris infection is not uncommon.

Treatment

In the case of concurrent infestation with ascaris or hookworm, which is not uncommon, treat these infections first and strongyloidiasis afterward.

A. Thiabendazole (Thibenzole®, Mintezol®): This is the drug of choice. Give 25 mg/kg body weight orally twice daily for 2 days. Side-effects, including headache, weakness, nausea, vomiting, vertigo, and decreased mental alertness, are very common and may be severe. Crystalluria and leukopenia have been reported.

B. Dithiazanine iodide (Abminthic®, Delvex®) is a toxic drug that has been withdrawn from the market in the USA. It should be used only for heavy and clinically significant infections, if at all, and the patient must be followed closely.

C. Stilbazium iodide (Monopar®) shows promise and may be given in a dosage of 4 gm in divided doses over 3–4 days. It colors the stools red.

Prognosis

Favorable except in massive infections, usually resulting from auto-infection, which may result in intractable diarrhea, severe debilitation, and complications as noted above.

Amir-Ahmadi, H., & others: Strongyloidiasis at the Boston City Hospital: Emphasis on gastrointestinal pathophysiology and successful therapy with thiabendazole. Am J Digest Dis 13:959–973, 1968.
Cruz, T., & others: Fatal strongyloidiasis in patients receiving corticosteroids. New England J Med 275:1093–1096, 1966.
Rivera, E., & others: Hyperinfection syndrome with *Strongyloides stercoralis.* Ann Int Med 72:199–204, 1970.

ENTEROBIASIS
(Pinworm Infection)

Essentials of Diagnosis

- Perianal pruritus, usually nocturnal, associated with insomnia and restlessness.
- Vague gastrointestinal symptoms.
- Adult worms in stool; eggs on skin of perianal area.

General Considerations

Enterobius vermicularis, a short spindle-shaped roundworm often called the pinworm, is worldwide in distribution and the most common cause of helminthic infection of man in the USA. Man is the only host for the parasite. Children are more often affected than adults. The adult worms inhabit the cecum and adja-cent bowel areas, lying with their heads loosely attached to the mucosa. When the fertilized female worms become gravid they migrate down the colon and out onto the skin, where eggs are deposited in large numbers. The females die after oviposition. The eggs become infective in a few hours and may then infect man if transferred to the mouth by inhalation or, more commonly, by hand, food, or drink contamination. The eggs are resistant to household disinfectants and drying, and may remain infective in dust for a considerable time. Retroinfection occasionally occurs when the eggs hatch on the perianal skin and the larvae migrate through the anus into the large intestine. If infective eggs are swallowed they hatch in the duodenum and the larvae migrate down to the cecum, moulting twice en route. The development of a mature ovipositing female from an ingested egg requires about 2 months.

Clinical Findings

A. Symptoms and Signs: The most common and most important symptom is pruritus of the perianal area, particularly at night. This must be distinguished from similar pruritus due to mycotic infections, allergies, and psychologic disorders. Insomnia, restlessness, enuresis, and irritability are common symptoms, particularly in children. Many mild gastrointestinal symptoms—abdominal pain, nausea, vomiting, diarrhea, anorexia—have also been attributed to enterobiasis, although the association is difficult to prove. It is claimed that these symptoms result from mucosal irritation by the adult worms in the cecum, appendix, and surrounding portions of the bowel.

B. Laboratory Findings: Except for a modest eosinophilia (4–12%), the blood picture is usually normal. The diagnosis depends upon finding adult worms in the stool or eggs on the perianal skin. Eggs are seldom found on stool examination. The most reliable diagnostic technic consists of applying a short strip of pressure-sensitive cellulose tape to the perianal skin and spreading it on a slide for study. Three such preparations made on consecutive mornings before bathing or defecation will establish the diagnosis in about 90% of cases. Five to 7 such examinations are necessary before the diagnosis can be ruled out.

Complications

It has been postulated that the presence of large numbers of worms in the cecum may predispose to appendicitis, but the evidence for this is inconclusive. Female worms occasionally migrate into the vagina, uterus, and fallopian tubes, where they may encyst.

Treatment

A. General Measures: Treat all infected members of the family and other groups of close contacts, since reinfection from nontreated contacts is frequent. Hygienic instruction is of particular importance, eg, careful washing of hands with soap and water after defecation, and again before meals. Fingernails should be kept trimmed close and clean, and the patient should abstain from scratching involved areas and should not put his fingers in his mouth. Carbolated petrolatum should be applied to the anal region after defecation, and the anal region should be washed thoroughly in the morning with soap and water. Toilet seats should be scrubbed with soap and water daily, and bed linens boiled twice a week. Pajamas (or "sleepers" for children) should be worn to prevent manual contact with anal region during sleep. Raise the temperature of the bedroom as high as possible for 1 hour every day and then air thoroughly.

B. Specific Measures: (In order of effectiveness.)

1. Piperazine citrate—Available in syrup containing 100 mg/ml or as tablets of 250 or 500 mg. The dosage for a course of 8 days is as follows:

> Up to 15 lb: 250 mg daily
> 15–30 lb: 250 mg twice daily
> 30–60 lb: 500 mg twice daily
> Over 60 lb: 1 gm twice daily

2. Pyrvinium pamoate in syrup, single dose of 5 mg/kg body weight (maximum of 0.25 gm), repeated after 2 weeks. It may cause nausea and vomiting, and turns the stools red.

3. Thiabendazole—Give 25 mg/kg body weight twice daily for 1 day and repeat after 1 week (see Strongyloidiasis, above).

4. Stilbazium iodide (Monopar®), single dose of 10–15 mg base/kg body weight, in enteric-coated capsules. The stools become colored red.

5. Methylrosaniline chloride (4-hour enteric-coated tablets), 1 mg/lb body weight in 3 divided doses daily before meals. Give for 8–10 days and repeat course after an interval of 1 week.

Prognosis

Although annoying, the infection is benign. Cure is readily attainable with one of several effective drugs, but reinfection is a major problem in many households. Thus the general measures cited above are of great importance.

Bumbalo, T.S.: Single-dose regimen in treatment of pinworm infection. New York J Med 65:248–251, 1965.

Davis, J.H.: Newer drugs in therapy of pinworm infestation. M Clin North America 51:1203–1212, 1967.

Mayers, C.P., & R.J. Purvis: Manifestations of pinworms. Canad MAJ 103:489–493, 1970.

HOOKWORM DISEASE

Essentials of Diagnosis

- Weakness, fatigue, pallor, palpitation, dyspnea associated with a hypochromic, microcytic anemia.
- Diarrhea, flatulence, abdominal discomfort, weight loss.
- Transient episodes of coughing, with sore throat and bloody sputum.
- Pruritic, erythematous, maculopapular or vesicular dermatitis.
- Characteristic eggs in the stool; guaiac-positive stool.

General Considerations

Hookworm disease, widespread in the tropics and subtropics, is caused by *Ancylostoma duodenale* and *Necator americanus*. In the Western Hemisphere necator is the prevailing genus. The adult worms, approximately 1 cm (3/8 inch) long, attach themselves to the mucosa of the small intestine, where they suck blood and mucosal substances. Symptomatology and pathology are proportionate to the number of worms infecting the patient. A burden of at least 100 worms is necessary to produce anemia and symptoms in an adult. Eggs produced by the female worms are passed in the stool, which must fall on warm, moist soil if larval development is to take place. Infective larvae remain in the soil until they come in contact with human skin. After penetrating the skin the larvae migrate through the lungs and eventually reach the small intestine where final development into adult worms takes place.

Clinical Findings

A. Symptoms and Signs: Ground itch, the first manifestation of hookworm infection, is a pruritic erythematous dermatitis, either maculopapular or vesicular, associated with the invasion of infective larvae. Strongyloides infection and creeping eruption caused by nonhuman hookworm species must be considered in the differential diagnosis at this stage. The severity of the dermatitis is a function of the number of invading larvae and the sensitivity of the host. The pulmonary phase of the disease is a transient reaction to larval migration through the lungs. Bloody sputum and cough result from damage caused by larvae breaking into alveoli from small blood vessels. Two or more weeks after the skin invasion, and depending upon the number of worms present, abdominal discomfort, flatulence, diarrhea, and other symptoms of intestinal irritation may appear as worms begin to attach themselves to the mucosa. Anemia appears 10–20 weeks after infection. The severity of the anemia depends upon the worm burden: more than 500 worms are necessary to produce profound anemia. The patient's nutritional status will also influence the severity of the anemia.

B. Laboratory Findings: The diagnosis ultimately depends upon demonstration of characteristic eggs in the stool. This can often be done on microscopic examination, but a better technic is to make thick smears of feces on blotting strips and place them in tubes so that the fecal material is held clear of 1 cm of water in the bottom of the tube. The eggs hatch at room temperature, and identifiable larvae migrate to the water. Larvae may occasionally be discovered in either the stool or sputum. The stool contains occult blood. The severity of the hypochromic microcytic anemia will depend upon the worm burden, which can be estimated by egg counting technics. Eosinophilia is usually present, particularly in the early months of the infection.

Complications

The skin lesions may become secondarily infected. In highly sensitive individuals the allergic reaction to the invading and migrating larvae may be so severe as to require treatment. With profound anemia there may be cardiac decompensation with edema and ascites, mental retardation, stunting of growth, and impaired renal function.

Treatment

A. General Measures: Estimation of the need for treatment should be based upon quantitative counts of the eggs in the stools. Light infections require no treatment, particularly if it occurs after treatment of heavy infection. It is often impossible to completely eradicate the infection.

Provide an adequate high-protein diet with supplementary iron medication. Rule out the possibility of coincidental ascariasis. If ascariasis is present, or when diagnostic facilities are limited, give piperazine or hexylresorcinol as prescribed for ascariasis (see above). Tetrachloroethylene stimulates ascaris activity, which occasionally results in intestinal obstruction. If large numbers of hookworms are still present following the administration of hexylresorcinol, wait 1 week following the last dose and give tetrachloroethylene.

B. Specific Measures:

1. Tetrachloroethylene is the drug of choice for necator (but see bephenium, below). *Caution:* Be sure to correct malnutrition and anemia before giving this drug. Tetrachloroethylene is contraindicated in patients with alcoholism, chronic gastrointestinal disorders, severe constipation, hepatic disease, and in patients undergoing heavy metal therapy.

Give 30 gm magnesium sulfate in water or 240 ml magnesium citrate solution the night before drug therapy. Eliminate alcohol and fatty foods for 48 hours before medication, give a light evening meal, and give no more food until after medication and the subsequent purge. Give tetrachloroethylene, 0.12 ml/kg body weight (not more than 5 ml) in soluble gelatin capsules containing 1 ml, in the morning on an empty stomach. Saline purgation is no longer recommended. Examine stools 1 week later on 3 successive days to determine efficacy of treatment. Repeat treatment in 2 weeks if stools are positive. Ferrous sulfate, 0.2–0.3 gm 3 times daily after meals, is usually indicated for anemia.

2. Bephenium hydroxynaphthoate (Alcopara®), relatively nontoxic, is the drug of choice for ancylostoma and for mass treatment of children. It is to be preferred for severely debilitated children but may cause nausea and vomiting. Suspend the bitter granules in a flavored vehicle. For ancylostoma, give 5 gm orally twice daily for 1 day, repeating in a few days if necessary. For children weighing less than 22 kg, give half this dose. For necator, the same dose for 3 days may reduce the worm load to acceptable levels. *Do not follow with a purge.*

3. Hexylresorcinol may be used if tetrachloroethylene is contraindicated, ineffective, or not available. It should be given on 3 successive mornings (see Ascariasis, above).

Prognosis

If the disease is recognized before serious secondary complications appear, the prognosis is favorable. With iron therapy, improved nutrition, and administration of an anthelmintic, complete recovery is the rule. The persistence of a few eggs in the stool of an asymptomatic person who is not anemic is not an indication for repeated treatments.

Roche, M., & M. Layrisse: The nature of "hookworm anemia." Am J Trop Med 15:1032–1102, 1966.

Salem, H.H., & others: Clinical trials with bephenium hydroxynaphthoate against *Ancylostoma duodenale* and other intestinal helminths. J Trop Med 68:21–25, 1965.

Stoll, N.R.: For hookworm diagnosis, is finding an egg enough? Ann New York Acad Sc 98:712–724, 1962.

Sturrock, R.F.: Chemical control of hookworm larvae. Lancet 2:1256–1257, 1966.

•   •   •

VISCERAL LARVA MIGRANS

Infection by the larval dog and cat ascarids, *Toxocara canis* and *T cati,* usually occurs in young children as a result of dirt eating. The larvae, unable to mature in an abnormal host, migrate through the body and lodge in various organs, particularly the lungs, liver, and brain. Because the disease is difficult to diagnose its distribution is not well known, but it is probably cosmopolitan.

Fever, cough, hepatomegaly, and nervous symptoms are the commonest clinical findings. A variety of other symptoms may occur when such organs as the heart, eyes, and kidneys are invaded. Many infections are asymptomatic. Eosinophil counts of 30–80% and leukocytosis are common. Hyperglobulinemia occurs when the liver is extensively invaded.

There is no specific treatment, but thiabendazole should be tried. The cortisones, antibiotics, antihistamines, and analgesics may be needed to provide symptomatic relief. Symptoms may persist for months, but the ultimate prognosis is usually good.

Beaver, P.C.: The nature of visceral larva migrans. J Parasitol 55:3–12, 1969.

Huntley, C., Costas, M.C., & A. Lyerly: Visceral larva migrans syndrome: Clinical characteristics and immunologic studies in 51 patients. Pediatrics 36:523–536, 1965.

Kagan, I.G.: Serologic diagnosis of visceral larva migrans. Clin Pediat 7:508–509, 1968.

Woodruff, A.W.: Toxocariasis. Brit MJ 3:663–669, 1970.

INTESTINAL CAPILLARIASIS

A few fatal cases of human infection by the liver parasite *Capillaria hepatica* have been recorded in the past, but the syndrome of intestinal capillariasis recently recognized in the northern Philippines is a new clinical entity. The parasite, *C filippinensis,* is found in the mucosa of the small intestine, especially the jejunum. Infection presents as an intractable diarrhea and many cases have been fatal. At least 127 cases (77 fatal) have been recognized since 1965. Malabsorption is a feature of the disease. Adult nematodes and eggs can be found in the stool. Thiabendazole and dithiazanine are under investigation as aids in treatment.

Dauz, U., Cabrera, B.D., & B.D. Canlas, Jr.: Human intestinal capillariasis. Acta med philippina 4:72–83, 84–91, 92–103, 1967.

FILARIASIS

Essentials of Diagnosis

- Recurrent attacks at irregular intervals of lymphangitis, lymphadenitis, fever, orchitis.
- Hydrocele, chyluria, elephantiasis of legs, arms, genitalia, or breasts.
- Characteristic microfilariae in the blood.
- Eosinophilia; positive skin or complement fixation tests.

General Considerations

Filariasis is caused by infection with one of 2 filarial nematodes, *Wuchereria bancrofti,* and *Brugia malayi.* Infective larvae of *B malayi* are transmitted to man by the bite of certain Mansonia and Anopheles mosquitoes of south India, Ceylon, south China, and southeast Asia. *W bancrofti,* widely distributed in the tropics and subtropics of both hemispheres, is transmitted by certain Culex and Aedes mosquitoes. Over a period of months, adult worms of both species mature in or near the superficial and deep lymphatics and lymph nodes. The adults produce large numbers of motile larvae (microfilariae), which appear in the peripheral blood. Microfilariae of *W bancrofti* are found in the blood chiefly at night (nocturnal periodicity), except for a nonperiodic variety in the South Pacific. *B malayi* microfilariae are usually nocturnally periodic but may be semi-periodic (present at all times with a slight nocturnal rise). While man is the only vertebrate host for *W bancrofti,* cats, monkeys, and other animals may harbor *B malayi.* Several other species of filarial worms infect man without causing important signs or symptoms. The microfilariae of 2 of these, *Tetrapetalonema perstans* (African and South American tropics) and *Mansonella ozzardi* (West Indies and South America), appear in the blood and must be differentiated from those of the pathogenic species. There have been a few reports of accidental and, usually, inconsequential human infections by filarial worms of the genus Dirofilaria.

Clinical Findings

A. Symptoms and Signs: The early clinical manifestations are inflammatory; those of the later stages are obstructive. Episodes of fever, with or without inflammation of lymphatics and nodes, occur at irregular intervals in typical early cases. Persistent lymph node enlargement is most common in *B malayi* infections but occurs in some *W bancrofti* endemic areas. Funiculitis and orchitis are common and abscesses may form at sites of lymphatic inflammation. Such episodes may occur intermittently for months or years before the first obstructive signs appear. The number and severity of these attacks, and the extent of the later changes, depends primarily upon the intensity of the infection, which in turn is related to the length of residence in an endemic area. Obstructive phenomena, arising from interference with normal lymphatic flow, include hydrocele, scrotal lymphedema, lymphatic varices, and elephantiasis. Chyluria may result from rupture of distended lymphatics into the urinary tract. In the early stages of elephantiasis the tissues of the affected part are edematous and soft; later, with skin hypertrophy and subcutaneous connective tissue proliferation, the part becomes hard. As the swelling enlarges, sometimes to enormous size, the skin surface folds and fissures. Bancroftian elephantiasis frequently involves the legs and genitalia, less often the arms and breasts; in *B malayi* infections elephantiasis of the legs below the knees is most common and genital structures are rarely affected.

Hydrocele and elephantoid tissue changes in persons residing in endemic areas are usually filarial in origin. Elephantiasis in those who have visited endemic areas only briefly is rarely due to filariasis. Many infections are asymptomatic and detected only by blood examination.

B. Laboratory Findings: Eosinophilia (10–30%, higher with *B malayi*) is usual in the early stages; the count falls, sometimes to normal, as elephantiasis develops. Microfilariae are rare in the blood in the first 2–3 years after infection, abundant as the disease progresses, and again rare in the advanced obstructive stage. Laboratory diagnosis usually requires demonstration of microfilariae, which must be differentiated from the nonpathogenic species. Both day and night blood specimens should be examined. Diagnosis can also be made by finding adult worms in biopsy specimens, but these should be taken only from lymphatics of the extremities. Removal of nodes may further impair drainage from the affected area. When microfilariae cannot be found, skin and complement fixation tests are fairly satisfactory for diagnosis. Skin tests are the more reliable (only 10% false-positive).

Differential Diagnosis

Diagnosis of the early febrile and inflammatory episodes may be difficult, particularly when the patient has moved away from an endemic area, because attacks of lymphangitis, adenitis, and fever are transitory and microfilariae may be rare in the blood. Filarial funiculitis, orchitis, and epididymitis may suggest gonococcal infection, but there is no urethral discharge in the uncomplicated case. Among the late manifestations, elephantiasis may be confused with hernia, Milroy's disease, multiple lipomatosis, severe congestive heart failure, venous thrombosis, and obstructive lesions of the lymphatics, which may produce nonfilarial elephantiasis of the extremities. The last 3 named can be distinguished readily from filariasis. Multiple lipomas may produce a massive soft lumpy swelling of the proximal part of a limb. In contrast, the filarial lesion starts distally and becomes hard as it enlarges. Milroy's congenital elephantiasis usually involves both legs below the knees. The skin is smooth, there is no eosinophilia, and the patient often has never visited the tropics.

Treatment

A. General Measures: Bed rest is indicated during febrile and local inflammatory episodes. Antibiotics should be given for secondary infections, particularly abscesses over inflamed nodes. Suspensory bandaging is a valuable palliative measure for orchitis, epididymitis, and scrotal lymphedema. Treat mild edema of a limb with rest, elevation, and firm bandaging. Chyluria usually requires no treatment except rest.

B. Surgical Measures: Surgical removal of the elephantoid scrotum, vulva, or breast is relatively easy, and the results are usually satisfactory. Surgery for limb elephantiasis is difficult and the results are often disappointing. Attempt operation only if the swollen limb severely limits the patient's ability to earn a living.

C. Specific Measures: Diethylcarbamazine (Hetrazan®) is the drug of choice. The usual dosage is 2–3 mg of the citrate/kg body weight orally 3 times daily for 14 (sometimes 21) days. Use a single dose on the first day and regulate subsequent dosage to minimize allergic reactions, common early in treatment as microfilariae are killed. The drug itself is nontoxic in usual doses. Microfilariae are rapidly destroyed, but the drug has only a limited action on the adult worms. Since microfilarial relapses often occur 3–12 months after treatment, control of the infection may require several courses over 1–2 years. The principal value of the drug is in eliminating the patient as a source of infection. Drug treatment will not significantly influence the course of advanced filariasis.

Prognosis

In early and mild cases the prognosis is good if the patient leaves the endemic area or if transmission in the area is reduced by control measures (mosquito control and drug treatment of human infections). Surgical treatment of genital elephantiasis often produces satisfactory results. For severe elephantiasis of a limb the prognosis is less favorable.

Beaver, P.C., & T.C. Orihel: Human infection with filariae of animals in the United States. Am J Trop Med 14:1010–1029, 1965.

Wijetunge, H.P.A.: Clinical manifestations of early bancroftian filariasis. J Trop Med 70:90–94, 1967.

Wilson T.: Filariasis in Malaya: A general review. Tr Roy Soc Trop Med Hyg 55:107–129, 1961.

LOIASIS

Loiasis is a common and distinctive disease of tropical Africa caused by the filarial nematode, *Loa loa*. The intermediate host, Chrysops, a biting fly, carries the infection from man or monkey to man. Infective larvae, introduced by the biting fly, develop into adult worms in about 12 months. It is the adult worms migrating through subcutaneous tissues which cause the symptoms of loiasis, not the larval microfilariae in the bloodstream.

Many infected persons remain symptom-free; others develop severe allergic reactions to the infection and sometimes emotional disturbances. The first definite sign of the disease is the appearance of a Calabar swelling or the migration of a worm across the eye. The swelling is a temporary, usually painless, subcutaneous edematous reaction often several inches in diameter. The overlying and surrounding skin is often reddened, irritated, and pruritic. The swelling may migrate a few inches before disappearing; more often it remains in one place for several days and then subsides. The reaction occurs most frequently on the hands, forearms, and around the eyes, but it may appear anywhere. Some patients experience Calabar swellings at infrequent intervals, others as often as twice a week. Migration of the worm across the eye produces a foreign body sensation, often with considerable irritation. Migrating worms are sometimes visible in subcutaneous tissues elsewhere in the body. Generalized urticaria, edema of a whole limb, extensive erythema, and generalized pruritus have been reported in some patients.

The adult worm may be recovered from the eye or skin (rarely), or microfilariae may be found in daytime blood films (20–30% of patients). Complement fixation and skin tests are often useful in diagnosis. The eosinophil count is elevated, varying between 10–40% or more.

Surgical removal of adult worms is sometimes possible, but the most satisfactory treatment is with diethylcarbamazine (Hetrazan®), a relatively nontoxic drug. Optimal dosage is 2–3 mg/kg body weight 3 times daily after meals for 14 days. Because allergic reactions (fever, urticaria, rashes, pruritus) are common early in treatment (probably as a result of rapid killing of microfilariae) use only a single dose on the first day of treatment and regulate subsequent dosage according to the patient's reaction. Antihistamine therapy is often helpful early in the course of treatment.

The prognosis is good with treatment. Without treatment, loiasis is annoying and uncomfortable but rarely life-endangering. Fatal encephalitis rarely occurs.

Cahill, K.M.: Other filarial infections of man. New York J Med 63:1551–1554, 1963.

Gordon, R.M., & others: The problem of loiasis in West Africa. Tr Roy Soc Trop Med Hyg 44:11–41, 1950.

ONCHOCERCIASIS

Man and Simulium black flies are the natural hosts of *Onchocerca volvulus,* a filarial nematode found in many parts of tropical Africa and in localized areas of Central America and northern South America, including southern Mexico, the highlands of Guatemala, and eastern Venezuela. The biting fly introduces infective larvae which develop slowly in the cutaneous and subcutaneous tissues of man. Flies are infected in turn by picking up microfilariae while biting. Adult worms may live for years, frequently in fibrous nodules which develop around one or more of the parasites. Microfilariae, motile and migratory, may be found in the skin, subcutaneous tissues, lymphatics, the conjunctivas, and other structures of the eye.

Clinical Findings

A. Symptoms and Signs: Intensity of infection determines the extent and severity of the clinical picture. After an incubation period of several months to 1 year, skin manifestations appear in up to 40% of patients. Localized or generalized pruritus is common, usually causing scratching and skin excoriation. Pigmentary changes, skin thickening, and lichenification may appear later. Erysipeloid or papulovesicular eruptions are sometimes seen. Subcutaneous nodules develop around adult worms; hence they appear at a later stage of the infection. The nodules, usually painless, consist of fibrous tissue surrounding one or many living or dead worms. Common sites are over bony prominences on the trunk, thighs, shoulders, arms, and head. Few patients have more than 3–6 nodules. The most common early ocular finding is a superficial punctate keratitis. Vascular pannus, iritis, and cyclitis are serious later manifestations. While certain retinal changes, atrophic choroiditis, and optic atrophy are seen in patients with onchocerciasis, some investigators doubt that these lesions are actually due to the infection.

B. Laboratory Findings: Eosinophilia of 15–50% is common. Aspiration of nodules will usually reveal eggs and microfilariae, and adult worms may be demonstrated in excised nodules. Microfilariae are not found in the blood, but can be identified in skin or conjunctival snips or in skin shavings. The snip is performed by tenting the skin with a needle and cutting off a bit of skin above the needle tip. A blood-free shaving may be cut with a razor blade from the top of a ridge of skin firmly pressed between thumb and forefinger. Cocaine improves rather than detracts from the value of conjunctival snips. The snip or shaving is examined in a drop of saline under a coverslip on a slide. Shavings or snips should be taken from several sites over bony prominences of the scapular region, hips, and thighs.

C. Special Examinations: In ocular onchocerciasis, slit lamp will usually reveal many microfilariae in the anterior chamber. Complement fixation and skin tests are of doubtful value because of high false-positive reaction rates.

Complications

Glaucoma and cataracts arising from iritis and cyclitis may cause blindness. Posterior segment lesions seen in patients with onchocerciasis may also cause blindness.

Treatment

A. Specific Measures:

1. Diethylcarbamazine (Hetrazan®, Banocide®) is almost nontoxic and effective against microfilariae but not the adult worms. Give 2–3 mg/kg body weight orally 3 times daily for 14–21 days. To prevent severe allergic symptoms which may be provoked early in therapy as microfilariae are rapidly killed, start treatment with small doses and increase dosage over 3–4 days. When the eyes are involved particular caution is necessary, starting with a single daily dose of 0.25 mg/kg. Use antihistamines to control allergic symptoms.

2. Suramin sodium is more effective than diethylcarbamazine in eradicating infection by killing the adult worms, but it has the disadvantage of potential renal toxicity (proteinuria, casts, red cells). Renal disease is a contraindication. For adults give 1 gm of a 10% solution in distilled water IV every 7 days to a total dose of 5–10 gm. Start treatment with a test dose of 0.2 gm.

B. Surgical Measures: Surgical removal of nodules is not curative, but removes many adult worms and is particularly justifiable when nodules are located close to the eyes. Nodulectomy may also be indicated for cosmetic reasons.

Prognosis

With chemotherapy, progression of all forms of the disease usually can be checked. The prognosis is unfavorable only for those patients seen for the first time with already far-advanced ocular onchocerciasis.

Duke, B.O.L.: Onchocerciasis. Brit MJ 1:301–304, 1968.

Woodruff, A.W., & others: Papers and discussion on onchocerciasis. Tr Roy Soc Trop Med Hyg 60:695–734, 1966.

DRACUNCULIASIS
(Guinea Worm Infection, Dracunculosis, Dracontiasis)

Dracunculus medinensis is a nematode parasite of man found through northern and central Àfrica, southern Asia, and northeastern South America. It occurs in the Caribbean but is not seen in the USA except in imported cases. Man is infected by swallowing water containing the infected intermediate host, the crustacean Cyclops, which is common in wells and ponds in the tropics. Larvae escape from the crustacean in the human host and mature in the connective tissues. After mating the male worm dies and the gravid female, now 1 meter (40 inches) or more in length, moves to the surface of the body. The head of the worm reaches the skin surface, a blister develops and ruptures, and the uterus discharges great numbers of larvae whenever the ulcer comes in contact with water. Larval discharge continues intermittently for as long as 3 weeks until the uterus is empty. The female worm then dies and is either extruded or absorbed. In the absence of secondary infection the ulceration heals in 4—6 weeks from onset.

Clinical Findings

A. Symptoms and Signs: Clinical effects are produced only by the female worm. Multiple infections occur, but the usual infection is with a single worm. Several hours before the head appears at the skin surface local erythema and tenderness often develop in the area where emergence is to take place. In some patients there may be systemic symptoms at this time, including urticaria, generalized pruritus, nausea, vomiting, and dyspnea. As the blister forms and ruptures these symptoms subside. The tissues surrounding the ulceration which remains after rupture of the blister frequently become indurated, reddened, and tender; and since 90% of the lesions appear on the leg or foot the patient often must give up walking and work. Uninfected ulcers heal in 4—6 weeks, but secondary infection is so common that the course is often prolonged.

Calcified guinea worms are occasionally revealed as chance findings during x-ray examination of persons in endemic areas.

B. Laboratory Findings: When a worm is not visible in the ulcer the diagnosis may be made by detection of larvae in fluid expressed from the moistened ulcer. A skin test is available, but its value as a diagnostic aid is not established. Eosinophilia of about 10% often accompanies the symptoms before blister formation.

Complications

Secondary infection is the rule and may cause development of an abscess which eventually involves deep structures. Ankle and knee joint infection and deformity is a common complication in some areas. If the worm is broken during removal sepsis almost always results, leading to cellulitis, abscess formation, or septicemia.

Treatment

A. General Measures: The patient should be at bed rest with the affected part elevated. Cleanse the lesion and control secondary infection with antibiotics. Apply wet compresses continuously to hasten discharge of all larvae from the uterus of the worm. This may require 1—2 days.

B. Specific Measures: Give niridazole (Ambilhar®), 25 mg/kg in divided doses daily for 7 days.

C. Surgical Removal: Make multiple incisions under local anesthesia along the worm tract, and remove the entire worm carefully. This method has the advantage of speed, but the disadvantage that x-ray

(using a contrast medium in the tract) is usually necessary to locate the worm. Give antihistamines preoperatively to control allergic symptoms arising from manipulation or rupture of the worm. Before surgery the worm may be killed by injections of mercury bichloride, acriflavine, or chloroform, but this is probably not necessary.

D. Removal by Extraction: With patience this time-honored method is safe and effective, but it has the disadvantage of being slow. The head of the worm is identified and tied to an applicator stick with a thread. The worm is gently wound on the stick, a little at a time. The extraction may require a week or more. Injections of phenothiazine in olive oil into the parasite are said to cause partial extrusion of the worm and hasten the extraction.

Hodgson, C., & D.F. Barrett: Chronic dracunculosis. Brit J Dermat 76:211—217, 1964.
Kothari, M.L., & others: Niridazole in dracunculiasis. Am J Trop Med 17:864—866, 1968.

CUTANEOUS LARVA MIGRANS
(Creeping Eruption)

Creeping eruption, prevalent throughout the tropics and subtropics, is caused by the larvae of the dog and cat hookworms, *Ancylostoma braziliense* and *A caninum.* It is a common infection of man in the southeastern USA, particularly where people come in contact with moist sandy soil (beaches, children's sand piles) contaminated by dog or cat feces. The larvae may invade any skin surface, but the hands or feet are usually affected. The larvae may remain active in the skin for several weeks or months, slowly advancing but rarely moving more than a few inches from the penetration site. Eventually, if not killed by treatment, the larvae die and are absorbed.

Soon after invasion of the skin, minute itchy erythematous papules appear at the sites of entry. Two or 3 days later characteristic serpiginous eruptions begin to form as larval migration starts. These intensely pruritic lesions may persist for several months as migration continues. The parasite usually lies slightly ahead of the advancing end of the eruption. Vesiculation and crusting commonly occur in the later stages. About 30% of patients develop transient pulmonary infiltrates and eosinophilia, possibly representing larval migration through the lungs. There are no consistent laboratory findings in most cases.

The early stages may be confused with hookworm ground itch, schistosoma dermatitis, skin reactions to larval strongyloides, and reactions to various larval fly infestations. After serpiginous lesions develop there should be little difficulty in diagnosis.

Simple transient cases usually do not require treatment. The larvae must be killed to provide relief in severe or persistent cases. Freezing ahead of the eruption with ethyl chloride spray is often effective. Thiabendazole, given as for strongyloidiasis or in single doses, is an effective drug. Progression of the lesions and itching are usually stopped within 48 hours. Other methods include local injections of chloroquine or quinacrine (Atabrine®) and application of ethyl acetate collodion to the skin widely around and in advance of the larvae. Systemic treatment with diethylcarbamazine (Hetrazan®) in doses of 2–4 mg/kg body weight provides relief but is not curative. Antihistamines are helpful in controlling pruritus, and antibiotic ointments may be necessary to treat secondary infections.

When treatment is unsuccessful, symptoms may persist for several months. Barring reinfection, however, eventual recovery is certain.

Larval stages (spargana) of some tapeworms may produce itching, tender, moving subcutaneous nodules.

Katz, R., & others: The natural course of creeping eruption and treatment with thiabendazole. Arch Dermat 91:420–424, 1965.

Stone, O.J., & J.F. Mullins: Thiabendazole effectiveness in creeping eruption. Arch Dermat 91:427–429, 1965.

GNATHOSTOMIASIS

Gnathostomiasis is an infection due to the nematode parasite, *Gnathostoma spinigerum,* which is found only in eastern and southern Asia. Dogs and cats are the normal hosts; the crustacean Cyclops and fish serve as intermediate hosts. Man is infected accidentally by eating infected raw fish. In man the immature worm migrates continually until it dies or is removed.

A single migratory subcutaneous swelling is the most common manifestation. The usually painless swelling, caused by the migrating worm, is firm, pruritic, and variable in size. It may appear anywhere on the body surface, remain in that area for days or weeks, or wander continually. Internal organs, the eye, and the cervix may also be invaded. Occasionally the worm becomes visible under the skin.

Spontaneous pneumothorax, leukorrhea, hematuria, hemoptysis, paroxysmal coughing, and edema of the pharynx with dyspnea have been reported as complications.

A high eosinophilia accompanies the infection. Specific skin testing antigens are available as a diagnostic aid, but final diagnosis usually rests upon identification of the worm.

Surgical removal of the worm when it appears close to the skin surface is the only effective treatment. Chemotherapy has not proved successful, although symptoms may be relieved by the use of diethylcarbamazine (Hetrazan®) as for filariasis.

The prognosis is usually good. However, complications such as pneumothorax and pharyngeal edema may be dangerous in the absence of good medical care.

Daengsvang, S.: Human gnathostomiasis in Siam with reference to the method of prevention. J Parasitol 35:116–121, 1949.

ANGIOSTRONGYLIASIS
(Eosinophilic Meningoencephalitis)

A nematode of rodents, *Angiostrongylus cantonensis,* is recognized as the causative agent of a form of meningoencephalitis now reported from Hawaii, other islands of the Pacific, and the mainland of Southeast Asia. Human infection results from the ingestion of raw slugs, snails, crayfish, or other invertebrates harboring infective larvae. The larvae usually invade the CNS, producing signs and symptoms of meningoencephalitis, including headache, fever, paresthesias, and back and neck stiffness. A characteristic feature is spinal fluid pleocytosis consisting largely of eosinophils. Cases of ocular infection have been reported from Thailand.

An angiostrongylus antigen has been developed for intradermal testing: a negative reaction appears to be reliable in ruling out the parasite as a cause of the meningitis.

Treatment has been largely supportive and symptomatic, and fatalities have been reported.

Rosen, L., & others: Eosinophilic meningoencephalitis caused by a metastrongylid lungworm of rats. JAMA 179:620–624, 1962.

Tangchai, P., Nye, S.W., & P.C. Beaver: Eosinophilic meningoencephalitis caused by angiostrongyliasis in Thailand. Autopsy report. Am J Trop Med 16:454–461, 1967.

ARTHROPOD INFECTIONS

MYIASIS

Myiasis is infestation with the larvae of various species of flies. Specific myiases, in which the fly larvae are parasitic, developing only in living flesh (eg, botflies, screw-worm flies), cause the most serious lesions. They are widely distributed (eg, horse, cattle, and sheep botflies), but a few species are prominent in specific geographic areas, eg, the flesh-fly *Wohlfahrtia vigil* of the northern USA and adjacent Canada, and the human botfly (*Dermatobia hominis*) in Mexico and tropical South America, which, like the tumbu-fly of Africa (*Cordylobia anthropophaga*), produces large boil-like swellings; and the primary screw-worm (*Callitroga hominivorax, Cochliomyia americana*), of tropical and subtropical America, which invades tissues with astonishing speed. In the so-called semispecific myiases, the larvae developing (usually) in decaying flesh may invade wounds or cavities. In intestinal or accidental myiases the larvae or eggs are ingested or the eggs are laid at the body orifices.

Nasal, oral, ocular, and aural myiases are produced by invasion of these tissues by larvae of the primary screw-worm (*C hominivorax,* warm parts of the western hemisphere), the Old World screw-worm (chrysomyia, oriental and Ethiopian), sheep botfly (*Oestrus ovis,* worldwide), or flesh-flies (*Wohlfahrtia magnifica,* Mediterranean to USSR). Other flies may invade secondarily. There may be extensive tissue destruction.

Intestinal myiasis (various species) is worldwide in distribution, but most cases have been recorded in India. Genitourinary myiasis due to migration of larvae (many species) into the bladder or vagina is rare.

The clinical manifestations are nonspecific, and are ascribable to progressive inflammation, often with great irritation of the appropriate cavity. Gastrointestinal disturbances may include vomiting and melena, and larvae are commonly passed in the feces spontaneously. In the conjunctival sac or lacrimal duct, the nasal cavity or sinuses, or the oral cavity, larvae may be seen by appropriate methods.

Removal of larvae by irrigation is frequently made more effective by instilling 5–10% chloroform in milk or light vegetable oil for 30 minutes. This is best done after a preliminary lavage. Continue with appropriate treatment to encourage healing. In intestinal myiasis, victims often also harbor one or more species of helminth. Purges and vermifuges should be accompanied by efforts to minimize further infestation.

Ocular Myiasis

Conjunctival infestation with fly larvae occurs frequently in the tropics but is rare in the USA. Several species of flies have been incriminated. Larvae invade the conjunctival sac and produce a nonspecific inflammatory reaction. If they spread throughout the eye and orbit, the inflammatory reaction and eventual necrosis become severe. Destruction of the orbital contents and bony walls of the orbit with invasion of the meninges may occur.

Extreme itching and irritation are the cardinal symptoms. The conjunctiva is red and excoriated. Numerous elongated white larvae are seen, especially in the fornices.

Treatment consists of mechanical removal of the larvae after first instilling cocaine, which has a paralyzing effect upon them. If the larvae can be removed when they are few in number, the course of the disease is automatically terminated. If further infestations are permitted, the prognosis is extremely poor inasmuch as the larvae invade the tissues out of reach of any form of treatment other than exploratory surgery. In such cases, destruction of the bony orbital wall and its contents frequently occurs.

James, M.T.: The flies that cause myiasis in man. Dept Agric Miscell Publ 631, 1947.

• • •

General Bibliography

Adams, A.R.D., & B.G. Maegraith: *Clinical Tropical Diseases,* 4th ed. Blackwell, 1966.

Brown, H.W.: *Basic Clinical Parasitology,* 3rd ed. Appleton-Century-Crofts, 1969.

Chernin, E.: Enterobiasis, trichinosis. Chap 32, pp 567–589, in: *Preventive Medicine.* Clark, D.W., & B. MacMahon (editors). Little, Brown, 1967.

Drugs for parasitic infections. Med Lett Drugs Ther 11:21–28, 1969.

Faust, E.C., Beaver, P.C., & R.C. Jung: *Animal Agents and Vectors of Human Disease,* 3rd ed. Lea & Febiger, 1968.

Faust, E.C., Russell, P.F., & R.C. Jung: *Craig and Faust's Clinical Parasitology,* 8th ed. Lea & Febiger, 1970.

Gordon, R.M., & M.M.J. Lavoipierre: *Entomology for Students of Medicine.* Blackwell, 1962.

Hunter, G.W., III, Frye, W.W., & J.C. Swartzwelder: *A Manual of Tropical Medicine,* 4th ed. Saunders, 1966.

Marsden, P.D., & M.G. Schultz: Intestinal parasites. Gastroenterology 57:724–750, 1969.

Parasitic Disease Drug Service, National Communicable Disease Center: See Public Health Reports 84:541, 1969.

The serologic diagnosis of parasitic disease. Med Lett Drugs Ther 13:15–16, 1971.

Woodruff, A.W.: Pathogenicity of intestinal helminthic infection. Tr Roy Soc Trop Med Hyg 59:585–606, 1965.

25...

Infectious Diseases: Mycotic*

Carlyn Halde

COCCIDIOIDOMYCOSIS

Essentials of Diagnosis

- Influenza-like illness with malaise, fever, backache, headache, and cough.
- Pleural pain.
- Arthralgia and periarticular swelling of knees and ankles.
- Erythema nodosum or erythema multiforme.
- Dissemination (rare) may result in meningitis or granulomatous lesions in any or all organs.
- X-ray findings vary widely from pneumonitis to cavitation.
- Positive skin test, serologic tests useful; spherules containing endospores demonstrable in sputum or tissues.

General Considerations

Coccidioidomycosis should be considered in the diagnosis of any obscure illness in a patient who has lived in or visited an endemic area.

Infection results from the inhalation of arthrospores or mycelial fragments of *Coccidioides immitis*, a fungus which grows in soil in certain arid regions of the southwestern United States, Mexico, and localized areas in Central and South America.

About 60% of infections are subclinical and unrecognized other than by the subsequent development of a positive coccidioidin skin test. In the remaining cases, symptoms may be of severity warranting medical attention. Fewer than 1% show dissemination, but among these patients the mortality rate is high.

Clinical Findings

A. Symptoms and Signs: Symptoms of primary coccidioidomycosis occur in about 40% of infections. These vary from mild to severe and prostrating and resemble those due to viral, bacterial, or other mycotic infections. The onset (after an incubation period of 10–30 days) is usually that of a respiratory tract illness with fever and occasionally chills. Pleural pain is common and usually severe. Muscular ache, backache, and headache may be severe. Nasopharyngitis may be followed by bronchitis accompanied by a dry or slight-

ly productive cough. Weakness and anorexia may become marked, leading to prostration. A morbilliform rash may appear 1–2 days after the onset of symptoms.

Arthralgia accompanied by periarticular swellings, often of the knees and ankles, is common. Erythema nodosum may appear 2–20 days after onset of symptoms. Erythema multiforme may appear on the upper extremities, head, or thorax. Breath sounds may become bronchial in nature, especially in the severely ill patient. Persistent pulmonary lesions, varying from cavities and abscesses to parenchymal nodular densities or bronchiectasis, occur in about 5% of diagnosed cases.

About 0.1% of white and 1% of nonwhite patients are unable to localize or control infection due to *C immitis*. Symptoms in progressive coccidioidomycosis depend upon the site of dissemination. Any or all organs may be involved. Pulmonary findings usually become more pronounced, with mediastinal and hilar lymph node enlargement, cough, and increased sputum production. Pulmonary abscesses may rupture into the pleural space, producing an empyema. Extension to bones and skin may take place, and pericardial and myocardial extension is not unusual.

Lesions in the bones are often in the bony prominences and the ends of long bones. The ankle, wrist, and elbow joints are commonly involved. Meningitis occurs in about 25% of disseminated cases. Subcutaneous abscesses and verrucous skin lesions are especially common in fulminating cases. Lymphadenitis may occur and may progress to suppuration. Mediastinal and retroperitoneal abscesses are not uncommon.

B. Laboratory Findings: In primary coccidioidomycosis there may be a moderate leukocytosis and eosinophilia. The sedimentation rate is elevated, returning to normal as the infection subsides. If the sedimentation rate persists or increases, there is a danger of progressive disease. A coccidioidin skin test becomes positive within 1–3 weeks after onset of symptoms. Precipitin antibodies appear in most symptomatic infections but disappear after 1–2 months. Complement-fixing antibodies appear later but persist longer. An initial eosinophilia of 15% or higher together with a persistent rising complement fixation titer is a bad prognostic sign. A rising complement fixation titer may herald dissemination weeks before it is otherwise evident. Demonstrable antibodies in spinal fluid are pathognomonic for coccidioidal meningitis. Spinal

*Superficial mycoses are discussed in Chapter 3.

fluid findings include increased cell count with lymphocytosis and reduced sugar. Spherules filled with endospores may be found in clinical specimens. These should be cultured only by trained technicians using safety precautions because of the danger of laboratory infection.

C. X-Ray Findings: X-ray findings vary, but patchy and nodular infiltrations are the most common. Hilar lymphadenopathy may be visible. There may be primary pleural effusion. Thin-walled cavities may appear.

Complications

Pulmonary infiltrations persisting for 6 or more weeks should be suspected of possible progression, especially with increase in area, enlargement of mediastinal and hilar nodes, cavity enlargement, and hemoptysis. Progressive disease is more likely to appear in Negroes, Filipinos, and Mexicans. Pregnant women of any race are also more vulnerable to dissemination.

Treatment

Bed rest is the most important therapeutic measure for the primary infection. This should be continued until there is a complete regression of fever, a normal sedimentation rate, clearing or stabilization of pulmonary radiologic findings, and a lowering of the complement fixation titer. These precautions are especially important for patients in whom the rate of dissemination is high. General symptomatic therapy is given as needed.

There is no specific therapy for patients with disseminated disease. Amphotericin B (Fungizone®) has proved effective in some patients and should be tried. The drug is suspended in 500 ml of 5% dextrose in distilled water (not saline) and administered IV over a 4–6 hour period. The adult dose is 0.5–1 mg/kg; however, since this drug has toxic properties (including renal toxicity), therapy should begin with 1 mg/day, increasing by 5 mg increments to 20 mg/day. Continue at this dosage, decreasing with poor tolerance or increasing with poor clinical response. Because intravenous amphotericin B therapy presents technical difficulties, preserve veins by using small needles and peripheral veins (hands, forearms), and heparin, 10–20 mg/500 ml, to reduce phlebitis. Premedication with aspirin, diphenhydramine (Benadryl®), chlorpromazine, and hydrocortisone succinate intravenously reduces the side-effects of the drug in some patients. Therapy should be continued for 1–2 months. Giving the drug on alternate days is usually well tolerated if toxic reactions are noted.

The best monitor of renal function is a creatinine clearance test done before treatment and once a week during treatment. Determine the BUN periodically.

Thoracic surgery is, indicated for giant, infected, or ruptured cavities. Surgical drainage is also useful for subcutaneous abscesses. Excisional surgery may be used to remove any focus or source of proliferating spherules. Amphotericin B should be given for 3–4 weeks before and after surgery.

Prognosis

The prognosis is good, but persistent pulmonary cavities may present complications. Nodules, cavities, and fibrotic residuals may rarely progress after long periods of stability or regression. Before amphotericin B became available the prognosis for disseminated coccidioidomycosis was poor, with a mortality rate approaching 50%.

Buechner, H.A.: *Management of Fungus Diseases of the Lungs.* Thomas, 1971.

Fiese, M.J.: *Coccidioidomycosis.* Thomas, 1958.

Winn, W.A.: Long term study of 300 patients with cavitary-abscess lesions of the lung of coccidioidal origin. Dis Chest 54:268–272, 1968.

HISTOPLASMOSIS

Essentials of Diagnosis

- Asymptomatic to severe respiratory symptoms with malaise, fever, cough, and chest pain.
- Ulceration of naso- and oropharynx.
- Hepatomegaly, splenomegaly, and lymphadenopathy.
- Anemia and leukopenia.
- Diarrhea in children.
- Positive skin test; positive serologic findings; small budding fungus cells found within reticuloendothelial cells; culture confirms diagnosis.

General Considerations

Histoplasmosis is caused by *Histoplasma capsulatum,* a fungus which has been isolated from soil in endemic areas (central and eastern United States, eastern Canada, Mexico, Central America, South America, Africa, and Southeast Asia). Infection takes place presumably by inhalation of spores or mycelial fragments. These convert into small budding cells which are engulfed by phagocytic cells in the lungs. The organism proliferates and may be carried by the blood to other areas of the body.

Clinical Findings

A. Symptoms and Signs: Most cases of histoplasmosis are asymptomatic or mild and so are unrecognized. Past infection is recognized by the development of a positive histoplasmin skin test and occasionally by pulmonary and splenic calcification. Symptomatic infections may present mild influenza-like characteristics, often lasting 1–4 days. Signs and symptoms of pulmonary involvement are usually absent even in patients who subsequently show areas of calcification on chest x-ray. Moderately severe infections are frequently diagnosed as atypical pneumonia. These patients have fever, cough, and mild chest pain lasting 5–15 days. Physical examination is usually negative. X-ray findings are variable and nonspecific.

Severe infections have been divided into 3 groups: (1) Acute histoplasmosis frequently occurs in epidemics. It is a severe disease with marked prostration, fever, and occasional chest pain, but no particular symptoms relative to the lungs even when x-rays show severe disseminated pneumonitis. The illness may last from 1 week to 6 months, but is almost never fatal. (2) Acute progressive histoplasmosis is usually fatal within 6 weeks or less. Symptoms usually consist of fever, dyspnea, cough, loss of weight, and prostration. Diarrhea is usually present in children. Ulcers of the mucous membranes of the oral pharynx may be present. The liver and spleen are nearly always enlarged, and all the organs of the body are involved. (3) Chronic progressive histoplasmosis may continue for years. It is usually seen in older patients in whom it has been mistaken for tuberculosis. The lungs show chronic progressive changes, often with cavities. The disease closely resembles chronic tuberculosis, and occasionally the patient has both diseases. Chronic histoplasmosis appears to be primarily confined to the lungs, but all organs of the body are involved in the terminal stage.

B. Laboratory Findings: In the moderately to severely ill patient the sedimentation rate is elevated. Leukopenia is present, with a normal differential count or neutropenia. Most patients with progressive disease show a progressive hypochromic anemia. Complement-fixing antibodies can be demonstrated, and a change in titer is of use in prognosis.

Treatment

There is no specific therapy. Bed rest and supportive care are indicated for the primary form. Normal activities should not be resumed until fever has subsided. Resection of lung tissue containing cavities has been useful. Amphotericin B (Fungizone®) (as for coccidioidomycosis) has proved useful for some patients with progressive histoplasmosis. Some children and adults with milder forms of acute primary or early chronic pulmonary disease respond to sulfadiazine therapy.

Prognosis

The prognosis is excellent for primary pulmonary histoplasmosis; only fair in localized infection; and poor in untreated generalized infection.

Bennett, D.E.: Histoplasmosis of the oral cavity and larynx. Arch Int Med 120:417–427, 1967.

Parker, J.D., & others: Treatment of chronic pulmonary histoplasmosis. New England J Med 283:225–229, 1970.

Vanek, J., & J. Schwarz: The gamut of histoplasmosis. Am J Med 50:89–104, 1971.

CRYPTOCOCCOSIS

Cryptococcosis, a chronic disseminated infection which frequently involves the CNS, is caused by *Cryptococcus neoformans.* This is an encapsulated, budding, yeast-like fungus which has been found in soil and in pigeon nests. Human infection is world-wide.

It is believed that most infections are acquired by inhalation. In the lung the infection may remain localized, heal, or disseminate. Upon dissemination lesions may form in any part of the body, but involvement of the CNS is most common and is the usual cause of death. Generalized meningoencephalitis occurs more frequently than localized granuloma in the brain or spinal cord. Solitary localized lesions may develop in the skin and rarely in the bones and other organs.

Cryptococcosis was at one time believed to be invariably fatal, but some cases (especially pulmonary) of spontaneous resolution have been reported. The incidence of fatal cases, on the other hand, is increasing as a result of increased numbers of infections in susceptible debilitated individuals.

In pulmonary cryptococcosis there are no specific signs or symptoms, and many patients are nearly asymptomatic. The patient may present a subacute respiratory infection with low-grade fever, pleural pain, and cough. There may be sputum production. Physical examination usually reveals signs of bronchitis or pulmonary consolidation. X-rays commonly show a solitary, moderately dense infiltration in the lower half of the lung field, with little or no hilar enlargement. More diffuse pneumonic infiltration, also in the lower lung fields, or extensive peribronchial infiltration or miliary lesions, may also occur.

CNS involvement usually presents a history of recent upper respiratory or pulmonary infection. Increasingly painful headache is usually the first and most prominent symptom. Vertigo, nausea, anorexia, ocular disorders, and mental deterioration develop. Nuchal rigidity is present, and Kernig's and Brudzinski's signs are positive. Patellar and Achilles reflexes are often diminished or absent.

Cutaneous lesions are variable in appearance. Acneiform lesions are more commonly seen. These enlarge slowly and ulcerate, often coalescing with other lesions to cover a large area. Bone lesions are painful, and the area is often swollen. Eye involvement may result from direct extension along the subarachnoid space into the optic nerve.

A mild anemia, leukocytosis, and increased sedimentation rate are found. Spinal fluid findings include increased pressure, many white cells (usually lymphocytes), budding encapsulated fungus cells, increased protein and globulin, and decreased sugar and chlorides. The organism is readily seen in an India ink preparation.

There is no specific therapy for cryptococcosis. Amphotericin B (Fungizone®) (as for coccidioidomycosis) and 5-fluorocytosine have been successful in some cases. Cisternal or Ommaya reservoir (ventricular) amphotericin B therapy has been used. Surgical resection of pulmonary granulomas has been successful.

Fass, R.J., & R.L. Perkins: 5-Fluorocytosine in the treatment of cryptococcal and candida mycoses. Ann Int Med 74:535–539, 1971.

Sarosi, G.A., & others: Amphotericin B in cryptococcal menin-
    gitis. Ann Int Med 71:1079–1087, 1969.

NORTH AMERICAN BLASTOMYCOSIS

Blastomyces dermatitidis causes this chronic
systemic fungus infection. The disease occurs more
often in men and in a geographically delimited area of
central and eastern United States and Canada. A few
cases have been found in Mexico, South America, and
Africa.

Mild or asymptomatic cases have not been found.
When dissemination takes place, lesions are most frequently seen on the skin, in bones, and in the CNS,
although any or all organs of the body may be attacked.

Little is known concerning the mildest pulmonary
phase of this disease. Cough, moderate fever, dyspnea,
and chest pain are evident in symptomatic patients.
These may disappear or may progress to a marked degree with bloody and purulent sputum production,
pleurisy, fever, chills, loss of weight, and prostration.
Radiologic studies usually reveal massive densities pro-
jecting irregularly from the mediastinal nodes, which
are markedly enlarged. Raised, verrucous cutaneous lesions which have an abrupt downward sloping border
are usually present in disseminated blastomycosis. The
surface is covered with miliary pustules. The border
extends slowly, leaving a central atrophic scar. In some
patients only cutaneous lesions are found. These may
persist untreated for long periods, with a gradual decline in the patient's health. Bones—often the ribs and
vertebrae—are frequently involved. These lesions appear both destructive and proliferative on x-ray.
Symptoms referable to CNS involvement appear in
about 1/3 of cases. The viscera may be invaded, but
rarely the gastrointestinal tract.

Laboratory findings usually include leukocytosis,
hypochromic anemia, and elevated sedimentation rate.
The organism is found in clinical specimens as a 5–20
μ, thick-walled cell which may have a single bud. It
grows readily on culture. Complement-fixing antibody
titer is variable but useful for prognosis.

There is no specific therapy for blastomycosis.
Amphotericin B (Fungizone®) (as for coccidioidomycosis) appears to be the best drug available for treatment. Surgical procedures may be successful for the
removal of cutaneous lesions, persistent cavities, or
other localized pulmonary lesions.

Careful follow-up for early evidence of relapse
should be made for several years so that amphotericin
B therapy may be resumed or instituted in those cases
which were initially treated with the less toxic
2-hydroxystilbamidine. Patients whose disease is limited to localized cutaneous lesions have the best prognosis in that they show a better immunologic response
to their infection.

Furcolow, M.L., & others: Some factors affecting survival in
    systemic blastomycosis. Dis Chest 54:285–291, 1968.
Witorsch, P., & J.P. Utz: American blastomycosis: A study of
    40 patients. Medicine 47:169–200, 1968.

SOUTH AMERICAN BLASTOMYCOSIS

Paracoccidioides brasiliensis infections have been
found only in patients who have resided in South or
Central America and Mexico.

Ulceration of the naso- and oropharynx is usually
the first symptom. Papules ulcerate and enlarge both
peripherally and deeper into the subcutaneous tissue.
Extensive coalescent ulcerations may eventually result
in destruction of the epiglottis, vocal cords, and uvula.
Extension to the lips and face may occur. Eating and
drinking are extremely painful. Skin lesions, usually on
the face, may occur. Variable in appearance, they may
have a necrotic central crater with a hard hyperkeratotic border. Lymph node enlargement always follows
mucocutaneous lesions, eventually ulcerating and
forming permanent draining sinuses. Lymph node enlargement may be the presenting symptom, with subsequent suppuration and rupture through the skin. In
some patients gastrointestinal disturbances are first
noted. Although the liver and spleen become enlarged,
there is a lack of specific gastrointestinal symptoms.
Cough, sometimes with sputum, indicates pulmonary
involvement, but the signs and symptoms are often
mild, even though x-ray findings indicate severe parenchymatous changes in the lungs.

The extensive ulceration of the entire gastrointestinal tract prevents sufficient intake and absorption
of food. Most patients become cachectic early. Death
usually results from associated malnutrition.

Laboratory findings include elevated sedimentation rate, leukocytosis with a neutrophilia showing a
shift to the left, and sometimes eosinophilia and monocytosis. Serologic results are variable. A high titer usually indicates progressive disease; a descending titer is a
favorable sign. The fungus is found in clinical specimens as a spherical cell which may have many buds
arising from it. Colonial and cellular morphology are
typical on culture.

The prognosis for South American blastomycosis
has been poor. Amphotericin B (Fungizone®) (as for
coccidioidomycosis) has been used recently with considerable success. Sulfadiazine and triple sulfonamides
in daily doses of 2–4 gm have been used for control,
and occasional cures have been reported following
months or years of therapy. Relapses are frequent
when the drug is stopped. Drug toxicity with prolonged high dosage is common. Rest and supportive
care are of value in promoting a favorable immunologic
response.

Restrepo, A., & others: Paracoccidioidomycosis (South Ameri-
    can blastomycosis): Study of 39 cases. Am J Trop Med
    19:68–76, 1970.

CANDIDIASIS

Candida albicans may be cultured from the mouth, vagina, and feces of about 65% of the population. It is more frequent in debilitated individuals. Thrush, vaginitis, cutaneous lesions (frequently in intertriginous areas), onychia, and paronychia are common. These are discussed elsewhere in this book. Systemic infection is usually found in patients with a history of other pulmonary disorders, diabetes mellitus, or general debilitation, or in those who have undergone prolonged antibiotic therapy. *Candida albicans* is a frequent secondary invader in other types of infection.

Systemic infection is of 2 types. Endocarditis, which almost always affects previously damaged heart valves, usually follows heart surgery or inoculation by contaminated needles or catheters. Splenomegaly and petechiae are usual, and emboli are common. In the other type of systemic infection the kidneys, myocardium, and brain are the usual sites of infection; this type frequently follows antibiotic and glucocorticosteroid therapy for serious debilitating disease. Upper gastrointestinal tract candidiasis is frequently the portal of entry. Splenomegaly and petechiae are rare. Fungiuria is usual in renal disease; however, especially in older persons, Candida organisms can be found in the bladder or as a urethral saprophyte.

It is doubtful if primary bronchial or pulmonary infection occurs. Infection in these areas is nearly always superimposed on other serious underlying disease.

Candida albicans is seen as gram-positive budding cells (2.5—6 μ) and as a pseudomycelium. It grows readily in culture. It is the most common cause of systemic disease, but *C tropicalis* is not uncommon. Many species may cause endocarditis.

Intravenous administration of amphotericin B (Fungizone®) (as for coccidioidomycosis) is necessary in serious systemic infections. Associated oral, gastrointestinal, and cutaneous lesions should be treated with amphotericin B or nystatin (Mycostatin®) mouthwash, tablets (500,000 units 3 times daily), and lotions. Gentian violet, 1%, in 10—20% alcohol, is also effective for oral, cutaneous, and vaginal lesions. Antibiotic therapy should be discontinued if possible. The correction of underlying factors may be sufficient to control candidiasis without specific therapy. All patients with candidiasis should be carefully examined for diabetes mellitus.

Response to amphotericin B is often poor in endocarditis. In other systemic infections the prognosis is generally good if the underlying predisposing factors are corrected.

Kay, J.H., & others: Surgical treatment of Candida endocarditis. JAMA 203:621—626, 1968.

Louria, D.B.: Pathogenesis of candidiasis. Pages 417—426 in: *Antimicrobial Agents and Chemotherapy, 1965.* American Society for Microbiology, 1966.

Tennant, F.S., Jr., & others: Primary renal candidiasis. Arch Int Med 122:435—440, 1968.

NOCARDIOSIS

Nocardia asteroides causes pulmonary and systemic nocardiosis. Other species of Nocardia are discussed in the section on mycetoma. The majority of patients with nocardiosis have serious underlying disorders, especially lymphoma, leukemia, and other neoplastic diseases.

Pulmonary involvement usually begins with malaise, loss of weight, fever, and night sweats. Cough and production of purulent sputum are the chief complaints. X-ray shows massive areas of consolidation, usually at the base of both lungs. Small areas of rarefaction caused by abscess formation within these consolidated masses may lead to multiple cavities. The lesions may penetrate to the exterior through the chest wall, invading the ribs. Pleural adhesions are common.

Dissemination may involve any organ. Lesions in the brain or meninges are most frequent, and such dissemination may occur following any minor pulmonary symptoms. Dissemination is common in debilitated patients.

An increased sedimentation rate and leukocytosis with increase in neutrophils are found in systemic nocardiosis. *N asteroides* is usually found as delicate, branching, gram-positive filaments which may be partially acidfast. Identification is made by culture.

Nocardiosis generally responds to sulfadiazine in a dosage sufficient to maintain a serum level of about 10 mg/100 ml (0.5—2 gm every 6 hours orally). Sensitivity tests should be used to determine the appropriate antibiotic, which should be administered concurrently in large dosage. Response is slow, and therapy should be continued for several months after all clinical manifestations have disappeared. Surgical procedures such as drainage and resection may be imperative.

The prognosis for systemic nocardiosis is poor when diagnosis and therapy are delayed.

Hoeprich, P.D., & others: Nocardial brain abscess cured with cycloserine and sulfonamides. Am J Med Sci 255:208—216, 1968.

ACTINOMYCOSIS

Actinomyces israelii occurs in the normal flora of the mouth and tonsillar crypts. It is an anaerobic, gram-positive, branching filamentous organism resembling bacteria in that the filaments (1 μ in diameter) readily fragment into bacillary forms. In diseased tissue these filaments are seen as a compact mass called a "sulfur granule." When introduced into tissue and associated with bacteria, *A israelii* becomes a pathogen. Hard, indurated, granulomatous, suppurative lesions develop which give rise to sinus tracts.

The most common site of infection is the cervicofacial area (about 60% of cases), and infection typically follows extraction of a tooth or other trauma. Lesions may develop in the gastrointestinal tract or lungs following ingestion or inhalation of the fungus from its endogenous source in the mouth.

Cervicofacial actinomycosis develops slowly. The area becomes markedly indurated and the overlying skin becomes reddish or cyanotic. The surface is irregular. Abscesses developing within and eventually draining to the surface persist for long periods. Sulfur granules may be found in the pus. There is usually little pain unless there is marked secondary infection. Trismus indicates that the muscles of mastication are involved. X-ray reveals eventual involvement of the bone with rarefaction as well as some proliferation of the underlying bone.

Abdominal actinomycosis usually causes pain in the ileocecal region, spiking fever and chills, intestinal colic, vomiting, and weight loss. Irregular masses in the ileocecal area or elsewhere in the abdomen may be palpated. Sinuses draining to the exterior may develop. X-ray may reveal the mass or enlarged viscera. Vertebrae and pelvic bones may be invaded.

Thoracic actinomycosis begins with fever, cough, and sputum production. The patient becomes weak, loses weight, may have night sweats and dyspnea. Pleural pain may be present. Dysphagia can result from mediastinal involvement. Multiple sinuses may extend through the chest wall, to the heart, or into the abdominal cavity. Ribs may be involved. X-ray shows massive areas of consolidation, frequently at the bases of the lungs.

The sedimentation rate may be elevated in patients with progressive disease. Anemia and leukocytosis are usually present. The anaerobic, gram-positive organism may be demonstrated as a granule or as scattered branching gram-positive filaments in the pus. Anaerobic culture is necessary to distinguish *A israelii* from Nocardia species. Specific identification by culture is necessary to avoid confusion with nocardiosis because specific therapy differs radically.

Penicillin G is the drug of choice. Ten to 20 million units are given via a parenteral route for 4–6 weeks. Continue treatment with penicillin V orally. Prolonged massive therapy is necessary in order to push effective levels of the drug into the abscesses where the organism is found. Sulfonamides may be added to the regimen, as well as streptomycin, which will control associated gram-negative organisms. Broad-spectrum antibiotics should be considered only if sensitivity tests show that the organism is resistant to penicillin. Immediate amelioration of symptoms or prompt improvement cannot be expected because of the chronic nature of this disease. Therapy should be continued for weeks to months after clinical manifestations have disappeared in order to ensure cure. Surgical procedures such as drainage and resection are of great benefit.

With penicillin and surgery, the prognosis is good. The difficulties of diagnosis, however, may permit extensive destruction of tissue before therapy is started.

McQuarrie, D.G., & W.H. Hall: Actinomycosis of the lung and chest wall. Surgery 64:905–911, 1968.

SPOROTRICHOSIS

Sporotrichosis is a chronic fungal infection caused by *Sporotrichum schenkii*. It is world-wide in distribution; most patients are people whose occupation brings them in contact with soil, plants, or decaying wood. Infection takes place when the organism is introduced by trauma into the skin, often on the hand, arm, or foot.

The most common form of sporotrichosis begins with a hard, nontender subcutaneous nodule. This later becomes adherent to the overlying skin, ulcerates (chancriform), and may persist for a long time. Within a few days to weeks, similar nodules usually develop along the lymphatics draining this area, and these may ulcerate. The lymphatic vessels become indurated and are easily palpable. The infection usually ceases to spread before the regional lymph nodes are invaded, and blood-borne dissemination is rare. The general health of the patient is not affected. Some patients complain of considerable pain. Skin infection may not spread through the lymphatics but may appear only as warty or papular, scaly lesions which may become pustular.

Pulmonary sporotrichosis presents no characteristic findings. Patients may be asymptomatic although pleural effusion, hilar adenopathy, fibrosis, caseous nodularity, and cavitation have been reported.

Disseminated sporotrichosis presents a picture of multiple, hard subcutaneous nodules scattered over the body. These become soft but rarely rupture spontaneously. Lesions may also develop in the bones, joints, muscles, and viscera.

There are no specific laboratory findings. Cultures are necessary to establish the diagnosis. A skin test with heat-killed vaccine or sporotrichin is positive.

Potassium iodide taken orally in increasing dosage promotes rapid healing, although the drug is not fungicidal. Give as the saturated solution, 5 drops 3 times a day, after meals, increasing by 1 drop per dose until 40 drops 3 times a day are being given. Continue for 2 weeks or until signs of the active disease have disappeared. The dosage is then decreased by 1 drop per dose until 5 drops are being given, and then is discontinued. Care must be taken to reduce the dosage if signs of iodism appear. Amphotericin B (Fungizone®) intravenously (as for coccidioidomycosis) has been effective in systemic infection. Surgery is usually contraindicated except for simple aspiration of secondary nodules.

The prognosis is good for all forms of sporotrichosis except the disseminated type, when decreased natural resistance probably plays a role.

Orr, E.R., & H.D. Riley: Sporotrichosis in childhood: Report of ten cases. J Pediat 78:951–957, 1971.

CHROMOBLASTOMYCOSIS

Chromoblastomycosis is a chronic, principally tropical fungal infection caused by several species of closely related fungi having a dark mycelium (Cladosporium [Hormodendrum] spp and Phialophora sp). In nature these fungi grow as filamentous saprophytes in soil and on decaying vegetation.

The disease progresses slowly before the development of clinically characteristic lesions.

Lesions occur most frequently on a lower extremity, but may occur on the hands, arms, and elsewhere. The lesion begins as a papule or ulcer. Over a period of months to years the lesions enlarge to become vegetating, papillomatous, verrucous, elevated nodules with a cauliflower-like appearance or wide-spread dry verrucous plaques. The latter lesions spread peripherally with a raised, verrucous border leaving central atrophic scarring. The surface of the active border contains minute abscesses. Satellite lesions may appear along the lymphatics. There may be extensive secondary bacterial infection with a resulting foul odor. Some patients complain of itching. Elephantiasis may result if there is marked fibrosis and lymph stasis in the limb.

The fungus is seen as brown, thick-walled, spherical, sometimes septate cells in pus. The type of spore formation found in culture determines the species.

Surgical excision and skin grafting have been necessary in the past; however, 1 mg of amphotericin B (Fungizone®) per ml of 5% dextrose injected directly into the lesion several times a week has proved curative. Tattooing a solution of amphotericin B into the lesion with a vibrapuncture apparatus or with a jet pressure gun has resulted in cure. Potassium iodide (as for sporotrichosis) and calciferol (50,000 units twice a week) have been reported to be useful in early cases when there is little fibrosis.

The prognosis is favorable if the disease is diagnosed and treated in its early stages.

Whiting, D.A.: Treatment of chromoblastomycosis with high local concentrations of amphotericin B. Brit J Dermat 79:345–351, 1967.

MYCETOMA
(Maduromycosis & Actinomycotic Mycetoma)

Maduromycosis is the term used to describe mycetoma caused by the true fungi. Actinomycotic mycetoma is caused by Nocardia and Streptomyces sp. The many species of causative fungi are found in soil. Organisms are introduced by trauma in barefoot people. Mycetoma may occur on the hand and other parts of the body also. With time, the subcutaneous lesions develop sinuses which drain to the surface as well as deep into muscle and bone. The fungus is compacted into a granule which drains out in the pus.

The disease begins as a papule, nodule, or abscess which over months to years progresses slowly to form multiple abscesses and sinus tracts ramifying deep into the tissue. The entire area becomes indurated, and the skin becomes discolored. Open sinuses or atrophic scars are scattered over its surface. Secondary bacterial infection may result in large open ulcers. When x-rayed, destructive changes are seen in the underlying bone. Extensive fibrosis in the tissue causes elephantiasis. Pain is not a serious complaint until the disease is far advanced.

The fungus occurs as white, yellow, red, or black granules in the tissue or pus. Microscopic examination assists in the diagnosis. The granules of nocardia and streptomyces consist of delicate, gram-positive branching filaments 1 μ in diameter. Maduromycosis caused by the true fungi has granules consisting of hyphae 5 μ in diameter interspersed with large thick-walled chlamydospores.

The prognosis is good for patients with actinomycotic mycetoma since they usually respond well to sulfonamides and sulfones, especially if treated early. Give sulfadiazine or triple sulfonamides, 4–5 gm daily, and increase to 10–12 gm daily if the patient is able to tolerate this dosage. Diaminodiphenylsulfone (Avlosulfon®), 100 mg twice daily after meals, or other sulfones have been reported to be effective. All of these medications must be taken for long periods of time and continued for several months after clinical cure to prevent a relapse. Surgical procedures such as drainage assist greatly in healing.

There is no specific therapy for maduromycosis, and at present the prognosis is poor. Sulfones have been reported to be effective in isolated cases. Surgical excision of early lesions may prevent spread. Amputation is necessary in far-advanced cases.

Zaias, N., & others: Mycetoma. Arch Dermat 99:215–225, 1969.

OPPORTUNISTIC FUNGUS INFECTIONS

Debilitating diseases and often the drugs used in their treatment (corticosteroids, antibiotics, antimetabolites), as well as pregnancy and other altered physiologic states, may render a patient susceptible to invasion by fungi which ordinarily are unable to cause disease. These factors may also cause infections due to the pathogenic fungi to be more serious.

The term **phycomycosis** (mucormycosis) is applied to infections caused by members of the genera Mucor, Absidia, Rhizopus, Mortierella, and Basidiobolus. These appear in tissue as broad, branching, nonseptate hyphae which may show a special affinity for blood vessels. Sinus, orbit, brain, lung, and digestive tract infections are often associated with diabetic acidosis. Control of the diabetic condition and antifungal therapy initiated early are essential. Amphotericin B (Fungizone®) (as for coccidioidomycosis), potassium iodide (as for sporotrichosis), nystatin, and surgery have been successful, but the prognosis is generally poor.

Aspergillosis may be caused by various species of Aspergillus. The colonization of an ectatic bronchus to form a compact mass of mycelium ("fungus ball") is usually associated with some immunity, and the fungus rarely adheres or penetrates the wall of the bronchus. *Aspergillus fumigatus* causes more serious infections. It invades necrotic tissue or pulmonary cavities produced by other causes, sometimes with subsequent radial extension into surrounding tissue and eventual hematogenous dissemination. The prognosis is poor although amphotericin B has been used successfully in some cases.

Aspergillus is recognized in tissue and sputum as dichotomously branched, septate hyphae. Spores may be formed in pulmonary cavities.

Mycotic keratitis has been caused by many species of normally saprophytic fungi. Trauma to the cornea followed by steroid and antibiotic therapy is the predisposing factor in most cases. Prompt withdrawal of corticosteroids, removal of the infected necrotic tissue, and application of fungicidal agents are essential for management.

Young, R.C., & others: Aspergillus lobar pneumonia. JAMA 208:1156–1162, 1969.

SYSTEMIC ANTIFUNGAL AGENTS*

AMPHOTERICIN B
(Fungizone®)

Amphotericin, derived from *Streptomyces nodosus,* is active against a wide variety of fungi causing

*Griseofulvin: See p 53.

systemic mycoses, and is indicated in severe systemic fungal infections.

Amphotericin B is poorly absorbed orally and should be given intravenously. The adult daily dosage is 0.5–1 mg/kg, but therapy should begin with 1 mg/day, increasing by 5 mg increments to 20 mg/day for 1–2 months. Clinical response and patient tolerance govern dosage change. Suspend the drug in 500 ml of 5% dextrose in distilled water (not saline) and give by slow intravenous drip. Preserve veins by using small needles and peripheral veins (hands, forearms). Heparin, 10–20 mg/500 ml, reduces phlebitis. Premedication with aspirin, diphenhydramine (Benadryl®), chlorpromazine, and hydrocortisone succinate intravenously reduces the side-effects of the drug in some patients.

Fungus drug sensitivity levels and serum assays for individualization of therapy allow lower drug dosage with fewer side-effects.

Toxicity includes chills, fever, malaise, renal and bone marrow damage, and thrombophlebitis. Monitor with creatinine clearance tests done before treatment, then weekly or biweekly; and with BUN determination.

Drutz, D.J., & others: Treatment of disseminated mycotic infections. A new approach to amphotericin B therapy. Am J Med 45:408–418, 1968.

NYSTATIN
(Mycostatin®)

Nystatin is derived from *Streptomyces noursei.* It is active against a wide variety of fungi and yeasts and is very poorly absorbed from the gastrointestinal tract, so that its activity is principally within the lumen of the bowel or wherever applied locally. Superinfection with candida caused by tetracycline therapy may be reduced by oral administration of nystatin. It may be used locally in candida infections of the mouth, genitalia, or skin.

The dosage is 500,000 units orally 3 times daily; 100,000 units locally as vaginal suppositories once or twice daily, or as ointment (100,000 units/gm).

• • •

General Bibliography

Campbell, C.C.: Use and interpretation of serologic and skin tests in the respiratory mycoses: Current considerations. Dis Chest 54:305–310, 1968.

Conant, N.F., & others: *Manual of Clinical Mycology.* Saunders, 1971.

Fetter, B.F., & others: *Mycoses of the Central Nervous System.* Williams & Wilkins, 1967.

Halde, C.: Systemic mycoses. Chap 23, pp 481–486, in: *Current Medical References,* 6th ed. Chatton, M.J., & P.J. Sanazaro (editors). Lange, 1970.

Hildick-Smith, G., & others: *Fungus Diseases and Their Therapy.* Little, Brown, 1964.

Louria, D.B.: Deep-seated mycotic infections: Allergy to fungi and mycotoxins. New England J Med 277:1065–1071, 1126–1134, 1967.

Rifkind, D., & others: Systemic fungal infections complicating renal transplantation and immunosuppressive therapy. Am J Med 43:28–38, 1967.

Schwarz, J., & K. Salfelder: Diagnosis of surgical deep mycoses. Surg Gynec Obst 128:259–274, 1969.

26...

Anti-Infective Chemotherapeutic & Antibiotic Agents

Ernest Jawetz

Some Rules for Antimicrobial Therapy

Antimicrobial drugs are used on a very large scale, and their proper use results in striking therapeutic results. On the other hand, they can give rise to serious complications and should therefore be administered only upon proper indication.

Drugs of choice and second-line drugs are presented in Table 26–3.

The following steps merit consideration in each patient.

A. Etiologic Diagnosis: Formulate an etiologic diagnosis based on clinical observations. Microbial infections are best treated early. Therefore, the physician must attempt to decide on clinical grounds (1) whether the patient has a microbial infection that can probably be influenced by antimicrobial drugs, and (2) the most probable kind of microorganisms causing this type of infection.

B. "Best Guess": Select a specific antimicrobial drug on the basis of past experience (personal or in the literature). Based on a "best guess" about the probable cause of the patient's infection, the physician should choose a drug that is likely to be effective against the suspected microorganism.

C. Laboratory Control: Before beginning antimicrobial drug treatment, obtain meaningful specimens for laboratory examination to determine the causative infectious organism and, if desirable, its susceptibility to antimicrobial drugs.

D. Clinical Response: Based on the clinical response of the patient, evaluate the laboratory reports and consider the desirability of changing the antimicrobial drug regimen. Laboratory results should not automatically overrule clinical judgment. The isolation of an organism that reinforces the initial clinical impression is a useful confirmation. Conversely, laboratory results may contradict the initial clinical impression and may force its reconsideration. If the specimen was obtained from a site which is normally devoid of bacterial flora and not exposed to the external environment (eg, blood, CSF, pleural fluid, joint fluid), the recovery of a microorganism is a significant finding even if the organism recovered is different from the clinically suspected etiologic agent and may force a change in antimicrobial treatment. On the other hand, the isolation of unexpected microorganisms from the respiratory tract, gut, or surface lesions (sites that have a complex flora) must be critically evaluated before drugs are abandoned which were judiciously selected on the basis of an initial "best guess."

E. Drug Sensitivity Tests: Some microorganisms are fairly uniformly susceptible to certain drugs; if such organisms are isolated from the patient, they need not be tested for drug susceptibility. For example, pneumococci, group A hemolytic streptococci, and clostridia respond predictably to penicillin. On the other hand, some kinds of microorganisms (eg, coliform gram-negative rods) are sufficiently variable in their response to warrant drug susceptibility testing whenever they are isolated from a significant specimen.

Antimicrobial drug susceptibility tests (commonly called "disk tests") usually give valuable results. Occasionally there is a marked discrepancy between the results of the test and the clinical response of the patient. The following possible explanations (among others) of such discrepancies may have to be considered:

1. Failure to drain a collection of pus or to remove a foreign body.

2. Failure of a poorly diffusing drug to reach the site of infection (eg, joint cavity, pleural space) or to reach intracellular phagocytized bacteria.

3. Superinfection in the course of prolonged chemotherapy. After suppression of the original infection or of normal flora, a second type of microorganism may establish itself against which the originally selected drug is ineffective.

4. Emergence of drug-resistant mutants from a large microbial population.

5. Participation of 2 or more microorganisms in the infectious process of which only one was originally detected and used for drug selection.

F. Adequate Dosage: To determine whether the proper drug is being used in adequate dosage, a serum assay can be performed. Two or 3 days after a drug regimen is established, serum is obtained from the patient. Dilutions of this serum are set up against the microorganism originally isolated from the patient's infection and the antibacterial activity estimated. If an adequate dose of a proper drug is being employed, the serum should be markedly bactericidal in vitro. In infections limited to the urinary tract, the antibacterial activity of urine can be estimated.

G. Oral Antibiotics: The absorption of oral penicillins, tetracyclines, lincomycin, etc is impaired by food. Therefore, these oral drugs must be given between meals.

TABLE 26—1. Incompatibilities between antimicrobial drugs and other agents.

Antimicrobial Drug	Other Agent	Result
In Vitro Incompatibilities When Mixed for Intravenous Administration*		
Amphotericin B	Benzylpenicillin, tetracyclines	Precipitate
Cephalosporins	Calcium gluconate or calcium chloride, polymyxin B, erythromycin, tetracyclines	Precipitate
Chloramphenicol	Polymyxin B, tetracyclines, vancomycin, hydrocortisone, B complex vitamins	Precipitate
Methicillin	Any acidic solution, tetracyclines	Inactivation in 6 hours
Nafcillin	Any acidic solution, B complex vitamins	Inactivation in 12 hours
Oxacillin	Any acidic solution, B complex vitamins	Inactivation in 12 hours
Penicillin G	Any acidic solution, B complex vitamins, amphotericin B, chloramphenicol, tetracyclines, vancomycin, metaraminol, phenylephrine	Inactivation in 12 hours, precipitate
Polymyxin B	Cephalothin, tetracyclines	Precipitate
Tetracyclines	Calcium-containing solutions, amphotericin B, cephalosporins, heparin, hydrocortisone, polymyxin B, chloramphenicol, any divalent cations	Chelation, inactivation, precipitate
Vancomycin	Heparin, penicillins, hydrocortisone, chloramphenicol	Precipitate
Physiologic Drug Interactions		
Chloramphenicol	Diphenylhydantoin, tolbutamide	Increased concentration in blood
Griseofulvin	Anticoagulants	Decreased anticoagulant effect
Kanamycin, streptomycin, neomycin, gentamicin, polymyxins	Curare	Increased curare effect
Sulfonamides, chloramphenicol, tetracyclines	Anticoagulants	Increased anticoagulant effect (probably due to inhibition of intestinal flora, which produces vitamin K)
Sulfonamides	Sulfonylurea Methenamine (oral)	Hypoglycemia Insoluble compound in urine

*Many other incompatibilities may occur.

H. Adverse Reactions: The administration of antimicrobial drugs is commonly associated with untoward reactions. These fall into several groups. (1) Hypersensitivity: The most common hypersensitivity reactions are fever and skin rashes. Hematologic or hepatic disorders and anaphylaxis are rare. (2) Direct toxicity: Most common are nausea, vomiting, and diarrhea. More serious toxic reactions are impairment of renal, hepatic, or hematopoietic functions or damage to the 8th nerve. (3) Suppression of normal microbial flora and "superinfection" by drug-resistant microorganisms, or continued infection with the initial pathogen through the emergence of drug-resistant mutants.

In each case, the physician must evaluate the desirability of continuing a given drug regimen against the risk of discontinuing it. He must evaluate the severity and prognosis of each untoward reaction and choose between continuing a probably offending drug and discontinuing the drug but risking uncontrolled infection. An effective antimicrobial drug regimen which evokes hypersensitivity reactions can sometimes be continued with the simultaneous use of corticosteroids. In the presence of impaired renal function, toxic accumulation of drugs is likely. Therefore, reduction in dosage or frequency of medication is often necessary in renal failure (Table 26—2).

I. Discontinue Treatment: If the patient is responding favorably to the administration of antimicrobial drugs as judged by appropriate clinical or laboratory findings, treatment should be discontinued as soon as possible to minimize untoward drug reactions.

Jawetz, E.: General principles of anti-infective therapy. Chapter 48, pp 461—466, in: Meyers, F.H., Jawetz, E., & A. Goldfien: *Review of Medical Pharmacology*, 2nd ed. Lange, 1970.

Weinstein, L.: Common sense (clinical judgment) in the diagnosis and antibiotic therapy of etiologically undefined infections. P Clin North America 15:141—156, 1968.

PENICILLINS

The penicillins comprise a large group of antimicrobial substances some of which are natural products of molds and others semisynthetic compounds. They share a common chemical nucleus (6-aminopenicillanic acid) and a common mode of antibacterial action—the inhibition of cell wall mucopeptide (peptidoglycan) synthesis. The penicillins are in 1971 the

TABLE 26-2. Antibiotic dosage in renal failure.

Drug	Principal Mode of Excretion or Detoxification	Approximate Half-Life in Serum		Proposed Dosage Regimen in Renal Failure†	
		Normal	Renal Failure*	Initial Dose and Route*	Give Half the Initial Dose at Intervals Of
Penicillin G	Tubular secretion	0.5 hours	10 hours	6 gm IV	8-12 hours
Ampicillin	Tubular secretion	0.5 hours	10 hours	6 gm IV	8-12 hours
Methicillin	Tubular secretion	0.5 hours	10 hours	6 gm IV	6-8 hours
Cephalothin	Tubular secretion	0.8 hours	15 hours	8 gm IV	12 hours
Cephalexin	Tubular secretion and glomerular filtration	1 hour	15 hours	2 gm orally	8-12 hours
Streptomycin	Glomerular filtration	2.5 hours	3-4 days	1 gm IM	3-4 days
Kanamycin	Glomerular filtration	3 hours	3-4 days	1 gm IM	3-4 days
Gentamicin	Glomerular filtration	2.5 hours	3-4 days	2 mg/kg IM	3-4 days
Vancomycin	Glomerular filtration	6 hours	8-9 days	0.5 gm IV	8-10 days
Polymyxin B	Glomerular filtration	5 hours	2-3 days	2.5 mg/kg IV	2-4 days
Colistimethate	Glomerular filtration	3 hours	2-3 days	3.5 mg/kg IM	2-4 days
Tetracyclines	Glomerular filtration and liver	8 hours	3 days	1 gm orally, or 0.5 gm IV	3 days
Chloramphenicol	Liver and glomerular filtration	3 hours	4 hours	1 gm orally or IV	8 hours
Erythromycin	Liver and glomerular filtration	1.5 hours	5 hours	1 gm orally or IV	8 hours
Lincomycin	Glomerular filtration and liver	4.5 hours	10 hours	1 gm orally or IV	12 hours

*Considered here to be marked by creatinine clearance of 10 ml/minute or less.

†For a 60 kg adult with a serious systemic infection. The "initial dose" listed is administered as an intravenous infusion over a period of 1-8 hours, or as 2 intramuscular injections during an 8-hour period, or as 2-3 oral doses during the same period.

most important and most widely applicable group of antibacterial drugs. They can be arranged according to several major criteria:

(1) Susceptibility to destruction by penicillinase (ie, hydrolysis by the β-lactamase of bacteria).

(2) Susceptibility to destruction by acid pH (ie, relative stability to gastric acid).

(3) Relative efficacy against gram-positive versus gram-negative bacteria.

Antimicrobial Activity

All penicillins have the same mechanism of antibacterial action. They specifically inhibit the synthesis of bacterial cell walls which contain a complex mucopeptide (peptidoglycan). It is probable that they act by inhibiting the terminal cross-linking of linear glucopeptides and thus prevent the formation of a rigid cell wall. This leads to lysis of the cell in an isotonic environment and to the formation of "cell wall deficient" forms (L forms, protoplasts) in a hypertonic environment. Most penicillins are much more active against gram-positive than against gram-negative bacteria, probably because of chemical differences in cell wall structure. Penicillins are inactive against bacteria which are not multiplying and thus form no new cell walls ("persisters").

One million units of penicillin G equal 0.6 gm. Other penicillins are prescribed in grams. A blood serum level of 0.01-1 μg/ml penicillin G or ampicillin is lethal for a majority of susceptible microorganisms; methicillin and isoxazolylpenicillins are 1/5-1/50 as active.

Resistance

Resistance to penicillins falls into 4 different categories:

(1) Certain bacteria (eg, some staphylococci, gram-negative bacteria) produce enzymes (penicillinases, β-lactamases) which destroy penicillin G, ampicillin, and other penicillins. The genetic control of this enzyme in staphylococci resides in a "plasmid" which is transmissible to other bacteria of the same species via bacteriophage. Clinical penicillin resistance of staphylococci falls largely into this category.

(2) Certain bacteria (eg, coliform organisms) produce an enzyme (amidase) which can split off the side chain from the penicillin nucleus and thus destroy biologic activity.

(3) Certain bacteria are resistant to some penicillins although they do not produce enzymes destroying the drug. Clinical methicillin resistance falls into this category and may be due to cell wall change.

(4) Metabolically inactive organisms which make no new cell wall mucopeptide are temporarily resistant to penicillins. They can act as "persisters" and perpetuate infection during and after penicillin treatment. L-forms are in this category.

Absorption, Distribution, & Excretion

After parenteral administration, absorption of most penicillins is complete and rapid. Because of the irritation and consequent local pain produced by the intramuscular injection of large doses, administration by the intravenous route (continuous infusion, or intermittent addition to a continuous drip) is often preferred. After oral administration, only a portion of the dose is absorbed—from 1/3–1/20, depending upon acid stability, binding to foods, and the presence of buffers. In order to minimize binding to foods, oral penicillins should not be preceded or followed by food for at least 1 hour.

After absorption, penicillins are widely distributed in body fluids and tissues. This varies to some extent with the degree of protein binding exhibited by different penicillins. Penicillin G, methicillin, and ampicillin are moderately protein bound (depending upon the method of measurement, 30–60%), whereas the isoxazolylpenicillins are highly protein bound (90–98%). While the importance of serum binding is far from clear, it is probable that intensive protein binding diminishes the amount of drug available for antibacterial action in vivo and thus delays a therapeutic response. With parenteral doses of 3–6 gm (5–10 million units) of penicillin G, injected by continuous infusion or divided intramuscular injections, average serum levels of the drug reach 1–10 units (0.6–6 μg)/ml. A rough relationship of 6 gm given parenterally per day, yielding serum levels of 1–6 μg/ml, also applies to other penicillins. Naturally, the highly serum bound isoxazolylpenicillins yield, on the average, lower levels of free drug than less strongly bound penicillins.

Special dosage forms of penicillin have been designed for delayed absorption to yield low blood and tissue levels for long periods. The outstanding example is benzathine penicillin G. After a single intramuscular injection of 1.5 gm (2.4 million units), serum levels in excess of 0.03 unit/ml are maintained for 10 days and levels in excess of 0.005 unit/ml for 3 weeks. The latter is sufficient to protect against beta-hemolytic streptococcal infection; the former to treat an established infection with these organisms. Procaine penicillin also has delayed absorption, yielding levels for 24 hours.

In many tissues, penicillin concentrations are equal to those in serum. Much lower levels are found in the joints, eyes, and CNS. However, with active inflammation of the meninges, as in bacterial meningitis, penicillin levels in the CSF exceed 0.2 μg/ml with a daily parenteral dose of 12 gm. Thus, pneumococcal and meningococcal meningitis may be treated with systemic penicillin and there is no need for intrathecal injection.

Most of the absorbed penicillin is rapidly excreted by the kidneys into the urine; small amounts are excreted by other channels. About 10% of renal excretion is by glomerular filtration and 90% by tubular secretion, to a maximum of about 2 gm/hour in an adult. Tubular secretion can be partially blocked by probenecid (Benemid®) to achieve higher systemic levels. Renal clearance is less efficient in the newborn,

so that proportionately smaller doses result in higher systemic levels and are maintained longer than in the adult. Individuals with impaired renal function likewise tend to maintain higher penicillin levels longer.

Renal excretion of penicillin results in very high levels in the urine. Thus, systemic daily doses of 6 gm of penicillin may yield urine levels of 500–3000 μg/ml—enough to suppress not only gram-positive but also many gram-negative bacteria in the urine (provided they produce no β-lactamase or amidase).

Penicillin is also excreted into sputum and milk to levels of 3–15% of those present in the serum. This is the case in both man and cattle. The presence of penicillin in the milk of cows treated for mastitis presents a problem in allergy.

Indications, Dosages, & Routes of Administration

The penicillins are by far the most effective and the most widely used antimicrobial drugs. All oral penicillins must be given 1 hour away from meal times to reduce binding and acid inactivation. Blood levels of all penicillins can be raised by simultaneous administration of probenecid, 0.5 gm every 6 hours orally (10 mg/kg every 6 hours).

A. Penicillin G: This is the drug of choice for infections caused by gonococci, pneumococci, streptococci, meningococci, non–β-lactamase producing staphylococci, *Treponema pallidum* and many other spirochetes, *Bacillus anthracis* and other gram-positive rods, clostridia, listeria, and bacteroides.

1. Intramuscular or intravenous—Most of the above-mentioned infections respond to aqueous penicillin G in daily doses of 0.6–5 million units (0.36–3 gm) administered by intermittent IM injection every 4–6 hours. Much larger amounts (6–120 gm daily) can be given by continuous IV infusion in serious or complicated infections due to these organisms. Sites for such intravenous administration are subject to thrombophlebitis and superinfection and must be rotated every 2 days and kept scrupulously aseptic. In enterococcus endocarditis, kanamycin or streptomycin is given simultaneously with large doses of penicillin.

2. Oral—Buffered penicillin G (or penicillin V) is indicated only in minor infections (eg, of the respiratory tract or its associated structures) in daily doses of 1–4 gm (1.6–6.4 million units). About 1/5 of the oral dose is absorbed, but oral administration is subject to so many variables that it should not be relied upon in seriously ill patients.

3. Intrathecal—With high serum levels of penicillin, adequate concentrations reach the CNS and CSF for the treatment of meningitis. Therefore, and because injection of more than 10,000 units of penicillin G into the subdural space may cause convulsions, intrathecal injection has been virtually abandoned.

4. Topical—Penicillins have been applied to skin, wounds, and mucous membranes by compress, ointment, and aerosol. These applications are highly sensitizing and rarely warranted. Rarely, solutions of penicillin (eg, 100,000 units/ml) are instilled into joint or pleural space infected with susceptible organisms.

B. Benzathine Penicillin G: This penicillin is a salt of very low water solubility. It is injected intramuscularly to establish a depot which yields low but prolonged drug levels. A single injection of 2.4 million units IM is satisfactory for treatment of beta-hemolytic streptococcal pharyngitis and perhaps for early syphilis. An injection of 1.3–2.4 million units IM every 3–4 weeks provides satisfactory prophylaxis for rheumatics against reinfection with group A streptococci. There is no indication for using this drug by mouth. Procaine penicillin G is another repository form for maintaining drug levels for up to 24 hours. For highly susceptible infections, 300–600 thousand units IM are usually given once daily.

C. Ampicillin, Carbenicillin: These drugs differ from penicillin G in having greater activity against gram-negative bacteria, but, like penicillin G, they are destroyed by penicillinases.

Ampicillin is the drug of current choice for bacterial meningitis in small children, especially meningitis due to *H influenzae*; 150 mg/kg/day are injected IV. Ampicillin can be given orally in divided doses, 3–6 gm daily to treat urinary tract infections with coliform bacteria, enterococci, or *Proteus mirabilis*. It is ineffective against enterobacter and pseudomonas. In salmonella infections, ampicillin, 6–12 gm daily orally, can be effective in suppressing clinical disease (second choice to chloramphenicol in acute typhoid or paratyphoid) and may eliminate salmonellae from some chronic carriers. Ampicillin is more effective than penicillin G against enterococci and may be used in such infections in combination with streptomycin, kanamycin, or gentamicin. Carbenicillin is more active against pseudomonas, but resistance emerges rapidly. Therefore, a combination with gentamicin is suggested in pseudomonas sepsis. Hetacillin is converted in vivo to ampicillin and should not be used.

D. Penicillinase-Resistant Penicillins: Methicillin, oxacillin, cloxacillin, dicloxacillin, nafcillin, and others are relatively resistant to destruction by β-lactamase. The only indication for the use of these drugs is infection by β-lactamase producing staphylococci.

1. Oral—Oxacillin, cloxacillin, dicloxacillin (the isoxazolylpenicillins), or nafcillin may be given in doses of 0.25–0.5 gm every 4–6 hours in mild or localized staphylococcal infections (50–100 mg/kg/day for children). Food must not be given in proximity to these doses because it will markedly interfere with absorption.

2. Intravenous—For serious systemic staphylococcal infections, methicillin, 8–16 gm, or nafcillin, 6–12 gm, is administered IV, usually by injecting 1–2 gm during 20–30 minutes every 2 hours into a continuous infusion of 5% dextrose in water or physiologic salt solution. The dose for children is methicillin, 100–300 mg/kg/day, or nafcillin, 50–100 mg/kg/day.

Adverse Effects

The penicillins undoubtedly possess less direct toxicity than any other antibiotics. Most of the serious side-effects are due to hypersensitivity.

A. Allergy: All penicillins are cross-sensitizing and cross-reacting. Any preparation containing penicillin may induce sensitization, including foods or cosmetics. In general, sensitization occurs in direct proportion to the duration and total dose of penicillin received in the past. The responsible antigenic determinants appear to be degradation products of penicillins, particularly penicilloic acid and products of alkaline hydrolysis bound to host protein. Skin tests with penicilloyl-polylysine, with alkaline hydrolysis products, and with undegraded penicillin will identify many hypersensitive individuals. Among positive reactors to skin tests, the incidence of subsequent penicillin reactions is high. Although many persons develop antibodies to antigenic determinants of penicillin, the presence of such antibodies is not correlated with allergic reactivity (except rare hemolytic anemia), and serologic tests have little predictive value. A history of a penicillin reaction in the past is not reliable; however, in such cases the drug should be administered with caution.

Allergic reactions may occur as typical anaphylactic shock, typical serum sickness type reactions (urticaria, fever, joint swelling, angioneurotic edema, intense pruritus, and respiratory embarrassment occurring 7–12 days after exposure), and a variety of skin rashes, oral lesions, fever, nephritis, eosinophilia, hemolytic anemia, other hematologic disturbances, and vasculitis. LE cells are sometimes found. The incidence of hypersensitivity to penicillin is estimated to be 5–10% among adults in the USA, but is negligible in small children. Acute anaphylactic life-threatening reactions are fortunately very rare. Ampicillin produces skin rashes (mononucleosis-like) 3–5 times more frequently than other penicillins.

Individuals known to be hypersensitive to penicillin can at times tolerate the drug during corticosteroid administration. "Desensitization" with gradually increasing doses of penicillin is also occasionally attempted but is not without hazard.

B. Toxicity: Since the action of penicillin is directed against a unique bacterial structure, the cell wall, it is virtually without effect on animal cells. The toxic effects of penicillin G are due to the direct irritation caused by intramuscular or intravenous injection of exceedingly high concentrations (eg, 1 gm/ml). Such concentrations may cause local pain, induration, thrombophlebitis, or degeneration of an accidentally injected nerve. All penicillins are irritating to the CNS. There is little indication for intrathecal administration at present. In rare cases a patient receiving more than 50 gm of penicillin G daily parenterally has exhibited signs of cerebrocortical irritation, presumably as a result of the passage of unusually large amounts of penicillin into the CNS. With doses of this magnitude, direct cation toxicity (Na^+, K^+) can also occur. Potassium penicillin G contains 1.7 mEq of K^+ per million units (2.8 mEq/gm), and potassium may accumulate in the presence of renal failure. Carbenicillin contains 4.7 mEq of Na^+ per gram—a risk in heart failure.

Large doses of penicillins given orally may lead to gastrointestinal upset, particularly nausea and diarrhea.

Oral therapy may also be accompanied by luxuriant overgrowth of staphylococci, pseudomonas, proteus, or yeasts, which may occasionally cause enteritis. Superinfections in other organ systems may occur with penicillins as with any antibiotic therapy. Methicillin and isoxazolylpenicillins have occasionally caused granulocytopenia, especially in children. Carbenicillin can cause transaminase elevations in serum.

Barrett, F.F., & others: Methicillin-resistant *Staphylococcus aureus* at Boston City Hospital. New England J Med 279:441–448, 1968.
Grieco, M.H.: Cross-allergenicity of the penicillins and the cephalosporins. Arch Int Med 119:141–146, 1967.
Kunin, C.M.: Clinical pharmacology of the new penicillins. Clin Pharmacol & Therap 7:166–179, 1966.
Martin, W.J.: Newer penicillins. M Clin North America 51:1107–1126, 1967.
Pines, A., & others: Treatment of severe pseudomonas infections. Brit MJ 1:663–665, 1970.

CEPHALOSPORINS

Cephalosporins are a group of compounds closely related to the penicillins. In place of 6-aminopenicillanic acid, cephalosporins have a nucleus of 7-aminocephalosporanic acid. The mode of action is the same as that of penicillins, there is some (limited) cross-allergenicity, and they are resistant to destruction by β-lactamase.

Antimicrobial Activity

Cephalosporins inhibit the synthesis of bacterial cell wall mucopeptide in a fashion analogous to that of penicillins. They are resistant to destruction by β-lactamase, but they can be hydrolyzed by a cephalosporinase produced by certain microorganisms. The cephalosporins are bactericidal in vitro in concentrations of 1–20 μg/ml against most gram-positive microorganisms, except *Streptococcus faecalis*, and in concentrations of 5–30 μg/ml against many gram-negative bacteria, except pseudomonas, herellea, proteus, and enterobacter. There is at least partial cross-resistance between cephalosporins and β-lactamase resistant penicillins. Thus, methicillin-resistant staphylococci are also resistant to cephalosporins.

Absorption, Distribution, & Excretion

Cephalothin and cephaloridine are not significantly absorbed from the gut. After parenteral injection, they are distributed widely, and 20–60% of the drugs in serum are protein-bound. Concentrations in synovial fluid, CNS, and CSF are low after parenteral injection. Thus, cephalothin is not a drug of choice in meningitis. Excretion of cephalosporins is primarily by tubular secretion into the urine.

Urine levels may reach 200–1000 μg/ml. In the presence of impaired renal function, very high blood and tissue levels of cephalosporins may accumulate and exert toxic effects.

Cephaloglycine and cephalexin are somewhat better absorbed from the gut, and therapeutic urine levels are reached after oral doses.

Indications, Dosages, & Routes of Administration

A. Oral: Cephaloglycine, 0.5 gm 4 times daily orally, yields urine concentrations of 50–500 μg/ml—sufficient for treatment of urinary tract infections due to coliform organisms. Cephalexin, 0.5 gm orally 4 times daily (50 mg/kg/day), can be used in urinary or respiratory tract infections due to susceptible organisms.

B. Intravenous: Cephalothin (Keflin®), 8–16 gm daily (for children, 50–100 mg/kg/day) by continuous drip, gives serum concentrations of 5–20 μg/ml. This is adequate for the treatment of gram-negative bacteremia or staphylococcal sepsis, or as a substitute for penicillin in serious infections caused by susceptible organisms in persons allergic to penicillin (although some cross-hypersensitivity exists). Cephaloridine (Keflordin®, Loridine®), 4 gm daily (for children, up to 100 mg/kg/day) IV, gives serum levels of 10–25 μg/ml. It is used for the same indications.

C. Intramuscular: Cephaloridine, 0.5–1 gm IM every 6 hours, is used for the same indications as above in less severely ill patients. Cephalothin is too painful when injected intramuscularly.

Adverse Effects

A. Allergy: Cephalosporins are sensitizing and a variety of hypersensitivity reactions occur, including anaphylaxis, fever, skin rashes, granulocytopenia, and hemolytic anemia. Cross-allergy also exists with penicillins and can produce the same hypersensitivity reactions. Perhaps 10–30% of penicillin-allergic persons are also hypersensitive to cephalosporins.

B. Toxicity: Local pain after intramuscular injection, thrombophlebitis after intravenous injection. Cephaloridine can cause renal damage with tubular necrosis and uremia.

Griffith, R.S., & H.R. Black: Cephalexin. M Clin North America 54:1229–1244, 1970.
Meyers, B.R., & others: Cephalexin. Clin Pharmacol Therap 10:810–816, 1969.
Steigbigel, N.H., & others: Clinical evaluation of cephaloridine. Arch Int Med 121:24–38, 1968.
Thoburn, R., & others: The relationship of cephalothin and penicillin allergy. JAMA 198:345–348, 1966.

ERYTHROMYCIN GROUP
(Macrolides)

The erythromycins are a group of closely related compounds characterized by a macrocyclic lactone ring to which sugars are attached. There are several different members of the group.

Erythromycins inhibit protein synthesis and are bacteriostatic or bactericidal against gram-positive organisms—especially pneumococci, streptococci, staphylococci, and corynebacteria—in concentrations of 0.02–2 μg/ml. Neisseriae and mycoplasmas are also susceptible. Activity is enhanced at alkaline pH. Resistant mutants occur in microbial populations, including pneumococci and mycoplasmas, and tend to emerge during prolonged treatment. There is complete cross-resistance among all members of the erythromycin group. Absorption of these drugs varies greatly. Basic erythromycins are destroyed by stomach acids. Erythromycin stearate is acid-resistant. The propionyl ester of erythromycin (erythromycin estolate) and the triacetyl ester of oleandomycin are among the best absorbed oral preparations. Oral doses of 2 gm/day result in blood levels of up to 2 μg/ml, and there is wide distribution of the drug in all tissues except the CNS. Erythromycins are excreted largely in bile; only 5% of the dose is excreted into the urine. Alkaline pH enhances activity.

Erythromycins are the drugs of choice in corynebacterial infections (diphtheroid sepsis, erythrasma) and in mycoplasmal pneumonia. They are most useful as substitutes for penicillin in persons with streptococcal and pneumococcal infections who are allergic to penicillin.

Dosages

A. Oral: Erythromycin base, stearate, succinate, or estolate, or triacetyloleandomycin, 0.5 gm every 6 hours (for children, 40 mg/kg/day).

B. Intravenous: Erythromycin lactobionate or gluceptate, 0.5 gm every 12 hours.

Adverse Effects

Nausea, vomiting, and diarrhea may occur after oral intake. Erythromycin estolate or triacetyloleandomycin can produce acute cholestatic hepatitis (fever, jaundice, impaired liver function). Most patients recover completely. Upon readministration, the hepatitis promptly recurs. It is probably a hypersensitivity reaction.

TETRACYCLINE GROUP

The tetracyclines are a large group of drugs with common basic chemical structures, antimicrobial activity, and pharmacologic properties. Microorganisms resistant to this group show complete cross-resistance to all tetracyclines.

Antimicrobial Activity

Tetracyclines are inhibitors of protein synthesis and are bacteriostatic for many gram-positive and gram-negative bacteria, including anaerobes, and are strongly inhibitory for the growth of mycoplasmas, rickettsiae, chlamydiae (psittacosis-LGV-trachoma agents), and some protozoa (eg, amebas). Equal concentrations of all tetracyclines in blood or tissue have approximately equal antimicrobial activity. Such differences in activity as may be claimed for individual tetracycline drugs are of no practical importance. However, there are great differences in the susceptibility of different strains of a given species of microorganism, and laboratory tests are therefore important. Because of the emergence of resistant strains, tetracyclines have lost some of their former usefulness. Proteus and pseudomonas are regularly resistant; among coliform bacteria, pneumococci, and streptococci, resistant strains are increasingly common.

Absorption, Distribution, & Excretion

Tetracyclines are absorbed somewhat irregularly from the gut. Absorption is limited by the low solubility of the drugs and by chelation with divalent cations, eg, Ca^{++} or Fe^{++}. A large proportion of orally administered tetracycline remains in the gut lumen, modifies intestinal flora, and is excreted in feces. Of the absorbed drug, 20–50% is protein bound in the blood. With full systemic doses (2 gm/day), levels of active drug in serum reach 2–10 μg/ml. The drugs are widely distributed in tissues and body fluids, but the levels in CNS, CSF, and joint fluids are only 3–10% of serum levels. Tetracyclines are specifically deposited in growing bones and teeth, bound to calcium.

Absorbed tetracyclines are excreted mainly in bile and urine. Up to 20% of oral doses may appear in the urine after glomerular filtration. Urine levels may be 5–50 μg/ml or more. With renal failure, doses of tetracyclines must be reduced or intervals between doses increased. Up to 80% of an oral dose appears in the feces.

Demethylchlortetracycline, methacycline, and doxycycline are well absorbed from the gut but are excreted much more slowly than others, leading to accumulation and prolonged blood levels. Specially formulated buffered tetracycline solutions can be injected parenterally.

Indications, Dosages, & Routes of Administration

At present, tetracyclines are the drugs of choice in cholera, mycoplasmal pneumonia, infections with chlamydiae (psittacosis-LGV-trachoma), and infections with some rickettsiae. They may be used in various bacterial infections provided the organism is susceptible, and in amebiasis.

A. Oral: Tetracycline hydrochloride, oxytetracycline, and chlortetracycline are dispensed in 250 mg capsules. Give 0.25–0.5 gm orally every 6 hours (for children, 20–40 mg/kg/day). In acne vulgaris, 0.25 gm once or twice daily for many months is prescribed by dermatologists.

Demethylchlortetracycline and methacycline are long-acting tetracyclines available in capsules containing 50 or 150 mg. Give 0.15–0.3 gm orally every 6 hours (for children, 12–20 mg/kg/day). Doxycycline is available in capsules containing 50 or 100 mg or as powder for oral suspension. Give 100 mg every 12 hours on the first day and 100 mg/day in 1 or 2 doses for maintenance.

B. Intramuscular or Intravenous: Several tetracyclines are formulated for intramuscular or intravenous injection. Give 0.1–0.5 gm every 6–12 hours in individuals unable to take oral medication (for children, 10–15 mg/kg/day).

C. **Topical:** Topical tetracycline, 1%, in ointment, can be applied to conjunctival infections.

Adverse Effects

A. **Allergy:** Hypersensitivity reactions with fever or skin rashes are uncommon.

B. **Gastrointestinal Side-Effects:** Gastrointestinal side-effects, especially diarrhea, nausea, and anorexia, are common. These can be diminished by reducing the dose or by administering tetracyclines with food or carboxymethylcellulose, but sometimes they force discontinuance of the drug. After a few days of oral use, the gut flora is modified so that drug-resistant bacteria and yeasts become prominent. This may cause functional gut disturbances, anal pruritus, and even enterocolitis with shock and death.

C. **Bones and Teeth:** Tetracyclines are bound to calcium deposited in growing bones and teeth, causing fluorescence, discoloration, enamel dysplasia, deformity, or growth inhibition. Therefore, tetracyclines should not be given to pregnant women or small children.

D. **Liver Damage:** Tetracyclines can impair hepatic function or even cause liver necrosis, particularly during pregnancy, in the presence of preexisting liver damage, or with doses of more than 3 gm IV.

E. **Kidney Damage:** Outdated tetracycline preparations have been implicated in renal tubular acidosis and other forms of renal damage.

F. **Other:** Tetracyclines, principally demethylchlortetracycline, may induce photosensitization, especially in blonds. Intravenous injection may cause thrombophlebitis, and intramuscular injection may induce local inflammation with pain.

Kunin, C.M.: The tetracyclines. P Clin North America 15:43–56, 1968.

CHLORAMPHENICOL

Chloramphenicol is a synthetic drug and potent inhibitor of bacterial protein synthesis which inhibits the growth of many bacteria and rickettsiae in concentrations of 0.5–10 μg/ml. Resistant mutants occur in most susceptible species. There is no cross-resistance with other drugs.

After oral administration chloramphenicol is rapidly and completely absorbed. Administration of 2 gm/day orally to adults results in blood levels of 20 μg/ml. In children, chloramphenicol palmitate, 50 mg/kg/day orally, is hydrolyzed in the gut to yield free chloramphenicol and gives a blood level of 10 μg/ml. Chloramphenicol succinate, 25–50 mg/kg/day IM or IV, yields free chloramphenicol by hydrolysis and gives blood levels comparable to those achieved by oral administration. After absorption, chloramphenicol is widely distributed to all tissues, including the CNS and CSF. It penetrates cells readily. About 50% of drug in the serum is protein-bound. Chloramphenicol is inactivated either by conjugation with glucuronic acid in the liver or by reduction to inactive aryl amines. In hepatic insufficiency, the drug may accumulate to toxic levels. Only 10% of active drug is excreted by glomerular filtration in the urine.

Because of its potential toxicity, chloramphenicol is at present a possible drug of choice only in the following cases: (1) symptomatic salmonella infection, eg, typhoid fever; (2) *Hemophilus influenzae* meningitis, laryngotracheitis, or pneumonia that does not respond to ampicillin; (3) occasional gram-negative bacteremia; (4) severe rickettsial infection; and (5) meningococcal infection in patients hypersensitive to penicillin. It is occasionally used topically in ophthalmology.

In serious systemic infection, the dose is 0.5 gm orally every 4–6 hours (for children, 30–50 mg/kg/day) for 7–21 days. Similar amounts are given intravenously.

Adverse Effects

Nausea, vomiting, and diarrhea occur infrequently. The most serious adverse effects pertain to the hematopoietic system. Adults taking chloramphenicol in excess of 50 mg/kg/day regularly exhibit disturbances in red cell maturation after 1–2 weeks of blood levels above 25 μg/ml. There is anemia, rise in serum iron concentration, reticulocytopenia, and the appearance of vacuolated nucleated red cells in the bone marrow. These changes regress when the drug is stopped and are not related to the rare aplastic anemia.

Serious aplastic anemia is a rare consequence of chloramphenicol administration and represents a specific, probably genetically determined individual defect. It is not related to dose or time of intake but is seen more frequently with either prolonged or repeated use. It tends to be irreversible and fatal. It is estimated that fatal aplastic anemia occurs 13 times more frequently after the use of chloramphenicol than as a spontaneous occurrence. Hypoplastic anemia may be followed by the development of leukemia.

Chloramphenicol inhibits the metabolism of certain drugs. Thus, it may prolong the action and raise blood concentration of tolbutamide or diphenylhydantoin.

Chloramphenicol is specifically toxic for newborns. Because they lack the mechanism for detoxification of the drug in the liver, the drug may accumulate, producing the highly fatal "gray syndrome" with vomiting, flaccidity, hypothermia, and collapse. Chloramphenicol should only rarely be used in infants, and the dose must be limited to less than 50 mg/kg/day in full-term infants and less than 30 mg/kg/day in prematures.

Ingall, D., & J.D. Sherman: Chloramphenicol. P Clin North America 15:57–72, 1968.

Wallerstein, R.O., & others: Statewide study of chloramphenicol therapy and fatal aplastic anemia. JAMA 208:2045–2050, 1969.

AMINOGLYCOSIDES

Aminoglycosides are a group of drugs with similar chemical, antimicrobial, pharmacologic, ototoxic, and nephrotoxic characteristics. Important members are streptomycin, neomycin, kanamycin, and gentamicin. All of the aminoglycosides inhibit microbial protein synthesis by attaching to the 30S unit of microbial ribosomes and causing a misreading of the genetic message.

1. STREPTOMYCIN

Streptomycin is a product of *Streptomyces griseus*. Dihydrostreptomycin was derived from it by chemical reduction, but it is no longer used because of serious ototoxicity. Streptomycin can be bactericidal for gram-positive and gram-negative bacteria and for *Mycobacterium tuberculosis*. Its antituberculosis activity is described below.

In all bacterial strains there are mutants which are 10–1000 times more resistant to streptomycin than the remainder of the microbial population. These are selected out rapidly in the presence of streptomycin. Treatment with streptomycin for 4–5 days thus results either in eradication of the infecting agent or the emergence of resistant infection which is untreatable with the drug. For this reason, streptomycin is usually employed in combination with another drug to delay the emergence of resistance. Streptomycin may enhance the bactericidal action of penicillins, particularly against *Streptococcus faecalis*.

Streptomycin is not significantly absorbed from the gut. After intramuscular injection, it is rapidly absorbed and widely distributed in body fluids and tissues except the CNS and CSF. Streptomycin does not penetrate well into living cells. Thus it is only slightly active against intracellular phagocytized bacteria and fails to eradicate those chronic infections in which most organisms are intracellular. With 2 gm given IM daily, serum levels reach 20 μg/ml.

Streptomycin is excreted mainly by glomerular filtration into the urine, where the concentration may be 5–50 times higher than in serum. In renal failure, excretion of streptomycin is impaired and accumulation to toxic levels occurs unless the dose is greatly reduced and the intervals between injections are lengthened.

Indications & Dosages

The principal indications for streptomycin at present are (1) serious active tuberculosis (see p 825); (2) plague, tularemia, or occasional gram-negative sepsis; (3) acute brucellosis (used in conjunction with tetracycline); (4) bacterial endocarditis caused by *Streptococcus faecalis* or *S viridans* (used in conjunction with penicillin).

The dose in the nontuberculous infections is 0.5–1 gm IM every 6–12 hours (for children, 20–40 mg/kg/day), depending on severity of the disease.

Adverse Effects

Allergic reactions, including skin rashes and fever, may occur upon prolonged contact with streptomycin, eg, in personnel preparing solutions. The principal side-effects are nephrotoxicity and ototoxicity. Renal damage with nitrogen retention occurs mainly after prolonged high doses or in persons with preexisting impairment of renal function. Damage to the 8th nerve manifests itself mainly by tinnitus, vertigo, ataxia, loss of balance, and occasionally loss of hearing. Chronic vestibular dysfunction is most common after prolonged use of streptomycin. Streptomycin, 2–3 gm/day for 4 weeks, has been used to purposely damage semicircular canal function in the treatment of Ménière's disease.

Streptomycin should not be used concurrently with other aminoglycosides, and great caution is necessary in persons with impaired renal function.

2. KANAMYCIN

Kanamycin is an aminoglycoside for systemic use in gram-negative sepsis. Kanamycin is bactericidal for many gram-positive (except enterococci) and gram-negative bacteria in concentrations of 1–10 μg/ml. Activity is enhanced at alkaline pH. Some strains of proteus are susceptible, but pseudomonas and serratia are often resistant. In susceptible bacterial populations, resistant mutants are rare. Kanamycin exhibits complete cross-resistance with neomycin but not with gentamicin.

Kanamycin is not significantly absorbed from the gut. After intramuscular injection (0.5 gm every 6–12 hours), serum levels may reach 5–10 μg/ml. The drug is distributed widely in tissues but does not reach significant concentrations in the CSF, joints, or pleural fluid unless injected locally. Excretion is mainly by glomerular filtration into the urine, where levels of 10–50 μg/ml are reached, and into the bile. In the presence of renal insufficiency, the drug may accumulate rapidly and reach toxic levels.

Indications & Dosages

The principal indication for systemic kanamycin is bacteremia caused by gram-negative enteric organisms or, occasionally, serious urinary tract infection with enterobacter, proteus, or other "difficult" organisms. The IM dose is 0.5 gm every 6–12 hours (15 mg/kg/day). In renal failure, the dose is reduced and the interval between injections prolonged (see p 817).

Adverse Effects

Like all aminoglycosides, kanamycin is ototoxic and nephrotoxic. At present, kanamycin is believed to be less toxic than neomycin. Proteinuria and nitrogen retention occur commonly during treatment. This must be monitored and the dose or frequency of injection adjusted when creatinine clearance falls. In general, these nephrotoxic effects are reversible upon discontinuance of the drug. The auditory portion of the 8th nerve can be selectively and irreversibly damaged by kanamycin. The development of deafness is proportionate to the level of drug and the time of its administration, but it can occur unpredictably even after a short course of treatment. Loss of perception of high frequencies in audiograms may be a warning sign. Ototoxicity is a particular risk in patients with impaired kidney function. The sudden absorption of large amounts of kanamycin (or any other aminoglycoside) can lead to respiratory arrest. This has occurred after the instillation of 3–5 gm of kanamycin (or neomycin) into the peritoneal cavity following bowel surgery. Neostigmine is a specific antidote.

3. NEOMYCIN

Neomycin is analogous in all pharmacologic and antibacterial characteristics to kanamycin. However, it is believed at present to be somewhat more toxic when given parenterally and is therefore used mainly for topical application and for oral administration.

Indications, Dosages, & Routes of Administration

After oral intake, only a minute portion of neomycin is absorbed. Most of the drug remains in the gut lumen and alters intestinal flora. For preoperative reduction of the gut flora, give neomycin, 1 gm orally every 4–6 hours for 2–3 days before surgery. In hepatic coma, ammonia intoxication can be reduced by suppressing the coliform flora of the gut with neomycin, 1 gm orally every 6–8 hours, and limiting the protein intake. Oral neomycin, 50–100 mg/kg/day, is effective against enteropathic *Escherichia coli.* To control surface infections of the skin (pyoderma), ointments containing neomycin, 1–5 mg/gm, are applied several times daily. Solutions containing 10 mg/ml of neomycin can be instilled (up to a total of 0.5 gm/day) into infected joints, pleura, or tissue spaces. Paromomycin (Humatin®), a close relative of neomycin, is given in a dosage of 1 gm orally every 6 hours for the treatment of intestinal amebiasis.

Adverse Effects

All topically administered forms of neomycin may produce sensitization. Hypersensitivity reactions occur particularly in the eye and skin after repeated use of neomycin ointments. Topical or oral neomycin rarely produces systemic toxicity. However, oral neomycin alters the intestinal flora and thus predisposes to superinfection. Staphylococcal enterocolitis, occasion-

ally fatal, has followed the use of neomycin for preoperative "bowel sterilization."

4. GENTAMICIN

Gentamicin is an aminoglycoside antibiotic which shares many properties with kanamycin but differs in antimicrobial activity. In concentrations of 0.5–5 μg/ml, gentamicin is bactericidal not only for staphylococci and coliform organisms but also for many strains of pseudomonas, proteus, and serratia. Enterococci are resistant. Gentamicin is not significantly absorbed after oral intake. After intramuscular injection, gentamicin is rapidly absorbed and widely distributed except into the CNS. Thirty percent of the drug in serum is protein-bound. With full doses (3 mg/kg/day), serum levels reach 3–5 μg/ml, and the serum half-life is 2 hours. In the presence of renal failure, there is marked accumulation of the drug to toxic levels. Gentamicin is excreted by glomerular filtration into the urine, where levels are 10–100 times higher than in the serum. Gentamicin activity is greatly enhanced at alkaline pH.

Indications, Dosages, & Routes of Administration

Gentamicin is used in severe infections caused by gram-negative bacteria which are likely to be resistant to other, less toxic drugs. Included are sepsis, infected burns, pneumonia and other serious infections due to coliform organisms, klebsiella-enterobacter, proteus, pseudomonas, and serratia. The dosage is 2–3 mg/kg/day IM in 3 equal doses for 7–10 days. In life-threatening infections, 5–7 mg/kg/day have been given. In urinary tract infections caused by these organisms, 0.8–1.2 mg/kg/day is given IM for 10 days or longer. It is necessary to monitor renal, auditory, and vestibular functions and to lengthen the interval between doses if renal function declines (see p 817).

For infected burns or skin lesions, creams containing 0.1% gentamicin are used. In meningitis due to gram-negative bacteria, 0.1–1 mg gentamicin has been injected daily intrathecally. For endophthalmitis, 10 mg can be injected subconjunctivally.

Renal function must be monitored by repeated creatinine clearance tests, although nephrotoxicity is said to be infrequent with recommended doses and in the absence of preexisting renal damage. About 2–3% of patients develop vestibular dysfunction (perhaps because of destruction of hair cells), and occasional cases of loss of hearing have been reported.

Finland, M. (editor): International symposium on gentamicin. J Infect Dis 119:335–540, 1969.

Mann, C.H. (editor): Kanamycin: appraisal after 8 years of clinical application. Ann New York Acad Sc 132:771–1090, 1966.

Weinstein, L.: Streptomycin. Chapter 58, pp 1230–1240, *in:* Goodman, L.S., and A. Gilman (editors): *The Pharmacological Basis of Therapeutics,* 3rd ed. Macmillan, 1965.

POLYMYXINS

The polymyxins are a group of basic polypeptides bactericidal for most gram-negative bacteria except proteus and especially useful against pseudomonas. Only 2 drugs are used: polymyxin B sulfate and colistin (polymyxin E) methanesulfonate.

Polymyxins are not absorbed from the gut. After parenteral injection they are distributed in some tissues but do not reach the CNS, CSF, joints, or ocular tissues unless injected locally. Blood levels usually do not exceed $1-2$ $\mu g/ml$. Polymyxins are excreted into the urine (colistin more rapidly than polymyxin B), where concentrations of $25-300$ $\mu g/ml$ may be reached. Excretion is impaired in renal insufficiency, so that accumulation to toxic levels can occur unless the dose is drastically reduced and the interval between doses lengthened (see Table 26–2).

Indications, Dosages, & Routes of Administration

Polymyxins are indicated in serious infections due to pseudomonas and other gram-negative bacteria which are resistant to other antimicrobial drugs.

A. Intramuscular: The injection of polymyxin B is painful. Therefore, colistimethate, which contains a local anesthetic and is more rapidly excreted in the urine, is given IM $2.5-5$ mg/kg/day, for urinary tract infection.

B. Intravenous: In pseudomonas sepsis, polymyxin B sulfate, 2.5 mg/kg/day, is injected by continuous IV infusion.

C. Intrathecal: In pseudomonas meningitis, give polymyxin B sulfate, $2-10$ mg once daily for $2-3$ days, and then every other day for $2-3$ weeks. (Colistimethate must not be given intrathecally.)

D. Topical: Solutions of polymyxin B sulfate, 1 mg/ml, can be applied to infected surfaces, injected into joint spaces, intrapleurally or subconjunctivally, or inhaled as aerosols. Ointments containing 0.5 mg/gm polymyxin B sulfate in a mixture with neomycin or bacitracin are often applied to infected skin lesions. Solutions containing polymyxin B, 20 mg/liter, and neomycin, 40 mg/liter, can be used for continuous irrigation of the bladder with an indwelling catheter and a closed drainage system.

Adverse Effects

The toxicities of polymyxin B and colistimethate are similar. With the usual blood levels there are paresthesias, dizziness, flushing, and incoordination. These disappear when the drug has been excreted. With unusually high levels, respiratory arrest and paralysis can occur. Depending upon the dose, all polymyxins are nephrotoxic, producing tubular injury. Proteinuria, hematuria, and cylindruria tend to be reversible, but nitrogen retention or severe electrolyte disturbances may force reduction in dose or discontinuance of the drug. In individuals with preexisting renal insufficiency, kidney function must be monitored (preferably by creatinine clearance) and the dose reduced or the interval between injections increased (see p 817).

Jawetz, E.: Polymyxin, colistin, bacitracin and vancomycin. P Clin North America 15:85–94, 1968.

Ryan, K.J., & others: Colistimethate toxicity: report of a fatal case. JAMA 207:2099–2101, 1969.

ANTITUBERCULOSIS DRUGS

Singular problems exist in the treatment of tuberculosis and other mycobacterial infections. They tend to be exceedingly chronic but may give rise to hyperacute lethal complications. The organisms are frequently intracellular, have long periods of metabolic inactivity, and tend to develop resistance to any one drug. Combined drug therapy is often employed to delay the emergence of this resistance. "First line" drugs, often employed together in tuberculous meningitis, miliary dissemination, or severe pulmonary disease, are streptomycin, isoniazid, ethambutol, and aminosalicylic acid. A series of "second line" drugs will be mentioned only briefly.

1. STREPTOMYCIN

The general pharmacologic features and toxicity of streptomycin are described above. Streptomycin, $1-10$ $\mu g/ml$, is inhibitory and bactericidal for most tubercle bacilli, whereas most "atypical" mycobacteria are resistant. All large populations of tubercle bacilli contain some streptomycin-resistant mutants, which tend to emerge during prolonged treatment with streptomycin alone and result in "treatment resistance" within $2-4$ months. This is the main reason why streptomycin is usually employed in combination with another antituberculosis drug.

Streptomycin penetrates poorly into cells and exerts its action mainly on extracellular tubercle bacilli. Since at any moment 90% of tubercle bacilli are intracellular and thus unaffected by streptomycin, treatment for many months is required.

For combination therapy in tuberculous meningitis, miliary dissemination, and severe organ tuberculosis, streptomycin is given IM, 1 gm daily (30 mg/kg/day for children) for weeks or months. This is followed by streptomycin, 1 gm IM $2-3$ times a week for months or years. In tuberculous meningitis, intrathecal injections ($1-2$ mg/kg/day) are sometimes given in addition.

The vestibular dysfunction resulting from prolonged streptomycin treatment results in inability to maintain equilibrium. However, some compensation usually occurs so that patients can function fairly well.

2. ISONIAZID (INH)

Isoniazid is the hydrazide of isonicotinic acid (INH), the most active antituberculosis drug. INH inhibits most tubercle bacilli in a concentration of 0.2 μg/ml or less. However, most "atypical" mycobacteria are resistant. In susceptible large populations of *Mycobacterium tuberculosis*, INH-resistant mutants occur. Their emergence is delayed in the presence of a second drug. There is no cross-resistance between INH, streptomycin, PAS, or ethambutol.

INH is well absorbed from the gut and diffuses readily into all tissues, including the CNS, and into living cells. A dose of 8 mg/kg/day results in blood levels of 2 μg/ml or more. The inactivation of INH— particularly its acetylation—is under genetic control. In "rapid inactivators," plasma levels are 0.2 μg/ml or less 6 hours after ingestion of 4 mg/kg INH, whereas in "slow inactivators" plasma levels at that time are 0.8 μg/ml or more. INH and its conjugates are excreted mainly in the urine.

Indications, Dosages, & Routes of Administration

INH is the most widely used drug in tuberculosis. INH should not be given as the sole drug in active tuberculosis. This favors emergence of resistance (up to 20% in some countries). In active, clinically manifest disease, it is given in conjunction with streptomycin and PAS or ethambutol. The initial dose is 8–10 mg/kg/day orally (up to 20 mg/kg/day in small children); later, the dosage is reduced to 5–7 mg/kg/day.

Children (or young adults) converting from a tuberculin-negative to tuberculin-positive skin test may be given 10 mg/kg/day (maximum: 300 mg/day) for 1 year as prophylaxis against the 5–15% risk of meningitis or miliary dissemination. For this "prophylaxis," INH is given as the sole drug.

Toxic reactions to INH include insomnia, restlessness, dysuria, hepatitis, hyperreflexia, and even convulsions and psychotic episodes. Some of these are attributable to a relative pyridoxine deficiency and peripheral neuritis and can be prevented by the administration of pyridoxine, 100 mg/day. INH can reduce the metabolism of diphenylhydantoin, increasing its blood level and toxicity.

3. AMINOSALICYLIC ACID (PAS)

p-Aminosalicylic acid, closely related to *p*-aminobenzoic acid, inhibits most tubercle bacilli in concentrations of 1–5 μg/ml but has no effect on other bacteria. Resistant *Mycobacterium tuberculosis* emerges rapidly unless another antituberculosis drug is present.

PAS is readily absorbed from the gut. Doses of 8–12 gm/day orally give blood levels of 10 μg/ml. The drug is widely distributed in tissues (except the CNS) and rapidly excreted into the urine. To avoid crystalluria, the urine should be kept alkaline.

Common side-effects include anorexia, nausea, diarrhea, and epigastric pain. These may be diminished by taking PAS with meals and with antacids, but peptic ulceration may occur. Sodium PAS may be given parenterally. Hypersensitivity reactions include fever, skin rashes, granulocytopenia, lymphadenopathy, and arthralgias.

4. ETHAMBUTOL

This is a synthetic, water-soluble, heat-stable compound, dispensed as the hydrochloride.

Many strains of *Mycobacterium tuberculosis* are inhibited in vitro by ethambutol, 1–5 μg/ml. The mechanism of action is not known.

Ethambutol is well absorbed from the gut. Following ingestion of 25 mg/kg, a blood level peak of 2–5 μg/ml is reached in 2–4 hours. About 20% of the drug is excreted in feces and 50% in the urine, in unchanged form. Excretion is delayed in renal failure. About 15% of absorbed drug is metabolized by oxidation and conversion to a dicarboxylic acid. In meningitis, ethambutol appears in the CSF.

Resistance to ethambutol emerges fairly rapidly among mycobacteria when the drug is used alone. Therefore, ethambutol is best given in combination with other antituberculosis drugs, most commonly INH. In combined therapy, ethambutol effectively replaces PAS and is better tolerated than PAS by most patients.

Ethambutol, 15 mg/kg, is usually given as a single daily dose in combination with INH. At times, the dose is 25 mg/kg/day.

Hypersensitivity to ethambutol occurs infrequently. The commonest side-effects are visual disturbances: reduction in visual acuity, optic neuritis, and perhaps retinal damage occur in some patients on full doses given for several months. Most of these changes apparently regress when ethambutol is discontinued. However, periodic visual acuity testing is mandatory during treatment.

5. ALTERNATIVE DRUGS IN TUBERCULOSIS TREATMENT

The drugs listed alphabetically below are usually considered only in cases of drug resistance (clinical or laboratory) to "first line" drugs and when expert guidance is available to deal with toxic side-effects.

Capreomycin, 0.5–1.5 gm/day IM, can perhaps substitute for streptomycin in combined therapy. It is not commercially available. It is nephrotoxic and ototoxic.

Cycloserine (Seromycin®), 0.5–1.0 gm/day orally, has been used alone or with INH. It can induce a variety of CNS dysfunctions and psychotic reactions. In smaller doses (15–20 mg/kg/day) it has been used in urinary tract infections.

Ethionamide (Trecator®), 0.5–gm/day orally, has been used in combination therapy but produces marked gastric irritation.

Pyrazinamide (PZA, Aldinamide®), 2–3 gm/day orally, has been used in combination therapy but may produce serious liver damage.

Rifampin is a semisynthetic derivative of rifamycin. Rifampin, 1 μg/ml or less, inhibits many gram-positive cocci, meningococci, and tubercle bacilli in vitro. Gram-negative organisms are often more resistant. Highly resistant mutants occur relatively frequently in susceptible microbial populations. Rifampin is also active against chlamydiae and poxviruses.

Rifampin binds strongly to DNA-dependent bacterial RNA polymerase and thus inhibits RNA synthesis in bacteria and chlamydiae. It blocks a late stage in the assembly of poxviruses.

Rifampin given orally is well absorbed and widely distributed in tissues. It is excreted mainly through the liver and to a lesser extent in the urine. With oral doses of 600 mg, serum levels exceed 5 μg/ml for 4–6 hours, and urine levels may be 10–100 times higher.

In the treatment of tuberculosis, a single oral dose of 600 mg is given daily (0.45–0.9 gm/day). Because of the rapid emergence of resistant microorganisms, combined treatment with ethambutol or another antituberculous drug is required. Rifampin, 600 mg daily, has also succeeded in eradicating the meningococcal carrier state and has shown promise in leprosy.

In urinary tract infections and in chronic bronchitis, rifampin has not given encouraging results.

Rifampin imparts an orange color to urine and sweat. Occasional adverse effects include rashes, thrombocytopenia, and transient elevations of SGOT, alkaline phosphatase, and serum bilirubin.

Viomycin (Vinactane®, Viocin®), 2 gm IM every 3 days, can occasionally substitute for streptomycin in combination therapy. It is nephrotoxic and ototoxic.

Curry, F.J.: Prophylactic effect of isoniazid in young tuberculin reactors. New England J Med 277:562–567, 1967.

Dans, P.E., & others: Rifampin: Antibacterial activity, absorption and excretion. Am J M Sc 259:120–131, 1970.

Ferebee, S.H.: Controlled chemoprophylaxis trials in tuberculosis. Advances Tuberc Res 17:28–106, 1969.

Mitchell, R.S.: Control of tuberculosis. New England J Med 276:842–848, 905–911, 1967.

Place, V.A., & others: Ethambutol in tuberculous meningitis. Am Rev Resp Dis 99:783–785, 1969.

SULFONAMIDES & SULFONES

Since the demonstration, in 1935, of the striking antibacterial activity of sulfanilamide, the molecule has been drastically altered in many ways. More than 150 different sulfonamides have been marketed at one time or another, the modifications being designed principally to achieve greater antibacterial activity, a wider anti-

bacterial spectrum, greater solubility, or more prolonged action. Because of their low cost and their relative efficacy in some common bacterial infections, sulfonamides are still used widely in many parts of the world. However, the increasing emergence of sulfonamide resistance (eg, among streptococci, meningococci, and shigellae) and the higher efficacy of other antimicrobial drugs have drastically curtailed the number of specific indications for sulfonamides as drugs of choice. The present indications for the use of these drugs can be summarized as follows:

(1) First (previously untreated) infection of the urinary tract: Many coliform organisms, which are the most common causes of urinary infections, are still susceptible to sulfonamides.

(2) Chlamydial infections of the trachoma-inclusion conjunctivitis-LGV group: Sulfonamides are often as effective as tetracyclines in suppressing clinical activity, and they may be curative in acute infections. However, they often fail to eradicate chronic infection.

(3) Parasitic and fungal diseases: In combination with pyrimethamine, sulfonamides are used in toxoplasmosis. In combination with trimethoprim, sulfonamides are sometimes effective in falciparum malaria. Alone or in combination with cycloserine, sulfonamides may be active in nocardiosis.

(4) Bacterial infections: In underdeveloped parts of the world, sulfonamides, because of their availability and low cost, may still be useful for the treatment of pneumococcal or staphylococcal infections; bacterial sinusitis, bronchitis, or otitis media; bacillary (shigella) dysentery; and meningococcal infections. In most developed countries, however, sulfonamides are not the drugs of choice for any of these conditions, and sulfonamide resistance of the respective etiologic organisms is widespread.

(5) Leprosy: Certain sulfones are the drugs of choice in leprosy.

Antimicrobial Activity

The action of sulfonamides is bacteriostatic and is reversible upon removal of the drug or in the presence of an excess of *p*-aminobenzoic acid (PABA). Susceptible microorganisms require extracellular PABA in order to synthesize folic acid, an essential step in the formation of purines. Sulfonamides are structural analogues of PABA, can enter into the reaction in place of PABA competing for the enzyme involved, and can form nonfunctional analogues of folic acid. As a result, further growth of the microorganism is inhibited. Animal cells and some sulfonamide-resistant microorganisms are unable to synthesize folic acid from PABA but depend on exogenous sources of preformed folic acid. Other microorganisms may be sulfonamide-resistant because they produce a large excess of PABA.

Trimethoprim can inhibit the step in bacterial purine synthesis (dihydrofolic acid reductase) which follows the step blocked by sulfonamides. Trimethoprim plus sulfonamides can therefore produce sequential blocking of purine synthesis. Such "synergism" has been used in bacterial urinary tract infection and in malaria.

Pharmacologic Properties

The soluble sulfonamides are readily absorbed from the gut, distributed widely in tissues and body fluids, and excreted primarily by glomerular filtration into the urine. Varying amounts of sulfonamides are acetylated by the liver or bound to plasma protein. A portion of the drug in the urine is acetylated, but enough active drug remains in the urine to permit effective treatment of urinary tract infections (usually 10–20 times the concentration present in the blood). In order to be therapeutically effective for systemic therapy, a sulfonamide must achieve a concentration of 8–12 mg/ml of blood. This is accomplished by full systemic doses listed below.

"Long-acting" sulfonamides (eg, sulfamethoxy-pyridazine, sulfadimethoxine, sulfameter) are readily absorbed after oral intake, but urinary excretion is very slow, resulting in prolonged blood levels. "Intermediate-acting" sulfonamides (eg, sulfamethoxazole) are also excreted relatively slowly. All of these compounds may have a convenience factor but cause a higher incidence of severe toxic reactions.

"Insoluble" sulfonamides (eg, succinylsulfathiazole) are absorbed only slightly after oral administration and are largely excreted in the feces. Their action is mainly on the intestinal flora.

For parenteral (usually intravenous) administration, sodium salts of several sulfonamides are used because of their greater solubility. Their distribution and excretion are similar to those of the orally administered, absorbed sulfonamides.

Dosages & Routes of Administration

A. Topical: The application of sulfonamides to skin, wounds, or mucous membranes is undesirable because of the high risk of allergic sensitization or reaction and the low antimicrobial activity. Exceptions are the application of sodium sulfacetamide solution (30%) or ointment (10%) to the conjunctivas, or mafenide acetate cream (Sulfamylon®) to burned surfaces.

B. Oral: For systemic disease, the soluble, rapidly excreted sulfonamides (eg, sulfadiazine, sulfisoxazole) are given in an initial dose of 2–4 gm (40 mg/kg) followed by a maintenance dose of 0.5–1 gm (20 mg/kg) every 4–6 hours. Trisulfapyrimidines USP may be given in the same total doses. Urine must be kept alkaline.

For urinary tract infections (first attack, not previously treated), trisulfapyrimidines, sulfisoxazole, or another sulfonamide with equally high solubility in urine are given in the same (or somewhat lower) doses as shown above. Following one course of sulfonamides, resistant organisms usually prevail. Simultaneous administration of sulfadiazine, 2 gm/day orally, and trimethoprim, 400 mg/day orally, may be more effective in urinary or respiratory tract infections than sulfonamide alone.

For "intestinal surgery prophylaxis," insoluble sulfonamides (eg, succinylsulfathiazole, phthalylsulfathiazole), 8–15 gm/day, are given for 5–7 days before operations on the bowel. Salicylazosulfapyridine, 6 gm/day, has been given in ulcerative colitis, but there is little evidence of its efficacy.

"Long-acting" and "intermediate-acting" sulfonamides (eg, sulfamethoxypyridazine, sulfadimethoxine, sulfamethoxazole) can be used in doses of 0.5–1 gm/day (10 mg/kg) for prolonged maintenance therapy (eg, trachoma) or for the treatment of minor infections. These drugs have a significantly higher rate of toxic effects than the "short-acting" sulfonamides.

C. Intravenous: Sodium sulfadiazine and other sodium salts can be injected intravenously in 0.5% concentration in 5% dextrose in water, physiologic salt solution, or other diluent in a total dose of 6–8 gm/day (120 mg/kg/day). This is reserved for comatose individuals or those unable to take oral medication.

Adverse Effects

Sulfonamides produce a wide variety of side-effects—due partly to hypersensitivity, partly to direct toxicity—which must be considered whenever unexplained symptoms or signs occur in a patient who may have received these drugs. Except in the mildest reactions, fluids should be forced, and—if symptoms and signs progressively increase—the drugs should be discontinued. Precautions to prevent complications (below) are important.

A. Systemic Side-Effects: Fever, skin rashes, urticaria; nausea, vomiting, or diarrhea; stomatitis, conjunctivitis, arthritis, exfoliative dermatitis; hematopoietic disturbances, including thrombocytopenia, hemolytic (in G6PD deficiency) or aplastic anemia, granulocytopenia, leukemoid reactions; hepatitis, polyarteritis nodosa, vasculitis, Stevens-Johnson syndrome; psychosis; and many others.

B. Urinary Tract Disturbances: Sulfonamides may precipitate in urine, especially at neutral or acid pH, producing hematuria, crystalluria, or even obstruction. They have also been implicated in various types of nephritis and nephrosis. Sulfonamides and methenamine salts should not be given together.

Precautions in the Use of Sulfonamides

(1) There is cross-allergenicity among all sulfonamides. Obtain a history of past administration or reaction. Observe for possible allergic responses.

(2) Keep the urine volume above 1500 mg/day by forcing fluids. Check urine pH—it should be 7.5 or higher. Give alkali by mouth (sodium bicarbonate or equivalent, 5–15 gm/day). Examine fresh urine for crystals and red cells every 2–4 days.

(3) Check hemoglobin, white blood cell count, and differential count every 3–5 days to detect possible disturbances early.

Weinstein, L., Madoff, M.A., & C.M. Samet: The sulfonamides. New England J Med 263:900–907, 952–956, 1960.

SULFONES USED IN
THE TREATMENT OF LEPROSY

A number of drugs closely related to the sulfon-amides have been used effectively in the long-term treatment of leprosy. The clinical manifestations of both lepromatous and tuberculoid leprosy can often be suppressed by treatment extending over several years.

Absorption, Metabolism, & Excretion

All of the sulfones are well absorbed from the intestinal tract, are distributed widely in all tissues, and tend to be retained in skin, muscle, liver, and kidney. Skin involved by leprosy contains 10 times more drug than normal skin. Sulfones are excreted into the bile and reabsorbed by the intestine. Consequently, blood levels are prolonged. Excretion into the urine is vari-able and occurs mostly as a glucuronic acid conjugate. Some persons acetylate sulfones slowly and others rapidly, and this requires dosage adjustment.

Adverse Effects

The sulfones may cause any of the side-effects listed above for sulfonamides. Anorexia, nausea, and vomiting are common. Hemolysis, methemoglobine-mia, or agranulocytosis may occur.

Dosages & Routes of Administration

A. Diaminodiphenylsulfone (DDS, dapsone, Avlo-sulfon®) is the most widely used and least expensive drug. It is given orally, beginning with a dosage of 25 mg twice weekly and gradually increasing to 100 mg 3–4 times weekly and eventually to 300 mg twice weekly.

B. Sulfoxone sodium (Diasone®) is given orally in corresponding dosage.

C. Solapsone (Sulphetrone®), a complex substitu-ted derivative of DDS, is given initially in a dosage of 0.5 gm 3 times daily orally. The dose is then gradually increased until a total daily dose of 6–10 gm is reached.

D. Other classes of drugs are used uncommonly. An ethyl mercaptan (Ditophal®) may be applied to the skin. Thiosemicarbazones (eg, amithiozone, Tibione®) permit the rapid emergence of resistance if used alone. Therefore, if administered, they are given with a sul-fone.

SPECIALIZED DRUGS AGAINST
GRAM-POSITIVE BACTERIA

1. BACITRACIN

This polypeptide antibiotic is selectively active against gram-positive bacteria, including penicillinase-producing staphylococci, in concentrations of 0.1–20 units/ml. Bacitracin is very little absorbed from gut,

skin, wounds, or mucous membranes. Topical applica-tion results in local effects without significant toxicity. Bacitracin, 500 unit/gm in ointment base, is often combined with polymyxin or neomycin for the sup-pression of mixed bacterial flora in surface lesions. Systemic administration of bacitracin has been aban-doned because of its severe nephrotoxicity.

2. LINCOMYCIN & CLINDAMYCIN

These drugs resemble erythromycin (although different in structure) and are active against gram-posi-tive organisms (except enterococci) in concentrations of 0.5–5 µg/ml. Lincomycin, 0.5 gm orally every 6 hours (30–60 mg/kg/day for children), or clindamy-cin, 0.15–0.3 gm orally every 6 hours, yields serum concentrations of 2–5 µg/ml. The drugs are widely distributed in tissues. Excretion is through bile and urine. Lincomycin, 0.6 gm, can also be injected IM or IV every 8–12 hours. The drugs are alternatives to erythromycin as a substitute for penicillin. Success in staphylococcal bone infections has been reported.

Common side-effects are diarrhea and nausea. Impaired liver function and neutropenia have been noted. If 3–4 gm are given rapidly intravenously, cardiorespiratory arrest may occur. Clindamycin may have a lower incidence of gastrointestinal side-effects than lincomycin.

3. NOVOBIOCIN

Many gram-positive cocci are inhibited by novo-biocin, 1–5 µg/ml, but resistant variants tend to emerge rapidly during treatment. Novobiocin, 0.5 gm orally every 6 hours (30 mg/kg/day for children), yields serum concentrations of 2–5 µg/ml. It is widely distributed in tissues and excreted in urine and feces. It can also be given intramuscularly or intravenously. In the past, a possible indication for novobiocin was infection caused by penicillinase-producing staphylo-cocci. However, many better drugs are now available, so that no clear indication for novobiocin exists.

Skin rashes, drug fever, and granulocytopenia are common side-effects; many others have been observed occasionally.

4. VANCOMYCIN

This drug is bactericidal for most gram-positive organisms, particularly staphylococci and enterococci, in concentrations of 0.5–10 µg/ml. Resistant mutants are rare, and there is no cross-resistance with other

TABLE 26–3. Drug selections, 1971–1972.

Suspected or Proved Etiologic Agent	Drug(s) of First Choice	Alternative Drug(s)
Gram-negative cocci		
Gonococcus	Penicillin[1], ampicillin	Erythromycin[2], tetracycline[3]
Meningococcus	Penicillin[1]	Tetracycline, chloramphenicol
Gram-positive cocci		
Pneumococcus	Penicillin[1]	Erythromycin, lincomycin
Streptococcus, hemolytic groups A,B,C	Penicillin[1]	Erythromycin, lincomycin
Streptococcus viridans	Penicillin[1]	Cephalosporin[4], vancomycin
Staphylococcus, nonpenicillinase-producing	Penicillin[1]	Cephalosporin, vancomycin, lincomycin
Staphylococcus, penicillinase-producing	Penicillinase-resistant penicillin[5]	Cephalosporin, vancomycin, lincomycin
Streptococcus faecalis (enterococcus)	Ampicillin plus streptomycin or kanamycin	Penicillin plus kanamycin or gentamicin
Gram-negative rods		
Aerobacter (Enterobacter)	Kanamycin or gentamicin	Tetracycline, chloramphenicol, polymyxin
Bacteroides	Tetracycline	Ampicillin, chloramphenicol
Brucella	Tetracycline plus streptomycin	Streptomycin plus sulfonamide[6]
Escherichia		
E coli sepsis	Kanamycin	Cephalothin, ampicillin
E coli urinary tract infection (first attack)	Sulfonamide[7]	Ampicillin, cephalexin
Hemophilus (meningitis, respiratory infections)	Ampicillin	Chloramphenicol
Klebsiella	Cephalosporin or kanamycin	Gentamicin, chloramphenicol
Mima-Herellea	Kanamycin	Tetracycline, gentamicin
Pasteurella (plague, tularemia)	Streptomycin plus tetracycline	Sulfonamide[6]
Proteus		
P mirabilis	Penicillin or ampicillin	Kanamycin, gentamicin
P vulgaris and other species	Kanamycin or carbenicillin	Chloramphenicol, gentamicin
Pseudomonas		
Ps aeruginosa	Polymyxin or gentamicin	Carbenicillin
Ps pseudomallei (melioidosis)	Chloramphenicol	Rifampin, tetracycline
Ps mallei (glanders)	Streptomycin plus tetracycline	
Salmonella	Chloramphenicol	Ampicillin
Serratia	Gentamicin	Kanamycin
Shigella	Ampicillin	Tetracycline, kanamycin
Vibrio (cholera)	Tetracycline	Chloramphenicol
Gram-positive rods		
Actinomyces	Penicillin[1]	Tetracycline, sulfonamide
Bacillus (eg, anthrax)	Penicillin[1]	Erythromycin
Clostridium (eg, gas gangrene, tetanus)	Penicillin[1]	Tetracycline, erythromycin
Corynebacterium	Erythromycin	Penicillin, cephalosporin
Acid-fast rods		
Mycobacterium tuberculosis	INH plus PAS plus streptomycin	Other antituberculosis drugs
Mycobacterium leprae	Dapsone or sulfoxone	Other sulfones
Nocardia	Sulfonamide[6]	Tetracycline, cycloserine
Spirochetes		
Borrelia (relapsing fever)	Tetracycline	Penicillin
Leptospira	Penicillin	Tetracycline
Treponema (syphilis, yaws)	Penicillin	Erythromycin, tetracycline
Mycoplasma	Tetracycline	Erythromycin
Psittacosis-lymphogranuloma-trachoma agents (chlamydiae)	Tetracycline, sulfonamide[6]	Erythromycin, chloramphenicol
Rickettsiae	Tetracycline	Chloramphenicol

[1] Penicillin G is preferred for parenteral injection; penicillin G (buffered) or penicillin V for oral administration. Only highly sensitive microorganisms should be treated with oral penicillin.

[2] Erythromycin estolate and triacetyloleandomycin are the best absorbed oral forms.

[3] All tetracyclines have the same activity against microorganisms and all have comparable therapeutic activity and toxicity. Dosage is determined by the rates of absorption and excretion of different preparations.

[4] Cephalothin and cephaloridine are the best accepted cephalosporins at present.

[5] Parenteral methicillin, nafcillin, or oxacillin. Oral dicloxacillin or other isoxazolylpenicillin.

[6] Trisulfapyrimidines have the advantage of greater solubility in urine over sulfadiazine for oral administration; sodium sulfadiazine is suitable for intravenous injection in severely ill persons.

[7] For previously untreated urinary tract infection, a highly soluble sulfonamide such as sulfisoxazole or trisulfapyrimidines is the first choice.

antimicrobial drugs. Vancomycin is not absorbed from the gut. It is given orally (3–4 gm/day) only for the treatment of staphylococcal enterocolitis. For systemic effect the drug must be administered intravenously. After IV injection of 0.5 gm over a period of 20 minutes, blood levels of 10 μg/ml are maintained for 1–2 hours. Vancomycin is largely excreted into the urine. In the presence of renal insufficiency, marked accumulation may occur and have toxic consequences.

The only indications for vancomycin are serious staphylococcal infection or enterococcal endocarditis untreatable with penicillins. Vancomycin, 0.5 gm, is injected IV over a 20-minute period every 6–8 hours (for children, 20–40 mg/kg/day). It can also be given by continuous intravenous infusion.

Vancomycin is intensely irritating to tissues. Intramuscular injection or extravasation from intravenous injection sites is very painful. Chills, fever, and thrombophlebitis commonly follow intravenous injection. The drug is both nephrotoxic and ototoxic, and renal function must be monitored.

Friedberg, C.K., & others: Vancomycin therapy for enterococcal and *Streptococcus viridans* endocarditis. Arch Int Med 21:134–140, 1968.

Kirby, W.M.M., & others: Treatment of staphylococcal septicemia with vancomycin: Report of 33 cases. New England J Med 262:49–55, 1960.

Wallace, J.F., & others: Oral administration of vancomycin in the treatment of staphylococcal enterocolitis. New England J Med 272:1014–1015, 1965.

URINARY ANTISEPTICS

These drugs exert antimicrobial activity in the urine but have little or no systemic antibacterial effect. Their usefulness is limited to urinary tract infections.

1. NITROFURANTOIN
(Furadantin®)

Nitrofurantoin is bacteriostatic and bactericidal for both gram-positive and gram-negative bacteria in concentrations of 10–500 μg/ml. The activity of nitrofurantoin is greatly enhanced at pH 6.5 or lower.

Nitrofurantoin is rapidly absorbed from the gut. The drug is bound so completely to serum protein that no antibacterial effect occurs in the blood. Nitrofurantoin has no systemic antibacterial activity. In kidney tubules, the drug is separated from carrier protein and excreted in urine where concentrations may be 200–400 μg/ml.

The average daily dose in urinary tract infections is 100 mg orally 4 times daily (for children, 5–10 mg/kg/day), taken with food. If oral medication is not feasible, nitrofurantoin can be given by continuous IV infusion, 180–360 mg/day.

Oral nitrofurantoin often causes nausea and vomiting. Hemolytic anemia occurs in G6PD deficiency. Hypersensitivity may produce skin rashes and pulmonary infiltration.

2. NALIDIXIC ACID
(NegGram®)

This synthetic urinary antiseptic inhibits many gram-negative bacteria in concentrations of 1–50 μg/ml but has no effect on pseudomonas. In susceptible bacterial populations, resistant mutants emerge fairly rapidly.

Nalidixic acid is readily absorbed from the gut. In the blood, virtually all drug is firmly bound to protein. Thus there is no systemic antibacterial action. About 20% of the absorbed drug is excreted in the urine in active form to give urine levels of 10–150 μg/ml, which may produce false-positive tests for glucose.

The dose in urinary tract infections is 1 gm orally 4 times daily (for children, 55 mg/kg/day). Adverse reactions include nausea, vomiting, skin rashes, drowsiness, visual disturbances, and, rarely, increased intracranial pressure with convulsions.

3. METHENAMINE MANDELATE
(Mandelamine®)
& METHENAMINE HIPPURATE

These are salts of methenamine and mandelic acid or hippuric acid. The action of the drug depends on the liberation of formaldehyde and of acid in the urine. The urinary pH must be below 5.5, and sulfonamides must not be given at the same time. The drug inhibits a variety of different microorganisms except those (eg, proteus) which liberate ammonia from urea and produce strongly alkaline urine. The dosage is 2–6 gm orally daily.

4. ACIDIFYING AGENTS

Urine with a pH below 5.5 tends to be antibacterial. Many substances can acidify urine and thus produce antibacterial activity. Ammonium chloride, ascorbic acid, methionine, and mandelic acid are sometimes used. The dose has to be established for each patient by testing the urine for acid pH with test paper at frequent intervals.

SYSTEMICALLY ACTIVE DRUGS IN URINARY TRACT INFECTIONS

Many antimicrobial drugs are excreted in the urine in very high concentration. For this reason, low and relatively nontoxic amounts of aminoglycosides, polymyxins, and cycloserine (see Antituberculosis Drugs, above) can produce effective urine levels. Many penicillins and cephalosporins can reach very high urine levels and can thus be effective in urinary tract infections.

Meyers, F., & others: *Review of Medical Pharmacology*, 2nd ed. Lange, 1970.

Turck, M., & others: Relapse and reinfection in chronic bacteriuria. New England J Med 275:70–73,1966.

ANTIFUNGAL DRUGS

Most antibacterial substances have no effect on pathogenic fungi. Only a few drugs are known to be therapeutically useful in mycotic infections. Penicillins and sulfonamides are used to treat actinomycosis; sulfonamides and cycloserine have been employed in nocardiosis.

1. AMPHOTERICIN B

Amphotericin B, 0.1–0.8 μg/ml, inhibits in vitro several organisms producing systemic mycotic disease in man, including histoplasma, cryptococcus, coccidioides, candida, blastomyces, sporotrichum, and others. Amphotericin B, 100 gm IV, results in average blood and tissue levels of 1–2 μg/ml and thus can be used for treatment of these systemic fungal infections. Intrathecal administration is necessary for the treatment of meningitis.

Amphotericin B solutions, 0.1 mg/ml in 5% dextrose in water, are given IV by slow infusion. The initial dose is 1–5 mg/day, increasing daily by 5 mg increments until a final dosage of 1–1.5 mg/kg/day is reached. This is usually continued for many weeks. In fungal meningitis, amphotericin B, 0.5 mg, is injected intrathecally 3 times weekly; continuous treatment (many weeks) with an Ommaya reservoir is sometimes employed. Relapses of fungal meningitis occur commonly.

The intravenous administration of amphotericin B usually produces chills, fever, vomiting, and headache. Tolerance may be enhanced by temporary lowering of the dose or administration of corticosteroids. Therapeutically active amounts of amphotericin B commonly impair kidney and liver function and produce anemia. Electrolyte disturbances, shock, and a variety of neurologic symptoms also occur.

2. GRISEOFULVIN

Griseofulvin is an antibiotic that can inhibit the growth of some dermatophytes but has no effect on bacteria or on the fungi that cause deep mycoses. Absorption of microsized griseofulvin, 1 gm/day, gives blood levels of 0.5–1.5 μg/ml. The absorbed drug has an affinity for skin and is deposited there, bound to keratin. Thus, it makes keratin resistant to fungal growth and the new growth of hair or nails is first freed of infection. As keratinized structures are shed, they are replaced by uninfected ones. The bulk of ingested griseofulvin is excreted in the feces. Topical application of griseofulvin has little effect.

Oral doses of 0.5–1 gm/day (for children, 15 mg/kg/day) must be given for 6 weeks if only the skin is involved and for 3–6 months or longer if the hair and nails are involved. Griseofulvin is most successful in severe dermatophytosis, particularly if caused by trichophyton or microsporon. Some strains of fungi are resistant.

Side-effects include headache, nausea, diarrhea, photosensitivity, fever, skin rashes, and disturbances of hepatic, nervous, and hematopoietic systems. Griseofulvin increases the metabolism of coumarin so that higher doses of the anticoagulant are needed.

3. NYSTATIN

Nystatin inhibits candida species upon direct contact. The drug is not absorbed from mucous membranes or gut. Nystatin in ointments, suspensions, etc can be applied to buccal or vaginal mucous membranes to suppress a local candida infection. After oral intake of nystatin, candida in the gut is suppressed while the drug is excreted in feces. However, there is no good indication for the use of nystatin orally because increase in gut candida is rarely associated with disease.

Butler, W.T.: Pharmacology, toxicity and therapeutic usefulness of amphotericin B. JAMA 195:371–375, 1966.

Sarosi, G.A., & others: Cryptococcal meningitis: Amphotericin therapy. Ann Int Med 71:1079–1087, 1969.

4. FLUOROCYTOSINE

5-Fluorocytosine inhibits some candida and cryptococcus strains. Dosages of 3–8 gm daily orally have produced clinical remissions in cases of meningitis or sepsis. Resistant organisms may appear, and toxic effects (bone marrow depression, loss of hair) are common.

ANTIVIRAL CHEMOTHERAPY

Several compounds are now available which can influence viral replication and the development of viral disease.

Amantadine hydrochloride (Symmetrel®), 200 mg orally daily for 2—3 days before and 6—7 days after influenza A infection, reduces the incidence and severity of symptoms. The most marked untoward effects are insomnia, dizziness, and ataxia.

Idoxuridine (Herplex®, Stoxil®), 0.1% solution or 0.5% ointment, can be applied topically every 2 hours to acute dendritic herpetic keratitis to enhance healing. It is also used, in conjunction with corticosteroids, for stromal disciform lesions of the cornea to reduce the chance of acute epithelial herpes. It may have some toxic effects on the cornea and should probably not be used for more than 2—3 weeks. Intravenous injection of idoxuridine (100—400 mg/kg/day for 5 days, not to exceed 30 gm) has been proposed for herpetic encephalitis.

Cytosine arabinoside (cytarabine, Cytosar®) also inhibits DNA viruses. It has been applied topically in herpetic keratitis due to idoxuridine-resistant virus. Cytosine arabinoside, 0.3—2 mg/kg as a single daily dose IV for 5 days, has been given in disseminated herpes simplex and in disseminated varicella.

Methisazone (Marboran®) can inhibit the growth of smallpox virus in man if administered to exposed persons within 1—2 days after exposure. Methisazone, 2—4 gm daily orally (for children, 100 mg/kg/day), gives striking protection against the development of clinical smallpox and permits an asymptomatic, immunizing infection. Methisazone can also inhibit the growth of vaccinia virus and is used for the treatment of complications of smallpox vaccination (eg, progressive vaccinia). The most pronounced toxic effect is profuse vomiting.

Nolan, D.C., & others: Herpesvirus encephalitis in Michigan. New England J Med 282:10—13, 1970.

● ● ●

General Bibliography

Garrod, L.P., & F. O'Grady: *Antibiotics and Chemotherapy,* 3rd ed. Livingstone, 1971.

Kagan, B.M. (editor): *Antimicrobial Therapy.* Saunders, 1970.

27...
Disorders Due to Physical Agents

Milton J. Chatton & John L. Wilson

DISORDERS DUE TO COLD

The response to very low temperatures may be either quantitative or qualitative. Some persons have an "allergy" to cold and may develop urticaria upon even limited exposure to a cold wind. Actual immersion in cold water may result in severe systemic symptoms, including shock. In many patients, cold hypersensitivity is an autosomal dominant hereditary disorder. Familial cold urticaria, manifested as a burning sensation of the skin occurring about ½ hour after exposure to cold, does not seem to be a true urticarial disorder. In some patients, however, cold urticaria may be due to an underlying disease (eg, collagen disease, lymphoma, multiple myeloma) associated with cryoglobulinemia, which often results in purpura, Raynaud's phenomenon, and leg ulceration. Cold urticaria may also be associated with cold hemoglobinuria (see Table 9–3) as a complication of syphilis or for unknown reasons.

Newborn infants, especially if premature, may be particularly sensitive to cold injury with serious consequences, including hypothermia, lethargy, malnutrition, gastrointestinal hemorrhage, edema, and convulsions.

In the normal individual, exposure to cold produces immediate localized vasoconstriction followed by generalized vasoconstriction. When the skin temperature falls to 25° C (77° F), tissue metabolism is slowed but the demand for oxygen is greater than the slowed circulation can supply and the area becomes cyanotic. At 15° C (59° F), tissue metabolism is markedly decreased and the dissociation of oxyhemoglobin is reduced, which gives a pink, well oxygenated appearance to the skin. Tissue survival at this temperature is slight. Tissue death may be caused by ischemia and thromboses in the smaller vessels or by actual freezing. Freezing (frostbite) does not occur until the skin temperature drops to –4 to –10° (25–14° F) or even lower, depending on such factors as wind, mobility, venous stasis, malnutrition, and occlusive arterial disease.

Prevention of Cold Injury

"Keep warm, keep moving, and keep dry." Individuals should wear warm, dry clothing, preferably several layers, with a windproof outer garment. Wet clothing, socks, and shoes should be removed as soon as possible and replaced with dry ones. Extra socks, mittens, and insoles should always be carried in a pack when in cold or icy areas. Cramped positions, constricting clothing, and prolonged dependency of the feet are to be avoided. Exercising arms, legs, fingers, and toes to maintain circulation is essential. Avoiding wet and muddy ground and keeping sheltered from wind are important. Good nutrition and skin cleanliness are necessary. Tobacco and alcohol should be avoided when the danger of frostbite is present.

Rogers, M.C., Greenberg, M., & J.J. Alpert: Cold injury of the newborn. New England J Med 285:332–334, 1971.

Tindall, J.P., Beeker, S.K., & W.F. Rosse: Familial cold urticaria. Arch Int Med 124:129–134, 1969.

CHILBLAIN
(Pernio)

Chilblains are red, itching skin lesions, usually on the extremities, caused by exposure to cold without actual freezing of the tissues. They may be associated with edema or blistering and are aggravated by warmth. With continued exposure, ulcerative or hemorrhagic lesions may appear and progress to scarring, fibrosis, and atrophy.

Treatment consists of elevating the affected part slightly and allowing it to warm gradually at room temperature. Do not rub or massage injured tissues or apply ice or heat. Protect the area from trauma and secondary infection.

FROSTBITE

Frostbite is injury of the superficial tissues due to freezing; it may be divided into 3 grades of severity: (1) **First degree:** freezing without blistering or peeling; (2) **second degree:** freezing with blistering or peeling; and (3) **third degree:** freezing with death of skin and perhaps the deeper tissues.

In mild cases the symptoms are numbness, prickling, and itching. With increasing severity there may be paresthesia and stiffness. Thawing causes tenderness and burning pain. The skin is white or yellow, loses its elasticity, and becomes immobile. Edema, blisters, necrosis, and gangrene may appear.

Treatment

A. Immediate Treatment:

1. Rewarming—The value of rewarming has not been conclusively established since patients are seldom seen while the tissues are still frozen. Superficial frostbite (frostnip) of extremities in the field can be treated by firm, steady pressure (without rubbing), by placing fingers in the armpits, and, in the case of the toes or heels, by removing footwear, drying feet, rewarming, and covering with adequate dry socks or other protective footwear. Rapid thawing at temperatures slightly above body heat may significantly decrease tissue necrosis. It has been suggested that rewarming is best accomplished by immersing the frozen portion of the body for several minutes in water heated to 40.6° C (105° F) *(not warmer)*. After thawing has occurred and the part has returned to normal temperature (usually in ½ to 1½ hours), discontinue external heat. Do not permit the patient to walk on thawed feet or toes since this is likely to cause serious tissue destruction. Never permit rewarming by exercise or thawing by rubbing with snow or ice-water. The patient's whole body temperature should be maintained by wrapping him in a blanket to keep him warm (not hot).

2. Protection of the part—Avoid trauma, eg, pressure or friction. Physical therapy is contraindicated in the early stage. Keep the patient at bed rest with the affected parts elevated and uncovered at room temperature. Do not apply casts, dressings, or bandages.

3. Anti-infective measures—Prevention of infection after the rewarming process is of great importance. Protect skin blebs from physical contact. Local infections may be treated with mild soaks. Prophylactic antibiotics are probably advisable. If ulceration has occurred, antitetanus immunization is warranted.

4. Anticoagulants—If anticoagulants are to be of value they must be given within 24 hours after thawing. Rapid-acting heparin sodium to prolong the clotting time for about 1 week may be useful in preventing secondary thromboses in surrounding areas.

B. Follow-Up Care: Gentle progressive physical therapy to promote circulation is important as the healing process occurs. Buerger's exercises should be instituted as soon as tolerated.

C. Surgery: Immediate regional sympathectomy has been reported to protect against early and late sequelae of frostbite. In general, other surgical intervention is to be avoided. *Amputation should not be considered until it is definitely* established that the tissues are dead. Tissue necrosis (even with black eschar formation) may be quite superficial and the underlying skin may heal well spontaneously.

Knize, D.M., & others: Prognostic factors in the management of frostbite. J Trauma 9:749–759, 1969.

Martinez, A., & others: The specific arterial lesions in mild and severe frostbite: Effect of sympathectomy. J Cardiovas Surg 7:495–503, 1966.
Paton, B.C.: The patient who came in from the cold. Emergency Med 2:12–17, Nov 1970.

IMMERSION SYNDROME
(Immersion Foot or Trench Foot)

Immersion foot (or hand) is caused by prolonged immersion in cool or cold water or mud. The affected parts are first cold and anesthetic; become hot with intense burning and shooting pains during the hyperemic period; and pale or cyanotic with diminished pulsations during the vasospastic period; later followed by blistering, swelling, redness, heat, ecchymoses, hemorrhage, or gangrene and secondary complications such as lymphangitis, cellulitis, and thrombophlebitis.

Treatment is best instituted during stage of reactive hyperemia. Immediate treatment consists of protecting the extremities from trauma and secondary infection and gradual rewarming by exposure to cool air (not ice or heat). Do not massage or moisten the skin or immerse the part in water. Bed rest is required until all ulcers have healed. Keep the affected parts elevated to aid in removal of edema fluid, and protect pressure sites (eg, heels) with pillows. Penicillin should be used if infection develops.

Later treatment is as for Buerger's disease.

Keatinge, W.R.: *Survival in Cold Water: The Physiology and Treatment of Immersion Hypothermia and of Drowning.* Davis, 1969.

DISORDERS DUE TO HEAT

Exposure to excessive heat results in prompt peripheral vasodilatation, increased cardiac output, and sweating. The resultant circulatory instability may lead to syncope if the patient remains erect and immobile, but muscular activity usually prevents syncope.

Fluid loss through sweating may amount to 3–4 liters/hour with heavy work at high temperatures. The salt content of sweat increases to 0.2–0.5% with rising temperatures.

Acclimatization usually results after 8–10 days of exposure to high temperatures; but even a fully acclimatized person may suffer a disorder in the event of excessive fatigue, severe infection, alcohol intoxication, use of belladonna-like drugs, or failure to maintain hydration, salt intake, or caloric intake. Elderly or obese persons and those with chronic debilitating diseases are most susceptible to disorders due to sustained climatic heat. Breakdown may be due to circulatory failure or failure of the sweating mechanism. Cessation of sweating may indicate impending stroke or collapse.

Prevention of Disorders Due to Heat

Avoid unnecessary exposure to heat and maintain adequate fluid and salt intake, using 0.1% saline as drinking water or salt tablets and water. Activity should be increased slowly until acclimatized. Clothing should be loose-fitting (preferably white) and permeable to moisture. Avoid alcoholic indulgence, excessive fatigue, and infections. Maintain good nutrition.

Leithead, C.S., & A.R. Lind: *Heat Stress and Heat Disorders.* Davis, 1964.

HEAT EXHAUSTION
(Heat Prostration)

Heat exhaustion is due to inadequacy or collapse of the peripheral circulation secondary to salt depletion and dehydration. The condition usually occurs in patients with underlying cardiac, cerebral, or systemic disease. The symptoms are weakness, dizziness, stupor, and headache, with or without muscle cramps. The skin is cool and pale and there is profuse perspiration, oliguria, tachycardia, and hypotension. Mental confusion and muscular incoordination may occur. Laboratory studies reveal hemoconcentration and salt depletion.

Place the patient at rest in a cool place, elevate feet, and massage his legs. Unless the patient is in danger of cardiac failure, give sodium chloride, 0.1% solution, by mouth, or physiologic saline, 1000–2000 ml IV. Treat shock when present (see Chapter 1). Avoid immediate reexposure to heat.

Ansari, A., & G.E. Burch: Influence of hot environments on the cardiovascular system. Arch Int Med 123:371–378, 1969.

HEAT STROKE
(Sunstroke)

Heat stroke is a rare disorder but a medical emergency characterized by sudden loss of consciousness and by failure of the heat-regulating mechanism as manifested by high fever and cessation of sweating. The condition often afflicts the elderly or those with cardiovascular or debilitating disease. There may be premonitory headache, dizziness, nausea, convulsions, and visual disturbances. The skin is hot, flushed, and dry; the pulse rapid, irregular, and weak; and the blood pressure is low. The rectal temperature may be as high as 108–112° F (42–44° C). Hydration and salt content of the body are normal.

Treatment is aimed first at reducing high temperature. Place the patient in a shady, cool place and remove his clothing. Cool him by fanning after sprinkling with water. As soon as possible, immerse him in cold water or use ice packs or ice water enemas. Do not lower the rectal temperature below 102° F (39° C) too rapidly. Massage the extremities to maintain circulation. Repeated small doses of chlorpromazine intravenously may be required to control delirium and shivering and to make treatment more tolerable for the conscious patient. Maintain an adequate airway and administer oxygen to combat further tissue hypoxia. Systemic heparin may be given for intravascular coagulation. Do not use dextran. Sedatives are to be avoided unless the patient is having convulsions, since they further disturb the heat-regulating mechanism. Give physiologic saline solution, 1000 ml *very slowly* IV. Observe for systemic infection and give appropriate treatment. Isoproterenol might be necessary for the treatment of shock (see Chapter 1).

Patients with heat stroke should avoid immediate reexposure to heat. Hypersensitivity to high temperatures may remain for a considerable time. It may be expedient to move to a more moderate climate in order to prevent a further episode of heat stroke.

Burch, G.E., & T.D. Giles: The burden of a hot and humid environment on the heart. Mod Concepts Cardiovas Dis 39:115–120, 1970.
Levine, J.A.: Heat stroke in the aged. Am J Med 47:251–258, 1969.

HEAT CRAMPS

Heat cramps are painful spasms of the involuntary muscles of the abdomen and extremities, due primarily to salt depletion. The skin is moist and cool, and muscle twitchings may be present. The temperature is normal or only slightly increased. Laboratory studies reveal hemoconcentration and low serum sodium.

Sodium chloride, 1 gm every ½–1 hour with large amounts of water, or physiologic saline solution by mouth or intravenously, usually relieves the attack promptly. Place the patient in a cool place and massage sore muscles gently. Rest should be continued for 1–3 days depending upon the severity of the attack.

BURNS

Burns may be caused by a wide variety of agents, including flame, hot water, steam, chemicals, electricity, or radiation. The general principles of management are the same in all types. There is considerable difference of opinion about what constitutes the optimal type of treatment for burns.

Evaluation of the Patient

A. General Condition of the Patient: Treatment and prognosis depend upon the severity of the burns, the time elapsed before proper treatment, the age of the patient (outlook is less favorable in elderly patients), and whether or not there are complicating medical disorders (eg, diabetes, cardiovascular, and renal disease). Inhalation of smoke and fumes can cause serious respiratory obstruction or pulmonary edema. Shock may appear quite early, and if not treated promptly can progress rapidly to stupor, coma, and death. Shock should be anticipated in all patients with burns involving more than 15–20% of the body surface area.

B. Depth or Degree of Burns:

1. **First degree**—Erythema without blistering.
2. **Second degree**—Erythema with blistering.
3. **Third degree**—Destruction of full thickness of skin and often of deeper tissues.

C. Estimate of Extent of Burn: The amount of body surface burned and the depth of the burn determine the fluid losses. The "rule of nines" is a useful means of estimating the percentage of total body surface involved by second or third degree burns of specific skin areas (see Fig 27–1). The extent of burn is commonly overestimated. Second and third degree burns of over 15–20% of total body surface (10% in children and the elderly) usually cause marked fluid loss which results in burn shock. Burn mortality is markedly influenced by the depth and extent of the burn and the age of the patient. Burns of over 50% of

body surface are frequently fatal, especially in children and the older age group.

D. Clinical Observations: Vital signs (pulse, temperature, respiration, and blood pressure) should be recorded hourly for the first 24 hours and at appropriate intervals thereafter. The general status of the patient should be carefully evaluated frequently; observe especially for evidence of shock, infection, or respiratory embarrassment. Fluid intake and output must be carefully recorded.

E. Special Laboratory Examinations: In severe burns, determine the hematocrit repeatedly as a guide to fluid therapy. Blood typing and cross-matching should be done in preparation for whole blood transfusion if needed.

Symptoms of Fluid Deficiency in Burns

Very close attention to clinical signs and symptoms is of great importance, particularly during the first 24 hours after the burn has occurred. Excessive thirst, vomiting, restlessness, disorientation, and mania—together with increase in pulse rate, decrease in blood pressure, collapsed veins, and oliguria—are indications that fluid losses have exceeded the rate of fluid replacement. During this critical early phase the adequacy of treatment is best judged by the urinary output, which should ideally be 30–50 ml/hour. If the rate of urinary excretion is below these suggested volumes, it is important to exclude acute renal insufficiency as a cause of the oliguria before increasing fluid intake.

Urine volumes greater than 100 ml/hour indicate that too much fluid has been given, but after 48 hours the urinary output is completely unreliable as a guide to therapy. In part this is due to the release of nitrogenous wastes from the burned tissues, which act as diuretics; in addition, electrolyte deficits may force compensatory elimination of water, as in the developing phase of a low-salt syndrome. Under these conditions, therapy is guided almost exclusively by clinical signs and symptoms, using enough fluid to maintain normal turgor of the unburned skin, fullness of the veins, and moisture of the oral mucosa. The quantities of fluid required to accomplish this may be surprisingly large. However, care must be taken to avoid simple overhydration with edema of the unburned tissues or water intoxication, which may lead to coma or death.

Fluid may be administered to the acute burn patient intravenously or by mouth. Severely burned patients often vomit when given significant amounts of oral fluids and usually require intravenous therapy. However, the oral route of fluid administration is preferred and oral should be substituted for intravenous fluids as soon as possible.

Intravenous Replacement Therapy

The objective of fluid therapy in acute burns is to maintain adequate tissue perfusion as indicated by blood pressure, pulse, urine output, acid-base balance, and the clinical state of consciousness and hydration of

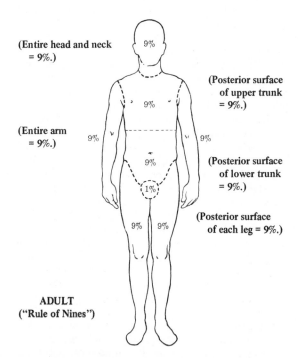

(Entire head and neck = 9%.)

9%

(Posterior surface of upper trunk = 9%.)

9%

(Entire arm = 9%.)

9%   9%

9%

(Posterior surface of lower trunk = 9%.)

1%

9%   9%

(Posterior surface of each leg = 9%.)

ADULT
("Rule of Nines")

FIG 27–1. Estimation of body surface area in burns. (Reproduced, with permission, from J.L. Wilson (editor): *Handbook of Surgery*, 4th ed. Lange, 1969.)

the patient. The volume of fluid required can be calculated initially in a variety of ways provided that the replacement program is adjusted in accordance with the clinical response of the patient. With this principle in mind, the following formula can be used to make a preliminary estimate of fluid needs:

During the first 24 hours after a severe burn, give 1 ml of plasma and 1 ml of balanced electrolyte solution (eg, lactated Ringer's injection USP) for each 1% of body surface burned and each kg of body weight. In addition, adults require 1000–2000 ml of balanced electrolyte solution to replace insensible loss.

Example: 70 kg man with a 40% burn.

1. Plasma: $1 \times 70 \times 40$ =   2800 ml
2. Electrolyte solution: $1 \times 70 \times 40$ =   2800 ml
3. Insensible loss (electrolyte solution) =   1400 ml

   Total fluids first 24 hours: 7000 ml
   During second 24 hours, give ½ this amount.

If more than 50% of the body surface is burned, calculations should be based on only 50% involvement. In no case should more than 10,000 ml of fluid be given in the first 24-hour period. In fact, 100 ml/kg body weight is usually sufficient as a maximum. Excess fluid in the early post-burn period serves to increase the amount of edema formation and exerts little or no effect on blood volume. For this reason, the hematocrit may remain elevated during the first day and fluid intake should not be increased with a view to restoring the hematocrit rapidly to normal.

Experience shows that an electrolyte solution such as lactated Ringer's can usually be substituted for plasma in the above formula in burns of less than 35–40% of body surface.

Acidosis is frequently present and may be corrected by administration of 0.5 mEq of $NaHCO_3$/kg body weight per mEq/liter decrease in plasma bicarbonate. Isotonic $NaHCO_3$ solution containing the calculated mEq of $NaHCO_3$ required for treatment of the acidosis can be substituted for an equivalent volume of balanced electrolyte solution in the fluid replacement formula. After the first few days, potassium loss is usually marked, making it advisable to give about 100 mEq potassium ion per day intravenously or by mouth.

Destruction of erythrocytes occurs in deep burns, but blood replacement is rarely required early in the post-burn period. Later, 3–5 days after the burn, transfusion of whole blood or packed red cells may be used to correct a reduced red cell mass.

Oral Replacement Therapy

Fluid and electrolyte replacement by the oral route can frequently be employed, alone or as a supplement to the intravenous route. For oral administration, a solution containing 5.5 gm/liter of sodium chloride (93 mEq Na^+/93 mEq Cl^-) and 4 gm/liter of

sodium bicarbonate (47 mEq Na^+/47 mEq HCO_3^-) may be used. This mixture contains 140 mEq/liter of sodium and is usually well tolerated if given slowly as repeated sips.

Guides to Fluid Therapy

Patients with burns over more than 25% of the body will probably require intravenous therapy—at least initially—because of their tendency to vomit. In such patients an intravenous catheter for infusion and an inlying bladder catheter for bladder drainage should be promptly inserted. Elderly patients and those with extensive burns should have a jugular catheter inserted for determination of central venous pressure. Fluid therapy and bladder drainage should be instituted before care of the burn wound is begun.

The objectives of fluid administration are to maintain plasma volume, urinary output, and blood pressure at satisfactory levels. Initially, lactated Ringer's solution is administered rapidly during the first 2 hours until a urinary output of 30–50 ml/hour is established. Plasma may then be administered simultaneously with the electrolyte solution, the rate being determined by the volume of fluid required to maintain the urinary output. Central venous pressure is monitored to avoid circulatory overloading, especially in elderly patients or when there is pre-existing cardiovascular disease.

When urinary output lags below the optimum of 30–50 ml/hour, the rate of administration of the electrolyte solution may be doubled and the urinary response noted. Hypotension as a cause of the oliguria must be ruled out; plasma must be administered rapidly if hypotension occurs or is suspected. If urinary output remains low in spite of satisfactory venous and arterial pressure and a presumably adequate fluid intake, it may be helpful to give 40 gm of urea in 4% solution IV over a 30-minute period as a diuretic. Ten grams of urea may usually be administered safely in children. A marked increase in urinary output, lasting several hours, generally follows the urea injection, and it may be repeated in 4 hours if necessary. Urea should not be given early in the post-burn period before an adequate amount of electrolyte solution has been given to expand the circulating blood volume.

The hematocrit rises in severe burns and may reach 60–65%. Adequate fluid therapy will control the rising hematocrit, but it is unnecessary and unwise to push fluids during the first 24–48 hours with the primary objective of lowering the hematocrit. It will come down spontaneously as edema fluid is returned to the circulation from the burn site. The most important parameters to observe in following the burn patient are the urinary output, the central venous and arterial blood pressures, and the clinical condition. Determination of pH and electrolyte values on blood and urine will serve as a guide to the adjustment of the electrolyte composition of the intravenous fluids. In respiratory tract burns, arterial pH, P_{CO_2}, and P_{O_2} aid in early detection and management of respiratory insufficiency.

EARLY CARE OF THE BURN WOUND

First Aid

Immersion of small or minor burned areas in cold water for ½ hour immediately after the burn, if feasible, will relieve pain and reduce cell damage.

A. First degree burns require no treatment.

B. Minor second degree burns may be washed with bland soap and water. Large blebs should be punctured aseptically but not removed. The wound is then covered with sterile petrolatum gauze and a pressure dressing. Change the dressing every 5–8 days. Healing usually takes about 2 weeks.

C. Severe burns should not be washed, greased, powdered, or painted with medication of any kind. Wrap the burned area in clean towels or sheets and transfer the patient to a hospital immediately.

Surgical Measures in Severe Burns

A. Control pain, which is usually marked, with morphine sulfate, 10–15 mg IV or IM, or other narcotic. General anesthesia is unnecessary for the initial cleansing and dressing of severe burns if a narcotic is used and procedures are done gently.

B. Treatment of Burned Area: Aseptic technic is essential. Wear cap, mask, sterile gown, and gloves when dressing burns. Sterile linen, instruments, and dressings are required. Cleanse burn and surrounding area with bland or hexachlorophene soap and sterile warm water. Wash gently with gauze sponges. Remove grease or oil with ether or benzene. Debride carefully. Remove only loose and necrotic tissue. Puncture blebs aseptically and leave them in place as protective coverings.

1. Closed treatment—Apply petrolatum gauze and a pressure dressing. Place a single layer of petrolatum (or Xeroform®) gauze smoothly over the burn, cover this with soft pads or other absorbent dressings, and secure firmly in place with stockinet or elastic or gauze bandage.

A variation of the closed technic consists of application to the burned areas of gauze roller bandages kept saturated with 0.5% silver nitrate solution. Dressings are changed daily. This method of burn treatment has not been widely used and may involve a hazard of systemic toxicity and sodium depletion.

2. Exposure treatment—In this form of treatment, no dressings or medications are applied to the burn after cleansing and debridement. On exposure to air a coagulum of serum seals the burn wound. This is the preferred method of treating burns of the head, neck, genitalia, and perineum. It is also suitable for limited burns on one side of the trunk or extremity. In mass casualties it may be necessary to treat the burns in this manner. The patient is placed on clean sheets. He must be turned frequently when burns encircle the body in order to avoid maceration. If infection occurs beneath the coagulum, it should be removed and warm saline compresses applied to the area.

C. Prevention of Infection: Reliance is placed on thorough cleansing of the burn and on aseptic dressing technics. Prophylactic antibiotics are rarely used. Cultures are obtained from exudates, and specific antibiotics chosen on the basis of sensitivity studies when signs of infection appear. Thorough but gentle daily bathing of the patient, followed by applications, during the day, of mafenide (Sulfamylon®, a sulfonamide derivative), is reported to control surface infection when used in conjunction with the exposure method of treatment.

Immunization against tetanus should be given during the first 24 hours in all major burns.

Burns of Specific Anatomic Areas

(1) Respiratory tract burns should be suspected in burns of the head and neck and when burns are sustained in a closed space. Inhalation of flame or hot gases produces severe tracheobronchitis and pneumonitis. Obstructive laryngeal edema may develop rapidly, preceded by stridor, copious respiratory tract secretions, dyspnea, and cyanosis. Tracheostomy should be done without delay if there is significant obstruction or retained secretions. Oxygen, humidification, and intravenous corticosteroids may be required. Pulmonary edema is treated by careful fluid restriction, diuretics, anticongestive drugs, and positive pressure ventilation. In cases of respiratory tract burns (when pneumonia is suspected), give penicillin until sputum cultures can be obtained and a specific antibiotic chosen.

(2) Head and neck burns are treated by exposure (see above). They are often less deep than suspected initially, and rapid healing is favored by the great vascularity of the region. Early grafting of eyelid burns is important to avoid ectropion and corneal ulceration due to exposure.

(3) Hand burns must be carefully cleansed and the fingers dressed individually with petrolatum gauze. Remove rings. Immobilize the entire hand in the position of function by pressure dressings and splints. Soon after the first redressing, which is done 5–8 days after the burn, areas of third degree burn should be excised in a bloodless field (using a pneumatic tourniquet) and a skin graft applied in order to obtain the earliest possible restoration of function.

(4) Joints should be maintained in optimal position and all third degree involvement grafted early to avoid disabling contractures.

(5) Perineum and genitalia burns are left exposed and cleansed with soap and water when they become soiled with feces or urine. An inlying Foley catheter for constant drainage of the bladder may be advisable in genital burns.

LATER CARE OF THE BURN WOUND

Redressing and Reevaluation

Observe strict aseptic technic in all burn dressings. Remove the original burn dressing down to the petrolatum gauze after 5–8 days. The depth and extent of the burn can be accurately determined at this time. Second degree burns require only reapplication of the pressure dressing and should heal in about 2 weeks. Third degree burns require special management.

Treatment of Third Degree Burns

A. **Removal of Slough:** The necrotic surface of a third degree burn usually does not separate for many weeks. Significant areas of slough or necrosis should therefore be removed in the operating room under general anesthesia 10–14 days after the burn if the patient's general condition allows. Burns of the face permit more conservative debridement since slough separates rapidly in this region.

B. **Skin Grafting:** Early skin grafting (preferably within the first few weeks following the burn) is essential to avoid chronic sepsis, malnutrition, and scar contractures. Skin grafting should be started as soon after removal of slough as possible. The denuded granulating surface should be firm and bright red, with a minimum of exudate. Warm saline dressings (changed several times daily) may be of assistance in the preparation of the burn wound for skin grafting. Homografts or heterografts, when used as temporary cover of the burn wound, may minimize fluid loss and infection while the patient is being prepared for autografting.

C. **Control of Infection:** Signs of infection include rising temperature, tachycardia, general toxicity, local pain and tenderness, and increased drainage. Pockets of pus trapped beneath slough must be sought and liberated by debridement. Warm saline dressings (changed several times daily) are applied to infected areas. Cultures are taken and antibiotic chosen by sensitivity studies. Prolonged antibiotic therapy is not necessary if drainage and dressings are adequate. Skin grafts will not survive in the presence of a virulent, invasive infection, but grafting should be done as soon as the infection is under control. A daily tub bath in warm water with hexachlorophene soap may be helpful in cleaning up a chronically septic burn. Bland ointment dressings can be soaked off relatively painlessly in the tub and reapplied after the bath. Continuous dressings soaked repeatedly with 0.5% silver nitrate solution between daily tub baths are an effective means of controlling surface infection.

General Supportive Measures

Chronic infection, exudative loss of protein, catabolic response to stress, and anorexia and depression caused by pain and toxemia can produce rapid nutritional depletion in the severely burned patient. The anemia that is often present is usually the result of hemolysis at the time of burning with subsequent inhibition of erythropoiesis by infection. The most effective supportive measures are a high-caloric, high-protein intake at the outset of therapy, vitamin supplements, and blood transfusions to keep the hemoglobin above 12 gm/100 ml.

The excretion of potassium is high during the acute phase of burns and may remain elevated for several weeks. In addition, a poor food intake at this time will prevent adequate replacement of potassium. Beginning on the third or fourth day of treatment, give potassium chloride, 3–4 gm orally (not in tablet form) in fruit juice or broth 3 times a day until a full normal diet is taken.

Artz, C.P., & J.A. Moncrief: *The Treatment of Burns.* Saunders, 1969.

Berens, J.J.: Thermal contact burns from streets and highways. JAMA 214:2025–2027, 1970.

Boswick, J.A. (editor): Symposium: Sixth National Burn Seminar. J Trauma 7:67–158, 1967.

Boswick, J.A., Jr., & N.H. Stone: Methods and materials in managing the severely burned patient. S Clin North America 48:177–190, 1968.

Boswick, J.A., Jr., (editor): Symposium on surgery of burns. S Clin North America 50:1191–1446, 1970.

Fox, C.L., Jr.: Treatment of burns. Mod Treat 4:1195–1313, 1967.

Herrin, J.T., & others: Care of the critically ill child: Major burns. Pediatrics 45:449–455, 1970.

Monafo, W.W.: The treatment of burns with compresses wet with 0.5% silver nitrate solution. S Clin North America 47:1029–1038, 1967.

Moncrief, J.A.: Topical therapy of the burn wound: Present status. Clin Pharmacol Therap 10:439–448, 1969.

Polk, H.C. Monafo, W.W., & C.A. Moyer: Human burn survival: Study of the efficacy of 0.5% aqueous silver nitrate. Arch Surg 98:262–265, 1969.

Stone, H.H., & J.D. Martin, Jr.: Pulmonary injury associated with thermal burns. Surg Gynec Obst 129:1242–1246, 1969.

WARM WATER IMMERSION FOOT SYNDROME

When individuals are unable to adequately dry their feet for several days as a result of prolonged immersion in warm water, such as might occur in the tropics, the feet become wrinkled, white, and so painful that walking is difficult. Infection may complicate the clinical picture. This condition should not be confused with the injury that follows exposure to a wet, cold environment.

If there are proper facilities and time to care for the feet, the condition will not develop. There are situations (eg, combat) when this is not feasible or practical. Whenever possible, the feet should be dried 3 times daily and overnight. A silicone cream applied to the bottom of the feet daily markedly retards or prevents the development of the syndrome for periods of up to 5 days.

Buckels, L.J., Gill, K.A., Jr., & G.T. Anderson: Prophylaxis of warm-water-immersion foot. JAMA 200:681–683, 1967.

DROWNING

Drowning is the 4th leading cause of accidental death in the USA. The number of deaths due to drowning could undoubtedly be significantly reduced if adequate preventive and first aid instruction programs were instituted. Swimming instruction should be given to as many people as possible at an early age. Private swimming pools should be properly enclosed, public pools should have trained life-guards, and hazardous swimming areas should be properly posted. As many individuals as possible should be taught the proper technic of artificial respiration. Compulsory teaching of artificial respiration to school children has been suggested. Swimmers should be cautioned against hyperventilation as a means of prolonging underwater swimming because of the possibility of inducing unconsciousness.

Spontaneous recovery usually occurs in victims of near drowning. If the victim is not breathing, clear the pharynx with the fingers and institute immediate artificial respiration by fully extending the victim's head and blowing intermittently through his mouth or nose (see Appendix). (Attempts to "drain water" from the victim are of doubtful value and may waste valuable time.) The prone position is not superior to the supine position with respect to drainage of water from the lungs. If intermittent positive pressure equipment is available, administration of 100% oxygen may be of considerable value. Mouth-to-mouth respiration should never be delayed or discontinued during transportation of the patient or in attempting to procure oxygen apparatus, airways, a defibrillator, or other equipment. Artificial respiration should be continued as long as the heart is still beating, no matter how weakly. If carotid pulsations cease, give simultaneous artificial ventilation and external cardiac massage (see Appendix). Summon an emergency vehicle for transportation to a hospital. Do not interrupt resuscitation for even a few seconds. Because metabolic acidosis is almost a constant finding, it is recommended that all patients be given sodium bicarbonate, 1 mEq/kg body weight IV, as soon as possible. Additional bicarbonate should be given as required.

Since fresh water is hypotonic and salt water is hypertonic, the pathophysiology of drowning in the 2 circumstances is markedly different and treatment varies accordingly.

In fresh water drowning, asphyxia, metabolic acidosis, ventricular fibrillation, reflex pulmonary hypertension, hemodilution, hypervolemia, hemolysis, and hyponatremia occur. Treatment includes artificial ventilation, cardiac resuscitation, and correction of the circulatory changes, blood hemolysis, and electrolyte imbalance. It has recently been reported that the pneumonitis due to fresh water aspiration may be improved by the administration of corticosteroids, greatly enhancing the possibility of recovery.

In salt water drowning, the pathologic findings consist of asphyxia, metabolic acidosis, pulmonary edema, hemoconcentration, hypovolemia, hypoproteinemia, and hypernatremia. Acute renal failure may occur. Treat pulmonary edema by positive pressure breathing (100% oxygen) and correct plasma deficiency.

When near drowning occurs in chlorinated fresh water, the most serious problem appears to be pulmonary edema and resultant hypoxia and metabolic acidosis. Hemolysis also occurs, but is less severe and slower in onset than when pure fresh water is aspirated. Treatment is directed primarily at the pulmonary edema, aspiration pneumonitis, and hypoxia. Mechanical intermittent positive pressure 100% oxygen therapy should be instituted as soon as possible.

Careful monitoring of cardiorespiratory function, measurement of urine output, and serial determination of blood gases and electrolytes are required. Supportive measures to correct hypoxia and acid-base, electrolyte, and circulatory disturbances should be continued until the victim is clearly out of danger.

Prophylactic antibiotics have been suggested for the prevention of aspiration pneumonia.

Grausz, H., Amend, W.J.C., Jr., & L.E. Early: Acute renal failure complicating submersion in sea water. JAMA 217:207–209, 1971.
Modell, J.H.: The pathophysiology and treatment of drowning. Acta anaesth scandinav 29 (Suppl):263–271, 1968.
Sladen, A., & H.L. Zauder: Methylprednisolone therapy for pulmonary edema following near drowning. JAMA 215:1793–1795, 1970.

ELECTRIC SHOCK

Direct current is much less dangerous than alternating current. Alternating current of high frequency or high voltage may be less dangerous than low frequency or low voltage. With alternating currents of 25–300 cycles, low voltages (below 220) tend to produce ventricular fibrillation; high voltages (over 1000), respiratory failure; intermediate voltages (220–1000), both. Electric burns are usually sharply demarcated, round or oval, painless gray areas with inflammatory reaction. Little happens to them for several weeks; sloughing then occurs slowly over a fairly wide area. Electric shock may produce momentary or prolonged loss of consciousness. With recovery there may be muscular pain, fatigue, headache, and nervous irritability. The physical signs vary according to the action of the current. With ventricular fibrillation no heart sounds or pulse can be found and the patient is unconscious. The respirations continue for a few minutes, becoming exaggerated as asphyxia occurs and then ceasing as death intervenes. With respiratory failure, respirations are absent and the patient is unconscious; the pulse can be felt, but there is a marked fall in blood pressure and the skin is cold and cyanotic. Electric shock may be a hazard in routine hospital equipment which is usually considered to be harmless (eg, electrocardiographs, suction machines, electrically operated beds, x-ray units). Proper installation, utilization, and maintenance by qualified personnel should minimize this hazard. Battery operated devices provide the maximum protection from accidental electric shock. Electrochemical cutaneous burns have been reported with direct current voltages as low as 3 volts.

Treatment

A. Emergency Measures: Free the victim from the current at once. This may be done in many ways, but the rescuer must protect himself. Turn off the power, sever the wire with a dry wooden-handled axe, make a proper ground to divert the current, or drag the victim carefully away by means of dry clothing or a leather belt.

Artificial respiration must be started immediately (see Appendix) if breathing is depressed or absent, and continued until spontaneous breathing returns or rigor mortis sets in.

Perform precordial compression (see Appendix) for ventricular fibrillation or arrest. Artificial respiration will not restore normal heart action, and other measures may not either. Incision of the chest and manual pumping of the heart may be employed as a last resort. Electric defibrillators may be employed if available.

Treat shock promptly.

Positive pressure oxygen with CO_2 may be used when available; or oxygen and CO_2 by mask combined with artificial respiration.

B. Hospital Measures: Hospitalize the patient when revived and observe for sudden cardiac dilatation or secondary hemorrhage.

Perform lumbar puncture if signs of increased intracranial pressure are noted.

Treat burns conservatively. The direction and extent of tissue injury may not be apparent for weeks. Infection is usually not a problem early. Patience and delay are important in treatment; allow granulation tissue to be well established before attempting surgery. Hemorrhage may occur late and may be severe.

Franco, S.C.: Electric shock and cardiopulmonary resuscitation. Arch Envir Health 19:261–264, 1969.

Starmer, C.F., McIntosh, H.D., & R.E. Whalen: Electrical hazards and cardiovascular function. New England J Med 284:181–186, 1971.

IRRADIATION REACTIONS

The effects of radiation may develop during or after the course of therapeutic x-ray or radium administration or after any exposure to ionizing radiation (eg, x-rays, neutrons, gamma rays, alpha or beta particles). The harmful effects of radiation are determined by the degree of exposure, which in turn depends not only upon the quantity of radiation delivered to the body but also the type of radiation, which tissues of the body are exposed, and the duration of exposure. Three hundred to 500 r (400–600 rads) of x-ray or gamma radiation applied to the entire body at one time would probably be fatal. (For purposes of comparison, a routine chest x-ray delivers about 0.3 r.) Tolerance to radiation is difficult to define and there is no firm basis for evaluating radiation effects for all types and levels of irradiation. The maximum permissible daily occupational total body exposure for radiation workers has been established at 5 rem/year (multiplied by number of years of age > 18) by the Federal Radiation Council (May, 1960).

Behrens, C.F., & E.R. King (editors): *Atomic Medicine,* 5th ed. Williams & Wilkins, 1969.

ACUTE (IMMEDIATE) RADIATION EFFECTS ON NORMAL TISSUES

Clinical Findings

A. Injury to Skin and Mucous Membranes: Irradiation causes erythema, epilation, destruction of fingernails, or epidermolysis, depending upon the dose.

B. Injury to Deep Structures:

1. Hematopoietic tissues—Injury to the bone marrow may cause diminished production of blood elements. Lymphocytes are most sensitive, polymorphonuclear leukocytes next most sensitive, and erythrocytes least sensitive. Damage to the blood-forming organs may vary from transient depression of one or more blood elements to complete destruction.

2. Blood vessels—Smaller vessels (the capillaries and arterioles) are more readily damaged than larger blood vessels. If injury is mild, recovery occurs.

3. Gonads—In males, small single doses of radiation (200–300 r) cause aspermatogenesis and larger doses (600–800 r) may cause sterility. In females, single doses of 200 r may cause temporary cessation of menses and 500–800 r may cause permanent castration. Moderate to heavy radiation of the embryo in utero results in injury to the fetus or to embryonic death and abortion.

4. Lungs—High or repeated moderate doses of radiation may cause pneumonitis.

5. The salivary glands may be depressed by radiation, but relatively large doses may be required.

6. Stomach—Gastric secretion may be temporarily (occasionally permanently) inhibited by moderately high doses of radiation.

7. Intestines—Inflammation and ulceration may follow moderately large doses of radiation.

8. Endocrine glands and viscera—The normal thyroid, pituitary, liver, pancreas, adrenals, and bladder are relatively resistant to radiation.

9. The brain and spinal cord may be damaged by high doses of radiation because of impaired blood supply.

10. Peripheral and autonomic nerves are highly resistant to radiation.

C. Systemic Reaction (Radiation Sickness): The basic mechanisms of radiation sickness are not known. Anorexia, nausea, vomiting, weakness, exhaustion, lassitude, and in some cases prostration may occur, singly or in combination. Radiation sickness associated with x-ray therapy is most likely to occur when the therapy is given in large dosage to large areas over the abdomen, less often when given over the thorax, and rarely when therapy is given over the extremities. With protracted therapy, this complication is rarely significant. The patient's psychologic reaction to his illness or to the treatment plays an important role in aggravating or minimizing such effect.

Prevention

Persons handling radiation sources can minimize exposure to radiation by recognizing the importance of time, distance, and of shielding. Areas housing x-ray and nuclear materials must be properly shielded. Untrained or poorly trained personnel should not be permitted to work with x-ray and nuclear radiation. Any unnecessary exposures, diagnostic or therapeutic, should be avoided. X-ray equipment should be periodically checked for reliability of output, and proper filters should be employed. When feasible, it is advisable to shield the gonads, especially of young persons. Fluoroscopic examination should be performed as rapidly as possible, using an optimal combination of beam characteristics and filtration; the tube-to-table distance should be at least 18 inches, and the beam size should be kept to a minimum required by the examination. Special protective clothing may be necessary to protect against contamination with radioisotopes. In the event of accidental contamination, removal of all clothing and vigorous bathing with soap and water should be followed by careful instrument (Geiger counter) check for localization of ionizing radiation.

Active research is being conducted on the use of pharmacologic radioprotectant agents (eg, glycine, alloxan, polyethylene), but no safe and effective drugs are as yet available for this purpose.

Treatment

There is no specific treatment for the biologic effects of ionizing radiation. The success of treatment of local radiation effects will depend upon the extent, degree, and location of tissue injury. Treatment is supportive and symptomatic.

A systemic radiation reaction following radiation therapy (radiation sickness) is preferably prevented, but when it does occur it is treated symptomatically and supportively. The antinauseant drugs, eg, dimenhydrinate (Dramamine®), 100 mg, or perphenazine (Trilafon®), 4–8 mg, 1 hour before and 1 hour and 4 hours after radiation therapy—or 4 times daily—may be of value. Whole blood transfusions may be necessary if anemia is present. Transfusion of marrow cells has been employed recently. Disturbances of fluid or electrolyte balance require appropriate treatment. Antibiotics may be of use in the event of secondary infection.

Chu, F.C.H., & others: A controlled clinical study of metopimazine and perphenazine in treatment of radiation nausea and vomiting. Clin Pharmacol Therap 10:800–809, 1969.

DELAYED (CHRONIC) EFFECTS OF EXCESSIVE DOSES OF IONIZING RADIATION

Clinical Findings

A. Somatic Effects: Skin scarring, atrophy, and telangiectases, obliterative endarteritis, pulmonary fibrosis, intestinal stenosis, and other late effects may occur.

Cataracts may occur following irradiation of the lens.

Leukemia may occur, perhaps only in susceptible individuals, many years following radiation. Under the usual conditions of radiation therapy this is rare; the incidence of cataracts in properly protected radiation workers should be about the same as in the general population.

The incidence of neoplastic disease is increased in persons exposed to large amounts of radiation, particularly in areas of heavy damage.

Microcephaly and other congenital abnormalities may occur in children exposed in utero, especially if the fetus was exposed during the first 4 months of pregnancy.

B. Genetic Effects: Alteration of the sex ratio at birth (fewer males than females) suggests genetic damage. The incidence of congenital abnormalities, stillbirths, and neonatal deaths when conception occurs after termination of radiation exposure is apparently not increased.

Ackay, M.M., & others: A new quantitative external monitoring technique. Internat J Appl Rad 17:261–268, 1966.
Barber, D.E.: Measurement of the performance of film badge services. Am Indust Hyg A J 27:243–251, 1966.
Behrens, C.F., & E.R. King (editors): *Atomic Medicine,* 5th ed. Williams & Wilkins, 1969.
Doolittle, D.P., & others: Protection from radiation lethality by alloxan. Internat J Radiat Biol 11:389–391, 1966.

· · ·

DECOMPRESSION SICKNESS
(Caisson Disease, Bends)

Decompression sickness has long been known as an occupational hazard of professional divers who are involved in deep-water exploration, rescue, salvage, or construction, and professional divers and their surface supporting teams are familiar with the prevention, recognition, and treatment of this disease. In recent years the sport of scuba (self-contained underwater breathing apparatus) diving has become very popular, and a large number of untrained individuals are exposed to, but unfamiliar with, the hazards of decompression sickness.

At low depths the greatly increased pressure (eg, at 100 feet the pressure is 4 times greater than at the surface) compresses the respiratory gases into the blood and other tissues. During ascent from depths greater than 30 feet, gases dissolved in the blood and other tissues escape as the external pressure decreases. The appearance of symptoms is dependent upon the depth and duration of submersion, the degree of physical exertion, the age, weight, and physical condition of the diver, and the rate of ascent. The size and number of the gas bubbles (notably nitrogen) escaping from the tissues is dependent upon the difference between the atmospheric pressure and the partial pressure of the gas dissolved in the tissues. It is the release of gas bubbles, and particularly the location of their release, which determines the symptoms.

Decompression sickness may also occur in rapid ascents from sea level to high altitudes when there is no adequate pressurizing protection.

The onset of symptoms occurs within 30 minutes in ½ of cases and almost invariably within 6 hours. Symptoms, which are highly variable, include pain (largely in the joints), pruritic rash, visual disturbances, weakness or paralysis, dizziness or vertigo, headache, dyspnea, paresthesias, aphasia, and coma.

Early recognition and prompt treatment are extremely important. Continuous administration of oxygen is indicated as a first aid measure, whether or not cyanosis is present. Aspirin may be given for pain, but narcotics should be used very cautiously since they may obscure the patient's response to recompression. Rapid transportation to a treatment facility for recompression is necessary not only to relieve symptoms but to prevent permanent impairment. The physician should be familiar with the nearest recompression center. The local public health department or nearest naval facility should be able to provide such information. The importance of treating plasma deficit has been recently emphasized. Hypothermia may also be indicated.

Lambertson, C.J., & others: Symposium on undersea-aerospace medicine: Modern aspects of treatment of decompression sickness. Aerospace Med 39:1055–1093, 1968.

Miles, S.: *Underwater Medicine,* 3rd ed. Lippincott, 1969.

MOUNTAIN SICKNESS

Modern, rapid means of transportation have increased the number of unacclimatized individuals who are exposed to the effects of high altitude. Lack of sufficient time for acclimatization, increased physical activity, and varying degrees of health may be responsible for the acute and chronic disturbances which result from hypoxia at altitudes of greater than 7000 feet. Marked individual differences of tolerance to hypoxia exist.

Acute Mountain Sickness

Initial manifestations include dizziness, headache, lassitude, drowsiness, chilliness, nausea and vomiting, facial pallor, dyspnea, and cyanosis. Later, there is facial flushing, irritability, difficulty in concentrating, vertigo, tinnitus, visual and auditory disturbances, anorexia, insomnia, increased dyspnea and weakness on exertion, increased headaches, palpitations, tachycardia, Cheyne-Stokes breathing, and weight loss. Voluntary, periodic hyperventilation may relieve symptoms. In most individuals symptoms clear within 24–48 hours, but in some instances the symptoms may be sufficiently persistent or severe to require return to lower altitudes. If necessary, administration of oxygen will promptly relieve acute symptoms. Judicious use of sedatives may be of value for some adults with irritability and insomnia. Preventive measures include adequate rest and sleep the day before travel, reduced food intake, and avoidance of alcohol, tobacco, and unnecessary physical activity during travel.

Acute High-Altitude Pulmonary Edema

This serious complication usually occurs at levels above 10,000 feet. Early symptoms of pulmonary edema may appear within 6–36 hours after arrival to a high-altitude area—dry, incessant cough, dyspnea at rest, and substernal oppression. Later, wheezing, orthopnea, and hemoptysis may occur. Physical findings include tachycardia, mild fever, tachypnea, cyanosis, and rales and rhonchi. The patient may become confused or even comatose, and the entire clinical picture may resemble severe pneumonia. The white count is often slightly elevated, but the blood sedimentation rate is usually normal. Chest x-ray findings vary from irregular patchy exudate in one lung to nodular densities bilaterally or with transient prominence of the central pulmonary arteries. Transient, nonspecific ECG changes, occasionally showing right ventricular strain, may occur. Pulmonary arterial blood pressure is elevated, whereas pulmonary wedge pressure is normal. Treatment consists of bed rest in the semi-Fowler position and continuous oxygen administration by tent or mask at 6–8 liters/hour. Subjective discomfort is relieved within 30 minutes to 2 hours, and recovery is usually complete within 2–3 days. If treatment facilities are not available and safe transportation is feasible, the patient should be moved to lower altitudes as soon as possible. If response to oxygen is not complete, or if oxygen is not available, rapid intravenous digitalization has been recommended. Improvement of overall gas exchange by the use of diuretic drugs has been reported. If bacterial pneumonia exists, appropriate antibiotic therapy should be given.

Preventive measures include education of prospective mountaineers regarding the possibility of serious pulmonary edema; optimal physical conditioning before travel; gradual ascent to permit acclimatization;

a period of rest and inactivity for 1–2 days after arrival at high altitudes; prompt medical attention if respiratory symptoms develop; and, in the case of individuals with a history of high-altitude pulmonary edema, routine hospitalization with special observation for tachycardia and cough. Mountaineering parties at levels of 10,000 feet or greater, if hospital facilities are not available, should carry a supply of oxygen and equipment sufficient for several days. Persons with symptomatic cardiac or pulmonary disease should avoid high altitudes.

Subacute Mountain Sickness

This occurs most frequently in unacclimatized individuals and at altitudes above 15,000 feet. Symptoms, which are probably due to CNS anoxia without associated alveolar hyperventilation, are similar to but more persistent and severe than those of acute mountain sickness. There are additional problems of dehydration, skin dryness, and pruritus. The hematocrit may be elevated, and there may be ECG and chest x-ray evidence of right ventricular hypertrophy. Treatment consists of rest, oxygen administration, and return to lower altitudes.

Chronic Mountain Sickness

This uncommon condition, which is encountered in individuals living in high-altitude communities for prolonged periods, is difficult to differentiate clinically from chronic pulmonary disease. The disorder is characterized by somnolence, mental depression, cyanosis, clubbing of fingers, polycythemia (hematocrit often > 75%), signs of right ventricular failure, ECG evidence of right axis deviation and right atrial and ventricular hypertrophy, and x-ray evidence of right heart enlargement and central pulmonary vessel prominence. There is no x-ray evidence of structural pulmonary disease. Pulmonary function tests usually disclose alveolar hypoventilation and elevated CO_2 tension but fail to reveal defective oxygen transport. There is a diminished respiratory response to CO_2. Almost complete disappearance of all abnormalities eventually occurs when the patient returns to sea level.

Lenfant, C., & K. Sullivan: Adaptation to high altitudes. New England J Med 284:1298–1309, 1971.
Singh, I., & others: Acute mountain sickness. New England J Med 280:175–184, 1969.

MEDICAL EFFECTS OF AIR TRAVEL & SELECTION OF PATIENTS FOR AIR TRAVEL

The decision about whether or not it is advisable for a patient to travel by air depends not only upon the nature and severity of the illness but also upon such factors as the duration of flight, the altitude to be flown, pressurization, the availability of supplementary oxygen, the presence of trained nursing attendants, and other special considerations. Medical hazards or complications of modern air travel are remarkably uncommon; unless there is some specific contraindication, air transportation is the best means of moving patients for distances over 200 miles. The Air Transport Association of America defines an incapacitated passenger as "one who is suffering from a physical or mental disability and who, because of such disability or the effect of the flight on the disability, is incapable of self-care; would endanger the health or safety of such person or other passengers or airline employees; or would cause discomfort or annoyance of other passengers."

Cardiovascular Disease

A. Cardiac Decompensation: Patients in congestive failure should not be permitted to fly until they are compensated by appropriate treatment, or unless they are in a pressurized plane with 100% oxygen therapy available during the entire flight.

B. Compensated Valvular or Other Heart Disease: Patients should not fly over 8000–9000 feet unless aircraft is pressurized and oxygen is administered at altitudes approaching or above 8000 feet.

C. Acute Myocardial Infarction, Convalescent and Asymptomatic: At least 6–8 weeks of convalescence are recommended even for asymptomatic patients if flying is contemplated. Ambulatory, stabilized, and compensated patients tolerate air travel well. Oxygen should be available.

D. Angina Pectoris: If slight physical exertion produces anginal pain, air travel is inadvisable. In mild to moderate cases of angina, air travel may be permitted, especially in pressurized planes. Oxygen should be available.

E. Hypertension: Ordinarily, there are no contraindications to air travel for hypertensive patients unless there are symptoms or signs of impending cerebrovascular accident. Mild sedatives are recommended for most patients.

Respiratory Disease

A. Asthma: Patients with mild asthma can travel without difficulty. Patients with status asthmaticus should not be permitted to fly.

B. Pneumonia: Unless there is marked impairment of pulmonary function, pneumonia patients may fly if oxygen is available.

C. Tuberculosis: Patients with active, communicable tuberculosis or pneumothorax should not be permitted to travel by air.

D. Other Pulmonary Disorders: Bronchiectasis, pulmonary abscess, or lung cancer patients may be flown safely unless there is marked impairment of pulmonary function.

Anemia

If hemoglobin is less than 8–9 gm/100 ml, oxygen should be available. Patients with severe anemia should not travel until hemoglobin has been raised to a reasonable level. Patients with sickle cell anemia appear to be particularly vulnerable.

Diabetes Mellitus

Diabetics who do not need insulin or who can administer their own insulin during flight may fly safely. "Brittle" diabetics who are subject to frequent episodes of hypoglycemia should be in optimal control before flying and should carry sugar or candy in case hypoglycemic reactions occur.

Contagious Diseases

Patients with contagious diseases are not permitted to travel by scheduled passenger airlines at any time.

Postoperative Patients

Patients convalescing from thoracic or abdominal surgery should not fly until 10 days after surgery, and then only if their wound is healed and there is no drainage.

Colostomy

Patients may be permitted to travel by air providing they are nonodorous and colostomy bags are emptied before flight.

Hernias

Patients with large hernias, unsupported by a truss or binder, should not be permitted to fly in nonpressurized aircraft because of an increased danger of strangulation.

Postsurgical or Posttraumatic Eye Cases

Pressurized cabins and oxygen therapy are necessary to avoid retinal damage due to hypoxia.

Psychoses

Severely psychotic, agitated, or disturbed patients should not be permitted to fly even when accompanied by a medical attendant.

Neuroses

Extremely nervous or apprehensive patients may travel by air if they receive adequate sedatives or tranquilizers before and during flight.

Motion Sickness

Patients subject to motion sickness should receive either sedatives or antihistamines (eg, dimenhydrinate [Dramamine®] or meclizine [Bonine®]), 50 mg 4 times daily, before and during the flight. Small meals of easily digested food before and during flight may reduce the tendency to nausea and vomiting.

Pregnancy

Pregnant women may be permited to fly during the first 8 months of pregnancy unless there is a history of habitual abortion or premature birth. During the 9th month of pregnancy a statement must be furnished that delivery is not due within 72 hours of destination time.

Early Infancy

Infants less than 1 week old should not be flown at high altitudes or for long distances.

Committee on Medical Criteria of the Aerospace Medical Association: Medical criteria for passenger flying: Scheduled commercial airlines. Arch Envir Health 2:124–138, 1961.

• • •

28...

Poisons

Robert H. Dreisbach

DIAGNOSIS OF POISONING

The diagnosis of poisoning, when not obvious, depends in great measure upon considering the possibility that poisoning has occurred. Once the physician includes poisoning in his differential diagnosis, he will be more likely to take the necessary steps to confirm or reject this possibility.

In general, the steps leading to a diagnosis of poisoning are as follows:

(1) Question the patient or his relatives or co-workers carefully concerning the presence of poisons in the environment.

(2) Take a careful history and perform a complete physical examination.

(3) Take samples for laboratory evaluation of damage to specific organs and to confirm or rule out exposure to specific poisons.

Cases of poisoning generally fall into 3 categories: (1) exposure to a known poison, (2) exposure to an unknown substance which may be a poison, and (3) disease of undetermined etiology in which poisoning must be considered as part of the differential diagnosis.

EXPOSURE TO KNOWN POISONS

In most cases of poisoning, the agent responsible is known and the physician's only problem is to determine whether the degree of exposure is sufficient to require more than emergency or first aid treatment. The exact quantity of poison absorbed by the patient will probably not be known, but the physician may be able to estimate the greatest amount which the patient could have absorbed by examining the container from which the poison was obtained and comparing the missing quantity with the known fatal dose. Reported minimum lethal doses are useful indications of the relative hazards of poisonous substances, but the fatal dose may vary greatly. If the poison is known to have caused serious or fatal poisoning, treatment for exposure to any quantity must be vigorous.

EXPOSURE TO SUBSTANCES WHICH MAY BE POISONOUS

If a patient has been exposed to a substance whose ingredients are not known, the physician must identify the contents without delay. The following sources are suggested for identifying the contents of trade-named mixtures.

Call Poison Information Center

Obtain the telephone number of the nearest Poison Information Center from the local medical society. Make certain that 24-hour service is available. Poison information centers are in most cases able to identify the ingredients of trade-named mixtures, give some estimate of their toxicity, and suggest the necessary treatment.

Books

Since available proprietary mixtures number in the hundreds of thousands, it is impractical to include all of these names in a single reference work. However, a number of books are useful in determining the contents of mixtures and should be available to every physician:

1. Frear, D.E.F.: *Pesticide Handbook* (annual publication). College Science Publishers. (Lists 9000 pesticide mixtures.)

2. Gleason, M.N., Gosselin, R.E., Hodge, H.C., & R.P. Smith: *Clinical Toxicology of Commercial Products,* 3rd ed. Williams & Wilkins, 1969. (Lists ingredients of about 17,000 household products.)

3. *The Merck Index,* 8th ed. Merck, 1968.

4. *American Drug Index* (annual). Lippincott.

5. *Physician's Desk Reference* (annual publication). Medical Economics, Inc. (Tablet and capsule identification guide.)

6. Dreisbach, R.H.: *Handbook of Poisoning: Diagnosis & Treatment,* 7th ed. Lange, 1971. (Lists 6000 poisons and trade-named mixtures.)

7. Hayes, W.J.: *Clinical Handbook on Economic Poisons.* US Public Health Service Publ No. 476. Government Printing Office, 1963.

8. Griffenhagen, G.B. (editor): *Handbook of Non-Prescription Drugs.* American Pharmaceutical Association, 1971.

9. Berg, G.L. (editor): *Farm Chemicals Handbook.* Meister, 1971.

The Manufacturer or His Local Representative

Another way to identify the contents of a substance is to telephone the manufacturer or his representative. He should have information concerning the type of toxic hazard to be expected from the material in question and will know what treatment should be given.

DIFFERENTIAL DIAGNOSIS OF DISEASES WHICH MAY BE THE RESULT OF POISONING

In any disease state of questionable etiology, poisoning must be considered as part of the differential diagnosis. For example, the high incidence of cases of lead poisoning which have been discovered in a few medical centers in recent years indicates that many cases must go unrecognized. Some of these patients had symptoms for more than a year and had been seen by several physicians before the diagnosis was made. Admittedly, the diagnosis of lead poisoning is difficult, but the possibility of this disorder must be considered before the necessary steps to confirm the diagnosis can be taken. Most important of the confirmatory steps in any case of poisoning is the discovery of a source of the poison and a history of exposure to it.

In making the differential diagnosis of a disease which may be the result of poisoning, the number of poisons which must be considered in any particular case can be reduced by classifying exposure possibilities. A convenient classification based on exposure consists of the following groups: (1) household, (2) medicinal, (3) industrial, (4) agricultural, and (5) natural.

HISTORY & PHYSICAL EXAMINATION

Symptom History
A. General Health:
1. Weight loss—Any chronic poisoning, but especially lead, arsenic, dinitrophenol, thyroid, mercury, and chlorinated hydrocarbons.
2. Asthenia—Lead, arsenic, mercury, chlorinated organic compounds.
3. Loss of appetite—Trinitrotoluene.
B. Head and CNS:
1. Delirium, hallucinations—Alcohol, antihistamines, atropine and related drugs, camphorated oil, lead, cannabis (marihuana), cocaine, amphetamine, bromides, quinacrine, ergot, santonin, rauwolfia, salicylates, phenylbutazone, methyl bromide, chlorophenothane (DDT), chlordane.
2. Depression, drowsiness, coma—Barbiturates or other hypnotics, alcohol, solvents, antihistamines, insecticides or rodenticides, atropine or related drugs,

cationic detergents, lead, opium and opium derivatives, paraldehyde, cyanides, carbon monoxide, alcohols, phenol, chenopodium, santonin, aspidium, salicylates, chlorpromazine, akee.
3. Muscular twitchings and convulsions—Insecticides, strychnine and brucine, camphor, atropine, aspidium, cyanides, santonin, ethylene glycol, nicotine, black widow spider.
4. Headache—Glyceryl trinitrate (nitroglycerin), nitrates, nitrites, hydralazine, trinitrotoluene.
C. Eyes:
1. Blurred vision—Atropine, physostigmine, phosphate ester insecticides, cocaine, solvents, dinitrophenol, nicotine, aspidium, methyl alcohol.
2. Colored vision—Santonin, aspidium, digitalis.
3. Double vision—Alcohol, barbiturates, nicotine, phosphate ester insecticides.
D. Ears:
1. Tinnitus—Quinine, salicylates, quinidine.
2. Deafness or disturbances of equilibrium—Streptomycin, dihydrostreptomycin, quinine.
E. Nose:
1. Anosmia—Phenol nose-drops, chromium.
2. Fetor nasalis—Chromium.
F. Mouth:
1. Loosening of teeth—Mercury, lead, phosphorus.
2. Painful teeth—Phosphorus, mercury, bismuth.
3. Dry mouth—Atropine and related drugs.
4. Salivation—Lead, mercury, bismuth, thallium, phosphate ester insecticides, other heavy metals.
G. Cardiorespiratory System:
1. Respiratory difficulty, including dyspnea on exertion and chest pain—Phosphate ester insecticides, salicylates, botulism, nickel carbonyl, black widow spider, scorpion, shellfish, fish, physostigmine, silicosis, other pneumoconioses, cyanide, carbon monoxide, atropine, strychnine.
2. Palpitation—Nitrites, glyceryl trinitrate (nitroglycerin), organic nitrates; sympathomimetics, including isoproterenol.
3. Cough—Smoke, dust, silica, beryllium.
H. Gastrointestinal System:
1. Vomiting, diarrhea, abdominal pain—Caused by almost all poisons, particularly corrosive acids or alkalies, metals, phenols, medicinal irritants, solvents, cold wave neutralizer, food poisoning.
2. Jaundice—Chlorinated compounds, arsenic and other heavy metals, chromates, cinchophen, neocinchophen, mushrooms, phenothiazine, sulfonamides, chlorpromazine, ethylene chlorhydrin, trinitrotoluene, aniline.
3. Blood in stools—Warfarin.
I. Genitourinary:
1. Anuria—Mercurials, bismuth, sulfonamides, carbon tetrachloride, formaldehyde, phosphorus, ethylene chlorhydrin, turpentine, oxalic acid, chlordane, castor bean, jequirity bean, trinitrotoluene.
2. Polyuria—Lead.
3. Menstrual irregularities—Estrogens, lead, bismuth, mercurials, other heavy metals.

4. **Color of urine**—Warfarin (red), fava beans (red), hepatotoxins (orange).

J. Neuromuscular System:

1. **Muscular weakness or paralysis**—Lead, arsenic, botulism, poison hemlock (*Conium maculatum*), organic mercurials, thallium, tri-orthocresyl phosphate, chlorophenothane (DDT), chlordane, shellfish.

2. **Muscle fasciculations**—Phosphate ester insecticides, nicotine, black widow spider, scorpion.

K. Endocrine System:

1. **Libido decreased**—Lead, mercury, other heavy metals, sedatives and hypnotics.

2. **Breast enlargement**—Estrogens.

L. Anemia: Lead, benzene, chloramphenicol.

Physical Examination

A. General:

1. **Blood pressure fall**—Nitrates, nitrites, glyceryl trinitrate (nitroglycerin), veratrum, cold wave neutralizer, acetanilid, chlorpromazine, quinine, chenopodium, volatile oils, aconite, disulfiram, iron salts, methyl bromide, arsine, phosphine, nickel carbonyl, stibine.

2. **Blood pressure rise**—Epinephrine or substitutes, veratrum, ergot, cortisone, vanadium, lead, nicotine.

3. **Tachycardia**—Potassium bromate.

4. **Bradycardia**—Veratrum, zygadenus.

5. **Fever**—Dinitrophenol or other nitrophenols, jimson weed (atropine), boric acid.

6. **Hypothermia**—Akee.

B. Skin:

1. **Cyanosis in the absence of respiratory depression or shock**—Methemoglobinemia from aniline, nitrobenzene, acetanilid, phenacetin, nitrate from well water or food, bismuth subnitrate, cloth marking ink (aniline), chloramine-T.

2. **Dryness**—Atropine and related compounds.

3. **Increased perspiration**—Alcohol, aspirin, arsenic, fluorides, insulin, mercuric chloride, muscarine, organic phosphates (parathion), pilocarpine.

4. **Corrosion or destruction**—Acids or alkalies, permanganate.

5. **Jaundice from liver injury**—Chlorinated compounds, arsenic, chromates, cinchophen, neocinchophen, mushrooms, phenothiazine, and sulfonamides.

6. **Jaundice from hemolysis**—Aniline, nitrobenzene, pamaquine, pentaquine, primaquine, benzene, castor beans, jequirity beans, fava beans, phosphine, arsine, nickel carbonyl.

7. **Redness**—Carbon monoxide, cyanide.

8. **Staining of skin**—Iodine (black), nitric acid (yellow), silver nitrate (blue-black).

9. **Rash**—Bromides, sulfonamides, antibiotics, poison oak, hair preparations, photographic developers, salicylates, trinitrotoluene, chromium, phenothiazine, gold salts, chlorinated compounds.

10. **Loss of hair**—Thallium, arsenic, sulfides, radiation.

C. Eyes:

1. **Dilated pupils**—Atropine and related drugs, cocaine, nicotine, solvents, amphetamines, hallucinogens, depressants.

2. **Contracted pupils**—Morphine and related drugs, physostigmine and related drugs, phosphate ester insecticides.

3. **Pigmented scleras**—Quinacrine, santonin, jaundice from hemolysis or liver damage.

4. **Pallor of optic disk**—Quinine, nicotine, carbon disulfide.

D. Perforated Nasal Septum: Chromium.

E. Mouth:

1. **Black line on gums**—Lead, mercury, arsenic, bismuth.

2. **Inflammation of gums**—Lead, mercury, arsenic, bismuth, other heavy metals.

3. **Salivation**—Phosphate ester insecticides, mercury, mushrooms.

4. **Breath odor**—Recognizable as such (alcohol, ether, paraldehyde, phenols and cresols, sulfides), garlic odor (arsenic, parathion, phosphorus), bitter almonds (cyanides).

F. Lungs:

1. **Wheezing**—Phosphate ester insecticides, physostigmine, neostigmine, mushrooms (*Amanita muscaria*).

2. **Decreased vital capacity**—Silica, beryllium dusts, other dusts.

3. **Rapid respirations**—Cyanide, atropine, cocaine, carbon monoxide, carbon dioxide.

4. **Slow respirations**—Cyanide, carbon monoxide, barbiturates, morphine, botulism, aconite, magnesium.

5. **Pulmonary edema**—Metal fumes, hydrogen sulfide, methyl bromide, methyl chloride.

G. Central Nervous System:

1. **Convulsions**—Insecticides, strychnine, camphor, atropine.

2. **Depression, drowsiness, coma**—Barbiturates or other hypnotics, alcohol, solvents, antihistamines, insecticides or rodenticides, atropine or related drugs, lead, opium and derivatives, paraldehyde, cyanides, carbon monoxide, phenol.

3. **Deafness or disturbances of equilibrium**—Streptomycin, dihydrostreptomycin, neomycin, quinine.

4. **Mental deterioration**—Alcohols, thallium, lead, mercury.

H. Muscles:

1. **Muscle weakness or paralysis (may be limited to a single muscle or muscle group)**—Lead, arsenic, botulism, poison hemlock (*Conium maculatum*), organic mercurials, tri-orthocresyl phosphate, carbon disulfide, insecticides.

2. **Muscle twitching**—Insecticides, nicotine, manganese, shellfish, chlorophenothane (DDT).

LABORATORY EXAMINATION

Simplified Laboratory Tests

A. Salicylates in Urine: To 5 ml of acidified urine add 10% tincture ferric chloride drop-by-drop until precipitation ceases. A purple color indicates a positive

First Aid Measures in Poisoning

The following summary is provided for the physician's use in giving instructions for first aid treatment in response to an emergency inquiry. With the exceptions noted under Ingested Poison, any of these procedures can be carried out by laymen.

Ingested Poison

Lay persons should not attempt treatment if the patient is convulsing or unconscious. If the patient has ingested corrosives (acid or alkali) or petroleum products (kerosene, gasoline, paint thinner, lighter fluid, etc), the procedures described in paragraph 3 below should not be used.

1. Have the patient drink one of the following to dilute the poison and slow absorption: milk, beaten eggs, a suspension of flour, starch, or mashed potatoes in water, or water.
2. Give activated charcoal if available.
3. Stimulate vomiting by rubbing the pharynx and the back of the tongue with a finger or spoon handle. If vomiting cannot be started in this way, give 1 tsp of powdered mustard in a glass of water or 15 ml (½ oz) syrup of ipecac in ½ glass of water.
4. Give a cathartic—One heaping tbsp of sodium sulfate (Glauber's salt) dissolved in ½ glass of water by mouth.
5. Conserve body warmth by applying blankets. Avoid external heat.

Inhaled Poisons

1. Carry the victim to fresh air immediately; loosen tight clothing.
2. Give artificial respiration by direct inflation (see p 926) if respiration is depressed. Remove any objects from the patient's mouth, hold his chin up, tilt his head back as far as possible, and blow into his mouth or nose until his chest rises. Repeat 20 times/minute. Obtain a resuscitator from the police department, fire department, or medical supply service company to facilitate oxygen administration.

Skin Contamination

1. Drench skin with water in tub or shower.
2. Direct a stream of water onto the skin while removing the patient's clothing.
3. Do not use chemical antidotes.

Eye Contamination

1. Holding the lids apart, wash the eye for 5 minutes with running water at eye fountain or with gentle stream of water from a hose or tap.
2. Do not use chemical antidotes.

Snake, Insect, or Arachnid Bite

1. Immobilize patient immediately.
2. Give specific antiserum as soon as possible.
3. If the patient must be moved, carry him on a stretcher as gently as possible.
4. Incision and suction will remove up to 10% of injected snake venom in the first half hour.

Injected Poisons (Overdosage of Drugs)

1. Make the patient lie down.
2. Apply a rubber band tourniquet (1 X 24 inches) proximal to the injection. The pulse should not disappear in vessels beyond the tourniquet, nor should a throbbing sensation be felt by the patient. Loosen tourniquet for 1 minute in every 15.

Identification of Unknown Toxic Agent

The following information is useful in attempting to identify a toxic agent. It should be available when you call your Poison Information Center.

1. Physical state (solid, liquid, gas).
2. Odor.
3. Trade-name.
4. Use.
5. Presence of poison label.
6. Inflammability warning.

---

test. (Boiling the urine eliminates diacetic acid, which also gives a positive test.)

B. Blood Bromide: The La Motte Chemical Company, Towson, Baltimore, Maryland 21204, has available a simplified procedure for determining blood bromide levels. The test is carried out by adding gold chloride reagent to 2 ml of deproteinized blood serum. The resulting color reaction is compared with a known bromide standard until a color match is obtained. The blood bromide concentration is then derived by reading directly from the standard color tube. An instruc-

tion book gives each step in detail. Blood bromide levels above 150 mg/100 ml of serum produce symptoms of intoxication; levels above 200 mg/100 ml are associated with serious toxicity.

C. Urine Bromide and Iodine: To 10 ml of urine add a few drops of fuming nitric acid and 5 ml of chloroform; mix gently and let stand 3 minutes. The chloroform settles to the bottom and takes on a pink to violet color in the presence of iodides or a yellow color in the presence of bromides. A positive test is not an indication of poisoning but only of absorption of bromide. The blood bromide test indicates the seriousness of poisoning.

D. **Urine Phenothiazine Tranquilizers:** Add 1 ml of a test solution containing 5 parts 5% ferric chloride, 45 parts 20% perchloric acid, and 50 parts 50% nitric acid to 1 ml of urine. A pink to red-purple color develops immediately that is proportionate to the daily dose of drug. All colors appearing after 10 seconds should be disregarded.

E. **Iron in Gastric Contents:** Dilute gastric contents or vomitus with sufficient water to make the specimen fluid. Filter and test the filtrate with 1 ml of 10% potassium ferricyanide solution. An intense blue color indicates the presence of ferrous salts. Repeat the test with 10% potassium ferrocyanide solution, which gives a similar blue color with ferric salts.

Special Examinations

Special chemical examinations for lead or other heavy metals, insecticides, cholinesterase, barbiturates, alkaloids, etc, may be necessary in the differential diagnosis of poisoning. The following laboratories are suggested for the performance of such analyses. It is wise to make prior arrangements with the laboratory to make certain that they will accept samples for analyses.

(1) County coroner's laboratory—Heavy metals, blood alcohol, barbiturates, alkaloids.

(2) City, county, or state police laboratory—Blood alcohol, barbiturates, other poisons.

(3) State toxicologist's office—As under (1). Analyses in connection with criminal poisonings.

(4) Federal Bureau of Investigation Laboratory, Washington, DC (only through local police).

(5) State departments of public health will usually perform analyses relating only to cases of occupational poisoning: insecticides, heavy metals.

(6) County hospital laboratory—Lead, barbiturates, alkaloids, blood alcohol.

(7) Private laboratories—Heavy metals, barbiturates.

(8) Technical Development Laboratory, United States Public Health Service, PO Box 769, Savannah, Georgia—Insecticides in blood, body fat, blood cholinesterase. (Send weighed, frozen sample.)

Kaye, S.: Bedside toxicology. P Clin North America 17:515–524, 1970.

PRINCIPLES OF TREATMENT OF POISONING
(See also First Aid Measures, p 850.)

In the emergency treatment of any poisoning in which the toxin has been taken by mouth, the following general procedures should be carried out: (1) Remove poison by emesis, lavage, catharsis, or diuresis as soon as possible. (2) Inactivate poison with specific or general antidote. Follow with lavage. (3) Combat shock, collapse, and specific manifestations as they arise. (4) Protect mucous membranes with demulcents.

Removal of Poison

Caution: Do not use stomach tubes or emetics in poisonings due to strong acids or alkalies or other corrosive agents; they may cause gastric perforation.

A. **Adsorption:** Activated charcoal is effective for adsorbing almost all poisons. Ten to 15 gm should be administered for each 1 gm of poison. Nuchar C® (West Virginia Pulp and Paper Co), Darco G60® (Atlas), and Norit A® (American Norit Co) are suitable products. Prepare ahead several 500 ml polyethylene bottles, each containing 50 gm charcoal. For use, add 400 ml distilled water and shake. Give orally or use as lavage fluid.

B. **Emesis:** This is the quickest way to evacuate gastric contents.

1. **Indications**—For removal of excess poison in cooperative patients, or for convenience when a stomach tube is unavailable or the patient is unable to take stomach tube.

2. **Contraindications**—(1) Drowsy or unconscious patients (danger of aspiration of stomach contents). (2) Ingestion of corrosive poisons, kerosene, or convulsants.

3. **Technic**—Introduce a finger into the throat, or give an emetic and follow with copious quantities of warm water. The most useful preparation is syrup (**not** fluidextract) of ipecac, 15 ml, and repeat in 20 minutes if necessary. Ipecac is not effective after charcoal. Apomorphine hydrochloride, 0.03 mg/lb IM, will often quiet the patient and will usually induce vomiting. Apomorphine is itself a depressant, with effects similar to those of morphine. Do not use if discolored. After vomiting begins, give levallorphan tartrate, 0.01 mg/lb IM, to antagonize apomorphine. Powdered mustard, 1–3 tsp in a glass of lukewarm water, is an uncertain and unpleasant emetic, but it has the advantage of being generally available.

Emesis should be continued until gastric contents are clear.

C. **Gastric Aspiration and Lavage:**

1. **Indications**—(1) Removal of excess of noncorrosive poisons which may later be absorbed from the gastrointestinal tract. (2) Removal of CNS depressant poisons when vomiting does not occur (vomiting center paralyzed). (3) For collection and examination of gastric contents for identification of poison. (4) For convenient administration of antidotes.

2. **Contraindications**—(1) Corrosion of tissues by poison. (2) Struggling, delirious, stuporous, or comatose patients, because of danger of aspiration pneumonia. (3) Kerosene or other hydrocarbons.

3. **Technic**—Gently insert a lubricated, soft but noncollapsible stomach tube through the mouth or nose into the stomach. Lavage copiously, but do not distend the stomach. Under some conditions it is better to lavage with a small quantity of fluid at frequent intervals. Always remove excess of lavage solution.

Collect and save washings in clean containers for toxicologic examination when indicated. In forensic cases, seal with sealing wax and place in a locked refrigerator; deliver to toxicologist personally and get a signed receipt. If refrigeration is lacking, preserve the specimen with equal quantities of 95% alcohol; do not use formalin, as this interferes with toxicologic examination.

4. Gastric lavage fluids—(1) Warm tap water or 1% salt solution. (2) Activated charcoal: Use 50 gm in 400 ml water and stir until completely wet. The suspension should have a slightly thickened consistency. (3) Thin soluble starch paste. (4) Sodium bicarbonate, 1%. (5) Sodium thiosulfate, 1%.

D. Catharsis: Sodium sulfate, 30 gm in 200 ml of water, may be effective in retarding absorption.

Inactivation by Demulcents

Demulcents precipitate metals and also help to limit the absorption of many poisons. These bland agents are also soothing to inflamed mucous membranes. Use the whites of 3 or 4 eggs beaten in 500 ml of milk or water, skimmed milk, or thin flour or starch solution (boiled, if possible). Follow with gastric lavage.

Supportive & Symptomatic Measures

The victim of acute poisoning must be kept under close observation in order to anticipate the immediate and delayed complications of the poisoning. Suicidal patients may need special surveillance and should be placed under the care of a psychiatrist.

A. Circulatory Failure:

1. Shock (see p 3)—The principal measures include recumbent position, warmth, and blood and parenteral fluids.

2. Cardiac failure (see p 203)—The principal measures include rest, oxygen, and digitalis.

3. Pulmonary edema—Give 100% oxygen by mask. If pulmonary edema is due to gaseous irritants, give aminophylline, 0.5 gm IV, to relieve associated bronchial constriction. Pulmonary edema due to heart failure is an emergency requiring morphine, oxygen, and digitalis. Pulmonary foaming may be reduced by using 20% ethyl alcohol in the oxygen humidifier. The oxygen should be given at slightly increased pressure by means of a mask with an adjustable exit valve.

B. Respiratory Abnormalities:

1. Respiratory obstruction—Correct by oropharyngeal airway, intratracheal intubation, or tracheostomy.

2. Respiratory depression—Remove from toxic atmosphere. Administer artificial respiration as needed. A resuscitator or other means of automatic ventilation may be employed but requires constant supervision. Stimulants (analeptic drugs) are of questionable value even for poisoning with CNS depressant drugs.

3. Hypostatic pneumonia—The principal measures include antibiotics and intratracheal aspiration as needed.

C. CNS Involvement:

1. CNS excitement—Use hypnotic or anticonvulsant drugs: (1) Amobarbital sodium (Amytal®), 250–500 mg as fresh 10% solution IM or IV. (2) Paraldehyde, 5–15 ml orally in cracked ice with milk, fruit juice, or whisky; or 5–30 ml rectally in an equal quantity of vegetable or mineral oil. Maintain respiration.

2. CNS depression—Maintain respiration.

D. Agranulocytosis: In the presence of fever, sore throat, or other signs of infection, give penicillin, 1 million units daily, or a broad-spectrum antibiotic in maximum doses until infection is controlled. Give repeated fresh blood transfusions.

E. Methemoglobinemia: Give 100% oxygen by mask, and methylene blue, 5–25 ml of 1% solution slowly IV.

Increased Drug Excretion

A. Diuretics: Osmotic diuretics (eg, mannitol, urea, hypertonic glucose) or saluretic agents (eg, ethacrynic acid, furosemide) may increase drug excretion in cases of serious poisoning with drugs primarily excreted by the kidney (eg, salicylates and long-acting barbiturates). The clearance of phenobarbital can be increased considerably by mannitol or urea diuresis. Osmotic diuretics may also relieve cerebral edema (eg, in lead poisoning). Forced diuresis requires an adequate osmotic load and appropriate parenteral fluids. It may be necessary to regulate urinary pH to ensure optimum excretion of different drugs. Basic drugs (eg, amphetamines, strychnine) are best excreted by maintaining an acid urine. Weakly acidic drugs (eg, salicylates, long-acting barbiturates) are best excreted with an alkaline urine. Contraindications to osmotic diuresis include renal insufficiency, pulmonary edema, cardiac insufficiency, and severe hypotension despite adequate fluid replacement.

B. Dialysis: Early enthusiasm for treating acute poisoning of all types with peritoneal dialysis or hemodialysis has been tempered by 2 decades of clinical experience. Assuming that technical and professional resources are available for prompt and safe dialysis, the indications for it can now be summarized as follows: (1) Known or suspected potentially lethal amounts of a dialyzable drug (Table 28–1). (2) Poisoning with deep coma, apnea, severe hypotension, fluid and electrolyte or acid-base disturbance, or extreme body temperature changes which cannot be corrected by conventional measures. (3) Poisoning in patients with severe renal, cardiac, pulmonary, or hepatic disease, and poisoning in patients who are pregnant.

Careful observation and treatment of the patient are required before, during, and after dialysis. Constant monitoring of vital signs, central venous pressure, and frequent laboratory determinations of fluids, electrolytes, and blood gases are required.

Peritoneal dialysis will continue to be the principal method of dialysis employed for acute poisonings not requiring maximally rapid dialysis.

TABLE 28–1. Toxic agents for which peritoneal dialysis or hemodialysis may be indicated.*

Sedative-hypnotics	**Other metals**
Alcohols	Calcium
Chloral hydrate	Lithium
Ethanol	Magnesium
Ethchlorvynol (Placidyl®)	Potassium
Ethylene glycol	
Methanol	**Halides**
Barbiturates	Bromides
Carbamates	Fluorides
Ethinamate (Valmid®)	Iodides
Meprobamate (Equanil®,	
Miltown®)	**Alkaloids**
Paraldehyde	Quinidine
	Quinine
Nonnarcotic analgesics	Strychnine
Acetaminophen	
Aspirin	**Miscellaneous**
Methyl salicylate	Anilines
Phenacetin	Antibiotics
	Borates
Amphetamines	Boric acid
	Carbon tetrachloride
Heavy metals	Chlorates
Arsenicals	Dichromate
Arsine	Diphenylhydantoin
Arsenic (after	(Dilantin®)
dimercaprol)	Ergotamine
Iron (after deferoxamine)	Isoniazid
Lead (after edetate)	Mushroom *(Amanita*
Mercury (after	*phalloides)*
dimercaprol)	Nitrobenzenes
	Nitrofurantoin
	Sulfonamides
	Thiocyanates

*Dialysis has *not* proved especially useful for the following compounds:

Amitriptyline (Elavil®)	Hallucinogens
Anticholinergics	Heroin
Atropine	Imipramine (Tofranil®)
Antidepressants	Methaqualone (Quaalude®)
Antihistamines	Methyprylon (Noludar®)
Chlordiazepoxide	Nortriptyline (Aventyl®)
(Librium®)	Oxazepam (Serax®)
Diazepam (Valium®)	Phenelzine (Nardil®)
Digitalis	Phenothiazines
Diphenoxylate (Lomotil®)	Propoxyphene (Darvon®)
Glutethimide (Doriden®)	

Dialysis should usually augment rather than be used in lieu of well established emergency and supportive measures.

Cashman, T.M., & H.C. Shirkey: Emergency management of poisoning. P Clin North America 17:525–534, 1970.

TREATMENT OF COMMON SPECIFIC POISONINGS (ALPHABETICAL ORDER)

ACIDS, CORROSIVE

The strong mineral acids exert primarily a local corrosive effect on the skin or mucous membranes. In severe burns, circulatory collapse may result. Symptoms include severe pain in the throat and upper gastrointestinal tract, marked thirst, bloody vomitus; difficulty in swallowing, breathing, and speaking; discoloration and destruction of skin and mucous membranes in and around the mouth; and shock.

The MLD is 1 ml of concentrated acid.

Inhalation of volatile acids, fumes, or gases such as chlorine, fluorine, bromine, or iodine cause severe irritation of the throat and chest with paroxysmal coughing and inhibition of respiration, followed by pulmonary edema.

Treatment

A. Ingested: Dilute immediately by giving 200 ml of milk of magnesia, aluminum hydroxide gel, milk, or water to drink; give beaten eggs (at least 12) as a demulcent. Pass a nasogastric tube gently and lavage with 2–4 liters of milk of magnesia in 100 ml portions. Leave the tube in place until the extent of the injury is known. Do not give bicarbonate or carbonates.

Relieve pain and treat shock. Administer corticosteroids.

B. Skin Contact: Flood with water for 15 minutes. Use no chemical antidotes; the heat of the reaction may cause additional injury. Relieve pain and treat shock.

C. Eye Contact: Flood with water for 5 minutes, holding the eyelids open. Relieve pain by use of local anesthetic agent.

D. Inhalation: Remove from further exposure to fumes or gas. Treat pulmonary edema.

ALCOHOL, ETHYL

Beverages containing ethyl alcohol have been widely used and abused throughout history. Although the acute and chronic toxic effects of alcohol are principally on the nervous and gastrointestinal systems, it may be seen from Table 28–2 that many other parts of the body are also susceptible to the potentially harmful effects of this agent.

The principal manifestation of ethyl alcohol poisoning is CNS depression and gastric irritation, with nausea and vomiting. Other manifestations include hypoglycemia, convulsions, fever to 40–42° C

TABLE 28–2. Toxicity of alcohol.

Psychoneurologic syndromes
Acute alcoholism
    Alcoholic intoxication
    Alcoholic hypoglycemia
    Alcoholic coma
Withdrawal syndromes
    Alcoholic hallucinosis
    Alcoholic seizures ("rum fits")
    Delirium tremens
Nutritional syndromes
    Wernicke-Korsakoff syndrome
    Pellagra
	Thrombocytopenia
	Defective granulocyte mobilization
	
	Neuromuscular syndromes
	Peripheral polyneuropathy
	Acute and chronic alcoholic myopathy
	
	Cardiovascular syndromes
	Alcoholic cardiomyopathy
	Quebec beer drinker's cardiomyopathy

Gastrointestinal syndromes Acute and chronic gastritis Malabsorption syndrome Alcoholic fatty liver Alcoholic cirrhosis Zieve's syndrome (jaundice, hemolytic anemia, and hyperlipidemia) Acute and chronic pancreatitis	**Metabolic syndromes** Lactic acidosis Hypoglycemia Hypomagnesemia **Conditions aggravated by alcohol** Traumatic encephalopathy Epilepsy Hodgkin's disease Porphyria Peptic ulcer
Hematologic syndromes Anemia due to acute or chronic blood loss Cytoplasmic vacuolization of erythroid precursors Megaloblastic marrow alterations (inhibition of folate metabolism) with anemia Sideroblastic marrow abnormalities Stomatocytic erythrocyte changes Hemolytic anemia	**Drugs which contraindicate concomitant use of alcohol** Disulfiram Sedatives Hypnotics Tranquilizers Phenformin

(104–108° F), and cerebral edema with severe headache.

Differentiate from barbiturate or paraldehyde poisoning, head injury, mental disorders, and insulin hypoglycemia.

The MLD is 300 ml.

Treatment of Acute Alcoholic Intoxication*

A. Emergency Measures: Remove unabsorbed alcohol by gastric lavage with tap water. Instill 4 gm of sodium bicarbonate.

B. General Measures: (Similar to those for barbiturate poisoning.)

1. Maintain the airway and respiration and keep the patient warm.

2. If the patient is comatose and areflexic, treat as for barbiturate poisoning.

3. For intractable retching or acute alcoholic excitation, give a phenothiazine tranquilizer (eg, chlorpromazine, 25–50 mg IM or orally) or a sedative-hypnotic (eg, paraldehyde, 15 ml orally or rectally) every 3–6 hours until symptoms have subsided. Two ml of paraldehyde may be administered deeply IM, avoiding nerve trunks. Sloughs occur, but only rarely.

Becker, C.E.: The clinical pharmacology of alcohol. California Med 113:37–45, Sept 1970.

Forney, R.B., & R.N. Harger: Toxicology of ethanol. Ann Rev Pharmacol 9:379–392, 1969.

Hines, J.D., & D.H. Cowan: Pathogenesis of alcohol-induced sideroblastic bone-marrow abnormalities. New England J Med 283:441–446, 1970.

Lieber, C.S., & E. Rubin: Alcoholic fatty liver. New England J Med 280:705–708, 1969.

McDonald, C.D., Burch, G.E., & J.J. Walsh: Alcoholic cardiomyopathy managed with prolonged bed rest. Ann Int Med 74:681–691, 1971.

Mendelson, J.H.: Biological concomitants of alcoholism. New England J Med 283:24–32, 71–81, 1970.

Mitchell, J.H., & L.S. Cohen: Alcohol and the heart. Mod Concepts Cardiovas Dis 39:109–113, 1970.

Moss, M.H.: Alcohol-induced hypoglycemia and coma caused by alcohol sponging. Pediatrics 46:445–447, 1970.

Myerson, R.M., & J.S. Lafair: Alcoholic muscle disease. M Clin North America 54:723–730, 1970.

Rubin, E., & C.S. Lieber: Alcoholism, alcohol and drugs. Science 172:1097–1102, 1971.

*See also discussion of alcoholism in Chapter 17.

ALCOHOL, METHYL

Methyl alcohol is a CNS depressant which produces specific damage to the retinal cells. Its end-products cause a metabolic acidosis. The MLD is 30–60 ml. Symptoms include headache, abdominal pain, dyspnea, nausea, vomiting, and blindness. Examination reveals flush or cyanosis, excitement or depression, delirium, coma, and convulsions.

Treatment
Lavage well with 1–2% sodium bicarbonate solution. Keep the patient in a dark room. Check CO_2 combining power. Give intravenous fluids to combat metabolic acidosis, and sodium bicarbonate, 5–15 gm orally every 2–3 hours. Give ethyl alcohol, 100 proof (50%), 0.5 ml/kg orally every 2 hours for 3–4 days, to block the metabolism of methyl alcohol until it is excreted. Dialysis is useful.

Closs, K., & C.O. Solberg: Methanol poisoning. JAMA 211:497–499, 1970.
Kane, R.L., & others: A methanol poisoning outbreak in Kentucky. Arch Envir Health 17:119–129, 1968.

ALKALIES

The strong alkalies are common ingredients of household cleaning compounds and may be detected by their "soapy" texture. They exert a local corrosive effect on mucous membranes and may produce circulatory failure. Symptoms include burning pain in the upper gastrointestinal tract, nausea, vomiting, and difficulty in swallowing and breathing. Examination reveals destruction and edema of the affected skin and mucous membranes, and bloody vomitus and stools. The MLD is 1 gm.

Treatment
A. Ingested: Immediate esophagoscopy in order to irrigate injured areas directly with 1% acetic acid until neutralized and to evaluate the extent of damage is the treatment of choice. Dilute immediately with 500 ml of dilute vinegar (1 part vinegar to 4 parts water) or citrus juice.

Relieve pain and treat shock.

Corticosteroids help prevent esophageal strictures or stenosis. The suggested drug for ages 1–4 is prednisolone, 10–15 mg 4 times a day, for about 2 weeks.

B. Skin Contact: Wash with running water until the skin no longer feels soapy. Relieve pain and treat shock.

C. Eye Contact: Wash with water continuously for 15 minutes, holding the lids open. Relieve pain. Have the eye examined by an ophthalmologist to determine the extent of damage.

Asch, M.J., & F.P. Herter: Lye ingestion causing pyloric stenosis without esophageal injury. New York J Med 71:455–457, 1971.
Leape, L.L., & others: Liquid lye. New England J Med 284:578–581, 1971.
Middelkamp, J.N., & others: The management and problems of caustic burns in children. J Thoracic Cardiovas Surg 57:341–347, 1969.

ANTICOAGULANTS

Bishydroxycoumarin, ethyl biscoumacetate, phenindione, and warfarin are used medically to inhibit the clotting mechanism by inhibiting prothrombin formation in the liver. Abnormal bleeding occurs only after prolonged administration. The MLD of bishydroxycoumarin and warfarin is 0.1 gm; of phenindione, 0.2 gm; of ethyl biscoumacetate, 0.6 gm. The pathologic findings consist of numerous gross and microscopic hemorrhages.

Clinical Findings
A. Symptoms and Signs: The principal manifestation of poisoning with the anticoagulants is bleeding: hemoptysis, hematuria, bloody stools, hemorrhages into organs, widespread bruising, and bleeding into joint spaces. Phenindione may also cause jaundice, hepatomegaly, skin rash, and agranulocytosis.

B. Laboratory Findings: The prothrombin concentration is lowered after administration of coumarin and indandione anticoagulants. Gross or microscopic hematuria may be present. The red cell count may also be reduced. The white count may be decreased after phenindione administration.

Treatment
A. Emergency Measures: Discontinue the drug at the first sign of bleeding. If ingestion of more than 10 times a daily therapeutic dose is discovered within 2 hours, remove by gastric lavage and catharsis.

B. General Measures: Give menadiol sodium diphosphate, 75 mg IM 1–3 times daily. For more rapid effect, give 50–150 mg of phytonadione (Aqua-Mephyton®) IV as the diluted emulsion. Give transfusions of fresh blood or plasma if hemorrhage is severe. Absolute bed rest must be maintained to prevent further hemorrhages.

Gazzaniga, A.B., & D.R. Stewart: Possible quinidine-induced hemorrhage in a patient on warfarin sodium. New England J Med 280:711–712, 1969.
Macon, W.L., Morton, J.H., & J.T. Adams: Significant complications of anticoagulant therapy. Surgery 68:571–582, 1970.
Sellers, E.M., Koch-Weser, J., & M.L. Lang: Potentiation of warfarin-induced hypoprothrombinemia by chloral hydrate. New England J Med 283:827–831, 1970.

ARSENIC

Arsenic is found in pesticides and industrial chemicals. Symptoms of poisoning usually appear within 1 hour after ingestion but may be delayed as long as 12 hours. They include abdominal pain, difficulty in swallowing, persistent vomiting, diarrhea, urinary suppression, and skeletal muscle cramps. Later findings are severe thirst and shock.

The MLD is 0.1 gm.

Treatment

A. Emergency Measures: Induce vomiting. Follow with 500 ml of milk. Lavage with 2–4 liters of warm tap water, 200 ml at a time. Treat shock.

B. Antidote: Give dimercaprol injection (BAL), 10% solution in oil. The side-effects include nausea, vomiting, headache, generalized aches, and burning sensations around the head and face. These usually subside in 30 minutes. Either ephedrine, 25 mg orally, or an antihistamine such as diphenhydramine (Benadryl®), 25–50 mg orally, will reduce the side-effects if given 30 minutes before dimercaprol.

1. Severe poisoning—Give IM, 3 mg/kg for each injection (1.8 ml/60 kg). **First and second days:** One injection every 4 hours day and night. **Third day:** One injection every 6 hours. **Fourth to 14th day:** One injection twice a day until recovery is complete.

2. Mild poisoning—2.5 mg/kg/dose (1.5 ml/60 kg). **First and second days:** One injection every 4 hours for 4 doses. **Third day:** One injection twice a day. **Fourth and subsequent days:** One injection once or twice a day for 10 days or until recovery is complete.

C. General Measures: Relieve pain and treat diarrhea. Hemodialysis will speed the removal of arsenic combined with dimercaprol.

Chhuttani, P.N., Chawla, L.S., & T.D. Sharma: Arsenical neuropathy. Neurology 17:269–274, 1967.

St. Petery, J., Gross, C., & B.E. Victorica: Ventricular fibrillation caused by arsenic poisoning. Am J Dis Child 120:367–371, 1970.

BARBITURATES & OTHER DEPRESSANTS
(Sedative-Hypnotics & Tranquilizers)

The barbiturates are among the most common offenders in accidental as well as suicidal poisoning. Other (or multiple) sedative-hypnotic drugs—particularly alcohol—may be involved. Obtain data on the drug and its dosage and time of ingestion from the patient, relatives, friends, or attending physician when possible.

Symptoms of mild poisoning consist of drowsiness, mental confusion, and headache. There may be euphoria or irritability. Moderate or severe poisoning causes delirium, stupor, shallow and slow respirations, circulatory collapse, cold clammy skin, cyanosis, pulmonary edema, dilated and nonreacting pupils, hyporeflexia, coma, and death.

The MLD is 0.5–2 gm. The lethal serum level in unsupported patients who have taken short-acting barbiturates is about 3.5 mg/100 ml; and with long-acting barbiturates, the lethal level is about 8 mg/100 ml.

Treatment

Note: The critical factor in the management of barbiturate poisoning is constant medical and nursing attendance to maintain physiologic responses until the danger of respiratory failure and circulatory depression has passed.

A. Mild Poisoning: Induce vomiting and give symptomatic and supportive nursing care. Keep the patient under observation until he is out of danger. Place suicidal patients under psychiatric care.

B. Moderate or Marked Poisoning: Most patients will survive even days of unconsciousness if the airway is kept open (usually requires tracheostomy) and if artificial respiration is maintained with a tank respirator, IPPB, or other mechanical ventilating apparatus. The patient should be hospitalized, and antishock measures instituted. Examine the patient and record the following at intervals of 1–4 hours (or oftener if the patient's condition is very poor): temperature, pulse, respiration, and blood pressure; mental status or state of consciousness, skin color (cyanosis or pallor), lung bases (pulmonary edema), reflexes (corneal, pupillary, gag, patellar), and sensation (response to pain).

1. Airway—Aspirate mucus, pull tongue forward, and insert oropharyngeal airway. Intratracheal or tracheostomy intubation and mechanical assistance to ensure adequate ventilation may be required. Serial determinations of blood gases is of great value.

2. Lavage with 2–4 liters of warm tap water, preferably containing activated charcoal. This is of doubtful value and may be dangerous if done after the patient has become drowsy or comatose. *Caution:* The danger of aspiration pneumonia is great in stuporous or comatose patients.

3. Excretion can be increased by alkalinization of the urine or administration of mannitol or urea. If renal function is adequate, give sodium lactate or sodium bicarbonate orally or intravenously.

4. Insert an indwelling catheter and save all urine for 48 hours for toxicologic study.

5. Parenteral fluids—Monitor central venous pressure. If cardiac failure is absent and renal function is adequate, give 1 liter of 0.45% sodium chloride solution and 1–2 liters of 5% dextrose solution IV daily to maintain a urine output of 1–1.5 liters/day. Unless fluid loss has been excessive, restrict fluids to 2–3 liters during the first 24 hours to reduce danger of pulmonary edema. In phenobarbital overdosage, if renal function is adequate, give up to 100 ml/kg of fluid daily, 1/3 as 20% mannitol, 1/3 as 10% dextrose in distilled water, and 1/3 as 0.145 M sodium bicarbonate (1.2%), plus 5 mEq/liter of potassium chloride. The amount of fluids should not exceed insensible losses (800–1000 ml/24 hours) plus the urine output.

In the event of shock, give plasma or other fluids intravenously in order to maintain a satisfactory blood pressure.

6. CNS stimulants (analeptics or convulsant drugs)—Picrotoxin, pentylenetetrazol, amphetamine, ephedrine, methamphetamine, strychnine, and bemegride (Megimide®) have been used, but they are not true antidotes. They do not shorten the duration of effect of poisoning and, if convulsions occur, postconvulsive depression will add to the severity of barbiturate depression. Hyperthermia and cardiac arrhythmias are also dangers.

7. Hemodialysis or peritoneal dialysis is indicated in severe cases when the necessary equipment and trained personnel are available. This is usually reserved for patients with hepatic or renal diseases. Dialysis is of doubtful value in glutethimide (Doriden®) poisoning.

Bloomer, H.A., & others: Rapid diagnosis of sedative intoxication by gas chromatography. Ann Int Med 72:223—228, 1970.

Comstock, E.G.: Glutethimide intoxication. JAMA 215:1668, 1971.

Mann, J.B., & D.H. Sandberg: Therapy of sedative overdosage. P Clin North America 17:617—628, 1970.

Mandelbaum, J.M., & N.M. Simon: Methyprylon poisoning treated by hemodialysis. JAMA 216:139—140, 1971.

Nordenberg, A., Delisle, G., & T. Izukawa: Cardiac arrhythmia in a child due to chloral hydrate ingestion. Pediatrics 47:134—135, 1971.

Shubin, H., & M.H. Weil: Shock associated with barbiturate intoxication. JAMA 215:263—268, 1971.

Wright, N., & P. Roscoe: Acute glutethimide poisoning. JAMA 214:1704—1706, 1970.

BELLADONNA DERIVATIVES
(Atropine & Scopolamine)

The belladonna alkaloids are parasympathetic depressants with variable CNS effects. The patient complains of dryness of the mouth, thirst, difficulty in swallowing, and blurring of vision. The physical signs include dilated pupils, flushed skin, tachycardia, fever, delirium, delusions, paralysis, stupor, and a rash on the face, neck, and upper trunk.

The MLD of atropine is 2—10 mg.

Treatment
Remove the poison by lavage and catharsis, and counteract excitement.

A. Emergency Measures: Induce vomiting and lavage with 2—4 liters of water, preferably containing activated charcoal. Follow lavage with sodium sulfate, 30 gm in 200 ml of water.

B. General Measures: Short-acting barbiturates such as secobarbital (Seconal®), 0.1 gm by mouth may be used if the patient is excitable. Treat respiratory difficulty as for barbiturate poisoning. Alcohol or cold water sponge baths are indicated to control high temperatures. Maintain blood pressure. Give physostigmine salicylate, 1—2 mg IM, to reverse the central and peripheral effects of atropine.

Duvoisin, R.C., & R. Katz: Reversal of central anticholinergic syndrome in man by physostigmine. JAMA 206:1963—1966, 1968.

BROMIDES

Bromides are CNS depressants still found in hypnotic and anticonvulsant preparations. Acute poisoning is rare. The symptoms include anorexia, constipation, drowsiness, apathy, and hallucinations. The physical examination reveals dermatitis, conjunctivitis, foul breath, furred tongue, sordes, unequal pupils, ataxia, abnormal reflexes (often bizarre), toxic psychosis, delirium, and coma.

The MLD is 10 gm or more.

Treatment
A. Emergency Measures: Lavage copiously with saline to remove unabsorbed bromides and later to remove those excreted into the stomach. Follow with sodium sulfate, 30 gm in 200 ml of water for catharsis.

B. General Measures: Give sodium chloride in addition to the regular dietary salt intake: (1) 1000 ml of physiologic saline IV or rectally once or twice daily; or (2) 1—2 gm as salt tablets every 4 hours orally. Continue until the blood bromide level is below 50 mg/100 ml.

Force fluids to 4 liters daily.

Diuretics will aid excretion of bromide.

Wooster, A.G., Dunlop, N., & R.A. Joske: Use of an oral diuretic (Doburil®) in treatment of bromide intoxication. Am J Med Sc 253:23—26, 1967.

Ziai, M., & A.C. Tahernia: Bromide intoxication in infants. Clin Pediat 6:365—367, 1967.

CARBON MONOXIDE

Carbon monoxide poisoning resulting from the use of unvented gas or coal-burning heaters is an important cause of accidental death. Voluntary inhalation of carbon monoxide in exhaust fumes is often used for suicidal purposes. The gas exerts its toxic effect by combining with hemoglobin to form a relatively stable compound (carboxyhemoglobin) which secondarily causes tissue anoxia. Manifestations are headache, faintness, giddiness, tinnitus, vomiting, cherry-red skin, vertigo, loss of memory, fainting, collapse, paralysis, and unconsciousness. Subclinical toxicity has been reported in dense traffic situations.

Treatment

Remove the patient from the toxic atmosphere. Loosen his clothing and keep him warm and at rest. Give artificial respiration with 100% oxygen for at least 1 hour. Give 50 ml of 50% glucose IV for cerebral edema as needed. Maintain body warmth and blood pressure. Reduce hyperthermia by cooling applications.

Beard, R.R., & G.A. Wertheim: Behavioural impairment associated with small doses of carbon monoxide. Am J Pub Health 57:2012–2022, 1967.

Bour, H., & I.M. Ledingham: Carbon monoxide poisoning. *Progress in Brain Research.* Vol 24. Elsevier, 1967.

Cohen, S.I., & others: Carbon monoxide uptake by inspectors at a United States—Mexico border station. Arch Envir Health 22:47–54, 1971.

Kokame, G.M., & S.E. Shuler: Hyperbaric oxygenation in carbon monoxide poisoning. Arch Surg 96:211–215, 1968.

CARBON TETRACHLORIDE

Carbon tetrachloride is a local irritant and cellular poison which when ingested or inhaled may severely damage the heart, liver, and kidneys. The effects are increased by ingestion of alcohol. Manifestations include headache, hiccup, nausea, vomiting, diarrhea, abdominal pain, drowsiness, visual disturbances, neuritis, and intoxication. Early signs are jaundice, liver tenderness, oliguria, and uremia. Nephrosis and cirrhosis may occur later.

The MLD is 3 ml.

Treatment

A. Emergency Measures: Remove the patient from exposure and keep him recumbent and warm. For poisoning due to ingestion, lavage copiously with tap water, and give sodium sulfate, 30 gm, in 200 ml of water. Do not give stimulants.

B. General Measures: Give inhalations of 100% oxygen by mask for 1 hour and artificial respiration if respirations are depressed. Treat cardiac, hepatic, and renal complications symptomatically. Do not give alcoholic beverages or stimulants. Maintain urine output at 4 liters daily by osmotic diuresis if renal function is normal.

Barnes, R., & R.C. Jones: Carbon tetrachloride poisoning. Am Indust Hyg AJ 28:557–560, 1967.

Clearfield, H.R.: Hepatorenal toxicity from sniffing spot-remover (trichloroethylene). Am J Digest Dis 15:851–856, 1970.

Miller, V., Dobbs, R.J., & S.I. Jacobs: Ethylene chlorohydrin intoxication with fatality. Arch Dis Childhood 45:589–590, 1970.

Recknagel, R.O.: Carbon tetrachloride hepatotoxicity. Pharmacol Rev 19:145–208, 1967.

Stewart, R.D.: Methyl chloroform intoxication. JAMA 215:1789–1792, 1971.

CHLORINATED INSECTICIDES
(Chlorophenothane [DDT], Lindane, Toxaphene, Chlordane, Aldrin, Endrin)

DDT and other chlorinated insecticides are CNS stimulants which can cause poisoning by ingestion, inhalation, or direct contact. The MLD is about 20 gm for DDT, 3 gm for lindane, 2 gm for toxaphene, 1 gm for chlordane, and less than 1 gm for endrin and aldrin. Poisoning following ingestion of DDT solution usually results from the organic solvent, whereas fatalities from the other chlorinated insecticides have resulted from the insecticide alone. The manifestations of poisoning are tired and aching limbs, nervous irritability, mental sluggishness, muscle twitchings, convulsions, and coma.

Treatment

A. Emergency Measures: (Avoid epinephrine, which may cause ventricular fibrillation.) Give activated charcoal at once if available, lavage with large quantities of warm tap water, and give sodium sulfate, 30 gm in 200 ml of water as cathartic.

B. General Measures: Pentobarbital sodium, 0.1 gm orally, may be sufficient to calm the patient. For convulsions give amobarbital sodium (Amytal®), 0.25–0.5 gm as fresh 10% solution slowly IV or IM. Maintain the airway and give oxygen. Avoid stimulants.

Conney, A.H., & others: The effect of pesticides on drug and steroid metabolism. Clin Pharmacol Therap 8:2–10, 1967.

Deichmann, W.B., & J.L. Radomski: Retention of pesticides in human adipose tissue: Preliminary report. Indust Med Surg 37:218–221, 1968.

CYANIDES: HYDROCYANIC ACID
(Prussic Acid, Rat Poison, Cyanogas®, Cyanogen)

Hydrocyanic acid and the cyanides cause death by inactivation of the respiratory enzyme, preventing utilization of oxygen by the tissues. The clinical combination of cyanosis, asphyxia, and the odor of bitter almonds on the breath is diagnostic. Respiration is first stimulated and later depressed. A marked drop in blood pressure may occur.

The MLD is 0.05 gm.

Treatment

A. Emergency Measures: *Act quickly.* Use nitrites to form methemoglobin, which combines with cyanide to form nontoxic cyanmethemoglobin. Then give thiosulfates to convert the cyanide released by dissociation of cyanmethemoglobin to thiocyanate.

1. Poisoning by inhalation—Place patient in open air in recumbent position. Remove contaminated clothing. Give artificial respiration.

2. Poisoning by ingestion—Induce vomiting immediately with a finger down the patient's throat. Do not wait until lavage tube has arrived; death may occur within a few minutes.

3. Give amyl nitrite inhalations for 15—30 seconds every 2 minutes.

B. Antidote: Give both of the following at once and repeat if symptoms recur: Sodium nitrite, 3%, 10—15 ml IV, or 1%, 50 ml IV, taking 2—4 minutes to give injection while monitoring blood pressure; and sodium thiosulfate, 25%, 50 ml IV. Repeat half these doses if symptoms recur. Cobalt ethylenediamine tetraacetate has also been used.

C. General Measures: Combat shock and give 100% oxygen by forced ventilation.

Berlin, C.M., Jr.: The treatment of cyanide poisoning in children. Pediatrics 46:793—796, 1970.

Lee-Jones, M., Bennett, M.A., & J.M. Sherwell: Cyanide self-poisoning. Brit MJ 4:780—781, 1970.

Trapp, W.G.: Massive cyanide poisoning with recovery: A boxing day story. Canad MAJ 102:517, 1970.

DIGITALIS

Because digitalis, digitoxin, and related drugs have a prolonged action, poisoning is most likely to occur when large doses are given to patients who have previously received digitalis drugs. Digitalizing doses should therefore be given only to patients who have not received digitalis for at least 1 week.

Clinical Findings

The principal manifestations of digitalis poisoning are vomiting and irregular pulse. Other signs include anorexia, nausea, diarrhea, yellow vision, delirium, slow pulse, fall of blood pressure, and ventricular fibrillation. The ECG may show lengthened P-R interval, heart block, ventricular extrasystoles, ventricular tachycardia, and a depressed ST segment.

The MLD of digitalis is 3 gm; of digitoxin, 3 mg.

Treatment

A. Emergency Measures: Delay absorption by giving tap water, milk, or activated charcoal and then remove by gastric lavage or emesis followed by catharsis. Do not give epinephrine or other stimulants. These may induce ventricular fibrillation.

B. General Measures: Give potassium chloride, 2 gm dissolved in water, every hour orally; or 0.3% in 5% dextrose slowly IV during ECG monitoring until the ECG shows improvement or evidence of potassium intoxication. If kidney function is impaired, serum potassium must be determined before potassium chloride is given.

Beller, G.A., & others: Digitalis intoxication: Clinical correlations with serum levels. New England J Med 284:989—997, 1971.

Jellife, R.W., & others: Death from weight-control pills (containing digitalis). JAMA 208:1843—1847, 1969.

Kastor, J.A., & P.M. Yurchak: Recognition of digitalis intoxication in the presence of atrial fibrillation. Ann Int Med 67:1045—1054, 1967.

Muggia, F.M.: Hemorrhagic necrosis of the intestine: Its occurrence with digitalis intoxication. Am J Med Sc 253:263—271, 1967.

FLUORIDES SOLUBLE IN WATER
(Insect Powders)

Symptoms include vomiting, diarrhea, salivation; shallow, rapid, and difficult respirations; convulsive seizures; rapid pulse; coma, and cyanosis. Interference with calcium metabolism causes severe damage to the vital centers and may result in death due to respiratory failure.

The MLD is 1 gm.

Treatment

A. Emergency Measures: Lavage with lime water; 1% calcium chloride, calcium lactate, or calcium gluconate; or large quantities of milk to form insoluble calcium fluoride. Give calcium gluconate, 10%, 10—20 ml IV; or calcium chloride, 5%, 10—20 ml IV for convulsions. Give sodium sulfate, 30 gm, in 200 ml of water as cathartic, and egg whites beaten in milk as demulcent.

B. General Measures: Treat shock and give supportive measures.

Eagers, R.Y.: *Toxic Properties of Inorganic Fluoride Compounds.* Elsevier, 1969.

Hodge, H.C., & F.A. Smith: Fluorides and man. Ann Rev Pharmacol 8:395—408, 1968.

IODINE

The clinical features of iodine poisoning include a characteristic stain of the mouth and odor of the breath, yellow or bluish vomitus, pain and burning in the pharynx and esophagus, marked thirst, diarrhea (stools may be bloody), weakness, dizziness, syncope, and convulsions.

The MLD is 2 gm.

Treatment

A. Emergency Measures: Give 15 gm cornstarch or flour in 500 ml of water or, if available, 250 ml of 1% sodium thiosulfate in water. Follow with an emetic or remove by lavage with sodium thiosulfate solution, 1%, and repeat until evidence of iodine has disappeared from the gastric contents. Then give demulcents, eg, milk or barley water.

B. General Measures: Maintain blood pressure and respiration.

IRON POISONING

Iron salts are used extensively as antianemic agents in a large number of prescription and over-the-counter "blood tonic" drugs. They are responsible for many instances of mild to severe acute poisoning as well as chronic poisoning.

Acute poisoning is manifested by lethargy, nausea, vomiting, tarry stools, diarrhea, fast and weak pulse, hypotension, and coma within ½−1 hour following ingestion of iron salts. If this is not fatal, the symptoms may clear in a few hours and the patient may be asymptomatic for 12−24 hours. Symptoms then return, with cyanosis, pulmonary edema, shock, and death in coma within 24−48 hours. The MLD is 5−10 gm.

Chronic poisoning may follow prolonged excess dosage of parenteral iron, causing exogenous hemosiderosis with damage to the liver and pancreas.

Treatment

Delay absorption of ingested iron by giving water, milk, or activated charcoal and then remove the gastric contents with syrup of ipecac or apomorphine. Use gastric lavage if emesis cannot be induced. Follow with catharsis. Then give 1 cup of milk, alternating with bismuth subcarbonate, every hour to relieve gastrointestinal irritation. Suction secretions and maintain an open airway. Give oxygen by inhalation. Prevent or control shock (see p 2).

The iron chelating agent deferoxamine mesylate (Desferal®), although an "antidote," is an adjunct to and not a substitute for the above general measures. If shock is not present, give deferoxamine, 0.25−1 gm IM initially and follow with 0.25−0.5 gm IM every 4 hours for 2 doses. The dose should not exceed 80 mg/kg in the first 24 hours and 50 mg/kg/day thereafter. If the patient is in shock, give 1 gm in normal saline solution or lactated Ringer's injection slowly IV at a rate not greater than 15 mg/kg/hour. This may be followed by 0.5 gm IV every 4 hours for 2 doses. Depending upon the clinical response, give 0.5 gm every 4−12 hours for a total treatment period of about 3 days. Deferoxamine is contraindicated in patients with severe renal disease or anuria.

James, J.A.: Acute iron poisoning: Assessment of severity and prognosis. J Pediat 77:117−119, 1970.

Movassaghi, N., Purugganan, G.G., & S. Leikin: Comparison of exchange transfusion and deferoxamine in the treatment of acute iron poisoning. J Pediat 75:604−608, 1969.

KEROSENE & RELATED COMPOUNDS
(Petroleum Ether, Charcoal Lighter Fluid, Paint Thinner, Benzine, Gasoline, Etc)

Kerosene poisoning results from ingestion. Gasoline or other volatile hydrocarbons can also cause poisoning by inhalation. Ingestion is especially dangerous because aspiration leads to pulmonary irritation. Acute manifestations are vomiting, pulmonary edema, bronchial pneumonia, vertigo, muscular incoordination, weak and irregular pulse, twitchings, and convulsions. Chronic poisoning causes also headache, drowsiness, dim vision, cold and numb hands, weakness, loss of memory, loss of weight, tachycardia, mental dullness or confusion, sores in the mouth, dermatoses, and anemia.

The MLD is 10−50 ml.

Treatment

Remove the patient to fresh air. Since aspiration during vomiting is a great danger, use of lavage or emesis induced by syrup of ipecac is controversial. Removal of ingested hydrocarbon is only suggested if the amount exceeds 1 ml/kg. If lavage is done, take extreme care to prevent aspiration. Use warm saline and leave 60 ml salad oil in stomach. Follow with sodium sulfate, 30 gm in 200 ml of water. Give prednisolone, 2−10 mg every 6 hours orally to reduce the pulmonary reaction. Watch closely for 3−4 days for symptoms of respiratory involvement. Treat pulmonary edema by positive pressure oxygen administration. If fever occurs, give antibiotics.

Knox, J.W., & J.R. Nelson: Permanent encephalopathy from toluene inhalation. New England J Med 275:1494−1496, 1966.

Shirkey, H.C.: Treatment of petroleum distillate ingestion. Mod Treat 4:697−709, 1967.

Wolfe, R.R., & others: Pneumatoceles complicating hydrocarbon pneumonitis. J Pediat 71:711−714, 1967.

LEAD

Lead poisoning may occur by ingestion or by inhalation of lead dust or fumes. Poisoning is manifested by a metallic taste, anorexia, irritability, apathy, abdominal colic, vomiting, diarrhea, constipation, headache, leg cramps, black stools (lead sulfide), oliguria, stupor, convulsions, palsies, and coma. Chronic lead poisoning causes variable involvement of the CNS, the blood-forming organs, and the gastrointestinal tract.

Diagnostic laboratory tests include blood lead (> 80 μg/100 ml), urine coproporphyrin (> 500 μg/ liter), urine δ-aminolevulinic acid (> 13 mg/liter), x-ray of abdomen (radiopaque paint), and x-ray of long bones (lead line).

The MLD is 0.5 gm of absorbed lead.

Treatment

A. Acute Poisoning:

1. Establish adequate urine flow (0.5–1 ml/minute). Give dextrose in water (10%, 10–20 ml/kg body weight) over 1–2 hours, or mannitol solution (20%) at a rate of 1 ml/minute until 10 ml/kg have been given. Daily urine output should be 350–500 ml/sq M.

2. Control convulsions with paraldehyde and phenobarbital.

3. For symptomatic children, including those with lead encephalopathy, give BAL (dimercaprol) and EDTA (calcium disodium edathamil) as follows: Begin first with BAL, 4 mg/kg IM, and repeat every 4 hours for 5 days (30 doses). Four hours after the first BAL injection, give EDTA, 12.5 mg/kg (20% solution, with 0.5% procaine added) IM, in a different site from BAL. Repeat every 4 hours for 5 days (30 doses). If symptoms have not improved by the 4th day, extend treatment to 7 days (42 doses each of both BAL and EDTA). If blood lead is still above 80 μg/100 ml 14 days later, repeat the 5-day course of both drugs.

4. For asymptomatic children, if blood lead is above 100 μg/100 ml, give a 5-day course of BAL-EDTA as above. If blood lead is below this level, give EDTA intramuscularly alone every 6 hours for 5-day course (20 injections).

5. For adults with encephalopathy, painful neuropathy, or abdominal symptoms, give BAL-EDTA intramuscularly as above or, if the patient is BAL-intolerant, give 50 mg/kg EDTA IV as 0.5% solution over not less than 8 hours.

6. Follow-up therapy (all cases)—Give penicillamine (Cuprimine®) orally daily in 2 doses ½ hour before meals. The dosage is 25 mg/kg for children and 500–750 mg for adults. Therapy should be continued for 1–2 months for adults and for 3–6 months for children. Do not give oral therapy if ingestion of lead is possible. Blood lead should be below 60 μg/100 ml at the end of treatment.

B. Chronic Poisoning: Remove permanently from exposure and give an adequate diet with vitamin supplements. Courses of oral penicillamine as for acute poisoning may be employed, especially when hematologic complications have occurred.

Cheatham, J.S., & E.F. Chobot, Jr.: The clinical diagnosis and treatment of lead encephalopathy. South MJ 16:529–531, 1968.

Chisolm, J.J., Jr.: The use of chelating agents in the treatment of acute and chronic lead intoxication in childhood. J Pediat 73:1–38, 1968.

Klein, M., & others: Earthenware containers as a source of fatal lead poisoning. New England J Med 283:669–672, 1970.

MERCURY

Acute poisoning (by ingestion or inhalation) is manifested by a metallic taste, salivation, thirst, a burning sensation in the throat, discoloration and edema of oral mucous membranes, abdominal pain, vomiting, bloody diarrhea, anuria, and shock. Chronic poisoning causes weakness, ataxia, intention tremors, irritability, depression, and muscle cramps. Chronic intoxication in children may be a cause of acrodynia.

The MLD is about 70 mg of mercury bichloride.

Treatment

A. Acute Poisoning: Give whites of eggs beaten with water or skimmed milk as precipitant; dimercaprol (BAL) at once as for arsenic poisoning; and sodium sulfate, 30 gm in 200 ml of water as cathartic. Maintain fluid output with 1000 ml of physiologic saline solution intravenously at once and repeat as necessary. Treat oliguria and anuria if they occur. Hemodialysis can be used to speed the removal of mercury combined with dimercaprol.

B. Chronic Poisoning: Remove from exposure.

Arena, J.N.: Treatment of mercury poisoning. Mod Treat 4:734–740, 1967.

Eyl, T.B.: Organic mercury food poisoning. New England J Med 284:706–709, 1971.

Hammond, A.L.: Mercury in the environment: Natural and human factors. Science 171:788–789, 1971.

Nelson, N., & others: Hazards of mercury. Envir Res 4:1–69, 1971.

Snyder, R.D.: Congenital mercury poisoning. New England J Med 284:1014–1016, 1971.

MORPHINE & OTHER NARCOTIC ANALGESICS

Morphine acts primarily on the CNS, causing depression and narcosis. The manifestations of poisoning with morphine and its substitutes, heroin, meperidine (Demerol®), propoxyphene (Darvon®), and methadone (Dolophine®), are headache, nausea, excitement, convulsions, depression, pin-point pupils, slow respirations, apnea, rapid and feeble pulse, shock, and coma.

The MLD is 65 mg in susceptible individuals.

Treatment

As an antidote for overdosage, give nalorphine hydrochloride (Nalline®), 0.1 mg/kg IV, or levallorphan (Lorfan®), 0.02 mg/kg IV. If effective increase in pulmonary ventilation is not achieved with the first dose, the dose may be repeated every 15 minutes until respirations return to normal and the patient responds to stimuli.

Maintain adequate ventilation with artificial respiration, using oxygen if necessary. Lavage stomach well (prevent aspiration) with activated charcoal at short intervals. Morphine is excreted into the stomach. Give sodium sulfate, 30 gm in 200 ml of water as cathartic.

Ament, M.E.: Diphenoxylate poisoning in children. J Pediat 74:462–464, 1969.

Gardner, R.: Methadone misuse and death by overdosage. Brit J Addict 65:113–118, 1970.

Kahn, E.J., Neumann, L.L., & G. Polk: The course of the heroin withdrawal syndrome in newborn infants treated with phenobarbital or chlorpromazine. J Pediat 75:495–500, 1969.

Litt, I.F., Colli, A.S., & M.I. Cohen: Diazepam in the management of heroin withdrawal in adolescents: Preliminary report. J Pediat 78:692–696, 1971.

Richards, L.G., & E.E. Carroll: Illicit drug use and addiction in the United States. Pub Health Rep 85:1035–1041, 1970.

MUSHROOMS

The Amanita genus of mushrooms accounts for almost all cases of fungus poisoning in the United States. *Amanita muscaria* poisoning, of rapid onset, responds promptly to atropine if treatment is given early, whereas *A phalloides* is more often of slow onset and many symptoms do not respond to atropine. (See Table 28–3.)

Tholen, H., & others: Early haemodialysis in poisoning by *Amanita phalloides.* German Med Monthly 11:89–90, 1966.

OXALIC ACID

Oxalic acid, a component of bleaching powder, is a corrosive which also precipitates ionized calcium. Poisoning is manifested by burning in the mouth and throat, violent abdominal pains, bloody vomitus, dyspnea, tremors, oliguria, and circulatory collapse.

The MLD is 4 gm.

Treatment

A. Emergency Measures: Give at once one of the following to precipitate as insoluble calcium oxalate: (1) Calcium lactate or other calcium salt, 30 gm in 200 ml of water; or (2) large amounts of milk. Give whites of eggs beaten in milk as demulcent.

B. General Measures: Give calcium gluconate or calcium lactate, 10 ml of 10% solution IV, and calcium orally, 1–2 gm 4 times daily. Institute supportive measures as required.

PHENOLS & DERIVATIVES

The phenols are present in carbolic acid, lysol, cresol, and creosote. They are local corrosives and also have marked systemic effects on the nervous and circulatory systems. Manifestations include burning in the upper gastrointestinal tract, thirst, nausea and vomiting, erosions of mucous membranes, dark vomitus, oliguria, muscle spasms, circulatory collapse, and respiratory failure.

The MLD is 2 gm.

TABLE 28–3. Mushroom poisoning.

	Amanita Muscaria	*Amanita Phalloides, A Brunnescens, A Verna*
Pharmacologic action	Muscarinic or atropine-like effects.	Direct toxic action on almost all cells, especially the liver, heart, and kidneys.
Onset	Sudden (1–2 hours).	Delayed (12–24 hours).
Symptoms and signs	Confusion, excitement, thirst, nausea and vomiting, diarrhea, wheezing, salivation, slow pulse, small pupils (muscarine), dilated pupils (atropine), tremors, weakness, collapse, and even death.	Confusion, depression, headache, convulsions, coma, nausea and vomiting, bloody vomitus and stools, painful enlargement of liver, jaundice, oliguria, pulmonary edema.
Treatment	(1) Remove gastrointestinal contents by emesis and lavage followed by catharsis. (2) Antidote: Atropine sulfate, 1–2 mg subcut, and repeat every 30 minutes as needed if signs of muscarine intoxication occur. (3) Give barbiturate sedatives for excitement. (4) Force fluids by oral and parenteral routes. (5) Treat shock.	(1) Remove gastrointestinal contents by emesis and lavage followed by catharsis. (2) Treat nonspecific parasympathetic autonomic effects with atropine sulfate, 1–2 mg subcut at once and repeat every 30 minutes as needed. (3) Relieve pain with narcotics as needed. (4) Maintain blood sugar with 4–5 liters of 5% dextrose solution every 24 hours if renal function is adequate. (5) Treat shock. (6) Institute hemodialysis immediately.

Treatment

A. Ingestion: Delay absorption by giving tap water, milk, or activated charcoal and then remove by repeated gastric lavage with tap water or by inducing vomiting. Then give castor oil, 60 ml, followed by sodium sulfate, 30 gm, in 200 ml of water. Do not give mineral oil and do not use alcohol for lavage. Give supportive measures as outlined on p 852.

B. External Burns: Wash with rubbing alcohol and then soap and water. Remove contaminated clothing.

Armstrong, R.W., & others: Pentachlorophenol poisoning in a nursery for newborn infants. II. Epidemiologic and toxicologic studies. J Pediat 75:317–325, 1969.

Robson, A.H., & others: Pentachlorophenol poisoning in a nursery for newborn infants. I. Clinical features and treatment. J Pediat 75:309–316, 1969.

PHENOTHIAZINE TRANQUILIZERS
(Chlorpromazine, Promazine, Prochlorperazine, Etc)

Chlorpromazine and related drugs are synthetic chemicals derived in most instances from phenothiazine. They are used as antiemetics and psychic inhibitors and as potentiators of analgesic and hypnotic drugs.

The acute fatal dose for these compounds appears to be above 50 mg/kg. Fatal poisoning from ingestion of approximately 75 mg/kg of chlorpromazine has been reported.

Clinical Findings

A. Symptoms and Signs: Minimum doses induce drowsiness and mild hypotension in as many as 50% of patients. Larger doses cause drowsiness, severe postural hypotension, tachycardia, dryness of the mouth, nausea, ataxia, anorexia, nasal congestion, fever, constipation, tremor, blurring of vision, stiffness of muscles, and coma. Intravenous injection of solutions containing more than 25 mg/ml of these drugs causes thrombophlebitis and cellulitis in a small number of patients.

Prolonged administration may cause leukopenia or agranulocytosis, jaundice, and generalized maculopapular eruptions; overdosage causes a syndrome similar to paralysis agitans, with spasmodic contractions of the face and neck muscles, extensor rigidity of the back muscles, carpopedal spasm, motor restlessness, salivation, and convulsions.

B. Laboratory Findings:

1. Liver function tests indicate the presence of obstructive jaundice.

2. Urine—Phenothiazine compounds in urine acidified with dilute nitric acid can be detected by the addition of a few drops of tincture of ferric chloride. A violet color results.

Treatment

Remove overdoses by gastric lavage or emesis. For severe hypotension, shock treatment may be necessary. Avoid the use of pressor drugs. Control convulsions with pentobarbital. Avoid other depressant drugs.

Give antiparkinsonism drugs. In the presence of fever, sore throat, pulmonary congestion, or other signs of infection, give penicillin, 1 million units daily, or a broad-spectrum antibiotic in maximum doses until infection is controlled. No measures have been helpful for jaundice other than discontinuing the drug.

Giles, T.D., & R.K. Modlin: Death associated with ventricular arrhythmia and thioridazine hydrochloride. JAMA 205:108–110, 1968.

Gupta, J.M., & F.H. Lovejoy, Jr.: Acute phenothiazine toxicity in childhood: A five-year survey. Pediatrics 39:771–773, 1967.

Moore, M.T., & M.H. Book: Sudden death in phenothiazine therapy. Psychiat Quart 44:389–402, 1970.

Prien, R.F., & others: Ocular changes occurring with prolonged high dose chlorpromazine therapy: Results from a collaborative study. Arch Gen Psychiat 23:464–468, 1970.

PHOSPHATES, ORGANIC
(Pesticide Sprays: Parathion, TEPP, Malathion, Thimet, Phosdrin, Systox, HETP, EPN, OMPA, Etc)

Inhalation, skin absorption, or ingestion of organic phosphorus causes marked depression of cholinesterase, resulting in continuous and excessive stimulation of the parasympathetic nervous system. Manifestations of acute poisoning appear within hours after exposure and include headache, sweating, salivation, lacrimation, vomiting, diarrhea, muscular twitchings, convulsions, dyspnea, and blurred vision. Pulse and blood pressure can be extremely variable. Contracted pupils with the above symptoms and signs and a history of exposure during the past 24 hours warrant therapy.

The MLD is 0.02–1 gm.

Treatment

A. Emergency Measures: If the material has been ingested, remove poison by inducing vomiting or gastric lavage with tap water. Remove from the skin (especially the hair and under the fingernails) by washing copiously. Counteract parasympathetic stimulation by giving atropine sulfate, 2 mg IM every 3–8 minutes until symptoms are relieved or signs of atropinization (dilated pupils, dry mouth) appear. Repeat as necessary to maintain complete atropinization. As much as 12 mg of atropine has been given safely in the first 2 hours. Give pralidoxime (Protopam®), 1 gm slowly IV in aqueous solution. Repeat after 30 minutes if respiration does not improve.

B. General Measures: Give oxygen under positive pressure if pulmonary edema or respiratory difficulty appears. Prolonged artificial respiration may be necessary. Take a blood sample for determination of red cell cholinesterase levels. (This is of no practical value in immediate diagnosis or treatment of the acute episode, but aids in confirmation of the diagnosis.)

Eitzman, D.V., & S.L. Wolfson: Acute parathion poisoning in children. Am J Dis Child 114:397–400, 1967.

Namba, T., Greenfield, M., & D. Grob: Malathion poisoning. Arch Envir Health 21:533–541, 1970.

West, I.: Sequelae of poisoning from phosphate ester pesticides. Indust Med 37:832–836, 1968.

Wyckoff, D.W., & others: Diagnostic and therapeutic problems of parathion poisonings. Ann Int Med 68:875–882, 1968.

Zavon, M.R.: Treatment of organophosphorus and chlorinated hydrocarbon insecticide intoxications. Mod Treat 4:625–632, 1967.

PHOSPHORUS, INORGANIC
(Rat Paste, Fireworks, Matches)

Phosphorus poisoning may result from contact, ingestion, or inhalation. Phosphorus is a local irritant and systemic toxin which acts on the liver, kidneys, muscles, bones, and cardiovascular system. Toxicity is manifested early by a garlic taste, pain in the upper gastrointestinal tract, vomiting, and diarrhea. Other symptoms and signs are headache, pleuritis, extreme weakness, jaundice, oliguria, petechiae, prostration, and cardiovascular collapse.

The MLD is 50 mg.

Treatment

A. Emergency Measures: Lavage with 5–10 liters of tap water or induce emesis with 0.5–1 liter volumes at least 3 times. Give sodium sulfate, 30 gm in 200 ml of water; and liquid petrolatum, 120 ml. (No other oils may be used.) Give whites of eggs beaten in milk as demulcent.

B. General Measures: Observe carefully for several days, and treat as for acute hepatitis if signs of jaundice or liver involvement appear.

Marin, G.A., & others: Evaluation of corticosteroid and exchange-transfusion treatment of acute yellow phosphorus intoxication. New England J Med 284:125–128, 1971.

Pietras, R.J., & others: Phosphorus poisoning simulating acute myocardial infarction. Arch Int Med 122:430–434, 1968.

SALICYLATE POISONING

Salicylate poisoning is most commonly caused by aspirin ingestion. Effects include acid-base disturbances, hypoprothrombinemia, and gastroenteritis. The acid-base disturbances are the most dangerous. Respiratory alkalosis appears first, followed by metabolic acidosis.

Salicylates stimulate the respiratory center, producing hyperpnea, CO_2 loss, a falling serum CO_2 content, a normal or high arterial blood pH; this combination represents respiratory alkalosis. In an effort to compensate, the kidneys excrete increased amounts of bicarbonate, potassium, and sodium, but retain chloride. The chief dangers during this stage are hypokalemia and dehydration. Salicylates also interfere with carbohydrate metabolism, which results in the formation of fixed acids, probably ketones.

When the patient is first seen he may be in alkalosis or acidosis. Diagnosis and treatment are dependent upon determination of serum CO_2 content, potassium, sodium and chloride, and arterial pH. The urine is unreliable as an indication of acidosis or alkalosis.

Salicylates are potent stimulators of metabolism, and hyperthermia may result.

The clinical picture includes a history of salicylate ingestion, hyperpnea, flushed face, hyperthermia, tinnitus, abdominal pain, vomiting, dehydration, spontaneous bleeding, twitchings, convulsions, pulmonary edema, uremia, and coma. Salicylates may give a false-positive ketonuria and glycosuria, or true ketonuria and glycosuria may be present.

The MLD is 5–10 gm.

Treatment

A. Emergency Measures: Aspirate the gastric contents first without using additional fluids, and then lavage with 2–4 liters of warm tap water containing activated charcoal.

B. General Measures: Treat dehydration and alkalosis with physiologic saline solution and added potassium as indicated. Treat acidosis with sodium bicarbonate, 7.5% solution (44.6 mEq/50 ml), 3–5 mEq/kg orally or IV over 2–4 hours. Maintenance of alkaline urine greatly speeds the excretion of salicylates. Administer alkalinizing agents intravenously to infants with great caution. Adjustment of sodium and potassium in fluids should be based on serum sodium and potassium determinations. Serial ECG's may be of value in controlling hypokalemia. Specific treatment of the alkalosis of salicylate intoxication is seldom required.

Phytonadione (AquaMephyton®), 50 mg IV, should be given once for hypoprothrombinemia. Whole blood or platelet transfusion is recommended for thrombocytopenia. Peritoneal dialysis or an artificial kidney may be lifesaving for critically ill patients with a high serum salicylate concentration or renal insufficiency.

Treat fever with cold water (10° C) sponge baths.

Bleyer, W.A., & R.T. Breckenridge: Studies on the detection of adverse drug reactions in the newborn. II. The effects of prenatal aspirin on newborn hemostasis. JAMA 213:2049–2053, 1970.

Boxer, L., Anderson, F.P., & D.S. Rowe: Comparison of ipecac-induced emesis with gastric lavage in the treatment of acute salicylate ingestion. J Pediat 74:800–803, 1969.

Decker, W.J., & others: Inhibition of aspirin absorption by activated charcoal and apomorphine. Clin Pharmacol Therap 10:710–713, 1969.

Done, A.K.: Treatment of salicylate poisoning. Mod Treat 4:648–670, 1967.

Done, A.K.: Treatment of salicylate poisoning: Review of personal and published experiences. Clin Toxicol 1:451, 1968.

Done, A.K., & A.L. Jung: A realistic approach to the prevention of childhood poisoning with special emphasis on aspirin. Clin Toxicol 1:63–70, 1968.

Ferguson, R.K., & A.M. Boutros: Death following self-poisoning with aspirin. JAMA 213:1186–1188, 1970.

Maclean, D., & others: Treatment of acute paracetamol [acetaminophen] poisoning. Lancet 2:849–851, 1968.

SNAKE (& GILA MONSTER) BITES

The venom of poisonous snakes and lizards may be predominantly neurotoxic or predominantly hemotoxic (cytolytic). Neurotoxins cause respiratory paralysis; hemotoxins cause hemorrhage due to hemolysis and destruction of the endothelial lining of the blood vessels. The manifestations are local pain, thirst, profuse perspiration, nausea, vomiting, stimulation followed by depression, local redness, swelling, extravasation of blood, and collapse.

Treatment

A. Emergency Measures: Immobilize the patient and the bitten part immediately. Avoid manipulation of the bitten area. Use of tourniquet and incision and suction will remove up to 10% of venom if done in the first 30 minutes. Incisions should be 1/8 inch deep and 1/4 inch long in the area of the bite. Do not allow the patient to walk or run or take alcoholic beverages or stimulants. Give specific antiserum subcut, after testing for serum sensitivity with 0.02 ml of 1:100 dilution of antiserum in 0.9% saline. (Follow printed instructions.) Carry the patient to a car and transport him to a hospital or other medical facility for definitive treatment. Maintain blood pressure by giving blood transfusions. Cortisone or substitutes in large doses will relieve symptoms temporarily but may not reduce the mortality rate. Corticosteroids should not be given if the patient is receiving antiserum. If marked swelling occurs in an extremity, with indication of nerve compression, relieve pressure in fascial spaces by incision.

B. General Measures: Give plenty of warm fluids. Use barbiturates as necessary for sedation.

McCollough, N.C., & J.F. Gennaro: Treatment of venomous snakebite in the United States. Clin Toxicol 3:483–500, 1970.

Reid, H.A.: The principles of snakebite treatment. Clin Toxicol 3:473–482, 1970.

Russell, F.E.: Clinical aspects of snake venom poisoning in North America. Toxicon 7:33–38, 1969.

Sadan, N., & B. Soroker: Observations on the effects of the bite of venomous snakes on children and adults. J Pediat 76:711–715, 1970.

SPIDER BITES & SCORPION STINGS

The toxin of the less venomous species of spiders and scorpions causes only local pain, redness, and swelling. That of the more venomous species, including black widow spiders (*Latrodectus mactans*), causes generalized muscular pains, convulsions, nausea and vomiting, variable CNS involvement, and shock.

Treatment

A. Emergency Measures: As for snake bite (see above), except that incision and suction are probably useless. If absorption has occurred, give calcium gluconate, 10%, 10 ml IV or IM, or mephenesin, 10–30 ml of 2% IV and repeat as necessary. Patients under 14 years of age should receive specific antiserum. Corticotropin or the corticosteroids may be of value in severe cases.

B. General Measures: Hot baths are of value for relief of pain. For local pain with no systemic involvement apply cold compresses. Give adequate sedation and institute supportive measures as indicated. Early excision of the necrotic lesion of the brown spider bite has been recommended.

Devi, C.S., & others: Defibrination syndrome due to scorpion venom poisoning. Brit MJ 1:345–347, 1970.

Gorham, J.R., & T.B. Rheney: Envenomation by spiders. JAMA 206:1958–1962, 1968.

Lyon, J.B.: Insect bites and stings. Practitioner 200:670–677, 1968.

Masso, H.L.: Scorpion bite treatment with chlorpromazine. JAMA 212:2122, 1970.

STIMULANTS: STRYCHNINE

Strychnine poisoning may result from ingestion or injection. The manifestations are convulsions, opisthotonos, dyspnea, foaming at the mouth, and asphyxia.

Treatment

A. Emergency Measures: Keep the patient quiet in a darkened room. Give amobarbital sodium (Amytal®) or an equivalent barbiturate sedative, 0.5 gm **at once** in 10–20 ml of water slowly IV. If amobarbital for injection is not available, give the drug orally in doses up to 5 times the hypnotic dose. Repeat in 30 minutes if necessary. Control convulsions with succinylcholine (Anectine®) and give artificial respiration and oxygen. Diazepam (Valium®), 10 mg IV, and repeated every 30 minutes, is reported to be effective. If possible, lavage gently with activated charcoal before symptoms appear. Do not lavage after twitching or convulsions have appeared unless succinylcholine is being given.

B. General Measures: Inhalation of ether or chloroform may be used to quiet the patient.

Coull, D.C., & others: Amitryptyline and cardiac disease: Risk of sudden death identified by monitoring system. Lancet 2:590–591, 1970.

Maron, B.J., Krupp, J.R., & B. Tune: Strychnine poisoning successfully treated with diazepam. J Pediat 78:697–699, 1971.

Sueblinvong, V., & J.F. Wilson: Myocardial damage due to imipramine intoxication. J Pediat 74:475–478, 1969.

Teitelbaum, D.T.: Treatment of imipramine intoxication. J Pediat 75:523–524, 1969.

WASP, BEE, YELLOW JACKET, & HORNET STINGS

Stings of these common insects, although locally painful, usually cause only mild symptoms of brief duration. Local cold compresses, application of baking soda solution, and oral salicylates or antihistamines are sufficient treatment. Multiple stings may cause a shock-like reaction with hemoglobinuria. Sensitive individuals may develop an acute allergic or even fatal anaphylactic response after a single sting.

Treatment

A. Emergency Measures: Give epinephrine hydrochloride, 1:1000 solution, 0.2–0.5 ml subcut or IM; and then diphenhydramine hydrochloride (Benadryl®), 5–20 mg slowly IV. Treat shock.

B. General Measures: Corticotropin (ACTH) or the corticosteroids intramuscularly may be necessary to support shock therapy.

Barnard, J.H.: Allergic and pathologic findings in fifty insect-sting fatalities. J Allergy 40:107–114, 1967.

Barnard, J.H.: Severe hidden delayed reactions from insect stings. New York J Med 66:1206–1210, 1966.

Combined Staff Clinic: Poisoning by venomous animals. Am J Med 42:107–128, 1967.

PSYCHOTOMIMETIC AGENTS

Classification

1. LSD (lysergic acid diethylamide): Semisynthetic, from ergot.
2. DMT (dimethyltryptamine): Synthetic and from a South American plant (*Piptadenia peregrina*).
3. DET (diethyltryptamine): Synthetic.
4. "STP," DOM (2,5-dimethoxy-4-methylamphetamine): Synthetic.
5. Marihuana: One active principle is tetrahydrocannabinol. From the Indian hemp plant (*Cannabis sativa*).
6. Mescaline (3,4,5-trimethoxyphenethylamine): Synthetic; also from peyote, a cactus (mescal, *Lophophora williamsii*).
7. Psilocybin and psilocin: Derivatives of 4-hydroxytryptamine. Synthetic; also from a mushroom (*Psilocybe mexicana*).
8. Bufotenine (dimethyl serotonin): Synthetic; also from *Piptadenia peregrina, Amanita muscaria,* and the skin of a toad (*Bufo marinus*).
9. Ibogaine: From the plant *Tabernante iboga.*
10. Harmine and harmaline: From plants (*Peganum harmala* and *Banisteria caapi*).
11. Ditran and phencyclidine (Sernyl®): Synthetic.
12. Amphetamine and related drugs: See below.
13. MDA (methylene dioxyamphetamine): Synthetic.

Clinical Findings

Manifestations requiring medical intervention are hyperexcitability, uncontrollability, ataxia, hypertension or hypotension, coma, and prolonged psychotic states.

Treatment

Give chlorpromazine, 0.5–2 mg/kg IM, to control the acute phase. (In STP poisoning, the combination is reported to be hazardous.) Treat coma as for barbiturate poisoning.

Brill, N.Q.: The marijuana problem. Ann Int Med 73:449–465, 1970.

Grinspoon, L.: Marihuana. Sc Am 221:17–25, June 1969.

Kolansky, H.: & W.T. Moore: Effect of marihuana on adolescents and young adults. JAMA 216:486–492, 1971.

Lieberman, C.M., & B.W. Lieberman: Marihuana: A medical review. New England J Med 284:88–91, 1971.

Louria, D.B.: Lysergic acid diethylamide. New England J Med 278:435–438, 1968.

Milman, D.H.: The role of marihuana in patterns of drug abuse by adolescents. J Pediat 74:283–290, 1969.

Van Dusen, W., & R. Metzner: The long-term effects of psychedelics. Clin Toxicol 1:227–234, 1968.

TREATMENT OF LESS COMMON SPECIFIC POISONINGS (ALPHABETICAL ORDER)

Acetaldehyde (Industrial)

Inhalation of acetaldehyde vapors causes severe irritation of mucous membranes with coughing, pulmonary edema, followed by narcosis. Ingestion causes narcosis and respiratory failure. The MLD in adults is about 5 gm.

Remove from exposure or remove ingested poison by gastric lavage or emesis followed by catharsis. Give oxygen for respiratory difficulty. Treat pulmonary edema.

Aconite (Liniment)

Manifestations are burning followed by numbness and tingling of the mouth, throat, and hands; blurred vision; weak pulse; fall of blood pressure; shallow respirations; convulsions; and respiratory or cardiac failure. The MLD is 1 gm of aconite or 2 mg of aconitine.

Remove ingested poison by gastric lavage or emesis followed by catharsis. Give artificial respiration or oxygen as necessary. Give digitalis to counteract cardiac depression. Treat convulsions. Give atropine, 1 mg to prevent vagal slowing of the heart.

Akee (Tree)

Manifestations are abdominal discomfort, vomiting, convulsions, coma, hypothermia, and fall of blood pressure. Jaundice may appear during the recovery phase.

Remove ingested akee by gastric lavage or emesis followed by catharsis. Control convulsions. Give carbohydrates as 5% glucose intravenously or as sugar dissolved in fruit juice orally to protect from liver damage.

Aminopyrine, Antipyrine, Phenylbutazone
(Analgesics)

Manifestations are dizziness, cyanosis, coma, and convulsions. Prolonged administration causes epigastric pain, urticaria, leukopenia, liver damage, exfoliative dermatitis, gastric or duodenal erosion, adrenal necrosis. The MLD is 5–30 gm.

Treat acute poisoning as for salicylates. Treat chronic poisoning by discontinuing drug.

Amphetamine, Methamphetamine, Dextroamphetamine, and Ephedrine
(Sympathomimetics)

Manifestations are tachycardia, dilated pupils, blurred vision, spasms, convulsions, gasping respirations, cardiac arrhythmias, psychosis, and respiratory failure. The blood pressure is elevated initially but below normal later. The MLD is 120 mg.

Remove ingested drug by emesis or gastric lavage followed by catharsis. Give artificial respiration if cyanosis is present. Maintain blood pressure in cardio-vascular collapse by the administration of fluids. Give chlorpromazine (Thorazine®), 1 mg/kg IM (or half that amount if these drugs have been taken with sedative-hypnotics).

Espelin, D.E., & A.K. Done: Amphetamine poisoning: Effectiveness of chlorpromazine. New England J Med 278:1361–1365, 1968.

Aniline (Industrial or cloth-marking ink)

Manifestations are cyanosis, shallow respirations, fall of blood pressure, convulsions, and coma. Blood methemoglobin, as determined photometrically, may reach 60% or more of total hemoglobin. The MLD is 1 gm.

Remove aniline from skin by washing thoroughly with soap and water or, if ingested, remove by emesis, gastric lavage, and catharsis. Give fluids and oxygen if respiration is shallow or if there is evidence of air hunger. As antidote for methemoglobinemia give methylene blue, 10–50 ml of 1% solution IV.

Antimony (Paint)

Manifestations are severe diarrhea with mucus followed by blood, hemorrhagic nephritis, and hepatitis. The MLD is 100 mg.

Remove ingested poison by gastric lavage, emesis, and catharsis. Treat as for arsenic poisoning.

Arsine (Industrial)
(See also Arsenic, p 856.)

Manifestations are pyrexia, cough, abdominal pain, hemolytic anemia, hemoglobinuria, anuria, methemoglobinemia, and diarrhea.

Alkalinize urine as for fava bean poisoning. Give blood transfusions if anemia is severe. Treat anuria.

Aspidium (Anthelmintic)

Manifestations are progressive vomiting, colored or blurred vision, tremors, convulsions, and respiratory failure. The urine may show protein, red cells, and casts. Jaundice and blindness may complicate recovery from nonfatal poisoning. The MLD is 4 gm.

Treat as for chenopodium poisoning.

Barium (Rodenticide)

Manifestations are tightness of the muscles of the face and neck, fibrillary muscular tremors, weakness, difficulty in breathing, irregularity of the heart, convulsions, and cardiac and respiratory failure. The MLD is 1 gm.

Give 10 ml of 10% sodium sulfate slowly IV and repeat every 15 minutes until symptoms subside. Give 30 gm sodium sulfate in 200 ml of water orally or by gastric tube and repeat in 1 hour.

Benzene (Solvent)

Manifestations are visual blurring, tremors, shallow and rapid respiration, ventricular irregularities, unconsciousness, and convulsions. Repeated exposure results in aplastic anemia and abnormal bleeding. The MAC is 35 ppm.

Remove patient from contaminated air and give artificial respiration with oxygen. Treat ingested poison as for gasoline poisoning.

Beryllium (Industrial)

Manifestations include acute pneumonitis; chest pain, bronchial spasm, fever, dyspnea, cough, and cyanosis. Right heart failure may occur. Pulmonary granulomatosis with weight loss and marked dyspnea may occur years after initial exposure. X-ray examination reveals diffuse increase in density of the lung fields or snowstorm appearance. No degree of exposure is safe.

Place the patient at complete bed rest and administer 60% oxygen by mask for cyanosis. EDTA has been suggested. The administration of corticosteroid or related drugs gives symptomatic relief but is not curative.

Bismuth Compounds (Medicinal)

Manifestations are skin eruptions, liver damage, anuria, cardiovascular collapse, proteinuria, hematuria, and liver function impairment. The MLD is 0.5 gm.

Give dimercaprol (BAL) and atropine, 1 mg subcut, to relieve gastrointestinal discomfort. Give fluids, 2–4 liters daily, if kidney function is not impaired. Treat anuria.

Bleaching Solutions (Household)

Clorox®, Purex®, Sani-Clor®, etc cause irritation and corrosion of mucous membranes with edema of the pharynx and larynx. Perforation of the esophagus or stomach is rare. The MLD is 15 ml.

Remove ingested solution by gastric lavage or emesis, using a solution of milk of magnesia or, preferably, sodium thiosulfate, 30–50 gm/liter, or milk. After emesis or lavage, give a cathartic consisting of sodium sulfate, 30 gm, and sodium thiosulfate, 10 gm, in 250 ml of milk or water. *Caution:* Do not use acid antidotes. Treat as for sodium hydroxide poisoning.

Boric Acid (Antiseptic)

Manifestations from ingestion or skin application are fever, anuria, and flushing of the skin followed by desquamation, lethargy, and convulsions. The MLD is 5–15 gm.

Remove ingested boric acid by emesis or gastric lavage followed by catharsis. Maintain urine output by giving liquids orally or, in the presence of vomiting, by giving 5% dextrose intravenously. Control convulsions by the cautious administration of ether. Remove circulating boric acid by peritoneal dialysis or with an artificial kidney. Treat anuria as for mercury poisoning.

Bromates (Cold wave neutralizer)

Manifestations are vomiting, abdominal pains, oliguria, coma, convulsions, fall of blood pressure, hematuria, and proteinuria. The MLD is 4 gm.

Remove poison by gastric lavage, emesis, and catharsis. Give sodium thiosulfate, 1–5 gm IV as a 10% solution. Treat shock by administration of repeated small blood transfusions.

Cadmium (Metal plating)

Ingestion causes diarrhea, vomiting, muscular aches, salivation, and abdominal pain. Inhalation causes shortness of breath, pain in the chest, foamy or bloody sputum, muscular aches. Chronic exposure produces, in addition, anemia, and x-ray examination indicates lung consolidation. A sulfosalicylic acid precipitable protein is present in the urine. The MLD is about 10 mg.

Treat pulmonary edema and give calcium edathamil. Remove ingested poison by emesis or gastric lavage followed by catharsis.

Caffeine, Aminophylline (Stimulants)

Manifestations are sudden collapse and cardiac arrest within 1–2 minutes after intravenous or rectal administration, and convulsions. The MLD is 1 gm.

Give oxygen by artificial respiration with forced ventilation, maintain blood pressure, remove rectally administered aminophylline by enema, and control convulsions as for strychnine poisoning.

Camphor (Stimulant)

Manifestations are a feeling of tension, dizziness, irrational behavior, rigidity, tachycardia, twitching of the facial muscles, and generalized convulsions. The MLD is 1 gm.

Remove ingested poison by gastric lavage or emesis followed by catharsis. Control convulsions.

Cantharidin (Irritant)

Manifestations are severe vomiting, diarrhea, fall of blood pressure, hematuria, and death in respiratory failure or uremia. The MLD is 10 mg.

Remove ingested poison by gastric lavage or emesis followed by catharsis. Treat cardiovascular collapse by blood transfusions and intravenous saline. Treat anuria.

Castor Beans (Plant)

Manifestations are vomiting, diarrhea, severe abdominal pain, cyanosis, circulatory collapse, and oliguria. Urine may show protein, casts, red blood cells, and hemoglobin. The MLD is 1 bean.

Remove ingested beans by gastric lavage or emesis followed by catharsis. Maintain blood pressure by blood transfusions. Alkalinize urine by giving 5–15 gm of sodium bicarbonate daily to prevent precipitation of hemoglobin or hemoglobin products in the kidneys. Treat anuria.

Chloramine-T (Disinfectant)

Manifestations are cyanosis, frothing at the mouth, and respiratory failure within a few minutes to 1 hour after ingestion. The MLD is 0.5 gm.

Remove ingested chloramine-T by gastric lavage or emesis followed by catharsis. Give antidotes as for cyanide poisoning.

Chlorates (Disinfectant)

Manifestations are cyanosis, hemolysis, anuria, and convulsions. The MLD is 15 gm. Laboratory findings include methemoglobinemia, anemia of the hemolytic type, and elevation of serum potassium.

Remove ingested chlorate by gastric lavage or emesis followed by catharsis. Treat methemoglobinemia with methylene blue. Force fluids to 2—4 liters daily to remove chlorate if urine output is adequate.

Chlorinated Hydrocarbons

For volatile chlorinated hydrocarbons, see Carbon Tetrachloride; for nonvolatile chlorinated hydrocarbons, see Chlorophenothane (DDT).

Chlorinated Naphthalene (Insulator)

The principal manifestation is a papular, acneform eruption which progresses to pustule formation. Jaundice, enlargement of the liver, and weakness also occur. Impairment of hepatic cell function is revealed by appropriate tests.

Treat liver damage as outlined under carbon tetrachloride poisoning.

Chromium & Chromate (Rustproofing)

Ingestion causes abdominal pain, vomiting, shock, and oliguria or anuria. Skin contact leads to incapacitating eczematous dermatitis and ulceration. Ulceration and perforation of the nasal septum also occur. Acute hepatitis has been observed. Examination of the urine reveals proteinuria and hematuria. The MLD of soluble chromate is 5 gm.

Remove ingested chromate by gastric lavage, emesis, and catharsis. Treat oliguria and liver damage.

Cinchophen & Neocinchophen (Analgesics)

Acute poisoning is similar to that due to the salicylates. Prolonged administration leads to jaundice, anorexia, abdominal discomfort, and painful enlargement of the liver. Progression to hepatic insufficiency is relatively common. Gastric perforation has also occurred. The MLD is 5—30 gm.

Treat as for salicylate poisoning. Treat hepatic insufficiency as for carbon tetrachloride poisoning.

Cocaine (Local anesthetic)

Manifestations are restlessness, excitability, hallucinations, irregular respirations, convulsions, and circulatory failure. The MLD is 30 mg.

Remove the drug from the skin or mucous membranes by washing with tap water or normal saline. Remove ingested cocaine by gastric lavage or emesis followed by catharsis. Limit absorption from an injection site by a tourniquet or ice pack. Control convulsions by giving thiopental sodium (Pentothal®). Prevent hypoxia by the administration of oxygen.

Colchicine (Gout remedy)

Manifestations are burning in the throat, watery to bloody diarrhea, cardiovascular collapse, and oliguria. The MLD is 6 mg.

Remove ingested poison by emesis or gastric lavage followed by catharsis. Give oxygen for respiratory difficulty. Treat oliguria.

Croton Oil (Irritant)

Manifestations are burning pain in the mouth and stomach, tenesmus, watery or bloody diarrhea, fall of blood pressure, and coma. The MLD is 1 gm.

Remove ingested croton oil by gastric lavage or emesis followed by saline catharsis. Treat shock. Maintain hydration by giving fluids orally or intravenously. Relieve pain with morphine sulfate, 10 mg.

Detergents (Soaps, detergents, and antiseptics.)

A. Cationic Detergents: These include the antiseptics of the quaternary ammonium type (Zephiran®, Diaperene®, Phemerol®). Manifestations are severe vomiting, shock, convulsions, and death within 1—4 hours. The MLD is 1—3 gm.

Remove unabsorbed detergent by emesis or gastric lavage. Ordinary face soap is an effective antidote for unabsorbed cationic detergent but is not effective against the systemic effects. Treat respiratory embarrassment or shock with appropriate supportive measures. Short-acting barbiturates should be used to control convulsions.

B. Anionic or Nonionic Detergents: These compounds, which are present in general laundry detergents and dishwashing solutions, are less toxic than the cationic detergents. Certain laundry compounds and electric dishwasher detergents may contain alkalies, however, and their ingestion requires immediate treatment for caustic poisoning. Poisoning with certain phosphate additives to some detergents requires treatment with parenteral calcium.

Dinitrophenol (Insecticide)

Manifestations are fever, prostration, thirst, excessive perspiration, difficulty in breathing, muscular tremors, and coma. Cataracts occur after repeated ingestion. The MLD is 100 mg.

Remove ingested poison by emesis, gastric lavage, and catharsis. If the body temperature is elevated, reduce to normal by immersion in cold water or by applying cold packs.

Dioxane (Solvent)

Prolonged exposure may lead to kidney and liver damage and pulmonary edema.

Remove from further exposure and treat symptomatically.

Disulfiram (Antabuse®) Plus Alcohol
(Alcohol sensitizer)

Manifestations are flushing, sweating, tachycardia, fall of blood pressure, cardiac arrhythmias, air hunger, and cardiac pain.

Give artificial respiration with oxygen, and ephedrine, 25 mg subcut to maintain normal blood pressure.

Ergotamine (Migraine remedy)

Manifestations are rise or fall of blood pressure, weak pulse, convulsions, and loss of consciousness. Prolonged administration causes numbness and coldness of the extremities, tingling, pain in the chest, gangrene of the fingers and toes, contractions of the facial muscles, and convulsions. The maximum safe dose is 6 mg/day.

Remove ingested drug by emesis or gastric lavage followed by catharsis. Treat convulsions as for strychnine poisoning.

Estrogens (Female sex hormones)

Manifestations are excessive vaginal bleeding and enlargement of the breasts. Discontinue further administration.

Ethylene Chlorohydrin (Fumigant)

Manifestations are abdominal pain, excitability, delirium, respiratory slowing, fall of blood pressure, twitching of muscles, cyanosis, and coma with respiratory and circulatory failure. The MLD is 5 ml.

Remove from further exposure and remove ingested poison by emesis, gastric lavage, and catharsis. Treat as for methyl bromide poisoning.

Ethylene Glycol (Anti-freeze)

The initial symptoms in massive dosage (over 100 ml in a single dose) are those of alcoholic intoxication. These symptoms then progress to stupor, anuria, and unconsciousness with convulsions. Smaller amounts (10–30 ml) result in anuria beginning 24–72 hours after ingestion. The urine may show calcium oxalate crystals, protein, red cells, and casts.

Remove ingested glycol by gastric lavage or emesis and catharsis. Give calcium gluconate, 10 ml of 10% solution IV, to precipitate oxalate. Give artificial respiration, using oxygen for depressed respiration. In the absence of renal impairment, force fluids to 4 liters or more daily to increase excretion of glycol. Give ethyl alcohol as in methyl alcohol poisoning. Treat uremia as for carbon tetrachloride poisoning.

Fava Beans (Plant)

Manifestations are fever, jaundice, dark urine, oliguria, and pallor. The urine may show presence of hemoglobin.

Give blood transfusions until anemia is corrected. Alkalinize urine with 5–15 gm of sodium bicarbonate every 4 hours to prevent the precipitation of hemoglobin in the kidneys. In the presence of normal kidney function, maintain urine output by giving 2–4 liters of fluid daily orally or IV. Give cortisone, 25–100 mg daily. Treat anuria.

Fish Poisoning

Manifestations are vomiting and muscular weakness progressing to paralysis, abdominal pain, and convulsions.

Remove ingested fish by gastric lavage or emesis followed by catharsis. Maintain adequate airway or give artificial respiration. Treat convulsions.

Fluoroacetate (Rodenticide)

Symptoms begin within minutes to hours with vomiting, excitability, convulsions, irregularity of the heart, and depression of respiration. The fatal dose is estimated to be 50–100 mg.

Remove ingested poison by emesis, gastric lavage, and catharsis. Control convulsions as for strychnine poisoning. Monoacetin (commercial 60% glycerol monoacetate) has been suggested as an antidote. The dosage is 0.1–0.5 ml/kg diluted in 5 parts of saline solution IV.

Food Poisoning: Bacterial

Manifestations are nausea, vomiting, diarrhea, and weakness progressing for 12–24 hours. Abdominal pain may be severe. Fever, shock, and dehydration occur rarely.

Remove toxin from gastrointestinal tract by gastric lavage or emesis. If diarrhea is not present, a saline cathartic may be given. Give nothing by mouth until vomiting has subsided. Then give oral fluids as tolerated for 12–24 hours before beginning a regular diet. If vomiting and diarrhea are severe, maintain fluid balance by giving 5% dextrose in saline intravenously. Give codeine phosphate, 30 mg orally or subcut, or paregoric, 4–12 ml after each bowel movement. Give atropine sulfate, 1 mg subcut, if gastrointestinal hyperactivity persists. Give bismuth subcarbonate, 1 gm after each bowel movement.

Food Poisoning: Nitrites

Manifestations are flushing of the skin, vomiting, dizziness, marked fall of blood pressure, cyanosis, and respiratory paralysis. The MLD is 2 gm.

Remove ingested poison by gastric lavage or emesis followed by catharsis. Maintain blood pressure by the injection of epinephrine, 1 ml of 1:1000 solution subcut, or levarterenol. Treat methemoglobinemia by the administration of methylene blue, 5–25 ml of 1% solution slowly IV.

Formaldehyde (Disinfectant)

Manifestations are severe abdominal pain followed by cardiovascular collapse, loss of consciousness, anuria, and circulatory failure. The MLD is 60 ml.

Remove ingested poison by gastric lavage or emesis followed by catharsis, preferably with 1% ammonium carbonate solution. Treat shock by administration of fluids.

Gold Salts (Antirheumatic)

Manifestations are skin rash, itching, eruptions, metallic taste, hepatitis, granulocytopenia, and aplastic anemia. Give dimercaprol (BAL).

Hydralazine (Hypotensive)

Manifestations are fever, diffuse erythematous facial dermatitis, lymph gland enlargement, splenomegaly, arthralgia, and simulated disseminated lupus erythematosus.

Discontinue further use at the first indication of joint involvement or rash. Give aspirin, 1–3 gm daily, or cortisone, 50–150 mg daily, until symptoms regress.

Hydrogen Sulfide & Carbon Disulfide (Fumigants)

Manifestations are painful conjunctivitis, appearance of a halo around lights, anosmia, pulmonary edema, restlessness, blurred vision, unconsciousness, and paralysis of respiration. Prolonged exposure causes persistent low blood pressure, impaired gait and balance, memory loss, mental depression, and parkinsonian tremor. The MAC is 20 ppm.

Remove from further exposure. Treat pulmonary edema.

Hydroquinone (Photo developer)

Repeated exposure will produce skin sensitivity reactions. Ingestion of 10 gm will cause symptoms similar to those due to phenol poisoning. Treat as for phenol poisoning.

Ipecac, Emetine (Emetics)

Manifestations are fatigue, dyspnea, tachycardia, low blood pressure, unconsciousness, and death from heart failure. The ECG reveals depressed T waves and arrhythmias. The MLD of emetine is 1 gm.

Remove ingested poison by gastric lavage or emesis followed by catharsis. Cautious digitalization may be helpful for myocardial weakness.

Iproniazid, Isocarboxazid, Pheniprazine, Nialamide, Phenelzine (Stimulants)

Overdoses cause ataxia, stupor excitement, fall of blood pressure, tachycardia, and convulsions. Repeated administration may cause weakness, hallucinations, mania, urine retention, liver injury with nausea, and vomiting. The MLD is 5 gm.

Remove ingested drug by gastric lavage, emesis, and catharsis. Give artificial respiration if respiration is depressed. Maintain blood pressure. Do not give stimulants. Discontinue administration at the first appearance of jaundice. Treat liver impairment as for carbon tetrachloride poisoning.

Larkspur (Liniment)

Manifestations are tingling and burning sensations of the mouth and skin, vomiting, diarrhea, fall of blood pressure, weak pulse, and convulsions.

Remove ingested poison by gastric lavage or emesis followed by saline catharsis. Give atropine, 2 mg subcut. Give artificial respiration. Maintain blood pressure.

Magnesium Salts (Cathartic)

Manifestations are watery diarrhea, gastrointestinal irritation, vomiting, tenesmus, collapse, flaccid paralysis, and, in the presence of impaired renal function, severe fall of blood pressure. The MLD is 30–60 gm.

Dilute orally or rectally administered magnesium sulfate by giving tap water. Give artificial respiration if necessary. Give calcium gluconate, 10 ml of 10% solution IV slowly, as a specific antidote.

Manganese (Industrial)

Ingestion causes lethargy, edema, and symptoms of extrapyramidal tract lesions. Inhalation causes bronchitis, pneumonia, and liver enlargement. Signs of parkinsonism also occur. Hepatic cell function tests may be impaired. The MAC is 6 mg/cu mm.

Remove from further exposure. Give EDTA.

Meprobamate (Sedative)

Manifestations are drowsiness and incoordination progressing to coma with cyanosis and respiratory depression. The MLD is 12 gm.

Remove ingested drug by gastric lavage or emesis followed by catharsis. Use resuscitative measures as for barbiturates if respiratory depression is present.

Metal Fumes (Industrial)

Inhalation of zinc oxide or other metal fumes causes fever, chills, muscular aches, and weakness. Pulmonary edema may follow.

Treat pulmonary edema. Bed rest and administration of analgesics will ordinarily relieve generalized symptoms.

Metaldehyde (Snail bait)

Manifestations are severe vomiting, abdominal pains, temperature elevation, muscular rigidity, convulsions, coma, and death from respiratory failure up to 48 hours after ingestion. The MLD for adults is about 5 gm.

Treat as for acetaldehyde poisoning, but note that snail bait commonly also contains arsenic.

Methenamine (Urinary antiseptic)

Manifestations are skin rash, kidney and bladder irritation, hematuria, and vomiting.

Discontinue further administration.

Methyl Bromide & Methyl Chloride (Fumigants)

Manifestations are dizziness, drowsiness, fall of blood pressure, coma, convulsions, and pulmonary edema after a latent period of 1–4 hours.

Treat convulsions as for strychnine poisoning. Treat pulmonary edema by administering 60% oxygen by face mask. Humidify inspired oxygen by using 20% ethyl alcohol in humidifier or nebulizer.

Methyl Sulfate (Industrial)

Ingestion or contact causes corrosion equivalent to that from sulfuric acid. Vapor exposure causes irritation and erythema of the eyes, pulmonary edema, proteinuria, and hematuria. The MLD for adults is about 1 gm.

Treat as for corrosive acid poisoning.

Methysergide Maleate (Sansert®)
(Migraine remedy)

Methysergide, which has been effectively employed in the prevention of migraine attacks, may cause hazardous fibrotic disorders involving primarily the retroperitoneal areas (retroperitoneal fibrosis) but also suggestive fibrotic changes affecting the aorta, heart valves, and lungs. Manifestations may include chest pain, dyspnea, fever, pleural effusion; pain in the back, abdomen, and pelvis; hydronephrosis, renal insufficiency, intermittent claudication, and edema of the lower extremities.

Cessation of methysergide therapy results in partial or complete remission of the disorder. Surgical removal of adhesions may be necessary.

Metol (Photo developer)

Repeated exposure may cause skin sensitivity reactions characterized by weeping and crusting. Ingestion may cause methemoglobinemia with cyanosis similar to that from antipyrine.

Remove from further exposure. Treat ingestion as for antipyrine.

Naphthalene (Moth balls)

Manifestations are diarrhea, oliguria, anemia, jaundice, pain on urination, and anuria. The MLD for adults is about 2 gm.

Remove ingested naphthalene by gastric lavage or emesis followed by catharsis. Alkalinize urine by giving sodium bicarbonate, 5 gm orally every 4 hours or as necessary to maintain alkaline urine. Give repeated small blood transfusions until hemoglobin is 60–80% of normal.

Naphthol (Industrial)

Acute poisoning is the same as that with phenol. Prolonged contact may cause bladder tumors, hemolytic anemia, and cataracts. Addition of ferric chloride to acidified urine gives a violet or blue color indicating the presence of a phenolic compound. The MLD is 2 gm.

Treat as for phenol poisoning.

Naphthylamine (Industrial)

Repeated exposure may cause skin sensitivity reactions with weeping and crusting. Exposure to large amounts may cause methemoglobinemia with cyanosis.

Remove from further exposure. Treat cyanosis as for aniline poisoning.

Nickel Carbonyl (Industrial)

Immediate symptoms are cough, dizziness, and weakness. Delayed reactions are characterized by dyspnea, cyanosis, rapid pulse, and respiratory embarrassment. The MAC is 1 ppm.

Treat cyanosis and dyspnea by giving 100% oxygen by mask. Treat pulmonary edema. Give sodium diethyldithiocarbamate, 50–100 mg/kg orally or IM.

Nicotine (Tobacco)

Manifestations are respiratory stimulation, nausea, diarrhea, tachycardia, elevation of blood pressure, salivation, and, with large doses, rapid progression to prostration, convulsions, respiratory slowing, cardiac irregularity, and coma. The fatal dose of pure nicotine is about 1 mg/kg. The MLD of tobacco is 5 gm.

Remove nicotine from skin by scrubbing or, if ingested, remove by thorough gastric lavage. Inject hexamethonium chloride, 25–50 mg subcut. Repeat

each hour until blood pressure falls to normal. Treat convulsions as for strychnine poisoning.

Oil of Chenopodium (Anthelmintic)

Manifestations are severe gastrointestinal irritation, difficult swallowing, collapse, convulsions, and coma. The urine may show red cells and protein. The MLD is 3 gm.

Remove by gastric lavage or emesis followed by catharsis. Treat convulsions and anuria.

Pamaquine (Anthelmintic)

Hemolytic anemia and methemoglobinemia occur most commonly in Negroes. Gastric distress and weakness occur after large doses.

Reduce dosage or discontinue drug. Treat hemolytic anemia by the administration of sodium bicarbonate to alkalinize the urine and prevent the precipitation of acid hematin. Give blood transfusions if anemia is severe.

Paraldehyde (Hypnotic)

Manifestations are deep sleep with ordinary doses and respiratory or cardiac depression occasionally with doses over 10 ml.

Treat as for acetaldehyde or barbiturate poisoning.

Pentylenetetrazol (Stimulant)

Manifestations are increased respiration, twitching, convulsions, and respiratory failure beginning within minutes after administration. The MLD by the intravenous route is 1 gm.

Treat as for strychnine poisoning.

Permanganate (Antiseptic)

Ingestion of solid or concentrated permanganate causes laryngeal edema, necrosis of oral mucosa, slow pulse, and cardiovascular collapse. Anuria may occur. The MLD is 10 gm.

Remove ingested poison by gastric lavage or emesis followed by catharsis. Treat shock and anuria.

Phenacetin & Acetanilid (Analgesics)

Acute poisoning is similar to that due to salicylates. Prolonged administration leads to renal impairment, cyanosis, hemolytic anemia, and skin eruptions. The MLD is 5–20 gm.

Treat as for salicylate poisoning. Treat methemoglobinemia by giving methylene blue, 5–25 ml of 1% solution slowly IV.

Phenolphthalein (Laxative)

Manifestations are erythematous, itching skin rash, or purging, collapse, and fall of blood pressure.

Prevent further use. Treat blood pressure fall by administration of fluids.

Phenylenediamine (Hair dye)

Repeated exposure may cause sensitivity dermatitis with itching. Remove from further exposure.

Physostigmine, Neostigmine, & Related Drugs
(Parasympathomimetics)

Manifestations are tremors, marked peristalsis, involuntary defecation and urination, pin-point pupils, difficult breathing, convulsions and severe respiratory difficulty. The MLD is 6 mg.

Give atropine sulfate, 2 mg IV or IM every 2–4 hours as necessary to relieve respiratory difficulty and other symptoms.

Picrotoxin (Stimulant)

Manifestations are increased respiration, twitching, convulsions, and respiratory failure, beginning 20 minutes to 1 hour after exposure and persisting up to 24 hours. The MLD is 20 mg.

Remove ingested poison by gastric lavage or emesis followed by catharsis in the absence of convulsions. Treat convulsions as for strychnine poisoning.

Poison Hemlock (Plant)

Manifestations are gradually increasing muscular weakness followed by paralysis with respiratory failure. Proteinuria also occurs.

Treat respiratory failure by artificial respiration with oxygen. Remove ingested poison by gastric lavage or emesis followed by catharsis.

Poison Ivy, Poison Oak (Plants)

Local effects begin after a delay of hours to days and include itching, swelling, vesiculation, generalized edema, proteinuria, and microscopic hematuria.

Minimize skin contamination by washing with strong soap and water. Remove ingested plant material by gastric lavage or emesis followed by saline catharsis. Treat exudative stage by exposure to air or with wet dressings of aluminum acetate, 1%. Generalized reactions may be treated with cortisone or related steroids to relieve symptoms.

Procaine (Local anesthetic)

Manifestations are dizziness, weakness, fall of blood pressure, muscular tremors, convulsions, and cardiovascular collapse. The MLD is 1 gm.

Treat as for cocaine poisoning.

Propylthiouracil (Antithyroid)

Manifestations are skin rash, urticaria, joint pains, fever, and leukopenia.

Treat agranulocytosis by the administration of large doses of penicillin or broad-spectrum antibiotics to control intercurrent infections.

Quinidine (Antifibrillatory)

Manifestations are tinnitus, diarrhea, dizziness, severe fall of blood pressure with disappearance of pulse, respiratory failure, thrombocytopenic purpura after prolonged use, urticaria, and anaphylactoid reactions. The ECG may show widening of QRS complex, lengthened Q–T interval, premature ventricular beats, and lengthened P–R interval. The MLD is 1 gm.

Remove ingested drug by gastric lavage or emesis followed by catharsis. Raise blood pressure by intravenous saline or blood transfusions or with levarterenol. The administration of sixth-molar sodium lactate solution intravenously is said to reduce the cardiotoxic effects of quinidine.

Quinine, Quinacrine, Chloroquine
(Antimalarials)

Manifestations are progressive tinnitus, blurring of vision, weakness, fall of blood pressure, anuria, and cardiac irregularities. Repeated ingestion of quinine causes visual loss associated with pallor of optic disks, narrowing of retinal vessels, and papilledema. Quinacrine causes hepatitis, aplastic anemia, psychosis, and jaundice. Chloroquine causes dizziness and blurred vision. The urine may show red cells, protein, and casts. The MLD is 1 gm.

Remove ingested drug by gastric lavage or emesis followed by catharsis. Treat shock. Give 2–4 liters of fluids daily to promote renal excretion. Treat anuria.

Rauwolfia (Antihypertensive)

Manifestations are diarrhea, nasal stuffiness, cardiac pain, extrasystoles, congestive failure, tremors, and emotional depression.

Discontinue further administration.

Santonin (Anthelmintic)

Manifestations are yellow vision, vomiting, confusion, hallucinations, convulsions, and respiratory or circulation failure. Urine shows hematuria, casts, and proteinuria. The MLD is 0.1 gm.

Remove ingested poison by gastric lavage or emesis followed by catharsis. Control convulsions and maintain blood pressure.

Shellfish

Manifestations are numbness and tingling of lips, tongue, face, and extremities, respiratory weakness or paralysis, and convulsions.

Remove ingested shellfish by gastric lavage or emesis followed by catharsis. Give artificial respiration with oxygen, and maintain blood pressure.

Silver Nitrate (Antiseptic)

Silver nitrate is a protein precipitant. Poisoning is manifested by nausea, vomiting, diarrhea, bloody stools, blue discoloration about the mouth, and shock.

Lavage with saline solution to precipitate silver chloride. Give whites of eggs beaten in milk as demulcent, and sodium sulfate, 30 gm in 200 ml of water as cathartic. Institute supportive measures.

Dimercaprol (BAL) has not proved effective.

Stibine (Industrial)

Manifestations are weakness, jaundice, anemia, and weak pulse. The MAC is 0.1 ppm.

Treat by blood transfusion and alkalinization of the urine.

Streptomycin (Antituberculosis)

Manifestations are 8th nerve injury with tinnitus, deafness, loss of sense of balance, and vertigo.

Discontinue administration at the first sign of 8th nerve injury.

Sulfonamides (Antibacterial)

Manifestations are skin eruptions, fever, hematuria, and oliguria or anuria with azotemia. The urine shows crystals, red cells, and protein.

If kidney function is normal, force fluids to 4 liters daily to speed excretion of sulfonamides. Treat anuria.

Talc (Dusting powder)

Prolonged inhalation causes fine fibrosis of the lungs and calcification of the pericardium.

Remove from further exposure. Treat as for silicosis.

Tetrachloroethane (Solvent)

Manifestations are irritation of the eyes and nose, headache, nausea, abdominal pain, jaundice, and anuria. Hepatic cell impairment may be revealed by appropriate tests. The urine may show proteins, red cells, or casts. The MLD is 1 gm.

Treat as for carbon tetrachloride poisoning.

Thallium (Rodenticide)

Thallium poisoning is characterized by slow onset of ataxia, pains and paresthesias of the extremities, bilateral ptosis, loss of hair, fever, and abdominal pains. Progression of poisoning is indicated by lethargy, jumbled speech, tremors, convulsions and cyanosis, pulmonary edema and respiratory difficulty. The MLD is 1 gm.

Remove ingested poison by emesis, gastric lavage, and catharsis. The administration of dimercaprol or dithizon, 20 mg/kg/day orally for 5 days, has been suggested. Maintain urine output at 1 liter or more daily unless renal insufficiency appears, in which contingency only sufficient fluid to replace losses is given. Maintain blood pressure.

Thanite (Insecticide)

Manifestations are respiratory difficulty and convulsions.

Remove ingested poison by emesis or gastric lavage. Treat convulsions as for strychnine poisoning.

Thiocyanates (Insecticides)

Manifestations are disorientation, weakness, low blood pressure, psychotic behavior, and convulsions. The fatal serum level of thiocyanate is 20 mg/100 ml.

Remove ingested thiocyanate by gastric lavage or emesis followed by catharsis. Give 2–4 liters of fluid orally or IV daily to maintain adequate urine output. Remove thiocyanate by peritoneal dialysis or by hemodialysis if necessary.

Thioglycollate (Cold wave)

Repeated application to the skin may cause sensitivity dermatitis with edema, itching, burning, and rash.

Discontinue use.

Thyroid (Medicinal)

Manifestations are fever, tachycardia, hypertension, and cardiovascular collapse at doses of 0.3 gm/kg.

Maintain normal body temperature and force fluids. Digitalize if cardiac weakness is present.

Trichloroethylene (Solvent)

Manifestations are dizziness, headache, excitement, loss of consciousness. Irregular pulse may occur. The MLD is 5 ml.

Remove the patient to fresh air and give artificial respiration. Do not give epinephrine or other stimulants.

Trinitrotoluene (Explosive)

Manifestations are jaundice, dermatitis, cyanosis, pallor, loss of appetite, and oliguria or anuria. The liver may be enlarged or atrophic. Hepatic cell injury may be revealed by appropriate tests. The MLD is 1 gm.

Remove from skin by thorough washing with soap and water. Remove swallowed trinitrotoluene by gastric lavage or emesis and catharsis. Protect liver by giving 10 ml of 10% calcium gluconate IV 3 times daily and a high-carbohydrate and high-calcium diet, including at least 1 quart of skimmed milk daily. Give vitamin D in high doses daily.

Tri-orthocresyl Phosphate (Plasticizer)

After 1–30 days' delay, weakness of the distal muscles develops, with foot drop, wrist drop, and loss of plantar reflex. Death may occur from respiratory muscle paralysis. The MLD for adults is about 5 gm.

Remove by gastric lavage or emesis followed by catharsis. Maintain respiration if necessary by tank respirator.

Vanadium (Industrial)

Manifestations are rhinorrhea, sneezing, sore chest, dyspnea, bronchitis, and pneumonitis.

Give ascorbic acid, 1 gm/day.

Veratrum, Zygadenus (Plants)

Manifestations are nausea, severe vomiting, muscular weakness, slow pulse, and low blood pressure. Excessive amounts may cause marked rise in blood pressure.

Remove ingested poison by gastric lavage or emesis followed by catharsis. Atropine, 2 mg subcut, will block the reflex fall of blood pressure and the bradycardia. Elevation of blood pressure is treated by the administration of phentolamine hydrochloride, 25 mg subcut repeated every 4 hours.

Volatile Anesthetics: Ether, Chloroform, Halothane, Divinyl Ether, Cyclopropane, Ethyl Chloride, Ethylene, Nitrous Oxide

Manifestations are excitement, unconsciousness, depression and paralysis of respiration. Cardiac irregularities occur with cyclopropane, chloroform, and halothane. Severe fall of blood pressure or cardiac arrest may also occur. The MLD is 1–30 ml.

Remove volatile anesthetic by artificial respiration. Maintain blood pressure by intravenous saline, blood transfusions, and levarterenol. Prevent hypoxia by administering oxygen.

Volatile Oils: Turpentine, Pine Oil, Menthol, Absinthe, Savin, Pennyroyal, Eucalyptus

Manifestations are vomiting, diarrhea, unconsciousness, shallow respiration, hematuria, and convulsions. The MLD is 15 gm.

Give 60–120 ml of liquid petrolatum or castor oil and then remove oils by gastric lavage, taking care to prevent aspiration. Follow with a saline cathartic. Give artificial respiration if necessary. Give fluids, 2–4 liter daily if kidney function is normal after the danger of pulmonary edema has passed.

Water Hemlock (Plant)

Manifestations are abdominal pain, vomiting, diarrhea, convulsions, cyanosis, and respiratory failure.

Treat as for hemlock poisoning.

Zinc Stearate (Dusting powder)

Inhalation causes fever, dyspnea, cyanosis, and bronchial pneumonia.

Give penicillin, 1 million units IM daily, or a broad-spectrum antibiotic to prevent bronchial pneumonia.

Zinc Sulfate (Astringent)

Manifestations are burning pain in the mouth and throat, vomiting, diarrhea, anuria, and cardiovascular collapse. The MLD is 30 gm.

Give milk or starch drinks to dilute the poison and remove by gastric lavage. Replace fluid loss with 5% dextrose in saline. Relieve pain by giving morphine sulfate, 10 mg.

· · ·

AIR POLLUTION

There is considerable evidence that the present levels of atmospheric contaminants which exist in many larger urban areas are sufficient to cause discomfort or significantly impair health. Air pollution is increasing, and it is presumed that the associated health hazard will also increase. Toxicologic and epidemiologic studies suggest that the noxious nature of the atmosphere is usually due to a complex mixture of pollutants and to meteorologic factors.

It is difficult to identify the irritant or toxic potential of single pollutants in the urban atmosphere. The large number of organic and inorganic compounds found in urban air may vary considerably according to the nature, source, and volume of emitted pollutants (eg, industrial processes, automotive exhaust, domestic heating and incineration) and climatic influences (eg, temperature, sunshine, humidity, barometric pressure, wind currents).

Air pollutants are usually divided into 2 broad classes: (1) particulates (smoke, dust, ash, mists, and fumes which exist in the atmosphere in either a solid or liquid state) and (2) gases (eg, carbon monoxide, sulfur oxides, hydrogen sulfide, nitrogen oxides, and carbon compounds—particularly those reacting in the atmosphere to form photochemical smog).

Air pollution is not believed to be the cause of specific illnesses which may result in death, but it may seriously aggravate preexisting respiratory and cardiac conditions. The irritating effects of air pollution on the eye and upper respiratory tract are well known. Inhalation of irritant materials may interfere with lung function, aggravating chronic bronchitis, chronic constrictive ventilatory disease, pulmonary emphysema, and bronchial asthma. Carbon monoxide, which may eventually become the greatest pollution problem, can interfere with oxygen delivery to the heart and to the brain—perhaps a critical factor in patients with coronary artery disease or in police and motorists in city traffic whose mental functioning is impaired by cerebral hypoxia.

The ill effects of atmospheric pollution are most obvious during acute episodes of unusually high pollution. Marked increases in the incidence of illnesses and deaths due to cardiorespiratory damage were reported in the Meuse Valley in Belgium in 1930, in Donora, Pennsylvania, in 1948, and in London in 1952 and 1962.

The insidious long-term toxic potential of exposure to single or multiple air pollutants is not known.

Casarett, L.J.: Toxicology: The respiratory tract. Ann Rev Pharmacol 11:425–446, 1971.

Glasser, M., & L. Greenburg: Air pollution, mortality, and weather: New York City 1960–1964. Arch Envir Health 22:334–343, 1971.

Higgins, I.T.T.: Effects of sulfur oxides and particulates on health. Arch Envir Health 22:584–590, 1971.

Menzel, D.B. (editor): Symposium on pollution and lung biochemistry. Arch Int Med 127:845–902, 1971.

Menzel, D.B.: Toxicity of ozone, oxygen, and radiation. Ann Rev Pharmacol 10:379–394, 1970.

Pearlman, M.E., & others: Nitrogen dioxide and lower respiratory illness. Pediatrics 47:391–398, 1971.

· · ·

General Bibliography

Arena, J.M. (editor): Symposium on advances in the treatment of poisoning. Mod Treat 4:597–740, 1967.

Coleman, A.B., & J.J. Alpert (editors): Symposium on poisoning in children. P Clin North America 17:471–758, 1970.

Goodman, L.S., & A. Gilman (editors): *The Pharmacological Basis of Therapeutics,* 4th ed. Macmillan, 1970.

Hardin, J.W., & J.M. Arena: *Human Poisoning From Native and Cultivated Plants.* Duke University, 1969.

Lampe, K.F., & R. Fagerström: *Plant Toxicity and Dermatitis: A Manual for Physicians.* Williams & Wilkins, 1968.

Liebowitz, M.R., & others: The clinical use of hemodialysis and peritoneal dialysis. Proc Rudolph Virchow Med Soc NY 25:29–41, 1966.

Maher, J.F., & G. Schreiner: The dialysis of poisons and drugs. Trans Am Soc Artific Int Organs 15:461–477, 1969.

Matthew, H., & A.A. Lawson: *Treatment of Common Acute Poisonings.* Livingstone, 1967.

Miller, R.B., & C.R. Tassistro: Peritoneal dialysis. New England J Med 281:945–949, 1969.

Reid, D.H.S.: Treatment of the poisoned child. Arch Dis Child 45:428–433, 1970.

Robertson, W.O.: Poisoning in childhood. Northwest Med 69:95–98, 1970.

Wilkinson, G.R.: Treatment of drug intoxication: A review of some scientific principles. Clin Toxicol 3:249–265, 1970.

Selected References on Adverse Reactions to Drugs.

Adverse Reactions. A monthly report of adverse reactions to drugs and therapeutic devices by the Adverse Reactions Branch, Food and Drug Administration, US Department of Health, Education, and Welfare, Washington, DC.

Clin-Alert. A weekly to fortnightly serial publication of all adverse drug reactions reported in the international medical literature. Science Editors, Inc., Louisville, Kentucky.

The Medical Letter on Drugs and Therapeutics. A valuable fortnightly periodical presenting brief, current clinical evaluations of drugs, including adverse reactions. Therapeutic Information, Inc., New York, New York.

Meyler, L.: *Side Effects of Drugs.* Vol V. Excerpta Medica, 1966.

Meyler, L., & H.M. Peck (editors): *Drug-Induced Diseases,* Vol 3. Excerpta Medica Foundation, 1968.

Moser, R.H.: *Diseases of Medical Progress: Present Status.* Abstracts of published adverse reactions to drugs appearing monthly in Clinical Pharmacology and Therapeutics.

29...

Medical Genetics

Margaret S. Kosek

The rapid advance of the science of genetics in recent years has so many applications to clinical medicine that a knowledge of basic genetic principles is now a necessity for diagnostic purposes. Many cases of mental retardation, infertility, dwarfism, habitual abortion, and multiple congenital anomalies are associated with specific chromosomal defects. Cells of certain tumors have an abnormal chromosomal composition, in some instances a specific one. Many of the metabolic disorders are hereditary, and even in the case of some drug reactions the problem lies not only with the drug but also with the patient who has inherited an enzymatic defect which prevents normal detoxification. Future genetic investigation promises to increase our understanding of the causes and the mechanisms of individual responses to disease.

GENERAL CONSIDERATIONS

Inherited characteristics are carried from generation to generation by the **chromosome**, a complex protein structure in the nucleus of the cell. Man normally has 46 chromosomes, which are arranged in 23 pairs. One of these pairs determines the sex of the individual; these are the **sex chromosomes**, which are designated as XX (female) and XY (male). The remaining 22 pairs are called **autosomes** (not sex determiners). Pairs of autosomes are **homologous**, ie, each member of a pair has the same configuration and genetic material as the other member of the pair. The sex chromosomes, on the other hand, are **heterologous**, ie, the X chromosome differs both in size and total function from the Y chromosome.

The X chromosome is roughly 5 times the size of the Y chromosome. Both the X and Y chromosomes have a genetic as well as sex determining aspect, but the genetic information is more extensive on the X chromosome. With the Y chromosome, the genetic information is so limited that it has only been recently discovered.

GENES

Chromosomes are composed of thousands of **genes**, which are the basic units of heredity. It is the gene which is the information area for the transmission of an inherited trait. The genes are arranged in a linear fashion on the chromosomes. The exact location of a gene on a chromosome is its **locus**. Each chromosome has thousands of loci arranged in a definite manner, and the number and arrangement of genes on homologous chromosomes are identical. Genes which occupy homologous loci are **alleles**, or partner genes. Each individual, therefore, has 2 of each kind of gene, one on each pair of chromosomes.

Although genes usually remain stable from generation to generation, it is possible for them to undergo a change, or **mutation**, and thereby to transmit a new or altered trait. This change will then be transmitted to future generations. Mutation may occur spontaneously or may be induced by such environmental factors as radiation, medication, or viral infections.

THE CHEMICAL BASIS OF HEREDITY (THE GENETIC CODE)

Chromosomes are composed of many deoxyribonucleic acid (DNA) molecules, each of which is a gene. DNA has 2 functions. First, it is able to synthesize or **replicate** itself, thereby assuring the integrity of hereditary transmission to future generations. Second, the sequential order of the bases (cytosine, guanine, adenine, thymine) of DNA acts as the **genetic code** that determines the development and metabolism of cells. DNA accomplishes this by directing the synthesis of ribonucleic acid (RNA). RNA, by its base sequence, determines the amino acid composition of proteins, and this in turn determines the function of proteins. The location of these proteins (which include the enzymes) determines the function of cells.

MODES OF INHERITANCE

The essential definitions of modes of inheritance can be illustrated by studying the inheritance of a **single** characteristic carried by only **one** gene and not influenced by environmental factors.

Syndactyly (webbed fingers or toes) is a clinical example of this. Fig 29–1 illustrates a family tree with

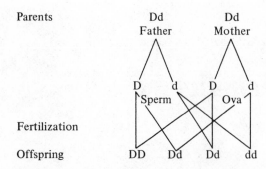

FIG 29—1. Mode of inheritance of syndactyly.

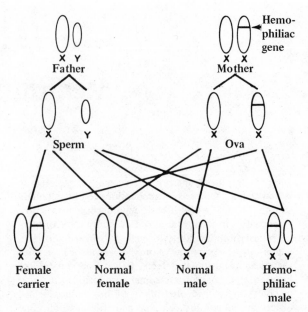

FIG 29—2. The inheritance of hemophilia from a female carrier, illustrating "mother-to-son" inheritance of X-linked recessive disease.

the abnormality. The gene for syndactyly is represented as **D** and the gene for normal interdigital spaces as **d**.

Each parent is represented by 2 genes, each of which they received from their mother and father, respectively. Their genetic constitution has arbitrarily been designated Dd. The male parent (Dd) will be able to produce sperm that are either D or d. The female parent will be able to produce ova that are either D or d. The possible offspring are DD, Dd or dd.

If we examine the parents and offspring for the presence of syndactyly, we find it in both parents (Dd and Dd) and 3 (DD, Dd, Dd) of the 4 offspring. Since these people have the same physical characteristic, ie, syndactyly, they are said to have the same **phenotype**. Their genetic composition, or **genotype**, is different, for it may be either Dd or DD. The genotype, therefore, may be the same as the phenotype, but it does not have to be. Since syndactyly is present if D is one gene of a pair of genes (Dd) as well as both genes (DD), it is a **dominant** trait. Normal digital spaces (d) are present only if d is on both genes (dd) and is a **recessive** trait. If an individual's genetic constitution for syndactyly contains similar genes (DD, dd), the person is a **homozygote**; if it contains dissimilar genes (Dd), the person is a **heterozygote**.

In addition to dominant and recessive inheritance, an **intermediate** inheritance may also occur. Hemoglobin S disease is an example of this. The S homozygote has sickle cell anemia; the S heterozygote has sickle cell trait; and the patient without S is normal.

Inheritance is either **autosomal** or **X-linked (sexlinked)** depending on the chromosomal location of the gene. In investigating family trees for genetic disease, certain inheritance patterns with distinct features become evident. **Autosomal dominant inheritance** has 3 criteria: (1) every affected person has an affected parent; (2) every affected person that marries a normal person has a 1:2 chance of having each offspring affected; and (3) every normal child of an affected person will have normal offspring. With **autosomal recessive inheritance**, many characteristics are present. The vast majority of affected persons have parents who are normal in all outward appearances. In affected families, each child has a 1:4 chance of having a genetic defect. When an affected person and a normal

person marry, their offspring will be normal in most cases. If their offspring is affected, the "normal" parent is a heterozygote. When 2 affected parents marry, all their children will be affected. Lastly, the rarer the defect, the more likely it is that there is consanguinity in the family tree.

With **X-linked recessive inheritance**, there are 2 main characteristics: the defect is carried by women and exhibited by men; and affected men can pass the disease only through their daughters. Hemophilia is an important clinical example of this (Fig 29—2). The female with her 2 X chromosomes must have the gene for hemophilia present in each X chromosome to have this recessive disease. Since the frequency of this gene in the population is low, the chances of 2 affected X chromosomes occurring together, although possible, is highly unlikely. Therefore, hemophilia is very rare in females. Males, with their XY chromosome composition, need the hemophilia gene present only on one chromosome (the X) to have it expressed clinically, for there is no homologous locus in the Y chromosome to neutralize the effect of the hemophiliac gene. Since the Y chromosome had to come from the father, the affected X chromosome was from the mother, thereby giving the "mother-to-son" inheritance pattern. In the case of **X-linked dominant inheritance,** no fully dominant X-linked gene has been discovered in humans.

Genes do not always have an "all or none" action. A certain number of offspring may fail to show expression of a gene even though the gene may be a dominant or homozygous recessive. **Penetrance** is the statistical concept that refers to the frequency with which a gene or genotype is morphologically manifest in the offspring. A comparable term, **expressivity**, refers to the degree of phenotypic expression of a trait (ie, forme fruste vs full expression). These variables make genetic analysis far more difficult.

The genetic disorders carried by a single gene have been most completely studied. They frequently have a characteristic somatic or biochemical defect that can be readily traced in many generations. On the whole, these genetic disorders are rare. It is much more difficult to determine the mode of inheritance of the common diseases of possible genetic background (eg, arteriosclerosis) because the disease may be the result not only of genetic constitution but also of environmental factors (eg, diet).

Some Diseases With Known Modes of Inheritance

AD = Autosomal dominant
AR = Autosomal recessive
SD = Sex-linked (X-linked) dominant
SR = Sex-linked (X-linked) recessive

Central Nervous System
A. Diffuse cerebral sclerosis (Pelizaeus-Merzbacher type): SD?, SR?
B. Diffuse cerebral sclerosis (Sholz type): SD?, SR?
C. Lowe's ocular cerebral renal disease: SR
D. Retinoblastoma: AD

Digestive System
A. Cystic fibrosis of the pancreas: AR
B. Hyperbilirubinemia:
  1. Congenital nonhemolytic jaundice with kernicterus (Crigler-Najjar): AR
  2. Familial nonhemolytic jaundice (Gilbert's disease): AD
  3. Chronic idiopathic jaundice (Dubin-Johnson): Probably AD
  4. Chronic familial nonhemolytic jaundice (Rotor's syndrome): AD

Genitourinary System
A. Cystinosis: AR
B. Cystinuria: AR
C. Fanconi's syndrome (infantile and adult): AR
D. Hartnup disease: AR
E. Nephrogenic diabetes insipidus: SR
F. Renal glycosuria: AD
G. Vitamin D-resistant rickets: SD

Skin
A. Albinism: AR
B. Anhidrotic ectodermal dysplasia: AR?
C. Xeroderma pigmentosum: AR

Hematologic System
A. Cell Disorders:
  1. Congenital nonspherocytic hemolytic anemia (pyruvate kinase deficiency): AR
  2. Sickle cell disease (homozygous hemoglobin S): AD

  3. Sickle cell trait (heterozygous hemoglobin S): AD
  4. Spherocytosis: AD
  5. Thalassemia major (homozygous): AD
  6. Thalassemia minor (heterozygous): AD
B. Plasma Disorders:
  1. Congenital agammaglobulinemia: SR
  2. Congenital afibrinogenemia: AR
  3. Hemophilia A (AHG deficiency): SR
  4. Hemophilia B (PTC deficiency): SR
  5. Hemophilia C (PTA deficiency): AD
  6. Deficiency of Hageman factor (factor XII): AR
  7. Deficiency of labile factor (factor V, plasma accelerator globulin, plasma AC globulin): AR
  8. Deficiency of stabile factor (factor VII, serum prothrombin conversion accelerator, SPCA): AR
  9. Deficiency of Stuart-Prower factor (factor X): AR
  10. Von Willebrand's disease (factor VIII deficiency): AD

Musculoskeletal System
A. Severe generalized familial muscular dystrophy (Duchenne's pseudohypertrophic muscular dystrophy): SR
B. Muscular dystrophy (facioscapulohumeral syndrome of Landouzy-Dejerine): AD
C. Progressive dystrophia ophthalmoplegica: AD
D. Myotonia atrophica: AD
E. Progressive muscular dystrophy (tardive type of Becker): SR
F. Charcot-Marie-Tooth peroneal muscular atrophy: AD, AR
G. Pseudohypoparathyroidism: SR
H. Periodic paralysis:
  1. Hyperkalemic: AD
  2. Hypokalemic: AD
  3. Normokalemic: AD

Endocrine System
A. Pituitary:
  1. Pituitary diabetes insipidus: AD
B. Thyroid:
  1. Familial cretinism with goiter—
    a. Iodide trapping defect: AR
    b. Iodide organification defect: AR?, AD?
    c. Iodotyrosyl coupling defect: AR?
    d. Deiodinase defect: AR
    e. Abnormal serum iodoprotein: AR
C. Adrenal:
  1. Congenital virilizing adrenal hyperplasia: AR

Metabolic Disorders
A. Carbohydrate:
  1. Idiopathic spontaneous hypoglycemia: AR
  2. Diabetes mellitus: AR
  3. Galactosemia: AR

4. Glycogen storage disease (types 1, 2, 3, 4, 5, 6) (Von Gierke's disease): AR
5. Gargoylism (lipochondrodystrophy) (Hurler's disease): AR, SR
6. Hyperoxaluria: AR
7. Hereditary fructose intolerance and essential fructosuria: AR
8. Hereditary lactose intolerance: AR
9. Hereditary disaccharide intolerance: AR
10. Monosaccharide malabsorption: AR
11. Mucopolysaccharidoses—
   a. Type 1. Hurler's disease: AR
   b. Type 2. Hurler's disease: SR
   c. Type 3. Sanfilippo syndrome (heparitinuria): AR
   d. Type 4. Morquio's disease: AR
   e. Type 5. Scheie's syndrome: AR

B. Fat:
   1. Idiopathic hyperlipemia (Buerger-Grutz disease): AR
   2. Familial high density lipoprotein disease (Tangier disease): AR
   3. Abetalipoproteinemia (acanthocytosis): AR
   4. Primary hypercholesterolemia: AD
   5. Gaucher's disease (cerebroside lipidosis): AR, AD
   6. Niemann-Pick disease (sphingomyelin lipidosis): AR
   7. Tay-Sachs disease (infantile amaurotic idiocy): AR
   8. Vogt-Spielmeyer disease (juvenile amaurotic idiocy): AR
   9. Metachromatic leukodystrophy (sulfatide lipidosis): AR
   10. Fabry's disease (glycolipid lipidosis): SR

C. Protein:
   1. Amino acids—
   a. Arginosuccinic aciduria: AR
   b. β-Aminoisobutyric aciduria: AR
   c. Citrullinemia: AR
   d. Cystathioninemia: AR
   e. Glucoglycinuria: AD
   f. Glycinuria: AR
   g. Histidinemia: AR
   h. Homocystinuria: AR
   i. Hydroxykynureninuria: AR
   j. Hydroxyprolinemia: AR
   k. Hyperlysinemia: AR
   l. Hyperprolinemia: AR
   m. Hypervalinemia: AR
   n. Isovaleric acidemia: AR
   o. Maple syrup urine disease: AR
   p. Phenylketonuria: AR
   q. Tryptophanuria: AD (?)
   r. Tyrosinosis: AR
   2. Porphyrias—
   a. Congenital erythropoietic porphyria: AR
   b. Erythropoietic porphyria: AR
   c. Acute intermittent porphyria: AD
   d. Porphyria cutanea tarda hereditaria: AD

3. Other—
   a. Hypophosphatasia: AR
   b. Deficiency of pseudocholinesterase: AR
   c. Deficiency of glucose-6-phosphate dehydrogenase: SD
   d. Acatalasia: AR
   e. Alkaptonuria: AR
   f. Congenital methemoglobinemia: AR
   g. Hyperuricemia: AD
   h. Hereditary orotic aciduria: AR
D. Minerals:
   1. Hepatolenticular degeneration (Wilson's disease): AR
   2. Hemochromatosis: AD, AR

McKusick, V.A.: *Mendelian Inheritance in Man: Catalogs of Autosomal Dominant, Autosomal Recessive and X-linked Phenotypes,* 2nd ed. Johns Hopkins Univ Press, 1968.

CYTOGENETICS

Cytogenetics is the study of the chromosomal structure of cells. Because of the constancy of chromosomal number and morphology, classification of chromosomes is possible. The basic characteristics of chromosomes are (1) total length, (2) position of the centromere, (3) the length of the arms, and (4) the presence or absence of satellites.

The 2 halves of the chromosome are called **chromatids**. A palely staining cross-over point or primary constriction called the **centromere** (centrosome) divides the chromosome into 2 arm lengths. Chromosomes are described according to the position of the centromere. If the centromere is at the middle of the chromosome, it is a **metacentric** chromosome; if near the middle of the chromosome, it is **submetracentric**; and if near the end of the chromosome, it is **acrocentric**. On some chromosomes there is a secondary constriction. The chromosomal material distal to this constriction is called a **satellite**.

In the Denver classification, chromosomes are arranged in 7 groups according to descending total length: group A (chromosomes 1–3); group B (chromosomes 4, 5); group C (chromosomes 6–12); group D (chromosomes 13–15); group E (chromosomes 16–18); group F (chromosomes 19, 20); and group G (chromosomes 21, 22). The X chromosome is in group C and the Y chromosome is in group G. All investigators can agree on which group a specific chromosome belongs in, but they may not be able to agree which specific chromosome of the group it is. The most readily identifiable chromosomes are 1, 2, 3, 16, and often Y. The most difficult group for specific chromsome identification is group C. Morphologically, X chromosome probably occurs between chromosomes 6 and 7, although it is often not possible to specifically identify it.

Autoradiographic studies of DNA with ^{3}H (tritium)-labeled thymidine show that there is a consistent and definite sequence to the order in which chromosomes begin and end their DNA replication. This enables identification of each chromosome. So far, the method is a research tool.

The chromosomal analysis is recorded by a uniform system of notation. First, there is the total chromosome count, followed by the sex chromosomes, and then any abnormalities thereafter. The autosomes are all designated by their number (1−22), and, if the autosomes cannot be identified, the involved chromosome group is identified by its letter (A−G). A plus (+) or minus (−) sign indicates, respectively, a gain or loss of chromosomal material. The letter *p* represents the short arm of the chromosome and the letter *q* represents the long arm. Other common symbols are *i* for isochromosome; *r* for ring chromosome; *s* for satellite; *t* for translocation; *inv* for inversion, *mar* for marker and *end* for endoreduplication. *Examples:* The normal male is 46,XY; a girl with Down's syndrome is 47,XX,G(+); a boy with cat cry syndrome is 46,XY,5p(−).

Chicago Conference: Standardization in human cytogenetics. Birth Defects 2:2−21, 1966.

Methods of Cellular Division

Cells divide in one of 2 ways: by **mitosis** (Fig 29−3) or by **meiosis** (Fig 29−6). In mitosis a mother cell divides longitudinally to produce 2 daughter cells of exactly the same chromosomal number and composition as the mother cell. This type of cellular division is purely multiplicative (1 cell → 2 cells → 4 cells → 8 cells, etc). Meiosis occurs in the ovary or testis and involves 2 separate steps. The first step is **reduction-division**, in which the germ cell with a **diploid (2n)** number of chromosomes (46) produces 2 cells with a **haploid (n)** number of chromosomes (23). During this step chromosomal material is exchanged between like chromosomes, thereby accounting for the random distribution of maternal and paternal genes. The second step is **equational division**, in which 4 daughter cells with a haploid number of chromosomes are formed by longitudinal division of the chromosomes produced in the first step of meiotic division. In the male, the 4 haploid cells are sperm. In the female, one of the 4 haploid cells is large and matures to form an ovum. The other 3 haploid cells are small cells called polar bodies, and undergo spontaneous degeneration.

TYPES OF CHROMOSOMAL ABNORMALITIES

Chromosomal abnormalities can be those of number, structure, or a combination of both. They affect the autosomes as well as the sex chromosomes. Often they are associated with such factors as advanced maternal age, radiation exposure, certain viral infections, and membership in a family with multiple cytogenetic defects. Once produced, these abnormalities are capable of perpetuating themselves.

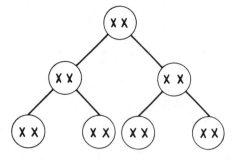

FIG 29−3. Normal mitoses (female).

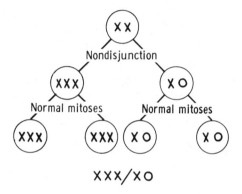

FIG 29−4. Formation of mosaic with 2 stem cells.

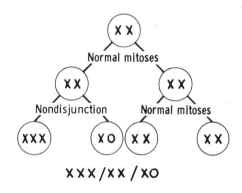

FIG 29−5. Formation of mosaic with 3 stem cells.

Abnormalities of Morphology

A. Nondisjunction: (See Figs 29−3 to 29−9.) Nondisjunction is failure of a chromatid pair to separate in a dividing cell. If it occurs in either the first or second divisions of meiosis, this results in gametes with abnormal chromosomal patterns. If it occurs in mitosis, **mosaic** patterns occur, ie, one area of an organism will have one genetic pattern and another area of the same organism another genetic pattern.

In medical practice, patients with a mosaic genetic constitution present an incomplete and variable clinical picture with features of each of the genetic syndromes represented in the mosaic.

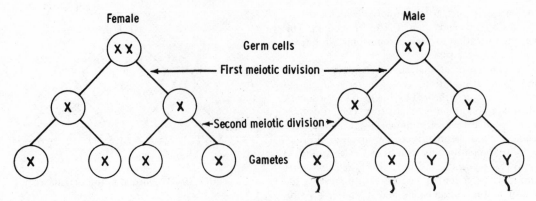

FIG 29–6. Normal meiosis.

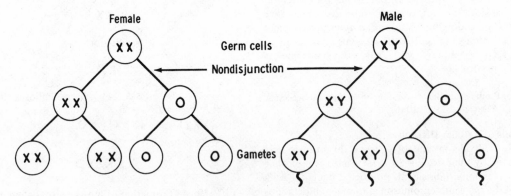

FIG 29–7. Formation of abnormal gametes by nondisjunction in first meiotic division.

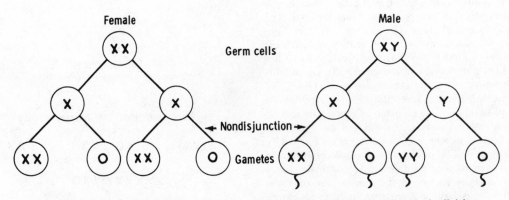

FIG 29–8. Formation of abnormal gametes by nondisjunction in second meiotic division.

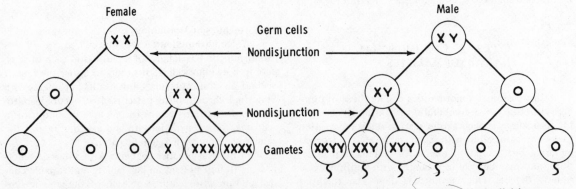

FIG 29–9. Formation of abnormal gametes by nondisjunction in first and second meiotic division.

TRANSLOCATION CHROMOSOME

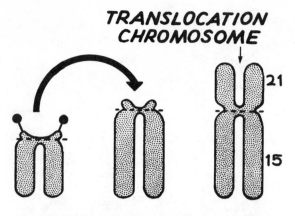

21

15

FIG 29–10. Diagrammatic representation of chromosomes 21 and 15 to show how one kind of translocation chromosome probably forms. A normal chromosome 21 is shown at left; the part above the stippled line breaks off (and is lost) as the translocation chromosome forms. A normal chromosome 15 is shown in the center; again the part above the stippled line breaks off and is lost. The abnormal translocation chromosome is shown being formed by end-to-end fusion of parts (below the stippled line) of chromosomes 21 and 15. (Redrawn and reproduced, with permission, from K.L. Moore: Human chromosomes. Review article. Canad MAJ 88:1071–1079, 1963.)

B. Translocation: (See Fig 29–10.) In translocation there is an exchange of chromosomal material between 2 nonhomologous chromosomes.

C. Deletion: In deletion there is a loss of chromosomal material due to breakage of a chromatid during cell division.

D. Duplication: If breakage occurs in a chromatid during cell division, the broken portion may realign itself so that many loci are duplicated on one chromosome and are entirely absent from the other member of the pair of chromosomes.

E. Occurrence of Isochromosomes: An isochromosome is a chromosome in which the arms on either side of the centromere have the same genetic material in the same order.

F. Inversion: Inversion occurs if, after fracture of a chromatid, the fragment reattaches itself to the same chromosome in an upside down manner. The same genetic material is present but is distributed in a different order.

Abnormalities of Chromosomal Number (Aneuploidy)

A. Monosomy: (Chromosomal number is 45.) In monosomy, only one member of a pair of chromosomes is present. *Example:* Stillborns, monosomy 21–22.

B. Trisomy: (Chromosomal number is 47.) Trisomy is caused by nondisjunction of a chromosome pair during the first meiotic division, with the result that 3 chromosomes are present instead of the usual 2. *Example:* Trisomy 13–15; 17–18; 21.

C. Polysomy: (Chromosomal number is 48 or more.) Polysomy occurs when one chromosome is represented 4 or more times. *Example:* XXXXY.

D. Complex Aneuploidy: In complex aneuploidy, 2 or more chromosomes have an abnormal variation in number; the structure of these chromosomes is normal. *Example:* Trisomy 21 and XXX in the same patient.

METHODS OF STUDY OF CHROMOSOMAL ABNORMALITIES

Several laboratory tests are available for the study of patients with known or suspected chromosomal aberrations: (1) the analysis of mature neutrophils for the presence of a nuclear appendage, the drumstick; (2) the study of cells for the presence of sex chromatin bodies (Barr bodies) in their nuclei; (3) analysis of chromosomes for fluorescence after treatment with quinacrine mustard; and (4) counting the chromosomes in the cells. The first 2 tests are easily obtainable, relatively inexpensive, and used for screening tests. The quinacrine mustard test is new. It is adaptable for a rapid screening test for the Y chromosome and, in its complete form, can be used for identifying all chromosomes. The chromosome count is a reliable but expensive test which at present can only be done by highly trained personnel in medical centers.

Peripheral Smear (See Fig 29–11.)

In a stained peripheral blood smear, the mature neutrophil may have a nuclear appendage called a drumstick–a solid, round, discrete head joined by a single thin strand of chromatin to a lobe of the neutrophil. It is approximately 1.5 μ in diameter and is visible at a magnification of × 90. It represents the sex chromatin. Normal females have a 1–3% incidence of drumsticks; normal males have none. (See Table 29–1.) A minimum of 200 mature neutrophils should be counted.

Sex Chromatin Analysis (See Fig 29–11.)

The sex chromatin (Barr) body is a solid, well defined planoconvex mass, approximately 1 μm in diameter, which is near or at the inner surface of the nuclear membrane. It is visible by light microscopy and, with proper staining, can be identified in all tissues of the body. The most frequent source of specimens for study is in the desquamated cells–buccal, vaginal, and amniotic. The sex chromatin body represents the heterochromatic X chromosome. The number of these chromatin bodies in a cell is one less than the number of X chromosomes in that cell. Females have an incidence of 40–60% and are "chromatin positive." Males do not possess these sex chromatin bodies and are therefore "chromatin negative." For an unknown reason, sex chromatin bodies are diminished in the first

TABLE 29–1. Sex chromosome abnormalities.*

Pheno-type	Drum-sticks	Sex Chromatin	Sex Chromosome	Chromosome Number	Clinical Picture
Female	Yes	Positive	XX	46	Normal female.
Female	No	Few smaller than normal Barr bodies (7%)	Xx (partial deletion)	46	Streak gonads. No 2° sex character-istics. Amenorrheic.
Female	No	Negative	XO	45	Turner's syndrome.
Female	Yes	Positive for 2 Barr bodies	XXX	47	Usually normally appearing female with mental retardation. Occasion-al menstrual disturbances and ab-sence of 2° sex characteristics.
Female	Yes	Positive for 3 Barr bodies	XXXX	48	Normal female with mental retarda-tion.
Female	Yes	Positive for 4 Barr bodies	XXXXX	49	Mental retardation with mongoloid facies and simian palmar crease.
Hermaph-rodite	Yes	Positive	XX	46	Variable phenotype. Both testicular and ovarian tissue in gonads.
Male	No	Negative	XY	46	Normal male.
Male	Yes	Positive for 1 Barr body	XXY	47	Klinefelter's syndrome.
Male	No	Negative	XYY	47	Undescended testes, ± mental retar-dation, irregularity of teeth. Tall (> 6 feet).
Male	No	Negative	XYYY	48	Mild psychomotor retardation, ingui-nal hernia, undescended testes, pul-monary stenosis, simian lines, den-tal dysplasia.
Male	Yes	Positive for 1 Barr body	XXYY	48	Klinefelter's syndrome.
Male	Yes	Positive for 2 Barr bodies	XXXY	48	Klinefelter's with more mental re-tardation and testicular atrophy.
Male	Yes	Positive for 3 Barr bodies	XXXXY	49	Mental retardation, hypoplastic ex-ternal genitals, and skeletal defects. Facies suggestive of Down's syn-drome.

*Normal male and normal female included for comparison.

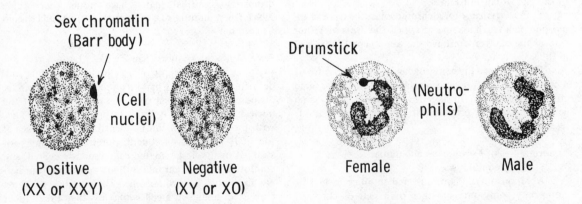

FIG 29–11. Normal chromatin and drumstick patterns. (Redrawn and reproduced, with permission, from R.R. Eggen: Cytogenetics: Review of newest advances in a new field of clinical pathology. Am J Clin Path 39:3–37, 1963.)

few days of life and during treatment with corticotropin, corticosteroids, testosterone, and progesterone. Diethylstilbestrol, on the other hand, causes a significant increase in sex chromatin bodies. The sex chromatin can be seen in the trophoblast at the 12th day, and in the embryo itself at the 16th day. Analysis of amniotic cells for sex chromatin can predict the sex of the unborn child.

The Quinacrine Mustard Test

Quinacrine mustard, a fluorescent material, binds itself to chromosomal DNA and gives each chromosome a characteristic fluorescent pattern that can be identified by photoelectric sensors. Since the fluorescence of the distal portion of the Y chromosome is characteristically the brightest, visual identification of Y is possible and reliable. This is the basis of the new and first screening test for the Y chromosome. It is applicable to all cells of the body.

Editorial: Dyeing the Y chromosome. Lancet 1:275, 1971.

Chromosomal Analysis

Chromosome analyses are done by growing cells of a biopsy in tissue culture, chemically inhibiting their mitoses at a specific phase (metaphase), and then sorting and counting the chromosomes. Specimens are most often taken from the peripheral blood, bone marrow, skin, and testes. A statistically significant number of cells must be counted.

The results of these analyses appear in the literature as either a karyotype or an idiogram. A **karyotype** (see Fig 29–12) is a drawing or photograph of a systematized array of chromosomes of a single cell. An **idiogram** is a diagrammatic arrangement of chromosomes which may be derived from one or many cells,

from the same or similar cases, and from one or many authors. Usually only one member of a pair of chromosomes is shown.

The present indications for this highly technical procedure are as follows: (1) Patients with malformations consistent with autosomal trisomy or deletion syndromes. (2) Parents of patients with a trisomy syndrome if the mother is younger than 30 years of age or if there are other similarly affected siblings. (3) Parents of all children with Down's syndrome who are found to be of the translocation or mosaic type. (4) Patients with an abnormality on drumstick or sex chromatin analysis. (5) Children who are grossly retarded physically or mentally, especially if there are associated anomalies. (6) All cases of intersex. (7) All females with evidence of Turner's syndrome, whether they are chromatin positive or chromatin negative. (8) All males with Klinefelter's disease, whether they are chromatin positive or chromatin negative. (9) Tall males (over 6 feet) with behavioral disorders.

AMNIOCENTESIS

Intrauterine diagnosis of certain chromosomal and genetic disorders is possible by cytogenetic and biochemical studies of amniotic cells obtained by transabdominal amniocentesis at about the 15th week of pregnancy. Chromosomal analysis detects the sex of the fetus and numerical or structural chromosomal defects whereas biochemical analysis uncovers certain inherited enzymatic disorders (Table 29–2). Indications for amniocentesis are as follows:

(1) Translocation carriers. *Example:* Down's syndrome from 15/21 translocation.

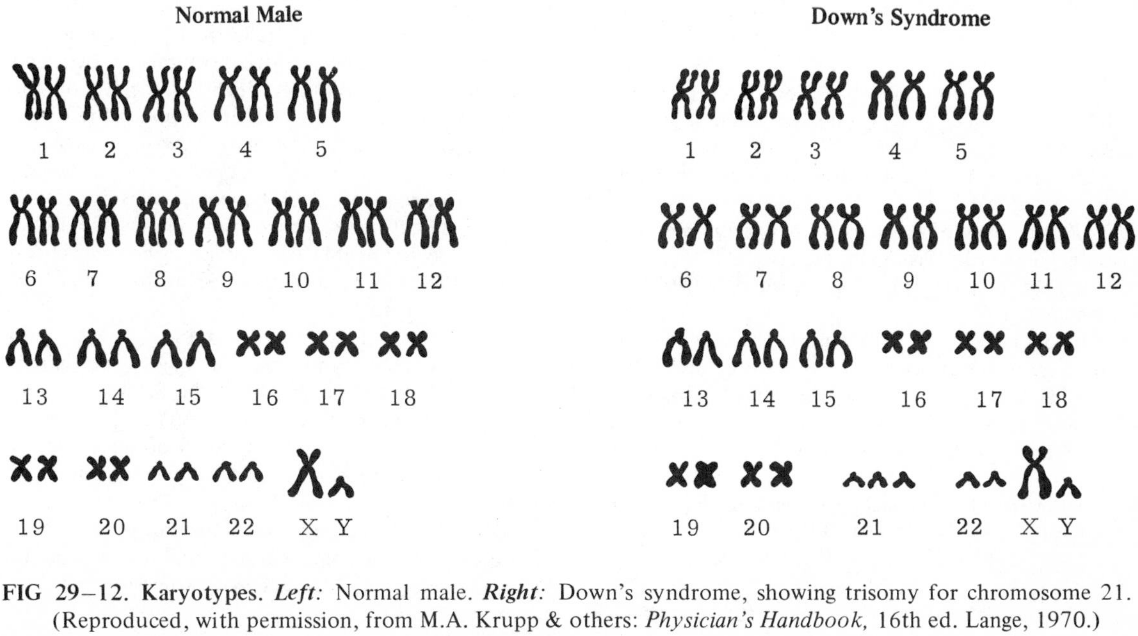

FIG 29–12. Karyotypes. *Left:* Normal male. *Right:* Down's syndrome, showing trisomy for chromosome 21. (Reproduced, with permission, from M.A. Krupp & others: *Physician's Handbook,* 16th ed. Lange, 1970.)

TABLE 29–2. Familial metabolic disorders
which have been detected in utero.*

Disorder	Method
Amniotic fluid	
Pompe's disease	Deficiency of a-1,4-glucosidase
Tay-Sachs disease	Deficiency of hexosaminidase A
Mucopolysaccharidosis	Quantitative and qualitative change in the mucopolysaccharides
Methylmalonic aciduria	Increased amounts of methylmalonate
Adrenogenital syndrome	Increased 17-ketosteroids and pregnanetriol
Uncultured amniotic fluid cells	
Pompe's disease	Deficiency of a-1,4-glucosidase; ultrastructural changes
Tay-Sachs disease	Deficiency of hexosaminidase A
Cultivated amniotic fluid cells	
Pompe's disease	Deficiency of a-1,4-glucosidase; ultrastructural changes
Galactosemia	Deficiency of galactose-1-phosphate uridyl transferase
X-linked uric aciduria	Autoradiography
Niemann-Pick disease	Deficiency of sphingomyelinase
Lysosomal acid phosphatase deficiency	Deficiency of lysosomal acid phosphatase
Fabry's disease	Deficiency of ceramide trihexosidase
Metachromatic leukodystrophy	Deficiency of aryl sulfatase A
Mucopolysaccharidosis	Metachromatic granules; abnormal $^{35}SO_4$-kinetics
Cystic fibrosis	Metachromatic granules
Marfan syndrome	Metachromatic granules
Tay-Sachs disease	Deficiency of hexosaminidase A
Miscellaneous material	
Methylmalonic aciduria	Methylmalonate excretion
Adrenogenital syndrome	Urinary estriol

*Reproduced, with permission, from H.L. Nadler: Indications for amniocentesis in early prenatal detection of genetic disorders. Birth Defects 7:7, 1971.

(2) Mothers over age 40. (There is an increasing incidence of Down's syndrome in infants born of women in this age group.)

(3) Carrier of X-linked disease. *Example:* Hemophilia.

(4) Members of families with certain metabolic disorders. *Example:* Tay-Sachs disease.

(5) Mother with previous trisomic Down's syndrome child.

In approximately 500 reported cases, the morbidity rate of the procedure was 1%. For the mother, the problem is infection, bleeding, and possible blood group sensitization. For the fetus, the risk is abortion, induced malformation, and puncture.

Milunsky, A., & others: Prenatal genetic diagnosis. New England J Med 283:1370, 1441, 1498, 1970.

CHROMOSOMAL DISORDERS

Frequency

Chromosomal anomalies occur surprisingly often. In studies of spontaneous abortions, 10–20% of the cases have chromosomal anomalies, the most frequent of which are triploidy, trisomy 18, and XO. With live births, trisomy of the sex chromosomes is most frequent. The XXX genotype is 1 per 1000 female births and the XXY is 2 per 1000 male births. Down's syndrome (trisomy 21) is the most frequent autosomal anomaly. Its incidence is 1 per 2000 if the mother is 25 and 1 per 100 if the mother is 40 or over. Trisomy 13 and 18 are 0.3 and 0.2 per 1000 live births, respectively.

Dhadial, D.E.L., Machin, A.M., & S.M. Tait: Chromosomal anomalies in spontaneously aborted fetuses. Lancet 1:20–21, 1970.

DISORDERS DUE TO ABNORMALITIES OF THE X & Y CHROMOSOMES

Most disorders of the sex chromosomes (Table 29–1) are compatible with life and do not display marked phenotypic abnormalities. With the exception of Turner's syndrome (XO), these disorders are due to an excess number of sex chromosomes. Both the multiple X and multiple Y syndromes have diverse clinical features. These include (singly or in combination) such problems as mental retardation, sterility, abnormal sex characteristics, and skeletal anomalies. Abnormal stature may also be associated with the sex chromosomes, since patients with Turner's syndrome are usually under 5 feet tall and those with a multiple Y syndrome are over 6 feet tall. In 1966, a study of inmates in maximum security hospitals in Scotland demonstrated an unusually high frequency of the multiple Y syndrome. This raised the possibility of the association of criminal behavior with a specific chromosomal defect. As more population surveys were done, it is now apparent that these conclusions reflect only the defects in selective sampling in the initial study. There is possibly an increase in behavioral disorders in the multiple Y syndrome, but these need not be criminal in nature.

At present, there are far more patients with known multiple X syndromes than with multiple Y syndromes. This may only reflect the fact that screening procedures for the X chromosomes have been available over 10 years whereas methods of screening for the Y chromosome have been available for only 1–2 years.

The **Lyon hypothesis** states that for patients with multiple X chromosome constitutions (including the normal female), only one X chromosome is genetically

TABLE 29–3. Autosomal disorders.

Type	Synonym	Signs
Monosomy		
Monosomy 21–22	. . .	Moderate mental retardation, antimongoloid slant of eyes, flared nostrils, small mouth, low-set ears, spade hands.
Trisomy		
Trisomy 13	Trisomy D: the "D" syndrome, Patau's syndrome	Severe mental retardation, congenital heart disease (77%), polydactyly, cerebral malformations, especially aplasia of olfactory bulbs, eye defects, low-set ears, cleft lip and palate, low birth weight, characteristic dermatoglyphic pattern.
Trisomy 18	Trisomy E: the "E" syndrome, Edward's syndrome	Severe mental retardation, long narrow skull with prominent occiput, congenital heart disease, flexion deformities of fingers, narrow palpebral fissures, low-set ears, harelip and cleft palate, characteristic dermatoglyphics, low birth weight.
Trisomy 21	Mongolism, Down's syndrome	Mental retardation, brachycephaly, prominent epicanthal folds, Brushfield spots, poor nasal bridge development, congenital heart disease, hypotonia, hypermobility of joints, characteristic dermatoglyphics.
Translocations		
15/21	Mongolism, Down's syndrome	Same as trisomy 21.
21/21	Mongolism, Down's syndrome	Same as trisomy 21.
22/21	Mongolism, Down's syndrome	Same as trisomy 21.
Deletions		
Short arm Chromosome 4 (4p–)	Wolf's syndrome	Severe growth and mental retardation, midline scalp defects, seizures, deformed iris, beak nose, hypospadias.
Short arm Chromosome 5 (5p–)	Cri du chat syndrome	Microcephaly, cat-like cry, hypertelorism with epicanthus, low-set ears, micrognathia, abnormal dermatoglyphics, low birth weight.
Long arm Chromosome 13 (13q–)	. . .	Microcephaly, psychomotor retardation, eye and ear defects, hypoplastic or absent thumbs.
Short arm Chromosome 18 (18p–)	. . .	Severe mental retardation, hypertelorism, low-set ears, flexion hand deformities.
Long arm Chromosome 18 (18q–)	. . .	Severe mental retardation, microcephaly, hypotonus, congenital heart disease, marked dimples at elbows, shoulders, knees.
Long arm Chromosome 21 (21q–)	. . .	Associated with chronic myelogenous leukemia.

active and capable of transmitting its information; the others became genetically inactive early in embryonic formation by an unknown mechanism. The same is suspected to be true for the multiple Y chromosome states, but there is no evidence to support this as yet.

Marinello, M.J., & others: A study of the XYY syndrome in tall men and juvenile delinquents. JAMA 208:321–325, 1969.

AUTOSOMAL DISORDERS

Although autosomes far outnumber the sex chromosomes, very few disorders are attributed to autosomal aberrations. The problem is in part due to the absence of a rapid screening test and in part due to the limitations of technologic methods which make it possible to detect only major chromosomal defects.

A few disorders can be recognized clinically (Table 29–3). Their chromosomal defects include monosomy, trisomy, translocations, and deletions. Other autosomal defects have been described, but there is no clearcut clinical description as yet. These include ring chromosomes of 13 and of 18; non-mongoloid trisomy G, and isochromosomes of D and possibly G.

The most prevalent autosomal disorder is Down's syndrome or mongolism. Ninety-five percent of cases are due to trisomy 21 and the remaining 5% are due to translocations of 15/21, 21/21, and 22/21 types. The trisomy 21 cases have an increasing frequency with advancing maternal age. The translocation cases account for the carrier state of Down's syndrome, for familial Down's syndrome, and the occurrence of Down's syndrome in younger mothers. Physical examination cannot distinguish between trisomy and translocation Down's syndrome.

Al-Aish, M.S., & others: Autosomal monosomy in man. New England J Med 277:777–784, 1967.

Allerdice, P.W., & others: The 13q deletion syndrome. Am J Human Genet 21:499–512, 1969.

De Grouchy, J.: The 18p-18q-18r syndromes. Birth Defects 5:74–87, 1969.

Lozzio, C.B.: Nonmongoloid trisomy G. Birth Defects 5:64–66, 1969.

Miller, D.J., Warburton, D., & W.R. Breg: Deletions of group B chromosomes. Birth Defects 5:100–105, 1969.

Polani, P.E.: Autosomal imbalance and its syndromes, excluding Down's. Brit M Bull 25:81–91, 1969.

Wolstenholme, G.E.W., & R. Porter: *Mongolism.* Ciba Foundation Study Group No. 25. Little, Brown, 1967.

CANCER

Studies of cancer patients indicate that genetic factors play a role in only a small percentage of cases. With carcinoma of the stomach, breast, colon, prostate, and endometrium, a hereditary factor with a site-specific basis is operating, for relatives of a patient with these malignancies have a 3-fold higher risk of having the same malignancy. Only rarely do the mendelian laws of inheritance appear. In general, the majority of cases of cancer are of unknown cause.

Chromosomes & Malignancy

A. Chromosome Breakage Syndromes: Three rare autosomal recessive diseases—Bloom's syndrome, Fanconi's anemia, and Mme Louis-Bar syndrome (ataxia-telangiectasia) have a tendency to chromosomal breakage and rearrangement in vitro. In addition, each of these diseases has a relatively high incidence of neoplasia, primarily leukemia and lymphoma. At this time, the role of chromosomal breakage in the production of malignancy is speculative.

B. Leukemia: Cytogenetic studies of leukemias reveal many abnormalities, but only with chronic myelogenous leukemia (see below) are the findings consistent and significant. In acute leukemias, about 50% of the reported cases with cytogenetic studies have chromosomal abnormalities. These are usually aneuploidy, mainly diploidy. No specific chromosome or group of chromosomes is involved. In a given case, the defect persists for the duration of the disease, and if it disappears with remission, the same defect recurs with the reappearance of leukemia. In chronic lymphocytic leukemia, again no specific abnormality is noted. The Christchurch (Ch) chromosome, initially implicated, is now recognized as a family marker chromosome. Other myeloproliferative syndromes have no consistent cytogenetic defect.

In **chronic myelogenous leukemia,** many patients have an abnormal (Ph) chromosome in their leukemic cells in the peripheral blood and bone marrow, both before and after treatment. This chromosome is most likely number 21 with its long arms shortened. Patients with chronic myelogenous leukemia can be divided into 2 groups on the basis of this chromosomal defect. Those that have the defect (Ph-positive) have clinical and hematologic features of typical chronic myelogenous leukemia, respond rapidly to chemotherapy, and are easily controlled therapeutically. Their average age at time of diagnosis is 52, and their survival is longer than that of Ph-negative patients. The Ph-negative group are clinically and hematologically, heterogenous, with an average age of 65. Most respond poorly to treatment and die in the first year of their disease. Although the Ph chromosome appears to have this diagnostic and prognostic value, the exact significance of its presence is not known.

C. Lymphoma: Lymphomas resemble other solid tumors in having no characteristic karyotype. Most chromosome counts are in the hyperploid range. Recently, Spiers found a deletion of the short and long arms of chromosome E17–18 in a few cases of Hodgkin's disease, follicular lymphoma, and reticulum cell sarcoma. This defect is called the Melbourne chromosome, and a relationship to the tumors is suggested.

D. Solid Tumors: The presence of nuclear hyperchromatism and abnormal mitotic figures in tumor cells has led many investigators to undertake the chromosomal analysis of solid malignant tumors. No consistent chromosomal pattern occurs in any type of malignant tumor, but certain generalities emerge from these studies.

1. Abnormalities in chromosomal number and structure—The chromosomal count is usually greater than 46 and is most often polyploidy or near polyploidy, ie, a multiple of the haploid number 23. Most of the additional number of chromosomes fit into the known chromosomal groups. Occasionally an abnormally shaped chromosome (ring, etc) called a "marker" is present and is able to perpetuate itself. The latter probably arises from abnormal chromosomal breakage and union.

2. Wide scatter of the chromosome count—Unlike normal tissue, tumor tissue shows a wide scatter of the chromosomal count around the modal chromosome number. The modal number is not specific for any particular tumor.

3. One of 2 stemline cells is present in each tumor—Stemline cells are cells with identical numerical or structural features that represent the largest percentage of the cell population. These stemline cells remain constant for a given tumor and are not altered by treatment. The chromosomal structure of tumor cells of malignant effusions and metastases is usually the same as that of the parent tumor. Interestingly, another tumor of the same pathologic diagnosis may have different stemline cells.

Conen, P.E.: Chromosome studies in leukemia. Canad MAJ 96:1599–1604, 1967.

German, J.: Bloom's syndrome. I. Genetical and clinical observations in the first 27 patients. Am J Human Genet 21:196–227, 1969.

Hecht, F., & others: Leukemia and lymphocytes in ataxia-telangiectasia. Lancet 2:1193, 1966.

Sandberg, A.A., & D.K. Hossfield: Chromosomal abnormalities in human neoplasia. Ann Rev Med 21:379–408, 1970.

Sandberg, A.A., & others: Chromosomes and the causation of human cancer and leukemia. V. Karyotypic aspects of acute leukemia. Cancer 22:1268–1282, 1968.

Spiers, A., & A.G. Baikie: Cytogenetic studies in malignant lymphomas and related neoplasms: Results in 27 cases. Cancer 22:193–217, 1968.

CHROMOSOMES & IONIZING RADIATION

The major problem of ionizing radiation is not the danger of lethal doses but of small doses that allow the cells to multiply after permanent alteration of their genetic material.

Detectable chromosomal changes occur after diagnostic and therapeutic x-ray as well as with beta and gamma radiation (^{131}I, ^{32}P). These usually persist for a few hours to several weeks. In vitro studies reveal a direct relationship between the dose of ionizing radiation and the number of chromosomal abnormalities.

Spar, I.L.: Genetic effects of radiation. M Clin North America 53:965, 1969.

Uchida, I., Holunga R., & C. Lawler: Maternal radiation and chromosomal aberrations. Lancet 2:1045–1048, 1968.

VIRUSES, CHEMICALS, & CHROMOSOMES

For more than half a century, viruses and chemicals have been known to induce chromosomal aberrations in plants and animals. Only in the past decade have human chromosomal defects been proved to be caused by these agents. The measles and chickenpox viruses may cause chromosomal aberrations in the leukocytes which may persist for several months after the clinical illness. Drugs such as ozone, analogous and intermediary metabolites of nucleic acids, and alkylating agents have deleterious effects on chromosomes. A recent study of workers exposed to the leukemogen, benzene, reveals an increased amount of structural chromosomal abnormalities in their peripheral blood cells.

It is hoped that these new findings will add to our understanding of "spontaneous" chromosomal changes as well as chemical carcinogenesis.

Shaw, M.W.: Chromosomal damage by chemical agents. Ann Rev Med 21:409–431, 1970.

GENETIC COUNSELING

Genetic counseling is available in many medical centers to inform members of a family with an inherited disorder of the recurrence risk. In certain disorders, intrauterine diagnosis by amniocentesis (see above) can clarify the problem. Otherwise, the first prerequisite is a definite diagnosis, since closely related disorders, especially biochemical defects, may have a markedly different prognosis and mode of inheritance. It is well to examine as many members of a family as possible for evidence of the disorder in order to clarify the pattern of inheritance. This includes normals as well as suspects.

When the diagnosis of a genetic disorder has been established, the physician is obliged to inform the family of its heritable nature, to mention the chance of recurrence, and to explain the range of possible defects. Above all, common sense must guide the counselor in explanation and recommendation to the family. With this information, the parents can better decide whether or not to have more children.

Reisman, L.E., & A.P. Malheny, Jr.: *Genetics & Counseling in Medical Practice.* Mosby, 1969.

●　　●　　●

General Bibliography

(For additional references, see Chapter 19.)

Bartolos, M.: *Genetics in Medical Practice.* Lippincott, 1968.

Carter, C.O.: An ABC of medical genetics. Lancet 1:1014–1016, 1041–1044, 1087–1090, 1139–1141, 1203–1206, 1252–1256, 1303–1305, 1969. [Also available in book form, published by Little, Brown, 1969.]

Ford, C.E., & H. Harris (editors): New aspects of human genetics. Brit M Bull 25:1–118, 1969.

Hamerton, J.L.: *Human Cytogenetics.* Vol 1. Academic Press, 1971.

Hsia, D.Y.-Y.: The diagnosis of carriers of disease-producing genes. Ann New York Acad Sc 134:946–964, 1966.

Hsia, D.Y.-Y., & T. Inouye: *Inborn Errors of Metabolism.* Part 1. Year Book, 1966.

McKusick, V.A.: *Heritable Disorders of Connective Tissue,* 3rd ed. Mosby, 1966.

McKusick, V.A.: *Human Genetics,* 2nd ed. Prentice Hall, 1969.

McKusick, V.A.: Human genetics. In: *Annual Review of Genetics.* Vol 4. H.L. Roman (editor). Annual Reviews, 1970.

Roberts, J.A.: *An Introduction to Medical Genetics,* 5th ed. Oxford Univ Press, 1970.

Rowley, J.D.: Cytogenetics in clinical medicine. JAMA 207:914–919, 1969.

Stanbury, J.B., Wyngaarden, J.B., & D.S. Fredrickson (editors): *The Metabolic Basis of Inherited Disease.* McGraw-Hill, 1966.

Stevenson, A.C., & B.C.C. Davison: *Genetic Counselling.* Lippincott, 1970.

Titus, J.L., & R.V. Pierre: Chromosomal analysis in clinical medicine. M Clin North America 54:1009–1028, 1970.

Townes, P.L. (editor): Genetics in clinical medicine. M Clin North America 53:739–1015, 1969.

Townes, P.L., & M.S. Adams: Cytogenetics and genetics. P Clin North America 15:493–512, 1968.

Turpin, R., & J. Lejeune: *Human Afflictions and Chromosomal Aberrations.* Pergamon, 1969.

30 . . .
Malignant Disorders

Sydney E. Salmon

Although neoplastic disorders have been discussed in the context of the organ system of their origin elsewhere in this book, certain general features of malignancy as a systemic disease which have relevance to a variety of neoplasms require special emphasis. These features include (1) unusual symptoms and syndromes which may be important in the diagnosis and management of cancer, (2) the diagnosis and treatment of emergency problems and complications of malignancy, and (3) cancer chemotherapy.

THE PARANEOPLASTIC SYNDROMES

The clinical manifestations of malignancy usually appear to be due to pressure effects of local tumor growth or to infiltration or metastatic deposition of tumor cells in a variety of organs in the body, or to certain systemic symptoms. Except in the case of functioning tumors such as those of the endocrine glands, systemic symptoms of malignancies usually are not specific and often consist of weakness, anorexia, and weight loss. In the paraneoplastic syndromes ("beyond tumor growth"), rather bizarre symptoms and signs may occur, producing clinical findings resembling those of primary endocrine, metabolic, hematologic, or neuromuscular disorders. At present, the possible mechanisms for such effects can be classed in 3 groups: (1) effects initiated by a tumor product (eg, carcinoid syndrome), (2) effects of destruction of normal tissues by tumor (eg, hypercalcemia with osteolytic skeletal metastases), and (3) effects due to unknown mechanisms (eg, osteoarthropathy with bronchogenic carcinoma). In some of the paraneoplastic syndromes associated with ectopic hormone production, tumor tissue itself has been found to contain and secrete the hormone which produces the syndrome.

The paraneoplastic syndromes are of considerable clinical importance for the following reasons:

(1) They sometimes accompany relatively limited neoplastic growth and may provide the clinician with an early clue to the presence of certain types of cancer. In some cases, early diagnosis may favorably affect the prognosis.

(2) The pathologic (metabolic or toxic) effects of the syndrome may constitute a more urgent hazard to the patient's life than the underlying malignancy (eg, hypercalcemia, hyponatremia) and may respond to treatment even though the underlying neoplasm does not.

(3) Effective treatment of the tumor should be accompanied by resolution of the paraneoplastic syndrome, and, conversely, recurrence of the cancer may be heralded by return of the systemic symptoms.

Not all endocrine or metabolic syndromes associated with cancer are necessarily "paraneoplastic." In some instances, the secretory product or syndrome results from the continuation of function of the normal precursor cell type which became malignant. In these instances, the function of the tumor cell may be a normal one exaggerated enormously in magnitude (eg, adrenal carcinoma, insulinoma, and carcinoid syndrome) by the increased number of functioning cells. Although the details of the mechanism of some metabolic effects are not known, in some instances the identical symptom complex (eg, hypercalcemia) may be induced by entirely different mechanisms. Hypercalcemia may in some instances be due to parathormone production by the tumor or to direct invasion of the skeleton by metastases of the tumor; in still other cases (eg, breast cancer), osteolytic sterols produced by the tumor have been implicated in the development of osteolysis and hypercalcemia. In each of these situations, effective treatment of the malignancy is usually associated with normalization of the serum calcium, although nonspecific supportive measures may also be of benefit.

Frequently reported paraneoplastic syndromes and endocrine secretions associated with certain functional malignancies are summarized in Table 30–1. Although this list is not complete, it indicates the variety of syndromes and abnormalities which have been described. The pathophysiologic explanation for many of these abnormalities remains unclear; however, recognition of such associations can be quite useful.

Bower, B., & G. Gordan: Endocrine effects of non-endocrine tumors. Ann Rev Med 16:83, 1965.

Brain, W.R.B., & F.H. Norris: *The Remote Effects of Cancer on the Nervous System.* Grune & Stratton, 1965.

Liddle, G.W., & others: Clinical and laboratory studies of ectopic humoral syndromes. Recent Progr Hormone Res 25:283–314, 1969.

TABLE 30–1. Paraneoplastic syndromes and certain endocrine secretions associated with cancer.

Hormone Excess or Syndrome	Bronchogenic Carcinoma	Breast Carcinoma	Renal Carcinoma	Adrenal Carcinoma	Hepatoma	Multiple Myeloma	Lymphoma	Thymoma	Prostatic Carcinoma	Pancreatic Carcinoma	Choriocarcinoma
Hypercalcemia	++	++++	++	++	+	++++	+	+	++	+	+
Cushing's syndrome	+++		+	+++				++	+	++	
Inappropriate ADH secretion	+++									+	
Hypoglycemia				+	++		+				
Gonadotropins	+				+						++++
Thyrotropin											+++
Polycythemia			+++		++						
Erythroid aplasia								++			
Fever			+++		++		+++	++		+	
Neuromyopathy	++	+						++	+	+	
Dermatomyositis	++	+								+	
Coagulopathy	+	++			+	+			+++	+++	
Thrombophlebitis			+						+	+++	
Immunologic deficiency						+++	+++	+++			

DIAGNOSIS & TREATMENT OF EMERGENCIES & COMPLICATIONS OF MALIGNANT DISEASE

Malignancies are chronic diseases, but acute emergency complications do develop. Such complications may be due either to local accumulations of tumor, as in spinal cord compression, superior vena cava syndrome, and malignant effusions; or to more generalized, systemic effects of cancer, as in hypercalcemia, septicemia and opportunistic infections, disseminated intravascular coagulation, hyperuricemia, and carcinoid syndrome. Although some of these acute problems arise in nonmalignant disorders, their severity and treatment are often somewhat different. Obviously, the acute complications of neoplastic disease must be treated even if the underlying malignancy is incurable. Indeed, one of the most important aspects of management of the patient with advanced cancer is the recognition and effective treatment of such acute problems.

Relatively few complications of malignancy are true emergencies—ie, it is not often essential to institute antineoplastic therapy within minutes. However, they should be recognized and treated promptly. Complications which may require true emergency management include hypercalcemia, severe hyperuricemia, severe carcinoid symptoms, and rapidly forming effusions in the pericardium or pleural space.

SPINAL CORD COMPRESSION

Spinal cord compression due to tumor is manifested by progressive weakness and sensory changes in the lower extremities, back pain, and blockage of contrast material as shown by myelography. It occurs as a complication of lymphoma or multiple myeloma, carcinomas of the lung, prostate, breast, and colon, and certain other neoplasms. Back pain at the level of the lesion occurs in 80% of cases. Since involvement is usually extradural, a mixture of nerve root and spinal cord symptoms often develops.

The initial findings of impending cord compression may be quite subtle, and this possibility should always be considered when patients with malignancy develop unexplained weakness of the lower extremities or back pain. Prompt diagnosis and therapy are essential if paraplegia, quadriglegia, or other types of permanent residual or spinal cord damage are to be prevented. Once paralysis develops, it is usually irreversible. Conversely, patients who are treated promptly may have complete return of function and may respond favorably to subsequent therapy of the malignancy.

The management of spinal cord compression often requires prompt intervention by a team of specialists: The patient's primary physician or a medical oncologist should coordinate the diagnostic and therapeutic program with the help of the radiologist, radiotherapist, and neurosurgeon. When the symptoms and the results of the neurologic examination are consistent with a diagnosis of cord compression, an emergency myelogram should be performed, usually by a neurosurgeon, who then also follows the patient in case decompression laminectomy becomes necessary. If a block is demonstrated on myelography, the contrast medium is often left in the spinal canal, so that alleviation of the block can subsequently be demonstrated on follow-up x-rays after treatment.

Emergency treatment consists of (1) mechlorethamine (nitrogen mustard, Mustargen®), freshly mixed, 0.4 mg/kg IV; (2) prednisone, 60 mg/day orally for 5–7 days, with subsequent tapering; and (3) radiotherapy to the involved area, usually initiated within 24 hours and continued to tolerance in a relatively short intensive course.

If treatment is begun promptly, decompression laminectomy is rarely indicated except in patients with extremely rapid progression of signs and symptoms. Patients must be followed closely, as occasional patients may require surgical intervention.

When the block is relieved, the flow of contrast in the remainder of the canal should be assessed, as blocks due to tumor (especially lymphoma) often are multiple.

Once the cord problem has subsided, systemic chemotherapy for the malignancy is indicated.

SUPERIOR VENA CAVA SYNDROME

Superior vena cava syndrome is a potentially fatal complication of bronchogenic carcinoma, occasional lymphomas, and certain other neoplasms which metastasize to the mediastinum. It is characterized by brawny edema and flushing of the head and neck and dilated neck and arm veins. The onset of symptoms is acute or subacute. Venous pressure in the upper extremities is increased, and bilateral brachial venography demonstrates a block to the flow of contrast material into the right heart as well as large collateral veins. The patient is often in a state of low cardiac output and is at risk of sudden death from cardiovascular collapse. Although the underlying carcinoma is usually incurable when the syndrome develops, emergency therapy for this complication can provide effective palliation for 6 months or more and is not necessarily a terminal event. Since this complication may be rapidly fatal, treatment should be initiated within

hours of recognition. Treatment is sometimes indicated even when the diagnosis of cancer has not been confirmed histologically since the syndrome is almost always due to cancer and thoracotomy would likely lead to fatality. In such unproved cases of cancer, the block should be unequivocally demonstrated angiographically, and other signs of tumor should be present on chest x-ray as well.

Emergency treatment consists of (1) administration of freshly mixed mechlorethamine, 0.4 mg/kg IV, to initiate tumor shrinkage; (2) intravenous injection of a potent parenteral diuretic (eg, ethacrynic acid) to relieve the edematous component of vena caval compression; and (3) mediastinal irradiation, starting within 24 hours, with a treatment plan designed to give a high daily dose but a short total course of therapy to rapidly shrink the local tumor even further. Intensive combined therapy will reverse the process in up to 90% of patients.

The ultimate prognosis depends on the nature of the primary neoplasm. Even in bronchogenic carcinoma, occasional patients have slowly growing tumors which may not cause further symptoms for considerable periods of time.

MALIGNANT EFFUSIONS

The development of effusions in closed compartments such as the pleural, pericardial, and peritoneal spaces presents significant diagnostic and therapeutic problems in patients with advanced neoplasms. Most malignant effusions are not acute emergencies, but they can be if they accumulate unusually rapidly or occur in the pericardial space. Although direct involvement (thickening) of the serous surface with tumor appears to be the most frequent initiating factor in such cases, not all effusions in cancer patients are malignant. Benign processes such as congestive heart failure, pulmonary embolus, trauma, and infection (eg, tuberculosis) may be responsible, mimicking the effects of a neoplasm. Bloody effusions are usually malignant but occasionally are due to embolus with infarction or trauma. Cytology or cell block of the fluid—or hook needle biopsy (eg, with the Cope pleural biopsy needle)—should be used to prove that the effusion is truly neoplastic before local therapy is employed to prevent recurrence. Pericardial effusions should be tapped with continuous ECG monitoring by means of a V lead attached to the pericardiocentesis needle so that the epicardium will be detected should it be contacted.

The management of malignant effusions should be appropriate to the severity of involvement. Effusions due to lung, ovarian, and breast carcinoma often require more than simple drainage. In other neoplasms, simple drainage is sometimes sufficient, especially if it coincides with the initiation of effective systemic chemotherapy. Drainage of a large pleural effusion can be accomplished rapidly and with relative safety with a closed system using a disposable phlebotomy set which is connected to a vacuum phlebotomy bottle after the needle has been passed through the skin of the thorax. Thoracentesis performed in this fashion requires very little manipulation of the patient and prevents the problems of inadvertent pneumothorax associated with multiple changes of a stopcock connected to a syringe. Nonetheless, post-tap films are indicated after thoracentesis to assess the results and to rule out pneumothorax.

Recurrent effusions which do not respond to repeated taps may often be controlled by instillation of either mechlorethamine or quinacrine (Atabrine®). Mechlorethamine injection will eliminate or suppress an effusion in 2/3 of patients with effusions due to carcinoma. The alkylating agent triethylenethiophosphoramide (Thio-TEPA®) appears to be preferable for suppression of ascites since it produces less local pain and discomfort in the peritoneum than do the other agents.

The procedure is as follows: Most of the pleural, ascitic, or pericardial fluid is withdrawn. While a free flow of fluid is still present, mechlorethamine is instilled into the cavity. The dose employed is 0.4 mg/kg, or a total dose of 20–30 mg in the usual patient. The solution should be freshly mixed at the time of injection to avoid hydrolysis prior to administration. After the drug is injected and the needle withdrawn, the patient is placed in a variety of positions in order to distribute the drug throughout the cavity. On the following day, the remaining fluid is withdrawn from the body cavity. Inasmuch as mechlorethamine and triethylenethiophosphoramide are absorbed systemically from the cavity, this treatment is not advised for patients who already have significant pancytopenia or bone marrow depression due to prior chemotherapy. In such cases, quinacrine is substituted for the alkylating agent inasmuch as it does not produce hematopoietic depression. Quinacrine is usually administered into the cavity in a dose of 200 mg/day for 5 days, with daily drainage of residual fluid.

Nausea and vomiting commonly follow the instillation of mechlorethamine but can often be controlled with prophylactic administration of an antiemetic prior to the procedure and at intervals afterward. Pleural pain and fever may occur after intracavitary administration of either alkylating agents or quinacrine but are more common with the latter compound. Narcotic analgesics are indicated for pain during the acute period; however, the need for these usually abates within several days. Once a pleural space or other potential space has been effectively sealed with such drug treatments, recurrent effusion is usually not a problem.

Dollinger, M.R., Krakoff, I.H., & D.A. Karnofsky: Quinacrine (Atabrine) in the treatment of neoplastic effusions. Ann Int Med 66:249–257, 1967.

HYPERCALCEMIA

Hypercalcemia secondary to malignancy is a fairly common medical emergency. It is particularly frequent in breast carcinoma and multiple myeloma but occurs also with a variety of other cancers, all of which need not metastasize to bone to initiate the syndrome. The typical findings consist of anorexia, nausea, vomiting, constipation, muscular weakness and hyporeflexia; confusion, psychosis, tremor, and lethargy; and elevated serum calcium. However, a wide range of symptom complexes may be observed, and sometimes the only abnormal finding will be an elevated serum calcium. ECG often shows a shortening of the Q–T interval. When the serum calcium rises above 12 mg/100 ml, sudden death due to cardiac arrhythmia or asystole may occur. The tragic medical and social consequences of untreated hypercalcemia are best illustrated in the instance of the young mother with breast cancer who dies of unrecognized hypercalcemia. Inasmuch as the underlying cancer can often be palliated for many years after an episode of hypercalcemia, this complication of malignancy need not indicate a poor prognosis and should be treated as a medical emergency.

In the absence of signs or symptoms of hypercalcemia, an elevated serum calcium should be repeated immediately to exclude the possibility of laboratory error.

Emergency treatment for hypercalcemia due to malignancy consists of (1) intravenous fluids, 3–4 liters/day (including saline infusions); (2) low-calcium diet; (3) prednisone, 60–80 mg/day orally for 4–5 days, followed by tapering; (4) intravenous administration of a potent diuretic (eg, ethacrynic acid [Edecrin®]) once saline infusion has been initiated; and (5) for severe hypercalcemia (greater than 15 mg/100 ml), mithramycin (Mithracin®), 25 μg/kg/day by slow IV infusion for 3–4 days. Although mithramycin therapy is often effective in relieving hypercalcemia and can be used less frequently for chronic management, the drug has significant toxicities, including a potential hemorrhagic syndrome. In most instances, however, only several doses are required, and these complications are unlikely to occur. At present, the use of mithramycin must be limited to cases of very severe or refractory hypercalcemia for which other treatment is not effective.

If alternative therapy is needed for refractory cases, intravenous 8–10 hour infusions of isotonic sodium sulfate, once daily for 1 or 2 days, will often reduce the serum calcium very rapidly. Patients treated with sodium sulfate will receive extremely large sodium loads with this treatment inasmuch as the isotonic solution used for infusion contains 38.9 gm of sodium sulfate per liter and up to 3 liters have been given. Such treatment, although effective, may induce hypernatremia, and the patient's condition must be such that a sodium load can be tolerated. Patients with uremia may be made worse, and the serum sodium may climb to 160 mEq/liter. Patients with cardiac disease who are susceptible to congestive failure may be pushed into overt heart failure. Thus, there is no standard dosage, and the patient must be both carefully selected and closely watched. Sodium phosphate infusions are not advisable since they are associated with extreme danger of metastatic calcification in addition to the hypernatremic effects.

Once the acute hypercalcemic episode has been treated, it is usually appropriate to begin systemic chemotherapy. In the instance of breast cancer, hypercalcemia may appear as a "flare" after initiation of estrogen therapy. In most instances, it is advisable to discontinue the estrogen and change to a different form of chemotherapy. If chronic hypercalcemia persists—even if only to a moderate degree—the patient should be treated with small doses of prednisone or oral sodium phosphate supplements (1—2 gm/day) and encouraged to maintain a high fluid intake in the hope of preventing renal damage. When phosphate is used, if no alternative source of phosphate is available, disposable Fleet's Phospho-Soda® enemas can be given orally. (*Caution:* Excessive dosage will lead to diarrhea.) In most instances, when the malignancy responds to chemotherapy, hypercalcemia subsides.

Chakmakian, Z.H., & J.E. Bethune: Sodium sulfate treatment of hypercalcemia. New England J Med 275:862, 1966.
Perlia, C.P., & others: Mithramycin in the treatment of hypercalcemia. Cancer 25:389, 1970.

HYPERURICEMIA &
ACUTE URATE NEPHROPATHY

Increased blood levels of uric acid are often observed in patients with neoplasms who are receiving cancer chemotherapy. In this circumstance, hyperuricemia should more appropriately be viewed as a preventable complication rather than an acute emergency, inasmuch as uric acid formation can be inhibited prophylactically. At present, hematologic neoplasms such as leukemia, lymphoma, and myeloma most frequently present the problem of hyperuricemia after therapy, but hyperuricemia may occur with any form of malignancy which undergoes rapid destruction and release of nucleic acid constituents, and in some instances prophylaxis will not have been given. Less commonly, certain rapidly proliferating neoplasms with a high nucleic acid turnover (eg, acute leukemia) may be present with hyperuricemia even in the absence of prior chemotherapy. If the patient is also receiving a thiazide diuretic, the problem may be compounded by decreased urate excretion. Routine follow-up of patients receiving cancer chemotherapy should include measurements of serum uric acid and creatinine as well as complete blood counts. Rapid elevation of the serum uric acid concentration usually does not produce gouty arthritis in these patients but does present

the danger of acute urate nephropathy. In this form of acute renal failure, uric acid crystallizes in the distal tubules, the collecting ducts, and the renal parenchyma. The danger of uric acid nephropathy is present when the serum urate concentration is above 15 mg/100 ml, and in some instances it may rise to as high as 80 mg/100 ml.

Prophylactic therapy consists of the administration of allopurinol (Zyloprim®), 200 mg 3 times daily, starting 1 day prior to the initiation of chemotherapy. Administration of allopurinol inhibits xanthine oxidase and prevents conversion of the highly soluble hypoxanthine and xanthine to the relatively insoluble uric acid. Patients who are to receive mercaptopurine (Purinethol®) for cancer chemotherapy should have its dose reduced to 25—35% of the usual dose if they are also receiving allopurinol, inasmuch as the latter drug potentiates both the effects and toxicity of mercaptopurine.

Emergency therapy for established severe hyperuricemia consists of (1) hydration with 3—4 liters of fluid per day; (2) alkalinization of the urine with 6—8 gm of sodium bicarbonate per day (in order to enhance urate solubility); (3) allopurinol (Zyloprim®), 200 mg 4 times daily orally; and (4) in severe cases, with serum urate levels above 25—30 mg/100 ml, emergency hemodialysis or peritoneal dialysis. *Caution:* Once the uropathy is established, items 1—3 are in fact dangerous until some means of getting rid of excess fluid is assured.

Since patients who suffer from this complication are often in the process of entering a stage of complete remission of the neoplasm, the prognosis is good if renal damage can be prevented.

BACTERIAL SEPSIS IN
CANCER PATIENTS

Many patients with disseminated neoplasms have increased susceptibility to infection. In some instances this results from impaired host defense mechanisms (eg, acute leukemia, Hodgkin's disease, multiple myeloma, chronic lymphocytic leukemia); in other patients it results from the myelosuppressive and immunosuppressive effects of cancer chemotherapy or a combination of these factors. In patients with acute leukemia and in those with granulocytopenia (less than 600 granulocytes per cu mm), infection is a medical emergency. Although fever alone does not prove the presence of infection, in these patients as well as in patients with multiple myeloma or chronic lymphocytic leukemia fever is virtually pathognomonic of infection. While infections in patients with myeloma or chronic leukemia are often due to pneumococcus or other sensitive organisms, patients with leukemia or pancytopenia are far less fortunate, as resistant gram-negative organisms are more often responsible. Appropriate cultures (eg, blood, sputum, urine, CSF) should always be obtained prior to initiation of therapy; however, one usually cannot await the results of these studies before initiating bactericidal antibiotic therapy. The results of Gram stains may be quite rewarding if they clearly show a predominant organism in the sputum, urine, or CSF.

Emergency Treatment

In the absence of granulocytopenia and in nonleukemic patients, the empirical combination of cephalosporin (Keflin®) and kanamycin (Kantrex®) has proved exceedingly useful for patients with acute bacteremia. Therapy with combinations of this nature must be given judiciously, as they are of very broad spectrum; they should always be replaced by the most appropriate antibiotics as soon as culture data become available. The combination of cephalosporin and kanamycin is ineffective against pseudomonas infection. In the current era of intensive chemotherapy of cancer, bacteremic infection with pseudomonas is now the most frequent infection in granulocytopenic patients and is all too often fulminant and fatal within 72 hours. Recent observations suggest that prompt institution of combination therapy with gentamicin (Garamycin®) and carbenicillin (Geopen®, Pyopen®) offers the best chance of curing pseudomonas bacteremia in cancer patients. Because of drug interactions, these 2 compounds cannot be mixed but must be administered separately. This combination is of lesser efficacy against *Escherichia coli* sepsis and should not be used for that purpose.

Granulocyte transfusions have recently been proved to have significant value in the treatment of granulocytopenic cancer patients with sepsis; however, at the present time, the complex procurement procedures have limited their availability almost entirely to large regional cancer institutes.

Schimpff, S., & others: Empiric therapy with carbenicillin and gentamicin for febrile patients with cancer and granulocytopenia. New England J Med 284:1061, 1971.

OPPORTUNISTIC INFECTIONS

Unusual infections also worthy of mention include *Pneumocystis carinii*, disseminated herpes zoster, and candida sepsis. These infections are due to "opportunistic pathogens" and virtually always occur in impaired hosts (eg, Hodgkin's disease or immunosuppression). The diagnosis of pneumocystis infection is currently difficult to establish short of lung biopsy (serologic tests may be available soon). Although pneumocystis usually occurs during chemotherapy, it has been seen in patients who have recently attained complete remission of malignancy. Once the diagnosis of pneumocystis infection is established, treatment with pentamidine isethionate (Lomidine®) is indicated and may be curative. This drug, although not commercially

available, can be obtained from the US Public Health Service in Atlanta. Also recently made available from this source is zoster-immune globulin (ZIG). Although chickenpox is normally a benign illness and herpes zoster is usually uncomplicated although painful, the varicella virus can cause extensive skin involvement, pneumonia, encephalitis, hemorrhage, and other manifestations of dissemination in patients with Hodgkin's disease and other malignancies. The efficacy of ZIG in such circumstances remains to be established, although it is likely to be of some benefit.

The diagnosis of candida sepsis can often be based on blood culture, urine culture, or liver biopsy.

Cancer chemotherapy should usually be discontinued temporarily when one of these bizarre infections arises and usually can be reinstituted once the infection has been treated and has resolved.

Goodell, B.W., & others: *Pneumocystis carinii:* The spectrum of diffuse interstitial pneumonia in patients with neoplastic diseases. Ann Int Med 72:337–340, 1970.
Lehrer, R.I.: The role of phagocyte function in resistance to infection. California Med 114:17, June 1971.

CARCINOID SYNDROME

Although tumors of argentaffin cells are rare and usually slow-growing, they synthesize and secrete a variety of vasoactive materials including serotonin, histamine, catecholamines, and vasoactive peptides. These substances are capable of initiating acute severe vascular changes which may be fatal.

Carcinoid tumors usually arise from either the ileum, the stomach, or the bronchus, and tend to metastasize relatively early, even though they may grow at an indolent pace.

The manifestations of carcinoid syndrome include facial flushing, edema of the head and neck (especially severe with bronchial carcinoid), abdominal cramps and diarrhea, asthmatic symptoms, cardiac lesions (pulmonary or tricuspid stenosis or insufficiency), telangiectases, and increased urinary 5-hydroxyindoleacetic acid (5-HIAA). Acute and particularly severe symptoms occur in patients with bronchial carcinoids and usually begin with a period of disorientation and tremulousness followed by fever and flushing episodes which may last 3 or 4 days. Hypotension and pulmonary edema have also been observed. Even a small coin lesion on chest x-ray may be capable of producing the entire syndrome and may not be recognized until after the diagnosis of carcinoid has been established biochemically. The biochemical diagnosis should be sought in all patients with such symptoms, even if the responsible tumor cannot be located. A qualitative test for urinary 5-HIAA is positive in most instances and indicates that the patient is probably secreting 25–30 mg of 5-HIAA per day. False negatives may occur in patients receiving phenothiazines, and false positives have been observed after ingestion of serotonin-rich foods such as bananas or walnuts or in patients taking cough syrups containing glycerol guaiacolate. Ideally, the patient should be taken off all drugs for several days prior to the urine collection.

A provocative test for the induction of the flush can be performed by injecting 5 μg of epinephrine (0.5 ml of 1:1000 solution diluted 100 times) IV. If positive, the facial flush and some dyspnea usually appear within several minutes.

Emergency therapy is indicated in patients with bronchial carcinoids and prolonged flushing episodes and consists of the administration of prednisone, 15–30 mg orally daily. This treatment has a dramatic effect and is usually continued for prolonged periods. The flushing itself may well be due to kinins rather than serotonin, and corticosteroids often do not change the effects of other mediators of the syndrome. These other manifestations may require additional treatment. The abdominal cramps and diarrhea can usually be managed with tincture of opium or diphenoxylate (Lomotil®), alone or in combination with an antiserotonin agent such as methysergide maleate (Sansert®).

Phenothiazines may also be of some benefit in relieving the symptoms of flushing.

Patients with intestinal carcinoids may do satisfactorily for 10–15 years with supportive therapy, and in these instances cancer chemotherapy may not always be indicated. Because of the more aggressive symptomatology of the bronchial lesions, if they cannot be resected or have metastasized, chemotherapy with an alkylating agent should also be considered.

Melmon, K.L.: The endocrinologic manifestations of the carcinoid tumor. Chap 17, pp 1161–1180, in: *Textbook of Endocrinology,* 4th ed. R.H. Williams (editor). Saunders, 1968.

Saterlee, W.G., Serpick, A., & J.R. Bianchine: The carcinoid syndrome: Chronic treatment with para-chlorophenylalanine. Ann Int Med 72:919–922, 1970.

CANCER CHEMOTHERAPY

Administration of cytotoxic drugs and hormones has become a highly specialized and increasingly effective means of treating advanced cancer patients with a variety of malignancies. Treatment is optimally directed by a medical oncologist or cancer chemotherapist who either provides primary care for such patients or serves as a consultant to the patient's family physician. The aim of this section is to provide the non-specialist with useful information about the types of advanced cancer which are likely to respond to currently available chemotherapeutic agents, about the pharmacology and toxicity of the agents, and to assist in the evaluation of response to treatment.

Cancer chemotherapy is usually curative only in choriocarcinoma in women and in Burkitt's lymphoma; occasionally in certain testicular tumors; and in rare cases of acute leukemia, insulinoma, and certain other tumors. Combined with surgery and irradiation, chemotherapy also increases the cure rate in Wilms's tumor. Chemotherapeutic management also provides significant palliation of symptoms along with prolongation of survival in many children with acute leukemia, adults with Hodgkin's disease, multiple myeloma, macroglobulinemia, and carcinomas of the breast, endometrium, and prostate. Patients with carcinoma of the colon, ovary, and larynx and the chronic leukemias also achieve some relief of symptoms with treatment, although significant prolongation of survival has yet to be demonstrated. Present therapy is usually unsuccessful in most cases of cancer of the lungs, kidneys, and certain other carcinomas, as well as sarcomas such as osteogenic sarcoma.

A summary of malignancies responsive to chemotherapy appears in Table 30–2. Table 30–3 outlines the currently used dosage schedules and the toxicities of the cancer chemotherapeutic agents. The dosage schedules given are for single agent therapy. Combination therapy, as is now used in advanced Hodgkin's disease, testicular tumors, and certain other neoplasms, requires downward modifications of the dosages shown—otherwise, the combined toxicity would be prohibitive. Such combination therapy should be attempted only by specialists who have adequate supportive services available (eg, platelet transfusions) for use as necessary.

TOXICITY & DOSE MODIFICATION OF CHEMOTHERAPEUTIC AGENTS

A number of cancer chemotherapeutic agents have cytotoxic effects on rapidly proliferating normal cells in the bone marrow, mucosa, and skin. Still other drugs such as the vinca alkaloids produce neuropathy, and the hormones often have psychic effects. Acute and chronic toxicities of the various drugs are summarized in Table 30–3. Early recognition of significant toxicity is important to make certain that the ratio of benefit to toxic effects of treatment remains favorable. Appropriate dose modification usually minimizes these side-effects, so that therapy can be continued with relative safety.

Bone Marrow Toxicity

Depression of the bone marrow is usually the most significant limiting toxicity in cancer chemotherapy.

Commonly used short-acting drugs which affect the bone marrow are the oral alkylating agents (eg, cyclophosphamide, melphalan, chlorambucil), procarbazine, mercaptopurine, methotrexate, vinblastine, and fluorouracil. The standard dosage schedules which produce tumor responses with these agents often do

TABLE 30–2. Malignancies responsive to chemotherapy.

Diagnosis	Alkylating Agents	Antimetabolites	Steroid Hormones	Miscellaneous Drugs
Acute lymphocytic leukemia	Cyclophosphamide	Mercaptopurine, thioguanine, methotrexate, ARA-C	Prednisone	Vincristine, asparaginase,* daunorubicin* (daunomycin)
Acute myelocytic leukemia		Thioguanine, ARA-C, mercaptopurine	Prednisone	Vincristine, allopurinol†
Chronic myelocytic leukemia	Busulfan, melphalan	Mercaptopurine, thioguanine		Vincristine, allopurinol†
Chronic lymphocytic leukemia	Chlorambucil, cyclophosphamide, triethylenethiophosphor-amide	Methotrexate	Prednisone	
Hodgkin's disease	Chlorambucil, mechlorethamine, cyclophosphamide, triethylenethiophosphor-amide		Prednisone	Vinblastine, vincristine, procarbazine, BCNU*, Bleomycin®*
Lymphosarcoma and reticulum cell sarcoma	Chlorambucil, cyclophosphamide, mechlorethamine		Prednisone	Vincristine
Multiple myeloma	Melphalan, cyclophosphamide		Prednisone, androgens†	BCNU*
Macroglobulinemia	Chlorambucil			
Polycythemia vera	Busulfan, chlorambucil			Allopurinol†
Carcinoma of lung	Cyclophosphamide, mechlorethamine	Methotrexate	Prednisone	Atabrine†
Carcinoma of larynx and other "head and neck" tumors		Methotrexate, fluouracil		Bleomycin®*
Carcinoma of endo-metrium			Progestins	
Carcinoma of ovary	Triethylenethiophosphor-amide, cyclophosphamide, chlorambucil	Fluorouracil		
Breast carcinoma	Cyclophosphamide, chlorambucil, mechlorethamine	Fluorouracil, methotrexate	Estrogens, androgens, Δ'-testonolactone, prednisone	Vincristine
Choriocarcinoma (trophoblastic neo-plasms)	Chlorambucil	Methotrexate, mercaptopurine		Dactinomycin, vinblastine, vincristine
Carcinoma of testis	Cyclophosphamide, chlorambucil	Methotrexate		Dactinomycin, vincristine, mithramycin
Carcinoma of prostate	Analine mustard*		Estrogens	
Wilms's tumor (children)	Mechlorethamine, cyclophosphamide		Prednisone	Dactinomycin, vincristine
Neuroblastoma	Cyclophosphamide			Vincristine
Carcinoma of adrenal				o,p'DDD*
Carcinoma of colon		Fluorouracil		
Carcinoid	Cyclophosphamide			Dactinomycin
Insulinoma				Streptozotocin*
Miscellaneous sarcomas and carcinomas	Mechlorethamine, cyclophosphamide, chlorambucil	Fluorouracil, methotrexate	Prednisone	Dactinomycin, vincristine

*Investigational agent.

†Valuable supportive agent, not oncolytic.

induce some bone marrow depression. In such instances, if the drug is not discontinued or its dosage reduced, severe bone marrow aplasia can develop and may result in pancytopenia, bleeding, or infection. Simple guidelines to therapy can usually prevent severe marrow depression.

Complete blood counts (white blood counts, differential, hematocrit or hemoglobin, and platelet count) should be obtained frequently. With chronic daily or weekly chemotherapy, counts should be obtained initially at weekly intervals; the frequency of counts may be reduced only after the patient's sensitivity to the drug can be well predicted (eg, 3–4 months) and cumulative toxicity excluded.

In patients with normal blood counts, drugs should usually be started at their full dosage and tapered if need be, rather than starting at a lower dose and escalating the dose to hematologic tolerance. When the dose is escalated, toxicity often cannot be adequately anticipated, especially if it is cumulative, and marrow depression is often more severe.

Drug dosage can usually be tapered on a fixed schedule as a function of the peripheral white blood count or platelet count (or both). In this fashion, smooth titration control of drug administration can usually be attained for oral alkylating agents or antimetabolites. A scheme for dose modifications is shown in Table 30–4.

Drugs with delayed hematologic toxicities do not always fit into such a simple scheme, and in general they should only be administered by specialists who are quite familiar with specific toxicities. Drugs which require more special precautions regarding toxicity include busulfan, cytosine arabinoside, and mithramycin, as well as the investigational agents BCNU (1,3-bis]2-chloroethyl]-1-nitrosourea), daunorubicin, and bleomycin.

Gastrointestinal & Skin Toxicity

Since antimetabolites such as methotrexate and fluorouracil act only on rapidly proliferating cells, they damage the cells of mucosal surfaces such as the gastrointestinal tract. Methotrexate has similar effects on the skin. These toxicities are at times more significant than those which have occurred in the bone marrow, and they should be looked for routinely when these agents are used.

Erythema of the buccal mucosa is an early sign of mucosal toxicity. If therapy is continued beyond this point, oral ulceration will develop. In general, it is wise to discontinue therapy at the time of appearance of early oral ulceration. This finding usually heralds the appearance of similar but potentially more serious ulceration at other sites lower in the gastrointestinal tract. Therapy can usually be reinstituted when the oral ulcer heals (within 1 week to 10 days). The dose of drug used may need to be modified downward at this point, with titration to an acceptable level of effect on the mucosa.

Miscellaneous Drug-Specific Toxicities

The toxicities of individual drugs have been summarized in Table 30–3; however, several of these warrant additional mention since they occur with frequently administered agents. Discussion of one investigational drug (bleomycin) is also included because of its potentially wide clinical application.

A. Cyclophosphamide-Induced Hemorrhagic Cystitis: Metabolic products of cyclophosphamide which retain cytotoxic activity are excreted into the urine. Some patients appear to metabolize more of the drug to these active excretory products; if their urine is concentrated, severe bladder damage may result. In general, it is wise to advise patients receiving cyclophosphamide to maintain a large fluid intake. Early symptoms include dysuria and frequency despite the absence of bacteriuria. Such symptoms develop in about 20% of patients who receive the drug. Should microscopic hematuria develop, it is advisable to stop the drug temporarily or switch to a different alkylating agent, increase fluid intake, and administer a urinary analgesic such as phenazopyridine (Pyridium®). With severe cystitis, large segments of bladder mucosa may be shed and the patient may have prolonged gross hematuria. Such patients should be observed for signs of urinary obstruction and may require cystoscopy for removal of obstructing blood clots. Patients whose tumors respond to cyclophosphamide who develop severe cystitis should stop taking all drugs until the syndrome clears and should then be given different alkylating agents (eg, chlorambucil, melphalan, mechlorethamine), which lack this toxicity, as they are likely to be equally effective against the tumor.

B. Vincristine Neuropathy: Neuropathy is a toxic side-effect which is peculiar to the vinca alkaloid drugs and is particularly observed with vincristine. The peripheral neuropathy can be sensory, motor, autonomic, or a combination of these effects. In its mildest form it consists of paresthesias ("pins and needles") of the fingers and toes. With continued vincristine therapy, the paresthesias extend to the proximal interphalangeal joints, hyporeflexia appears in the lower extremities, and significant weakness develops in the quadriceps muscle group. At this point, it is wise to discontinue vincristine therapy until the neuropathy has subsided somewhat. A useful means of judging whether the peripheral motor neuropathy is significant enough to warrant stopping treatment is to have the patient attempt to do deep knee bends or get up out of a chair without using his arms.

Constipation is the most common symptom of the autonomic neuropathy which occurs with vincristine therapy. This symptom should always be dealt with prophylactically, ie, patients receiving vincristine should be started on stool softeners and mild cathartics when therapy is instituted. If this potential complication is neglected, severe impaction may result in association with an atonic bowel.

More serious autonomic involvement can lead to acute intestinal obstruction with signs indistinguishable from those of an acute abdomen. Bladder neuropathies are uncommon but may be severe.

TABLE 30–3. Dosage and toxicity of cancer chemotherapeutic agents.

Chemotherapeutic Agent	Usual Adult Dosage	Acute Toxicity	Delayed Toxicity
Alkylating agents			
Mechlorethamine (nitrogen mustard, HN$_2$, Mustargen®)	0.4 mg/kg IV in single or divided doses.	Nausea and vomiting	Moderate depression of peripheral blood count.
Chlorambucil (Leukeran®)	0.1–0.2 mg/kg/day orally; 6–12 mg/day.	None	Excessive doses produce severe bone marrow depression with leukopenia, thrombocytopenia, and bleeding. Alopecia and hemorrhagic cystitis are peculiar toxicities of cyclophosphamide.
Cyclophosphamide	3.5–5 mg/kg/day orally for 10 days; 40 mg/kg IV as single dose.	Nausea and vomiting	
Melphalan (Alkeran®)	0.1 mg/kg/day orally for 7 days; 2–4 mg/day as maintenance dose.	None	
Triethylenethiophosphoramide (Thio-TEPA®)	0.2 mg/kg IV for 5 days.	None	
Busulfan (Myleran®)	2–8 mg/day orally; 150–250 mg/course.	None	
Structural analogues or antimetabolites			
Methotrexate (amethopterin, MTX)	2.5–5 mg/day orally; 5 mg intrathecally 1–2 times weekly. 15 mg IM twice weekly is well tolerated and may be preferable.	None	Oral and gastrointestinal tract ulceration, bone marrow depression, leukopenia, thrombocytopenia.
Mercaptopurine (Purinethol®, 6-MP)	2.5 mg/kg/day orally.	None	Usually well tolerated. Larger dosages may cause bone marrow depression.
Thioguanine (6-TG)	2 mg/kg/day orally.	None	Usually well tolerated. Larger dosages may cause bone marrow depression.
Fluorouracil (5-FU)	15 mg/kg/day IV for 3–5 days, or 15 mg/kg weekly for at least 6 weeks.	None	Nausea, oral and gastrointestinal ulceration, bone marrow depression.
Arabinosylcytosine (ARA-C, Cytosar®)	1–3 mg/kg IV by rapid injection or over 24 hours for up to 10 days.	None	Nausea and vomiting, bone marrow depression, megaloblastosis, leukopenia, thrombocytopenia.
Hormonal agents			
Androgens:			
Testosterone propionate	100 mg IM 3 times weekly.	None	Fluid retention, masculinization.
Fluoxymesterone (Halotestin®)	10–20 mg/day orally.	None	
Estrogens:			
Diethylstilbestrol	1–5 mg 3 times a day orally.	Occasional nausea and vomiting	Fluid retention, feminization, uterine bleeding.
Ethinyl estradiol (Estinyl®)	3 mg/day orally.	None	
Progestins:			
Hydroxyprogesterone caproate (Delalutin®)	1 gm IM twice weekly.	None	Occasional fluid retention.
Medroxyprogesterone (Provera®)	100–200 mg/day orally; 200–600 mg orally twice weekly.	None	
Adrenocorticosteroids:			
Prednisone	20–100 mg/day orally or, when effective, 50–100 mg every other day orally as single dose.	None	Fluid retention, hypertension, diabetes, increased susceptibility to infection, "moon facies," osteoporosis.

TABLE 30–3 (cont'd). Dosage and toxicity of cancer chemotherapeutic agents.

Chemotherapeutic Agent	Usual Adult Dosage	Acute Toxicity	Delayed Toxicity
Miscellaneous drugs			
Vinblastine (Velban®)	0.1–0.2 mg/kg IV weekly.	Nausea and vomiting	Alopecia, loss of reflexes, bone marrow depression.
Vincristine (Oncovin®)	0.015–0.05 mg/kg IV weekly.	None	Areflexia, muscular weakness, peripheral neuritis, paralytic ileus, mild bone marrow depression.
Dactinomycin (actinomycin D, Cosmegen®)	0.01 mg/kg day IV for 5 days, or 0.04 mg/kg IV weekly.	Nausea and vomiting	Stomatitis, gastrointestinal tract upset, alopecia, bone marrow depression.
Mithramycin (Mithracin®)	0.50 mg/kg IV every other day for 4 doses.	Nausea and vomiting, diarrhea	Bone marrow depression, hemorrhagic syndrome, hypocalcemia.
Procarbazine (N-methylhydrazine, Matulane®)	50–300 mg/day orally.	Nausea and vomiting	Bone marrow depression, mental depression, monoamine oxidase inhibition.
Bleomycin	15–30 mg 2 or 3 times weekly IV to a total of 200–300 mg.	Allergic reactions	Fever, dermatitis, pulmonary fibrosis.
o,p'DDD	6–12 gm/day orally.	Nausea and vomiting	Dermatitis, diarrhea, mental depression, muscle tremors.
Supportive agents			
Allopurinol (Zyloprim®)	300–800 mg/day orally for prevention or relief of hyperuricemia.	None	Usually none. Enhances effects and toxicity of mercaptopurine when used in combination.
Quinacrine (Atabrine®)	100–200 mg/day by intracavitary injection for 5 days.	Local pain and fever	None.

These 2 complications are absolute contraindications to continued vincristine therapy.

C. Busulfan Toxicity: The alkylating agent busulfan, which is frequently used for treatment of chronic myelogenous leukemia, has curious delayed toxicities, including (1) increased skin pigmentation, (2) a wasting syndrome reminiscent of adrenal insufficiency, and (3) progressive pulmonary fibrosis. Patients who develop either of the latter 2 problems should be taken off busulfan and switched to a different drug (eg, melphalan) when additional therapy is needed. The pigmentary changes are innocuous, and will usually regress slowly after treatment is discontinued; in this instance, change to a different compound is optional.

D. Bleomycin-Induced Squamous Cell Toxicity: This investigational agent appears likely to find increasing application in cancer chemotherapy in view of its striking effects on squamous cell carcinomas (as well as Hodgkin's disease). The bizarre toxicities of bleomycin are most striking in the skin, where it produces edema of the interphalangeal joints and hardening of the palmar and plantar skin, as well as sometimes also inducing a serious or fatal pulmonary fibrosis (seen especially in elderly patients receiving a total dose of over 300 mg). Development of nonproductive cough, fever, or dyspnea is an indication to discontinue the drug and institute antibiotic and corticosteroid therapy.

TABLE 30–4. Scheme for dose modification of cancer chemotherapeutic agents.

White Count (1 cu mm)	Platelet Count (1 cu mm)	Suggested Drug Dosage (% of full dose)
> 5000	> 100,000	100%
4000–5000		75%
3000–4000	75,000–100,000	50%
2000–3000	50,000–75,000	25%
< 2000	< 50,000	0%

EVALUATION OF TUMOR RESPONSE

Inasmuch as cancer chemotherapy can induce clinical improvement, significant toxicity, or both, it is extremely important to critically assess the beneficial effects of treatment to determine that the net effect is favorable. The most valuable signs to follow during therapy include the following:

A. Tumor Size: Demonstration of significant shrinkage in tumor size on physical examination, chest film or other x-ray, or special scanning procedure.

B. Marker Substances: Significant decrease in the quantity of a tumor product or marker substance which reflects the amount of tumor in the body. Examples of such markers include the paraproteins in the serum or urine in multiple myeloma and macroglobulinemia, chorionic gonadotropin in choriocarcinoma, urinary steroids in adrenal carcinoma and paraneoplastic Cushing's syndrome, and 5-hydroxyindoleacetic acid in carcinoid syndrome. Secreted tumor antigens are becoming of increasing importance with the recent recognition of alpha$_1$ fetoprotein in hepatoma and the carcinoembryonic antigen in carcinoma of the colon. Technics for measurement of these 2 fetal proteins are not yet generally available.

C. Organ Function: Normalization of function of organs which were previously impaired as a result of the presence of a tumor is a useful indicator of drug effectiveness. Examples of such improvement include the normalization of liver function (eg, increased serum albumin) in patients known to have liver metastases and improvement in neurologic findings in patients with cerebral metastases. Disappearance of the signs and symptoms of the paraneoplastic syndromes often falls in this general category and can be taken as indication of tumor response.

D. General Well Being and Performance Status: A valuable sign of clinical improvement is that of the general well being of the patient. Although this finding is a combination of subjective and objective factors and may be subject to placebo effects, it nonetheless serves as an obvious and useful sign of clinical improvement and can be used in reassessment of some of the objective observations listed above. Factors included in the assessment of general well being include improved appetite and weight gain and increased "performance status" (eg, ambulatory versus bedridden). Evaluation of factors such as activity status has the advantage of summarizing beneficial and toxic effects of chemotherapy and enables the physician to judge whether the net effect of chemotherapy is worthwhile palliation.

•   •   •

MANIFESTATIONS OF PARASITIC DISEASES SIMULATING NEOPLASTIC DISEASES

Hepatoma: Clonorchiasis, schistosomiasis.

Carcinoma (urinary bladder): Schistosomiasis haemotobium.

Carcinoma (colon or rectum): Schistosomiasis mansoni, japonicum; confusion with ameboma.

•   •   •

General Bibliography

Brodsky, I., & B.S. Kahn: *Cancer Chemotherapy.* Grune & Stratton, 1967.

Brown, J.H., & B.J. Kennedy: Mithramycin in the treatment of disseminated testicular neoplasms. New England J Med 272:111–118, 1965.

Brunner, K.W., & C.W. Young: A methyl-hydrazine derivative in Hodgkin's disease and other malignant neoplasms: Therapeutic and toxic effects studied in 51 patients. Ann Int Med 63:69–86, 1965.

Cancer Chemotherapy Reports. National Cancer Institute. US Department of Health, Education, & Welfare. US Public Health Service. Bethesda, Maryland 20014.

Cline, M.J.: *Cancer Chemotherapy.* Saunders, 1971.

Dameshek, W., & F. Gunz: *Leukemia,* 2nd ed. Grune & Stratton, 1964.

Salmon, S.E., & N.L. Petrakis: Cancer chemotherapy. Chap 45, pp 427–445, in: *Review of Medical Pharmacology,* 2nd ed. Meyers, F.H., Jawetz, E., & A. Goldfein (editors). Lange, 1970.

Spratt, J.S., & W.L. Donegan: *Cancer of the Breast.* Saunders, 1967.

Van Duren, B.J. (editor): Biological effects of alkylating agents. Ann New York Acad Sc 163:589–1029, 1969.

Appendix

MEDICAL RECOMMENDATIONS FOR FOREIGN TRAVEL

Medical advice for the traveler will naturally vary with the geographic destination, the length and nature of the trip, the health of the patient, and the adequacy of medical resources in the areas to be visited. When contemplating foreign travel, it is always advisable to plan well ahead (eg, about 2 months, especially for required inoculations).

A thorough current physical examination is advisable not only for health reasons but also for certification of freedom from physical, mental, or communicable disease, which may be required in certain countries. A current dental examination and needed dental care is recommended prior to travel.

Active Immunization Against Infectious Diseases

Every individual, child or adult, should be adequately immunized against infectious diseases. The biologic products used for active immunization are frequently modified. The schedule of administration, dose, and recommended method of choice vary with each product and change often. Always consult the manufacturer's package insert and follow its recommendations.

The schedule for active immunizations in childhood (Table 1) is adapted from: *Report,* 16th ed, by the Committee on Control of Infectious Diseases, American Academy of Pediatrics, 1970.

Regularly Prescribed Medications

The traveler should take along a sufficient quantity of chronically required nonperishable medications to cover his entire trip plus an adequate reserve supply in case of delays, loss, or breakage. Although the same drugs are available in most countries, they frequently

TABLE 1. Recommended schedule for active immunization and skin testing of children.

Age	Product Administered	Test Recommended
2−3 months	DPT[1] Oral poliovaccine[2], trivalent or type 1	
3−4 months	DPT Oral poliovaccine, trivalent or type 3	
4−5 months	DPT Oral poliovaccine, trivalent or type 2	
10−12 months		Tuberculin test
12 months	Measles vaccine[3]	
15−19 months	DPT Oral poliovaccine, trivalent	
3−4 years	DPT Rubella vaccine[5]	Tuberculin test[4]
6 years	TD[6] Oral poliovaccine, trivalent	Tuberculin test[4]
8−10 years	Mumps vaccine[7]	Tuberculin test[4]
12−14 years	TD	Tuberculin test

[1] **DPT**: Toxoids of diphtheria and tetanus, alum-precipitated or aluminum hydroxide absorbed, combined with pertussis bacterial antigen. Suitable for young children. Three doses of 0.5 ml IM at intervals of 4−8 weeks. Fourth injection of 0.5 ml IM given about 1 year later.

[2] **Oral live poliomyelitis virus vaccine**: Either trivalent (types 1, 2, and 3 combined) or single type. Trivalent given 3 times at intervals of 6−8 weeks and then as a booster 1 year later. Monovalent type 1, then type 3, then type 2 given at 6-week intervals, then trivalent vaccine as a booster 1 year later. Inactive (Salk type) trivalent vaccine is available but not recommended.

[3] **Live measles virus vaccine**, 0.5 ml IM. When using attenuated (Edmonston) strain, give human gamma globulin, 0.01 ml/lb, injected into the opposite arm at the same time, to lessen the reaction to the vaccine. This is not advised with "further attenuated" (Schwarz) strain. Inactivated measles vaccine should not be used.

[4] The frequency with which **tuberculin tests** are administered depends on the risk of exposure, ie, the prevalence of tuberculosis in the population group.

[5] **Rubella live virus vaccine (attenuated)** can be given between age 1 year and puberty, but preferably prior to entry into kindergarten. The entire contents of a single-dose vaccine vial, reconstituted from the lyophilized state, are injected subcutaneously. The vaccine must *not* be given to women who are pregnant or are likely to become pregnant within 3 months of vaccination. Adult women must also be warned that there is a 40% likelihood of developing arthralgias and arthritis (presumably self-limited) within 4 weeks of vaccination.

[6] **Tetanus toxoid** and **diphtheria toxoid**. purified, suitable for adults, given to adults every 10 years.

[7] **Live mumps virus vaccine (attenuated)**, 0.5 ml IM.

have unfamiliar names, may require prescriptions from local physicians, and may be of variable quality.

Patients with "chronic" illnesses which require treatment (eg, diabetes mellitus, heart disease) should be given a concise statement of their condition and treatment regimen which can be shown to a physician in case of need. A medical identification tag, bracelet, or card (eg, diabetes mellitus, drug allergy) should be carried. Advise diabetic patients that insulin preparations require refrigeration. Advance inquiry about the availability of the prescribed type of insulin and facilities for refrigeration is essential. Travel agents and consular representatives can provide the names of physicians or hospitals in the vicinity.

Contingency Drugs & Supplies

A. Systemic Anti-infectives: If exposure to infectious and parasitic diseases (eg, malaria) is a prominent risk in the areas to be visited, appropriate drugs should be carried together with instructions for use.

B. Local Anti-infectives and Protectives: Topical anti-infective ointments (eg, bacitracin, neomycin) and adhesive bandages are all that is necessary for minor cuts and abrasions. Prevent sunburn with protective lotions or creams. Use dusting powder in humid climates, especially in socks.

C. Antinauseants: Any of several motion sickness remedies can be used. For best effect they should be taken ½ hour before departure.

D. Antacids: For minor gastric upsets due to overindulgence or unfamiliar foods.

E. Antidiarrheal Precautions:

1. **Preventive**—Minor gastrointestinal disturbances are usually physiologic responses to changing timetables and habits. If water is of doubtful purity, halo-

gen or iodine preparations should be used as directed below.

2. Therapeutic—Diphenoxylate (Lomotil®), 2.5 mg following each liquid bowel movement, or 3—4 times daily as needed. Give codeine, 30 mg, for severe diarrhea, severe cramps, or tenesmus.

F. Sedatives: Sedative-hypnotic drugs can be used for very nervous, anxious patients who are fearful of flying, or for sleep.

G. Analgesics: Aspirin for headache or moderate pain. If codeine is carried as an antidiarrheal agent, it can be used if a stronger analgesic is required. An anesthetic ointment may be useful for burns or pruritus.

H. Eyeglasses: Either a prescription or an extra pair of glasses should be carried.

I. Dentures: If dentures are required, spare dentures should be carried.

J. A supply of commercial handwashing packets should be carried.

K. Insect Repellents: These may not only provide comfort against annoying insects but may prevent serious diseases transmitted by insects. Many such preparations are available (eg, Off®, 612®). Apply repeatedly to exposed skin.

Food and Water Safety

A. Water Purification: A dropper bottle filled with ordinary household sodium hypochlorite bleaching solution (eg, Clorox®, Purex®) can be used to make water safer for drinking. One drop to 1 glass of water will serve for water that is not grossly contaminated. Allow to stand for 15 minutes before drinking. Muddy water or water containing organic material should be filtered or allowed to clarify for several hours and decanted into a clean glass. Two drops of sodium hypochlorite solution are then added. Allow to stand for 15 minutes before drinking.

Globaline®, an iodine compound, may be used to purify drinking water. It is available in tablet form. Add 1 tablet per pint of water and let stand at least 3 minutes. It may cause a brown precipitate.

Precautions: Water or ice of doubtful purity should not be used. Bottled or pure water should be used for drinking and brushing teeth.

B. Food Safety: Unless in an area with high sanitary standards, it is generally inadvisable to eat local raw fruits and vegetables. Hot foods, thoroughly cooked (especially in the case of pork), are the safest; avoid stews and chopped meats when questionable. Dairy products which require pasteurization, as well as all meats or other proteins, may be dangerous if not kept under refrigeration.

C. Swimming Safety: Water may not be safe for swimming purposes in either natural water resources or in swimming pools in certain areas. It is best to check with responsible local health authorities.

RECOMMENDED IMMUNIZATION OF ADULTS FOR TRAVEL

Every adult, whether traveling or not, must be immunized with tetanus toxoid. Purified toxoid "for adult use" must be used to avoid reactions. Every adult should also receive primary vaccination for poliomyelitis (oral live trivalent vaccine) and for diphtheria (use purified toxoid "for adult use"). Every traveler must fulfill the immunization requirements of the health authorities of different countries. These are listed in *Immunization Information for International Travel,* USPHS, Division of Foreign Quarantine, 7915 Eastern Ave., Silver Spring, Maryland 20910.

The following are suggestions for travel in different parts of the world.

Tetanus

Booster injection of 0.5 ml tetanus toxoid, for adult use, every 7—10 years, assuming completion of primary immunization. (All countries.)

Smallpox

Vaccination or revaccination with live smallpox vaccine (vaccinia virus) by multiple pressure method is required for entry or reentry into the USA from smallpox endemic areas. WHO certificate requires registration of batch number of vaccine. The physician should ascertain a "take" by observing vesicle formation after administration of either liquid or freeze-dried effective vaccine. (All countries.)

Typhoid

Suspension of killed *Salmonella typhi*. For primary immunization, inject 0.5 ml subcut (0.25 ml for children under 10 years) twice at an interval of 4—6 weeks. For booster, inject 0.5 ml subcut (or 0.1 ml intradermally) every 3 years. (All countries.)

Paratyphoid vaccines are not recommended and are probably ineffective at present.

Yellow Fever

Live attenuated yellow fever virus, 0.5 ml subcut. WHO certificate requires registration of batch number of vaccine. Vaccination available in USA only at approved centers. Vaccination must be repeated at intervals of 10 years or less. (Africa, South America.)

Cholera

Suspension of killed vibrios, including prevalent antigenic types. Two injections of 0.5 and 1 ml are given IM 4—6 weeks apart. This must be followed by 0.5 ml booster injections every 6 months during periods of possible exposure. Protection depends largely on booster doses. WHO certificate is valid for 6 months only. (Middle Eastern countries, Asia, occasionally others.)

Plague

Suspension of killed plague bacilli given IM, 2 injections of 0.5 ml each, 4—6 weeks apart, and a third injection 6 months later. (Middle Eastern countries, Asia, occásionally South America and others.)

Typhus

Suspension of inactivated typhus rickettsiae given IM, 2 injections of 0.5 ml each, 4–6 weeks apart. Booster doses of 0.5 ml every 6 months may be necessary. (Southeastern Europe, Africa, Asia.)

Hepatitis

No active immunization available. Temporary passive immunity may be induced by the IM injection of human gamma globulin, 0.02 ml/kg every 2–3 months, or 0.1 ml/kg every 6 months.

Committee on Control of Infectious Diseases: *Report,* 16th ed. American Academy of Pediatrics, 1970.

Immunization Information for International Travel. USPHS, Division of Foreign Quarantine, 7915 Eastern Ave., Silver Spring, Maryland 20910.

Peebles, T.C., & others: Tetanus toxoid emergency boosters: A reappraisal. New England J Med 280:575–581, 1969.

Tahernia, A.C.: Diphtheria: Still lethal. Clin Pediat 8:508–511, 1969.

Woodson, R.D., & others: Hepatitis prophylaxis abroad. JAMA 209:1053–1055, 1969.

HYPERSENSITIVITY
TESTS & DESENSITIZATION

Tests for Hypersensitivity

Before injecting antitoxin or similar material derived from animal sources, always perform the following tests for hypersensitivity. If both tests are negative, desensitization is not necessary and a full dose of the antitoxin may be given. If one or both of the tests are positive, desensitization is necessary.

A. Intradermal Test: Inject 0.1 ml of a 1:10 dilution of the antitoxin intradermally on the flexor surface of the forearm. A large wheal and surrounding areola appearing within 5–20 minutes constitute a positive test.

B. Conjunctival Test: Instill 1 drop of a 1:10 dilution of the antitoxin into the conjunctival sac of one eye as a test dose and 1 drop of physiologic saline into the other eye as a control. Conjunctival redness, itching, and lacrimation appearing within 5–20 minutes in the test eye constitute a positive test.

Desensitization

A. Precautionary Measures:

1. An antihistaminic drug should be administered before beginning desensitization in order to lessen any reaction that might occur.

2. Epinephrine, 0.5–1 ml of 1:1000 solution, must be ready in a syringe for immediate administration.

B. Desensitization Method: The following plan may be used in desensitization. Give doses of antitoxin intramuscularly at 30-minute intervals and observe closely for reactions.

1st dose: 0.1 ml (1:10 dilution)
2nd dose: 0.2 ml (1:10 dilution)
3rd dose: 0.5 ml (1:10 dilution)
4th dose: 0.1 ml (undiluted)
5th dose: 0.2 ml (undiluted)
6th dose: 0.5 ml (undiluted)
7th dose: 1 ml (undiluted)
8th and subsequent doses: 1 ml (undiluted) every 30 minutes until the total amount of antitoxin is given.

Treatment of Reactions

A. Mild: If a mild reaction occurs, drop back to the next lower dose and continue with desensitization. If a severe reaction occurs, administer epinephrine (see below) and discontinue the antitoxin unless treatment is urgently needed. If desensitization is imperative, continue slowly, increasing the dosage of the antitoxin more gradually.

B. Severe: If manifestations of a severe reaction appear, give 0.5–1 ml of 1:1000 epinephrine subcut at once. The symptoms include urticaria, angioneurotic edema, dyspnea, coughing, choking, and shock. Observe the patient closely, and repeat epinephrine as necessary.

Corticosteroids may be used (eg, hydrocortisone, 100 mg IV).

Brown, E.A.: The conjunctival test. Ann Allergy 20:608–628, 674–701, 1962.

Hartman, M.M.: Capabilities and limitations of major drug groups in allergy: The role within current theories. Ann Allergy 27:164–181, 1969.

Samter, M., & others: Answers to questions on allergic emergencies. Hosp Med 4:61–74, 1968.

Sherman, W.B.: *Hypersensitivity: Mechanism and Management.* Saunders, 1968.

CHEMICAL CONSTITUENTS
OF BLOOD & BODY FLUIDS

Interpretation of laboratory tests: Normal values are those that fall within 2 standard deviations from the mean value for the normal population. This normal range encompasses 95% of the population. Many factors may affect values and influence the normal range; by the same token, various factors may produce values that are normal under the prevailing conditions but outside the 95% limits determined under other circumstances. These factors include age, race, sex, environment, and diurnal and other cyclic variations.

Normal values vary with the method employed, the laboratory, and conditions of collection and preservation of specimens. With increasing awareness of the proper application of laboratory control of performance and of method, variations in normal values occur less frequently. The normal values established by individual laboratories should be clearly expressed to ensure proper interpretation by the physician.

Interpretation of laboratory results must always be related to the condition of the patient. A low value may be the result of deficit or of dilution of the substance measured, eg, low serum sodium. Deviation from normal may be associated with a specific disease or with some drug consumed by the subject—eg, gout and treatment with chlorothiazides or with antineoplastic agents are associated with elevated serum uric acid concentrations. (See Tables 2 and 3.)

Values may be influenced by the method of collection of the specimen. Inaccurate collection of a 24-hour urine specimen, variations in concentration of the randomly collected urine specimen, hemolysis in a blood sample, addition of an inappropriate anticoagulant to a blood sample, and contaminated glassware or other apparatus are examples of causes of erroneous results.

Note: Whenever an unusual or abnormal result is obtained, all possible sources of error must be considered before responding with therapy based on the laboratory report. Laboratory medicine is a specialty, and experts in the field should be consulted whenever results are unusual or in doubt.

Albumin, Serum: See Protein, serum.

Aldolase, Serum: Normal: 3–8 units/ml (Bruns). Males, < 33 units; females, < 19 units (Warburg and Christian). 0–8 IU/liter.

A. Precautions: Serum should be separated promptly. If there is to be any delay in the determination, the serum should be frozen.

B. Physiologic Basis: Aldolase, also known as zymohexase, splits fructose-1, 6-diphosphate to yield dihydroxyacetone phosphate and glyceraldehyde-3-phosphate. Because it is present in higher concentration in tissue cells than in serum, destruction of tissue results in elevation of serum concentration.

C. Interpretation: Elevated levels in serum occur in myocardial infarction, muscular dystrophies, hemolytic anemia, metastatic prostatic carcinoma, leukemia, acute pancreatitis, and acute hepatitis. In obstructive jaundice or cirrhosis of the liver, serum aldolase is normal or only slightly elevated.

Ammonia, Blood: Normal (Conway): 40–70 μg/100 ml whole blood.

A. Precautions: Do not use anticoagulants containing ammonia. Suitable anticoagulants include potassium oxalate, EDTA, and heparin that is ammonia-free. The determination should be done immediately after drawing blood. If the blood is kept in an ice-water bath it may be held for up to 1 hour.

B. Physiologic Basis: Ammonia present in the blood is derived from 2 principal sources: (1) In the large intestine, putrefactive action of bacteria on nitrogenous materials releases significant quantities of ammonia. (2) In the process of protein metabolism, ammonia is liberated. Ammonia entering the portal vein or the systemic circulation is rapidly converted to urea in the liver. Liver insufficiency may result in an increase in blood ammonia concentration, especially if protein consumption is high or if there is bleeding into the bowel.

C. Interpretation: Blood ammonia is elevated in hepatic insufficiency or with liver by-pass in the form of a portacaval shunt, particularly if protein intake is high or if there is bleeding into the bowel.

D. Drug Effects on Laboratory Results: Elevated by methicillin, ammonia cycle resins, chlorthalidone, spironolactone. Decreased by monoamine oxidase inhibitors, oral antimicrobial agents.

Amylase, Serum: Normal: 80–180 Somogyi units/100 ml serum. (One Somogyi unit equals amount of enzyme which will produce 1 mg of reducing sugar from starch at pH 7.2.) 0.8–3.2 IU/liter.

A. Precautions: If storage for more than 1 hour is necessary, blood or serum must be refrigerated.

B. Physiologic Basis: Normally, small amounts of amylase (diastase) originating in the pancreas and salivary glands are present in the blood. Inflammatory disease of these glands or obstruction of their ducts results in regurgitation of large amounts of enzyme into the blood.

C. Interpretation:

1. **Elevated** in acute pancreatitis, obstruction of pancreatic ducts (carcinoma, stone, stricture, duct sphincter spasm after morphine), mumps, occasionally in the presence of renal insufficiency, occasionally in diabetic acidosis, and occasionally with inflammation of the pancreas from a perforating peptic ulcer.

2. **Decreased** in hepatitis, acute and chronic; pancreatic insufficiency, and occasionally in toxemia of pregnancy.

D. Drug Effects on Laboratory Results: Elevated by morphine, codeine, meperidine, methacholine, pancreozymin, sodium diatrizoate, cyproheptadine, perhaps by pentazocine, thiazide diuretics. Pancreatitis may be induced by indomethacin, furosemide, chlorthalidone, ethacrynic acid, corticosteroids, histamine, salicylates, and tetracyclines. Decreased by barbiturate poisoning.

Amylase, Urine: Normal: Varies with method. 40–250 Somogyi units/hour.

A. Precautions: If the determination is delayed more than 1 hour after collecting the specimen, urine must be refrigerated.

B. Physiologic Basis: See Amylase, Serum. If renal function is adequate, amylase is rapidly excreted in the urine. A timed urine specimen (ie, 2, 6, or 24 hours) should be collected and the rate of excretion determined.

C. Interpretation: Elevation of the concentration of amylase in the urine occurs in the same situations in which serum amylase concentration is elevated. Urinary amylase concentration remains elevated for up to

TABLE 2. Drugs interfering directly with chemical tests.*

Many drugs and metabolites react with ferric chloride and affect tests for ketone bodies, phenylpyruvic acid, homogentisic acid, and melanogen. Dyes (eg, methylene blue, phenazopyridine, BSP, phenolsulfonphthalein, indigocarmine, indocyanine green, azure A) color plasma and urine; they affect most colorimetric procedures. Some drugs act as indicators (eg, phenolphthalein, vegetable laxatives) and affect tests carried out at a particular pH.

Test	Drug	Effect†	Cause
Bilirubin	Caffeine, theophylline	−	Color reaction depressed
BSP	Dyes (eg, phenazopyridine)	+	Interfering color
Calcium	Edathamil (EDTA)	−	Interferes with dye-binding methods; no effect on flame methods
Chloride	Bromide	+	Reacts like chloride
Cholesterol	Bromide	+	Enhances color when iron reagent used
	Metandienone	+	Interferes with Zimmerman reaction
Glucose	Dextran	+	Copper complex in copper reduction methods
Iron	Intravenous iron-dextran	+	Total iron increased
Iron-binding capacity (unsaturated)	Intravenous iron-dextran	−	Available transferrin saturated
Protein	Dextran	−	Hemodilution
Quinidine	Triamterene	+	Interfering fluorescence
Uric acid	Ascorbic acid, theophylline	+	Phosphotungstic acid reduced
Urine			
Catecholamines	Erythromycin, methyldopa, tetracyclines, quinine, quinidine, salicylates, hydralazine, B vitamins (high dose)	+	Interfering fluorescence
Chloride	Bromide	+	Reacts like chloride
Creatinine	Nitrofuran derivatives	+	React with color reagent
Glucose	Some vaginal powders	+	Contain glucose: urine contaminated
(Benedict's test)	Drugs excreted as glucuronates	+	Reduce Benedict's reagent
	Salicylates	+	Excreted as salicyluric acid
	Ascorbic acid (high doses)	+	Reduces Benedict's reagent
	Chloral hydrate	+	Metabolites reduce
	Nitrofuran derivatives	+	Metabolites reduce
	Cephalothin	+	Black-brown color
5-HIAA	Phenothiazines	−	Inhibit color reaction
	Mephenesin, methocarbamol	+	Similar color reaction
17-OH steroids, 17-Ketogenic steroids	Meprobamate, phenothiazines, spironolactone, penicillin G		
17-Ketosteroids		+	Similar color reactions
	Cortisone	+	Mainly 17-OH and 17-KGS
Pregnanediol	Mandelamine	+	Unknown
Protein	Tolbutamide	+	Metabolite precipitated by salicylsulfonic acid and by heat and acetic acid
Phenolsulfonphthalein	Dyes and BSP	+	Interfering colors
Uric acid	Theophylline, ascorbic acid	+	Phosphotungstic acid reduced
Vanilmandelic acid	Mandelamine	+	Similar color

*Reproduced, with permission, from Lubran, M.: The effects of drugs on laboratory values. M Clin North America 53:211–222, 1969.

†+ indicates a false-positive or enhanced effect; − a false-negative or diminished effect.

**TABLE 3. Drugs affecting prothrombin time (Quick one-stage test)
of patients on anticoagulant therapy with coumarin or
phenindione derivatives.***

Prothrombin Time Increased By	Prothrombin Time Decreased By
Heparin	Vitamin K (in polyvitamin preparations and
Salicylates (in excess of 1 gm per day)	some diets)
Phenylbutazone, oxyphenbutazone	Corticosteroids
Oral sulfonamides	Mineral oil
Broad-spectrum antibiotics (eg, tetracyclines)	Barbiturates
Hydroxyzine	Antihistamines
Clofibrate	Diuretics
Diphenylhydantoin	Digitalis (in cardiac failure)
D-Thyroxine	Griseofulvin
Thyroid hormones	Glutethimide
Anabolic steroids (eg, norethandrolone)	Oral contraceptives
Metandienone	Xanthines (eg, caffeine)
Cholestyramine	
Indomethacin	
Quinine, quinidine	
Methylthiouracil, propylthiouracil	
Phenyramidol	
Amidopyrin	
Benziodarone	
ACTH	
Alcohol (in large amounts)	
Para-aminosalicylic acid	
Mefenamic acid	
Chloral hydrate	

*Slightly modified and reproduced, with permission, from Lubran, M.: The effects of drugs on
laboratory values. M Clin North America 53:211–222, 1969.

7 days after serum amylase levels have returned to normal following an attack of pancreatitis. Thus the determination of urinary amylase may be useful if the patient is seen late in the course of an attack of pancreatitis. An elevated serum amylase with normal or low urine amylase excretory rate may be seen in the presence of renal insufficiency.

Bicarbonate, Serum or Plasma (measured as CO_2 content): Normal: 24–28 mEq/liter or 55–65 vol %.

A. Precautions: Plasma or serum is preferably drawn under oil and handled anaerobically.

B. Physiologic Basis: Bicarbonate-carbonic acid buffer is one of the most important buffer systems in maintaining normal pH of body fluids. Bicarbonate and pH determinations on plasma serve as a basis for assessing "acid-base balance."

C. Interpretation:

1. Elevated in—

(a) **Metabolic alkalosis** (arterial blood pH increased) due to ingestion of large quantities of sodium bicarbonate, protracted vomiting of acid gastric juice, accompanying potassium deficit.

(b) **Respiratory acidosis** (arterial blood pH decreased) due to pulmonary emphysema or hypoventilation due to oversedation, narcotics, or inadequate artificial respiration (elevated P_{CO_2}).

2. Decreased in—

(a) **Metabolic acidosis** (arterial blood pH decreased) due to diabetic ketosis, starvation, persistent diarrhea, renal insufficiency, ingestion of excess acidifying salts, or salicylate intoxication.

(b) **Respiratory alkalosis** (arterial blood pH increased) due to hyperventilation (decreased P_{CO_2}).

Bilirubin, Serum: Normal: Direct (glucuronide), 0.1–0.4 mg/100 ml. Indirect (unconjugated), 0.2–0.7 mg/100 ml.

A. Precautions: The fasting state is preferred to avoid turbidity of serum. For optimal stability of stored serum, samples should be frozen and stored in the dark.

B. Physiologic Basis: Destruction of hemoglobin yields bilirubin, which is conjugated in the liver to the diglucuronide and excreted in the bile. Bilirubin accumulates in the plasma when liver insufficiency exists, biliary obstruction is present, or the rate of hemolysis increases. Rarely, abnormalities of enzyme systems involved in bilirubin metabolism in the liver (eg, absence of glucuronyl transferase) result in abnormal bilirubin concentrations.

C. Interpretation:

1. Direct and indirect forms of serum bilirubin are elevated in acute or chronic hepatitis, biliary tract obstruction (cholangiolar, hepatic, or common ducts),

toxic reactions to many drugs, chemicals, and toxins, and Dubin-Johnson and Rotor's syndromes.

2. Indirect serum bilirubin is elevated in hemolytic diseases or reactions and absence or deficiency of glucuronyl transferase, as in Gilbert's disease and Crigler-Najjar syndrome.

D. Drug Effects on Laboratory Results: Elevated by acetaminophen, chlordiazepoxide, novobiocin, acetohexamide. Many drugs produce impairment of liver function.

Calcium, Serum: Normal: 9–10.6 mg/100 ml or 4.5–5.3 mEq/liter.

A. Precautions: Glassware must be free of calcium. The patient should be fasting. Serum should be promptly separated from the clot.

B. Physiologic Basis: Endocrine, renal, gastrointestinal, and nutritional factors normally provide for precise regulation of calcium concentration in plasma and other body fluids. Since some calcium is bound to plasma protein, especially albumin, determination of the plasma albumin concentration is necessary before the clinical significance of abnormal serum calcium levels can be interpreted accurately.

C. Interpretation:

1. **Elevated** in hyperparathyroidism, secretion of parathyroid-like hormone by malignant tumors, vitamin D excess, milk-alkali syndrome, osteolytic disease such as multiple myeloma, invasion of bone by metastatic cancer; Paget's disease of bone, Boeck's sarcoid, and immobilization.

2. **Decreased** in hypoparathyroidism, vitamin D deficiency (rickets, osteomalacia), renal insufficiency, hypoproteinemia, malabsorption syndrome (sprue, ileitis, celiac disease, pancreatic insufficiency), and severe pancreatitis with pancreatic necrosis.

Calcium, Urine, Daily Excretion: Ordinarily there is a moderate continuous urinary calcium excretion of 50–150 mg/24 hours, depending upon the intake.

A. Procedure: The patient should remain upon a diet free of milk or cheese for 3 days prior to testing; for quantitative testing a neutral ash diet containing about 150 mg calcium per day is given for 3 days. Quantitative calcium excretion studies may be made on a carefully timed 24-hour urine specimen. The screening procedure with the Sulkowitch reagent is simple and useful.

B. Interpretation: On the quantitative diet a normal person secretes 125± 50 mg of calcium per 24 hours. Normally, a slight (1+) cloud reaction (Sulkowitch) occurs if milk and cheese are not present in the diet. In hyperparathyroidism, the urinary calcium excretion usually exceeds 200 mg/24 hours. Urinary calcium excretion is elevated in almost all situations in which serum calcium is high.

Carbon Dioxide Combining Power, Serum or Plasma: Normal: 24–29 mEq/liter or 55–75 vol/100 ml.

Plasma or serum CO_2 combining power is elevated or decreased in the same clinical circumstances as plasma or serum bicarbonate. Anerobic handling of the specimen is not necessary. The method is the same as for bicarbonate determination except that the serum or plasma is exposed to an "alveolar" air concentration of CO_2 (ie, 40–50 mm Hg partial pressure or 5–6% CO_2) prior to the determination.

See Bicarbonate, above, for interpretation.

Ceruloplasmin and Copper, Serum: Normal: Ceruloplasmin, 27–37 mg/100 ml; copper, 70–165 μg/100 ml.

A. Precautions: None.

B. Physiologic Basis: About 5% of serum copper is loosely bound to albumin and 95% to ceruloplasmin, an oxidase enzyme that is an alpha$_2$ globulin with a blue color. In Wilson's disease, serum copper and ceruloplasmin are low and urinary levels of copper are high.

C. Interpretation:

1. **Elevated** in pregnancy, hyperthyroidism, infection, aplastic anemia, acute leukemia, cirrhosis of the liver, and with use of oral contraceptives.

2. **Decreased** in Wilson's disease and accompanied by increased urinary excretion of copper.

Chloride, Serum or Plasma: Normal: 100–106 mEq/liter or 350–375 mg/100 ml.

A. Precautions: Determination on whole blood yields lower results than those obtained using serum or plasma as the specimen. Always use serum or plasma.

B. Physiologic Basis: Chloride is the principal inorganic anion of the extracellular fluid. It is important in maintenance of acid-base balance even though it exerts no buffer action. When chloride as HCl or NH_4Cl is lost, alkalosis follows; when chloride is retained or ingested, acidosis follows. Chloride (with sodium) plays an important role in control of osmolarity of body fluids.

C. Interpretation:

1. **Elevated** in renal insufficiency (when Cl intake exceeds excretion), nephrosis (occasionally), renal tubular acidosis, ureterosigmoid anastomosis (reabsorption from urine in gut), dehydration (water deficit), and overtreatment with saline solution.

2. **Decreased** in gastrointestinal disease with loss of gastric and intestinal fluids (vomiting of acid gastric juice, diarrhea, gastrointestinal suction), renal insufficiency (with salt deprivation), overtreatment with diuretics, chronic respiratory acidosis (emphysema), diabetic acidosis, excessive sweating, adrenal insufficiency (NaCl loss), hyperadrenocorticism (chronic K$^+$ loss), and metabolic alkalosis (NaHCO$_3$ ingestion; K$^+$ deficit).

Chloride, Urine:

Urine chloride content varies with dietary intake, acid-base balance, endocrine "balance," body stores of other electrolytes, and water balance. Relationships and responses are so variable and complex that there is little clinical value in urine chloride determinations other than in balance studies.

Cholesterol, Plasma or Serum: Normal: 150–280 mg/100 ml.

A. Precautions: The fasting state is preferred.

B. Physiologic Basis: Cholesterol concentrations are determined by metabolic functions which are influenced by heredity, nutrition, endocrine function, and integrity of vital organs such as the liver and kidney. Cholesterol metabolism is intimately associated with lipid metabolism.

C. Interpretation:

1. Elevated in familial hypercholesterolemia (xanthomatosis), hypothyroidism, poorly controlled diabetes mellitus, nephrotic syndrome, chronic hepatitis, biliary cirrhosis, obstructive jaundice, hypoproteinemia (idiopathic, with nephrosis or chronic hepatitis), and lipemia (idiopathic, familial).

2. Decreased in acute hepatitis and Gaucher's disease, occasionally in hyperthyroidism, acute infections, anemia, malnutrition.

D. Drug Effects on Laboratory Results: Elevated by bromides, anabolic agents, trimethadione, oral contraceptives. Decreased by cholestyramine resin, haloperidol, nicotinic acid, salicylates, thyroid hormone, estrogens, clofibrate, chlorpropamide, phenformin, kanamycin, neomycin, phenyramidol.

Cholesterol Esters, Plasma or Serum: Normal: 65–75% of total serum or plasma cholesterol.

A. Precautions: None.

B. Physiologic Basis: Cholesterol is esterified in the intestinal mucosa and in the liver. Cholesterol exists in plasma or serum as the free form (25–33% of total) and as the ester (67–75% of total). In the presence of acute hepatic insufficiency (as in acute hepatitis), the concentration of esters is reduced.

C. Interpretation:

1. Elevated along with cholesterol in absence of hyperbilirubinemia (see Cholesterol, above). The ratio of ester/total cholesterol under these circumstances is normal. With hyperbilirubinemia, absolute values may be elevated, but not in the same proportion as total cholesterol, so that the ester/total cholesterol ratio is less than 65%.

2. Decreased in acute hepatitis. Cholesterol esters may be decreased also in chronic hepatitis and chronic biliary obstruction; in these situations the decrease in cholesterol ester exceeds the decrease in total cholesterol, which results in an ester/total cholesterol ratio of less than 65%.

Creatine Phosphokinase (CPK): Normal: Varies with method. 10–50 IU/liter.

A. Precautions: The enzyme is unstable, and the red cell content inhibits enzyme activity. Serum must be removed from the clot promptly. If assay cannot be done soon after drawing blood, serum must be frozen.

B. Physiologic Basis: CPK splits creatine phosphate in the presence of ADP to yield creatine + ATP. Skeletal and heart muscle and brain are rich in the enzyme.

C. Interpretation: Normal values vary with the method.

1. Elevated in the presence of muscle damage such as with myocardial infarction, trauma to muscle, muscular dystrophies, polymyositis, severe muscular exertion, and hypothyroidism. Following myocardial infarction, serum CPK concentration increases rapidly (within 3–5 hours), and remains elevated for a shorter time after the episode (2 or 3 days) than does GOT or LDH.

2. Not elevated in pulmonary infarction or parenchymal liver disease.

Creatine, Urine (24 Hours): Normal: See Table 4.

TABLE 4. Urine creatine and creatinine, normal values (24 hours).

	Creatine	Creatinine
Newborn	4.5 mg/kg	10 mg/kg
1–7 months	8.1 mg/kg	12.8 mg/kg
2–3 years	7.9 mg/kg	12.1 mg/kg
4–4½ years	4.5 mg/kg	14.6 mg/kg
9–9½ years	2.5 mg/kg	18.1 mg/kg
11–14 years	2.7 mg/kg	20.1 mg/kg
Adult male	0–50 mg	25 mg/kg
Adult female	0–100 mg	21 mg/kg

A. Precautions: Collection of the 24-hour specimen must be accurate. The specimen may be refrigerated or preserved with 10 ml of toluene or 10 ml of 5% thymol in chloroform.

B. Physiologic Basis: Creatine is an important constituent of muscle, brain, and blood; in the form of creatine phosphate it serves as a source of high-energy phosphate. Normally, small amounts of creatine are excreted in the urine, but in states of elevated catabolism and in the presence of muscular dystrophies, the rate of excretion is increased.

C. Interpretation:

1. Elevated in muscular dystrophies such as progressive muscular dystrophy, myotonia atrophica, and myasthenia gravis; muscle wasting, as in acute poliomyelitis, amyotrophic lateral sclerosis, and myositis manifested by muscle wasting; starvation and cachectic states, hyperthyroidism, and febrile diseases.

2. Decreased in hypothyroidism, amyotonia congenita, and renal insufficiency.

Creatinine, Plasma or Serum: Normal 0.7–1.5 mg/100 ml.

A. Precautions: Other materials than creatinine may react to give falsely high results.

B. Physiologic Basis: Creatinine, which is derived from creatine, is excreted by filtration through the glomeruli of the kidney. Endogenous creatinine is apparently not excreted by renal tubules. Retention of creatinine is thus an index of glomerular insufficiency. Creatinine clearance closely approximates the inulin clearance and is an acceptable measure of filtration rate.

C. Interpretation: Creatinine is elevated in acute or chronic renal insufficiency, urinary tract obstruction, and impairment of renal function induced by some drugs. Values of less than 0.8 mg/100 ml are of no known significance.

D. Drug Effects on Laboratory Results: Elevated by ascorbic acid, barbiturates, sulfobromophthalein, methyldopa, and phenolsulfonphthalein, all of which interfere with the determination of the alkaline picrate method (Jaffe reaction).

Creatinine, Urine: See Table 4 for normal values.

Enzymes, Serum: See specific enzyme.

Globulin, Serum: See Proteins, below.

Glucose, Whole Blood, Plasma, Serum: Normal: Fasting blood glucose (Folin), 80–120 mg/100 ml. Fasting blood glucose (true), 60–100 mg/100 ml. Plasma and serum levels are slightly higher than those of whole blood, ie, true glucose, 70–110 mg/100 ml.

A. Precautions: If determination is delayed beyond 1 hour, sodium fluoride, about 3 mg/ml blood, should be added to the specimen. The filtrates may be refrigerated for up to 24 hours. Errors in interpretation may occur if the patient has eaten sugar or received glucose solution parenterally just prior to the collection of what is thought to be a "fasting" specimen. Whole blood, plasma, or serum may be used.

B. Physiologic Basis: The glucose concentration in extracellular fluid is normally closely regulated, with the result that a source of energy is available to tissues and no glucose is excreted in the urine. Hyperglycemia and hypoglycemia are nonspecific signs of abnormal glucose metabolism.

C. Interpretation:

1. Elevated in diabetes mellitus, hyperthyroidism, adrenocortical hyperactivity (cortical excess), hyperpituitarism, and hepatic disease (occasionally).

2. Decreased in hyperinsulinism, adrenal insufficiency, hypopituitarism, hepatic insufficiency (occasionally), functional hypoglycemia, and by hypoglycemic agents.

D. Drug Effects on Laboratory Results: Elevated by corticosteroids, chlorthalidone, thiazide diuretics, furosemide, ethacrynic acid, triamterene, indomethacin, oral contraceptives (estrogen-progestin combinations), isoniazid, nicotinic acid (large doses), phenothiazines, and paraldehyde. Decreased by acetaminophen, phenacetin, cyproheptadine, pargyline, and propranolol.

Iodine, Protein-bound (PBI), Butanol Extractable (BEI), Organic; Serum: Normal: PBI, 4–8 μg/100 ml; BEI, 3–6.5 μg/100 ml. (See tests of thyroid function, pp 570–573.) Thyroxine (T_4), 2.9–6.4 μg/100 ml.

A. Precautions: Avoid iodine contamination of glassware and the use of iodine on the skin prior to venipuncture. The patient need not be fasting.

B. Physiologic Basis: Thyroid hormone is normally the only organic iodine compound present in blood in significant concentration. The protein-bound iodine is, therefore, a measure of circulating thyroxine.

C. Interpretation:

1. Elevated in hyperthyroidism, thyroiditis (during active stage), and pregnancy. Factitiously high levels may result from (1) administration of large doses of thyroid hormone (desiccated thyroid, thyroxine), (2) ingestion of inorganic and organic iodides, and (3) administration of organic iodides used in x-ray diagnostic tests (cholecystograms, urograms, myelograms, bronchograms, uterosalpingograms). These diagnostic compounds may produce elevated iodine levels for 1 year or more.

2. Decreased in hypothyroidism, after use of mercurial diuretics (effect is only of few days' duration), during administration of reserpine, or during administration of triiodothyronine (which suppresses thyroxine production by the thyroid gland).

D. Drug Effects on Laboratory Results: Elevated by sulfobromophthalein, oral contraceptives (estrogen-progestin combinations), estrogens, pyrazinamide, chlormadinone, and Metrecal®. Decreased by salicylates, anabolic steroids, progestogens, bishydroxycoumarin, diphenylhydantoin, para-aminobenzoic acid, tolbutamide, tolazamide, and thiocyanate.

Iron, Serum: Normal: 50–175 μg/100 ml.

A. Precautions: Syringes and needles must be iron-free. Hemolysis of blood must be avoided. The serum must be free of hemoglobin.

B. Physiologic Basis: Iron concentration in the plasma is determined by several factors, including absorption from the intestine, storage in intestine, liver, spleen, and marrow, breakdown or loss of hemoglobin, and synthesis of new hemoglobin.

C. Interpretation:

1. Elevated in hemochromatosis, hemosiderosis (multiple transfusions, excess iron administration), hemolytic disease, pernicious anemia, hypoplastic anemias, often in viral hepatitis. Spuriously elevated if patient has received parenteral iron during the 2–3 months prior to determination.

2. Decreased in iron deficiency with infections, nephrosis, and chronic renal insufficiency, and during periods of active hematopoiesis.

Iron-binding Capacity, Serum: Normal: Total, 300–360 μg/100 ml. Unsaturated, 150–300 μg/100 ml.

A. Precautions: None.

B. Physiologic Basis: Iron is transported as a complex of the metal binding globulin transferrin or siderophilin. Normally this transport protein carries an amount of iron which represents about 30–40% of its capacity to combine with iron. Thus the "unsaturated" iron binding capacity is normally 60–70% of the total capacity.

C. Interpretation of Unsaturated Iron Binding Capacity:

1. **Elevated** in the presence of low serum iron or iron deficiency anemia, acute or chronic blood loss, pregnancy, acute hepatitis, and ingestion of oral contraceptive drugs.

2. **Decreased** in the presence of high serum iron, hemochromatosis, hemosiderosis, hemolytic disease, pernicious anemia, acute and chronic infections, cirrhosis of the liver, uremia, and malignancy.

Lactate Dehydrogenase, Serum, Serous Fluids, Spinal Fluid, Urine: Normal: Serum, 200–450 units (Wrobleski), 60–100 units (Wacker), 90–200 IU/liter. Serous fluids, lower than serum. Spinal fluid, 15–75 units (Wrobleski); 6.3–30 IU/liter. Urine, less than 8300 units/8 hours (Wrobleski).

A. Precautions: Any degree of hemolysis must be avoided because the concentration of LDH within red blood cells is 100 times that in normal serum. Heparin and oxalate may inhibit enzyme activity.

B. Physiologic Basis: LDH catalyzes the interconversion of lactate and pyruvate in the presence of NADH or $NADH_2$. It is distributed generally in body cells and fluids.

C. Interpretation: Elevated in all conditions accompanied by tissue necrosis, particularly those involving acute injury of the heart, red cells, kidney, skeletal muscle, liver, lung, and skin. Marked elevations accompany hemolytic anemias, and the anemias of vitamin B_{12} and folate deficiency, and polycythemia rubra vera. The course of rise in concentration over 3–4 days followed by a slow decline during the following 5–7 days may be helpful in confirming the presence of a myocardial infarction; however, pulmonary infarction, neoplastic disease, and megaloblastic anemia must be excluded. Although elevated during the acute phase of infectious hepatitis, enzyme activity is seldom increased in chronic liver disease.

Lactate Dehydrogenase Isoenzymes: Normal serum levels are as follows:

	Isoenzyme	Percentage of Total (and Range)
(Fastest)	1 (a_1)	28 (15–30)
	2 (a_2)	36 (22–50)
	3 (β)	23 (15–30)
	4 (γ_1)	6 (0–15)
(Slowest)	5 (γ_2)	6 (0–15)

A. Precautions: As for LDH (see above).

B. Physiologic Basis: LDH consists of 5 separable proteins, each made of tetramers of 2 types or subunits, H and M. The 5 isoenzymes can be distinguished by kinetics, electrophoresis, chromatography, and immunologic characteristics. By electrophoretic separation, the mobility of the isoenzymes corresponds to serum proteins α_1, α_2, β, γ_1, and γ_2. These are usually numbered 1 (fastest moving), 2, 3, 4, and 5 (slowest moving). Isoenzyme 1 is present in high concentrations in heart muscle (tetramer H H H H) and in erythrocytes and kidney cortex. Isoenzyme 5 is present in high concentrations in skeletal muscle (tetramer M M M M) and liver.

C. Interpretation: In myocardial infarction, the α isoenzymes are elevated–particularly LDH 1–to yield a ratio of LDH 1:2 of > 1.0. Similar α isoenzyme elevations occur in renal cortex infarction and with hemolytic anemias.

LDH 5 and 4 are relatively increased in the presence of acute hepatitis, acute muscle injury, dermatomyositis, and muscular dystrophies.

D. Drug Effects on Laboratory Results: Decreased by clofibrate.

Lipase, Serum: Normal: 0.2–1.5 units.

A. Precautions: None. The specimen may be refrigerated up to 24 hours prior to the determination.

B. Physiologic Basis: A low concentration of fat splitting enzyme is present in circulating blood. In the presence of pancreatitis, pancreatic lipase is released into the circulation in higher concentrations, which persist, as a rule, for a longer period than does the elevated concentration of amylase.

C. Interpretation: Serum lipase is elevated in acute or exacerbated pancreatitis and in obstruction of pancreatic ducts by stone or neoplasm.

Magnesium, Serum: Normal: 1.5–2.5 mEq/liter.

A. Precautions: None.

B. Physiologic Basis: Magnesium is primarily an intracellular electrolyte. In extracellular fluid it affects neuromuscular irritability and response. Magnesium deficit may exist with little or no change in extracellular fluid concentrations. Low magnesium levels in plasma have been associated with tetany, weakness, disorientation, and somnolence.

C. Interpretation:

1. **Elevated** in renal insufficiency and in overtreatment with magnesium salts intravenously or intramuscularly.

2. **Decreased** in chronic diarrhea, acute loss of enteric fluids, starvation, chronic alcoholism, chronic hepatitis, and hepatic insufficiency. May be decreased in and contribute to persistent hypocalcemia of hypoparathyroidism (especially after surgery for hyperparathyroidism) and when large doses of vitamin D and calcium are being administered.

Nonprotein Nitrogen (NPN), Blood, Plasma, or Serum: Normal: 15–35 mg/100 ml.

A. Precautions: See Urea, below.

B. Physiologic Basis and Interpretation: See Urea, below, and Creatinine, above.

Phosphatase, Acid, Serum: Normal: Bodansky units, 0.5–2; King-Armstrong, 1–5; Gutman, 0.5–2; Shinowara, 0–1.1; Bessey-Lowry, 0.1–0.63. Females: 0.2–9.5 IU/liter. Males: 0.5–11 IU/liter.

A. Precautions: Avoid hemolysis of the specimen, which releases erythrocyte phosphatase to give factitiously high results. Serum may be refrigerated 24–48 hours prior to determination.

B. Physiologic Basis: Phosphatase active at pH 4.9 is present in high concentrations in the prostate gland and in erythrocytes. In the presence of carcinoma of the prostate which has gone beyond the capsule of the gland or has metastasized, serum acid phosphatase concentration is increased.

C. Interpretation: Increased in carcinoma of the prostate, metastatic or invasive beyond the capsule of the gland, and occasionally in acute myelocytic leukemia.

Phosphatase, Alkaline, Serum: Normal: Bodansky, 2–5 units; King-Armstrong, 5–13 units; Gutman, 3–10 units; Shinowara, 2.2–8.6 units; Bessey-Lowry, children, 2.8–6.7 units; Bessey-Lowry, adults, 0.8–2.3 units. 30–85 IU/liter.

A. Precautions: Serum may be kept in refrigerator 24–48 hours, but values may increase slightly (10%). The specimen will deteriorate if not refrigerated. Do not use fluoride or oxalate.

B. Physiologic Basis: Alkaline phosphatase is present in high concentration in growing bone, in bile, and in the placenta. The phosphatase in serum consists of a mixture of isoenzymes not yet clearly defined. It appears that the enzyme of hepatic origin is resistant to heat; that of osseous origin is sensitive to heat.

C. Interpretation:

1. Elevated in—

a. Children (normal growth of bone).

b. Osteoblastic bone disease—Hyperparathyroidism, rickets and osteomalacia, neoplastic bone disease (osteosarcoma, metastatic neoplasms), ossification as in myositis ossificans, Paget's disease (osteitis deformans), and Boeck's sarcoid.

c. Hepatic duct or cholangiolar obstruction due to stone, stricture, or neoplasm.

d. Hepatic disease resulting from drugs such as chlorpromazine, methyltestosterone.

e. With no clinical correlate to account for an elevated enzyme level in the serum, an indication of the source of the increased concentration may be obtained by measuring activity before and after heating the serum at 56° C for 10 minutes.

Bone: residual activity < 25% of control.

Hepatic: residual activity > 35% of control.

"Normal" or "mixed": residual activity 25–30% of control.

2. Decreased in hypothyroidism and in growth retardation in children.

D. Drug Effects on Laboratory Results: Elevated by acetohexamide, tolazamide, tolbutamide, chlorpropamide, allopurinol, sulfobromophthalein, carbamazepine, cephaloridine, furosemide, methyldopa, phenothiazine, and oral contraceptives (estrogen-progestin combinations).

Phosphorus, Inorganic, Serum: Normal: Children, 4–7 mg/100 ml. Adults, 3–4.5 mg/100 ml or 0.9–1.5 mM/liter.

A. Precautions: Glassware cleaned with phosphate cleaners must be thoroughly rinsed. The fasting state is necessary to avoid postprandial depression of phosphate associated with glucose transport and metabolism.

B. Physiologic Basis: The concentration of inorganic phosphate in circulating plasma is influenced by parathyroid gland function, intestinal absorption, renal function, bone metabolism, and nutrition.

C. Interpretation:

1. Increased in renal insufficiency, hypoparathyroidism, and hypervitaminosis D.

2. Decreased in hyperparathyroidism, hypovitaminosis D (rickets, osteomalacia), malabsorption syndrome (steatorrhea), some forms of renal tubular insufficiency, postprandial state, and after insulin.

Potassium, Serum or Plasma: Normal: 3.5–5 mEq/liter; 14–20 mg/100 ml.

A. Precautions: Avoid hemolysis, which releases erythrocyte potassium. Serum must be separated promptly from the clot or plasma from the red cell mass to prevent diffusion of potassium out of erythrocytes.

B. Physiologic Basis: Potassium concentration in plasma determines the state of neuromuscular and muscular irritability. Elevated or decreased concentrations of potassium impair the capability of muscle to contract.

C. Interpretation:

1. Increased in renal insufficiency (especially in the presence of increased rate of protein or tissue breakdown); adrenal insufficiency; and too rapid administration of potassium salts, especially intravenously and with spironolactone (Aldactone®) administration.

2. Decreased in—

a. Inadequate intake (starvation).

b. Inadequate absorption or unusual enteric losses—Vomiting, diarrhea, or malabsorption syndrome.

c. Unusual renal loss—Secondary to hyperadrenocorticism (especially hyperaldosteronism) and to adrenocorticosteroid therapy, metabolic alkalosis, use of diuretics such as chlorothiazide and its derivatives and the mercurials, and renal tubular defects such as the De Toni-Fanconi syndrome and renal tubular acidosis.

d. Abnormal redistribution between extracellular and intracellular fluids—Familial periodic paralysis, testosterone administration.

D. Drug Effects on Laboratory Results: Elevated by triamterene, phenformin. Decreased by degraded tetracycline, phenothiazines, and sodium polystyrenesulfonate resin.

Proteins, Serum or Plasma (Includes Fibrinogen): Normal: See Interpretation, below.

A. Precautions: Serum or plasma must be free of hemolysis. Since fibrinogen is removed in the process of coagulation of the blood, fibrinogen determinations cannot be done on serum.

B. Physiologic Basis: Concentration of protein determines colloidal osmotic pressure of plasma. The concentration of protein in plasma is influenced by the nutritional state, hepatic function, renal function, occurrence of disease such as multiple myeloma, and metabolic errors. Variations in the several fractions of plasma proteins may signify the presence of specific disease.

C. Interpretation:

1. Total protein, serum—Normal: 6–8 gm/100 ml. See albumin and globulin fractions, below.

2. Albumin, serum or plasma—Normal: 3.5–5.5 gm/100 ml.

a. Elevated in dehydration, shock, hemoconcentration, administration of large quantities of concentrated albumin "solution" intravenously.

b. Decreased in malnutrition, malabsorption syndrome, acute or chronic glomerulonephritis, nephrosis, acute or chronic hepatic insufficiency, neoplastic diseases, and leukemia.

3. Globulin, serum or plasma—Normal: 1.5–3 gm/100 ml.

a. Elevated in hepatic disease, infectious hepatitis, cirrhosis of the liver, biliary cirrhosis, and hemochromatosis; disseminated lupus erythematosus; acute or chronic infectious diseases, particularly lymphopathia venereum, typhus fever, leishmaniasis, schistosomiasis, and malaria; multiple myeloma; and Boeck's sarcoid.

b. Decreased in malnutrition, congenital agammaglobulinemia, acquired hypogammaglobulinemia, and lymphatic leukemia.

4. Fibrinogen, plasma—Normal: 0.2–0.6 gm/100 ml.

a. Elevated in glomerulonephritis, nephrosis (occasionally), and infectious diseases.

b. Decreased in disseminated intravascular coagulation (accidents of pregnancy including placental ablation, amniotic fluid embolism, violent labor, meningococcal meningitis, metastatic carcinoma of the prostate and occasionally of other organs, and leukemia), acute and chronic hepatic insufficiency, and congenital fibrinogenopenia.

TABLE 5. Protein fractions as determined by electrophoresis.

	Percentage of Total Protein
Albumin	52–68
α_1 globulin	2.4–4.4
α_2 globulin	6.1–10.1
β globulin	8.5–14.5
γ globulin	10–21

Sodium, Serum or Plasma: Normal: 136–145 mEq/liter.

A. Precautions: Glassware must be completely clean.

B. Physiologic Basis: Sodium constitutes 140 of the 155 mEq of cation in plasma. With its associated anions it provides the bulk of osmotically active solute in the plasma, thus affecting the distribution of body water significantly. A shift of sodium into cells or a loss of sodium from the body results in a decrease of extracellular fluid volume with consequent effect on circulation, renal function, and nervous system function.

C. Interpretation:

1. Increased in dehydration (water deficit), CNS trauma or disease, and hyperadrenocorticism due to hyperaldosteronism or to corticosterone or corticosteroid excess.

2. Decreased in adrenal insufficiency; renal insufficiency, especially with inadequate sodium intake; renal tubular acidosis; as a physiologic response to trauma or burns (sodium shift into cells); unusual losses via the gastrointestinal tract, as in acute or chronic diarrhea, intestinal obstruction or fistula, and in unusual sweating with inadequate sodium replacement. In some patients with edema associated with cardiac or renal disease, serum sodium concentration is low even though total body sodium content is greater than normal; water retention and abnormal distribution of sodium between intracellular and extracellular fluid contribute to this paradoxical situation. Hyperglycemia occasionally results in shift of intracellular water to the extracellular space, producing a dilutional hyponatremia.

Transaminase Enzyme Tests, Serum or Serous Fluid: Normal: Glutamic-oxaloacetic transaminase (SGOT), 5–40 units (6–25 IU/liter). Glutamic-pyruvic transaminase (SGPT), 5–35 units (3–26 IU/liter).

A. Precautions: None.

B. Physiologic Basis: Glutamic oxaloacetic transaminase, glutamic pyruvic transaminase, and lactic dehydrogenase are all intracellular enzymes involved in amino acid or carbohydrate metabolism. The enzymes are present in high concentrations in muscle, liver, and brain. Elevations of concentrations of these enzymes in the blood indicate necrosis or disease, especially of these tissues.

C. Interpretation: Elevated in myocardial infarction; acute infections or toxic hepatitis; cirrhosis of the liver; liver neoplasm, metastatic or primary; and in transudates associated with neoplastic involvement of serous cavities. SGOT is elevated in muscular dystrophy, dermatomyositis, and paroxysmal myoglobinuria.

D. Drug Effects on Laboratory Results: Elevated by a host of drugs, including anabolic steroids, androgens, clofibrate, erythromycin (especially estolate) and other antibiotics, isoniazid, methotrexate, methyldopa, phenothiazines, oral contraceptives, salicylates, acetaminophen, phenacetin, indomethacin, acetohexamide, allopurinol, bishydroxycoumarin, carbamazepine, chlordiazepoxide, desimipramine, codeine, morphine, meperidine, tolazamide, propranolol, and guanethidine.

Triglycerides, Serum: Normal: < 165 mg/100 ml.

A. Precautions: Subject must be in a fasting state (preferably for at least 16 hours). The determination may be delayed if the serum is promptly separated from the clot and refrigerated.

B. Physiologic Basis: Dietary fat is hydrolyzed in the small intestine, absorbed and resynthesized by the mucosal cells, and secreted into lacteals in the form of chylomicrons. Triglycerides in the chylomicrons are cleared from the blood by tissue lipoprotein lipase (mainly adipose tissue) and the split products absorbed and stored. Free fatty acids derived mainly from adipose tissue are precursors of the endogenous triglycerides produced by the liver. Transport of endogenous triglycerides is in association with β lipoproteins, the very low density lipoproteins. (For further details, see pp 180 and 182.) In order to assure measurement of endogenous triglycerides, blood must be drawn in the postabsorptive state.

C. Interpretation: The concentrations of triglycerides, cholesterol, and the lipoprotein fractions (very low density, low density, and high density) are interpreted collectively. Disturbances in normal relationships of these lipid moieties may be primary or secondary.

1. **Elevated (hyperlipoproteinemia)—**

a. **Primary—**Type II hyperbetalipoproteinemia, type III broad beta hyperlipoproteinemia, type I hyperlipoproteinemia (exogenous hyperlipidemia), type IV hyperlipoproteinemia (endogenous hyperlipidemia), and type V hyperlipoproteinemia (mixed hyperlipidemia).

b. **Secondary—**Hypothyroidism, diabetes mellitus, nephrotic syndrome, chronic alcoholism with fatty liver, ingestion of contraceptive steroids, biliary obstruction, stress.

2. **Decreased (hypolipoproteinemia)—**

a. **Primary—**Tangier disease (a-lipoprotein deficiency), abetalipoproteinemia, and a few rare, poorly defined syndromes.

b. **Secondary—**Malnutrition, malabsorption, and occasionally with parenchymal liver disease.

Urea & Urea Nitrogen, Blood, Plasma, or Serum: Normal: BUN, 8–20 mg/100 ml.

A. Precautions: *Do not use* ammonium oxalate or "double oxalate" as anticoagulant, for the ammonia will be measured as urea (see Method). Do not use too much oxalate, for it will impair urease activity.

B. Physiologic Basis: Urea, an end-product of protein metabolism, is excreted by the kidney. In the glomerular filtrate the urea concentration is the same as in the plasma. Tubular reabsorption of urea varies inversely with rate of urine flow. Thus urea is a less useful measure of glomerular filtration than is creatinine, which is not reabsorbed. BUN varies directly with protein intake and inversely with the rate of excretion of urea.

C. Interpretation:

1. **Elevated in—**

a. Renal insufficiency—Nephritis, acute and chronic; acute renal failure (tubular necrosis), urinary tract obstruction.

b. Increased nitrogen metabolism associated with diminished renal blood flow or impaired renal function—Dehydration from any cause, gastrointestinal bleeding (combination of increased protein absorption from digestion of blood, plus decreased renal blood flow).

c. Decreased renal blood flow—Shock, adrenal insufficiency, occasionally congestive heart failure.

2. **Decreased in** hepatic failure, nephrosis not complicated by renal insufficiency, and cachexia.

D. Drug Effects on Laboratory Results: Elevated by many antibiotics that impair renal function, guanethidine, methyldopa, indomethacin, isoniazid, propranolol, and potent diuretics (decreased blood volume and renal blood flow).

Uric Acid, Serum or Plasma: Normal: 3–7.5 mg/100 ml.

A. Precautions: If plasma is used, lithium oxalate should be used as the anticoagulant; potassium oxalate may interfere with the determination.

B. Physiologic Basis: Uric acid, an end-product of nucleoprotein metabolism, is excreted by the kidney. Gout, a genetically transmitted metabolic error, is characterized by an increased plasma or serum uric acid concentration, an increase in total body uric acid, and deposition of uric acid in tissues. An increase in uric acid concentration in plasma and serum may accompany increased nucleoprotein catabolism (blood dyscrasias, therapy with antileukemic drugs), thiazide diuretics, or decreased renal excretion.

C. Interpretation:

1. **Elevated** in gout, toxemia of pregnancy (eclampsia), leukemia, polycythemia, therapy with antileukemic agents, and renal insufficiency.

2. **Decreased** in acute hepatitis (occasionally), treatment with allopurinol, probenecid.

D. Drug Effects on Laboratory Results: Elevated by thiazide diuretics, ethacrynic acid, spironolactone, furosemide, and triamterene. Decreased by salicylates (small doses), methyldopa, ascorbic acid, clofibrate, phenylbutazone, cincophen, sulfinpyrazone, and phenothiazines.

•　　•　　•

General Bibliography

Caraway, W.T.: Sources of Error in Clinical Chemistry. Pp 19–30 in: *Standard Methods of Clinical Chemistry,* vol 5. Academic, 1965.

Castleman, B., & B.U. McNeely: Normal laboratory values. New England J Med 276:167–174, 1967.

Elking, M.P., & H.F. Kabat: Drug induced modification of laboratory test values. Amer J Hosp Pharm 25:485–519, 1968.

Henry, R.J.: *Clinical Chemistry: Principles and Technics.* Hoeber, 1964.

Lubran, M.: The effects of drugs on laboratory values. M Clin North America 53:211–222, 1969.

Meyers, F.H., Jawetz, E., & A. Goldfien: *Review of Medical Pharmacology,* 2nd ed. Lange, 1970. [See Appendix.]

Winston, S.: Collection and Preservation of Specimens. Pp 1–17 in: *Standard Methods of Clinical Chemistry,* vol 5. Academic, 1965.

Wirth, W.A., & R.L. Thompson: The effect of various conditions and substances on the results of laboratory procedures. Am J Clin Path 43:579–590, 1965.

NORMAL VALUES

HEMATOLOGY

Bleeding time: 1–7 minutes (Ivy).

Cellular measurements of RBC: Average diameter = 7.3 μ (5.5–8.8 μ).
Mean corpuscular volume (MCV): 82–92 cμ
Mean corpuscular hemoglobin (MCH): 28–32 $\gamma\gamma$
Mean corpuscular hemoglobin concentration (MCHC): 32–37%
Color, saturation, and volume indices: 1 (0.9–1.1)

Clot retraction: Begins in 1–3 hours; complete in 24 hours.

Coagulation time (Lee-White): At 37°, 6–12 minutes; at room temperature, 10–18 minutes.

Fragility of red cells: Begins at 0.45–0.38% NaCl; complete at 0.36–0.3% NaCl.

Hematocrit (PCV): Men, 40–54%; women, 37–47%.

Hemoglobin [B]: Men, 14–18 gm/100 ml; women, 12–16 gm/100 ml. (Serum hemoglobin: 2–3 mg/100 ml.)

Platelets: 200–400 thousand/cu mm.

Prothrombin [P]: 75–125%.

Red blood count (RBC): Men, 4.5–6.2 million/cu mm; women, 4–5.5 million/cu mm.

Reticulocytes: 0.5–1.5% of red cells.

Sedimentation rate: Less than 20 mm/hour (Westergren); 0–10 mm/hour (Wintrobe).

White blood count (WBC) and differential: 5–10 thousand/cu mm.

Myelocytes	0 %
Juvenile neutrophils	0 %
Band neutrophils	0–5 %
Segmented neutrophils	40–60%
Lymphocytes	20–40%
Eosinophils	1–3 %
Basophils	0–1 %
Monocytes	4–8 %

BLOOD (B), PLASMA (P), OR SERUM (S): CHEMICAL CONSTITUENTS

Below are listed the specimen used, the amount of blood[[B], plasma [P], or serum [S] needed to provide an adequate specimen, the fasting state, and the normal values. Values vary with the procedure employed.

Acetone bodies: [P, 2 ml] 0.3–2 mg/100 ml.

Aldolase: [S, 4 ml] 3–8 units/ml (Bruns). Men, < 33 units; women, < 19 units (Warburg and Christian). 0–8 IU/liter.

Aldosterone: [P] 0.003–0.01 μg/100 ml.

Amino acid nitrogen: [P, 2 ml fasting] 3–5.5 mg/100 ml.

Ammonia*: [B, 2 ml] 40–70 μg/100 ml.

Amylase: [S, 2 ml] 80–180 units/100 ml (Somogyi). 0.8–3.2 IU/liter.

Ascorbic acid: [P, 7 ml] 0.4–1.5 mg/100 ml.

Base, total serum: [S, 2 ml] 145–160 mEq/liter.

*Do not use anticoagulant containing ammonium oxalate.

Bilirubin: [S, 3 ml]. (Van den Bergh test.) Direct, 0.1–0.4 mg/100 ml. Indirect, 0.2–0.7 mg/100 ml.

Calcium: [S, 2 ml fasting] 9–10.6 mg/100 ml; 4.5–5.3 mEq/liter (varies with protein concentration).

CO_2 Combining power: [S or P, 1 ml] 55–75 Vol%.

CO_2 Content: [S or P, 1 ml] 24–29 mEq/liter; 55–65 Vol%.

Carotenoids: [S, 2 ml fasting] 50–300 μg/100 ml.

Ceruloplasmin: [S, 2 ml] 27–37 mg/100 ml.

Chloride: [S, 1 ml] 100–106 mEq/liter; 350–375 mg/100 ml (as chloride).

Cholesterol: [S, 1 ml] 150–280 mg/100 ml.

Cholesterol esters: [S, 1 ml] 50–65% of total cholesterol.

Copper: [S, 5 ml] 100–200 μg/100 ml.

Cortisol: [P] 4–18 μg/100 ml (circadian variation).

Creatine phosphokinase: [S, 3 ml] 0–4.5 units (Hughes). 10–50 IU/liter.

Creatinine: [B or S, 1 ml] 0.7–1.5 mg/100 ml.

Epinephrine: [P] < 0.1 μg/liter.

Folic acid: [S, 4 ml] > 5–24 μg/ml.

Glucose (Folin): [B, 0.1–1 ml fasting] 80–120 mg/100 ml.

Glucose (true): [B, 0.1–1 ml fasting] 60–100 mg/100 ml.

Glucose tolerance: See p 609.

Iodine, butanol-extractable (BEI): [S, 10 ml] 3–6.5 μg/100 ml.

Iodine, protein-bound (thyroid hormone, PBI): [S, 5 ml] 4–8 μg/100 ml.

Iodine, thyroxine: [S, 5 ml] 2.9–6.4 μg/100 ml.

Iron: [S, 2 ml] 65–175 μg/100 ml.

Iron-binding capacity, total: [S, 2 ml] 250–410 μg/100 ml.

Lactic acid: [B, 2 ml in iodoacetate] 0.44–1.8 mM/liter; 4–16 mg/100 ml.

Lactate dehydrogenase (SLDH): [S, 2 ml] 215–450 units (Wrobleski). 90–200 IU/liter.

Lipase: [S, 2 ml] 0.2–1.5 units (ml of tenth normal NaOH).

Lipids, total: [S] 500–600 mg/100 ml.

Magnesium: [S, 2 ml] 1.5–2.5 mEq/liter.

Nonprotein nitrogen (NPN)*: [S or B, 1 ml] 15–35 mg/100 ml.

Norepinephrine: [P] < 0.5 μg/liter.

Osmolality: [S, 5 ml] 285–295 mOsm/kg water.

Oxygen:
  Capacity: [B, 5 ml] 16–24 Vol% (varies with hemoglobin concentration).
  Arterial content: [B, 5 ml] 15–23 Vol% (varies with hemoglobin concentration).
  Arterial % saturation: 94–100% of capacity.
  Arterial P_{O_2}: 95–100 mm Hg.

P_{CO_2}: [Arterial blood, 5 ml] 35–45 mm Hg.

pH (reaction): [P (arterial), 1 ml] 7.35–7.45.

Phosphatase, acid: [S, 2 ml] 1–5 units (King-Armstrong), 0.5–2 units (Bodansky), 0.5–2 units (Gutman), 0–1.1 units (Shinowara), 0.1–0.63 units (Bessey-Lowry). Females: 0.2–9.5 IU/liter. Males: 0.5–11 IU/liter.

Phosphatase, alkaline: [S, 2 ml] 5–13 units (King-Armstrong), 2–4.5 units (Bodansky), 3–10 units (Gutman), 2.2–8.6 units (Shinowara). Adults, 0.8–2.3 units (Bessey-Lowry); children, 2.8–6.7 units (Bessey-Lowry). Adults, 30–85 IU/liter.

Phosphorus, inorganic: [S, 1 ml fasting] 3–4.5 mg/100 ml (children, 4–7 mg); 0.9–1.5 mM/liter.

Phospholipid: [S, 2 ml] 145–200 mg/100 ml.

Potassium: [S, 1 ml] 2.5–5 mEq/liter; 14–20 mg/100 ml.

Protein:
  Total: [S, 1 ml] 6–8 gm/100 ml.
  Albumin: [S, 1 ml] 3.5–5.5 gm/100 ml.
  Globulin: [S] 1.5–3 gm/100 ml.
  Fibrinogen: [P, 1 ml] 0.2–0.6 gm/100 ml.
  Separation by electrophoresis: See Table 5.

Prothrombin clotting time: [P, 2 ml] By control.

Pyruvic acid: [B, 2 ml] 0.07–0.22 mM/liter; 0.6–2 mg/100 ml.

Serotonin: [B] 0.05–0.20 μg/ml.

Sodium: [S, 1 ml] 136–145 mEq/liter; 310–340 mg/100 ml (as Na).

*Do not use anticoagulant containing ammonium oxalate.

Specific gravity:
[B, 0.1 ml] 1.056 (varies with hemoglobin and protein concentration).
[S, 0.1 ml] 1.0254–1.0288 (varies with protein concentration).

Sulfate: [P or S, 2 ml] 0.5–1.5 mEq/liter.

Thyroxine: See Iodine, thyroxine.

Transaminases: [S, 2 ml]
Glutamic-oxaloacetic (SGOT), 5–40 units; 6–25 IU/liter.
Glutamic-pyruvic (SGPT), 5–35 units; 3–26 IU/liter.

Triglycerides: [S, 1 ml] < 165 mg/100 ml.

Triiodothyronine uptake (T_3): [S, 3 ml] 10–14.6%.

Urea nitrogen*: [S or B, 1 ml] 8–20 mg/100 ml.

Uric acid: [S, 1 ml] 3–7.5 mg/100 ml.

Vitamin B_{12}: [S, 2 ml] > 100 $\mu\mu$g ml.

Volume, blood (Evans blue dye method): Adults, 2990–6980 ml. Women, 46.3–85.5 ml/kg; men, 66.2–97.7 ml/kg.

LIVER FUNCTION TESTS†

Cephalin flocculation: [S] Up to ++ in 48 hours.

Galactose tolerance: Administer galactose, 0.5 gm/kg IV; the blood should contain less than 5 mg/100 ml at 75 minutes. Administer 40 gm orally; less than 3 gm should be excreted in the urine at 75 minutes.

Hippuric acid: Give sodium benzoate, 1.77 gm IV; more than 0.7 gm should be excreted in the urine in 1 hour.

Sulfobromophthalein (Bromsulphalein®): Give 5 mg/kg IV; less than 5% should be retained in the serum 45 minutes after the injection. Give Bromsulphalein®, 2 mg/kg IV; less than 5% should be retained in the serum 30 minutes after the injection.

Thymol turbidity: [S] Maximum, 5 units.

Zinc turbidity (gamma globulin): [S] Maximum, 12 units.

NORMAL CSF VALUES

Appearance: Clear and colorless.

Chlorides (as NaCl): 700–750 mg/100 ml; 120–130 mEq/liter.

Colloidal gold (gold sol): 0000110000.

Globulin: 0–6 mg/100 ml.

Glucose: 50–85 mg/100 ml.

Cells: Adults, 0–5 mononuclears/cu mm. Infants, 0–20 mononuclears/cu mm.

Pressure (reclining): Newborn, 30–80 mm water. Children, 50–100 mm water. Adults, 70–200 mm water (avg = 125).

Proteins, total: 20–45 mg/100 ml in lumbar CSF.

Specific gravity: 1.003–1.008.

RENAL FUNCTION TESTS

p-Aminohippurate (PAH) clearance (RPF): Men, 560–830 ml/minute; women, 490–700 ml/minute.

Creatinine clearance, endogenous (GFR): Approximates inulin clearance (see below).

Filtration fraction (FF): Men, 17–21%; women, 17–23%. (FF = GFR/RPF.)

Inulin clearance (GFR): Men, 110–150 ml/minute; women, 105–132 ml/minute (corrected to 1.73 square meters surface area).

Maximal glucose reabsorptive capacity (Tm_G): Men, 300–450 mg/minute; women, 250–350 mg/minute.

Maximal PAH excretory capacity (Tm_{PAH}): 80–90 mg/minute.

Phenolsulfonphthalein (PSP, phenol red): Administer 1 ml IV. In first 15 minutes, 25% or more should be excreted; in 30 minutes, 40% or more; in 2 hours, 55% or more.

Specific gravity of urine: 1.003–1.030.

Urea clearance (C_u): Standard, 40–65 ml/minute; maximal, 60–100 ml/minute.

---

*Do not use anticoagulant containing ammonium oxalate.
†See also Table 10–2.

MISCELLANEOUS NORMAL VALUES

Addis urine sediment test: Maximum values/24 hours are as follows:
Red cells, 1 million
White and epithelial cells, 2 million
Casts, 100 thousand
Protein, 30 mg.

Aldosterone, urinary: 2–26 μg/24 hours; varies slightly with sodium and potassium intake.

Catecholamines, urine: < 10 μg epinephrine; < 100 μg norepinephrine; varies with method.

Congo red test: [S] More than 60% retention in serum after 1 hour.

Fecal fat: Less than 30% dry weight.

Follicle-stimulating hormone (FSH), urinary: Before puberty, less than 5 mouse units/24 hours; after puberty, 5–50 mouse units/24 hours; after menopause, up to 150 mouse units/24 hours.

11,17-Hydroxycorticoids, urinary: Men, 4–12 mg/24 hours; women, 4–8 mg/24 hours. Varies with method used.

Insulin tolerance: [B] Glucose level decreases to half of fasting level in 20–30 minutes; returns to fasting level in 90–120 minutes.

17-Ketosteroids, urinary: Under 8 years, 0–2 mg/24 hours; adolescents, 2–20 mg/24 hours. Men, 10–20 mg/24 hours; women, 5–15 mg/24 hours. Varies with method used.

Lead, urine: 0–0.12 mg/24 hours.

Urobilinogen, fecal: 40–280 mg/24 hours.

Urobilinogen, urine: 0–4 mg/24 hours.

Vanillylmandelic acid (VMA), urine: Up to 9 mg/24 hours.

• • •

Centigrade/Fahrenheit Temperature Conversion

F°	C°	F°	C°	F°	C°	F°	C°
90 =	32.2	95 =	35.0	100 =	37.8	105 =	40.6
91 =	32.8	96 =	35.6	101 =	38.3	106 =	41.1
92 =	33.3	97 =	36.1	102 =	38.9	107 =	41.7
93 =	33.9	98 =	36.7	103 =	39.4	108 =	42.2
94 =	34.4	99 =	37.2	104 =	40.0	109 =	42.8

Milliequivalent Conversion Factors

mEq/liter of:	Divide mg/100 ml or Vol% by:
Calcium	2.0
Chloride (from Cl)	3.5
(from NaCl)	5.85
CO_2 combining power	2.222
Magnesium	1.2
Phosphorus	3.1 (mM)
Potassium	3.9
Sodium	2.3

Desirable Weight Tables (Pounds)

Men (Age 25 and Over)					Women (Age 25 and Over)				
Height*		Small Frame	Medium Frame	Large Frame	Height†		Small Frame	Medium Frame	Large Frame
Feet	Inches				Feet	Inches			
5	2	112–120	118–129	126–141	4	10	92– 98	96–107	104–119
5	3	115–123	121–133	129–144	4	11	94–101	98–110	106–122
5	4	118–126	124–136	132–148	5	0	96–104	101–113	109–125
5	5	121–129	127–139	135–152	5	1	99–107	104–116	112–128
5	6	124–133	130–143	138–156	5	2	102–110	107–119	115–131
5	7	128–137	134–147	142–161	5	3	105–113	110–122	118–134
5	8	132–141	138–152	147–166	5	4	108–116	113–126	121–138
5	9	136–145	142–156	151–170	5	5	111–119	116–130	125–142
5	10	140–150	146–160	155–174	5	6	114–123	120–135	129–146
5	11	144–154	150–165	159–179	5	7	118–127	124–139	133–150
6	0	148–158	154–170	164–184	5	8	121–131	128–143	137–154
6	1	152–162	158–175	168–189	5	9	126–135	132–147	141–158
6	2	156–167	162–180	173–194	5	10	130–140	136–151	145–163
6	3	160–171	167–185	178–199	5	11	134–144	140–155	149–168
6	4	164–175	172–190	182–204	6	0	138–148	144–159	153–173

*With shoes with 1-inch heels.

*For women between 18 and 25, subtract 1 lb for each year under 25.
†With shoes with 2-inch heels.

*This table was derived primarily from data of the Build and Blood Pressure Study, 1959, Society of Actuaries. A useful discussion is presented in Seltzer, C.C., & J. Mayer: How representative are the weights of insured men and women? JAMA 201:221–224, 1967.

Metric		Apothecary		Metric		Apothecary	
30	gm	1	oz	75	mg	1 1/4	gr
6	gm	90	gr	60	mg	1	gr
5	gm	75	gr	50	mg	3/4	gr
4	gm	60	gr	40	mg	2/3	gr
3	gm	45	gr	30	mg	1/2	gr
2	gm	30	gr	25	mg	3/8	gr
1.5	gm	22	gr	20	mg	1/3	gr
1	gm	15	gr	15	mg	1/4	gr
0.75	gm	12	gr	12	mg	1/5	gr
0.6	gm	10	gr	10	mg	1/6	gr
0.5	gm	7 1/2	gr	8	mg	1/8	gr
0.4	gm	6	gr	6	mg	1/10	gr
0.3	gm	5	gr	5	mg	1/12	gr
0.25	gm	4	gr	4	mg	1/15	gr
0.2	gm	3	gr	3	mg	1/20	gr
0.15	gm	2 1/2	gr	2	mg	1/30	gr
0.12	gm	2	gr	1.5	mg	1/40	gr
0.1	gm	1 1/2	gr	1.2	mg	1/50	gr
				1	mg	1/60	gr
				0.8	mg	1/80	gr
				0.6	mg	1/100	gr
				0.5	mg	1/120	gr
				0.4	mg	1/150	gr
				0.3	mg	1/200	gr
				0.25	mg	1/250	gr
				0.2	mg	1/300	gr
				0.15	mg	1/400	gr
				0.12	mg	1/500	gr
				0.1	mg	1/600	gr

Pounds to Kilograms
(1 kg = 2.2 lb; 1 lb = 0.45 kg)

lb	kg	lb	kg	lb	kg	lb	kg	lb	kg
5	2.3	50	22.7	95	43.1	140	63.5	185	83.9
10	4.5	55	25.0	100	45.4	145	65.8	190	86.2
15	6.8	60	27.2	105	47.6	150	68.0	195	88.5
20	9.1	65	29.5	110	49.9	155	70.3	200	90.7
25	11.3	70	31.7	115	52.2	160	72.6	205	93.0
30	13.6	75	34.0	120	54.4	165	74.8	210	95.3
35	15.9	80	36.3	125	56.7	170	77.1	215	97.5
40	18.1	85	38.6	130	58.9	175	79.4	220	99.8
45	20.4	90	40.8	135	61.2	180	81.6		

Feet and Inches to Centimeters
(1 cm = 0.39 in; 1 in = 2.54 cm)

ft	in	cm	ft	in	cm	ft	in	cm	ft	in	cm	ft	in	cm
0	6	15.2	2	4	71.1	3	4	101.6	4	4	132.0	5	4	162.6
1	0	30.5	2	5	73.6	3	5	104.1	4	5	134.6	5	5	165.1
1	6	45.7	2	6	76.1	3	6	106.6	4	6	137.1	5	6	167.6
1	7	48.3	2	7	78.7	3	7	109.2	4	7	139.6	5	7	170.2
1	8	50.8	2	8	81.2	3	8	111.7	4	8	142.2	5	8	172.7
1	9	53.3	2	9	83.8	3	9	114.2	4	9	144.7	5	9	175.3
1	10	55.9	2	10	86.3	3	10	116.8	4	10	147.3	5	10	177.8
1	11	58.4	2	11	88.8	3	11	119.3	4	11	149.8	5	11	180.3
2	0	61.0	3	0	91.4	4	0	121.9	5	0	152.4	6	0	182.9
2	1	63.5	3	1	93.9	4	1	124.4	5	1	154.9	6	1	185.4
2	2	66.0	3	2	96.4	4	2	127.0	5	2	157.5	6	2	188.0
2	3	68.6	3	3	99.0	4	3	129.5	5	3	160.0	6	3	190.5

ABBREVIATIONS

Å, angstrom

a̅a̅, of each

AA, Alcoholics Anonymous

a c, before meals

ACD, anterior chest diameter

ACTH, adrenocorticotropic hormone

ADH, antidiuretic hormone

A/G ratio, albumin-globulin ratio

AHF, antihemophilic factor

AHG, antihemophilic globulin

APC, aspirin, phenacetin, and caffeine

ASO, arteriosclerosis obliterans

A-V, arteriovenous

AV, atrioventricular

BAL, British anti-Lewisite (dimercaprol)

BBB, bundle branch block (R or L)

BBT, basal body temperature

BCG, bacille Calmette-Guérin

BEI, butanol-extractable iodine

b i d, twice a day

BLB, Boothby-Lovelace-Bulbulian (oxygen mask)

BMR, basal metabolic rate

BP, blood pressure

BUN, blood urea nitrogen

BSP, Bromsulphalein®

Cal, Calorie (ie, large calorie, or 1000 calories)

CBC, complete blood count

C-F, complement fixation test

CHO, carbohydrate

CNS, central nervous system

COPD, chronic obstructive pulmonary disease

CPK, creatine phosphokinase

CSF, cerebrospinal fluid

CVA, cerebrovascular accident

CVP, central venous pressure

D & C, dilatation and curettage

DDS, diaminodiphenylsulfone

DDT, diphenylthiourea

DPT, diphtheria-pertussis-tetanus

ECG, electrocardiogram, electrocardiography

ECT, electroconvulsive therapy

ECW, extracellular water

EDTA, calcium disodium edetate

EEG, electroencephalogram, electroencephalography

EFA, essential fatty acids

Eq, equivalent

EMG, electromyography

ESR, erythrocyte sedimentation rate

EST, electroshock therapy

FF, filtration fraction

FSH, follicle-stimulating hormone

FTA, fluorescent treponemal antibody

GFR, glomerular filtration rate

gm, gram

gr, grain

Hct, hematocrit

Hgb, hemoglobin

^{131}I, radioactive iodine

ICS, intercostal space

ICSH, interstitial cell–stimulating hormone

ICW, intracellular water

IDU, 5-iodo-2-deoxyuridine

IM, intramuscularly

INH, isonicotinic acid hydrazide, isoniazid

IPPB, intermittent positive pressure breathing

IQ, intelligence quotient

ISW, interstitial water

IU, international unit

IV, intravenously

IVP, intravenous pyelogram

kg, kilogram

KW, Keith-Wagener (ophthalmoscopic findings)

LA, left atrium

LATS, long-acting thyroid stimulator

LDH, lactic acid dehydrogenase

LE, lupus erythematosus

LMP, last menstrual period

LSD, lysergic acid diethylamide

LVH, left ventricular hypertrophy

M, molar

MAC, maximum allowable concentration

mcg, μg, microgram

MCH, mean corpuscular hemoglobin

MCHC, mean corpuscular hemoglobin concentration

MCV, mean corpuscular volume

MCL, midcostal line

mEq, milliequivalent

mg, milligram

MLD, minimum lethal dose

mM, millimols

mOsm, milliosmols

mrem, 1/1000 rem

NPH, neutral protamine Hagedorn (isophane insulin)

NPN, nonprotein nitrogen

OT, old tuberculin

^{32}P, radioactive phosphorus

PA, posteroanterior

PABA, para-aminobenzoic acid

PAM, penicillin with aluminum monostearate in oil

2-PAM, pyridine-2-aldoxime methochloride (pralidoxime)

PAS, para-aminosalicylic acid

PBI, protein-bound iodine

p c, after meals

P_{CO_2}, carbon dioxide partial pressure

PCV, packed cell volume

PGH, pituitary growth hormone

pH, hydrogen ion concentration

PID, pelvic inflammatory disease

PIE, pulmonary infiltration with eosinophilia

pK, dissociation constant

PKU, phenylketonuria

PMI, point of maximal impulse

PMN, polymorphonuclear neutrophil

PMP, past menstrual period

PPD, purified protein derivative

ppm, parts per million

p r n, as needed

PSP, phenolsulfonphthalein

PTA, plasma thromboplastic antecedent

PTC, plasma thromboplastin component

PZI, protamine zinc insulin

q s ad, to a sufficient quantity

q i d, 4 times daily

r, roentgen

RA, right atrium

rad, an energy transfer of 100 ergs/gm of irradiated object

RBC, red blood count

Rh, rhesus factor (blood group)

RPF, renal plasma flow

RVH, right ventricular hypertrophy

S-A, sino-atrial

SBE, subacute bacterial endocarditis

SGOT, serum glutamic-oxaloacetic transaminase

SGPT, serum glutamic-pyruvic transaminase

stat, immediately

STS, serologic tests for syphilis

subcut, subcutaneously

T_3, triiodothyronine

T_4, thyroxine

TAO, thromboangiitis obliterans

TBW, total body water

$TCID_{50}$, 1/50 of the tissue culture immunizing dose

TEM, triethylenemelamine

TIBC, total iron-binding capacity

t i d, 3 times daily

TPI, *Treponema pallidum* immobilization

TSH, thyroid-stimulating hormone

Vol, volume

Vol%, volumes percent

VC, vena cava

VDRL, Venereal Disease Research Laboratories

VMA, vanillylmandelic acid

WBC, white blood count

WBPTT, whole blood partial thromboplastin time

HEART-LUNG RESUSCITATION
(Modified after Safar.)

Phase I: First Aid (Emergency Oxygenation of the Brain)

Must be instituted within 3–4 minutes for optimal effectiveness and to minimize the possibility of permanent brain damage.

Step 1: Place patient supine on a firm surface (not a bed). (4 × 6′ plywood sheet to be placed under the patient should be available in emergency care centers.)

Step 2: Tilt head far backward and maintain in this hyperextended position. Keep mandible displaced forward by pulling strongly at the angle of the jaw.

If Victim Is Not Breathing:

Step 3: Clear mouth and pharynx of mucus, blood, vomitus, or foreign material.

Step 4: Separate lips and teeth to open oral airway.

Step 5: If steps 2–4 fail to open airway, forcibly blow air through mouth (keeping nose closed) or nose (keeping mouth closed) and inflate the lungs 3–5 times. Watch for chest

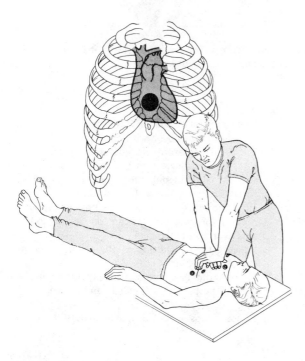

Technic of Closed Chest Cardiac Massage. Heavy circle in heart drawing shows area of application of force. Circles on supine figure show points of application of electrodes for defibrillation.

movement. If this fails to clear the airway immediately and if pharyngeal or tracheal tubes are available, use them without delay. Tracheostomy may be necessary.

Step 6: Feel the carotid artery for pulsations.

a. If Carotid Pulsations Are Present:

Give lung inflation by mouth-to-mouth breathing (keeping patient's nostrils closed) or mouth-to-nose breathing (keeping patient's mouth closed) 12–15 times per minute—allowing about 2 seconds for inspiration and 3 seconds for expiration—until spontaneous respirations return. Continue as long as the pulses remain palpable and previously dilated pupils remain constricted. Bag-mask technics for lung inflation should be reserved for experts. If pulsations cease, follow directions as in 6b, below.

b. If Carotid Pulsations Are Absent:

Alternate cardiac compression (closed heart massage) and pulmonary ventilation as in 6a, above. Place the heel of one hand on the sternum just above the xiphoid. With the heel of the other hand on top of it, apply firm vertical pressure sufficient to force the sternum about 2 inches downward (less in children) about once every second. For children, use only one hand; for babies, use only 2 fingers of one hand, compressing 80–100 times per minute. After 15 sternal compressions, alternate with 3–5 deep lung inflations. Repeat and continue this alternating procedure until it is possible to obtain additional assistance and more definitive care. If 2 operators are available, pause after every 5th compression while partner gives mouth-to-mouth inflation. Check carotid pulse after 1 minute and every 5 minutes thereafter. Resuscitation must be continuous during transportation to the hospital.

Phase II: Restoration of Spontaneous Circulation

Until spontaneous respiration and circulation are restored, there must be no interruption of artificial ventilation and cardiac massage while steps 7–13 (below) are being carried out. Three basic questions must be considered at this point:

(1) What is the underlying cause, and is it correctable?

(2) What is the nature of the cardiac arrest?

(3) What further measures will be necessary? The physician must plan upon the assistance of

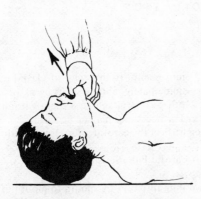

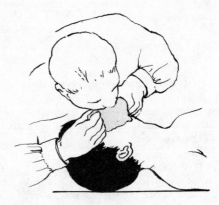

Method A: Clear mouth and throat. Place patient supine. Insert left thumb between patient's teeth, grasp mandible firmly in midline, and draw it forward (upward) so that the lower teeth are leading. Close patient's nose with right hand. Gauze (as shown) or airway may be used but is not necessary.

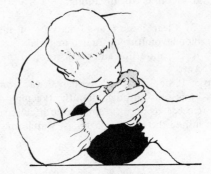

Method B: Clear mouth and throat. Place patient supine. Pull strongly forward at angle of mandible. Close patient's nose with your cheek. Gauze (as shown) or airway may be used but is not necessary.

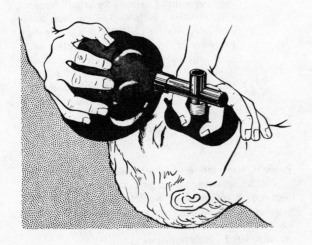

Instructions for Use of Manual Resuscitator

1. Lift the victim's neck with one hand.
2. Tilt head backward into maximum neck extension. Remove secretions and debris from mouth and throat, and pull the tongue and mandible forward as required to clear the airway.
3. Hold the mask snugly over the nose and mouth, holding the chin forward and the neck in extension as shown in diagram.
4. Squeeze the bag, noting inflation of the lungs by the rise of the chest wall.
5. Release the bag, which will expand spontaneously. The patient will exhale and the chest will fall.
6. Repeat steps 4 and 5 approximately 12 times per minute.

trained hospital personnel,* an ECG, a defibrillator, and emergency drugs.

Step 7: If a spontaneous effective heartbeat is not restored after 1–2 minutes of cardiac compression, have an assistant give epinephrine (adrenaline), 0.5–1 mg (0.5–1 ml of 1:1000 aqueous solution) IV or by the intracardiac route every 3–5 minutes as indicated. Epinephrine may be given intratracheally if necessary.

Step 8: Promote venous return and combat shock by elevating legs or placing patient in the Trendelenburg position, and give intravenous fluids as available and indicated. The use of tourniquets on the extremities may be of value.

Step 9: If the victim is pulseless for more than 5 minutes, give sodium bicarbonate solution, 3–4 gm/50 ml (1.5–2 gm/50 ml in children) IV to combat impending metabolic acidosis. Repeat every 5–10 minutes as indicated.

Step 10: If pulsations still do not return, determine the type of "cardiac arrest" by ECG: (1) Asystole, (2) shock (electrical activity without effective mechanical contraction), or (3) ventricular fibrillation. In case of asystole and shock, continue artificial respiration and external cardiac compression, epinephrine, and sodium bicarbonate. Give also calcium chloride, 5–10 ml (0.5–1 gm) of 10% solution IV every 5–10 minutes as indicated.

Step 11: If ECG demonstrates ventricular fibrillation, maintain respiration and external cardiac massage until just before giving an external defibrillating shock. Become familiar with the manufacturer's recommendations for each type of defibrillator. A 200–400 watt-second DC shock is given across the heart, eg, with one electrode firmly applied to the skin over the apex of the heart and the other over the sternal notch. (If an AC defibrillator is used, 440–1000 volts AC are given for 0.1–0.25 second.) Monitor with ECG. If cardiac function is not restored, resume external massage and repeat 3 or more shocks at intervals of 1–3 minutes. If cardiac action is reestablished but remains weak, give calcium chloride as above. If fibrillation persists or recurs, give lidocaine hydrochloride (Xylocaine®), 50–100 mg IV and repeat if necessary. It may be necessary in such cases also to use a pacemaker to capture or override the abnormal rhythm. In some instances of cardiac arrest with electrical bradycardia,

atropine sulfate, 0.4–0.6 mg IV, may be of value.

Step 12: Thoracotomy and open heart massage may be considered (but only in a hospital) if cardiac function fails to return after all of the above measures have been used.

Step 13: If cardiac, pulmonary, and CNS functions are restored, the patient should be carefully observed for shock and complications of the precipitating cause.

Phase III: Follow-up Measures

When cardiac and pulmonary function have been reestablished and satisfactorily maintained, evaluation of CNS function deserves careful consideration. Decision as to the nature and duration of subsequent treatment must be individualized. The physician must decide if he is "prolonging life" or simply "prolonging dying." Complete CNS recovery has been reported in a few patients unconscious up to a week after appropriate treatment.

Step 14: If circulation and respiration are restored but there are no signs of CNS recovery within 30 minutes, hypothermia at 30° C for 2–3 days may lessen the degree of brain damage.

Step 15: Support ventilation and circulation. Treat any other complications which might arise. Do not overlook the possibility of complications of external cardiac massage (eg, broken ribs, ruptured viscera).

Step 16: Meticulous post-resuscitation care is required, particularly for the first 48 hours after recovery. Observe carefully for possible multiple cardiac arrhythmias, especially recurrent fibrillation or cardiac standstill.

Step 17: Consider the use of assisted circulation in selected cases. A few patients who cannot be salvaged by conventional cardiopulmonary resuscitation may be saved by the addition of partial cardiopulmonary bypass measures.

Green, H.L., Hieb, G.E., & I.J. Schatz: Electronic equipment in critical care areas: Status of devices currently in use. Circulation 43:A101–A122, 1971.

Grossman, J.I., & I.L. Rubin: Cardiopulmonary resuscitation. Am Heart J 78:569–572, 709–714, 1969.

Jude, J.R., Bolooki, H., & E.L. Nagel: Cardiac resuscitation in the operating room: Current status. Ann Surg 171:948–955, 1970.

Jude, J.R., & E.L. Nagel: Cardiopulmonary resuscitation 1970. Mod Concepts Cardiovas Dis 39:133–139, 1970.

Lund, I., & B. Lind (editors): Aspects of resuscitation. Proceedings of the Second International Symposium on Emergency Resuscitation. Acta anaesth scandinav, Suppl 29, 1968.

Todd, J.S. (editor): Intensive care units. M Clin North America 55:1081-1374, 1971.

---

*In the hospital a physician able to intubate the trachea will quickly visualize the larynx, suck out all foreign material, pass a large cuffed endotracheal tube and attach the airway to an IPPB or anesthesia machine for adequate ventilation. Serial arterial blood gas, pH, and bicarbonate determinations are important.

Index

Stephen M. Stahl

METRIC SYSTEM PREFIXES
(Small Measurement)

In accordance with the decision of several scientific societies to employ a universal system of metric nomenclature, the following prefixes have become standard in many medical texts and journals.

k	kilo	10^3
c	centi	10^{-2}
m	milli	10^{-3}
μ	micro	10^{-6}
n	nano (formerly millimicro, mμ)	10^{-9}
p	pico (formerly micromicro, $\mu\mu$)	10^{-12}
f	femto	10^{-15}
a	atto	10^{-18}